HANDBOOK OF NEUROSCIENCE FOR THE BEHAVIORAL SCIENCES

HANDBOOK OF NEUROSCIENCE FOR THE BEHAVIORAL SCIENCES

Volume 2

Edited by

GARY G. BERNTSON

JOHN T. CACIOPPO

John Wiley & Sons, Inc.

Library of Congress Cataloging-in-Publication Data:

Handbook of neuroscience for the behavioral sciences / edited by Gary G.
Berntson, John T. Cacioppo.
  p. ; cm.
Includes bibliographical references and index.
ISBN 978-0-470-08355-0 (set) (cloth : alk. paper)—ISBN 978-0-470-08356-7
(v. 1) (cloth : alk. paper)—ISBN 978-0-470-08357-4 (v. 2) (cloth : alk. paper)
1. Neurosciences—Handbooks, manuals, etc. 2. Neuropsychology—Handbooks,
manuals, etc. I. Berntson, Gary G. II. Cacioppo, John T.
[DNLM: 1. Psychophysiology. 2. Behavior--physiology. 3. Mental Processes—physiology. WL 103 H2361 2009]
RC343.4.H36 2009
616.89—dc22
                                                                      2008042940

Printed in the United States of America.

10 9 8 7 6 5 4 3 2 1

Contents

VOLUME 1

VOLUME 2

Preface

The notion that 100 billion neurons give rise to human behavior proved daunting up through the twentieth century because neuroscientists were limited by existing technologies to studying the properties of single neurons or small groups of neurons. Characterizing simple neural circuits has led to an understanding of a variety of sensory processes, such as the initial stages in vision, and relatively simple motor processes, such as the generation of locomotion patterns. However, unraveling the neural substrates of more complex behaviors, such as the ability of an animal to navigate in its environment, to pay attention to relevant events in its surroundings, to perceive and communicate mental states including the beliefs and desires of others and to form and maintain interpersonal and group relationships remains one of the major challenges for the neurosciences in the twenty-first century. In contrast to more elementary behaviors, these complex behavioral processes depend on interactions within elaborate networks extending across distinct brain structures. Elucidating the neural bases of complex behaviors, therefore, may require sophisticated approaches and methods that have only recently, or have yet to be, developed. These include the ability to record electrical brain activity with multi-electrode arrays in freely behaving animals or humans, neuroimaging methods that can noninvasively monitor brain activity, and an increasing cornucopia of technologies from molecular biology and genetics that allow investigators to analyze the cellular bases of behaviors. These approaches are not only revealing the underlying neurobiology of behavior, but are establishing the foundation for an understanding for the biological bases of a variety of physical and mental health problems.

As a result of these developments, the neurosciences are reshaping the landscape of the behavioral sciences, and the behavioral sciences are of increasing importance to the neurosciences, especially for the rapidly expanding investigations into the highest level functions of the brain. The *Handbook of Neurosciences for the Behavioral Sciences* provides an introduction to graduate students and scholars in the neurosciences and behavioral sciences and informs about relevant theory, methods, and research in these two increasingly synergistic disciplines. The *Handbook* is designed to make neuroscience accessible to psychologists and other behavioral scientists with minimal background in biology or neuroscience, while at the same time offering information, constructs and approaches that will enhance the knowledge, teaching and research of active investigators at the intersection of psychology and neuroscience. In addition, the *Handbook* is designed to provide an accessible background in and to highlight currently active areas within the behavioral sciences for neuroscientists, who may have a minimal background in behavioral sciences.

To accomplish the dual purposes of exposing behavioral scientists to neuroscience and neuroscientists to psychology, we have adopted a unique organization in this two volume *Handbook*. The first volume includes a *Foundations* section that features a set of chapters that provide brief introductions to major questions and approaches at distinct levels of analysis. These include topics such as the logical basis of integrative neuroscience, developmental processes, comparative approaches, biological rhythms, neuropharmacology, neuroendocrinology, neuroimmunology, neuroanatomy, neuropsychology, and functional neuroimaging. These chapters are overviews that provide the reader with a basic conceptual orientation to the types of approaches and measures available and how they can be applied and interpreted. These chapters provide the basic background to allow the reader to comprehend and evaluate the subsequent chapters of the handbook, as well as the broader neuroscience literature.

The subsequent sections are comprised of groups of chapters organized around major psychological themes. In Volume 1, these include: *Sensation and Perception, Attention and Cognition,* and *Learning and Memory*. This organization carries over to Volume 2, with major sections being: *Motivation and Emotion, Social Processes, Psychological Disorders* and *Health and Aging*.

Throughout the *Handbook,* the goal has been to integrate information across disciplines and levels of organization/ analyses, from the cellular/molecular to systems to behavioral/social levels. The organization of the *Handbook* thus avoids artificial dichotomies such as lower level vs. higher level processes, or neuroscience vs. behavioral science sections. Coverage of motor systems, for example, is included in the section on *Attention and Cognition* and discussion of somatovisceral function is included in the context of *Motivation and Emotion,* providing the reader with the broadest and most interdisciplinary perspectives on a given topic. Cross referencing across chapters has been emphasized, to underscore the fact that a neuroscientific perspective may illuminate connections across areas of study in psychology, where none may have traditionally been recognized.

The intended audience for the *Handbook* is broad, including graduate students, psychologists and other behavioral scientists who seek knowledge and understanding about neuroscience. It is a resource for active behavioral neuroscientists as well as those with minimal background in the biological sciences. It should also be of interest to neuroscientists who want an introduction to contemporary psychological issues, presented in a neuroscientific context.

None of this would be possible without the tremendous efforts and high quality of the chapter authors. We thank them all for their contributions and we hope you will find this Handbook of value in understanding the behavioral neurosciences.

GARY G. BERNTSON
JOHN T. CACIOPPO

Contributors to Volume 2

Maria T. Acosta, MD
Department of Neurology
Children's National Medical Center
Washington, DC

Ralph Adolphs, PhD
Emotion and Social Cognition Laboratory
California Institute of Technology
Pasadena, California

David G. Amaral, PhD
The MIND Institute
University of California, Davis
Davis, California

Mauricio Arcos-Burgos, MD, PhD
Department of Psychiatry and Behavioral Sciences
University of Miami
Miami, Florida

Lauren Y. Atlas, MA
Department of Psychology
Columbia University
New York, New York

Antoine Bechara, PhD
Brain and Creativity Institute
University of Southern California
Los Angeles, California

Vaughan Bell, PhD
Institute of Psychiatry
Cardiff University
Cardiff, United Kingdom

Edward M. Bernat, PhD
Department of Psychology
University of Minnesota
Minneapolis, Minnesota

Gary G. Berntson, PhD
Department of Psychology, Psychiatry & Pediatrics
Ohio State University
Columbus, Ohio

Elizabeth H. Blackburn, PhD
Department of Biochemistry and Biophysics
University of California, San Francisco
San Francisco, California

D. Caroline Blanchard, PhD
Department of Neurobiology
University of Hawaii
Honolulu, Hawaii

Robert J. Blanchard, PhD
Department of Psychology
University of Hawaii, Manoa
Honolulu, Hawaii

Dorret I. Boomsma, PhD
Department of Biological Psychology
Vrije University
Amsterdam, Netherlands

David E. A. Bush, PhD
Center for Neural Science
New York University
New York, New York

John T. Cacioppo, PhD
Department of Psychology
University of Chicago
Chicago, Illinois

Cameron S. Carter, MD
Department of Psychiatry
University of California, Davis
Davis, California

Lisa M. Christian, PhD
Department of Psychology
The Ohio State University
Columbus, Ohio

Philip J. Corr, PhD
School of Social Work and Psychology
University of East Anglia
Norwich, United Kingdom

William A. Cunningham, PhD
Department of Psychology
Ohio State University
Columbus, Ohio

Katharine P. Dahl, BA
Department of Psychology
Columbia University
New York, New York

Jean Decety, PhD
Department of Psychology
University of Chicago
Chicago, Illinois

Nathan T. Deichert, PhD
Institute for Behavioral Medicine Research
Ohio State University
Columbus, Ohio

Boadie W. Dunlop, MD
Mood and Anxiety Disorders Program
Emory University, School of Medicine
Atlanta, Georgia

Elissa S. Epel, PhD
Department of Psychiatry
University of California, San Francisco
San Francisco, California

Emma Ferneyhough, BA
Department of Psychology
New York University
New York, New York

Susan T. Fiske, PhD
Department of Psychology
Princeton University
Princeton, New Jersey

Philip Gerrans, PhD
Department of Philosophy
University of Adelaide
Adelaide, Australia

Joshua Goh, MA
Beckman Institute
University of Illinois at Urbana-Champaign
Urbana, Illinois

Jean-Philippe Gouin, MPs
Department of Psychology
Ohio State University
Columbus, Ohio

Jennifer E. Graham, PhD
Department of Biobehavioral Health
Pennsylvania State University
University Park, Pennsylvania

Josée Guindon, PhD
Department of Psychology
The University of Georgia
Athens, Georgia

Peter W. Halligan, PhD
School of Psychology
Cardiff University
Cardiff, United Kingdom

Gregor Hasler, MD
Department of Psychiatry
Zurich University Hospital
Zurich, Switzerland

Todd F. Heatherton, PHD
Department of Psychological and Brain Sciences
Dartmouth College
Hanover, New Hampshire

Andrea G. Hohmann, PhD
Department of Psychology
The University of Georgia
Athens, Georgia

Peter W. Kalivas, PhD
Department of Physiology
Medical University of Southern Carolina
Charleston, South Carolina

Nancy Kanwisher, PhD
Department of Brain and Cognitive Sciences
Massachusetts Institute of Technology
Cambridge, Massachusetts

Janice K. Kiecolt-Glaser, PhD
Department of Psychiatry
Ohio State University
Columbus, Ohio

Clifford M. Knapp, PhD
Department of Psychiatry
Boston University, School of Medicine
Boston, Massachusetts

Conan Kornetsky, PhD
Department of Psychiatry
Boston University, School of Medicine
Boston, Massachusetts

Anne C. Krendl, PhD
Department of Psychology
Tufts University
Medford, Massachusetts

Morten L. Kringelbach, PhD
Department of Psychiatry
University of Oxford
Oxford, United Kingdom

Claus Lamm, PhD
Departments of Psychology and Psychiatry
The University of Chicago
Chicago, Illinois

Joseph E. LeDoux, PhD
New York University
Center for Neural Science
New York, New York

Jue Lin, PhD
Department of Biochemistry and Biophysics
University of California, San Francisco
San Francisco, California

Yoav Litvin, MA
Department of Psychology
University of Hawaii at Manoa
Honolulu, Hawaii

Daniel Margoliash, PhD
University of Chicago
Department of Organismal Biology and Anatomy
Chicago, Illinois

Bruce S. McEwen, PhD
Lab of Neuroendocrinology
The Rockefeller University
New York, New York

Michael J. McKinley, PhD
Howard Florey Institute
University of Melbourne
Victoria, Australia

Neil McNaughton, PhD
Department of Psychology
University of Otago
Dunedin, New Zealand

Christel M. Middeldorp, MD, PhD
Department of Biological Psychology
Vrije Universiteit, Amsterdam
Amsterdam, Netherlands

Michael Minzenberg, MD
Department of Psychiatry
University of California, Davis
Davis, California

Maximilian Muenke, MD
Medical Genetics Branch
National Human Genome Research Institute
Bethesda, Maryland

Dennis L. Murphy, MD
Laboratory of Clinical Science
National Institute of Mental Health
Bethesda, Maryland

Nasir Naqvi, MD, PhD
Brain and Creativity Institute
University of Southern California
Los Angeles, California

Charles B. Nemeroff, MD, PhD
Emory University, School of Medicine
Department of Psychiatry and Behavioral Sciences
Atlanta, Georgia

Greg J. Norman, PhD
Department of Psychology
The Ohio State University
Columbus, Ohio

Howard C. Nusbaum, PhD
University of Chicago
Department of Psychology
Chicago, Illinois

Arne Öhman, PhD
Department of Clinical Neuroscience-Psychology
Karolinska Institute and Hospital
Stockholm, Sweden

Andreas Olsson, PhD
Department of Clinical Neuroscience-Psychology
Karolinska Institute and Hospital
Stockholm, Sweden

Denise C. Park, PhD
Beckman Institute
University of Illinois at Urbana-Champaign
Urbana, Illinois

Christopher J. Patrick, PhD
Department of Psychology
University of Minnesota
Minneapolis, Minnesota

Nathan S. Pentkowski, PhD
Department of Psychology
University of Hawaii at Manoa
Honolulu, Hawaii

Elizabeth A. Phelps, PhD
Department of Psychology
New York University
New York, New York

Terry L. Powley, PhD
Department of Psychological Sciences
Purdue University
West Lafayette, Indiana

Christina Riccardi, BA
Department of Psychology
Florida State University
Tallahassee, Florida

Sally J. Rogers, PhD
MIND Institute
University of California, Davis
Davis, California

John L. R. Rubenstein, MD, PhD
Center for Neurobiology and Psychiatry
University of California, San Francisco
San Francisco, California

Glenn E. Schafe, PhD
Department of Psychology
Yale University
New Haven, Connecticut

Norman B. Schmidt, PhD
Department of Psychology
Florida State University
Tallahassee, Florida

Edward E. Smith, PhD
Department of Psychology
Columbia University
New York, New York

Michael Spezio, PhD
Emotion and Social Cognition Laboratory
California Institute of Technology
Pasadena, California

Damian Stanley, PhD
Department of Psychology
New York University
New York, New York

Edward Taub, PhD
Department of Psychology
University of Alabama, Birmingham
Birmingham, Alabama

Kiara R. Timpano, PhD
Department of Psychology
Florida State University
Tallahassee, Florida

Mary M. Torregrossa, PhD
Department of Psychiatry
Yale University
New Haven, Connecticut

Gitendra Uswatte, PhD
Department Psychology
University of Alabama, Birmingham
Birmingham, Alabama

Jay J. Van Bavel, PhD
Department of Psychology
Ohio State University
Columbus, Ohio

Tor D. Wager, PhD
Department of Psychology
Columbia University
New York, New York

Jong H. Y. Yoon, MD
Department of Psychiatry
University of California at Davis
Davis, California

Galit Yovel, PhD
Department of Brain and Cognitive Sciences
Massachusetts Institute of Technology
Cambridge, Massachusetts

PART V

Motivation and Emotion

Chapter 32

Evaluative Processes

GARY G. BERNTSON, GREG J. NORMAN, AND JOHN T. CACIOPPO

Natural selection has tailored the computational capacities of the brain to promote survival and maximize reproduction. This evolutionary pressure has led to the ability to quickly evaluate situations in which an organism must delineate between hostile and hospitable stimuli and select appropriate responses. The behavioral output of such evaluations may manifest in approach or avoidance dispositions that promote survival and minimize negative consequences. Although approach and avoidance dispositions often synergistically promote a common behavioral outcome, at times they may come into conflict (e.g., tolerating an unpalatable taste in order to obtain nutrients). Moreover, evaluative processes are represented in distributed systems at multiple levels of the neuraxis, and this multiple-level processing may also give rise to conflicts (e.g., suppressing pain-withdrawal reflexes to remove an embedded sliver).

Despite potential complexities of central evaluative substrates, behavioral manifestations are constrained—an organism cannot simultaneously approach and avoid a goal object. Such physical constraints may belie the underlying structure of central evaluative processes and have led to theoretical models, typically based on behavioral measures that characterize evaluative processes as points along a bipolar (positive to negative) dimension of valence (Osgood, Suci, & Tannenbaum, 1957; Posner, Russell, & Peterson, 2005; Russell, 2003; Watson, Wiese, Vaidya, & Tellegen, 1999). This is often considered to be mediated by a single neural integrator responsible for valence integration (Allport, 1935). Although useful in many contexts, models of evaluative processes that assume reciprocity among positive and negative valence and homogeneity of neural substrates are likely too simplistic. Based on evolutionary, neurobiological, and psychological considerations, Cacioppo and Berntson (1994; Cacioppo, Gardner, & Berntson, 1997; Larsen, McGraw, & Cacioppo, 2001) have proposed a more complex, bivariate space model of evaluative processes. This model recognizes distinct positive and negative evaluative systems that can function in a reciprocal or coactive fashion (e.g., in ambivalence) and embraces the multiple-level representations of

evaluative systems and the increasing complexity of these networks at higher levels of the neuraxis that can sustain at least partially independent activations. Such patterns allow for more flexible outputs, such as cautious approach during anxiety-like states (see Chapter 36), capable of developing over different temporal dimensions. We review evidence that evaluative processes are well conserved throughout ontogeny and phylogeny, represented throughout multiple levels of the neuraxis, and organized along a cardinal dimension of evaluative bivalence (i.e., approach vs. avoidance, positivity vs. negativity).

LEVELS OF ORGANIZATION IN THE NERVOUS SYSTEM

Levels of Evaluative Function: Lower-Level and Spinal Reflexes

Spinal reflexes are among the lowest levels of organization in the central nervous system, and their relative simplicity allows for fast and efficient adaptive response to environmental stimuli. Although capable of operating independently of higher levels, spinal reflexes also provide critical functional support for higher-level functions, an issue to which we return later.

In his treatise *The Integrative Action of the Nervous System* (1906), Sir Charles Sherrington detailed spinal organizations that contribute to postural regulation and provide the basic neurological support for locomotion. He also described spinal substrates for basic, low-level evaluative reactions. Among the most salient of spinal reflexes is the flexor (pain) withdrawal reflex, which represents a primitive but effective evaluative mechanism for protection against noxious or injurious stimuli. Nociceptive signals carried by somatosensory afferents activate flexor neuron pools via interneuron circuits within the spinal cord, resulting in flexor withdrawal responses (Craig, 2003; Lundberg, 1979; Sandrini et al., 2005; Schouenborg, Holmberg, & Weng, 1992).

Although appetitive reflexes may be less obvious than aversive reflexes at the level of the spinal cord, primitive approach/engagement dispositions are also apparent in spinal extensor reflexes. Sherrington (1906) described extensor thrust reflexes to Palmer contact that represent low-level reflexive dispositions promoting contact and engagement with the external environment. These approach/engagement reflexes are supplemented by suckling and ingestive reflexes of brain stem origin, which are considered later in this chapter.

At a trivial level, flexor and extensor reflexes promote diametrically opposing motoric dispositions. The spinal circuits for these reflexes are distinct and separately organized, and they include differences in peripheral sensory receptors, afferent axonal populations, central interneuronal pathways, and motoneuron output pools.

This is not to say that flexor/extensor reflexes are entirely independent. Although the primary neural circuits underlying flexor and extensor reflexes are parallel and distinct, there are rich interactions among these networks—an organizational pattern that Sherrington referred to as the *alliance of reflexes.* Examples include the *crossed-extension* reflex, in which activation of the flexor reflex in one limb is associated with a reflex extension of the opposite limb. Sherrington also described interactions among networks for opponent flexor and extensor reflexes for a given limb as a pattern of reciprocal innervation. *Reciprocal innervation* is the property by which spinal reflex networks that activate a specific outcome (e.g., limb flexion) also tend to inhibit opponent (e.g., extensor) muscles, which synergistically promote the target response. These organizational patterns are not unique to spinal circuits but represent general neuroarchitectural features that may inform the operations of higher-level systems as well. Behavioral manifestations of the principle of reciprocal innervation, for example, can be seen even at a cognitive level. One example comes from the cognitive dissonance literature, where the mere selection of an item from among several choices results in increased cognitive valuation of the chosen item and concurrent devaluation of the nonselected items (Aronson & Carlsmith, 1963; Egan, Santos, & Bloom, 2007).

The integrative outputs of spinal approach/withdrawal circuits may provide a basic model for understanding higher-level evaluative processes. For example, flexor withdrawal and extensor approach reflexes are not symmetrical in strength because flexor withdrawal reflexes are significantly more potent than their antagonistic extensor (approach) reflexes and recover more rapidly after spinal transection. As is considered later, asymmetric strength of evaluative systems is also apparent at higher levels of the neuraxis where avoidance reactions (anxiety, fear) tend to have a stronger hold on affect when compared to approach reactions (incentive, reward). This makes adaptive sense because a single failure of the avoidance system can lead to subsequent injury or death. Natural selection may have tuned the avoidance system for preferential control of behavior. The bias toward avoidance reactions represents a occurring theme at all levels of the neuraxis and has been termed the *negativity bias* (Cacioppo & Berntson, 1999; Cacioppo, Larsen, Smith, & Berntson, 2004).

Despite this negativity bias, flexor/withdrawal reflexes are not always dominant over their opponent processes because extensor/approach reflexes can take precedence over withdrawal processes at lower levels of stimulation or activation. This disposition toward approach behaviors in the context of low levels of activation has been termed the *positivity offset* (Cacioppo & Berntson, 1999; Cacioppo et al., 2004) and characterizes the operations of evaluative processes at multiple levels of the neuraxis. As we consider later, the asymmetry of neurobehavioral dispositions can lead to a context-dependent outcome because approach dispositions may predominate at lower levels of evaluative activation but can be trumped by avoidance or withdrawal (negativity bias) at higher levels of evaluative activation.

Spinal flexor and extensor reflexes have separate, although interacting, circuitries and thus can operate in parallel within the constraints of those neural interactions. Despite this underlying bivalence, the behavioral output of opponent extensor/flexor networks may lie along a bipolar continuum from flexion to extension, the output being constrained by the mechanical coupling of the extensor and flexor muscles around a specific point of articulation at a joint.

Neural Hierarchies

Multilevel perspectives of neuronal organization have been emphasized by scientists and philosophers alike, among the more influential of whom was the nineteenth-century neurologist John Hughlings Jackson. In his essay "Evolution and Dissolution of the Nervous System," Jackson (1884/1958) laid the groundwork for multilevel characterization of neuronal organization. Jackson argued that the evolutionary emergence of higher levels of neuronal organizations does not involve a replacement or displacement of lower levels. Rather, evolutionary development entails a re-representation and elaboration of functions at progressively higher levels of the nervous system. Although rostral levels were thought to be characterized by elaborate networks capable of more sophisticated functions, they were not seen to replace lower levels but in fact remain highly dependent on lower neuraxial substrates. For example, the critical spinal networks and related locomotor reflexes for stepping constitute essential lower processing circuits that support outputs from higher motor systems. In Jackson's view, the proper interpretation of the consequences of brain injuries is that these injuries are not optimally defined by the functions that are lost but rather in the reversion (dissolution) of those functions to lower levels of neural organization.

It is now apparent that the neuraxis is replete with hierarchical organizations composed of simple reflex-like circuits at the lowest levels, such as the brain stem and spinal cord, and neural networks for more integrative computations at higher levels (for reviews, see Berntson, Boysen, & Cacioppo, 1993; Berntson & Cacioppo, 2000; Berridge, 2004). The relatively simple neural circuitry characteristic of lower levels of the neuraxis is essential for survival because it allows for rapid computations and subsequent motor outputs. The adaptive function of such circuits is obvious because it may be more important in some circumstances to perform a rapid but imperfect response rather than a more elaborate and protracted performance that may produce a more elaborate outcome. The additional time consumed by such processes could lead to a negative outcome. As environmental challenges grow increasingly complex, more integrated neuronal processing may be more adaptive, and higher level analytical and response mechanisms may come into play. Moreover, learned anticipatory processes may promote more strategic avoidance of adaptive challenges prior to their occurrence. The increasing amount of information that must be processed and integrated by progressively higher-level systems may lead to neurocomputational bottlenecks that require a slower and more serial mode of processing. Based on hierarchical interconnections, higher-level systems may depend heavily on lower-level systems for the transmission and preliminary processing and filtering of afferent sensory and perceptual data and for the implementation of sensorimotor subroutines that support executive outputs. The advantages and disadvantages associated with higher-level (integrative, flexible, but capacity-limited) and lower-level (rapid, efficient, but rigid) processing were a likely source of evolutionary pressure for the preservation of lower-level substrates, despite higher-level elaborations and re-representations (Berntson & Cacioppo, in press). Together these interacting hierarchical structures allow neural systems to rapidly respond through low-level processing (e.g., pain-withdrawal reflexes), whereas more rostral neural substrates permit a more elaborate response over time and allow for evaluation of future strategies and subsequent consequences. Hierarchical representations do not merely reflect theoretical models or cognitive curiosities but are empirically documented by neuroanatomical and functional analyses of neural systems throughout the brain (Berntson et al., 1993; Figure 32.1).

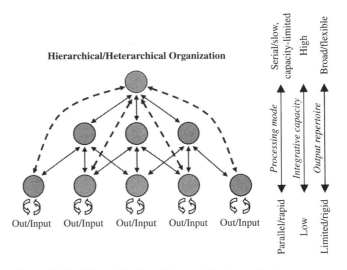

Figure 32.1 Hierarchical and heterarchical organizations.

Note: A heterarchy differs from a hierarchy (illustrated by solid arrows) by the additional presence of long ascending and descending pathways that span intermediate levels (dashed arrows). Properties of the levels in both classes of organizations lie along the illustrated continua of processing mode, integrative capacity, and output repertoire. Heterarchical organizations have greater integrative capacity and output flexibility because the long ascending and descending projections provide inputs and outputs that are not constrained by intermediate levels.

Neural Heterarchies

Additional neuroarchitectural complexities exist beyond strict hierarchical organization patterns because long descending pathways exist that bypass intermediate levels and directly synapse onto lower levels of the neuraxis (Porter, 1987; Wakana, Jiang, Nagae-Poetscher, Zijl, & Mori, 2004). This type of organization is documented by the existence of direct, long descending projections from higher neuraxial systems to lower motor neurons, effectively bypassing intermediate levels. In addition to the well-known anatomy of somatomotor systems (Porter, 1987; Wakana et al., 2004), this pattern of organization is also apparent in the autonomic nervous system (Berntson & Cacioppo, 2000). As illustrated in Figure 32.2, for example, the baroreflex is a tightly organized brain stem–mediated reflex system that serves to maintain blood pressure homeostasis. Increases in blood pressure activate specialized cardiovascular mechanoreceptors, which then feed back into brain stem reflex circuitry, leading to reciprocal increases in vagal cardiac output and decreases in sympathetic cardiac and vascular tone. These responses collectively lead to decreases in heart rate, cardiac output, and vascular tone, which synergistically compensate for the blood pressure perturbation. In contrast to this lower-level, homeostatic reflex regulation, higher-level systems (e.g., with even mild psychological stress) are capable of overriding the baroreflex and yielding concurrent increases in

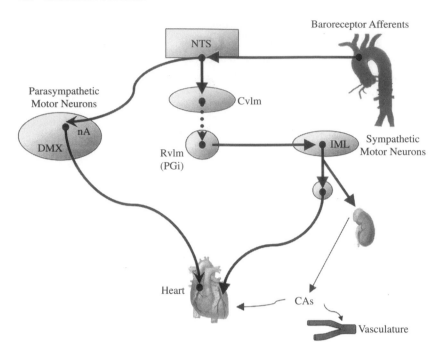

Figure 32.2 (**Figure C. 34** in color section) Summary of brain stem systems underlying the baroreceptor cardiac reflex.

Note: Baroreceptor afferents project to nucleus tractus solitarius (NTS), which in turn leads to activation of parasympathetic motor neurons in the nucleus ambiguus (nA) and dorsal motor nucleus of the vagus (DMX). The NTS also activates the caudal ventrolateral medulla (Cvlm), which in turn inhibits the rostral ventrolateral medulla (Rvlm), leading to a withdrawal of excitatory drive on the sympathetic motor neurons in the intermediolateral cell column of the spinal cord (IML). CAs = Catecholamines; PGi = Nucleus paragigantocellaris (coextensive with Rvlm).

blood pressure and heart rate. This nonhomeostatic modulation of cardiovascular may arise in part from descending inhibition of brain stem baroreflex networks. It also likely reflects the actions of long descending projections from higher neurobehavioral substrates that bypass intermediate reflex circuits and project monosynpatically to lower autonomic source nuclei (see Figure 32.3). As a result, cortical and limbic structures are able to bypass intermediate hierarchical elements and directly control lower levels (see Berntson et al., 1994).

The presence of long ascending and descending pathways in neural organizational patterns, combined with lateral interconnections between levels, has previously been described as a *neural heterarchy* (see Berntson et al., 1993; Berntson & Cacioppo, 2000). Heterarchical organization patterns have the components of hierarchical systems, as higher levels are in continuous communication with lower-level systems via intermediate levels, but they have the additional capacity to interact over widely separated levels via direct connections. Direct neuronal projections from higher brain systems to lower-level systems allow for manifestations of higher computational re-representative networks that are not constrained by intermediate-level organizations. This affords cognitive and behavioral flexibility when needed but also allows for intermediate-level processing when necessary. The multiple levels of organization and associated functional flexibility come with a disadvantage because a heterarchical organization opens the possibility for functional conflicts between distinct levels of processing (e.g., when an organism must inhibit pain

withdrawal to achieve a higher-order goal). We return to this issue later.

Levels of Evaluative Function: Intermediate Levels—Decerebration

Although primitive approach/withdrawal dispositions are represented at spinal levels, they are substantially developed and elaborated at brain stem levels. Classical demonstrations of the functional capacity of brain stem networks come from studies of experimental isolation of the brain stem and spinal cord (i.e., *decerebration*) and from tragic cases of human decerebration (Berntson & Micco, 1976; Berntson, Tuber, Ronca, & Bachman, 1983; Harris, Kelso, Flatt, Bartness, & Grill, 2006; Ronca, Berntson, & Tuber, 1986; Tuber, Berntson, Bachman, & Allen, 1980; Yates, Jakus, & Miller, 1993). Although acute postsurgical somatomotor rigidity historically obscured the behavioral capacities of the experimental decerebrate, with longer survival times and the resolution of this rigidity a great deal of organizational capacity is apparent at brain stem levels (Bard & Macht, 1958; Berntson & Micco, 1976; Norman, Buchwald, & Villablanca, 1977). Decerebrate animals, for example, can right themselves and locomote; eat and drink on encountering appropriate goal objects; groom; and display aggressive, defensive, and escape behaviors to noxious stimuli (see Adams, 1979; Berntson & Micco, 1976; Norman et al., 1977).

Considerable functional capacity is also apparent in tragic cases of human decerebration (anencephaly and

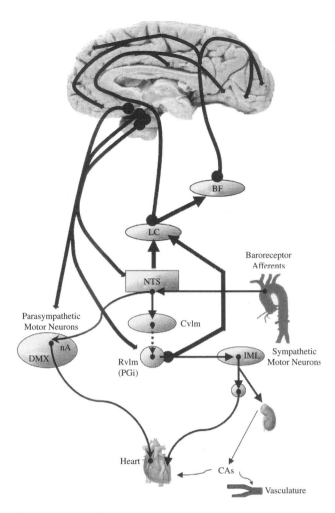

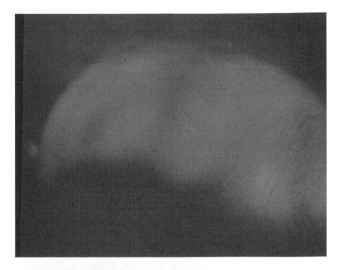

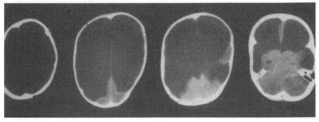

Figure 32.3 (**Figure C. 33** in color section) Expansion of the baroreflex circuit of Figure 32.2 to illustrate the ascending and descending pathways to and from rostral neural areas such as the medial prefrontal cortex, hypothalamus, and amygdala.

Note: Ascending systems include routes from the rostral ventrolateral medulla (Rvlm) and the nucleus of the tractus solitarius (NTS) to the locus coeruleus (LC) noradrenergic system and indirectly to the basal forebrain (BF) cortical cholinergic system. CAs = Catecholamines; Cvlm = Caudal ventrolateral medulla; DMX = Dorsal motor nucleus of the vagus; IML = Intermediolateral cell column of the spinal cord; nA = Nucleus ambiguus; PGi = Paragigantocullar nucleus (partially coextensive with Rvlm).

hydranencephaly), generally resulting from a failure of cell migration early in neurodevelopment. Although these infants generally do not survive for more than a few weeks after birth, they show a relatively intact array of infantile reflexes, including flexor and extensor reflexes, stepping reflexes, and a wide range of brain stem reflexes including tonic neck reflexes and suckling reflexes, among others.

Figure 32.4 illustrates transillumination of the scalp and a representative CAT scan from a decerebrate human infant. Despite the virtual lack of any neural tissue above the diencephalon, this infant showed basic manifestations of evaluative processing. In addition to displaying typical pain-withdrawal reflexes, she would fuss and cry in

Figure 32.4 Neurological status of a decerebrate infant.

Note: **Top:** Results of transillumination of the head (viewed posteriorly—tip of left ear on leftward side). The dark region toward the base of the head is the cerebellum; note that there is little to occlude the light above that level. **Bottom:** Results of CAT scan at four horizontal planes of the head (front of the head is up) from dorsal (left) to ventral (right). Light areas indicate more radiodense areas such as bone and neural tissue, dark regions more radiolucent areas. Note the clear appearance of the skull but the absence of brain tissue on the left. In the two middle planes, the cerebellum is apparent posteriorly (bottom of the cranial vault). In the lowest plane (right), diencephalic and other brain stem tissue is present.

response to noxious stimuli and could be quieted and comforted with contact and rocking. This infant also showed typical appetitive responses and would suckle and ingest milk sufficient to maintain body weight.

It is worth noting that brain stem neurobehavioral substrates do not entail a mere assemblage of rigidly regulated and tightly organized reflex networks because both decerebrate animals (Mauk & Thompson, 1987; Norman et al., 1977) and humans (Berntson et al., 1983; Tuber et al., 1980) display neural plasticity and associative learning.

Intake/Rejection Responses and Taste Hedonics

Among the more thoroughly studied brain stem evaluative processes are those supporting approach/avoidance action dispositions related to taste hedonics. Similar to the organization of the spinal cord, the neuroarchitectures underlying approach vs. avoidance dispositions appear to be relatively independent and under separate control in brain stem circuitry (Berntson et al., 1993; Berridge & Grill,

1984; Steiner, Glaser, Hawilo, & Berridge, 2001). Taste hedonics and associated intake/rejection responses offer a prime example of brain stem evaluative systems. Orofacial displays to taste, represented by stereotyped, reflex-like negative rejection/ejection responses to aversive stimuli (gaping, tongue protrusion) and positive intake responses (smiling, licking, swallowing) are well conserved in mammals. Such responses can be seen early in development and are readily apparent in decerebrate organisms. The positive and negative responses to gustatory stimuli mirror the evaluative reflexes of the spinal cord in that they reflect opposing patterns of approach/avoidance dispositions. Similar to spinal reflexes, the behavioral output of these systems cannot be interpreted as lying along a single bipolar continuum extending from approach (highly positive) to avoidance (highly negative). Although this depiction can be useful, it belies the underlying complexity of hedonic processes because experimental evidence suggests that gustatory approach/withdrawal systems are partially independent and do not converge on a single hedonic integrator (Berridge & Grill, 1984).

Just as a person can tighten extensor and flexor muscles simultaneously, intake and rejection responses are not incompatible and can become coactive. For example, although the probability of rejection responses to a glucose solution increases following the addition of a bitter compound, this can occur without a reciprocal reduction in probability of intake responses. Similarly, increasing both bitter and sweet concurrently leads to increases in both intake and rejection responses. Thus, it is clear that taste preference, as measured by behavioral consumption and represented on a bipolar scale, does not always represent the underlying bivariate hedonic state. This does not rule out interaction between the approach/avoidance responses, but suggests that the mixing positive and negative valences of hedonic stimuli do not simply yield a null average of the two or a state of indifference (Berridge & Grill, 1984).

Gustatory approach/avoidance responses are represented by distinct positive and negative hedonic dimensions that conform to the positivity offset and negativity bias as described previously. Gustatory evaluative processes mediated by brain stem systems are more complex than their behavioral output (total intake continuum), and knowledge of this fact facilitates a more accurate description of evaluative processes based on the underlying bivariate substrates.

Levels of Function: Higher-Level Rerepresentations

As we move to the highest levels of the neuraxis, the rerepresentation and elaboration of evaluative processes becomes ever more apparent, and neuron-organizational complexity expands dramatically. The brain stem and spinal cord are highly sensitive to aversive and hedonic stimuli and can yield appropriate behavioral responses, but this so-called reptilian brain (MacLean, 1985) lacks much of the behavioral flexibility and adaptability characteristic of intact organisms. Although decerebrates may ingest palatable foods, they do not display typical goal-seeking behavior in the absence of a food stimulus but rather are prisoners of the momentary stimulus or environmental context (see Berntson et al., 1993; Berntson & Micco, 1976). Decerebrates lack the flexibility and variety of behavior seen in intact animals because of the devolution of the nervous system to its more primitive representations. It is not until the development of the paleomammalian brain (limbic system and archicortex) and the neomammalian brain (neocortex) that we see the full evolution and elaboration of evaluative processes (MacLean, 1985). It is with the development of rostral brain structures that we begin to see the emergence of goal-directed behaviors that reflect anticipatory processes and expectancies that liberate the organism from the immediate exigencies of this stimulus or that.

In view of the expanding complexity of rostral evaluative substrates, it seems unlikely that these networks would simplify from the basic bivariate evaluative structure of lower substrates to become a single bipolar hedonic integrator. In contrast, with the expanding cognitive and computational complexity of evaluative processes at higher neuraxial levels, there is a parallel expansion of the complexity of the underlying mediating neural systems. Higher evaluative processes entail planning, strategizing, and engaging in anticipatory processes that can require access to associative networks, attentional and computational resources, and so on. Moreover, whereas lower evaluative substrates may entail simple approach/withdrawal dispositions, higher motivational processes become further differentiated and nuanced. Berridge (1996) characterized the "liking" aspects of motivation as those that entail the hedonic and response-eliciting properties of a stimulus or motivational context. These are apparent in the orofacial intake/ingestive responses to positive hedonic tastes as described previously for the decerebrate organism. The decerebrate, however, largely lacks what Berridge termed the *wanting* aspects of motivation, which entail an attentional focus on, and goal-seeking behaviors directed toward, a desired stimulus, state, or context. This latter aspect of evaluative processes is heavily dependent on the increased computational capacity of higher levels of the neuraxis and is mediated by more elaborate neural circuitry.

It should not be surprising that the neuroarchitecture of higher evaluative processes entails more complex and distributed networks that are not as readily dichotomized into positive and negative substrates as is the case with lower level representations. Indeed, many computational, attentional, and memorial processes may be commonly deployed for positive and/or negative evaluative processing. Moreover, the further development and elaboration of evaluative systems, such as that between "liking" and "wanting," may entail added neuroanatomical complexity. Historically, the nucleus accumbens (nACC) has been depicted as a neural integrator of reward and positive hedonic states (Berridge & Grill, 1984; Hoebel, Rada, Mark, & Pothos, 1999; Koob, 1992). In the 1940s, Robert Heath, working on psychiatric patients with indwelling electrical brain stimulators, showed that patients would report pleasurable states and would self-administer stimulation to various brain regions, especially areas in and around the nACC (Heath, 1972). More recently, electrical stimulation of the nACC has been reported to elicit a smile associated with euphoric responses (Okun et al., 2004). It is now clear that nearly all rewarding stimuli or positive hedonic states are associated with dopamine release in the nACC, and lesions or blockage of dopamine receptors in the nACC reduces rewards and positive hedonics (Hoebel et al., 1999; Robinson & Berridge, 2003; Wise, 2006; see also Chapter 40). In this regard, the nACC contrasts with the amygdala, which has generally been implicated in fear conditioning, negative affect, and aversive states (see Chapter 39), a topic to which we return.

Although these findings are consistent with a differentiation of positive and negative neural substrates at higher levels of the neuraxis, similar to that seen at lower levels, there are added complexities in higher substrates. The nACC, in fact, may not be a simple monolithic reward integrator. Recent work has suggested important phenomenological and computational distinctions within the nACC. For example, the liking (positive hedonic effect, reward) and wanting (incentive salience, goal striving) aspects of hedonic states are mediated by distinct anatomical regions of the nACC (Berridge, 1996; Pecina & Berridge, 2005). Moreover, negative stimuli may also activate the nACC, and other distinct areas may be involved in suppression of negative evaluative processing (Pecina & Berridge, 2005). These complexities caution against the overly simplistic ascription of discrete neural loci to the mediation of complex neuropsychological phenomena. Nevertheless, there remain clear differentiations between higher neural substrates mediating positive and negative evaluative processes.

A hemispheric lateralization of positive and negative evaluative processes has been reported, with the right hemisphere implicated more in negative affective processing or avoidance dispositions and the left hemisphere involved more in positive affect or approach dispositions (Cacioppo & Gardner, 1999; Davidson, 1990; Harmon-Jones, Vaughn,

Mohr, Sigelman, & Harmon-Jones, 2004). For example, positive affective stimuli induce greater activation in the left hemisphere (Canli, Desmond, Zhao, Glover, & Gabrieli, 1998; Davidson, 1998, 2004; Lee et al., 2004; Nitschke, Sarinopoulos, Mackiewicz, Schaefer, & Davidson, 2006; Pizzagalli, Sherwood, Henriques, & Davidson, 2005), and patients with damage to the left hemisphere have a higher probability of experiencing depression and overall negative affect (Davidson, 1998). Similarly, facial expression and reaction time data suggest a left hemisphere predominance for positive affect and a greater right hemisphere representation for negative affect (Davidson, Shackman, & Maxwell, 2004; Root, Wong, & Kinsbourne, 2006). The relative right hemispheric bias for withdrawal/avoidance reactions may be related to the right lateralization of visceral/nociceptive afferent projections (Craig, 2005) and is consistent with the finding that left insula stimulation gives rise to parasympathetic cardiac activation whereas right insula stimulation induces sympathetic activation (Oppenheimer, 1993, 2006).

Furthermore, within-hemisphere differentiation is also apparent in cortical representations. Pleasantness rating of odors, for example, was related to the degree of medial orbitofrontal activation as measured by fMRI, whereas unpleasantness was more related to activation of the dorsal anterior cingulate (Grabenhorst, Rolls, Margot, da Silva, & Velazco, 2007). Similarly, deciding on the lesser of two punishments yielded greater activation in the dorsal anterior cingulate, whereas deciding between the larger of two rewards yielded greater activation in the ventromedial prefrontal cortex (Blair et al., 2006).

The amygdala has been especially implicated in fear and negative affect since the classic studies of Walter Rudolf Hess (1954) on brain stimulation in the waking animal. The amygdala appears to be a critical nodal point in subcortical circuits that allow for rapid detection and response to threat and for the learning of fear-related cues (LeDoux, 1996; Öhman & Mineka, 2001). These circuits allow for more elaborate processing of threat-related cues than do lower-level brain stem substrates but remain highly efficient because they can operate without the need for extensive cortical processing (Larson et al., 2006; LeDoux, 1996; Öhman & Mineka, 2001; Tooby & Cosmides, 1990). Although the amygdala may also participate in classical thalamo-cortical-limbic circuits, direct thalamo-amygdala pathways are a sufficient substrate for fear reactions and simple fear conditioning, providing for a "quick and dirty transmission route" (LeDoux, 2000). The thalamo-amygdala subcortical circuit may support simple fear conditioning and fear reactions in the absence of awareness ("blindsight") following visual cortical injuries (see De Gelder, Vroomen, Pourtois, & Weiskrantz, 1999; Pegna,

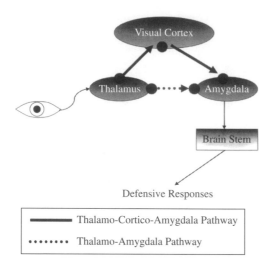

Figure 32.5 Schematic representation of the classical thalamo-cortical visual pathway, where afferent information is conveyed to the cortex via the relay nucleus of the thalamus (lateral geniculate nucleus).

Note: Also illustrated is an alternative thalamo-amygdala route that can bypass the cortex and mediate rapid fear and defensive responses to certain classes of aversive stimuli (see LeDoux, 2003).

Khateb, Lazeyras, & Seghier, 2005; Weiskrantz, 1986). In contrast, relational learning (e.g., contextual conditioning) and the processing of more complex threat-related cues may be more dependent on higher-level cortical processing (Berntson, Sarter, & Cacioppo, 1998; see also Chapter 39). Recent research supports this heterarchical organization showing that auditory fear conditioning induces plasticity in amygdala neurons prior to apparent changes in cortical areas, suggesting that early plasticity in amygdala neurons results from direct thalamo-amygdala projections (Öhman & Mineka, 2001; Quirk, Armony, & LeDoux, 1997; Quirk, Repa, & LeDoux, 1995; see Figure 32.5).

The more direct, efficient, but relatively limited direct thalamo-amygdala and the more elaborate, integrative, and flexible thalamo-cortical-amygdala circuits represent distinct heterarchical levels of processing.

Fear versus Anxiety

Fear is a reaction to an explicit threatening stimulus, with escape or avoidance the outcome of increased cue proximity (see Chapter 49). *Anxiety* is a more general state of distress, typically longer lasting, prompted by less explicit or more generalized cues, and involving physiological arousal but often without organized functional behavior (Berntson et al., 1998; Lang, Davis, & Ohman, 2000).

The amygdala appears to be especially critical for simple fear conditioning and fear potentiation of startle (LeDoux, 2003; Phelps & LeDoux, 2005; Walker, Toufexis, & Davis, 2003). Inactivation of the lateral nucleus of the

amygdala, for example, blocks the conditioned fear response in rats and attenuates fear-potentiated startle (LeDoux, 2003; Walker et al., 2003). Conversely, although the amygdala may play a role in anxiety-like responses, inactivation of the central nucleus of the amygdala does not attenuate anxiety-like behavior in mice (Walker & Davis, 1997). Rather, the bed nucleus of the stria terminalis and the medial prefrontal cortex may be more specifically involved in anxiety-like reactions to longer-lasting, more generalized threat cues. Lesions of the bed nucleus of the stria terminalis, for example, disrupt light-induced startle potentiation (which has been suggested to be a model for anxiety) but largely spare simple, conditioned fear-potentiated startle (Walker & Davis, 1997; Walker et al., 2003). Furthermore, lesions of the basal forebrain cortical cholinergic pathway or its termination in the medial prefrontal cortex disrupt anxiety-like responses but spare simple fear conditioning (Berntson et al., 1998; Hart, Sarter, & Berntson, 1999). Whereas cortical systems may not be necessary in explicit fear responses, they appear to be critical for the processing of more complex stimuli and for contextual fear conditioning (Knox & Berntson, 2006; LeDoux, 2000; Phillips & LeDoux, 1992; Stowell, Berntson, & Sarter, 2000).

Mental imagery or anticipation of aversive or anxiogenic contexts induces activation in the bed nucleus of the stria terminalis as well as in cortical areas, including the medial prefrontal cortex and the anterior cingulate cortex (Kosslyn et al., 1996; Shin et al., 2004; Straube, Mentzel, & Miltner, 2007). Gray and McNaughton (2000) incorporated much of this information into a two-dimensional defense system model that makes clear anatomical, behavioral, and functional distinctions between fear and anxiety. The first dimension is a qualitative distinction between systems controlling defensive avoidance (fear) and defensive approach (anxiety). The two states often display opposite characteristics—fear produces speed toward or away from a stimulus whereas anxiety produces slowness, caution, and deliberation (see also Chapter 36). The second dimension is based on functional and organizational properties inherent to the neuroarchitectural substrates involved in the two qualitative distinctions. These distinctions are characterized in a hierarchical manner whereby substantial overlap between the two systems exists at caudal levels (periaqueductal gray and medial hypothalamus). As one moves rostrally, some differentiation may emerge (e.g., anterior cingulate for defensive avoidance and posterior cingulate for defensive approach), but the more significant perspective concerns the level of requisite processing (see Chapter 36). This is consistent with the present heterarchical model.

The multiple heterarchical levels represent at least partially distinct processing substrates and may function in partial independence from other levels (Berntson et al., 1998). This is an issue to which we return (see "Multilevel Organization and Its Conflicts"). Generally, however, different levels are in constant reciprocal communication with one another and are capable of shifting from approach to avoidance defensive strategies at a moment's notice and displaying coactivity of substrates (Gray & McNaughton, 2000). The multiplicity in heterarchical levels may preclude simple isomorphic mappings between affect in the psychological domain and neural substrates in the biological domain (Berntson, 2006). The complexity in brain–behavior mapping in affective processes is illustrated by recent findings on the role of the amygdala.

The Amygdala

The amygdala is one of the most well-studied neural structures. It has been the subject of neuroscientific as well as psychological research for decades and is central to many theories of affect and evaluative processing. In general accord with animal studies, imaging studies in humans have reported amygdala activation during emotion, especially with negative emotions (Critchley et al., 2005; Irwin et al., 1996; Sabatinelli, Bradley, Fitzsimmons, & Lang, 2005; Zald & Pardo, 1997), and patients with amygdala damage show attenuated negative affect (Tranel, Gullickson, Koch, & Adolphs, 2006) and deficits in emotional memory (Buchanan, Tranel, & Adolphs, 2006; LaBar & Cabeza, 2006; Phelps, 2006; Phelps & LeDoux, 2005). Although the amygdala has been implicated in a range of processes extending from fear conditioning to emotional memory to aversive reactions, the precise role of this structure has not been fully clarified.

This issue was pursued in a recent study of patients with amygdala damage (Berntson, Berchara, Damasio, Tranel, & Cacioppo, 2007). Participants rated a set of images from the International Affective Picture System (Lang, Bradley, & Cuthbert, 1999) on perceived valence (extending from highly positive to highly negative picture content) and on affective intensity (i.e., how aroused the images made them feel). As illustrated in Figure 32.6, patients with damage to the amygdala were comparable on their ratings of valence of the picture content to persons in a norm group and to control patients with lesions that spared the amygdala. Patients were quite capable of recognizing and appropriately labeling positive and negative aspects of the stimuli. When compared to other groups, however, amygdala lesion patients significantly differed on their ratings of emotional arousal or intensity (see Figure 32.6). Control patients and the norm group showed the expected increases in arousal ratings as the images approached either positive or negative extremes. Amygdala patients also displayed an increase in arousal to the more positive images. They did not, however, show a parallel arousal gradient to negative stimuli. Although the amygdala patients clearly recognized and labeled the negative images, they did not display the expected affective response.

These findings are in agreement with a previously reported double dissociation between cognitive and affective processes in brain-damaged patients (Bechara et al., 1995). Consistent with the animal literature, a patient with amygdala damage failed to develop a typical conditioned autonomic response to a conditioned stimulus that was paired with a loud noise, despite the fact that this patient acquired declarative knowledge about the relation between the conditioned stimulus and the noise. This parallels the dissociation between the cognitive and arousal dimensions in the affective picture task of the Berntson et al. (2007) study. In contrast, a patient with damage to the hippocampus (sparing the amygdala) developed a conditioned autonomic response to the conditioned stimulus but could not cognitively describe the experimental contingencies (Bechara et al., 1995).

These dissociations between cognitive knowledge and affective/autonomic responses reflect the multiple levels at which evaluative processing can occur. They also document the further differentiation between dimensions of evaluative processing, even within a given valence, at higher neural levels. In view of this elaboration and differentiation, it is highly unlikely the basic delineation between positive/approach and negative/withdrawal dispositions would devolve into a single affective continuum. Although there may be a perceived continuum between positive and negative affect, this perception may not accurately reflect the distinct neural substrates for these affective dimensions.

In a recent fMRI study, Grabenhorst et al. (2007) reported that pleasant (jasmine) and unpleasant (indole) odors resulted in similar activations in primary olfactory areas (pyriform cortex), with these activations being correlated with odor intensity. The pleasant and unpleasant odors, however, differentially activated other distinct brain regions (e.g., medial orbitofrontal cortex and dorsal anterior cingulate cortex, respectively). Although a mixture of the two odors was rated as pleasant, it continued to show distinct activations in both the medial orbitofrontal cortex (where activations were correlated with pleasantness) and the anterior cingulate (where activations were correlated with unpleasantness). The authors concluded, "Mixtures that are found pleasant can have components that are separately pleasant and unpleasant, and the brain can separately and simultaneously represent the positive and negative hedonic value." (p. 13532).

Differential activation of positive and/or negative evaluative substrates may guide behavior even in the absence

(A) Amygdala Lesion

(B) Contrast Lesion

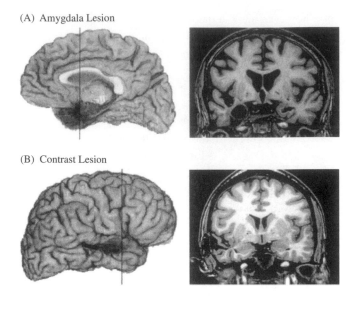

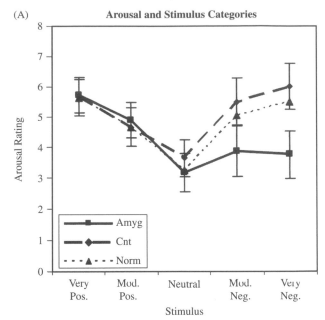
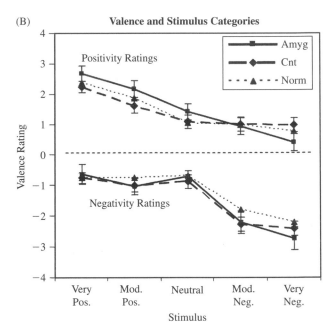

Figure 32.6   **A**: Lesions and arousal and valence ratings in the evaluative picture-rating study; **B**: Mean (*SEM*) arousal (I) and valence (II) ratings across stimulus categories for patients with amygdala lesions compared with the clinical contrast group and normative control data.

Note: (A) (I) Illustrative bilateral lesion of the amygdala secondary to herpes simplex encephalitis. (II) Example of one of the smaller lesions in the lesion contrast group that spared the amygdala. All groups effectively discriminated the stimulus categories and applied valance ratings accordingly. (B) All groups also displayed comparable arousal functions to positive stimuli, but the amygdala group showed diminished arousal selectively to the negative stimuli. Neg = Negative; Pos = Positive. From "Amygdala Contribution to Selective Dimensions of Emotion," by G. G. Berntson, A. Bechara, H. Damasio, D. Tranel, and J. T. Cacioppo, 2007, *Social Cognitive and Affective Neuroscience, 2,* pp. 123–129, pp. 3 & 5. Reprinted with permission.

of awareness. This is consistent with a report that a patient with damage to the primary gustatory cortex (and other areas) was unable to recognize or even distinguish sweet (positive) from saline (aversive) solutions and would drink either avidly. When given a choice between the two, however, this patient would consistently choose the sweet solution, although he could not explain why (Adolphs, Tranel, Koenigs, & Damasio, 2005). In this case, higher-level substrates for cognitive recognition and labeling were disrupted, but lower heterarchical systems were able to guide behavioral choice in the absence of cognitive awareness.

MULTILEVEL ORGANIZATIONS AND THEIR CONFLICTS

Evaluative processes evidence a cardinal feature of bivalence in their functional architecture and are represented at multiple levels of the neuraxis. Although these bivalent substrates may interact, they retain at least some degree of independence and separability. Substrates at differing levels of the neuraxis also interact in a heterarchical fashion, but they, too, entail at least partially distinct organizations with differential processing capacities and differential access to sensory, perceptual, memorial, and cognitive information. The lowest heterarchical levels provide for rapid, albeit rather inflexible, information processing and adaptive reflexive reactions. Higher levels are capable of broader integration of information, expanded neural computations, and a richer and more flexible array of actions and outputs. An important question concerns the determinants of the level or levels of processing that are deployed in a given situation. In their *elaboration likelihood model,* Cacioppo and Petty (1984; Petty, Cacioppo, Strathman, & Priester, 2005) distinguish between what they term *central* and *peripheral routes* to persuasion and attitude dispositions. The central route is characterized by higher-level cognitive deliberation, whereas the peripheral route is less processing dependent and entails appeal to authority, reliance on preexisting biases or prejudices, and so on. In this model, important determinants of which route will predominate are the availability information as well as cognitive resources and motivation for deliberative consideration that are necessary to support the central, as opposed to the peripheral, processing route.

Processing may also occur at multiple levels, with the output or action reflecting some aggregate manifestation or the predominance of one or another level. As discussed previously, higher neural systems can inhibit or override lower-level substrates, but more typically, complex interactions and recurrent processing may occur across levels. In their *iterative processing model,* Cunningham and Zelazo (2007) propose recurrent, reciprocal communications across processing levels. In this scheme, lower level substrates may provide affectively laden information regarding the valance and the arousal dimensions of a particular stimulus or context to higher evaluative processing substrates, which in turn can then modulate lower-level processing systems.

In some cases, the bivalent organization and multiple levels in evaluative processing substrates may lead to conflicts. The coexistence of both positive and negative attributes to an object or outcome does not necessarily result in a neutral dispositional state, as might be implied by a bipolar evaluative model. Ambivalence is not the simple equivalent of indifference. Ambivalence may reflect the coactivation of both positive and negative evaluations.

In his classic studies on conflict, Neal Miller (1959, 1961) used behavioral measures (e.g., running speed or the strength of pull on a tether to approach a reward or avoid a noxious stimulus) to assess motivational dispositions in rats. A typical gradient of an approach disposition to a food reward is illustrated in Figure 32.7 as a function of the proximity of the animal to the goal box. Similarly

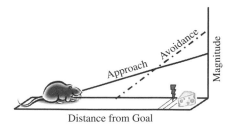

Figure 32.7 Miller's (1959, 1961) approach/avoidance conflict.
Note: Approach (solid line) and avoidance (dashed line) gradients as a function of distance from the goal. Goal items include food (positive incentive) and shock (negative incentive). The avoidance gradient has a steeper slope and predominates as the goal box is approached (negativity bias), whereas at more remote loci, the approach gradient is higher than the avoidance gradient (positivity offset). The intersection of the gradients represents the maximal conflict point, where approach and avoidance dispositions are equivalent.

illustrated is the avoidance disposition away from a shock grid at the goal box, as measured independently. Miller generally observed that the slope of the avoidance gradient tended to be steeper than that of the approach gradient, so that at a distance from the goal, the approach disposition was greater than the avoidance disposition, and vice versa at proximate locations. The two motivational dispositions (approach and avoidance) were then invoked simultaneously, by the presence of both the food and the shock grid. This introduced what Miller termed an *approach/avoidance conflict.* The animal would approach the goal box if placed remotely in the apparatus, but as it approached the goal, the relative strength of the avoidance disposition increased (see Figure 32.7) and the approach disposition was overcome by avoidance. At that point, the animal was in what Miller referred to as a *stable* conflict. Any further approach would lead to an increment in avoidance, and any movement away would lead to a relative predominance of approach. Indeed, animals showed agitation and vacillation at an intermediate distance from the goal, and that point could be predicted by the relative magnitudes of the approach and avoidance gradients as measured independently.

For Miller's rats, the aggregate effect of a positive motivation and a concurrent negative disposition was not evaluative neutrality and sanguinity—it was ambivalence, agitation, and vacillation.

Conceptually similar findings have emerged from studies on humans (Larsen, McGraw, Mellers, & Cacioppo, 2004). Good outcomes that could have been better (i.e., disappointing wins) and bad outcomes that could have been worse (i.e., relieving losses) are rated by participants toward the middle or neutral point of bipolar emotion scales (i.e., ratings along a positive to negative continuum). This might suggest that such outcomes are associated with the absence of affect or indifference. If participants are presented with continuous unipolar measures of positive and negative affect, however, a very different picture emerges. When rating positive and negative separately, participants indicate the coactivation of both positive and negative affect. The participants are not indifferent—they are ambivalent (from the Latin, "both valences or vigors").

There is a conceptual parallel in this study with Miller's (1959, 1961) rats. Although behavioral or measurement constraints may make it appear that positive and negative evaluative dispositions lie on a continuum, these appearances may belie the underlying bivalence of the neurobehavioral substrates. In the Miller study, physical constraints precluded the concurrent motor expressions of approach and avoidance. A rat cannot simultaneously approach and avoid the same place at the same time, although it may serially express the underlying bivalent affect states in its vacillation around the equilibrium point of two opposing evaluative dispositions. In the Larsen, McGraw, Mellers, & Cacioppo (2004) study, behavioral constraints were not imposed because the two (positive and negative) unipolar affect ratings were done sequentially. With a bipolar rating scale, however, a constraint is imposed by the measurement instrument, which is grounded on a spurious bipolar theory about the underlying evaluative structure.

Because of the inherent complexity in higher levels of evaluative processes, as well as physical and measurement constraints, basic positive (generally associated with approach) and negative (generally associated with avoidance) evaluative systems may not always be readily discernable in behavior. Although affective states may at times appear to lie along a continuum from positive to negative, the fundamental underlying substrates evidence a bivalent organization, even at the highest levels of the neuraxis.

The cortical system represents the ultimate level of neuronal complexity and processing capacity. The mammalian neocortical system includes networks responsible for the most complex of sensory and perceptual processes, associative learning, memory, attentional focus, contextual awareness, strategizing, and outcome monitoring. In primates, the expanded cortex allows for even more elaborate processing. The additional computational power of primate neocortical structures allows for intricate social interactions that are dependent on the ability to anticipate future outcomes, run cognitive simulations, and manage social alliances. Although such complex neuropsychological phenomena would not be possible without the highest-level brain systems, these functions have more primitive representations at lower levels of the neuraxis and, in many cases, are derivative of the lower substrates.

EVALUATIVE SPACE AND THE NEUROARCHITECTURE OF EVALUATIVE PROCESSES

Wundt (1896) and Thurstone (1931) were early champions of the bipolar model of affect, in which the momentary affective states could be characterized as lying along a bipolar continuum extending from positive to negative. This view has also been incorporated into contemporary models of emotion, including the circumplex model of Russell and others (Russell, 1980, 1983; see also Posner et al., 2005). Cacioppo and Berntson have proposed an alternative, bivariate model of affect whereby the positive and negative dimensions are at least partially independent in both their conceptual and neurological bases (Cacioppo & Berntson, 1994; Cacioppo, Gardner, & Berntson, 1997; Cacioppo et al., 2004). As illustrated in Figure 32.8, this *evaluative space model* subsumes the bipolar model as the reciprocal diagonal and also offers a more comprehensive representative of affective states. Whereas bipolar models are unable to represent states of ambivalence, the evaluative space model readily accounts for such states as a manifestation of coactivation of both positive and negative affect. It is also in accord with the finding that positive and negative emotions are not always correlated (Larsen et al., 2004).

The evaluative space model illustrates how neuroevolutionary and neurobehavioral frameworks can guide and constrain theories and models of higher neuropsychological functioning. Moreover, behavioral findings and features may inform neurobehavioral theories as well, in a reciprocal fashion. The fact that neuronal substrates of approach and avoidance are at least partially independent allows for evolutionary pressures to sculpt these circuits independently.

Because the driving force in evolution is the ability to pass on genetic information, avoiding noxious or potentially lethal stimuli may assume greater adaptive importance, especially at close proximities, than approaching positive or rewarding stimuli. The latter can always be pursued subsequently if the organism lives to see another day. This may be the evolutionary basis for the negativity bias in evaluative processing, as is apparent in lower reflex substrates discussed previously. It is also apparent from the steeper slope of the avoidance gradient in Neal Miller's (1959, 1961) behavioral studies of conflict. Additional research utilizing event-related potentials has demonstrated a similar negativity bias in early stages of evaluative processing in humans (Cacioppo et al., 2004).

Miller also observed what has been termed a *positivity offset* in his conflict paradigm. This refers to the fact that the approach gradient often surpasses the avoidance gradient as the distance to the goal increases beyond the equilibrium point (see Figure 32.9). Both the positivity offset and

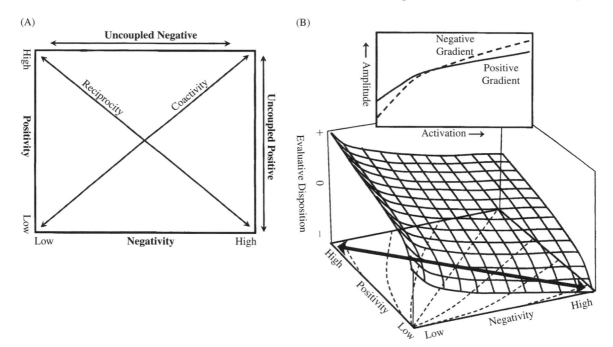

Figure 32.8   Bivariate evaluative space. **A:** The bivariate evaluative plane. **B:** A three-dimensional depiction of evaluative space, where the surface overlying the bivariate plane represents the net approach/avoidance disposition for any location on that plane.

Note: (A) The *y* axis represents the level of activation of positive evaluative processes (Positivity), and the *x* axis represents the level of activation of the negative evaluative process (Negativity). The reciprocity diagonal represents the classical bipolar model of valence that extends from high positivity (upper left) to high negativity (lower right) along a single evaluative continuum. The coactivity diagonal represents an alternative mode where both evaluative dimensions (conflict, ambivalence) are coactivated.

The arrows outside of the box represent uncoupled changes in positive or negative evaluative processing. This evaluative plane provides a more comprehensive model of evaluative processes that subsumes the bipolar model as one reciprocal. (B) The insert on this figure illustrates activation functions along the positivity and negativity axes. Differences in the slopes and intercepts of these functions depict the positivity offset (higher intercept) and negativity bias (higher slope). From "Relationship between Attitudes and Evaluative Space: A Critical Review, with Emphasis on the Separability of Positive and Negative Substrates," by J. T. Cacioppo and G. G. Berntson, 1994, *Psychological Bulletin, 115,* p. 412. Adapted with permission.

negativity bias are apparent in numerous behavioral contexts (see Ito & Cacioppo, 2005, for a review and empirical studies). As depicted in Figure 32.8, the negativity bias and the positivity offset are reflected in the differential slopes of the positivity and negativity functions in the evaluative space model. The overlying surface of Figure 32.8 represents the net action dispositions on both the positivity and negativity continua. Movement along the positivity axis represents the positive or approach gradient, movement along the negativity axis represents the negative or avoidance gradient, and the surface in between these extremes represents varying degrees of ambivalence. The evaluative space model in Figure 32.8 is useful in describing and explaining overall action dispositions. It should be noted, however, that this characterization could be applied to distinct levels within the evaluative heterarchy, with the overall action disposition representing a composite or aggregate of the multiple processing levels. This aggregate function, therefore, may well be dynamic, as differing levels of processing may come into play depending on the situation or context.

MULTILEVEL INTERACTIONS: EXAMPLES FROM THE AUTONOMIC NERVOUS SYSTEM

The evaluative space model in Figure 32.8 may provide a broader framework for conceptualizing other neurobiological processes that have a fundamental bivariate structure. One example is the autonomic nervous system (ANS) and its neurobehavioral control (Berntson et al., 1998). Mirroring the bipolar conceptualizations of evaluative processes, historical depictions of the sympathetic and parasympathetic branches of the ANS have been of a reciprocally regulated system, with increases in activity of one branch associated with decreases in the other (Berntson, Cacioppo, & Quigley, 1991). This bipolar conceptualization arose largely out of research on basic autonomic reflexes that, like the flexor–extensor circuits, are rather rigid and lack the range and flexibility of control characteristic of more rostral systems. The efferent arm of the baroreceptor heart rate reflex, for example, entails a notable reciprocal regulation of the sympathetic and parasympathetic branches of the ANS. Baroreceptor afferents

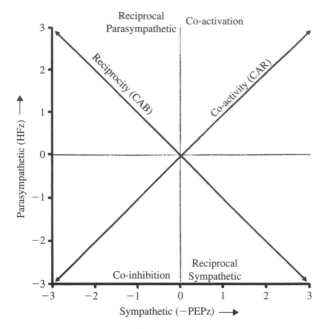

Figure 32.9 Distribution of normalized parasympathetic cardiac control (as indexed by HF [HFz]) and sympathetic cardiac control (as indexed by PEP [-PEPz]) scores across the CHASRS population, and their relation to the derived CAR and CAB metrics.

Note: The overall distribution deviates considerably from the reciprocal diagonal representing a bipolar model. Individuals in the reciprocal parasympathetic quadrant would have relatively high CAB scores, whereas those in the reciprocal sympathetic quadrant would have relatively low CAB scores. An additional dimension is reflected along the coactivity diagonal. Individuals in the coactivation quadrant would have relatively high CAR scores, whereas those in the co-inhibition quadrant would have relatively low CAR scores. CAB = Cardiac autonomic balance; CAR = Cardiac autonomic regulatory capacity; CHASRS = Chicago Health and Social Relations Study; HF = High-frequency heart rate variability; PEP = Preejection period. From "Cardiac Autonomic Balance versus Cardiac Regulatory Capacity," by G. G. Berntson, G. J. Norman, L. C. Hawkley, and J. T. Cacioppo, 2008, *Psychophysiology, 45,* p. 646. Reprinted with permission.

increase their rate of firing in response to mechanical distortion associated with an increase in blood pressure, and this afferent signal is conveyed to the nucleus tractus solitarius in the medulla, which is the primary visceral receiving area of the brain. The nucleus tractus solitarius subsequently issues direct and indirect excitatory projections to vagal motor neurons in the nucleus ambiguous and dorsal motor nucleus, leading to a reflexive increase in parasympathetic outflow. This yields a decrease in heart rate and a reduction in cardiac output, which tends to normalize or oppose the pressor perturbation. Projections from the nucleus tractus solitarius also indirectly suppress sympathetic outflow via inhibition of the sympathoexcitatory neurons in the rostral ventrolateral medulla. This sympathetic withdrawal acts to further slow the beat of the heart as well as to decrease myocardial contractility. Thus, the reciprocal actions of the individual branches of the ANS synergistically contribute to the homeostatic regulation of blood pressure.

The baroreceptor heart rate reflex represents a prototypic, reciprocally regulated system, having a bipolar action disposition extending from sympathetic to parasympathetic dominance. Although descriptive of some basic autonomic reflexive circuits, this characterization belies the true complexity of autonomic control of cardiovascular function.

Higher-level brain structures are capable of modulating ANS activity via direct projections from forebrain structures such as the cingulate cortex (Critchley et al., 2005), amygdala (LeDoux, Iwata, Cicchetti, & Reis, 1988), and insular cortex (Oppenheimer, 1993) to autonomic brain stem nuclei (see also Berntson et al., 1998). Stimulation and lesion studies of rostral structures have shown that higher systems can facilitate, inhibit, or even bypass basic brain stem autonomic reflexes and thereby modulate autonomic outflow directly (Sévoz-Couche, Comet, Hamon, & Laguzzi, 2003). It is not likely a coincidence that many of these same brain structures may be the substrates for higher-level functions, including evaluative processes. These descending pathways are the conduit by which psychological stressors can yield anti-homeostatic effects on the ANS, including concurrent increases in blood pressure and heart rate (in opposition to baroreflex control).

Direct stimulation of the hypothalamus, for example, can invoke each of the basic modes (see Figure 32.9) of reciprocal, coactive, or independent changes in the activity of the autonomic branches (Koizumi & Kollai, 1981; Shih, Chan, & Chan, 1995). The ability of higher-level systems to flexibly modulate activities in the autonomic branches has required an expansion of simple, reciprocally regulated homeostatic models. Given the research on evaluative processes, it has now also become clear that simple bipolar conceptualizations of the ANS are inadequate. Contemporary systems models recognize the basic bivariate organization of the ANS and include concepts such as heterostasis, allostasis, and allodynamic regulation that recognize the greater breadth and flexibility of autonomic control associated with rostral regulatory substrates (Berntson, Norman, Hawkley, & Cacioppo, 2008; McEwen, 2004).

Theories about both evaluative processes and autonomic control have significance for the kinds of data scientists collect and for scientists' understanding of the basic neurobiology of these processes. Bipolar theories of affect, for example, lead to the development of bipolar scales of valence that obscure the underlying bivariate nature of evaluative processes. Similarly, the reciprocal model of autonomic control biases toward particular conceptions of psychosomatic relations that may impact research and understanding of disease processes.

Concepts of a reciprocally regulated, homeostatic system have limited understanding of the ANS and lead to models of autonomic contributions to disease states as reflecting a homeostatic failure. Although there are homeostatic features to some aspects of autonomic control, the ANS is not a universally homeostatic system. The concurrent increase in blood pressure and heart rate during stress is not a homeostatic response—it is explicitly anti-homeostatic. But it may be nevertheless highly adaptive, at least in the short term, in preparing for action. The multiplicity of the modes of autonomic control (see Figure 32.9) may have important health implications.

Berntson et al. (1994) found substantial individual differences in patterns of stress reactivity, and such differences may play an important role in the susceptibility to disease (see Cacioppo et al., 1998). The understanding and measurement of these patterns, however, is heavily dependent on models of autonomic control. An index of autonomic balance could be derived from a bipolar conception of autonomic control as a scale extending from maximal sympathetic activation at one end to maximal parasympathetic activation at the other (i.e., along the reciprocal diagonal of Figure 32.9). A measure of cardiac autonomic balance (CAB) was so derived from normalized measures of high-frequency heart rate variability (which provides a relatively pure index of parasympathetic cardiac control) and preejection period (which provides a relatively pure index of sympathetic cardiac control). Although this index was not correlated with most aspects of health and disease in a population-based sample (i.e., the Chicago Health and Social Relations Study), it was predictive of diabetes mellitus and independent of demographics and health behaviors (Berntson et al., 2008).

Other conceptualizations of psychosomatic relations have emphasized not so much the state of sympathetic/parasympathetic balance but rather the overall capacity for autonomic control as indexed by autonomic flexibility and variability. This concept, together with the demonstration of the basic bivariate structure of autonomic control, suggests an alternative metric to CAB. An index of cardiac autonomic regulatory capacity (CAR) was derived as the sum of activities of the autonomic branches, again based on normalized high-frequency heart rate variability and preejection period measures. In contrast to the reciprocal diagonal represented by CAB, CAR as a metric captures the coactivity diagonal of Figure 32.9. Analysis of the Chicago Health and Social Relations Study sample revealed that CAR was a better predictor of overall health status and was a significant predictor of the prior occurrence of myocardial infarction, whereas the reciprocity metric (CAB) was not (Figure 32.10). These results suggest that distinct patterns of modes of autonomic control may be associated with distinct health dimensions. A bipolar conception of autonomic control, however, admits theory and measurement only of CAB and would occlude the relationships between CAR and health. In contrast, the broader and more comprehensive bivariate model of auto-

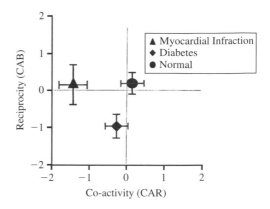

Figure 32.10 CAR and CAB in disease states.

Note: Data points illustrate means and standard errors of CAR and CAB as a function of participant group, relative to the population. Compared to other participants, those with a prior myocardial infarction (MI) had lower CAR scores, indicating lower overall cardiac regulatory capacity, but were not highly deviant on CAB. In contrast, those with diabetes showed a lower CAB score, reflective of a predominant sympathetic balance, but were not highly deviant on CAR. CAB = Cardiac autonomic balance; CAR = Cardiac autonomic regulatory capacity. From "Cardiac Autonomic Balance versus Cardiac Regulatory Capacity," by G. G. Berntson, G. J. Norman, L. C. Hawkley, and J. T. Cacioppo, 2008, *Psychophysiology, 45,* p. 649. Reprinted with permission.

nomic control subsumes CAB as one diagonal (reciprocal diagonal of Figure 32.9) and captures CAR as the coactivity diagonal. Theories impact understandings, and specious or oversimplified theories may obscure lawful relationships.

SUMMARY

With recent theoretical and technological advances, scientifically relevant conceptualizations of affective processes and their neural substrates are now possible. Utilizing strong evidence from fields such as genetics, evolutionary biology, neurobiology, and psychology provides points of convergence where interdisciplinary perspectives complement one another. The bivariate multilevel model of evaluation allows for the inclusion of new theoretical constructs and empirical evidence that can resolve competing hypotheses, generate new and testable hypotheses, and increase theoretical breadth and depth, leading to better conceptualizations of affective phenomena. Theories that assume strictly bipolar (valence) mechanisms underlying affective responses have difficulty accounting for evidence from the neurosciences that shows distinct neural substrates are coactivated in the presence of appetitive and aversive stimuli. Nor do these theories incorporate the influence of evaluative mechanisms organized at lower levels of the neuraxis. The evaluative space model provides a more comprehensive conception of evaluative processes and subsumes, rather than discards, more simplistic models based on bipolar conceptualizations of affect.

REFERENCES

Adams, D. B. (1979). Brain mechanisms for offense, defense, and submission. *Behavioral and Brain Sciences, 2,* 201–241.

Adolphs, R., Tranel, D., Koenigs, M., & Damasio, A. R. (2005). Preferring one taste over another without recognizing either. *Nature Neuroscience, 7,* 860–861.

Allport, G. W. (1935). *Attitudes.* In C. Murchison (Ed.), *Handbook of social psychology* (Vol. 2, pp. 798–884). Worchester, MA: Clark University Press.

Aronson, E., & Carlsmith, J. M. (1963). Effect of severity of threat on the devaluation of forbidden behavior. *Journal of Abnormal and Social Psychology, 66,* 584–588.

Bard, P., & Macht, M. B. (1958). The behavior of chronically decerebrate cats. In G. E. W. Wolsten-Holme & C. M. O'Connor (Eds.), *Neurological basis of behavior* (pp. 55–75). London: Churchill.

Bechara, A., Tranel, D., Damasio, H., Adolphs, R., Rockland, C., & Damasio, A. R. (1995, August 25). Double dissociation of conditioning and declarative knowledge relative to the amygdala and hippocampus in humans. *Science, 269,* 1115–1118.

Berntson, G. G. (2006). Reasoning about brains. In J. T. Cacioppo, P. S. Visser, & C. L. Pickett (Eds.), *Social neuroscience: People thinking about thinking people* (pp. 1–11). Cambridge, MA: MIT Press.

Berntson, G. G., Bechara, A., Damasio, H., Tranel, D., & Cacioppo, J. T. (2007). Amygdala contribution to selective dimensions of emotion. *Social Cognitive and Affective Neuroscience, 2,* 123–129.

Berntson, G. G., Boysen, S. T., & Cacioppo, J. T. (1993). Neurobehavioral organization and the cardinal principle of evaluative bivalence. *Annals of the New York Academy of Science, 702,* 75–102.

Berntson, G. G., & Cacioppo, J. T. (2000). From homeostasis to allodynamic regulation. In J. T. Cacioppo, L. G. Tassinary, & G. G. Berntson (Eds.), *Handbook of psychophysiology* (pp. 459–481). Cambridge, England: Cambridge University Press.

Berntson, G. G., & Cacioppo, J. T. (2008). The neuroevolution of motivation. In J. Shah & W. Gardner (Eds.), *Handbook of motivation science* (pp. 188–200). New York: Guilford Press.

Berntson, G. G., Cacioppo, J. T., Binkley, P. F., Uchino, B. N., Quigley, K. S., & Fieldstone, A. (1994). Autonomic cardiac control: III. Psychological stress and cardiac response in autonomic space as revealed by pharmacological blockades. *Psychophysiology, 31,* 599–608.

Berntson, G. G., Cacioppo, J. T., & Quigley, K. S. (1991). Autonomic determinism: The modes of autonomic control, the doctrine of autonomic space, and the laws of autonomic constraint. *Psychological Reviews, 98,* 459–487.

Berntson, G. G., & Micco, D. J. (1976). Organization of brainstem behavioral systems. *Brain Research Bulletin, 1,* 471–483.

Berntson, G. G., Norman, G. J., Hawkley, L. C., & Cacioppo, J. T. (2008). Cardiac autonomic balance versus cardiac regulatory capacity. *Psychophysiology, 45,* 643–652.

Berntson, G. G., Sarter, M., & Cacioppo, J. T. (1998). Anxiety and cardiovascular reactivity: The basal forebrain cholinergic link. *Behavioural Brain Research, 94,* 225–248.

Berntson, G. G., Tuber, D. S., Ronca, A. E., & Bachman, D. S. (1983). The decerebrate human: Associative learning. *Experimental Neurology, 81,* 77–88.

Berridge, K. C. (1996). Food reward: Brain substrates of wanting and liking. *Neuroscience Biobehavioral Review, 20,* 1–25.

Berridge, K. C. (2004). Motivation concepts in behavioral neuroscience. *Physiology and Behavior, 81,* 179–209.

Berridge, K. C., & Grill, H. J. (1984). Idohedonic tastes support a two-dimensional hypothesis of palatability. *Appetite, 5,* 221–231.

Blair, K., Marsh, A. A., Morton, J., Vythilingam, M., Jones, M., Mondillo, K., et al. (2006). Choosing the lesser of two evils, the better of two goods: Specifying the roles of ventromedial prefrontal cortex and dorsal anterior cingulate in object choice. *Journal of Neuroscience, 26,* 11379–11386.

Buchanan, T. W., Tranel, D., & Adolphs, R. (2006). Memories for emotional autobiographical events following unilateral damage to medial temporal lobe. *Brain, 129,* 115–127.

Cacioppo, J. T., & Berntson, G. G. (1994). Relationship between attitudes and evaluative space: A critical review, with emphasis on the separability of positive and negative substrates. *Psychological Bulletin, 115,* 401–423.

Cacioppo, J. T., & Berntson, G. G. (1999). The affect system: Architecture and operating characteristics. *Current Directions in Psychological Science, 8,* 133–137.

Cacioppo, J. T., Berntson, G. G., Malarkey, W. B., Kiecolt-Glaser, J. K., Sheridan, J. F., Poehlmann, K. M., et al. (1998). Autonomic, neuroendocrine, and immune responses to psychological stress: The reactivity hypothesis. *Annals of the New York Academy of Sciences, 840,* 664–673.

Cacioppo, J. T., & Gardner, W. L. (1999). Emotion. *Annual Review of Psychology, 50,* 191–214.

Cacioppo, J. T., Gardner, W. L., & Berntson, G. G. (1997). The affect system has parallel and integrative processing components: Form follows function. *Journal of Personality and Social Psychology, 76,* 839–855.

Cacioppo, J. T., Larsen, J. T., Smith, N. K., & Berntson, G. G. (2004). The affect system: What lurks below the surface of feelings. In A. S. R. Manstead, N. Frijda, & A. Fischer (Eds.), *Feelings and emotions* (pp. 221–240). Cambridge, England: Cambridge University Press.

Cacioppo, J. T., & Petty, R. E. (1984). The elaboration likelihood model of persuasion. *Advances in Consumer Research, 11,* 673–675.

Canli, T., Desmond, J. E., Zhao, Z., Glover, G., & Gabrieli, J. D. (1998). Hemispheric asymmetry for emotional stimuli detected with fMRI. *NeuroReport, 9,* 3233–3239.

Craig, A. D. (2003). Pain mechanisms: Labeled lines versus convergence in central processing. *Annual Review of Neuroscience, 26,* 1–30.

Craig, A. D. (2005). Forebrain emotional asymmetry: A neuroanatomical basis? *Trends in Cognitive Sciences, 9,* 566–571.

Critchley, H. D., Taggart, P., Sutton, P. M., Holdright, D. R., Batchvarov, V., Hnatkova, K., et al. (2005). Activity in the human brain predicting differential heart rate responses to emotional facial expressions. *NeuroImage, 24,* 751–762.

Cunningham, W. A., & Zelazo, P. D. (2007). Attitudes and evaluations: A social cognitive neuroscience perspective. *Trends in Cognitive Sciences, 11,* 97–104.

Davidson, R. J. (1990). Approach-withdrawal and cerebral asymmetry: Emotional expression and brain physiology. *Journal of Personality and Social Psychology, 58,* 330–341.

Davidson, R. J. (1998). Anterior electrophysiological asymmetries, emotion, and depression: Conceptual and methodological conundrums. *Psychophysiology, 35,* 607–614.

Davidson, R. J. (2004). What does the prefrontal cortex "do" in affect: Perspectives on frontal EEG asymmetry research. *Biological Psychology, 67,* 219–233.

Davidson, R. J., Shackman, A. J., & Maxwell, J. S. (2004). Asymmetries in face and brain related to emotion. *Trends in Cognitive Science, 8,* 389–391.

De Gelder, B., Vroomen, J., Pourtois, G., & Weiskrantz, L. (1999). Non-conscious recognition of affect in the absence of striate cortex. *NeuroReport, 10,* 3759–3763.

Egan, L. C., Santos, L. R., & Bloom, P. (2007). The origins of cognitive dissonance: Evidence from children and monkeys. *Psychological Science, 18,* 978–983.

Grabenhorst, F., Rolls, E. T., Margot, C., da Silva, M. A., & Velazco, M. I. (2007). How pleasant and unpleasant stimuli combine in different brain regions: Odor mixtures. *Journal of Neuroscience, 27,* 13532–13540.

Gray, J. A., & McNaughton, N. (2000). *The neuropsychology of anxiety: An enquiry into the functions of the septo-hippocampal system.* Oxford, England: Oxford University Press.

Harmon-Jones, E., Vaughn, K., Mohr, S., Sigelman, J., & Harmon-Jones, C. (2004). The effect of manipulated sympathy and anger on left and right frontal cortical activity. *Emotion, 4,* 95–101.

Harris, R. B., Kelso, E. W., Flatt, W. P., Bartness, T. J., & Grill, H. J. (2006). Energy expenditure and body composition of chronically maintained decerebrate rats in the fed and fasted condition. *Endocrinology, 147,* 1365–1376.

Hart, S., Sarter, M., & Berntson, G. G. (1999). Cholinergic inputs to the rat medial prefrontal cortex mediate potentiation of the cardiovascular defensive response by the anxiogenic benzodiazepine receptor partial inverse agonist FG 7142. *Neuroscience, 94,* 1029–1038.

Heath, R. G. (1972). Pleasure and brain activity in man: Deep and surface electroencephalograms during orgasm. *Journal of Nervous and Mental Diseases, 154,* 3–18.

Hess, W. R. (1954). Diencephalon: Autonomic and extrapyramidal functions. Monographs in biology and medicine: Vol. III. New York: Grune & Stratton.

Hoebel, B. G., Rada, P. V., Mark, G. P., & Pothos, E. N. (1999). Neural systems for reinforcement and inhibition of behavior: Relevance to eating, addiction, and depression. In D. Kahneman, E. Diener, & N. Schwarz (Eds.), *Well-being: The foundations of hedonic psychology* (pp. 558–572). New York: Russell Sage Foundation.

Irwin, W., Davidson, R. J., Lowe, M. J., Mock, B. J., Sorenson, J. A., & Turski, P. A. (1996). Human amygdala activation detected with echo-planar functional magnetic resonance imaging. *NeuroReport, 7,* 1765–1769.

Ito, T. A., & Cacioppo, J. T. (2005). Variations on a human universal: Individual differences in positivity offset and negativity bias. *Cognition and Emotion, 19,* 1–26.

Jackson, J. H. (1958). Evolution and dissolution of the nervous system (Croonian Lectures). In J. Taylor (Ed.), *Selected writings of John Hughlings Jackson* (pp. 45–63). New York: Basic Books. (Original work published 1884.)

Knox, D., & Berntson, G. G. (2006). Effect of nucleus basalis magnocellularis cholinergic lesions on fear-like and anxiety-like behavior. *Behavioral Neuroscience, 120,* 307–312.

Koizumi, K., & Kollai, M. (1981). Control of reciprocal and non-reciprocal action of vagal and sympathetic efferents: Study of centrally induced reactions. *Journal of the Autonomic Nervous System, 3,* 483–501.

Koob, G. F. (1992). Drugs of abuse: Anatomy, pharmacology, and function of reward pathways. *Trends in Pharmacological Sciences, 13,* 177–184.

Kosslyn, S. M., Shin, L. M., Thompson, W. L., McNally, R. J., Rauch, S. L., Pitman, R. K., et al. (1996). Neural effects of visualizing and perceiving aversive stimuli: A PET investigation. *NeuroReport, 7,* 1569–1576.

LaBar, K. S., & Cabeza, R. (2006). Cognitive neuroscience of emotional memory. *Nature Reviews Neuroscience, 7,* 54–64.

Lang, P. J., Bradley, M. M., & Cuthbert, B. N. (1999). *International affective picture system (IAPS): Instruction manual and affective ratings.* [Technical report A-4.] Gainsville, FL: University of Florida, Center for Research in Psychophysiology.

Lang, P. J., Davis, M., & Ohman, A. (2000). Fear and anxiety: Animal models and human cognitive psychophysiology. *Journal of Affective Disorders, 61,* 137–159.

Larsen, J. T., McGraw, A. P., & Cacioppo, J. T. (2001). Can people feel happy and sad at the same time? *Journal of Personality and Social Psychology, 81,* 684–696.

Larsen, J. T., McGraw, A. P., Mellers, B. A., & Cacioppo, J. T. (2004). The agony of victory and thrill of defeat: Mixed emotional reactions to disappointing wins and relieving losses. *Psychological Science, 15,* 325–330.

Larson, C. L., Schaefer, H. S., Siegle, G. J., Jackson, C. A., Anderle, M. J., & Davidson, R. J. (2006). Fear is fast in phobic individuals: Amygdala activation in response to fear-relevant stimuli. *Biological Psychiatry, 60,* 410–417.

LeDoux, J. E. (1996). *The emotional brain: The mysterious underpinnings of emotional life.* New York: Simon & Schuster.

LeDoux, J. (2000). Emotion circuits in the brain. *Annual Review of Neuroscience, 23,* 155–184.

LeDoux, J. (2003). The emotional brain, fear, and the amygdala. *Cellular and Molecular Neurobiology, 23,* 727–738.

LeDoux, J. E., Iwata, J., Cicchetti, P., & Reis, D. J. (1988). Different projections of the central amygdaloid nucleus mediate autonomic and behavioral correlates of conditioned fear. *Journal of Neuroscience, 8,* 2517–2529.

Lee, G. P., Meador, K. J., Loring, D. W., Allison, J. D., Brown, W. S., Paul, L. K., et al. (2004). Neural substrates of emotion as revealed by functional magnetic resonance imaging. *Cognitive and Behavioral Neuroscience, 17,* 9–17.

Lundberg, A. (1979). Multisensory control of spinal reflex pathways. *Progress in Brain Research, 50,* 11–28.

MacLean, P. D. (1985). Evolutionary psychiatry and the triune brain. *Psychological Medicine, 15,* 219–221.

Mauk, M., & Thompson, R. F. (1987). Retention of classically conditioned eyelid responses following acute decerebration. *Brain Research, 403,* 89–95.

McEwen, B. (2004). Protection and damage from acute and chronic stress: Allostasis and allostatic overload and relevance to the pathophysiology of psychiatric disorders. *Annals of the New York Academy of Sciences, 1032,* 1–7.

Miller, N. E. (1959). Liberalization of basic S-R concepts: Extensions to conflict behavior, motivation and social learning. In S. Koch (Ed.), *Psychology: A study of a science* (pp. 196–292). New York: McGraw-Hill.

Miller, N. E. (1961). Some recent studies on conflict behavior and drugs. *American Psychologist, 16,* 12–24.

Nitschke, J. B., Sarinopoulos, I., Mackiewicz, K. L., Schaefer, H. S., & Davidson, R. J. (2006). Functional neuroanatomy of aversion and its anticipation. *NeuroImage, 29,* 106–116.

Norman, R. J., Buchwald, J. S., & Villablanca, V. J. (1977, April 29). Classical conditioning with auditory discrimination of the eye blink in decerebrate cats. *Science, 196,* 551–553.

Öhman, A., & Mineka, S. (2001). Fears, phobias, and preparedness: Toward an evolved module of fear and fear learning. *Psychological Review, 108,* 438–522.

Okun, M. S., Bowers, D., Springer, U., Shapira, N. A., Malone, D., & Rezai, A. R. (2004). What's in a 'smile'? Intra-operative observations of contralateral smiles induced by deep brain stimulation. *Neurocase, 10,* 271–279.

Oppenheimer, S. (1993). The anatomy and physiology of cortical mechanisms of cardiac control. *Stroke, 24,* 13–15.

Oppenheimer, S. M. (2006). Cerebrogenic cardiac arrhythmias: Cortical lateralization and clinical significance. *Clinical Autonomic Research, 16,* 1619–1560.

Osgood, C., Suci, G., & Tannenbaum, P. (1957). *The measurement of meaning.* Urbana: University of Illinois.

Pecina, S., & Berridge, K. C. (2005). Hedonic hot spot in the nucleus accumbens shell: where do mu-opiods cause increased hedonic impact of sweetness? *Journal of Neuroscience, 25,* 11777–11787.

Pegna, A. J., Khateb, A. A., Lazeyras, F., & Seghier, M. L. (2005). Discriminating emotional faces without primary visual cortices involves the right amygdala. *Nature Neuroscience, 8,* 24–25.

Petty, R. E., Cacioppo, J. T., Strathman, A. J., & Priester, J. R. (2005). To think or not to think: Exploring two routes to persuasion. In S. Shavitt & T. C. Brock (Eds.), *Persuasion: Psychological insights and perspectives* (2nd ed., pp. 81–116). New York: Allyn & Bacon.

Phelps, E. A. (2006). Emotion and cognition: Insights from studies of the human amygdala. *Annual Review of Psychology, 57,* 27–53.

Phelps, E. A., & LeDoux, J. E. (2005). Contributions of the amygdala to emotion processing: From animal models to human behavior. *Neuron, 48,* 175–187.

Phillips, R. G., & LeDoux, J. E. (1992). Differential contribution of amygdala and hippocampus to cued and contextual fear conditioning. *Behavioral Neuroscience, 106,* 274–285.

Pizzagalli, D. A., Sherwood, R. J., Henriques, J. B., & Davidson, R. J. (2005). Frontal brain asymmetry and reward responsiveness: A source-localization study. *Psychological Science, 16,* 805–813.

Porter, R. (1987). Functional studies of motor cortex. *Ciba Foundation Symposium, 132,* 83–97.

Posner, J., Russell, J. A., & Peterson, B. S. (2005). The circumplex model of affect: An integrative approach to affective neuroscience, cognitive development, and psychopathology. *Development and Psychopathology, 173,* 715–734.

Quirk, G. J., Armony, J. L., & LeDoux, J. E. (1997). Fear conditioning enhances different temporal components of tone-evoked spike trains in auditory cortex and lateral amygdala. *Neuron, 19,* 613–624.

Quirk, G. J., Repa, C., & LeDoux, J. E. (1995). Fear conditioning enhances short-latency auditory responses of lateral amygdala neurons: Parallel recordings in the freely behaving rat. *Neuron, 15,* 1029–1039.

Robinson, T. E., & Berridge, K. C. (2003). Addiction. *Annual Review of Psychology, 54,* 25–53.

Ronca, A. E., Berntson, G. G., & Tuber, D. A. (1986). Cardiac orienting and habituation to auditory and vibrotactile stimuli in the infant decerebrate rat. *Developmental Psychobiology, 18,* 79–83.

Root, J. C., Wong, P. S., & Kinsbourne, M. (2006). Left hemisphere specialization for response to positive emotional expressions: A divided output methodology. *Emotion, 6,* 473–483.

Russell, J. A. (1980). A circumplex model of affect. *Journal of Personality and Social Psychology, 39,* 1161–1178.

Russell, J. A. (1983). Pancultural aspects of human conceptual organization of emotions. *Journal of Personality and Social Psychology, 45,* 1281–1288.

Russell, J. A. (2003). Core affect and the psychological construction of emotion. *Psychological Review, 110,* 145–172.

Sabatinelli, D., Bradley, M. M., Fitzsimmons, J. R., & Lang, P. J. (2005). Parallel amygdala and inferotemporal activation reflect emotional intensity and fear relevance. *NeuroImage, 24,* 1265–1270.

Sandrini, G., Serrao, M., Rossi, P., Romaniello, A., Cruccu, G., & Willer, J. C. (2005). The lower limb flexion reflex in humans. *Progress in Neurobiology, 77,* 353–395.

Schouenborg, J., Holmberg, H., & Weng, H. R. (1992). Functional organization of the nociceptive withdrawal reflexes: II. Changes of excitability and receptive fields after spinalization in the rat. *Experimental Brain Research, 90,* 469–478.

Sévoz-Couche, C., Comet, M. A., Hamon, M., & Laguzzi, R. (2003). Role of nucleus tractus solitarius 5-HT3 receptors in the defense reaction-induced inhibition of the aortic baroreflex in rats. *Journal of Neurophysiology, 90,* 2521–2530.

Sherrington, C. S. (1906). *The integrative action of the nervous system.* New Haven, CT: Yale University Press.

Shih, C. D., Chan, S. H., & Chan, J. Y. (1995). Participation of hypothalamic paraventricular nucleus in locus ceruleus-induced baroreflex suppression in rats. *American Journal of Physiology: Heart and Circulatory Physiology, 269,* H46–H52.

Shin, L. M., Orr, S. P., Carson, M. A., Rauch, S. L., Macklin, M. L., Lasko, N. B., et al. (2004). Regional cerebral blood flow in the amygdala and medial prefrontal cortex during traumatic imagery in male and female Vietnam veterans with PTSD. *Archives of General Psychiatry, 61,* 168–176.

Steiner, J. E., Glaser, D., Hawilo, M. E., & Berridge, K. C. (2001). Comparative expression of hedonic impact: Affective reactions to taste by human infants and other primates. *Neuroscience and Biobehavioral Reviews, 25,* 53–74.

Stowell, J. R., Berntson, G. G., & Sarter, M. (2000). Attenuation of the bidirectional effects of chlordiazepoxide and FG 7142 on conditioned response suppression and associated cardiovascular reactivity by loss of cortical cholinergic inputs. *Psychopharmacology, 150,* 141–149.

Straube, T., Mentzel, H. J., & Miltner, W. H. (2007). Waiting for spiders: Brain activation during anticipatory anxiety in spider phobics. *NeuroImage, 37,* 1427–1436.

Thurstone, L. L. (1931). The measurement of attitudes. *Journal of Abnormal Psychology, 26,* 249–269.

Tooby, J., & Cosmides, L. (1990). The past explains the present: Emotional adaptations and the structure of ancestral environment. *Ethology and Sociobiology, 11,* 375–424.

Tranel, D., Gullickson, G., Koch, M., & Adolphs, R. (2006). Altered experience of emotion following bilateral amygdala damage. *Cognitive Neuropsychiatry, 11,* 219–232.

Tuber, D. S., Berntson, G. G., Bachman, D. S., & Allen, J. N. (1980, November 28). Associative learning in premature hydranencephalic and normal twins. *Science, 210,* 1035–1037.

Wakana, S., Jiang, H., Nagae-Poetscher, L. M., Zijl, P. C., & Mori, S. (2004). Fiber tract based atlas of human white matter anatomy. *Radiology, 230,* 77–87.

Walker, D. L., & Davis, M. (1997). Double dissociation between the involvement of the bed nucleus of the stria terminalis and the central nucleus of the amygdala in light-enhanced versus fear potentiated startle. *Journal of Neuroscience, 17,* 9375–9383.

Walker, D. L., Toufexis, D. J., & Davis, M. (2003). Role of the bed nucleus of the stria terminalis versus the amygdala in fear, stress, and anxiety. *European Journal of Pharmacology, 463,* 199–216.

Watson, D., Wiese, D., Vaidya, J., & Tellegen, A. (1999). The two general activation systems of affect: Structural findings, evolutionary considerations, and psychobiological evidence. *Journal of Personality and Social Psychology, 76,* 820–838.

Weiskrantz, L. (1986). *Blindsight: A case study and implications.* Oxford, England: Oxford University Press.

Wise, R. A. (2006). Role of brain dopamine in food reward and reinforcement. *Philosophical Transactions of the Royal Society of Biological Sciences, 361,* 1149–1158.

Wundt, W. (1896). *Outlines of psychology.* Leipzig, Germany: Engelmann.

Yates, B. J., Jakus, J., & Miller, A. D. (1993). Vestibular effects on respiratory outflow in the decerebrate cat. *Brain Research, 3,* 209–217.

Zald, D. H., & Pardo, J. V. (1997). Emotion, olfaction, and the human amygdala: Amygdala activation during aversive olfactory stimulation. *Proceedings of the National Academy of Sciences, USA, 94,* 4119–4124.

Pain: Mechanisms and Measurement

JOSÉE GUINDON AND ANDREA G. HOHMANN

DEFINITION OF PAIN

The word *pain* comes from the Latin word *peona* meaning punishment or penalty. Pain is an unpleasant, complex, personal, and subjective experience that can range in intensity from slight through severe to indescribable. In the general population of the United States, the two most common forms of pain involve headaches and back pain that affect 45 and 9 million people, respectively. The management of moderate and severe chronic pain is the main concern and burden of patients and clinicians. Despite improvements in our understanding of neural circuits contributing to pain transmission and modulation, the need for safe and effective approaches for pain relief remains predominant.

The mission of defining pain is a complicated one (for review, see Brennan, Carr, & Cousins, 2007; Price, 1999). This definition has evolved through time together with advances in both our understanding of the neural circuits implicated in pain transmission and modulation and ongoing improvements in the evaluation of its effects. It is now generally acknowledged that pain comprises sensory-discriminative, motivational-affective, and cognitive-evaluative dimensions (Figure 33.1). In the mid-1990s, pain was defined by the International Association of the Study of Pain (IASP) as "an unpleasant sensory and emotional experience associated with actual or potential tissue damage, or described in terms of such damage" (Merskey & Bogduk, 1994, pp. 209–214). This definition raised questions because it is possible to experience an injury without pain and pain can also be experienced in the absence of any apparent injury. For example, people born with congenital analgesia exhibit profound insensitivity to pain even in the presence of serious injury (e.g., fractures, burns, appendicitis; Comings & Amromin, 1974; Manfredi et al., 1981; Waxman, 2007). The cause underlying congenital analgesia until recently has remained elusive.

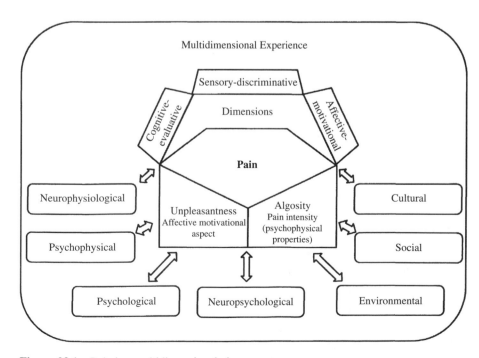

Figure 33.1 Pain is a multidimensional phenomenon.

A mutation in the SCN9A gene, which is linked to chromosome 2q24.3 and results in nonfunctional Na$_v$1.7 channels, has been implicated in congenital insensitivity to pain (Cox et al., 2006; Waxman, 2007). Furthermore, causes underlying the two most common forms of pain in the population, headaches (Moskowitz, 1992; Villalon, Centurion, Valdivia, de Vries, & Saxena, 2003) and back pain (Loeser, 2001), remain poorly understood. In many cases, pain is felt without any sign of injury causing controversy and speculation about the pathophysiology of these conditions. Furthermore, it is also possible for motorcycle accident victims to experience pain after healing the avulsion of the brachial plexus (Wynn Parry, 1980). Therefore, another definition of pain was proposed by Price (1999). According to this definition, pain is a somatic perception containing: (a) a bodily sensation with qualities like those reported during tissue-damaging stimulation, (b) an experienced threat associated with this sensation, and (c) a feeling of unpleasantness or other negative emotion based on this experienced threat. This definition doesn't require the demonstration of tissue damage or the association between sensation and tissue lesion. However, unpleasant somatic sensation (e.g., itch) is not necessarily associated with pain. Therefore, pain may more appropriately be defined with the association of two somatosensory qualities: unpleasantness (affective-motivational aspect) and algosity (a unique quality of pain that allows it to be unequivocally identified). The psychophysics and neural mechanisms may differ for each of these dimensions. These dimensions are distinct in their intensity-based sensory discriminations. Moreover, the magnitude of unpleasantness can be dissociated from the pain intensity (algosity magnitude; Fields, 1999). Pain remains a complex multidimensional experience related to sensory-discriminative, cognitive-evaluative, and motivational-affective dimensions which, by its complexity, cannot be solely explained by social, cultural, environmental, neurophysiological, psychophysical, psychological, or neuropsychological aspects (Melzack & Katz, 1999; Melzack & Wall, 1991; Price, 1999). Interactions between these aspects are also likely to occur (Figure 33.1).

THE CONCEPTUALIZATION OF PAIN HAS EVOLVED

The concept of pain has evolved over time (for a review, see Melzack & Wall, 1991). The ancient Greeks grouped pain with the emotions or appetites and not with sensation. They considered pain to be the opposite of pleasure (Dallenbach, 1939; Livingstone, 1998; Marshall, 1894). The view of pain as pure emotion went into decline in the seventeenth century with the advent of *specificity theory*. This theory postulates that a specific pain system carries a message from pain receptors in the skin to a pain center in the brain. The best classical description of this theory comes from Descartes (1664) who conceived of the pain system as a straight-through channel from the skin to the brain (Figure 33.2). Different qualities of sensation were not recognized in this early conceptualization. Müller's (1842) doctrine of specific nerve energies postulated that the qualities of experience were associated with the properties of sensory nerves. Müller proposed that the brain receives information about external objects only by way of the sensory nerves and five classical senses were recognized: seeing, hearing, taste, smell, and touch. The theory of cutaneous senses was established by Max von Frey between 1894 and 1895. Von Frey's designation of the free nerve endings as pain receptors is the basis of the specificity theory (Boring, 1942; Figure 33.2). A "solution" to the puzzle of pain was explained by the existence of specific pain receptors in the body tissue traveling via pain fibers and a pain pathway to a pain center in the brain (Boring, 1942). It was later proposed that the amount and quality of perceived pain were modulated by many psychological variables in addition to the sensory input. For example, dogs that received electric shocks, burns, or cuts followed by the presentation of food eventually responded to these noxious stimuli as signals for food and most notably failed to show any signs of pain (Pavlov, 1927).

Goldscheider (1894) was the first to propose that stimulus intensity and central summation are the critical determinants of pain. This conceptualization represented the *origin of pattern theory*. Goldscheider concluded that mechanisms of central summation, which were postulated to be localized in the dorsal horn of the spinal cord, were essential for any understanding of pain mechanisms. Livingstone (1943) proposed that pathological stimulation of sensory nerves (e.g., peripheral nerve damage) initiates activity in reverberatory circuits in the gray matter of the spinal cord. This abnormal activity could be triggered by normally nonnoxious inputs and generates volleys of nerve impulses that are interpreted centrally as pain (Figure 33.2). The simplest form of pattern theory deals with peripheral instead of central patterning. According to this theory, the pattern of pain is produced by an intense stimulation of nonspecific receptors (Sinclair, 1955; Weddell, 1955). Note that in this conceptualization, all fiber endings (except those innervated by hair cells) were believed to be alike.

The *sensory interaction theory* developed by Noordenbos (1959) suggests that the small diameter fibers exist to carry nerve impulse patterns that produce pain, whereas the large fibers inhibit this transmission. Therefore, a shift in

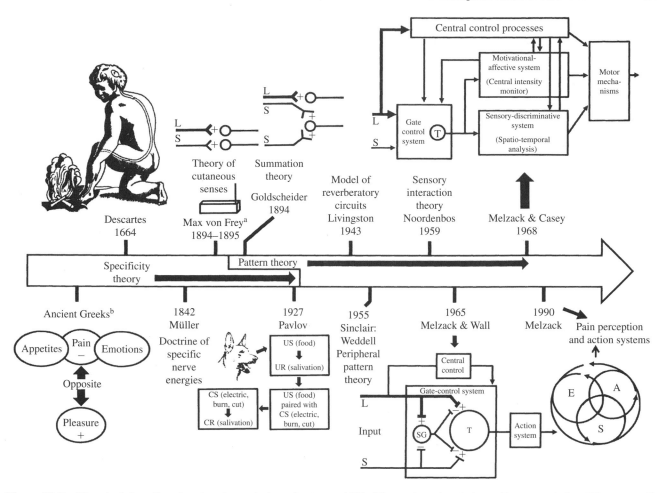

Figure 33.2   Historical time line showing the evolution of pain theories.

Note: A = Affective-motivational; CR = conditioned response; CS = conditioned stimuli; E = evaluative-cognitive; L = large diameter fiber; S = small diameter fiber = SD = sensory-discriminative for Melzack, 1990; SG = substantia gelatinosa; T = transmission; US = unconditioned stimuli; UR = unconditioned response.

Data source: [a]Boring (1942), Melzack and Wall (1991); [b]Marshall (1894), Dallenbach (1939), Livingstone (1998).

the ratio toward small fibers would result in an increase in neural transmission, summation, and excessive pathological pain. Finally, the *gate-control theory* postulated that the perception of pain is determined by interactions between different types of fibers, both small-diameter pain transmitting and large-diameter nonpain transmitting fibers. This theory asserted that activation of the large diameter (fast-conducting) nonpain transmitting fibers could indirectly inhibit signals from small-diameter (slow-conducting) pain transmitting fibers and block the transmission and perception of pain (Melzack & Wall, 1965; Figure 33.2). Under pathological conditions, the fast system loses its dominance over the slow one, resulting in slow pain (Bishop, 1946), diffuse burning pain (Bishop, 1959), or hyperalgesia (Noordenbos, 1959). This model was updated by Melzack and Casey (1968) as a conceptual model of the sensory, motivational, and central control determinants of pain. In this conceptualization, the

output of the transmission (T) cells of the gate-control system projects to the sensory-discriminative system (via the neospinothalamic fibers) and the motivational-affective system (via the paramedical ascending system). The central control trigger projects back to the gate-control system, the sensory-discriminative system, and the motivational-affective system. These three systems interact and project to the motor system to influence motor responses to pain (Figure 33.2). *Body-self matrix theory* developed from attempts to explain the neurophysiology of phantom limb pain (Melzack, 1990a, 1999). According to this theory, a genetically built-in matrix of neurons for the whole body comprises a widely distributed neural network that incorporates somatosensory, limbic, and thalamocortical components. These components contain smaller parallel networks that contribute to sensory-discriminative, affective-motivational, and evaluative-cognitive dimensions of pain experience as the neuromatrix. According to this theory, the cyclical processing and synthesis of nerve impulses in the neuromatrix imposes a characteristic output pattern or a neurosignature that is perceived as pain (Melzack, 1990a; Figure 33.2). The conceptualization of pain is likely to continue to evolve over time together with advances in our understanding of pain transmission and modulation.

TRANSIENT PAIN

Transient pain is defined by the brief duration of the experienced pain sensation. It is the feeling commonly experienced with minor injuries (e.g., a stubbed toe, a mild burn, the itching of sunburn). Transient pain has no long-term consequence because it is associated with almost no tissue damage. Transient pain is not typically accompanied by anxiety (Melzack & Wall, 1991). In this situation, a first pain is felt which is well localized and relatively mild (Table 33.1). This is followed shortly by a second pain that distracts attention from the person's previous activity and decreases in intensity until it fades away (Marchand, 1998; Melzack & Wall, 1991; Table 33.1).

ACUTE PAIN

Acute pain (e.g., such as that felt after twisting an ankle or cutting your finger) is a more intense sensation than transient pain. This experience is marked by intense consciousness of the event and a penetrating sensation that is accompanied by alertness and orientation toward the affected region. This painful experience contains a sequence of perceptions, evaluations, and emotions (Price, 1999). Perception and evaluation are mostly related to examination of the injury itself but can be influenced by previous experiences (e.g., a prior history of similar experiences) or the personality of the injured (Melzack & Wall, 1991; Price, 1999). The emotional component of acute pain may be related to fear or anxiety emanating from the body following the injury and includes autonomic activation. Furthermore, after some delay, thoughts and concerns regarding pain become more elaborated, reflective, and directed toward the long-term consequences of this injury (e.g., activities and responsibilities that will be unattended) and anxiety about the healing process. The immediate and late stage of this acute pain experience involves two main aspects: the desire to avoid harm due to the injury and the expectation that you will succeed in preventing harm (Price, 1999). Expectations can also be focused on the healing process and anxiety/fear can be experienced

if these expectations are not met. Thus, acute pain can reiterate some of the complexities of the multidimensional experience that represents persistent pain.

PAIN AS A RECUPERATIVE HEALING MECHANISM

Transient and acute pain is adaptive in that it serves a protective function and enables the affected individual to learn to avoid serious injuries in the future. A sequence of change occurs after an injury on several levels: physiological, biological, neurological, and behavioral. A relationship exists between the behavioral and biological events to ensure subsequent recuperation and healing after injury. Individuals born with congenital insensitivity to pain often sustain serious injuries, providing a rather extreme illustration of the useful functions of pain to warn, protect, and heal injured tissue (Fields, 1987; Melzack & Wall, 1983).

Wall (1979) proposed that three phases of pain behavior— immediate, acute, and chronic—follow an injury in both animals and humans. The *immediate phase* of pain behavior is the first period corresponding to the activation of nociceptive afferent neurons and is related to autonomic responses (e.g., fight-or-flight responses) combined with emotions (e.g., fear or anger). It is possible that pain is not felt at this moment if the subject is caught in a stressful situation where it is necessary to escape or find safety. The *acute phase* of pain behavior corresponds to the behavior associated with the recovery process. At this point, the subject will feel pain and will have to cope with it (i.e., find treatment and prepare for recovery). This phase can be accompanied by anxiety and distress about the injury. Finally, the *chronic phase* of pain consists of quiet inactivity and related behavior related to rest, inactivation, recuperation, and healing. Long-term changes in the nervous system induced by the failure or delays in complete healing of the injury where pain is no longer a symptom of an injury, but rather becomes a serious medical syndrome, may contribute to the development of chronic pain syndromes in humans (Price, 1999; Wall, 1979).

LONG-TERM OR CHRONIC PAIN

The fact that long-term or chronic pain is accepted and recognized as a distinct medical entity represents a major breakthrough in the field of pain (Bonica, 1953, 1974). A few decades ago, people who felt pain long after healing had occurred were frequently sent to psychiatric hospitals. Misdiagnosis and mistreatment resulted from an utter lack

TABLE 33.1 Characterization of different types of afferent fibers and their relationship to first and second pain

Fibre Type		Myelinated	Diameter	Conduction Velocity	Receptor Type	Respond To
Aβ		Yes	5 – 15 μm	30 – 100 m/sec	Specialized and free	Light pressure or touch
Aδ		Yes	1 – 5 μm	6 – 30 m/s	Free	Light pressure Heavy pressure Heat (45°C +)
C		No	0.25 – 1.5 μm	1.0 – 2.5 m/s	Free	Light pressure Heavy pressure Heat (45°C +) Chemicals Warmth

of knowledge regarding the pathophysiology of chronic pain. Chronic pain is defined as pain that persists after all possible healing has occurred or long after pain can serve any useful function. Thus, chronic pain is no longer a symptom of injury or disease but is a medical problem in its own right that requires urgent attention to alleviate unnecessary suffering (Melzack & Wall, 1991). Feelings of fear, anxiety, and anger characterizing the earliest phase of the pain experience are transformed into despair, frustration, hopelessness, and depression that can develop later (Cohen, Patel, Khetpal, Peterson, & Kimmel, 2007; Price, 1999; Scholl & Allen, 2007). Such changes are understandable and may be related to reflections about the interference of pain in everyday life, difficulty of enduring such pain, and the ultimate negative consequences of enduring this persistent pain (Price, 1988, 1999). Moreover, treatments that are usually beneficial for most acute pains are not necessarily effective for chronic pain (Guindon, Walczak, & Beaulieu, 2007). Chronic pain is perceived as intractable and becomes intolerable because existing pharmacotherapies show only limit efficacy for pain management and adverse side-effects constrain therapeutic dosing. Many factors interact and negatively contribute to chronic pain including psychological factors that can lead to depression in both adults (Chenot et al., 2008; Cohen et al., 2007) and children (Scholl & Allen, 2007). Future research aimed at further elucidating mechanisms underlying transmission and modulation of pain, especially chronic pain, are required to eliminate unnecessary suffering in affected patients.

PATHWAYS CONTRIBUTING TO THE TRANSMISSION AND MODULATION OF PAIN

The trajectory of nociceptive information traveling from the periphery through sensory nerve fibers to the central nervous system after an injury is characterized by a series of chemical and electrical reactions. These reactions may be divided into four steps (Fields, 1987). The first step is *transduction,* which corresponds to the transformation of the chemical, thermal, or mechanical stimulus into energy (action potentials) in sensory nerve endings. For example, when an individual burns a finger, intense heat energy from the burn will be converted into electrical nerve impulses at the free nerve endings in the skin (Melzack & Wall, 1991; Price, 1999). In this case, any skin damage will activate these networks and initiate the *transmission* (second step) of trains of neural impulses along sensory nerve fibers (known as primary afferent neurons) running from the periphery (skin) to the spinal cord. Then, the signal moves along secondary projection neurons via ascending pathways that originate in the spinal cord and innervate the brain stem and thalamus. Thalamic neurons subsequently convey this information to diverse cortical regions (Fields, 1987). The third step is the *modulation* of neurons responsible for the transmission of nociceptive information from the periphery to the central nervous system by descending projections from the brain. These descending processes may either inhibit or facilitate pain (Bie & Pan, 2007; Garcia-Larrea & Magnin, 2008; Mason, 2005). The fourth step refers to the *perception* of pain. This phenomenon corresponds to the finality of the nociceptive experience that can be influenced by emotional state and previous experience (Fields, 1987).

Transduction

Nociceptive information is perceived by the application of a stimulus capable of harming the integrity of the organism (e.g., burning a finger with fire). Note that the same stimulus will be ignored by some receptors and perceived by others. The latter receptors, better known as nociceptors (responding to noxious stimulation), are bushy networks of fibers that penetrate many layers of the skin, muscles, articulations, and visceral structures (Melzack & Wall, 1991; Price, 1999). These nociceptive receptors are sensitive to stimuli of various kinds (chemical, thermal, or mechanical) and transduce this stimulus energy into actions potentials. Transmission of this information is linked to the intensity of nociceptive stimulation and is encoded by the frequency and pattern of firing of nociceptive afferent neurons (Fields, 1987; Julius & Basbaum, 2001; Price, 1999). These primary afferents consequently mediate both transduction and transmission of pain (Fields, 1987; Millan, 1999). These nociceptive receptors are also described as nerve endings linked to sensory nerve fibers. The primary afferent sensory fibers include A (large myelinated), $A\beta$ (small myelinated), and C fibers (thin unmyelinated), which are classified based on their fiber diameters and conduction velocities (Table 33.1). These fibers are tuned precisely to begin firing nerve impulses when a particular event occurs (depending on the fiber recruited) in the region of their terminals. For example, $A\beta$ fibers start firing when skin is cooled by a fraction of a degree and $A\beta/C$ fibers largely respond to an increase in temperature. A single painful stimulus evokes two successive and qualitatively different pain sensations, termed *first* and *second pain.* First pain is mediated by $A\beta$ fibers and is characterized by a brief, well-localized sensation whereas second pain is mediated by C fibers and is associated by a later, longer lasting burning and more diffusely localized sensation (Melzack & Wall, 1991; Price, Hu, Dubner, & Gracely, 1977; Table 33.1).

Transmission

The transmission of nociceptive information from the periphery to the central nervous system constitutes a first line of defense to minimize damage to the organism. This process is more complex than described previously by early pain theories due to the multiplicity of different receptors, overlap in receptive fields of afferent fibers, and involvement of multiple ascending nociceptive pathways (for a review, see Julius & Basbaum, 2001; Melzack & Wall, 1991; Millan, 1999; Price, 1999). Skin damage initiates trains of nerve impulses along primary afferent fibers that are running from the periphery to the spinal cord. The primary nociceptive afferent neurons enter the spinal cord via the dorsal roots to converge on and synaptically excite neurons in the grey matter of the dorsal horn of the spinal cord. The cells in the grey matter of the spinal cord are arranged in laminae (or layers) in a dorsal ventral direction running the entire length of the spinal cord (Rexed, 1952). A total of 10 laminae have been described, of which 6 are found in the dorsal horn (Figure 33.3). Laminae II may be further subdivided into laminae II inner and outer, which receive different primary afferent inputs (Julius & Basbaum, 2001; Marker, Lujan, Colon, & Wickman, 2006). In general, nociceptive afferent C fibers and some Aβ fibers terminate in laminae

I and II, whereas other A fibers penetrate deeper into the dorsal horn (laminae V).

The second-order neurons in the dorsal horn of the spinal cord cross over (decussate) to the contralateral side and ascend to innervate the thalamus via the spinothalamic tract (neospinothalamic and paleospinothalamic), the major ascending central pathway for pain (Melzack & Wall, 1991; Price, 1999). The neospinothalamic pathway originates in part from laminae I of the spinal cord that receives input from Aβ fibers responsible for rapid and well-localized pain (for review, see Besson & Chaouch, 1987; Julius & Basbaum, 2001; Kandel, 1985; Melzack, 1990b).

At least four classes of spinal and medullary dorsal horn neurons have been identified. These include low threshold mechanosensitive (LTM), thermoreceptive (warm and cold), wide dynamic range (WDR), and nociceptive specific (NS) cells. WDR neurons respond with increasing action potential frequency to stimulation ranging from nonnoxious to noxious. These neurons, which receive input from both large diameter (A) and small diameter (Aδ and C) fibers, code information about stimulus intensity. Nociceptive specific cells, which receive input from small diameter (Aδ mechanosensitive, Aδ heat, and C polymodal), respond exclusively to noxious stimuli. By contrast, low-threshold mechanosensitive cells, which receive input

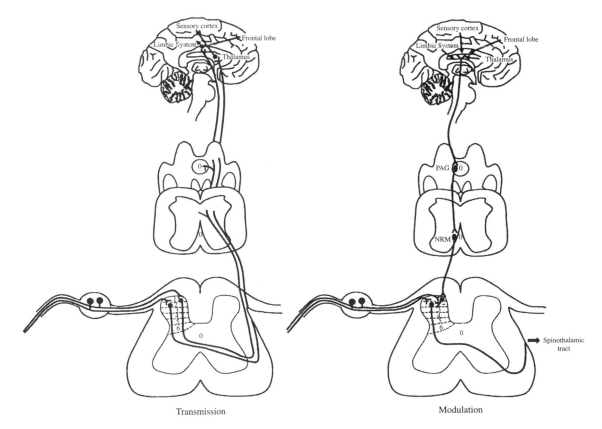

Transmission   Modulation

Figure 33.3 Circuitry mediating transmission (from the periphery to the brain) and modulation (from the brain to the periphery) of pain.

from large-diameter A fibers, respond to light touch, pressure, and hair movement. Few of these fibers project into the spinothalamic tract. Thermoreceptive cells respond exclusively to either warming or cooling of the receptive field. Several lines of evidence specifically support a role for WDR and NS cells in pain discrimination (see Price & Dubner, 1977, for a review): (a) selective stimulation of these fibers produces sensations of pain, (b) these neurons exhibit maximal responses to noxious (as opposed to nonnoxious) levels of stimulation, (c) manipulations that reduce neural responses in these cells produce concomitant reductions in pain sensation, and (d) these neurons exhibit anatomical connections consistent with a role in pain transmission.

Nociceptive dorsal horn neurons project to the ventro-posterolateral (VPL) nucleus of the thalamus. VPL neurons subsequently relay the transmitted information to the sensory cortex. The rapid conduction of Aβ fibers and the small receptive fields of the neospinothalamic pathway are essential qualities that permit the physical or sensory-discriminative aspects of pain (localization and perception; Figure 33.3). The paleospinothalamic tract is located on the median position of the thalamus. This tract is mainly innervated by dorsal horn neurons that receive afferent input from C fibers that transmit slow and diffuse pain. Synapses converge principally on the nucleus of the reticular formation of the cerebral trunk and the median nucleus of the thalamus whose neurons subsequently project to the frontal cortex and limbic system. These latter regions are also implicated in emotion and memory (Kandel, 1985; Melzack, 1990b). The slow conduction of C fibers, the diffuse aspect of the receptive fields, and the higher cerebral structures implicated in the paleospinothalamic pathway support a role for this pathway in motivational-affective (e.g., unpleasantness) aspects of pain perception (Figure 33.3).

Modulation

Nociceptive information traveling from the periphery to the central nervous system can be modulated by inhibition or facilitation from pathways that descend from the brain to the spinal cord. Descending inhibition occurs at any moment of the transmission of nerve impulse. Three main mechanisms describe this modulation: the gate-control theory (Melzack & Wall, 1965), the descending inhibitory control system (Basbaum & Fields, 1978; Bie & Pan, 2007; Garcia-Larrea & Magnin, 2008; Millan, 2002; Reynolds, 1969), and the inhibitory control produced by higher centers of the central nervous system (Bie & Pan, 2007; Craig & Bushnell, 1994; Garcia-Larrea & Magnin,

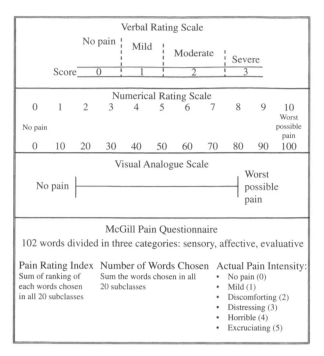

Figure 33.4 Four valid tools (or instruments) to measure pain in humans: (1) Verbal Rating Scale, (2) Numerical Rating Scale, (3) Visual Analogue Scale, and (4) McGill Pain Questionnaire.

2008; Hagbarth & Kerr, 1954; Mason, 2005; Melzack, Stotler, & Livingston, 1958; Figure 33.3). The gate-control theory (see Figure 33.2) proposes the existence of a rapidly conducting fiber system (referring to A fibers), which inhibits the synaptic transmission at laminae I and II of the dorsal horn of the spinal cord of a more slowly conducting system (Aβ and C fibers) that carries the signal for pain (Melzack & Wall, 1965). The existence of a descending inhibitory control system was first described by Reynolds (1969), who hypothesized that electrical stimulation of a small area of the grey matter surrounding the cerebral aqueduct—the periaqueductal grey area (PAG)—could enhance descending inhibition and produce analgesia. His hypothesis was borne out as electrical stimulation of the PAG induced sufficient analgesia to perform an invasive surgery (laparotomy) on otherwise awake rats. Later, it was discovered that brain stem inhibitory fibers descend through a distinct pathway in the dorsolateral spinal cord called the dorsolateral funiculus (Basbaum, Marley, O'Keefe, & Clanton, 1977). The PAG was a key component of this descending system (Fields, Basbaum, & Heinricher, 2006). The PAG receives input from many different brain regions (e.g., hypothalamus, cortex, thalamus) and is implicated in the mechanism whereby cortical and other inputs act to control the nociceptive gate in the dorsal horn. PAG neurons activate neurons in the nucleus raphe magnus (NRM), an area of the rostral medulla close to the midline, which in turn project via the dorsolateral funiculus of the spinal cord to make synaptic connections on dorsal horn interneurons (Basbaum & Fields, 1978; Fields, Basbaum, & Heinricher, 2006). Inhibitory control produced by higher centers of the central nervous system was first demonstrated by the fact that responses evoked in the ventrolateral spinal cord could be virtually abolished by the stimulation of different brain structures including the reticular formation, the cerebellum, and the cerebral cortex (Hagbarth & Kerr, 1954). The clear implications of this demonstration were that these neural structures exert an inhibitory control over the transmission of pain in the dorsal horn. This hypothesis was confirmed by the demonstration that lesions of a small area of the reticular formation (the central tegmental tract adjacent to the lateral PAG) produced hyperalgesia in cats. This area was postulated to exert a tonic inhibitory control over the pain signals because ablation of this structure produced hyperresponsiveness to pain. Thus, removal of inhibition allows pain signals to travel unchecked to the brain and can even permit summation of nonnoxious signals to produce spontaneous pain (Melzack et al., 1958).

Chronic pain is also known to be actively facilitated by descending projections from the nucleus raphe magnus (Bie & Pan, 2007; Garcia-Larrea & Magnin, 2008). Mechanisms underlying descending inhibition (see reviews by Bie & Pan, 2007; Fields, Basbaum, & Heinricher, 2006; Garcia-Larrea & Magnin, 2008; Mason, 2005; Melzack & Wall, 1991; Price, 1999) and descending facilitation (Garcia-Larrea & Magnin, 2008; Mason, 2005) of pain

are reviewed elsewhere. Pathophysiologic modifications that can contribute to pain and the attenuation of spinal inhibition include selective neuronal loss and subsequent development of inflammatory phenomena (e.g., cytokine secretion by macrophages and glial cells). These observed changes in the dorsal horn can modify the activity of projections neurons to the brain stem, thereby increasing spinal hyperactivity (DeLeo & Yezierski, 2001; Garcia-Larrea & Magnin, 2008; Pruimboom & vanDam, 2007).

Perception

The personal interpretation of a nociceptive stimulus that is associated with an emotional state of mind (or situation) or past experiences is described as the perception of pain. Note that a similar stimulus may provoke different sensations in different individuals, suggesting that pain is highly modifiable. Many psychological, neurophysiological, and psychophysical factors can modulate and influence the perception of pain, thereby altering the effectiveness of the treatment (Greenwald, 1991; Guindon, Walczak, & Beaulieu, 2007; see Table 33.2). Thus, early imaging studies using positron emission tomography (PET) and, more recently, functional magnetic resonance imaging (fMRI) hold significant promise for identifying networks of interconnected cerebral structures implicated in the affective component of pain (Bingel, Schoell, & Büchel, 2007; Craggs, Price, Verne, Perlstein, & Robinson, 2007; Moisset & Bouhassira, 2007; Rainville, Duncan, Price, Carrier, & Bushnell, 1997).

TABLE 33.2 Drugs commonly used in the treatment of pain

Classical analgesics and new adjuvants

Opioids	*NSAIDs*	*Antidepressants*	*Local anesthetics*
• Morphine	• Diclofenac	• Venlaflaxine	• Bupivacaine
• Hydromorphone	• Ketorolac	• Imipramine	• Ropivacaine
• Fentanyl	• Ketoprofen	• Duloxetine	• Levobupivacaine
• Remifentanil	• Ibuprofen	• Bupropion	• Lidocaine 5%
• Alfentanil	• Naproxen	*Anticonvulsants*	
• Sufentanil		• Gabapentin	*Others*
• Meperidine	*COXIBS*	• Pregabalin	• Acetaminophen
• Buprenorphine	• Celecoxib	• Lamotrigine	(paracetamol)
• Butorphanol	• Etoricoxib	*Cannabinoids*	• Ketamine
• Nalbuphine	• Lumiracoxib	• Cannabis	• Nefopam
• Oxycodone	• Parecoxib	• Δ^9-THC/CBD	• Clonidine
• Tramadol		• Nabilone	• Neostigmine
• Methadone		• Dronabinol	• Magnesium
		• Adjulemic Acid	

PAIN MEASUREMENT IN HUMANS

The development of valid instruments for measuring pain in humans is critical to effectively quantify the intensity, quality, and duration of pain. Measurement of pain in humans is important for diagnosis, choice of therapy, and evaluation of the relative effectiveness of different therapies (Guarino & Myers, 2007; Melzack & Katz, 1999). The varieties of pain experience can be assessed by a description of the qualities of pain experienced within three (i.e., sensory-discriminative, motivational-affective, and cognitive-evaluative) dimensions (Melzack, 2005). However, it may be difficult to describe pain experience because these words are not often used and it seems impossible to actively capture such abstract sensations as the shooting pain felt by neuropathic patients (Melzack & Katz, 1999; Melzack & Wall, 1991). In the past, pain was measured with respect to a single unique quality: the variation in intensity (Beecher, 1959). Methods used included verbal rating, numerical rating, and visual analogue scales (Figure 33.4). Verbal rating scales consist of a series of verbal pain descriptors ordered from the least to the most intense sensation (no pain, mild, moderate, severe; Daoust, Beaulieu, Manzini, Chauny, & Lavigne, 2008; Jensen & Karoly, 1992). The patient reads the list and chooses the one word that most closely describes his momentary pain (e.g., a score of zero to the lowest rank descriptor, a score of one for the next lowest rank descriptor, and so on). Numerical rating scales are described as a series of numbers from 0 to 10 or 0 to 100 with endpoints intended to represent the extremes of the pain experience, such as no pain and worst possible pain, respectively (Jensen & Karoly, 1992; Molton, Jensen, Nielson, Cardenas, & Ehde, 2008). In this case, the patient has to decide the number that best corresponds to the intensity of his or her actual pain. These two methods are simple to administer, reliable, and valid. Visual analogue scales remain the measurement instrument of choice for pain assessment when unidimensional levels of pain are assessed. The visual analogue scale consists of a 10-cm horizontal (Daoust et al., 2008; Huskisson, 1983; Joyce, Zutshi, Hrubes, & Mason, 1975) or vertical (Sriwatanakul et al., 1983) line with the two endpoints marked as no pain and worst pain ever (or other similar descriptors). The patient is asked to place a mark on the line at the point that best describes the level of the pain intensity experienced. The distance from the low end to the mark is used as a numerical index. This method is particularly valuable because it can be used to assess unpleasantness of the pain experience (Nielsen, Price, Vassend, Stubhaug, & Harris, 2005; Price, Harkins, & Baker, 1987; Price, Harkins, Rafii, & Price, 1986) separately from intensity, is sensitive to pharmacological and nonpharmacological procedures that alter pain experience (Bélanger, Melzack, & Lauzon, 1989; Choinière, Melzack, Girard, Rondeau, & Paquin, 1990; Price, Harkins, & Baker, 1987), and correlates well with verbal and numerical rating scales measuring pain (Daoust et al., 2008; Ekblom & Hansson, 1988; Kremer & Atkinson, 1983). This method was improved by Choinière and Amsel (1996) with their development of a visual analogue thermometer. This instrument consists of a rigid plastic horizontal scale of 10 cm with a band that slides from the left (no pain) to the right (worst pain ever) with a tab on the back of the thermometer; the patient places the cursor at the point referring to his or her pain intensity. However, in some elderly patients who lack manual dexterity, this method is not optimal and numerical or verbal rating scales are more reliable (Gagliese & Melzack, 1997). The visual analogue scale has been used to measure pain affect (or unpleasantness), although it corresponds to only one dimension of pain experience leaving the two other dimensions to be assessed separately. The complexity of pain necessitates describing it in terms of three dimensions to adequately capture the pain experience. The McGill Pain Questionaire (MPQ; Melzack, 1975) was developed to better specify the qualities of pain. This questionnaire developed from choosing 102 words from the literature and categorizing them into three major classes related to the three dimensions of pain: (1) sensory descriptors that describe the sensory qualities of the pain experience in terms of temporal, spatial, pressure, thermal, or other such qualities; (2) affective descriptors that assess the affective qualities in terms of tension, fear, and autonomic properties that are part of the pain experience; and (3) evaluative descriptors that describe the subjective overall intensity of the total pain experience (Melzack, 2005; Melzack & Torgerson, 1971). The words were divided in three major classes, and further separated into 16 subclasses. The intensity of each word was subsequently rated using a numerical scale ranging from least to worst pain by physicians, patients, and university graduates. Some key words were considered missing by patients and a fourth supplementary class (adding 4 subclasses) called miscellaneous was added to the lists of pain descriptors (Melzack & Torgerson, 1971). The descriptor lists of the MPQ are read to the patient who is instructed to choose only the words that describe the feelings and sensations at that precise moment (Melzack, 1975). The questionnaire gives the clinicians three major indices: (1) the pain rating index that corresponds to the sum of ranking of each word chosen in all 20 subclasses (the word in each subclass implying the least pain is given a score of 1, the next word a score of 2, and so on); (2) the number of words that are chosen; (3) the actual pain intensity when the questionnaire is administered from no pain (score 0) to excruciating pain (score 5; Melzack, 1975, 2005). The MPQ has been demonstrated to be a reliable, consistent, valid, and useful tool for clinicians to assess pain qualities in each patient (Chapman et al., 1985; Love, Leboeuf, & Crisp, 1989; Melzack, 1983; Wilkie, Savedra, Holzemier, Tesler, & Paul, 1990). The MPQ is sensitive enough to measure decreases in pain behavior following analgesic treatments in patients with wounds (Briggs, 1996) or breast cancer (Eija, Tiina, & Pertti, 1996) pain and also measure decreases comparable to those detected using visual analogue or verbal rating scales following oral analgesics treatments in postoperative pain (Jenkinson et al., 1995). Since its introduction in 1975, the MPQ has been used in several hundred studies of pain and translated into several languages (Melzack & Katz, 1999). A short version of the MPQ was subsequently developed to better suit project research or emergency situations where the time available to obtain information is limited and critical (Melzack, 1987). This short version consists of 15 words taken from the longer version (11 words from the sensory and 4 words from the affective categories), and is accompanied by a present pain intensity score and a visual analogue scale rating (Cook et al., 2004; Melzack, 1987). Although pain is a private and personal experience, patients suffering the same or similar pain syndromes can characterized their pain by a distinctive constellation of words. Patients with similar conditions but sometimes divergent backgrounds show remarkable consistency in this choice of words (Grushka & Sessle, 1984; Katz, 1992; Katz & Melzack, 1991; Melzack, 2005). Thus, the MPQ enables different pain syndromes to be reliably discriminated (Dubuisson & Melzack, 1976). However, high levels of anxiety in a patient can diminish the discriminative capacity of the instrument (Atkinson, Kremer, & Ignelzi, 1982; Bélanger et al., 1989; Melzack, Wall, & Ty, 1982). Behavioral approaches such as those used to measure pain in animals are relied on to assess pain in infants and preverbal children, and also in adults with poor language capacity or mental confusion (Chapman et al., 1985; Marinov, Mandadjieva, & Kostianev, 2008; McGrath & Unruh, 2002; Ross & Ross, 1984). However, behavioral measures of pain should not replace self-rated measures if the patient is able to rate his or her subjective state of pain. Someone else's pain cannot be described completely by anyone other than the inflicted individual (Melzack & Katz, 1999). Some patients may be stoic in response to pain and outwardly exhibit a calm demeanor even while experiencing excruciating pain accompanied by autonomic activation, whereas other patients may exaggerate pain behaviors but in fact experience less pain. Therefore, concordance in the assessment of pain may vary between the patient and health care professionals, effects that may be attributed to the personal and private nature of the pain experience (Choinière et al., 1990). In some cases, physiological approaches (e.g., heart rate, blood pressure, electrodermal activity) can also be used to better correlate pain experience with its behavioral counterpart in patients and elucidate mechanisms associated with the painful experience (al'Absi, Petersen, & Wittmers, 2002; Chapman et al., 1985; Price, 1988). Nonetheless, it must be noted that even though many physiological and endocrine events can be measured and occur concurrently with pain experience, many of these events are not exclusively related to pain and may appear in response to stress rather than pain per se (Christensen, Brandt, Rem, & Kehlet, 1982).

PAIN MEASUREMENT IN ANIMALS

Early studies on pain were performed in anaesthetized animals and used transient stimuli to produce pain in order to avoid tissue damage. In the past decade, many animal pain models have been developed to study mechanisms underlying persistent pain in awake behaving animals (for a review, see Dubner & Ren, 1999). Animal subjects are necessary in pain research because they permit manipulation of experimental variables that can lead to a better understanding of pain mechanisms at cellular and subcellular levels and improve analgesic therapies. Moreover, animal models can be used to model certain human pathological conditions (Chapman et al., 1985). The main purpose of these studies is to further elucidate the physiopathological aspect of pain conditions found in humans and permit preclinical validation of novel analgesic targets. Experimental pain may be induced in animals with different modalities of noxious stimulation (e.g., heat, mechanical, electrical and chemical stimulation; for reviews, see Chapman et al., 1985; Dubner & Ren, 1999; Hogan, 2002; Ren & Dubner, 1999; Whiteside, Adedoyin, & Leventhal, 2008). Although animals lack the ability to verbally communicate their pain, they exhibit the same motor behaviors and physiological responses demonstrated by humans following pain stimulation (Chapman et al., 1985; Dubner & Ren, 1999; Whiteside et al., 2008). However, for ethical reasons, animals should be exposed to the minimal pain necessary to carry out the experiment (Dubner, 1983) and they should not be exposed to pain greater than humans themselves would tolerate (Bowd, 1980). Finally, animal studies on pain employ behavioral measures of two types: simple reflex measures and more complex voluntary and intentional behaviors that can be either unlearned or learned (Chapman et al., 1985).

Simple Reflex Measures

Simple reflex measures include the tail-flick, the hot-plate, the mechanical withdrawal reflex, the Hargreaves, and the paw pressure tests (Table 33.3). In most cases, latency to withdraw/escape from noxious stimulation is assessed. The tail-flick test measures the latency for a rodent to withdraw his tail from a heat source (radiant heat or hot water immersion) focused on the tail (D'Amour & Smith, 1941). The hot-plate test measures the latency to escape (licking, lifting, paw fluttering) when the animal is placed on a preheated plate (van Eick, 1967). In the mechanical withdrawal test, thermal, mechanical, or electrical stimuli may be employed (Chaplan, Bach, Pogrel, Chung, & Yaksh, 1994). The Hargreaves test measures the latency to paw withdrawal following application of radiant heat to the plantar surface of the paw through the floor of a glass platform (Hargreaves, Dubner, Brown, Flores, & Joris, 1988). One advantage of this latter method is that animals do not need to be restrained, but rather may be placed underneath an inverted plastic cage positioned on the glass platform so that they may move freely. The paw pressure test measures the latency to struggle or vocalization following application of a constant, or more frequently, an increasing mechanical pressure applied to the hind limb (Randall & Selitto, 1957). It is important to note that in all these simple reflex measures the animal has control over the intensity and duration of the stimulus ensuring that the animal is not exposed to intolerable levels of pain (Dubner & Ren, 1999).

Organized Unlearned Behaviors

Complex organized unlearned behaviors may be assessed to measure pain because these behaviors require supraspinal sensory processing rather than relying exclusively on simple reflexes (Chapman et al., 1985). Commonly associated behaviors are used to assess nocifensive manifestation following inflammatory, neuropathic, visceral, cancer, or postoperative pain (Bennett & Xie, 1988; Brennan, Vandermeulen, & Gebhart, 1996; Hargreaves et al., 1988; Ness, 1999; Pogatzki, Niemeier, & Brennan, 2002; Schwei et al., 1999; Wacnik et al., 2003). In these models, pain is produced that cannot be controlled by the animal. Therefore, it is important that investigators assess the level of pain in these animals and provide analgesics when it doesn't interfere with the experiment (Dubner & Ren, 1999).

Organized Learned Behaviors

Organized learned behaviors are considered as a separate category because pain is inferred from an animal's learned or operant responses to escape noxious stimulation. Indeed, the most common method involves an animal escaping from a noxious stimulus by initiating a learned behavior such as crossing a barrier or pressing a bar. For example, electric shock can be delivered to a grid floor in a cage and the animal can learn to jump over a barrier partition to escape this stimulus. It is important to note that these learning procedures give the animal control over the painful stimulus of the experiment (Dubner & Ren, 1999).

Tissue Injury Models of Persistent Pain

Animal models of tissue injury and inflammation have been developed to reproduce features of clinical pain conditions (Whiteside et al., 2008). The formalin test (Dubuisson & Dennis, 1977) and the orofacial formalin test (Clavelou, Dallel, Orliaguet, Woda, & Raboisson, 1995; Clavelou, Pajot, Dallel, & Raboisson, 1989) are commonly employed examples. Other models of more persistent pain employ irritants (e.g., capsaicin, bee venom) or inflammatory agents (e.g., carrageenan or complete Freund's adjuvant; Hargreaves et al., 1988; LaMotte, Shain, Simone, & Tsai, 1991; Stein, Millan, & Herz, 1988). Animal models of polyarthritis and arthritis have also been developed to attempt to mimic these human conditions (Coderre & Wall, 1987; De Castro Costa, DeSutter, Gybels, & Van Hees, 1981; Okuda, Nakahama, Miyakawa, & Shima, 1984; Schaible, Schmidt, & Willis, 1987; Table 33.4). Furthermore, visceral pain (Chernov, Wilson, Fowler, & Plummer, 1967; Ness & Gebhart, 1988; Table 33.5), cancer pain (Medhurst et al., 2002; Wacnik et al., 2001; Table 33.6), and postoperative pain (Brennan et al., 1996; Pogatzki et al., 2002; Table 33.7) models have been developed as well. These models are well characterized and remain sensitive to analgesics that are effective for suppressing similar pain states in humans.

Nerve Injury Models of Persistent Pain

Nerve injury models have been developed to better understand the mechanisms involved in the development of neuropathic pain in humans. Several models of nerve ligation have been developed over the past 20 years (Bennett & Xie, 1988; Decosterd & Woolf, 2000; Kim & Chung, 1992; Seltzer, Dubner, & Shir, 1990) and have improved our understanding of mechanisms (e.g., central sensitization; Woolf & Thompson, 1991) that contribute to neuropathic pain states (Table 33.8). Bennett and Xie (1988) developed the first animal model of neuropathic pain, known as the chronic constriction injury (CCI) of the sciatic nerve. The development of animal models of neuropathic pain has had a monumental impact on the pain field, both by spurring research on the underlying mechanisms, by encouraging the development of additional animal models, and by enabling preclinical validation of novel analgesics that have shown efficacy

TABLE 33.3 Methods for measurement of acute pain in animals

	Test	Description	Dependent Measures	Commentary	References
Thermal	Tail-flick test	• Radiant heat is focused on the tail • The tail can also be immersed in hot water	• Measure the latency for the animal to remove it's tail from the heat source	• Simple method that measures spinal nociceptive reflex • Sensitive to analgesics	D'Amour & Smith, 1941
	Hot-plate test	• Animal is placed on a metal surface that is either preheated to a noxious temperature or progressively increases in temperature	• Measure the latency to the appearance of evoked responses from the animal (lick, bite, fluttering of hindpaws, and/or jump)	• Licking is a reflex • Jump reflects an integrated response at the supraspinal level • Sensitive to analgesics	van Eick, 1967
	Hargreaves test	• Heat is applied to the plantar surface of the hind paw through the floor of a glass platform	• Measure the latency for the animal to withdraw its paw from a heat source	• Animal is not manually restrained during assessment • Sensitive to analgesics	Hargreaves et al., 1988
Mechanical	Von Frey filament test	• Application of filaments of different calibers (force) are typically applied to the plantar surface of the paw • Filaments applied through the floor of a wire mesh platform	• The threshold of paw withdrawal is related to the force applied by the filament • Frequency of paw withdrawal to a given filament (force)	• Animal is not manually restrained during assessment • Sensitive to analgesics	Chaplan et al, 1994
	Paw pressure test	• A mechanical simulator is used to apply a constant noxious pressure or, more often, an increasing pressure to the hind paw of the animal	• Behavioral assessments: freezing (no movement), withdrawal of the paw, and vocalization produced by the animal	• Animal must be manually restrained for assessment • Sensitive to analgesics	Randall & Selitto, 1957

TABLE 33.4 Animal models of tissue injury-induced persistent pain

Test	Description	Dependent Measures	Commentary	References
Formalin test	• Subcutaneous (dorsal surface) or intraplantar (plantar surface) injection of formalin in the paw • Injection is unilateral	• Duration of licking/biting, lifting, and favoring the injected paw is measured • A weighted pain score may be calculated based on time spent in each category of behavior	• Biphasic pain response, characterized by acute and inflammatory phases • This model is commonly used in rats and in mice	Dubuisson & Dennis, 1977; Watson, Sufka, Coderre, 1997
Orofacial formalin test	• Injection of formalin into the upper lip of a rodent	• Duration of time spent rubbing the injected upper lip	• Biphasic response similar to that observed following formalin injection in the paw • Reliable method to assess trigeminal pain	Clavelou et al., 1989; Clavelou et al., 1995
Capsaicin	• Intraplantar injection of capsaicin in rodents • Intradermal injection of capsaicin into forearm of humans	• Nocifensive behavior (licking, biting, and flinching injected paw) • Mechanical and thermal hypersensitivity (assessed in rodents with von Frey filaments and Hargreaves testing)	• This model is used in rats, mice and human and nonhuman primates	Simone, Ngeow, Putterman, LaMotte, 1987; LaMotte et al., 1991
Carrageenan	• Intraplantar injection of carrageenan	• Mechanical and thermal hypersensitivity • Edema	• Behavioral changes maximal at 2 hr post-injection and typically persist for 24 to 96 hr • Used in rats and mice	Hargreaves et al., 1988
Complete Freund's adjuvant	• Intraplantar injection of complete Freund's adjuvant (CFA) in rodents	• Mechanical and thermal hypersensitivity • Edema	• Inflammation appears 2 hr after injection and is maximal after 6–8 hr	Stein, Millan, Herz, 1988; Iadarola et al., 1988
Acute arthritis	• Intrajoint injection of sodium urate crystals, carrageenan, kaolin, or other irritants provoke acute inflammation of the joint	• Degree of flexion of the joint • Circumference of the joint • Mechanical and thermal hypersensitivity	• Sodium urate crystal-induced arthritis is fully developed within 24 hr	Okuda et al., 1984; Coderre & Wall, 1987; Schaible et al., 1987
Polyarthritis	• CFA injected into the tail induces a delayed hypersensitivity • Inflammation and hyperalgesia of multiple joints occurs after 10 days to 3 weeks	• Scratching behavior • Reduction in motor activity • Mechanical and thermal hypersensitivity	• Systemic disease develops and includes: skin lesions, destruction of bones and cartilage, liver impairment, and lymphadenopathy	De Castro Costa et al., 1981

TABLE 33.5 Animal models of visceral pain

Test	Description	Dependent Measures	Commentary	References
Writhing test	• Injection (i.p.) of noxious irritants such as acetic acid produces a characteristic response (e.g., arched back, abdominal contractions, rolling on one side)	• Abdominal contractions and stretching of the body	• Inflammation of the visceral organs and abdominal wall • Used in mice and rats	Chernov, Wilson, Fowler, Plummer, 1967; Helfer & Jaques, 1970; Vyklicky, 1979
Colorectal distension	• Colorectal distension induced by an inflatable device • Additionally used on anaesthetized animals to measure tachycardia simultaneously	• Muscle contraction or behavioral reaction is measured • Tachycardia grade related to increasing colorectal distension	• Stimulus more natural than injections of irritants • Strong clinical relevance • Attenuated by analgesics	Ness & Gebhart, 1988; Ness, Randich, Gebhart, 1991, Ness, 1999
Bladder distension	• Distension of the bladder in anaesthetized animals	• Physiological responses or activation of micturition reflex	• Observed cardiovascular or visceromotor responses are reliable and reproducible	Gosling, Dixon, Dunn, 1977; Ness, 1999
Cystitis	• Cystitis is induced in mice, and rats by i.p. injection of cyclophosphamide (anticancer substance) with adverse effects affecting the bladder • Mustard oil, acetic acid, and other compounds have been used to induce cystitis	• In rats, pain behavior (licking, abdominal contraction, piloerection, arched back) are commonly evaluated • In mice, mechanical allodynia and locomotion behavior are commonly measured	• The stimulus is known to affect only one viscera organ, the bladder • Strong clinical relevance	McMahon & Abel, 1987; Lanteri-Minet, Don, de Pommery, Michiels, Menetrey, 1995
Ureteral calculosis	• Artificial stone (made using dental cement) is implanted in rat ureteral tract • Animals show discomfort (abdominal contraction and hind limb extension) during 4 days following the implantation	• Muscular lumbar hyperalgesia is demonstrated by vocalization of the animal following electrical stimulation of lumbar muscle	• Strong clinical relevance	Giamberardino, Vecchiet, Albe-Fessard, 1990; Giamberardino, Valente, de Bigontina, Vecchiet, 1995
Myocardial ischemia	• Temporary obstruction of coronary artery or application of algogenic substances to epicardium of anaesthetized animal	• Recordings of neuronal electrical activity	• This model is used to elucidate pain mechanisms related to angina	Kumar et al., 1970; Pan & Chen, 2002

TABLE 33.6   Animal models of cancer pain

Test	Description	Dependent Measures	Commentary	References
Carcinoma	• Neoplasia cells (from mammary gland) are injected into the tibia • Bone destruction is observed between 10 and 14 days; bone integrity is compromised after 20 days	• Mechanical hypersensitivity	• This metastasis cancer model is proposed to study new therapeutic treatments for metastasis pain • Metastatic bone pain is difficult to control due to fast progression and difficulty in predicting onset and severity	Medhurst et al., 2002; Walker et al., 2002
Fibrosarcoma	• Malignant neoplasia cells are injected into the humerus of mice • Hyperalgesia appears on the third day after injecting the cells and progresses with tumor development • Malignant neoplasia cells may also be injected into the calcaneus bone • Destruction is appearing after six days	• Hypersensitivity related to movement • Mechanical and thermal hypersensitivity	• Humerus cancer model permits evaluation of hypersensitivity in movement	Wacnik et al., 2001, Wacnik et al., 2003
Osteosarcoma	• Malignant neoplasia cells are injected inside the femur of mice • Cancer pain lesions are developing and are destroying the bone	• Mechanical hypersensitivity	• Injecting cancer cells in the femur of mice was the first cancer pain model to be developed • This model suggests that cancer pain is different from inflammatory or neuropathic pain	Schwei et al., 1999; Wang & Wang, 2003
Neuropathic cancer pain	• Sarcoma cells are injected at the proximity of the sciatic nerve in mice • Tumor growth compresses the nerve	• Mechanical and thermal hypersensitivity	• Nerve damage appears progressively by compression and better represents neuropathic cancer pain observed clinically	Shimoyama, Tanaka, Hasue, Shimoayama, 2002

TABLE 33.7   Animal models of postoperative pain

Test	Description	Dependent Measures	Commentary	References
Plantar hindpaw incision	• 1 cm incision is made on the plantar surface of the hindpaw in rats • Plantar muscle is cut parallel to muscle fiber	• Mechanical hypersensitivity	• Nociceptive behavior and mechanical hypersensitivity is similar to human reaction to wound • Pain is elevated after surgery and decreases 7 to 10 days later • Local morphine or anesthetics reduce pain behavior	Brennan et al., 1996; Brennan, 1999
Gastrocnemius muscles paw incision	• Gastrocnemius muscles of the rat paw are sectioned under general anesthesia	• Thermal and mechanical hypersensitivity on the plantar face	• This model permits evaluation of mechanisms responsible for secondary hypersensitivity and its role in postoperative persistent pain • Opiate administration reduces pain behavior	Pogatzki et al., 2002
Ovariohysterectomy	• Removal of ovaries and uterus in rodents • Pain behavior associated with abdominal contractions and stretching of the body	• Mechanical and thermal hypersensitivity • Painful behaviors are evaluated with a rating scale	• Strong clinical relevance • Visceral or peritoneal pain may increase painful behaviors • Analgesics reduce these abnormal behaviors	Lascelles, Waterman, Cripps, Livingston, Henderson, 1995; Gonzalez, Field, Bramwell, McCleary, Singh, 2000

TABLE 33.8A   Animal models of neuropathic pain: traumatic nerve injury

Test	Description	Dependent Measures	Commentary	References
Chronic construction of sciatic nerve	• Three loosely constrictive ligatures are placed around the common sciatic nerve • Animals develop nociceptive behaviors (protection and reduction of weight on the affected limb and lameness)	• Mechanical and thermal hypersensitivity • Cold allodynia • Spontaneous pain	• Hypersensitivity develops between 10 and 14 days and persists for 8 weeks • Used in rats and mice • Termed CCI model	Bennett & Xie, 1988
Partial sciatic nerve injury	• The sciatic nerve is exposed at high-thigh level and 1/3–1/2 of the dorsal thickness of the nerve is trapped in a ligature • Animals develop nociceptive behaviors (protection and licking of the affected limb)	• Mechanical and thermal hypersensitivity • Ipsilateral and contralateral deficits	• Hypersensitivity can persist for many months • Used in mice and rats	Seltzer et al., 1990
Spinal nerve ligation	• L5 and L6 spinal nerves are ligated and sectioned distal to the dorsal root ganglion; L4 spinal nerve is intact • Animals develop nociceptive behaviors (protection and reduction of weight on the affected limb and lameness)	• Mechanical and thermal hypersensitivity • Spontaneous pain	• Thermed SNL (Chung) model • The SNL model (with the CCI and partial ligation of the sciatic nerve) constitute the three most widely used neuropathic pain models	Kim & Chung, 1992
Spared nerve injury	• Two of the three terminal branches of the sciatic nerve (tibial and common peroneal nerves) are ligated and sectioned. The third branch, the sural nerve, is left intact • Animals develop chronic nociceptive behaviors (modification of position and reduction of weight on the affected limb)	• Mechanical and thermal hypersensitivity • Cold allodynia • Spontaneous pain	• This model shows that sensitivity of intact small nerve is modified by section of an adjacent nerve fiber • Rapid onset of cutaneous hypersensitivity	Decosterd & Woolf, 2000
Neuritis-induced neuropathic pain	• Application of complete Freund's adjuvant to the nerve (usually at the periphery of the sciatic nerve)	• Mechanical and thermal hypersensitivity • Cold allodynia	• This model assesses the contribution of inflammation to the development of neuropathic pain	Bennett et al., 2000; Bennett, Everhart, Hulsebosch, 2000
Saphenous nerve partial ligation	• 1/3–1/2 of the saphenous nerve is ligated (via three loose ligatures around the circumference of the saphenous nerve) • Neuropathic pain behaviors are observed 3 to 5 days after surgery	• Mechanical and thermal hypersensitivity	• This model is also used in mice; known as chronic constriction of the saphenous nerve	Walczak, Pichette, Leblond, Desbiens, Beaulieu, 2005, 2006

TABLE 33.8B   Animal models of neuropathic pain: metabolic and toxic neuropathies

Test	Description	Dependent Measures	Commentary	References
Diabetic neuropathy	• Injection (i.p.) of streptozotocine in rats provokes destruction of β cells in the pancreas and subsequent development of diabetes type 1 • Rats develop reductions in locomotor activity	• Mechanical and thermal hypersensitivity	• This model is controversial because observations are difficult to attribute to neuropathy because rats show impaired health and obvious signs of discomfort	Rakieten, Rakieten, Nadkarni, 1963; Wuarin Bierman, Zahnd, Kaufmann, Burcklen, Adler, 1987
Chemotherapy-evoked toxic neuropathy	• Repeated injections of antitumor agents (vincristine, paclitaxel, or cisplatin) change responsiveness to mechanical and sometimes thermal (cold or heat) stimulation	• Mechanical hypersensitivity always observed • Thermal hyperalgesia or hypoalgesia may be absent or present depending on agent and dose used	• These models are useful for understanding neuropathy induced in patients by treatment with chemotherapeutic agents	Aley, Reichling, Levine, 1996; Authier, Coudore, Eschalier, Fialip, 1999; Polomano & Bennett, 2001

for treating neuropathic pain in humans (e.g., gabapentin). The development of neuropathy following neuritis (Bennett, Chastain, & Hulsebosch, 2000), metabolic challenges (Rakieten, Rakieten, & Nadkarni, 1963; Wuarin Bierman, Zahnd, Kaufmann, Burcklen, & Adler, 1987), and chemotherapeutic treatment (Aley, Reichling, & Levine, 1996; Authier, Coudore, Eschalier, & Fialip, 1999; Polomano & Bennett, 2001) have also been studied (Table 33.8).

PHARMACOLOGICAL MANAGEMENT OF PAIN

The main concern of clinical health professionals is to improve the management of pain in their patients. However, available pharmacotherapies for the management of pain are inadequate and require that multiple factors (e.g., unwanted side-effect profiles) also be considered (Table 33.9) to optimize the efficacy of the treatment. Pain is a multifactorial phenomenon requiring interdisciplinary approaches. Multimodal analgesia is an approach that involves the combination of several analgesics administered by the same or different routes to achieve better, more effective relief than analgesics administered separately. Thus, the combination of desipramine (an antidepressant) with morphine enhances the efficacy of the narcotic analgesic for the control of postoperative pain (Levine, Gordon, Smith, & McBryde, 1986). Furthermore, low back pain is well relieved by the combination of tramadol with acetaminophen (Perrot, Krause, Crozes, & Naïm, 2006). Musculoskeletal pain is similarly reduced by the combination of acetaminophen with hydrocodone (Hewitt et al., 2007). Different pharmacological approaches exist for the treatment of pain such as the use of opioids or nonsteroidal anti-inflammatory drugs

(NSAIDs), anticonvulsants, antidepressants, ketamine, and others (for review, see Guindon, Walczak, & Beaulieu, 2007) although adverse side-effects remain the main constraint (Table 33.10). Furthermore, along with standard routes of administration, novel drug delivery approaches have become available in the past few years, including transdermal patches, oral mucosal sprays, intranasal instillation, rectal suppositories, and others (Table 33.10). The literature has indicated that multimodality approaches are associated with an increase in patient satisfaction and a reduction in side-effects compared to those resulting from single analgesic techniques in pain management (Brodner et al., 2001; Mugabure Bujedo, Tranque Bizueta, Gonzalez Santos, & Adrian Garde, 2007; Pyati & Gan, 2007).

NONPHARMACOLOGICAL MANAGEMENT OF PAIN

Less than 50 years ago, neurosurgery was a common approach employed to manage severe or chronic pain. Indeed, the destruction of peripheral nerves by a meticulous surgery that excise the injured area and include grafting of a new nerve section was performed frequently. However, this procedure failed to alleviate pain and in some cases exacerbated it (Noordenbos & Wall, 1981). In addition, the cordotomy procedure (cutting tracts of the spinal cord) was used on terminally ill cancer patients to reduce severe cancer pain (Ischia, Ischia, Luzzani, Toscano, & Steele, 1985; Ischia, Luzzani, Ischia, & Pacini, 1984). This procedure was recommended only to terminal cancer patients because the pain returns and is frequently accompanied by unpleasant sensations and incontinence (Ischia et al., 1984, 1985). However, surgery infrequently achieves long-term control of pain and resumption of pain is common. This finding is unsurprising because surgical section disrupts the normal patterns of input to the central nervous system (e.g., resulting in abnormal bursting activity in the deafferented central cells that persists long after the surgery; Melzack & Loeser, 1978). Morever, the complexity of brain activity and its plasticity contradict a simple surgical solution for pain problems. Therefore, a more promising approach consists of continuous nerve blockage to reduce evoked pain. This technique reduces nausea and vomiting in patients receiving continuous peripheral nerve blocks while increasing their satisfaction. In this case, rehabilitation is improved and incidence of postsurgery chronic pain syndromes is greatly decreased (Boezaart, 2006). In home treatments are also possible, increasing patient satisfaction and comfort (Ilfed & Enneking, 2005). Furthermore, the use of nonpharmacological options such as massage, acupuncture, heat therapy, relaxation, and

TABLE 33.9 Multiple factors influencing pharmacological treatment of pain

- Cultural and religious belief
- Personal experience
- Social/family environment
- Previous medical history
- Pain intensity
- Reduced work status
- Interference with leisure activity
- Other diseases interacting
- Interactions with other drugs
- Toxicity
- Cost
- Patient acceptance and compliance
- Patient expectations and beliefs about the cause of pain

TABLE 33.10 Different pharmacological treatments and administrations for pain relief

Drug	Indications	Route of Administration	Adverse Effects	Contraindications
Opioids Morphine (or alternative opioid: hydromorphone, fentanyl, remifentanil, alfentanil, sufentanil, meperidine, buprenorphine, butorphanol, etc.)	Treatment of pain such as: • Neuropathic • Inflammatory • Cancer • Acute • Post-operative	• Oral • Intravenous • Transdermal (patch) • Sublingual spray • Intranasal spray • Oral transmucosal • Pulmonary • Microspheres	• Respiratory depression • Sedation • Nausea and vomiting • Constipation • Cognitive dysfunction • Pruritus • Tolerance/dependence • Euphoria	• Screen patients for alcohol/substance abuse; co-administer preemptive stool softeners and antiemetics
NSAIDs _Traditional_: diclofenac, ketorolac, ketoprofen, ibuprofen, naproxen _Coxibs_: celecoxib, etoricoxib, lumiracoxib, parecoxib	• Analgesics • Anti-inflammatory agents Relief of: • Osteoarthritis • Rheumatoid arthritis • Acute or postoperative pain	• Oral • Topical	• Gastrointestinal disturbances • Renal • Skin reactions • Cardiac (myocardial infarction and stroke) • Gastrointestinal associated with long-term use • Renal (acute renal failure)	• Patients with gastrointestinal and renal complications • Patients with cardiovascular and cerebrovascular disease • Carefulness in patients with hypertension, hyperlipidaemia, diabetes, arterial disease, or smoking
Antidepressants _Tricyclic_ (imipramine) _Newer_ (venlaflaxine, duloxetine, bupropion)	• Neuropathic pain	• Oral	• Sedation • Constipation • Dry mouth • Orthostatic hypotension • Weight gain with _tricyclic_ • Ataxia, nausea, and anorexia using _newer antidepressants_	• Patients with glaucoma and/or taking monoamine oxidase inhibitors • Duloxetine has been approved by US FDA for use in diabetic, neuropathy
Anticonvulsants Gabapentin, pregabalin, lamotrigine	• Diabetic neuropathy • Postherpetic neuralgia • Trigeminal neuralgia	• Oral	• Sedation • Ataxia • Edema • Diplopia • Weight gain	• Patients with renal dysfunction need a dose adjustment
Cannabinoids Cannabis, nabilone, dronabinol, Δ^9-THC/CBD	• Acute • Chronic pain	• Oral • Sublingual spray • Inhalation	• Euphoria • Tachycardia • Tolerance • Memory impairment	• Patients with hypertension and ischemic heart disease
Local anesthetics Lidocaine, bupivacaine, and others	• Blocking evoked pain	• Local/regional • Transdermal (patch) • Intravenous • Neuroaxial (spinal, epidural)	• Convulsions • Coma • Skin erythema • Rash • Cardiorespiratory depression with increasing doses	• Locoregional anesthesia problems: non-consenting patients, local infection, coagulation disorders, inadequate monitoring

transcutaneous electrical nerve stimulation (TENS) as adjuvants to conventional analgesia can also be considered and incorporated to achieve an effective and successful pain management regimen in some patients (Pyati & Gan, 2007). It is also possible to reduce clinical pain by using cognitive therapies although these therapies are not exclusive and need to be used in conjunction with the proper medication. For example, in patients suffering from post-traumatic stress syndrome (Muse, 1985, 1986) and ovarian cancer (Montazeri, McEwen, & Gillis, 1996), psychological counseling is validated to improve quality of life and reduce pain. However, there are no perfect therapies and the effectiveness of each can vary depending on the disease and the patient. Although each therapy has its own specific limitations related to the disease/patient context (see Table 33.10), it is highly significant that the effects of two or more therapies given in combination can produce additive or synergistic effects.

SUMMARY

Great advances have been made in the past several decades in defining pain and understanding its underlying mechanisms. Further research is nonetheless necessary to reduce unnecessary suffering in chronic pain patients. Although many treatment modalities are being used to reduce and alleviate pain, many basic research and clinical questions remain unanswered. These gaps in our knowledge base may be attributed to the complexity of pain mechanisms that are involved. Filling these gaps may identify previously unrecognized therapeutic targets. In the coming years, advances in our preclinical and clinical understanding of pain mechanisms are expected, which should provide an impetus for improving pharmacotherapies for chronic pain. Treatment paradigms are shifting from single to multiple therapies that combine medications with distinct mechanisms of action and/or combine medications with nontraditional therapies. Targeting multiple analgesic mechanisms simultaneously holds promise for attaining a more complete attenuation of pain with a more limited spectrum of unwanted side-effects.

REFERENCES

al'Absi, M., Petersen, K. L., & Wittmers, L. E. (2002). Adrenocortical and hemodynamic predictors of pain perception in men and women. *Pain, 96,* 197–204.

Aley, K. O., Reichling, D. B., & Levine, J. D. (1996). Vincristine hyperalgesia in the rat: A model of painful vincristine neuropathy in humans. *Neuroscience, 73,* 259–265.

Atkinson, J. H., Kremer, E. F., & Ignelzi, R. J. (1982). Diffusion of pain language with affective disturbance confounds differential diagnosis. *Pain, 12,* 375–384.

Authier, N., Coudore, F., Eschalier, A., & Fialip, J. (1999). Pain related behavior during vincristine-induced neuropathy in rats. *NeuroReport, 10,* 965–968.

Basbaum, A. I., & Fields, H. L. (1978). Endogenous pain control mechanisms: Review and hypothesis. *Annals of Neurology, 4,* 451–462.

Basbaum, A. I., Marley, N. J. E., O'Keefe, J., & Clanton, C. H. (1977). Reversal of morphine and stimulus produced analgesia by subtotal spinal cord lesions. *Pain, 3,* 43–56.

Beecher, H. K. (1959). *Measurement of subjective responses.* New York: Oxford University Press.

Bélanger, E., Melzack, R., & Lauzon, P. (1989). Pain of first-trimester abortion: A study of psychosocial and medical predictors. *Pain, 36,* 339–350.

Bennett, A. D., Chastain, K. M., & Hulsebosch, C. E. (2000). Alleviation of mechanical and thermal allodynia by CGRP(8–37) in a rodent model of chronic central pain. *Pain, 86,* 163–175.

Bennett, A. D., Everhart, A. W., & Hulsebosch, C. E. (2000). Intrathecal administration of an NMDA or a non-NMDA receptor antagonist reduces mechanical but not thermal allodynia in a rodent model of chronic central pain after spinal cord injury. *Brain Research, 859,* 72–82.

Bennett, G. J., & Xie, Y. K. (1988). A peripheral mononeuropathy in rat that produces disorders of pain sensation like those seen in man. *Pain, 33,* 87–107.

Besson, J. M., & Chaouch, A. (1987). Peripheral and spinal mechanisms of nociception. *Physiological Reviews, 67,* 67–186.

Bie, B., & Pan, Z. Z. (2007). Trafficking of central opioid receptors and descending pain inhibition. *Molecular Pain, 3,* 37.

Bingel, U., Schoell, E., & Büchel, C. (2007). Imaging pain modulation in health and disease. *Current Opinion in Neurology, 20,* 424–431.

Bishop, G. H. (1946). Neural mechanisms of cutaneous sense. *Physiological Reviews, 26,* 77–102.

Bishop, G. H. (1959). The relation between nerve fiber size and sensory modality: Phylogenetic implications of the afferent innervations of the cortex. *Journal of Nervous and Mental Diseases, 128,* 89–114.

Boezaart, A. P. (2006). Perineural infusion of local anesthetics. *Anesthesiology, 104,* 872–880.

Bonica, J. J. (1953). *The management of pain.* Philadelphia: Lea and Febiger.

Bonica, J. J. (1974). Organization and function of a pain clinic. In J. J. Bonica (Ed.), *Advances in neurology* (pp. 433–443). New York: Raven Press.

Boring, E. G. (1942). *Sensation and perception in the history of experimental psychology.* New York: Appleton-Century-Crofts.

Bowd, A. D. (1980). Ethics and animal experimentation. *American Psychologist, 35,* 224–225.

Brennan, F., Carr, D. B., & Cousins, M. (2007). Pain management: A fundamental human right. *Anesthesia and Analgesia, 105,* 205–221.

Brennan, T. J. (1999). Postoperative models of nociception. Animal models of pain. *ILAR Journal, 40,* 129–136.

Brennan, T. J., Vandermeulen, E. P., & Gebhart, G. F. (1996). Characterization of a rat model of incisional pain. *Pain, 64,* 493–501.

Briggs, M. (1996). Surgical wound pain: A trial of two treatments. *Journal of Wound Care, 5,* 456–460.

Brodner, G., Van Aken, H., Hertle, L., Fobker, M., Von Eckardstein, A., Goeters, C., et al. (2001). Multimodal perioperative management: Combining thoracic epidural analgesia, forced mobilization, and oral nutrition: Reduces hormonal and metabolic stress and improves convalescence after major urologic surgery. *Anesthesia and Analgesia, 92,* 1594–600.

Chaplan, S. R., Bach, F. W., Pogrel, J. W., Chung, J. M., & Yaksh, T. L. (1994). Quantitative assessment of tactile allodynia in the rat paw. *Journal of Neuroscience Methods, 53*, 55–63.

Chapman, C. R., Casey, K. L., Dubner, R., Foley, K. M., Gracely, R. H., & Reading, A. E. (1985). Pain measurement: An overview. *Pain, 22*, 1–31.

Chenot, J. F., Leonhardt, C., Keller, S., Scherer, M., Donner-Banzhoff, N., Pfingsten, M., et al. (2008). The impact of specialist care for low back pain on health service utilization in primary care patients: A prospective cohort study. *European Journal of Pain, 12*, 275–283.

Chernov, H. I., Wilson, D. E., Fowler, W. F., & Plummer, A. J. (1967). Non-specificity of the mouse writhing test. *Archives Internationales de Pharmacodynamie et de Thérapie, 167*, 171–178.

Choinière, M., & Amsel, R. (1996). A visual analogue thermometer for measuring pain intensity. *Journal of Pain and Symptom Management, 11*, 299–311.

Choinière, M., Melzack, R., Girard, N., Rondeau, J., & Paquin, M. J. (1990). Comparisons between patients and nurses assessments of pain and medication efficacy in severe burn injuries. *Pain, 40*, 143–152.

Christensen, P., Brandt, M. R., Rem, J., & Kehlet, H. (1982). Influence of extradural morphine on the adrenocortical and hyperglycaemic response to surgery. *British Journal of Anaesthesia, 54*, 23–27.

Clavelou, P., Dallel, R., Orliaguet, T., Woda, A., & Raboisson, P. (1995). The orofacial formalin test in rats: Effects of different formalin concentrations. *Pain, 62*, 295–301.

Clavelou, P., Pajot, J., Dallel, R., & Raboisson, P. (1989). Application of the formalin test to the study of orofacial pain in the rat. *Neuroscience Letters, 103*, 349–353.

Coderre, T. J., & Wall, P. D. (1987). Ankle joint urate arthritis (AJUA) in rats: An alternative animal model of arthritis to that produced by Freund's adjuvant. *Pain, 28*, 379–393.

Cohen, S. D., Patel, S. S., Khetpal, P., Peterson, R. A., & Kimmel, P. L. (2007). Pain, sleep disturbance, and quality of life in patients with chronic kidney disease. *Clinical Journal of the American Society of Nephrology, 2*, 919–925.

Comings, D. E., & Amromin, G. D. (1974). Autosomal dominant insensitivity to pain with hyperplastic myelinopathy and autosomal dominant indifference to pain. *Neurology, 24*, 838–848.

Cook, A. J., Roberts, D. A., Henderson, M. D., VanWinkle, L. C., Chastain, D. C., & Hamill-Ruth, R. J. (2004). Electronic pain questionnaires: A randomized, crossover comparison with paper questionnaires for chronic pain assessment. *Pain, 110*, 310–317.

Cox, J. J., Reimann, F., Nicholas, A. K., Thornton, G., Roberts, E., Springell, K., et al. (2006, August 24). An SCN9A channelopathy causes congenital inability to experience pain. *Nature, 444*, 894–898.

Craggs, J. G., Price, D. D., Verne, G. N., Perlstein, W. M., & Robinson, M. M. (2007). Functional brain interactions that serve cognitive-affective processing during pain and placebo analgesia. *NeuroImage, 38*, 720–729.

Craig, A. D., & Bushnell, M. C. (1994, July 8). The thermal grill illusion: Unmasking the burn of cold pain. *Science, 265*, 252–255.

Dallenbach, K. M. (1939). Pain: History and present status. *American Journal of Psychology, 52*, 331–347.

D'Amour, F. E., & Smith, D. L. (1941). A method for determining loss of pain sensation. *Journal of Pharmacology and Experimental Therapeutics, 72*, 74–79.

Daoust, R., Beaulieu, P., Manzini, C., Chauny, J. M., & Lavigne, G. (2008). Estimation of pain intensity in emergency medicine: A validation study. *Pain, 138*, 565–570.

De Castro Costa, M., DeSutter, P., Gybels, J., & Van Hees, J. (1981). Adjuvant-induced arthritis in rats: A possible animal model of chronic pain. *Pain, 10*, 173–186.

Decosterd, I., & Woolf, C. J. (2000). Spared nerve injury: An animal model of persistent peripheral neuropathic pain. *Pain, 87*, 149–158.

DeLeo, J. A., & Yezierski, R. P. (2001). The role of inflammation and neuroimmune activation in persistent pain. *Pain, 201*, 1–6.

Descartes, R. (1664). L'homme translated by M. Foster in 1901. *Lectures on the history of physiology during 16th, 17th, and 18th centuries*. Cambridge: Cambridge University Press.

Dubner, R. (1983). Pain research in animals. *Annals of the New York Academy of Sciences, 406*, 128–132.

Dubner, R., & Ren, K. (1999). Assessing transient and persistent pain in animals. In P. D. Wall & R. Melzack (Eds.), *Textbook of pain* (4th ed., pp. 359–369). London: Churchill Livingstone.

Dubuisson, D., & Dennis, S. G. (1977). The formalin test: A quantitative study of the analgesic effects of morphine, meperidine, and brain stem stimulation in rats and cats. *Pain, 4*, 161–174.

Dubuisson, D., & Melzack, R. (1976). Classification of clinical pain descriptors by multiple group discriminant analysis. *Experimental Neurology, 51*, 480–487.

Eija, K., Tiina, T., & Pertti, N. J. (1996). Amitriptyline effectively relieves neuropathic pain following treatment of breast cancer. *Pain, 64*, 293–302.

Ekblom, A., & Hansson, P. (1988). Pain intensity measurements in patients with acute pain receiving afferent stimulation. *Journal of Neurology, Neurosurgery, and Psychiatry, 51*, 481–486.

Fields, H. L. (1987). *Pain*. New York: McGraw-Hill.

Fields, H. L. (1999). Pain: An unpleasant topic. *Pain* (Suppl. 6), S61–S69.

Fields, H. L., Basbaum, A. I., Heinricher, M. M. (2006). Central nervous system mechanisms of pain modulation. In S. B. McMahon & M. Koltzenburg (Eds.), *Wall & Melzack's Textbook of pain*, 5th edition (pp. 125–142). Edinburgh: Elsevier.

Gagliese, L., & Melzack, R. (1997). Age differences in the quality of chronic pain: A preliminary study. *Pain Research and Management, 2*, 157–162.

Garcia-Larrea, L., & Magnin, M. (2008). Pathophysiology of neuropathic pain: Review of experimental models and proposed mechanisms. *Presse Médicale, 37*, 315–340.

Giamberardino, M. A., Valente, R., de Bigontina, P., & Vecchiet, L. (1995). Artificial ureteral calculosis in rats: Behavioral characterization of visceral pain episodes and their relationship with referred lumbar muscle hyperalgesia. *Pain, 61*, 459–469.

Giamberardino, M. A., Vecchiet, L., & Albe-Fessard, D. (1990). Comparison of the effects of ureteral calculosis and occlusion on muscular sensitivity to painful stimulation in rats. *Pain, 43*, 227–234.

Goldscheider, A. (1894). *Uber den Schmerz in physiologischer und klinischer hinsichl*. Berlin, Germany: Hirschwald.

Gonzalez, M. I., Field, M. J., Bramwell, S., McCleary, S., & Singh, L. (2000). Ovariohysterectomy in the rat: A model of surgical pain for evaluation of pre-emptive analgesia? *Pain, 88*, 79–88.

Gosling, J. A., Dixon, J. S., & Dunn, M. (1977). The structure of the rabbit urinary bladder after experimental distension. *Investigative Urology, 14*, 386–389.

Greenwald, H. P. (1991). Interethnic differences in pain perception. *Pain, 44*, 157–163.

Grushka, M., & Sessle, B. J. (1984). Applicability of the McGill Pain Questionnaire to the differentiation of toothache pain. *Pain, 19*, 49–57.

Guarino, A. H., & Myers, J. C. (2007). An assessment protocol to guide opioid prescriptions for patients with chronic pain. *Missouri Medicine, 104*, 513–516.

Guindon, J., Walczak, J. S., & Beaulieu, P. (2007). Recent advances in the pharmacological management of pain. *Drugs, 67*, 2121–2133.

Hagbarth, K. E., & Kerr, D. I. (1954). Central influences on spinal afferent conduction. *Journal of Neurophysiology, 17*, 295–307.

Hargreaves, K., Dubner, R., Brown, F., Flores, C., & Joris, J. (1988). A new and sensitive method for measuring thermal nociception in cutaneous hyperalgesia. *Pain, 32*, 77–88.

Helfer, H., & Jaques, R. (1970). The duration of action of antinociceptive agents ad determined in mice using the arachidonic acid writhing test. *Pharmacology, 4*, 163–168.

Hewitt, D. J., Todd, K. H., Xiang, J., Jordan, D. M., Rosenthal, N. R., & CAPSS-216 Study Investigators. (2007). Tramadol/acetaminophen or hydrocodone/acetaminophen for the treatment of ankle sprain: A randomized, placebo-controlled trial. *Annals of Emergency Medicine, 49*, 468–480.

Hogan, Q. (2002). Animal pain models. *Regional Anesthesia and Pain Medicine, 27*, 385–401.

Huskisson, E. C. (1983). *Visual analogue scales*. In R. Melzack (Ed.), *Pain measurement and assessment* (pp. 33–37). New York: Raven Press.

Iadarola, M. J., Brady, L. S., Draisci, G., & Dubner, R. (1988). Enhancement of dynorphin gene expression in spinal cord following experimental inflammation: Stimulus specificity, behavioral parameters and opioid receptor binding. *Pain 1 35*, 313–326.

Ilfeld, B. M., & Enneking, F. K. (2005). Continuous peripheral nerve blocks at home: A review. *Anesthesia and Analgesia, 100*, 1822–1833.

Ischia, S., Ischia, A., Luzzani, A., Toscano, D., & Steele, A. (1985). Results up to death in the treatment of persistent cervico-thoracic (Pancoast) and thoracic malignant pain by unilateral percutaneous cervical cordotomy. *Pain, 21*, 339–355.

Ischia, S., Luzzani, A., Ischia, A., & Pacini, L. (1984). Role of unilateral percutaneous cervical cordotomy in the treatment of neoplastic vertebral pain. *Pain, 19*, 123–131.

Jenkinson, C., Carroll, D., Egerton, M., Frankland, T., McQuay, H., & Nagle, C. (1995). Comparison of the sensitivity to change of long and short form pain measures. *Quality of Life Research, 4*, 353–357.

Jensen, M. P., & Karoly, P. (1992). Self-report scales and procedures for assessing pain in adults. In D. C. Turk & R. Melzack (Eds.), *Handbook of pain assessment* (pp. 135–151). New York: Guilford Press.

Joyce, C. R., Zutshi, D. W., Hrubes, V., & Mason, R. M. (1975). Comparison of fixed interval and visual analogue scales for rating chronic pain. *European Journal of Clinical Pharmacology, 8*, 415–420.

Julius, D., & Basbaum, A. I. (2001, July 21). Molecular mechanisms of nociception. *Nature, 413*, 203–210.

Katz, J. (1992). Psychophysical correlates of phantom limb experience. *Journal of Neurology, Neurosurgery, and Psychiatry, 55*, 811–821.

Katz, J., & Melzack, R. (1991). Auricular TENS reduces phantom limb pain. *Journal of Pain and Symptom Management, 6*, 73–83.

Kandel, E. R. (1985). Central representations of pain and analgesia. In E. R. Kandel & J. H. Schwartz (Eds.), *Principles of neural science* (pp. 331–343). New York: Elsevier.

Kim, S. H., & Chung, J. M. (1992). An experimental model for peripheral neuropathy produced by segmental spinal nerve ligation in the rat. *Pain, 50*, 355–363.

Kremer, E., & Atkinson, J. H. (1983). Pain language as a measure of effect in chronic pain patients. In R. Melzack (Ed.), *Pain measurement and assessment* (pp. 119–127). New York: Raven Press.

Kumar, B., Hood, W. B., Jr., Joison, J., Gilmour, D. P., Norman, J. C., & Abelmann, W. H. (1970). Experimental myocardial infarction: VI. Efficacy and toxicity of digitalis in acute and healing phase in intact conscious dogs. *Journal of Clinical Investigation, 49*, 358–364.

LaMotte, R. H., Shain, C. N., Simone, D. A., & Tsai, E. F. (1991). Neurogenic hyperalgesia: Psychophysical studies of underlying mechanisms. *Journal of Neurophysiology, 66*, 190–211.

Lanteri-Minet, M., Bon, K., dePommery, J., Michiels, J. F., & Menetrey, D. (1995). Cyclophosphamide cystitis as a model of visceral pain in rats: Model elaboration and spinal structures involved as revealed by the expression of c-Fos and Krox-24 proteins. *Experimental Brain Research, 105*, 220–232.

Lascelles, B. D., Waterman, A. E., Cripps, P. J., Livingston, A., & Henderson, G. (1995). Central sensitization as a result of surgical pain: Investigation of the pre-emptive value of pethidine for ovariohysterectomy in the rat. *Pain, 62*, 201–212.

Levine, J. D., Gordon, N. C., Smith, R., & McBryde, R. (1986). Desipramine enhances opiate postoperative analgesia. *Pain, 27*, 45–49.

Livingstone, W. K. (1943). *Pain mechanisms*. New York: Macmillan.

Livingstone, W. K. (1998). *Pain and suffering*. Seattle: IASP Press.

Loeser, J. D. (2001). Tic douloureux. *Pain Research and Management, 6*, 156–165.

Love, A., Leboeuf, D. C., & Crisp, T. C. (1989). Chiropractic chronic low back pain sufferers and self-report assessment methods: Pt. I. A reliability study of the Visual Analogue Scale, the pain drawing and the McGill Pain Questionnaire. *Journal of Manipulative and Physiological Therapeutics, 12*, 21–25.

Manfredi, M., Bini, G., Cruccu, G., Accornero, N., Berardelli, A., & Medolago, L. (1981). Congenital absence of pain. *Archives of Neurology, 38*, 507–511.

Marchand, S. (1998). *Le phénomène de la douleur*. Montreal, Ontario, Canada: Chenelière/McGraw-Hill.

Marinov, B., Mandadjieva, S., & Kostianev, S. (2008). Pictorial and verbal category-ratio scales for effort estimation in children. *Child: Care, Health, and Development, 34*, 35–43.

Marker, C. L., Lujan, R., Colon, J., & Wickman, K. (2006). Distinct populations of spinal cord lamina II interneurons expressing G-protein-gated potassium channels. *Journal of Neuroscience, 26*, 12251–12259.

Marshall, H. R. (1894). *Pain, pleasure and aesthetics*. London: Macmillan.

Mason, P. (2005). Ventromedial medulla: Pain modulation and beyond. *Journal of Comparative Neurology, 493*, 2–8.

McGrath, P. J., & Unruh, A. M. (2002). The social context of neonatal pain. *Clinics in Perinatology, 29*, 555–572.

McMahon, S. B., & Abel, C. (1987). A model for the study of visceral pain states: Chronic inflammation of the chronic decerebrate rat urinary bladder by irritant chemicals. *Pain, 28*, 109–127.

Medhurst, S. J., Walker, K., Bowes, M., Kidd, B. L., Glatt, M., Muller, M., et al. (2002). A rat model of bone cancer pain. *Pain, 96*, 129–140.

Melzack, R. (1975). The McGill Pain Questionnaire: Major properties and scoring methods. *Pain, 1*, 277–299.

Melzack, R. (1983). *Pain measurement and assessment*. New York: Raven Press.

Melzack, R. (1987). The short-form McGill Pain Questionnaire. *Pain, 30*, 191–197.

Melzack, R. (1990a). Phantom limbs and the concept of a neuromatrix. *Trends in Neuroscience, 13*, 88–92.

Melzack, R. (1990b). The tragedy of needless pain. *Scientific American, 262*, 27–33.

Melzack, R. (1999). From the gate to the neuromatrix. *Pain* (Suppl. 6), S121–S126.

Melzack, R. (2005). The McGill Pain Questionnaire: From description to measurement. *Anesthesiology, 103*, 199–202.

Melzack, R., & Casey, K. L. (1968). Sensory, motivational, and central control determinants of pain: A new conceptual model. In D. Kenshalo (Ed.), *The skin senses* (pp. 422–443). Springfield: Thomas.

Melzack, R., & Katz, J. (1999). Pain measurement in persons in pain. In P. D. Wall & R. Melzack (Eds.), *Textbook of pain* (4th ed., pp. 409–426). London: Churchill Livingstone.

Melzack, R., & Loeser, J. D. (1978). Phantom body pain in paraplegics: Evidence for a central "pattern generating mechanism" for pain. *Pain, 4*, 195–210.

Melzack, R., Stotler, W. A., & Livingston, W. K. (1958). Effects of discrete brainstem lesions in cats on perception of noxious stimulation. *Journal of Neurophysiology, 21,* 353–367.

Melzack, R., & Torgerson, W. S. (1971). On the language of pain. *Anesthesiology, 34,* 50–59.

Melzack, R., & Wall, P. D. (1965, November 19). Pain mechanisms: A new theory. *Science, 150,* 971–979.

Melzack, R., & Wall, P. D. (1983). *The challenge of pain.* New York: Basic Books.

Melzack, R., & Wall, P. D. (1991). *The challenge of pain.* London: Penguin Books.

Melzack, R., Wall, P. D., & Ty, T. C. (1982). Acute pain in an emergency clinic: Latency of onset and description patterns related to different injuries. *Pain, 14,* 33–43.

Merskey, H., & Bogduk, N. (1994). Part III: Pain terms, a current list with definitions and notes on usage. In H. Merskey & N. Bogduk (Eds.), *Classification of chronic pain,* 2nd edition (pp. 209–214). Seattle, WA: IASP Press.

Millan, M. J. (1999). The induction of pain: An integrative review. *Progress in Neurobiology, 57,* 1–164.

Millan, M. J. (2002). Descending control of pain. *Progress in Neurobiology, 66,* 355–474.

Moisset, X., & Bouhassira, D. (2007). Brain imaging of neuropathic pain. *NeuroImage, 37* (Suppl. 1), S80–S88.

Molton, I. R., Jensen, M. P., Nielson, W., Cardenas, D., & Ehde, D. M. (2008). A preliminary evaluation of the motivational model of pain self-management in persons with spinal cord injury-related pain. *Journal of Pain, 9,* 606–612.

Montazeri, A., McEwen, J., & Gillis, C. R. (1996). Quality of life in patients with ovarian cancer: Current state of research. *Support Care Cancer, 4,* 169–179.

Moskowitz, M. A. (1992). Neurogenic versus vascular mechanisms of sumatriptan and ergot alkaloids in migraine. *Trends in Pharmacological Sciences, 13,* 307–311.

Müller, J. (1842). *Elements of physiology.* London: Taylor.

Mugabure Bujedo, B., Tranque Bizueta, I., Gonzalez Santos, S., & Adrian Garde, R. (2007). Multimodal approaches to postoperative pain management and convalescence. *Revista Española de Anestesiología y Reanimación, 54,* 29–40.

Muse, M. (1985). Stress-related, postraumatic chronic pain syndrome: Criteria for diagnosis, and preliminary report on prevalence. *Pain, 23,* 295–300.

Muse, M. (1986). Stress-related, postraumatic chronic pain syndrome: Behavioral treatment approach. *Pain, 25,* 389–394.

Ness, T. J. (1999). Models of visceral nociception. *ILAR Journal, 40,* 119–128.

Ness, T. J., & Gebhart, G. F. (1988). Colorectal distension as a noxious visceral stimulus: Physiologic and pharmacologic characterization of pseudaffective reflexes in the rat. *Brain Research, 450,* 153–169.

Ness, T. J., Randich, A., & Gebhart, G. F. (1991). Further behavioral evidence that colorectal distension is a "noxious" visceral stimulus in rats. *Neuroscience Letters, 131,* 113–116.

Nielsen, C. S., Price, D. D., Vassend, O., Stubhaug, A., & Harris, J. R. (2005). Characterizing individual differences in heat-pain sensitivity. *Pain, 119,* 65–74.

Noordenbos, W. (1959). *Pain.* Amsterdam: Elsevier Press.

Noordenbos, W., & Wall, P. D. (1981). The failure of nerve grafts to relieve pain following nerve injury. *Journal of Neurology, Neurosurgery, and Psychiatry, 44,* 1008–1073.

Okuda, K., Nakahama, H., Miyakawa, H., & Shima, K. (1984). Arthritis induced in cats by sodium urate: A possible animal model for chronic pain. *Pain, 18,* 287–297.

Pan, H. L., & Chen, S. R. (2002). Myocardial ischemia recruits mechanically insensitive cardiac sympathetic afferents in cats. *Journal of Neurophysiology, 87,* 660–668.

Pavlov, I. P. (1927). *Conditioned reflexes.* Oxford: Humphrey Milford.

Perrot, S., Krause, D., Crozes, P., Naïm, C., & GRTF-ZAL-1 Study Group. (2006). Efficacy and tolerability of paracetamol/tramadol (325 mg/37.5 mg) combination treatment compared with tramadol (50 mg) monotherapy in patients with subacute low back pain: A multicenter, randomized, double-blind, parallel-group, 10-day treatment study. *Clinical Therapeutics, 28,* 1592–1606.

Pogatzki, E. M., Niemeier, J. S., & Brennan, T. J. (2002). Persistent secondary hyperalgesia after gastrocnemius incision in the rat. *European Journal of Pain, 6,* 295–305.

Polomano, R. C., & Bennett, G. J. (2001). Chemotherapy-evoked painful peripheral neuropathy. *Pain Medicine, 2,* 8–14.

Price, D. D. (1988). *Psychological and neural mechanisms of pain.* New York: Raven Press.

Price, D. D. (1999). *Psychological mechanisms of pain and analgesia: Progress in pain research and management.* Seattle, WA: IASP Press.

Price, D. D., & Dubner, R. (1977). Neurons that subserve the sensory-discriminative aspects of pain. *Pain, 3,* 307–338.

Price, D. D., Harkins, S. W., & Baker, C. (1987). Sensory-affective relationships among different types of clinical and experimental pain. *Pain, 28,* 297–307.

Price, D. D., Harkins, S. W., Rafii, A., & Price, C. (1986). A simultaneous comparison of fentanyl's analgesic effects on experimental and clinical pain. *Pain, 24,* 197–203.

Price, D. D., Hu, J. W., Dubner, R., & Gracely, R. H. (1977). Peripheral suppression of first pain and central summation of second pain evoked by noxious heat pulses. *Pain, 3,* 57–68.

Pruimboom, L., & vanDam, A. C. (2007). Chronic pain: A non-use disease. *Medical Hypotheses, 68,* 506–511.

Pyati, S., & Gan, T. J. (2007). Perioperative pain management. *CNS Drugs, 21,* 185–211.

Rainville, P., Duncan, G. H., Price, D. D., Carrier, B., & Bushnell, M. C. (1997, August 15). Pain affect encoded in human anterior cingulate but not somatosensory cortex. *Science, 277,* 968–971.

Rakieten, N., Rakieten, L., & Nadkarni, M. V. (1963). Studies on the diabetogenic action of streptozotocin. *Cancer Chemotherapy Reports, 29,* 91–98.

Randall, L. O., & Selitto, J. J. (1957). A method for measurement of analgesic activity on inflamed tissue. *Archives Internationales de Pharmacodynamie et de Thérapie, 111,* 409–419.

Ren, K., & Dubner, R. (1999). Inflammatory models of pain and hyperalgesia. *ILAR Journal, 40,* 111–118.

Rexed, B. (1952). The cytoarchitectonic organization of the spinal cord in the cat. *Journal of Comparative Neurology, 96,* 415–495.

Reynolds, D. V. (1969, April 25). Surgery in the rat during electrical analgesia induced by focal brain stimulation. *Science, 164,* 444–445.

Ross, D. M., & Ross, S. A. (1984). Childhood pain: The school-aged child's viewpoint. *Pain, 20,* 179–191.

Schaible, H. G., Schmidt, R. F., & Willis, W. D. (1987). Enhancement of the responses of ascending tract cells in the cat spinal cord by acute inflammation of the knee joint. *Experimental Brain Research, 66,* 489–499.

Scholl, J., & Allen, P. J. (2007). A primary care approach to functional abdominal pain. *Pediatric Nursing, 33,* 247–254.

Schwei, M. J., Honore, P., Rogers, S. D., Salak-Johnson, J. L., Finke, M. P., Ramnaraine, M. L., et al. (1999). Neurochemical and cellular reorganization of the spinal cord in a murine model of bone cancer pain. *Journal of Neuroscience, 19,* 10886–10897.

Seltzer, Z., Dubner, R., & Shir, Y. (1990). A novel behavioral model of neuropathic pain disorders produced in rats by partial sciatic nerve injury. *Pain, 43*, 205–218.

Shimoyama, M., Tanaka, K., Hasue, F., & Shimoyama, N. (2002). A mouse model of neuropathic cancer pain. *Pain, 99*, 167–174.

Simone, D. A., Ngeow, J. Y., Putterman, G. J., & LaMotte, R. H. (1987). Hyperalgesia to heat after intradermal injection of capsaicin. *Brain Research, 418*, 201–203.

Sinclair, D. C. (1955). Cutaneous sensation and the doctrine of specific nerve energies. *Brain, 78*, 584–614.

Sriwatanakul, K., Kelvie, W., Lasagna, L., Calimlim, J. F., Weis, O. F., & Mehta, G. (1983). Studies with different types of visual analog scales for measurement of pain. *Clinical Pharmacology and Therapeutics, 34*, 234–239.

Stein, C., Millan, M. J., & Herz, A. (1988). Unilateral inflammation of the hindpaw in rats as a model of prolonged noxious stimulation: Alterations in behavior and nociceptive thresholds. *Pharmacology, Biochemistry, and Behavior, 31*, 455–461.

van Eick, A. J. (1967). A change in the response of the mouse in the "hot plate" analgesia-test, owing to a central action of atropine and related compounds. *Acta Physiologica et Pharmacologica Neerlandica, 14*, 499–500.

Villalon, C. M., Centurion, D., Valdivia, L. F., de Vries, P., & Saxena, P. R. (2003). Migraine: Pathophysiology, pharmacology, treatment and future trends. *Current Vascular Pharmacology, 1*, 71–84.

Vyklicky, L. (1979). Techniques for the study of pain in animals. In J. J. Bonica, J. C. Liebeskind, & D. G. Albe-Fessard (Eds.), *Advances in pain research and therapy* (Vol. 3, pp. 727–745). New York: Raven Press.

Wacnik, P. W., Eikmeier, L. J., Ruggles, T. R., Ramnaraine, M. L., Walcheck, B. K., Beitz, A. J., et al. (2001). Functional interactions between tumor and peripheral nerve: Morphology, algogen identification, and behavioral characterization of a new murine model of cancer pain. *Journal of Neuroscience, 21*, 9355–9366.

Wacnik, P. W., Kehl, L. J., Trempe, T. M., Ramnaraine, M. L., Beitz, A. J., & Wilcox, G. L. (2003). Tumor implantation in mouse humerus evokes movement-related hyperalgesia exceeding that evoked by intramuscular carrageenan. *Pain, 101*, 175–186.

Walczak, J. S., Pichette, V., Leblond, F., Desbiens, K., & Beaulieu, P. (2005). Behavioral, pharmacological and molecular characterization of the saphenous nerve partial ligation: A new model of neuropathic pain. *Neuroscience, 132*, 1093–1102.

Walczak, J. S., Pichette, V., Leblond, F., Desbiens, K., & Beaulieu, P. (2006). Characterization of chronic constriction of the saphenous nerve, a model of neuropathic pain in mice showing rapid molecular and electrophysiological changes. *Journal of Neuroscience Research, 83*, 1310–1322.

Walker, K., Medhurst, S. J., Kidd, B. L., Glatt, M., Bowes, M., Patel, S., et al. (2002). Disease modifying and anti-nociceptive effects of the bisphosphonate, zoledronic acid in a model of bone cancer pain. *Pain, 100*, 219–229.

Wall, P. D. (1979). On the relation of injury to pain [The first John J. Bonica Lecture]. *Pain, 6*, 253–264.

Wang, L. X., & Wang, Z. J. (2003). Animal and cellular models of chronic pain. *Advanced Drug Delivery Reviews, 55*, 949–965.

Watson, G. S., Sufka, K. J., & Coderre, T. J. (1997). Optimal scoring strategies and weights for the formalin test in rats. *Pain, 70*, 53–58.

Waxman, S. G. (2007). Nav1.7, its mutations, and the syndromes that they cause. *Neurology, 69*, 505–507.

Weddell, G. (1955). Somesthesis and the chemical senses. *Annual Review of Psychology, 6*, 119–136.

Whiteside, G. T., Adedoyin, A., & Leventhal, L. (2008). Predictive validity of animal pain models? A comparison of the pharmacokinetic-pharmacodynamic relationship for pain drugs in rats and humans. *Neuropharmacology, 54*, 767–775.

Wilkie, D. J., Savedra, M. C., Holzemier, W. L., Tesler, M. D., & Paul, S. M. (1990). Use of the McGill Pain Questionnaire to measure pain: A meta-analysis. *Nursing Research, 39*, 36–41.

Woolf, C. J., & Thompson, S. W. N. (1991). The induction and maintenance of central sensitization is dependent on N-methyl-D-aspartic acid receptor activation; implications for the treatment of post-injury pain insensitivity states. *Pain, 44*, 293–299.

Wuarin Bierman, L., Zahnd, G. R., Kaufmann, F., Burcklen, L., & Adler, J. (1987). Hyperalgesia in spontaneous and experimental animal models of diabetic neuropathy. *Diabetologia, 30*, 653–658.

Wynn Parry, C. B. (1980). Pain in avulsion lesions of the brachial plexus. *Pain, 9*, 41–53.

You, H. J., Dahl Morch, C., Chen, J., & Arendt-Nielsen, L. (2003). Simultaneous recordings of wind up of paired spinal dorsal horn nociceptive neuron and nociceptive flexion reflex in rats. *Brain Research, 960*, 235–245.

Chapter 34

Hunger

TERRY L. POWLEY

The neural basis of ingestive behavior is a central topic of behavioral neuroscience. Brain mechanisms of feeding have been discussed in clinical neurology for well over a century, and they have been the subject of intensive experimental scrutiny for more than six decades. Much has been learned. Crucial hypothalamic circuits have been delineated. Key brain stem mechanisms have been identified. Important limbic and telencephalic networks have been described. In addition, extensive autonomic control loops connecting the brain with the periphery have been defined, and batteries of gut-brain peptides, hormones, cytokines, and other signals reflecting energy balance have been identified and shown to affect feeding. Adipose tissue and other energy stores have also been shown to be innervated, to be actively regulated, and to generate feedback signals influencing feeding.

But much remains to be explained. Perhaps the most sobering gauge of the adequacy of current models of central nervous system (CNS) mechanisms of ingestion is the fact that these accounts, to date, have not produced effective therapies for any of the major eating disorders, including anorexia, bulimia, and obesity that occur in epidemic proportions.

Obesity, because of its prevalence, is the most widely targeted disorder. And, ironically, the most successful interventions for obesity yet devised are radical bariatric surgeries (Thomas, 1995). Such treatments do not draw on what is known about the brain mechanisms of feeding, rather they revise gastrointestinal (GI) physiology and feedback signals. The irony that these peripheral interventions were not formulated from an understanding of brain feeding circuits is accentuated by the likelihood that, as advances are made in understanding the neurobiology of ingestion, radical bariatric surgery will one day be considered gastroenterology's frontal lobotomy.

A survey of the research on the neural basis of energy intake underscores the conclusion that different neuroscience methods have generated different—in some cases conflicting, in some cases complementary—views of the neural mechanisms of feeding. These disparate perspectives produced with different methods have yet to be synthesized into a coherent account of hunger and satiety. Until there is better integration, effective treatments for eating disorders may continue to elude both researchers and those suffering from the disorders.

FOOD INTAKE: THE TERMINOLOGY AND CONSTRUCTS OF HUNGER AND SATIETY

The behavioral neuroscience of ingestion employs, for the most part, a terminology of eating drawn from the popular vernacular (e.g., hunger, satiety, appetite, anorexia). With this lay vocabulary comes excess baggage—the terminology carries multiple connotations and incorporates assumptions, a "folk psychology" of feeding. These implications embedded in the language can have ramifications for investigations designed to produce a neuroscience of feeding.

Early investigations of the neural bases of feeding focused on ingestion as a motivated behavior and used food intake as a prototype for motivations associated with homeostasis. With this traditional emphasis on explaining intake in terms of motivation, many experiments measured behavior (feeding or feeding cessation) while making assumptions about internal motivational processes (hunger or satiety, respectively) and, in turn, then making inferences about how those imputed motivations might be organized in terms of their neural circuitry.

Both the concept of *hunger,* the motivation to seek and ingest food that occurs when an individual is in negative energy balance, and the concept of *satiety,* the motivation to refrain from ingesting nutrients in the face of either a net positive energy balance or a substantial energy load in the GI tract, are constructs or intervening variables (cf. Blundell, 1980). For research purposes, since hunger and satiety cannot typically, if ever, be directly observed, investigators rely on operational definitions. In the behavioral neuroscience of ingestion, hunger is usually gauged by the amount a subject will spontaneously consume (or the amount of time the subject is deprived); satiety is used synonymously with the cessation of consumption (or an absence of deprivation). These conventions are used provisionally in this chapter.

It should be stressed, though, that factors other than what most investigators would recognize as the experiential elements of hunger and satiety can also affect food intake. If an experimenter holds the energy balance of an animal or human subject constant while varying the subject's stress, fatigue, distractions, hydrational status, arousal, nociceptive stimulation, social contingencies, or any number of other altered states, the investigator can affect the subject's intake of nutrients and thus confound operational definitions of hunger and satiety.

When a researcher does a feeding experiment, he or she tries, of course, to control the environment and hold extraneous variables constant. When an experimenter manipulates an animal's brain or physiology, however, it is far more difficult to establish that the manipulation does not indirectly affect feeding by altering one or more of the myriad conditions that can circuitously influence energy balance or its effects on feeding.

DIFFERENT METHODS, DIFFERENT MODELS OF NEURAL FEEDING MECHANISMS

This chapter emphasizes two aspects of the literature on the neural models of feeding, or hunger and satiety. The first aspect relates to methods; the second to the evolution of the problem. Both are useful in terms of understanding the sources of current ideas and appreciating the limitations of these ideas.

It is an axiom of science that experimental answers reflect the techniques that are used in the experiment. Techniques limit what can be measured and hence what results are obtained, but they also mold the interpretations of those results. The point is as true for the behavioral neuroscience of ingestion as for any science. Assessing or rethinking a particular observation and its common interpretation is often aided by a reconsideration of the selectivities and biases inherent in the methods used to generate the observation.

It is also axiomatic that the scientific understanding of a problem does not develop against a static background. Techniques evolve as do experimental and conceptual paradigms. Experimental questions reflect these changes. Understanding the context or state of the science at the time a particular model of feeding was developed is another way of appreciating both the limitations and strengths of that model.

As neuroscience has grown exponentially, its ideas about neural organization and function have changed, and with the transformations, the models of behavioral neuroscience have also changed. Questions about the neural basis of behavior, for example, are not framed the same way they were decades ago, and newer results (e.g., Holstege, Bandler, & Saper, 1996; Janig, 2006; Swanson, 2000) are not interpreted the same way they would have been. Thinking in terms of CNS "centers" dominated the early work on the behavioral neuroscience of ingestion; "distributed circuits" and "networks" are more consonant with neuroscience's present view of the CNS (e.g., Berthoud, 2002; Holstege et al., 1996; Sawchenko, 1998; van den Pol, 2003). These trends are illustrated in our survey of the neuroscience of feeding according to a rough chronology reflecting the introduction of different techniques.

HYPOTHALAMUS: FEEDING CENTER OR NETWORK NODE?

The neuroscience of ingestive behavior has long focused on the hypothalamus as the hub of CNS feeding circuitry. Beginning with early clinical observations on Froehlich's syndrome over a century ago and extending through the past six or more decades of experimental analysis, it is clear that damage to the basomedial hypothalamus can produce the classic "ventromedial hypothalamic syndrome" distinguished by hyperphagia and obesity. The syndrome is also characterized by a sensitivity of the hyperphagia to particular diets (e.g., high fat diets), a "finickiness," as well as by other symptoms (e.g., disruptions of reproductive functions, changes in temperament; Corbit & Stellar, 1964; Hetherington & Ranson, 1942; King & Cox, 1973) that are usually presumed to be incidental to the ingestive disorder.

In contrast, bilateral damage to the lateral hypothalamus often leads to an aphagia and/or anorexia with an associated reduction in body weight (Teitelbaum & Epstein, 1962). This lateral hypothalamic syndrome encompasses other symptoms including an exaggerated dependence of ingestion on the palatability of the diet and other consequences that are generally presumed to be incidental to the dramatic feeding effects (e.g., an adipsia).

In a number of ways, these two classic hypothalamic syndromes appear to be mirror images or reciprocals of each other. And soon after the patterns of symptoms were initially characterized, investigators concluded that the intact ventromedial hypothalamus apparently comprises a "satiety center" and the lateral hypothalamus a "hunger center" (e.g., Anand & Brobeck, 1951). These observations and the center analysis were made not long after Sherrington's (1906) seminal delineation of the reciprocal and antagonist operations of spinal motor neuron pools innervating flexors and extensors had been incorporated into physiological and behavioral thinking, and the center models were cast in terms analogous to cross-linked and opposing Sherringtonian reflexes. These postulated reciprocally acting feeding centers were taken as a prototype for Stellar's (1954) classical and highly influential description of hypothalamic mechanisms of motivated behaviors, and his schematic summary (Figure 34.1) captures the general outline articulated for feeding as well as other motivations.

The signals most often postulated to supply the feedback to the hypothalamus from metabolic or energy balance were blood glucose (the "glucostatic" hypothesis formalized by Mayer, 1953) or lipids (the "lipostatic" hypothesis articulated by Kennedy, 1953). Another alternative was that the thermic effects of metabolism influenced hypothalamic functions not only to regulate body temperature, but also energy balance (the "thermostatic" hypothesis considered by Brobeck, 1957), but much of the evidence initially obtained [based on parabiosis experiments (discussed later in this chapter—see Figure 34.7), infusions of metabolites, glucoprivation experiments, gold thioglucose lesion selectivity, etc.] was used to support one or another variant of the glucostatic or lipostatic hypotheses.

Though the initial analyses of the syndromes resulting from basomedial hypothalamic damage and lateral hypothalamic lesions emphasized the feeding alterations and interpreted the associated changes in body weight that occurred (obesity or excessive leanness, respectively) as secondary to changes in appetite or satiety and hunger, subsequent experimentation challenged the conclusions that the distorted motivation to feed was a primary effect of the lesion and the corresponding change in body weight was secondary. In the case of both the ventromedial hypothalamic and lateral hypothalamic syndromes, experimentally displacing an animal's body weight to the plateau that would be achieved by the animal after it sustained hypothalamic damage, but doing so prior to the production of the lesions, was found to eliminate the dramatic hyperphagia or aphagia, respectively, that typically occurred after the hypothalamic damage (Hoebel & Teitelbaum, 1966; Powley & Keesey, 1970). The observations suggested that the affected hypothalamic areas might play a role in the long-term regulation of energy balance and body energy stores and that the areas might modulate, directly or indirectly, feeding behavior so as to regulate body weight or adiposity.

The idea that hunger and satiety, the motivational substrates of ingestion, were organized within the hypothalamus in a manner similar to Sherringtonian motor neuron pools also frayed as additional experimentation on the feeding syndromes appeared. The ventromedial syndrome was often far from dramatic and robust, depending heavily on animal strain, gender, diet conditions, and other factors (Corbit &

Stellar, 1964; Teitelbaum, 1955). Many of the motivational and behavioral changes associated with hypothalamic damage also appeared to be secondary consequences of more proximal autonomic and endocrine adjustments occasioned by the hypothalamic manipulation (Powley, 1977). The lateral hypothalamic syndrome in some cases seemed produced by or reinforced by either sensory neglect (Marshall, Turner, & Teitelbaum, 1971) or dyskinesias or akinesias resulting from disruptions of nigrostriatal circuitry in addition to hypothalamic circuitry (Marshall, Richardson, & Teritelbaum, 1974; Ungerstedt, 1970).

Furthermore, the nature of the hypothalamic role in feeding was also questioned by the realization that hypothalamic outflows are only one or two synapses upstream of both pituitary endocrine effectors and autonomic preganglionic motor neurons, whereas hypothalamic efferents are far less directly linked to somatic or skeletal motor neuron pools. As discussed in more detail later in this chapter, subsequent neuroanatomical developments failed to delineate obvious structural counterparts of the "final common path" to behavior posited by Stellar and others (see Figure 34.1). The patterns of connectivity discovered raised the possibility that the hypothalamus might operate to effect autonomic and endocrine control of energy handling, that is, "physiological energy balance," and that the influences on ingestion, that is, "behavioral energy balance," might either be coordinated in parallel or might be secondary effects that occurred as energy partitioning changed (Figure 34.2). Any path to behavior was not a "final common path" but rather an output relayed circuitously through polysynaptic networks with myriad opportunities for further modulation or neural editing (Figure 34.3).

Consistent with the idea that much of the hypothalamic role in feeding was secondary to endocrine or autonomic adjustments, pair-feeding experiments indicated that animals with basomedial hypothalamic lesions fattened, even when energy intake was tightly clamped at control levels and even when both the amount of food and pattern of meal taking were both controlled (Walgren & Powley, 1985). Similarly, animals with lateral hypothalamic damage defend their altered body weight levels with physiological energy balance responses when caloric intake is experimentally controlled (Hirvonen & Keesey, 1996; Keesey, Powley, & Kemnitz, 1976).

Such assessments also make the point that feeding represents one side of the energy balance equation. Energy homeostasis is the product of both intake and expenditure, and expenditure is affected by behaviors other than feeding (e.g., activity, nursing young) and by various anabolic processes that promote energy conversation and storage (e.g., slowing metabolic rate and growth) and catabolic processes that stimulate energy expenditure (e.g., thermogenesis).

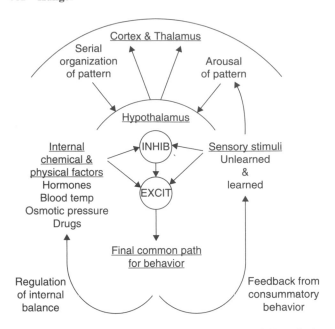

Figure 34.1 Stellar's classical formulation (1954) of the hypothalamic control of motivated behaviors, including feeding.

Note: Eliot Stellar developed his pivotal theory to account for motivated behaviors generally (hunger, sexual behavior, sleep, thirst, etc.), but he drew on early work concluding that the hypothalamus contained hunger and satiety centers. He also drew on the Sherringtonian physiology of spinal motor neurons, including the "final common path" concept. In the case specifically of feeding, the lateral hypothalamus was posited to issue an excitatory (EXCIT) command to feed by way of a "final common path for behavior." In this explanation of feeding, the basomedial hypothalamus was postulated to inhibit (INHIB) feeding by acting as a brake on the excitatory outflow from the lateral hypothalamus. In this hypothalamic model, which dominated early experimentation on the neural basis of feeding, internal humoral signals, sensory information from the environment, arousal and patterning inputs from the forebrain were all envisioned to converge on the hypothalamic centers. These centers in turn were assumed to integrate these inputs and adjust feeding according to need. From "The Physiology of Motivation," by E. Stellar, 1954, *Psychological Review, 61,* pp. 6. Reprinted with permission.

Two corollaries of the insight about energy balance are particularly relevant to attempts to understand feeding. First, not only can feeding not be fully appreciated without reference to the other factors in the equation, but, in terms of experimental analyses, it is important to recognize that alterations in feeding can in some cases be secondary to changes in other anabolic or catabolic adjustments. Second, the extensive participation of hypothalamic mechanisms in both endocrine and autonomic systems suggests that hypothalamic feeding effects will almost unavoidably be nested within more global neural programs of energy homeostasis broadly defined—energy homeostasis integrating the demands of growth, reproduction, thermogenesis, activity, and so on. This last point is particularly important in terms of the ongoing searches for therapeutic pharmacological interventions to manage feeding disorders because interventions targeted to the hypothalamic control of feeding

may ramify to interact with the physiologies of growth, reproduction, arousal, and so on.

Other sets of observations based on more recently introduced methodologies (see discussions that follow) have further reshaped our understanding of the role of the hypothalamus—as well as other brain mechanisms—in controlling food intake. Before surveying some of these contributions, however, it is useful to reconsider the way in which methods in behavioral neuroscience shape our explanations of behavior. Lesions, localized and nonspecific tissue damage, and macro stimulation, involving relatively large electrodes in the case of electrical stimulation or large cannulas in the case of chemical delivery, were the most widely used techniques in behavioral neuroscience during the era of the hypothalamic feeding center analyses.

These techniques, however, in no small measure were responsible for generating the models. Just as to a hammer every problem is a nail, so to a lesion (or conventional stimulation procedure) every problem is a neural center. If not a center, then a fiber bundle that can be interrupted by a focal manipulation. The conventional lesion and stimulation techniques employed in early investigations of the hypothalamus were biased to locate concentrations or nexuses of neural tissue. At the same time, though, by their focal nature, they were also biased to overlook or miss diffusely distributed and redundantly organized neural systems.

Both because of the dramatic nature of the symptoms that occurred following hypothalamic manipulations and because the hypothalamus was easily accessible and a convenient size for the neuroscience techniques of the time, it was particularly easy to ignore the limitations and complexities of interpreting lesions and to fall into the trap that every lesion "syndrome" uncovered a "center" (Glassman, 1978). And, additionally, because of the prevalence of the faculty psychology of the era, a psychology that posited centers for behavioral faculties or constructs such as hunger, the behavioral neuroscience of the feeding was preoccupied with the hypothalamus until roughly three decades ago.

FOOD INTAKE WITHOUT THE HYPOTHALAMUS: CAUDAL BRAIN STEM CIRCUITS

The early monopoly of the hypothalamus in the behavioral neuroscience of ingestion was challenged by a key series of experiments that demonstrated the capacity of other CNS sites, specifically regions of the caudal brain stem, to organize feeding behavior without hypothalamic influence. In this series, to explore what controls of ingestion were still functional in long-term decerebrate rats, Grill and Norgren (1978) capitalized on the fact that the behavior of

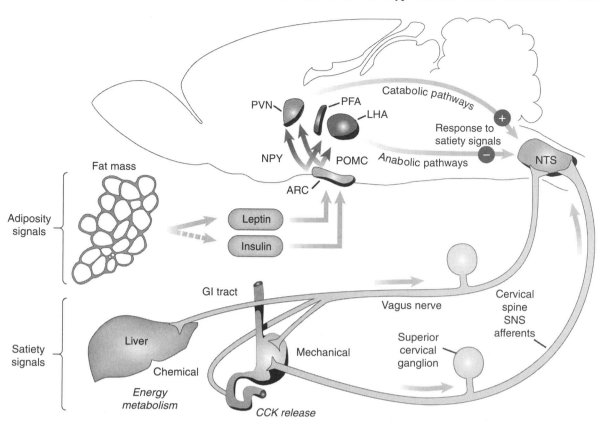

Figure 34.2   The endocrine and autonomic core of the visceral neuroaxis.

Note: This neuroaxis coordinates endocrine and autonomic responses participating in overall energy balance and thus, through its modulation of anabolic and catabolic conditions and the resulting energy homeostasis, generates many of the signals that determine feeding decisions. These signals include not only the exemplars of leptin, insulin, and CCK noted in the figure, but also an extensive battery of peptides released in both gut and brain. Furthermore, other signals such as chemical and mechanical signals from the GI tract are generated in the periphery and affect central integration by way of centripetal neural projections (e.g., afferents of the vagus nerve) through the visceral neuroaxis. Receptors for gut-brain peptides are expressed throughout this visceral neuroaxis, thus establishing a distributed network involved in processing and integrating energy balance signals. This extended visceral neuroaxis in turn is reciprocally and extensively interconnected rostrally with the limbic and telencephalic sites (not illustrated) that have been implicated in feeding and energy balance. ARC = Arcuate nucleus; LHA = Lateral hypothalamic area; NPY = Neuropeptide Y; NTS = Nucleus of the solitary tract; PFA = Perifornical area; POMC = Proopiomelanocortin; PVN = Paraventricular nucleus = SNS = Sympathetic nervous system. From "Central Nervous System Control of Food Intake," by M. W. Schartz, S. C. Woods, D. Porte Jr., R. J. Seeley, and Baskin, D. G., 2000, *Nature, 404* pp. 668. Reprinted with permission.

chronically decerebrate animals cannot be organized exclusively by the hypothalamus (or any other diencephalic or telencephalic regions) and must reflect the potential of the caudal brain stem. Though such animals do not seem to evidence long-term regulation of body weight (a function that can potentially still be ascribed to the hypothalamus), they do display the capacity to increase and decrease their ingestion in response to a variety of the short-term signals that control intake in intact or control animals. Grill and Norgren, in their reassessment of what they described as the "hypothalamic hegemony" over the neuroscience of feeding, argued persuasively for a more hierarchical view of feeding circuitry, one more consistent with a Jacksonian hierarchy in which functions are redundantly organized or "re-represented" at multiple levels of the neuroaxis, than with a "center" organization.

Thus, the caudal brain stem possesses many of the capacities to generate feedings responses and affect energy homeostasis that had long been attributed exclusively to the hypothalamus. Though many more recent research efforts still—or again—focus on the ventral diencephalic networks and even though the hypothalamic melanocortin system and the rest of the ventral diencephalic ingestive circuitry is clearly critically implicated in feeding (see later discussion), it has also been established that that the caudal brain stem independently possesses many of the same capacities attributed to hypothalamic circuits. Stated differently, hypothalamic circuitry must not be necessary or uniquely organized for many ingestive functions since a decerebrate animal can perform the functions even when the hypothalamus (and indeed the forebrain) is no longer connected to the brain stem.

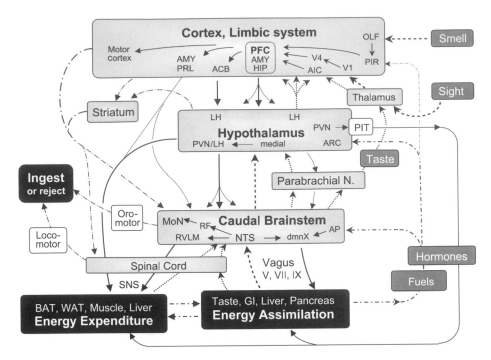

Figure 34.3 Neural networks responsible for feeding and energy balance.

Note: The schematic summarizes numerous projections and inputs that have been identified and characterized with modern neuroscience mapping tools. *Dotted lines with arrows* are used to designate signals from the environment and/or the internal milieu that converge on the central nervous system. *Solid lines with arrows* identify centrifugal projections to effector organs or sites. *Stippled lines with arrows* designate motor pathways. ACB = Nucleus accumbens; AIC = Agranular insular cortex; AMY = Amygdala; AP = Area postrema; ARC = Arcuate nucleus; dmnX = Dorsal motor nucleus of the vagus; HIP = Hippocampus; LH = Lateral hypothalamus; MoN = Motor nuclei for oromotor control; NTS = Nucleus of the solitary tract; OLF = Olfactory bulb; PFC = Prefrontal cortex; PIR = Piriform cortex; PIT = Pituitary gland; PRL = Prelimbic cortex; PVN = Paraventricular nucleus of the hypothalamus; RF = Medullary reticular formation; RVLM rostroventrolateral medulla; SNS = Sympathetic nervous system; V1/V4 = Visual processing areas 1 and 4; VII = Facial nerve; V = Trigeminal nerve; IX = Glossopharyngeal nerve. From "Mind versus Metabolism in the Control of Food Intake and Energy Balance," by H.-R. Berthoud, 2004, *Physiology and Behavior, 81,* pp. 785. Reprinted with permission.

A second type of observation, one based on receptor mapping studies, reinforces the point that the caudal brain stem contains the circuitry necessary to control feeding. As more recent research (see discussion that follows) has focused on key roles of cholecystokinin (CCK), leptin, insulin, ghrelin, and other peripheral hormones in feeding, the initial tendency has naturally been to focus on the hypothalamus, given its well-established involvement in ingestive behavior. The lack of a complete blood-brain barrier in the basomedial hypothalamus, the early demonstrations of receptors for the metabolic hormones in arcuate and other hypothalamic nuclei, and the delineation of the melanocortin circuitry in the hypothalamus all converged on a hypothalamic account of the feeding effects elicited by humoral signals.

In spite of these several observations tending to reinforce what has been characterized as a "hypothalamocentric" model of feeding, parallel observations on both the blood-brain barrier of the dorsal vagal complex and the key hormones signaling energy conditions indicated that this brain stem vagal trigone area possessed the same features as the basomedial hypothalamus. Like the basomedial hypothalamus, the nucleus of the solitary tract/area postrema region possesses a leaky blood-brain area that gives circulating humoral factors access to the parenchyma of the dorsal vagal complex. In addition, like the basomedial hypothalamus, the dorsal vagal complex densely expresses receptors for CCK (Zarbin, Innis, Wamsley, Snyder, & Kuhar, 1983), leptin (Funahashi, Yada, Suzuki, & Shioda, 2003), ghrelin (Zigman, Jones, Lee, Saper, & Elmquist, 2006), insulin (Hill, Lesniak, Pert, & Roth, 1986; Kar, Chabot, & Quirion, 1993), melanocortin-4 (Kishi et al., 2003), and many of the other gut or gut-brain hormones and neuropeptides that also modulate central feeding systems.

A complementary set of experiments, based on yet a different experimental strategy, also indicates that the receptors for gut-brain neuropeptides and metabolic hormones are not only present in the caudal brain stem, but that these receptors do apparently mediate many of the same ingestive responses previously ascribed to the basomedial hypothalamus. These experiments involve infusing the different neuropeptides and hormones directly into the brain stem or floor of the fourth ventricle and measuring ingestive responses. Indeed, in a series of experiments that have infused candidate signals directly into the fourth ventricle (since CSF flows caudally within the ventricular system, fourth ventricle infusions should produce negligible rostral effects) and compared the efficacies of this route of administration with those of more rostral infusions, Grill and colleagues (Grill & Kaplan, 1990) as well as others (reviewed in Blessing, 1997) have found that fourth ventricular stimulation is as effective or even, in some cases, more effective than third ventricular stimulation at mobilizing appropriate feeding responses.

Such experiments find a foundation in the general point that many earlier infusion experiments designed to probe the role of the hypothalamus in organizing feeding in response to different humoral signals (and interpreted in terms of a hypothalamo-centric model) did not necessarily limit the administration of the signals to the hypothalamus. The most commonly used protocol for probing the humoral sensitivity of the hypothalamus has been to cannulate a lateral ventricle or the third ventricle and to infuse the signal, say leptin, into the ventricle. If we adopt a hypothalamo-centric model and assume the target receptors and target tissues are in the arcuate nucleus or infundibular hypothalamus, then such ventricular infusions will apparently have their effects at these diencephalic sites and diffusion or spillage to other sites will be inconsequential. Alternatively (if the hypothalamo-centric assumption about limited distribution of receptors is wrong, as it has proven to be), since the flow of CSF is caudal toward the fourth ventricle, any receptors in dorsal vagal complex or other periventricular sites might also be activated.

Two key perspectives emerge from the observations establishing that the lower brain stem contains the neural circuitry sufficient to control feeding: First, observations on the ingestive behavior evidence by decerebrate animals also suggest that metabolic signals are detected not exclusively by the hypothalamus, but also, in parallel, by other regions of the visceral neuroaxis including the caudal brain stem and even the primary afferents that innervate the viscera (see Figure 34.2; also see Figure 34.5). The evidence indicates that there is considerable redundancy in the CNS in terms of the metabolic signals that influence feeding—the role of the hypothalamus (and that of the caudal brain stem as well) is more one of a *cooperative* part of a distributed network, rather than a monolithic *control* center. Second, much of the neural apparatus controlling feeding must be organized in the caudal brain stem, thus suggesting

that these particular elements of ingestive behavior are not uniquely and/or exclusively organized in the hypothalamus. By extension, the point suggests, as discussed previously, that the hypothalamic circuits implicated in feeding may be committed more to monitoring humoral and endocrine signals and integrating them into coordinated autonomic or neuroendocrine adjustments associated with energy balance.

LESSONS FROM ANATOMICAL MAPPING AND TRACING TECHNOLOGIES: DISTRIBUTED NEURAL NETWORKS COOPERATE TO CONTROL OF FEEDING AND ENERGY REGULATION

Anatomical analyses have implications for functional interpretations and define boundary conditions within which behavioral systems presumably operate. It is possible, in broad terms, to reverse engineer the types of operations that are likely to occur from the structural organization that exists, that is, to infer function from form. If, for example, there are no neural connections between two regions, then any interactions or communications must either (1) be non-neural (e.g., hormonal or humoral), or (2) possibly not occur. Strong projections between a site and a target, on the other hand, suggest substantial neural interactions. Or, yet again, sites or circuits that express a particular receptor presumably respond to the corresponding ligand.

Often such constraints of structure influence behavioral neuroscience analyses and models without much explicit discussion. For example, the limited anatomical information about hypothalamic projections and interconnections that was available at the middle of the past century made it reasonable at the time to consider hypothalamic sites implicated in feeding behavior as executive centers that operated more or less autonomously. Similarly, with relatively few energy-balance feedback signals recognized at the time, and with those known (e.g., the glucostatic and lipostatic mechanisms) seemingly effective in the hypothalamus, it was reasonable for investigators to conclude that the few humoral signals and an equally limited number of visceral afferent inputs converged on the hypothalamus that then controlled feeding and the physiology of energy balance in a top-down executive program.

By comparison with today's information, knowledge about brain circuitry was quite limited when the original hypothalamic feeding center models were developed. Much of what was then known about neural circuits was inferred from staining procedures that delineated Nissl patterns of conspicuous clusters of neurons, nuclei, and the more conspicuous and coherent fiber tracts, either in relief or in myelin staining. These nissl-and-myelin maps were supplemented by information from notoriously capricious silver methods for degeneration and limited tracing methods, mainly retrograde degeneration that is often illusive and rarely works in polysynaptic chains. Thus, the limited anatomical appreciation of the extent of the interconnectivity of the hypothalamus—and for that matter, the caudal brain stem—with other brain sites made it reasonable, and even necessary, to consider the hypothalamus in terms of overly simplified assumptions of inputs and outputs. These unrealistic expectations were then incorporated into many models and schematics (see, for example, Figure 34.1).

The past decades, however, have seen the development of an enormous battery of tools for delineating the details of neural circuits. Hundreds of neural tracing techniques have been developed (e.g., Zaborszky, Wouterlood, & Lanciego, 2006) and used to specify myriad interconnections and projections that were unknown when lesion studies initially concentrated on the hypothalamus. Similarly, an equal or larger number of histochemical and immunocytochemical protocols have been developed and used to recognize pathways expressing particular neurotransmitters, peptides, or receptors (e.g., Bjorklund, Hokfelt, & Owman, 1988).

As these mapping tools have been applied, much has been learned about just how extensive the interconnections of the different sites implicated in the control of feeding actually are.

The developments include the recognition that the hypothalamus is reciprocally and multiply interconnected with the caudal brain stem sites implicated in feeding (Broberger & Hokfelt, 2001; Sawchenko, 1998). Furthermore, the mapping experiments indicate that both of these hubs of feeding circuitry are embedded in extensive, often parallel and redundant, circuitry that welds the two complex stations into a massively cross-linked system of re-entrant connections involving most, and probably all, of the brain (e.g., Berthoud, 2002, 2004; Holstege et al., 1996; see also Figure 34.3).

Parallel discoveries, with the different mapping techniques have also produced a corresponding rethinking of the peripheral nervous system and have indicated both the complexity of autonomic circuitry in the viscera and the extensive afferent and efferent projections by which the CNS is linked to that peripheral circuitry. The enteric nervous system of the gut is now widely recognized as being complexly interconnected and containing so many neurons (equivalent to the total number in the spinal cord) that it is often considered a "second brain" or a "little brain" organized in a distributed fashion throughout the gut.

Correspondingly, the extrinsic pathways that connect the CNS to the enteric nervous system or "brain" in the gut are now similarly realized to be both more numerous and more highly organized than previously presumed. Autonomic efferents project densely to the GI tract (Holst, Kelly, & Powley, 1997), and, within the organs of digestion, visceral afferents supply a profuse network formed of a number of different specialized endings (Powley & Phillips, 2002). The autonomic efferents and afferents interconnecting the brain of the CNS with the little brain of the GI tract are so extensive that, from the functional perspective, it is even in all likelihood misleading functionally to compartmentalize and separate CNS and peripheral nervous system (PNS).

As structural experiments revealed the ubiquitous cross-linkages throughout both the central and peripheral components of the visceral neuroaxis, two other aspects of the changing views of energy-balance signaling have reinforced the conclusion that the visceral neural network is distributed and decentralized with cross-linked control loops controlling energy balance and feeding. One of the developments was the recognition that, in contrast to the assumptions of early models of feeding, the peripheral organs that participated in energy metabolism and energy regulation also have much richer local control networks of not only neural, but also endocrine and paracrine, coordination that effect regulation of the energy economy in the periphery, presumably without hypothalamic executive intervention.

The second change in the perspective on energy balance to develop was the realization of how extensive a battery of hormones and cytokines the organs of digestion and metabolism release in the course of executing the local regulation of the different phases of metabolism. In the middle of the twentieth century, when the hypothalamic feeding center model was proposed, only two or three GI hormones had been identified and characterized. In contrast, it is now appreciated that the gut is the largest endocrine organ in the body and that it orchestrates much of energy balance with the releases of over 30 peptide hormones that serve as endocrine signals reflecting anabolic and catabolic events (e.g., Rehfeld, 1998; also see Figures 34.4 and 34.5). The GI tract, for example, elaborates, among others, CCK, leptin, ghrelin, glucagon-like peptide-1 (GLP1), peptide YY (PYY), gastrin, secretin, obestatin, numerous other hormones, and a number of cytokines. These hormones commonly serve as paracrine and neurocrine factors influencing local physiology and thus, indirectly, produce additional feedback and feed forward to neural circuits. Similarly, adipose tissue is now realized to be an active, dynamic system with its own regulatory loops as well as to be innervated (Badman & Flier, 2007; Powell, 2007). In its decentralized orchestration of metabolism, adipose tissue synthesizes and releases leptin, adiponectin, resistin, estradiol, angiotensin, and cytokines such as interleukin-6 (IL-6) and tumor-necrosis factor-alpha (TNF-a).

Concomitantly, with the recognition that there is considerable local integration and control and that a substantial number of potential signals is generated in the process of local control of the viscera, came recognition (a) that many peptide hormones produced by the gut were actually gut-brain hormones (Figure 34.4) elaborated by both the viscera and the brain and (b) that the receptors for many of these signals could be found throughout the visceral neuroaxis (Figure 34.5).

As the enormously wide distributions of receptors for the multiplicity of endocrine and humoral factors influencing energy balance was recognized (Funahashi et al., 2003; Hill, Lesniak, Pert, & Roth, 1986; Kar et al., 1993; Kishi et al., 2003; Zarbin et al., 1983, 2006), the simplifying proposition that any one hormone might code for or signal a particular function (e.g., ghrelin for hunger or CCK for satiety) became untenable. The hormones affecting energy balance also operate in many physiological and behavioral systems, not merely ingestion (see Figure 34.6). Leptin, for example, does not simply modulate feeding, it participates in, *inter alia,* immune function, inflammation, learning processes, cardiovascular function, reproduction, and

bone metabolism as well (Harvey & Ashford, 2003). That signaling associated with a single hormone cuts across so much physiology tends, of course, to confound the search for function-specific pharmacological treatments.

With all of the new observations, the idea that the hypothalamus, among neural sites, might have near-exclusive access to the putative humoral signals and that it must therefore act as a top-down controller failed to square with (a) complex regulatory loops discovered in the periphery, (b) the rich flux of potential signals elaborated by these regulatory loops, (c) the fact that receptors for the putative signals are widely distributed throughout the visceral neuroaxis, and (d) the evidence that the signals set and bias the gains of the regulatory circuitry. Indeed, the amount of integration and local regulation that is now known to occur in the GI tract and other viscera makes it possible to assert persuasively that the control of feeding involves as much bottom-up regulation and integration (e.g., Cummings & Overduin, 2007) as it does top-down programming by hypothalamic circuits.

What modern neuroanatomical methods have *not* revealed is also instructive. As mentioned, many early versions (and even recent versions) of the hypothalamic feeding center model implicitly or even explicitly (see Figure 34.1; also, for comparison, see Figure 34.8) considered the

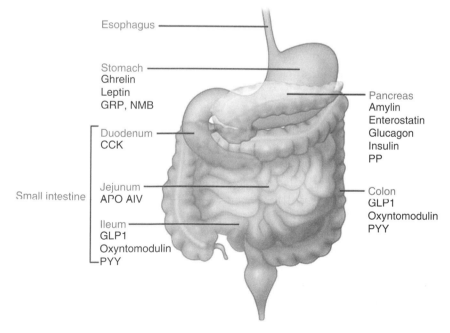

Figure 34.4 Principal peripheral sites of synthesis of gut-brain peptides or gastrointestinal peptides that influence feeding.

Note: Signals are depicted in terms of the main gut location of production, though many of the peptides are produced at multiple sites. Importantly, most of these peptides (i.e, CCK, APO AIV, GLP1, oxyntomodulin, PYY, enterostatin, ghrelin, gastrin-releasing peptide [GRP], neuromedin B [NMB], and possibly pancreatic polypeptide [PP]) are synthesized within the brain as well as within the gut. Gut peptides that influence feeding,

but that do not appear to be synthesized in CNS include leptin, insulin, glucagon, and amylin. Additional abbreviations are given in Figure 34.6. APO AIV = Apolipoprotein A-IV; CCK = Cholecystokinin; GLP1 = glucagon-like peptide-1 ; GRP = Gastrin-releasing peptide; NMB = Neuromedin B; PP = pancreatic polypeptide; PYY = peptide YY. "Gastrointestinal Regulation of Food Intake," by D. E. Cummings and J. Overduin, 2007, *Journal of Clinical Investigation, 117,* pp. 14. Reprinted with permission.

Selected GI and pancreatic peptides that regulate food intake

Peptide	Main site of synthesis	Receptors mediating feeding effects	Sites of action of peripheral peptides germane to feeding			Effect on food intake[A]
			Hypothalamus	Hindbrain	Vagus nerve	
CCK	Proximal intestinal I cells	CCK1R	X	X	X	↓
GLP1	Distal-intestinal L cells	GLP1R	X?	X?	X	↓
Oxyntomodulin	Distal-intestinal L cells	GLP1R and other	X			↓
PYY$_{3-36}$	Distal-intestinal L cells	Y2R	X		X	↓
Enterostatin	Exocrine pancreas	F1-ATPase β subunit			X	↓
APO AIV	Intestinal epithelial cells	Unknown	X		X	↓
PP	Pancreatic F cells	Y4R, Y5R		X	X	↓
Amylin	Pancreatic β cells	CTRs, RAMPs	X	X		↓
GRP and NMB	Gastric myenteric neurons	GRPR		X	X	↓
Gastric leptin	Gastric chief and P cells	Leptin receptor	?	?	X	↓
Ghrelin	Gastric X/A–like cells	Ghrelin receptor	X	X	X	↑

Figure 34.5 A partial list of selected gastrointestinal and pancreatic gut-brain peptides that influence food intake.

Note: The primary site of synthesis of the peptide and its receptor mediating its effects on ingestion are summarized, as is the orexic or anorexic influence that the peptide has on intake. In addition, known nervous system sites of action of the peptides are indicated with "Xs." Even with an absence of evidence for some peptides at some sites (the blank spaces), as of yet, it is clear the majority of the peptides bind with their receptors throughout the visceral neuroaxis—in the vagus nerve and brain stem as well as in the hypothalamus. APO AIV = Apolipoprotein A-IV; CCK = Cholecystokinin; CTRs = Calcitonin receptors; GLP-1 = Glucagon-like peptide 1; GRP = Gastrin-releasing peptide; GRPR = GRP receptor; NMB = Neuromedin B; RAMPs = Receptor activity-modifying proteins. From "Gastrointestinal Regulation of Food Intake," by D. E. Cummings and J. Overduin, 2007, *Journal of Clinical Investigation, 117*, pp. 15. Reprinted with permission.

hypothalamic mechanisms an integrative center that generates executive motor decisions to feed or not to feed. These models, in the spirit of a Sherringtonian final common path or a command neuron output, often hypothesize a key output pathway to brain stem motor centers that would ultimately organize the behaviors. In contrast to the direct efferent access to the pituitary and autonomic preganglionics, such posited pathways from hypothalamic circuitry to brain stem and spinal cord motor neurons pools have not, however, been verified in the extensive tracing and mapping analyses that have now been done.

Overall, the new insights to have emerged from modern mapping strategies have necessitated a rethinking of the neural basis of feeding. Such a reframing is still very much ongoing, though. For example, by one construction, each of the multiple sites associated with feeding could be considered a specialized processor or module—multiple specialized processors, each contributing unique analyses or syntheses to the enterprise of energy balance. Such a view has been adopted or discussed in recent reviews (Berthoud, 2002, 2004; Saper, Chou, & Elmquist, 2002; Williams et al., 2001). In contrast, however, another construction of the decentralized network delineated by the newer mapping analyses would be that there is an extensive amount of redundancy and overlap of functional capacity among the distributed sites. Presently available observations on the neural substrate of feeding neither firmly reject either of the constructions nor unequivocally establish the validity of either perspective.

NEUROPHYSIOLOGY OF SINGLE CELLS: ANOTHER DISTRIBUTED-NETWORK VIEW OF BRAIN FEEDING MECHANISMS

Single-unit electrophysiology has provided another important window on how the nervous system integrates the signals of energy balance and organizes feeding responses. The contributions of single-cell recording experiments to the neurobiology of feeding might be viewed as paralleling chronologically the development and application of the neural tracing technologies just discussed. Like anatomical mapping techniques, electrophysiological analyses have evolved considerably in terms of their sensitivity and scope. For purposes of this brief survey, the evolution might be considered to encompass three stages: an initial period in which recording needed to be performed in animals that were extensively restrained or, even more often, anesthetized; a later phase in which unit recording was practical in awake, freely behaving animals; and a final stage in which multiple units of circuits or ensembles could be simultaneously recorded during behavior.

In the earliest electrophysiological work, recording experiments were perhaps most commonly designed to corroborate the hypothalamic feeding center model. Recording typically did not take place during behavior, and the animal subject was anesthetized and/or paralyzed. Many of the experiments were focused on the hypothalamus, with little or no sampling of neurons in other regions, and often explored the types of signals (glucose, other metabolites,

Selected appetite-modifying peptides, illustrating their central effects on energy balance and other physiological activities

Peptide	Effects on Energy Balance			Examples of Other Physiological Actions
	Feeding	Thermogenesis	Body Weight	
NPY	↑↑	↓	↑	Blood pressure regulation, circadian rhythmicity, and memory processing
MCH	↑	?	→	Locomotion and regulation of skin colour
Orexin A	↑	→	→	Wakefulness and alertness
Galanin	↑	↓	→	Reproduction
Opioids	↑	↓	↑	Locomotion and reproductive behavior
α-MSH	↓	↑	↓	Grooming and blood pressure regulation
5-HT	↓	↑	↓	Mood regulation and behavioral responses
GLP-1	↓	→	↓	Regulation of blood glucose and gut motility
CCK	↓	→	→	Grooming and blood pressure regulation

Figure 34.6 Some of the most common neuropeptides implicated in the control of food intake.

Note: These neuropeptides are widely expressed in the hypothalamus and rest of the CNS, as well as in the periphery. Arrows summarize dominant directions of effect exerted by the neuropeptides (decreases, increases, no clear increase or decrease). As the table organization illustrates, many of the neuropeptides influence both feeding (as well as body weight) and energy expenditure or thermogenesis. In addition, notably, as summarized in the right-hand column, all of the neuropeptides also influence other physiological systems, not merely energy homeostasis. From "The Hypothalamus and the Control of Energy Homeostasis: Different Circuits, Different Purposes" by G. Williams et al., 2004, *Physiology and Behavior*, 81, p. 212. Reprinted with permission.

gustatory and visceral afferent inputs, etc.) that would affect hypothalamic unit activity. In this phase, most of the electrophysiology was designed to confirm and to elucidate the hypothalamic center model, and the resulting observations were generally consistent the proposition that the hypothalamus received (and therefore, at least in principle could integrate) humoral, gustatory, and visceral inputs (presumably in the service of decisions to feed or not to feed).

As single-unit techniques evolved and could be used practically to monitor neuronal traffic in awake, behaving subjects, however, a picture of a more extensive circuitry of feeding emerged. In part perhaps because the power of the newer electrophysiological paradigms permitted recording from awake, behaving animals and in part because the proposition that feeding was virtually a hypothalamic prerogative had already begun to wane, unit recording began to describe a much more distributed network of sites participating in the control of feeding. Individual units throughout much of the limbic system, and particularly in the orbitofrontal cortex, were found (Rolls, 2005) to have firing patterns associated with deprivation, repletion, food choice, palatability, and other conditions classically ascribed to the hypothalamic feeding centers. Similarly, neurons throughout the gustatory and visceral neuroaxes,

including even first-, but particularly second- and all higher-order neurons of the neuroaxes displayed evidence that their respective activities were modulated by signals (e.g., energy infusions) or conditions (e.g., deprivation or hunger, refeeding or satiety) that often had been attributed to hypothalamic processing (Scott, Yan, & Rolls, 1995). The organizational pattern suggested by the results was more consonant overall with the distributed network ideas that were emerging in the neural tracing developments (see previous discussion) occurring in parallel.

Even more recently, in what might be considered the third stage of development, the further evolution of techniques for the recording of cells in behaving animals, the introduction of "multi-trode" or multiple electrode recording simultaneously from large numbers or ensembles of individual neurons combined with the increased availability of hardware and software for massive computation has made it feasible to monitor systems or networks of neurons in behaving animals. For example, Araujo and co-workers (2006), based on concomitant recordings from the lateral hypothalamus, amygdala, insular cortex, and orbitofrontal cortex through a complete feeding-satiety-feeding cycle, argued that hunger may be organized in terms of a "distributed population code."

Too few electrophysiological observations—certainly too few cases examining neurons in multiple sites for long intervals—are yet available to yield a complete perspective on the prospect of ensemble coding of hunger and satiety. Furthermore, the exquisitely high temporal and spatial resolution that unit recording achieves, often comes at the price of limited windows of time for observation (gauged by the length of a feeding bout or the duration of an inter-meal interval). Because of the temporal constraints and sampling limitations, only relatively phasic and potentially unrepresentative subsets of neurons from the entire population of the viscera neuroaxis can be readily characterized. Nonetheless, it is the case that as single-neuron electrophysiology has developed, it has come to portray an extensive and distributed network of neurons that are active during the execution of feeding behavior.

ECOLOGICAL OBSERVATIONS: ENVIRONMENTAL CONTINGENCIES HAVE SHAPED NEURAL MECHANISMS OF FEEDING

Applications of newly developed neuroscience technologies have driven most of the evolution in ideas about the neurobiology of feeding. Nonetheless, advances have come from other biological fields as well. Two ecological analyses have been particularly instructive. The first analysis deals with rethinking regulatory mechanisms that determine hunger and satiety; the second addresses the issue of brain networks implicated in feeding behavior. These ecological perspectives developed initially independently of, and in parallel with, the neuroscience of feeding. More recently, though, the ecological and neural perspectives have begun to merge.

Thrifty Gene Hypothesis

The first ecological analysis challenges traditional views about the operations of the regulatory mechanisms controlling feeding. This viewpoint is associated with the *thrifty gene hypothesis* introduced by Neel (1962). The concept can be appreciated by contrasting it with the ideas about the control of energy balance that were common prior to Neel's articulating the hypothesis. Early feeding models assumed, in effect, that hunger and satiety mechanisms are organized in a symmetrical manner, much like Sherrington's agonists and antagonists or flexors and extensors, around a point of energy balance. Specifically, the models often assumed that the control function gains of the neural mechanisms translating energy perturbations into responses that correct deficits and surpluses, respectively, are comparable.

Neel and other investigators who explored the thrifty gene concept noted, however, that a symmetry assumption is not consistent with observations on the biological adaptations of most species (Bjorntorp, 2001; Coleman, 1979; Schwartz et al., 2003). Behavioral and physiological mechanisms that redress energy deficits and their counterpart mechanisms that correct energy surpluses are not controls of comparable efficiency organized in mirror-image symmetry around an equilibrium point at which intake is matched to expenditure.

While there presumably have been many imperative selection pressures to avoid energy deficits, analyses suggest that there have not been equally strong pressures to avoid positive energy balances. Even more specifically, Neel noted that evolution in demanding environments would have selected for genes that are "thrifty" and promote efficient storage of calories that may mitigate times of intermittent food availability or famine. The more unpredictable and/or hostile the environment, the more advantage in having such thrifty genes promoting energy storage.

Procreation requires not starving to death before you can pass on your genes. Falling into energy deficit can easily be fatal and thus thwart propagating one's genes, while having plenty—perhaps even excesses—of calories stored may well see members of the species through their reproductive age. Even if energy surpluses are not optimal for avoiding diseases of old age (Neel focused on Type II diabetes and obesity) or for longevity, they make good reproductive sense. Indeed, too effective a set of defenses mobilized against any stored energy excess would be maladaptive, and reserves that were so tightly regulated that they could not fluctuate would be something of an oxymoron.

Hence, from a thrifty gene vantage point, animals benefit from stringent hunger mechanisms and defenses against energy deficits, while they also benefit (at least reproductively) from elastic, flexible, and more limited satiety mechanisms and defenses against positive energy balance and storage. These functional asymmetries can elucidate how control mechanisms are structured. They also can partially explain why numerous challenges from dietary manipulations to even subtle metabolic disorders easily produce obesity and excessive energy storage conditions but less readily yield anorexias and wasting disorders.

Feeding Complexities, Brain Mass, and Brain Circuits

The second perspective, which emerges from neuroecology, reinforces the inferences about distributed networks that have emerged from anatomical mapping experiments (see earlier section) and have been emerging from both electrophysiological mapping experiments (see earlier discussion) and functional scanning studies as well (discussed in the next section). The perspective grows out of the widely accepted evidence that the brain sizes of different species are proportional to the variety, complexity, or unpredictability in space and time of their respective food supplies. Omnivores, active predators, and generalist species living in problematic environments, all have relatively larger brains (even once the contribution of factors such as body mass that also predict a portion of brain mass are accounted for). Herbivores with simple diets, animals adapted to predictable environments with ready sources of nutrients, and monophagous species have relatively smaller brains for their respective body sizes.

The brain-environmental-demand correlation can be decomposed into two more particular relationships, each with implications for a neurobiology of feeding behavior. First, there is a correlation between the behavioral specializations species use in feeding and the relative size of the different sensory, motor, and "cognitive" neural systems that hypertrophy in those species. Raptors and other predators that rely on sight, for example, have more extensive visual systems; caching species that must remember storage sites have larger hippocampi; species that devise novel feeding solutions have larger forebrains and cortical association areas. Such observations are numerous, and they have been documented for a variety of different taxa and families, including fish, birds, rodents, and primates (see, e.g., Iwaniuk & Hurd, 2005; Lefebvre, Reader, & Sol, 2004; Nicolakakis & Lefebvre, 2000; Timmermans, Lefebvre, Boire, & Basu, 2000). Conspicuously—and tellingly—in its absence, hypothalamic hypertrophy has not been correlated with demanding environments.

The second, and more general, correlation between brain mass and feeding complexity is that, even after the increases associated with general factors such as body size and with the specific factors of sensory or motor or cognitive systems have all been partialled out, there is still an underlying residual positive correlation between overall brain mass and the complexity of the ecological niche for feeding. Bigger brains are found in species with complex feeding patterns adapted to challenging environments. This more general relationship also appears to hold for a variety of taxa and families (e.g., Aboitiz, 1996; Bernard & Nurton, 1993; but also see Healy & Rowe, 2007).

Though there are a number of interpretations we might apply to these observations, this general correlation is consistent with the implication suggested by the neuroanatomical mapping, electrophysiological, and functional mapping (see discussion that follows) literatures implicating many distributed CNS sites as a neural network active and involved in hunger and satiety. The two neuroecological correlations taken together point to a complex neural network involved in ingestive behavior. They also serve as a reminder to neurobiological analyses of ingestion of just how pervasive feeding behavior is in most species' lives and just how much of the CNS is preoccupied with ingestive behavior. Though

animal or human subjects and nutritional neuroscientists who study them are, typically, buffered from the exigencies of their hunter-gatherer roots, most species expend most of their energy most of the time making feeding decisions in challenging environments where it is necessary to obtain nutrients while evading predation, conserving calories, balancing multiple homeostatic needs, maintaining physiological vigilance for microbes and toxins that often occur in potential food sources, and juggling resource unpredictabilities. A consideration of these environmental and physiological contingencies (for instructive discussions, see Collier & Johnson, 2004; Garcia, Hankins, & Coil, 1977; Harris & Ross, 1987; Rozin, 1976; Woods, 1991) and the multidimensional demands they place on sensory, motor, memory, and planning operations explains why a multiplicity of brain sites increase in mass in challenging environments.

Neurobiology of Ingestive Mechanisms from the Environmental Perspective

Ecology, in stepping back from a short-sighted focus on neural machinery and in considering the environment to which the circuitry is adapted, offers other lessons as well. Such examinations have forced a more general recognition that the mechanisms of energy homeostasis did not evolve in vacuums. Neural controls carry the stamp of the environment and the diets that species have evolved to exploit. This realization has spotlighted the fact that feeding strategies and the neural control mechanisms that were shaped for the Paleolithic era or before may be inefficient—or even pathological—in negotiating the dietary, nutritional and energetic contingencies of the twenty-first century. Just as the physiological disturbances that astronauts experience in zero gravity have emphasized that mechanisms selected for an earth-bound gravitational environment do not perform optimally in all environments, so the obesity epidemic and other modern feeding disorders would seem to suggest there are limits of energy-balance mechanisms that were selected for the environmental challenges faced by man's hunter-gatherer ancestors (Eaton, Eaton, & Konner, 1999; Pollan, 2006). Certainly the environments in which feeding mechanisms evolved did not include ready surpluses of energy-dense, highly-processed sources of nutrients.

Finally, ecological observations also add an instructive methodological footnote that applies to many feeding experiments in behavioral neuroscience. Laboratory experiments on feeding typically employ highly simplified, rigidly predictable environments and testing regimens. Such is the nature of good experimental control. Paradoxically, though, in establishing experimental control, laboratory research removes or clamps many of the challenges that the nervous system has evolved to negotiate when the individual feeds. Thus, experiments often remove many of the sensory, motor, memory, and planning demands the animal more typically faces. In essence, to study, say, the hypothalamus, we remove the challenges for the association cortex, frontal lobe, parietal lobe, cingulate cortex, and cerebellum from the contingencies the animal encounters. Not surprisingly (though seldom actually discussed), such a paradigm accentuates, or even exaggerates, the apparent role of the hypothalamus by deemphasizing the operations of the other stations of the neural network. Simplify the environment enough, engineer most of the normal environmental contingencies out of the task, and employ tests selected to tap hypothalamic processing, and it is likely that the hypothalamus will appear to operate like an executive center controlling feeding.

HYPOTHALAMIC CIRCUITS OF INGESTION AND THEIR SIGNALS CHARACTERIZED WITH MOLECULAR BIOLOGY

As previously outlined, early behavioral neuroscience explained the control of food intake and energy balance in terms of hypothalamic hunger and satiety centers. These ideas, though, seemed to lose much of their explanatory validity in the research of the past three decades of the twentieth century. The unique and executive preeminence originally assigned to the hypothalamus became unsupportable as different technologies such as decerebration techniques, anatomical mapping, and single unit electrophysiology were applied. Simultaneously, the hypothalamic center idea also seemed less accurate as neuroscientific explanations of a variety of motivated behaviors (e.g., reproductive behavior—see Chapters 5, 6, 24, and 35), including feeding, evolved.

As better understanding of motivational mechanisms accumulated (see also Chapter 36), there was a growing recognition that the uncritical invocation of *hunger* and *satiety* mechanisms, as frequently had occurred, amounted to invoking a folk or faculty psychology to account for feeding. Behavioral "faculties" were simply mapped, particularly in some of the earlier brain behavior analyses, onto regions of the brain in a one-to-one phrenological fashion. But, unless the operation of neural region can be specified at the neuronal level, treating a region as a proverbial black box and invoking the idea of a hunger center to explain *hunger* is tautological, and positing a satiety center to explain *satiety* is hollow.

In the past decade or so, in terms of experimental focus, the research pendulum has swung back to a strongly renewed interest in the hypothalamus (Elmquist, Elias, & Saper, 1999; King, 2006; Marx, 2003; Schwartz, Woods,

Porte, Seeley, & Baskin, 2000; Woods, Schwartz, Baskin & Seeley, 2000). Though the reversal is by no means complete, the hypothalamus has been implicated as a crucial hub in the control of feeding by new methodologies that provide some of the previously unavailable neuronal-level specification of mechanism, thus offering critical information to escape the circularity just discussed. At least three complementary types of investigations, emerging in large part from the revolution in molecular biology and applications of new genetic tools to the epidemic of obesity and other eating disorders, have again refocused considerable experimental effort on the hypothalamic mechanisms that affect ingestive behavior. An understanding of the circulating signals, the circuits, and the neuropeptides expressed in the hypothalamic network have developed synergistically.

Earlier studies, and in particular experiments that combined genetically obese mutant *ob/ob* and *db/db* mice in parabiotic pairs (see Figure 34.7; see also Coleman, 1973; Coleman & Hummel, 1969), had implicated a lipostatic signal in the adiposity disorders, but the exact mechanism remained obscure. When the *ob* gene was eventually cloned and determined to encode leptin and the *db* gene was found to code for the leptin receptor (Tartaglia et al., 1995; Zhang et al., 1994), it rapidly emerged that the hormone leptin, produced primarily by adipocytes, served as a lipostatic signal, that receptors for the signal were expressed in the hypothalamus, that leptin was transported across the weak blood-brain barrier of the basomedial hypothalamus, and that appropriate manipulations of the hormone and receptor could variously produce phenocopies of the *ob/ob* mice or correct the disturbances caused by the mutation (Friedman & Halaas, 1998).

With a key role for leptin established, receptor mapping studies of the hypothalamus indicated that leptin receptors were found through the tuberal hypothalamic nuclei implicated in feeding (including the ventromedial nucleus and lateral hypothalamus as well as the paraventricular, dorsomedial, and arcuate nuclei), with particularly heavy expression found in the arcuate nucleus (Barsh & Schwartz, 2002; Elmquist et al., 1999; Sawchenko, 1998; van den Pol, 2003).

As investigations focused on the arcuate nucleus, the outlines of the intrahypothalamic circuitry implicated in energy balance, a network now recognized as a melanocortin system, emerged (see Figure 34.8). The arcuate nucleus contains two distinct types of neurons, both expressing the leptin receptor and both releasing the inhibitory transmitter gamma-aminobutyric acid (GABA), which through the neuropeptide modulators they produce and also release, have opposite effects (through the melanocortin system) on feeding. One class of arcuate neurons expresses both proopiomelanocortin (POMC) and cocaine-amphetamine regulated transcript (CART). POMC is cleaved into a number of products including melanocyte-stimulating hormones, adrenocorticotropic hormone, and β-endorphin. When these POMC/CART neurons are activated, they affect melanocortin receptors (particularly the subtypes 3 and 4, or MC3R and MC4R) expressed through the paraventricular nucleus, lateral hypothalamus, dorsal hypothalamic nucleus, and arcuate. Such activation when elicited by leptin or other stimulation or when achieved by the appropriate pharmacological challenges reduces food intake and body weight while simultaneously increasing energy expenditure.

The second class of arcuate neurons, intermingled with the first, has reciprocal effects. This second class also releases GABA, but produces and secretes the neuropeptides neuropeptide Y (NPY) and agouti gene-related transcript (AgRP). The peptides are endogenous antagonists of the MC3R and MC4R, thereby blocking the activation of the melanocortin receptors by α-MSH and other products of the POMC/CART neurons. NPY and AgRP release with its blockade

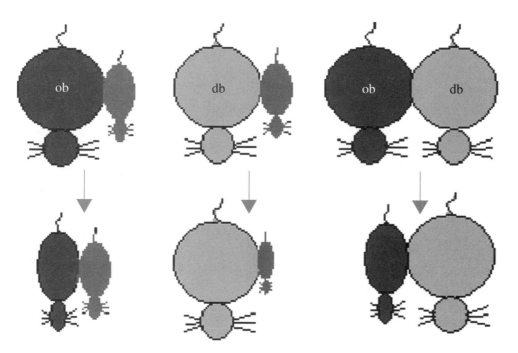

Figure 34.7 The parabiosis method and a classical illustration of the technique used to demonstrate a lipostatic signal (i.e., leptin).

Note: Parabiosis is the condition in which two animals are conjoined surgically, typically side-to-side. The surgical union is commonly performed so that the animals exchange blood through vascular anastomoses. This experimental analogue of Siamese twins thus provides a preparation in which hormonal and other blood-borne signals pass between the pair of animals (but, of course, their neural pathways remain separate). The demanding surgical and maintenance requirements have limited the use of the technique, but the method can, in some cases, provide particularly definitive tests.

In classical experiments performed 25 years before the *ob* and *db* genes were cloned and determined to code for leptin and the leptin receptor, respectively, Coleman and his colleagues (Coleman, 1973; Coleman & Hummel, 1969) were able to predict the existence of the adipocyte hormone and its receptor and partially describe the unknown hormone's physiology through experiments using parabiosis. Three of the surgical pairings that the Coleman laboratory employed are illustrated in the top row of this figure; the experimental outcomes of the different unions are illustrated in the bottom row. When (in the left column) an obese *ob/ob* mouse (dark gray) was joined parabiotically to a normal control mouse (medium gray), the *ob/ob* mouse reduced its food intake and dieted down, suggesting that the normal-weight control animal was producing a lipostatic signal (now known to be leptin) that the *ob/ob* mouse could detect, but not produce. When (in the middle column) a fat *db/db* mouse (light gray) was joined to a control mouse (medium gray), the control mouse reduced its food intake below normal and dieted down, suggesting that the obese *db/db* mouse was producing high levels of a lipostatic signal (leptin, as it turns out), which it did not detect but which the normal control mouse interpreted as excess adiposity. When (in the right-hand column) an obese *ob/ob* mouse (dark gray) was parabiosed with a similarly obese *db/db* mouse (light gray), the *ob/ob* mouse reduced its intake and dieted down while the *db/db* mouse remained fat, suggesting again that the *ob/ob* mouse was sensitive to, or had the receptor for, a circulating lipostatic factor produced by the *db/db* mouse. The *db/db* mouse of the pair remained obese, consistent with the conclusion that this animal lacked the receptor for the lipostatic hormone. From "Genetics of food intake, body weight and obesity," By R. Bowen(2001). Web publication: http://www.vivo.colostate.edu/hbooks/pathphys/digestion/pregastric/fatgenes.html. Reprinted with permission.

As the Coleman experiment illustrates, the parabiosis method can yield compelling analyses of humoral factors (see also Martin, White, & Hulsey, 1991, for a review of additional demonstrations). Variants of the surgical protocol can also be employed to particular effect. In one such variant, it is possible to cross not only the blood supplies of parabiotic twins, but also segments of their gastrointestinal tracts. Koopmans, McDonald, and DiGirolamo (1997), for example, have done a number of experiments with parabiotic "intestines-crossed" rats in which food ingested and then partially digested by one animal can be diverted from its proximal intestines into the distal intestines of its parabiotic partner (and vice versa).

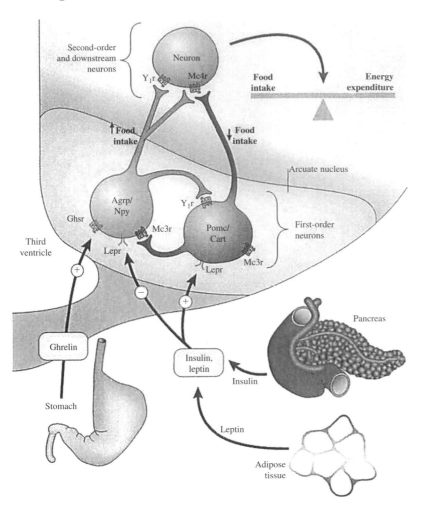

Figure 34.8 Hypothalamic circuitry controlling food intake and energy balance, as delineated with molecular biological and other modern neuroscience tools.

Note: The model includes two set of neurons in the arcuate nucleus—Agrp/Npy and Pomc/Cart neurons—that are regulated by circulating anabolic and catabolic hormones. Ghsr = Growth hormone secretagogue receptor; Lepr = Leptin receptor; Mc3r/Mc4r = Melanocortin 3/4 receptor; Y_1r = Neuropeptide Y1 receptor. From "Genetic Approaches to Studying Energy Balance: Perception and Integration," by G. S. Barsh and M. W. Schwartz, 2002, *Nature Reviews: Genetics, 3,* pp. 592. Reprinted with permission.

of the MC3/4R system leads to increased food intake and weight gain as well a corresponding energy conservation. The orexigenic NPY/AgRP neurons of the arcuate nucleus also project onto local anorexigenic POMC/CART neurons, where their GABA release effectively inhibits the anorexigenic neurons.

With their somata in the median eminence and with the tuberal region's fenestrated capillaries and weak blood-brain barrier, the reciprocally organized or push-pull orexigenic NPY/AgRP neurons and the anorexigenic POMC/CART neurons are viewed as first-order neurons that transduce circulating hormonal and humoral signals reflecting energy balance conditions. The neurons express receptors not only for leptin, but also for ghrelin and insulin and numerous other metabolic hormones. Thus, the neuropeptidergic arcuate neurons are situated to transduce and integrate hormones that reflect the energy regulation at the level of the fat pad (e.g., leptin), stomach (e.g., ghrelin), and pancreas (e.g., insulin).

The first-order arcuate NPY/AgRP and POMC/CART neurons project to second-order melanocortin system neurons distributed within paraventricular nucleus (PVN) and perifornical and lateral hypothalamic regions of the hypothalamus. In the case of the lateral hypothalamus, two subpopulations of neurons have been implicated in feeding. One group expresses the neuropeptide hypocretin (or orexin); the other group expresses melanin-concentrating hormone (MCH). Both subpopulations have wide projection fields throughout the brain, suggesting that they modulate arousal, motivation, emotion, and motor systems. In terms of their projections and effects, the two subpopulations seem to operate independently, perhaps coordinating different responses that synergize in complementary responses appropriate to energy balance status. The ventromedial nucleus of the hypothalamus also receives inputs from, and reciprocally projects to, both NPY/AgRP and POMC/CART arcuate neurons.

In their strategic location to monitor signals of metabolic status and with their demonstrated effects on feeding and body weight, the arcuate nucleus neurons and the hypothalamic neurons of the melanocortin system have become the subject of impressive and intense research efforts. Neurons of the local hypothalamic circuitry bind not only leptin, insulin, and ghrelin, they also bind many, if not most, hormones that impact catabolic or anabolic processes. A partial list includes glucocorticoids, estrogen, prolactin, and interleukins. In addition, neurons within the circuitry, through their intracellular utilization, also appear to monitor circulating fuels including glucose and fatty acids. The intracellular signaling cascades initiated by leptin and ghrelin receptor binding in the hypothalamic neurons have been particularly thoroughly delineated, because of the strategic position for transducing the many signals reflecting energy status.

It is appropriate to consider these observations on hypothalamic circuitry and the signals involved in the context of other observations, some already surveyed and others discussed next. Like the dramatic symptoms elicited from the hypothalamus by lesions during the early feeding center analyses, the striking feeding effects that can be elicited by genetic and molecular manipulations (gene knockouts, peptide infusions, etc.) at a first look seem to substantiate the early feeding center description of hypothalamic function. Rather than seeing the hypothalamus as merely one important station among others in a multiplicity of complex circuits operating cooperatively to organize energy balance, it is tempting to return to the idea that it is the critical, executive node in the neural feeding apparatus. As mentioned, a number of reports have suggested that there is a "renaissance" of the hypothalamic feeding model (Elmquist et al., 1999; King, 2006). Similarly, many of the schematic summaries of feeding emphasize the hypothalamic circuitry while they reduce the contributions of the rest of the nervous system to a few vectors or arrows (e.g., see schematics in Figures 34.1, 34.3, and 34.8). Although there is a widespread reluctance to speak in terms of "center," some analyses appear to circumvent the negative connotations of the term not by moving to a noncenter analysis but by stripping terms such as "circuit" or "network" of much of their meaning and using them as circumlocutions, in effect, for centers.

Such views are at risk of being myopic. As discussed earlier, many of the receptors manipulated and discussed in terms of their hypothalamic expression are actually broadly distributed throughout the nervous system, many of the manipulations (e.g., peptide infusions) directed at the hypothalamus are not limited to the hypothalamus, and many of the feeding or energy balance effects that have been ascribed to the hypothalamus can be elicited from the caudal brain stem when infusions or other manipulations of the peptide systems are confined to the medulla. In this regard, it should be noted that a number of syntheses in which the hypothalamic circuitry is more explicitly integrated into or with the caudal brain stem and other CNS circuitries implicated in feeding have been suggested (e.g., Berthoud, 2002, 2004; Broberger & Hokfelt, 2001; Williams et al., 2001). The risk of short-sightedness is also underscored by the recent realization that the hypothalamic mechanisms are not highly stable hardwired circuits, but

rather neural pathways capable of synaptic plasticity and reorganization in response to different demands (Horvath & Diano, 2004).

Another methodological footnote is appropriate here: Gene knockouts and mutations are fundamentally lesions. They are molecular lesions, but they are lesions just as surely as are ablative lesions and space-occupying lesions. Though they are often interpreted—as are other types of lesions—as revealing the function of the disabled or destroyed element, or in this case protein product, the effects that these molecular lesions cause may, of course, result from any of the convoluted, potentially distorted, and compensatory adjustments they occasion (Glassman, 1978). Knocking out or mutating, say the *ob* gene for leptin, does not illustrate by any simple subtractive logic the normal function of leptin. Instead, it illustrates how the organism is able to develop, adapt, compensate, and adjust in the absence of that gene.

There have been repeated reminders that inferences from mutation effects back to normal function can be problematic. Loss-of-function lesions of the gene for leptin lead to dramatic obesity in rodents and humans, and this observation was initially used to support the conclusion that leptin operates as a critical negative feedback signal to inhibit excess positive energy balance, obesity, and overconsumption. Ironically, though, leptin administration to obese rodents or humans typically produces relatively subtle—or no—effects on the positive energy balance conditions (except for, of course, those few rodents and humans with loss-of-function mutations of the *ob* gene). And conversely, there are many other examples where a given neuropeptide or gene product has one effect when administered to intact individuals, but loss of the gene product produces very different and asymmetrical effects. NPY, for example, administered into the hypothalamus produces dramatic feeding, an effect that led to the conclusion that the peptide is a transmitter coding for feeding, but loss-of-function mutations or knockouts of the NPY gene have marginal to no effects on feeding (Qian et al., 2002). Or, for a final example, the orexigenic gut peptide hormone ghrelin is secreted by the stomach in a pattern that tracks hunger (by increasing) and satiety (by decreasing), and administration of the peptide elicits food intake, yet molecular "lesions" that eliminate ghrelin have little to no effect on feeding (Sun, Ahmed, & Smith, 2003).

Finally, the risk of a myopia or a tunnel vision can be appreciated by comparison with other neural systems. The successes of modern molecular techniques in unraveling the neural connectivities and neurochemistries of the hypothalamic sites implicated in feeding have been dramatic. Nonetheless, most of the recent scrutiny of the circuitry of feeding focuses on first-order arcuate neurons that detect circulating hormones and metabolites and second-order hypothalamic neurons (the paraventricular, ventromedial, dorsomedial, etc. neurons) and treats them as an integrative system, or as a simple system—a simulacrum standing in for all the extended neural machinery of feeding. All the rest of the nervous system and other peripheral signals tend to be subsumed into schematic input and output vectors (see, for example, Figure 34.8). Clearly, though, treating a two- or three-neuron chain of afferents as an executive site responsible for all the integration and analysis of the body's energy economy is unrealistic. Relegating the rest of the neural trafficking to flowchart vectors begs questions of how feeding is orchestrated by the nervous system. It is hard to imagine anyone attempting to explain visual perception or visually guided behavior in terms of only a simplified circuitry consisting of retinal amacrine and bipolar cells, with the rest of the visual system reduced to schematic arrows.

NEUROIMAGING IDENTIFIES DISTRIBUTED CORTICAL AND DIENCEPHALIC SITES PARTICIPATING IN INGESTIVE BEHAVIOR

The recent revolution in noninvasive neuroimaging techniques provides yet another perspective on the neural circuitry of feeding. As subjects—typically human subjects in this case—are presented with food cues or feeding opportunities while they are under either fasting or sated conditions, patterns of neural activity can be assessed. Within-subject comparisons can be made of the different neural signatures that characterize hunger and satiety by comparing the dynamic differences that occur when the subjects' fasted trials are compared with their sated trials. Alternative, between-subject comparisons (obese vs. normal-weight subjects, anorexics vs. controls, etc.) can also be made. With the high temporal resolution permitted by current scanning techniques, the patterns of brain activation can be examined essentially in real time.

Deprivation that presumably makes subjects hungry generally increases regional cerebral blood flow and hence regional activity in a variety of limbic, paralimbic, and cortical sites. Details of the pattern of activation vary to some extent between subject populations and between laboratories, but activation is commonly observed in the orbitofrontal and anterior cingulate cortex, as well as in visceral sensory cortex, including most particularly insular and piriform cortex (Tataranni et al., 1999; Wang et al., 2004). Notably, activity in the orbitofrontal cortex tends to correlate particularly well with self-reports and ratings of hunger (Wang et al., 2004). Additionally, during fasting, increased activation is also often seen in the amygdala, hippocampus, and parahippocampal regions, the striatum, and the cerebellum, among other sites (Arana et al., 2003; Morris & Dolan, 2001; Tataranni et al., 1999). Increases in activation are also occasionally, but not always, seen in the region of the hypothalamus as well (Tataranni et al., 1999).

Repletion or satiety or, even more operationally, the consumption of a test meal or nutrient load tends to be associated with increases in activation in prefrontal cortex and the inferior parietal lobe.

Neuroimaging experiments also commonly assay the CNS response to external stimuli such as to taste stimuli or to food-related stimuli under different conditions such as fasted or fed state. Food stimuli routinely activate the insula and neighboring superior temporal cortex as well as the orbitofrontal cortex. Amygdaloid, temporal lobe, and parahippocampal lobe activity appears to be particularly sensitive to stimulus properties, including the attractiveness or salience of food stimuli (Morris & Dolan, 2001; Wang et al., 2004).

Scanning methods have also been employed to evaluate how brain activity varies as a function of internal visceral and hormonal signals. Visceral inputs such as gastric stimulation also tend to activate the insula, amygdala, and hippocampus (Wang et al., 2006).

As another means of appreciating the neural mechanisms of feeding and disturbances in these mechanisms that must cause and/or reflect common eating disorders, neuroimaging studies have also begun to characterize how patterns of regional blood flow vary between normal-weight and overweight populations or between health control populations and those with anorexia or bulimia or other feeding disorders (Kaye et al., 2005; Liu & Gold, 2003).

Whereas most other neuroscience techniques have focused—or been focused—on the hypothalamus and the caudal brain stem, the functional scanning literature implicates limbic regions of the diencephalon and telencephalon in hunger, satiety, and food selection, many of these same limbic regions are also implicated in a variety of emotional and motivational behaviors (see Chapters 36 and 38). The pattern suggests that the processing associated with feeding shares common circuitry with other motivated behavior—that, in essence, feeding programs run on the same processors as other functional motivational systems, not on a dedicated feeding processor.

Something of an apparent paradox in the scanning literature is the fact that the hypothalamus appears to have a much less conspicuous and prominent pattern of activation than might be inferred from the lesion and hormone binding analyses on the structure. Several factors—some methodological, but some perhaps substantive—may explain the apparent paradox. Such a lack of a hypothalamic signature may, in some cases, merely reflect the limits of spatial resolution of current scanning protocols and equipment. Furthermore, as Liu, Gao, Liu, and Fox (2000) have suggested, activation patterns within the distributed network that seems to organize ingestive behavior may have complex phasic temporal and spatial patterns, and only analyses that examine the spatial and temporal parcellations will be able to capture all the local transients. Alternatively, the lack of a conspicuous involvement may also reflect the possibilities that the hypothalamus is more heavily involved in longer-term regulatory adjustments of energy balance that eventually modulate feeding, and less involved in the real-time organization of feeding behavior. Finally, scanning experiments may be, perhaps very correctly, suggesting that the hypothalamic role in hunger and satiety has historically been blown out of proportion in respect to the roles of the various limbic, cortical, diencephalic, mesencephalic, and rhombencephalic circuits that recent research has implicated in ingestive behavior.

In summary, sensitive neuroimaging techniques that have recently become available, have begun to delineate a picture of the neural substrate of ingestion that is quite different from that which was concentrated on the hypothalamus. Scanning work describes dynamic and distributed patterns of activation more adequately characterized by Sherrington's "enchanted loom" weaving "dissolving pattern(s)," always "meaningful," never "abiding," than by executive centers in the hypothalamus.

SUMMARY

Behavioral neuroscience has yet to produce, as measured by its unsatisfactory record in predicting effective therapies for eating disorders, a completely coherent account of food intake. The different methods employed in the neurosciences generate distinctly different, sometimes even conflicting, views of the neural basis of food intake. These disparate views serve as reminders that, while our models affect our choice of methods, our methods also shape our models.

Since the era of the early experimental formulations that accounted for feeding and energy balance in terms of hypothalamic centers, neuroscience has discovered a much more extensive and distributed network of sites participating in feeding. This network or visceral neuroaxis includes a multiplicity of CNS sites from the caudal brain stem to the frontal cortex. This visceral network also includes the enteric nervous system or "little brain" in the gut, and the autonomic efferents and visceral afferents linking the enteric network to the CNS, all extensively interconnected by multiple pathways. In addition, a diverse battery of gut-brain and adipocyte hormones, paracrine factors, neurocrine factors, cytokines, and other signals modulate or set the gains on neurons throughout the entire span of the visceral neuroaxis.

Experimental protocols that employ limited environments, paradigms with tight experimental control, and techniques biased toward localization outcomes (e.g., lesions, focal stimulation) have tended to support the inference that the brain is organized with compartmentalized centers specialized for the control of feeding or body weight. And this center paradigm has provided a convenient, accessible, and simplifying model of ingestive behavior. Though experimentally and conceptually tractable, the model appears, in some cases, to beg the questions it purports to answer and, in other cases, to be inaccurate and invalid.

In contrast, tests that employ more complex environmental situations or stimuli, experimental paradigms designed to provide subjects with more opportunities or options, and techniques adapted to characterizing distributed networks (e.g., nervous-system-wide mapping of receptors or neuronal connections, functional scanning techniques) have tended to support the conclusion that feeding and body weight regulation are organized by an extensive network of decentralized sites throughout the central—as well as peripheral and enteric—nervous systems, with substantial interconnections and parallel architectures. Additionally, these open-architecture techniques challenge the idea that the brain "wetware" can be compartmentalized with any one area dedicated to, or specialized for, a single type of behavior such as feeding.

In the immediate future, a major—perhaps *the* major—goal for the neuroscience of feeding behavior may be to better reconcile and synthesize the multiple dissimilar views of the neural circuitry of ingestion suggested by the disparate techniques now in use. To achieve this end, it will be particularly useful to weigh the influences—and recognize the biases—of the different methodologies on both the data collected and the interpretations generated.

REFERENCES

Aboitiz, F. (1996). Does bigger mean better? Evolutionary determinants of brain size and structure. *Brain, Behavior and Evolution, 47,* 225–245.

Anand, B. K., & Brobeck, J. R. (1951). Localization of a "feeding center" in the hypothalamus of the rat. *Proceedings of the Society of Experimental Biology and Medicine, 77,* 323–324.

Arana, F. S., Parkinson, J. A., Hinton, E., Holland, A. J., Owen, A. M., & Roberts, A. C. (2003). Dissociable contributions of the human amygdala and orbitofrontal cortex to incentive motivation and goal selection. *Journal of Neuroscience, 23,* 9632–9638.

Araujo, I. E., Gutierrez, R., Oliveira-Maia, A. J., Pereira, A., Jr., Nicolelis, M. A. L., & Simon, S. A. (2006). Neural ensemble coding of satiety states. *Neuron, 51,* 483–494.

Badman, M. K., & Flier, J. S. (2007). The adipocyte as an active participant in energy balance and metabolism. *Gastroenterology, 132,* 2103–2115.

Barsh, G. S., & Schwartz, M. W. (2002). Genetic approaches to studying energy balance: Perception and integration. *Nature Reviews: Genetics, 3,* 589–600.

Bernard, R. T. F., & Nurton, J. (1993). Ecological correlates of relative brain size in some South-African rodents. *South African Journal of Zoology, 28,* 95–98.

Berthoud, H.-R. (2002). Multiple neural systems controlling food intake and body weight. *Neuroscience and Biobehavioral Reviews, 26,* 393–428.

Berthoud, H.-R. (2004). Mind versus metabolism in the control of food intake and energy balance. *Physiology and Behavior, 81,* 781–793.

Bjorklund, A., Hokfelt, T., & Owman, C. (Eds.). (1988). *Handbook of chemical neuroanatomy: Vol. 6. The peripheral nervous system.* Amsterdam: Elsevier.

Bjorntorp, P. (2001). Thrifty genes and human obesity: Are we chasing ghosts? *Lancet, 358,* 1006–1008.

Blessing, W. W. (1997). *The lower brainstem and bodily homeostasis.* New York: Oxford University Press.

Blundell, J. E. (1980). Hunger, appetite and satiety: Constructs in search of identities. In M. Turner (Ed.), *Nutrition and lifestyles* (pp. 21–42). London: Applied Science.

Bowen, R. (2001). *Genetics of food intake, body weight and obesity.* Retrieved (April 23, 2008) from www.vivo.colostate.edu/hbooks/pathphys/digestion/pregastric/fatgenes.html.

Brobeck, J. R. (1957). Neural control of hunger, appetite, and satiety. *Yale Journal of Biology and Medicine, 29,* 566–574.

Broberger, C., & Hokfelt, T. (2001). Hypothalamic and vagal neuropeptide circuitries regulating food intake. *Physiology and Behavior, 74,* 669–682.

Coleman, D. L. (1973). Effects of parabiosis of obese with diabetes and normal mice. *Diabetologia, 9,* 294–298.

Coleman, D. L. (1979, February 16). Obesity genes: Beneficial effects in heterozygous mice. *Science, 203,* 663–665.

Coleman, D. L., & Hummel, K. P. (1969). Effects of parabiosis of normal with genetically diabetic mice. *American Journal of Physiology, 217,* 1298–1304.

Collier, G., & Johnson, D. F. (2004). The paradox of satiation. *Physiology and Behavior, 82,* 149–153.

Corbit, J. D., & Stellar, E. (1964). Palatability, food intake, and obesity in normal and hyperphagic rats. *Journal of Comparative and Physiological Psychology, 58,* 63–67.

Cummings, D. E., & Overduin, J. (2007). Gastrointestinal regulation of food intake. *Journal of Clinical Investigation, 117,* 13–23.

Eaton, S. B., Eaton, S. B. III, & Konner, M. J. (1999). Paleolithic nutrition revisited. In W. R. Trevathan, E. O. Smith, & J. J. McKenna (Eds.), *Evolutionary medicine* (pp. 313–332). New York: Oxford University Press.

Elmquist, J. K., Elias, C. F., & Saper, C. B. (1999). From lesions to leptin: Hypothalamic control of food intake and body weight. *Neuron, 22,* 221–232.

Friedman, J. M., & Halaas, J. L. (1998, October 22). Leptin and the regulation of body weight in mammals. *Nature, 395,* 763–770.

Funahashi, H., Yada, T., Suzuki, R., & Shioda, S. (2003). Distribution, function, and properties of leptin receptors in the brain. *International Review of Cytology, 224,* 1–27.

Garcia, J., Hankins, W. G., & Coil, J. D. (1977). Koalas, men, and other conditioned gastronomes. In N. W. Milgram, L. Krames, & T. M. Alloway (Eds.), *Food aversion learning* (pp. 196–218). New York: Plenum Press.

Glassman, R. B. (1978). The logic of the lesion experiment and its role in the neural sciences. In S. Finger (Ed.), *Recovery from brain damage: Research and theory* (pp. 3–31). New York: Plenum Press.

Grill, H. J., & Kaplan, J. M. (1990). Caudal brainstem participates in the distributed neural control of feeding. In E. M. Stricker (Ed.), *Handbook of behavioral neurobiology: Vol. 10, Neurobiology of Food and Fluid Intake,* (pp. 125–149). New York: Plenum Press.

Grill, H. J., & Norgren, R. (1978, July 21). Chronically decerebrate rats demonstrate satiation but not bait shyness. *Science, 201,* 267–269.

Harris, M., & Ross, E. B. (Eds.). (1987). *Food and evolution: Toward a theory of human food habits.* Philadelphia: Temple University Press.

Harvey, J., & Ashford, M. L. J. (2003). Leptin in the CNS: Much more than a satiety signal. *Neuropharmacology, 44,* 845–854.

Healy, S. D., & Rowe, C. (2007). A critique of comparative studies of brain size. *Proceedings of the Royal Society, B, 274,* 453–464.

Hetherington, A. W., & Ranson, S. W. (1942). The relation of various hypothalamic lesions to adiposity in the rat. *Journal of Comparative Neurology, 76,* 475–499.

Hill, J. M., Lesniak, M. A., Pert, C. B., & Roth, J. (1986). Autoradiographic localization of insulin receptors in rat brain: Prominence in olfactory and limbic areas. *Neuroscience, 17,* 1127–1138.

Hirvonen, M. D., & Keesey, R. E. (1996). Chronically altered body protein levels following lateral hypothalamic lesions in rats. *American Journal of Physiology-Regulatory, Integrative and Comparative Physiology, 270,* R738–R743.

Hoebel, B. G., & Teitelbaum, P. (1966). Weight regulation in normal and hypothalamic hyperphagic rats. *Journal of Comparative and Physiological Psychology, 61,* 189–193.

Holst, M.-C., Kelly, J. B., & Powley, T. L. (1997). Vagal preganglionic projections to the enteric nervous system characterized with PHA-L. *Journal of Comparative Neurology, 381,* 81–100.

Holstege, G., Bandler, R., & Saper, C. B. (Eds.). (1996). The emotional motor system. *Progress in Brain Research, 107,* (pp. 1–627). Amsterdam: Elsevier Press.

Horvath, T. L., & Diano, S. (2004). The floating blueprint of hypothalamic feeding circuits. *Nature Reviews: Neuroscience, 5,* 662–667.

Iwaniuk, A. N., & Hurd, P. L. (2005). The evolution of cerebrotypes in birds. *Brain, Behavior and Evolution, 65,* 215–230.

Janig, W. (2006). *The integrative action of the autonomic nervous system: Neurobiology of homeostasis.* Cambridge, MA: Cambridge University Press.

Kar, S., Chabot, J. G., & Quirion, R. (1993). Quantitative autoradiographic localization of [I-125] insulin-like growth factor-I, I[I-125] insulin-like growth factor-II, and [I-125] insulin-receptor binding sites in developing and adult rat brain. *Journal of Comparative Neurology, 333,* 375–397.

Kaye, W. H., Frank, G. K., Bailer, U. F., Henry, S. E., Meltzer, C. C., Price, J. C., et al. (2005). Serotonin alterations in anorexia and bulimia nervosa: New insights from imaging studies. *Physiology and Behavior, 85,* 73–81.

Keesey, R. E., Powley, T. L., & Kemnitz, J. W. (1976). Prolonging lateral hypothalamic anorexia by tube-feeding. *Physiology and Behavior, 17,* 367–371.

Kennedy, G. C. (1953). The role of depot fat in the hypothalamic control of food intake in the rat. *Proceedings of the Royal Society, B., 140,* 578–592.

King, B. M. (2006). The rise, fall, and resurrection of the ventromedial hypothalamus in the regulation of feeding behavior and body weight. *Physiology and Behavior, 87,* 221–244.

King, J. M., & Cox, V. C. (1973). The effects of estrogens on food intake and body weight following ventromedial hypothalamic lesions. *Physiological Psychology, 1,* 261–264.

Kishi, T., Aschkenasi, C. J., Lee, C. E., Mountjoy, K. G., Saper, C. B., & Elmquist, J. K. (2003). Expression of melanocortin 4 receptor mRNA in the central nervous system of the rat. *Journal of Comparative Neurology, 457,* 213–235.

Koopmans, H. S., McDonald, T. J., & DiGirolamo, M. (1997). Morphological and metabolic changes associated with large differences in daily food intake in crossed-intestines rats. *Physiology and Behavior, 62,* 129–136.

Lefebvre, L., Reader, S. M., & Sol, D. (2004). Brains, innovations and evolution in birds and primates. *Brain, Behavior and Evolution, 63,* 233–246.

Liu, Y., Gao, J. H., Liu, H. L., & Fox, P. T. (2000, June 29). The temporal responses of the brain after eating revealed by functional MRI. *Nature, 405,* 1058–1062.

Liu, Y., & Gold, M. S. (2003). Human functional magnetic resonance imaging of eating and satiety in eating disorders and obesity. *Psychiatric Annals, 33,*127–132.

Marshall, J. F., Richardson, J. S., & Teitelbaum, P. (1974). Nigrostriatal bundle damage and the lateral hypothalamic syndrome. *Journal of Comparative and Physiological Psychology, 87,* 808–830.

Marshall, J. F., Turner, B. H., & Teitelbaum, P. (1971, October 29). Sensory neglect produced by lateral hypothalamic damage. *Science, 174,* 523–525.

Martin, R. J., White, B. D., & Hulsey, M. G. (1991). The regulation of body weight. *American Scientist, 79,* 528–541.

Marx, J. (2003, February 7). Cellular warriors at the battle of the bulge. *Science, 299,* 846–849.

Mayer, J. (1953). Glucostatic mechanisms of regulation of food intake. *New England Journal of Medicine, 249,* 13–16.

Morris, J. S., & Dolan, R. J. (2001). Involvement of human amygdala and orbitofrontal cortex in hunger-enhanced memory for food stimuli. *Journal of Neuroscience, 21,* 5304–5310.

Neel, J. V. (1962). Diabetes mellitus: A "thrifty" genotype rendered detrimental by "progress"? *American Journal of Human Genetics, 14,* 353–362.

Nicolakakis, N., & Lefebvre, L. (2000). Forebrain size and innovation rate in European birds: Feeding, nesting and confounding variables. *Behaviour, 137,* 1415–1429.

Pollan, M. (2006). *The omnivore's dilemma.* New York: Penguin Press.

Powell, K. (2007, May 31). The two faces of fat. *Nature, 447,* 525–527.

Powley, T. L. (1977). The ventromedial hypothalamic syndrome, satiety, and a cephalic phase hypothesis. *Psychological Review, 84,* 89–126.

Powley, T. L., & Keesey, R. E. (1970). Relationship of body weight to the lateral hypothalamic syndrome. *Journal of Comparative and Physiological Psychology, 70,* 25–36.

Powley, T. L., & Phillips, R. J. (2002). Musings on the wanderer: What's new in our understanding of vago-vagal reflexes? Pt. I. Morphology and topography of vagal afferents innervating the GI tract. *American Journal of Physiology, 283,* G1217–G1225.

Qian, S., Chen, H., Weingarth, D., Trumbauer, M. E., Novi, D. E., Guan, X., et al. (2002). Neither agouti-related protein nor neuropeptide Y is critically required for the regulation of energy homeostasis in mice. *Molecular and Cellular Biology, 22,* 5027–5035.

Rehfeld, J. F. (1998). The new biology of gastrointestinal hormones. *Physiological Reviews, 78,* 1087–1108.

Rolls, E. T. (2005). Taste, olfactory, and food texture processing in the brain, and the control of food intake. *Physiology and Behavior, 85* 45–56.

Rozin, P. (1976). The selection of foods by rats, humans, and other animals. In J. Rosenblatt, R. A. Hide, C. Beer, & E. Shaw (Eds.), *Advances in the study of behavior*, Volume 6 (pp. 21–76). New York: Academic Press.

Saper, C. B., Chou, T. C., & Elmquist, J. K. (2002). The need to feed: Homeostatic and hedonic control of eating. *Neuron, 36,* 199–211.

Sawchenko, P. E. (1998). Toward a new neurobiology of energy balance, appetite, and obesity: The anatomist weighs in. *Journal of Comparative Neurology, 402,* 435–441.

Schwartz, M. W., Woods, S. C., Porte, D., Jr., Seeley, R. J., & Baskin, D. G. (2000, April 6). Central nervous system control of food intake. *Nature, 404,* 661–671.

Schwartz, M. W., Woods, S. C., Seeley, R. J., Barsh, G. S., Baskin, D. G., & Leibel, R. L. (2003). Is the energy homeostasis system inherently biased toward weight gain? *Diabetes, 52,* 232–238.

Scott, T. R., Yan, J., & Rolls, E. T. (1995). Brain mechanisms of satiety and taste in macaques. *Neurobiology, 3,* 281–292.

Sherrington, C.S. (1906). *The integrative action of the nervous system.* New York: Charles Scribner's Sons.

Stellar, E. (1954). The physiology of motivation. *Psychological Review, 61,* 5–22.

Sun, Y., Ahmed, S., & Smith, R. G. (2003). Deletion of ghrelin impairs neither growth nor appetite. *Molecular and Cellular Biology, 23,* 7973–7981.

Swanson, L. W. (2000). Cerebral hemisphere regulation of motivated behavior. *Brain Research, 886,* 113–164.

Tartaglia, L. A., Dembski, M., Weng, X., Deng, N., Culpepper, J., Devos, R., et al. (1995). Identification and expression cloning of a leptin receptor, OB-R. *Cell, 83,* 1263–1271.

Tataranni, P. A., Gautier, J.-F., Chen, K., Uecker, A., Bandy, D., Salbe, A. D., et al. (1999). Neuroanatomical correlates of hunger and satiation in humans using positron emission tomography. *Proceedings of the National Academy of Sciences, USA, 96,* 4569–4574.

Teitlebaum, P. (1955). Sensory control of hypothalamic hyperphagia. *Journal of Comparative and Physiological Psychology, 48,* 156–163.

Teitelbaum, P., & Epstein, A. N. (1962). The lateral hypothalamic syndrome: Recovery of feeding and drinking after lateral hypothalamic lesions. *Psychological Review, 69,* 74–90.

Thomas, P. R. (Ed.). (1995). *Weighing the options: Criteria for evaluating weight-management programs.* Washington, DC: National Academy Press.

Timmermans, S., Lefebvre, L., Boire, D., & Basu, P. (2000). Relative size of the hyperstriatum ventrale is the best predictor of feeding innovation rate in birds. *Brain, Behavior, and Evolution, 56,* 196–203.

Ungerstedt, U. (1970). Is interruption of the nigro-striatal dopamine system producing the "lateral hypothalamus syndrome"? *Acta Physiologica Scandinavia, 80,* A35–A36.

van den Pol, A. N. (2003). Weighing the role of hypothalamic feeding centers. *Neuron, 40,* 1059–1061.

Walgren, M. C., & Powley, T. L. (1985). Effects of intragastric hyperalimentation on pair-fed rats with ventromedial hypothalamic lesions. *American Journal of Physiology, 248,* R172–R180.

Wang, G.-J., Volkow, N. D., Telang, F., Jayne, M., Ma, J., Rao, M., et al. (2004). Exposure to appetitive food stimuli markedly activates the human brain. *NeuroImage, 21,* 1790–1797.

Wang, G.-J., Yang, J., Volkow, N. D., Telang, F., Ma, Y., Zhu, W., et al. (2006). Gastric stimulation in obese subjects activates the hippocampus and other regions involved in brain reward circuitry. *Proceedings of the National Academy of the Sciences, USA, 103,* 15641–15645.

Williams, G., Bing, C., Cai, X. J., Harrold, J. A., King, P. J., & Liu, X. H. (2001). The hypothalamus and the control of energy homeostasis: Different circuits, different purposes. *Physiology and Behavior, 74,* 683–701.

Williams, G. Cai, X. J., Elliott, J. C., & Harrold, J. A. (2004). Anabolic neuropeptides. *Physiology & Behavior, 81,* 211–222.

Woods, S. C. (1991). The eating paradox: How we tolerate food. *Psychological Review, 98,* 488–505.

Woods, S. C., Schwartz, M. W., Baskin, D. G., & Seeley, R. J. (2000). Food intake and the regulation of body weight. *Annual Review of Psychology, 51,* 255–277.

Zaborszky, L., Wouterlood, F. G., & Lanciego, J. L. (Eds.). (2006). *Neuroanatomical tract-tracing 3: Molecules, neurons, and systems.* New York: Springer.

Zarbin, M. A., Innis, R. B., Wamsley, J. K., Snyder, S. H., & Kuhar, M. J. (1983). Autoradiographic localization of cholecystokinin receptors in rodent brain. *Journal of Neuroscience, 3,* 877–906.

Zhang, Y., Proenca, R., Maffei, M., Barone, M., Leopold, L., & Friedman, J. M. (1994, December 1). Positional cloning of the mouse obese gene and its human homologue. *Nature, 372,* 425–432.

Zigman, J. M., Jones, J. E., Lee, C. E., Saper, C. B., & Elmquist, J. K. (2006). Expression of ghrelin receptor mRNA in the rat and mouse brain. *Journal of Comparative Neurology, 494,* 528–548.

Chapter 35

Thirst

MICHAEL J. MCKINLEY

THE NATURE OF THIRST

A Homeostatic Emotion

Thirst is an impelling urge to drink water or aqueous fluids. As a private, subjective state, thirst is difficult to define. Yet few who read this chapter have not experienced thirst. It can be classified with the urge to inhale air, the desire for sleep, feeling hot or cold, pain, hunger, fatigue, full bladder or bowel, and nausea as essential motivating emotions arising from interoceptive signals that lead subsequently to appropriate behavior to correct bodily deficits or surfeits, thereby restoring normal physiological set points. Thirst is an essential homeostatic emotion (Craig, 2003).

Some have defined thirst as a disposition to drink (Booth, 1991), but such a definition includes the motivation to drink resulting from habit, advice, ritual, or social, cultural, and psychotic drives. Such dispositions to drink almost certainly do not reflect the same motivational emotion that arises from bodily dehydration and they should be differentiated from the homeostatic emotion of thirst that is the subject of this chapter. An essential feature of thirst is a degree of discomfort or craving, so that as thirst intensifies, it becomes more distressing, tormenting, and ultimately agonizing and overwhelming. Fortunately, most people will not experience thirst of this severity.

It is not surprising that as fluid deficits increase, thirst and the motivation to ingest water increase concomitantly. Water is by far the most abundant molecule in the body, being 60% of its weight but approximately 98% of all the molecules in the body. Adequate intracellular water is essential for maintaining intracellular concentrations of dissolved enzymes, substrates, and ions that allow maximal functioning of cellular activity. Adequate extracellular water is essential for maintaining the integrity of the cardiovascular system and for thermoregulation. Obligatory losses of water from the body occur continually from the respiratory and gastrointestinal tracts, kidney, and skin. To replace these losses, some water is ingested in the form of food and some obtained from metabolic reactions, however, the drinking of aqueous fluid is the main source for replacing fluid deficits. While much of fluid intake is of a social, habitual, and prandial nature, rather than a response to thirst, if these sources of fluid are inadequate, thirst provides the fail-safe system to ensure that fluid deficits are replaced. No matter how effectively the kidney can concentrate urine and reduce water lost therein, this mechanism does not replace the obligatory fluid deficits mentioned. Analogous to the hunger for air ensuring sufficient oxygen intake and survival in the short term, thirst is a homeostatic emotion essential for survival in the longer term (Cannon, 1919).

Concepts of Thirst

The development of ideas on how thirst is generated has been described in some detail by Fitzsimons (1979). At the beginning of the twentieth century, Mayer (1900) proposed that thirst was a sensation that arose essentially as a result of the osmotic pressure of the body fluids and tissues increasing. In attempting to define thirst, Cannon (1919) proposed a somatosensory explanation, attributing dryness in the pharynx and mouth as the essential feature of thirst. However, if dry mouth and throat are experimentally contrived by pharmacological means, subjects are not rendered thirsty, arguing against this explanation. Thus, the idea of thirst as a specific somatic sensation in the mouth and throat has lost favor. Following the demonstration that water drinking could be evoked by chemical or electrical stimulation of the hypothalamus (Andersson, 1953;

The author was supported by an Australian NHMRC Fellowship (ID 454369), and grants from the NHMRC (Project Grant ID 350437), Australian Research Council, the Robert J. Jr. & Helen C. Kleberg Foundation, and the G. Harold and Leila Y. Mathers Charitable Foundation. Thanks to Dr. Robin McAllen for comments and Julianna McKinley for artwork.

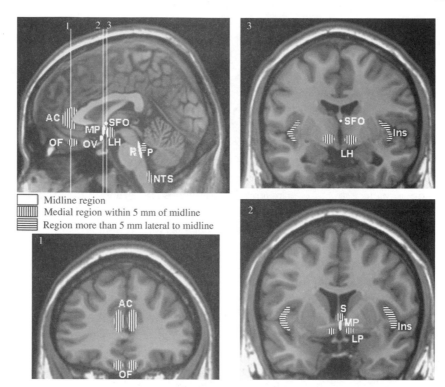

Figure 35.1 (**Figure C. 34** in color section) A guide to the location within the brain of regions implicated in the generation and regulation of thirst.

Note: **Top left panel:** specific regions are projected onto a longitudinal magnetic resonance (MR) image of the midline of the human brain. The other panels show several of these regions in transverse MR images of the same brain at three rostro-caudal levels (1,2,3) that are indicated by the white vertical lines in panel A. AC = Anterior cingulate cortex; INS = Insula; LH = Lateral hypothalamic area; LP = Lateral preoptic area; MP = Median preoptic nucleus; NTS = Nucleus of the solitary tract; OF = Orbito-frontal cortex; OV = Organum vasculosum of the lamina terminalis; P = Parabrachial nucleus; R = Midbrain raphé (dorsal and medial nuclei); S = Septal region; SFO = Subfornical organ.

Andersson & McCann, 1955; Greer, 1955) and hypothalamic lesions caused adipsia (Teitelbaum & Epstein, 1962), a hypothalamic thirst center became a popular theme, although the idea of a brain center mediating thirst had been advocated earlier by Nothnagel (1881) and Mayer (1900). In the past half century, identification of several relevant brain regions, hormonal stimuli, and neural pathways linking sensor and integrative regions have been elucidated. Nowadays, the concept that thirst is an emotion generated centrally by the integration within the brain stem, hypothalamus, and preoptic area of neural, osmotic, and hormonal signals, transmitted via multiple neural pathways to produce neural outputs that are distributed to cortical effector sites, holds sway. A guide to the cerebral locations of a number of brain regions implicated in the generation and regulation of thirst is provided in Figure 35.1.

REGULATORY THIRST

The Dual Depletion Theory

Reduction in the volume of either the intracellular or extracellular fluid generates an urge to ingest water. Satisfaction of this urge by drinking fluid can replenish both of these fluid compartments. When a mammal is deprived of water and becomes dehydrated, water is usually lost from both intracellular and extracellular compartments. Separate bodily sensors detect changes in intracellular and extracellular volumes, and signals from these sensors subsequently initiate homeostatic responses that include thirst. Therefore, a dual depletion mechanism to drive thirst mechanisms in dehydrated animals has been advanced. The sensor and signaling mechanisms that respond to such "dual depletion" are discussed in the following section.

Osmoregulatory Thirst and Intracellular Dehydration

Under normal physiological conditions, the osmolality (i.e., total concentration of dissolved solutes in a liquid) of plasma is maintained within a narrow range in most mammals (280 to 290 mosmol/kg). Plasma osmolality will increase if ingested solutes such as sodium chloride are absorbed into the bloodstream, or if evaporative dehydration occurs. In both conditions, as the effective osmotic pressure of the circulating and interstitial fluids (i.e., the extracellular fluid within tissues) increases, water will move by osmosis from the interior of cells to the extracellular space, causing depletion of the intracellular fluid.

There is considerable evidence to show that depletion of the intracellular compartment is associated with thirst, and that specific brain sensors (osmoreceptors) detect intracellular dehydration and initiate compensatory mechanisms such as water drinking, vasopressin secretion, and natriuresis, all of which act to reduce the hypertonicity (McKinley et al., 1987a; Verney, 1947; Wolf, 1950).

Investigation of the thirst-stimulating effects of intravenous infusions of hypertonic solutions led to the concept of osmoregulatory thirst. Intravenous infusion of concentrated solutions of sodium chloride, sucrose, fructose, or mannitol increase the tonicity of plasma and stimulate water drinking in species as diverse as dogs, rats, goats, sheep, iguanas, pigs, and pigeons (Fitzsimons, 1979). Because it is not possible to truly know the subjective perception experienced by animals that lead them to drink water, it is assumed that such drinking is the result of a thirst being generated in these species. However, in the case of human studies, thirst ratings can be obtained from experimental subjects, and the results are consistent with the animal investigations. Increasing the effective osmotic pressure of plasma by means of intravenous infusion of hypertonic sodium chloride (Figure 35.2), sorbitol, or mannitol stimulates thirst in humans (Wolf, 1950; Zerbe & Robertson, 1983).

Not all types of systemically infused hyperosmolar solutions stimulate drinking or strong thirst. When concentrated solutions of urea, glycerol, glucose, or isomannide are administered systemically, thirst ratings or the volume of water drunk are considerably less than those observed with infusion of equivalent amounts of hypertonic saline, sorbitol, fructose, mannitol, or sucrose solutions (Fitzsimons, 1963; Gilman, 1937; Holmes & Gregerson, 1950; McKinley, Denton, & Weisinger, 1978; Olsson, 1972; Zerbe & Roberston, 1983). The solutes that are effective dipsogenic agents are those that do not readily permeate into cells (sodium chloride, sucrose, fructose, mannitol) so that an osmotic gradient is established across the semi-permeable cell membranes. As a consequence of this gradient, movement of water out of cells by osmosis results in cellular dehydration. The movement of smaller solutes such as urea and glycerol into cells via specific urea and glycerol channels and glucose via a glucose transporter is relatively rapid, so that an osmotic gradient from outside to inside of the cell is not maintained, and significant cellular dehydration does not occur. Therefore, thirst is stimulated acutely by increases in the effective osmotic pressure (the tonicity) of plasma, a condition that causes cellular dehydration. As expressed initially by Gilman (1937), "The logical conclusion to draw from the above results is that *cellular* dehydration rather than an increase in cellular osmotic pressure *per se* is the stimulus of true thirst." Olsson (1972) also showed that infusions of hypertonic sodium chloride or fructose into the carotid artery were far more effective than equivalent infusions into the jugular vein, indicating that the osmosensors were probably located in the brain. Contemporaneous with the investigations of Gilman, Wolf, and others on osmoregulatory thirst was the discovery of osmoreceptors that regulate the secretion of the antidiuretic hormone, more commonly termed *vasopressin* (Verney, 1947). Cellular dehydration

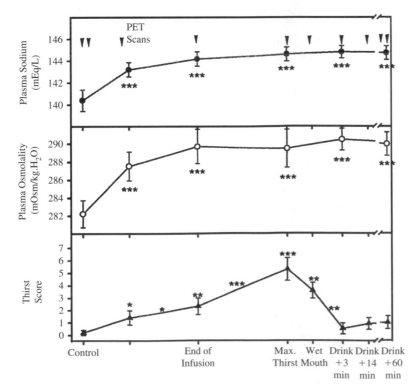

Figure 35.2 Increase of plasma sodium concentration, plasma osmolality, and thirst rating during an intravenous infusion of 0.51 mol/l saline for 25 or 50 minutes in 10 healthy adult human subjects, then subsequently after rinsing the mouth with water, and drinking water to satiate thirst.

Note: The subjects were asked to rate thirst on a scale of 0 to 10 with 0 being no thirst, and 10 the thirstiest they had ever experienced. These data were obtained while subjects underwent positron emission topography scans indicated by the arrowheads. Asterisks at points indicate significant difference from control, and those between points indicate significant difference between those two observations. From "The Correlation of Regional Blood Flow (rCBF) and Plasma Sodium Concentration during Genesis and Satiation of Thirst," by D. A. Denton et al., 1999, *Proceedings of the National Academy of Sciences, USA, 96,* p. 2533, Fig. 1. Reprinted with permission.

was shown to stimulate vasopressin release from the posterior pituitary, and in addition, the location of the relevant osmoreceptors was shown to be within the hypothalamic region of the brain (Jewell & Verney, 1957). Renal water retention under the regulation of vasopressin is the complementary arm of body fluid homeostasis, in that although fluid losses from the body are not restored by vasopressin action on the kidney, further obligatory fluid losses in urine are minimized. The integrated neural and endocrine regulation of body fluids is summarized in Figure 35.3.

Location of Osmoreceptors for Thirst

Following the discovery of a cerebral location for osmoreceptors that regulate vasopressin secretion (Verney, 1947), interest focused on the hypothalamus as a probable site of osmoreceptors that drive thirst. Consistent with this idea was the observation that injection of a small amount of hypertonic sodium chloride into the hypothalamus in the region of the mammillothalamic tract stimulated copious water drinking in water-replete goats (Andersson, 1953). Relative to the physiological concentration of sodium

chloride in the extracellular fluid of the brain (0.15 M), the high concentrations of sodium chloride that were injected in these experiments may have nonspecifically stimulated neurons or fibers subserving drinking, or spread the stimulus to an adjacent brain region. Therefore, Andersson was conservative in the interpretation of these experiments, having reservations that the injection regions were the sites of thirst osmoreceptors. Subsequently, investigators in Sweden (Andersson, Leksell, & Lishajko, 1975; Rundgren & Fyhrquist, 1978) showed that ablation of a region rostral to these hypothalamic sites, the anterior wall of the third ventricle, resulted in adipsia in goats. As well, they observed that infusions of hypertonic saline but not hypertonic saccharide solutions into the third cerebral ventricle stimulated drinking. As a result, they proposed that cerebral sodium receptors located in the anterior wall of the third ventricle of the brain mediated osmoregulatory thirst, rather than hypothalamic osmoreceptors. However, injection of hypertonic sucrose into the third ventricle does stimulate drinking (in sheep) if the sucrose is prepared in an artificial cerebrospinal fluid (CSF), although the response was less than that with hypertonic saline injection

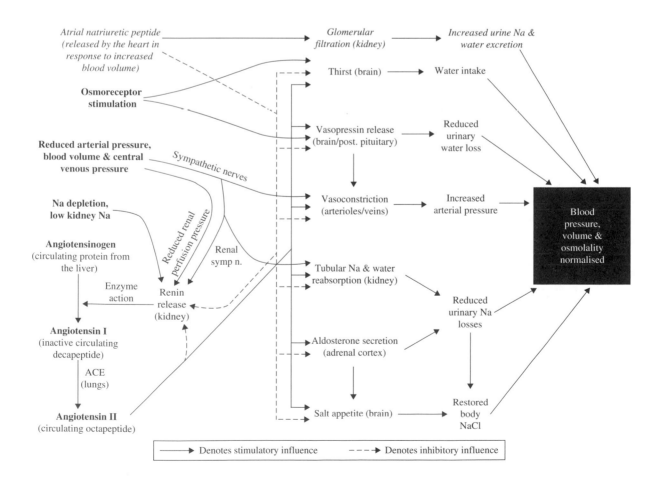

Figure 35.3   Diagrammatic summary of the main hormonal regulators of body fluid homeostasis in mammals.

Note: ACE = Angiotensin converting enzyme.

(McKinley, Blaine, & Denton, 1974). Thus, while central osmoreceptors were indicated by this result, a specific effect of sodium chloride was also evident. Observations that ablation of the medial preoptic region including lamina terminalis or anteroventral third wall of the third ventricle (AV3V) region disrupted osmoregulatory thirst in rats (Black, 1976; Johnson & Buggy, 1978) were consistent with the evidence in goats of a role of the anterior wall of the third ventricle in osmoregulatory thirst.

Osmoreceptors in the Lamina Terminalis

To test the hypothesis that brain sodium receptors are responsible for thirst (Andersson, 1978), studies were made in conscious sheep of the effects of infusions of various hypertonic solutions into the carotid artery on water intake and on CSF sodium concentration (McKinley et al., 1978). Infusions of hyperosmolar sodium chloride, sucrose, or urea into the carotid arterial blood supply to the brain all increased CSF Na concentration, even though plasma sodium concentration increased only with hypertonic saline. The increased CSF sodium levels occurring with all three solutes was attributed to the exclusion of urea as well as sodium chloride and sucrose from the brain interstitium by the blood-brain barrier (Oldendorf, 1971), creating an osmotic gradient, resulting in osmotic movement of water from brain interstitium to the bloodstream. The increased CSF sodium concentration was indicative that the brain had been osmotically dehydrated by all three infusions, but only two of the infusions rapidly stimulated drinking—hypertonic saline and sucrose. Hyperosmolar urea was much less effective as a dipsogen. While these results did not support a role for sodium sensors in osmoregulatory thirst, there was a paradox. Why do only hypertonic sucrose and sodium chloride stimulate drinking, while all three solutions dehydrate the brain? Therefore, it was proposed that at least some osmoreceptors must be located in regions of the brain devoid of a blood-brain barrier—specifically circumventricular organs such as the organum vasculosum of the lamina terminalis (OVLT) or subfornical organ (see Figure 35.1 for locations) which lack a blood-brain barrier. Within these sites, it should be possible for osmoreceptors to distinguish the different solutes (McKinley et al., 1978).

Subsequent studies in sheep (McKinley et al., 1982) and dogs (Thrasher, Keil, & Ramsay, 1982b) showed that ablation of the OVLT reduced drinking responses to systemic infusion of hypertonic saline, consistent with the presence of thirst osmoreceptors in the OVLT. Complete ablation of the OVLT did not totally abolish osmoregulatory drinking. Injection of hypertonic 0.2 M sodium chloride into the subfornical stimulates drinking (Camargo, Menani, Saad, & Saad, 1984), and ablation of the subfornical organ in the rat and sheep (but not dog) has been shown to reduce

osmotically stimulated drinking also (Hosutt, Rowland, & Stricker, 1978; Lind, Thunhorst, & Johnson, 1984; Thrasher, Simpson, & Ramsay, 1982). Combined ablation of the subfornical organ and OVLT severely reduces osmoregulatory drinking (Figure 35.4) in sheep, but does not abolish it (McKinley, Mathai, Pennington, Rundgren, & Vivas, 1999). Only total or near total ablation of the lamina terminalis (i.e., subfornical organ, median preoptic nucleus, and OVLT) prevents drinking responses to acute intravenous infusion of hypertonic saline in sheep (Figure 35.4), and it was suggested that there may be considerable redundancy within the lamina terminalis for osmoreceptor function (McKinley et al., 1999). It is unlikely that the other sensory circumventricular organ, the area postrema (located in the hindbrain immediately dorsal to the nucleus of the solitary tract; see Figure 35.1), is a site of thirst osmoreceptors, because ablation of this structure had no inhibitory effect on drinking in response to intravenous hypertonic saline in sheep (Slavin & McKinley, 1989, unpublished observations). However, ablation of the area postrema does alter hypothalamic and drinking responses to intragastric or ingested hypertonic saline (Carlson, Collister, & Osborn, 1998; Curtis, Huang, Sved, Verbalis, & Stricker, 1999) suggesting it may relay signals from visceral osmoreceptors that could influence thirst.

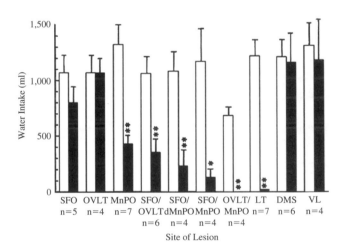

Figure 35.4 Effect of ablation of different parts of the lamina terminalis, alone or in combination, on water drinking of sheep in response to intravenous infusion of hypertonic 4 mol/l saline at 1.3 ml/min that increased plasma osmolality by 12 mosmol/kg over 30 minutes.

Note: Open bars show the drinking responses prelesion and the filled bars the postlesion responses. DB = Diagonal band; dMnPO = Dorsal median preoptic nucleus; LT = Total lamina terminalis; MS = Medial septum; OVLT = Organum vasculosum of the lamina terminalis; T = Septal triangularis nucleus; vMnPO = Ventral median preoptic nucleus; SFO = Subfornical organ; VL = Lateral to MnPO. From Figure 35.6, "The Effect of Individual or Combined Ablation of the Nuclear Groups of the Lamina Terminalis on Water Drinking in Sheep," by M. J. McKinley, M. L. Mathai, G. L. Pennington, Rundgren M., and L. Vivas, 1999, *American Journal of Physiology, 276,* p. R678. Reprinted with permission.

In regard to the other anatomical component of the lamina terminalis, the median preoptic nucleus (see Figure 35.1), which is behind the blood-brain barrier, ablation of this nucleus by either electrolytic or neurotoxin (ibotenic acid) techniques severely disrupts acute osmoregulatory water drinking (Cunningham et al., 1991; Mangiapane, Thrasher, Keil, Simpson, & Ganong, 1983; McKinley et al., 1999). While the median preoptic nucleus receives neural input from both the subfornical organ and OVLT (Miselis, 1981; Saper & Levisohn, 1983), and this may be the cause of the reduced osmoregulatory drinking when it is ablated, it seems likely that the median preoptic nucleus is also a sensor region for hypertonicity. This is because ablation of both OVLT and subfornical organ in combination do not completely abolish osmoregulatory drinking, and the residual response is abolished if the median preoptic nucleus (see Figure 35.1) is ablated as well (McKinley et al., 1999). Neurons within the median preoptic nucleus are responsive to directly applied hypertonic saline in vitro, although they are inhibited by hypertonicity and excited by hypotonicity (Travis & Johnson, 1993). Studies of c-fos expression, show median preoptic neurons are activated in vivo by systemic infusion of hypertonic saline when the subfornical organ and OVLT have been ablated (Hochstenbach & Ciriello, 1996). There is also reason to believe that some osmoreceptors exist on the brain side of the blood-brain barrier. For example, osmoreceptors may reside in the median preoptic nucleus, and these sensors could explain why intracarotid infusions of urea cause a dipsogenic response of much slower onset and much lesser magnitude, than the responses to hypertonic saline, sucrose, or fructose mentioned previously. Intracarotid infusion of hypertonic glucose is invariably ineffective as a dipsogen (McKinley et al., 1978; Olsson, 1972), infusions of hypertonic urea increase the sodium chloride concentration, and therefore the effective osmotic pressure, of the brain extracellular fluid (except in the circumventricular organs) whereas infusions of hypertonic glucose do not because it is rapidly transported across the blood-brain barrier as well as into cells (McKinley et al., 1978). An osmoreceptor (or sodium sensor) for thirst in the median preoptic nucleus should respond to hypertonic urea but not to hypertonic glucose infusion, while osmoreceptors in the subfornical organ and OVLT would not respond to either. This arrangement would explain the moderate drinking response to urea but the lack of response to glucose.

Immunohistochemical detection of Fos, a protein that influences gene transcription in the nucleus of the cell, and identifies neurons that have been activated in response to a particular stimulus (Sagar, Sharp, & Curran, 1988), has allowed histological identification of the neurons within the lamina terminalis that respond to systemic hypertonicity. This method shows that intravenously infused solutions of hypertonic saline or sucrose activate neurons throughout the lamina terminalis of the rat (Oldfield, Bicknell, McAllen, Weisinger, & McKinley, 1991); so too does dehydration resulting from water deprivation for 24 to 48 hours (McKinley, Hards, & Oldfield, 1994). However, in the rat, osmotically stimulated neurons are concentrated particularly in the dorsal cap of the OVLT, the periphery of the subfornical organ (Figure 35.5), and throughout the median preoptic nucleus (McKinley et al., 1994). Intense Fos immunoreactivity induced in mouse OVLT in response to an intraperitoneal injection of hypertonic saline can be seen in Figure 35.6. These results are consistent with earlier electrophysiological studies that all parts of the lamina terminalis are responsive to systemically infused hypertonic stimuli (Gutman, Ciriello, & Mogenson, 1988; McAllen, Pennington, & McKinley, 1990; Vivas, Chiaraviglio, & Carrer, 1990). Functional brain imaging studies in human subjects infused systemically with hypertonic saline also show the lamina terminalis (Figure 35.7) to be activated by hypertonicity (Egan et al., 2003).

In contrast to the effects on dipsogenic responses to acute hypertonicity, drinking following water deprivation for 48 hours was not inhibited by ablation of considerable parts of the lamina terminalis; it was reduced but not abolished by complete destruction of the lamina terminalis (McKinley et al., 1999). These observations show that other brain regions may have a role in osmoregulatory thirst. They also indicate that the mechanism of the acute thirst response to hypertonicity, largely under the control of the lamina terminalis, may be different to the mechanism regulating thirst in response to long-term hypertonicity.

Lateral Preoptic Area

Another region that has been implicated as a site of thirst osmoreceptors is the lateral preoptic region (see panel 2 of Figure 35.1). Injections of hypertonic saline or sucrose, but not urea, into the lateral preoptic area stimulates drinking in rats and rabbits, while ablation of the lateral preoptic area disrupts osmoregulatory drinking in a 4-hour test following intraperitoneal injection of hypertonic saline. Drinking following 24-hour water deprivation was not affected by lateral preoptic lesions (Blass & Epstein, 1971; Peck & Novin, 1971). More detailed mapping studies using the microinjection technique showed that osmotically stimulated drinking sites in the preoptic region were more widespread than initially observed (Peck & Blass, 1975). Osmosensitive neurons have been detected in the lateral preoptic area (Malmo & Mundl, 1975). However, osmoregulatory thirst is delayed rather than blocked by ablation of the lateral preoptic area; as well, appropriate drinking

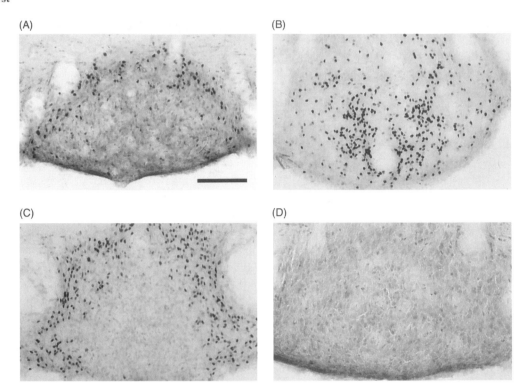

Figure 35.5 Activated neurons in coronal sections of the subfornical organ of rats as shown by Fos-immunoreactivity (black dots) induced by intravenous infusion of hypertonic saline (A), intravenous infusion of angiotensin II (B), intravenous infusion of relaxin (C), and control infusion of isotonic 0.15 mol/l saline.

Note: Magnification bar = 100 μm. Infusion of hypertonic saline or relaxin activated neurons mainly in the periphery of the subfornical organ, while angiotensin II stimulated neurons throughout this region.

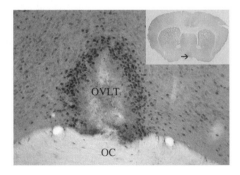

Figure 35.6 Activated neurons, shown by intense Fos-immunreactivity (black dots), in the OVLT of a mouse brain 2 hours after an intraperitoneal injection of hypertonic saline (0.8 mol/l).

Note: The arrow in the inset indicates the site of the OVLT in the coronal section of the mouse brain. OC = Optic chiasma; OVLT = Organum vasculosum of the lamina terminalis.

occurs in lateral preoptic-lesioned rats in response to intravenous infusion of hypertonic saline, increased dietary sodium chloride intake, or water deprivation (Coburn & Stricker, 1978). It is proposed that neurons within the lateral preoptic area and the lamina terminalis may interact in the regulation of thirst (Camargo et al., 1984), but the relationship of putative osmoreceptors in the lateral preoptic area with those in the lamina terminalis remains to be elucidated.

Hepatic or Gastrointestinal Osmoreceptors

Osmoreceptors in the hepatic portal vein or liver have been shown to influence vasopressin secretion and urine output (Baertschi & Vallet, 1981; Haberich, 1971). In regard to thirst, infusion of water but not saline into the portal vein inhibits water intake of dehydrated rats (Kobashi & Adachi, 1992). As well, water drinking by rats administered intragastric loads of hypertonic saline occurs before any measurable change in systemic plasma osmolality, suggesting that gastrointestinal or hepato-portal osmoreceptors may regulate thirst (Kraly, Kim, Dunham, & Tribuzio, 1995). Further support for this idea comes from studies in which intragastric hypertonic saline loads caused a potentiation of water drinking in response to dehydration or intravenous hypertonic saline infusion (Stricker, Callahan, Huang, & Sved, 2002). These investigators suggested that signals from central osmoreceptors interact with those from peripheral osmoreceptors, depending on the animal's hydration state; the peripheral sensors providing early signaling of ingested fluid before any change in the tonicity of the general circulation occurs. Signals from portal or gastrointestinal osmoreceptors may be relayed via the area postrema (Curtis et al., 1999; Stricker et al., 2002). There is evidence that osmoreceptors within the lamina terminalis influence these signals (Freece, Van Bebber, Zierath, & Fitts, 2005).

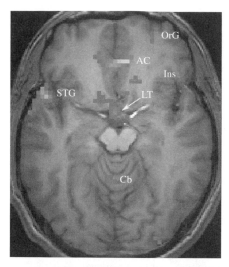

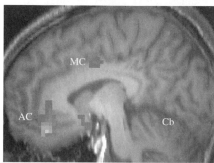

Figure 35.7 (**Figure C. 35** in color section) Functional magnetic resonance imaging (BOLD signal) sections of a conscious subject experiencing maximum thirst resulting from intravenous infusion of hypertonic saline.

Note: Activations (light gray regions): ACC − Anterior cingulate cortex; Cb = Cerebellum; Ins = Insula; LT = Lamina terminalis; MC = Orbital gyrus, mid cingulate region, posterior part; OrG = Orbital gyrus; STG = Superior temporal gyrus. From Figure 35.3, "Neural Correlates of the Emergence of Consciousness of Thirst," by G. Egan et al., 2003, *Proceedings of the National Academy of Sciences, USA, 100,* p. 15245. Reprinted with permission.

TRPV Channels and Osmosensory Transduction

Identification of the molecular characteristics of thirst osmoreceptors has been advanced recently with the discovery that ion channels of the transient receptor potential vanilloid (TRPV) class may play a role in transducing osmosensory function. Both TRPV1 and TRPV4 channels have been implicated in osmoregulatory transduction because they are located within osmosensory neurons of the lamina terminalis, and deletion of genes encoding these TRPV channels moderately reduces osmoregulatory drinking in mice (Ciura & Bourque, 2006; Liedtke, 2007).

HYPOVOLEMIC THIRST AND EXTRACELLULAR FLUID DEPLETION

Thirst and drinking of fluids can also result from depletion of the extracellular fluid without any intracellular

dehydration. Loss of fluid from the extracellular compartment (hypovolemia) may occur naturally under physiological or pathophysiological conditions that include hemorrhage, vomiting, diarrhea, burns, or sweating. If there is sufficient loss of extracellular fluid, thirst results that drives fluid intake (Fitzsimons, 1961). In the laboratory, several strategies have been employed in experimental animals to deplete the extracellular fluid without any apparent depletion of the intracellular compartment. These include hemorrhage, subcutaneous injection of colloid (e.g., polyethylene glycol) causing sequestration of extracellular fluid under the skin, diuretic treatment, peritoneal dialysis, diuretics, hemofiltration or loss of saliva from a parotid fistula (Abraham et al., 1976; Anderson & Houpt, 1990; Fitzsimons, 1961; Rabe, 1975; Stricker, 1966; Zimmerman, Blaine, & Stricker, 1981). These procedures are associated with increased water intake, although hemorrhage is an inconsistent dipsogenic stimulus (Fitzsimons, 1979; Wolf, 1958). The extracellular compartment is comprised of fluid within the circulation (plasma) and the interstices of tissues (interstitial fluid). When the extracellular compartment is depleted, the volume of fluid within the circulation falls, particularly on the venous side of the heart, resulting in reduced central venous pressure and reduced venous return to the heart. Experimental procedures (e.g., constriction of the vena cava) that mimic the changes in pressures that occur within the great veins returning blood to the heart during hypovolemic conditions also stimulate thirst and water intake (Thrasher, Keenan, & Ramsay, 1999).

Sodium Appetite

If there is depletion of the extracellular fluid without a concomitant increase of extracellular concentration of sodium chloride, a deficit in whole body sodium chloride as well as water occurs. Therefore, while ingestion of water may restore the volume of fluid lost, unless sodium chloride is also ingested, restoration of both volume and ionic concentrations of extracellular fluid will not result. Thus, it is not surprising that extracellular hypovolemia is also associated with the development of an appetite that is specific for sodium salts. Sodium appetite is much slower in onset than thirst, developing over several hours following the loss of extracellular fluid (Fitzsimons, 1979). Endocrine signaling mechanisms play a major role in the generation of sodium appetite during conditions of hypovolemia. Blood concentrations of both angiotensin II and aldosterone increase and may act synergistically within the brain to generate an appetite for salt (Figure 35.3). It is beyond the scope of this chapter to review the physiological mechanisms subserving sodium appetite and more details can be found in number of excellent reviews and monographs (Denton, 1982; Fitzsimons, 1979; Johnson & Thunhorst, 1997).

Additivity of Hyperosmotic and Hypovolemic Dipsogenic Signals

As stated earlier, in a condition of dehydration, water is withdrawn from both intracellular and extracellular compartments of the body. Signals from both osmoreceptors and volume sensors contribute to the resultant thirst. While osmotic signals account for the majority of the dipsogenic response to dehydration, volume signals make a significant contribution (Ramsay, Rolls, & Wood, 1977). Further, studies in which simultaneous delivery of an osmotic load with a hypovolemic stimulus resulted in water intake that was the sum of that attributable to each independent stimulus show the probable additivity of hypovolemic and osmotic stimuli mediating dehydrational thirst (Blass & Fitzsimons, 1970; Fitzsimons, 1979).

Sensors and Afferent Signaling of Hypovolemic Thirst

With only a few exceptions, studies of the afferent signaling mechanisms mediating water drinking in response to hypovolemia have been confined to rats and dogs. The experimental model of hypovolemia that has been studied in the dog is constriction or obstruction of the inferior vena cava (caval ligation) to reduce venous return to the heart, lowering central venous pressure and arterial pressure. In the rat, subcutaneous sequestration of extracellular fluid under the skin has been utilized as a means of producing systemic hypovolemia.

Neural Signaling

Hypovolemic thirst results from both hormonal and neural signals being transmitted to the brain. These signals may act either singly, or in combination to generate thirst. Stretch receptors in the heart and blood vessels provide the neural signals that relate information to the CNS on the degree of filling and pressures within the circulation. These afferent signals, which are stimulated by increases in pressure and reduced when pressure decreases, are carried largely by the vagus and glossopharyngeal nerves and terminate in the nucleus of the solitary tract in the medulla oblongata (Dampney, 1994; see Figure 35.1, panel A). From there, polysynaptic neural pathways, that involve both excitatory and inhibitory synapses, relay signals to other sites that control a number of functions that include the baroreceptor reflex, vasopressin secretion, and thirst. It is possible that neural relays via the A1 cell group in the caudal ventrolateral medulla, and/or other hindbrain and midbrain sites send signals to neurons in the lamina terminalis to influence drinking (Johnson, Cunningham, & Thunhorst, 1996). However, the participation of these pathways in hypovolemic thirst remains to be proven.

Angiotensin-Mediated Hormonal Signaling

When blood volume, arterial pressure and central venous pressure fall, circulating concentrations of angiotensin II increase (see Figure 35.3). The initial step in the generation of angiotensin II, the effector peptide of the renin-angiotensin system, is the release of the proteolytic enzyme renin from the kidney. The signals that drive renin secretion in hypovolemic states are increased renal sympathetic nerve activity, reduced renal perfusion pressure, and altered sodium load at the macula densa of the distal tubule of the kidney. Once released into the bloodstream, renin catalyzes the formation of the decapeptide molecule angiotensin I in the circulation by cleaving it from a large (40,000 Dalton) plasma protein, angiotensinogen that is synthesized in the liver. Angiotensin converting enzyme (ACE) mainly in the lung, but also in other tissues, then splits off two more amino acids from the carboxyl terminus of angiotensin I causing the formation of the biologically active octapeptide angiotensin II (see Montani & Van Vliet, 2004, for a review).

In regard to the humoral signals for hypovolemic thirst, evidence in both rat and dog favors a significant role for the renin-angiotensin system in thirst associated with depletion of the extracellular fluid. There are compelling data favoring a role for circulating angiotensin II, at least in combination with neural signals, in the genesis of hypovolemic thirst. First, removal by bilateral nephrectomy of the source of renin, the enzyme needed for generation of angiotensin I, reduces drinking in response to caval ligation in rats (Fitzsimons, 1969). Second, peripheral administrations of inhibitors of angiotensin converting enzyme (ACE inhibitors) or angiotensin receptor antagonists reduce drinking responses to caval ligation in dog or rat (Fitzsimons & Elfont, 1982; Fitzsimons & Moore-Gillon, 1980; Thrasher, Keil, & Ramsay, 1982). Third, the blood levels of angiotensin II that are reached following subcutaneous injection of polyethylene glycol (a large colloidal molecule) or caval ligation are above the threshold plasma concentrations of angiotensin II for drinking achieved by intravenous infusion of angiotensin II (Johnson & Thunhorst, 1997). Fourth, ablation of the subfornical organ, the site of angiotensin receptors mediating the dipsogenic action of this octapeptide, inhibits water intake in response to hypovolemia (Lind et al., 1984; Stratford & Wirtshafter, 2000).

Intrathoracic Receptors Signaling Hypovolemia

It is also clear that other signaling mechanisms besides the renin-angiotensin system play an important role in hypovolemic thirst. Data from three studies of the dipsogenic effect of caval ligation in the dog are particularly relevant to this point. First, significant drinking in response to caval ligation is still evident in dogs in which angiotensin receptors have been totally blocked pharmacologically (Thrasher, Simpson, et al., 1982). Second, the drinking response to caval ligation was reduced by approximately half when the heart was denervated so that putative low pressure atrial stretch receptors no longer send signals to the brain. Denervation of the high pressure baroreceptors in the aortic arch and carotid sinus also substantially reduced such drinking while combined cardiac and arterial baroreceptor denervation totally abolished the dipsogenic effect of caval ligation, despite high circulating angiotensin II levels being maintained (Quillen, Keil, & Reid, 1990). These data indicate that signals from baroreceptors in the heart and carotid sinus and aortic arch have an important role in mediating hypovolemic thirst in the dog. More recently, Thrasher et al. (1999) performed a series of intrathoracic vascular ligations of the inferior vena cava (IVC), the pulmonary artery, or the ascending aorta in conscious dogs so that blood pressure at the arterial baroreceptors fell by 25 mm Hg in each case. As expected, constriction of the IVC reduced left atrial, right atrial, and mean arterial pressure and stimulated drinking. So too did constriction of the pulmonary artery that reduced left atrial and arterial pressure, but increased right atrial pressure. However, constriction of the ascending aorta that also reduced arterial pressure and right atrial pressure, but increased left atrial pressure, did not stimulate thirst in the dogs. These results show either that loading left atrial receptors can override signals from other baroreceptors, or it is possible that unloading of low-pressure stretch receptors in the left atrium of the heart in combination with unloading of high-pressure arterial baroreceptors is the cause of hypovolemic thirst in the dog (Thrasher et al., 1999). In sheep, a crushing injury to the left atrial appendage caused hypovolemia-induced water intake to be depressed, evidence supporting a role for left atrial receptors mediating hypovolemic thirst in this species (Zimmerman et al., 1981). There are stretch receptors in the ventricles of the heart and coronary arteries as well as the atria that could also have role in mediating hypovolemic thirst; investigations have yet to be made in this regard.

In rats, the right atrium appears to play an important sensor role for hypovolemic thirst. Since nephrectomized, polyethylene glycol-treated (i.e., hypovolemic) rats that cannot increase blood angiotensin II levels still increase water intake, nonangiotensin signaling must be involved (Fitzsimons, 1961). Inflation of a balloon at the junction of the superior vena cava and the right atrium abolished drinking responses to intraperitoneal polyethylene glycol, reduced dehydration-induced drinking, or the spontaneous overnight water intake, but had no effect on the drinking response to intravenous infusion of hypertonic saline (Kaufman, 1984). An interesting aspect of this study was that atrial stretch reduced the volume of water drunk in

response to 24 hours of water-deprivation by 30%, which is the proportion of water intake of dehydrated rats that Ramsay et al. (1977) attributed to the reduced extracellular volume, the rest being osmotically stimulated. Alternatively, drinking in response to subcutaneous injection of polyethylene glycol was totally blocked, consistent with this stimulus being a pure hypovolemia. Kaufman (1984) proposed that a direct nervous input from the right atrium to the central nervous system mediated hypovolemic drinking. However, it is also possible that release of atrial natriuretic peptide from the heart contributes to the inhibition of hypovolemic thirst by atrial balloon inflation.

HORMONAL INFLUENCES ON THIRST

Angiotensin II

Following the discovery of a renal dipsogen that appeared to be renin (Fitzsimons, 1969), rapid progress was made in identifying the thirst-stimulating properties of angiotensin II, and the evidence for its role as a dipsogenic hormone has been detailed previously. Systemic administration of components of the renin-angiotensin system—renin, angiotensin I, or angiotensin II—stimulates water drinking in many mammals and reptiles (Fitzsimons, 1979). In some species (e.g., sheep, humans), the blood levels of infused angiotensin II needed to stimulate drinking were found to be high relative to the levels observed physiologically during hypovolemia (Abraham, Baker, Blaine, Denton, & McKinley, 1975; Phillips, Rolls, Ledingham, Morton, & Forsling, 1985). However, it is likely that in these species, the dipsogenic effect of angiotensin II that would occur normally during intravenous infusion of this octapeptide is offset by the simultaneous rise in blood pressure that inhibits thirst by stimulation of arterial baroreceptors (Evered, 1992; Klingbeil, Brooks, Quillen, & Reid, 1991). Because arterial pressure does not increase during hypovolemia, such an inhibitory influence on the dipsogenic action of angiotensin II is not a consideration in this condition and lower circulating levels of the peptide should induce thirst.

Site in the Brain of the Dipsogenic Action of Angiotensin II

Hydrophilic peptide molecules like angiotensin II do not normally gain rapid passage into the brain interstitium from the bloodstream because of the blood-brain barrier. Following the discovery of the dipsogenic action of angiotensin II, the question soon arose as to how a polar molecule like angiotensin II could act on the brain to stimulate thirst if did not cross the blood-brain barrier. Experiments in the rat showed that angiotensin II from the bloodstream acted on neurons located in the subfornical organ to stimulate drinking behavior (Simpson & Routtenberg, 1973). This circumventricular organ lacks a normal blood-brain barrier (Wislocki & Leduc, 1952) and neurons within it express high concentrations of angiotensin AT_1 receptors in all species studied (Allen et al., 2000) including humans (McKinley, Allen, Clevers, Paxinos, & Mendelsohn, 1987). Angiotensin II, directly applied or from blood, stimulates action potentials in subfornical neurons (Felix & Schlegel, 1978; Gutman et al., 1988) and circulating angiotensin II activates neurons throughout the subfornical organ (Figure 35.5B) as indicated by expression of the proto-oncogene c-fos (McKinley, Badoer, & Oldfield, 1992). For water drinking, the rat subfornical organ is exquisitely sensitive to minute quantities of directly injected angiotensin II, while ablation of the subfornical organ prevents drinking in response to intravenously infused angiotensin II and some hypovolemic stimuli (Simpson, Epstein, & Camardo, 1978).

Paradoxical Potentiation of Thirst by Angiotensin Converting Enzyme Inhibitors

An interesting aspect of angiotensin action on the subfornical organ is the very high concentrations of angiotensin converting enzyme (ACE) present there (Brownfield, Reid, Ganten, & Ganong, 1982). These high concentrations of ACE allow angiotensin I originating from the systemic circulation to be converted to angiotensin II locally within the subfornical organ. This probably explains why lower doses of ACE inhibitors, such as captopril, that block peripheral generation of angiotensin II, not only do not block drinking responses, but actually potentiate them (Lehr, Goldman, & Casner, 1973). This paradox arises because although peripheral ACE blockade reduces circulating angiotensin II levels, the concentration of blood-borne angiotensin I increases dramatically. This angiotensin I can then be converted to angiotensin II locally in the subfornical organ to stimulate thirst, because the doses of ACE inhibitors used may not be sufficient to block the high concentrations of ACE in the subfornical organ. In line with this interpretation, administration of a much higher concentration of ACE inhibitor directly into the subfornical organ, blocks drinking responses (Thunhorst, Fitts, & Simpson, 1989).

Relaxin

Source of Relaxin and Effects on Fluid Balance

Relaxin is a peptide hormone that is synthesized in the corpus lutea of the ovary and secreted into the systemic circulation during most of pregnancy in many mammals. In addition to its actions on reproductive tissues (e.g., inhibition of uterine contractions, ripening of the cervix, and mammary duct development), relaxin can stimulate water drinking and the secretion of vasopressin. Intravenous infusion of relaxin (Sinnayah, Burns, Wade, Weisinger, & McKinley, 1999) or direct injection into the brain ventricles (Thornton & Fitzsimons, 1995) stimulates water drinking by rats of either sex.

Administration of relaxin-neutralizing antibodies to pregnant rats reduced water intake during the second half of pregnancy in these animals, indicating a likely role for relaxin in their fluid intake (Zhao, Malmgren, Shanks, & Sherwood, 1985). Blood concentrations of angiotensin II as well as relaxin increase during pregnancy and a synergy between circulating angiotensin II and relaxin to stimulate water drinking in rats has been demonstrated (Sinnayah et al., 1999). Circulating relaxin also stimulates vasopressin secretion (Parry, Poterski, & Summerlee, 1994) and in combination with its dipsogenic action, relaxin would be expected to promote a positive fluid balance. Indeed, pregnancy is characterized by a reduction in plasma osmolality in many mammals, and it has been suggested that a resetting of the osmostat occurs (Durr, Stamotsos, & Lindheimer, 1981). It seems likely that this so-called resetting of the osmostat is due in part to the dipsogenic action of relaxin to maintain water intake in pregnancy despite the hyponatremia and hypotonicity of body fluids.

Site in the Brain of the Dipsogenic Action of Relaxin

The relaxin receptor (LGR-7) is present at relatively high concentrations in several regions of the brain that include the subfornical organ and OVLT, sites devoid of a blood-brain barrier and accessible to circulating relaxin (Osheroff & Phillips, 1991). The dipsogenic action of relaxin is almost certainly initiated via a group of relaxin-sensitive neurons in the periphery of the subfornical organ because (a) relaxin acts directly on neurons of the isolated subfornical organ in vitro to increase the frequency of action potentials; (b) intravenous infusion of relaxin activates subfornical organ neurons as indicated by the increased expression of c-fos in a subgroup of neurons within its periphery (Figure 35.5C); and (c) ablation of the subfornical organ (but not the OVLT) abolishes drinking in response to systemically infused relaxin (Sunn et al., 2002). The efferent neural pathways from the subfornical organ mediating this relaxin-induced drinking are unknown.

Atrial Natriuretic Peptide

Atrial natriuretic peptide (ANP) is one of three closely related natriuretic peptides released from cardiac myocytes in conditions of increased extracellular fluid volume (see Figure 35.3). As befits its release during states of fluid loading, ANP inhibits water drinking. ANP exerts inhibitory actions on angiotensin-related drinking and dehydration-induced drinking in rats (Antunes-Rodrigues, McCann, Rogers, & Sampson, 1985) and inhibits osmoregulatory thirst in humans (Burrell, Lambert, & Bayliss, 1991). The actions of ANP on thirst are probably due to a direct inhibitory action on neurons of the subfornical organ because ANP, directly applied to subfornical neurons, inhibits their firing rate and excitatory response to angiotensin II (Hattori, Kasai, Uesugi, Kawata, & Yamashita, 1988); and direct injection of ANP into the subfornical organ of rats reduces water intake in response to water deprivation or angiotensin (Ehrlich & Fitts, 1990).

Estrogen

Ovarian steroid hormones such as estrodiol probably have a physiological role in regulating thirst in females. Day-to-day water drinking changes during the course of the estrus cycle in animals, and these alterations can be abolished by oophorectomy (Findlay, Fitzsimons, & Kucharczyk, 1979; Michell, 1979). If estrodiol benzoate is implanted into ovariectomized female rats, water intake falls, as it does in intact female rats at estrus when blood levels of endogenous estrogen increase (Findlay et al., 1979). Estrogen (but not progesterone) treatment in ovariectomized rats causes a reduction in water drinking elicited by angiotensin II administered peripherally or centrally, but does not affect osmoregulatory drinking (Findlay et al., 1979; Fregly, 1980; Kisley, Sakai, Ma, & Fluharty, 1999). A likely explanation of the estrogen-induced reduction in angiotensin-related drinking is a down regulation of angiotensin AT$_1$ receptors in the subfornical organ. AT$_1$ receptors are co-located on many neurons that also express estrogen receptors in the periphery of the subfornical organ of ovariectomized rats. The expression of AT$_1$ receptors on these neurons is greatly reduced following estrogen administration for 5 days (Rosas-Arellano, Solano-Flores, & Ciriello, 1999). It has been shown also that estrogen treatment reduces the angiotensin responsiveness of subfornical neurons from ovariectomized rats (Tanaka, Miyakubo, Okamura, Sakamaki, & Hayashi, 2001). Water intake in response to injection of angiotensin II directly into the subfornical was attenuated in estrogen- treated rats, whereas these rats drank normally in response to injections of angiotensin II into the median preoptic nucleus. The authors propose that estrogen depresses the activity of angiotensin-responsive neurons in the subfornical organ projecting to the median preoptic nucleus (Tanaka, Miyakubo, Fujisawa, & Nomura, 2003). The estrogen receptor ER-α is expressed in osmoresponsive neurons in the periphery of the subfornical organ and dorsal cap of the OVLT, and this expression is greatly increased by hypertonicity resulting from water deprivation (Somponpun, Johnson, Beltz, & Sladek, 2004), however

estrogen does not seem to affect osmotically stimulated drinking (Findlay et al., 1979).

Other Hormones

Vasopressin

Systemically infused vasopressin has been observed to increase the osmotic responsiveness of dogs to drink (Szczepanska-Sadowska, Sobocinska, & Sodowski, 1982). Despite the obvious association of vasopressin secretion and thirst, there is little if any evidence in other species to suggest that vasopressin is a dipsogenic hormone.

Hormones Associated with Feeding

Much of the normal day-to-day water drinking of mammals is closely associated with feeding, and it is possible that hormones from the gastrointestinal region may influence thirst and water intake (Kraly, 1991). Amylin is a hormone secreted from pancreatic islet beta cells following the intake of food. When administered peripherally, it stimulates water drinking in rats. Amylin causes excitation of neurons in the subfornical organ in vitro, and it has been suggested that it is a dipsogenic hormone that acts via the subfornical organ to stimulate prandial drinking (Riediger, Rauch, & Schmid, 1999). Amylin also stimulates renin secretion from the kidney (Wookey, Cao, & Cooper, 1998) and its dipsogenic action could also be mediated in part via increased angiotensin II levels in the circulation.

Obestatin, a peptide from the gastrointestinal tract, is a posttranslational variant of the ghrelin gene. It inhibits drinking following feeding or centrally administered angiotensin II in rats. Obestatin depresses the activity of subfornical organs in vitro, suggesting that its antidipsogenic action may be mediated via an action on this circumventricular organ (Samson, White, Price, & Ferguson, 2007). Its physiological significance as an antidipsogenic hormone requires further evaluation.

INTEGRATIVE BRAIN REGIONS RELAYING THIRST SIGNALS

Neural signals from peripheral and central sensors are relayed and integrated within the central nervous system to generate the conscious emotion of thirst. Major neural pathways are summarized in Figure 35.8.

Nucleus of the Soltary Tract and Area Postrema

Vagal and glossopharyngeal afferent nerves transmitting sensory signals from visceral sensors that include baroreceptors, stretch receptors in the gastrointestinal tract, and

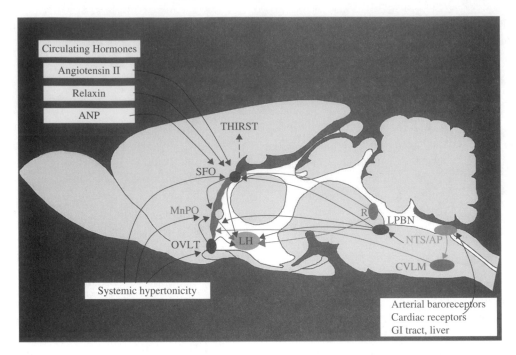

Figure 35.8 A diagram of major neural pathways (excitatory or inhibitory) linking sensors in the lamina terminalis for osmoreception and circulating hormones, regions of the medulla that receive afferent neural input from arterial baroreceptors, the heart, gastrointestinal tract, and liver, with integrative regions in the midbrain and hypothalamus.

Note: The influence of ANP (interrupted arrow) on the subfornical organ is inhibitory. ANP = Atrial natriuretic peptide; AP = Area postrema; CVLM = Caudal ventrolateral medulla; GI = Gastrointestinal; LH = Lateral hypothalamic area; LPBN = Lateral parabrachial nucleus; MnPO = Median preoptic nucleus; NTS = Nucleus of the solitary tract; OVLT = Organum vasculosum of the lamina terminalis; R = Midbrain raphe; SFO = Subfornical organ.

taste receptors terminate within the nucleus of the soltary tract (NTS) and area postrema (Contreras, Beckstead, & Norgren, 1982) and may influence thirst. Combined ablation of the area postrema and adjacent NTS increased water intake in response to angiotensin-related dipsogenic stimuli in rats (Edwards & Ritter, 1982; Ohman & Johnson, 1989). This effect was less if the lesion was restricted more to the area postrema, and greater if a larger proportion of the NTS was ablated (T. Wang & Edwards, 1997). It is proposed that signals from the viscera, that have an influence on thirst, are relayed via the NTS to more rostral brain regions via the lateral parabrachial nucleus and ventrolateral medulla (Johnson & Thunhorst, 1997). Ad libitum water drinking, or that resulting from hypovolemia, was not affected by lesions of the NTS designed to destroy neural input from intrathoracic baroreceptors, and it has been suggested that neural input from ascending spinal pathways transmitting signals from renal sensors could be influencing thirst in these animals (Schreihofer et al., 1999).

Lateral Parabrachial Nucleus

The lateral parabrachial nucleus (LPBN) in the dorsolateral midbrain is the major efferent target of neurons within

the NTS relaying afferent nerve signals from the viscera (Herbert, Moga, & Saper, 1991). In turn, neurons within the LPBN project efferent nerve fibers to regions known to influence thirst such as the median preoptic nucleus and subfornical organ in the lamina terminalis and the lateral hypothalamic area (Herbert, et al., 1991; Saper & Levisohn, 1983). Ablation of the LPBN, by either electrolysis or injection of neurotoxin, enhanced water intake in response to angiotensin-mediated dipsogenic stimuli, but did not change day-to-day water intake, or drinking responses to systemic hypertonicity or polyethylene glycol-induced hypovolemia (Edwards & Johnson, 1991; Ohman & Johnson, 1989). Therefore, neurons within the LPBN do not seem to influence ad libitum water drinking, but may relay signals that inhibit water drinking associated with angiotensin's dipsogenic action, possibly preventing excessive water intake in response to angiotensin. It is possible that the LPBN restricts water drinking by engaging neural mechanisms mediating satiety. Microinjection of the GABA agonist muscimol into the LPBN to inhibit its neural activity in water-sated rats causes a small but significant increase in drinking, consistent with the idea that LPBN neurons play a role in thirst satiety.

Another interesting aspect of LPBN function in relation to thirst mechanisms is the apparent switching of a thirst to an appetite for salt when serotonergic antagonists are injected into the LPBN of rats administered various dipsogenic stimuli (Menani, Columbari, Beltz, Thunhorst, & Johnson, 1998).

Midbrain Raphé Nuclei

Located in the dorsal midline of the midbrain (see Figure 35.1, panel A), the dorsal and median raphé nuclei probably relay neural signals that exert inhibitory serotonergic influences on thirst mechanisms. Ablation of the dorsal raphé nucleus causes increased water intake in response to dehydration or an angiotensin II–mediated stimulus (isoproterenol treatment), and also changes the sodium/water preference of rats resulting in large increases in both salt and water intake (Olivares, Costa-e-Sousa, & Cavalcante-Limal 2003).

In regard to the median raphé nucleus, ablation of serotonergic neurons therein resulted in a gradual increase in water intake of rats (Barofsky, Grier, & Pradhan, 1980), while acute inhibition of neurons within this brain region by microinjection of muscimol (a drug that inhibits neurons by acting at GABA receptors) into it caused a rapid drinking response in normally hydrated rats. Inhibitory neural pathways from median raphé to the subfornical organ and/or lateral hypothalamic area may mediate its inhibitory influence on thirst because ablation of either of these regions disrupts the dipsogenic effect of injections of muscimol into the median raphé nucleus (Stratford & Wirtshafter, 2000).

Zona Incerta

Located ventral to the thalamus, the zona incerta has been implicated in thirst mechanisms because its ablation disrupts drinking responses. However, results are inconsistent as to the type of drinking that is affected by ablation of the zona incerta. Grossman (1984) reported that osmoregulatory but not hypovolemic drinking was inhibited by lesions in the rostral zona incerta, whereas Evered and Mogenson (1976) observed that water intake in response to hypertonicity or hypovolemia was normal in rats with zona incerta lesions, but secondary, nonhomeostatic drinking was impaired. The zona incerta is connected to many brain regions, including the subfornical organ, lateral hypothalamic area, and several thalamic sites (Miselis, Weiss, & Shapiro, 1987; Ricardo, 1981) and is well positioned to relay neural signals for thirst.

Lateral Hypothalamic Area

As mentioned in an earlier section, stimulation of the lateral hypothalamus (LH) stimulates drinking (Andersson & McCann, 1955; Greer, 1955), while ablation of the LH caused severe hypodipsia and hypophagia (Teitelbaum & Epstein, 1962). The disruption of ascending catecholaminergic fibers of passage in the medial forebrain bundle passing through the LH was considered a crucial factor in the cause of adipsia and aphagia of the LH syndrome (Ungerstedt, 1971). However, later investigations in rats, in which the excitotoxin kainic acid was used to ablate LH neurons but leave fibers of passage intact, revealed that osmoregulatory, hypovolemic, and angiotensin-stimulated water-drinking responses were severely disrupted, but drinking following water deprivation was not (Stricker, Swerdloff, & Zigmond, 1978; Winn, Tarbuck, & Dunnett, 1984). The LH receives a strong afferent neural input from the lamina terminalis, LPBN, and midbrain raphe (Berk & Finkelstein, 1981; Herbert et al., 1991; Miselis et al., 1987) and has numerous efferent connections to thalamic and cortical regions. It is possible that it could relay thirst related signals to these cortical regions from sensors in the lamina terminalis.

Median Preoptic Nucleus

The median preoptic nucleus, located in the lamina terminalis between the subfornical organ and OVLT, has direct neural links with many brain regions that have been implicated in the control of body fluid homeostasis. These include a rich reciprocal neural connectivity with the OVLT and subfornical organ, neural input from the LPBN, ventrolateral medulla, midbrain raphé, and hypothalamic paraventricular nucleus (Saper & Levisohn, 1983; Zardetto-Smith & Johnson, 1995). As well, its strong efferent links to the lateral preoptic and lateral hypothalamic areas, parastrial nucleus, supraoptic nucleus, magno- and parvocellular parts of the hypothalamic paraventricular nucleus, midbrain and medullary raphé, periaqueductal grey, bed nucleus of the stria terminalis, and amygdala (Gu & Simerly, 1997) emphasize the potential of this nucleus for an integrative role in the regulation of thirst.

Evidence that is consistent with an integrative role of the median preoptic nucleus in thirst is the severe disruption of osmoregulatory, angiotensin-stimulated or hypovolemic drinking responses caused by ablation of this nucleus by either neurotoxin or electrolytic methods (Cunningham et al., 1991; Johnson et al., 1996; Mangiapane et al., 1983; McKinley et al., 1999). Neurons within the median preoptic nucleus are activated when animals are dehydrated, infused systemically with hypertonic saline or angiotensin II, or intracerebroventricularly with angiotensin II or relaxin, which are all dipsogenic stimuli (Herbert, Forsling, Howes, Stacey, & Shiers, 1992;

McAllen et al., 1990; McKinley et al., 1992, 1994, 1997). Severing the neural connections between the subfornical organ and median preoptic nucleus disrupts drinking in response to systemically administered angiotensin II, as does cutting the efferent neural output from the median preoptic nucleus (Eng & Miselis, 1981; Lind & Johnson, 1982). The high concentration of angiotensin AT_1 receptors in the median preoptic nucleus (Allen et al., 2000) that would not be directly accessed by circulating angiotensin II (because of the blood-brain barrrier), indicate that it probably receives afferent angiotensinergic input. It has been proposed that angiotensin-senstive neurons in the subfornical organ that are stimulated by blood-borne angiotensin relay neural signals out of the lamina terminalis via an angiotensergic synapse in the median preoptic nucleus (Johnson et al., 1996).

Septal Nuclei

Harvey and Hunt (1965) showed initially that ablation of the septum (see Figure 35.1, panel 2 for location) could cause large, prolonged (over months) increases in daily fluid intake in rats (termed *septal hyperdipsia*), suggesting that this region may relay inhibitory neural signals related to thirst. Polydipsia resulting from septal lesions persisted in rats with the ureter ligated to prevent urine loss, demonstrating that a primary polydipsia occurs with septal lesions (Blass & Hanson, 1970). In rats, day-to-day drinking increases, and angiotensin-stimulated but not osmoregulatory drinking is potentiated (Blass, Nussbaum, & Hanson, 1974). In sheep with septal lesions, neither angiotensin- or osmotically stimulated drinking is potentiated, but daily water intake may more than double. Such water drinking continues during the day when plasma osmolality has decreased below the normal set point (Smardencas & McKinley, 1994). It is possible that normal inhibitory influences of hypotonicity or hypovolemia on thirst may be relayed via the septum, being disrupted when the septal region is ablated. There is also evidence of a relay via the nucleus of the diagonal band from the hindbrain that is involved in hypovolemic thirst (Sullivan et al., 2003).

EFFECTOR REGIONS FOR THIRST IN THE CEREBRAL CORTEX

Unlike vasopressin secretion, where the neuroendocrine motor output from neurons in the supraoptic and paraventricular nucleus is well defined, the effector sites in the brain that generate the emotion of thirst remain clouded in uncertainty. Thirst demands a behavioral response— fluid ingestion. As a function of the conscious brain, the emotion of thirst has been assumed to be generated by the cerebral cortex.

Cortical Stimulation

In a survey of the cerebral cortex of conscious monkeys, Robinson and Mishkin (1966) electrically stimulated many cortical loci and obtained drinking responses at several sites. These included the substantia innominata, putamen, substantia nigra, preoptic region, lateral hypothalamus, and ventral tegmentum, but the region that most reliably yielded drinking behavior when stimulated was the anterior cingulate cortex. In the classical studies of Penfield and colleagues, many different superficial sites in the cerebral cortex of conscious human surgical patients were electrically stimulated, and their subjective responses recorded. The subjects, with scalp and skull locally anesthetized, although reporting many somatic and visceral sensations, rarely mention the induction of thirst during these stimulations (Penfield & Faulk, 1955; Penfield & Rasmussen, 1950). However, in two epileptic subjects, thirst or a need for water was associated with stimulation of the superior temporal gyrus (Penfield & Jasper, 1954).

Brain Imaging Studies

Functional brain imaging studies in human subjects infused intravenously with hypertonic saline to induce thirst have also provided information in this regard. Both positron emission tomography (PET) and functional magnetic resonance imaging (fMRI) that reflect changes in regional blood flow in the brain, show that the anterior cingulate region (see Figure 35.1, panels A and 1 for location) is activated in subjects made thirsty by this procedure (Figure 35.7), and that satiation of thirst by drinking, quickly led to this activation being extinguished (Denton et al., 1999; Egan et al., 2003). Activation of the anterior cingulate region was also correlated with thirst in another group of subjects (de Araujo, Kringelbach, Rolls, & McGlone, 2003). Activations in the posterior cingulate, parahippocampal gyrus, insular cortex (Figure 35.7), precentral gyrus, orbital gyrus, superior temporal gyrus (Figure 35.7), anterior perforated substance, and regions within the cerebellum also correlated with thirst scores. While the activity of several brain regions correlated with the thirst score, such correlations do not allow the precise function of these regions to be specified from these imaging experiments. The superior temporal region was implicated in thirst by Penfield and Jasper (1954). Three of the regions mentioned—,the anterior cingulate, insular and orbito-frontal cortices—have been implicated in the generation of homeostatic emotions (Craig, 2002).

Anterior Cingulate Cortex

The brain imaging investigations in human subjects, and electrical stimulation studies in monkeys mentioned, consistently link the anterior cingulate cortex with thirst mechanisms. The anterior cingulate region has been shown to be activated by sensory (e.g., pain, temperature), emotional (e.g., depression), cognitive (e.g., mental arithmetic), autonomic and reward based stimuli (Bush, Luu & Posner, 2000; Craig, 2002; Critchley, Corfield, Chandler, Mathias, & Dolan, 2000; Gehring & Taylor, 2004; Mayberg et al., 1999). It appears to be activated when an adverse condition occurs and a decision regarding a response strategy needs to be made (Gehring & Taylor, 2004). A characteristic of humans and rats that have undergone destruction of the anterior cingulate region is an apparent apathy, or lack of concern to rectify an adverse condition (Eslinger & Damasio, 1985; Johansen, Fields, & Manning, 2001). Although there appears to have been no investigation of thirst in patients who have undergone surgical cingulotomy, reports of dehydration or disordered fluid homeostasis in such patients are not readily found. It is possible that the role of the anterior cingulate is to provide the motivational or impelling aspect of the emotion of thirst that will result in the drinking of water.

Insular Cortex

The insular cortex (see Figure 35.1, panels 2 and 3) receives visceral afferent sensory input via synapses in the NTS, parabrachial nucleus, and thalamus (Saper, 2002). The parasympathetic afferents carry neural signals to the anterior insular cortex from many different sensors that include baroreceptors and receptors in the gastrointestinal tract that are known to influence thirst. In the schema proposed by Craig (2003), the role of the insula in the generation of specific homeostatic emotions, such as thirst, is to give specificity to the emotion in regard to the homeostatic perturbation—the subjective feeling of a person's homeostatic state.

Orbito-Frontal Cortex

de Araujo et al. (2003) utilized fMRI to show that water in the mouth activated part of the orbito-frontal cortex of thirsty subjects, but not water-replete subjects. The location of this region is shown in Figure 35.1 (panels A and 1). They interpreted this result as an indication that the orbito-frontal cortex provided a hedonic component to the behavioral response of drinking. Water in the mouth is pleasant if the subject is thirsty, but less so if the subject is not thirsty. Craig (2002) concluded that as the anterior cingulate and insular cortices are connected to the orbito-frontal cortex, sensory signals relating to the homeostatic state of the individual will reach this region and be interpreted there as to their pleasantness or reward value. In this schema, the

cortical generation of the emotion of thirst would involve activations of neurons within the anterior cingulate cortex for motivational intensity, the insula for homeostatic specificity, and the orbito-frontal region for reward.

NEUROCHEMISTRY OF THIRST

Neurotransmitters

Glutamate

Glutamatergic neural pathways are likely to have an important role in mediating thirst. Intracerebroventricular injection of the NMDA receptor antagonist MK801 blocks drinking responses stimulated by angiotensin II, intragastric hypertonic saline or water deprivation for 22 hours. Increased c-fos expression in the median preoptic nucleus, but not the subfornical organ, in response to angiotensin II and water deprivation was reduced by the MK801 (Xu & Herbert, 1998; Xu, Lane, Zhu, & Herbert, 1997), suggesting that a glutamatergic input to the median preoptic nucleus mediates both osmoregulatory and angiotensin-stimulated thirst. The vesicular glutamate transporter vGlut2, a marker of glutamatergic neurons, is expressed in the median preoptic nucleus, periphery of the subfornical organ, and dorsal cap of the OVLT, consistent with excitatory glutamatergic output from each of these regions of the lamina terminalis (Grob, Trottier, Drolet, & Mouginot, 2003). The non-NMDA receptor antagonist drug CNQX stimulates drinking in the rat (Xu & Johnson, 1998), suggesting that a glutamatergic pathway also drives an inhibitory input to thirst.

Acetylcholine

Acetylcholine has long been considered to have a role as a neurotransmitter in the neural circuitry subserving thirst. Microinjection of acetylcholine or the cholinergic agonist carbachol into several regions of the brain that include the LH, the preoptic and septal regions, hypothalamic paraventricular nucleus, and the subfornical organ stimulates water intake in rats (Fisher & Levitt, 1967; Grossman, 1960; Mangiapane & Simpson, 1983; Swanson & Sharpe, 1973). Systemic administration of the cholinergic muscarinic receptor blocking drug atropine sulphate, that has passage across the blood-brain barrier, inhibits but does not abolish water drinking in response to hypertonicity resulting from either intraperitoneal injection of hypertonic saline or water deprivation, hypovolemia resulting from polyethylene glycol injection, or day to water drinking in normal and lactating rats (Blass & Chapman, 1971; Fitzsimons & Setler, 1975; Speth, Smith, & Grove, 2002). Whether acetylcholine has a role in thirst in species other than the rat has yet to be proven.

Regarding the dipsogenic action of carbachol on the subfornical organ of the rat (Mangiapane & Simpson, 1983), neurons within the outer annulus of the subfornical organ receive a strong cholinergic innervation (Xu, Pekarek, Ge, & Yao, 2001). This cholinergic input originates from the medial septal nucleus and diagonal band, exerting direct excitatory actions on subfornical neurons via the M3 muscarinic receptor subtype (Honda et al., 2003). Acetylcholine could also affect thirst by a presynaptic action to reduce GABAergic influences on the subfornical organ (Xu, Honda, Ono, & Inenaga, 2001).

Dopamine

Interest in possible dopaminergic involvement in thirst mechanisms has resulted from observations that polydipsia that is often observed in psychotic states is modified by neuroleptic drugs (Canuso & Goldman, 1996). Injection of dopamine intracerebroventricularly at relatively large dosage (Setler, 1973) or peripheral dopaminergic agonists (pergolide, bromocriptine) that enter the brain (Fregly & Rowland, 1988; Zabik, Sprague, & Odio, 1993) will either stimulate or augment water drinking in rats, although another dopaminergic agonist, quinpirole hydrochloride, inhibits a number of dipsogenic responses (Fregly & Rowland, 1986). Systemic administration of dopaminergic D_2 receptor blocking drugs such as haloperidol, pimozide, or spiperone inhibit water intake in response to several different dipsogenic stimuli in rats (Fitzsimons & Setler, 1975; Fregly & Rowland, 1986, 1988; Zabik et al., 1993). However, while these data show that dopamine is probably influential in neural pathways of thirst, drawing any firm conclusions in regard to its exact role and locus of action as a transmitter in thirst circuitry is fraught with difficulty. This is because of the multiplicity of neural systems (e.g., sensory-motor, reward, neuroendocrine pathways) they influence and the lack of receptor specificity of most dopaminergic antagonists.

Noradrenaline

Noradrenergic pathways may influence thirst at more than one level of organization. Peripheral administration of clonidine, the presynaptically acting ·2-adrenoceptor agonist has a strong inhibitory action on drinking responses to osmoregulatory and hypovolemic dipsogenic stimuli in the rat. These actions are blocked by the α2-antagonist yohimbine, and this drug also augments angiotensin-induced thirst (Fregly, Kelleher, & Greenleaf, 1981; Fregly & Rowland, 1986). As stimulation of ·2-adrenoceptors reduces the presynaptic release of noradrenaline at nerve terminals, these data suggest an important function of noradrenaline release within neural pathways of thirst, that may be regulated by adrenergic α2-autoreceptors. In regard to central sites of noradrenaline action, depletion of catecholamines within the ventral lamina terminalis region by injections of the neurotoxin 6-hydroxydopamine therein disrupts angiotensin-stimulated drinking, and this effect is due to loss of noradrenergic rather than dopaminergic neurons (Bellin, Landas, & Johnson, 1988; Cunningham & Johnson, 1989, 1991). The origin of the noradrenergic input to the median preoptic nucleus is likely to be the A1 group in the caudal ventrolateral medulla (Kawano & Masuko, 1999), and it is proposed that this noradrenergic input combines an angiotensinergic pathway to drive thirst responses (Johnson & Thunhorst, 1997). There is also evidence of an ascending noradrenergic input from the A2 group in the nucleus of the solitary tract to the subfornical organ that could influence thirst (Tanaka, Hayashi, Shimamune, & Nomura, 1997).

Serotonin

Pharmacological studies of serotonergic agonist and antagonists injected into the CNS show that drinking responses can be influenced by these agents. They are particularly effective when injected into the lateral parabrachial nucleus in the midbrain where the nonselective serotonin-blocking drug methysergide causes enhanced angiotensin-induced water drinking, while injection there of serotonin agonists depress water drinking (Menani & Johnson, 1995).

Gamma Amino Butyric Acid

Inhibitory neural pathways influencing thirst presumably have an important role in satiety and baroreceptor inhibition of thirst, and gamma amino butyric acid (GABA) neurotransmission is likely to mediate these inhibitory influences. GABAergic mechanisms appear to play an important role within the lamina terminalis. The median preoptic nucleus receives GABAergic input from the subfornical organ as well as other brain regions. GABA may act presynaptically via $GABA_B$ receptors, and at postsynaptic sites through $GABA_A$ receptors in the median preoptic nucleus (Kolaj, Bai, & Renaud, 2004). GABAergic neurons are present in the median preptic nucleus (Grob et al., 2003), providing a significant output from it to vasopressin-containing neurons in the supraoptic nucleus (Nissen & Renaud, 1994), and possibly also to regions that influence thirst.

Nitric Oxide

Nitrous oxide (NO) may have a role as an inhibitory neurotransmitter or locally released influence on thirst. The enzyme that facilitates its production, neuronal nitric oxide synthase, is found in high concentration within the thirst-mediating regions of the subfornical organ, OVLT, and median preoptic nucleus (Jurzak, Schmid, & Gerstberger,

1994). Water intake in response to angiotensin II or water deprivation is inhibited by central administration of l-arginine from which NO is synthesized, and this effect is blocked by inhibitors of nitric oxide synthase (Calapai & Caputi, 1996). Direct application of nitroprusside, an NO donor, to angiotensin-sensitive subfornical organ neurons in vitro depresses their electrical activity (Rauch, Schmid, DeVente, & Simon, 1997), showing it likely that NO exerts its action on thirst by inhibiting angiotensin-sensitive neurons in the lamina terminalis. On the other hand, it has also been shown that centrally administered inhibitors of neuronal nitric oxide synthase also cause an inhibition of angiotensin drinking in the rat (Kadekaro & Summy-Long, 2000), which is not consistent with the theory that NO inhibits thirst. However, results from experiments employing centrally administered nitric oxide synthase inhibitors should be viewed with caution because reduction in fluid intakes caused by central administration of these drugs could be secondary to other effects such as hyperthermia (Mathai, Arnold, Febbraio, & McKinley, 2004) and increased arterial pressure (Kadekaro & Summy-Long, 2000) that also result from NOS inhibition.

Neuropeptides

A number of neuropeptides have been reported to influence water drinking when injected into the brain (Table 35.1). However, the physiological role in thirst of most of these peptides is still unclear. Angiotensin II is by far the most widely studied of the dipsogenic neuropeptides.

Angiotensin II

In addition to its function as the circulating effector hormone of the peripheral renin-angiotensin system, the octapetide angiotensin II is generated within the brain independently of the peripheral renin-angiotensin system. All components of a brain renin-angiotensin system (peptides, enzymes and receptors) exist within the brain. While astrocytes are the main site for synthesis in the brain of the precursor peptide angiotensinogen (Lynch, Hawelu-Johnson, & Guyenet, 1987), angiotensin peptides are probably generated within neurons. Angiotensin receptors, both AT_1 and AT_2 subtypes, are located on neurons in many brain regions associated with body fluid and cardiovascular homeostasis (Allen et al., 2000; Lenkei, Palkovits, Corvol, & Llorens-Cortes, 1997). Except for those receptors in the circumventricular organs that have been described in an earlier section of this chapter, these receptor sites are within the blood barrier. Therefore, they are not influenced directly by blood-borne angiotensin II, but are likely to have brain-generated angiotensin as their endogenous ligand.

One of the most powerful of all experimental dipsogenic procedures, and one of the most investigated, is the injection of angiotensin II into the ventricular system or specific regions of the brain, whether the subject be rat, dog, goat, sheep, cow, or monkey (Fitzsimons, 1998). This effect is mediated largely by AT1 receptors in the region of the anteroventral wall of the third ventricle (AV3V region), and not the subfornical organ, the site that transduces the drinking response to circulating angiotensin II (Buggy & Johnson, 1978). Neurons within the median

TABLE 35.1   Neuropeptides that influence water intake when injected into the cerebral ventricles or specific brain regions.

Neuropeptide	Effect on Water Intake	Reference
Adrenomedullin	Inhibition	Murphy & Samson (1995)
Angiotensin II	Stimulation	Fitzsimons (1998)
Angiotensin III	Stimulation	Wilson et al. (2005)
Appelin	Stimulation	Taheri et al. (2002)
Atrial natriuretic peptide	Inhibition	Antunes-Rodrigues et al. (1985)
Brain natriuretic peptide	Inhibition	Itoh et al. (1988)
Corticotropin-releasing hormone	Inhibition	Van Gaalen et al. (2002)
Dermorphin	Inhibition	De Caro (1986)
β-endorphin	Inhibition	Summy-Long et al. (1981)
Leu-enkephalin	Inhibition	Summy-Long et al. (1981)
Met-enkephalin	Inhibition	Summy-Long et al. (1981)
Endothelin	Inhibition	Samson et al. (1991)
Galanin	Inhibition	Brewer et al. (2005)
Melanin-concentrating hormone	Stimulation	Clegg et al. (2002)
Orexin A	Stimulation	Kunii et al. (1999)
Substance P	Inhibition (mammals)	De Caro (1986)

preoptic nucleus, which is situated within the AV3V region, are activated by intracerebroventricular angiotensin II (Herbert et al., 1992), and direct injection of angiotensin II into the median preoptic nucleus of the rat causes water drinking (O'Neill & Brody, 1987). Most likely, intracerebroventricularly injected angiotensin II acts on the median preoptic nucleus to stimulate drinking and mimics the effect of synaptically released angiotensin II at this site. Angiotensin III, the heptapeptide formed by degradation of angiotensin II is also dipsogenic when administered centrally (Wright, Morseth, Abhold, & Harding, 1985) and may act also at central angiotensinergic receptors for thirst.

In regard to central angiotensinergic relays mediating thirst, an angiotensergic synapse within the median preoptic nucleus relaying signals to it from angiotensin II stimulated neurons in the subfornical organ has been proposed (Johnson et al., 1996). Pharmacological blockade of AT_1 receptors in the brain by losartan inhibits water drinking in the rat in response to intracerebroventricular infusion of hypertonic saline in several species, suggesting that a central angiotensinergic relay mediates osmoregulatory drinking (Blair-West et al., 1994). However, recent observations that osmoregulatory drinking is entirely intact in genetically modified mice totally lacking angiotensin peptides due to deletion of the gene encoding angiotensinogen are not in agreement with this suggestion (McKinley, Alexiou, et al., 2006).

SATIATION OF THIRST

Satiation of thirst, at least initially, is more than just an absence of thirst. The act of drinking by the thirsty person is pleasurable, and this response appears to be more than just the mere removal of the tormenting aspects of thirst. It is likely that extinguishing thirst involves the activation of dopaminergic reward pathways in the brain (Ettenberg & Camp, 1986). The Swedish explorer Sven Hedin (1865–1952) gives an account (cited by Wolf, 1958) of the exhilaration and joy that came from finding and ingesting water when he was extremely thirsty during a harsh journey through the arid Taklamakan desert of western China. He relates "I stood on the brink of a little pool of water—beautiful water! ... I took the tin box out of my pocket and filled it, and drank. How sweet that water tasted! Nobody can conceive it who has not been within an ace of dying of thirst. I lifted the tin to my lips, calmly, slowly, deliberately, and drank, drank, drank, time after time. How delicious! What exquisite pleasure! The noblest wine pressed out of the grape, the divinest nectar ever made, was never half so sweet."

Thirst satiety provides the signal that prevents excessive hydration, and this satiety usually occurs before systemic absorption of ingested water. The consequences of overhydration—hyponatremia and cerebral oedema—can be as lethal as severe dehydration. Thus, this satiating mechanism is a crucial homeostatic emotion that contributes to accurate repletion of body fluids without overhydration following a period of dehydration.

Voluntary Dehydration

The speed at which water is drunk and thirst quenched following a period of water deprivation varies considerably across mammals. Some species (e.g., dog, camel, sheep, goats, deer) when dehydrated, replace fluid deficits immediately on gaining access to drinking water. Others (e.g., rats, humans, horse) replace their fluid deficit more slowly and may take several hours to restore fluid balance (Adolph, 1950). In this latter group, after an initial drinking bout that is not sufficient to replace all the fluid lost, but sufficient to cause temporary satiety or loss of thirst, intermittent drinking bouts occur over a few hours until rehydration is complete. This phenomenon has been termed "voluntary dehydration." The gradual replenishment of a fluid deficit may be protective against rapidly occurring hyponatremia and cerebral oedema.

Scientific investigation of the signals that bring about thirst satiety goes back to Claude Bernard who studied the effects of "sham drinking" in dehydrated dogs with an esophageal fistula. This phenomenon has been investigated in several species (dog, rat, sheep, monkey, man) and it is clear that animals drink considerably more than their fluid deficit if the water imbibed immediately leaves the body through an oesophageal or gastric fistula (Bott, Denton, & Weller, 1965; Towbin, 1949; Wood, Maddison, Rolls, Rolls, & Gibbs, 1980). Indeed, animals with an open fistula will continue to drink until they appear fatigued from the effort. Therefore, the act of drinking and swallowing water per se is an insufficient stimulus to satiate thirst. Yet, if a quantity of water equivalent to a dehydrational deficit is placed by tube directly in the stomach without it touching the mouth, pharynx, and esophagus, thirst will not be relieved for some time (Figaro & Mack, 1997; Thrasher, Nistal-Herrera, Keil, & Ramsay, 1981). However, an essential aspect of the initial thirst-satiating mechanism is that fluid remains in the stomach after it has been ingested (Blass & Hall, 1976; Gibbs, Rolls, & Rolls, 1986). Therefore, a combination of oropharyngeal, esophageal, and gastric signals, in appropriate temporal sequence, appear to be necessary for thirst satiety to be achieved in the short term.

The amount of water ingested during the initial rehydrating bout does not depend on its temperature or composition—water, isotonic saline, or isotonic glucose are similarly ingested (Appelgren, Thrasher, Keil, & Ramsay, 1991; Hoffman, DenBleyker, Smith, & Stricker, 2005). These data suggest that mechanical distention signals from the throat, esophagus, and stomach mediate the initial stop signal for drinking. Capsaicin treatment, which damages vagal afferent nerves from the gut in rats, leads to lack of thirst satiation initially (Curtis & Stricker, 1997), suggesting that these neural signals are carried via this nerve to the brain. These preabsorptive signals from the gastrointestinal tract also influence other homeostatic responses; they rapidly suppress vasopressin release and stimulate sweating in humans and panting in animals when they rehydrate (Appelgren et al., 1991; Baker & Turlejska, 1989; Figaro & Mack, 1997; Takamata, Mack, Gillen, Jozsi, & Nadel, 1995; Thrasher et al., 1981). Thereafter, absorption of ingested water in the duodenum also provides a satiating signal for thirst (Gibbs et al., 1986) that could be vagally mediated because selective hepatic vagotomy causes dehydrated rats to overdrink (Smith & Jerome, 1983). In the longer term, absorption of fluid into the systemic circulation and reduction of plasma osmolality makes a minor contribution to satiety (Wood et al., 1980).

PHYSIOLOGICAL AND PATHOPHYSIOLOGICAL CONDITIONS INFLUENCING THIRST

Pregnancy

Pregnancy is a condition that alters body fluid balance. Plasma osmolality falls by approximately 10 mosmol/kg within 5 to 10 weeks following conception; the reduced plasma osmolality is maintained throughout pregnancy (Davison, Gilmore, Durr, Robertson, & Lindheimer, 1984). Plasma osmolality also falls during pregnancy in rats, yet vasopressin continues to be secreted, as it does in pregnant women, in the face of the plasma hypotonicity. It is proposed that the osmostat for vasopressin secretion is reset to a lower level (Davison et al., 1984; Durr et al., 1981). Despite plasma osmolality falling, animals increase daily water intake during pregnancy (Denton, McKinley, Nelson, & Weisinger, 1977; Richter & Barelare, 1938), which suggests that the osmoreceptor for thirst is also reset during pregnancy. The observation that pregnant homozygous Brattleboro rats, which are devoid of vasopressin, double daily water intake and lower plasma osmolality from 310 to 292 mosmol/kg, is consistent with a resetting of the thirst osmostat in these animals. The threshold osmolality for thirst in pregnant women is 10 mosmol/kg lower than it is preconception or postpartum (Davison, Shiells, Phillips, & Lindheimer, 1988). The same authors have shown also that

treatment with human chorionic gonadotrophin reduces the thirst threshold in mothers, and have suggested that this hormone has a signaling role in resetting the osmoreceptor. Relaxin may have a similar role in rats (Weisinger, Burns, Eddie, & Wintour, 1993).

Lactation

Lactation involves loss of fluid by mothers in the form of milk. This fluid loss needs to be replaced if dehydration is to be prevented and adequate milk supply maintained. There are many anecdotal reports of thirst being experienced by nursing mothers, and the daily water intake of animals with multiple offspring such as rats and rabbits increases considerably during lactation (Denton, et al., 1977; Richter & Barelare, 1938). Inhibition of the increased daily water intake in lactating rats by a centrally administered angiotensin antagonist suggests a role for brain angiotensinergic pathways in lactation-induced thirst (Speth et al., 2002). James, Irons, Holmes, Drewett, and Bayliss (1995) observed that thirst and water intake increased during suckling periods in 10 nursing mothers, and the increased thirst corresponded with oxytocin secretion and milk letdown. No change in plasma osmolality or vasopressin levels occurred. These investigators suggested that suckling may send afferent nerve signals to the hypothalamus that generate thirst as well as oxytocin secretion.

Age

As animals and humans age, thirst may become impaired. As a consequence, they drink less fluid in response to being dehydrated, and this impaired thirst renders them liable to the deleterious effects of dehydration such as heat stroke in hot weather.

The reasons for the waning of thirst with age are unclear. Some but not all investigators report that thirst ratings and amount of water drunk in response to a purely osmotic stimulus (e.g., intravenous infusion of hypertonic saline) are depressed in elderly subjects (Kenney & Chiu, 2001; Phillips et al., 1984). More consistent are observations that thirst and fluid intake following a period of water deprivation are less intense in elderly subjects in comparison to young adults (Kenney & Chiu, 2001).

Animal models of the influence of aging on thirst have been described recently. Brown-Norway and Munich Wistar (but not Sprague Dawley or Fischer 344) strains of rat exhibit progressively impaired drinking responses to water deprivation and hypertonicity as they age, while hypovolemic thirst was not reduced until advanced age. The dipsogenic reponse to angiotensin II, however, was not diminished with age (McKinley, Denton, et al., 2006;

Thunhorst & Johnson, 2003). Several influences on thirst are changed with age (Ferrari, Radaelli, & Centola, 2003; Kenney & Chiu, 2001), and could contribute to age-impaired thirst. First, cardiovascular reflexes arising from arterial baroreceptors and cardiopulmonary receptors are known to be reduced in elderly humans and this may depress thirst in response to hypovolemia; second, elevated plasma concentrations of atrial natriuretic peptide have been observed in aged humans and rats; third, the renin-angiotensin system is depressed in the aged, and this may influence thirst mechanisms in older subjects.

In a recent study (Farrell et al., in press), young adults and elderly human subjects were infused intravenously with hypertonic saline, then allowed to satiate their thirst while undergoing PET imaging of the brain. Both groups reported similar thirst ratings as a result of the hypertonic stimulus, but the elderly only drank half the volume of water to quench their thirst and reduce activity in the cingulate cortex compared to the younger group. The results suggest that mechanisms of thirst satiety change with age; this may contribute to the susceptibility of the elderly to become dehydrated.

An increase in core body temperature induces evaporative cooling responses of sweating and panting (depending on the species) that result in loss of fluid from the body. If thirst is a response to increased core temperature, resulting fluid intake could be an anticipatory mechanism to prevent dehydration. While most water intake that occurs with hyperthermia is secondary to dehydration (Barney & Folkerts, 1995; Hainsworth, Stricker, & Epstein, 1968), there is evidence that direct thermal stimulation of the preoptic-hypothalamic region of the brain can stimulate water drinking (Andersson & Larsson, 1961). An increase of 0.8°C in core temperature potentiated the thirst and water ingested by human subjects in response to intravenous hypertonic saline (Takamata, Mack, Stachenfeld, & Nadel, 1995), suggesting that there is a physiological effect of increased body temperature to enhance thirst.

Thirst in Some Disease States

Diabetes Insipidus

The water intake of patients with diabetes insipidus is enormous, often exceeding 12 litres per day (Blotner, 1951). It is driven by thirst that arises from continual dehydration caused by excessive loss of dilute urine due to lack of vasopressin (cranial diabetes insipidus) or insensitivity of the kidney to its action (nephrogenic diabetes insipidus). Administration of pitressin or the vasopressin analogue dDAVP ameliorates the diuresis of central diabetes insipidus and fluid intake correspondingly decreases. The sensitivity of the thirst mechanism to hypertonicity is normal in patients with diabetes insipidus (Thompson & Bayliss, 1987). Indeed, normal thirst and subsequent fluid intake are essential for preventing lethal dehydration in untreated diabetes insipidus.

Diabetes Mellitus

Untreated diabetes mellitus (type 1 or 2) is characterized by strong thirst, often the first indication of its onset. Excessive urine output in the form of a glycosuria also occurs due to failure of the kidney to reabsorb the high filtered glucose load that results from lack of insulin, or insensitivity of tissues to insulin. Dehydration of both intracellular and extracellular compartments may result, but because high blood glucose levels do not usually stimulate thirst, diabetic thirst has been considered more likely to be the result of extracellular fluid loss (Fitzsimons, 1998). A recent study of water intake in rats with diabetes mellitus (induced by treatment with the drug streptozotocin) showed that systemic administration of an angiotensin antagonist had only a small inhibitory effect on their water drinking. Increased expression of c-fos was observed in osmoregulatory regions of the lamina terminalis: the dorsal cap of the OVLT, periphery of subfornical organ, and median preoptic nucleus. Moreover, while intravenous infusion of hypertonic glucose is not normally dipsogenic, it does stimulate drinking in diabetic rats, suggesting that diabetic thirst involves osmoreceptor stimulation (McKinley, Burns, Oldfield, Sunigawa, & Weisinger, 2004). Intracellular dehydration of the osmoreceptor could occur in diabetic rats because the osmoreceptor's glucose transporter is saturated by high plasma glucose concentrations, and/or it is normally insulin sensitive. If so, when insulin is absent or ineffective, hypertonic glucose would be excluded from the osmoreceptor thereby creating an osmotic gradient and cellular dehydration.

Heart Failure

When the left ventricle of the heart is damaged and fails to adequately perfuse the tissues of the body with blood, compensatory autonomic and neuroendocrine mechanisms are engaged. These include increased activity of sympathetic nerves and the renin-angiotensin-aldosterone system, and vasopressin release. Congestive heart failure is characterized by excessive fluid retention and hyponatremia, that together with increased sympathetic- and angiotensin-mediated vasoconstriction, deleteriously increase the load on the failing heart (Kalra, Anker, & Coats, 2001; Packer, 1992). Fluid intake is maintained in the face of low plasma osmolality, high blood levels of ANP, and expanded extracellular fluid volume. Studies of thirst in such patients have not been undertaken, but it has been shown in rats with heart failure caused experimentally by coronary artery ligation, that water intake in response to dehydration is excessive (De Smet, Menadue, Oliver, & Phillips, 2003). The authors suggested that increased sensitivity of the osmoreceptor, increased blood angiotensin II levels, or changed baroreceptor stimulation could be driving the increased thirst in these animals.

Fever

There are reports that administration of the pyrogenic agent lipopolysaccharide (a molecule derived from bacterial cell walls) stimulates drinking behavior, particularly in the early phase of fever (Szczepanska-Sadowska, Sobocinska, & Kozlowski, 1979; Wang & Evered, 1993). However, once lipopolysaccharide-induced fever has peaked and stabilized, thirst is depressed (Nava, Calapai, De Sarro, & Caputi, 1996; Szczepanska-Sadowska et al., 1979). The inhibition of thirst that occurs following pyrogen administration can be dissociated from the febrile response in that repeated treatment with pyrogen can result in tolerance to fever, but not to the antidipsogenic action of lipopolysaccharide (Nava & Carta, 2000). While a centrally administered interleukin-1 antagonist blocked pyrogen-induced fever, it did not block its antidipsogenic effect (Nava et al., 1996). Central administration of the nitric oxide oxide synthase inhibitor L-NAME, while normally inhibitory to thirst, has been shown to reverse the inhibition of dehydration-induced thirst caused by fever in rats (Raghavendra, Agrewala, & Kulkarni, 1999), suggesting that an inhibitory influence of NO on the neural circuitry of thirst results from the administration of a pyrogen.

Syndrome of Inappropriate Antidiuretic Hormone Secretion

The syndrome of inappropriate antidiuretic hormone secretion (SIADH) is characterized by hyponatremia, normovolemia, and abnormally high plasma vasopressin concentrations relative to the low plasma osmolality. This condition is associated with various diseases such as lung cancer, pancreatic cancer, and bronchiectasis and is side effect of some therapeutic drugs (Robertson, 1989; Smith, Moore, Tormey, Bayliss, & Thompson, 2004). While vasopressin secretion is excessive relative to plasma osmolality (approximately 270 mosmol/kg) in SIADH, the maintenance of normal fluid intake and thirst by SIADH patients is also inappropriate. Smith et al. (2004) studied thirst in eight patients with SIADH of varying etiology, and consistently observed that the osmotic threshold for thirst was reduced from 288 in normal control subjects to 270 mosmol/kg in SIADH. The intensity of thirst increased from these different thresholds similarly in both groups, and the drinking of water immediately and normally suppressed thirst in both groups. Therefore, in SIADH, the thirst mechanism operates normally around a lower set point of plasma osmolality. The cause of the alteration in thirst threshold plasma osmolality in SIADH is unknown.

Hemodialysis

Many patients with end stage renal failure undergoing hemodialysis report strong thirst, water drinking, weight gain, and extracellular fluid volume expansion between periods of dialysis. There is evidence that high plasma angiotensin II levels contribute to this thirst because it has been eliminated by bilateral nephrectomy (Rogers & Kurtzman, 1973) and reduced by treatment with an angiotensin converting enzyme inhibitor (Oldenburg, MacDonald, & Shelley, 1988). Increase of plasma sodium and urea concentrations during the interdialytic period, and the concentration of sodium in the dialysis fluid may also be dipsogenic factors in these patients (Giovannetti et al., 1994).

Schizophrenia

Compulsive water drinking is observed in 10% to 20% of schizophrenic subjects. Excessive water drinking and fluid retention can lead to lethal hyponatremia in these patients (Illowski & Kirch, 1988). Whether the compulsion to drink water is the result of altered thirst is debatable (Goldman, Robertson, Luchin, & Hedeker, 1996). However, it has been reported that thirst ratings in compulsive water drinkers in response to infusion of hypertonic saline are higher than normal, and remained elevated following drinking episodes, unlike control subjects in which drinking quickly reduced the thirst rating (Thompson, Edwards, & Bayliss, 1991).

SUMMARY

This chapter focused on the physiological mechanisms that regulate the emotion of thirst. However, in regard to the physiological and psychological mechanisms regulating the amount of water ingested by humans and animals, thirst is but one of a number of interacting factors that determine fluid intake. In some instances, thirst may have no influence at all on the amount of water ingested. A striking and tragic example of this in recent times is the slavish adherence to advice of some athletes to drink excessive amounts of water prior to endurance sporting events. Fluid intake in the face of overhydration, and therefore lack of any thirst, has caused severe hyponatremia (low plasma sodium concentration), cerebral edema, and rapid death in some cases (Noakes et al., 2005; Verbalis, Goldsmith, Greenberg, Schrier, & Sterns, 2007). The popular belief that it is necessary to ingest eight glasses of water per day, regardless of physical activity or ambient temperature, is another example, albeit less dangerous, of water intake based not on thirst, but on advice that appears to lack supporting empirical evidence (Valtin, 2002).

In many human societies, water is ingested most often in the form of beverages. While thirst may drive the intake of beverages in certain circumstances, most often such intake is determined by reward aspects of the ingested fluid. Taste, odor, and temperature of ingested beverages can be reinforcers of beverage ingestion, as can the pharmacological properties of alcohol- and caffeine-containing drinks and the social consequences of drinking behavior (Booth, 1991). Learning also probably plays an important role in determining regulatory (homeostatic) and nonregulatory drinking behavor. Complex neural pathways involving the orbito-frontal cortex and amygdala (McDannald, Saddoris, Gallagher, & Holland, 2005; Rolls, 2000) as well as mesolimbic dopaminergic and opiate reward system (Kelley & Berridge, 2002; Wise, 2002) may drive a large part of the fluid intake of sedentary humans. Nevertheless, a major proportion of the world's population still resides in tropical and subtropical climates and participates in relatively intense physical activity in the course of earning a living or recreational pursuits. It is in conditions where nonregulatory intake of fluid as a beverage fails to deliver sufficient water to maintain adequate fluid balance, that the emotion of thirst provides the fail-safe signal to ingest fluid and restore a water deficit. The remarkable constancy of plasma osmolality that occurs throughout life, and across many mammalian species, attests to the effectiveness of the neural, endocrine and behavioral mechanisms (Figure 35.3) that regulate body fluid homeostasis. Thirst has a pivotal role in these mechanisms.

REFERENCES

Abraham, S. F., Baker, R. M., Blaine, E. H., Denton, D. A., & McKinley, M. J. (1975). Water drinking induced in sheep by angiotensin: A physiological or pharmacological effect? *Journal of Comparative and Physiological Psychology, 88,* 503–518.

Abraham, S. F., Coghlan, J. P., Denton, D. A., McDougall, J. G., Mouw, D. R., & Scoggins, B. A. (1976). Increased water drinking induced by sodium depletion in sheep. *Quarterly Journal of Experimental Physiology, 61,* 185–192.

Adolph, E. F. (1950). Thirst and its inhibition in the stomach. *American Journal of Physiology, 161,* 374–386.

Allen, A. M., Oldfield, B. J., Giles, M. E., Paxinos, G., McKinley, M. J., & Mendelsohn, F. A. O. (2000). Localization of angiotensin receptors in the nervous system. In R. Quirion, A. Bjorklund, & T. Hokfelt (Eds.), *Handbook of chemical neuroanatomy: Peptide Receptors, Pt. I* (Vol. 16, pp. 79–124). Amsterdam: Elsevier Science.

Anderson, C. R., & Houpt, T. R. (1990). Hypertonic and hypovolemic stimulation of thirst in pigs. *American Journal of Physiology, 258,* R149–R154.

Andersson, B. (1953). The effect of injections of hypertonic NaCl solutions into different parts of the hypothalamus of goats. *Acta Physiologica Scandinavica, 81,* 188–201.

Andersson, B. (1978). Regulation of water intake. *Physiological Reviews, 58,* 582–683.

Andersson, B., & Larsson, S. (1961). Influence of local temperature changes in the preoptic area and rostral hypothalamus on the regulation of food and water intake. *Acta Physiologica Scandinavica, 52,* 75–89.

Andersson, B., & McCann, S. M. (1955). A further study of polydipsia evoked by hypothalamic stimulation. *Acta Physiologica Scandinavica, 33,* 333–346.

Andersson, B., Leksell, L. G., & Lishajko, F. (1975). Perturbations in fluid balance induced by medially placed forebrain lesions. *Brain Research, 99,* 261–275.

Antunes-Rodrigues, J., McCann, S. M., Rogers, L. C., & Sampson, W. K. (1985). Atrial natriuretic factor inhibits dehydration and angiotensin II-induced water intake in the conscious unrestrained rat. *Proceedings of the National Academy of Sciences, USA, 82,* 8720–8723.

Appelgren, B. H., Thrasher, T. N., Keil, L. C., & Ramsay, L. C. (1991). Mechanism of drinking: Induced inhibition of vasopressin secretion in dehydrated dogs. *American Journal of Physiology, 261,* R1226–R1233.

Baertschi, A. J., & Vallet, P. G. (1981). Osmosensitivity of the hepatic portal vein area and vasopressin release in rats. *Journal of Physiology, 215,* 217–230.

Baker, M. A., & Turlejska, E. (1989). Thermal panting in dehydrated dogs: Effects of plasma volume expansion and drinking. *Pflugers Archive, 413,* 511–515.

Barney, C. C., & Folkerts, M. M. (1995). Thermal dehydration-induced thirst in rats: Role of body temperature. *American Journal of Physiology, 269,* R557–R564.

Barofsky, A. L., Grier, H. C., & Pradhan, T. K. (1980). Evidence for regulation of water intake by median raphe serotoninergic neurons. *Physiology and Behavior, 24,* 951–955.

Bellin, S. I., Landas, S. K., & Johnson, A. K. (1988). Selective catecholamine depletion of structures along the ventral lamina terminalis: Effects on experimentally induced drinking and pressor responses. *Brain Research, 456,* 9–16.

Berk, M. L., & Finkelstein, J. A. (1981). Afferent projections to the preoptic and hypothalamic regions of the rat brain. *Neuroscience, 6,* 1601–1624.

Black, S. L. (1976). Preoptic hypernatremic syndrome and the regulation of water balance in the rat. *Physiology and Behavior, 17,* 473–482.

Blair-West, J. R., Burns, P., Denton, D. A., Ferraro, T., McBurnie, M. I., Tarjan, E., et al. (1994). Thirst induced by increasing brain sodium concentration is mediated by brain angiotensin. *Brain Research, 637,* 335–338.

Blass, E. M., & Chapman, H. W. (1971). An evaluation of cholinergic mechanisms to thirst. *Physiology and Behavior, 7,* 679–686.

Blass, E. M., & Epstein, A. N. (1971). A lateral preoptic osmosensitive zone for thirst in the rat. *Journal of Comparative and Physiological Psychology, 76,* 378–394.

Blass, E. M., & Fitzsimons, J. T. (1970). Additivity of effect and interaction of a cellular and an extracellular stimulus of drinking. *Journal of Comparative and Physiological Psychology, 70,* 200–205.

Blass, E. M., & Hall, W. G. (1976). Drinking termination: Interactions among hydrational, orogastric, and behavioural controls in rats. *Psychological Review, 83,* 356–374.

Blass, E. M., & Hanson, D. G. (1970). Primary hyperdipsia in the rat following septal lesions. *Journal of Comparative and Physiological Psychology, 70,* 87–93.

Blass, E. M., Nusssbaum, A. I., & Hanson, D. G. (1974). Septal hyperdipsia: Specific enhancement of drinking to angiotensin in rats. *Journal of Comparative and Physiological Psychology, 87,* 422–439.

Blotner, H. (1951). *Diabetes insipidus.* New York: Oxford University Press.

Booth, D. (1991). Influences on human fluid consumption. In D. J. Ramsay & D. A. Booth (Eds.), *Thirst: Physiological and psychological aspects* (pp. 53–73). London: Springer Verlag.

Bott, E., Denton, D. A., & Weller, S. (1965). Water drinking in sheep with oesophageal fistulae. *Journal of Physiology, 176,* 323–336.

Brewer, A., Langel, U., & Robinson, J. K. (2005). Intracerebroventricular administration of galanin decreases free water intake and operant water reinforcer efficacy in water-restricted rats. *Neuropeptides, 39,* 117–124.

Brownfield, M. S., Reid, I. A., Ganten, D., & Ganong, W. F. (1982). Differential distribution of immunoreactive angiotensin and angiotensin-converting enzyme in rat brain. *Neuroscience, 7,* 1759–1769.

Buggy, J. W., & Johnson, A. K. (1978). Angiotensin induced thirst: Effects of third ventricular obstruction and periventricular ablation. *Brain Research, 149,* 117–128.

Burrell, L. M., Lambert, H. J., & Bayliss, P. H. (1991). Effect of atrial natriuretic peptide on thirst and arginine vasopressin release in humans. *American Journal of Physiology, 260,* R475–R479.

Bush, G., Luu, P., & Posner, M. I. (2000). Cognitive and emotional influences in anterior cingulate cortex. *Trends in Cognitive Science, 4,* 215–222.

Calapai, G., & Caputi, A. P. (1996). Nitric oxide and drinking behaviour. *Regulatory Peptides, 66,* 117–121.

Camargo, L. A. A., Menani, J. V., Saad, W. A., & Saad, W. A. (1984). Interaction between areas of the central nervous system in the control of water intake and arterial pressure in rats. *Journal of Physiology, 350,* 1–8.

Cannon, W. B. (1919). The physiological basis of thirst. *Proceedings of the Royal Society, B, 90,* 283–301.

Canuso, C. M., & Goldman, M. B. (1996). Does minimizing neuroleptic dosage influence hyponatremia. *Psychiatry Research, 63,* 227–229.

Carlson, S. H., Collister, J. P., & Osborn, J. W. (1998). The area postrema modulates hypothalamic fos responses to intragastric hypertonic saline in conscious rats. *American Journal of Physiology, 275,* R1921–R1927.

Ciura, S., & Bourque, C. W. (2006). Transient receptor vanilloid I is required for intrinsic osmoreceptionin organum vasculosum lamina terminalis neurons for normal thirst responses to systemic hyperosmolalit. *Journal of Neuroscience, 26,* 9069–9075.

Clegg, D. J., Air, E. L., Benoit, S. C., Sakai, R. S., Seeley, R. J., & Woods, S. C. (2003). Intraventricular melanin-concentrating hormone stimulates water intake independently of food intake. *American Journal of Physiology, 284,* R494–R499.

Coburn, P. C., & Stricker, E. M. (1978). Osmoregulatory thirst after lateral preoptic lesions. *Journal of Comparative and Physiological Psychology, 92,* 350–361.

Contreras, R. J., Beckstead, R. M., & Norgren, R. (1982). The central projections of the trigeminal, facial, glossopharyngeal and vagus nerves: An autoradiographic study in the rat. *Journal of the Autonomic Nervous System, 6,* 303–322.

Craig, A. D. (2002). How do you feel? Interoception: The sense of the physiological condition of the body. *Nature Reviews Neuroscience, 3,* 655–666.

Craig, A. D. (2003). A new view of pain as a homeostatic emotion. *Trends in Neurosciences, 26,* 303–307.

Critchley, H. D., Corfield, D. R., Chandler, M. P., Mathias, C. J., & Dolan, R. J. (2000). Cerebral correlates of autonomic cardiovascular arousal: A functional neuroimaging investigation in humans. *Journal of Physiology, 523,* 259–270.

Cunningham, J. T., & Johnson, A. K. (1989). Decreased norepinephrine in the ventral lamina terminalis region is associated with angiotensin II drinking response deficits following local 6-hydroxydopamine injections. *Brain Research, 480,* 65–71.

Cunningham, J. T., & Johnson, A. K. (1991). The effects of central norepinephrine infusions on drinking behaviour induced by angiotensin after 6-hydroxydopamine injections into the anteroventral region of the third ventricle (AV3V). *Brain Research, 558,* 112–116.

Cunningham, J. T., Sullivan, M. J., Edwards, G. L., Farinpour, R., Beltz, T., & Johnson, A. K. (1991). Dissociation of experimentally induced drinking behavior by ibotenate injection into the median preoptic nucleus. *Brain Research, 554,* 153–158.

Curtis, K. S., Huang, W., Sved, A. F., Verbalis, J. G., & Stricker, E. M. (1999). Impaired osmoregulatory responses in rats with area postrema lesions. *American Journal of Physiology, 277,* R209–R219.

Curtis, K., & Stricker, E. M. (1997). Enhanced fluid intake by rats after capsaicin treatment. *American Journal of Physiology, 272,* R704–R709.

Dampney, R. A. (1994). Functional organization of central pathways regulating the cardiovascular system. *Physiological Reviews, 74,* 323–364.

Davison, J. M., Gilmore, E. A., Durr, J., Robertson, G. L., & Lindheimer, M. D. (1984). Altered osmotic thresholds for vasopressin secretion and thirst in human pregnancy. *American Journal of Physiology, 247,* F105–F109.

Davison, J. M., Shiells, E. A., Phillips, P. R., & Lindheimer, M. D. (1988). Serial release of vasopressin and thirst in human pregnancy: Role of human gonadotrophin in the osmoregulatory changes of gestation. *Journal of Clinical Investigation, 81,* 798–806.

de Araujo, I. E. T., Kringelbach, M. L., Rolls, E. T., & McGlone, F. (2003). Human cortical reponses to water in the mouth and the effects of thirst. *Journal of Neurophysiology, 90,* 1865–1876.

De Caro, G. (1986). Effects of peptides of the gut-brain-skin-triangle on drinking behaviour ofv rats and birds. In G. de Caro, A. N. Epstein, & M. Massi (Eds.), *The physiology of thirst and sodium appetite* (pp. 213–226). New York: Plenum Press.

Denton, D. A. (1982). *The hunger for salt.* Berlin: Springer.

Denton, D. A., McKinley, M. J., Nelson, J. F., & Weisinger, R. S. (1977). Pregnancy, lactation and hormone induced mineral appetite. In Y. Katsuki, M. Sato, S. Takagi, & Y. Oomura (Eds.), *Food intake and chemical senses* (pp. 247–262). Tokyo: Japan Scientific Societies Press.

Denton, D. A., Shade, R., Zamarippa, F., Egan G., Blair-West, J., McKinley, M., et al. (1999). The correlation of regional blood flow (rCBF) and plasma sodium concentration during genesis and satiation of thirst. *Proceedings of the National Academy of Sciences, USA, 96,* 2532–2537.

De Smet, H. R., Menadue, M. F., Oliver, J. R., & Phillips, P. A. (2003). Increased thirst and vasopressin secretion after myocardial infarction in rats. *American Journal of Physiology, 285,* R1203–R1211.

Durr, J. A., Stamotsos, B., & Lindheimer, M. D. (1981). Osmoregulation durng pregnancy in the rat: Evidence of the resetting of the threshold for vasopressin secretion during gestation. *Journal of Clinical Investigation, 68,* 337–346.

Edwards, G. L., & Johnson, A. K. (1991). Enhanced drinking after excitotoxic lesions of the parabrachial nucleus in the rat. *American Journal of Physiology, 261,* R1039–R1044.

Edwards, G. L., & Ritter, R. C. (1982). Area postrema lesions increase drinking to angiotensin and extracellular dehydration. *Physiology and Behavior, 29,* 943–947.

Egan, G., Silk, T., Zammaripa, F., Williams, J., Federico, P., Cunnington, R., et al. (2003). Neural correlates of the emergence of consciousness of thirst. *Proceedings of the National Academy of Sciences, USA, 100,* 15241–15246.

Ehrlich, K. J., & Fitts, D. A. (1990). Atrial natriuretic peptide in the subfornical organ reduces drinking induced by angiotensin or in response to water deprivation. *Behavioral Neuroscience, 104,* 365–372.

Eng, R., & Miselis, R. R. (1981). Ploydipsia and abolition of angiotensin-induced drinking after transections of subfornical organ efferent projections in the rat. *Brain Research, 225,* 200–206.

Eslinger, P. J., & Damasio, A. R. (1985). Severe disturbance of higher cognition after bilateral frontal lobe ablation: Patient EVR. *Neurology, 35,* 1731–1741.

Ettenberg, A., & Camp, C. H. (1986). A partial reinforcement extinction effect in water-reinforced rats intermittently treated with haloperidol. *Pharmacology, Biochemistry and Behavior, 25,* 1231–1235.

Evered, M. D. (1992). Investigating the role of angiotensin II in thirst: Interactions between arterial pressure and the control of drinking. *Canadian Journal of Physiology and Pharmacology, 70,* 791–797.

Evered, M. D., & Mogenson, G. J. (1976). Regulatory and secondary water intake in rats with lesions of the zonz incerta. *American Journal of Physiology, 230,* 1049–1057.

Farrell, M. J., Zamarripa, F., Shade, R., Phillips, P. A., McKinley, M., Fox, P. T., et al. (in press). Effect of ageing on regional cerebral blood flow responses associated with osmotic thirst and its satiation by water drinking: A PET study. *Proceedings of the National Academy of Sciences, USA.*

Felix, D., & Schlegel, W. (1978). Angiotensin receptive neurons in the subfornical organ: Structure activity relations. *Brain Research, 149,* 107–116.

Ferrari, A. U., Radaelli, A., & Centola, M. (2003). Aging and the cardovascular system. *Journal of Applied Physiology, 95,* 2591–2597.

Figaro, M. K., & Mack, G. W. (1997). Regulation of fluid intake in dehydrated humans: Role of oropharyngeal stimulation. *American Journal of Physiology, 272,* R1740–R1746.

Findlay, A. L. R., Fitzsimons, J. T., & Kucharczyk, J. (1979). Dependence of spontaneous and angiotensin-induced drinking in the rat upon the oestrous cycle and ovarian hormones. *Journal of Endocrinology, 82,* 215–225.

Fisher, A. N., & Levitt, R. A. (1967). Drinking induced by carbachol: Thirst circuit or ventricular modification? *Science, 157,* 839–841.

Fitzsimons, J. T. (1961). Drinking by rats depleted of body fluid without increase in osmotic pressure. *Journal of Physiology, 159,* 297–309.

Fitzsimons, J. T. (1963). The effects of slow infusions of hypertonic solutions on drinking and drinking thresholds in rats. *Journal of Physiology, 167,* 344–354.

Fitzsimons, J. T. (1969). The role of a renal thirst factor in drinking induced by extracellular stimuli. *Journal of Physiology, 201,* 349–368.

Fitzsimons, J. T. (1979). *The physiology of thirst and sodium appetite.* Cambridge: Cambridge University Press.

Fitzsimons, J. T. (1998). Angiotensin, thirst and sodium appetite. *Physiological Reviews, 78,* 583–686.

Fitzsimons, J. T., & Elfont, R. M. (1982). Angiotensin does contribute to drinking induced by caval ligation in rat. *American Journal of Physiology, 243,* R558–R562.

Fitzsimons, J. T., & Moore-Gillon, M. J. (1980). Drinking and antidiuresis in response to reductions in venous return in the dog: Neural and endocrine mechanisms. *Journal of Physiology, 308,* 403–416.

Fitzsimons, J. T., & Setler, P. (1975). The relative importance of central nervous catecholaminergic and cholinergic mechanisms in drinking in response to angiotenein and other thirst stimuli. *Journal of Physiology, 250,* 613–631.

Freece, J. A., Van Bebber, J. E., Zierath, D. K., & Fitts, D. A. (2005). Subfornical organ disconnection alters Fos expression in the lamina terminalis, supraoptic nucleus, and area postrema after intragastric hypertonic NaCl. *American Journal of Physiology, 288,* R947–R955.

Fregly, M. J. (1980). Effect of chronic treatment with estrogen on the dipsogenic response of rats to angiotensin. *Pharmacology Biochemistry and Behavior, 12,* 131–136.

Fregly, M. J., Kelleher, D. L., & Greenleaf, J. E. (1981). Antidipsogenic effect of clonidine on angiotensin II-, hypertonic saline-, pilocarpine-, and dehydration-induced water intakes. *Brain Research Bulletin, 7,* 661–664.

Fregly, M. J., & Rowland, N. E. (1986). Role for ·2 adrenoceptors in experimentally-induced drinking in rats. In G. de Caro, A. N. Epstein, & M. Massi (Eds.), *The physiology of thirst and sodium appetite* (pp. 509–519). New York: Plenum Press.

Fregly, M. J., & Rowland, N. E. (1988). Augmentation of isoproterenol-induced drinking by acute treatment with certain dopaminergic agonists. *Physiology and Behavior, 44,* 473–481.

Gehring, W. J., & Taylor, S. F. (2004). When the going gets tough, the cingulate gets going. *Nature Neuroscience, 7,* 1285–1287.

Gibbs, J., Rolls, B. J., & Rolls, E. T. (1986). Preabsorptive and postabsorptive factors in termination of drinking in the rhesus monkey. In G. de Caro, A. N. Epstein, & M. Massi (Eds.), *The physiology of thirst and sodium appetite* (pp. 287–294). New York: Plenum Press.

Gilman, A. (1937). The relation between blood osmotic pressure, fluid distribution and voluntary water intake. *American Journal of Physiology, 120,* 323–328.

Giovannetti, S., Barsotti, G., Cupista, A., Morelli, E., Agostini, B., Posella, L., et al. (1994). Dipsogenic factors operating in chronic uremics on maintenance hemodialysis. *Nephron, 66,* 413–420.

Goldman, M. B., Robertson, G. L., Luchin, D. J., & Hedeker, D. (1996). The influence of polydipsia on water excretion in hyponatremic, polydipsic, schizophrenic patients. *Journal of Clinical and Endocrinology and Metabolism, 81,* 1465–1470.

Greer, M. A. (1955). Suggestive evidence of a primary "drinking center." *Proceedings of the Society of Experimental Biology, 89,* 59–62.

Grob, M., Trottier, J.-F., Drolet, G., & Mouginot, D. (2003). Characterization of the neurochemical content of neuronal populations of the lamina terminalis activated by acute hydromineral challenge. *Neuroscience, 122,* 247–257.

Grossman, S. P. (1960, July 29). Eating or drinking elicited by direct adrenergic or cholinergic stimulation of the lateral hypothalamus. *Science, 132,* 301–302.

Grossman, S. P. (1984). A reassessment of the brain mechanisms that control thirst. *Neuroscience Biobehavioral Review, 8,* 95–104.

Gu, G. B., & Simerly, R. B. (1997). Projections of the sexually dimorphic anteroventral periventricular nucleus in the female rat. *Journal of Comparative Neurology, 384,* 142–164.

Gutman, M. B., Ciriello, J., & Mogenson, G. J. (1988). Effects of plasma angiotensin: Pt. II. Hypernatremia on subfornical organ neurons. *American Journal of Physiology, 254,* R746–R754.

Haberich, F. J. (1971). Osmoreceptors in the portal circulation and their significance for the regulation of water balance. *Triangle, 10,* 123–130.

Hainsworth, F. R., Stricker, E. M., & Epstein, A. N. (1968). Water metabolism of rats in the heat. *American Journal of Physiology, 214,* 983–989.

Harvey, J. A., & Hunt, H. F. (1965). Effect of septal lesions on thirst in the rat as indicated by water consumption and operant responding for water reward. *Journal of Comparative and Physiological Psychology, 59,* 49–56.

Hattori, Y., Kasai, M., Uesugi, S., Kawata, M., & Yamashita, H. (1988). Atrial natriuretic polypeptide depresses angiotensin II-induced excitation of neurons in the rat subfornical organ in vitro. *Brain Research, 443,* 355–359.

Herbert, H., Moga, M. M., & Saper, C. B. (1991). Connections of the parabrachial nucleus with the nucleus of the solitary tract and medullary reticular formation in the rat. *Journal of Comparative Neurology, 293,* 540–580.

Herbert, J., Forsling, M. L., Howes, S. R., Stacey, P. M., & Shiers, H. M. (1992). Regional expression of *c-fos* antigen in the basal forebrain following intraventricular infusions of angiotensin and its modulation by drinking either water or saline. *Neuroscience, 51,* 857–882.

Hochstenbach, S. L., & Ciriello, J. (1996). Effect of lesions of forebrain circumventricular organs on c-fos expression in the central nervous system to plasma hypernatremia. *Brain Research, 713,* 17–28.

Hoffman, M. L., DenBleyker, M., Smith, J. C., & Stricker, E. M. (2005). Inhibition of thirst when dehydrated rats drink water or saline. *American Journal of Physiology, 290,* R1199–R1207.

Holmes, J. H., & Gregerson, M. I. (1950). Observations on drinking induced by hypertonic solutions. *American Journal of Physiology, 162,* 326–337.

Honda, E., Ono, K., Toyono, T., Kawano, H., Masuko, S., & Inenaga, K. (2003). Activation of muscarinic receptors in rat subfornical organ neurones. *Journal of Neuroendocrinology, 15,* 770–777.

Hosutt, J. A., Rowland, N., & Stricker, E. M. (1978). Impaired drinking responses of rats with lesions of the subfornical organ. *Journal of Comparative and Physiological Psychology, 95,* 104–113.

Illowski, B. P., & Kirch, D. G. (1988). Polydipsia and hyponatremia in psychiatric patients. *American Journal of Psychiatry, 145,* 675–683.

Itoh, H., Nakao, K., Yamada, T., Shirakami, G., Kangawa, K., Minamino, N., et al. (1988). Antidipsogenic activity of a novel peptide, "brain natriuretic peptide" in rats. *European Journal of Pharmacology, 150,* 193–196.

James, R. J. A., Irons, D. W., Holmes, C., Drewett, R. F., & Bayliss, P. H. (1995). Thirst induced by a suckling episode during breast feeding and its relation with plasma vasopressin, oxytocin and osmoregulation. *Clinical Endocrinology, 43,* 277–282.

Jewell, P. A., & Verney, E. B. (1957). An experimental attempt to determine the site of the neurohypohysial osmoreceptors in the dog. *Philosophical Transactions of the Royal Society. Series B, Biological Sciences, 240,* 197–324.

Johansen, J. P., Fields, H. L., & Manning, B. H. (2001). The affective component of pan in rodents: Direct evidence for a contribution of the anterior cingulate cortex. *Proceedings of the National Academy of Sciences, USA, 98,* 8077–8082.

Johnson, A. K., & Buggy, J. (1978). Periventricular preoptic-hypothalamus is vital for thirst and normal water economy. *American Journal of Physiology, 23,* R122–R129.

Johnson, A. K., Cunningham, J. T., & Thunhorst, R. L. (1996). Integrative role of the lamina terminalis in the regulation of cardiovascular and body fluid homeostasis. *Clinical and Experimental Pharmacology and Physiology, 23,* 183–191.

Johnson, A. K., & Thunhorst, R. L. (1997). The neuroendocrinoloy of thirst and salt appetite: Visceral sensory signals and mechanisms of central integration. *Frontiers in Neuroendocrinology, 18,* 292–353.

Jurzak, M., Schmid, H., & Gerstberger R. (1994). NADPH-diaphorase staining and NO-synthase immunoreactivity in circumventricular organs of the rat brain. In K. Pleschka & R. Gerstberger (Eds.), *Integrative and cellular aspects of autonomic functions: Temperature and osmoregulation* (pp. 451–459). Paris: John Libbey Eurotext.

Kadekaro, M., & Summy-Long, J. (2000). Centrally produced nitric oxide and the regulation of body fluid and blood pressure homeostasis. *Clinical and Experimental Pharmacology and Physiology, 27,* 450–459.

Kalra, P. R., Anker, S. D., & Coats, A. J. S. (2001). Water and sodium regulation in chronic heart failure: The role of natriuretic peptides and vasopressin. *Cardiovascular Research, 51,* 495–509.

Kaufman, S. (1984). Role of right atrial receptors in the control of drinking in the rat. *Journal of Physiology, 349,* 389–396.

Kawano, H., & Masuko, S. (1999). Synaptic contacts between nerve terminals originating from the ventrolateral medullary catecholaminergic area and median preoptic neurons projecting to the paraventricular hypothalamic nucleus. *Brain Research, 817,* 110–116.

Kelley, A. E., & Berridge, K. C. (2002). The neuroscience of natural rewards: Relevance to addictive drugs. *Journal of Neuroscience, 22,* 3306–3311.

Kenney, W. L., & Chiu, P. (2001). Influence of age on thirst and fluid intake. *Medical Science Sports Exercise, 33,* 1524–1532.

Kisley, L. R., Sakai, R. R., Ma, L. Y., & Fluharty, S. J. (1999). Ovarian steroid regulation of angiotensin II-induced water intake in the rat. *American Journal of Physiology, 276,* R90–R96.

Klingbeil, C. K., Brooks, V. L., Quillen, E. W., & Reid, I. A. (1991). Effect of baroreceptor denervation on stimulation of drinking by angiotensin II in conscious dogs. *American Journal of Physiology, 260,* E333–E337.

Kobashi, M., & Adachi, A. (1992). Effect of hepatic portal infusion of water on water intake by water-deprived rats. *Physiology and Behavior, 52,* 885–888.

Kolaj, M., Bai, D., & Renaud, L. P. (2004). GABA$_B$ receptor modification of rapid inhibitory and excitatory neurotransmission from the subfornical organ and other afferents tomedian preoptic nucleus neurons. *Journal of Neurophysiology, 92,* 111–122.

Kraly, F. S. (1991). Effects of eating on drinking. In D. J. Ramsay & D. A. Booth (Eds.), *Thirst: Physiological and psychological aspects* (pp. 296–312). London: Springer Verlag.

Kraly, F. S., Kim, Y. M., Dunham, L. M., & Tribuzio, R. A. (1995). Drinking after intragastric NaCl without increase in systemic plasma osmolality in rats. *American Journal of Physiology, 276,* R1085–R1092.

Kunii, K., Yamanaka, A., Nambu, T., Matsuzaki, I., Goto, K., & Sakurai, T. (1999). Orexins/hypocretins regulate drinking behaviour. *Brain Research, 842,* 256–261.

Lehr, D., Goldman, H. W., & Casner, P. (1973, December 7). Renin angiotensin role in thirst: Paradoxical enhancement of drinking by angiotensin converting enzyme inhibitor. *Science, 182,* 1031–1034.

Lenkei, Z., Palkovits, M., Corvol, P., & Llorens-Cortes, C. (1997). Expression of angiotensin type-1 (AT1) and type-2 (AT2) receptor mRNAs in the adult rat brain: A functional neuroanatomical review. *Frontiers in Neuroendocrinology, 18,* 383–439.

Liedtke, W. (2007). Role of TRPV ions channels in sensory transduction of osmotic stimuli in mammals. *Experimental Physiology, 92,* 507–512.

Lind, R. W., & Johnson, A. K. (1982). Subfornical organ-median preoptic connections and drinking and pressor responses to angiotensin II. *Journal of Neuroscience, 2,* 1043–1051.

Lind, R. W., Thunhorst, R. L., & Johnson, A. K. (1984). The subfornical organ and the integration of multiple factors in thirst. *Physiology and Behavior, 32,* 69–74.

Lynch, K. R., Hawelu-Johnson, C. L., & Guyenet, P. G. (1987). Localization of brain angiotensinogen mRNA by hybridization histochemistry. *Brain Research, 388,* 149–158.

Malmo, R. B., & Mundl, W. J. (1975). Osmosensitive neurons in the rat's preoptic area: Medial-lateral comparison. *Journal of Comparative and Physiological Psychology, 88,* 161–175.

Mangiapane, M. L., & Simpson, J. B. (1983). Drinking and pressor responses after acetylcholine injection into the subfornical organ. *American Journal of Physiology, 24,* R508–R513.

Mangiapane, M. L., Thrasher, T. N., Keil, L. C., Simpson, J. B., & Ganong, F. (1983). Deficits in drinking and vasopressin secretion after lesions of the nucleus medianus. *Neuroendocrinology, 37,* 73–77.

Mathai, M. L., Arnold, I., Febbraio, M. A., & McKinley, M. J. (2004). Central blockade of nitric oxide synthesis induces hyperthermia that is prevented by indomethacin in rats. *Journal of Thermal Biology, 29,* 401–405.

Mayberg, H. S., Liotti, M., Brannan, S. K., McGinnis, S., Mahurin, R. K., Jerabik, P. A., et al. (1999). Reciprocal limbic-cortical function and negative mood: Converging PET signals in depression and normal sadness. *American Journal of Psychiatry, 156,* 675–682.

Mayer, A. (1900). Variations de la tension osmotique du sang chez les animaux prives de liquids. *Comptes Rendus de la Société Biologie (Paris), 52,* 153–155.

McAllen, R. M., Pennington, G. L., & McKinley, M. J. (1990). Osmoresponsive units in sheep median preoptic nucleus. *American Journal of Physiology, 259,* R593–R600.

McDannald, M. A., Saddoris, M. P., Gallagher, M, & Holland, P. C. (2005). Lesions of orbitofrontal cortex impair rats' differential outcome expectancy learning but not conditioned stimulus-potentiated feeding. *Journal of Neuroscience, 25,* 4628–4632.

McKinley, M. J., Alexiou, T., Boon, W. M., Campbell, D. J., Denton, D. A., Dinicolantonio, R., et al. (2006). Osmoregulatory thirst in mice lacking angiotensin. *Proceedings of the Australian Neuroscience Society, 17,* 45.

McKinley, M. J., Allen, A. M., Clevers, J., Paxinos, G., & Mendelsohn, F. A. O. (1987). Angiotensin receptor binding in human hypothalamus: Autoradiographic localization. *Brain Research, 420,* 375–379.

McKinley, M. J., Badoer, E., & Oldfield, B. J. (1992). Intravenous angiotensin II induces Fos-immunoreactivity in circumventricular organs of the lamina terminalis. *Brain Research, 594,* 295–300.

McKinley, M. J., Blaine, E. H., & Denton, D. A. (1974). Brain osmoreceptors, cerebrospinal fluid electrolyte composition and thirst. *Brain Research, 70,* 532–537.

McKinley, M. J., Burns, P., Colvill, L. M., Oldfield, B. J., Wade, J. D., Weisinger, R. S., et al. (1997). Distribution of Fos immunoreactivity in the lamina terminalis and hypothalamus induced by centrally administered relaxin in conscious rats. *Journal of Neuroendocrinology, 9,* 431–438.

McKinley, M. J., Burns, P., Oldfield, B. J., Sunigawa, K., & Weisinger, R. S. (2004). Diabetic thirst: Osmoreceptor stimulation by hyperglycemia in streptozotocin-induced diabetic rats. *Appetite, 42,* 384.

McKinley, M. J., Denton, D. A., Coghlan, J. P., Harvey, R. B., McDougall, J. G., Rundgren, M., et al. (1987). Cerebral osmoregulation of renal sodium excretion: A response analogous to thirst and vasopressin release. *Canadian Journal of Physiology and Pharmacology, 65,* 1724–1729.

McKinley, M. J., Denton, D. A., Leksell, L. G., Mouw, D. R., Scoggins, B. A., Smith, M. H., et al. (1982). Osmoregulatory thirst in sheep is disrupted by ablation of the anterior wall of the optic recess. *Brain Research, 236,* 210–215.

McKinley, M. J., Denton, D. A., Thomas, C., Woods, R., & Mathai, M. L. (2006). Differential effects of aging on fluid intake in response to hypovolemia, hypertonicity and hormonal stimuli in hypertonicity and hormonal stimuli in Munich Wistar rats. *Proceedings of the National Academy of Sciences, USA, 103,* 3450–3455.

McKinley, M. J., Denton, D. A., & Weisinger, R. S. (1978). Sensors for thirst and antidiuresis: Osmoreceptors or CSF sodium detectors. *Brain Research, 141,* 89–103.

McKinley, M. J., Hards, D. K., & Oldfield, B. J. (1994). Identification of neural pathways activated in dehydrated rats by means of Fos-immunohistochemistry and neural tracing. *Brain Research, 653,* 305–314.

McKinley, M. J., Mathai, M. L., Pennington, G. L., Rundgren M., & Vivas, L. (1999). The effect of individual or combined ablation of the nuclear groups of the lamina terminalis on water drinking in sheep. *American Journal of Physiology, 276,* R673–R683.

Menani, J. V., Columbari, D. S. A., Beltz, T. G., Thunhorst, R. L., & Johnson, A. K. (1998). Salt appetite: Interaction of forebrain angiotensinergic and hindbrain serotonergic mechanisms. *Brain Research, 801,* 29–35.

Menani, J. V., & Johnson, A. K. (1995). Lateral parabrachial serotonergic mechanisms: Angiotensin-induced pressor and drinking responses. *American Journal of Physiology, 269,* R1044–R1049.

Michell, A. R. (1979). Water and electrolyte excretion during the oestrous cycle in sheep. *Quarterly Journal of Experimental Physiology, 64,* 79–88.

Miselis, R. R. (1981). The efferent projections of the subfornical organ of the rat: A circumventricular organ within a neural network subserving water balance. *Brain Research, 230,* 1–23.

Miselis, R. R., Weiss, M., & Shapiro, R. F. (1987). Modulation of the visceral neuraxis. In P. M. Gross (Ed.), *Circumventricular organs and body fluids* (Vol. III, pp. 143–162). Boca Raton: CRC Press.

Montani, J.-P., & Van Vliet, B. N. (2004). General physiology and pathophysiology of the renin-angiotensin system. In T. Unger & B. A. Scholkens (Eds.), *Handbook of experimental pharmacology* (Vol. 163, Angiotensin Vol. I, pp. 3–30). Berlin: Springer.

Murphy, T., & Samson, W. K. (1995). The novel vasoactive hormone, adrenomedullin, inhibits water drinking in the rat. *Endocrinology, 136,* 2459–2463.

Nava, F., Calapai, G., De Sarro, A., & Caputi, A. P. (1996). Interleukin-1 receptor antagonist does not reverse lipopolysaccharide-induced inhibition of water inake in rat. *European Journal of Pharmacology, 309,* 223–227.

Nava, F., & Carta, G. (2000). Repeated lipopolysaccharide administration produces tolerance to anorexia and fever but not to inhibition of thirst in rat. *International Journal of Immunopharmacology, 22,* 943–953.

Nissen, R., & Renaud, L. P. (1994). GABA receptor mediation of median preoptic nucleus-evoked inhibition of supraoptic neurosecretory neurones in rat. *Journal of Physiology, 479,* 207–216.

Noakes, T. D. (2003). Overconsumption of fluids by athletes. *British Medical Journal, 327,* 113–114.

Nothnagel, H. (1881). Durst und polydipsia. *Archiv fur pathologische Anatomie und Physiologie, 86,* 435–437.

Ohman, L. E., & Johnson, A. K. (1989). Brain stem mechanisms and the inhibition of angiotensin-induced drinking. *American Journal of Physiology, 256,* R264–R269.

Oldenburg, B., MacDonald, G. J., & Shelley, S. (1988). Controlled trial of enalapril inpatients with chronic fluid overload undergoing dialysis. *British Medical Journal, 296,* 1089–1091.

Oldendorf, W. H. (1971). Brain uptake of radiolabeled amino acids, amines, and hexoses after arterial injection. *American Journal of Physiology, 221,* 1629–1639.

Oldfield, B. J., Bicknell, R. J., McAllen, R. M., Weisinger, R. S., & McKinley, M. J. (1991). Intravenous hypertonic saline induces Fos immunoreactivity in neurons throughout the lamina terminalis. *Brain Research, 561,* 151–156.

Olivares, E. L., Costa-e-Sousa, R. H., & Cavalcante-Lima, H. R. (2003). Effect of electrolytic lesions of the dorsal raphe nucleus on water intake and sodium appetite. *Brazilian Journal of Medical Biological Research, 36,* 1709–1716.

Olsson, K. (1972). Dipsogenic effects of intracaotid infusions of various hypertosmolar solutions. *Acta Physiologica Scandinavica, 85,* 517–522.

O'Neill, T. P., & Brody, M. J. (1987). Role for the median preoptic nucleus in centrally evoked pressor responses. *American Journal of Physiology, 252,* R1165–R1172.

Osheroff, P. L., & Phillips, H. S. (1991). Autoradiographic localization of relaxin binding sites in rat brain. *Proceedings of the National Academy of Sciences, USA, 88,* 6413–6417.

Packer, M. (1992). The neurohumoral hypothesis: A theory to explain the mechanism of disease progression in heart failure. *Journal of the American College of Cardiology, 20,* 248–252.

Parry, L. J., Poterski, R. S., & Summerlee, A. J. (1994). Effects of relaxin on blood pressure and the release of vasopressin and oxytocin in anesthetised rats during pregnancy and lactation. *Biology of Reproduction, 50,* 622–628.

Peck, J. W., & Blass, E. M. (1975). Localization of thirst and antidiuretic osmoreceptors by intracranial injections in rats. *American Journal of Physiology, 228,* 1501–1509.

Peck, J. W., & Novin, D. (1971). Evidence that osmoreceptors mediating drinking are in the lateral preoptic area. *Journal of Comparative and Physiological Psychology, 74,* 134–147.

Penfield, W., & Faulk, M. E. (1955). The insula: Further observations on its function. *Brain, 78,* 445–470.

Penfield, W., & Jasper, H. (1954). *Epilepsy and the functional anatomy of the human brain.* Boston: Little, Brown.

Penfield, W., & Rasmussen, T. (1950). *The cerebral cortex of man.* New York: Macmillan.

Phillips, P. A., Rolls, B. J., Ledingham, J. G. G., Forsling, M. L., Morton, J. J., Crowe, M. J., et al. (1984). Reduced thirst after water deprivation in healthy elderly men. *New England Journal of Medicine, 311,* 753–759.

Phillips, P. A., Rolls, B. J., Ledingham, J. G. G., Morton, J. J., & Forsling, M. L. (1985). Angiotensin-induced thirst and vasopressin release in man. *Clinical Science, 68,* 669–674.

Quillen, E.W., Keil, L. C., & Reid, I. A. (1990). Effects of baroreceptor denervation on endocrine and drinking responses to caval constriction in dogs. *American Journal of Physiology, 259,* R618–R626.

Rabe, E. F. (1975). Relationship between absolute body deficits and fluid intake in the rat. *Journal of Comparative and Physiological Psychology, 89,* 468–477.

Raghavendra, V., Agrewala, J. N., & Kulkarni, S. K. (1999). Role of centrally administered melatonin and inhibitors of COX, and NOS in LPS-induced hyperthermia and adipsia. *Prostaglandins Leukotrienes Essential Fatty Acids, 60,* 249–253.

Ramsay, D. J., Rolls, B. J., & Wood, R. J. (1977). Body fluid changes which influence drinking in the water deprived rat. *Journal of Physiology, 266,* 453–469.

Rauch, M., Schmid, H., DeVente, J., & Simon, E. (1997). Electrophysiological and immunocytochemical evidence for a cGMP-mediated inhibition of subfornical organ neurons by nitric oxide. *Journal of Neuroscience, 17,* 363–371.

Ricardo, J. A. (1981). Efferent connections of the subthalamic region in the rat: Pt. II. The zona incerta. *Brain Research, 214,* 43–60.

Richter, C. P., & Barelare, B. (1938). Nutritional requirements of pregnant and lactating rats studied by self-selection method. *Endocrinology, 23,* 15–24.

Riediger, T., Rauch, M., & Schmid, H. A. (1999). Actions of amylin on subfornical organ neurons and on drinking behavior in rats. *American Journal of Physiology, 276,* R514–R521.

Robertson, G. L. (1989). Syndrome of inappropriate antidiuresis. *New England Journal of Medicine, 321,* 538–539.

Robinson, B. W., & Mishkin, M. (1966). Alimentary responses to forebrain stimulation in monkeys. *Experimental Brain Research, 4,* 330–366.

Rogers, P. W., & Kurtzman, N. A. (1973). Renal failure, uncontrollable thirst, and hyperreninaemia: Cessation of thirst with bilateral nephrectomy. *Journal of the American Medical Association, 225,* 1236–1238.

Rolls, E. T. (2000). The orbitofrontal cortex and rewaed. *Cerebral Cortex, 10,* 284–294.

Rosas-Arellano, M. P., Solano-Flores, L. P., & Ciriello, J. (1999). Co-localization of estrogen and angiotensin receptors within subfornical organ neurons. *Brain Research, 837,* 254–262.

Rundgren, M., & Fyhrquist, F. (1978). A study of permanent adipsia induced by medial forebrain lesions. *Acta Physiologica Scandinavica, 103,* 463–467.

Sagar, S. M., Sharp, F. R., & Curran, T. (1988, June 3). Expression of c-fos protein in brain: Metabolic mapping at the cellular level. *Science, 240,* 1328–1331.

Samson, W. K., Skala, K., Huang, F. L. S., Gluntz, S., Alexander, B., & Gomez-Sanchez, C. E. (1991). Central nervous system of endothelin-3 to inhibit water drinking in the rat. *Brain Research, 539,* 347–351.

Samson, W. K., White, M. M., Price, C., & Ferguson, A. V. (2007). Obestatin acts in the brain to inhibit thirst. *American Journal of Physiology, 292,* R637–R643.

Saper, C. B. (2002). The central autonomic nervous system: Conscious visceral perception and autonomic pattern generation. *Annual Review of Neuroscience, 25,* 433–469.

Saper, C. B., & Levisohn, D. (1983). Afferent connections of the median preoptic nucleus in the rat: Anatomical evidence for a cardiovascular integrative mechanism in the anteroventral third ventricular (AV3V) region. *Brain Research, 288,* 21–31.

Schreihofer, A. M., Anderson, B. K., Schiltz, J. C., Xu, L., Sved, A. F., & Stricker, E. M. (1999). Thirst and salt appetite elicited by hypovolemia in rats with chronic lesions of the nucleus of the solitary tract. *American Journal of Physiology, 276,* R251–R258.

Setler, P. (1973). The role of catecholamines in thirst. In A. N. Epstein, H. R. Kissileff, & E. Stellar (Eds.), *The neuropsychology of thirst: New findings and advances in concepts* (pp. 279–291). Washington, DC: Winston.

Simpson, J. B., Epstein, A. N., & Camardo, J. S. (1978). Localization of receptors for the dipsogenic action of angiotensin II in the subfornical organ of the rat. *Journal of Comparative and Physiological Psychology, 92,* 581–608.

Simpson, J. B., & Routtenberg, A. (1973). Subfornical organ: Site of dipsogenic action of angiotensin II. *Science, 181,* 1172–1175.

Sinnayah, P., Burns, P., Wade, J., Weisinger, R. S., & McKinley, M. J. (1999). Water drinking in rats resulting from intravenous relaxin and its modification by other dipsogenic factors. *Endocrinology, 140,* 5082–5086.

Slavin, A., & McKinley, M. J. (1989). [The physiology and anatomy of the area postrema of the sheep]Unpublished observations.

Smardencas, A, & McKinley, M. J. (1994). unpublished observations

Smith, D., Moore, K., Tormey, W., Bayliss, P. H., & Thompson, C. J. (2004). Downward resetting of the osmotic threshold for thirst in patients with SIADH. *American Journal of Physiology, 287,* E1019–E1023.

Smith, G. P., & Jerome, C. (1983). Effects on total and selective vagotomies on water intake in rats. *Journal of the Autonomic Nervous System, 9,* 259–271.

Somponpun, S. J., Johnson, A. K., Beltz, T., & Sladek, C. D. (2004). Estrogen receptor-alpha expression in osmosensitive elements of the lamina terminalis: Regulation by hypertonicity. *American Journal of Physiology, 287,* R661–R669.

Speth, R. C., Smith, M. S., & Grove, K. L. (2002). Brain angiotensinergic mediation of enhanced water consumption in lactating rats. *American Journal of Physiology, 282,* R695–R701.

Stratford, T. R., & Wirtshafter, D. (2000). Forebrain lesions differentially affect drinking eleicited by dipsogenic challenges and injections of muscimol into the median raphe nucleus. *Behavioral Neuroscience, 114,* 760–771.

Stricker, E. M. (1966). Extracellular fluid volume and thirst. *American Journal of Physiology, 211,* 232–238.

Stricker, E. M., Callahan, J. B., Huang, W., & Sved, A. F. (2002). Early osmoregulatory stimulation of neurohypohysial hormone secretion and thirst after gastric NaCl loads. *American Journal of Physiology, 282,* R1710–R1717.

Stricker, E. M., Swerdloff, A. F., & Zigmond, M. J. (1978). Intrahypothalamic injections of kainic acid produce feeding and drinking deficits in rat. *Brain Research, 158,* 470–473.

Sullivan, M. J., Cunningham, J. T., Mazzella, D., Allen, A. M., Nissen, R., & Renaud, L. P. (2003). Lesions of the diagonal band of Broca enhance drinking in the rat. *Journal of Neuroendocrinology, 15,* 907–915.

Summy-Long, J. Y., Keil, L. C., Deen, K., Rosella, L., & Severs, W. B. (1981). Endogenous opioid peptide inhibition of the central action of angiotensin. *Journal of Pharmacology and Experimental Therapeutics, 217*, 619–629.

Sunn, N., Egli, M., Burazin, T., Burns, P., Colvill, L., Davern, P., et al. (2002). Circulating relaxin acts on the subfornical organ to stimulate water drinking in the rat. *Proceedings of the National Academy of Sciences, USA, 99*, 1701–1706.

Swanson, L. W., & Sharpe, L. G. (1973). Centrally induced drinking: Comparison of angiotensin II- and carbachol-sensitive sites in rats. *American Journal of Physiology, 225*, 566–573.

Szczepanska-Sadowska, E., Sobocinska, J., & Kozlowski, S. (1979). Thirst and renal excretion of water and electrolytes during pyrogen fever in dogs. *Archives of the International Physiologie Biochimie, 87*, 673–686.

Szczepanska-Sadowska, E., Sobocinska, J., & Sadowski, S. (1982). Central dipsogenic effect of vasopressin. *American Journal of Physiology, 242*, R372–R379.

Taheri, S., Murphy, K., Cohen, M., Sujkovic, E., Kennedt, A., Dhillo, W., et al. (2002). The effects of centrally administered apelin-13 on food intake, water intake and pituitary hormone release in rats. *Biochemical Biophysical Research Communication, 291*, 1208–1212.

Takamata, A., Mack, G. W., Gillen, C. M., Jozsi, A. C., & Nadel, E. R. (1995). Osmoregulatory modulation of thermal sweating in humans: Reflex effects of drinking. *American Journal of Physiology, 268*, R414–R442.

Takamata, A., Mack, G. W., Stachenfeld, N. S., & Nadel, E. R. (1995). Body temperature modification of osmotically induced vasopressin secretion and thirst in humans. *American Journal of Physiology, 269*, R874–R880.

Tanaka, J., Hayashi, Y., Shimamune, S., Hori, K., & Nomura, H. (1997). Subfornical efferents enhance extracellular noradrenaline concentration in the median preoptic nucleus area of rats. *Neuroscience Letters, 230*, 171–174.

Tanaka, J., Miyakubo, H., Fujisawa, S., & Nomura, M. (2003). Reduced dipsogenic response to angiotensin II activation of subfornical organ projections to the median preoptic nucleus in estrogen-treated rats. *Experimental Neurology, 179*, 83–89.

Tanaka, J., Miyakubo, H., Okamura, T., Sakamaki, K., & Hayashi, Y. (2001). Estrogen decreases the responsiveness of subfornical organ neurons projecting to the hypothalamic paraventricular nucleus to angiotensin II in female rats. *Neuroscience Letters, 307*, 155–158.

Teitelbaum, P., & Epstein, A. N. (1962). The lateral hypothalamic syndrome: Recovery of feeding and drinking after lateral hypothalamic lesions. *Psychological Review, 69*, 74–90.

Thompson, C. J., & Bayliss, P. H. (1987). Thirst in diabetes insipidus: Clinical relevance of quantitative assessment. *Quarterly Journal of Medicine, 65*, 853–862.

Thompson, C. J., Edwards, C. R., & Bayliss, P. H. (1991). Osmotic and non-osmotic regulation of thirst and vasopressin secretion in patients with compulsive water drinking. *Clinical Endocrinology, 35*, 221–228.

Thornton, S. N., & Fitzsimons, J. T. (1995). The effects of centrally administered porcine relaxin on drinking behaviour in male and female rats. *Journal of Neuroendocrinology, 7*, 165–170.

Thrasher, T. N., Keenan, C. R., & Ramsay, D. (1999). Cardiovascular afferent signals and drinking in response to hypotension in dogs. *American Journal of Physiology, 277*, R795–R801.

Thrasher, T. N., Keil, L. C., & Ramsay, D. J. (1982a). Hemodynamic, hormonal, and drinking responses to reduced venous return in the dog. *American Journal of Physiology, 243*, R354–R362.

Thrasher, T. N., Keil, L. C., & Ramsay, D. (1982b). Lesions of the organum vasculosum of the lamina terminalis (OVLT) attenuate osmotically-induced drinking and vasopressin secretion in the dog. *Endocrinology, 110*, 1837–1839.

Thrasher, T. N., Nistal-Herrera, J. F., Keil, L. C., & Ramsay, D. J. (1981). Satiety and inhibition of vasopressin secretion after drinking in dehydrated dogs. *American Journal of Physiology, 240*, E394–E401.

Thrasher, T. N., Simpson, J. B., & Ramsay, D. J. (1982). Lesions of the subfornical organ block angiotensin-induced drinking in the dog. *Neuroendocrinology, 35*, 68–72.

Thunhorst, R. L., Fitts, D. A., & Simpson, J. B. (1989). Angiotensin-converting enzyme in subfornical organ mediates captopril- induced drinking. *Behavioral Neuroscience, 103*, 1302–1310.

Thunhorst, R. L., & Johnson, A. K. (2003). Thirst and salt appetite responses in young and old brown Norway rats. *American Journal of Physiology, 284*, R417–R327.

Towbin, E. J. (1949). Gastrc distention as a factor in the satiation of thirstin esophagostomized dogs. *American Journal of Physiology, 159*, 533–541.

Travis, K. A., & Johnson, A. K. (1993). In vitro sensitivity of median preoptic neurons to angiotensin II, osmotic pressure, and temperature. *American Journal of Physiology, 264*, R1200–R1205.

Ungerstedt, U. (1971). Adipsia and aphagia after 6-hydroxydopamine induced degeneration of the nigro-striatal dopamine system. *Acta Physiologica Scandinavica, 367*, 95–122.

Valtin, H. (2002). "Drink at least eight glasses of water a day." Really? Is there scientific evidence for "8 × 8"? *American Journal of Physiology, 283*, R993–R1004.

van Gaalen, M. M., Stenzel-Poore, M. P., Holsboer, F., & Steckler, T. (2002). Effects of transgenic overproduction of CRH on anxiety-like behaviour. *European Journal of Neuroscience, 15*, 2007–2015.

Verbalis, J., Goldsmith, S. R., Greenberg, A., Schrier, R. W., & Sterns, R. H. (2007). Hyponatremia treatment guidelines: Expert panel recommendations. *American Journal of Medicine, 120*, S1–S21.

Verney, E. B. (1947). The antidiuretic hormone and factors which determine its release. *Proceedings of the Royal Society, B, 135*, 25–106.

Vivas, L., Chiaraviglio, E., & Carrer, H. F. (1990). Rat organum vasculosum laminae terminalis in vitro: Responses to changes in sodium concentration. *Brain Research, 519*, 294–300.

Wang, K., & Evered, M. D. (1993). Endotoxin stimulates drinking in rat without changing dehydrational signals controlling thirst. *American Journal of Physiology, 265*, R1043–R1051.

Wang, T., & Edwards, G. L. (1997). Differential effects of dorsomedial medulla lesion size on ingestive behavior in rats. *American Journal of Physiology, 273*, R1299–R1308.

Weisinger, R. S., Burns, P., Eddie, L. W., & Wintour, E. M. (1993). Relaxin alters the plasma osmolality-arginine vasopressin relationship in the rat. *Journal of Endocrinology, 137*, 505–510.

Wilson, W. L., Roques, B. P., Llorens-Cortes, C., Speth, R. C., Harding, J. W., & Wright, J. W. (2005). Roles of brain angiotensins II and III in thirst and sodium appetite. *Brain Research, 1060*, 108–117.

Winn, P., Tarbuck, A., & Dunnett, S. B. (1984). Ibotenic acid lesions of the lateral hypothalamus: Comparison with the electrolytic syndrome. *Neuroscience, 12*, 225–240.

Wise, R. A. (2002). Brain reward circuitry: Insights from unsensed incentives. *Neuron, 36*, 229–240.

Wislocki, G. B., & Leduc, E. H. (1952). Vital staining of the hematoencephalic barrier by silver nitrate and trypan blue, and cytological comparisons of the neurohypophysis, pineal body, area postrema, intercolumnar tubercle and supraoptic crest. *Journal of Comparative Neurology, 96*, 371–414.

Wolf, A. V. (1950). Osmometric analysis of thirst in man and dog. *American Journal of Physiology, 161*, 75–86.

Wolf, A. V. (1958). *Thirst: Physiology of the urge to drink and problems of water lack.* Springfield, IL: Charles C Thomas.

Wood, R. J., Maddison, S., Rolls, E. T., Rolls, B. J., & Gibbs, J. (1980). Drinking in rhesus monkeys: Roles of presystemic and systemic factors in control of drinking. *Journal of Comparative and Physiological Psychology, 94,* 1135–1148.

Wookey, P. J., Cao, Z. & Cooper, M.E. (1998). Interaction of the renal amylin and renin-angiotensin system in animal models of diabetes and hypertension. *Mineral and Electrolyte Metabolism, 24,* 389–399.

Wright, J. W., Morseth, S. L., Abhold, R. H., & Harding, J. W. (1985). Pressor action and dipsogenicity induced by angiotensin: Pts. II & III in rats. *American Journal of Physiology, 249,* R514–R521.

Xu, D. S. H., Honda, E., Ono, K., & Inenaga, K. (2001). Muscarinic modulation of GABAergic transmission to neurons in the rat subfornical organ. *American Journal of Physiology, 280,* R1657–R1664.

Xu, J., Pekarek, E., Ge, J., & Yao, J. (2001). Functional relationship between subfornical organ cholinergic stimulation and cellular activation in the hypothalamus and AV3V region. *Brain Research, 922,* 191–200.

Xu, Z., & Herbert, J. (1998). Effects of intracerebroventricular dizocilpine (MK801) on dehydration-induced dipsogenic responses, plasma vasopressin and c-Fos expression in the rat forebrain. *Brain Research, 784,* 91–99.

Xu, Z., & Johnson, A. K. (1998). Non-NMDA receptor antagonist-induced drinking in rat. *Brain Research, 808,* 124–127.

Xu, Z., Lane, J. M., Zhu, B., & Herbert, J. (1997). Dizocilpine maleate an N-methyl-D-aspartate antagonist inhibits dipsogenic reponses and C-Fos expression induced by intracerebroventricular infusion of angiotensin Pt. II. *Neuroscience, 78,* 203–214.

Zabik, J. E., Sprague, J. E., & Odio, M. (1993). Interactive dopaminergic and noradrenergic systems in the regulation of thirst in the rat. *Physiology and Behavior, 54,* 29–33.

Zardetto-Smith, A. M., & Johnson, A. K. (1995). Chemical topography of efferent projections from the median preoptic nucleus to pontine monoaminergic groups in the rat. *Neuroscience Letters, 199,* 215–219.

Zerbe, R. L., & Robertson, G. L. (1983). Osmoregulation of thirst and vasopressin secretion in human subjects: Effect of various solutes. *American Journal of Physiology, 244,* E607–E614.

Zhao, S., Malmgren, C. H., Shanks, R. D., & Sherwood, O. D. (1985). Monclonal antibodies specific for rat relaxin: Pt. VII. Passive immunization with monoclonal antibodies throughout the second half of pregnancy reduces water consumption in rats. *Endocrinology, 136,* 1892–1897.

Zimmerman, M. B., Blaine, E. H., & Stricker, E. M. (1981, January 30). Water intake in hypovolemic sheep: Effects of crushing the left atrial appendage. *Science, 211,* 489–491.

Chapter 36

Central Theories of Motivation and Emotion

NEIL McNAUGHTON AND PHILIP J. CORR

The concept of emotion has aroused extreme theoretical positions: from Skinner's (1953) denouncement of it as a muddle-minded causal fiction to the view that it is fundamental to the whole of psychology (Panksepp, 1998). Although it is more than 120 years since William James (1884) asked, "What is an emotion?" the question proved so difficult to answer that for a long period the word *emotion* virtually disappeared from psychology textbooks and even from more specialized books on learning or cognition. For those with a strongly behaviorist perspective, there might seem to be no reason to regret this; nor, indeed, to concern yourself with theories, central or otherwise, of emotion and motivation. For those focusing on cognitive processes also, motivation and emotion may seem peripheral. However, we believe that behavioral observations can best be integrated, and cognitive processes best understood, if we see behavior as the result of activation of one or more of a set of distinct hierarchically organized systems in the brain, where each system has evolved under pressure from a different specific class of adaptive requirements. Critically, we believe we can identify the resultant emotion, and associated motivation, with the general adaptive function that defines a class of behaviors even when the specific behaviors produced differ across occasions or species. By this route, we can achieve theoretical integration along the phylogenetic scale. The emotion systems controlling such behaviors, and their interaction with cognitive processes, such as working memory, have now become the subject of intense and detailed study (LeDoux, 1993).

These adaptation-specific (emotional) systems are also connected with two general systems that control approach and avoidance motivations, respectively—as well as a third system that resolves conflicts between these motivations. In this context, *motivation* is an ambiguous term. A motivation (e.g., thirst) is specific and distinct from other motivations (e.g., hunger). But the specificity is most obvious in terms of elicited behavior and, when we talk about motivation rather than emotion, we are most often thinking of it in terms of general approach and avoidance tendencies, or positive and negative reinforcement, ignoring the specific nature of the reinforcer. Further, it is variation in the sensitivities of the systems that control positive and negative affect generally that appears to make the greatest contribution to human personality and to the risk of psychopathology—areas of human psychology where we clearly see the importance, or at least the prominence, of emotion and motivation.

In this chapter, we present emotion as a cluster of reactions, including motivation, that are linked to specific classes of affordances (the aspects of an object or situation that make certain actions available) of stimuli in the world—where both the nature of the external stimulus and the animal's internal state combine to determine the precise affordance at any particular point in time. In the process, it will be necessary to consider neural plasticity resulting from:

- *Simple association:* Where no specialized reinforcer is required to generate plasticity and where behavior undergoes relatively little modification but engages in stimulus substitution;
- *Stimulus-reinforcer pairing:* Where the result will often be observationally classical conditioning, but where response to the conditional stimulus may not be the same as those to the unconditional stimulus, and where the result can also be observationally instrumental conditioning; and
- *Stimulus-response-reinforcer pairings:* Where the result will be observationally instrumental conditioning.

Particularly in this latter case, learning itself is initially associated with strong emotional reactions but well-learned responding need not be. Thus, there is a strong link between emotion and motivation (with the latter apparently embedded in the former). But, emotional reactions have many semi- or actually independent parts and so, at the limit, all that may apparently be left is a motivation. The relation between motivation and emotion, as linguistic terms, may be murky but, as we shall see, the phenomenology, and the use of the terms, can be anchored through central (neurally based) theories.

VALUE OF CENTRAL (NEURALLY BASED) THEORIES

Recently, rather than being the topic that cannot be named, *emotion* (often without any definition of the term) has become a focus of study of a wide variety of phenomena in behavioral neuroscience. But there is still no consensus as to what an emotion *is* (and, as we shall see, the term may not refer to any single coherent internal entity). Motivation is also not clearly defined. The root of both words implies that the construct being referred to is something that produces movement—and yet most psychologists contrast emotion with motivation. Despite this, it is difficult to think of motivationally significant stimuli that are not characterized by the capacity to elicit emotion. In this chapter, we hope to show that a neuroscientific approach can clarify the nature of emotion, motivation, drive, and related constructs in ways that, if not impossible for a purely behaviorist approach, are at least very difficult if all that is measured is behavior.

The focus of this chapter on *central* theories of motivation and emotion is to a large extent predicated on taking a neuroscientific approach. Behaviorally-based theories of, for example, a *central motivational state* have been proposed in the past (Bindra, 1969). However, the dissection of the parts of which emotional and motivational reactions are composed and the linking of those parts into coherent, predictive theory is very difficult with purely behavioral methodologies. By contrast, a neuroscientist can, often literally, dissect classes of behavior and their control systems. They can also do so without first defining, or even proving the existence of, the higher order entity that they are dissecting. If a particular drug or brain lesion changes one set of behaviors, but not another, then clearly these sets represent different functional classes. That said, proper behavioral analysis will also then be required to determine the functional nature of the classes that have been so separated.

Neurally grounded theories of emotion and motivation have the key advantage, then, that they are anchored in specific anatomically identifiable systems. Their accounts do not depend on the superficial characters of behaviors and, indeed, can treat superficially quite different behaviors in different species as homologous. Neural homology and evolutionary (functional) homology, therefore, go hand in hand. When one is discerned, the other can usually be discovered—and vice versa. Evolutionary (and thus psychological function) become, then, things that must be extracted from the nature of known neural systems. With this approach, the definition of a psychological construct should map to a specific aspect of a coherent neural and functional system. In some cases, achieving this mapping requires elimination of an older psychological term and creation of a new one.

However, neural analysis cannot proceed by itself. While it can anchor and dissect constructs derived from the experimental analysis of behavior and from ethological analysis, the brain is so complex that, without preliminary behavioral analysis, functional systems cannot easily be identified. Neural analysis of circuits that show lateral inhibition, for example, allows explanation of a wide range of sensory illusions—including those where the presence of lateral inhibition in the relevant circuits is inferred rather than directly measured. However, one could not have easily predicted any of these illusions (or any aspect of our experience of "normal" perception) from the simple observation of lateral inhibition at the neural level.

So, central theories of emotion and motivation are the result of continuous interaction between behavioral and neuroscientific approaches. The neuroscientist provides anchors and mechanisms for genuine central (nervous system) theories of motivation and emotion; but, when these theories are properly developed, they are also central theories from a more psychological perspective. The patterns of activity in their higher order neural elements are central cognitive and emotional states. The behavioral neuroscientist, then, can integrate behavioral observations in terms of higher order internal states (something that all but the most radical behaviourist would see as desirable), but does so in terms of direct measures of those central states and so avoids the problems (which drove the development of the radical behaviourist philosophy) of inferring specific complex central states solely from patterns of behavior or, worse, introspection.

Perhaps the most important feature of central theories of motivation and emotion for higher-level psychological analysis is one that is usually implicit rather than explicit at the level of neuroscientific analysis. Central motivational-emotional states need to be viewed at the neural level as complex compounds. This is true in two senses. On the one hand, they are complexes of emotional reactions and motivation: Initial elicitation of emotional reactions also generates motivation; but, particularly with well-learned responses, motivation can drive behavior in the absence of major emotional reactions. On the other hand, an emotion can be the result of parallel independent processes rather than of output from a single central control system. It will be seen, later, that current central theories share a tendency to see the critical elements of neural/cognitive processing as "goals." Neither purely cognitive nor purely emotional/motivational attributes are given primacy; and simple stimulus-response reactions are rejected. The key drivers of behavior are seen as cognitive-emotional compounds (Hinde, 1998).

ROAD MAP TO CENTRAL THEORIES OF EMOTION AND MOTIVATION

We start with the esoteric and microscopic. We look at the bits and pieces from which evolution has formed emotions and motivations. We then move to the general, the basic reinforcement systems through which the stimuli that elicit highly specific "fixed action patterns" can, through learning, shape general, flexible, emotion-independent behavior. We then compare and contrast some current central theories of emotion and motivation that amalgamate these specific and general aspects of behavioral control. Finally, we indulge ourselves—and hopefully show that our previous dry, didactic analysis has significant mundane applications—by looking at some possibly unexpected implications of current central theories.

EMOTION, MOTIVATION, AND EVOLUTION

The behavioral neuroscientist thinks in terms of specific neural networks that deliver, often complex, patterns of behavior in response to appropriate environmental circumstance. Such networks cannot appear in evolution or development fully formed. They must result from progressive, incremental changes. In evolution, these changes occur as the result of random mutations interacting with selection pressures. As mentioned earlier, we would equate a specific emotion with the nature of the consistent selection pressure (functional requirement) that has driven the evolution of a set of reactions. But this means that the underlying control of behaviors (and other, e.g., autonomic, reactions) need not map simply to their superficial organization.

Evolution and "Rules of Thumb" as a Problem for Behavioral Analysis

The selection pressure driving evolution can be understood in terms of models such as those of optimal foraging theory. These are theoretical analyses that determine the behavioral rules required to maximize such things as the amount of food that an animal can obtain given specific starting assumptions about the environmental constraints (McNamara & Houston, 1980). It should be noted that these analyses are not predictions as to the rules that an animal will use, but define the boundary conditions toward which an animal should evolve if there is sufficient mutation and if selection of advantageous mutations is not blocked in some way.

The important concept here is that the animal can use rules of thumb (ROT) of a relatively simple sort to achieve behavior, under normal ecological conditions, that

approaches optimality—but where, in phylogenetically unusual conditions, responding may be suboptimal. For example, the parasite *Nemeritis canescens* "allocates its searching time in relation to host density approximately as predicted by an optimal foraging model [but] the decision rule used by *Nemeritis* . . . is a simple mechanism based on habituation to host scent—a far cry from the Lagrange multipliers and Newton's iterative approximations used by the theorist to solve the problem" (Krebs, Stephens, & Sutherland, 1983, p. 188).

ROT originate because, in the absence of any adaptive behavior, any mutation that results in any increase in adaptive value, however limited, will be selected. A later mutation can then provide a further increase in adaptive value—and so on. The result is that emotional control mechanisms may involve both serial and parallel ROT. In some cases, specific ROT may produce conflicting responses to the same stimulus (freezing and escape when faced with a threat, for example). These present no problem for behavior analysis as the distinct behaviors can be analyzed separately. In other cases, specific ROT may not conflict but may nonetheless fulfill quite different functions (increased blood-clotting factor is only required if escape is not successful). Again, because the responses are different, they can be identified as such and analyzed separately. The critical problem for behavior analysis is that in some cases multiple ROT can deliver essentially the same superficial behavior. They then provide the appearance, but not actuality, of a single generalized pattern of adaptive responding resulting from the application of a single, higher order, functional rule. This is exemplified by the partial reinforcement extinction effect.

The Partial Reinforcement Extinction Effect and Serial ROT

The partial reinforcement extinction effect (PREE) is a greater persistence of responding in extinction after prior training on partial (intermittent) reinforcement than after prior training with continuous (consistent) reinforcement. It is one of the more reliable phenomena in behavioral analysis. McNamara and Houston (1980) analyzed the general problem of how long to persist when responses no longer yield rewards. They looked at the specific case (which occurs with extinction of any positively reinforced response) of a number of initial responses that are rewarded with some probability p that are followed by a number of later responses that deliver no reward. The response is assumed to have some cost (e.g., loss of energy in making the response).

Absolute optimality (which cannot be achieved in the real world without precognition) is to cease responding as soon as reward is no longer available. The theoretical optimality problem is, then, to determine the rule that defines the point when an animal should decide that reward has actually become unavailable rather than the alternative possibility that it is faced with an unusually long run of non-rewarded responses in a sequence with average probability *p*. The precise answer to this question depends on the cost of responding and the value of *p*. Under realistic conditions, the value of *p* is not known and so it must be estimated from the pattern of rewards. Further *p*—and reward value and even cost value—are likely to vary from response to response. This presents a highly complex set of adaptive requirements. However, it turns out that "regardless of the exact [values of these parameters], the optimal policy for this sort of problem involves persisting for far more trials in the face of failure if [the original] *p* [of reward] is low. This provides an explanation of the PREE in terms of optimality theory" (McNamara & Houston, 1980, p. 687).

The explanation of the PREE by optimality theory is not a mechanistic explanation. It is, rather, a description of the general functional requirements that provide a background against which any mechanism that results in persistent responding will be selected. It is not a prediction as to how an animal will actually solve the problem. Further, it does not give us any insight into what ROT the animal uses; whether more than one ROT is required; or even whether extinction and resistance to extinction are derived from the same ROT. This is where attempts to determine the central mechanisms underlying the PREE provide some surprising answers.

Behavioral analysis of the PREE suggested that it could depend on simple associative effects (Sutherland, 1966), including those based on conditioning to the after-effects of reward and nonreward (Capaldi, 1967) or, alternatively, could involve more emotionally mediated effects resulting from the generation, by nonreward, of frustration (Amsel, 1992). Consistent with the idea that independent ROT can control apparently similar behavior under different conditions, the PREE is differentially sensitive to drugs. With short inter-trials intervals (when associative explanations appear to explain the behavioral phenomena best) the PREE is not sensitive to anxiolytic drugs; whereas at long inter-trial intervals (when frustration appears to explain the behavioral phenomena best) the PREE can be essentially eliminated by anxiolytic drugs (Feldon, Guillamon, Gray, De Wit, & McNaughton, 1979; Ziff & Capaldi, 1971).

However, if we ask about the psychological nature of the neural systems specifically affected by these drugs, we discover some interesting properties of the processes involved.

Emotional explanations of the PREE have often focused on counterconditioning—the reduction in negative affective value when negative stimuli are paired with positive ones. Anxiolytic drugs do not reduce counterconditioning (McNaughton & Gray, 1983). The drugs appear, instead, to reduce a nonassociative "toughening up" process (McNaughton, 1989b, chap. 7). Further, although the drugs affect both extinction (which could be viewed as dependent on conditioned frustration) and the PREE (which could be viewed as dependent on toughening up to the experience of conditioned frustration) in ways that could seem to depend simply on changes in sensitivity to the emotional experience of conditioned frustration, it turns out that extinction and the PREE depend on quite distinct neural systems and are, in a sense, unrelated to each other (Gray & McNaughton, 2000, appendix 9, table 1). Extinction in continuously reinforced rats is retarded by fiber-sparing lesions of the hippocampus proper, which do not reduce the PREE. Conversely, extinction in continuously reinforced rats is unaffected by lesion of the pathway connecting the subiculum of the hippocampus to the nucleus accumbens but these same lesions abolish the PREE.

Thus, both extinction and the PREE each appear to depend on a number of mechanisms (each one based on a particular ROT) and, in at least some cases, the mechanisms delivering extinction are quite distinct from those delivering the PREE. We thus have evidence for a variety of parallel ROT delivering adaptive extinction responding under a variety of situational circumstances (in particular, varying schedules of reward and reward omission).

Separation Anxiety and Parallel ROT

In one sense, the idea of parallel ROT—that is parallel systems concurrently activated—seems trivial. Autonomic and skeletal reactions, for example, must have evolved separately and are certainly represented in separate parts of the brain once we get "below" command centers such as the periaqueductal grey (Bandler, Keay, Floyd, & Price, 2000; Bandler, Price, & Keay, 2000). However, this issue is only trivial if a single command center controls both aspects of output. At least in the case of separation anxiety, this is not the case.

Separation anxiety is clearly identifiable, both by the means of producing it (removal of the primary caregiver, usually the mother) and by its characteristic pattern of autonomic and behavioral changes. It can be seen, in much the same form, in human children and the young of other mammals, such as rats, dogs, and primates. When the "reaction is beyond that expected for the child's developmental level," it becomes Separation Anxiety Disorder (American Psychiatric Association, 1987).

The behavioral and autonomic components of this emotion give the appearance of joint outputs from a single command center—and, if either output were missing, the result would not be what is generally recognized as separation anxiety. However, it has been shown that, in rats, the behavioral reactions (locomotion, grooming, defecation, and urination elicited by a novel environment) can be eliminated by the presence of a nonlactating foster mother, whereas the autonomic reaction (a reduction in heart rate) can be eliminated by regular feeding with milk—but not, in either case, vice versa (Hofer, 1972). Thus, the two effector aspects of the one emotion can be doubly dissociated in the laboratory.

It appears that rather than available stimuli each activating a single cognitive center (detecting, say, threat in general), it is possible that each recognizable aspect of an emotion could result from a different aspect of the available stimulus input (Figure 36.1). Each emotion could consist of multiple parallel ROT. As with serial ROT, this does not create a problem for our naming of the phenomena. *Separation anxiety* remains a nameable set of entities that are coherent under normal ecological circumstances and our analysis does not require any change in the everyday use of the term. But, for scientific purposes, we must view the term

as grounded in a particular class of evolutionarily recurring situations (loss of parents) that give rise to a consistent set of adaptive requirements and so a usually consistent effector pattern (behavioral and autonomic) that constitutes a fairly consistent distributed central state—but without the need for a single command center or any other internal link between the components.

Evolution, ROT and Functional Definitions of Emotional Systems

If parts of a functional system can be independent, whether as a result of serial or parallel ROT, how can we understand or define the system—or even refer to it as a system at all? Rather than being a major problem, inverting this question allows us not only a convenient way to refer to, and to distinguish among, central emotional and motivational systems but also as well as a means of dealing with the fact that these systems involve multiple hierarchically organized layers:

> [This] approach to [emotion] stems from analysis of its possible functional significance. This approach is based on the premise that important and pervasive human action tendencies, particularly those which occur across a wide range of cultures and specific learning situations, are very likely to have their origin in the functionally significant behavior patterns of nonhuman animals. . . . This approach, working through the characteristic behavior patterns seen in response to important ecological demands (e.g., feeding, reproduction, defense) when animals are given the rather wide range of behavioral choices typical of most natural habitats, is called ethoexperimental analysis. It involves a view that the functional significance of behavior attributed to anxiety (or other emotions) needs to be taken into account; and that this functional significance reflects the dynamics of that behavior in interaction with the ecological systems in which the species has evolved, implying that these dynamics . . . can be determined far more efficiently when the behavior is studied under conditions typical of life for the particular species. (R. J. Blanchard & Blanchard, 1990b, p. 125)

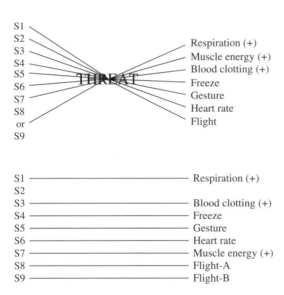

Figure 36.1   The extremes of the possible neural relations that could have evolved to control responses to threat.

Note: The top half of the figure shows the functional relations linking stimuli (S1–S9) to responses where the stimuli are either regular predictors of threat (S1–S7) or where different stimuli are predictive of threat at different times (S8, S9). It can also be viewed as a representation of the simplest view of emotional states, namely that all stimuli activate a single neural representation of threat and this in turn activates the separate response systems. The bottom half of the figure shows, in its most extreme form, the opposite type of neural organization suggested by Hofer's experiments (see text). Here, each response system is under its own private stimulus control. Some stimuli (S2) may have not acquired control over any response system and some stimuli (S8, S9) may have acquired control over a particular response (flight) but only under some circumstances (-A, -B). Redrawn from "Anxiety: One label for many processes." *New Zealand Journal of Psychology, 18,* Figure 1, p53 by McNaughton, 1989a.

Detailed ethological analysis of defensive responses obtained under experimentally controlled conditions by the Blanchards has demonstrated a categorical separation of a set of reactions that can be grouped together under the rubric of "fear" from a quite distinct "anxiety" set (R. J. Blanchard & Blanchard, 1988; R. J. Blanchard & Blanchard, 1989, 1990a, 1990b; R. J. Blanchard, Griebel, Henrie, & Blanchard, 1997).

The Blanchards elicited their set of "fear" behaviors with a predator. These behaviors, originally all linked solely through ethology, turn out to be sensitive to drugs that are panicolytic but not to those that are only anxiolytic

(R. J. Blanchard et al., 1997). The Blanchards elicited their set of "anxiety" behaviors (especially risk assessment; see Chapter 49) with stimuli that only suggested the potential presence of a predator. These behaviors, again originally all linked solely through ethology, turn out to be sensitive to anxiolytic drugs. The Blanchards' detailed analysis, and its pharmacological validation, provides a basis for coherent conceptualization of a vast animal literature. For example, their analysis of fear predicts the well-demonstrated insensitivity to anxiolytic drugs of active avoidance in a wide variety of species and of phobia in humans (Sartory, MacDonald, & Gray, 1990). Because of the detailed effects of anxiolytic drugs on operant and other behavior (Gray, 1977), we have argued (Gray & McNaughton, 2000; McNaughton & Corr, 2004) that the key factor distinguishing fear and anxiety is one of "defensive direction." Fear is that set of reactions that have evolved to allow the animal to leave a dangerous situation (predator escape; operant active avoidance); anxiety is that set of reactions that have evolved to allow the animal to enter a dangerous situation (e.g., cautious "risk assessment" approach behavior) or to withhold entrance (passive avoidance).

Evolution, ROT and Hierarchical Organization

With the PREE, we simply accepted the fact that, where there is a single high-level general rule for optimal behavior, there may be multiple ROT that deliver the appropriate behavior under different circumstances. However, when the functional requirement is something as general as "escape," different circumstances may not only require different ROT to produce essentially the same behavior pattern under those different circumstances but also require noticeably different behavior patterns to achieve the result.

Here we can link the evolution of serial ROT to the hierarchical organization of emotional systems. At the perceptual level, there are both "quick and dirty" as well as "slow and sophisticated" sensory mechanisms for detecting predators (LeDoux, 1994). There are also simpler and more complex behaviors that can be generated depending on the time available for execution (and other constraints). We can see all these mechanisms as parallel ROT that have evolved to improve survival in the face of threat, each new one filling a gap left by existing mechanisms.

But these ROT have not evolved entirely independently of each other. First, simpler mechanisms will have evolved before more complex ones, providing a substrate for the development of the more complex and also providing a partial solution to the global problem that leaves a gap in adaptive advantage that later ROT must fill. Second, it makes no sense to have available a slow and sophisticated

strategy for, say, escape if an evolutionarily older panic reaction takes command of the motor apparatus. When it is activated, a higher and slower mechanism must be capable of inhibiting inconvenient aspects of the lower and faster mechanisms. The result, with defensive behavior, has been the evolution of a hierarchically ordered series of defensive reactions (each appropriate to a particular "defensive distance," see the discussion that follows) that, in turn, map to lower and higher levels of the nervous systems, respectively. While behaviorally and neurally complex, all these reactions fulfill the same basic function and so can all be seen as part of a single "fear system."

The Blanchards developed the concept of defensive distance as part and parcel of their analysis of the differences between fear and anxiety, mentioned earlier. Operationally, with the most basic defensive reactions, it can be viewed as the literal distance between the subject and a predator. It is a dimension controlling the type of defensive behavior observed—that is, specific behaviors appear consistently at particular distances. In the case of defensive avoidance, the smallest defensive distances result in explosive attack, intermediate defensive distances result in freezing and flight, and very great defensive distances (i.e., absence of the predator) result in normal nondefensive behavior. However, defensive distance is not related directly to distance per se. It operationalizes an internal cognitive construct of intensity of perceived threat. For a particular individual in a particular situation, defensive distance equates with real distance. But, in a more dangerous situation, a greater real distance will be required to achieve the same defensive distance. Likewise, in the same situation, but with a braver individual, a smaller real distance will be required to achieve the same defensive distance.

This concept can resolve otherwise unexpected findings in, for example, behavioral pharmacology. It is tempting for those who focus on behavior as the thing to be studied in itself, as opposed to being a sign of states within the organism, to expect particular pharmacological interventions to affect specific behaviors in a consistent way. That this is not the case is shown by the effects of anti-anxiety drugs on risk assessment behavior. If perceived intensity of threat is high (small defensive distance), an undrugged rat is likely to remain still. Under these conditions, an anxiolytic drug will increase risk assessment (this will increase approach to the source of threat). But, if perceived threat is medium, an undrugged rat is likely to engage in risk assessment behavior. Under these conditions, an anxiolytic drug will decrease risk assessment (which again increases approach to the source of threat as it releases normal appetitive behavior). Thus, the drug does not alter specific observable risk assessment behaviors consistently but instead produces changes in behavior that depend on the animal's initial state and are consistent with a pharmacological increase in defensive distance (R. J. Blanchard & Blanchard, 1990; R. J. Blanchard, Blanchard, Tom, & Rodgers, 1990).

This leaves us with a picture of ROT (in this case various levels of defense reaction) that have accumulated hierarchically. Their evolution has been accompanied not only by mechanisms controlling *which* ROT control behavior at any particular moment in time but also by mechanisms that can adjust which *level* of the system is selected by any particular external stimulus configuration (or rather the cognitions engendered by the stimuli).

In the case of the defense system, the hierarchical levels of responding can be mapped to levels of the nervous system and, at least, some of the overall control mechanisms identified. This is shown in Figure 36.2. The precise details contained in the figure are not important for our current argument and are dealt with in detail elsewhere (Gray & McNaughton, 2000; McNaughton & Corr, 2004; see Chapter 36) and are also briefly summarized in the section on specific central theories that follows. The important point is that a central theory of emotion, such as this, can treat different classes of behavior as, in one sense, discrete—each controlled by a particular different part of the brain—but at the same time can show that these different classes contribute to a more generalized functional system with control of the different parts that is at least sometimes integrated.

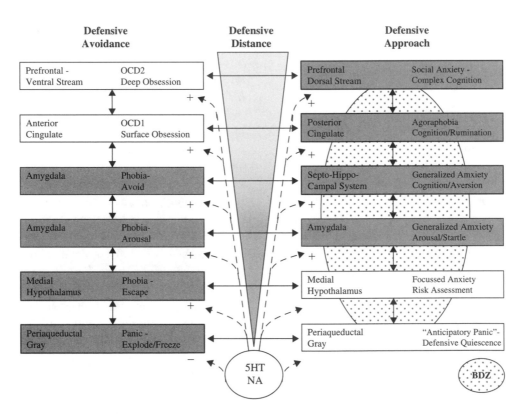

Figure 36.2   The two-dimensional defense system.

Note: The two columns of structures represent subsystems controlling defensive avoidance and defensive approach, respectively. Each subsystem is divided, from top to bottom, into a number of hierarchical levels, both with respect to neural level (and cytoarchitectonic complexity) and to functional level (i.e., defensive distance—small at the bottom, large at the top). Each level is associated with specific classes of normal behavior and so, also, symptom and syndrome of abnormal behavior. Each level is interconnected with adjacent levels (vertical arrows shown) and also with higher and lower levels (connections not shown) and these connections allow integrated control of the whole subsystem. The subsystems are also connected with each other (horizontal arrows shown) allowing for control of behavior to pass between one and the other. Superimposed on the levels of each system is input from monoamines systems. The monoamines modulate activity, essentially altering defensive distance generally, and so which level of a subsystem will be in control of behavior at any particular point in time. Endogenous hormones binding to the benzodiazepine receptor (BDZ) can similar alter defensive distance but only in relation to structures in the defensive approach subsystem and to a lesser extent at the highest and lowest levels of the system than at the middle levels (as indicated by the width of the stippled oval as it intersects a structure). NA 5 Noradrenaline; 5HT 5 Serotonin. For details see "A Two-Dimensional Neuropsychology of Defense: Fear/Anxiety and Defensive Distance," by McNaughton and Corr, 2004, *Neuroscience and Biobehavioral Reviews, 28,* pp. 285–305. Adapted with permission from Figure 3, p. 293.

EMOTION, MOTIVATION, AND LEARNING

Emotional systems have multiple parts that are several and distinct. Each involves a particular proximal form of appetitive or aversive behavior. But emotional stimuli are also reinforcing and, here, there is a surprising functional unity. Before proceeding to a consideration of the link between motivation and emotion, it will be helpful to clarify what modern neuroscience can tell us about the central mechanisms of reinforcement. Much analysis of emotion and motivation in the experimental literature has used learned responses because of their analytical simplicity. This can create problems when we attempt to link emotional concepts developed via ethological analysis with theories of learning and motivation developed via the experimental analysis of behavior.

Association versus Classical Conditioning versus Instrumental Conditioning at the Neural Level

The dominant paradigm for the study of synaptic processes underlying learning and memory is long-term potentiation (LTP), a phenomenon discovered by Bliss and Lomo (Bliss, Gardner-Medwin, & Lomo, 1973; Bliss & Lomo, 1973). Although LTP is usually studied electrophysiologically by high-frequency stimulation of a single neural pathway, its molecular mechanisms can clearly support strengthening of a single synapse that is driven by the coincidence of a previously weak input at that synapse with the firing of the cell produced by a strong input.

The key aspect of this strengthening (which at most junctions depends on a specific receptor, the NMDA receptor) is that it is associative. Only currently active synapses (essentially acting as CS+) are strengthened and other inputs to the same target cell that are not active (CS−) are not strengthened. This strengthening appears, ultimately, to involve structural changes in the synapses and not merely depend on modification of biochemical pathways (see Chapter 27).

LTP has attracted particular attention because it conforms very tightly to the requirements for memory formation postulated of cortical neural processes by Hebb (1949). Hebb's rule (as it has come to be known) can be summarized as "cells that fire together wire together" and was postulated simply on the basis of psychological findings with no evidence for a matching real neural process until the discovery of LTP.

An important point to note is that Hebb's original example discussed the linking of two stimuli within the visual cortex. His postulated mechanism was, therefore, purely associative, requiring no additional reinforcer to strengthen the connection. A light paired with a light would become associated via connections within the visual cortex, as could a light with a tone—given the existence of "silent" connections between visual and auditory areas (Figure 36.3).

Thus Hebbian learning is best exemplified by what is normally known as "sensory preconditioning." ("Sensory preconditioning" is essentially a misnomer based on the, false, assumptions that learning requires a reinforcer and that without a change in behavior conditioning has not occurred.) The typical sensory preconditioning experiment can be confusing because it requires a reinforcer in order to demonstrate learning that did not itself depend on one. (With humans, we can omit the reinforcer by asking people to report their knowledge verbally.) The typical phases of a sensory preconditioning experiment are:

Phase 1: Stimulus A (a light) is paired with stimulus B (a tone) in a series of classical (Pavlovian) conditioning-like trials. Neither A nor B produces any observable response, before or after the conditioning-like trials.

Phase 2: Stimulus B (the tone) is next paired with a food in a series of conditioning trials. Initially, the subject salivates when the food is presented; after a number of trials, they salivate when B is presented.

Phase 3: Stimulus A is now presented to the subject without any previous pairing of A with food. In experiments of this type it is usually found that the subject will salivate when A is presented. Yet, A has never been paired with food.

The conclusion from these results has to be that, during Phase 1, an association was formed between A and B. In Hebb's version of events, there initially exists a weak connection between a cell assembly activated by A and a cell assembly activated by B. When A is presented close in time to B, its weak synapses on the cell assembly encoding B will be activated at the same time that the cell assembly fires and so the connection will be strengthened. On later presentation of A, this connection activates (at least partially) the B cell assembly—and so produces, although perhaps weakly, the neural effects of the presentation of B (Figure 36.3A).

In Phase 2, stimulus B acquires observable consequences. These consequences are therefore likely to follow from the subsequent activation of the A assembly even in the absence of direct input by the B stimulus to the B assembly. This effect of A is demonstrated in Phase 3.

The purely associative process of long-term potentiation can also explain "classical conditioning" involving

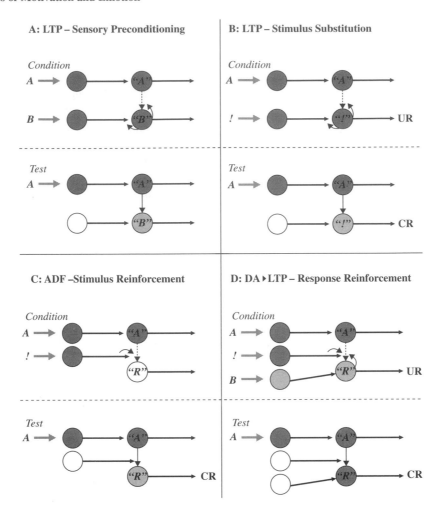

Figure 36.3   Different ways in which neural plasticity can result in associative learning.

Note: **A:** Long-term potentiation (LTP) resulting in sensory preconditioning. Pairing of a neutral stimulus A with a second neutral stimulus B strengthens the connection between the representation of A and B such that presentation of A activates the representation of B when B is not physically present. **B:** As in A but with the second neutral stimulus (B) substituted by a reinforcer. The unconditioned response (UR) to ! undergoes Pavlovian stimulus substitution with the result that it, or some component of it, appears as the conditioned response (CR) when A is later presented alone. **C:** Activity dependent facilitation (ADF) as a basis for reinforced classical conditioning. Pairing of a neutral stimulus with a reinforcer results in strengthening of the connection of A with the neural representation of a response (R), independent of whether the response is currently activated. The result is classical conditioning that can produce a response that was not elicited by the unconditioned stimulus and so need not involve stimulus substitution. **D:** Dopamine-dependent-LTP (DA▶LTP) as a basis for reinforcement of instrumental responding. A low baseline emission of an operant response R is supported by the presence of an eliciting stimulus B. A conditional stimulus A is paired with the delivery of reinforcement (!) when the response is emitted as a UR. This strengthens the connection between the neural representation of A and the neural center controlling the emission of the response. This results in the response being emitted as a conditioned response when A is presented in future.

Pavlovian stimulus substitution without the need to invoke a specific reinforcement process (Figure 36.3B). If B is a motivationally significant stimulus prior to pairing with A, then activation of its stimulus representation by A will result in the same responses to A as previously occurred to B. This is like sensory preconditioning but with the link between B and an observable response having been established previously by evolution rather than later by an experimenter. In the case of tone-shock conditioning, the specific synaptic junction generating the conditioned fear reaction has been identified as a monosynaptic connection between the thalamus (containing the tone representation) and the amygdala (which is activated by the shock and generates the unconditioned response). Injection of an NMDA antagonist into the amygdala blocks LTP and so acquisition of the conditioned response but has no effect if injected once conditioning is complete (LeDoux, 1994; for a more detailed analysis of fear conditioning see Chapter 39; for a comparison of the neural circuits involved in fear conditioning and eyeblink conditioning see Chapter 26).

Simple LTP-based association can also explain what appears to be instrumental conditioning but is in fact disguised classical conditioning with stimulus substitution. Pigeons are typically conditioned to peck keys that are lit prior to delivery of the reward. Under these conditions, autoshaping occurs. The pigeon comes to peck the key, essentially because its lit state predicts reward and not because the pecking is instrumentally reinforced. This is shown by two pieces of evidence. First, autoshaping with a superimposed instrumental omission contingency (which pits classical autoshaping against instrumental omission of reward if the pigeon pecks the key) results in behavior cycling between pecking and not pecking. The attractiveness of the lit key overrides any instrumental learning that pecking cancels reward; and the cyclical loss of responding can be attributed to extinction of the classical contingency rather than any effect of the instrumental one. Second, the nature of the key peck is determined by the reinforcer. The pigeon, effectively "drinks" a key paired with water and "eats" a key paired with food (Jenkins & Moore, 1973).

With so much possible with simple LTP-dependent association and its resultant stimulus substitution, we might be inclined to abandon the idea of reinforcement altogether. However, neuroscience provides at least two cases where true reinforcement mechanisms can be invoked.

The first reinforcement mechanism has been demonstrated in classical conditioning in the sea slug *Aplysia californica*. This animal is so simple that specific neurons can be identified and named reliably from animal to animal and be shown to control the same responses in each individual. This has allowed detailed analysis of the entire neural circuit involved in conditioning (Chapter 27; Kandel & Hawkins, 1992). Shock to the tail activates a single neuron that can release transmitter presynaptically onto the terminals connecting sensory neurons with a motor neuron that controls gill withdrawal. Pairing of a light touch to the mantle of *Aplysia* with a shock to the tail can then strengthen the connection between a sensory neuron that detects the touch and the motor neuron—a process referred to as activity dependent facilitation (ADF). The activity dependence of ADF results in a conditioned withdrawal of the gill to subsequent touching of the mantle (the CS+), but not of other sensory inputs, for example, a touch to the siphon. As with LTP, ADF is truly associative in that previous CS− can be conditioned if they are later paired with the shock. An important feature of ADF is that, in contrast to LTP, it allows true reinforcement in the sense of production of a new response that is not elicited by the unconditional stimulus (e.g., freezing to a CS for a shock, in contrast to the movement and vocalization normally produced by the shock).

The second reinforcement mechanism combines features of both standard LTP and ADF (Figure 36.3D). Like LTP, it requires the coincidence of the release of transmitter from the presynaptic neuron with the firing of the postsynaptic cell. However, in addition, LTP only occurs if dopamine is released presynaptically as a result of activation of the brain's "reward system" (Reynolds, Hyland, & Wickens, 2001). Notably the postsynaptic cell controls responding rather than encoding a stimulus. Its initial activation (on which responding and so reward-delivery are dependent) results from the presence in the environment of appropriate eliciting stimuli (unless the response can be spontaneously generated). As discussed next, this allows responses to continue to be produced on some occasions even when reinforcement conditions are changed or when the reinforcer is devalued. That is, a response can be habitual and its cessation will depend on active extinction as a result of negative reinforcement rather than simply fading away in the absence of significant events. (The phasic release of dopamine, relating to reinforcement and tonic release that can be identified with hedonic changes appear to activate different networks; and dopamine may not underlie all rewarding effects, see Chapter 40).

From Emotion to Motivation

Our argument, so far, is that specific ROT (controlled by specific neural mechanisms) have evolved in a not entirely piecemeal fashion so that, in at least some cases, they become organized into functional systems. In the case of defensive avoidance, we have a hierarchically organized system, each part of which can generate appropriate defensive behavior (e.g., freezing, aggression, escape, avoidance) within a specific range of environmental circumstances.

A large part of the theoretical structure of Figure 36.2 is devoted to an account of a fairly large number of particular situation-typical behaviors, which we group together not because of their specific form but because they share the same general function: removing the animal from danger. Aversive stimuli—both natural stimuli, such as a cat, and artificial stimuli, such as presentation of a shock, as well as the omission of expected rewards (frustrative nonreward)—all tend to have similar eliciting properties. Presentation of a cat elicits autonomic arousal, freezing, or attack, if defensive distance is short, and escape where this is possible. Much the same pattern is produced by both presentation of shock and frustrative nonreward: autonomic arousal, attack if there is a conspecific close by to attack, and escape if this is available (Gray, 1987, chap. 10). More general avoidance behavior is appropriate not only for a wide range of dangers, in the sense of things that can cause pain, but also for other stimuli that are merely disgusting, or even simply of no current interest.

Fear conditioning, learned escape, and learned avoidance of the simplest sort can all be viewed, in this context, as the result of simple Pavlovian stimulus substitution. Pure associative conditioning results in a previously neutral stimulus becoming a signal for an upcoming noxious event and resulting in the class of defensive response appropriate to the level of threat signaled.

Whether the unconditioned stimulus is the presentation of a natural or artificial punishment or the removal of a natural or artificial reward, we can view avoidance behavior in general as resulting from activity in what has been known as the fight-flight system (Gray, 1987) but is probably better called the fight-flight-freeze system (FFFS; Gray & McNaughton, 2000).

It is at this point that we must distinguish between two quite distinct ways in which the words *fear* and *conditioning* can be combined. In the first conjunction of fear and conditioning, *fear conditioning,* a neutral stimulus is paired with a shock and responses such as freezing are conditioned. Critically, the shock is inescapable and so the conditioned form of the previously unconditioned fear responses remains even after many trials. This conditioning is purely associative, as with the learning of a light-tone pairing of the type evidenced in experiments on sensory preconditioning. It is dependent simply on the coincidence of the two critical stimuli that then become associated via the process of long term potentiation (Fanselow & LeDoux, 1999). The stimulus we often refer to as the *reinforcer* is necessary if a response of some type is to be observed but the learned association can be formed even with neutral stimuli and so does not depend on reinforcement in the strict Pavlovian meaning of the term. In the second conjunction of fear and conditioning, *conditioning of avoidance by fear* (with, for example, a lever press as the avoidance response), something quite different happens. In the initial phases of training, there is both a high level of autonomic arousal and the release of the stress hormone corticosterone (Brady, 1975a, 1975b). However, once avoidance is well established, all these signs of emotional reaction disappear and the only obvious difference in behavior, as compared with behavior observed before training, is that the avoidance response is reliably produced.

This leaves us in the apparently odd situation of maintaining that although an avoidance response is being made (as a result of the motivation of fear) the animal is not afraid (in the sense of showing emotional reactions). The commonsense view is that there is no reason for the animal to be afraid because it knows the avoidance response will prevent it from receiving a shock. There are two levels at which we need to take this idea seriously.

The more trivial level at which a learned avoidance response is not driven by fear is that well-learned responses are, in a very real sense, habits. Even with positive reinforcers that are physically present on every trial (such as food for a hungry animal), sufficiently long training results in the animal continuing to respond even when the reinforcer is devalued. The "rewarded response" is made but the reward itself is not consumed (Dickinson, 1980). With successful avoidance responses the reinforcer is never present and so responding can be even more resistant to extinction. The same is true of the conditioned suppression of behavior by anxiety. After extended training, the suppression becomes insensitive to anxiolytic drugs (McNaughton, 1985).

The deeper level at which a learned avoidance response is not driven by fear rests in the fact that, unlike fear conditioning, it is not the presentation of shock that "reinforces" learning: rather it is the omission of shock. Continued responding is driven by relief, not fear. This is not mere semantic quibbling. In the same way that omission of reward has the same reinforcing properties (and many of the same eliciting properties) as the presentation of punishment—the "fear = frustration hypothesis" (Gray, 1987)—omission of punishment has the same reinforcing properties as the presentation of reward—the "hope = relief hypothesis" (Gray, 1987). As we shall see, below, we can attribute the learning of new responses to the release of dopamine and, consistent with this, dopamine is involved in avoidance conditioning (Sokolowski, McCullough, & Salamone, 1994; Stark, Bischof, & Scheich, 1999). Omission of punishment is, thus, truly rewarding.

Here we should notice an asymmetry in the types of released behaviors associated with approach reactions compared to those associated with avoidance. Avoidance involves, in general, a hierarchically organized set of released action patterns that do not vary much with the specific eliciting stimulus and that vary with "defensive distance"; approach involves, in general, released action patterns only in contact with the eliciting stimulus and then produces stimulus-specific responses. (Avoidance also involves stimulus-specific responses with contacting stimuli: for example attack of a predator is replaced with defensive burying of a shock probe—but these are not as many or various as the stimulus-specific responses produced by contact with appetitive stimuli. Likewise, there is little difference in principle between an appetitive-conditioned jaw movement response and an aversive-conditioned eyeblink response.)

The specific behaviors observed in the context of active avoidance (when the animal moves away from a localized aversive stimulus) are suprisingly general and depend much more on defensive distance than on the specific nature of the aversive stimulus. Thus, both punishment and frustration will generally increase aggressive responses within and between many species, including humans (Renfrew & Hutchinson, 1983) and, in humans, will even increase aggressive responses directed at completely innocent inanimate objects (Kelly & Hake, 1970). Defensive behaviors, then, give the appearance of output from a single, fairly homogenous, system—with specific released, as opposed to learned, behaviors varying mainly with the defensive distance.

By contrast, the proximal behaviors required to consummate the approach to an appetitive stimulus are entirely stimulus specific. We eat food and mount a sexual partner, but not vice versa. There has not been reported, however, a hierarchical series of standard behaviors required for approach that varies with "appetitive distance." It may simply be that there has been a lack of appropriate ethological analysis of such approach behavior. However, the behaviors required to approach an appetitive stimulus (other than simple locomotion) are unique to each situation and driven by the specifics of the situation rather than the nature of the appetitive stimulus. Indeed, the most obvious fundamental requirement is the learning of whatever new and, in evolutionary terms, completely arbitrary responses are required to achieve the goal. There are, then, no emotion-general innate reactions that characterize a specific appetitive distance.

This not to say that there is no dimension of appetitive distance. Appetitive goals produce a systematic, distance-related, effect. But the evidence is that variation in distance between an organism and an appetitive goal drives the quantity or intensity of behavior, but not its quality. The intensity with which approach behavior is executed increases the closer an animal is to the goal, as if there is a "goal gradient" (Hull, 1952)—but this is as true of lever pressing on a fixed interval schedule in an operant chamber as of running in runway on a continuous reinforcement schedule.

We have, therefore, two fundamental systems: one that controls the avoidance of specific stimuli (including reward omission) and one that controls approach to specific stimuli (including safety). Each of these is linked to systems that determine the specific aversive (e.g., defensive burying) or appetitive (e.g., eating) behavior that will be released by contact with a motivationally significant stimulus. But each is also more fundamentally a generic system devoted to avoidance or approach, respectively. Because of the asymmetry in functional requirements noted previously, the avoidance system has been named in terms of some common discrete elicited behaviors (fight, flight, freeze); while the approach system has been named generically *the Behavioral Approach System* (Gray, 1982) or Behavioral Activation System (Smits & Boeck, 2006)—with the abbreviation, BAS, designating the same appetitive neural system in both cases.

Here we come to the nub of the relationship between the central control of emotion and that of motivation. To a first approximation, when we talk about emotion, we are talking about the elicitation of particular patterns of internal (autonomic) and external (skeletal) behavior; when we talk about motivation, we are talking about the production of generalized approach or avoidance tendencies. Motivation, in this sense, cannot exist without emotion—at least in the initial phases of learning. But, in stable environments, with habitual responses reliably delivering appropriate appetitive stimuli or apparently successfully avoiding aversive stimuli, emotional reactions are minimized.

We need to clear up a common misconception: There can be a tendency to link aversive stimuli and avoidance to emotion and to see them as distinct from appetitive stimuli and an approach that just involves motivation. This tendency results from the fact that the usual way to study aversive stimuli in the laboratory is to deliver electric shock (which requires no prior deprivation of some need for it to be effective); while the usual way to study appetitive stimuli is to deliver food to a hungry animal or water to a thirsty animal. It is common to see the eliciting stimulus of shock as creating the motivational state that drives behavior in the aversive case but to see deprivation, rather than the appetitive stimulus, as driving the motivational state in the appetitive case.

Positive motivation does not, however, require a state of deprivation of some basic need. Female rats can often appear relatively passive during copulation—albeit showing receptive behavior linked to the phase of their ovarian cycle. However, not only does their receptive phase involve permitting the male to mount, it turns out that it involves more active tendencies when appropriate.

> Male (rats) normally pause for a while after intromissions, and for a longer time after intromissions that culminate in ejaculation. . . . Bermant (1961a, 1961b) provided female rats with a lever they could press to produce a male rat. After a mount (regardless of whether it resulted in intromission) the male was removed. The females quickly pressed the lever after the male was removed following a mount (without intromission), paused a bit more after an intromission (without ejaculation), and waited the longest time before summoning a male rat after ejaculation. Thus it appears that male and female rats prefer the same frequency of sexual contact. (Carlson, 1980, p. 333)

Here the reaction of the female rat to the male (albeit approach) is essentially the same class of reaction as that of a rat to a cat (albeit avoidance). The availability of the motivationally significant stimulus—and interactions with it—drives the behavior. One could argue that there is a background level of preparedness on the part of the female rat driven by the ovarian cycle—but there are also variations in fearfulness within rats from time to time and between rats, and the same is true for humans—especially with sexual receptivitiy.

Even with hunger, it should be noted that the normal experience of hunger is linked as much or more to the availability of palatable food, or some other external or temporal cue for eating, than it is related to tissue need or level of deprivation (Pinel, 1997). For example, if a rat is provided for some time with six meals a day that are spaced irregularly but signaled by a buzzer and light stimulus and is then placed on free food so that it is satiated, presentation of the buzzer and light will elicit eating of as much as 20% of their daily food intake (Weingarten, 1983). (The total amount eaten over a day was not changed as later free feeding adjusted for the extra meal.) Likewise, if we see hunger as an essentially emotional rather than homeostatic state, we can understand its links with emotional disorder: the life-threatening reductions in weight that can occur in anorexia nervosa and the health-threatening increases in weight that can occur in depression.

Likewise, simple rewarded responding can depend, like simple fear conditioning, on stimulus substitution. As we noted earlier, in experiments with autoshaped responses, pigeons produce stereotyped responses that show they are effectively drinking the key when they are thirsty and eating the key when they are hungry (Jenkins & Moore, 1973). Further, if the autoshaping schedule (which pairs a lit key with the reward) has added to it an instrumental omission contingency (so that pecking cancels food), the pigeon goes through cycles of responding and nonresponding corresponding to the simple associative contingencies in the situation, unlike a rat that ceases responding and reacts to the reinforcement contingencies (see Millenson & Leslie, 1979).

SOME CURRENT CENTRAL THEORIES OF MOTIVATION AND EMOTION

There are many specific hypotheses currently being advanced by neuroscientists in relation to detailed aspects of the control of specific emotional reactions, motivational control systems, and learning and memory. For the behavioral scientist wanting to enter this field (which can appear like a minefield of novel jargon and mind-boggling detail), it is probably most important to note that the many detailed issues can be dealt with one at a time. You can focus on the detail that pertains only to the current issue. In essence, one is dealing with the neural specifics of particular ROT. Provided one has been warned about the capacity of ROT to be nested both in serial and parallel, it is not difficult to accept the bits of the jigsaw piecemeal and leave integration until sufficient bits have been obtained to make the overall puzzle worth solving. The most important thing is to not believe that the solution to the puzzle is obvious

and to wait for a sufficient number of the pieces to become available.

Partly because they deal with the neural instantiation of ROT, neuroscientists seldom integrate their findings on emotion and motivation into grand overall theoretical schemes. They do use global, apparently integrative, concepts. But these concepts are usually taken directly from behavior analysis and so subsume ROT within what are effectively clusters (such as the PREE and instrumental learning) based on overall evolutionary function. This may give the impression that they are ascribing to ROT a specific source of integrated control but, as we have seen, this need not be the case. Instead, the use value of this approach is to gather together phenomena that may have some, albeit loose, integrated control—or that may have the appearance of control as an emergent property of the interaction of multiple ROT.

There are, nonetheless, neuroscientifically grounded theories that attempt to provide more wholistic, integrated perspectives. In this section, we briefly describe some of these and show how the architecture of each maps to the basic ideas we have presented above.

Gray and McNaughton

We have based a number of the concepts we have already presented on one such theory—the idea, originally proposed by Jeffrey Gray (1982), that behavior is primarily controlled by a Fight-Flight-Freeze System (FFFS) and a Behavioral Approach System (BAS) with, linked to these, and controlling conflict between approach and avoidance, a Behavioral Inhibition System (BIS). This theory has clear links with the idea of multiple ROT, especially in its more recent development (Gray & McNaughton, 2000; McNaughton & Corr, 2004). Multiple ROT are instantiated in the mixture of levels and streams of Figure 36.2, which shows the FFFS and BIS, and in the matching levels of the separate stream of structures controlling the BAS (not shown). It also has at its core the idea that, in general, approach and avoidance behavior are each controlled in fundamentally the same way independent of the specific source of motivation for that approach or avoidance.

Rolls

This latter perspective is presented in perhaps an even stronger way by Edmund Rolls (1990, 2000) in his general theory of the control of emotion and motivation by the brain. He sees evolution as starting with simple ROT in the form of taxes that attract simple animals (including those with no nervous system) toward items that promote survival and reproduction and that drive them away from items with the opposite consequences. He argues that:

> brains are designed around reward- and punishment-evaluation systems, because this is how genes can build a complex system that will produce appropriate but flexible behavior to increase fitness. . . . If arbitrary responses are to be made by the animals, rather than just preprogrammed movements such as tropisms and taxes, [is] there any alternative to such a reward/punishment based systems in this evolution by natural selection situation? It is not clear that there is, if the genes are efficiently to control behavior. The argument is that genes can specify actions that will increase fitness if they specify the goals for action. It would be very difficult for them in general to specify in advance the particular response to be made to each of a myriad of different stimuli. . . . Outputs of the reward and punishment system must be treated by the action systems as being the goals for action. (Rolls, 2000, pp. 190, 183, 191).

Rolls could, at first blush, appear to be taking an excessively binary view. He states, for example, that "emotions can usefully be defined as states elicited by rewards and punishments, including changes in rewards and punishments" (Rolls, 2000, p. 178). He also argues that "the amygdala and orbitofrontal cortex . . . [are] of great importance for emotions, in that they are involved, respectively in the elicitation of learned emotional responses and in the correction or adjustment of these emotional responses as the reinforcing value of the environmental stimuli alters" (Rolls, 1990, p. 161). This perspective seems to force all emotion into either a reward or a punishment box with variation in behavior simply being the results of the learning of arbitrary responses.

However, on closer inspection of the details of Rolls' theory, it is clear that he allows not only for multiple ROT in terms of elements of behavior but also in terms of the separation of, for example, autonomic from behavioral aspects of emotional response. In his view, there are three major, neurally separate, classes of output available for any emotion: There are autonomic and endocrine outputs that optimize the state of the animal for particular types of action; there are *implicit* behavioral responses; and there are *explicit* behavioral responses. Implicit behavioral responses are controlled "via brain systems that have been present . . . for millions of years and can operate without conscious control. These systems include the amygdala and, particularly well developed in primates, the orbitofrontal cortex. They provide information about the possible goals for action based on their decoding of primary reinforcers taking into account the current motivational state, and on their decoding of whether stimuli have been associated by previous learning with reinforcement." This clearly encompasses a wide range of emotion-specific and innately elicited responses. The control of explicit behavioral responses, by contrast,

"involves a computation with many 'if . . . then' statements, to implement a plan to obtain a reward or to avoid a punisher." Here the behavior controlled is clearly general in its form and largely based on strategies for simple approach or avoidance. He locates the highest levels of this control in the dorsolateral prefrontal cortex—where they are strongly related to the processing of shortterm (or "active") memory.

Despite Rolls' somewhat different perspective compared to Gray and McNaughton, he is like them in seeing orbitofrontal cortex as, in essence, coding "what" a stimulus is. "What" here has the sense of what specific class of reinforcer such as food, drink, or sex it is that the stimulus represents—and compounds "sensory integration, emotional processing, and hedonic experience" (see Chapter 41). Dorsolateral frontal cortex, by contrast, codes "where" a stimulus is. Thus both theories see a distinction between a reactive and excitatory orbital system and a prospective and inhibitory dorsolateral system.

Critically, in the context of ROT, Rolls (2000) warns that "these three systems do not necessarily act as an integrated whole. Indeed, insofar as the implicit system may be for immediate goals, and the explicit system is computationally appropriate for deferred longer terms goal, they will not always indicate the same action. Similarly, the autonomic system does not use entirely the same neural systems . . . and will not always be an excellent guide to the emotional state of the animal, which the above argument in any case indicates is not unitary" (pp. 188–189).

There is a strong link between emotion and motivation for Rolls, in both their more innate and more conditioned forms. While starting from the position that "emotions can usefully be considered as states produced by reinforcing stimuli" (Rolls, 1990), he sees the particular value of those states as involving elicitation of autonomic and hormonal responses and, in learning experiments, in the production of various conditioned emotional responses. Emotion, viewed in this light, provides a basis for the facilitation of memory storage and for the immediate elicitation of flexible responding when conditions change. The blocking of a learned response by new circumstances leaves intact the conditioned emotional response, which then provides the basis for the development of new behavior. Background autonomic and hormonal reactions provide the basis for the storage of such strategies as then prove successful.

Ledoux

For many years, Joe Ledoux has been developing a theory of fear, and consequentially, anxiety that is more limited in terms of the emotions analyzed but potentially deeper in the picture it presents of the details of the emotional systems. This can be seen as dovetailing to some extent with both the theoretical positions we have described so far.

While Gray and McNaughton focus on hierarchy in terms of the specific elicited behaviors associated with specific defensive distances, Ledoux can be thought of as focusing more on hierarchies of stimulus analysis that are to some extent also selected by defensive distance. He has contrasted "quick and dirty" threat detection systems (operating via the thalamus) with slower and more sophisticated ones operating through sensory cortex (Ledoux, 1994) and more recently (Ledoux, 2002) has laid emphasis on the even slower, and potentially more sophisticated, mechanisms that reside in frontal cortex and are linked to working memory and that form of planning that we can call "worry."

At first, his theory appears to be at total variance with that of Gray and McNaughton. However, when we look at the neural details, we discover that the discrepancy is not great; and we demonstrate a major advantage of a central/neural approach to emotion and motivation. The details of the theories are linked to neural reality very tightly and this allows one to resolve, relatively easily, issues that depend much more on arbitrary linguistic definitions than scientific facts.

Ledoux (2002) argues to some extent that anxiety is really fear but represented differently in consciousness. Thus:

anxiety, in my view, is a cognitive state in which working memory is monopolized by fretful, worrying thoughts. The difference between an ordinary state of mind (of working memory) and an anxious one is that, in the latter case, systems involved in emotional processing, such as the amygdala, have detected a threatening situation, and are influencing what working memory attends to and processes. This in turn will affect the manner in which executive functions select information from other cortical networks and from memory systems and make decisions about the course of action to take. . . . I believe that the hippocampus is involved in anxiety not because it processes threat, as Gray suggests, but instead because it supplies working memory with information about stimulus relations in the current environmental context, and about past relations stored in explicit memory. . . . When the organism, through working memory, conceives that it is facing a threatening situation and is uncertain about what is going to happen or about the best course of action to take, anxiety occurs. (p. 288)

Ledoux's very influential theory of the neural processing of fear was essentially incorporated into Gray's (1982) original, essentially amygdala-free, theory in its revision by Gray and McNaughton (2000). So, as far as fear goes, there is essentially general agreement among the theories of Ledoux, Gray and McNaughton, and Rolls. It is in dealing with anxiety that he sees the Gray and McNaughton theory as underemphasizing working memory and worry, "in my opinion, it still gives the septum and hippocampus too prominent a role, at the expense of the amygdala and prefrontal cortex" (p. 288).

In resolving the differences, let us first note that Gray and McNaughton's theory is anchored primarily in the effects of anxiolytic drugs. The link between anxiolytic action and effects on hippocampal electrical activity have been ever more firmly established (McNaughton, Kocsis, & Hajós, 2007). However, as Gray and McNaughton noted in their introduction:

"psychosurgery"—lesions of the cingulate or prefrontal cortex—has been used as a treatment with some degree of success. So these cortical areas could well mediate extreme (Marks, Birley, & Gelder, 1966) or complex forms of anxiety, especially . . . in the case of obsessive-compulsive disorder (Rapoport, 1989). (Gray & McNaughton, 2000, p. 5)

Gray and McNaughton (2000) have a theory of "anxiolytic-sensitive anxiety" that necessarily separates this from the processes of anxiety (or fear or obsession) that are controlled by frontal cortex. What of their view of frontal and cingulate cortex—on which Ledoux focuses:

We view them . . . as being hierarchically organized areas which deal (in their successively "higher" layers) with progressively higher levels of anticipation of action. . . . In the same way, then, that we distinguished the role of the hippocampus (in resolving concurrent goal-goal conflict) from the role of the defense system and other motor systems in resolving motor program conflicts without goal conflict, so we must distinguish its role from that of prefrontal and cingulate cortex. In our view these cortical areas are involved, quite independently of the hippocampus, in the resolution (i.e., ordering) of conflicts between successive sub-goals in a task. In the case of prefrontal cortex this amounts to saying that it is concerned with plans more than goals as such. However, where (as is common in certain types of working memory task) there is concurrent goal conflict within such a task, both the septo-hippocampal system and the prefrontal cortex are likely to be involved. (p. 5)

This view is not far from that expressed by Ledoux 2 years later, if we do not try and force the word "anxiety" to mean the same thing in the two cases. Gray and McNaughton focus on approach-avoidance conflict; something that can occur as a result of the apposition of two classes of innate releasing stimulus, with no requirement for learning or working memory. Ledoux focuses on "worry," the maintaining of a perception of threat in working memory (with no necessary requirement for anything other than pure avoidance). The two theories are talking about different processes in different structures— and Gray and McNaughton have much the same view of the operations of frontal cortex and of the amygdala as Ledoux. Both theories agree that "the amygdala and hippocampus normally cooperate in the intact brain to store different components of the fear learning experience" (see Chapter 39).

There is perhaps one area where discrepency may remain and where further experiment (or theoretical analysis) may be required to integrate the theories. Gray and McNaughton see the personality factor of neuroticism as being linked to frontal cortex, and as predisposing to both fear (threat avoidance) and anxiety (threat approach) disorders. Although they do not explicitly do so, they should link this personality factor to worry. For them worry is something that, if excessive, can lead to both pathological fear and pathological anxiety. These two states would appear to not only be conflated in Ledoux's analysis but also to be consequences not causes. Ledoux sees threat, detected in the amygdala, as infecting working memory processes and resulting in worry. There is evidence that worry is not directly aligned with anxiety as measured by standard anxiety scales (Meyer, Miller, Metzger, & Borkovec, 1999) and that worry can result in intrusive negative thoughts (Borkovec, Robinson, Pruzinsky, & DePree, 1983).* This suggests that, provided we use the words "worry" and "anxiety" with sufficiently restricted definitions, we can see Ledoux's theory as being more focused on a cause of pathological anxiety (and fear and depression), and their etiology, and Gray and McNaughton's as providing a view of state fear and state anxiety that encompasses both normal and pathological examples of these emotions but distinguishes between them.

Many of the differences between these three theories of central emotional and motivational states are more apparent (through variations in the use and meanings of words) than real. Critically, when what each theorist says of the mechanisms and psychological constructs associated with a particular neural structure is compared with the others, their fundamental message is very similar. They all believe that central states are fundamental to emotion and motivation, either in its normal or pathological form.

We would also agree with Ledoux (2002) when he states, "I don't study behavior to understand behavior so much as to understand how processes in the brain work" (p. 209). To this we, personally, would add the coda that we want to understand the processes in the brain because these anchor our understanding of the workings of the mind.

Damasio

While it is not a full theory of emotion, mention should also be made here of Damasio's somatic marker hypothesis (Damasio, 1995, 1996). This is a partial theory of how emotion or motivation can interact with cognition. It is

intended to be an account of only one of several ways that affect can influence decision making and focuses primarily on the operation of the ventromedial prefrontal cortex, to the exclusion of other frontal areas. It is of interest here for two reasons: First, its view of emotional influence is different from the theories we have discussed so far. Second, its view of somatic phenomena is broader ranging.

Damasio's theory (Damasio 1995, 1996; for a critical review, see Dunn, Dalgleish, & Lawrence, 2006; also see Chapter 38) originated in an attempt to account for the effects of ventromedial prefrontal damage. His patients showed severe impairments in decision making and in social choices but have intact IQ, learning, and retention of knowledge (including social knowledge) and skills, logical analysis, and language skills. They also perform normally on the Wisconsin Card Sorting Test that is normally affected by frontal damage. The abnormal decision making and social choices of these patients were accompanied by abnormalities in emotion and feeling and Damasio postulated that these emotional changes were the cause of the abnormal decision making.

"The somatic marker hypothesis proposes that 'somatic marker' biasing signals from the body are represented and regulated in the emotion circuitry of the brain . . . to help regulate decision-making in situations of complexity and uncertainty" (Dunn et al., 2006, p. 240). The presence of what is, in effect, a somatic image called up by a situation constrains decision making and limits the amount of processing required of cognitive mechanisms either by explicitly labeling a scenario as negative or positive; or implicitly biasing decision mechanisms in a positive or negative direction.

The somatic marker hypothesis differs from the other theories we have discussed in that it keeps the encoding of emotion (or strictly soma, see discussion that follows) distinct from the encoding of the information on which cognitive processes act, even at the prefrontal level. That is, emotional information can supplant, or bias, the processing of other types of information and is only integrated with them by altering their processing. The other theories, by and large, operate in terms of goals—compounds of cognitive (situational) and affective (affordance) information. It remains to be seen (Dunn et al., 2006) how far a somatic marker system in the ventromedial prefrontal cortex can be distinguished from some specific aspect of goal processing and how far it is qualitatively distinct from the other classes of processing that the hypothesis allows occur in other areas of frontal cortex.

The somatic marker hypothesis is also broader ranging than conventional postive/negative valence approaches. Here it departs both from the other theories and from more conventional behaviorist perspectives. Damasio (1996) holds:

that the results of emotion are primarily represented in the brain in the form of transient changes in the activity patterns

---

* We thank Rama Ganesan for bringing this literature to our notice.

of *somato-sensory* structures. I designated the emotional changes under the umbrella term 'somatic state'. Note that by somatic I refer to the musculoskeletal, visceral and internal milieu components of the soma rather than just to the musculoskeletal aspect; and note also that a somatic signal or process, although related to structures which represent the body and its states does not need to originate in the body in every instance. (p. 1412, italics added for emphasis)

Thus, somatic markers are not the simple assignment of valence or even of specific motivation to a stimulus. They are the perception or recall of a quite specific and detailed somatic image. There is no question that we can encode such images, and rehearse in our "mind's eye" the somatic experience of, say, a competition dive. However, to see this image as the basis of a background biasing of a cognitive decision about whether to make a particular bet in Damasio's paradigm task, the Iowa Gambling Task, is a radical departure from most other views of decision making and goal processing.

Central Theories of Emotion and Motivation—Some Broad Conclusions

The details, perspectives, and specific assignment of functions to structures by the theories we have considered differ. However, they all share a picture of the control of behavior by multiple serial and parallel ROT by hierarchically organized systems in the brain. They thus account for (without producing a complete explanation of) the apparent theoretical impenetrability of emotion.

No two emotions need be constructed or controlled in the same way as each other. No single emotion need have a unitary control. Rather, an emotion, as normally identified, may be an emergent structure deriving much of its superficial unity from the evolutionary path that has shaped the various component reactions. That said, the adaptive requirements facing, for example, the autonomic nervous system are sufficiently similar across the different emotions that at the general, as opposed to specific, level they can be seen to have many common features. Critically, neural analysis can determine the similarities and differences in the control of both superficially similar and superficially different reactions.

The theories also share a common picture of a variety of emotions being linked to two broad classes of general behavioral tendency: approach and avoidance. These have their origin, as emphasized by Rolls, in the fundamental properties of taxes—which are defined in terms of their being the result of the simplest stimuli generating, in the simplest way, either approach or avoidance—these ideas follow from Gray's early articulation of the same basic principles. Thus, while affective stimuli will define specific goals (and, with the possible exception of Damasio, the theories all see behavior as goal directed), a behavior such as a lever press can result in food, delivery of a mate, safety from shock, or a variety of other specific results—but in all cases (including relief from nonpunishment) it is reinforced in the same basic way, by the release of dopamine. The control of distal behavior, then, depends on systems fundamentally devoted to approach, in general, and avoidance, in general. To these basic systems, Gray and McNaughton add an additional system that resolves conflict between the approach and avoidance systems—but their view of the basic approach and avoidance systems is essentially similar to that of Rolls and their view of the basic control of avoidance is much the same as that of Ledoux.

FUTURE DIRECTIONS

So far, it might be thought that our analysis has not produced much of an advance, from a behaviorist perspective, beyond confirming the unsurprising conclusions that different stimuli elicit different proximal behaviors, and that behavioral plasticity can be understood in terms of positive and negative reinforcement. However, there are a number of points where neural analysis provides specific departures from any simple form of these conclusions and where it leads, in extreme cases, to unexpected conclusions.

Beyond the Basics—The Potential for Unexpected Conclusions

Perhaps the most important conclusion that neural analysis allows is that what is paradigmatically conditioning does not necessarily require explicit reinforcement. As we noted, sensory preconditioning and Pavlovian fear conditioning both involve the same basic form of stimulus-stimulus association in which simple long-term potentiation is all that is required for the strengthening of connections. The specific site of this potentiation, for fear conditioning, has been identified as the input from the thalamus (which encodes the conditional stimulus) to the amygdala (which generates the unconditioned, and then conditioned, responses). We have also argued that this purely associative, nonreinforced, type of learning underlies what often appears to be instrumental learning in cases, such as a pigeon pressing a lit key, where the behavior is autoshaping in disguise—although it has not yet been proved that this involves long-term potentiation.

Following on from this conclusion is the fact that true reinforcement in the classic sense intended by Pavlov, while strengthening neural connections, need not reinforce a previously occurring response. This provides a simple explanation of the fact that, for example, the conditioned response to a stimulus that predicts shock (usually freezing) is not simply the unconditioned response to the shock (vocalization, movement) moved forward in time. Indeed, while there will not be a perfect match between dependence on association rather than reinforcement and the occurrence of stimulus substitution, the neural data suggest that association rather than reinforcement should be suspected whenever the conditioned response (including those that are superficially the result of instrumental conditioning) can be accounted for by stimulus substitution.

A related issue, with instrumental reinforcement, is the demonstration that punishers release dopamine. The broad two-dimensional affective model we presented is, admittedly, derived originally from learning theoretic analysis (Gray, 1975). In this analysis, the omission of expected, or termination of, punishment is functionally equivalent to the presentation of rewarding stimuli; and in a symmetrical manner, the omission of expected, or termination of, reward is functionally equivalent to the presentation of punishment. But the demonstration of a link between punishment and dopamine, and of the role of dopamine in controlling instrumental reinforcement (Reynolds et al., 2001), has two important consequences for this model. First, it means we can be sure that, at a mechanistic level, the effects of reward and punishment omission are identical—they both change behavior by releasing dopamine. It is not the case that they happen to coincidentally produce the same superficial effects on behavior through independent mechanisms. Second, we can link both normal reward and normal punishment omission directly to explanations of addiction—where all addictive drugs (and some addictive-like behavior) have been shown to support continued behavior by the release of dopamine (but see also Chapter 40). We use this fact to provide potential explanations of some behaviors that might not be expected from the perspective of a simple reinforcement theory.

A final point we need to consider before moving on to some specific scenarios is the nature of the interaction between reward and punishment—where we again need to take into account the tendency of evolution to select multiple ROT rather than producing integrated control systems. In terms of simple decision making, for example, reward and punishment systems suppress each other. However, with respect to arousal, and so sometimes the vigor of production of responses, they can summate (Gray & Smith, 1969). These are quite distinct computations and, in terms of the effect of anxiolytic drugs on approach-avoidance conflict, can be shown to be processed in quite different parts of the brain. The inhibitory effect of punishment on rewarded behavior is mediated via the hippocampus, while the excitatory effect of punishment on reward-elicited arousal is mediated via the amygdala and not, in either case, vice versa (Gray & McNaughton, 2000). As a result, the addition of negative reinforcement can increase the levels of behavior generated by a positive reinforcer (e.g., in behavioral contrast). More peripheral theories of emotion and motivation would struggle to account for such findings.

In the sections that follow, we speculatively consider the possible insight that these features of the reward and punishment systems can offer into some of the more perplexing behaviors shown by human beings. (For a higher level view of apparently irrational behavior patterns, see Chapter 37.)

Relief of Nonpunishment: Gambling

We have already considered the complex mechanisms underlying the partial reinforcement extinction effect—where we argued that the phenomena are generally adaptive in that they conform to optimal foraging analyses. Here we consider cases of pathological gambling where persistence in the face of intermittent reinforcement is, in optimal foraging terms, maladaptive.

According to standard behavioral accounts, pathological gambling should not develop very easily and should extinguish fast. That is, engaging in a behavior that provides a high ratio of punishment to reward should led to avoidance behavior, which of course it does in the majority of the population. However, in a significant minority of people, pathological gambling behavior develops. That is, the behavior entails high monetary losses leading to personal, family, and societal problems.

We could attempt to explain this maladaptive behavior using standard learning theory. There is intermittent positive reinforcement, and the ratio and pattern of reward to response are carefully chosen to produce robust conditioning and maximum resistance to extinction. To some extent, this can explain gambling. But it seems not to be a sufficient explanation of normal gambling far less its pathological form. First, in animals simply subjected to intermittent schedules, as we noted earlier, the level of behavior conforms approximately to optimality—with over-responding being present only while information about a new reward density is being gathered. Second, quite apart from the local preponderance of negative reinforcement for the behavior, there is usually additional negative reinforcement in terms of the effect on other aspects of life, and this should produce robust avoidance behavior. Third, there is the brute fact that the majority of people who engage in recreational gambling do not develop pathological gambling behavior. These facts suggest that we must look elsewhere for a sufficient explanation of this form of counterproductive behavior.

One alternative theory is to assume that people prone to pathological gambling have biased cognitions (e.g., "The more I lose, the more chance of have of winning"). We may suppose that such biases are important in maintaining pathological gambling, but such explanations are high on description but low on powers of explanation, and specifically fail to reveal *why* such cognitive biases exists, let alone *how* they relate to reinforcement sensitivity (which we know is important in gambling behavior). Nor do they explain the intensity of the behavior.

A possibility suggested by our current analysis is that pathological gambling develops as a as a form of self-defeating dopamine-mediated approach behavior. On this view, punishment summates with the expectation of rare, large rewards, to create a high level of arousal. It thus energies and invigorates behavior. Even if the schedule of reinforcement were net positive for the player (as it can be with games such as "21") it involves a background of fairly steady punishment, in the form of loss of the stake and reward omission. This means that when a reward occurs its effect is supercharged by the positive effects of relieving nonpunishment. The resultant physiological arousal acts in the same way as a drug, such as amphetamine, to create an emotional high that produces rapid and resistant conditioning (e.g., to the paraphilia of the gambling context). These emotional "highs", that are *predicted* by the higher-density of punishments, can become associated with it and so, through counterconditioning, reduce its negative reinforcing value (which is weak at the level of the individual response). The overall picture, as with chemical addiction, is an overriding of background negative stimuli by occasional powerful stimulation of the dopamine system.

As yet these behavioral processes, and the apparently paradoxical fact that punishment in gambling seems to maintain pathological gambling itself, does not make much sense in traditional Skinnerian terms, but it finds a natural explanation within the context of the known properties of the dopamine system—and with the low level of genuine "pleasure" in those addicted to drugs.

Reward-Punishment Mutual Inhibition: Romantic Partner Abuse

A similar process to that seen in pathological gambling may also operate in romantic partners who suffer long-term abuse but who are reluctant to escape their abusing partner (i.e., are reluctant to engage in FFFS-mediated avoidance of the threat stimulus). Putting aside other relevant factors involved in such situations (e.g., children and financial dependence), some abused partners (both males as well as females—here the forms of abuse may differ) repeatedly fail to leave their partners who, on the one hand, they openly declare are abusing them, but, on the other hand, find it difficult to break away (even where there do not exist an financial, or other, objective reason, for doing so).

Partner abuse should be expected to activate the FFFS (as well as the BIS due to the likelihood of conflict) leading to punishment-mediated behaviors (in this case fear, tension, attempts to avoid/escape abuse). When the abusive partner reconciles, the abused partner will not only experience an absence of punishment (itself a good thing in terms of reduced FFFS activity), but also a strong boost to the BAS in the form of release of suppression of the reward system by the punishment (FFFS/BIS) system. As in the case of gambling (see above), relief of nonpunishment processes may also be assumed to operate. This release, and the subsequent rebound effects, would be expected to lead to a heightened BAS activity and an emotional high, which would stamp in, via conditioning, behaviors immediately preceding it, namely the partner's reconciliation behavior and associated stimuli—Konorski (1967) made a similar claim about the rebound effects in romantic "making-up" behavior.

Once again, the FFFS/BIS-induced arousal would serve further to augment the rebound of the BAS, increasing the subjective intensity of the positive emotional high. (Rebound effects are also suggested by anti-anxiety drugs that are traded illegally for the highs they produce in some people.)

There is a further theoretical twist that would make an additional contribution to this BAS-mediated emotional high and resulting approach behavior (e.g., making up). The mutual inhibition of the reward and punishment systems would mean that the previous negative emotion and behavior associated with the punishment system would now itself be suppressed, making the abused partner, emotionally speaking, to forget (or, at least, attenuate the strength of) the previous punishment delivered by the partner.

Thus, we may predict that one of the major factors contributing to the continuation of abusive relationships is that the abused partner has a strong mutual inhibition between their reward and punishment systems, rendering a supercharged BAS input from the abusive partner's reconciliation behavior. It might be the case that the abusive partner learns how to manipulate the emotions of the abused partner, and this would contribute to the cycle of abuse.

SUMMARY

In our discussion of central states and theories of emotion and motivation, we ranged freely from the exotic, but fairly well established, theories of the partial reinforcement extinction effect (PREE) to the prosaic, but not clearly understood, behavior of pathological gambling and romantic partner relations. We attempted to show that neural analysis can, and has, generated quite distinct theories that not only have the advantage of being tied to neural and pharmacological reality (and so are less subject to the whims of verbal definition) but also have the advantage of throwing into strong relief some of the less obvious properties of emotional and motivational systems. These properties derive from the fact the emotion and motivation involve multiple serial and parallel ROT, each of which has evolved separately but nonetheless regularly co-occurs with and is often seamlessly integrated with others.

The existence of multiple ROT itself creates an environment in which higher order control mechanisms can evolve. The addition of later, complex, ROT to sets of simpler ones has also tended to produce hierarchical structures with the quickest, dirtiest, and phylogenetically earliests mechanisms located at lower levels of the neuraxis and progressively slower and more sophisticated mechanism located at progressively higher levels.

We considered a number of current central theories of emotion and motivation. These differ in detail and even in their use of terms. But they can all be seen as sharing a fundamentally Hebbian (purely associative, as opposed to reinforced) view of basic memory processes; a picture of two fundamental reinforcement systems—with dopaminergic systems reinforcing specific responses whether these produce reward or relieving nonpunishment; a distinction between ventral ("what") and dorsal ("where") processing streams; a view that behavior results from neural processing of goals (stimulus/response or, better, occasion/affordance compounds); and a view of prefrontal cortex as holding potential or intended goals in mind (i.e., in "working" or "active" memory).

The take-home message is that emotion and motivation are intertwined and each is multifaceted. This is often blindingly obvious at the neural level—but still goes against the grain of our normal use of emotional terms. As we have seen, what is meant by "anxiety" can differ even among neurally driven theorists—making it unclear how far disagreements are about real facts or arbitrary definitions. What is needed, then, is recursive processing of neural and behavioral information. When the resultant "psychological" constructs are also firmly tied down to particular neural instantiations then we will be in a position to say that we truly understand the resultant structure of the behaviors emitted by the organism—and will be on the way to understanding our own minds from an objective standpoint.

REFERENCES

American Psychiatric Association. (1987). *Diagnostic and statistical manual of mental disorders* (3rd ed., rev.). Washington, DC: Author.

Amsel, A. (1992). *Frustration theory: An analysis of dispositional learning and memory.* Cambridge: Cambridge University Press.

Bandler, R., Keay, K. A., Floyd, N., & Price, J. (2000). Central circuits mediating patterned autonomic activity during active vs. passive emotional coping. *Brain Research Bulletin, 53*(1), 95–104.

Bandler, R., Price, J. L., & Keay, K. A. (2000). Brain mediation of active and passive emotional coping. *Progress in Brain Research, 122,* 331–347.

Bindra, D. (1969). A unified interpretation of emotion and motivation. *Annals of the New York Academy of Sciences, 159,* 1071–1083.

Blanchard, D. C., & Blanchard, R. J. (1988). Ethoexperimental approaches to the biology of emotion. *Annual Review of Psychology, 39,* 43–68.

Blanchard, D. C., & Blanchard, R. J. (1990). Effects of ethanol, benzodiazepines and serotonin compounds on ethopharmacological models of anxiety. In N. McNaughton & G. Andrews (Eds.), *Anxiety* (pp. 188–199). Dunedin: Otago University Press.

Blanchard, D. C., Blanchard, R. J., Tom, P., & Rodgers, R. J. (1990). Diazepam changes risk assessment in an anxiety/defense test battery. *Psychopharmacology (Berl), 101,* 511–518.

Blanchard, R. J., & Blanchard, D. C. (1989). Antipredator defensive behaviors in a visible burrow system. *Journal of Comparative Psychology, 103*(1), 70–82.

Blanchard, R. J., & Blanchard, D. C. (1990a). Anti-predator defense as models of animal fear and anxiety. In P. F. Brain, S. Parmigiani, R. J. Blanchard, & D. Mainardi (Eds.), *Fear and defence* (pp. 89–108). Chur: Harwood.

Blanchard, R. J., & Blanchard, D. C. (1990b). An ethoexperimental analysis of defense, fear and anxiety. In N. McNaughton & G. Andrews (Eds.), *Anxiety* (pp. 124–133). Dunedin: Otago University Press.

Blanchard, R. J., Griebel, G., Henrie, J. A., & Blanchard, D. C. (1997). Differentiation of anxiolytic and panicolytic drugs by effects on rat and mouse defense test batteries. *Neuroscience and Biobehavioral Reviews, 21*(6), 783–789.

Bliss, T. V. P., Gardner-Medwin, A. R., & Lomo, T. (1973). Synaptic plasticity in the hippocampus. In G. B. Ansell & P. B. Bradley (Eds.), *Macromolecules and behaviour* (pp. 193–203). London: Macmillan.

Bliss, T. V. P., & Lomo, T. (1973). Long-lasting potentiation of synaptic transmission in the dentate area of the anaethsetised rabbit following stimulation of the perforant path. *Journal of Physiology (Lond), 232,* 331–356.

Borkovec, T. D., Robinson, E., Pruzinsky, T., & DePree, J. A. (1983). Preliminary exploration of worry: Some characteristics and processes. *Behaviour Research and Therapy, 21*(1), 9–16.

Brady, J. V. (1975a). Conditioning and emotion. In L. Levi (Ed.), *Emotions: Their parameters and measurement* (pp. 309–340). New York: Raven Press.

Brady, J. V. (1975b). Toward a behavioural biology of emotion. In L. Levi (Ed.), *Emotions: Their parameters and measurement* (pp. 17–46). New York: Raven Press.

Capaldi, E. J. (1967). A sequential hypothesis of instrumental learning. In K. W. Spence & J. T. Spence (Eds.), *The psychology of learning and motivation* (pp. 67–156). New York: Academic Press.

Carlson, N. R. (1980). *Physiology of behavior.* Boston: Allyn & Bacon.

Damasio, A. R. (1995). On some functions of the human prefrontal cortex. *Annals of the New York Academy of Sciences, 769,* 241–251.

Damasio, A. R. (1996). The somatic marker hypothesis and the possible functions of the prefrontal cortex. *Philosophical Transactions of the Royal Society of London. Series B, Biological Sciences, 351,* 1413–1420.

Dickinson, A. (1980). *Contemporary animal learning theory*. Cambridge: Cambridge University Press.

Dunn, B. D., Dalgleish, T., & Lawrence, A. D. (2006). The somatic marker hypothesis: A critical evaluation. *Neuroscience and Biobehavioral Reviews, 30*(2), 239–271.

Fanselow, M. S., & LeDoux, J. E. (1999). Why we think plasticity underlying pavlovian fear conditioning occurs in the basolateral amygdala. *Neuron, 23*(2), 229–232.

Feldon, J., Guillamon, A., Gray, J. A., De Wit, H., & McNaughton, N. (1979). Sodium amylobarbitone and responses to nonreward. *Quarterly Journal of Experimental Psychology, 31*, 19–50.

Gray, J. A. (1975). *Elements of a two-process theory of learning*. London: Academic Press.

Gray, J. A. (1977). Drug effects on fear and frustration: Possible limbic site of action of minor tranquilizers. In L. L. Iversen, S. D. Iversen, & S. H. Snyder (Eds.), *Handbook of psychopharmacology, drugs, neurotransmitters and behaviour* (Vol. 8, pp. 433–529). New York: Plenum Press.

Gray, J. A. (1982). *The neuropsychology of anxiety: An enquiry in to the functions of the septo-hippocampal system*. Oxford: Oxford University Press.

Gray, J. A. (1987). *The psychology of fear and stress*. London: Cambridge University Press.

Gray, J. A., & McNaughton, N. (2000). *The neuropsychology of anxiety: An enquiry into the functions of the septo-hippocampal system*. Oxford: Oxford University Press.

Gray, J. A., & Smith, P. T. (1969). An arousal-decision model for partial reinforcement and discrimination learning. In R. Gilbert & N. S. Sutherland (Eds.), *Animal discrimination learning* (pp. 243–272). London: Academic Press.

Hebb, D. O. (1949). *The organization of behavior: A neuropsychological theory*. New York: Wiley-Interscience.

Hinde, R. A. (1998). *Animal behaviour*. New York: McGraw-Hill.

Hofer, M. A. (1972). Physiological and behavioural processes in early maternal deprivation. In R. Porter & J. Knight (Eds.), *Physiology, emotion and psychosomatic illness* (pp. 175–186). Ciba symposium No. 8 (new series). Elsevier.

Hull, C. L. (1952). *A behavior system*. Yale University Press.

James, W. (1884). What is an emotion? *Mind, 9*, 188–205.

Jenkins, H. M., & Moore, B. R. (1973). The form of the auto-shaped response with food or water reinforcers. *Journal of the Experimental Analysis of Behavior, 20*, 163–181.

Kandel, E. R., & Hawkins, R. D. (1992). The biological basis of learning and individuality. *Scientific American, 267*, 79–86.

Kelly, J. F., & Hake, D. F. (1970). An extinction-induced increase in an aggressive response with humans. *Journal of the Experimental Analysis of Behavior, 14*, 153–164.

Konorski, J. (1967). *Integrative activity of the brain: An interdisciplinary approach*. Chicago: University of Chicago Press.

Krebs, J. R., Stephens, D. W., & Sutherland, W. J. (1983). Perspectives in optimal foraging. In G. A. Clark & A. H. Brush (Eds.), *Perspectives in ornithology* (pp. 165–221). Cambridge: Cambridge University Press.

LeDoux, J. E. (1993). Emotional memory systems in the brain. *Behavioural Brain Research, 58*, 69–79.

LeDoux, J. E. (1994). Emotion, memory and the brain. *Scientific American, 270*, 50–59.

LeDoux, J. E. (2002). *Synaptic self*. Harmondsworth: Viking Penguin.

McNamara, J., & Houston, A. (1980). The application of statistical decision theory to animal behaviour. *Journal of Theoretical Biology, 85*, 673–690.

McNaughton, N. (1985). Chlordiazepoxide and successive discrimination: Different effects on acquisition and performance. *Pharmacology, Biochemistry and Behavior, 23*, 487–494.

McNaughton, N. (1989a). Anxiety: One label for many processes. *New Zealand Journal of Psychology, 18*, 51–59.

McNaughton, N. (1989b). *Biology and emotion*. Cambridge: Cambridge University Press.

McNaughton, N., & Corr, P. J. (2004). A two-dimensional neuropsychology of defense: Fear/anxiety and defensive distance. *Neuroscience and Biobehavioral Reviews, 28*, 285–305.

McNaughton, N., & Gray, J. A. (1983). Pavlovian counterconditioning is unchanged by chlordiazepoxide or by septal lesions. *Quarterly Journal of Experimental Psychology, 35B*, 221–233.

McNaughton, N., Kocsis, B., & Hajós, M. (2007). Elicited hippocampal theta rhythm: A screen for anxiolytic and pro-cognitive drugs through changes in hippocampal function? *Behavioural Pharmacology, 18*, 329–346.

Meyer, T. J., Miller, M. L., Metzger, R. L., & Borkovec, T. D. (1999). Development and validation of the Penn state worry questionnaire. *Behaviour Research and Therapy, 28*, 487–495.

Millenson, J. R., & Leslie, J. C. (1979). *Principles of behavior analysis*. New York: MacMillan.

Panksepp, J. (1998). *Affective neuroscience: The foundations of human and animal emotions*. New York: Oxford University Press.

Pinel, J. P. J. (1997). *Biopsychology*. Boston: Allyn & Bacon.

Renfrew, J. W., & Hutchinson, R. R. (1983). Motivation The motivation of aggression. In E. Satinoff & P. Teitelbaum (Eds.) *Handbook of Behavioural Neurobiology*, (Vol. 6, pp. 511–541). Plenum Press.

Reynolds, J. N. J., Hyland, B. I., & Wickens, J. R. (2001, August 23). A cellular mechanism of reward-related learning. *Nature, 413*(6851), 67–70.

Rolls, E. T. (1990). A theory of emotion, and its application to understanding the neural basis of emotion. *Cognition and Emotion, 4*, 161–190.

Rolls, E. T. (2000). On the brain and emotion. *Behavioral and Brain Sciences, 23*(2), 219–228.

Sartory, G., MacDonald, R., & Gray, J. A. (1990). Effects of diazepam on approach, self-reported fear and psychophysological responses in snake phobics. *Behaviour Research and Therapy, 28*(4), 273–282.

Skinner, B. F. (1953). *Science and human behavior*. New York: Macmillan.

Smits, D. J. M., & Boeck, P. D. (2006). From BIS/BAS to the big five. *European Journal of Personality, 20*, 255–270.

Sokolowski, J. D., McCullough, L. D., & Salamone, J. D. (1994). Effects of dopamine depletions in the medial prefrontal cortex on active avoidance and escape in the rat. *Brain Research, 651*, 293–299.

Stark, H., Bischof, A., & Scheich, H. (1999). Increase of extracellular dopamine in prefrontal cortex of gerbils during acquisition of the avoidance strategy in the shuttle-box. *Neuroscience Letters, 264*(1–3), 77–80.

Sutherland, N. S. (1966). Partial reinforcement and the breadth of learning. *Journal of Experimental Psychology, 18*, 289–301.

Weingarten, H. P. (1983). Conditioned cues elicit feeding in sated rats: A role for learning in meal initiation. *Science, 220*(4595), 431–433.

Ziff, D. R., & Capaldi, E. J. (1971). Amytal and the small trial partial reinforcement effect: Stimulus properties of early trial nonrewards. *Journal of Experimental Child Psychology, 87*, 263–269.

Chapter 37

The Affective Neuroscience of Emotion: Automatic Activation, Interoception, and Emotion Regulation

ANDREAS OLSSON AND ARNE ÖHMAN

Emotions sometimes appear mysterious. They can appear unmistakably clear, yet at the same time elusive. In our daily lives we often define the basic goals of human striving in terms of emotion: We yearn for happiness and do our best to avoid misery. But making the distinction between positive and negative emotions is not as simple as saying that we seek the former and shun the latter. Peace Corps workers, parachute jumpers, and snake handlers might seek situations that most of us fear. Likewise, we may indulge in behaviors such as passionate love, overeating, drinking too much, and substance abuse even when it brings misery. At times we may simultaneously experience two conflicting emotions about another person, pulling us in opposite directions, and after a separation we may find that our current emotions are not as abyssal as we forecasted them to be some time ago. In many of the most common psychological disorders—depression, anxiety disorders, and phobias—individuals find that their emotional lives defy reason and rational thought. Still, for most of us, life without emotion would not be worth living.

Conflicts are not only abundant in our everyday experience of emotions. The landscape of scientific theories aspiring to describe and explain emotion is also riddled with conflicts. However, these often opposing theories of emotion have over the past century inspired various research paradigms in the behavioral and neurosciences that have contributed importantly to what we know about emotions today. In this chapter we revisit a selection of the most influential

approaches to emotion to discuss findings that are enlightening in terms of the link between behavior and its neural bases. A greater appreciation of the link between emotional behavior and its biological bases is critical for a more complete understanding of emotion and its conflicting nature.

UNDERSTANDING EMOTION THROUGH THE BRAIN–BEHAVIOR LINK

The Neuroscience of Emotion

Psychological research on emotion basically is a multivariate enterprise seeking to develop theories that relate emotion-provoking circumstances to verbal reports of emotion, psychophysiological data, and behavioral responses. An important contribution of this research is that it has made sophisticated methodologies available for manipulating and measuring emotion in the psychological laboratory (see Coan & Allen, 2007). Neuroscience offers unique prospects for a deeper understanding of emotion by revealing the neural underpinnings of the relationships revealed in the psychological laboratory.

Imaging Emotion

Animal research over the past century laid the foundation for understanding some of the basic neural mechanisms of emotion. However, the recent development of techniques to image the healthy human brain in vivo has provided an unprecedented opportunity to directly study the neural elements of emotional responses and experiences. Through imaging, the workings of the emotional brain can now be observed independently of people's introspective accounts of their emotional states. Together with our already quite sophisticated knowledge of the peripheral psychophysiology of emotional responses, descriptions of neural processes are helping us to understand the specific mechanisms

The authors are also affiliated with the NIHM Center for the Study of Emotion and Attention at the University of Florida–Gainesville and the NOS-HS Center of Excellence on Cognitive Control. Arne Öhman is the recipient of a grant for Long-Term Support of Leading Investigators from the Swedish Science Research Council. Address for both authors: Section of Psychology, Department of Clinical Neuroscience, Karolinska University Hospital, Solna.

underlying emotions. In turn, mechanistic accounts provide a biological grounding that can be used to constrain alternative models and theories of emotion. Moreover, knowledge about which psychological processes involve similar and different neurobiological processes allows us to use neurobiology to carve the nature of emotion at its joints. For example, brain imaging research has confirmed that negative attitudes to members belonging to a racial group other than one's own has an immediate, nonconscious emotional component, which is modulated by prefrontal influences (Cunningham, Johnson, Gatenby, Gore, & Banaji, 2004; Phelps et al., 2000).

The rapidly growing body of knowledge about the workings of the human brain has made it possible to compare and integrate this knowledge with what we know about the brain–behavior link in other animals. Comparisons across species make it possible to use experimental paradigms in nonhuman animals, which would not be ethically feasible in humans, to learn more about human emotions. As a result, evolutionary theory has gained increasing influence as a unifying theory in psychology, solidifying its place within the realm of biological sciences. This development has facilitated scientific accounts of emotional behavior comprising both its proximate mechanisms and evolutionary functions (Damasio, 1994; LeDoux, 1996; Öhman, 1986; Rolls, 1999).

Limitations of Imaging

It should be remembered that neuroimaging has inherent limitations because of its correlational nature. For example, it can tell us which brain areas are involved in an emotional response, but it remains silent on what neural processes are necessary for a specific response, which is a critical step in inferring causality. To learn about the causal links between brain functions and behavior we need observations of the effects on behavior when the functioning of well-defined functional neural circuitry is impaired. To this end, systematic studies of patients with localized brain damage have proven invaluable. Lately a new technique, transcranial magnetic stimulation, has gained popularity. This technique has been developed to induce temporary and completely reversible brain lesions in healthy volunteers through the application of strong magnetic fields to specific cortical areas. Although there are several limitations to this technique, such as its being applicable only to cortical regions, it has been successfully used to examine the causal link between brain and behavior in humans. Nevertheless, to overcome the limitations associated with experimentation in humans, the study of other animals will remain imperative in our quest for a full understanding of emotion.

Implicit and Explicit Measures of Emotion

As stated earlier, neural activation, whether central or peripheral, can be assessed independently of the individual's verbal accounts of emotional experiences. Measures of emotional responses that are nonverbal in nature are often referred to as "implicit," in contrast to "explicit," verbal accounts. Whereas implicit measures assess responses of which the individual often lacks introspective awareness, explicit measures tap responses dependent of linguistic processes, such as reflective reasoning. Because of their relative insensitivity to demand characteristics, implicit responses are critical in cross-species comparisons of emotion. Particularly informative are implicit responses that can be dissociated from the emoter's explicit reports. There are good reasons for assuming that these responses provide a window into the workings of phylogenetically older mechanisms, drawing on brain systems that are partially independent from more recently evolved systems that are responsible for linguistic processing (LeDoux, 1996; Öhman, 1986; Öhman & Wiens, 2003). Although our current understanding of implicit emotional responses relies on recent technological advancements, the interest in different, separable nuances of emotional responses is ancient.

TWO EMOTIONAL MOVEMENTS

More than 2,000 years ago Greek philosophers belonging to the Stoic tradition proposed an interesting separation between what they called the first and second "movements" of an emotion (Oatley, 2004). This would turn out to be prophetic about an important distinction in modern emotion research: automatic versus controlled emotional processing, or primary versus secondary appraisal. The first movement is rapid and reflexive, such as when we freeze when we are confronted with a snake or a fearful other whose fear expression might be informative about an imminent danger (Figure 37.1). The second movement is what we make of this instinctive response and how we appraise the current situation: Is the snake poisonous? Why is the other expressing fear? How does this fit into the surrounding context (Figure 37.1)? What are his or her intentions? This evaluative or reflective process depends mainly on voluntary mental activity. Reflecting about the properties of a stimulus is likely to change our emotional experience without our intending to do so. However, reflection can also be intentionally used to change our emotional responses. For example, you might want to curb the empathic response you feel for a terrified child who is about to receive an injection (Figure 37.1)—especially if you are the doctor who has to administer the injection with acute precision. An emotional response can be down-regulated in various ways, such as by shifting one's attention to something less evocative or by reinterpreting the meaning of the situation. For the purpose of this chapter, and to maintain the Stoic terminology, we have tentatively called this intentional regulation the "third movement."

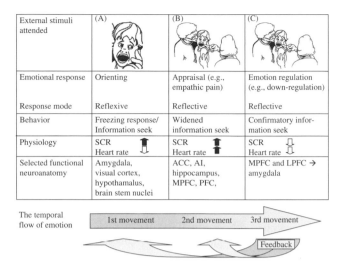

External stimuli attended	(A)	(B)	(C)
Emotional response	Orienting	Appraisal (e.g., empathic pain)	Emotion regulation (e.g., down-regulation)
Response mode	Reflexive	Reflective	Reflective
Behavior	Freezing response/ Information seek	Widened information seek	Confirmatory information seek
Physiology	SCR ⬆ Heart rate ⬆	SCR ⬆ Heart rate ⬆	SCR ⬇ Heart rate ⬇
Selected functional neuroanatomy	Amygdala, visual cortex, hypothalamus, brain stem nuclei	ACC, AI, hippocampus, MPFC, PFC,	MPFC and LPFC → amygdala

The temporal flow of emotion: 1st movement — 2nd movement — 3rd movement — Feedback

Figure 37.1   The temporal flow of emotion.

Note. This figure illustrates how an emotional situation (a fearful child anticipating an injection) gives rise to the unfolding of a series of emotional responses in a perceiver. The temporal flow of these responses and a selection of the associated functional neuroanatomy is divided into three hypothetical stages, approximating the first (A), second (B), and third (C) emotional movements. (A) Initially, the fearful face of the child is encountered, giving rise to a reflexive orienting response, which mobilizes the perceiver to search of the environment for potential threats that could have caused the child's fear expression. The attentional focus on the fearful face produces heart rate deceleration and an increased arousal response (SCR). These primary responses are predominantly mediated by a subcortical neural circuitry centered on the amygdala, which affects behavior through hypothalamic and brain stem nuclei. (B) As additional information becomes available to the perceiver, the situation is appraised in terms of its context and memories of similar situations. For example, facilitated by an automatically triggered mirroring of the child's emotional responses, the reflective attribution of pain might produce an empathic response in the perceiver, which leads to an increase in physiological arousal. Apart from the subcortical circuitry described (A), this process is likely to draw on both regions involved in the retrieval of episodic memories, such as the hippocampus, sensory, and frontal regions responsible for the empathic experience of and reflection about the child's emotional state. (C) The empathic response can be intentionally down-regulated through reappraisal of the situation. For example, reminding oneself of the long-term benefits to the child from receiving a life-saving vaccination or attending to his or her soothing parent might mitigate the perceiver's emotional response. This regulatory process can be facilitated by selectively attending information that confirms one's reappraisal of the situation. Emotion regulation has been shown to involve prefrontal influences on the subcortical circuitry described in A. As illustrated by the arrows at the bottom of the figure, the reflective appraisals of the situation described in B and C are likely to affect the initial response to new stimuli through top-down modulation of primary appraisals, supported by bidirectional neural connections. ACC = Anterior cingulate cortex; AI = Anterior insula; LPFC = Lateral prefrontal cortex; MPFC = Medial prefrontal cortex; PFC = Prefrontal cortex; SCR = Skin conductance response.

By making the second movement the essence of emotion, the Stoics changed the meaning of emotion from an automatic and involuntary response to something individuals could consciously control and take responsibility for. The distinction between the first and second movements is reminiscent of today's accounts of dual processing of emotion that comes in many guises. Common to all of them is the suggestion that two distinct kinds of processes, resembling the two movements, are responsible for different aspects of emotional responses. Recent neuroscientific research has substantiated dual processing by describing two general types of processes, engaging partially separated but, under normal circumstances, interacting neural systems. The first system comprises reflexive, automatic responses that are implicitly expressed; the second comprises more reflective processes that can be affected by voluntary control.

The First Movement of Emotion

Automatic Appraisal

In 1980 Robert Zajonc and colleagues proposed a conceptualization of the first movement of emotion in terms of an automatic affective response that was primary to, and independent of, cognitive responses to the stimulus (Kunst-Wilson & Zajonc, 1980). Succinctly summarized, Zajonc claimed that we are sure of what we like, even though we may not know why we like it, or even what it is that we like. This proposal was backed up by an extensive series of studies examining the liking of stimuli as a function of repeated exposure (see Zajonc, 2004, for a concise summary). For example, Kunst-Wilson and Zajonc presented Chinese ideograms at durations as short as a few milliseconds to make them unrecognizable. Even though the data confirmed their unrecognizability, the participants liked previously shown (but nonseen) more than new ideograms.

The Neural Bases of Automatic Appraisal

LeDoux (1996) suggested that the automatic affective response described by Zajonc (1980) was related to the very fast brain activation he and his colleagues had demonstrated through a direct route between sensory thalamic nuclei and the amygdala, a conglomerate of subnuclei bilaterally located in the medial temporal lobes, which has long been considered a central substrate of emotion (Klüver & Bucy, 1939; Weiskrantz, 1956). It has been argued that this neural system evolved to cope with rapidly emerging dangers, quickly relaying crude representations of potentially threatening stimuli to the amygdala, bypassing the cortex (Adolphs, 2001; de Gelder, Snyder, Greve, Gerard, & Hadjikhani, 2004; LeDoux, 1996, 2000; Morris, Öhman, & Dolan, 1999; Öhman & Mineka, 2001; Whalen et al., 1998).

In an extensive research program, LeDoux (1996, 2000) and others (see Davis & Whalen, 2001) have demonstrated that the amygdala is the hub of this automatic and phylogenetically ancient neural circuitry centered on subcortical regions, controlling fear responses to threatening stimuli. The lateral nucleus of the amygdala receives input from the external world via the direct thalamic route and via the classical sensory pathways through sensory thalamic nuclei and the primary and secondary sensory cortices. This information is forwarded to the central nucleus, which has efferent connections to areas involved in emotional expression, such as the hypothalamus (sympathetic branch of the autonomic nervous system), and midbrain and brain stem nuclei related to fear behavior (periaqueductal gray), defensive reflexes (such as startle), and facial expression (facial nucleus). Although involved in many emotionally relevant processes, the primary function of this network is to quickly enhance attention to evaluate a potential threat by means of ramping up activation in a distributed network of functional brain systems (Davis & Whalen, 2001). It is also critical to the acquisition, retention, and expression of basic emotional forms of learning (Phelps & LeDoux, 2005) and certain social functions (Adolphs, 2001; Adolphs et al., 2005).

Consistent with the role of this neural system in assembling perceptual and attentional resources and to prepare for action, the processing of emotionally significant stimuli that is known to involve the amygdala has been reported to influence early visual and attentional processing (Anderson & Phelps, 2001; Morris, Friston, et al., 1998; Phelps, Ling, & Carrasco, 2006; Vuilleumier, Richardson, Armony, Driver, & Dolan, 2004; see also Volume II, Section V, Chapter 11 of this handbook [D'Stanley, Ferneyhough & Phelps]) and action representations (de Gelder et al., 2004). However, the precise mechanisms underlying the amygdala's influence on a widely distributed network of cortical areas have not yet been specified. These issues are currently attracting much research and debate (McGaugh, 2004; Phelps, 2006).

Data Supporting the Concept of Automatic Appraisal

Supporting the concept of a first automatic stage in emotion activation are both behavioral and neuroimaging indicators of immediate nonconscious emotional responses to unseen images presented very briefly and effectively masked from conscious perception by an immediate masking picture. For example, participants fearful of snakes and spiders responded with enhanced skin conductance responses (SCRs) to pictorial representations of the feared animals even when pictures of the animals were unseen (masked; Öhman & Soares, 1994). These behavioral data have been supported by brain imaging studies showing amygdala activations to masked snakes and spiders in fearful individuals

(Carlsson et al., 2004; Figure 37.2), to masked fearful faces (Whalen et al., 1998), and to aversively conditioned masked angry faces (Morris, Öhman, & Dolan, 1998). Furthermore, two studies have reported reliable amygdala activation to suppressed pictures of fearful faces in a binocular rivalry paradigm (Pasley, Mayes, & Schultz, 2004; Williams, Morris, McGlone, Abbott, & Mattingley, 2004), thus providing converging evidence that the amygdala can be activated by "unseen" visual stimuli.

There is also suggestive evidence that visual information may take a direct route to the amygdala, bypassing the cortex. Morris, Öhman, & Dolan (1999) examined the neural connectivity between the amygdala and other brain regions when the amygdala was activated by masked stimuli. They reported that such activation could be reliably predicted from activation of subcortical way stations in the visual systems, such as the superior colliculus and the right pulvinar nucleus of the thalamus, but not from any cortical regions. The superior colliculus and the pulvinar are both involved in attentional processes, the superior colliculus

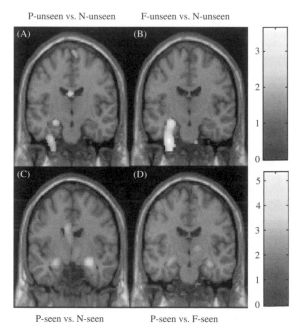

Figure 37.2 Amygdala activations to masked and nonmasked pictures of snakes and spiders in individuals fearful of snakes or spiders.

Note. Upper panels (A–B) show coronal views ($y = -4$) of activation maps for unseen (masked) phobic stimuli (e.g., picture of a snake) contrasted with an unseen neutral stimulus (a picture of a mushroom) (P-unseen versus N-unseen) and a fear-relevant but nonfeared (e.g., a spider) stimulus (F-unseen versus N-unseen). Note the left-lateralized amygdala activations in both conditions. Lower panels (C–D) show contrasts between seen (nonmasked) phobic and neutral stimuli (P-seen versus N-seen, $y = -8$) and between phobic and fear-relevant but nonfeared stimuli (P-seen versus F-seen, $y = -4$). Note the bilateral amygdala activations seen in both contrasts. From "Fear and the Amygdala: Manipulation of Awareness Generates Differential Cerebral Responses to Phobic and Fear-Relevant (but Nonfeared) Stimuli," by Carlsson et al., 2004, *Emotion, 4,* p. 345. Reprinted with permission.

in eye movement control and shifts of attention and the pulvinar in monitoring attentional salience.

Liddell et al. (2005) examined the effect of masked fearful versus masked neutral faces on anatomically defined regions of interest. Confirming the connectivity data reported by Morris, Öhman, et al. (1999), they found reliable activation to masked fearful faces in the left superior colliculi, the left pulvinar, and the bilateral amygdala. In addition they found activation in the locus coeruleus and the anterior cingulate cortex.

The visual resolution that can be achieved by this route is likely to be quite restricted. Vuilleumier, Armony, Driver, and Dolan (2003) suggested that it operates primarily on gross, low-frequency information. Accordingly, they filtered the spatial frequency of pictures of faces to produce facial stimuli that retained only high- or low-frequency spatial information. Their results showed that amygdala responses were larger for low-frequency faces provided that they showed expressions of fear. Moreover, these researchers demonstrated activation of the pulvinar and superior colliculus by low-frequency but not high-frequency fearful faces. Thus these results suggest that there is a distinct superior colliculus-pulvinar pathway to the amygdala that operates primarily on low-frequency information.

Appraising Reward

Whereas the amygdala has been primarily implicated in the processing of aversive information (although evidence for its involvement in appetitive processing is accumulating; see, e.g., Murray, 2007; Sabatinelli, Bradley, Fitzsimmons, & Lang, 2005), the striatum has been singled out as critical for the automatic processing of appetitive stimuli and the generation of implicit positive emotional responses. Research has shown that the striatum can be engaged in a variety of different, but often related, tasks, such as the processing of reward stimuli (Cromwell & Schultz, 2003; Knutson, Adams, Fong, & Hommer, 2001), error-driven learning (O'Doherty et al., 2004; Schultz, 2002), novelty seeking (Bevins et al., 2002), and the initiation of instrumental behaviors (Rolls, 1999).

With regard to appetitive emotional stimuli, Berridge and Winkielman (2003) showed that perceptually masked pictures of happy faces facilitated fluid consumption in thirsty participants who remained completely unaware of the emotional faces and any relationship between them and the drinking task. Angry faces had the opposite effect.

Pessiglione et al. (2007) demonstrated that the striatum was critical in mediating motivation to perform in a task reinforced by monetary incentives. They provided masked or nonmasked information to their participants about how much money they could earn by exerting maximal hand-grip force. Even when pictures of expected monetary gain (a pound or a penny) were blocked from awareness by masking stimuli, activation in the ventral striatum was larger and the force exerted higher when the potential gain was large rather than small. Thus, whereas the amygdala can be nonconsciously activated to mediate fear, the striatum can be nonconsciously activated to mediate reward and positive emotion. There is converging evidence, therefore, that rapid, automatic processes operate both in aversive and appetitive circumstances to result in immediate and unconscious emotional activation.

At this point a caveat is in place. Although we have focused on two core functional regions (the amygdala and the striatum), both aversive and reward processes normally draw on a widely distributed network of neural systems. This is discussed in greater detail later.

Automatic Appraisal in Social Contexts

Designed by Evolution

Evolutionary scientists commonly assume that the pressure of complex social organization catalyzed the rapid enlargement of the human brain during the past million years. Robinson Crusoe, as Nicholas Humphrey once remarked, illustrates this model of human evolution: The real challenge for Crusoe was not to survive alone on the island but to survive the relationship with his man, Friday (Humphrey, 1983). Compared to the physical environment, our social milieu is more complex, less predictable, and, importantly, more responsive to our behavior. These characteristics, especially the benefits associated with social reciprocity and the dangers linked to interpersonal aggression, are thought to have driven the evolution of emotional responses to social cues. In light of this, it is not surprising that emotional and social tasks to a large extent recruit overlapping regions of the brain, engaging both subcortical and more posterior regions of the brain that traditionally have been ascribed a role in more reflexive emotional functions, as well as more anterior-medial cortices supporting reflective emotional functions (Ochsner et al., 2004a; Olsson & Ochsner, 2008). Indeed, there are both ontogenetic and phylogenetic reasons for why emotional and social processes should be intimately intertwined at all levels of explanation: the behavioral, the experiential, and the neural. Next we consider emotions in the social domain to illustrate the unfolding of the two movements and the dynamic interplay between them.

Automatic Appraisal of Social Threat

Our social environment is the source of our happiest moments, but also our greatest fears, and the emotional value of social stimuli can change within fractions of a second. Indeed, the swift alternation of facial expressions in a conspecific, signaling a shift from benevolent to adversary intentions, illustrates rapidly occurring changes that may have fatal implications for the individual if not adaptively responded to immediately. Under these circumstances it is critical to make a rapid evaluation of emotionally relevant cues around us, as well as of the current social context (Figure 37.1).

As discussed earlier, the amygdala has been shown to play a role in the automatic appraisal of biologically relevant cues, such as fearful and angry faces (Morris et al., 1998). Adding importantly to our knowledge about the role of the amygdala in social emotions, a study on brain-damaged patients suggested that the amygdala not only is sensitive to fear and other expressions, but may also contribute to the generation of actions favoring the detection of fear (Adolphs et al., 2005). This study reported that the inability to recognize fear expressions in a patient with bilateral amygdala lesions was due to the patient's inability to make spontaneous use of information in the eye region, a region that is particularly diagnostic for fear expressions. These results remind us about the importance of complementing imaging work with research on patients with specific brain damages.

Naturally our social environment contains significant cues other than emotional expressions, which can trigger a fast emotional response in the perceiver. Based on the significance of the sex and group belonging of others, signaling a potential mate, friend, or foe, it is reasonable that these categories are evaluated quickly. Indeed, research has shown that these categories are coded instantly, giving rise to a reflexive response. For example, there are now numerous demonstrations that unknown racial outgroup members, that is, individuals not belonging to one's own racial group, can elicit a rapid threat response associated with the amygdala (Cunningham et al., 2004; Phelps et al., 2000). Pointing to the possibility of a hard-wired disposition to develop xenophobic responses, when associated with something aversive, male outgroup members elicit a stronger implicit fear response that is more persistent than that produced by male ingroup members. Interestingly, this effect has been demonstrated to be independent of explicit attitudes as well as previous exposure to the racial outgroup, with the exception of having outgroup dating experience, which abolishes the effect (Navarrete et al., 2009; Olsson, Ebert, Banaji, & Phelps, 2005).

Automatic Appraisal of Traits

People's evaluations of each other often involve more complex judgments that are detached from the physical features of the target individual. Research has shown that even thin temporal slices of visual information can result in social evaluations that are quite sophisticated and surprisingly reliable. For example, a recent study shows that viewing times as short as 100 ms allow a person to form an impression about a target person's likeability, trustworthiness, competence, and aggressiveness that are highly correlated with impressions made in the absence of time constraints (Willis & Todorov, 2006). This resonates well with previous imaging (Winston, Strange, O'Doherty, & Dolan, 2002) and neuropsychological (Adolphs, 2001) studies reporting that the amygdala is involved in automatic evaluation of trustworthiness. That some of these immediate evaluations can have real and important behavioral implications outside the laboratory is evidenced by the fact that impression of competence formed about a face within 1 second has been shown to predict U.S. congressional elections better than chance (Todorov, Mandisodza, Goren, & Hall, 2005).

Automatic Appraisal of Social Rewards

Because danger in an evolutionary perspective was defined by agile, hungry predators and attacking conspecifics, with potentially deadly consequences, there was a high premium on responding quickly to these kinds of stimuli. Missing out on positive resources such as mates and meals, on the other hand, typically involved a missed opportunity rather than the end of a genetic lineage. In this perspective, it is hardly surprising that "negative information weighs more heavily on the brain" (Ito, Larsen, Smith, & Cacioppo, 1998, p. 887). Naturally, social stimuli can also trigger rapid reward-related emotional responses, although the heavy research bias on studying aversive responses appears to suggest something else. For example, attractive faces are instantly responded to even when the perceiver's attentional resources are consumed by some other explicit task. These emotional responses are tracked by the striatum (Childress et al., 2008; Cloutier, Heatherton, Whalen, & Kelley, 2008). Not only facial displays are instantly registered. Other physical traits signaling fertility and biological aptness, such as symmetry and body proportions, are also registered by the striatum even when the perceiver is lacking awareness of these cues (Cornwell et al., 2004; Schützwohl, 2006). Research has shown that unseen social rewards (erotica) can also affect our behavior (Jiang, Costello, Fang, Huang, & He, 2006).

Mirroring Emotions

To predict the potential threat or reward value of another individual, information about his or her emotional state and intentions is critical. To this end people might benefit from an experiential sharing of the other's emotional state. Apart form enhancing the predictability of others' behavior, this might also facilitate our social interaction.

Supporting these assumptions, it has been shown that humans spontaneously imitate emotional facial expressions. Experimenters using masking stimuli have even observed unconscious imitation responses (as assessed by electrophysiological measurements of facial muscles) to both angry and happy faces (Dimberg, Thunberg, & Elmehed, 2000). Without knowing it, we respond with minuscule facial gestures, which adds emotional color to our social interactions. In addition, social psychologists have demonstrated that whether we feel relaxed or uncomfortable with some people is affected by nonconscious emotional cues (Chartrand & Bargh, 1999).

Mirror Neurons

The discovery of so-called mirror neurons in the motor cortex that represent both one's own and the corresponding actions in others has led to the suggestion that these reflexive responses play a key role in the understanding of actions and intentions (Gallese, Keysers, & Rizzolatti, 2004; Iacoboni & Dapretto, 2006). Inspired by this development, it has been proposed that shared representations of one's own and others' emotional experiences provide the reflexive basis for emotional empathy. This logic has guided subsequent studies of the direct experience and observation of pain or emotion showing activation of overlapping neural systems, mainly two cortical regions receiving ascending viscerosensory inputs: the anterior insula (AI) and the mid portion of the anterior cingulate cortex (ACC; Carr, Iacoboni, Dubeau, Mazziotta, & Lenzi, 2003; Decety & Jackson, 2007; Gallese et al., 2004; Iacoboni & Dapretto, 2006; Morrison, Lloyd, di Pellegrino, & Roberts, 2004; Singer, et al., 2004; Zaki, Ochsner, Hanelin, Wager, & Mackey, 2007). The AI is thought to support affective experience in part by providing awareness of these body state inputs (Craig, 2002; Critchley, Wiens, Rotshtein, Öhman, & Dolan, 2004), and the ACC is believed to code affective attributes of pain, such as perceived unpleasantness as opposed to sensory-discriminative properties, such as location and intensity (Eisenberger, Lieberman, & Williams, 2003; Hutchison, Davis, Lozano, Tasker, & Dostrovsky, 1999; Wager et al., 2004), and motivate appropriate behavior via projections to brain regions supporting motor and autonomic output (Critchley et al., 2004). The engagement of the AI, ACC, and other regions supporting the automatic sharing of, and hence an experiential understanding of, the intentions behind others' emotional behaviors may in turn provide a substrate for the empathic responses underlying prosocial behaviors (Decety & Jackson, 2007; Lamm, Batson, & Decety, 2007; Singer et al., 2004).

Of course, emotion understanding isn't always so simple. Nonverbal emotional cues are often ambiguous, and additional information is needed to constrain attributions about someone's emotional state and intentions. Our prior experience with that person and knowledge about antecedent events and the wider surrounding context are important sources of information (Figure 37.1). For example, wide-open eyes could mean someone is either afraid or surprised—triggering amygdala activity accordingly—depending on our knowledge of what has just happened to him or her (Kim, Somerville, Johnstone, Alexander, & Whalen, 2003). Similarly, activation of shared representations—and presumably empathic responses—may be blocked if one perceives another to be a past or potential competitor (Batson, Thompson, & Chen, 2002; Singer et al., 2006) or the situation makes an emotional response inappropriate (Figure 37.1). Indeed, our understanding of the context and our expectations about the future (e.g., others' behavior) are important determinants in our experience of a situation, which brings us to the next step of emotional processing.

The Second Movement of Emotion

Secondary Appraisal

Automatic emotional activation provides input to the next stage of emotional processing, which we have called the *second movement of emotion* (Oatley, 2004). This is a more sluggish activity, which is responsive to reflection and explicit mental processes. It depends on more flexible neural mechanisms, primarily drawing on regions in sensory and prefrontal cortices as well as regions responsible for episodic memories, such as the hippocampus (Tulving, 2002). Of course, in our daily lives, which for most people is predominantly spent outside the laboratory, distant from experimenters' surreptitious attempts to artificially tease apart different kinds of emotional processes, there is a constant interplay between rapid, reflexive processes on the one hand and slower reflective processes on the other. Providing the basis for this cross-talk, the amygdala and the striatum are reciprocally connected with cortical brain regions with a more recent evolutionary past.

Constructing Emotions

The second movement is the driving force behind the fact that people tend to construct their emotions. Depending on our previous experiences, we may respond in vastly different ways to the same emotional stimulus (Figure 37.1). Following this, some researchers have argued that the perceived meaning of the situation is the central determinant of the emotional response. And emotional meaning, it is claimed, results from an appraisal process (Scherer, Schorr, & Johnstone, 2001). To distinguish this from the automatic processes that provide an immediate evaluation of a stimulus, these appraisal processes should be called *secondary appraisal*.

Input from Automatic to Secondary Appraisal

There are different kinds of input from automatic to secondary appraisal. A major part concerns outputs from preliminary sensory processing. For example, these outputs may segregate the perceptual field into central figures and background, provide preliminary identification of the figures, and command attention to them for further processing. More important in the present context, the automatic processes of the amygdala and the striatum provide emotional coloring of the stimulus even before it is identified. The primary result of this evaluation is an estimate of the "goodness" and the "badness" of the stimulus, relating to a behavioral posture of approach or avoidance (e.g., Lang, Bradley, & Cuthbert, 1998).

Interoceptive Input to Emotion

What is the medium for conveying the emotional tone between the automatic and secondary appraisal stages? Conceptualizing the interface between the two processes in this way invites resurrecting the basic idea of the James-Lange theory of emotion: Feedback from the emotional response is a central stimulus source for emotion (and emotional experience). Concisely put, we do not cry because we feel sad; we feel sad because we cry. This idea has been in disrepute for close to a century after Cannon's (1927) devastating critique. Cannon's basic argument was that the physiological activation seen in intense emotion is too crude and too slow to account for the richness and nuance of emotional experience. Indeed, Cannon himself demonstrated that the patterns of physiological responses observed in anger and fear are indistinguishable and that it takes several seconds (and sometimes even tens of seconds) for the autonomic response to reach its maximum after an emotional provocation.

Given what we know today, this critique is not as damaging as once perceived. Emotional information may reach the amygdala and start activating the bodily response within some 10 ms after it reaches sensory receptors and before it reaches the adequate cortical areas for identification. Feedback from facial responses is highly patterned and available within a few hundred milliseconds. Furthermore, facial feedback remains available even after surgery that blocks information from the body from reaching the brain. This may help explain why animals with such surgery (and humans with spinal chord damage that blocks feedback from the body) still appear to have emotion (thus rebutting another of Cannon's [1927] critiques of the James-Lange theory).

Feedback from the slow autonomic responses may not have to await the full-blown peripheral responses but may start coming in as soon as the relevant brain nuclei are activated. As Damasio (1999) pointed out, actual bodily feedback may not always be necessary, because there may be "as-if body loops" that provide central simulations of previously experienced "real" emotional body loops in compressed time scales. Thus the brain may have quite specific information from the body early enough to make it a factor in shaping emotional experience and behavior. Indeed, Damasio and coworkers (2000) showed that simple instructions to recall different emotional episodes activated distinct patterns of activity in brain structures that regulate and represent bodily states. Such patterns provide "neural maps" that differ among emotions. According to Damasio, feelings can be understood as mental images arising from changes in such neural maps representing bodily activations brought about by emotional stimuli. He further speculated that these neural maps may be stored in the anterior insula, which is located in the convoluted cortex between the temporal and frontal lobes and which contains topographical maps of the viscera (see also Craig, 2002, 2004).

Critchley et al. (2004) provided experimental data consistent with these conjectures when participants "listened for their heartbeats." Participants listened to a sequence of tones that were either directly elicited by their heartbeats or were delayed by half a second from the heartbeats, which perceptually disconnected them from the heart. Their task was to decide whether the tones were synchronous with or independent from their heartbeats. In a control task, the participants listened for a tone that was fainter than the others. Compared to the control task, listening for the heartbeats produced activations in the insula, somatomotor, and cingulated cortex (Figure 37.3). Activity in the anterior insula predicted accuracy of heartbeat perception, and self-rated anxiety was related both to insula activation and to accurate heartbeat detection. Gray matter volume in the insula was correlated with heartbeat perception and with self-reported awareness of bodily changes. These data provide a quite compelling case for giving the insula a central role in perception and awareness of bodily changes (Craig, 2004). In addition, there are masking studies suggesting that the anterior insula is one of the brain areas that is exclusively correlated with conscious recognition of emotional stimuli (Critchley, Mathias, & Dolan, 2002).

The exact role of bodily input to emotional processing remains to be determined. Because automatic appraisal decides that a stimulus is relevant for well-being, the associated bodily activation provides a critical signal that something should be done about the situation. In most cases, the reason for this activation should be readily appreciated from available contextual information, which also will support appropriate action. However, as we have seen, conscious perception of the eliciting stimulus is not necessary, which means that there might be instances when an emotional arousal is activated in the absence of a readily

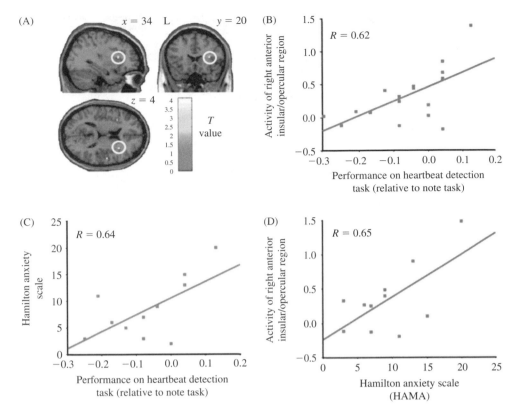

Figure 37.3 Functional neural correlates of interoceptive sensitivity.

Note. **A:** Activation of the right anterior insula/opercular area is illustrated as a contrast between activities in the heartbeat auditory detection tasks. The anatomical location is mapped on orthogonal sections of a template brain, with coordinates in mm from anterior commissure. **B:** Activity within right insular/opercular cortex during interoceptive trials is plotted against interoceptive accuracy (relative to exteroceptive accuracy, to control for nonspecific detection difficulty in the noisy scanning environment). The Pearson correlation coefficient (*R*) is given in the plot. **C:** Subject scores on the Hamilton Anxiety Scale are plotted against relative interoceptive awareness to illustrate the correlation in these subjects between sensitivity to bodily responses and subjective emotional experience, particularly of negative emotions. **D:** Activity in right anterior insula/opercular activity during interoception also correlated with anxiety score, suggesting that emotional feeling states are supported by explicit interoceptive representations within the right insula cortex. From "Neural Systems Supporting Interoceptive Awareness," by Critchley et al., 2004, *Nature Neuroscience, 7,* p. 192. Reprinted with permission.

available explanation. Such unexplained arousal is a powerful motivation to search for explanations (Schachter & Singer, 1962), which will affect how the situation is interpreted. Thus, there may be spillover effects that influence the way the situation is emotionally interpreted. For example, running up stairs triggers an activation of the cardiovascular system. However, the emotional ramification of this activation is very different if we do it for exercise, to meet a lover waiting at the top of the stairs, or to escape a man chasing us with an axe. Although we discuss appraisal processes in terms of explicit mental activity, they need not be conscious. Although originally conscious activities, appraisals, particularly immediate ones, may become automatized to work outside of awareness (Lieberman, 2007).

Secondary Appraisal in Social Contexts

The range of reflective emotional processes is, if anything, both larger and more complex than the first movement of emotional responses. People use conscious reflection to understand both their own and others' emotional states. As discussed earlier, interoception provides a key component in reflecting about one's own emotional state. Because we have already elaborated interoceptive input to the understanding of one's own emotions was quite extensively, we focus next on reflection about others' emotions.

Appraising Others' Emotions

The ability to understand another individual's emotional states is essential for virtually all aspects of social behavior and is likely to depend on both the reflexive emotional empathic responses discussed here and the attribution of mental states. Indeed, emotion understanding by definition requires a causal attribution about the intentions behind an action. As we have seen, people understand others' emotions partly through the operation of rapid reflexive processes, such as the automatic appraisal of facial expressions and the sharing of emotional states. However, when

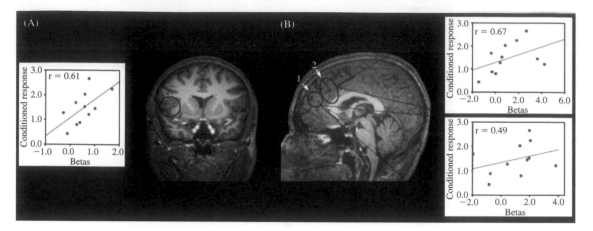

Figure 37.4   Functional activation during an observational fear-learning task.

A: A coronal view of activation in the right anterior insula, AI (–28, 15, –4)[a] when observing the pain response of a learning model to a shock. The adjacent graph shows that the magnitude of this activation predicts the strength of the conditioned response (indexed by the SCR) at a later time to a cue associated with the pain of the learning model. **B:** A sagittal view of activation in the (1) MPFC (1,46,24)[a] and (2) the ACC (3,27,32)[a] during the observation of the pain response of a learning model to a

shock. As in A, adjacent graphs display the positive relationship between the magnitude of activation during observation and the subsequent conditioned response. From "The Role of Social Cognition in Emotion," by Olsson and Ochsner, 2008, *Trends in Cognitive Sciences, 12,* pp. 65–71. Reprinted with permission.

[a] x, y, z coordinates for local maxima in Talairach space.

stimulus-driven processing of information is not sufficient, more reflective mental state attributions may be needed to understand another individual's emotional state. These controlled attributions allow us to actively take other people's perspectives and make judgments about their emotions or diagnostic elements of their emotional dispositions, thereby changing empathic responding (Batson et al., 2002) and recruitment of the anterior insula and the ACC (Lamm et al., 2007). These reflective processes have been shown to depend on a network of regions, including the right temporal parietal junction and dorsal regions of the medial prefrontal cortex (MPFC), including Brodmann area 10 (BA 10; Mitchell, Macrae, & Banaji, 2006; Ochsner et al., 2004a; Saxe, Moran, Scholz, & Gabrieli, 2006). Interestingly, a recent meta-analysis singles out BA 10, which is especially developed in humans, as particularly sensitive to tasks involving *both* emotions and mental state attributions (Gilbert et al., 2006). Taken together, these lines of work suggest that if the ACC and AI support direct experiential awareness of intentional states, the MPFC network might support the metacognitive reflective awareness of these experiences.

The function of appropriately attributing emotional states to others is not limited to understanding, and thus responding to, their emotional expressions in the present moment, but additionally helps us to learn about the events causing others' emotional responses. Previous behavioral research across primates has suggested that learning through observation draws on overlapping neural processes as classical conditioning (Mineka & Cook, 1993; Olsson & Phelps, 2004). Indeed, these findings were corroborated in

an imaging study demonstrating that overlapping regions of the amygdala, AI, and ACC were active during both observational learning and subsequent expression of fear responses (Olsson, Nearing, & Phelps, 2007). In contrast, the dorsal MPFC was active only during observation of another's distress. Importantly, the magnitude of the conditioned response was predicted by activity in the AI, ACC, and dorsal MPFC, suggesting that shared representations supporting experiential understanding of emotion, as well as regions supporting reflective mental state attributions, together support social-emotional learning (Figure 37.4).

REGULATING OUR EMOTIONAL RESPONSES: A "THIRD MOVEMENT"?

An important role of reflective emotional processes is to regulate one's own emotional responses. Once an emotional response has arisen, there are several ways it can be affected through top-down control (Ochsner & Gross, 2005). It has been argued that primitive regulatory processes that do not need voluntary effort, such as the extinction of a conditioned response, involve the down-regulation of amygdala activity by means of ventral and medial regions of the prefrontal cortex (PFC) across species (Quirk, Garcia, & Gonzalez-Lima, 2006). In contrast, depending on the strategy, voluntary up or down-regulation of amygdala-based emotions have been shown to draw on more dorsal medial and lateral regions, which have been implicated in executive control (Kalisch et al., 2005; Ochsner & Gross, 2005; Ochsner et al., 2004b).

The most basic way of intentionally regulating one's emotional response is to divert one's attention away from the emotion-provoking stimuli. However, the flexibility of the human mind allows people to reappraise, or reinterpret, the situation in light of other knowledge. For example, if an emotion is evoked by another individual's emotional expression, one strategy is to reinterpret the situational meaning of the other's intentions or feelings, as when thinking positively or negatively about the dispositions ("He is hearty [or weak]") and future emotions ("Receiving the injection will inflict pain [or make him healthy]"; Figure 37.1). Interestingly, recent work suggests that simply making an attribution about the feelings of another person can have the unintended consequence of disrupting amygdala-mediated negative evaluations of him or her (Harris, Todorov, & Fiske, 2005; Lieberman, 2007). One reason for this may be that the attribution of emotional states can direct attention to the nonthreatening intentions (e.g., thinking about his or her food preferences) of a social target, thereby disambiguating the individual as a potential source of threat. This regulatory strategy can modulate amygdala activity through primarily ventrolateral PFC regions used to select from memory information that helps interpret another's feelings (Ochsner et al., 2004a). It is suggested that similar areas inhibit the enhanced amygdala response of nonprejudiced White participants exposed to masked Black faces (indicating an implicit racial bias) when the masking interval was extended to allow conscious recognition (Amodio, Devine, & Harmon-Jones, 2008).

The Power of Language

Humans are prone to retrospective justifications. As dramatically stated by V. S. Ramachandran (2004, p. 1), "Your conscious life . . . is nothing but an elaborate posthoc rationalization of things you really do for other reasons." Famous examples of this process were inspired by Leon Festinger's (1957) theory of cognitive dissonance, which stated that humans seek balance and consistency in their belief systems. As a consequence, we are motivated to restore balance when there are conflicts between beliefs or between belief and action. For example, when persuaded by shrewd social psychologists to publicly express a view that was inconsistent with their beliefs, research participants were more likely to actually change their beliefs if paid a small rather than a large sum of money. With a big reward, participants could explain away the dissonant action as "I only did it for the money," whereas with a trivial reward, justifying the action was more likely to require a change in conviction (Festinger & Carlsmith, 1959).

Similar processes may be at work in emotion. Even though specific stimuli automatically activate emotions, this automatic response often merely sets the constructive mind to work. We feel pressed to understand and to justify our emotions ("The man was so scary, what could I do but try to escape?" or "As adorable as she was, I just fell helplessly in love"), and we retrospectively manipulate emotion to justify our action ("I hit him because he made me so mad" or "I certainly must be madly in love to act this stupidly"). This was illustrated in a choice experiment in which subjects had to choose the most attractive face from two presented alternatives. Unbeknown to the subjects, a card trick made them believe that they had chosen the face they actually had not chosen. Not only did the surreptitious manipulation go unnoticed, but the vast majority of subjects also provided quite elaborated motivations for what they thought were their choices (Johansson, Hall, Sikstrom, & Olsson, 2005).

Largely based on his research on split-brain patients, who have had their two cerebral hemispheres surgically disconnected from each other as a treatment for epilepsy, Michael Gazzaniga (1998, 2000) argued that the pressure to justify one's actions reflects the operation of "an interpreter system" housed in the left frontal cerebral hemisphere. According to this view, the brain automatically takes care of most of the exigencies raised by the interaction of person and environment. The fundamental interpretive component of the human mind comes in late to make sense of the unfolding scenario mindlessly managed by the brain, to fit it into one's worldview and self-image, and to keep constructing the narrative that we take to be our lives. Unlike all other creatures, humans can, by their access to language, keep a running commentary on their lives. As a consequence, we are prone to mixing up the commentary and the commented-on events in our memories, which may explain the unreliability of our memories (Loftus, 2005). But the commentary is not merely epiphenomenal activity. Rather, it gives consistency to the world and to our actions in it, and it helps us to cope with new situations by time-proven (and largely culturally and socially determined) formulas. In doing its work, the interpreter tries hard to be rational. Indeed, Gazzaniga claims that the interpreter is behind the human adoration of reason. Indeed, this mechanism might also explain the way emotions sometimes appear disconnected from our rational thinking.

SUMMARY AND CONCLUSIONS

Our aim in this chapter has been to provide a selective overview of research that illuminates the link between emotional behavior and its neural substrate. To this end we have drawn on various streams of work within the realms of affective and cognitive neuroscience. Providing a rough framework for this endeavor, we have revisited the ancient division of emotion into two separable movements. To this division, which was originally proposed by the Stoics more than 2,000 years ago (Oatley, 2004), we have added another stage that we have called the *third movement*. Recent behavioral, psychophysiological, and neural data have validated these distinctions.

The first movement describes the initial surge of rapid, automatic, often implicit emotional responses to a stimulus or event, whereas the second movement captures the slower unfolding of a more nuanced repertoire of emotional responses that are dependent on conscious appraisals. Unlike the initial response, these secondary appraisals are shaped by situational factors, our explicit memories, and reflective reasoning.

The amygdala has been identified as a core region in neural circuitry responsible for the automatic appraisal of emotionally relevant, especially potentially threatening stimuli. Providing further rapid information and connecting us with our social environment, another network of cortical regions, including the so-called mirror neurons system and the AI, is believed to support rapid mimicking of others' emotional expressions and experiential sharing of their emotions.

These neural systems supporting the first emotional movement contribute important input to a more widely distributed neural network underlying the second emotional movement. For example, the AI provides interoceptive information about one's own emotional state, and together with prefrontal regions, such as the ACC and medial region of the PFC, it provides the basis for reflections about both one's own and others' emotional states. Thanks to the reciprocal connectivity between these more recently evolved prefrontal circuits and evolutionarily older circuits supporting automatic appraisal, emotional responses can not only be spontaneously regulated, but can be shaped by volitional strategies. The reinterpretation of the emotional value of a situation is one such strategy that has received much attention lately and has been shown to involve medial and lateral prefrontal regions.

In a way, this prefrontally driven regulation extends the ancient Stoic description of emotions by adding a third movement to the two existing ones. A third movement closes the circle and provides for a loop of neural activation that can be continuously calibrated to produce the currently most adaptive emotional response. In humans language brings about a uniquely flexible tool kit for up or down-regulation of emotional responses. Indeed, the flexibility of symbols can sometimes play tricks on us, such as when our verbal reports of emotions or reflective reasoning stand in conflict with our own emotional experience or behavior. Although much work remains before we can fully understand the nature of emotion, this chapter

has shown that we have made good progress so far. With the rapid development of techniques to map the functional activity of the human brain, it will continue to be imperative to link these data with their physiological and behavioral correlates. Only this way will emotion—as we known it—appear less mysterious.

REFERENCES

Adolphs, R. (2001). The neurobiology of social cognition. *Current Opinion in Neurobiology, 11,* 231–239.

Adolphs, R., Gosselin, F., Buchanan, T. W., Tranel, D., Schyns, P., & Damasio, A. R. (2005, January 20). A mechanism for impaired fear recognition after amygdala damage. *Nature, 433,* 68–72.

Amodio, D. M., Devine, P. G., & Harmon-Jones, E. (2008). Individual differences in the regulation of intergroup bias: The role of conflict monitoring and neural signals for control. *Journal of Personality and Social Psychology, 94,* 60–74.

Anderson, A. K., & Phelps, E. A. (2001, May 17). Lesions of the human amygdala impair enhanced perception of emotionally salient events. *Nature, 411,* 305–309.

Batson, C. D., Thompson, E. R., & Chen, H. (2002). Moral hypocrisy: Addressing some alternatives. *Journal of Personality and Social Psychology, 83,* 330–339.

Berridge, K. C., & Winkielman, P. (2003). What is an unconscious emotion? (The case for unconscious "liking"). *Cognition and Emotion, 17,* 181–211.

Bevins, R. A., Besheer, J., Palmatier, M. I., Jensen, H. C., Pickett, K. S., & Eurek, S. (2002). Novel-object place conditioning: Behavioral and dopaminergic processes in expression of novelty reward. *Behavioral Brain Research, 129,* 41–50.

Cannon, W. (1927). The James-Lange theory of emotions: A critical examination and an alternative theory. *American Journal of Psychology, 39,* 106–124.

Carlsson, K., Petersson, K. M., Lundqvist, D., Karlsson, A., Ingvar, M., & Öhman, A. (2004). Fear and the amygdala: Manipulation of awareness generates differential cerebral responses to phobic and fear-relevant (but nonfeared) stimuli. *Emotion, 4,* 340–353.

Carr, L., Iacoboni, M., Dubeau, M. C., Mazziotta, J. C., & Lenzi, G. L. (2003). Neural mechanisms of empathy in humans: A relay from neural systems for imitation to limbic areas. *Proceedings of the National Academy of Sciences, USA, 100,* 5497–5502.

Chartrand, T. L., & Bargh, J. A. (1999). The chameleon effect: The perception-behavior link and social interaction. *Journal of Personality and Social Psychology, 76,* 893–910.

Childress, A. R., Ehrman, R. N., Wang, Z., Li, Y., Sciortino, N., Hakun, J., et al. (2008). Prelude to passion: Limbic activation by "unseen" drug and sexual cues. *PLoS ONE, 3,* 1506.

Cloutier, J., Heatherton, T. F., Whalen, P. J., & Kelley, W. M. (2008). Are attractive people rewarding? Sex differences in the neural substrates of facial attractiveness. *Journal of Cognitive Neuroscience, 20,* 941–951.

Coan, J. A., & Allen, J. J. B. (Eds.). (2007). *Handbook of emotion elicitation and assessment.* New York: Oxford University Press.

Cornwell, R. E., Boothroyd, L., Burt, D. M., Feinberg, D. R., Jones, B. C., Little, K., et al. (2004). Concordant preferences for opposite-sex signals? Human pheromones and facial characteristics. *Proceedings of the Royal Society: Biological Science, 271,* 635–640.

Craig, A. D. (2002). How do you feel? Interoception: The sense of the physiological condition of the body. *Nature Reviews, 3,* 655–666.

Craig, A. D. (2004). Human feelings: Why are some more aware than others? *Trends in Cognitive Science, 8,* 239–241.

Critchley, H., Mathias, C., & Dolan, R. J. (2002). Fear conditioning in humans: The influence of awareness and autonomic arousal on functional neuroanatomy. *Neuron, 33,* 653–663.

Critchley, H. D., Wiens, S., Rotshtein, P., Öhman, A., & Dolan, R. J. (2004). Neural systems supporting interoceptive awareness. *Nature Neuroscience, 7,* 189–195.

Cromwell, H. C., & Schultz, W. (2003). Effects of expectations for different reward magnitudes on neuronal activity in primate striatum. *Journal of Neurophysiology, 89,* 2823–2838.

Cunningham, W. A., Johnson, M. K., Gatenby, J. C., Gore, J. C., & Banaji, M. R. (2003). Neural components of social evaluation. *Journal of Personality and Social Psychology, 85,* 639–649.

Cunningham, W. A., Johnson, M. K., Raye, C. L., Gatenby, J., Gore, J. C., & Banaji, M. R. (2004). Separable neural components in the processing of Black and White faces. *Psychological Science, 15,* 806–313.

Damasio, A. (1994). *Descartes' error: Emotion, reason, and the human brain.* New York: Avon Books.

Damasio, A. (1999). *The feeling of what happens: Body and emotion in the making of consciousness.* New York: Harcourt Brace.

Damasio, A. R., Grabowski, T. J., Bechara, A., Damasio, H., Ponto, L. L., Parvizi, J., Hichwa, R. D. (2000). Subcortical and cortical brain activity during the feeling of self-generated emotions. *Nature Neuroscience, 3,* 1049–1056.

Davis, M., & Whalen, P. J. (2001). The amygdala: Vigilance and emotion. *Molecular Psychiatry, 6,* 13–34.

Decety, J., & Jackson, P. L. (2007). The functional architecture of human empathy. *Behavioral and Cognitive Neuroscience Reviews, 3,* 71–100.

de Gelder, B., Snyder, J., Greve, D., Gerard, G., & Hadjikhani, N. (2004). Fear fosters flight: A mechanism for fear contagion when perceiving emotion expressed by a whole body. *Proceedings of the National Academy of Sciences, USA, 101,* 16701–16706.

Dimberg, U., Thunberg, M., & Elmehed, K. (2000). Unconscious facial reactions to emotional facial expressions. *Psychological Science, 11,* 86–89.

Eisenberger, N. I., Lieberman, M. D., & Williams, K. D. (2003, October 10). Does rejection hurt? An FMRI study of social exclusion. *Science, 302,* 290–292.

Festinger, L. (1957). A theory of cognitive dissonance. Evanston, IL: Row, Peterson.

Festinger, L., & Carlsmith, C. (1959). Cognitive consequences of forced compliance. *Journal of Abnormal and Social Psychology, 58,* 203–210.

Gallese, V., Keysers, C., & Rizzolatti, G. (2004). A unifying view of the basis of social cognition. *Trends in Cognitive Science, 8,* 396–403.

Gazzaniga, M. (1998). *The mind's past.* Berkeley: University of California Press.

Gazzaniga, M. (2000). Cerebral specialization and interhemispheric communication: Does the corpus callosum enable the human condition? *Brain, 123,* 1293–1326.

Gilbert, S. J., Spengler, S., Simons, J. S., Steele, J. D., Lawrie, S. M., Frith, C. D., Burgess, P. W. (2006). Functional specialization within rostral prefrontal cortex (area 10): A meta-analysis. *Journal of Cognitive Neuroscience, 18,* 932–948.

Harris, L. T., Todorov, A., & Fiske, S. T. (2005). Attributions on the brain: Neuro-imaging dispositional inferences, beyond theory of mind. *NeuroImage, 28,* 763–769.

Humphrey, N. (1983). *Consciousness regained: Chapters in the development of mind.* Oxford University Press.

Hutchison, W. D., Davis, K. D., Lozano, A. M., Tasker, R. R., & Dostrovsky, J. O. (1999). Pain-related neurons in the human cingulate cortex. *Nature Neuroscience, 2,* 403–405.

Iacoboni, M., & Dapretto, M. (2006). The mirror neuron system and the consequences of its dysfunction. *Nature Reviews Neuroscience, 7,* 942–951.

Ito, T. A., Larsen, J. T., Smith, N. K., & Cacioppo, J. T. (1998). Negative information weighs more heavily on the brain: The negativity bias in evaluative categorizations. *Journal of Personality and Social Psychology, 75,* 887–900.

Jiang, Y., Costello, P., Fang, F., Huang, M., & He, S. A. (2006). A gender- and sexual orientation-dependent spatial attentional effect of invisible images. *Proceedings of the National Academy of Science, USA, 103,* 1748–1752.

Johansson, P., Hall, L., Sikstrom, S., & Olsson, A. (2005, October 7). Failure to detect mismatches between intention and outcome in a simple decision task. *Science, 310,* 116–119.

Kalisch, R., Wiech, K., Critchley, H. D., Seymour, B., O'Doherty, J. P., Oakley, D. A., Allen, P., & Dolan, R. J. (2005). Anxiety reduction through detachment: Subjective, physiological, and neural effects. *Journal of Cognitive Neuroscience, 17,* 874–883.

Kim, H., Somerville, L. H., Johnstone, T., Alexander, A. L., & Whalen, P. J. (2003). Inverse amygdala and medial prefrontal cortex responses to surprised faces. *NeuroReport, 14,* 2317–2322.

Klüver, H., & Bucy, P. (1939). Preliminary analysis of functioning of the temporal lobes in monkeys. *Archives of Neurological Psychiatry, 42,* 979–1000.

Knutson, B., Adams, C. M., Fong, G. W., & Hommer, D. (2001). Anticipation of increasing monetary reward selectively recruits nucleus accumbens. *Journal of Neuroscience, 21,* 1–5.

Kunst-Wilson, W. R., & Zajonc, R. B. (1980, February 1). Affective discrimination of stimuli that cannot be recognized. *Science, 207,* 557–558.

Lamm, C., Batson, C. D., & Decety, J. (2007). The neural substrate of human empathy: Effects of perspective-taking and cognitive appraisal. *Journal of Cognitive Neuroscience, 19,* 42–58.

Lang, P. J., Bradley, M. M., & Cuthbert, B. N. (1998). Emotion, motivation, and anxiety: Brain mechanisms and psychophysiology. *Biological Psychiatry, 44,* 1248–1263.

LeDoux, J. E. (1996). *The emotional brain.* New York: Simon & Schuster.

LeDoux, J. E. (2000). Emotion circuits in the brain. *Annual Review of Neuroscience, 23,* 155–184.

Liddell, B. J., Brown, K. J., Kemp, A. H., Barton, M. J., Das, P., Peduto, A., et al. (2005). A direct brainstem-amygdala-cortical "alarm" system for subliminal signals of fear. *Neuroimage, 24,* 235–243.

Lieberman, M. D. (2007). Social cognitive neuroscience: A review of core processes. *Annual Review of Psychology, 58,* 259–289.

Loftus, E. (2005). Planting misinformation in the human mind: A 30-year investigation of the malleability of memory. *Learning and Memory, 12,* 361–366.

McGaugh, J. L. (2004). The amygdala modulates the consolidation of memories of emotionally arousing experiences. *Annual Review of Neuroscience, 27,* 1–28.

Mineka, S., & Cook M. (1993). Mechanisms involved in the observational conditioning of fear. *Journal of Experimental Psychology, 122,* 23–38.

Mitchell, J. P., Macrae, C. N., & Banaji, M. R. (2006). Dissociable medial prefrontal contributions to judgments of similar and dissimilar others. *Neuron, 50,* 655–663.

Morris, J. S., Friston, K. J., Buchel, C., Frith, C. D., Young, A. W., Calder, A. J., et al. (1998). A neuromodulatory role for the human amygdala in processing emotional facial expressions. *Brain, 121,* 47–57.

Morris, J. S., Öhman, A., & Dolan, R. J. (1998, June 4). Conscious and unconscious emotional learning in the amygdala. *Nature, 393,* 467–470.

Morris, J. S., Öhman, A., & Dolan, R. J. (1999). A subcortical pathway to the right amygdala mediating "unseen" fear. *Proceedings of the National Academy of Sciences, USA, 96,* 1680–1685.

Morrison, I., Lloyd D., di Pellegrino, G., & Roberts, N. (2004). Vicarious responses to pain in anterior cingulate cortex: Is empathy a multisensory issue? *Cognitive, Affective and Behavioral Neuroscience, 4,* 270–278.

Murray, E. A. (2007). The amygdala, reward and emotion. *Trends in Cognitive Sciences, 11,* 489–497.

Navarrete, C. D., Olsson, A., Ho, A., Mendes, W., Thomsen, L., & Sidanius, J. (2009). The roles of race and gender in the persistence of learned fear. *Psychological Science, 20,* 155–158.

Oatley, K. (2004). *Emotions: A brief history.* Toronto: University of Toronto Press.

Ochsner, K. N., & Gross, J. J. (2005). The cognitive control of emotion. *Trends in Cognitive Sciences, 9,* 242–249.

Ochsner, K. N., Ray, R. D., Cooper, J. C., Robertson, E. R., Chopra, S., Gabrieli, J. D., et al. (2004a). For better or for worse: Neural systems supporting the cognitive down- and up-regulation of negative emotion. *NeuroImage, 23,* 483–499.

Ochsner, K. N., Ray, R. D., Cooper, J. C., Robertson, E. R., Chopra, S., Gabrieli, J. D., et al. (2004b). Reflecting upon feelings: An fMRI study of neural systems supporting the attribution of emotion to self and other. *Journal of Cognitive Neuroscience, 16,* 1746–1772.

O'Doherty, J., Dayan, P., Schultz, J., Deichmann, R., Friston, K., & Dolan, R. J. (2004, April 16). Dissociable roles of ventral and dorsal striatum in instrumental conditioning. *Science, 304,* 452–454.

Öhman, A. (1986). Face the beast and fear the face: Animal and social fears as prototypes for evolutionary analyses of emotion. *Psychophysiology, 23,* 123–145.

Öhman, A., & Mineka, S. (2001). Fears, phobias, and preparedness: Toward an evolved module of fear and fear learning. *Psychological Review, 108,* 483–522.

Öhman A., & Soares, J. J. (1994). "Unconscious anxiety": Phobic responses to masked stimuli. *Journal of Abnormal Psychology, 103,* 231–240.

Öhman, A., & Soares, J. J. F. (1998). Emotional conditioning to masked stimuli: Expectancies for aversive outcomes following non-recognized fear-relevant stimuli. *Journal of Experimental Psychology: General, 127,* 69–82.

Öhman, A., & Wiens, S. (2003). On the automaticity of autonomic responses in emotion: An evolutionary perspective. In R. J. Davidson, K. Scherer, & H. H. Goldsmith (Eds.), *Handbook of affective sciences* (pp. 256–275). New York: Oxford University Press.

Olsson, A., Ebert, J. P., Banaji, M. R., & Phelps, E. A. (2005, July 29). The role of social groups in the persistence of learned fear. *Science, 309,* 785–787.

Olsson, A., Nearing, K. I., & Phelps, E. A. (2007). Learning fears by observing others: The neural systems of social fear transmission. *Social Cognitive and Affective Neuroscience, 2,* 3–11.

Olsson, A., & Ochsner, K. N. (2008). The role of social cognition in emotion. *Trends in Cognitive Sciences, 12,* 65–71.

Olsson, A., & Phelps, E. A. (2004). Learned fear of "unseen" faces after Pavlovian, observational, and instructed fear. *Psychological Science, 15,* 822–828.

Pasley, B. N., Mayes, L. C., & Schultz, R. T. (2004). Subcortical discrimination of unperceived objects during binocular rivalry. *Neuron, 42,* 163–172.

Pessiglione, M., Schmidt, L., Draganski, B., Kalisch, R., Lau, H., Dolan, R. J., et al. (2007, May 11). How the brain translates money into force: A neuroimaging study of subliminal motivation. *Science, 316,* 904–906.

Phelps, E. A. (2006). Emotion and cognition: Insights from studies of the human amygdala. *Annual Review of Psychology, 24,* 27–53.

Phelps, E. A., & LeDoux, J. E. (2005). Contributions of the amygdala to emotion processing: From animal models to human behavior. *Neuron, 48,* 175–187.

Phelps, E. A., Ling, S., & Carrasco, M. (2006). Emotion facilitates perception and potentiates the perceptual benefit of attention. *Psychological Science, 17,* 292–299.

Phelps, E. A., O'Connor, K. J., Cunningham, W. A., Funayma, E. S., Gatenby, J. C., Gore, J. C., et al. (2000). Performance on indirect measures of race evaluation predicts amygdala activity. *Journal of Cognitive Neuroscience, 12,* 1–10.

Quirk, G. J., Garcia, R., & Gonzalez-Lima, F. (2006). Prefrontal mechanisms in extinction of conditioned fear. *Biological Psychiatry, 60,* 337–643.

Ramachandran, V. S. (2004). *A brief tour of human consciousness.* New York: Pi Press.

Rolls, E. T. (1999). *The brain and emotion.* New York: Oxford University Press.

Sabatinelli, D., Bradley, M. M., Fitzsimmons, J. R., & Lang, P. J. (2005). Parallel amygdala and inferotemporal activation reflect emotional intensity and fear relevance. *NeuroImage, 24,* 1265–1270.

Saxe, R., Moran, J. M., Scholz, J. K., & Gabrieli, J. D. E. (2006). Overlapping and non-overlapping brain regions for theory of mind and self reflection in individual subjects. *Social Cognitive Affective Neuroscience, 1,* 229–234.

Schachter, S., & Singer, J. E. (1962). Cognitive, social, and physiological determinants of emotional state. *Psychology Review, 69,* 379–399.

Scherer, K. R., Schorr, A., & Johnstone, T. (Eds.). (2001). *Appraisal processes in emotion: Theory, methods, and research.* New York: Oxford University Press.

Schultz, W. (2002). Getting formal with dopamine and reward. *Neuron, 36,* 241–263.

Schützwohl, A. (2006). Judging female figures: A new methodological approach to male attractiveness judgments of female waist-to-hip ratio. *Biological Psychology, 71,* 223–229.

Singer, T., Seymour, B., O'Doherty, J., Kaube, H., Dolan, R. J., & Frith, C. D. (2004, February 20). Empathy for pain involves the affective but not sensory components of pain. *Science, 303,* 1157–1162.

Singer, T., Seymour, B., O'Doherty, J., Stephan, K. E., Dolan, R. J., & Frith, C. D. (2006, January 26). Empathic neural responses are modulated by the perceived fairness of others. *Nature, 439,* 466–469.

Todorov, A., Mandisodza, A. N., Goren, A., & Hall, C. C. (2005, June 10). Inferences of competence from faces predict election outcomes. *Science, 308,* 1623–1626.

Tulving, E. (2002). Episodic memory: From mind to brain. *Annual Review of Psychology, 53,* 1–25.

Vuilleumier, P., Armony, J. L., Driver, J., & Dolan, R. J. (2003). Distinct spatial frequency sensitivities for processing faces and emotional expressions. *Nature Neuroscience, 6,* 624–631.

Vuilleumier, P., Richardson, M. P., Armony, J. L., Driver, J., & Dolan, R. J. (2004). Distant influences of amygdala lesion on visual cortical activation during emotional face processing. *Nature Neuroscience, 7,* 1271–1278.

Wager, T. D., Rilling, J. K., Smith, E. E., Sokolik, A., Casey, K. L., Davidson, R. J., Kosslyn, S. M., Rose, R. M, Cohen, J. D. (2004, February 20). Placebo-induced changes in fMRI in the anticipation and experience of pain. *Science, 303,* 1162–1167.

Weiskrantz, L. (1956). Behavioral changes associated with ablation of the amygdaloid complex in monkeys. *Journal of Comparative Physiological Psychology, 49,* 381–391.

Whalen, P. J., Rauch, S. L., Etcoff, N. L., McInerney, S. C., Lee, M. B., & Jenike, M. A. (1998). Masked presentations of emotional facial expressions modulate amygdala activity without explicit knowledge. *Journal of Neuroscience, 18,* 411–418.

Williams, M. A., Morris, A. P., McGlone, F., Abbott, D. F., & Mattingley, J. B. (2004). Amygdala responses to fearful and happy facial expressions under conditions of binocular suppression. *Journal of Neuroscience, 24,* 2898–2904.

Willis, J., & Todorov, A. (2006). First impressions: Making up your mind after a 100-ms exposure to a face. *Psychological Science, 17,* 592–598.

Winston, J. S., Strange, B. A., O'Doherty, J., & Dolan, R. J. (2002). Automatic and intentional brain responses during evaluation of trustworthiness of faces. *Nature Neuroscience, 5,* 277–283.

Zajonc, R. B. (2004). Exposure effects: An unmediated phenomenon. In A. S. R. Manstead, N. Frijda, & A. Fischer (Eds.), *Feelings and emotions,* (pp. 194–203). Amsterdam Symposium: Cambridge: Cambridge University Press.

Zajonc, R. B. (1980). Feeling and thinking: Preferences need no inferences. *American Psychologist, 1980, 35,* 151–175.

Zaki, J., Ochsner, K. N., Hanelin, H., Wager, T. D., & Mackey, S. (2007). Different circuits for different pain: Patterns of functional connectivity reveal distinct networks for processing pain in self and others. *Social Neuroscience, 2,* 276–291.

Chapter 38

The Somatovisceral Components of Emotions and Their Role in Decision Making: Specific Attention to the Ventromedial Prefrontal Cortex

ANTOINE BECHARA AND NASIR NAQVI

The orbital and mesial prefrontal cortices have been implicated in a range of affective processes, including hedonic and anticipatory responses to reward and punishment, subjective states of desire, and basic as well as social emotions. Changes in the visceral state may be considered a form of anticipation of the bodily impact of objects and events in the world. Visceral responses to biologically relevant stimuli allow an organism to maximize the survival value of situations that may impact the state of the internal milieu. These include events that promote homeostasis, such as an opportunity to feed or engage in social interaction, as well as events that disrupt homeostasis, such as a physical threat or a signal of social rejection. Visceral responses are just one component of a broader emotional response system that also includes changes in the endocrine and skeletomotor systems, as well as changes within the brain that alter the perceptual processing of biologically relevant stimuli (A. R. Damasio, 1994).

William James (1884) initially proposed that visceral responses to biologically relevant stimuli are a necessary component of the subjective experience of emotion. More specifically, suppose you saw the person you love bringing you flowers. The encounter may cause your heart to race, your skin to flush, and your facial muscles to contract with a happy expression. The encounter may also be accompanied by some body sensations, such as hearing your heartbeat and sensing "butterflies" in your stomach. However, there is also another kind of sensation: the emotional feeling of love, ecstasy, and elation directed toward your loved one. Since James's initial proposal, neuroscientists and philosophers have debated whether these two sensations are fundamentally the same. The psychological view of James-Lange (James, 1884) implied that the two were

the same. However, philosophers argued that emotions are not just bodily sensations; the two have different objects. Body sensations are about awareness of the internal state of the body. Emotional feelings are directed toward objects in the external world. Neuroscientific evidence based on functional magnetic resonance imaging (fMRI) tend to provide important validation of the theoretical view of James-Lange that neural systems supporting the perception of body states provide a fundamental ingredient for the subjective experience of emotions. This is consistent with contemporary neuroscientific views (e.g., see Craig, 2002), which suggest that the anterior insular cortex, especially on the right side of the brain, plays an important role in the mapping of bodily states and their translation into emotional feelings. The view of A. R. Damasio (1999, 2003) is consistent with this notion, but it suggests further that emotional feelings are not just about the body, but they are also about things in the world. In other words, sensing changes in the body requires neural systems, in which the anterior insular cortex is a critical substrate. However, the feelings that accompany emotions require additional brain regions. In Damasio's view, feelings arise in conscious awareness through the representation of bodily changes in relation to the object or event that incited the bodily changes. This second-order mapping of the relationship between organism and object occurs in brain regions that can integrate information about the body with information about the world. Such regions include the anterior cingulate cortex (Figure 38.1), especially its dorsal part.

According to A. R. Damasio (1994, 1999, 2003), there is an important distinction between *emotions* and *feelings*. Emotions are a collection of changes in body and brain states triggered by a dedicated brain system that responds

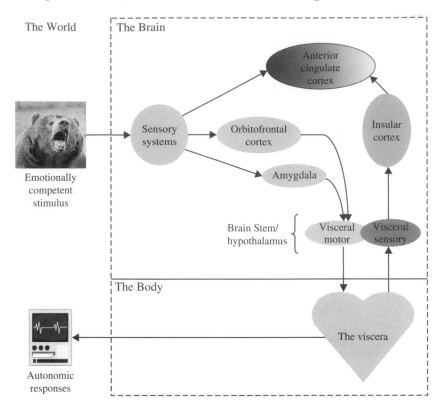

Figure 38.1 Information related to the emotionally competent object is represented in one or more of the brain's sensory processing systems.

Note: This information, which can be derived from the environment or recalled from memory, is made available to the amygdala and the orbitofrontal cortex, which are trigger sites for emotion. The emotion execution sites include the hypothalamus, the basal forebrain, and nuclei in the brain stem tegmentum. Only the visceral response is represented, although emotion comprises endocrine and somatomotor responses as well. Visceral sensations reach the anterior insular cortex by passing through the brain stem. Feelings result from the re-representation of changes in the viscera in relation to the object or event that incited them. The anterior cingulate cortex is a site where this second-order map is realized.

to the content of one's perceptions of a particular entity or event. The responses toward the body proper enacted in a body state involve physiological modifications that range from changes that are hidden from an external observer (e.g., changes in heart rate, smooth muscle contraction, endocrine release) to changes that are perceptible to an external observer (e.g., skin color, body posture, facial expression). The signals generated by these changes toward the brain itself produce changes that are mostly perceptible to the individual in whom they were enacted, which then provide the essential ingredients for what is ultimately perceived as a feeling. Thus, *emotions* are what an outside observer can see, or at least can measure through neuroscientific tools. *Feelings* are what the individual senses or subjectively experiences.

An emotion begins with a stimulus (imagined or perceived), such as a snake, a speaking engagement, or the person you are in love with. In neural terms, images related to the emotional stimulus are represented in one or more of the brain's sensory processing systems. Regardless of how short this presentation is, signals related to the

presence of that stimulus are made available to a number of emotion-triggering sites elsewhere in the brain. Two of these emotion-triggering sites are the amygdala and the orbitofrontal cortex (Figure 38.1). Evidence suggests that there may be some difference in the way the amygdala and the orbitofrontal cortex process emotional information: The amygdala is more engaged in the triggering of emotions when the emotional stimulus is present in the environment; the orbitofrontal cortex is more important when the emotional stimulus is recalled from memory (Bechara, Damasio, & Damasio, 2003).

To create an emotional state, the activity in triggering sites must be propagated to execution sites by means of neural connections. The emotion execution sites are visceral motor structures that include the hypothalamus, the basal forebrain, and some nuclei in the brain stem tegmentum (Figure 38.1).

Feelings result from neural patterns that represent changes in the body's response to an emotional object. Signals from body states are relayed back to the brain, and representations of these body states are formed at the level of visceral sensory nuclei in the brain stem. Representations of these body signals also form at the level of the insular cortex and lateral somatosensory cortex (Figure 38.1). It is most likely that the reception of body signals at the level of the brain stem does not give rise to conscious feeling as we know it, but the reception of these signals at the level of the cortex does so. The anterior insular cortex plays a special role in mapping visceral states and in bringing interoceptive signals to conscious perception. It is less clear whether the anterior insular cortex also plays a special role in translating the visceral states into subjective feeling and self-awareness. In A. R. Damasio's (1999) view, feelings arise in conscious awareness through the representation of bodily changes in relation to the emotional object (present or recalled) that incited the bodily changes. A first-order mapping of self is supported by structures in the brain stem, insular cortex, and somatosensory cortex. However, additional regions, such as the anterior cingulate cortex, are required for a second-order mapping of the relationship between organism and emotional object, and the integration of information about the body with information about the world.

According to the somatic marker hypothesis (A. R. Damasio, 1994), the sensory mapping of visceral responses not only contributes to feelings, but is also important for the execution of highly complex, goal-oriented behavior. In this view, visceral responses function to mark potential choices as advantageous or disadvantageous. This process aids in decision making in which there is a need to weigh positive and negative outcomes that may not be predicted decisively through cold rationality alone. Both the Jamesian view and the somatic marker hypothesis hold that the brain contains a system that translates the sensory properties of external stimuli into changes in the visceral state that reflect their biological relevance. We propose that this is the essential function of the ventromedial prefrontal cortex (vmPFC), a function that ties control of the visceral state to decision making and affect.

In this chapter we review evidence that the vmPFC plays a role in eliciting visceral responses that are related to the value of objects and events in the world. We start by discussing anatomical and physiological evidence that the vmPFC can both influence the state of the viscera and also register changes in the viscera elicited by biologically relevant stimuli. We then review the results of lesion studies in humans showing that the vmPFC is necessary for eliciting visceral responses to certain forms of emotional stimuli. Finally, we review evidence supporting the somatic marker hypothesis, showing that the visceral responses that are controlled by the vmPFC play a role in guiding decision making in the face of uncertain reward and punishment.

It is important to clarify up front that although the Jamesian and the Damasio views have insinuated that different emotions and bodily states (or somatic states) are characterized by a unique signature of visceral responses (see Rainville et al., 2006, for an example), the fact remains that the preponderance of evidence does not seem to support this depiction (for reviews, see, e.g., Cacioppo, Berntson, Larsen, Poehlmann, & Ito, 2000; Cacioppo, Klein, Berntson, & Hatfield, 1993). However, the cumulative evidence suggesting that there are no physiological response profiles that differentiate discrete emotions is not necessarily fatal to the concept of the somatic marker hypothesis, as interoception from visceral responses is still likely to be playing a role (see the discussion of the somatovisceral afference model of emotion, SAME, which was first proposed in 1992 to explain precisely how the undifferentiated visceral responses might produce immediate, discrete, and indubitable emotions; Cacioppo et al., 1993, 2000). Thus, somatic markers can be viewed as becoming differentiated at the level of the central nervous system and not necessarily in the periphery, although peripheral visceral input still plays a key role.

VISCERAL FUNCTIONS OF THE vmPFC

The terms *ventromedial prefrontal cortex* and *orbitofrontal cortex* (OFC) are often used interchangeably in the literature, even though they do not refer to identical regions. For this reason it is necessary to clarify exactly what we mean when we use these terms. The OFC is the entire cortex occupying the ventral surface of the frontal lobe, dorsal to the orbital plate of the frontal bone. We have used the term *vmPFC* to designate a region that encompasses medial portions of the OFC along with ventral portions of the medial prefrontal cortex. The vmPFC is an anatomical designation that has arisen because lesions that occur in the basal portions of the anterior fossa, which include meningiomas of the cribiriform plate and falx cerebri, and aneurysms of the anterior communicating and anterior cerebral arteries, frequently lead to damage in this area (Figure 38.2). Often this damage is bilateral. With respect to the cytoarchitectonic fields identified in the human orbitofrontal and medial prefrontal cortices by Price and colleagues (Ongur & Price, 2000), the vmPFC comprises Brodmann area (BA) 14 and medial portions of BA 11 and 13 on the orbital surface and BA 25 and 32 and caudal portions of BA 10 on the mesial surface. The vmPFC excludes lateral portions of the OFC, namely BA 47/12, as well as more dorsal and posterior regions of BA 24 and 32 of the medial prefrontal cortex. The vmPFC is thus a relatively large and heterogeneous area.

(A)

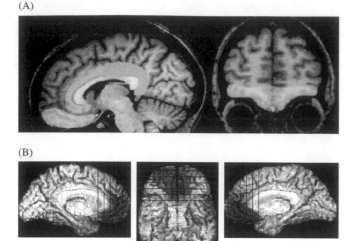

(B)

Figure 38.2   (Figure C. 36 in color section) **A:** The orbitofrontal cortex. **B:** The location of the vmPFC as defined in our lesion studies and in this chapter.

Note: (A) On the sagittal section (left), the medial sector of the orbitofrontal cortex is depicted on the area of the brain highlighted in yellow. On the coronal slice (right), both the medial and lateral areas of the orbitofrontal cortex are depicted on the area of the brain highlighted in yellow. (B) A map showing areas of the brain that are damaged in patients who show impairments in visceral response and decision making. The colors reflect the number of subjects with damage in a given voxel. The region of greatest overlap is the vmPFC. Note the involvement of medial wall and medial orbitofrontal areas and the relative absence of involvement of the lateral orbitofrontal areas.

Viewing the vmPFC as a single region may blur the distinction between functions subserved by the OFC on the one hand and the ventral portion of the medial prefrontal cortex on the other. Recent evidence in both rodents (Chudasama & Robbins, 2003) and nonhuman primates (Pears, Parkinson, Hopewell, Everitt, & Roberts, 2003) suggests that these regions subserve distinct motivational and learning functions. Thus, lesions of the vmPFC in humans may disrupt more than one process. This is important to keep in mind when inconsistencies arise between animal studies and human studies. These differences are also important when comparing human lesion studies, which tend to examine the functions of relatively large regions, and functional imaging studies, which reveal more focused patterns of activity.

The vmPFC encompasses different regions that have been identified in functional imaging studies. The vmPFC includes the medial prefrontal area identified as being deactivated by a broad range of cognitive tasks that require focused attention, reflecting a high level of resting activity that is suspended during goal-directed behavior (Raichle et al., 2001). Other investigators have argued that the

vmPFC encompasses the medial orbitofrontal area, in which activity is consistently related to the "reward value" of hedonically positive stimuli (Kringelbach & Rolls, 2004). In addition, the vmPFC includes the subgenual cingulate cortex (Figure 38.2), an area that has been implicated through functional imaging studies in the pathogenesis of mood disorders (Drevets et al., 1997). It remains to be seen whether these seemingly distinct functions reflect the operation of a single brain area that can be called the *vmPFC,* or instead are due to separate mental processes mediated by three functionally distinct areas encompassed by the vmPFC.

There are two points that need to be considered when interpreting functional imaging studies of the vmPFC. First, as with all cognitive functions, activation or deactivation may show that this region is engaged by a particular function, but does not mean that it is necessary for the function to be performed. Thus, even though activity in the vmPFC can be shown to correlate with the reward value of hedonically positive stimuli, it still remains to be seen whether lesions in the human vmPFC disrupt the subjective experience of, for example, pleasure. Second, in fMRI studies the vmPFC undergoes significant BOLD signal dropout due to its location near an air–tissue interface. For this reason, the failure to detect activation or deactivation of the vmPFC using fMRI should not be taken as evidence that the vmPFC is not involved in the function under investigation, unless special procedures have been implemented to overcome signal dropout. For example, an fMRI study of decision making (Fukui, Murai, Fukuyama, Hayashi, & Hanakawa, 2005) using a task (the Iowa Gambling Task) on which subjects with vmPFC damage are impaired did not show activation of the vmPFC. An earlier positron emission tomography (PET) study (Ernst et al., 2002) using the same task did find activation in the vmPFC. Although one may cite differences in the experimental conditions or data analysis to explain this discrepancy, perhaps the most parsimonious explanation is that the Fukui et al. study did not use procedures to counteract BOLD signal dropout in the vmPFC, which was not an issue in the Ernst et al. study. This points to the larger possibility that the vmPFC is involved in a broader set of functions than would be indicated by fMRI studies alone.

Nauta (1971) and then Neafsey (1990) proposed that the ventral prefrontal cortex represents a distinct visceromotor output region. Price and colleagues (Ongur & Price, 2000) later refined this concept, synthesizing the previous anatomic literature on the prefrontal cortex with their own anatomical studies in macaques. In their conception, the ventral prefrontal cortex (a region they term "the orbito-medial prefrontal cortex") is composed of functionally distinct orbital and medial networks. The orbital network is essentially a sensory input area that receives afferents from late sensory cortices for vision, audition, olfaction, taste, and visceral sensation and has reciprocal connections with the dorsolateral prefrontal cortex. The medial network is essentially a visceromotor output area that sends projections to subcortical structures that are involved in emotional and motivational processes, such as the amygdala and the nucleus accumbens, as well as regions of the brain stem and hypothalamus that directly govern the state of the viscera. In between the orbital and medial networks lies a transitional zone that is interconnected with both the orbital and medial networks that may function to transfer information between those networks. According to this scheme, the vmPFC, as we define it, corresponds largely to the medial and intermediate networks, areas that are largely concerned with translating highly processed sensory inputs into visceromotor output.

Much of the early evidence for the role of the vmPFC in the control of visceral functions came from studies examining the cardiorespiratory effects of stimulation in this area in cats and macaques, but further support for the role of the vmPFC in visceral motor functions also comes from lesion studies. Early studies in humans (Luria, Pribram, & Homskaya, 1964) examined the effects of relatively large lesions of the frontal lobes on visceral functions. Our own laboratory has performed studies examining the effects of lesions in an array of cortical areas on visceral responses (Tranel & Damasio, 1994). These studies demonstrated that a number of cortical regions, including the vmPFC but also the anterior cingulate cortex and the right inferior parietal cortex, are necessary for the generation of visceral responses to sensory stimuli. These studies also showed that the role of the vmPFC in governing visceral responses is specific to stimuli with emotional or social content.

More recent evidence for the visceral functions of the vmPFC comes from functional imaging studies. One study showed that neural activity in the vmPFC covaries with visceral responses, this time with skin conductance response during anticipation and receipt of monetary rewards (Critchley, Elliott, Mathias, & Dolan, 2000). In this study, skin conductance responses were modeled as discrete events, which allowed for the correlation with brain activity both preceding and following the responses. Using this approach it was possible to show that activity in the vmPFC was related to both the generation of skin conductance responses as well as the afferent mapping of skin conductance responses, indicating both visceral motor and visceral sensory functions for the vmPFC. Using fMRI it has also been shown that activity in vmPFC is correlated with skin conductance response across a variety of cognitive

states, including the resting state (Nagai, Critchley, Featherstone, Trimble, & Dolan, 2004; Patterson, Ungerleider, & Bandettini, 2002). These studies suggest that the visceral functions of the vmPFC are not specific to emotional stimuli, contrary to the results of the lesion studies described earlier. However, just because activity in the vmPFC is related to visceral responses in a given context does not mean that it is necessary for the generation of visceral responses in that context.

Both the somatic marker hypothesis and the Jamesian view of emotion place importance on the sensory representations of the visceral responses that are elicited by biologically relevant stimuli. An important question, therefore, regards how visceral responses, once generated by the vmPFC and deployed in the body, are mapped in the brain. Visceral sensations are represented at multiple levels of the neuraxis, including the spinal cord, brain stem, hypothalamus, thalamus, and cortex (Craig, 2002). Each of these stages of visceral representation may have a specific role to play in affective and executive processes.

The sensory representation of the viscera within the insular cortex, in particular the right anterior insular cortex, has been proposed to play a special role in conscious emotional feelings (Craig, 2002; Damasio et al., 2000). The right insular cortex, along with the right somatosensory cortices, have also been proposed by A. R. Damasio (A. R. Damasio, 1994) to be a component of the somatic marker network for decision making. The anterior (agranular) insular cortex projects to a number of areas involved in emotion and motivation, including the amygdala and the nucleus accumbens. The anterior insular cortex also projects to the vmPFC, both via the orbital network and through direct projections to medial network areas (Flynn, Benson, & Ardila, 1999). In addition, recent anatomical evidence suggests that the right anterior insular cortex has evolved special functions in higher primates (Craig, 2002), consistent with a role in conscious feelings. Indeed, the right anterior insular cortex has been shown to be active during a number of subjective feeling states (Critchley, Wiens, Rotshtein, Ohman, & Dolan, 2004; A. R. Damasio et al., 2000; Lane, Reiman, Ahern, Schwartz, & Davidson, 1997). Thus, the visceral sensory representation within the right anterior insular cortex may play a role in the feelings that accompany decision making, such as hunches and gut feelings that may guide decision making in the face of uncertainty.

According to the somatic marker hypothesis (Bechara & Damasio, 2005), visceral sensory signals can also influence decision making by acting on brain stem nuclei for ascending neurotransmitter systems, including dopaminergic, serotonergic, and noradrenergic systems. These neurotransmitter systems exert widespread influence on the function of the prefrontal cortex, including the dorsolateral, medial, and orbital prefrontal cortices, and on subcortical structures, including the amygdala and the ventral and dorsal striata. Through these projections, ascending neurotransmitter systems play a role in multiple attentional, executive, and motivational processes (Berridge & Robinson, 1998; Rahman, Sahakian, Cardinal, Rogers, & Robbins, 2001). There is evidence for direct visceral sensory inputs to these nuclei and that visceral states can influence neurotransmitter release from these nuclei (Berntson, Sarter, & Cacioppo, 2003). The somatic marker hypothesis holds that visceral states, via their influence on ascending neurotransmitter systems, can influence decision making both by promoting the maintenance of specific goals in working memory and by biasing of behavior toward these goals. In this framework, brain stem neurotransmitter nuclei may also be engaged by "as if" loops. Here, areas such as the vmPFC, instead of triggering visceral responses in the body that feed back to brain stem neurotransmitter nuclei, facilitate neurotransmitter release via direct brain stem projections that bypass the body. This triggers neurotransmitter release as if a visceral response had been expressed in the body.

As discussed earlier, functional imaging evidence (Critchley et al., 2000) indicates that the vmPFC, in addition to its role in the generation of visceral responses, plays a role in the sensory representation of the visceral state. The vmPFC may receive visceral sensory information from the insular cortex or via ascending neurotransmitter systems. One function of the visceral sensory inputs to the vmPFC may be to represent the visceral responses that are themselves induced within the vmPFC, amygdala, or other areas that trigger visceral responses to biologically relevant stimuli. This function may allow the vmPFC to compare the sensory representations of the visceral state with an efferent copy of the visceral response evoked by a biologically relevant stimulus. Differences between these two inputs may signal that a goal has been achieved; that is, a consummatory event has occurred that has altered the state of the viscera.

The vmPFC has available to it information regarding the sensory consequences of innately pleasurable consummatory behaviors that impinge directly on the viscera, such as feeding, as well as innately aversive bodily states that result from actual or potential tissue damage (nociception). For example, it has been shown that activity in the vmPFC is correlated with the subjective pleasantness of stimuli such as taste (Kringelbach & Rolls, 2004), the oral sensations elicited by water (Denton et al., 1999a, 1999b), and pleasant touch (Rolls, 2000). In addition, activity in the vmPFC is correlated with subjective ratings of the intensity of thermal pain (Craig, 2002). All of these

stimuli have direct homeostatic relevance and are signaled through a distinct sensory channel that includes the insular cortex (Craig, 2002). This suggests that the vmPFC represents the hedonic value of the visceral sensory signals generated by innately rewarding or punishing consummatory behavior (so-called primary reinforcers; Kringelbach & Rolls, 2004). These representations may be important for the feelings of pleasure and pain that accompany good and bad outcomes. However, there is a lack of human lesion evidence that indicates that the vmPFC mediates the subjective hedonic impact of interoceptive stimuli. Another possibility is that interoceptive or visceral signals within the vmPFC may be important for learning to associate the hedonic consequences of behavior with the particular courses of action that precede them. This is supported by the findings from functional imaging studies that the vmPFC is activated when feedback indicating a correct choice is signaled specifically via an interoceptive route (Hurliman, Nagode, & Pardo, 2005). In this way, interoceptive signals generated by primary reinforcers may form the basis for representations of more abstract rewards and punishments that are elicited within the vmPFC.

DECISION-MAKING FUNCTIONS OF THE vmPFC

Our laboratory's interest in the functions of the vmPFC was fueled by observations in neurological patients that lesions in this area led to profound impairments in personality and real-life decision-making capabilities. One of the first and most famous cases of the so-called frontal lobe syndrome was the patient Phineas Gage, a railroad construction worker who survived an explosion that blasted an iron tamping bar through the front of his head (Harlow, 1848). Before the accident Gage was a man of normal intelligence, energetic and persistent in executing his plans of operation. He was responsible, sociable, and popular among peers and friends. After the accident his medical recovery was remarkable. He survived the accident with normal intelligence, memory, speech, sensation, and movement. However, his behavior changed completely. He became irresponsible, untrustworthy, and impatient of restraint or advice when it conflicted with his desires. Using modern neuroimaging techniques, H. Damasio and colleagues (H. Damasio, Grabowski, Frank, Galburda, & Damasio, 1994) have reconstituted the accident by relying on measurements taken from Gage's skull. The key finding of this neuroimaging study was that the most likely placement of Gage's lesion included the vmPFC region, bilaterally.

The case of Phineas Gage paved the way for the notion that the frontal lobes were linked to social conduct, judgment, decision making, and personality. A number of instances similar to Gage's case have since appeared in the literature (Ackerly & Benton, 1948; Brickner, 1932; Welt, 1888). Interestingly, these cases received little attention for many years. Over the years, we have studied numerous patients with this type of lesion. Such patients with damage to the vmPFC develop severe impairments in personal and social decision making, in spite of otherwise largely preserved intellectual abilities. These patients had normal intelligence and creativity before their brain damage. After the damage they begin to have difficulties planning their workday and future and difficulties in choosing friends, partners, and activities. The actions they elect to pursue often lead to losses of diverse order, for example, financial losses, losses in social standing, losses of family and friends. The choices they make are no longer advantageous and are remarkably different from the kinds of choices they were known to make in the premorbid period. These patients often decide against their best interests. They are unable to learn from previous mistakes, as reflected by repeated engagement in decisions that lead to negative consequences. In striking contrast to this real-life decision-making impairment, problem-solving abilities in laboratory settings remain largely normal. As noted, the patients have normal intellect, as measured by a variety of conventional neuropsychological tests (Bechara, Damasio, Tranel, & Anderson, 1998; A. R. Damasio, Tranel, & Damasio, 1990; Eslinger & Damasio, 1985; Saver & Damasio, 1991).

The Genesis of the Somatic Marker Hypothesis

When we first observed the real-life decision-making deficits of patients with vmPFC damage, a good deal of evidence for the visceral motor functions of the vmPFC, described earlier, had already accumulated. The question then arose as to whether the decision-making deficits caused by vmPFC damage were related to its visceromotor functions. Nauta (1971) had by then proposed that the guidance of behavior by the frontal lobes was linked to the interoceptive and visceromotor functions of this area. Specifically, he proposed that the prefrontal cortex, broadly defined, functioned to compare the affective responses evoked by the various choices for behavior and to select the option that "passed censure by an interoceptive sensorium." (p. 172). According to Nauta, the "interoceptive agnosia" suffered by patients with frontal lobe damage could explain their impairments in real life, as well as their poor performance on various tests of executive function, including the Wisconsin card sort task. This model was meant to explain the function of the prefrontal cortex as a whole. Furthermore, it was meant as a broad explanation of executive function deficits, not of a specific deficit in decision making within the social and personal domains. However, the deficits of patients with damage in the vmPFC were limited to the personal and social domains; patients with focal vmPFC damage showed marked impairments in their real-life personal and social functioning but had intact intelligence. Indeed, these patients performed normally on standard laboratory tests of executive function such as the Wisconsin card sort task.

This background helped to shape a more specific formulation, deemed the "somatic marker hypothesis" (A. R. Damasio, 1994; A. R. Damasio, Tranel, & A. R. Damasio, 1991). According to this hypothesis, patients with damage in the vmPFC make poor decisions in part because they are unable to elicit somatic (visceral) responses that mark the consequences of their actions as positive or negative. In this framework, the vmPFC functions to elicit visceral responses that reflect the anticipated value of the choices. Though this function is specific to the vmPFC, it draws on information about the external world that is represented in multiple higher order sensory cortices. Furthermore, this function is limited to specific types of decision making, in particular those situations where the meaning of events is implied and the consequences of behavior are uncertain. These are situations, such as social interactions and decisions about one's personal and financial life, where the consequences of behavior have emotional value; that is, they can be experienced as subjective feelings and can also increase or decrease the likelihood of similar behavior in the future (they are rewarding or punishing). Furthermore, these are situations where the rules of behavior are not explicit but yet require some form of mental deliberation in real time in order to navigate them successfully. This form of reasoning is distinct from reasoning that does not require the weighing of positive and negative consequences, or in which the outcomes of decisions are known with a high degree of certainty. In addition to explaining the specificity of the impairments in patients with vmPFC damage, the somatic marker framework leads to testable hypotheses about the kinds of information represented within the vmPFC and the relationship of this information to the state of the viscera.

Lesions of the vmPFC Impair Visceral Responses to Emotional Stimuli

One of the first empirical tests of the somatic marker hypothesis came from studies examining the effects of vmPFC lesions on the visceral response to complex visual stimuli (A. R. Damasio et al., 1990). Though it was known that the vmPFC played a role in the elicitation of visceral responses, the precise behavioral context in which visceral functions were engaged by the vmPFC was not known. In other words, it was possible that the vmPFC functioned to elicit visceral responses to all forms of stimuli, or only certain types of stimuli, such as those that, like social signals, possess emotional value that is often largely implicit. According to the somatic marker hypothesis, the visceral responses that were mediated by the vmPFC were especially related to the implied meaning of social stimuli.

To address this hypothesis, one study examined the visceral responses of a group of patients with damage in the vmPFC, all of whom showed a pattern of behavior that reflected an inability to make advantageous decisions in the personal and social realms despite intact intellectual functioning. The subjects were shown a series of affectively charged pictures, including pictures of mutilations, disasters, and sexual images, along with a series of neutral pictures. The patients were tested in two conditions, one in which they watched the stimuli passively and another in which they were asked to describe the pictures in terms of their emotional content. After each stimulus, the skin conductance response (SCR), an index of sympathetic arousal, was measured. In addition, SCRs to orienting stimuli, including loud noises and deep breaths, were measured. The responses of patients with vmPFC damage were compared to the responses of patients with damage to regions outside the vmPFC as well as the responses of neurologically intact comparison subjects.

It was found that patients with vmPFC damage were significantly impaired in their visceral responses to emotional pictures when required to view them passively, compared to both neurologically intact and brain-damaged comparison subjects. However, when required to comment on the content of the pictures, the visceral responses of the vmPFC patients to the emotional pictures were largely intact. In addition, the vmPFC patients showed intact SCRs to orienting stimuli. These results indicate that the vmPFC plays a role in the elicitation of visceral responses to biologically relevant stimuli. This impairment is specific to stimuli for which emotional meaning must be decoded through cognitive processes and does not extend to stimuli that elicit visceral responses because they are innately aversive or arousing (e.g., a loud noise) or to stimuli that are physiological elicitors of visceral responses (e.g., a deep breath). The results also imply that the vmPFC mediates the visceral response to emotional stimuli when the evaluation of these stimuli does not require verbal mediation, that is, when it is implicit.

Lesions in the vmPFC Lead to Impairments in the Iowa Gambling Task

Once it was known that patients with vmPFC damage were abnormal both in their capacity to make decisions and in their ability to respond viscerally to the emotional meaning of certain stimuli, it still remained to be shown that these two abnormalities were linked. Up to this point, the behavioral abnormalities of these patients, which were striking in real life, had largely eluded conventional neuropsychological and laboratory tests. Thus, it was important to develop a laboratory test that simulated the real-life decisions in which patients with vmPFC damage failed. This test factored in reward and punishment, as well as the uncertainty and risk that accompany many real-life decisions. In addition, this test required participants to reason and deliberate the outcome of choices in real time.

The Iowa Gambling Task

The Iowa Gambling Task (IGT; Bechara, Damasio, Damasio, & Anderson, 1994; Bechara, Tranel, & Damasio, 2000) uses four decks of cards, named A, B, C, and D. The goal in the task is to maximize profit on a loan of play money. Subjects are required to make a series of 100 card selections. However, they are not told ahead of time how many card selections they are going to make. Subjects can select one card at a time from any deck they choose, and they are free to switch from any deck to another at any time and as often as they wish. However, the subject's decision to select from one deck versus another is largely influenced by various schedules of immediate reward and future punishment. These schedules are preprogrammed and known to the examiner but not to the subject, and they entail the following principles.

Every time the subject selects a card from deck A or deck B, the subject gets $100. Every time the subject selects a card from deck C or deck D, the subject gets $50. However, in each of the four decks, subjects encounter unpredictable punishments (money loss). The punishment is set to be higher in the high-paying decks A and B and lower in the low-paying decks C and D. For example, if one picks 10 cards from deck A, one would earn $1,000. However, in those 10 card picks, five unpredictable punishments would be encountered, ranging from $150 to $350, bringing a total cost of $1,250. Deck B is similar: Every 10 cards picked from deck B would earn $1,000; however, these 10 card picks would encounter one high punishment of $1,250. On the other hand, every 10 cards from deck C or D earn only $500, but they cost only $250 in punishment. Hence, decks A and B are disadvantageous because they cost more in the long run; that is, one loses $250 every 10 cards. Decks C and D are advantageous because they result in an overall gain in the long run; that is, one wins $250 every 10 cards.

We investigated the performance of normal controls and patients with vmPFC lesions on this task. Normal subjects avoided the bad decks A and B and preferred the good decks C and D. In sharp contrast, the vmPFC patients did not avoid the bad decks A and B; indeed, they preferred those decks (Figure 38.3). From these results we suggested that the patients' performance profile is comparable to their real-life inability to decide advantageously. This is especially true in personal and social matters, a domain for which, in life, as in the task, an exact calculation of the future outcomes is not possible and choices must be based on hunches and gut feelings.

Lesions in the vmPFC Disrupt Visceral Responses during the Iowa Gambling Task

In light of the finding that the IGT is an instrument that detects the decision-making impairment of vmPFC patients in the laboratory, we went on to address the next question: whether the impairment is linked to a failure in somatic signaling (Bechara, Tranel, Damasio, & Damasio, 1996). To address this question, we added a physiological measure to the IGT. The goal was to assess somatic state activation while subjects were making decisions during performance of the task. We studied two groups: normal subjects and vmPFC patients. We had them perform the IGT while we recorded their electrodermal activity (SCRs). As the body begins to change after a thought, and as a given somatic state begins to be enacted, the autonomic nervous system begins to increase the activity in the skin's sweat glands. Although this sweating activity is relatively small and not observable by the naked eye, it can be amplified and recorded by a polygraph as a wave. The amplitude of this wave can be measured and thus provide an indirect measure of the somatic state experienced by the subject.

Both normal subjects and vmPFC patients generated SCRs after they had picked a card and were told that they won or lost money. The most important difference, however, was that normal subjects, as they became experienced with the task, began to generate SCRs *prior* to the selection of any cards, that is, during the time they were pondering which deck to choose. These anticipatory SCRs were more pronounced before picking a card from the risky decks A and B when compared to the safe decks C and D. In other words, these anticipatory SCRs were like gut feelings that warned the subject against picking from the bad decks. Patients with vmPFC damage failed to generate such SCRs before picking a card. This failure to generate anticipatory SCRs *before* picking cards from the bad decks correlates with their failure to avoid these bad decks and choose advantageously in this task (Figure 38.4). These results provide strong support for the notion that decision making is guided by emotional signals (gut feelings) that are generated in anticipation of future events.

An important question regards the information content of visceral responses that are elicited by the vmPFC. If somatic markers are to be useful in guiding decision-making processes involving uncertain reward and punishment, then they should provide information about both the valence of an anticipated outcome (e.g., whether a choice will result in winning or losing money) and the magnitude of the anticipated outcome (e.g., how much money will be won or lost). Our results using the IGT show that the vmPFC triggers anticipatory visceral responses to both the advantageous and the disadvantageous decks. These responses are larger for disadvantageous decks than for advantageous decks, though they are still deployed for the advantageous decks. Further experiments from our laboratory (Bechara, Dolan, & Hindes, 2002) and others (Tomb, Hauser, Deldin, & Caramazza, 2002) have shown that when the reward-punishment contingencies are reversed, with the disadvantageous decks paying out

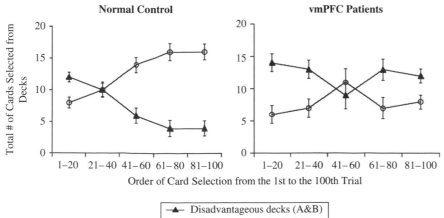

Figure 38.3 Card selection on the Iowa Gambling Task as a function of group (normal control, vmPFC), deck type (disadvantageous versus advantageous), and trial block.

Note: Normal control subjects shifted their selection of cards to the advantageous decks. The vmPFC prefrontal patients did not make a reliable shift and opted for the disadvantageous decks.

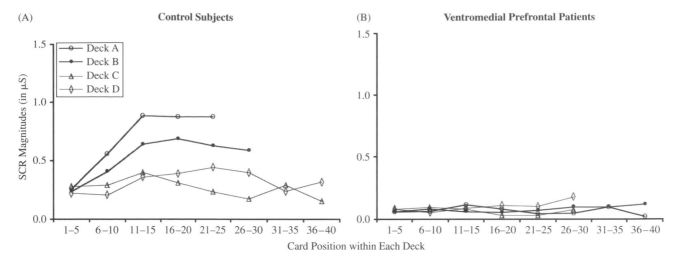

Figure 38.4 Magnitudes of anticipatory SCRs as a function of group (control **[A]** versus vmPFC **[B]**), deck, and card position within each deck.

Note: Control subjects gradually began to generate high-amplitude SCRs to the disadvantageous decks. The vmPFC patients failed to do so.

a lower quantity of reward rather than doling out a higher punishment, the SCRs are now greater to the advantageous decks than to the disadvantageous decks. This suggests that SCR is not merely an index of the potential "badness" of choices. Rather, SCR can index the magnitude of both the anticipated negative and the anticipated positive outcomes of a choice. It seems, however, that SCR does not differentiate the anticipated valence of the outcomes. This is consistent with work by others (Lang, Bradley, Cuthbert, & Patrick, 1993) showing that SCR does not differentiate the hedonic valence of emotional stimuli but does index the magnitude of the arousal that they elicit. This would mean that some other signal is required in order to assess the valence of the anticipated outcome. Although our laboratory (Rainville et al., 2006) has provided preliminary evidence that cardiovascular responses, such as changes in heart rate, can provide information that distinguishes between positive and negative emotional states, the fact remains that the preponderance of evidence speaks to the lack of such a distinction at the peripheral visceral level (Cacioppo et al., 1993, 2000). Although it is possible that such signals can combine with those reflected in the SCR to provide information about both the perceived valence and the perceived magnitude of the future outcome of a choice, there is a strong likelihood that this discrimination is not achieved until the signals reach the central nervous system. Indeed, the somatovisceral afference model of emotion does provide an explanation for how undifferentiated visceral responses might produce distinguishable emotions (Cacioppo et al., 1993, 2000). Perhaps somatic markers operate in a fashion that is consistent with that model. Future experiments may examine at what level of the brain the visceral signals reflecting different channels

of autonomic outflow become differentiated in such a manner to exert influence on decision making.

Visceral Responses That Signal the Correct Strategy Do Not Need to Be Conscious

According to the somatic marker hypothesis, the vmPFC mediates an implicit representation of the anticipated value of choices that is distinct from an explicit awareness of the correct strategy. To test this idea, we performed a study (Bechara, Damasio, Tranel, & Damasio, 1997) in which we examined the development of SCRs over time in relation to subjects' knowledge of the advantageous strategy in the IGT. In this study the IGT was administered as before, but this time the task was interrupted at regular intervals and the subjects were asked to describe their knowledge about what was going on in the task and their feelings about the task. Normal subjects began to choose preferentially from the advantageous decks before they were able to report why these decks were preferred. They then began to form hunches about the correct strategy, which corresponded to their choosing more from the advantageous decks than from the disadvantageous decks. Finally, some subjects reached a conceptual stage where they possessed explicit knowledge about the correct strategy (i.e., to choose from decks C and D because, although they pay less, they result in less punishment). As before, normal subjects developed SCRs preceding their choices that were larger for the disadvantageous decks than for the advantageous decks. This time it was also found that the SCR discrimination between advantageous and disadvantageous decks preceded the development of conceptual knowledge of the correct strategy. In fact, the SCR discrimination between advantageous and disadvantageous decks even preceded the development of hunches about the correct strategy.

In contrast to the normal subjects, subjects with damage in the vmPFC failed to switch from the disadvantageous decks to the advantageous decks, as in the previous study. In addition, subjects in this group again failed to develop anticipatory responses that discriminated between the disadvantageous and advantageous decks. Furthermore, patients with vmPFC damage never developed hunches about the correct strategy.

Together, these results suggest that anticipatory visceral responses that are governed by the vmPFC precede emergence of advantageous choice behavior, which itself precedes explicit knowledge of the advantageous strategy. This further suggests that signals generated by the vmPFC, reflected in visceral states, may function as a nonconscious bias toward the advantageous strategy.

More recently, other investigators have questioned whether it is necessary to invoke visceral responses as constituting nonconscious biasing signals (Maia & McClelland, 2004). By using more detailed questions to probe subjects' awareness of the attributes of each of the decks in the IGT, this study showed that subjects possess explicit knowledge of the advantageous strategy at an earlier stage in the task than was shown in the Bechara et al. (1997) study. Furthermore, the Maia and McClelland study found that subjects began to make advantageous choices at around the same time that they reported knowledge of the correct strategy. Based on these findings, it was argued that nonconscious somatic marker processes are not *required* in order to explain how decision making occurs.

A response to this study has been published elsewhere (Bechara, Damasio, Tranel, & Damasio, 2005), along with a rebuttal by Maia and McClelland (2005). Two points bear discussion here. First, because this study did not measure visceral responses and did not examine the effects of brain damage, it does not disprove the hypothesis that somatic markers mediated by the vmPFC play a role in decision making; it only shows that conscious awareness of the correct strategy occurs at around the same time as advantageous decision making. Second, both the Bechara et al. (1997) study and the Maia and McClelland (2005) study found that some subjects continue to make disadvantageous choices despite being able to report the correct strategy. This pattern bears an uncanny resemblance to the way subjects with lesions in the vmPFC are able to report the correct strategies for personal and social decision making, despite their severe deficits in the actual execution of personal and social behavior in real life. Indeed, this clinical observation provided the initial impetus to hypothesize a role for covert biasing processes in decision making in the first place. This indicates that,

in both the IGT and in real life, conscious knowledge of the correct strategy may not be enough to guide advantageous decision making.

Thus, some process that operates independently of conscious knowledge of the correct strategy (i.e., somatic markers) must be invoked to explain fully how individuals make advantageous decisions. Indeed, it seems likely that this process can sometimes bias behavior that goes against what a person consciously thinks to be the correct strategy. That nonconscious biasing processes may not precede conscious knowledge in time is potentially an important finding, but it does not provide a basis for rejection of the fundamental role of somatic markers as nonconscious biases of behavior.

The Decision-Making Functions of the vmPFC Are Different from the Decision-Making Functions of the Amygdala

Like patients with damage to the vmPFC, patients with bilateral damage to the amygdala also demonstrate impairments in their ability to make advantageous choices in their personal and social lives (A. R. Damasio, 1994). The amygdala, like the vmPFC, has been strongly implicated in emotional and motivational processes (Cardinal, Parkinson, Hall, & Everitt, 2002; LeDoux, 1996). There is much in common between the amygdala and the vmPFC in terms of cortical and subcortical connectivity. In particular, the amygdala receives information from higher order sensory cortices for vision, olfaction, audition, and visceral sensation (Amaral, Price, Pitkanen, & Carmichael, 1992) and sends output to subcortical sites that regulate the state of the viscera, including nuclei of the brain stem and hypothalamus. Thus, like the vmPFC, the amygdala is positioned to receive multiple sensory inputs pertaining to biologically relevant stimuli and to trigger changes in the visceral state. This suggests that the amygdala plays a role similar to that of the vmPFC in decision making. However, there are important differences between the amygdala and the vmPFC in terms of their visceral and decision-making functions.

One source of evidence regarding these distinct roles comes from an experiment in which we administered the IGT to a group of subjects with bilateral amygdala damage (Bechara, Damasio, Damasio, & Lee, 1999). Their performance on this task, along with their SCRs, were compared to a group of subjects with vmPFC damage and a group of neurologically intact subjects. Similar to subjects with vmPFC damage, subjects with damage to the amygdala performed poorly on the IGT, failing to shift toward choosing more frequently from the advantageous decks. When examining the SCRs, however, there were different patterns of deficit in amygdala-lesioned subjects versus vmPFC-lesioned subjects. As discussed earlier, patients with vmPFC damage fail to deploy anticipatory visceral responses before their choices, responses that, in normal subjects, are larger before choosing from the disadvantageous decks than before choosing from the advantageous decks. As also noted previously, vmPFC-lesioned subjects continue to have normal SCRs in response to receiving reward and punishment. In contrast, patients with amygdala damage fail to deploy SCRs during both the anticipatory period and in response to receiving rewards and punishments. These data are shown in Figure 38.5. This suggests that the decision-making deficit in patients with amygdala damage is due to an inability to respond viscerally to rewards and punishments. This is different from the deficit in patients with vmPFC damage, who possess an inability to viscerally anticipate uncertain rewards and punishments but who are normal in their ability to respond viscerally to rewards and punishments once they are received.

To examine further the distinction between the affective-visceral functions of the amygdala and the vmPFC, the same subjects underwent a Pavlovian conditioning paradigm (Bechara et al., 1999). Here it was found that patients with bilateral amygdala damage failed to acquire conditioned SCRs. In contrast, patients with vmPFC damage were not different from neurologically intact subjects in their ability to produce conditioned SCRs. Both the amygdala and the vmPFC patients were normal in their SCRs in response to the unconditioned stimulus. This indicates that the amygdala, but not the vmPFC, is required for the acquisition of Pavlovian conditioning. In other words, the visceral responses to stimuli that acquire hedonic value through simple associative learning processes are not mediated by the vmPFC but are mediated by the amygdala. This parallels the dissociation between the amygdala and the vmPFC with respect to the visceral response to reward and punishment in the IGT.

The distinction between the affective-visceral functions of the amygdala and the vmPFC may be conceptualized in

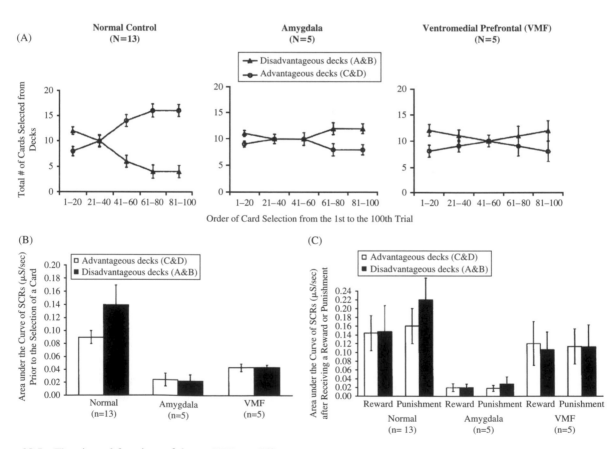

Figure 38.5   The visceral functions of the vmPFC are different from those of the amygdala.

Note: **A:** Behavioral performance on the IGT. Both vmPFC- and amygdala-lesioned subjects fail to switch to choosing preferentially from the advantageous decks. **B:** Both vmPFC and amygdala-lesioned subjects fail to produce anticipatory SCRs. **C:** vmPFC-lesioned subjects produce normal SCRs in response to reward and punishment, but amygdala lesioned subjects fail to produce SCRs in response to reward and punishment.

Error bars represent the standard error of the mean. Not depicted are results showing that vmPFC-lesioned subjects produce normal SCRs to a classically conditioned stimulus, whereas amygdala-lesioned subjects fail to produce classically conditioned SCRs. From "Different Contributions of the Human Amygdala and Ventromedial Prefrontal Cortex to Decision-Making," by A. Bechara, H. Damasio, A. R. Damasio, and G. P. Lee, 1999, *Journal of Neuroscience, 19,* pp. 5473–5481. Reprinted with permission.

terms of the demands of processing biologically relevant stimuli on attention and working memory. In this view, the amygdala triggers visceral responses to stimuli whose biological significance can be decoded in relatively automatic fashion, such as winning or losing money, conditioned stimuli that reliably predict aversive and pleasurable events in the future, and stimuli with innate biological significance, such as the sight of spiders and snakes and facial expressions of fear. We refer to this class of stimuli as "primary inducers." The visceral responses to primary inducers can be elicited quickly and without thought or complex attention. The vmPFC, in contrast, triggers visceral responses to stimuli whose biological significance must be decoded through a deliberative process. We refer to this class of stimuli as "secondary inducers." This includes thoughts of future loss or gain, particularly when loss or gain is uncertain, as well as the recollection of pleasant and unpleasant events from the past. Secondary inducers, which may not be present within the sensory field, must be brought to mind to elicit a visceral response. Thus, vmPFC functions are related to attention and working memory and also to the recall of episodic memories.

SUMMARY

The Somatic Maker Hypothesis

Somatic Markers as Executive Processes

According to the somatic marker hypothesis (A. R. Damasio, 1994), the visceral response elicited during decision making, both during the contemplation of the future outcome of a choice and after the outcome of a choice has been signaled, aid in guiding decisions toward advantageous choices and away from disadvantageous choices. The process that is assessed by the IGT is ultimately a learning process, one in which knowledge of the correct strategy evolves over time. In this view, visceral responses to receiving reward and punishment, which are mediated by the amygdala, contribute to the encoding of the predictive value of the sensory cues and actions that preceded reward and punishment. Over time, through this encoding, subjects learn the association between a given choice and its outcome. This learning may precede explicit awareness of the contingencies between specific choices and their outcome. This learning is expressed by the vmPFC, which evokes learned representations of the predictive value of a choice in the period before a choice is made, when the outcomes of various choices are weighed against each other as they are held in mind. The representation of predictive value is based on the visceral response that is triggered within the vmPFC, an emotional response that marks the value of options for behavior based on past experience.

Within the somatic marker framework, then, the vmPFC functions as a system that holds the affective-visceral properties of objects in mind during the planning and organization of behavior that is directed toward courses of action that are in the overall best interests of the organism. This function falls into the broader executive role of the prefrontal cortex, of which the vmPFC is a part. This role is supported by connections between the vmPFC and higher order sensory cortices, as well as connections between the vmPFC and the dorsolateral prefrontal cortex (both of which are mediated by the orbital network). The connections with higher order sensory cortices provide a route for highly processed information about the sensory properties of biologically relevant stimuli to reach the vmPFC. The connections with the dorsolateral prefrontal cortex link the functions of the vmPFC to executive processes that guide attention and prioritize action, allowing the vmPFC to serve as a buffer for the maintenance of information pertaining to the homeostatic value of goal objects (i.e., predictive value). Thus, the vmPFC is not involved in regulating global working memory processes, as indicated by the finding that damage to the vmPFC does not disrupt performance on broad tasks of working memory (Bechara et al., 1998). However, vmPFC function does require intact working memory processes, as indicated by the finding that damage in regions of the prefrontal cortex that play a global role in working memory impairs performance on the IGT (Bechara, 2004; Clark, Cools, & Robbins, 2004).

Some tasks that call on representations of predictive reward value but that do not require this information to be held in working memory may also engage the vmPFC. For example, one study has shown that damage to the vmPFC disrupts both reversal learning and IGT performance (Fellows & Farah, 2005). In contrast, damage to the dorsolateral prefrontal cortex impairs performance on the IGT but does not impair reversal learning. An important caveat in the comparison of this study with studies from our laboratory is that the Fellows and Farah study examined damage in posterior regions of vmPFC that also impinged on basal forebrain structures, such as the nucleus accumbens. Our studies, in contrast, have found that lesions restricted to more anterior regions of the vmPFC that do not include the basal forebrain can alter performance on the IGT (Bechara et al., 1998). Thus, it is possible that the reversal learning deficits found in the Fellows and Farah study are attributable to damage in the basal forebrain rather than to damage in the vmPFC. Notwithstanding this, it is possible that both reversal learning and the IGT require an ability to register that the predictive reward value of a stimulus has changed, as well as an ability to inhibit a previously rewarded response. However, unlike the IGT, reversal learning does not require that information about the predictive reward value of a stimulus be held in working memory. Thus, the vmPFC may be engaged by processes that invoke representations of predictive reward value as well as by processes that require inhibition of a previously rewarded response. Such processes, which may themselves rely on somatic markers, could operate independently of working memory under certain experimental situations, such as reversal learning. In real life, however, where decision making usually requires holding representations of predictive reward value in mind over a delay, they are likely to work in concert with working memory processes.

The Role of Feedback of Somatic Markers in Decision Making

According to the somatic marker hypothesis, the afferent feedback of visceral responses is an important component of the decision-making process. In other words, the visceral responses during the contemplation of choices are necessary for biasing behavior in the advantageous direction, as well as for gut feelings and hunches related to choices. The question arises, then, as to whether the visceral responses induced by the vmPFC are actually necessary for decision making or are merely an epiphenomenal bodily reflection of the operation of certain mental processes.

One way to address this question is to directly manipulate the sensory feedback of the visceral state during performance of the IGT. A number of studies have attempted to do this. For example, one study has examined how cervical transection of the spinal cord affects performance on the IGT (North & O'Carroll, 2001). This study found no effect of the manipulation on performance on the IGT. Because the spinal cord carries somatosensory and interoceptive information from the body to the brain (Craig, 2002), this may be taken as evidence that the sensory feedback of bodily states does not contribute to decision making. However, a great deal of the information about visceral states is conveyed to the central nervous system via the vagus nerve, which is spared by spinal transection. If visceral states play a special role in signaling homeostatic processes, which we believe they do, then it is not surprising that spinal transection has a limited effect on decision making. Another study (Heims, Critchley, Dolan, Mathias, & Cipolotti, 2004) examined more specifically the role of visceral states in decision making. This study showed that patients with pure autonomic failure, a peripheral nervous disorder that broadly disrupts the ability to deploy visceral responses, do not demonstrate impaired performance on the IGT. This can also be taken as evidence that visceral responses are not necessary for decision making. However, this study did not actually measure visceral responses during the IGT, so it is possible that subjects still produced some form of visceral response during the task. Also, it is possible that, because pure autonomic failure develops slowly and manifests later in life, significant neural reorganization may take place in subjects with this disease, altering the normal mechanism of decision making. Yet another study (Martin, Denburg, Tranel, Granner, & Bechara, 2004) showed that electrical stimulation of the vagus nerve during the IGT, which largely affects visceral-afferent signaling, can actually improve performance. This can be taken as evidence that visceral states do play a role in decision making. However, this study was limited by the fact that most of the subjects suffered long-standing epilepsy, and many of them had lower than normal decision-making ability to begin with.

Functional imaging studies have provided circumstantial evidence of the role of visceral states in decision making. As discussed earlier, the insular cortex is a visceral sensory region that has been hypothesized to play a role in decision making by mapping the visceral responses that are induced by the vmPFC and the amygdala. A number of studies (Craig, 2002) have shown that activity in the insular cortex is correlated with changes in the visceral state. The insular cortex is also activated by decision-making tasks that involve uncertain reward and punishment and an evaluation of emotional information. For example, a PET study (Ernst et al., 2002) has shown that performance of the IGT, in addition to activating the vmPFC, also activates the insular cortex. Moreover, this study found that activity in the insular cortex was correlated with performance on the IGT. The insular cortex has also been shown using fMRI to be activated during other decision-making tasks that involve uncertain reward and punishment (Critchley, Mathias, & Dolan, 2001). In addition, one study (Sanfey, Hastie, Colvin, & Grafman, 2003) found that the insular cortex is activated by the evaluation of the fairness of offers of money. Here activity in the insular cortex was shown to be correlated with the tendency to reject unfair offers. Although these studies did not examine visceral responses directly, they show that the insular cortex, an area that has previously been established as a visceral sensory representation area, is engaged during decision making, particularly when the decisions require an evaluation of emotional consequences that are uncertain.

Thus, on balance, the evidence seems to favor the role of visceral states in decision making; however, more definitive evidence is required to establish exactly how and under what circumstances visceral states contribute to decision making. Though certain forms of decision making may engage somatic marker processes, it may be that not all forms of decision making require the elicitation and sensory mapping of visceral states. Indeed, the somatic marker hypothesis maintains that, under some conditions, as-if representations of the visceral state, mediated by direct connections between the vmPFC and brain stem neurotransmitter nuclei, may be sufficient to guide decision making in the advantageous direction. Also, decisions that do not require the weighing of rewarding or punishing consequences or in which the outcome is relatively certain may not engage somatic marker processes at all.

Why Somatic Markers?

A strictly computational approach to decision making may not require that the brain represent signals that are expressed within the body in order to compute the anticipated value of options for behavior (Maia & McClelland, 2004, 2005; Rolls, 1999). It is important to keep in mind, however, that human brains differ from computers in many ways, not the least of which is a concern for the promotion of survival through regulation of the internal milieu—which is the regulation of bodily processes. All nervous systems contain representations of basic bodily processes, such as those that regulate energy demands, reproduction, fluid balance, temperature, and the response to sickness and injury. Survival requires precise control over the state of these processes in order to maintain them within the narrow range that is compatible with life (i.e., homeostasis). The autonomic nervous system functions to make relatively rapid adjustments in the visceral state that maximize the survival value of events in the world that have the potential to impact homeostasis.

It can be argued that visceral responses operate merely as reflexes, acting independently of higher order cognitive processes. Indeed, visceral reflexes that are implemented at the level of the spinal cord and brain stem do provide some benefit after the fact for reacting to events that challenge homeostasis. However, it is more advantageous to be able to predict the impact of events on the internal milieu before they occur. To do this the brain must connect sensory and motor representations of the viscera with processes that govern perception, learning, memory, and goal-directed behavior. It is clear, based on a multitude of studies, many of which are reported in this volume, that the vmPFC plays a role in a number of cognitive processes. It is also clear that the vmPFC plays a role in the control and mapping of visceral states. The most parsimonious explanation would seem to be that the cognitive processes that are mediated by the vmPFC and the visceral functions mediated by this area are somehow linked.

According to the somatic marker hypothesis, the integration of visceral states into higher cognitive functions, such as decision making, is the function of the vmPFC. This function has expanded in evolution, allowing for the planning of behaviors that are executed further into the future and for which the outcomes of behavior in terms of rewards and punishments are more abstract. In humans, as well as in nonhuman primates and rodents, the vmPFC is involved in the planning of behaviors related to the most immediate and basic needs, such as food, water, and sex. In humans the vmPFC also plays a role in guiding behaviors for which choosing advantageously requires a deliberate concern for one's long-term well-being as well as knowledge of cultural norms and expectations. In this way the vmPFC may function to link highly evolved human faculties, such as moral behavior, altruism, financial reasoning, creativity, and a sense of purpose in one's work life and social relationships, to the basic mechanisms that govern survival and the maintenance of homeostasis.

REFERENCES

Ackerly, S. S., & Benton, A. L. (1948). Report of a case of bilateral frontal lobe defect. *Proceedings of the Association for Research in Nervous and Mental Disease (Baltimore)*, *27*, 479–504.

Amaral, D. G., Price, J. L., Pitkanen, A., & Carmichael, S. T. (1992). Anatomical organization of the primate amygdaloid complex. In J. P. Aggleton (Ed.), *The amygdala: Neurobiological aspects of emotion, memory, and mental dysfunction* (pp. 1–66). New York: Wiley-Liss.

Bechara, A. (2004). The role of emotion in decision-making: Evidence from neurological patients with orbitofrontal damage. *Brain and Cognition*, *55*, 30–40.

Bechara, A., & Damasio, A. R. (2005). The somatic marker hypothesis: A neural theory of economic decision. *Games and Economic Behavior*, *52*, 336–372.

Bechara, A., Damasio, A. R., Damasio, H., & Anderson, S. W. (1994). Insensitivity to future consequences following damage to human prefrontal cortex. *Cognition*, *50*, 7–15.

Bechara, A., Damasio, H., & Damasio, A. R. (2003). The role of the amygdala in decision-making. In P. Shinnick-Gallagher, A. Pitkanen, A. Shekhar, & L. Cahill (Eds.), *The amygdala in brain function: Basic and clinical approaches* (Vol. 985, pp. 356–369). New York: Annals of the New York Academy of Sciences.

Bechara, A., Damasio, H., Damasio, A. R., & Lee, G. P. (1999). Different contributions of the human amygdala and ventromedial prefrontal cortex to decision-making. *Journal of Neuroscience*, *19*, 5473–5481.

Bechara, A., Damasio, H., Tranel, D., & Anderson, S. W. (1998). Dissociation of working memory from decision making within the human prefrontal cortex. *Journal of Neuroscience*, *18*, 428–437.

Bechara, A., Damasio, H., Tranel, D., & Damasio, A. R. (1997, February 28). Deciding advantageously before knowing the advantageous strategy. *Science*, *275*, 1293–1295.

Bechara, A., Damasio, H., Tranel, D., & Damasio, A. R. (2005). The Iowa Gambling Task (IGT) and the somatic marker hypothesis (SMH): Some questions and answers. *Trends in Cognitive Sciences*, *9*, 159–162.

Bechara, A., Dolan, S., & Hindes, A. (2002). Decision-making and addiction: Pt. II. Myopia for the future or hypersensitivity to reward? *Neuropsychologia*, *40*, 1690–1705.

Bechara, A., Tranel, D., & Damasio, H. (2000). Characterization of the decision-making impairment of patients with bilateral lesions of the ventromedial prefrontal cortex. *Brain*, *123*, 2189–2202.

Bechara, A., Tranel, D., Damasio, H., & Damasio, A. R. (1996). Failure to respond autonomically to anticipated future outcomes following damage to prefrontal cortex. *Cerebral Cortex*, *6*, 215–225.

Berntson, G. G., Sarter, M., & Cacioppo, J. T. (2003). Ascending visceral regulation of cortical affective information processing. *European Journal of Neuroscience, 18*, 2103–2109.

Berridge, K. C., & Robinson, T. E. (1998). What is the role of dopamine in reward: Hedonic impact, reward learning, or incentive salience? *Brain Research Reviews, 28*, 309–369.

Brickner, R. M. (1932). An interpretation of frontal lobe function based upon the study of a case of partial bilateral frontal lobectomy: Localization of function in the cerebral cortex. *Proceedings of the Association for Research in Nervous and Mental Disease (Baltimore), 13*, 259–351.

Cacioppo, J., Berntson, G., Larsen, J., Poehlmann, K., & Ito, T. (2000). The psychophysiology of emotion. In M. Lewis & J. Haviland-Jones (Eds.), *The handbook of emotion* (2nd ed., pp. 173–191). New York: Guilford Press.

Cacioppo, J., Klein, D. J., Berntson, G. G., & Hatfield, E. (1993). The psychophysiology of emotion. In M. Lewis & J. M. Haviland (Eds.), *The handbook of emotion* (pp. 119–148). New York: Guilford Press.

Cardinal, R. N., Parkinson, J. A., Hall, J., & Everitt, B. J. (2002). Emotion and motivation: The role of the amygdala, ventral striatum and prefrontal cortex. *Neuroscience and Biobehavioral Reviews, 26*, 321–352.

Chudasama, Y., & Robbins, T. W. (2003). Dissociable contributions of the orbitofrontal and infralimbic cortex to Pavlovian autoshaping and discrimination reversal learning: Further evidence for the functional heterogeneity of the rodent frontal cortex. *Journal of Neuroscience, 23*, 8771–8780.

Clark, L., Cools, R., & Robbins, T. (2004). The neuropsychology of ventral prefrontal cortex: Decision-making and reversal learning. *Brain and Cognition, 55*, 41–53.

Craig, A. D. (2002). How do you feel? Interoception: The sense of the physiological condition of the body. *Nature Reviews: Neuroscience, 3*, 655–666.

Critchley, H., Elliott, R., Mathias, C. J., & Dolan, R. J. (2000). Neural activity relating to generation and representation of galvanic skin conductance responses: A functional magnetic resonance imaging study. *Journal of Neuroscience, 20*, 3033–3040.

Critchley, H., Mathias, C., & Dolan, R. (2001). Neuroanatomical basis for first- and second-order representations of bodily states. *Nature Neuroscience, 4*, 207–212.

Critchley, H., Wiens, S., Rotshtein, P., Ohman, A., & Dolan, R. (2004). Neural systems supporting interoceptive awareness. *Nature Neuroscience, 7*, 189–195.

Damasio, A. R. (1994). *Descartes' error: Emotion, reason, and the human brain*. New York: Grosset/Putnam.

Damasio, A. R. (1999). *The feeling of what happens: Body and emotion in the making of consciousness*. New York: Harcourt.

Damasio, A. R. (2003). *Looking for Spinoza: Joy, sorrow, and the feeling brain*. New York: Harcourt.

Damasio, A. R., Grabowski, T. G., Bechara, A., Damasio, H., Ponto, L. L. B., Parvizi, J., et al. (2000). Subcortical and cortical brain activity during the feeling of self-generated emotions. *Nature Neuroscience, 3*, 1049–1056.

Damasio, A. R., Tranel, D., & Damasio, H. (1990). Individuals with sociopathic behavior caused by frontal damage fail to respond autonomically to social stimuli. *Behavioral Brain Research, 41*, 81–94.

Damasio, A. R., Tranel, D., & Damasio, H. (1991). Somatic markers and the guidance of behavior: Theory and preliminary testing. In H. S. Levin, H. M. Eisenberg, & A. L. Benton (Eds.), *Frontal lobe function and dysfunction* (pp. 217–229). New York: Oxford University Press.

Damasio, H., Grabowski, T., Frank, R., Galburda, A. M., & Damasio, A. R. (1994, May 20). The return of Phineas Gage: Clues about the brain from the skull of a famous patient. *Science, 264*, 1102–1104.

Denton, D., Shade, R., Zamarippa, F., Egan, G., Blair-West, J., McKinley, M., et al. (1999a). Correlation of regional cerebral blood flow and change of plasma sodium concentration during genesis and satiation of thirst. *Proceedings of the National Academy of Sciences, USA, 96*, 2532–2537.

Denton, D., Shade, R., Zamarippa, F., Egan, G., Blair-West, J., McKinley, M., et al. (1999b). Neuroimaging of genesis and satiation of thirst and an interoceptor-driven theory of origins of primary consciousness. *Proceedings of the National Academy of Sciences, USA, 96*, 5304–5309.

Drevets, W. C., Price, J. L., Simpson, J. R., Todd, R. D., Reich, T., Vannier, M., et al. (1997, April 24). Subgenual prefrontal cortex abnormalities in mood disorders. *Nature, 386*, 824–827.

Ernst, M., Bolla, K., Moratidis, M., Contoreggi, C. S., Matochick, J. A., Kurian, V., et al. (2002). Decision-making in a risk taking task. *Neuropsychopharmacology, 26*, 682–691.

Eslinger, P. J., & Damasio, A. R. (1985). Severe disturbance of higher cognition after bilateral frontal lobe ablation: Patient evr. *Neurology, 35*, 1731–1741.

Fellows, L. K., & Farah, M. J. (2005). Different underlying impairments in decision making following ventromedial and dorsolateral frontal lobe damage in humans. *Cerebral Cortex, 15*, 58–63.

Flynn, F. G., Benson, D. F., & Ardila, A. (1999). Anatomy of the insula: Functional and clinical correlates. *Aphasiology, 13*(1), 55–78.

Fukui, H., Murai, T., Fukuyama, H., Hayashi, T., & Hanakawa, T. (2005). Functional activity related to risk anticipation during performance of the Iowa Gambling Task. *NeuroImage, 24*, 253–259.

Harlow, J. M. (1848). Passage of an iron bar through the head. *Boston Medical and Surgical Journal, 39*, 389–393.

Heims, H. C., Critchley, H. D., Dolan, R., Mathias, C. J., & Cipolotti, L. (2004). Social and motivational functioning is not critically dependent on feedback of autonomic responses: Neuropsychological evidence from patients with pure autonomic failure. *Neuropsychologia, 42*, 1979–1988.

Hurliman, E., Nagode, J. C., & Pardo, J. V. (2005). Double dissociation of exteroceptive and interoceptive feedback systems in the orbital and ventromedial prefrontal cortex of humans. *Journal of Neuroscience, 25*, 4641–4648.

James, W. (1884). What is an emotion? *Mind, 9*, 188–205.

Kringelbach, M. L., & Rolls, E. T. (2004). The functional neuroanatomy of the human orbitofrontal cortex: Evidence from neuroimaging and neuropsychology. *Progress in Neurobiology, 72*(5), 341–372.

Lane, R., Reiman, E., Ahern, G., Schwartz, G., & Davidson, R. (1997). Neuroanatomical correlates of happiness, sadness, and disgust. *American Journal of Psychiatry, 154*, 926–933.

Lang, P. J., Bradley, M. M., Cuthbert, B. N., & Patrick, C. J. (1993). Emotion and psychopathology: A startle probe analysis. In L. J. Chapman, J. P. Chapman, & D. C. Fowles (Eds.), *Experimental personality and psychopathology research* (Vol. 16, pp. 163–199). New York: Spring Publishing.

LeDoux, J. (1996). *The emotional brain: The mysterious underpinnings of emotional life*. New York: Simon & Schuster.

Luria, A. R., Pribram, K. H., & Homskaya, E. D. (1964). An experimental analysis of the behavioral disturbance produced by a left frontal arachnoidal endothelioma (meningioma). *Neuropsychologia, 2*, 257–280.

Maia, T. V., & McClelland, J. L. (2004). A reexamination of the evidence for the somatic marker hypothesis: What participants really know in the Iowa Gambling Task. *Proceedings of the National Academy of Sciences, USA, 101*, 16075–16080.

Maia, T. V., & McClelland, J. L. (2005). The somatic marker hypothesis: Still many questions but no answers: Response to Bechara et al. *Trends in Cognitive Sciences, 9*, 162–164.

Martin, C., Denburg, N., Tranel, D., Granner, M., & Bechara, A. (2004). The effects of vagal nerve stimulation on decision-making. *Cortex, 40,* 1–8.

Nagai, Y., Critchley, H. D., Featherstone, E., Trimble, M. R., & Dolan, R. J. (2004). Activity in ventromedial prefrontal cortex covaries with sympathetic skin conductance level: A physiological account of a "default mode" of brain function. *NeuroImage, 22,* 243–251.

Nauta, W. J. H. (1971). The problem of the frontal lobes: A reinterpretation. *Journal of Psychiatric Research, 8,* 167–187.

Neafsey, E. J. (1990). Prefrontal cortical control of the autonomic nervous system: Anatomical and physiological observations. In H. B. M. Uylings, C. G. Van Eden, J. P. C. De Bruin, M. A. Corner, & M. G. P. Feenstra (Eds.), *Progress in brain research* (Vol. 85, pp. 147–166). New York: Elsevier.

North, N. T., & O'Carroll, R. E. (2001). Decision making in patients with spinal cord damage: Afferent feedback and the somatic marker hypothesis. *Neuropsychologia, 39,* 521–524.

Ongur, D., & Price, J. L. (2000). The organization of networks within the orbital and medial prefrontal cortex of rats, monkeys and humans. *Cerebral Cortex, 10,* 206–219.

Patterson, J. C., Ungerleider, L. G., & Bandettini, P. A. (2002). Task-independent functional brain activity correlation with skin conductance changes: An fMRI study. *NeuroImage, 17,* 1797–1806.

Pears, A., Parkinson, J. A., Hopewell, L., Everitt, B. J., & Roberts, A. C. (2003). Lesions of the orbitofrontal but not medial prefrontal cortex disrupt conditioned reinforcement in primates. *Journal of Neuroscience, 23,* 11189–11201.

Rahman, S., Sahakian, B. J., Cardinal, R. N., Rogers, R. D., & Robbins, T. W. (2001). Decision making and neuropsychiatry. *Trends in Cognitive Sciences, 6,* 271–277.

Raichle, M. E., MacLeod, A. M., Snyder, A. Z., Powers, W. J., Gusnard, D. A., & Shulman, G. L. (2001). A default mode of brain function. *Proceedings of the National Academy of Sciences, USA, 98,* 676–682.

Rainville, P., Bechara, A., Naqvi, N., Virasith, A., Bilodeau, M., & Damasio, A. R. (2006). Basic emotions are associated with distinct patterns of cardiorespiratory activity. *International Journal of Psychophysiology, 61,* 5–18.

Rolls, E. T. (1999). *The brain and emotion.* Oxford: Oxford University Press.

Rolls, E. T. (2000). The orbitofrontal cortex and reward. *Cerebral Cortex, 10,* 284–294.

Sanfey, A., Hastie, R., Colvin, M., & Grafman, J. (2003). Phineas Gage: Decision-making and the human prefrontal cortex. *Neuropsychologia, 41,* 1218–1229.

Saver, J. L., & Damasio, A. R. (1991). Preserved access and processing of social knowledge in a patient with acquired sociopathy due to ventromedial frontal damage. *Neuropsychologia, 29,* 1241–1249.

Tomb, I., Hauser, M., Deldin, P., & Caramazza, A. (2002). Do somatic markers mediate decisions on the gambling task? *Nature Neuroscience, 5,* 1103–1104.

Tranel, D., & Damasio, H. (1994). Neuroanatomical correlates of electrodermal skin conductance responses. *Psychophysiology, 31,* 427–438.

Welt, L. (1888). Uber charaktervaranderungen des menschen infoldge von lasionen des stirnhirns. *Dutsch Archives of Klinical Medicine, 42,* 339–390.

Chapter 39

Neural Basis of Fear Conditioning

DAVID E. A. BUSH, GLENN E. SCHAFE, AND JOSEPH E. LEDOUX

Emotion affects behavior in numerous ways. Emotion increases arousal, triggers hormonal stress responses, and alters motivation. Emotion can also alter how well something is learned and the strength of memory storage. But it is important to keep in mind that for these things to occur there needs to be a mechanism that assesses whether a given stimulus should trigger an emotional response in the first place. The problem is not so difficult for biologically significant unconditioned stimuli, such as an electric shock or the taste of a sweet food, because these stimuli are already hardwired to produce emotional responses. However, in everyday life we have emotional responses to all sorts of stimuli that are not innately aversive or appetitive. This is important because organisms need to respond to stimuli that predict dangerous or desirable events. Emotional stimuli thus serve as guides to direct behavior in adaptive directions. Novel stimuli acquire emotional significance through *emotional learning*. Emotional learning shares many characteristics with other forms of learning, especially at cellular and molecular levels, but there are also important differences. These differences exist essentially because of the distinct brain circuitry that underlies the interpretation and encoding of emotional information: the inputs, outputs, and processing resources in between.

Fear conditioning is the best studied example of emotional learning. In this chapter we therefore focus on our current understanding of fear conditioning. However, it is important to keep in mind that fear is just one example of emotion. Emotional learning can also involve stimuli that predict positive or appetitive emotional properties. As we will see, the amygdala has emerged as a structure that is crucial for fear learning, but the role of the amygdala in appetitive emotional memories is still not well understood.

Although studies using appetitive conditioning in animals and humans find involvement of the amygdala, other studies that have examined humans with amygdala damage have found a selective role of the amygdala in negative emotion (Berntson, Bechara, Damasio, Tranel, & Cacioppo, 2007). For an in-depth survey of aspects of emotional learning related to positive or appetitive conditioning, see reviews by Balleine and Dickinson (1998), Cardinal, Parkinson, Hall, and Everitt (2002), and Holland and Gallagher (2004).

AN OVERVIEW OF FEAR CONDITIONING

In fear conditioning, the subject, typically a rat, is placed in an experimental chamber and given paired presentations of an innocuous conditioned stimulus (CS), such as a tone, together with an aversive unconditioned stimulus (US), such as a brief footshock. The CS does not elicit defensive behavior before fear conditioning, but after even a single CS-US pairing the animal begins to exhibit a range of conditioned responses (CRs), both to the CS and to the context (i.e., the conditioning chamber) in which conditioning occurs. In rats these responses include freezing or immobility (a species-typical behavioral response that makes a rodent less easily detected by predators), autonomic and endocrine responses (such as changes in heart rate and blood pressure, defecation, and increased levels of circulating stress hormones), and the potentiation of reflexes, such as the acoustic startle response (Blanchard & Blanchard, 1969; Davis, Walker, & Lee, 1997; Kapp, Frysinger, Gallagher, & Haselton, 1979; LeDoux, Iwata, Cicchetti, & Reis, 1988; Roozendaal, Koolhaas, & Bohus, 1991; Smith, Astley, Devito, Stein, & Walsh, 1980). Thus, as the result of a simple associative pairing, the CS comes to elicit many of the same defensive responses that are elicited by naturally aversive or threatening stimuli (see Figure 39.1). Similar responses occur in other mammals, including humans, allowing the fear conditioning procedure to be used to compare brain mechanisms across species.

This work was supported in part by National Institutes of Health grants MH 46516, MH 00956, MH 39774, and MH 11902, and a grant from the W. M. Keck Foundation to New York University.

(A)

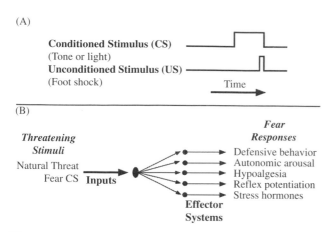

(B)

Figure 39.1 Pavlovian fear conditioning.

Note: Fear conditioning involves the presentation of an initially innocuous stimulus, such as a tone (conditioned stimulus; CS), that is paired or associated with a noxious stimulus, such as a brief electric shock to the feet (unconditioned stimulus; US). Before conditioning, the CS elicits little response from the animal. After conditioning, the CS elicits a wide range of behavioral and physiological responses, including freezing, that are characteristically elicited by naturally aversive or threatening stimuli.

THE NEURAL CIRCUITRY OF FEAR CONDITIONING

The fear conditioning paradigm has enabled researchers to be systematic about studying the way that emotional stimuli are processed in the brain, and this research has implicated the amygdala as a region that is crucial for assessing fear CS inputs, and then coordinating outputs to brain regions that mediate fear responses. In the sections that follow we review how auditory CS information reaches the amygdala, how this information then flows through different amygdala subregions, and how amygdala outputs coordinate fear responses.

Input Pathways to the Amygdala

The neural circuitry underlying Pavlovian fear conditioning, particularly auditory fear conditioning, has been well characterized (Figure 39.2). Cells in the lateral amygdala (LA) receive excitatory, glutamatergic projections (Farb, Aoki, Milner, Kaneko, & LeDoux, 1992; LeDoux & Farb, 1991) from areas of the auditory thalamus, including the medial division of the thalamic medial geniculate body (MGm) and the posterior intralaminar nucleus (PIN), and also from the auditory cortex (area TE3; Bordi & LeDoux, 1992; Doron & LeDoux, 1999; LeDoux, Farb, & Romanski, 1991; LeDoux, Ruggerio, & Reis, 1985; McDonald, 1998; Romanski & LeDoux, 1993). Thus, there are two general routes: a direct subcortical route from the auditory thalamus (MGm/PIN) and a more indirect route that continues from the thalamus to the cortex before descending to the amygdala from cortical regions (e.g., TE3). Thalamic and cortical inputs to the

LA, both capable of mediating fear learning (Romanski & LeDoux, 1992b), are believed to carry different types of information to the LA. The thalamic route (often called the "low road") is believed to be critical for rapidly transmitting crude aspects of the CS to the LA, whereas the cortical route (known as the "high road") is believed to carry highly refined information to the amygdala (LeDoux, 2000). Interestingly, whereas pretraining lesions of MGm/PIN impair auditory fear conditioning (LeDoux, Iwata, Pearl, & Reis, 1986; LeDoux, Sakaguchi, & Reis, 1984), similar lesions of the auditory cortex do not (LeDoux et al., 1984; Romanski & LeDoux, 1992a). Thus, the thalamic pathway between the MGm/PIN and the LA appears to be particularly important for auditory fear conditioning. This is not to say that the cortical input to the LA is not involved. Electrophysiological responses of cells in the auditory cortex are modified during fear conditioning (Edeline, Pham, & Weinberger, 1993), and posttraining lesions of the insular cortex attenuate auditory fear conditioning (Brunzell & Kim, 2001), suggesting that cortical inputs to the LA contribute to fear memory in the intact brain. Indeed, when conditioning depends on the ability of the animal to make fine discriminations between different auditory CSs, or when the CS is a complex auditory cue, such as an ultrasonic vocalization, then cortical regions appear to be crucial (Jarrell, Gentile, Romanski, McCabe, & Schneiderman, 1987; Lindquist & Brown, 2004).

Recent evidence suggests that thalamic and cortical inputs terminate on different dendritic sites and have different

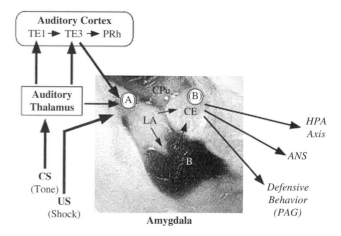

Figure 39.2 Anatomy of the fear system.

Note: **A:** Auditory fear conditioning involves the transmission of CS sensory information from areas of the auditory thalamus and cortex to the lateral amygdala (LA), where it can converge with incoming somatosensory information from the foot shock US. It is in the LA that alterations in synaptic transmission are thought to encode key aspects of the learning. **B:** During fear expression the LA engages the central nucleus of the amygdala (CE), which projects widely to many areas of the forebrain and brain stem that control the expression of fear CRs, including freezing, hypothalamic-pituitary-adrenal axis activation, and alterations in cardiovascular activity.

cellular properties (Humeau & Lüthi, 2007). Nevertheless, the inputs from MGm/PIN and TE3 converge onto single cells in the LA (Li, Stutzmann, & LeDoux, 1996), and these same cells are also responsive to the footshock US (Romanski, Clugnet, Bordi, & LeDoux, 1993). Thus, individual cells in the LA are well suited to integrate information about the tone and shock during fear conditioning, which highlights the LA as a likely locus of the cellular events underlying fear acquisition. Consistent with this, behavioral studies have demonstrated that acquisition of auditory fear conditioning is disrupted both by conventional electrolytic or neurotoxic lesions of the LA and by reversible inactivation of LA cellular activity (Campeau & Davis, 1995; Helmstetter & Bellgowan, 1994; Kim, Rison, & Fanselow, 1993; LeDoux, Cicchetti, Xagoraris, & Romanski, 1990; Muller, Corodimas, Fridel, & LeDoux, 1997; Wilensky, Schafe, & LeDoux, 2000).

Output Pathways from the Amygdala

Although the LA is important for fear acquisition, its connections with other amygdaloid nuclei (Paré, Smith, & Paré, 1995; Pitkänen, Savander, & LeDoux, 1997), including the basal nucleus (B) and the central nucleus (CE), are essential for fear expression. During retrieval or expression of a fear memory, activation of the LA is thought to control CE activity through activation of B and/or the GABAergic intercalated cell masses situated along the lateral CE border (Paré, Quirk, & LeDoux, 2004). Auditory fear conditioning is disrupted by damage confined only to the LA and CE (Amorapanth, LeDoux, & Nader, 2000; Nader, Majidishad, Amorapanth, & LeDoux, 2001), suggesting that communication between the LA and the CE is sufficient to mediate fear conditioning.

The connectivity of the CE with downstream brain regions is consistent with the traditional view that it serves as a principal output nucleus of the fear learning system. The CE projects to areas of the forebrain, the hypothalamus, and the brain stem, regions that control behavioral, endocrine, and autonomic CRs associated with fear learning (Davis, 1997; Davis et al., 1997; Kapp, Frysinger, Gallagher, & Haselton, 1979; LeDoux et al., 1988; Roozendaal et al., 1991). Projections from the CE to the midbrain periaqueductal gray, for example, have been shown to be particularly important for mediating behavioral and endocrine responses such as freezing and hypoalgesia (De Oca, DeCola, Maren, & Fanselow, 1998; Helmstetter & Landeira-Fernandez, 1990; Helmstetter & Tershner, 1994; LeDoux et al., 1988), and projections to the lateral hypothalamus have been implicated in the control of conditioned cardiovascular responses (Iwata, LeDoux, & Reis, 1986; LeDoux et al., 1988). Importantly, whereas lesions of these individual areas can selectively impair expression of individual

CRs, damage to the CE interferes with the expression of all fear CRs (LeDoux, 2000). Thus, the CE is typically thought of as the principal output nucleus of the fear system that acts to orchestrate the collection of hardwired, and typically species-specific responses that underlie defensive behavior.

Pretraining electrolytic lesions of the B, unlike lesions of the LA and the CE, do not disrupt fear conditioning, which suggests that the B is not essential for fear conditioning (Amorapanth et al., 2000). However, one study observed deficits in auditory and contextual fear conditioning when pretraining lesions were localized to the anterior, but not posterior, divisions of the B (Goosens & Maren, 2001). Thus, although not essential, projections from the LA to the B may be important under some circumstances. In support of this, if B lesions occur after fear conditioning rather than before, fear memory expression is impaired (Anglada-Figueroa & Quirk, 2005), which indicates that the B participates in fear memory when it is intact at the time of conditioning. Interestingly, the B is also important for mediating more complex responses to fear stimuli, such as the performance of instrumental responses that actively avoid or escape a threatening stimulus (Amorapanth et al., 2000). We will return to this topic in a later section.

AMYGDALA SYNAPTIC PLASTICITY AND FEAR CONDITIONING

Synaptic plasticity is believed to be a neural mechanism that underlies learning, as was discussed in detail in Chapter 1. Considerable evidence shows that synapses in the LA are plastic, which could enable the LA to store memories for fear conditioning by altering connections between converging CS and US inputs. Unlike most other brain regions, synaptic plasticity in the amygdala has been directly related to learning. Consequently, this research has facilitated research not only on fear and emotion, but also on learning and memory.

Synaptic Plasticity in the Lateral Amygdala Induced by Fear Conditioning

Individual cells in the LA alter their response properties after a CS and US are paired during fear conditioning. The LA cells that are only weakly responsive to auditory input prior to conditioning will respond vigorously to the same input after fear conditioning (Goosens, Hobin, & Maren, 2003; Goosens & Maren, 2004; Maren, 2000; Quirk, Armony, & LeDoux, 1997; Quirk, Repa, & LeDoux, 1995). Thus, as a consequence of the training, a change occurs in the response of LA cells to the auditory CS, which is consistent with the view that neural plasticity in the LA encodes key aspects of fear learning and memory storage (Blair, Schafe, Bauer, Rodrigues, & LeDoux, 2001; Fanselow & LeDoux, 1999;

Maren, 1999; Quirk, Armony, Repa, Li, & LeDoux, 1997; for review, see Maren & Quirk, 2004).

Interestingly, single-unit studies have suggested that there are at least two populations of LA cells that undergo plastic changes during fear conditioning in unique ways (Repa et al., 2001). The first is a more dorsal population (near the border of the caudate/putamen) that shows enhanced firing to the CS in the initial stages of training and testing and is sensitive to fear extinction (see Figure 39.3; Repa et al., 2001). These so-called transiently plastic cells exhibit short-latency changes (within 10 to 15 ms after tone onset). These short latencies are consistent with a rapid, monosynaptic thalamic input. The second population of LA cells occupies a more ventral position. In contrast to the transiently plastic cells, the more ventral cells exhibit enhanced firing to the CS throughout training and testing and do not appear to be sensitive to

extinction. Further, these long-term plastic cells exhibit longer latencies (within 30 to 40 ms after tone onset), which indicates a polysynaptic pathway. Thus, it has been hypothesized that a dorsal-to-ventral network of neurons within the LA is responsible for triggering and storing fear memories, respectively (Medina, Repa, & LeDoux, 2002; Radwanska, Nikolaev, Knapska, & Kaczmarek, 2002; Repa et al., 2001).

Long-Term Potentiation as a Mechanism for Lateral Amygdala Synaptic Plasticity Underlying Fear Conditioning

The change in the responsiveness of LA cells during fear conditioning suggests that alterations in excitatory transmission between LA synapses might be critical for fear conditioning. Many of the recent studies that have examined

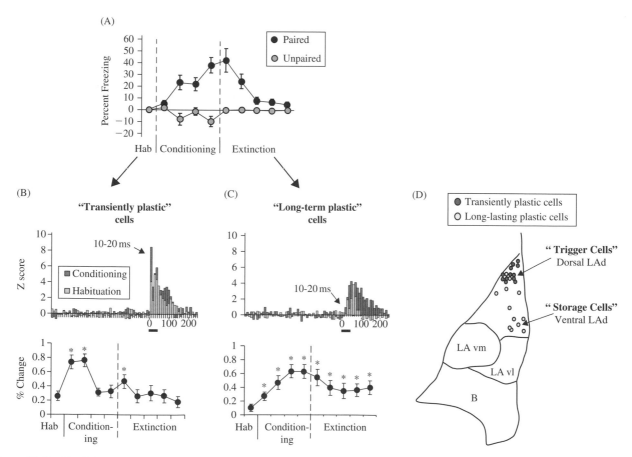

Figure 39.3 Plasticity in the LA during fear conditioning.

Note: Pairing of CS and US during fear conditioning leads to changes in fear behavior **A:** and also to changes in the responsiveness of single LA cells to auditory stimuli. During fear conditioning there are two populations of cells that undergo plastic change. **B:** Transiently plastic cells are generally short latency and show enhanced firing shortly after training and during the initial phases of extinction, but not at other times. **C:** Long-term plastic cells are generally longer latency and show enhanced firing throughout training and extinction. **D:** Transiently plastic cells are generally found in the dorsal tip of the lateral amygdala (LAd), where they may serve to trigger the initial stages of memory formation. Long-term plastic cells, on the other hand, are found in the ventral regions of the LAd and may be important for long-term, extinction-resistant memory storage. From "Two Different Lateral Amygdala Cell Populations Contribute to the Initiation and Storage of Memory," by Repa et al., 2001, *Nature Neuroscience, 4*, pp. 724–731. Adapted with permission.

the biochemical basis of fear conditioning have drawn on a larger literature that has focused on the biochemical events that underlie long-term potentiation (LTP), an activity-dependent form of synaptic plasticity that was initially discovered in the hippocampus (Bliss & Lømo, 1973). Importantly, LTP has also been demonstrated, both in vivo and in vitro, in each of the major auditory input pathways to the LA, including the thalamic and cortical auditory pathways (Chapman, Kairiss, Keenan, & Brown, 1990; Clugnet & LeDoux, 1989; Huang & Kandel, 1998; Rogan & LeDoux, 1995; Weisskopf, Bauer, & LeDoux, 1999; Weisskopf & LeDoux, 1999). This includes tetanus-induced LTP, which appears to

depend on activation of the glutamatergic NMDA receptor (Bauer, Schafe, & LeDoux, 2002; Huang & Kandel, 1998), and also associative LTP, which is induced following pairing of subthreshold presynaptic auditory inputs with postsynaptic depolarizations of LA cells (Bauer et al., 2002; Huang & Kandel, 1998; Weisskopf et al., 1999). Unlike LTP induced by a tetanus, associative LTP in the LA is dependent on L-type voltage-gated calcium channels (VGCCs; Bauer et al., 2002; Humeau & Lüthi, 2007; Weisskopf et al., 1999).

A number of findings have converged to support the hypothesis that fear conditioning is mediated by an associative LTP-like process in the LA (see Figure 39.4). First,

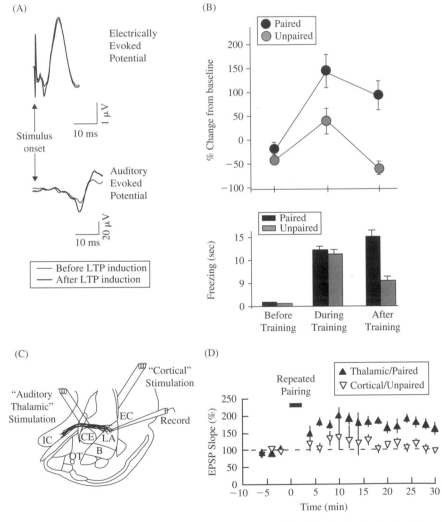

Figure 39.4 LTP in the LA.

Note: **A:** (top) LTP is induced in the LA following high-frequency electrical stimulation of the MGm/PIN. The trace represents a stimulation-evoked field potential in the LA before and after LTP induction. (bottom) Following artificial LTP induction, processing of naturalistic auditory stimuli is also enhanced in the LA. The trace represents an auditory-evoked field potential in the LA before and after LTP induction. **B:** (top) Fear conditioning leads to electrophysiological changes in the LA in a manner similar to LTP. The figure represents a percentage change in the slope of the auditory-evoked field potential in the LA before, during, and after conditioning in both paired and unpaired rats. (bottom) Freezing behavior across training and

testing periods. Note that both paired and unpaired groups show equivalent freezing behavior during training, but only the paired group shows an enhanced neural response. **C:** Associative LTP is induced in the amygdala slice by pairing trains of presynaptic stimulation of fibers coming from the auditory thalamus with depolarization of LA cells. Stimulation of fibers coming from cortical areas serves as a control for input specificity. **D:** LTP induced by pairing as measured by the change in the slope of the excitatory postsynaptic potential (EPSP) over time. In this case, the thalamic pathway received paired stimulation, whereas the cortical pathway received unpaired stimulation (i.e., trains and depolarizations, but in a noncontingent manner). The black bar represents the duration of the pairing.

LTP induction at thalamic inputs to the LA has been shown to enhance auditory processing, and thus natural information flow within the LA (Rogan & LeDoux, 1995). Second, fear conditioning has been shown to lead to electrophysiological changes in the LA in a manner that is very similar to those observed following artificial LTP induction, and these changes persist over days (McKernan & Shinnick-Gallagher, 1997; Rogan, Staubli, & LeDoux, 1997). Third, associative LTP in the LA has been shown to be sensitive to the same contingencies as fear conditioning. That is, LTP is strong when presynaptic trains precede the onset of postsynaptic depolarizations 100% of the time. However, LTP is much weaker if noncontingent depolarizations of the postsynaptic LA cell are interleaved within the same number of contiguous pairings (Bauer, LeDoux, & Nader, 2001). Thus, the LTP-induced change in synaptic efficacy within the LA depends on the contingency between pre- and postsynaptic activity rather than simply on temporal contiguity. Importantly, it is contingency, rather than temporal pairing, that is known to be critical for associative learning, including fear conditioning (Rescorla, 1968). Fourth, fear conditioning and LTP induction have been characterized by a common pharmacological and biochemical substrate. Fear conditioning, for example, has been shown to be impaired by pharmacological blockade of both NMDA receptors (Kim, DeCola, Landeira-Fernandez, & Fanselow, 1991; Miserendino, Sananes, Melia, & Davis, 1990; Rodrigues, Schafe, & LeDoux, 2001) and L-type VGCCs (Bauer et al., 2002) in the amygdala.

Training-induced elevations in Ca^{2+} through both NMDA and L-type VGCCs in the LA appear to set in motion a process that is essential for both synaptic plasticity and fear memory formation, and this process appears to share essential features with that underlying LTP in the hippocampus and in other systems. Recent studies, for example, have demonstrated the involvement of Ca^{2+}-regulated intracellular signaling cascades, including protein kinase A (PKA) and the mitogen-activated protein kinase (MAPK) in synaptic plasticity in fear memory consolidation. Each of these signaling cascades is thought to promote long-term synaptic plasticity and memory formation, in part, by activating transcription factors in the nucleus, including the cyclic adenosine monophosphate (cAMP)-response element binding (CREB) protein. In turn, CREB and cAMP-response element (CRE)-mediated transcription is thought to promote the long-term structural and functional changes underlying memory formation. Many of these recent studies have used molecular genetic methods in which the molecules of interest have been manipulated in knockout or transgenic mouse lines (Abel et al., 1997; Bourtchuladze et al., 1994; Brambilla et al., 1997). Other recent studies have used pharmacological or viral transfection methods to examine the involvement of these molecules specifically in the amygdala. For example, recent studies have shown that infusions of drugs into the LA that specifically block RNA or protein synthesis or PKA activity impair the formation of fear memories (Bailey, Kim, Sun, Thompson, & Helmstetter, 1999; Schafe & LeDoux, 2000). Further, extracellular signal-regulated kinase (ERK)/MAPK is activated in the LA following fear conditioning, and pharmacological blockade of this activation via localized infusions of ERK/MAPK inhibitors impairs fear conditioning (Schafe et al., 2000). Another recent study has shown that overexpression of the transcription factor CREB in the LA facilitates formation of fear memories (Josselyn et al., 2001). Thus, as shown in Figure 39.5 (Rodrigues, Schafe, & LeDoux, 2004; Huang, Martin, & Kandel, 2000), similar biochemical signaling pathways and molecular events that are involved in amygdala LTP are also necessary for fear conditioning.

Most studies have emphasized the role of postsynaptic processes in fear conditioning. However, recent studies suggest that LTP at LA synapses may involve pre- as well as postsynaptic mechanisms (Apergis-Schoute, Debiec, Doyère, LeDoux, & Schafe, 2005; Humeau, Shaban, Bissière, & Lüthi, 2003; Schafe et al., 2005).

BEYOND THE SIMPLE FEAR CONDITIONING CIRCUIT

Fear conditioning to a discrete cue is probably the simplest form of emotional learning, but most emotions are far more complex. Stimuli that trigger fear responses can involve much more than a pure tone. Also, regardless of the trigger stimulus, emotions can lead to a wide range of responses beyond the initial fear reaction, including active responses that help the animal cope with the stimulus, as well as other mechanisms that help to reduce the intensity of fear reactions. In the sections that follow we first examine neural circuitry that is thought to underlie the processing of more complex stimuli, and then consider how established fear memories can be modified and diminished.

Contextual Fear Conditioning

In a typical auditory fear conditioning experiment, the animal learns to fear not only the footshock-paired tone, but also the context in which conditioning occurs. Contextual fear is also learned when footshock stimuli are presented in the absence of a discrete CS. With contextual fear conditioning, fear to the context is later measured by returning the rat to the conditioning chamber on the test day and measuring the CR, including freezing behavior (Blanchard, Dielman, & Blanchard, 1968; Fanselow, 1980).

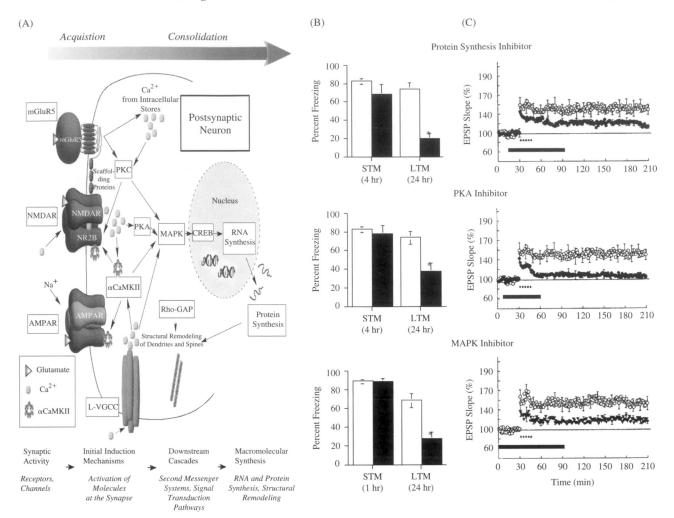

Figure 39.5   Molecular pathways underlying fear conditioning.

Note: **A:** Illustration of the molecular pathways within cells of the LA that are needed for the acquisition and consolidation of fear conditioning and also for LA LTP. Both fear conditioning and LTP involve the release of glutamate and Ca^{2+} influx through either NMDA receptors or L-type VGCCs. The increase in intracellular Ca^{2+} leads to the activation of protein kinases, such as PKA and ERK/MAPK. Once activated, these kinases can translocate to the nucleus, where they activate transcription factors such as CREB. The activation of CREB by PKA and ERK/MAPK promotes CRE-mediated gene transcription and the synthesis of new proteins. From Figure 2, page 85 in "Molecular mechanisms underlying emotional learning and memory in the lateral amygdala," by Rodrigues et al., 2004, *Neuron, 44,* pp. 75–91. Adapted with permission. **B:** Disruption of these molecular pathways in the LA interferes with fear memory formation. In these studies, rats received intra-amygdala infusions of anisomycin (a protein synthesis inhibitor; B-Top), Rp-cAMPS (a PKA inhibitor; B-Middle), or U0126 (a MEK inhibitor, which is an upstream regulator of ERK/MAPK activation; B-Bottom) at or around the time of training and were assayed for both short-term memory (1 to 4 hours later) and long-term memory (24 hours later) of auditory fear conditioning. In each figure vehicle-treated rats are represented by the gray bars, and drug-treated animals are represented by the black bars. $*p < .05$ relative to vehicle controls. **C:** Amygdala LTP has been shown to require the same biochemical processes. In these studies amygdala slices were treated with either anisomycin (C-Top), KT5720 (a PKA inhibitor; C-Middle), or PD098059 (a MEK inhibitor; C-Bottom) prior to and during tetanus of the thalamic pathway. In each experiment field recordings were obtained from the LA and expressed across time as a percentage of baseline. From "Both Protein Kinase A and Mitogen-Activated Protein Kinase Are Required in the Amygdala for the Macromolecular Synthesis-Dependent Late Phase of Long-Term Potentiation," by Huang et al., 2000, *Journal of Neuroscience, 20,* pp. 6317–6325. Copyright 2000 by the Society for Neuroscience. Reprinted with permission.

In comparison to auditory fear conditioning, much less is known about the neural systems underlying contextual fear. Substrates of contextual fear have been identified primarily through the use of lesion methods, and, as in auditory fear conditioning, the amygdala appears to play an essential role. For example, lesions of the amygdala, including the LA and B, have been shown to disrupt both the acquisition and the expression of contextual fear conditioning (Kim et al., 1993; Maren, 1998; Phillips & LeDoux, 1992). Reversible inactivation, usually achieved by microinjecting muscimol or tetrodotoxin into the LA, has similar effects (Muller et al., 1997). Contextual fear conditioning is also impaired by infusion of NMDA receptor antagonists, RNA and protein synthesis inhibitors, and inhibitors of PKA into the amygdala (Bailey et al., 1999; Goosens, Holt, & Maren, 2000; Huff & Rudy, 2004; Kim et al., 1991; Rodrigues et al., 2001; but see Walker, Paschall, & Davis, 2005). Collectively these findings suggest that essential aspects of the memory are encoded and stored in the amygdala. At this time, however, there is little evidence that allows us to distinguish between the involvement of different amygdala subnuclei in contextual fear, although recent lesion evidence suggests that the LA and anterior B, but not the posterior regions of the B, are critical (Goosens & Maren, 2001). The CE is, of course, also essential for the expression of contextual fear, as it is for auditory fear conditioning (Goosens & Maren, 2001). However, although lesions of the CE disrupt both cued and contextual fear, lesion studies suggest that other brain regions, including the bed nucleus of the stria terminalis, appear to be required only for the expression of contextual (not cued) fear (Sullivan et al., 2004).

The hippocampus has also been implicated in contextual fear conditioning, although its exact role has been difficult to define. A number of studies have shown that electrolytic and neurotoxic lesions of the hippocampus disrupt contextual, but not auditory, fear conditioning (see Figure 39.6, Kim & Fanselow, 1992; Kim et al., 1993; Maren, Aharonov, & Fanselow, 1997; Phillips & LeDoux, 1992). However, only lesions given shortly after training disrupt contextual fear conditioning (Frankland, Cestari,

Filipkowski, McDonald, & Silva, 1998). If rats are given hippocampal lesions 28 days after training, there is no memory impairment (Kim & Fanselow, 1992). This "retrograde gradient" of recall suggests that hippocampal-dependent memories are gradually transferred over time to other regions of the brain for permanent storage, an idea that is consistent with the findings of hippocampal-dependent episodic memory research in humans (Milner, Squire, & Kandel, 1998).

It is clear, however, that the hippocampus undergoes plastic changes during fear conditioning, some of which may be necessary for memory formation of contextual fear. For example, intrahippocampal infusion of the NMDA receptor antagonist APV impairs contextual fear conditioning (Stiedl, Birkenfeld, Palve, & Spiess, 2000; Young, Bohenek, & Fanselow, 1994). Also, fear conditioning to a context, but not to an auditory CS, is impaired in mice that lack the NR1 subunit of the NMDA receptor exclusively in area CA1 of the hippocampus (Rampon et al., 2000). Fear conditioning also leads to increases in the activation of Calmodulin-dependent Protein Kinase II (CaMKII), PKC, ERK/MAPK, and CRE-mediated gene expression in the hippocampus (Atkins, Selcher, Petraitis, Trzaskos, & Sweatt, 1998; Hall, Thomas, & Everitt, 2000; Impey et al., 1998). These findings add support to the notion that NMDA receptor-dependent plastic changes in the hippocampus, in addition to the amygdala, are required for

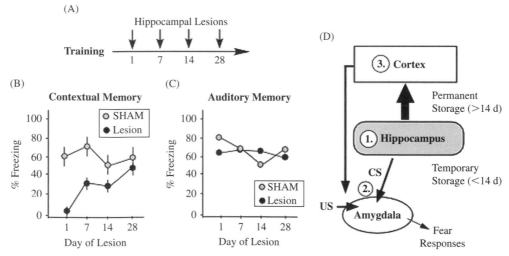

Figure 39.6 Hippocampal-dependent contextual fear.

Note: Contextual fear conditioning requires the dorsal hippocampus, but only for a limited time. A: Experimental protocol from Kim and Fanselow (1992), where rats were trained with tone-shock pairings and then given lesions of the dorsal hippocampus either 1, 7, 14, or 28 days later. B: Contextual memory was impaired when lesions were given 1 day after training, but not if given 28 days after training. C: Auditory fear conditioning was not affected by hippocampal lesions. In each panel, the lesioned rats are represented by the black circles. From "Modality-Specific Retrograde Amnesia of Fear," by J. J. Kim, and M. S. Fanselow, *Science, 256,* May 1, 1992, p. 676. Copyright 1992 by the American Association for the Advancement of Science (AAAS). Reprinted with permission. D: A model of the neural system underlying contextual fear conditioning. The hippocampus (1) is necessary for forming an initial representation of the context and for providing that information as a CS to the amygdala (2) during fear conditioning. In the amygdala, the contextual CS can converge with the footshock US, and it is here that the memory of contextual fear is thought to be formed. Over time, however, the contextual memory formed by the hippocampus is transferred to the cortex (3) for permanent storage. At this point, the hippocampus is not necessary to retrieve the memory.

contextual fear conditioning. However, it should be emphasized that the exact contribution of these plastic changes to contextual fear conditioning remains unclear. Most of these studies cannot distinguish between a role for NMDA receptor-mediated plasticity in fear memory formation and in the formation of contextual representations that then serve as the fear CS (Rudy, Huff, & Matus-Amat, 2004). Further, regulation of intracellular signaling cascades in the hippocampus by fear conditioning, though potentially indicative of some type of memory storage, does not necessarily indicate that these changes are related to the acquisition of *fear* memories. They may be related to episodic memories of the training experience that are acquired at the same time as fearful memories (LeDoux, 2000; and see later discussion). Indeed, a number of studies have shown that hippocampal cells undergo plastic changes during and after fear conditioning (Doyère et al., 1995; Moita, Rosis, Zhou, LeDoux, & Blair, 2003), including auditory fear conditioning, which is spared following hippocampal lesions (Kim & Fanselow, 1992).

Although auditory fear conditioning can be learned independently of the hippocampus, it has recently been shown that hippocampal involvement is recruited with weaker fear conditioning protocols that involve low footshock intensity and few training trials (Quinn, Wied, Ma, Tinsley, & Fanselow, 2008). Thus, the amygdala and hippocampus normally cooperate in the intact brain to store different components of the fear learning experience. The amygdala independently stores the direct association between the cue and the footshock, and the hippocampus stores more general features of the conditioning episode that can contribute to the fear memory.

Altering Established Fear Memories

Thus far we have focused on how a fear memory is formed. But what happens after a fear memory has been retrieved? Two paradigms have been used to examine how fear memories change with retrieval: reconsolidation and extinction.

Reconsolidation Blockade

The traditional way of thinking about memory formation is that memories are laid down by a time-dependent process, called consolidation, that stabilizes the neuronal representation of the memory trace. Newly acquired memories, for example, are thought to be inherently unstable, acquiring stability only over time as RNA and protein synthesis-dependent processes kick in. According to this view, after the memory has been consolidated retrieval simply involves going back and reactivating the original trace. However, over the years a number of studies have challenged this linear notion of memory formation and retrieval. In these studies, manipulations that are known to disrupt memory

consolidation when given around the time of initial learning have also been found to disrupt the integrity of an established memory when given around the time of memory *retrieval* (see Sara, 2000). These findings suggest that the retrieval process renders a memory susceptible to disruption, similar to the susceptibility that exists prior to the consolidation of a newly formed memory.

Recent studies using the fear conditioning paradigm have rekindled interest in this phenomenon. For example, infusion of the protein synthesis inhibitor anisomycin into the amygdala immediately after retrieval of an auditory fear memory was shown to impair memory retrieval on subsequent tests (Nader, Schafe, & LeDoux, 2000). This effect was clearly dependent on retrieval of the memory because no subsequent memory deficit was observed if the CS exposure was omitted. Further, the anisomycin-induced memory deficit was observed not only when the initial CS exposure was given shortly after training (i.e., 1 day), but also when the CS exposure was given 14 days after initial training, suggesting that the effect could not be attributable to disruption of late phases of protein synthesis necessary for consolidation. Thus, following active retrieval of a previously consolidated fear memory, that memory appears to undergo a second stabilization process (so-called reconsolidation) that requires protein synthesis in the amygdala. There is much that remains unknown about reconsolidation, but recent work has extended these findings by showing that amygdala CREB activation is also required for reconsolidation, because transient overexpression of a dominant negative isoform of CREB at the time of memory retrieval disrupts memory for both auditory and contextual fear conditioning (Kida et al., 2002), suggesting that a nuclear event is involved. Recent studies have demonstrated a similar role for activation of the ERK/MAPK pathway in the LA. Interestingly, postretrieval blockade of ERK/MAPK signaling in the LA not only disrupts fear memory consolidation, but also reverses the fear retrieval-induced potentiation of LA field potentials that accompanies the fear response (Doyère, Debiec, Monfils, Schafe, & LeDoux, 2007). In essence, reconsolidation blockade is associated not only with disruption of the fear memory, but also with disruption of the potentiated electrophysiological response that is associated with the retrieved memory.

The therapeutic implications of this ability to disrupt fear memory reconsolidation still need to be explored. Of course, protein synthesis inhibition, or even disruption of ERK/MAPK and CREB signaling, is not likely to be useful for reconsolidation-based fear reduction manipulations in the clinic. Therefore, based on reconsolidation experiments in rats with other kinds of memories (Sara, 2000), it has recently been shown that beta-adrenergic receptor antagonists (e.g., propranolol), which are already used in humans for other purposes, can also disrupt fear memory reconsolidation (Debiec & LeDoux, 2004). This suggests that beta blockers, given in conjunction with the retrieval of traumatic memories, might be able to reduce the potency of fear-related pathologies, such as Posttraumatic Stress Disorder (Debiec & LeDoux, 2006).

Extinction

Extinction is a more traditional way of decreasing the potency of established fear memories. Extinction is a process whereby repeated presentations of the CS in the absence of the US lead to a weakening of the expression of conditioned responding. Unlike reconsolidation blockade, which is thought to disrupt the original memory trace, extinction involves the formation of a new *inhibitory* memory (i.e., a CS-No US trace) that competes with the original trace for control over behavior. Extinction of conditioned fear has been well documented in the behavioral literature, but we know comparatively little about its neurobiological substrate. However, research over the past 2 decades has implicated a circuit that involves complex interactions among the amygdala, the ventral medial prefrontal cortex (mPFC), and the hippocampus in fear extinction learning and retrieval.

Early studies showed that selective lesions of the ventral mPFC retard the extinction of fear to an auditory CS, while having no effect on initial fear acquisition (Morgan & LeDoux, 1995; Morgan, Romanski, & LeDoux, 1993; but see Gewirtz, Falls, & Davis, 1997). Further, neurons in the mPFC alter their response properties as a result of extinction (Garcia, Vouimba, Baudry, & Thompson, 1999; Herry, Vouimba, & Garcia, 1999). However, recent work suggests that the role of the ventral mPFC in extinction is complex. Briefly, the mPFC may not be necessary for the initial *acquisition* of fear extinction, but rather in the posttraining storage of information needed later to rapidly retrieve extinction learning under appropriate circumstances (see Figure 39.7; Quirk, Russo, Barron, & Lebron, 2000; Milad & Quirk, 2002). For example, rats with mPFC lesions are able to extinguish within a session but show impaired extinction retrieval when tested in a later session (Quirk et al., 2000). Further, neurons in the mPFC fire strongly to a tone CS after behavioral extinction has occurred, and artificial stimulation of the mPFC that resembles responding in an extinguished rat is sufficient to inhibit behavioral expression of fear in non-extinguished rats (Milad & Quirk, 2002). Consistent with this, blockade of mPFC NMDA receptors shortly *after* extinction

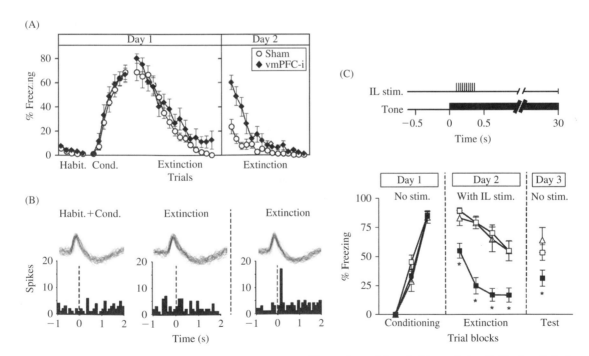

Figure 39.7 The role of the medial prefrontal cortex (mPFC) in long-term retention of fear extinction.

Note: **A:** Rats with lesions of the mPFC can acquire and extinguish auditory fear conditioning normally (Day 1). However, they cannot retain their memory for extinction (Day 2; 24 hours later). In each panel, the lesioned animals are represented by the black circles. From "The Role of Ventromedial Prefrontal Cortex in the Recovery of Extinguished Fear," by G. J. Quirk, G. K. Russo, J. L. Barron, and K. Lebron, 2000, *Journal of Neuroscience, 20,* p. 6227. Copyright 2000 by the Society for Neuroscience. Adapted with permission. **B:** Single cells in the mPFC are generally unresponsive to tones during training and extinction (Day 1), but signal vigorously during long-term recall of extinction (Day 2; 24 hours later). **C:** Direct stimulation of the mPFC during the early phases of extinction (Day 2) results in a dramatic reduction in fear, which is long-lasting (Day 3; 24 hours later). In each figure the stimulated animals are represented by the black squares. From "Neurons in Medial Prefrontal Cortex Signal Memory for Fear Extinction," by M. R. Milad and G. J. Quirk, November 7, 2002, *Nature, 420,* pp. 70–74. Copyright 2002 by Macmillan Publishers Ltd. Adapted with permission.

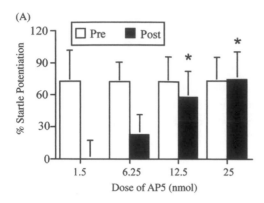

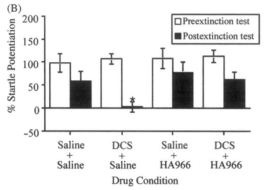

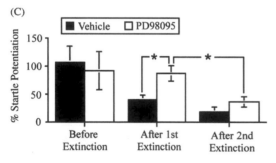

Figure 39.8 The amygdala and fear extinction.

Note: Extinction of fear-potentiated startle (FPS) can be impaired or facilitated by pharmacological manipulations of the amygdala. **A:** Extinction of FPS is impaired in a dose-dependent manner following infusion of AP5, an NMDA receptor antagonist, into the amygdala. White bars represent preextinction startle baselines; black bars represent the amount of startle potentiation after an extinction session in each group. Note that with increasing doses there is less extinction. From "Extinction of Fear-Potentiated Startle: Blockade by Infusion of an NMDA Antagonist into the Amygdala," by W. A. Falls, M. J. Miserendino, and M. Davis, 1992, *Journal of Neuroscience, 12*, pp. 854–863. Copyright 1992 by the Society for Neuroscience. Adapted with permission. **B:** Extinction of FPS can be facilitated by infusion of a partial agonist of the NMDA receptor in the amygdala. Rats that were given intra-amygdala infusions of D-cycloserine (DCS; DCS/saline), a partial agonist of the glycine recognition site of the NMDA receptor, had facilitated extinction relative to controls (saline/saline). This effect could be reversed by HA966 (DCS/HA966), an antagonist of the glycine recognition site that has no effect on extinction itself (saline/HA966). In each group white bars represent preextinction startle baselines, and black bars represent the amount of startle potentiation after drug treatment and an extinction session. From "Facilitation of Conditioned Fear Extinction by Systemic Administration or Intra-Amygdala Infusions of D-Cycloserine as Assessed with Fear-Potentiated Startle in Rats," by D. L. Walker, K. J. Ressler, K.-T. Lu, and M. Davis, 2002, *Journal of Neuroscience, 22*, pp. 2343–2351. Copyright 2002 by the Society for Neuroscience. Adapted with permission. **C:** Intra-amygdala

training disrupts the subsequent retrieval of the extinction memory (Burgos-Robles, Vidal-Gonzalez, Santini, & Quirk, 2007), suggesting that cells in the mPFC store features of the fear extinction experience after training is complete.

Importantly, extinction is known to be context-specific. That is, if a fear-conditioned rat is given fear extinction training in one context (Context A), the ability to inhibit fear is apparently linked to that context because *renewal* of the fear response occurs if the rat is presented with the CS outside of the extinction context (Bouton & Ricker, 1994). This fact, together with the finding that fully extinguished memories are capable of reinstating upon presentation of the US (Rescorla & Heth, 1975), has led to the long-held view that extinction does not result in the erasure of the original memory trace but is instead a new kind of learning that serves to inhibit expression of the old memory (Pavlov, 1927). Not surprisingly, recent studies have indicated that the hippocampus plays an important role in the contextual modulation of fear extinction. Maren and colleagues (Hobin, Goosens, & Maren, 2003), for example, have shown that training-induced neurophysiological responses in the LA readily extinguish within a fear extinction session, but that this neural representation of extinction, like the behavior itself, is specific to the context in which extinction has taken place. Further, functional inactivation of the hippocampus using the GABA-A agonist muscimol can impair the context-specific expression of fear extinction (Corcoran & Maren, 2001). The requirements for both hippocampal and mPFC activity in extinction suggest that connections from the hippocampus to the mPFC are important for encoding contextual constraints on fear extinction learning. Beyond this, these findings have led researchers to propose a broad circuit model for fear extinction that involves projections from the hippocampus to the mPFC, and from the mPFC to the amygdala. The hippocampal-mPFC connection is needed to appropriately contextualize extinction, and the mPFC-amygdala connection is needed to express extinction by inhibiting fear outputs from the fear circuitry of the amygdala (LA/B–intercalated cell masses–CE) that was discussed earlier in this chapter (Corcoran & Quirk, 2007; Hobin et al., 2003; Maren & Quirk, 2004; Paré et al., 2004; Quirk & Mueller, 2008; Sotres-Bayon, Bush, & LeDoux, 2004).

infusion of a MAP kinase inhibitor (PD98095) blocks extinction of FPS. Rats were infused with PD98095 before the 1st extinction session. The 2nd extinction session was given drug-free. Note the absence of extinction on the 1st session. In each group, black bars represent preextinction startle baselines, and white bars represent the amount of startle potentiation after an extinction session. From "Mitogen-Activated Protein Kinase Cascade in the Basolateral Nucleus of Amygdala Is Involved in Extinction of Fear-Potentiated Startle," by K. T. Lu, D. L. Walker, and M. Davis, 2001, *Journal of Neuroscience, 21*, RC162. Copyright 2001 by the Society for Neuroscience. Adapted with permission.

These advances in our understanding of hippocampal and mPFC control over extinction retrieval have been important steps for the field. But questions about the neural mechanisms that underlie the actual formation of the extinction memory are not explained by this model. Insights into this problem come from a number of studies that have implicated the amygdala as an essential site of plasticity for the acquisition of fear extinction (Figure 39.8; Falls, Miserendino, & Davis, 1992; Lu, Walker, & Davis, 2001; Walker, Ressler, Lu, & Davis, 2002). Infusions of NMDA receptor antagonists or ERK/MAPK inhibitors into the amygdala have been shown to impair fear extinction (Davis, 2002; Falls et al., 1992; Lu et al., 2001). Conversely, both systemic and intra-amygdala infusions of partial agonists of the NMDA receptor facilitate fear extinction (Walker et al., 2002). These experiments suggest that some type of activity-dependent synaptic plasticity must take place in the amygdala during extinction learning, as it does during initial learning. In fact, unlike the mPFC, the amygdala appears to be necessary for the *acquisition* of fear extinction because blockade of NR2B-containing NMDA receptors in the LA prevents rats from the fear extinction learning that occurs across trials within a single extinction training session (Sotres-Bayon, Bush, & LeDoux, 2007). In contrast, disruption of BDNF-TrkB signaling with viral vector-mediated amygdala expression of dominant-negative TrkB was found to disrupt the consolidation, but not the acquisition, of fear extinction, suggesting that BDNF participates in the consolidation of the extinction memory within the intrinsic circuitry of the amygdala (Chhatwal, Stanek-Rattiner, Davis, & Ressler, 2006). When considered together with the systems-level circuit discussed earlier, these findings suggest that fear extinction is first encoded in the amygdala during extinction training, and subsequently the amygdala trains the hippocampal-mPFC circuit so that the extinction memory can be later retrieved under contextually appropriate circumstances. The mechanisms for this systems-level consolidation process are not yet understood but may involve an amygdala-driven rehearsal of the extinction training experience via reciprocal connections from the amygdala to the hippocampus and mPFC.

Fear-Motivated Instrumental Learning

Reconsolidation blockade and extinction both represent mechanisms for diminishing the intensity of fear memories. Active coping is yet another mechanism for reducing the behavioral and emotional impact of fear. Pavlovian fear conditioning is useful for learning to detect a dangerous object or situation, but animals must also be able to use this information to guide ongoing behavior that is instrumental in avoiding that danger. Successful avoidance, made possible by Pavlovian associations that provide advance warning of danger, is therefore a potentially positive (and behaviorally reinforcing) outcome following CS exposure. In experimental situations this type of learning can be modeled by requiring the animal to make a response (i.e., move away, press a bar, turn a wheel) that will allow it to avoid presentation of a shock or danger signal, a form of learning known as "active avoidance." In other experimental situations, the animal can be required to learn *not* to respond, known as "passive avoidance." Both of these are examples of instrumental conditioning, and the amygdala, cooperating with other brain regions, plays a vital role in each.

Previously, we mentioned that only the LA and CE were critical for Pavlovian fear conditioning. However, we have recently begun to appreciate the significance of projections from the LA to the basal nucleus of the amygdala (B, as defined earlier). Studies that employ fear learning tasks that require rats to learn both classical and instrumental components have begun to develop our knowledge of how emotional information can be used to motivate goal-directed responses (Amorapanth et al., 2000; Killcross, Robbins, & Everitt, 1997). Amorapanth et al., for example, first trained rats to associate a tone with footshock (the Pavlovian component). Next, rats learned to move from one side of a 2-compartment box to the other to avoid presentation of the tone (the instrumental component), a so-called escape-from-fear task. Findings showed that whereas lesions of the LA impaired both types of learning, lesions of the CE impair only the Pavlovian component (i.e., the tone-shock association). Conversely, lesions of the B impaired only the instrumental component (learning to move to the second compartment). Thus, different outputs of the LA appear to mediate Pavlovian and instrumental behaviors elicited by a fear-arousing stimulus (Amorapanth et al., 2000). It is important to note, however, that these findings do not indicate that the B is a site of motor control or a locus of memory storage for instrumental learning. Rather, the B likely guides fear-related behavior and reinforcement learning via its projections to nearby striatal regions that are known to be necessary for instrumental learning and reward processes (Everitt, Cador, & Robbins, 1989; Everitt et al., 1999; Robbins, Cador, Taylor, & Everitt, 1989). Our knowledge of how the amygdala transfers emotional information to brain regions involved in motivation and instrumental learning is still in its infancy. Research that addresses this issue is needed to unite these two related but sparsely integrated disciplines within behavioral neuroscience.

Modulation of Explicit Memory by Fear Arousal

Pavlovian fear conditioning is an implicit form of learning and memory. However, during most emotional experiences, including fear conditioning, explicit or conscious memories are also formed (LeDoux, 1996). These occur through the operation of the medial temporal lobe memory system involving the hippocampus and related cortical areas (Eichenbaum, 2000; Milner et al., 1998). The role of the hippocampus in the explicit memory of an emotional experience is much the same as its role in other kinds of experiences, with one important exception. During fearful or emotionally arousing experiences, the amygdala activates neuromodulatory systems in the brain and hormonal systems in the body via its projections to the hypothalamus, which can drive the hypothalamic-pituitary-adrenal (HPA) axis. Neurohormones released by these systems can, in turn, feed back to modulate the function of forebrain structures such as the hippocampus and serve to enhance the storage of the memory in these regions (McGaugh, 2000).

The primary support for this model comes from studies of *inhibitory avoidance learning,* a type of passive avoidance learning, briefly introduced in the preceding section, whereby the animal must learn to not enter a chamber in which it previously received a shock. In this paradigm, various pharmacological manipulations of the amygdala that affect neurotransmitter or neurohormonal systems modulate the strength of the memory. For example, immediate posttraining blockade of intra-amygdala noradrenergic or glucocorticoid receptors impairs retention of inhibitory avoidance, whereas facilitation of these systems in the amygdala enhances acquisition and memory storage (McGaugh, 2000; McGaugh et al., 1993). The exact subnuclei in the amygdala that are critical for memory modulation remain unknown, as do the areas of the brain where these amygdala projections influence memory storage. Candidate areas include the hippocampus and entorhinal and parietal cortices (Izquierdo et al., 1997). Indeed, it would be interesting to know whether the changes in unit activity, or the activation of intracellular signaling cascades, in the hippocampus during and after fear conditioning, as discussed earlier, might be related to formation of such explicit memories, and how regulation of these signals depends on the integrity of the amygdala and its neuromodulators. Interestingly, it has been shown that stimulation of the B can modulate the persistence of LTP in the hippocampus (Frey, Bergado-Rosado, Seidenbecher, Pape, & Frey, 2001), which provides a potential mechanism whereby the amygdala can modulate hippocampal-dependent memories (Roozendaal, Barsegyan, & Lee, 2008; Roozendaal, Okuda, de Quervain, & McGaugh, 2006).

FEAR CONDITIONING IN HUMANS

Studies of fear conditioning in humans have corroborated the findings from fear conditioning research in rodents.

In general, advances in our understanding of the brain's contributions to human emotions have come from two broad categories of neuropsychology research: studies in patients with damage to localized brain regions and studies that involve brain imaging in healthy subjects. The former provide evidence for a causal link between loss of function and region-specific damage, but the extent of brain damage cannot be easily controlled. The latter provide greater spatial and temporal precision.

Neuropsychology of Fear in Brain-Lesioned Patients

One of the most important insights gained from studies in brain-lesioned patients is that emotional learning and conscious awareness are dissociable phenomena. Patients with damage to the medial temporal lobe region, including the amygdala, show deficits in the ability to acquire conditioned fear responses, even when conscious awareness of the fear conditioning experience is intact. Conversely, patients with selective damage to the hippocampus and related areas of the medial temporal lobe show the opposite pattern: impaired declarative memory for the fear conditioning experience but intact implicit emotional responses to the CS (Bechara et al., 1995; Hamann, Monarch, & Goldstein, 2002; LaBar, LeDoux, Spencer, & Phelps, 1995). Hippocampal damage also appears to remove contextual constraints on fear extinction (LaBar & Phelps, 2005). In addition to the hippocampus, damage to the ventral mPFC also produces fear extinction deficits (Bechara, Damasio, Damasio, & Anderson, 1994; Davidson, Putnam, & Larson, 2000; Rolls, Hornak, Wade, & McGrath, 1994), which corresponds to deficits observed in rats with ventral mPFC lesions (Lebron, Milad, & Quirk, 2004; Morgan & LeDoux, 1995; Morgan et al., 1993; Morgan, Schulkin, & LeDoux, 2003; Quirk et al., 2000; Sierra-Mercado, Corcoran, Lebron-Milad, & Quirk, 2006).

Functional Brain Imaging of Fear in Healthy Subjects

Functional imaging during fear conditioning of healthy volunteers consistently reveals increased amygdala activation during fear conditioning and early phases of extinction (Buchel, Dolan, Armony, & Friston, 1999; Buchel, Morris, Dolan, & Friston, 1998; Cheng, Knight, Smith, Stein, & Helmstetter, 2003; Knight, Cheng, Smith, Stein, & Helmstetter, 2004; LaBar, Gatenby, Gore, LeDoux, & Phelps, 1998; Phelps, Delgado, Nearing, & LeDoux, 2004). In fact, individual differences in fear have been found to correlate with the degree of amygdala activity (Cheng et al., 2003; Furmark, Fischer, Wik, Larsson, & Fredrikson, 1997; LaBar et al., 1998). Interestingly, the strongest amygdala activation is observed during the early phase of conditioning (Buchel et al., 1998; LaBar et al., 1998), which is reminiscent of the transiently plastic cells observed in the dorsal regions of the LA in the rat (Repa et al., 2001).

In addition to learning about danger from direct contact with an unconditioned stimulus, humans also learn in indirect ways. This is illustrated by a paradigm called "instructed fear," whereby the subjects are told that one stimulus may be paired with a shock, but the subjects never receive a shock. Nevertheless, the CS leads to amygdala activation (Phelps et al., 2001), and damage to the amygdala disrupts the expression of the CS-elicited autonomic responses (Funayama, Grillon, Davis, & Phelps, 2001). Another way that fear is learned indirectly is by observation; that is, subjects who observe others being conditioned also develop conditioned responses to the CS. Such a CS then leads to amygdala activation (Olsson & Phelps, 2007).

Fear conditioning leads to CS-induced amygdala activation even when subjects are unaware of the CS due to subliminal presentation techniques (Morris, Ohman, & Dolan, 1999). Similarly, a subliminal CS elicits amygdala activation after observational learning but not after instructed fear conditioning (Olsson & Phelps, 2004). Examples of fMRI imaging of amygdala activity after fear conditioning, instructed fear, and observational fear are shown in Figure 39.9 (courtesy of Elizabeth A. Phelps).

Clinical Implications

The close correspondence between the brain regions involved in rodent and human fear conditioning suggests that insights gained from animal studies can be applied to the clinical setting. Exposure therapy is procedurally similar to fear extinction training and is currently the most effective method for treating anxiety disorders, especially phobias. However, similar to the postextinction renewal of fear seen in rat studies, when the CS is presented outside the extinction training context, patients often experience relapse of fear symptoms when they leave the therapeutic setting (Rodriguez, Craske, Mineka, & Hladek, 1999). Because animal studies conducted by Davis and colleagues have shown that partial NMDA agonists can facilitate fear extinction (Walker et al., 2002), the same group was able to use a similar pharmacological treatment and successfully enhance the clinical efficacy of exposure therapy in human patients (Ressler et al., 2002). This kind of translational research is becoming an increasingly important emphasis in emotion research.

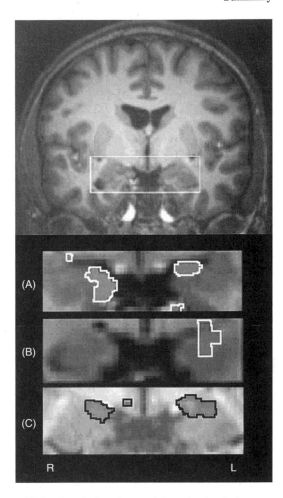

Figure 39.9   Fear-induced amygdala activation in humans.

Note: CS presentations to humans cause similar increases in amygdala activation after **A:** fear conditioning, in which subjects are given paired presentations of the CS and US, **B:** instructed fear, in which subjects are instructed about the CS-US association but do not directly experience the association, and **C:** observational fear learning, in which subjects observe someone else undergoing fear conditioning. Figure shows structural MRI of the human brain. Figure courtesy of Elizabeth A. Phelps.

SUMMARY

In just over 2 decades we have seen a remarkable resurgence of interest in emotion research. Advances in brain research have been systematically combined with the fear conditioning paradigm, which has enabled us to trace how stimuli are attributed with fear-eliciting properties through their temporal association with innately aversive events. The amygdala has emerged as a crucial site of convergence for CS and US input pathways, and we now have knowledge of the cellular and molecular events that are needed to encode and store fear memories. This has led to important discoveries about the different ways and mechanisms through which an established fear memory can be modified, including reconsolidation, extinction, and the learning of active coping responses. These discoveries, in turn, have provided empirical data that indicate a separation of the brain mechanisms that mediate emotion and conscious awareness, as well as improved understanding of how these dissociable processes interact. Finally, these insights have begun to suggest new methods that can be introduced into the clinical setting.

REFERENCES

Abel, T., Nguyen, P. V., Barad, M., Deuel, T. A., Kandel, E. R., & Bourtchouladze, R. (1997). Genetic demonstration of a role for PKA in the late phase of LTP, and in hippocampus-based long-term memory. *Cell, 88*, 615–626.

Amorapanth, P., LeDoux, J. E., & Nader, K. (2000). Different lateral amygdala outputs mediate reactions and actions elicited by a fear-arousing stimulus. *Nature Neuroscience, 3*, 74–79.

Anglada-Figueroa, D., & Quirk, G. J. (2005). Lesions of the basal amygdala block expression of conditioned fear but not extinction. *Journal of Neuroscience, 25*, 9680–9685.

Apergis-Schoute, A. M., Debiec, J., Doyère, V., LeDoux, J. E., & Schafe, G. E. (2005). Auditory fear conditioning and long-term potentiation in the lateral amygdala require ERK/MAP kinase signaling in the auditory thalamus: A role for presynaptic plasticity in the fear system. *Journal of Neuroscience, 25*, 5730–5739.

Atkins, C. M., Selcher, J. C., Petraitis, J. J., Trzaskos, J. M., & Sweatt, J. D. (1998). The MAPK cascade is required for mammalian associative learning. *Nature Neuroscience, 1*, 602–609.

Bailey, D. J., Kim, J. J., Sun, W., Thompson, R. F., & Helmstetter, F. J. (1999). Acquisition of fear conditioning in rats requires the synthesis of mRNA in the amygdala. *Behavioral Neuroscience, 113*, 276–282.

Balleine, B. W., & Dickinson, A. (1998). Goal-directed instrumental action: Contingency and incentive learning and their cortical substrates. *Neuropharmacology, 37*(4–5), 407–419.

Bauer, E. P., LeDoux, J. E., & Nader, K. (2001). Fear conditioning and LTP in the lateral amygdala are sensitive to the same stimulus contingencies. *Nature Neuroscience, 4*, 687–688.

Bauer, E. P., Schafe, G. E., & LeDoux, J. E. (2002). NMDA receptors and L-type voltage-gated calcium channels contribute to long-term potentiation and different components of fear memory formation in the lateral amygdala. *Journal of Neuroscience, 22*, 5239–5249.

Bechara, A., Damasio, A. R., Damasio, H., & Anderson, S. W. (1994). Insensitivity to future consequences following damage to human prefrontal cortex. *Cognition, 50*(1/3), 7–15.

Bechara, A., Tranel, D., Damasio, H., Adolphs, R., Rockland, C., & Damasio, A. R. (1995, August 25). Double dissociation of conditioning and declarative knowledge relative to the amygdala and hippocampus in humans. *Science, 269*, 1115–1118.

Berntson, G. G., Bechara, A., Damasio, H., Tranel, D., & Cacioppo, J. T. (2007). Amygdala contribution to selective dimensions of emotion. *Social Cognitive and Affective Neuroscience, 2*, 123–129.

Blair, H. T., Schafe, G. E., Bauer, E. P., Rodrigues, S. M., & LeDoux, J. E. (2001). Synaptic plasticity in the lateral amygdala: A cellular hypothesis of fear conditioning. *Learning and Memory, 8*, 229–242.

Blanchard, R. J., & Blanchard, D. C. (1969). Crouching as an index of fear. *Journal of Comparative Physiological Psychology, 67*, 370–375.

Blanchard, R. J., Dielman, T. E., & Blanchard, D. C. (1968). Postshock crouching: Familiarity with the shock situation. *Psychonomic Science, 10*, 371–372.

Bliss, T. V. P., & Lømo, T. (1973). Long-lasting potentiation of synaptic transmission in the dentate area of the anaesthetized rabbit following stimulation of the perforant path. *Journal of Physiology, 232*, 331–356.

Bordi, F., & LeDoux, J. E. (1992). Sensory tuning beyond the sensory system: An initial analysis of auditory properties of neurons in the lateral amygdaloid nucleus and overlying areas of the striatum. *Journal of Neuroscience, 12*, 2493–2503.

Bourtchuladze, R., Frenguelli, B., Blendy, J., Cioffi, D., Schutz, G., & Silva, A. J. (1994). Deficient long-term memory in mice with a targeted mutation of the cAMP-responsive element-binding protein. *Cell, 79*, 59–68.

Bouton, M. E., & Ricker, S. T. (1994). Renewal of extinguished responding in a second context. *Animal Learning and Behavior, 22*, 317–324.

Brambilla, R., Gnesutta, N., Minichiello, L., White, G., Roylance, A. J., Herron, C. E., et al. (1997, November 20). A role for the ras signaling pathway in synaptic transmission and long-term memory. *Nature, 390*, 281–286.

Brunzell, D. H., & Kim, J. J. (2001). Fear conditioning to tone, but not to context, is attenuated by lesions of the insular cortex and posterior extension of the intralaminar complex in rats. *Behavioral Neuroscience, 115*, 365–375.

Buchel, C., Dolan, R. J., Armony, J. L., & Friston, K. J. (1999). Amygdala-hippocampal involvement in human aversive trace conditioning revealed through event-related functional magnetic resonance imaging. *Journal of Neuroscience, 19*, 10869–10876.

Buchel, C., Morris, J., Dolan, R. J., & Friston, K. J. (1998). Brain systems mediating aversive conditioning: An event-related fMRI study. *Neuron, 20*, 947–957.

Burgos-Robles, A., Vidal-Gonzalez, I., Santini, E., & Quirk, G. J. (2007). Consolidation of fear extinction requires NMDA receptor-dependent bursting in the ventromedial prefrontal cortex. *Neuron, 53*, 871–880.

Campeau, S., & Davis, M. (1995). Involvement of the central nucleus and basolateral complex of the amygdala in fear conditioning measured with fear-potentiated startle in rats trained concurrently with auditory and visual conditioned stimuli. *Journal of Neuroscience, 15*, 2301–2311.

Cardinal, R. N., Parkinson, J. A., Hall, J., & Everitt, B. J. (2002). Emotion and motivation: The role of the amygdala, ventral striatum, and prefrontal cortex. *Neuroscience and Biobehavioral Reviews, 26*, 321–352.

Chapman, P. F., Kairiss, E. W., Keenan, C. L., & Brown, T. H. (1990). Long-term synaptic potentiation in the amygdala. *Synapse, 6*, 271–278.

Cheng, D. T., Knight, D. C., Smith, C. N., Stein, E. A., & Helmstetter, F. J. (2003). Functional MRI of human amygdala activity during Pavlovian fear conditioning: Stimulus processing versus response expression. *Behavioral Neuroscience, 117*, 3–10.

Chhatwal, J. P., Stanek-Rattiner, L., Davis, M., & Ressler, K. J. (2006). Amygdala BDNF signaling is required for consolidation but not encoding of extinction. *Nature Neuroscience, 9*, 870–872.

Clugnet, M. C., & LeDoux, J. E. (1989). Synaptic plasticity in fear conditioning circuits: Induction of LTP in the lateral nucleus of the amygdala by stimulation of the medial geniculate body. *Journal of Neuroscience, 10*, 2818–2824.

Corcoran, K. A., & Maren, S. (2001). Hippocampal inactivation disrupts contextual retrieval of fear memory after extinction. *Journal of Neuroscience, 21*, 1720–1726.

Corcoran, K. A., & Quirk, G. J. (2007). Recalling safety: Cooperative functions of the ventromedial prefrontal cortex and the hippocampus in extinction. *CNS Spectrums, 12*(3), 200–206.

Davidson, R. J., Putnam, K. M., & Larson, C. L. (2000). Dysfunction in the neural circuitry of emotion regulation: A possible prelude to violence. *Science, 289*, 591–594.

Davis, M. (1997). Neurobiology of fear responses: The role of the amygdala. *Journal of Neuropsychiatry and Clinical Neurosciences, 9*, 382–402.

Davis, M. (2002). Role of NMDA receptors and MAP kinase in the amygdala in extinction of fear: Clinical implications for exposure therapy. *European Journal of Neuroscience, 16*, 395–398.

Davis, M., Walker, D. L., & Lee, Y. (1997). Roles of the amygdala and bed nucleus of the stria terminalis in fear and anxiety measured with the acoustic startle reflex: Possible relevance to PTSD. *Annals of the New York Academy of Sciences, 821,* 305–331.

Debiec, J., & LeDoux, J. E. (2004). Disruption of reconsolidation but not consolidation of auditory fear conditioning by noradrenergic blockade in the amygdala. *Neuroscience, 129,* 267–272.

Debiec, J., & LeDoux, J. E. (2006). Noradrenergic signaling in the amygdala contributes to the reconsolidation of fear memory: Treatment implications for PTSD. *Annals of the New York Academy of Sciences, 1071,* 521–524.

De Oca, B. M., DeCola, J. P., Maren, S., & Fanselow, M. S. (1998). Distinct regions of the periaqueductal gray are involved in the acquisition and expression of defensive responses. *Journal of Neuroscience, 18,* 3426–3432.

Doron, N. N., & LeDoux, J. E. (1999). Organization of projections to the lateral amygdala from auditory and visual areas of the thalamus in the rat. *Journal of Comparative Neurology, 412,* 383–409.

Doyère, V., Debiec, J., Monfils, M. H., Schafe, G. E., & LeDoux, J. E. (2007). Synapse-specific reconsolidation of distinct fear memories in the lateral amygdala. *Nature Neuroscience, 10,* 414–416.

Doyère, V., Redini-Del Negro, C., Dutrieux, G., Le Floch, G., Davis, S., & Laroche, S. (1995). Potentiation or depression of synaptic efficacy in the dentate gyrus is determined by the relationship between the conditioned and unconditioned stimulus in a classical conditioning paradigm in rats. *Behavioural Brain Research, 70,* 15–29.

Edeline, J.-M., Pham, P., & Weinberger, N. M. (1993). Rapid development of learning-induced receptive field plasticity in the auditory cortex. *Behavioral Neuroscience, 107,* 539–551.

Eichenbaum, H. (2000). A cortical-hippocampal system for declarative memory. *Nature Reviews: Neuroscience, 1,* 41–50.

Everitt, B. J., Cador, M., & Robbins, T. W. (1989). Interactions between the amygdala and ventral striatum in stimulus-reward associations: Studies using a second-order schedule of sexual reinforcement. *Neuroscience, 30,* 63–75.

Everitt, B. J., Parkinson, J. A., Olmstead, M. C., Arroyo, M., Robledo, P., & Robbins, T. W. (1999). Associative processes in addiction and reward: The role of amygdala-ventral striatal subsystems. *Annals of the New York Academy of Sciences, 877,* 412–438.

Falls, W. A., Miserendino, M. J., & Davis, M. (1992). Extinction of fear-potentiated startle: Blockade by infusion of an NMDA antagonist into the amygdala. *Journal of Neuroscience, 12,* 854–863.

Fanselow, M. S. (1980). Conditional and unconditional components of postshock freezing. *Pavlovian Journal of Biological Science, 15,* 177–182.

Fanselow, M. S., & LeDoux, J. E. (1999). Why we think plasticity underlying Pavlovian fear conditioning occurs in the basolateral amygdala. *Neuron, 23,* 229–232.

Farb, C. R., Aoki, C., Milner, T., Kaneko, T., & LeDoux, J. E. (1992). Glutamate immunoreactive terminals in the lateral amygdaloid nucleus: A possible substrate for emotional memory. *Behavioural Brain Research, 593,* 145–158.

Frankland, P. W., Cestari, V., Filipkowski, R. K., McDonald, R. J., & Silva, A. J. (1998). The dorsal hippocampus is essential for context discrimination but not for contextual conditioning. *Behavioral Neuroscience, 112,* 863–874.

Frey, S., Bergado-Rosado, J., Seidenbecher, T., Pape, H. C., & Frey, J. U. (2001). Reinforcement of early long-term potentiation (early-LTP) in dentate gyrus by stimulation of the basolateral amygdala: Heterosynaptic induction mechanisms of late-LTP. *Journal of Neuroscience, 21,* 3697–3703.

Funayama, E. S., Grillon, C., Davis, M., & Phelps, E. A. (2001). A double dissociation in the affective modulation of startle in humans: Effects of unilateral temporal lobectomy. *Journal of Cognitive Neuroscience, 13,* 721–729.

Furmark, T., Fischer, H., Wik, G., Larsson, M., & Fredrikson, M. (1997). The amygdala and individual differences in human fear conditioning. *NeuroReport, 8,* 3957–3960.

Garcia, R., Vouimba, R. M., Baudry, M., & Thompson, R. F. (1999, November 18). The amygdala modulates prefrontal cortex activity relative to conditioned fear. *Nature, 402,* 294–296.

Gewirtz, J. C., Falls, W. A., & Davis, M. (1997). Normal conditioned inhibition and extinction of freezing and fear-potentiated startle following electrolytic lesions of medial prefrontal cortex in rats. *Behavioral Neuroscience, 111,* 712–726.

Goosens, K. A., Hobin, J. A., & Maren, S. (2003). Auditory-evoked spike firing in the lateral amygdala and Pavlovian fear conditioning: Mnemonic code or fear bias? *Neuron, 40,* 1013–1022.

Goosens, K. A., Holt, W., & Maren, S. (2000). A role for amygdaloid, PKA and PKC in the acquisition of long-term conditional fear memories in rats. *Behavioural Brain Research, 114*(1–2), 145–152.

Goosens, K. A., & Maren, S. (2001). Contextual and auditory fear conditioning are mediated by the lateral, basal, and central amygdaloid nuclei in rats. *Learning and Memory, 8,* 148–155.

Goosens, K. A., & Maren, S. (2004). NMDA receptors are essential for the acquisition, but not expression, of conditional fear and associative spike firing in the lateral amygdala. *European Journal of Neuroscience, 20,* 537–548.

Hall, J., Thomas, K. L., & Everitt, B. J. (2000). Rapid and selective induction of BDNF expression in the hippocampus during contextual learning. *Nature Neuroscience, 3,* 533–535.

Hamann, S., Monarch, E. S., & Goldstein, F. C. (2002). Impaired fear conditioning in Alzheimer's disease. *Neuropsychologia, 40,* 1187–1195.

Helmstetter, F. J., & Bellgowan, P. S. (1994). Effects of muscimol applied to the basolateral amygdala on acquisition and expression of contextual fear conditioning in rats. *Behavioral Neuroscience, 108,* 1005–1009.

Helmstetter, F. J., & Landeira-Fernandez, J. (1990). Conditional hypoalgesia is attenuated by naltrexone applied to the periaqueductal gray. *Brain Research, 537,* 88–92.

Helmstetter, F. J., & Tershner, S. A. (1994). Lesions of the periaqueductal gray and rostral ventromedial medulla disrupt antinociceptive but not cardiovascular aversive conditional responses. *Journal of Neuroscience, 14,* 7099–7108.

Herry, C., Vouimba, R. M., & Garcia, R. (1999). Plasticity in the mediodorsal thalamo-prefrontal cortical transmission in behaving mice. *Journal of Neurophysiology, 82,* 2827–2832.

Hobin, J. A., Goosens, K. A., & Maren, S. (2003). Context-dependent neuronal activity in the lateral amygdala represents fear memories after extinction. *Journal of Neuroscience, 23,* 8410–8416.

Holland, P. C., & Gallagher, M. (2004). Amygdala-frontal interactions and reward expectancy. *Current Opinion in Neurobiology, 4,* 148–155.

Huang, Y. Y., & Kandel, E. R. (1998). Postsynaptic induction and PKA-dependent expression of LTP in the lateral amygdala. *Neuron, 21,* 169–178.

Huang, Y. Y., Martin, K. C., & Kandel, E. R. (2000). Both protein kinase A and mitogen-activated protein kinase are required in the amygdala for the macromolecular synthesis-dependent late phase of long-term potentiation. *Journal of Neuroscience, 20,* 6317–6325.

Huff, N. C., & Rudy, J. W. (2004). The amygdala modulates hippocampus-dependent context memory formation and stores cue-shock associations. *Neuroscience, 118,* 53–62.

Humeau, Y., & Lüthi, A. (2007). Dendritic calcium spikes induce bi-directional synaptic plasticity in the lateral amygdala. *Neuropharmacology, 52,* 234–243.

Humeau, Y., Shaban, H., Bissière, S., & Lüthi, A. (2003, December 18). Presynaptic induction of heterosynaptic associative plasticity in the mammalian brain. *Nature, 426,* 841–845.

Impey, S., Smith, D. M., Obrietan, K., Donahue, R., Wade, C., & Storm, D. R. (1998). Stimulation of cAMP response element (CRE)-mediated transcription during contextual learning. *Nature Neuroscience, 1,* 595–601.

Iwata, J., LeDoux, J. E., & Reis, D. J. (1986). Destruction of intrinsic neurons in the lateral hypothalamus disrupts the classical conditioning of autonomic but not behavioral emotional responses in the rat. *Behavioural Brain Research, 368,* 161–166.

Izquierdo, I., Quillfeldt, J. A., Zanatta, M. S., Quevedo, J., Schaeffer, E., Schmitz, P. K., et al. (1997). Sequential role of hippocampus and amygdala, entorhinal cortex and parietal cortex in formation and retrieval of memory for inhibitory avoidance in rats. *European Journal of Neuroscience, 9,* 786–793.

Jarrell, T. W., Gentile, C. G., Romanski, L. M., McCabe, P. M., & Schneiderman, N. (1987). Involvement of cortical and thalamic auditory regions in retention of differential bradycardia conditioning to acoustic conditioned stimuli in rabbits. *Brain Research, 412,* 285–294.

Josselyn, S. A., Shi, C., Carlezon, W. A., Jr., Neve, R. L., Nestler, E. J., & Davis, M. (2001). Long-term memory is facilitated by cAMP response-element binding protein overexpression in the amygdala. *Journal of Neuroscience, 21,* 2404–2412.

Kapp, B. S., Frysinger, R. C., Gallagher, M., & Haselton, J. R. (1979). Amygdala central nucleus lesions: Effect on heart rate conditioning in the rabbit. *Physiology and Behavior, 23,* 1109–1117.

Kida, S., Josselyn, S. A., de Oritz, S. P., Kogan, J. H., Chevere, I., Masushige, S., et al. (2002). CREB required for the stability of new and reactivated fear memories. *Nature Neuroscience, 5,* 348–355.

Killcross, S., Robbins, T. W., & Everitt, B. J. (1997, July 24). Different types of fear-conditioned behaviour mediated by separate nuclei within amygdala. *Nature, 388,* 377–380.

Kim, J. J., DeCola, J. P., Landeira-Fernandez, J., & Fanselow, M. S. (1991). N-Methy-D-Aspartate receptor antagonist APV blocks acquisition but not expression of fear conditioning. *Behavioral Neuroscience, 105,* 126–133.

Kim, J. J., & Fanselow, M. S. (1992, May 1). Modality-specific retrograde amnesia of fear. *Science, 256,* 675–677.

Kim, J. J., Rison, R. A., & Fanselow, M. S. (1993). Effects of amygdala, hippocampus, and periaqueductal gray lesions on short- and long-term contextual fear. *Behavioral Neuroscience, 107,* 1–6.

Knight, D. C., Cheng, D. T., Smith, C. N., Stein, E. A., & Helmstetter, F. J. (2004). Neural substrates mediating human delay and trace fear conditioning. *Journal of Neuroscience, 24,* 218–228.

LaBar, K. S., Gatenby, J. C., Gore, J. C., LeDoux, J. E., & Phelps, E. A. (1998). Human amygdala activation during conditioned fear acquisition and extinction: A mixed-trial fMRI study. *Neuron, 20,* 937–945.

LaBar, K. S., LeDoux, J. E., Spencer, D. D., & Phelps, E. A. (1995). Impaired fear conditioning following unilateral temporal lobectomy in humans. *Journal of Neuroscience, 15,* 6846–6855.

LaBar, K. S., & Phelps, E. A. (2005). Reinstatement of conditioned fear in humans is context dependent and impaired in amnesia. *Behavioral Neuroscience, 119,* 677–686.

Lebron, K., Milad, M. R., & Quirk, G. J. (2004). Delayed recall of fear extinction in rats with lesions of ventral medial prefrontal cortex. *Learning and Memory, 11,* 544–548.

LeDoux, J. E. (1996). *The emotional brain.* New York: Simon & Schuster.

LeDoux, J. E. (2000). Emotion circuits in the brain. *Annual Review of Neuroscience, 23,* 155–184.

LeDoux, J. E., Cicchetti, P., Xagoraris, A., & Romanski, L. M. (1990). The lateral amygdaloid nucleus: Sensory interface of the amygdala in fear conditioning. *Journal of Neuroscience, 10,* 1062–1069.

LeDoux, J. E., & Farb, C. R. (1991). Neurons of the acoustic thalamus that project to the amygdala contain glutamate. *Neuroscience Letters, 134,* 145–149.

LeDoux, J. E., Farb, C. R., & Romanski, L. M. (1991). Overlapping projections to the amygdala and striatum from auditory processing areas of the thalamus and cortex. *Neuroscience Letters, 134,* 139–144.

LeDoux, J. E., Iwata, J., Cicchetti, P., & Reis, D. J. (1988). Different projections of the central amygdaloid nucleus mediate autonomic and behavioral correlates of conditioned fear. *Journal of Neuroscience, 8,* 2517–2529.

LeDoux, J. E., Iwata, J., Pearl, D., & Reis, D. J. (1986). Disruption of auditory but not visual learning by destruction of intrinsic neurons in the rat medial geniculate body. *Behavioural Brain Research, 371,* 395–399.

LeDoux, J. E., Ruggerio, D. A., & Reis, D. J. (1985). Projections to the subcortical forebrain from anatomically defined regions of the medial geniculate body in the rat. *Journal of Comparative Neurology, 242,* 182–213.

LeDoux, J. E., Sakaguchi, A., & Reis, D. J. (1984). Subcortical efferent projections of the medial geniculate nucleus mediate emotional responses conditioned by acoustic stimuli. *Journal of Neuroscience, 4,* 683–698.

Li, X. F., Stutzmann, G. E., & LeDoux, J. E. (1996). Convergent but temporally separated inputs to lateral amygdala neurons from the auditory thalamus and auditory cortex use different postsynaptic receptors: In vivo intracellular and extracellular recordings in fear conditioning pathways. *Learning and Memory, 3*(2/3), 229–242.

Lindquist, D. H., & Brown, T. H. (2004). Temporal encoding in fear conditioning revealed through associative reflex facilitation. *Behavioral Neuroscience, 118,* 395–402.

Lu, K. T., Walker, D. L., & Davis, M. (2001). Mitogen-activated protein kinase cascade in the basolateral nucleus of amygdala is involved in extinction of fear-potentiated startle. *Journal of Neuroscience, 21,* RC162.

Maren, S. (1998). Overtraining does not mitigate contextual fear conditioning deficits produced by neurotoxic lesions of the basolateral amygdala. *Journal of Neuroscience, 18,* 3088–3097.

Maren, S. (1999). Long-term potentiation in the amygdala: A mechanism for emotional learning and memory. *Trends in Neuroscience, 22,* 561–567.

Maren, S. (2000). Auditory fear conditioning increases CS-elicited spike firing in lateral amygdala neurons even after extensive overtraining. *European Journal of Neuroscience, 12,* 4047–4054.

Maren, S., Aharonov, G., & Fanselow, M. S. (1997). Neurotoxic lesions of the dorsal hippocampus and Pavlovian fear conditioning in rats. *Behavioural Brain Research, 88,* 261–274.

Maren, S., & Quirk, G. J. (2004). Neuronal signaling of fear memory. *Nature Reviews: Neuroscience, 5,* 844–852.

McDonald, A. J. (1998). Cortical pathways to the mammalian amygdala. *Progress in Neurobiology, 55,* 257–332.

McGaugh, J. L. (2000, January 14). Memory: A century of consolidation. *Science, 287,* 248–251.

McGaugh, J. L., Introini-Collison, I. B., Cahill, L. F., Castellano, C., Dalmaz, C., Parent, M. B., et al. (1993). Neuromodulatory systems and memory storage: Role of the amygdala. *Behavioural Brain Research, 58,* 81–90.

McKernan, M. G., & Shinnick-Gallagher, P. (1997, December 11). Fear conditioning induces a lasting potentiation of synaptic currents in vitro. *Nature, 390,* 607–611.

Medina, J. F., Repa, J. C., & LeDoux, J. E. (2002). Parallels between cerebellum- and amygdala-dependent conditioning. *Nature Reviews: Neuroscience, 3,* 122–131.

Milad, M. R., & Quirk, G. J. (2002, November 7). Neurons in medial prefrontal cortex signal memory for fear extinction. *Nature, 420,* 70–74.

Milner, B., Squire, L. R., & Kandel, E. R. (1998). Cognitive neuroscience and the study of memory. *Neuron, 20,* 445–468.

Miserendino, M. J. D., Sananes, C. B., Melia, K. R., & Davis, M. (1990, June 21). Blocking of acquisition but not expression of conditioned fear-potentiated startle by NMDA antagonists in the amygdala. *Nature, 345,* 716–718.

Moita, M. A., Rosis, S., Zhou, Y., LeDoux, J. E., & Blair, H. T. (2003). Hippocampal place cells acquire location-specific responses to the conditioned stimulus during auditory fear conditioning. *Neuron, 37,* 485–497.

Morgan, M. A., & LeDoux, J. E. (1995). Differential contribution of dorsal and ventral medial prefrontal cortex to the acquisition and extinction of conditioned fear in rats. *Behavioral Neuroscience, 109,* 681–688.

Morgan, M. A., Romanski, L. M., & LeDoux, J. E. (1993). Extinction of emotional learning: Contribution of medial prefrontal cortex. *Neuroscience Letters, 163,* 109–113.

Morgan, M. A., Schulkin, J., & LeDoux, J. E. (2003). Ventral medial prefrontal cortex and emotional perseveration: The memory for prior extinction training. *Behavioural Brain Research, 146*(1/2), 121–130.

Morris, J. S., Ohman, A., & Dolan, R. J. (1999). A subcortical pathway to the right amygdala mediating "unseen" fear. *Proceedings of the National Academy of Sciences, USA, 96,* 1680–1685.

Muller, J., Corodimas, K. P., Fridel, Z., & LeDoux, J. E. (1997). Functional inactivation of the lateral and basal nuclei of the amygdala by muscimol infusion prevents fear conditioning to an explicit conditioned stimulus and to contextual stimuli. *Behavioral Neuroscience, 111,* 683–691.

Nader, K., Majidishad, P., Amorapanth, P., & LeDoux, J. E. (2001). Damage to the lateral and central, but not other, amygdaloid nuclei prevents the acquisition of auditory fear conditioning. *Learning and Memory, 8,* 156–163.

Nader, K., Schafe, G. E., & LeDoux, J. E. (2000, August 17). Fear memories require protein synthesis in the amygdala for reconsolidation after retrieval. *Nature, 406,* 722–726.

Olsson, A., & Phelps, E. A. (2004). Learned fear of "unseen" faces after Pavlovian, observational, and instructed fear. *Psychological Sciences, 15,* 822–828.

Olsson, A., & Phelps, E. A. (2007). Social learning of fear. *Nature Neuroscience, 10,* 1095–1102.

Paré, D., Quirk, G. J., & LeDoux, J. E. (2004). New vistas on amygdala networks in conditioned fear. *Journal of Neurophysiology, 92,* 1–9.

Paré, D., Smith, Y., & Paré, J. F. (1995). Intra-amygdaloid projections of the basolateral and basomedial nuclei in the cat: Phaseolus vulgaris-leucoagglutinin anterograde tracing at the light and electron microscopic level. *Neuroscience, 69,* 567–583.

Pavlov, I. P. (1927). *Conditioned reflexes.* London: Oxford University Press.

Phelps, E. A., Delgado, M. R., Nearing, K. I., & LeDoux, J. E. (2004). Extinction learning in humans: Role of the amygdala and vmPFC. *Neuron, 43,* 897–905.

Phelps, E. A., O'Connor, K. J., Gatenby, J. C., Gore, J. C., Grillon, C., & Davis, M. (2001). Activation of the left amygdala to a cognitive representation of fear. *Nature Neuroscience, 4,* 437–441.

Phillips, R. G., & LeDoux, J. E. (1992). Differential contribution of amygdala and hippocampus to cued and contextual fear conditioning. *Behavioral Neuroscience, 106,* 274–285.

Pitkänen, A., Savander, V., & LeDoux, J. E. (1997). Organization of intra-amygdaloid circuitries in the rat: An emerging framework for understanding functions of the amygdala. *Trends in Neuroscience, 20,* 517–523.

Quinn, J. J., Wied, H. M., Ma, Q. D., Tinsley, M. R., & Fanselow, M. S. (2008). Dorsal hippocampus involvement in delay fear conditioning depends upon the strength of the tone-footshock association. *Hippocampus, 18,* 640–654.

Quirk, G. J., Armony, J. L., & LeDoux, J. E. (1997). Fear conditioning enhances different temporal components of tone-evoked spike trains in auditory cortex and lateral amygdala. *Neuron, 19,* 613–624.

Quirk, G. J., Armony, J. L., Repa, J. C., Li, X.-F., & LeDoux, J. E. (1997). Emotional memory: A search for sites of plasticity. *Cold Spring Harbor Symposia on Biology, 61,* 247–257.

Quirk, G. J., & Mueller, D. (2008). Neural mechanisms of extinction learning and retrieval. *Neuropsychopharmacology, 33,* 56–72.

Quirk, G. J., Repa, C., & LeDoux, J. E. (1995). Fear conditioning enhances short-latency auditory responses of lateral amygdala neurons: Parallel recordings in the freely behaving rat. *Neuron, 15,* 1029–1039.

Quirk, G. J., Russo, G. K., Barron, J. L., & Lebron, K. (2000). The role of ventromedial prefrontal cortex in the recovery of extinguished fear. *Journal of Neuroscience, 20,* 6225–6231.

Radwanska, K., Nikolaev, E., Knapska, E., & Kaczmarek, L. (2002). Differential response of two subdivisions of lateral amygdala to aversive conditioning as revealed by c-Fos and P-ERK mapping. *NeuroReport, 13,* 2241–2246.

Rampon, C., Tang, Y. P., Goodhouse, J., Shimizu, E., Kyin, M., & Tsien, J. Z. (2000). Enrichment induces structural changes and recovery from nonspatial memory deficits in CA1 NMDAR1-knockout mice. *Nature Neuroscience, 3,* 238–244.

Repa, J. C., Muller, J., Apergis, J., Desrochers, T. M., Zhou, Y., & LeDoux, J. E. (2001). Two different lateral amygdala cell populations contribute to the initiation and storage of memory. *Nature Neuroscience, 4,* 724–731.

Rescorla, R. A. (1968). Probability of shock in the presence and absence of CS in fear conditioning. *Journal of Comparative Physiological Psychology, 66,* 1–5.

Rescorla, R. A., & Heth, C. D. (1975). Reinstatement of fear to an extinguished conditioned stimulus. *Journal of Experimental Psychology: Animal Behavior Processes, 1*(1), 88–96.

Ressler, K. J., Rothbaum, B. O., Tannenbaum, L., Anderson, P., Graap, K., Zimand, E., et al. (2002). Cognitive enhancers as adjuncts to psychotherapy: Use of D-cycloserine in phobic individuals to facilitate extinction of fear. *Archives of General Psychiatry, 61,* 1136–1144.

Robbins, T. W., Cador, M., Taylor, J. R., & Everitt, B. J. (1989). Limbic-striatal interactions in reward-related processes. *Neuroscience Biobehavioral Reviews, 13,* 155–162.

Rodrigues, S. M., Schafe, G. E., & LeDoux, J. E. (2001). Intraamygdala blockade of the NR2B subunit of the NMDA receptor disrupts the acquisition but not the expression of fear conditioning. *Journal of Neuroscience, 21,* 6889–6896.

Rodrigues, S. M., Schafe, G. E., & LeDoux, J. E. (2004). Molecular mechanisms underlying emotional learning and memory in the amygdala. *Neuron, 44,* 75–91.

Rodriguez, B. I., Craske, M. G., Mineka, S., & Hladek, D. (1999). Context-specificity of relapse: Effects of therapist and environmental context on return of fear. *Behaviour Research and Therapy, 37,* 845–862.

Rogan, M., & LeDoux, J. E. (1995). LTP is accompanied by commensurate enhancement of auditory-evoked responses in a fear conditioning circuit. *Neuron, 15,* 127–136.

Rogan, M., Staubli, U., & LeDoux, J. E. (1997, December 11). Fear conditioning induces associative long-term potentiation in the amygdala. *Nature, 390,* 604–607.

Rolls, E. T., Hornak, J., Wade, D., & McGrath, J. (1994). Emotion-related learning in patients with social and emotional changes associated with frontal lobe damage. *Journal of Neurology, Neurosurgery, and Psychiatry, 57,* 1518–1524.

Romanski, L. M., Clugnet, M. C., Bordi, F., & LeDoux, J. E. (1993). Somatosensory and auditory convergence in the lateral nucleus of the amygdala. *Behavioral Neuroscience, 107,* 444–450.

Romanski, L. M., & LeDoux, J. E. (1992a). Bilateral destruction of neo-cortical and perirhinal projection targets of the acoustic thalamus does not disrupt auditory fear conditioning. *Neuroscience Letters, 142,* 228–232.

Romanski, L. M., & LeDoux, J. E. (1992b). Equipotentiality of thalamo-amygdala and thalamo-cortico-amygdala circuits in auditory fear conditioning. *Journal of Neuroscience, 12,* 4501–4509.

Romanski, L. M., & LeDoux, J. E. (1993). Information cascade from primary auditory cortex to the amygdala: Corticocortical and corticoamygdaloid projections of temporal cortex in the rat. *Cerebral Cortex, 3,* 515–532.

Roozendaal, B., Barsegyan, A., & Lee, S. (2008). Adrenal stress hormones, amygdala activation, and memory for emotionally arousing experiences. *Progressive Behavioural Brain Research, 167,* 79–97.

Roozendaal, B., Koolhaas, J. M., & Bohus, B. (1991). Attenuated cardiovascular, neuroendocrine, and behavioral responses after a single footshock in central amygdaloid lesioned male rats. *Physiology and Behavior, 50,* 771–775.

Roozendaal, B., Okuda, S., de Quervain, D. J., & McGaugh, J. L. (2006). Glucocorticoids interact with emotion-induced noradrenergic activation in influencing different memory functions. *Neuroscience, 138,* 901–910.

Rudy, J. W., Huff, N. C., & Matus-Amat, P. (2004). Understanding contextual fear conditioning: Insights from a two-process model. *Neuroscience and Biobehavioral Reviews, 28,* 675–685.

Sara, S. J. (2000). Retrieval and reconsolidation: Toward a neurobiology of remembering. *Learning and Memory, 7,* 73–84.

Schafe, G. E., Atkins, C. M., Swank, M. W., Bauer, E. P., Sweatt, J. D., & LeDoux, J. E. (2000). Activation of ERK/MAP kinase in the amygdala is required for memory consolidation of Pavlovian fear conditioning. *Journal of Neuroscience, 20,* 8177–8187.

Schafe, G. E., Bauer, E. P., Rosis, S., Farb, C. R., Rodrigues, S. M., & LeDoux, J. E. (2005). Memory consolidation of Pavlovian fear conditioning requires nitric oxide signaling in the lateral amygdala. *European Journal of Neuroscience, 22,* 201–211.

Schafe, G. E., & LeDoux, J. E. (2000). Memory consolidation of auditory Pavlovian fear conditioning requires protein synthesis and protein kinase A in the amygdala. *Journal of Neuroscience, 20,* RC96.

Sierra-Mercado, D., Jr., Corcoran, K. A., Lebron-Milad, K., & Quirk, G. J. (2006). Inactivation of the ventromedial prefrontal cortex reduces expression of conditioned fear and impairs subsequent recall of extinction. *European Journal of Neuroscience, 24,* 1751–1758.

Smith, O. A., Astley, C. A., Devito, J. L., Stein, J. M., & Walsh, R. E. (1980). Functional analysis of hypothalamic control of the cardiovascular responses accompanying emotional behavior. *Federation Proceedings, 39,* 2487–2494.

Sotres-Bayon, F., Bush, D. E. A., & LeDoux, J. E. (2004). Emotional perseveration: An update on prefrontal-amygdala interactions in fear extinction. *Learning and Memory, 11,* 525–535.

Sotres-Bayon, F., Bush, D. E. A., & LeDoux, J. E. (2007). Acquisition of fear extinction requires activation of NR2B-containing NMDA receptors in the lateral amygdala. *Neuropsychopharmacology, 32,* 1929–1940.

Stiedl, O., Birkenfeld, K., Palve, M., & Spiess, J. (2000). Impairment of conditioned contextual fear of C57BL/6J mice by intracerebral injections of the NMDA receptor antagonist APV. *Behavioural Brain Research, 116,* 157–168.

Sullivan, G. M., Apergis, J., Bush, D. E. A., Johnson, L. R., Hou, M., & LeDoux, J. E. (2004). Lesions in the bed nucleus of the stria terminalis disrupt corticosterone and freezing responses elicited by a contextual but not by a specific cue-conditioned fear stimulus. *Neuroscience, 128,* 7–14.

Walker, D. L., Paschall, G. Y., & Davis, M. (2005). Glutamate receptor antagonist infusions into the basolateral and medial amygdala reveal differential contributions to olfactory vs. context fear conditioning and expression. *Learning and Memory, 12,* 120–129.

Walker, D. L., Ressler, K. J., Lu, K.-T., & Davis, M. (2002). Facilitation of conditioned fear extinction by systemic administration or intra-amygdala infusions of D-cycloserine as assessed with fear-potentiated startle in rats. *Journal of Neuroscience, 22,* 2343–2351.

Weisskopf, M. G., Bauer, E. P., & LeDoux, J. E. (1999). L-type voltage-gated calcium channels mediate NMDA-independent associative long-term potentiation at thalamic input synapses to the amygdala. *Journal of Neuroscience, 19,* 10512–10519.

Weisskopf, M. G., & LeDoux, J. E. (1999). Distinct populations of NMDA receptors at subcortical and cortical inputs to principal cells of the lateral amygdala. *Journal of Neurophysiology, 81,* 930–934.

Wilensky, A. E., Schafe, G. E., & LeDoux, J. E. (2000). The amygdala modulates memory consolidation of fear-motivated inhibitory avoidance learning but not classical fear conditioning. *Journal of Neuroscience, 20,* 7059–7066.

Young, S. L., Bohenek, D. L., & Fanselow, M. S. (1994). NMDA processes mediate anterograde amnesia of contextual fear conditioning induced by hippocampal damage: Immunization against amnesia by context preexposure. *Behavioral Neuroscience, 108,* 19–29.

Chapter 40

Neural Basis of Pleasure and Reward

CLIFFORD M. KNAPP AND CONAN KORNETSKY

Rewarding stimuli all share the properties of engendering approach behaviors and of being able to act as unconditioned stimuli. Natural rewards include food, water, and copulation, all of which are closely linked to the survival of a species. Food and water will serve as motivators of animals to expend energy in tasks such as lever pressing. Similar behaviors are produced by certain artificial rewarding stimuli that include pharmacological agents such as cocaine and heroin and the electrical stimulation of select brain areas.

Human experience indicates that interaction with rewarding stimuli is frequently associated with the experiencing of both short-lived pleasurable sensations and longer lasting periods of elevated mood. We can infer from the behavior of animals that they may also experience the hedonic effects of rewarding stimuli. This inference is strengthened by evidence that many of the systems that have been implicated in the experience of pleasure in humans are similar to their counterparts in other mammals. One example of this arises from the finding that the electrical stimulation of what were characterized as "septal" areas in humans in early experiments produce reports of pleasurable responses (Bishop, Elder, & Heath, 1963), while the delivery of brain stimulation to comparable regions in the rat is rewarding enough to maintain sustained responding for this stimulation (J. Olds & Milner, 1954). What had been called septal areas have now been identified as regions linked to the functioning of mesocorticolimbic systems. These systems have been implicated in the regulation of reward-related behavior.

Within these mesocorticolimbic systems the ventral tegmental area (VTA) sends neuronal projections to other mesocorticolimbic structures, most notably the nucleus accumbens and the prefrontal cortical (see Figure 40.1; Emson & Koob, 1978; Hasue & Shammah-Lagnado, 2002). These projections are from cells that contain the neurotransmitter dopamine. When released from these cells, dopamine may interact with five types of receptors,

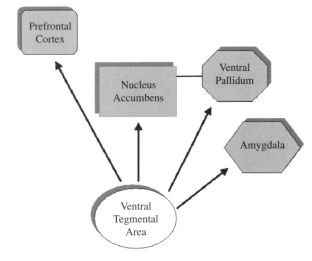

Figure 40.1 Simplified schematic of projections of dopaminergic neurons (arrows) from the ventral tegmental area to target structures within the mesocorticolimbic system.

which are divided into two basic classes. One class includes the dopamine D_1-like receptors (the D_1 and D_5 receptors), and the second consists of D_2-like receptors (the D_2, D_3, and D_4 receptors).

Several approaches are used to measure the hedonic effects of rewarding stimuli in human subjects. Such measures have been extensively developed in the field of drug abuse studies. Subjects may be asked to place a mark on visual analogue scales (i.e., Likert scales) to indicate to what degree they like a drug or experience a high after receiving a drug (Fischman & Foltin, 1991). Questionnaires have been developed based on the responses of drug users to series of questions that allow for the measure of different aspects of the subjective effects of drugs. The Addiction Research Center Inventory is one such questionnaire that allows rating of euphoric responses to drugs using the Morphine Benzedrine Group scale (ARCI-MBG) of the inventory (Haertzen, Hill, & Belleville, 1963).

The likelihood that a drug will be abused is related to the ability of the drug to produce elevations in subjective scales of drug liking and euphoric effects as assessed using scales such as the ARCI-MBG. All of the commonly abused drugs, including amphetamine, heroin, and morphine, produce such elevations in recovering addict populations (Preston & Jasinski, 1991). Although these findings indicate that the hedonic effects of abused drugs play a role in the development of drug dependence, the determination of the precise role of these effects in this process remains a challenge.

The study of the hedonic effects of stimuli in animals requires less direct approaches than are used for human subjects because hedonic value of any stimulus in an animal is based on inference. Measuring response rates for rewards delivered under schedules of reinforcement has been one approach to assessing the extent of reward produced by these stimuli. The progressive ratio schedule, which allows the determination of a break point, that is, the point of maximal response to obtain a reward (Roberts, Loh, & Vickers, 1989), is an example of such a schedule. Rates of response remain an indirect measure of reward value because responding may be driven in some cases by negative reinforcement, such as withdrawal symptoms, or may be depressed by conditions that involve impairment of motor function. In the conditioned place-preference approach, the amount of time that an animal will spend in an area that has been paired with a rewarding stimulus is regarded as another measure of the reward produced by a stimulus. Several factors, however, other than the degree of reward produced by a stimulus can influence conditioned place preference. These include factors that regulate learning, memory, and responsiveness to conditioned cues.

Measures of level of currents that will maintain responding for brain stimulation offer a more direct means of examining the effects of rewarding stimuli on brain reward systems than do other behavioral measures. This is because responding for brain stimulation reward (BSR) involves responses to direct activation of the brain's reward systems. Sensitivity to brain stimulation reward, as reflected in the lowering of current thresholds for brain stimulation reward responding, is increased by a variety of commonly abused drugs, such as alcohol, cocaine, and morphine (Kornetsky, 2004), that have hedonic effects in humans. An example of the effects of three of these drugs—heroin, methamphetamine, and nicotine—on brain stimulation reward thresholds is shown in Figure 40.2.

Sensitivity to rewarding brain stimulation is measured by determining thresholds for some level of responding for this stimulation. One method of determining thresholds involves determining the current intensity or frequency at which animals will exhibit a half-maximal response for

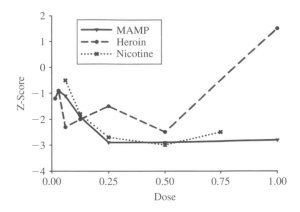

Figure 40.2   The effects of heroin, methamphetamine (MAMP), and nicotine on brain stimulation reward thresholds as a function of dose.

Note: Current thresholds, determined by the rate-independent method, are expressed as standardized z-scores using performance on saline as the baseline condition. Consequently, a value of zero represents the threshold obtained when saline was administered. A z-score of 2 or greater represents a significant change from the saline condition, with $p < .05$. Note that at the highest dose tested heroin raised the reward threshold, indicating what is often a common U-shaped dose-response.

rewarding stimulation. An alternative method of determining brain stimulation thresholds involves the use of classic psychophysics to generate a rate-independent threshold (Kornetsky, 2004). This approach involves the presentation of different current intensities during discrete trials; the threshold is taken to be the current intensity at which responding is maintained 50% of the time for a certain level of stimulation. The rate-independent method for assessing BSR thresholds is less influenced by the effects of drugs on motor behaviors and thus in some circumstances may more accurately reflect the effects of drugs on reward systems than do rate-dependent methods (Markou & Koob, 1992).

Fundamental questions remain unanswered with respect to the neural basis of the hedonic effects of rewarding stimuli. It is not clear to what extent there is overlap in the neuronal networks that produce the hedonic effects associated with the wide variety of types of rewarding stimuli. For example, how similar are the neuronal networks that mediate the hedonic effects of natural rewards such as food compared to those of drugs, or those involved in the hedonic actions of psychomotor stimulants such as cocaine compared to other classes of drugs such as the opioids? Studies using multiple electrodes to detect the firing of individual neurons in the nucleus accumbens, a central structure in the mesolimbic system, indicate that distinct neuron populations encode information about cocaine-related reward compared to natural rewards such as food and water (Carelli & Wondolowski, 2003; Deadwyler,

Hayashizaki, Cheer, & Hampson, 2004). Distinct patterns of discharge have been observed in the nucleus accumbens for the time preceding response for a reward and the period after the reward delivery (Deadwyler et al., 2004). The actual response of the brain to rewarding stimuli most likely involves extensively distributed networks of neurons that consist of, at least, thousands of cells. It is not clear, then, that studies in which the activity of only a few cells is monitored can provide a comprehensive picture of the changes in neuronal activity that occur following exposure to rewarding stimuli.

One problem that makes it difficult to identify the neuronal networks involved in the production of the hedonic effects of rewarding stimuli is that many rewarding stimuli have a diverse range of actions other than activation of reward processes. Drugs such as cocaine, for example, in addition to their rewarding effects, can produce anxiety, enhance locomotor activity, and increase arousal levels. One approach to dealing with this problem is to examine the effects of brain stimulation on changes in regional brain activity. The advantages of this approach are, first, that brain stimulation reward can be delivered to discrete brain regions and, second, that the stimulation is presumed to activate regions directly involved in the production of rewarding effects. Changes in neuronal activity result in alterations of glucose metabolism that can be monitored using 2-[^{14}C]deoxyglucose autoradiography. This technique offers the advantage of allowing identification of changes of neuronal activity throughout the brain. Rewarding brain stimulation delivered to the medial forebrain bundle at the level of the lateral hypothalamus resulted in increases in metabolic activity in several discrete brain regions (Porrino, Huston-Lyons, Bain, Sokoloff, & Kornetsky, 1990). These included the nucleus accumbens, olfactory tubercle, lateral septum, medial prefrontal cortex, and VTA. The olfactory tubercle appears to be functionally linked to the nucleus accumbens (Ikemoto, 2007). Overall, then, these findings implicate the mesocorticolimbic systems as being activated by rewarding brain stimulation.

One limitation of the 2-[^{14}C]deoxyglucose method is that it does not provide spatial resolution down to the cellular level. This limitation is not associated with techniques in which the product of the immediate early gene c-Fos is measured using immunohistochemical techniques. Increased Fos levels are indicative of enhanced neuronal activity. The number of Fos-positive cells has been found to be greater in several brain regions in animals receiving brain stimulation reward delivered to the medial forebrain bundle, the ventral pallidum, and the medial prefrontal cortex. Fos-like immunoreactivity is increased by brain stimulation delivered to the medial forebrain bundle in many of the structures that were also found to be increased

in regional glucose metabolism studies. These structures included the nucleus accumbens shell, medial prefrontal cortex, VTA, and lateral septum (Hunt & McGregor, 1998). Other structures in which Fos-like immunoreactivity increased were the locus coeruleus, bed nucleus of the stria terminalis, and central nucleus of the amygdala. The ventral pallidum, which receives projections from the nucleus accumbens, will also support responding for brain stimulation reward (Panagis et al., 1997). Self-stimulation of this structure has been found to produce elevations in Fos-like immunoreactivity in the medial prefrontal cortex, nucleus accumbens, and posterior lateral hypothalamus (Panagis et al., 1997). A slightly different pattern of increases in Fos-like immunoreactivity has been seen as a consequence of self-stimulation of the medial prefrontal cortex. These increases were found to be located in the prelimbic cortex, cingulate cortex, nucleus accumbens, lateral hypothalamus, amygdala, and anterior portion of the VTA (Arvanitogiannis, Tzschentke, Riscaldino, Wise, & Shizgal, 2000).

An alternative approach to establishing which brain regions are involved in the production of rewarding effects is to identify discrete regions of the brain into which animals will micro-inject pharmacologically active agents. In an early study, for example, it was shown that rats will self-administer heroin directly into the nucleus accumbens, establishing this structure as important in the production of the rewarding effects of μ-opioid receptor agonists (M. E. Olds, 1982). Another example of the infusion mapping approach includes findings that rats also will self-administer amphetamine into the nucleus accumbens (McBride, Murphy, & Ikemoto, 1999), particularly the medial shell of this structure (Ikemoto, Qin, & Liu, 2005). Amphetamine administration by rats into the nucleus accumbens is antagonized by the concurrent infusion of either dopamine D_1 or D_2 receptor antagonists, suggesting that dopamine receptors mediate the rewarding effects of amphetamine. Rats will also self-administer high concentrations of cocaine into the shell of the nucleus accumbens (Ikemoto et al., 2005). The ventral olfactory tubercle will also support cocaine self-administration (Ikemoto, 2003). Both cocaine and morphine increase the rate of glucose utilization in the olfactory tubercle (Kornetsky, Huston-Lyons, & Porrino, 1991) in rats responding for brain stimulation reward. This suggests that structure may play an important role in reward processes, at least in rodents.

Functional magnetic resonance imaging (fMRI) is another approach used to identify areas in human subjects that may play a role in mediating the hedonic effects of rewarding stimuli. Functional MRI can provide information concerning changes in regional blood flow in the brain that may reflect changes in neuronal activity. For example, the presentation of pleasant images of erotic and romantic interactions between couples were found to produce increases in activity in the nucleus accumbens and medial prefrontal cortex of healthy subjects (Sabatinelli, Bradley, Lang, Costa, & Versace, 2007). In contrast, unpleasant but arousing and neutral pictures failed to produce this effect. When a single dose (0.6 mg/kg) of cocaine was administered to cocaine-dependent subjects, fMRI signals increased in the nucleus accumbens, putamen, ventral tegmentum, cingulate prefrontal, and temporal cortices, and several other regions (Breiter et al., 1997). Subjects in this study first experienced sensations of "rush" and "high" that were then followed by feeling of "craving" and "low." During the repeated self-administration of cocaine by subjects dependent on this drug, self-ratings on the intensity of the drug-induced high were found to correlate with decreased activity in several brain regions, including the nucleus accumbens, frontal cortical areas, and the anterior cingulate (Risinger et al., 2005). These subjects received doses of cocaine of 20 mg/70 kg up to six times. Functional MRI signals were found to be increased in smokers following the intravenous injection of nicotine in the nucleus accumbens, amygdala, cingulate, and frontal lobes (Stein et al., 1998). These changes occurred in association with feelings of "rush" and "high" and a sustained feeling of pleasantness. When administered to healthy volunteers, morphine produced a different pattern of changes in regional brain activity (Becerra, Harter, Gonzalez, & Borsook, 2006). A low dose of morphine that produced mild euphoria in subjects increased activity in the nucleus accumbens, the hippocampus, the hypothalamus, the orbitofrontal cortex, and the putamen. Morphine administration also resulted in the decreased activation of several cortical structures, including the dorso-lateral prefrontal cortex, the temporal lobe, and the anterior cingulate.

Overall, the results of these mapping approaches demonstrate that mesocorticolimbic structures play a key role in the processing of rewarding stimuli. While dopamine in the mesocorticolimbic systems has been regarded as a key neurotransmitter in the processing of rewarding stimuli, clearly many other systems are involved because activity within brain neuronal networks is always the product of the interaction of a wide variety of neurotransmitters. In addition to dopaminergic receptors, cholinergic, GABAergic, glutamatergic, opioid, and serotonergic systems have been implicated in regulating the actions of rewarding stimuli. In this chapter we consider the putative roles of these receptor systems in regulating reward processes. Much of our emphasis is on the actions of brain stimulation reward and drugs of abuse on brain receptor systems. Other reviews are available that have a greater focus on the neural basis of the rewarding effects of food (see, e.g., Kelley, Baldo, Pratt, & Will, 2005; Rolls, 2006).

MESOLIMBIC DOPAMINE AND REWARD

The nucleus accumbens may play a key role in the processing of rewarding stimuli. This structure receives information concerning rewarding stimuli from both cortical and limbic structures and appears to integrate this information to regulate reward-related behaviors. The nucleus accumbens receives dense dopaminergic innervation from VTA afferents (see Figure 40.1). It also receives glutamatergic afferents that originate from the prefrontal cortex, amygdala, hippocampus, and thalamus (see Figure 40.3; Groenewegen, Wright, Beijer, & Voorn, 1999). Dopaminergic and glutamatergic systems interact to regulate activity within the nucleus accumbens by influencing a network of medium spiny neurons located in this structure (West, Floresco, Charara, Rosenkranz, & Grace, 2003). This network processes incoming information and sends out afferent projections that release the inhibitory neurotransmitter gamma amino butyric acid (GABA) to the ventral pallidum and the VTA. The ventral pallidum provides feedback from the nucleus accumbens to cortical areas via the mediodorsal thalamus (O'Donnell, Lavín, Enquist, Grace, & Card, 1997).

Dopaminergic neurons in the mesocorticolimbic systems may serve a number of functions. One may involve the processing of reward-predictive signals. Midbrain dopaminergic neurons exhibit phasic (i.e., short-duration) activation following the presentation of stimuli that predict the availability of a reward (Schultz, 2007). A second possible and related function of dopaminergic neurons is to elicit drug-seeking behavior. Animals trained to self-administer drugs will stop responding if saline is substituted for the drug. Exposure to a priming dose of the drug will reinstate responding. Cocaine actions result, in part, from the blockade of the reuptake of dopamine, norepinephrine, and serotonin by binding to monoamine transporter proteins. Evidence of the involvement of dopamine in reinstatement of responding for cocaine

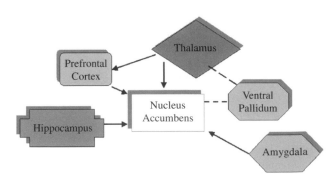

Figure 40.3 Simplified schematic of glutamatergic neuron projections to the nucleus accumbens from cortical and limbic structures (arrows).

Note: Dashed lines indicate nonglutamatergic connections between structures.

includes the finding that responding on a lever previously associated with cocaine administration is reinstated by the administration of dopamine transporter (DAT) but not norepinephrine transporter (NET) or serotonin transporter (SERT) protein inhibitors (Schmidt & Pierce, 2006). Similar effects are produced by the infusion of selective dopamine D_1 and D_2 receptor agonists into the shell of the nucleus accumbens (Schmidt, Anderson, & Pierce, 2006).

A third function of mesocorticolimbic dopaminergic neurons may be the modulation and possibly the direct activation of reward systems resulting in the production of hedonic effects. An increase in the extracellular concentrations of dopamine in the nucleus accumbens has been observed following exposure to a wide variety of rewarding stimuli (see Table 40.1). These elevations occur over time spans of minutes to tens of minutes that may produce changes in the tonic activity of neurons in the accumbens. The administration of amphetamine, cocaine, and morphine has been found to produce more pronounced increases in dopamine extracellular concentrations in the shell as compared to the core of the nucleus accumbens (Pontieri, Tanda, & Di Chiara, 1995). The chronic self-administration of cocaine (Lecca, Cacciapaglia, Valentini, Acquas, & Di Chiara, 2007), heroin (Lecca, Valentini, Cacciapaglia, Acquas, & Di Chiara, 2007), or nicotine (Lecca et al., 2006) preferentially increased extracellular dopamine levels in the shell as compared to the core of the nucleus accumbens.

Clinical studies implicate drug-induced elevation in ventral striatal dopamine levels in the production of drug-related hedonic effects. Dopamine release in the human brain can be assessed by measuring the displacement of highly selective dopamine ligands produced by the administration of indirect dopamine agonists such as amphetamine

or cocaine that increase extracellular dopamine levels. Such displacement can be detected by labeling drugs with high affinities for a particular dopamine receptor subtype with a radioactive isotope such as carbon 11 (^{11}C). The concentration of this radio-labeled drug in the brain can be measured using positron emission tomography (PET). Displacement of the dopamine D_2 receptor selective agent raclopride in the striatum is produced by the intravenous administration of the psychomotor stimulant methylphenidate to healthy subjects (Volkow et al., 1999). The magnitude of this displacement was found to correlate with increased ratings of sensations of "high" and "rush." Similarly, amphetamine-induced displacement of raclopride in the ventral striatum was found to correlate with increases in ratings of euphoric feelings in healthy subjects (Drevets et al., 2001; Martinez et al., 2003; Oswald et al., 2005). Reductions in the binding of raclopride in the ventral striatum have also been found to correlate with hedonic responses to nicotine delivered in cigarette smoke (Barrett, Boileau, Okker, Pihl, & Dagher, 2004).

The administration of a variety of abused drugs and selective dopamine and opioid agonists has been found to lower thresholds for rewarding brain stimulation delivered to the medial forebrain bundle (see Table 40.2). This suggests that agents that either promote dopamine release into the nucleus accumbens or directly stimulate dopamine receptors act to enhance the sensitivity of the brain to rewarding stimuli. This link is supported by the observations that the infusion of amphetamine directly into the nucleus accumbens results in a lowering of brain stimulation reward thresholds (Knapp, Lee, Foye, Ciraulo, & Kornetsky, 2001) and in enhanced rates of responding for brain stimulation reward (Broekkamp, Pijnenburg, Cools, & Van Rossum, 1975).

Perhaps the clearest evidence that dopaminergic receptor stimulation results in rewarding effects is that administration of either the direct dopamine D_2 receptor agonist bromocriptine (Knapp & Kornetsky, 1994; Steiner, Katz, & Carroll, 1980) or the selective DAT inhibitor GBR 12909 (Baldo, Jain, Veraldi, Koob, & Markou, 1999; Maldonado-Irizarry, Stellar, & Kelley, 1994) enhances the effects of rewarding brain stimulation. Also, the selective DAT inhibitor GBR 12783 will produce conditioned placed preference (Le Pen, Duterte-Boucher, & Costentin, 1996). Finally, rats and monkeys (Wise, Murray, & Bozarth, 1990; Woolverton, Goldberg, & Ginos, 1984) will self-administer bromocriptine, and rhesus monkeys will respond for GBR 12909 (Stafford, LeSage, Rice, & Glowa, 2001; Wojnicki & Glowa, 1996), which is also consistent with these agents having rewarding actions.

The administration of dopamine receptor antagonists would be expected to attenuate the effects of rewarding

TABLE 40.1 Example of rewards that produce sustained elevations in nucleus accumbens extracellular dopamine concentrations during consummatory or self-administration periods

Reward	Class	Reference
Food	Natural	Martel & Fantino (1996)
Sucrose	Natural	Hajnal et al. (2004)
Copulation	Natural	Fiorino et al. (1997)
Brain stimulation	Artificial stimulant	Hernandez et al. (2006)
Amphetamine	Psychomotor stimulant	Ranaldi et al. (1999)
Cocaine	Psychomotor stimulant	Bradberry et al. (2000)
Nicotine	Nicotinic agonist	Lecca et al. (2006)
Heroin	Opioid agonist	Lecca et al. (2007)
Ethanol	Positive GABA$_A$ receptor modulator	Doyon et al. (2003)

TABLE 40.2 Drugs that produce lowering of brain stimulation reward thresholds

Drug	Class	Reference
Amphetamine	Psychomotor stimulant	Kornetsky & Esposito (1979)
Cocaine	Psychomotor stimulant	Gill et al. (2004)
MDMA	Psychomotor stimulant	Hubner et al. (1988)
Bromocriptine	D_2 receptor agonist	Knapp & Kornetsky (1994)
GBR 12909	Selective DAT inhibitor	Baldo et al. (1999)
Buprenorphine	Opioid agonist	Hubner & Kornetsky (1988)
Heroin	Opioid agonist	Hubner & Kornetsky (1992)
Morphine	Opioid agonist	Esposito & Kornetsky (1977)
DAMGO	Mu-receptor opioid agonist	Duvauchelle, Fleming, & Kornetsky (1997)
DPDPE	Delta-receptor opioid agonist	Duvauchelle et al. (1997)
Nicotine	Nicotinic agonist	Huston-Lyons, Sarkar, & Kornetsky (1993)
Ethanol	Positive $GABA_A$ modulator	Kornetsky, Moolten, & Bain (1991)

brain stimulation if dopamine receptor systems acted to positively modulate these effects. Experimental results concerning the actions of dopamine receptor antagonist administration on responding for brain stimulation reward may be influenced by the nonspecific effects of these agents on cognitive and motor performance. Treatment with the dopamine D_2 selective antagonist pimozide, however, was found to increase reward threshold levels at doses that did not influence attentional processes (Bird & Kornetsky, 1990). The administration of the dopamine receptor antagonist haloperidol elevated reward thresholds for BSR at doses that did not influence a measure of motor performance, that is, latency of response (Esposito, Faulkner, & Kornetsky, 1979). Similar effects were produced by the administration of the selective dopamine D_1 receptor antagonist SCH 23390. It has not, however, always been possible to separate blockade of rewarding stimulation from impairment of motor effects. Administration of the D_2 selective antagonist raclopride, for example, was shown to increase response latencies as it elevated brain stimulation reward thresholds (Baldo, Jain, Veraldi, Koob, & Markou, 1999).

The infusion of dopamine antagonists into discrete brain areas would be expected to produce less nonselective disruption of responding for rewarding brain stimulation than does systemic administration of these drugs. Microinjection of the dopamine antagonist cis-flupenthixol into the nucleus accumbens attenuated the effects of brain stimulation reward (Stellar & Corbett, 1989). Infusion of the dopamine D_1 receptor antagonist SCH 23390 into the nucleus accumbens decreased rates of responding for rewarding brain stimulation, but administration of the D_2 receptor selective antagonist raclopride did not produce a significant effect (Cheer et al., 2007). Interestingly, microinjection of SCH 23390 into the nucleus accumbens elevated brain stimulation thresholds; in contrast, thresholds were lowered when this drug was administered into the prefrontal cortex (Duvauchelle, Fleming, & Kornetsky, 1998).

Pharmacological agents that block dopamine receptors can be considered to have only relative selectivity for the different dopamine receptor subtypes. Attempts have been made to address this problem by using animals in which the genes that express the proteins needed to form a particular type of receptor have been deleted or rendered inactive. This typically involves the use of transgenic mice. A transgenic mouse is one that carries a foreign gene that has been inserted into its genome. The foreign gene is constructed using recombinant DNA. In knockout mice the replacement gene (or null gene) is nonfunctional. In homozygous mice, who receive the null gene from both parents, the expression of a specific protein may be completely absent. In heterozygotic animals, in which the null gene is received from only one parent, the level expression of the protein is greatly reduced. Wild-type animals have parents that are both nontransgenic.

Selective deletion of specific dopamine receptor proteins in knockout mice allows for the assessment of brain stimulation reward in animals in whom the expression of specific dopamine receptor subtypes has been blocked. One group of researchers found that thresholds for brain stimulation were elevated in dopamine D_1 receptor knockout mice compared to thresholds obtained for wild-type mice (Tran et al., 2005). This finding implicates dopamine D_1 receptors in the regulation of responses to brain stimulation reward. In contrast, this same group of investigators reported that responding for brain stimulation reward was unaltered in dopamine D_2 receptor knockout mice compared to wild-type animals (Tran et al., 2002). This suggests that dopamine D_2 receptors do not play an essential role in the maintenance of baseline levels of responding for brain stimulation. Other researchers, however, have found that significantly higher levels of current intensity are needed to maintain responding for brain stimulation to obtain stimulation in D_2 receptor knockout mice than was required for wild-type mice (Elmer et al., 2005).

Knockout mice have been used to examine the role played by dopamine receptor systems in mediating the rewarding effects of drugs of abuse. Dopamine D_2 receptor knockout mice will self-administer cocaine (Caine et al., 2002). The intake of cocaine by these animals is higher at high doses of cocaine than for wild-type mice. These results indicate that dopamine D_2 receptors may not be essential for mediating the rewarding effects of cocaine. Cocaine-induced conditioned place preference was not found to differ significantly in either dopamine D_1 receptor or dopamine D_3 receptor knockout mice compared to that seen in wild-type animals (Karasinska, George, Cheng, & O'Dowd, 2005). Dopamine D_1 receptor knockout mice, however, failed to reliably self-administer cocaine (Caine et al., 2007). Overall these studies tentatively suggest that the dopamine D_2 receptor may not be essential for the induction of cocaine's rewarding actions, whereas D_1 receptors might play a critical role in these actions.

If the rewarding effects of cocaine are related to increases in extracellular levels of dopamine in the brain, then the DAT protein would be expected to be the site of action at which this drug would bind to produce these increases. However, DAT knockout mice will self-administer cocaine (Rocha et al., 1998). Cocaine administration also has been found to induce conditioned place preference in DAT knockout mice (Sora et al., 1998). These results are not consistent with a role for DAT in mediating the rewarding effects of cocaine. There is evidence, however, that the regulation by neurotransmitters of reward system function is altered in DAT knockout mice. Most notably, nisoxetine, a NET inhibitor, and fluoxetine, a SERT inhibitor, both produce conditioned place preference in DAT knockout mice, although they do not have similar actions in wild-type animals (Hall et al., 2002). In an attempt to circumvent the problems associated with neuronal development in animals that never express DAT, one group of researchers has developed a strain of DAT knockin mice in which DAT that has a low affinity for cocaine is expressed (R. Chen et al., 2006). The DAT expressed in these animals remains functional with respect to the transport of dopamine, but it does not interact with cocaine. In the DAT knockin mice cocaine administration failed to produce conditioned place preference. This result supports the idea that DAT is involved in mediating the rewarding effects of cocaine in animals in which this transporter protein remains functional.

In clinical studies the role of dopamine receptors in mediating the hedonic effects of commonly abused stimulants has been assessed by examining how these effects are modified by the administration of dopamine receptor antagonists. In one study, an injection of the dopamine antagonist haloperidol had no effect on the sensation of "rush" produced by intravenous cocaine, but ratings of "good" feelings and "high" were significantly diminished (Sherer,

Kumor, & Jaffe, 1989) by administration of this drug. In another study, haloperidol administration blocked euphoria induced by the stimulant methylphenidate in manic-depressive subjects (Wald, Ebstein, & Belmaker, 1978). Ratings of "high" and "good effects" produced by cocaine were reduced by concurrent treatment with the dopamine D_1 antagonist ecopipam (Romach et al., 1999). Administration of the atypical neuroleptic clozapine to cocaine-dependent individuals reduced cocaine-induced increases in feelings of "high" and "rush" (Farren et al., 2000). Haloperidol administration also was found to decrease the euphoric and stimulant effects of ethanol in social drinkers, suggesting that dopamine antagonists can block the hedonic effects of abuse drugs that are not stimulants (Enggasser & de Wit, 2001).

Not all findings are consistent with the notion that the administration of dopamine antagonists will block the hedonic effects of drugs of abuse. Amphetamine-induced euphoria was not blocked by administration of the dopamine D_2 antagonist pimozide (Brauer & DeWit, 1997). Administration of either haloperidol or the atypical neuroleptic risperidone did not alter the subjective response of healthy volunteers to methamphetamine (Wachtel, Ortengren, & de Wit, 2002). Findings from a few studies suggest that dopamine receptor antagonists may not block the hedonic effects of nicotine. The positive subjective effects produced by nicotine have not been reduced by the administration of either ecopipam (Chausmer, Smith, Kelly, & Griffiths, 2003) or haloperidol (Walker, Mahoney, Ilivitsky, & Knott, 2001). Whether differences in factors such as drug doses used can explain the discrepancies among studies concerning the effects of dopamine antagonists on drug-induced hedonic effects remains to be determined.

GABA AND REWARD

GABA may act on both $GABA_A$ and $GABA_B$ receptors within the brain to regulate the effects of rewarding stimuli. The ventral pallidum is a subcortical structure that receives GABAergic input from the nucleus accumbens. This structure sends inhibitory GABAergic projections into the VTA (Wu, Hrycyshyn, & Brudzynski, 1996). GABA released within the VTA may act on $GABA_A$ receptors located on interneurons in the VTA. This may result in an inhibition of release of GABA from these interneurons. GABA released from interneurons in the VTA interacts with $GABA_B$ receptors located on dopamine neurons to inhibit the activity of dopaminergic neurons (Kalivas, Duffy, & Eberhardt, 1990). Thus, activation of $GABA_A$ neurons within the VTA may lead to a disinhibition of dopaminergic activity by indirectly preventing the stimulation of $GABA_B$ receptors located on dopamine neurons.

There also appear to be extensive interactions between dopaminergic and GABAergic systems within the structures that regulate reward in the nucleus accumbens (Geldwert et al., 2006). Coinfusion of either bicuculline, a $GABA_A$ receptor antagonist, or the $GABA_B$ antagonist phaclofen with the selective DAT inhibitor GBR 12909 leads to increases in dopamine concentrations within the nucleus accumbens significantly above those seen with GBR 12909 alone (Rahman & McBride, 2002). These results suggest that the GABA receptors regulate the release of dopamine within the nucleus accumbens.

Rats will self-administer the $GABA_A$ receptor agonist muscimol into the VTA, suggesting that stimulation of $GABA_A$ receptors in this structure produces rewarding effects (Ikemoto, Murphy, & McBride, 1998). The finding that muscimol injection into the VTA can result in conditioned place preference is consistent with this idea (Laviolette & van der Kooy, 2001). Place preference resulting from intra-VTA muscimol administration was blocked by treatment with the dopamine antagonist α-flupenthixol (Laviolette & van der Kooy, 2001), indicating that muscimol-rewarding actions may be linked to dopaminergic-related reward processes.

The infusion of muscimol into the rostral portion of the VTA has been found to increase break points for cocaine delivered under a progressive ratio schedule (D. Y. Lee et al., 2007). This is consistent with muscimol activating the same reward pathways as does cocaine. This activation may result from stimulation of $GABA_A$ receptors located on interneurons in the VTA that, in turn, leads to inhibitory effects that block the release of GABA from these neurons (Kalivas et al., 1990).

GABA is metabolized in the brain by the enzyme GABA transaminase. Inhibition of this enzyme can be produced by administration of the GABA transaminase inhibitor vigabatrin, resulting in marked elevations in brain GABA levels. Treatment with vigabatrin results in the blockade of increases in nucleus accumbens dopamine levels that are produced by the administration of methamphetamine, heroin, or ethanol (Gerasimov et al., 1999). Vigabatrin, then, would be expected to block the rewarding effects of many commonly abused drugs by suppressing the increased release of dopamine that would otherwise occur when they are administered. This drug has been found to decrease the self-administration of cocaine, ethanol, and morphine (Buckett, 1981; Stromberg, Mackler, Volpicelli, O'Brien, & Dewey, 2001) and block heroin-induced place preference (Paul, Dewey, Gardner, Brodie, & Ashby, 2001). Break points for cocaine self-administration are decreased by concurrent treatment with vigabatrin, indicating a reduction in cocaine's rewarding effects (Kushner, Dewey, & Kornetsky, 1999). In addition, the administration of vigabatrin

blocks cocaine-induced lowering of brain stimulation reward thresholds (Kushner, Dewey, & Kornetsky, 1997). Vigabatrin administration also decreases responding for food, which has led some investigators to question the specificity of its effects (Barrett, Negus, Mello, & Caine, 2005).

Both the $GABA_B$ receptor agonist baclofen and the positive modulator of $GABA_B$ activity GS39783 will attenuate cocaine-induced enhancement of animals' sensitivity to brain stimulation reward (Slattery, Markou, Froestl, & Cryan, 2005). When administered alone at a higher dose baclofen will significantly elevate brain stimulation reward thresholds. These results are in accord with the view that $GABA_B$ receptors may act to inhibit the rewarding effects of both brain stimulation and cocaine. This may be related to inhibition of mesolimbic dopamine release produced by the activation of $GABA_B$ receptors located on dopaminergic neurons.

Cocaine self-administration is inhibited by the systemic administration of the $GABA_A$ agonist muscimol or the $GABA_B$ receptor agonist baclofen (Barrett et al., 2005). These findings suggest that both the $GABA_A$ and $GABA_B$ receptors may have inhibitory actions on the rewarding effects of cocaine. This finding also indicates that systemically administered muscimol may have actions distinct from those caused by the infusion of this drug into the VTA. It should also be noted that baclofen and muscimol decreased cocaine self-administration only at doses that also decreased food-maintained responding, which raises the question of whether these GABA agonists when administered systemically selectively act on cocaine-induced reward (Barrett et al., 2005). These agents also either may have nonselective effects on lever pressing or may alter the rewarding effects of food (Barrett et al., 2005).

Both barbiturates and benzodiazepine sedative-hypnotics act at the $GABA_A$ receptor complex to enhance the effects of GABA on this complex. Clinical studies indicate that the administration of barbiturates, including pentobarbital (Carter, Richards, Mintzer, & Griffiths, 2006) and butabarbital (Zawertailo, Busto, Kaplan, Greenblatt, & Sellers, 2003), produce elevations in ratings of drug liking and other measures of pleasant drug effects in subjects with a history of recreational sedative use. Similar effects are seen following the administration of benzodiazepines to sedative users (Carter et al., 2006; Zawertailo et al., 2003), abstinent alcoholics (Ciraulo et al., 1997), and children of alcoholics (Ciraulo, Barnhill, Ciraulo, Greenblatt, & Shader, 1989; Ciraulo et al., 1996). Thus, sedative-hypnotics that enhance the activity of $GABA_A$ receptors produce rewarding actions in human subjects. Treatment with pentobarbital, however, did not result in alterations in brain stimulation reward thresholds (Kornetsky, 2004). When administered systemically the benzodiazepines diazepam (Invernizzi, Pozzi, & Samanin, 1991) and midazolam (Finlay, Damsma, & Fibiger, 1992) both decreased dopamine concentrations in the nucleus accumbens. These results suggest that the hedonic effects of barbiturates and benzodiazepines may result from dopamine-independent processes.

OPIOID SYSTEMS AND REWARD

There are three types of opioid receptors: the μ, δ, and κ, receptors (De Vries & Shippenberg, 2002). Most commonly used opioid analgesics act at the μ-receptor, producing elevation of mood and euphoria in many individuals. A few of the available opioid analgesics act by stimulating κ-receptors, but these drugs may sometimes produce unpleasant (dysphoric) feelings. Endogenous opioids known as the enkephalins activate δ-receptors. The administration of opioid drugs with μ-opioid receptor agonist effects can result in lowering brain stimulation reward thresholds (see Table 40.2). In contrast, the administration of the selective opioid κ-receptor agonist U-69593 may elevate brain stimulation reward thresholds (Todtenkopf, Marcus, Portoghese, & Carlezon, 2004). The κ-receptor agonist ethylketocyclazocine, on the other hand, has been found to have no effect on these thresholds (Unterwald, Sasson, & Kornetsky, 1987).

Several findings indicate that changes in dopaminergic activity can influence the effects of μ-opioid receptor agonists on brain stimulation thresholds, suggesting that this neurotransmitter may be a mediator of the effects of these agents on reward systems. Injection of morphine into the VTA enhances the effects of brain stimulation reward (Broekkamp & Phillips, 1979). This action may result from morphine-induced increases in the firing of dopaminergic cells within the VTA (Gysling & Wang, 1983; Kiyatkin & Rebec, 1997). Opioid-induced increases in VTA dopamine cell firing may account for the increase in dopamine efflux in the nucleus accumbens that occurs during the administration of either morphine (Pontieri et al., 1995) or heroin (Lecca et al., 2007).

The increase in firing produced by opioid administration may result from the suppression of GABA release from interneurons that act to inhibit dopaminergic neuronal activity in the VTA (Bergevin, Girardot, Bourque, & Trudeau, 2002; Kalivas et al., 1990; Klitenick, DeWitte, & Kalivas, 1992). Evidence of this inhibitory effect includes the finding that the firing rate of GABA neurons in the VTA is reduced following the self-administration of heroin (Steffensen et al., 2006). The infusion of vigabatrin into either the VTA or ventral pallidum resulted in the suppression of heroin self-administration (Xi & Stein, 2000).

Systemic administration of the GABA$_B$ receptor antagonist 2-OH-saclofen antagonized the inhibitory effects of vigabatrin administered into the VTA on heroin self-administration (Xi & Stein, 2000). This finding suggests that the activation of GABA$_B$ receptors in the VTA may antagonize the rewarding effects of opioid agonists.

Evidence of the involvement of the dopaminergic systems in the interaction between opioids and brain stimulation reward includes the finding that low doses of apomorphine, which may act presynaptically to block dopamine release, blocks morphine-induced lowering of brain stimulation reward thresholds (Knapp & Kornetsky, 1996). Also, the systemic administration of the nonselective dopamine antagonist cis-flupenthixol blocked the stimulation reward threshold lowering effects produced by the microinjection into the accumbens of either the μ-opioid receptor agonist DAMGO or the δ-opioid agonist DPDPE (Duvauchelle, Fleming, & Kornetsky, 1997). Finally, in dopamine D$_2$ receptor knockout mice, morphine administration produces an elevation as opposed to a decrease in frequency thresholds for rewarding brain stimulation, suggesting that the rewarding effects of morphine do not occur in these animals (Elmer et al., 2005). In a complementary self-administration study, dopamine D$_2$ receptor knockout mice did not show greater responses for morphine than they did for saline (Elmer et al., 2002). This result is consistent with the notion that dopamine D$_2$ receptor systems are needed for the production of the rewarding actions of opioids.

There are some findings that do not support the idea that dopamine is needed for the production of the rewarding effects of opioids. Heroin self-administration has been found to persist in animals in which dopamine terminals in the nucleus accumbens have been destroyed using 6-hydroxydopamine (Pettit, Ettenberg, Bloom, & Koob, 1984). Injection of the dopamine antagonist α-flupenthixol into the nucleus accumbens failed to block morphine-induced conditioned place preference in opioid-naive rats (Laviolette, Nader, & van der Kooy, 2002). Morphine-induced conditioned place preference also is produced in dopamine-deficient mutant mice (Hnasko, Sotak, & Palmiter, 2005). At present it is hard to reconcile the inconsistent evidence concerning the role of dopamine in the production of the rewarding effects of opioids. One likely possibility is that opioid-induced reward may be mediated by both dopamine-dependent and dopamine-independent mechanisms.

Several studies implicate CB$_1$ cannabinoid receptor systems in the regulation of the rewarding effects of opioids. Administration of the CB$_1$ receptor antagonist SR1451716A produces a decrease in the break points for heroin delivered under a progressive ratio schedule

(Caillé & Parsons, 2003; De Vries, Homberg, Binnekade, Raasø, & Schoffelmeer, 2003). The administration of this antagonist also blocked morphine-induced place preference (Mas-Nieto et al., 2001; Navarro et al., 2001). Other evidence of involvement of CB_1 receptors in modulating the rewarding effects of opioids includes findings that morphine self-administration is not seen in CB_1 receptor knockout mice (Cossu et al., 2001). Acquisition of morphine-induced place preference may be blocked in these animals (Martin, Ledent, Parmentier, Maldonado, & Valverde, 2000), although this has not been a consistent finding (Rice, Gordon, & Gifford, 2002). The lack of rewarding effects of morphine in CB_1 receptor knockout mice may be related to a reduction of morphine-induced accumbens dopamine release in these animals (Mascia et al., 1999).

The threshold lowering of several psychomotor stimulants, including cocaine (Bain & Kornetsky, 1987), d-amphetamine (Esposito, Perry, & Kornetsky, 1980), amfonelic acid (Knapp & Kornetsky, 1989), and 3,4-methlenedioxymethamphetamine (Hubner, Bird, Rassnick, & Kornetsky, 1988), are attenuated by the concurrent administration of high doses of the opioid antagonist naloxone. Treatment with naloxone will significantly decrease response rates for the self-administration of cocaine (Kiyatkin & Brown, 2003). When microinjected into the ventral pallidum, naloxone also blocks cocaine-induced place preference (Skoubis & Maidment, 2003). These results suggest that endogenous opioid peptides may play a role in the modulation of the rewarding actions of psychomotor stimulants.

The μ-opioid receptor has been implicated as the opioid receptor subtype that regulates drug-induced reward. Evidence of this includes the finding that intracerebroventricular infusion of the selective μ-receptor antagonist CTAP prevents the development of cocaine-induced conditioned place preference (Schroeder et al., 2007). Selective deletion of the OPRM1 (i.e., the μ-opioid receptor) gene from mice results in the failure of cocaine to produce conditioned place preference (Becker et al., 2002; Hall, Goeb, Li, Sora, & Uhl, 2004). The finding that ethanol reward and ethanol-induced place preference are attenuated in OPRM1 knockout mice suggests that this opioid receptor is also involved in mediating the rewarding effects of alcohol (Hall, Sora, & Uhl, 2001).

Several studies have examined the interaction between the opioid antagonist naltrexone and commonly abused drugs on the subjective response of human subjects to these agents. Treatment with naltrexone decreased ratings of "high" but not ratings of "like the drug" in healthy volunteers challenged with a dose of amphetamine (Jayaram-Lindström, Wennberg, Hurd, & Franck, 2004). Ratings of cocaine's "good effects" were decreased by naltrexone administration in crack cocaine users (Sofuoglu et al., 2003). In contrast, in one study with subjects with a history of cocaine and heroin use, naltrexone treatment had no significant effect on ratings of either cocaine-associated "high," "good effects," or "liking" (Walsh, Sullivan, Preston, Garner, & Bigelow, 1996).

The administration of opioid antagonists may attenuate the hedonic effects of rewarding substances other than cocaine, including those of food. Administration of naltrexone reduced ratings of the pleasantness of food (M. R. Yeomans & Gray, 1996, 1997). The euphoria-inducing effects of nicotine gum in smokers were blocked by pretreatment with naltrexone (Knott & Fisher, 2007). Treatment with naltrexone reduced ratings by alcoholic subjects of ethanol-induced "high" (Volpicelli, Watson, King, Sherman, & O'Brien, 1995) and by heavy drinkers of ratings of alcohol "liking" (McCaul, Wand, Eissenberg, Rohde, & Cheskin, 2000). In alcoholic individuals the initial stimulatory effects of ethanol are decreased by the administration of either naltrexone or the opioid antagonist nalmefene (Drobes, Anton, Thomas, & Voronin, 2004).

SEROTONIN AND NOREPINEPHRINE AND REWARD

At least 14 subtypes of receptors have been identified as mediating the effects of serotonin (Hoyer, Hannon, & Martin, 2002). Many of these are located within the brain, including the 5-HT_{1A}, 5-HT_{1B}, 5-HT_{2A}, 5-HT_{2B}, 5-HT_{2C}, and 5-HT_3 subtypes. This extensive diversity of serotonin receptor subtypes in the brain has complicated the task of characterizing the role of serotonin receptors in the regulation of reward system activity. The nonselective stimulation of serotonin receptors produced by the administration of the SERT inhibitor fluoxetine has been found to reduce the sensitivity of rats to rewarding brain stimulation (Harrison & Markou, 2001; K. Lee & Kornetsky, 1998). Treatment with fluoxetine has been found to decrease the positive effects of intravenous cocaine administration on mood (Walsh, Preston, Sullivan, Fromme, & Bigelow, 1994). In the squirrel monkey administration of the SERT inhibitor alaproclate both reduces cocaine self-administration and blocks cocaine-induced elevation in extracellular dopamine concentrations in the nucleus accumbens (Czoty, Ginsburg, & Howell, 2002). These results suggest that the increase in serotonin levels produced by acute SERT inhibitor administration may attenuate the rewarding effects of both brain stimulation reward and cocaine. The actions of alaproclate suggest that SERT inhibitors can block cocaine-induced increases in extracellular dopamine levels within the nucleus accumbens, an effect that would explain how they block the effects of rewarding stimuli. This explanation conflicts, however, with evidence that fluoxetine administration enhances cocaine-induced elevations in nucleus accumbens dopamine in the rat (Bubar, McMahon, De Deurwaerdere, Spampinato, & Cunningham, 2003).

The 5-HT$_1$ serotonin receptors appear to regulate the reward processes that are activated by rewarding brain stimulation. In one study 5-HT$_{1A}$ and 5-HT$_{1/B}$ agonists elevated brain stimulation reward thresholds (see Table 40.3). When microinjected in the median raphe or when administered in low doses the 5-HT$_{1A}$ agonist 8-OH-DPAT produced a lowering of reward thresholds. Both reward threshold lowering and elevating effects of 8-OH-DPAT are blocked by the administration of the selective 5-HT$_{1A}$ antagonist p-MMPI. It has been suggested that the threshold-lowering effect of 8-OH-DPAT results from 5-HT$_{1A}$ autoreceptor-mediated reductions in serotonin release from median raphe neurons (Harrison & Markou, 2001).

The 5-HT$_{1B}$ receptor gene can be incorporated into a viral DNA that can then enter a neuron to increase the expression of that gene in the transfected neuronal cell. Viral-mediated gene transfer–induced increases in 5-HT$_{1B}$ receptor expression in accumbens neurons enhanced the sensitivity of rats to the place-preference-inducing actions of cocaine (Barot, Ferguson, & Neumaier, 2007). Administration of 5-HT$_{1B}$ agonists may increase the break point for self-administered cocaine (see Table 40.3). These results suggest that the stimulation of 5-HT$_{1B}$ receptors may enhance the rewarding actions of cocaine. Elevation in extracellular dopamine levels in the accumbens produced

by cocaine administration is enhanced by the infusion of the 5-HT$_{1B}$ agonist CP 93,129 (O'Dell & Parsons, 2004). Infusion of this agonist into the nucleus accumbens increased extracellular dopamine in this structure (Yan & Yan, 2001). Serotonin 5-HT$_{1B}$-mediated enhancement of cocaine's rewarding actions, then, may be due to facilitation of dopamine release by this receptor.

The various subtypes of 5-HT$_2$ receptors may differ in how they modulate the actions of rewarding stimuli. Administration of the 5-HT$_{2A}$ receptor antagonist M100907 may not alter brain stimulation thresholds or cocaine self-administration responding (see Table 40.3). These results suggest that 5-HT$_{2A}$ receptors are not involved in the modulation of the rewarding effects of either brain stimulation or cocaine. In contrast, the 5-HT$_{2C}$ receptors appear to regulate the rewarding effects of many commonly abused drugs and of food. The administration of 5-HT$_{2C}$ agonists reduces self-administration responding for a variety of rewarding substances (see Table 40.3), suggesting that activation of these receptors decreases the effects of rewarding stimuli. This idea is supported by evidence showing that mutant mice with deletions of the protein for 5-HT$_{2C}$ receptors exhibited higher break points for cocaine than did wild-type mice (Rocha et al., 2002). This may have occurred because cocaine-induced increases in extracellular dopamine levels were greater in these mutant mice compared to wild-type animals. Consistent with the idea that 5-HT$_{2C}$ receptors attenuate the rewarding actions of cocaine is evidence that treatment with the 5-HT$_{2C}$ antagonists may produce a leftward shift in the dose-response curve for cocaine self-administration. These agents enhance

TABLE 40.3   Effects of systemically administered serotonin receptor subtype selective drugs on rewarding stimuli

Receptor	Drug	Class	Effect	Reference
5-HT$_{1A}$	8-OH-DPAT	Agonist	↑ BSR	Harrison & Markou (2001)
5-HT$_{1A/B}$	Ru 24969	Agonist	↑ BSR	Harrison, Parsons, Koob, & Markou (1999)
5-HT$_{1B}$	CP 94,253	Agonist	↑ BP Cocaine SA	Parsons, Weiss, & Koob (1998)
5-HT$_{2A}$	M100907	Antagonist	0 BSR Threshold	Benalioud, Kapur, & Rompré (2007)
5-HT$_{2A}$	M100907	Antagonist	0 Cocaine SA	Fletcher, Grottick, & Higgins (2002)
5-HT$_{2C}$	SB242,084	Antagonist	↑ Cocaine SA	Fletcher et al. (2002)
5-HT$_{2C}$	R0 60-0175	Agonist	↓ Cocaine SA	Grottick, Fletcher, & Higgins (2000)
5-HT$_{2C}$	R0 60-0175	Agonist	↓ Nicotine SA	Grottick, Corrigall, & Higgins (2001)
5-HT$_{2C}$	R0 60-0175	Agonist	↓ Ethanol SA	Tomkins et al. (2002)
5-HT$_{2C}$	R0 60-0175	Agonist	↓ Food SA	Grottick et al. (2000)
5-HT$_3$	Y-25130	Antagonist	0 BSR	Kelley & Hodge (2003)
5-HT$_3$	Ondansetron	Antagonist	0 BSR	Herberg, De Belleroche, Rose, & Montgomery (1992)
5-HT$_3$	Ondansetron	Antagonist	0 Cocaine SA	Lane et al. (1992)
5-HT$_3$	Ondansetron	Antagonist	↓ Cocaine BP	Davidson, Lee, Xiong, & Ellinwood (2002)
5-HT$_3$	GBR 38032F	Antagonist	0 Cocaine SA	Peltier & Schenk (1991)
5-HT$_3$	MDL 72222	Antagonist	↓ Cocaine SA	Kankaanpää, Meririnne, & Seppälä (2002)

↑ BP SA = Increase in break point for self-administration; ↓ BP SA = Decrease in breakpoint for self-administration; 0 BSR = No change in sensitivity to brain stimulation ↑ reward; BSR = Increase in sensitivity to brain stimulation reward; 0 SA = No change in self-administration; ↑ SA = Increased self-administration; ↓ SA = Decreased self-administration; 8-O-DPAT = 8-hydroxy-2-(di-n-propyl-amino) tetralin hydrobromide.

cocaine-induced elevations in extracellular dopamine in the nucleus accumbens (Navailles, De Deurwaerdere, Porras, & Spampinato, 2004).

The 5-HT$_3$ antagonists have not been found to alter the effects of rewarding brain stimulation. Treatment with the 5-HT$_3$ antagonist Y-25130, however, attenuated the threshold-lowering effects of cocaine (S. P. Kelley & Hodge, 2003). Co-administration of the serotonin 5-HT$_3$ antagonist ICS 205,930 blocks the self-administration of cocaine into the posterior portion of the VTA (Rodd et al., 2005). Results concerning the effects of systemically administered 5-HT$_3$ antagonists on cocaine self-administration, however, are inconsistent (see Table 40.3). The 5-HT$_3$ antagonist ondansetron reverses both cocaine- and amphetamine-induced increases in extracellular dopamine levels in the nucleus accumbens (Kankaanpää, Lillsunde, Ruotsalainen, Ahtee, & Seppälä, 1996). In contrast, MDL 72222, a different 5-HT$_3$ antagonist, failed to have similar effects on cocaine's action on accumbens dopamine levels (De Deurwaerdère, Moison, Navailles, Porras, & Spampinato, 2005). Thus, some findings indicate that the stimulation of 5-HT$_3$ receptors may somehow facilitate the rewarding effects of psychomotor stimulants, possibly through the modulation of mesolimbic dopamine levels. Other results, though, have failed to support this view.

Evidence that noradrenergic systems are involved in the regulation of the actions of rewarding stimuli is inconsistent. Recently it has been shown that the noradrenergic α$_1$ receptor antagonist terazosin, when infused into the locus coeruleus, produces a rightward shift in rate-frequency curves for brain stimulation reward responding (Y. Lin, de Vaca, Carr, & Stone, 2007). As mentioned earlier, nisoxetine administration will induce conditioned place preference in mice with DAT deletions (Hall et al., 2002). Findings implicating noradrenergic receptors in the regulation of drug-induced reward is provided by observation of drug effects in mutant mice deficient in the α$_1$b-noradrenergic receptor (Drouin et al., 2002). These mice failed to exhibit morphine-induced conditioned place preference or a preference for orally administered cocaine. In mice lacking the gene for beta-hydroxylase, the enzyme needed to synthesize norepinephrine, the administration of either cocaine or morphine fails to induce conditioned place preference (Jasmin, Narasaiah, & Tien, 2006). Other evidence of the noradrenergic system's involvement in the production of cocaine's rewarding actions includes the finding that dose-response curves for cocaine self-administration may be shifted to the right in NET knockout mice compared to wild-type mice (Rocha, 2003).

In contrast to the studies just discussed, there are results suggesting that noradrenergic receptor systems are not involved in facilitating the effects of rewarding stimuli. This includes evidence that the administration of the selective NET inhibitor nisoxetine did not alter brain stimulation reward thresholds in the rat (Izenwasser & Kornetsky, 1989). Also, monkeys will not self-administer nisoxetine (Woolverton, 1987). Treatment with the α$_1$ noradrenergic receptor antagonist prazosin has not been shown to significantly influence patterns of cocaine self-administration by monkeys (Woolverton, 1987). Sensitivity to the conditioned-place-preference-inducing effects of cocaine was found to be enhanced in NET knockout mice (Xu et al., 2000).

MUSCARINIC AND NICOTINIC RECEPTORS AND REWARD

The neurotransmitter acetylcholine stimulates both muscarinic and nicotinic types of receptors. Different types of muscarinic receptors exist, including the M1 and M2 types. Nicotinic receptors are composed of different subunits, such as the α$_7$ subunit. Both muscarinic and nicotinic receptors have been found to modulate the actions of rewarding stimuli. The stimulation of acetylcholine receptors within the VTA may result in rewarding effects. Rats will self-administer the nonselective cholinergic agonist carbachol directly into the VTA (Ikemoto & Wise, 2002). They will also administer the acetylcholinesterase inhibitor neostigmine, which increases intracellular levels of acetylcholine into the posterior region of the VTA. The self-administration of carbachol into the VTA is blocked by treatment with either scopolamine, a muscarinic receptor antagonist, or dihydro-β-erythroidine, a nicotinic receptor antagonist. These results provide evidence that both muscarinic and nicotinic receptors in the VTA are implicated in mediating the rewarding actions of cholinergic agonists in the VTA.

The finding that the administration of the muscarinic receptor antagonists atropine and scopolamine results in an elevation of brain stimulation reward thresholds supports the idea that muscarinic receptors are involved in regulating the effects of rewarding stimulation (Kornetsky, 2004). Further evidence of this is supplied by the finding that infusion of the muscarinic M5 receptor oligonucleotide antisense into the VTA resulted in elevation of brain stimulation reward thresholds (J. S. Yeomans et al., 2000).

Findings that nicotine receptors also may regulate the actions of rewarding stimulation include results showing that brain stimulation reward thresholds are lowered by the administration of nicotine (Huston-Lyons, Sarkar, & Kornetsky, 1993; Ivanová & Greenshaw, 1997). The nicotinic receptor antagonist dihydro-β-erythroidine blocks nicotine-induced lowering of brain stimulation reward thresholds (Harrison, Gasparini, & Markou, 2002). The threshold-lowering effects of nicotine are potentiated by the concurrent administration of either amphetamine or morphine (Huston-Lyons et al., 1993). These effects of nicotine are blocked by the co-administration of the dopamine D_2 receptor antagonist pimozide (Huston-Lyons et al., 1993), the nonselective dopamine antagonist haloperidol (Ivanová & Greenshaw, 1997), and the dopamine D_1 receptor antagonist SCH 23390 (Harrison et al., 2002). These findings suggest that nicotine interacts with brain stimulation reward in a manner similar to many other commonly abused drugs.

The systemic administration of nicotine produces an increase in dopamine release in the nucleus accumbens (Imperato, Mulas, & Di Chiara, 1986). This action may be explained by the observation that the intravenous administration of nicotine results in short-lasting inhibition of dopamine neurons in the VTA, which is followed by increased rates of firing (Erhardt, Schwieler, & Engberg, 2002). Mice will self-administer nicotine into the VTA, indicating that this structure may be an important site for the mediation of the rewarding effects of this compound (David, Besson, Changeux, Granon, & Cazala, 2006). The excitatory effects of nicotine may be related to an increase of glutamate release within the VTA. The release of glutamate may lead to the activation of NMDA receptors (Chergui et al., 1993). Presynaptic nicotine receptors that contain the α_7 nicotinic receptor subunit appear to regulate the release of glutamate within the VTA. Microinjection of the α_7 nicotine receptor subunit antagonist methyllycaconitine blocks both nicotine- and food-induced dopamine release in the nucleus accumbens (Schilström, Svensson, Svensson, & Nomikos, 1998). Methyllycaconitine administration into the VTA will attenuate the threshold-lowering effects of nicotine, suggesting that the α_7 nicotine receptor subunit is involved in mediating the effects of nicotine on reward pathways (Panagis, Kastellakis, Spyraki, & Nomikos, 2000). Infusion of this antagonist into the VTA has also been demonstrated to block cocaine-induced lowering of brain stimulation reward thresholds (Panagis et al., 2000). This finding suggests that α_7 nicotine-containing receptors may also regulate the rewarding actions of psychomotor stimulants.

The VTA receives input from the laterodorsal and pedunculopontine tegmental nuclei in the rostral midbrain. These structures contain cholinergic neurons that project to the VTA (Oakman, Faris, Kerr, Cozzari, & Hartman, 1995). The pedunculopontine tegmental nucleus itself receives projections from the lateral hypothalamus (Semba & Fibiger, 1992). Self-stimulation of the lateral hypothalamus leads to enhanced release of acetylcholine in both the pedunculopontine tegmental nucleus and the VTA (Chen, Nakamura, Kawamura, Takahashi, & Nakahara, 2006;

Rada, Mark, Yeomans, & Hoebel, 2000). Acetylcholine levels in the VTA are also elevated in food- or water-deprived animals after they start to eat or drink, respectively (Rada et al., 2000). Microinjection of the muscarinic antagonist scopolamine into the pedunculopontine tegmental nucleus will lower thresholds for rewarding stimulation, possibly by blocking inhibition of presynaptic neurotransmitter release. The nicotine receptor antagonist mecamylamine, when infused into the VTA, does not significantly alter brain stimulation reward thresholds. Nicotine-induced lowering thresholds for rewarding brain stimulation, however, are blocked by infusion of mecamylamine into the pedunculopontine tegmental nucleus (Chen et al., 2006).

Acetylcholine receptors in the nucleus accumbens may regulate extracellular dopamine levels within the nucleus accumbens. Cocaine-induced increases in nucleus accumbens dopamine levels in mice are decreased by infusion of mecamylamine into this structure (Zanetti, Picciotto, & Zoli, 2007). Increases in extracellular dopamine concentrations induced by the local infusion of the selective DAT inhibitor GBR 12909 within the nucleus accumbens are attenuated by the administration of either scopolamine or mecamylamine (Rahman & McBride, 2002). These findings are consistent with the involvement of both nicotinic and muscarinic receptors in the regulation of nucleus accumbens dopamine concentrations acting via an inhibitory feedback mechanism. The involvement of muscarinic receptors in regulating dopamine levels within the nucleus accumbens may partly explain why the self-administration of cocaine is attenuated by the concurrent administration of scopolamine (Ranaldi & Woolverton, 2002).

Both the M1 and M5 muscarinic receptor subtypes have been implicated in the regulation of drug-induced reward. Sensitivity to either cocaine or morphine in the production of conditioned place preference is attenuated in muscarinic M1 receptor knockout mice (Carrigan & Dykstra, 2007). Administration of the selective M1 receptor antagonist pirenzepine has been shown to antagonize the induction of conditioned place preference produced by the administration of either cocaine or morphine (Carrigan & Dykstra, 2007). Deletion of the M_5 muscarinic receptor from mice resulted in a marked reduction in either cocaine- (Fink-Jensen et al., 2003) or morphine-induced conditioned place preference (Basile et al., 2002). Break points for low but not high doses of self-administered cocaine are lower for M_5 knockout mice than they are for wild-type mice, suggesting that cocaine's rewarding actions are altered in the absence of the M_5 receptor but that they are still retained at higher doses of this drug (Thomsen et al., 2005).

GLUTAMATE AND REWARD

Glutamate acts at the ionotropic glutamate receptors that include the *N*-methyl-D-aspartate (NMDA), α-amino-3-hydroxy-5-methylisoxazole-4-propionic acid (AMPA), and kainate receptors. Glutamate also interacts with several types of metabotropic receptors (mGluR) that influence intraneuronal activity via second messenger systems, such as the cyclic adenosine monophosphate (cAMP) signaling pathway. As discussed earlier, glutamatergic neurons project from limbic and cortical areas to the nucleus accumbens. The VTA also receives glutamatergic inputs from the medial prefrontal cortex and the pedunculopontine nucleus (Meltzer, Christoffersen, & Serpa, 1997; Sesack & Pickel, 1992). Given that glutamatergic neurons project into mesolimbic areas, it would be expected that glutamate receptor systems are involved in the regulation of the effects of rewarding stimuli.

The systemic administration of NMDA receptor antagonists can result in a lowering of brain stimulation reward thresholds (see Table 40.4). Microinjections of phencyclidine or other NMDA receptor antagonists, including dizocilpine and CPP [3-((±) 2-carboxypiperazin-4-yl) propyl-1-phosphonate], into the nucleus accumbens produce a decrease in frequency thresholds for rewarding brain stimulation (Carlezon & Wise, 1996; Clements & Greenshaw, 2005). These findings indicate that the NMDA receptors may have an inhibitory influence on rewarding stimulation. Intracerebroventricular infusion of the competitive NMDA receptor antagonist LY235959 increases break points for self-administered cocaine (Allen, Uban, Atwood, Albeck, & Yamamoto, 2007). This finding indicates that NMDA receptors may also have an inhibitory influence on the rewarding actions of cocaine.

Infusion of either of the AMPA/kainate antagonists CNQX or NBQX did not significantly alter the rewarding effects of brain stimulation delivered to the VTA (Choi, Clements, & Greenshaw, 2005). When administered in combination with the $D_{2/3}$ dopamine receptor agonist 7-OH-DPAT, these agents produced an elevation in frequency thresholds. Other evidence of the role of AMPA receptors in regulating the actions of rewarding stimulation includes the finding that this stimulation alters the levels of expression of different AMPA receptor subunits. These subunits, which combine to form AMPA receptors, include the GluR1 and GluR2 subunits. Increasing the expression of the GluR2 AMPA receptor subunit in the shell of the nucleus accumbens using viral vectors results in a decrease in brain stimulation reward thresholds (Todtenkopf et al., 2006). Opposite effects are produced by the enhanced expression of the GluR1 subunit in the accumbens shell (Todtenkopf et al., 2006).

Group I metabotropic receptors (mGluR1 and mGluR5) stimulate the second messenger phospholipase C and activate phosphoinositide hydrolysis (Kew & Kemp, 2005). Null mutant mice lacking mGluR5 receptors will not self-administer cocaine (Chiamulera et al., 2001). Cocaine and nicotine self-administration and break points for cocaine, nicotine, and food administered under progressive ratio schedules are decreased by treatment with the mGluR5 antagonist MPEP, [2-methyl-6-(phenylethynyl)-pyridine] (see Table 40.4). When administered into the ventricles of the brain, this antagonist also blocks the development of morphine-induced conditioned place preference (Aoki, Nirata, Shibasaki, & Suzuki, 2004). These findings suggest that mGluR5 receptors contribute to the rewarding effects of many abused drugs. The administration of a mGluR5 antagonist produces elevations in brain stimulation reward thresholds, which again implicates mGluR5 receptors in the production of the hedonic effects of rewarding stimuli. Administration of MPEP attenuates increases in sensitivity to rewarding brain stimulation that are produced by

TABLE 40.4 Effects of systemically administered glutamate receptor agents on rewarding stimuli

Receptor	Drug	Class	Effect	Reference
NMDA	PCP	Antagonist	↑ BSR	Kornetsky & Esposito (1979)
mGluR5	MPEP	Antagonist	↓ Cocaine SA	Kenny, Boutrel, Gasparini, Koob, & Markou (2005)
mGluR5	MPEP	Antagonist	↓ BP Cocaine SA	Paterson & Markou (2005)
mGluR5	MPEP	Antagonist	↓ BP Nicotine SA	Paterson & Markou (2005)
mGluR5	MPEP	Antagonist	↓ BP Food SA	Paterson & Markou (2005)
mGluR5	MPEP	Antagonist	↓ BSR	Harrison, Gasparini, & Markou (2002)
mGluR5	MPEP	Antagonist	↓ Nicotine SA	Liechti & Markou (2007)
mGluR2/3	LY379268	Agonist	↓ Nicotine SA	Liechti, Lhuillier, Kaupmann, & Markou (2007)

↑ BP SA = Increase in break point for self-administration; ↓ BP = Decrease in breakpoint for self-administration; 0 BSR = No change in sensitivity to brain stimulation reward; ↑ BSR = Increase in sensitivity to brain stimulation reward; ↓ BSR = Decreased sensitivity to brain stimulation reward; MPEP = 2-methyl-6-(phenylethynyl)-pyridine; PCP = Phencyclidine; ↑ SA = Increased self-administration; ↓ SA = Decreased self-administration.

cocaine administration (Kenny, Boutrel, Gasparini, Koob, & Markou, 2005).

Group II metabotropic receptors (mGluR2 and mGluR3) inhibit the formation of the second messenger cAMP (Kew & Kemp, 2005). Release of dopamine and glutamate within the nucleus accumbens (Greenslade & Mitchell, 2004; Xi, Baker, Shen, Carson, & Kalivas, 2002) is regulated by mGluR2/3 receptors, and so it would be expected that these receptors can modulate the effects of rewarding stimuli. The self-administration of nicotine, but not food, is decreased by mGluR2/3 agonist administration. This suggests that the stimulation of Group II metabotropic glutamate receptors can attenuate the rewarding actions of nicotine. The role these receptors play in regulating the rewarding effects of psychomotor stimulants is, at present, less clear. Antagonism of Group II receptors produced by the injection of the antagonist (2 S)-α-ethylglutamic acid resulted in the blockade of amphetamine-induced conditioned place preference (Gerjikov & Beninger, 2006). Stimulation of these receptors with the mGluR2/3 agonist LY379268 was found to decrease cocaine self-administration, but only when this agent was administered at higher doses (Baptista, Martin-Fardon, & Weiss, 2004). Exactly why both blockade and stimulation of Group II receptors appear to decrease the rewarding effects of psychomotor stimulants remains to be elucidated.

SIGNAL TRANSDUCTION PATHWAYS AND REWARD

The D_1 receptor agonists produce increases in intracellular levels of the second messenger cAMP. In addition to dopamine D_1 receptors, cAMP acts as a second messenger for a variety of other types of receptors, including adenosine A_2, serotonin 5-HT_4, and $GABA_B$ receptors. Activation of cAMP-dependent protein kinase (PKA) produced by the stimulation of dopamine D_1 receptors can lead to phosphorylation of a wide variety of proteins that regulate cellular function. The catabolism of cAMP is catalyzed by Type IV phosphodiesterase enzymes. Administration of the Type IV phosphodiesterase inhibitor rolipram into the nucleus accumbens resulted in a lowering of brain stimulation reward thresholds (Knapp et al., 2001). This suggests that acute elevations of cAMP levels in the nucleus accumbens may produce rewarding effects. When rolipram infused into accumbens and in combination with systemically administered cocaine was administered, brain stimulation reward thresholds were lowered in what was at least an additive fashion. Infusion of the PKA inhibitor R_p-cAMPS into the nucleus accumbens produces a blockade of amphetamine-induced conditioned place preference

(Beninger, Nakonechny, & Savina, 2003; Gerdjikov, Giles, Swain, & Beninger, 2007). This would suggest that the activation of PKA contributes to the rewarding effects of amphetamine.

In seeming contradiction to the studies just discussed, the results of other studies indicate that the activation of cAMP pathways may have an inhibitory action on reward processes, whereas inhibition of these pathways has the opposite effect. Infusion of the PKA activating agent S_p-cAMPS also results in a reduction of amphetamine-induced place preference (Beninger et al., 2003). Other investigators have found that infusion of S_p-cAMPS into the nucleus accumbens shifts to the right dose-response curves for self-administered cocaine (Self et al., 1998). The PKA inhibitor R_p-cAMPS was shown to shift to the left cocaine self-administration dose-response curves (Self et al., 1998). This result would suggest that activation of cAMP systems attenuates the rewarding effects of cocaine. The systemic administration of rolipram has been found to attenuate both cocaine- and morphine-induced place preference (Thompson, Sachs, Kantak, & Cherry, 2004), a finding consistent with the idea that stimulation of PKA can block the rewarding effects of either cocaine or opioids.

At present it is not clear why different manipulations of cAMP pathways have very different effects on rewarding stimuli. Factors that might explain these discrepancies include the differences in the time course of the effects of the agents used to activate or inhibit PKA activity, the existence of several isoforms of PKA, and the diverse nature of the function of cAMP pathways in different cell types.

Calcium-dependent protein kinase (PKC) is another enzyme that may play an important role in signal transduction pathways that regulate the actions of rewarding stimuli. The concurrent administration of the PKC inhibitor NPC 1537 blocks conditioned place preference produced by the infusion of amphetamine into the nucleus accumbens (Aujla & Beninger, 2003). Intracerebroventricular infusion of the PKC inhibitor calphostin C has been found to dose-dependently block morphine-induced conditioned place preference (Narita, Aoki, Ozaki, Yajima, & Suzuki, 2001).

Calcium-dependent protein kinase consists of a series of isoenzymes. Of these, the epsilon and gamma isoforms have been implicated in regulating the rewarding effects of drugs of abuse. In mice, morphine-induced conditioned place preference results in an increase in the limbic forebrain of the gamma isoform of PKC (Aoki et al., 2004). The morphine-induced increase in this isoform of PKC is antagonized by the administration of the mGluR5 antagonist MPEP (Aoki et al., 2004). The administration of this antagonist also blocks morphine-induced place preference. Genetic deletion of the gamma isoform of PKC in mice results in an increase in ethanol consumption (P. M. Newton & Ron, 2007). In contrast, mice deficient in the epsilon form of PKC showed reduced intake of self-administered ethanol compared to wild-type mice (Olive, Mehmert, Messing, & Hodge, 2000). The PKC epsilon-deficient mice fail to show an increase in nucleus accumbens dopamine concentrations after the administration of ethanol. This may be an important factor as to why these mice exhibit patterns of low ethanol intake.

The cAMP response element binding protein (CREB) is a transcription factor that is activated by several signal-transduction pathways, including cAMP signaling pathways. CREB is activated by its transformation into phospho-CREB. Phospho-CREB regulates gene expression via interactions with CREs (cAMP response elements that regulate transcription). Exposure to amphetamine, cocaine, or morphine can produce activation of CREB (Konradi, Cole, Heckers, & Hyman, 1994; Walters, Kuo, & Blendy, 2003). This effect is important because CREB may be involved in regulating the rewarding effects of both the opioids and the psychomotor stimulants. Down regulation of CREB-regulated gene transcription by the infusion of CREB antisense into the nucleus accumbens produces a downward shift in cocaine self-administration, suggesting a reduction in the rewarding effects of this drug (Choi, Whisler, Graham, & Self, 2006). Mutant mice lacking the alpha and delta isoforms of CREB show diminished sensitivity to low-dose morphine in conditioned place-preference experiments (Walters & Blendy, 2001). These animals, in comparison to wild-type mice, displayed a positive place-preference response to high-dose morphine (Walters, Godfrey, Li, & Blendy, 2005). This suggests that the loss of the alpha and delta isoforms may produce a rightward shift in the dose-response curve for morphine-induced conditioned place preference.

While CREB has been implicated in the production of the rewarding effects of cocaine and morphine, this protein has been shown to have different, regionally specific actions that are dependent on the level of expression of CREB in a particular region. Increased expression of CREB in the shell of the nucleus accumbens produced by the injection of a viral vector has reduced the sensitivity of rats to the rewarding effects of cocaine (Carlezon et al., 1998). In contrast, increased expression of CREB in the lateral hypothalamus greatly increases the sensitivity of animals to the rewarding effects of morphine in place-preference experiments (Olson, Green, Neve, & Nestler, 2007). Viral-mediated expression of CREB in this structure also enhanced food consumption. In the rostral portion of the VTA, increased CREB expression induced by a viral vector increased sensitivity to the rewarding effects of either cocaine or morphine (Olson et al., 2005).

A different effect resulted from the injection of a CREB-enhancing viral vector into the caudal portion of the VTA, with low doses of either cocaine or morphine producing conditioned place aversion.

ADDICTION AND CHRONIC EXPOSURE TO REWARDING STIMULI

The major theories concerning the development of drug addiction differ in basic assumptions concerning how the hedonic effects of drugs of abuse change following periods of chronic drug exposure. The hedonic theory of drug addiction posits that the hedonic effects of drugs act as a persistent factor in both drug abuse and dependence, and so involves the assumption that drugs continue to produce rewarding effects in drug-using populations (Kornetsky & Bain, 1987). The incentive-salience theory of addiction (Robinson & Berridge, 2003) sees a diminished role for the hedonic effects of drugs in addiction, with a greater role played by salient conditioned stimuli. Thus, this theory emphasizes the development of tolerance to the hedonic effects of drugs as drug dependence progresses. The hedonic dysregulation theory of drug addiction holds that there are decreases in the basal activity of reward processes as a consequence of chronic drug use and an accompanying onset of negative emotions, such as anhedonia and depression (Le Moal & Koob, 2007). Drugs are then used by dependent individuals to counter this dysregulation of reward processes.

The results of numerous studies indicate that the rewarding effects of drugs remain essentially unaltered when they are administered chronically, at least under certain schedules of drug administration (see Table 40.5). The repeated daily administration of morphine over a period of several weeks did not result in a loss in the ability of this agent to produce lowering of reward threshold levels (Esposito & Kornetsky, 1977). This occurred despite the development of physical dependence in the animals that were treated with morphine. The findings of some investigations, however, suggest that the chronic administration of psychomotor stimulants produces either sensitization or tolerance to the effects of these drugs on brain stimulation reward. Overall it appears that whether the chronic administration of psychomotor stimulants produces the development of sensitization or tolerance or no effect at all in the sensitivity of animals to brain stimulation reward may be related to the history of drug exposure of the animal.

Data from human drug users indicate that many continue to experience the hedonic effects of drugs. For subjects with a history of heavy cocaine use or cocaine dependence, subjective measures of drug "liking" and drug

TABLE 40.5 Effects of chronic administration of several drugs of abuse on sensitivity to the effects of rewarding brain stimulation

Effect	Drug	Schedule	Reference
None	Morphine	Daily	Esposito & Kornetsky (1977)
	GBR 12909	Every other day	Melnick, Maldonado-Vlaar, Stellar, & Trzcinska (2001)
	Cocaine	Daily	Frank, Manderscheid, Panicker, Williams, & Kokoris (1992)
	Cocaine	3 times daily or every other day	Bauco & Wise (1997)
	Phencyclidine	Intermittent	Carlezon & Wise (1993)
	Nicotine	Daily	Bauco & Wise (1994)
Sensitization	Amphetamine	Once every 5 days	Lin, Koob, & Markou (2000)
	Amphetamine	Twice daily for 5 days	Kokkinidis & Zacharko (1980)
Tolerance	Cocaine	Multiple times daily	Frank, Manderscheid, Panicker, Williams, & Kokoris (1992)
	Amphetamine	Increasing dose or high dose twice daily	Kokkinidis & Zacharko (1980); Leith & Barrett (1976)
	Cocaine/methylphenidate	Postamphetamine	Leith & Barrett (1981)

"high" become elevated during cocaine self-administration sessions (Foltin & Fischman, 1992; Lynch et al., 2006). Similarly, in heroin-dependent individuals this drug produces dose-dependent increases in measures of euphoria, "good" drug effects, and "high" during periods of heroin self-administration testing (Comer, Collins, MacArthur, & Fischman, 1999; Comer et al., 1998). Evidence that individuals with a history of dependence on psychomotor stimulants or opioids remain able to derive pleasure from these drugs provides allowance for the theory that hedonic drug effects are a major factor underlying the development and continuation of drug abuse.

Although drug users remain sensitive to the hedonic effects of drugs of abuse there is evidence that this sensitivity can decrease during periods of sustained drug use. During testing in a "binge" cocaine self-administration session, subjects with a history of cocaine use developed acute tolerance to several of the subjective effects produced by this drug (Ward, Haney, Fischman, & Foltin, 1997). In cocaine users subjective feelings of "high" and euphoria were found to be diminished as concentrations of cocaine remained at sustained levels in the plasma (Foltin & Fischman, 1991). This finding is also consistent with the development of acute tolerance.

Animal studies of the effects of prolonged exposure to drugs of abuse on brain stimulation reward threshold show changes in baseline sensitivities to this stimulation. The repeated daily administration of amphetamine was found to result in an elevation in brain stimulation reward threshold levels at times subsequent to lowering of thresholds produced by this agent (D. Lin, Koob, & Markou, 2000). This effect may be related to alteration in reward system function following acute drug withdrawal. Similar elevations in stimulation threshold levels have been observed during acute withdrawal from ethanol (Schulteis, Markou, Cole, & Koob, 1995) and heroin (Kenny, Chen, Kitamura,

Markou, & Koob, 2006). Brain stimulation reward thresholds have become elevated above baseline levels at 2 hours after the self-administration of 40 and 80 injections (0.25 mg/injection) of cocaine, but not after 10 or 20 self-administered injections of this agent (Kenny, Polis, Koob, & Markou, 2003). These threshold elevations persist for 24 to 48 hours after the administration of higher doses of cocaine. Following the administration of 40 or fewer injections of cocaine, the threshold-lowering effects of this drug were still evident 15 minutes after the end of self-administration sessions.

Rats allowed to self-administer cocaine or heroin during short intervals of 1 to 3 hours show stable levels of intake of this drug. In contrast, cocaine intake has been found to escalate in rats given access to this agent for extended intervals of 6 hours or more (Ahmed & Koob, 1998). Baseline brain stimulation reward thresholds remain stable in rats given access to cocaine or heroin for only short intervals. Long-term access to either cocaine or heroin results in an elevation in threshold levels (Ahmed, Kenny, Koob, & Markou, 2002; Ahmed, Walker, & Koob, 2000). This effect persists for several days when animals first given prolonged access to cocaine are then allowed access to this stimulant for only short intervals. Acute cocaine administration resulted in a decrease in brain stimulation reward thresholds from elevated levels observed in rats given prolonged access to cocaine (Ahmed et al., 2002). This may indicate that the rewarding actions of cocaine may remain in animals in which prolonged exposure to cocaine has decreased basal levels of sensitivity to brain stimulation reward.

It has been suggested that prolonged exposure to many drugs of abuse results in persistent deficits in the regulation of brain reward function. This deficit is postulated to contribute to the compulsive use of drugs and to be related to decreased activity in mesolimbic dopaminergic systems. Evidence of reduced dopamine neurotransmission has been demonstrated in clinical studies in some drug-using populations. Cocaine-dependent individuals show a marked reduction in amphetamine-induced dopamine release in the ventral striatum and the anterior cingulate, assessed using PET imaging (Martinez et al., 2007). This has also been seen in the ventral striatum of alcohol-dependent subjects (Martinez et al., 2005).

Deficits in brain reward function are postulated to be related to the occurrence of anhedonia and related depressive symptoms in drug-using populations. It has been suggested that the administration of abusable drugs may reverse anhedonia that occurs during drug withdrawal, and that this may be a contributing factor to the development of addiction. Consistent with this hypothesis, smokers with high scores on ratings of anhedonia, compared to subjects with low scores, had greatly enhanced increases in the levels of positive affect produced by pleasurable memories and music when challenged with nicotine (Cook, Spring, & McChargue, 2007). In related findings, high levels of apathy or depressive symptoms in cocaine-dependent subjects were associated with the experience of a greater "high" after cocaine administration than were low levels of apathy or depression (T. F. Newton, Kalechstein, De La Garza, Cutting, & Ling, 2005; Uslaner, Kalechstein, Richter, Ling, & Newton, 1999). Negative emotions such as clinically significant depression, however, have yet to be identified as occurring in a substantial number of individuals who are drug-dependent (Darke & Ross, 1997; Gawin & Kleber, 1986; Grant et al., 2004). Serious questions therefore remain as to what role the negative affective states play in the development of addictive disorders.

SUMMARY

The evidence presently available indicates that sustained elevations of dopamine levels within the nucleus accumbens are associated with the production of hedonic effects by a variety of rewarding stimuli, ranging from natural stimuli such as sucrose to artificial rewards such as heroin. Changes in the phasic activity of dopaminergic neurons, in contrast, have been linked to behaviors associated with functions such as prediction of reward. The sustained elevations in mesolimbic dopamine levels that result from exposure to rewarding stimuli may activate different networks that are involved in the production of hedonic effects.

Dopaminergic receptor systems, however, constitute only one element of the network of neurons that support pleasurable experiences. It is clear that the hedonic effects of rewarding stimuli reflect the interactions of a large variety of neurotransmitters. The existing evidence suggests that the rewarding effects of opioid agonists and GABA agonists, in addition to resulting from modulation of mesocorticolimbic dopaminergic activity, might also produce reward through dopamine-independent mechanisms. Indeed, some authors have argued that the hedonic effects of palatable foods are dopamine-independent and involve primarily opioid-related mechanisms (A. E. Kelley et al., 2005).

Of critical importance to our understanding of how disorders that involve the compulsive use of rewarding substances develop is knowledge concerning how the hedonic effects associated with such use change over time. Individuals with histories of use of sedative agents, psychomotor stimulants, and opioids report experiencing the hedonic effects of these drugs under laboratory situations. This suggests that the mood-elevating and pleasurable actions of abused drugs could continue to exert some influence on the behavior of individuals with prolonged histories of drug use. This does not, however, mean that factors such as conditioned stimuli associated with drug use or negative mood states observed after intense periods of drug use are never involved in the development of addictive disorders. Determining how these factors interact to regulate drug self-administration may require more sophisticated modeling of patterns of use in drug-dependent individuals.

REFERENCES

Ahmed, S. H., Kenny, P. J., Koob, G. F., & Markou, A. (2002). Neurobiological evidence for hedonic allostasis associated with escalating cocaine use. *Nature Neuroscience, 5*, 625–626.

Ahmed, S. H., & Koob, G. F. (1998, October 9). Transition from moderate to excessive drug intake: Change in hedonic set point. *Science, 282*, 298–300.

Ahmed, S. H., Walker, J. R., & Koob, G. F. (2000). Persistent increase in the motivation to take heroin in rats with a history of drug escalation. *NeuroPsychopharmacology, 22*, 413–421.

Allen, R. M., Uban, K. A., Atwood, E. M., Albeck, D. S., & Yamamoto, D. J. (2007). Continuous intracerebroventricular infusion of the competitive NMDA receptor antagonist, LY235959, facilitates escalation of cocaine self-administration and increases break point for cocaine in Sprague-Dawley rats. *Pharmacology Biochemistry and Behavior, 88*, 82–88.

Aoki, T., Nirata, M., Shibasaki, M., & Suzuki, T. (2004). Metabotropic glutamate receptor 5 localized in the limbic forebrain is critical for the development of morphine-induced rewarding effect in mice. *European Journal of Neuroscience, 20*, 1633–1638.

Arvanitogiannis, A., Tzschentke, T. M., Riscaldino, L., Wise, R. A., & Shizgal, P. (2000). Fos expression following self-stimulation of the medial prefrontal cortex. *Behavioral Brain Research, 107*, 123–132.

Aujla, H., & Beninger, R. J. (2003). Intra-accumbens protein kinase C inhibitor NPC 15437 blocks amphetamine-produced conditioned place preference in rats. *Behavioral Brain Research, 147*, 41–48.

Bain, G. T., & Kornetsky, C. (1987). Naloxone attenuation of the effect of cocaine on rewarding brain stimulation. *Life Sciences, 40*, 1119–1125.

Baldo, B. A., Jain, K., Veraldi, L., Koob, G. F., & Markou, A. (1999). A dopamine D1 agonist elevates self-stimulation thresholds: Comparison to other dopamine-selective drugs. *Pharmacology Biochemistry and Behavior, 62*, 659–672.

Baptista, M. A., Martin-Fardon, R., & Weiss, F. (2004). Preferential effects of the metabotropic glutamate 2/3 receptor agonist LY379268 on conditioned reinstatement versus primary reinforcement: Comparison between cocaine and a potent conventional reinforcer. *Journal of Neuroscience, 24*, 4723–4727.

Barot, S. K., Ferguson, S. M., & Neumaier, J. F. (2007). 5-HT(1B) receptors in nucleus accumbens efferents enhance both rewarding and aversive effects of cocaine. *European Journal of Neuroscience, 25*, 3125–3131.

Barrett, A. C., Negus, S. S., Mello, N. K., & Caine, S. B. (2005). Effect of GABA agonists and GABA-A receptor modulators on cocaine- and food-maintained responding and cocaine discrimination in rats. *Journal of Pharmacology and Experimental Therapeutics, 315*, 858–871.

Barrett, S. P., Boileau, I., Okker, J., Pihl, R. O., & Dagher, A. (2004). The hedonic response to cigarette smoking is proportional to dopamine release in the human striatum as measured by positron emission tomography and [11C]raclopride. *Synapse, 54*, 65–71.

Basile, A. S., Fedorova, I., Zapata, A., Liu, X., Shippenberg, T., Duttaroy, A., et al. (2002). Deletion of the M5 muscarinic acetylcholine receptor attenuates morphine reinforcement and withdrawal but not morphine analgesia. *Proceedings of the National Academy of Sciences, USA, 99*, 11452–11457.

Bauco, P., & Wise, R. A. (1994). Potentiation of lateral hypothalamic and midline mesencephalic brain stimulation reinforcement by nicotine: Examination of repeated treatment. *Journal of Pharmacology and Experimental Therapeutics, 271*, 294–301.

Bauco, P., & Wise, R. A. (1997). Synergistic effects of cocaine with lateral hypothalamic brain stimulation reward: Lack of tolerance or sensitization. *Journal of Pharmacology and Experimental Therapeutics, 283*, 1160–1167.

Becerra, L., Harter, K., Gonzalez, R. G., & Borsook, D. (2006). Functional magnetic resonance imaging measures of the effects of morphine on central nervous system circuitry in opioid-naive healthy volunteers. *Anesthesia and Analgesia, 103*, 208–216.

Becker, A., Grecksch, G., Kraus, J., Loh, H. H., Schroeder, H., & Höllt, V. (2002). Rewarding effects of ethanol and cocaine in mu opioid receptor-deficient mice. *Naunyn Schmiedebergs Archives of Pharmacology, 365*, 296–302.

Benaliouad, F., Kapur, S., & Rompré, P. P. (2007). Blockade of 5-HT2a receptors reduces haloperidol-induced attenuation of reward. *NeuroPsychopharmacology, 32*, 51–61.

Beninger, R. J., Nakonechny, P. L., & Savina, I. (2003). CAMP-dependent protein kinase and reward-related learning: Intra-accumbens Rp-cAMPS blocks amphetamine-produced place conditioning in rats. *Psychopharmacology, 170*, 23–32.

Bergevin, A., Girardot, D., Bourque, M. K., & Trudeau, L. E. (2002). Presynaptic muopioid receptors regulate a late step of the secretory process in rat ventral tegmental area GABAergic neurons. *Neuropharmacology, 42*, 1065–1078.

Bird, M., & Kornetsky C. (1990). Dissociation of the attentional and motivational effects of pimozide on the threshold for rewarding brain stimulation. *NeuroPsychopharmacology, 3*, 33–40.

Bishop, M. P., Elder, S. T., & Heath, R. G. (1963, April 26). Intracranial self-stimulation in man. *Science, 140*, 394–396.

Bradberry, C. W., Barrett-Larimore, R. L., Jatlow, P., & Rubino, S. R. (2000). Impact of self-administered cocaine and cocaine cues on extracellular dopamine in mesolimbic and sensorimotor striatum in rhesus monkeys. *Journal of Neuroscience, 20*, 3874–3883.

Brauer, L. H., & DeWit, H. (1997). High dose pimozide does not block amphetamine-induced euphoria in normal volunteers. *Pharmacology Biochemistry and Behavior, 56*, 265–272.

Breiter, H. C., Gollub, R. L., Weisskoff, R. M., Kennedy, D. N., Makris, N., Berke, J. D., et al. (1997). Acute effects of cocaine on human brain activity and emotion. *Neuron, 19*, 591–611.

Broekkamp, C. L., & Phillips, A. G. (1979). Facilitation of self-stimulation behavior following intracerebral microinjections of opioids into the ventral tegmental area. *Pharmacology Biochemistry and Behavior, 11*, 289–295.

Broekkamp, C. L., Pijnenburg, A. J., Cools, A. R., & Van Rossum, J. M. (1975). The effect of microinjections of amphetamine into the neostriatum and the nucleus accumbens on self-stimulation behaviour. *Psychopharmacologia, 28*, 179–183.

Bubar, M. J., McMahon, L. R., DeDeurwaerdere, P., Spampinato, U., & Cunningham, K. A. (2003). Selective serotonin reuptake inhibitors enhance cocaine-induced locomotor activity and dopamine release in the nucleus accumbens. *Neuropharmacology, 44*, 342–353.

Buckett, W. R. (1981). The influence of a GABA transaminase inhibitor, gamma-vinyl GABA, on voluntary morphine consumption in the rat. *Psychopharmacology, 75*, 214–216.

Caillé, S., & Parsons, L. H. (2003). SR141716A reduces the reinforcing properties of heroin but not heroin-induced increases in nucleus accumbens dopamine in rats. *European Journal of Neuroscience, 18*, 3145–3149.

Caine, S. B., Negus, S. S., Mello, N. K., Patel, S., Bristow, L., Kulagowski, J., et al. (2002). Role of dopamine D2-like receptors in cocaine self-administration: Studies with D2 receptor mutant mice and novel D2 receptor antagonists. *Journal of Neuroscience, 22*, 2977–2988.

Caine, S. B., Thomsen, M., Gabriel, K. I., Berkowitz, J. S., Gold, L. H., Koob, G. F., et al. (2007). Lack of self-administration of cocaine in dopamine D1 receptor knock-out mice. *Journal of Neuroscience, 27*, 13140–13150.

Carelli, R. M., & Wondolowski, J. (2003). Selective encoding of cocaine versus natural rewards by nucleus accumbens neurons is not related to chronic drug exposure. *Journal of Neuroscience, 23*, 11214–11223.

Carlezon, W. A., Jr., Thome, J., Olson, V. G., Lane-Ladd, S. B., Brodkin, E. S., Hiroi, N., et al. (1998, December 18). Regulation of cocaine reward by CREB. *Science, 282*, 2272–2275.

Carlezon, W. A., Jr., & Wise, R. A. (1993). Phencyclidine-induced potentiation of brain stimulation reward: Acute effects are not altered by repeated administration. *Psychopharmacology, 111*, 402–408.

Carlezon, W. A., Jr., & Wise, R. A. (1996). Microinjections of phencyclidine (PCP) and related drugs into nucleus accumbens shell potentiate medial forebrain bundle brain stimulation reward. *Psychopharmacology, 128*, 413–420.

Carrigan, K. A., & Dykstra, L. A. (2007). Behavioral effects of morphine and cocaine in M1 muscarinic acetylcholine receptor-deficient mice. *Psychopharmacology, 191*, 985–993.

Carter, L. P., Richards, B. D., Mintzer, M. Z., & Griffiths, R. R. (2006). Relative abuse liability of GHB in humans: A comparison of psychomotor, subjective, and cognitive effects of supratherapeutic doses of triazolam, pentobarbital, and GHB. *NeuroPsychopharmacology, 31*, 2537–2551.

Chausmer, A. L., Smith, B. J., Kelly, R. Y., & Griffiths, R. R. (2003). Cocaine-like subjective effects of nicotine are not blocked by the D1 selective antagonist ecopipam (SCH 39166). *Behavioral Pharmacology, 14*, 111–120.

Cheer, J. F., Aragona, B. J., Heien, M. L., Seipel, A. T., Carelli, R. M., & Wightman, R. M. (2007). Coordinated accumbal dopamine release and neural activity drive goal-directed behavior. *Neuron, 54*, 237–244.

Chen, J., Nakamura, M., Kawamura, T., Takahashi, T., & Nakahara, D. (2006). Roles of pedunculopontine tegmental cholinergic receptors in brain stimulation reward in the rat. *Psychopharmacology, 184*, 514–522.

Chen, R., Tilley, M. R., Wei, H., Zhou, F., Zhou, F. M., Ching, S., et al. (2006). Abolished cocaine reward in mice with a cocaine-insensitive dopamine transporter. *Proceedings of the National Academy of Sciences, USA,* *103,* 9333–9338.

Chergui, K., Charléty, P. J., Akaoka, H., Saunier, C. F., Brunet, J. L., Buda, M., et al. (1993). Tonic activation of NMDA receptors causes spontaneous burst discharge of rat midbrain dopamine neurons in vivo. *European Journal of Neuroscience, 5,* 137–144.

Chiamulera, C., Epping-Jordan, M. P., Zocchi, A., Marcon, C., Cottiny, C., Tacconi, S., et al. (2001). Reinforcing and locomotor stimulant effects of cocaine are absent in mGluR5 null mutant mice. *Nature Neuroscience, 4,* 873–874.

Choi, K. H., Clements, R. L., & Greenshaw, A. J. (2005). Simultaneous AMPA/kainate receptor blockade and dopamine D(2/3) receptor stimulation in the nucleus accumbens decreases brain stimulation reward in rats. *Behavioral Brain Research, 158,* 79–88.

Choi, K. H., Whisler, K., Graham, D. L., & Self, D. W. (2006). Antisense-induced reduction in nucleus accumbens cyclic AMP response element binding protein attenuates cocaine reinforcement. *Neuroscience, 137,* 373–383.

Ciraulo, D. A., Barnhill, J. G., Ciraulo, A. M., Greenblatt, D. J., & Shader, R. I. (1989). Parental alcoholism as a risk factor in benzodiazepine abuse: A pilot study. *American Journal of Psychiatry, 146,* 1333–1335.

Ciraulo, D. A., Barnhill, J. F., Ciraulo, A. M., Sarid-Segal, O., Knapp, C., Greenblatt, D. J., et al. (1997). Alterations in pharmacodynamics of anxiolytics in abstinent alcoholic men: Subjective responses, abuse liability, and electroencephalographic effects of alprazolam, diazepam, and buspirone. *Journal of Clinical Pharmacology, 37,* 64–73.

Ciraulo, D. A., Sarid-Segal, O., Knapp, C., Ciraulo, A. M., Greenblatt, D. J., & Shader, R. I. (1996). Liability to alprazolam abuse in daughters of alcoholics. *American Journal of Psychiatry, 153,* 956–958.

Clements, R. L., & Greenshaw, A. J. (2005). Facilitation of brain stimulation reward by MK-801 (dizocilpine) may be independent of D2-like dopamine receptor stimulation in rats. *Psychopharmacology, 182,* 65–74.

Comer, S. D., Collins, E. D., MacArthur, R. B., & Fischman, M. W. (1999). Comparison of intravenous and intranasal heroin self-administration by morphine-maintained humans. *Psychopharmacology, 143,* 327–338.

Comer, S. D., Collins, E. D., Wilson, S. T., Donovan, M. R., Foltin, R. W., & Fischman, M. W. (1998). Effects of an alternative reinforcer on intravenous heroin self-administration by humans. *European Journal of Pharmacology, 345,* 13–26.

Cook, J. W., Spring, B., & McChargue, D. (2007). Influence of nicotine on positive affect in anhedonic smokers. *Psychopharmacology, 192,* 87–95.

Cossu, G., Ledent, C., Fattore, L., Imperato, A., Böhme, G. A., Parmentier, M., et al. (2001). Cannabinoid CB1 receptor knockout mice fail to self-administer morphine but not other drugs of abuse. *Behavioral Brain Research, 118,* 61–65.

Czoty, P. W., Ginsburg, B. C., & Howell, L. L. (2002). Serotonergic attenuation of the reinforcing and neurochemical effects of cocaine in squirrel monkeys. *Journal of Pharmacology and Experimental Therapeutics, 300,* 831–837.

Darke, S., & Ross, J. (1997). Polydrug dependence and psychiatric comorbidity among heroin injectors. *Drug and Alcohol Dependence, 48,* 135–141.

David, V., Besson, M., Changeux, J. P., Granon, S., & Cazala, P. (2006). Reinforcing effects of nicotine microinjections into the ventral tegmental area of mice: Dependence on cholinergic nicotinic and dopaminergic D1 receptors. *Neuropharmacology, 50,* 1030–1040.

Davidson, C., Lee, T. H., Xiong, Z., & Ellinwood, E. H. (2002). Ondansetron given in the acute withdrawal from a repeated cocaine sensitization dosing regimen reverses the expression of sensitization and inhibits self-administration. *Neuropsychopharmacology, 27,* 542–553.

Deadwyler, S. A., Hayashizaki, S., Cheer, J., & Hampson, R. E. (2004). Reward, memory and substance abuse: Functional neuronal circuits in the nucleus accumbens. *Neuroscience and Biobehavioral Review, 27,* 703–711.

De Deurwaerdère, P., Moison, D., Navailles, S., Porras, G., & Spampinato, U. (2005). Regionally and functionally distinct serotonin3 receptors control in vivo dopamine outflow in the rat nucleus accumbens. *Journal of Neurochemistry, 94,* 140–149.

De Vries, T. J., Homberg, J. R., Binnekade, R., Raasø, H., & Schoffelmeer, A. N. (2003). Cannabinoid modulation of the reinforcing and motivational properties of heroin and heroin-associated cues in rats. *Psychopharmacology, 168,* 164–169.

De Vries, T. J., & Shippenberg, T. S. (2002). Neural systems underlying opiate addiction. *Journal of Neuroscience, 22,* 3321–3325.

Doyon, W. M., York, J. L., Diaz, L. M., Samson, H. H., Czachowski, C. L. & Gonzales, R. A. (2003). Dopamine activity in the nucleus accumbens during consummatory phases of oral ethanol self administration. *Alcoholism Clinical and Experimental Research, 27,* 1573–1582.

Drevets, W. C., Gautier, C., Price, J. C., Kupfer, D. J., Kinahan, P. E., Grace, A. A., et al. (2001). Amphetamine-induced dopamine release in human ventral striatum correlates with euphoria. *Biological Psychiatry, 49,* 81–96.

Drobes, D. J., Anton, R. F., Thomas, S. E., & Voronin, K. (2004). Effects of naltrexone and nalmefene on subjective response to alcohol among non-treatment-seeking alcoholics and social drinkers. *Alcoholism Clinical and Experimental Research, 28,* 1362–1370.

Drouin, C., Darracq, L., Trovero, F., Blanc, G., Glowinski, J., Cotecchia, S., et al. (2002). Alpha1b-adrenergic receptors control locomotor and rewarding effects of psychostimulants and opiates. *Journal of Neuroscience, 22,* 2873–2884.

Duvauchelle, C. L., Fleming, S. M., & Kornetsky, C. (1997). DAMGO and DPDPE facilitation of brain stimulation reward thresholds is blocked by the dopamine antagonist cis-flupenthixol. *Neuropharmacology, 36,* 1109–1114.

Duvauchelle, C. L., Fleming, S. M., & Kornetsky, C. (1998). Prefrontal cortex infusions of SCH 23390 cause immediate and delayed effects on ventral tegmental area stimulation reward. *Brain Research, 811,* 57–62.

Elmer, G. I., Pieper, J. O., Levy, J., Rubinstein, M., Low, M. J., Grandy, D. K., et al. (2005). Brain stimulation and morphine reward deficits in dopamine D2 receptor-deficient mice. *Psychopharmacology, 182,* 33–44.

Elmer, G. I., Pieper, J. O., Rubinstein, M., Low, M. J., Grandy, D. K., & Wise, R. A. (2002). Failure of intravenous morphine to serve as an effective instrumental reinforcer in dopamine D2 receptor knock-out mice. *Journal of Neuroscience, 22,* RC224 1–6.

Emson, P. C., & Koob, G. F. (1978). The origin and distribution of dopamine-containing afferents to the rat frontal cortex. *Brain Research, 142,* 249–267.

Enggasser, J. L., & de Wit, H. (2001). Haloperidol reduces stimulant and reinforcing effects of ethanol in social drinkers. *Alcoholism Clinical and Experimental Research, 25,* 1448–1456.

Erhardt, S., Schwieler, L., & Engberg, G. (2002). Excitatory and inhibitory responses of dopamine neurons in the ventral tegmental area to nicotine. *Synapse, 43,* 227–237.

Esposito, R., Faulkner, W., & Kornetsky, C. (1979). Specific modulation of brain stimulation reward by haloperidol. *Pharmacology Biochemistry and Behavior, 10,* 937–940.

Esposito, R., & Kornetsky C. (1977, January 14). Morphine lowering of self-stimulation thresholds: Lack of tolerance with long-term administration. *Science, 195,* 189–191.

Esposito, R., Perry, W., & Kornetsky, C. (1980). Effects of d-amphetamine and naloxone on brain stimulation reward. *Psychopharmacology, 69,* 187–191.

Farren, C. K., Hameedi, F. A., Rosen, M. A., Woods, S., Jatlow, P., & Kosten, T. R. (2000). Significant interaction between clozapine and cocaine in cocaine addicts. *Drug and Alcohol Dependence, 59,* 153–163.

Fink-Jensen, A., Fedorova, I., Wörtwein, G., Woldbye, D. P., Rasmussen, T., Thomsen, M., et al. (2003). Role for M5 muscarinic acetylcholine receptors in cocaine addiction. *Journal of Neuroscience Research, 74,* 91–96.

Finlay, J. M., Damsma, G., & Fibiger, H. C. (1992). Benzodiazepine-induced decreases in extracellular concentrations of dopamine in the nucleus accumbens after acute and repeated administration. *Psychopharmacology, 106,* 202–208.

Fiorino, D. F., Coury, A., & Phillips, A. G. (1997). Dynamic changes in nucleus accumbens dopamine efflux during the Coolidge effect in male rats. *Journal of Neuroscience, 17,* 4849–4855.

Fischman, M. W., & Foltin, R. W. (1991). Utility of subjective-effects measurements in assessing abuse liability of drugs in humans. *British Journal of Addiction, 86,* 1563–1570.

Fletcher, P. J., Grottick, A. J., & Higgins, G. A. (2002). Differential effects of the 5-HT(2A) receptor antagonist M100907 and the 5-HT(2C) receptor antagonist SB242084 on cocaine-induced locomotor activity, cocaine self-administration and cocaine-induced reinstatement of responding. *NeuroPsychopharmacology, 27,* 576–586.

Foltin, R. W., & Fischman, M. W. (1991). Smoked and intravenous cocaine in humans: Acute tolerance, cardiovascular and subjective effects. *Journal of Pharmacology and Experimental Therapeutics, 257,* 247–261.

Foltin, R. W., & Fischman, M. W. (1992). The cardiovascular and subjective effects of intravenous cocaine and morphine combinations in humans. *Journal of Pharmacology and Experimental Therapeutics, 261* 623–632.

Frank, R. A., Manderscheid, P. Z., Panicker, S., Williams, H. P., & Kokoris, D. (1992). Cocaine euphoria, dysphoria, and tolerance assessed using drug-induced changes in brain-stimulation reward. *Pharmacology Biochemistry and Behavior, 42,* 771–719.

Gawin, F. H., & Kleber, H. D. (1986). Abstinence symptomatology and psychiatric diagnosis in cocaine abusers. Clinical observations. *Archives of General Psychiatry, 43,* 107–113.

Geldwert, D., Norris, J. M., Feldman, I., Schulman, J. J., Joyce, M. P., & Rayport S. (2006). Dopamine presynaptically and heterogenously modulates nucleus accumbens medium-spiny neuron GABA synapses in vitro. *BMC Neuroscience, 7,* 53.

Gerasimov, M. R., Ashby, C. R. Jr., Gardner, E. L., Mills, M. J., Brodie, J. D., & Dewey, S. L. (1999). Gamma-vinyl GABA inhibits methamphetamine, heroin, or ethanol-induced increases in nucleus accumbens dopamine. Synapse, *34,* 11–19.

Gerdjikov, T. V., & Beninger, R. J. (2006). Place preference induced by nucleus accumbens amphetamine is impaired by local blockade of Group II metabotropic glutamate receptors in rats. *BMC Neuroscience, 7,* 43.

Gerdjikov, T. V., Giles, A. C., Swain, S. N., & Beninger, R. J. (2007). Nucleus accumbens PKA inhibition blocks acquisition but enhances expression of amphetamine-produced conditioned activity in rats. *Psychopharmacology, 190,* 65–72.

Gill, B. M., Knapp, C. M., & Kornetsky, C. (2004). The effects of cocaine on the rate independent brain stimulation reward threshold in the mouse. *Pharmacology Biochemistry and Behavior, 79,* 165–170.

Grant, B. F., Stinson, F. S., Dawson, D. A., Chou, S. P., Dufour, M. C., Compton, W., et al. (2004). Prevalence and co-occurrence of substance use disorders and independent mood and anxiety disorders: Results from the National Epidemiologic Survey on Alcohol and Related Conditions. *Archives of General Psychiatry, 61,* 807–816.

Greenslade, R. G., & Mitchell, S. N. (2004). Selective action of (-)-2-oxa-4-aminobicyclo[3.1.0]hexane-4, 6-dicarboxylate (LY379268), a group II metabotropic glutamate receptor agonist, on basal and phencyclidine-induced dopamine release in the nucleus accumbens shell. *Neuropharmacology, 47,* 1–8.

Groenewegen, H. J., Wright, C. I., Beijer, A. V., & Voorn, P. (1999). Convergence and segregation of ventral striatal inputs and outputs. *Annals of the New York Academy of Sciences, 877,* 49–63.

Grottick, A. J., Corrigall, W. A., & Higgins, G. A. (2001). Activation of 5-HT(2C) receptors reduces the locomotor and rewarding effects of nicotine. *Psychopharmacology, 157,* 292–298.

Grottick, A. J., Fletcher, P. J., & Higgins, G. A. (2000). Studies to investigate the role of 5-HT(2C) receptors on cocaine- and food-maintained behavior. *Journal of Pharmacology and Experimental Therapeutics, 295,* 1183–1191.

Gysling, K., & Wang, R. Y. (1983). Morphine-induced activation of A10 dopamine neurons in the rat. *Brain Research, 277,* 119–127.

Haertzen, C. A., Hill, H. E., & Belleville, R. E. (1963). Development of the Addiction Research Center Inventory (ARCI): Selection of items that are sensitive to the effects of various drugs. *Psychopharmacologia, 4,* 155–166.

Hajnal, A., Smith, G. P., & Norgren, R. (2004). Oral sucrose stimulation increases accumbens dopamine in the rat. *American Journal Physiology Regulatory Integrative and Comparative Physiology, 286,* R31–R37.

Hall, F. S., Goeb, M., Li, X, Sora, I., & Uhl, G. (2004). Mu-opioid receptor knockout mice display reduced cocaine conditioned place preference but enhanced sensitization of cocaine-induced locomotion. *Brain Research Molecular Brain Research, 121,* 123–130.

Hall, F. S., Li, X. F., Sora, I., Xu, F., Caron, M., Lesch, K. P., et al. (2002). Cocaine mechanisms: Enhanced cocaine, fluoxetine and nisoxetine place preferences following monoamine transporter deletions. *Neuroscience, 115,* 153–161.

Hall, F. S., Sora, I., & Uhl, G. R. (2001). Ethanol consumption and reward are decreased in mu-opiate receptor knockout mice. *Psychopharmacology, 154,* 43–49.

Harrison, A. A., Gasparini, F., & Markou, A. (2002). Nicotine potentiation of brain stimulation reward reversed by DH beta, E and SCH 23390, but not by eticlopride, LY 314582 or MPEP in rats. *Psychopharmacology, 160,* 56–66.

Harrison, A. A., & Markou, A. (2001). Serotonergic manipulations both potentiate and reduce brain stimulation reward in rats: Involvement of serotonin-1A receptors. *Journal of Pharmacology and Experimental Therapeutics, 297,* 316–325.

Harrison, A. A., Parsons, L. H., Koob, G. F., & Markou, A. (1999). RU 24969, a 5-HT1A/1B agonist, elevates brain stimulation reward thresholds: An effect reversed by GR 127935, a 5-HT1B/1D antagonist. *Psychopharmacology, 141,* 242–250.

Hasue, R. H., & Shammah-Lagnado, S. J. (2002). Origin of the dopaminergic innervation of the central extended amygdala and accumbens shell: A combined retrograde tracing and immunohistochemical study in the rat. *Journal of Comparative Neurology, 454,* 15–33.

Herberg, L. J., De Belleroche, J. S., Rose, I. C., & Montgomery, A. M. (1992). Effect of the 5-HT3 receptor antagonist ondansetron on hypothalamic self-stimulation in rats and its interaction with the CCK analogue caerulein. *Neuroscience Letters, 140,* 16–18.

Hernandez, G., Hamdani, S., Rajabi, H., Conover, K., Stewart, J., Arvanitogiannis, A., et al. (2006). Prolonged rewarding stimulation of the rat medial forebrain bundle: Neurochemical and behavioral consequences. *Behavioral Neuroscience, 120,* 888–904.

Hnasko, T. S., Sotak, B. N., & Palmiter, R. D. (2005, December 8). Morphine reward in dopamine-deficient mice. *Nature, 438,* 854–857.

Hoyer, D., Hannon, J. P., & Martin, G. R. (2002). Molecular, pharmacological and functional diversity of 5-HT receptors. *Pharmacology Biochemistry and Behavior, 71,* 533–554.

Hubner, C. B., Bird, M., Rassnick, S., & Kornetsky, C. (1988). The threshold lowering effects of MDMA (ecstasy) on brain-stimulation reward. *Psychopharmacology, 95,* 49–51.

Hubner, C. B., & Kornetsky, C. (1988). The reinforcing properties of the mixed agonist-antagonist buprenorphine as assessed by brain-stimulation reward. *Pharmacology Biochemistry and Behavior, 30,* 195–197.

Hubner, C. B., & Kornetsky, C. (1992). Heroin, 6-acetylmorphine and morphine effects on threshold for rewarding and aversive brain stimulation. *Journal of Pharmacology and Experimental Therapeutics, 260,* 562–567.

Hunt, G. E., & McGregor, I. S. (1998). Rewarding brain stimulation induces only sparse Fos-like immunoreactivity in dopaminergic neurons. *Neuroscience, 83,* 501–515.

Huston- Lyons, D., Sarkar, M., & Kornetsky, C. (1993). Nicotine and brain-stimulation reward: Interactions with morphine, amphetamine and pimozide. *Pharmacology Biochemistry and Behavior, 46,* 453–457.

Ikemoto, S. (2003). Involvement of the olfactory tubercle in cocaine reward: Intracranial self-administration studies. *Journal of Neuroscience, 23,* 9305–9311.

Ikemoto, S. (2007). Dopamine reward circuitry: Two projection systems from the ventral midbrain to the nucleus accumbens-olfactory tubercle complex. *Brain Research Reviews, 56,* 27–78.

Ikemoto, S., Murphy, J. M., & McBride, W. J. (1998). Regional differences within the rat ventral tegmental area for muscimol self-infusions. *Pharmacology Biochemistry and Behavior, 61,* 87–92.

Ikemoto, S., Qin, M., & Liu, Z. H. (2005). The functional divide for primary reinforcement of D-amphetamine lies between the medial and lateral ventral striatum: Is the division of the accumbens core, shell, and olfactory tubercle valid? *Journal of Neuroscience, 25,* 5061–5065.

Ikemoto, S., & Wise, R. A. (2002). Rewarding effects of the cholinergic agents carbachol and neostigmine in the posterior ventral tegmental area. *Journal of Neuroscience, 22,* 9895–9904.

Imperato, A., Mulas, A., & Di Chiara, G. (1986). Nicotine preferentially stimulates dopamine release in the limbic system of freely moving rats. *European Journal of Pharmacology, 132,* 337–338.

Invernizzi, R., Pozzi, L., & Samanin, R. (1991). Release of dopamine is reduced by diazepam more in the nucleus accumbens than in the caudate nucleus of conscious rats. *Neuropharmacology, 30,* 575–578.

Ivanová, S., & Greenshaw, A. J. (1997). Nicotine-induced decreases in VTA electrical self-stimulation thresholds: Blockade by haloperidol and mecamylamine but not scopolamine or ondansetron. *Psychopharmacology, 134,* 187–192.

Izenwasser, S., & Kornetsky, C. (1989). The effect of amfonelic acid or nisoxetine in combination with morphine on brain-stimulation reward. *Pharmacology Biochemistry and Behavior, 32,* 983–986.

Jasmin, L., Narasaiah, M., & Tien, D. (2006). Noradrenaline is necessary for the hedonic properties of addictive drugs. *Vascular Pharmacology, 45,* 243–250.

Jayaram-Lindström, N., Wennberg, P., Hurd, Y. L., & Franck, J. (2004). Effects of naltrexone on the subjective response to amphetamine in healthy volunteers. *Journal of Clinical Psychopharmacology, 24,* 665–669.

Kalivas, P. W., Duffy, P., & Eberhardt, H. (1990). Modulation of A10 dopamine neurons by gamma-aminobutyric acid agonists. *Journal of Pharmacology and Experimental Therapeutics, 253,* 858–866.

Kankaanpää, A., Lillsunde, P., Ruotsalainen, M., Ahtee, L., & Seppälä, T. (1996). 5-HT3 receptor antagonist MDL 72222 dose-dependently attenuates cocaine- and amphetamine-induced elevations of extracellular dopamine in the nucleus accumbens and the dorsal striatum. *Pharmacology and Toxicology, 78,* 317–321.

Kankaanpää, A., Meririnne, E., & Seppälä, T. (2002). 5-HT3 receptor antagonist MDL 72222 attenuates cocaine- and mazindol-, but not methylphenidate-induced neurochemical and behavioral effects in the rat. *Psychopharmacology, 159,* 341–350.

Karasinska, J. M., George, S. R., Cheng, R., & O'Dowd, B. F. (2005). Deletion of dopamine D1 and D3 receptors differentially affects spontaneous behaviour and cocaine-induced locomotor activity, reward and CREB phosphorylation. *European Journal of Neuroscience, 22,* 1741–1750.

Kelley, A. E., Baldo, B. A., Pratt, W. E., & Will, M. J. (2005). Corticostriatal-hypothalamic circuitry and food motivation: Integration of energy, action and reward. *Physiology and Behavior, 86,* 773–795.

Kelley, S. P., & Hodge, C. W. (2003). The 5-HT3 antagonist Y-25130 blocks cocaine-induced lowering of ICSS reward thresholds in the rat. *Pharmacology Biochemistry and Behavior, 74,* 297–302.

Kenny, P. J., Boutrel, B., Gasparini, F., Koob, G. F., & Markou, A. (2005). Metabotropic glutamate 5 receptor blockade may attenuate cocaine self-administration by decreasing brain reward function in rats. *Psychopharmacology, 179,* 247–254.

Kenny, P. J., Chen, S. A., Kitamura, O., Markou, A., & Koob, G. F. (2006). Conditioned withdrawal drives heroin consumption and decreases reward sensitivity. *Journal of Neuroscience, 26,* 5894–5900.

Kenny, P. J., Polis, I., Koob, G. F., & Markou, A. (2003). Low dose cocaine self-administration transiently increases but high dose cocaine persistently decreases brain reward function in rats. *European Journal of Neuroscience, 17,* 191–195.

Kew, J. N., & Kemp, J. A. (2005). Ionotropic and metabotropic glutamate receptor structure and pharmacology. *Psychopharmacology, 179,* 4–29.

Kiyatkin, E. A., & Brown, P. L. (2003). Naloxone depresses cocaine self-administration and delays its initiation on the following day. *NeuroReport, 14,* 251–255.

Kiyatkin, E. A., & Rebec, G. V. (1997). Activity of presumed dopamine neurons in the ventral tegmental area during heroin self-administration. *NeuroReport, 8,* 2581–2585.

Klitenick, M. A., DeWitte, P., & Kalivas, P. W. (1992). Regulation of somatodendritic dopamine release in the ventral tegmental area by opioids and GABA: An in vivo microdialysis study. *Journal of Neuroscience, 12,* 2623–2632.

Knapp, C. M., & Kornetsky, C. (1989). The effects of amfonelic acid alone and in combination with naloxone on brain-stimulation reward. *Pharmacology Biochemistry and Behavior, 32,* 977–982.

Knapp, C. M., & Kornetsky, C. (1994). Bromocriptine, a D2 receptor agonist, lowers the threshold for rewarding brain stimulation. *Pharmacology Biochemistry and Behavior, 49,* 901–904.

Knapp, C. M., & Kornetsky, C. (1996). Low-dose apomorphine attenuates morphine-induced enhancement of brain stimulation reward. *Pharmacology Biochemistry and Behavior, 55,* 87–91.

Knapp, C. M., Lee, K., Foye, M., Ciraulo, D. A., & Kornetsky, C. (2001). Additive effects of intra-accumbens infusion of the cAMP-specific phosphodiesterase inhibitor, rolipram and cocaine on brain stimulation reward. *Life Sciences, 69,* 1673–1682.

Knott, V. J., & Fisher, D. J. (2007). Naltrexone alteration of the nicotine-induced EEG and mood activation response in tobacco-deprived cigarette smokers. *Experimental and Clinical Psychopharmacology, 15,* 368–381.

Kokkinidis, L., & Zacharko, R. M. (1980). Enhanced lateral hypothalamic self-stimulation responding after chronic exposure to amphetamine. *Behavioral Neural Biology, 29,* 493–497.

Konradi, C., Cole, R. L., Heckers, S., & Hyman, S. E. (1994). Amphetamine regulates gene expression in rat striatum via transcription factor CREB. *Journal of Neuroscience, 14,* 5623–5634.

Kornetsky, C. (2004). Brain-stimulation reward, morphine-induced oral stereotypy, and sensitization: Implications for abuse. *Neuroscience and Biobehavioral Reviews, 27,* 777–786.

Kornetsky, C., & Bain, G. (1987). Neuronal bases for hedonic effects of cocaine and opiates. In S. Fisher, A. Raskin, & E. H. Uhlenhuth (Eds.), *Cocaine: Clinical and biobehavioral aspects* (pp. 66–82). New York: Oxford University Press.

Kornetsky, C., & Esposito, R. U. (1979). Euphorigenic drugs: Effects on the reward pathways of the brain. *Federation Proceedings, 38,* 2473–2476.

Kornetsky, C., Huston-Lyons, D., & Porrino, L. J. (1991). The role of the olfactory tubercle in the effects of cocaine, morphine and brain-stimulation reward. *Brain Research, 541*, 75–81.

Kornetsky, C., Moolten, M., & Bain, G. (1991). Ethanol and rewarding brain stimulation. In R. E. Meyer, M. J. Lewis, S. M. Paul, & G. F. Koob (Eds.), *Neuropharmacology of ethanol: New approaches* (pp. 179–199). Boston: Birkhäuser.

Kushner, S. A., Dewey, S. L., & Kornetsky, C. (1997). Gamma-vinyl GABA attenuates cocaine-induced lowering of brain stimulation reward thresholds. *Psychopharmacology, 133*, 383–388.

Kushner, S. A., Dewey, S. L., & Kornetsky, C. (1999). The irreversible gamma-aminobutyric acid (GABA) transaminase inhibitor gamma-vinyl-GABA blocks cocaine self-administration in rats. *Journal of Pharmacology and Experimental Therapeutics, 290*, 797–802.

Lane, J. D., Pickering, C. L., Hooper, M. L., Fagan, K., Tyers, M. B., & Emmett-Oglesby, M. W. (1992). Failure of ondansetron to block the discriminative or reinforcing stimulus effects of cocaine in the rat. *Drug and Alcohol Dependence, 30*, 151–162.

Laviolette, S. R., Nader, K., & van der Kooy, D. (2002). Motivational state determines the functional role of the mesolimbic dopamine system in the mediation of opiate reward processes. *Behavioral Brain Research, 129*, 17–29.

Laviolette, S. R., & van der Kooy, D. (2001). GABAA receptors signal bidirectional reward transmission from the ventral tegmental area to the tegmental pedunculopontine nucleus as a function of opiate state. *European Journal of Neuroscience, 20*, 2179–2187.

Lecca, D., Cacciapaglia, F., Valentini, V., Acquas, E., & Di Chiara, G. (2007). Differential neurochemical and behavioral adaptation to cocaine after response contingent and noncontingent exposure in the rat. *Psychopharmacology, 191*, 653–667.

Lecca, D., Cacciapaglia, F., Valentini, V., Gronli, J., Spiga, S., & Di Chiara, G. (2006). Preferential increase of extracellular dopamine in the rat nucleus accumbens shell as compared to that in the core during acquisition and maintenance of intravenous nicotine self-administration. *Psychopharmacology, 184*, 435–446.

Lecca, D., Valentini, V., Cacciapaglia, F., Acquas, E., & Di Chiara, G. (2007). Reciprocal effects of response contingent and noncontingent intravenous heroin on in vivo nucleus accumbens shell versus core dopamine in the rat: A repeated sampling microdialysis study. *Psychopharmacology, 194*, 103–116.

Lee, D. Y., Guttilla, M., Fung, K. D., McFeron, S., Yan, J., & Ranaldi, R. (2007). Rostral-caudal differences in the effects of intra-VTA muscimol on cocaine self-administration. *Pharmacology Biochemistry and Behavior, 86*, 542–549.

Lee, K., & Kornetsky, C. (1998). Acute and chronic fluoxetine treatment decreases the sensitivity of rats to rewarding brain stimulation. *Pharmacology Biochemistry and Behavior, 60*, 539–544.

Leith, N. J., & Barrett, R. J. (1976). Amphetamine and the reward system: evidence for tolerance and post-drug depression. *Pharmacologia, 46*, 19–25.

Leith, N. J., & Barrett, R. J. (1981). Self-stimulation and amphetamine: Tolerance to d and l isomers and cross tolerance to cocaine and methylphenidate. *Psychopharmacology, 74*, 23–28.

Le Moal, M., & Koob, G. F. (2007). Drug addiction: Pathways to the disease and pathophysiological perspectives. *European Neuropsychopharmacology, 17*, 377–393.

Le Pen, G., Duterte-Boucher, D., & Costentin, J. (1996). Place conditioning with cocaine and the dopamine uptake inhibitor GBR12783. *NeuroReport, 7*, 2839–2842.

Liechti, M. E., Lhuillier, L., Kaupmann, K., & Markou, A. (2007). Metabotropic glutamate 2/3 receptors in the ventral tegmental area and the nucleus accumbens shell are involved in behaviors relating to nicotine dependence. *Journal of Neuroscience, 27*, 9077–9085.

Liechti, M. E., & Markou, A. (2007). Interactive effects of the mGlu5 receptor antagonist MPEP and the mGlu2/3 receptor antagonist LY341495 on nicotine self-administration and reward deficits associated with nicotine withdrawal in rats. *European Journal of Pharmacology, 554*, 164–174.

Lin, D., Koob, G. F., & Markou, A. (2000). Time-dependent alterations in ICSS thresholds associated with repeated amphetamine administrations. *Pharmacology Biochemistry and Behavior, 65*, 407–417.

Lin, Y., de Vaca, S. C., Carr, K. D., & Stone, E. A. (2007). Role of alpha(1)-adrenoceptors of the locus coeruleus in self-stimulation of the medial forebrain bundle. *NeuroPsychopharmacology, 32*, 835–841.

Lynch, W. J., Sughondhabirom, A., Pittman, B., Gueorguieva, R., Kalayasiri, R., Joshua, D., et al. (2006). A paradigm to investigate the regulation of cocaine self-administration in human cocaine users: A randomized trial. *Psychopharmacology, 185*, 306–314.

Maldonado-Irizarry, C. S., Stellar, J. R., & Kelley, A. E. (1994). Effects of cocaine and GBR-12909 on brain stimulation reward. *Pharmacology Biochemistry and Behavior, 48*, 915–920.

Markou, A., & Koob, G. F. (1992). Construct validity of a self-stimulation threshold paradigm: Effects of reward and performance manipulations. *Physiology and Behavior, 51*, 111–119.

Martel, P., & Fantino, M. (1996). Mesolimbic dopaminergic system activity as a function of food reward: A microdialysis study. *Pharmacology Biochemistry and Behavior, 53*, 221–226.

Martin, M., Ledent, C., Parmentier, M., Maldonado, R., & Valverde, O. (2000). Cocaine, but not morphine, induces conditioned place preference and sensitization to locomotor responses in CB1 knockout mice. *European Journal of Neuroscience, 12*, 4038–4046.

Martinez, D., Gil, R., Slifstein, M., Hwang, D. R., Huang, Y., Perez, A., et al. (2005). Alcohol dependence is associated with blunted dopamine transmission in the ventral striatum. *Biological Psychiatry, 58*, 779–786.

Martinez, D., Narendran, R., Foltin, R. W., Slifstein, M., Hwang, D. R., Broft, A., et al. (2007). Amphetamine-induced dopamine release: Markedly blunted in cocaine dependence and predictive of the choice to self-administer cocaine. *American Journal of Psychiatry, 164*, 622–629.

Martinez, D., Slifstein, M., Broft, A., Mawlawi, O., Hwang, D. R., Huang, Y., et al. (2003). Imaging human mesolimbic dopamine transmission with positron emission tomography: Pt. II. Amphetamine -induced dopamine release in the functional subdivisions of the striatum. *Journal of Cerebral Blood Flow Metabolism, 23*, 285–300.

Mascia, M. S., Obinu, M. C., Ledent, C., Parmentier, M., Böhme, G. A., Imperato, A., et al. (1999). Lack of morphine-induced dopamine release in the nucleus accumbens of cannabinoid CB(1) receptor knockout mice. *European Journal of Pharmacology, 383*, R1–R2.

Mas-Nieto, M., Pommier, B., Tzavara, E. T., Caneparo, A., Da Nascimento, S., Le Fur, G., et al. (2001). Reduction of opioid dependence by the CB(1) antagonist SR141716A in mice: Evaluation of the interest in pharmacotherapy of opioid addiction. *British Journal of Pharmacology, 132*, 1809–1816.

McBride, W. J., Murphy, J. M., & Ikemoto, S. (1999). Localization of brain reinforcement mechanisms: Intracranial self-administration and intracranial place-conditioning studies. *Behavioral Brain Research, 101*, 129–152.

McCaul, M. E., Wand, G. S., Eissenberg, T., Rohde, C. A., & Cheskin, L. J. (2000). Naltrexone alters subjective and psychomotor responses to alcohol in heavy drinking subjects. *Neuropsychopharmacology, 22*, 480–492.

Melnick, S. M., Maldonado-Vlaar, C. S., Stellar, J. R., & Trzcinska, M. (2001). Effects of repeated GBR 12909 administration on brain stimulation reward. *European Journal of Pharmacology, 419*, 199–205.

Meltzer, L. T., Christoffersen, C. L., & Serpa, K. (1997). Modulation of dopamine neuronal activity by glutamate receptor subtypes. *Neuroscience Biobehavioral Reviews, 21*, 511–518.

Narita, M., Aoki, T., Ozaki, S., Yajima, Y., & Suzuki, T. (2001). Involvement of protein kinase C gamma isoform in morphine-induced reinforcing effects. *Neuroscience, 103,* 309–314.

Navailles, S., De Deurwaerdere, P., Porras, G., & Spampinato, U. (2004). In vivo evidence that 5-HT2C receptor antagonist but not agonist modulates cocaine-induced dopamine outflow in the rat nucleus accumbens and striatum. *NeuroPsychopharmacology, 29,* 319–326.

Navarro, M., Carrera, M. R., Fratta, W., Valverde, O., Cossu, G., Fattore, L., et al. (2001). Functional interaction between opioid and cannabinoid receptors in drug self-administration. *Journal of Neuroscience, 21,* 5344–5350.

Newton, P. M., & Ron, D. (2007). Protein kinase C and alcohol addiction. *Pharmacological Research, 55,* 570–577.

Newton, T. F., Kalechstein, A. D., De La Garza, R. Jr., Cutting, D. J., & Ling, W. (2005). Apathy predicts hedonic but not craving response to cocaine. *Pharmacology Biochemistry and Behavior, 82,* 236–240.

Oakman, S. A., Faris, P. L., Kerr, P. E., Cozzari, C., & Hartman, B. K. (1995). Distribution of pontomesencephalic cholinergic neurons projecting to substantia nigra differs significantly from those projecting to ventral tegmental area. *Journal of Neuroscience, 15,* 5859–5869.

O'Dell, L. E., & Parsons, L. H. (2004). Serotonin1B receptors in the ventral tegmental area modulate cocaine-induced increases in nucleus accumbens dopamine levels. *Journal of Pharmacology and Experimental Therapeutics, 311,* 711–719.

O'Donnell, P., Lavín, A, Enquist, L. W., Grace, A. A., & Card, J. P. (1997). Interconnected parallel circuits between rat nucleus accumbens and thalamus revealed by retrograde transsynaptic transport of pseudorabies virus. *Journal of Neuroscience, 17,* 2143–2167.

Olds, J., & Milner, P. (1954). Positive reinforcement produced by electrical stimulation of septal area and other regions of rat brain. *Journal of Comparative Physiological Psychology, 47,* 419–427.

Olds, M. E. (1982). Reinforcing effects of morphine in the nucleus accumbens. *Brain Research, 237,* 429–440.

Olive, M. F., Mehmert, K. K., Messing, R. O., & Hodge, C. W. (2000). Reduced operant ethanol self-administration and in vivo mesolimbic dopamine responses to ethanol in PKCepsilon-deficient mice. *European Journal of Neuroscience, 12,* 4131–4140.

Olson, V. G., Green, T. A., Neve, R. L., & Nestler, E. J. (2007). Regulation of morphine reward and feeding by CREB in the lateral hypothalamus. *Synapse, 61,* 110–113.

Olson, V. G., Zabetian, C. P., Bolanos, C. A., Edwards, S., Barrot, M., Eisch, A. J., et al. (2005). Regulation of drug reward by cAMP response element-binding protein: Evidence for two functionally distinct subregions of the ventral tegmental area. *Journal of Neuroscience, 25,* 5553–5562.

Oswald, L. M., Wong, D. F., McCaul, M., Zhou, Y., Kuwabara, H., Choi, L., et al. (2005). Relationships among ventral striatal dopamine release, cortisol secretion, and subjective responses to amphetamine. *NeuroPsychopharmacology, 30,* 821–832.

Panagis, G., Kastellakis, A., Spyraki, C., & Nomikos, G. (2000). Effects of methyllycaconitine (MLA), an alpha 7 nicotinic receptor antagonist, on nicotine- and cocaine-induced potentiation of brain stimulation reward. *Psychopharmacology, 149,* 388–396.

Panagis, G., Nomikos, G. G., Miliaressis, E., Chergui, K., Kastellakis, A., Svensson, T. H., et al. (1997). Ventral pallidum self-stimulation induces stimulus dependent increase in c-fos expression in reward-related brain regions. *Neuroscience, 77,* 175–186.

Parsons, L. H., Weiss, F., & Koob, G. F. (1998). Serotonin1B receptor stimulation enhances cocaine reinforcement. *Journal of Neuroscience, 18,* 10078–10089.

Paterson, N. E., & Markou, A. (2005). The metabotropic glutamate receptor 5 antagonist MPEP decreased break points for nicotine, cocaine and food in rats. *Psychopharmacology, 179,* 255–261.

Paul, M., Dewey, S. L., Gardner, E. L., Brodie, J. D., & Ashby, C. R. Jr., (2001). Gamma-vinyl GABA (GVG) blocks expression of the conditioned place preference response to heroin in rats. *Synapse, 41,* 219–220.

Peltier, R., & Schenk, S. (1991). GR38032F, a serotonin 5-HT3 antagonist, fails to alter cocaine self-administration in rats. *Pharmacology Biochemistry and Behavior, 39,* 133–136.

Pettit, H. O., Ettenberg, A., Bloom, F. E., & Koob, G. F. (1984). Destruction of dopamine in the nucleus accumbens selectively attenuates cocaine but not heroin self-administration in rats. *Psychopharmacology, 84,* 167–173.

Pontieri, F. E., Tanda, G., & Di Chiara, G. (1995). Intravenous cocaine, morphine, and amphetamine preferentially increase extracellular dopamine in the "shell" as compared with the "core" of the rat nucleus accumbens. *Proceedings of the National Academy of Sciences, USA, 92,* 12304–12308.

Porrino, L. J., Huston-Lyons, D., Bain, G., Sokoloff, L., & Kornetsky, C. (1990). The distribution of changes in local cerebral energy metabolism associated with brain stimulation reward to the medial forebrain bundle of the rat. *Brain Research, 511,* 1–6.

Preston, K. L., & Jasinski, D. R. (1991). Abuse liability studies of opioid agonist-antagonists in humans. *Drug and Alcohol Dependence, 28,* 49–82.

Rada, P. V., Mark, G. P., Yeomans, J. J., & Hoebel, B. G. (2000). Acetylcholine release in ventral tegmental area by hypothalamic self-stimulation, eating, and drinking. *Pharmacology Biochemistry and Behavior, 65,* 375–379.

Rahman, S., & McBride, W. J. (2002). Involvement of GABA and cholinergic receptors in the nucleus accumbens on feedback control of somatodendritic dopamine release in the ventral tegmental area. *Journal of Neurochemistry, 80,* 646–654.

Ranaldi, R., Pocock, D., Zereik, R., & Wise, R. A. (1999). Dopamine fluctuations in the nucleus accumbens during maintenance, extinction, and reinstatement of intravenous D-amphetamine self-administration. *Journal of Neuroscience, 19,* 4102–4109.

Ranaldi, R., & Woolverton, W. L. (2002). Self-administration of cocaine: Scopolamine combinations by rhesus monkeys. *Psychopharmacology, 161,* 442–448.

Rice, O. V., Gordon, N., & Gifford, A. N. (2002). Conditioned place preference to morphine in cannabinoid CB1 receptor knockout mice. *Brain Research, 945,* 135–138.

Risinger, R. C., Salmeron, B. J., Ross, T. J., Amen, S. L., Sanfilipo, M., Hoffmann, R. G., et al. (2005). Neural correlates of high and craving during cocaine self-administration using BOLD fMRI. *NeuroImage, 26,* 1097–1108.

Roberts, D. C., Loh, E. A., & Vickers, G. (1989). Self-administration of cocaine on a progressive ratio schedule in rats: Dose-response relationship and effect of haloperidol pretreatment. *Psychopharmacology, 97,* 535–538.

Robinson, T. E., & Berridge, K. C. (2003). Addiction. *Annual Reviews of Psychology, 54,* 25–53.

Rocha, B. A. (2003). Stimulant and reinforcing effects of cocaine in monoamine transporter knockout mice. *European Journal of Pharmacology, 479,* 107–115.

Rocha, B. A., Fumagalli, F., Gainetdinov, R. R., Jones, S. R., Ator, R., Giros, B., et al. (1998). Cocaine self-administration in dopamine-transporter knockout mice. *Nature Neuroscience, 1,* 132–137.

Rocha, B. A., Goulding, E. H., O'Dell, L. E., Mead, A. N., Coufal, N. G., Parsons, L. H., et al. (2002). Enhanced locomotor, reinforcing, and neurochemical effects of cocaine in serotonin 5-hydroxytryptamine 2C receptor mutant mice. *Journal of Neuroscience, 22,* 10039–10045.

Rodd, Z. A., Bell, R. L., Kuc, K. A., Zhang, Y., Murphy, J. M., & McBride, W. J. (2005). Intracranial self-administration of cocaine within the posterior ventral tegmental area of Wistar rats: Evidence for involvement of serotonin-3 receptors and dopamine neurons. *Journal of Pharmacology and Experimental Therapeutics, 313,* 134–145.

Rolls, E. T. (2006). Brain mechanisms underlying flavour and appetite. *Philosophical Transactions of the Royal Society of London. Series B, 361,* 1123–1136.

Romach, M. K., Glue, P., Kampman, K., Kaplan, H. L., Somer, G. R., Poole, S., et al. (1999). Attenuation of the euphoric effects of cocaine by the dopamine D1/D5 antagonist ecopipam (SCH 39166). *Archives of General Psychiatry, 56,* 1101–1106.

Sabatinelli, D., Bradley, M. M., Lang, P. J., Costa, V. D., & Versace, F. (2007). Pleasure rather than salience activates human nucleus accumbens and medial prefrontal cortex. *Journal of Neurophysiology, 98,* 1374–1379.

Schilström, B., Svensson, H. M., Svensson, T. H., & Nomikos, G. G. (1998). Nicotine and food induced dopamine release in the nucleus accumbens of the rat: Putative role of alpha7 nicotinic receptors in the ventral tegmental area. *Neuroscience, 85,* 1005–1009.

Schmidt, H. D., Anderson, S. M., & Pierce, R. C. (2006). Stimulation of D1-like or D2 dopamine receptors in the shell, but not the core, of the nucleus accumbens reinstates cocaine-seeking behaviour in the rat. *European Journal of Neuroscience, 23,* 219–228.

Schmidt, H. D., & Pierce, R. C. (2006). Systemic administration of a dopamine, but not a serotonin or norepinephrine, transporter inhibitor reinstates cocaine seeking in the rat. *Behavioral Brain Research, 175,* 189–194.

Schroeder, J. A., Hummel, M., Simpson, A. D., Sheikh, R., Soderman, A. R., & Unterwald, E. M. (2007). A role for mu opioid receptors in cocaine-induced activity, sensitization, and reward in the rat. *Psychopharmacology, 195,* 26–272.

Schulteis, G., Markou, A., Cole, M., & Koob, G. F. (1995). Decreased brain reward produced by ethanol withdrawal. *Proceedings of the National Academy of Sciences, USA, 92,* 5880–5884.

Schultz, W. (2007). Behavioral dopamine signals. *Trends in Neuroscience, 30,* 203–210.

Self, D. W., Genova, L. M., Hope, B. T., Barnhart, W. J., Spencer, J. J., & Nestler, E. J. (1998). Involvement of cAMP-dependent protein kinase in the nucleus accumbens in cocaine self-administration and relapse of cocaine-seeking behavior. *Journal of Neuroscience, 18,* 1848–1859.

Semba, K., & Fibiger, H. C. (1992). Afferent connections of the laterodorsal and the pedunculopontine tegmental nuclei in the rat: A retro- and antero-grade transport and immunohistochemical study. *Journal of Comparative Neurology, 323,* 387–410.

Sesack, S. R., & Pickel, V. M. (1992). Prefrontal cortical efferents in the rat synapse on unlabeled neuronal targets of catecholamine terminals in the nucleus accumbens septi and on dopamine neurons in the ventral tegmental area. *Journal of Comparative Neurology, 320,* 5–60.

Sherer, M. A., Kumor, K. M., & Jaffe, J. H. (1989). Effects of intravenous cocaine are partially attenuated by haloperidol. *Psychiatry Research, 27,* 117–125.

Skoubis, P. D., & Maidment, N. T. (2003). Blockade of ventral pallidal opioid receptors induces a conditioned place aversion and attenuates acquisition of cocaine place preference in the rat. *Neuroscience, 119,* 241–249.

Slattery, D. A., Markou, A., Froestl, W., & Cryan, J. F. (2005). The GABAB receptor-positive modulator GS39783 and the GABAB receptor agonist baclofen attenuate the reward-facilitating effects of cocaine: Intracranial self-stimulation studies in the rat. *NeuroPsychopharmacology, 30,* 2065–2072.

Sofuoglu, M., Singha, A., Kosten, T. R., McCance-Katz, F. E., Petrakis, I., & Oliveto, A. (2003). Effects of naltrexone and isradipine, alone or in combination, on cocaine responses in humans. *Pharmacology Biochemistry and Behavior, 75,* 801–808.

Sora, I., Wichems, C., Takahashi, N., Li, X., Zeng, Z., Revay, R., et al. (1998). Cocaine reward models: Conditioned place preference can

be established in dopamine- and in serotonin-transporter knockout mice. *Proceedings of the National Academy of Sciences, USA, 95,* 7699–7704.

Stafford, D., LeSage, M. G., Rice, K. C., & Glowa, J. R. (2001). A comparison of cocaine, GBR 12909, and phentermine self-administration by rhesus monkeys on a progressive-ratio schedule. *Drug and Alcohol Dependence, 62,* 41–47.

Steffensen, S. C., Stobbs, S. H., Colago, E. E., Lee, R., Koob, G. F., Gallegos, R. A., et al. (2006). Contingent and non-contingent effects of heroin on mu-opioid receptor-containing ventral tegmental area GABA neurons. *Experimental Neurology, 202,* 139–151.

Stein, E. A., Pankiewicz, J., Harsch, H. H., Cho, J. K., Fuller, S. A., Hoffmann, R. G., et al. (1998). Nicotine-induced limbic cortical activation in the human brain: A functional MRI study. *American Journal of Psychiatry, 155,* 1009–1015.

Steiner, M., Katz, R. J., & Carroll, B. J. (1980). Behavioral effects of dopamine agonists across the estrous cycle in rats. *Psychopharmacology, 71,* 147–151.

Stellar, J. R., & Corbett, D. (1989). Regional neuroleptic microinjections indicate a role for nucleus accumbens in lateral hypothalamic self-stimulation reward. *Brain Research, 477,* 126–143.

Stromberg, M. F., Mackler, S. A., Volpicelli, J. R., O'Brien, C. P., & Dewey, S.L. (2001). The effect of gamma-vinyl-GABA on the consumption of concurrently available oral cocaine and ethanol in the rat. *Pharmacology Biochemistry, and Behavior, 68,* 291–299.

Thompson, B. E., Sachs, B. D., Kantak, K. M., & Cherry, J. A. (2004). The Type IV phosphodiesterase inhibitor rolipram interferes with drug-induced conditioned place preference but not immediate early gene induction in mice. *European Journal of Neuroscience, 19,* 2561–2568.

Thomsen, M., Woldbye, D., Wörtwein, G., Fink-Jensen, A., Wess, J., & Caine, S. (2005). Reduced cocaine self-administration in muscarinic M5 acetylcholine receptor-deficient mice. *Journal of Neuroscience, 25,* 8141–8149.

Todtenkopf, M. S., Marcus, J. F., Portoghese, P. S., & Carlezon, W. A. (2004). Effects of kappa-opioid receptor ligands on intracranial self-stimulation in rats. *Psychopharmacology, 172,* 463–470.

Todtenkopf, M. S., Parsegian, A., Naydenov, A., Neve, R. L., Konradi, C., & Carlezon, W. A., Jr. (2006). Brain reward regulated by AMPA receptor subunits in nucleus accumbens shell. *Journal of Neuroscience, 26,* 11665–11669.

Tomkins, D. M., Joharchi, N., Tampakeras, M., Martin, J. R., Wichmann, J., & Higgins, G. A. (2002). An investigation of the role of 5-HT(2C) receptors in modifying ethanol self-administration behaviour. *Pharmacology Biochemistry and Behavior, 71,* 735–744.

Tran, A. H., Tamura, R., Uwano, T., Kobayashi, T., Katsuki, M., Matsumoto, G., et al. (2002). Altered accumbens neural response to prediction of reward associated with place in dopamine D2 receptor knockout mice. *Proceedings of the National Academy of Sciences, USA, 99,* 8986–8991.

Tran, A. H., Tamura, R., Uwano, T., Kobayashi, T., Katsuki, M., & Ono, T. (2005). Dopamine D1 receptors involved in locomotor activity and accumbens neural responses to prediction of reward associated with place. *Proceedings of the National Academy of Sciences, USA, 102,* 2117–2122.

Unterwald, E., Sasson, S., & Kornetsky, C. (1987). Evaluation of the supraspinal analgesic activity and abuse liability of ethylketocyclazocine. *European Journal of Pharmacology, 133,* 275–281.

Uslaner, J., Kalechstein, A., Richter, T., Ling, W., & Newton, T. (1999). Association of depressive symptoms during abstinence with the subjective high produced by cocaine. *American Journal of Psychiatry, 156,* 1444–1446.

Volkow, N. D., Wang, G. J., Fowler, J. S., Logan, J., Gatley, S. J., Wong, C., et al. (1999). Reinforcing effects of psychostimulants in humans are associated with increases in brain dopamine and occupancy of D(2) receptors. *Journal of Pharmacology and Experimental Therapeutics, 291*, 409–415.

Volpicelli, J. R., Watson, N. T., King, A. C., Sherman, C. E., & O'Brien, C. P. (1995). Effect of naltrexone on alcohol "high" in alcoholics. *American Journal of Psychiatry, 152*, 613–615.

Wachtel, S. R., Ortengren, A., & de Wit, H. (2002). The effects of acute haloperidol or risperidone on subjective responses to methamphetamine in healthy volunteers. *Drug and Alcohol Dependence, 68*, 23–33.

Wald, D., Ebstein, R. P., & Belmaker, R. H. (1978). Haloperidol and lithium blocking of the mood response to intravenous methylphenidate. *Psychopharmacology, 57*, 83–87.

Walker, D., Mahoney, C., Ilivitsky, V., & Knott, V. J. (2001). Effects of haloperidol pretreatment on the smoking-induced EEG/mood activation response profile. *Neuropsychobiology, 43*, 102–112.

Walsh, S. L., Preston, K. L., Sullivan, J. T., Fromme, R., & Bigelow, G. E. (1994). Fluoxetine alters the effects of intravenous cocaine in humans. *Journal of Clinical Psychopharmacology, 14*, 396–407.

Walsh, S. L., Sullivan, J. T., Preston, K. L., Garner, J. E., & Bigelow, G. E. (1996). Effects of naltrexone on response to intravenous cocaine, hydromorphone and their combination in humans. *Journal of Pharmacology and Experimental Therapeutics, 279*, 524–538.

Walters, C. L., & Blendy, J. A. (2001). Different requirements for cAMP response element binding protein in positive and negative reinforcing properties of drugs of abuse. *Journal of Neuroscience, 21*, 9438–9444.

Walters, C. L., Godfrey, M., Li, X., & Blendy, J. A. (2005). Alterations in morphine-induced reward, locomotor activity, and thermoregulation in CREB-deficient mice. *Brain Research, 1032*, 193–199.

Walters, C. L., Kuo, Y. C., & Blendy, J. A. (2003). Differential distribution of CREB in the mesolimbic dopamine reward pathway. *Journal of Neurochemistry, 87*, 1237–1244.

Ward, A. S., Haney, M., Fischman, M. W., & Foltin, R. W. (1997). Binge cocaine self-administration in humans: Intravenous cocaine. *Psychopharmacology, 132*, 375–381.

West, A. R., Floresco, S. B., Charara, A., Rosenkranz, J. A., & Grace, A. A. (2003). Electrophysiological interactions between striatal glutamatergic and dopaminergic systems. *Annals of the New York Academy of Sciences, 1003*, 53–74.

Wise, R. A., Murray, A., & Bozarth, M. A. (1990). Bromocriptine self-administration and bromocriptine-reinstatement of cocaine-trained and heroin-trained lever pressing rats. *Psychopharmacology, 100*, 355–360.

Wojnicki, F. H., & Glowa, J. R. (1996). Effects of drug history on the acquisition of responding maintained by GBR 12909 in rhesus monkeys. *Psychopharmacology, 123*, 34–41.

Woolverton, W. L. (1987). Evaluation of the role of norepinephrine in the reinforcing effects of psychomotor stimulants in rhesus monkeys. *Pharmacology Biochemistry and Behavior, 26*, 835–839.

Woolverton, W. L., Goldberg, L. I., & Ginos, J. Z. (1984). Intravenous self-administration of dopamine receptor agonists by rhesus monkeys. *Journal of Pharmacology and Experimental Therapeutics, 230*, 678–683.

Wu, M., Hrycyshyn, A. W., & Brudzynski, S. M. (1996). Subpallidal outputs to the nucleus accumbens and the ventral tegmental area: Anatomical and electrophysiological studies. *Brain Research, 740*, 151–161.

Xi, Z. X., Baker, D. A., Shen, H., Carson, D. S., & Kalivas, P. W. (2002). Group II metabotropic glutamate receptors modulate extracellular glutamate in the nucleus accumbens. *Journal of Pharmacology and Experimental Therapeutics, 300*, 162–171.

Xi, Z., & Stein, E. A. (2000). Increased mesolimbic GABA concentration blocks heroin self-administration in the rat. *Journal of Pharmacology and Experimental Therapeutics, 294*, 613–619.

Xu, F., Gainetdinov, R. R., Wetsel, W. C., Jones, S. R., Bohn, L. M., Miller, G. W., et al. (2000). Mice lacking the norepinephrine transporter are supersensitive to psychostimulants. *Nature Neuroscience, 3*, 465–471.

Yan, Q. S., & Yan, S. E. (2001). Activation of 5-HT(1B/1D) receptors in the mesolimbic dopamine system increases dopamine release from the nucleus accumbens: A microdialysis study. *European Journal of Pharmacology, 418*, 55–64.

Yeomans, J. S., Takeuchi, J., Baptista, M., Flynn, D. D., Lepik, K., Nobrega, J., et al. (2000). Brain-stimulation reward thresholds raised by an antisense oligonucleotide for the M5 muscarinic receptor infused near dopamine cells. *Journal of Neuroscience, 20*, 8861–8867.

Yeomans, M. R., & Gray, R. W. (1996). Selective effects of naltrexone on food pleasantness and intake. *Physiology and Behavior, 60*, 439–446.

Yeomans, M. R., & Gray, R. W. (1997). Effects of naltrexone on food intake and changes in subjective appetite during eating: Evidence for opioid involvement in the appetizer effect. *Physiology and Behavior, 62*, 15–21.

Zanetti, L., Picciotto, M. R., & Zoli, M. (2007). Differential effects of nicotinic antagonists perfused into the nucleus accumbens or the ventral tegmental area on cocaine-induced dopamine release in the nucleus accumbens of mice. *Psychopharmacology, 190*, 189–199.

Zawertailo, L. A., Busto, U. E., Kaplan, H. L., Greenblatt, D. J., & Sellers, E. M. (2003). Comparative abuse liability and pharmacological effects of meprobamate, triazolam, and butabarbital. *Journal of Clinical Psychopharmacology, 23*, 269–280.

Chapter 41

Neural Basis of Mental Representations of Motivation, Emotion, and Pleasure

MORTEN L. KRINGELBACH

Motivation and emotion govern our lives for better and sometimes for worse (Kringelbach, 2005). The underlying hedonic processing is arguably at the heart of what makes us human, but at the same time it is also one of the most important factors keeping us from staying healthy (Kringelbach, 2004b; Saper, Chou, & Elmquist, 2002). A better understanding of the underlying brain mechanisms can therefore help us understand and potentially treat the serious problems of affective disorders, such as unipolar depression, bipolar disorder, chronic pain, and eating disorders.

This review is centered on the functional neuroanatomy of pleasure and hedonic processing in general, where pleasure is defined as one of the positive dimensions of the more general category of hedonic processing, which also includes other negative and unpleasant dimensions such as pain (Berridge & Kringelbach, 2008; Kringelbach & Berridge, 2009; see Figure 41.1). Malignant affective disorders such as depression, chronic pain, and eating disorders are characterized by the lowered or missing ability to experience pleasure, anhedonia. The evidence reviewed comes from human neuroimaging, neuropsychology, and neurosurgery. This chapter concentrates on the evidence linking the orbitofrontal cortex to reward and hedonic processing (see Figure 41.2).

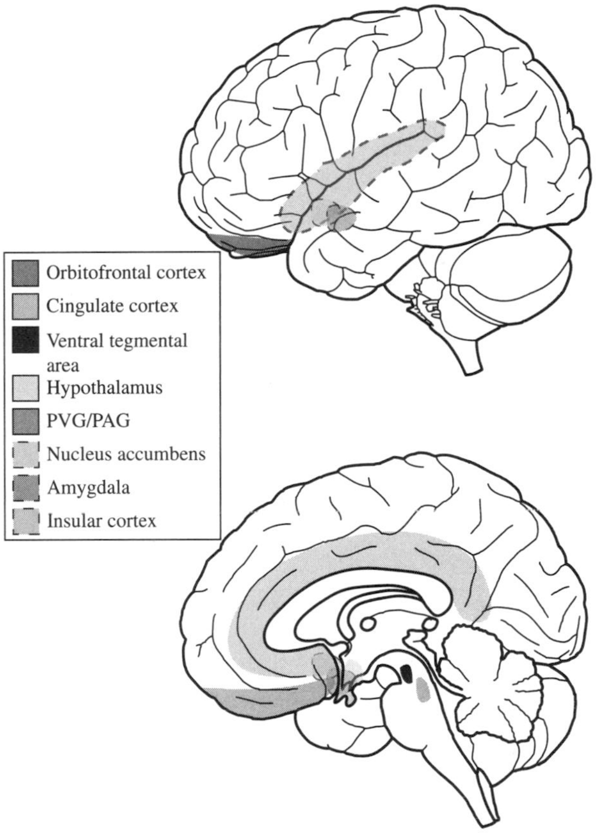

EMOTION AND MOTIVATION

Emotion and motivation remained for many years elusive scientific topics and were generally defined in opposition to cognition as that which move us in some way, as implied by the Latin root *movere,* to move. Owing primarily to its perceived subjective nature, the scientific study of emotion

This research was supported by TrygFonden Charitable Foundation, MRC, and Wellcome Trust.

Figure 41.1 (**Figure C.38** in color section) Some important brain structures in the pleasure brain.

Note: The human brain seen from the side (top) and split in the middle (bottom) overlaid with the important brain structures of the pleasure brain. These include the orbitofrontal cortex (grey), the cingulate cortex (light blue), ventral tegmental area in the brain stem (light red), hypothalamus, periventricular gray/periacqueductal gray (PVG/PAG, green), nucleus accumbens (in the temporal lobes, light green), amygdala (in the temporal lobes, light red) and the insular cortices (buried between the prefrontal and temporal lobes, orange).

was stunted despite ideas put forward by pioneering individuals such as Charles Darwin (1872), who examined the evolution of emotional responses and facial expressions, and suggested that emotions allow an organism to make

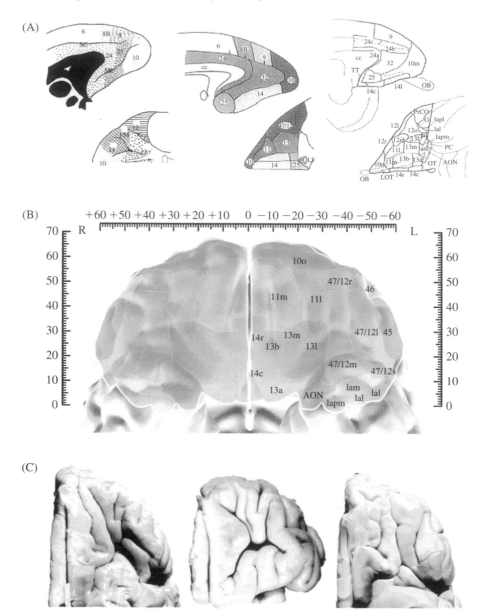

Figure 41.2 The orbitofrontal cortex.

Note: **A:** The primate orbitofrontal was subdivided to reflect its heterogeneity, as first proposed by the maps by Walker (1940), with the areas in the monkey Macaca fascicularis shown in views of the medial wall and the ventral surface. Walker proposed a further parcellation of the orbitofrontal cortex into five areas (areas 10, 11, 12, 13, and 14) (leftmost). Walker's nomenclature was then reconciled with that used in Brodmann's primate and human brain by Petrides and Pandya (1994), with lateral parts of the orbitofrontal cortex designated area 47/12 (middle). Even further subdivisions of the orbitofrontal cortex were subsequently proposed by Carmichael and Price (Carmichael & Price, 1994; rightmost). **B:** The human cytoarchitectonic maps of the orbitofrontal cortex rendered on the orbital surface in normalized space. From "The Functional Neuroanatomy of the Human Orbitofrontal Cortex: Evidence from Neuroimaging and Neuropsychology," by M. L. Kringelbach and E. T. Rolls, 2004, *Progress in Neurobiology, 72,* pp. 341–372. Based on a template provided by the Montreal Neurological Institute. Adapted with permission. **C:** The sulcal variability of the human orbitofrontal cortex is demonstrated with ventral views of the three main types taken from the left hemisphere. From "Orbitofrontal Sulci of the Human and Macaque Monkey Brain," by M. M. Chiavaras and M. Petrides, 2000, *Journal of Comparative Neurology, 422,* pp. 35–54. Adapted with permission. It is clear that this variability poses substantial challenges for normalization across brains, but some possible strategies have been offered in a recent article (Kringelbach & Rolls, 2004).

adaptive responses to salient stimuli in the environment, thus enhancing its chances of survival.

A highly successful scientific strategy has been to divide the concept of emotion into two parts: the *emotional state* that can be measured through physiological changes such as visceral and endocrine responses, and *feelings*, seen as the subjective experience of emotion (Kringelbach, 2004a). This allows emotional states to be measured in animals using, for example, conditioning, and most subsequent research has regarded emotions as states elicited by rewards and punishments (which, of course, is a rather circular definition; Weiskrantz, 1968). Emotional stimuli (primary and secondary reinforcers) are represented by brain structures, depending on the kind of reinforcer. Reinforcers are defined such that positive reinforcers (rewards) increase the frequency of behavior leading to their acquisition, while negative reinforcers (punishers) decrease the frequency of behavior leading to their encounter and increase the frequency of behavior leading to their avoidance.

The subsequent emotional processing is a multistage process mediated by networks of brain structures. The results of this processing influence which behavior is selected, which autonomic responses are elicited, and which conscious feelings are produced (at least in humans).

An early, contrasting but still influential, theory of emotion was proposed independently by William James (1890) and Carl Lange (1887) who proposed that rather than emotional experience being a response to a stimulus, it is the perception of the ensuing physiological bodily changes. The James-Lange theory of emotion suggests that contrary to popular perception we do not run from the bear because we are afraid but that we *become* afraid because we run.

Several scientists have remained skeptical of such bodily theories of emotion. One of the initial main proponents, William Cannon (1927), offered a detailed critique of the James-Lange theory. He showed that surgical disruption of the peripheral nervous system in dogs did not eliminate emotional responses as would have been predicted by the theory. Further investigations by Schachter and Singer (1962) suggested that bodily states must be accompanied by cognitive appraisal for an emotion to occur. However, this research did not fully resolve the basic question of the extent to which bodily states influence emotion and feelings.

The James-Lange theory was resurrected first by Walla Nauta (1971) with his *interoceptive* markers, and since—to far more popular acclaim—by Antonio Damasio (1994) in the form of his somatic marker hypothesis, in which feedback from the peripheral nervous system controls the *decision* about the correct behavioral response rather than the *emotional feelings* as postulated in the James-Lange theory.

Among the objections to these and other bodily theories of emotion are that they are underspecified with regard to what constitute emotional stimuli; that signals from the body are noisy and it is not clear whether they can distinguish the different emotions; and that animals and humans with severe spinal cord damage appear to have normal emotions. Some of these objections are addressed in the somatic marker theory that includes an as-if loop for those decision-making situations with relatively low uncertainty that allows the brain to bypass the role of body (Damasio, 1996). It has also been argued that emotions are constituted in large measure by visceral and endocrine responses rather than through the spinal cord. The orbitofrontal cortex certainly has the connectivity to receive and integrate visceral sensory signals to influence ongoing behavior, and although it is not clear how this information is integrated, it remains possible that these signals have a significant role in decision making and emotion (Craig, 2002). It should also be noted that most primary reinforcers are signaled via an interoceptive route and that this is likely to be essential for hedonic experience.

At the same time, it is clear from the evidence of, for example, successful use of various beta blockers in alleviating stage fright, anxiety, and panic attacks in stage musicians and other world-class performers that the body clearly must play a role in the regulation of emotions. Some observers have therefore suggested that the role of the body in emotion is perhaps more akin to an amplifier than to a generator.

There are close links between body and brain, as was fully clear to even Descartes who is otherwise widely seen as one of the main proponents for the mind-body split. It is at best misleading to assign Descartes such a simple-minded dualistic position (Descartes, 1649; Sutton, 2001)— although he was clearly on the wrong track when he named the pineal gland as the seat of the soul. Later research has shown that this brain structure is a key structure in the control of hormones and thus an unlikely contributor to the metaphysical construction of the soul.

On Hedonic Processing Past and Present

From an evolutionary perspective, reward, pleasure, and hedonic processing have important roles in helping with the Darwinian imperative of survival and procreation. It has proven useful to divide hedonic processing into at least two categories: basic and higher pleasures (Kringelbach & Berridge, 2009). The basic pleasures are linked to survival and include sensory pleasures such as food as well as sex (Berridge, 1996; Kringelbach, 2004b). Similarly, the basic pleasures are linked to both survival and procreation since the social interactions with conspecifics may potentially lead to the propagation of genes. This has probably been selected for in evolution, which means that social pleasures are also likely to be part of our repertoire of basic pleasures (Kringelbach & Rolls, 2003). In the development of the social pleasures, the early attachment bonds between parents and infants are likely to be extremely important (Stein et al., 1991). In fact, in social species such as humans, it might well be that the social pleasures are at least as pleasurable as the sensory pleasures.

In addition to these basic sensory and social pleasures, there are a large number of higher-order pleasures, including monetary, artistic, musical, altruistic, and transcendent pleasures. Such higher-order pleasures might be conceptualized as higher-dimensional combinations of the basic pleasures and as such may re-use some of the same brain mechanisms.

Over the past century, a large corpus of animal experimentation has investigated reward processing in the brain. Many people have subsequently defined pleasure to be the conscious experience of reward but it is questionable whether such a narrow definition is meaningful or indeed useful. Such a definition would limit pleasure to conscious organisms, which is problematic for a number of reasons, not the least being that we do not have a good definition of consciousness.

Pleasure is not a sensation because it does not fit most common definitions of sensations, as pointed out by Ryle (1954). Instead, pleasure would appear to be part of the subsequent valuation of sensory stimuli needed in decision making, including most importantly the hedonic valence, and as such may well be present in many species.

While the pleasure—or hedonic impact—of a reward such as sweetness can be measured by verbal reports in conscious humans, this hedonic processing is not dependent on the presence of language. In most nonlinguistic mammals, pleasure will also elicit "acceptance wriggles" that add a hedonic gloss to the sensation which we experience as conscious pleasure. Pleasure-elicited behaviors (such as protruding tongue movements to sweet foods) are present in other animals including rodents and has been proposed as an objective measure of the pleasure elicited (Steiner, Glaser, Hawilo, & Berridge, 2001). While human infants initially exhibit similar kinds licking of their lips for sweet foods, these stereotyped behaviors disappear after a while.

Humans do, however, exhibit much pleasure behavior, from the carefree smiles and laughter of pleasant social interactions to the deep groans of sensory and sexual pleasure (James, 1890). Most people instinctively feel that our pleasures would somehow not be quite the same without these pleasure-elicited behaviors.

At the same time, much of our brain activity is not available for conscious introspection and the neuroscientific evidence from humans and other animals has made it clear that nonconscious brain activity is essential for controlling our behavior. Some of this nonconscious brain activity is related to hedonic processing and may lead to hedonic reactions, where we are not conscious of their origin but where we are nevertheless happy to confabulate about the causes (Kringelbach, 2004c).

Similarly to how it is has proven useful to divide emotion into the nonconscious and conscious subcomponents of emotions and feelings, it might be useful and meaningful to divide pleasure into nonconscious and conscious subcomponents

of evaluative hedonic processing (Kringelbach, 2004a). Such a definition would hold that while pleasure plays a central role for emotions and conscious feelings, it is not itself a conscious feeling.

Reward and hedonic processing are closely linked with motivation and emotion. Historically, early drive theories of motivation proposed that need potentiated previously learned habits, and that need reduction strengthened new stimulus-response habit bonds (Hull, 1951). This was then taken to mean that hedonic behavior is controlled by need states. But these theories do not, for example, explain why people still continue to eat when sated. This led to theories of incentive motivation where hedonic behavior is mostly determined by the incentive value of a stimulus or its capacity to function as a reward (Bindra, 1978). Need states such as hunger are still important but only work indirectly on the stimulus' incentive value. *Alliesthesia* is the principle of modulation of the hedonic value of a consummatory sensory stimulus by homeostatic factors (Cabanac, 1971).

A useful distinction has been proposed between two aspects of reward: hedonic impact and incentive salience, where the former refers to the liking or pleasure related to the reward, and the latter to the wanting or desire for the reward (Berridge, 1996; Berridge & Robinson, 1998). In order to provide hedonic evaluation of stimuli, the brain regions implicated in hedonic assessment must receive salient information about stimulus identity from the primary and secondary sensory cortices.

Neuroimaging offers a powerful way to investigate both the liking and wanting components in the human brain. One way to investigate liking is to take subjective hedonic ratings throughout a human neuroimaging experiment and then correlate these ratings with changes in activity in the human brain (De Araujo, Kringelbach, Rolls, & McGlone, 2003; De Araujo, Rolls, Kringelbach, McGlone, & Phillips, 2003; Kringelbach, O'Doherty, Rolls, & Andrews, 2003). This allows for a unique window on the hedonic processes evaluating the pleasantness of salient stimuli and has pointed to the central role of the orbitofrontal cortex.

THE PRIMATE ORBITOFRONTAL CORTEX

The human orbitofrontal cortex has received relatively little attention in studies of the prefrontal cortex, and many of its functions remain enigmatic (Kringelbach, 2005). During primate evolution, the orbitofrontal cortex has developed considerably, and although some progress has been made through neurophysiological recordings in nonhuman primates, it is only during the past couple of years that evidence has converged from neuroimaging, neuropsychology, and neurophysiology to allow a better understanding of the functions of the human orbitofrontal cortex. These studies indicate that the orbitofrontal cortex is a nexus for sensory integration, the modulation of autonomic reactions, and participation in learning, prediction, and decision making for emotional and reward-related behaviors. The orbitofrontal cortex functions as part of various networks that include regions of the medial prefrontal cortex, hypothalamus, amygdala, insula/operculum, dopaminergic midbrain, and areas in the basal ganglia including the ventral and dorsal striatum. These additional areas have been investigated in detail in rodents and other animals, and have been described in other reviews (Cardinal, Parkinson, Hall, & Everitt, 2002; Holland & Gallagher, 2004). Here the focus is on the functions of the *human* orbitofrontal cortex because the phylogenetic expansion and heterogeneous nature of this brain region mean that a full understanding of its functions must be informed by evidence from human neuroimaging and neuropsychology studies.

Neuroimaging studies have found that the reward value (Kringelbach, O'Doherty, Rolls, & Andrews, 2000; O'Doherty et al., 2000), the expected reward value (Gottfried, O'Doherty, & Dolan, 2003), and even the subjective pleasantness of foods (Kringelbach et al., 2003) and other reinforcers are represented in the orbitofrontal cortex. Such findings could provide a basis for further exploration of the brain systems involved in the conscious experience of pleasure and reward and, as such, provide a unique method for studying the hedonic quality of human experience.

Neuroanatomy of the Orbitofrontal Cortex

The orbitofrontal cortex occupies the ventral surface of the frontal part of the brain (see Figures 40.1 and 40.2). It is defined as the part of the prefrontal cortex that receives projections from the magnocellular, medial, nucleus of the mediodorsal thalamus (Fuster, 1997). This is in contrast to areas of the prefrontal cortex that receive projections from other parts of the mediodorsal thalamus. For example, the dorsolateral prefrontal cortex (Brodmann area [BA] 46/9) receives projections from the parvocellular, lateral, part of the mediodorsal thalamic nucleus, whereas the frontal eye fields in the anterior bank of the arcuate sulcus (BA 8) receive projections from the paralamellar part of the mediodorsal thalamic nucleus. This is a broad connectional topography, in which each specific portion of the mediodorsal thalamus is connected to more than one architectonic region of the prefrontal cortex (Pandya & Yeterian, 1996), and a better definition therefore includes the cortical area's corticocortical connectivity and morphological features.

Brodmann (1909) carried out one of the first comprehensive cytoarchitectural analyses of both the human and the primate (*Cercopithecus*) brain, in which different cytoarchitectonic areas were assigned unique numbers. Unfortunately, he did not investigate the orbitofrontal cortex in detail, and his maps of the human brain include only three orbitofrontal cortical areas, 10, 11, and 47. In addition, his nomenclature was not consistent across species: Area 11 in the primate map is extended laterally, and area 12 has taken over the medial area occupied by area 11 in the human map, whereas area 47 is not included at all in the nonhuman primate map.

Walker (1940) provided some clarification of the cross-species inconsistencies present in Brodmann's maps in his investigation of the monkey species *Macaca fascicularis*. He found the orbitofrontal cortex to be much less homogeneous than Brodmann specified, and he proposed to parcellate the primate orbital surface into five distinct areas (areas 10, 11, 12, 13, and 14; see Figure 41.2A). Walker's areas 12 and 13 occupy the lateral and medial orbital surface, respectively, whereas area 14 is on the ventromedial convexity near the gyrus rectus. More anteriorly, area 10 occupies the frontal pole, whereas area 11 occupies the remaining anterior orbital surface.

However, this left the problem of area 47 from the human map, which was still not included in Walker's map. Petrides and Pandya (1994) subsequently tried to reconcile the remaining inconsistencies between the human and monkey cytoarchitectonic maps by labeling the lateral parts of the orbitofrontal gyri as 47/12. Even further subdivisions of the orbitofrontal cortex were subsequently proposed using nine different histochemical and immunohistochemical stains (Carmichael & Price, 1994).

Two important cytoarchitectonic features of the orbitofrontal cortices are the phylogenetic differences and the considerable variability between individuals (Chiavaras & Petrides, 2000, 2001). The former poses potential problems when trying to understand functional relationships across species, and the latter poses interesting methodological challenges for those who hope to normalize individual brains to a template brain to explore the functional anatomy of the human orbitofrontal cortex.

The orbitofrontal cortex receives inputs from the classic five sensory modalities: gustatory, olfactory, somatosensory, auditory, and visual (Carmichael & Price, 1995b). It also receives visceral sensory information, and all this input makes the orbitofrontal cortex perhaps the most polymodal region in the entire cortical mantle, with the possible exception of the rhinal regions of the temporal lobes (Barbas, 1988).

The orbitofrontal cortex also has direct reciprocal connections with other brain structures, including the amygdala (Amaral & Price, 1984; Carmichael & Price, 1995a), cingulate cortex (Öngür & Price, 2000; Van Hoesen, Morecraft, & Vogt, 1993), insula/operculum (Mesulam & Mufson, 1982), hypothalamus (Rempel-Clower & Barbas, 1998), hippocampus (Cavada, Company, Tejedor, Cruz Rizzolo, & Reinoso Suarez, 2000), striatum (Eblen & Graybiel, 1995), periaqueductal grey (Rempel-Clower & Barbas, 1998), and dorsolateral prefrontal cortex (Barbas & Pandya, 1989; Carmichael & Price, 1995b).

FUNCTIONAL NEUROANATOMY OF THE HUMAN ORBITOFRONTAL CORTEX

In terms of its neuroanatomical connectivity, the orbitofrontal cortex is uniquely placed to integrate sensory and visceral motor information to modulate ongoing behavior through both visceral and motor systems. This has led to the proposal that the orbitofrontal cortex is an important part of the networks involved in emotional and hedonic processing (Nauta, 1971; E. T. Rolls, 1999). The orbitofrontal cortex has direct connections to the basolateral amygdala, and these two brain areas probably have an important role in goal-directed behavior (E. T. Rolls, 1999).

The orbitofrontal cortex is a comparatively large brain area in nonhuman primates and humans and is heterogeneous in terms of its connectivity and morphological features, so its constituent parts probably have different functional roles. One proposal based on neuroanatomical and neurophysiological evidence from nonhuman primates is that the orbitofrontal cortex should be viewed as part of a functional network known as the orbital and medial prefrontal cortex (OMPFC; Öngür & Price, 2000). This network includes both the orbitofrontal cortex and parts of the anterior cingulate cortex, and has distinct connections to other parts of the brain. The *orbital* network includes areas 11, 13, and 47/12 of the orbitofrontal cortex and receives input from all the sensory modalities, including visceral afferents and is proposed to be important for the regulation of food intake. The *medial* network (which includes medial areas 11, 13, 14, and lateral area 47/12s of the orbitofrontal cortex as well as areas 25, 32, and 10 on the medial wall) has extensive visceromotor outputs. The two networks might therefore serve as a crucial sensory-visceromotor link for consummatory behaviors. It should be noted that the definition of the medial network partly overlaps with the *ventromedial prefrontal cortex* as utilized by Bechara, Damasio, Damasio, and Anderson (1994), but the latter does not include lateral regions of the orbitofrontal cortex.

Another proposal extends the OMPFC network, based on evidence from human neuroimaging and neuropsychology studies, to suggest that there are medial-lateral and posterior-anterior distinctions within the human orbitofrontal cortex (Kringelbach & Rolls, 2004). A large meta-analysis of the existing neuroimaging data was used to show that activity in the medial orbitofrontal cortex is related to the monitoring, learning, and memory of the reward value of reinforcers, whereas lateral orbitofrontal cortex activity is related to the evaluation of punishers, which can lead to a change in ongoing behavior. There was also a posterior-anterior distinction, with more complex or abstract reinforcers (such as monetary gain and loss) represented more anteriorly in the orbitofrontal cortex than less complex reinforcers (such as taste).

Other proposed functions of the orbitofrontal cortex include a role for the lateral parts in response inhibition (Elliott, Dolan, & Frith, 2000), based on the observation that humans and nonhuman primates will perseverate in choosing a previously, but no-longer rewarded, stimulus in object-reversal learning tasks (Dias, Robbins, & Roberts, 1996; E. T. Rolls, Hornak, Wade, & McGrath, 1994). There is now strong evidence that this inhibition cannot be a simple form of response inhibition. Lesion studies in monkeys have shown that errors on reversal-learning tasks may not be caused by perseverative responses, but can be caused by failure to learn to respond to the currently rewarded stimulus (Iversen & Mishkin, 1970). Similarly, simple response inhibition cannot account for the severe impairment on the reversal part of an object-reversal learning task shown by patients with discrete bilateral surgical lesions to the lateral orbitofrontal cortex (Hornak et al., 2004). It is possible that the orbitofrontal cortex has a role in more complex behavioral changes that could be interpreted as being inhibitory to behavior, and that this behavior arises in conjunction with activity in other brain structures such as the anterior cingulate cortex, as discussed later.

These influential proposals share some similarities and conclusions, but the exact functions and underlying mechanisms of the various parts of the orbitofrontal cortex have yet to be discovered. Here I consider new evidence from neuroimaging and neuropsychology studies that can help to illuminate the functions of the orbitofrontal cortex in sensory integration, reward processing, decision making, reward prediction, and subjective hedonic processing. It is important to remember that studies using fMRI are prone to signal dropout, geometric distortion, and susceptibility artefacts in the orbitofrontal cortex due to its close proximity to the air-filled sinuses (Deichmann, Josephs, Hutton, Corfield, & Turner, 2002; Wilson et al., 2002), so negative findings should be treated with caution.

SENSORY PLEASURES: INTEGRATION AND REWARD VALUE

Neurophysiological recordings have found that the nonhuman primate orbitofrontal cortex receives input from all of the five senses (E. T. Rolls, 1999), and neuroimaging has confirmed that the human orbitofrontal cortex is activated by auditory (Frey, Kostopoulos, & Petrides, 2000), gustatory (Small et al., 1999), olfactory (Zatorre, Jones-Gotman, Evans, & Meyer, 1992), somatosensory (E. T. Rolls, O'Doherty, Kringelbach, Francis, Bowtell, & McGlone, 2003), and visual (Aharon et al., 2001) inputs. This cortical region also receives information from the visceral sensory system (Critchley, Mathias, & Dolan, 2002), and even abstract reinforcers such as money can activate the human orbitofrontal cortex (O'Doherty, Kringelbach, Rolls, Hornak, & Andrews, 2001; Thut et al., 1997).

Four computational principles have been proposed for the interaction between sensory and hedonic processing in humans: (1) motivation-independent processing of identity and intensity; (2) formation of learning-dependent multimodal sensory representations; (3) reward representations using state-dependent mechanisms including selective satiation; and (4) representations of hedonic experience, monitoring/learning or direct behavioral change (Kringelbach, 2006).

Sensory inputs enter the orbitofrontal cortex mostly through its posterior parts (see next section). Here they are available for multisensory integration (DeAraujo, Rolls, et al., 2003; Kringelbach et al., 2003; Small, Jones-Gotman, Zatorre, Petrides, & Evans, 1997) and subsequent encoding of the reward value of the stimulus. One approach to demonstrate the encoding of the reward value of a stimulus is by a manipulation called selective or sensory-specific satiety (B. J. Rolls, Rolls, Rowe, & Sweeney, 1981), which is a form of reinforcer devaluation. This approach was used in neuroimaging experiments on hungry human subjects who were scanned while being presented with two food-related stimuli. Subjects were then fed to satiety on one of the corresponding stimuli, which led to a selective decrease in reward value of the food eaten, and scanned again in their satiated state using exactly the same procedure. The neuroimaging experiments using olfactory (O'Doherty et al., 2000) and whole-food (Kringelbach et al., 2000, 2003) stimuli showed that the activity in more anterior parts of the orbitofrontal cortex tracks the changes in reward value of the two stimuli such that the activity selectively decreases for the food eaten but not for the other food.

This is compatible with studies in nonhuman primates where monkeys with lesions to the orbitofrontal cortex responded normally to associations between food and conditioners but failed to modify their behavior to the cues when the incentive value of the food was reduced (Butter, Mishkin, & Rosvold, 1963), and where lesions to the orbitofrontal cortex altered food preferences in monkeys (Baylis & Gaffan, 1991). Similarly, unilateral crossed lesions between the orbitofrontal cortex and the

basolateral part of the amygdala in monkeys disrupted devaluation effects in a procedure in which the incentive value of a food was reduced by satiation on that specific food (Baxter, Parker, Lindner, Izquierdo, & Murray, 2000).

A malfunction of these satiation mechanisms could explain the profound changes in eating habits (escalating desire for sweet food coupled with reduced satiety) that are often followed by enormous weight gain in patients with frontotemporal dementia, a progressive neurodegenerative disorder associated with major and pervasive behavioral changes in personality and social conduct resembling those produced by orbitofrontal lesions (Rahman, Sahakian, Hodges, Rogers, & Robbins, 1999; although it should be noted that more focal lesions to the orbitofrontal cortex have not to date been associated with obesity).

Further evidence for the representation of the reward value of more abstract reinforcers comes from neuroimaging studies of, for example, social judgments (Farrow et al., 2001) and music (Blood, Zatorre, Bermudez, & Evans, 1999). A meta-analysis of neuroimaging studies found that abstract reinforcers such as money are represented more anteriorly in the orbitofrontal cortex than less complex reinforcers such as taste (Kringelbach & Rolls, 2004). These studies show that the orbitofrontal cortex represents the affective value of both primary and abstract secondary reinforcers.

SOCIAL PLEASURES: FACE PROCESSING

Humans are intensely social, and experiments have shown time and again that our preferred route to health, pleasure, and perhaps even happiness is through social relationships with other people (Layard, 2005). Human social relationships are very rich and complex, and we have only started to understand some of the underlying brain processes (Adolphs, 2003).

In humans and other primates, facial expressions act as important social cues to regulate behavior (Darwin, 1872; Ekman & Friesen, 1971). Much is known about the neural correlates of the decoding of face expressions from neurophysiological studies in nonhuman primates (Bruce, Desimone, & Gross, 1981; Desimone & Gross, 1979; Hasselmo, Rolls, Baylis, & Nalwa, 1989; Perrett, Rolls, & Caan, 1982) and from human lesion (Adolphs, Tranel, Damasio, & Damasio, 1994; Bodamer, 1947; Sergent & Villemure, 1989) and imaging studies (Haxby et al., 1994), but very little is known about the neural correlates of how face expressions govern human social behavior. In addition, it is clear that infant faces serve an important role in the early attachment between parents and children, which is the foundation of our hedonic brain.

Infant and Infantile Faces as a Tool for Understanding Social Attachment

The scientific interest in the infant faces started with Charles Darwin (1872) who pointed out that in order for infants to survive and to perpetuate the human species, adults need to respond and care for their young. The Nobel Prize winner Konrad Lorenz (1971) proposed that it is the specific structure of the infant face that serves to elicit these parental responses, but the biological basis for this has remained elusive. Lorenz argued that infantile features serve as "innate releasing mechanisms" for affection and nurturing in adult humans and that most of these features are evident in the face including a relatively large head, predominance of the brain capsule, large and low-lying eyes and bulging cheek region. Thus, it is argued that these "babyish" features of infants increase the infant's chance of survival by evoking parental responses (Bowlby, 1957, 1969), and the parents' ability to respond is important for the survival of the species (Darwin, 1872).

Although a considerable body of research has focused on how the human brain processes adult faces, much less research has investigated the processing of infant faces (Frith, 2006). A number of studies have used fMRI to examine parental responses to children's faces, which has advanced our understanding of some of the underlying neural circuitry (Swain, Lorberbaum, Kose, & Strathearn, 2007). Most studies have compared parental responses to their own children with their responses to other children. It has been found that there is stronger activity to one's own children compared to other infants in striate and extrastriate visual areas and in reward-related areas such as the nucleus accumbens, anterior cingulate and amygdala (Ranote et al., 2004; Swain et al., 2007).

While these studies have substantially increased our general knowledge of the parental neural responses to children faces, there are a number of reasons why a substantial test of the Lorenz's theory of the specificity of infant faces requires a direct comparison between matched adult and infant faces from the first year of life; preferably where the faces are unfamiliar and using neuroimaging techniques that permit the temporal progression of brain activity to be studied.

We used magnetoencephalography (MEG) to investigate the temporal and spatial distribution of the underlying neural systems for these facial responses in 12 adult human participants (Kringelbach, Lehtonen, et al., 2007; Kringelbach et al., 2008). Consistent with previous findings, we found that face processing of both adult and infant faces elicits a wave of activity starting in the striate cortices and spreading along ventral and dorsal pathways (Blair, 2003).

In addition, however, we found that at around 130 ms after presentation of the infant faces, activity occurred in the medial orbitofrontal cortex identifying for the first time a neural basis for this vital evolutionary process (see Figure 41.3). This was not evident in response to the adult faces. Since the infant and adult faces used in the present study were carefully matched by independent panels of participants for emotional valence and arousal, and attractiveness, the findings provide evidence that it is the distinct features of the infant faces compared to adult faces that are important, rather than evaluative subjective processing such as attractiveness or emotional valence.

These specific responses to unfamiliar infant faces occur so fast that they are almost certainly quicker than anything under conscious control suggesting that they are automatized. The findings are therefore potentially of interest in that they suggest a temporally earlier role than previously thought for the medial orbitofrontal cortex in guiding affective reactions, which may even be nonconscious.

The medial orbitofrontal cortex may thus provide the necessary attentional—and perhaps hedonic—tagging of infant faces that predisposes humans to treat infant faces as special and elicits caring, as suggested by Lorenz. It would be of considerable interest to investigate the brain responses to infants of other species to see whether a similar effect is present.

Overall, these neuroimaging studies demonstrate that faces are important stimuli to help understand how the social pleasures might govern behavior. In particular, they show that the sensory and social pleasures share a similar network of interacting brain regions.

DECISION MAKING AND PREDICTION

In decision making, the brain must compare and evaluate the predicted reward value of various behaviors. This processing can be complex because the estimations will vary in quality depending on the sampling rate of the behavior and the variance of reward distributions. It is hard to provide a reliable estimate of the reward value of a food that appears to be highly desirable and is high in nutritional value but is only rarely available and varies significantly in quality. This raises the classic problem in animal learning of how to optimize behavior such that the amount of exploration is balanced with the amount of exploitation, where exploration is the time spent sampling the outcome of different behaviors and exploitation is the time spent using existing behaviors with known reward values. Food-related behaviors have to be precisely controlled because the decision to swallow toxins, microorganisms, or nonfood objects on the basis of erroneously determining the sensory properties of the food can be fatal. Humans and other animals have therefore developed elaborate food-related behaviors to balance conservative risk-minimizing and life-preserving strategies (exploitation) with

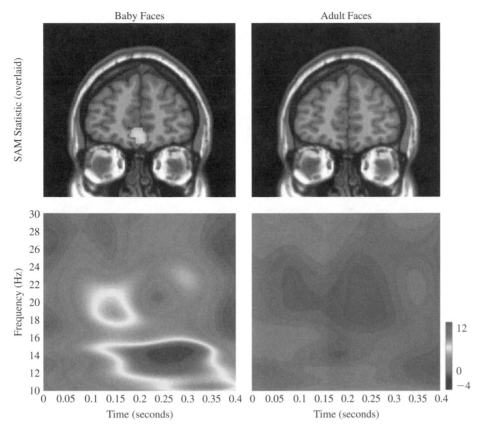

Figure 41.3 Infant faces elicited an early neural signature.

Note: (Top Row) Significant activity was present from around 130 ms in the medial orbitofrontal cortex when viewing infant faces but not when viewing adult faces. (Bottom Row) Time-frequency representations of the normalized evoked average group responses to baby and adult faces from the virtual electrodes show that the initial response to infant faces is present in the 12 to 20 Hz band from around 130 ms—and not present in adult faces. From "A Specific and Rapid Neural Signature for Parental Instinct," by Kringelbach et al., 2008, *PLoS ONE.* 3(2): e1664. Reprinted with permission.

occasional novelty seeking (exploration) in the hope of discovering new, valuable sources of nutrients (Rozin, 2001).

The orbitofrontal and anterior cingulate cortices were implicated in decision making by the classic case of Phineas Gage, whose frontal lobes were penetrated by a metal rod (Harlow, 1848). Gage survived but his personality and emotional processing were changed completely (although the case should be viewed with caution because the available information is limited; Macmillan, 2000). In more recent cases of orbitofrontal cortex damage, patients have often shown problems with decision making, a lack of affect, and social inappropriateness and irresponsibility (S. W. Anderson, Bechara, Damasio, Tranel, & Damasio, 1999; Blair & Cipolotti, 2000; Hornak et al., 2003; E. T. Rolls et al., 1994). Such patients are impaired in identifying social signals that are important for decision making, including, for example, face and voice expressions (Hornak et al., 2003; Hornak, Rolls, & Wade, 1996).

Reliable prediction underlies decision making (Schultz & Dickinson, 2000), and neuroimaging has been used to investigate the predicted reward value of rewarding and punishing stimuli. Often this is done using classical conditioning paradigms, in which an arbitrary neutral stimulus is paired with a reward or punishment. After learning, the arbitrary stimulus takes on the predictive value of the specific reward value of the unconditioned stimulus, but

it can also code for various aspects of the sensory or general affective properties of the unconditioned stimulus. In an fMRI study using selective satiation, subjects were presented with predictive cues associated with one of two food-related odors (Gottfried et al., 2003). By comparing the brain activity in response to the cues before and after devaluation (by feeding to satiety) of the associated food, it was found that neural responses in the orbitofrontal cortex, amygdala, and ventral striatum tracked the relative changes in the specific predictive reward value of the odors.

When the specific predictive reward values of different behaviors are in place, comparison and evaluation mechanisms must choose between them to optimize behavior. Bechara and colleagues developed a gambling task in which subjects were asked to select cards from four decks and maximize their winnings (Bechara et al., 1994). After each selection of a card, facsimile money is lost or won. Two of the four packs produce large payouts with larger penalties (and can thus be considered high-risk), whereas the other two packs produce small payouts but smaller penalties (low-risk). The most profitable strategy is therefore to select cards from the two low-risk decks; this strategy is adopted by normal control subjects. During the task, electrodermal activity (skin conductance responses, SCR) of the subject is measured as an index of visceral sensory arousal. Patients with damage to the ventromedial prefrontal cortex (including parts of the medial orbitofrontal cortex), but not the dorsolateral prefrontal cortex, persistently draw cards from the high-risk packs, and lack anticipatory SCRs while they consider risky choices (Bechara, Damasio, Tranel, & Anderson, 1998; but see also a recent critique of this experiment; Maia & McLelland, 2004).

In another decision-making task, a visual discrimination reversal task, subjects had to associate an arbitrary stimulus with monetary wins or losses, and then rapidly reverse these associations when the reinforcement contingencies altered. Probabilistic reward and punishment schedules were used such that selecting either the currently rewarded stimulus or the unrewarded stimulus can lead to a monetary gain or loss, but only consistent selection of the currently rewarded stimulus results in overall monetary gain. An fMRI study of this task in normal subjects found a dissociation of activity in the medial and lateral parts of the orbitofrontal cortex: Activity in the medial orbitofrontal cortex correlated with how much money was won on single trials, and activity of the lateral orbitofrontal cortex correlated with how much money was lost on single trials (O'Doherty et al., 2001). Another PET study also found that predominantly lateral parts of the orbitofrontal cortex were significantly activated during decision making (Rogers et al., 1999).

Other studies have since confirmed the role of the medial orbitofrontal cortex in monitoring and learning about the reward value of stimuli that have no immediate behavioral consequences (see Figure 41.4). Neuroimaging experiments have found activations in the medial orbitofrontal cortex that monitor the affective properties of olfaction (A. K. Anderson et al., 2003; E. T. Rolls, Kringelbach, & De Araujo, 2003), gustation (Small et al., 2003), somatosensory (E. T. Rolls, O'Doherty, et al., 2003), and multimodal (De Araujo, Rolls, et al., 2003) stimuli. This monitoring process is consistent with intriguing findings in spontaneously confabulating patients with lesions to the medial orbitofrontal cortex (Schnider, 2003; Schnider & Ptak, 1999). A PET study has found that the medial orbitofrontal cortex monitors outcomes even when no reward is at stake (Schnider, Treyer, & Buck, 2005).

In contrast, the lateral orbitofrontal cortex is often co-active with the anterior cingulate cortex when subjects evaluate punishers, which, when detected, can lead to a change in behavior (see Figure 41.5). A PET study investigating analgesia and placebo found that the lateral orbitofrontal and anterior cingulate cortices were co-active in subjects who responded to the placebo, suggesting that the pain relief effect of the placebo might be related to the co-activation of these two brain areas (Petrovic & Ingvar, 2002; Petrovic, Kalso, Petersson, & Ingvar, 2002). Another neuroimaging study found evidence that the lateral orbitofrontal cortex is related to changing behavior, in this case

when there were unexpected breaches in expectation in a visual attention task (Nobre, Coull, Frith, & Mesulam, 1999).

A direct investigation of the role of the lateral orbitofrontal cortex was carried out using a face reversal–learning task that solved the problem inherent in the monetary reversal-learning task (mentioned previously; O'Doherty et al., 2001), in which the probabilistic nature of the task meant that the magnitude of negative reinforcers (money loss) was slightly confounded by the reversal event per se. This new reversal-learning study showed that the lateral orbitofrontal cortex and a region of the anterior cingulate cortex are together responsible for supporting general reversal learning in the human brain (Kringelbach, 2004d; Kringelbach & Rolls, 2003; see Figure 41.6). This is consistent with the finding that passively presenting angry facial expressions—a signal that ongoing social behavior should be changed—activates the orbitofrontal and anterior cingulate cortices (Blair, Morris, Frith, Perrett, & Dolan, 1999). Further strong, causal evidence has come from a similar reversal-learning experiment in patients with discrete, surgical lesions to the orbitofrontal cortex, in which bilateral lesions to the lateral orbitofrontal cortex—but not unilateral lesions to medial parts of the orbitofrontal cortex—produce significant impairments in reversal learning (Hornak et al., 2004).

A recent fMRI study investigated the interaction between decision making and performance monitoring (Walton, Devlin, & Rushworth, 2004). The orbitofrontal cortex was more involved in outcome monitoring for the externally instructed condition than in the internally generated volition condition. In contrast, the anterior cingulate cortex was more active when the selected response was internally generated than when it was externally instructed by the experimenter.

In summary, decision making, performance, and outcome monitoring require complex processing that relies strongly on frontal cortical areas, and in particular on interactions between the orbitofrontal and anterior cingulate cortices. Different parts of these cortical regions have been implicated in different aspects and timings of decision making and outcome monitoring (Ullsperger & von Cramon, 2004). In particular, there is now evidence from a large meta-analysis of the neuroimaging literature for the differential roles of the medial and lateral parts of the orbitofrontal cortex (Kringelbach & Rolls, 2004). Activity in the medial orbitofrontal cortex is related to the monitoring, learning, and memory of the reward value of reinforcers, whereas activity in the lateral orbitofrontal cortex is related to the evaluation of punishers, which can lead to a change in behavior. As already mentioned, the meta-analysis also found evidence for a posterior-anterior distinction between more complex or abstract and less complex reinforcers.

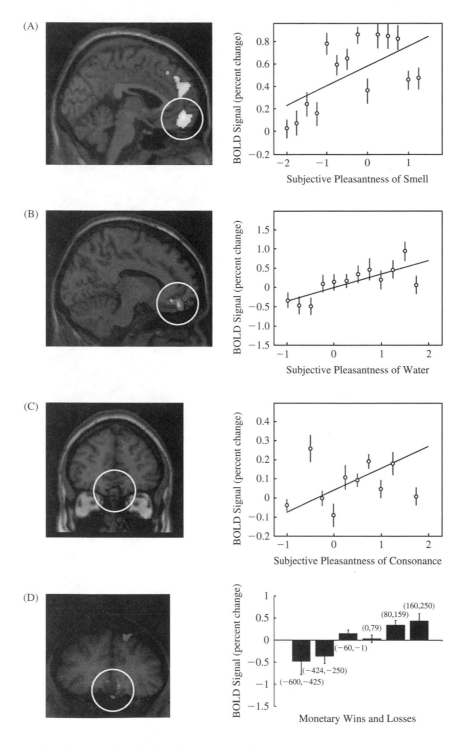

Figure 41.4 Valence coding in medial orbitofrontal cortex (OFC).

Note: **A:** The activity in medial OFC correlates with the subjective ratings of pleasantness in an experiment with three pleasant and three unpleasant odors (Rolls, Kringelbach, et al., 2003). **B:** Similarly, the activity in medial OFC was also correlated with the subjective pleasantness ratings of water in a thirst experiment (De Araujo, Kringelbach, Rolls, & McGlone, 2003). A correlation in a very similar part of medial OFC was found with the pleasantness of other pure tastants used in the experiment (not shown).

C: This corresponded to the findings in an experiment investigating taste and smell convergence and consonance, which found that activity in the medial OFC was correlated to subjective consonance ratings (De Araujo, Rolls, et al., 2003). **D:** Even higher-order rewards such as monetary reward was found to correlate with activity in the medial OFC. From "Abstract Reward and Punishment Representations in the Human Orbitofrontal Cortex," by J. O'Doherty, M. L. Kringelbach, E. T. Rolls, J. Hornak, and C. Andrews, 2001, *Nature Neuroscience, 4,* p. 99. Reprinted with permission.

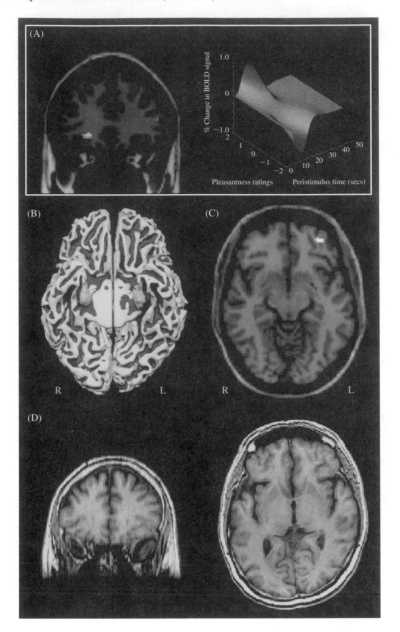

Figure 41.5   (**Figure C.38** in color section) Hedonic experience.

Note: **A:** A neuroimaging study using selective satiation found that mid-anterior parts of the orbitofrontal cortex are correlated with the subjects' subjective pleasantness ratings of the foods throughout the experiment. On the right is shown a plot of the magnitude of the fitted haemodynamic response from a representative single subject against the subjective pleasantness ratings (on a scale from –2 to +2) and peristimulus time in seconds. From "Activation of the Human Orbitofrontal Cortex to a Liquid Food Stimulus Is Correlated with Its Subjective Pleasantness," by M. L. Kringelbach, J. O'Doherty, E. T. Rolls, and C. Andrews, 2003, *Cerebral Cortex, 13,* p. 1067. Reprinted with permission. **B:** Additional evidence for the role of the orbitofrontal cortex in subjective experience comes from another neuroimaging experiment investigating the supra-additive effects of combining the *umami* tastants monosodium glutamate and inosine monophosphate. The figure shows the region of mid-anterior orbitofrontal cortex showing synergistic effects (rendered on the ventral surface of human cortical areas with the cerebellum removed). The perceived synergy is unlikely to be expressed in the taste receptors themselves and the activity in the orbitofrontal cortex may thus reflect the subjective enhancement of *umami* taste that must be closely linked to subjective experience. From "The Representation of Umami Taste in the Human Brain," by I. E. De Araujo, M. L. Kringelbach, E. T. Rolls, and P. Hobden, 2003, *Journal of Neurophysiology, 90,* p. 316. Reprinted with permission. **C:** Adding strawberry odor to a sucrose taste solution makes the combination significantly more pleasant than the sum of each of the individual components. The supralinear effects reflecting the subjective enhancement were found to significantly correlate with the activity in a lateral region of the left anterior orbitofrontal cortex, which is remarkably similar to that found in the other experiments. From "Taste-olfactory convergence, and the representation of the pleasantness of flavour, in the human brain," by I. E. T. De Araujo, E. T. Rolls, M. L. Kringelbach, F. McGlone, and N. Phillips, *European Journal of Neuroscience, 18,* p. 2064. Reprinted with permission. **D:** These findings were strengthened by findings using deep brain stimulation (DBS) and magnetoencephalography (MEG). Pleasurable subjective pain relief for chronic pain in a phantom limb in a patient was causally induced by effective deep brain stimulation in the PVG/PAG part of the brain stem. When using MEG to directly measure the concomitant changes in the rest of the brain, a significant change in power was found in the mid-anterior OFC. From "Deep Brain Stimulation for Chronic Pain Investigated with Magnetoencephalography," by M. L. Kringelbach, N. Jenkinson, A. L. Green, et al., 2007, *NeuroReport, 18,* p. 224. Reprinted with permission.

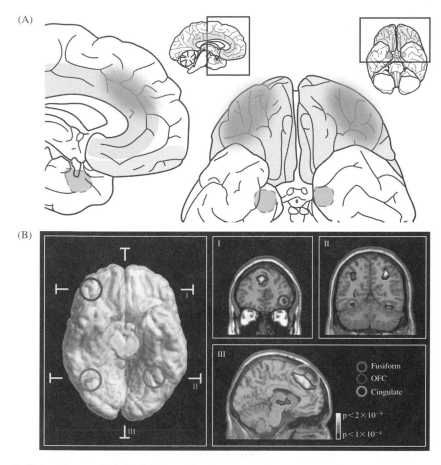

Figure 41.6 (**Figure C.39** in color section) Social interactions and the case of reversal learning.

Note: **A:** The lateral orbitofrontal and parts of the anterior cingulate cortices in the rostral cingulate zone are often found to be co-active in neuroimaging studies (with the regions superimposed in red). Most often this is found in tasks where the subjects have to evaluate negative stimuli which when detected may lead to a change in current behavior. **B:** A recent neuroimaging study found that the lateral orbitofrontal and the anterior cingulate/paracingulate cortices are together responsible for changing behavior in an object-reversal task. This task was setup to model aspects of human social interactions (see text for full description of task). Subjects were required to keep track of the faces of two people and to select the happy person, who would change mood after some time, and subjects had to learn to change, reverse, their behavior to choose the other person. The most significant activity during the reversal phase was found in the lateral orbitofrontal and cingulate cortices (red and green circles), while the main effects of faces were found to elicit activity in the fusiform gyrus and intraparietal sulcus (blue circles). From "Neural Correlates of Rapid Context-Dependent Reversal Learning in a Simple Model of Human Social Interaction," by M. L. Kringelbach and E. T. Rolls, 2003, *NeuroImage, 20,* p. 1375. Reprinted with permission.

SUBJECTIVE PLEASANTNESS

Using food as stimuli in neuroimaging has proved to be an interesting avenue for studying the hedonic quality of life, which is perhaps not surprising given that the essential energy to sustain life is obtained from food intake, as is much of the pleasure of life (especially on an empty stomach; Kringelbach, 2004b). Food intake in humans is not only regulated by homeostatic processes, as illustrated by our easy overindulgence on sweet foods and by rising obesity levels, but relies on the interactions between homeostatic regulation and hedonic experience (Saper et al., 2002). This complex subcortical and cortical processing involves higher-order processes such as learning, memory, planning, and prediction, and gives rise to conscious experience of not only the sensory properties of the food (such as the identity, intensity, temperature, fat content, and viscosity) but also the valence elicited by the food (including, most importantly, the hedonic experience).

In humans and higher primates, the orbitofrontal cortex receives multimodal information about the sensory properties of food and is therefore a candidate region for representing the incentive salience, the hedonic impact and the subjective hedonic experience hereof. A sensory-specific satiety neuroimaging study of activity in the mid-anterior region of the orbitofrontal cortex showed not only a sensory-specific decrease in the reward value of the whole food eaten to satiety (and *not* of the whole food not eaten), but also a correlation between brain activity and pleasantness ratings (see Figure 41.5A; Kringelbach et al., 2003).

This indicates that the reward value of the taste, olfactory, and somatosensory components of a whole food are represented in the orbitofrontal cortex, and that the subjective pleasantness of food might be represented here.

As mentioned, a related fMRI study found that activity in adjacent mid-anterior parts of the orbitofrontal cortex was selectively decreased in response to an arbitrary visual cue linked to an odor that had been devalued using a selective satiation paradigm in which subjects were fed on the associated food (Gottfried et al., 2003). Another recent PET study found that the extrinsic incentive value of foods was located in a similar part of the orbitofrontal cortex (Hinton et al., 2004).

Further evidence of neural correlates of subjective experience was found in an fMRI experiment investigating true taste synergism (De Araujo, Kringelbach, Rolls, & Hobden, 2003). The results of the study showed that the strong subjective enhancement of *umami* taste was correlated with increased activity in a mid-anterior part of the orbitofrontal cortex (see Figure 41.5B). The perceived synergy is unlikely to be expressed in the taste receptors themselves and the activity in the orbitofrontal cortex might thus reflect the subjective enhancement of umami taste. Similarly, a neuroimaging study showed that the synergistic enhancement of a matched taste and retronasal smell (where the multimodal combination was significantly more pleasant than the sum of the unimodal stimuli) correlated with activity in a mid-anterior region of the orbitofrontal cortex (De Araujo, Kringelbach, Rolls, & Hobden, 2003; see Figure 41.5C).

Other neuroimaging studies have directly correlated brain activity with the subjective ratings of the pleasantness and intensity of different positive and negative reinforcers, but crucially without devaluing or otherwise manipulating the reinforcers to change their valence during the course of the experiment. The results of these correlations are therefore perhaps better thought of in terms of the monitoring processing in the orbitofrontal cortex, described previously. Consistent with this suggestion, correlations with pleasantness have been found almost exclusively in the medial orbitofrontal cortex. Pleasantness but not intensity ratings were correlated with activity in the medial orbitofrontal and anterior cingulate cortices for taste (De Araujo, Kringelbach, Rolls, & McGlone, 2003), odor (Anderson et al., 2003; E. T. Rolls, O'Doherty, et al., 2003), chocolate (Small, Zatorre, Dagher, Evans, & Jones-Gotman, 2001), and stimulus fat content (independent of viscosity; De Araujo & Rolls, 2004). In addition, a study of thermal stimulation showed that the perceived thermal intensity was correlated with activity in the insula and orbitofrontal cortices (Craig, Chen, Bandy, & Reiman, 2000). A correlation was also recently found between a reliable index of the rush of intravenous met-amphetamine in drug-naive subjects and activity in the medial orbitofrontal cortex (Völlm et al., 2004). In addition, activation of the orbitofrontal cortex correlates with the negative dissonance (pleasantness) of musical chords (Blood et al., 1999), and intensely pleasurable responses, or chills, that are elicited by music are correlated with activity in the orbitofrontal cortex, ventral striatum, cingulate, and insula cortex (Blood & Zatorre, 2001).

Supporting evidence for the interpretation that the medial orbitofrontal cortex implements monitoring processing of the incentive salience comes from the study mentioned previously with patients with damage to the ventromedial prefrontal cortex who have been reported to have relatively intact SCRs when receiving the monetary rewards and punishments (Bechara et al., 1994). This monitoring process is in contrast, as shown earlier, to the mid-anterior parts of the orbitofrontal cortex which correlate directly with the subjective hedonic impact. It would thus appear that dissociable regions of the human orbitofrontal cortex represent both the wanting and the liking aspect of reward.

These exciting findings from neuroimaging extend previous findings in nonhuman primates of reinforcer representations to representations of the *subjective affective value* of these reinforcers. One has to be careful not to overinterpret mere correlations with the elusive qualities of subjective experience, and it is unlikely that hedonic experience depends on only one cortical region. Even so, it would be interesting to obtain more evidence on this issue by investigating patients with selective lesions to these areas to investigate whether their subjective affective experiences have changed. Some evidence has already been obtained to suggest that this is the case (Hornak et al., 2003).

DEEP BRAIN PLEASURES

The sensory and social pleasures can be bypassed by direct stimulation of the brain (Kringelbach, Jenkinson, Owen, & Aziz, 2007). Deep brain stimulation (DBS) is generally thought to have started with the demonstration of the localized electrical excitability of the motor cortex by Fritsch and Hitzig (1870). It was, however, only with the invention of the Horsley-Clarke frame for stereotactic neurosurgery (Horsley & Clarke, 1908) that DBS became practical for subcortical structures and the full potential awaited the adaptation of this frame for humans by Spiegel, Wycis, Mark, and Lee (1947). New targets were mostly inspired by animal experiments such as the pioneering studies by Hess and Hassler during the 1940s, and by Olds and Milner in the 1950s (Gildenberg, 2005). Early usage in humans included alleviation of movement disorders, where mostly the globus pallidus and the ventral thalamus were targeted (Bechtereva, Bondartchuk, & Smirnov, 1972; Hassler, 1955; Hassler, Riechert, Mundinger, Umbach, & Ganglberger, 1960). In parallel, human psychosurgery from Egas Moniz' and Walter Freeman's lobotomies to Heath's electrical stimulation in schizophrenics and homosexuals drew sharp public criticism (Baumeister, 2000; Valenstein, 1973). Most of this research in both animals and humans proceeded without the use of a stereotactic frame and the exact brain targets of these early electrical stimulation studies were never clear (Peciña, Smith, & Berridge, 2006).

After an initial flourish, stereotactic surgery for Parkinson's disease was largely abandoned in the 1960s when the link was found to the degeneration of the dopamine cells of the substantia nigra pars compacta and L-Dopa became widely used for treatment. However, L-Dopa often has very serious side effects and in the 1990s lesions of the globus pallidus internus (GPi) were reintroduced for PD dyskinesia. Lesions of the subthalamic nucleus (STN) can cause hemiballismus, and instead DBS of the STN and GPi at 130–180 Hz has been shown as effective and comparably safe (Aziz, Peggs, Sambrook, & Crossman, 1991).

The current DBS targets for pain are in the brain stem (periventricular gray, PVG, and periaqueductal gray, PAG) and thalamus (Nandi, Liu, Joint, Stein, & Aziz, 2002). The targets for PD are in the STN (Bittar, Burn, et al., 2005), GPi (Bittar, Burn, et al., 2005; Krack et al., 2003), and pedunculopontine nucleus in the brain stem (Jenkinson, Nandi, Aziz, & Stein, 2005; Mazzone et al., 2005; Plaha & Gill, 2005). The current target for cluster headache is in the hypothalamus (Leone, Franzini, Broggi, May, & Bussone, 2004). Some promising targets for depression have been found in the inferior thalamic peduncle (Andy & Jurko, 1987), the nucleus accumbens (Schlaepfer et al., 2007), and the subgenual cingulate cortex (Mayberg et al., 2005). Programmable stimulators are implanted subcutaneously and thousands of patients have been restored to near normal lives (Perlmutter & Mink, 2006).

Mood changes linked to changes in reward and hedonic processing such as unipolar depression are found in up to 40% of PD patients often starting before the onset of PD symptoms (Cummings, 1992). This is perhaps not surprising given the important role of the basal ganglia not only in movement but also in affect. The technique of stereotactic DBS thus has wide-reaching therapeutic applications clinically and in the neurosciences generally.

Patients with chronic pain who have DBS of the PVG/PAG report experiencing much less pain (Bittar, Kar-Purkayastha et al., 2005; Bittar, Otero, Carter, & Aziz, 2005). The PVG/PAG receives noxious input from ascending spinothalamic pathways and descending regulatory input from higher brain structures such as the orbitofrontal cortex. Electrical stimulation of the PAG induces stimulation-produced analgesia in animals and humans (Boivie & Meyerson, 1982; Reynolds, 1969). This effect is ascribed to a release of endogenous opioids because the effects are reversible with the administration of the opioid antagonist naloxone (Akil, Mayer, & Liebeskind, 1976; Hosobuchi, Adams, & Linchitz, 1977), and also to the activation of descending inhibitory systems that depress spinal noxious transmission (Fields & Basbaum, 1999).

Measuring Whole Brain Activity Elicited by Deep Brain Stimulation

What is particularly exciting about DBS is that it offers the potential for *causally* changing brain activity and thus potentially can inform us about the fundamental mechanisms of brain function (Kringelbach, Jenkinson, Owen, et al., 2007). This is particularly true when combined with a noninvasive whole-brain neuroimaging technique such as MEG (Kringelbach, Jenkinson, Green, et al., 2007).

In some select patients, this chronic pain can be significantly changed over a short period of time with DBS. This subjective change can be measured with MEG when changing DBS from effective to noneffective, while acquiring repeated subjective measurements on a visual scale. This can then be used in the data analysis to reveal the brain regions that mediate the change in subjective hedonic experience.

We were the first group to use MEG to make direct measurements of the whole brain elicited by DBS. When DBS was turned off, the participant reported significant increases in subjective pain. During the pain relief, we found corresponding significant changes in brain activity in a network that comprises the regions of the hedonic brain and includes the mid-anterior orbitofrontal and subgenual cingulate cortices (see Figure 41.5D; Kringelbach, Jenkinson, Green, et al., 2007). We found similar brain changes in a patient with depression and in a patient with intractable cluster headache (Ray et al., 2007).

This finding is strong evidence linking the orbitofrontal cortex to pain relief. These findings raise some pertinent questions about the nature of DBS. While stimulation of the PVG/PAG clearly brings about pain relief, which is clearly pleasurable, it is not clear if this would also be the case in humans without chronic pain. It is well known that while low-frequency stimulation of the PVG/PAG can bring about pain relief in chronic pain patients, high-frequency stimulation has the opposite effect and actually makes the pain worse (Kringelbach, Jenkinson, Green, et al., 2007). Anecdotally, some DBS patients with chronic pain relief report that the pain is still there but that DBS makes them care less about the pain (Aziz, personal communication).

A PET study investigating analgesia and placebo found that the opioid-rich brain structures lateral orbitofrontal and anterior cingulate cortices are co-active in placebo-responders, suggesting that the pain relief effect of the placebo might be related to these two brain areas being co-active (Petrovic & Ingvar, 2002; Petrovic, Kalso, Petersson, & Ingvar, 2002).

It is also potentially of interest to note that lesions to an output structure of the orbitofrontal cortex, the ventral pallidum (Öngür & Price, 2000), can lead to anhedonia (Miller et al., 2006). Similar evidence of anhedonia linked to lesions of some parts of the pallidum was also found in a large case series of 117 patients undergoing pallidotomies for movement disorders (Aziz, personal communication). This is of particular importance since lesions of the posterior ventral pallidum in rats abolishes and replaces liking reactions to sweetness with bitter-type disliking instead (e.g., gapes; Cromwell & Berridge, 1993).

Similar, DBS of the nucleus accumbens, which is another output structure of the orbitofrontal cortex, can alleviate anhedonia in patients with treatment-resistant depression (Schlaepfer et al., 2007). These results are not surprising given the animal literature on lesions and brain stimulation effects, where studies of rodents have indicated pleasure (liking) reactions to be generated by a network of hedonic hotspots distributed across the brain (Peciña & Berridge, 2005). Hotspot sites include cubic-millimeter localizations in nucleus accumbens, ventral pallidum, and possibly other forebrain and limbic cortical sites, and also deep brain-stem sites including the parabrachial nucleus in the pons (Peciña et al., 2006). Each hotspot is capable of supporting opioid-mediated, endocannabinoid-mediated, or other neurochemical enhancements of liking reactions to a sensory pleasure such as sweetness (Smith & Berridge, 2005). Only one hedonic hotpot so far appears to be strongly necessary to normal pleasure, in the sense that only damage to it abolishes and replaces liking reactions to sweetness with bitter-type disliking instead (e.g., gapes). This essential hotspot appears to be in the posterior ventral pallidum, and perhaps adjacent areas in substantia innominata, extended amygdala, and lateral hypothalamus (Cromwell & Berridge, 1993).

These findings open up a number of interesting avenues of human research, and it would be of considerable interest to investigate the effects of DBS on the mid-anterior orbitofrontal cortex as well as on the ventral pallidum.

But does DBS actually produce pleasure? One could plausibly argue that DBS may help to modulate otherwise malignant oscillatory activity in the brain, based on what is known about the neural mechanisms of DBS (Kringelbach, Jenkinson, Owen, et al., 2007). The evidence would suggest that although DBS may help to restore the brain's normal equilibrium in pathological states, DBS might have little effect on long-term pleasure in the normal brain. It might be possible for DBS to perturb the brain's equilibrium in the normal state, but such perturbations are likely to be short lived, similar to those induced by various drugs. For now, DBS remains a very useful technique for alleviating the acute symptoms of anhedonia so that people can again appreciate normal sensory and social pleasures.

SUMMARY

The scientific study of emotion, motivation, pleasure, and hedonic processing in humans remains in its infancy. Some progress has been made in understanding the putative brain structures involved in emotion and pleasure, mostly based on animal models but also to some extent based on human neuroimaging studies. Animal models using primarily rodents have convincingly shown that the hypothalamus, nucleus accumbens, ventral pallidum, and various brainstem nuclei such as the periaqueductal grey are important for hedonic processing (Berridge, 1996; Peciña et al., 2006). Human neuroimaging research has implicated primarily the orbitofrontal and cingulate cortices as well as the amygdala and the insular cortices. The subcortical brain regions identified with animal models (such as the nucleus accumbens and the ventral pallidum) provide some of the necessary input and output systems for multimodal association regions such as the orbitofrontal cortex that are involved in representing and learning about the reinforcers that elicit emotions and conscious feelings (Kringelbach, 2005).

The recent convergence of findings from neuroimaging, neuropsychology, neurophysiology, and neurosurgery has demonstrated that the human orbitofrontal cortex is best thought of as an important nexus for sensory integration, emotional processing, and hedonic experience (see Figure 41.7).

A model for the functions of the orbitofrontal cortex could be following: The posterior parts process the sensory information for further multimodal integration. The reward value of the reinforcer is assigned in more anterior parts of the orbitofrontal cortex from where it can be modulated by hunger and other internal states, and can be used to influence subsequent behavior (in lateral parts of the anterior orbitofrontal cortex with connections to anterior cingulate cortex), stored for monitoring, learning, and memory (in medial parts of the anterior orbitofrontal cortex), and made available for subjective hedonic experience (in mid-anterior orbitofrontal cortex). At all times, there is important reciprocal information flowing between the various regions of the orbitofrontal cortex and other brain regions subserving hedonic processing including the anterior cingulate cortex, the amygdala, the nucleus accumbens, and the ventral pallidum. Lateralization does not appear to play a major

(A)

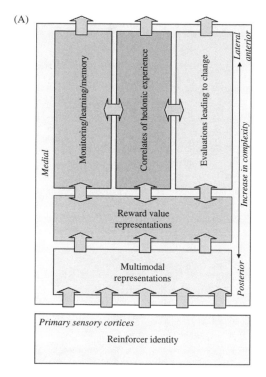

(B)

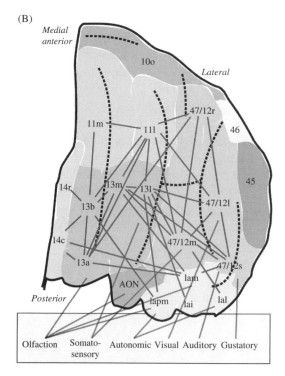

Figure 41.7   Model of the functions of the orbitofrontal cortex.

Note: The proposed model shows the interactions between sensory and hedonic systems in the orbitofrontal cortex using as an example one hemisphere of the orbitofrontal cortex. Information is flowing from bottom to top on the figure. Sensory information arrives from the periphery to the primary sensory cortices, where the stimulus identity is decoded into stable cortical representations. This information is then conveyed for further multimodal integration in brain structures in the posterior parts of the orbitofrontal cortex. The reward value of the reinforcer is assigned in more anterior parts of the orbitofrontal cortex from where it can then be used to influence subsequent behavior (in lateral parts of the anterior

orbitofrontal cortex with connections to anterior cingulate cortex), stored for learning/memory (in medial parts of the anterior orbitofrontal cortex), and made available for subjective hedonic experience (in mid-anterior orbitofrontal cortex). The reward value and the subjective hedonic experience can be modulated by hunger and other internal states. In addition, there is important reciprocal information flowing between the various regions of the orbitofrontal cortex and other brain regions involved in hedonic processing. From "Food for Thought: Hedonic Experience beyond Homeostasis in the Human Brain," by M. L. Kringelbach, 2004b, *Neuroscience, 126*, p. 815. Reprinted with permission.

role for the functions of the human orbitofrontal cortex as shown by the largest meta-analysis of its involvement by neuroimaging studies (Kringelbach & Rolls, 2004).

This model does not posit that medial orbitofrontal cortex only codes for the valence of positive reinforcers and vice versa for the lateral parts. Instead, the evidence from neuroimaging would seem to suggest that the valence of pleasures can be represented differently in different subparts of the orbitofrontal cortex. The activity (as indexed by the blood level dependent [BOLD]signal as measured with fMRI) in the medial orbitofrontal cortex would appear to correlate with the valence of reinforcers such that positive reinforcers elicit a higher BOLD signal than negative reinforcers, which is consistent with a monitoring role for the medial orbitofrontal cortex. The inverse appears to be true for the lateral parts of the orbitofrontal cortex, but with the important caveat that only the lateral parts are mostly concerned with those negative reinforcers that can bring about a change in behavior. Finally, the mid-anterior

region of the orbitofrontal cortex would appear to integrate the valence with state-dependent mechanisms such as selective satiation and is thus a candidate region for taking part in the mediation of subjective hedonic experience.

The proposed link to subjective hedonic processing places the orbitofrontal cortex as an important gateway to subjective conscious experience. One possible way to conceptualize the role of the orbitofrontal and anterior cingulate cortices would be as part of a global workspace for access to consciousness with the specific role of evaluating the affective valence of stimuli (Dehaene, Kerszberg, & Changeux, 1998). In this context, the medial parts of the orbitofrontal cortex are part of a proposed network for the baseline activity of the human brain at rest (Gusnard & Raichle, 2001) placing the orbitofrontal cortex as a key node in the network subserving consciousness. This could potentially explain why all experiences have an emotional tone.

There are many interesting and important issues in pleasure research that are not yet fully understood. We have still to understand the exact interactions and oscillations of the network of brain regions subserving hedonic processing. In particular, it is presently unclear which brain regions are necessary and sufficient for pleasure. Although conscious appraisal of pleasure is usually what we mean by referring to pleasure, many emotional stimuli can be processed on a nonconscious level as demonstrated by subliminal priming (Naccache et al., 2005; Winkielman, Berridge, & Wilbarger, 2005).

The most difficult question facing pleasure research remains the nature of the subjective experience of pleasure, and while some progress has been made, it is important not to over-interpret mere correlations from neuroimaging with the elusive qualities of subjective experience.

In summary, pleasure, motivations, and emotions are evolutionarily important for animals (including humans) in evaluating and preparing for appropriate actions. The evolution of conscious pleasure and emotion in humans could be adaptive because they allow us to consciously appraise our emotions and actions, and subsequently to learn to manipulate these appropriately. Pleasure and emotion may be some of evolution's most productive breakthroughs, constantly reminding us that we are still animals at heart, but endowed with the possibility of enjoying our limited time on this planet and with the enhanced control of our subjective experience that comes with it.

REFERENCES

Adolphs, R. (2003). Cognitive neuroscience of human social behaviour. *Nature Reviews: Neuoscience, 4*, 165–178.

Adolphs, R., Tranel, D., Damasio, H., & Damasio, A. (1994, December 15). Impaired recognition of emotion in facial expressions following bilateral damage to the human amygdala. *Nature, 372*, 669–672.

Aharon, I., Etcoff, N., Ariely, D., Chabris, C. F., O'Connor, E., & Breiter, H. C. (2001). Beautiful faces have variable reward value: FMRI and behavioral evidence. *Neuron, 32*, 537–551.

Akil, H., Mayer, D. J., & Liebeskind, J. C. (1976, March 5). Antagonism of stimulation-produced analgesia by naloxone, a narcotic antagonist. *Science, 191*, 961–962.

Amaral, D. G., & Price, J. L. (1984). Amygdalo-cortical projections in the monkey (Macaca fascicularis). *Journal of Comparative Neurology, 230*, 465–496.

Anderson, A. K., Christoff, K., Stappen, I., Panitz, D., Ghahremani, D. G., Glover, G., et al. (2003). Dissociated neural representations of intensity and valence in human olfaction. *Nature Neuroscience, 6*, 196–202.

Anderson, S. W., Bechara, A., Damasio, H., Tranel, D., & Damasio, A. R. (1999). Impairment of social and moral behavior related to early damage in human prefrontal cortex. *Nature Neuroscience, 2*, 1032–1037.

Andy, O. J., & Jurko, F. (1987). Thalamic stimulation effects on reactive depression. *Applied Neurophysiology, 50*(1–6), 324–329.

Aziz, T. Z., Peggs, D., Sambrook, M. A., & Crossman, A. R. (1991). Lesion of the subthalamic nucleus for the alleviation of 1-methyl-4-phenyl-1, 2, 3, 6-tetrahydropyridine (MPTP)-induced parkinsonism in the primate. *Movement Disorders, 6*, 288–292.

Barbas, H. (1988). Anatomic organization of basoventral and mediodorsal visual recipient prefrontal regions in the rhesus monkey. *Journal of Comparative Neurology, 276*, 313–342.

Barbas, H., & Pandya, D. N. (1989). Architecture and intrinsic connections of the prefrontal cortex in the rhesus monkey. *Journal of Comparative Neurology, 286*, 353–375.

Baumeister, A. A. (2000). The Tulane Electrical Brain Stimulation Program a historical case study in medical ethics. *Journal of the History of the Neurosciences, 9*, 262–278.

Baxter, M. G., Parker, A., Lindner, C. C., Izquierdo, A. D., & Murray, E. A. (2000). Control of response selection by reinforcer value requires interaction of amygdala and orbital prefrontal cortex. *Journal of Neuroscience, 20*, 4311–4319.

Baylis, L. L., & Gaffan, D. (1991). Amygdalectomy and ventromedial prefrontal ablation produce similar deficits in food choice and in simple object discrimination learning for an unseen reward. *Experimental Brain Research, 86*, 617–622.

Bechara, A., Damasio, A. R., Damasio, H., & Anderson, S. W. (1994). Insensitivity to future consequences following damage to human prefrontal cortex. *Cognition, 50*, 7–15.

Bechara, A., Damasio, H., Tranel, D., & Anderson, S. W. (1998). Dissociation of working memory from decision making within the human prefrontal cortex. *Journal of Neuroscience, 18*, 428–437.

Bechtereva, N. P., Bondartchuk, A. N., & Smirnov, V. M. (1972). Therapeutic electrostimulations of the deep brain structures. *Vopr Neirokhir, 1*, 7–12.

Berridge, K. C. (1996). Food reward: Brain substrates of wanting and liking. *Neuroscience and Biobehavioral Reviews, 20*, 1–25.

Berridge, K. C., & Kringelbach, M. L. (2008). Affective neuroscience of pleasure: Reward in humans and animals. *Psychopharmacology, 199*, 457–480.

Berridge, K. C., & Robinson, T. E. (1998). What is the role of dopamine in reward: Hedonic impact, reward learning, or incentive salience? *Brain Research Reviews, 28*, 309–369.

Bindra, D. (1978). How adaptive behavior is produced: A perceptual-motivational alternative to response-reinforcement. *Behavioral and Brain Sciences, 1*, 41–91.

Bittar, R. G., Burn, S. C., Bain, P. G., Owen, S. L., Joint, C., Shlugman, D., et al. (2005). Deep brain stimulation for movement disorders and pain. *Journal of Clinical Neuroscience, 12*, 457–463.

Bittar, R. G., Kar-Purkayastha, I., Owen, S. L., Bear, R. E., Green, A., Wang, S., et al. (2005). Deep brain stimulation for pain relief: A meta-analysis. *Journal of Clinical Neuroscience, 12*, 515–519.

Bittar, R. G., Otero, S., Carter, H., & Aziz, T. Z. (2005). Deep brain stimulation for phantom limb pain. *Journal of Clinical Neuroscience, 12*, 399–404.

Blair, R. J. (2003). Facial expressions, their communicatory functions and neuro-cognitive substrates. *Philosophical Transactions of the Royal Society of London. Series B, 358*, 561–572.

Blair, R. J., & Cipolotti, L. (2000). Impaired social response reversal. A case of "acquired sociopathy." *Brain, 123*, 1122–1141.

Blair, R. J., Morris, J. S., Frith, C. D., Perrett, D. I., & Dolan, R. J. (1999). Dissociable neural responses to facial expressions of sadness and anger. *Brain, 122*(Pt. 5), 883–893.

Blood, A. J., & Zatorre, R. J. (2001). Intensely pleasurable responses to music correlate with activity in brain regions implicated in reward and emotion. *Proceedings of the National Academy of Sciences, USA, 98*, 11818–11823.

Blood, A. J., Zatorre, R. J., Bermudez, P., & Evans, A. C. (1999). Emotional responses to pleasant and unpleasant music correlate with activity in paralimbic brain regions. *Nature Neuroscience, 2*, 382–387.

Bodamer, J. (1947). Die prosop-agnosie. *Archiv für Psychiatrie und Nervenkrankheiten, 179*, 6–53.

Boivie, J., & Meyerson, B. A. (1982). A correlative anatomical and clinical study of pain suppression by deep brain stimulation. *Pain*, *13*, 113–126.

Bowlby, J. (1957). An ethological approach to research in child development. *British Journal of Medical Psychother*, *30*, 230–240.

Bowlby, J. (1969). *Attachment and Loss: Vol. 1. Attachment*. London: Hogarth Press.

Brodmann, K. (1909). *Vergleichende Lokalisationslehre der Grosshirnrinde in ihren Prinzipien dargestellt auf Grund des Zellenbaues*. Leipzig, Germany: Barth.

Bruce, C., Desimone, R., & Gross, C. G. (1981). Visual properties of neurons in a polysensory area in superior temporal sulcus of the macaque. *Journal of Neurophysiology*, *46*, 369–384.

Butter, C. M., Mishkin, M., & Rosvold, H. E. (1963). Conditioning and extinction of a food-rewarded response after selective ablations of frontal cortex in rhesus monkeys. *Clinical and Experimental Neurology*, *7*, 65–75.

Cabanac, M. (1971, September 17). Physiological role of pleasure. *Science*, *173*, 1103–1107.

Cannon, W. B. (1927). The James-Lange theory of emotion. *American Journal of Psychology*, *39*, 106–124.

Cardinal, R. N., Parkinson, J. A., Hall, J., & Everitt, B. J. (2002). Emotion and motivation: The role of the amygdala, ventral striatum, and prefrontal cortex. *Neuroscience and Biobehavioural Reviews*, *26*, 321–352.

Carmichael, S. T., & Price, J. L. (1994). Architectonic subdivision of the orbital and medial prefrontal cortex in the macaque monkey. *Journal of Comparative Neurology*, *346*, 366–402.

Carmichael, S. T., & Price, J. L. (1995a). Limbic connections of the orbital and medial prefrontal cortex in macaque monkeys. *Journal of Comparative Neurology*, *363*, 615–641.

Carmichael, S. T., & Price, J. L. (1995b). Sensory and premotor connections of the orbital and medial prefrontal cortex of macaque monkeys. *Journal of Comparative Neurology*, *363*, 642–664.

Cavada, C., Company, T., Tejedor, J., Cruz Rizzolo, R. J., & Reinoso Suarez, F. (2000). The anatomical connections of the macaque monkey orbitofrontal cortex. A review. *Cerebral Cortex*, *10*, 220–242.

Chiavaras, M. M., & Petrides, M. (2000). Orbitofrontal sulci of the human and macaque monkey brain. *Journal of Comparative Neurology*, *422*, 35–54.

Chiavaras, M. M., & Petrides, M. (2001). Three-dimensional probabilistic atlas of the human orbitofrontal sulci in standardized stereotaxic space. *NeuroImage*, *13*, 479–496.

Craig, A. D. (2002). Opinion: How do you feel? Interoception: The sense of the physiological condition of the body. *Nature Reviews: Neuroscience*, *3*, 655–666.

Craig, A. D., Chen, K., Bandy, D., & Reiman, E. M. (2000). Thermosensory activation of insular cortex. *Nature Neuroscience*, *3*, 184–190.

Critchley, H. D., Mathias, C. J., & Dolan, R. J. (2002). Fear conditioning in humans: The influence of awareness and autonomic arousal on functional neuroanatomy. *Neuron*, *33*, 653–663.

Cromwell, H. C., & Berridge, K. C. (1993). Where does damage lead to enhanced food aversion: The ventral pallidum/substantia innominata or lateral hypothalamus? *Brain Research*, *624*(1–2), 1–10.

Cummings, J. L. (1992). Depression and Parkinson's disease: A review. *American Journal of Psychiatry*, *149*, 443–454.

Damasio, A. R. (1994). *Descartes' error*. New York: Putnam.

Damasio, A. R. (1996). The somatic marker hypothesis and the possible functions of the prefrontal cortex. *Philosophical Transactions of the Royal Society of London. Series B*, *351*, 1413–1420.

Darwin, C. (1872). *The expression of the emotions in man and animals* (3rd ed.). Chicago: University of Chicago Press.

De Araujo, I. E., Kringelbach, M. L., Rolls, E. T., & Hobden, P. (2003). The representation of umami taste in the human brain. *Journal of Neurophysiology*, *90*, 313–319.

De Araujo, I. E., Kringelbach, M. L., Rolls, E. T., & McGlone, F. (2003). Human cortical responses to water in the mouth, and the effects of thirst. *Journal of Neurophysiology*, *90*, 1865–1876.

De Araujo, I. E., & Rolls, E. T. (2004). Representation in the human brain of food texture and oral fat. *Journal of Neuroscience*, *24*, 3086–3093.

De Araujo, I. E., Rolls, E. T., Kringelbach, M. L., McGlone, F., & Phillips, N. (2003). Taste-olfactory convergence, and the representation of the pleasantness of flavour, in the human brain. *European Journal of Neuroscience*, *18*, 2059–2068.

Dehaene, S., Kerszberg, M., & Changeux, J. P. (1998). A neuronal model of a global workspace in effortful cognitive tasks. *Proceedings of the National Academy of Sciences, USA*, *95*, 14529–14534.

Deichmann, R., Josephs, O., Hutton, C., Corfield, D. R., & Turner, R. (2002). Compensation of susceptibility-induced BOLD sensitivity losses in echo-planar fMRI imaging. *NeuroImage*, *15*, 120–135.

Descartes, R. (1649). *Les passions de l'âme*. [The passions of the Soul] Paris: Henry LeGras.

Desimone, R., & Gross, C. G. (1979). Visual areas in the temporal cortex of the macaque. *Brain Research*, *178*(2–3), 363–380.

Dias, R., Robbins, T., & Roberts, A. (1996, March 7). Dissociation in prefrontal cortex of affective and attentional shifts. *Nature*, *380*, 69–72.

Eblen, F., & Graybiel, A. M. (1995). Highly restricted origin of prefrontal cortical inputs to striosomes in the macaque monkey. *Journal of Neuroscience*, *15*, 5999–6013.

Ekman, P., & Friesen, W.-V. (1971). Constants across cultures in the face and emotion. *Journal of Personality and Social Psychology*, *17*, 124–129.

Elliott, R., Dolan, R. J., & Frith, C. D. (2000). Dissociable functions in the medial and lateral orbitofrontal cortex: Evidence from human neuroimaging studies. *Cerebral Cortex*, *10*, 308–317.

Farrow, T. F., Zheng, Y., Wilkinson, I. D., Spence, S. A., Deakin, J. F., Tarrier, N., et al. (2001). Investigating the functional anatomy of empathy and forgiveness. *NeuroReport*, *12*, 2433–2438.

Fields, H. L., & Basbaum, A. (1999). Central nervous system mechanisms of pain modulation. In P. D. Wall & R. Melzack (Eds.), *Textbook of pain* (pp. 309–329). Edinburgh, Scotland: Churchill Livingstone.

Frey, S., Kostopoulos, P., & Petrides, M. (2000). Orbitofrontal involvement in the processing of unpleasant auditory information. *European Journal of Neuroscience*, *12*, 3709–3712.

Frith, C. D. (2006). The value of brain imaging in the study of development and its disorders. *Journal of Child Psychology and Psychiatry*, *47*, 979–982.

Fritsch, G., & Hitzig, E. (1870). Über die elektrische Erregbarkeit des Grosshirns. *Archives of Anatomica Physiology*, *37*, 300–332.

Fuster, J. M. (1997). *The prefrontal cortex* (3rd ed.). New York: Raven Press.

Gildenberg, P. L. (2005). Evolution of neuromodulation. *Stereotactic and Functional Neurosurgery*, *83*(2–3), 71–79.

Gottfried, J. A., O'Doherty, J., & Dolan, R. J. (2003, August 22). Encoding predictive reward value in human amygdala and orbitofrontal cortex. *Science*, *301*, 1104–1107.

Gusnard, D. A., & Raichle, M. E. (2001). Searching for a baseline: Functional imaging and the resting human brain. *Nature Reviews: Neuroscience*, *2*, 685–694.

Harlow, J. M. (1848). Passage of an iron rod through the head. *Boston Medical and Surgical Journal*, *39*, 389–393.

Hasselmo, M. E., Rolls, E. T., Baylis, G. C., & Nalwa, V. (1989). Object-centred encoding by face-selective neurons in the cortex in the superior temporal sulcus of the the monkey. *Experimental Brain Research*, *75*, 417–429.

Hassler, R. (1955). The influence of stimulations and coagulations in the human thalamus on the tremor at rest and its physiopathologic mechanism. *Proceedings of the Second International Congress of Neuropathology, 2,* 637–642.

Hassler, R., Riechert, T., Mundinger, F., Umbach, W., & Ganglberger, J. A. (1960). Physiological observations in stereotaxic operations in extrapyramidal motor disturbances. *Brain, 83,* 337–350.

Haxby, J. V., Horwitz, B., Ungerleider, L. G., Maisog, J. M., Pietrini, P., & Grady, C. L. (1994). The functional organization of human extrastriate cortex: A PET-rCBF study of selective attention to faces and locations. *Journal of Neuroscience, 14,* 6336–6353.

Hinton, E. C., Parkinson, J. A., Holland, A. J., Arana, F. S., Roberts, A. C., & Owen, A. M. (2004, September). Neural contributions to the motivational control of appetite in humans. *European Journal of Neuroscience, 20,* 1411–1418.

Holland, P. C., & Gallagher, M. (2004, April). Amygdala-frontal interactions and reward expectancy. *Current Opinion in Neurobiology, 14,* 148–155.

Hornak, J., Bramham, J., Rolls, E. T., Morris, R. G., O'Doherty, J., Bullock, P. R., et al. (2003). Changes in emotion after circumscribed surgical lesions of the orbitofrontal and cingulate cortices. *Brain, 126,* 1671–1712.

Hornak, J., O'Doherty, J., Bramham, J., Rolls, E. T., Morris, R. G., Bullock, P. R., et al. (2004). Reward-related reversal learning after surgical excisions in orbitofrontal and dorsolateral prefrontal cortex in humans. *Journal of Cognitive Neuroscience, 16,* 463–478.

Hornak, J., Rolls, E. T., & Wade, D. (1996). Face and voice expression identification in patients with emotional and behavioural changes following ventral frontal lobe damage. *Neuropsychologia, 34,* 247–261.

Horsley, V., & Clarke, R. H. (1908). The structure and functions of the cerebellum examined by a new method. *Brain, 31,* 45–124.

Hosobuchi, Y., Adams, J. E., & Linchitz, R. (1977, July 8). Pain relief by electrical stimulation of the central gray matter in humans and its reversal by naloxone. *Science, 197,* 183–186.

Hull, C. L. (1951). *Essentials of behavior.* New Haven, CT: Yale University Press.

Iversen, S. D., & Mishkin, M. (1970). Perseverative interference in monkeys following selective lesions of the inferior prefrontal convexity. *Experimental Brain Research, 11,* 376–386.

James, W. (1890). *The principles of psychology.* New York: Henry Holt.

Jenkinson, N., Nandi, D., Aziz, T. Z., & Stein, J. F. (2005). Pedunculopontine nucleus: A new target for deep brain stimulation for akinesia. *NeuroReport, 16,* 1875–1876.

Krack, P., Batir, A., Van Blercom, N., Chabardes, S., Fraix, V., Ardouin, C., et al. (2003). Five-year follow-up of bilateral stimulation of the subthalamic nucleus in advanced Parkinson's disease. *New England Journal of Medicine, 349,* 1925–1934.

Kringelbach, M. L. (2004a). Emotion. In R. L. Gregory (Ed.), *The Oxford companion to the mind* (2nd ed., pp. 287–290). Oxford: Oxford University Press.

Kringelbach, M. L. (2004b). Food for thought: Hedonic experience beyond homeostasis in the human brain. *Neuroscience, 126,* 807–819.

Kringelbach, M. L. (2004c). *Hjernerum: Den følelsesfulde hjerne.* Copenhagen, Denmark: People's Press.

Kringelbach, M. L. (2004d). Learning to change. *PLoS Biology, 2*(5), e140.

Kringelbach, M. L. (2005). The orbitofrontal cortex: Linking reward to hedonic experience. *Nature Reviews: Neuroscience, 6,* 691–702.

Kringelbach, M. L. (2006). Cortical systems involved in appetite and food consumption. In S. J. Cooper & T. C. Kirkham (Eds.), *Appetite and body weight: Integrative systems and the development of anti-obesity drugs* (pp. 5–26). London: Elsevier.

Kringelbach, M. L., & Berridge, K. C. (2009). *Pleasures of the brain.* New York: Oxford University Press.

Kringelbach, M. L., Jenkinson, N., Green, A. L., Owen, S. L. F., Hansen, P. C., Cornelissen, P. L., et al. (2007). Deep brain stimulation for chronic pain investigated with magnetoencephalography. *NeuroReport, 18,* 223–228.

Kringelbach, M. L., Jenkinson, N., Owen, S. L. F., & Aziz, T. Z. (2007). Translational principles of deep brain stimulation. *Nature Reviews: Neuroscience, 8,* 623–635.

Kringelbach, M. L., Lehtonen, A., Squire, S., Harvey, A. G., Craske, M. G., Holliday, I. E., et al. (2007). Infant faces evoke a highly specific and rapid neural signature in the human brain. *Society for Neuroscience,* 782.1.

Kringelbach, M. L., Lehtonen, A., Squire, S., Harvey, A. G., Craske, M. G., Holliday, I. E., et al. (2008). A specific and rapid neural signature for parental instinct. *PLoS ONE. 3*(2): e1664.

Kringelbach, M. L., O'Doherty, J., Rolls, E. T., & Andrews, C. (2000). Sensory-specific satiety for the flavour of food is represented in the orbitofrontal cortex. *NeuroImage, 11,* S767.

Kringelbach, M. L., O'Doherty, J., Rolls, E. T., & Andrews, C. (2003). Activation of the human orbitofrontal cortex to a liquid food stimulus is correlated with its subjective pleasantness. *Cerebral Cortex, 13,* 1064–1071.

Kringelbach, M. L., & Rolls, E. T. (2003). Neural correlates of rapid context-dependent reversal learning in a simple model of human social interaction. *NeuroImage, 20,* 1371–1383.

Kringelbach, M. L., & Rolls, E. T. (2004). The functional neuroanatomy of the human orbitofrontal cortex: Evidence from neuroimaging and neuropsychology. *Progress in Neurobiology, 72*(5), 341–372.

Lange, C. G. (1887). *Über Gemüstbewegungen. (Org. Om Sindsbevægelser).* Leipzig, Germany: Thomas Theodor.

Layard, R. (2005). *Happiness: Lessons from a new science.* London: Penguin Press.

Leone, M., Franzini, A., Broggi, G., May, A., & Bussone, G. (2004). Long-term follow-up of bilateral hypothalamic stimulation for intractable cluster headache. *Brain, 127,* 2259–2264.

Lorenz, K. (1971). *Studies in animal and human behavior* (Vol. 2). London: Methuen.

Macmillan, M. (2000). *An odd kind of fame: Stories of Phineas Gage.* Cambridge, MA: MIT Press.

Maia, T. V., & McLelland, J. L. (2004). A reexamination of the evidence for the somatic marker hypothesis: What participants really know in the Iowa gambling task. *Proceedings of the National Academy of Sciences, USA, 101,* 16075–16080.

Mayberg, H. S., Lozano, A. M., Voon, V., McNeely, H. E., Seminowicz, D., Hamani, C., et al. (2005). Deep brain stimulation for treatment-resistant depression. *Neuron, 45,* 651–660.

Mazzone, P., Lozano, A. M., Stanzione, P., Galati, S., Scanati, E., Peppe, A., et al. (2005). Implantation of human pedunculopontine nucleus: A safe and clinically relevant target in Parkinson's disease. *NeuroReport, 16,* 1877–1881.

Mesulam, M.-M., & Mufson, E. J. (1982). Insula of the old world monkey: Pt. III. Efferent cortical output and comments on function. *Journal of Comparative Neurology, 212,* 38–52.

Miller, J. M., Vorel, S. R., Tranguch, A. J., Kenny, E. T., Mazzoni, P., van Gorp, W. G., et al. (2006). Anhedonia after a selective bilateral lesion of the globus pallidus. *American Journal of Psychiatry, 163,* 786–788.

Naccache, L., Gaillard, R., Adam, C., Hasboun, D., Clemenceau, S., Baulac, M., et al. (2005). A direct intracranial record of emotions evoked by subliminal words. *Proceedings of the National Academy of Sciences, USA, 102,* 7713–7717.

Nandi, D., Liu, X., Joint, C., Stein, J., & Aziz, T. (2002). Thalamic field potentials during deep brain stimulation of periventricular gray in chronic pain. *Pain, 97*(1/2), 47–51.

Nauta, W. J. (1971). The problem of the frontal lobe: A reinterpretation. *Journal of Psychiatric Research, 8,* 167–187.

Nobre, A. C., Coull, J. T., Frith, C. D., & Mesulam, M. M. (1999). Orbitofrontal cortex is activated during breaches of expectation in tasks of visual attention. *Nature Neuroscience, 2,* 11–12.

O'Doherty, J., Kringelbach, M. L., Rolls, E. T., Hornak, J., & Andrews, C. (2001). Abstract reward and punishment representations in the human orbitofrontal cortex. *Nature Neuroscience, 4,* 95–102.

O'Doherty, J., Rolls, E. T., Francis, S., Bowtell, R., McGlone, F., Kobal, G., et al. (2000). Sensory-specific satiety-related olfactory activation of the human orbitofrontal cortex. *NeuroReport, 11,* 893–897.

Öngür, D., & Price, J. L. (2000, March). The organization of networks within the orbital and medial prefrontal cortex of rats, monkeys and humans. *Cerebral Cortex, 10,* 206–219.

Pandya, D. N., & Yeterian, E. H. (1996). Comparison of prefrontal architecture and connections. *Philosophical Transactions of the Royal Society of London, Series B, 351,* 1423–1432.

Peciña, S., & Berridge, K. C. (2005). Hedonic hot spot in nucleus accumbens shell: Where do mu-opioids cause increased hedonic impact of sweetness? *Journal of Neuroscience, 25,* 11777–11786.

Peciña, S., Smith, K. S., & Berridge, K. C. (2006). Hedonic hot spots in the brain. *Neuroscientist, 12,* 500–511.

Perlmutter, J. S., & Mink, J. W. (2006). Deep brain stimulation. *Annual Reviews of Neuroscience, 29,* 229–257.

Perrett, D. I., Rolls, E. T., & Caan, W. (1982). Visual neurons responsive to faces in the monkey temporal cortex. *Experimental Brain Research, 47,* 329–342.

Petrides, M., & Pandya, D. N. (1994). Comparative cytoarchitectonic analysis of the human and the macaque frontal cortex. In F. Boller & J. Grafman (Eds.), *Handbook of neuropsychology* (Vol. 9, pp. 17–58). Amsterdam: Elsevier.

Petrovic, P., & Ingvar, M. (2002). Imaging cognitive modulation of pain processing. *Pain, 95*(1/2), 1–5.

Petrovic, P., Kalso, E., Petersson, K. M., & Ingvar, M. (2002, March 1). Placebo and opioid analgesia: Imaging a shared neuronal network. *Science, 295,* 1737–1740.

Plaha, P., & Gill, S. G. (2005). Bilateral deep brain stimulation of the pedunculopontine nucleus for idiopathic Parkinson's disease. *NeuroReport, 16,* 1883–1887.

Rahman, S., Sahakian, B. J., Hodges, J. R., Rogers, R. D., & Robbins, T. W. (1999). Specific cognitive deficits in mild frontal variant frontotemporal dementia. *Brain, 122,* 1469–1493.

Ranote, S., Elliott, R., Abel, K. M., Mitchell, R., Deakin, J. F., & Appleby, L. (2004). The neural basis of maternal responsiveness to infants: An fMRI study. *NeuroReport, 15,* 1825–1829.

Ray, N. J., Kringelbach, M. L., Jenkinson, N., Owen, S. L. F., Davies, P., Wang, S., et al. (2007). Using magnetoencephalography to investigate deep brain stimulation for cluster headache. *Biomedical Imaging and Intervention Journal, 3,* e25.

Rempel-Clower, N. L., & Barbas, H. (1998). Topographic organization of connections between the hypothalamus and prefrontal cortex in the rhesus monkey. *Journal of Comparative Neurology, 398,* 393–419.

Reynolds, D. V. (1969, April 25). Surgery in the rat during electrical analgesia induced by focal brain stimulation. *Science, 164,* 444–445.

Rogers, R. D., Owen, A. M., Middleton, H. C., Williams, E. J., Pickard, J. D., Sahakian, B. J., et al. (1999). Choosing between small, likely rewards and large, unlikely rewards activates inferior and orbital prefrontal cortex. *Journal of Neuroscience, 19,* 9029–9038.

Rolls, B. J., Rolls, E. T., Rowe, E. A., & Sweeney, K. (1981). Sensory specific satiety in man. *Physiology and Behavior, 27,* 137–142.

Rolls, E. T. (1999). *The brain and emotion.* Oxford: Oxford University Press.

Rolls, E. T., Hornak, J., Wade, D., & McGrath, J. (1994). Emotion-related learning in patients with social and emotional changes associated with frontal lobe damage. *Journal of Neurology, Neurosurgery, and Psychiatry, 57,* 1518–1524.

Rolls, E. T., Kringelbach, M. L., & De Araujo, I. E. T. (2003). Different representations of pleasant and unpleasant odors in the human brain. *European Journal of Neuroscience, 18,* 695–703.

Rolls, E. T., O'Doherty, J., Kringelbach, M. L., Francis, S., Bowtell, R., & McGlone, F. (2003). Representations of pleasant and painful touch in the human orbitofrontal and cingulate cortices. *Cerebral Cortex, 13,* 308–317.

Rozin, P. (2001). Food preference. In N. J. Smelser & P. B. Baltes (Eds.), *International encyclopedia of the social and behavioral sciences* (pp. 5719–5722). Amsterdam: Elsevier.

Ryle, G. (1954). Pleasure. *Proceedings of the Aristotelian Society, 28,* 135–146.

Saper, C. B., Chou, T. C., & Elmquist, J. K. (2002). The need to feed: Homeostatic and hedonic control of eating. *Neuron, 36,* 199–211.

Schachter, S., & Singer, J. (1962). Cognitive, social and physiological determinants of emotional state. *Psychological Review, 69,* 387–399.

Schlaepfer, T. E., Cohen, M. X., Frick, C., Kosel, M., Brodesser, D., Axmacher, N., et al. (2007). Deep brain stimulation to reward circuitry alleviates anhedonia in refractory major depression. *Neuropsychopharmacology, 22,* 368–377.

Schnider, A. (2003, August). Spontaneous confabulation and the adaptation of thought to ongoing reality. *Nature Reviews: Neuroscience, 4,* 662–671.

Schnider, A., & Ptak, R. (1999). Spontaneous confabulators fail to suppress currently irrelevant memory traces. *Nature Reviews: Neuroscience, 2,* 677–681.

Schnider, A., Treyer, V., & Buck, A. (2005). The human orbitofrontal cortex monitors outcomes even when no reward is at stake. *Neuropsychologia, 43,* 316–323.

Schultz, W., & Dickinson, A. (2000). Neuronal coding of prediction errors. *Annual Review of Neuroscience, 23,* 473–500.

Sergent, J., & Villemure, J. G. (1989). Prosopagnosia in a right hemispherectomized patient. *Brain, 112,* 975–995.

Small, D. M., Gregory, M. D., Mak, Y. E., Gitelman, D., Mesulam, M. M., & Parrish, T. (2003). Dissociation of neural representation of intensity and affective valuation in human gustation. *Neuron, 39,* 701–711.

Small, D. M., Jones-Gotman, M., Zatorre, R. J., Petrides, M., & Evans, A. C. (1997). Flavor processing: More than the sum of its parts. *NeuroReport, 8,* 3913–3917.

Small, D. M., Zald, D. H., Jones-Gotman, M., Zatorre, R. J., Pardo, J. V., Frey, S., et al. (1999). Human cortical gustatory areas: A review of functional neuroimaging data. *NeuroReport, 10,* 7–14.

Small, D. M., Zatorre, R. J., Dagher, A., Evans, A. C., & Jones-Gotman, M. (2001). Changes in brain activity related to eating chocolate: From pleasure to aversion. *Brain, 124,* 1720–1733.

Smith, K. S., & Berridge, K. C. (2005). The ventral pallidum and hedonic reward: Neurochemical maps of sucrose "liking" and food intake. *Journal of Neuroscience, 25,* 8637–8649.

Spiegel, E. A., Wycis, H. T., Marks, M., & Lee, A. J. (1947, October 10). Stereotaxic apparatus for operations on the human brain. *Science, 106,* 349–350.

Stein, A., Gath, D. H., Bucher, J., Bond, A., Day, A., & Cooper, P. J. (1991). The relationship between post-natal depression and mother-child interaction. *British Journal of Psychiatry, 158,* 46–52.

Steiner, J. E., Glaser, D., Hawilo, M. E., & Berridge, K. C. (2001). Comparative expression of hedonic impact: Affective reactions to taste by human infants and other primates. *Neuroscience and Biobehavioral Reviews, 25,* 53–74.

Sutton, J. (2001). Descartes, René. In *Encyclopedia of life sciences*. Retrieved November 14, 2008, from http://doi.wiley.com/10.1038/npg.els.0002472.

Swain, J. E., Lorberbaum, J. P., Kose, S., & Strathearn, L. (2007). Brain basis of early parent-infant interactions: Psychology, physiology, and in vivo functional neuroimaging studies. *Journal of Child Psychology and Psychiatry, 48*(3/4), 262–287.

Thut, G., Schultz, W., Roelcke, U., Nienhusmeier, M., Missimer, J., Maguire, R. P., et al. (1997). Activation of the human brain by monetary reward. *NeuroReport, 8*, 1225–1228.

Ullsperger, M., & von Cramon, D. Y. (2004). Decision making, performance and outcome monitoring in frontal cortical areas. *Nature Neuroscience, 7*, 1173–1174.

Valenstein, E. S. (1973). *Brain control: A critical examination of brain stimulation and psychosurgery*. London: Wiley-Interscience.

Van Hoesen, G. W., Morecraft, R. J., & Vogt, B. A. (1993). Connections of the monkey cingulate cortex. In B. A. Vogt & M. Gabriel (Eds.), *The Neurobiology of the cingulate cortex and limbic thalamus: A comprehensive handbook* (pp. 249–284). Boston: Birkhäuser.

Völlm, B. A., de Araujo, I. E. T., Cowen, P. J., Rolls, E. T., Kringelbach, M. L., Smith, K. A., et al. (2004). Methamphetamine activates reward circuitry in drug naïve human subjects. *Neuropsychopharmacology, 29*, 1715–1722.

Walker, A. E. (1940). A cytoarchitectural study of the prefrontal area of the macaque monkey. *Journal of Comparative Neurology, 73*, 59–86.

Walton, M. E., Devlin, J. T., & Rushworth, M. F. (2004, November). Interactions between decision making and performance monitoring within prefrontal cortex. *Nature Neuroscience, 7*, 1259–1265.

Weiskrantz, L. (1968). Emotion. In L. Weiskrantz (Ed.), *Analysis of behavioural change* (pp. 50–90). New York and London: Harper & Row.

Wilson, J., Jenkinson, M., de Araujo, I. E. T., Kringelbach, M. L., Rolls, E. T., & Jezzard, P. (2002). Fast, fully automated global and local magnetic field optimization for fMRI of the human brain. *NeuroImage, 17*, 967–976.

Winkielman, P., Berridge, K. C., & Wilbarger, J. L. (2005). Unconscious affective reactions to masked happy versus angry faces influence consumption behavior and judgments of value. *Personality and Social Psychology Bulletin, 31*, 121–135.

Zatorre, R. J., Jones-Gotman, M., Evans, A. C., & Meyer, E. (1992, November 26). Functional localization and lateralization of human olfactory cortex. *Nature, 360*, 339–340.

Chapter 42

Neural Perspectives on Emotion: Impact on Perception, Attention, and Memory

DAMIAN STANLEY, EMMA FERNEYHOUGH, AND ELIZABETH A. PHELPS

In behavioral science, investigations of the structure and impact of emotion have traditionally occurred within the domains of social, personality, or clinical psychology. Studies of cognition, inspired by the computer metaphor and the information processing approach (Miller, 2003), have generally focused on characterizing functions such as perception, attention, and memory assuming little role for emotion. This traditional divide between emotion and cognition has been debated in psychological science (Lazarus, 1984; Zajonc, 1984). Underlying these debates is the notion that the mechanisms of emotion and cognition can be separated and investigated independently.

This assumption has been challenged as behavioral science has started to incorporate methods from neuroscience. One of the striking characteristics of the brain is the extensive connectivity between regions thought to underlie independent processes. This is particularly apparent in studies of emotion. Investigations of neural connectivity have shown that the amygdala, a region thought to be more or less specialized for emotion, has extensive connections throughout the brain (Young, Scannell, Burns, & Blakemore, 1994). The amygdala is a small, almond-shaped structure in the medial temporal lobe that both receives input from and projects to a wide array of brain regions implicated in cognitive processes, including those underlying perception, attention, and memory. What is the role of these connections? An examination of neural circuitry suggests that emotion and cognition are intertwined at several stages of stimulus processing. From an evolutionary perspective, this makes sense. The purpose of emotion is to highlight what is relevant (Frijda, 1986) and potentially important for survival. Given this, we might expect the mechanisms of cognition to be tuned to highlight emotional events.

In this chapter, we review recent research exploring the relation between cognition and emotion that has been informed by advances in cognitive neuroscience. Although the range of processes that comprise emotion (e.g., Scherer, 2005) is represented in several regions and circuits of the brain (Dagleish, 2004), we focus on insights from studies of the amygdala. The amygdala, because of its wide connectivity, is suggested to play a primary role in the modulation of cognition in the presence of emotional events (Anderson & Phelps, 2000). Furthermore, due to its prominence in studies of emotion across species, the amygdala is one of the most thoroughly investigated brain regions in studies of emotion (e.g., Aggleton, 1992; LeDoux, 1996). In particular, we focus on how studies of the human amygdala have enhanced our understanding of emotion's impact on perception, attention, and memory.

EMOTION'S INFLUENCE ON ATTENTION AND PERCEPTION

The influence of emotional stimuli on attention and perception has been documented using a variety of techniques. Emotion is thought to influence attention and perception in two distinct ways. First, emotion has been found to enhance or facilitate attentional and perceptual processes, thereby increasing the salience of emotional stimuli. Second, emotion has been shown to capture our attention, leading to impaired processing of nonemotional stimuli present in the environment.

Emotion Enhances Attention and Perception

A number of psychological and psychophysical paradigms have demonstrated emotion's facilitation of attention and perception. Often these are paradigms used by vision and attention researchers to show that a particular stimulus or class of stimuli has preferential access to awareness as a result of its saliency. One example is visual search, in which observers search for a target in an array of distracters. When the target and the distracters are equally salient, people take longer to find the target because they must inspect each item in the array to determine whether it is a target or a distracter. However, when a target is salient compared to surrounding distracters, it is immediately distinguishable and is said to "pop out" (Treisman & Gelade, 1980). Ohman and colleagues (Ohman, Flykt, & Esteves, 2001; Ohman, Lundqvist, & Esteves, 2001) used the visual search paradigm to show that emotional targets (e.g., threatening faces, snakes, or spiders) pop out when embedded in an array of neutral distracters (e.g., friendly faces, flowers, or mushrooms) but the reverse is not true for neutral targets. It is proposed that an enhanced ability to detect a snake in a field of flowers may have been advantageous to survival and subject to evolutionary pressures. A similar ability to detect a flower in a pit of snakes would confer little evolutionary advantage on the possessor.

Other studies demonstrating emotion's facilitation of attention have adopted paradigms used by vision researchers to suppress awareness of visual stimuli in order to determine whether affective stimuli are less susceptible to such suppression. The attentional blink (AB; Raymond, Shapiro, & Arnell, 1992) is one such paradigm. In the AB, observers view a continuous stream of rapidly changing stimuli (e.g., 6 to 20 items per second) and indicate when one of two target stimuli appears. Typically, observers experience an attentional blink for a short period (180 to 450 ms) during which the presentation of a second target goes unnoticed. Researchers interested in the influence of emotion on attention have manipulated the affective value of the targets in the AB paradigm. Anderson and Phelps (2001) found that when the target presented during the AB period is an emotionally significant word, it is often detected, suggesting that emotional stimuli have preferential access to awareness at times when attention is limited (Anderson, 2005; Anderson & Phelps, 2001). Interestingly, Anderson and Phelps (2001) also found that patients with lesions of the amygdala do not show enhanced detection of emotional stimuli, indicating a role for the amygdala in our enhanced sensitivity to affectively salient events.

Another visual suppression paradigm used to demonstrate that emotional stimuli receive preferential access to awareness (Yang, Zald, & Blake, 2007) is continuous flash suppression (CFS; Tsuchiya & Koch, 2005), a variant of binocular rivalry. In binocular rivalry, two different images are presented simultaneously, one to each eye, in overlapping regions of visual space. The brain, unable to merge the dissimilar images, compromises by switching between the two so that only one is perceived at a time. If the images are equally salient, the dominant percept will switch back and forth between the two images. If the images are not equally salient, then one will tend to dominate over the other. In CFS, the visual properties of the stimulus presented to one eye are manipulated so that it is constantly dominant—preventing the input to the other eye from reaching awareness. Yang et al. (2007) used this paradigm to show that fearful faces (both upright and inverted) were less susceptible to CFS than neutral or happy ones. Other studies involving binocular rivalry and emotional faces or aversively conditioned stimuli have found similar effects in that the emotional stimuli dominate perception compared to their neutral counterparts (Alpers & Gerdes, 2007; Alpers, Ruhleder, Walz, Mühlberger, & Pauli, 2005).

These studies demonstrate that when attentional resources are limited, emotional stimuli have preferential access to awareness. Emotion's facilitation of attention also extends to the perception of nonemotional stimuli in the vicinity of emotional stimuli. This was demonstrated using an attentional cuing paradigm (Posner, 1980) in which fearful or neutral faces were used to cue the location of a subsequent target (Phelps, Ling, & Carrasco, 2006). The target was a simple gabor patch that varied in its visibility from trial to trial by altering its contrast. Observers had to indicate the orientation of the target. Cuing with a fearful face enhanced the perceived contrast of the subsequent target relative to cuing with a neutral face. That is, observers were able to identify the orientation of lower contrast targets when they were preceded by a fearful cue. There was an overall effect of the fear face cues on perception as well as a positive interaction between emotion and attention, providing support for separate but interacting mechanisms through which emotion and attention enhance perception. Orientation discrimination is a basic perceptual function known to rely on early visual cortex for processing. This suggests that one mechanism whereby emotion enhances perception and interacts with attention may be through the modulation of early visual areas by attentional and emotional systems.

An examination of the connectivity of the brain also suggests the amygdala may play a role in modulating the visual cortex at multiple levels. As displayed in Figure 42.1, tract-tracing studies in macaque monkeys found that the majority of the ventral visual sensory cortex (from area V1 to area TE) receives direct, topographically organized projections from the amygdala (Amaral, Behniea, & Kelly, 2003). This topographic organization indicates that the amygdala's input to the visual cortex does not serve as a diffuse, general modulator, but rather it has the spatial specificity to selectively activate different (presumably stimulus-relevant) visual regions. Further study of the termination pattern of the amygdala projections to visual cortices has revealed that they are most likely excitatory and modulatory in nature (Freese & Amaral, 2005, 2006), resembling other feedback projections into the visual

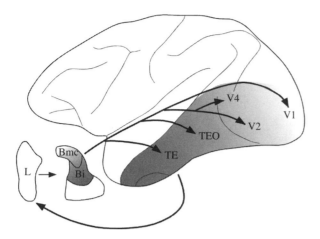

Figure 42.1 The connectivity of subregions of the amygdala (L, Bi, Bmc), and ventral visual cortical regions (V1, V2, V4, TEO, TE) in the macaque monkey.

Note: From "The Organization of Projections from the Amygdala to Visual Cortical Areas TE and V1 in the Macaque Monkey," by J. L. Freese and D. G. Amaral, 2005, *Journal of Comparative Neurology, 486,* p. 314. Reprinted with permission.

cortex that are known to facilitate neuronal responses to visual stimuli (Hupé et al., 1998, 2001). This pattern of connectivity between the amygdala and the sensory cortex is not unique to vision. Other neuroanatomical studies have found a similar topographic pattern of amygdala input to the sensory auditory cortex (Yukie, 2002) and evidence of projections to the early somatosensory cortex (Amaral & Price, 1984).

These anatomical studies suggest a pathway by which the amygdala may facilitate attention and perception in the presence of emotional stimuli by modulating processing in sensory cortices. Consistent with this, functional brain imaging studies have shown amygdala involvement in the enhancement of responses to emotional stimuli in the visual cortex. Morris and colleagues (Morris, Buchel, & Dolan, 2001; Morris, Friston, et al., 1998) reported a correlation between the magnitude of amygdala activation in response to fearful faces and fear-conditioned stimuli, relative to neutral stimuli, and the magnitude of the enhanced response to these emotional stimuli in the visual cortex. Vuilleumier, Armony, Driver, and Dolan (2001) found that activation in the fusiform face area (FFA), a region in the ventral visual stream involved in face processing (Kanwisher, McDermott, & Chun, 1997), was modulated both by attention and emotion. They also looked for regions in which there was an interaction between emotion and attention and found that this was the case in the primary visual cortex. These functional imaging studies show a correlation between amygdala activation and enhanced responses in the visual cortex to emotional stimuli, but do not indicate that the amygdala is mediating this enhanced

cortical response. By combining lesion and brain imaging techniques, Vuilleumier, Richardson, Armony, Driver, and Dolan (2004) were able to demonstrate that the enhanced response in the visual cortex to emotional stimuli may be the result of feedback from the amygdala. They showed a lack of visual cortex activation to fearful versus neutral faces in patients with focal damage to the amygdala. This finding supports the proposed role of the amygdala suggested by the anatomical connectivity studies and strongly implicates the amygdala in the enhancement of sensory cortical responses to emotionally salient stimuli.

One possible means by which the amygdala may modulate sensory cortical regions is through reciprocal connections. The amygdala receives input from the sensory cortex that allows the detection of an emotionally salient event and then, in turn, it modulates further perceptual processing. However, findings that emotionally salient stimuli both induce and, *almost simultaneously,* are the target of their *own* modulatory influences on perception and attention imply that the amygdala might also receive information about these stimuli rapidly so that it can act on early sensory representations. Researchers investigating auditory fear conditioning in rats have identified a critical, rapid, subcortical route to the amygdala from the auditory thalamus (see Phelps & LeDoux, 2005, for a review). The existence of a similar visual subcortical route from the retina to the amygdala via the superior colliculus and pulvinar nucleus of the thalamus has been suggested (see Ohman, Carlsson, Lundqvist, & Ingvar, 2007, for a review). In support of this subcortical visual pathway for the rapid detection of emotional events, studies in monkeys have shown that the earliest neural responses in the amygdala to visual stimuli occur 60 ms after the presentation of the stimulus, which suggests little-to-no cortical processing (Nakamura, Mikami, & Kubota, 1992).

In humans, strong evidence of a subcortical route for conveying the emotional nature of visual stimuli to the amygdala has been difficult to obtain because of the correlational nature of functional imaging techniques and the difficulty in interpreting null results. However, some studies have reported responses to fear faces in the proposed subcortical route (i.e., pulvinar and superior colliculus) and not in cortical regions to subliminal, unseen stimuli, as well as increased functional connectivity between the amygdala and these subcortical nuclei for unseen versus seen stimuli (Lidell et al., 2005; Morris, Friston, & Dolan, 1997; Morris, Ohman, & Dolan, 1998, 1999). Another imaging study by Vuilleumier, Armony, Driver, and Dolan (2003) took advantage of the hypothesis that a subcortical route would be more sensitive to crude, low spatial frequency visual information, whereas visual cortical processing is necessary to detect detailed, high-spatial frequency information. They showed that the superior colliculus, the pulvinar nucleus, and the amygdala are all preferentially sensitive to differences in low-spatial frequency information between emotional and neutral faces. In contrast, visual areas involved in face processing were more sensitive to the high-spatial frequency content of emotional faces. These imaging studies provide some support for the existence of a visual subcortical route and indicate that it may be an important component of the amygdala's sensitivity to emotional stimuli. However, they are correlative in nature and therefore cannot be used to establish causality.

The strongest evidence for the existence of a visual subcortical route involved in the processing of emotional stimuli comes from patient studies involving blindsight. Patients with blindsight have lesions in their primary visual cortex and as a result are unaware of stimuli that are presented to the corresponding visual field. However, they maintain a residual ability to discriminate certain stimuli in the absence of conscious perception (Weiskrantz, 1990). This residual visual ability is thought to rely on the retinocolliculo-pulvinar pathway. De Gelder, Vroomen, Pourtois, and Weiskrantz (1999) showed that a patient with blindsight was able to distinguish between faces with different emotional facial expressions presented in the blind visual field. Morris, DeGelder, Weiskrantz, and Dolan (2001) used functional imaging in the same patient to demonstrate that amygdala sensitivity to fearful faces presented in the blind field remained intact while sensitivity in cortical regions involved in face processing did not. Moreover, the authors found that this amygdala sensitivity to subliminal, unseen fearful faces was correlated with activity in the superior colliculus and pulvinar, further supporting a role for these subcortical regions in the processing of emotional stimuli.

Emotion Captures Attention, Impairing Perception

The majority of work examining the effects of emotion on attention and perception has focused on the enhanced processing of emotional stimuli. However, this enhancement does not come without a price. Much like talking on a mobile phone while driving impairs one's driving ability (Strayer, Drews, & Johnston, 2003), focusing attention on one stimulus often comes at the perceptual cost of others (e.g., Carrasco, 2006; Pestilli & Carrasco, 2005). Is the attentional facilitation observed for emotional stimuli accompanied by an attentional cost for other, nonemotional, stimuli in the environment? A few studies have examined this question and found that perception of neutral stimuli is indeed impaired in the presence of emotional

stimuli, a phenomenon referred to as the *emotional capture of attention*.

As discussed, previous research has shown that emotional stimuli are more resistant to the attentional blink than neutral stimuli (Anderson & Phelps, 2001). Using modified versions of this task, other research groups have found that emotional stimuli can also exacerbate the AB. The important difference between these two types of findings lies in the placement of the emotional stimulus. In contrast to the AB paradigm used by Andersen and Phelps (2001), Most, Chun, Widders, and Zald (2005) placed emotional stimuli in a stream of distracters and investigated what would happen when an emotional distracter preceded a neutral target. They found that observers detected the target less often when it followed an emotional distracter at a delay of 200 ms, but not at a delay of 800 ms. A second study by the same group (Smith, Most, Newsome, & Zald, 2006) found a similar impairment for targets following an aversively conditioned stimulus. These findings not only provide support for the emotional capture of attention, but they also show that this capture is transient, lasting less than 800 ms. The effects of this emotional capture may be reduced using cognitive strategies, though the rate of success depends on observers' propensity to avoid harm (Most et al., 2005).

The emotional capture of attention, as demonstrated by the impaired processing of neutral stimuli, has been observed in a range of paradigms (e.g., Mathews & MacLeod, 1985), but these studies do not isolate the component of attention that is mediating this effect. In an effort to determine if emotion results in faster shifts of attention, or perhaps a difficulty in disengaging from a detected emotional stimulus to process other stimuli, spatial attention was examined with the Posner cuing paradigm (Posner, 1980). Observers fixate on a central point while a stimulus is briefly flashed (100 ms) on either the left or right side of the screen. This stimulus automatically shifts covert attention to that side of the screen. Immediately after, a target dot appears on either the left or right side, and the observer's task is to indicate on which side the target appeared. The dependent measure is reaction time, which is expected to be longer for invalid trials (when the location of the stimulus and target are not the same). Fox, Russo, Bowles, and Dutton (2001) used this paradigm to present neutral, positive, or negative words and examine whether the affective value of the words altered observers' ability to detect the subsequent target dot. They found that on valid trials, where the target appeared in the same location as the words, there was no difference in reaction time for the three types of words. This suggests that emotion does not result in faster shifts of attention to the target location. However, on invalid trials, reaction times were significantly longer for trials with negative words compared to those with neutral or positive words. This finding indicates that once attention has shifted to the location of a negative stimulus, it is harder to disengage attention from this location to respond to nonemotional targets elsewhere. They also found that this disengagement cost for threat-related stimuli was greater in subjects who scored highly on scales of state-anxiety.

There have been very few studies of neurobiological mechanisms mediating the capture of attention, and it is not yet known precisely what role the amygdala may play in this effect (Pessoa, 2008). However, a study by Pourtois and Vuilleumier (2006) identified one component of the neural circuitry underlying the emotional capture of attention. They used electroencephalography (EEG), which provides high-resolution temporal information about neural events, and functional magnetic resonance imaging (fMRI) in two experiments using a Posner-style cuing paradigm. They found that enhanced EEG responses to targets following valid fearful faces in early visual cortex were preceded by heightened responses in regions of contralateral parietal lobe that are known to be involved in attentional control to that region of visual space. This suggests that emotional stimuli can modulate attentional control mechanisms. In addition, in the fMRI study, they found evidence of an "invalidity" effect. When a face was flashed to one side of the screen, the region of the parietal attentional control network that would be engaged in shifting attention to the other side of the screen showed less activation when this face had a fearful expression (relative to neutral). In other words, fearful faces on invalid trials captured attention, producing disengagement costs reflected in fMRI activity in the parietal cortex and resulting in impaired processing of the target. These data provide convincing evidence that emotional stimuli can modulate the neural systems involved in attentional control, effectively capturing attention and impairing processing for other, nonemotional, stimuli in the environment.

EMOTION'S INFLUENCE ON MEMORY

In the *Principles of Psychology,* William James (1890) suggested, "An impression may be so exciting emotionally as almost to leave a scar upon the cerebral tissues" (p. 670). James was reflecting on the common insight that emotion creates memories that have unique qualities and are often perceived to be more vivid and accurate than memories for mundane events. Both psychological and neuroscience studies of emotion have specified a number of ways emotion can change memory. It has been proposed that emotion can alter all three stages of memory: encoding, storage,

and retrieval. Episodic memory depends on the orchestration of a number of brain regions, most critically the hippocampal complex (Eichenbaum, 2002; Squire & Zola-Morgan, 1991), which lies adjacent to the amygdala in the medial temporal lobe (see Figure 42.2). In the presence of emotional events, the amygdala may modulate the neural circuitry of memory by influencing a range of mnemonic functions.

Emotion's Impact on Encoding

The first stage of memory, encoding, refers to the processes that occur when a stimulus is first encountered. At encoding, factors that influence attention and perception will also influence later memory (Craik, Govoni, Naveh-Benjamin, & Anderson, 1996). As outlined, emotion can influence attention in two ways. Emotion facilitates attention and perception for emotional events, or those cued by emotion, and also captures attention resulting is less processing of some other, nonemotional aspects of the environment. In memory research, it has been proposed that this resulting "narrowing-of-attention" around the emotional aspects of an event results in enhanced memory for details within this narrow focus of attention and worse memory for other details (Easterbrook, 1959). This pattern of memory performance has been observed in a number of psychological studies (Heuer & Reisberg, 1992). For instance, studies of weapon focus have demonstrated how the presence of a threatening stimulus in a scene, such as a gun, can result in enhanced memory for details of the gun and stimuli in close proximity, and impaired memory for

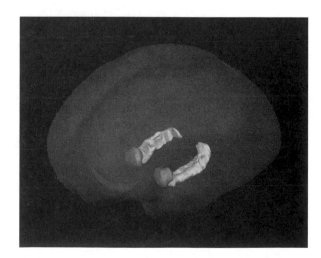

Figure 42.2   (**Figure C. 40** in color section) The amygdala (left, darker grey) and hippocampus (right, lighter grey).

Note: Adapted from "The Human Amygdala and Awareness: Interaction of the Amygdala and Hippocampal Complex," by E. A. Phelps, 2004, *Current Opinion in Neurobiology, 14,* p. 199. Reprinted with permission.

other scene details, such as the face of the person holding the gun (Kramer, Buckhout, & Eugenio, 1990). A study by Adolphs, Tranel, and Buchanan (2005) found that the amygdala may mediate this trade-off in memory for details. They observed that patients with amygdala damage fail to show the normal memory enhancement for details of the gist of the central aspects of an emotional scene, with no difference in memory for peripheral details.

Emotion Modulates Consolidation

By influencing encoding, emotion is altering the nature of the stimuli that are available for the second stage of memory: retention or storage. Although the storage stage is essentially passive in that it is simply the interval between encoding and retrieval and requires no action or thought, the existing evidence suggests that it is actually a neurobiologically active process. For a period of time after encoding, the neural representation that leads to a lasting memory trace can either be strengthened, in which case the event is available for later retrieval, or weakened, in which case the event may be forgotten. This time-dependent process that helps strengthen or solidify memories is consolidation. One of the primary means by which emotion can influence memory is by enhancing the consolidation or storage of emotional events (McGaugh, 2000).

Kleinsmith and Kaplan (1963) demonstrated the impact of emotion on memory storage in a classic study in which subjects were presented with word-digit pairs. The words varied in how arousing they were. At later testing, subjects were presented each word and asked to recall the digit. Some subjects were given the memory test immediately after encoding and others were given the memory test after a variety of delays ranging from 20 minutes to 1 week. When comparing recall for the digits paired with the high-versus low-arousal words, arousal impaired the immediate cued recall of the digits, but by 45 minutes after encoding, memory for digits paired with high-arousal words was significantly enhanced. This effect emerged because recall for digits paired with high-arousal words did not decline, and even improved slightly, whereas recall for the digits paired with the low-arousal words showed the standard delay dependent decay in memory (Ebbinghaus, 1885/2003). This enhanced retention with arousal is consistent with an active storage process that is modulated by emotion (see also Berlyne, 1969; Heuer & Reisberg, 1992).

In an elegant series of studies in nonhuman animals, McGaugh (2000) outlined the neural mechanism mediating this enhanced retention for arousing events. Physiological arousal is linked to the release of stress hormones from the adrenal gland, including epinephrine and cortisol, a glucocorticoid. Epinephrine indirectly activates β-adrenergic receptors in the amygdala, which in turn play an important role in mediating the impact of arousal on glucocorticoid receptors in the hippocampus. This critical role for the amygdala in modulating hippocampal consolidation has been demonstrated with a range of neuroscience techniques that impact the different components of this proposed neural mechanism. The evidence that the amygdala's modulatory role impacts the consolidation or storage of hippocampal-dependent memories comes from studies showing that influencing β-adrenergic receptors or lesioning the amygdala immediately *after* memory encoding alters arousal's impact on memory consolidation. McGaugh suggested that a possible role for a slow consolidation process is to allow the emotional impact of an event, which may unfold after the event occurs, to modulate subsequent memory. In this way, emotional events, which may provide important lessons for future survival, are more likely to be retained.

Evidence from studies with humans suggesting a role for the amygdala in the modulation of hippocampal consolidation has been observed with a number of cognitive neuroscience techniques. Brain imaging studies have reported that activation of the amygdala at encoding can predict later memory for emotional stimuli (Cahill et al., 1996; Canli, Zhao, Brewer, Gabrieli, & Cahill, 2000). The amygdala has direct projections to the anterior portion of the hippocampus (Stefanacci, Suzuki, & Amaral, 1996). The activation of the amygdala and anterior hippocampus is correlated during the encoding of emotional scenes that were later remembered (Dolcos, LaBar, & Cabeza, 2004). Although these studies do not indicate if the enhanced amygdala activation observed at encoding is related to altered encoding or consolidation processes, it has been demonstrated that this activation is more strongly correlated with delayed compared to immediate recall (Hamann, Ely, Grafton, & Kilts, 1999). It has also been reported that patients with amygdala damage fail to show the normal enhancement of memory with arousal (Cahill, Babinsky, Markowitsch, & McGaugh, 1995). Amygdala damage results in similar forgetting curves for arousing and neutral stimuli, in contrast to normal control subjects who show enhanced retention for arousing stimuli. This lack of a retention difference for arousing and neutral stimuli is consistent with a role for the amygdala in modulating storage or consolidation (LaBar & Phelps, 1998). Finally, in a direct test of the neurochemical mechanisms thought to mediate the amygdala's influence on hippocampal consolidation, Cahill, Prins, Weber, and McGaugh (1994) administered a drug that blocked β-adrenergic receptors. The administration of this drug also blocked the normal enhanced memory observed for arousing stimuli, consistent with animal models.

One of the difficulties in isolating an effect of altered storage or consolidation for arousal on memory performance is separating encoding from consolidation because memory retrieval reflects their combined effects. In a clever series of studies, Cahill, Gorski, and Le (2003) were able to isolate an effect of arousal on memory consolidation in humans by manipulating arousal immediately *after* stimulus encoding. In these studies, subjects were presented with scenes that had an emotional meaning (valence), but did not elicit a strong arousal response. Immediately after these scenes were encoded, half of the subjects were given an arousal manipulation and the other half a control manipulation. In one study, this arousal manipulation required subjects to place their arms in freezing water (cold pressor stress), while control subjects were required to place their arms in warm water. In a second study, subjects were given a drug that elicits physiological arousal (epinephrine), while control subjects were given a placebo (Cahill & Alkire, 2003). Both arousal manipulations resulted in enhanced memory for the low-arousal scenes immediately followed by arousal relative to the control manipulation. This effect of postencoding arousal on later memory only emerged for scenes that have an emotional meaning or valence. Memory for neutral scenes did not improve as a result of postencoding arousal. These results are consistent with the proposal that arousal modulates the consolidation or storage of events independent of emotion's impact on encoding, but suggests some limits on the types of stimuli that can elicit this effect.

Emotion Enhances the Subjective Sense of Remembering at Retrieval

Through its impact on attention, emotion facilitates encoding of salient aspects of the environment, sometimes at the decrement of nonemotional details. Those details that are encoded are then more likely to be retained via arousal's influence on memory consolidation. The results of these combined processes are observed at the final stage of memory, retrieval. However, studies of the retrieval of emotional events have also reported an effect of emotion on memory that is not readily apparent from its influence on encoding and consolidation. Independent of its effect on memory accuracy, emotion also enhances the subjective sense of remembering. Remembering is not only accompanied by the retrieval of past events, but also by the subjective judgment that the memory is or is not vivid, detailed, and held with confidence in its accuracy. These qualities make up the subjective sense of remembering.

Brown and Kulik (1977) coined the term "flashbulb memory" to describe the impact of emotion on recollection. By examining memories for highly emotional, public events, such as the assassination of John F. Kennedy, they determined that emotion results in highly vivid, detailed,

and confident memories, almost as if one is looking at a picture taken with a flashbulb. Brown and Kulik assumed these vivid recollections were also highly accurate because memory confidence is generally linked to memory accuracy (Lindsay, Read, & Sharma, 1998). However, when researchers examined memories for emotional public events over time, they found that these memories were often highly inaccurate in their details and were distinguished primarily by their sense of vividness and confidence in their accuracy (Neisser & Harsch, 1992; Talarico & Rubin, 2003). In other words, the subjective sense of remembering was enhanced for emotion, even when accuracy for details of the memory was not. Laboratory studies have reported a similar effect. When subjects are asked to indicate if they "remember" previously presented emotional or neutral scenes along with details of the encoding context, or simply "know" that the scene is familiar, they are more likely to indicate they "remember" emotional scenes, even when there is no difference in overall accuracy for emotional and neutral scenes (Ochsner, 2000; Sharot, Delgado, & Phelps, 2004).

The neural systems mediating the impact of emotion on the subjective sense of remembering have been explored using this remember/know paradigm. Studies examining both memory encoding (Dolcos et al., 2004) and retrieval (Sharot et al., 2004) have reported that different neural mechanisms may mediate the subjective judgment of remembering for emotional and neutral scenes. For neutral scenes judged as "remembered," stronger activation is observed in the posterior parahippocampal cortex, relative to those judged as "known." This region of the parahippocampal cortex is also known as the parahippocampal place area (PPA; Epstein & Kanwisher, 1998) and has been shown to be involved in the processing of scenes and the encoding of scene details (Kohler, Crane, & Milner, 2002). Because subjects in this task are asked to judge if their recollection of the scene is accompanied by encoding details, it is not surprising that activation of this region would be linked to this judgment. What is surprising is that emotional scenes judged as "remembered" versus "known" do not show differential activation in this region. Instead, activation of the amygdala differentiates this mnemonic judgment for emotional scenes. In other words, there is a double dissociation. Even though subjects are making the same subjective assessment of their memory, different medial temporal lobe structures seem to be mediating this judgment for emotional and neutral stimuli.

A similar pattern was observed when examining memories for September 11, 2001 (Sharot, Martorella, Delgado, & Phelps, 2007). Subjects who were in Manhattan on 9/11 were asked to retrieve personal autobiographical events from that day or the summer of 2001. They then rated these memories for arousal, vividness, confidence, sense of reliving, and "remembering." About half of the participants showed enhanced ratings for the 9/11 versus summer memories. What differentiated those subjects whose 9/11 memories yielded these "flashbulb" qualities is proximity to the World Trade Center (WTC) during the terrorist attack. Those closest to the WTC not only rated their memories as more vivid, but also were more likely to report experiencing threat and direct sensory experience of the attack (e.g., seeing, hearing, smelling). An examination of the neural systems underlying the retrieval of 9/11 versus summer memories revealed that proximity was correlated with greater amygdala activation and decreased posterior parahippocampal activation, mirroring the pattern observed in laboratory studies using the remember/know paradigm.

The enhanced subjective sense of memory for emotional events suggests a possible functional role for this mnemonic judgment. Our judgments about our memories can influence how we use them to guide our future actions. If we are confident in the accuracy of a memory for an event in the past, we may act decisively when encountering a similar situation in the future. However, if a memory is held with less confidence, we might seek to gather more information before acting. It has been proposed that emotion's impact on the subjective sense of remembering, in the absence of absolute veridicality, may serve to promote faster and less ambiguous action in the face of familiar, emotional situations (Phelps & Sharot, 2008). Even if a memory is inaccurate in its details, the strong memory for the gist of an emotional event may be sufficient to enhance the vividness and confidence of memory and allow for fast action in a similar circumstance in the future.

SUMMARY

By incorporating neuroscience methods in our efforts to understand human behavior a different perspective on behavioral science is beginning to emerge. Psychologists and other behavioral scientists have divided the study of human behavior into distinct domains, which have yielded unique subsets of academic departments, conferences, and journals. These boundaries, however, are not recognized by the brain. As the range of behavioral disciplines incorporating neuroscience methods expands, so does the necessity to adopt a broader and more integrative approach to the study of human behavior.

In this chapter, we highlighted how neuroscience research has informed our understanding of the relation between emotion and cognition. In light of our knowledge of the brain and its connectivity, it no longer appears feasible to clearly differentiate emotion processes from cognitive functions.

Emotion and cognition interact at all stages of information processing, from early perception to higher reasoning. By highlighting what is important, emotion provides a framework by which cognition can be tuned to respond adaptively to environmental demands.

REFERENCES

Adolphs, R., Tranel, D., & Buchanan, T. W. (2005). Amygdala damage impairs emotional memory for gist but not details of complex stimuli. *Nature Neuroscience, 8,* 512–518.

Aggleton, J. P. (1992). *The amygdala: Neurobiological aspects of emotion, memory, and mental dysfunction.* New York: Wiley-Liss.

Alpers, G. W., & Gerdes, A. B. M. (2007). Here is looking at you: Emotional faces predominate in binocular rivalry. *Emotion, 7,* 495–506.

Alpers, G. W., Ruhleder, M., Walz, N., Mühlberger, A., & Pauli, P. (2005). Binocular rivalry between emotional and neutral stimuli: A validation using fear conditioning and EEG. *International Journal of Psychophysiology, 57,* 25–32.

Amaral, D. G., Behniea, H., & Kelly, J. L. (2003). Topographic organization of projections from the amygdala to the visual cortex in the macaque monkey. *Neuroscience, 118,* 1099–1120.

Amaral, D. G., & Price, J. L. (1984). Amygdalo-cortical projections in the monkey. *Journal of Comparative Neurology, 230,* 465–496.

Anderson, A. K. (2005). Affective influences on the attentional dynamics supporting awareness. *Journal of Experimental Psychology: General, 134,* 258–281.

Anderson, A. K., & Phelps, E. A. (2000). Perceiving emotion: There's more than meets the eye. *Current Biology, 10,* R551–R554.

Anderson, A. K., & Phelps, E. A. (2001, May 17). Lesions of the human amygdala impair enhanced perception of emotionally salient events. *Nature, 411,* 305–309.

Berlyne, D. E. (1969). Arousal, reward and learning. *Annals of the New York Academy of Sciences, 159,* 1059–1070.

Brown, R., & Kulik, J. (1977). Flashbulb memories. *Cognition, 5,* 73–99.

Cahill, L., & Alkire, M. T. (2003). Epinephrine enhancement of human memory consolidation: Interaction with arousal at encoding. *Neurobiololgy of Learning and Memory, 79,* 194–198.

Cahill, L., Babinsky, R., Markowitsch, H. J., & McGaugh, J. L. (1995, September 28). The amygdala and emotional memory. *Nature, 377,* 295–296.

Cahill, L., Gorski, L., & Le, K. (2003). Enhanced human memory consolidation with post-learning stress: Interaction with the degree of arousal at encoding. *Learning and Memory, 10,* 270–274.

Cahill, L., Haier, R. J., Fallon, J., Alkire, M. T., Tang, C., Keator, D., et al. (1996). Amygdala activity at encoding correlated with long-term, free recall of emotional information. *Proceedings of the National Academy of Sciences, USA, 93,* 8016–8021.

Cahill, L., Prins, B., Weber, M., & McGaugh, J. L. (1994, October 20). Beta-adrenergic activation and memory for emotional events. *Nature, 371,* 702–704.

Canli, T., Zhao, Z., Brewer, J., Gabrieli, J. D., & Cahill, L. (2000). Event-related activation in the human amygdala associates with later memory for individual emotional experience. *Journal of Neuroscience, 20,* RC99.

Carrasco, M. (2006). Covert attention increases contrast sensitivity: Psychophysical, neurophysiological and neuroimaging studies. *Progress in Brain Research, 154,* 33–70.

Craik, F. I. M., Govoni, R., Naveh-Benjamin, M., & Anderson, N. D. (1996). The effects of divided attention on encoding and retrieval processes in human memory. *Journal of Experimental Psychology. General, 125,* 159–180.

Dagleish, T. (2004). The emotional brain. *Nature Reviews: Neuroscience, 5,* 582–589.

de Gelder, B., Vroomen, J., Pourtois, G., & Weiskrantz, L. (1999). Non-conscious recognition of affect in the absence of striate cortex. *NeuroReport, 10,* 3759–3763.

Dolcos, F., LaBar, K. S., & Cabeza, R. (2004). Interaction between the amygdala and the medial temporal lobe memory system predicts better memory for emotional events. *Neuron, 42,* 855–863.

Easterbrook, J. A. (1959). The effect of emotion on cue utilization and the organization of behavior. *Psychological Review, 66,* 183–201.

Ebbinghaus, H. (1885/2003). *Memory: A contribution to experimental psychology.* New York: Cosmo Publications.

Eichenbaum, H. (2002). The hippocampal system and declarative memory in animals. *Journal of Cognitive Neuroscience, 4,* 217–231.

Epstein, R., & Kanwisher, N. (1998, April 9). A cortical representation of the local visual environment. *Nature, 392,* 598–601.

Fox, E., Russo, R., Bowles, R., & Dutton, K. (2001). Do threatening stimuli draw or hold visual attention in subclinical anxiety? *Journal of Experimental Psychology: General, 130,* 681–700.

Freese, J. L., & Amaral, D. G. (2005). The organization of projections from the amygdala to visual cortical areas TE and V1 in the macaque monkey. *Journal of Comparative Neurology, 486,* 295–317.

Freese, J. L., & Amaral, D. G. (2006). Synaptic organization of projections from the amygdala to visual cortical areas, T E, & V1 in the macaque monkey. *Journal of Comparative Neurology, 496,* 655–667.

Frijda, N. H. (1986). *The emotions.* Cambridge: Cambridge University Press.

Hamann, S. B., Ely, T. D., Grafton, S. T., & Kilts, C. D. (1999). Amygdala activity related to enhanced memory for pleasant and aversive stimuli. *Nature Neuroscience, 2,* 289–293.

Heuer, F., & Reisberg, D. (1992). *Emotion, arousal, and memory for detail.* In S. Christianson (Ed.), *The handbook of emotion and memory* (pp. 151–164). Hillsdale, NJ: Erlbaum.

Hupé, J. M., James, A. C., Girard, P., Lomber, S. G., Payne, B. R., & Bullier, J. (2001). Feedback connections act on the early part of the responses in monkey visual cortex. *Journal of Neurophysiology, 85,* 134–145.

Hupé, J. M., James, A. C., Payne, B. R., Lomber, S. G., Girard, P., & Bullier, J. (1998, August 20). Cortical feedback improves discrimination between figure and background by V1, V2 and V3 neurons. *Nature, 394,* 784–787.

James, W. (1890). *The principles of psychology.* New York: Dover.

Kanwisher, N., McDermott, J., & Chun, M. M. (1997). The fusiform face area: A module in human extrastriate cortex specialized for face perception. *Journal of Neuroscience, 17,* 4302–4311.

Kleinsmith, L. J., & Kaplan, S. (1963). Paired-associate learning as a function of arousal and interpolated interval. *Journal of Experimental Psychology, 65,* 190–193.

Kohler, S., Crane, J., & Milner, B. (2002). Differential contributions of the parahippocampal place area and the anterior hippocampus to human memory for scenes. *Hippocampus, 12,* 718–723.

Kramer, T. H., Buckhout, R., & Eugenio, P. (1990). Weapon focus, arousal, and eyewitness memory: Attention must be paid. *Law and Human Behavior, 14,* 167–184.

LaBar, K. S., & Phelps, E. A. (1998). Arousal-mediated memory consolidation: Role of the medial temproal lobe in humans. *Psychological Science, 9,* 490–493.

Lazarus, R. S. (1984). On the primacy of cognition. *American Psychologist, 39,* 124–129.

LeDoux, J. E. (1996). *The emotional brain.* New York: Simon & Schuster.

Liddell, B. J., Brown, K. J., Kemp, A. H., Barton, M. J., Das, P., Peduto, A., et al. (2005). A direct brainstem-amygdala-cortical "alarm" system for subliminal signals of fear. *NeuroImage, 24,* 235–243.

Lindsay, D. S., Read, J. D., & Sharma, K. (1998). Accuracy and confidence in person identification: The relationship is strong when witnessing conditions vary widely. *Psychological Science, 9,* 215–218.

Mathews, A. M., & MacLeod, C. (1985). Selective processing of threat cues in anxiety states. *Behavioral Research Therapy, 23,* 563–569.

McGaugh, J. L. (2000, January 14). Memory: A century of consolidation. *Science, 287,* 248–251.

Miller, G. A. (2003). The cognitive revolution: A historical perspective. *Trends in Cognitive Neuroscience, 7,* 141–144.

Morris, J. S., Buchel, C., & Dolan, R. J. (2001). Parallel neural responses in amygdala subregions and sensory cortex during implicit fear conditioning. *Neuroimage, 13,* 1044–1052.

Morris, J. S., DeGelder, B., Weiskrantz, L., & Dolan, R. J. (2001). Differential extrageniculostriate and amygdala responses to presentation of emotional faces in a cortically blind field. *Brain, 124,* 1241–1252.

Morris, J. S., Friston, K. J., Büchel, C., Frith, C. D., Young, A. W., Calder, A. J., et al. (1998). A neuromodulatory role for the human amygdala in processing emotional facial expressions. *Brain, 121,* 47–57.

Morris, J. S., Friston, K. J., & Dolan, R. J. (1997). Neural responses to salient visual stimuli. *Proceedings of the Royal Society, B, Biological Sciences, 264,* 769–775.

Morris, J. S., Ohman, A., & Dolan, R. J. (1998, June 4). Conscious and unconscious emotional learning in the human amygdala. *Nature, 393,* 467–470.

Morris, J. S., Ohman, A., & Dolan, R. J. (1999). A subcortical pathway to the right amygdala mediating "unseen" fear. *Proceedings of the National Academy of Sciences, USA, 96,* 1680–1685.

Most, S. B., Chun, M. M., Widders, D. M., & Zald, D. H. (2005). Attentional rubbernecking: Cognitive control and personality in emotion-induced blindness. *Psychonomic Bulletin and Review, 12,* 654–661.

Nakamura, K., Mikami, A., & Kubota, K. (1992). Activity of single neurons in the monkey amygdala during performance of a visual discrimination task. *Journal of Neurophysiology, 67,* 1447–1463.

Neisser, U., & Harsch, N. (1992). Phantom flashbulbs: False recollections of hearing news about the Challenger. In E. Winograd & U. Neisser (Eds.), *Affect and accuracy in recall: Studies of "flashbulb" memories* (pp. 9–31). Cambridge: Cambridge University Press.

Ochsner, K. N. (2000). Are affective events richly recollected or simply familiar? The experience and process of recognizing feelings past. *Journal of Experimental Psychology: General, 129,* 242–261.

Ohman, A., Carlsson, K., Lundqvist, D., & Ingvar, M. (2007). On the unconscious subcortical origin of human fear. *Physiology and Behavior, 92,* 180–185.

Ohman, A., Flykt, A., & Esteves, F. (2001). Emotion drives attention: Detecting the snake in the grass. *Journal of Experimental Psychology: General, 130,* 466–478.

Ohman, A., Lundqvist, D., & Esteves, F. (2001). The face in the crowd revisited: A threat advantage with schematic stimuli. *Journal of Personality and Social Psychology, 80,* 381–396.

Pessoa, L. (2008). On the relationship between emotion and cognition. *Nature Reviews: Neuroscience, 9,* 148–158.

Pestilli, F., & Carrasco, M. (2005). Attention enhances contrast sensitivity at cued and impairs it at uncued locations. *Vision Research, 45,* 1867–1875.

Phelps, E. A. (2004). The human amygdala and awareness: Interaction of the amygdala and hippocampal complex. *Current Opinion in Neurobiology, 14,* 198–202.

Phelps, E. A., & LeDoux, J. E. (2005). Contributions of the amygdala to emotion processing: From animal models to human behavior. *Neuron, 48,* 175–187.

Phelps, E. A., Ling, S., & Carrasco, M. (2006). Emotion facilitates perception and potentiates the perceptual benefits of attention. *Psychological Science, 17,* 292–299.

Phelps, E. A., & Sharot, T. S. (2008). How (and why) emotion enhances the subjective sense of recollection. *Current Directions in Psychological Science, 17,* 147–152.

Posner, M. I. (1980). Orienting of attention. *Quarterly Journal of Experimental Psychology, 32,* 3–25.

Pourtois, G., & Vuilleumier, P. (2006). Dynamics of emotional effects on spatial attention in the human visual cortex. *Progress in Brain Research, 156,* 67–91.

Raymond, J. E., Shapiro, K. L., & Arnell, K. M. (1992). Temporary suppression of visual processing in an RSVP task: An attentional blink? *Journal of Experimental Psychology: Human Perception and Performance, 18,* 849–860.

Scherer, K. R. (2005). What are emotions? And how can they be measured? *Social Science Information, 44,* 695–729.

Sharot, T., Delgado, M. R., & Phelps, E. A. (2004). How emotion enhances the feeling of remembering. *Nature Neuroscience, 7,* 1376–1380.

Sharot, T., Martorella, E. A., Delgado, M. R., & Phelps, E. A. (2007). Remembering 9/11: How personal experience modulates the neural circuitry of recollection. *Proceedings of the National Academy of Sciences, USA, 104,* 389–394.

Smith, S. D., Most, S. B., Newsome, L. A., & Zald, D. H. (2006). An emotion-induced attentional blink elicited by aversively conditioned stimuli. *Emotion, 6,* 523–527.

Squire, L. R., & Zola-Morgan S. (1991, September 20). The medial temporal lobe memory system. *Science, 253,* 1380–1386.

Stefanacci, L., Suzuki, W. A., & Amaral, D. G. (1996). Organization of connections between the amygdaloid complex and the perirhinal and parahippocampal cortices in macaque monkeys. *Journal of Comparative Neurology, 375,* 552–582.

Strayer, D. L., Drews, F. A., & Johnston, W. A. (2003). Cell phone-induced failures of visual attention during simulated driving. *Journal of Experimental Psychology: Applied, 9,* 23–32.

Talarico, J. M., & Rubin, D. C. (2003). Confidence, not consistency, characterizes flashbulb memories. *Psychological Science, 14,* 455–461.

Treisman, A., & Gelade, G. (1980). A feature integration theory of attention. *Cognitive Psychology, 12,* 97–136.

Tsuchiya, N., & Koch, C. (2005). Continuous flash suppression reduces negative afterimages. *Nature Neuroscience, 8,* 1096–1101.

Vuilleumier, P., Armony, J. L., Driver, J., & Dolan, R. J. (2001). Effects of attention and emotion on face processing in the human brain: An event-related fMRI study. *Neuron, 30,* 829–841.

Vuilleumier, P., Armony, J. L., Driver, J., & Dolan, R. J. (2003). Distinct spatial frequency sensitivities for processing faces and emotional expressions. *Nature Neuroscience, 6,* 624–631.

Vuilleumier, P., Richardson, M. P., Armony, J. L., Driver, J., & Dolan, R. J. (2004). Distant influences of amygdala lesion on visual cortical activation during emotional face processing. *Nature Neuroscience, 7,* 1271–1278.

Weiskrantz, L. (1990). *Blindsight: A case study and its implications.* (New Ed.). Oxford: Oxford University Press.

Yang, E., Zald, D. H., & Blake, R. (2007). Fearful expressions gain preferential access to awareness during continuous flash suppression. *Emotion, 7,* 882–886.

Young, M. P., Scannell, J. W., Burns, G. A., & Blakemore, C. (1994). Analysis of connectivity: Neural systems in the cerebral cortex. *Reviews in the Neurosciences, 5,* 227–250.

Yukie, M. (2002). Connections between the amygdala and auditory cortical areas in the macaque monkey. *Neuroscience Research, 42,* 219–229.

Zajonc, R. B. (1984). On the primacy of affect. *American Psychologist, 39,* 117–123.

PART VI

Social Processes

Chapter 43

Face Perception

NANCY KANWISHER AND GALIT YOVEL

For highly social organisms like us, faces reign supreme among visual stimuli. Faces inform us not only about a person's identity, but also about his or her mood, sex, age, and direction of gaze. The ability to extract this information within a fraction of a second of viewing a face is crucial for normal social interactions and has likely played a critical role in the survival of our primate ancestors. Considerable evidence from behavioral, neuropsychological, and neurophysiological investigations supports the hypothesis that the perception of faces is conducted by specialized cognitive and neural machinery distinct from that engaged in the perception of objects (the face specificity hypothesis). This fact has important implications for social cognition. It shows that at least one aspect of social cognition is domain specific (Fodor, 1983): Fundamentally different mental processes apparently go on, and different neural systems become engaged, when we think about people compared to objects (see also Downing, Jiang, Shuman, & Kanwisher, 2001; Saxe & Powell, 2006). The domain specificity of face perception invites a much broader investigation of domain specificity of other aspects of social cognition (Saxe & Powell, 2006).

In this chapter, we review the literature on the three main cortical regions engaged in face perception in humans. We begin with a broad survey of the evidence from multiple methods for the face specificity hypothesis.

SPECIALIZED MECHANISMS FOR FACE PERCEPTION: EVIDENCE FROM NEUROPSYCHOLOGY, BEHAVIOR, ELECTROPHYSIOLOGY, AND NEUROIMAGING

Evidence from neuropsychology, behavior, electrophysiology, and neuroimaging supports the hypothesis that special mechanisms are engaged for the perception of faces.

Evidence from Neuropsychology: Prosopagnosia and Agnosia

The first evidence that face perception engages specialized machinery distinct from that engaged during object perception came from the syndrome of acquired prosopagnosia, in which neurological patients lose the ability to recognize faces after brain damage. Prosopagnosia is not a general loss of the concept of the person because prosopagnosic subjects can easily identify individuals from their voice or from a verbal description of the person. Impairments in face recognition are often accompanied by deficits in other related tasks such as object recognition, as expected given the usually large size of lesions relative to functional subdivisions of the cortex. However, a few prosopagnosic patients show very selective impairments in which face recognition abilities are devastated despite the lack of discernible deficits in the recognition of nonface objects (Wada & Yamamoto, 2001). Some prosopagnosic subjects have a preserved ability to discriminate between exemplars within a category (Duchaine, Yovel, Butterworth, & Nakayama, 2006; Henke, Schweinberger, Grigo, Klos, & Sommer, 1998; McNeil & Warrington, 1993), including objects of expertise (Sergent & Signoret, 1992) arguing against the idea that mechanisms of face perception are engaged more broadly on any visual stimuli requiring fine-grained discrimination. Some cases of "developmental prosopagnosia" (Duchaine et al., 2006), a lifelong impairment in face recognition (Behrmann & Avidan, 2005) with no apparent neurological lesion, show remarkably specific deficits in face perception only (Duchaine et al., 2006).

Is face recognition merely the most difficult visual recognition task we perform, and hence the most susceptible to

We thank Bettiann McKay for help with manuscript preparation. This research was supported by NIH grant EY13455 and a grant from the Ellison Foundation to Nancy Kanwisher.

brain damage? Apparently not: The striking case of patient CK (Moscovitch, Winocur, & Behrmann, 1997; see also McMullen, Fisk, Phillips, & Maloney, 2000), who had shown deficits in object recognition but normal face recognition, indicates a double dissociation between the recognition of faces and objects. Further, patient CK, who had been a collector of toy soldiers, lost his ability to discriminate these stimuli, showing a further dissociation between face recognition (preserved) and visual expertise (impaired). Thus, taken together, these selective cases of prosopagnosia and agnosia support the face specificity hypothesis and are inconsistent with its domain-general alternatives.

Behavioral Signatures of Face-Specific Processing

Classic behavioral work in normal subjects has also shown dissociations between the recognition of faces and objects by demonstrating a number of differences in the ways that these stimuli are processed. Best known among these signatures of face-specific processing is the face inversion effect, in which the decrement in performance that occurs when stimuli are inverted (i.e., turned upside-down) is greater for faces than for nonface stimuli (Yin, 1969). Other behavioral markers include the "part-whole" effect (Tanaka & Farah, 1993), in which subjects are better able to distinguish which of two face parts (e.g., two noses) appeared in a previously shown face when they are presented in the context of the whole face than when they are shown in isolation, and the "composite effect" (Young, Hellawell, & Hay, 1987), in which subjects are slower to identify one half of a chimeric face if it is aligned with an inconsistent other half-face than if the two half-faces are misaligned. Consistent with the holistic hypothesis, the probability of correctly identifying a whole face is greater than the sum of the probabilities of matching each of its component face halves (Yovel, Paller, & Levy, 2005). Taken together, these effects suggest that upright faces are processed in a distinctive "holistic" manner (McKone, Martini, & Nakayama, 2001; Tanaka & Farah, 2003), that is, that faces are processed as wholes rather than as sets of parts processed independently. All the holistic effects mentioned are either absent or reduced for inverted faces and nonface objects (Robbins & McKone, 2007; Tanaka & Farah, 1993), indicating that this holistic style of processing is specific to upright faces.

According to one alternative to the face specificity hypothesis, it is our extensive experience with faces that leads us to process them in this distinctive holistic and orientation-sensitive fashion. The original impetus for this hypothesis came from Diamond and Carey's (1986) classic report that dog experts show inversion effects for dog stimuli (see Figure 43.1). Since then, claims that nonface objects of expertise exhibit facelike processing have been widespread. However, an extensive effort to replicate the original Diamond and Carey result met with total failure (Robbins & McKone, 2007). Further, McKone, Kanwisher, and Duchaine (2007) reviewed all of the relevant published behavioral experiments (including those that claim to support the expertise hypothesis) and found no evidence for facelike processing of objects of expertise (see Figure 43.1).

Electrophysiology in Humans

Face-selective electrophysiological responses occurring 170 ms after stimulus onset have also been measured in humans using scalp electrodes (Bentin, Allison, Puce, Perez, & McCarthy, 1996; Downing, Chan, Peelen, Dodds, & Kanwisher, 2006; Jeffreys, 1996). These results have been replicated with both ERPs and MEG in numerous studies that show face-selective responses both as early as 100 ms after stimulus onset (Itier & Taylor, 2004; Liu, Harris, & Kanwisher, 2002), and around 170 ms after stimulus onset (Halgren, Raij, Marinkovic, Jousmaki, & Hari, 2000; Liu et al., 2002). Although it has been claimed that the face-selective N170 response is sensitive to visual expertise with nonface stimuli (Gauthier, Curran, Curby, & Collins, 2003; Rossion, Curran, & Gauthier, 2002; Tanaka & Curran, 2001), these studies are hard to interpret because none of them include all three critical conditions: faces, objects of expertise, and control objects (McKone & Kanwisher, 2005). The one published study that included all three conditions investigated the face-selective magnetic (M170) response (Halgren et al., 2000; Liu et al., 2002) and found no elevated response to cars in car experts, and no trial-by-trial correlation between the amplitude of the M170 response and successful identification of cars by car experts (Xu, 2005) . Thus, the N170 and M170 appear to be truly face-selective and at least the M170 response is not consistent with any alternative domain-general hypotheses.

What is the nature of the face representation that is manifested by the N170? Initial studies suggested that the N170 is not sensitive to identity information, but instead primarily reflects structural encoding of facial information (Bentin & Deouell, 2000). However, other studies have shown that the N170 amplitude is smaller for subsequent presentation of similar faces (within the perceptual category boundary) than different identity faces (Jacques & Rossion, 2006), which suggest that identity is processed by 170 ms after stimulus onset. (For further discussion of the logic of adaptation studies, see the discussion that follows.) Importantly, this adaptation of the N170 to identity information (i.e., the lower response for repeated compared to unrepeated face stimuli) is shown for upright faces but not inverted faces (Jacques, d'Arripe, & Rossion, 2007). Evidence for holistic processing at 170 ms after stimulus

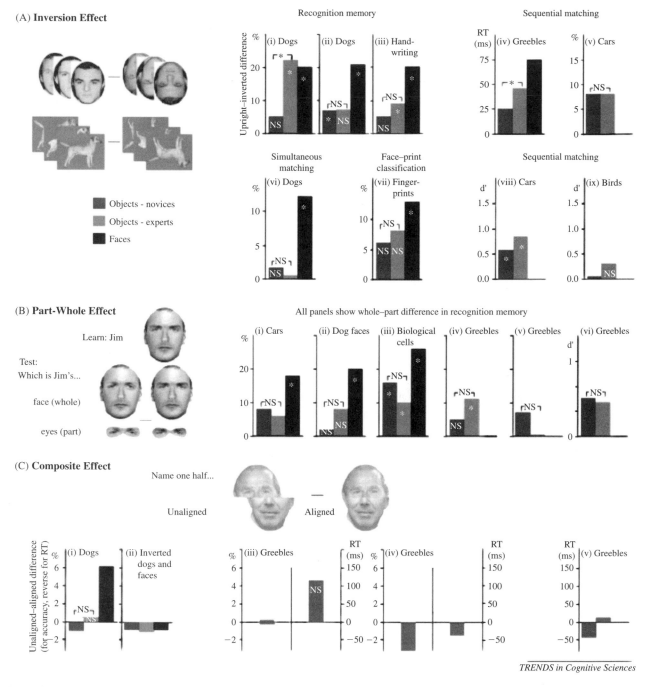

Figure 43.1 The available data reveal no evidence for holistic processing of objects of expertise.

Note: **A:** Inversion effects for homogeneous objects increase little with expertise and do not become facelike, even in a recent direct replication (aii) of the classic Diamond & Carey experiment using dogs (ai). (Instead, in most studies, experts improve relative to novices for both upright and inverted stimuli, which suggests expertise in part-based processing.) **B:** The part-whole effect does not increase with expertise and does not become facelike; unlike inversion, this task is a direct measure of measures holistic processing directly. **C:** The composite effect is not found for objects of expertise, despite strong effects for upright faces. The two double-panel plots in (iii) and (iv) show cases where both accuracy (% correct) and reaction time (RT) were reported. For further details and references, see McKone et al. (2007). NS = $p > .05$. From "Can Generic Expertise Explain Special Processing for Faces?" by E. McKone, N. Kanwisher, and B. C. Duchaine, 2007, *Trends in Cognitive Sciences, 11*, p. 9. Reprinted with permission.

* $p < .05$.

onset has been recently demonstrated in another adaptation study that revealed a composite effect on the N170 (Jacques et al., 2007; for more information, see Schiltz & Rossion, 2006, for similar findings with functional magnetic resonance imaging or fMRI). Taken together, these

findings suggest that by 170 ms a face-specific holistic representation, which includes all aspects of facial information, is already generated.

One important unanswered question concerns the neural source of the face-selective electrophysiological responses, which could be either the fusiform face area (FFA; Halgren et al., 2000) and/or the superior temporal sulcus (STS) (Bentin et al., 1996). Although this question is difficult to answer given the relatively low spatial resolution of event-related potentials (ERP) and magnetoencephalography (MEG), subdural ERP measurements in epilepsy patients have shown strongly face-selective responses in discrete patches of the temporal lobe (Allison et al., 1994; Allison, Puce, Spencer, & McCarthy, 1999). Further, a powerful demonstration of the causal role of these regions in face perception comes from two studies demonstrating that electrical stimulation of these ventral temporal sites can produce a transient inability to identify faces (Mundel et al., 2003; Puce, Allison, & McCarthy, 1999).

Neurophysiology and Functional Magnetic Resonance Imaging in Monkeys

Face specificity has been demonstrated in monkeys at both the single-cell level and at the level of cortical regions. Numerous studies dating back decades have reported face-selective responses from single neurons (face cells) in the temporal lobes of macaques (Desimone, Albright, Gross, & Bruce, 1984). Face-selective regions have been reported in macaques using fMRI (Pinsk, DeSimone, Moore, Gross, & Kastner, 2005; Tsao, Freiwald, Knutsen, Mandeville, & Tootell, 2003) and in vervets using a novel dual-activity mapping technique based on induction of the immediate early gene zif268 (Zangenehpour & Chaudhuri, 2005).

Strong claims of face selectivity entail the prediction that no nonface stimulus will ever produce a response as strong as a face; because the set of nonface stimuli is infinite, there is always some possibility that a future study will show that a putative face-selective cell or region actually responds more to some previously untested stimulus (say, armadillos) than to faces. However, studies in neurophysiology have addressed this problem about as well as can practically be hoped for. Foldiak, Xiao, Keysers, Edwards, and Perrett (2004) used rapid serial visual presentation (RSVP) to test each cell on over 1,000 natural images, and found some cells that were truly face-selective: For some cells, the 70 stimuli producing the strongest responses all contained faces, and the next best stimuli produced less than one-fifth the maximal response.

Although these data demonstrate individual cells that are strikingly face-selective, they don't address the face selectivity of whole regions of the cortex. However, a more recent study demonstrates a spectacular degree of selectivity of whole regions of the cortex. Tsao, Freiwald, Tootell, and Livingstone (2006) directed eletrodes into the face-selective patches they had previously identified

with fMRI (Tsao et al., 2003), and found that 97% of the visually responsive cells in these regions responded selectively (indeed, for most cells, exclusively) to faces. These stunning data suggest that the weak responses of the FFA to nonface stimuli may result from "partial voluming," that is, from the inevitable blurring of face-selective and non-face-selective regions that arise when voxel sizes are large relative to the size of the underlying functional unit. Thus, these data provide some of the strongest evidence to date on the extreme selectivity of some cortical regions for face processing (Kanwisher, 2006).

Brain Imaging in Humans

In the early 1990s, positron emission tomography (PET) studies showed activation of the ventral visual pathway, especially the fusiform gyrus, in a variety of face perception tasks (Haxby et al., 1991; Sergent, Ohta, & MacDonald, 1992). fMRI studies of the specificity of these cortical regions for faces per se began in the mid-1990s, with demonstrations of fusiform regions that responded more strongly to faces than to letterstrings and textures (Puce, Allison, Asgari, Gore, & McCarthy, 1996), flowers (McCarthy, Puce, Gore, & Allison, 1997), and other stimuli, including mixed everyday objects, houses, and hands (Kanwisher, McDermott, & Chun, 1997). Although face-specific fMRI activations could also be seen in many subjects in the region of the face-selective STS (fSTS) and in the occipital lobe in a region named the occipital face area (OFA), the most consistent and robust face-selective activation was located on the lateral side of the mid-fusiform gyrus in a region we named the fusiform face area (FFA; Kanwisher et al., 1997; see Figure 43.2).

One of the most consistent findings about face-selective activations in the occipital-temporal cortex is its hemispheric asymmetry. All three face-selective regions are larger over the right than the left hemisphere. Furthermore, this asymmetry is stable across sessions (even when they take place more than 1 year apart) in particular for the FFA (Yovel, Tambini, & Bradman, 2008). This asymmetric response to faces is consistent with the finding that right hemisphere damage is necessary (though not always sufficient) for prosopagnosia (Barton, Press, Keenan, & O'Connor, 2002; Sergent & Signoret, 1992). We recently assessed whether individual differences in the asymmetric brain response to faces is associated with the behavioral left visual field superiority for face recognition. Numerous behavioral laterality studies have shown that normal individuals recognize better faces that are presented in the left visual field that projects directly to the right hemisphere than the right visual field that projects directly to the left

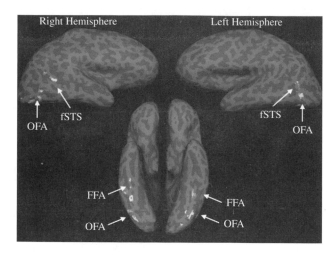

Figure 43.2 Face-selective activation (faces > objects, $p < .0001$) on an inflated brain of one subject, shown from lateral and ventral views of the right and left hemispheres.

Note: Three face-selective regions are typically found: the FFA in the fusiform gyrus along the ventral part of the brain, the OFA in the lateral occipital area, and the fSTS in the posterior region of the superior temporal sulcus.

hemisphere (Rhodes, 1985; Sergent & Bindra, 1981). The known right-hemisphere dominance for face processing has been suggested to account for this behavioral laterality effect. However, this association has never been demonstrated directly. We recently found that the asymmetry of the volume of the FFA was correlated across subjects with the magnitude of the behavioral asymmetry that was collected on a different session outside the scanner. That is, subjects who showed better performance for right- than left-side faces also had a larger FFA over the right than left hemisphere. This correlation was not found with the laterality of the occipital face area or with nearby object-selective regions (lateral occipital complex or LOC). These findings suggest that the asymmetric response of the brain to faces is a stable characteristic of each individual, which is manifested both at the neural and the behavioral level (Yovel et al., 2008).

The FFA region can be reliably identified in almost every normal subject in a short "localizer" fMRI scan contrasting the response to faces versus objects. In the functional region of interest (fROI) approach, the FFA is first functionally localized in each individual, then its response magnitude is measured in a new set of experimental conditions; this method enables the FFA to be studied directly despite its anatomical variability across subjects, in a statistically powerful yet unbiased fashion (Saxe, Brett, & Kanwisher, 2006). In contrast, group studies often cannot identify the FFA at all because of the variability in its precise location across subjects. Because the FFA is the most robust of the three face-selective regions (Kanwisher et al., 1997; Yovel &

Kanwisher, 2004), it has been investigated most fully, more is known about it, and we focus on it in this section. We return to other face-selective regions later in the chapter.

Three lines of evidence indicate that the FFA responds specifically to faces and not to lower-level stimulus features usually present in faces (such as a pair of horizontally arranged dark regions). First, the FFA responds strongly and similarly to a wide variety of face stimuli that would appear to have few low-level features in common, including front and profile photographs of faces (Tong, Nakayama, Moscovitch, Weinrib, & Kanwisher, 2000), line drawings of faces (Spiridon & Kanwisher, 2002), cat faces (Tong et al., 2000), and two-tone stylized Mooney faces. Second, the FFA response to upright Mooney faces is almost twice as strong as the response to inverted Mooney stimuli in which the face is difficult to detect (Kanwisher, Tong, & Nakayama, 1998; Rhodes, Byatt, Michie, & Puce, 2004), even though most low-level features (such as spatial frequency composition) are identical in the two stimulus types. Finally, for bistable stimuli such as the illusory face-vase (Hasson, Hendler, Ben Bashat, & Malach, 2001), or for binocularly rivalrous stimuli in which a face is presented to one eye and a nonface is presented to the other eye (Pasley, Mayes, & Schultz, 2004; Tong, Nakayama, Vaughan, & Kanwisher, 1998; Williams, Moss, & Bradshaw, 2004), the FFA responds more strongly when subjects perceive a face than when they do not see a face even though the retinal (Andrews, Schluppeck, Homfray, Matthews, & Blakemore, 2002) stimulation is unchanged. For all these reasons, it is difficult to account for the selectivity of the FFA in terms of lower-level features that covary with faceness. Instead, these findings support the face specificity hypothesis.

However, before the specificity of the FFA can be accepted, several other alternatives must be considered. First, is the FFA engaged whenever subjects must discriminate between similar exemplars within a category, whether or not the stimulus is a face (Gauthier, Behrmann, & Tarr, 1999)? No: When subjects perform within-category discrimination for faces and houses that have been matched for discriminability, the FFA still responds about three times as strongly during face discrimination as house discrimination (Yovel & Kanwisher, 2004). This experiment also rules out a second alternative to the face specificity hypothesis, according to which the FFA is involved in domain-general configural processing of any stimulus types: The FFA response was no higher when subjects discriminated faces or houses on the basis of the spacing between parts than when they discriminated faces or houses based on the appearance of the parts. Thus, the FFA is not involved in a domain-general way in either fine-grained discrimination, or configural processing, or any stimulus type; instead, it is specific for faces per se.

In the most widely discussed third alternative hypothesis, it is claimed that the FFA is not face specific because it responds more strongly to objects of expertise than to control objects. However, this effect is in fact significant in only three (Gauthier, Skudlarski, Gore, & Anderson, 2000; Gauthier et al., 1999; Xu, 2005) of the nine studies that have tested the hypothesis (see also Grill-Spector, Knouf, & Kanwisher, 2004; Jiang et al., 2007; Moore, Cohen, & Ranganath, 2006; Op de Beeck, Baker, DiCarlo, & Kanwisher, 2006; Rhodes et al., 2004; Yue, Tjan, & Biederman, 2006). A plausible alternative account of this weak and unreliable effect is that it reflects a general increase in attentional engagement for objects of expertise compared to control objects, not a special role of face regions in expertise. This alternative attentional account predicts that increased responses to objects of expertise should be found not only in the FFA but in nearby object-processing regions such as the LOC. Indeed, all four studies that have tested for effects of expertise in both the FFA and the LOC find *larger effects* of expertise in the LOC than in the FFA (Jiang et al., 2007; Moore et al., 2006; Op de Beeck et al., 2006; Yue et al., 2006). These findings are inconsistent with the expertise hypothesis, instead supporting the face specificity hypothesis (see also Kanwisher & Yovel, 2006; McKone et al., 2007).

Summary

Taken together, these lines of research make a compelling case for the existence of specialized cognitive and neural machinery for face perception per se (the face specificity hypothesis), and argue against a variety of alternative hypotheses. First, neuropsychological double dissociations exist between face recognition and visual expertise for nonface stimuli, casting doubt on the claim that these two phenomena share processing mechanisms. Second, behavioral data from normal subjects show a number of "signatures" of holistic face processing that are not observed for other stimulus classes, such as inverted faces and objects of expertise. Third, electrophysiological measurements indicate face-specific processing at or before 200 ms after stimulus onset (N170). Fourth, fMRI and physiological investigations in monkeys show strikingly selective (and often exclusive) responses to faces both within individual neurons, and more recently also within cortical regions. Finally, extensive investigation of the most robust face-selective cortical region in humans, the FFA, supports the face specificity hypothesis (see also Kanwisher & Yovel, 2006) . This strong evidence for face-specific mechanisms invites a more detailed investigation of the precise nature of the computations and representations extracted in each of the face-selective regions of the cortex, which we turn to next.

THE NATURE OF THE FACE REPRESENTATIONS IN THE FUSIFORM FACE AREA

Many experiments implicate the FFA in determining face identity, that is, in extracting the perceptual information used to distinguish between individual faces. For example, we showed a higher FFA response on trials in which subjects correctly identified a famous face than on trials in which they failed to recognize the same individual (Grill-Spector et al., 2004), implicating this region in the extraction of information about face identity. (No comparable correlation between the FFA response and performance was seen for identification of specific types of cars, guitars, buildings, etc.) Further evidence that the FFA is critical for distinguishing between individual faces comes from studies that use fMRI-adaptation, discussed later. Finally, the critical lesion site for prosopagnosia is very close to the FFA (Barton et al., 2002; Bouvier & Engel, 2006). However, these results tell us nothing about the nature of the representations extracted from faces in the FFA, which we turn to next.

Invariances of Face Representations

To understand the representations of faces extracted by the FFA, we need to determine their equivalence classes. If the FFA is involved in discriminating between individuals, then it must extract different representations for different individuals. But are these representations invariant across images of the same face that differ in size, position, view, and so on?

The best current method for approaching this problem with fMRI is fMRI-adaptation (Grill-Spector et al., 1999; Kourtzi & Kanwisher, 2001), in which the blood-oxygen-level dependent (BOLD) response to two (or more) stimuli in a given region of the brain is lower when they are the same than when they are different, indicating a sensitivity of that brain region to that stimulus difference. This sensitivity to the sameness of two stimuli enables us to ask each brain region which stimulus pairs it takes to be the same and which it takes to be different, that is, to discover equivalence classes and invariances in neural representations of faces. Several studies have found robust fMRI-adaptation for faces in the FFA, that is a lower response to identically repeated faces than to new faces (e.g., Avidan, Hasson, Malach, & Behrmann, 2005; Eger, Schweinberger, Dolan, & Henson, 2005; Gauthier & Nelson, 2001; Pourtois, Schwartz, Seghier, Lazeyras, & Vuilleumier, 2005; Rotshtein, Henson, Treves, Driver, & Dolan, 2005; Yovel & Kanwisher, 2004). Does this adaptation reflect a representation of face identity that is invariant across different images of the same person? Several studies have found adaptation across repeated images of the same face even when those images differ in position (Grill-Spector et al., 1999), image size (Andrews & Schluppeck, 2004; Grill-Spector et al., 1999), and spatial scale (Eger, Schyns, & Kleinschmidt, 2004). Further, Rotshtein et al. (2005) used categorical perception of morphed faces to show adaptation across physically different images that were perceived to be the same (i.e., two faces that were on the same side of a perceptual category boundary), but not across physically different images that were perceived to be different (i.e., two faces that straddled the category boundary). A similar study with unfamiliar morphed faces also revealed a close correspondence between the perceptual boundary and the magnitude of adaptation (Gilaie-Dotan & Malach, 2007). Thus, representations in the FFA are not tied to low-level image properties, but instead show at least partial invariance to simple image transformations.

However, representations in the FFA do not appear to be invariant to nonaffine changes such as changes in lighting direction (Bradshaw, 1968), viewpoint (Pourtois et al., 2005; Warrington, Logue, & Pratt, 1971), and combinations thereof (Avidan et al., 2005; Pourtois et al., 2005). Fang, Murray, and He (2007) found sharp view-specific tuning in the FFA and STS. View-specific tuning in the FFA was more precise after very long presentations of the adaptor (25 sec) than after shorter presentations (0.3 sec). These studies indicate that the FFA treats two images of the same face that differ in viewpoint and lighting as two different images.

In sum, studies conducted to date converge on the conclusion that neural representations of faces in the FFA discriminate between faces of different individuals and are partly tolerant to simple image transformations including size, position, and spatial scale. However, these representations are not invariant to nonaffine changes in viewpoint or lighting.

Discriminating between Familiar and Unfamiliar Faces

A finding that the FFA responds differently to familiar and unfamiliar faces would support the role of this region in face recognition (though it is not required by this hypothesis as discussed shortly). Several fMRI studies have investigated this question (George et al., 1999; Gorno-Tempini et al., 1998; Haxby et al., 1999; Henson, Shallice, Gorno-Tempini, & Dolan, 2002; Leveroni et al., 2000; Sergent et al., 1992; Wiser et al., 2000) using as familiar faces either famous faces or faces studied in the lab.

Two studies that investigated faces learned in the lab found opposite results, one showing an increase in the response to familiar compared to unfamiliar faces in the FFA (Lehmann et al., 2004) and the other (using PET) found a decrease in the response to familiar faces (Rossion, Schiltz, & Crommelinck, 2003). Although this discrepancy may be due to the use of different tasks in the two experiments (Rossion et al., 2003; see also Henson et al., 2002), studies of famous faces, which provide a stronger manipulation of familiarity, do not give a much clearer picture. One study found a small but significant increase in the response to famous compared to nonfamous faces (Avidan et al., 2005) but two other studies found no difference in the response to famous versus nonfamous faces in the FFA (Eger et al., 2005; Pourtois et al., 2005; see also Gorno-Tempini & Price, 2001; Gorno-Tempini et al., 1998). Taken together, these studies do not show a consistently different FFA response for familiar versus unfamiliar faces. Although these studies do not strengthen the case that the FFA is important for face recognition, it is important to note that they do not provide evidence against this hypothesis either. These results may simply show that the FFA merely extracts a perceptual representation from faces in a bottom-up fashion, with actual recognition (i.e., matching to stored representations) occurring at a later stage of processing. It is also possible that information about face familiarity is represented not by an overall difference in the mean response but by the pattern of response across voxels within the FFA (Haxby et al., 2001; but see Kriegeskorte, Formisano, Sorger, & Goebel, 2007).

Studies of face familiarity do however enable us to address a different question about the FFA—its role in processing of nonvisual semantic information about people. Because famous faces are associated with rich semantic information about the person, but nonfamous faces are not, the lack of a consistently and robustly higher response for famous rather than nonfamous faces in the FFA casts doubt on the idea espoused by some (Martin & Chao, 2001), that this region is engaged in processing not only perceptual but also semantic information about people (Turk, Rosenblum, Gazzaniga, & Macrae, 2005).

Face Inversion Effect and Holistic Processing

As described previously, behavioral studies have discovered distinctive "signatures" of face-like processing, including the face inversion effect (Yin, 1969) and the composite effect. Does the FFA mirror these behavioral signatures of face-specific processing?

Early studies of the face inversion effect in the FFA found little (Haxby et al., 1999; Kanwisher, Stanley, & Harris, 1999) or no (Aguirre, Singh, & D'Esposito, 1999; Leube et al., 2003) difference in the response to upright and inverted faces. However, we reported a substantially higher FFA response for upright compared to inverted faces (Yovel et al., 2004). Further, in a subsequent study, we (Yovel & Kanwisher, 2005) reported that the FFA-face inversion effect was correlated across subjects with the behavioral face inversion effect. That is, subjects who showed a large increment in performance for upright versus inverted faces also showed a large increment in the FFA response to upright versus inverted faces (see Figure 43.3). Second, we found greater fMR-adaptation for upright than inverted faces, indicating that the FFA is more sensitive to identity information in upright than in inverted faces (Yovel & Kanwisher, 2005; see also Mazard, Schiltz, & Rossion, 2006). Thus, consistent with the behavioral face inversion effect, the FFA better discriminates faces when they are upright than when they are inverted. Importantly, this pattern of response was specific to the FFA studies (see discussion of OFA and STS that follows). In summary, in contrast to previous findings that found only a weak relationship between the FFA and the face inversion effect, our findings show a close link between these behavioral and neural markers of specialized face processing.

The larger behavioral inversion effect for faces rather than objects has been taken as evidence for holistic processing of upright but not inverted faces (Farah, Tanaka, & Drain, 1995). However, more direct evidence for holistic processing comes from the composite effect (Young et al., 1987) in which subjects are not able to process the upper or lower half of a composite face independently from the other half of the face even when instructed to do so, unless the two halves are misaligned. This effect is found for upright but not inverted faces. If the FFA is engaged in holistic processing of faces, then we might expect it to show an fMRI correlate of the composite effect. One study used fMRI adaptation to show evidence for a composite face effect in the FFA (Schiltz & Rossion, 2006). In particular, the FFA only showed adaptation across two identical top halves of a face (compared to two different top halves) when the bottom half of the face was also identical, consistent with the behavioral composite face effect. As with the behavioral composite effect, the fMRI composite effect was found only for upright faces and was absent for inverted faces or misaligned faces.

Thus, fMRI measurements from the FFA show neural correlates of the classic behavioral signatures of face-like processing, including the face inversion effect and the composite effect. These findings link the behavioral evidence on face-specific processing with research on the FFA, as well as helping to characterize the operations and representations that occur in the FFA.

Representation of Configuration and Parts of Faces

Three prominent features of face stimuli are the classic frontal face configuration (the arrangement of two horizontally and symmetrically placed parts above two vertically placed parts), the presence of specific face parts (eyes, nose, mouth), and the bounding contour of a roughly oval shape with hair on the top and sides. Which of these stimulus properties are important in driving the response of the FFA? Liu and colleagues (Liu et al., 2003) created stimuli in which each of these three attributes were orthogonally varied. The face configuration was either canonical or scrambled (with face parts rearranged to occur in different positions), veridical face parts were either present or absent (i.e., replaced by black ovals), and external features were either present or absent (with a rectangular frame showing only internal features, omitting chin and hairline). This study found that the FFA responds to all three kinds of face properties.

A prominent theory (Maurer, LeGrand, & Mondloch, 2002) suggests that the spacing among face parts plays a privileged role in our representation of faces, dissociable from the representation of the shape of the parts. However, fMRI studies consistently lead to the conclusion that the FFA is involved in processing both the parts and the spacing among the parts of faces (Maurer et al., 2007; Rotshtein, Geng, Driver, & Dolan, 2007; Yovel & Kanwisher, 2004). First, Yovel and Kanwisher (2004) scanned subjects while they performed a successive discrimination task on pairs of faces that differed in either the individual parts, or in the configuration (i.e., spacing) of those parts. Subjects were informed in advance of each block which kind of discrimination they should perform. The FFA response was similar and strong in both conditions, again indicating a role of the FFA in the discrimination of both face parts and face configurations. Second, two fMRI studies that examined the brain response when subjects discriminated faces that differ in spacing or parts also support the hypothesis that the FFA is involved in processing both spacing and part information in faces. Although Maurer et al. (2007) reported some regions that were differentially sensitive to spacing information or to part-based information, these fusiform activations were located *outside* the FFA and therefore do not argue against our contention that the FFA is engaged in both processes. A close examination of the face-selective region in their study did not reveal any difference between the response to spacing and parts even when very low threshold levels were applied. Similarly, Rotshtein et al. (2007) examined repetition effects for faces that differ in spacing and parts. Several regions outside face-selective regions showed differential sensitivity to

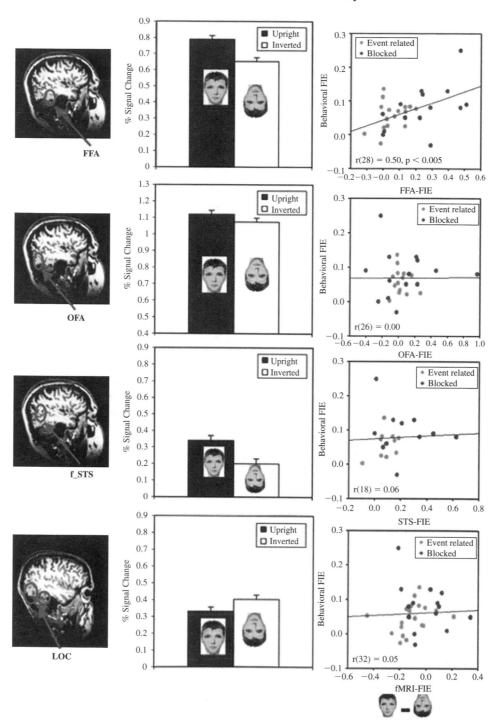

Figure 43.3 The magnitude of the face inversion effect in the FFA (but not the OFA, fSTS, or LOC) is correlated across subjects with the magnitude of the behavioral face inversion effect.

Note: From "A Whole Face Is More Than the Sum of Its Halves: Interactive Processing in Face Perception," by Yovel, et al. (2005). The neural basis of the FIE *Current Biology, pp. 15,* 2256–2262, Figure 2.

spacing versus parts, whereas an area that overlapped with the face-selective fusiform area was sensitive to repetition of parts and was correlated with performance on the spacing discrimination task. The authors concluded that information about spacing and parts may converge in the FFA.

Taken together, these studies show that the FFA is not sensitive to only a few specific face features, but instead seems to respond generally to a wide range of features spanning the whole face. Whereas several brain regions do show dissociated responses to information about spacing or parts, the FFA seems instead to generate an integrated representation that includes all aspects of face information. These findings are consistent with a recent behavioral study that found a positive correlation across subjects between performance on discrimination of spacing and discrimination of parts only for upright faces, not for inverted faces or houses (Yovel & Kanwisher, 2008). Thus, although spacing and part-based information about objects are processed by distinct mechanisms, information about the spacing and parts of upright faces are integrated into a common, holistic representation.

Norm-Based Coding of Faces

The power of caricatures to capture the likeness of a face suggests that face identity is coded in terms of deviation from the norm or average face, a hypothesis supported by behavioral studies (Leopold, O'Toole, Vetter, & Blanz, 2001; Rhodes, Brennan, & Carey, 1987). One fMRI study found higher FFA responses to atypical compared to average faces, implicating the FFA in such norm-based coding of face identity (Loffler, Yourganov, Wilkinson, & Wilson, 2005). However, efforts in this study to unconfound such face typicality effects from the greater adaptation effects expected between highly similar faces (in the average-face condition) versus very different faces (in the atypical face condition) were not entirely satisfactory. Therefore, the interesting hypothesis that the FFA codes faces in terms of deviation from the average face remains to be fully tested and explored.

Top-Heavy Figures

Although several studies have found that newborns look preferentially at facelike images (Johnson, Dziurawiec, Ellis, & Morton, 1991), this preference may reflect a more general preference for top-heavy figures (Cassia, Turati, & Simion, 2004). Top-heavy figures are similar to faces in that they contain more information in their upper half. To assess whether the FFA shows a similar preference to such figures, Caldara and colleagues (2006) presented head-shape and square-shape figures that included more information in their upper or lower halves. The right FFA showed the highest response to head-shape top-heavy stimuli. The response of the right FFA to a top-heavy square and bottom-heavy stimuli was similar and lower. This pattern is consistent with behavioral ratings of faceness on these stimuli. The left FFA and the OFA showed similar responses to top and bottom-heavy stimuli. Thus, only the right FFA shows a higher sensitivity to the type of stimuli that elicit longer looking time during the first 24 hours of life.

Fusiform Face Area and Facial Expression Information

fMRI studies of face expression have primarily focused on the amygdala (e.g., Glascher, Tuscher, Weiller, & Buchel, 2004; Williams et al., 2004). However, studies that have investigated the response of the temporal cortex have also found higher responses to emotional rather than neutral faces in the fusiform gyrus (Breiter et al., 1996; Dolan, Morris, & de Gelder, 2001; Vuilleumier, Armony, Driver, & Dolan, 2001, 2003; Williams et al., 2004). It has been suggested that this effect is modulated by connections from the amygdala (Dolan et al., 2001). Consistent with this hypothesis, effects of facial expression (in contrast to face identity) are not specific to the FFA. Given the higher arousal generated by emotional faces, the higher response to expressive than neutral faces in the FFA may reflect a general arousal effect rather than specific representation of facial expression. Indeed, one fMRI-adaptation study (Winston, Vuilleumier, & Dolan, 2003), in which expression and identity were manipulated in a factorial manner, did not find significant fMRI-adaptation to expression information in the fusiform gyrus, but did find fMRI-adaptation to face expression in regions in the STS. These findings are consistent with the idea that the FFA is involved in the extraction of identity but not expression information, whereas the STS shows the opposite pattern of response (Haxby, Hoffman, & Gobbini, 2000). However, another study found a higher FFA response during expression judgments and identity judgments that were done on separate blocks on the same face stimuli (Ganel, Valyear, Goshen-Gottstein, & Goodale, 2005), casting some doubt on the simple idea that the FFA is involved exclusively in processing face identity information.

Further evidence for the possible role of the FFA in expression processing comes from a recent developmental fMRI study in which adults, teenagers (13 to 17 years), and children (8 to 11 years) were asked to classify facial expressions for upright or inverted faces (Passarotti, Smith, DeLano, & Huang, 2007). Just as for face identity findings (Yovel & Kanwisher, 2005), adults showed higher responses to upright than inverted stimuli in regions that overlap with face-selective regions in the fusiform gyrus and the STS (a face localizer was not included in Passarotti et al., 2007). In contrast, teenagers and children showed weaker or absent fMRI-face inversion effects in these regions. Finally, only in adults and only in the area that overlapped with the right FFA, a correlation across subjects was found between the fMRI and behavioral inversion effects. This finding suggests that the FFA may play some role in extracting information about emotional expressions in faces.

Summary

The results reviewed in this section provide the beginnings of a characterization of the computations and representations that occur in the FFA. The FFA is implicated in face detection and face discrimination, but evidence on the role of the FFA in discriminating familiar from unfamiliar faces or in discriminating emotional expressions in faces is inconsistent. Representations of faces in the FFA are partly invariant to simple image transformations such as changes in size, position, and spatial scale, but largely noninvariant to changes in most viewpoints and lighting direction of the face image. The FFA shows both a face inversion effect (i.e., a higher response for upright than inverted faces) and holistic processing of faces, as expected if this region plays a major role in face-processing phenomena established in previous behavioral work.

Although the FFA is by far the most robust and hence most studied of the face-selective regions of the cortex, two other face-selective regions have also been investigated, the OFA in the lateral occipital cortex and what we call the fSTS (a face-selective region in the posterior part of the superior termporal gyrus). Figure 43.2 shows these face-selective activations on an inflated brain from one subject. Ongoing work has begun to reveal a functional division of labor between these three cortical regions.

FUNCTION OF THE FACE-SELECTIVE OCCIPITAL FACE AREA

Situated just posterior and lateral to the FFA, the most natural hypothesis is that the OFA is an earlier stage of the face-processing network that sends its output to the FFA. Although the responses of the OFA are in many ways similar to responses of the FFA, they do differ in some telling respects that are largely consistent with this hypothesis. First, the OFA has a stronger contralateral-field bias than the FFA (Hemond, Kanwisher, & Op de Beeck, 2007). Second, Rotshtein et al. (2005) showed that a posterior face-sensitive region in the inferior occipital gyrus, presumably the OFA, is sensitive to physical changes in the face stimulus, independent of whether those changes are perceived as a change in face identity, whereas a face-sensitive region in the right fusiform gyrus, presumably the FFA, is sensitive only to perceived changes in face identity. Third, Yovel and Kanwisher (2005) found that the OFA showed a similar response to upright and inverted faces, and there was no correlation across subjects between the magnitude of the behavioral face inversion effect and the difference in the response of the OFA to upright and inverted faces (OFA–face inversion effect). In contrast, the FFA showed higher response to upright than inverted faces and this difference was correlated across subjects with the behavioral face inversion effect. Finally, whereas the FFA responds to first-order stimulus information about both face parts and face configurations, the OFA is sensitive only to face parts (Liu et al., 2003). Consistent with these findings, a transcranial magnetic stimulation (TMS) study (Pitcher, Walsh, Yovel, & Duchaine, 2007) showed that that OFA stimulation that takes place 60 to 100 ms after stimulus onset disrupts discrimination of faces that differ in parts but not in spacing among them (Pitcher, Garrido, Walsh, & Duchaine, 2008). Taken together, these findings suggest that the OFA constitutes an earlier stage of face processing, which represents information that is more closely tied to the face stimulus, whereas the FFA represents the perceived identity of the face.

However, all of the data just summarized is based on the functional properties of the OFA and FFA. What do we know about the critical question of how these regions are connected? Efforts to answer this question using functional connectivity (Fairhall & Ishai, 2007) are suggestive but not yet conclusive, and fiber-tracing methods cannot distinguish direct connections between the OFA and FFA from other nearby fibers. However, evidence from disruption methods shows that the OFA is a necessary stage in the face-processing network. First, patient PS with no right OFA but intact right FFA was severely prosopagnosic (Rossion et al., 2003). Although this result by itself makes sense, a puzzle arises from the fact that the same patient shows a face-selective activation in the fusiform gyrus (FFA) in fMRI. One possibility is that the right FFA receives input form the left OFA. However, a study of another patient (DF) with bilateral lesions in the OFA also shows apparently intact face-selective activation in the FFA (Steeves et al., 2006). These data suggest that the FFA gets face input from early visual areas outside the OFA (Dricot, Sorger, Schiltz, Goebel, & Rossion, 2008). However, this input does not generate an intact representation of identity information in the FFA. fMRI adaptation has shown that the FFA in patient PS does not discriminate between individual faces (Schiltz, Sorger, Ahmed, Mayer, & Goebel, 2006), suggesting that interaction with the OFA is necessary for normal functioning of the FFA. In a follow-up study that tested adaptation to faces in nearby nonface-selective regions, the absence of adaptation for face identity in the FFA was replicated, but intact adaptation effect to faces in nearby object processing regions was observed. These findings suggest that the OFA is associated with the FFA but not with nearby nonface-selective regions that show normal adaptation response even when the OFA is damaged (Dricot et al., 2008). Finally, as mentioned previously, TMS to the OFA selectively disrupts perception of face parts (Pitcher et al., 2007).

In sum, the OFA appears to constitute an early stage of face processing necessary for the perception of face parts, and most likely connecting directly to the FFA, but not processing the only input to the FFA.

FUNCTION OF THE FACE-SELECTIVE REGION IN THE SUPERIOR TEMPORAL SULCUS

Although the FFA can be found in essentially all normal subjects, the face-selective region in the STS (fSTS) is less reliable; it is found in only half (Kanwisher et al., 1997) to three quarters (Yovel & Kanwisher, 2005) of subjects scanned individually. For this reason, this region has been studied less extensively than the FFA, although numerous studies investigate responses in the STS to face stimuli. Nonetheless, evidence suggests important functional distinctions between the fSTS and other face-selective regions of the cortex, with the fSTS more involved in processing dynamic and social aspects of faces such as emotional expression and gaze (Haxby et al., 2000).

First, the fSTS does not show the same involvement in the detection of faces and the perceptual analysis of face identity that has been found in the FFA. Two studies have found that the FFA but not the fSTS is correlated with successful face detection. Andrews and Schulppeck (2004) presented ambiguous stimuli (Mooney faces) that on some trials were perceived as faces but on others were perceived as novel blobs. Whereas the FFA response was stronger for face than blob percepts (see also Kanwisher et al., 1998), the fSTS showed no difference between the two types of trials. These findings are consistent with Grill-Spector et al. (2004) who found that the response of the FFA was correlated with successful detection of faces in brief masked stimuli, but the response of the fSTS was not. The failure to find a correlation with successful face detection in the fSTS when stimuli are held constant (or are similar) is somewhat surprising given that this region by definition responds more strongly when faces are present than when they are not. In any event, the correlation with successful face detection of the FFA but not fSTS, which was found in both studies, shows a dissociation between the two regions.

Given the findings just described, it is not surprising that the fSTS shows no sensitivity to face identity information. For example, Grill-Spector et al. (2004) found no correlation of the fSTS response with successful identification of faces. Similarly, studies that used fMRI-adaptation found sensitivity to face identity in the FFA but not in the fSTS (Andrews & Schluppeck, 2004; Yovel & Kanwisher, 2005). Several studies have found a robust face inversion effect (higher response to upright than inverted faces) in the fSTS (Haxby et al., 1999; Leube et al., 2003; Yovel & Kanwisher, 2005). However, in contrast to the FFA, this difference between upright and inverted faces was not correlated with the behavioral face inversion effect measured in a face identity discrimination task (Yovel & Kanwisher, 2005; see Figure 43.3). These findings are consistent with the idea that the fSTS is not involved in extracting individual identity from faces. Its higher response to upright rather than inverted faces may suggest that the computations that are done in the fSTS to extract dynamic aspects of facial information are specific to upright faces.

Several studies have provided compelling evidence that the fSTS is involved in the processing of eye gaze, emotional expression, and dynamic information about faces. First, Hoffman and Haxby (2000) showed that although the FFA responds more strongly when subjects performed a one-back task on face identity rather than gaze information, the fSTS showed a higher response for the gaze task than the identity task. Second, an fMRI-adaptation study (Winston et al., 2003), in which expression and identity were manipulated in a factorial manner, found significant sensitivity to information about emotional expression in faces in the fSTS but none in the fusiform gyrus (see also Andrews & Ewbank, 2004). Other studies have shown strong responses in the fSTS to dynamic face stimuli in which expression or gaze changes (Calvert & Campbell, 2003; Thompson, Hardee, Panayiotou, Crewther, & Puce, 2007).

Is an intact OFA necessary for an fSTS activation? fMRI studies of patients with unilateral (Sorger, Goebel, Schiltz, & Rossion, 2007) and bilateral OFA (Steeves et al., 2006) lesions show intact fSTS activation in these patients, which suggests that the fSTS gets face input from areas outside the OFA. It is still not known, however, whether more subtle fMRI measures of the fSTS activation during expression and gaze processing may be intact in these patients.

In sum, whereas the FFA and OFA appear to be more involved in the analysis of face identity, the STS is more involved in the analysis of social and dynamic information in faces such as gaze, expression, and movement (Haxby et al., 2000).

ORIGINS OF FACE PROCESSING

How do face-selective cortical regions and adult-like face processing arise in development? Are they constructed by a process of experience-dependent cortical self-organization (Jacobs, 1997)? Are some aspects of face processing partly innately specified? For the case of faces, these questions have been hard to answer because both experiential and evolutionary arguments are plausible. Evidence from individuals with face impairments due to developmental prosopagnosia and congenital cataracts are suggestive (for a review, see Kanwisher & Yovel, 2006; McKone et al., 2007), but do not yet provide definitive answers to these questions (but see Duchaine, Germine, & Nakayama, 2007; Grueter et al., 2007). However, clues are beginning to emerge from a number of recent studies.

Ongoing work is characterizing the developmental trajectory of face perception abilities, and the face-selective cortex, in increasing detail. Neuroimaging studies show that the FFA is still developing into the early teenage years (Aylward et al., 2005; Golarai et al., 2007; Passarotti et al., 2003; Scherf, Behrmann, Humphrey, & Luna, 2007). In contrast, behavioral work shows that all of the key behavioral signatures of adult-like face processing are qualitatively present by 4 years of age (Kanwisher & Yovel, 2006; McKone et al., 2007). A major puzzle for future research will be to understand why the FFA changes at least twofold in volume between age 7 and adulthood, after face perceptual abilities are largely in place. Whatever the ultimate answer to this question, it is important to note that late development of face perception (whether by 4 or 14 years of age) need not indicate a critical role for experience in the construction of the FFA; maturation could explain some of all of this developmental change. To understand how face-processing mechanisms arise, we must turn to other methods.

At least some aspects of face perception appear to be innately specified because infants less than 24 hours old preferentially track schematic faces compared to visually similar scrambled or inverted faces (Cassia et al., 2004; Johnson, Dziurawiec, Ellis, & Morton, 1991). Experience also affects face perception, as evidenced by the "other race effect," in which neural responses (Golby, Gabrieli, Chiao, & Eberhardt, 2001) and behavioral performance (Malpass & Kravitz, 1969; Meissner & John, 2001) are higher for faces of a familiar than for an unfamiliar race, even if (in the latter case) the relevant experience occurs after age 3 (Sangrigoli, Pallier, Argenti, Ventureyra, & de Schonen, 2005). However, these two observations leave open a vast space of possible scenarios in which genes and environment interact in the construction of a selective region of cortex such as the FFA. Two recent findings suggest a greater role for genes than many would have guessed.

First, Polk, Park, Smith, and Park (2007) compared the spatial distribution of response to various stimulus categories across the ventral visual pathway in twins. They found that for faces and places the pattern of response was more similar for monozygotic than dizygotic twins, whereas

for pseudowords and chairs, it was not. This result indicates that differences between individuals in the pattern of response to faces in the ventral visual pathway are due in part to genes. However, note that this result does not argue against a role for experience in the construction of the FFA. Although genes might exert some kind of direct control over neural connectivity, another possibility is that genes that affect social behavior lead some individuals to look at faces more than others do, and this differential experience itself affects neural responses to these categories. Although this study presents some of the first evidence we know of for a genetic influence on the cortical machinery of face perception (see also Duchaine et al., 2007; Grueter et al., 2007), that evidence does not necessarily argue against a role for experience in the construction of the FFA. There are many possible causal pathways from genes to neural architecture, some of which crucially implicate experience as the key intervening variable.

Another recent study argues that experience with faces may not be necessary for the construction of face-processing machinery. Sugita (2008) raised baby monkeys without ever allowing them to see faces, from birth to the age of 6, 12, or 24 months. The monkeys lived in enriched visual environments and were cared for by human caretakers who wore hoods over their faces at all times while in the presence of the monkeys. Astonishingly, when the monkeys were first tested on face perception, even after 2 years of deprivation, they showed the standard preference to look at static photographs of faces over novel object photographs. Even more surprising, they showed adult-like sensitivity to differences between faces: Given a choice between a face they had just habituated to, and a new face, they looked more at the new face, even though the differences between faces were very subtle. These findings leave little room for a role of face experience in the construction of adult face-processing performance, at least in monkeys. Crucial future work should use even more subtle tests to ask whether these monkeys have truly normal face perception abilities. Also of great interest is the question of whether these monkeys who never saw faces in the first 2 years of life nonetheless have normal face-selective cortical regions (Tsao et al., 2003), and if so, how quickly these arise after exposure to faces.

Although we still don't know how the machinery of face processing arises during development, new evidence suggests that experience with faces may not be necessary.

SUMMARY

In this chapter, we described the current state of knowledge about face-selective regions of cortex in humans and their role in face perception. Current evidence supports the hypothesis that the FFA is specifically involved in face perception per se. The division of labor between the three face-selective cortical regions is beginning to come into focus, with the OFA apparently more involved in the analysis of face parts, the FFA involved in the construction of perceptual descriptions of faces used in face identity discrimination, and the fSTS involved in discriminating social/dynamic information in faces such as eye gaze direction and perhaps also emotional expression. Further work is characterizing the representations of faces extracted in each of these regions, though much remains to be done. Finally, although the FFA is clearly influenced both by experience and by genes, very recent work opens up the surprising possibility that experience with faces may not be necessary for the construction of adult-like face-processing abilities.

Despite the wealth of knowledge accrued from the past decade of research into the cortical regions involved in face perception, fundamental questions remain unanswered. First, we have only begun to scratch the surface in understanding what information is represented in each of these regions, and we have no idea at all about the neural circuits that give rise to these representations. Second, virtually nothing is known about the connections between each of these regions, or between these regions and the rest of the brain. Third, although current methods of human cognitive neuroscience can tell us about time (via ERPs and MEG) or about space (via fMRI), we have almost no data that can tell us about the precise time course of response in specific spatially resolved regions of the brain (for powerful but rare data on this question, see Mundel et al., 2003; Puce et al., 1999). For example, despite the many fMRI studies of the FFA using fMRI, it is unknown which of its response properties arise during the initial feedforward response to a stimulus, and which may arise hundreds of milliseconds later. Fourth, with few exceptions (Afraz, Kiani, & Esteky, 2006; Pitcher et al., 2007; Puce et al., 1999), we know very little about the causal structure of the face-processing system: which regions play a necessary role in which aspects of face perception. Finally, we know next to nothing about why face-selective regions land so systematically where they do in the cortex, or about the mechanisms that wire this system up during development.

These questions remain largely unanswered because current methods of human cognitive neuroscience cannot answer them. However, the bright light on the horizon is the fact that monkeys too have face-selective regions of the cortex and methods exist to tackle most of these questions in macaques. Indeed, the combination of behavioral, neuroimaging, and physiological studies in monkeys (Tsao & Livingstone, 2008) is likely to prove very powerful over the next decade.

REFERENCES

Afraz, S.-R., Kiani, R., & Esteky, H. (2006, August 10). Microstimulation of inferotemporal cortex influences face categorization. *Nature, 442,* 692–695.

Aguirre, G. K., Singh, R., & D'Esposito, M. (1999). Stimulus inversion and the responses of face and object-sensitive cortical areas. *NeuroReport, 10,* 189–194.

Allison, T., Ginter, H., McCarthy, G., Nobre, A. C., Puce, A., Luby, M., et al. (1994). Face recognition in human extrastriate cortex. *Journal of Neurophysiology, 71,* 821–825.

Allison, T., Puce, A., Spencer, D. D., & McCarthy, G. (1999). Electrophysiological studies of human face perception: Pt. I. Potentials generated in occipitotemporal cortex by face and non-face stimuli. *Cerebral Cortex, 9,* 415–430.

Andrews, T. J., & Ewbank, M. P. (2004). Distinct representations for facial identity and changeable aspects of faces in the human temporal lobe. *NeuroImage, 23,* 905–913.

Andrews, T. J., & Schluppeck, D. (2004). Neural responses to Mooney images reveal a modular representation of faces in human visual cortex. *NeuroImage, 21,* 91–98.

Andrews, T. J., Schluppeck, D., Homfray, D., Matthews, P., & Blakemore, C. (2002). Activity in the fusiform gyrus predicts conscious perception of Rubin's vase-face illusion. *NeuroImage, 17,* 890–901.

Avidan, G., Hasson, U., Malach, R., & Behrmann, M. (2005). Detailed exploration of face-related processing in congenital prosopagnosia: Pt. 2. Functional neuroimaging findings. *Journal of Cognitive Neuroscience, 1,* 1150–1167.

Aylward, E. H., Park, J. E., Field, K. M., Parsons, A. C., Richards, T. L., Cramer, S. C., et al. (2005). Brain activation during face perception: Evidence of a developmental change. *Journal of Cognitive Neuroscience, 17,* 308–319.

Barton, J. J., Press, D. Z., Keenan, J. P., & O'Connor, M. (2002). Lesions of the fusiform face area impair perception of facial configuration in prosopagnosia. *Neurology, 58,* 71–78.

Behrmann, M., & Avidan, G. (2005). Congenital prosopagnosia: Face-blind from birth. *Trends in Cognitive Sciences, 9,* 180–187.

Bentin, S., Allison, T., Puce, A., Perez, E., & McCarthy, G. (1996). Electrophysiological studies of face perception in humans. *Journal of Cognitive Neuroscience, 8,* 551–565.

Bentin, S., & Deouell, L. Y. (2000). Structural encoding and identification in face processing: ERP evidence for separate mechanisms. *Cognitive Neuropsychology, 17*(1/3), 35–54.

Bouvier, S. E., & Engel, S. A. (2006). Behavioral deficits and cortical damage loci in cerebral achromatopsia. *Cerebral Cortex, 16,* 183–191.

Bradshaw, J. L. (1968). Load and pupillary changes in continuous processing tasks. *British Journal of Psychology, 59,* 265–271.

Breiter, H. C., Etcoff, N. L., Whalen, P. J., Kennedy, W. A., Rauch, S. L., Buckner, R. L., et al. (1996). Response and habituation of the human amygdala during visual processing of facial expression. *Neuron, 17,* 875–887.

Caldara, R., Seghier, M. L., Rossion, B., Lazeyras, F., Michel, C., & Hauert, C. A. (2006). The fusiform face area is tuned for curvilinear patterns with more high-contrasted elements in the upper part. *NeuroImage, 31,* 313–319.

Calvert, G. A., & Campbell, R. (2003). Reading speech from still and moving faces: The neural substrates of visible speech. *Journal of Cognitive Neuroscience, 15,* 57–70.

Cassia, V. M., Turati, C., & Simion, F. (2004). Can a nonspecific bias toward top-heavy patterns explain newborns' face preference? *Psychological Sciencse, 15,* 379–383.

Desimone, R., Albright, T. D., Gross, C. G., & Bruce, C. (1984). Stimulus-selective properties of inferior temporal neurons in the macaque. *Journal of Neuroscience, 4,* 2051–2062.

Diamond, R., & Carey, S. (1986). Why faces are and are not special: An effect of expertise. *Journal of Experimental Psychology: General, 115,* 107–117.

Dolan, R. J., Morris, J. S., & de Gelder, B. (2001). Crossmodal binding of fear in voice and face. *Proceedings of the National Academy of Sciences, USA, 98,* 10006–10010.

Downing, P. E., Chan, A. W., Peelen, M. V., Dodds, C. M., & Kanwisher, N. (2006). Domain specificity in visual cortex. *Cerebral Cortex, 16,* 1453–1461.

Downing, P. E., Jiang, Y., Shuman, M., & Kanwisher, N. (2001, September 28). A cortical area selective for visual processing of the human body. *Science, 293,* 2470–2473.

Dricot, L., Sorger, B., Schiltz, C., Goebel, R., & Rossion, B. (2008) The roles of "face" and "non-face" areas during individual face perception: Evidence by fMRI adaptation in a brain-damaged prosopagnosic patient. *Neuorimage, 40,* 318–332.

Duchaine, B., Germine, L., & Nakayama, K. (2007). Family resemblance: Ten family members with prosopagnosia and within-class object agnosia. *Cognitive Neuropsychology, 24,* 419–430.

Duchaine, B., Yovel, G., Butterworth, E., & Nakayama, K. (2006). Prosopagnosia as an impairment to face-specific mechanisms: Elimination of the alternative hypotheses in a developmental case. *Cognitive Neuropsychology, 23,* 714–747.

Eger, E., Schweinberger, S. R., Dolan, R. J., & Henson, R. N. (2005). Familiarity enhances invariance of face representations in human ventral visual cortex: FMRI evidence. *Neuroimage, 26,* 1128–1139.

Eger, E., Schyns, P. G., & Kleinschmidt, A. (2004). Scale invariant adaptation in fusiform face-responsive regions. *Neuroimage, 22,* 232–242.

Fairhall, S. L., & Ishai, A. (2007). Effective connectivity within the distributed cortical network for face perception. *Cerebral Cortex, 17,* 2400–2406.

Fang, F., Murray, S. O., & He, S. (2007). Duration-dependent FMRI adaptation and distributed viewer-centered face representation in human visual cortex. *Cerebral Cortex, 17,* 1402–1411.

Farah, M. J., Tanaka, J. W., & Drain, H. M. (1995). What causes the face inversion effect? *Journal of Experimental Psychology: Human Perception and Performance, 21,* 628–634.

Fodor, J. A. (1983). *The modularity of mind.* Cambridge, MA: MIT Press.

Foldiak, P., Xiao, D., Keysers, C., Edwards, R., & Perrett, D. I. (2004). Rapid serial visual presentation for the determination of neural selectivity in area STSa. *Progress in Brain Research, 144,* 107–116.

Ganel, R., Valyear, K. F., Goshen-Gottstein, Y., & Goodale, M. A. (2005). The involvement of the "fusiform face area" in processing facial expression. *Neuropsychologia, 43,* 1645–1654.

Gauthier, I., Behrmann, M., & Tarr, M. J. (1999). Can face recognition really be dissociated from object recognition? *Journal of Cognitive Neuroscience, 11,* 349–370.

Gauthier, I., Curran, T., Curby, K. M., & Collins, D. (2003). Perceptual interference supports a non-modular account of face processing. *Nature Neuroscience, 6,* 428–432.

Gauthier, I., & Nelson, C. A. (2001). The development of face expertise. *Current Opinion in Neurobiology, 11,* 219–224.

Gauthier, I., Skudlarski, P., Gore, J. C., & Anderson, A. W. (2000). Expertise for cars and birds recruits brain areas involved in face recognition. *Nature Neuroscience, 3,* 191–197.

Gauthier, I., Tarr, M. J., Anderson, A. W., Skudlarski, P., & Gore, J. C. (1999). Activation of the middle fusiform 'face area' increases with expertise in recognizing novel objects. *Nature Neuroscience, 2,* 568–573.

George, N., Dolan, R. J., Fink, G. R., Baylis, G. C., Russell, C., & Driver, J. (1999). Contrast polarity and face recognition in the human fusiform gyrus. *Nature Neuroscience, 2,* 574–580.

Gilaie-Dotan, S., & Malach, R. (2007). Sub-exemplar shape tuning in human face-related areas. *Cerebral Cortex, 17,* 325–338.

Glascher, J., Tuscher, O., Weiller, C., & Buchel, C. (2004). Elevated responses to constant facial emotions in different faces in the human amygdala: An fMRI study of facial identity and expression. *BMC Neuroscience, 5,* 45.

Golarai, G., Ghahemani, D. G., Whitfield-Gabrieli, S., Reiss, A., Eberhardt, J. L., Gabrieli, J. D., et al. (2007). Differential development of high-level visual cortex correlates with category-specific recognition memory. *Nature Neuroscience, 10,* 512–522.

Golby, A. J., Gabrieli, J. D., Chiao, J. Y., & Eberhardt, J. L. (2001). Differential responses in the fusiform region to same-race and other-race faces. *Nature Neuroscience, 4,* 775–776.

Gorno-Tempini, M. L., & Price, C. J. (2001). Identification of famous faces and buildings: A functional neuroimaging study of semantically unique items. *Brain, 124*(Pt. 10), 2087–2097.

Gorno-Tempini, M. L., Price, C. J., Josephs, O., Vandenberghe, R., Cappa, S. F., Kapur, N., et al. (1998). The neural systems sustaining face and proper-name processing. *Brain, 121,* 2103–2118.

Grill-Spector, K., Knouf, N., & Kanwisher, N. (2004). The fusiform face area subserves face perception, not generic within-category identification. *Nature Neuroscience, 7,* 555–562.

Grill-Spector, K., Kushnir, T., Edelman, S., Avidan, G., Itzchak, Y., & Malach, R. (1999). Differential processing of objects under various viewing conditions in the human lateral occipital complex. *Neuron, 24,* 187–203.

Grueter, M., Grueter, T., Bell, V., Horst, J., Laskowski, W., Sperling, K., et al. (2007). Hereditary prosopagnosia: The first case series. *Cortex, 43,* 734–749.

Halgren, E., Raij, T., Marinkovic, K., Jousmaki, V., & Hari, R. (2000). Cognitive response profile of the human fusiform face area as determined by MEG. *Cerebral Cortex, 10,* 69–81.

Hasson, U., Hendler, T., Ben Bashat, D., & Malach, R. (2001). Vase or face? A neural correlate of shape-selective grouping processes in the human brain. *Journal of Cognitive Neuroscience, 13,* 744–753.

Haxby, J. V., Gobbini, M. I., Furey, M. L., Ishai, A., Schouten, J. L., & Pietrini, P. (2001, September 28). Distributed and overlapping representations of faces and objects in ventral temporal cortex. *Science, 293,* 2425–2430.

Haxby, J. V., Grady, C. L., Horwitz, B., Ungerleider, L. G., Mishkin, M., Carson, R. E., et al. (1991). Dissociation of object and spatial visual processing pathways in human extrastriate cortex. *Proceedings of the National Academy of Sciences, USA, 88,* 1621–1625.

Haxby, J. V., Hoffman, E. A., & Gobbini, M. I. (2000). The distributed human neural system for face perception. *Trends in Cognitive Sciences, 4,* 223–233.

Haxby, J. V., Ungerleider, L. G., Clark, V. P., Schouten, J. L., Hoffman, E. A., & Martin, A. (1999). The effect of face inversion on activity in human neural systems for face and object perception. *Neuron, 22,* 189–199.

Hemond, C. C., Kanwisher, N., & Op de Beeck, H. P. (2007). A preference for contralateral stimuli in human object- and face-selective cortex. *PLoS ONE, 2*(6), e574.

Henke, K., Schweinberger, S. R., Grigo, A., Klos, T., & Sommer, W. (1998). Specificity of face recognition: Recognition of exemplars of non-face objects in prosopagnosia. *Cortex, 34,* 289–296.

Henson, R. N., Shallice, T., Gorno-Tempini, M. L., & Dolan, R. J. (2002). Face repetition effects in implicit and explicit memory tests as measured by fMRI. *Cerebral Cortex, 12,* 178–186.

Hoffman, E. A., & Haxby, J. V. (2000). Distinct representations of eye gaze and identity in the distributed human neural system for face perception. *Nature Neuroscience, 3,* 80–84.

Itier, R. J., & Taylor, M. J. (2004). N170 or N1? Spatiotemporal differences between object and face processing using ERPs. *Cerebral Cortex, 14,* 132–142.

Jacobs, R. A. (1997). Nature, nurture, and the development of functional specializations: A computational approach. *Psychological Bulletin and Review, 4,* 2999–2309.

Jacques, C., d'Arripe, O., & Rossion, B. (2007). The time course of the inversion effect during individual face discrimination. *Journal of Vision, 7,* 1–9.

Jacques, C., & Rossion, B. (2006). The speed of individual face categorization. *Psychological Science, 17,* 485–492.

Jeffreys, D. A. (1996). Evoked potential studies of face and object processing. *Visual Cognition, 3,* 1–38.

Jiang, X., Bradley, E., Rini, R., Zeffiro, T., VanMeter, J., & Riesenhuber, M. (2007). Categorization training results in shape- and category-selective human neural plasticity. *Neuron, 53,* 891–903.

Johnson, M. H., Dziurawiec, S., Ellis, H., & Morton, J. (1991). Newborns' preferential tracking of face-like stimuli and its subsequent decline. *Cognition, 40*(1/2), 1–19.

Kanwisher, N. (2006, February 3). Neuroscience: What's in a face? *Science, 311,* 617–618.

Kanwisher, N., McDermott, J., & Chun, M. M. (1997). The fusiform face area: A module in human extrastriate cortex specialized for face perception. *Journal of Neuroscience, 17,* 4302–4311.

Kanwisher, N., Stanley, D., & Harris, A. (1999). The fusiform face area is selective for faces not animals. *NeuroReport, 10,* 183–187.

Kanwisher, N., Tong, F., & Nakayama, K. (1998). The effect of face inversion on the human fusiform face area. *Cognition, 68,* B1–B11.

Kanwisher, N., & Yovel, G. (2006). The fusiform face area: A cortical region specialized for the perception of faces. *Philosophical Transactions of the Royal Society of London. Series B, 361,* 2109–2128.

Kourtzi, Z., & Kanwisher, N. (2001, August 24). Representation of perceived object shape by the human lateral occipital complex. *Science, 293,* 1506–1509.

Kriegeskorte, N., Formisano, E., Sorger, B., & Goebel, R. (2007). Individual faces elicit distinct response patterns in human anterior temporal cortex. *Proceedings of the National Academy of Sciences, USA, 104,* 20600–20605.

Lehmann, C., Mueller, T., Federspiel, A., Hubl, D., Schroth, G., Huber, O., et al. (2004). Dissociation between overt and unconscious face processing in fusiform face area. *NeuroImage, 21,* 75–83.

Leopold, D. A., O'Toole, A. J., Vetter, T., & Blanz, V. (2001). Prototype-referenced shape encoding revealed by high-level aftereffects. *Nature Neuroscience, 4,* 89–94.

Leube, D. T., Yoon, H. W., Rapp, A., Erb, M., Grodd, W., Bartels, M., et al. (2003). Brain regions sensitive to the face inversion effect: A functional magnetic resonance imaging study in humans. *Neuroscience Letters, 342,* 143–146.

Leveroni, C. L., Seidenberg, M., Mayer, A. R., Mead, L. A., Binder, J. R., & Rao, S. M. (2000). Neural systems underlying the recognition of familiar and newly learned faces. *Journal of Neuroscience, 20,* 878–886.

Liu, J., Harris, A., & Kanwisher, N. (2002). Stages of processing in face perception: An MEG study. *Nature Neuroscience, 5,* 910–916.

Liu, J., Harris, A., Mangini, M., Wald, L., Kwong, K. K., & Kanwisher, J. W. (2003). *Distinct representations of faces in the FFA and the OFA: An fMRI study.* Paper presented at the 33rd Annual Society for Neuroscience, New Orleans, LA.

Loffler, G., Yourganov, G., Wilkinson, F., & Wilson, H. R. (2005). FMRI evidence for the neural representation of faces. *Nature Neuroscience, 8,* 1386–1390.

Malpass, R. S., & Kravitz, J. (1969). Recognition for faces of own and other race. *Personality and Social Psychology, 13,* 330–334.

Martin, A., & Chao, L. L. (2001). Semantic memory and the brain: Structure and processes. *Current Opinion in Neurobiology, 11,* 194–201.

Maurer, D., LeGrand, R., & Mondloch, J. (2002). The many faces of configural processing. *Trends in Cognitive Sciences, 6,* 225–260.

Maurer, D., O'Craven, K. M., Le Grand, R., Mondloch, C. J., Springer, M. V., Lewis, T. L., et al. (2007). Neural correlates of processing facial identity based on features versus their spacing. *Neuropsychologia, 45,* 1438–1451.

Mazard, A., Schiltz, C., & Rossion, B. (2006). Recovery from adaptation to facial identity is larger for upright than inverted faces in the human occipito-temporal cortex. *Neuropsychologia, 44,* 912–922.

McCarthy, Puce, A. Gore, J., & Allison, T. (1997). Infrequent events transiently activate human prefrontal and parietal cortex as measured by functional MRI. *Journal of Neurophysiology, 77,* 1630–1634.

McKone, E., & Kanwisher, N. (2005). Does the human brain process objects of expertise like faces? A review of the evidence. In S. Dehaene, J. R. Duhamel, M. Hauser, & G. Rizzolatti (Eds.), *From monkey brain to human brain* (pp. 339–356). Cambridge, MA: MIT Press.

McKone, E., Kanwisher, N., & Duchaine, B. C. (2007). Can generic expertise explain special processing for faces? *Trends in Cognitive Sciences, 11,* 8–15.

McKone, E., Martini, P., & Nakayama, K. (2001). Categorical perception of face identity in noise isolates configural processing. *Journal of Experimental Psychology: Human Perception and Performance, 27,* 573–599.

McMullen, P. A., Fisk, J. D., Phillips, S. J., & Maloney, W. J. (2000). Apperceptive agnosia and face recognition. *Neurocase, 6,* 403–414.

McNeil, J. E., & Warrington, E. K. (1993). Prosopagnosia: A face-specific disorder. *Quarterly Journal of Experimental Psychology: A Human Experimental Psychology, 46,* 1–10.

Meissner, C. A. B., & John, C. (2001). Thirty years of investigating the own-race bias in memory for faces: A meta-analytic review. *Psychology, Public Policy, and Law, 7*(1), 3–35.

Moore, C. D., Cohen, M. X., & Ranganath, C. (2006). Neural mechanisms of expert skills in visual working memory. *Journal of Neuroscience, 26,* 11187–11196.

Moscovitch, M., Winocur, G., & Behrmann, M. (1997). What is special about face recognition? Nineteen experiments on a person with visual object agnosia and dyslexia but normal face recognition. *Journal of Cognitive Neuroscience, 9,* 555–604.

Mundel, T., Milton, J. G., Dimitrov, A., Wilson, H. W., Pelizzari, C., Uftring, S., et al. (2003). Transient inability to distinguish between faces: Electrophysiologic studies. *Journal of Clinical Neurophysiology, 20,* 102–110.

Op de Beeck, H. P., Baker, C. I., DiCarlo, J. J., & Kanwisher, N. G. (2006). Discrimination training alters object representations in human extrastriate cortex. *Journal of Neuroscience, 26,* 13025–13036.

Pasley, B. N., Mayes, L. C., & Schultz, R. T. (2004). Subcortical discrimination of unperceived objects during binocular rivalry. *Neuron, 42,* 163–172.

Passarotti, A., Paul, B., Bussiere, J., Buxton, R., Wong, E., & Stiles, J. (2003). The development of face and location processing: An fMRI study. *Developmental Science, 6*(1), 100–117.

Passarotti, A., Smith, J., DeLano, M., & Huang, J. (2007). Developmental differences in the neural bases of the face inversion effect show progressive tuning of face-selective regions to the upright orientation. *NeuroImage, 34,* 1708–1722.

Pinski, M. A., DeSimone, K., Moore, T., Gross, C. G., & Kastner, S. (2005). Representations of faces and body parts in macaque temporal cortex: A functional MRI study. *Proceedings of the National Academy Sciences, USA, 102,* 6996–7001.

Pitcher, D., Garrido, L., Walsh, V., & Duchaine, B. (2008) TMS disrupts the perception and embodiment of facial expressions. *Journal of Neuroscience, 28,* 8929–8933.

Pitcher, D., Walsh, V., Yovel, G., & Duchaine, B. (2007). TMS evidence for the involvement of the right occipital face area in early face processing. *Current Biology, 17,* 1568–1573.

Polk, T. A., Park, J., Smith, M. R., & Park, D. C. (2007). Nature versus nurture in ventral visual cortex: A functional magnetic resonance imaging study of twins. *Journal of Neuroscience, 27,* 13921–13925.

Pourtois, G., Schwartz, S., Seghier, M. L., Lazeyras, F., & Vuilleumier, P. (2005). Portraits or people? Distinct representations of face identity in the human visual cortex. *Journal of Cognitive Neuroscience, 17,* 1043–1057.

Puce, A., Allison, T., Asgari, M., Gore, J. C., & McCarthy, G. (1996). Differential sensitivity of human visual cortex to faces, letterstrings, and textures: A functional magnetic resonance imaging study. *Journal of Neuroscience, 16,* 5205–5215.

Puce, A., Allison, T., & McCarthy, G. (1999). Electrophysiological studies of human face perception: Pt. III. Effects of top-down processing on face-specific potentials. *Cerebral Cortex, 9,* 445–458.

Rhodes, G. (1985). Lateralized processes in face recognition. *British Journal of Psychology, 76,* 249–271.

Rhodes, G., Brennan, S., & Carey, S. (1987). Identification and ratings of caricatures: Implications for mental representations of faces. *Cognitive Psychology, 19,* 473–497.

Rhodes, G., Byatt, G., Michie, P. T., & Puce, A. (2004). Is the fusiform face area specialized for faces, individuation, or expert individuation? *Journal of Cognitive Neuroscience, 16,* 189–203.

Robbins, R., & McKone, E. (2007). No face-like processing for objects-of-expertise in three behavioural tasks. *Cognition, 103,* 34–79.

Rossion, B., Curran, T., & Gauthier, I. (2002). A defense of the subordinate-level expertise account for the N170 component. *Cognition, 85,* 189–196.

Rossion, B., Schiltz, C., & Crommelinck, M. (2003). The functionally defined right occipital and fusiform "face areas" discriminate novel from visually familiar faces. *NeuroImage, 19,* 877–883.

Rotshtein, P., Geng, J. J., Driver, J., & Dolan, R. J. (2007). Role of features and second-order spatial relations in face discrimination, face recognition, and individual face skills: Behavioral and functional magnetic resonance imaging data. *Journal of Cognitive Neuroscience, 19,* 1435–1452.

Rotshtein, P., Henson, R. N., Treves, A., Driver, J., & Dolan, R. J. (2005). Morphing Marilyn into Maggie dissociates physical and identity face representations in the brain. *Nature Neuroscience, 8,* 107–113.

Sangrigoli, S., Pallier, C., Argenti, A. M., Ventureyra, V. A., & de Schonen, S. (2005). Reversibility of the other-race effect in face recognition during childhood. *Psychological Sciences, 16,* 440–444.

Saxe, R., Brett, M., & Kanwisher, N. (2006). Divide and conquer: A defense of functional localizers. *NeuroImage, 3,* 1088–1096.

Saxe, R., & Powell, L. J. (2006). It's the thought that counts: Specific brain regions for one component of theory of mind. *Psychological Science, 17,* 692–699.

Scherf, K. S., Behrmann, M., Humphrey, K., & Luna, B. (2007). Visual category-selectivity for faces, places and objects emerges along different developmental trajectories. *Developmental Science, 10*(4), F15–F30.

Schiltz, C., & Rossion, B. (2006). Faces are represented holistically in the human occipito-temporal cortex. *NeuroImage, 32,* 1385–1394.

Schiltz, C., Sorger, B. R. C., Caldara, R., Ahmed, F., Mayer, E., Goebel, R., et al. (2006). Impaired face discrimination in acquired prosopagnosia is associated with abnormal response to individual faces in the right middle fusiform gyrus. *Cerebral Cortex, 16,* 574–586.

Sergent, J., & Bindra, D. (1981). Differential hemispheric processing of faces: Methodological considerations and reinterpretation. *Psychological Bulletin, 89,* 541–554.

Sergent, J., Ohta, S., & MacDonald, B. (1992). Functional neuroanatomy of face and object processing: A positron emission tomography study. *Brain, 115,* 15–36.

Sergent, J., & Signoret, J. L. (1992). Implicit access to knowledge derived from unrecognized faces in prosopagnosia. *Cerebral Cortex, 2,* 389–400.

Sorger, B., Goebel, R., Schiltz, C., & Rossion, B. (2007). Understanding the functional neuroanatomy of acquired prosopagnosia. *NeuroImage, 35,* 836–852.

Spiridon, M., & Kanwisher, N. (2002). How distributed is visual category information in human occipito-temporal cortex? An fMRI study. *Neuron, 35,* 1157–1165.

Steeves, J. K., Culham, J. C., Duchaine, B. C., Pratesi, C. C., Valyear, K. F., Schindler, I., et al. (2006). The fusiform face area is not sufficient for face recognition: Evidence from a patient with dense prosopagnosia and no occipital face area. *Neuropsychologia, 44,* 594–609.

Sugita, Y. (2008). Face perception in monkeys reared with no exposure to faces. *Proceedings of the National Academy of Sciences, USA, 105,* 394–398.

Tanaka, J. W., & Curran, T. (2001). A neural basis for expert object recognition. *Psychological Science, 12,* 43–47.

Tanaka, J. W., & Farah, M. J. (1993). Parts and wholes in face recognition. *Quarterly Journal of Experimental Psychology: A Human Experimental Psychology, 46,* 225–245.

Tanaka, J. W., & Farah, M. (2003). Holistic face recognition. In M. Peterson & G. Rhodes (Eds.), *Analytic and holistic processes in the perception of faces, objects and scenes* (Vol. 2, pp. 53–74). New York: Oxford University Press.

Thompson, J. C., Hardee, J. E., Panayiotou, A., Crewther, D., & Puce, A. (2007). Common and distinct brain activation to viewing dynamic sequences of face and hand movements. *NeuroImage, 37,* 966–973.

Tong, F., Nakayama, K., Moscovitch, M., Weinrib, O., & Kanwisher, N. (2000). Response properties of the human fusiform face area. *Cognitive Neuropsychology, 17*(1/3), 257–279.

Tong, F., Nakayama, K., Vaughan, J. T., & Kanwisher, N. (1998). Binocular rivalry and visual awareness in human extrastriate cortex. *Neuron, 21,* 753–759.

Tsao, D. Y., Freiwald, W. A., Knutsen, T. A., Mandeville, J. B., & Tootell, R. B. (2003). Faces and objects in macaque cerebral cortex. *Nature Neuroscience, 6,* 989–995.

Tsao, D. Y., Freiwald, W. A., Tootell, R. B., & Livingstone, M. S. (2006, February 3). A cortical region consisting entirely of face-selective cells. *Science, 311,* 670–674.

Tsao, D. Y., & Livingstone, M. S. (2008). Mechanisms of face perception. *Annual Review of Neuroscience, 31,* 411–437.

Turk, D. J., Rosenblum, A. C., Gazzaniga, M. S., & Macrae, C. N. (2005). Seeing John Malkovich: The neural substrates of person categorization. *NeuroImage, 24,* 1147–1153.

Vuilleumier, P., Armony, J. L., Driver, J., & Dolan, R. J. (2001). Effects of attention and emotion on face processing in the human brain: An event-related fMRI study. *Neuron, 30,* 829–841.

Vuilleumier, P., Armony, J. L., Driver, J., & Dolan, R. J. (2003). Distinct spatial frequency sensitivities for processing faces and emotional expressions. *Nature Neuroscience, 6,* 624–631.

Wada, Y., & Yamamoto, T. (2001). Selective impairment of facial recognition due to a haematoma restricted to the right fusiform and lateral occipital region. *Journal of Neurology, Neurosurgery, and Psychiatry, 71,* 254–257.

Warrington, E. K., Logue, V., & Pratt, R. T. C. (1971). The anatomical localisation of selective impairment of auditory-verbal short-term memory. *Neuropsychologia, 9,* 377–387.

Williams, M. A., Moss, S. A., & Bradshaw, J. L. (2004). A unique look at face processing: The impact of masked faces on the processing of facial features. *Cognition, 91,* 155–172.

Winston, J. S., Vuilleumier, P., & Dolan, R. J. (2003). Effects of low-spatial frequency components of fearful faces on fusiform cortex activity. *Current Biology, 13,* 1824–1829.

Wiser, A. K., Andreasen, N., O'Leary, D. S., Crespo-Facorro, B., Boles-Ponto, L. L., Watkins, G. L., et al. (2000). Novel vs. well-learned memory for faces: A positron emission tomography study. *Journal of Cognitive Neuroscience, 12,* 255–266.

Xu, Y. (2005). Revisiting the role of the fusiform face area in visual expertise. *Cerebral Cortex, 15,* 1234–1242.

Yin, R. (1969). Looking at upside down faces. *Journal of Experimental Psychology, 81,* 141–145.

Young, A. W., Hellawell, D., & Hay, D. C. (1987). Configurational information in face perception. *Perception, 16,* 747–759.

Yovel, G., & Kanwisher, N. (2004). Face perception domain specific, not process specific. *Neuron, 44,* 889–898.

Yovel, G., & Kanwisher, N. (2005). The neural basis of the behavioral face-inversion effect. *Current Biology, 15,* 2256–2262.

Yovel, G., & Kanwisher, N. (2008) The representations of spacing and part-based information are associated for upright faces but dissociated for objects: Evidence from individual differences. *Psychonomics Bulletin and Review, 15,* 933–939.

Yovel, G., Paller, K. A., & Levy, J. (2005). A whole face is more than the sum of its halves: Interactive processing in face perception. *Visual Cognition, 12,* 337–352.

Yovel, G., Tambini, A., & Brandman, T. (2008) The asymmetry of the fusiform face area is a stable individual characteristic which underlies the left visual field superiority for faces. *Neuropsychologia, 46,* 3061–3068.

Yue, X., Tjan, B. S., & Biederman, I. (2006). What makes faces special? *Vision Research, 46,* 3802–3811.

Zangenehpour, S., & Chaudhuri, A. (2005). Patchy organization and asymmetric distribution of the neural correlates of face processing in monkey inferotemporal cortex. *Current Biology, 15,* 993–1005.

Chapter 44

Self versus Others/Self-Regulation

ANNE C. KRENDL AND TODD F. HEATHERTON

Humans are fundamentally social beings. Collectively, we crave social interactions and actively seek them out whenever possible (Baumeister & Leary, 1995). In fact, social interactions are so vital to our physical and mental well-being that being without them has grave consequences. For instance, social isolation can lead to severe depression and loneliness (Rubin & Mills, 1988) and is a major risk factor for mortality (Cacioppo, Hughes, Waite, Hawkley, & Thisted, 2006; House, Landis, & Umberso, 1988).

As humans, we expend a great deal of energy on maintaining and promulgating our social groups. Many of the most popular modern technological advances serve the sole purpose of increasing the quantity of our social interactions. For instance, there has been an unprecedented increase in chat rooms, online gaming, and virtual reality worlds that center around promoting social interactions on the Internet. Meanwhile, increasing obsessions with personal digital assistants, e-mail, text messaging, and cell phones allow us to maintain constant social contact at all times, no matter where we are physically located.

Arguably, a primary cause for the amount of effort we exert on maintaining social interactions stems from the fact that human social interactions are remarkably complex. Determining when someone might have a crush on you, when your friends are no longer your friends, and the best time to ask your boss for a raise each involves highly developed levels of social awareness. Understanding the social rules required to successfully navigate through these myriad social interactions requires complex levels of cognitive processing. It is therefore not surprising that the brain has developed an intricate system of neural networks to support and facilitate social interactions. In this chapter,

we describe the fundamental psychological components necessary for social behavior and we review what is currently known regarding known neural correlates. Before we begin our review, it is important to emphasize that the social brain is not located in one discrete location in the brain. Rather, it is comprised of multiple systems throughout the brain. Although we describe each of these systems separately, we do so with the following two caveats: First, each of the subcomponents of the social brain serve multiple functions, many of them overlapping; second, these subcomponents work together to give rise to the social brain as a whole. As we argue in this chapter, damage to any one system leads to profound social deficits. We begin by describing the theoretical basis of our model and then discuss relevant research.

THE SOCIAL BRAIN

Our overall approach follows a social brain sciences perspective that merges evolutionary theory, experimental social cognition, and neuroscience to elucidate the neural mechanisms that support social behavior (Adolphs, 2003; Heatherton, Macrae, & Kelley, 2004). Initial findings using neuroimaging have shown that unique neural substrates are associated with processing social information as compared to general semantic knowledge. For instance, Mitchell, Heatherton, and Macrae (2002) showed that when participants make semantic judgments about words that could either describe a person (e.g., assertive, fickle) or an object such as fruit (e.g., sundried, seedless), two separate networks were engaged. One system was activated when participants made judgments about objects (e.g., left inferior prefrontal cortex and left posterior parietal cortex), and a separate network was engaged when they made judgments about people (e.g., left temporal sulcus, medial prefrontal cortex, and fusiform gyrus; Figure 44.1). Similarly, Mason, Banfield, and Macrae (2004) found that when participants made judgments about whether an action (e.g., running,

The work described in this chapter was supported by an NSF Graduate Fellowship to ACK and NIMH 59282, NIDA 022582 and NSF BCS 0354400 to TH. We acknowledge our group members of the Dartmouth Center for Social Brain Sciences as collaborators on much of the research described.

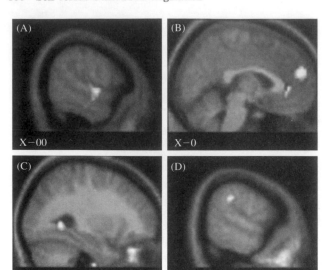

Figure 44.1 Activation maps show brain areas to be more active during person trials than during object trials.

Note: Regions of modulation included **A:** the left temporal sulcus **B:** the dorsal and ventral mPFC **C:** the right fusiform gyrus, and **D:** the right parietal temporal occipital junction.

sitting, or biting) could be performed by a person or a dog, they showed dissociable patterns of neural activation. When making judgments about people, participants revealed a distinct pattern of activation in the prefrontal cortex (e.g., right middle frontal gyrus and medial prefrontal cortex) as compared to when they made judgments about dogs (e.g., occipital and parahippocampal gyri). There are countless other examples of discrete neural networks being recruited to process social as compared to nonsocial information, several of which we explore in more detail throughout this chapter.

From an evolutionary perspective, the brain is an organ that has evolved over millions of years to solve problems related to survival and reproduction. Those ancestors who were able to solve survival problems and adapt to their environments were most likely to reproduce and pass along their genes. Whether certain aspects of the social brain (i.e., a sense of self) truly are adaptive is open to some debate (Leary, 2005), although there is ample evidence that the ability to engage in social interactions provided considerable advantages over the course of evolution, such as facilitating communication and cooperation with group members (Sedikides & Skowronski, 1997). From the social brain sciences perspective, just as there are dedicated brain mechanisms for breathing, walking, and talking, the brain has evolved specialized mechanisms for processing information about the social world. It is important to emphasize here that we are not suggesting that there is a specific "social" module or region of the brain. Rather, psychological processes are distributed throughout the brain, with contributions from multiple subcomponents

determining discrete mental activities that come together to support the social brain (Turk, Heatherton, Macrae, Kelley, & Gazzaniga, 2003). Various cognitive, sensory, motor, somatosensory, and affective processes are essential to the successful navigation of social interactions, and these processes reflect the contribution of several cortical and subcortical regions.

Much of our approach relies on the idea that humans have evolved a fundamental need to belong, which encourages behavior that prevents people from being evicted from their social groups (Baumeister & Leary, 1995; Bowlby, 1969). According to the need-to-belong theory, the need for interpersonal attachments is a fundamental motive that has evolved for adaptive purposes. Over the course of human evolution, those who lived with others were more likely to survive and pass along their genes. Adults who were capable of developing long-term committed relationships were more likely to reproduce and also more likely to have their offspring survive to reproduce. Effective groups shared food, provided mates, and helped care for offspring. As such, human survival has long depended on living within groups; banishment from the group was effectively a death sentence. Baumeister and Leary (1995) argued that the need to belong is a basic motive that activates behavior and influences cognition and emotion, and that it leads to ill effects when not satisfied. Even today not belonging to a group increases a person's risk for a number of adverse consequences, such as illnesses and premature death (see Cacioppo et al., 2000, 2006).

In essence, the social brain allows individuals to operate as effective group members, which allows them to maintain their status within the group as well as cooperate with other group members in service of the group's survival needs. Such a system requires four components, each of which is likely to have a discrete neural signature. First, people need self-awareness—to be aware of their behavior so as to gauge it against societal or group norms. Both the psychologist William James and the sociologist George Herbert Mead differentiated between the self as the knower ("I") and the self as the object that is known ("me"). In the sense of the knower, the self is the subject doing the thinking, feeling, and acting, which we will consider later as part of the executive self. In the sense of the objectified self, the self consists of the knowledge that people hold about themselves, as when they contemplate their best and worst qualities. The experience of self as the object of attention is the psychological state known as self-awareness, which allows people to reflect on their actions and understand the extent to which those actions match both personal values and beliefs as well as group standards. For instance, people who violate societal rules (i.e., by using more than their fair share of resources by cheating their group mates) tend to feel ashamed of their behavior.

In order to experience social emotions, such as shame, people need to understand how people are reacting to their behavior so as to predict how others will respond to them (Heatherton & Krendl, 2007). In other words, they need the capacity to attribute mental states to others so that they are able to accurately interpret the beliefs and emotional states of those individuals. For instance, to feel guilty about hurting a loved one, people need to understand that other people have feelings. All social emotions related to empathy require the capacity to attribute specific mental states to others (Heatherton & Krendl, 2007). Similarly, feeling shy is the belief that one is being evaluated by others (thereby giving rise to emotions such as embarrassment), which at its core means recognizing that other people make evaluative judgments. The ability to infer the mental states of others is commonly referred to as mentalizing, or having the capacity for theory of mind (ToM). ToM enables the ability to empathize and cooperate with others, interpret other people's behavior, and even deceive others when necessary. This capacity is vital to ensure that people understand how others are viewing them in the group.

One value of having ToM is that it supports a third mechanism—threat detection—especially in complex situations. If humans have a fundamental need to belong, then there ought to be mechanisms for detecting inclusionary status (Leary, Tambor, Terdal, & Downs, 1995; Macdonald & Leary, 2005). Put another way, given the importance of group inclusion, humans need to be sensitive to signs that the group might exclude them. There is evidence that people feel anxious when they face exclusion from their social groups. Thus, feeling socially anxious or worrying about potential rejection should lead to heightened social sensitivity. Research has demonstrated that people who worry most about social evaluation (i.e., the shy and lonely) show enhanced memory for social information, are more empathetically accurate, and show heightened abilities to decode social information (Gardner, Pickett, & Brewer, 2000; Gardner, Pickett, Jefferis, & Knowles, 2005; Pickett, Gardner, & Knowles, 2004).

Not all threats, however, are related to social exclusion. Just as people naturally fear dangerous animals (i.e., poisonous snakes and spiders, tigers, and wolves), they also fear (and encounter) harm from other humans. Other group members can transmit disease, act carelessly to place bystanders at risk, waste or steal vital group resources, or poach one's mate. Similarly, people from other groups also can be dangerous; over the course of human evolution, competition between small groups over scarce resources led to intergroup violence. Hence, there is also a need for mechanisms that detect threats from people from other groups. We argue that threatening people are accorded a special status that identifies them as potentially burdensome or dangerous—they are stigmatized. Thus, as research in social psychology has documented, humans quickly and efficiently categorize others based on information that is evolutionarily meaningful (Macrae & Bodenhausen, 2000).

Finally, there needs to be a mechanism for resolving discrepancies between self-knowledge and social expectations or norms, thereby motivating behavior to resolve any conflict that exists. This executive aspect of self (the "I" as knower) is responsible for ensuring that behaviors that might lead one to be expelled from the group are discouraged and, conversely, that behaviors that promote harmonious social relations within the group are encouraged. The control of one's own behavior is known as *self-regulation,* which is the process by which people change themselves, including their thoughts, their emotions and moods, their impulsive acts, and their performance at school or work. Although people can delay gratification, control appetites and impulses, and persevere in order to attain goals, many people have difficulties with self-regulation from time to time. Failures of self-regulation are implicated in most of the major problems of contemporary society, including addiction, obesity, risky sex, drunk driving, alcohol abuse, excessive gambling, spiraling consumer debt, marital infidelity, impulsive crimes, and school violence. Many of these behaviors threaten group inclusion; accordingly, understanding their neural basis is of considerable importance.

We do not contend that other psychological processes are unimportant for social functioning. Capacities such as language, memory, vision, along with motivational and basic emotional states, are generally important for functioning within the social group. However, they are not necessary for a person to be a good group member; the blind and deaf can contribute substantially to their groups. By contrast, people with fundamental disturbances in the primary components of self, ToM, threat detection, or self-regulation have fundamental and often specific impairments in social function. The literature is replete with case studies of individuals with brain injuries who suffer social impairments while having other capacities intact (e.g., Phineas Gage). Likewise, individuals with a disturbed sense of self often have interpersonal problems (Stuss & Alexander, 1994): Those who have difficulties with ToM (i.e., autistics) or impoverished empathy (i.e., psychopaths) are socially impaired, and those who fail to regulate their behavior are often ostracized and even imprisoned. Although space limitations preclude a theory discussion of social impairments, our contention is that many of them are due to fundamental problems with one of the core processes we have identified.

Thus, according to our model, the brain has evolved distinct mechanisms for knowing ourselves (self-awareness), knowing how others respond to us (which requires theory of mind), detecting threats from within our social group and beyond, and regulating our actions in order to avoid being ejected from our social groups. Together, these abilities form the foundation of the social brain. In the next few sections, we consider how neuroimaging can elucidate each of these discrete processes.

Self-Reflection and Awareness

The concept of self forms the foundation of the social brain. The self-concept consists of all that we know about ourselves, including things such as name, race, likes, dislikes, beliefs, values, and even whether we possess certain personality traits. According to Baumeister (1998), "the capacity of the human organism to be conscious of itself is a distinguishing feature and is vital to selfhood" (p. 683). Given that self-knowledge plays a critical role in understanding who we are, researchers have long debated whether the brain gives privileged status to information that is self-relevant or alternatively if information processed about the self is treated in the same manner as any other type of information (Bower & Gilligan, 1979; Klein & Kihlstrom, 1986; Klein & Loftus, 1988; Maki & McCaul, 1985; Markus, 1977; Rogers, Kuiper, & Kirker, 1977). This is the key issue underlying the question of whether self is "special" in any meaningful way. Gillihan and Farah (2005) argue that the majority of the patient and neuroimaging research does not provide sufficient support to conclude that self-relevant information is processed in any "special" way. In this section, we explore several studies that argue that self-relevant information is given a unique and "special" status in the brain.

Perhaps one of the most striking examples of the uniqueness of self is reflected in the self-relevant memory enhancement effect. A seminal study by Timothy Rogers and colleagues (1977) found a memory advantage for information encoded with reference to self. They found that asking people to make personal judgments on trait adjectives (e.g., "Are you mean?") produced significantly improved memory for the words than if the participants were asked to make semantic judgments (e.g., "Define the word mean"). This self-reference memory enhancement effect has been observed in many contexts, such as when people remember information processed with reference to self better than information processed with reference to other people (Symons & Johnson, 1997). The overall picture that emerges is that self-relevant information is especially memorable. Even people who can remember very little can often remember information that is self-relevant. For

instance, patients who suffer from severe amnesia (resulting from brain injury, developmental disorders, or Alzheimer's disease) retain the ability to accurately describe whether specific traits are true of the self (Klein, 2004). Klein provides the example of patient K.C., who showed a preserved ability to accurately identify his "new" personality traits after becoming profoundly amnesic and undergoing a radical personality change following a motorcycle accident (Tulving, 1993). Even patients with Alzheimer's disease who suffer severe temporal disorientation and have difficulty recognizing their own family have shown evidence of self-knowledge. Patient K.R., for instance, suffered from profound Alzheimer's disease, yet she was still able to identify self-relevant personality traits accurately (Klein, Cosmides, & Costabile, 2003). But why is information about the self particularly memorable?

During the 1980s, research in social cognition examined the self-reference superiority effect in memory. Although it was undeniable that memory was better for self-relevant information, it was widely debated whether self-relevant information was supported by discrete cognitive systems (Rogers, Kuiper, & Kirker, 1977), or if superior memory could occur simply because people had greater knowledge about the self, which in turn could produce more elaborate encoding and, hence, better memory (Greenwald & Banaji, 1989; Klein & Kihlstrom, 1986). Neuroimaging techniques are exceptionally positioned to resolve the debate regarding the self-reference effect in memory. The first group to use brain imaging to examine this question was Fergus Craik and his colleagues at the University of Toronto. Using positron emission tomography (PET), Craik et al. (1999) examined brain activity while participants rated personality traits for the self or for a familiar other (in this case, the Canadian Prime Minister). These researchers did not replicate the self-relevant memory enhancement effect, but they did observe distinct activations for self-referential material in frontal regions, notably medial prefrontal cortex (mPFC) and areas of the right prefrontal cortex.

Using rapid event-related functional magnetic resonance imaging (fMRI), we asked participants to judge 270 trait adjectives in one of three ways: self ("Does the trait describe you?"); other ("Does the trait describe George Bush?"); and case ("Is the trait presented in uppercase letters?"; Kelley et al., 2002). The expected self-relevant enhancement effect was observed in this study, and a direct comparison of "self" trials to "other" trials revealed heightened activation in a number of different brain regions, most notably the mPFC (Figure 44.2). We conducted a subsequent study that showed that mPFC activity during the encoding of self-relevant words later predicted memory for these words (i.e., the greater the mPFC activity during the encoding of each item, the more likely that item was to be remembered;

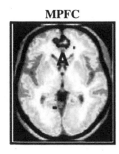

MPFC

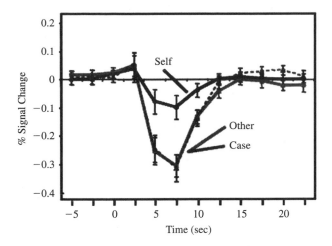

Figure 44.2 Statistical activation maps comparing self and other trials demonstrated greater activity during self-encoding trials in the mPFC.

Note: Displayed at the left is the axial through the activation foci averaged across participants. The left side of the image corresponds to the left side of the brain. Time courses (right panel) were computed for each condition within a 3-D region surrounding the peak voxel identified all contiguous voxels within the 10 mm of the peak that reached the significance level ($p < .0001$). Bars indicate standard error of the mean (SEM). Activity in the mPFC was uniquely sensitive to self-encoding trials.

Macrae, Moran, Heatherton, Banfield, & Kelley, 2004). Thus, we were able to demonstrate that mPFC contributes to the formation of self-relevant memories. This supports our contention that self-referential processing is functionally dissociable from general semantic processing. In other words, the brain has discrete neural substrates that give rise to the self.

The extent to which we include others in our self-concept has been a topic of particular interest for social psychologists. Theories of intimacy and personal relationships might suggest that the self-reference effect is affected by the closeness of a relationship with the other used as a target. Aron and colleagues define closeness as the extension of self into other and suggest that one's cognitive processes about a close other develop in a way so as to include that person as part of the self (Aron & Aron, 1996; Aron, Aron, Tudor, & Nelson, 1991; Aron & Fraley, 1999). Consistent with this idea, the memorial advantage afforded to self-referenced material can be diminished or eliminated when the comparison target is an intimate other such as a parent, friend, or spouse (Bower & Gilligan, 1979; Keenan & Baillet, 1980).

To address this question, we conducted a study nearly identical to the Kelley et al. (2002) method, but this time we had people make judgments for their best friend rather than for George Bush (Heatherton et al., 2006). Although differences in recognition memory performance for self and intimate other judgments were modest, neural response differences in the mPFC were robust, with self showing much greater activity in mPFC than for best friend or case judgments, which did not differ from one another. These results indicate an mPFC response that is self-specific; that is, in the brain, judgments pertaining to the self were distinct from those made for friends.

Our findings diverge from others that have been reported in which mPFC activity was similar for self and intimate others (Ochsner et al., 2005; Schmitz, Kawahara-Baccus, & Johnson, 2004; Seger, Stone, & Keenan, 2004). Two methodological issues may account for this discrepancy. First, the three previous studies used block designs with fairly long intertrial intervals, whereas our study used an event-related design; the former may obscure single-trial events because brain activity is averaged across the entire block. It is possible that participants engaged in self-reflection between trials within the blocks, thereby mixing self-referential processing with judgments about the intimate others (e.g., such as recalling episodes in which the person acted in accordance with the trait during an interaction with the subject). We also used an unusually large number of research participants ($N = 30$) and therefore we had the power to detect differences between self and other; the finding of no difference between self and other in the previous studies might be due to power issues. Further research is necessary to resolve the importance of these methodological factors.

Considered together, the findings from our three studies support the idea that mPFC is involved in self-referential processing, and that the actions of this region support greater memory for material encoded with reference to self. These findings are also consistent with those obtained by other researchers (Gusnard, 2005). For instance, Gusnard, Akbudak, Shulman, and Raichle (2001) used a blocked-design fMRI paradigm to examine judgments about affectively normed pictures and observed mPFC activity that was preferentially associated with self-referential judgments. Johnson et al. (2002) asked participants to respond to a series of questions that demanded access to either personal knowledge (e.g., "I have a quick temper") or general semantic knowledge (e.g., "Ten seconds is more than a minute"). Their results revealed that self-reflective thought was accompanied by activity in anterior regions of mPFC. Cabeza et al. (2004) found heightened mPFC activation for episodic memory retrieval of autobiographical events. In the study, participants were presented with photographs that either they had taken around campus, or that someone else had taken. The participants showed heightened mPFC activity for photographs they themselves had taken. More recently, Mitchell, Banaji, and Macrae (2005) showed participants a series of faces and asked them to judge physical (i.e., how symmetrical the face appeared) or mental features (i.e., how pleased the people were to have their photographs taken). They found that the activity in mPFC was correlated with the extent to which participants judged the people in the photographs to be similar to them, but only for the mentalizing task.

The mPFC has also been implicated in autobiographical memory, an important component of self-awareness. Knowing yourself requires remembering events unique to your own past experiences. These memories play a large role in your understanding of who you are. Steinvorth, Corkin, and Halgren (2006) asked participants to recall past autobiographical memories (e.g., "A birthday party: Who spilled wine on your pants?") as well as semantic memories (e.g., "A cartoon figure: What is the color of the fur on Garfield?"). They found that participants engaged mPFC when recalling autobiographical memories, but not for semantic memories. Further, Addis, Wong, and Schacter (2006) found that ruminating on future biographical events (i.e., "Imagine your future child") also elicited activation in the mPFC.

Thus, the imaging literature is quite clear regarding tasks that involve self-reflection; they activate mPFC (Gusnard, 2005). The view that mPFC plays a prominent role in self-referential processing is also supported by neuropsychological evidence of patients with frontal lobe injuries (Feinberg & Keenan, 2005; Stuss & Benson, 1984; Wheeler, Stuss, & Tulving, 1997). However, this is not to suggest that the mPFC is the only neural region that selectively responds to self-relevant information. For instance, Northoff and Bermpohl (2004) suggest that the parietal cortex is vital to understanding the location of self in space (Vogeley & Fink, 2003) and the orbitomedial prefrontal cortex tags incoming information as self-relevant so it can be processed by the appropriate system (see also Schore, 2003). The mPFC, however, plays an important role in

self-awareness and extensive literature has consistently implicated this region as being particularly important to processing self-relevant information.

Emerging evidence suggests that the same areas implicated in processing self-relevant information also appear to be tonically active when the brain is "at rest"; that is, not performing a cognitive task (Raichle et al., 2001). This so-called "default state" includes the same network of regions observed when participants perform self-relevant processing tasks—mPFC, precuneus, and posterior cingulate (Gusnard et al., 2001). This finding has led to the supposition that when people are "doing nothing," the default state of the brain is to self-reflect (Gusnard et al., 2001; Kelley et al., 2002; Mason, Norton, Van Horn, Wegner, Grafton, & Macrae, 2007).

The converging evidence the studies described in this section suggests that mPFC plays a critical role in the social brain by giving rise to the execution and storage of self-relevant information. Self-awareness provides the ability us with the necessary information to understand our own social goals in the world. This necessitates being able to take the perspective of another. In the next section, we review the findings from emerging neuroimaging research attempting to isolate the neural mechanisms engaged in theory of mind.

Theory of Mind

The social brain requires more than just being aware of our own mental states and feelings. A vital component of the social brain is the ability to recognize the mental states of others so we can engage in deception, empathize and cooperate with others, and accurately interpret other people's behavior (Gallagher & Frith, 2003). Our ability to infer the mental states of others is commonly referred to as theory of mind (ToM). The extent to which ToM is a uniquely human trait is highly contentious, and evidence on this point is mixed.

Primitive forms of apparent mentalizing have been recorded in the animal literature, but it is widely debated whether these studies demonstrate ToM or just learned behavior (for review, see Seyfarth & Cheney, 2003). For instance, research with baboons has shown that if a dominant female grunts to a subordinate following aggression, the subordinate's behavior immediately changes (Cheney & Seyfarth, 1997). Based on this observation, the authors posit two possible explanations: First, the subordinate has recognized a change in the dominant's attitude toward her (e.g., the dominant is trying to make the subordinate feel less anxious), so the subordinate baboon changes her behavior accordingly (an explanation that necessitates ToM). The second possible explanation for this behavioral change is that it simply reflects a learned behavior—the subordinate baboon has learned through experience that this type of grunt typically leads to reduced aggression (an explanation that does not require ToM).

Of the extant animal literature, the most compelling evidence for ToM has been observed in chimpanzees (for review, see Seyfarth & Cheney, 2003). Unlike other non-human primates, chimpanzees are able to recognize intentional gestures such as pointing. Povinelli, Nelson, and Boysen (1990) found that when chimpanzees were given clues by two different experimenters as to where food was hidden, they would follow the hints of the experimenter whom they had observed hide the food, instead of the clues provided by the second experimenter who had waited outside the room while the food was hidden. The authors argued that the chimpanzees' ability to correctly determine that the person they had seen hide the food would know its true location is clear evidence that the chimpanzees possess ToM. Additionally, chimpanzees follow the gaze of a human or other group member to a specific location, an action that, when observed in children, is believed to be evidence of ToM (Tomasello, Hare, & Agnetta, 1999). However, not all research with chimpanzees points to evidence that they have acquired ToM. Chimpanzees exhibit no preference between begging an experimenter who could plainly see them for food, or begging another experimenter whose face or eyes were covered, and therefore could not see them (Povinelli & Eddy, 1996).

Emerging research on ToM in humans has sought to identify the neural correlates that are selectively engaged during mentalizing tasks. These studies have consistently implicated a network of brain areas, including mPFC, posterior cingulate, and tempero-parietal junction, as the central components of ToM. Of central interest in this work has been the role of the mPFC in ToM tasks. As discussed in the previous section, the mPFC plays a central role in processing self-relevant information. It is therefore not surprising that the same region that supports our ability to determine our own mental states would be involved in our ability to infer the mental states of others.

Compelling evidence has emerged in the patient literature to support the assertion that the mPFC plays a central role in ToM. For instance, research with people who are either autistic or suffer from Asperger's syndrome (which both have impairments in the ability to mentalize) has revealed that the deficits may result, at least in part, from deficiencies in the mPFC (Gallagher & Frith, 2003). Further, Stuss, Gallup, and Alexander (2001) found that patients with frontal lobe lesions (particularly to the right mPFC) were unable to detect deception, a task requiring ToM.

The advent of PET and fMRI has allowed researchers to examine the neural correlates engaged in ToM tasks in healthy participants. In one of the first attempts to identify brain regions involved in ToM, Fletcher and colleagues (1995) measured neural activity while participants made judgments (based on ToM reasoning) about the motivations of an actor's behavior. For example, participants had to work out that an actor's behavior (giving himself up to the police) was based on his assumption about the policeman's beliefs (the policeman knew he had robbed a shop). Because the policeman's beliefs were not made explicit in the story, mental state attribution (i.e., ToM reasoning) was required to perform the task. These researchers found that these mental state attributions were accompanied by a relative increase in activation in mPFC. Activation in the mPFC has also been observed in ToM paradigms that use pictures that require mental state attribution to be understood (Gallagher et al., 2000).[1]

mPFC activation has been observed even in contrived tasks in which participants are led believe they must infer the mental states of others. Gallagher, Jack, Roepstorff, and Frith (2002) had participants play a game of "rock, paper, scissors" while in the PET scanner. Participants were told during some blocks that they were playing against the experimenter, and in others that they were playing against the computer. In truth, they received randomly generated stimuli from the computer throughout the experiment. However, on trials during which participants believed they were playing the experimenter, they showed robust activation in the mPFC (suggesting they were using ToM to determine how the experimenter might play the next hand), whereas they did not show this activation when they believed they were playing the computer. Similarly, mPFC activation was observed on tasks in which cooperation was required among team members. McCabe, Houser, Ryan, Smith, and Trouard (2001) had participants compete in a trust game with either human or computer partners. The authors found that participants showed heightened activation in mPFC when they were cooperating with a human partner. They argue that such cooperation requires ToM because participants must be able to infer the mental states

---

[1]In several studies described in this chapter, changes in mPFC activity often appear to be decreases in activity from an arbitrary baseline. As discussed earlier in this chapter, mPFC is tonically active when the brain is at rest. In other words, when the brain is engaged in cognitive tasks, mPFC activity appears to decrease relative to resting state (which is measured by the arbitrary baseline) because its most active state occurs at rest (for a more detailed discussion of the default state and mPFC, please see Raichle et al., 2001). Thus, for the sake of clarity, our use the term "activations" in this chapter refers to changes in neural activity that are significantly greater in the experimental than control conditions.

of their partners in order to form mutual expectations of making cooperative choices.

Thus, the mPFC can be engaged when perceivers either are interacting with another human, or simply believe that they are. Further, the extent to which the perceiver can identify with an individual with whom he is interacting may also modulate the extent to which mPFC is engaged. Mitchell, Macrae, and Banaji (2006) had participants who were self-proclaimed liberals and conservatives make judgments about themselves, other liberals, or other conservatives (e.g., "Would this individual enjoy having a roommate from a different country?" "Would this individual drive a small car entirely for environmental reasons?"). The authors found that the activation in the ventral mPFC was greater for judgments made about individuals that participants perceived to be similar to themselves (i.e., participants who were identified as liberals by a measure of implicit political bias showed heightened vmPFC when making judgments about other liberals than when evaluating conservatives), whereas activation was greater in the dorsal mPFC for individuals that participants perceived as being dissimilar to themselves (e.g., liberals evaluating conservatives).

Although the extant literature on ToM has clearly emphasized the role of the mPFC in mentalizing tasks, emerging research has also implicated the tempero-parietal junction (TPJ) in inferring mental states. Saxe and Kanwisher (2003) observed heightened activation in this region when participants read stories that uniquely described the goals or beliefs of an individual (a task that requires ToM), as opposed to when participants read stories that simply described people in physical detail (a task that does not require ToM). In a later study, Saxe and Wexler (2005) had participants make judgments about the mental states of others who either came from similar (familiar) or dissimilar (foreign) backgrounds. In both cases, participants were given a short story about an individual with either a familiar (e.g., Your friend is happily married) or foreign (e.g., Your friend belongs to a cult that promotes extramarital affairs) background. Each story then had a "normal" (e.g., Your friend confided that he hoped his wife never cheated on him) or "norm-violating" (e.g., Your friend confided that he hoped his wife would have a relationship outside of marriage) desire. The authors found that the right TPJ was recruited when perceivers were trying to reconcile incongruent information (e.g., a protagonist from a foreign background who expressed a "normal" mental state), which they argued requires greater mentalizing. The mPFC, however, did not discriminate between stories that would require differing levels of mentalizing. Thus, the authors argue that the right TPJ, not the mPFC, is uniquely engaged in the attribution of mental states.

To further explore the possibly diverging roles of the TPJ and mPFC, Saxe and Powell (2006) gave participants stories that described either the appearance of a person (e.g., "Joe was a heavy-set man, with a gut that fell over his belt. He was balding and combed his blonde hair over the top of his head. His face was pleasant, with large brown eyes"), a bodily sensation (e.g., "Sheila skipped breakfast because she was late for the train to her mother's. By time she got off the train, she was starving. Her stomach was rumbling, and she could smell food everywhere"), or thoughts (e.g., "Nicky knew that his sister's flight from San Francisco was delayed 10 hours. Only one flight was delayed so much that night, so when he got to the airport, he knew that flight was hers"). The authors found that only the TPJ (bilaterally) and posterior cingulate were selectively recruited when participants read stories about a protagonist's thoughts or beliefs (the only task that would require ToM), but not in the other two conditions. They observed similar patterns of mPFC activation in all three conditions. In other words, participants recruited mPFC equally when they were reading any story describing an individual, and not just in conditions in which they were making mental state inferences. The authors therefore argue that the TPJ is uniquely engaged in mentalizing tasks, whereas the mPFC may play a broader role in social processing.

Although the findings suggest that TPJ is involved in mentalizing, its precise role in theory of mind is widely debated. Gobbini, Koralek, Bryan, Montgomery, and Haxby (2007) presented participants with false belief stories and pictures of geometric shapes moving in a socially relevant manner: two tasks that both require mentalizing. They only observed TPJ activation in the story condition, not in the social animation condition. Based on these findings, the authors argue that TPJ may play a role in interpreting "covert mental states" to help predict future behavior, but that it is not involved in interpreting beliefs and actions based on perceived actions. In an attempt to dissociate the recruitment of TPJ from mPFC in theory of mind tasks, Ciaramidaro and colleagues (2007) presented participants with cartoons depicting unique actions with disparate goals: private intentions (i.e., fixing a broken light bulb to read), prospective social intentions (i.e., observing a single person prepare dinner for someone else, reflecting a social intention to engage in a social interaction), and communicative intention (i.e., observing person A obtain a glass of water for person B after being asked to do so). The authors found that the right TPJ was active for all three conditions relative to control scenarios, whereas mPFC was only active for the social intention conditions, and not the private intentions. Importantly, the authors found a functional dissociation within the TPJ in that right TPJ in engaged in processing all intentions, but left TPJ is only engaged in processing discrete social intentions (communicative intentions). Together, these findings suggest that the neural network engaged during theory of mind tasks may be more complex than previously thought.

Although the studies discussed in this section reveal conflicting evidence for identifying the central mechanisms that give rise to ToM, one point remains clear: The brain has a specialized network engaged in mentalizing tasks. This key ingredient to the social brain allows us to engage in complex social interactions involving cooperation, deception, and empathy. ToM provides us a specialized tool by which to detect threats from within our social group. For instance, the ability to understand when you have committed a social error, and then determine how to overcome that social error, requires ToM. Successfully detecting threats from the environment—both from within the social group and beyond—is an important aspect of the social brain. We explore the unique mechanisms dedicated to threat detection in the next section.

Threat Detection

An important aspect of the social brain is the ability to detect threats in the environment. These threats can be threats to our physical self (i.e., quickly detecting when a predator is pursuing us or recognizing individuals who may threaten our social group or resources) or they may be threats to our psychological self (i.e., threats that affect our status within our social group via social rejection or social exclusion). It is apparent that the brain has developed an efficient system to respond to threats from the environment. For instance, the superior temporal sulcus is uniquely sensitive to detecting biological motion (i.e., movement of the eyes, mouth, hands, and body; Allison, Puce, & McCarthy, 2000; Grezes et al., 2001). However, the amygdala is central to this threat detection system (for review, see Whalen, 1998). The amygdala automatically detects potentially aversive stimuli in the environment, sometimes causing us to jump away from an object that resembles a threat (i.e., a curved branch in the forest that we mistake for a snake) even without knowing what it is.

Research with nonhuman primates has shown that amygdala lesions impair appropriate fear responses to novel stimuli (Amaral, 2002). For instance, Amaral showed that primates with amygdala lesions approach and play with a toy snake, while primates with intact amygdala cower from the toy. Evidence from patient research with humans suggests that the amygdala damage impairs patients' ability to accurately identify the arousal associated with negative stimuli. Intriguingly, however, patients with amygdala damage are able to accurately identify the valence of positive and negative stimuli (Bernston, Bechara, Damasio, Tranel, & Cacioppo, 2007).

The amygdala may also play an important role in social threats. The amygdala shows heightened activation in response to fearful faces (Whalen, 1998). Research has shown that people are remarkably adept at recognizing fearful faces (Schubo, Gendolla, Meinecke, & Abele, 2006), and this ability is pervasive over the life span (Mather & Knight, 2006). Chiu, Ambady, and Deldin (2004) demonstrated that high-prejudiced White individuals more quickly evaluated angry Black faces as compared to happy Black faces. In other words, high-prejudice participants in this study could more quickly detect and evaluate an outgroup member when that individual conveyed threat (i.e., via an angry facial expression). Norris, Chen, Zhu, Small, and Cacioppo (2004) demonstrated that images with social and emotional content have an additive effect on the amygdala. They showed participants images that contained (a) social information only, (b) emotional information only, and (c) social and emotional information together along with neutral controls. They found the amygdala activation was significantly stronger in response to the pictures that conveyed both social and emotional information as compared to all other conditions. A similar finding emerged from a study by Ito and Cacioppo (2000) using event-related potentials. They found that negative images with social information (e.g., negative pictures that included people) received heightened processing as compared to images that were void of social information. Together these findings suggest that negative social information elicits heightened neural activation as compared to negative nonsocial information, particularly in the amygdala.

Given the important role of the amygdala in detecting threats in the environment, it is not surprising that the amygdala also is largely involved in our ability to detect social threats. Emerging research on threat detection from outgroup members has focused primarily on the role of the amygdala in automatically detecting threats from the environment (for review, see Eberhardt, 2005). We next explore these findings in more detail.

Threats from Outgroups

There is a ubiquitous tendency among humans to stigmatize outgroup members (Kurzban & Leary, 2001). Stigma refers to an attribute that renders individuals "devalued, spoiled or flawed in the eyes of others" (Crocker, Major, & Steele, 1998). Broadly defined, common stigmas include people of different races, people who are physically disabled (e.g., paraplegics), or people with mental disabilities (i.e., schizophrenics; Goffman, 1963). Extensive research has revealed that stigmas automatically elicit powerful and often negative responses from perceivers (for review, see Crocker et al., 1998).

Kurzban and Leary (2001) argued that outgroup members are stigmatized as a way of helping social groups protect themselves from outside threats. Emerging neuroscience research has focused primarily on the stigma of race and has revealed that the amygdala plays a central role in perceiving other races (Cunningham et al., 2004; Hart et al., 2000; Lieberman, Hariri, Jarcho, Eisenberger, & Bookheimer, 2005; Phelps et al., 2000; Richeson et al., 2003). However, it remains an open question what role the amygdala is playing in perceiving outgroup members. Specifically, is the amygdala responding because we experience negative emotions upon seeing outgroup members, or is the amygdala simply responding to the novelty of the outgroup member?

Phelps and colleagues (2000) found a strong positive correlation between heightened amygdala activation of White participants to their anti-Black bias (as measured by the Implicit Association Test; Greenwald, McGhee, & Schwartz, 1998), which may suggest that the amygdala's role in perceiving race is more emotion based. Conversely, Hart and colleagues (2000) demonstrated the amygdala activation of White participants habituated to the presentation of White, but not Black, faces over time, suggesting that the amygdala simply responds to the novelty of the social stimulus. Further suggesting a more subtle role of the amygdala in processing outgroup members, Wheeler and Fiske (2005) found that the types of judgments that participants make about faces affects amygdala activity. For instance, when White participants were asked to evaluate Black faces, amygdala activity was observed only when the target was socially categorized (e.g., "Is this individual over 21 years old?"), and not when participants were asked to individuate the target ("Would this individual like this vegetable?").

The amygdala is only one of several neural areas engaged during the evaluation of an outgroup member. Emerging research from neuroimaging has revealed that areas of the prefrontal cortex involved in cognitive control are also engaged in these tasks. For instance, Cunningham and colleagues (2004) showed that the amygdala responded to pictures of Black faces when presented very quickly (30 ms). However, when the faces were presented longer (525 ms), the amygdala response was dampened, and instead increased activation was observed in the prefrontal cortex. The authors argue that the heightened activation in the prefrontal cortex may have been inhibiting the automatic response elicited by the amygdala.

Richeson and colleagues (2003) also found that White participants engage prefrontal control mechanisms (i.e., dorsolateral prefrontal cortex and anterior cingulate cortex) in response to viewing Black faces (Figure 44.3). However, they found that the activation of these areas was positively correlated with anti-Black bias. In other words, they found that White individuals with greater anti-Black bias recruit some of these cognitive control areas to a greater extent than White individuals with less anti-Black bias. They argue that this heightened activation results from the higher bias Whites' attempts to mask their prejudice (see also Richeson & Shelton, 2003).

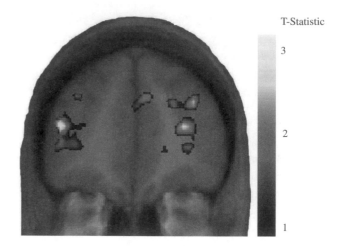

Figure 44.3 Statistical activation maps of Black faces versus White faces contrast, showing regions in right and left middle frontal gyri, as well as right anterior cingulate cortex.

Neuroscience research on nonrace stigmas is scant, but two studies examine the neural mechanisms engaged in perceiving nonrace stigmas (Harris & Fiske, 2006; Krendl, Macrae, Kelley, Fugelsang, & Heatherton, 2006). Krendl and colleagues (2006) examined the neural mechanisms engaged during explicit (conscious) and implicit (unconscious) evaluations of socially stigmatized individuals (e.g., people who are unattractive or who have numerous facial piercings). We demonstrated that individuals also engaged inhibitory mechanisms in response to viewing socially stigmatized targets, even when the perceivers were unaware that they were evaluating the targets. We also showed that stigmas that were explicitly rated as being more aversive elicited heightened amygdala response (Figure 44.4).

Harris and Fiske (2006) examined nonrace stigmas from the perspective of mentalizing. Specifically, they sought to identify whether activation in the medial prefrontal cortex (mPFC) is modulated by the type of stigma group being evaluated. They found that the mPFC was less active than when participants evaluated "extreme outgroup members" (homeless people, drug addicts) as compared to other stigmatized groups (e.g., older adults, disabled people). However, in a subsequent study, they found that the activity of mPFC was further modulated by the type of judgment individuals made about the stigmatized individuals (Harris & Fiske, 2007). For instance, making judgments about whether individuals would like certain vegetables elicited heightened mPFC activity in response to both extreme outgroup members and other stigmatized individuals as compared to making age judgments about the individuals.

Considered as a whole, these results revealed two important points: (1) outgroup members appear to automatically activate aversive responses in perceivers, particular when the perceiver is high in prejudice; and (2) perceivers

(A)

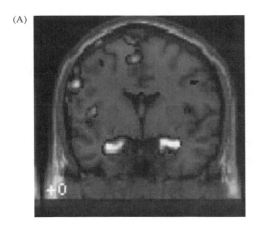

(B)

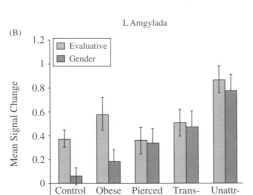

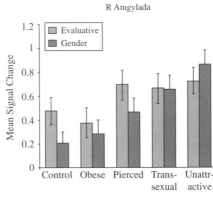

Figure 44.4 Parametric modulation of disgust ratings: Analysis conducted with individual disgust ratings modeled linearly as a covariate of interest.

Note: **A:** Coronal slice at the 0 point on the *z*-axis shows robust activity in the bilateral amygdala (L: –18, –4, –17; R: 18, –4, –17) and left insula (BA 13: –42, –3, 9). **B:** Plots show change in signal amplitude across conditions relative to a baseline control condition (fixating a cross-hair). Error bars indicate SEM. Left amygdala (left panel) demonstrated sensitivity to highly negative stigmas as compared to controls in the evaluative (explicit) condition, but only to the most negative stigma (unattractive) in the gender (implicit) condition. Right amygdala (right panel) demonstrated sensitivity to stigma conditions in both the evaluative and gender conditions.

must successfully engage cognitive control mechanisms to inhibit aversive responses to stigmatized outgroup members. Together these studies reveal a unique social function for the amygdala and prefrontal cortex in detecting threats from outgroup members. In the next section, we explore the manner in which the social brain can detect threats from the ingroup.

Threat from Ingroups

Ingroup threats (i.e., social rejection or isolation) pose arguably the most potential harm to group members because they can result in ejection from one's social group. There are several possible causes for ingroup threat. For instance, Kurzban and Leary (2001) argue that individuals will be ostracized from the social group if they endanger the group (i.e., they have a disease that poses a risk to the group) or if they do not contribute to the group (i.e., they are missing a limb and thereby unable to help gather resources). Such individuals, according to Kurzban and Leary, are stigmatized and socially isolated from the group. Further, they argue that individuals who directly violate the rules of the group are subjected to social isolation. In other words, people who steal from the group or intentionally harm other group members will be ejected from the group. Thus, to maintain group membership, one must adhere to

the social norms of the group. It is on this final point that we focus most of our attention in this section.

Violations of social norms are met with harsh punishment or ostracism, even among nonhuman primates. Rhesus macaques, for instance, will unleash significantly more aggression on group members who find food and do not share it with their cohort (Hauser, 1992). For humans, such deviations from social group norms may result in social rejection, or even ejection from one's social group (Kurzban & Leary, 2001), a punishment most individuals want to avoid at all costs. Thus, the social brain has evolved an extensive network to detect violations of social group norms, thereby serving to protect our membership in the group.

The ability to detect ingroup social threats appears to rely, at least in part, on the anterior cingulate cortex (ACC), a region that has been implicated in conflict resolution (Kerns et al., 2004). The ACC has been implicated in responding to social interactions that provide conflicting social feedback (Eisenberger, Lieberman, & Williams, 2003). Somerville, Heatherton, and Kelley (2006) provided subjects with false feedback that was either negative or positive (rejection or not), and also that was incongruent or congruent with their expectations (expectancy violation or not). Results revealed a double dissociation between dorsal and ventral ACC regions. The dorsal ACC (dACC) was uniquely sensitive to expectancy violations, and ventral (vACC) was uniquely sensitive to social feedback (Figure 44.5), with significantly greater response to negative feedback than positive feedback, irrespective of expectancy violations.

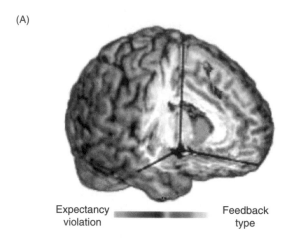

(A)

Expectancy violation ————— Feedback type

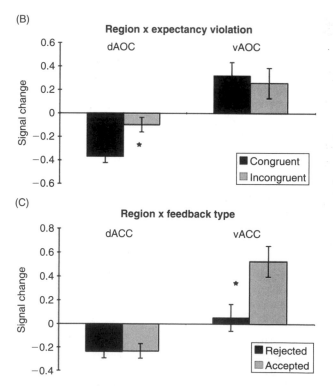

(B)

Region x expectancy violation

(C)

Region x feedback type

Figure 44.5 (**Figure C.41** in color section) Differential ACC response to expectancy violation and social feedback.

Note: **A:** A three-dimensional rendering of the medial surface of the brain illustrates a functional dissociation between dorsal (dACC0) and ventral (vACC) anterior cingulate. A whole-brain voxel-by-voxel analysis of variance (ANOVA) was used to identify voxels that showed a significant main effect ($p < .001$, uncorrected) of expectancy violation (blue) and a main effect of feedback (yellow). B–C: Voxels in the dACC (BA 32: −6, 28, 32; 13 voxels) demonstrated greater sensitivity to expectancy violation (incongruent > congruent) (B) whereas voxels in the vACC (BA 32/10: −6, 49, −13: 16 voxels) demonstrated greater sensitivity to feedback (accepted > rejected). (C) Error bars denote s.e.m.

Similarly, Krendl, Richeson, Kelley, and Heatherton (2008) found vACC activation during a social threat task. We conducted an fMRI study in which women were reminded of gender stereotypes about math ability while they were completing difficult math problems. Women showed an increase in vACC activity while performing difficult math problems after a social threat was induced (reminding them of gender stereotypes), whereas in the absence of social threat, women instead showed heightened activation over time in regions associated with math learning, and no change in vACC activation (Figure 44.6). Not surprisingly, women who were threatened exhibited a decrease in math performance over time whereas women who were not threatened improved in performance over time. Based on these findings, we conclude that the vACC is engaged in social and emotional processing.

Perhaps one of the most immediate sources of ingroup threats stems from violating social norms. In order to protect against such threats, the social brain has developed an intricate network of aptly named social emotions to warn us when we have violated social norms. Social emotions are complex emotions (e.g., admiration, jealousy, envy, irritation, flirtatiousness) that promote long-term social relationships and interactions. These emotions are critical in ensuring that we adhere to social norms in social interactions.

Powerful social emotions commonly referred to as moral emotions are engaged to identify when we have acted inappropriately and violated a social norm. These emotions include guilt, pity, embarrassment, shame, pride, awe, contempt, indignation, moral disgust, and gratitude (Moll, de Oliveira-Souza, Zahn, & Grafman, 2008). Their purpose is to elicit negative reactions that will (hopefully) prevent us from committing the violation in the future. Emerging neuroimaging research has begun to identify the unique neural mechanisms that are selectively engaged to process social and moral emotions. Not surprisingly, social and moral emotions engage many of the same structures activated by basic emotions (e.g., anger, fear), but they also selectively engage neural networks involved in assessing affect (e.g., amygdala, orbitofrontal cortex), as well as those regions that are involved in building cognitive schemas about the social world (left prefrontal cortex, right parietal cortex, anterior and posterior cingulate cortex; Adolphs, 2003).

The role of the amygdala in processing social emotions is a recent and novel finding that has emerged from patient and neuroimaging research. For instance, Adolphs, Baron-Cohen, and Tranel (2002) presented facial expressions of social emotions (arrogant, guilt, admiration, flirtatiousness) to patients with amygdala damage. Patients with unilateral or bilateral amygdala damage were impaired when recognizing those specific emotions; moreover, they were

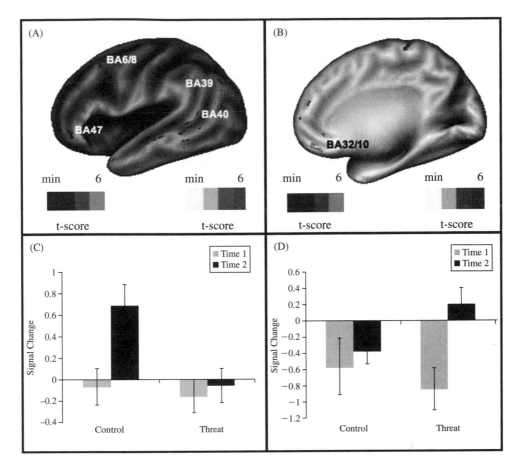

Figure 44.6 (**Figure C.42** in color section)   Changes in neural activation over time for controls and threatened participants.

Note: Statistical maps **A:** lateral view of the left hemisphere of an inflated brain, **B:** medial view of the right hemisphere of an inflated brain) depicting neural regions that are more active during the second math task than the first for both controls and threatened participants. Activation for controls is depicted in blue, whereas activation for threatened participants is depicted in orange. Images are thresholded at $p < .001$ uncorrected, with a minimum t of 3.5 and maximum of 6.0 for all. **C and D:** signal change from a fixation control task for left inferior prefrontal cortex (C: BA 47) and ventral anterior cingulate cortex (D: BA 32/10). Controls recruited greater activity in the left inferior prefrontal cortex, whereas the threatened participants showed no change in activation in this region. Conversely, threatened participants recruited greater ventral anterior cingulate activity over time, whereas controls did not.

more impaired at recognizing social emotions than basic emotions.

Ruby and Decety (2004) conducted a PET study in which participants were asked to choose the appropriate reaction (from varying perspectives) to sentences that represented different social emotions (embarrassment, pride, shame, guilt, admiration, irritation), or nonsocial emotions and nonemotional sentences. Results revealed heightened amygdala activation during the processing of all social emotions, regardless of the perspective taken during the task. However, it is important to note that the authors do not dissociate between types of social emotions in the task. Thus, it is unclear whether the amygdala activation observed was driven by a specific emotion.

Berthoz, Grezes, Armony, Passingham, and Dolan (2006) conducted an fMRI study to examine intentional violations of social norms. In the study, participants were presented with stories (e.g., "You are invited for a Japanese dinner at your friend's house"), and one of three endings: one was descriptive of normal social behavior (e.g., "You have a bite of the first course, like it, and congratulate your friend for her good cooking"); one that described an embarrassing conclusion (e.g., "You have a bite of the first course, you choke and spit out the food while you are coughing"); or one in which the protagonist violated a social norm (e.g., "You have a bite of the first course, but do not like it and spit the food back into your plate"). Participants evaluated the statements from their own perspective, or someone else's. When taking their own perspective, participants showed greater amygdala activation in response to intentional violations of social norms.

However, the amygdala is only one part of the neural network engaged in perceiving social and moral emotions. Shin and colleagues (2000) used PET to isolate the neural correlates of guilt, a moral emotion. Prior to the PET scan, participants were asked to provide written accounts of three distinct events: one involving the most guilt the participant had ever experienced, and two additional events involving no clear emotion. During the scan, a tape-recording of the autobiographical events was presented aurally to participants, and they were asked to reexperience the event to which they were listening. Direct comparisons between guilt-induction conditions versus neutral elicited heightened activation in anterior cingulate gyrus and left anterior insula.

A recent fMRI study on embarrassment, also a moral emotion, found that the anterior cingulate cortex was activated when it was clear that a social norm had been violated. Berthoz, Armony, Blair, and Dolan (2002) used fMRI to investigate the neural systems supporting embarrassing situations and violations of social norms using the same paradigm described previously. Violation of social norms yielded greater activation in the anterior cingulate than embarrassment. Both violation of social norms and embarrassment led to greater activation in the medial prefrontal cortex (such as observed in self-awareness and ToM tasks) and the left orbitofrontal cortex.

mPFC activation was also observed in an fMRI study by Takahashi and colleagues (2004) when they compared guilt and embarrassment to neutral emotions. In the study, participants were shown sentences that had been previously rated as inducing guilt (e.g., "I shoplifted a dress from the store"), embarrassment (e.g., "I soiled my underwear"), or no emotion (neutral; e.g., "I washed my clothes"). Both guilt and embarrassment elicited mPFC activation, but direct comparisons between the two revealed heightened activation for mPFC in the guilt condition as compared to embarrassment. The involvement of mPFC in social and moral emotions suggests that these emotions may uniquely engage some form of mentalizing in order to be effective.

One possible explanation for why social and moral emotions may engage an extensive network of activation is that simply experiencing social emotions does not make them effective. Instead, social emotions must inform the perceiver of what social norms were followed or violated and provide either a reward or punishment (respectively) to encourage or deter future reoccurrences. However, in order to be effective, the perceiver of the social emotion must possess self-awareness and ToM. For instance, when we commit a social error during a social interaction, we may feel embarrassed. However, to recognize that we are embarrassed because of the social error, we must have self-awareness. Conversely, we may recognize the social error first by realizing that the person to whom our comment was directed is upset by our remark. This recognition may then lead to a feeling of embarrassment. In this case, we would assess violations of social norms by making an inference about the mental state of someone else, which requires ToM.

Possessing self-awareness and ToM only allow us to understand when a social norm has been violated and does little to prevent us from committing the errors in the future. Here is where self-regulation plays a vital role in the social brain. Self-regulation allows us to control our behavior to ensure that we do not violate social norms. We next explore how the social brain gives rise to self-regulation.

Self-Regulation

A unique aspect of human behavior is the ability to regulate and control thoughts and actions, an ability commonly referred to as self-regulation. Self-regulation allows us to make plans, choose from alternatives, focus attention on pursuit of goals, inhibit competing thoughts, and regulate social behavior (Baumeister, Heatherton, & Tice, 1994; Baumeister & Vohs, 2004; Metcalfe & Mischel, 1999; Wegner, 1994). Extensive evidence from neuroimaging and patient research demonstrates that the prefrontal cortex is imperative in successfully engaging self-regulatory processes, as befitting its label as "chief executive" of the brain (Goldberg, 2001). The vital role of the prefrontal cortex in self-regulation was famously observed in the case of Phineas Gage, who suffered profound frontal lobe damage when a railroad spike misfired into his head. Formerly described by friends as dependable, polite, and hardworking, Gage became capricious and volatile after the accident. Gage's failure to regulate his social behavior after his injury was among the first lines of evidence that the prefrontal cortex supports the inhibitory mechanisms necessary to regulate behavior.

Since Gage's accident, abundant patient and neuroimaging research has identified discrete brain regions within prefrontal cortex that are critical for self-regulation (for review, see Banfield, Wyland, Macrae, Münte, & Heatherton, 2004), primarily the dorsolateral prefrontal cortex (DLPFC; involved in modulating of cognitive control), the orbitofrontal cortex (OFC; involved in integrating cognitive and affective information), and the anterior cingulate cortex (ACC; involved in conflict resolution).

The DLPFC has been associated with planning, novelty processing, choice, the control of memory, and working memory and language function (see D'Esposito et al., 1995; Dronkers, Redfern, & Knight, 2000; Fuster, Brodner, & Kroger, 2000; Goldman-Rakic, 1987). Damage to this area often results in patients' experiencing an inability to inhibit certain behaviors (Pandya & Barnes, 1987). Damage to the OFC, which controls our behavioral and emotional output and how we interact with others (Dolan, 1999), often results in striking, and sometimes aggressive, behavioral changes (e.g., Rolls, Hornak, Wade, & McGrath, 1994). Damage to the OFC usually results in personality changes such as indifference, impaired social judgment and responsiveness, poor self-regulation, lack of impulse control, and poor judgment and insight (Damasio, 1994; Stone, Baron-Cohen, & Knight, 1998; Stuss & Alexander, 2000). Patients with OFC damage often cannot inhibit desires for instant gratification and thus may commit thefts or sexually aggressive behavior (Blumer & Benson, 1975; Grafman et al., 1996).

The ACC is essential for initiating actions, evaluating conflicts, and also inhibiting prepotent responses, processes heavily involved in self-regulation (Kerns et al., 2004). The ACC is functionally dissociated into the dorsal ACC that evaluates cognitive conflict, and the ventral ACC that evaluates emotional conflict (Bush, Luu, & Posner, 2000). The ACC is often engaged whenever any kind of "supervisory input" is required (Badgaiyan & Posner, 1998). In fact, it is widely accepted that the ACC is somehow involved in evaluating the degree and nature of conflict, whereas other parts of the brain (particularly the PFC) may be involved in resolving the conflict itself (Botvinick, Cohen, & Carter, 2004; Cohen, Botvinick, & Carter, 2000; Kerns et al., 2004).

Emerging neuroimaging research has sought to more clearly identify the neural structures in self-regulation by examining the structures engaged in emotion and cognitive regulation. Ochsner, Bunge, Gross, and Gabrieli (2002) showed participants highly negative pictures and instructed them either to "attend" (study the picture and be aware of, but not try to alter, their feelings toward it) or "reappraise" (reinterpret the picture in such a way that it would no longer elicit a negative response) the photograph. The authors found that reappraising the photographs led to decreased subjective negative affect, and this was reflected in a reduction of activity in the amygdala (a region implicated in processing fear) and OFC, and increased activation in the lateral and medial prefrontal cortex, as well as in the anterior cingulate cortex.

In a later study, Ochsner and colleagues (2004) instructed participants to increase negative affect toward the image (by imagining themselves or a loved one as the central figure in a highly negative photograph) or decrease their negative affect to the photograph (by psychologically distancing themselves from it). Here, the authors found that extensive networks in the prefrontal cortex (left prefrontal cortex, dorsal anterior cingulate, and dorsal mPFC) were engaged when participants were using self-regulatory processes either to increase or decrease their affective response to the photographs. They observed that enhancing negative emotions engaged primarily left-lateralized prefrontal regions, whereas suppressing negative affect engaged bilateral prefrontal regions. Importantly, they also observed that activity in the amygdala decreased when participants actively decreased their negative affect to the picture, and increased when they increased their negative affect.

Self-regulation research has not been limited to modulating negative affect. Kim and Hamann (2007) observed increased activation in the left prefrontal cortex when participants were asked to increase either positive or negative affective responses to stimuli, and predominantly bilateral prefrontal activity in response to suppressing positive or negative affect. Importantly, the dorsal mPFC and the OFC were engaged for regulating both positive and negative emotions. Activation of the amygdala increased during the increase condition for both positive and negative pictures, and decreased in the suppress conditions in response to both positive and negative stimuli as well. Beauregard, Levesque, and Bourgouin (2001) had male participants view erotic films clips while undergoing fMRI. Participants were instructed either to allow themselves to become aroused during the clips, or to suppress any arousal they might be feeling. The authors found that suppressing arousal resulted in heightened activation in the right superior prefrontal and right anterior cingulate cortices with no accompanying activation in the limbic areas (e.g., amygdala, hypothalamus) that were active during the arousal condition.

Together, these findings have had important implications in patient populations. For instance, emerging research on patients with severe depression has revealed that their prefrontal cortex is unable to suppress amygdala activation in emotion regulation tasks (Johnstone, van Reekum, Urry, Kalin, & Davidson, 2007). When depressed patients are asked to suppress negative affect to highly aversive pictures, depressed patients show a positive correlation between the amygdala and vmPFC, whereas controls demonstrate a negative correlation between the two. In other words, the more controls engage vmPFC to suppress negative affect, the greater decrease is observed in activity in the amygdala. However, the more depressed patients try to suppress negative affect, the greater the activity in their amygdala.

Another important form of self-regulation that is critical for daily living is mental control. Successfully controlling the contents of consciousness is a difficult task—worries intrude when people least desire them and it is not uncommon for the mind to wander when people should be focused on a particular task or objective. Research by Wegner (1994) demonstrated that trying to suppress a particular thought can paradoxically lead to an increase in the very thought one is attempting to suppress. One open question is whether cognitive control of thoughts and actions involves similar component processes and therefore recruits common brain regions. If so, one might expect to observe ACC activity during attempts to control thoughts. To address this issue, we conducted an fMRI study of attempted thought suppression (Wyland, Kelley, Macrae, Gordon, & Heatherton, 2003). Participants were each asked to provide a personally relevant thought that was especially salient to them at that moment (e.g., "study for an exam" or "a phone call with a distant girlfriend"). During the scan, they were given visual prompts that instructed them to: (a) suppress the personally relevant thought they had generated before the task ("suppress"), (b) think about nothing ("clear"), or (c) think about anything ("free thought"). Both the "suppress" and "clear" conditions required a form of thought suppression. To dissociate these two processes, no overt behavioral response was collected (e.g., pushing a button to index thought intrusions) as such a requirement contaminates thought suppression with response generation. Moreover, we were not concerned with failures of cognitive control per se, but rather the ongoing process of mental regulation.

The results indicated that the brain regions previously implicated in the suppression of overt behavior were also active during attempts to control the emergence of unwanted thoughts. Specifically, we found greater activation in the ACC for the "suppress" condition than for the "free thought" condition. When the "clear" and "free thought" conditions were compared, a more diverse pattern of neural activation was observed. Specifically, greater activation was observed in the anterior cingulate, left inferior frontal cortex, right insula, right parietal cortex, and right medial frontal cortex in the "clear" as compared to the "free thought" condition. The greater activity for the "clear" condition may have occurred because it is more difficult to suppress all thoughts than to suppress a specific thought. Our participants reported having a great deal of difficulty with this condition (the interested reader should go ahead and try this; it is nearly impossible). As previously demonstrated by Wegner and his colleagues (1989), suppressing a specific thought can be achieved relatively easily by thinking of something else, especially if that other thought captures attention.

Because we are also interested in examining failures of mental control, we conducted a second study in which participants were asked to suppress the specific thought of white bears (Mitchell, Heatherton, Kelley, Wyland, and Macrae (2006). In this study, participants were scanned while alternatively trying to suppress the thought of a white bear or freely thinking about anything that came to mind; in either case, they pressed a button to indicate a white bear thought (we also had a third condition in between blocks that required participants to press a key when a yellow light appeared in order to control for simple motor movement). We found that right dorsolateral prefrontal cortex showed a sustained response when participants were attempting to suppress thoughts (i.e., the tonic state), whereas the ACC was activated by the intrusion of forbidden thoughts (i.e., transient events). This pattern of results is consistent with neural models of cognitive control that emphasize the interplay between PFC and ACC in cognitive control (Kerns et al., 2004) as well as with the Wegner's (1994) model of mental control. The use of imaging is well suited to contribute to our ability to examine theoretical models of self-regulation, both in emotion and mental regulation tasks.

SUMMARY

In this chapter, we described how neuroimaging has informed our knowledge of the unique components of the social brain. Our research has identified a number of frontal lobe regions that appear to subserve important human talents, such as the ability to introspect, evaluate ourselves and others, detect social threats around us, and to purposefully modify our thoughts and behaviors in the pursuit of goals. Knowing where in the brain something happens doesn't by itself tell you very much. But, knowing that there are consistent patterns of brain activation associated with specific psychological tasks provides evidence that the two are connected, and provides an opportunity to identify component processes that might be important for a full understanding of mental constructs. We believe that a social brain sciences approach will be useful for understanding the nature of the social brain.

Now that we have identified various regions of the brain that comprise the social brain, one next logical step is to try to identify the specific role of these regions. Many of the regions discussed in this chapter (e.g., the amygdala, ACC, DLPFC) have been implicated in nonsocial tasks. It would therefore be misleading to suggest that these regions are solely "social brain areas." More than likely, these regions have a broader role in the brain (e.g., threat detection, conflict resolution) that renders them useful both in certain cognitive and social tasks.

However, the role of the mPFC in the social brain is particularly puzzling because it is robustly activated during self-relevant and theory of mind tasks, but otherwise it is deactive during most cognitive tasks (Raichle et al., 2001). It is thus thought that the mPFC is engaged when the brain is "inactive," suggesting perhaps that the "default state" of the brain is introspection (Raichle et al., 2001). One possible explanation for this is that the deactivations observed in mPFC during cognitive tasks are due to the fact that available neural resources are required to perform the task at hand, and therefore fewer are available for inward reflection, thus causing a decline in activity in the mPFC (Gusnard, 2005). Another possibility is that mPFC operates by binding together various physical experiences and cognitive operations that have implications for self. The prefrontal cortex receives input from all sensory modalities, and is therefore the brain region where inputs from internal sources conjoin with information received from the outside world. This region may act in a metacognitive fashion to monitor all stimuli, whether internal or external, so that our conscious sense of self at any particular moment reflects a workspace determined by which brain regions are most active.

Finally, evidence is accumulating that the medial prefrontal cortex is important not only for processing information about the self, but also for inferring mental states in others (Macrae et al., 2004; Mitchell et al., 2005). This raises the possibility that having a self might be adaptive because it allows us to simulate the mental lives of others, thereby allowing us to better know others and predict their behavior. Functionally, having ToM allows us to be good group members because we can predict how others will respond to our actions and ensure that we act in accordance with group norms and values. Such a theory is consistent with the argument that a symbolic self is adaptive (Sedikides & Skowronski, 1997). These and other theories will inspire further research on the social brain.

REFERENCES

Addis, D. R., Wong, A. T., & Schacter, D. L. (2006). Remembering the past and imagining the future: Common and distinct neural substrates during event construction and elaboration. *Neuropsychologia, 45,* 1363–1377.

Adolphs, R. (2003). Cognitive neuroscience of human social behaviour. *Nature Reviews: Neuroscience, 4,* 165–178.

Adolphs, R., Baron-Cohen, S., & Tranel, D. (2002). Impaired recognition of social emotions following amygdala damage. *Journal of Cognitive Neuroscience, 14,* 1264–1274.

Allison, T., Puce, A., & McCarthy, G. (2000). Social perception from visual cues: Role of the STS region. *Trends in Cognitive Sciences, 4,* 267–278.

Amaral, D. G. (2002). The primate amygdala and the neurobiology of social behavior: Implications for understanding social anxiety. *Biological Psychiatry, 51,* 11–17.

Aron, A., & Aron, E. N. (1996). *Self and self-expansion in relationships.* Hillsdale, NJ: Erlbaum.

Aron, A., Aron, E. N., Tudor, M., & Nelson, G. J. (1991). Close relationships as including other in the self. *Journal of Personality and Social Psychology, 60,* 241–253.

Aron, A., & Fraley, B. (1999). Relationship closeness as including other in the self: Cognitive underpinnings and measures [Special issue: Social Cognition and Relationships]. *Social Cognition, 17,* 140–160.

Badgaiyan, R., & Posner, M. (1998). Mapping the cingulate cortex in response selection and monitoring. *NeuroImage, 7,* 255–260.

Banfield, J. F., Wyland, C. L., Macrae, C. N., Münte, T. F., & Heatherton, T. F. (2004). *The cognitive neuroscience of self-regulation.* New York: Guilford Press.

Baumeister, R. F. (1998). *The self* (4th ed. Vol. 2). New York: McGraw-Hill.

Baumeister, R. F., Heatherton, T. F., & Tice, D. M. (1994). *Losing control: How and why people fail at self-regulation.* San Diego, CA: Academic Press.

Baumeister, R. F., & Leary, M. R. (1995). The need to belong: Desire for interpersonal attachments as a fundamental human motivation. *Psychological Bulletin, 117,* 497–529.

Baumeister, R. F., & Vohs, K. D. (2004). *Handbook of self-regulation: Research, theory, and applications.* New York: Guilford Press.

Beauregard, M., Levesque, J., & Bourgouin, P. (2001). Neural correlates of conscious self-regulation of emotion. *Journal of Neuroscience, 21,* 1–5.

Bernston, G. G., Bechara, A., Damasio, H., Tranel, D., & Cacioppo, J. T. (2007). Amygdala contribution to selection dimensions of emotion. *Social Cognitive and Affective Neuroscience, 2,* 123–129.

Berthoz, S., Armony, J. L., Blair, R. J., & Dolan, R. J. (2002). An fMRI study of intentional and unintentional (embarrassing) violations of social norms. *Brain, 125,* 1696–1708.

Berthoz, S., Grezes, J., Armony, J. L., Passingham, R. E., & Dolan, R. J. (2006). Affective response to one's own moral violations. *NeuroImage, 31,* 945–950.

Blumer, D., & Benson, D. (1975). *Personality changes with frontal and temporal lesions.* New York: Grune & Stratton.

Botvinick, M. M., Cohen, J. D., & Carter, C. S. (2004). Conflict monitoring and anterior cingulate cortex: An update. *Trends in Cognitive Sciences, 8,* 539–546.

Bower, G. H., & Gilligan, S. G. (1979). Remembering information related to one's self. *Journal of Research in Personality, 13,* 420–432.

Bowlby, J. (1969). *Attachment and loss* (Vol. 1). New York: Basic Books.

Bush, G., Luu, P., & Posner, M. I. (2000). Cognitive and emotional influences in anterior cingulate cortex. *Trends in Cognitive Sciences, 4,* 215–222.

Cabeza, R., Prince, S. E., Daselaar, S. M., Greenberg, D. L., Budde, M., Dolcos, F., et al. (2004). Brain activity during episodic retrieval of autobiographical and laboratory events: An fMRI study using a novel photo paradigm. *Journal of Cognitive Neuroscience, 16,* 1583–1594.

Cacioppo, J. T., Ernst, J. M., Burleson, M. H., McClintock, M. K., Malarkey, W. B., Hawkley, L. C., et al. (2000). Lonely traits and concomitant physiological processes: The MacArthur social neuroscience studies. *International Journal of Pshchophysiology, 35,* 143–154.

Cacioppo, J. T., Hughes, M. E., Waite, L. J., Hawkley, L. C., & Thisted, R. A. (2006). Loneliness as a specific risk factor for depressive symptoms: Cross sectional and longitudinal analyses. *Psychology and Aging, 21,* 140–151.

Cheney, D. L., & Seyfarth, R. M. (1997). Reconciliatory grunts by dominant female baboons influence victims' behavior. *Animal Behaviour, 54,* 409–418.

Chiu, P., Ambady, N., & Deldin, P. (2004). Contingent negative variation to emotional in- and out-group stimuli differentiates high- and low-prejudiced individuals. *Journal of Cognitive Neuroscience, 16,* 1830–1839.

Ciaramidaro, A., Adenzato, M., Enrici, I., Erk, S., Pia, L., Bara, B. G., et al. (2007). The intentional network: How the brain reads varieties of intentions. *Neuropsychologia, 45,* 3105–3113.

Cohen, J. D., Botvinick, M., & Carter, C. S. (2000). Anterior cingulate and prefrontal cortex: Who's in control? *Nature Neuroscience, 3,* 421–423.

Craik, F. I. M., Moroz, T. M., Moscovitch, M., Stuss, D. T., Winocur, G., Tulving, E., et al. (1999). In search of the self: A positron emission tomograph study. *Psychological Science, 10,* 26–34.

Crocker, J., Major, B., & Steele, C. (1998). *Social stigma* (Vol. 2, 4th ed.). New York: McGraw-Hill.

Cunningham, W. A., Johnson, M. K., Raye, C. L., Gatenby, C. J., Gore, J. C., & Banaji, M. R. (2004). Separable neural components in the processing of black and white faces. *Psychological Sciences, 15,* 806–813.

Damasio, A. R. (1994). Descartes' error and the future of human life. *Scientific American*, *271*, 144.

D'Esposito, M., Detre, J. A., Alsop, D. C., Shin, R. K., Atlas, S., & Grossman, M. (1995, November 16). The neural basis of the central executive system of working memory. *Nature*, *378*, 279–281.

Dolan, R. J. (1999). On the neurology of morals. *Nature Neuroscience*, *2*, 927–929.

Dronkers, N. F., Redfern, B. B., & Knight, R. T. (2000). *The neural architecture of language disorders*. Cambridge, MA: MIT Press.

Eberhardt, J. L. (2005). Imaging race. *American Psychologist*, *60*, 181–190.

Eisenberger, N. I., Lieberman, M. D., & Williams, K. D. (2003, October 10). Does rejection hurt? An fMRI study of social exclusion. *Science*, *302*, 290–292.

Feinberg, T. E., & Keenan, J. P. (2005). *The lost self: Pathologies of the brain and identity*. New York: Oxford University Press.

Fletcher, P. C., Happe, F., Frith, U., Baker, S. C., Dolan, R. J., Frackowiak, R. S., et al. (1995). Other minds in the brain: A functional imaging study of "theory of mind" in story comprehension. *Cognition*, *57*, 109–128.

Fuster, J. M., Brodner, M., & Kroger, J. K. (2000, May 18). Cross-modal and cross-temporal associations in neurons of frontal cortex. *Nature*, *405*, 347–351.

Gallagher, H. L., & Frith, C. D. (2003). Functional imaging of 'theory of mind.' *Trends in Cognitive Sciences*, *7*, 77–83.

Gallagher, H. L., Happe, F., Brunswick, N., Fletcher, P. C., Frith, U., & Frith, C. D. (2000). Reading the mind in cartoons and stories: An fMRI study of 'theory of mind' in verbal and nonverbal tasks. *Neuropsychologia*, *38*, 11–21.

Gallagher, H. L., Jack, A. I., Roepstorff, A., & Frith, C. D. (2002). Imaging the intentional stance in a competitive game. *NeuroImage*, *3*, 814–821.

Gardner, W. L., Pickett, C. L., & Brewer, M. B. (2000). Social exclusion and selective memory: How the need to belong influences memory for social events. *Personality and Social Psychology Bulletin*, *26*, 486–496.

Gardner, W. L., Pickett, C. L., Jefferis, V., & Knowles, M. (2005). On the outside looking in: Loneliness and social monitoring. *Personality and Social Psychology Bulletin*, *31*, 1549–1560.

Gillihan, S. J., & Farah, M. J. (2005). Is self special? A critical review of evidence from experimental psychology and cognitive neuroscience. *Psychological Bulletin*, *13*, 76–97.

Gobbini, M. I., Koralek, A. C., Bryan, R. E., Montgomery, K. J., & Haxby, J. V. (2007). Two takes on the social brain: A comparison of theory of mind tasks. *Journal of Cognitive Neuroscience*, *19*, 1803–1814.

Goffman, E. (1963). *Stigma: Notes on the management of spoiled identity*. New York: Simon & Schuste.

Goldberg, E. (2001). *The executive brain: The frontal lobes and the civilized mind*. New York: Oxford University Press.

Goldman-Rakic, P. S. (1987). Development of cortical circuitry and cognitive function. *Child Development*, *58*, 601–622.

Grafman, J., Schwab, K., Warden, D., Pridgen, A., Brown, H. R., & Salazar, A. M. (1996). Frontal lobe injuries, violence, and aggression: A report of the Vietnam Head Injury Study. *Neurology*, *46*, 1231–1238.

Greenwald, A. G., & Banaji, M. R. (1989). The self as a memory system: Powerful, but ordinary. *Journal of Personality and Social Psychology*, *57*, 41–54.

Greenwald, A. G., McGhee, D. E., & Schwartz, J. L. K. (1998). Measuring individual differences in implicit cognition: The implicit association test. *Journal of Personality and Social Psychology*, *74*, 1464–1480.

Grezes, J., Fonlupt, P., Bertenthal, B., Delon-Martin, C., Segebarth, C., & Decety, J. (2001). Does perception of biological motion rely on specific brain regions? *NeuroImage*, *13*, 775–785.

Gusnard, D. A. (2005). Being a self: Considerations from functional imaging. *Consciousness and Cognition*, *14*, 679–697.

Gusnard, D. A., Akbudak, E., Shulman, G. L., & Raichle, M. E. (2001). Medial prefrontal cortex and self-referential mental activity: Relation to a default mode of brain function. *Proceedings of the National Academy of Sciences, USA*, *98*, 4259–4264.

Harris, L. T., & Fiske, S. T. (2006). Dehumanizing the lowest of the low: Neuroimaging responses to extreme out-groups. *Psychological Science*, *17*, 847–853.

Harris, L. T., & Fiske, S. T. (2007). Social groups that elicit disgust are differentially processed in mPFC. *Social Cognitive and Affective Neuroscience*, *2*, 45–51.

Hart, A. J., Whalen, P. J., Shin, L. M., McInerney, S. C., Fischer, H., & Rauch, S. L. (2000). Differential response in the human amygdala to racial outgroup vs ingroup face stimuli. *NeuroReport*, *11*, 2351–2355.

Hauser, M. D. (1992). Costs of deception: Cheaters are punished in rhesus monkeys (Macaca mulatta). *Proceedings of the National Academy of Sciences, USA*, *89*, 12137–12139.

Heatherton, T. F., & Krendl, A. C. (2007). *Social emotions: Imaging social emotions*. New Encyclopedia of Neuroscience. Oxford: Elsevier.

Heatherton, T. F., Macrae, C. N., & Kelley, W. M. (2004). What the social brain sciences can tell us about the self. *Current Directions in Psychological Science*, *13*, 190–193.

Heatherton, T. F., Wyland, C., Macrae, C. N., Denny, B. T., Demos, K. D., & Kelley, W. M. (2006). *Friends among us? Medial prefrontal activity is specific for self-referential processing*. Unpublished manuscript.

House, J. S., Landis, K. R., & Umberso, D. (1988, July 29). Social relationships and health. *Science*, *241*, 540–545.

Ito, T. A., & Cacioppo, J. T. (2000). Electrophysical evidence of implicit and explicit categorization processes. *Journal of Experimental Social Psychology*, *36*, 660–676.

Johnson, S. C., Baxter, L. C., Wilder, L. S., Pipe, J. G., Heiserman, J. E., & Prigatano, G. P. (2002). Neural correlates of self-reflection. *Brain*, *125*, 1808–1814.

Johnstone, T., van Reekum, C. M., Urry, H. L., Kalin, N. H., & Davidson, R. J. (2007). Failure to regulate: Counterproductve recruitment of top-down prefrontal-subcortical circuitry in major depression. *Journal of Neuroscience*, *27*, 8877–8884.

Keenan, J. M., & Baillet, S. D. (1980). *Memory for personally and socially significant events*. Hillsdale, NJ: Erlbaum.

Kelley, W. M., Macrae, C. N., Wyland, C. L., Caglar, S., Inati, S., & Heatherton, T. F. (2002). Finding the self?: An event-related fMRI study. *Journal of Cognitive Neuroscience*, *14*, 785–794.

Kerns, J. G., Cohen, J. D., MacDonald, A. W., III, Cho, R. Y., Stenger, V. A., & Carter, C. S. (2004, February 13). Anterior cingulate conflict monitoring and adjustments in control. *Science*, *303*, 1023–1026.

Kim, S. H., & Hamann, S. (2007). Neural correlates of positive and negative emotion regulation. *Journal of Cognitive Neuroscience*, *19*, 776–798.

Klein, S. B. (2004). *The cognitive neuroscience of knowing one's self* (Vol. 3). Cambridge, MA: Institute of Technology.

Klein, S. B., Cosmides, L., & Costabile, K. A. (2003). Preserved knowledge of self in a case of Alzheimer's dementia. *Social Cognition*, *21*, 157–165.

Klein, S. B., & Kihlstrom, J. F. (1986). Elaboration, organization, and the self-reference effect in memory. *Journal of Experimental Psychology: General*, *115*, 26–38.

Klein, S. B., & Loftus, J. (1988). The nature of self-referent encoding: The contributions of elaborative and organizational processes. *Journal of Personality and Social Psychology*, *55*, 5–11.

Krendl, A. C., Macrae, C. N., Kelley, W. M., Fugelsang, J. F., & Heatherton, T. F. (2006). The good, the bad, and the ugly: An fMRI investigation of the functional anatomic correlates of stigma. *Social Neuroscience*, *1*, 5–15.

Krendl, A. C., Richeson, J. A., Kelley, W. M., & Heatherton, T. F. (2008). The negative consequences of threat: An fMRI investigation of the neural mechanisms underlying women's underperformance in math. *Psychological Science, 19,* 168–175.

Kurzban, R., & Leary, M. R. (2001). Evolutionary origins of stigmatization: The functions of social exclusion. *Psychological Bulletin, 127,* 187–208.

Leary, M. R. (2005). *Interpersonal cognition and the quest for social acceptance: Inside the sociometer.* New York: Guilford Press.

Leary, M. R., Tambor, E. S., Terdal, S. K., & Downs, D. L. (1995). Self-esteem as an interpersonal monitor: The sociometer hypothesis. *Journal of Personality and Social Psychology, 68,* 518–530.

Lieberman, M. D., Hariri, A., Jarcho, J. M., Eisenberger, N. I., & Bookheimer, S. Y. (2005). An fMRI investigation of race-related amygdala activity in African-American and Caucasian-American individuals. *Nature Neuroscience, 8,* 720–722.

Macdonald, G., & Leary, M. R. (2005). Why does social exclusion hurt? The relationship between social and physical pain. *Psychological Bulletin, 131,* 202–223.

Macrae, C. N., & Bodenhausen, G. V. (2000). Social cognition: Thinking categorically about others. *Annual Review of Psychology, 51,* 93–120.

Macrae, C. N., Moran, J. M., Heatherton, T. F., Banfield, J. F., & Kelley, W. M. (2004). Medial prefrontal activity predicts memory for self. *Cerebral Cortex, 14,* 647–654.

Maki, R. H., & McCaul, K. D. (1985). The effects of self-reference versus other reference on the recall of traits and nouns. *Bulletin of the Psychonomic Society, 23,* 169–172.

Markus, H. (1977). Self-schemata and processing information about the self. *Journal of Personality and Social Psychology, 35,* 63–78.

Mason, M. F., Banfield, J. F., & Macrae, C. N. (2004). Thinking about actions: The neural substrates of person knowledge. *Cerebral Cortex, 14,* 209–214.

Mason, M. F., Norton, M. I., Van Horn, J. D., Wegner, D. M., Grafton, S. T., & Macrae, C. N. (2007). Wandering minds: The default network and stimulus independent thought. *Science, 315,* 393–395.

Mather, M., & Knight, M. R. (2006). Angry faces get noticed quickly: Threat detection is not impaired among older adults. *Journals of Gerontology. Series B, Psychological Sciences, 61*(1), P54–P57.

McCabe, K., Houser, D., Ryan, L., Smith, V., & Trouard, T. (2001). A functional imaging study of cooperation in two-person reciprocal change. *Proceedings of the National Academy of Sciences, USA, 98,* 11832–11835.

Metcalfe, J., & Mischel, W. (1999). A hot/cool-system analysis of delay of gratification: Dynamics of willpower. *Psychological Review, 106,* 3–19.

Mitchell, J. P., Banaji, M. R., & Macrae, C. N. (2005). General and specific contributions of the medial prefrontal cortex to knowledge about mental states. *NeuroImage, 28,* 757–762.

Mitchell, J. P., Heatherton, T. F., Kelley, W. M., Wyland, C. L., & Macrae, C. N. (2006). *Controlling the contents of consciousness: The neural substrates of thought suppression.* Unpublished manuscript.

Mitchell, J. P., Heatherton, T. F., & Macrae, C. N. (2002). Distinct neural systems subserve person and object knowledge. *Proceedings of the National Academy of Sciences, USA, 99,* 15238–15243.

Mitchell, J. P., Macrae, C. N., & Banaji, M. R. (2006). Dissociable medial prefrontal contributions to judgments of similar and dissimilar others. *Neuron, 50,* 655–663.

Moll, J., de Oliveira-Souza, R., Zahn, R., & Grafman, J. (2008). *The cognitive science of morality* (Vol. 2). Cambridge, MA: MIT Press.

Norris, C. J., Chen, E. E., Zhu, D. C., Small, S. L., & Cacioppo, J. T. (2004). The interaction of social and emotional processes in the brain. *Journal of Cognitive Neuroscience, 16,* 1818–1829.

Northoff, G., & Bermpohl, F. (2004). Cortical midline structures and the self. *Trends in Cognitive Sciences, 8,* 102–107.

Ochsner, K. N., Beer, J. S., Robertson, E. R., Cooper, J. C., Gabrieli, J. D., Kihsltrom, J. F., et al. (2005). The neural correlates of direct and reflected self-knowledge. *NeuroImage, 28,* 797–814.

Ochsner, K. N., Bunge, S. A., Gross, J. J., & Gabrieli, J. D. (2002). Rethinking feelings: An FMRI study of the cognitive regulation of emotion. *Journal of Cognitive Neuroscience, 14,* 1215–1229.

Ochsner, K. N., Ray, R. D., Cooper, J. C., Robertson, E. R., Chopra, S., Gabrieli, J. D. E., et al. (2004). For better or for worse: Neural systems supporting the cognitive dow- and up-regulation of negative emotion. *NeuroImage, 2,* 483–499.

Pandya, D. N., & Barnes, C. L. (1987). *Architecture and connections of the frontal lobe.* New York: IRBN Press.

Phelps, E. A., O'Connor, K. J., Cunningham, W. A., Funayama, E. S., Gatenby, J. C., Gore, J. C., et al. (2000). Performance on indirect measures of race evaluation predicts amygdala activation. *Journal of Cognitive Neuroscience, 12,* 729–738.

Pickett, C. L., Gardner, W. L., & Knowles, M. (2004). Getting a cue: The need to belong and enhanced sensitivity to social cues. *Personality and Social Psycgology Bulletin, 30,* 1095–1107.

Povinelli, D. J., & Eddy, T. J. (1996). What chimpanzees know about seeing. *Monographs of the Society for Reseach in Child Development, 61,* 1–152.

Povinelli, D. J., Nelson, K. E., & Boysen, S. T. (1990). Inferences about guessing and knowing by chimpanzees (Pan troglodytes). *Journal of Comparative Psychology, 104,* 203–210.

Raichle, M. E., MacLeod, A. M., Snyder, A. Z., Powers, W. J., Gusnard, D. A., & Shulman, G. L. (2001). A default mode of brain function. *Proceedings of the National Academy of Sciences, USA, 98,* 676–682.

Richeson, J. A., Baird, A. A., Gordon, H. L., Heatherton, T. F., Wyland, C. L., Trawalter, S., et al. (2003). An fMRI investigation of the impact of interracial contact on executive function. *Nature Neuroscience, 6,* 1323–1328.

Richeson, J. A., & Shelton, J. N. (2003). When prejudice does not pay: Effects of interracial contact on executive function. *Psychological Science, 14,* 287–290.

Rogers, T. B., Kuiper, N. A., & Kirker, W. S. (1977). Self-reference and the encoding of personal information. *Journal of Personality and Social Psychology, 35,* 677–688.

Rolls, E. T., Hornak, J., Wade, D., & McGrath, J. (1994). Emotion-related learning in patients with social and emotional changes associated with frontal lobe damage. *Journal of Neurology, Neurosurgery, and Psychiatry, 57,* 1518–1524.

Rubin, K. H., & Mills, R. S. (1988). The many faces of social isolation in childhood. *Journal of Consulting and Clinical Psychology, 56,* 916–924.

Ruby, P., & Decety, J. (2004). How would you feel versus how do you think she would feel? A neuroimaging study of perspective-taking with social emotions. *Journal of Cognitive Neuroscience, 16,* 988–999.

Saxe, R., & Kanwisher, N. (2003). People thinking about people: The role of the termpero-parietal junction in "theory of mind." *NeuroImage, 19,* 1835–1842.

Saxe, R., & Powell, L. J. (2006). It's the thought that counts: Specific brain regions for one component of theory of mind. *Psychological Science, 17,* 692–699.

Saxe, R., & Wexler, A. (2005). Making sense of another mind: The role of the right tempero-parietal junction. *Neuropsychologia, 43,* 1391–1399.

Schmitz, T. W., Kawahara-Baccus, T. N., & Johnson, S. C. (2004). Metacognitive evaluation, self-relevance, and the right prefrontal cortex. *NeuroImage, 22,* 941–947.

Schore, A. N. (2003). *Affect regulation and repair of the self.* New York: W. W. Norton.

Schubo, A., Gendolla, G. H., Meinecke, C., & Abele, A. E. (2006). Detecting emotional faces and features in a visual search paradigm: Are faces special? *Emotion, 6,* 246–256.

Sedikides, C., & Skowronski, J. J. (1997). The symbolic self in evolutionary context. *Personality and Social Psychology Review, 1*, 80–102.

Seger, C. A., Stone, M., & Keenan, J. P. (2004). Cortical activations during judgments about the self and an other person. *Neuropsychologia, 42*, 1168–1177.

Seyfarth, R. M., & Cheney, D. L. (2003). Signalers and receivers in animal communcation. *Annual Review of Psychology, 54*, 145–173.

Shin, L. M., Dougherty, D. D., Orr, S. P., Pitman, R. K., Lasko, M., Macklin, M. L., et al. (2000). Activation of anterior paralimbic structures during guilt-related script-driven imagery. *Biological Psychiatry, 48*, 43–50.

Somerville, L. H., Heatherton, T. F., & Kelley, W. M. (2006). Dissociating expectancy violation from social rejection. *Nature Neuroscience, 9*, 1007–1008.

Steinvorth, S., Corkin, S., & Halgren, E. (2006). Ecphory of autobiographical memories: An fMRI study of recent and remote memory retrieval. *NeuroImage, 30*, 285–298.

Stone, V. E., Baron-Cohen, S., & Knight, R. T. (1998). Does frontal lobe damage produce theory of mind impairment? *Journal of Cognitive Neuroscience, 10*, 640–656.

Stuss, D. T., & Alexander, M. P. (1994). *Functional and anatomical specificity of frontal lobe functions*. New York: Plenum Press.

Stuss, D. T., & Alexander, M. P. (2000). Executive functions and the frontal lobes: A conceptual view. *Psychology Research, 63*(3–4), 289–298.

Stuss, D. T., & Benson, D. F. (1984). Neuropsychological studies of the frontal lobes. *Psychological Bulletin, 95*, 3–28.

Stuss, D. T., Gallup, G. G., & Alexander, M. P. (2001). The frontal lobes are necessary for 'theory of mind.' *Brain, 124*, 279–286.

Symons, C. S., & Johnson, B. T. (1997). The self-reference effect in memory: A meta-analysis. *Psychological Bulletin, 121*, 371–394.

Takahashi, H., Yahata, N., Koeda, M., Matsuda, T., Asai, K., & Okubo, Y. (2004). Brain activation associated with evaluative processes of guilt and embarassment: An fMRI study. *NeuroImage, 23*, 967–974.

Tomasello, M., Hare, B., & Agnetta, B. (1999). Chimpanzees follow gaze direction geometrically. *Animal Behaviour, 58*, 769–777.

Tulving, E. (1993). *Self-knowledge of an amnesic individual is represented abstractly*. Hillsdale, NJ: Erlbaum.

Turk, D. J., Heatherton, T. F., Macrae, C. N., Kelley, W. M., & Gazzaniga, M. S. (2003). Out of contact, out of mind: The distributed nature of the self. *Annals of the New York Academy of Sciences, USA, 1001*, 65–78.

Vogeley, K., & Fink, G. R. (2003). Neural correlates of first-person perspective. *Trends in Cognitive Sciences, 7*, 38–42.

Wegner, D. M. (1989). *White bears and other unwanted thoughts: Suppression, obsession, and the psychology of mental control*. New York: Penguin Press.

Wegner, D. M. (1994). Ironic processes of mental control. *Psychological Review, 101*, 34–52.

Whalen, P. J. (1998). Fear, vigilance, and ambiguity: Initial neuroimaging studies of the human amygdala. *Current Directions in Psychological Science, 7*, 177–188.

Wheeler, M. A., Stuss, D. T., & Tulving, E. (1997). Toward a theory of episodic memory: The frontal lobes and autonoetic consciousness. *Psychological Bulletin, 121*, 331–354.

Wheeler, M. E., & Fiske, S. T. (2005). Controlling racial prejudice: Social-cognitive goals affect amygdala and stereotype activation. *Psychological Sciences, 16*, 56–63.

Wyland, C. L., Kelley, W. M., Macrae, C. N., Gordon, H. L., & Heatherton, T. F. (2003). Neural correlates of thought suppression. *Neuropsychologia, 41*, 1863–1867.

Chapter 45

Language Processes

HOWARD C. NUSBAUM AND DANIEL MARGOLIASH

Although physicists have debated the possibility of action at a distance for quite some time, the biological form of action at a distance is well established, as achieved through vocal communication in an extremely broad range of behaviors and settings. Many species of fish, amphibians, reptiles, birds, and mammals commonly exchange information at a distance through their calls. The learned songs (and some calls) of songbirds are particularly rich sources of information, conveying to the receiver individual identity and a host of other characteristics of the sender (Kroodsma & Miller, 1996). Frogs are generally characterized by their low frequency hearing, yet some species have evolved ultrasonic communication to communicate in high noise environments near streams and waterfalls (Feng et al., 2006). Some mammals exchange information at great distances through calling behavior. Humpback whale (Megaptera novaeangliae) vocalizations are perceived over extremely long distances and may be used to maintain social groups at distances as great as 5 km (Frankel, Clark, Herman, & Gabriele, 1995). African elephants (Loxodonta africana) can recognize friends and relatives from their calls at a distance of 2.5 km (McComb, Reby, Baker, Moss, & Sayialel, 2003). Among the nonhuman primates, flanged male orangutans (Pongo pygmaeus) are notable for maintaining spacing with other males and advertising for receptive females over distances of at least 1 km with their long calls (Galdikas, 1983; MacKinnon, 1974). Human sheepherders keep each other company from the top of one mountain to another in the Canary Islands using a whistled language called *Silbo Gomero* (Busnel & Classe, 1976). Whether for purposes of mating, threat, warning, or social organization, conveying information regarding location, identity, and motivation, and directed at one individual or toward far-flung groups, vocal communication plays an important role in the social connection and behavior of a great number of vertebrate species. This affords insight into biological constraints on the evolution of vocal communication systems.

HUMAN UNIQUENESS AND COMPUTATIONAL MECHANISMS

The differences often loom larger when we compare human spoken language with nonhuman vocal communication. Certainly, the issue of the "human uniqueness" of language, whether taken broadly across a variety of properties (e.g., Pinker & Jackendoff, 2005) or defined minimally (Hauser, Chomsky, & Fitch, 2002; Hauser, Barner, & O'Donnell, 2007) has become a point of substantial controversy (see Gentner, Fenn, Margoliash, & Nusbaum, 2006). An extreme view, primarily attributed to Chomsky (1988), Piattelli-Palmarini (1989), and by Pinker (2003) to Gould (1997), is that language "could not" have evolved because certain aspects of language such as recursive processing in grammar could not have emerged gradually. This argumentation unwittingly supports "creation science" (see Bates, Thal, & Marchman, 1991), and appropriately so—it is wholly ignorant of evolutionary process whereby radical specialization can emerge. Consider, for example, the existence of ultrasonic frogs, or recursive processing in other human cognitive domains.

By contrast, Pinker (2003) and Pinker and Bloom (1990) argue that language is the result of evolution through adaptation. Pinker contrasts this with the idea that language is manifest as the result of more general cognitive evolution. In other words, from the Chomskian perspective, language emerged without evolutionary antecedents. But from Pinker's perspective, language evolved, and Pinker and Bloom (1990) assert the possibility of natural selection operating as the basis for the intelligent "design" of the syntactic complexity demonstrated in human language. According to this argument, comparative biology is not helpful in understanding this evolutionary development because it all occurred over the 200,000 to 300,000 generations that have occurred since our divergence from our common ancestor with modern apes (Pinker, 2003). Thus, the theoretical sanctity of human uniqueness is entirely preserved by the evolutionary isolation of humans from other species from that point on, as is true during the course of evolution as each species emerges at the point of reproductive isolation. Human vocalizations do not leave a fossil image, but neither do those vocalizations of other animals whose behavior has been usefully analyzed from an evolutionary perspective. Those who write with confidence regarding the kind of evidence that future research will bring to bear on the notion of human uniqueness do so with unjustified confidence.

The issue of the human uniqueness of language is fundamentally not a deep philosophical problem, but a pragmatic problem of a sparse evolutionary history (one surviving species of Homo) during a period of rapid evolutionary change. Imagine if we could investigate the vocal repertoire of Cro Magnum and Neanderthal. So far we cannot, so it is unlikely that there will be a simple resolution to this debate because psychologists are obligated to investigate the internal "mental" states (goals etc.) to understand deeply what could be communicated among nonhuman animals. However, we do know that the set of communications (regularly used, differentiable vocalizations) is substantially restricted in nonhuman species compared to humans and the flexibility in the circumstances of the use of these vocalizations appears much more restricted (Hauser, 1996). Thus, regardless of the ultimate theoretical or empirical resolution to the human uniqueness debate, humans appear to have more things to talk about and use more ways to say the same thing when compared with nonhuman vocal communication systems. This enormous breadth (perhaps unlimited) of vocal repertoire in speech is attributed to a core property of language to generate entirely novel utterances to express new concepts.

The productivity of human language is one of its most interesting properties, which contrasts with vocal communication systems in other species that are much smaller, and often fixed throughout adult life. In human language, there is a system for producing new patterns from some foundation of shared knowledge and a way for recipients to understand these entirely new communication patterns. Animals have a much smaller range of variation in this context, but it is not zero. Some species such as mockingbirds (Mimus polyglottus) acquire new vocalizations throughout life, and birds such as thrushes (e.g., American robin, Turdus migratorius) produce continually variable song patterns, albeit how much information is conveyed in that variation remains unresolved. With a fixed message set, communication systems can (but need not be) relatively simple using specific predetermined motor plans for production and matching communicative signals to previously learned templates or patterns. However, when the communicative needs of a novel situation demand expression, new

utterances must be generated from idiosyncratic experience, but these messages must be understandable to a listener without the same prior experience.

For human language, Hockett (1960) considered this one of the fundamental "design" principles. The property of productivity (producing novel utterances) can be thought of as resulting from the property called "duality of patterning" together with the property of arbitrariness (the pattern of an expression is arbitrary in relation to the meaning of an expression). Duality of patterning refers to the fact that, in language, pattern elements without intrinsic meaning (i.e., phonemes) combine to make meaningful patterns (i.e., words), and meaningful patterns can be combined to make other meaningful patterns (e.g., sentences). Given that the meaning of patterns is arbitrary with respect to the form of the pattern itself, it is possible to make new meaning patterns by different combinations of existing meaningful units (e.g., to make new sentences) or by novel combinations of the meaningless units to make new meaningful units (e.g., novel words). As a result, the range of expression for human language is not bounded by a fixed set of vocalization patterns. Moreover, based on the principle of arbitrariness, a language can be constructed on the basis of almost any set of intrinsically meaningless elements that can be combined, thus licensing sign languages and printed languages. New words can be coined and combined in novel ways and these two levels of analysis—the lexical and syntactic—have thus been the focus of much language research.

Indeed, Pinker (2003) distinguishes two attributes of language—word recognition and grammar—with respect to the importance of evolution and human uniqueness. From his perspective, words are simply a memorized pairing of pattern form (e.g., sound pattern) with meaning. Therefore, this kind of associative system, which is found in many animals, is not the locus of the intelligent design of language through adaptation (Pinker & Bloom, 1990). Several studies (e.g., Cohen & Dehaene, 2004; Cohen, Jobert, LeBihan, & Dehaene, 2004; Vinckier et al., 2007) have examined the role of a part of the fusiform gyrus in recognizing visual word forms. This work suggests that visual word recognition may be understood as an exaptation (Gould, 1991; Gould & Vrba, 1982) of visual object recognition processing (Dehaene & Cohen, 2007). Similarly, spoken word recognition may be viewed as arising from the neural mechanisms involved in general auditory and conceptual processing (see Price, Thierry, & Griffiths, 2005) and thus as an exaptation of more general auditory pattern recognition and cognitive processes.

According to Pinker (2003), it is grammar that provides Hockett's (1960) productivity. Grammar consists of syntax, morphology, and phonology. Syntax is the rule system that governs the ordering of words into linguistically acceptable sentences. Morphology is the rule system that governs affixing and the extensibility of lexical forms. Phonology is the rule system that governs the sound patterns of a language. Together these rule systems provide for the productive extensibility that comes from creating words and creating sentences. It is the grammar that is viewed as unique to humans and has evolved uniquely to suit the specific information and social demands of humans.

These descriptions define a complexity of human vocalizations beyond those of nonhuman species, but not categorically so. For example, the songs of European starlings (Sturnus vulgaris) comprise sequences of motifs, and different motifs comprise sequences of notes. Notes apparently are arbitrary, but motifs have meaning if not semantic value, in the sense that motifs appear to be the fundamental unit that drives vocal recognition. There is an overall structure to the sequence of motifs within song (whistles, variable phrases, rattles, and high-frequency phrases) but this varies from one song rendition to the next (Adret-Hausberger & Jenkins, 1988; Eens, Pinxten, & Verheyen, 1989). Again, the full extent of information conveyed in all this variation is unknown, but there is good evidence that at least some features of variation carry information (Gentner & Hulse, 2000).

In communication systems with a fixed vocal repertoire, utterance recognition could be quite simple, at least when described abstractly in a pristine research setting isolated from the real world. A set of pattern templates can be compared to auditory transforms (minimizing distortion and noise by filtering) of utterances and the closest match selected similar to the way the first small vocabulary speech recognition systems operated. This vastly oversimplifies real vocal recognition because multiple signals can overlap in time, vocalizations show variations due to the individual and the environment that can defeat linear separability of even a small set of patterns unless constructed robustly by design. These limitations hampered the success of even small vocabulary speech recognition systems (e.g., Nusbaum & Pisoni, 1987) for human speech. However, the problems become insurmountable when small fixed-vocabulary recognition problems become open-ended, fluent continuous spoken language understanding problems (cf. Klatt, 1977). Small vocabulary recognition systems are successful because of the constraints provided by the task at hand (which could be limited to flight status or account numbers) and the choice of vocabulary (that can be prompted within the task) using highly discriminable items. The validity of this viewpoint is best tested with the more complex animal vocalizations such as those of starlings or mockingbirds, which have much larger repertoires and greater variability than single-song fixed repertoire species, but far less variation than do humans. In principle,

it should be possible to design a highly accurate song recognition system for such species of birds, but so far none have yet been reported (c.f. Kogan & Margoliash, 1998; Tao, Johnson, & Osiejuk, 2008).

When expanded beyond these bounds, the recognition possibilities increase dramatically and a different approach is needed (Klatt, 1977) that is more about language and less about task constraints. Moreover, if not all utterances we understand have been heard previously (even if many of them have been heard) and thus cannot be stored in some form ahead of time, it becomes necessary to compose new interpretations out of utterance parts. This suggests that the computational demands of recognition for spoken language might well be different from the computational requirements of recognizing a limited set of possible utterances, or in the case of some species, presumptively limited recognition within a large possible set of utterances. This places constraints on what can be gained from a comparative neuroethology of vocal communication.

PRODUCTION AND COMPREHENSION

The functional linkage between production and perception of biologically significant signals has often suggested that there should be interactions among the underlying neural systems, whether in crickets (Hoy & Paul, 1973), songbirds (Gentner & Margoliash, 2002; Margoliash, 2002; Marler & Peters, 1980), bats (e.g., Moss & Sinha, 2003), or humans (Liberman & Mattingly, 1985). When signal producers are also signal perceivers, there is a tendency to assume that some kind of common processing system may underlie aspects of both. From an engineering perspective, if one were building a device to both produce and interpret a set of signals, there needs to be a way to relate the meaning of signals, even if the generation of a signal is physically different from the sensory encoding of a signal. However, for organisms, the common principles derive not only from the physical constraints of the environments and the signals (which engineers will know about), but also from evolutionary constraints (which engineers will not know about). This can have unexpected consequences. For example, in the electric fish, "timed" electric pulses are used as a kind of sonar system for perceiving the environment, and when two fish are close, their signals can interfere. To avoid this interference, the fish that is sending lower-frequency signals reduces frequency and the higher-frequency sender increases signal frequency. One might assume that part of this jamming avoidance response depends on the use of a common "pacer" or "clock" neuron both in production and perception, but this is not correct—the system is much more complicated (Heiligenberg, 1991; Nelson & MacIver,

2006). This suggests the cautionary point that the assumption of processing commonality between production and perception simply on the face of apparent similarity can be wholly misleading.

Theories of speech perception that depend on the motor system have a long history in modern speech research (at least over the past 40 years). For example, Liberman and his colleagues (e.g., Liberman, Cooper, Shankweiler, & Studdert-Kennedy, 1967; Liberman & Mattingly, 1985) argued that speech *perception* could only be accounted for by the involvement of the motor system. In the most general terms, the theory was intended to account for our ability to recognize phonemes in spite of the many-to-many relationship between acoustic patterns and linguistic categories. This lack of invariance between acoustic patterns and phonetic categories is observed, for example, for vowel categories between speakers (Peterson & Barney, 1952) and for stop consonants across vowel contexts (Liberman et al., 1967) and for consonants at different rates of speech (Francis & Nusbaum, 1996). A particular acoustic pattern for a phoneme (e.g., the second formant transition for the consonant /d/) may be different in two contexts (e.g., /i/ and /u/) and yet listeners hear the same phoneme regardless of context. Moreover, the same acoustic pattern (e.g., formant transition rate) may indicate two different phonemes (e.g., /b/ or /w/) depending on context (e.g., speaking rate). In theoretical terms, perhaps the most critical feature of the lack of invariance problem is that it makes speech recognition an inherently nondeterministic process (see Nusbaum & Magnuson, 1997).

A deterministic process is one in which the prior history, the current state of the system, and the current input to the system uniquely specify a single next state for the system. In a simple case, each unique input pattern has a unique corresponding invariant interpretation. By contrast, a nondeterministic process is one in which there is more than one possible state even given the prior history, current state, and input state. As pointed out by Nusbaum and Henly (unpublished manuscript), this is a general problem for language at all levels of analysis: The phonetic interpretation of acoustic speech patterns, the lexical interpretation of phonetic sequences, and the sentential interpretation of lexical sequences all have a many-to-many mapping that makes the process of interpreting linguistic patterns nondeterministic.

NONDETERMINISM AND ACTIVE PROCESSES

To understand the significance of this, we need to consider briefly the definition of a finite state automaton (Gross,

1972; Hopcroft & Ullman, 1969). A finite state automaton is an abstract computational mechanism that can represent (in terms of computational theory) a broad class of different "real" computational processes. A finite state automaton consists of a set of states (that differ from each other), a vocabulary of symbols, a mapping process that denotes how to change to a new state given an old state and an input symbol, a starting state, and a set of ending states. Finite state automata have been used to represent and analyze grammars (e.g., Gross, 1972) and other formal computational problems (Hopcroft & Ullman, 1969). For our purposes, the states can be thought of as representing internal linguistic states such as phonetic features or categories and the symbols can be thought of as acoustic properties present in an utterance. The possible orderings of permissible states in the automaton can be thought of as the phonotactic constraints inherent in language. The transition from one state to another that determines those orderings is based on acoustic input with acoustic cues serving as the input symbols to the system. This is actually a relatively uncontroversial conceptualization of speech recognition (e.g., Klatt, 1979; Levinson, Rabiner, & Sondhi, 1983; Lowerre & Reddy, 1980) and is similar to the use of finite state automata in other areas of language processing such as syntactic analysis (e.g., Charniak, 1993; Woods, 1973).

A deterministic finite state automaton changes from one state to another such that the new state is uniquely determined by the information (i.e., next symbol) that is processed. In speech, this means that if there were a one-to-one relationship between acoustic information and the phonetic classification of that information (i.e., each acoustic cue denotes one and only one phonetic category or feature), a wide variety of relatively simple deterministic computational mechanisms (e.g., some simple context-free grammars, Chomsky, 1957; feature detectors, Abbs & Sussman, 1971) could be invoked to explain the apparent ease with which we recognize speech. As we know all too well by now, this is not the case. Instead, there is a many-to-many mapping between acoustic patterns and phonetic categories, which is referred to as the *lack of invariance problem.*

Theories of Perceptual Invariance

Any particular phonetic category (or feature) may be instantiated acoustically by a variety of different acoustic patterns. Conversely, any particular acoustic pattern may be interpreted as a variety of different phonetic categories (or features). Although a many-to-one mapping can still be processed by a deterministic finite state automaton because each new category or state is still uniquely determined, albeit by different symbols or information (e.g., the set of different cues any one of which could denote a particular feature), the one-to-many mapping represents a nondeterministic problem. Given the current state of the system and the acoustic information, there are multiple possible states to which the system could change. There is nothing inherent in the input symbol or acoustic information, or in the system itself, that uniquely determines the classification of that information (i.e., the next state of the system). In other words, there is a computational ambiguity that is unresolvable given just the information that describes the system. Thus, interpreting speech sounds and linguistic structure depends on additional information. What form that information takes and to what degree it is innately specified or acquired and modified during development represent issues of central importance for language research.

Motor theory originally proposed that knowledge of the process of articulation could be used in resolving this computational ambiguity (Liberman, Cooper, Harris, & MacNeilage, 1962). Subsequently, the motor theory was revised (Liberman & Mattingly, 1985) to suggest that the sound patterns of speech are not the proximal stimuli for phoneme perception; rather listeners directly perceive the motor gestures that gave rise to the sounds. Under this revised version, speech perception is treated as a module (see Fodor, 1983) that is explicitly independent of other processes involved in auditory perception or cognition.

However, none of these approaches has been entirely successful or convincing in explaining phonetic constancy. All depend on the assumption that the appropriate kind of (e.g., motor) knowledge or representation will be sufficient to restructure the nondeterministic relationship between the acoustic patterns of speech and the linguistic interpretation into a deterministic relationship. Measures of speech production show as much lack of invariance in the motor system as there is in the relationship between acoustics and phonetics (e.g., MacNeilage, 1970). As noted earlier, there is as much lack of invariance between sound patterns and larger linguistic units (e.g., syllables, words) as there is with phonemes or phonetic features. And the perspective that better acoustic knowledge would provide an invariant mapping has failed as well.

One interpretation of the problem of lack of invariance is that the kinds of acoustic analyses being carried out in typical acoustic-phonetic research (e.g., spectrographs for examining time-frequency-amplitude plots of speech patterns) do not reveal acoustic invariance that other types of analyses might show. For example, Stevens and Blumstein (1978, 1981) provided evidence that when the power spectrum of the initial 25.6 ms of the release of a stop consonant (e.g., /b/ or /d/) is examined, the distribution of energy is invariant with respect to place of articulation (e.g., /d/ or /t/ versus /b/ or /p/), and listeners can use this

to classify the speech. The argument was that this energy distribution would provide an invariant acoustic signature for one important phonetic aspect of consonants previously thought to show lack of invariance (Liberman et al., 1967). However, when the putative spectral invariant cue was tested directly against the variable cue formant patterns over time, Walley and Carrell (1983) demonstrated that listeners carry out phonetic classification by using the noninvariant portions of the signal rather than the invariant portions. Listeners appear to use context-dependent acoustic information even when context-independent cues are present.

Theories of speech perception have largely failed to explain phonetic constancy given the problem of lack of invariance because they have taken the wrong tack on analyzing the problem (see Nusbaum & Magnuson, 1997). Although place of articulation is taken as the paradigm case of lack of invariance, the same issues hold for vowel perception and talker variability (Nusbaum & Morin, 1992) and for speaking rate and manner (Francis & Nusbaum, 1996). Theories focus on addressing one particular limited aspect of lack of invariance and then in broad strokes assume that other aspects of the problem will be addressed similarly in spite of important differences among these problems. By focusing on a content analysis of the lack of invariance problem, these theories have tried to specify the type of information or knowledge that would permit accurate recovery of phonetic structure from acoustic patterns. In other words, there is an assumption that if we only had the right acoustic analysis (e.g., onset power spectrum), the right decoding information (e.g., the motor codebook), or some broader rule-based knowledge (e.g., syntactic structure), the lack of invariance problem would disappear. However, there is no reason to believe that these approaches can basically change what is fundamentally a nondeterministic problem into a deterministic problem that could be solved by a simple computational architecture like a finite-state automaton.

To understand the process of speech perception, it may be critical to analyze the computational considerations inherent in a nondeterministic system. The point of this section has been to argue that it is important to shift the focus of theories from a consideration of the problem of lack of invariance as a matter of determining the correct representation of the information in speech to a definition of the problem in computational terms. We claim speech perception is a nondeterministic computational problem. Furthermore, we claim that deterministic mechanisms and passive systems are incapable of accounting for phonetic constancy. Human speech perception requires an active control system in order to resolve the fundamental lack of invariance between acoustic patterns and phonetic categories. By focusing on an analysis of the specific nature of the active system used in speech perception, it will be possible to develop theories that provide better explanations of phonetic constancy.

Active systems have been proposed as explanations of speech perception in the past (see Nusbaum & Schwab, 1986), including analysis-by-synthesis (Stevens & Halle, 1967) and Trace (McClelland & Elman, 1986). These theories have acknowledged the importance of complex control systems in accounting for phonetic constancy. However, even in these theories, the focus has been on the nature of the information (e.g., articulatory in analysis-by-synthesis and acoustic-phonetic, phonological, and lexical in Trace); the active control system has subserved the role of delivering the specific information at the appropriate time or in the appropriate manner. Unfortunately, from our perspective, these earlier theories took relatively restricted views of the problem of lack of invariance. Although all theories of speech perception have generally acknowledged that lack of invariance arises from variation in phonetic context, speaking rate, and the vocal characteristics of talkers, most theories have focused on the problem of variation in phonetic context alone. By focusing on the specific knowledge or representations needed to maintain phonetic constancy over variability in context, these theories developed highly specific approaches that do not generalize to problems of talker variability or variability in speaking rate (e.g., see Klatt, 1986, for a discussion of this problem in Trace). For these theories, there is no clear set of principles for dealing with nondeterminism in speech that would indicate how to generalize these theories to other sources of variability such as talker variability.

However, the theory of analysis by synthesis (Stevens & Halle, 1967) presented an active theory of speech perception in which the motor system was invoked in service of resolving the lack of invariance between acoustic patterns and phonetic categories. In this theory, the auditory transforms of acoustic speech patterns were matched against stored representations of phonetic categories. When a clear match could be made, the phoneme was recognized. However, when there was a problem matching the pattern to a single phonetic category due to lack of invariance, a motor simulation of speech production was carried out internally to synthesize the patterns that would arise in the context that had been recognized. This is a kind of internal active processing similar to active processing seen in other species for resolving complex sensory inputs (e.g., Moss, Bohn, Gilkenson, & Surlykke, 2006; Nelson & McIver, 2006).

Although proponents of motor theory have argued that there is substantial behavioral evidence supporting motor theory (e.g., Liberman & Mattingly, 1985), alternative theories based only on passive auditory processes (e.g., Diehl, Lotto, & Holt, 2004) can account for much of the same data. In many respects, this situation parallels the debate about the representation of mental imagery in terms of perceptual processes or propositional-symbolic processes; behavioral data can be explained by very different alternative theories and neurophysiological evidence was viewed as the only basis for testing among the theories (see Anderson, 1978). The parallel deficits in perception and mental imagery for patients with visual agnosia (Farah, 1984) provided strong evidence in support of the perceptual representation theory. Furthermore, neuroimaging data showing activity in visual areas during mental imagery (Kosslyn & Sussman, 1994; Kosslyn, Thompson, & Alpert, 1997) converges with the neuropsychology data to strongly support this type of theory. Thus, neurophysiological evidence can be critical to testing specific aspects of psychological theories when behavioral evidence is equivocal. However, this takes a very narrow view of the role of neuroscience in understanding biologically important processes such as vocal communication.

Metaphors and Mechanisms

Perhaps a more important role for neuroscience is to offer new ways to understand behavior such as vocal communication. Psychological explanations and theories derive metaphors from a wide range of human experience, from steam engines to telephone switchboards to digital computers. However, neuroscience offers new metaphors and mechanisms to explain psychological processes (cf. Churchland, 1999). Historically, some research has tried to impose linguistic analyses on specific brain regions, whereas other research has tried to use language-processing deficits associated with brain injuries as the basis for neuroscience theories. By using research on neurophysiology as a basis for theory and by understanding the systems neuroscience research of other complex behaviors, it is possible that new theories of language processing may be developed.

Researchers often make strong theoretical pronouncements about the mechanisms of speech perception with little or no empirical support but based on a functionalist analysis and introspection. For over half a century, the scientific study of language has been strongly influenced by the perspective of linguistics (e.g., Chomsky, 1957). Note that linguistic investigation represents just one way to study language, and that psychology, sociology, computer science, anthropology, neurobiology, and philosophy all play important roles in understanding language. During this time, two basic assumptions shaped a broad range of language research particularly in psychology and neurobiology. The first assumption is that we can separate out the study of language as an object of inquiry from the study of language use. The competence/performance distinction is rooted in the notion that there is a Platonic idealization of language that can be studied independent of the moment-by-moment limitations, distractions, and disturbances to which all human performance is subject. In other words, language can be studied independently of other aspects of psychology including cognitive processing, social interaction, and affective processing, and language areas of the brain can be understood apart from other complementary regions and networks, such as the motor system or the limbic system. It is this perspective—separating language from all of psychology and much of biology—that allows extreme views to arise (such as the claim that language could not have evolved).

The second assumption derives from the notion that we can analytically separate putative language functions from each other, and having done so, empirically study each as if truly dissociated from other language functions. The prototypical example is syntax. Chomsky (1957) initially viewed the explanation of syntactic processing as a component of the language system that was scientifically tractable and isolatable from other aspects of language. One aspect of Chomsky's work was an attempt to outline the way in which competing theories of syntax could be tested under the assumption that the problem of syntax was sufficiently tractable that it would give rise to a number of such theories. Unfortunately, given the lack of any sufficient theory of syntax, testing among equally competent theories has not been a serious problem for linguistics. But we infer that the entire enterprise of isolating for analysis a psychological process that appears to be tractable on its own terms may be misleading. If the fundamental assumption of an area of inquiry is flawed, progress, even considerable progress, can be made within that area, but with the underlying errors unchallenged.

Consider attempts to understand airflow over the wing of an airplane (see Gleick, 1987). Under some conditions, airflow over a wing is smooth and laminar whereas under other conditions, airflow is noisy and turbulent. For a long time, these two types of physical behavior were viewed as having entirely different theoretic explanations, one being simple and linear and the other complex and nonlinear. However, this separation into systems based on apparently different modes of behavior led researchers away from a single, simpler explanation in terms of a chaotic dynamical system.

These are not just philosophical considerations of metaphorical examples, but are highly relevant to understanding behavior at all levels of analysis. In the neurosciences, sensory processing had long been analyzed with far greater attention paid to *ascending* than to *descending connections.* Yet, we now know that in the auditory system, descending input from the cortex fundamentally shapes the receptive field properties of subcortical neurons (e.g., Yan & Suga, 1996). Thus, auditory receptive fields can be studied ignoring the role of descending inputs, but this will limit the understanding of time-domain, frequency domain, and attentional influences. In the visual system, it is established that principle ascending connections to the cortex arising from the thalamus account for approximately 5% of all input to cortical cells (Douglas & Martin, 1991). Receptive fields can be studied ignoring the role of descending inputs and intercortical connections, but this will limit the understanding of numerous psychophysical phenomena such as illusory contours (von der Heydt, Peterhans, & Baumgartner, 1984). In many areas of inquiry, neurobiology has been highly successful taking the approach to study isolated systems, but behavior is the sum total of the interactions of all those systems. This perspective helps to motivate neuroethological studies, which tend to be more holistic.

These examples help to emphasize that it is deeply problematic to assume that because we can be analytically introspective about syntactic structure or any particular psychological process, it has an independent psychological and biological reality from other psychological processes. As described by Fodor (1983), the notion of an autonomous, biologically fixed, evolutionarily expert, mandatory, and automatic syntactic processor has given rise to a great deal of research and controversy (e.g., Appelbaum, 1998; Garfield, 1987; Sperber, 2001). As in the case of all language processing modules (e.g., lexical module), the controversy has generally focused on whether processing falling within the domain of expertise of the putative module interacts with other kinds of processing outside the module (beyond the operation of a discrete input and output stage). Proponents of modularity deny such interaction whereas opponents support it.

Theoretical considerations aside, this kind of debate has had important practical consequences, limiting experimental design and isolating theory from verification and falsification. Language processing is often studied independent of context and separately for each putative unit of analysis—syllables, words, or sentences. Language processing is typically studied without much consideration for the relationship of the interlocutors to each other in a conversation—in those relatively rare instances when actual face-to-face conversation is studied (see Pickering & Garrod, 2004). Language processing is often studied as independent of other cognitive, affective, and social mechanisms. Language processing is studied without consideration for the speaker's intentions or goals or the listener's intentions or goals. In theoretic terms, it is generally accepted in much of language research that messages can be understood independent of situation (i.e., pragmatic context) or even independent of the contents of the message. In other words, it is assumed that the possible importance (i.e., personal relevance) of a message's meaning to a listener has little or no bearing on the way the message is processed as language. Understanding the message is typically viewed as independent of what we understand about the person who was talking (although, e.g., see Holtgraves, 1994). On the one hand, the assumption of modular language mechanisms is often viewed as a "null hypothesis" to be rejected by specific experiments and therefore only a testable theoretic proposition. On the other hand, this is a theoretic foundation that shifts research away from the basic evolutionary forces that actually shaped the biological development of linguistic communication—the need for social interaction between people. This limits the potential impact of the large body of ethological and neuroethological literature investigating the vocal communication and social interaction for understanding language processing.

Dewey (1896) pointed out that although researchers can analytically decompose a mental process into separated components, the reality of such components is not substantiated by that analysis. Furthermore, just starting with the assumption of separability or isolability leads to research questions and methods that would not otherwise be employed but that could distort, in various ways, our understanding of a psychological system such as language. Dewey recognized that in many cases goals and motives may actually determine (i.e., restructure or change) the nature of the entire processing system rather than simply affect the outcome of processing. This notion goes well beyond the standard view of interactions in which one process provides inputs to another process. Instead, this is closer to the idea emerging from some neuroscience research (e.g., Barrie, Freeman, & Lenhart, 1996; Freeman, 2003; Freeman & Skarda, 1990), that neural processes and representations are context-sensitive and can change dynamically with goals and motivations and experience.

Churchland (1999) has argued that we need to move from a theoretical vocabulary rooted in functionalism to a new "eliminative materialism" in which explanations would be grounded directly in the theoretical constructs of neuroscience. It is possible by examining the functional anatomy of vocal communication, we may come to a different parsing of language processing, one grounded in neurobiological operation and structure, rather than introspection and analysis. Of course, there is a long history of theories of spoken language use that is grounded in neuroscience.

NEURAL MECHANISMS OF LANGUAGE USE

Before we had the technology to systematically measure brain responses during psychological processing, the primary method of studying neural mechanisms was through intervention by natural accident or surgery. Thus, Broca (1861) described a patient Leborgne who had severe brain damage to the left side of his brain (see Figure 45.1) and as a result could only utter a single nonsense syllable. Broca's aphasia, widely associated with damage to the left inferior frontal gyrus (IFG, although damage is seldom confined to that region) has long been identified as "expressive aphasia." An aphasia is defined as a selective disruption of a language function and expressive aphasia was described as selective damage to the ability to produce language.

Wernicke (1874) subsequently identified damage to a posterior region of the superior temporal gyrus but extending into the parietal cortex (see Figure 45.1, although c.f. Bogen & Bogen, 1976) with a selective loss of comprehension or "receptive aphasia." This led to a proposed neural model of language processing in which the respective functions of talking and understanding were assigned to different cortical areas, one in the IFG and one in the posterior (pSTG)/inferior parietal region. Lichtheim (1885) developed a more elaborated model of language use that related neural mechanisms for production, comprehension, and conceptual representation and their relationships in processing. This relatively simple view of the neural mechanisms of language processing was being advocated as late as the 1970s (Geschwind, 1970), suggesting little theoretical development in the neuroscience of language over 100 years.

While subjectively the difference between talking and listening (expressive and receptive language processing) seems like a plausible division of language function, this is a very different view of the parts of language than has developed in either modern linguistics or psychology.

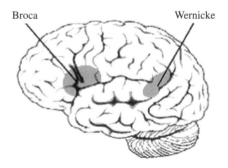

Figure 45.1 Left lateral surface of the brain showing (roughly) the location of Broca's area (inferior frontal gyrus or IFG) and Wernicke's area (posterior superior temporal gyrus, or pSTG, and inferior parietal, or iPL).

Areas of language "competence" such as phonetics, phonology, morphology, semantics, syntax, and pragmatics represent the divisions that linguists view as domains of research, whereas psychological research at these levels of analysis considers aspects of processing such as speech perception, word recognition, syntactic constraint, and so on.

The behavioral approach has long guided the neuroethological branch of auditory research (Capranica, 1972; Roeder, 1964), and in visual science, animal neurophysiological research has more recently emerged as providing potent evidence to guide psychophysical and perceptual theory and interpretation (e.g., von der Heydt et al., 1984; Newsome, Shadlen, Zohary, Britten, & Movshon, 1995; Teller, 1984) and vice versa (see Chalupa & Werner, 2003). Similarly, for issues of low-level speech processing, animal models have provided valuable guidance. Evidence for categorical perception *and thus an aspect of phonetic constancy* in nonhuman mammals (Kuhl & Miller, 1975) and in birds (Kluender, Diehl, & Killeen, 1987) helped to evaluate claims of human uniqueness for those attributes of speech perception. Analysis of peripheral representations of speech signals (e.g., Sachs & Young, 1979) informed theories of population coding of speech. Analysis of sensitivity of neurons to missing fundamentals has identified a region of auditory cortex in monkeys and humans specialized for pitch processing (Bendor & Wang, 2005). A state-dependent neuronal replay phenomenon (Dave & Margoliash, 2000; Dave, Yu, & Margoliash, 1998) has stimulated research on the role of sleep in vocal learning (Derégnaucourt, Mitra, Feher, Pytte, & Tchernichovski, 2005; Shank & Margoliash, in press), and the role of sleep in speech perceptual learning (Fenn, Nusbaum, & Margoliash, 2003).

A similar approach has not been exploited for language processing. Neuroimaging data makes it possible to compare neurophysiological measures in humans and animals further advancing research. Without a clear animal model and without direct neurophysiological measures, however, the neuroscience of language has until recently been constrained to study patients with brain damage and some interventions in clinical patients such as electrical stimulation.

The advent of neuroimaging and other modern neuroscience methods (e.g., transcranial magnetic stimulation, human electrophysiology) has changed the scientific and conceptual landscape of human neuroscience research. Neuroimaging methods make it possible to relate specific ongoing psychological processing to patterns of brain activity (electrical, hemodynamic, or metabolic) in particular anatomical regions. This minimally provides a common theoretical reference for cognitive neuroscientists, in terms of brain anatomy. By identifying brain regions that,

through damage, transcranial magnetic stimulation (TMS; see Devlin & Watkins, 2007), or electrical stimulation (e.g., Ojemann & Mateer, 1979), affect behavior and that are activated in association with behavior and that can be related to research on animals, it becomes possible to develop a more coherent neuroscientific explanation of psychological processing in language.

TOWARD A NEW MOTOR THEORY OF SPEECH PERCEPTION

As noted, the neuroscience of language processing has long been shaped by studies of patients with relatively focal brain lesions. In many areas of cognitive and social neuroscience (e.g., memory and behavioral regulation), research has been influenced by notable patients such as HM and Phineas Gage (e.g., see Farah & Feinberg, 2000). However, this foundation has always been tempered by animal models of perception, memory, and even aspects of behavioral control and emotion that make possible neurophysiological measures and intervention that could not be carried out with human participants until recently. However, a different approach to thinking about the neuroscience of communication has emerged from research on the motor system.

This research indicated that neurons previously thought to play a role in the production of action also play a role in understanding observed action. Rizzolatti and colleagues (see Rizzolatti & Craighero, 2004; Rizzolatti, Fogassi, & Gallese, 2002) demonstrated that some neurons that fire during execution of a learned action also fire during observation of that action. In other words, when learning to perform a behavior, some parts of the motor system that fire during performance also respond during perception of that specific action. These neurons, located in area F5 of the macaque cortex, respond in an effector specific manner (mouth actions different from hand actions) to observed action (Gallese, Fadiga, Fogassi, & Rizzolatti, 1996) and are putatively sensitive to the goal of the action rather than the specific motor behavior (Rizzolatti, Fogassi, & Gallese, 2001). Based on these findings, this observation has given rise to the mirror neuron hypothesis (Rizzolatti & Craighero, 2004) in which such neurons are responsible for comprehension of such observed actions. Moreover, this theory of the mirror system has been extended more broadly to include understanding social cognition and others' behavior more broadly (Gallese, Keysers, & Rizzolatti, 2004). While other research has suggested substantially greater limits on the role this system may play in empathy and social cognition (e.g., Decety & Lamm, 2006), the recognition of the importance of motor mimicry (e.g., Lakin & Chartrand, 2003) in interpersonal interaction is growing, even in respect to language processing (Giles, Mulac, Bradac, & Johnson, 1987; Pickering & Garrod, 2004).

Rizzolatti and Arbib (1998) have suggested that the mirror neuron system may provide an evolutionary foundation for human language. Rather than ground language in a vocal communication process, they take the genesis of language to be the comprehension of other people's actions through mirror neurons. Thus, vocal sound production and perception is not the basis for language. Instead, they start with the assumption that mirror neurons serve to decode observed actions and that gestures or symbolic actions (e.g., iconic gestures, McNeill, 2007) abstracted actions into communication. From this abstraction, gestures were presumably conventionalized initially to share a common form vocabulary. Mouth gestures (e.g., lip smacks) that were produced along with manual gestures then presumably evolved into an acoustic basis for language when the sounds accompanying the mouth gestures provided additional communicative utility.

According to this view, language processing is a form of action understanding. The actions involved are abstractions from the real behavioral actions one might engage in. Nonetheless, this suggests a view of language processing that is based on a projection from sensory areas of the brain in the visual cortex and auditory cortex to motor areas of the brain. Understanding then becomes a kind of motor resonance with sound patterns and visual patterns that correspond to articulatory gestures and manual gestures localizing the seat of comprehension (if such a thing were to exist) in posterior portions of the inferior frontal gyrus (homologue of macaque F5) and premotor cortex which are purported to code for the goals of actions (Rizzolatti & Craighero, 2004; Wilson & Iacoboni, 2006).

This presents a very different view of the evolution of language from a more traditional view in which language evolved by the refinement of vocal communication systems from other species. The model of language processing as grounded in action production and perception is quite different from the more traditional linguistic view of language as a conventional system of symbol use and organization that evolved from the communicative signs of other species. On a linguistic analysis, the fundamental properties of language consist of the meaningless form elements (e.g., phonemes or syllables) organized into hierarchically meaningful symbolic patterns (e.g., words and sentences). This suggests that the sound patterns of speech must be recognized and combined according to abstract rules that allow for the generativity of any novel legal utterance (Hockett, 1960). This view of language processing has a large group

of proponents (e.g., Caplan, 1996; Friederici, Fiebach, et al., 2006), who espouse a view of spoken language understanding that progresses from auditory patterns to phonological analysis in the superior temporal gyrus (Hickok & Poeppel, 2004) to lexical processing in the more posterior regions proximal to traditional Wernicke's area, to syntactic processing in Broca's area (Friederici, Bahlmann, et al., 2006) and sentence understanding (Hagoort, 2005).

Indeed, this is essentially the model that Hickok and Poeppel (2004) present as the "ventral stream" in speech perception. They suggest that speech perception is mediated by networks that are similar to the ventral/dorsal pathway difference in vision (Goodale & Milner, 1992; Mishkin, Ungerleider, & Macko, 1983). In vision, these two systems are respectively viewed as important for object recognition (ventral stream) and for object location or object-oriented action (dorsal stream). Although others (e.g., Rauschecker, 1998) have argued for a ventral/dorsal distinction in auditory processing, Hickok and Poeppel specifically make this distinction for speech perception. The ventral stream, projecting from the primary auditory cortex ventrally and laterally to the posterior inferior temporal cortex is responsible for mapping sound onto meaning, ultimately projecting to anterior temporal cortex (aSTS) for sentence processing. This represents a kind of bottom-up sound-to-phoneme-to-word-to-sentence mapping process that bears some general similarity to the traditional neural models of vision in which simple features map to complex features which map onto object form and then visual memory in a progression along the ventral visual stream. By contrast, the dorsal speech stream, projects from auditory areas to parietal cortex to the IFG and premotor cortex, is functionally more vague. Hickok and Poeppel allude to its role in language development and maintaining information in working memory though the use of the "phonological loop" to subvocalize (Baddeley & Hitch, 1974). In other words, according to this model, speech perception is fundamentally a bottom-up process of progressive interpretation within the ventral stream, while the dorsal stream projection to the premotor system plays little or no role in normal speech understanding.

There has been one longstanding distinction among theories of speech perception. On the one hand, auditory theories (e.g., Diehl & Kluender, 1989; Diehl et al., 2004; Fant, 1967; Stevens & Blumstein, 1981) view speech perception as a purely auditory process in which acoustic features are coded and matched to stored representations of phonetic categories that are then mapped onto words and so on. On the other hand, motor theory (Liberman & Mattingly, 1985) and analysis-by-synthesis (Stevens & Halle, 1967) have viewed speech perception as involving the motor system as part of the recognition process (albeit in very different ways). Neuroimaging methods have begun to present evidence that increasingly supports the involvement of the motor system in the process of speech perception. The enthusiasm to embrace this new evidence for motor theory needs to be tempered by the fact that the same neuroimaging methods implicate broader arrays of cortical activation than previously anticipated for numerous tasks. If so, then the new data help to define language mechanisms, placing them in the context of other perceptual processes (e.g., Price et al., 2005).

If Rizzolatti and Arbib (1998) are correct in their view of the evolution of spoken language, then face-to-face communication is a much better match to the conditions under which language emerged than long-range communication (as might be exemplified by the telephone model investigated in most speech research). If spoken language understanding is an abstracted form of action understanding, we might expect to see evidence of ventral premotor activity (corresponding to mouth movements) when a talking face is visible. However, the ventral stream described by Hickok and Poeppel does not involve the premotor cortex. There is no reason why seeing the face of a talker should necessarily recruit the premotor cortex in service of speech perception, given that the ventral stream is responsible for understanding spoken language. Skipper, Nusbaum, and Small (2005) examined patterns of neural activity while listeners heard auditory-only spoken stories or watched and heard an audio-video recording of a person telling stories. Hearing and seeing someone tell stories significantly increases ventral premotor activity compared to either the speech alone or the talking face with no speech. In addition, hearing and seeing the talker significantly increased neural activity in the superior temporal cortex as well. Moreover, for stories with greater viseme content (visual mouth shapes that are informative about the phonetic structure of speech), premotor activity was greater than for stories with less viseme content. This suggests that the premotor activity was specifically related to phonetic information visible in the talker's mouth movements.

Sumby and Pollack (1954) demonstrated that speech presented in noise is significantly more intelligible when the talking face can be seen by listeners. Clearly, there is phonetically useful information in the visible mouth movements made during speech production. In fact, McGurk and MacDonald (1976) demonstrated that visible mouth movements dramatically change the perception of the acoustic speech signal. For example, when an acoustic recording of /pa/ is dubbed onto a video recording of a face producing /ka/, listeners often perceive an illusory syllable /ta/. The increased activity in the ventral premotor region during audiovisual speech perception may indicate a mechanism by which this illusion is created. This mechanism

may operate in much the same way that Stevens and Halle (1967) suggested in analysis-by-synthesis.

Skipper, Nusbaum, and Small (2006) suggested that the motor system may operate as part of the active process of speech perception (see Nusbaum & Schwab, 1986). Sensory information from visual and auditory representations in the occipital and temporal cortex are decoded into motor representations in the premotor cortex. These motor representations can feedback to the sensory systems as part of a distributed recognition network. This suggests that the sensory and motor cortex may interact over time to determine the phonetic percept experienced by the observer (see Figure 45.2).

To test this, Skipper, van Wassenhove, Nusbaum, and Small (2007) examined patterns of neural activity during the perception of the McGurk illusion. The time course of BOLD response to audiovisual /pa/, /ta/, and /ka/ in the right ventral premotor, left supermarginal, and right middle occipital cortices were measured as estimated population responses to these syllables. The correlation between the McGurk syllable (audio /ka/ and visual /pa/) and each of these population responses was measured to determine how similar the neural response to the McGurk syllable was to each of the three consistent audiovisual syllables. The results (see Figure 45.3) showed that in the ventral premotor region, /ta/ (consistent with the actual percept) was the best fitting representation of the McGurk syllable, whereas in the supermarginal gyrus, the initial best fitting syllable was /pa/ (consistent with the acoustic signal) which then shifted to fitting best with /ta/. In the middle occipital gyrus, the initial best fit was to /ka/ (consistent with visual information about the mouth movements) which shifted to /ta/. Thus, in the sensory cortex, the best fitting representations for the McGurk stimulus started out consistent with their respective sensory input signals but then shifted to fit best with the percept. However, in the ventral premotor region, the /ta/ representation fit best throughout the entire time course of processing. This is consistent with the hypothesis that visual and auditory information, when fed to the premotor cortex give rise to an activity pattern consistent with the McGurk illusion that then may interact with sensory cortices resulting in a final activity pattern consistent across all regions with the McGurk percept.

These results are entirely consistent with an active theory of perception by which the lack of invariance between acoustic patterns and phonetic categories is resolved by an interaction between articulatory knowledge in the premotor representation of speech and the sensory representation of speech. One interpretation of this kind of interaction is the notion of covert motor simulation: The activity within the premotor region leads to associated sensory activity that would be associated with the actual act of speech

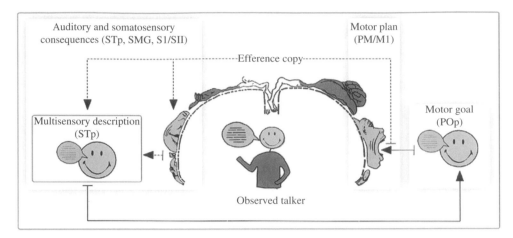

Figure 45.2 A model of sensory-motor interaction.

Note: Sensory information from the sounds and sight of an observed talker result in a multisensory description in the posterior STG (from primary auditory and visual cortex) that activates pars opercularis in the IFG that gives rise to associated sensory activity. From "Hearing lips and seeing voices: How cortical areas support speech production mediate audiovisual speech perception," by J. I. Skipper, V. van Wassenhove, H. C. Nusbaum, and S. L. Small, S. L.,2007, *Cerebral Cortex, 17,* p. 2388. Reprinted with permission.

production (Skipper et al., 2006). The premotor representation can be taken as a kind of "hypothesis" regarding the phonetic interpretation of sensory input and this hypothesis can constrain the alternative interpretations possible given the sensory representations alone. This is exactly the kind of mechanism described by Nusbaum and Magnuson (1997) in considering how an active process might resolve the nondeterministic relationship between acoustic speech patterns and the possible phonetic interpretations of those patterns, although it was not clear that articulatory knowledge would provide sufficient phonetic constraint. Cross-modal interactions are typically poorly explored but there is increasing evidence for such interactions (Bensmaïa, Killebrew, & Craig, 2006). Thus, this new perspective on language processing may be illuminating general properties of cortical organization, not those that are unique to language.

One apparent problem with this active theory of speech perception, by contrast to Hickok and Poeppel's dual pathway model, is that the supporting evidence derives largely from audiovisual speech perception. Although the support from audiovisual speech is consistent with the idea that speech has evolved as face-to-face communication (and thus audiovisual speech may be the "ethologically appropriate" stimulus), the ventral stream of the dual pathway does not really use any premotor processing. Thus, if the dorsal stream were modified to play a role in speech recognition when face information is present, the dual pathway model would be largely unchanged. Moreover, this raises the question as to whether there is any role for premotor processing when face information is not present. Can premotor activity serve as a constraint on phonetic interpretation even without visual input about mouth movements? Part of the motivation for the revision of the motor theory proposed by Liberman and Mattingly (1985) was to assert the proximal equivalence of mouth movements and acoustic patterns in speech perception given the McGurk effect. Although this also entailed the theoretically implausible claim that auditory sensory processing plays no role in speech perception, the notion was that motor knowledge should be important in speech perception whether a face is seen or not. If we take seriously the current premise that covert motor simulation (or prior associations between speech production experiences and the sensory consequences of production) provide a constraint on phonetic interpretation that can reduce acoustic-phonetic uncertainty, there should be evidence of premotor activity even without face input. Indeed, there is a substantial body of research on motor imagery that demonstrates substantial premotor activity during imagery that overlaps with motor execution (see Hanakawa et al., 2003; Jeannerod, 1994). Moreover, this evidence of premotor simulation during imagery has been functionally interpreted as relevant to understanding others' actions (Decety & Grezes, 2006).

Fadiga, Craighero, Buccino, and Rizzolatti (2002) showed some evidence for the involvement of the premotor system in speech perception, even without input from the mouth movements seen while watching a talker's face. Audio-only speech perception alone was not sufficient to produce peripheral electromyography (EMG) signals in tongue muscles, nor did single-shot TMS to the ventral premotor region alone produce a tongue EMG. However, the combination of speech input and premotor TMS did produce measurable tongue EMG. Fadiga et al. suggested

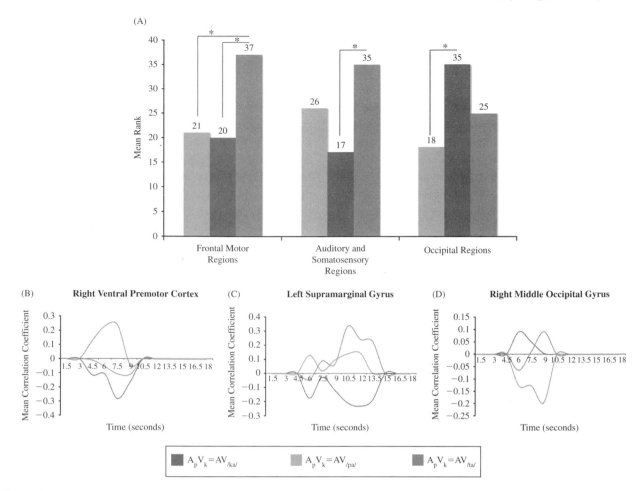

Figure 45.3 Population code representations in the ventral premotor, supramarginal, and middle occipital cortex during the McGurk stimulus (audio /p/, visual /k/).

Note: **A:** The McGurk stimulus produces patterns of activity that are most like the audiovisual /ta/ (which is the perception of this stimulus) in motor regions and the auditory and somatosensory cortex whereas the activity in occipital cortex is more like the visual channel of input or an audiovisual /ka/. **B:** Time course of the mean correlation coefficient for the activity associated with the McGurk stimulus with each of the three audiovisual syllables (/pa/, /ta/, and /ka/) indicating how the population response in ventral PM is most similar to the perceptual experience over the entire time course of processing. **C:** The time course of population response indicates that initially the McGurk stimulus activates the left supramar-

ginal gyrus most like the consistent audiovisual /pa/ but then changes to match the audiovisual /ta/. This suggests the initial interpretation is most like the audio portion of the McGurk stimulus but it changes to match the interpretation in the vPM cortex. **D:** The time course of processing in the middle occipital cortex suggests an initial population response to the McGurk stimulus is based on visual information (best match to audiovisual /ka/) but this changes to match the perceived category of /ta/ becoming consistent with the vPM region. From "Hearing lips and seeing voices: How cortical areas support speech production mediate audiovisual speech perception," by J. I. Skipper, V. van Wassenhove, H. C. Nusbaum, and S. L. Small, S. L., 2007, *Cerebral Cortex, 17*, p. 2394. Reprinted with permission.

that during audio-only speech perception, premotor cortex is active but well below the threshold to produce a peripheral EMG in articulators. However the addition of TMS-induced neural activity in the premotor system was sufficient to produce measurable EMG.

Wilson, Saygin, Sereno, and Iacoboni (2004) presented acoustic speech syllables to listeners (with no visual information) and found evidence for ventral premotor activity. Subsequently, Wilson and Iacoboni (2006) presented listeners with familiar phonemes and unfamiliar phonemes from other languages and measured brain activity during passive listening (no classification task involved). They

reported significantly more premotor activity for unfamiliar phonemes although this activity did not change with producibility of the speech. They interpret this result, along with activity in the superior temporal gyrus as evidence for the role of ventral premotor activity in speech perception. Specifically, they interpret their data as suggesting that premotor categorizations serve as phonetic hypotheses that are tested against auditory representations in sensory areas arguing for speech perception as a neither purely sensory nor purely motor but instead a sensorimotor process.

Hasson, Skipper, et al. (2007) investigated the neural representation of abstract phonetic categories. In the

McGurk percept, we have an experience that does not correspond to either the acoustic information or the visual information, but transcends them as an abstraction. By examining the effects of perceiving one syllable on the neural activity associated with perception of a subsequent syllable, it is possible to investigate the neural representation of the the phonetic information carried over in processing. When a stimulus is repeated, the neural response to the second occurrence is typically reduced (called *repetition suppression*) compared to the activity associated with the first occurrence (see Grill-Spector, Henson, & Martin, 2006). To the extent that this repetition suppression occurs between syllables that do not share sensory components, but do share the same perceptual experience or phonetic category, it is possible to assess how such sensory-independent phonetic information is represented. By examining how brain activity is suppressed in the McGurk illusory /ta/ by an antecedent audiovisual /ta/ we provided evidence demonstrating that the "abstract" phonetic representations of speech that are independent of sensory information are distributed between the posterior part of the inferior frontal gyrus (pars opercularis) in the motor system and the planum polare. This indeed demonstrates that phonetic representation has both a motor and sensory aspect.

BEYOND SPEECH PERCEPTION TO SPOKEN LANGUAGE UNDERSTANDING

The proposal of language understanding as symbolic action understanding has broader support than simply the evolutionary arguments made by Rizzolatti and Arbib (1998). There is a growing body of research on embodied cognition that understanding is grounded in aspects of concrete sensorimotor representation. Barsalou (1999) has argued for sensory and motor simulation as a fundamental basis for conceptual representation. Glenberg and Kaschak (2002) demonstrated that motor responses are facilitated or inhibited when they are directionally compatible versus different from the directionality inherent the main verb of a stimulus sentence (toward or away from oneself). This suggests that the semantics of verbs are closely linked to our understanding of motor plans.

Tettamanti et al. (2005) demonstrated that listening to sentences describing action increases brain activity in the motor system in pars opercularis and the premotor cortex. Similarly, Hauk, Johnsrude, and Pulvermüller (2004) showed that reading action words that are specific to the hand, foot, or mouth (e.g., grasp, kick, kiss) activate a pattern of cortical activity in the premotor cortex that displays somatopic organization similar to the performance of those actions. These studies demonstrate that there is a close correspondence between the patterns of cortical activity seen in the motor system when understanding the meaning of action words and sentences and when engaged in motor behavior.

In the anatomical model of neural language processing derived from Broca, Wernicke, and Lichtheim, the conceptual representation of word and sentence meaning was not considered to be in the motor system (e.g., see Geschwind, 1970; Pulvermuller, 2003). In the model proposed by Hickok and Poeppel (2004), within the ventral stream where sentences are understood, meaning is not represented in the motor system either. Given the kind of evidence for motor system activity during word and sentence comprehension, it is unlikely there is a single amodal conceptual representation system. An abstract conceptual representational system alone cannot account for why the motor system would be involved in comprehending language. Barsalou's (1999) view of a sensory and motor grounded conceptual system seems much more consistent the behavioral and neural evidence regarding embodied comprehension.

Moreover, this kind of semantic system appears to be relatively plastic both in the long term and in the short term. Holt and Beilock (2006) have shown that expert sports players (hockey or football) understand sentences containing sport-specific objects or actions differently from people with little or no experience in that sport. In recognizing whether an object was named in a sentence (cf. Zwaan, Stanfield, & Yaxley, 2002), Holt and Beilock showed that amount of sports expertise interacted with the response time to make that decision about compatibility of the depiction of the sport object with the rest of the sentence. This interaction is not found for nonsport-specific sentences indicating that it is the domain of expertise that is determining this comprehension effect: Long-term experience with an action domain shapes the understanding and representations we draw from utterances. Beilock, Lyons, Mattarella-Micke, Nusbaum, and Small (2008) used fMRI neuroimaging data to show that the effect of hockey expertise in understanding hockey sentences is entirely mediated by premotor activity. Thus, even among adults, increased experience in a domain of action can significantly modify the neural processing of language to recruit more strongly brain areas that are not part of the traditional language network (i.e., IFG and pSTG). This suggests that many neural models of language processing need to consider how other domains of experience and cognitive processing may operate during language understanding.

Hasson, Nusbaum, and Small (2007) investigated the neural activity associated with discourse comprehension. Specifically, they examined how a sentence at the end of a story was processed if the sentence was informative in the context of the antecedent discourse. Two different neural networks were identified as relevant to discourse understanding and memory: A fronto-temporal network overlapping with regions involved in language comprehension and working memory increased in activity with improved memory for discourse and a second network, often called the *default network* or *resting state network* (e.g., Gusnard & Raichle, 2001), showed a biphasic relationship between activity and subsequent memory. Within this default network, often considered to reflect "mind wandering" or diffuse cognitive processes, memory for informative sentences was predicted by increased activity but increased activity also predicted forgetting for uninformative sentences. These data suggest that comprehension of language is closely tied to memory (seen in an overlap between regions sensitive to discourse semantics and those that predicted subsequent recall). Moreover, it is interesting to note that contrasting informative and uninformative story endings revealed activity in a set of brain regions often associated with attention including the right SFG and MFG, superior parietal, and the thalamus. This suggests a close coupling between the more traditional fronto-temporal (IFG, STG) language areas and areas more typically associated with general cognitive processes of attention and memory.

Even in considering aspects of speech perception, there is evidence of the involvement of other cognitive processes not typically considered part of language processing. As discussed earlier, the problem of nondeterministic mapping of acoustic patterns onto phonetic categories may require an active system of hypothesis testing to resolve phonetic ambiguity (see Nusbaum & Magnuson, 1997). This problem has traditionally been discussed as a lack of invariance between acoustic patterns and phonetic patterns that motor theory was originally proposed to resolve (Liberman et al., 1967). The problem of lack of invariance has typically been attributed to the process of speech production. Phonemes are coarticulated with each other, meaning that the articulatory gestures used to produce speech sounds are not discrete and separable from one another. The physics and neurophysiology of motor control result in temporal overlap of the articulatory gestures in speech production—one mouth movement comes from another and must anticipate future movements. This means that the acoustic patterns at any point in time are shaped by previous and subsequent phonemes. Moreover, as the rate of speech production changes, this coarticulation changes as well so that acoustic patterns can be dilated or compressed in time. Different talkers, with different vocal tract architectures and different motor systems, will respond to and produce phonemes in different ways. As a result, the relationship between any particular acoustic pattern and phonetic categories is nondeterministic.

Nusbaum and Morin (1992) examined the way listeners adjust to the differences between talkers. Using a speeded target-monitoring paradigm, comparing recognition for speech produced by a single talker with recognition for speech produced by a mix of talkers, they reported that talker variability slowed recognition time reliably (about 20 to 40 ms) for consonants, vowels, and words (see also Mullennix & Pisoni, 1990). Moreover, they showed that this increase in recognition time was due to an increase in cognitive load demonstrated by an interaction between a secondary working memory load and talker variability. Furthermore, they showed that when there was talker variability, listeners directed attention to specific cues (fundamental frequency and formants above F2) as a way of providing information about talker vocal characteristics; the absence of these cues significantly reduced recognition accuracy but only when there was talker variability. Francis and Nusbaum (1996) found that speaking rate variability produced similar results, slowing recognition and interacting with a working memory load.

These studies suggest that resolving the nondeterministic mapping between acoustic patterns and phonetic categories is an active attention-demanding process (see Nusbaum & Schwab, 1986). Listeners shift attention to different acoustic cues in order to reduce the increased working memory demands of alternative phonetic interpretations under conditions of increased acoustic-phonetic variability. Moreover, Magnuson and Nusbaum (2007) demonstrated that talker calibration is not an automatic bottom-up process, but can be driven by listeners' expectations about the interpretation of a talker-specific cue such as voice fundamental frequency.

If relatively fast calibration to a talker's voice occurs as a result of shifting attention to different cues in speech, there should be evidence for this in terms of the recruitment of neural mechanisms involved in attention. Just as we saw evidence for the recruitment of cortical and subcortical brain areas typically involved in attention in processing informative versus noninformative sentences, there should be evidence of attention processing in speech perception when there is talker variability. Wong, Nusbaum, and Small (2004) presented neuroimaging evidence that talker variability significantly increases cognitive demands and recruits brain areas involved in attention that are not typically involved in language processing. Talker variability increases neural activity in the STG and in superior parietal cortex. Given the hypothesized role of the premotor cortex in generating phonetic hypotheses described earlier, we might expect to see increased premotor activity as well. Moreover, we might predict that there should be a significant covariance relationship between activity within the attention network and the premotor activity. Unfortunately, this study was run with a lower strength scanner (1.5 T compared to 3 T more typically used) and the evidence for premotor activity was not reliable. As a result, it will be necessary to replicate this study at a higher field strength to test this prediction.

However, it is clear that language processing takes place in a much broader network that has been typically considered. Speech perception may draw on the motor system and attention mechanisms. Word and sentence understanding may also depend on the use of the motor system, although in different ways from phoneme perception. Finally, discourse comprehension, and the comprehension of sentences in the context of discourse also may recruit attention and memory systems. These kinds of results suggest that the basic processing of language depends broadly on neural networks subserving more general cognitive processes than would be considered under the rubric of "neural mechanisms of language comprehension."

A BROADER VIEW OF NEURAL LANGUAGE PROCESSING

Bar (2003) speculated on a direct connection between the ventral and dorsal pathway in vision. Rather than view these as playing functionally distinct roles in vision (ventral = recognition and dorsal = action), he suggested that the dorsal route may represent a coarse route to object recognition that connects through goal-directed attention systems linked to working memory to affective-modulation systems that may bias responses. The dorsal route projects through motor, attention, affective, and working memory systems and then projects back to the inferior temporal cortex to constrain aspects of perceptual analysis carried out in parallel by the ventral pathway. Given the proximity (even overlap) in brain systems involved in emotion, executive function and behavioral control, working memory, and attention, and the relationship between these systems and other aspects of perceptual processing, it seems surprising that this kind of proposal has not been made previously. Moreover, it raises the possibility of thinking about language networks in much the same way.

Roland (1993) argued that the frontal cortex can generate sensory expectations that can "tune" the sensitivity of more posterior areas. Bar's (2003) argument is that affective goals and evaluations are important in shifting attention for perception. This process of shifting attention involves frontal and prefrontal systems changing the sensitivity of posterior sensory processes, presumably by modifying receptive fields (e.g., Moran & Desimone, 1985). This could be the way in which visual information about mouth movements during speech production changes

neural population responses in the superior temporal cortex during comprehension of the talker's speech.

To postulate that goals, motives, and expectations may change the processing of auditory information goes well beyond the notion that immediately available visual information about motor movements changes phonetic perception. Goals, motivation, and expectations are not manifest in the sensory signal about the articulations underlying speech production—they are completely endogenous information. Consider that seeing the race of a talker's face (shown as a static image) can change the perception of the talker's speech (Rubin, 1992) and the gender of a talker's face can change interpretation of speech (Johnson, Strand, & D'Imperio, 1999). These effects are driven by expectations of the listener rather than the sensory information from a talker's mouth movements. Even without dynamic real-time perceptual input about a talker's mouth movements, expectations can change the interpretation of speech. Furthermore, language processing is shaped by expectations even when they do not involve information about a talker's face. As noted previously, Magnuson and Nusbaum (2007) showed the expectations about the importance of an acoustic fundamental frequency difference can drive a low-level perceptual process such as calibrating to the vocal characteristics of a talker.

However, the impact of listener expectations is much broader and deeper than just calibrating talker differences. Remez, Rubin, Pisoni, and Carrell (1981) demonstrated that when presented with sinusoidal replicas of a sentence, listeners generally report that these signals sound like nonspeech bird chirps but when told that the signals are language, listeners can correctly understand the speech. Wymbs, Nusbaum, and Small (2004) measured the cortical activity of listeners presented with sinewave speech before and after language instructions. The results showed that linguistic expectations activate an attentional-motor network involving the inferior frontal gyrus and superior parietal cortex. Changing a listener's expectations about speech fundamentally changes the pattern of cortical processing that mediates perception of speech.

How can we explain the role of expectations in recognizing and understanding speech? One approach would be to posit two different systems, a cognitive system for maintaining and applying expectations (e.g., working memory and attention) and a sensory system for speech perception. This approach would be consistent with the kind of theory proposed by Hickock and Poeppel in that recognition within the ventral stream (speech recognition) would then be modulated by processing within the dorsal stream (working memory and attention). However, as described, this model does not make clear how such interactions would take place. Indeed, the model itself does not specifically try to explain how expectations might play a role in speech perception. In general, expectations, attention, and other processes that are not specifically linguistic in nature are treated as external to a language processing system, even given the evidence that such processes might be critical to understanding language comprehension. Social expectations (e..g., Johnson et al., 1999; Rubin, 1992) and emotional expectations (Luks, Nusbaum, & Levy, 1998) seem to interact with the basic processes of phonetic and prosodic recognition. This would suggest a more direct interaction akin to Bar's (2003) model of vision. Indeed, Erthal et al. (2005) demonstrated how attentional load can down regulate affective and perceptual responses to emotional faces. Increasing demands on perceptual attention can reduce amygdale and visual cortex responses to fear faces. This kind of research is needed to begin to investigate the interrelationship of cognitive and affective and social information in language.

The shift to consider information beyond the propositional content of utterances, such as social and emotional information leads to a consideration of prosody. While the linguistic categories used in the "message" content of speech are considered discrete (Hockett, 1960), speech also conveys less categorical and more continuous information in prosody. Although there is a general assumption that much of the processing of prosodic information is carried out by the right hemisphere whereas the categorical information of a linguistic message is carried out in the left hemisphere, this seems to be an oversimplification. For example, Luks et al. (1998) investigated the cortical lateralization of intonation information relevant to emotion and syntactic judgments using a behavioral method similar to research investigating the lateralization of phonetic processing. (It is important to point out that, with recent neuroimaging methods, such lateralization results seem to reflect more a subtle shift in the balance of cortical processing rather than strong evidence that mechanisms in just one hemisphere are carrying out the perceptual task.) When judging whether a sentence was spoken in an angry or sad intonation, there was a reliable left ear advantage, suggesting greater right hemisphere processing. In contrast, when listeners made decisions about whether a sentence was a question or a statement (based on rising or falling intonation of the same declarative syntactic form), there was no advantage in processing sentences in either ear, suggesting both right and left hemispheres were contributing to processing equally. However, when the same sentences that differed in rising or falling pitch were judged as indicating either surprise or neutral attitude (thus the same speech signals with a different listener decision), a left ear advantage was found. This suggests that the way listeners attend to the speech determines aspects of the neural processing of the speech.

Although there has been some research using neuroimaging to measure brain responses to emotional speech (e.g., Schirmer & Kotz, 2006; Wildgruber et al., 2004), it is not yet clear how attention modulates this kind of processing (cf. Sander et al., 2005). Because we know that variation in working memory load does affect behavioral measures of processing in talker variability (Nusbaum & Morin, 1992) it seems plausible that it might affect other aspects of speech perception. Similarly, there is evidence that perceptual load affects other aspects of auditory processing (e.g., Watkins, Dalton, Lavie, & Rees, 2007), and it seems plausible that varying perceptual load may affect our perception of emotional speech. Given the social importance of language and faces, it is surprising that there has been relatively little research on the role of face information beyond phonetic processing (although see Massaro, 1998). It is important to go beyond the long-standing limited linguistic notions of the meaning of language and start to develop an understanding of the emotional and social impact of language use and how this impact is realized in terms of neural mechanisms.

The interaction between affective systems and cognitive systems also raises the question of understanding the relationship between cortical and subcortical mechanisms. Subcortical structures are clearly important in a number of psychological processes such as attention (thalamus), emotion and reward (ventral striatum), and motor control (basal ganglia) and are heavily connected to cortical systems that are typically studied in language processing. However, few studies have explicitly investigated the relationship between subcortical and cortical processing of language. Musacchia et al. (Musacchia, Sams, Nicol, & Kraus, 2006; Musacchia, Sams, Skoe, & Kraus, 2007) demonstrated that auditory brain stem responses are shaped by higher-order sensory inputs so that visual information such as seeing a talker's mouth produce speech sharpens the subcortical coding of auditory information such as speech. This suggests that neural theories such as Suga's corticofugal (e.g., Suga & Ma, 2003) model of bat echolocation may provide new insights about active processing in speech perception.

PLASTICITY AND DEVELOPMENT

There is great potential for the neuroscience of language processing to be informed by the research in neuroethology. However, it also possible that in some cases comparisons among species may be taken directly in a way that could be misleading. The notion of a developmentally critical period, derived from ethology (see Michel & Tyler, 2005) was applied as a theory about the development of language (Lenneberg, 1967). This theory states that there is a biologically determined limited time for the "natural development" of a native language (e.g., see Johnson & Newport, 1989). This can be seen as similar to the critical period in the development of bird song (Marler, 1970; Thorpe, 1961). Although we understand much about the neural mechanisms underlying the development of bird song, we understand little about the neural mechanisms underlying human language acquisition.

Prather, Peters, Nowicki, and Mooney (2008) demonstrated the existence of "mirror neurons" in the swamp sparrow forebrain area HVC that respond in the same way when a bird sings or hears the same song (see also Dave & Margoliash, 2000). These HVC neurons innervate neurons in area X (which includes the song system part of the avian basal ganglia) that are important in song acquisition. The authors suggested that one important role for such mirror neurons is to guide the development of bird song.

Although the suggestion of mirror neurons operating in speech perception is more specifically linked to the problem of recognizing speech rather than learning to recognize speech, it is possible that they may play an analogous role in birds and humans. Rosenblum, Miller, and Sanchez (2007), showed that the experience of lip-reading a talking face without hearing the speech can aid in recognizing subsequent novel speech (without the face) from the same talker. Given the evidence that phonetic categorization can take place within the motor system (Hasson, Skipper, et al., 2007) it seems entirely plausible that this plasticity of subsequent auditory recognition of speech is mediated in part by activity within the motor system.

While this might seem to be a special case of spoken language plasticity in the short term, and thus not germane to native language learning, there is now substantial evidence for robust language learning abilities in the adult human. For example, after eight one-hour sessions of being trained on computer-generated (synthetic speech) words and sentences, never hearing the same words twice, adults show huge improvements from 20% correct word identification to almost 70% correct (Schwab, Nusbaum, & Pisoni, 1985). Even after 6 months without subsequent exposure, when tested on a new set of words not heard during training, listeners retain most of what they have learned. This is substantial, robust, generalized, and long-lasting learning of the phonetic properties of speech that results from a perceptual reorganization of the phonetic space (see Francis, Fenn, & Nusbaum, 2007). This perceptual reorganization suggests that listeners change the way they direct attention to the speech signal as a result of learning. Francis, Baldwin, and Nusbaum (2000) showed experimentally that the kind of feedback presented to listeners in this type of training can direct attention to specific acoustic cues, even when listeners are not subjectively aware of those cues, and thus change the phonetic classification of speech sounds.

Although this work focuses on perceptual learning of new acoustic patterns from computer-generated synthetic speech rather than learning new phonetic categories, a similar process seems to be at work in learning a new phonology. Yamada and Tohkura (1992) showed that the reason that the /r/-/l/ distinction is difficult for Japanese listeners is because, compared to American English listeners, they direct attention to different acoustic cues in this speech that are not the ones used in English. In learning a new phonological category, listeners must learn to shift attention from one set of cues to another (see Nusbaum & Lee, 1992). Francis and Nusbaum (2002) showed that listeners can do this with appropriate training: American English listeners have a single phonetic dimension which they apply to Korean stop consonants that Korean listeners perceive as having two phonetic dimensions. Following appropriate training, American English listeners learn to redirect attention to the speech signal and induce the second dimension. This means that listeners can show substantial flexibility, with appropriate feedback and training, in shifting attention to the acoustic properties of speech either to adapt to a novel talker (such as a computer) or to a new phonological system. The problems in acquiring a new phonological system may be more a result of the critical mass of first language knowledge we have that, as a system, may direct attention to different acoustic properties than are needed for a new phonological system (see Nusbaum & Lee, 1992).

Studies of birdsong share at least some of the same flavor. The original concept of a fixed critical period for auditory exposure has been modified. In general, the early laboratory studies failed to identify the much richer context in the field of song learning, where there are multiple influences on the sensitivity and duration to song exposure (Beecher, 1996). Memory acquisition is sensitive to social cues (e.g., Baptista & Petrinovich, 1984; Payne, 1981). The duration of the sensitive phase for song memory acquisition depends not only on timely sensory exposure (Marler, 1970), but depends strongly on environmental factors that vary throughout the year (Kroodsma & Pickert, 1980). Songs memories are not simple veridical templates but may be laid down in packages or "chunks" (Hultsch & Todt, 1989; Williams & Staples, 1992). Memory representations of the tutor songs are associative in nature (Rose et al., 2004). Many songbird species retain plasticity into adulthood, but this can be affected by the quality of developmental song learning. Most generally, there are some 3,500 species of songbirds that learn to sing, so picking a simple early model of song memorization born of laboratory observation of a few species in an attempt to model human language acquisition may arrive at only limited success. We need to think about song and language learning in a broader biological context than the simple notion of a genetically programmed critical period suggests.

If we take language acquisition as a learning process, rather than a result of a critical period of developmental plasticity, why does this learning persist? The critical period hypothesis suggests that acquisition can only occur for a limited time and then sensitivity to new language forms shuts down after this period. However, a learning model for language acquisition does not by itself indicated why this learning is retained, even for adult learners. What makes synthetic speech learning by adults robust over long time periods such as 6 months without subsequent training? The answer may come from understanding the biological mechanisms involved in the consolidation of learning (McGaugh, 2000). Consolidation is the process whereby learning becomes robust against subsequent interference and decay. One of the primary candidate processes for consolidation of learning is sleep, although the actual mechanism by which sleep might consolidate learning is a topic of intense research and speculation (e.g., see Huber, Ghilardi, Massimini, & Tononi, 2004; Tononi & Cirelli, 2001; Walker & Stickgold, 2006; Shank & Margoliash, in press).

Although much of the research showing sleep consolidation of learning has focused on rote learning of a specific stimulus or a particular single motor behavior, there is evidence that sleep consolidates perceptual learning of speech. Fenn, Nusbaum, and Margoliash (2003) examined the effects of sleep on perceptual learning of synthetic speech. Unlike the prior studies of sleep consolidation, participants never heard the same words twice. In a one-hour training session, participants improved in recognizing novel words in synthetic speech by 20 percentage points. After a 12-hour waking retention interval, performance dropped by almost half suggesting that over this waking period, experience with spoken language may have interfered with learning. By comparison, a 12-hour period that included sleep did not show a similar reduction in performance on a subsequent posttest. Moreover, by comparing two different 24-hour retention groups, it was possible to see that sleep had two different benefits for consolidation of learning: First, sleep actually could restore performance following a waking interval suggesting that what appeared to be lost due to interference could actually be regained simply through sleep. Second, sleep prior to a waking retention interval inoculated the learner against loss during the waking interval. Clearly then, sleep consolidation plays an important role in making generalized learning of phonetic information robust and may contribute to maintaining the robustness and resilience of native language learned early.

However, learning language is not simply a matter of learning the phonetic constituents of speech. Saffran (2003) demonstrated that learning the phonotactic patterns of a language can be thought of as a statistical learning process that is not specific to language. Similarly, Gentner et al. (2006) demonstrated that learning complex syntactic patterns is not unique to humans nor specific to language. If starlings can learn finite state and context-sensitive grammars and can generalize this learning to patterns and pattern lengths with which they have no prior experience, it seems that the mechanisms needed to learn complex hierarchical patterns are quite general. Moreover, there is some evidence that sleep may play a role in consolidating this kind of rule-based abstraction, at least for human infants (see Gomez, Bootzin, & Nadel, 2006). Thus, learning syntactic patterns may reflect a combination of memory for specific instances and generalization and abstraction over those instances.

This suggests that there should be some enduring trace of the processing of a sentence that can form part of the basis for generalization. In some sense, we might think of sentences as objects in their own right. Hasson, Nusbaum, and Small (2007) showed that repeating the same sentence resulted in repetition suppression—a reduction in neural activity for the second occurrence (see Grill-Spector et al., 2006). This change in neural processing resulting from previous experience occurred primarily in the middle temporal gyrus for passive listening. However, with more specific processing goals the change in neural processing was seen in a broader network, including the IFG. Thus, there is indeed a trace of prior processing of a specific sentence and the nature of this effect depends on the cognitive processing carried out. This may provide a neural basis for subsequent generalization and abstraction of sentence properties such as syntax.

SUMMARY

Rather than think about language simply as a signal (multimodal rather than just acoustic, of course) for transmitting information, we can think about the communicative interaction itself as a psychologically significant act that was part of the basic force shaping the evolution of the brain. By this construal, the listener's goal may not be to interpret the linguistic message but to interact with the interlocutor in a way that satisfies specific social goals and motives. This would suggest that communicative behavior—broadly construed—should be affected by a conversational partner's behavior, even beyond the simple process of interpretation.

There is substantial evidence to support this hypothesis. Giles (1973; Giles & Smith, 1979) has demonstrated speech accommodation in conversations, in which one interlocutor (or both) converges on the speech of the other, in terms of speaking patterns. This kind of vocal accommodation or indexical mimicry is increased between members of the same social group and decreased between groups (Giles & Coupland, 1991). It is also increased, when one interlocutor is trying to persuade the other of something (Giles & Coupland, 1991). Moreover, this kind of behavioral convergence in a conversation is not restricted to speech patterns. Chartrand and Bargh (1999) demonstrated that other motor behaviors that are not speech related show similar accommodation between conversational partners and depend on social goals. One conversational partner tapping her foot can start the other partner tapping as well even though this is not a linguistically relevant behavior. And this can serve to socially link the interlocutors, increasing the sense of interpersonal affiliation (Lakin & Chartrand, 2003) as well as shifting attention from one's self to the broader environment (Van Baaren, Horgan, Chartrand, & Dijkmans, 2004).

The work by Giles (1973; Giles et al., 1987; Giles, Taylor, & Bourhis, 1973) on speech accommodation—the convergence of speech patterns between conversational partners—reflects a kind of short-term interactive plasticity in language use that suggests that spoken language use is always sensitive to the inputs that occur in conversations. Moreover, the motor mimicry research that suggests that there is a social connection that is formed on this basis (Lakin & Chartrand, 2003) reflects that this as unconscious communication and adaptive plasticity that is always present in conversations. If we take the view that language evolved in the context of face-to-face interaction seriously, then understanding this kind of behavioral plasticity simply echoes the role of the motor system in spoken language comprehension. Rizzolatti and Arbib (1998) suggested that language evolved based on the availability of the mirror neuron system as a way of understanding goal-directed action. Although the observation of mirror neurons has been extended into theories of empathy (Decety & Jackson, 2006; Decety & Lamm, 2006) and social understanding (Gallese et al., 2004), the notion that the motor system may aid in spoken language understanding has received empirical support in recent neuroimaging studies. Moreover, there is also a shift in the paradigms used to study language processing, moving from isolated sentences to conversational interaction (Pickering & Garrod, 2004) and from the study of decontextualized reading to contextualized spoken language that refers to an immediately present real world (Sedivy, Tanenhaus, Chambers, & Carlson, 1999; Tanenhaus, Spivey-Knowlton, Eberhard,

& Sedivy, 1995). Taken together with the growing interest in understanding cognition as embodied and grounded in sensory and motor representations, neuroscience researchers are becoming more focused on understanding real face-to-face communication rather than linguistic competence.

There is much more information in conversations than is represented in the propositional utterances and the prosodic expression of speaker attitude and emotion. In addition to the mouth movements that correspond to articulatory gestures, speakers routinely make manual gestures accompanying speech (see McNeill, 1992). These hand movements represent a channel of information that is not entirely independent of speech but not completely redundant either. McNeill argued that the gestures accompanying speech present more continuous and analogical representations of information than discrete and conventionalized linguistic forms. It seems entirely plausible that such gestures are processed using neural mechanisms in the dorsal premotor region, given the representation of hand movements in that area and there is some evidence suggesting that this may be the case. Gestures, more than other nongesture hand movements, differentially activate the dorsal premotor and have increased connectivity to the anterior portion of the STG which is associated with sentence processing (Skipper, Goldin-Meadow, Nusbaum, & Small, 2007a, 2007b). This suggests that gesture may be understood through the use of sensorimotor networks that, in some sense, parallel the sensorimotor networks that process spoken language.

If gestures represent a first abstraction of observed action, and the underpinning of speech, then perhaps there should be some form of speech that is more similar to gesture. In other words, is there a vocal signal that is descriptive and referential, as is true of the propositional content of language, but is also continuous (as opposed to the discrete representation in language) and analogical rather than arbitrary (as are words and sentences)? Speech researchers typically describe the arbitrary-discrete and analogical-continuous aspects of language as corresponding to the propositional content in words and the attitude and affect content in prosody. However, Shintel, Nusbaum, and Okrent (2006) described a third channel of spoken language that may serve as a kind of "missing link" between manual gesture and propositional speech. They showed that when speakers are asked to describe a dot moving up or down or moving fast or slow, they modulate the fundamental frequency of their voice or speaking rate to refer to these events. Speakers do this even without instruction and even when the propositional content is about a different aspect of the event. Speakers can say "It's going right" quickly or slowly to indicate dot speed, even when the task is to describe dot direction. Furthermore, this information is communicative for listeners who can decide what the speaker was referring to. Shintel and Nusbaum (2007) demonstrated that this kind of analogue acoustic expression or spoken gesture can actually create an image in the head of the listener so that describing a horse with a fast rate of speech implies to the listener a horse in motion. Finally, listeners' interpretation of spoken gesture is not a simple motor resonance with the articulatory gestures that produced the speech. Shintel and Nusbaum (2008) showed that the interpretation of spoken gesture depends on the discourse context that preceded it. Thus, as with all other aspects of spoken language, there is no unique and invariant interpretation of the acoustic signature of spoken gesture.

Spoken language understanding is not a process of determining an objectively specified meaning for a particular utterance. It is a process of construing the intended meaning of an utterance as a construction within the context of a social interaction. The listener must bring to bear a broad set of mechanisms including some that are language specific and some that are more general to cognition such as attention and memory and some that are more general still to social interaction and affective evaluation. The primary function of language is as a social signal. As social communication, it may share much in common with the vocal communication systems of other species, even if the evolutionary history of those systems is quite different. Although much of the research in the neuroscience of language started from a traditional linguistic perspective that separates out the propositional content from other aspects of communication such as manual gesture, spoken gesture, and emotional information, by understanding spoken language use as social communication, we may derive new insights into the neural basis of language.

REFERENCES

Abbs, J. H., & Sussman, H. M. (1971). Neurophysiological feature detectors and speech perception: A discussion of theoretical implications. *Journal of Speech and Hearing Research, 14,* 23–36.

Adret-Hausberger, M., & Jenkins, P. F. (1988). Complex organization of the warbling song in the European Starling (Sturnus vulgaris). *Behaviour, 107,* 138–156.

Anderson, J. R. (1978). Arguments concerning representations for mental imagery. *Psychological Review, 85,* 249–277.

Appelbaum, I. (1998). Fodor, modularity, and speech perception. *Philosophical Psychology, 11,* 317–330.

Baddeley, A. D., & Hitch, G. (1974). *Working memory.* In G. H. Bower (Ed.), *The psychology of learning and motivation: Advances in research and theory* (Vol. 8, pp. 47–89). New York: Academic Press.

Baptista, L. F., & Petrinovich, L. (1984). Social interaction, sensitive phrases and the song template hypothesis in the white-crowned sparrow. *Animal Behaviour, 32,* 172–181.

Bar, M. (2003). A cortical mechanism for triggering top-down facilitation in visual object recognition. *Journal of Cognitive Neuroscience, 15,* 600–609.

Barrie, J. M., Freeman, W. J., & Lenhart, M. D. (1996). Spatiotemporal analysis of prepyriform, visual, auditory, and somesthetic surface EEGs in trained rabbits. *Journal of Neurophysiology, 76,* 520–539.

Barsalou, L. (1999). Perceptual symbol systems. *Behavioral and Brain Sciences, 22,* 577–660.

Bates, E., Thal, D., & Marchman, V. (1991). *Symbols and syntax: A Darwinian approach to language development.* In N. Krasnegor, D. Rumbaugh, R. Schiefelbusch, & M. Studdert-Kennedy (Eds.), *Biological and behavioral determinants of language development* (pp. 29–65). Hillsdale, NJ: Erlbaum.

Beecher, M. D. (1996). *Birdsong learning in the laboratory and field.* In D. E. Kroodsma & E. H. Miller (Eds.), *Ecology and evolution of acoustic communication in birds* (pp. 61–78). Ithaca, NY: Cornell University Press.

Beilock, S. L., Lyons, I., Mattarella-Micke, A., Nusbaum, H., & Small, S. (2008). *Sports experience changes the neural processing of language.* Paper to be presented at the 15th Annual Meeting of the Cognitive Neuroscience Society, San Francisco.

Bendor, D., & Wang, X. (2005). The neuronal representation of pitch in primate auditory cortex. *Nature, 436,* 1161–1165.

Bensmaïa, S. J., Killebrew, J. H., & Craig, J. C. (2006). Influence of visual motion on tactile motion perception. *Journal of Neurophysiology, 96,* 1625–1637.

Bogen, J. E., & Bogen, G. M. (1976). Wernicke's region: Where is it? *Annals of the New York Academy of Sciences, 280,* 834–843.

Broca, P. P. (1861). Nouvelle observation d'aphémie produite par une lesion de la partie postérieure des deuxième et troisième circonvolutions frontales. [New observation of aphemia produced by a lesion in the posterior half of the second and third frontal convolution.]. *Bulletins de la Societe Anatomique, 6,* 398–407.

Busnel, R. G., & Classe, A. (1976). *Whistled languages.* New York: Springer-Verlag.

Caplan, D. (1996). *Language: Structure, processing, and disorders.* Cambridge, MA: MIT Press.

Capranica, R. R. (1972). Why auditory neurophysiologists should be more interested in animal sound communication. *Physiologist, 15*(2), 55–60.

Chalupa, L. M., & Werner, J. S. (Eds.). (2003). *Visual neurosciences.* Cambridge, MA: MIT Press.

Charniak, E. (1993). *Statistical language learning.* Cambridge, MA: MIT Press.

Chartrand, J. L., & Bargh, J. A. (1999). The chameleon effect: The perception-behavior link and social interaction. *Journal of Personality and Social Psychology, 76,* 893–910.

Chomsky, N. (1957). *Syntactic structures.* Hague: Mouton.

Chomsky, N. (1988). *Language and problems of knowledge:* The managua lectures. (Current studies in linguistics series 16). Cambridge, MA: MIT Press.

Churchland, P. M. (1999). Eliminative materialism and the propositional attitudes. In W. G. Lycan (Ed.), *Mind and cognition: An anthology* (2nd ed., pp. 120–132). Malden, MA: Blackwell Publishers.

Cohen, L., & Dehaene, S. (2004). Specialization within the ventral stream: The case for the visual word form area. *NeuroImage, 22,* 466–476.

Cohen, L., Jobert, A., LeBihan, D., & Dehaene, S. (2004). Distinct unimodal and multimodal regions for word processing in the left temporal cortex. *NeuroImage, 23,* 1256–1270.

Dave, A. S., & Margoliash, D. (2000). Song replay during sleep and computational rules for sensorimotor vocal learning. *Science, 290,* 812–816.

Dave, A. S., Yu, A. C., & Margoliash, D. (1998). Behavioral state modulation of auditory activity in a vocal motor system. *Science, 282,* 2250–2254.

Decety, J., & Grezes, J. (2006). The power of simulation: Imagining one's own and other's behavior. *Brain Research, 1079*, 4–14.

Decety, J., & Jackson, P. L. (2006). A social neuroscience perspective on empathy. *Current Directions in Psychological Science, 15*, 54–58.

Decety, J., & Lamm, C. (2006). Human empathy through the lens of social neuroscience. *Scientific World Journal, 6*, 1146–1163.

Dehaene, S., & Cohen, L. (2007). Cultural recycling of cortical maps. *Neuron, 56*, 384–398.

Derégnaucourt, S., Mitra, P. P., Feher, O., Pytte, C., & Tchernichovski, O. (2005). How sleep affects the developmental learning of bird song. *Nature, 433*, 710–716.

Devlin, J. T., & Watkins, K. E. (2007). Stimulating language: Insights from TMS. *Brain, 130*, 610–622.

Dewey, J. (1896). The reflex arc concept in psychology. *Psychological Review, 3*, 357–370.

Diehl, R. L., & Kluender, K. R. (1989). On the objects of speech perception. *Ecological Psychology, 1*(2), 121–144.

Diehl, R. L., Lotto, A. J., & Holt, L. L. (2004). Speech perception. *Annual Review of Psychology, 55*, 149–179.

Douglas, R. J., & Martin, K. A. (1991). Opening the grey box. *Trends in Neurosciences, 14*, 286–293.

Eens, M., Pinxten, R., & Verheyen, R. F. (1989). Temporal and sequential organization of song bouts in the starling. *Ardea, 77*, 75–86.

Erthal, F. S., Oliveira, L., Mocaiber, I., Pereira, M. G., Machado-Pinheiro, W., Volchan, E., et al. (2005). Load-dependent modulation of affective picture processing. *Cognitive, Affective, and Behavioral Neuroscience, 5*, 388–395.

Fadiga L., Craighero L., Buccino G., & Rizzolatti G. (2002). Speech listening specifically modulates the excitability of tongue muscles: A TMS study. *European Journal of Neuroscience, 15*, 399–402.

Fant, G. (1967). Sound, features and perception. *STL-QPSR (Quarterly Progress and Status Report), 2*, 1–14.

Farah, M. J. (1984). The neurological basis of mental imagery: A componential analysis. *Cognition, 18*, 245–272.

Farah, M. J., & Feinberg, T. E. (Eds.). (2000). *Patient-based approaches to cognitive neuroscience.* Cambridge, MA: MIT Press.

Feng, A. S., Narins, P. M., Xu, C. H., Lin, W. Y., Yu, Z. L., Qiu, Q., et al. (2006). Ultrasonic communication in frogs. *Nature, 440*, 333–336.

Fenn, K. M., Nusbaum, H. C., & Margoliash, D. (2003). Consolidation during sleep of perceptual learning of spoken language. *Nature, 425*, 614–616.

Fodor, J. A. (1983). *The modularity of mind.* Cambridge, MA: MIT Press.

Francis, A. L., Baldwin, K., & Nusbaum, H. C. (2000). Learning to listen: The effects of training on attention to acoustic cues. *Perception and Psychophysics, 62*, 1668–1680.

Francis, A., Fenn, K., & Nusbaum, H. (2007). Effects of training on the acoustic-phonetic representation of synthetic speech. *Journal of Speech, Language, and Hearing Research, 50*, 1445–1465.

Francis, A., & Nusbaum, H. C. (1996). Paying attention to speaking rate. *Proceedings of the International Conference on Spoken Language Processing,* SaA2L2.5.

Francis, A., & Nusbaum, H. C. (2002). Selective attention and the acquisition of new phonetic categories. *Journal of Experimental Psychology: Human Perception and Performance, 28*, 349–366.

Frankel, A. S., Clark, C. W., Herman, L. M., & Gabriele, C. M. (1995). Spatial distribution, habitat utilization, and social interactions of humpback whales, Megaptera novaeangliae, off Hawaii, determined using acoustic and visual techniques. *Canadian Journal of Zoology, 73*, 1134–1146.

Freeman, W. J. (2003). Neurodynamic models of brain in psychiatry. *Neuropsychopharmacology, 28*, S54–S63.

Freeman, W. J., & Skarda, C. A. (1990). Representations: Who needs them. In J. L. McGaugh, N. M. Weinberger (Eds.), *Brain organization and memory: Cells, systems, and circuits* (pp. 375–380). New York: Oxford University Press.

Friederici, A. D., Bahlmann, J., Heim, S., Schubotz, R. I., & Anwander, A. (2006). The brain differentiates human and non-human grammars: Functional localization and structural connectivity. *Proceedings of the National Academy of Sciences, USA, 103*, 2458–2463.

Friederici, A. D., Fiebach, C. J., Schlesewsky, M., Bornkessel, I., & von Cramon, D. Y. (2006). Processing linguistic complexity and grammaticality in the left frontal cortex. *Cerebral Cortex, 16*, 1709–1714.

Galdikas, B. M. F. (1983). The orangutan long call and snag crashing at Tanjung Puting reserve. *Primates, 24*, 371–384.

Gallese, V., Fadiga, L., Fogassi, L., & Rizzolatti, G. (1996). Action recognition in the premotor cortex. *Brain, 119*, 593–609.

Gallese, V., Keysers, C., & Rizzolatti, G. (2004). A unifying view of the basis of social cognition. *Trends in Cognitive Sciences, 8*, 396–403.

Garfield, J. L. (Ed.). (1987). *Modularity in knowledge representation and natural-language understanding.* Cambridge, MA: MIT Press.

Gentner, T. Q., & Hulse, S. H. (2000). Perceptual classification based on the component structure of song in European starlings. *Journal of the Acoustical Society of America, 107*, 3369–3381.

Gentner, T. Q., Fenn, K. M., Margoliash, D., & Nusbaum, H. C. (2006). Recursive syntactic pattern learning by songbirds. *Nature, 440*, 1204–1207.

Gentner, T. Q., & Margoliash, D. (2002). The neuroethology of vocal communication: Perception and cognition [Acoustic communication]. In A. Megela-Simmons, A. N. Popper, & R. R. Fay (Eds.), p.3 *Springer handbook of auditory research* (Vol. 16, pp. 324–386).

Geschwind, N. (1970). The organization of language and the brain. *Science, 170*, 940–944.

Giles, H. (1973). Accent mobility: A model and some data. *Anthropological Linguistics, 15*, 87–105.

Giles, H., & Coupland, N. (1991). *Language: Contexts and consequences.* Pacific Grove: Brooks/Cole.

Giles, H., Mulac, A., Bradac, J. J., & Johnson, P. (1987). Speech accommodation theory: The first decade and beyond. In M. McLaughlin (Ed.), *Communication yearbook* (Vol. 10, pp. 13–48). Newbury Park, CA: Sage.

Giles, H., & Smith, P. (1979). Accommodation theory: Optimal levels of convergence. In H. Giles & R. N. St. Clair (Eds.), *Language and social psychology* (pp. 45–65). Baltimore: University Park Press.

Giles, H., Taylor, D. M., & Bourhis, R. Y. (1973). Towards a theory of interpersonal accommodation through speech: Some Canadian data. *Language in Society, 2*, 177–192.

Gleick, J. (1987). *Chaos: Making a new science.* New York: Viking.

Glenberg, A. M., & Kaschak, M. P. (2002). Grounding language in action. *Psychonomic Bulletin and Review, 9*, 558–565.

Gomez, R. L., Bootzin, R. R., & Nadel, L. (2006). Naps promote abstraction in language-learning infants. *Psychological Science, 17*, 670–674.

Goodale, M. A., & Milner, A. D. (1992). Separate visual pathways for perception and action. *Trends in Neurosciences, 15*, 20–25.

Gould, S. J. (1991). Exaptation: A crucial tool for evolutionary psychology. *Journal of Social Issues, 47*, 43–65.

Gould, S. J. (1997). Darwinian fundamentalism. *New York Review of Books,* 34–37.

Gould, S. J., & Vrba, E. S. (1982). Exaptation: A missing term in the science of form. *Paleobiology, 8*, 4–15.

Grill-Spector, K., Henson, R., & Martin, A. (2006). Repetition and the brain: Neural models of stimulus-specific effects. *Trends in Cognitive Sciences, 10*, 14–23.

Gross, M. (1972). *Mathematical models in linguistics*. Englewood Cliffs, NJ: Prentice-Hall.

Gusnard, D. A., & Raichle, M. E. (2001). Searching for a baseline: Functional imaging and the resting human brain. *Nature Reviews: Neuroscience, 2*, 685–694.

Hagoort, P. (2005). On broca, brain, and binding: A new framework. *Trends in Cognitive Sciences, 9*, 416–423.

Hanakawa, T., Immisch, I., Toma, K., Dimyan, M. A., Van Gelderen, P., & Hallett, M. (2003). Functional properties of brain areas associated with motor execution and imagery. *Journal of Neurophysiology, 89*, 989–1002.

Hasson, U., Nusbaum, H. C., & Small, S. L. (2007). Brain networks subserving the extraction of sentence information and its encoding to memory. *Cerebral Cortex, 17*, 2899–2913.

Hasson, U., Skipper, J. I., Nusbaum, H. C., & Small, S. L. (2007). Abstract coding of audiovisual speech: Beyond sensory representation. *Neuron, 56*, 1116–1126.

Hauk, O., Johnsrude, I., & Pulvermüller, F. (2004). Somatotopic representation of action words in human motor and premotor cortex. *Neuron, 41*, 301–307.

Hauser, M. D. (1996). *The evolution of communication*. Cambridge, MA: MIT Press.

Hauser, M. D., Barner, D., & O'Donnell, T. (2007). Evolutionary linguistics: A new look at an old landscape. *Language Learning and Development, 2*, 101–132.

Hauser, M. D., Chomsky, N., & Fitch, T. (2002). The faculty of language: What is it, who has it, and how did it evolve? *Science, 298*, 1569–1579.

Heiligenberg, W. F. (1991). *Neural nets in electric fish*. Cambridge, MA: MIT Press.

Hickok, G., & Poeppel, D. (2004). Dorsal and ventral streams: A framework for understanding aspects of the functional anatomy of language. *Cognition, 92*, 67–99.

Hockett, C. F. (1960). The origin of speech. *Scientific American, 203*, 88–96.

Holt, L. E., & Beilock, S. L. (2006). Expertise and its embodiment: Examining the impact of sensorimotor skill expertise on the representation of action-related text. *Psychonomic Bulletin and Review, 13*, 694–701.

Holtgraves, T. (1994). Communication in context: Effects of speaker status on the comprehension of indirect requests. *Journal of Experimental Psychology: Learning, Memory, and Cognition, 20*, 1205–1218.

Hopcroft, J. E., & Ullman, J. D. (1969). *Formal languages and their relation to automata*. Reading, MA: Addison-Wesley.

Hoy, R. R., & Paul, R. C. (1973). Genetic control of song specificity in crickets. *Science, 180*, 82–83.

Huber, R., Ghilardi, M. F., Massimini, M., & Tononi, G. (2004). Local sleep and learning. *Nature, 430*, 78–81.

Hultsch, H., & Todt, D. (1989). Memorization and reproduction of songs in nightingales (Luscinia megarhynchos): Evidence for package formation. *Journal of Comparative Psychology, 165*, 197–203.

Jeannerod, M. (1994). The representing brain: Neural correlates of motor intention and imagery. *Behavioral and Brain Science, 17*, 187–245.

Johnson, J. S., and Newport, E. L. (1989). Critical period effects in second language learning: The influence of maturational state on the acquisition of English as a second language. *Cognitive Psychology, 21*, 60–99.

Johnson, K., Strand, E. A., & D'Imperio, M. (1999). Auditory: Visual integration of talker gender in vowel perception. *Journal of Phonetics, 27*, 359–384.

Klatt, D. H. (1977). Review of the ARPA speech understanding project. *Journal of the Acoustic Society of America, 62*, 1345–1366.

Klatt, D. H. (1979). Speech perception: A model of acoustic-phonetic analysis and lexical access. *Journal of Phonetics, 7*, 279–312.

Klatt, D. H. (1986). Comment. In J. S. Perkell & D. H. Klatt (Eds.), *Invariance and variability in speech processes* (pp. 381–382). Hillsdale, NJ: Erlbaum.

Kluender, K. R., Diehl, R. L., & Killeen, P. R. (1987). Japanese quail can learn phonetic categories. *Science, 237*, 1195–1197.

Kogan, J., & Margoliash, D. (1998). Automated recognition of bird song elements from continuous recordings using dynamic time warping and hidden Markov models: A comparative study. *Journal of the Acoustical Society of America, 103*, 2185–2196.

Kosslyn, S. M., & Sussman, A. L. (1994). Roles of imagery in perception: Or, there is no such thing as immaculate perception. In M. S. Gazzaniga (Ed.), *The cognitive neurosciences* (pp. 1035–1042). Cambridge, MA: MIT Press.

Kosslyn, S. M., Thompson, W. L., & Alpert, N. M. (1997). Neural systems shared by visual imagery and visual perception: A positron emission tomography study. *NeuroImage, 6*, 320–334.

Kroodsma, D. E., & Miller, E. H. (Eds.). (1996). *Ecology and evolution of acoustic communication in birds*. Ithaca, NY: Cornell University Press.

Kroodsma, D. E., & Pickert, R. (1980). Environmentally dependent sensitive periods for avian vocal learning. *Nature, 288*, 477–479.

Kuhl, P. K., & Miller, J. D. (1975). Speech perception by the chinchilla: Voiced-voiceless distinction in alveolar plosive consonants. *Science, 190*, 69–72.

Lakin, J., & Chartrand, T. L. (2003). Using nonconscious behavioral mimicry to create affiliation and rapport. *Psychological Science, 14*, 334–339.

Lenneberg, E. H. (1967). *Biological foundations of language*. New York: Wiley.

Levinson, S. E., Rabiner, L. R., & Sondhi, M. M. (1983). An introduction to the application of the theory of probabilistic functions of a Markov process to automatic speech recognition. *Bell System Technical Journal, 62*, 1035–1074.

Liberman, A. M., Cooper, F. S., Harris, K. S., & MacNeilage, P. F. (1962). *A motor theory of speech perception*. Proceedings of the Speech Communication Seminar (Vol. 2). Stockholm: Royal Institute of Technology.

Liberman, A. M., Cooper, F. S., Shankweiler, D. P., & Studdert-Kennedy, M. (1967). Perception of the speech code. *Psychological Review, 74*, 431–461.

Liberman, A. M., & Mattingly, I. G. (1985). The motor theory of speech perception revised. *Cognition, 21*, 1–36.

Lichtheim, L. (1885). On aphasia. *Brain, 7*, 433–484.

Lowerre, B., & Reddy, R. (1980). The Harpy speech understanding system. In W. A. Lea (Ed.), *Trends in speech recognition* (pp. 340–360). Englewood Cliffs, NJ: Prentice-Hall.

Luks, T. L., Nusbaum, H. C., & Levy, J. (1998). Hemispheric involvement in the perception of syntactic prosody is dynamically dependent on task demands. *Brain and Language, 65*, 313–332.

MacKinnon, J. (1974). The behaviour and ecology of wild orang-utans (*Pongo pygmaeus*). *Animal Behaviour, 22*, 3–74.

MacNeilage, P. F. (1970). Motor control of serial ordering of speech. *Psychological Review, 77*, 182–196.

Magnuson, J. S., & Nusbaum, H. C. (2007). Acoustic differences, listener expectations, and the perceptual accommodation of talker variability. *Journal of Experimental Psychology: Human Perception and Performance, 33*, 391–409.

Margoliash, D. (2002). Evaluating theories of bird song learning: Implications for future directions. *Journal of Comparative Physiology, 188*, 851–866.

Marler, P. (1970). A comparative approach to vocal learning: Song learning in white-crowned sparrows. *Journal of Comparative Physiological Psychology*, *71*, 1–25.

Marler, P., & Peters, S. (1980). Birdsong and speech: Evidence for special processing. In P. Eimas & J. Miller (Eds.), *Perspectives on the study of speech* (pp. 75–112). Hillsdale, NJ: Erlbaum.

Massaro, D. W. (1998). *Perceiving talking faces: From speech perception to a behavioral principle.* Cambridge, MA: MIT Press.

McClelland, J. L., & Elman, J. L. (1986). The TRACE model of speech perception. *Cognitive Psychology*, *18*, 1–86.

McComb, K., Reby, D., Baker, L., Moss, C., & Sayialel, S. (2003). Long-distance communication of acoustic cues to social identity in African elephants. *Animal Behaviour*, *65*, 317–329.

McGaugh, J. L. (2000). Memory: A century of consolidation. *Science*, *287*, 248–251.

McGurk, H., & MacDonald, J. (1976, December 23). Hearing lips and seeing voices. *Nature*, *264*, 746–748.

McNeill, D. (1992). *Hand and mind: What gestures reveal about thought.* Chicago: University of Chicago Press.

McNeill, D. (2007). *Gesture and thought.* Chicago: University of Chicago Press.

Michel, G. F., & Tyler, A. N. (2005). Critical period: A history of the transition from questions of when, to what, to how. *Developmental Psychobiology*, *46*(3), 156–162.

Mishkin, M., Ungerleider, L. G., & Macko, K. A. (1983). Object vision and spatial vision: Two cortical pathways. *Trends in Neurosciences*, *6*, 414–417.

Moran, J., & Desimone, R. (1985). Selective attention gates visual processing in the extrastriate cortex. *Science*, *229*, 782–784.

Moss, C. F., & Sinha, S. R. (2003). Neurobiology of echolocation in bats. *Current Opinion in Neurobiology*, *13*, 755–762.

Moss, C. F., Bohn, K., Gilkenson, H., & Surlykke, A. (2006). Active listening for spatial orientation in a complex auditory scene. *Public Library of Science Biology*, *4*, 615–626.

Mullennix, J. W., & Pisoni, D. B. (1990). Stimulus variability and processing dependencies in speech perception. *Perception and Psychophysics*, *47*, 379–380.

Musacchia, G., Sams, M., Nicol, T. G., & Kraus, N. (2006). Seeing speech affects acoustic information processing in the human brainstem. *Experimental Brain Research*, *168*, 1–10.

Musacchia, G., Sams, M., Skoe, E., & Kraus, N. (2007). Musicians have enhanced subcortical auditory and audiovisual processing of speech and music. *Proceedings of the National Academy of Sciences, USA*, *104*, 15894–15898.

Nelson, M. E., & MacIver, M. A. (2006). Sensory acquisition in active sensing systems. *Journal of Comparative Physiology*, *192*, 573–586.

Newsome, W. T., Shadlen, M. N., Zohary, E., Britten, K. H., & Movshon, J. A. (1995). Visual motion: Linking neuronal activity to psychophysical performance. In M. S. Gazzaniga (Ed.), *The cognitive neurosciences* (pp. 401–414). Cambridge, MA: MIT Press.

Nusbaum, H. C., & Henly, A. S. (unpublished manuscript). Understanding speech perception from the perspective of cognitive psychology. In J. Charles-Luce, P. A. Luce, & J. R. Sawusch (Eds.), *Spoken language processing*. Newark, NJ: Ablex.

Nusbaum, H. C., & Lee, L. (1992). Learning to hear phonetic information. In Y. Tohkura, E. Vatikiotis-Bateson, & Y. Sagisaka (Eds.), *Speech perception, production, and linguistic structure* (pp. 265–273). Tokyo: Ohmsha.

Nusbaum, H. C., & Magnuson, J. S. (1997). Talker normalization: Phonetic constancy as a cognitive process. In K. A. Johnson & J. W. Mullennix (Eds.), *Talker variability in speech processing* (pp. 109–132). New York: Academic Press.

Nusbaum, H. C., & Morin, T. M. (1992). Paying attention to differences among talkers. In Y. Tohkura, E. Vatikiotis-Bateson, & Y. Sagisaka (Eds.), *Speech perception, production, and linguistic structure* (pp. 113–134). Tokyo: OHM.

Nusbaum, H. C., & Pisoni, D. B. (1987). Automatic measurement of speech pp.109-132 recognition performance: A comparison of six speaker-dependent recognition devices. *Computer Speech and Language*, *2*, 87–108.

Nusbaum, H. C., & Schwab, E. C. (1986). The role of attention and active processing in speech perception. In E. C. Schwab & H. C. Nusbaum (Eds.), *Pattern recognition by humans and machines: Speech perception* (Vol. 1, pp. 113–157). San Diego, CA: Academic Press.

Ojemann, G., & Mateer, C. (1979). Human language cortex: Localization of memory, syntax, and sequential motor-phoneme identification systems. *Science*, *205*, 1401–1403.

Payne, R. B. (1981). Song learning and social interaction in indigo buntings. *Animal Behaviour*, *29*, 688–697.

Peterson, G., & Barney, H. (1952). Control methods used in a study of the vowels. *Journal of the Acoustical Society of America*, *24*, 175–184.

Piattelli-Palmarini, M. (1989). Evolution, selection, and cognition: From "learning" to parameter setting in biology and the study of language. *Cognition*, *31*, 1–44.

Pickering, M. J., & Garrod, S. (2004). Towards a mechanistic Psychology of dialogue. *Behavioral and Brain Sciences*, *27*, 169–226.

Pinker, S. (2003). Language as an adaptation to the cognitive niche. In M. Christiansen & S. Kirby (Eds.), *Language evolution: States of the Art* (pp. 16–37). New York: Oxford University Press.

Pinker, S., & Bloom, P. (1990). Natural language and natural selection. *Behavioral and Brain Sciences*, *13*, 707–784.

Pinker, S., & Jackendoff, R. (2005). The faculty of language: What's special about it? *Cognition*, *95*, 201–236.

Prather, J. F., Peters, S., Nowicki, S., & Mooney, R. (2008). Precise auditory: Vocal mirroring in neurons for learned vocal communication. *Nature*, *451*, 305–310.

Price, C., Thierry, G., & Griffiths, T. (2005). Speech-specific auditory processing: Where is it? *Trends in Cognitive Sciences*, *9*, 271–276.

Pulvermuller, R. (2003). *The neuroscience of language.* Cambridge, MA: Cambridge University Press.

Rauschecker, J. P. (1998). Cortical processing of complex sounds. *Current Opinion in Neurobiology*, *8*, 516–521.

Remez, R. E., Rubin, P. E., Pisoni, D. B., & Carrell, T. I. (1981). Speech perception without traditional speech cues. *Science*, *212*, 947–950.

Rizzolatti, G., & Arbib, M. A. (1998). Language within our grasp. *Trends in Neurosciences*, *21*, 188–194.

Rizzolatti, G., & Craighero, L. (2004). The mirror-neuron system. *Annual Review of Neuroscience*, *27*, 169–192.

Rizzolatti, G., Fogassi, L., & Gallese, V. (2001). Neurophysiological mechanisms underlying the understanding and imitation of action. *Nature Review Neuroscience*, *2*, 661–670.

Rizzolatti, G., Fogassi, L., & Gallese, V. (2002). Motor and cognitive functions of the ventral premotor cortex. *Current Opinion in Neurobiology*, *12*, 149–154.

Roeder, K. D. (1964). Aspects of the noctuid tympanic nerve response having significance in the avoidance of bats. *Journal of Insect Physiology*, *10*, 529–546.

Roland, P. (1993). *Brain activation.* New York: Wiley-Liss.

Rose, G. J., Goller, F., Gritton, H. J., Plamondon, S. L., Baugh, A. T., & Cooper, B. G. (2004). Species-typical songs in white-crowned sparrows tutored with only phrase pairs. *Nature*, *432*, 753–758.

Rosenblum, L. D., Miller, R. M., & Sanchez, K. (2007). Lip-read me now, hear me better later: Cross-modal transfer of talker-familiarity effects. *Psychological Science*, *18*, 369–468.

Rubin, D. L. (1992). Nonlanguage factors affecting undergraduates' judgments of nonnative English-speaking teaching assistants. *Research in Higher Education, 33*, 511–531.

Sachs, M. B., & Young, E. D. (1979). Encoding of steady-state vowels in the auditory nerve: Representation in terms of discharge rate. *Journal of the Acoustical Society of America, 66*, 470–479.

Saffran, J. R. (2003). Statistical language learning: Mechanisms and constraints. *Current Directions in Psychological Science, 12*, 110–114.

Sander, D., Grandjean, D., Pourtois, G., Schwartz, S., Seghier, M., Scherer, K. R., et al. (2005). Emotion and attention interactions in social cognition: Brain regions involved in processing anger prosody. *NeuroImage, 28*, 848–858.

Schirmer, A., & Kotz, S. A. (2006). Beyond the right hemisphere: Brain mechanisms mediating vocal emotional processing. *Trends in Cognitive Sciences, 10*, 24–30.

Schwab, E. C., Nusbaum, H. C., & Pisoni, D. B. (1985). Effects of training on the perception of synthetic speech. *Human Factors, 27*, 395–408.

Sedivy, J. E., Tanenhaus, M. K., Chambers, C. G., & Carlson, G. N. (1999). Achieving incremental interpretation through contextual representation: Evidence from the processing of adjectives. *Cognition, 71*, 109–147.

Shank, S., & Margoliash, D. (in press). Sleep, sensorimotor integration, and early vocal learning. *Nature*.

Shintel, H., & Nusbaum, H. C. (2007). The sound of motion in spoken language: Visual information conveyed by acoustic properties of speech. *Cognition, 105*, 681–690.

Shintel, H., & Nusbaum, H. C. (2008). Moving to the speed of sound: Context modulation of the effect of acoustic properties of speech. *Cognitive Science, 32*, 1063–1074.

Shintel, H., Nusbaum, H. C., & Okrent, A. (2006). Analog acoustic expression in speech communication. *Journal of Memory and Language, 55*, 167–177.

Skipper, J. I., Goldin-Meadow, S., Nusbaum, H. C., & Small, S. L. (2007a). *Observed iconic and metaphoric speech-associated gestures are processed differently by ventral and dorsal premotor cortex.* Paper presented at the 14th Annual Meeting of the Cognitive Neuroscience Society, New York, NY, USA.

Skipper, J. I., Goldin-Meadow, S., Nusbaum, H. C., & Small, S. L. (2007b). Speech-associated gestures, Broca's area, and the human mirror system. *Brain and Language, 101*, 260–277.

Skipper, J. I., Nusbaum, H. C., & Small, S. L. (2005). Listening to talking faces: Motor cortical activation during speech perception. *NeuroImage, 25*, 76–89.

Skipper, J. I., Nusbaum, H. C., & Small, S. L. (2006). Lending a helping hand to hearing: Another motor theory of speech perception. In M. A. Arbib (Ed.), *Action to language via the mirror neuron system* (pp. 250–285). New York: Cambridge University Press.

Skipper, J. I., van Wassenhove, V., Nusbaum, H. C., & Small, S. L. (2007). Hearing lips and seeing voices: How cortical areas support speech production mediate audiovisual speech perception. *Cerebral Cortex, 17*, 2387–2399.

Sperber, D. (2001). In defense of massive modularity. In E. Dupoux (Ed). *Language, brain, and cognitive development: Essays in honor of Jacques Mehler* (pp. 47–57). Cambridge, MA: MIT Press.

Stevens, K. N., & Blumstein, S. E. (1978). Invariant cues for place of articulation in stop consonants. *Journal of the Acoustical Society of America, 64*, 1358–1368.

Stevens, K. N., & Blumstein, S. E. (1981). The search for invariant acoustic correlates of phonetic features. In P. D. Eimas & J. Miller (Eds.), *Perspectives on the study of speech* (pp. 1–38). Hillsdale, NJ: Erlbaum.

Stevens, K. N., & Halle, M. (1967). Remarks on analysis by synthesis and distinctive features. In W. Walthen-Dunn (Ed.), *Models for the perception of speech and visual form* (pp. 88–102). Cambridge, MA: MIT Press.

Suga, N., & Ma, X. (2003). Multiparametric corticofugal modulation and plasticity in the auditory system. *Nature Reviews: Neuroscience, 4*, 783–794.

Sumby, W. H., & Pollack, I. (1954). Visual contribution of speech intelligibility in noise. *Journal of the Acoustical Society of America, 26*, 212–215.

Tanenhaus, M. K., Spivey-Knowlton, M., Eberhard, K., & Sedivy, J. C. (1995). Integration of visual and linguistic information is spoken-language comprehension. *Science, 268*, 1632–1634.

Tao, J., Johnson, M. T., & Osiejuk, T. S. (2008). Acoustic model adaptation for ortolan bunting (Emberiza hortulana L.) song-type classification. *Journal of the Acoustical Society of America, 123*, 1582–1590.

Teller, D. Y. (1984). Linking propositions. *Vision Research, 24*, 1233–1246.

Tettamanti, M., Buccino, G., Saccuman, M. C., Gallese, V., Danna, M., Scifo, P., et al. (2005). Listening to action-related sentences activates fronto-parietal motor circuits. *Journal of Cognitive Neuroscience, 17*, 273–281.

Thorpe, W. H. (1961). *Bird-song: The biology of vocal communication and expression in birds.* Cambridge, MA: Cambridge University Press.

Tononi, G., & Cirelli, C. (2001). Some consideration on sleep and neural plasticity. *HCN Italian Archives of Biology, 139*, 221–241.

Van Baaren, R. B., Horgan, T. G., Chartrand, T. L., & Dijkmans, M. (2004). The forest, the trees and the chameleon: Context-dependency and mimicry. *Journal of Personality and Social Psychology, 86*, 453–459.

Vinckier, F., Dehaene, S., Jobert, A., Dubus, J. P., Sigman, M., & Cohen, L. (2007). Hierarchical coding of letter strings in the ventral stream: Dissecting the inner organization of the visual word-form system. *Neuron, 55*, 143–156.

von der Heydt, R., Peterhans, E., & Baumgartner, G. (1984). Illusory contours and cortical neuron responses. *Science, 224*, 1260–1262.

Walker, M. P., & Stickgold, R. (2006). Sleep, memory, and plasticity. *Annual Review of Psychology, 57*, 139–166.

Walley, A. C., & Carrell, T. D. (1983). Onset spectra and formant transitions in the adult's and child's perception of place of articulation in stop consonants. *Journal of the Acoustical Society of America, 73*, 1011–1022.

Watkins, S., Dalton, P., Lavie, N., & Rees, G. (2007). Brain mechanisms mediating auditory attentional capture in humans. *Cerebral Cortex, 17*, 1694–1700.

Wernicke, C. (1874). *Der aphasische symptomenkomplex.* [HCN The aphasia symptom complex.]. Breslau: Cohn & Weigert.

Wildgruber, D., Hertrich, I., Riecker, A., Erb, M., Anders, S., Grodd, W., et al. (2004). Distinct frontal regions subserve evaluation of linguistic and emotional espects of speech sntonation. *Cerebral Cortex, 14*, 1384–1389.

Williams, H., & Staples, K. (1992). Syllable chunking: In zebra finch taeniopygia-guttata song. *Journal of Comparative Psychology, 106*, 278–286.

Wilson, S. M., & Iacoboni, M. (2006). Neural responses to non-native phonemes varying in producibility: Evidence for the sensorimotor nature of speech perception. *NeuroImage, 33*, 316–325.

Wilson, S. M., Saygin, A. P., Sereno, M. I., & Iacoboni, M. (2004). Listening to speech activates motor areas involved in speech production. *Nature Neuroscience, 7*, 701–702.

Wong, P. C. M., Nusbaum, H. C., & Small, S. L. (2004). Neural bases of talker normalization. *Journal of Cognitive Neuroscience, 16*, 1173–1184.

Woods, W. A. (1973). An experimental parsing system for transition network grammars. In R. Rustin (Ed.), *Natural language processing* (pp. 111–145). New York: Algorithmics Press.

Wymbs, N. F., Nusbaum, H. C., & Small, S. L. (2004). *The informed perceiver: Neural correlates of linguistic expectation and speech perception.* Paper presented to the 11th Annual Meeting of the Cognitive Neuroscience Society, March, San Francisco.

Yamada, R. A., & Tohkura, Y. (1992). Perception of American English and native speakers of Japanese. In Y. Tohkura, E. Vatikiotis-Bateson, & Y. Sagisaka (Eds.), *Speech perception, production and linguistic structure* (pp. 155–174). Tokyo: Ohmsha.

Yan, J., & Suga, N. (1996). Corticofugal modulation of time-domain processing of biosonar information in bats. *Science, 273,* 1100–1103.

von der Heydt, R., Peterhans, E., & Baumgartner, G. (1984). Illusory contours and cortical neuron responses. *Science, 224,* 260–1262.

Zwaan, R. A., Stanfield, R. A., & Yaxley, R. H. (2002). Language comprehenders mentally represent the shape of objects. *Psychological Science, 13,* 168–171.

Chapter 46

Imitation and Theory of Mind

PHILIP GERRANS

THEORY OF MIND, SIMULATION, AND IMITATION

In 1985, Simon Baron-Cohen, Uta Frith, and Alan Leslie published the influential paper, "Does the autistic child lack a theory of mind" (Baron-Cohen, Leslie, & Frith, 1985). What they called *theory of mind* (TOM) is the ability to conceive of mental states as internal representations that stand for objects in the world and, in doing so, may misrepresent it (Perner, 1991). Acquiring this concept of mental states allows the child to become a competent *mind reader*—to use the felicitous expression of S. Baron-Cohen (1995)—able to treat other people as agents animated by an inner mental life instead of as organisms directly coupled to the world by shallow perception-action loops.

The expression "theory of mind" is sometimes used synonymously with "mind reading" to refer to the ability to attribute mental states, but it is in fact a theory about the cognitive processes on which mind reading depends. The essence of TOM is the idea that mind reading depends on *metarepresentation,* the representation of the relationship between a representation and its object. Metarepresentation allows the child to *decouple* the concept of a mental state from the world by thinking of mental states as possibly false or inaccurate (Leslie, 1994).

The main competitor for TOM is the simulation theory of mind reading. Instead of using TOM to mind-read, we *simulate* the psychology of others by pretending to be them or imaginatively projecting ourselves into their situation (Goldman, 2006; Heal, 1996). And, intuitively, it seems that there are occasions when we simulate other people to read their minds. When playing chess or bidding against another person at an auction, we imagine ourselves in their situation to anticipate their next move. The attraction of the simulation alternative to TOM is that simulation is less conceptually demanding than theoretically embedded metarepresentation. Just as we can use a model plane or boat to make predictions in the absence of a detailed theory about how it works, we can use our own psychology to

simulate others in the absence of a psychological theory about the relationship between inner mental states and actions. This argument suggests that simulation is a mechanism that enables direct apprehension of mental states embodied in behavior rather than inference-based attribution of mental states hypothesized as underlying causes of behavior (Gordon, 1986). The notion of simulation unites philosophical arguments about direct perception of mental states with a Gibsonian strand in psychology which also argues that perception is part of a sensory motor continuum that couples an agent to the world (Gallese & Goldman, 1998). Of course, the coupling involved in simulation is only partial: The simulator *imagines* performing the action, which takes the action offline (Nichols, Stich, Leslie, & Klein, 1996). Hence, it is also a mechanism of decoupling, but less abstract and theoretical than the TOM idea that decoupling requires amodal forms of representation not essentially linked to action.

If we understand other people by simulating them, there is an intuitive link with the concept of imitation (Byrne, 2005; Carpenter, Call, & Tomasello, 2005; Meltzoff & Decety, 2003; Sommerville & Decety, 2006; Wolpert, Doya, & Kawato, 2003; Zaitchik, 1990). One way to simulate other people is to *imagine imitating them;* that is, performing the same action. If imagined performance automatically induces the same mental states in the simulator as the target, then imitation can be a mechanism of mental state simulation.

Simulation theorists were therefore keen to recruit research in cognitive neuroscience, which showed automatic imitation of perceived actions such as smiles and tongue protrusion in human neonates (Meltzoff & Moore, 1983) and mirror phenomena in monkeys and humans (Rizzolatti & Craighero, 2004). In mirror phenomena, third-person observation of an action produces activation of the same premotor and parietal circuitry involved in first-person execution of the action (Gallese, Fadiga, Fogassi, & Rizzolatti, 1996; Gallese, Keysers, & Rizzolatti, 2004; Rizzolatti & Craighero, 2004; Rizzolatti, Ferrari,

Rozzi, & Fogassi, 2006). Simulationists suggested that these types of involuntary motor imitation, which are best described as *motor contagion,* could be a developmental basis for simulation and ultimately for mind reading. Goldman and Gallese suggested, "Mirror Neurons represent a primitive version, or possibly a precursor in phylogeny of a simulation heuristic that might underlie mind-reading" (Gallese et al., 2004, p. 498).

Results such as these combined with an increasing number of imaging and lesion studies of mind reading shifted the terrain of the debate between TOM and simulation theorists (Davies & Stone, 1995). The neural rather than conceptual basis of mind reading is now the focus with a priori and conceptual arguments restricted to providing hypotheses about the cognitive role played by different neural systems. No one now doubts that there is a *conceptual* difference between simulation and TOM-based mind reading, but a crucial question is whether the temporo-parietal junction (TPJ) activation elicited in some mind reading studies is computing the metarepresentation of mental states (Saxe, 2005, 2006; Saxe, Carey, & Kanwisher, 2004; Saxe & Wexler, 2005) or is involved in some less specialized integrative functions (Decety & Lamm, 2007; Stone & Gerrans, 2006a) that could be assimilated to the simulation paradigm (Decety & Lamm, 2007).

THEORY OF MIND: BEHAVIORAL PARADIGMS AND NEURAL CORRELATES

The ability to decouple mental states arrives at different times for different states. Children can decouple emotions, perceptions, desires, and pretend states well before they can decouple beliefs. In effect, this means that a child can understand that another person can have different emotions, perceptual experiences, and desires from those of the child and that these states can be entertained even in the absence of their intentional object. Not only that, but children as young as 2 years old seem to have a naive psychological understanding in which these decoupled states are understood to fit together coherently. Children aged 2 years understand the relationship between desire and emotion. Asked to choose a picture that predicts the responses of a child who wanted a puppy and either did or did not get one, 2-year-olds chose pictures of happy and sad faces respectively (Wellman & Woolley, 1990).

So it is not quite correct to say that toddlers cannot mind read. However, their mind reading undergoes a dramatic transformation between the ages of three and five. By the age of five, the neurotypical child can attribute *beliefs* understood as decoupled representations, completing the repertoire required for adult mind reading and expanding her capacities

for social cognition. Thus some theorists have distinguished between early TOM and late or mature TOM in which the child can attribute decoupled beliefs. Others refer to social cognition as a general phenomenon of which TOM is a discrete component. Thus the acid test for the TOM interpretation of mind reading is the false belief test.

In the classic false belief test, a child is seated at a table that contains two containers and a toy, opposite a partner (A). The partner leaves the room and the experimenter moves the toy from one container to another. The child is then asked, "Where will A look for the toy?" The correct answer is the previous location. Five-year-olds pass this test; 3-year-olds fail it. The 3-year-old does not seem to understand that the partner has a false belief based on perceptual information which has been falsified (Baron-Cohen et al., 1985).

There are many versions of the test but a recent one by Ziv and Frye captures both the synchronic and diachronic aspects of TOM. In this test, children are read two short stories about characters called Duck and Cat and their belongings, a book and a ball. In change-of-location stories, Duck puts his ball in a bag, then leaves the room. While he is away, Cat removes the ball, in some cases replacing it with a book. The child is then asked, "Where does Duck think the ball is?/want the ball to be?" The results are the same as earlier. Three-year-olds pass the desire test but fail the belief test, 5-year-olds pass them both. In change-of-object stories, the child is asked, "What is in the bag? What does Duck think is in the bag? What does Duck want to be in the bag?" The conceptual advance of the 5-year-old is the ability to understand that someone may have a representation of the world that *misrepresents* it (Baron-Cohen et al., 1985; Wellman & Lagattuta, 2000; Ziv & Frye, 2003).This is consistent with findings that 3-year-olds have difficulty with the appearance/reality distinction. Shown a sponge painted as a rock, 3-year-olds will say both that it is a sponge *and* that it looks like a sponge (Astington, 1993).

The other classic experiment recruited as evidence for TOM is the false photograph test in which the child watches while a Polaroid camera is used to take a photo of a scene containing an object. While the picture is developing, the object is moved and the child is asked, "Where will the object be in the photograph?" replicating the change-of-location problem in the false belief test. Unlike the false belief test, 3-year-olds have no trouble with the false photo task. Another crucial finding is that children with autism, a developmental disorder characterized by a range of impairments in social cognition, typically pass the false photo test but have impaired performance on the false belief test. Autistic and normal children exhibit the reverse pattern of performance on false belief and false photo tasks (Zaitchik, 1990).

These basic paradigms establish the framework against which the neural correlates of TOM and mind reading are investigated. All studies correlate neural activity revealed by imaging methodologies or focal lesions with performance on tasks that require the ability to attribute beliefs. Before we look at those studies, there are two important points to note, both relating to the possible *modularity* of TOM.

Baron-Cohen et al. interpreted the false belief test as evidence that the 5-year-old forms a belief about a false belief and hence that metarepresentation of beliefs is the key to passing the false belief test. If this is the case, mind reading should develop in tandem with the development of metarepresentational capacities, scaffolded by other high-level capacities such as recursion (the embedding of one representation inside another) and executive function. Executive function, a developmental prerequisite for all forms of high-level domain-general cognition, involves the ability to selectively inhibit some representations while flexibly manipulating others. Executive function seems important to false belief tasks because the child has to inhibit the perceptual information about the new location while retrieving the memory of the original location that supplies the content for the false belief (Carlson & Moses, 2001; Moses, 2001; Perner & Lang, 1999).

Another high-level ability that integrates seamlessly with executive and metarepresentational capacities arriving at about this time is a capacity for mental time travel, the use of episodic memory and imagination to plan, deliberate, and ruminate (Suddendorf & Busby, 2005; Suddendorf & Corballis, 2007). The name Mental Time Travel captures the idea that a combination of episodic memory and imagination under executive control allows a person to project herself forward and backward in time. Mental time travel appears to be a crucial cognitive adaptation, enhancing planning and deliberation by allowing a subject to simulate and evaluate contingencies in the Cartesian privacy of her own mind.

Brain imaging and lesion studies indicate that episodic memory and prospection (imaginative rehearsal of future experience) recruit similar mechanisms and strongly overlapping neural systems. Rather than thinking of memory and imagination as different abilities, we should conceive them as part of a unified capacity for the construction of imagery that underwrites both episodic memory and prospection required for planning and problem solving. As Schacter et al. put it in a recent review: "[T]he medial temporal lobe system which has long been considered to be crucial for remembering the past might actually gain adaptive value through its ability to provide details that serve as building blocks of future event simulations" (Addis, Wong, & Schacter, 2007; Hassabis, Kumaran, & Maguire, 2007; Hassabis & Maguire, 2007).

Some theorists note that in preschoolers, improved executive capacities consequent on maturation of prefrontal

areas coincide with the installation of a capacity for voluntary episodic memory and (fragile) capacity for planning using prospection (Gerrans, 2002; Miller & Cohen, 2001). If this is correct, the precocious role of pretense in human cognitive development seems less anomalous (Gerrans, 1998; Leslie, 1994). Sophisticated pretend play, often taken to be an important precursor of TOM in virtue of its metarepresentational structure, can be seen as a socially sculpted mental time travel and perhaps assimilated by simulationists as a landmark in the development of third-person simulation.

Thus one view of TOM is that it results from the ability to deploy a suite of higher level capacities, of which executive function and metarepresentation are perhaps the most important, to the task of understanding other minds.

A mainstream view of TOM, following two decades of further research, however, is that it is a domain-specific cognitive adaptation for metarepresentation of mental states implemented in a specialized neural circuit: a "TOM module" as it is known. The initial impetus for the modular theory was the behavioral double dissociation elegantly demonstrated by Zaitchek (1990). Modular theorists treat it as evidence for the inference that the tasks are subserved by different cognitive subsystems or modules or, at the very least, for partitioning of metapresentational abilities.

A stronger *nativist* modular hypothesis is that the development of this specialized neural circuitry is genetically specified. For nativists, TOM implemented in the TPJ or MPFC is akin to language: a universal cognitive adaptation that develops relatively autonomously. For modular nativists, impairments in social cognition characteristic of autism result from the developmental dissociation of a TOM module (Gerrans & Stone, 2008; Leslie & Thaiss, 1992; Scholl & Leslie, 2001).

Thus when studies show selective activation of neural circuitry in mind-reading tasks, the role of that circuitry has been interpreted in different ways: as evidence for the modular hypothesis (Happé et al., 1996; Saxe et al., 2004; Saxe & Wexler, 2005); or as evidence that the child's higher order intellectual capacities are focused on a mind-reading task. In the latter case, the onus is on the theorist to show that the neural systems recruited by the experimental task are *not* specialized for TOM but have some more general, possibly executive or metarepresentational role. Apperly, Samson, Chiavarino, Bickerton, & Humphreys, 2007; (Apperly, Samson, Chiavarino, & Humphreys, 2004; Stone & Gerrans, 2006a, 2006b).

Distinguishing these hypotheses is not an insuperable task: It seems to require that activation elicited by the hypothesized TOM task be compared with that produced by a task with the same conceptual structure and matched for executive and metarepresentational demands. For this reason, versions of the false photo and false belief task matched for difficulty have been used to pry apart the contribution to mind reading of domain general and domain specific cognitive systems (Apperly et al., 2004). Another important strategy is to examine cases of lesion to areas putatively identified by other studies as specialized for TOM. If they are specialized for TOM, we should expect (*modulo* the usual caveats about the distributed nature of higher level cognition and the difficulty of inferring cognitive specialization from neural localization; Saxe, 2006), that damage to them should lead to selective impairment in mind reading (Apperly et al., 2007).

The other important point to note before we turn to the neural correlates of TOM is that mind reading builds on earlier developmental stages called *precursors,* characterized by specific forms of behavior underwritten by specialized cognitive systems. Gaze tracking, joint attention, and social referencing are precursors to mind reading in the sense that children who do not exhibit them subsequently have delays or impairments in mind reading. A satisfactory explanation of mind reading would show how the cognitive structure of precursor states produces the cognitive structure of mind reading. There are two main possibilities: In the first, weak, sense precursors are important early inputs to development of another cognitive process. This seems to be the sense in which domain general metarepresentational theorists of TOM conceive the role of early quasi-perceptual precursors such as intention detecting or social referencing: They provide social information that becomes evidence for a domain general inference system.

The second, strong, sense of a precursor is that it is an earlier state of the same cognitive process (in this case mind reading), which is the *explanandum.* The syntactic structure of language has been proposed as a precursor to TOM in this strong sense because embedded complement clauses (he *said* that . . . , she *saw* that . . . , he is *pretending* that . . .) have the argument structure required for metarepresentation of mental states (she believes *that* . . .) (de Villiers, 2007). Alan Leslie followed a similar strategy in his suggestion that pretense is an important precursor of mind reading because pretense has the same argument structure as belief (S pretends of x that it is F; S believes of x that it is F; Leslie, 1994).

Common to all accounts of mind reading is the idea that it requires *prior* development of a suite of specialized lower-level cognitive mechanisms. These precursor mechanisms, whether understood as weak or strong precursors of mind reading, represent vital information about the social world of infants and toddlers and mediate their earliest interactions with others. These mechanisms enable face processing, representations of gaze direction, gaze monitoring, detection of animacy, tracking of intentions and goals, and

joint attention (Baron-Cohen, 1995; Carpenter et. al., 2001; Charman et al., 2000; Crichton & Lange-Kuttner, 1999; Csibra, Biro, Koos, & Gergely, 2003; Dawson, Meltzoff, et al., 1998; Hare, Call, Agnetta, & Tomasello, 2000; Saxe et al., 2004; Schultz, 2005; Stone, 2005; Woodward, 2003). These capacities seem to be specific to social stimuli, are shared with other primates, and appear to depend on neural circuitry that responds specifically to social stimuli (Blakemore & Decety, 2001; Campbell, Heywood, Cowey, Regard, & Landis, 1990; Csibra et al., 2003; Hare et al., 2000; Kumashiro et al., 2003; Povinelli & Vonk, 2003; Tomasello, Call, & Hare, 2003). Gaze monitoring seems to involve specific regions of the superior temporal sulcus that respond to the stimulus of eye gaze direction but not to other stimuli, even other stimuli that are physically similar to images of eyes (Campbell et al., 1990; Haxby, Hoffman, & Gobbini, 2000; Perrett, Hietanen, Oram, Benson, & Rolls, 1992). Assessing others' goals and intentions seems to depend on specific representations of certain movement patterns—limb movement, combined with gaze, head, or body orientation—and involves both superior temporal sulcus and superior parietal and lateral frontal areas (Blakemore & Decety, 2001; Jellema, Baker, Wicker, & Perrett, 2000).

These precursor mechanisms are not superseded by mind reading. Mature social cognition integrates these mechanisms together with mind-reading systems to allow a person to parse the social world. To understand an implied threat requires both an understanding of the literal meaning of the sentence as well as the contrary belief or desire expressed. Crucial clues may be given by vocalization, subtle gestures or expressions, and the overall context. People are very good at integrating this information, which requires a variety of mechanisms functioning in harmony. Any mind-reading task will activate many components of this suite of systems so a problem for an experimenter is to distinguish the contribution to the task of early components of social cognition from TOM or simulation.

Given the centrality of the TOM hypothesis to many research programs, ranging from evolutionary psychology to developmental psychology and psychopathology, there are relatively few imaging studies using standardized tasks designed to elicit attribution of belief. This is in some ways unsurprising given the range of conditions under which belief attribution is normally elicited. Prediction, as in false belief contexts, is one instance, but communication, cooperation, and deception in verbal and nonverbal contexts involving shared or nonshared goals are all situations in which humans need to attribute beliefs. Versions of all these situations have been used as paradigms to elicit belief attribution. Table 46.1 summarizes the results of some studies (see also Figure 46.1).

TABLE 46.1 Imaging studies of belief attribution.

Study/Method	Task	Neural Correlate of TOM Condition
Goel et al. (1995) PET[^{15}O]H$_2$O	Infer others' attribution of function to novel object Control: visual and semantic knowledge of objects	Left medial frontal lobe Left temporal lobe
Fletcher et al. (1995) PET[^{15}O]H$_2$O	Story comprehension Control: stories not requiring mental state attribution	Left medial frontal gyrus Posterior cingulate cortex
Gallagher et al. (2000) fMRI	Story and cartoon comprehension	Medial prefrontal cortex (PFC; especially paracingulate gyrus)
Brunet et al. (2000) PET[^{15}O]H$_2$O	Nonverbal comic strips Completion required attributing intentions, physical logic, or semantic knowledge	Right medial and middle PFC Inferior and superior temporal gyrus Left cerebellum, anterior cingulate middle temporal gyri
Russell et al. (2000) fMRI	Reading the Mind in the Eyes Test	Left inferior frontal gyrus medial frontal lobes Left middle and superior gyrus
McCabe et al. (2001) fMRI	Two-person trust and reciprocity games with human or computer counterpart	For cooperators, PFC more active when playing a human
Vogeley et al. (2001) fMRI	TOM stories, physical stories, self- and other ascription stories, and self-ascription stories	Anterior cingulate gyrus Self condition: temporo-parietal junction and anterior cingulate cortex (ACC)
Calder et al. (2002) PET[^{15}O]H$_2$O	Eye gaze direction: 100% direct, 50% direct, 100% averted from subject	Medial prefrontal cortex with direct gaze Middle and superior temporal gyri
Ferstl & Von Cramon (2002) fMRI	Logical or TOM explanation of sentence pairs	Frontal medial cortex
Calarge et al. (2003) PET[^{15}O]H$_2$O	Invent TOM story	Medial frontal cortex, superiori and inferior frontal regions, paracingulate and cingulated gyrus Anterior pole of temporal lobe Right cerebellum
Nieminen-von Wendt et al. (2003) PET[^{15}O]H$_2$O	Heard TOM and physical (control) stories	Neurotypical subjects showed higher activation in medial prefrontal areas than Asperger's subjects
Saxe & Kanwisher (2003) fMRI	Visual stories of false belief, mechanical inference, action, and nonhuman objects	TPJ bilaterally only in false-belief condition Left TPJ objects and photos, right TPJ people
Walter et. al. (2004) fMRI	Comic strips requiring inference of intention in social and nonsocial actions Future intentional action	Anterior paracingulate gyrus in current and prospective intention STS and ACC in physical action condition
Grezes et al. (2004) fMRI	Videos of action (lifting and carrying) Infer expectations of weight from action	Dorsal premotor, left frontal operculum, left intraparietal sulcus, left cerebellum Earlier onset for observation of self than other
Rilling et al. (2004) fMRI	Feedback from computer or partner in game theoretic interactions Prisoner's dilemma Ultimatum game	Right mid STS in both tasks Ultimatum game with computers only activated dorsomedial PFC rostral ACC
German et al. (2004) fMRI	Video of actions and pretend actions	Medial PFC Inferior frontal gyrus, TPJ
Harris et al. (2005) fMRI	Inferring dispositions in high and low consensus conditions	Medial PFC in conditions of low consensus
Saxe & Powell (2005) fMRI	Parse "early" versus "late" social cognition stories	Medial PFC for all story conditions TPJ bilaterally for "late": inferring thoughts or socially relevant information
Kobayashi et al. (2006) fMRI	Verbal and nonverbal false-belief tasks with children (8–12) and adults	TPJ bilaterally and right inferior parietal lobule for both groups Age-related differences in inferior frontal gyrus and left TPJ
Sommer et al. (2007) fMRI	Nonverbal false-belief test (cartoon) contrast with true-belief test	False belief versus true belief activated dorsal ACC Right lateral rostral PFC and right TPJ
Mitchell (2007) fMRI	Nonsocial attentional reorienting task Aim to see whether TPJ recruited	Attentional reorienting recruits the TPJ
Wakusawa et al. (2008) fMRI	Detection of irony	Medial orbitofrontal cortex (OFC)
Abraham et al. (2008) fMRI	Infer intentional versus nonintentional relations between people	Precuneus, temporal poles medial prefrontal cortex
Lissek et al. (2008) fMRI	Detecting cooperation and deception in cartoon scenarios	Both conditions activated TPJ parietal in cingulate regions Deception alone OFC and medial PFC

ACC = Anterior cingulate cortex; OFC = Orbitofrontal cortex; PFC = Prefontal cortex; STS = Superior temporal sulcus; TOM = Theory of Mind; TPJ = Temporo-parietal junction.

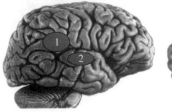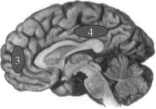

Figure 46.1 (**Figure C.43** in color section) Lateral and medial view of the human brain showing main areas activated in belief attribution tasks summarized in Table 46.1.

Note: **1:** bilateral temporo-parietal junction (TPJ). **2:** right anterior superior temporal sulcus (STS). **3:** medial prefrontal cortex (MPFC). **4:** posterior cingulate. Of these areas, the MPFC and TPJ have received the most recent attention as proposed neural substrates for TOM.

SUMMARY OF IMAGING STUDIES OF TOM

A brief summary suggests that early studies from approximately the 1990s to early 2000s found that the area most consistently activated in conditions requiring the attribution of mental states was the medial prefrontal cortex (MPFC; Calarge, Andreasen, & O'Leary, 2003; Ferstl & von Cramon, 2002; Fletcher et al., 1995; Gallagher et al., 2000; Happé et al., 1996; McCabe, Houser, Ryan, Smith, & Trouard, 2001; Nieminen-von Wendt et al., 2003; Vogeley et al., 2001). Other areas that figure consistently in these studies are paracingulate gyrus and temporal poles. Thus many commentators converged on the idea that the MPFC plays an important role in mind reading and this hypothesis is still strongly favored, at least to the extent that activation in this area is interpreted as evidence that the task involved requires mental state inferences (Decety & Lamm, 2006; Moriguchi, Ohnishi, Mori, Matsuda, & Komaki, 2007; Sommer et al., 2007). The precise nature of those inferences is difficult to determine given that the studies used different paradigms (e.g., verbal and nonverbal story completion and comprehension or games of deception and cooperation) as well as more classic false belief–type scenarios (Vogeley et al., 2001).

Another pattern emerges from studies conducted since the early 2000s that contrast the false belief and false photograph task. These studies elicit the involvement of the temporo-parietal junction (TPJ) sometimes bilaterally and sometimes, the right TPJ. Saxe et al. (2004) found that the TPJ bilaterally was activated more strongly for false belief than false photo tasks and that there was a lateralization effect for inferences involving people (right) and objects and photos (left). Other studies since then have found TPJ activation correlated with parsing scenarios that require the attribution of false beliefs or contrasts between true and false belief (Kobayashi, Glover, & Temple, 2007; Sommer et al., 2007).

Advocates of the modular and nonmodular versions of TOM and simulationists naturally give different interpretations of these results. Rather than try to adjudicate disputes within a research program that is in its infancy, we can note issues that will no doubt figure in future studies.

The first is an elegant explanation of the roles of both TPJ and MPFC proposed by Saxe and Powell (advocates of the idea that TPJ is the neural substrate of TOM inference). They suggested that the MPFC takes input from early precursor subsystems involved in social cognition and hence will be activated by any scenario that involves metarepresentation of precursors to TOM (e.g., conceptualizing behavior in terms of intentions or goals). The TPJ in contrast is specialized for aspects of social cognition requiring the metarepresentation of beliefs, or what they call "late" social cognition. This may be consistent with a finding by Moriguchi et al. that maturation of the prefrontal cortex is associated with different patterns of activation in the MPFC for TOM tasks. They noted an age-related shift from the ventral to the dorsal part of the MPFC during late childhood and adolescence. Perhaps this shift is associated with the recruitment of the TPJ for metarepresentation of belief that reduces processing demands on MPFC (Moriguchi et al., 2007).

Another way to establish the role of circuits identified by fMRI is to look at lesion studies. If the MPFC and TPJ are specialized for TOM, lesions to those areas should produce selective deficits in TOM.

Subjects with medial frontal damage who have TOM deficits all have accompanying executive function deficits (Happé et al., 2001; Stone, 2005). Furthermore, extensive medial frontal damage does not necessarily cause impairment in TOM (Bird, Castelli, Malik, Frith, & Husain, 2004). The patient in this case had extensive medial frontal damage with characteristic executive impairments but "no significant impairment on tasks requiring her to construct a theory of mind." Hence while MPFC is recruited during TOM tasks, its contribution does not seem to be specific to TOM inferences.

Similarly a hypothesis that TPJ is the site of the TOM module suggests that TPJ patients should have specific TOM deficits. Indeed, initial research with TPJ patients showed deficits on false belief tasks and not other EF tasks even when the general demands of executive function were controlled for (Apperly et al., 2004). However, more recent research shows that all TPJ lesion patients who performed below chance on false belief tasks also performed poorly on a false photograph task (Apperly et al., 2007). Thus, there is as yet no conclusive evidence from neurological patients that supports the claim that the TPJ is the site of a domain-specific mechanism dedicated to TOM inferences.

Just as the idea that MPFC is not specialized for TOM fits with general considerations about its executive role, general anatomical and processing considerations support a similar domain general interpretation of TPJ function. Mitchell (2008) found that the TPJ was preferentially activated by the Posner cueing task in which subjects are required to attend to predicted or unpredicted cues. This finding is not inconsistent with a role for TPJ in false belief tasks, only with the idea that the TPJ is somehow specialized for TOM. Decety and Lamm in a meta-analysis of fMRI studies of the TPJ (Decety & Lamm, 2007) concluded that it has a role in low level (bottom up) processes associated with the sense of agency and attention to salient stimuli. Once again, these results are not inconsistent with Saxe's findings that TPJ is more activated by false belief than by nonsocial representations, just the idea that it is only activated by false belief stories. A speculative interpretation consistent with Decety and Lamm's findings is that the TPJ is recruited by tasks that involve comparison of predicted and actual states. The comparison can be between intrapersonal perceptual modalities (giving rise to the sense of agency); interpersonally, between self and other perspectives, or even between beliefs entertained by self and other where attribution requires comparison of perceptually acquired information as in false belief tests.

While mind reading constitutes a specific cognitive domain constituted by interacting subsystems, the jury is still out on whether one of those components is subserved by a neural circuitry (typically hypothesized to lie in the MPFC or TPJ) specialized for the metarepresentation of mental states.

CONTAGION, IMITATION, SIMULATION

Most of the interest in imitation involves the idea that it might be an important precursor of simulation in the strong sense; that is, the cognitive architecture of imitation is transformed in development into an architecture supporting imitation-based simulation. Combined with the idea that mind reading depends on simulation rather than TOM, imitation could thus be a crucial cognitive bridge between early social cognition and mind reading.

For this strategy to work, the simulation theorist needs to challenge the conception of decoupling that subtends the TOM interpretation of the false belief test. Imitation is at heart a motor phenomenon, the reproduction of a movement or an action. Thus the simulation theorist needs to build a cognitive bridge between motor cognition and social cognition.

The attraction of this approach is that it fits well with the idea that the brain evolved as a control system for sensorimotor cognition, which, in species like ours, developed

special adaptations for increasingly complex forms of social cognition. The TOM theory tends to approach mind reading by conceptualizing it as an application of abstract theorizing about unobservable causes: a unique human achievement that seems to have no essential connection to the sensorimotor cognition. Each conception has different problems. For TOM, it is closing the conceptual gap between TOM and the affectively scaffolded sensorimotor precursors. For the simulation theory, it is showing how cognition can move from being essentially tied to action interpretation and prediction to the level of abstraction implied by success on the false belief task.

Theorists in this camp suggest that the issue can be approached by situating both imitation and simulation on the other side of a contrast with TOM drawn by Sommerville and Decety this way:

> Traditional theories of knowledge assume that knowledge consists of amodal redescriptions of sensory motor and introspective states . . . knowledge exists independently of these states and operates according to different principles. In contrast embodied theories of cognition construe knowledge as partial simulations of these sensory, motor, and introspective states. (Sommerville & Decety, 2006, p. 180)

The most promising approach for simulationists is therefore to conceive mind reading not as a theoretical achievement but as essentially a motor phenomenon of action synchronization (Byrne, 2005; Jackson & Decety, 2004; Jackson, Meltzoff, & Decety, 2006; Meltzoff & Decety, 2003; Ruby & Decety, 2004; Sommerville & Decety, 2006). This approach emphasizes that action has both a strictly motor component (controlling the trajectory of bodily movement) *and* an intentional one, the representation of the goal achieved by that movement (Chaminade, Meltzoff, & Decety, 2002). Imitation of *action* requires the representation of goals as well as motor mimicry and hence could be a way for a subject to become aware of another's goals, an important step on the path to mind reading (Decety, Chaminade, Grezes, & Meltzoff, 2002; Iacoboni et al., 1999; Jackson et al., 2006; Meltzoff & Decety, 2003; Oztop, Kawato, & Arbib, 2006). If it is the case that imitating action also rehearses the appropriate intention, simulation could provide access to intentions. It would be a further step from simulation-based knowledge of intention to knowledge of beliefs, but imitation of this kind could take the subject part of the way toward a conception of decoupled mental states.

This promising idea faces a problem that it will be helpful to keep in mind. I see a swimmer moving his arm back and forth. Why is he doing this? Is he drowning and signaling for help or waving in exuberance? Perhaps I could solve this problem or get some vital information by mentally imitating him. However, if I simply reproduce the *movement,* the trajectory of his arm, by motor mimicry, the problem remains the same as before. I have reproduced the means to an end: calling for help or waving a greeting, but I need to know the end communicated by this movement. The same is true if observing his movement activates the same motor circuit that I would use to produce the movement via motor contagion. Wittgenstein is no longer the flavor of the month in philosophy of mind, but he did point out that we do not solve the problem of determining the meaning of a perceived object (in this case a movement) by associating it with a mental image of that object (in this case motor

representation of the mimicked movement). On the one hand, we need to represent the end as well as the means to understand action. On the other hand, if I imitate waving or signalling for help rather than the bodily movement common to both, I have already solved my problem because to do either I must represent the ends as well as the means.

So it is helpful to build the case for simulation by trying to understand how mechanisms which mimic movements could be part of cognitive systems that give rise to simulation-based knowledge of intentions and ultimately beliefs. In other words, we describe a transition from conceptualizing mechanisms in terms of contagion, to imitation and, ultimately, to simulation (Fig. 46.2.)

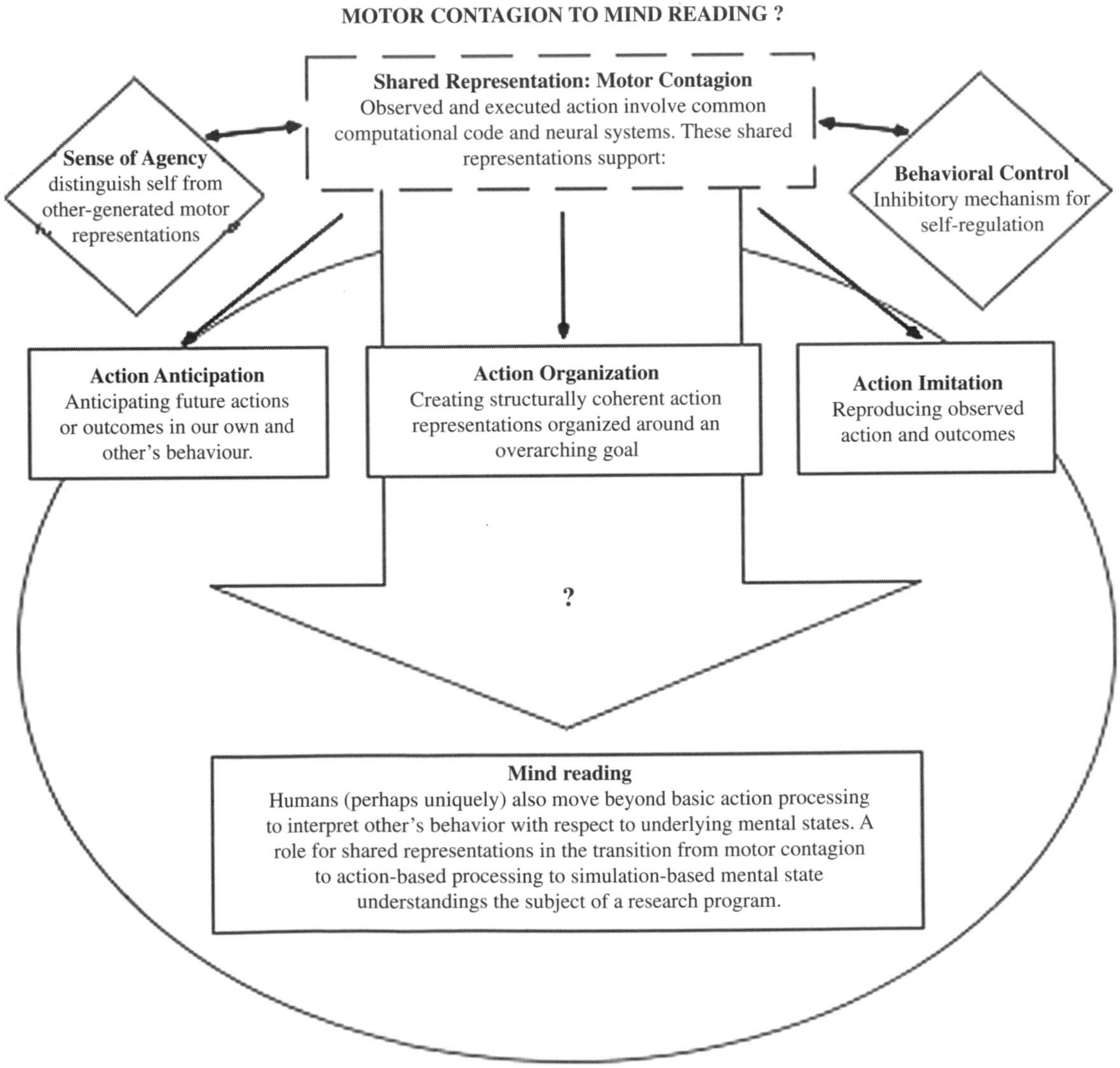

MOTOR CONTAGION TO MIND READING ?

Sense of Agency
distinguish self from other-generated motor representations

Shared Representation: Motor Contagion
Observed and executed action involve common computational code and neural systems. These shared representations support:

Behavioral Control
Inhibitory mechanism for self-regulation

Action Anticipation
Anticipating future actions or outcomes in our own and other's behaviour.

Action Organization
Creating structurally coherent action representations organized around an overarching goal

Action Imitation
Reproducing observed action and outcomes

?

Mind reading
Humans (perhaps uniquely) also move beyond basic action processing to interpret other's behavior with respect to underlying mental states. A role for shared representations in the transition from motor contagion to action-based processing to simulation-based mental state understandings the subject of a research program.

Figure 46.2   This diagram captures the idea that higher order social cognition emerges from the recruitment of motor cognition into systems that perform increasingly sophisticated forms of social cognition culminating in mind reading.

Note: As Sommerville and Decety note in their review, while the mechanisms of motor cognition are well specified, a role for these mechanisms in mind reading has not been conclusively established. From "Weaving the Fabric of Social Interaction: Articulating Developmental Psychology and Cognitive Neuroscience in the Domain of Motor Cognition," by J. A. Sommerville and J. Decety, 2006, *Psychonomic Bulletin and Review, 13,* pp. 179–200. Adapted with permission.

CONTAGION

The attempt to bridge the gap between ends and means naturally starts from cases in which the gap is small, such as the induction of emotion from perception. If the child sees a parent's fearful or happy expression when confronted with an ambiguous stimulus and her own fearful or happy expression or feeling state is automatically evoked, the child will be in a similar state as the parent in relation to the stimulus (Decety & Lamm, 2006; Gallese et al., 2004; Goldman & Sripada, 2005; Ruby & Decety, 2004; Saxe et al., 2004; Wicker et al., 2003). Of course, the child will not thereby gain conceptual knowledge that fear represents danger or happiness pleasure. To do so, she would have to metarepresent the relationship between the mental state that produces the expression and its object. We might say of an infant who turned up her nose at a dirty diaper and simultaneously felt the sensation of disgust, as a result of automatically imitating her parent's expression, "She thinks her mum thinks the diaper is disgusting" without being committed to the view that she metarepresents. Once again, however, a simulationist would argue that the explanandum here is the ability to coordinate appropriate responses to disgusting objects rather than the ability to metarepresent emotions.

The same problem of inferring what, if anything, is represented by a state automatically evoked by perception appears in the case of motor contagion as the difficulty of finding out the intention realized by the bodily movement (Oztop et al., 2006). Even if perceiving an action automatically rehearses the observer's motor circuitry, which we can call a form of automatic motor imitation, a question remains: Is action or movement being imitated?

A role for imitation in development of mind reading was initially suggested by Meltzoff and Moore who observed neonatal imitation of facial gestures such as tongue protrusion within an hour of birth. This was consistent with films of infants dating from the 1970s showing preferential attention to and mimicry of facial expressions. As Meltzoff and Moore observed, this type of imitation requires the infant to map perception of another's movements onto her own motor system to reproduce the observed action (Meltzoff & Moore, 1983).

Interestingly, this type of motor contagion has two properties not shared by all mirror systems. It is *overt* in that it proceeds all the way to behavior: The neonate reproduces the behavior she observes. And it is *intransitive*. Transitive actions have a goal or target. Reaching and grasping for example are aimed at a target. Tongue protrusion is a gesture without a target but it is mirrored nonetheless.

Sommerville and Decety (2006) have suggested that overt intransitive imitation is a consequence of the lack of prefrontal inhibition of sensory motor processes. The ability to inhibit overt action or to imitate more selectively is something that arrives later as prefrontal cortical connectivity matures. Until then, observation rehearses some motor schemas all the way to completion.

A parsimonious interpretation of the role of neonatal imitation and emotional contagion is therefore that they are weak precursors of mind reading. Infants who lack them will lose an important developmental resource.

Interest in motor contagion as a possible strong precursor of mind reading was ignited by the discovery of mirror neurons in the premotor and parietal cortices of macaque monkeys in the 1990s. Some cells in the ventral premotor cortex, area F5, fire both when an action is observed and when the same action is executed by the monkey. Observation and execution of hand and mouth grasping will produce firing of the same premotor neurons involved in grasp. Some of these neurons fire even when the target of an action is occluded. Other neurons in the posterior parietal cortex (area PF) fire when the consequence of an action, such as tearing paper or breaking a peanut is perceived through another modality such as audition (Gallese et al., 1996, 2004; Grezes, Armony, Rowe, & Passingham, 2003; Iacoboni et al., 2005).

These monkey mirror neurons are all transitive: They fire only when the action has a target or object and not when objectless gestures are perceived although they will fire when observing the last segment of reach to a previously seen currently occluded target (Umilta et al., 2001).

Because single neuron studies are not performed on humans, an homologous mirror system in humans has been discovered through MEG and fMRI studies that have shown overlapping activation in the premotor and parietal cortices for both observation and execution of both transitive and (some) intransitive actions (Iacoboni et al., 2005; Rizzolatti & Craighero, 2004). A final piece of evidence about the human mirror systems is that premotor and parietal areas show overlapping activation for execution and for *imagination* of actions (Decety, et. al. 1997; Fig. 46.3).

Thus there is strong evidence for shared circuits activated by third-person observation and first-person production of actions (Currie & Ravenscroft, 2002; Hurley & Chater, 2005; Jeannerod, 2006).

Some theorists have suggested as a consequence that mirror neurons provide a neural basis for imitation, and hence for imitation-based simulation. However, as Oztop et al. point out, "Neurophysiological data simply show that a mirror neuron fires when a monkey [or human in the case of mirror circuitry] fires both when the monkey executes a certain action and when he observes a more or less congruent action" (Chaminade, Oztop, Cheng, & Kawato, 2008; Oztop et al., 2006).

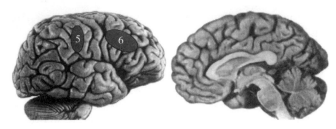

Figure 46.3 (**Figure C.44** in color section) The human mirror system.

Note. Areas activated in both performance and observation of actions. **5:** Right inferior parietal cortex. **6:** Inferior frontal gyrus.

To show that motor contagion also plays an important role in imitation, we need to understand its role in imitation.

IMITATION

The human ability to imitate as opposed to emulate arrives quite early. Infants 12 to 18 months old who observe an action such as hopping a mouse across a rug into a house will reproduce both ends and means. If the means are unavailable, they will reproduce the ends only, placing the mouse in the house (Carpenter et al., 2005). By contrast, chimpanzees will not reproduce the means. If a rake is used to pull a banana toward the demonstrator, a child who watches will use the rake. A chimpanzee will obtain the banana by other means (although a more recent experiment found some ability of chimpanzees to use the observed means; Buttelmann, Carpenter, Call, & Tomasello, 2007; Carpenter et al., 2005).

Infants of about 9 months can also detect if they are being imitated, and toddlers engage in games of reciprocal imitation. Imaging studies with adults suggest that reciprocal imitation engages the STS (an area known to be involved in response to goal-directed movement) as well as left inferior parietal cortex when the participant imitates the other and right parietal cortex when the participant is imitated by the other (Decety et al., 2002). This is consistent with many other studies which detect lateralization for representation of self and other produced actions in the inferior parietal cortex. These studies suggest that a sense of agency, that is of being the initiator and controller of an action, is associated with activity in the right inferior parietal cortex (Blakemore, Oakley, & Frith, 2003; Uddin, Molnar-Szakacs, Zaidel, & Iacoboni, 2006; Vosgerau & Newen, 2007).

Imaging studies of adult imitation following observation of means (arm and hand movements without the completion of the action) and goals (building a house out of LEGO blocks) suggest imitation of goals and means recruits different circuitry. The medial prefrontal cortex was involved in imitating means only, whereas the imitation

of goals produced activation in left premotor cortex. The experimenters suggested that dorsolateral prefrontal cortex and cerebellum are active in imitating both ends and means (Chaminade et al., 2002).

In fact, the human capacity for imitation cannot depend *essentially* on mirror circuits homologous to those of macaques. Macaques, who possess mirror neurons cannot imitate. When they are presented with a novel action and are rewarded for performing it, they cannot reproduce the action (Oztop et al., 2006; although see Kumashiro et al., 2003). This may be a consequence of the fact that mirror neuron firing in monkeys is limited to *learned* goal-directed action, and when presented with a novel action, they cannot readily infer the goal. Similarly, when presented with an intransitive action, chimpanzees cannot imitate it (Myowa-Yamakoshi & Matsuzawa, 2000). This suggests that what is driving the chimpanzee is an attempt to acquire a salient object rather than reproduce the motor component of an action.

Monkeys and apes *emulate* rather than imitate. If they can infer a goal, they can produce an action from their motor repertoire to pursue the goal as a means. A monkey prevented from grasping by mouth will reach by hand for a target after observing a conspecific grasp the target by mouth. Thus they fail to meet the first two of the three essential conditions for imitation proposed by Tomasello et al.:

1. The behavior should be novel.
2. The behavior must reproduce the observed behavior.
3. The behavior should share the same final goal.

Consequently, the consensus is that "imitation and language are not inherent in a macacque-like mirror system but instead depend on the embedding of circuitry homologous to that of the macaque in *more extended systems in the human brain*" (Oztop et al., 2006 p. 255, my italics).

Thus to understand the contribution of mirror neurons to human imitation, it becomes important to understand the nature and contribution of the delete wider system in which the mirror systems are embedded. An interesting finding is that neural network models trained to imitate, or that evolve from a starting state to an end state in which they reproduce transitive actions, also show mirror properties. Cells in the middle layers are activated by both observation and production of target action see (Oztop et al., 2006) for a review. These results are consistent with findings that imitation of actions produces activation of the mirror systems in humans, Iacoboni et al. found that the left pars opercularis of the inferior frontal gyrus (considered to be an homologue of the monkey F5 area) was more active in an imitation than an observation condition for simple finger movements (Iacoboni et al., 1999). In another important experiment, Decety et al. (1997) asked participants to observe an action in two conditions: one for later reproduction of the action (imitation), and another for later recognition of the action. In the imitation condition, elements of the mirror systems were active (relevant to a control condition in which static postures were shown). In the action recognition condition, the contrast with the control was in different areas: inferior frontal gyrus STS, posterior STS, and parietal cortex.

Recognizing a movement as intentional, purposeful movement, seems to involve the superior temporal sulcus (STS) rather than the motor mirror system. A series of experiments have shown that STS neurons, which have *no motor properties,* respond to goal-directed movement such as reaching when the actor is looking at the target. That the STS seems to play a crucial role in the detection of purposeful bodily movement is also shown in experiments involving point light displays of human movement and Heider and Simmel type experiments in which subjects overattribute intentions to moving geometric shapes. Watching a montage of moving shapes, they say the triangle is "chasing" the circle and so on. When these tasks were contrasted with false belief tests, the STS was activated by the moving shape task, and as predicted by the TPJ hypothesis of mind reading, the TPJ was activated by false belief tasks (Gobbini, Koralek, Bryan, Montgomery, & Haxby, 2007).

These cases are particularly interesting since no motor or mirror activity is evoked by perception of geometric shapes (the human motor system is indifferent to the trajectories of geometric shapes), and yet the subjects still attribute goals to the triangles, squares, and circles purely in virtue of their trajectories.

This last finding is important because it suggests that the mirror system is not required for action recognition and classification. Although recruited by imitation of action, which requires recognizing an action *qua* action, it seems that the role of the mirror system is different. What then is the mirror system doing during imitation of observed actions?

One suggestion is that mirror neurons are *essentially motor control neurons.* They encode movement kinematics, not intended goals. If that is the case, why do they exist and what is their role in the distinctively human capacity for imitation? It is necessary to encode motor trajectories for control of first-person action, but why should mechanisms evolved for that purpose also respond to observation of actions?

An answer is provided by the forward model hypothesis of action control. On that hypothesis, to control action we need perceptual information to check that our movements are correct. In reaching to pick up a glass, we use perceptual information, first to calculate the difference between the current state of the system and the goal state (e.g., if the target is 30cm from the hand, we need to move the hand

30 cm to pick it up); this is known as an *inverse* model. We then use the inverse model to create an instruction to produce the instrumental movements necessary to achieve the goal. In this case, move the hand 30 cm. This instruction is then executed by motor systems that decompose it into elements executable by different subsystems that control force, trajectory of limb movement, power, and precision grip. These instructions are used to create a series of *forward models* that include predictions of the outcome of movements. The forward model for the whole movement predicts that the target will be grasped. The forward model for precision grip predicts the consequences for the fingertips of fine motor movements. The prediction made by the forward model is then compared with the perceived actual state of the system that results from the movement. If there is a mismatch, the procedure is repeated until the error signal is zero. If motor prediction was that the hand projects 30 cm but we see it overshoot the target by 5 cm, we can produce another instruction to withdraw the hand 5 cm closer to the body (Blakemore & Decety, 2001; Miall, 2003; Wolpert et al., 2003; Wolpert & Kawato, 1998).

This is a description of a process whose actual cognitive architecture is the topic of ongoing computational modelling that tries to replicate actual neurocognitive processes (Oztop et al., 2006). Despite controversy, one conclusion can be drawn. The comparison process decomposes the action into a series of finer-grained forward models. Only at the top level are goals represented. To determine whether the intention to pick up the cup is fulfilled, we compare perception of the action to the intention. At lower levels, the comparison is between perceptual information and motor information, to which the goal is irrelevant. This is made clear by consideration of cases in which the same motor movement can implement two different intentions/goals. Tracing a horizontal line on a page can be the completion of an architectural plan or an underlining of text. But the motor representations of the movement are the same in each case. The perceptual information used to *control the movement* is compared with the motor representation, not the overarching goal.

A persuasive suggestion about mirror neurons is that they are part of the system implementing the predictive component of the forward model (Oztop et al., 2006). When a canonical representation of a movement is produced, a prediction of the consequences (motor and perceptual) is also created. The mirror neurons in F5 premotor cortex are not canonical neurons but part of this predictive system (Grezes et al., 2003). This is shown by experiments in which canonical neurons are deactivated, leading to inability to produce movement. Deactivating mirror neurons does not affect movement. In essence, the prediction is a copy of the motor representation not used for action but as the basis for subsequent comparison with sensory feedback. The parietal cortex is a sensory integration area that maps perceptual to motor information as part of the process of controlling movement (Rizzolatti et al., 2006). This is why the mirror neurons are activated by perception of goal-directed movement: They help implement the comparison of the predictive motor representation to perceptual feedback.

Consequently, mirror systems will be active in imitation because they encode the motor component of the imitated action, which is shared between both perceiver and target. They are indifferent to whether the movement originates with the first or third person because they encode kinematic information. When subjects imitate a perceived intransitive movement, the contralateral sensory motor cortex is more active if that movement is presented from the first-person perspective (Jackson et al., 2006). Presumably this is because the mapping from first-person perspective to a copy of a first-person motor prediction requires less transformation than the mapping from third- to first-person perspective.

Thus it is entirely consistent with the finding that mirror neurons are active during imitation and are activated by goal-directed movement that their role should be essentially motor control rather than the "mentalistic" aspects of social cognition such as inferring intentions and goals. The fact that mirror neurons fire for goal-directed action does not mean that they encode the goal of the action. The evidence we have reviewed suggests that goal representation is subserved by different circuitry that operates in harmony with the mirror system. The information encoded by the mirror system is part of a hierarchy of representations involved in producing and reproducing action. A recent imaging study parsed the action understanding system into different levels of representational complexity and content and mapped those components to different areas of a distributed motor system (Lestou, Pollick, & Kourtzi, 2008). The experimenters summarized their findings this way:

> [T]he ventral premotor cortex *encodes the physical similarity* between movement trajectories and action goals that are important for exact copying of actions and the acquisition of complex motor skills. In contrast, whereas parietal regions and the superior temporal sulcus process the perceptual similarity between movements and may support the perception and imitation of *abstract action goals* and movement styles. Thus, our findings propose that fronto-parietal and visual areas involved in action understanding mediate a cascade of visual-motor processes at different levels of action description from *exact movement copies to abstract action goals* achieved with different movement styles. (p. 324, my italics)

This is consistent with the findings of Decety and collaborators, who found that imitation of action requires frontal and executive control as well as the integration of perceptual and motor information (Decety et al., 1997). In fact, this is what we could expect of imitation: Motor aspects need to be controlled by higher level plans (Decety et al., 1997; Jeannerod, 2006; Pacherie, 2006). The intention to imitate a movement must be decomposed into less complex intentions and ultimately to motor plans executable by the motor systems. The representations encoded by the mirror system are of movement kinematics necessary to compare observed movement with intended movements, not with intentions.

This minimal interpretation of the role of mirror systems is not unanimous. Rizzolatti and Craighero and Iacoboni et al. argue that mirror systems have an important role in inferring intentions (Iacoboni et al., 2005; Rizzolatti & Craighero, 2004). The basic reason is for this interpretation is that mirror neurons are selectively activated by different types of action (reaching and grasping) rather than intransitive movements. As Octopi et al. remark, however, it is not clear why this interpretation rather than the narrower one should be accepted.

One possibility is that mirror neurons could function not only as part of a forward model which transforms intentions to motor commands to movements and compares actual to intended movements but as a part of an *inverse model* that maps perceived movements to (stored copies of) motor commands to intentions. This comparator system thus *could* be used to gain knowledge of third-person intentions if (a), the movement kinematics and hence motor representations are the same in observer and actor and (b), there is *correspondence* between the movement kinematics and the representations of action. In such a case, recovering the intention governing a perceived action would be a matter of retracing the path from perceived action to intention via the mirror system. In effect, this strategy uses mirror neurons, not only as part of a forward model for controlling movements, but as part of an inverse model for discovering intentions (Blakemore & Decety, 2001; Iacoboni et al., 2005; Miall, 2003; Rizzolatti et al., 2006). It is worth noting that conditions (a) and (b) seem to be met in the case of reaching tasks for monkeys. The movements made by target and subject are the same and, given that there are only a small number of movements (mouth and hand grasping) and one action (grasping), it should be possible to recover the intention from the perception of an action via the motor system, which encodes the movements (Fig. 46.4).

A difficulty with this idea is that it could not work for novel intentions or actions, so as a general analysis of imitation and learning by imitation, it is unsatisfactory. Consequently, if we conceive of imitation as the attainment of an already understood or novel goal by copying the means to that goal, motor contagion cannot be the basis for

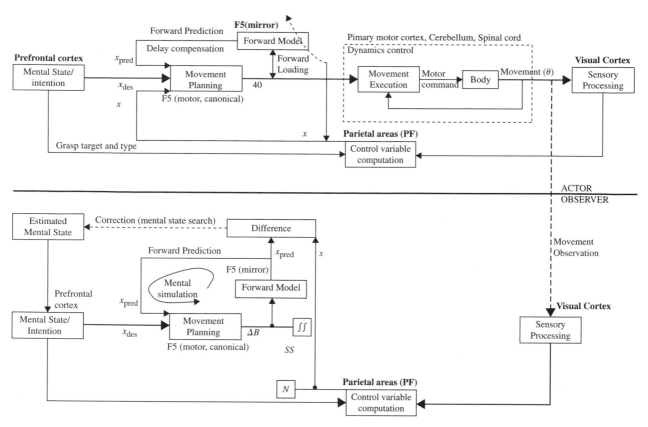

Figure 46.4   This diagram shows how mirror neurons fit into the forward model for action monitoring.

Note: The bottom half of the diagram shows how an observer's motor systems mirror those of the target: The same predictive circuitry is activated by both observation and performance. The crucial question raised by models such as these is whether the observer's mirror system does in fact play a role in inferring the mental state expressed by the imitated action. From "Mirror Neurons and Imitation: A Computationally Guided Review," by E. Oztop, M. Kawato, and M. Arbib, 2006, *International Neural Network Society, 19,* 254–271. p. 264. Reprinted with permission.

imitation. However, such imitation will inevitably involve mirroring to the extent that the encoding of the kinematics of the action copied is neutral between first and third person. We should expect to see mirror activity in the premotor cortex and parietal lobule (PF) of someone learning a musical instrument, such as a guitar, by imitation because the kinematics are similar for observer and actor (Vogt et al., 2007). Even in cases such as this, however, it seems that the first-person perspective recruits the motor system more extensively, which suggests that the motor representations are not completely neutral between perspectives. It might be advantageous to teach your child to tie her shoes, not by having her observe you but by reaching around her from behind and tying them yourself so that, from her perspective, the action looks as if she were doing it.

Consequently, despite the suggestiveness of links between motor contagion, imitation, simulation, and mind reading, there is as yet no evidence that they share a common computational structure. Motor contagion is *embedded within* imitation and imitation-based simulation but does not provide information about the crucial aspect that transforms movement to action: the mental states that provide the intentions and goals to which the movement is a means.

SIMULATION

Initial discussion of simulation focused on the case of explicit simulation involving imagination or pretence. The problem arising automatically is that where the target of a simulation has different beliefs and desires to the simulator, the simulation will be inaccurate. If the simulator likes chocolate and the target is allergic to it, simulation will produce an inaccurate prediction about the response to a gift of an Easter egg. Both children and adults make egocentric errors of this kind all the time, but we also compensate for them, and the ability to compensate seems to require precisely the kind of abstract amodal theorizing that led to the TOM theory.

We could refine the simulation in this case by imagining that the person did not like chocolate, or believed that the chocolate contains allergens, but that kind of refinement seems to involve possession of the concepts simulation was proposed to explain

This is the main objection to hybrid theories in which simulation is the *default* process involved in mind reading and TOM is engaged to resolve errors of prediction or interpretation in the same way aeronautical engineers resort to theory to explain unpredicted results produced by their simulations. The hybrid theory needs to explain why, if we already possess the TOM concepts and can employ them as backup, we do not simply employ them in the first instance. And indeed, rather than simulate and then compensate for errors using TOM, children and adults often use naive psychological theories about others' beliefs to understand them.

In one experiment, a child and an adult observer (A) are seated in front of two dishes of beads. The round dish contains red and green beads, but the square dish contains only yellow. The child and A watch while an assistant moves a bead from the round dish into an opaque bag. The child, but not A, sees that the bead is green. When the child is asked, "What color does A think the bean in the bag is?" the typical reply is "red." Surely if the child was simulating, she would say red or green. The TOM theorist suggests that the child is using a theoretical rule of thumb: "ignorance equals wrong." Whether that is correct, the error made by the child is not easy to explain as the result of conflating first- and third-person perspectives (Ruffman, 1996) .

Adults also make errors in situations that require them to make inferences about the mental states of other people. Saxe suggests that a large body of research in social psychology on reasoning errors is best explained in terms of reliance on intuitive theories of psychology: that is as stereotyping, categorization, biases, and heuristics. People's ratings of their own trustworthiness, responsibility, and fidelity often differ from their predictions about others (Epley, Keysar, Van Boven, & Gilovich, 2004; Gilovich, 1993; Kahneman, Slovic, & Tversky, 1982; Malle, 2004; Pronin, 2002; Pronin, Gilovich, & Ross, 2004; Ross, Amabile, & Steinmetz, 2005). These differences seem to result from beliefs about other people's mental states and character traits.

Of itself, egocentric bias in social judgment is not evidence for either TOM or simulation. The difference between first- and third-person judgments of say trustworthiness could result from egocentric bias, a version of an availability heuristic, that makes us rely on stereotypes about others while taking a more sympathetic and nuanced, if often wrong, view about ourselves. This is consistent with the idea that in our own case we imagine or remember details about our character or dispositions to predict our behavior, using mental time travel to simulate outcomes, while invoking theory-based stereotypes to explain others.

The concept of simulation seems to require that that we imaginatively project ourselves into others' situations to predict their behavior: exporting our egocentric biases so to speak and assimilating others to ourselves. Noting that we have egocentric biases does not refute the "argument from error" against simulation. The simulationist might reply that perhaps what we do is inhabit the shoes of the other person by slightly changing some parameters ("If I were stressed and had just lost my job, I would . . .") but if those parameters are mental states, the simulationist needs an account of mental states fed into any simulation that does not beg the question against competing theories (Fig. 46.5).

In an imaging study (Delgado, Frank, & Phelps, 2005) of subjects playing a game involving trust (a classic situation in which one might project oneself into the other's situation to predict a response to an offer), participants choices reflected knowledge acquired about the other person's traits. Their choices about whether to make large or small offers varied according to the content of stories describing the character and previous actions of the other participant. These varied independently of the rewards obtained in the game for "good" and "bad" partners suggesting that preexisting beliefs about the other person's mental states overrode quite powerful reinforcement mechanisms (which were operative in the case of "neutral" partners).

We cannot use the fact that we make egocentric errors to support a simulation case for mind reading. However, that still leaves many issues unresolved. A stronger argument against pure simulation-based mind reading is suggested by the discussion of relationship between mirror neurons and imitation. We considered the hypothesis that we could recover intentions from observation of an action by retracing the path from effect (perceived action) to intentional cause via the mirror system. We noted that movements are the means and the goal of an action is the end, but that the inverse modeling approach would not work unless the representation of the means also carried information about the end. And, as we saw previously, ends and means are represented by different neural systems. As part of their elegant and exhaustive review of the relationship between motor and social cognition, Sommerville and Decety (2006) noted, "[A]lthough goals and means are closely intertwined in the act of imitation they are, to some extent dissociable and may therefore tap partly distinct neural processes" (p. 190). Consequently, we do not need to use the computationally baroque method of inferring ends from means via the mirror system.

The same is true for imitation-based simulation. If we want to find out the mental states of someone performing an action, we cannot simply rehearse the relevant

(A)

Pure simulation:

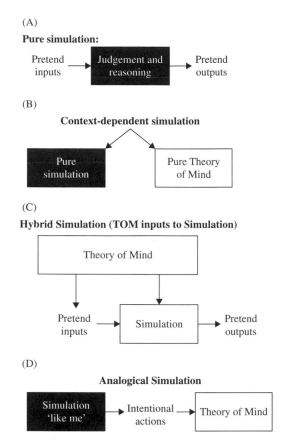

(B)

Context-dependent simulation

(C)

Hybrid Simulation (TOM inputs to Simulation)

(D)

Analogical Simulation

Figure 46.5   Varieties of simulation.

Note: In the simplest case **(A)**, we predict others mental states by pretending to be them. We use our own psychology as a black box. **(B)** describes the case where we alternate between simulation and TOM as required by the context. Perhaps we use more theoretically based knowledge for situations in which we are aware that the other person is unlikely to behave like us or that our own database is inadequate. **(C)** is only weakly a simulation alternative to TOM. It suggests that we simulate using inputs characterized in TOM terms (If I believed that P and desired that Q I would . . .). **(D)** suggests that we could use simulations to provide inputs to TOM processing using a "like me" heuristic. Once again, the hard work is being done by the metarepresentation of mental states and their representational properties.

movement and read off the ends to which it is a means. Jacob and Jeannerod give an example that dramatizes the point. Dr. Jekyll and Mr. Hyde are names for two personalities who inhabit the mind of one person. One is a caring and competent surgeon who never manifests emotions for fear of compromising the quality of his work, the other is a cold-blooded sadist. When we observe Jekyll/Hyde vivisecting a patient, how can we tell whether what we are watching is surgery or torture? The motor component is identical. Even if observation rehearses our own motor systems so that we simulate movements involved in incisions and excisions, how could we use that rehearsal to recover the mental states involved; that is, to tell whether Dr. Jekyll or Mr. Hyde is wielding the scalpel? Their answer is that we cannot (Jacob & Jeannerod, 2005).

SUMMARY

There is no undisputed signature for either TOM or imitation/simulation. Even putatively clear candidates for the neural substrate of TOM such as the TPJ have been disputed by theorists arguing that the role played by the TPJ is a component process such as attention switching or expectation-matching, which is consistent with a role in simulation.

Attempts to determine experimentally whether mind reading depends on pure TOM, pure simulation, or a hybrid in which inputs to the simulation or its outputs are characterized using TOM concepts tend to founder on the difficulty of operationalizing a TOM or simulation concept of belief for both first and third persons. Is there a clear behavioral and neural difference between belief that it is hot in Ecuador, reached by *imagining* being in Ecuador (simulation), and the same belief reached by inference from the fact that it is on the equator (theory-based inference)? Most of the experiments on perspective taking recruited by simulationists are, for good methodological reasons, unable to address this type of question. Similarly, can we operationalize differences between tacit, explicit, and dispositional (long-term memory) or occurrent (working memory and executive function) beliefs? Many beliefs seem to depend on a mixture of theoretical inference and imaginative simulation. To decide whether it is hot in Quito, I might infer that it is hot in Ecuador from background knowledge but then remember freezing at the high altitude of Quito. This is a real difficulty for TOM experiments that must probe possession of beliefs using nonverbal paradigms (Apperly, 2008). Recognizing this, some theorists in both camps hoped that neuroscience might distinguish theoretically based inference from simulation by finding a neural signature for each type of process. While there is no overlap between mirror circuits in the motor cortex and circuits activated in false belief tasks, we are a long way from determining whether attribution of mental states is essentially a matter of TOM or imitation-based simulation.

False belief experiments, still the gold standard for mind reading, present the subjects with vignettes, stories, and psychodramas and ask them to predict or interpret the target's actions. We report the results in folk psychological vocabulary. If Sally predicts that James will say an animal lives in the zoo with the tigers, we might report Sally's prediction using the sentence, "Sally believes that James believes the cat is a tiger." The deep issue here is whether the neurocomputational processes performed by neural circuits recruited in that type of prediction have the conceptual structure and logical syntax of the sentence that reports it. Oztop et al. (2006) complained with justification that theories about the role of mirror neurons in imitation were unsupported by neurally constrained computational models of the development and deployment of imitation. The same complaint could be made about the inference to the computational nature of the systems involved in false belief tests (Addis et al., 2007). Ian Apperly has made the same point about simulation and TOM in general, "[O]n the basis of the current literature it seems possible that these theories will become redundant as new findings about TOM motivate the development of new models based on well characterized cognitive and neural processes" (Apperly, 2008, p282).

REFERENCES

Abraham, A., Werning., M., Rakoczy, H., von Cramon, Y., & Schubotz, R. I., (2008). Minds, persons, and space: An fMRI investigation into the relational complexity of higher-order intentionality. *Consciousness and Cognition, 17,* 438–450.

Addis, D. R., Wong, A. T., & Schacter, D. L. (2007). Remembering the past and imagining the future: Common and distinct neural substrates during event construction and elaboration. *Neuropsychologia, 45,* 1363–1377.

Apperly, I. A. (2008). Beyond simulation-theory and theory-theory: Why social cognitive neuroscience should use its own concepts to study "theory of mind." *Cognition, 107,* 266–283.

Apperly, I. A., Samson, D., Chiavarino, C., Bickerton, W. L., & Humphreys, G. W. (2007). Testing the domain-specificity of a theory of mind deficit in brain-injured patients: Evidence for consistent performance on non-verbal, "reality-unknown" false belief and false photograph tasks. *Cognition, 103,* 300–321.

Apperly, I. A., Samson, D., Chiavarino, C., & Humphreys, G. W. (2004). Frontal and temporo-parietal lobe contributions to theory of mind: Neuropsychological evidence from a false-belief task with reduced language and executive demands. *Journal of Cognitive Neuroscience, 16,* 1773–1784.

Astington, J. W. (1993). *The child's discovery of the mind.* Cambridge, MA: Harvard University Press.

Baron-Cohen, S. (1995). *Mindblindness: An essay on autism and theory of mind.* Cambridge, MA: MIT Press.

Baron-Cohen, S., Leslie, A., & Frith, U. (1985). Does the autistic child have a theory of mind? *Cognition, 21,* 37–46.

Bird, C. M., Castelli, F., Malik, O., Frith, U., & Husain, M. (2004). The impact of extensive medial frontal lobe damage on "theory of mind" and cognition. *Brain, 127,* 914–928.

Blakemore, S. J., & Decety, J. (2001). From the perception of action to the understanding of intention. *Nature Reviews: Neuroscience, 2,* 561–567.

Blakemore, S. J., Oakley, D. A., & Frith, C. D. (2003). Delusions of alien control in the normal brain. *Neuropsychologia, 41,*1058–1067.

Brunet, E., Sarfati, Y., Hardy-Bayle, M., & Decety, J. (2000). A PET investigation of the attribution of intentions with a nonverbal task. *NeuroImage, 11,* 157–166.

Buttelmann, D., Carpenter, M., Call, J., & Tomasello, M. (2007). Enculturated chimpanzees imitate rationally. *Developmental Science, 10*(4), F31–F38.

Byrne, R. W. (2005). Social cognition: Imitation, imitation, imitation. *Current Biology, 15,* R498–R500.

Calarge, C., Andreasen, N. C., & O'Leary, D. S. (2003). Visualizing how one brain understands another: A PET study of theory of mind. *American Journal of Psychiatry, 160,* 1954–1964.

Calder, A. J., Lawrence, A. D., Keane, J., Scott, S. K., Owen, A. M., Christoffels, I., & Young, A. W. (2002). Reading the mind from eye gaze. *Neuropsychologia, 40,* 1129–1138.

Campbell, R., Heywood, C. A., Cowey, A., Regard, M., & Landis, T. (1990). Sensitivity to eye gaze in prosopagnosic patients and monkeys with superior temporal sulcus ablation. *Neuropsychologia, 28,* 1123–1142.

Carlson, S. M., & Moses, L. J. (2001). Individual differences in inhibitory control and children's theory of mind. *Child Development, 72,* 1032–1053.

Carpenter, M., Call, J., & Tomasello, M. (2005). Twelve- and 18-month-olds copy actions in terms of goals. *Developmental Science, 8*(1), F13–F20.

Chaminade, T., Meltzoff, A. N., & Decety, J. (2002). Does the end justify the means? A PET exploration of the mechanisms involved in human imitation. *Neuroimage, 15,* 318–328.

Chaminade, T., Oztop, E., Cheng, G., & Kawato, M. (2008). From self-observation to imitation: Visuomotor association on a robotic hand. *Brain Research Bulletin, 75,* 775–784.

Charman, T., S. Baron-Cohen, et al. (2000). Testing joint attention, imitation, and play as infancy precursors to language and theory of mind. *Cognitive Development* 15(4), 481–498.

Crichton, M. T. and C. Lange-Kuttner (1999). Animacy and propulsion in infancy: Tracking, waving and reaching to self-propelled and induced moving objects. *Developmental Science,* 2(3), 318–324.

Csibra, G., Biro, S., Koos, O., & Gergely, G. (2003). One-year-old infants use teleological representations of actions productively. *Cognitive Science, 27,* 111–133.

Currie, G., & Ravenscroft, I. (2002). *Recreative minds: Imagination in philosophy and psychology.* New York: Oxford University Press.

Davies, M., & Stone, T. (1995). *Mental simulation.* Cambridge, MA: Blackwell.

Decety, J., Chaminade, T., Grezes, J., & Meltzoff, A. N. (2002). A PET exploration of the neural mechanisms involved in reciprocal imitation. *NeuroImage, 15,* 265–272.

Decety, J., Grezes, J., Costes, N., Perani, D., Jeannerod, M., Procyk, E., et al. (1997). Brain activity during observation of actions: Influence of action content and subject's strategy. *Brain, 120,* 1763.

Decety, J., & Lamm, C. (2006). Human empathy through the lens of social neuroscience. *Scientific World Journal, 6,* 1146–1163.

Decety, J., & Lamm, C. (2007). The role of the right temporoparietal junction in social interaction: How low-level computational processes contribute to meta-cognition. *Neuroscientist, 13,* 580–593.

Delgado, M. R., Frank, R. H., & Phelps, E. A. (2005). Perceptions of moral character modulate the neural systems of reward during the trust game. *Nature Neuroscience, 8,* 1611–1618.

de Villiers, J. (2007). The interface of language and theory of mind. *Lingua, 117,* 1858–1878.

Epley, N., Keysar, B., Van Boven, L., & Gilovich, T. (2004). Perspective taking as egocentric anchoring and adjustment. *Journal of Personality and Social Psychology, 87,* 327–339.

Ferstl, E. C., & von Cramon, D. Y. (2002). What does the frontomedian cortex contribute to language processing: Coherence or theory of mind? *NeuroImage, 17,* 1599–1612.

Fletcher, P. C., Happé, F., Frith, U., Baker, S. C., Dolan, R. J., Frackowiak, R. S., et al. (1995). Other minds in the brain: A functional imaging study of "theory of mind" in story comprehension. *Cognition, 57,* 109–128.

Gallagher, H. L., Happé, F., Brunswick, N., Fletcher, P. C., Frith, U., & Frith, C. D. (2000). Reading the mind in cartoons and stories: An fMRI study of "theory of mind" in verbal and nonverbal tasks. *Neuropsychologia, 38,* 11–21.

Gallese, V., Fadiga, L., Fogassi, L., & Rizzolatti, G. (1996). Action recognition in the premotor cortex. *Brain, 119,* 593–609.

Gallese, V., & Goldman, A. (1998). Mirror neurons and the simulation theory of mind-reading. *Trends in Cognitive Sciences, 2,* 493–501.

Gallese, V., Keysers, C., & Rizzolatti, G. (2004). A unifying view of the basis of social cognition. *Trends in Cognitive Sciences, 8,* 396–403.

German, T. P., Niehaus, J. L., Roarty, M. P., Giesbrecht, B., Miller, M. B. (2004). Neural correlates of detecting pretense: Automatic engagement of the intentional stance under covert conditions. *Journal of Cognitive Neuroscience, 16,* 1805–1817.

Gerrans, P. (1998). The norms of cognitive development. *Mind and Language, 13,* 56–75.

Gerrans, P. (2002). The theory of mind module in evolutionary psychology. *Biology and Philosophy, 17,* 305–321.

Gerrans, P. & Stone V. (2008). Generous or Parsimonious Cognitive Architecture. Cognitive Neuroscience and Theory of Mind. *The British Journal for the Philosophy of Science,* 59(2), 121–141.

Gilovich, T. (1993). *How we know what isn't so: The fallibility of human reason in everyday life.* New York: Free Press.

Gobbini, M. I., Koralek, A. C., Bryan, R. E., Montgomery, K. J., & Haxby, J. V. (2007). Two takes on the social brain: A comparison of theory of mind tasks. *Journal of Cognitive Neuroscience, 19,* 1803–1814.

Goel, V., Grafman, J., Sadato, N., & Hallett, M. (1995). Modeling other minds. *NeuroReport, 6,* 1741–1746.

Goldman, A. I. (2006). *Simulating minds: The philosophy, psychology, and neuroscience of mindreading.* New York: Oxford University Press.

Goldman, A. I., & Sripada, C. S. (2005). Simulationist models of face-based emotion recognition. *Cognition, 94,* 193–213.

Gordon, R. M. (1986). Folk psychology as simulation. *Mind and Language, 1,* 158–171.

Grezes, J., Armony, J. L., Rowe, J., & Passingham, R. E. (2003). Activations related to "mirror" and "canonical" neurones in the human brain: An fMRI study. *NeuroImage, 18,* 928–937.

Happé, F., Ehlers, S., Fletcher, P., Frith, U., Johansson, M., Gillberg, C., et al. (1996). "Theory of mind" in the brain: Evidence from a PET scan study of Asperger syndrome. *NeuroReport, 8,* 197–201.

Happé, F., H. Brownell, et al. (1999). Acquired 'theory of mind' impairments following stroke. *Cognition, 70,* 211–240.

Hare, B., Call, J., Agnetta, B., & Tomasello, M. (2000). Chimpanzees know what conspecifics do and do not see. *Animal Behaviour, 59,* 771–785.

Harris, L. R., Todorov, T., & Fiske, S. T. (2005). Attributions on the brain: Neuro-imaging dispositional inferences, beyond theory of mind. *NeuroImage, 28,* 763–769

Hassabis, D., Kumaran, D., & Maguire, E. A. (2007). Using imagination to understand the neural basis of episodic memory. *Journal of Neuroscience, 27,* 14365–14374.

Hassabis, D., & Maguire, E. A. (2007). Deconstructing episodic memory with construction. *Trends in Cognitive Sciences, 11,* 299–306.

Haxby, J. V., Hoffman, E. A., & Gobbini, M. I. (2000). The distributed human neural system for face perception. *Trends in Cognitive Sciences, 4,* 223–233.

Hogrefe, G.-J., H. Wimmer, et al. (1986). Ignorance versus False Belief: A Developmental Lag in Attribution of Epistemic States. *Child Development, 57,* 567–82.

Heal, J. (1996). Simulation, theory, and content. In Peter Carruthers & Peter Smith (Eds.), *Theories of Theories of Mind,* Cambridge, CUP. 75–89.

Hurley, S., & Chater, N. (2005). *Perspectives on imitation: From cognitive neuroscience to social science.* New York: Cambridge University Press.

Iacoboni, M., Molnar-Szakacs, I., Gallese, V., Buccino, G., Mazziotta, J. C., & Rizzolatti, G. (2005). Grasping the intentions of others with one's own mirror neuron system. *PLoS Biology, 3*(3), e79.

Iacoboni, M., Woods, R. P., Brass, M., Bekkering, H., Mazziotta, J. C., & Rizzolatti, G. (1999, December 24). Cortical mechanisms of human imitation. *Science, 286,* 2526–2528.

Jackson, P. L., & Decety, J. (2004). Motor cognition: A new paradigm to study self-other interactions. *Current Opinion in Neurobiology, 14,* 259–263.

Jackson, P. L., Meltzoff, A. N., & Decety, J. (2006). Neural circuits involved in imitation and perspective-taking. *NeuroImage, 31,* 429–439.

Jacob, P., & Jeannerod, M. (2005). The motor theory of social cognition: A critique. *Trends in Cognitive Sciences, 9,* 21–25.

Jeannerod, M. (2006). *Motor cognition: What actions tell the self.* Oxford, New York: Oxford University Press.

Jellema, T., Baker, C. I., Wicker, B., & Perrett, D. I. (2000). Neural representation for the perception of the intentionality of actions. *Brain and Cognition, 44*(2), 280–302.

Kahneman, D., Slovic, P., & Tversky, A. (1982). *Judgment under uncertainty: Heuristics and biases:* New York: Cambridge University Press.

Keisuke Wakusawa, K., Sugiura, M., Sassa, Y., Jeong, H., Horie, K., Sato, S., Yokoyama, H., Tsuchiya, S., Inuma, K., & Kawashima, R., (2007). Comprehension of implicit meanings in social situations involving irony: A functional MRI study. *NeuroImage 37,* 1417–1426

Kobayashi, C., Glover, G. H., & Temple, E. (2007). Children's and adults' neural bases of verbal and nonverbal "theory of mind." *Neuropsychologia, 45,* 1522–1532.

Kobayashi, C., Gary, H., Glover, G. H., & Temple, E. (2007). Children's and adults' neural bases of verbal and nonverbal 'theory of mind.' *Neuropsychologia, 45,* 1522–1532.

Kumashiro, M., Ishibashi, H., Uchiyama, Y., Itakura, S., Murata, A., & Iriki, A. (2003). Natural imitation induced by joint attention in Japanese monkeys. *International Journal of Psychophysiology, 50*(1/2), 81–99.

Leslie, A. and Thaiss, L. (1992). Domain specificity in conceptual development: evidence from autism. *Cognition, 43,* 225–251.

Leslie, A. M. (1994). Pretending and believing: Issues in the theory of ToMM. *Cognition 50,* 211–238.

Leslie, A. M. (1994). Pretending and believing: Issues in the theory of ToMM. *Cognition, 50*(1/3), 211–238.

Lestou, V., Pollick, F. E., & Kourtzi, Z. (2008). Neural substrates for action understanding at different description levels in the human brain. *Journal of Cognitive Neuroscience, 20,* 324–341.

Lissek, S., Peters, S., Fuchs, N., Witthaus, H., Nicolas, V., et al. (2008). Cooperation and deception recruit different subsets of the theory-of-mind network. *PLoS ONE 3:* e2023. doi:10.1371/journal.pone.000202

Malle, B. F. (2004). *How the mind explains behavior: Folk explanations, meaning, and social interaction.* Bradford Books.

McCabe, K., Houser, D., Ryan, L., Smith, V., & Trouard, T. (2001). A functional imaging study of cooperation in two-person reciprocal exchange. *Proceedings of the National Academy of Sciences, USA, 98,* 11832–11835.

Meltzoff, A. N., & Decety, J. (2003). What imitation tells us about social cognition: A rapprochement between developmental psychology and cognitive neuroscience. *Philosophical Transactions of the Royal Society of London. Series B, 358,* 491–500.

Meltzoff, A. N., & Moore, M. K. (1983). Newborn infants imitate adult facial gestures. *Child Development, 54,* 702–709.

Miall, R. C. (2003). Connecting mirror neurons and forward models. *NeuroReport, 14,* 2135–2137.

Miller, E. K., & Cohen, J. D. (2001). An integrative theory of prefrontal cortex function. *Annual Review of Neuroscience, 24,* 167–202.

Mitchell, J. P. (2008). Activity in right temporo-parietal junction is not selective for theory-of-mind. *Cereb Cortex, 18,* 262–271.

Moriguchi, Y., Ohnishi, T., Mori, T., Matsuda, H., & Komaki, G. (2007). Changes of brain activity in the neural substrates for theory of mind during childhood and adolescence. *Psychiatry and Clinical Neuroscience, 61,* 355–363.

Moses, L. J. (2001). Executive accounts of theory-of-mind development. *Child Development, 72,* 688–690.

Myowa-Yamakoshi, M., & Matsuzawa, T. (2000). Imitation of intentional manipulatory actions in chimpanzees (Pan troglodytes). *Journal of Comparative Psychology, 114,* 381–391.

Nichols, S., Stich, S., Leslie, A., & Klein, D. (1996). Varieties of off-line simulation. *Theories of Theories of Mind, 24,* 39–74.

Nieminen-von Wendt, T., Metsahonkala, L., Kulomaki, T., Aalto, S., Autti, T., Vanhala, R., et al. (2003). Changes in cerebral blood flow in Asperger syndrome during theory of mind tasks presented by the auditory route. *European Child and Adolescent Psychiatry, 12*(4), 178–189.

Oztop, E., Kawato, M., & Arbib, M. (2006). Mirror neurons and imitation: A computationally guided review. *International Neural Network Society, 19*, 254–271.

Pacherie, E. (2006). Towards a dynamic theory of intentions: *Does consciousness cause behavior?* 145–167.

Perner, J. (1991). *The representational theory of mind.* Cambridge, MA: MIT Press.

Perner, J., & Lang, B. (1999). Development of theory of mind and executive control. *Trends in Cognitive Sciences, 3*, 337–344.

Perrett, D. I., Hietanen, J. K., Oram, M. W., Benson, P. J., & Rolls, E. T. (1992). Organization and functions of cells responsive to faces in the temporal cortex [and discussion]. *Philosophical Transactions of the Royal Society of London, Series B, 335*, 23–30.

Povinelli, D. J., & Vonk, J. (2003). Chimpanzee minds: Suspiciously human? *Trends in Cognitive Sciences, 7*, 157–160.

Pronin, E. (2002). Understanding mindreading: Social psychological perspectives: Heuristics and biases. *Psychology of Intuitive Judgment, 636–665.*

Pronin, E., Gilovich, T., & Ross, L. (2004). Objectivity in the eye of the beholder: Divergent perceptions of bias in self versus others. *Psychological Review, 111*, 781–799.

Rilling, J. K., Sanfey, A. G., Aronson, J. A., Nystrom, L. E., & Cohen, J. D. (2004). Opposing bold responses to reciprocated and unreciprocated altruism in putative reward pathways. *NeuroReport, 15*, 2539–2543.

Rizzolatti, G., & Craighero, L. (2004). The mirror-neuron system. *Annual Reviews of Neuroscience, 27*, 169–192.

Rizzolatti, G., Ferrari, P. F., Rozzi, S., & Fogassi, L. (2006). The inferior parietal lobule: Where action becomes perception. *Novartis Foundation Symposium, 270*, 129–140; discussion 140–125, 164–129.

Ross, L. D., Amabile, T. M., & Steinmetz, J. L. (2005). Social roles, social control, and biases in social-perception processes. In David Hamilton (Ed.), *Social Cognition: Key Readings.* Psycholgy Press. Hove.

Ruby, P., & Decety, J. (2004). How would you feel versus how do you think she would feel? A neuroimaging study of perspective-taking with social emotions. *Journal of Cognitive Neuroscience, 16*, 988–999.

Ruffman, T. E. D. (1996). Do children understand the mind by means of simulation or a theory? Evidence from their understanding of inference. *Mind and Language, 11*, 388–414.

Russell, T. A., Rubia, K., Bullmore, E. T., Soni, W., Suckling, J., Brammer, M. J., Simmons, A., Williams, S. C. R., & Sharma, T. Exploring the social brain in schizophrenia: Left prefrontal underactivation during mental state attribution. *American Journal of Psychiatry, 157*, 2040–2042.

Saxe, R., & Kanwisher, N. (2003). People thinking about thinking people: The role of the temporo-parietal junction in theory of mind. *NeuroImage, 9*, 1835–1842.

Saxe, R., & Powell, L. (2006). It's the thought that counts: Specific brain regions for one component of Theory of Mind. *Psychological Science, 17*, 692–699.

Saxe, R. (2005). Against simulation: The argument from error. *Trends in Cognitive Sciences, 9*, 174–179.

Saxe, R. (2006). Why and how to study theory of mind with fMRI. *Brain Research,*

Saxe, R., Carey, S., & Kanwisher, N. (2004). Understanding other minds: Linking developmental psychology and functional neuroimaging. *Annual Reviews of Psychology, 55*, 87–124.

Saxe, R., & Wexler, A. (2005). Making sense of another mind: The role of the right temporo-parietal junction. *Neuropsychologia, 43*, 1391–1399.

Schultz, J., Friston, K. J. et al. (2005). Activation in posterior superior temporal sulcus parallels parameter inducing the percept of animacy. *Neuron, 45*, 625–635.

Sommer, M., Dohnel, K., Sodian, B., Meinhardt, J., Thoermer, C., & Hajak, G. (2007). Neural correlates of true and false belief reasoning. *Neuroimage, 35*, 1378–1384.

Sommerville, J. A., & Decety, J. (2006). Weaving the fabric of social interaction: Articulating developmental psychology and cognitive neuroscience in the domain of motor cognition. *Psychonomic Bulletin and Review, 13*, 179–200.

Stone, V. E., & Gerrans, P. (2006a). Does the normal brain have a theory of mind? *Trends in Cognitive Sciences, 10*, 3–4.

Stone, V. E., & Gerrans, P. (2006b). What's domain-specific about theory of mind? *Social Neuroscience, 1*, 309–319.

Stone, V., Cosmides, L., Tooby, J., Kroll, N., & Knight, R (2002). Selective impairment of reasoning about social exchange in a patient with bilateral limbic system damage. *Proceedings of the National Academy of Sciences, 99*, 11531–11536.

Suddendorf, T., & Busby, J. (2005). Making decisions with the future in mind: Developmental and comparative identification of mental time travel. *Learning and Motivation, 36*, 110–125.

Suddendorf, T., & Corballis, M. C. (2007). The evolution of foresight: What is mental time travel, and is it unique to humans? *Behavioral and Brain Sciences, 30*, 299–313.

Tomasello, M., Call, J., & Hare, B. (2003). Chimpanzees understand psychological states: The question is which ones and to what extent. *Trends in Cognitive Sciences, 7*, 153–156.

Uddin, L. Q., Molnar-Szakacs, I., Zaidel, E., & Iacoboni, M. (2006). RTMS to the right inferior parietal lobule disrupts self-other discrimination. *Social Cognitive and Affective Neuroscience, 1*, 65–71.

Umilta, M. A., Kohler, E., Gallese, V., Fogassi, L., Fadiga, L., Keysers, C., et al. (2001). I know what you are doing: A neurophysiological study. *Neuron, 31*, 155–165.

Vogeley, K., Bussfeld, P., Newen, A., Herrmann, S., Happé, F., Falkai, P., et al. (2001). Mind reading: Neural mechanisms of theory of mind and self-perspective. *Neuroimage, 14*, 170–181.

Vogt, S., Buccino, G., Wohlschlager, A. M., Canessa, N., Shah, N. J., Zilles, K., et al. (2007). Prefrontal involvement in imitation learning of hand actions: Effects of practice and expertise. *NeuroImage, 37*, 1371–1383.

Vosgerau, G., & Newen, A. (2007). Thoughts, motor actions, and the self. *Mind and Language, 22*, 22–43.

Walter, H., Adenzato, M., Ciaramidaro, A., Enrici, I., Pia, L., Bara, B. G. (2004). Understanding intentions in social interaction: The role of the anterior paracingulate cortex. *Journal of Cognitive Neuroscience, 16*, 1854–1863.

Wellman, H. M., & Woolley, J. D. (1990). From simple desires to ordinary beliefs: The early development of everyday psychology. *Cognition, 35*, 245–275.

Wellman, H. L. (2000). Developing Understandings of Mind. Understanding Other Minds. H. T. F. D. C. S Baron-Cohen. Oxford, Oxford University Press.

Wicker, B., Keysers, C., Plailly, J., Royet, J. P., Gallese, V., & Rizzolatti, G. (2003). Both of us disgusted in my insula: The common neural basis of seeing and feeling disgust. *Neuron, 40*, 655–664.

Wolpert, D. M., Doya, K., & Kawato, M. (2003). A unifying computational framework for motor control and social interaction. *Philosophical Transactions of the Royal Society of London. Series B, 358*, 593–602.

Wolpert, D. M., & Kawato, M. (1998). Multiple paired forward and inverse models for motor control. *International Neural Network Society, 11*, 1317–1329.

Woodward, A. L. (2003). Infants'developing understanding of the link between looker and object. *Developmental Science, 6*(3), 297–311.

Zaitchik, D. (1990). When representations conflict with reality: The preschooler's problem with false beliefs and "false" photographs. *Cognition, 35*, 41–68.

Ziv, M., & Frye, D. (2003). The relation between desire and false belief in children's theory of mind: No satisfaction? *Developmental Psychology, 39*, 859–876.

Chapter 47

Social Cognition

RALPH ADOLPHS AND MICHAEL SPEZIO

WHAT IS SOCIAL COGNITION?

As the name says, social cognition pertains to the cognitive processing of socially relevant information. The meaning of the term *social* is clear enough, although there is debate about its boundaries and properties: It is that domain relating to other people. Social cognition may come into play even when the stimuli are not people as such, but are animals, computers, or nonsocial stimuli about which we anthropomorphize (Heberlein & Adolphs, 2004). Nonetheless, processing under these circumstances would be "social" in the sense that it is derivatively social. There is yet another wrinkle: There is some evidence that the brain's default mode of processing stimuli may be to treat stimuli as social. Many of the brain structures implicated in social processing, such as the medial prefrontal cortex, are activated at rest, remain activated when social stimuli are processed, and become deactivated when nonsocial stimuli are processed (Mitchell, Heatherton, & Macrae, 2002; Raichle et al., 2001). Thus, at least one contribution to the observed differences in regional brain activation between social and nonsocial stimuli appears to arise from an evoked deactivation to the nonsocial stimuli.

The meaning of the term *cognition* is more problematic. A standard view of cognition is that it is the level of processing that is inferential, going beyond the simple transformation of stimulus-response processing that would be seen in reflexes, and involving the kind of creative modeling of the world that is typical of human thought. Under this interpretation, emotional appraisal is cognitive. It is important not to equate cognition with consciousness—although there are interesting relationships between the two, a large research effort is in fact directed at elucidating the extent to which social cognition can occur without conscious awareness of the stimuli, the processing, or even the behavioral consequences of such processing (Tsuchiya & Adolphs, 2007). It may be more relevant to associate cognition with attention, and certainly with "top-down" attentional effects that are not driven solely by the saliency of the stimuli per se.

(It is noteworthy that attention and consciousness are also separable; Koch & Tsuchiya, 2006.)

Examples perhaps provide the best way to characterize social cognition. When we recognize someone from their face, voice, or gait; when we think about how we feel about someone; when we empathize with them; when we ponder how we can outsmart them: These are aspects of social cognition. Some aspects are rapid, some slow, some involve conscious access, and some do not. This variety may seem bewildering, but it can be placed in an overall processing hierarchy. Roughly, early perception feeds into identification and recognition, which feed into memory and decision making. Modulating these levels of processing are arousal, attention, and emotion. This level at which we identify social cognition does not preclude specializations at other levels that also show differentiation among social and nonsocial stimuli. There are receptors in the olfactory epithelium and in the vomeronasal organ already specialized for smelling certain socially informative conspecific molecules, and indeed there are highly specific routes of social information transmission whereby a specific molecule (called a pheromone) can bind to a specific receptor and elicit a specific social behavior (e.g., aggressive behavior; Chamero et al., 2007). Similarly, the auditory system of many mammals shows some specialization for representing sound frequencies that are the most important in social communication already at the level of the cochlea (e.g., in humans, we are most sensitive to, and our auditory system overrepresents, frequencies around 4 kHz). Nonetheless, while these peripheral specializations certainly contribute to the bandwidth of stimuli to which an organism is sensitive and can emphasize the processing of socially relevant stimuli, they are not generally thought of as cognitive, because they do not involve the flexible, inferential central processing that is the hallmark of cognition. In addition to being central in this sense of being post early perception and prior to action, social cognition in particular also offers several distinctive features—these all these come into play for cognition more generally, but arguably more so for social cognition.

A feature that has received considerable attention because of its relevance to psychopathology is self-regulation: our ability (in healthy adults, and with notable individual differences) to reinterpret and control social information processing, at least to some degree (Ochsner, Bunge, Gross, & Gabrieli, 2002; Ochsner & Gross, 2005). Many of the cultural norms for appropriate social behavior that are internalized over a lifetime depend on successful self-regulation for their implementation (cf. Chapter 51, this volume), and this aspect shows pronounced changes during development and into old age (cf. the sections on Development and Aging, Part VIII) as does the associated brain region thought to be most important for these processes: the prefrontal cortex. Social cognition is thus in part distinguished from other aspects of cognition by its high level of cultural internalization and the rich interplay between automatic and effortful processing, exemplified by emotion regulation in social contexts.

Another important feature of social cognition is its reliance on long-term future planning, counterfactual, and strategic thinking. To anticipate other people's behavior, to prepare our own, and to navigate a complex and interactive social environment, we need to imagine what others are up to, and how they will react to what we do. This aspect has also received a lot of interest, with some speculation that

episodic memory, thinking about the future, and the ability to imagine what goes on in other people's minds might all have neural substrates in common (Buckner & Carroll, 2006; D. T. Gilbert & Wilson, 2007). Intriguingly, some of these same neural substrates are the ones mentioned at the outset of this chapter, such as the medial prefrontal cortex, that appear to correspond to a default mode of processing. Perhaps the best quick definition of social cognition, then, is "thinking about people" (D. T. Gilbert, 1998), with the understanding that this aspect of thinking features an especially prominent component of control and regulation, and that it requires especially rich inferences to go from the behavior that we observe in others to the internal states that we attribute to them. Some of the component processes, and a preview of the neural structures that we discuss in more detail in the next section, are given in Figures 47.1 and 47.2.

The preceding short introduction to the domain of social cognition also points toward aspects that make its investigation difficult. It is complex; it shows large individual differences; it shows large context effects; and for all these reasons, it is difficult to elicit validly and to study quantitatively in the laboratory. None of these hurdles, however, has stopped neurobiologists from investigating the topic, or social psychologists from using neuroscience tools. The

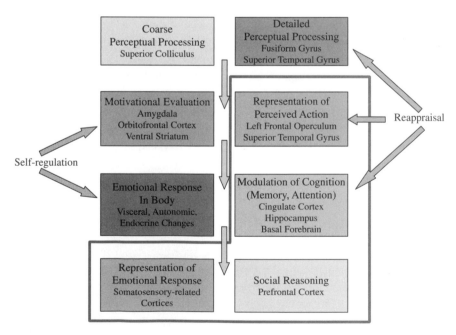

Figure 47.1 Processes that participate in social cognition.

Note: Some of the processes involved are indicated in the boxes, together with some of the structures thought to participate in their implementation. The schematic is divided into those processes more aligned with emotional reactions, on the left, and those more aligned with aspects other than emotion, on the right. Self-regulation and reappraisal operate to

control processing in each of these streams, respectively. The set of processes inside the larger L-shaped box are perhaps the best candidates for contributing directly to conscious experience. From "Is the Human Amygdala Specialized for Social Cognition" (pp. 326–340), by R. Adolphs, in *The Amygdala in Brain Function,* volume 985, S.-G. et al. (Eds.), 2003c, New York: Annals of the New York Academy of Sciences. Adapted with permission.

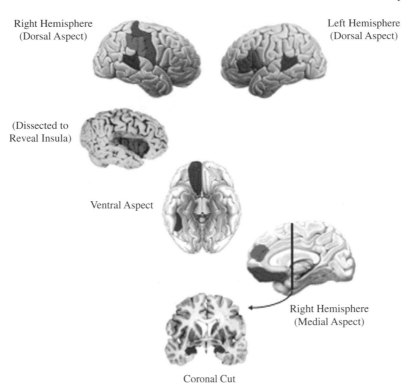

Right Hemisphere
(Dorsal Aspect)

Left Hemisphere
(Dorsal Aspect)

(Dissected to
Reveal Insula)

Ventral Aspect

Right Hemisphere
(Medial Aspect)

Coronal Cut

Figure 47.2   Neuroanatomy of social cognition.

Note: Shown on various images of brains are subsets of the structures involved in social cognition that we discuss in this chapter. (A) This right lateral view of a brain shows somatosensory cortices and superior temporal gyrus regions; roughly between them and posterior would be the TPJ, which is not shaded to preserve clarify of the figure. (B) Left prefrontal regions are also involved in making personality attributions to others, and indicated again here is the superior temporal gyrus, involved in processes such as biological motion. (C) This picture of the insula is revealed when the frontal operculum is removed. (D) A ventral view of the brain shows the medial prefrontal cortex (in this ventral view, medial OFC) and, more posteriorly, the fusiform gyrus, involved in face processing. (E) A medial view of the right hemisphere shows the anterior cingulate and again the medial PFC. (F) A coronal section along the line indicated reveals the amygdala in the medial temporal lobe.

use of neuroscience methods to investigate social cognition has rapidly become a hot topic, in good part due to the enthusiasm with which many social psychologists have made use of fMRI, ERPs and other tools. The field of *social neuroscience* (Cacioppo et al., 2001) and, within it, social *cognitive* neuroscience (Ochsner & Lieberman, 2001), has fostered numerous books and meetings, and is now the target of some focused graduate programs. The tools and approaches needed to investigate social cognition remain a topic of lively debate (Adolphs, 2003b), but as this volume demonstrates, the wisest strategy is to know something about behavioral social science, and to know something about cognitive neuroscience: Put the two together (often collaboratively), and you're doing social neuroscience. The hope of the field is that the complexity of the processes under investigation will yield best to a multi-pronged attack from multiple disciplines, and that the neuro-science data will help us constrain, and ultimately understand, the process models that compose social cognition.

Needless to say, we cannot review all social cognition in a chapter, and we also wish to avoid redundancy with some of the contributions in this volume that overlap considerably with social cognition. We highlight some examples where the cognitive neuroscience of a higher social process is relatively well understood, while giving the reader a sense for the diversity of approaches and topics out there. This includes our own work on the amygdala, and some suggestions for future directions that have been underemphasized.

NEUROANATOMY OF SOCIAL COGNITION

Given the multiple aspects of social cognition at the process level, it should come as no surprise that it draws on a large array of brain structures, some of which are shown in Figure 47.2. In this section, we provide a brief overview of the neuroanatomy of social cognition, and we give examples of recent studies that have explored specific structures or social processes.

Brain regions demonstrating a differential sensitivity for social cognition, as identified by the lesion method and by neuroimaging, include the amygdala, the cingulate gyrus (CingG), the fusiform gyrus, the insula (Ins), the orbitofrontal cortex (OFC), the somatosensory cortex (SSC), the superior temporal sulcus (STS), the supramarginal gyrus (SMG), the temporo-parietal junction (TPJ), and the ventromedial prefrontal cortex (vmPFC), among many others (Adolphs, 2003a; also see Figure 47.2). The FG is reviewed in Chapter 43 (Kanwisher and Yovel), this volume, and we provide a detailed discussion of the amygdala in the following section; here we review the other structures.

The CingG is a large structure that is typically subdivided into sectors from anterior to posterior. Posterior cingulate gyrus and adjacent retrosplenial cortex constitute a complex array of several cytoarchitectonic regions that are implicated in self-referential processing and autobiographical memory, as well as spatial cognition (Maddock, 1999); the region is known to participate in a widely distributed anatomical network for processing emotional and self-related information (Parvizi, Van Hoesen, Buckwalter, & Damasio, 2006). Ochsner et al. (2004) found that the posterior cingulate was differentially activated when making judgments about oneself compared with making judgments of others. Saxe and Powell (2006) sought to test the hypothesis that thinking about another agent's thoughts drives this activation. They found that PCC was differentially activated when participants actively considered the thoughts of the protagonist in a story (what another person was believing and thinking about), compared with when they processed other information relating to the subjective states or other social information about a person (such as their appearance or whether they felt hungry or sick). While the posterior cingulate cortex has become a topic of interest recently, it is fair to say that it remains fairly poorly understood.

Considerably more is known about the functions of the anterior subdivisions of the CingG, which has been associated with cognitive conflict monitoring and anticipation of cognitive conflict (Botvinick, Cohen, & Carter, 2004; Sohn, Albert, Jung, Carter, & Anderson, 2007). The fMRI actions within it have been associated also with ERP responses that can be measured at the scalp. In addition, there are lesion studies that more definitively point toward its possible functions. Macaque monkeys with bilateral lesions to the anterior cingulate cortex (ACC) exhibit deficits in social behaviors, such as fewer social interactions, reduced time near conspecifics, and fewer vocalizations (Hadland, Rushworth, Gaffan, & Passingham, 2003). At the same time, the lesioned monkeys showed increases in manipulating inanimate objects, so the social deficits were not the result of an overall decrease in activity. ACC, particularly ventral ACC, has been associated with affective/emotional processing (Devinsky, Morrell, & Vogt, 1995)

and shows differential activation for empathy, social intuition (Vollm et al., 2006), and cooperation (Rilling et al., 2002). From monkey lesion studies, there is evidence that the ACC contributes more to impairments in social behavior than does the orbitofrontal cortex (Rudebeck, Buckley, Walton, & Rushworth, 2006), a nearby region that is often damaged together with the ACC in humans who have lesions of the prefrontal cortex. The ACC has long been known to be involved in pain perception (its white matter connections are a target of neurosurgery for treating intractable pain; neurosurgical recordings in humans have documented single neurons that response to pain; Hutchison, Davis, Lozano, Tasker, & Dostrovsky, 1999) and motivated behavior more generally (Vogt, 2005). A clinical outcome of acute bilateral lesions to the anterior cingulate cortex is a phenomenon called *akinetic mutism*—a complete lack of willed, volitional behavior. Such patients can perceive stimuli in their environment, and they are not paralyzed, but they lack any motivation to behave. All these findings taken together argue that the involvement of the ACC in social cognition is related to the strong motivation to behave and the need to monitor conflict, both of which may feature more prominently, on average, in social behavior than in other aspects of behavior.

The SSC and SMG have both been demonstrated to be associated with decisions about the emotion in a face. Adolphs, Damasio, Tranel, Cooper, and Damasio (2000) demonstrated that lesions to the right SSC and the right SMG severely impaired performance on a task in which participants judged emotion from facial expression in static images. Keysers et al. (2004) showed that "tactile empathy," in which someone reports feeling what they see happen to another person, associates with differential activation in secondary, but not primary, SSC. These findings support the notion that social cognition about others draws upon emotional information in the form of body-state representations, and is related to the by now very large literature on simulation and mirror neurons. While this literature has emphasized the motor aspects of mirroring other people, the involvement of the SSC argues also for sensory components of this mechanism.

The TPJ is a structure most frequently associated with thought about another's state of mind (Saxe & Kanwisher, 2003; Saxe & Wexler, 2005; but see Mitchell, 2007). Saxe and Wexler (2005) found that the right TPJ was more differentially selective for the attribution of mental states than even other areas known to be associated with representing another's mind, such as the PCC and the mPFC. There is an active debate about how to interpret the activations in the TPJ that have been observed—whether they are specific to social processing or reflect a more general, but correlated process. On the one side, Rebecca Saxe (Saxe & Powell,

2006) has argued that the TPJ is activated relatively specifically when we attribute beliefs to others; on the other side, Jason Mitchell (Mitchell, 2007) has argued that its activation reflects more general (not specifically social) attentional orienting—a process that certainly also comes into play when we attribute beliefs to others, but that is by no means unique to it. The debate is a good example of an attempt to find a socially specific function for a brain region (Saxe, 2006), similar in spirit to the much longer standing debates about whether ventral regions of the temporal lobe are specialized for processing faces (Kanwisher, 2000; Tarr & Gauthier, 2000).

Throughout the literature, there is a close association between social cognition and emotion. Those brain regions that most consistently show an association between emotional experience and social processing are the ventromedial prefrontal cortex, the right insula, and right somatosensory cortices, and the amygdala. Bar-On, Tranel, Denburg, and Bechara (2003) tested 6 subjects with bilateral focal lesions of anterior and posterior vmPFC, 3 subjects with unilateral lesions of the right Ins and SSC, and 3 subjects with unilateral lesions of the Amy on emotional intelligence (Bar-On, 1997) and social functioning (Tranel, Bechara, & Denburg, 2002). They compared performance of these groups with a group of control subjects who had lesions that did not involve the vmPFC, the right Ins and SSC, or the Amy. The study found no differences between any of the experimental groups and control group on full IQ, executive function, perception, or memory, nor were there any indications of psychopathology. But each experimental group was significantly impaired on emotional intelligence compared with the control group. Combining all three experimental groups yielded significant deficits in social functioning compared with controls.

The vmPFC was one of the first brain regions to catch the attention of neuroscientists with respect to regulating social behavior, in large part because of several highly influential lesion studies. The landmark case is that of Phineas Gage, a nineteenth-century railroad worker who had an iron rod blasted longitudinally through the front of his head in an explosives accident (A. R. Damasio, 1994; H. Damasio, Grabowski, Frank, Galaburda, & Damasio, 1994). Not only did Gage survive, but the only notable enduring effect of Gage's head injury was a change in personality. Gage changed from shrewd, persistent, and respectable to profane, capricious, and unreliable (although the historical details of this account have been the topic of some debate; MacMillan, 2000). The association of impairments in social behavior with ventromedial prefrontal cortex (VMPC) damage has since been investigated in much greater detail. Perhaps the most illustrative modern example of this phenomenon is patient EVR (A. R. Damasio,

Tranel, & Damasio, 1990). At age 35, EVR underwent resection of a bilateral orbitofrontal meningioma. Mesial orbital and lower mesial frontal cortices (collectively referred to as ventromedial prefrontal cortex; VMPC) were excised with the tumor. Following the surgery, EVR exhibited a remarkable decline in his personal and professional life, including two divorces, the loss of his job, and bankruptcy. Despite the gross alteration of his social conduct and decision making, neuropsychological testing indicates EVR's intellectual abilities remained superior (Saver & Damasio, 1991). While striking, EVR is not an isolated case. Subsequent group studies of VMPC patients have identified typical personality changes associated with VMPC damage: blunted affect, poor frustration tolerance, impaired goal-directed behavior, inappropriate social conduct, and marked lack of insight into these changes (Barrash, Tranel, & Anderson, 2000). Further experimental work has demonstrated that VMPC damage impairs subjective and autonomic responses to emotionally charged pictures (e.g., mutilated bodies, nudes) and to emotional memories. Studies involving gambling games indicate that VMPC patients experience diminished emotional arousal before making risky choices (Bechara, Damasio, Damasio, & Anderson, 1994), as well as diminished regret when considering alternate outcomes after making risky choices (Camille et al., 2004). In such games, VMPC patients persistently make disadvantageous choices. These results suggest that emotional signals mediated by VMPC may be a critical influence on social conduct and decision making (Bechara, Damasio, & Damasio, 2000).

Experimental tests that directly assess social knowledge provide further support for the role of VMPC in social cognition. VMPC patients have deficits in interpreting nonverbal social information such as facial expression, gestures, or body posture. VMPC patients typically have preserved declarative knowledge of basic social and moral norms, but detection of complex verbal social information, such as faux pas, sarcasm, and aspects of moral judgment, may be impaired (Koenigs et al., 2007; Saver & Damasio, 1991). Studies of moral cognition underscore the importance of VMPC in social decision making. Functional imaging experiments reveal that areas within VMPC are active during viewing of unpleasant moral pictures and judgment of moral statements (Moll, Zahn, de Oliveira-Souza, Krueger, & Grafman, 2005). When evaluating hypothetical moral dilemmas, patients with VMPC damage exhibit an abnormally utilitarian pattern of moral judgments, basing their judgments more on the consideration of outcomes than on the moral permissibility of the means to obtain the outcomes (Koenigs et al., 2007).

Shamay-Tsoory, Tomer, Berger, and Aharon-Peretz (2003) tested 12 subjects with focal lesions to the vmPFC on empathy and the recognition of social faux pas. They found that these subjects, as a group, provided significantly lower empathy scores and were significantly more impaired at recognizing social faux pas than age-matched (but not IQ-matched) controls and people with unilateral lesions to the posterior cortex of the brain. To test if this was due primarily to impairments in emotional processing, Shamay-Tsoory and coworkers (Shamay-Tsoory, Tomer, Berger, Goldsher, & Aharon-Peretz, 2005) conducted another study in which they used a second-order false belief task, an ironic utterance task, and a social faux pas task, and compared the performance of participants with lesions localized to the vmPFC with that of participants with lesions localized to the dorsolateral PFC or to the posterior cortex. In line with their hypothesis that vmPFC contributes to social cognition primarily via affective/emotional processing, vmPFC lesions did not impair second-order belief formation, but severely impaired performance in detection of irony and social faux pas, compared with the controls.

While the majority of studies have focused on, and the largest effects have been found, for patients who have bilateral damage to the vmPFC, unilateral damage also causes the pattern of impairments previously described, only more mildly. There appears to be an interesting asymmetry in that unilateral right-sided lesions seem to cause a more severe impairment than do unilateral left-sided lesions. A further wrinkle on this story is that unilateral right lesions are more severe than left in males, whereas unilateral left lesions may be more severe than right in females (Tranel, Damasio, Denburg, & Bechara, 2005).

Patients with early onset damage involving VMPC are a unique resource for investigating the development of social cognition. Like patients with adult-onset damage, individuals acquiring VMPC damage in infancy or early childhood manifest defects in social conduct and decision making despite intact language, memory, and IQ. However, the social defects following early onset VMPC damage appear more severe than in the adult-onset cases. Common features include apathy and unconcern; lack of guilt, empathy, or remorse; violent outbursts; lewd and irresponsible behavior; petty criminal behavior; and lack of awareness of behavioral problems (S. W. Anderson, Damasio, Tranel, & Damasio, 2000). Unlike adult-onset cases, early onset VMPC patients may have impaired knowledge of social/moral conventions (S. W. Anderson, Bechara, Damasio, Tranel, & Damasio, 1999). These results indicate that VMPC is critically involved in the acquisition of social and moral knowledge during development. Adult-onset VMPC patients, who presumably undergo normal social development, retain declarative access to social/moral facts, but they appear to lose access to emotional signals that are necessary to guide appropriate social and decision-making

behavior in real-life situations. Early-onset VMPC patients seem to have never acquired appropriate levels of factual social knowledge, nor do they have access to normal "on-line" emotional processing, resulting in an even greater level of social impairment.

As the review and these brief examples illustrate, some regions of the brain are certainly more important for social cognition than others, and there is good evidence to suggest that there is a network, or networks, for social cognition. Yet this does not mean that the structure or the network in question is limited in its function to social cognition, nor even that it is disproportionately involved in social cognition. Attempts to demonstrate such a disproportionate involvement have either all met with deconstructions that reduce higher-order and domain-specific social processes to simpler, domain-general processing, or else they are still under active debate. The difficulty is that it is impossible, merely from investigating a structure in one species at one point in time, to gain much insight into its function in a teleological sense. That requires information from development and from comparative studies; the former is well represented in this *Handbook*, and we provide next a brief review of the latter.

EVOLUTION OF SOCIAL COGNITION: THE SOCIAL BRAIN HYPOTHESIS

The social brain hypothesis attempts to explain the extraordinary size and complexity of the human brain (Barrett & Henzi, 2005; Barrett, Henzi, & Dunbar, 2003; Bradbury, 2005; Byrne & Whiten, 1988; Dunbar & Shultz, 2007a; Roth & Dicke, 2005; Whiten & Byrne, 1997). The evolution of human brain size to its present 1.3 kg has been relatively stable within the past 100,000 to 150,000 years, with some evidence of a slight decline between 70,000 and 50,000 years ago (Ruff, Trinkaus, & Holliday, 1997). By contrast, the brain size of the great ape species closest in evolution to humans, such as chimpanzees (*Pan troglodytes*) and bonobos (*Pan paniscus*), is only 25% to 35% of this size (about the size of the brain our hominid ancestors would likely have had about 4 million years ago), while body size is comparable (~100 pounds; Bradbury, 2005; see Figure 47.3). Given the increased maternal investment required to produce offspring with large brains (Martin, 2007), and the increased metabolic costs of maintaining a large brain (Isler & van Schaik, 2006), the central puzzles of human brain evolution are—why so large and how could this possibly have taken place as recently as 100,000 years ago?

Responses to these puzzles have included a focus on ethology, with attention to problem solving in a complex

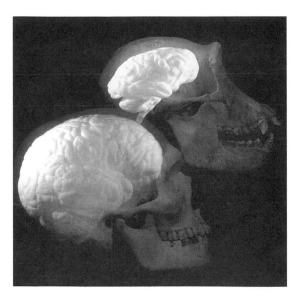

Figure 47.3   Comparison of brains.

Note: **Top**: The brain and skull of a modern chimpanzee. **Bottom**: A human brain. The chimp brain is only a quarter or so the size of the human brain.

environment, a focus on developmental costs, and a focus on social cognition, with attention to problem solving in a complex social environment (Dunbar & Shultz, 2007b). Byrne and Whiten (1988) were among the first to propose the so-called Machiavellian Intelligence hypothesis to argue in favor of complex social environments being the primary selective pressure for human brain size. They contended that individuals who could navigate the complexity required to maintain group cohesion in challenging environments would enjoy a strong evolutionary advantage over individuals who could not. Despite the title of their first edited volume, Byrne and Whiten included all aspects of social problem solving, both prosocial and deceitful, in their proposal. Subsequently, they and others renamed this approach to explaining human brain evolution the "social brain hypothesis" (Whiten & Byrne, 1997).

One class of empirical tests for this hypothesis seeks to determine whether those regions where the human brain differs most in size from brains of apes correspond to regions important for social cognition in humans. Zilles and coworkers operationalized regional size similarity by the level of deformation a region requires when spatially transforming an ape brain into human brain space (Bradbury, 2005). They found that the regions requiring the largest spatial transformations were in ventromedial and orbitofrontal cortex, frontopolar cortex (e.g., BA 10), and regions for hypothalamic and neuroendocrine function (Bradbury, 2005). Though the frontal cortex as a whole is not differentially enlarged in humans compared with that of apes (Semendeferi & Damasio, 2000; Semendeferi,

Damasio, Frank, & Van Hoesen, 1997), humans were shown to have greater complexity in orbitofrontal cortex rostral to BA 13, compared with other apes (Semendeferi, Armstrong, Schleicher, Zilles, & Van Hoesen, 1998). Additionally, BA 10 in humans was found to be enlarged and to show increased specialization for communication with other higher order association areas (Allman, Hakeem, & Watson, 2002; Semendeferi, Armstrong, Schleicher, Zilles, & Van Hoesen, 2001). Finally, evidence suggests that in humans, the insula is relatively larger than in apes, after overall brain size is controlled for (Semendeferi & Damasio, 2000). Besides being a brain region involved in social cognition, the anterior insula is also known to contain von Economo neurons, spindle-like neurons observed thus far among primates only in humans and some ape species, whose proportional representation in the brain increases with brain size (Allman et al., 2002; Nimchinsky et al., 1999). This class of neurons has been proposed to underlie complex social functioning, such as social intuition (Allman, Watson, Tetreault, & Hakeem, 2005), and it is intriguing to note that they may also be present in some other mammals known to have complex social behavior, such as whales and elephants.

Additional empirical tests of the social brain hypothesis focus on operationalizing social complexity in ways that include size of the overall group, size of an average grooming clique, size and frequency of temporally limited subgroups (e.g., coalitions), number and complexity of mating strategies, frequency and complexity of social play, frequency and complexity of deception, and the extent of any social learning (Dunbar & Shultz, 2007b). Some of these operationalizations have parallels in the study of social capital in human communities (Putnam, 2000; Veenstra, 2002). In general, results from these empirical investigations are consistent with the social brain hypothesis, not just in primates but across species (Dunbar & Shultz, 2007a, 2007b). That is, the more social the species (e.g., high pair-bonding), the greater the brain volume. Evidence suggests that prevalence of prosocial behaviors, specifically pair-bonding behaviors, explains more variance in brain size than do other types of social complexity (R. Dunbar & Shultz, 2007).

A third class of empirical test of the social brain hypothesis proceeds by agent-based modeling (ABM), in which computer models of reproducing individual agents, and their interactions, are built to study whether pressures from social complexity do in fact result in increased cognitive complexity, increased cooperative behavior, and so on (Bryson, Ando, & Lehmann, 2007; Burtsev & Turchin, 2006; Conte, 2002; N. Gilbert & Bankes, 2002). Gavrilets and Vose (2006) investigated the evolution of cognitive capacity due to social pressure by constructing a model that focused on male mating strategies in a sexually diploid population. They modeled the genetic control of each individual's ability to learn new strategies (learning ability) and capacity to store learned strategies (cerebral capacity) using separate, independent loci that were equal in effect on survival. They chose these two traits specifically because of their association with increased brain size and complexity. The model also used an overall carrying capacity to control the size of the modeled population of agents, which was kept to between 50 and 150 individuals. The authors used small, constant rates to model an individual's forgetting of learned strategies and invention of new strategies, and they classified each strategy according to its "Machiavellian fitness" and complexity. Machiavellian fitness was just their measure of how well an individual did in competition with other individuals for mates. Complexity regulated how easily the strategy could be learned. The rate of learning a strategy was proportional to learning ability, and inversely proportional to the strategy's complexity and the number of strategies already learned. The fitness of an individual was just the sum of the fitnesses of all the strategies the individual learned, and the probability of winning a contest with another individual depended on the difference in fitness values. Offspring of matings were produced probabilistically using naturalistic models of recombination, segregation, and random mutation.

With this model, in which social intelligence and social pressure were the operative forces, the authors demonstrated that the number of total strategies, the average learning ability, the average cerebral capacity, and the average fitness all increased substantially in only 10–20 thousand generations (~150,000 to 300,000 years). Notably, however, the model did not explicitly model the kind of pair-bonding that may be more relevant to recent associations between social complexity and brain size in apes (Dunbar & Shultz, 2007b). This suggests directions for future work using agent-based modeling more tightly constrained by research findings in the social cognition of nonhuman primates.

A final point of interest that brings together evolutionary and developmental aspects of human brain size is that humans are highly altricial: At birth, we are helpless, and our development, notably including social development, occurs over a protracted period lasting many years. One way of appreciating this statement is to note that human brains are only about 25% their adult volume at birth—constraints imposed in part by our bipedal nature and the evolution of the female pelvis, with the consequence that infant human brains are highly immature. By comparison, chimpanzee brains are nearly 50% their adult size at birth, and macaque monkey brains are about 70% of their adult size at birth. These differences in the size of the neonatal brain relative to the adult brain mirror the species

differences in the length of their development and their dependency on social support during this development. A recently found skull from a 1.8 million-year-old hominid child provided evidence that our ancestors 1.8 MY ago had a cranial capacity at birth that is essentially like that of apes, rather than like that of modern humans, arguing that this developmental shift occurred relatively recently and may be one of the features that contributed to the evolution of *homo sapiens* (Coqueugnlot, Hublin, Vellon, Houet, & Jacob, 2004).

THE AMYGDALA: FROM EMOTION TO SOCIAL ATTENTION

Much of our own work has been on the amygdala, and this together with other recent findings in both animals and humans has yielded a fairly detailed compendium of what it is that the amygdala might contribute to social cognition. If we look at the history of work on the amygdala, it appears to follow two largely independent paths. One begins with the classical studies of Kluver and Bucy (although there were even earlier studies; Brown & Shafer, 1888) who made large bilateral lesions of the temporal lobes in monkeys. The syndrome that was named after them features a mixture of impairments due to amnesia, agnosia, and also emotional changes (Kluver & Bucy, 1939). A small number of investigators have modernized these early studies and made more selective lesions of the amygdala in monkeys by injecting a neurotoxin, ibotenic acid. This achieves a focal lesion of the amygdala that spares surrounding structures (unlike Kluver and Bucy's very large lesions that did not permit any specific conclusions to be drawn about the amygdala per se), and importantly, it also spares fibers of passage—white matter coursing near or within a structure whose destruction (e.g., by electrolytic or aspiration lesions) would additionally introduce impairments due to disconnection of distal structures that normally communicate through these fibers. These much more selective ibotenic-acid lesions of the amygdala have revealed that amygdala damage in primates is subtle and also sensitive to the context and species (Machado & Bachevalier, 2006). In general, the animals still appear to have a normal repertoire of social behaviors (Amaral et al., 2003), but they don't apply them normally. They fail to take into account the circumstances and behave in social inappropriate ways, often appearing very passive and tame (Emery et al., 2001). Moreover, the effects of amygdala damage depend critically on the age at which the lesions are introduced—lesioning the amygdala in infant monkeys actually induces a social phobia of sorts (Prather et al., 2001), which has made this of some interest as a possible model for autism (see Chapter 52, Section VII, this volume). We take up the human analogue of such lesion studies in detail later in this chapter.

The second and parallel effort of studies on the amygdala, one which has involved a much larger number of laboratories and which has focused mostly on rodents, is the amygdala's role in associative emotional memory—specifically, its role in fear conditioning (although its role in the modulation of declarative memory by emotion has also received some attention—see Chapter 31, Volume 1). This line of work has investigated how an animal learns that a stimulus or context is potentially aversive, and how it learns to avoid the stimulus as a consequence (Davis, 2000). There remains debate over the precise role of the amygdala in learned fear, but it is clear that it plays an important role. This line of work has used selective lesions of nuclei within the amygdala in rodents (although monkeys have also been investigated), and it has been borne out (at a much coarser level of anatomical and process resolution) also in humans. The human amygdala appears necessary for normal fear conditioning (Bechara et al., 1995) and is activated during the acquisition of such conditioning (Buechel, Morris, Dolan, & Friston, 1998). These studies in humans have now been taken also into neuroeconomics, which provides a mathematical framework for analyzing the decisions people make on the basis of the prior outcomes they have experienced. Some of this work has also examined the connections between multiple structures known to be important to decision making, such as those between the amygdala and prefrontal cortex.

Fear conditioning, social behavior, and decision making seem to be a disparate batch of processes, and it has been hard to come up with any unified view of amygdala function. In part, this problem is real, and it is not surprising. After all, the primate amygdala consists of over a dozen nuclei, and the more detailed studies of fear conditioning in rodents have demonstrated that these nuclei all subserve different functions. They receive inputs from different parts of the brain, they send output to different parts, and they have different internal connectivity (Amaral, Price, Pitkanen, & Carmichael, 1992; Figure 47.4). The basolateral nucleus is the primary source of cortical sensory input to the amygdaloid complex, whereas the central nucleus is a main source of output to autonomic control centers. The individual roles of particular nuclei have often not been studied in primate studies of social behavior, and also not in studies in humans, certainly accounting for some of the discrepancies in the literature.

Nonetheless, there is a common theme in functions assigned to the amygdala: its role related to prioritizing information processing and allocating attention (Adolphs & Spezio, 2006). This idea goes back to earlier proposals

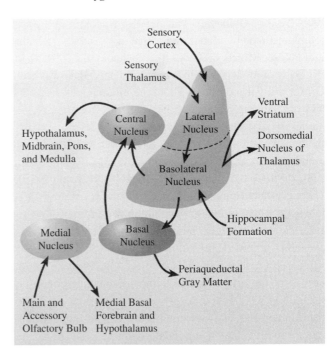

Figure 47.4 Amygdala nuclei.

Note: A schematic showing some of the inputs and outputs, as well as intrinsic connections, of the primate amygdala. Note that none of the arrows are intended to denote monosynaptic connections. A major input nucleus is the basolateral region, whereas a major output for eliciting emotional reactions is the central nucleus.

by Paul Whalen, that the amygdala is involved in detecting ambiguous stimuli in the environment about which an organism must find out more—stimuli that are potentially threatening and dangerous, and toward which processing resources and attention must be directed (Davis & Whalen, 2001; Whalen, 1999). The amygdala's modulation of attention had also been studied in rats (Holland & Gallagher, 1999), and was consistent with large number of studies in primates including humans. A recent neuroeconomics study found amygdala activation under decision-making circumstances where the outcomes of a choice were especially uncertain: The odds of getting a particular outcome weren't even known (Hsu, Bhatt, Adolphs, Tranel, & Camerer, 2005). Assigning a function to the amygdala for detecting highly uncertain, unpredictable, and potentially important events ties together a lot of findings in the literature.

Our own studies of the consequences of amygdala lesions in humans, complemented by those of others, followed a similar development from a role in basic emotion processing toward a more cognitive role in allocating processing resources and attention, and we review this next.

Several lesion studies (Adolphs, Tranel, Damasio, & Damasio, 1994; A. K. Anderson & Phelps, 2000; A. K. Anderson, Spencer, Fulbright, & Phelps, 2000; Calder et al.,

1996; Young, Hellawell, Van de Wal, & Johnson, 1996), complemented by functional imaging studies (Breiter et al., 1996; Morris et al., 1996; Whalen et al., 2001), had originally demonstrated that the human amygdala was critical for normal judgments about the internal states of others from viewing pictures of their facial expressions. Some studies have found a disproportionately severe impairment in recognizing fear (Adolphs, Tranel, Damasio, & Damasio, 1995; A. K. Anderson & Phelps, 2000; Broks et al., 1998; Calder et al., 1996; Sprengelmeyer et al., 1999), whereas others found evidence for a broader or more variable impairment in recognizing multiple emotions of negative valence in the face, including fear, anger, disgust, and sadness (Adolphs, 1999; Adolphs et al., 1999; Schmolck & Squire, 2001; Siebert, Markowitsch, & Bartel, 2003). Across the majority of studies, impairments in recognition of emotion were found despite an often normal ability to discriminate perceptually among the same stimuli. Many patients with bilateral amygdala damage perform in the normal range on the Benton Face Matching Task (Benton, Hamsher, Varney, & Spreen, 1983), in which subjects are asked to match different views of the same, unfamiliar person's face, and they also perform normally in discriminating subtle changes in facial expression, even for facial expressions that they are nonetheless unable to recognize (Adolphs & Tranel, 2000; Adolphs, Tranel, & Damasio, 1998).

Back in the early 1990s, one of us (R.A.) studied in detail a rare subject, SM, who has been especially informative because of the specificity of both her lesion and her impairment (Adolphs & Tranel, 2000; Tranel & Hyman, 1990). SM is a 42-year-old woman who has complete bilateral amygdala damage resulting from a rare disease (Urbach-Wiethe disease; Hofer, 1973). On a series of tasks, she shows a relatively disproportionate impairment in recognizing the intensity of fear from faces alone, and a lesser impairment also in recognizing the intensity of related emotions such as surprise and anger (Adolphs et al., 1994).

A further role for the amygdala in processing aspects of faces comes from studies of the interaction between facial emotion and eye gaze. The direction of eye gaze in other individuals' faces is an important source of information about their emotional state, intention, and likely future behavior. Eye gaze is a key social signal in many species (Emery, 2000), especially apes and humans, whose white sclera makes the pupil more easily visible and permits better discrimination of gaze. Human viewers make preferential fixations onto the eye region of others' faces (Janik, Wellens, Goldberg, & Dell'Osso, 1978), a behavior that appears early in development and may contribute to the socioemotional impairments seen in developmental

disorders like autism (Baron-Cohen, 1995). Eyes signal important information about emotional states, and there is evidence from functional imaging studies that at least some of this processing recruits the amygdala (Baron-Cohen et al., 1999; Kawashima et al., 1999; Wicker, Perrett, Baron-Cohen, & Decety, 2003). The interaction between facial emotion and direction of eye gaze has been explored. It was found that direct gaze facilitated processing of approach-oriented emotions such as anger, whereas averted gaze facilitated the processing of avoidance-oriented emotions such as fear (Adams & Kleck, 2003) and that this processing facilitation correlated with increased activation of the amygdala in a functional imaging study (Adams, Gordon, Baird, Ambady, & Kleck, 2003).

The amygdala's role is not limited to making judgments about basic emotions, but includes a role in making social judgments. This fact was already suggested by the earlier studies in nonhuman primates alluded to earlier (Kling & Brothers, 1992; Kluver & Bucy, 1937; Rosvold, Mirsky, & Pribram, 1954), which demonstrated impaired social behavior following amygdala damage, confirmed to some extent by the more recent studies that produced a more restricted set of impairments with more anatomically restricted damage to the amygdala (Emery & Amaral, 1999; Emery et al., 2001). What is the analogue in humans? Some studies of the human amygdala suggest a general role for the amygdala in the collection of abilities whereby we attribute internal mental states, intentions, desires, and emotions to other people ("theory of mind"; Baron-Cohen et al., 2000; Fine, Lumsden, & Blair, 2001). Relatedly, the amygdala shows differential habituation of activation to faces of people of another race (Hart et al., 2000), and amygdala activation has been found to correlate with race stereotypes of which the viewer may be unaware (Phelps et al., 2000). However, the amygdala's role in processing information about race is still unclear: Other brain regions, in extrastriate visual cortex, are also activated differentially as a function of race (Golby, Gabrieli, Chiao, & Eberhardt, 2001), and lesions of the amygdala do not appear to impair race judgments (Phelps, Cannistraci, & Cunningham, 2003).

The preceding findings support the simulation view of how emotional expressions might be recognized, an issue we briefly mentioned when discussing somatosensory cortices. The story roughly runs like this. Visual cortices in the temporal lobe would be involved in perceptual processing of facial features, would then convey a perceptual representation of the face to the basolateral amygdala, which in turn would associate it with its emotional response, likely effected by amygdala nuclei and corresponding to changes in a number of measures. One such change would be the somatic response triggered by the central nucleus of the amygdala (e.g., changes in autonomic tone). These emotional responses, in turn, would be perceived and represented in somatosensory cortices including insula, and would for the direct substrate for sharing the observed person's feeling of the emotion.

The preceding account of how we might infer another's emotional state via simulation (Goldman & Sripada, 2005) has turned out to be an incomplete picture. A more recent study from our lab gave the surprising finding that the amygdala comes into play in a more abstract, and earlier, processing component (Adolphs et al., 2005; see Figure 47.5). Amygdala damage was found to impair the ability to use information from a diagnostic facial feature—the eye region of the face. Following amygdala damage, the eye region of faces was no longer used effectively by the viewer to discriminate fear. These findings were consistent with other results showing amygdala activation to fearful eyes (Morris, deBonis, & Dolan, 2002), or only to the briefly presented whites of eyes (Whalen et al., 2004).

The experiment that demonstrated this finding used a new technique, called "bubbles," in which small portions of an image of a face were revealed to viewers. On a particular trial, a viewer might see only the ear of an underlying face, or perhaps part of the cheek and part of the forehead. Some quick reflection immediately suggests that not all regions of the face would be equally informative about the emotion: Seeing part of an ear does not distinguish emotions, whereas seeing part of the eyes or the mouth is much more discriminative. We can take advantage of this fact using a procedure similar to reverse correlation. When shown these randomly revealed pieces of faces, subjects are asked to judge the emotion. Those trials they get correct are all summed, and we now subtract all those trials (those pieces of faces) that they get incorrect. This procedure (or its continuous analogue, regressing performance accuracy on the regions of the face that are revealed in each trial) generates a so-called classification image that denotes the regions of the face on the basis of which subjects can discriminate the emotion.

Perhaps not too surprisingly, the classification image for discriminating fear from happiness (the particular discrimination we used in our experiment) prominently shows the eyes and the mouth. However, when the same experiment was conducted in subject SM, mentioned earlier, who has

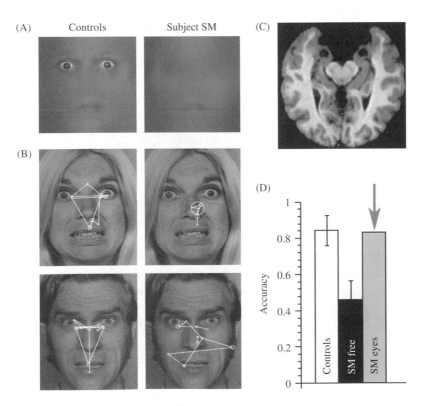

Figure 47.5 Bilateral amygdala lesions impair the use of the eyes and gaze to the eyes during emotion judgment.

Note: Applying the bubbles method (see Adolphs et al., 2005) to identify face areas used during emotion judgment, patient SM (brain shown in C) differed from controls such that controls exhibited much greater use of the eyes than SM, whereas SM did not rely more on any area of the face than did controls (A). While looking at whole faces, SM exhibited abnormal face gaze (B), making far fewer fixations to the eyes than did controls. This was observed across emotions (free viewing, emotion judgment, gender discrimination). When SM was instructed to look at the eyes (D, "SM eyes") in a whole face, she could do this, resulting in a remarkable recovery in ability to recognize the facial expression of fear. From "A Mechanism for Impaired Fear Recognition after Amygdala Damage," by R. Adolphs et al., January 6, 2005, *Nature, 433*, pp. 68–72. Reprinted with permission.

bilateral amygdala damage, the classification image did not contain as much of the eyes. In fact, the impaired use of visual information from the face in subject SM was specific: She failed to make use of high spatial frequency information from the eye region of faces.

In fact, the deficit was even more basic than that: Information about the eye region was not used effectively in subject SM because the eye region was not fixated in the first place. A second experiment measured viewers' eye movements as they judged the emotion shown in facial expressions. While healthy individuals spend a lot of time fixating the eye region of faces, subject SM failed to do so. Thus, her impaired use of visual information about the eye region of the face was likely derivative to an impaired ability to allocate visual attention and fixate the eye region in the first place. Her brain did not possess the mechanism to decide which regions of a face to explore preferentially to glean relevant information about the emotion.

The preceding findings could provide the basis for impaired fear recognition following amygdala damage. Since the eye region of faces is most important to distinguish fear from other emotions, and since SM fails to fixate and make use of information about the eye region of faces, her impaired fear recognition apparently results from her impaired fixation of the eyes in faces. A final experiment tested this interpretation directly: We instructed SM to direct her gaze onto the eyes of other people's faces, and found that this manipulation temporarily allowed her to generate a normal performance on a fear recognition task in which she was otherwise severely impaired.

It is worth noting two key further results from this study. First, SM failed to fixate the eyes in any face, not just facial expressions of fear. In fact, she simply failed to explore faces in general, which included a failure to direct her gaze toward the eye region. Similarly, the abnormal use of information from the eye region held for happy faces as well as for fearful faces. So the impairment in use of information from, and fixation onto, the eyes in faces was general for faces. This general impairment resulted in a relatively specific impairment in fear recognition because the eye region of the face was in fact the most diagnostic for signaling fear, rather than other emotions. Given the recognition tasks we used, this resulted in a severe impairment in recognizing fear, but not in recognizing other emotions. (Interestingly, unpublished data indicate that the same subject does fixate the eye region when the faces are shown inverted. So, while the brain does not need to know that the face is showing fear for the impaired eye fixations to occur, it apparently does need to know that the stimulus is a face; the impairment in fixation does not seem to generalize to objects other than faces, including inverted faces.)

Another point worth noting is that the explicit instruction to fixate the eyes in faces, while rescuing SM's impaired recognition of fear, did so only transiently (as long as that block of the experiment lasted). When later asked to view faces, SM spontaneously reverted to her lack of exploration of the face, and once again showed impaired fear recognition. It may well be that the improvement was not more permanent because SM was not given additional information about her impairment. She was unaware that she failed to fixate the eyes, as she was unaware that her performance in fear recognition was impaired. This raises further questions: Why did she not ask about her performance, why did she not notice that she failed to fixate the eyes? These questions may point toward a broader interpretation of the impairment. SM, as a result of damage to the amygdala, lacked a normal mechanism to explore the environment. An aspect of such an impairment was a failure to fixate the eyes in faces, to explore them normally with her gaze. Another aspect of the impairment was a failure to question what was going on in the experiment in any way, or to monitor her own performance during it. In both cases, there remains a passive ability to process sensory information, but the instrumental component of seeking out such information in the first place has been severely compromised.

A study carried out in rodents and humans provides yet further detail to this picture. The study suggests that the amygdala can respond to stimuli on the basis of their unpredictability alone, apparently without any emotional significance (Herry et al., 2007). In this study, sequences of tones that were unpredictable in time (jittered randomly around a mean intertone interval) activated the amygdala more in both mice and humans and resulted in anxiety-like consequences on cognition and behavior in both species. There was nothing emotional about the tones (they had not been paired with shock, they were not dissonant or particularly loud, and there was nothing else about the experiment that would be expected to make the tones emotional, let alone to make the jittered tones differentially emotional with respect to the regular tones). Yet the mere unpredictability in time of the jittered tones appeared to be sufficient to activate the amygdala (by a cellular mechanism likely relying on differential habituation) and to induce anxiety-like consequences.

This example brings us back to our question about the domain-specificity of social cognition—are there structures for social cognition? Or can all aspects of social cognition ultimately be reduced to more basic and more abstract computations that have nothing to do with the social or with emotions, but merely happen to be important also for those domains (Adolphs, 2003c)? As noted, to fully understand this issue, we would need comparative and developmental studies that can shed light on the evolution of the amygdala's role in social behavior, and the emergence of its function in childhood and adolescence—studies that are now beginning to appear in the literature. There also remain important open questions about the story thus far: While the amygdala indeed appears to respond to unpredictable and ambiguous stimuli, it is unclear whether this needs to be temporal (rather than unpredictable sequences of tones in time, could we perhaps test stimuli that are unpredictable in space?) or is really independent of emotion. (So far, all the unpredictable and ambiguous stimuli used have also been aversive to some extent—is it possible to devise unpredictable yet completely neutral, or even pleasant, stimuli? Would those still activate the amygdala?) Perhaps the most important open question is the relationship between unpredictability and informativeness. It is unclear to what extent unpredictable tone sequences are stimuli that an animal is desperately trying to figure out and to predict, trying to glean information from a stimulus that is in fact uninformative. Perhaps the conjunction of trying hard to predict a stimulus and continuously failing at that effort is driving the saliency of the unpredictable stimuli in the preceding experiment. What would happen if we presented the same kind of unpredictable stimuli but in a context (or, for humans, perhaps with explicit instructions) that makes them uninteresting, so that the animal or the human does not try to process them? Some stimuli in the environment are important if they are unpredictable; they are then surprising. But other stimuli may be boring if they unpredictable because they are deemed to be uninformative noise. Without any basis for making the distinction between these two possibilities, it may be that the brain defaults to assuming the stimuli could be informative, and that is the reason for the observed effects.

SUMMARY

We began this chapter by suggesting ways in which social cognition was distinguished from cognition in general (self-regulation and counterfactual thinking among them), and we have had space only to review the main underpinnings of social cognition. In closing, we want to point toward another distinguishing feature of social cognition that bears considerably on psychopathology: individual differences. It is now commonplace to see neuroimaging studies show at least some figures in which regional brain activation is correlated with a personality dimension, or shown to vary with a genetic polymorphism. Most of these investigations—and much of the history of neuroscientific exploration of social cognition generally—has focused on the implications for pathology. Essentially every psychiatric disorder involves impairments in social behavior and

functioning of some kind—autism, schizophrenia, depression, and anxiety disorders are obvious examples (Cacioppo et al., 2007). Yet, work on individual differences has pointed to the importance of looking for deviations from the norm in the opposite direction as well: What about people who are especially socially skilled, especially empathic, or especially sensitive to social information?

This last question has been taken up by only a handful of investigators (it is telling that the last two chapters of this volume are about pathology, and about avoiding pathology, but not about being "extrasocial"). Two case studies in this literature are worth highlighting—one genetic, the other largely acquired (although this is unclear). The genetic example comes from Williams syndrome, a multisystemic disorder due to a hemideletion of a set of contiguous genes on chromosome 7 (Ewart et al., 1993), all of which have been mapped and are being explored for the individual contributions to the phenotype (Korenberg et al., 2000). In addition to deleterious consequences on organs like the heart (supravalvular aortic stenosis is one aspect of the phenotype that often kills patients relatively early in life), people with Williams syndrome show an unusual cognitive profile: Although language function and face processing are relatively spared, they are devastated in visuospatial cognition (Meyer-Lindenberg et al., 2004). But perhaps most intriguing is their hypersocial behavior: They are extremely interested in other people, take a great interest in how others feel, and use unusual attention-getting devices in their speech.

The interest that people with Williams syndrome show for others is certainly not normal, and it is unlikely that it represents very prosocial behavior on a continuum with normal individual differences. Rather, it seems to arise from dysfunction in specific neural structures such as the amygdala and the prefrontal cortex, that results in an absence of fear of strangers and a disinhibition of approach behaviors. People with Williams syndrome fail to show normal amygdala activation to social stimuli such as fearful facial expressions, yet show exaggerated amygdala activation to nonsocial fearful stimuli, consistent with the high incidence of anxiety and specific phobias in the disorder (Meyer-Lindenberg et al., 2005). Neuropsychological studies have suggested that a failure to inhibit normal social approach behaviors (e.g., caution when approaching strangers) may arise also from frontal lobe dysfunction (Porter, Coltheart, & Langdon, 2007). All these findings argue that hypersociability here is not really an aspect of unusually positive, healthy social behavior; rather, it is pathological social behavior that superficially shows some of the attributes that we would thing of as prosocial.

There are, of course, examples of truly exemplary prosocial behavior—accounts of people who sacrificed their lives to help others are known well enough, and they remain perhaps the strongest examples of truly altruistic behavior in humans. Yet, next to nothing is known about either the processes or the neural substrates behind those individual differences. Are they genetic? Are they learned? Can the behavior be explained by the current frameworks that explain nonreciprocal altruism, and is it mediated by reward and motivation-related structures in the brain that are the same as those revealed in all other studies of motivated instrumental behavior? Or are there examples of prosocial behavior in humans that are really of a different kind? These are provocative questions, and given the increasingly global effects of human social interaction, there is a sense of urgency about gaining insight into them. The next generation of young investigators in social cognitive neuroscience should rise to the challenge.

REFERENCES

Adams, R. B., Gordon, H. L., Baird, A. A., Ambady, N., & Kleck, R. E. (2003, June 6). Effects of gaze on amygdala sensitivity to anger and fear faces. *Science, 300,* 1536.

Adams, R. B., & Kleck, R. E. (2003). Perceived gaze direction and the processing of facial displays of emotion. *Psychological Science, 14,* 644–647.

Adolphs, R. (1999). The human amygdala and emotion. *Neuroscientist, 5,* 125–137.

Adolphs, R. (2003a). Cognitive neuroscience of human social behavior. *Nature Reviews: Neuroscience, 4,* 165–178.

Adolphs, R. (2003b). Investigating the cognitive neuroscience of social behavior. *Neuropsychologia, 41,* 119–126.

Adolphs, R. (2003c). Is the human amygdala specialized for social cognition. In Shinnick-Gallagher et al., (Eds.), *The amygdala in brain function* (Vol. 985, pp. 326–340). New York: Annals of the New York Academy of Sciences.

Adolphs, R., Damasio, H., Tranel, D., Cooper, G., & Damasio, A. R. (2000). A role for somatosensory cortices in the visual recognition of emotion as revealed by 3-D lesion mapping. *Journal of Neuroscience, 20,* 2683–2690.

Adolphs, R., Gosselin, F., Buchanan, T. W., Tranel, D., Schyns, P. G., & Damasio, A. (2005, January 6). A mechanism for impaired fear recognition after amygdala damage. *Nature, 433,* 68–72.

Adolphs, R., & Spezio, M. L. (2006). Role of the amygdala in processing visual social stimuli. *Progressive Brain Research, 156,* 363–378.

Adolphs, R., & Tranel, D. (2000). Emotion recognition and the human amygdala. In J. P. Aggleton (Ed.), *The amygdala: A functional analysis* (pp. 587–630). New York: Oxford University Press.

Adolphs, R., Tranel, D., & Damasio, A. R. (1998, June 4). The human amygdala in social judgment. *Nature, 393,* 470–474.

Adolphs, R., Tranel, D., Damasio, H., & Damasio, A. (1994, December 15). Impaired recognition of emotion in facial expressions following bilateral damage to the human amygdala. *Nature, 372,* 669–672.

Adolphs, R., Tranel, D., Damasio, H., & Damasio, A. R. (1995). Fear and the human amygdala. *Journal of Neuroscience, 15,* 5879–5892.

Adolphs, R., Tranel, D., Hamann, S., Young, A., Calder, A., Anderson, A., et al. (1999). Recognition of facial emotion in nine subjects with bilateral amygdala damage. *Neuropsychologia, 37,* 1111–1117.

Allman, J. M., Hakeem, A., & Watson, K. (2002). Two phylogenetic specializations in the human brain. *Neuroscientist, 8,* 335–346.

Allman, J. M., Watson, K. K., Tetreault, N. A., & Hakeem, A. (2005). Intuition and autism: A possible role for von economo neurons. *Trends in Cognitive Sciences, 9,* 367–373.

Amaral, D. G., Capitanio, J. P., Jourdain, M., Mason, W. A., Mendoza, S. P., & Prather, M. (2003). The amygdala: Is it an essential component of the neural network for social cognition? *Neuropsychologia, 41,* 235–240.

Amaral, D. G., Price, J. L., Pitkanen, A., & Carmichael, S. T. (1992). Anatomical organization of the primate amygdaloid complex. In J. P. Aggleton (Ed.), *The amygdala: Neurobiological aspects of emotion, memory, and mental dysfunction* (pp. 1–66). New York: Wiley-Liss.

Anderson, A. K., & Phelps, E. A. (2000). Expression without recognition: Contributions of the human amygdala to emotional communication. *Psychological Science, 11,* 106–111.

Anderson, A. K., Spencer, D. D., Fulbright, R. K., & Phelps, E. A. (2000). Contribution of the anteromedial temporal lobes to the evaluation of facial emotion. *Neuropsychology, 14,* 526–536.

Anderson, S. W., Bechara, A., Damasio, H., Tranel, D., & Damasio, A. R. (1999). Impairment of social and moral behavior related to early damage in human prefrontal cortex. *Nature Neuroscience, 2,* 1032–1037.

Anderson, S. W., Damasio, H., Tranel, D., & Damasio, A. R. (2000). Long-term sequelae of prefrontal cortex damage acquired in early childhood. *Developmental Neuropsychology, 18,* 281–296.

Bar-On, R. (1997). *The Bar-On Emotional Quotient Inventory (EQ-i): A test of emotional intelligence.* Toronto, Ontario, Canada: Multi-Health Systems.

Bar-On, R., Tranel, D., Denburg, N., & Bechara, A. (2003). Exploring the neurological substrate of emotional and social intelligence. *Brain, 126,* 1790–1800.

Baron-Cohen, S. (1995). *Mindblindness: An essay on autism and theory of mind.* Cambridge, MA: MIT Press.

Baron-Cohen, S., Ring, H. A., Bullmore, E. T., Wheelwright, S., Ashwin, C., & Williams, S. C. R. (2000). The amygdala theory of autism. *Neuroscience and Biobehavioral Reviews, 24,* 355–364.

Baron-Cohen, S., Ring, H. A., Wheelwright, S., Bullmore, E. T., Brammer, M. J., Simmons, A., et al. (1999). Social intelligence in the normal and autistic brain: An fMRI study. *European Journal of Neuroscience, 11,* 1891–1898.

Barrash, J., Tranel, D., & Anderson, S. W. (2000). Acquired personality disturbances associated with bilateral damage to the ventromedial prefrontal region. *Developmental Neuropsychology, 18,* 355–381.

Barrett, L., & Henzi, P. (2005). The social nature of primate cognition. *Proceedings: Biological Sciences, 272,* 1865–1875.

Barrett, L., Henzi, P., & Dunbar, R. (2003). Primate cognition: From "what now?" to "what if?" *Trends in Cognitive Sciences, 7,* 494–497.

Bechara, A., Damasio, A. R., Damasio, H., & Anderson, S. W. (1994). Insensitivity to future consequences following damage to human prefrontal cortex. *Cognition, 50,* 7–15.

Bechara, A., Damasio, H., & Damasio, A. R. (2000). Emotion, decision-making, and the orbitofrontal cortex. *Cerebral Cortex, 10,* 295–307.

Bechara, A., Tranel, D., Damasio, H., Adolphs, R., Rockland, C., & Damasio, A. R. (1995, August 25). Double dissociation of conditioning and declarative knowledge relative to the amygdala and hippocampus in humans. *Science, 269,* 1115–1118.

Benton, A. L., Hamsher, K., Varney, N. R., & Spreen, O. (1983). *Contributions to neuropsychological assessment.* New York: Oxford University Press.

Botvinick, M. M., Cohen, J. D., & Carter, C. S. (2004). Conflict monitoring and anterior cingulate cortex: An update. *Trends in Cognitive Sciences, 8,* 539–546.

Bradbury, J. (2005). Molecular insights into human brain evolution. *PLoS Biology, 3*(3), e50.

Breiter, H. C., Etcoff, N. L., Whalen, P. J., Kennedy, W. A., Rauch, S. L., Buckner, R. L., et al. (1996). Response and habituation of the human amygdala during visual processing of facial expression. *Neuron, 17*, 875–887.

Broks, P., Young, A. W., Maratos, E. J., Coffey, P. J., Calder, A. J., Isaac, C., et al. (1998). Face processing impairments after encephalitis: Amygdala damage and recognition of fear. *Neuropsychologia, 36*, 59–70.

Brown, S., & Shafer, E. A. (1888). An investigation into the functions of the occipital and temporal lobes of the monkey's brain. *Philosophical Transactions of the Royal Society of London. Series B, 179*, 303–327.

Bryson, J. J., Ando, Y., & Lehmann, H. (2007). Agent-based modelling as scientific method: A case study analysing primate social behaviour. *Philosophical Transactions of the Royal Society of London. Series B, 362*, 1685–1698.

Buckner, R. L., & Carroll, D. C. (2006). Self-projection and the brain. *Trends in Cognitive Sciences, 11*, 49–57.

Buechel, C., Morris, J., Dolan, R. J., & Friston, K. J. (1998). Brain systems mediating aversive conditioning: An event-related fMRI study. *Neuron, 20*, 947–957.

Burtsev, M., & Turchin, P. (2006, April 20). Evolution of cooperative strategies from first principles. *Nature, 440*, 1041–1044.

Byrne, R., & Whiten, A. (Eds.). (1988). *Machiavellian intelligence: Social expertise and the evolution of intellect in monkeys, apes, and humans.* Oxford: Clarendon Press.

Cacioppo, J. T., Amaral, D. G., Blanchard, J. J., et al. (2007). Social neuroscience: Progress and implications for mental health. *Social Neuroscience, 2*, 99–123.

Cacioppo, J. T., Berntson, G. G., Adolphs, R., Carter, C. S., Davidson, R. J., McClintock, M. K., et al. (Eds.). (2001). *Foundations in social neuroscience.* Cambridge, MA: MIT Press.

Calder, A. J., Young, A. W., Rowland, D., Perrett, D. I., Hodges, J. R., & Etcoff, N. L. (1996). Facial emotion recognition after bilateral amygdala damage: Differentially severe impairment of fear. *Cognitive Neuropsychology, 13*, 699–745.

Camille, N., Coricelli, G., Sallet, J., Pradat-Diehl, P., Duhamel, J.-R., & Sirigu, A. (2004, May 21). The involvement of the orbitofrontal cortex in the experience of regret. *Science, 304*, 1167–1170.

Chamero, P., Marton, T. F., Logan, D. W., Flanagan, K., Cruz, J. R., Saghatelian, A., et al. (2007, December 6). Identification of protein pheromones that promote aggressive behavior. *Nature, 450*, 899–902.

Conte, R. (2002). Agent-based modeling for understanding social intelligence. *Proceedings of the National Academy of Sciences, USA, 99*, 7189–7190.

Coqueugnlot, H., Hublin, J.-J., Vellon, F., Houet, F., & Jacob, T. (2004, September 16). Early brain growth in *homo erectus* and implications for cognitive ability. *Nature, 431*, 299–332.

Damasio, A. R. (1994). *Descartes' error: Emotion, reason, and the human brain.* New York: Grosset/Putnam.

Damasio, A. R., Tranel, D., & Damasio, H. (1990). Individuals with sociopathic behavior caused by frontal damage fail to respond autonomically to social stimuli. *Behavioral Brain Research, 41*, 81–94.

Damasio, H., Grabowski, T., Frank, R., Galaburda, A. M., & Damasio, A. R. (1994, May 20). The return of Phineas Gage: Clues about the brain from the skull of a famous patient. *Science, 264*, 1102–1104.

Davis, M. (2000). The role of the amygdala in conditioned and unconditioned fear and anxiety. In J. Aggleton (Ed.), *The amygdala. A functional analysis* (pp. 213–288). New York: Oxford University Press.

Davis, M., & Whalen, P. J. (2001). The amygdala: Vigilance and emotion. *Molecular Psychiatry, 6*, 13–34.

Devinsky, O., Morrell, M. J., & Vogt, B. A. (1995). Contributions of anterior cingulate cortex to behavior. *Brain, 118*, 279–306.

Dunbar, R. & Shultz, S. (2007a, September 7). Evolution in the social brain. *Science, 317*, 1344–1347.

Dunbar, R., & Shultz, S. (2007b). Understanding primate brain evolution. *Philosophical Transactions of the Royal Society of London. Series B, 362*, 649–658.

Emery, N. J. (2000). The eyes have it: The neuroethology, function and evolution of social gaze. *Neuroscience and Biobehavioral Reviews, 24*, 581–604.

Emery, N. J., & Amaral, D. G. (1999). The role of the amygdala in primate social cognition. In R. D. Lane & L. Nadel (Eds.), *Cognitive neuroscience of emotion* (pp. 156–191). Oxford: Oxford University Press.

Emery, N. J., Capitanio, J. P., Mason, W. A., Machado, C. J., Mendoza, S. P., & Amaral, D. G. (2001). The effects of bilateral lesions of the amygdala on dyadic social interactions in rhesus monkeys. *Behavioral Neuroscience, 115*, 515–544.

Ewart, A. K., Morris, C. A., Atkinson, D., Jin, W., Sternes, K., Spallone, P., et al. (1993). Hemizygosity at the elastin locus in a developmental disorder, Williams syndrome. *Nature Genetics, 5*, 11–16.

Fine, C., Lumsden, J., & Blair, R. J. R. (2001). Dissociation between "theory of mind" and executive functions in a patient with early left amygdala damage. *Brain, 124*, 287–298.

Gavrilets, S., & Vose, A. (2006). The dynamics of machiavellian intelligence. *Proceedings of the National Academy of Sciences, USA, 103*, 16823–16828.

Gilbert, D. T. (1998). Ordinary personology. In S. T. Fiske, D. T. Gilbert, & G. Lindzey (Eds.), *The handbook of social psychology* (pp. 89–150). New York: McGraw-Hill.

Gilbert, D. T., & Wilson, T. D. (2007, September 7). Prospection: Experiencing the future. *Science, 317*, 1351–1354.

Gilbert, N., & Bankes, S. (2002). Platforms and methods for agent-based modeling. *Proceedings of the National Academy of Sciences, USA, 99*, 7197–7198.

Golby, A. J., Gabrieli, J. D. E., Chiao, J. Y., & Eberhardt, J. L. (2001). Differential responses in the fusiform region to same-race and other-race faces. *Nature Neuroscience, 4*, 845–850.

Goldman, A. I., & Sripada, C. S. (2005). Simulationist models of face-based emotion recognition. *Cognition, 94*, 193–213.

Hadland, K. A., Rushworth, M. F., Gaffan, D., & Passingham, R. E. (2003). The effect of cingulate lesions on social behaviour and emotion. *Neuropsychologia, 41*, 919–931.

Hart, A. J., Whalen, P. J., Shin, L. M., McInerney, S. C., Fischer, H., & Rauch, S. L. (2000). Differential response in the human amygdala to racial outgroup vs ingroup face stimuli. *NeuroReport, 11*, 2351–2355.

Heberlein, A. S., & Adolphs, R. (2004). Impaired spontaneous anthropomorphizing despite intact social knowledge and perception. *Proceedings of the National Academy of Sciences, 101*, 7487–7491.

Herry, C., Bach, D. R., Esposito, F., DiSalle, F., Perrig, W. J., Scheffler, K., et al. (2007). Processing of temporal unpredictability in human and animal amygdala. *Journal of Neuroscience, 27*, 5958–5966.

Hofer, P.-A. (1973). Urbach-Wiethe disease: A review. *Acta Derm Venerol, 53*, 5–52.

Holland, P. C., & Gallagher, M. (1999). Amygdala circuitry in attentional and representational processes. *Trends in Cognitive Sciences, 3*, 65–73.

Hsu, M., Bhatt, M., Adolphs, R., Tranel, D., & Camerer, C. F. (2005, December 9). Neural systems responding to degrees of uncertainty in human decision-making. *Science, 310*, 1680–1683.

Hutchison, W. D., Davis, K. D., Lozano, A. M., Tasker, R. R., & Dostrovsky, J. O. (1999). Pain-related neurons in the human cingulate cortex. *Nature Neuroscience, 2*, 403–405.

Isler, K., & van Schaik, C. P. (2006). Metabolic costs of brain size evolution. *Biology Letters, 2*, 557–560.

Janik, S. W., Wellens, A. R., Goldberg, M. L., & Dell'Osso, L. F. (1978). Eyes as the center of focus in the visual examination of human faces. *Perceptual and Motor Skills, 47*, 857–858.

Kanwisher, N. (2000). Domain specificity in face perception. *Nature Neuroscience, 3,* 759–763.

Kawashima, R., Sugiura, M., Kato, T., Nakamura, A., Natano, K., Ito, K., et al. (1999). The human amygdala plays an important role in gaze monitoring. *Brain, 122,* 779–783.

Keysers, C., Wicker, B., Gazzola, V., Anton, J.-L., Fogassi, L., & Gallese, V. (2004). A touching sight: SII/PV activation during the observation and experience of touch. *Neuron, 42,* 335–346.

Kling, A. S., & Brothers, L. A. (1992). The amygdala and social behavior. In J. P. Aggleton (Ed.), *The amygdala: Neurobiological aspects of emotion, memory, and mental dysfunction* (pp. 353–378). New York: Wiley-Liss.

Kluver, H., & Bucy, P. C. (1937). Psychic blindness and other symptoms following bilateral temporal lobectomy in rhesus monkeys. *American Journal of Physiology, 119,* 352–353.

Kluver, H., & Bucy, P. C. (1939). Preliminary analysis of functions of the temporal lobes in monkeys. *Archives of Neurology and Psychiatry, 42,* 979–997.

Koch, C., & Tsuchiya, N. (2006). Attention and consciousness: Two distinct brain processes. *Trends in Cognitive Sciences, 11,* 16–22.

Koenigs, M., Young, L., Adolphs, R., Tranel, D., Cushman, F., Hauser, M., et al. (2007, April 19). Damage to the prefrontal cortex increases utilitarian moral judgments. *Nature, 446,* 908–911.

Korenberg, J. R., Chen, X.-N., Hirota, H., Lai, Z., Bellugi, U., Burian, D., et al. (2000). Genome structure and cognitive map of Williams syndrome. *Journal of Cognitive Neuroscience, 12,* 89–107.

Machado, C. J., & Bachevalier, J. (2006). The impact of selective amygdala, orbital frontal cortex, or hippocampal formation lesions on established social relationships in rhesus monkeys. *Behavioral Neuroscience, 120,* 761–786.

MacMillan, M. (2000). *An odd kind of fame: Stories of Phineas Gage.* Cambridge, MA: MIT Press.

Maddock, R. J. (1999). The retrosplenial cortex and emotion: New insights from functional neuroimaging of the human brain. *Trends in Neurosciences, 22,* 310–316.

Martin, R. D. (2007). The evolution of human reproduction: A primatological perspective. *American Journal of Physical Anthropology, 134*(Suppl. 45), 59–84.

Meyer-Lindenberg, A., Hariri, A., Munoz, K. E., Mervis, C. B., Mattay, V. S., Morris, C. A., et al. (2005). Neural correlates of genetically abnormal social cognition in Williams syndrome. *Nature Neuroscience, 8,* 991–993.

Meyer-Lindenberg, A., Kohn, P., Mervis, C. B., Kippenhan, J. S., Olsen, R. K., Morris, C. A., et al. (2004). Neural basis of genetically determined visuospatial construction deficit in Williams syndrome. *Neuron, 43,* 623–631.

Mitchell, J. P. (2007). Activity in right temporo-parietal junction is not selective for theory-of-mind. *Cereb Cortex, 18,* 262–271.

Mitchell, J. P., Heatherton, T. F., & Macrae, C. N. (2002). Distinct neural systems subserve person and object knowledge. *Proceedings of the National Academy of Sciences, 99,* 15238–15243.

Moll, J., Zahn, R., de Oliveira-Souza, R., Krueger, F., & Grafman, J. (2005). The neural basis of human moral cognition. *Nature Reviews: Neuroscience, 6,* 799–809.

Morris, J. S., deBonis, M., & Dolan, R. J. (2002). Human amygdala responses to fearful eyes. *NeuroImage, 17,* 214–222.

Morris, J. S., Frith, C. D., Perrett, D. I., Rowland, D., Young, A. W., Calder, A. J., et al. (1996, October 31). A differential neural response in the human amygdala to fearful and happy facial expressions. *Nature, 383,* 812–815.

Nimchinsky, E. A., Gilissen, E., Allman, J. M., Perl, D. P., Erwin, J. M., & Hof, P. R. (1999). A neuronal morphologic type unique to humans and great apes. *Proceedings of the National Academy of Sciences, 96,* 5268–5273.

Ochsner, K. N., Bunge, S. A., Gross, J. J., & Gabrieli, J. D. E. (2002). Rethinking feelings: An fMRI study of the cognitive regulation of emotion. *Journal of Cognitive Neuroscience, 14,* 1215–1229.

Ochsner, K. N., & Gross, J. J. (2005). The cognitive control of emotions. *Trends in Cognitive Sciences, 9,* 242–249.

Ochsner, K. N., Knierim, K., Ludlow, D. H., Hanelin, J., Ramachandran, T., Glover, G., et al. (2004). Reflecting upon feelings: An fMRI study of neural systems supporting the attribution of emotion to self and other. *Journal of Cognitive Neuroscience, 16,* 1746–1772.

Ochsner, K. N., & Lieberman, M. D. (2001). The emergence of social cognitive neuroscience. *American Psychologist, 56,* 717–734.

Parvizi, J., Van Hoesen, G. W., Buckwalter, J., & Damasio, A. R. (2006). Neural connections of the posteromedial cortex in the macaque. *Proceedings of the National Academy of Sciences, USA, 103,* 1563–1568.

Phelps, E. A., Cannistraci, C. J., & Cunningham, W. A. (2003). Intact performance on an indirect measure of race bias following amygdala damage. *Neuropsychologia, 41,* 203–209.

Phelps, E. A., O'Connor, K. J., Cunningham, W. A., Funayama, E. S., Gatenby, J. C., Gore, J. C., et al. (2000). Performance on indirect measures of race evaluation predicts amygdala activation. *Journal of Cognitive Neuroscience, 12,* 729–738.

Porter, M. A., Coltheart, M., & Langdon, R. (2007). The neuropsychological basis of hypersociability in Williams and Down syndrome. *Neuropsychologia, 45,* 2839–2849.

Prather, M. D., Lavenex, P., Mauldin-Jourdain, M. L., Mason, W. A., Capitanio, J. P., Mendoza, S. P., et al. (2001). Increased social fear and decreased fear of objects in monkeys with neonatal amygdala lesions. *Neuroscience, 106,* 653–658.

Putnam, R. D. (2000). *Bowling alone: The collapse and revival of American community.* New York: Simon & Schuster.

Raichle, M. A., Macleod, A. M., Snyder, A. Z., Powers, W. J., Gusnard, D. A., & Shulman, G. L. (2001). A default mode of brain function. *Proceedings of the National Academy of Sciences, USA, 98,* 676–682.

Rilling, J., Gutman, D., Zeh, T., Pagnoni, G., Berns, G., & Kilts, C. (2002). A neural basis for social cooperation. *Neuron, 35,* 395–405.

Rosvold, H. E., Mirsky, A. F., & Pribram, K. (1954). Influence of amygdalectomy on social behavior in monkeys. *Journal of Comparative and Physiological Psychology, 47,* 173–178.

Roth, G., & Dicke, U. (2005). Evolution of the brain and intelligence. *Trends in Cognitive Sciences, 9,* 250–257.

Rudebeck, P. H., Buckley, M. J., Walton, M. E., & Rushworth, M. F. (2006). A role for the macaque anterior cingulate gyrus in social valuation. *Science, 313,* 310–313.

Ruff, C. B., Trinkaus, E., & Holliday, T. W. (1997, May 8). Body mass and encephalization in pleistocene homo. *Nature, 387,* 173–176.

Saver, J. L., & Damasio, A. R. (1991). Preserved access and processing of social knowledge in a patient with acquired sociopathy due to ventromedial frontal damage. *Neuropsychologia, 29,* 1241–1249.

Saxe, R. (2006). Why and how to study theory of mind with fMRI. *Brain Research, 1079,* 57–65.

Saxe, R., & Kanwisher, N. (2003). People thinking about thinking people: The role of the temporo-parietal junction in theory of mind. *NeuroImage, 19,* 1835–1842.

Saxe, R., & Powell, L. J. (2006). It's the thought that counts: Specific brain regions for one component of theory of mind. *Psychological Sciences, 17,* 692–699.

Saxe, R., & Wexler, A. (2005). Making sense of another mind: The role of the right temporo-parietal junction. *Neuropsychologia, 43,* 1391–1399.

Schmolck, H., & Squire, L. R. (2001). Impaired perception of facial emotions following bilateral damage to the anterior temporal lobe. *Neuropsychology, 15,* 30–38.

Semendeferi, K., Armstrong, E., Schleicher, A., Zilles, K., & Van Hoesen, G. W. (1998). Limbic frontal cortex in hominoids: A comparative study of area 13. *American Journal of Physical Anthropology, 106,* 129–155.

Semendeferi, K., Armstrong, E., Schleicher, A., Zilles, K., & Van Hoesen, G. W. (2001). Prefrontal cortex in humans and apes: A comparative study of area 10. *American Journal of Physical Anthropology, 114,* 224–241.

Semendeferi, K., & Damasio, H. (2000). The brain and its main anatomical subdivisions in living hominoids using magnetic resonance imaging. *Journal of Human Evolution, 38,* 317–332.

Semendeferi, K., Damasio, H., Frank, R., & Van Hoesen, G. W. (1997). The evolution of the frontal lobes: A volumetric analysis based on three-dimensional reconstructions of magnetic resonance scans of human and ape brains. *Journal of Human Evolution, 32,* 375–388.

Shamay-Tsoory, S. G., Tomer, R., Berger, B. D., & Aharon-Peretz, J. (2003). Characterization of empathy deficits following prefrontal brain damage: The role of the right ventromedial prefrontal cortex. *Journal of Cognitive Neuroscience, 15,* 324–337.

Shamay-Tsoory, S. G., Tomer, R., Berger, B. D., Goldsher, D., & Aharon-Peretz, J. (2005). Impaired "affective theory of mind" is associated with right ventromedial prefrontal damage. *Cognitive and Behavioral Neurology, 18*(1), 55–67.

Siebert, M., Markowitsch, H. J., & Bartel, P. (2003). Amygdala, affect and cognition: Evidence from 10 patients with Urbach-Wiethe disease. *Brain, 126,* 2627–2637.

Sohn, M. H., Albert, M. V., Jung, K., Carter, C. S., & Anderson, J. R. (2007). Anticipation of conflict monitoring in the anterior cingulate cortex and the prefrontal cortex. *Proceedings of the National Academy of Sciences, USA, 104,* 10330–10334.

Sprengelmeyer, R., Young, A. W., Schroeder, U., Grossenbacher, P. G., Federlein, J., Buttner, T., et al. (1999). Knowing no fear. *Philosophical Transactions of the Royal Society, Series B, Biological Sciences, 266,* 2451–2456.

Tarr, M. J., & Gauthier, I. (2000). FFA: A flexible fusiform area for subordinate-level visual processing automatized by expertise. *Nature Neuroscience, 3,* 764–769.

Tranel, D., Bechara, A., & Denburg, N. L. (2002). Asymmetric functional roles of right and left ventromedial prefrontal cortices in social conduct, decision-making, and emotional processing. *Cortex, 38,* 589–612.

Tranel, D., Damasio, H., Denburg, N., & Bechara, A. (2005). Does gender play a role in functional asymmetry of ventromedial prefrontal cortex? *Brain, 128,* 2872–2881.

Tranel, D., & Hyman, B. T. (1990). Neuropsychological correlates of bilateral amygdala damage. *Archives of Neurology, 47,* 349–355.

Tsuchiya, N., & Adolphs, R. (2007). Emotion and consciousness. *Trends in Cognitive Sciences, 11,* 158–167.

Veenstra, G. (2002). Explicating social capital: Trust and participation in the civil space. *Canadian Journal of Sociology, 27,* 547–572.

Vogt, B. A. (2005). Pain and emotion interactions in subregions of the cingulate gyrus. *Nature Reviews: Neuroscience, 6,* 533–544.

Vollm, B. A., Taylor, A. N., Richardson, P., Corcoran, R., Stirling, J., McKie, S., et al. (2006). Neuronal correlates of theory of mind and empathy: A functional magnetic resonance imaging study in a nonverbal task. *NeuroImage, 29,* 90–98.

Whalen, P. J. (1999). Fear, vigilance, and ambiguity: Initial neuroimaging studies of the human amygdala. *Current Directions in Psychological Science, 7,* 177–187.

Whalen, P. J., Kagan, J., Cook, R. G., Davis, F. C., Kim, H., Polis, S., et al. (2004, December 17). Human amygdala responsivity to masked fearful eye whites. *Science, 306,* 2061.

Whalen, P. J., Shin, L. M., McInerney, S. C., Fischer, H., Wright, C. I., & Rauch, S. L. (2001). A functional MRI study of human amygdala responses to facial expressions of fear versus anger. *Emotion, 1,* 70–83.

Whiten, A., & Byrne, R. (Eds.). (1997). *Machiavellian intelligence: Pt. II. Extensions and evaluations.* Cambridge, England: Cambridge University.

Wicker, B., Perrett, D. I., Baron-Cohen, S., & Decety, J. (2003). Being the target of another's emotion: A PET study. *Neuropsychologia, 41,* 139–146.

Young, A. W., Hellawell, D. J., Van de Wal, C., & Johnson, M. (1996). Facial expression processing after amygdalotomy. *Neuropsychologia, 34,* 31–39.

Chapter 48

Empathy and Intersubjectivity

JEAN DECETY AND CLAUS LAMM

Human beings are intrinsically social. Our survival critically depends on social interactions with others, the formation of alliances, and accurate social judgments (Cacioppo, 2002). We are motivated to form and maintain positive and significant relationships (Baumeister & Leary, 1995), and most of our actions are directed toward or are responses to others (Batson, 1990). No single factor can account for human social cognitive evolution (e.g., diet and climate), but the single most important factor is the increasing complexity of hominid social groups (Bjorklund & Bering, 2003). It is therefore logical that dedicated mechanisms have evolved to perceive, understand, predict, and respond to the internal states (subjective in nature) of other individuals.

The construct of empathy accounts for a fundamental aspect of social interaction (see Table 48.1 for definitions). Philosophers and psychologists have long debated the nature of empathy (e.g., Ickes, 2003; Smith, 1790; Thompson, 2001), and whether the capacity to share and understand other people's emotions sets humans apart from other species (e.g., de Waal, 2005). Here, we consider empathy as a construct accounting for a sense of similarity in feelings experienced by the self and the other, without confusion between the two individuals (Decety & Jackson, 2004; Decety & Lamm, 2006; Eisenberg, Spinrad, & Sadovsky, 2006). The experience of empathy can lead to sympathy (concern for another based on the apprehension or comprehension of the other's emotional state or condition), or even personal distress (an aversive, self-focused emotional reaction to the apprehension or comprehension of another's emotional state or condition) when there is confusion between self and other. Knowledge of empathic behavior is essential for an understanding of human social and moral development (Eisenberg et al., 1994). It is generally assumed that people who experience others' emotion and feel concerned for them are motivated to help (Hoffman, 2000). Furthermore, psychopathologies are marked by

empathy deficits, and a wide array of psychotherapeutic approaches stress clinical empathy as a fundamental component of treatment (Farrow & Woodruff, 2007). These are all good reasons to investigate the computational and biological mechanisms that underpin the processes involved in interpersonal sensitivity and intersubjectivity.

There has been a great upsurge in neuroimaging investigations of empathy. Most of these investigations reflect the approach of social neuroscience, which combines research designs and behavioral measures used in social psychology with neuroscience markers (Cacioppo, 2002; Cacioppo, Berntson, Sheridan, & McClintock, 2000). Such an approach plays an important role in disambiguating competing theories in social psychology in general and in empathy-related research in particular (Decety & Hodges, 2006). For example, a critical question debated among social psychologists is whether perspective-taking instructions induce empathic concern or personal distress, and to what extent prosocial motivation springs from self-other overlap.

In this chapter, we focus on social neuroscience research exploring how people respond behaviorally and neurally to the pain of others. The perception of pain in others constitutes an ecologically valid way to investigate the mechanisms underpinning the experience of empathy for two reasons: First everybody knows what pain is—it is a common and universal experience—and knows its physical and psychological manifestations; second, we have good knowledge about the neurophysiological pathways involved in processing nociceptive information.

Findings from recent functional neuroimaging studies of pain empathy demonstrate that an observer's mere perception of another individual in pain results in the activation of the neural network involved in processing the firsthand experience of pain. This intimate (yet not complete) overlap between the neural circuits responsible for our ability to perceive the pain of others and those underpinning our own self-experience of pain supports the shared-representation theory of social cognition (Decety & Sommerville, 2003). This theory posits that perceiving someone else's emotion

The writing was supported by grant #BCS-0718480 to Dr. Jean Decety from the National Science Foundation.

TABLE 48.1   Despite the abundance of definitions of empathy, it is possible and recommended to differentiate emotional contagion, empathy, sympathy, and personal distress.

Term	Definition
Emotional contagion	The tendency to automatically mimic and synchronize facial expressions, vocalizations, postures, and movements with those of another individual.
Empathy	An emotional response that stems from another's state and is congruent with the other's emotional state. It involves at least a minimal distinction between self and other. Empathy is not a separate emotion, but a kind of induction process by which emotions, both positive and negative, are shared.
Personal distress	An aversive state (e.g., anxiety, worry) that is not congruent with the other's state and that leads to a self-oriented, egoistic reaction.
Sympathy (or empathic concern)	A reference to feelings of sorrow or of being sorry for another. It is often the consequence of empathy, although it is possible that sympathy results from cognitive perspective taking. Sympathy is believed to involve an other-oriented, altruistic motivation.
Emotion	A process that facilitates appropriate physiological responses to aid the survival of the organism.

and having an emotional response or subjective feeling state fundamentally draw on the same computational processes and rely on somatosensory and motor representations (Sommerville & Decety, 2006). However, a complete self-other overlap in neural circuits can lead to personal distress and possibly be detrimental to empathic concern and prosocial behavior. Personal distress may even result in a more egoistic motivation to reduce it by withdrawing from the stressor, thereby decreasing the likelihood of prosocial behavior (Tice, Bratslavsky, & Baumeister, 2001).

The chapter starts with a discussion of the evolutionary origins of empathy focusing on the role of the autonomic nervous system, followed by a section on the role of hormones. Then, we review the empirical evidence that supports the notion of shared neural circuits for the generation of behavior in oneself and its perception from others. We emphasize recent functional neuroimaging studies showing the involvement of shared neural circuits during the observation of pain in others and during the experience of pain in the self. Next, we discuss how perspective taking and the ability to differentiate the self from the other affect this sharing mechanism. Finally, we examine how some interpersonal variables modulate empathic concern and personal distress. The chapter concludes with cautionary considerations about the social neuroscience approach to intersubjective processes.

THE EVOLUTIONARY ORIGINS OF EMPATHY

Natural selection has fine-tuned the mechanisms that serve the specific demands of each species' ecology. MacLean (1985) has proposed that empathy emerged in relation with the evolution of mammals (180 million years ago). In the evolutionary transition from reptiles to mammals, three

key developments were (1) nursing, in conjunction with maternal care; (2) audiovocal communication for maintaining maternal-offspring contact; and (3) play. The development of this behavioral triad may have depended on the evolution of the thalamocingulate division of the limbic system, a derivative from early mammals. The thalamocingulate division (which has no distinctive counterpart in the reptilian brain) is, in turn, geared in with the prefrontal neocortex that, in human beings, may be inferred to play a key role in familial acculturation. When mammals developed parenting behavior, the stage was set for increased exposure and responsiveness to emotional signals of others including signals of pain, separation, and distress. Indeed, parenting involves the protection and transfer of energy, information, and social relations to offspring. African hominoids, including chimpanzees *(Pan troglodytes),* gorillas *(Gorilla gorilla),* and humans *(Homo sapiens),* share a number of parenting mechanisms with other placental mammals, including internal gestation, lactation, and attachment mechanisms involving neuropeptides such as oxytocin (Geary & Flinn, 2001).

The phylogenic origin of behaviors associated with social engagement has been linked to the evolution of the autonomic nervous system and how it relates to emotion. According to Porges (2001), social approach or withdrawal stems from the implicit computation of feelings of safety, discomfort, or potential danger. He proposed that the evolution of the autonomic nervous system (sympathetic and parasympathetic systems) provides a means to understand the adaptive significance of mammalian affective processes including empathy and the establishment of lasting social bonds. These basic evaluative systems are associated with motor responses that aid the adaptive responding of the organism. At this primitive level, appetitive and aversive behavioral responses are modulated by specific neural circuits in the brain that share common neuroarchitectures among mammals (Parr & Waller, 2007). These brain systems are genetically hardwired to enable animals to respond unconditionally to threatening, or appetitive, stimuli using specific response patterns that are most adaptive to the particular species and environmental condition. The limbic system, which includes the hypothalamus, the parahippocampal cortex, the amygdala, and several interconnected areas (septum, basal ganglia, nucleus accumbens, insula, retrospenial cingulate cortex, and prefrontal cortex) is primarily responsible for emotion processing. What unites these regions are their roles in motivation and emotion, mediated by connections with the autonomic system. The limbic system also projects to the cingulate and orbitofrontal cortices, which are involved with the regulation of emotion.

There is evidence for a lateralization of emotion processing in humans and primates that has been marshaled under two distinct theories. One theory states that the right hemisphere is primarily responsible for emotional processing (Cacioppo & Gardner, 1999), whereas another one suggests that the right hemisphere regulates negative emotion and the left hemisphere regulates positive emotion (Davidson, 1992). This asymmetry is anatomically based on an asymmetrical representation of homeostatic activity that originates from asymmetries in the peripheral autonomic nervous system, and fits well with the homeostatic model of emotional awareness, which posits that emotions are organized according to the fundamental principle of autonomic opponency for the management of physical and mental energy (Craig, 2005). Supporting evidence for the lateralization of emotion comes from neuroimaging studies and neuropsychological observations with brain-damaged patients, as well as studies in nonhuman primates. In one study, tympanic membrane temperature (Tty) was used to assess asymmetries in the perception of emotional stimuli in chimpanzees (Parr & Hopkins, 2000). The tympanic membrane is an indirect, but reliable, site from which to measure brain temperature and is strongly influenced by autonomic and behavioral activity. In that study, chimpanzees were shown positive, neutral, and negative emotional videos depicting scenes of play, scenery, and severe aggression, respectively. During the negative emotional condition, right Tty was significantly higher than the baseline temperature. This effect was relatively stable, long lasting, and consistent across individuals. Temperatures did not change significantly from baseline in the neutral or positive emotion condition, although a significant number of measurements showed increased left Tty during the neutral emotion condition. These data suggest that viewing emotional stimuli results in asymmetrical changes in brain temperature (in particular increased right Tty during the negative emotion condition), providing evidence of emotional

arousal in chimpanzees and support for right hemispheric asymmetry in our closest living ancestor.

At the behavioral level, it is evident from the descriptions of comparative psychologists and ethologists that behaviors homologous to empathy can be observed in other mammalian species. Notably, reports on ape empathic reactions suggest that, apart from emotional connectedness, apes have an explicit appreciation of the other's situation (de Waal, 1996). A good example is consolation, defined as reassurance behavior by an uninvolved bystander toward one of the combatants in a previous aggressive incident (de Waal & van Roosmalen, 1979). De Waal (1996) has convincingly argued that empathy is not an all-or-nothing phenomenon, and many forms of empathy exist between the extremes of mere agitation at the distress of another and full understanding of their predicament. Many other comparative psychologists view empathy as a kind of induction process by which emotions, both positive and negative, are shared, and by which the probabilities of similar behavior are increased in the participants. In the view developed in this chapter, this is a necessary but not a sufficient mechanism to account for the full-blown ability of human empathy. It does provide the basic primitive, yet crucial mechanism on which empathy develops. Some aspects of empathy are present in other species, such as motor mimicry and emotion contagion (see de Waal & Thompson, 2005). Parr (2001) conducted an experiment in which peripheral skin temperature (indicating greater negative arousal) was measured in chimpanzees while they were exposed to emotionally negative video scenes. Results demonstrate that skin temperature decreased when subjects viewed videos of conspecifics injected with needles or videos of the needles themselves, but not videos of a conspecific chasing the veterinarian. Thus, when chimpanzee are exposed to meaningful emotional stimuli, they are subject to physiological changes similar to those observed during fear in humans, which is similar to the dispositional effects of emotional contagion (Hatfield, 2009).

In humans, the construct of empathy accounts for a more complex psychological state than the one associated with the automatic sharing of emotions. As in other species, emotions and feelings may be shared between individuals, but humans also can intentionally "feel for" and act on behalf of other people whose experiences may differ greatly from their own (Batson et al., 1991; Decety & Hodges, 2006). This phenomenon, called *empathic concern* or *sympathy,* is often associated with prosocial behaviors such as helping kin, and has been considered as a chief enabling process for altruism. According to Wilson (1988), empathic helping behavior has evolved because of its contribution to genetic fitness (kin selection). In humans and other mammals, an impulse to care for offspring is almost certainly genetically hardwired. It is far less clear that an impulse to care for siblings, more remote kin, and similar nonkin is genetically hardwired (Batson, 2006). The emergence of altruism, of empathizing with and caring for those who are not kin is thus not easily explained within the framework of neo-Darwinian theories of natural selection. Social learning explanations of kinship patterns in human helping behavior are thus highly plausible.

One of the most striking aspects of human empathy is that it can be felt for virtually any target—even targets of a different species. In addition, as emphasized by Harris (2000), humans, unlike other primates, can put their emotions into words, allowing them not only to express emotion but also to report on current as well as past emotions. These reports provide an opportunity to share, explain, and regulate emotional experience that is not found in other species. Conversation helps to develop empathy, for it is often here that people learn of shared experiences and feelings. Moreover, this self-reflexive capability (which includes emotion regulation) may be an important difference between humans and other animals (Povinelli, 2001).

Two key regions, the anterior insula and anterior cingulate cortex (ACC), involved in affective processing in general and empathy for pain in particular, have singularly evolved in apes and humans. Cytoarchitectonic work by Allman, Watson, Tetreault, and Hakeem (2005) indicates that a population of large spindle neurons is uniquely found in the anterior insula and anterior cingulate of humanoid primates. Most notably, they reported a trenchant phylogenetic correlation, in that spindle cells are most numerous in aged humans, but progressively less numerous in children, gorillas, bonobos and chimpanzees, and nonexistent in macaque monkeys. Craig (2007) recently suggested that these spindle neurons interconnect the most advanced portions of limbic sensory (anterior insula) and limbic motor (ACC) cortices, both ipsilaterally and contralaterally. This is in sharp contrast to the tightly interconnected and contiguous sensorimotor cortices, which are situated physically far apart as a consequence of the pattern of evolutionary development of limbic cortices. Thus, the spindle neurons could enable fast, complex, and highly integrated emotional behaviors. In support of this view, convergent functional imaging findings reveal that the anterior insula and the anterior cingulate cortices are conjointly activated during all human emotions. According to Craig (2002), this indicates that the limbic sensory representation of subjective feelings (in the anterior insula) and the limbic motor representation of volitional agency (in the anterior cingulate) together form the fundamental neuroanatomical basis for all human emotions, consistent with the definition of an emotion in humans as both a feeling and a motivation with concomitant autonomic sequelae (Rolls, 1999).

Overall, this evolutionary conceptual view is compatible with the hypothesis that advanced levels of social cognition may have arisen as an emergent property of powerful executive functioning assisted by the representational properties of language (Barrett, Henzi, & Dunbar, 2003). These higher levels operate on previous levels of organization and should not be seen as independent of, or conflicting with one another. Evolution has constructed layers of increasing complexity, from nonrepresentational (e.g., emotion contagion) to representational and meta-representational mechanisms (e.g., sympathy), which need to be taken into account for a full understanding of human empathy.

NEUROENDOCRINOLOGICAL ASPECTS

Although we prefer to believe that our behavior is largely dependent on the processes in the central nervous system, other factors such as hormonal status or autonomic nervous system activity have to be taken into account if we want to achieve an accurate understanding of human social interaction. Hormones affect the body and the nervous system in various ways and shape the way in which our bodies and minds are affected by social interactions. As will be exemplified later in this chapter, individual differences in stress coping mechanisms may determine how we respond to another's distress. A potential mechanism for these individual differences is the release of stress hormones such as cortisol, which has been shown to affect approach and withdrawal responses to threatening social stimuli (Roelofs, Elzinga, & Rotteveel, 2005). In a similar vein, the neuropeptides oxytocin (OT) and vasopressin (VP) have been repeatedly associated with individual differences in social cognition and behaviors. In nonhuman mammals, oxytocin is a key mediator of complex emotional and social behaviors, including attachment, social recognition, and aggression. It has been shown in prairie voles (Microtus ochrogaster) that OT facilitates positive social behaviors and promotes social attachment, such as parental and pair bonding behavior (Carter, Williams, Witt, & Insel, 1992). Among other mechanisms, OT seems to exert these effects by enabling a more adaptive response of the organism to stressful events. OT achieves this by modulating autonomic arousal, in particular by reducing activity of the hypothalamic-pituitary-adrenal (HPA) axis. The HPA axis strongly affects how we react to stressors by increasing sympathetic arousal via the release of stress hormones such as cortisol in humans or corticosterone in rodents. Importantly, the effects of the HPA axis are rather slow and tonic and sometimes persist over extended periods—acting via changes in gene expression both in the body and in the brain. This is in contrast to the second system involved in stress responses, the sympathetic-adrenomedullary system, which triggers fast mobilization of vital resources by the release of adrenalin and noradrenalin (Gunnar & Quevedo, 2007, for review).

Interestingly, OT and VP receptors are found in areas of the nervous system associated with regulation of HPA axis and autonomic nervous system activity. In addition, OT and VP receptors in brain structures associated with social behaviors and emotional processing might be the central nervous system substrates for the facilitating effects these hormones have on social interactions. For example, OT receptors are found in the amygdala, the medial prefrontal cortex, and the septum. Selective effects of OT on these regions have been demonstrated both in nonhuman mammals and in humans. The amygdala plays a central role in autonomic function and has been linked to fear and associated automatic responses to environmental threats (e.g., LeDoux, 2000). The anxiolytic and calming role of OT might be achieved by acting on receptors in this subcortical structure. Microinjections of OT in the central nucleus of the amygdala inhibit aggressive maternal behavior in female rats (Consiglio, Borsoi, Pereira, & Lucion, 2005), in line with the finding that OT excites inhibitory neurons in the central amygdala (Huber, Veinante, & Stoop, 2005). In humans, neuroimaging demonstrates reduced amygdala responses to social and nonsocial stimuli after intranasal administration of OT (Kirsch et al., 2005). Individual OT levels also seem to be related to human trust and trustworthiness—as shown by a higher level of trust in an economic exchange game requiring participants to accept social risks (Kosfeld, Heinrichs, Zak, Fischbacher, & Fehr, 2005) or as expressed by higher OT levels with higher intentional trust in a similar experimental context (Zak, Kurzban, & Matzner, 2005).

The effects of OT in promoting social attachment led to speculations that it also plays a role for empathic concern, sympathy, and prosocial behavior. OT and VP are also potential candidates to explain the etiology of autism spectrum disorders (Carter, 2007, for review). ASD are characterized by deficits in social behavior and communication, with one distinctive feature being deficits in theory of mind (the ability to reason about intentions and beliefs of others) and empathy. In line with this idea, preliminary evidence from a small sample of ASD participants showed better comprehension of affective speech and the assignment of emotional significance to speech intonation with OT administration (Hollander et al., 2007). In the normal behavioral spectrum, OT enhanced the ability to infer others' mental states by interpreting subtle social cues expressed in the eye region. Notably, this effect was only observed for more difficult emotional-social expressions

(Domes, Heinrichs, Glascher, et al., 2007). In a companion study, the same group demonstrated that activation in the right (but not the left) amygdala is reduced when presenting facial displays of emotions—irrespective of their valence (Domes, Heinrichs, Michel, Berger, & Herpertz, 2007). A potential mechanism of OT in enabling empathy and reading the intentions of others might be a general reduction of arousal and anxiety usually triggered by social and nonsocial stressors. This should allow for a more controlled processing of social cues and a more adaptive response to the emotional state of others. This hypothesis would be in line with evidence from social psychology showing that the need to belong to others—which can be interpreted as a measure of social attachment or the motivation for it—correlates with higher empathic accuracy for both positive and negative affective information (Pickett, Gardner, & Knowles, 2004). Alternatively, and as speculated by Domes and colleagues, OT-induced increases in empathy and mind reading might reduce social ambiguity and by this means encourage social approach and trusting behavior.

While research on OT and human social behavior is still in its infancy, future investigations will have to show which neural and neuronal-hormonal mechanisms are at play when it exerts its effects. The available evidence indicates a promising role of OT for promoting intersubjective understanding and prosocial behavior.

SHARED NEURAL CIRCUITS BETWEEN SELF AND OTHER

It has long been suggested that empathy involves resonating with another person's unconscious affect. Ax in 1964 proposed that empathy can be thought of as an autonomic nervous system state that tends to simulate the state of another person. In the same vein, Basch (1983) speculated that, because their respective autonomic nervous systems are genetically programmed to respond in a similar fashion, a given affective expression by a member of a particular species can trigger similar responses in other members of that species. This idea fits neatly with the notion of embodiment, which refers both to actual bodily states and to simulations of experience in the brain's modality-specific systems for perception, action, and the introspective systems that underlie conscious experiences of emotion, motivation, and cognitive operations (Niedenthal, Barsalou, Winkielman, Krauth-Gruber, & Ric, 2005). Furthermore, the view that unconscious automatic mimicry of a target generates in the observer the autonomic response associated with that bodily state and facial expression subsequently received empirical support from behavioral and physiological studies marshaled under the perception-action coupling account of empathy (Preston & de Waal, 2002). The core assumption of the perception-action model of empathy is that perceiving a target's state automatically activates the corresponding representations of that state in the observer, which in turn activates somatic and autonomic responses. The discovery of sensory-motor neurons (called *mirror neurons*) in the premotor and posterior parietal cortex discharging both during the production of a given action and the perception of the same action performed by another individual provides the physiological mechanism for this direct link between perception and action (Rizzolatti & Craighero, 2004).

In line with the perception-action matching mechanism, a number of behavioral and electromygraphic studies demonstrated that viewing facial expressions triggers similar expressions on viewer's own face, even in the absence of conscious recognition of the stimulus (Hatfield, Cacioppo, & Rapson, 1994). While watching someone smile, the observer activates the same facial muscles involved in producing a smile at a subthreshold level, and this would create the corresponding feeling of happiness in the observer. There is evidence for such a mechanism in the recognition of emotion from facial expression. Viewing facial expressions triggers expressions on one's own face, even in the absence of conscious recognition of the stimulus (Dimberg, Thunberg, & Elmehed, 2000). Making a facial expression generates changes in the autonomic nervous system and is associated with feeling the corresponding emotion. In a series of experiments, Levenson, Ekman, and Friesen (1990) instructed participants to produce facial configurations for anger, disgust, fear, happiness, sadness, and surprise while heart rate, skin conductance, finger temperature, and somatic activity were monitored. They found that such a voluntary facial activity produced significant levels of subjective experience of the associated emotions as well as specific and reliable autonomic measures. A functional magnetic resonance imaging (fMRI) experiment extended these results by showing that when participants are required to observe or to imitate facial expressions of various emotions, increased neurodynamic activity is detected in the brain regions implicated in the facial expressions of these emotions, including the superior temporal sulcus, the anterior insula, and the amygdala, as well as specific areas of the premotor cortex (Carr, Iacoboni, Dubeau, Mazziotta, & Lenzi, 2003).

Accumulating evidence suggests that a mirroring or resonance mechanism is also at play both when one experiences sensory and affective feelings in the self and perceives them in others. Even at the level of the somatosensory cortex, seeing another's neck or face being touched elicits appropriately organized somatotopic activations in the mind of the observer (Blakemore, Bristow, Bird, Frith, & Ward, 2005). Robust support for the involvement of shared neural circuits in the perception of affective states comes from recent neuroimaging and transcranial magnetic stimulation (TMS). The firsthand experience of disgust and the sight of disgusted facial expressions in others both activate the anterior insula (Wicker et al., 2003). Similarly, the observation of hand and face actions performed with an emotion engages regions that are also involved in the perception and experience of emotion and communication (Grosbras & Paus, 2006).

PERCEIVING OTHERS IN PAIN

Pain is conceived as a subjective experience triggered by the activation of a mental/neural representation of actual or potential tissue damage. This representation involves somatic sensory features, as well as affective-motivational reactions associated with the promotion of protective or recuperative visceromotor and behavioral responses. It is the affective experience of pain that signals an aversive state and motivates behavior to terminate, reduce, or escape exposure to the source of noxious stimulation (Price, 2000). The expression of pain also provides a crucial signal that can motivate soothing and caring behaviors in others. It is therefore a valuable and ecologically valid means to investigate the mechanisms underlying the experience of empathy.

A growing body of research demonstrates shared physiological mechanisms for the firsthand experience of pain and the perception of pain in others (Figure 48.1). A specific indication for such a shared neural mechanism comes from a single-cell recordings study in neurological patients by Hutchison, Davis, Lozano, Tasker, and Dostrovsky (1999). These authors recorded with microelectrodes from the dorsal ACC as several types of painful stimuli were delivered to the patients' hands, and found stimulus-specific pain responses in Brodmann area 24. Some of these cells displayed mirror-like properties, as they responded to the pinprick whether it was administered to the patient's own hand or to that of the experimenter.

The first functional MRI experiment that investigated neural responses to both the firsthand experience of pain and perception of pain in others was conducted by Morrison, Lloyd, di Pellegrino, and Roberts (2004). Study participants were scanned during a condition of feeling a moderately painful pinprick stimulus to the fingertips and another condition in which they watched another person's hand undergo similar stimulation. Both conditions resulted in common hemodynamic activity in a pain-related area in the right dorsal ACC. In contrast, the primary somatosensory cortex showed significant activations in response to noxious tactile, but not visual, stimuli.

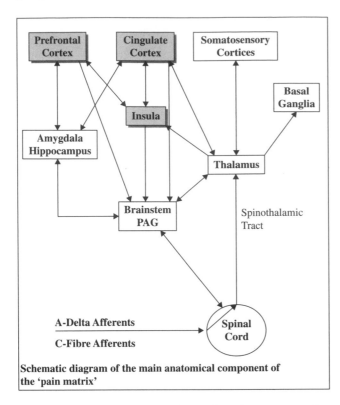

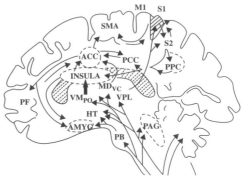

→ **The primary (SI) and secondary (SII) sensory cortices are** involved in the sensory-discriminative aspect of pain, e.g., the bodily location and intensity of the stimulus.

→ **ACC and insula** subserve the affective-motivational component, i.e., the evaluation of subjective discomfort and response preparation in the context of painful or aversive stimuli

Figure 48.1 Neurophysiological research on pain points out a distinction between the sensory-discriminative aspect of pain processing and the affective-subjective one.

Note: These two aspects are underpinned by discrete yet interacting neural networks. A growing number of neuroimaging studies recently demonstrated that the observation of pain in others recruits brain areas chiefly involved in the affective and motivational processing of direct pain perception (areas colored in gray).

Another fMRI study demonstrated that the dorsal ACC, the anterior insula, cerebellum, and brain stem were activated when healthy participants experienced a painful stimulus, as well as when they observed a signal indicating that another person was receiving a similar stimulus. However, only the actual experience of pain resulted in activation in the somatosensory cortex and a more ventral region of the ACC (Singer et al., 2004). The different response patterns in the two areas are consistent with the ACC's role in coding the motivational-affective dimension of pain, which is associated with the preparation of behavioral responses to aversive events. These findings are supported by an fMRI study in which participants were shown still photographs depicting right hands and feet in painful or neutral everyday-life situations, and asked to imagine the level of pain that these situations would produce (Jackson, Meltzoff, & Decety, 2005). Significant activation in regions involved in the affective aspects of pain processing, notably the dorsal ACC, the thalamus, and the anterior insula was detected, but no activity in the somatosensory cortex. Moreover, the level of activity within the dorsal ACC was strongly correlated with participants' mean ratings of pain attributed to the different situations.

Crying is a universal vocalization in human infants as well as in the infants of other mammals (Newman, 2007). In all studied mammals, young infants emit a species-specific cry when in distress, and mothers generally respond with caretaking behavior (e.g., Bell & Ainsworth, 1972). A functional MRI study measured brain activity in healthy, breastfeeding first-time mothers with young infants while they listened to infant cries, white noise control sounds, and a rest condition (Lorberbaum et al., 2002). Signal increase was detected in ACC, anterior insula, the medial thalamus, and medial prefrontal and right orbitofrontal cortices. Several other structures thought important in rodent maternal behavior also displayed increased activity, including the midbrain, hypothalamus, dorsal and ventral striatum, and the vicinity of the lateral septal region.

Facial expressions of pain constitute an important category of facial expression that is readily understood by observers. One study investigated the neural response to pain expressions by performing functional magnetic resonance imaging (fMRI) as subjects viewed short video sequences showing faces expressing either moderate pain or, for comparison, no pain (Botvinick et al., 2005). In alternate blocks, the same subjects received both painful and nonpainful thermal stimulation. Facial expressions of pain were found to engage cortical areas also engaged by the firsthand experience of pain, including the anterior cingulate cortex and anterior insula.

Using fMRI, Saarela and colleagues (2006) showed that not only the presence of pain but also the intensity of the observed pain is encoded in the observer's brain—as occurs during the observer's own pain experience. When subjects observed pain from the faces of chronic pain patients, activations in bilateral anterior insula, left anterior cingulate cortex, and left inferior parietal lobe in the observers' brains correlated with their estimates of the intensity of observed pain. Furthermore, the strengths of activation in the left anterior insula and left inferior frontal gyrus during observation of intensified pain correlated with subjects' self-rated empathy.

Overall, these fMRI studies consistently detected activation of the anterior insula and dorsal ACC (two key regions that belong to the processing of the affective-motivational dimension of pain) during the perception of pain in others, and thus lend support to the idea that common neural substrates are involved in representing one's own and others' affective states. Most of these neuroimaging studies (except Moriguchi et al., 2007) did not report significant signal change in the somatosensory cortex/posterior insula (the region involved in the sensory discriminative dimension of pain). This result seems at odds with the perception-action coupling mechanism (mirror-neuron system) that underlies the automatic resonance between self and others. The somatosensory cortex/posterior dorsal insula contributes to the sensory discriminative dimension of pain as demonstrated by neuroimaging investigations and lesion studies (e.g., Symonds, Gordon, Bixby, & Mande, 2006).

Two recent studies indicate involvement of motor cortex during the perception of pain in others. These studies used transcranial magnetic stimulation (TMS) and found changes in the corticospinal motor representations of hand muscles in individuals observing needles penetrating hands or feet of a human model (Avenanti, Bueti, Galati, & Aglioti, 2005). Using electroencephalography (EEG), another study found modulation of somatosensory cortex activity contingent on observation of others' pain (Bufalari, Aprile, Avenanti, Di Russo, & Aglioti, 2007). Two possibilities can explain the discrepancy of the EEG and TMS with the fMRI studies. One is that the TMS and EEG methods can sense subtle changes in the sensorimotor cortex that are below the significance threshold in fMRI techniques. The other possibility is that attending to a specific body part elicits somatosensory activity in the corresponding brain region. This has been demonstrated in a positron emission tomography study in which participants were instructed

to focus their attention either on the unpleasantness or on the location of the noxious stimuli delivered on the participants' hands (Kulkarni et al., 2005), with the latter condition resulting in increased regional cerebral blood flow in the contralateral primary somatosensory cortex.

To test if the perception of pain in others involves the somatosensory cortex, Cheng, Yang, Lin, Lee, and Decety (2008) measured neuromagnetic oscillatory activity from the primary somatosensory cortex in participants while they observed static pictures depicting body parts in painful and nonpainful situations. The left median nerve was stimulated at the wrist, and the poststimulus rebounds of the ~10-Hz somatosensory cortical oscillations were quantified. Compared with the baseline condition, the level of the ~10-Hz oscillations was suppressed during both observational situations, indicating activation of the somatosensory cortex. Importantly, watching painful compared with nonpainful situations suppressed somatosensory oscillations to a significantly stronger degree. In addition, these suppressions negatively correlated with the perspective taking subscale of the interpersonal reactivity index. These results, consistent with the mirror-neuron system, demonstrate that the perception of pain in others modulates neural activity in somatosensory cortex and supports the idea that the perception of pain in others elicits subtle somatosensory activity that may be difficult to detect by fMRI techniques.

Most neuroimaging studies that have explored the overlap in brain response between the observation of behavior performed by others and the generation of the same behavior in self have relied on simple subtraction methods and generally highlight the commonalities between self and other processing, and ignore the differences. This is particularly true for the recent series of fMRI studies that have reported shared neural circuits for the firsthand experience of pain and the perception of pain in others (see Jackson, Rainville, & Decety, 2006). It is possible, as argued by Zaki, Ochsner, Hanelin, Wager, and Mackey (2007), that common activity in ACC and AI may reflect the operation of distinct but overlapping networks of regions that support perception of self or other pain. To address this issue, they scanned participants while they received noxious thermal stimulation (self pain condition) or watched short videos of other people sustaining painful injuries (other pain condition). Analyses identified areas whose activity covaried with ACC and AI activity during self or other pain either across time (intraindividual connectivity) or across participants (interindividual connectivity). Both connectivity analyses identified clusters in the midbrain and periaqueductal gray with greater connectivity to the AI during self-pain as opposed to other pain. The opposite pattern was found in the dorsal medial prefrontal cortex, which showed greater connectivity to the ACC and AI during other pain than during self-pain using both types of analysis. Intraindividual connectivity analyses also revealed regions in the superior temporal sulcus, posterior cingulate, and precuneus that became more connected to ACC during other pain compared with self-pain. The results of this experiment document distinct neural networks associated with ACC and anterior insula in response to firsthand experience of pain and response to seeing other people in pain. These networks could not have been detected in prior work that examined overlap between self and other pain in terms of average activity, but not connectivity. Morrison and Downing's (2007) analyses of single-subject data in generic space similarly suggest that distinct neural networks in anterior and medial cingulate cortex (MCC) are activated during the firsthand versus thirdhand experience of pain. This is in line with a quantitative meta-analysis of published studies on empathy for pain versus pain in the self using Activation Likelihood Estimation. This analysis

reveals distinct subclusters in both ACC/MCC and the insular cortices (Figures 48.2 and 48.3). While activation in MCC seems to be more left-lateralized, caudal, and dorsal during empathy for pain, a rostro-caudal activation gradient is evident in the insular cortex. These distinct activation patterns suggest the involvement of only partially overlapping neural subpopulations and indicate the involvement of distinct cognitive and affective processes. It should also be kept in mind that the effective spatial resolution of fMRI, the different experimental paradigms as well as the inherently complex mapping from cognitive to neural/hemodynamic processes make it difficult to achieve a definite conclusion about how much of the activation during empathy for pain can be attributed to shared neural and mental representations.

Summing up, current neuroscientific evidence suggests that merely perceiving another individual in a painful situation yields responses in the neural network associated with the coding of the motivational-affective and the sensory dimensions of pain in oneself. It is worth noting that vicariously instigated activations in the pain matrix are not necessarily specific to the emotional experience of pain, but to other processes such as somatic monitoring, negative stimulus evaluation, and the selection of appropriate skeletomuscular movements of aversion. Thus, the shared neural representations in the affective-motivational part of the pain matrix might not be specific to the sensory qualities of pain, but instead might be associated with more general survival mechanisms such as aversion and withdrawal.

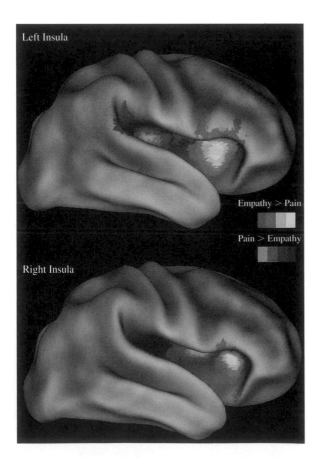

Figure 48.2 (**Figure C.45** in color section) Results of a meta-analysis comparing empathy for pain with the first experience of pain.

Note: Activation differences are projected onto a flattened representation of the left and right hemispheres. Observe that empathy predominantly activates the anterior parts of the insula while pain sensations lead to more rostral activation—especially in the contralateral (left) hemisphere.

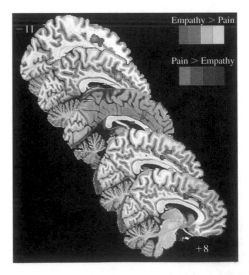

Figure 48.3 (**Figure C.46** in color section) Results of the same meta-analysis for the MCC/ACC.

Note: Observe the more left-lateralized and dorsal activations for empathy for pain.

PERSPECTIVE-TAKING

There is consensus among theorists that the ability to adopt and entertain the psychological perspective of others has important consequences in social interaction. Well-developed perspective-taking abilities allow us to overcome our usual egocentrism and tailor our behaviors to others' expectations (Davis, Conklin, Smith, & Luce, 1996). Further, successful role-taking has been linked to moral reasoning and altruism (Batson et al., 1991). Adopting another person's perspective involves more than simply focusing our attention on the other. It involves imagining how that person is affected by his or her situation without confusion between the feelings experienced by the self versus feelings experienced by the other person (Decety, 2005).

We see others as similar to ourselves on a variety of dimensions and consequently assume that they act as we act, know what we know, and feel what we feel. This default mode is based on a shared representations mechanism between self and other (Decety & Sommerville, 2003) driven by the automatic link between perception and action (Jackson & Decety, 2004). Thus, for successful social interaction, and empathic understanding in particular, an adjustment must operate on the shared representations that are automatically activated through the perception-action coupling mechanism. Whereas the projection of self-traits onto the other does not necessitate any significant storage of knowledge about the other, empathic understanding requires the inclusion of other characteristics within the self. An essential aspect of empathy is to recognize the other person as being like ourselves, while maintaining a clear separation between ourselves and other. Hence, mental flexibility and self-regulation are important components of empathy. We need to calibrate our own perspective that has been activated by the interaction with the other, or even by its mere imagination. Such calibration requires the prefrontal cortex executive resources in conjunction with the temporo-parietal junction, as demonstrated by neuroimaging experiments in healthy participants as well as lesion studies in neurological patients.

Several neuroimaging studies have consistently reported that the medial prefrontal cortex is specifically involved in tasks requiring the processing of information relevant to the self, such as traits and attitudes (e.g., Johnson et al., 2002). An fMRI study investigated the neural regions mediating self-referential processing of emotional stimuli and explored how these regions are influenced by the emotional valence of the stimulus (Fossati et al., 2003). Results showed that the self-referential condition induced bilateral activation in the dorsomedial prefrontal cortex, whereas the other referential condition induced activation in lateral prefrontal areas. Activation in the right dorsomedial prefrontal cortex was specific to the self-referential condition

regardless of the valence of the words. The authors of that study proposed that a specific role of the right dorsomedial prefrontal cortex is to represent states of an emotional episodic self and then to process emotional stimuli with a personally relevant perspective. This proposition is in line with studies showing activations within both the left and right dorsomedial prefrontal cortex during "theory of mind" tasks (Brunet-Gouet & Decety, 2006). Because emotions generally signal issues related to the self, subjects may use emotional cues during some theory of mind tasks to differentiate self from other; this self-related emotional processing is indicated by an increase of activity in the right dorsomedial prefrontal cortex.

The medial prefrontal cortex is involved not only when we reflect on ourselves, but also when individuals imagine the subjective perspective of others. Using mental imagery to take the perspective of another is a powerful way to place ourselves in the situation or emotional state of that person. Mental imagery not only enables us to see the world of our conspecifics through their eyes or in their shoes, but may also result in similar sensations as the other person's (Decety & Grèzes, 2006). A series of neuroimaging studies with healthy volunteers investigated the neural underpinning of perspective taking in three different modes (motor, conceptual, and emotional) of self-other representations. In a first study, participants were scanned while they were asked to either imagine themselves performing everyday actions (e.g., winding up a watch), or to imagine another individual performing similar actions (Ruby & Decety, 2001). Both conditions were associated with common activation in the supplementary motor area (SMA), premotor cortex, and the TPJ region. This neural network corresponds to the shared motor representations between the self and the other. Taking the perspective of the other to simulate his or her behavior resulted in selective activation of the frontopolar cortex and right inferior parietal lobule. In a second study, medical students were shown a series of affirmative health-related sentences (e.g., taking antibiotic drugs causes general fatigue) and were asked to judge their truthfulness either according to their own perspective (as experts in medical knowledge) or according to the perspective of a layperson (Ruby & Decety, 2003). The set of activated regions recruited when the participants put themselves in the shoes of a layperson included the medial prefrontal cortex, the frontopolar cortex, and the right TPJ. In a third study, the participants were presented with short written sentences that depicted real-life situations (e.g., someone opens the toilet door that you have forgotten to lock), which are likely to induce social emotions (e.g., shame, guilt, pride), or other situations that were emotionally neutral (Ruby & Decety, 2004). In one condition, they were asked to imagine how they would feel if they were experiencing these situations. And in another condition, they were asked to imagine how their mothers would feel in those situations. Reaction times were prolonged when participants imagined emotional-laden situations compared with neutral ones, both from their own perspective and from the perspective of their mothers. Neurodynamic changes were detected in the frontopolar cortex, the ventromedial prefrontal cortex, the medial prefrontal cortex, and the right inferior parietal lobule when the participants adopted the perspective of their mothers, regardless of the affective content of the situations depicted. Cortical regions that are involved in emotional processing, including the amygdala and the temporal poles, were found activated in the conditions that integrated emotional-laden situations.

A recent functional MRI study used a factorial design to examine the neural correlates of self-reflection and perspective taking (D' Argembeau et al., 2007). Participants were asked to judge the extent to which trait adjectives described their own personality (e.g., "Are you sociable?") or the personality of a close friend (e.g., "Is Caroline sociable?") and were also asked to put themselves in the place of their friend (to take a third-person perspective) and estimate how this person would judge the adjectives, with the target of the judgments again being either the self (e.g., "According to Caroline, are you sociable?") or the other person (e.g., "According to Caroline, is she sociable?"). The results showed that self-referential processing (judgments targeting the self versus the other person) was associated with activation in the ventral and dorsal anterior MPFC, whereas perspective taking (adopting the other person's perspective, rather than their own, when making judgments) resulted in activation in the posterior dorsal MPFC; the interaction between the two dimensions yielded activation in the left dorsal MPFC. Findings from this study indicate that self-referential processing and perspective taking recruit distinct regions of the MPFC and suggest that the left dorsal MPFC may be involved in decoupling a person's own perspective from other people's perspectives on the self.

Social psychology has for a long time been interested in the distinction between imagining the other and imagining oneself, and in particular in the emotional and motivational consequences of these two perspectives. A number of these studies show that focusing on another's feelings may evoke stronger empathic concern, whereas explicitly putting oneself into the shoes of the target (imagine self) induces both empathic concern and personal distress.

Batson, Early, and Salvarini (1997) investigated the affective consequences of different perspective-taking instructions when participants listened to a story about Katie Banks, a young college student struggling with her life after the death of her parents. This study demonstrated that different instructions had distinct effects on how participants perceived the target's situation. Participants imagining themselves in Katie's place showed stronger signs of discomfort and personal distress as participants focusing on the target's responses and feelings (imagine other), or as participants instructed to take on an objective, detached point of view. Also, both perspective-taking instructions differed from the detached perspective by resulting in higher empathic concern. This observation may help explain why observing a need situation does not always yield to prosocial behavior: If perceiving another person in an emotionally or physically painful circumstance elicits personal distress, then the observer may tend not to fully attend to the other's experience and as a result lack sympathetic behaviors.

Two functional MRI studies recently investigated the neural mechanisms subserving the effects of perspective-taking during the perception of pain in others.

One study used pictures of hands and feet in painful scenarios and instructed the participants to imagine and rate the level of pain perceived from two different perspectives (self versus other; Jackson, Brunet, Meltzoff, & Decety, 2006). Results indicated that both the self and the other perspectives are associated with activation in the neural network involved in the processing of the affective aspect of pain, including the dorsal ACC and the anterior insula. However, the self-perspective yielded higher pain ratings and involved the pain matrix more extensively, including the secondary somatosensory cortex, the mid-insula, and the caudal part of the anterior cingulate cortex. Adopting the perspective of the other was associated with increased activation in the right temporo-parietal junction and precuneus. In addition, distinct subregions were activated within the insular cortex for the two perspectives (anterior aspect for others and more posterior for self). These neuroimaging data highlight both the similarities and the distinctiveness of self and other as important aspects of human empathy. The experience of pain in oneself is associated with more caudal activations (within area 24), consistent with spino-thalamic nociceptive projections, whereas the perception of pain in others is represented in more rostral (and dorsal) regions (within area 32). A similar rostro-caudal organization is observed in the insula, which is consistent with its anatomical connectivity and electrophysiological properties (Jackson, Rainville, & Decety, 2006). Painful sensations are evoked in the posterior part of the insula (and not in the anterior part) by direct electrical stimulation of the insular cortex in neurological patients (Ostrowsky et al., 2002). Altogether, these findings are in agreement with the fact that indirect pain representations (as elicited by the observation of pain in others) are qualitatively different from the actual experiences of pain.

In a second neuroimaging study, the distinction between empathic concern and personal distress was investigated more specifically by using a number of behavioral measures and a set of ecological and extensively validated dynamic stimuli (Lamm, Batson, & Decety, 2007). Participants watched a series of video-clips featuring patients undergoing painful medical treatment. They were asked to either put themselves explicitly in the shoes of the patient (imagine self), or to focus on their feelings and affective expressions (imagine other). The behavioral data confirmed that explicitly projecting oneself into an aversive situation leads to higher personal distress, whereas focusing on the emotional and behavioral reactions of another's plight is accompanied by higher empathic concern and lower personal distress. The neuroimaging data are consistent with this finding and provide some insights into the neural correlates of these distinct behavioral responses. The self-perspective evoked stronger hemodynamic responses in brain regions involved in coding the motivational-affective dimensions of pain, including bilateral insular cortices, anterior MCC, the amygdala, and various structures involved in action control (Figure 48.4). The amygdala plays a critical role in fear-related behaviors, such as the evaluation of actual or potential threats. Imagining oneself to be in a painful and potentially dangerous situation might therefore have triggered a stronger fearful or aversive response than imagining someone else to be in the same situation.

This pattern of results fits well with the pioneering research of Stotland (1969) on the effects of perspective taking on empathy and distress. Participants observed an individual experiencing a painful diathermy using either an imagine self or an imagine other instruction. Stotland found higher vasoconstriction for the other-perspective, and more palmar sweat and higher tension and nervousness in the self-perspective. This finding was interpreted as being more in resonance with the feelings of the target when focusing on his affective expressions and motor responses (imagine other), whereas the first-person perspective led to more self-oriented responding that was less closely matched to the actual feelings of the target.

Corresponding with Jackson and colleagues (2006), the insular activation found by Lamm & coworkers was also located in a more posterior, mid-dorsal subsection of this area. The mid-dorsal part of the insula plays a role in coding the sensory-motor aspects of painful stimulation, and it has strong connections with the basal ganglia where activity was also higher during the self-perspective (see also Figure 48.2). Taken together, it appears that the insular activity during the self-perspective reflects simulation of sensory aspects of the painful experience. Such a simulation might serve to mobilize motor areas for the preparation of defensive or withdrawal behaviors, as well as instigate the interoceptive monitoring associated with autonomic changes evoked by this simulation process (Critchley, Wiens, Rotshtein, Öhman, & Dolan, 2005). Finally, the higher activation in premotor structures might connect with a stronger mobilization of motor representations by the more stressful and discomforting first-person perspective. Further support for this interpretation is provided by a positron emission tomography study investigating the relationship between situational empathic

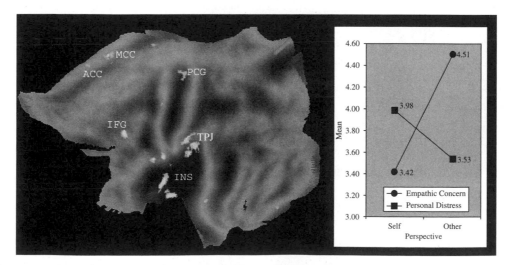

Figure 48.4 Neural and behavioral consequences of two different perspective-taking instructions.

Note: (adapted from Lamm et al., 2007). The flat-map representation of the left hemisphere shows higher activations during the self-perspective in limbic/paralimbic (medial and anterior cingulate cortex MCC and ACC, insula INS) and cortical brain structures (temporo-parietal junction TPJ, inferior frontal gyrus IFG, postcentral gyrus PCG). From "The Neural Basis of Human Empathy: Effects of Perspective-Taking and Cognitive Appraisal," by C. Lamm, C. D. Batson, and J. Decety, 2007, *Journal of Cognitive Neuroscience, 19,* p. 49. Adapted with permission.

accuracy and brain activity, which also found higher activation in medial premotor structures, partially extending into MCC, when participants witnessed the distress of others (Shamay-Tsoory et al., 2005). This study also pointed to the importance of prefrontal areas in the understanding of distress.

Altogether, the available empirical findings reveal important differences between the neural systems involved in first- and third-person perspective-taking and contradict the hypothesis/notion that the self and other completely merge in empathy. The specific activation differences in both the affective and sensorimotor aspects of the pain matrix, along with the higher pain and distress ratings, reflect the self-perspective's need for more direct and personal involvement. A key region that might facilitate self versus other distinctions is the right temporo-parietal junction (TPJ). The TPJ is activated in most neuroimaging studies on empathy (Decety & Lamm, 2007) and seems to play a decisive role in self-awareness and the sense of agency (the awareness of oneself as an agent who is the initiator of actions, desires, thoughts, and feelings). Agency is essential for a successful navigation of shared representations between self and other.

Decety and Lamm (2007) conducted a quantitative meta-analysis of 70 functional neuroimaging studies on agency, empathy, theory of mind, as well as on reorienting of attention. The results demonstrate a substantial overlap in brain activation between low-level processing such as reorienting of attention or the sense of agency and higher-level social-cognitive abilities such as empathy or theory of mind (see Figure 48.5). These results provide strong empirical support for a domain-general mechanism implemented in the right TPJ, and show that this area is also engaged in lower-level (bottom-up) computational processes associated with the sense of agency and in reorienting attention to salient stimuli.

Thus, self-awareness and a sense of agency both play pivotal roles in empathy and significantly contribute to social interaction. These important aspects are likely to be involved in distinguishing emotional contagion, which relies heavily on the automatic link between perceiving the emotions of another and our own experience of the same emotion, from empathic responses that call for a more detached and aware relation. The neural responses identified in these studies as nonoverlapping between self and other may take advantage of available processing capacities to plan appropriate future actions concerning the other. Furthermore, awareness of our own feelings and the ability to (consciously and automatically) regulate our own emotions may allow us to disconnect empathic responses to others from our own personal distress, with only the former leading to prosocial behavior.

MODULATION OF EMPATHIC RESPONDING

Although the mere perception of the behavior of others activates similar circuits in the self, and in the case of empathy for pain neural circuits involved in the first-hand experience of pain, there is also evidence that this unconscious level can be modulated by situational and dispositional variables. Research in social psychology has identified these factors, such as the relationship between target and empathizer, the empathizer's dispositions, and the context in which the social interaction takes place. Therefore, whether observing the distress of a close friend results in empathic concern and helping behavior or withdrawal from the situation is influenced by the complex interaction between these factors.

Emotion regulation seems to have a particularly important role in social interaction, and it has a clear adaptive function for both the individual and the species (Ochsner & Gross, 2005). It has been demonstrated that individuals who can regulate their emotions are more likely to experience empathy, and also to interact in morally more desirable ways with others (Eisenberg et al., 1994). In contrast, people who experience their emotions intensely, especially negative emotions, are more prone to personal distress, an aversive emotional reaction, such as anxiety or discomfort based on the recognition of another's emotional state or condition.

In the case of perception of others in pain, the ability to downregulate our emotions is particularly valuable when the distress of the target becomes overwhelming. A mother alarmed by her baby's cries at night has to cope with her

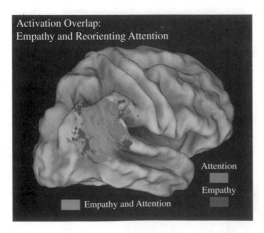

Figure 48.5 (**Figure C.47** in color section) Activation overlap in right TPJ for empathy for pain and reorienting of attention/change detection.

Note: From "The Role of the Right Temporoparietal Junction in Social Interaction: How Low-Level Computational Processes Contribute to Meta-Cognition," by J. Decety and C. Lamm, 2007, *Neuroscientist, 13,* 580–593. Adapted with permission.

own discomfort to provide appropriate care for her distressed offspring. A strategy to regulate emotions is based on cognitive reappraisal. This involves reinterpreting the valence of a stimulus to change the way that we respond to it. It can either be intentionally achieved or result from additional information provided about the emotion-eliciting stimulus. By providing different context information about the consequences of the observed pain, we investigated the effects of cognitive appraisal on the experience of empathy in the previously mentioned fMRI study by Lamm and colleagues (2007). The observed target patients belonged to two different groups. In one group, health and quality of life improved after the painful therapy, while members of the other group did not benefit from the treatment. Thus, stimuli of identically arousing and negatively valenced emotional content were watched with different possibilities to appraise the patients' pain. The results confirmed our hypotheses and demonstrated that appraisal of an aversive event can considerably alter our responses to it. Patients undergoing noneffective treatment were judged to experience higher levels of pain, and personal distress in the observers was more pronounced when watching videos of these patients. Brain activation was modulated in two subregions of the orbitofrontal cortex (OFC) and the rostral part of aMCC. The OFC is known to play an important role in the evaluation of positive and negative reinforcements and is also involved in emotion reappraisal. Activity in the OFC may thus reflect valence evaluations of the presented stimuli. Interestingly, watching effectively versus noneffectively treated patients did not modulate hemodynamic changes in either the visual-sensory areas or the insula. This suggests that both patient groups triggered an emotional reaction, and that top-down mechanisms did not alter stimulus processing at an early perceptual stage.

Since the mere perception of others in pain may lead to personal distress and discomfort, regulatory mechanisms must operate in people who inflict painful procedures in their practice with patient populations to prevent their distress from impairing their ability to be of assistance. In one functional MRI study, physicians who practice acupuncture were compared with naive participants (matched for age, gender, and level of academic education) while observing animated visual stimuli depicting needles being inserted into different body parts including the mouth region, hands, and feet (Cheng, Lin, et al., 2008). Results indicate that the anterior insula, periaqueductal gray, and anterior cingulate cortex were significantly activated in the control participants, but not in the expert participants, who instead showed activation of the medial prefrontal cortices and right inferior parietal lobule. This study establishes that the perception of pain can be modulated by the expertise of the observer.

Another intrapersonal factor affecting the empathic response is the emotional background state of the observer (Niedenthal, Halberstadt, Margolin, & Innes-Ker, 2000). A depressive mood can affect the way we perceive the expression of emotions by others. In a developmental neuroscience study, limbic structures such as the amygdala and the nucleus accumbens became hyperactive when participants with pediatric bipolar disorder attended to the facial expression of emotion (Pavuluri, O'Connor, Harral, & Sweeney, 2007). Similarly, patients with generalized social phobia show increased amygdala activation when exposed to angry or contemptuous faces (Stein, Goldin, Sareen, Zorrilla, & Brown, 2002).

Whether individual differences in dispositional empathy and personal distress modulate the occurrence and intensity of self- versus other-centered responding is currently a matter of debate. Several recent neuroimaging studies demonstrate specific relationships between questionnaire measures of empathy and brain activity. Both Singer and colleagues (2004) and Lamm and colleagues (2007) detected significantly increased activation in insular and cingulate cortices in participants with higher self-reported empathy during perception. This shows modulation of neural activity in the very brain regions that are involved in coding the affective response to the other's distress. No such correlations were found in a similar study (Jackson et al., 2005). Also, no correlations with self-report data on personal distress were observed by Lamm et al. (2007) or Jackson, Rainville, and Brunet (2006). However, Lawrence and collaborators (2006) did report such correlations in cingulate and prefrontal regions of participants labeling a target's mental and affective state. Part of this discrepancy between neuroscience research and dispositional measures may be related to the low validity of self-report measures in predicting actual empathic behavior (Davis & Kraus, 1997). Brain-behavior correlations should be treated with caution, and care must be taken to formulate specific hypotheses about the neural correlates of the dispositional measures as well as what the questionnaire actually measures. The personal distress subscale of the Interpersonal Reactivity Index (Davis et al., 1996) showed correlations close to zero with the experimentally derived distress measures and no significant correlations with brain activation. This indicates that the subscale is probably not an appropriate measure of situative discomfort evoked by the observation of another's distress.

The effects of *interpersonal* factors—such as the similarity or closeness of empathizer and target—have been investigated at the behavioral, psychophysiological, and neural levels. Cialdini, Brown, Lewis, Luce, and Neuberg (1997) have documented that perceived oneness—that is, the perceived overlap between self and other—is an important predictor of helping behavior and correlates strongly with empathic concern. The work of Lanzetta and Englis (1989) made interesting observations concerning the effects of attitudes on social interaction. Their studies show that, in a competitive relationship, observation of joy can result in distress, while pain in the competitor leads to positive emotions. These findings reflect an important and often ignored aspect of empathy, that this ability can also be used in a malevolent way—as when knowledge about the emotional or cognitive state of competitors is used to harm them. The study by Singer and colleagues (2006) revealed the neural correlates of such counterempathic responding. In that study, participants were first engaged in a sequential prisoner's dilemma game with confederate targets who were playing the game either fairly or unfairly. Following this behavioral manipulation, fMRI measures were taken during the observation of fair and unfair players receiving painful stimulation. Compared with the observation of fair players, activation in brain areas coding the affective components of pain was significantly reduced when participants observed unfair players in pain. This effect, however, was detected in male participants only, who also exhibited a concurrent increase of activation in reward-related areas.

In sum, there is strong behavioral evidence demonstrating that the experience of empathy and personal distress can be modulated by social-cognitive factors. In addition, a few recent neuroscience studies indicate that such a modulation leads to activity changes in the neural systems that process social information. Further studies are required to increase our knowledge about the various factors, processes, and neural and behavioral effects involved in and resulting from the modulation of empathic responses. This knowledge will inform us how empathy can be promoted to ultimately increase humankind's ability to act in more prosocial and altruistic ways.

SUMMARY

In the recent decades, there has been an increased interest in the biological mechanisms that underpin the experience of empathy (shared feelings without confusion between self and others). Much of this new work relies on functional neuroimaging studies with an emphasis on the perception of pain. The combined results of these studies demonstrate that when individuals perceive others in pain or distressful situations, they use the same neural mechanisms as when they are in painful situations themselves. Such a shared neural mechanism offers an interesting foundation for intersubjectivity because it provides a functional bridge between first-person information and third-person information, is

grounded in self-other equivalence (Decety & Sommerville, 2003; Sommerville & Decety, 2006), allows analogical reasoning, and offers a possible route to understanding others. Yet a minimal distinction between self and other is essential for social interaction in general and for empathy in particular, and new work in social neuroscience has demonstrated that the self and other are distinguished at both the behavioral and neural levels. A handful of cognitive neuroscience studies also indicate that the neural response to others in pain can be modulated by situational and dispositional variables.

Taken together, these data support the view that empathy (at least for pain) operates by way of conscious as well as automatic processes, which far from functioning independently, represent different aspects of a common subjective experience. These accounts of empathy are in harmony with theories of embodied cognition, which contend that cognitive representations and operations are fundamentally grounded in bodily states and in the brain's modality-specific systems (Niedenthal et al., 2005).

Future research should continue to investigate which pain-related brain areas are active in response to the perception of pain in others, and which are not, to help determine what aspects of pain are involved in the experience of empathy.

Another interesting issue is whether there are gender differences in empathy. If so, are they learned or related to hormonal and innate differences in the way our brain is shaped? The work in social psychology, though not entirely conclusive, has seriously questioned the alleged female-superiority in empathic understanding, suggesting motivational differences between the genders instead (Ickes, 2003). More specific differences might be biologically based, as suggested by the results of a recent fMRI study that investigated neural response in men and women to infant crying and laughing showing significant differences between the two groups (Seifritz et al., 2003). Women but not men, independent of their parental status, showed neural deactivation in the anterior cingulate cortex in response to infant crying and laughing. In addition, the response pattern in the amygdala and interconnected limbic structures changed fundamentally with parental experience in both men and women. Nonparents showed stronger activation from laughing, whereas parents showed stronger activation for crying. These results seem to demonstrate that the emotion-sharing component may be subjected to personal experience, and that emotion regulation is differently prepared biologically in men and women.

Finally, it is often assumed that empathy is a necessary prerequisite for altruism and compassion, and that we are, by nature, moral creatures. Despite this supposed link between empathy and prosocial behavior, no neuroscience evidence as yet demonstrates the existence of such a link. Empathy may well be viewed as a neutral capacity whose outcome, depending on a complex interplay of situational and personality factors, will result in positive or negative consequences for the target. One of the challenges for a social neuroscience approach to empathy and prosocial behavior is the difficulty of taking into account situational variables. To provide interpretable data, neuroscience experiments—especially functional neuroimaging studies—require intraindividual comparisons and repeated-measures designs. To be financially feasible, they require small samples. These conditions limit opportunities to study the effects of potentially important situational variables. This is but one example of the perennial challenge objective science faces in the attempt to understand human subjectivity in all its richness and complexity.

REFERENCES

Allman, J. M., Watson, K. K., Tetreault, N. A., & Hakeem, A. Y. (2005). Intuition and autism: A possible role for von economo neurons. *Trends in Cognitive Sciences, 9,* 367–373.

Avenanti, A., Bueti, D., Galati, G., & Aglioti, S. M. (2005). Transcranial magnetic stimulation highlights the sensorimotor side of empathy for pain. *Nature Neuroscience, 8,* 955–960.

Ax, A. F. (1964). Goals and methods of psychophysiology. *Psychophysiology, 62,* 8–25.

Barrett, L., Henzi, P., & Dunbar, R. I. M. (2003). Primate cognition: From what now to what if. *Trends Cognitive Sciences, 7,* 494–497.

Basch, M. F. (1983). Empathic understanding: A review of the concept and some theoretical considerations. *Journal of the American Psychoanalytic Association, 31,* 101–126.

Batson, C. D. (1990). How social an animal? *American Psychologist, 45,* 336–346.

Batson, C. D. (2006). Folly bridges. In P. A. M. van Lange (Ed.), *Bridging social psychology* (pp. 59–64). Mahwah, NJ: Erlbaum.

Batson, C. D., Batson, J. G., Singlsby, J. K., Harrell, K. L., Peekna, H. M., & Todd, R. M. (1991). Empathic joy and the empathy-altruism hypothesis. *Journal of Personality and Social Psychology, 61,* 413–426.

Batson, C. D., Early, S., & Salvarini, G. (1997). Perspective taking: Imagining how another feels versus imagining how you would feel. *Personality and Social Personality Bulletin, 23,* 751–758.

Baumeister, R. F., & Leary, M. R. (1995). The need to belong: Desire for interpersonal attachments as a fundamental human motivation. *Psychological Bulletin, 117,* 497–529.

Bell, S., & Ainsworth, M. (1972). Infant crying and maternal responsiveness. *Child Development, 43,* 1171–1190.

Bjorklund, D. F., & Bering, J. M. (2003). Big brains, slow development and social complexity: The development and evolutionary origins of social cognition. In M. Brune, H. Ribbert, & W. Schiedfenhovel (Eds.), *The social brain: Evolution and pathology* (pp. 113–151). Hoboken, NJ: Wiley.

Blakemore, S.-J., Bristow, D., Bird, G., Frith, C., & Ward, J. (2005). Somatosensory activations during the observation of touch and a case of vision-touch synaesthesia. *Brain, 128,* 1571–1583.

Botvinick, M., Jha, A. P., Bylsma, L. M., Fabian, S. A., Solomon, P. E., & Prkachin, K. M. (2005). Viewing facial expressions of pain engages cortical areas involved in the direct experience of pain. *NeuroImage, 25,* 312–319.

Brunet-Gouet, E., & Decety, J. (2006). Social brain dysfunctions in schizophrenia: A review of neuroimaging studies. *Psychiatry Research, 148,* 75–92.

Bufalari, I., Aprile, T., Avenanti, A., Di Russo, F., & Aglioti, S. M. (2007). Empathy for pain and touch in the human somatosensory cortex. *Cerebral Cortex, 17,* 2553-2561.

Cacioppo, J. T. (2002). Social neuroscience: Understanding the pieces fosters understanding the whole and vice versa. *American Psychologist, 57,* 819–831.

Cacioppo, J. T., Berntson, G. G., Sheridan, J. F., & McClintock, M. K. (2000). Multilevel integrative analyses of human behavior: Social neuroscience and the complementing nature of social and biological approaches. *Psychological Bulletin, 126,* 829–843.

Cacioppo, J. T., & Gardner, W. L. (1999). Emotion. *Annual Review of Psychology, 50,* 191–214.

Carr, L., Iacoboni, M., Dubeau, M. C., Mazziotta, J. C., & Lenzi, G. L. (2003). Neural mechanisms of empathy in humans: A relay from neural systems for imitation to limbic areas. *Proceedings of the National Academy of Sciences, USA, 100,* 5497–5502.

Carter, C. S. (2007). Sex differences in oxytocin and vasopressin: Implications for autism spectrum disorders? *Behavioral Brain Research, 176,* 170–186.

Carter, C. S., Williams, J. R., Witt, D. M., & Insel, T. R. (1992). Oxytocin and social bonding. *Annals of the New York Academy of Sciences, 652,* 204–211.

Cheng, Y., Lin, C. P., Liu, H. L., Hsu, Y., Hung, D., & Decety, J. (2008). *Expertise modulates the perception of pain in others.* Submitted.

Cheng, Y., Yang, C. Y., Lin, C. P., Lee, P. R., & Decety, J. (2008). *The perception of pain in others suppresses somatosensory oscillations: A MEG study.* Manuscript submitted for publication.

Cialdini, R. B., Brown, S. L., Lewis, B. P., Luce, C., & Neuberg, S. L. (1997). Reinterpreting the empathy-altruism relationship: When one into one equals oneness. *Journal of Personality and Social Psychology, 73,* 481–494.

Consiglio, A., Borsoi, A., Pereira, G., & Lucion, A. (2005). Effects of oxytocin microinjected into the central amygdaloid nucleus and bed nucleus of stria terminalis on maternal aggressive behavior in rats. *Physiology and Behavior, 85,* 354–362.

Craig, A. D. (2002). How do you feel? Interoception: The sense of the physiological condition of the body. *Nature Reviews: Neuroscience, 3,* 655–666.

Craig, A. D. (2005). Forebrain emotional asymmetry: A neuroanatomical basis? *Trends in Cognitive Sciences, 9,* 566–571.

Craig, A. D. (2007). Interoception and emotion: A neuroanatomical perspective. In M. Lewis, J. M. Haviland-Jones, & L. F. Barrett (Eds.), *Handbook of emotion* (3rd ed., pp. 272-288). New York: Guilford Press.

Critchley, H. D., Wiens, S., Rotstein, P., Öhman, A., & Dolan, R. D. (2005). Neural systems supporting interoceptive awareness. *Nature Neuroscience, 7,* 189–195.

D'Argembeau, A., Ruby, P., Collette, F., Degueldre, C., Balteau, E., Luxen, A., et al. (2007). Distinct regions of the medial prefrontal cortex are associated with self-referential processing and perspective taking. *Journal of Cognitive Neuroscience, 19,* 935–944.

Davidson, R. J. (1992). Anterior cerebral asymmetry and the nature of emotion. *Brain and Cognition, 20,* 125–151.

Davis, M. H., Conklin, L., Smith, A., & Luce, C. (1996). Effect of perspective taking on the cognitive representation of persons: A merging of self and other. *Journal of Personality and Social Psychology, 70,* 713–726.

Davis, M. H., & Kraus, L. A. (1997). Personality and empathic accuracy. In W. Ickes (Ed.), *Empathic accuracy* (pp. 144–168). New York: Guilford Press.

Decety, J. (2005). Perspective taking as the royal avenue to empathy. In B. F. Malle & S. D. Hodges (Eds.), *Other minds: How humans bridge the divide between self and other* (pp. 135–149). New York: Guilford Press.

Decety, J., & Grèzes, J. (2006). The power of simulation: Imagining one's own and other's behavior. *Brain Research, 1079,* 4–14.

Decety, J., & Hodges, S. D. (2006). A social cognitive neuroscience model of human empathy. In P. A. M. van Lange (Ed.), *Bridging social psychology: Benefits of transdisciplinary approaches* (pp. 103–109). Mahwah, NJ: Erlbaum.

Decety, J., & Jackson, P. L. (2004). The functional architecture of human empathy. *Behavioral and Cognitive Neuroscience Reviews, 3,* 71–100.

Decety, J., & Lamm, C. (2006). Human empathy through the lens of social neuroscience. *Scientific World Journal, 6,* 1146–1163.

Decety, J., & Lamm, C. (2007). The role of the right temporoparietal junction in social interaction: How low-level computational processes contribute to meta-cognition. *Neuroscientist, 13,* 580–593.

Decety, J., & Sommerville, J. A. (2003). Shared representations between self and others: A social cognitive neuroscience view. *Trends in Cognitive Sciences, 7,* 527–533.

de Waal, F. B. M. (1996). *Good natured: The origins of right and wrong in humans and other animals.* Harvard: Harvard University Press.

de Waal, F. B. M. (2005). Primates, monks and the mind. *Journal of Consciousness Studies, 12,* 1–17.

de Waal, F. B. M., &, Thompson, E. (2005). Primates, monks and the mind: The case of empathy. *Journal of Consciousness Studies, 12,* 38–54.

de Waal, F. B. M., & van Roosmalen, A. (1979). Reconciliation and consolation among chimpanzees. *Behavioral Ecology and Sociobiology, 5,* 55–66.

Dimberg, U., Thunberg, M., & Elmehed, K. (2000). Unconscious facial reactions to emotional facial expressions. *Psychological Science, 11,* 86–89.

Domes, G., Heinrichs, M., Glascher, J., Buchel, C., Braus, D. F., & Herpertz, S. C. (2007). Oxytocin attenuates amygdala responses to emotional faces regardless of valence. *Biological Psychiatry, 62,* 1197–1190.

Domes, G., Heinrichs, M., Michel, A., Berger, C., & Herpertz, S. C. (2007). Oxytocin improves mind-reading in humans. *Biological Psychiatry, 61,* 731–733.

Eisenberg, N., Fabes, R. A., Murphy, B., Karbon, M., Maszk, P., Smith, M., et al. (1994). The relations of emotionality and regulation to dispositional and situational empathy-related responding. *Journal of Personality and Social Psychology, 66,* 776–797.

Eisenberg, N., Spinrad, T. L., & Sadovsky, A. (2006). Empathy-related responding in children. In M. Killen & J. Smetana (Eds.), *Handbook of moral development* (pp. 517–549). Mahwah, NJ: Erlbaum.

Farrow, T., & Woodruff, P. W. (2007). *Empathy in mental illness and health.* Cambridge, MA: Cambridge University Press.

Fossati, P., Hevenor, S. J., Graham, S. J., Grady, C., Keightley, M. L., Craik, F., et al. (2003). In search of the emotional self: An fMRI study using positive and negative emotional words. *American Journal of Psychiatry, 160,* 1938–1945.

Geary, D. C., & Flinn, M. (2001). Evolution of human parental behavior and the human family. *Parenting: Science and Practice, 1,* 5–61.

Grosbras, M. H., & Paus, T. (2006). Brain networks involved in viewing angry hands or faces. *Cerebral Cortex, 16,* 1087–1096.

Gunnar, M., & Quevedo, K. (2007). The neurobiology of stress and development. *Annual Review of Psychology, 58,* 145–173.

Harris, P. L. (2000). Understanding emotion. In M. Lewis & J. M. Haviland-Jones (Eds.), *Handbook of emotions* (pp. 281–292). New York: Guilford Press.

Hatfield, E. (2009). Emotional contagion and empathy. In J. Decety & W. Ickes (Eds.), *the social neuroscience of empathy* (pp. 19–30). Cambridge, MA: MIT Press.

Hatfield, E., Cacioppo, J., &, Rapson, R. (1994). *Emotional contagion.* New York: Cambridge University Press.

Hoffman, M. L. (2000). *Empathy and moral development: Implication for caring and justice.* Cambridge, MA: Cambridge University Press.

Hollander, E., Bartz, J., Chaplin, W., Phillips, A., Sumner, J., Soorya, L., et al. (2007). Oxytocin increases retention of social cognition in autism. *Biological Psychiatry, 61,* 498–503.

Huber, D., Veinante, P., & Stoop, R. (2005, April 8). Vasopressin and oxytocin excite distinct neuronal populations in the central amygdala. *Science, 308,* 245–249.

Hutchison, W. D., Davis, K. D., Lozano, A. M., Tasker, R. R., & Dostrovsky, J. O. (1999). Pain-related neurons in the human cingulate cortex. *Nature Neuroscience, 2,* 403–405.

Ickes, W. (2003). *Everyday mind reading: Understanding what other people think and feel.* Amherst, NY: Prometheus Books.

Jackson, P. L., Brunet, E., Meltzoff, A. N., & Decety, J. (2006). Empathy examined through the neural mechanisms involved in imagining how I feel versus how you feel pain. *Neuropsychologia, 44,* 752–761.

Jackson, P. L., & Decety, J. (2004). Motor cognition: A new paradigm to study self other interactions. *Current Opinion in Neurobiology, 14,* 259–263.

Jackson, P. L., Meltzoff, A. N., & Decety, J. (2005). How do we perceive the pain of others: A window into the neural processes involved in empathy. *NeuroImage, 24,* 771–779.

Jackson, P. L., Rainville, P., & Decety, J. (2006). From nociception to empathy: The neural mechanism for the representation of pain in self and in others. *Pain, 125,* 5–9.

Johnson, S. C., Baxter, L. C., Wilder, L. S., Pipe, J. G., Heiserman, J. E., & Prigatano, G. P. (2002). Neural correlates of self-reflection. *Brain, 125,* 1808–1814.

Kirsch, P., Esslinger, C., Chen, Q., Mier, D., Lis, S., & Siddhanti, S. (2005). Oxytocin modulates neural circuitry for social cognition and fear in humans. *Journal of Neuroscience, 25,* 11489–11493.

Kosfeld, M., Heinrichs, M., Zak, P. J., Fischbacher, U., & Fehr, E. (2005, June 2). Oxytocin increases trust in humans. *Nature, 435,* 673–676.

Kulkarni, B., Bentley, D. E., Elliott, R., Youell, P., Watson, A., Derbyshire, S. W., et al. (2005). Attention to pain localization and unpleasantness discriminates the functions of the medial and lateral pain systems. *European Journal of Neuroscience, 21,* 3133–3142.

Lamm, C., Batson, C. D., & Decety, J. (2007). The neural basis of human empathy: Effects of perspective-taking and cognitive appraisal. *Journal of Cognitive Neuroscience, 19,* 42–58.

Lanzetta, J. T., & Englis, B. G. (1989). Expectations of cooperation and competition and their effects on observers' vicarious emotional responses. *Journal of Personality and Social Psychology, 56,* 543–554.

Lawrence, E. J., Shaw, P., Giampietro, V. P., Surguladze, S., Brammer, M. J., & David, A. S. (2006). The role of "shared representations" in social perception and empathy: An fMRI study. *NeuroImage, 29,* 1173–1184.

LeDoux, J. E. (2000). Emotion circuits in the brain. *Annual Review of Neuroscience, 23,* 155–184.

Levenson, R. W., Ekman, P., & Friesen, W. V. (1990). Voluntary facial action generates emotion-specific autonomic nervous system activity. *Psychophysiology, 27,* 363–384.

Lorberbaum, J. P., Newman, J. D., Horwitz, A. R., Dubno, J. R., Lydiard, R. B., Hammer, M. B., et al. (2002). A potential role for thalamocingulate circuitry in human maternal behavior. *Biological Psychiatry, 51,* 431–445.

MacLean, P. D. (1985). Brain evolution relating to family, play, and the separation call. *Archives of General Psychiatry, 42,* 405–417.

Moriguchi, Y., Decety, J., Ohnishi, T., Maeda, M., Matsuda, H., & Komaki, G. (2007). Empathy and judging other's pain: An fMRI study of alexithymia. *Cerebral Cortex, 9,* 2223–2234.

Morrison, I., & Downing, P. E. (2007). Organization of felt and seen pain responses in anterior cingulate cortex. *NeuroImage, 37,* 642–651.

Morrison, I., Lloyd, D., di Pellegrino, G., & Roberts, N. (2004). Vicarious responses to pain in anterior cingulate cortex: Is empathy a multisensory issue? *Cognitive and Affective Behavioral Neuroscience, 4,* 270–278.

Newman, J. D. (2007). Neural circuits underlying crying and cry responding in mammals. *Behavioural Brain Research, 182,* 155–165.

Niedenthal, P. M., Halberstadt, J. B., Margolin, J., & Innes-Ker, A. H. (2000). Emotional state and the detection of change in the facial expression of emotion. *European Journal of Social Psychology, 30,* 211–222.

Niedenthal, P.M., Barsalou, L.W., Winkielman, P., Krauth-Gruber, S., & Ric, F. (2005). Embodiment in attitudes, social perception, and emotion. *Personality and Social Psychology Review, 9,* 184–211.

Ochsner, K. N., & Gross, J. J. (2005). The cognitive control of emotion. *Trends in Cognitive Sciences, 9,* 242–249.

Ostrowsky, K., Magnin, M., Ryvlin, P., Isnard, J., Guenot, M., & Mauguiere, F. (2002). Representation of pain and somatic sensation in the human insula: A study of responses to direct electrical cortical stimulation. *Cerebral Cortex, 12,* 376–385.

Parr, L. A. (2001). Cognitive and physiological markers of emotional awareness in chimpanzees (Pan troglodytes). *Animal Cognition, 4,* 223–229.

Parr, L. A., & Hopkins, W. D. (2000). Brain temperature asymmetries and emotional perception in chimpanzees (Pan troglodytes). *Physiology and Behavior, 71,* 363–371.

Parr, L. A., &, Waller, B. (2007). The evolution of human emotion. In J. Kaas (Ed.), *Evolution of the nervous system* (Vol. 5, pp. 447–472). New York: Elsevier.

Pavuluri, M. N., O'Connor, M. M., Harral, E., & Sweeney, J. A. (2007). Affective neural circuitry during facial emotion processing in pediatric bipolar disorder. *Biological Psychiatry, 62,* 158–167.

Pickett, C. L., Gardner, W. L., & Knowles, M. (2004). Getting a cue: The need to belong and enhanced sensitivity to social cues. *Personality and Social Psychology Bulletin, 30,* 1095–1107.

Porges, S. W. (2001). The polyvagal theory: Phylogenetic substrates of a social nervous system. *International Journal of Psychophysiology, 42,* 123–146.

Povinelli, D. J. (2001). *Folk physics for apes.* New York: Oxford University Press.

Preston, S. D., & de Waal, F. B. M. (2002). Empathy: Its ultimate and proximate bases. *Behavioral and Brain Sciences, 25,* 1–72.

Price, D. D. (2000, June 9). Psychological and neural mechanisms of the affective dimension of pain. *Science, 288,* 1769–1772.

Rizzolatti, G., & Craighero, L. (2004). The mirror-neuron system. *Annual Review in Neuroscience, 27,* 169–192.

Roelofs, K., Elzinga, B.M., & Rotteveel, M. (2005). The effects of stress-induced cortisol responses on approach–avoidance behavior. *Psychoneuroendocrinology, 30,* 665–677.

Rolls, E. T. (1999). *The brain and emotion.* Oxford: Oxford University Press.

Ruby, P., & Decety, J. (2001). Effect of subjective perspective taking during simulation of action: A PET investigation of agency. *Nature Neuroscience, 4,* 546–550.

Ruby, P., & Decety, J. (2003). What you believe versus what you think they believe? A neuroimaging study of conceptual perspective taking. *European Journal of Neuroscience, 17,* 2475–2480.

Ruby, P., & Decety, J. (2004). How would you feel versus how do you think she would feel? A neuroimaging study of perspective taking with social emotions. *Journal of Cognitive Neuroscience, 16,* 988–999.

Saarela, M. V., Hluschuk, Y., Williams, A. C., Schurmann, M., Lalso, E., & Hari, R. (2006). The compassionate brain: Humans detect intensity of pain from another's face. *Cerebral Cortex, 17,* 230–237.

Seifritz, E., Esposito, F., Neuhoff, J. G., Lüthi, A., Mustovic, H., Dammann, G., et al. (2003). Differential sex-independent amygdala response to infant crying and laughing in parents versus nonparents. *Biological Psychiatry, 54,* 1367–1375.

Shamay-Tsoory, S. G., Lester, H., Chisin, R., Israel, O., Bar-Shalom, R., Peretz, A., et al. (2005). The neural correlates of understanding the other's distress: A positron emission tomography investigation of accurate empathy. *NeuroImage, 15,* 468–472.

Singer, T., Seymour, B., O'Doherty, J., Kaube, H., Dolan, R. J., & Frith, C. D. (2004, February 20). Empathy for pain involves the affective but not the sensory components of pain. *Science, 303,* 1157–1161.

Singer, T., Seymour, B., O'Doherty, J. P., Stephan, K. E., Dolan, R. J., & Frith, C. D. (2006, January 26). Empathic neural responses are modulated by the perceived fairness of others. *Nature, 439,* 466–469.

Smith, A. (1790). *The theory of moral sentiments.* London: Millar.

Sommerville, J. A., & Decety, J. (2006). Weaving the fabric of social interaction: Articulating developmental psychology and cognitive neuroscience in the domain of motor cognition. *Psychonomic Bulletin and Review, 13,* 179–200.

Stein, M. B., Goldin, P. R., Sareen, J., Zorrilla, L. T., & Brown, G. G. (2002). Increased amygdala activation to angry and contemptuous faces in generalized social phobia. *Archives of General Psychiatry, 59,* 1027–1034.

Stotland, E. (1969). Exploratory investigations of empathy. In L. Berkowitz (Ed.), *Advances in experimental social psychology* (Vol. 4, pp. 271–313). New York: Academic Press.

Symonds, L. L., Gordon, N. S., Bixby, J. C., & Mande, M. M. (2006). Right-lateralized pain processing in the human cortex: An FMRI study. *Journal of Neurophysiology, 95,* 3823–3830.

Thompson, E. (2001). Empathy and consciousness. *Journal of Consciousness Studies, 8,* 1–32.

Tice, D. M., Bratslavsky, E., & Baumeister, R. F. (2001). Emotional distress regulation takes precedence over impulse control: If you feel bad, do it! *Journal of Personality and Social Psychology, 80,* 53–67.

Van Essen, D. C., Dickson, J., Harwell, J., Hanlon, D., Anderson, C. H., & Drury, H. A. (2001). An integrated software system for surface-based analyses of cerebral cortex. *Journal of American Medical Informatics Association, 41,* 1359–1378.

Wicker, B., Keysers, C., Plailly, J., Royet, J. P., Gallese, V., & Rizzolatti, G. (2003). Both of us disgusted in my insula: The common neural basis of seeing and feeling disgust. *Neuron, 40,* 655–664.

Wilson, E. O. (1988). *On human nature.* Cambridge, MA: Harvard University Press.

Zak, P. J., Kurzban, R., & Matzner, W. T. (2005). Oxytocin is associated with human trustworthiness. *Hormones and Behavior, 48,* 522–552.

Zaki, J., Ochsner, K. N., Hanelin, J., Wager, T. D., & Mackey, S. C. (2007). Different circuits for different pain: Patterns of functional connectivity reveal distinct networks for processing pain in self and others. *Social Neuroscience, 2,* 276–291.

Chapter 49

Defense and Aggression

D. CAROLINE BLANCHARD, YOAV LITVIN, NATHAN S. PENTKOWSKI, AND ROBERT J. BLANCHARD

DEFENSE

The Functions of Defense

Defensive behaviors constitute the immediate and direct behavioral response to threats to life and bodily safety (D. C. Blanchard & Blanchard, 2008). For most species, including many mammals, defensive behaviors are less dependent on individual learning than on evolved responses to the stimuli and situations that were frequent dangers in the evolutionary histories of that species (see Chapter 36, this volume). They have evolved because of the differential survival/reproductive success that such behaviors afford to individuals displaying them appropriately. In this context, "appropriately" means not only that the defenses be well executed, but that each individual defensive behavior has been particularly successful in response to that particular type of threat and in that particular type of situation. The notion that defensive behaviors reflect evolved neurobehavioral systems, rather than a set of purely learned responses based on pain (see Chapter 39, this volume) is crucial for understanding their cross-species commonalities, and their propensity to emerge in the absence of experience that would permit such learning.

How successful is defensive behavior? One index of this is the success of predation. Overall and across species, most predators kill prey on less than 50% of their encounters with them (Vermeij, 1982), attesting to the value of prey behavior in thwarting such predatory attacks. In mammals, much of what we know about the efficacy of defensive behavior is based on estimates of the success of hunts by lions, cheetahs, and the like. This information, which may or may not be generalized to other predator-prey relationships, is available largely because such predators, and their prey, are large and live in open areas where visibility is good and the outcome of a hunt relatively easy to determine. Estimates that only about 1 in 3 hunts ends in a kill (Schaller, 1972, pp. 251–255) suggest that while lion hunting success may vary considerably with type of habitat

and the composition of the hunting group, the defensive behaviors of the prey in these hunts are quite successful. Looking at this from a slightly different angle, the world is a dangerous place, and has been so throughout evolution. The remarkable fact is that each of us is the product of an incredibly long line of ancestors, each of whom showed successful defensive behavior to all the threats they encountered, at least until the individuals were old enough to reproduce the next in the line of our ancestors. As a result of this heritage, mechanisms related to defense are widely represented in the nervous systems of higher animals, providing a substrate for normal defensive behavior as well as a potential site for abnormal functioning.

Types of Defensive Behavior

Flight, avoidance, freezing, defensive threat, defensive attack, and risk assessment to threatening stimuli have been characterized in a variety of species (e.g., D. C. Blanchard, 1997), as have some other behaviors (e.g., burying of novel, aversive, or potentially dangerous objects; Treit, Pinel, & Fibiger, 1981) that may be functional in particular threat situations, or functionally related to one or more of the preceding defense patterns. Alarm cries warning potentially related conspecifics of the presence of danger are also adaptive, insofar as the increased safety to genetic relatives exceeds the risk of damage to the alarm caller. Thus alarm cries would be expected to occur more frequently in species in which related conspecifics typically live in close proximity (Litvin, Blanchard, & Blanchard, 2007). Reducing attention to oneself (e.g., rat pups cease separation/distress vocalizations in the presence of an adult male; Takahashi, 1992), is also a common element of defense across many species and situations.

Although the category of defense remains somewhat open-ended, typical forms of defense are common to most if not all mammalian species (Edmunds, 1974; Hedinger, 1969) and to many nonmammals as well. Virtually all vertebrates and many invertebrates show some form of flight, avoidance, or hiding, while most also show freezing, defensive threat, and defensive attack. Although no single defensive behavior is yet recognized as genuinely "species-specific," or restricted to a single species, some defense-related behaviors such as stotting, shooting poison liquids at the threat source, or rolling up into a ball are restricted to a few species. In addition, the functions of some of these rare defenses are not always clear, as the conditions of observation in free-living animals typically do not facilitate analysis of the relationship between these behaviors and their outcomes in terms of success or failure. However, most defensive behaviors are common to many or most vertebrate species: The threat stimuli that higher animals face have a good deal in common, such that appropriate and effective responses to them show many parallels from one species to another.

Threat Stimuli and Their Impact on Defensive Behaviors

Endler (1986) divided the types of threat stimulus that animals are likely to encounter into three categories: predators, attack by conspecifics, and dangerous features of the environment. It is probably safe to say that all these classes of threat are relevant to the overwhelming majority of animal species living now or in the past.

Predators

Of the three types of threat, predators may show the most variation across prey species. Small animals all tend to be preyed on by something, regardless of whether they may themselves be predators of something else. The prototypical evolved response to this situation for terrestrial invertebrates, all of which are quite small, has been structural, involving the development of armor for protection; cryptic coloration or patterning for concealment; or bad tastes or poison to reduce palatability. Immobility and habitat choices provide some behavioral additions to this armamentarium, but the range of behavioral defenses of invertebrates is impoverished compared with that of vertebrates, and especially in comparison to mammals. Small mammals have relatively few structural defenses. Only pangolins and armadillos have sufficient armor to be effective, and it is questionable whether any mammals taste bad enough or are poisonous enough on consumption to make them immune to predator attack. Crypsis remains an important mode of defense, although utilized as much by stealth predators as by prey. Nonetheless, mammals overwhelmingly defend themselves from predators by their actions, not their body parts.

A core feature of the analysis of antipredator defense is that different types of attack call for different defenses:

As the abilities and hunting styles of predator species differ widely, it is important that heavily predated animals show appropriately different responses to different types of predators. Seyfarth and Cheney (2003) point out that some birds and mammals, including vervet and diana monkeys, have distinct alarm cries or calls to terrestrial, aerial, and even subterranean predators, and that these cries in turn produce different and appropriate defensive responses in the recipients. Suricates (meerkats) also have different cries for different types of predator and can acoustically signal the urgency of danger, as indexed by the distance between the threat stimulus and the caller (Manser, Seyfarth, & Cheney, 2002). This urgency factor for an alarm vocalization may contribute to an important motivational or emotional response parameter that results in lesser or greater strength of responding by the recipient. Ydenberg and Dill (1986) have shown that prey flight speed increases in response to decreases in the distance to a chasing predator. In the present context, such phenomena provide evidence that many animals can differentiate predators in terms of characteristics that impact the most appropriate form of defense, and respond suitably to this differentiation.

Conspecific Threat

Responses to conspecific threat vary in several ways from those to predators. First, conspecific defenses are responsive to an adaptive peculiarity of conspecific attack that, particularly in social species, such attack tends to be aimed at nonlethal targets on the body of the defender (see Offensive Aggression, later in this chapter, for details). This provides an additional mode of defense; concealment of these specific nonlethal targets, a strategy that can sharply reduce the effectiveness of conspecific attack in reaching its targets. This specific mode of defense is prominent in conspecific defense but useless, indeed counterproductive, in defense against predators, as it involves the interposition of more vulnerable sites such as the ventrum, to conspecific attack. While these coordinated target-concealing movements may occur in naive animals of some species, they also improve with practice, such that experienced fighter rats can better avoid being bitten by a conspecific attacker, even though the basic patterns of defense that they use are similar to those of inexperienced males (R. J. Blanchard, Fukunaga, Blanchard, & Kelley, 1975).

A second feature of the conspecific defense situation is that conspecific relationships may be neutral, or amiable, rather than engendering defense. From an experimental or analytic perspective, pure defensive behaviors to a conspecific may be more difficult to elicit than defensive responses to a predator, and conspecific interactions may reflect more complex motivations than simple attack and defense. For example, male rats and mice do not attack females with the same intensity as they attack sexually mature males. However, they may attack females if the female fails to cooperate with a sexual advance by the male (Arakawa, Blanchard, & Blanchard, 2007).

A third complexity, particularly in the analysis of conspecific and also antipredator defense, is that domestication has resulted in a profound reduction in defensiveness of rats and mice due to selection against animals showing strong defensiveness to handling; an effect paralleled in programs of deliberate selection of "tame" animals (Naumenko, Popova, & Nikulina, 1989; see Figure 49.1). The selection associated with domestication was informal and variable but mainly involved rejection of animals showing defensive actions that humans interpreted as aggressive (Stone, 1932). This was measured in response to human handling, a situation that elicits defensive rather than offensive attack, with the consequence that defensive attack is sharply reduced in laboratory rats whereas offensive attack appears to be little changed (Takahashi & Blanchard, 1982). Thus, laboratory rats seldom show defense prior to being attacked by a conspecific, and defensive attack to any threat stimulus is virtually absent unless

the rat is actually subjected to a sharp pain, such as shock or a bite (R. J. Blanchard, Blanchard, & Takahashi, 1978). This, plus the fact that the majority of defense-related tests are run in small chambers where flight is impossible, avoidance difficult, and risk assessment simply doesn't get measured, leaves freezing as the major measure of defensiveness for most studies of both conditioned and unconditioned defense. This is particularly true for research using rats, as domesticated (laboratory) rats show no diminution in freezing, although other defenses may be profoundly reduced. The situation is different in mice, as lab mice tend to freeze less than their wild congeners, in line with a more general though quantitatively less profound reduction in many aspects of defensiveness with domestication for this species (Figure 49.1).

Environmental Threats

The more common environmental features that pose a threat to animals in natural situations, such as spreading fire, floods, and earth movements have seldom been investigated in a laboratory context. The most prominent exception was the "visual cliff" (Walk, Gibson, & Tighe,

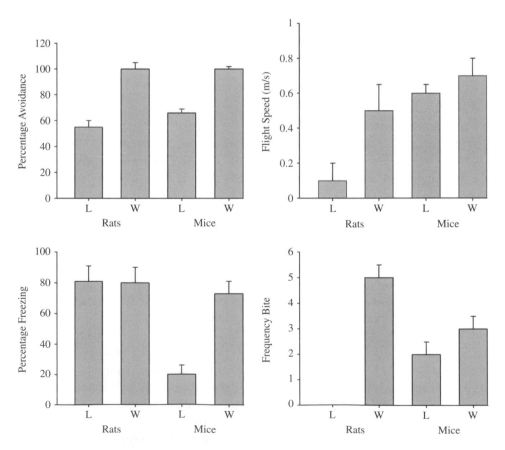

Figure 49.1 A comparison of defensive behaviors in laboratory (L) and wild (W) rats and mice demonstrates the effects of domestication.

1957) in which young animals were placed on the edge of a high table and their avoidance responses to this drop evaluated. Although innate avoidance of stepping onto an apparent drop is common in young mammals, dangerous environmental stimuli are unlikely to have had as specific and robust an effect on the shaping of defensive behaviors as have animate stimuli; that is, predators or conspecifics. This is because many environmental threats are either virtually inescapable (e.g., erupting volcanoes; earthslides; rapidly spreading fires), and leave no survivors to enjoy differential reproductive success; or they are relatively easy to avoid (bodies of water; individual stationary fires; high places), putting little emphasis on rapid and appropriate responding to threat. Potentially dangerous situations, however, including those that are novel, too dark, too light, or too open, or have other unsettling associations (e.g., problematic odors or sounds), all require some degree of vigilance to facilitate early detection of danger and preparation for appropriate reactions to it.

The traditional and still most commonly used threat stimulus for laboratory research, pain, may be associated with any of these stimuli. Predators bite or slash, as do attacking conspecifics. Fire burns, thorns cut and sting, and falls break bones. By far the most effective way to deal with all such potentially painful events is to avoid them. On an evolutionary basis, the more predictable is pain from a particular source, the more adaptive it is to simply avoid that source. This fits well with findings that predators and stimuli associated with the presence of predators (e.g., predator odors) elicit strong avoidance, even in naive laboratory animals (R. J. Blanchard, Blanchard, Rodgers, & Weiss, 1990; Dielenberg & McGregor, 1999; Zangrossi & File, 1992), whereas stimuli associated with conspecifics are more varied (Arakawa et al., 2007), befitting the wider range of behaviors that conspecifics elicit.

Threat Stimulus Characteristics

In addition to the type of threat stimulus, several characteristics of threat stimuli may have a strong impact on the success or failure of specific defensive responses. Two of these are threat ambiguity and threat distance, that is, the distance between the threatening stimulus and the threatened subject.

Threat Ambiguity

Many threats are not obvious, at least until it is too late for any specific antipredator defenses to have a good chance of success. Stealth predators are successful insofar as they can remain undetected until they reach striking distance to the prey. Also, both conspecifics and predators typically form part of the landscape for many animals so that the

detection of danger from such a source is different and more specific than simply detecting its presence. A sleeping lion poses little threat, but one that is systematically moving is to be watched very carefully!

This careful watching is labeled "vigilance" in field studies. It is often measured by the animal's activity and orientation: Nondefensive animals have clear patterns of behaviors such as foraging/eating, conspecific interactions including sexual behavior and care of young, and self-care, including grooming and sleeping. In the presence of potential danger, such activities abruptly cease, to be replaced by a "heads up" posture and scanning or sniffing the environment. If a possible danger has been spotted, the subject will orient fixedly toward it, and may even approach. In laboratory studies, the combination of orientation, sensory attention (scanning; ears forward; sniffing) and sometimes approach are labeled "risk assessment" (RA) behaviors. In rodents, RA is typically measured by the subject's assumption of a stretched posture oriented to threat, or by stretched approach to the threat source; both may include scanning and sniffing (R. J. Blanchard, Blanchard, & Hori, 1989; Pinel, Mana, & Ward, 1989). Extensions of these analyses have suggested that the division between approaching (as in RA) or avoiding aversive stimuli may provide an important factor in conceptualization of defense (McNaughton & Corr, 2004).

RA and its sequelae constitute a dynamic event. Novelty, including new places, objects, sounds, and smells, often induces initial RA, with subsequent habituation of these behaviors if no actual danger is found. This is in contrast to actual predator stimuli, to which much less habituation is seen (R. J. Blanchard et al., 1998; Dielenberg & McGregor, 1999). Although information-gathering is certainly involved in other situations as well, the stealthy postures involved in rodent RA are not seen during foraging for food. These actions appear to be functional in reducing the animal's visibility to others, while enabling it to focus on and approach, the potential threat. RA is strongly associated with learning about stimuli associated with danger (Pinel et nb al., 1989).

Threat Distance

The distance between an animal and a threat stimulus also strongly impacts the magnitude (Ydenberg & Dill, 1986) or type of defense offered. In fact, Fanselow and Lester (1988) have conceptualized a "predatory imminence" organization for defense, based largely on this relationship, with "preencounter," "postencounter," and "circa-strike" components; freezing, flight, and defensive attack, respectively. This is in general agreement with findings that, in wild rats, decreasing separation between subject and threat is an extremely robust determinant of defensive threat

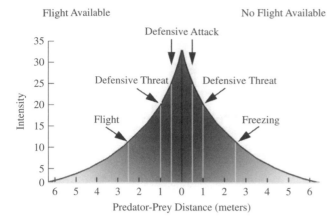

Figure 49.2 Defensive behaviors of wild rats to an approaching human are modulated by availability of escape and predator-prey distance.

(at approximately 1 m separation from predator) and defensive attack (approximately 0.5 m separation from predator) (D. C. Blanchard, Williams, & Blanchard, 1981). However, the determination of flight versus freezing appears to involve additional factors; in particular, the presence or absence of an escape route from the area where the encounter is taking place (see Figure 49.2).

Situational Stimuli That Facilitate or Hamper the Success of Specific Defenses

Features of the environment, as well as of the threat stimulus strongly influence the success or failure of particular defensive behaviors. For an optimal outcome, each such behavior should represent the most effective defense possible, given the specific features of the situation in which the threat is encountered. Flight, defined as rapid locomotion away from a threat, is possible in even relatively small

enclosures. It is only effective, however, when there is a way for the subject to actually escape the enclosure; when no way out is possible, flight simply presents the attacker with a clear shot at a particularly poorly armed portion of the defender's body, its back and rump. Other defenses, such as freezing, followed by defensive threat and attack, may be more effective when escape is impossible, and the switch from flight to the freezing/threat/attack sequence when an escape route is blocked can be demonstrated in rats (D. C. Blanchard, 1997). Other enabling stimuli include the presence of a concealing or protecting area, crucial for hiding or sheltering to be effective, and the presence of conspecifics, necessary for alarm cries to fulfill the function of alerting relatives to the presence of danger.

Conspecific presence has indeed been shown to facilitate rat ultrasonic alarm calls after encountering a cat (R. J. Blanchard, Blanchard, Agullana, & Weiss, 1991). As with flight from an inescapable situation, it is certainly possible for animals to make alarm cries when no conspecifics are present: The actions involved in defensive attack (e.g., lunging and biting) are possible even when the threat is at such a distance that these behaviors are totally ineffective. But they don't occur at such ineffective (large) distances. Instead defensive behaviors of even naive rats show extremely consistent relationships to such features as defensive distance, ambiguity of threat, and the presence of an escape route; attesting to the strong evolutionary relationship between threat and situational features, on the one hand, and the effectiveness of particular defenses, on the other. Some of these relationships are outlined in Table 49.1.

Defensive Threat and Attack

Defensive aggression, a term that tends to include both defensive threat and defensive attack, is marked out for special attention here because it is frequently and incorrectly

TABLE 49.1   Defensive behaviors as a function of threat certainty, its proximity, and presence of particular enabling stimuli

Source of Threat (and distance)	Enabling Stimuli	Behavior	Typical Outcomes
Discrete	"Way out" available	Flight	Escapes
Discrete	No means of escape	Freezing	Reduces attack
Discrete	Conspecifics nearby	Alarm cry	Warn conspecifics
Discrete	Hiding place available	Hides	No detection/access
Discrete (close in)		Defensive threat	Threatens attacker
Discrete (contact)		Defensive attack	Hurts attacker
Discrete (contact)		Startle	Startles attacker
Ambiguous (potential)		Risk assessment	Localize, identify threat
Ambiguous (potential)	Substrate	Defensive burying	Elicit animate movement

conflated with offensive aggression and needs to be differentiated from the latter. Defensive attack has different antecedents than offense, responding to threat of bodily harm or death, rather than to challenge over resources. Whereas offensive attack is reduced by fear (R. J. Blanchard, Kleinschmidt, Flannelly, & Blanchard, 1988; Harcourt & de Waal, 1992; Leyhausen, 1979), defensive attack may be enhanced by it. The circumstances under which defensive attack is most likely to occur, including close proximity or contact with a predator or conspecific attacker, or pain from this attack, are such as to maximize fear (D. C. Blanchard et al., 1981). Defensive threat signals include loud vocalizations in a range likely to be audible to predators; display of weapons such as teeth or claws (see Figure 49.3); and body orientations and distensions that enhance the animal's apparent size; all useful in indicating the defensive capabilities of the defending animal. These are highly salient signals and generally impossible to ignore. However, mammalian threat activities appear to be more than displays (Szamado, 2003). In addition to indicating (and possibly exaggerating) the capabilities and determination of the defensive animal, these actions also present weapon systems in a state of readiness, constituting preparation for the species-typical fighting techniques that will be used if the display is not effective. In all these particulars, except for body size enhancements, offense is different. Offensive threat tends to be quieter, including, in cats, a low growl rather than the scream of the defensive cat, and to involve simple approach rather than the dramatic and sometimes contorted movements of the defensive animal (Leyhausen, 1979). In addition, as noted, the target sites for attack are different from those for offensive attack in animals of the same species: Defensive attack is aimed at particularly vulnerable sites, whereas offensive attack involves targets where damage is less lethal, or that are

Figure 49.3 A territorial aggressive display in an African Hippopotamus (*Hippopotamus amphibious*).

protected by defensive structures such as the lion's mane or the rat's vibrissae.

The role of defensive threat and attack has been somewhat neglected in recent years, for several reasons. First, its role in antipredator behavior can be seen only when the predator is allowed to carry out an attack on a prey animal, an event that is seldom allowed in most contemporary laboratories: Second, because of selective breeding, in lab rats defensive attack is typically elicited only by painful contact with an attacker, usually occurring only as the immediate and direct response to a bite; making defensive attack a much less prominent component in lab rat defense. This very limited role for defensive attack is misleading, as wild-trapped and first generation lab-bred wild *R. norvegicus* show high levels of defensive threat and considerable defensive attack to human handling (Takahashi & Blanchard, 1982). However, because of its rarity in lab rats, it is often ignored as a separate type of aggression. When it does appear in consequence of manipulations such as brain stimulation or lesions, it is often interpreted as offensive aggression or, more commonly, simply as aggression, with no distinction between the two forms of attack. The so-called septal syndrome is frequently associated with aggression, but if septal-lesioned rats are allowed to escape the stranger with which they are paired, they will do so, rather than attacking it. In this case, attack occurs if the two rats are forced into close proximity by a small enclosure, whereas there is no attack by the septal-lesioned animal when the same opponent is encountered in a large cage (D. C. Blanchard, Blanchard, Takahashi, & Takahashi, 1977).

While defensive behaviors are obviously fascinating as examples of the strength and specificity of adaptive mechanisms in evolution, they have recently come to serve in a different, although related, capacity, as potential models for defense-related psychopathologies such as anxiety disorders (R. J. Blanchard et al., 2008). Their value in this capacity is that instead of measuring a global or amorphous concept of stress response or anxiety, they may provide behavioral measures that are, in some cases, similar to the behaviors that serve as core symptoms of specific anxiety disorders. One case in which this appears to be working well, in terms of both behavioral and drug response criteria, relates to flight and panic disorder (D. C. Blanchard et al., 2001; Pinheiro, Zangrossi, Del-Ben, & Graeff, 2007).

AGGRESSION

Anger and Aggression

Anger can be defined as motivation to harm another individual, and aggression as the pattern of behavior directly expressing that motive. This conceptualization works very well in the context of human behavior, in which anger has a strong subjective component, and angry individuals are capable of providing a verbal description and confirmation of it in the absence of any overt aggressive action (Averill, 1982). Neuroscience research, however, is largely done on nonhuman animals, for which there is no robust and specific measure of anger except that of aggressive behavior, so the anger component is generally omitted, and emphasis placed on aggressive behaviors. An additional consideration in the analysis of aggression is that, this definition of aggression notwithstanding, the concept of aggression has gone through many phases, definitions, and value-judgments in the history of psychology, and its basic status as an evolved and generally adaptive biobehavioral system has taken a long time to be recognized. Aggression—like defense, sexual behavior, eating, and other generally adaptive action patterns—is elicited and modulated by a range of biological, experiential, and environmental factors. There are many ways in which these eliciting and modulatory factors can prove dysfunctional, resulting in disordered aggression or, disordered defensive behavior, sexual behavior, consummatory behavior, and the like. This chapter presents the basic patterns of aggression (and defense) and merely notes that their dysfunctional aspects may be related to a range of human psychopathologies.

Offensive aggressive behaviors are associated with anger, directly or indirectly motivated by resource control, and particularly elicited by challenge to such control. In contrast, defensive aggression is associated with high levels of fear, directly motivated by danger of harm or death to the individual, and is directed at the source of the danger. Other behaviors share some similarities with either the motivations or the behaviors of these two patterns, but typically are not included under the rubric of aggression. Predation is excluded on the basis that it is aimed at consumption of the opponent, not on hurting or killing it, per se. While the act of killing appears to have positive valence for at least some predators (Kruuk, 1972), most appear to be uninterested unless they or their offspring are hungry. Also, predation does not appear to be influenced by a history of either successful or unsuccessful fighting with members of the same species (e.g., Kemble, Flannelly, Salley, & Blanchard, 1985), making it different from conspecific offensive aggression. Finally, the neural systems underlying predation appear to be different from those in aggression directed toward either conspecifics, or predators (Canteras, Ribeiro-Barbosa, & Comoli, 2001). Similarly, "play fighting" during early ontogeny does not usually produce any harm to the opponent, and both members of the interacting dyad appear to regard the activity as rewarding (see Pellis & Pellis, 1998, for review).

Although the categories of offensive and defensive aggression are typically applied to animal research and analysis, a rather different schema, of reactive versus instrumental aggression is more often utilized in human studies. This difference has had unfortunate effects on attempts to link the two fields of endeavor, as the category of reactive aggression appears to make no distinction between aggression as a reaction to the sorts of provocation that elicit offensive attack in animals, and those that elicit defensive attack. Instrumental aggression means aggression based on external rewards. Although such aggression is undoubtedly common in human life, it is not clear how this category is importantly different from other actions aimed at the acquisition of extraneous rewards, such as what might be termed "instrumental sex" (prostitution), "instrumental mothering" (nanny or nursemaid), or "instrumental allo-grooming" (hairdresser or masseuse); all of which, along with "instrumental aggression," constitute human occupational categories. Indeed, the category of "actor" makes it clear that humans can emit, convincingly and effectively, virtually any behavior for extraneous rewards. Aggression may be an easy pattern to acquire in this context, reflecting its normal role in resource competition—that the victor receives or controls the disputed resource—but the fact that aggression responds to reward says nothing exceptional about aggression.

Animal aggression has also been categorized on specific antecedents or on the types (e.g., gender, gestational status, age) of animals involved, such as male-male fighting; isolation-induced aggression, or maternal aggression (see Crabtree & Moyer, 1981, for specific categories). Some of these categories exemplify offensive aggression, elicited or modulated by specific stimuli, but some may reflect defense, or a combination of offensive and defensive aggression. Many specific agonistic situations involve mixtures of offensive and defensive aggression. In both natural and laboratory situations, aggression is a dynamic event. In intense dyadic interactions, brief perturbations can dramatically alter the motives of the interacting individuals. In particular, pain can elicit defense in an animal that had initially shown high levels of offensive attack motivation, producing a switch from offensive to defensive behavior. When two animals dispute over an important resource, both with initially high levels of offensive aggressive motivation, the typical outcome of victory for one and defeat for the other involves a switch from predominantly offensive to predominantly defensive behavior on the part of the latter; this switch is often triggered by the level of pain or damage experienced. Figure 49.4 shows a play fighting encounter between immature chacma baboons. The smaller animal is additionally showing signs of fear or defensiveness. This interpretation was confirmed

Figure 49.4 Conspecific play fighting in young chacma baboons (Papio ursinus). Kruger National Park, South Africa.

shortly after the photograph was taken by its flight and vocalization behaviors.

Mixed motivations to offense and defense also occur in laboratory tests, depending on conditions: Attacks by postparturient female rats on intruder females are typically offensive (and respond to antiaggressive drugs), whereas attacks by the same females to adult male intruders are more defensive in terms of behavior and are less responsive to drugs that are specifically effective against offensive attack (Parmigiani, Ferrari, & Palanza, 1998; Parmigiani, Rodgers, Palanza, Mainardi, & Brain, 1989). This situation of a mixture of core motivations or elements is hardly unique to aggression and defense. Being wet and being cold can easily be separated by appropriate manipulations, but under normal circumstances such as being caught in the rain or swimming in the ocean, being wet often involves being cold as well. The trick—easier for wet and cold than for offense and defense—is to find ways of separating the two for purposes of analysis.

OFFENSIVE AGGRESSION

Antecedents to Offensive Aggression

The core factor in offensive aggression is resource control. Resources may be functionally defined as objects or relationships that facilitate the enhanced representation of an individual's genes in the next generation, that is, reproductive success. Offensive aggression represents a direct approach to resource control through defeating or intimidating the other combatant into abandoning its claims to that resource. In offensive aggression, the resource control benefit comes at the expense of the other individual. This nonzero sum game approach reflects that many resources can only be used once, at least in terms of a particular episode. Food is eaten and disappears; a nest or denning site will accommodate only a single individual or a mated pair and their offspring; an impregnated female is not available to productively breed again for quite a long time.

Most offensive aggression is aimed at conspecifics. One reason for this is proximity; that conspecifics of social species are more or less constantly present and ready to use the same resources as the focal animal. Another aspect is that the adaptive resources of a focal individual are the same as those of its conspecifics of similar age and sex, bringing them into conflict over such resources when the latter are limited and sequesterable. A particularly important reason that offensive aggression is largely confined to conspecifics is that the most direct determinant of a focal animal's reproductive, adaptive success is sexual access to an opposite-sex conspecific in breeding condition. Such a resource is of limited value to a nonconspecific, as interspecies hybrids are almost always sterile, and many species that are capable of interbreeding have evolved elaborate patterns of courtship activities and displays that serve to limit breeding to conspecific individuals (Krohmer, 2004). This core resource for animals of the same sex and species is therefore of little value to animals of other species, sharply limiting the motivation for interspecies offensive attack. It is interesting, however, to note reports of fighting between Atlantic spotted dolphins and bottlenose dolphins. These species have been reported to produce viable, though not necessarily fertile, hybrids in the wild, suggesting that reproductive access may be a contested resource for them (Herzing, Moewe, & Brunnick, 2003).

The degree to which a resource can be sequestered, or set apart and protected by an individual animal, is also especially high in the case of reproduction. A female in breeding condition is a particularly valuable resource that can, in principle, be totally sequestered from competitors if sufficient time, muscle, energy, and skill are put into the effort. At the other extreme, while air to breathe is the most immediate and necessary of all resources, it is very difficult indeed to sequester. Food has a variable position along this continuum of sequesterability, with discrete items like larger-sized prey being high, and small and scattered items like grass or small insects being low on the continuum. The propensity of individuals of a given species to fight over food is highly correlated with its sequesterability. While predators or scavengers on larger prey frequently fight over food, ungulates, and other grazers show little tendency to do so, even when these small food items are also scarce: It is less productive to fight over these resources than to spend the time finding and consuming them.

The Super Resources—Dominance and Territoriality

Dominance hierarchies and territoriality are believed to have evolved because they are adaptive in facilitating access to a wide range of resources for the dominant or the territory holder, while reducing fights over specific resources. They serve as highly desirable and defensible "super resources" that initially must be gained in the same manner as other resources, through competition and, usually, fighting. Once a dominance hierarchy or a territory has been established, it often confers priority or sole access to important resources without additional fighting unless the resource holder is specifically challenged. Territoriality involves a space that may be marked (e.g., scent marks in many rodents, visual or auditory displays in many other mammalian species) and patrolled by the territory-holder to deny entry to same sex conspecifics (see Stamps & Buechner, 1985, for review). Variants to this pattern are frequent, including tolerance of same-sex individuals until they are mature; or even tolerance of sexually mature same-sex conspecifics unless they make sexual overtures to the females living in the territory. The importance of fighting over females, that is, the degree to which such fighting results in reproductive advantage in a particular species, is mirrored in the degree of sexual dimorphism of that species. Harem-holding species, in which a few dominant males strongly monopolize the reproductive services of females while nondominant males are much less likely to breed at all, show strong sexual dimorphism: Males are larger than females, and the larger the male, the more likely it is to be dominant. In contrast, monogamous species, in which male-male fighting plays a much smaller role in reproduction, tend to show little sexual size dimorphism.

For animals that do not have a specific home area but roam over a number of sites, individual territoriality is more difficult: Among social species, a dominance hierarchy is likely to be the result (Abbott et al., 2003). Dominance relationships may also be more common than territoriality in situations in which the presence of a cohesive group is advantageous and the driving away of subordinates might be detrimental; such subordinates might serve as alternative targets for predators, or lend numbers to intergroup raids (Wrangham, 1999). Thus, unlike strict territoriality, dominance hierarchies usually include tolerance of the presence of sexually mature same-sex individuals (male except for a few species, such as spotted hyenas, where females are dominant; Glickman et al., 1992), so long as these animals do not present challenges to the dominant. For species living in large groups, and with a definite breeding season, dominance hierarchies may be manifest only during such a rutting period, sometimes in a territory that is defended only during this season.

While dominance confers enhanced access to some or many resources, strategies to circumvent the dominant's priority of access have also evolved. Until recently, access to breeding females was considered a major sinecure for dominants of many species, but DNA analyses have made it clear that "sneak mating strategies" result in a substantial portion of foreign or subordinate males siring offspring in some territorial or dominance hierarchy species (Bishop, Jarvis, Spinks, Bennett, & O'Ryan, 2004; Marvan et al., 2006).

Offensive Aggression: Behaviors and Targets

When laboratory animals are maintained in small groups and the status of each animal within the group is well established, dominant male rats show a highly organized form of offensive attack, with bites aimed at the back of the attacked (typically male) animal, a site in which bites are unlikely to cause debility or death (R. J. Blanchard et al., 1975). This provides a means of delivering pain to nondominant males and encouraging them to leave the group, but without much risk of killing or damaging the reproductive potential of an animal that is likely in nature to be one of the dominant's own maturing male offspring. The same system, a bite or blow that will hurt but not kill, is also useful in species such as chimpanzees, where the continued presence of subordinate adult males in a group is important to the continuation of the group (Wrangham, 1999), and it is notable that primates as well as rodents appear to show a targeting of attack bites and blows (Adams, 1979).

While target sites for bites and blows appear to be characteristic also of less social species such as mice, mice are less inhibited about making bites to potentially dangerous sites such as the ventrum or genitals than are rats (R. J. Blanchard, O'Donnell, & Blanchard, 1979; Litvin, Blanchard, Pentkowski, & Blanchard, 2007), suggesting that the dangerousness of the attack seen in conspecific fighting may be a particularly important determinant of the degree to which that species maintains stable social groups. At one end of this continuum of dangerousness may be fights involving targets for which there are specific protective structures, that is, where protective structures have evolved to protect the recipient of blows. Many ungulates aim conspecific blows at the antlers or horns of the opponent, a site where blows are seldom (although not always) without damage to the recipient. These structures may be especially necessary in species that are equipped with very dangerous weaponry. Thus lions, the only large cats to live in social groups, have a mane over the back of the head and the neck that is not found in other large (but solitary-living) cats (see Figure 49.5).

Figure 49.5 African lions (*Panthera leo*).

Note: These males were two of a group of three brothers that hunted together and had recently killed the dominant male of a pride (Chobe National Park, Botswana).

As bites or blows (depending on the weapon system used) are aimed at specific target sites on the body of the opponent, and inhibited toward other sites, a highly effective defense by the recipient is to conceal or remove these targets by body manipulations or contortions. In rats, this involves "back-defense" behaviors including upright facing of the attacker, interposing the defender's face (which is protected by long vibrissae, another structural protection for an area that would otherwise be a target of attack; R. J. Blanchard, Blanchard, Takahashi, & Kelley, 1977) and ventrum (an area that is highly vulnerable and not attacked), between the attacker's jaws and the defender's own vulnerable dorsal (back) area. The attacker counters this defense by attempting to lunge around the defender to reach its target: The defender pivots in the same direction, to continue to face the attacker, and so on. When the attack becomes very pressing, the defender may slip backward to lie on its back, additionally rolling toward the attacker if the latter attempts to dig under for a bite. That these attack and defensive behaviors function to facilitate or deny, respectively, access to specific target sites may be seen in findings that they occur together for the two members of an attack/defense dyad, with the form of defense

typically serving to drive the specific actions involved in attack (Takahashi & Blanchard, 1982).

While targets of aggressive attack and strategies to defend them have been specifically investigated in only a few species, targeting appears to be a widespread phenomenon among mammals, and targets of play fighting have been described in a wide range of both mammals and primates (Pellis & Pellis, 1987).

The tenet that damaging behaviors such as bites and blows tend to be aimed at less vulnerable sites on the opponent during intraspecific offensive attack, with this tendency higher in social species, is important to understanding a number of factors in aggression. First, it represents an important enabling factor for the adaptive value of aggression to be realized while avoiding damage to conspecific opponents. Second, it provides an explanation for the specific form of a number of attack (and defensive) behaviors seen during intraspecific fighting. Third, it is highly compatible with findings of structural adaptations for intraspecific fighting, including manes and ruffs, antlers, horns, and the like. Fourth, it provides a means of evaluating whether a specific harm-delivering action represents offensive or defensive aggression. As Pellis and Pellis (1987) note, the target site strategy applies to play fighting as well, but the targets of play fights tend to be different from those in either offensive or defensive attack.

The second of these considerations, that target sites for attack provide an explanation for the specific form of attack (and also defense) in some species, is also of interest in terms of the more traditional ethological interpretation that many of these same actions represent signals to the opposing combatant (see Figure 49.6). Instead, a target site view suggests that many such movements represent offensive strategies adaptive in gaining access to the targets of attack, or defensive strategies useful in denying the opponent such access (R. J. Blanchard et al., 1977). If a particular intraspecific aggressive or defensive action demonstrably does not aid in the attainment or denial of such access, it might be examined for its potential status as a signal. Thus piloerection, erection of hairs making the combatant appear larger, might well be regarded as sending a (false or exaggerated) signal of the animal's size.

As discussed later, there is a clear and important use of target sites for offensive versus defensive attack to determine, within a paradigm or in an individual fighting sequence, what pattern of aggression is being demonstrated. This should be a particularly important consideration in work on the neural systems or neurotransmitters involved in offensive versus defensive aggression. In practice, the requirement of separating offensive from defensive attack has largely involved use of paradigms such as the resident-intruder model, in which these patterns should

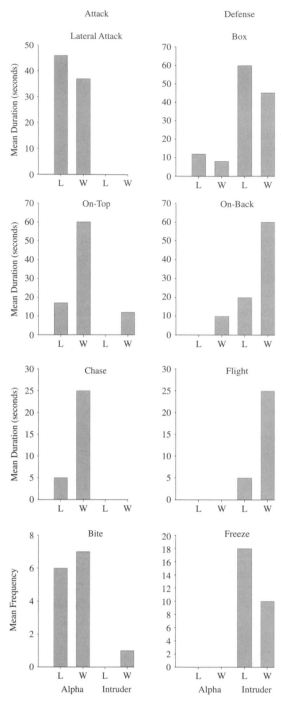

Figure 49.6 Attack and defensive behaviors of laboratory (L) or wild (W) dominant rats (two left bars of each graph) and intruder (L or W right bars of each graph) during conspecific fighting of *Rattus norvegicus*. Behaviors in the left column (attack, on top, chase and bite) are associated with offensive attack, whereas those in the right column (box, on back, flight, and freeze) are associated with defense. These durations or frequencies were measured in within-strain (L or W) encounters in which lateral attack (dominant) and boxing (subordinate) occur as dyads, as do on top and on back, or chase and flight. Bite and freeze, however, are unrelated behaviors.

Note: From "Attack and Defense in Laboratory and Wild Norway and Black Rats," by L. K. Takahashi and R. J. Blanchard, 1982, *Behavioral Processes, 7,* pp. 49–62. Adapted with permission.

be polarized, but without necessarily checking individual behaviors to determine that they do represent either offensive or defensive behavior, a situation that has resulted in some potential confusion with reference to the biology of offensive and defensive aggression.

Offensive Interspecies Fighting

Descriptions of interspecies aggression distinct from predator-prey relationships are increasing in frequency, and these are increasingly recognized as having important effects on species ecology and distributions. Among mammalian carnivores, competition over food or territories appears to be particularly common (and deadly), suggesting that these represent interspecies offensive aggression. Thus wolves and bears have been shown to contest kills in areas of low prey availability, while lions, leopards, cheetahs, and wild dogs all have been noted in altercations over food (Ballard, 1982). These interactions may be symmetrical (both species attack the other), as with hyenas and lions, in which the initial direction of attack depends on the numbers of each species involved; or asymmetrical, when one species usually dominates over the other in such interactions (e.g., lions attack cheetahs and the latter flee). That this is not a normal predation situation is reflected in the rarity of consumption of the loser by the victor. In fact, the usual outcome is that the loser flees and the victor, failing to chase, consumes the spoils of victory, the carcass of the prey.

Strategies for minimizing interspecific aggression over resources include spatial and temporal differences in habitat usage. Interspecies aggressive interactions have a pronounced effect on the spatial distribution of animals, sometimes forcing the weaker participant species to completely withdraw from a given habitat. Cheetahs and wild dogs show avoidance of areas characterized by high prey densities which in turn attract the top carnivores (hyenas and lions; Caro, 1994; Creel & Creel, 1996). They thus survive and reproduce most successfully in areas of low prey and competitor density. Adults of one species may target only the young of the competing species (Palomares & Caro, 1999). In areas where arctic and red foxes are sympatric, red foxes have been shown to kill juvenile arctic foxes (Tannerfeldt & Elmhagen, 2002). As a result, arctic foxes avoid red foxes by forming dens in areas poor in resources; namely those in higher altitudes. Temporal differences in habitat usage may include seasonal as well as daily activity pattern variations. In Chile, the sympatric grey and culpeo foxes display differential daily activity patterns, with the former preferring the summer and fall seasons and the latter winter and spring (Johnson & Franklin, 1994). In Kruger National Park in South Africa, lions, wild dogs, and cheetahs show a preference for different hunting times. Schaller (1972) proposed that cheetahs in the Serengeti prefer hunting at midday due to reduced interference from lions and hyenas at this time.

Such interspecific aggression between predators may be an important determinant of densities of other species than the combatants. Red foxes, which aggressively interact with coyotes, feed on duck nests. A decrease in coyotes produces an increase in red foxes, which ultimately leads to dramatic decreases in duck populations (Sovada, Sargeant, & Grier, 1995). Coyote-wolf interactions have an impact on populations of San Joaquin kit foxes, with predation by coyotes responsible for over 75% of kit fox mortality (Cypher & Scrivner, 1992; Linnell & Strand, 2000; Ralls & White, 1995). Thus, wolf extermination directly affects coyote numbers, which in turn negatively affect the kit fox population.

Interspecific offensive aggression would be expected to be different from intraspecies offense in respect to the role of mechanisms reducing damage to the opponent. While this has not been examined systematically, the not uncommon findings of lethal attack during intraspecific fighting of predators over prey (e.g., Lawick-Goodall, 1971, p. 185) is consonant with a view that such fighting is neither inhibited nor is its lethality reduced by targeting of nonvulnerable structures, such as may occur in intraspecies fighting.

Neural Systems: Defense

The neural systems involved in conditioned aspects of defense appear to encompass a much wider array of structures than do those underlying unconditioned defensive behaviors (for reviews, see Chapter 39, this volume, or Myers & Davis, 2008). The present material will be confined to neural systems involved in unconditioned defense.

A productive approach to this issue involves evaluation of intermediate early gene (c-fos) activation patterns in rodents following exposure to predators (Canteras & Goto, 1999) or predator odors (Dielenberg et al., 2001). These show a high degree of agreement, indicating the involvement of several forebrain, midbrain, and hindbrain structures, including the hypothalamus (anterior hypothalamic nucleus [AHN], dorsomedial part of the ventromedial nucleus [VMHdm], and the dorsal premamillary nucleus [PMd]); the posteroventral portion of the medial nucleus of the amygdala (MeApl); the bed nucleus of the stria terminalis (BNST); and the periaqueductal gray (PAG).

The Medial Hypothalamic Zone

Canteras (2008) proposed that the anterior hypothalamic nucleus (AHN), the dorsomedial part of the ventromedial nucleus (VMHdm), and the dorsal premamillary nucleus (PMd) of the hypothalamus serve as an integrating medial hypothalamic zone (MHZ) for the regulation of defense, with input from the amygdala, reflecting olfactory, and other predator-related sensory information, and from the septohippocampal system. The latter may supply information related to contextual or spatial orientation, a crucial factor in determining the form of defensive behavior. The MHZ is reciprocally connected, via the thalamus, to the cortex (Risold, Thompson, & Swanson, 1997), providing a potential avenue for cortical modulation of this level of integration. Finally, the MHD may initiate defensive responses through descending projections to brain stem regions, specifically the PAG, for which there has long been independent evidence of involvement in defensive behavior (reviewed by Bandler & Keay, 1996). Lesion studies support the involvement of many of these structures in defense (Canteras & Goto, 1999; Dielenberg, Hunt, & McGregor, 2001; Markham, Blanchard, Canteras, Cuyno, & Blanchard, 2004), with particularly strong reductions in unconditioned defensive behaviors seen following lesions of the PMd (for summary see Figure 49.7).

The Hippocampus

The hippocampus (HPC) is the topic of an immense literature on aversive situational conditioning (for review see Fanselow & Ponnusamy, 2008) and lesions in the ventral HPC reduce unconditioned defensive behaviors of rats to a cat (Pentkowski, Blanchard, Lever, Litvin, & Blanchard, 2006). The hippocampus sends projections to the MHD system by way of two main pathways. First, to the dorsal region of the ventrolateral zone of the rostral part of the lateral septal nucleus (LSrvld; Risold & Swanson, 1997), which then projects to the AHN and PMd (Comoli, Ribeiro-Barbosa, & Canteras, 2000; Risold, Canteras, & Swanson, 1994). The LSrvld contains gaba-aminobutyric acid (GABA)ergic neurons that may provide inhibitory inputs to circuits mediating defense (Canteras, 2002). Second, projections to the lateral, medial, and posterior basomedial and basolateral amygdala nuclei (Canteras & Swanson, 1992; Petrovic, Risold, & Swanson, 1996, 2001; Pikkarainen, Ronkko, Savander, Insausti, & Pitkanen, 1999), which then project through the BNST to the VMHdm and AHN, may be involved in the integration of sensory information impacting defense (Canteras, 2002).

Amygdala

The amygdala has long been known as a key structure in the expression of innate defensive responses of a rat to a predator, a cat (D. C. Blanchard & Blanchard, 1972). The medial amygdala, with strong projections to both the VMH and the AHN is involved in unconditioned fear responses of rats to cat odor, likely through its mediation of odor information from the accessory olfactory system

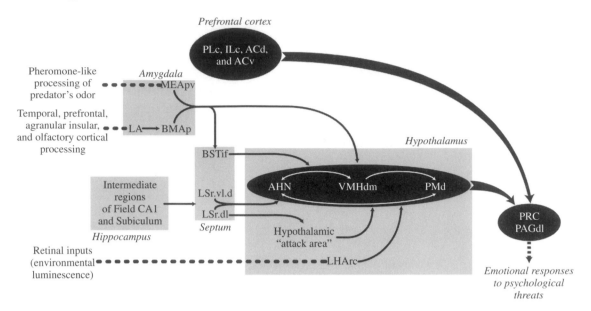

Figure 49.7 Summary diagram showing the organization of major parallel prosencephalic pathways involved in the control of innate fear responses to psychological threats.

Note: Acd = Anterior cingulate area, dorsal part; Acv = Anterior cingulate area, ventral part; AHN = Anterior hypothalamic nucleus; BMAp = Basomedial amygdalar nucleus, posterior part; BSTif = Bed nuclei of the stria terminalis, interfascicular nucleus; Ilc = Imfralimbic area, caudal part; LA = Lateral amygdalar nucleus; LHArc = Lateral hypothalamic area, retinoceptive region; LSr.dl = Lateral septal nucleus, rostral part, dorsolateral zone; LSr.vl.d = Lateral septal nucleus, rostral part, ventrolateral zone, dorsal region; MEApv = Medial amygdalar nucleus, posteroventral part; PAGdl = Periaqueductal gray, dorsolateral part; PLc = Prelimbic area, caudal part; PMd = Dorsal premammillary nucleus; PRC = Precommissural nucleus; VMHdm = Ventromedial hypothalamic nucleus, dorsomedial part.

(Staples, McGregor, Apfelbach, & Hunt, 2007). An n-methyl-d-aspartate (NMDA)-dependent pathway from the central amygdala to the lateral PAG may mediate lasting anxiogenic behaviors in the elevated plus maze (EPM) following predator stress (R. Adamec, 2001; R. E. Adamec, Blundell, & Burton, 2005).

The periaqueductal grey (PAG) has a rostrocaudal columnar organization, with four columns: the dorsolateral (dlPAG), dorsomedial (dmPAG), lateral (lPAG), and ventrolateral (vlPAG) (Bandler & Keay, 1996). The MHZ has extensive projections to the PAG: From VMH to all parts of the PAG; from PMd to the dlPAG; and from AHN to dmPAG and vlPAG (Cameron, Khan, Westlund, & Willis, 1995; Canteras, 2002; Vianna & Brandao, 2003). Chemical or electrical stimulation of the PAG and some surrounding areas (e.g., superior and inferior colliculi; cuneiform nucleus) produces defensive behaviors such as freezing, arousal and escape, defecation, analgesia, and changes in autonomic measures (see Bandler & Keay, 1996, and Vienna & Bandao, 2003, for review). In particular, flight responses from activation of the dorsal PAG have been suggested to serve as an important mechanism in panic attacks (Graeff, Guimarães, De Andrade, & Deakin, 1996). Microinjection of excitatory amino acids (EAA) into the vlPAG evoked a passive coping reaction characterized by quiescence, decreased vigilance, hypotension, and bradycardia (Bandler & Carrive, 1988; Bandler, Depaulis, & Vergnes, 1985; Bandler & Keay, 1996; Bandler & Shipley, 1994; Depaulis, Bandler, & Vergnes, 1989; Depaulis & Vergnes, 1986; Zhang, Bandler, & Carrive, 1990; Zhang, Davis, Bandler, & Carrive, 1994; but see Mongeau, De Oca, Fanselow, & Marsden, 1998, for a different view).

Neural Systems for Offensive and Defensive Aggression

At first glance, the neural systems associated with aggression, for example, hypothalamus, septum, periaqueductal grey (PAG), amygdala, bed nucleus of the stria terminalis (BNST), and frontal cortex (Delville, De Vries, & Ferris, 2000; Nelson & Trainor, 2007) appear to be virtually identical to those involved with defense. Immunostaining for c-Fos has shown increased labeling in the MeA, septum, BNST, hypothalamus, and amygdala during displays of intermale aggression (e.g., Veening et al., 2005), with relatively similar Fos activation patterns for rats (Halasz, Liposits, Meelis, Kruk, & Haller, 2002; Veening et al., 2005) hamsters (Delville et al., 2000; Kollack-Walker & Newman, 1995) and mice (Haller, Toth, Halasz, & De Boer, 2006). In particular, aggression appears to be associated with enhanced vasopressin representation in an anterior hypothalamus–medial preoptic area (AHN) in hamsters (Ferris, Axelson, Martin, & Roberge, 1989) while the "hypothalamic attack area" (HAA) in rats consists of the intermediate hypothalamic area (IHA) and the ventrolateral pole of the ventromedial nucleus of the hypothalamus (VMHvl). The view that the HAA (rats) and AHN (hamsters) are central sites in mediating rodent aggression (Delville et al., 2000; Risold et al., 1994) is supported by findings that both share reciprocal neural connections with the LS, MeA, PAG, and BNST (Coolen & Wood, 1998; Risold & Swanson, 1997; Roeling et al., 1994) sites that are commonly associated with aggressive behaviors.

However, the apparent overlap between neural systems for aggression and for defense may be misleading, as different sites or systems within these brain areas may differentially mediate defensive and offensive behaviors. The posteroventral portion of the medial amygdala (MeApv) and the dorsomedial division of the VMH (VMHdm) have been implicated in mediating defensive behaviors (Canteras, 2002), whereas it is the posterodorsal region of the MeA (MeApd) and the ventrolateral section of the VMH (VMHvl) that may be components of the neural circuit subserving the expression of aggression (Kollack-Walker & Newman, 1995; Swanson, 2000; Veening et al., 2005). In addition, the overlap is hardly complete: The PMd, an area in which particularly robust effects on defense to stimuli have been obtained (see Markham et al., 2004, for review) appears not to be involved in aggression.

An additional complication of these analyses is that the behavior changes associated with lesions and stimulations of these structures are sometimes ambiguous in terms of a distinction between offensive and defensive attack. Thus stimulation of the HAA produces a violent attack on conspecifics in rats, but Kruk (1991) makes the important observation that such hypothalamic attack is insensitive to many drugs that do affect naturally elicited attack in rats, and that it does not involve the same target-attack behaviors, such as lateral attack to obtain access to the back, that is typical of normal aggression. Similarly, electrical stimulation of the VMH in the cat produces a pattern of ear retraction, growling, hissing, and retreat intermixed with paw attack (Sweidan, Edinger, & Siegel, 1991), that the authors appropriately interpret as reflecting affective defense: In terms of behaviors of nonmanipulated cats in agonistic encounters, each of these components (except for growling, which may be seen in either situation) reflects defensive attack, rather than offensive attack (Leyhausen, 1979). This may represent cross-species variation in the organization of such behaviors or may suggest that there is an important defensive attack component to the aggression seen after stimulation of the VMH.

The differentiation between defensive and offensive aggression, often not clearly made in the context of brain stimulation studies, may also be of interest in the context of aggression that is sharply enhanced by genetic, endocrine, drug, or experiential manipulations. For at least some of these aggression enhancements (e.g., aggression escalated by alcohol. See Miczek et al., 2007, for review), changes in serotonergic and GABAergic systems leading to reductions of cortical inhibitory influences appear to be important. Decreases in GABA activity resulting in lowered PFC inhibition may also be involved in the enhanced attack seen in adrenalectomized male rats maintained on low (and unchanging) levels of glucocorticoids. This aggression was characterized by attacks aimed at vulnerable body targets including the head, throat, and belly, and thus was more suggestive of a defensive attack pattern than of offense (Halasz, Totha, Kallob, Liposits, & Haller, 2006). Attack accompanying unilateral electrical stimulation of the hypothalamic attack area (HAA) and also aimed at vulnerable body sites was associated with increased activation of the central amygdala (CeA), the mediodorsal thalamus (MD), and several cortical areas (Halasz et al., 2002). These and other methods of enhancing aggression have seen a strong upsurge of attention. It will be of considerable interest to determine if the behaviors involved in these enhancements and the neural systems underlying them can illuminate not only patterns of offensive and defensive attack, but also how changes in (inhibitory?) factors can alter some of the constraints that normally differentiate the two types of aggression.

While it is striking that there is so much overlap in brain systems associated with offense and defense, in rodents, this should be viewed in the context of other behaviors such as reproduction, parenting, and sociality, which often involve many of the same brain areas (e.g., De Vries & Panzica, 2006). A major organizing factor for behaviors involving interactions with conspecifics and other animals is olfaction. For macrosmatic rodents, the subjects for the vast majority of these research programs, olfaction is perhaps the core sensory system in recognizing and responding to biologically important, animate stimuli. These are mediated by the main and the accessory olfactory systems (for reviews, see Bakker, 2003; Keller, Douhard, Baum, & Bakker, 2006), which, along with their connections, comprise the rhinencephalic brain; traditionally the seat of the emotions. While, as noted for the MeA and the VMH, different types of input (in this case, odors of predator versus adult male conspecific) may produce within-area differentiations in activity, the gross areas affected may be similar, representing a particular sequence in an only partly differentiated olfactory input. This analysis, while crude, has an important corollary, that understanding of the systems underlying defense and aggression will require a great deal more specific attention to functional hodology, as well as to the crucial minutiae of behavior.

REFERENCES

Abbott, D. H., Kerverne, E. B., Bercovitch, F. B., Shively, C. A., Mendoza, S. P., Saltzman, W., et al. (2003). Are subordinates always stressed? A comparative analysis of rank differences in cortisol levels among primates. *Hormones and Behavior, 43,* 67–82.

Adamec, R. E. (2001). Does long term potentiation in periacqueductal gray (PAG) mediate lasting changes in rodent anxiety-like behavior (ALB) produced by predator stress?: Effects of low frequency stimulation (LFS) of PAG on place preference and changes in ALB produced by predator stress. *Behavioural Brain Research, 120,* 111–135.

Adamec, R. E., Blundell, J., & Burton, P. (2005). Neural circuit changes mediating lasting brain and behavioral response to predator stress. *Neuroscience and Biobehavioral Reviews, 29,* 1225–1241.

Adams, D. B. (1979). Brain mechanisms for offense, defense and submission. *Behavioral and Brain Sciences, 2,* 201–241.

Arakawa, H., Blanchard, D. C., & Blanchard, R. J. (2007). Colony formation of C57BL/6J mice in visible burrow system: Identification of eusocial behaviors in a background strain for genetic animal models of autism. *Behavioural Brain Research, 176,* 27–39.

Averill, J. R. (1982). *Anger and aggression: An essay on emotion.* New York: Springer-Verlag.

Bakker, J. (2003). Sexual differentiation of the neuroendocrine mechanisms regulating mate recognition in mammals. *Journal of Neuroendocrinology, 15,* 615–621.

Ballard, W. B. (1982). Gray wolf-brown bear relationships in the Nelchina Basin of South-Central Alaska. In F. H. Harrington & P. C. Paquet (Eds.), *Wolves of the world: Perspectives of behavior, ecology and conservation* (pp. 71–80). Park Ridge, NJ: Noyes Publications.

Bandler, R., & Carrive, P. (1988). Integrated defence reaction elicited by excitatory amino acid microinjection in the midbrain periaqueductal grey region of the unrestrained cat. *Brain Research, 439*(1–2), 95–106.

Bandler, R., Depaulis, A., & Vergnes, M. (1985). Identification of midbrain neurones mediating defensive behaviour in the rat by microinjections of excitatory amino acids. *Behavioural Brain Research, 15,* 107–119.

Bandler, R., & Keay, K. A. (1996). Columnar organization in the midbrain periaqueductal gray and the integration of emotional expression. *Progress in Brain Research, 107,* 285–300.

Bandler, R., & Shipley, M. T. (1994). Columnar organization in the midbrain periaqueductal gray: Modules for emotional expression? *Trends in Neurosciences, 17,* 379–389.

Bishop, J. M., Jarvis, J. U. M., Spinks, A. C., Bennett, N. C., & O'Ryan, C. (2004). Molecular insights into patterns of colony composition and paternity in the common mole-rat *Cryptomys hottentotus hottentotus. Molecular Ecology, 15,* 1217–1229.

Blanchard, D. C. (1997). Stimulus, environmental and pharmacological control of defensive behaviors. In M. Bouton & M. S. Fanselow (Eds.), *Learning, motivation and cognition: The functional behaviorism of Robert C. Bolles* (pp. 283–305). Washington, DC: American Psychological Association.

Blanchard, D. C., & Blanchard, R. J. (1972). Innate and conditioned reactions to threat in rats with amygdaloid lesions. *Journal of Comparative and Physiological Psychology, 81,* 281–290.

Blanchard, D. C., & Blanchard, R. J. (2008). Defensive behaviors, fear and anxiety. In R. J. Blanchard, D. C. Blanchard, G. Griebel, & D. J. Nutt (Eds.), *Hand book of anxiety and fear* (pp. 63–80). Amsterdam: Elsevier Academic Press.

Blanchard, D. C., Blanchard, R. J., Takahashi, L. K., & Takahashi, T. (1977). Septal lesions and aggressive behavior. *Behavioral Biology, 21,* 157–161.

Blanchard, D. C., Williams, G., & Blanchard, R. J. (1981). Taming of wild rattus norvegicus by lesions of the mesencephalic central gray. *Physiological Psychology, 9,* 157–163.

Blanchard, R. J., Blanchard, D. C., Agullana, R., & Weiss, S. M. (1991). Twenty-two kHz alarm cries to presentation of a predator, by laboratory rats living in visible burrow systems. *Physiology and Behavior, 50,* 967–972.

Blanchard, R., Blanchard, D.C., Griebel, G., and Nutt, D. (2007). *Handbook of Anxiety and Fear.* London: Elsevier.

Blanchard, R. J., Blanchard, D. C., & Hori, K. (1989). An ethoexperimental approach to the study of defense. In R. J. Blanchard, P. F. Brain, D. C. Blanchard, & S. Parmigiani (Eds.), *Ethoexpermental approaches to the study of behavior* (Vol. 48, pp. 114–136). Boston: Kluver Academic.

Blanchard, R. J., Blanchard, D. C., Rodgers, J., & Weiss, S. M. (1990). The characterization and modelling of antipredator defensive behavior. *Neuroscience and Biobehavioral Reviews, 14,* 463–472.

Blanchard, R. J., Blanchard, D. C., & Takahashi, L. K. (1978). Pain and aggression in the rat. *Behavioral Biology, 23,* 291–305.

Blanchard, R. J., Blanchard, D. C., Takahashi, T., & Kelley, M. J. (1977). Attack and defensive behaviour in the albino rat. *Animal Behaviour, 25,* 622–634.

Blanchard, R. J., Fukunaga, K., Blanchard, D. C., & Kelley, M. J. (1975). Conspecific aggression in the laboratory rat. *Journal of Comparative and Physiological Psychology, 89,* 1204–1209.

Blanchard, R. J., Kleinschmidt, C. K., Flannelly, K. J., & Blanchard, D. C. (1988). Fear and aggression in the rat. *Aggressive Behavior, 10,* 309–315.

Blanchard, R. J., Nikulina, J. N., Sakai, R. R., McKittrick, C., McEwen, B., & Blanchard, D. C. (1998). Behavioral and endocrine change following chronic predatory stress. *Physiology and Behavior, 63,* 561–569.

Blanchard, R. J., O'Donnell, V., & Blanchard, D. C. (1979). Attack and defensive behaviors in the albino mouse (*Mus musculus*). *Aggressive Behavior, 5,* 341–352.

Cain, C. K., & LeDoux, J. E. (2008). Brain mechanisms of Pavlovian and instrumental aversive conditioning. In R. J. Blanchard, D. C. Blanchard, G. Griebel, & D. J. Nutt (Eds.), *Handbook of anxiety and fear* (pp. 103–124). Amsterdam: Elsevier Academic Press.

Cameron, A. A., Khan, I. A., Westlund, K. N., & Willis, W. D. (1995). The efferent projections of the periaqueductal gray in the rat: A phaseolus vulgaris-leucoagglutinin study: Pt. II. Descending projections. *Journal of Comparative Neurology, 351,* 585–601.

Canteras, N. S. (2002). The medial hypothalamic defensive system: Hodological organization and functional implications. *Pharmacology, Biochemistry, and Behavior, 71,* 481–491.

Canteras, N. S. (2008). Neural systems activated in response to predators and partial predator stimuli. In R. J. Blanchard, D. C. Blanchard, G. Griebel, & D. J. Nutt (Eds.), *Handbook of anxiety and fear* (pp. 125–140). Amsterdam: Elsevier Academic Press.

Canteras, N. S., & Goto, M. (1999). Fos-like immunoreactivity in the periaqueductal gray of rats exposed to a natural predator. *NeuroReport, 10,* 413–418.

Canteras, N. S., Ribeiro-Barbosa, E. R., & Comoli, E. (2001). Tracing from the dorsal premammillary nucleus prosencephalic systems involved in the organization of innate fear responses. *Neuroscience and Biobehavioral Reviews, 25*(7–8), 661–668.

Canteras, N. S., & Swanson, L. W. (1992). Projections of the ventral subiculum to the amygdala, septum, and hypothalamus: A PHAL anterograde tracttracing study of the rat. *Journal of Comparative Neurology, 324,* 180–194.

Caro, T. M. (1994). *Cheetahs of the Serengeti Plains*. Chicago: Chicago University Press.

Comoli, E., Ribeiro-Barbosa, E. R., & Canteras, N. S. (2000). Afferent connections of the dorsal premammillary nucleus. *Journal of Comparative Neurology, 423*, 83–98.

Coolen, L. M., & Wood, R. I. (1998). Bidirectional connections of the medial amygdaloid nucleus in the Syrian hamster brain: Simultaneous anterograde and retrograde tract tracing. *Journal of Comparative Neurology, 399*, 189–209.

Crabtree, J. M., & Moyer, K. E. (1981). *Bibliography of aggressive behavior: A reader's guide to the research literature*. New York: Alan R. Liss.

Creel, S., & Creel, N. M. (1996). Limitation of African wild dogs by competition with larger carnivores. *Conservation Biology, 10*, 526–538.

Cypher, B. L., & Scrivner, J. H. (1992). Coyote control to protect endangered San Joaquin kit foxes at the naval petroleum reserves, California. *Proceedings of the Vertebrate Pest Conference, 15*, 42–47.

Delville, Y., De Vries, G. J., & Ferris, C. F. (2000). Neural connections of the anterior hypothalamus and agonistic behavior in golden hamsters. *Brain, Behavior and Evolution, 55*, 53–76.

Depaulis, A., Bandler, R., & Vergnes, M. (1989). Characterization of pretentorial periaqueductal gray matter neurons mediating intraspecific defensive behaviors in the rat by microinjections of kainic acid. *Brain Research, 486*, 121–132.

Depaulis, A., & Vergnes, M. (1986). Elicitation of intraspecific defensive behaviors in the rat by microinjection of picrotoxin, a gamma-aminobutyric acid antagonist, into the midbrain periaqueductal gray matter. *Brain Research, 367*(1–2), 87–95.

De Vries, G. J., & Panzica G. C. (2006). Sexual differentiation of central vasopressin and vasotocin systems in vertebrates: Different mechanisms, similar endpoints. *Neuroscience, 138*(3), 947–55.

Dielenberg, R. A., Hunt, G. E., & McGregor, I. S. (2001). "When a rat smells a cat": The distribution of fos immunoreactivity in rat brain following exposure to a predatory odor. *Neuroscience, 104*, 1085–1097.

Dielenberg, R. A., & McGregor, I. S. (1999). Low-dose midazolam attenuates predatory odor avoidance in rats. *Pharmacology, Biochemistry, and Behavior, 62*, 197–201.

Edmunds, M. (1974). *Defence in animals: A survey of anti-predator defences*. New York: Longman Group.

Endler, J. A. (1986). *Defense against predators*. Chicago: University of Chicago Press.

Fanselow, M. S., & Lester, L. S. (1988). A functional behaviouristic approach to aversively motivated behavior: Predatory imminence as a determinant of the topography of defensive behavior. In R. C. Bolles & M. D. Beecher (Eds.), *Evolution and learning* (pp. 185–199). Mahwah, NJ: Erlbaum.

Fanselow, M. S., & Ponnusamy, R. (2008). The use of conditioning tasks to model fear and anxiety. In R. J. Blanchard, D. C. Blanchard, G. Griebel, & D. J. Nutt (Eds.), *Handbook of anxiety and fear* (pp. 29–48). Amsterdam: Elsevier Academic Press.

Ferris, C. F., Axelson, J. F., Martin, A. M., & Roberge, L. F. (1989). Vasopressin immunoreactivity in the anterior hypothalamus is altered during the establishment of dominant/subordinate relationships between hamsters. *Neuroscience, 29*, 675–683.

Glickman, S. E., Frank, L. G., Licht, P., Yalcinkaya, T., Siiteri, P. K., & Davidson, J. (1992). Sexual differentiation of the female spotted hyena: One of nature's experiments. *Annals of the New York Academy of Sciences, 662*, 135–159.

Graeff, F. G., Guimarães, F. S., De Andrade, T. G., & Deakin, J. F. (1996). Role of 5-HT in stress, anxiety, and depression. *Pharmacology, Biochemistry, and Behavior, 54*(1), 129–141.

Halasz, J., Liposits, Z., Meelis, W., Kruk, M. R., & Haller, J. (2002). Hypothalamic attack area-mediated activation of the forebrain in aggression. *NeuroReport, 13*, 1267–1270.

Halasz, J., Totha, M., Kallob, I., Liposits, Z., & Haller, J. (2006). The activation of prefrontal cortical neurons in aggression: A double labeling study. *Behavioural Brain Research, 175*, 166–175.

Haller, J., Toth, M., Halasz, J., & De Boer, S. F. (2006). Patterns of violent aggression-induced brain c-fos expression in male mice selected for aggressiveness. *Physiology and Behavior, 88*(1–2), 173–182.

Harcourt, A. H., & de Waal, F. B. M. (1992). *Coalitions and alliances in humans and other animals*. New York: Oxford University Press.

Hedinger, H. (1969). *The psychology of animals in zoos and circuses*. New York: Dover Publications.

Herzing, D. L., Moewe, K., & Brunnick, B. J. (2003). Interspecies interactions between Atlantic spotted dolphins, Stenella frontalis and bottlenose dolphins, *Tursiops truncatus*, on Great Bahama Bank, Bahamas. *Aquatic Mammals, 29*, 335–341.

Johnson, W. E., & Franklin, W. L. (1994). Spatial resource partitioning by sympatric grey fox (Dusicyon griseus) and culpeo fox (Dusicyon culpaeus) in southern Chile. *Canadian Journal of Zoology, 72*, 1788–1793.

Keller, M., Douhard, Q., Baum, M. J., & Bakker, J. (2006). Destruction of the main olfactory epithelium reduces female sexual behavior and olfactory investigation in female mice. *Chemical Senses, 31*, 315–323.

Kemble, E. D., Flannelly, K. J., Salley, H., & Blanchard, R. J. (1985). Mouse killing, insect predation, and conspecific attack by rats with differing prior aggressive experience. *Physiology and Behavior, 34*, 645–648.

Kollack-Walker, S., & Newman, S. W. (1995). Mating and agonistic behavior produce different patterns of fos immunolabeling in the male syrian hamster brain. *Neuroscience, 66*, 721–736.

Krohmer, R. W. (2004). The male red-sided garter snake (*Thamnophis sirtalis parietalis*): Reproductive pattern and behavior. *ILAR Journal, 45*, 54–74.

Kruk, M. R. (1991). Ethology and pharmacology of hypothalamic aggression in the rat. *Neuroscience and Biobehavioral Reviews, 15*, 527–538.

Kruuk, H. (1972). *The spotted hyena: A study of predation and social behavior*. Chicago: University of Chicago press.

Lawick-Goodall, J. (1971). *In the shadow of man*. Boston: Houghton Mifflin.

Leyhausen, P. (1979). *Cat behavior: The predatory and social behavior of domestic and wild cats*. New York & London: Garland STPM Press.

Linnell, J. D. C., & Strand, O. (2000). Interference interactions, co-existence and conservation of mammalian carnivores. *Diversity and Distributions, 6*, 169–176.

Litvin, Y., Blanchard, D. C., & Blanchard, R. J. (2007). Rat 22kHz ultrasonic vocalizations as alarm cries. *Behavioural Brain Research, 182*, 166–172.

Litvin, Y., Blanchard, D. C., Pentkowski, N. S., & Blanchard, R. J. (2007). A pinch or a lesion: A reconceptualization of biting consequences in mice. *Aggressive Behavior, 33*, 1–7.

Manser, M. B., Seyfarth, R. M., & Cheney, D. L. (2002). Suricate alarm calls signal predator class and urgency. *Trends in Cognitive Sciences, 6*, 55–57.

Markham, C. M., Blanchard, D. C., Canteras, N. S., Cuyno, C. D., & Blanchard, R. J. (2004). Modulation of predatory odor processing following lesions to the dorsal premammillary nucleus. *Neuroscience Letters, 372*(1–2), 22–26.

Marvan, R., Stevens, J. M., Roeder, A. D., Mazura, I., Bruford, M. W., & de Ruiter, J. R. (2006). Male dominance rank, mating and reproductive success in captive bonobos *(Pan paniscus)*. *Folia Primatologica: International Journal of Primatology, 77*, 364–376.

McNaughton, N., & Corr, P. J. (2004). A two-dimensional neuropsychology of defense: Fear/anxiety and defensive distance. *Neuroscience and Biobehavioral Reviews, 28*, 285–305.

Miczek, K. A., de Almeida, R. M., Kravitz, E. A., Rissman, E. F., de Boer, S. F., & Raine, A. (2007). Neurobiology of escalated aggression and violence. *Journal of Neuroscience, 27*(44), 11803-6.

Mongeau, R., De Oca, B. M., Fanselow, M. S., & Marsden, C. A. (1998). Differential effects of neurokinin-1 receptor activation in subregions of the periaqueductal gray matter on conditional and unconditional fear behaviors in rats. *Behavorial Neurosci 112*(5), 1125–35.

Myers, K. M., & Davis, M. (2008). Extinction of fear: From animal studies to clinical interventions. In R. J. Blanchard, D. C. Blanchard, G. Griebel, & D. J. Nutt (Eds.), *Handbook of anxiety and fear* (pp. 000–000). Amsterdam: Elsevier Academic Press.

Naumenko, E. V., Popova, N. K., & Nikulina, W. M. (1989). Behavior, adrenocortical activity, and brain monoamines in Norway rats selected for reduced aggressiveness towards man. *Pharmacology, Biochemistry, and Behavior, 33,* 85–91.

Nelson, R. J., & Trainor, B. C. (2007). Neural mechanisms of aggression. *Nature Reviews: Neuroscience, 8,* 536–546.

Palomares, F., & Caro, T. M. (1999). Interspecific killing among mammalian carnivores. *American Naturalist, 153,* 492–508.

Parmigiani, S., Ferrari, P. F., & Palanza, P. (1998). An evolutionary approach to behavioral pharmacology: Using drugs to understand proximate and ultimate mechanisms of different forms of aggression in mice. *Neuroscience and Biobehavioral Reviews, 23,* 143–153.

Parmigiani, S., Rodgers, R. J., Palanza, P., Mainardi, M., & Brain, P. F. (1989). The inhibitory effects of fluprazine on parental aggression in female mice are dependent upon intruder sex. *Physiology and Behavior, 46,* 455–459.

Pellis, S. M., & Pellis, V. C. (1987). Play fighting differs from serious fighting in both target of attack and tactics of fighting in the laboratory rat *(Rattus norvegicus). Aggressive Behavior, 13,* 227–242.

Pellis, S. M., & Pellis, V. C. (1998). Play fighting of rats in comparative perspective: A schema for neurobehavioral analyses. *Neuroscience and Biobehavioral Reviews, 23,* 87–101.

Pentkowski, N. S., Blanchard, D. C., Lever, C., Litvin, Y., & Blanchard, R. J. (2006). Effects of lesions to the dorsal and ventral hippocampus on defensive behaviors in rats. *European Journal of Medicine, 23,* 2185–2196.

Petrovic, G. D., Risold, P. Y., & Swanson, L. W. (1996). Organization of the projections of the basomedial nucleus of the amygdala: A PHAL study in the rat. *Journal of Comparative Neurology, 374,* 387–420.

Petrovic, G. D., Risold, P. Y., & Swanson, L. W. (2001). Combinatorial amygdalar inputs to hippocampal domains and hypothalamic behavior systems. *Brain Research: Brain Research Reviews, 38,* 247–289.

Pikkarainen, M., Ronkko, S., Savander, V., Insausti, R., & Pitkanen, A. (1999). Projections from the lateral, basal, and accessory basal nuclei of the amygdala to the hippocampal formation in rat. *Journal of Comparative Neurology, 403,* 229–260.

Pinel, J. P. J., Mana, M. J., & Ward, J. A. (1989). Stretched-approach sequences directed at a localized shock source by *Rattus-norvegicus. Journal of Comparative Psychology, 103,* 140–148.

Pinheiro, S. H., Zangrossi, H. H., Jr., Del-Ben, C. M., & Graeff, F. G. (2007). Elevated mazes as animal models of anxiety: Effects of serotonergic agents. *Anais da Academia Brasileira de Ciencias, 79*(1), 71–85.

Ralls, K., & White, P. J. (1995). Predation on San Joaquin kit foxes by larger canids. *Journal of Mammology, 76,* 723–729.

Risold, P. Y., Canteras, N. S., & Swanson, L. W. (1994). Organization of projections from the anterior hypothalamic nucleus: A phaseolus vulgaris leucoagglutinin study in the rat. *Journal of Comparative Neurology, 348,* 1–40.

Risold, P. Y., & Swanson, L. W. (1997). Connections of the rat lateral septal complex. *Brain Research: Brain Research Reviews, 24*(2–3), 115–195.

Risold, P. Y., Thompson, R. H., & Swanson, L. W. (1997). The structural organization of connections between hypothalamus and cerebral cortex. *Brain Research: Brain Research Reviews, 24*(2–3), 197–254.

Roeling, T. A. P., Veening, J. G., Kruk, M. R., Peters, J. P. W., Vermelis, M. E. J., & Nieuwenhuys, R. (1994). Efferent connections of the hypothalamic "aggression area" in the rat. *Neuroscience, 59,* 1001–1024.

Schaller, G. B. (1972). *The serengeti lion: A study of predator-prey relations.* Chicago: University of Chicago Press.

Seyfarth, R. M., & Cheney, D. L. (2003). Meaning and emotion in animal vocalizations. *Annals of the New York Academy of Sciences, 1000,* 32–55.

Sovada, M. A., Sargeant, A. B., & Grier, J. W. (1995). Differential effects of coyotes and red foxes on duck nest success. *Journal of Wildlife Management, 59,* 1–9.

Stamps, J. A., & Buechner, M. (1985). The territorial defense hypothesis and the ecology of insular vertebrates. *Quarterly Review of Biology, 60,* 155–181.

Staples, L. G., McGregor, I. S., Apfelbach, R., & Hunt, G. E. (2007). Cat odor, but not trimethylthiazoline (fox odor), activates accessory olfactory and defense-related brain regions in rats. *Neuroscience, 151,* 937–947.

Stone, C. P. (1932). *Wildness and savageness in rats of different strains.* Chicago: University of Chicago Press.

Swanson, L. W. (2000). Cerebral hemisphere regulation of motivated behavior. *Brain Research, 886*(1–2), 113–164.

Sweidan, S., Edinger, H., & Siegel, A. (1991). D2 dopamine receptor-mediated mechanisms in the medial preoptic-anterior hypothalamus regulate effective defense behavior in the cat. *Brain Research, 549,* 127–137.

Szamado, S. (2003). Threat displays are not handicaps. *Journal of Theoretical Biology, 221,* 327–348.

Takahashi, L. K. (1992). Ontogeny of behavioral inhibition induced by unfamiliar adult male conspecifics in preweanling rats. *Physiology and Behavior, 52,* 493–498.

Takahashi, L. K., & Blanchard, R. J. (1982). Attack and defense in laboratory and wild Norway and black rats. *Behavioural Processes, 7,* 49–62.

Tannerfeldt, M., & Elmhagen, B. (2002). Exclusion by interference competition? The relationship between red and arctic foxes. *Oecologia, 132,* 213–220.

Treit, D., Pinel, J. P., & Fibiger, H. C. (1981). Conditioned defensive burying: A new paradigm for the study of anxiolytic agents. *Pharmacology, Biochemistry, and Behavior, 15,* 619–626.

Veening, J. G., Coolen, L. M., de Jong, T. R., Joosten, H. W., De Boer, S. F., Koolhaas, J. M., et al. (2005). Do similar neural systems subserve aggressive and sexual behaviour in male rats? Insights from c-Fos and pharmacological studies. *European Journal of Pharmacology, 526*(1–3), 226–239.

Vermeij, G. J. (1982). Unsuccessful predation and evolution. *American Naturalist, 120,* 701–720.

Vianna, D. M., & Brandao, M. L. (2003). Anatomical connections of the periaqueductal gray: Specific neural substrates for different kinds of fear. *Brazilian Journal of Medical and Biological Research, 36,* 557–566.

Walk, R. D., Gibson, E. J., & Tighe, T. J. (1957, July 12). Behavior of light- and dark-reared rats on a visual cliff. *Science, 126,* 80–81.

Wrangham, R. W. (1999). Evolution of coalitionary killing. *American Journal of Physical Anthropology, 29,* 1–30.

Ydenberg, R. C., & Dill, L. M. (1986). The economics of fleeing from predators. *Advances in the Study of Behavior, 16,* 229–249.

Zangrossi, H., Jr., & File, S. E. (1992). Behavioral consequences in animal tests of anxiety and exploration of exposure to cat odor. *Brain Research Bulletin, 29*(3–4), 381–388.

Zhang, S. P., Bandler, R., & Carrive, P. (1990). Flight and immobility evoked by excitatory amino acid microinjection within distinct parts of the subtentorial midbrain periaqueductal gray of the cat. *Brain Research, 520*(1–2), 73–82.

Zhang, S. P., Davis, P. J., Bandler, R., & Carrive, P. (1994). Brain stem integration of vocalization: Role of the midbrain periaqueductal gray. *Journal of Neurophysiology, 72,* 1337–1356.

Chapter 50

A Neural Analysis of Intergroup Perception and Evaluation

WILLIAM A. CUNNINGHAM AND JAY J. VAN BAVEL

In an era of increasing globalization, social and economic harmony depends on the ability of people to cooperate with others from a variety of ethnic, geographic, and religious backgrounds. A trend toward explicitly egalitarian attitudes among North Americans has been accompanied (and motivated) by legislation that makes discrimination a crime and public scrutiny that makes a single racist statement a major political liability. Yet, although a majority of Americans now report nonprejudiced attitudes and strong motivations to respond without prejudice, investigations over the past few decades have shown that the majority still have lingering automatic and perhaps unconsciously activated negative responses toward many minorities and socially disadvantaged groups (Nosek, Banaji, & Greenwald, 2002). These subtle prejudices have been shown to activate even among individuals with egalitarian motivations, and appear to take considerable cognitive effort to control once released. These prejudices have also been shown to directly predict discrimination, including negative nonverbal behavior and biased hiring decisions toward racial and other social groups (Dovidio, Kawakami, & Gaertner, 2002; Dovidio, Kawakami, Johnson, Johnson, & Howard, 1997). In a recent meta-analysis, these automatic forms of prejudice were stronger predictors of discrimination than self-report when there was a strong desire to hide or conceal one's attitude (Greenwald, Poehlman, Uhlmann, & Banaji, in press). To deal with these challenges, basic research is needed to understand the structures and mechanisms that promote social prejudice: from large societal structures and historical events, to the genetic and neural mechanisms that provide the basic machinery humans use to understand and navigate their complex social worlds.

Although research examining the neural bases of prejudice using neuroscience methods has a relatively short history, this research has already made dramatic progress. Looking across several key studies, one conclusion can be easily drawn—the processing of social group membership (typically investigated in a racial context) appears to influence nearly all aspects of brain function from early visual processing to higher order aspects of executive function and deliberate thought. The widely distributed patterns of brain activity found to covary with the processing of social groups suggest that the simple categorization of people into groups influences not a single group perception system, but rather a constellation of processes that collectively give rise to a multitude of social biases. Although the processes underlying social perception require further specification, initial neuroscience research on social prejudice provides important hints for our understanding of the mechanisms of prejudice and intergroup discrimination.

SOCIAL COGNITIVE PERSPECTIVE

The study of prejudice has been at the forefront of social psychology for over a half century. Ever since Allport (1954) wrote his classic book, *The Nature of Prejudice*, and placed research on prejudice firmly within mainstream social psychology, psychologists have sought to understand prejudice and find effective means for its elimination. For obvious reasons, much of this work studied overt acts of discrimination and verbally reported statements of prejudiced attitudes. However, evidence shows that people may also spontaneously evaluate social objects along a good-bad dimension, without necessarily being aware that they are doing so (Bargh, Chaiken, Govender, & Pratto, 1992; Fazio, Sanbonmatsu, Powell, & Kardes, 1986). Given such findings, models of social attitudes suggest at least two modes of evaluation: one that involves conscious and controlled modes of thinking and another that involves relatively automatic processes that operate without deliberate thought and sometimes without conscious awareness (Greenwald & Banaji, 1995; Nisbett & Wilson, 1977). Importantly, an evaluation following more controlled processing may differ from an evaluation based only on more automatic processing. On indirect or implicit measures that tap automatic associations, many White participants show negativity toward Blacks, the elderly, or foreigners compared with Whites, the young, or Americans, respectively; yet they report unbiased attitudes on questionnaires that allow more controlled or conscious evaluations of the same groups (Cunningham, Nezlek, & Banaji, 2004; Devine, 1989; Nosek et al., 2002). When the social context discourages expressions of prejudice, automatic biases can be a stronger predictor of discrimination than self-report measures, particularly of subtle, nonverbal acts (Greenwald et al., in press).

Evidence that prejudice can operate automatically has led researchers to the troubling conclusion that verbal reports are not always bona fide indicators of prejudice. If people cannot fully report on the ways that prejudice influences their thoughts, feelings, and behaviors, then the extent to which group biases permeate social cognition may be underestimated. With this in mind, it is necessary to examine the ways that prejudice, both in its conscious and unconscious forms, influences each step of social perception, all the way from early visual processing where social categories are initially encoded and applied, to the reflective processing used to generate more or less biased perceptions as a function of high-order goals and values. Using the classic computer metaphor in cognitive science in which the mind processes information in a serial sequence of processing stages, this chapter examines how social categories shape each stage of social perception. Information processing at each stage is dependant on information outputted from preceding stages, which implies that small biases occurring during initial stages may have dramatic downstream effects. Thus, although later consciously accessible evaluative processes feel as if they are under our deliberate control, they can be heavily biased by automatic forms of prejudice that influence processing and behavior prior to conscious reflection.

"THEY ALL LOOK ALIKE TO ME": PERCEPTION AND CATEGORIZATION

The unfortunate, yet too often overheard, phrase in the title of this section underscores that prejudices can influence the very way that individuals see the world; and specifically, that people appear to be better at processing and remembering people from their own race than from other races—an effect that has been termed the *same-race bias* (Malpass & Kravitz, 1969). Although the same-race bias may seem relatively harmless at first glance, it can have serious implications for crucial decisions in the real world.

With eyewitness testimony being among the most compelling pieces of evidence in criminal trials, the misidentification of a suspect from another race can literally lead to a death sentence for an innocent person (Brigham & Ready, 2005), especially when paired with certain societal stereotypes and prejudices (e.g., Seeleman, 1940).

If people are less likely to identity outgroup relative to ingroup members, it is possible that this bias occurs in the early stages of visual processing—outgroup faces may not be processed at the same level of detail as ingroup faces. One brain region that has been proposed as particularly important for perceptual biases in social processing is an area of visual cortex known as the fusiform gyrus (see Figure 50.1). In particular, the fusiform face area (FFA), has been shown to respond preferentially to faces (as contrasted with almost any other type of visual stimulus) (Kanwisher, McDermott, & Chun, 1997) and involves in the extraction of low-level perceptual features that can allow for individuation. To examine the role of the FFA in the same-race effect Golby, Gabrieli, Chiao, and Eberhardt (2001) used fMRI to examine the brain regions associated with facial processing while participants viewed same-race and other-race faces, as well as objects (radios). Black and White participants viewed pictures of Black and White faces to compare the processing of ingroup and outgroup members. As expected, the FFA was more sensitive to ingroup than outgroup faces for both Black and White participants (see also Lieberman, Hariri, Jarcho, Eisenberger, & Bookheimer, 2005). Moreover, on a subsequent memory test, the degree of same-race bias (superior memory for same-race over other-race faces) was predicted by fusiform gyrus activation to racial ingroup members at encoding.

Although this research provides an important link between early perceptual processing and racial biases in memory, these data are silent with regard to the psychological mechanism(s) that give rise to the difference (Levin, 2000; Sporer, 2001). On the one hand, it is possible that the same-race bias is the result of familiarity with same-race faces. According to this view, people have a lifetime of experience interacting with family, friends, and acquaintances of the same race, and consequently become experts at automatically processing and distinguishing members of their race. As such, the bias is not necessarily motivational, but rather the consequence of long accrued perceptual experience. On the other hand, it is also possible that this bias is the result of motivated social perception (Balcetis & Dunning, 2006); categorizing others as ingroup or outgroup members may alter the depth of processing that they receive. People might view ingroup members as more important and be more likely to process them as individuals, in contrast to less relevant outgroup members who are lumped together (even perceptually) simply as "them." Thus, while

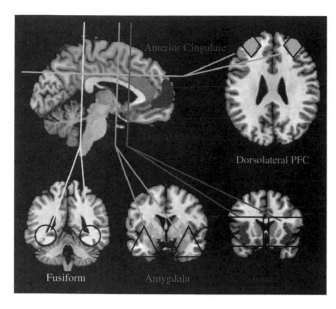

Figure 50.1

Note: **Circle:** Fusiform gyrus: Involved in visual perception and recognition. A subregion of the fusiform, known as the fusiform face area, has been shown to be particularly active to presentations of faces, and face-like stimuli. Beyond just faces, this region appears to play a role in making distinctions within categories of stimuli (e.g., cars), especially among experts. **Triangle:** Amygdala: A small structure in the medial temporal lobe that plays a role in the encoding and processing of affective representations. Activation in the amygdala is commonly found following the presentation of affectively intense stimuli (e.g., fear), although a more general role for the processing of any motivationally significant stimulus has been proposed. **Rectangle:** Insula: A region located within the somatosensory cortex. The anterior insula, in particular, receives direct input about homeostatic and visceral information from the body and sends output to other limbic (including amygdala) and cortical regions. The insula has been linked to the experience of disgust and other emotional states. **Dark grey.** Medial prefrontal cortex: The medial region of the anterior frontal lobes. The medial PFC has been implicated in social and affective processes, including self-referential processing and simulating the mental states of other (termed *mentalizing*). **Gray:** Anterior cingulate: A functionally heterogeneous region of the cingulate cortex. The anterior ACC—especially the dorsal region—appears to play a key role in monitoring for cognitive conflict. **Diamond:** Dorsolateral prefrontal cortex: The lateral regions of the anterior frontal lobes. The lateral PFC appears to play an important role in cognitive control and executive function, including the processes involved in working memory.

a lifetime of greater experience with one's own groups may help give rise to or enhance the same-race bias, the simple categorization of others into an ingroup or outgroup may be *sufficient* to generate biases in intergroup perception and memory (Bernstein, Young, & Hugenberg, 2007).

A recent study tested these competing hypotheses by randomly assigning participants to one of two novel groups: the Leopards or Tigers (Van Bavel, Packer, & Cunningham, 2008). After participants learned the members of each group, they were presented with the same faces during fMRI. Importantly, participants had equal prescanning exposure to the ingroup and outgroup faces. To the extent

that differences in group processing in the fusiform gyrus occur simply because of perceptual familiarity, no differences to ingroup and outgroup faces should be found. In contrast, if fusiform activity is sensitive to motivated aspects of social perception, including current self-categorization, then we should expect greater fusiform activity to ingroup as opposed to outgroup faces. Results supported the second hypothesis: The fusiform gyrus was more sensitive to novel ingroup than outgroup faces. This study suggests that the individuation of ingroup members as opposed to outgroup members may begin at the earliest stages of information processing and that this differentiation can be driven by the simple classification of others into groups.

Together, these data are consistent with the idea that ingroup members may be processed at a more individuated level than outgroup members even at the earliest stages of information processing (Rhodes, Byatt, Michie, & Puce, 2004). Whereas ingroup members are processed as individuals, extracting information about what makes each person unique, outgroup members are processed as interchangeable members of a general social category (see also Outgroup Homogeneity Effect; Ostrom & Sedikides, 1992). As such, outgroup members are more likely to be stereotyped, and these stereotypes are less likely to be disconfirmed by individuating information. Consistent with this idea and complementing the individuation of ingroup members, people are faster to categorize other-race faces according to their race than own-race faces—an effect that has been labeled the *other-race* categorization advantage (Levin, 1996; Valentine & Endo, 1992). Using event-related potentials (ERPs), Caldara, Rossion, Bovet, and Hauert (2004) showed that the brain response to categorizing other-race faces (Asian faces) was about 20 ms faster than for own-race faces. Remarkably, these effects were seen a mere 240 ms after stimulus presentation, providing strong evidence for rapid and automatic differences in the processing and categorization of social groups.

These studies indicate the extent to which race and group membership influence early aspects of social perception. From an information processing perspective, initial perceptual processes can influence subsequent processes and ultimately lead to discrimination and injustice. If group membership influences the way that we see the social world and how we unconsciously divide others into meaningful categories, it should not be surprising that these early processes are going to affect downstream evaluations and behavior.

AFFECTIVE EVALUATIONS AND PREJUDICE

A central focus of the neuroscience research on intergroup relations has been prejudice—the (typically negative) affective response people have to social groups as a whole, as well as individual members of those groups. Although the neural networks involved in an affective evaluative response are likely diffuse (Cunningham & Zelazo, 2007; Cunningham, Zelazo, Packer, & Van Bavel, 2007), initial research began with a focus on the amygdala. The amygdala is a small structure in the temporal lobe linked to an array of social and affective processes, including learning emotional information (Phelps, 2006), perceiving emotional faces (Whalen et al., 1998), and directing attention to important stimuli (Vuilleumier, 2005). More directly, with its tight connection to fear conditioning, threat processing, and negative affect more generally (Phelps, 2006), the amygdala was a logical starting place to investigate social prejudice. Importantly for the study of automatic affective biases, amygdala activation to negative emotional expressions (e.g., greater to fearful than to neutral facial expressions) has been found to be similar whether stimuli are presented at durations long enough for the stimuli to be consciously seen (Morris et al., 1996) or more briefly (33 ms and masked) (Whalen et al., 1998). This suggests that the amygdala may play a critical role in rapid and unconscious evaluation of the environment.

In the first fMRI study of prejudice, Hart and colleagues (2000) showed Black and White participants blocks of Black and White faces. While this initial study revealed greater amygdala activation to outgroup than to ingroup faces (White participants viewing Black faces and Black participants viewing White faces), these results were qualified by a small sample size ($N = 8$) and relatively weak effects (the reported pattern was only observed in the second half of the study). Armed with a larger sample size, Lieberman, Hariri, Jarcho, Eisenberger, and Bookheimer (2005) replicated these results for White participants, but found the opposite pattern for Black participants, who also showed greater amygdala activation to Black than White faces. Despite the discrepancies between these initial studies, they provided evidence of a link between the processing of social group membership and a subcortical (perhaps automatic and unconscious) affective response.

To directly investigate the relationship between prejudiced attitudes and amygdala activity, subsequent research examined the relationship between amygdala activation and behavioral measures of prejudice. Phelps and colleagues (Phelps et al., 2000) presented White participants with Black and White faces while their amygdala was scanned during fMRI. Following the scanning procedure, participants completed both indirect (reaction time and physiological) and direct (self-report) measures of prejudice. If the amygdala was involved in prejudice, it was

hypothesized that more prejudiced participants would show greater amygdala response to Black than White faces. Further, because the amygdala has been shown to be involved in unconscious evaluation and there tends to be greater variability on automatic/indirect than self-report measures of prejudice, it was hypothesized that a stronger relationship would be observed for the indirect than the direct measures. Although the study did not find overall greater amygdala activation to Black than White faces, both the reaction time measure (the Implicit Association Test; Greenwald, McGhee, & Schwartz, 1998) and the physiological measure (startle eyeblink) were significantly correlated with more amygdala activity to Black than White faces. Further, the explicit measure of prejudice was uncorrelated with amygdala activity.

Although Phelps et al. provided evidence for an important link between individual differences in automatic prejudice and amygdala activation, several important questions remained. Most importantly, if automatic evaluative biases are so pervasive, why were there no main effects of amygdala activation? In a follow-up study, Cunningham, Johnson, and colleagues (2004) reasoned that paradigms used in previous fMRI studies of race bias may confound multiple processes and may obscure the full power of unconscious bias. Specifically, because long blocks of Black and White faces were presented supraliminally, participants may automatically evaluate the Black faces more negatively than White faces, but may also then try to control or suppress their responses (discussed later in this chapter). To more closely examine unconscious race bias, the participants were presented with Black and White faces subliminally (for 30 ms), so that only automatic, unconscious processes could be used to evaluate the stimuli. Further confirming the role of the amygdala in the automatic evaluative processing of social groups, significantly greater amygdala activity was found for subliminal Black than White faces in all participants but one. In addition, this differential amygdala activation was correlated ($r = .79$) with the Implicit Association Test, the same indirect measure of prejudice used by Phelps and colleagues (2000).

Although these studies link the amygdala to automatic racial bias, the exact role the amygdala plays in prejudice remains unclear. For example, a patient with bilateral amygdala damage has shown racial bias on the IAT, demonstrating that the amygdala is not necessary for the expression of automatic prejudice (Phelps, Cannistraci, & Cunningham, 2003). Moreover, a valence-specific conceptualization of amygdala activation has been called into question by studies showing that positive as well as negative stimuli both evoke amygdala activity (Hamann, Ely,

Hoffman, & Kilts, 2002). Further research will be critical in determining the role of amygdala when processing social group membership. These studies not only will lead to a better understanding of prejudice, but will also aid in our understanding of amygdala function per se.

Power of the Ingroup

Perhaps because negative visceral aspects of prejudice are the most frightening and salient to observers, dislike of outgroups has received much more attention than the reciprocal form of prejudice—positive associations toward ingroup members. However, the history of intergroup conflict provides strong evidence that ingroup love is a more common root of discrimination than "outgroup hate" (Brewer, 1999). Moreover, in contexts where discrimination arises as a result of differential evaluations of two groups, ingroup bias can lead to the same patterns of discrimination as outgroup derogation (e.g., in the context of a hiring decision, ingroup bias and outgroup derogation would both lead a White candidate to be hired over a Black candidate). Although these decisions are the result of quite different affective processes, the result is identical—a Black candidate is treated unfairly and the cycle of discrimination continues.

Recent research has begun to dissociate the neural processes involved in ingroup and outgroup biases. In one study, participants were asked to think about the opinions and preferences of a person who had a similar or dissimilar political affiliation (Mitchell, Macrae, & Banaji, 2006). In the current partisan political landscape in the United States, it was assumed that more politically identified participants would process the similar person as an ingroup member, and therefore activate brain areas that have been linked to self-referential processing. Liberals were expected to be more motivated to understand the mental states of another liberal than a conservative, and the converse was expected for conservatives. This is exactly what was found. Considering the mental state of a similar other lead to activity in ventral areas of medial prefrontal cortex (PFC), whereas considering the mental state of a dissimilar other lead to activity in more dorsal areas of medial PFC. Interestingly, individuals who strongly self-categorized with a political group, as measured by an implicit measure, had greater *ventral* medial activity to politically similar others and less *dorsal* medial PFC activity to dissimilar others. Because regions of medial PFC have previously been implicated in building mental models of other minds and simulating the thoughts and feelings of other people (called *mentalizing,* Mitchell, 2006), with more ventral areas being more involved in

the processing of self-relevant information (Kelley et al., 2002), the authors concluded that although similar and dissimilar others both recruit regions involved in understanding others, similar others were more likely to be processed like the self.

If people are more willing or able to mentalize about people with whom they share a group membership, especially a group identity they highly value, certain outgroup members may not receive this processing. Consistent with this hypothesis, Harris and Fiske (2006) found that when participants viewed members of social outgroups that typically arouse feelings of contempt, such as drug users, less ventral medial prefrontal cortex activation was observed. Instead, for these stigmatized group members, the insula—a brain area associated with the emotion of disgust (Phillips et al., 1997)—showed more activation. This pattern of data is consistent with the idea that not only can negative emotions be activated in response to outgroup members, but there may be certain aspects of prejudice marked by less processing for outgroups compared with ingroups. People may use less mentalization for certain groups of people over others (Cortes, Demoulin, Rodriguez, Rodriguez, & Leyens, 2005; Vaes, Paladino, Castelli, Leyens, & Giovanazzi, 2003).

UNDOING THE AUTOMATIC: THE DELIBERATE CONTROL OF PREJUDICE

With a large body of research demonstrating that people are evaluated as members of social groups automatically, unconsciously, and sometimes unfairly, one might be inclined to take a pessimistic view of human nature. More optimistically, however, research has also documented that, at least under some circumstances, people can control automatic responses, and sometimes even replace evaluations of one valence (a negative affective response) with another (a positive affective response). Among the more cherished aspects of human cognition is its ability to use controlled processing and abstraction to escape immediate stimulus-response contingencies and generate more nuanced evaluations and judgments in the service of long-term goals and values (Cunningham & Zelazo, 2007; Greenwald & Banaji, 1995). Behavioral research provides evidence for this suggestion, showing that when people have the motivation and opportunity to use more deliberate forms of cognitive processing, the influence of automatically activated stereotypes and prejudice is dramatically reduced (Devine, 1989; Dovidio et al., 1997; Fazio, 1990; Fazio, Jackson, Dunton, & Williams, 1995). Thus, although initial intergroup categorization and evaluation have important implications for intergroup relations, human behavior is often driven by values, goals, and motivations.

Social cognitive studies of prejudice regulation have tended to focus on the inhibition or suppression of initial evaluations deemed inappropriate or suboptimal (Devine, 1989; Petty & Wegener, 1993). In this view, the automatic activation of prejudiced representations and biased processing leads to discriminatory behavior unless controlled intervention eliminates these biases. For this to be successful, two sets of processes are thought to be necessary—a *conflict-detection system* and a *regulatory control system*—each with different temporal dynamics and neural generators (Botvinick, Braver, Barch, Carter, & Cohen, 2001; Cohen, Botvinick, & Carter, 2000; MacDonald, Cohen, Stenger, & Carter, 2000). The conflict-detection system automatically monitors current representations and provides a signal that additional processing resources are required when incompatible representations are active. In the case of an egalitarian person, prejudiced representations that contrast with egalitarian goals would trigger this conflict detection system, which may then recruit the regulatory control system to update and modify prejudiced representations. The *conflict-detection* system is thought to be mediated by the anterior cingulate gyrus, and the slower, more reflective *regulation* system is thought to be mediated by regions of anterior and lateral PFC.

A study by Cunningham, Johnson, and colleagues (2004) provided evidence that these regulatory systems play an important role in modulating automatic affective responses to race. As noted in the section on evaluation, Cunningham, Johnson, and colleagues presented White participants with Black and White faces for 30 or 525 ms. Although these participants reported having strong egalitarian values, they also showed more automatically activated negative responses to the social category Black than White on an Implicit Association Test (IAT) (Greenwald et al., 1998). Showing that automatic prejudice operates unconsciously as well as that people can control this response White participants had greater amygdala activation to Black than to White faces (which were randomly intermixed), but only when the faces were presented subliminally (30 ms), such that participants did not report seeing the faces. In contrast, Black faces in the supraliminal (525 ms) condition were associated with activity in brain regions involved in controlled processing and executive function, such as the anterior cingulate cortex and lateral PFC. Moreover, the reduction in amygdala response during the supraliminal condition was inversely correlated with activity in these areas of anterior cingulate cortex and dorsolateral PFC. This pattern was consistent with the idea that people with the motivation and opportunity can control their automatic responses to social groups.

Providing further evidence that the PFC is involved in the regulation of prejudice and building on the idea that explicit linguistic processing generally inhibits affective processing (Lieberman, 2003), Lieberman and colleagues (2005) asked both Black and White participants to categorize Black and White faces according to linguistic labels ("African American" versus "Caucasian") or perceptual information (e.g., matching one Black face to another Black face). When participants categorized faces according to perceptual information, they had greater amygdala activity to Black than White faces. In contrast, there were no differences in amygdala activity when individuals categorized according to linguistic labels. Similar to the study by Cunningham, Johnson, and colleagues (2004), this lack of amygdala difference was accompanied by heightened lateral PFC to the Black than White faces, and this increase in lateral PFC activity was associated with the decrease in amygdala activation to Black faces. Again, these data show that the PFC is involved in modulating presumably more automatic responses under certain conditions.

Although these fMRI studies implicate the PFC in the regulation of prejudiced responses and show that these areas can decrease differential responses to Black and White faces in the amygdala, they are silent to how quickly these processes unfold. To study the temporal aspects of the *conflict-detection* system in prejudice control, Amodio and colleagues (2004) measured ERPs while participants categorized rapidly presented images as tools or guns. Immediately preceding each object, a Black or White face appeared (see Payne, 2001, for more details). The task was designed so that if a Black face automatically activated concepts of negativity (or the specific stereotype of violence), then participants would be more likely to make errors misidentifying a tool as a gun following the presentation of a Black face. For egalitarian participants, these errors should activate the conflict-detection system because their behavior (prejudiced response) would be incongruent with their values and ideals. As predicted, prejudicial errors among egalitarian participants were followed by an ERP signal that has been previously associated with the anterior cingulate in general, and the conflict detection system specifically—the ERN (error-related negativity). Importantly, the ERN in this study occurred within 200 ms of response errors, providing evidence that people do automatically monitor for unconscious prejudice and may be able to trigger corrective processes relatively automatically.[1]

Although deliberate control is typically associated with inhibition, reflective aspects of emotion regulation can also be involved in the maintenance or enhancement of affective states to construct a more intense explicit evaluation. Many social groups evoke negative affective responses without an increase in compunction or guilt (Crandall, Eshleman, & O'Brien, 2002). Few people attempt to mitigate their feelings or expressions of disgust toward child molesters, their anger at terrorists, or their distrust of particular politicians. Quite opposite to the controlled processes of inhibition, people are likely to desire to "upregulate" their emotional responses to feel more negative (or less positive) if they have the opportunity. Although these groups have received less attention, there is evidence that these normatively stigmatized groups (e.g., obese people) also lead to activity in brain regions associated with affective (amygdala and insula) and controlled processing (ACC and lateral PFC; Krendl, Macrae, Kelley, & Heatherton, 2006). Whereas Krendl and colleagues found greater amygdala and insula—a region linked to the intense feelings, including disgust (Phillips et al., 1997)—activation to stigmatized groups compared with controls, they reported that there was *also* greater activity to these groups in the lateral PFC. Although the positive relationship between affective and controlled brain regions was interpreted as a failed attempt to control negativity, work by Ochsner and colleagues (2004) on the upregulation of emotion raises the possibility that lateral PFC activity in this study reflected an effort to increase or maintain a negative response that is personally or culturally acceptable.

PROBLEMS WITH SUPPRESSION AND ALTERNATE APPROACHES TO REGULATION

For the most part, investigations of prejudice regulation have focused on the ways that people can suppress automatically activated affective and stereotypical responses. Yet, in his analysis of emotion regulation strategies, Gross (Gross, 1998; Gross & Thompson, 2007) provided a useful taxonomy in which response-focused emotion regulation strategies are contrasted with antecedent emotion regulation strategies. Whereas response-focused strategies typically involve the simple suppression of an affective response following its activation, antecedent focused strategies attempt to shape an affective response prior to activation, or quickly following activation through processes of reappraisal. Interestingly, in comparing the pros and cons of each class of regulation, Gross notes that whereas antecedent forms tend to provide strong and adaptive changes in affective experience, response-focused strategies (and suppression in particular) tend to work only for short periods of time, are associated with unhealthy physiological side effects (such as high blood pressure) and, most important, can backfire and result in rebound effects.

Thus, an unfortunate consequence of a desire to suppress all prejudiced thoughts and feelings is that, to the extent that automatic bias is pervasive, people will need to engage in the most effort to control these biases and may therefore be the ones who suffer the largest cognitive costs (Baumeister, Bratslavsky, Muraven, & Tice, 1998). Providing evidence for this hypothesis, Richeson and Shelton (2003) found that after White participants with high levels of automatic racial bias interacted with a Black individual, they subsequently performed worse on the Stroop task, which requires cognitive control. Presumably, White participants with racial bias on implicit measures had the most bias to control, and therefore were cognitively depleted following an interracial interaction. These studies suggest that people with automatic racial biases need to engage in greater levels of controlled processing to successfully navigate interracial interactions and these extra efforts lead to subsequent impairments in controlled processing, raising doubts about their ability to suppress bias for any extended period. Ironically,

---

[1] Not all people are motivated to control their prejudice to the same degree. Some people may strive to be egalitarian in all their thoughts and feelings, remaining vigilant at all times, whereas others may not care about their prejudiced reactions until they need to conceal it from others. Recent research explored the effect of internal versus external motivations to respond without prejudice on different aspects of controlled processing during the shooter task (Amodio & Devine, 2006). Replicating the previous research by Amodio and colleagues (Amodio et al., 2004), the more automatic dorsal ACC was linked to control of racial bias on the shooter task across conditions among White participants.

However, the later rostral ACC component was only associated with control in the shooter task among participants with a high external motivation when they were in a public situation that precluded racially biased responding. That is, people motivated for social reasons only engaged in controlled processing mediated by the rostral ACC when they were in a situation where social constraints were a factor, and this aspect of control took slightly longer. These data suggest that more automatic aspects of control (dACC) were rapidly engaged and insensitive to contextual pressures, whereas external motivations and contextual pressures triggered more delayed aspects of controlled processing (rACC).

people who try the hardest to suppress their biases may be the most likely to express these biases in later intergroup encounters.

In a follow-up fMRI study, Richeson and colleagues (2003) scanned White participants while they viewed Black and White faces during fMRI. Afterward, participants interacted with a Black confederate and then performed the Stroop task. As would be expected if participants were attempting to control prejudice while in the scanner, heightened activation to Black than White faces was observed in areas of right lateral PFC and ACC. More importantly, these levels of activation correlated with poorer performance on an executive function task (the Stroop task) following scanning. These patterns of results provide support both for the idea that nonprejudiced participants attempt to regulate their emotional responses to Black faces and that this regulation depletes executive functioning resources. As such, this provides strong evidence that the attempt to suppress by those most wanting to think and feel without prejudice may ironically be the ones who may be most likely to fall victim to automatic bias after their cognitive resources have been depleted.

Because suppression can lead to negative consequences, both for the social perceiver and the targets of prejudice, research is needed to examine alternative strategies for regulation that have the potential to avoid the unintended negative side effects of suppression. One unstudied but potentially promising approach is conscious reappraisal—the process of consciously changing the meaning and the appraisal of social groups and their members. Work by Kevin Ochsner and colleagues have consistently found that changing cognitions about an event or person changes affective responses (see Ochsner & Gross, 2005 for review). If people change their cognitions to feel more negative, greater amygdala activation is found, and if people change their cognitions to feel less negative, less amygdala activation is found (Ochsner, Bunge, Gross, & Gabrieli, 2002; Ochsner et al., 2004). This suggests that people can shape the contents of their mental space by foregrounding some pieces of information and backgrounding others to generate an emotional response that is consistent with their goals and values.

Another strategy for changing the way that evaluations unfold is for people to consciously change their processing goals (see Cunningham, Van Bavel, & Johnsen, 2008). A processing goal that may be particularly useful is an explicit motivation to individuate people and place less emphasis on group membership in person perception. In this context, one hypothesis is that having the goal to look for individuating characteristics may change the level of processing and may indirectly reduce the power of automatic stereotypes and prejudices. To test this prediction,

Wheeler and Fiske (2005) presented White participants with Black and White faces and had them engage in judgments that were designed to induce participants to either process the faces as individuals or as members of social groups. Consistent with previous research, when participants engaged in social categorization (e.g., classifying the faces by age), they showed greater amygdala activity to the Black than White faces. However, when participants were simply asked to decide whether each person preferred particular vegetables (a task thought to increase attention to individuating features), the amygdala no longer activated more to Black than White faces. To the extent that amygdala activation can be taken as affective bias, the simple act of individuation eliminated the standard race bias effect.

SUMMARY

The study of intergroup relations using neuroscience methods remains relatively young. Nevertheless, the past decade of research has revealed several important insights into the complexity of intergroup perception and evaluation. This research has provided exciting evidence of the automaticity of intergroup perception and evaluation, and the complex interactions between the component processes that guide behavior. These studies highlight the speed with which individuals distinguish different groups, their ability to do so without conscious awareness, and their ability to alter these initial processes according to motivations or goals. Improvements in technology and convergence across methods will add precision and contribute novel insights about an evaluative system that influences intergroup relations. In addition, the insights gleaned from a multilevel approach will eventually lead to novel predictions for traditional behavioral investigations and ultimately interventions that improve intergroup relations.

REFERENCES

Allport, G. W. (1954). *The nature of prejudice.* Reading, MA: Addison-Wesley.

Amodio, D. M., & Devine, P. G. (2006). Stereotyping and evaluation in implicit race bias: Evidence for independent constructs and unique effects on behavior. *Journal of Personality and Social Psychology, 91,* 652–661.

Amodio, D. M., Harmon-Jones, E., Devine, P. G., Curtin, J. J., Hartley, S. L., & Covert, A. E. (2004). Neural signals for the detection of unintentional race bias. *Psychological Science, 15,* 88–93.

Balcetis, E., & Dunning, D. (2006). See what you want to see: Motivational influences on visual perception. *Journal of Personality and Social Psychology, 91,* 612–625.

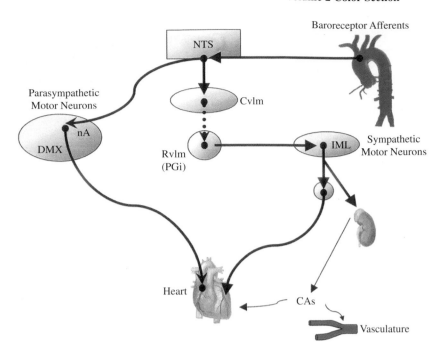

Figure C.32. Summary of brain stem systems underlying the baroreceptor cardiac reflex.

Note: Baroreceptor afferents project to nucleus tractus solitarius (NTS), which in turn leads to activation of parasympathetic motor neurons in the nucleus ambiguus (nA) and dorsal motor nucleus of the vagus (DMX). The NTS also activates the caudal ventrolateral medulla (Cvlm), which in turn inhibits the rostral ventrolateral medulla (Rvlm), leading to a withdrawal of excitatory drive on the sympathetic motor neurons in the intermediolateral cell column of the spinal cord (IML). CAs = Catecholamines; PGi = Nucleus paragigantocellaris (coextensive with Rvlm).

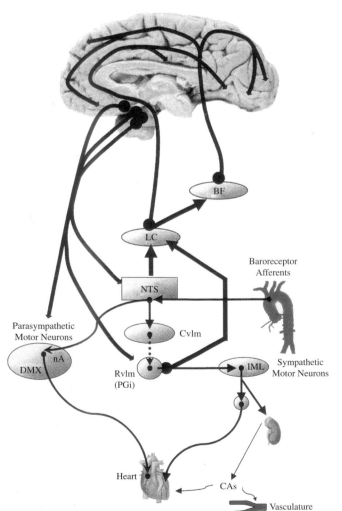

Figure C.33. Expansion of the baroreflex circuit of Figure 32.2 to illustrate the ascending and descending pathways to and from rostral neural areas such as the medial prefrontal cortex, hypothalamus, and amygdala.

Note: Ascending systems include routes from the rostral ventrolateral medulla (Rvlm) and the nucleus of the tractus solitarius (NTS) to the locus coeruleus (LC) noradrenergic system and indirectly to the basal forebrain (BF) cortical cholinergic system. CAs = Catecholamines; Cvlm = Caudal ventrolateral medulla; DMX = Dorsal motor nucleus of the vagus; IML = Intermediolateral cell column of the spinal cord; nA = Nucleus ambiguus; PGi = Paragigantocullar nucleus (partially coextensive with Rvlm).

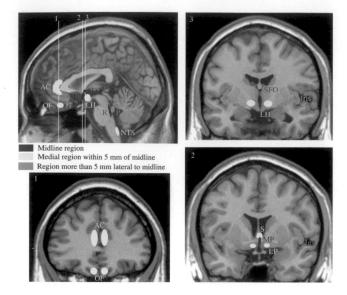

■ Midline region
□ Medial region within 5 mm of midline
▨ Region more than 5 mm lateral to midline

Figure C.34. A guide to the location within the brain of regions implicated in the generation and regulation of thirst. In the top left panel, specific regions are projected onto a longitudinal magnetic resonance (MR) image of the midline of the human brain. The other panels show several of these regions in transverse MR images of the same brain at three rostro-caudal levels (1,2,3) that are indicated by the white vertical lines in panel A. AC = Anterior cingulate cortex; I = Insula; LH = Lateral hypothalamic area; LP = Lateral preoptic area; MP = Median preoptic nucleus; NS = Nucleus of the solitary tract; OF = Orbito-frontal cortex; OV = Organum vasculosum of the lamina terminalis; P = Parabrachial nucleus; R = Midbrain raphé (dorsal and medial nuclei); S = Septal region; SF = Subfornical organ.

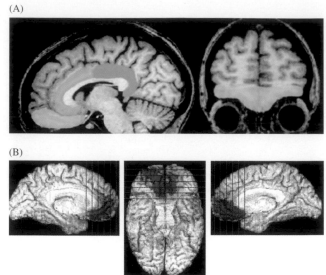

(A)

(B)

Figure C.36 (A) The orbitofrontal cortex. (B) The location of the vmPFC as defined in our lesion studies and in this chapter.

Note: **A:** On the sagittal section (left), the medial sector of the orbitofrontal cortex is depicted on the area of the brain highlighted in yellow. On the coronal slice (right), both the medial and lateral areas of the orbitofrontal cortex are depicted on the area of the brain highlighted in yellow. **B:** A map showing areas of the brain that are damaged in patients who show impairments in visceral response and decision making. The colors reflect the number of subjects with damage in a given voxel. The region of greatest overlap is the vmPFC. Note the involvement of medial wall and medial orbitofrontal areas and the relative absence of involvement of the lateral orbitofrontal areas.

Figure C.37 (Opposite page, top) Some important brain structures in the pleasure brain.
Note: The human brain seen from the side (**top**) and split in the middle (**bottom**) overlaid with the important brain structures of the pleasure brain. These include the orbitofrontal cortex (grey), the cingulate cortex (light blue), ventral tegmental area in the brain stem (light red), hypothalamus, periventricular gray/periacqueductal gray (PVG/PAG, green), nucleus accumbens (in the temporal lobes, light green), amygdala (in the temporal lobes, light red) and the insular cortices (buried between the prefrontal and temporal lobes, orange).

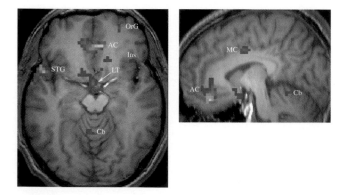

Figure C.35
Functional magnetic resonance imaging (BOLD signal) sections of a conscious subject experiencing maximum thirst resulting from intravenous infusion of hypertonic saline. Activations (red/yellow regions) in the anterior cingulate cortex (ACC), cerebellum (Cb), insula, (Ins) lamina terminalis (LT), orbital gyrus, mid cingulate region, posterior part (MC), orbital gyrus (OrG) and superior temporal gyrus (STG). Reproduced from Egan et al., 2003, (Fig. 3) with permission.

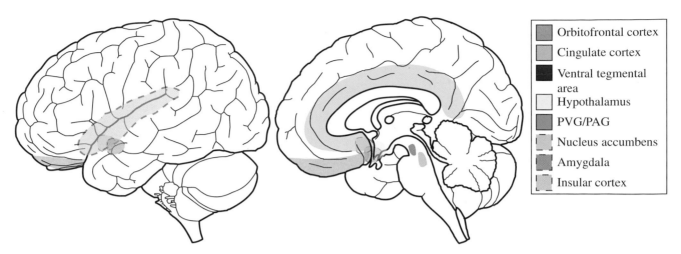

	Orbitofrontal cortex
	Cingulate cortex
	Ventral tegmental area
	Hypothalamus
	PVG/PAG
	Nucleus accumbens
	Amygdala
	Insular cortex

Figure C.38 (Right column) Hedonic experience.

Note: **A:** A neuroimaging study using selective satiation found that midanterior parts of the orbitofrontal cortex are correlated with the subjects' subjective pleasantness ratings of the foods throughout the experiment. On the right is shown a plot of the magnitude of the fitted haemodynamic response from a representative single subject against the subjective pleasantness ratings (on a scale from −2 to +2) and peristimulus time in seconds. From "Activation of the Human Orbitofrontal Cortex to a Liquid Food Stimulus Is Correlated with Its Subjective Pleasantness," by M. L. Kringelbach, J. O'Doherty, E. T. Rolls, and C. Andrews, 2003, *Cerebral Cortex,* 13, p. 1067. Reprinted with permission. **B:** Additional evidence for the role of the orbitofrontal cortex in subjective experience comes from another neuroimaging experiment investigating the supra-additive effects of combining the umami tastants monosodium glutamate and inosine monophosphate. The figure shows the region of mid-anterior orbitofrontal cortex showing synergistic effects (rendered on the ventral surface of human cortical areas with the cerebellum removed). The perceived synergy is unlikely to be expressed in the taste receptors themselves and the activity in the orbitofrontal cortex may thus reflect the subjective enhancement of umami taste that must be closely linked to subjective experience. From "The Representation of Umami Taste in the Human Brain," by I. E. De Araujo, M. L. Kringelbach, E. T. Rolls, and P. Hobden, 2003, *Journal of Neurophysiology,* 90, p. 316. Reprinted with permission. **C:** Adding strawberry odor to a sucrose taste solution makes the combination significantly more pleasant than the sum of each of the individual components. The supralinear effects reflecting the subjective enhancement were found to significantly correlate with the activity in a lateral region of the left anterior orbitofrontal cortex, which is remarkably similar to that found in the other experiments. From "Tasteolfactory convergence, and the representation of the pleasantness of flavour, in the human brain," by I. E. T. De Araujo, E. T. Rolls, M. L. Kringelbach, F. McGlone, and N. Phillips, *European Journal of Neuroscience,* 18, p. 2064. Reprinted with permission. **D:** These findings were strengthened by findings using deep brain stimulation (DBS) and magnetoencephalography (MEG). Pleasurable subjective pain relief for chronic pain in a phantom limb in a patient was causally induced by effective deep brain stimulation in the PVG/PAG part of the brain stem. When using MEG to directly measure the concomitant changes in the rest of the brain, a significant change in power was found in the mid-anterior OFC. From "Deep Brain Stimulation for Chronic Pain Investigated with Magnetoencephalography," by M. L. Kringelbach, N. Jenkinson, A. L. Green, et al., 2007, *NeuroReport,* 18, p. 224. Reprinted with permission.

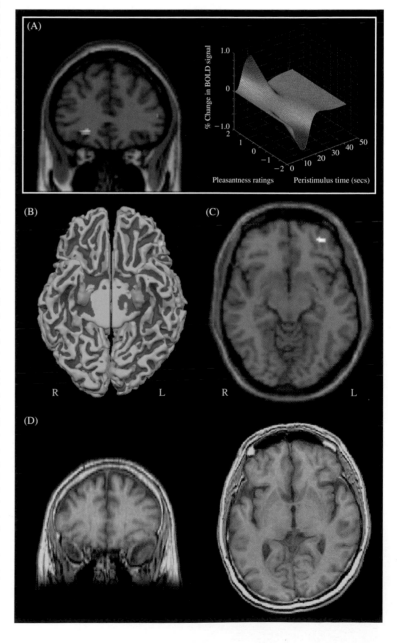

(A)

(B)

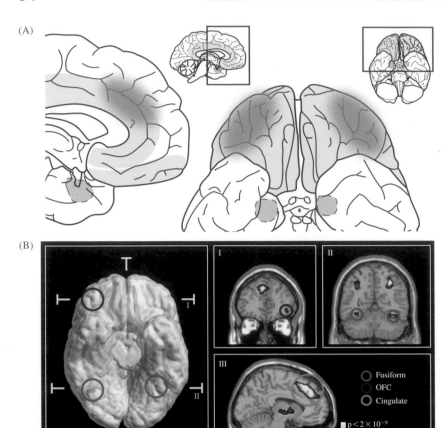

Figure C.39   Social interactions and the case of reversal learning.

Note: **A:** The lateral orbitofrontal and parts of the anterior cingulate cortices in the rostral cingulate zone are often found to be co-active in neuroimaging studies (with the regions superimposed in red). Most often this is found in tasks where the subjects have to evaluate negative stimuli which when detected may lead to a change in current behavior. **B:** A recent neuroimaging study found that the lateral orbitofrontal and the anterior cingulate/paracingulate cortices are together responsible for changing behavior in an object reversal-task. This task was setup to model aspects of human social interactions (see text for full description of task). Subjects were required to keep track of the faces of two people and to select the happy person, who would change mood after some time, and subjects had to learn to change, reverse, their behavior to choose the other person. The most significant activity during the reversal phase was found in the lateral orbitofrontal and cingulate cortices (red and green circles), while the main effects of faces were found to elicit activity in the fusiform gyrus and intraparietal sulcus (blue circles). From "Neural Correlates of Rapid Context-Dependent Reversal Learning in a Simple Model oHuman Social Interaction," by M. L. Kringelbach and E. T. Rolls, 2003, *Neuroimage, 20,* p. 1375. Reprinted with permission.

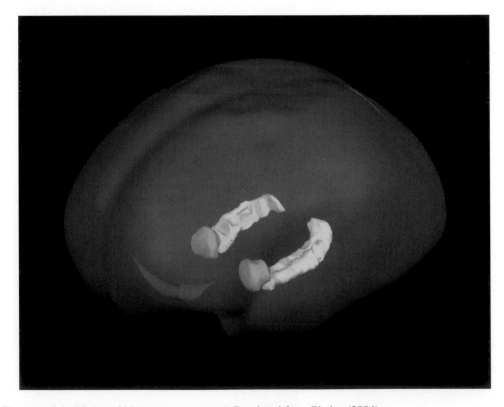

Figure C.40   The amygdala (blue) and hippocampus (green). Reprinted from Phelps (2004).

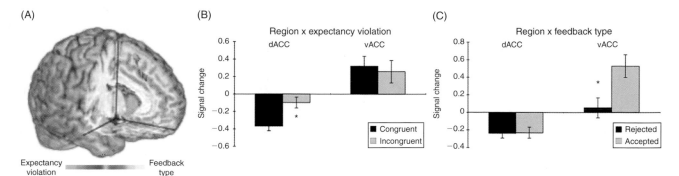

Figure C.41 Differential ACC response to expectancy violation and social feedback.

Note: **A:** A three-dimensional rendering of the medial surface of the brain illustrates a functional dissociation between dorsal (dACC0) and ventral (vACC) anterior cingulate. A whole-brain voxel-byvoxel analysis of variance (ANOVA) was used to identify voxels that showed a significant main effect (p < .001, uncorrected) of expectancy violation (blue) and a main effect of feedback (yellow). **B–C:** Voxels in the dACC (BA 32: –6, 28, 32; 13 voxels) demonstrated greater sensitivity to expectancy violation (incongruent > congruent) (B) whereas voxels in the vACC (BA 32/10: –6,49, –13: 16 voxels) demonstrated greater sensitivity to feedback (accepted > rejected). (C) Error bars denote s.e.m.

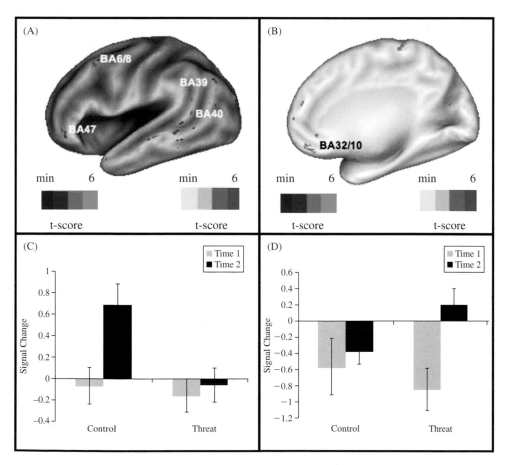

Figure C.42 Changes in neural activation over time for controls and threatened participants.

Note: Statistical maps **A:** lateral view of the left hemisphere of an inflated brain, **B:** medial view of the right hemisphere of an inflatedbrain) depicting neural regions that are more active during the second math task than the first for both controls and threatened participants. Activation for controls is depicted in blue, whereas activation for threatened participants is depicted in orange. Images are thresholded at p < .001 uncorrected, with a minimum t of 3.5 and maximum of 6.0 for all. Panels **C** and **D** depict signal change from a fixation control task for left inferior prefrontal cortex (C: BA 47) and ventral anterior cingulate cortex (D: BA 32/10). Controls recruited greater activity in the left inferior prefrontal cortex, whereas the threatened participants showed no change in activation in this region. Conversely, threatened participants recruited greater ventral anterior cingulate activity over time, whereascontrols did not.

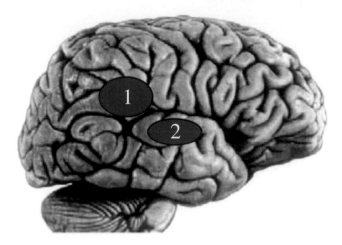 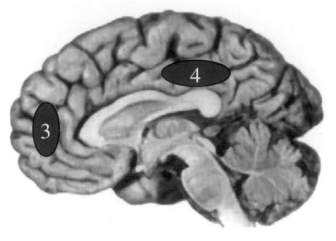

Figure C.43 Lateral and medial view of the human brain showing main areas activated in belief attribution tasks summarized in Table 46.1 .

Note: **(1)** bilateral temporo-parietal junction (TPJ). **(2)** right anterior superior temporal sulcus (STS). **(3)** medial prefrontal cortex (MPFC). **(4)** posterior cingulate. Of these areas, the MPFC and TPJ have received the most recent attention as proposed neural substrates for TOM.

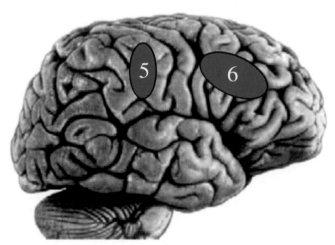 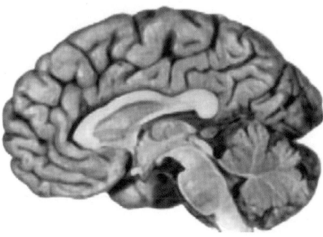

Figure C.44 The human mirror system.

Note. Areas activated in both performance and observation of actions. **(5)** Right inferior parietal cortex. **(6)** Inferior frontal gyrus.

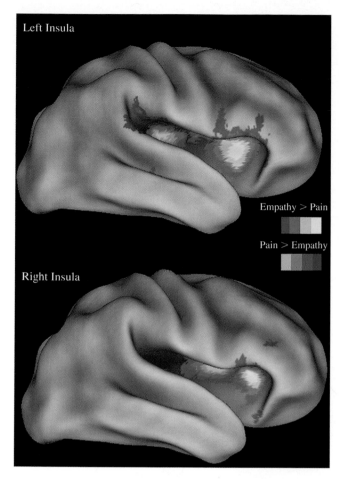

Left Insula

Empathy > Pain

Pain > Empathy

Right Insula

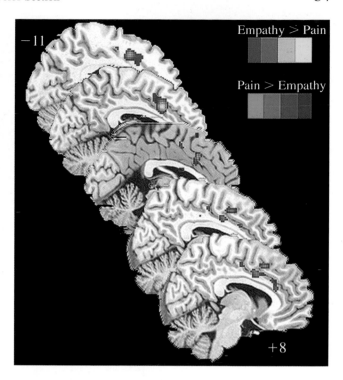

−11

Empathy > Pain

Pain > Empathy

+8

Figure C.46   Results of the same meta-analysis for the MCC/ACC.
Note: Observe the more left-lateralized and dorsal activations for empathy for pain.

Figure C.45   Results of a meta-analysis comparing empathy for pain with the 1st pain experience of pain.
Note: Activation differences are projected onto a flattened representation of the left and right hemispheres. Observe that empathy predominantly activates the anterior parts of the insula while pain sensations lead to more rostral activation—especially in the contralateral (left) hemisphere.

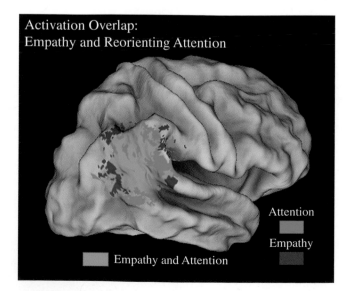

Activation Overlap:
Empathy and Reorienting Attention

Attention

Empathy

Empathy and Attention

Figure C.47   Activation overlap in right TPJ for empathy for pain and reorienting of attention/change detection.
Note: From "The Role of the Right Temporoparietal Junction in Social Interaction: How Low-Level Computational Processes Contribute to Meta-Cognition," by J. Decety and C. Lamm, 2007, Neuroscientist, 13, 580–593. Adapted with permission.

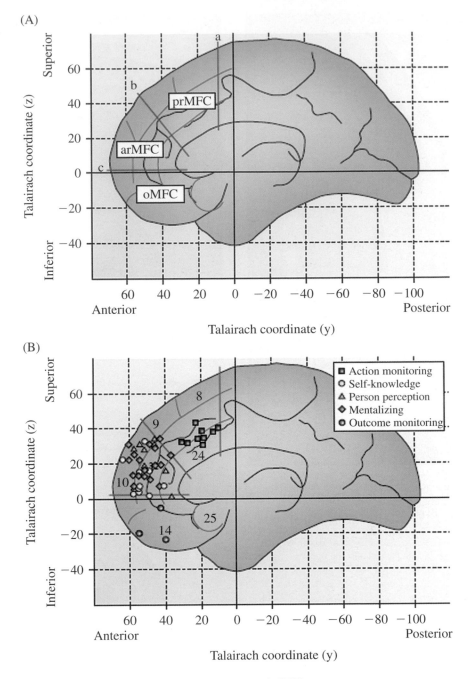

Figure C.48 Some functional divisions of the medial prefrontal cortex (mPFC).
Note: According to meta-analyses, more cognitive tasks such as action-monitoring often implicate the posterior rostral MFC (also called dorsal MPFC). More potentially emotional tasks such as emotion-ratings, self-knowledge, person perception, and mentalizing (imagining another's mind) often implicate the more anterior rostral MFC (also sometimes called dorsal MPFC, but a relatively more ventral location). Finally, the most orbital MFC (oMPFC) is implicated in outcome-monitoring. Figure C.48A labels these areas and C.48B locates the specific studies. For purposes of these diagrams, per the authors, the MPFCincludes the ACC (anterior cingulate cortex). From "Meeting of Minds: The Medial Frontal Cortex and Social Cognition," by D. M. Amodio and C. D. Frith, 2006, *Nature Reviews Neuroscience,* 7, pp. 268-277. Reprinted with permission.

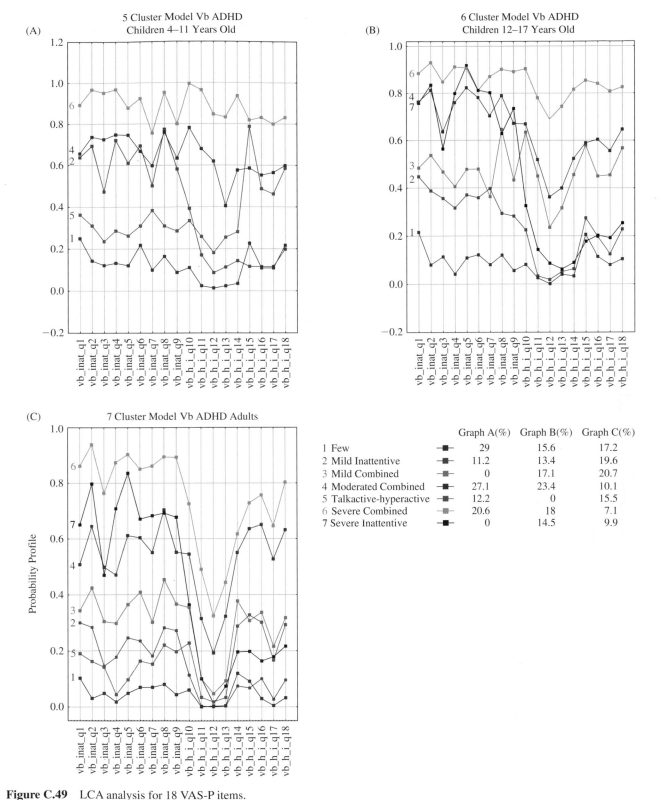

Figure C.49 LCA analysis for 18 VAS-P items.
Note: (**A**) for children (**B**) adolescents, and (**C**) adults. Each figure shows the latent classes endorsement probabilities (y-axes) for every VAS-P item (symptoms)

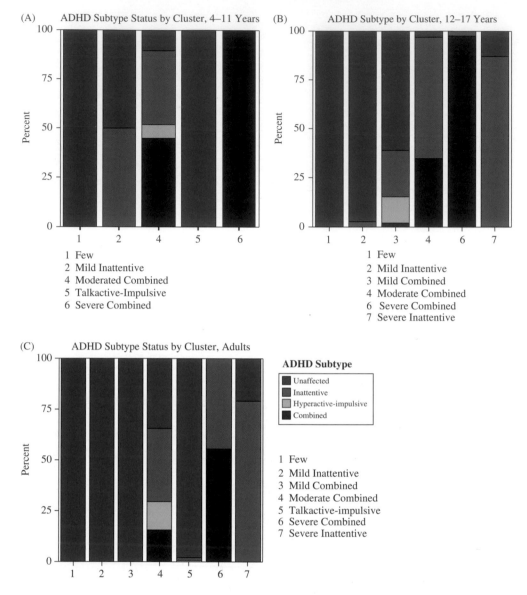

Figure C.50 Comparison of ADHD status as defined by the DSM-IV best estimate, and posterior cluster membership (each cluster adds to 100%).

New classifications and definitions of ADHD (e.g., upcoming *DSM-V*) should consider the wide diversity of symptoms and manifestations throughout the life span. Advances in understanding the neurobiology and the clinical manifestations will help to develop a more comprehensive set of diagnostic tools for primary ADHD patients.

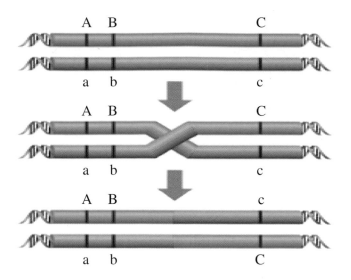

Figure C.51

The maternal and paternal alleles are mixed during a normal recombination process. If a specific disease gene is identified (gene A) recombination is likely to occur much more frequently between A and C than it is between A and B.

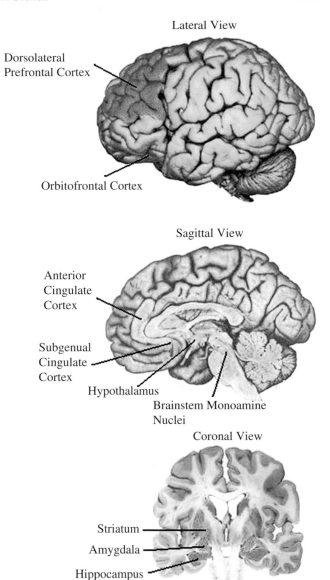

Figure C.53 Brain regions important in the pathophysiology of major depressive disorder.

Note: Three views of the brain, identifying regions considered to be important in the pathophysiology of depression. Brodmann area 25 (BA25) is part of the subgenual cingulate cortex. The brain-stem monoamine nuclei of importance include the dorsal raphe (serotonin), the locus ceruleus (norepinephrine) and the ventral tegmental area (dopamine). The striatum is a component of the basal ganglia, and includes the caudate nucleus and putamen.

From "Depression: Perspectives from Affective Neuroscience," by R. J. Davidson, D. Pizzagalli, J. B. Nitschke, and K. M. Putnam, 2002, *Annual Review of Psychology, 53,* pp. 545-574. Reprinted with permission, from the Annual Review of Psychology, Volume 53 © 2002 by Annual Reviews www.annualreviews.org.

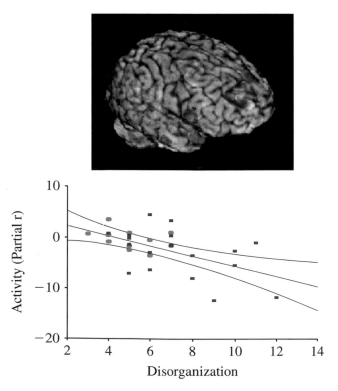

Figure C.52 Decreased Prefrontal Cortical Function in First Episode Schizophrenia.

Note: From MacDonald et al. (2005).

(A)

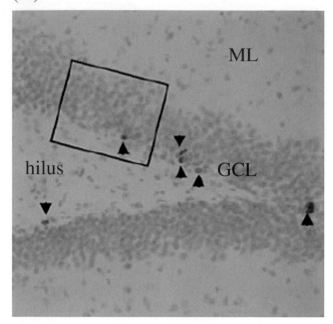

(B)

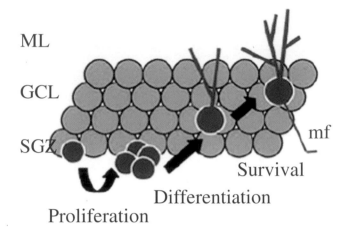

Figure C.54 Neurogenesis in hippocampus.
Note: **A:** The dark cells indicated by arrowheads are bromodeoxy uridine-labeled newborn neurons in the rat adult hippocampus. **B:** Newborn neurons in the subgranular zone (SGZ) undergo proliferation, an effect enhnaced by antidepressants. The new cells migrate to the granular cell layer (GCL), and mature to become granule cells, forming dendritic connections in the molecular layer (ML) and extending axons into the CA3 pyramidal cell layer through the mossy fiber pathway (mf). From "Hippocampal Neurogenesis: Opposing Effects of Stress and Antidepressant Treatment," by J. L. Warner-Schmidt and R. S. Duman, 2006, *Hippocampus, 16,* p. 241. Reprinted with permission.

(A)   (B)

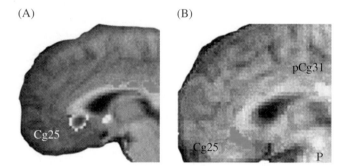

Figure C.55 Subgenual anterior cingulate cortex activation in depressive states.
Note: **A:** The subgenual cingulate cortex (Cg25) increases in activity (red) during the induction of transient sadness in healthy control subjects. **B:** Chronic treatment with fluoxetine for depression induces a reduction in activity (green). From "Targeting Abnormal Neural Circuits in Mood and Anxiety Disorders: from the Laboratory to the Clinic," by K. J. Ressler and H. S. Mayberg, 2007, *Nature Neuroscience, 10,* p. 1117. Reprinted with permission.

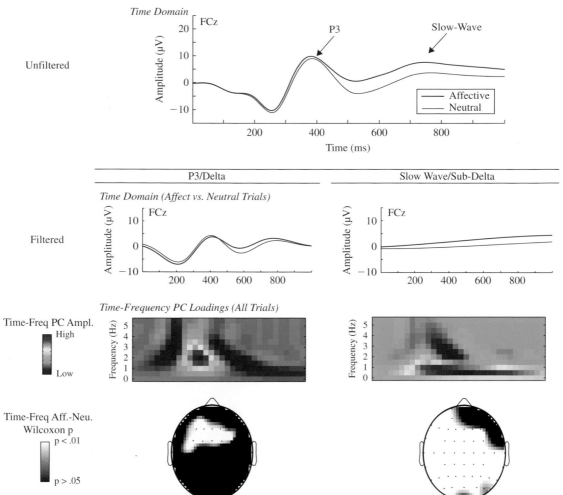

Figure C.56 Time-frequency (TF) decomposition of average ERP responses to affective versus neutral pictures presented as novel-nontargets in a three-stimulus visual oddball task.

Note: The data are for a sample of 149 undergraduate participants. Waveform plots depict results for electrode site FCz. The plot at the top depicts unfiltered ERP averages for the affective and neutral picture conditions. The waveform plots immediately below this show time-domain averages for affective versus neutral conditions that have been frequency-filtered using third-order Butterworth filters to approximate the TF components (discussed below) in a more familiar waveform representation. Activity in the delta (0.5 to 3 Hz bandpass) range corresponding to P3 response is depicted in the left plot, and activity in the subdelta (0.5 Hz lowpass) range corresponding to the ERP slow-wave response is depicted in the right plot. The two-color surface plots depict principal component scores reflecting the P3/delta and slow-wave/subdelta activity contained in the ERP signal, derived from a TF decomposition of the EEG data across all picture trials. Statistical maps at the bottom depict the scalp topography distribution of the difference in amplitude of ERP response to affective versus neutral picture stimuli in the P3/delta TF component (left map) and in the slow-wave subdelta component (right map).

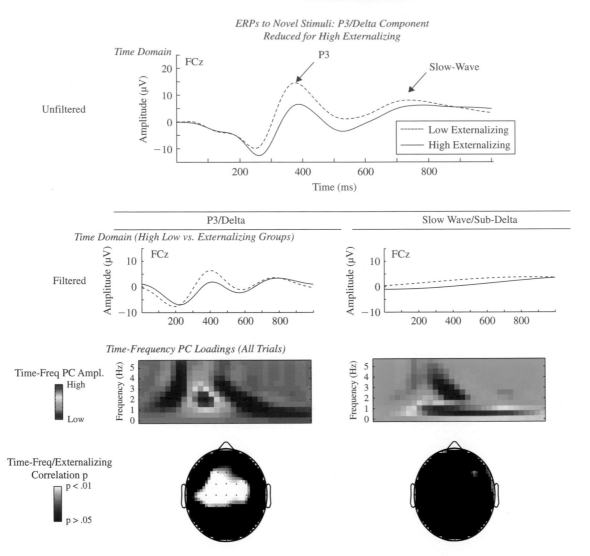

Figure C.57   Results from a time-frequency (TF) decomposition of average ERP responses to pictures presented as novel stimuli in a visual oddball task, displayed separately for subgroups of high versus low externalizing participants.

Note: High and low externalizing participant groups are as described in Figure 57.3. Waveform plots depict results for electrode site FCz. The plot at the top depicts unfiltered ERP averages across all novel picture trials for these high and low externalizing subgroups. The waveform plots immediately below this show time-domain averages for the two subgroups that have been frequency-filtered using third-order Butterworth filters. Activity in the delta (0.5 to 3 Hz bandpass) range corresponding to the

P3 response is depicted in the left plot, and activity in the subdelta (0.5 Hz low pass) range corresponding to the ERP slow-wave response is depicted in the right plot. The two color surface plots depict principal component scores reflecting the P3/delta and slow-wave/subdelta activity contained in the ERP signal, derived from a TF decomposition of the EEG data across all picture trials. Statistical maps at the bottom depict, for the overall test sample (N = 149) that included these extreme subgroups, the scalp topography distribution of the negative association between externalizing scores and amplitude of ERP response to novel pictures in the P3/delta TF component (left map) and in the slow-wave subdelta component (right map).

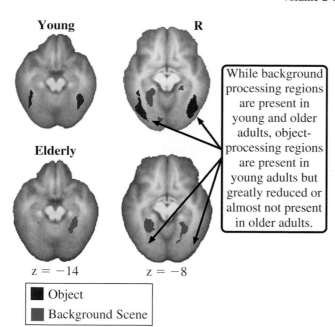

While background processing regions are present in young and older adults, object-processing regions are present in young adults but greatly reduced or almost not present in older adults.

Figure C.58 Object and background-scene processing areas identified in young and older adults during passive viewing of complex pictures.

Note: Background processing regions are present in the parahippocampal area in both young and older adults, but object regions in the lateral occipital area are greatly reduced in older adults. From "Age-Related Changes in Object Processing and Contextual Binding Revealed Using FMR Adaptation," by M. Chee et al., p. 501. Copyright 2006 from MIT Press. Reprinted with permission.

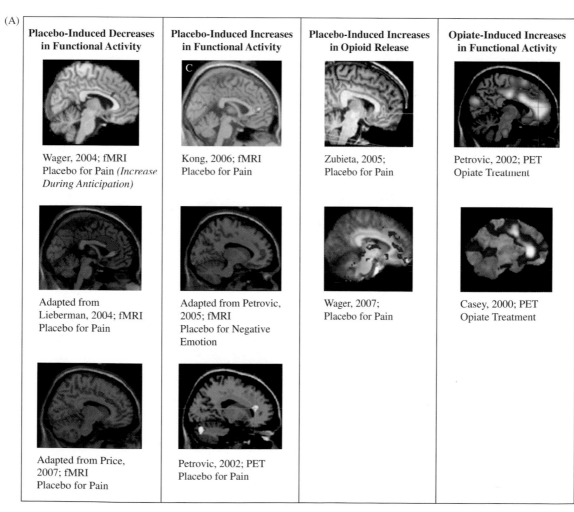

Figure C.59A Consistency of placebo results across studies.
Note: Neuroimaging studies of the placebo response and related processes reveal certain commonalities that provide synergistic insight into the mechanisms underlying the placebo response across domains. **A:** Many studies reveal placebo-induced modulation of dorsal rostral anterior cingulate (rACC) a region involved in regulating affect and appraisal. **B: on overleaf)** Numerous studies also reveal placebo increases in lateral orbitofrontal cortex (OFC), a region highly involved in cognitive control and evaluative processing.

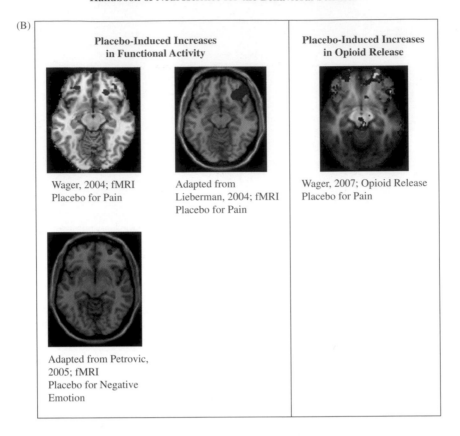

(B)

Placebo-Induced Increases in Functional Activity

Wager, 2004; fMRI
Placebo for Pain

Adapted from
Lieberman, 2004; fMRI
Placebo for Pain

Adapted from Petrovic,
2005; fMRI
Placebo for Negative
Emotion

Placebo-Induced Increases in Opioid Release

Wager, 2007; Opioid Release
Placebo for Pain

Figure C.59B

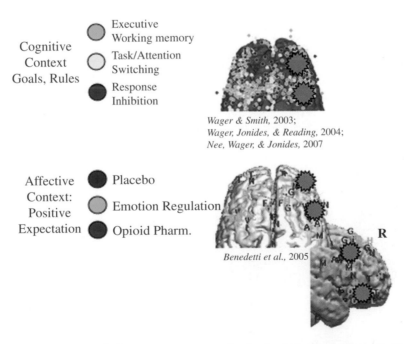

Cognitive
Context
Goals, Rules

Executive
Working memory

Task/Attention
Switching

Response
Inhibition

*Wager & Smith, 2003;
Wager, Jonides, & Reading, 2004;
Nee, Wager, & Jonides, 2007*

Affective
Context:
Positive
Expectation

Placebo

Emotion Regulation

Opioid Pharm.

Benedetti et al., 2005

R

Figure C.60　Prefrontal regulation of pain and affect.
Note: Meta-analyses of neuroimaging studies (Benedetti, Mayberg, Wager, Stohler, & Zubieta, 2005; Nee, Wager, & Jonides, 2007; Wager, Jonides, & Reading, 2004; Wager & Smith, 2003) that examined regulation of cognitive and affective context: Each point shows results from a study. Overlap between cognitive and affective regulation can be seen in dorsolateral prefrontal cortex (DLPFC) and lateral orbitofrontal cortex (OFC). These regions likely support central modulatory mechanisms of placebo, providing placebo-induced regulation of domain-specific processes.

Bargh, J. A., Chaiken, S., Govender, R., & Pratto, F. (1992). The generality of the automatic attitude activation effect. *Journal of Personality and Social Psychology, 62,* 893–912.

Baumeister, R. F., Bratslavsky, E., Muraven, M., & Tice, D. M. (1998). Ego depletion: Is the active self a limited resource? *Journal of Personality and Social Psychology, 74,* 1252–1265.

Bernstein, M., Young, S., & Hugenberg, K. (2007). The cross-category effect: Mere social categorization is sufficient to elicit an own-group bias in face recognition. *Psychological Science, 18,* 709–712.

Botvinick, M. M., Braver, T. S., Barch, D. M., Carter, C. S., & Cohen, J. D. (2001). Conflict monitoring and cognitive control. *Psychological Review, 108,* 624–652.

Brewer, M. B. (1999). The psychology of prejudice: Ingroup love or out-group hate? *Journal of Social Issues, 55,* 429–444.

Brigham, J. C., & Ready, D. J. (2005). Own-race bias in lineup construction. *Law and Human Behavior, 9,* 415–424.

Caldara, R., Rossion, B., Bovet, P., & Hauert, C. A. (2004). Event-related potentials and time course of the "other-race" face classification advantage. *NeuroReport, 15,* 905–910.

Cohen, J. D., Botvinick, M., & Carter, C. S. (2000). Anterior cingulate and prefrontal cortex: Who's in control? *Nature Neuroscience, 3,* 421–423.

Cortes, B. P., Demoulin, S., Rodriguez, R. T., Rodriguez, A. P., & Leyens, J.-P. (2005). Infrahumanization or familiarity?: Attribution of uniquely human emotions to the self, the ingroup, and the outgroup. *Personality and Social Psychology Bulletin, 31,* 243–253.

Crandall, C. S., Eshleman, A., & O'Brien, L. (2002). Social norms and the expression and suppression of prejudice: The struggle for internalization. *Journal of Personality and Social Psychology, 82,* 359–378.

Cunningham, W. A., Johnson, M. K., Raye, C. L., Gatenby, J. C., Gore, J. C., & Banaji, M. R. (2004). Separable neural components in the processing of Black and White Faces. *Psychological Science, 15,* 806–813.

Cunningham, W. A., Nezlek, J. B., & Banaji, M. R. (2004). Implicit and explicit ethnocentrism: Revisiting the ideologies of prejudice. *Personality and Social Psychology Bulletin, 30,* 1332–1346.

Cunningham, W. A., Van Bavel, J. J., & Johnsen, I. R. (2008). Affective flexibility: Evaluative processing goals shape amygdala activity. *Psychological Science, 19,* 152–160.

Cunningham, W. A., & Zelazo, P. D. (2007). Attitudes and evaluations: A social cognitive neuroscience perspective. *Trends in Cognitive Sciences, 11,* 97–104.

Cunningham, W. A., Zelazo, P. D., Packer, D. J., & Van Bavel, J. J. (2007). The iterative reprocessing model: A multi-level framework for attitudes and evaluation. *Social Cognition, 25,* 736–760.

Devine, P. G. (1989). Stereotypes and prejudice: Their automatic and controlled components. *Journal of Personality and Social Psychology, 56,* 5–18.

Dovidio, J. F., Kawakami, K., & Gaertner, S. L. (2002). Implicit and explicit prejudice and interracial interaction. *Journal of Personality and Social Psychology, 82,* 62–68.

Dovidio, J. F., Kawakami, K., Johnson, C., Johnson, B., & Howard, A. (1997). On the nature of prejudice: Automatic and controlled processes. *Journal of Experimental Social Psychology, 33,* 510–540.

Fazio, R. H. (1990). Multiple processes by which attitudes guide behavior: The MODE model as an integrative framework. In M. P. Zanna (Ed.), *Advances in experimental social psychology* (Vol. 23, pp. 75–109). New York: Academic Press.

Fazio, R. H., Jackson, J. R., Dunton, B. C., & Williams, C. J. (1995). Variability in automatic activation as an unobtrusive measure of racial attitudes: A bona fide pipeline? *Journal of Personality and Social Psychology, 69,* 1013–1027.

Fazio, R. H., Sanbonmatsu, D. M., Powell, M. C., & Kardes, F. R. (1986). On the automatic activation of attitudes. *Journal of Personality and Social Psychology, 50,* 229–238.

Golby, A. J., Gabrieli, J. D. E., Chiao, J. Y., & Eberhardt, J. L. (2001). Differential fusiform responses to same- and other-race faces. *Nature Neuroscience, 4,* 845–850.

Greenwald, A. G., & Banaji, M. R. (1995). Implicit social cognition: Attitudes, self-esteem, and stereotypes. *Psychological Review, 102,* 4–27.

Greenwald, A. G., McGhee, D. E., & Schwartz, J. L. K. (1998). Measuring individual differences in implicit cognition: The Implicit Association Test. *Journal of Personality and Social Psychology, 74,* 1464–1480.

Greenwald, A. G., Poehlman, T. A., Uhlmann, E., & Banaji, M. R. (in press). Understanding and using the Implicit Association Test: Pt. III. Meta-analysis of predictive validity. *Journal of Personality and Social Psychology.*

Gross, J. J. (1998). Antecedent- and response-focused emotion regulation: Divergent consequences for experience, expression, and physiology. *Journal of Personality and Social Psychology, 74,* 224–237.

Gross, J. J., & Thompson, R. A. (2007). Emotion regulation: Conceptual foundations. In J. J. Gross (Ed.), *Handbook of emotion regulation* (pp. 3–24). New York: Guilford Press.

Hamann, S. B., Ely, T. D., Hoffman, J. M., & Kilts, C. D. (2002). Ecstasy and agony: Activation of the human amygdala in positive and negative emotion. *Psychological Science, 13,* 135–141.

Harris, L. T., & Fiske, S. T. (2006). Dehumanizing the lowest of the low: Neuroimaging responses to extreme out-groups. *Psychological Science, 17,* 847–853.

Hart, A. J., Whalen, P. J., Shin, L. M., McInerney, S. C., Fischer, H., & Rauch, S. L. (2000). Differential response in the human amygdala to racial outgroup versus ingroup face stimuli. *NeuroReport, 11,* 2351–2355.

Kanwisher, N., McDermott, J., & Chun, M. (1997). The fusiform face area: A module in human extrastriate cortex specialized for the perception of faces. *Journal of Neuroscience, 17,* 4302–4311.

Kelley, W. M., Macrae, C. N., Wyland, C. L., Caglar, S., Inati, S., & Heatherton, T. F. (2002). Finding the self? An event-related fMRI study. *Journal of Cognitive Neuroscience, 14,* 785–794.

Krendl, A. C., Macrae, C. N., Kelley, W. M., & Heatherton, T. F. (2006). The good, the bad, and the ugly: An fMRI investigation of the functional anatomic correlates of stigma. *Social Neuroscience, 1,* 5–15.

Levin, D. T. (1996). Classifying faces by race: The structure of face categories. *Journal of Experimental Psychology: Learning, Memory, and Cognition, 22,* 1364–1382.

Levin, D. T. (2000). Race as a visual feature: Using visual search and perceptual discrimination tasks to understand face categories and the cross-race recognition deficit. *Journal of Experimental Psychology: General, 129,* 559–574.

Lieberman, M. D. (2003). Reflective and reflexive judgment processes: A social cognitive neuroscience approach. In J. P. Forgas, K. D. Williams, & W. von Hippel (Eds.), *Social judgments: Explicit and implicit processes* (pp. 44–67). New York: Cambridge University Press.

Lieberman, M. D., Hariri, A., Jarcho, J. M., Eisenberger, N. I., & Bookheimer, S. Y. (2005). An fMRI investigation of race-related amygdala activity in African-American and Caucasian-American individuals. *Nature Neuroscience, 8,* 720–722.

MacDonald, A. W., Cohen, J. D., Stenger, V. A., & Carter, C. S. (2000, June 9). Dissociating the role of the dorsolateral prefrontal and anterior cingulate cortex in cognitive control. *Science, 288,* 1835–1838.

Malpass, R. S., & Kravitz, J. (1969). Recognition for faces of own and other "race." *Journal of Personality and Social Psychology, 13,* 330–334.

Mitchell, J. P. (2006). Mentalizing and marr: An information processing approach to the study of social cognition. *Brain Research, 1079,* 66–75.

Mitchell, J. P., Macrae, C. N., & Banaji, M. R. (2006). Dissociable medial prefrontal contributions to judgments of similar and dissimilar others. *Neuron, 50,* 655–663.

Morris, J. S., Frith, C. D., Perrett, D. I., Rowland, D., Young, A. W., Calder, A. J., et al. (1996, October 31). A differential neural response in the human amygdala to fearful and happy facial expressions. *Nature, 383,* 812–815.

Nisbett, R. E., & Wilson, T. D. (1977). Telling more than we can know: Verbal reports on mental processes. *Psychological Review, 84,* 231–259.

Nosek, B. A., Banaji, M. R., & Greenwald, A. G. (2002). Harvesting intergroup attitudes and stereotypes from a demonstration website. *Group Dynamics, 6*(1), 101–115.

Ochsner, K. N., Bunge, S. A., Gross, J. J., & Gabrieli, J. D. E. (2002). Rethinking feelings: An fMRI study of the cognitive regulation of emotion. *Journal of Cognitive Neuroscience, 14,* 1215–1299.

Ochsner, K. N., & Gross, J. J. (2005). The cognitive control of emotion. *Trends in Cognitive Sciences, 9,* 242–249.

Ochsner, K. N., Ray, R. D., Robertson, E. R., Cooper, J. C., Chopra, S., Gabrieli, J. D. E., et al. (2004). For better or for worse: Neural systems supporting the cognitive down- and up-regulation of negative emotion. *NeuroImage, 23,* 483–499.

Ostrom, T. M., & Sedikides, C. (1992). Out-group homogeneity effects in natural and minimal groups. *Psychological Bulletin, 112,* 536–552.

Payne, B. K. (2001). Prejudice and perception: The role of automatic and controlled processes in misperceiving a weapon. *Journal of Personality and Social Psychology, 81,* 181–192.

Petty, R. E., & Wegener, D. T. (1993). Flexible correction processes in social judgment: Correcting for context-induced contrast. *Journal of Experimental Social Psychology, 29,* 137–165.

Phelps, E. A. (2006). Emotion and cognition: Insights from studies of the human amygdala. *Annual Review of Psychology, 24,* 27–53.

Phelps, E. A., Cannistraci, C. J., & Cunningham, W. A. (2003). Intact performance on an indirect measure of race bias following amygdala damage. *Neuropsychologia, 41,* 203–208.

Phelps, E. A., O'Connor, K. J., Cunningham, W. A., Funayama, E. S., Gatenby, J. C., Gore, J. C., et al. (2000). Performance on indirect measures of race evaluation predicts amygdala activation. *Journal of Cognitive Neuroscience, 12,* 729–738.

Phillips, M. L., Young, A. W., Senior, C., Brammer, M., Andrew, C., Calder, A. J., et al. (1997, October 2). A specific neural substrate for perceiving facial expressions of disgust. *Nature, 389,* 495–498.

Rhodes, G., Byatt, G., Michie, P. T., & Puce, A. (2004). Is the fusiform face area specialized for faces, individuation, or expert individuation? *Journal of Cognitive Neuroscience, 16,* 189–203.

Richeson, J. A., Baird, A. A., Gordon, H. L., Heatherton, T. F., Wyland, C. L., Trawalter, S., et al. (2003). An fMRI examination of the impact of interracial contact on executive function. *Nature Neuroscience, 6,* 1323–1328.

Richeson, J. A., & Shelton, J. N. (2003). When prejudice does not pay: Effects of interracial contact on executive function. *Psychological Science, 14,* 287–290.

Seeleman, V. (1940). The influence of attitude upon the remembering of pictorial material. *Archives of Psychology, 36,* 6–69.

Sporer, S. L. (2001). Recognizing faces of other ethnic groups: An integration of theories. *Psychology, Public Policy, and Law, 7,* 36–97.

Vaes, J., Paladino, M. P., Castelli, L., Leyens, J.-P., & Giovanazzi, A. (2003). On the behavioral consequences of infrahumanization: The implicit role of uniquely human emotions in intergroup relations. *Journal of Personality and Social Psychology, 85,* 1016–1034.

Valentine, T., & Endo, M. (1992). Towards an exemplar model of face processing: The effects of race and distinctiveness. *Quarterly Journal of Experimental Psychology: Human Experimental Psychology, 44A,* 671–703.

Van Bavel, J. J., Packer, D. J, & Cunningham, W. A. (2008). The Neural substrates of in-group bias: A functional magnetic resonance imaging investigation. *Psychological Science, 19,* 1131–1139.

Vuilleumier, P. (2005). How brains beware: Neural mechanisms of emotional attention. *Trends in Cognitive Sciences, 9,* 585–594.

Whalen, P. J., Rauch, S. L., Etcoff, N. L., McInerney, S. C., Lee, M., & Jenike, M. A. (1998). Masked presentations of emotional facial expressions modulate amygdala activity without explicit knowledge. *Journal of Neuroscience, 18,* 411–418.

Wheeler, M. E., & Fiske, S. T. (2005). Controlling racial prejudice: Social-cognitive goals affect amygdala and stereotype activation. *Psychological Science, 16,* 56–63.

Chapter 51

Cultural Processes

SUSAN T. FISKE

"Cultural neuroscience" is almost an oxymoron. The Venn diagrams for cultural psychology and neuroscience at present show scant overlap, as revealed by online searches and other reviews (Chiao & Ambady, 2007). At first glance, the difficulty of joining the two fields boggles the mind. How do we undertake complex neural measurements in separate cultures, given all the paraphernalia involved? Thoughts of researchers in jeeps toting fMRI magnets to remote villages somehow defy plausibility. What's more, cultural psychology and hard-core neuroscience often caricature each other as respectively imprecise and reductionist, among more polite terms. Are the obstacles insurmountable?

No. Culture constitutes a natural and even feasible topic for behavioral neuroscience. Despite the past misguided wars between those who study culture and those who study more biological factors, this marriage can work. People are biologically adapted to acquire a culture because they must coordinate with other people (A. P. Fiske, 2002); people are predisposed to acquire any of a variety of culturally specific languages, relationships, rituals, and other elements of human sociality. The a priori proclivity of people to absorb culture makes no adaptive sense without the human cultures to acquire, and the human cultures cannot be efficiently transmitted without the biological attunements to acquire them. People are biologically prepared for a cultural niche (Li, 2003).

Cultures are stored in people's brains. And people's cultural niche reciprocally affects their brain development. The field of neuroecology dates back decades, to the interspecies comparative approaches of ethology (for a recent review, see Sherry, 2006). Here we see the mutual influence of neocortex size and social group size in primates (e.g., Dunbar, 2001; Whiten & Byrne, 1997). In humans and our ancestors, neocortex capacity and group size track each other over evolutionary time (Donald, 1991; Dunbar, 1993; Massey, 2005). People simply need more brain power to deal with the exponential increase in numbers of dyadic relationships as group size increases, let alone the complexities of social structure and culture that grow with ever-larger societies.

Ample evidence indicates that humans do orient to other humans. Social psychologists have lately described this as a need to belong (Baumeister & Leary, 1995), describing it as the most basic, core motive (S. T. Fiske, 2004). Essentially, other people constitute our adaptational niche. People survive and thrive best when immersed in social relationships; isolation risks both physical and mental illness, even mortality (Cacioppo et al., 2006; Hawkley, Burleson, Berntson, & Cacioppo, 2003). Some have argued that the neural signature for social isolation mimics that for physical pain (Eisenberger, Lieberman, & Williams, 2003); at a minimum, social exclusion activates areas implicated in conflict and problem-solving (anterior cingulate cortex) as well as emotion regulation (right ventral prefrontal cortex) (see Figure 51.1). As another illustration, people's neural resting state, the so-called default network, may indicate a background preoccupation with people (Iacoboni et al., 2004). People's neural responses tune acutely to social interaction, perhaps because it is adaptive to get along with one's group.

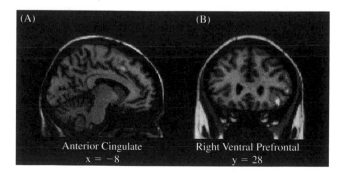

Figure 51.1 **A:** Increased activity in anterior cingulate cortex (ACC) during exclusion relative to inclusion. **B:** Increased activity in right ventral prefrontal cortex (RVPFC) during exclusion relative to inclusion.

Note: From "Does Rejection Hurt? An fMRI Study of Social Exclusion," N. I. Eisenberger, M. D. Lieberman, and K. D. Williams, 2003, *Science, 302*, p. 291. Reprinted with permission.

People's brains thus are based in their physical and social environment—we know this from the enlarged navigation-oriented hippocampi of taxi drivers (Maguire et al., 2000), from blind individuals' increased sensori-motor representation of their braille-reading finger (Hamilton & Pascual-Leone, 1998), from early training in stringed-instruments predicting enlarged cortical representations of the left playing hand (Elbert, Pantev, Weinbruch, Rockstroh, & Taub, 1995), and from neural regional intensity changes in adolescents transitioning to college (Bennett & Baird, 2006), all compared with controls not experiencing those environments. To the extent that cultures are influenced by physical environments and certainly create social environments, then culture will be reflected in brain structure, both within individuals and as an adaptive response across generations abiding in that physical and social niche. The review returns to these themes in the context of specific cultural neuroscience research.

Because of the nascent state of cultural neuroscience, this review essentially makes a promissory note to the future. This IOU will focus in turn on (a) some initially identified cultural differences in social responses that implicate neural systems, (b) some candidates for future research in these areas, and (c) some universal dimensions in culture that are likely candidates for neuroscience exploration. The review closes by (d) addressing theoretical and methodological challenges to cultural neuroscience. The review focuses on a few key areas most likely to interest behavioral scientists; it excludes cultural differences in patient populations responding to brain injury, cultural differences in neurological testing, and clinical population variance in genetic testing. Instead, specific topics include social cognitive processes such as perceiving and considering self, others, faces, races, and social structure, all critical indicators of culture.

CULTURAL VARIATION IN COGNITIVE AND AFFECTIVE NEURAL PROCESSES, WITH IMPLICATIONS FOR SOCIAL COGNITION

In considering cultural variations, this section moves from the bottom up, from attentional focus, through visual processing, to attributions of causality, to language and other cultural artifacts, to social interaction. Some intermittent themes contrast independent-interdependent cultural emphases, as well as behavioral approach and behavioral inhibition systems.

Attention

From the earliest moments of perception onward, culture impacts how the brain responds to stimuli. Behavioral inhibition systems (BIS) and behavioral approach systems (Carver & White, 1994) provide a contrast in people's earliest orientation to stimuli. The development of attentional networks reflects culture from an early age (Posner & Rothbart, 2007). A cultural route to attentional socialization may operate by sensitively activating the amygdala's vigilance response to other people's emotional expressions; this would be a social caution-related route that would emphasize noticing other people's subtle emotions and avoiding harm that would reactivate the amygdala response system. This route relies on amygdala-related distress and empathy; these children socialize relatively easily and readily internalize moral principles. Another cultural route to socialization, in this view, would move slightly downstream to emphasize anterior cingulate cortex, which typically responds to discrepancies and triggers problem solving. This route would emphasize self-regulation and conscience in regard to others, to avoid harm (Posner & Rothbart, 2007). This route relies on effortful control and internalized conscience.

It might seem that the caution-related route would more often characterize Eastern cultures, whereas the conscience-related route would more often characterize Western cultures. If so, this would fit respectively a more reactive, hesitant, and shame-oriented socialization, compared with a more effortful, conscious, and guilt-oriented socialization. All these processes would operate on early attentional processes.

Visual Processing

Once attending, encoding processes also appear to be shaped by culture, here highlighting the independence-interdependence theme. Westerners tend to operate with more analytic, piecemeal, and context-independent perceptual processes, focusing on single salient objects. Easterners tend to operate more holistically, in a more integrative, context-sensitive mode, attending to relationships between objects and their settings (Nisbett, 2003; Nisbett & Masuda, 2003; Nisbett & Miyamoto, 2005). Thus Westerners more readily recognize an object out of context, but they do not as readily recall its relationships to the other objects or the original context, compared with Easterners. Consistent with this idea, East Asians show more eye fixations on backgrounds than Americans do (Chua, Boland, & Nisbett, 2005).

Illustrating these ideas with activation patterns in specific neural regions, Americans engage more object-processing areas in the ventral visual cortex, compared with Chinese participants (Gutchess, Welsh, Boduroglu, & Park, 2006). If culture affects neural activation patterns and even the size of various neural structures, then older adults should show more cultural differences in the brain than would younger adults (D. C. Park & Gutchess, 2002). Indeed, young Americans and young Singaporeans of Chinese descent show few object-processing differences in the lateral occipital cortex, but older adults show the predicted cultural differences (Chee et al., 2006).

Attributions of Causality

These visual processing differences may underlie cultural patterns of causal attributions for other people's behavior. Americans tend to show a dispositional bias in explaining others' behavior, whereas East and South Asians tend to emphasize situational causality to a greater extent (Nisbett, 2003). This corresponds to the independent American relative emphasis on isolated targets (whether human or not) and interdependent Asian relative emphasis on context. Other research documents neural markers of dispositional attributions (Harris, Todorov, & Fiske, 2005), specifically MPFC and STS activity to specific combinations of information that produce dispositional inferences (but not to other, non-dispositional combinations of the same information; see Figure 51.2). Thus, cultural differences in context-sensitive, situational versus object-oriented, dispositional attributions may well have similar neural signatures emphasizing MPFC and STS. An individual's cumulative life experience in a particular culture permanently marks the brain.

Language

Language, the basic cultural experience, creates culture-specific perceptual attunements as early as infancy (Aslin, 1981; Cheour et al., 1998; Kuhl, Williams, Lacerda, Stevens, & Lindblom, 1992; Näätänen et al., 1997). Language then leaves neural traces as well (Neville et al., 1998). The left hemisphere activations of bilinguals for their native language overlaps their second language only for early bilingual learners, and less so for late learners (Kim, Relkin, Lee, & Hirsch, 1997; Neville & Bavelier, 1998; Weber-Fox & Neville, 1996). As another example, color perception varies with language, and neuropsychology backs up the neural traces of culturally influenced processing (Davidoff, 2001).

Reading likewise reflects culture, both in language and orthography (Schlaggar & McCandliss, 2007). A meta-analysis of largely Western studies implicates the left visual word-form area, supporting perceptual expertise for words, and especially the left phonological system, linking word forms and sounds (Bolger, Perfetti, & Schneider, 2005). Activations differ depending on the language's complexity of letter-sound mappings (e.g., Italian is consistent; English is inconsistent; Paulesu et al., 2001), but the same areas activate consistently within culture. In contrast, Chinese logography activates phonology less, but orthography and word meaning more (Tan, Spinks, Eden, Perfetti, & Siok, 2005). Where Western reading links words and sounds, Chinese reading implicates words and space, with corresponding shifts in brain activity (Siok, Perfetti, Zhen, & Tan, 2004).

Cultural differences in writing-reading direction (left to right or vice versa) apparently have ramifications for social perception. In Western, left-to-right settings, stereotypically more agentic group members (e.g., men) are more often represented visually to the left of less agentic group members (e.g., women) (Maass, Suitner, Favaretto, & Cignacchi, 2009). In art, photographs, and cartoons, this spatial agency bias occurs unless the man in the couple is perceived to be less agentic, and it correlates with an artist's own beliefs in the agency of men. Europeans show this bias, whereas Arabic speakers tend to show the opposite bias, reflecting their written language's right-to-left direction. This implicates culturally dictated forms of reading and writing in social perception. Such basic social perceptual processes likely implicate neural activations as well, but that research remains to be done.

Cultural Artifacts

Beyond language, specific cultural artifacts can mediate the impact of culture on neural functioning in surprisingly specific ways. Expertise on the East Asian abacus facilitates related visuospatial tasks (Hatano, Miyake, & Binks, 1977), although it also creates vulnerabilities to such distracters in the same modality (Hatano, Amaiwa, & Shimizu, 1987). Numerical memory span appears to be influenced by the logic of Chinese number words, giving an advantage to Chinese over Americans at an early age (Geary, Bow-Thomas, Fan, & Siegler, 1993; Miller, Smith, Zhu, & Zhang, 1995; Stigler, Lee, & Stevenson, 1986). Neuroimaging has differentiated numerical representations of Chinese and English native speakers (Tang et al., 2006), with the English-speakers more linguistic and cortical, and the Chinese speakers more visual-premotor. Reading experiences, language acquisition, and mathematics instruction all are implicated in these cultural differences.

Another specifically neural impact of a numerical cultural artifact appears in Canadian postal workers, who sort zip codes that combine letters and numbers, showing less representational distinction in the left inferior occipitotemporal cortex between digit and letters, in comparison with coworkers who do not sort mail (Polk & Farah, 1998). Language may or may not play a role in numeracy (Gelman & Butterworth, 2005).

Social Interaction

Finally, moving from cognition, perception, and language directly to social interaction, recent research implicates

(A)

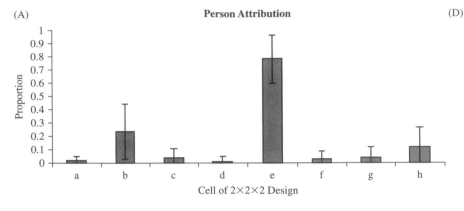

Person Attribution

(D)

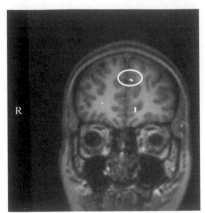

(B)

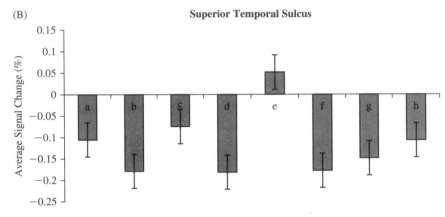

Superior Temporal Sulcus

(C)

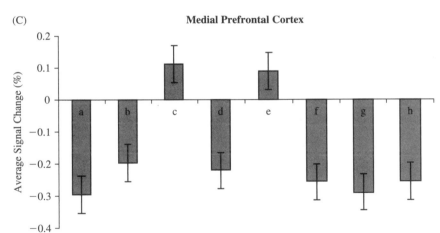

Medial Prefrontal Cortex

Figure 51.2 **A:** Proportion of person attributions, by $2 \times 2 \times 2$ condition. **B:** Superior temporal sulcus. **C:** Left medial prefrontal cortex. **D:** Left medial prefrontal cortex.

Note: (A) Dispositional attribution predicted for cell e (high consistency, low consensus, low distinctiveness). From "Attributions on the Brain: Neuro-Imaging Dispositional Inferences, beyond Theory of Mind," by L. T. Harris, A. Todorov, S. T. Fiske, 2005, *NeuroImage, 28*, pp. 766. (B) STS reflects intent, trajectory, goal-directed motion. From "Attributions on the Brain: Neuro-Imaging Dispositional Inferences, beyond Theory of Mind," by L. T. Harris, A. Todorov, S. T. Fiske, 2005, *NeuroImage, 28,* p. 767 (C) MPFC reflects mentalizing, considering others' minds; cell c represents conditions similar to cell e, except consensus, which is often ignored in attributions, considering what everyone including the target does under similar circumstances. From "Attributions on the Brain: Neuro-Imaging Dispositional Inferences, beyond Theory of Mind," by L. T. Harris, A. Todorov, S. T. Fiske, 2005, *NeuroImage, 28,* p. 767(D) Locations of signal change. From "Attributions on the Brain: Neuro-Imaging Dispositional Inferences, beyond Theory of Mind," by L. T. Harris, A. Todorov, S. T. Fiske, 2005, *NeuroImage, 28,* p. 768. Reprinted with permission.

cultural differences in independent-interdependent responses to social support under stress. Some individuals are homozygous for the short allele (s/s) of the serotonin transporter gene-linked polymorphic region, and this s/s combination is particularly over-represented in Asian populations. The s/s combination, in a gene-by-environment interaction, puts people particularly at risk for depression when they have had a stressful early family environment or recent adversity (Taylor et al., 2006). The authors speculate that the robust cultural difference in interdependence between Asians and Westerners (e.g., Markus & Kitayama, 1991) might have developed partly in response to Asians' greater genetic risk

factors for stress, by encouraging a supportive family and social network.

Other gene-by-environment interactions appear in risk factors for aggression. Prior research indicates a relationship between the monoamine oxidase-A gene and aggression (Caspi et al., 2002; Nelson & Trainor, 2007; Shih, Chen, & Ridd, 1999). Individuals with the low-expression version of this MAO-A gene report a potentially volatile combination (Eisenberger, Way, Taylor, Welch, & Lieberman, 2007): (a) higher chronic levels of aggression, (b) hypersensitivity to interpersonal events, and (c) increased response to social rejection in the anterior cingulate cortex, which has been implicated both in processing of discrepancies (Botvinick, Cohen, & Carter, 2004) and in social and physical pain (Eisenberger et al., 2003). To the extent that aggression results from failed interpersonal control—that is, a perceived lack of correlation between an individual's interpersonal behavior and outcomes (S. T. Fiske, 2004, chap. 10; Malamuth & Addison, 2001)—this possibly creates an aggression-prone gene-by-environment interaction. Individuals differ widely in MAO-A gene activity, but reviews do not yet indicate known population differences. Nevertheless, with time, a complex interplay may document such genetic population differences, environmental factors modulating expression, and cultural factors for coping with its expression.

Focusing just on environments, some cultures mandate elaborate interpersonal signals, often heavy politeness norms, possibly to mute aggressive reactions to rejection (Cohen, Vandello, Puente, & Rantilla, 1999). Example environments would include cultures of honor (Nisbett & Cohen, 1996), in historically frontier, herding societies such as the southern United States, Euro-Mediterranean countries, and the northern British Isles. These cultural variations in environment may differentially affect people with individual variations in the MAO-A gene, even absent any differences in population distributions.

Summary

Cultural variation in perceptual-cognitive-affective processes, with implications for social perception and cognition, appear from the earliest moments of perception through to the most complex social-emotional responses, all with neural markers. Different routes to socialization speculatively might especially implicate either the amygdala, causing a more inhibition-oriented and interdependent, cautious, preoccupied approach to others, or alternatively, the anterior cingulate cortex, reflecting a more approach-oriented and independent, agentic but conscience-driven process. Relatively more holistic Eastern perception focuses more on environments and relationships among objects and people, whereas a relatively more target-oriented Western perceptual process focuses more on isolated objects and people; this would help explain cultural patterns of causal attribution that rely respectively more on situations versus the dispositions of individual actors. Cultural variations in acquiring numeracy, literacy, and spoken languages also may create long-term neural patterns that reflect persistent cultural patterns of social communication. And cultural differences in social interdependence may even reflect population distributions of certain genetic predispositions. Notably, all these studies involve neural moderators or mediators of cultural patterns.

Notably, also, these studies almost all contrast Asians and Europeans or Americans. Future cultural neuroscience research must eventually expand to other regions and cultures.

CANDIDATES FOR FUTURE RESEARCH ON NEURAL REFLECTIONS OF CULTURAL VARIATION

Given the promissory nature of most avenues for cultural neuroscience, this section explores some candidate cultural variations that may lend themselves to neural explorations. The most prominent classic variable in cultural psychology for many years was individualism-collectivism (Triandis, 1990), with Westerners scoring higher on individualism, defined as a focus on the autonomous person, and Asians, South Americans, and Africans scoring higher on collectivism, emphasizing groups such as the family, community, or organization. Individualism-collectivism varies regionally even in the United States (Vandello & Cohen, 1999). The Rocky Mountains and Great Plains tend to show the most individualism, whereas collectivism more characterizes immigrant-destinations such as Hawaii, California, New York, and New Jersey, or religion-centered areas such as the Deep South and Utah.

More individualist cultures put each person's own needs over the group's needs, whereas more collectivist cultures put group needs over individual needs. A related description, interdependent versus independent selves (Markus & Kitayama, 1991) also contrasts East-West cultural orientations toward autonomous versus socially embedded selves. In individualist (independent self) settings, both theories imply interpersonal perception more focused on the isolated, agentic self and autonomous others, consistent with the earlier-cited Western attributional focus on individual dispositions. This fits Western neural patterns described earlier, and complementary neural states that fit the contrasting Eastern focus on situations and relationships. We next consider other candidates for future research on neural reflections of cultural variation.

Default, Resting-State Activity

The individual-collective (independent-interdependent) dimension implies untapped directions that extend far beyond attribution, such as when people's minds wander and their brains rest in a default network (Mason et al., 2007). Among many intriguing leads, the cultural tendencies toward individualist versus collectivist focus should appear in default, resting-state preoccupation with self and others. Self-referential activation appears in resting, default state activations for Americans (Gusnard, Akbudak, Shulman, & Raichle, 2001). If people spontaneously think about themselves as agents in more individualist cultures, then resting-state thoughts should focus especially on self in Westerners. For example, thought-listing studies suggest that among Westerners, much thought is operant: instrumental, problem solving, and volitional (Klinger, 1978; see S. T. Fiske & Taylor, 2008, pp. 36–41, for a review). All this centers on the self-as-agent, an essentially Western perspective.

A more recent imaging study suggests a specific way to test this differential focus; it manipulates people's reflective tasks (thinking about self, another person, social issues), compared with resting state in Dutch participants (D'Argembeau et al., 2005). More self-reported self-referential thought occurs in the self task, but also more in resting states than in thinking about others. According to PET data, the self task also activates ventral medial prefrontal cortex (VMPFC) more than all the other tasks, and the resting state more than the society task or other task. Crucially, the VMPFC areas overlapping self and resting activation then turn out to correlate with participant reports of self-referential thought during the tasks. In contrast, more dorsal MPFC characterizes all three reflective tasks compared with rest; the DMPFC often activates when people are thinking about (their own or others') mental states, as discussed later (e.g., Amodio & Frith, 2006).

To the extent that self-reflection and similar-other activation is more ventral and dissimilar other-activation is more dorsal in the MPFC (Mitchell, Banaji, & Macrae,

2005; Mitchell, Macrae, & Banaji, 2006; see Figure 51.3), these patterns might distinguish relatively individualist and collectivist participants. In an individualist culture, resting (default) activity might focus more on self (ventral). In a more collectivist culture, people in a resting state might spontaneously think more about other people (dorsal).

At least among American participants, self and intimate others activate proximate but distinct areas of MPFC (Heatherton et al., 2006). Thus, in an individualist culture, people might differentiate self from both similar and dissimilar others more than people in a collectivist culture, so the ventral-dorsal MPFC axis for self and dissimilar others might be exaggerated for individualists.

Still another possibility would be differences in perspective-taking for self-other judgments, with collectivist cultures showing more activation in the posterior dorsal MPFC and individualist cultures showing more anterior MPFC activations. This would extend experimental manipulations showing self-other and perspective-taking differential activations in MPFC (D'Argembeau et al., 2007).

Self Representations

Consistent with some of these ideas, MPFC (and anterior cingulate cortex, ACC) activated for both Chinese and Western participants judging traits of self, compared with others. However, Chinese participants also activated MPFC for judging their mother's traits, suggesting a more interdependent self-representation in an overlap not shown

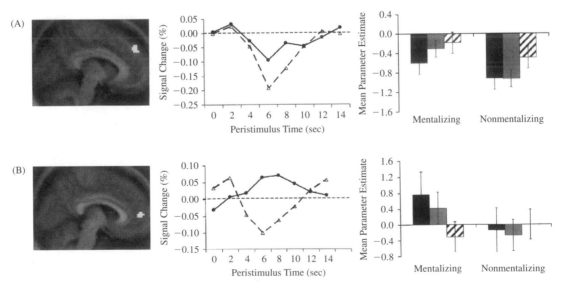

Figure 51.3 Two MPFC regions reflect more broadly **A:** dorsal (dissimilar others) and **B:** ventral (similar others) social cognition.

Note: Specifically, the top panels (A) contrast mentalizing (closed circles in the time course) versus not (open circles); overall, not-mentalizing reduces dorsal MPFC activation compared with mentalizing, so mentalizing relatively activates dorsal MPFC. The relative activation under mentalizing tends to be exaggerated for less similar others (striped bars, mentalizing condition). In a more ventral area of MPFC, panels (B) indicate activation above resting baseline in the mentalizing condition only; this activation correlates with others' similarity ranging from most (dark bars on the bar graph) to least similar (striped bars). From "The Link between Social Cognition and Self-Referential Thought in the Medial Frontal Cortex," by J. P. Mitchell, M. R. Banaji, and C. N. Macrae, 2005, *Journal of Cognitive Neuroscience, 17*, p. 1308. Reprinted with permission.

by Western participants (Zhu, Zhang, Fan, & Han, 2007). Some of the first cognitive social neuroimaging studies focused on self-representations (Heatherton, Macrae, & Kelley, 2004). Showing that MPFC activity predicts both self-referential judgments and memory early established the link that later research has exploited so well (Macrae, Moran, Heatherton, Banfield, & Kelley, 2004).

Self-referential processing in the MPFC differs according to task but not the modality, according to narrative and meta-analytic literature reviews (Northoff & Bermpohl, 2004; Northoff et al., 2006): As Figure 51.4 indicates: (a) Representation of self-relatedness implicates orbitoMPFC and paraACC (ventral MPFC); this fits the Mitchell et al. distinction between more ventral processing for self and similar others; (b) evaluation and emotional reappraisal implicate DMPFC. (Two other processes are not discussed here but are common in the literature: [c] monitoring implicates anterior cingulate cortex and [d] integration with autobiographical memory implicates the posterior CC/precuneus.) These cortical midline structures, ranging from ventral to dorsal to posterior, might show cultural variations in relative emphases ranging from immediate representation, to emotional loadings, to long-term memory for self. Interdependent selves might show less integration of new inputs with individual autobiographical long-term memory.

Self-evaluations reliably activate MPFC regions (e.g., Ochsner et al., 2004, 2005). These researchers distinguish

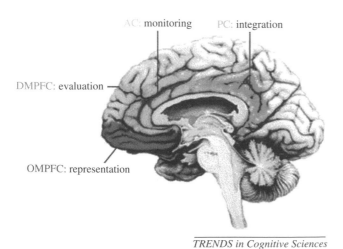

AC: monitoring   PC: integration

DMPFC: evaluation

OMPFC: representation

TRENDS in Cognitive Sciences

Figure 51.4   Processing of self-referential stimuli in the cortical midline structures (CMS).

Note: Orbitomedial prefrontal cortex (OMPFC; sometimes called ventromedial PFC), dorsomedial prefrontal cortex (DMPFC), anterior cingulate cortex, particularly the supragenual region (AC), posterior cingulate cortex (PC) including the adjacent retrosplenial cortex. The four hypothesized subprocesses of self-referential processing associated with each region are shown. From "Cortical Midline Structures and the Self," by G. Northoff and F. Bermpohl, 2004, *Trends in Cognitive Sciences, 8,* p. 104. Reprinted with permission.

two kinds of self-appraisals: direct (one's own self-evaluation) and reflected (one's representation of others' appraisals of self). These direct (self) and indirect (social) appraisals show different activation patterns. They further might respectively receive priority for independent versus interdependent selves. Perhaps cultural variations in autonomous self-focus would appear also in these activation patterns.

Similarly, independent selves tend to self-enhance more than interdependent selves (Heine, Lehman, Markus, & Kitayama, 1999; Taylor & Brown, 1988), and these differences might be reflected in variations between orbital and less ventral PFC (Beer, 2007). Many avenues of cultural variation in self-representation would be open for the next level of cultural neuroscience.

Mimicry: Bridging Self and Other

We have just explored cortical midline structures that might reflect cultural differences, focusing on the MPFC, as well as anterior and posterior cingulate cortex; broadly speaking, these are implicated in abstract representations of self and others. Other brain systems bridge self and others in a more somatosensory/motoric mode, by observation and imitation (see Chapter 16, Volume 1, plus Rizzolatti & Craighero, 2004; Uddin, Iacoboni, Lange, & Keenan, 2007; see also Figure 51.5). Two right lateral cortical areas—inferior frontal and rostral inferior parietal lobule—are implicated in the human mirror neuron system (MNS). This right frontoparietal system activates for its own actions as well as the comparable actions of others. The MNS apparently supports the motor simulation of imitation in gesture, instrumental action, and language, all fundamental components of culture. One lesson from the human MNS is our neural readiness to acquire culture by observation and imitation of others. Another is the possibility of cultural differences in attunement to others, again contrasting more interdependent and independent stances. Finally, cultural differences in power distance and the importance of status might predict differences in subordinate attunement to powerful others.

Regulation and Suppression

Cultures differ dramatically in their degree of self-monitoring and emotional expressiveness (e.g., Mesquita & Frijda, 1992; Pennebaker, Rimé, & Blankenship, 1996). We might therefore expect neural reflections of these patterns. At a minimum, behavioral inhibition systems (BIS) may dominate behavioral activation systems (BAS) (Carver & White, 1994), and vice versa, correlated with cultural variations in self-regulation and mental suppression (BIS) versus agency and approach (BAS).

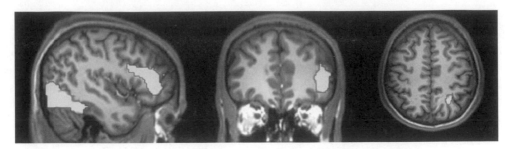

Figure 51.5   Overlap between areas involved in self-recognition and mirror-neuron areas.

Note: Self-recognition seems to engage mirror-neuron areas in the right hemisphere. Tasks of self-recognition produce activations that significantly overlap with those from tasks that involve imitation and action observation. Frontal and parietal areas of overlapping activity for the two tasks are shown. From "The Self and Social Cognition: The Role of Cortical Midline Structures and Mirror Neurons," by L. O. Uddin, M. Iacoboni, C. Lange, and J. P. Keenan, 2007, *Trends in Cognitive Sciences, 11,* p. 155. Reprinted with permission.

Orbitofrontal cortex plays a role in emotion regulation, according to patient brain-damage studies (Beer, Heerey, Keltner, Scabini, & Knight, 2003; Beer, John, Scabini, & Knight, 2006; Beer, Knight, & D'Esposito, 2006; Roberts et al., 2004). As noted, amygdala responses to emotionally significant stimuli might well also vary across cultures, in line with socialization to emotional expression and response. Hence, we might expect cultural variations in activation and development of the relevant networks, with more inhibition-shame-regulated cultures developing more sensitive neural systems of emotion regulation. In contrast, more approach-guilt-unregulated cultures might develop agentic, approach systems to a greater extent, in the management of emotion.

Not only emotions, but also sheer thought can be targeted for suppression. Two of the cognitive phenomena involved in thought suppression are working memory load and interference; these activate overlapping prefrontal areas (Bunge, Ochsner, Desmond, Glover, & Gabrieli, 2001). Dorsolaterial PFC activates to sustained efforts at thought and memory control, whereas ACC signals transient thought control (Anderson et al., 2004; Mitchell et al., 2007; Wyland, Kelley, Macrae, Gordon, & Heatherton, 2003), in line with its more general involvement in discrepancy detection (Botvinick et al., 2004). To the extent that people regulate unwanted thoughts, they tend to be more optimistic. And indeed, the right lateral PFC activation correlates with individual differences in agreeableness, which can be viewed as skillfully regulating negative affect (Haas, Omura, Constable, & Canli, 2007). To the extent that some cultures emphasize control, whereas others emphasize expression, neural activations might reflect those cultural proclivities.

Racial Cues

In U.S. culture, a major target of thought control and expression is racism. Race is a cultural phenomenon in several respects. First, the definition of race is culture-dependent, and reactions to race are certainly determined by culture (e.g., Fredrickson, 2002; Jones, 1997; Sears, 1998). What's more, norms around expressions of those reactions are culture-specific.

Because Americans usually try to suppress racist expression, American social psychologists quickly turned to implicit, unexamined, and automatic forms of racism to explain continuing discrimination and disparities (S. T. Fiske, 1998; Mays, Cochran, & Barnes, 2007). Prominent among these indicators, lately, have been neural correlates of racial perception (Eberhardt, 2005). A variety of approaches have focused, first, on event-related potentials indicating extremely early responses to race and, second, on imaging studies variously implicating the amygdala, the fusiform face area, and dlPFC.

People categorize other people by race, age, and gender early and often (S. T. Fiske, 1998). Categorical information is extracted from faces more readily than individuating information (Cloutier, Mason, & Macrae, 2005) and implicates the left hemisphere (Mason & Maccrae, 2004). Early processes differentiate ingroup ("us") from outgroup ("them") and good from bad (Ito, Thompson, & Cacioppo, 2004). Black targets preferentially draw attention as early as 100 msec into stimulus exposure (Ito & Urland, 2003), although racially ambiguous faces may be differentiated as late as 500 msec after stimulus exposure (Willadsen-Jensen & Ito, 2006). The early reactions are consequential, translating to racial biases in simulated shoot/no-shoot responses (Correll, Urland, & Ito, 2006).

Both affective and cognitive information influence racial categorization from its earliest moments. Phenotypically irrelevant affect-laden information (such as individual liking and disliking) influences racial categorization (Richeson & Trawalter, 2005a). Stereotypic racial assumptions affect early visual processing of race in faces, especially for visually typical racial appearances (Eberhardt, Goff, Purdie, & Davies, 2004). For some less flexible perceivers (so-called entity theorists), memory for racially ambiguous faces reverts to more racially prototypical faces, especially given a racial label for the face (Eberhardt, Dasgupta, & Banaszynski, 2003). Racial prototypicality correlates with harsher sentences in capital crimes, even controlling for relevant features of the crime (Eberhardt, Davies, Purdie-Vaughns, & Johnson, 2006), so racial appearance matters from early perception through consequential life-and-death decisions.

Locating some of these early features of racial perception has proved fruitful, ever since the earliest forays into social neuroscience. Same-race faces are more memorable than other-race faces, and this correlates with degree of activation in the fusiform face area (FFA; Golby, Gabrieli, Chiao, & Eberhardt, 2001). Such attunement should differ with culture, intergroup experience, and cross-cultural experience, a cultural neuroscience avenue worth pursuit. Cultural variations in the definition of race should determine people's tendency to include a face as "own race." And given that the FFA responds to other types of perceptual expertise besides faces (Gauthier, Skudlarski, Gore, & Anderson, 2000), culturally based variations in intergroup experience will determine perceptual expertise and FFA response.

Another index of early attunement to race is the vigilance system involving amygdala activation, which supports the heavy emotional loading of interracial interactions in the United States, and which could index cultural variability in such responses. Some of the most provocative early work on the neuroscience of interracial reactions documented amygdala responses correlated with negative implicit associations (IAT) but also with startle-eyeblink indicators of a defensive motivational orientation, especially in Whites responding to Blacks (Cunningham, Johnson, et al., 2004; Hart et al., 2000; Lieberman, Hariri, Jarcho, Eisenberger, & Bookheimer, 2005; Phelps et al., 2000; Wheeler & Fiske, 2005). Among Whites intrinsically concerned about prejudice (high in internal but low in external motivation to control their prejudice), their startle-eyeblink response to Black faces revealed lower automatic affective bias, compared with other participants (Amodio, Harmon-Jones, & Devine, 2003).

Other neuro-related evidence converges on the immediate affective loading of interracial encounters, especially for Whites. Facial muscle activity (subtle expressive movements not yet visible but tracked electromyographically) indicates subtle racial bias (Vanman, Paul, Ito, & Miller, 1997). Whites inexperienced at interacting with Blacks show cardiovascular reactivity consistent with threat in cross-racial interactions (Blascovich, Mendes, Hunter, Lickel, & Kowai-Bell, 2001; Mendes, Blascovich, Lickel, & Hunter, 2002). They then perform poorly on subsequent cognitive tasks, consistent with other evidence that executive control over prejudiced responses has mental costs (Richeson & Shelton, 2003; Richeson & Trawalter, 2005b). Conversely, Blacks who especially favor their ingroup also incur costs after interracial interaction (Richeson, Trawalter, & Shelton, 2005).

Nevertheless, Whites' successful control over racially biased responses still leaves neural traces, implicating dlPFC, among other indicators (Amodio et al., 2004; Cunningham, Johnson, et al., 2004; Lieberman et al., 2005; Richeson et al., 2003). American Whites apparently respond immediately to Blacks as emotionally significant and often negative, but they also quickly invoke controlled processes.

Dehumanization

Excluded groups vary by culture, though many cultures seem to disdain poor people, and social class can trump even race (Cuddy et al., 2009). In the United States, drug addicts and homeless people are among the lowest of the low, allegedly possessing no redeeming features. These extreme outgroups, compared with more ambivalently perceived, less extreme outgroups, and compared with all ingroups, elicit a unique neural signature: They alone fail to activate MPFC significantly above baseline (Harris & Fiske, 2006). Earlier, we noted that MPFC regions reliably activate to representations of one's own and other people's minds; specifically, MPFC activates when people consider other people's dispositions (Harris et al., 2005) or form impressions of other people (Mitchell, Macrae, & Banaji, 2004). Apparently "other people" does not include some extreme outgroups such as the homeless.

Reduced MPFC activity to extreme outgroups correlates with increased insula and amygdala activity to them, consistent with ratings of these people as disgusting and to be avoided (Harris & Fiske, 2008). The dimensions that typically control MPFC activity in the social neuroscience literature—similarity, familiarity, intelligence, empathy— are rated low for these targets, and people do not spontaneously mentalize them (think about their minds). All this fits the idea that the decreased MPFC activity reflects a form of dehumanization. Furthermore, a manipulation that asks perceivers to think about these targets' preferences brings the MPFC back online (Harris & Fiske, 2007). Other allegedly disgusting stigmas (e.g., obesity, facial piercings, transsexuality, ugliness) show similar patterns of decreased MPFC activation along with increased insula and amygdala activation (Krendl, Macrae, Kelley, Fugelsang, & Heatherton, 2006). Extreme forms of prejudice, under the wrong conditions, can lead to extreme behavior (S. T. Fiske, Harris, & Cuddy, 2004). The reliability of MPFC, insula, and amygdala as neural correlates of extreme prejudice suggests that they might serve as a comparative measure of each culture's untouchables.

More broadly, ventral MPFC operates in reward processing, though it is particularly tuned to rewarding people (Harris, McClure, van den Bos, Cohen, & Fiske, 2007; van den Bos, McClure, Harris, Fiske, & Cohen, 2007). It plays a role in more affective theory of mind reasoning (Shamay-Tsoory, Tibi-Elhanay, & Aharon-Peretz, 2006). Just as this area can differentiate depressed and healthy individuals (Keedwell, Andrew, Williams, Brammer, & Phillips, 2005), so it might differentiate more and less optimistic cultural outlooks.

CULTURAL UNIVERSALS AS CANDIDATES FOR CULTURAL NEUROSCIENCE

The previous section examined some reliable cultural variations as candidates for cultural neuroscience research. This section examines two kinds of social cultural universals as candidates for future social-cultural-neural research: the importance of perceived interpersonal intent and status.

Inferring Intent: The Warmth Dimension

The earliest adaptive judgment about another being is its intent toward oneself, for good or ill. The sentries' cry "Friend or foe?" captures this basic question. Much evidence now supports the rapid early judgment of friendliness, trustworthiness, warmth, and good intention (versus hostility, untrustworthiness, coldness, and bad intention) as the first dimension of interpersonal and intergroup judgment, across cultures (S. T. Fiske, Cuddy, & Glick, 2007).[1]

A focal stimulus for inferring hostile or benign intent is the face. Affective reactions to others' behaviors bind to the other's face (Todorov, Gobbini, Evans, & Haxby,

---

[1] This is not equivalent to a simple valence judgment for objects or words, which are not intentional agents, and some evidence indicates these judgments operate somewhat differently. For example, pure evaluative space probably operates more by independent negative and positive dimensions (Cacioppo & Berntson, 1999). Social cognition differs from object cognition in a number of respects (S. T. Fiske & Taylor, 2008). The amygdala may reflect intensity in a valence x intensity space, in judgments of socially relevant words; in that setting, the insula and orbital frontal cortex correlate with valence (e.g., Cunningham, Raye, & Johnson, 2004; Lewis, Critchley, Rotshtein, & Dolan, 2007). The exception seems to be famous names of people, wherein amygdala apparently codes for valence, as in its reactivity to trustworthiness in actual faces (Cunningham, Johnson, Gatenby, Gore, & Banaji, 2003).

2007), and extracting person knowledge from faces occurs unintentionally (Macrae, Quinn, Mason, & Quadfleig, 2005). Judging another person's trustworthiness—a key element of the warmth dimension—occurs within 50 msec of exposure to the face and correlates with unconstrained longer exposures (Willis & Todorov, 2006), but is not equivalent to global face evaluation (Todorov & Pakrashi, 2008). Features of the face that create consensus about trustworthiness best correlate with amygdala activation (Engell, Haxby, & Todorov, 2007), and these facial features resemble extreme versions of emotions: happiness (trustworthiness) and anger (untrustworthiness; Todorov, Baron, & Oosterhof, 2008). Faces depicting anger are detected faster than other expressions, and again implicate the amygdala (Green & Phillips, 2004). Amygdala lesions damage the ability to detect social threat from faces (Adolphs, Tranel, & Damasio, 1998; Amaral, 2002). Systems involving the amygdala selectively respond to threatening faces, in effect assigning a certain aspect of emotional value (Frith, 2007). All this fits the role of the amygdala in alerting to emotionally important stimuli.

Judging another person's predispositions also implicates the MPFC (as noted: e.g., Harris, Todorov, & Fiske, 2005; Mitchell, Cloutier, Banaji, & Macrae, 2006; see Figure 51.6). A variety of work on intentionality implicates the precuneus, temporoparietal junction (TPJ), and the paraACC (e.g., Ciaramidaro et al., 2007; Saxe & Kanwisher, 2003; Saxe & Powell, 2006; Saxe & Wexler, 2005). Imputing social intentions appears to differ from imputing private, nonsocial intentions (Walter et al., 2004). And the false-belief paradigms so prevalent in theory-of-mind studies activate different systems (e.g., pACC, precuneus, TPJ) than do interacting animated shapes (pSTS, frontal orperculum, inferior parietal lobule; Gobbini, Koralek, Bryan, Montgomery, & Haxby, 2007). The STS seems particularly involved in biological motion and gaze shifts (e.g., Pelphrey, Morris, & McCarthy, 2004), which might be subsumed under the notion of human trajectory. So at least three systems need to be sorted out, centered respectively on MPFC, TPJ, and STS (cf. Frith, 2007). As research accumulates, clarity and nuance will doubtless emerge.

Meanwhile, promising avenues open up for exploring the universal human need to understand other people's intentions. Cultural similarities in some systems (vMPFC and precuneus) can contrast with differences in other systems (TPJ and inferior frontal gyrus) (Kobayashi, Glover, & Temple, 2007).

People infer intent from others' structural position as cooperator or competitor, another apparent cultural universal (Caprariello, Cuddy, & Fiske, 2008; Cuddy et al.,

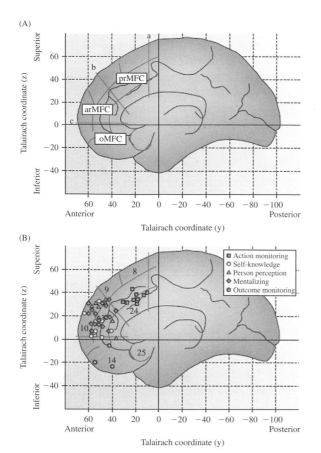

Figures 51.6 (**Figure C.48** in color section) Some functional divisions of the medial prefrontal cortex (mPFC).

Note: According to meta-analyses, more cognitive tasks such as action-monitoring often implicate the posterior rostral MFC (also called dorsal MPFC). More potentially emotional tasks such as emotion-ratings, self-knowledge, person perception, and mentalizing (imaging another's mind) often implicate the more anterior rostral MFC (also sometimes called dorsal MPFC, but a relatively more ventral location). Finally, the most orbital MFC (oMPFC) is implicated in outcome-monitoring. Figure 51.6A labels these areas and 51.6B /C.32 (*See insert for color figure*) locates the specific studies. For purposes of these diagrams, per the authors, the MPFC includes the ACC (anterior cingulate cortex). From "Meeting of Minds: The Medial Frontal Cortex and Social Cognition," by D. M. Amodio and C. D. Frith, 2006, *Nature Reviews Neuroscience, 7*, pp. 268–277. Reprinted with permission.

2009; S. T. Fiske, Cuddy, Glick, & Xu, 2002; Russell & Fiske, 2008). Arguably, people's neurocognitive systems evolved to detect other people's intents toward social exchange (Cosmides & Tooby, 1989; Cosmides, Tooby, Fiddick, & Bryant, 2005). People find another's cooperative intentions rewarding, as indicated by both self-reports and neural systems activated, and especially for human cooperators (Rilling et al., 2002; Rilling, Sanfey, Aronson, Nystrom, & Cohen, 2004; Walter, Abler, Ciaramidaro, & Erk, 2005). Again, cultural universals in preferences for cooperative versus competitive interaction partners might show similar neural signatures, with cultural variations.

Inferring Ability to Act on Intent: Status and Competence

Having inferred another's intent for good or ill, survival dictates inferring the other's ability to enact that intent, and accordingly, competence is the second apparently universal dimension of social perception (S. T. Fiske et al., 2007; Judd, James-Hawkins, Yzerbyt, & Kashima, 2005). Of these two universal dimensions, competence is a slightly slower, lower-priority judgment than warmth, but still incredibly fast (e.g., Hack, Goodwin, & Fiske, 2008; Willis & Todorov, 2006).

Inferred competence correlates highly with the structural variable of perceived status, across the world (Cuddy et al., 2009). Evolutionary psychology often singles out status/dominance hierarchies as basic to interpersonal interaction (e.g., Buss & Kenrick, 1998), and perceived competence predicts consequential status-related outcomes, such as elections (Todorov, Mandisodza, Goren, & Hall, 2005). Hence, one might expect neurocognitive systems for detecting competence/status. They differ in one being a trait (competence) and the other being a social structural relationship (status), so it is not surprising that they also differ in the relevant perceptual cues. Perceived competence, inferred from faces, correlates with facial maturity (Zebrowitz & Montepare, 2005). Perceived status correlates with size, height, numerosity, and precedence (Chiao, Bordeaux, & Ambady, 2004; A. P. Fiske, 2004).

A related dimension, perceived dominance, correlates with direct eye gaze, among other nonverbal cues (Hall, Coats, & LeBeau, 2005). Direct eye gaze facilitates person perception, that is, both categorization and category-based associations (Macrae, Hood, Milne, Rowe, & Mason, 2002; Mason, Hood, & Macrae, 2004). And direct versus averted gaze interacts with neural activation patterns to angry versus fearful faces (Adams, Gordon, Baird, Ambady, & Kleck, 2003). This matters to dominance because anger is an emotion of the powerful (Tiedens, Ellsworh, & Mesquita, 2000), whereas fear is an emotion of the subordinate. Consistent with this direct-gaze-anger-dominance configuration is work showing that anger is an approach emotion (Harmon-Jones & Allen, 1998; Harmon-Jones & Sigelman, 2001) because power broadly activates the behavioral approach system (BAS; Guinote, 2007; Keltner, Gruenfeld, & Anderson, 2003). Altogether, then, a variety of results suggest a dominance configuration that implicates anger, BAS, and the neural concomitants associated with left frontal activity (Harmon-Jones & Sigelman, 2001; Putman, Hermans, & van Honk, 2004).

In contrast, fear and anxiety, subordinate emotions, implicate the behavioral inhibition system (BIS; Keltner et al., 2003) with fallout for executive control (Putman et al., 2004). Low-status also interferes with executive control (Inzlicht, McKay, & Aronson, 2006) and correlates with reduced pACC volume (Gianaros et al., 2007). Fear and vigilance also reliably involve the amygdala (Phelps, 2006). One might also predict activation in brain areas implicated in vigilance (amygdala) because people attend to high-power others (S. T. Fiske, 1993), as well as medial prefrontal cortex because people want to know the intentions of high-power others (S. T. Fiske, 1993), and possibly anterior cingulate cortex because successful outgroup members present a cognitive conflict (Botvinick et al., 2004).

In general, the cultural universal here is likely to be BIS/BAS and some of their affective and neural correlates. Fear is socially learned (Olsson, Nearing, & Phelps, 2007), and as noted, some cultural settings might exaggerate the BIS, orienting toward deference, whereas others exaggerate the BAS, orienting toward dominance. Neurotransmitters such as serotonin (lower for low-status) and dopamine are likely to be implicated in status systems as well (Moskowitz, Pinard, Zuroff, Annable, & Young, 2001; S. B. Park et al., 1994; Raleigh, Mcguire, Brammer, & Yuwiler, 1984).

Even cultural universals, such as amygdala-fear linkages, are likely to have some cultural specificity (Chiao et al., 2006). Europeans respond to fearful faces with more activation in posterior cingulate, supplementary motor cortex, and amygdala, which could be interpreted as more direct, emotional way, whereas Japanese responded with more activation in right inferior frontal, premotor cortex, and left insula, which could be interpreted as more indirect, template matching way (Moriguchi et al., 2005). Another likely cultural universal would be thinking more abstractly when in power (Smith & Trope, 2006; Smith, Wigboldus, & Dijksterhuis, 2008).

CHALLENGES TO CULTURAL NEUROSCIENCE

Cultural neuroscience presents both huge opportunities and huge challenges. There is a reason cultural neuroscience is almost an oxymoron. A number of opportunities appear in prior sections, and we must collectively pursue them. They provide a unique opportunity to observe the interplay between brains and environments. Cultural similarities and differences in neural system responses offer an exciting chance to explore putative universals and cultural adaptations.

How to do cultural neuroscience is another question. Short of toting magnets (or less bulky luggage such as EEG caps) about the world, we can coordinate across cultures, as we do in many cultural studies, working with existing research groups who use similar equipment and methodologies across cultures. In social cultural neuroscience, the same problems arise as in any cultural psychology study: translation and cultural fit of stimulus materials and self-report measures, controlling for culture/method confounds, experimenter differences, and so on (for a review, see Kitayama & Cohen, 2007). Nevertheless, neuroscience equipment can add a layer of bias, due to the idiosyncrasies of particular machines and centers, which go beyond the issues for paper-and-pencil or even web studies.

Cultural researchers can hold constant particular, inevitably idiosyncratic equipment and staff if they conduct all their research in one spot but compare participants who are native-born residents versus those newly arrived from elsewhere. Of course, self-selection contaminates the subset of any given culture who choose to travel or emigrate.

A promising avenue for cultural research is priming dimensions in either monocultural individuals or more often, bicultural individuals (Oyserman & Lee, 2008). Effect sizes for priming individualism and collectivism are moderate for relationality and cognition, suggesting that this is a viable route that complements the other methods.

This exciting area of research is wide open for enterprising exploration. Cultural comparisons can inform our growing knowledge about brain functions, and neuroscience can inform our quest to better understand cultural universals and variations. Two words to the wise: "cultural neuroscience."

REFERENCES

Adams, R. B., Jr., Gordon, H. L., Baird, A. A., Ambady, N., & Kleck, R. E. (2003, June 6). Effects of gaze on amygdala sensitivity to anger and fear faces. *Science, 300,* 1536.

Adolphs, R., Tranel, D., & Damasio, A. R. (1998, June 4). The human amygdala in social judgment. *Nature, 393,* 470–474.

Amaral, D. G. (2002). The primate amygdala and the neurobiology of social behavior: Implications for understanding social anxiety. *Biological Psychiatry, 51,* 11–17.

Amodio, D. M., & Frith, C. D. (2006). Meeting of minds: The medial frontal cortex and social cognition. *Nature Reviews Neuroscience, 7,* 268–277.

Amodio, D. M., Harmon-Jones, E., & Devine, P. G. (2003). Individual differences in the activation and control of affective race bias as assessed by startle eyeblink response and self-report. *Journal of Personality and Social Psychology, 84,* 738–753.

Amodio, D. M., Harmon-Jones, E., Devine, P. G., Curtin, J. J., Hartley, S. L., & Covert, A. E. (2004). Neural signals for the detection of unintentional race bias. *Psychological Science, 15,* 88–93.

Anderson, M. C., Ochsner, K. N., Kuhl, B., Cooper, J., Robertson, E., Gabrieli, S. W., et al. (2004, January 9). Neural systems underlying the suppression of unwanted memories. *Science, 303,* 232–235.

Aslin, R. N. (1981). Experiential influences and sensitive periods in perceptual development: A unified model. In R. N. Aslin, J. R.

Alberts, & M. R. Petersen (Series Eds.), *Development of perception: Psychobiological perspectives: The visual system* (Vol. 2). New York: Academic Press.

Baumeister, R. F., & Leary, M. R. (1995). The need to belong: Desire for interpersonal attachments as a fundamental human motivation. *Psychological Bulletin, 117,* 497–529.

Beer, J. S. (2007). The default self: Feeling good or being right? *Trends in Cognitive Sciences, 11,* 187–189.

Beer, J. S., Heerey, E. A., Keltner, D., Scabini, D., & Knight, R. T. (2003). The regulatory function of self-conscious emotion: Insights from patients with orbito-frontal damage. *Journal of Personality and Social Psychology, 85,* 594–604.

Beer, J. S., John, O. P., Scabini, D., & Knight, R. T. (2006). Orbito-frontal cortex and social behavior: Integrating self-monitoring and emotion-cognition interactions. *Journal of Cognitive Neuroscience, 18,* 871–879.

Beer, J. S., Knight, R. T., & D'Esposito, M. (2006). Controlling the integration of emotion and cognition: The role of frontal cortex in distinguishing helpful from hurtful emotional information. *Psychological Science, 17,* 448–453.

Bennett, C. M., & Baird, A. A. (2006). Anatomical changes in the merging adult brain: A voxel-based morphometry study. *Human Brain Mapping, 27,* 766–777.

Blascovich, J., Mendes, W. B., Hunter, S. B., Lickel, B., & Kowai-Bell, N. (2001). Perceiver threat in social interactions with stigmatized others. *Journal of Personality and Social Psychology, 80,* 253–267.

Bolger, D. J., Perfetti, C. A., & Schneider, W. (2005). Cross-cultural effect on the brain revisited: Universal structures plus writing system variation. *Human Brain Mapping, 25,* 92–104.

Botvinick, M. M., Cohen, J. D., & Carter, C. S. (2004). Conflict monitoring and anterior cingulate cortex: An update. *Trends in Cognitive Sciences, 8,* 539–546.

Bunge, S. A., Ochsner, K. N., Desmond, J. E., Glover, G. H., & Gabrieli, J. D. E. (2001). Prefrontal regions involved in keeping information in and out of mind. *Brain: A Journal of Neurology, 124,* 2074–2186.

Buss, D. M., & Kenrick, D. T. (1998). Evolutionary social psychology. In D. T. Gilbert, S. T. Fiske, & G. Lindzey (Eds.), *Handbook of social psychology* (4th ed., Vol. 2, pp. 982–1026). New York: McGraw-Hill.

Cacioppo, J. T., & Berntson, G. G. (1999). The affect system: Architecture and operating characteristics. *Current Directions in Psychological Science, 8,* 133–137.

Cacioppo, J. T., Hawkley, L. C., Ernst, J. M., Burleson, M., Berntson, G. G., Nouriani, B., et al. (2006). Loneliness within a nomological net: An evolutionary perspective. *Journal of Research in Personality, 40,* 1054–1085.

Caprariello, P. A., Cuddy, J. C., & Fiske, S. T. (2008). *Social structure shapes cultural stereotypes and emotions: A causal test of the stereotype content model.* Manuscript under review.

Carver, C. S., & White, T. L. (1994). Behavioral inhibition, behavioral activation, and affective responses to impending reward and punishment: The BIS/BAS Scales. *Journal of Personality and Social Psychology, 67,* 319–333.

Caspi, A., McClay, J., Moffitt, T. E., Mill, J., Martin, J., & Craig, I. W., et al. (2002, August 2). Role of genotype in the cycle of violence in maltreated children. *Science, 297,* 851–854.

Chee, M. W. L., Goh, J. O. S., Venkatraman, V., Tan, J. C., Gutchess, A., Sutton, B., et al. (2006). Age-related changes in object processing and contextual binding revealed using fMR adaptation. *Journal of Cognitive Neuroscience, 18,* 495–507.

Cheour, M., Ceponiene, R., Lehtokoski, A., Luuk, A., Allik, J., Ahlo, K., et al. (1998). Development of language-specific phoneme representations in the infant brain. *Nature Neuroscience, 1,* 351–353.

Chiao, J. Y., & Ambady, N. (2007). Cultural neuroscience: Parsing universality and diversity across levels of analysis. In S. Kitayama &

D. Cohen (Eds.), *Handbook of cultural psychology* (pp. 237–254). New York: Guilford Press.

Chiao, J. Y., Bordeaux, A. R., & Ambady, N. (2004). Mental representations of social status. *Cognition, 93,* B49–B57.

Chiao, J. Y., Iidaka, T., Gordon, H. L., Nogawa, J., Bar, M., Aminoff, E., et al. (2006). *Cultural specificity in amygdala response to fear faces.* Poster presented at the Cognitive Neuroscience Society meeting, San Francisco.

Chua, H. F., Boland, J. E., & Nisbett, R. E. (2005). Cultural variation in eye movements during scene perception. *Proceedings of the National Academy of Sciences, USA, 102,* 12629–12633.

Ciaramidaro, A., Adenzato, M., Enrici, I., Erk, S., Pia, L., Bara, B. G., et al. (2007). The intentional network: How the brain reads a variety of intentions. *Neuropsychologia, 45,* 3105–3113.

Cloutier, J., Mason, M. F., & Macrae, C. N. (2005). The perceptual determinants of person construal: Reopening the social-cognitive toolbox. *Journal of Personality and Social Psychology, 88,* 885–894.

Cohen, D., Vandello, J., Puente, S., & Rantilla, A. (1999). "When you call me that, smile!" How norms for politeness, interaction styles, and aggression work together in Southern culture. *Social Psychology Quarterly, 62,* 257–275.

Correll, J., Urland, G. R., & Ito, T. A. (2006). Event-related potentials and the decision to shoot: The role of threat perception and cognitive control. *Journal of Experimental Social Psychology, 42,* 120–128.

Cosmides, L., & Tooby, J. (1989). Evolutionary psychology and the generation of culture: Pt. II. Case study: A computational theory of social exchange. *Ethology and Sociobiology, 10,* 51–97.

Cosmides, L., Tooby, J., Fiddick, L., & Bryant, G. A. (2005). Detecting cheaters: Comment. *Trends in Cognitive Sciences, 9,* 505–506.

Cuddy, A. J. C., Fiske, S. T., Kwan, V. S. Y., Glick, P., Demoulin, S., Leyens, J.-Ph., et al. (2009). Is the stereotype content model culture-bound? A cross-cultural comparison reveals systematic similarities and differences. *British Journal of Social Psychology.*

Cunningham, W. A., Johnson, M. K., Gatenby, J. C., Gore, J. C., & Banaji, M. R. (2003). Neural components of social evaluation. *Journal of Personality and Social Psychology, 85,* 639–649.

Cunningham, W. A., Johnson, M. K., Raye, C. L., Gatenby, J. C., Gore, J. C., & Banaji, M. R. (2004). Separable neural components in the processing of black and white faces. *Psychological Science, 15,* 806–813.

Cunningham, W. A., Raye, C. L., & Johnson, M. K. (2004). Implicit and explicit evaluation: FMRI correlates of valence, emotional intensity, and control in the processing of attitudes. *Journal of Cognitive Neuroscience, 16,* 1717–1729.

D'Argembeau, A., Collette, F., Van der Linden, M., Laureys, S., Del Fiore, G., Degueldre, C., et al. (2005). Self-referential reflective activity and its relationship with rest: A PET study. *NeuroImage, 25,* 616–624.

D'Argembeau, A., Ruby, P., Collette, F., Degueldre, C., Balteau, E., Luxen, A., et al. (2007). Distinct regions of the medial prefrontal cortex are associated with self-referential processing and perspective taking. *Journal of Cognitive Neuroscience, 19,* 935–944.

Davidoff, J. (2001). Language and perceptual categorisation. *Trends in Cognitive Sciences, 5,* 382–387.

Donald, M. (1991). *Origins of the modern mind: Three states in the evolution of culture and cognition.* Cambridge, MA: Harvard University Press.

Dunbar, R. (1993). Co-evolution of neocortical size, group size, and language in humans. *Behavioral and Brain Sciences, 16,* 681–735.

Dunbar, R. (2001). Brains on two legs: Group size and the evolution of intelligence. In F. B. M. de Waal (Ed.), *Tree of origin: What primate behavior can tell us about human social evolution* (pp. 175–191). Cambridge, MA: Harvard University Press.

Eberhardt, J. L. (2005). Imaging race. *American Psychologist, 60,* 181–190.

Eberhardt, J. L., Dasgupta, N., & Banaszynski, T. L. (2003). Believing is seeing: The effects of racial labels and implicit beliefs on face perception. *Personality and Social Psychology Bulletin, 29,* 360–370.

Eberhardt, J. L., Davies, P. G., Purdie-Vaughns, V. J., & Johnson, S. L. (2006). Looking deathworthy: Perceived stereotypicality of black defendants predicts capital-sentencing outcomes. *Psychological Science, 17,* 383–386.

Eberhardt, J. L., Goff, P. A., Purdie, V. J., & Davies, P. G. (2004). Seeing black: Race, crime, and visual processing. *Journal of Personality and Social Psychology, 87,* 876–893.

Eisenberger, N. I., Lieberman, M. D., & Williams, K. D. (2003, October 10). Does rejection hurt? An fMRI study of social exclusion. *Science, 302,* 290–292.

Eisenberger, N. I., Way, B. M., Taylor, S. E., Welch, W. T., & Lieberman, M. D. (2007). Understanding genetic risk for aggression: Clues from the brain's response to social exclusion. *Biological Psychiatry, 61,* 1100–1108.

Elbert, T., Pantev, C., Weinbruch, C., Rockstroh, B., & Taub, E. (1995, October 13). Increased cortical representation of the fingers of the left hand in string players. *Science, 270,* 305–307.

Engell, A. D., Haxby, J. V., & Todorov, A. (2007). Implicit trustworthiness decisions: Automatic coding of face properties in the human amygdala. *Journal of Cognitive Neuroscience, 19,* 1508–1519.

Fiske, A. P. (2002). Complementarity theory: Why human social capacities evolved to require cultural complements. *Personality and Social Psychology Review, 4,* 76–94.

Fiske, A. P. (2004). Four modes of constituting relationships: Consubstantial assimilation; space, magnitude, time and force; concrete procedures; abstract symbolism. In N. Haslam (Ed.), *Relational models theory: A contemporary overview* (pp. 61–146). Mahwah, NJ: Erlbaum.

Fiske, S. T. (1993). Controlling other people: The impact of power on stereotyping. *American Psychologist, 48,* 621–628.

Fiske, S. T. (1998). Stereotyping, prejudice, and discrimination. In D. T. Gilbert, S. T. Fiske, & G. Lindzey (Eds.), *Handbook of social psychology* (4th ed., Vol. 2, pp. 357–411). New York: McGraw-Hill.

Fiske, S. T. (2004). *Social beings.* Hoboken, NJ: Wiley.

Fiske, S. T., Cuddy, A. J. C., & Glick, P. (2007). Universal dimensions of social perception: Warmth and competence. *Trends in Cognitive Sciences, 11,* 77–83.

Fiske, S. T., Cuddy, A. J., Glick, P., & Xu, J. (2002). A model of (often mixed) stereotype content: Competence and warmth respectively follow from perceived status and competition. *Journal of Personality and Social Psychology, 82,* 878–902.

Fiske, S. T., Harris, L. T., & Cuddy, A. J. C. (2004, November 26). Why ordinary people torture enemy prisoners. *Science, 306,* 1482–1483.

Fiske, S. T., & Taylor, S. E. (2008). *Social cognition: From brains to culture.* New York: McGraw-Hill.

Fredrickson, G. M. (2002). *Racism: A short history.* Princeton, NJ: Princeton University Press.

Frith, C. D. (2007). The social brain? *Philosophical Transactions of the Royal Society, B: Biological Sciences, 362,* 671–678.

Gauthier, I., Skudlarski, P., Gore, J. C., & Anderson, A. W. (2000). Expertise for cars and birds recruits brain areas involved in face recognition. *Nature Neuroscience, 3,* 191–197.

Geary, D. C., Bow-Thomas, C. C., Fan, L., & Siegler, R. S. (1993). Even before formal instruction, Chinese children outperform American children in mental addition. *Cognitive Development, 8,* 517–529.

Gelman, R., & Butterworth, B. (2005). Number and language: How are they related? *Trends in Cognitive Sciences, 9,* 6–10.

Gianaros, P. J., Horenstein, J. A., Cohen, S., Matthews, K. A., Brown, S. M., Flory, J. D., et al. (2007). Perigenual anterior cingulate morphology covaries with perceived social standing. *Social Cognitive and Affective Neuroscience, 2,* 161–173.

Gobbini, M. I., Koralek, A. C., Bryan, R. E., Montgomery, K. J., & Haxby, J. V. (2007). Two takes on the social brain: A comparison of theory of mind tasks. *Journal of Cognitive Neuroscience, 19,* 1803–1814.

Golby, A. J., Gabrieli, J. D. E., Chiao, J. Y., & Eberhardt, J. L. (2001). Differential responses in the fusiform region to same-race and other-race faces. *Nature Neuroscience, 4,* 845–850.

Green, M. J., & Phillips, M. L. (2004). Social threat perception and the evolution of paranoia. *Neuroscience and Biobehavioral Reviews, 28,* 333–342.

Guinote, A. (2007). Power and goal pursuit. *Personality and Social Psychology Bulletin, 33,* 1076–1087.

Gusnard, D. A., Akbudak, E., Shulman, G. L., & Raichle, M. E. (2001). Medial prefrontal cortex and self-referential mental activity: Relation to a default mode of brain function. *Proceedings of the National Academy of Sciences, USA, 98,* 4259–4264.

Gutchess, A. H., Welsh, R. C., Boduroglu, A., & Park, D. C. (2006). Cultural differences in neural function associated with object processing. *Cognitive, Affective and Behavioral Neuroscience, 6,* 102–109.

Haas, B. W., Omura, K., Constable, R. T., & Canli, T. (2007). Is automatic emotion regulation associated with agreeableness?: A perspective using a social neuroscience approach. *Psychological Science, 18,* 130–132.

Hack, T. E., Goodwin, S. A., & Fiske, S. T. (2008). *Warmth trumps competence in social evaluations.* Manuscript under review.

Hall, J. A., Coats, E. J., & LeBeau, L. S. (2005). Nonverbal behavior and the vertical dimension of social relations: A meta-analysis. *Psychological Bulletin, 13,* 898–924.

Hamilton, R. H., & Pascual-Leone, A. (1998). Cortical plasticity associated with Braille learning. *Trends in Cognitive Sciences, 2,* 168–174.

Harmon-Jones, E., & Allen, J. J. B. (1998). Anger and frontal brain activity: EEG asymmetry consistent with approach motivation despite negative affective valence. *Journal of Personality and Social Psychology, 74,* 1310–1316.

Harmon-Jones, E., & Sigelman, J. (2001). State anger and prefrontal brain activity: Evidence that insult-related relative left-prefrontal activation is associated with experienced anger and aggression. *Journal of Personality and Social Psychology, 80,* 797–803.

Harris, L. T., & Fiske, S. T. (2006). Dehumanizing the lowest of the low: Neuro-imaging responses to extreme outgroups. *Psychological Science, 17,* 847–853.

Harris, L. T., & Fiske, S. T. (2007). Social groups that elicit disgust are differentially processed in mPFC. *Social Cognitive and Affective Neuroscience, 2,* 45–51.

Harris, L. T., & Fiske, S. T. (2008). *Dehumanized perception: Less mentalizing and more avoidance of disgusting people.* Manuscript under review.

Harris, L. T., McClure, S. M., van den Bos, W., Cohen, J. D., & Fiske, S. T. (2007). Regions of mPFC differentially tuned to affective and social stimuli. *Cognitive and Behavioral Neuroscience.*

Harris, L. T., Todorov, A., & Fiske, S. T. (2005). Attributions on the brain: Neuro-imaging dispositional inferences, beyond theory of mind. *NeuroImage, 28,* 763–769.

Hart, A. J., Whalen, P. J., Shin, L. M., McInerney, S. C., Fischer, H., & Rauch, S. L. (2000). Differential response in the human amygdala to racial outgroup vs ingroup face stimuli. *NeuroReport, 11,* 2351–2355.

Hatano, G., Amaiwa, S., & Shimizu, K. (1987). Formation of a mental abacus for computation and its use as a memory device for digits: A developmental study. *Developmental Psychology, 23,* 832–839.

Hatano, G., Miyake, Y., & Binks, M. G. (1977). Performance of expert abacus operators. *Cognition, 15,* 95–110.

Hawkley, L. C., Burleson, M. H., Berntson, G. G., & Cacioppo, J. T. (2003). Loneliness in everyday life: Cardiovascular activity, psychosocial context, and health behaviors. *Journal of Personality and Social Psychology, 85,* 105–120.

Heatherton, T. F., Macrae, C. N., & Kelley, W. M. (2004). What the social brain sciences can tell us about the self. *Current Directions in Psychological Science, 13,* 190–193.

Heatherton, T. F., Wyland, C. L., Macrae, C. N., Demos, K. E., Denny, B. T., & Kelley, W. M. (2006). Medial prefrontal activity differentiates self from close others. *Social Cognitive and Affective Neuroscience, 1,* 18–25.

Heine, S. J., Lehman, D. R., Markus, H. R., & Kitayama, S. (1999). Is there a universal need for positive self-regard? *Psychological Review, 106,* 766–794.

Iacoboni, M., Lieberman, M. D., Knowlton, B. J., Molnar-Szakacs, I., Moritz, M., Throop, C. J., et al. (2004). Watching social interactions produces dorsomedial prefrontal and medial parietal BOLD fMRI signal increases compared to a resting baseline. *NeuroImage, 21,* 1167–1173.

Inzlicht, M., McKay, L., & Aronson, J. (2006). Stigma as ego depletion: How being the target of prejudice affects self-control. *Psychological Science, 17,* 262–269.

Ito, T. A., Thompson, E., & Cacioppo, J. T. (2004). Tracking the time-course of social perception: The effects of racial cues on event-related brain potentials. *Personality and Social Psychology Bulletin, 30,* 1267–1280.

Ito, T. A., & Urland, G. R. (2003). Race and gender on the brain: Electrocortical measures of attention to the race and gender of multiply categorizable individuals. *Journal of Personality and Social Psychology, 85,* 616–626.

Jones, J. M. (1997). *Prejudice and racism* (2nd ed.). New York: McGraw-Hill.

Judd, C. M., James-Hawkins, L., Yzerbyt, V., & Kashima, Y. (2005). Fundamental dimensions of social judgment: Understanding the relations between judgments of competence and warmth. *Journal of Personality and Social Psychology, 89,* 899–913.

Keedwell, P. A., Andrew, C., Williams, S. C. R., Brammer, M. J., & Phillips, M. L. (2005). A double dissociation of ventromedial prefrontal cortical responses to sad and happy stimuli in depressed and healthy individuals. *Biological Psychiatry, 58,* 495–503.

Keltner, D., Gruenfeld, D. H., & Anderson, C. (2003). Power, approach, and inhibition. *Psychological Review, 110,* 265–284.

Kim, K. H. S., Relkin, N. R., Lee, K. M., & Hirsch, J. (1997, July 10). Distinct cortical areas associated with native and second languages. *Nature, 388,* 171–174.

Kitayama, S., & Cohen, D. (Eds.). (2007). *Handbook of cultural psychology.* New York: Guilford Press.

Klinger, E. (1978). Modes of normal conscious flow. In K. S. Pope & J. L. Singer (Eds.), *The stream of consciousness: Scientific investigations into the flow of human experience* (pp. 225–258). New York: Plenum Press.

Kobayashi, C., Glover, G. H., & Temple, E. (2007). Cultural and linguistic effects on neural bases of "theory of mind" in American and Japanese children. *Brain Research, 1164,* 95–107.

Krendl, A. C., Macrae, C. N., Kelley, W. M., Fugelsang, J. A., & Heatherton, T. F. (2006). The good, the bad and the ugly: An fMRI investigation of the functional correlates of stigma. *Social Neuroscience, 1,* 5–15.

Kuhl, P. K., Williams, K. A., Lacerda, F., Stevens, K. N., & Lindblom, B. (1992, January 31). Linguistic experience alters phonetic perception in infants by 6 months of age. *Science, 255,* 606–608.

Lewis, P. A., Critchley, H. D., Rotshtein, P., & Dolan, R. J. (2007). Neural correlates of processing valence and arousal in affective words. *Cerebral Cortex, 17,* 742–748.

Li, S. (2003). Biocultural orchestration of developmental plasticity across levels: The interplay of biology and culture in shaping the mind and behavior across the life span. *Psychological Bulletin, 129,* 171–194.

Lieberman, M. D., Hariri, A., Jarcho, J. M., Eisenberger, N. I., & Bookheimer, S. Y. (2005). An fMRI investigation of race-related amygdala activity in African-American and Caucasian-American individuals. *Nature Neuroscience, 8,* 720–722.

Maass, A., Suitner, C., Favaretto, X., & Cignacchi, M. (2009). Groups in space: Stereotypes and the spatial agency bias. *Journal of Experimental Psychology.*

Macrae, C. N., Hood, B. M., Milne, A. B., Rowe, A. C., & Mason, M. F. (2002). Are you looking at me? Eye gaze and person perception. *Psychological Science, 13,* 460–464.

Macrae, C. N., Moran, J. M., Heatherton, T. F., Banfield, J. F., & Kelley, W. M. (2004). Medial prefrontal activity predicts memory of self. *Cerebral Cortex, 14,* 647–654.

Macrae, C. N., Quinn, K. A., Mason, M. F., & Quadfleig, S. (2005). Understanding others: The face and person construal. *Journal of Personality and Social Psychology, 89,* 686–695.

Malamuth, N. M., & Addison, T. (2001). Integrating social psychological research on aggression within an evolutionary-based framework. In G. J. O. Fletcher & M. S. Clark (Eds.), *Blackwell handbook of social psychology: Interpersonal processes* (pp. 129–161). Malden, MA: Blackwell.

Maguire, E. A., Gadian, D. G., Johnsrude, I. S., Good, C. D., Ashburner, J., Frackowiak, R. S. J., et al. (2000). Navigation-related structural change in the hippocampi of taxi drivers. *Proceedings of the National Academy of Sciences, USA, 97,* 4398–4403.

Markus, H. R., & Kitayama, S. (1991). Culture and the self: Implications for cognition, emotion, and motivation. *Psychological Review, 98,* 224–253.

Mason, M. F., Hood, B. M., & Macrae, C. N. (2004). Look into my eyes: Gaze direction and person memory. *Memory, 12,* 637–643.

Mason, M. F., & Macrae, C. N. (2004). Categorizing and individuating others: The neural substrates of person perception. *Journal of Cognitive Neuroscience, 16,* 1785–1795.

Mason, M. F., Norton, M. I., Van Horn, J. D., Wegner, D. M., Grafton, S. T., & Macrae, C. N. (2007, January 19). Wandering minds: The default network and stimulus-independent thought. *Science, 315,* 393–395.

Massey, D. S. (2005). *Strangers in a strange land: Humans in an urbanizing world.* New York: Norton.

Mays, V. M., Cochran, S. D., & Barnes, N. W. (2007). Race, race-based discrimination, and health outcomes among African Americans. *Annual Review of Psychology, 58,* 201–225.

Mendes, W. B., Blascovich, J., Lickel, B., & Hunter, S. (2002). Challenge and threat during social interaction with White and Black men. *Personality and Social Psychology Bulletin, 28,* 939–952.

Mesquita, B., & Frijda, N. H. (1992). Cultural variations in emotions: A review. *Psychological Bulletin, 112,* 179–204.

Miller, K. F., Smith, C. M., Zhu, J., & Zhang, H. (1995). Preschool origins of cross-national differences in mathematical competence: The role of number-naming systems. *Psychological Science, 6,* 56–60.

Mitchell, J. P., Banaji, M. R., & Macrae, C. N. (2005). The link between social cognition and self-referential thought in the medial frontal cortex. *Journal of Cognitive Neuroscience, 17,* 1306–1315.

Mitchell, J. P., Cloutier, J., Banaji, M. R., & Macrae, C. N. (2006). Medial prefrontal dissociations during processing of trait diagnostic and nondiagnostic person information. *Social Cognitive and Affective Neuroscience, 1,* 49–55.

Mitchell, J. P., Heatherton, T. F., Kelley, W. M., Wyland, C. L., Wegner, D. M., & Macrae, C. N. (2007). Separating sustained from transient aspects of cognitive control during thought suppression. *Psychological Science, 18,* 292–297.

Mitchell, J. P., Macrae, C. N., & Banaji, M. R. (2004). Encoding-specific effects of social cognition on the neural correlates of subsequent memory. *Journal of Neuroscience, 24,* 4912–4917.

Mitchell, J. P., Macrae, C. N., & Banaji, M. R. (2006). Dissociable medial prefrontal contributions to judgments of similar and dissimilar others. *Neuron, 50,* 655–663.

Moriguchi, Y., Ohnishi, T., Kawachi, T., Mori, T., Hirakata, M., Yamada, M., et al. (2005). Specific brain activation in Japanese and Caucasian people to fearful faces. *NeuroReport, 16,* 133–136.

Moskowitz, D. S., Pinard, G., Zuroff, D. C., Annable, L., & Young, S. N. (2001). The effect of tryptophan on social interaction in everyday life: A placebo-controlled study. *Neuropsychopharmacology, 25,* 277–289.

Näätänen, R., Lehtokoski, A., Lennes, M., Cheour, M., Huotilainen, M., Iivonen, A., et al. (1997, January 30). Language-specific phoneme representations revealed by electric and magnetic brain responses. *Nature, 385,* 432–434.

Nelson, R. J., & Trainor, B. C. (2007). Neural mechanisms of aggression. *Nature Reviews Neuroscience, 8,* 536–546.

Neville, H. J., & Bavelier, D. (1998). Neural organization and plasticity of language. *Current Opinion in Neurobiology, 8,* 254–258.

Neville, H. J., Bavelier, D., Corina, D., Rauschecker, J., Karni, A., Lalwani, A., et al. (1998). Cerebral organization for language in deaf and hearing subjects: Biological constraints and effects of experience. *Proceedings of the National Academy of Sciences, USA, 95,* 922–929.

Nisbett, R. E. (2003). *The geography of thought: How Asians and Westerners think differently . . . and why.* London: Nicholas Brealey.

Nisbett, R. E., & Cohen, D. (1996). *Culture of honor: The psychology of violence in the south.* Boulder, CO: Westview Press.

Nisbett, R. E., & Masuda, T. (2003). Culture and point of view. *Proceedings of the National Academy of Sciences, USA, 100,* 11163–11170.

Nisbett, R. E., & Miyamoto, Y. (2005). The influence of culture: Holistic versus analytic perception. *Trends in Cognitive Sciences, 9,* 467–473.

Northoff, G., & Bermpohl, F. (2004). Cortical midline structures and the self. *Trends in Cognitive Sciences, 8,* 102–107.

Northoff, G., Heinzel, A., de Greck, M., Bermpohl, F., Dobrowolny, H., & Panksepp, J. (2006). Self-referential processing in our brain: A meta-analysis of imaging studies on the self. *NeuroImage, 31,* 440–457.

Ochsner, K. N., Beer, J. S., Robertson, E. R., Cooper, J. C., Gabrieli, J. D. E., Kihlstrom, J. F., et al. (2005). The neural correlates of direct and reflected self-knowledge. *NeuroImage, 28,* 797–814.

Ochsner, K. N., Knierim, K., Ludlow, D. H., Hanelin, J., Ramachandran, T., Glover, G., et al. (2004). Reflecting upon feelings: An fMRI study of neural systems supporting the attribution of emotion to self and other. *Journal of Cognitive Neuroscience, 16,* 1746–1772.

Olsson, A., Nearing, K. I., & Phelps, E. A. (2007). Learning fears by observing others: The neural systems of social fear transmission. *Social Cognitive and Affective Neuroscience, 2,* 3–11.

Oyserman, D., & Lee, S. W. S. (2008). Does culture influence what and how we think? Effects of priming individualism and collectivism. *Psychological Bulletin.*

Park, D. C., & Gutchess, A. H. (2002). Aging, cognition, and culture: A neuroscientific perspective. *Neuroscience and Biobehavioral Reviews, 26,* 859–867.

Park, S. B., Coull, J. T., McShane, R. H., Young, A. H., Sahakian, B. J., Robbins, T. W., et al. (1994). Tryptophan depletion in normal volunteers produces selective impairments in learning and memory. *Neuropharmacology, 33,* 575–588.

Paulesu, E., Demonet, J. F., Fazio, F., McCrory, E., & Chanoine, V., et al. (2001, March 16). Dyslexia: Cultural diversity and biological unity. *Science, 291,* 2064–2065.

Pelphrey, K. A., Morris, J. P., & McCarthy, G. (2004). Grasping the intentions of others: The perceived intentionality of an action influences activity in the superior temporal sulcus during social perception. *Journal of Cognitive Neuroscience, 16,* 1706–1716.

Pennebaker, J. W., Rimé, B., & Blankenship, V. E. (1996). Stereotypes of emotional expressiveness of Northerners and Southerners: A cross-cultural test of Montesquieu's hypotheses. *Journal of Personality and Social Psychology, 70,* 372–380.

Phelps, E. A. (2006). Emotion and cognition: Insights from studies of the human amygdala. *Annual Review of Psychology, 57,* 27–53.

Phelps, E. A., O'Connor, K. J., Cunningham, W. A., Funayama, E. S., Gatenby, J. C., Gore, J. C., et al. (2000). Performance on indirect measures of race evaluation predicts amygdala activation. *Journal of Cognitive Neuroscience, 12,* 729–738.

Polk, T. A., & Farah, M. J. (1998). The neural development and organization of letter recognition: Evidence from functional neuroimaging, computational modeling and behavioral studies. *Proceedings of National Academy of Sciences, USA, 95,* 847–852.

Posner, M. I., & Rothbart, M. K. (2007). Research on attention networks as a model for the integration of psychological science. *Annual Review of Psychology, 58,* 1–23.

Putman, P., Hermans, E., & von Honk, J. (2004). Emotion Stroop performance for masked angry faces: It's BAS, Not BIS. *Emotion, 4,* 305–311.

Raleigh, M. J., McGuire, M. T., Brammer, G. L., & Yuwiler, A. (1984). Social and environmental influences on blood serotonin concentrations in monkeys. *Archives of General Psychiatry, 41,* 405–410.

Richeson, J. A., Baird, A. A., Gordon, H. L., Heatherton, T. F., Wyland, C. L., Trawalter, S., et al. (2003). An fMRI investigation of the impact of interracial contact on executive function. *Nature Neuroscience, 6,* 1323–1328.

Richeson, J. A., & Shelton, J. N. (2003). When prejudice does not pay: Effects of interracial contact on executive function. *Psychological Science, 14,* 287–290.

Richeson, J. A., & Trawalter, S. (2005a). On the categorization of admired and disliked exemplars of admired and disliked racial groups. *Journal of Personality and Social Psychology, 89,* 517–530.

Richeson, J. A., & Trawalter, S. (2005b). Why do interracial interactions impair executive function? A resource-depletion account. *Journal of Personality and Social Psychology, 88,* 934–947.

Richeson, J. A., Trawalter, S., & Shelton, J. N. (2005). African Americans' implicit racial attitudes and the depletion of executive function after interracial internactions. *Social Cognition, 23,* 336–352.

Rilling, J., Gutman, D., Zeh, T., Pagnoni, G., Berns, G., & Kilts, C. (2002). A neural basis for social cooperation. *Neuron, 18,* 395–405.

Rilling, J., Sanfey, A. G., Aronson, J. A., Nystrom, L. E., & Cohen, J. D. (2004). The neural correlates of theory of mind within interpersonal interactions. *NeuroImage, 22,* 1694–1703.

Rizzolatti, G., & Craighero, L. (2004). The mirror-neuron system. *Annual Review of Neuroscience, 27,* 169–192.

Roberts, N. A., Beer, J. S., Werner, K. H., Scabini, D., Levens, S. M., Knight, R. T., et al. (2004). The impact of orbital prefrontal cortex damage on emotional activation to unanticipated and anticipated acoustic startle stimuli. *Cognitive, Affective, and Behavioral Neuroscience, 4,* 307–316.

Russell, A. M., & Fiske, S. T. (2008). *It's all relative: Social position and interpersonal perception.* Manuscript under review.

Saxe, R., & Kanwisher, N. (2003). People thinking about thinking people. The role of the temporo-parietal junction in "theory of mind." *Neuroimage, 19,* 1835–1842.

Saxe, R., & Powell, L. J. (2006). It's the thought that counts: Specific brain regions for one component of theory of mind. *Psychological Science, 17,* 692–699.

Saxe, R., & Wexler, A. (2005). Making sense of another mind: The role of the right temporo-parietal junction. *Neuropsychologia, 43,* 1391–1399.

Schlaggar, B. L., & McCandliss, B. D. (2007). Development of neural systems for reading. *Annual Review of Neuroscience, 30,* 475–503.

Sears, D. O. (1998). Racism and politics in the United States. In J. L. Eberhardt & S. T. Fiske (Eds.), *Confronting racism: The problem and the response* (pp. 76–100). Thousand Oaks, CA: Sage.

Shamay-Tsoory, S. G., Tibi-Elhanay, Y., & Aharon-Peretz, J. (2006). The ventromedial prefrontal cortex is involved in understanding affective but not cognitive theory of mind stories. *Social Neuroscience, 1,* 149–166.

Sherry, D. F. (2006). Neuroecology. *Annual Review of Psychology, 57,* 167–197.

Shih, J. C., Chen, K., & Ridd, M. J. (1999). Monoamine oxidase: From genes to behavior. *Annual Review of Neuroscience, 22,* 197–217.

Siok, W. T., Perfetti, C. A., Zhen, J., & Tan, L. H. (2004, September 3). Biological abnormality of impaired reading is constrained by culture. *Nature, 431,* 71–76.

Smith, P. K., & Trope, Y. (2006). You focus on the forest when you're in charge of the trees: Power priming and abstract information processing. *Journal of Personality and Social Psychology, 90,* 578–596.

Smith, P. K., Wigboldus, D. H. J., & Dijksterhuis, A. (2008). Abstract thinking increases one's sense of power. *Journal of Experimental Social Psychology, 44,* 378–385.

Stigler, J. W., Lee, S.-Y., & Stevenson, H. W. (1986). Digit memory in Chinese and English: Evidence for a temporally limited store. *Cognition, 23,* 1–20.

Tan, L. H., Spinks, J. A., Eden, G. F., Perfetti, C. A., & Siok, W. T. (2005). Reading depends on writing, in Chinese. *Proceedings of National Academy of Sciences, USA, 102,* 8781–8785.

Tang, Y., Zhang, W., Chen, K., Feng, S., Ji, Y., Shen, J., et al. (2006). Arithmetic processing in the brain shaped by cultures. *Proceedings of National Academy of Sciences, USA, 103,* 10775–10780.

Taylor, S. E., & Brown, J. D. (1988). Illusion and well-being: A social psychological perspective on mental health. *Psychological Bulletin, 103,* 193–210.

Taylor, S. E., Way, B. M., Welch, W. T., Hilmert, C. J., Lehman, B. J., & Eisenberger, N. I. (2006). Early family environment, current adversity, the serotonin transporter promoter polymorphism, and depressive symptomatology. *Biological Psychiatry, 60,* 671–676.

Tiedens, L. Z., Ellsworth, P. C., & Mesquita, B. (2000). Stereotypes about sentiments and status: Emotional expectations for high- and low-status group members. *Personality and Social Psychology Bulletin, 26,* 560–574.

Todorov, A., Baron, S. G., & Oosterhof, N. N. (2008). Evaluating face trustworthiness: A model based approach. *Social Cognitive and Affective Neuroscience, 3,* 119–127.

Todorov, A., Gobbini, M. I., Evans, K. K., & Haxby, J. V. (2007). Spontaneous retrieval of affective person knowledge in face perception. *Neuropsychologia, 45,* 163–173.

Todorov, A., Mandisodza, A. N., Goren, A., & Hall, C. C. (2005, June 10). Inferences of competence from faces predict election outcomes. *Science, 308,* 1623–1626.

Todorov, A., & Pakrashi, M. (2008). *Trait judgments from faces: Rapid, unreflective, and robust.* Manuscript under review.

Triandis, H. C. (1990). Cross-cultural studies of individualism and collectivism. In J. Berman (Ed.), *Nebraska symposium on motivation* (pp. 41–133). Lincoln: University of Nebraska Press.

Uddin, L. O., Iacoboni, M., Lange, C., & Keenan, J. P. (2007). The self and social cognition: The role of cortical midline structures and mirror neurons. *Trends in Cognitive Sciences, 11,* 153–157.

van den Bos, W., McClure, S. M., Harris, L. T., Fiske, S. T., & Cohen, J. D. (2007). Dissociating affective evaluation and social cognitive processes in ventral medial prefrontal cortex. *Cognitive and Behavioral Neuroscience.*

Vandello, J. A., & Cohen, D. (1999). Patterns of individualism and collectivism across the United States. *Journal of Personality and Social Psychology, 77,* 279–292.

Vanman, E. J., Paul, B. Y., Ito, T. A., & Miller, N. (1997). The modern face of prejudice and structural features that moderate the effect of cooperation on effect. *Journal of Personality and Social Psychology, 73,* 941–959.

Walter, H., Abler, B., Ciaramidaro, A., & Erk, S. (2005). Motivating forces of human actions: Neuroimaging reward and social interaction. *Brain Research Bulletin, 15,* 368–381.

Walter, H., Adenzato, M., Ciaramidaro, A., Enrici, I., Pia, L., & Bara, B. G. (2004). Understanding intention in social perception: The role of the anterior paracingulate cortex. *Journal of Cognitive Neuroscience, 16,* 1854–1863.

Weber-Fox, C., & Neville, H. J. (1996). Maturational constraints on functional specializations for language processing: ERP and behavioral evidence in bilingual speakers. *Journal of Cognitive Neuroscience, 8,* 231–256.

Wheeler, M. E., & Fiske, S. T. (2005). Controlling racial prejudice: Social cognitive goals affect amygdala and stereotype activation. *Psychological Science, 16,* 56–63.

Whiten, A., & Byrne, R. W. (Eds.). (1997). *Machiavellian intelligence: Pt. II. Extensions and evaluations.* Cambridge, England: Cambridge University Press.

Willadsen-Jensen, E. C., & Ito, T. A. (2006). Ambiguity and the timecourse of racial perception. *Social Cognition, 24,* 580–606.

Willis, J., & Todorov, A. (2006). First impressions: Making up your mind after a 100-ms exposure to a face. *Psychological Science, 17,* 592–598.

Wyland, C. L., Kelley, W. M., Macrae, C. N., Gordon, H. L., & Heatherton, T. F. (2003). Neural correlates of thought suppression. *Neuropsychologia, 41,* 1863–1867.

Zebrowitz, L. A., & Montepare, J. M. (2005). Appearance does matter. *Science, 308,* 1565–1566.

Zhu, Y., Zhang, L., Fan, J., & Han, S. (2007). Neural basis of cultural influence on self-representation. *NeuroImage, 34,* 1310–1316.

PART VII

Psychological Disorders

Chapter 52

Autism

DAVID G. AMARAL, JOHN L. R. RUBENSTEIN, AND SALLY J. ROGERS

Autism or autistic spectrum disorders (ASD) are a group of neurodevelopmental disorders with varying degrees of behavioral impairment. The cause(s) of autism are unknown though it is now generally believed that there are multiple forms of autism with multiple etiologies. Many in the field refer to autism*s* rather than autism. Diagnosis, which generally occurs prior to 3 years of age, is based on observing behavioral impairments in three categories: (1) social behavior, (2) verbal and nonverbal communication, and (3) stereotyped, repetitive behaviors and interests (American Psychiatric Association, 1994). The disorder ranges from the lower functioning end of the spectrum with comorbid mental retardation, to the higher functioning end of the spectrum with normal IQ, to Asperger syndrome with normal to high IQ and relatively normal language development. Because of this heterogeneity, it is perhaps preferable to refer to autism spectrum disorders rather than autism. There are comorbid conditions at all levels of the spectrum including epilepsy, anxiety, gastrointestinal problems, sleep disorders and the inability to modulate sensory input. Current estimates of prevalence are on the order of 1:150 children. Males are four times as likely to have an autistic spectrum disorder as females.

Autism was first described in 1943 by Leo Kanner, a psychiatrist at Johns Hopkins University (Kanner, 1943). He identified common features of 11 children whom he treated over a 5-year period "whose condition differ[ed] so markedly and uniquely from anything reported so far" (p. 217). Kanner described a set of core features, the most important of which was "the children's inability to relate themselves in an ordinary way to people and situations from the beginning of life" (p. 242). The parental phrases that he quoted: "happiest when left alone, acting as if people weren't there, oblivious to everything around him" are common even now when clinicians interview parents during the diagnostic process. Kanner (1971) followed 9 of the 11 children into adulthood. While there was some improvement in all symptoms, the individuals all continued to have problems engaging in normal social relations. Only two adults were eventually employed but both remained single and lived with their parents.

Hans Asperger, an Austrian pediatrician, wrote a paper roughly at the same time as that of Kanner (Asperger, 1944), and the parallels of his independent observations were striking. Asperger also used the term "autistic" to refer to his patients and also emphasized their social impairments. Asperger emphasized that the syndrome was present from early in life but not progressive. He underscored the pervasive nature of the condition: "[I]t totally colours affect, intellect, will, and action" (p. 39). Unlike Kanner, Asperger noted that several of his patients demonstrated high intellectual ability in math and reading. Asperger also described circumscribed interests in particular objects or topic areas leading often to lengthy monologues about these special interests. This description has spawned the term *little professors* in many descriptions of Asperger syndrome. Currently, the term *Asperger syndrome* is typically reserved for those individuals who have normal or even superior intellectual abilities and little or no evidence of language impairment while retaining social impairments and limited interests and behaviors.

EPIDEMIOLOGY OF AUTISM

The current rate of autism, particularly the perceived increase in the rate portrayed by advocates, has generated substantial attention both in the popular press and in scientific and educational agencies. Prevalence estimates have increased in the past 20 years by more than tenfold (Chakrabarti & Fombonne, 2005) from a widely accepted figure of 5 cases per 10,000 in the 1980s to current estimates of 1 in 150 (Kuehn, 2007) for autism spectrum disorders. Some have claimed that we are in the midst of an autism epidemic and have blamed environmental factors and current medical practices as the culprits. There is currently inadequate scientific evidence to determine the real magnitude of the increase in autism spectrum disorders.

Some of the increased prevalence is due to both increased sensitivities in diagnosis (Fombonne, 2005; Newschaffer et al., 2007) and the widening of diagnostic criteria. While definitions of autism 20 years ago reflected the classic, severe form of the disorder, the current *DSM-IV-TR* classification system (American Psychiatric Association, 1994) now includes children who meet full criteria for Autistic Disorder (AD), as well as those who do not meet stringent criteria and are given the diagnosis of Asperger's Disorder or even the less specified diagnosis of Pervasive Developmental Disorder—Not Otherwise Specified (PDD-NOS). Epidemiological studies generally find that the prevalence of children diagnosed with PDD-NOS is higher than those with classic autism (Baker, 2002; Chakrabarti & Fombonne, 2005; Yeargin-Allsopp et al., 2003). Thus, the group of persons now being counted in prevalence studies includes many who would not have been counted previously based on earlier diagnostic definitions of autism.

A variety of environmental and biological causes have also been suggested to account for some of the increasing prevalence rates of autism spectrum disorders (Altevogt, Hanson, & Leshner, 2008). Environmental exposures, particularly mercury exposure through vaccinations, dental procedures, and environmental contaminants, increased use of fertility treatments, interactions between immune abnormalities in mother or child and exposure to immune challenges in the uterine or postuterine environments, air and environmental pollutants such as heavy metals and PCBs (Newschaffer et al., 2007) have increased significantly in the past decade. The science of understanding autism is reliant on a true appreciation of the real increased prevalence of autism. The prospective epidemiological studies needed to get a scientifically valid appreciation of increased incidence have not yet been completed. While autism has a substantial genetic component, there is also evidence for environmental contributions to the etiology of autism. If autism is truly undergoing a substantial increase in prevalence, this would tend to point to environmental factors as critically important (Bello, 2007).

DIAGNOSIS AND BEHAVIORAL FEATURES

Core Behavioral Features of Autism

Kanner described that his patients were oblivious to the social world; not unaware, but uninterested. They ignored speech, such as calling their names, to such an extent that some were considered to be deaf, though none had a hearing impairment. The children ignored their parents, the presence of strangers, and the presence of other children (Kanner, 1943). Kanner described what is now considered to be the most severe form of a continuum of impairment in reciprocal social relatedness. Subsequently, Wing (1981) has fractionated the social impairments into three main types: aloof (as Kanner described), passive (responsive to others' interactions but not initiating interactions themselves), and active but odd (clearly interested in social interaction but unusual or inappropriate in the way they go about it).

Children demonstrate social reciprocity in a variety of ways, including making eye contact, sharing emotional expressions, and executing typical social body postures and gestures. This capacity is present in human development in the first few months of life in gestures like raising arms up to be lifted and using facial expressions directed to others to communicate feelings (D. Stern, 1985; Trevarthen & Aitken, 2001). All these forms of social expression are affected in autism across age and spectrum of ability (Hobson & Lee, 1999; Wimpory, Hobson, Williams, & Nash, 2000).

Abnormal development or use of language is another key feature of autism. A significant number of persons with autism do not acquire speech. This group typically does not develop an alternative communication system without extensive instruction. Thus, this subgroup often lacks verbal and nonverbal communication. For those who develop speech in the preschool period, speech appears less a system for sharing thoughts, feelings, desires, and experiences with others and more a system of naming objects. Children with autism rely much more heavily on repetition, or echolalia, for language learning than others. Development of sentences is typically delayed and marked by echolalia (repetition of others' words or sentences); pronoun confusion is also common. Verbal children eventually master syntactic rules but their language is literal and they often have difficulty with metaphor, irony, and humor (Tager-Flusberg, Paul, & Lord, 2005).

A third area of impairment relates to the repetition of behaviors and the limited scope of interests. Children with autism have a narrow range of activities and interests and devote large amounts of time to repetitive and ritualized behaviors. Motor stereotypies such as hand flapping, toe walking, finger movements, odd visual behaviors, and repetitive words or other vocalizations are also common. Rituals and routines may involve consistent patterns of grouping objects. It is often upsetting if objects on a child's desk or within a child's room are moved from their typical location or configuration. This feature was quite evident in Kanner's first patients (Kanner, 1943), and these behaviors continue to be an important part of the diagnostic picture (*DSM-IV-TR*, APA, 1994).

Many children and adults with autism have unusual reactions to the sensory world. Many children with autism respond strongly to loud noises and moving objects, though they themselves could make just as loud noises without being upset. Fascination with moving objects, water, watching the wheels of cars and trains spin, elevator doors, and feeling textures may go hand in hand with severe aversions to clothing textures, food textures, certain sounds, and negative reactions to haircuts or hair washing. Sensory over- or under-responsiveness may be seen in any sensory domain, and in the same child. The adult autobiographical literature gives vivid descriptions of the degree of difficulty this symptom can cause in everyday life (Grandin, 1992; Ratey, Grandin, & Miller, 1992; D. Williams, 1992).

Current Diagnostic Definitions

In the United States, the diagnosis of autistic spectrum disorder (ASD) is made according to the *DSM-IV-TR* criteria. Pervasive Developmental Disorders (the *DSM-IV-TR* generic term for ASD), involves five diagnostic groups: Autistic Disorder (AD), Asperger's Disorder (AS), Pervasive Developmental Disorder, not otherwise specified (PDD-NOS), Childhood Disintegrative Disorder (CDD), and Rett's Disorder. Childhood Disintegrative Disorder and Rett's Disorder are generally not currently considered part of the pervasive developmental disorder group. Rett syndrome is a single gene mutation involving the MECP2 gene. It affects mostly girls, is progressive in its course, and results in severe intellectual impairment and profound disability in all areas of functioning over time. Childhood Disintegrative Disorder is a very rare condition in which a fairly rapid regression occurs, generally between the third and fifth years, in children previously developing typically; and after that point, children appear indistinguishable from other children with fairly severe autistic disorder and intellectual deficits (Volkmar & Klin, 2005).

The diagnostic criteria for autistic disorder involve demonstrating a total of six or more of the symptoms listed in the *DSM-IV,* including two from the social communication category, one from language category, and one from the restricted and repetitive behaviors category. The diagnosis of autism is made from three types of diagnostic procedures: a detailed history from parental interviews, parental description of current functioning in typical situations, and clinical observation and assessment of the child's behavior. Recent developments in assessment tools have made the diagnosis of autism much more reliable. In fact, the diagnosis of autistic disorder among experienced clinicians has the highest rate of inter-rater agreement and the most stability of any of the psychiatric diagnoses (Lord, 2005). The most common tools for ascertaining autistic participants in research studies include the autism diagnostic inventory (ADI-R), an experimenter administered interview, the social communication questionnaire (SCQ), a parent questionnaire with key questions from the ADI-R, the autism diagnostic observational scale (ADOS), an interactive semistructured interview with the child or adult being diagnosed, and the childhood autism rating scales (CARS), an examiner behavior rating system completed after a developmental evaluation (Lord, 2005).

There has been substantial controversy concerning the heterogeneity of onset of autism. While initially disputed, it is now clear that there are multiple patterns of onset (Goldberg, Thorsen, Osann, & Spence, 2007; Ozonoff, Williams, & Landa, 2005; Richler et al., 2006). Based on parental report and analysis of first birthday videotapes, some children are showing signs of pathology at 12 months of age. However, it is equally clear that a second group of children are closely hitting normal developmental milestones until approximately 18 to 24 months when they regress into a form of autism that is largely indistinguishable from early onset autism. This is typically referred to as regressive autism. It is likely to be the case that a relatively small fraction of children with autism show early onset versus regressive forms of autism. Many children appear to undergo some delays with subsequent regressions.

COMORBID FEATURES OF AUTISM

The past decade of research and public scrutiny of autism has revealed that symptoms and difficulties are not confined to the nervous system. A number of common, comorbid features have become evident; some of these were already described by Kanner and Asperger.

Seizures

While epilepsy has long been associated with autism spectrum disorders, the proportion of patients reported to demonstrate comorbid seizure disorder varies from 5% to 44% (Tuchman & Rapin, 2002). Hara (2007) carried out a follow-up study of 135 patients with idiopathic autism. Of these, 25% exhibited epileptic seizures that had an onset between 8 and 26 years of age. While 18% of the nonepileptic group exhibited epileptic discharges on EEG, 68% of the epileptic group revealed epileptiform EEG findings before the onset of epilepsy. Some studies have found an association between low IQ and the occurrence of epilepsy (Pavone et al., 2004) or low IQ and motor deficit and epilepsy (Tuchman, Rapin, & Shinnar, 1991). Abnormal or epileptiform EEG is also observed in substantial numbers of individuals with autism who do not have seizures (Tuchman & Rapin, 1997; Tuchman et al., 1991). While the presence of seizure disorder and its association with other aspects of autism may provide interesting clues to the underlying pathophysiology, it remains unclear to what extent epileptiform activity contributes to the generation of the core features of autism.

Anxiety

In Kanner's (Kanner, 1943) original description of autism, he noted unusual fear or anxiety in several of his young patients. One child, Herbert, was "tremendously frightened by running water, gas burners, and many other things." He became upset by any change of an accustomed pattern. "If he notices change, he is very fussy and cries." Another child did a "good deal of worrying." He was upset because the moon did not always appear in the sky at night. He preferred to play alone and would get down from a play apparatus as soon as another child approached. Insistence on sameness leads children with autism to become greatly distressed when anything is broken or incomplete, and they demand consistency in the sequence of daily events.

Muris, Steerneman, Merckelbach, Holdrinet, and Meesters (1998) examined the presence of co-occurring anxiety symptoms in 44 children diagnosed with autism or pervasive developmental disorder. Using parental report, they found that 84.1% of the children met criteria for at least one anxiety disorder. Gillott, Furniss, and Walter (2001) compared high-functioning children with autism to two control groups including children with specific language impairment and normally developing children on measures of anxiety and social worry. Children with autism were found to be significantly more anxious on both indexes. More recently, this same group of investigators found that adults with autism were almost three times more anxious than a comparison group and gained significantly higher scores on anxiety subscales of panic and agoraphobia, separation anxiety, obsessive-compulsive disorder, and generalized anxiety disorder (Gillott & Standen, 2007).

Gastrointestinal Disorders

While research on gastrointestinal (GI) problems in children with autism is somewhat limited and conflicted (Erickson et al., 2005), it appears that autistic children have a higher incidence of GI problems than typically developing children or children with developmental delays (Valicenti-McDermott et al., 2006). GI problems are a common complaint of parents of children with autism, and this factor has prompted the use of complementary and alternative medicines (Harrington, Rosen, Garnecho, & Patrick, 2006). A number of clinicians have emphasized the need to investigate GI problems particularly in low-functioning children who cannot communicate their distress and for whom alleviation of the GI condition may appreciably improve the quality of life.

Autoimmune Disorders

Immune dysfunction may play an important role in a subset of autistic spectrum disorder cases (van Gent, Heijnen, & Treffers, 1997). Some individuals with autism demonstrate abnormalities and deficits of immune system function leading to inappropriate or ineffective immune response to pathogens (Ashwood & Van de Water, 2004a). Children with autism often have recurrent infections (L. Stern et al., 2005), peripheral immune abnormalities (Ashwood et al., 2003; Croonenberghs, Bosmans, Deboutte, Kenis, & Maes, 2002; Singh, 1996), or neuroinflammatory responses in the central nervous system (Vargas, Nascimbene, Krishnan, Zimmerman, & Pardo, 2005). In addition to general immune system dysfunction, evidence suggests that certain forms of autism are associated with an autoimmune condition (Ashwood & Van de Water, 2004a, 2004b). Autoimmunity occurs when the immune system inappropriately identifies and reacts to "self" components. Antibodies produced during an autoimmune response play a critical role in the pathogenesis of several peripheral neurological diseases, including myasthenia gravis (Lang, Dale, & Vincent, 2003; Lang, Pinto, Giovannini, Newsom-Davis, & Vincent, 2003; Lang & Vincent, 2003; Newsom-Davis et al., 2003; Scoppetta et al., 2003). Autoimmunity may also play a role in central nervous system diseases, notably psychological and neural disorders associated with streptococcal infections (PANDAS) which accounts for a subgroup of childhood-onset obsessive-compulsive disorders (OCD) and tic disorders (Snider & Swedo, 2003). Autoimmune disorders also appear to be more common in family members of ASD patients compared with typically developing controls. Mothers and first-degree relatives of children with autism are more likely to have an autoimmune disorder (16% and 21%) than controls (2% and 4%) (Comi, Zimmerman, Frye, Law, & Peeden, 1999). Similar results have been obtained in a study of autoimmune disorder frequency in families with children who have pervasive developmental disorders, including autism (Sweeten, Bowyer, Posey, Halberstadt, & McDougle, 2003). Regression in autism has been significantly associated with a family history of autoimmune disorders (Richler et al., 2006).

Antibodies directed against CNS proteins have been found in the sera of autistic children. Targets of autoantibodies in pervasive developmental disorder patients include neuron-axon filament protein (Singh, Warren, Averett, & Ghaziuddin, 1997), myelin basic protein (Singh, Warren,

Odell, Warren, Cole, 1993), serotonin receptor (Todd & Ciaranello, 1985), cerebellar neurofilaments (Plioplys, Greaves, Kazemi, & Silverman, 1994), nerve growth factor (Kozlovskaia et al., 2000), alpha-2-andrenergic binding sites (Cook, Perry, Dawson, Wainwright, & Leventhal, 1993b), and antibodies against the caudate nucleus (Singh & Rivas, 2004).

Maternal antibodies to fetal brain tissue may also play a role in a subset of pervasive developmental disorder cases (Vincent, Dalton, Clover, Palace, & Lang, 2003). Antibodies from serum of mothers who have children with pervasive developmental disorder have been shown to react to antigens on lymphocytes from their affected children (Warren et al., 1990). Because antigens expressed on lymphocytes are also found on cells of the central nervous system, aberrant maternal immunity may be associated with the development of some cases of autism. In support of this, the presence of antibodies against brain tissue was identified in the serum of a mother whose child has autism (P. Dalton et al., 2003). Van de Water and colleagues have identified a common pattern of autoantibody production to fetal brain tissue in the serum of mothers who have two or more children with pervasive developmental disorder (Braunschweig et al., 2008). Collectively, these studies suggest that an atypical maternal antibody response directed against the fetal brain during pregnancy may be present in a subset of individuals with autistic spectrum disorders.

Autism affects four times as many boys as girls, a consistent observation for which the mechanism remains elusive. Based on the concordance rates in monozygotic twins (~60% to 90%), which at least historically have been reported to be roughly 10-fold higher than in dizygotic twins and siblings, autism is considered to be the most heritable of neuropsychiatric disorders (Bailey et al., 1995; Smalley, Asarnow, & Spence, 1988). However, it is generally acknowledged that autism is genetically heterogeneous. The state of autism genetics has been cogently reviewed by Abrahams and Geschwind (2008). As they note, defined mutations, genetic syndromes, and *de novo* copy number variation probably account for about 10% to 20% of cases, with none of these known causes accounting for more than 1% to 2%. None of the molecules or syndromes currently linked to the autism spectrum disorders has been proven to selectively cause autism. It is generally believed that many cases of autism are due to more complex genetic mechanisms, including coinheritance of multiple alleles and/or epigenetic modifications (Freitag, 2007; Gupta & State, 2007). Approximately 10% of sporadic cases of autism are associated with de novo copy number variations in either single genes or sets of genes (Sebat et al., 2007). This finding raises the prospect that

de novo germ line mutations (mutations not seen in the parents) are a more significant risk for autism than previously appreciated. The mechanisms that cause these copy number variations are unknown, but, interestingly, paternal age appears to contribute to autism risk (Reichenberg et al., 2006). Perhaps increasing age leads to the accumulation of these de novo germ line mutations.

Autism is probably caused by alterations in the structural organization of neural systems that process social information, language, and sensorimotor integration. We have recently reviewed the components of these systems as a context for understanding the neuropathology of autism (Amaral, Schumann, & Nordahl, 2008). Neural system lesions can be localized or distributed (Rubenstein, 2006). A localized lesion that weakens or disables one component of a circuit can impede the function of the entire circuit, generating a behavioral phenotype. This phenotype can likewise be generated by defects in another component of the same circuit. Thus, related behavioral syndromes can be generated by different anatomical defects.

Distributed lesions can be caused by defects that are common to many regions of a given neural system, or to multiple neural systems. Mutation of a gene that is broadly expressed, such as those that cause fragile X mental retardation (FRAXA; FMR1), Rett syndrome (MeCP2), or tuberous sclerosis (TSC1 & 2), will disrupt neural function throughout the nervous system. Localized lesions are exemplified by mutation of genes that are expressed in neurons that share common features (such as neurotransmitter type or participation in a common circuit). Members of the Dlx homeobox gene family (which encode transcription factors) are expressed during development of most forebrain GABAergic neurons, and some Dlx genes are expressed in mature forebrain GABAergic neurons (Cobos et al., 2005). Mutations that simultaneously block the function of pairs of mouse Dlx genes disrupt development of most forebrain GABAergic neurons (Anderson et al., 1997). This has the potential to massively disrupt communication between the neocortex, basal ganglia, and thalamus and disrupt cognitive functions that are dependent on these brain regions. Furthermore, individual Dlx genes are required for survival of maturing cortical interneurons and loss of Dlx1 function can result in epilepsy (Cobos et al., 2005). While mutations in the Dlx genes have been detected in some autistic individuals, it is unknown whether these contribute to the development of the disorder (Hamilton et al., 2005) or comorbid symptoms such as epilepsy.

Developmental defects can alter the connectivity between brain regions or the function within a given region and thereby impair neural functions. Interregional connectivity defects can be caused by alterations in axon path finding and synapse choice. It is not known whether these types of abnormalities are found in autism, although there is evidence for connectivity defects from functional imaging studies (Kana, Keller, Cherkassky, Minshew, & Just, 2006; Minshew & Williams, 2007). The array of genes that either cause or predispose to autism speaks to the diversity of genetic and epigenetic mechanisms that can cause this heterogeneous disorder (Abrahams & Geschwind, 2008). While it is beyond the scope of this chapter to review all the genes that have been associated with autism spectrum disorders, some mechanistic themes are beginning to emerge.

Alterations of many of the genes associated with autism (FRMR1, MET, NGLN3/4, PTEN, Shank3, TSC1/2) lead to defects in molecular pathways that link synaptic and nonsynaptic signals with changes in protein synthesis that can modulate neural response properties. TSC1/TSC2 are integral regulators of signal-transduction cascades downstream of signaling pathways that activate receptor tyrosine kinases (Inoki, Corradetti, & Guan, 2005). These signals activate a family of phosphatidylinositol lipid kinases that in turn activate the serine-threonine kinase AKT, which then represses TSC1/TSC2 (Inoki et al., 2005). TSC1/TSC2 are also regulated by intracellular amino acid concentration and by the ATP/AMP ratio—the end product of this regulation is to promote appropriate levels of protein synthesis and cell size (Inoki et al., 2005). Neuroligins (NLGN3 and NLGN4) encode plasma membrane proteins that are implicated in regulating synapse development through binding neurexin proteins (Varoqueaux et al., 2006). In rare cases of autism, mutations in two X-linked neuroligins (NLGN3 and NLGN4; Xq13 and Xp22.33, respectively) have been found (Jamain et al., 2003). Furthermore, *neurexin1* (NRX1) disruptions have recently been identified in a pair of autistic individuals (Kim et al., 2008).

Other genetic alterations in genes such as DLX2/5, EN2, and MeCP2 lead to defects in transcriptional regulation of neural genes. MeCP2, the gene and protein linked to Rett syndrome, is a nuclear protein that binds to methylated CpG dinucleotides. It recruits a co-repressor complex that is implicated in transcriptional repression. This gene, therefore, has as its major function the regulation of other gene products. Defects in genes related to various ion channels also have been occasionally linked to autism. Mis-sense mutations in the L-type (CACNA1C, Cav1.2; 12p13.3) and the T-type (CACNA1H, Cav3.2) calcium channels have been identified in rare cases of autism (Splawski et al., 2004, 2006). Similarly rare mis-sense mutations have been identified in two sodium channel genes (SCN1A; 2q24; SCN2A; 2q23-q24.3) (Weiss et al., 2003).

Finally, genes associated with peptide and transmitter systems implicated in one or more of the relevant autistic behaviors have also demonstrated alterations in some cases of autism. Oxytocin and vasopressin peptides are neuromodulatory hormones that are produced by neurons in the hypothalamus and the amygdala. These neuropeptides have been implicated in the mediation of certain social behaviors particularly in the vole (Young, Murphy Young, & Hammock, 2005), and the receptors for oxytocin (OXTR; 3p25-p26) and arginine vasopressin 1a (AVPR1a; 12q14–15) are associated with autism (Wu et al., 2005; Yirmiya et al., 2006).

Serotonin has potent effects on many behavioral and developmental processes. One of the earliest biochemical indications that serotonin metabolism may be altered in autism was the finding of an increase in platelet serotonin levels in approximately 30% of individuals with autism (Cook et al., 1993). Although this is not a specific diagnostic finding, it increases the potential importance that some alleles of the serotonin transporter gene (SLC6A4, SERT; 17q11.2) might be associated with autism (Brune et al., 2006; Sutcliffe et al., 2005).

It will be critical to understand how these molecular lesions disrupt neural systems that process cognition and social behaviors. Mutations that alter the balance of excitatory and inhibitory synapses in key brain regions may impede the ability to detect salient sensory signals above ambient noise (Levitt, Eagleson, & Powell, 2004; Rubenstein & Merzenich, 2003). Mutations in many of the genes described earlier cause epilepsy that is a gross manifestation of dysregulated excitatory/inhibitory balance. One of the several questions raised by these genetic studies is whether certain brain regions or certain cell types are selectively affected in autism. We turn next to an overview of the neuropathology of autism.

NEUROPATHOLOGY

Magnetic Resonance Imaging Studies

While early computed axial tomography studies carried out on individuals with autism described abnormalities such as ventricular enlargement (Damasio, Maurer, Damasio, & Chui, 1980), later studies determined that there were no consistent tomographic findings in children with classic autism (Prior, Tress, Hoffman, & Boldt, 1984). The first magnetic resonance imaging (MRI) studies were carried out in the mid-1980s and publications began appearing around 1987 (Courchesne, Hesselink, Jernigan, & Yeung-Courchesn, 1987; Gaffney, Kuperman, Tsai, Minchin, & Hassanein, 1987). Early studies were based on the areal analysis of single, relatively thick sections through the brain and focused on differences of the ventricles, cerebellum, and brain stem. Courchesne, Yeung-Courchesne, Press, Hesselink, & Jernigan (1988) proposed that hypoplasia of cerebellar vermal lobules VI and VII was characteristic of autism. These findings, however, have generally not been replicated (Piven, Saliba, Bailey, & Arndt, 1997). In fact, an *increase* in total cerebellar volume is one of the more consistent findings from MRI studies (Brambilla et al., 2003; Sparks et al., 2002). Interestingly, even Courchesne's laboratory has reported substantial heterogeneity in cerebellar findings. In a study of 50 autistic patients ranging in age from 2 to 40 years (Courchesne et al., 1994), 86% of patients were reported to demonstrate vermal hypoplasia while 12% demonstrated vermal hyperplasia. Other brain regions that have been found to be abnormal in autism include the cerebral cortex (although the critical portion of the cerebral cortex varies from study to study), medial temporal lobe structures such as the amygdala and hippocampus, and the corpus callosum. In a comprehensive review of the structural MRI studies published up until May 2003, Brambilla et al. (2003) concluded:

> [D]espite a growing number of quantitative MRI studies, few robust findings have been observed. Structural abnormalities involving total brain volume, the cerebellum and, recently, corpus callosum have been consistently replicated. . . . In order to overcome design limitations of the previous morphometric neuroimaging reports, future quantitative MRI studies should focus on identifying possible morphological brain markers including homogeneous groups of well characterized individuals with autism and healthy controls, matched for age, gender, SES and IQ and should longitudinally investigate these groups. (p. 567).

We have recently reviewed the state of autism MRI studies through the end of 2007 (Amaral et al., 2008). We agree that previous studies were plagued by small numbers of participants, wide ranges of ages in each group and limited sampling of the autism spectrum. Since 1987, there have been 86 structural MRI publications. The largest sample in any of these studies was in Hashimoto et al. (Hashimoto et al., 1995) that evaluated 76 males with autism and 65 controls over a very large age range. The average sample size in the 86 publications was 24 individuals with autism and 20 typically developing controls for males and 3 girls with autism compared with 5 typically developing girls. Many studies included only high-functioning participants or studied participants from heterogeneous diagnostic categories ("autism" would often include individuals ranging from low functioning autism to Asperger syndrome). There is also very little longitudinal information on the development of the brain with autism. These findings have contributed to the current situation where relatively little can be said with confidence about neuropathology in the autistic brain. However, there is now reason to believe

that the trajectory of brain changes over time provides a clearer picture of brain alterations in autism.

The notion that cortical development may be altered in autism arose initially from clinical observations indicating that the head circumference of children with autism is larger than general population controls. Bailey et al. (1993) found that 37% of their subjects had a head circumference above the 97th percentile while Lainhart et al. (1997) found that 14% of autistic subjects had macrocephaly. Fombonne, Roge, Claverie, Courty, and Fremolle (1999) conducted a meta-analysis of published literature and concluded that an average estimate of macrocephaly in autism was 20.6%. These data would suggest that large head and thus brain size might be a common, though by no means universal, feature of individuals with autism.

Courchesne and colleagues have published a series of provocative studies that demonstrate abnormal brain growth in autism (Carper & Courchesne, 2005; Courchesne, Carper, & Akshoomoff, 2003; Courchesne et al., 2001; Redcay & Courchesne, 2005). They propose that the brains of children with autism are either of normal size or perhaps slightly smaller than typically developing children at birth. However, the cerebral cortex, and preferentially the frontal lobe, undergoes a rapid and precocious growth during the first 2 years of life. Subsequently, brain growth plateaus and the volume of the brains of typically developing children catch up. Thus, in older children with autism, the brain is either the same size or even slightly smaller than typically developing subjects. Importantly, this finding has recently been replicated by the Piven laboratory (Hazlett et al., 2005). However, in this replication study, the brains of children with autism were only larger relative to a developmentally delayed comparison; there was no significant enlargement relative to age-matched controls. However, there is at least some evidence in support of the idea that precocious brain growth begins around the emergence of symptoms (near the end of the first year of life and is evident by the second year of life).

Beyond the cerebral cortex, other brain regions have also been found to have an abnormal brain development. Perhaps most striking is the amygdala, a region of the temporal lobe that is involved in the detection of dangers in the environment and in modulating some forms of social interaction (Amaral, 2003). Interestingly, the amygdala undergoes a protracted development in boys (Giedd et al., 1996). It increases in size by nearly 40% between the ages of 8 and 18 years (Schumann et al., 2004). This is striking since the rest of the brain actually decreases in size during this same time period by about 10%. For boys who have been diagnosed with autism, the amygdala demonstrates precocious growth and has reached adult size by 8 years of age.

Many studies have gone beyond evaluating the volume of brain regions and have broken the tissue down into compartments representing gray matter and white matter. There have been some indications that alterations in white matter volumes may actually be a more sensitive indicator of pathology in autism than gray matter differences (Carper & Courchesne, 2005; Courchesne et al., 2001, 2003; Herbert, 2005; Herbert et al., 2004). In fact, some have proposed that the enlarged brain volume that has been reported can be accounted for, in large part, by disproportionate increases in the volume of white matter. There are reports of greater white matter volumes in boys with autism aged 2 to 3 years when compared with controls. Other analyses of white matter have suggested that those compartments of white matter that develop latest (the radiate regions that mature late in the first year and into the second postnatal year and beyond) are of greater volume than the earlier maturing sagittal and bridging fibers (Herbert et al., 2003). Recent studies using diffusion tensor weighted imaging of white matter indicate that in autism regionally specific disruptions of white matter integrity may persist into adulthood (Keller, Kana, & Just, 2007).

Despite the heterogeneity of findings, a few clear directions are emerging: First, autism is not a disorder that affects a single brain region; second, the kind of brain pathology in a particular individual may depend on the phenotypic characteristics of autism (e.g., presence vs. lack of developmental delays) as well as comorbid features of the disorder (e.g., seizures vs. no seizures); and third, the pathology of autism may not be apparent in the mature size and shape of the brain but in the time course of development of both the structure and connections of the brain.

Microscopic Neuropathology

There are no obvious lesions or clear pathology in the brains of individuals with autism. In fact, at first blush the brain looks remarkably normal. One consistent finding in autism has been a reduced number of Purkinje cells in the cerebellum (Ritvo & Garber, 1988). When using neural stains that mark cell bodies, there are noticeable gaps in the orderly arrays of Purkinje cells. Whether Purkinje cell loss is due to autism, epilepsy, or the co-occurrence of both disorders is not currently clear. It is also not clear whether loss of Purkinje cells is characteristic of autism or a more general finding in many neurodevelopmental disorders. Thus, cerebellar alterations have been reported in idiopathic mental retardation, Williams syndrome, and many other childhood disorders.

The cerebral cortex has also been reported to be abnormal at a microscopic level in autism. There have been some published examples of migration defects such as ectopias (Bailey et al., 1998). More recently, it has been proposed that the columnar organization of the cortex in autistic patients is abnormal (Casanova, 2006; Casanova, Buxhoeveden, Switala, & Roy, 2002). These provocative findings are awaiting confirmation in larger studies using sophisticated quantitative strategies. A quantitative neuroanatomical study has demonstrated that cells in the fusiform gyrus of the autistic brain are both smaller and fewer in number than age-matched control brains (van Kooten et al., 2008). The decrease in neurons was not seen in the primary visual cortex or when the entire cerebral cortex was analyzed. The fusiform gyrus is interesting because at least part of it is made up of the fusiform face area that appears to be involved in face processing. Finally, the amygdala has been found to have fewer neurons in the mature brain (Schumann & Amaral, 2006). Since this study was carried out with cases that did not have comorbid epilepsy, this appears to be a real component of autistic neuropathology.

FUNCTIONAL NEUROIMAGING

Another approach to establishing which brain regions are most impacted by autism is the use of functional magnetic resonance imaging (fMRI). While this literature is growing rapidly and has provided important insights into the neural impairments of autism, it also applies only to the high-functioning segment of the population who can be compliant with the demands of the behavioral and imaging conditions. Many of the functional imaging studies have focused on brain regions thought to be involved in social function, such as the frontal lobe and amygdala, and on behaviors thought to be selectively impaired in autism, such as perception of social stimuli and theory of mind. More than 400 papers have appeared in recent years dealing with functional imaging of individuals with autism; therefore we only briefly highlight some findings related to the amygdala that, as described earlier, is pathological in autism. For more extensive reviews of fMRI in autism, see Just, Cherkassky, Keller, Kana, and Minshew (2007) and Kana et al. (2006).

The amygdala has been the focus of many functional imaging studies in autism prompted, in part, by the "Amygdala Theory of Autism" proposed by Baron-Cohen and colleagues (2000). Functional neuroimaging studies have indicated that individuals with an autism spectrum disorder show abnormal patterns of amygdala activation (hypoactivation) in response to social stimuli. High-functioning adults with autism or Asperger syndrome demonstrate deficits in the ability to infer the mental state of another person by viewing images of their eyes (Baron-Cohen, Jolliffe, Mortimore, & Robertson, 1997). This task activates the amygdala and superior temporal gyrus in control subjects. In contrast, individuals with autism or Asperger syndrome activate the frontotemporal regions but not the amygdala when performing this task (Baron-Cohen et al., 1999). Pierce, Muller, Ambrose, Allen, and Courchesne (2001) found that the amygdala was activated when typically developing individuals viewed unfamiliar faces, but the amygdala was not activated in individuals with autism during this task. Children and adolescents with autism spectrum disorders show abnormal amygdala activation while matching faces by emotion and assigning a label to facial expressions (Wang, Dapretto, Hariri, Sigman, & Bookheimer, 2004). While children in the control group showed more amygdala activation when matching faces by emotion than when assigning a verbal label, the children with autism spectrum disorders did not demonstrate this pattern of task-dependent amygdala modulation.

A caveat to interpreting findings from face processing studies is that subjects with autism are reluctant to make eye contact and there is some controversy as to whether they are actually examining the face in a similar manner as controls (Davidson & Slagter, 2000). In fact, when viewing faces, individuals with autism show abnormal visual scan paths during eye-tracking studies, typically spending little time on the eyes (Klin, Jones, Schultz, & Volkmar, 2003; Pelphrey et al., 2002). Whether these findings represent active avoidance of the eye region, potentially involving the amygdala, or a more global lack of social interest or motivation is unclear. An emerging hypothesis is that the amygdala may play a role in mediating or directing visual attention to the eyes (Adolphs et al., 2005; Grelotti et al., 2005; Schultz, 2005).

Research from typically developing children indicates that children who are physiologically aroused by a distressing film are more likely to avert their gaze from the stimulus. It is plausible that children with autism use a similar strategy of gaze aversion in response to arousing social stimuli. Given the amygdala's role in fear and anxiety, we would predict heightened amygdala activation during eye contact in persons with autism if they found the eye contact aversive. Dalton and colleagues (K. M. Dalton et al., 2005) found that the amount of time persons with autism spent looking at the eye region of the face was strongly positively correlated with amygdala activation, but this was not the case in control subjects. The autism subjects also showed greater left amygdala activation relative to controls in response to unfamiliar faces and greater right amygdala activation in response to both familiar and unfamiliar faces. This suggests a heightened emotional, or even fearful, response when autistic individuals look at another person's eyes, regardless of whether they are familiar or a stranger. Nacewicz et al. (2006) recently found that

individuals with autism (8 to 25 years of age) who had a smaller amygdala were also slower to distinguish emotional from neutral expressions and showed least fixation on the eye regions of the face. These same individuals were also the most socially impaired in early childhood.

Ashwin, Baron-Cohen, Wheelwright, O'Riordan, and Bullmore (2007) found that during the perception of fearful faces, Asperger syndrome patients showed less activation in the left amygdala relative to controls. However, these results may again be due to the abnormal way in which individuals with autism view faces. Spezio, Adolphs, Hurley, and Piven (2007a, 2007b) confirmed that participants with autism show less fixation on the eyes and mouth, but also a greater tendency to saccade away from the eyes when information was present in those regions. This study provides insight into the aberrant manner in which people with autism view faces, which likely influences face processing and subsequent fMRI results. Additional studies would benefit from measuring the physiological responses associated with arousal and anxiety (increased heart rate, skin response) during face processing in individuals with autism.

BEHAVIORAL TREATMENT

Based on the experiences of the past 50 years, it is clear that autism is treatable. Early on in autism treatment, two main treatment approaches dominated the literature: treatment based on a psychodynamic conceptualization of autism (e.g., Bettelheim, 1967) and treatment based on the application of Skinnerian models of learning. The first empirically supported paper came from the latter tradition (Wolf, Risley, & Mees, 1964). The treatment was carried out virtually all day, every day, for several years in an institutional setting. The child eventually returned to his home, with greatly improved behavior, language, adaptive, and cognitive abilities. The teaching procedures involve massed trial teaching and many of the core approaches to teaching are still in use today (Leaf & McEachin, 2001; Lovaas, 1981). The view that autism is a neurobiological disorder (Rimland, 1964) had fundamental effects on treatments. Gradually, autism became viewed as a developmental disorder, like mental retardation, for which rehabilitation was the appropriate approach.

Three main philosophies guided the development of interventions. One strategy involved the continued application of learning theory to reduce behavioral deficits and to decrease behavioral excesses (Wolf et al., 1964). These strategies, under the umbrella of Applied Behavior Analysis, were applied in two basic forms. The first involved massed trials with high levels of adult control and direction (Lovaas, 1987; McEachin, Smith, & Lovaas, 1993).

A more naturalistic application of learning principles capitalized on children's own interests, preferences, and initiatives to assure high levels of motivation for learning. These approaches are best described in two well-known models, Incidental Teaching, first applied to autism by McGee, Krantz, Mason, & McClannahan (1991); McGee, Krantz, Mason, & McClannahan (1983); and Pivotal Response Training, as developed by Schriebman and Koegel (Koegel, O'Dell, & Dunlap, 1988; Schreibman & Pierce, 1993; J. A. Williams, Koegel, & Egel, 1981).

A second main approach was the Treatment and Education of Autistic and Related Communication Handicapped Children (TEACCH) model of intervention (Schopler, Mesibov, & Hearsey, 1995; Schopler, Mesibov, Shigley, & Bashford, 1984). This capitalized on teaching by directing tasks to children's visual-spatial skills. This approach focused on developing skills for independent work and independent functioning, minimized the need for ongoing social and verbal instruction, used visual communication systems to supplement verbal instruction, built a great deal of repetition and routine into the organization of the teaching, and reduced the sensory complexity of the environment to maximize attention. This approach also used parents as primary deliverers of the intervention.

The third main approach focuses on autism as a developmental deficit. It is based on the premise that early compromises in social and communicative development lead to large downstream effects that impair the development of social relations (Meyer & Hobson, 2004; Rogers & Pennington, 1991; Sigman & Capps, 1997). The developmental approaches have flourished and current models include the Floortime approach (Greenspan et al., 1997), Relationship Development Intervention (Gutstien, Burgess, & Montfort, 2007), the Denver Model (Rogers & Lewis, 1989), and the Social Communication, Emotional Regulation and Transactional Support (SCERTS) model (Prizant, Wetherby, Rubin, Laurent, & Rydell, 2006). These approaches strongly emphasize the quality of the relationship between child and the teacher as well as the child and parent. They use a child-centered approach based on following children's interests and initiatives, and strongly emphasize progress in social communication skills.

A fourth treatment orientation focuses on the sensory and motor differences characteristic of autism. Some practitioners think that the sensory differences in autism are the primary impairments, with the social, communicative, and behavioral abnormalities resulting from the intense distress or confusion that the sensory impairments cause (reviewed in Baranek, 2002).

Behavioral treatments may be delivered to change targeted symptoms. Virtually all the main symptoms of autism have been demonstrated to be modifiable with targeted treatments (Schreibman, 2005). Positive treatment outcomes for targeted skills have been documented across the entire age range and functioning range for persons with autism spectrum disorders. Moreover, the use of aversive consequences has largely disappeared as the field has become more sophisticated in the application of reinforcement strategies (Carr et al., 2002; Horner, Carr, Strain, Todd, & Reed, 2002; Howlin, 1998; Lalli, Casey, & Kates, 1995).

OTHER TREATMENTS

Psychopharmacological Treatments

Given the lack of specific brain or neurotransmitter systems as a target for pharmacological treatment, currently no psychopharmacological treatment is directed at the core symptoms of autism (Palermo & Curatolo, 2004). The atypical antipsychotics (olanzapine, ziprasidone, quetiapine, aripiprazole) have shown some efficacy in improving certain behavioral symptoms of autistic disorder such as aggressiveness, hyperactivity, and self-injurious behavior (Stachnik & Nunn-Thompson, 2007). Weight gain and sedation are frequently reported adverse consequences of these treatments. Risperidone has become the first approved drug for treatment of autism. Previously, risperidone was studied as an off-label medication to treat autism because of its increased safety and efficacy over conventional neuroleptics. Risperidone can be used as a potentially safe and effective treatment for disruptive behavioral symptoms in children with autism (West & Waldrop, 2006). The long-term use of these drugs in conjunction with the other alternative medications being used requires additional analysis pertaining to safety (McCracken, 2005).

Complementary Alternative Medicine Treatments

It would be fair to say that in no area of developmental pediatric practice is there more controversy than in the selection of treatments for children with autistic spectrum disorders. An increasing number of complementary and alternative medical therapies are often tried because they are perceived as treating the cause of the children's symptoms (Levy & Hyman, 2005). Current treatments range from various forms of restricted diet (such as gluten- and casein-free diets; Millward, Ferriter, Calver, & Connell-Jones, 2004) to hyperbaric oxygen treatment (Rossignol, 2007) to vitamin and mineral supplements (Hanson et al., 2007). Secretin provides a good example of how an incidental perception of behavioral improvement following treatment leads to widespread clinical use despite little or no scientific rationale for the therapy. And despite nearly unanimous negative results in placebo-controlled clinical trials (Esch & Carr, 2004), there still remains substantial parental interest in attempts at using secretin as a potential therapy. In many respects, this speaks to the desperate need of parents and practitioners alike to obtain more scientifically based approaches to the therapy of both the core and comorbid symptoms of autism.

SUMMARY

Autism is a spectrum disorder that is defined behaviorally as consisting of social and communication impairments, stereotyped behaviors, and circumscribed interests. There is consensus that autism has a variety of etiologies, each of which has different genetic and environmental contributions. While some 10% of autism cases are associated with a defined medical condition such as fragile X syndrome, the cause(s) of the remainder of idiopathic autism are currently unknown. Autism is often considered to be a polygenic disorder with multiple genes showing weak association. This may reflect the fact that better phenotyping of autism subtypes is essential before fruitful genotyping can be accomplished. Autism affects the development of several brain systems. The most common biological finding is precocious brain development of the cerebral cortex and amygdala. White matter may be more affected than gray matter. However, the neuropathology of autism is still at a very early stage of understanding, and additional structural MRI and postmortem studies are needed to better define the neural systems involved. Beyond the nervous system, there appears to be a variety of dysregulated functions in the immune system of some individuals with autism and some mothers of individuals with autism. Whether the immune dysregulation is a cause or effect of autism remains to be determined. Various behavioral therapies based on the operant conditioning literature are valuable for eliminating unwanted behaviors and bolstering language, social interaction, and pragmatic life skills. Finally, autism currently affects 1:150 children in the United States and other industrialized countries. While the increase in prevalence is due, in part, to increased public and professional awareness as well as the broadening of diagnostic criteria, there is also concern that the incidence of autism is truly increasing. This raises the prospect that environmental or other nongenetic factors may be increasingly impacting modern children. This highlights the important need for a better understanding of the biological underpinnings of autism and what factors may produce this complex disorder.

REFERENCES

Abrahams, B. S., & Geschwind, D. H. (2008). Advances in autism genetics: On the threshold of a new neurobiology. *Nature Reviews: Genetics, 9,* 341–355.

Adolphs, R., Gosselin, F., Buchanan, T. W., Tranel, D., Schyns, P., & Damasio, A. R. (2005, January 6). A mechanism for impaired fear recognition after amygdala damage. *Nature, 433,* 68–72.

Altevogt, B. M., Hanson, S. L., & Leshner, A. I. (2008). Autism and the environment: Challenges and opportunities for research. *Pediatrics, 121,* 1225–1229.

Amaral, D. G. (2003). The amygdala, social behavior, and danger detection. *Annals of the New York Academy of Sciences, 1000,* 337–347.

Amaral, D. G., Schumann, C. M., & Nordahl, C. W. (2008). Neuroanatomy of autism. *Trends in Neurosciences, 31,* 137–145.

American Psychiatric Association. (1994). *Diagnostic and statistical manual of mental disorders* (4th ed.). Washington, DC: Author.

Anderson, S. A., Qiu, M., Bulfone, A., Eisenstat, D. D., Meneses, J., Pedersen, R., et al. (1997). Mutations of the homeobox genes dlx-1 and dlx-2 disrupt the striatal subventricular zone and differentiation of late born striatal neurons. *Neuron, 19,* 27–37.

Ashwin, C., Baron-Cohen, S., Wheelwright, S., O'Riordan, M., & Bullmore, E. T. (2007). Differential activation of the amygdala and the "social brain" during fearful face-processing in Asperger syndrome. *Neuropsychologia, 45,* 2–14.

Ashwood, P., Anthony, A., Pellicer, A. A., Torrente, F., Walker-Smith, J. A., & Wakefield, A. J. (2003). Intestinal lymphocyte populations in children with regressive autism: Evidence for extensive mucosal immunopathology. *Journal of Clinical Immunology, 23,* 504–517.

Ashwood, P., & Van de Water, J. (2004a). Is autism an autoimmune disease? *Autoimmunity Reviews, 3*(7–8), 557–562.

Ashwood, P., & Van de Water, J. (2004b). A review of autism and the immune response. *Clinical and Developmental Immunology, 11,* 165–174.

Asperger, H. (1944). Die autistischen psychopathen im kindesalter. *Archiv fur Psychiatrie und Nervenkrankheiten, 117,* 76–136.

Bailey, A., Le Couteur, A., Gottesman, I., Bolton, P., Simonoff, E., Yuzda, E., et al. (1995). Autism as a strongly genetic disorder: Evidence from a British twin study. *Psychological Medicine, 25,* 63–77.

Bailey, A., Luthert, P., Bolton, P., Le Couteur, A., Rutter, M., & Harding, B. (1993). Autism and megalencephaly. *Lancet, 341,* 1225–1226.

Bailey, A., Luthert, P., Dean, A., Harding, B., Janota, I., Montgomery, M., et al. (1998). A clinicopathological study of autism. *Brain, 121*(Pt. 5), 889–905.

Baker, H. C. (2002). A comparison study of autism spectrum disorder referrals 1997 and 1989. *Journal of Autism and Developmental Disorders, 32,* 121–125.

Baranek, G. T. (2002). Efficacy of sensory and motor interventions for children with autism. *Journal of Autism and Developmental Disorders, 32,* 397–422.

Baron-Cohen, S., Jolliffe, T., Mortimore, C., & Robertson, M. (1997). Another advanced test of theory of mind: Evidence from very high functioning adults with autism or Asperger syndrome. *Journal of Child Psychology and Psychiatry, and Allied Disciplines, 38,* 813–822.

Baron-Cohen, S., Ring, H. A., Bullmore, E. T., Wheelwright, S., Ashwin, C., & Williams, S. C. (2000). The amygdala theory of autism. *Neuroscience and Biobehavioral Reviews, 24,* 355–364.

Baron-Cohen, S., Ring, H. A., Wheelwright, S., Bullmore, E. T., Brammer, M. J., Simmons, A., et al. (1999). Social intelligence in the normal and autistic brain: An fMRI study. *Supplement to the European Journal of Neuroscience, 11,* 1891–1898.

Bello, S. C. (2007). Autism and environmental influences: Review and commentary. *Reviews on Environmental Health, 22,* 139–156.

Bettelheim, B. (1967). *The empty fortress.* New York: Free Press.

Brambilla, P., Hardan, A., di Nemi, S. U., Perez, J., Soares, J. C., & Barale, F. (2003). Brain anatomy and development in autism: Review of structural MRI studies. *Brain Research Bulletin, 61,* 557–569.

Braunschweig, D., Ashwood, P., Krakowiak, P., Hertz-Picciotto, I., Hansen, R., Croen, L. A., et al. (2008). Autism: Maternally derived antibodies specific for fetal brain proteins. *Neurotoxicology, 29,* 226–231.

Brune, C. W., Kim, S. J., Salt, J., Leventhal, B. L., Lord, C., & Cook, E. H., Jr. (2006). 5-httlpr genotype-specific phenotype in children and adolescents with autism. *American Journal of Psychiatry, 163,* 2148–2156.

Carper, R. A., & Courchesne, E. (2005). Localized enlargement of the frontal cortex in early autism. *Biological Psychiatry, 57,* 126–133.

Carr, E., Dunlap, G., Horner, R., Koegel, L., Turnbill, A., Sailor, W., et al. (2002). Positive behavior support: Evolution of an applied science. *Journal of Positive Behavior Interventions, 4,* 4–16.

Casanova, M. F. (2006). Neuropathological and genetic findings in autism: The significance of a putative minicolumnopathy. *Neuroscientist, 12,* 435–441.

Casanova, M. F., Buxhoeveden, D. P., Switala, A. E., & Roy, E. (2002). Minicolumnar pathology in autism. *Neurology, 58,* 428–432.

Chakrabarti, S., & Fombonne, E. (2005). Pervasive developmental disorders in preschool children: Confirmation of high prevalence. *American Journal of Psychiatry, 162,* 1133–1141.

Cobos, I., Calcagnotto, M. E., Vilaythong, A. J., Thwin, M. T., Noebels, J. L., Baraban, S. C., et al. (2005). Mice lacking dlx1 show subtype-specific loss of interneurons, reduced inhibition, and epilepsy. *Nature Neuroscience, 8,* 1059–1068.

Comi, A. M., Zimmerman, A. W., Frye, V. H., Law, P. A., & Peeden, J. N. (1999). Familial clustering of autoimmune disorders and evaluation of medical risk factors in autism. *Journal of Child Neurology, 14,* 388–394.

Cook, E. H., Jr., Arora, R. C., Anderson, G. M., Berry-Kravis, E. M., Yan, S. Y., Yeoh, H. C., et al. (1993). Platelet serotonin studies in hyperserotonemic relatives of children with autistic disorder. *Life Sciences, 52,* 2005–2015.

Cook, E. H., Jr., Perry, B. D., Dawson, G., Wainwright, M. S., & Leventhal, B. L. (1993). Receptor inhibition by immunoglobulins: Specific inhibition by autistic children, their relatives, and control subjects. *Journal of Autism and Developmental Disorders, 23,* 67–78.

Courchesne, E., Carper, R., & Akshoomoff, N. (2003). Evidence of brain overgrowth in the first year of life in autism. *Journal of the American Medical Association, 290,* 337–344.

Courchesne, E., Hesselink, J. R., Jernigan, T. L., & Yeung-Courchesne, R. (1987). Abnormal neuroanatomy in a nonretarded person with autism: Unusual findings with magnetic resonance imaging. *Archives of Neurology, 44,* 335–341.

Courchesne, E., Karns, C. M., Davis, H. R., Ziccardi, R., Carper, R. A., Tigue, Z. D., et al. (2001). Unusual brain growth patterns in early life in patients with autistic disorder: An MRI study. *Neurology, 57,* 245–254.

Courchesne, E., Saitoh, O., Townsend, J. P., Yeung-Courchesne, R., Press, G. A., Lincoln, A. J., et al. (1994). Cerebellar hypoplasia and hyperplasia in infantile autism. *Lancet, 343,* 63–64.

Courchesne, E., Yeung-Courchesne, R., Press, G. A., Hesselink, J. R., & Jernigan, T. L. (1988). Hypoplasia of cerebellar vermal lobules vi and vii in autism. *New England Journal of Medicine, 318,* 1349–1354.

Croonenberghs, J., Bosmans, E., Deboutte, D., Kenis, G., & Maes, M. (2002). Activation of the inflammatory response system in autism. *Neuropsychobiology, 45,* 1–6.

Cunningham, W., A., Johnson, M. K., Raye, C. L., Gatenbyn, J. C., & Bunaji, M. R. (2004), Separable neural components in the processing of Black and White faces. *Psychological Science, 15,* 806–813.

Dalton, K. M., Nacewicz, B. M., Johnstone, T., Schaefer, H. S., Gernsbacher, M. A., Goldsmith, H. H., et al. (2005). Gaze fixation and the neural circuitry of face processing in autism. *Nature Neuroscience, 8,* 519–526.

Dalton, P., Deacon, R., Blamire, A., Pike, M., McKinlay, I., Stein, J., et al. (2003). Maternal neuronal antibodies associated with autism and a language disorder. *Annals of Neurology, 53,* 533–537.

Damasio, H., Maurer, R. G., Damasio, A. R., & Chui, H. C. (1980). Computerized tomographic scan findings in patients with autistic behavior. *Archives of Neurology, 37,* 504–510.

Davidson, R. J., & Slagter, H. A. (2000). Probing emotion in the developing brain: Functional neuroimaging in the assessment of the neural substrates of emotion in normal and disordered children and adolescents. *Mental Retardation and Developmental Disabilities Research Reviews, 6,* 166–170.

Erickson, C. A., Stigler, K. A., Corkins, M. R., Posey, D. J., Fitzgerald, J. F., & McDougle, C. J. (2005). Gastrointestinal factors in autistic disorder: A critical review. *Journal of Autism and Developmental Disorders, 35,* 713–727.

Esch, B. E., & Carr, J. E. (2004). Secretin as a treatment for autism: A review of the evidence. *Journal of Autism and Developmental Disorders, 34,* 543–556.

Fombonne, E. (2005). Epidemiology of autistic disorder and other pervasive developmental disorders. *Journal of Clinical Psychiatry, 66*(Suppl. 10), 3–8.

Fombonne, E., Roge, B., Claverie, J., Courty, S., & Fremolle, J. (1999). Microcephaly and macrocephaly in autism. *Journal of Autism and Developmental Disorders, 29,* 113–119.

Freitag, C. M. (2007). The genetics of autistic disorders and its clinical relevance: A review of the literature. *Molecular Psychiatry, 12,* 2–22.

Gaffney, G. R., Kuperman, S., Tsai, L. Y., Minchin, S., & Hassanein, K. M. (1987). Midsagittal magnetic resonance imaging of autism. *British Journal of Psychiatry, 151,* 831–833.

Giedd, J. N., Vaituzis, A. C., Hamburger, S. D., Lange, N., Rajapakse, J. C., Kaysen, D., et al. (1996). Quantitative MRI of the temporal lobe, amygdala, and hippocampus in normal human development: Ages 4–18 years. *Journal of Comparative Neurology, 366,* 223–230.

Gillott, A., Furniss, F., & Walter, A. (2001). Anxiety in high-functioning children with autism. *Autism, 5,* 277–286.

Gillott, A., & Standen, P. J. (2007). Levels of anxiety and sources of stress in adults with autism. *Journal of Intellectual Disabilities, 11,* 359–370.

Goldberg, W. A., Thorsen, K. L., Osann, K., & Spence, M. A. (2008). Use of home videotapes to confirm parental reports of regression in autism. *Journal of Autism and Developmental Disorders, 6,* 1136–1146.

Grandin, T. (1992). An inside view of autism. In E. Schopler & G. Mesibov (Eds.), *High-functioning individuals with autism* (pp. 105–126). New York: Plenum Press.

Greenspan, S., Kalmanson, B., Shahmoon-Shanok, R., Wieder, S., Gordon-Williamson, G., & Anzalone, M. (1997). *Assessing and treating infants and young children with severe difficulties in relating and communicating.* Washington, DC: Zero to Three.

Grelotti, D. J., Klin, A. J., Gauthier, I., Skudlarski, P., Cohen, D. J., Gore, J. C., et al. (2005). FMRI activation of the fusiform gyrus and amygdala to cartoon characters but not to faces in a boy with autism. *Neuropsychologia, 43,* 373–385.

Gupta, A. R., & State, M. W. (2007). Recent advances in the genetics of autism. *Biological Psychiatry, 61,* 429–437.

Gutstein S. E., Burgess A. F., & Montfort K. (2007) Evaluation of the relationship development intervention program. *Autism, 11,* 397–411.

Hamilton, S. P., Woo, J. M., Carlson, E. J., Ghanem, N., Ekker, M., & Rubenstein, J. L. (2005). Analysis of four dlx homeobox genes in autistic probands. *BMC Genetics, 6,* 52.

Hanson, E., Kalish, L. A., Bunce, E., Curtis, C., McDaniel, S., Ware, J., et al. (2007). Use of complementary and alternative medicine among children diagnosed with autism spectrum disorder. *Journal of Autism and Developmental Disorders, 37,* 628–636.

Hara, H. (2007). Autism and epilepsy: A retrospective follow-up study. *Brain and Development, 29,* 486–490.

Harrington, J. W., Rosen, L., Garnecho, A., & Patrick, P. A. (2006). Parental perceptions and use of complementary and alternative medicine practices for children with autistic spectrum disorders in private practice. *Journal of Developmental and Behavioral Pediatrics, 27*(Suppl. 2), S156–S161.

Hashimoto, T., Tayama, M., Murakawa, K., Yoshimoto, T., Miyazaki, M., Harada, M., et al. (1995). Development of the brainstem and cerebellum in autistic patients. *Journal of Autism and Developmental Disorders, 25,* 1–18.

Hazlett, H. C., Poe, M., Gerig, G., Smith, R. G., Provenzale, J., Ross, A., et al. (2005). Magnetic resonance imaging and head circumference study of brain size in autism: Birth through age 2 years. *Archives of General Psychiatry, 62,* 1366–1376.

Herbert, M. R. (2005). Large brains in autism: The challenge of pervasive abnormality. *Neuroscientist, 11,* 417–440.

Herbert, M. R., Ziegler, D. A., Deutsch, C. K., O'Brien, L. M., Lange, N., Bakardjiev, A., et al. (2003). Dissociations of cerebral cortex, subcortical and cerebral white matter volumes in autistic boys. *Brain, 126*(Pt. 5), 1182–1192.

Herbert, M. R., Ziegler, D. A., Makris, N., Filipek, P. A., Kemper, T. L., Normandin, J. J., et al. (2004). Localization of white matter volume increase in autism and developmental language disorder. *Annals of Neurology, 55,* 530–540.

Hobson, R. P., & Lee, A. (1999). Imitation and identification in autism. *Journal of Child Psychology and Psychiatry, and Allied Disciplines, 40,* 649–659.

Horner, R. H., Carr, E. G., Strain, P. S., Todd, A. W., & Reed, H. K. (2002). Problem behavior interventions for young children with autism: A research synthesis. *Journal of Autism and Developmental Disorders, 32,* 423–446.

Howlin, P. (1998). Practitioner review: Psychological and educational treatments for autism. *Journal of Child Psychology and Psychiatry, and Allied Disciplines, 39,* 307–322.

Inoki, K., Corradetti, M. N., & Guan, K. L. (2005). Dysregulation of the tsc-mtor pathway in human disease. *Nature Genetics, 37,* 19–24.

Jamain, S., Quach, H., Betancur, C., Rastam, M., Colineaux, C., Gillberg, I. C., et al. (2003). Mutations of the x-linked genes encoding neuroligins nlgn3 and nlgn4 are associated with autism. *Nature Genetics, 34,* 27–29.

Just, M. A., Cherkassky, V. L., Keller, T. A., Kana, R. K., & Minshew, N. J. (2007). Functional and anatomical cortical underconnectivity in autism: Evidence from an fMRI study of an executive function task and corpus callosum morphometry. *Cerebral Cortex, 17,* 951–961.

Kana, R. K., Keller, T. A., Cherkassky, V. L., Minshew, N. J., & Just, M. A. (2006). Sentence comprehension in autism: Thinking in pictures with decreased functional connectivity. *Brain, 129*(Pt. 9), 2484–2493.

Kanner, L. (1943). Autistic disturbances of affective contact. *Nervous Child, 2,* 217–250.

Kanner, L. (1971). Follow-up study of eleven autistic children originally reported in 1943. *Journal of Autism and Childhood Schizophrenia, 1,* 119–145.

Keller, T. A., Kana, R. K., & Just, M. A. (2007). A developmental study of the structural integrity of white matter in autism. *NeuroReport, 18,* 23–27.

Kim, H. G., Kishikawa, S., Higgins, A. W., Seong, I. S., Donovan, D. J., Shen, Y., et al. (2008). Disruption of neurexin 1 associated with autism spectrum disorder. *American Journal of Human Genetics, 82,* 199–207.

Klin, A., Jones, W., Schultz, R., & Volkmar, F. (2003). The enactive mind, or from actions to cognition: Lessons from autism. *Philosophical Transactions of the Royal Society of London, B: Biological Sciences, 358,* 345–360.

Koegel, R. L., O'Dell, M., & Dunlap, G. (1988). Producing speech use in nonverbal autistic children by reinforcing attempts. *Journal of Autism and Developmental Disorders, 18,* 525–538.

Kozlovskaia, G. V., Kliushnik, T. P., Goriunova, A. V., Turkova, I. L., Kalinina, M. A., & Sergienko, N. S. (2000). [nerve growth factor autoantibodies in children with various forms of mental dysontogenesis and in schizophrenia high risk group]. *Zhurnal nevrologii i psikhiatrii imeni S.S. Korsakova, 100*(3), 50–52.

Kuehn, B. M. (2007). Cdc: Autism spectrum disorders common. *Journal of the American Medical Association, 297,* 940.

Lainhart, J. E., Piven, J., Wzorek, M., Landa, R., Santangelo, S. L., Coon, H., et al. (1997). Macrocephaly in children and adults with autism. *Journal of the American Academy of Child and Adolescent Psychiatry, 36,* 282–290.

Lalli, J. S., Casey, S., & Kates, K. (1995). Reducing escape behavior and increasing task completion with functional communication training, extinction, and response chaining. *Journal of Applied Behavior Analysis, 28,* 261–268.

Lang, B., Dale, R. C., & Vincent, A. (2003). New autoantibody mediated disorders of the central nervous system. *Current Opinion in Neurology, 16,* 351–357.

Lang, B., Pinto, A., Giovannini, F., Newsom-Davis, J., & Vincent, A. (2003). Pathogenic autoantibodies in the Lambert-Eaton myasthenic syndrome. *Annals of the New York Academy of Sciences, 998,* 187–195.

Lang, B., & Vincent, A. (2003). Autoantibodies to ion channels at the neuromuscular junction. *Autoimmunity Reviews, 2*(2), 94–100.

Leaf, R., & McEachin, J. (2001). *A work in progress.* New York: DRL Books.

Levitt, P., Eagleson, K. L., & Powell, E. M. (2004). Regulation of neocortical interneuron development and the implications for neurodevelopmental disorders. *Trends in Neurosciences, 27,* 400–406.

Levy, S. E., & Hyman, S. L. (2005). Novel treatments for autistic spectrum disorders. *Mental Retardation and Developmental Disabilities Research Reviews, 11,* 131–142.

Lord, C. (2005). Diagnostic instruments in autistic spectrum disorders. In F. Volkmar, R. Paul, A. Klin, & D. Cohen (Eds.), *Handbook of autism and pervasive development disorders* (pp. 730–771). Hoboken, NJ: Wiley.

Lovaas, O. I. (1981). *Teaching developmentally disabled children: The me book.* Baltimore: University Park Press.

Lovaas, O. I. (1987). Behavioral treatment and normal educational and intellectual functioning in young autistic children. *Journal of Consulting and Clinical Psychology, 55,* 3–9.

McCracken, J. T. (2005). Safety issues with drug therapies for autism spectrum disorders. *Journal of Clinical Psychiatry, 66*(Suppl. 10), 32–37.

McEachin, J. J., Smith, T., & Lovaas, O. I. (1993). Long-term outcome for children with autism who received early intensive behavioral treatment. *American Journal of Mental Retardation, 97,* 359–372; 373–391.

McGee, G. G., Krantz, P. J., Mason, D., & McClannahan, L. E. (1983). A modified incidental-teaching procedure for autistic youth: Acquisition and generalization of receptive object labels. *Journal of Applied Behavior Analysis, 16,* 329–338.

McGee, G. G., Krantz, P. J., Mason, D., & McClannahan, L. E. (1991). A comparison of emotional facial display by children with autism and typical preschoolers. *Journal of Early Intervention, 15,* 237–245.

Meyer, J., & Hobson, R. P. (2004). Orientation in relation to self and other: The case of autism. *Interaction Studies, 5,* 221–244.

Millward, C., Ferriter, M., Calver, S., & Connell-Jones, G. (2004). Gluten- and casein-free diets for autistic spectrum disorder [CD003498]. *Cochrane Database of Systematic Reviews,*(2).

Minshew, N. J., & Williams, D. L. (2007). The new neurobiology of autism: Cortex, connectivity, and neuronal organization. *Archives of Neurology, 64,* 945–950.

Muris, P., Steerneman, P., Merckelbach, H., Holdrinet, I., & Meesters, C. (1998). Comorbid anxiety symptoms in children with pervasive developmental disorders. *Journal of Anxiety Disorders, 12,* 387–393.

Nacewicz, B. M., Dalton, K. M., Johnstone, T., Long, M. T., McAuliff, E. M., Oakes, T. R., et al. (2006). Amygdala volume and nonverbal social impairment in adolescent and adult males with autism. *Archives of General Psychiatry, 63,* 1417–1428.

Newschaffer, C. J., Croen, L. A., Daniels, J., Giarelli, E., Grether, J. K., Levy, S. E., et al. (2007). The epidemiology of autism spectrum disorders. *Annual Review of Public Health, 28,* 238–258.

Newsom-Davis, J., Buckley, C., Clover, L., Hart, I., Maddison, P., Tuzum, E., et al. (2003). Autoimmune disorders of neuronal potassium channels. *Annals of the New York Academy of Sciences, 998,* 202–210.

Ozonoff, S., Williams, B. J., & Landa, R. (2005). Parental report of the early development of children with regressive autism: The delays-plus-regression phenotype. *Autism, 9,* 461–486.

Palermo, M. T., & Curatolo, P. (2004). Pharmacologic treatment of autism. *Journal of Child Neurology, 19,* 155–164.

Pavone, P., Incorpora, G., Fiumara, A., Parano, E., Trifiletti, R. R., & Ruggieri, M. (2004). Epilepsy is not a prominent feature of primary autism. *Neuropediatrics, 35,* 207–210.

Pelphrey, K. A., Sasson, N. J., Reznick, J. S., Paul, G., Goldman, B. D., & Piven, J. (2002). Visual scanning of faces in autism. *Journal of Autism and Developmental Disorders, 32,* 249–261.

Pierce, K., Muller, R. A., Ambrose, J., Allen, G., & Courchesne, E. (2001). Face processing occurs outside the fusiform "face area" in autism: Evidence from functional MRI. *Brain, 124,* 2059–2073.

Piven, J., Saliba, K., Bailey, J., & Arndt, S. (1997). An MRI study of autism: The cerebellum revisited. *Neurology, 49,* 546–551.

Plioplys, A. V., Greaves, A., Kazemi, K., & Silverman, E. (1994). Lymphocyte function in autism and Rett syndrome. *Neuropsychobiology, 29,* 12–16.

Prior, M. R., Tress, B., Hoffman, W. L., & Boldt, D. (1984). Computed tomographic study of children with classic autism. *Archives of Neurology, 41,* 482–484.

Prizant, B., Wetherby, A., Rubin, E., Laurent, A., & Rydell, P. (2006). *The scerts model: A comprehensive educational approach for children with autism spectrum disorders.* Baltimore: Paul H. Brookes.

Ratey, J. J., Grandin, T., & Miller, A. (1992). Defense behavior and coping in an autistic savant: The story of Temple Grandin, PhD. *Psychiatry, 55,* 382–391.

Redcay, E., & Courchesne, E. (2005). When is the brain enlarged in autism? A meta-analysis of all brain size reports. *Biological Psychiatry, 58,* 1–9.

Reichenberg, A., Gross, R., Weiser, M., Bresnahan, M., Silverman, J., Harlap, S., et al. (2006). Advancing paternal age and autism. *Archives of General Psychiatry, 63,* 1026–1032.

Richler, J., Luyster, R., Risi, S., Hsu, W. L., Dawson, G., Bernier, R., et al. (2006). Is there a "regressive phenotype" of autism spectrum disorder associated with the measles-mumps-rubella vaccine? A CPEA study. *Journal of Autism and Developmental Disorders, 36,* 299–316.

Rimland, B. (1964). *Infantile autism.* New York: Appleton-Century-Crofts.

Ritvo, E. R., & Garber, H. J. (1988). Cerebellar hypoplasia and autism. *New England Journal of Medicine, 319,* 1152–1154.

Rogers, S. J., & Lewis, H. (1989). An effective day treatment model for young children with pervasive developmental disorders. *Journal of the American Academy of Child and Adolescent Psychiatry, 28,* 207–214.

Rogers, S. J., & Pennington, B. (1991). A theoretical approach to the deficits in infantile autism. *Development and Psychopathology, 3,* 137–162.

Rossignol, D. A. (2007). Hyperbaric oxygen therapy might improve certain pathophysiological findings in autism. *Medical Hypotheses, 68,* 1208–1227.

Rubenstein, J. L. (2006). Comments on the genetic control of forebrain development. *Clinical Neuroscience Research,* 169–177.

Rubenstein, J. L., & Merzenich, M. M. (2003). Model of autism: Increased ratio of excitation/inhibition in key neural systems. *Genes Brain Behavior, 2,* 255–267.

Schopler, E., Mesibov, G., & Hearsey, K. (1995). Structured teaching in the TEACCH system. In E. Schopler & G. Mesibov (Eds.), *Learning and cognition in autism* (pp. 243–268). New York: Plenum Press.

Schopler, E., Mesibov, G., Shigley, R., & Bashford, A. (1984). Helping autistic children through their parents: The TEACCH model. In E. Schopler & G. Mesibov (Eds.), *The effects of autism on the family* (pp. 65–81). New York: Plenum Press.

Schreibman, L. (2005). *The science and fiction of autism.* Boston: Harvard University Press.

Schreibman, L., & Pierce, K. (1993). Achieving greater generalization of treatment effects in children with autism: Pivotal response training and self management. *Clinical Psychologist, 46,* 184–191.

Schultz, R. T. (2005). Developmental deficits in social perception in autism: The role of the amygdala and fusiform face area. *International Journal of Developmental Neuroscience, 23*(2–3), 125–141.

Schumann, C. M., & Amaral, D. G. (2006). Stereological analysis of amygdala neuron number in autism. *Journal of Neuroscience, 26,* 7674–7679.

Schumann, C. M., Hamstra, J., Goodlin-Jones, B. L., Lotspeich, L. J., Kwon, H., Buonocore, M. H., et al. (2004). The amygdala is enlarged in children but not adolescents with autism: The hippocampus is enlarged at all ages. *Journal of Neuroscience, 24,* 6392–6401.

Scoppetta, C., Onorati, P., Eusebi, F., Fini, M., Evoli, A., & Vincent, A. (2003). Autoimmune myasthenia gravis after cardiac surgery. *Journal of Neurology Neurosurgery, and Psychiatry, 74,* 392–393.

Sebat, J., Lakshmi, B., Malhotra, D., Troge, J., Lese-Martin, C., Walsh, T., et al. (2007). Strong association of de novo copy number mutations with autism. *Science, 316,* 445–449.

Sigman, M., & Capps, L. (1997). *Children with autism: A developmental perspective.* Cambridge, MA: Harvard University Press.

Singh, V. K. (1996). Plasma increase of interleukin-12 and interferon-gamma: Pathological significance in autism. *Journal of Neuroimmunology, 66*(1–2), 143–145.

Singh, V. K., & Rivas, W. H. (2004). Prevalence of serum antibodies to caudate nucleus in autistic children. *Neuroscience Letters, 355*(1–2), 53–56.

Singh, V. K., Warren, R., Averett, R., & Ghaziuddin, M. (1997). Circulating autoantibodies to neuronal and glial filament proteins in autism. *Pediatric Neurology, 17,* 88–90.

Singh, V. K., Warren, R. P., Odell, J. D., Warren, W. L., & Cole, P. (1993). Antibodies to myelin basic protein in children with autistic behavior. *Brain, Behavior, and Immunity, 7,* 97–103.

Smalley, S. L., Asarnow, R. F., & Spence, M. A. (1988). Autism and genetics: A decade of research. *Archives of General Psychiatry, 45,* 953–961.

Snider, L. A., & Swedo, S. E. (2003). Post-streptococcal autoimmune disorders of the central nervous system. *Current Opinion in Neurology, 16,* 359–365.

Sparks, B. F., Friedman, S. D., Shaw, D. W., Aylward, E. H., Echelard, D., Artru, A. A., et al. (2002). Brain structural abnormalities in young children with autism spectrum disorder. *Neurology, 59,* 184–192.

Spezio, M. L., Adolphs, R., Hurley, R. S., & Piven, J. (2007a). Abnormal use of facial information in high-functioning autism. *Journal of Autism and Developmental Disorders, 37,* 929–939.

Spezio, M. L., Adolphs, R., Hurley, R. S., & Piven, J. (2007b). Analysis of face gaze in autism using "bubbles." *Neuropsychologia, 45,* 144–151.

Splawski, I., Timothy, K. W., Sharpe, L. M., Decher, N., Kumar, P., Bloise, R., et al. (2004). Ca(v)1.2 calcium channel dysfunction causes a multisystem disorder including arrhythmia and autism. *Cell, 119,* 19–31.

Splawski, I., Yoo, D. S., Stotz, S. C., Cherry, A., Clapham, D. E., & Keating, M. T. (2006). Cacna1h mutations in autism spectrum disorders. *Journal of Biological Chemistry, 281,* 22085–22091.

Stachnik, J. M., & Nunn-Thompson, C. (2007). Use of atypical antipsychotics in the treatment of autistic disorder. *Annals of Pharmacotherapy, 41,* 626–634.

Stern, D. (1985). *The interpersonal world of the human infant.* New York: Basic Books.

Stern, L., Francoeur, M. J., Primeau, M. N., Sommerville, W., Fombonne, E., & Mazer, B. D. (2005). Immune function in autistic children. *Annals of Allergy, Asthma and Immunology, 95,* 558–565.

Sutcliffe, J. S., Delahanty, R. J., Prasad, H. C., McCauley, J. L., Han, Q., Jiang, L., et al. (2005). Allelic heterogeneity at the serotonin transporter locus (slc6a4) confers susceptibility to autism and rigid-compulsive behaviors. *American Journal of Human Genetics, 77,* 265–279.

Sweeten, T. L., Bowyer, S. L., Posey, D. J., Halberstadt, G. M., & McDougle, C. J. (2003). Increased prevalence of familial autoimmunity in probands with pervasive developmental disorders. *Pediatrics, 112,* e420.

Tager-Flusberg, H., Paul, R., & Lord, C. (2005). Language and communication in autism. In F. Volkmar, R. Paul, A. Klin, & D. Cohen (Eds.), *Handbook of autism and pervasive developmental disorders* (pp. 335–364). Hoboken, NJ: Wiley.

Todd, R. D., & Ciaranello, R. D. (1985). Demonstration of inter- and intra-species differences in serotonin binding sites by antibodies from an autistic child. *Proceedings of the National Academy of Sciences, USA, 82,* 612–616.

Trevarthen, C., & Aitken, K. J. (2001). Infant intersubjectivity: Research, theory, and clinical applications. *Journal of Child Psychology and Psychiatry, and Allied Disciplines, 42,* 3–48.

Tuchman, R. F., & Rapin, I. (1997). Regression in pervasive developmental disorders: Seizures and epileptiform electroencephalogram correlates. *Pediatrics, 99,* 560–566.

Tuchman, R. F., & Rapin, I. (2002). Epilepsy in autism. *Lancet Neurology, 1,* 352–358.

Tuchman, R. F., Rapin, I., & Shinnar, S. (1991). Autistic and dysphasic children: Pt. II. Epilepsy. *Pediatrics, 88,* 1219–1225.

Valicenti-McDermott, M., McVicar, K., Rapin, I., Wershil, B. K., Cohen, H., & Shinnar, S. (2006). Frequency of gastrointestinal symptoms in children with autistic spectrum disorders and association with family history of autoimmune disease. *Journal of Developmental and Behavioral Pediatrics, 27*(Suppl 2), S128–S136.

van Gent, T., Heijnen, C. J., & Treffers, P. D. (1997). Autism and the immune system. *Journal of Child Psychology and Psychiatry, and Allied Disciplines, 38,* 337–349.

van Kooten, I. A., Palmen, S. J., von Cappeln, P., Steinbusch, H. W., Korr, H., Heinsen, H., et al. (2008). Neurons in the fusiform gyrus are fewer and smaller in autism. *Brain, 131*(Pt. 4), 987–999.

Vargas, D. L., Nascimbene, C., Krishnan, C., Zimmerman, A. W., & Pardo, C. A. (2005). Neuroglial activation and neuroinflammation in the brain of patients with autism. *Annals of Neurology, 57,* 67–81.

Varoqueaux, F., Aramuni, G., Rawson, R. L., Mohrmann, R., Missler, M., Gottmann, K., et al. (2006). Neuroligins determine synapse maturation and function. *Neuron, 51,* 741–754.

Vincent, A., Dalton, P., Clover, L., Palace, J., & Lang, B. (2003). Antibodies to neuronal targets in neurological and psychiatric diseases. *Annals of the New York Academy of Sciences, 992,* 48–55.

Volkmar, F., & Klin, A. (2005). Issues in the classification of autism and related conditions. In F. Volkmar, R. Paul, A. Klin, & D. Cohen (Eds.), *Handbook of autism and pervasive developmental disorders* (pp. 5–41). Hoboken, NJ: Wiley.

Wang, A. T., Dapretto, M., Hariri, A. R., Sigman, M., & Bookheimer, S. Y. (2004). Neural correlates of facial affect processing in children and adolescents with autism spectrum disorder. *Journal of the American Academy of Child and Adolescent Psychiatry, 43,* 481–490.

Warren, R. P., Cole, P., Odell, J. D., Pingree, C. B., Warren, W. L., White, E., et al. (1990). Detection of maternal antibodies in infantile autism. *Journal of the American Academy of Child and Adolescent Psychiatry, 29,* 873–877.

Weiss, L. A., Escayg, A., Kearney, J. A., Trudeau, M., MacDonald, B. T., Mori, M., et al. (2003). Sodium channels scn1a, scn2a and scn3a in familial autism. *Molecular Psychiatry, 8,* 186–194.

West, L., & Waldrop, J. (2006). Risperidone use in the treatment of behavioral symptoms in children with autism. *Pediatric Nursing, 32,* 545–549.

Williams, D. (1992). *Nobody nowhere.* New York: Times Books.

Williams, J. A., Koegel, R. L., & Egel, A. L. (1981). Response-reinforcer relationships and improved learning in autistic children. *Journal of Applied Behavior Analysis, 14,* 53–60.

Wimpory, D. C., Hobson, R. P., Williams, J. M., & Nash, S. (2000). Are infants with autism socially engaged? A study of recent retrospective parental reports. *Journal of Autism and Developmental Disorders, 30,* 525–536.

Wing, L. (1981). Language, social, and cognitive impairments in autism and severe mental retardation. *Journal of Autism and Developmental Disorders, 11,* 31–44.

Wolf, M., Risley, T., & Mees, H. (1964). Application of operant conditioning procedures to the behaviour problems of an autistic child. *Behavior Research and Therapy, 1,* 305–312.

Wu, S., Jia, M., Ruan, Y., Liu, J., Guo, Y., Shuang, M., et al. (2005). Positive association of the oxytocin receptor gene (oxtr) with autism in the Chinese Han population. *Biological Psychiatry, 58,* 74–77.

Yeargin-Allsopp, M., Rice, C., Karapurkar, T., Doernberg, T., Boyle, C., & Murphy, C. (2003). Prevalence of autism in a US metropolitan area. *Journal of the American Medical Association, 289,* 49–55.

Yirmiya, N., Rosenberg, C., Levi, S., Salomon, S., Shulman, C., Nemanov, L., et al. (2006). Association between the arginine vasopressin 1a receptor (avpr1a) gene and autism in a family-based study: Mediation by socialization skills. *Molecular Psychiatry, 11,* 488–494.

Young, L. J., Murphy Young, A. Z., & Hammock, E. A. (2005). Anatomy and neurochemistry of the pair bond. *Journal of Comparative Neurology, 493,* 51–57.

Chapter 53

Attention-Deficit/Hyperactivity Disorder

MARIA T. ACOSTA, MAURICIO ARCOS-BURGOS, AND MAXIMILIAN MUENKE

Attention-Deficit/Hyperactivity Disorder (ADHD), the most common behavioral disorder of childhood, affects 8% to 12% of children worldwide (Biederman, 2005). ADHD is defined as a persistent syndrome characterized by inattention, excessive motor activity, and impulsivity of a given developmental stage. ADHD is not only a behavioral trait carried by American children, as suggested in the past, but a human behavior variant that can be operatively defined in many populations worldwide (Faraone, Sergeant, Gillberg, & Biederman, 2003). Affected individuals are at increased risk for poor educational achievement, low income, underemployment, legal difficulties, and impaired social relationships (Faraone, Biederman, Mennin, Gershon, & Tsuang, 1996). A conservative estimate for an ADHD prevalence of 5% established that the costs attributable to ADHD in the United States are $42.5 billion per year (range $36 to $52.4 billion; Pelham, Foster, & Robb, 2007). As result of the high prevalence, life-span affection, and transcendent socioeconomic impact, ADHD is the best researched behavioral disorder of childhood (Pelham et al., 2007).

Despite the high social impact, it is unclear whether ADHD should be viewed as a nosological entity or as a common variant of human behavior. ADHD occurs as a single disorder in the minority of diagnosed individuals. In many patients, comorbidities such as Oppositional Defiant Disorder (ODD), Conduct Disorder (CD), alcohol or drug abuse, and anxiety or depression are strongly associated.

ADHD is more complex than was thought previously and the underlying neurobiology is not well understood. Several concepts have arisen in recent years; ADHD is a biological entity with a strong genetic component that is more heterogeneous than was previously considered. The better we understand the underlying etiology related to the clinical manifestations, the better we can design effective intervention programs. If we define human behaviors on a spectrum of hyperactive-hypoactive or hyperattentive to inattentive, there are several clusters of behavioral subtypes, categorically independent among them (Arcos-Burgos & Acosta, 2007). In this chapter, we focus on research data obtained from several lines of scientific evidence that shape our understanding of neurobiology and clinical presentation of ADHD.

HISTORY AND EPIDEMIOLOGY

Contrary to public belief, ADHD is not a new condition. Hippocrates in 493 BC described a condition that seems to be compatible with what we know as ADHD. He described patients who had "quickened responses to sensory experience, but also were less tenaciousness because the soul moves on quickly to the next impression." Hippocrates attributed this condition to an "overbalance of fire over water." In 1845, the German physician, Heinrich Hoffmann, wrote a series of children's stories with poems and illustrations about children with undesirable behaviors. Two of his characters in those books were boys he called "Johnny Head-in-the Air" and "Fidgety Philip." Their behavior could be interpreted as attributed to the inattentive or hyperactive/impulsive subtype of ADHD, respectively (Wortis, 1988). In 1902, George Sill, a British physician, delivered a series of lectures to the Royal College of Physicians in England and described a condition characterized by "lack of moral control" among children without noted physical impairments. He believed this behavior was caused by an innate hereditary dysfunction and not by poor rearing or other environment (Rowland, Lesesne, & Abramowitz, 2002). The condition we refer to as ADHD dates to the mid-twentieth century, when physicians developed a list of clinical observations that when they appeared in combination would receive a series of different names, including "minimal brain damage syndrome," "minimal brain dysfunction," and "hyperkinetic reaction of childhood." These names described the disorder that we know today as attention-deficit/hyperactivity disorder. Early attempts to link attention deficits and behavioral disturbances to brain dysfunction were shaped by the experience of the encephalitis epidemic of 1917–1918. Children who survived the infection experienced subsequent problems including hyperactivity, personality changes, and learning difficulties. However, despite many years of research attempting to identify specific etiologic correlates of the disorder, no single cause has been identified and ADHD is currently best understood as a group of behavioral symptoms that reflect excessive impulsivity, hyperactivity, or inattention.

The first empirically based official set of diagnostic criteria for ADHD was delineated in the American Psychiatric Association's *Diagnostic and Statistical Manual of Mental Disorders* (*DSM-III;* 1980). Early focus on hyperactivity symptoms and later shifts toward inattention and impulsivity symptoms are reflected in the changes to the *Diagnostic and Statistical Manual of Mental Disorders,* revised third edition (*DSM-III-R;* American Psychiatric Association, 1987). The current classification criteria of the *Diagnostic and Statistical Manual of Mental Disorders,* fourth edition (*DSM-IV-TR;* American Psychiatric Association, 2000) for ADHD allow diagnosis of subtypes as predominantly inattentive, predominantly hyperactive, or combined (see Table 53.1).

Although current diagnostic criteria include hyperactivity and impulsivity as does the nomenclature, attention deficit remains the core of the disorder. These successive changes in diagnostic criteria reflect a combination of empirical research findings and expert committee consensus. Taken as a whole, these criteria require an illness pattern that starts early, is enduring, and has led to impairment. To make this diagnosis correctly, the clinician must be familiar with normal development and behavior, gather information from several sources to evaluate the child's symptoms in different settings, and construct an appropriate differential diagnosis for the present complaints. It is important to distinguish children with ADHD from those children whose parents or teachers are mislabeling normal behavior as pathological—children who are truly unaffected. When used by appropriated trained examiners, the diagnostic criteria demonstrate high reliability on individual items for the overall diagnosis (Shaffer et al., 1996).

TABLE 53.1 Symptoms in the DSM IV-TR for ADHD: Diagnostic criteria for Attention-Deficit/Hyperactivity Disorder

Six or more of the following symptoms of Inattention and/or six or more symptoms of Hyperactivity-Impulsivity. symptoms have persisted for more than 6 months to a degree that is maladaptative and inconsistent with developmental level:

1. **Inattention symptoms:**

    Often fails to pay close attention to details or makes careless mistakes in schoolwork, work, or other activities

    Often has difficulty sustaining attention in tasks or play activities

    Often seems to not be listening when spoken to directly

    Often does not follow through on instructions and fails to finish schoolwork, chores, or duties in the workplace (not due to oppositional behavior or failure to understand instructions)

    Often has difficulty organizing tasks and activities

    Often avoids, dislikes, or is reluctant to engage in tasks that require sustained mental effort (such as schoolwork or homework)

    Often loses things necessary for tasks or activities (e.g., toys, school assignments, pencils, books, or tools)

    Is often easily distracted by extraneous stimuli

    Is often forgetful in daily activities

2. **Hyperactivity-Impulsivity symptoms**

    Often fidgets with hands or feet or squirms in seat

    Often leaves seat in classroom or in other situations in which remaining seated is expected

    Often runs about or climbs excessively in situations in which it is inappropriate (in adolescents or adults may be limited to subjective feeling of restlessness)

    Often has difficulty playing or engaging in leisure activities quietly

    Is often "on the go" or often acts as if "driven by a motor"

    Often talks excessively

3. **Impulsivity**

    Often blurts out answers before questions have been completed

    Often has difficulty awaiting a turn

    Often interrupts or intrudes on others (e.g., butts into conversations or games)

    Symptoms that cause impairment were present before age 7 years

    Some impairment from symptoms is present in two or more settings

Epidemiological research in ADHD has been hampered by difficulties involving the diagnosis of ADHD and the numerous changes in its definition over the past 20 years. It has become clear that individuals with ADHD comprise a heterogeneous population sharing a cluster of symptoms. The lack of available biological markers and variable definitions make an adequate comparison of epidemiological studies difficult. Despite these difficulties, rigorous estimates indicate that ADHD has been described almost everywhere around the world. Community studies have estimated prevalence ranging between 1.7% and 21%, depending on the population and the diagnostic methods used (Faraone et al., 2003).

These results suggest that across populations under diverse geographic, racial, ethnic, and socioeconomic conditions there is a sizable percentage of school-age children with ADHD. Furthermore, because the evolution of criteria from *DSM-III* to *DSM-IV* have broadened the limits of case definition, more children appear to be affected (Lahey, Schaughency, Hynd, Carlson, & Nieves, 1987). This is largely a function of the increased emphasis on attentional problems as opposed to a more narrow focus on hyperactivity in earlier diagnostic sets. As a result of these changes in definition, girls have been diagnosed as having ADHD more frequently than they were in the past (Biederman, 1998; Gaub & Carlson, 1997b). Caution must be used when comparing epidemiological data from different studies, because diverse instruments and questionnaires have been used in different trials and the *DSM-IV* definition of impairment is operationally vague. These issues are a source of subjective knowledge to the clinical evaluator when deciding the affection status. Furthermore, random selection of the sample versus "volunteer" participation could introduce a relevant bias in the estimation of epidemiological parameters (Acosta, Arcos-Burgos, & Muenke, 2004). On the one hand, stigmatization of ADHD patients and their families may lead to an underestimation of its prevalence. On the other hand, patients already under medication will exhibit less severe symptoms at the time of the screening. Differences in perception between parents and teachers should also be considered in ADHD studies. Teacher reports may be influenced by factors such as class size, teacher training, or disciplinary aptitudes and practices. Although the *DSM-IV* age criterion to establish the diagnosis is 7 years, new classifications should include a broad range of age for the diagnosis because preschoolers and adults clearly are part of the continuous spectrum of clinical manifestations in ADHD (Rowland et al., 2001).

DIAGNOSIS

The diagnosis of ADHD is made by obtaining a careful clinical history. A child with ADHD is characterized by a considerable degree of inattentiveness, distractibility, impulsivity, and often hyperactivity that is inappropriate for the developmental stage of the child. Current clinical definitions and diagnosis are done according to the guidelines and criteria for diagnosis established by the *DSMIV-TR* or *ICD-10* (Swanson & Castellanos, 1998). As noted, the criteria of the *Diagnostic and Statistical Manual of Mental Disorders,* Fourth Edition (*DSM-IV*) for ADHD allow for diagnosis of subtypes as predominantly inattentive, predominantly hyperactive, or combined.

Criteria for each *DSM-IV* subtype require positive identification of 6 or more of the 9 symptoms in each respective category. There are 4 additional criteria: age of onset by 7, ADHD-specific adaptive impairments, pervasiveness, and separation from other existing conditions.

The combined subtype is the most commonly represented subgroup accounting for 40% to 75% of all ADHD individuals, followed by the inattentive subtype (30% to 40%), and the hyperactive-impulsive subtype (less than 15%; Acosta et al., 2004, 2008; Gaub & Carlson, 1997a; Palacio et al., 2004). Alongside clinical interviews and direct observations, *DSM-IV* diagnosis of ADHD incorporates reports from parents and teachers. Under these diagnostic systems, individuals are classified as affected if they meet a specific number of criteria, determined with reliable and validated psychiatric instruments. Variations in interpretation of symptoms and total prevalence are influenced by cultural differences. ADHD, however, is a condition described worldwide (Faraone et al., 2003).

An important genetic component in ADHD is currently accepted. Multiple lines of evidence suggest that the relationship between risk genes and ADHD symptoms is likely to be pleiotropic, that is, the same gene or genes may be associated with different aspects of the phenotypes (Jain et al., 2007; Willcutt et al., 2002). Similarly, several studies have suggested that ADHD represents one extreme of the quantitative manifestation of normal behavior (Curran et al., 2003; Levy, Hay, McStephen, Wood, & Waldman, 1997; Arcos-Burgos & Acosta, 2007; Stevenson, 1992). These observations would imply that diagnosis of ADHD requires a better understanding and definition, not only in terms of categorical diagnostic criteria, but also of the continuous trait in the population. A specific number of positive symptoms are needed to reach the diagnosis of ADHD, according to the categorical diagnostic criteria used by the *DSM-IV.* In contrast, ADHD behavior can be considered as a continuous trait in the population with variations in clinical manifestation along the spectrum of clinical symptoms. This spectrum would vary from normal behavior to severe forms of symptoms associated with the diagnosis of ADHD. Based on these considerations, several researchers have concluded, [B]oth categorical (diagnostic) and continuous (quantitative trait) approaches to phenotypic dimension are valid and may be complimentary in molecular genetic studies on ADHD (Acosta et al., 2004; Curran et al., 2003).

Among statistical approaches, latent class analysis (LCA)—a categorical approach to ADHD applied to parent report rating scales—is often used. The goal of LCA is to identify naturally occurring clusters of symptoms without imposition of a cutoff for the number of positive symptoms required for diagnosis (as in *DSM-IV*). Applied to parent reports of ADHD symptoms, LCA (Magidson & Vermunt, 2003) has repeatedly yielded six to eight clusters that appear to consistently account for the distribution of ADHD-related symptomatology across cultures, types of samples, population type, and diagnostic methods (Rasmussen et al., 2002; Rohde et al., 2001; Todd et al., 2001). Indirect evidence for the neurobiological validity of the observed latent classes derives from the observation that these clusters show higher heritability estimates than *DSM-IV* subtypes, that is, monozygotic cotwins are significantly more likely to resemble one another in latent class membership than on *DSM-IV* subtype classification (Hudziak et al., 1998; Neuman et al., 2001; Rasmussen et al., 2002; Rohde et al., 2001; Todd et al., 2001; Volk, Neuman, & Todd, 2005). The six to eight clusters typically established in LCA include three that are particularly clinically relevant: severe inattentive, severe combined, and severe hyperactive. These three clusters correspond roughly to the typically defined *DSM-IV* subtypes (Lahey et al., 2004) However, subjects not meeting *DSM-IV* criteria are also often included in clusters. Subjects included in the *DSM-IV* predominantly inattentive ADHD subtype are found to be divided across several latent classes and the severe inattentive latent class contains some *DSM-IV* predominantly inattentive subtype cases. The inattentive and combined LCA-derived subtypes demonstrate clinical stability over time. In contrast, persons assigned to the predominantly hyperactive/impulsive subtype typically evolve to a different subtype over time. These findings suggest the presence of more subtle independent groups within the ADHD phenotype than those advocated by the classical categorical classification (Acosta et al., 2008; Rasmussen et al., 2002). Figures 53.1 and 53.2 from a recent publication, Acosta and colleagues (2008) show the group of different subtypes observed in a sample of families with one affected member with ADHD. A total of 6 to 8 clusters of symptoms are present. Similar observations have been published in other cross cultural studies. This figures shown that regardless of age, cluster classification follows similar patterns. In a sample of 1,010 individuals from a nationwide recruitment of unilineal families with at least one child with ADHD and another either affected or clearly unaffected with six to eight clusters similar to other cross-cultural studies. These figures shown that regardless of age, cluster classification follows similar patterns.

To add complexity to the diagnostic process in ADHD, it is important to understand that many other conditions may mimic ADHD, as the behavioral manifestations seen in ADHD are part of the spectrum of clinical presentation for those conditions. Differences in attention and activity level are part of numerous genetic conditions, some of which are listed in Table 53.2

These conditions share symptoms also present in ADHD. Thus the additional diagnosis and clinical components of the concomitant diagnosis rule out the diagnosis of primary ADHD. In contrast if ADHD is considered as a continuous trait, these associations are highly expected. In addition, recognition of the neurobiological deficits underlying the behavioral deficits in these entities may help to better understand the neurobiology in ADHD. Alcohol fetal syndrome (Nash et al., 2006; O'Malley & Nanson, 2002) and genetic disorders such as Turner syndrome (Russell et al., 2006), neurofibromatosis type 1(Acosta, Gioia, & Silva, 2006), and Klinefelter syndrome (Giedd et al., 2007; Simpson et al., 2003) are highly associated with ADHD symptoms. Understanding the impact of these and other genetic deficits on early brain development and brain function may also help our understanding of the mechanism underlying ADHD symptoms (Acosta et al., 2006).

Use of Scales for Diagnosis of ADHD

Current diagnosis of ADHD is based on use of different behavioral scales that adequately assess these dimensions of ADHD. Many scales are available for the evaluation of ADHD symptoms and classifications according with the subtypes mandated by the *DSM-IV*. Unlike many other neuropsychiatric conditions that use self-report scales for the diagnosis, ADHD scales are usually rating scales that are completed by an adult informant, such as teachers, parents, or other caregivers. This is particularly helpful as it reflects differences in the manifestation of externalizing symptoms such as disruptive behavior compared with internalizing symptoms. By definition, the assessment of internalizing and related symptoms requires information regarding a youth's internal experience. While internalizing symptoms may go unnoticed by caregivers, youths with externalizing behaviors are publicly observable and are typically referred because of the problems they pose to parents and teachers. In addition, although children and adolescents are the best reporters of their subjective experience, they tend to underestimate their externalizing behaviors. Thus, parents and teachers are the optimal informants (Loeber, Green, Lahey, & Stouthamer-Loeber, 1991). When a comprehensive clinical evaluation is the goal, then both teachers' and parents' reports should be included. Regardless of the basis for this discrepancy among informants, it highlights the need for multiinformant assessment, particularly as *DSM-IV* criteria require impairment across settings.

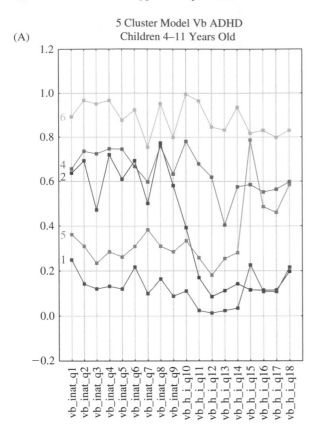

(A) 5 Cluster Model Vb ADHD
Children 4–11 Years Old

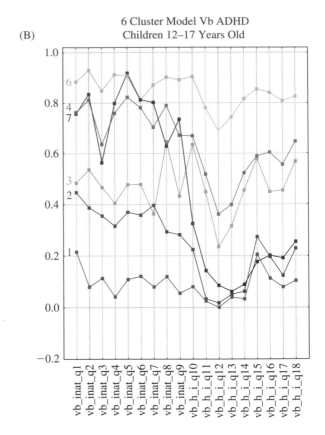

(B) 6 Cluster Model Vb ADHD
Children 12–17 Years Old

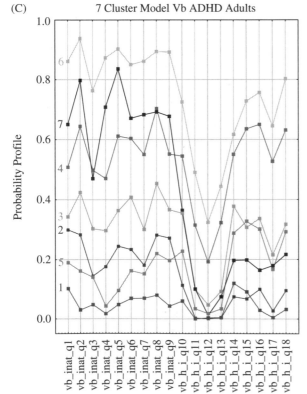

(C) 7 Cluster Model Vb ADHD Adults

		Graph A(%)	Graph B(%)	Graph C(%)
1	Few	29	15.6	17.2
2	Mild Inattentive	11.2	13.4	19.6
3	Mild Combined	0	17.1	20.7
4	Moderated Combined	27.1	23.4	10.1
5	Talkactive-hyperactive	12.2	0	15.5
6	Severe Combined	20.6	18	7.1
7	Severe Inattentive	0	14.5	9.9

Figure 53.1 (**Figure C.49** in color section) LCA analysis for 18 VAS-P items.

Note: **A:** for children **B:** adolescents, and **C:** adults. Each figure shows the latent classes endorsement probabilities (y-axes) for every VAS-P item (symptoms). From: Acosta, M.T., Castellanos, F. X., Kelly, M. D., Balog, J. Z., Eagen, P., et al. (2008). Latent class subtyping of attention-deficit/hyperactivity disorder and comorbid conditions. *Journal of the American Academy of child and Adolescent Psychiatry,* 47:7.

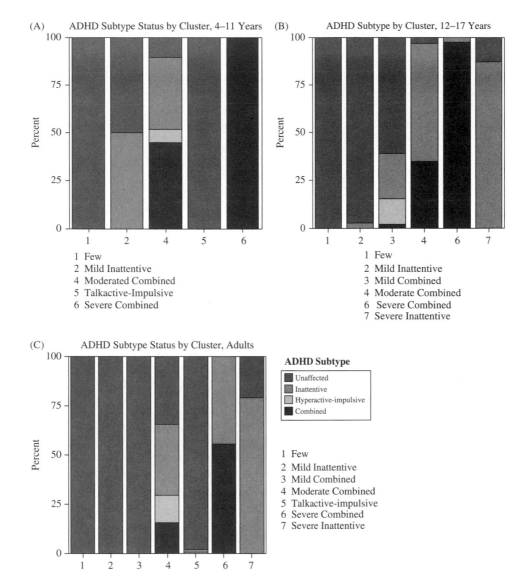

Figure 53.2 (**Figure C.50** in color section) Comparison of ADHD status as defined by the DSM-IV best estimate, and posterior cluster membership (each cluster adds to 100%).

New classifications and definitions of ADHD (e.g., upcoming DSM-V) should consider the wide diversity of symptoms and manifestations throughout the life span. Advances in understanding the neurobiology and the clinical manifestations will help to develop a more comprehensive set of diagnostic tools for primary ADHD patients. From: Acosta, M. T., Castellanos, F. X., Kelly, M. D., Balog, J. Z., Eagen, P., et al. (2008). Latent class subtyping of attention-deficit/hyperactivity disorder and comorbid conditions. *Journal of the American Academy of child and Adolescent Psychiatry,* 47:7.

Scales used for the diagnosis of ADHD may be classified as narrowband scales and broadband scales (Collett, Ohan, & Myers, 2003). Broadband scales cover several behaviors, symptoms, and diagnosis; thus, they are especially useful in the diagnosis of ADHD and the identification of comorbidities. Examples of these scales are the Child Behavior Checklist (Achenbach & Edelbrock, 1983; Achenbach & Ruffle, 2000) or the Behavioral Assessment System for Children (Reynolds & Kamphaus, 1992), DICA (Ezpeleta et al., 1997), DISC (Schwab-Stone et al., 1996; Shaffer et al., 1996) among others. The lengths of these instruments make them less useful for repeated measurements (e.g., when using scales for a monitored treatment response. In contrast, narrowband scales are quick to administer and useful for focused evaluation and repeated measurements (see Table 53.3).

Most of these scales have been designed and are highly suitable for school-age children. It is less clear whether they are equally appropriate for older and younger patients and for girls (several studies have demonstrated differences in scores in boys and girls; Arnold, 1996; Gaub & Carlson, 1997b). As mentioned, new classifications and tools for diagnosis are needed to better consider greater age ranges, including adults, and differences in gender—groups that are currently underdiagnosed by available tools.

TABLE 53.2   Selected genetic disorders associated with ADHD symptoms

Diagnosis	Genetic or Neurobiology Alteration	Cognitive Profile	References
Turner Syndrome	Deletion of part or all of one X chromosome	Normal verbal abilities, visuospatial deficits ADHD diagnosis 24%	Russell et al. (2006)
Neurofibromatosis type 1	Germ line mutations in the NF1 gene mapping to 17q11.2	ADHD symptoms 40%–60% Learning disabilities up to 80% Mental retardation 8%–10%	Acosta et al. (2006)
Williams syndrome	Microdeletion in at least 25 genes on chromosome 7q11.23	ADHD symptoms in 64.7% Relative strengths in verbal short-term memory and language and extreme weakness in visuospatial construction, including writing, drawing, and pattern construction Social interaction characteristic	Leyfer, Woodruff-Borden, Klein-Tasman, Fricke, & Mervis (2006)
Smith-Magenis syndrome	Interstitial deletion of chromosome 17p11.2.	Moderate to severe mental retardation IQ scores between 20 and 78 Relative weaknesses in sequential processing and short-term memory and relative strengths in long-term memory and perceptual closure Behavioral problems including ADHD symptoms in up to 80% Self-injurious behaviors	Smith, Dykens, & Greenberg (1998)
Fragile X syndrome	Mutation of a specific gene on the long arm of the X chromosome in which the number of cytosine-guanine-guanine (CGG) triplet repeats expands beyond normal	ADHD symptoms 55%–59% IQ from normal to mental retardation Executive function deficits Association with autism	Farzin et al. (2006); Sullivan et al. (2006)
Phenylketonuria	Aberrant or absent phenylalanine hydroxylase (PAH) gene	Mental retardation and autism spectrum without treatment Prefrontal system deficits main deficits Manifestations dependent on exposure timing: prenatal exposure is associated with a higher likelihood of expressing hyperactive/impulsive symptoms, and postnatal exposure is associated with a higher likelihood of expressing inattentive symptoms	Antshel & Waisbren (2003)
Fetal Alcohol syndrome	In utero exposure to alcohol	ADHD (41%), followed by learning disorder (17%), and oppositional-defiant/conduct disorder (16%) Prevalence rates of ADHD across the groups generally were high risk IQ variable from normal to mild to moderated deficits	Nash et al. (2006)
Klinnefelter syndrome	47,XXY, the occurrence of an additional X chromosome In males, aneuploidy and is found in between 1 of 6001,2 and 1 of 10003	Executive function impairments, high frequency ADHD symptoms IQ within normal limits to mild mental retardation	Giedd et al. (2007)

TABLE 53.3   Selected Narrowband scales for ADHD diagnosis

Scale	Administration Time	Ages	Scoring Items	Reference
Conners Rating Scales-Revised (CRS-R)	20–30 minutes	3–17 years	Parents: 80 items Teachers: 59 items Adolescents: 87 items	Conners et al. (1997)
IOWA Conners Teacher Rating Scales	5 minutes	6–12 years	10 items	Loney & Milich (1982)
The Swanson, Nolan and Phelam-IV Questionnaire (SNAP IV)	20–30 minutes full version	5–11 years	Full version: 90 items ADHD + ODD: 31 items	Gau et al. (2008); Swanson et al. (2001)
The Swanson, Kotkin, Atkins, M Flynn and Phelam Scale (SKAMP)	5 minutes	7–12 years	13 items	Wigal, Gupta, Guinta, & Swanson (1998)
Strengths and Weaknesses of ADHD symptoms and normal behavior (SWAN)	5 minutes	5–11 years	26 items	Hay, Bennett, Levy, Sergeant, & Swanson (2007)
ADHD Rating Scale IV (ADHD RS-IV)	5–10 minutes (Spanish translation)	5–18 years	18 items	DuPaul, Ervin, Hook, & McGoey (1998)
Vanderbilt ADHD Teacher and Parent Rating Scale (VADTRS & VADPRS)	10–15 minutes Spanish and German translations	6–12 years	43 items	Wolraich et al. (2003)
Brown Attention Deficit Disorder Scales for Children and Adolescents (BADDS)	10–15 minutes	3–12 years 8–18 years	3- to 7-year-olds with parent form & teacher form: 44 items 8- to 12-year-olds with parent and teacher forms and self-report: 50 items 12- to 18-year-olds self-report: 40 items	Brown et al. (2001)

The decision which scales to use depends of the length of the scale, the needs for additional information such as comorbidity, and the age of the patient. Narrowband scales are based on *DSM-IV* and have good face validity as their items are derived from a clear diagnosis construct for ADHD. It is difficult to establish any preference as comparisons between scales are very limited. In clinical settings, a combination of broadband scales and narrow scales are used for the initial evaluation. Narrowband scales are preferred for repetitive measurements, monitoring of treatment response, and longitudinal evaluation of ADHD symptoms.

In looking forward, there are proposals to expand the set of diagnostic symptoms to include executive functions (such as time management and multitasking), especially in older individuals (Barkley, Edwards, Laneri, Fletcher, & Metevia, 2001). In fact, the symptom "often has difficulties organizing" is the most complex *DSM* item and appeared for the first time in *DSM-IV*. New definitions also need to include age-related changes and manifestation according to gender, as well as a broader spectrum of severity that will include milder cases. Executive functions are currently considered a core symptom in the manifestation of ADHD. Observations and evaluations of these complex behaviors in the context of everyday life have become important for evaluation of the impact that ADHD behaviors have in daily performance. Evaluation scales like the Behavior Rating Inventory of Executive Function (BRIEF;

Gioia, Isquith, Kenworthy, & Barton, 2002; Gioia, Isquith, Retzlaff, & Espy, 2002), are used more frequently as a complementary evaluation to provide a more comprehensive overview of the impact of ADHD components in daily life and for follow-up assessment of intervention plans.

CLINICAL PRESENTATION

The diagnosis of ADHD is made by obtaining a careful clinical history. As mentioned, the child with ADHD is characterized by inattentiveness, distractibility, impulsivity, and often hyperactivity that is inappropriate for the developmental stage of the child. Although ADHD is often first observed in early childhood, many overactive toddlers will not develop ADHD. Other common symptoms include low tolerance to frustration, shifting activities frequently, difficulties in organization, and daydreaming. These symptoms are usually pervasive; however, they may not all occur in all settings. According to subtype, behavioral manifestations may be present or not. Children with predominantly inattentive subtype may have more school difficulties and fewer difficulties with peers or family. Conversely, children with excessive hyperactivity or impulsive symptoms may do relatively well in school, but have difficulties at home or in situations with less guidance and structure.

Factors such as environment, level of tolerance, parenting styles, IQ, and socioeconomic status may play a role in the age of diagnosis of the ADHD symptomatology. Internal factors related to the diagnosis (e.g., severity, subtype, comorbidities) are also fundamental at the age of presentation.

AGE OF ONSET

Even though *DSM-IV* requires the presence of the symptomatology compatible with the diagnosis of ADHD before age of 7 years, there is a consensus among clinicians about the enormous variability in the presentation and detection of symptoms. The symptoms of some patients are described by their parents as having been present "forever," even before birth, meaning that those patients have been extremely hyperactive, had early motor development, and were always "on-the-go." In other cases, the diagnosis is given several years after the cutoff of age 7 or even in adulthood. Those patients possibly can refer retrospectively to some vague symptomatology that was not severe enough to produce impairment or to diagnose this condition earlier.

There are significant differences between the hyperactive/impulsive type and the inattentive type in terms of the age at which symptoms emerge. Retrospective parent reports have demonstrated that children with ADHD become noticeably impaired around the age of 3 ½, with a median age of onset of the first ADHD symptoms appearing around 1 year later. The age of onset of the hyperactive type (mean 4.21 years) is earlier than that of the combined type, and both are earlier than the inattentive type. Virtually all children with the hyperactive/impulsive type and 83% of combined type are considered impaired before they reach the 7 years of age. By 9 years, all would meet formal ADHD criteria for diagnosis (Lahey et al., 2004).

In contrast, the developmental trajectory characterizing the inattentive type is quite different: ADHD of the inattentive type is often not apparent until around the first grade (mean age 6.1 years) and in some cases not until around 14 years will patients finally meet the criteria for diagnosis according to *DSM-IV* symptoms.

During the preschool years, symptoms like inattention without hyperactivity are less obvious and only around 50% of children will demonstrate some type of impairment by first grade. Even though up to 85% of children with inattentive type may have some symptoms before age 7, only less than 40% will have a real impairment by 7 years of age. Many children may continue having symptoms on and off, making adaptations on their own or taking advantage of environmental accommodations that allow them to go through the first years of education without a formal diagnosis. In some cases, only when they embark on demanding academic programs or in a profession, does the real impairment became evident.

Chronic symptoms of ADHD in adults can have a significant impairment in academic, social, work, and family functioning. Frequency of ADHD in adults has been estimated to be between 2.9% to 6% (Barkley, Fischer, Smallish, & Fletcher, 2002; Biederman, 2004; Faraone, Biederman, Spencer, et al., 2000). Adults must have childhood onset, persistent, and current symptoms of ADHD to be diagnosed with the disorder. Parent reports of persistence of symptoms in adulthood in previous diagnosed patients estimate that around 50% of children with diagnosis of ADHD will continue fulfilling the criteria for the diagnosis (Barkley et al., 2002). Adults with ADHD often present with marked inattention, distractibility, organization difficulties and poor efficiency, which culminate in life histories of academic and occupational failure (Barkley et al., 2002; Biederman, 2004; Faraone, Biederman, Spencer, et al., 2000). These findings are of considerable importance to the clinician. The clinician should be able to make the diagnosis of ADHD combined type or predominantly hyperactive type during the preschool years. In addition, the age of onset criteria specified in *DSM-IV* for ADHD of the inattentive type, which indicates that "symptoms need to be present before age 7" needs to be considered carefully as evidence of impairments may not be present until several years later. Adults with ADHD also need careful consideration, as there is not an absolute consensus about the best diagnostic pathway to follow in those cases that present with first-time evidence of impairment in adulthood. In retrospect, most of the symptoms have been present for a long time, but individual adaptations, different styles, or variability in demands contained the evidence of impairment until later in life.

GENDER

Only recently has it been recognized that girls and boys have similar risks for ADHD. It was believed that clinical manifestations were gender-specific, but it is now clear that boys and girls have a similar profile of social, behavioral, and academic performance impairment. Gender-specific differences have been observed among clinical samples and population-based samples. Externalized symptoms and behavioral problems are an important reason for early evaluation. Boys are more frequently referred for evaluation early in life than girls. In clinic-referred samples, girls more often present with inattention and internalizing symptoms and less aggression than boys with ADHD.

A meta-analysis (Gaub & Carlson, 1997b) compared ADHD symptoms, intellectual and academic functioning, comorbid behavioral problems, social behavior, and family problems in boys and girls. No differences were found in impulsivity, academic performance, social functioning, fine motor skills, parental education, or parental depression. Girls, however, were less hyperactive than boys, had fewer externalizing behaviors, and were more intellectually impaired. Additional differences were observed in associated comorbidities. Girls have a greater frequency of anxiety depression, low self-esteem, a sense of limited control, and significant difficulties in social environments. Boys present more often with signs of ODD and CD than girls (Hartung et al., 2002; Lahey et al., 2007).

A methodological review concluded that differences between boys and girls are not related to the diagnosis of ADHD, but are part of gender differences per se (Biederman et al., 2005). Boys and girls with ADHD do not have gender-specific differences in prefrontal executive function. When girls with ADHD are compared with controls, they have significant impairments in academic performance, behavioral problems, and disruptive behavioral disorders, and are more vulnerable to drug abuse and academic failure. Furthermore, girls with combined type of ADHD are more vulnerable to be abused and suffer more social rejection. Lastly, girls with the inattentive type have the tendency to be more isolated socially (Greene et al., 2001; Hinshaw, 2002; Hinshaw, Carte, Sami, Treuting, & Zupan, 2002; Rucklidge & Tannock, 2001).

In summary, findings from different studies have demonstrated that ADHD is more frequent in girls than was previously recognized. They have a similar profile of behavioral and academic problems when compared with boys who have ADHD. Girls may be less likely identified as they have fewer externalized symptoms than boys. Thus, differences in clinical manifestations are related to gender, not to the clinical components of ADHD symptoms.

COMORBIDITIES

Childhood ADHD

Through the life cycle, key clinical features observed in patients with ADHD are associated comorbidities. Externalizing and internalizing disorders vary in their frequencies in the ADHD population among different studies and populations (Pliszka, 2000; Sanders, Arduca, Karamitsios, Boots, & Vance, 2005). Externalizing disorders, such as CD and oppositional defiant disorder (ODD) occur with frequencies up to 50% (Palacio et al., 2004). An estimated 20% of children diagnosed with ADHD have CD, and 30% to 45% have ODD (Acosta et al., 2004; August, Realmuto, Joyce, & Hektner, 1999; Burke, Loeber, Lahey, & Rathouz, 2005; Palacio et al., 2004). Among the internalizing disorders, the prevalence of co-occurrence is somewhat lower with 10% to 20% of children with ADHD exhibiting mood disorder (Acosta et al., 2004; Eiraldi, Power, & Nezu, 1997; Sanders et al., 2005; Vance, Sanders, & Arduca, 2005). In addition, the association of ADHD with both depressive disorders and anxiety disorders has been replicated by new epidemiological studies (Angold, Costello, & Erkanli, 1999; Costello, Egger, & Angold, 2005). It is now clear that assessment of the underlying structure of these disorders, to discriminate natural symptom aggregation across ADHD domains and provide insight into the cause of comorbidity, is necessary to better understand the psychopathology of these entities.

Conduct Disorder and antisocial behaviors, as comorbidities in ADHD, have been better defined in terms of genetic association (Arcos-Burgos et al., 2004; Faraone, Biederman, & Monuteaux, 2001; Palacio et al., 2004). A recent study (Jain et al., 2007) supports the hypothesis that major genes underlie a broad behavioral phenotype in some families that may manifest as a range of symptoms including ADHD, disruptive behaviors, and alcohol abuse or dependence. These data are consistent with the notion that different behavioral phenotypes comprise a nosological entity and that the concept of comorbidity is inadequate (Jain et al., 2007; Palacio et al., 2004).

The picture is less clear for internalizing disorders. Anxiety and depression may have different phenotypic expressions modified by comorbidity with ADHD, or by genetic and environmental factors that alter the final phenotype (Kendler, 1996). Special consideration is necessary for ODD, which is not only highly comorbid with ADHD but is also a predictor of two different developmental trajectories ending in either CD or anxiety. The path that the ODD phenotype selects is dictated by complex interactions between genetics and environment (Burke et al., 2005; Lavigne et al., 2001).

As mentioned, variations of these comorbidities and their association with ADHD are also related with gender and age. In a systematic evaluation of the impact of gender on the clinical features of ADHD, Faraone et al. (Faraone, Biederman, Mick, et al., 2000) reported that girls with ADHD were at less risk for comorbid disruptive behavior disorder than boys with ADHD. Because disruptive behavioral disorder drives referral, this might explain the substantial discrepancy in the male/female ratio between clinic-referred (10:1) and community samples (3:1) of children with ADHD (Biederman et al., 2002). Furthermore, this gender discrepancy suggests that girls with ADHD might be underidentified and undertreated (Biederman et al., 2005)

Comorbidities in Adult ADHD

Follow-up studies have found that 5% to 66% of children with ADHD persist with this disorder in adulthood (Biederman, 1998; Weiss, Murray, & Weiss, 2002; Wilens et al., 2005). Current epidemiological studies estimate the prevalence of adult ADHD to be between 3% and 5% (Faraone & Biederman, 2005; Kessler et al., 2005). Furthermore, studies of referred and nonreferred adults with a clinical diagnosis of childhood onset and persistent ADHD revealed that clinical correlates—demographic, psychosocial, psychiatric, and cognitive features—mirrored well-documented findings among children with ADHD (Biederman, 2004).

A study (Acosta et al., 2008) using the 18 Vanderbilt Assessment Scale for Parents (VAS-P) items for inattention, impulsivity, and hyperactivity, produced similar clustering patterns—six to eight clusters and similar cluster definitions, as shown in other Latent Class Analysis (LCA) studies of ADHD symptoms (Hudziak et al., 1998; Neuman et al., 2001; Rasmussen et al., 2002; Rohde et al., 2001; Todd et al., 2001; Volk, Henderson, Neuman, & Todd, 2006). Since the VAS-P has not been used for this purpose in adults and symptom severities are known to differ among age groups, LCA was performed separately for children, adolescents, and adults. While the age groups differed on certain hyperactivity symptoms, overall the symptom-clustering patterns between age groups were strikingly similar. Adding comorbidities had little effect on the cluster distributions. This comparability of symptom profiles among age groups with a broad range of internalizing and externalizing symptoms supports the use of LCA in genetic cohorts that include both adults and children.

Lifetime prevalence rates of comorbid anxiety disorders in adults with ADHD approach 50%, whereas mood disorders, antisocial disorders, and alcohol or drugs dependency also show substantial prevalence rates (Biederman, 2004; Shekim, Asarnow, Hess, Zaucha, & Wheeler, 1990). It is clear that ADHD persists and is present in adulthood. Studies have demonstrated that ADHD in adults is similar in both genders and the validity of the diagnosis is supported (Biederman, 2004).

GENETIC STUDIES

Twin and Family Studies

Over the past decade, twin, adoption, family, and association studies have shown that genetic factors substantially contribute to the etiology of ADHD. Genetic studies in twins indicate a substantially high genetic (additive) contribution to phenotypic variation, reaching 0.91 (Levy et al., 1997). Adoption studies have also confirmed that genetics rather than shared environment cause familial clustering of ADHD (Faraone et al., 2005; Sprich, Biederman, Crawford, Mundy, & Faraone, 2000). Family studies have confirmed the increased recurrence risk by comparing the ratio of the prevalence of ADHD in various kinds of relatives with the population prevalence using the λ statistic (Faraone, Biederman, & Monuteaux, 2000; Faraone et al., 2005; Sprich et al., 2000). Independent complex segregation analyses consistently demonstrated that the model best fitting the data was that of a major autosomal dominant/codominant gene (Lopera et al., 1999; Maher, Marazita, Moss, & Vanyukov, 1999) Additionally, candidate genes selected because of their theoretical and empirical involvement in the physiopathogenesis of ADHD have shown significant association/linkage to ADHD even though they disclose very small effect sizes (reviewed in Acosta et al., 2004).

Linkage Studies

In linkage analysis, markers throughout the genome are screened systematically to identify chromosomal regions that are shared by affected relatives more often than expected by chance alone. In an attempt to find regions of chromosomes that might harbor genes for ADHD, four groups have conducted genome-wide linkage scans for ADHD in distinct populations. They have reported significant linkage to 4q, 5q, 5p, 11q, 16p, and 17p (Arcos-Burgos et al., 2004; Bakker et al., 2003; Fisher et al., 2002; Jain et al., 2007; Ogdie et al., 2003, 2006). Linkage to regions located in 5p, 11q, 16p, and 17p have been replicated by at least 2 studies (Arcos-Burgos et al., 2004; Bakker et al., 2003; Fisher et al., 2002; Jain et al., 2007; Ogdie et al., 2003, 2006; see Figure 53.3). Interpretations of these findings

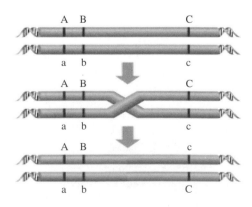

Figure 53.3 (**Figure C.51** in color section) Sample of linkage.

may be variable. Some authors consider that there is a lack of overlapping of the findings between studies, with the exception of regions like 17p11 and 5p13 and with regions in which candidate genes for ADHD are known to reside (Doyle et al., 2005; Faraone et al., 2005). Other interpretations of these linkage studies may consider that the overlaps represent a high degree of replication for this trait and therefore suggest some common susceptibility genes. That the studies have found potentially identical variants within those genes can be seen as evidence of the susceptibility for ADHD across various diverse populations (Arcos-Burgos & Acosta, 2007).

Evolutionary Forces in ADHD

Increase of Fitness

A different approach considers ADHD as a common phenotype with a common representation in the general population, instead of a rare one. This is also supported by the fact that genetic variants that have been associated with the physiopathology of ADHD (some described as candidate genes earlier) are common variants in the general population and possibly totally fixed in some of those populations (Arcos-Burgos & Acosta, 2007). A working hypothesis considers that ADHD as the most common neuropsychiatry disorder is in reality an evolutionary trait that conferred selective advantage and is the result of natural selection patterns (e.g., faster responses to predators, best hunting performance, more effective territorial defense, and improvement in the capacity of mobility and settling). All these factors may lead to an increase in fertility and survival. Studies in other psychiatric conditions such as schizophrenia and mood disorders have demonstrated lower fertility, not present in ADHD populations (Keller & Miller, 2006). As Arcos-Burgos and Acosta point out, these behavioral traits are now under scrutiny because of new emerging social necessities (Arcos-Burgos & Acosta, 2007). Previously, this trait was rewarded by natural selection over millions of years of human evolution; the fast revolution of human society during the past two centuries, however, brought new challenges rewarding behaviors such as planning, design, and attention while limiting rewards for the behaviors associated with ADHD (Arcos-Burgos & Acosta, 2007).

Comparing the frequency of some of the susceptibility variants throughout populations distributed worldwide, using ALFRED (allele frequency database) a resource of gene frequency data on human populations, it is possible to observe that allelic variants conferring susceptibility to ADHD are frequent in the population. This is the case for variants like the seven repeat (7R) allele of the human dopamine receptor D_4 (DRD4) gene, which was previously mentioned as a candidate gene for ADHD. It is especially prevalent in South America with a frequency as high as 80% of the population. Ding et al. (2002) showed that it is a young variant and it has been exposed to selective advantageous pressure because of genetic parameters such as a linkage disequilibrium (LD) extension and variability. Another example, the 10-repeat allele of a tandem repeat polymorphism located in the 3' untranslated region of SLC6A3 (DAT), which is also associated with ADHD susceptibility, is the most frequent throughout the world, reaching fixation (gene frequency of 1.0) in some American populations.

Even though clinical evidence has been used to justify the search for specific endophenotypes and related genes as potential explanations for the symptomatology in ADHD, the heterogeneity of the condition and the phenotypic differences have impacted our ability to find appropriate correlations. In pursuing the neurophysiological basis of the ADHD phenotype, definition of endophenotypes outlines a promising strategy to dissect biological causes of complex phenotypes. Following the operational definition of Castellanos and Tannock (Castellanos et al., 2002), endophenotypes are defined as heritable quantitative traits that index an individual's liability to develop or manifest a given disease, and they are thought to be more directly related than dichotomous diagnostic categories to etiological factors. In addition endophenotypes (a) are present with higher frequency or intensity in affected people; (b) segregate throughout generations; (c) are objective, feasible for quantification, reliable, and reproducible characteristics; and finally, (d) they can be present in unaffected family members, but significantly, in a lesser frequency or lower intensity. Several studies have proposed several traits accomplishing operational criteria that outline endophenotypes, that is, deregulation of executive and inhibitory brain mechanisms, stress aversion, novelty seeking, unexpected reward responses, working memory dysfunction as well as personal time perception with poor fitness to real chronometry and wait aversion. Additionally, cognitive effort and continuous vigilance have been considered as vulnerability traits underlying ADHD symptoms.

New research in genetics in ADHD needs to focus on genetic association of specific phenotypic profiles and markers. Phenomics (Bilder, 2008) is a new discipline that promises to advance our understanding of the genetics and phenotypic association in ADHD and other clinically complex behavioral and psychiatric conditions. It is perhaps the time to redefine ADHD from the clinical and neurobiological perspectives.

NONGENETIC ASPECTS IMPLICATED IN ADHD

Despite the evidence that ADHD carries a strong genetic component, it appears that the clinical manifestations in ADHD are the result of complex interactions between genetic and environmental factors. Several environmental factors have been considered as a potential explanation for ADHD symtomatology. A large body of literature suggests that maternal tobacco smoking and alcohol used during pregnancy have adverse effects and contribute to developing ADHD (Hill, Lowers, Locke-Wellman, & Shen, 2000; Knopik et al., 2005; Linnet et al., 2003; Mick, Biederman, Faraone, Sayer, & Kleinman, 2002). Tobacco smoking during pregnancy has also been associated in the offspring with many other behavioral outcomes, such as conduct disorder and antisocial behavior (Ernst, Heishman, Spurgeon, & London, 2001; Linnet et al., 2003; Thapar, van den Bree, Fowler, Langley, & Whittinger, 2006). Furthermore, studies of children whose mothers smoked during pregnancy have demonstrated neurocognitive deficits such as poor school performance and lower scores on intelligence and achievement tests. Few studies have investigated the effect of both genetic polymorphisms and prenatal smoking or alcohol use on ADHD (Brookes et al., 2006; Kahn, Khoury, Nichols, & Lanphear, 2003). Children with the DAT 480/480 homozygous genotype who were exposed to prenatal smoking had significantly elevated hyperactive—impulsive and oppositional scores on the Conners' Parent Rating Scale Revised-Long Version (Kahn et al., 2003). The most striking association was with oppositional-defiant behavior. Increased risk for ADHD was shown in two independent samples of children exposed to prenatal alcohol use and containing haplotypes with the DAT1 480 allele. Also ADHD, per se, is associated with increased risk for smoking (Becker, El-Faddagh, Schmidt, Esser, & Laucht, 2008). Thus it is not clear whether maternal smoking during pregnancy contributes to ADHD or whether it is really a proxy for ADHD in the mother that is being transmitted to the offspring.

Jain et al. (2007) studied a highly prevalent ADHD isolated population in South America. They found that ADHD cosegregates with disruptive behaviors, as well as alcohol and nicotine dependence. Furthermore, they found highly significant LOD scores and the presence of linkage homogeneity throughout all the sets of families suggesting pleiotropic expression of specific vulnerability genes. These results suggest that major genes may underlie a broad behavioral phenotype in these families that can manifest as a range of symptoms that includes ADHD, disruptive behaviors (ODD and CD), and alcohol abuse or dependence. Thus, ADHD, disruptive behav-

ior, and substance abuse due to specific genetic causes might be classified as a new disorder in the future. These findings would support the hypothesis that maternal smoking in a subset of ADHD patient may be related to the genetic component for ADHD rather than be the underlying etiology. However, in utero nicotine exposure by itself may also impact developmental pathways adding complexity to the definition of etiologic components in ADHD.

NEUROBIOLOGY OF ADHD

Attention is a complex mechanism that implies the perfectly orchestrated function of several brain areas and biological mechanisms. For a detailed review about more detailed aspects of attention mechanism, refer to Chapter 18 (Odluda & Posner) in this Handbook. Several components of attention task have been implicated in the pathophysiology of ADHD. Symptoms of ADHD have been attributed to deficits in frontal-striatal pathways, regions of the brain that underlie executive functions. Executive functions are capacities that allow a person to generate voluntary behaviors that are controlled and actively guided (Gioia et al., 2002). Current findings from studies on the neuropharmacology, genetics, neuropsychology, and neuroimaging of ADHD attribute a central role to frontostriatal pathway disruption. These data suggest that the disorder may result from a disruption in a more distributed circuitry including the frontal brain regions as well as the basal ganglia, the cerebellar hemispheres, and the cerebellar vermis (Kieling, Goncalves, Tannock, & Castellanos, 2008). Frontostriatal and frontoparietal networks supporting an array of top-down or executive processes, such as dorsolateral prefrontal cortices, anterior cingulated cortices, and associated striatal regions, have been extensively associated with ADHD dysfunction (Barkley, 1997; Castellanos & Tannock, 2002).

Recent advances of our neurobiological understanding of ADHD come from noninvasive neuroanatomic imaging, functional magnetic resonance imaging (fMRI) and neuropsychological studies (Dickstein, Bannon, Castellanos, & Milham, 2006; Willcutt, Doyle, Nigg, Faraone, & Pennington, 2005). In the following sections, we explore these advances in the comprehension of ADHD considering the neuropsychological components and anatomical neuroimaging aspects. In addition, we focus on neurotransmitters and special dopaminergic pathways and developmental trajectories. As genetic components are known to play a fundamental role in the pathophysiology of ADHD, they are discussed in an independent section.

Neuroimaging Studies: Morphometric Magnetic Resonance Imaging

While morphometric neuroimaging studies cannot be used to diagnose ADHD, they are ideal for testing hypotheses about the locus or loci of brain dysfunction in individuals with ADHD as they provide direct assessments of both brain structure and brain dysfunction in ADHD. Structural imaging studies using magnetic resonance imaging found evidence of structural brain abnormalities among ADHD patients. The most common findings in children with ADHD are smaller volumes in frontal cortex, cerebellum, and subcortical structures. Castellanos et al., in one of the largest and most important neuroimaging studies of ADHD, found smaller total cerebral brain volumes from childhood through adolescence in children with ADHD. This study suggests that genetic or early environmental influences on brain development in ADHD are fixed, nonprogressive, and unrelated to stimulant treatment (Castellanos et al., 2002). Limitations included the combining of longitudinal and cross-sectional assessments.

Brain-imaging studies fit well with the concept that dysfunctions in frontal subcortical structures (caudate, putamen, and globus pallidus) implicated by the imaging studies are part of the neural circuitry underlying motor control, executive functions, inhibition of behavior, and the modulation or reward pathways. These frontal-strial-pallidal-thalamic circuits provide feedback to the cortex for the regulation of behavior (Alexander, DeLong, & Strick, 1986).

Cerebellum and corpus callosum have also been implicated in the pathophysiology of ADHD. The cerebellum contributes significantly to cognitive functioning, presumably through cerebellar-cortical pathways involving the pons and the thalamus. The corpus callosum connects homotypic regions of the two cerebral hemispheres. Size variations in the callosum and volume differences in number of cortical neurons may degrade communications between these two hemispheres, which may account for some of the cognitive and behavioral symptoms of ADHD (Castellanos et al., 2002).

Overall, research in the past 2 decades has confirmed these original findings, and it is now accepted that the brains of children who have ADHD are significantly smaller, on average, than the brains of healthy controls throughout childhood and adolescence.

Neuropsychological Studies: Executive Function

Clinical manifestations of behavior in ADHD suggest deficits in the voluntary control of behavior. It is unclear, however, what core components in executive function (EF) command the clinical manifestations in ADHD. Barkley (1997) proposed a model of ADHD in which disinhibition is the core deficit, whereas others have proposed more generalized deficits in self-regulation (Houghton et al., 1999). In addition, working memory and temporal processing have also been considered as a potential core deficit (Castellanos & Tannock, 2002). Given both the strong association between executive function and the frontal lobes and the presence of executive dysfunction in ADHD, it is not surprising that nearly all neuroimaging studies have focused on cognitive paradigms assessing executive processes (Dickstein et al., 2006; Willcutt et al., 2005).

Neuropsychological studies alone or in combination with neuroimaging techniques have found, in general, dysfunction in EF tasks in ADHD patients. Moreover, functional imaging studies have shown that an expected increase in prefrontal metabolism during response inhibition tasks is reduced markedly in ADHD subjects (Dickstein et al., 2006; Kieling et al., 2008; Rubia et al., 1999). In fact, a recent meta-analysis of 16 published functional neuroimaging studies of ADHD revealed that significant patterns of frontal hypoactivity are detected across studies in patients who have ADHD, affecting anterior cingulate, dorsolateral prefrontal, and inferior prefrontal cortices (Dickstein et al., 2006).

A meta-analysis (Willcutt et al., 2005) of 83 studies that administered executive function measures to groups, for a total of 3,734 ADHD patients and 2,969 non-ADHD individuals found that, in general, ADHD individuals demonstrated weakness in several EF domains. The strongest and most consistent effects were obtained on measures of response inhibition, vigilance, spatial working memory, and some measures of planning. Executive function weaknesses are present in both clinic-referred and community samples and are not fully explained by group differences in intelligence, academic achievement, or symptoms of other disorders.

Executive dysfunction in domains such as response inhibition, planning, vigilance, and working memory plays an important role in the complex neuropsychology of ADHD. Because the spectrum is heterogeneous and complex, further evaluation is necessary to assess the impact of diagnostic and neuropsychological heterogeneity and to clarify the relations between various EF dimensions, as well as the relations between EF and other neurocognitive and emotion-motivation domains.

New Neuroimaging Techniques

Noninvasive neuroimaging techniques have allowed researchers to examine the neural correlates of ADHD, resulting in a rapidly growing literature. A recent publication (Bush,

Valera, & Seidman, 2005) surveyed over a dozen neuroimaging studies of ADHD encompassing functional imaging techniques (PET, SPECT, fMRI,1H-MRS, and EEG) and cognitive paradigms (e.g., inhibitory control, selective attention, working memory, and vigilance). The authors found a consistent pattern of frontal dysfunction with altered patterns of activity in anterior cingulate, dorsolateral prefrontal, and ventrolateral prefrontal cortices, as well as associated parietal, striatal, and cerebellar regions. Despite broad consistencies, multiple challenges are present when comparing results across studies; and interpretation is difficult due to small sample sizes and methodological issues related to statistical analysis.

To date, the most consistent findings in the neuroimaging literature of ADHD are deficits in neural activity within frontostriatal and frontoparietal circuits. The distributed natures of these results fail to support models emphasizing dysfunction in any one frontal subregion.

A complementary approach (Castellanos et al., 2008) is to examine the neural substrates of ADHD-relevant behaviors, such as attentional lapses, and then assess whether the underlying circuits are implicated in ADHD through analysis of the temporal correlations among distributed brain regions. This method of functional connectivity provides remarkably detailed spatial maps of putatively functionally related regions. This resting-state functional MRI technique demonstrated that adults who have ADHD exhibit decreased functional connectivity in long-range connections linking the anterior cingulate region and two posterior components of the so-called default-mode network (precuneus and posterior cingulated). These new findings in brain activation in addition to previous results in terms of variations in anatomic structures in individua with ADHD, may imply that the neural mechanism implicated in ADHD symptoms are more complex that was suggested before. Perhaps long-range connections, such as those linking dorsal anterior cingulate to posterior cingulate and precuneus should be considered as a candidate locus of dysfunction in ADHD (Castellanos et al., 2008). These are all new and exciting findings that deserve further investigation.

Proton magnetic resonance spectroscopy (¹H-MRS) is another noninvasive technique for evaluating brain chemistry in vivo (Sun et al., 2005). ¹H-MRS can obtain the spectra of metabolites linked directly as well as indirectly to neurotransmission pathways including N-acetylaspartate (NAA), Inositol (Ins), Choline (Cho), and Glutamate-Glutamine complex (Glx) to creatine (Cr) ratios. Such brain metabolic changes fundamentally reflect an ontogenic brain development status and an index of neuronal function, both events finally related to neuronal activity and viability number (Sun et al., 2005). These features make ¹H-MRS a promising technique to evaluate the

biochemical component of in vivo brain tissue.¹H-MRS preliminary studies in ADHD cases and controls have showed the presence of differences between ADHD cases and controls. Some studies have found differences in Glx-to-Cr ratio differences at the frontal-striatal region, and at the right dorsolateral frontal region (MacMaster, Carrey, Sparkes, & Kusumakar, 2003); lower NAA levels in the dorsolateral prefrontal cortex patients with ADHD (Hesslinger, Thiel, van Tebartz, Hennig, & Ebert, 2001); and a higher ratio of glutamate plus glutamine to *myo*-inositol-containing compounds in the anterior cingulate cortex (Moore et al., 2006).

This is a promising technique that provides information about in vivo biochemistry changes in brain development and function. In the immediate future, it might provide opportunities to integrate our current knowledge in neuroanatomy, function, connectivity and metabolic changes that could explain the behavioral aspects observed in individuals with ADHD. Figure 53.4, summarizes some of the most important neurobiological aspects that have been implicated in the pathophysiology of ADHD. The combination of neuroimaging data, clinical data, neuropsychological evaluations, genetic results, and the distribution of neurotransmitters have contributed to this hypothetical "map for ADHD."

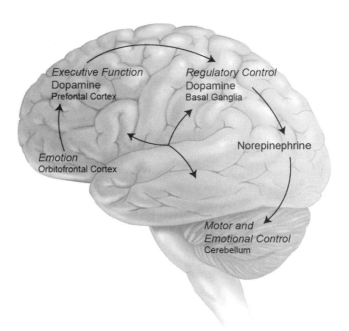

Figure 53.4 Fronto-striatal-Cerebellar pathways have strongly implicated in the physiopathology of ADHD. Anatomical, neurotransmitters and functional correlations in this pathway play a fundamental role.

Neurodevelopmental Hypothesis in ADHD: Are Brain Developmental Pathways Different in ADHD?

There is growing evidence that ADHD pathophysiology is strongly explained by changes and variations that primarily impact developmental trajectories (Arcos-Burgos & Acosta, 2007; Castellanos et al., 2002; Shaw et al., 2007; Sonuga-Barke, 2003). From the neuropsychological perspective, some researchers consider that ADHD should be better considered as a "developmental executive dysfunction." The prefrontal hypotheses of ADHD have primarily involved the dorsolateral prefrontal cortex. Some of the behaviors associated with these structures are associated with organization, planning, working memory, and attentional dysfunctions and orbital lesions associated with social disinhibition and impulse control disorders (Bush et al., 2005; Seidman, Valera, & Makris, 2005; Valera, Faraone, Biederman, Poldrack, & Seidman, 2005).

The frontosubcortical systems pathways associated with ADHD are rich in catecholamines, norepinephrine, and dopamine. A plausible model for the effects of medications in ADHD suggests that, through dopaminergic and/or noradrenergic pathways, these agents increase the inhibitory influences of frontal, cortical activity on subcortical structures (Pliszka, McCracken, & Maas, 1996; Zametkin & Rapoport, 1987). Furthermore, ADHD-associated dopaminergic deficits in the prefrontal cortex have been postulated (Sonuga-Barke, 2003). From this neurobiological evidence, it has been hypothesized that clinical manifestations and pharmacological responses to treatment could be explained by imbalances in dopaminergic and noradrenergic systems (Pliszka et al., 1996; Zametkin & Rapoport, 1987). During brain development, dopamine acts as a neuronal morphogen during frontal cortical development (Todd, 1992). Those findings together suggest that several components implied in the development of frontal cortex, including genetic markers, neurotransmitters, and formation of neural pathways could play an important role in the pathophysiology of ADHD. In addition, behavioral expressions of those variations in development are manifested as developmental components of executive functions.

Interactions between genetic background and environmental factors may also play a role in the modification of these developmental neural trajectories. A recent paper proposes that a synaptic model for prenatal nicotine exposure interacting with ADHD genotypes may modulate the risk for severe ADHD (Neuman et al., 2007).

ADHD symptoms are highly correlated with frontal lobe function and executive function manifestations. If ADHD is to be considered as a continuous trait in the population with a range of manifestation that goes from normal behavior to abnormal manifestations associated with social impairments, any advance in understanding the neurobiology of ADHD will advance our understanding of normal human behavior. Executive functions are a fundamental component of any cognitive process, and they can be the difference between failure and success for many individuals. It is also clear that they are impacted by many biological conditions. Advances in neuroimaging and genetics will help us to understand not only ADHD, but also the fundamental biological components of human behavior.

Brain imaging studies strongly support the following anatomical and developmental differences between ADHD cases and control individuals: (a) the caudate nucleus and globus pallidus are smaller in the ADHD than in the control groups; (b) ADHD groups have larger posterior brain regions and smaller anterior brain regions (Castellanos et al., 2002); (c) areas coordinating multiple brain regions as the rostrum and splenium of the corpus callosum and the cerebellum vermis lobules VIII-X are smaller in ADHD than in control groups (Swanson et al., 2007); and (d) presence of delay in the age of attaining peak cortical thickness in ADHD children when compared with controls throughout most of the cerebrum (Shaw et al., 2007). These established structural variations suggest variable brain neuronal regulation and function as well as different patterns of brain ontogeny between ADHD cases and controls.

TREATMENT

Pharmacological Treatment

Pharmacological treatment is currently considered a fundamental part of any intervention plan for ADHD children and adults. Dysfunction of noradrenergic and/or dopaminergic neurotransmission has been widely implicated in the manifestation of ADHD (Pliszka et al., 1996; Zametkin & Rapoport, 1987). Noradrenaline (NA) and dopamine (DA) exert neuromodulatory influences over behavior and cognition via fronto-striato-cerebellar circuitry (Alexander et al., 1986) and pharmacotherapy is thought to target these systems to ameliorate problems with impulsivity, inattention, and hyperactivity (Spencer et al., 2005; Spencer, Biederman, Wilens, & Faraone, 2002). Psychostimulants are widely used for ADHD and act to increase free brain levels of noradrenaline and dopamine by blocking reuptake and triggering release (Spencer et al., 2002, 2005). A wealth of evidence shows these agents to be effective in the treatment of ADHD for up to 80% of patients. (Biederman & Spencer, 2008).

The most commonly used compounds in this class include methylphenidate (Ritalin), d-methylphenidate (Focalin), d-amphetamine (Dexedrine), and a mixed-amphetamine product (Adderall). These drugs have been shown to enhance dopaminergic and noradrenergic transmission (Volkow et al., 2001). Treatment with stimulants improves not only abnormal behaviors of ADHD but also self-esteem, cognition, and social and family function. A new generation of highly sophisticated, well-developed, safe, and effective long-acting preparations of stimulant drugs has recently reached the market and revolutionized the treatment of ADHD (Biederman & Spencer, 2008).

The most commonly reported side effects associated with stimulant medication are appetite suppression and sleep disturbances. Although less commonly reported, mood disturbances ranging from increased tearfulness to a full-blown major depression-like syndrome can be associated with stimulant treatment. Other infrequent side effects include headaches, abdominal discomfort, increased lethargy, and fatigue (Biederman & Spencer, 2008). For an extensive review on ADHD pharmacological treatment, review Pliszka (2007) and Biederman and Spencer (2008).

In 1997, the Collaborative Multimodal Treatment Study of Children with ADHD (MTA) examined the long-term effectiveness of medication versus behavioral treatment versus both for treatment of ADHD and compared state-of-the-art treatment with routine community care (Arnold et al., 1997). After 14 months of treatment, patients assigned to the medication group showed superior responses compared with the group that received behavioral treatment. The combined treatment group (medication 1 behavioral treatment) did not show greater benefits than medication alone (MTA Study, 1999). These results made clear that pharmacological intervention was a fundamental part in the treatment of ADHD. Recently, however, some concern has been shown about the long-term efficacy of methylphenidate based on the 36-month data from the Multimodal Treatment Study of Children with ADHD study (Jensen et al., 2007). Comparison between groups showed that for the long-term prognosis, the superior improvement for the medication treatment group is less evident, and behavioral treatment also improves ADHD-related symptoms and prognosis over time.

Multiple nonstimulant compounds have been used as an alternative or complementary treatment in ADHD. Those more frequently used are presented in Table 53.4. Atomoxetine, approved in the United States for the treatment of ADHD in November 2002, is a nonstimulant that is thought to act presynaptically via the inhibition of norepinephrine reuptake. It is the most prescribed nonstimulant medication for treatment of ADHD. Atomoxetine has limited effect on the serotonin or dopamine transporters and has low affinity at dopaminergic, muscarinic-cholinergic, histaminic, serotonergic, and a_1- or a_2-adrenergic receptors. Multiple recent reports have provided evidence that this medication is safe and well tolerated. In addition to treating ADHD, atomoxetine was shown to improve depression or anxiety in a pediatric population (Kratochvil et al., 2005). Although a stimulant will be the first choice in most patients, atomoxetine may be preferred in some cases, particularly when substance abuse or comorbid tics are a problem, if a strong family preference exists for a nonstimulant, if 24-hour action is strongly required, or if comorbid anxiety is present. In the presence of adverse events while using stimulants, the next step often will be atomoxetine.

ADHD is a heterogeneous disorder with strong neurobiological basis that affects millions of individuals of all ages worldwide. Although the stimulants remain the mainstay of treatment for this disorder, a new generation of no-stimulant drugs is emerging that provides a viable alternative for patients and families. When assessing patients

TABLE 53.4   Most frequently used medications in ADHD

Medication Family	Brand and Generic name
Amphetamines (dextroanphetamine, mixed salts of amphetamine)	Short acting: Adderall (mixed salt amphetamines), Dexedrine, Dextrostat
	Long acting: Dexedrine Spansule, Adderall XR, Lisdexamfetamine
Methylphenidate	Short acting: Focalin (d-isomer), Methylin, Ritalin
	Intermediate acting: Metadate-ER, Methylin ER, Ritalin SR, Metadate CD, Ritalin LA
	Long acting: Concerta (OROS-MPH), Daytrana Patch (MPH Transdermal system), Focalin XR (d-isomer MPH)
Selective norepinephrine reuptake inhibitor	Strattera (Atomoxetine)
Antidepressants	Wellbutrin (Bupoprion), Tofranil (Imipramine), Pamelor (Nortriptyline)
α 2-Adrenergic agonist	Tenex (Guanfacine), Catapres (Clonidine)

who have ADHD, a careful differential diagnosis must be applied that considers psychiatric, social, cognitive, educational, and medical/neurological factors that may contribute to the clinical presentation. Realistic expectations of intervention, careful definition of target symptoms, and careful assessment of the potential risks and benefits of each type of intervention for these patients are major ingredients for success.

Genetic and neuroimaging studies are becoming more and more involved in the understanding of pharmacological and therapeutic responses. Medications with demonstrable efficacy in the treatment of ADHD act mainly on these systems and have been shown to exert beneficial effects on aspects of cognition (such as response inhibition) in proof-of-concept studies. Translational approaches are shedding light on the precise neurochemical mechanisms. The body of evidence also implicates subtle structural and functional abnormalities of fronto-striatal-cerebellar circuitry in the manifestation of the disorder. Pharmaco-fMRI should be used to investigate the effects of ADHD medications on neural activity during cognitive tests and to compare different agents. There is also a need for baseline factors influencing clinical outcomes to be explored. It will be critical to examine whether baseline cognitive function and the presence of different genetic polymorphisms modulate treatment outcomes. Research in these areas may contribute to the development of improved treatment algorithms for children and adults with ADHD, to reduce harm (side effects and abuse potential) and maximize clinical benefits.

Nonpharmacological Treatment: Complementary and Alternative Medical Therapies (CAM)

In the United States, an estimated 2.5 million children take stimulants (Nissen, 2006). Despite the evidence of the stimulant treatments' efficacy, many parents seek alternatives for their children because of their concern about giving their child a controlled substance or because of the changes in personality some parents report. Some parents worry that their child will develop drug abuse problems after using stimulants for ADHD, despite evidence to the contrary (Dosreis et al., 2003; Volkow et al., 2008). Parents and the medical communities often express concern about the number of children prescribed these controlled substances and question the possibility of misdiagnosis or overdiagnosis of ADHD. Further studies are needed to better understand the long-term effects of stimulant medications on the developing brain and the neuronal imprinting effects of these medications.

The frequency of use in children who have ADHD of complementary therapies ranges between 12% and 64%. Complementary alternative medical therapies include nutritional changes (Feingold diet, food sensitivities and sugar avoidance, essential fatty acid), herbal and natural health products, electroencephalographic feedback, massage and yoga, meditation, vitamins and minerals, homeopathy, and environmental issues (for an extensive review, see Weber & Newmark, 2007).

A search on the Internet for ADHD treatment provides hundreds of links to over-the-counter products and treatments that are being enthusiastically advertised as a "definitive cure" for ADHD. Most of these products and treatments have little if any research documenting their safety let alone their efficacy.

There is a significant gap between our current knowledge of CAM for ADHD and their use frequency. There is a large use rate compared with a very low number of well-controlled, large, randomized trials. It is essential for researchers to include a comparison group when studying natural treatments for these conditions, which often are based on parental or teacher reports. Without a control group, it is impossible to determine whether the improvement seen in a trial is the result of the natural course of the symptoms. Effective CAM treatments for ADHD are highly desired by parents who seek alternatives to stimulant medications. Clinical trials are needed to determine the safety and efficacy of these natural therapeutic options.

SUMMARY

ADHD is the most common behavioral disorder of childhood. It is more complex than was thought previously and the underlying neurobiology is not well understood. However, key elements of the neurobiological bases of ADHD are starting to be uncovered, as new neuroimaging and molecular techniques allow research to aim at increasingly sophisticated goals. Studies have identified relevant genetic and environmental risk factors for ADHD, making genes and exposures to substances, necessary study variables for subsequent etiologic research. Brain studies are proving to be an essential transitional point of analysis, building the necessary link between disease susceptibility and clinical expression, as researchers discover how specific combinations of genes relate to various abnormalities in brain-based functions. A translational approach to ADHD decipherment is essential for putting together neuroscience and nosology. The recognition of biological bases of behavioral processes might reduce the stigma associated with mental disorders. Most importantly, insights from the neurobiology of ADHD may strengthen its validity as a clinical syndrome and improve diagnosis and treatment. A growing scientific movement considers that despite the high social impact, it is unclear if ADHD should be considered as a nosological entity or as a common variant of human behavior. Our understanding of "normal" human behavior would help to clarify those questions. A promising strategy for future research is to integrate information from multiple levels of analysis, by studying genetic, neurophysiological, and clinical processes across the developmental continuum. Most importantly, insights from the neurobiology of ADHD may strengthen its validity as a clinical syndrome, and improve diagnosis and treatment. Interesting questions regarding the validity of nonpharmacological medical interventions are increasingly arising from parents and care providers.

REFERENCES

Achenbach, T., & Edelbrock, C. (1983). *Manual for the child behavior checklist and revised child behavior profile.* Burlington, VT: University of Vermont, Department of Psychiatry.

Achenbach, T. M., & Ruffle, T. M. (2000). The child behavior checklist and related forms for assessing behavioral/emotional problems and competencies. *Pediatrics in Review, 21,* 265–271.

Acosta, M. T., Castellanos, F. X., Bolton, K. L., Balog, J. Z., Eagan, P., Nee, L., et al. (2008). Latent class subtyping of attention-deficit/hyperactivity disorder and comorbid conditions. *Journal of the American Academy of Child and Adolescent Psychiatry, 47,*797–807.

Acosta, M. T., Gioia, G. A., & Silva, A. J. (2006). Neurofibromatosis type 1: New insights into neurocognitive issues. *Current Neurology and Neuroscience Reports, 6,* 136–143.

Acosta, M. T., Arcos-Burgos, M., & Muenke, M. (2004). Attention deficit/hyperactivity disorder (ADHD): Complex phenotype, simple genotype? *Genetics in Medicine, 6,* 1–15.

Alexander, G. E., DeLong, M. R., & Strick, P. L. (1986). Parallel organization of functionally segregated circuits linking basal ganglia and cortex. *Annual Review of Neuroscience, 9,* 357–381.

American Psychiatry Association. (1987). *Diagnostic and statistical manual of mental disorders: DSM III-R* (pp. 85–98). Washington DC, American Psychiatry Association.

American Psychiatric Association. (1980). *Diagnostic and statistical manual of mental disorders* (3rd ed.). Washington, DC: Author.

American Psychiatric Association. (2000). *Diagnostic and statistical manual of mental disorders* (4th ed., text rev.). Washington, DC: Author.

Angold, A., Costello, E. J., & Erkanli, A. (1999). Comorbidity. *Journal of Child Psychology and Psychiatry, 40,* 57–87.

Antshel, K. M., & Waisbren, S. E. (2003). Developmental timing of exposure to elevated levels of phenylalanine is associated with ADHD symptom expression. *Journal of Abnormal Child Psychology, 31,* 565–574.

Arcos-Burgos, M., & Acosta, M. T. (2007). Tuning major gene variants conditioning human behavior: The anachronism of ADHD. *Current Opinion in Genetics and Development, 17,* 234–238.

Arcos-Burgos, M., Castellanos, F. X., Pineda, D., Lopera, F., Palacio, J. D., Palacio, L. G., et al. (2004). Attention-deficit/hyperactivity disorder in a population isolate: Linkage to loci at 4q13.2, 5q33.3, 11q22, and 17p11. *American Journal of Human Genetics, 75,* 998–1014.

Arnold, L. E. (1996). Sex differences in ADHD: Conference summary. *Journal of Abnormal Child Psychology, 24,* 555–569.

Arnold, L. E., Abikoff, H. B., Cantwell, D. P., Conners, C. K., Elliott, G., Greenhill, L. L., et al. (1997). National institute of mental health collaborative multimodal treatment study of children with ADHD (the MTA): Design challenges and choices. *Archives of General Psychiatry, 54,* 865–870.

August, G. J., Realmuto, G. M., Joyce, T., & Hektner, J. M. (1999). Persistence and desistance of oppositional defiant disorder in a community sample of children with ADHD. *Journal of the American Academy of Child and Adolescent Psychiatry, 38,* 1262–1270.

Bakker, S. C., van der Meulen, E. M., Buitelaar, J. K., Sandkuijl, L. A., Pauls, D. L., Monsuur, A. J., et al. (2003). A whole-genome scan in 164 Dutch sib pairs with attention-deficit/hyperactivity disorder: Suggestive evidence for linkage on chromosomes 7p and 15q. *American Journal of Human Genetics, 72,* 1251–1260.

Barkley, R. A. (1997). Behavioral inhibition, sustained attention, and executive functions: Constructing a unifying theory of ADHD. *Psychological Bulletin, 121,* 65–94.

Barkley, R. A., Edwards, G., Laneri, M., Fletcher, K., & Metevia, L. (2001). Executive functioning, temporal discounting, and sense of time in adolescents with attention-deficit/hyperactivity disorder (ADHD) and oppositional defiant disorder (ODD). *Journal of Abnormal Child Psychology, 29,* 541–556.

Barkley, R. A., Fischer, M., Smallish, L., & Fletcher, K. (2002). The persistence of attention-deficit/hyperactivity disorder into young adulthood as a function of reporting source and definition of disorder. *Journal of Abnormal Psychology, 111,* 279–289.

Becker, K., El-Faddagh, M., Schmidt, M. H., Esser, G., & Laucht, M. (2008). Interaction of dopamine transporter genotype with prenatal smoke exposure on ADHD symptoms. *Journal of Pediatrics, 152,* 263–269.

Biederman, J. (1998). Attention-deficit/hyperactivity disorder: A life-span perspective. *Journal of Clinical Psychiatry, 59*(Suppl. 7), 4–16.

Biederman, J. (2004). Impact of comorbidity in adults with attention-deficit/hyperactivity disorder. *Journal of Clinical Psychiatry, 65*(Suppl. 3), 3–7.

Biederman, J. (2005). Attention-deficit/hyperactivity disorder: A selective overview. *Biological Psychiatry, 57,* 1215–1220.

Biederman, J., Kwon, A., Aleardi, M., Chouinard, V. A., Marino, T., Cole, H., et al. (2005). Absence of gender effects on attention-deficit/hyperactivity disorder: Findings in nonreferred subjects. *American Journal of Psychiatry, 162,* 1083–1089.

Biederman, J., Mick, E., Faraone, S. V., Braaten, E., Doyle, A., Spencer, T., et al. (2002). Influence of gender on attention-deficit/hyperactivity disorder in children referred to a psychiatric clinic. *American Journal of Psychiatry, 159,* 36–42.

Biederman, J., & Spencer, T. J. (2008). Psychopharmacological interventions. *Child and Adolescent Psychiatric Clinics of North America, 17,* 439–458.

Bilder, R. M. (2008). Phenomics: Building scaffolds for biological hypotheses in the post-genomic era. *Biological Psychiatry, 63,* 439–440.

Brookes, K. J., Mill, J., Guindalini, C., Curran, S., Xu, X., Knight, J., et al. (2006). A common haplotype of the dopamine transporter gene associated with attention-deficit/hyperactivity disorder and interacting with maternal use of alcohol during pregnancy. *Archives of General Psychiatry, 63,* 74–81.

Brown, R. T., Freeman, W. S., Perrin, J. M., Stein, M. T., Amler, R. W., Feldman, H. M., et al. (2001). Prevalence and assessment of attention-deficit/hyperactivity disorder in primary care settings. *Pediatrics, 107,* E43.

Burke, J. D., Loeber, R., Lahey, B. B., & Rathouz, P. J. (2005). Developmental transitions among affective and behavioral disorders in adolescent boys. *Journal of Child Psychology and Psychiatry, 46,* 1200–1210.

Bush, G., Valera, E. M., & Seidman, L. J. (2005). Functional neuroimaging of attention-deficit/hyperactivity disorder: A review and suggested future directions. *Biological Psychiatry, 57,* 1273–1284.

Castellanos, F. X., Lee, P. P., Sharp, W., Jeffries, N. O., Greenstein, D. K., Clasen, L. S., et al. (2002). Developmental trajectories of brain volume abnormalities in children and adolescents with attention-deficit/hyperactivity disorder. *Journal of the American Medical Association, 288,* 1740–1748.

Castellanos, F. X., Margulies, D. S., Kelly, C., Uddin, L. Q., Ghaffari, M., Kirsch, A., et al. (2008). Cingulate-precuneus interactions: A new locus of dysfunction in adult attention-deficit/hyperactivity disorder. *Biological Psychiatry, 63,* 332–337.

Castellanos, F. X., & Tannock, R. (2002). Neuroscience of attention-deficit/hyperactivity disorder: The search for endophenotypes. *Nature Reviews: Neuroscience, 3,* 617–628.

Collett, B. R., Ohan, J. L., & Myers, K. M. (2003). Ten-year review of rating scales: Pt. V. Scales assessing attention-deficit/hyperactivity disorder. *Journal of the American Academy of Child and Adolescent Psychiatry, 42,* 1015–1037.

Conners, C. K., Wells, K. C., Parker, J. D., Sitarenios, G., Diamond, J. M., & Powell, J. W. (1997). A new self-report scale for assessment of adolescent psychopathology: Factor structure, reliability, validity, and diagnostic sensitivity. *Journal of Abnormal Child Psychology, 25,* 487–497.

Costello, E. J., Egger, H. L., & Angold, A. (2005). The developmental epidemiology of anxiety disorders: Phenomenology, prevalence, and comorbidity 6. *Child and Adolescent Psychiatric Clinics of North America, 14,* 631–648.

Curran, S., Rijsdijk, F., Martin, N., Marusic, K., Asherson, P., Taylor, E., et al. (2003). CHIP: Defining a dimension of the vulnerability to attention-deficit/hyperactivity disorder (ADHD) using sibling and individual data of children in a community-based sample. *American Journal of Medical Genetics, Part B: Neuropsychiatric Genetics, 119,* 86–97.

Dickstein, S. G., Bannon, K., Castellanos, F. X., & Milham, M. P. (2006). The neural correlates of attention-deficit/hyperactivity disorder: An ALE meta-analysis. *Journal of Child Psychology and Psychiatry, 47,* 1051–1062.

Ding, Y. C., Chi, H. C., Grady, D. L., Morishima, A., Kidd, J. R., Kidd, K. K., et al. (2002). Evidence of positive selection acting at the human dopamine receptor D4 gene locus. *Proceedings of the National Academy of Sciences, USA, 99,* 309–314.

Dosreis, S., Zito, J. M., Safer, D. J., Soeken, K. L., Mitchell, J. W., Jr., & Ellwood, L. C. (2003). Parental perceptions and satisfaction with stimulant medication for attention-deficit/hyperactivity disorder. *Journal of Developmental and Behavioral Pediatrics, 24,* 155–162.

Doyle, A. E., Faraone, S. V., Seidman, L. J., Willcutt, E. G., Nigg, J. T., Waldman, I. D., et al. (2005). Are endophenotypes based on measures of executive functions useful for molecular genetic studies of ADHD? *Journal of Child Psychology and Psychiatry, 46,* 774–803.

DuPaul, G. J., Ervin, R. A., Hook, C. L., & McGoey, K. E. (1998). Peer tutoring for children with attention-deficit/hyperactivity disorder: Effects on classroom behavior and academic performance. *Journal of Applied Behavior Analysis, 31,* 579–592.

Eiraldi, R. B., Power, T. J., & Nezu, C. M. (1997). Patterns of comorbidity associated with subtypes of attention-deficit/hyperactivity disorder among 6- to 12-year-old children. *Journal of the American Academy of Child and Adolescent Psychiatry, 36,* 503–514.

Ernst, M., Heishman, S. J., Spurgeon, L., & London, E. D. (2001). Smoking history and nicotine effects on cognitive performance. *Neuropsychopharmacology, 25,* 313–319.

Ezpeleta, L., de la Cruz, O. N., Domenech, J. M., Navarro, J. B., Losilla, J. M., & Judez, J. (1997). Diagnostic agreement between clinicians and the Diagnostic Interview for Children and Adolescents (DICA-R): In an outpatient sample. *Journal of Child Psychology and Psychiatry, 38,* 431–440.

Faraone, S. V., & Biederman, J. (2005). What is the prevalence of adult ADHD? Results of a population screen of 966 adults. *Journal of Attention Disorders, 9,* 384–391.

Faraone, S. V., Biederman, J., Mennin, D., Gershon, J., & Tsuang, M. T. (1996). A prospective four-year follow-up study of children at risk for ADHD: Psychiatric, neuropsychological, and psychosocial outcome. *Journal of the American Academy of Child and Adolescent Psychiatry, 35,* 1449–1459.

Faraone, S. V., Biederman, J., Mick, E., Williamson, S., Wilens, T., Spencer, T., et al. (2000). Family study of girls with attention-deficit/hyperactivity disorder. *American Journal of Psychiatry, 157,* 1077–1083.

Faraone, S. V., Biederman, J., & Monuteaux, M. C. (2000). Attention-deficit disorder and conduct disorder in girls: Evidence for a familial subtype. *Biological Psychiatry, 48,* 21–29.

Faraone, S. V., Biederman, J., & Monuteaux, M. C. (2001). Attention deficit hyperactivity disorder with bipolar disorder in girls: Further evidence for a familial subtype? *Journal of Affective Disorders, 64,* 19–26.

Faraone, S. V., Biederman, J., Spencer, T., Wilens, T., Seidman, L. J., Mick, E., et al. (2000). Attention-deficit/hyperactivity disorder in adults: An overview. *Biological Psychiatry, 48,* 9–20.

Faraone, S. V., Perlis, R. H., Doyle, A. E., Smoller, J. W., Goralnick, J. J., Holmgren, M. A., et al. (2005). Molecular genetics of attention-deficit/hyperactivity disorder. *Biological Psychiatry, 57,* 1313–1323.

Faraone, S. V., Sergeant, J., Gillberg, C., & Biederman, J. (2003). The worldwide prevalence of ADHD: Is it an American condition? *World Psychiatry, 2,* 104–113.

Farzin, F., Perry, H., Hessl, D., Loesch, D., Cohen, J., Bacalman, S., et al. (2006). Autism spectrum disorders and attention-deficit/hyperactivity disorder in boys with the fragile X premutation. *Journal of Developmental and Behavioral Pediatrics, 27,* S137–S144.

Fisher, S. E., Francks, C., McCracken, J. T., McGough, J. J., Marlow, A. J., MacPhie, I. L., et al. (2002). A genomewide scan for loci involved in attention-deficit/hyperactivity disorder. *American Journal of Human Genetics, 70,* 1183–1196.

Gau, S. S., Shang, C. Y., Liu, S. K., Lin, C. H., Swanson, J. M., Liu, Y. C., et al. (2008). Psychometric properties of the Chinese version of the Swanson, Nolan, and Pelham, version IV Scale: Parent form. *International Journal of Methods in Psychiatric Research, 17,* 35–44.

Gaub, M., & Carlson, C. L. (1997a). Behavioral characteristics of DSM-IV ADHD subtypes in a school-based population. *Journal of Abnormal Child Psychology, 25,* 103–111.

Gaub, M., & Carlson, C. L. (1997b). Gender differences in ADHD: A meta-analysis and critical review. *Journal of the American Academy of Child and Adolescent Psychiatry, 36,* 1036–1045.

Giedd, J. N., Clasen, L. S., Wallace, G. L., Lenroot, R. K., Lerch, J. P., Wells, E. M., et al. (2007). XXY (Klinefelter syndrome): A pediatric quantitative brain magnetic resonance imaging case-control study. *Pediatrics, 119,* e232–e240.

Gioia, G. A., Isquith, P. K., Kenworthy, L., & Barton, R. M. (2002). Profiles of everyday executive function in acquired and developmental disorders. *Child Neuropsychology, 8,* 121–137.

Gioia, G. A., Isquith, P. K., Retzlaff, P. D., & Espy, K. A. (2002). Confirmatory factor analysis of the Behavior Rating Inventory of Executive Function (BRIEF) in a clinical sample. *Child Neuropsychology, 8,* 249–257.

Greene, R. W., Biederman, J., Faraone, S. V., Monuteaux, M. C., Mick, E., DuPre, E. P., et al. (2001). Social impairment in girls with ADHD: Patterns, gender comparisons, and correlates. *Journal of the American Academy of Child and Adolescent Psychiatry, 40,* 704–710.

Hartung, C. M., Willcutt, E. G., Lahey, B. B., Pelham, W. E., Loney, J., Stein, M. A., et al. (2002). Sex differences in young children who meet criteria for attention-deficit/hyperactivity disorder. *Journal of Clinical Child and Adolescent Psychology, 31,* 453–464.

Hay, D. A., Bennett, K. S., Levy, F., Sergeant, J., & Swanson, J. (2007). A twin study of attention-deficit/hyperactivity disorder dimensions rated by the strengths and weaknesses of ADHD-symptoms and normal-behavior (SWAN) scale. *Biological Psychiatry, 61,* 700–705.

Hesslinger, B., Thiel, T., van Tebartz, E. L., Hennig, J., & Ebert, D. (2001). Attention-deficit disorder in adults with or without hyperactivity: Where is the difference? A study in humans using short echo (1)H-magnetic resonance spectroscopy. *Neuroscience Letters, 304,* 117–119.

Hill, S. Y., Lowers, L., Locke-Wellman, J., & Shen, S. A. (2000). Maternal smoking and drinking during pregnancy and the risk for child and adolescent psychiatric disorders. *Journal of Studies on Alcohol, 61,* 661–668.

Hinshaw, S. P. (2002). Preadolescent girls with attention-deficit/hyperactivity disorder: Pt. I. Background characteristics, comorbidity, cognitive and social functioning, and parenting practices. *Journal of Consulting and Clinical Psychology, 70,* 1086–1098.

Hinshaw, S. P., Carte, E. T., Sami, N., Treuting, J. J., & Zupan, B. A. (2002). Preadolescent girls with attention-deficit/hyperactivity disorder: Pt. II. Neuropsychological performance in relation to subtypes and individual classification. *Journal of Consulting and Clinical Psychology, 70,* 1099–1111.

Houghton, S., Douglas, G., West, J., Whiting, K., Wall, M., Langsford, S., et al. (1999). Differential patterns of executive function in children with attention-deficit/hyperactivity disorder according to gender and subtype. *Journal of Child Neurology, 14,* 801–805.

Hudziak, J. J., Heath, A. C., Madden, P. F., Reich, W., Bucholz, K. K., Slutske, W., et al. (1998). Latent class and factor analysis of DSM-IV ADHD: A twin study of female adolescents. *Journal of the American Academy of Child and Adolescent Psychiatry, 37,* 848–857.

Jain, M., Palacio, L. G., Castellanos, F. X., Palacio, J. D., Pineda, D., Restrepo, M. I., et al. (2007). Attention-deficit/hyperactivity disorder and comorbid disruptive behavior disorders: Evidence of pleiotropy and new susceptibility loci. *Biological Psychiatry, 61,* 1329–1339.

Jensen, P. S., Arnold, L. E., Swanson, J. M., Vitiello, B., Abikoff, H. B., Greenhill, L. L., et al. (2007). 3-year follow-up of the NIMH MTA study. *Journal of the American Academy of Child and Adolescent Psychiatry, 46,* 989–1002.

Kahn, R. S., Khoury, J., Nichols, W. C., & Lanphear, B. P. (2003). Role of dopamine transporter genotype and maternal prenatal smoking in childhood hyperactive-impulsive, inattentive, and oppositional behaviors. *Journal of Pediatrics, 143,* 104–110.

Keller, M. C., & Miller, G. (2006). Resolving the paradox of common, harmful, heritable mental disorders: Which evolutionary genetic models work best? *Behavioral Brain Science, 29,* 385–404.

Kendler, K. S. (1996). Major depression and generalised anxiety disorder. Same genes, (partly) different environments: Revisited. *British Journal of Psychiatry, 30* (Suppl.), 68–75.

Kessler, R. C., Adler, L. A., Barkley, R., Biederman, J., Conners, C. K., Faraone, S. V., et al. (2005). Patterns and predictors of attention-deficit/hyperactivity disorder persistence into adulthood: Results from the national comorbidity survey replication. *Biological Psychiatry, 57,* 1442–1451.

Kieling, C., Goncalves, R. R., Tannock, R., & Castellanos, F. X. (2008). Neurobiology of attention-deficit/hyperactivity disorder. *Child and Adolescent Psychiatric Clinics of North America, 17,* 285–307.

Knopik, V. S., Sparrow, E. P., Madden, P. A., Bucholz, K. K., Hudziak, J. J., Reich, W., et al. (2005). Contributions of parental alcoholism, prenatal substance exposure, and genetic transmission to child ADHD risk: A female twin study. *Psychological Medicine, 35,* 625–635.

Kratochvil, C. J., Newcorn, J. H., Arnold, L. E., Duesenberg, D., Emslie, G. J., Quintana, H., et al. (2005). Atomoxetine alone or combined with fluoxetine for treating ADHD with comorbid depressive or anxiety symptoms. *Journal of the American Academy of Child and Adolescent Psychiatry, 44,* 915–924.

Lahey, B. B., Hartung, C. M., Loney, J., Pelham, W. E., Chronis, A. M., & Lee, S. S. (2007). Are there sex differences in the predictive validity of DSM-IV ADHD among younger children? *Journal of Clinical Child and Adolescent Psychology, 36,* 113–126.

Lahey, B. B., Pelham, W. E., Loney, J., Kipp, H., Ehrhardt, A., Lee, S. S., et al. (2004). Three-year predictive validity of DSM-IV attention-deficit/hyperactivity disorder in children diagnosed at 4–6 years of age. *American Journal of Psychiatry, 161,* 2014–2020.

Lahey, B. B., Schaughency, E. A., Hynd, G. W., Carlson, C. L., & Nieves, N. (1987). Attention deficit disorder with and without hyperactivity: Comparison of behavioral characteristics of clinic-referred children. *Journal of the American Academy of Child and Adolescent Psychiatry, 26,* 718–723.

Lavigne, J. V., Cicchetti, C., Gibbons, R. D., Binns, H. J., Larsen, L., & DeVito, C. (2001). Oppositional defiant disorder with onset in preschool years: Longitudinal stability and pathways to other disorders. *Journal of the American Academy of Child and Adolescent Psychiatry, 40,* 1393–1400.

Levy, F., Hay, D. A., McStephen, M., Wood, C., & Waldman, I. (1997). Attention-deficit/hyperactivity disorder: A category or a continuum? Genetic analysis of a large-scale twin study. *Journal of the American Academy of Child and Adolescent Psychiatry, 36,* 737–744.

Leyfer, O. T., Woodruff-Borden, J., Klein-Tasman, B. P., Fricke, J. S., & Mervis, C. B. (2006). Prevalence of psychiatric disorders in 4 to 16-year-olds with Williams syndrome. *American Journal of Medical Genetics: Part B, Neuropsychiatric Genetics, 141,* 615–622.

Linnet, K. M., Dalsgaard, S., Obel, C., Wisborg, K., Henriksen, T. B., Rodriguez, A., et al. (2003). Maternal lifestyle factors in pregnancy risk of attention-deficit/hyperactivity disorder and associated behaviors: Review of the current evidence. *American Journal of Psychiatry, 160,* 1028–1040.

Loeber, R., Green, S. M., Lahey, B. B., & Stouthamer-Loeber, M. (1991). Differences and similarities between children, mothers, and teachers as informants on disruptive child behavior. *Journal of Abnormal Child Psychology, 19,* 75–95.

Loney, J., & Milich, R. (1982). Hyperactivity, inattention and aggression in clinical practice. In D. Routh (Ed.), *Advances in behavioral pediatrics.* New York: Plenum Press.

Lopera, F., Palacio, L. G., Jimenez, I., Villegas, P., Puerta, I. C., Pineda, D., et al. (1999). Discrimination between genetic factors in attention deficit. *Revue Neurologique, 28,* 660–664.

MacMaster, F. P., Carrey, N., Sparkes, S., & Kusumakar, V. (2003). Proton spectroscopy in medication-free pediatric attention-deficit/hyperactivity disorder. *Biological Psychiatry, 53,* 184–187.

Magidson, J., & Vermunt, J. K. (2003). Latent class analysis . In D. Kaplan (Ed.), *Handbook of quantitative methodology for the social sciences* (Chapter 10 pp. 175–198). New burry Park, CA, Califorina: Sage Publications.

Maher, B. S., Marazita, M. L., Moss, H. B., & Vanyukov, M. M. (1999). Segregation analysis of attention-deficit/hyperactivity disorder. *American Journal of Medical Genetica, 88,* 71–78.

Mick, E., Biederman, J., Faraone, S. V., Sayer, J., & Kleinman, S. (2002). Case-control study of attention-deficit/hyperactivity disorder and maternal smoking, alcohol use, and drug use during pregnancy. *Journal of the American Academy of Child and Adolescent Psychiatry, 41,* 378–385.

Moore, C. M., Biederman, J., Wozniak, J., Mick, E., Aleardi, M., Wardrop, M., et al. (2006). Differences in brain chemistry in children and adolescents with attention-deficit/hyperactivity disorder with and without comorbid bipolar disorder: A proton magnetic resonance spectroscopy study. *American Journal of Psychiatry, 163,* 316–318.

Nash, K., Rovet, J., Greenbaum, R., Fantus, E., Nulman, I., & Koren, G. (2006). Identifying the behavioural phenotype in fetal alcohol spectrum disorder: Sensitivity, specificity and screening potential. *Archives of Women's Mental Health, 9,* 181–186.

Neuman, R. J., Heath, A., Reich, W., Bucholz, K. K., Madden, P. A. F., Sun, L., et al. (2001). Latent class analysis of ADHD and comorbid symptoms in a population sample of adolescent female twins. *Journal of Child Psychology and Psychiatry, 42,* 933–942.

Neuman, R. J., Lobos, E., Reich, W., Henderson, C. A., Sun, L. W., & Todd, R. D. (2007). Prenatal smoking exposure and dopaminergic genotypes interact to cause a severe ADHD subtype. *Biological Psychiatry, 61,* 1320–1328.

Nissen, S. E. (2006). ADHD drugs and cardiovascular risk. *New England Journal of Medicine, 354,* 1445–1448.

Ogdie, M. N., Bakker, S. C., Fisher, S. E., Francks, C., Yang, M. H., Cantor, R. M., et al. (2006). Pooled genome-wide linkage data on 424 ADHD ASPs suggests genetic heterogeneity and a common risk locus at 5p13. *Molecular Psychiatry, 11,* 5–8.

Ogdie, M. N., MacPhie, I. L., Minassian, S. L., Yang, M., Fisher, S. E., Francks, C., et al. (2003). A genomewide scan for attention-deficit/ hyperactivity disorder in an extended sample: Suggestive linkage on 17p11. *American Journal of Human Genetics, 72,* 1268–1279.

O'Malley, K. D., & Nanson, J. (2002). Clinical implications of a link between fetal alcohol spectrum disorder and attention-deficit/hyperactivity disorder. *Canadian Journal of Psychiatry, 47,* 349–354.

Palacio, J. D., Castellanos, F. X., Pineda, D. A., Lopera, F., rcos-Burgos, M., Quiroz, Y. T., et al. (2004). Attention-deficit/ hyperactivity disorder and comorbidities in 18 Paisa Colombian multi-generational families. *Journal of the American Academy of Child and Adolescent Psychiatry, 43,* 1506–1515.

Pelham, W. E., Foster, E. M., & Robb, J. A. (2007). The economic impact of attention-deficit/hyperactivity disorder in children and adolescents. *Journal of Pediatric Psychology, 32,* 711–727.

Pliszka, S. R. (2000). Patterns of psychiatric comorbidity with attention-deficit/hyperactivity disorder. *Child and Adolescent Psychiatric Clinics of North America, 9,* 525–540.

Pliszka, S. R. (2007). Pharmacologic treatment of attention-deficit/ hyperactivity disorder: Efficacy, safety and mechanisms of action. *Neuropsychology Review, 17,* 61–72.

Pliszka, S. R., McCracken, J. T., & Maas, J. W. (1996). Catecholamines in attention-deficit/hyperactivity disorder: Current perspectives. *Journal of the American Academy of Child and Adolescent Psychiatry, 35,* 264–272.

Rasmussen, E. R., Neuman, R. J., Heath, A. C., Levy, F., Hay, D. A., & Todd, R. D. (2002). Replication of the latent class structure of attention-deficit/hyperactivity disorder (ADHD) subtypes in a sample of Australian twins. *Journal of Child Psychology and Psychiatry, 43,* 1018–1028.

Reynolds, C. R., & Kamphaus, R. W. (1992). *Behavior assessment system for children (BASC).* Cicle Pines, MN: American Guidance Service.

Rohde, L. A., Barbosa, G., Polanczyk, G., Eizirik, M., Rasmussen, E. R., Neuman, R. J., et al. (2001). Factor and latent class analysis of DSM-IVADHD symptoms in a school sample of Brazilian adolescents. *Journal of the American Academy of Child and Adolescent Psychiatry, 40,* 711–718.

Rowland, A. S., Lesesne, C. A., & Abramowitz, A. J. (2002). The epide-miology of attention-deficit/hyperactivity disorder (ADHD): A pub-lic health view. *Mental Retardation and Developmental Disabilities Research Reviews, 8,* 162–170.

Rowland, A. S., Umbach, D. M., Catoe, K. E., Stallone, L., Long, S., Rabiner, D., et al. (2001). Studying the epidemiology of attention-deficit/hyperactivity disorder: Screening method and pilot results. *Canadian Journal of Psychiatry, 46,* 931–940.

Rubia, K., Overmeyer, S., Taylor, E., Brammer, M., Williams, S. C., Simmons, A., et al. (1999). Hypofrontality in attention-deficit/ hyperactivity disorder during higher-order motor control: A study with functional MRI. *American Journal of Psychiatry, 156,* 891–896.

Rucklidge, J. J., & Tannock, R. (2001). Psychiatric, psychosocial, and cognitive functioning of female adolescents with ADHD. *Journal of the American Academy of Child and Adolescent Psychiatry, 40,* 530–540.

Russell, H. F., Wallis, D., Mazzocco, M. M., Moshang, T., Zackai, E., Zinn, A. R., et al. (2006). Increased prevalence of ADHD in Turner syndrome with no evidence of imprinting effects. *Journal of Pediatric Psychology, 31,* 945–955.

Sanders, M., Arduca, Y., Karamitsios, M., Boots, M., & Vance, A. (2005). Characteristics of internalizing and externalizing disorders in medication-naive, clinically referred children with attention-deficit/hyperactivity disorder, combined type and dysthymic disorder. *Australian and New Zealand Journal of Psychiatry, 39,* 359–365.

Schwab-Stone, M. E., Shaffer, D., Dulcan, M. K., Jensen, P. S., Fisher, P., Bird, H. R., et al. (1996). Criterion validity of the NIMH Diagnostic Interview Schedule for Children Version 2.3 (DISC-2.3). *Journal of the American Academy of Child and Adolescent Psychiatry, 35,* 878–888.

Seidman, L. J., Valera, E. M., & Makris, N. (2005). Structural brain imaging of attention-deficit/hyperactivity disorder. *Biological Psychiatry, 57,* 1263–1272.

Shaffer, D., Fisher, P., Dulcan, M. K., Davies, M., Piacentini, J., Schwab-Stone, M. E., et al. (1996). The NIMH Diagnostic Interview Schedule for Children Version 2.3 (DISC-2.3): Description, acceptability, prev-alence rates, and performance in the MECA study: Methods for the epidemiology of child and adolescent mental disorders study. *Journal of the American Academy of Child and Adolescent Psychiatry, 35,* 865–877.

Shaw, P., Eckstrand, K., Sharp, W., Blumenthal, J., Lerch, J. P., Greenstein, D., et al. (2007). Attention-deficit/hyperactivity disorder is characterized by a delay in cortical maturation. *Proceedings of the National Academy of Sciences, USA, 104,* 19649–19654.

Shekim, W. O., Asarnow, R. F., Hess, E., Zaucha, K., & Wheeler, N. (1990). A clinical and demographic profile of a sample of adults with attention-deficit/hyperactivity disorder, residual state. *Comprehensive Psychiatry, 31,* 416–425.

Simpson, J. L., de la Cruz, C. F., Swerdloff, R. S., Samango-Sprouse, C., Skakkebaek, N. E., Graham, J. M., Jr., et al. (2003). Klinefelter syn-drome: Expanding the phenotype and identifying new research direc-tions. *Genetics in Medicine, 5,* 460–468.

Smith, A. C., Dykens, E., & Greenberg, F. (1998). Behavioral phenotype of Smith-Magenis syndrome (del 17p11.2). *American Journal of Medical Genetics, 81,* 179–185.

Sonuga-Barke, E. J. (2003). The dual pathway model of AD/HD: An elaboration of neuro-developmental characteristics. *Neuroscience and Biobehavior Reviews, 27,* 593–604.

Spencer, T. J., Biederman, J., Madras, B. K., Faraone, S. V., Dougherty, D. D., Bonab, A. A., et al. (2005). In vivo neuroreceptor imaging in attention-deficit/hyperactivity disorder: A focus on the dopamine transporter. *Biological Psychiatry, 57,* 1293–1300.

Spencer, T. J., Biederman, J., Wilens, T. E., & Faraone, S. V. (2002). Overview and neurobiology of attention-deficit/hyperactivity disorder. *Journal of Clinical Psychiatry, 63*(Suppl. 12), 3–9.

Sprich, S., Biederman, J., Crawford, M. H., Mundy, E., & Faraone, S. V. (2000). Adoptive and biological families of children and adolescents with ADHD. *Journal of the American Academy of Child and Adolescent Psychiatry, 39,* 1432–1437.

Stevenson, J. (1992). Evidence for a genetic etiology in hyperactivity in children. *Behavior Genetics, 22,* 337–344.

Sullivan, K., Hatton, D., Hammer, J., Sideris, J., Hooper, S., Ornstein, P., et al. (2006). ADHD symptoms in children with FXS. *American Journal of Medical Genetics, Part A, 140,* 2275–2288.

Sun, L., Jin, Z., Zang, Y. F., Zeng, Y. W., Liu, G., Li, Y., et al. (2005). Differences between attention-deficit disorder with and without hyperactivity: A 1H-magnetic resonance spectroscopy study. *Brain Development, 27,* 340–344.

Swanson, J. M., & Castellanos, F. X. (1998). Diagnosis and treatment of attention deficit hyperactivity disorder (ADHD). Biological bases of

ADHD: Neuroanatomy, genetics, and pathophysiology. In *NIH consensus development conference*, NIH consensus online. Nov 16–18; 16(2), 1–37

Swanson, J. M., Kinsbourne, M., Nigg, J., Lanphear, B., Stefanatos, G. A., Volkow, N., et al. (2007). Etiologic subtypes of attention-deficit/hyperactivity disorder: Brain imaging, molecular genetic and environmental factors and the dopamine hypothesis. *Neuropsychology Review, 17,* 39–59.

Swanson, J. M., Kraemer, H. C., Hinshaw, S. P., Arnold, L. E., Conners, C. K., Abikoff, H. B., et al. (2001). Clinical relevance of the primary findings of the MTA: Success rates based on severity of ADHD and ODD symptoms at the end of treatment. *Journal of the American Academy of Child and Adolescent Psychiatry, 40,* 168–179.

Thapar, A., van den Bree, B. M., Fowler, T., Langley, K., & Whittinger, N. (2006). Predictors of antisocial behaviour in children with attention-deficit/hyperactivity disorder. *European Child and Adolescent Psychiatry, 15,* 118–125.

The MTA Study. (1999). A 14-month randomized clinical trial of treatment strategies for attention-deficit/hyperactivity disorder. The MTA cooperative group: Multimodal treatment study of children with ADHD. *Archives of General Psychiatry, 56,* 1073–1086.

Todd, R. D. (1992). Neural development is regulated by classical neurotransmitters: Dopamine D2 receptor stimulation enhances neurite outgrowth. *Biological Psychiatry, 31,* 794–807.

Todd, R. D., Rasmussen, E. R., Neuman, R. J., Reich, W., Hudziak, J. J., Bucholz, K. K., et al. (2001). Familiality and heritability of subtypes of attention-deficit/hyperactivity disorder in a population sample of adolescent female twins. *American Journal of Psychiatry, 158,* 1891–1898.

Valera, E. M., Faraone, S. V., Biederman, J., Poldrack, R. A., & Seidman, L. J. (2005). Functional neuroanatomy of working memory in adults with attention-deficit/hyperactivity disorder. *Biological Psychiatry, 57,* 439–447.

Vance, A., Sanders, M., & Arduca, Y. (2005). Dysthymic disorder contributes to oppositional defiant behaviour in children with attention-deficit/hyperactivity disorder, combined type (ADHD-CT). *Journal of Affective Disorders, 86,* 329–333.

Volk, H. E., Henderson, C., Neuman, R. J., & Todd, R. D. (2006). Validation of population-based ADHD subtypes and identification of three clinically impaired subtypes. *American Journal of Medical Genetics, Part B: Neuropsychiatric Genetics, 141,* 312–318.

Volk, H. E., Neuman, R. J., & Todd, R. D. (2005). A systematic evaluation of ADHD and comorbid psychopathology in a population-based twin sample. *Journal of the American Academy of Child and Adolescent Psychiatry, 44,* 768–775.

Volkow, N. D., Wang, G., Fowler, J. S., Logan, J., Gerasimov, M., Maynard, L., et al. (2001). Therapeutic doses of oral methylphenidate significantly increase extracellular dopamine in the human brain. *Journal of Neuroscience, 21,* RC121.

Volkow, N. D., Wang, G. J., Telang, F., Fowler, J. S., Logan, J., Childress, A. R., et al. (2008). Dopamine increases in striatum do not elicit craving in cocaine abusers unless they are coupled with cocaine cues. *Neuroimage, 39,* 1266–1273.

Weber, W., & Newmark, S. (2007). Complementary and alternative medical therapies for attention-deficit/hyperactivity disorder and autism. *Pediatric Clinics of North America, 54,* 983–1006.

Weiss, M., Murray, C., & Weiss, G. (2002). Adults with attention-deficit/hyperactivity disorder: Current concepts. *Journal of Psychiatric Practice, 8,* 99–111.

Wigal, S. B., Gupta, S., Guinta, D., & Swanson, J. M. (1998). Reliability and validity of the SKAMP rating scale in a laboratory school setting. *Psychopharmacology Bulletin, 34,* 47–53.

Wilens, T. E., Kwon, A., Tanguay, S., Chase, R., Moore, H., Faraone, S. V., et al. (2005). Characteristics of adults with attention-deficit/hyperactivity disorder plus substance use disorder: The role of psychiatric comorbidity. *American Journal of Addictions, 14,* 319–327.

Willcutt, E. G., Doyle, A. E., Nigg, J. T., Faraone, S. V., & Pennington, B. F. (2005). Validity of the executive function theory of attention-deficit/hyperactivity disorder: A meta-analytic review. *Biological Psychiatry, 57,* 1336–1346.

Willcutt, E. G., Pennington, B. F., Smith, S. D., Cardon, L. R., Gayan, J., Knopik, V. S., et al. (2002). Quantitative trait locus for reading disability on chromosome 6p is pleiotropic for attention-deficit/hyperactivity disorder. *American Journal of Medical Genetics, 114,* 260–268.

Wolraich, M. L., Lambert, W., Doffing, M. A., Bickman, L., Simmons, T., & Worley, K. (2003). Psychometric properties of the Vanderbilt ADHD diagnostic parent rating scale in a referred population. *Journal of Pediatric Psychology, 28,* 559–567.

Wortis, J. (1988). Struwwelpeter Heinrich Hoffmann (1809–1894). *Biological Psychiatry, 24,* 615–618.

Zametkin, A. J., & Rapoport, J. L. (1987). Neurobiology of attention deficit disorder with hyperactivity: Where have we come in 50 years? *Journal of the American Academy of Child and Adolescent Psychiatry, 26,* 676–686.

Chapter 54

Schizophrenia

CAMERON S. CARTER, MICHAEL MINZENBERG, AND JONG H. Y. YOON

Schizophrenia is a serious, disabling lifelong mental disorder that affects men and women equally and 1% of the population worldwide. It is characterized by a range of striking disturbances in many aspects of mental life and behavior, including hallucinations and delusions, diminished emotional expression and motivation, cognitive deficits, and behavioral disorganization.

Schizophrenia has its onset typically during adolescence or early adulthood. Historically, a substantial majority of people with the illness have been unable to maintain independent living or gainful employment for any significant period of time in their lives after the onset of illness. Once a chronic course is established, patients generally suffer relapsing periods of overt psychotic symptoms, characterized by disruptions in the capacity to properly perceive the environment, maintain coherent thinking processes, or derive meaning in a manner that can properly guide thoughts, plans, and behaviors. During quiescent periods of the illness, patients continue to have cognitive and social disturbances that sharply limit their capacity for true recovery and reintegration into the community. Schizophrenia also has profound disruptive and demoralizing effects on the families who often struggle to help the affected individual cope with the illness.

Overall, the public health impact of schizophrenia is staggering. While the prevalence of the illness is approximately 1%, patients with schizophrenia occupy 25% of all inpatient hospital beds (Terkelsen & Menikoff, 1995) and represent 50% of all inpatient admissions (Geller, 1992). The total cost of the illness is estimated to be $44.9 billion in the United States for the year 1994 (Murray & Lopez, 1996). Schizophrenia is one of the top 10 causes of disability-adjusted life years (Murray & Lopez, 1996), representing 2.3% of the total burden of disease in developed countries (the fourth leading cause among persons ages 15 to 44) and 0.8% in developing countries (U.S. Institute of Medicine, 2001). Patients with schizophrenia are also disproportionately found among the chronically homeless, those who undergo the "revolving door" of repeated brief

hospitalizations with premature discharge and insufficient postdischarge care, and those in jails and prisons, suggesting a pervasive failure in contemporary society to adequately meet the needs of these patients.

OVERVIEW

Haslam, and independently Pinel, both in the early nineteenth century, wrote the earliest modern descriptions of individuals afflicted with the illness that we now recognize as schizophrenia. Later in the eighteenth century, Morel first used the term *dementia praecox* to describe schizophrenia as a premature dementia, emphasizing the early onset and progressive clinical decline. Kahlbaum categorized the symptoms and derived subtypes of schizophrenia, such as catatonia, and hebetic paraphrenia, later termed *hebephrenia* by Hecker. The German psychiatrist Kraepelin adopted the term *dementia praecox* and provided a detailed account of the clinical course and outcome of patients. He noted that the age of onset, family history, premorbid personality, and a deteriorating clinical course were useful in the distinction of dementia praecox from manic-depressive illness. Kraepein also emphasized hereditary factors, obstetrical complications, and physical abnormalities as potentially important etiological factors in the illness and indicated that clinical improvement in these patients should be considered temporary, as residual symptoms were ubiquitous, and relapse inevitable. In his later writings, however, came to acknowledge that some patients experienced a relatively later onset of illness and/or a significant measure of recovery (Adityanjee, Aderibigbe, Theodoridis, & Vieweg, 1999).

Eugen Bleuler, a Swiss psychiatrist introduced the term *schizophrenia*. He criticized the notion of dementia praecox, which he considered a heterogeneous group of disorders. Bleuler defined the primary features of schizophrenia as the "four As": (1) looseness of associations, (2) affective flattening, (3) autism, and (4) ambivalence. This is essentially an emphasis on cognition, apparent in the link between the term *schizophrenia*, or split mind, and the formal thought disorder manifest in disturbed associations. Importantly, he also recognized disturbances in emotion and motivation that were largely neglected by earlier theorists.

The other European figure whose work helped shape modern notions of schizophrenia is Schneider who outlined a set of "first-rank" symptoms that included many of the most extreme disruptions of reality, such as thought insertion and withdrawal, thought broadcasting, hallucinated voices in argument with each other, and some other more severe delusional and passivity experiences that patients with schizophrenia reported. This represented one of the first attempts at establishing a discrete criteria set for the diagnosis. This also had the effect of narrowing the diagnosis of schizophrenia, as the first-rank symptoms were clearly pathological, in comparison to some of Bleuler's symptoms, which appeared to be more continuously distributed in the general population. The ideas of Kraepelin, Bleuler, and Schneider remain highly influential to this day and helped shape the construct of schizophrenia as defined in the *DSM*, the diagnostic system of the American Psychiatric Association.

Symptoms

Schizophrenia is operationally defined by a large set of signs and symptoms cutting across diverse domains of behavior and mental processes. While there is still active debate on the relative merits and validity of the various symptom classification systems that have been proposed, in this chapter, we mostly rely on a scheme that segregates clinical findings into positive, negative, and disorganized symptoms or syndromes. This system is simple and has received empirical validation in factor analytic studies (Bilder, Mukherjee, Rieder, & Pandurangi, 1985; Liddle, 1987). The term *positive symptom* refers to the *presence* of abnormal mental processes. Positive symptoms include hallucinations, which may be experienced in any sensory modality and delusions, or false beliefs. Negative symptom refers to the *absence* of normal mental function, such as reduced emotional expression, decreased interest in social activities, and reduced motivation. The disorganized category refers to disturbances in language production (or thought disorder), gross distractibility, and odd or unusual behavior.

Cognitive Deficits

Kraeplin and Bleuler both emphasized cognitive impairments as a core aspect of this illness. With the emergence of modern cognitive science, it has become increasingly clear that patients with schizophrenia show a range of impaired higher cognitive functions including problems with attention, long-term memory, working memory, abstraction and planning, and language comprehension and production. These cognitive deficits present significant barriers to maintaining occupational and everyday function. Cognitive deficits may be the best predictor of functionality over and above other symptom clusters (Green, 1996).

Attention and memory problems are common in schizophrenia. Working memory, the capacity to maintain information on line to rapidly guide thoughts and behavior, has been proposed as a fundamental cognitive deficit in schizophrenia. These theories suggest that many of the clinical features of schizophrenia are manifestations of working memory deficits. For example, thought disorder can be conceived as the inability to maintain a communication goal in mind. Problems with multitasking, distractibility, and planning may also result from working memory problems. Long-term memory is also an important disability in schizophrenia. Memory problems are not progressive or as profound as in amnestic syndromes such as Alzheimer's disease and qualitatively resemble those seen in patients with frontal lobe injury rather than dementias resulting from injury to the medial temporal lobe. Common and clinically relevant manifestations of this impairment include forgotten appointments or medication directions, which may directly impact the treatment and stability of the patient.

DIAGNOSING SCHIZOPHRENIA

The *DSM-IV-TR* defines schizophrenia as an illness characterized by positive, negative, and/or disorganized symptoms that must be present for a significant portion of time during at least 1 month (unless the symptoms are successfully treated). These Criterion A symptoms are referred to as active-phase symptoms. There must be impairment in psychosocial function (work, interpersonal relationships, or self-care). To receive a diagnosis, some continuous signs of the disturbance must be evident for at least 6 months; this must include at least 1 month of active-phase symptoms but may include periods of prodromal or residual symptoms.

At the present time, the diagnostic process rests solely on the history of illness and a thorough mental status examination. No reliable laboratory tests have yet been established for this illness. The major task in differential diagnosis is to distinguish schizophrenia from a range of other psychiatric disorders that may also involve psychotic symptoms. These include schizoaffective disorder; major mood disorders that can present with psychotic features, such as major depression and acute mania among bipolar affective disorder type I patients; delusional disorder; and personality disorders. To rule out the major mood disorders or schizoaffective disorder, the active phase of psychosis should occur in the absence of an acute mood disorder episode, or alternatively the mood episodes should be relatively brief in relation to the total duration of the psychotic episode. Most mood disorder patients also maintain or recover significant levels of psychosocial function in between episodes of illness, as they do not experience continuous psychotic symptoms or persistently severe mood disturbance. Delusional disorder is distinguished by the lack of other psychotic symptoms, and the content of delusions tend not to be the bizarre thoughts or beliefs often observed in schizophrenia, such as beliefs that monitoring devices are implanted in the patient's body, or that the patient is communicating with other species. These individuals also tend to maintain a higher level of function because they largely experience only the circumscribed delusions that meet the criteria for the disorder. Schizophreniform disorder and brief psychotic disorder are also characterized by overt psychotic symptoms. If a clinician encounters the patient relatively early in the active psychotic phase of illness, one of these diagnoses (both with a briefer duration criterion then schizophrenia) is most appropriate to assign initially. However, if psychotic symptoms persist beyond 6 months, then the diagnosis of schizophrenia is most appropriate.

LONG-TERM OUTCOME OF SCHIZOPHRENIA

Numerous studies have been conducted in an attempt to characterize the long-term outcome of patients with schizophrenia. Hegarty, Baldessarini, Tohen, Waternaux, and Oepen (1994) reviewed 320 studies that included a total of 51,800 patients with schizophrenia, conducted between 1895 and 1992. Patients were followed approximately 6 years on average, and 40% were considered to have improved, as measured by recovery, remission, or becoming clinically stable with minimal symptoms. Those studies where patients were diagnosed with a more narrow criteria set showed lower rates of improvement, 27% on average, probably reflecting the more "Kraepelinian" deteriorating course associated with narrower definitions of the illness. In addition, the rate of improvement was greater for those patients identified after the middle of the twentieth century than those followed earlier, likely reflecting treatment advances in this period. Studies reported more recently have indicated lower rates of improvement, possibly reflecting again-narrowed criteria for the diagnosis, as well as more stringent criteria for clinical improvement as well.

Several studies have now been reported where patients with schizophrenia have been identified using contemporary diagnostic criteria, and follow-up obtained over at least

10 years (Jobe & Harrow, 2005). Most of these have been retrospective chart reviews, typically of patients who were identified initially upon hospitalization and then followed after discharge. The Iowa 500 study followed 500 psychiatric patients admitted to the Iowa State Psychiatric Hospital between 1934 and 1944, and used the Feighner (Feighner et al., 1972) criteria to identify schizophrenia patients, of whom 200 were followed an average of 35 years from the index hospitalization. These patients were followed in an era prior to modern antipsychotic medication or modern psychosocial treatment, therefore providing significant documentation of the untreated course of schizophrenia. In this study, the schizophrenia patients were observed to have poorer outcome on all measures, relative to other psychiatric patients and nonpsychiatric surgical patients. 54% had incapacitating symptoms, 67% never married, 18% were living in institutions, and over 10% had committed suicide (Tsuang & Winokur, 1975). The Chestnut Lodge study followed 532 patients discharged from this private hospital between 1950 and 1975, for an average of 15 years. Patients were diagnosed by less restrictive *DSM-III* criteria, yet the findings were broadly similar to those of the Iowa 500. The 163 schizophrenia patients as a group were found to have the following outcomes: 6% recovered, 8% good, 22% moderate, 23% marginal, and 41% continuously incapacitated (McGlashan, 1984). A study conducted at the New York State Psychiatric Institute included 552 patients who underwent treatment with psychoanalytically oriented psychotherapy, of whom 99 met *DSM-III* criteria for schizophrenia. With follow-up between 10 to 23 years, the schizophrenia patients showed poorer outcomes when compared with other psychiatric patients, had an average *DSM* GAF score of 39, and a completed suicide rate of 10% (Stone, 1986). While these studies largely emphasized the relatively poor prognosis of most schizophrenia patients, other studies identified subgroups with better outcomes. These studies include Vaillant's study in Boston, where the patients identified as completely remitted from an earlier study were then followed prospectively for 4 to 16 years. He found that 61% of these patients remained in remission. A study in Alberta found 58% of 92 patients diagnosed with *DSM-II* schizophrenia to experience full recovery, despite 45% of the full sample having discontinued their psychiatric medication in the 10 months after the index hospitalization. When this same sample was narrowed by using stricter diagnostic criteria, the percentage of those considered fully recovered was halved (Bland, Parker, & Orn, 1978).

Only two long-term follow-up studies were fully prospective in design. The Chicago Follow-up Study included 73 schizophrenia patients followed up to 20 years. This study found the schizophrenia patients to generally fluctuate between moderate and severe disability, though with over 40%

showing periods of recovery, which often lasted for several years (Harrow & Jobe, 2005). Some of these patients were able to function without the benefit of continuous antipsychotic treatment and tended to have better premorbid function. In addition, a large percentage of the full sample of schizophrenia patients (65%) had also experienced at least one depressive syndrome at 20-year followup; the completed suicide rate was 10% at 10 years and over 12% at 20 years. The other long-term prospective study of schizophrenia patients, conducted by Carpenter and Strauss (1991), followed 55 *DSM-III*-identified schizophrenia patients for 11 years, finding no change in their relatively poorer outcome status at 5 versus 10 years.

A number of long-term follow-up studies have been conducted outside of North America. These studies have typically used *ICD* criteria rather than *DSM* criteria to identify patients. Some of these studies have found women to have a relatively more benign course of illness compared to men (Angermeyer, Goldstein, & Kuehn, 1989). One particularly important study is the International Pilot Study of Schizophrenia sponsored by the WHO. A total of 1,633 subjects from 14 incidence cohorts and 4 prevalence cohorts, in 9 different nations were studied. The most dramatic finding was that outcome in schizophrenia was poorer in fully industrialized countries than in developing countries. Repeated psychotic episodes, for instance, was more common in the developed countries despite the greater availability of modern treatment. The range and severity of symptoms at initial enrollment was not significantly different between sites. This finding has been subject to a great deal of discussion. Some have suggested that a culture of tolerance and benevolence toward those with unusual thoughts and behaviors is more prevalent in developing countries, with a salutary effect of normalizing or "buffering" the patient's psychopathology, and maintaining integration in the local community. However, this does not appear to fully account for the differences between these groups of nations (McGrath et al., 2004). Others have suggested that economies that are not fully market-oriented place fewer psychological and practical demands on schizophrenia patients, with less illness exacerbation and less downward social drift as a result. On the whole, the strongest predictors of poor outcome in the WHO study were social isolation, duration of index episode, history of psychiatric treatment, unmarried status, and history of childhood behavioral problems. It is possible that these factors all reflect a more severe form of illness at outset.

ETIOLOGY AND PATHOPHYSIOLOGY

Modern psychiatric research has produced an abundance of evidence supporting the notion that schizophrenia is a disorder primarily related to brain dysfunction. The convergence of disparate modern investigative techniques into this question has revealed many important clues as to the neurobiological basis of this condition. However, despite these advances, the full understanding of the causes and the biological pathways leading to schizophrenia remains one of the most pressing challenges facing modern medicine.

Two concepts describe the generally accepted framework reflecting our current understanding of the etiology and pathophysiology of schizophrenia. The first is the view that schizophrenia is a neurodevelopmental disorder—that disturbances in the growth and maturation of neurons and neural pathways give rise to schizophrenia. The other overarching framework is the stress-diathesis model of schizophrenia. This model posits a dynamic interplay between environmental (stress) and heritable (diathesis) factors in determining whether any individual develops this illness. This model is consistent with available data showing that while the risk of developing schizophrenia is strongly influenced by genetics, the eventual development of this illness is also strongly modulated by the environmental factors (D. A. Lewis & Levitt, 2002; Lieberman et al., 2001).

Genetics

That schizophrenia has a strong genetic component is a readily accepted notion (see Chapter 60). The degree of risk is proportional to the degree of shared genes and twin studies show concordance rates between 25% and 50% (McGue & Gottesman, 1991). Adoption studies show an elevated risk for schizophrenia among the offspring of mothers with schizophrenia (Kety, Rosenthal, Wender, & Schulsinger, 1971). The exact manner in which schizophrenia is heritable and the identity of the specific genes that may give rise to schizophrenia, however, remain topics of significant debate and uncertainty. It is very evident that schizophrenia does not follow simple Mendelian principles of inheritance (McGue & Gottesman, 1989). This conclusion follows from the logic that inheritance patterns of diseases following simple Mendelian genetics are relatively easy to detect and no such pedigree has ever been described for schizophrenia. A complex genetic model of transmission is much more likely to be the case for schizophrenia. Complex diseases involve several genes, each with a modest effect on heritability, acting in concert, either in a linear or synergistic manner, to confer an overall disease risk (Risch, 1990). Additional complexity may arise from partial penetrance of these genes, interactions between genes, and epigenetic neurodevelopmental or environmental factors. The potential complexity of genetic and nongenetic factors in schizophrenia is illustrated by twin adoption studies. Several have been published, and on the whole, they have been remarkably consistent in demonstrating approximately 50% concordance rate for monozygotic twins. This result accentuates the importance of both the genetic and nongenetic factors in conferring disease risk. Despite the fact that two individuals share identical genetic makeup, there is only approximately 50% chance that both will develop schizophrenia. Consequently, nongenetic causes must account for this lack of full concordance. This elevated risk may be mediated in part by a stressful environment (Tienari et al., 1994). Similar models of gene-environment interaction leading to disease expression has received empirical validation in other psychiatric disorders (Moffitt, Caspi, & Rutter, 2005). In the epidemiology section, some of the more commonly cited nongenetic factors thought to explain this concordance rate are reviewed.

In the past 10 years, with the development of novel study designs and high throughput methods, we have witnessed a tremendous proliferation in the number of putative schizophrenia risk genes. An interesting aspect of this list is that many of these genes are related to neurodevelopmental processes involved in the establishment of neural networks, for example, neuronal migration and synapse formation and/or the regulation of synaptic transmission. One such gene that has received a lot of attention is dysbindin DTNBP1 (Straub et al., 2002). This gene product binds to components of the dystrophin complex, thought to be important in mediating neural synapse structure and function. Another putative schizophrenia gene is neuregulin (NGR1; Stefansson et al., 2002). It is located on 8p21–22 and it may exhibit a diverse range of roles in neural transmission, axonal development, and synaptogenesis (Corfas, Roy, & Buxbaum, 2004). Replications of findings from linkage studies have been relatively rare. However, this may be resolved by considering that several risk genes are involved, each with only modest effect. A recent meta-analysis of these linkage studies did show some support for the involvement of several regions (Badner & Gershon, 2002; C. M. Lewis et al., 2003). Follow-up association studies in many of these regions have been promising and they have identified several candidate schizophrenia risk genes (Owen, Craddock, & O'Donovan, 2005).

Environmental Factors

Because identical twins have a concordance rate of only 50%, it is eminently clear that nonheritable or environmental factors also play a significant role in the risk for developing schizophrenia. The idea that fetal neural development represents a vulnerable period for the genesis of schizophrenia is supported by observations of higher incidence of obstetric and perinatal complications in patients with schizophrenia in a number of studies. A recent meta-analytic review

has categorized these events as (a) complications of pregnancy, (b) abnormal fetal growth and development, and (c) complications of delivery (Cannon, Jones, & Murray, 2002). The meta-analysis indicates that each of these categories was significantly associated with increased risk, but that the effect sizes were generally modest. Another line of studies has found an association between maternal nutritional status and schizophrenia in the offspring. The Dutch Famine study examined the prevalence of schizophrenia among a cohort of births that occurred during the winter of 1944/1945, a period of severe malnutrition for most citizens in a region of the Netherlands (Susser et al., 1996). The study showed a two-fold increased risk for schizophrenia associated with extreme prenatal malnutrition.

Most epidemiologic studies investigating environmental risk factors for schizophrenia are limited by the retrospective manner in which data is collected. For example, in the case of maternal exposure to influenza, this information is usually obtained from participants' recollection of influenza infection during pregnancy or the association of a known influenza outbreak in a particular community within the period of pregnancy. The Prenatal Determinants of Schizophrenia (PDS) study addresses this limitation by relying on prospectively gathered data, which included maternal serum obtained during prenatal visits and demographic information of the participants (Susser, Schaefer, Brown, Begg, & Wyatt, 2000). From the cohort of roughly 12,000 pregnant women, potential cases of schizophrenia were identified from medical and pharmacy records. Of these potential cases, face-to-face diagnostic evaluations by research psychiatrists resulted in the identification of 71 subjects with schizophrenia. This study concluded that there is a seven-fold increased risk of schizophrenia and related disorders associated with influenza infection in the 1st trimester (Brown et al., 2004). Other possible pathogens that have been identified in the PDS study include toxoplasmosis and lead.

Another line of research has pointed to the importance of the physical environment and fetal exposures during gestation. Seasonal variation in the prevalence of births leading to schizophrenia has been identified, with an excess of births in winter and spring months (Davies, Welham, Chant, Torrey, & McGrath, 2003). A variety of theories attempting to account for this have been proposed—environmental factors that predisposed to schizophrenia development such as ambient temperature, exposure to infectious agents, and nutritional deficiencies; increased resistance to infections and other insults conferred by schizophrenia leading to increased survival in winter months.

Although the worldwide prevalence is thought to be equivalent across nations (Jablensky, 2000; Sartorius, Jablensky, & Shapiro, 1977), there have been numerous findings and theories suggesting a direct relationship between specific social and cultural factors and the development or severity of schizophrenia. Some of these factors include immigration status, urbanicity, and socioeconomic status. However, the results of studies examining these factors have either been inconsistent or complicated by confounds that make it very difficult to ascertain whether these factors are causes or effects of illness, for example, downward drift in socioeconomic status due to mental illness.

Neurochemical Abnormalities

Dopamine

Chlorpromazine was originally synthesized in the 1950s as an antihistamine for use as a preanesthetic agent. Upon noting its particularly striking calming effect on patients, the French surgeon Henri Laborit recommended chlorpromazine to his psychiatric colleagues for use with agitated patients. They quickly found it beneficial with patients with schizophrenia. They also noted Parkinsonian side effects with higher doses. They coined the term *neuroleptic*, literally translated from the French as "seizing the neuron," to reflect their intuition that the mechanism of action somehow involved neural modulation. The serendipitous discovery of the usefulness of chlorpromazine in schizophrenia led ultimately to the development of the dopamine hypothesis, one of the most influential theories on the etiology of schizophrenia. It posits that the symptoms of this illness are the byproducts of dysfunction of dopamine neurotransmission. The main lines of evidence supporting this role for dopamine came from work in the 1960s and 1970s. It was shown, for example, that the administration of phenothiazines in animals blocks the behavioral effects of dopamine agonists (such as amphetamine) and results in increased turnover of dopamine. Conversely, the administration of amphetamine, which was known to increase

synaptic levels of dopamine, resulted in behavioral abnormalities and symptoms reminiscent of schizophrenia. Later work further specified that the most important dopamine receptor may be the D2 subtype in that clinical potency is best correlated with binding to this receptor subtype (Creese, Burt, & Snyder, 1976).

Neuroimaging has made significant contributions to our evolving understanding of the neurochemical basis for schizophrenia. Imaging modalities such as positron emission tomography (PET) and single photon emission computed tomography (SPECT) are allowing researchers to assess the functional status of neurotransmitter systems (Figure 54.1). One line of PET studies has led to a more refined hypothesis of dopamine dysregulation. These studies indicate that the dopaminergic tone associated with schizophrenia may be more complex than previously thought. This newer hypothesis proposes a hyperdopamineragic state in the striatal D2 system (Abi-Dargham et al., 2000) giving rise to positive symptoms and a hypodopaminergic state in the prefrontal D1 system associated with higher-order cognitive deficits (Abi-Dargham et al., 2002).

As important as the dopamine hypothesis has been to schizophrenia research, modern psychiatry has appreciated the limitations of this theory. The challenge to the dopamine hypothesis comes from primarily two lines of evidence. First, the dopamine hypothesis does not account for negative symptoms, which are now acknowledged to be essential components of this illness. Dopamine blocking agents have not been shown to be effective in treating negative symptoms nor have dopaminergic agents been shown to induce negative symptoms. The second challenge to the dopamine hypothesis comes from the efficacy of the so-called atypical neuroleptics, medications that are thought to act through multiple neurotransmitter systems in addition to dopamine.

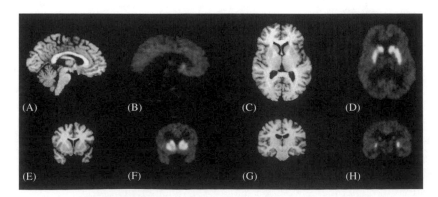

Figure 54.1 Evidence for increased dopamine release in schizophrenia

Note: From Abi-Dargham et al. 2002.

Other Monoamines

The observations that the prototypical "atypical" neuroleptic, clozapine, is often effective in patients who have symptoms refractory to the traditional D2 blocking agents and possesses high affinity for diverse monoaminergic receptors including serotonin, histamine, muscarinic, and alpha-adrenergic receptors, in addition to the D2 receptor, have led to the hypothesis that other neurotransmitter systems may be involved in the pathophysiology of schizophrenia. One of the most important of these other neurotransmitters is serotonin. Serotonin has been implicated by the clinical efficacy of the many atypical agents with high affinity for its receptors. There are 14 known serotonin receptor subtypes but some of the most important for schizophrenia include the 5HT-2C, -2A, and -1A subtypes. The acetylcholine system has been implicated in the pathophysiology of schizophrenia based initially on the observation that patients with schizophrenia exhibit high rates of use of tobacco products. This led to the hypothesis that the nicotine in tobacco provides some amelioration of symptoms through its action on the acetylcholine system. This hypothesis has received some support by work examining the effects of nicotine on early sensory deficits that were well documented in schizophrenia: Nicotine normalizes measures of deficient auditory gating in schizophrenia (Adler, Hoffer, Griffith, Waldo, & Freedman, 1992).

Glutamate/NMDA

Glutamate is the most prevalent excitatory neurotransmitter in the brain. Consequently, the function of glutamate is fundamentally different from dopamine and the other monoaminergic neurotransmitters, which are primarily modulators of excitatory or inhibitory neurotransmission. The involvement of the glutamate system in the pathophysiology of schizophrenia is inferred primarily from the observation that people intoxicated with agents acting on the glutamate receptor, phencyclidine (PCP) and ketamine, often exhibit a behavioral syndrome mimicking schizophrenia. This syndrome can include both positive and negative symptoms of schizophrenia (Javitt & Zukin, 1991). PCP and ketamine bind to the N-methyl-D-aspartate (NMDA) class of glutamate receptors and, consequently, the main focus of glutamate research has been on this receptor. The NMDA receptor regulation is highly complex with numerous sites of allosteric modulation. One of the most important in terms of psychopathology appears to be the glycine site. There have been several clinical trials examining partial (D-cycloserine) and full agonists (glycine, D-serine, and D-alanine) of this site. The pharmacodynamics of cycloserine with the NMDA receptor is complex with cycloserine acting as an agonist at low and an antagonist at high concentrations. One of the main current uses of cycloserine is treatment for tuberculosis in high doses and a relatively common side effect in this setting is psychosis. The results of clinical studies investigating the effects of glycine agonists have been mixed with some studies showing benefit for both positive and negative symptoms. However, due to the limited number of studies, understanding the importance of the glutamate/NDMA system in schizophrenia will require further studies.

GABA

The potential role for GABA in the pathophysiology of schizophrenia follows two separate but related lines of research involving inhibitory interneurons. In the first line of research, it is thought that the psychotomimetic effects of NMDA antagonists, such as PCP, are mediated through their action on GABA release. NMDA receptors are found on GABAergic inhibitory interneurons. Activation of these NMDA receptor results in increased GABA release, which then causes suppression of glutamate release from glutamatergic cells. The binding of an antagonist on the NMDA receptor on the inhibitory neurons ultimately results in a hyperglutamatergic state, which is presumed to cause symptoms of psychosis.

In the second line of research, it is thought that alterations in the neural circuitry of the prefrontal cortex, involving GABA, give rise to the higher-order cognitive deficits in schizophrenia. Theories on GABA dysfunction in schizophrenia center on the parvalbumin (PV) containing group of inhibitory interneurons. Studies showing reduction in the number of PV cells and under-expression of glutamic acid decarboxylase (GAD), a key enzyme in GABA synthesis (Akbarian et al., 1995; Volk, Austin, Pierri, Sampson, & Lewis, 2000) point to a functional deficit in GABA in the prefrontal cortex. PV cells can be further subdivided based on differences in histological and putative functional properties. Chandelier cell axons target the axonal initial segment (AIS) of pyramidal cells in the neocortex and show a limited coverage area of its axons. The wide arbor cells target the soma and proximal portions of the dendrites and, as its name implies, its axons cover a broad area. With the privileged position of its axonal cartridges, the chandelier cells are thought to potently regulate the timing of output of pyramidal cells within a column, while wide arbor cells are thought to inhibit pyramidal cells in neighboring columns (D. A. Lewis, 2000). Additionally, chandelier cells can terminate on several hundreds of pyramidal cells, setting the stage for the synchronization of many cells (Figure 54.2; Cobb, Buhl, Halasy, Paulsen, & Somogyi, 1995; Howard, Tamas, & Soltesz, 2005). Taken together, the chandelier and wide arbor cells are thought to coordinate the fine control of the synchrony and spatial extent of pyramidal cell

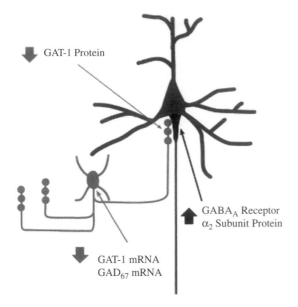

GAT-1 Protein

GABA$_A$ Receptor
α_2 Subunit Protein

GAT-1 mRNA
GAD$_{67}$ mRNA

Figure 54.2 Cortical microanatomy and schizophrenia

Note: From "Impaired Prefrontal Inhibition in Schizophrenia. Relevance for Cognitive Dysfunction," by D. Volk and D. A. Lewis, 2002, *Physiology and Behavior*, *77*, p. 503. Reprinted with permission.

activity in the prefrontal cortex. The disruption of these functions in schizophrenia would be expected to lead to the loss of temporal and spatial organization in neuronal activity necessary for higher order cognitive processes.

Anatomic and Histologic Studies

The study of structural abnormalities in brains of individuals with schizophrenia was once considered a "graveyard" for neuropathologists. The emergence of modern neuroimaging and molecular techniques has led to a renewed interest in this field. Neuroimaging studies have shown robust evidence of whole brain volume deficits while modern neuropathology studies have uncovered provocative clues pointing to alterations in the microscopic neuroanatomy in schizophrenia (Table 54.1).

The advent of modern neuroimaging techniques has allowed detailed analysis of brain structures and has significantly shaped our understanding of the neural basis of schizophrenia. Previously, the measurement of brain volumes could only be conducted in a reliable manner with postmortem samples. The relative ease of use has resulted in a proliferation of in vivo neuroimaging volumetric studies. Computed tomography (CT) studies documenting significant enlargement of cerebral ventricles and decrease in overall brain volume in subjects with schizophrenia (relative to healthy control subjects) have provided the first compelling neuroimaging results indicating that schizophrenia is a brain-based disorder (Johnstone, Crow, Frith,

Husband, & Kreel, 1976). These results remain the most reliable and robust volumetric findings in schizophrenia, with a median reduction in ventricular volume estimated to be 40% (Lawrie & Abukmeil, 1998). However, despite the large difference between patients and controls, there is substantial overlap between groups and this measure cannot be used to reliably differentiate between patients and controls. In other words, we do not yet have a good biological diagnostic marker for schizophrenia. More recent MRI volumetric studies have confirmed the results of these earlier CT studies. They have also identified several specific regions of decreased volume including the prefrontal, medial temporal structures, lateral temporal cortex, and thalamus (Harrison, 1999). The magnitude of volume difference between subjects with schizophrenia and healthy controls is generally modest in these regions and these results have not been as consistent as the ventricular and whole brain findings. A recent meta-analysis of MRI studies involving first episode subjects showed highly significant reductions in total brain and increased ventricular volume (Steen, Mull, McClure, Hamer, & Lieberman, 2006), suggesting that these findings are not just the result of disease chronicity or medication exposure.

Neuroimaging studies have strongly confirmed that brain abnormalities are indeed associated with schizophrenia. Consequently, there has been renewed interest in identifying microscopic neural abnormalities, with modern neuropathology studies revealing alterations not previously appreciated in the brains of individuals with schizophrenia. A review of the literature shows robust findings including reduction in cortical neuronal size, reduction in axonal and dendritic arborization, and reduction in the number of thalamic neurons. The latter study has shown highly significant loss in the number of neurons in the mediodorsal nucleus of the thalamus, particularly in the subnucleus that projects to the dorsolateral prefrontal cortex (Popken, Bunney, Potkin, & Jones, 2000).

The development of diffusion tensor imaging (DTI), an MR based technique, is allowing researchers to measure white fiber integrity in the brain. DTI has been quickly adopted by schizophrenia researchers to examine white fiber pathology (Kanaan et al., 2005), thereby testing the hypothesis that schizophrenia is a result of diminished connectivity between brain regions. A growing number of studies have reported loss of white fiber integrity in many areas, such as in tracts connecting the prefrontal and temporal cortices. However, as expected with such a new technique applied to a complex illness, there has yet to be a large body of studies replicating these early results. Consequently, the field will have to await future studies using this promising technology before we can assess the importance of this line of research.

TABLE 54.1 Summary of Structural Brain Abnormalities in Schizophrenia

Change in Brain Structure	Strength of Evidence
Macroscopic Findings	
Enlarged lateral and third ventricles	$++++$
Decreased cortical volume	$++++$
The above changes present in first-episode patients	$+++$
Disproportionate volume loss from temporal lobe (incl. hippocampus)	$+++$
Decreased thalamic volume	$++$
Cortical volume loss affects grey rather than white matter	$++$
Enlarged basal ganglia secondary to antipsychotic medication	$+++$
Histological Findings	
Absence of gliosis as an intrinsic feature	$+++$
Smaller cortical and hippocampal neurons	$+++$
Fewer neurons in dorsal thalamus	$+++$
Reduced synaptic and dendritic markers in hippocampus	$++$
Maldistribution of white matter neurons	$+$
Entorhinal cortex dysplasia	$\pm$
Cortical or hippocampal neuron loss	$\pm$
Disarray of hippocampal neurons	$\pm$
Miscellaneous	
Alzheimer's disease is not more common in schizophrenia	$++++$
Pathology interacts with cerebral asymmetries	$++$

$\pm$ = Weak; $+$ = Moderate; $++$ = Good; $+++$ = Strong; $++++$ = Shown by meta-analysis.

Note: From "The Neuropathology of Schizophrenia. A Critical Review of the Data and Their Interpretation," by P. J. Harrison, 1999, *Brain 122*(Pt. 4), pp. 593–624.

Cognitive and Information Processing Deficits

Cognitive deficits have been recognized as an important feature of schizophrenia since the beginning of efforts to systematically study this condition. About 100 years ago, Kraepelin referred to schizophrenia as *dementia praecox*, or premature dementia, to describe the prominent cognitive deficits that he thought formed the core of this condition. As noted earlier, the word *schizophrenia*, originally coined by Bleuler, is best translated from German as the "splitting of the mind," a term intended to capture the loss of integration of mental processes. The interest in cognition waned in the intervening years as other aspects of the illness became the focal point of research interest. However, in the past 20 years, there has been renewed interest in studying cognitive dysfunction in schizophrenia as a way to understand its pathophysiology. The logic is that cognitive abnormalities represent core deficits of schizophrenia and that the study of core deficits may provide a better index of underlying neural dysfunction. Evidence that cognition is a core feature of schizophrenia comes from many fronts. First, studies have documented a fairly strong correlation between cognitive deficits and functional status. This is in distinction to psychotic symptoms, which generally do not correlate well with functional status. Second, cognitive deficits are very common among individuals suffering from schizophrenia. Third, cognitive deficits appear to be an essential aspect of this condition because they predate the onset of psychotic symptoms, and they are present in unaffected first-degree relatives and identical twins. The study of cognition has the additional practical benefit that there is an abundance of paradigms amenable to experimental controls and manipulation and it is now possible to image brain activity using fMRI and other non invasive methods during the course of cognitive processing.

There is now an abundance of research indicating prominent deficits in higher-order cognition in schizophrenia.

Disturbances in cognitive control (the coordination of thought and actions), attention, language, and memory have been documented by a number of researchers using diverse paradigms. Some investigators have attempted to develop comprehensive cognitive models of schizophrenia that could explain many of the behavioral deficits and symptoms of schizophrenia. Goldman-Rakic proposed that working memory, the maintenance of information "on-line" to guide behavior, is the fundamental disturbance in schizophrenia. She further proposed that the cognitive deficits and symptoms such as disorganization in speech and actions are manifestations of working memory deficits Cohen and colleagues have proposed the context processing deficit model for schizophrenia (Cohen et al., 1999). Here context is defined as the conjunction of items, rules, and goals required to guide behavior or decisions. A real life example of context processing is the ability of a tourist from the United States, while visiting England, to avoid being hit by a car while crossing a street. He does so by realizing that one needs to look right first and then left before crossing a street in England. In this example, the conjunction of seeing the crossing signal and the rules of the road in England constitutes the context with which actions (looking right then left) are decided on. According to the context processing models, much of the diverse cognitive deficits seen in schizophrenia can be reduced to this inability to hold diverse representations in mind. Andreasen (1997, 2000) proposed the cognitive dysmetria model of schizophrenia in which the primary deficit is in the inability of patients to rapidly and efficiently coordinate mental activity in a task appropriate manner.

The first generation of cognitive neuroscience studies focused primarily on traditional areas of research in cognition, namely higher-order cognitive processes. More recently, the boundaries of inquiry have broadened to include virtually all domains of mental processes impaired in schizophrenia. Consequently, the term *information processing deficits* may be a more general and appropriate term to describe the diverse studies currently undertaken by schizophrenia researchers. These studies are revealing information processing deficits in early sensory, affective, and social domains.

Early Sensory Processing Deficits

While dysfunction in higher-order cognitive processes have now been firmly established, another line of research is investigating the hypothesis that deficits in early sensory processing is a fundamental aspect of schizophrenia. Some have proposed that these early sensory deficits may contribute to higher-order cognitive deficits and have significant impact on the functional status of the affected individuals (Brenner, Lysaker, Wilt, & O'Donnell,

2002; Javitt, Strous, Grochowski, Ritter, & Cowan, 1997; Saccuzzo & Braff, 1981). The visual and auditory systems have been the best studied. In the visual domain, studies examining the earliest processes in visual perception have demonstrated deficits in schizophrenia. For example, visual masking is a procedure in which the perception of a briefly presented object (target) is reduced by the presentation of another object (mask) shortly before or after. Numerous studies have demonstrated that patients exhibit visual masking deficits, meaning they have more difficulty, compared to healthy subjects, accurately perceiving the target when a mask is presented (Green & Walker, 1986). The visual masking deficit has been shown to correlate with negative symptoms (Green & Walker, 1986) and formal thought disorder (Perry & Braff, 1994). Another line of research has demonstrated neural correlates of deficits in early visual processing. Using evoked response potentials (ERP), several groups have demonstrated abnormalities in the P1 component of visual evoked responses in schizophrenia.

In the auditory domain, early sensory deficits have been found using auditory ERP. Patients exhibit abnormalities in the so-called P50 suppression. In healthy subjects, two sounds presented in rapid succession will produce a reduction in the amplitude of the P50 component of the auditory ERP elicited by the second sound (Adler et al., 1982). This can be viewed as a type of habituation in which the repetition of a sensory event results in a dampening of the neural response. It has been shown that patients do not exhibit this P50 suppression with the second auditory stimulus. This has been interpreted as the inability of patients to properly gate sensory information.

Patients have also been shown to exhibit deficits in mismatch negativity (MMN; Shelley et al., 1991). In healthy subjects, the presentation of an oddball tone, a deviant tone within a train of brief repetitions of a standard tone, elicits an auditory ERP that is different from the response elicited by the standard tone. Like the P50 suppression, it is thought that MMN is preattentive in that the MMN can be elicited regardless of whether the subject is attending to the stimulus.

Affect Processing

With the recognition of the importance of negative symptoms in schizophrenia, increasing attention is being paid to the study of affect and related processes in schizophrenia. In the past 10 years, we have witnessed an exponential increase in the number of studies focusing on this aspect of the illness. These affect studies can be further categorized as those focusing on emotional expression, recognition of emotional signals, and the subjective experiencing of emotions. Deficits in the emotional expressivity of patients, for example, blunted or flat affect, is perhaps the single most visibly apparent symptom of schizophrenia. Other than the distressed expressions associated with psychosis, there is a marked decrease in the emotional expressivity and responsivity of the face in schizophrenia (Berenbaum & Oltmanns, 1992). Contrary to the belief that diminished expression of emotion reflects diminished experience of emotion, patients, in general, appear not to have a subjective, experiential deficit (Berenbaum & Oltmanns, 1992; Earnst & Kring, 1999). This is true even in patients with the deficit syndrome or a predominance of blunted affect. In addition to deficits in the ability to express emotions, individuals with schizophrenia experience difficulty recognizing affect in others. A number of studies have found that when presented with a series of pictures of faces depicting the basic emotions, patients have difficulty naming the expressed emotion (Kohler, Bilker, Hagendoorn, Gur, & Gur, 2000; Schneider et al., 2006). Some researchers have hypothesized that this deficit is one of the basis of social communication problems that patients face in everyday life. An important factor yet to be clarified in this line of work is the specificity of the affect recognition deficit above and beyond a generalized cognitive deficit because some studies have shown the absence (Kohler et al., 2000; Salem, Kring, & Kerr, 1996) while others have shown the presence of a differential deficit (Schneider et al., 2006).

Social Cognition

As is the case with affect, there has been a great expansion in the interest in examining deficits in social functioning in schizophrenia. A strong argument can be made that the social deficits of schizophrenia constitutes a core feature of this illness based on the observations that abnormalities in social functions often occur during the prodromal phase (Davidson et al., 1999), at the time of initial diagnosis, and throughout the course of illness (Addington & Addington, 2000). Studies on social cognition have identified two general areas of abnormality in schizophrenia: theory of mind and social perceptions (Pinkham, Penn, Perkins, & Lieberman, 2003). Theory of mind refers to the capacity to (a) understand that the mental state (beliefs, intentions, and perspectives) of others is separate and distinct from one's own, and (b) the ability to make inferences about another's intentions. Theory-of-mind skills are higher-order cognitive processes requiring the integration of sensory inputs from multiple channels with contextual information. Studies have shown schizophrenia patients to be lacking in theory-of-mind skills (Corcoran, Mercer, & Frith, 1995; Frith & Corcoran, 1996). Social perception, the ability to recognize information governing appropriate social behavior, has also consistently been shown to be abnormal in schizophrenia patients. The facial affect recognition deficits previously discussed is

an important example of a social perception dysfunction. It is thought that deficits in affect recognition is the cause of schizophrenia patients' inability to decode the emotional state of the others. Deficits in social cue perception have been shown to be more acute for abstract compared to non-abstract information (Corrigan & Nelson, 1998).

Functional Neuroimaging

The discovery that the activity of specific brain regions could be imaged in awake and behaving subjects has been one of the most important developments in the history of psychiatric and schizophrenia research. Especially since the availability of functional magnetic resonance imaging (fMRI), functional neuroimaging has been widely adopted by researchers and is now a mainstream method in our search for the neurobiological basis of schizophrenia. By allowing researchers to assess the neural functional correlates of a given cognitive task, functional neuroimaging allows researchers to identify diseased brain regions and abnormal cognitive processes in schizophrenia. The identification of dysfunctional regions provides information that can inform and constrain hypotheses in studies utilizing other research methods. For example, the discovery of abnormal engagement of the DLPFC has been very important in guiding postmortem and genetic studies seeking the cellular and molecular basis of higher-order cognitive deficits in schizophrenia.

Functional Imaging Studies of Higher-Order Cognitive Deficits

Although modern functional neuroimaging studies are beginning to uncover the neural correlates of most clusters of clinical features of schizophrenia, including those associated with deficits in early sensory, affective, social processes mentioned previously, the majority of functional neuroimaging studies have historically focused on higher-order cognitive deficits. These studies point to abnormalities in several multimodal associative brain regions. These include deficits in the anterior cingulated cortex, superior temporal gyrus, and medial temporal cortex. Since the 1970s implementation of the earliest functional neuroimaging studies in schizophrenia (Ingvar & Franzen, 1974), there has been special interest in the DLPFC. The DLPFC is thought to be a key region subserving higher-order cognitive processing and, consequently, the DLPFC is hypothesized to be one of the most important sites of pathology in schizophrenia. Ingvar and Franzen, and later Weinberger, Berman, and colleagues, found that the DLPFC is hypoactive in schizophrenia (Berman, Zec, & Weinberger, 1986; Weinberger, Berman, & Zec, 1986). These results provide the basis for the "hypofrontality" hypothesis of schizophrenia. In the past 20 years, a large number of neuroimaging studies have generally supported the notion of a dysfunctional DLPFC in schizophrenia across different imaging modalities and cognitive paradigms (Callicott et al., 2000; Manoach et al., 2000; Perlstein, Carter, Noll, & Cohen, 2001).

Neural Basis of Symptoms

Although functional neuroimaging, particularly fMRI, is a relatively new investigative tool, it has already made significant contributions to our understanding of the neural basis of the clinical features of schizophrenia. Two such clinical features are cognitive disorganization and auditory hallucinations.

Broadly following the theories set forth by Goldman-Rakic and others that postulate that (a) the ability to maintain information "on-line" forms the basis for many higher-order cognitive processes and behaviors and (b) the DLPFC is the key brain region supporting the maintenance of information on-line, a series of functional imaging studies has demonstrated that the degree of activation of the DLPFC in schizophrenia is highly correlated with clinical measures of cognitive and behavioral disorganization (Figure 54.3).

Another series of studies is elucidating the neural basis of auditory hallucinations and thereby providing a neurobiological rational for an effective treatment for this symptom. Auditory hallucinations appear to be the result of abnormal activation of the neural system serving auditory sensory processing. In one study involving patients with schizophrenia with auditory hallucinations, the onset and offset of the hallucinations correlated with the engagement and disengagement of the primary auditory cortex (Dierks et al., 1999).

Functional neuroimaging studies, such as the one cited above, have provided support for a novel treatment strategy targeting auditory hallucinations refractory to medications. fMRI studies have shown over-activation in the temporal-parietal cortex during auditory hallucinations. Consequently, it would be logical to hypothesize that treatment of auditory hallucination could be effected through the deactivation of this region. Hoffman and colleagues (2005) have proposed to do this with repetitive transcranial magnetic stimulation (rTMS). RTMS is a procedure in which brief, repetitive pulses of a magnetic field is applied to a localized region of the cortex. It is thought that rTMS reduces excitability in the applied region. A large clinical study indicates that rTMS of the left temporal-parietal region is a safe and effective method to reduce the severity of AH in medication-resistant subjects with schizophrenia.

INTERVENTION AND MANAGEMENT

Antipsychotic Medications

Pharmacological agents have been the mainstay of schizophrenia treatment since the mid-twentieth century, though other medical approaches were in use prior to this time. Indeed, the modern history of approaches to schizophrenia treatment exemplifies the process of scientific discovery in clinical medicine, and the evolution of how this illness has been conceptualized (see Chapter 5). Early in the twentieth century, a variety of pharmacological interventions for schizophrenia were attempted and reported in the literature, including cocaine, manganese, castor oil, and sulfur oil. More widely known are the attempts to remediate symptoms of schizophrenia by induction of either sleep or insulin-induced coma, the latter of which dominated the treatment options for psychiatrists until the 1950s (Ban, 2004). As described earlier, the development of novel adjunct medication for anesthesia yielded the compound chlorpromazine, which was synthesized in 1950 and subsequently observed to induce conscious sedation in agitated patients. It was quickly adopted for use in

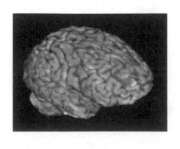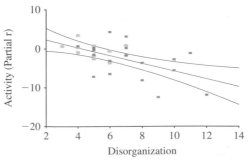

Figure 54.3 (**Figure C.52** in color section) Decreased Prefrontal Cortical Function in First Episode Schizophrenia
Note: From MacDonald et al. (2005).

agitated patients with schizophrenia and found by inpatient clinicians to decrease the need for physical restraint. This phenothiazine compound was the first medication for schizophrenia to be tested in placebo-controlled studies, with the landmark report of its superiority in the treatment of schizophrenia emerging several years later. In addition, reserpine (isolated from the Rauwolfia plant) was introduced in 1954, though its propensity to induce or worsen depressive symptoms was noted, leading to the examination of its monoaminergic actions and the subsequent articulation of the biogenic amine hypothesis of depression, which paralleled the dopaminergic hypothesis of schizophrenia. Haloperidol was synthesized in 1958 and introduced the following year; it remains one of the most widely prescribed antipsychotic medications.

Subsequent studies conducted in the 1960s and thereafter further specified the target symptoms responsive to these medications, rates of clinical response, and functional outcome of patients offered these treatments (detailed later). Basic science investigations established the neurochemical basis for the clinical efficacy of these medications. Initially, Carlsson and Lindqvist (1963) found that administration of these compounds to rodents led to increased levels of dopamine metabolites and antagonized the behavioral effects of dopamine agonists such as amphetamine and apomorphine. This led Snyder and colleagues to demonstrate that the clinical efficacy of existing antipsychotic medications was directly related to their potency in blocking dopamine receptors (Creese et al., 1976), thus refining the dopamine hypothesis of schizophrenia.

Mechanism of Antipsychotic Medication Action

To date, over 30 medications from 11 different chemical classes have been introduced worldwide for the treatment of schizophrenia (Ban, 2004). These are generally identified as first-generation (FGA) or second-generation antipsychotics (SGA), also commonly known as "atypical" antipsychotics. FGAs (typified by haloperidol) all have in common a high affinity for D_2 receptors, and the clinical efficacy of these medications is strongly related to binding affinity for these receptors (Seeman, Lee, Chau-Wong, & Wong, 1976). PET studies have demonstrated that clinical antipsychotic effects occur at doses where striatal D_2 receptor occupancy of 65% to 70%, whereas D_2 receptor occupancy above 80% is associated with significantly increased incidence of extrapyramidal symptoms (EPS; Remington & Kapur, 1999). These studies have also found that at therapeutic doses, FGAs block D_2-like receptors to an equal degree in limbic cortical areas and the striatum, which is also consistent with the relatively narrow range of antipsychotic efficacy in the absence of EPS (Xiberas

et al., 2001). The precise cellular feature of altered dopaminergic activity that provides the basis for clinical efficacy remains an active area of investigation. A leading hypothesis suggests that acute administration of these medications is associated with antagonism of D_2 autoreceptors on dopaminergic nerve terminals, leading to a depolarization inactivation of ion channels at those terminals and a resulting incapacity of propagating action potentials to further depolarize the terminal, thus chronically blocking dopamine release into the synapse (Grace, Bunney, Moore, & Todd, 1997). In contrast, the six SGAs that are currently available in the United States are more heterogeneous in their profile of dopamine receptor antagonism. Risperidone, for example, exhibits D_2 antagonism that is within the range of that for FGAs, and consequently at therapeutic doses is associated with rates of EPS intermediate between FGAs and other SGAs. Other SGAs, such as clozapine and quetiapine, exhibit minimal D_2 receptor binding at therapeutic doses (Miyamoto, Duncan, Marx, & Lieberman, 2005). These medications (including the other available SGAs, olanzapine, ziprasidone, and aripiprazole) show heterogeneous profiles of binding at other dopamine receptors as well. A leading current hypothesis (the "fast-off" hypothesis) suggests that the relative lack of EPS stemming from the use of these medications may be due to the relatively faster rate of dissociation of these agents from D_2 receptors. This faster dissociation rate would be expected to more optimally accommodate normal physiological dopamine transmission. In contrast, a competing hypothesis of what constitutes atypicality emphasizes the serotonergic receptor activity ($5HT_{2A}$ and $5HT_{2C}$ antagonism and $5HT_{1A}$ agonism) that is found among SGAs. These actions are associated with enhanced dopamine and glutamate in prefrontal relative to subcortical areas and, in particular, the ratio of $5HT_{2A}$ to D_2 blockade may prevent EPS and remediate negative symptoms of schizophrenia in a manner superior to the FGAs (Meltzer, Li, Kaneda, & Ichikawa, 2003). In addition, aripiprazole is unique as a D_2 partial agonist, which may stabilize elevated rates of dopamine transmission while avoiding a degree of dopamine blockade necessary for EPS. It should also be emphasized here that all antipsychotics (FGAs and SGAs) exhibit high-affinity binding at a range of other monoamine receptors in the brain, which may be partly responsible for their efficacy but are well-established as the basis for many of their side effects. This includes antagonism at muscarinic, histaminergic, and adrenergic receptors, with predictable autonomic effects. In addition, the monoaminergic transporter blocking effects and $5HT_{1A}$ receptor partial agonism or antagonism exhibited by some SGAs suggest that these medications may exert antidepressant and anxiolytic effects as well.

Despite the substantial basic pharmacological differences between FGAs and SGAs noted previously, recent effectiveness studies such as the NIMH sponsored CATIE study have highlighted the fact that in the context of those trials, the advantages, in terms of patient adherence, effects on cognition and so on are modest at best. The high discontinuation rates in this study highlight the limited effectiveness of modern antipsychotic treatment, the high prevalence of unpleasant side effects, and the need for the development of more effective and better tolerated therapies as well as more integrative approaches that combine pharmacotherapy with psychosoc1al interventions.

Importance of Integrated Schizophrenia Treatment

Psychosocial treatment is an essential element of the treatment needs of all patients with schizophrenia. In general, all of the interventions described next are compatible not only with each other but with pharmacological treatment as well (Lauriello, Lenroot, & Bustillo, 2003). As a complex disorder that affects virtually every psychological and functional domain, a comprehensive treatment approach to schizophrenia must necessarily address a broad spectrum of problems. Lehman (1999) has proposed a framework for evaluating outcomes in schizophrenia that is based on the findings of an NIMH expert panel. Four domains are identified: clinical, rehabilitative, humanitarian, and public welfare. The clinical domain includes psychopathology and treatment issues. The rehabilitative domain includes social and vocational function. The humanitarian domain includes quality of life, subjective well-being, and other patient-centered measures, and the public safety domain includes optimizing and resolving the rights of the patients with the welfare of the community at large. It is increasingly recognized that integration of care is associated with maximal benefit for patients with schizophrenia, particularly those who are the sickest and are the highest users of services (Lenroot, Bustillo, Lauriello, & Keith, 2003). A cornerstone of this perspective is the establishment and maintenance of the alliance not only with the patient but with families and other care and service providers as well. This is also of increasing importance given the progressive shifting of the locus of care for the most severely chronically disabled schizophrenia patients, from the large state hospitals of an earlier era to the community today.

Case Management/Assertive Community Treatment

Case management is fundamentally a method of coordinating services for the patient in the community. In this model, an individual case manager (typically a licensed social worker) serves a role somewhat analogous to a primary care physician, assessing and prioritizing the needs of the patient, developing an integrated care plan, arranging for provision of this care, and serving as the patient's primary point of contact in the mental health system. Case managers interact both with social service agencies and with clinicians, to achieve and maintain access to entitlements, social services, and clinical care. Case management aims to maintain the patient in the system of care, to permit the most efficacious treatment in the least restrictive setting, and to optimize outcome, particularly quality of life and social function.

Psychotherapy

Effective psychotherapies for schizophrenia include psychoeducation, cognitive behavior therapy targeted at coping with and reducing positive symptoms, social skills training, and cognitive rehabilitation. Successful intervention requires a multidisciplinary approach that focuses on engaging, educating, and supporting the family as well as on addressing specific needs of the patient. This extends beyond positive symptom control and relapse prevention, for which antipsychotic medications are effective when adherence is adequate, to include social, occupational, and cognitive deficits in the illness.

SUMMARY

Schizophrenia is a common, debilitating illness that presents a major burden for individuals, families, and society. Our understanding of schizophrenia has evolved significantly along with recent advances in neuroscience and genetics. This increased understanding includes significant refinement in how the illness is identified as well as a deeper understanding of its natural course, relationship to boundary conditions, the disturbances in brain structure and function that underlie cognitive and functional deficits, and the genetic and environmental factors that modify the appearance and clinical course of this illness. This advance in understanding is likely to accelerate in the coming years, with the promise of leading us toward more effective therapies and prevention strategies and improving the lives of patients and their families.

REFERENCES

Abi-Dargham, A., Mawlawi, O., Lombardo, I., Gil, R., Martinez, D., Huang, Y., et al. (2002). Prefrontal dopamine D1 receptors and working memory in schizophrenia. *Journal of Neuroscience*, *22*, 3708–3719.

Abi-Dargham, A., Rodenhiser, J., Printz, D., Zea-Ponce, Y., Gil, R., Kegeles, L. S., et al. (2000). Increased baseline occupancy of D2 receptors by dopamine in schizophrenia. *Proceedings of the National Academy of Sciences, USA, 97*, 8104–8109.

Addington, J., & Addington, D. (2000). Neurocognitive and social functioning in schizophrenia: A 2.5 year follow-up study. *Schizophrenia Research, 44*, 47–56.

Adityanjee, Aderibigbe, Y. A., Theodoridis, D., & Vieweg, V. R. (1999). Dementia praecox to schizophrenia: The first 100 years. *Psychiatry and Clinical Neurosciences, 53*(4), 437–448.

Adler, L. E., Hoffer, L. J., Griffith, J., Waldo, M. C., & Freedman, R. (1992). Normalization by nicotine of deficient auditory sensory gating in the relatives of schizophrenics. *Biological Psychiatry, 32*, 607–616.

Adler, L. E., Pachtman, E., Franks, R. D., Pecevich, M., Waldo, M. C., & Freedman, R. (1982). Neurophysiological evidence for a defect in neuronal mechanisms involved in sensory gating in schizophrenia. *Biological Psychiatry, 17*, 639–654.

Akbarian, S., Kim, J. J., Potkin, S. G., Hagman, J. O., Tafazzoli, A., Bunney, W. E., Jr., et al. (1995). Gene expression for glutamic acid decarboxylase is reduced without loss of neurons in prefrontal cortex of schizophrenics. *Archives of General Psychiatry, 52*, 258–266.

Andreasen, N. C. (1997). The evolving concept of schizophrenia: From Kraepelin to the present and future. *Schizophrenia Research, 28*, 105–109.

Andreasen, N. C. (2000). Schizophrenia: The fundamental questions. *Brain Research: Brain Research Reviews, 31*, 106–112.

Angermeyer, M. C., Goldstein, J. M., & Kuehn, L. (1989). Gender differences in schizophrenia: Rehospitalization and community survival. *Psychological Medicine, 19*, 365–382.

Badner, J. A., & Gershon, E. S. (2002). Meta-analysis of whole-genome linkage scans of bipolar disorder and schizophrenia. *Molecular Psychiatry, 7*, 405–411.

Ban, T. A. (2004). Neuropsychopharmacology and the genetics of schizophrenia: A history of the diagnosis of schizophrenia. *Progress in Neuro-Psychopharmacology and Biological Psychiatry, 28*, 753–762.

Berenbaum, H., & Oltmanns, T. F. (1992). Emotional experience and expression in schizophrenia and depression. *Journal of Abnormal Psychology, 101*, 37–44.

Berman, K. F., Zec, R. F., & Weinberger, D. R. (1986). Physiologic dysfunction of dorsolateral prefrontal cortex in schizophrenia: Pt. II. Role of neuroleptic treatment, attention, and mental effort. *Archives of General Psychiatry, 43*, 126–135.

Bilder, R. M., Mukherjee, S., Rieder, R. O., & Pandurangi, A. K. (1985). Symptomatic and neuropsychological components of defect states. *Schizophrenia Bulletin, 11*, 409–419.

Bland, R. C., Parker, J. H., & Orn, H. (1978). Prognosis in schizophrenia: Prognostic predictors and outcome. *Archives of General Psychiatry, 35*, 72–77.

Brenner, C. A., Lysaker, P. H., Wilt, M. A., & O'Donnell, B. F. (2002). Visual processing and neuropsychological function in schizophrenia and schizoaffective disorder. *Psychiatry Research, 111*, 125–136.

Brown, A. S., Begg, M. D., Gravenstein, S., Schaefer, C. A., Wyatt, R. J., Bresnahan, M., et al. (2004). Serologic evidence of prenatal influenza in the etiology of schizophrenia. *Archives of General Psychiatry, 61*, 774–780.

Callicott, J. H., Bertolino, A., Mattay, V. S., Langheim, F. J., Duyn, J., Coppola, R., et al. (2000). Physiological dysfunction of the dorsolateral prefrontal cortex in schizophrenia revisited. *Cerebral Cortex, 10*, 1078–1092.

Cannon, M., Jones, P. B., & Murray, R. M. (2002). Obstetric complications and schizophrenia: Historical and meta-analytic review. *American Journal of Psychiatry, 159*, 1080–1092.

Carlsson, A., & Lindqvist, M. (1963). Effect of chlorpromazine or haloperidol on formation of 3methoxytyramine and normetanephrine in mouse brain. *Acta Pharmacologica et Toxicologica, 20*, 140–144.

Carpenter, W. T., Jr., & Strauss, J. S. (1991). The prediction of outcome in schizophrenia: Pt. IV. Eleven-year follow-up of the Washington IPSS cohort. *Journal of Nervous and Mental Disease, 179*, 517–525.

Cobb, S. R., Buhl, E. H., Halasy, K., Paulsen, O., & Somogyi, P. (1995, November 2). Synchronization of neuronal activity in hippocampus by individual GABAergic interneurons. *Nature, 378*, 75–78.

Cohen, J.D., Barch, D.M., Carter, C.S. & Servan-Schreiber, D. (1999). Context processing deficits in schizophrenia: Converging evidence from three theoretically motivated cognitive tasks. *Journal of Abnormal Psychology, 108*, 120–133.

Corcoran, R., Mercer, G., & Frith, C. D. (1995). Schizophrenia, symptomatology and social inference: Investigating "theory of mind" in people with schizophrenia. *Schizophrenia Research, 17*, 5–13.

Corfas, G., Roy, K., & Buxbaum, J. D. (2004). Neuregulin 1-erbB signaling and the molecular/cellular basis of schizophrenia. *Nature Neuroscience, 7*, 575–580.

Corrigan, P. W., & Nelson, D. R. (1998). Factors that affect social cue recognition in schizophrenia. *Psychiatry Research, 78*, 189–196.

Creese, I., Burt, D. R., & Snyder, S. H. (1976, April 30). Dopamine receptor binding predicts clinical and pharmacological potencies of antischizophrenic drugs. *Science, 192*, 481–483.

Davidson, M., Reichenberg, A., Rabinowitz, J., Weiser, M., Kaplan, Z., & Mark, M. (1999). Behavioral and intellectual markers for schizophrenia in apparently healthy male adolescents. *American Journal of Psychiatry, 156*, 1328–1335.

Davies, G., Welham, J., Chant, D., Torrey, E. F., & McGrath, J. (2003). A systematic review and meta-analysis of northern hemisphere season of birth studies in schizophrenia. *Schizophrenia Bulletin, 29*, 587–593.

Dierks, T., Linden, D. E., Jandl, M., Formisano, E., Goebel, R., Lanfermann, H., et al. (1999). Activation of Heschl's gyrus during auditory hallucinations. *Neuron, 22*, 615–621.

Earnst, K. S., & Kring, A. M. (1999). Emotional responding in deficit and non-deficit schizophrenia. *Psychiatry Research, 88*, 191–207.

Feighner, J. P., Robins, E., Guze, S. B., Woodruff, R. A., Jr., Winokur, G., & Munoz, R. (1972). Diagnostic criteria for use in psychiatric research. *Archives of General Psychiatry, 26*, 57–63.

Frith, C. D., & Corcoran, R. (1996). Exploring 'theory of mind' in people with schizophrenia. *Psychological Medicine, 26*, 521–530.

Geller, J. L. (1992). A report on the "worst" state hospital recidivists in the US. *Hospital and Community Psychiatry, 43*, 904–908.

Grace, A. A., Bunney, B. S., Moore, H., & Todd, C. L. (1997). Dopamine-cell depolarization block as a model for the therapeutic actions of antipsychotic drugs. *Trends in Neurosciences, 20*, 31–37.

Green, M., & Walker, E. (1986). Symptom correlates of vulnerability to backward masking in schizophrenia. *American Journal of Psychiatry, 143*, 181–186.

Green, M. F. (1996). What are the functional consequences of neurocognitive deficits in schizophrenia? *American Journal of Psychiatry, 153*, 321–330.

Harrison, P. J. (1999). The neuropathology of schizophrenia: A critical review of the data and their interpretation. *Brain, 122*(Pt. 4), 593–624.

Harrow, M., & Jobe, T. H. (2005). Longitudinal studies of outcome and recovery in schizophrenia and early intervention: Can they make a difference? *Canadian Journal of Psychiatry, 50*, 879–880.

Hegarty, J. D., Baldessarini, R. J., Tohen, M., Waternaux, C., & Oepen, G. (1994). One hundred years of schizophrenia: A meta-analysis of the outcome literature. *American Journal of Psychiatry, 151*, 1409–1416.

Hoffman, R. E., Gueorguieva, R., Hawkins, K. A., Varanko, M., Boutros, N. N., Wu, Y. T., et al. (2005). Temporoparietal transcranial magnetic stimulation for auditory hallucinations: Safety, efficacy and moderators in a fifty patient sample. *Biological Psychiatry, 58*, 97–104.

Howard, A., Tamas, G., & Soltesz, I. (2005). Lighting the chandelier: New vistas for axo-axonic cells. *Trends in Neurosciences, 28*, 310–316.

Ingvar, D. H., & Franzen, G. (1974). Abnormalities of cerebral blood flow distribution in patients with chronic schizophrenia. *Acta Psychiatrica Scandinavica, 50*, 425–462.

Jablensky, A. (2000). Epidemiology of schizophrenia: The global burden of disease and disability. *European Archives of Psychiatry and Clinical Neuroscience, 250*, 274–285.

Javitt, D. C., Strous, R. D., Grochowski, S., Ritter, W., & Cowan, N. (1997). Impaired precision, but normal retention, of auditory sensory (echoic) memory information in schizophrenia. *Journal of Abnormal Psychology, 106*, 315–324.

Javitt, D. C., & Zukin, S. R. (1991). Recent advances in the phencyclidine model of schizophrenia. *American Journal of Psychiatry, 148*, 1301–1308.

Jobe, T. H., & Harrow, M. (2005). Long-term outcome of patients with schizophrenia: A review. *Canadian Journal of Psychiatry, 50*, 892–900.

Johnstone, E. C., Crow, T. J., Frith, C. D., Husband, J., & Kreel, L. (1976). Cerebral ventricular size and cognitive impairment in chronic schizophrenia. *Lancet, 2*, 924–926.

Kanaan, R. A., Kim, J. S., Kaufmann, W. E., Pearlson, G. D., Barker, G. J., & McGuire, P. K. (2005). Diffusion tensor imaging in schizophrenia. *Biological Psychiatry, 58*, 921–929.

Kety, S. S., Rosenthal, D., Wender, P. H., & Schulsinger, F. (1971). Mental illness in the biological and adoptive families of adpoted schizophrenics. *American Journal of Psychiatry, 128*, 302–306.

Kohler, C. G., Bilker, W., Hagendoorn, M., Gur, R. E., & Gur, R. C. (2000). Emotion recognition deficit in schizophrenia: Association with symptomatology and cognition. *Biological Psychiatry, 48*, 127–136.

Lauriello, J., Lenroot, R., & Bustillo, J. R. (2003). Maximizing the synergy between pharmacotherapy and psychosocial therapies for schizophrenia. *Psychiatric Clinics of North America, 26*, 191–211.

Lawrie, S. M., & Abukmeil, S. S. (1998). Brain abnormality in schizophrenia: A systematic and quantitative review of volumetric magnetic resonance imaging studies. *British Journal of Psychiatry, 172*, 110–120.

Lehman, A. F. (1999). Developing an outcomes-oriented approach for the treatment of schizophrenia. *Journal of Clinical Psychiatry, 60*(Suppl, 19), 30–35; discussion 36–37.

Lenroot, R., Bustillo, J. R., Lauriello, J., & Keith, S. J. (2003). Integrated treatment of schizophrenia. *Psychiatric Services, 54*, 1499–1507.

Lewis, C. M., Levinson, D. F., Wise, L. H., DeLisi, L. E., Straub, R. E., Hovatta, I., et al. (2003). Genome scan meta-analysis of schizophrenia and bipolar disorder: Pt. II. Schizophrenia. *American Journal of Human Genetics, 73*, 34–48.

Lewis, D. A. (2000). GABAergic local circuit neurons and prefrontal cortical dysfunction in schizophrenia. *Brain Research: Brain Research Reviews, 31*, 270–276.

Lewis, D. A., & Levitt, P. (2002). Schizophrenia as a disorder of neurodevelopment. *Annual Review of Neuroscience, 25*, 409–432.

Liddle, P. F. (1987). The symptoms of chronic schizophrenia: A re-examination of the positive-negative dichotomy. *British Journal of Psychiatry, 151*, 145–151.

Lieberman, J. A., Perkins, D., Belger, A., Chakos, M., Jarskog, F., Boteva, K., et al. (2001). The early stages of schizophrenia: Speculations on pathogenesis, pathophysiology, and therapeutic approaches. *Biological Psychiatry, 50*, 884–897.

MacDonald, A. W., Carter, C. S., Kerns, J. G., Ursu, S., Barch, D. M., Holmes, A. J., Stenger, V. A., & Cohen, J. D. (2005). Specificity of prefrontal dysfunction and context processing deficits to schizophrenia in never-medicated patients with first-episode psychosis. *American Journal of Psychiatry, 162*, 475–484.

Manoach, D. S., Gollub, R. L., Benson, E. S., Searl, M. M., Goff, D. C., Halpern, E., et al. (2000). Schizophrenic subjects show aberrant fMRI activation of dorsolateral prefrontal cortex and basal ganglia during working memory performance. *Biological Psychiatry, 48*, 99–109.

McGlashan, T. H. (1984). The Chestnut Lodge follow-up study: Pt. II. Long-term outcome of schizophrenia and the affective disorders. *Archives of General Psychiatry, 41*, 586–601.

McGrath, J., Saha, S., Welham, J., El Saadi, O., MacCauley, C., & Chant, D. (2004). A systematic review of the incidence of schizophrenia: The distribution of rates and the influence of sex, urbanicity, migrant status and methodology. *BMC Medicine, 2*, 13.

McGue, M., & Gottesman, I. I. (1989). A single dominant gene still cannot account for the transmission of schizophrenia. *Archives of General Psychiatry, 46*, 478–480.

McGue, M., & Gottesman, I. I. (1991). The genetic epidemiology of schizophrenia and the design of linkage studies. *Eur Arch Psychiatry Clin Neurosci., 240*, 174–181.

Meltzer, H. Y., Li, Z., Kaneda, Y., & Ichikawa, J. (2003). Serotonin receptors: Their key role in drugs to treat schizophrenia. *Progress in Neuro-Psychopharmacology and Biological Psychiatry, 27*, 1159–1172.

Miyamoto, S., Duncan, G. E., Marx, C. E., & Lieberman, J. A. (2005). Treatments for schizophrenia: A critical review of pharmacology and mechanisms of action of antipsychotic drugs. *Molecular Psychiatry, 10*, 79–104.

Moffitt, T. E., Caspi, A., & Rutter, M. (2005). Strategy for investigating interactions between measured genes and measured environments. *Archives of General Psychiatry, 62*, 473–481.

Murray, C. J., & Lopez, A. D. (1996, November 1). Evidence-based health policy: Lessons from the Global Burden of Disease Study. *Science, 274*, 740–743.

Owen, M. J., Craddock, N., & O'Donovan, M. C. (2005). Schizophrenia: Genes at last? *Trends Genet, 21*, 518–525.

Perlstein, W. M., Carter, C. S., Noll, D. C., & Cohen, J. D. (2001). Relation of prefrontal cortex dysfunction to working memory and symptoms in schizophrenia. *American Journal of Psychiatry, 158*, 1105–1113.

Perry, W., & Braff, D. L. (1994). Information-processing deficits and thought disorder in schizophrenia. *American Journal of Psychiatry, 151*, 363–367.

Pinkham, A. E., Penn, D. L., Perkins, D. O., & Lieberman, J. (2003). Implications for the neural basis of social cognition for the study of schizophrenia. *American Journal of Psychiatry, 160*, 815–824.

Popken, G. J., Bunney, W. E., Jr., Potkin, S. G., & Jones, E. G. (2000). Subnucleus-specific loss of neurons in medial thalamus of schizophrenics. *Proceedings of the National Academy of Sciences, USA, 97*, 9276–9280.

Remington, G., & Kapur, S. (1999). D2 and 5-HT2 receptor effects of antipsychotics: Bridging basic and clinical findings using PET. *Journal of Clinical Psychiatry, 60*(Suppl, 10), 15–19.

Risch, N. (1990). Genetic linkage and complex diseases, with special reference to psychiatric disorders. *Genet Epidemiol, 7*, 3–16; discussion 17–45.

Saccuzzo, D. P., & Braff, D. L. (1981). Early information processing deficit in schizophrenia: New findings using schizophrenic subgroups and manic control subjects. *Archives of General Psychiatry, 38*, 175–179.

Salem, J. E., Kring, A. M., & Kerr, S. L. (1996). More evidence for generalized poor performance in facial emotion perception in schizophrenia. *Journal of Abnormal Psychology, 105*, 480–483.

Sartorius, N., Jablensky, A., & Shapiro, R. (1977). Two-year follow-up of the patients included in the WHO international pilot study of schizophrenia. *Psychological Medicine, 7*, 529–541.

Schneider, F., Gur, R. C., Koch, K., Backes, V., Amunts, K., Shah, N. J., et al. (2006). Impairment in the specificity of emotion processing in schizophrenia. *American Journal of Psychiatry, 163*, 442–447.

Seeman, P., Lee, T., Chau-Wong, M., & Wong, K. (1976, June 24). Antipsychotic drug doses and neuroleptic/dopamine receptors. *Nature, 261,* 717–719.

Shelley, A. M., Ward, P. B., Catts, S. V., Michie, P. T., Andrews, S., & McConaghy, N. (1991). Mismatch negativity: An index of a preattentive processing deficit in schizophrenia. *Biological Psychiatry, 30,* 1059–1062.

Steen, R. G., Mull, C., McClure, R., Hamer, R. M., & Lieberman, J. A. (2006). Brain volume in first-episode schizophrenia: Systematic review and meta-analysis of magnetic resonance imaging studies. *British Journal of Psychiatry, 188,* 510–518.

Stefansson, H., Sigurdsson, E., Steinthorsdottir, V., Bjornsdottir, S., Sigmundsson, T., Ghosh, S., et al. (2002). Neuregulin 1 and susceptibility to schizophrenia. *American Journal of Human Genetics, 71,* 877–892.

Stone, M. H. (1986). Exploratory psychotherapy in schizophrenia-spectrum patients: A reevaluation in the light of long-term follow-up of schizophrenic and borderline patients. *Bulletin of the Menninger Clinic, 50,* 287–306.

Straub, R. E., Jiang, Y., MacLean, C. J., Ma, Y., Webb, B. T., Myakishev, M. V., et al. (2002). Genetic variation in the 6p22.3 gene DTNBP1, the human ortholog of the mouse dysbindin gene, is associated with schizophrenia. *American Journal of Human Genetics, 71,* 337–348.

Susser, E., Neugebauer, R., Hoek, H. W., Brown, A. S., Lin, S., Labovitz, D., et al. (1996). Schizophrenia after prenatal famine: Further evidence. *Archives of General Psychiatry, 53,* 25–31.

Susser, E. S., Schaefer, C. A., Brown, A. S., Begg, M. D., & Wyatt, R. J. (2000). The design of the prenatal determinants of schizophrenia study. *Schizophrenia Bulletin, 26,* 257–273.

Terkelsen, K. G., & Menikoff, A. (1995). Measuring the costs of schizophrenia: Implications for the post-institutional era in the US. *Pharmacoeconomics, 8,* 199–222.

Tienari, P., Wynne, L. C., Moring, J., Lahti, I., Naarala, M., Sorri, A., et al. (1994). The Finnish adoptive family study of schizophrenia: Implications for family research. *British Journal of Psychiatry, 23,* 20–26.

Tsuang, M. T., & Winokur, G. (1975). The Iowa 500: Field work in a 35-year follow-up of depression, mania, and schizophrenia. *Canadian Psychiatric Association Journal, 20,* 359–365.

Volk, D. W., Austin, M. C., Pierri, J. N., Sampson, A. R., & Lewis, D. A. (2000). Decreased glutamic acid decarboxylase67 messenger RNA expression in a subset of prefrontal cortical gamma-aminobutyric acid neurons in subjects with schizophrenia. *Archives of General Psychiatry, 57,* 237–245.

Volk, D., & Lewis, D. A. (2002). Impaired prefrontal inhibition in schizophrenia: Relevance for cognitive dysfunction. *Physiology and Behavior, 77,* 510–505.

Weinberger, D. R., Berman, K. F., & Zec, R. F. (1986). Physiologic dysfunction of dorsolateral prefrontal cortex in schizophrenia: Pt. I. Regional cerebral blood flow evidence. *Archives of General Psychiatry, 43,* 114–124.

Xiberas, X., Martinot, J. L., Mallet, L., Artiges, E., Loc, H. C., Maziere, B., et al. (2001). Extrastriatal and striatal D(2) dopamine receptor blockade with haloperidol or new antipsychotic drugs in patients with schizophrenia. *British Journal of Psychiatry, 179,* 503–508.

Chapter 55

Depression

BOADIE W. DUNLOP AND CHARLES B. NEMEROFF

A clinically depressed mood is found in several psychiatric disorders, including major depressive disorder (MDD), bipolar disorder, posttraumatic stress disorder, and dysthymia, as well as in substance-induced mood disorders, and mood disorders associated with comorbid medical illnesses, such as Parkinson's disease. These disorders all have distinguishing biological characteristics and treatment responsiveness, illustrating how the experience of a depressed mood may arise from a variety of biological sources. This chapter focuses on the findings of studies of MDD because it is the most common of these illnesses, has the greatest impact on public health, and has been the focus of the most extensive neuroscientific investigations.

It is difficult to overstate the public health importance of MDD. The lifetime prevalence of MDD is 16%, and the 12-month prevalence is 6.6% (Kessler et al., 2003). The lifetime risk for the illness in women is approximately double the risk in men. A widely cited study, the Global Burden of Disease, conducted by the World Bank, the World Health Organization, and the Harvard School of Public Health, predicts that by the year 2020, MDD will be the second leading cause of disability worldwide, trailing only cardiovascular disease (Murray & Lopez, 1996). MDD is also a leading cause of premature death due to suicide. Depressive symptoms contribute to risk for several other important diseases, including coronary artery disease and stroke (Anda et al., 1993; Jonas & Mussolino, 2000). MDD follows a chronic course in about 20% of those affected, and of those who remit, approximately 85% will experience another episode of depression within 15 years (Mueller et al., 1999). Finally, the economic burden of MDD is enormous, with conservatively estimated annual direct costs of $2.1 billion and indirect costs of $4.2 billion per year in the United States alone (Jones & Cockrum, 2000).

MDD, also known as *unipolar depression,* to distinguish it from depression occurring in bipolar disorder (manic-depressive illness), is a multidimensional disorder. Only one major depressive episode (see Table 55.1) is required for the diagnosis of MDD, though major depressive episodes can also occur in other disorders. The primary clinical characteristics that distinguish these disorders from MDD are presented in Table 55.2. The clinical diagnosis of a major depressive episode refers to a syndrome in which there is a significant change in (a) mood state: either prominent feelings of sadness and/or anhedonia, along with the presence of several other symptoms. These other symptoms can be grouped into additional categories; (b) neurovegetative systems: disturbances in sleep and appetite, and reductions in energy; (c) cognitive functions: excessive thoughts of guilt or worthlessness, poor concentration or indecisiveness, and thoughts of suicide; and (d) psychomotor performance: either slowed (retarded) or agitated. The symptoms in each of these categories have their own specific neurobiological basis. Because the diagnosis of a major depressive episode can be made when all four categories are present, or when as few as two categories of symptoms are present, great heterogeneity between equivalently diagnosed patients exists, both phenomenologically and biologically.

Dr. Dunlop is supported by 5K12RR017643 and 1KL2RR025009. Dr. Nemeroff was supported by NIH MH-42088, MH-39415, MH-77083, MH-69056, and MH-58922.

Disclosures of Possible Conflicts of Interest: Dr. Dunlop has received research support from AstraZeneca, Bristol-Myers Squibb, Cephalon, Forest, Janssen, Ono Pharmaceuticals, Novartis, and Takeda. He has served as a consultant to Cephalon, Shire, and Wyeth, and served on the speaker's bureau of Bristol-Myers Squibb.

Over the past 1.5 years, Dr. Nemeroff has served on the Scientific Advisory Board for Astra-Zeneca, Johnson & Johnson, Pharma Neuroboost, Forest Laboratories, Quintiles, and NARSAD. He is a grant recipient from NIH, NARSAD, and AFSP. He serves on the Board of Directors of AFSP, NovaDel Pharmaceuticals, Mt. Cook Pharma, Inc., and the George West Mental Health Foundation. He owns equity in CeNeRx and Reevax. He owns stock or stock options in Corcept and NovaDel.

TABLE 55.1   Diagnostic criteria for a major depressive episode

Symptom Category	Symptom
Mood change	1. Excessive sadness
	2. Anhedonia/loss of interest
Neurovegetative	3. Insomnia or hypersomnia
	4. Weight or appetite change
	5. Diminished energy
Cognitive	6. Poor concentration or indecisiveness
	7. Excessive guilt or worthlessness
	8. Thoughts of own death or suicide
Psychomotor speed	9. Psychomotor agitation or retardation

Note: To diagnose a major depressive episode, at least five of the listed symptoms must be present for most of the day, nearly every day for the past 2 weeks and the symptoms must cause some level of impairment. At least 1 of the symptoms must be either excessive sadness or anhedonia. One major depressive episode justifies the diagnosis of major depressive disorder, as long as criteria for other disorders higher in the diagnostic hierarchy are not met.

TABLE 55.2   Other *DSM-IV* diagnoses with prominent depression without psychotic symptoms

Diagnosis	Primary Characteristic Distinguishing from MDD
Bipolar disorder	If a major depressive episode is present, the patient has also experienced at least one episode of elevated, irritable, or expansive mood.
Dysthymia	Chronic ($\geq$ 2 years) of depressed mood with less intensity and associated depressive symptoms than a major depressive episode.
Post-traumatic stress disorder (PTSD)	In addition to symptoms of depression, the patient also experiences re-experiencing symptoms (e.g., nightmares, flashbacks, intrusive memories) of a traumatic life event. Patient may have both major depressive disorder (MDD) and PTSD, concurrently.
Substance-induced mood disorder	Depressed mood stemming directly from a state of intoxication or withdrawal from a substance (e.g., alcohol or cocaine).
Mood disorder due to a medical condition	Depressed mood derived directly from the pathophysiologic processes of a medical disorder (e.g., hypothyroidism).

HETEROGENEITY

Many efforts have been made to identify subtypes of MDD to address this heterogeneity. The first approaches attempted to distinguish depressed patients on clinical grounds. Although the categories have undergone revision over time, the clinical approach is still codified in the fourth edition of the *Diagnostic and Statistical Manual* (*DSM-IV*). The current *DSM-IV* clinical descriptors of a major depressive episode are:

Melancholic features: Near complete loss of pleasure or reactivity to stimuli.

In addition, three of the following 6 symptoms must also be present: distinct quality of depressed mood, anorexia or weight loss, early morning awakening, worse morning mood, psychomotor change, and excessive guilt.

Atypical features: Preserved mood reactivity to stimuli.

In addition, two of the following four symptoms must also be present: hypersomnia, heavy/leaden feeling in arms or legs, weight gain or increased appetite, and persistent sensitivity to feelings of rejection in relationships.

Psychotic features: Presence of delusions or hallucinations during the depressive episode (not better explained by another disorder; e.g., schizophrenia).

Catatonic features: Profound psychomotor disturbance during the depressive episode, characterized by severe motoric immobility or purposeless excessive activity, bizarre movements or posturing, echolalia or echopraxia, or profound negativism (i.e., mutism or resistance to being moved).

Postpartum onset: Onset of current depressive episode within 4 weeks postpartum.

Chronic: Full criteria for MDD met continuously for at least 2 years.

The episode may also be described in terms of its overall severity: mild, moderate, or severe.

There are precious few factors available today to guide clinician choices of treatments for MDD. Those that are used derive from clinical data, for example, a personal or family history of response to a specific treatment, presence of other medical or psychiatric disorders in addition to MDD, and a desire to avoid certain side effects. In the research arena, a renewed interest in identifying biologically based subtypes is emerging. This approach has not yet yielded any specific clinical benefits, but future progress toward developing more precise treatments will depend on gains in our understanding of the pathophysiology of the mood disorders.

The concept of endophenotypes, that is, subtypes of depression with specific clinical or biological features, may have particular relevance in our efforts to determine the neurobiological underpinnings of MDD. The clinical endophenotypes with the strongest data are those of anhedonia, increased stress sensitivity, and depressive mood bias. Biological endophenotypes identified include those depressed patients sensitive to tryptophan depletion and those with abnormal hypothalamic-pituitary-adrenal (HPA) axis function (Hasler, Drevets, Manji, & Charney, 2004). Table 55.3 lists the current clinical and biological endophenotypes in order of the strength of existing evidence.

This limitation of inadequately defined clinical and biological subtypes of major depression is a significant hindrance to identifying homogeneous samples of patients

TABLE 55.3　Putative Endophenotypes for Major Depressive Disorder

	Heritability	Description
Clinical Endophenotype		
Anhedonia	Yes	Prominent deficits in reward processing
Increased stress sensitivity	Yes	Heightened susceptibility to depression after exposure to stressful life events
Depressed mood bias	No	Prominent biasing of information processing toward negative (sad or unpleasant) content
Diurnal variation	Yes	Marked variability in symptoms related to disruptions in circadian rhythms
Executive cognitive function	Yes	Decreased speed of response on tasks of selecting strategies, planning, and monitoring performance
Biological Endophenotype		
Tryptophan depletion	Yes	Depressive symptoms emerging in state of reduced dietary tryptophan
Dex/CRH test	Yes	Elevated concentrations of ACTH and cortisol from CRH stimulation after dexamethasone dosing to suppress HPA axis
Catecholamine depletion	No	AMPT-induced exacerbation of mood symptoms
REM sleep abnormalities	Yes	Reduced REM latency, higher REM density and increased overall REM sleep
Altered subgenual PFC function	No	Volume loss and increased (volume corrected) metabolic processing in this component of the affective ACC
Reduced $5HT_{1A}$ receptor BP	Yes	Decreased expression or activity of $5HT_{1A}$ receptors
Increased cytokine activity	No	Increased concentrations of proinflammatory cytokines IL-1, IL-6, and TNF-α

Note: "Heritability" refers to whether there are published studies suggesting that variance in the endophenotypes is associated with genetic variance. ACC = anterior cingulate cortex; AMPT = α-methylparatyrosine; ACTH = adreoncorticotropin; BP = binding potential; Dex/CRH = dexamethasone/corticotropin releasing hormone challenge test; 5HT = 5-hydroxytryptophan; IL-1 = interleukin-1; IL-6 = interleukin-6; REM = rapid eye movement; TNF = tumor necrosis factor.

From "Discovering Endophenotypes for Major Depression," by G. Hasler, W. C. Drevets, H. K. Manji, and D. S. Charney, 2004, *Neuropsychopharmacology*, 29, pp. 1765–1781. Adapted with permission.

who may share the same pathobiology. Further heterogeneity is introduced by differences in family history (and thus genetic susceptibility) and presence of other psychiatric conditions that frequently co-occur with major depression, such as anxiety disorders, attention deficit hyperactivity disorder, substance abuse, and psychotic symptoms. Another ongoing challenge is separating state effects (i.e., those features of the biology present only during the depressive episode) from trait effects (i.e., the biological features that continue to be present both during an episode and in remission from the illness, perhaps representing some aspect of vulnerability to depression). The impact of age is an important confounder. Patients 50 years of age or older experiencing a first episode of depression are more likely to have cerebrovascular changes contributing to their depressive syndrome (Krishnan, Hays, & Blazer, 1997). Responsiveness to placebo treatment, and the naturally remitting nature of the illness further complicate the biological assessments of the specificity of treatments of MDD. Finally, adequately distinguishing between anxiety and depression is also challenging because these two forms of mental experience commonly co-occur and share some biological substrates. Anxiety is best conceived as a state of apprehension and hyperarousal related to perceived future threat or danger; depression is a state of reduced hedonic experience or excessive sadness. All these factors contribute to the substantial heterogeneity within MDD, and likely underlie the inconsistency of biological findings reported to date.

METHODS OF INVESTIGATION

The scientific study of major depression can be divided into four categories of approach: biochemistry, genetics, neuroimaging, and postmortem and animal studies.

Biochemistry

The first and most well-established approach, biochemistry, involves the analysis of various endogenous substances in the brain and body thought to be important in the regulation of mood and behavior. From the original discovery of the importance of monoamines in the regulation of mood, these neurochemistry approaches have broadened to include a large number of potentially important molecules, which will be discussed in the following section. Biochemical approaches include: (a) comparing the quantity or activity of a biological component or system in those with MDD and a group of healthy controls not afflicted with the illness; (b) challenging or stimulating a biological system through pharmacologic, psychologic, or other means, and comparing the results between MDD and control subjects, or within MDD subjects at two different time points; and (c) exploring the effects of treatment on biological systems of depressed patients. Measures that "normalize" to the levels of nonaffected individuals after remission from the episode identify state effects of the illness. Comparisons between subjects remitted from a depressive episode and never-depressed control groups are crucial for the identification of trait effects, which do not change significantly between ill and well phases of the illness. The argument that what works to treat an illness reflects the underlying pathophysiology of the illness is somewhat circular and not necessarily valid. Nevertheless, since the start of biological investigations of MDD, studies of the pathophysiology of MDD have been driven in part by studying the mechanisms of drugs found to provide relief from the illness. The first example was the catecholamine hypothesis of MDD, derived in large part from the finding that imipramine impeded norepinephrine reuptake from the synapse. Biochemical experiments in MDD have nearly always produced results for which the ranges of measurements overlap between the depressed and nondepressed groups, limiting their use as diagnostic tests, though insight into pathophysiology is possible.

Genetics

The rapidly advancing field of genetics constitutes the second major approach to the study of MDD. Genetic studies aim to identify alleles of genes that convey vulnerability or resilience to developing MDD. The heritability of MDD (i.e., the proportion of the variation in major depression attributable to genetic factors) is approximately one-third, with an even greater percentage present in cases of depression with an early age of onset (i.e., before age 40) that are recurrent (P. F. Sullivan, Neale, & Kendler, 2000). Family-based studies have found the relative risk of developing MDD for first-degree relatives of depressed individuals is nearly three times greater than the general population (Gershon et al., 1982; Maier et al., 1992).

MDD is almost certainly a complex polygenetic illness, with its phenotypic expression most often dependent on interactions between genes and the individual's environmental experiences (i.e., gene by environment interactions). This model implies that inheritance of specific alleles produces a trait of vulnerability (or resilience) to developing depression, which can become manifest after the individual experiences certain negative life events. In polygenetic illnesses, the effect size of any individual gene is likely to be small, and the same gene may produce vulnerability for other illnesses in addition to major depression. For example, MDD shares about 55% of the genetic risk with neuroticism (i.e., a personality type characterized by high degrees of dysphoria, tension, anxiety, and emotional reactivity; Kendler, Neale, Kessler, Heath, & Eaves, 1993). Generalized anxiety disorder also shares similar genetic factors with MDD, and some evidence links the genetics of panic disorder and social phobia to MDD (Mineka, Watson, & Clark, 1998; Weissman et al., 2005).

Association and linkage studies have identified many potential genetic contributors to MDD, though confirmatory studies often have failed to replicate the findings. Perhaps one of the most important reasons for this inconsistency is that the clinical syndrome of MDD can have significant symptomatic variation between individuals, suggesting that specific genes may exert variable effects depending on the form of depression under study. Incomplete penetrance of genes, such that individuals of the same genotype do not uniformly express the illness, is another complicating factor. For example, dysthymia and "subsyndromal" depression or "minor depression," in which a patient meets some by not all criteria for MDD, may reflect incomplete penetrance of MDD-related genes. The concept of incomplete penetrance of genes in MDD is concordant with the concept of gene by environment interactions, because in this model the gene only becomes "penetrant" if the individual experiences certain environmental adverse events. One potential mediator for variable gene expression is the role of DNA methylation patterns, which regulate the transcription of genes in response to environmental events (Abdolmaleky et al., 2004).

Neuroimaging

The third and most recent approach to the study of depression is the use of neuroimaging. The promise of neuroimaging approaches for depression is in elucidating specifically how brain function is disrupted in the diseased state. Neuroimaging approaches to depression fall into two main categories: (1) Structural imaging approaches identify how the morphology of the brain of depressed patients differs from that of healthy controls. (2) Functional neuroimaging examines patterns of brain activity of specific brain regions or circuits, either while the brain is "at rest" or engaged with the performance of a task.

Structural neuroimaging, originally employing computerized tomography (CT) and now magnetic resonance imaging (MRI) techniques, is useful for identifying abnormalities of the gross morphology of living subjects, and in doing so, identify structures that warrant further examination through other approaches. The structural approach is, however, somewhat limited because the gross morphological changes in major depression are relatively small, in contrast to the morphological changes observed in schizophrenia.

Functional imaging approaches offer the tantalizing promise of evaluating brain changes in real time. Three functional imaging approaches used in the study of depression are positron emission tomography (PET), single photon emission computerized tomography (SPECT), and functional MRI (fMRI). Due to its greater resolution, PET is superior to SPECT, though more expensive and difficult to conduct. PET and SPECT studies, using low levels of radioactive tracers, can be employed in two ways. First, by attaching a radioactive tag to molecules that bind to specific receptors or transporters (reuptake pumps) in the brain, the density of these proteins can be measured. This approach thus allows for the comparison of receptor densities between depressed and healthy control subjects, or in depressed subjects both before and after treatment or recovery from the episode of depression. Thus, biochemical theories of treatment-induced changes of receptor and transporter availability can be tested in the living patient. An important caveat of these studies is that binding does not necessarily reflect activity states of the protein. Thus, proteins (or components of proteins) that bind the tracer molecule may be present in the cytoplasm of the cell (i.e., internalized), and therefore not actively engaged in signal transduction on the cell surface. The other PET method is the use of radioisotopes of water (^{15}O) or glucose (^{18F}Glu) to measure cerebral blood flow and glucose metabolism, respectively. This approach thereby complements that of fMRI, which measures changes in blood flow over time. Functional imaging studies can be divided into *resting state* studies, in which subjects are imaged while simply lying down, relaxed, and not thinking of anything in particular, and *activation* studies, in which subjects are imaged prior, during, and after being prompted to engage in some observation or task.

Postmortem and Animal Studies

Research into the neurobiology of depression also relies on two other important approaches. Postmortem studies complement living-subject studies in that they allow for analysis of central nervous system (CNS) tissue from individuals who suffered from depression during life. There are several limitations to postmortem studies, including incomplete or uncertain diagnoses of the deceased, variability in the state and clinical features of the depressive illness during life, uncertainty about previous treatment and substance abuse, difficulty of separating suicidality from depression, and variation in agonal states.

Animal models of depression complement these human-subject study designs. Rodent models are by far the most commonly employed, but they present their own challenges. Most current models (e.g., learned helplessness, forced swim test, chronic mild stress, tail suspension test) focus on inducing a state of inescapable stress, whereas the bulbectomized rat model induces a state of dysregulated amygdala function and cortisol hypersecretion (O'Neill & Moore, 2003; Song & Leonard, 2005). The maternal deprivation model in rodents and nonhuman primates focuses on the now well-established observation that early life trauma is associated with a marked increase in risk for depression in adulthood (Kendler, Gardner, & Prescott, 2002). Due to the rodents' markedly less-developed prefrontal cortex compared to humans', rodent models cannot provide insight into the uniquely human cognitive experiences of guilt, suicidal thoughts, and poor concentration that occur in depression. Rather, these models have greater face validity with the more overt symptoms of depression, such as anhedonia, amotivation, and behavioral despair (helplessness). Despite their limitations, these models have been quite successful at identifying novel compounds that are effective antidepressants in humans.

Summary

The results of these scientific investigations into MDD have produced four main systems of interest relevant to the pathophysiology of depression. These systems will be discussed separately, though it should be emphasized that all of these systems have complex interactions with each other. We start with the limbic-HPA axis because current evidence suggests that this is the system closest to being the core disruption in most individuals with MDD. Subsequently, the roles of cytokines, monoamines, and brain-derived neurotrophic factor (BDNF) and neurogenesis is discussed. Other systems that are perhaps less central to the core pathophysiologies are then described, including the findings regarding thyroid and other endocrine systems, the fast-acting neurotransmitters glutamate and γ-amino butyric acid (GABA), and sleep. We also include a separate section on the neuroimaging findings in MDD, before concluding with examples of how these various systems interact. The brain regions considered to be of greatest importance to the pathophysiology of MDD are identified in Figure 55.1.

ROLE OF THE HYPOTHALAMIC-PITUITARY-ADRENAL AXIS

Particularly early in the course of MDD, depressive episodes often emerge in the wake of a significant life stressor. As the disease progresses, future episodes are less closely linked to adverse life experiences (Lewinsohn, Allen, Seeley, & Gotlib, 1999). This observation served as an important initial impetus for research on the HPA axis in MDD (Figure 55.2). One of the earliest biological findings in the study of the pathophysiology of depression were abnormalities in adrenocortical function in depressed

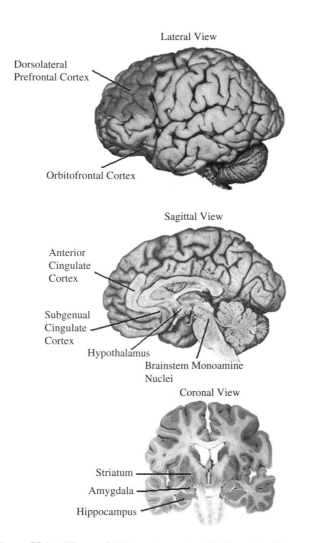

Lateral View

Dorsolateral
Prefrontal Cortex

Orbitofrontal Cortex

Sagittal View

Anterior
Cingulate
Cortex

Subgenual
Cingulate
Cortex

Hypothalamus

Brainstem Monoamine
Nuclei

Coronal View

Striatum

Amygdala

Hippocampus

Figure 55.1 (**Figure C.53** in color section) Brain regions important in the pathophysiology of major depressive disorder.

Note: Three views of the brain, identifying regions considered to be important in the pathophysiology of depression. Brodmann area 25 (BA25) is part of the subgenual cingulate cortex. The brain stem monoamine nuclei of importance include the dorsal raphe (serotonin), the locus ceruleus (norepinephrine) and the ventral tegmental area (dopamine). The striatum is a component of the basal ganglia, and includes the caudate nucleus and putamen. From "Depression: Perspectives from Affective Neuroscience," by R. J. Davidson, D. Pizzagalli, J. B. Nitschke, and K. M. Putnam, 2002, *Annual Review of Psychology, 53*, pp. 545–574. Reprinted, with permission, from the Annual Review of Psychology, Volume 53 ©2002 by Annual Reviews www.annualreviews.org.

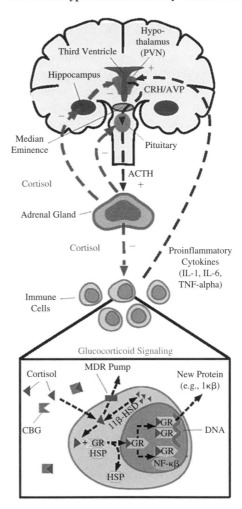

Figure 55.2   HPA axis and cytokine activity.

Note: Corticotropin releasing factor (hormone) (CRH) and vasopressin (AVP) secreted from the paraventricular nucleus of the hypothalamus control release of adrenocorticotropin (ACTH) from the pituitary. ACTH regulates cortisol release from the adrenal glands. Upon activation by cortisol, the glucocorticoid receptor (GR) dissociates from its chaperone heat shock protein (HSP) and translocates to the nucleus, where it interacts with other transcription factors or binds directly to DNA to influence gene transcription. Cortisol regulates its own production via negative feedback at the hippocampus, hypothalamus, and pituitary. CRH release can be stimulated by the proinflammatory cytokines, including interleukin-1 (IL-1), interleukin-6 (IL-6), and tumor necrosis factor (TNF). From "When Not Enough Is Too Much: The Role of Insufficient Glucocorticoid Signaling in the Pathophysiology of Stress-Related Disorders," by C. L. Raison and A. H. Miller, 2003, *American Journal of Psychiatry, 160*, 1554–1565. Reprinted with permission.

patients (J. L. Gibbons & McHugh, 1962). These early findings were subsequently confirmed, with elevated cortisol concentrations in the plasma and urine of patients with MDD now among the most reproducible findings in biologic psychiatry (Sachar, Hellman, Fukushima, & Gallagher, 1970). Some components of the HPA axis also demonstrate structural changes in depressed patients, including enlargement of the pituitary and adrenal glands (Krishnan et al., 1991; Nemeroff et al., 1992). Adrenal gland enlargement (due to adrenocortical, not adrenomedullary hypertrophy) likely results from adrenocorticotropic hormone (ACTH)

hypersecretion in depressed patients; it appears to be state-dependent because adrenal enlargement is correlated with symptomatic status of the patient (Nemeroff et al., 1992; Rubin, Phillips, Sadow, & McCracken, 1995).

Corticotropin-releasing factor (CRF), a 41 amino acid peptide, is synthesized in the diencephalon, primarily in the parvocellular neurons of the paraventricular nucleus (PVN) of the hypothalamus. Brain regions thought to be important in emotion processing, including the brain stem, amygdala, and the bed nucleus of the stria terminalis all project to the PVN CRF neurons (Hauger & Dautzenberg, 2000). The PVN CRF neurons have short projections to the median eminence of the hypothalamus, where they release CRF into the hypothalamo-hypophyseal portal system under conditions of stress. The released CRF is transported to the anterior pituitary where it binds to CRF receptors on corticotrophs. These pituicytes then synthesize pro-opiomelanocortin, the precursor of ACTH and β-endorphin, and release ACTH. Vasopressin (also known as antidiuretic hormone), which is secreted along with CRF from the hypothalamus, amplifies the effects of CRF at the pituitary. The ACTH secreted from the pituitary enters the systemic circulation and acts on the adrenal cortex to induce the production and release of cortisol. In the healthy state, cortisol then exerts negative feedback effects via binding to glucocorticoid (GC) receptors in the pituitary and hippocampus, resulting in a down-regulation of activity of the HPA axis. In many patients with depression, this negative feedback process does not occur, despite high levels of circulating cortisol.

Challenging the Hypothalamic-Pituitary Adrenal Axis

The dexamethasone suppression test (DST) was developed in the 1960s as a means of evaluating HPA axis function in patients with primary endocrine disorders such as Cushing's disease, and then adapted for use in the study of depression (Carroll, Martin, & Davies, 1968). The DST is typically conducted by administering an oral dose of 1.0 mg of dexamethasone at 11 PM, followed by measurement of plasma cortisol concentrations at various times the following day. In healthy controls, administration of dexamethasone (a synthetic glucocorticoid) suppresses endogenous cortisol via its cortisol-like negative feedback effects, primarily by action on the pituitary. By contrast, many patients with MDD fail to exhibit suppression of cortisol production; such subjects are referred to as *nonsuppressors*. Escape from the suppressive effects of cortisol or dexamethasone in depressed patients may be explained by impaired glucocorticoid receptor signaling at the level of the pituitary. This hypothesis is supported by a transgenic mouse model, producing mice with diminished glucocorticoid receptor function (Pepin, Pothier, & Barden, 1992). These transgenic mice demonstrate escape from dexamethasone suppression, which can be normalized after 10 days of treatment with the antidepressant imipramine.

Unfortunately, results of the DST have produced a sensitivity level too low for use as a screening test for major depression (Arana, Baldessarini, & Ornsteen, 1985). The test also has insufficient specificity for use as a confirmatory diagnostic test because several other medical conditions

and about 7% of normal controls were found to be non-suppressors (Janicak, Davis, Preskorn, & Ayd, 1997). In the 1980s, the amino acid sequence for CRF was identified, and a standardized CRF stimulation test was developed to assess HPA axis activity. In this test, a CRF dose of 1 μg/kg, or a fixed dose of 100 μg, is administered intravenously, and the concentrations of ACTH and cortisol are measured at 30-minute intervals over a 2- to 3-hour period (Holsboer, von Bardeleben, Wiedemann, Muller, & Stalla, 1987). Depressed patients demonstrate a blunted ACTH and β-endorphin response to CRF compared with nondepressed controls (Kathol, Jaeckle, Lopez, & Meller, 1989; Young et al., 1990). The attenuated ACTH response to CRF observed in depressed patients may result from down-regulation of CRF receptors in the anterior pituitary stemming from chronic CRF hypersecretion (Wynn, Harwood, Catt, & Aguilera, 1988).

An alternative hypothesis is that chronically elevated cortisol concentrations result in diminished ACTH release via negative feedback. However, the cortisol response in the CRF stimulation test does not consistently differ between patients and controls. The state of the art in assessing HPA axis function has now evolved into the combination of these two tests, which overcomes the limitations of the DST. In the dexamethasone/CRF test, at 3 PM on the day following the 1 mg dexamethasone dose, 100 μg of CRF is administered intravenously, with blood draws at 30-minute intervals for 2 hours to measure ACTH and cortisol plasma concentrations (Holsboer et al., 1987). This test has a diagnostic sensitivity in depression of up to 80% (Heuser, Yassouridis, & Holsboer, 1994). Depressed patients who are nonsuppressors in the dexamethasone/CRF test prior to treatment demonstrate a better response to antidepressant treatment than suppressors, that is, normal results on this test prior to treatment predict poor response to antidepressant medication. Additionally, failure to normalize HPA axis function from nonsuppression to suppression 2 to 3 weeks after starting antidepressant medication also predicts poor response, and a greater likelihood of depressive relapse among those who do clinically improve with treatment (Aubry et al., 2007).

Another test to assess HPA axis responsivity in a more naturalistic manner is the Trier social stress test (TSST; Kirschbaum, Pirke, & Hellhammer, 1993). This test requires subjects to perform a simulated 10-minute public speech and a very challenging mental arithmetic task in front of a small unsupportive audience. Performing the TSST reliably activates the HPA axis, as assessed by increases in ACTH and cortisol concentrations during the test. In the TSST, subjects with a history of early life abuse or neglect show particularly marked elevations of ACTH, but only subjects who have experienced abuse or neglect and are actively depressed also exhibit increased cortisol concentrations (Heim, Newport, Bonsall, Miller, & Nemeroff, 2001). The fact that actively depressed subjects without a history of abuse or neglect do not show elevations of ACTH or cortisol on the TSST greater than controls suggests that stress reactivity may be one means through which the pathophysiology of depression can be subtyped.

Corticotropin-Releasing Factor

Considerable attention to the CRF receptor as a novel target for intervention in depression has occurred over the past decade. Two CRF receptor subtypes have been identified, CRF_1 and CRF_2, that have a distinct neuro-anatomic localization and receptor pharmacology, have been identified in rats and humans (Hauger & Dautzenberg, 2000). Both receptors are G-protein coupled receptors and are positively coupled to adenylyl cyclase via the protein G_s. The CRF_1 subtype is considered to play a more central role in mediating depressive and anxious behaviors, and preclinical and clinical studies suggest that compounds that block this receptor may possess antidepressant and anxiolytic efficacy (Zobel et al., 2000).

In addition to their location in the hypothalamus, CRF-producing neurons are found in a variety of brain regions that regulate stress response and emotion processing, including the amygdala, thalamus, hippocampus and prefrontal cortex (Sanchez, Young, Plotsky, & Insel, 1999; Van Pett et al., 2000). CRF directly injected into the CNS of laboratory animals produces behaviors similar to those of MDD, including decreased libido, reduced appetite, weight loss, sleep disturbances, and neophobia (Owens & Nemeroff, 1991). Some of the extrahypothalamic CRF neurons project to the spinal cord (Kiss, Martos, & Palkovits, 1991) and brain stem nuclei (Swanson & Kuypers, 1980), including the locus ceruleus (LC) and dorsal raphe (Reyes, Valentino, Xu, & Van Bockstaele, 2005). This close anatomic proximity between the monoamine systems and CRF suggests a likely regulatory interaction between these two systems, and may be a mechanism by which antidepressants act upon the CRF system.

The potential role for extrahypothalamic CRF systems in the pathophysiology of MDD is supported by human studies demonstrating elevated CRF concentrations in the cerebrospinal fluid (CSF) of depressed patients (Banki, Bissette, Arato, O'Connor, & Nemeroff, 1987; France et al., 1988; Nemeroff et al., 1984), although discrepant results have been reported (Roy et al., 1987). Elevated CRF concentrations are also present in the CSF of depressed suicide victims (Arato, Banki, Bissette, & Nemeroff, 1989). Suicide victims also have elevated CRF concentrations and reduced CRF receptor binding density and expression in the frontal cortex compared with controls (Merali et al., 2006; Merali, Khan, Michaud, Shippy, & Anisman, 2004; Nemeroff, Owens, Bissette, Andorn, & Stanley, 1988). Reductions in CSF CRF concentrations occur in healthy volunteers administered the antidepressant desipramine (Veith et al., 1993) and in depressed patients treated with fluoxetine (De Bellis, Gold, Geracioti, Listwak, & Kling, 1993), amitriptyline (Heuser et al., 1998), or ECT (Nemeroff, Bissette, Akil, & Fink, 1991). These findings argue that elevated CSF CRF concentrations are a marker of the depressed state, rather than a trait marker, of many individuals with MDD.

A strongly supported endophenotype of MDD is one characterized by exaggerated stress sensitivity. Exposure to severe stress early in life may result in sensitization of the HPA axis and extrahypothalamic CRF neurons, thereby increasing the risk for these individuals to develop MDD after exposure to additional stressors later in life. Animal studies employing models of early life stress, such as removal of rat pups from their mothers for various periods of time, have demonstrated both acute and sustained changes in neuroendocrine and behavioral systems. In particular, rat pups exposed to maternal deprivation display hypersecretion of CRF, increased CRF mRNA expression, and increased CRF signal transduction when exposed to psychological stressors as adults (Newport, Stowe, & Nemeroff, 2002). In primate models of stress, mothers rearing their young in an environment of variable foraging demand (in which the food supply was unpredictable) provided less maternal care to their infants than mothers in situations where food supply was predictably plentiful or scarce. The offspring reared in the variable foraging demand condition had significantly elevated CRF concentrations which persist for years and abnormal functioning of both norepinephrine (NE) and serotonin systems in adulthood (Coplan et al., 1996, 2005).

Taken together, the neurochemical, postmortem, and pharmacological data is concordant with the hypothesis that CRF is hypersecreted in many patients with MDD. Conditions experienced during childhood may alter the set-point for the activity of CRF neurons and HPA axis activity when exposed to stress, which may form the basis for an endophenotype of MDD characterized by exaggerated stress sensitivity. It remains to be determined whether dysfunction of the CRF system is the primary pathophysiologic disturbance in MDD, or whether that dysfunction results from another dysregulated brain system.

CYTOKINES

The breadth of evidence supporting a central role for glucocorticoid resistance in the pathophysiology of many patients with MDD leads to the question of what process is responsible for the development of insensitivity to glucocorticoid feedback. Emerging data suggest that the source of the defect may be impaired glucocorticoid receptor function resulting, perhaps, from sustained elevated concentrations of inflammatory cytokines during medical illness or chronic stress exposure (Pace, Hu, & Miller, 2007). Several medical disorders, such as asthma, rheumatoid arthritis, and inflammatory bowel disease share the feature of excessive inflammation, and have been associated with diminished inhibitory effects of glucocorticoids (Raison & Miller, 2003). Glucocorticoids exert their effects via binding to glucocorticoid receptors (GRs) located in the cytoplasm, where they are usually maintained in a nonactive state through association with a chaperone protein complex containing heat shock proteins. Once the GR is bound by a glucocorticoid, it activates and translocates to the nucleus where it dimerizes. The resultant homodimers alter cellular function via binding to the glucocorticoid responsive promoter element of particular genes or interacting with other nuclear transcription factors. Through these mechanisms, glucocorticoid binding to GRs inhibits inflammatory cytokine signaling, CRF release, and the sympathetic nervous system (Pace et al., 2007).

The most well-replicated finding of immune system activation in MDD is increased plasma concentrations of interleukin (IL)-6 and its liver product, C-reactive protein (CRP). Other proinflammatory cytokines, including IL-1 and tumor necrosis factor (TNF)-α, have also been observed to be elevated in MDD (Raison, Capuron, & Miller, 2006). These cytokines can inhibit GR function by reducing GR nuclear translocation and by impairing activation of GR-inducible enzymes (A. H. Miller, Pariante, & Pearce, 1999). There are a large number of inflammatory and immune-regulating signaling pathways (e.g., the mitogen activated protein kinase pathway) that regulate GR function, and which are susceptible to disruption by proinflammatory cytokines. Another important component of the inflammatory response is a nuclear transcription factor, nuclear factor-$\kappa\beta$ (NF-$\kappa\beta$). This protein plays a key role in mediating inflammatory and immune responses to the proinflammatory cytokines IL-1, IL-6 and TNF-α. Once activated, NF-$\kappa\beta$ translocates to the nucleus and induces the transcription of specific genes, including the proinflammatory cytokines. In the previously described TSST paradigm, depressed patients with a history of early life trauma demonstrate significantly higher levels of IL-6 and activation of NF-$\kappa\beta$, than healthy controls (Pace et al., 2006). In the healthy state, glucocorticoids are potent inhibitors of NF-$\kappa\beta$, and consequently suppress inflammatory activity.

This model of the pathophysiology of MDD is particularly attractive as it identifies insufficient glucocorticoid signaling as the biological link that connects the high incidence of depression in medical disorders associated with inflammation, including diabetes, cancer and cardiovascular disease (Raison et al., 2006). Furthermore, administration of proinflammatory cytokines induces "sickness behavior" in animals and humans, characterized by disturbances in mood, cognition and neurovegetative behaviors that mimic to a considerable extent the syndrome of MDD (Dantzer, 2004). Patients with hepatitis C who receive interferon-α treatment frequently develop symptoms of MDD (Raison et al., 2006), which can be effectively treated with SSRI treatment (Musselman et al., 2001; Raison, Demetrashvili, Capuron, & Miller, 2005). Indeed, antidepressants have been found to exhibit anti-inflammatory activity, with clinical response correlated with reductions in cytokine levels (Raison, Marcin, & Miller, 2002).

Although much work needs to be done to clarify the relevant intracellular GR pathways disrupted in MDD, several antidepressants increase dexamethasone-induced GR-mediated gene transcription and GR translocation (Pariante & Miller, 2001). Thus, although antidepressant medications exert their initial effects on the cell surface, the effects on intracellular signaling pathways stemming from signal transduction of monoamine receptor binding is likely to be a crucial component of their antidepressant effects.

MONOAMINES

In the absence of a clear pathogenetic model of MDD, early clues about the biology of the illness were drawn from the study of the biological effects of treatments known to reduce the symptoms of the illness. The monoamine hypothesis of depression (also known as the biogenic amine hypothesis) derived from several observations in the 1950s. These included the depressogenic effects of reserpine, an antihypertensive agent that interferes with the vesicular storage of monoamines (Muller, Pryer, Gibbons, & Orgain, 1955; Shore, Silver, & Brodie, 1955); the antidepressant effects of iproniazid, an anti-tubercular drug that inhibits the monoamine oxidase activity (Bloch, Dooneief, Buchberg, & Spellman, 1954); and imipramine, an agent that blocks the reuptake of norepinephrine and serotonin (5-hydroxytryptophan, 5HT) developed as an anxiolytic to treat psychotic patients, enhanced the mood of depressed subjects (Glowinski & Axelrod, 1966; Glowinski, Snyder, & Axelrod, 1966; Sulser & Dingell, 1968). Imipramine was the first of the tricyclic antidepressants (TCAs, so named based on their three-ring hydrocarbon nucleus), which became the primary medication treatment for MDD until 1988, when the first of the selective serotonin reuptake inhibitors (SSRIs), fluoxetine, was introduced.

As it became clear that all of these medications altered the concentrations of the monoamines NE, 5HT, and/or dopamine (DA), several hypotheses were proposed suggesting that MDD resulted from depletions in these monoamines, though theories differed in their emphasis on NE (Bunney & Davis, 1965; Schildkraut, 1965) or 5HT (Coppen, 1967; Lapin & Oxenkrug, 1969). These theories shared the basic concept that MDD resulted from a deficiency of one or more monoamines, and that antidepressant treatment corrected this imbalance. These original formulations of the monoamine hypothesis faced several significant challenges. Most important is the generally observed delay in the onset of antidepressant action, despite the increase in synaptic concentrations of monoamines that occur within hours of the ingestion of the antidepressant. In addition, some studies of NE concentrations in CSF and plasma demonstrated increased noradrenergic activity in MDD, rather than deficiencies of the neurotransmitter (Veith et al., 1994; Wong et al., 2000). Consequently, the original monoamine hypothesis of MDD has undergone revision, with a focus on the regulation of neurotransmitter release by feedback at autoreceptors of monoamine neurons, on both the cell body and axon terminal. It is now generally believed that disrupted signaling of no single neurotransmitter is the etiologic agent for MDD because the monoamine systems interact extensively, both in the brain stem at the level of the cell bodies and in the terminal projection regions. Thus, alterations in the activity of one neurotransmitter will have an impact on the activity of other neurotransmitters. The nature and degree of the neurotransmitter disruptions likely has an impact on the specific depressive symptoms that become manifest in a particular patient. Monoamine functioning undergoes regulation at several levels, as indicated in Table 55.4.

The importance of monoamine degradation was recently revealed in a PET study using [^{11}C]harmine [a radioligand specific for the measurement of monoamine oxidase A (MAO-A) activity]. Depressed subjects demonstrated a dramatic 34% elevation in MAO-A activity in numerous brain regions when compared with control subjects (Meyer et al., 2006). MAO-A is responsible for catabolizing 5HT, NE, and, to a lesser extent, DA in the CNS. This finding suggests that elevated MAO-A levels may be an important contributor to reduced monoamine concentrations in MDD.

Serotonin

All 5HT in the CNS is synthesized in the raphe nuclei located in the brain stem. The serotonin hypothesis of depression posits that deficits in serotonergic signaling are either the proximate cause or represent a vulnerability factor for the development of MDD (Maes & Meltzer, 1995).

TABLE 55.4. Sites of regulation of monoamine neurotransmitter function

Site of Regulation	Examples
Precursor availability	Dietary tryptophan (5HT)
	Dietary tyrosine (NE, DA)
Synthesis of the monoamine	Tryptophan hydroxylase (5HT)
	Tyrosine hydroxylase (NE, DA)
Storage and release of the monoamine from synaptic vesicles	Vesicular transporters (5HT, NE, DA)
Postsynaptic signal transduction via receptor binding	5HT2 receptor (5HT)
	β_1 receptor (NE)
	D_2 receptor (DA)
Intracellular signal transduction	Adenylate cyclase; phopholipase C
Termination of monoamine signal via presynaptic reuptake	SERT (5HT)
	NET (NE)
	DAT (DA)
Feedback to monoamine cell firing via presynaptic receptors	5HT1a receptor (5HT)
	α_2 receptor (NE)
	D_2 receptor (DA)
Degradation of the monoamine after reuptake	Monoamine oxidase (5HT, NE, DA)

DA = dopamine; DAT = dopamine transporter; 5HT = 5-hydroxytryptophan (Serotonin); NE = norepinephrine; NET = norepinephrine transporter; SERT = serotonin transporter.

It is not possible in this review to comprehensively cover all of the research studies conducted on this topic. Rather we focus on those investigations that provide the most compelling argument for the neurotransmitter's involvement. Keep in mind that serotonergic function in depression has been difficult to keep completely distinct from its role in suicidality and impulsivity.

One of the most compelling pieces of evidence for the involvement of 5HT-containing circuits in the neurobiology of major depression arises from the efficacy of 5HT-altering agents in its treatment. SSRIs, including fluoxetine, fluvoxamine, sertraline, paroxetine, citalopram, and escitalopram, induce remission from depression in approximately one-third of patients, and significantly improve symptoms in another third (Trivedi et al., 2006). These agents act by blocking 5HT reuptake by the 5HT transporter (SERT) from the synapse into the presynaptic nerve terminal, thereby increasing intrasynaptic 5HT concentrations. Similarly, agents such as nefazodone and mirtazapine, that antagonize postsynaptic 5HT receptors, especially the 5-HT$_2$ subtypes, are also effective antidepressants.

The effort to develop 5HT-specific agents for the treatment of depression arose from several lines of research. The depletion of tryptophan (TRP), the aminoacid precursor in the synthesis of 5HT, was found to increase the rate of relapse in patients successfully treated with antidepressants. The risk of relapse was greatest for patients taking serotoninergic, as opposed to noradrenergic, antidepressants. Additionally, TRP depletion in first-degree relatives of depressed patients induces dysphoria, but not in relatives of nondepressed individuals (Benkelfat, Ellenbogen, Dean, Palmour, & Young, 1994).

CSF concentrations of the primary serotonin metabolite, 5-hydroxyindoleacetic acid (5-HIAA) have not revealed consistent differences between depressed and control subjects, though it is reduced in patients who attempt or die by suicide, particularly those employing a violent method (Asberg, Traskman, & Thoren, 1976; R. D. Gibbons & Davis, 1986; Roy, De Jong, & Linnoila, 1989), regardless of psychiatric diagnosis (Traskman, Asberg, Bertilsson, & Sjostrand, 1981; Van Praag, 1982). Overall the strongest association of low CSF 5-HIAA concentrations is with violent and/or impulsive behavior (Linnoila & Virkkunen, 1992). MDD with low CNS serotonin availability may result in a subtype of depression with significant impulsivity and risk for lethal suicide attempts.

There are a number of neuroendocrine challenge tests that have been used to assess activity of the 5HT system. The best replicated of these is the fenfluramine challenge test (Mitchell & Smythe, 1990). Fenfluramine, an appetite suppressant, induces a rapid release of 5HT from presynaptic terminals. In the anterior pituitary gland, 5HT binding to postsynaptic $5HT_{2a}$ and $-_{2c}$ receptors induces the release of prolactin into the systemic circulation. Thus, in healthy individuals, fenfluramine administration generally results in an increase in serum prolactin concentrations, an effect that is blunted in depressed subjects (O'Keane & Dinan, 1991). Unfortunately, the effects of antidepressant treatment on the fenfluramine challenge test are highly conflicting, with increases, decreases, and no changes from baseline reported in the literature (Kavoussi, Hauger, & Coccaro, 1999; Shapira, Cohen, Newman, & Lerer, 1993). The results of this test suggest that the serotonergic dysfunction in MDD stems either from diminished 5HT release from the presynaptic neuron or diminished postsynaptic $5HT_{2a}$ and $_{2c}$ responsiveness. Results from another challenge test, the m-chorophenylpiperazine (m-CPP) test suggests that the dysfunction results from presynaptic dysfunction (Anand et al., 1994) because m-CPP exerts mixed effects at postsynaptic 5HT receptors, most notably the $5-HT_2$ receptor family, and no differences in neuroendocrine responses have been found in depressed versus control subjects after m-CPP administration. However, it is uncertain the degree to which the activity of serotonin system in the hypothalamic-pituitary complex can be generalized to activity of 5HT-containing neurons elsewhere in the CNS.

The SSRIs act by blocking the SERT, thereby increasing 5HT concentrations in the synapse. Thus, the density or availability of the SERT on the cell membrane may be a key component in the pathophysiology of major depression. As discussed later, the genetic polymorphism for the SERT has been strongly implicated in the pathogenesis of major depression. Additional evidence of the importance of 5HT reuptake has come from the study of platelets, which also express the SERT. SERT density can be measured with $[^3H]$-imipramine binding and $[^3H]$-paroxetine binding. The functional capacity of platelet and CNS SERT is highly correlated, supporting the use of platelets as a surrogate measure for CNS SERT function, though there may be differences in how the SERT gene and protein are regulated between the two tissue types (Rausch et al., 2005). The great majority of studies of platelet SERT activity demonstrate both reduced 5HT uptake and density of SERT binding sites in depressed versus control subjects (Ellis & Salmond, 1994). This reduced 5HT binding is likely a state marker for depression because it improves with treatment, though all of these studies were conducted prior to the discovery of the SERT genetic polymorphism, which affects SERT binding and function.

The gene encoding the serotonin transporter (SLC6A4) was an obvious candidate gene for depression because it is the theorized site of action of SSRIs, and neuroimaging studies have demonstrated reduced SERT binding in depressed patients versus controls (see later discussion of findings from neuroimaging). Three functional genetic polymorphisms in the promoter region of the SERT gene have been identified (Heils et al., 1996; Hu, Zhu, Lipsky & Goldman, 2004). Initially only two alleles, the short (S) and long (L) forms of the promoter region of the gene were described, though subsequent work identified two functional variants of the long form: L_A, which results in greater SERT expression than the S form, and L_G, which expresses the SERT comparably to the S form. The S form of this polymorphism has been modestly associated with bipolar disorder, suicidal behavior, and depression-related trait scores, but association and linkage studies have reported mixed results for increased S form expression in patients with a diagnosis of MDD (Levinson, 2006). The inconsistency between studies may arise in part from variations in ethnicity between sampled populations because the effects of SERT promoter polymorphism on measures of CNS serotonergic function have been shown to vary by race in healthy subjects (Williams et al., 2003). The importance of the SERT promoter polymorphism is better established in studies exploring gene by environment interactions. Consistently, the S and L_G forms of the SERT polymorphisms have been found to convey increased risk for the development of MDD following stressful life events (Caspi et al., 2003; Kendler, Kuhn, Vittum, Prescott, & Riley, 2005). Several published studies have now confirmed this finding (Zammit & Owen, 2006).

PET imaging studies of SERT density have found a lower binding potential in depressed versus control subjects (Malison et al., 1998; Parsey et al., 2006), and individuals with the S form exhibit reduced SERT binding (Heinz et al., 2000). Discrepant SERT binding results have also been reported (Meyer et al., 2004). Postmortem brain tissue analyses of SERT binding in depressed and control brains have not been as consistent as the platelet binding data, likely due to the many confounding issues in postmortem tissue analysis (Bligh-Glover et al., 2000; Mann et al., 2000). The 5-HT$_{1A}$ receptors located on the cell body of serotonergic neurons control their rate of firing and consequently the availability of 5-HT in the synapse. Antidepressant treatment has been hypothesized to induce changes in the number or responsiveness of the 5-HT$_{1A}$ receptor, leading to an increase in the firing rate of the serotonergic neurons (Blier, deMontigny, & Chaput, 1990). Postmortem studies of 5-HT$_{1A}$ receptor density have not consistently found differences between the brains of depressed and control subjects (Lowther, De Paermentier, Crompton, Katona, & Horton, 1994; Mattsubara, Arora, & Meltzer, 1991). PET imaging using ligands specific to the 5-HT$_{1A}$ and 5-HT$_{2A}$ receptors now allow for in vivo studies (Fujita, Charney, & Innis, 2000). The ligand [^{11}C] WAY100635 has been consistently used to image the 5-HT$_{1A}$ receptor in PET studies. Reduced 5-HT$_{1A}$ receptor binding in depressed patients compared to their control groups has been reported in limbic and midbrain raphe regions (Hasler, et al., 2007; Sargent et al., 2000). However, another study reported increased 5-HT$_{1A}$ receptor binding in antidepressant naïve depressed patients versus control subjects, and no difference between previously treated depressed subjects and controls (Parsey et al., 2006). A persistent 17% decrease versus controls in cortical 5-HT$_{1A}$ receptor binding in treated male patients remitted from MDD has also been reported (Bhagwagar, Rabiner, Sargent, Grasby, & Cowen, 2004). These data do not resolve the question of whether reduced 5-HT$_{1A}$ expression is a trait marker for major depression, but they do suggest that antidepressant use may exert long-term effects on the 5-HT$_{1A}$ receptor.

The 5-HT$_{2A}$ receptors are located postsynaptically and are widely distributed with particularly high density in the frontal cortex, caudate nucleus, nucleus accumbens, and hippocampus. These receptors are involved in a variety of functions, including secretion of ACTH and cortisol and working memory and response execution. They are also suspected of being integral in response to antidepressant treatment, if not in the pathophysiology of MDD itself. Results from imaging studies of this receptor are also quite variable, probably due to methodological variability in the specific radioligand employed and inconsistent exposure of patients to psychotropic medications in relation to the time of scanning. Two studies have found significantly decreased 5-HT$_{2A}$ receptor binding in frontal cortical regions (Biver et al., 1997; Yatham et al., 2000). In the largest study to date, depressed subjects had 29% lower receptor binding in the hippocampus (Mintun et al., 2004). PET studies in which 5-HT$_2$ receptors were measured both pre- and posttreatment have produced highly inconsistent results that do not allow conclusions about the effects of antidepressants on 5-HT$_2$ receptor expression (Attar-Levy et al., 1999; Yatham et al., 1999). In a large study of antidepressant treatments, allelic variation in an intron of the gene for the 5-HT$_{2A}$ receptor was strongly correlated with antidepressant nonresponse. The allele predictive of nonresponse was six times more common among African-American depressed subjects than Caucasians (McMahon et al., 2006).

Tryptophan hydroxylase (TPH) is the rate-limiting enzyme in the synthetic pathway of 5HT. Despite numerous investigations, the TPH isoform 1 gene (TPH1) has not been consistently linked to the pathogenesis of depression. In 2003, a second isoform (TPH2) was discovered to be preferentially expressed in the brain, whereas TPH1 is mainly expressed in the periphery. A rare functional single nucleotide polymorphism (SNP) was initially identified in a sample of elderly, treatment-resistant subjects with major depression (Zhang et al., 2005). Although this polymorphism has not been replicated in other samples of depressed subjects, SNP and haplotype linkage analyses of the TPH2 gene have identified several polymorphisms and regions associated with increased risk for MDD, suicidality, and bipolar disorder (M. Harvey et al., 2004; van den Bogaert et al., 2006; Zill et al., 2004). A TPH2 polymorphism has also been correlated with lower CSF 5HIAA levels in depressed subjects (Zhou et al., 2005).

In conclusion, there is a large database that implicates disrupted serotonergic signaling in the pathophysiology of MDD. The most impressive component of the data is that many antidepressants apparently act by modifying the activity of serotonergic circuits. The degree to which changes in serotonergic signaling impact other important systems, such as the CRF/HPA axis and neurotrophic factors, will be a major focus of future research.

Norepinephrine

Measuring the concentration of NE in bodily fluids is difficult because it is rapidly catabolized. However, the principal metabolite, 3-methoxy-4-hydroxyphenylglycol (MHPG), is stable, allowing its concentration to be used as a surrogate measure of NE levels. Approximately 20% of urinary MHPG derives from the CNS pool, leading to the assumption that changes in urinary MHPG concentration reflect changes in the activity of NE neurons in the CNS (Potter, Karoum, & Linnoila, 1984). Although early investigations found lower urinary MHPG in depressed versus control subjects, subsequent studies have not replicated these findings, especially in studies where care was taken to exclude subjects with bipolar depression (Maas, Fawcett, & Dekirmenjian, 1972; Schildkraut, 1973). Urinary MHPG levels do not differentiate patients with MDD from healthy controls.

The utility of NE and MHPG concentrations may be greater for efforts to identify specific biological subtypes of MDD. CSF MHPG concentrations were found to be elevated in hospitalized depressed patients with high levels of anxiety, agitation, somatization, and sleep disturbance (Redmond et al., 1986). CSF NE concentrations measured hourly for 30 consecutive hours were significantly elevated in subjects with the melancholic subtype of depression compared to controls (Wong et al., 2000). A unique study of treatment-refractory MDD patients employing cannulas inserted into the internal jugular vein to measure veno-arterial neurotransmitter gradients found reduced venoarterial NE, MHPG, and dopamine gradients in the patients compared to the controls (Lambert, Johansson, Agren, & Friberg, 2000). These studies suggest that the study of NE concentrations and its metabolites may reflect differences in subtypes of MDD.

The activity of the CNS NE system can be reduced by the use of α-methyl-para-tyrosine (AMPT), a tyrosine hydroxylase (TH) inhibitor that transiently depletes CNS NE and other catecholamine (i.e., DA and epinephrine) stores. Healthy subjects with no history of depression who are administered AMPT experience no change in their mood state (Salomon, Miller, Krystal, Heninger, & Charney, 1997). Untreated depressed patients receiving AMPT also do not experience any worsening of core mood symptoms, but do have worsening of anergia (H. L. Miller et al., 1996). However, depressed patients responsive to desipramine or mazindol, which specifically inhibit NE reuptake from the synapse, suffer a significant return of depressive symptoms upon AMPT administration (Berman et al., 1999; H. L. Miller et al., 1996). Using PET imaging techniques, this AMPT-induced return of depressive symptoms was found to correlate with reduced brain metabolism in the dorsolateral prefrontal cortex (PFC), orbitofrontal cortex, and thalamus (Bremner et al., 2003). In contrast, SSRI-treated patients do not relapse when treated with AMPT. These findings parallel the findings of tryptophan depletion in SSRI-treated subjects, arguing that, regardless of the underlying pathobiology of depression, existing medication treatments require adequate neurotransmitter concentrations in the systems they are thought to alter in order to provide efficacy (Heninger, Delgado, & Charney, 1996).

The effects of NE are mediated at several different adrenergic receptor subtypes, which may contribute to the pathophysiology of depression and the mechanism of action of antidepressants (Duman & Nestler, 1995). Of particular importance is the α_2 receptor subtype. Postmortem studies of patients with MDD have elevated α_2 receptor densities in the locus ceruleus compared to controls (Ordway, Schenk, Stockmeier, May, & Klimek, 2003). The α_2 receptors in the locus ceruleus likely function as autoreceptors, inhibiting NE cell firing. Postmortem studies of α_2 receptor binding density in the cerebral cortex of depressed patients and healthy controls have had mixed results, with both elevations (Meana, Barturen, & Garcia-Sevilla, 1992), and unchanged levels reported (Arango, Ernsberger, Sved, & Mann, 1993; Klimek et al., 1999).

Platelets also express α_2 receptors, allowing their function to be studied as surrogates for CNS α_2 receptors. An increased density of α_2 receptors on the platelets of medication-free depressed patients have consistently been reported compared to control subjects (Garcia-Sevilla, Ulibarri, Ugedo, & Gutierrez, 1987; Garcia-Sevilla, Padro, Giralt, Guimon, & Areso, 1990; Gurguis, Vo, Griffith, & Rush, 1999), though discrepant reports have appeared (Maes, Gastel, Delmeire, & Meltzer, 1999). One of the functions of the platelet α_2 receptor is to mediate platelet aggregation, a response that is exaggerated in depressed patients (Musselman et al., 1996).

The functional state of signal transduction of CNS α_2 receptors may be indirectly assessed via the clonidine challenge test. Clonidine is an α_2 agonist that induces growth hormone (GH) release from the anterior pituitary gland, likely through a postsynaptic mechanism. The GH response to clonidine is blunted in acutely depressed patients versus controls (Amsterdam, Maislin, Skolnick, Berwish, & Winokur, 1989; Siever et al., 1984), as well as in patients treated with antidepressants, and in remitted patients (Mitchell, Bearn, Corn, & Checkley, 1988; Siever et al., 1992). Although tentative, these findings suggest that altered α_2 receptor function may be a trait characteristic of some depressed subjects. One limitation of these studies was the potential confounding effects of anxiety. In a recent study using the clonidine challenge test, depressed patients without anxiety were compared with anxious patients without depression or mixed anxious/depressed patients. Only the anxious or mixed anxiety/depression patients demonstrated a reduced GH response to clonidine (Cameron, Abelson, & Young, 2004).

β-Adrenergic receptors may also contribute to the pathophysiology of MDD and response to antidepressants. Postmortem brain tissue studies of suicide victims have alternately found both increases or no difference in β-adrenergic receptor density in depressed versus control subjects (Crow et al., 1984; de Paermentier, Cheetham, Crompton, Katona, & Horton, 1990; Mann, Stanley, McBride, & McEwen, 1986). Leukocytes also possess β-adrenergic receptors and equally mixed results have been obtained (Extein, Tallman, Smith, & Goodwin, 1979; Healy, Carney, O'Halloran, & Leonard, 1985). Down-regulation of β-adrenergic receptors has been postulated to be integral to antidepressant action (Banarjee, Kung, Riggi, & Chanda, 1977). In animal models, chronic, but not acute, treatment with tricyclic antidepressants consistently induces down-regulation of β-receptors and uncoupling of the receptors from their second messenger systems. This finding is specific for noradrenergic-acting antidepressants, because studies with primarily serotonergic agents have found no such effect (Nalepa & Vetulani, 1993; Ordway et al., 1991). In this way, the specificity of treatment effects is similar to the results of the monoamine depletion studies using tryptophan depletion and AMPT discussed earlier.

Taken together, results evaluating the expression and function of α- and β-adrenergic receptors present a mixed picture that is difficult to interpret. This variability may result from differences in methodology between studies, or from heterogeneity of patient populations. Given the importance of NE signaling in anxiety disorders such as PTSD and panic disorder (Ressler & Nemeroff, 2000), the most likely explanation for the findings may be that depression co-occurring with significant anxiety is the subtype most likely to demonstrate elevated noradrenergic activity.

Dopamine

With the exception of depression with psychotic features, where it has a fundamental role, DA has historically received scant consideration in the pathophysiology of depression. There is now increasing interest in the contribution of DA to depressive symptomatology, at least in a subset of patients. DA systems are well-established to play a seminal role in normal motivation, pleasure, psychomotor speed, and cognitive ability, all systems that may be disrupted in MDD. The psychostimulants d-amphetamine and methylphenidate increase DA signaling, resulting in improvements in energy, activation, and mood. However, when used as monotherapy, these agents do not consistently produce an antidepressant effect, unlike the NE- and 5HT-acting agents (Little, 1988). Nevertheless, many subjects with MDD do not achieve full remission with an SSRI or TCA, and may benefit from augmentation with DA-acting agents to achieve full recovery.

The activity of DA systems can be assessed by measuring concentrations of homovanillic acid (HVA), the major metabolite of DA, in bodily fluids. Most studies exploring CSF HVA concentrations in MDD reported lower concentrations in depressed patients compared to controls, particularly in patients with psychomotor retardation (Kapur & Mann, 1992). However, low CSF HVA concentrations are also present in Parkinson's (where there is a loss of DA neurons) and Alzheimer's diseases, both of which are characterized by psychomotor retardation (van Praag, Korf, Lakke, & Schut, 1975; Wolfe et al., 1990). Conversely, increased CSF HVA is present in agitated and manic patients further implicating CSF HVA levels and hence DA neurotransmission as a state marker for psychomotor activity more than for mood state (Willner, 1983). However, 5% to 10% of Parkinson's disease patients develop a major depressive episode, with another 10% to 30% developing subsyndromal depressive symptoms (Tandberg, Larsen, Aarsland, & Cummings, 1996). In these patients, depressive symptoms often precede the development of the physical manifestations of the disorder and do not appear to be related to the severity of disability stemming from Parkinson's disease itself (Guze & Barrio, 1991; van Praag et al., 1975).

Secretion of growth hormone releasing hormone (GHRH) from the arcuate nucleus of the hypothalamus, which regulates the release of GH from the anterior pituitary is in part mediated by DA receptor function. Apomorphine, an agonist at D_2/D_3 DA receptors, acts to induce secretion of GH via binding to postsynaptic DA receptors. Studies employing this test to assess CNS DA receptor function have overall found no differences between depressed and healthy control subjects in GH concentrations after apomorphine administration (McPherson, Walsh, & Silverstone, 2003). There is some data, however, to suggest that the apomorphine challenge test may distinguish between depressed patients with and without significant suicidality (D'Haenen & Bossuyt, 1994; Pitchot, Hansenne, et al., 2001; Pitchot, Reggers, et al., 2001; Shah, Ogilvie, Goodwin, & Ebmeier, 1997).

Neuroimaging studies of DA function in depressed subjects have produced inconclusive results, probably due to heterogeneity between patient samples. Elevated D_2 receptor binding in neuroimaging studies may result from increased numbers of D_2 receptors in MDD (perhaps reflecting a reduction in synaptic DA availability or increased affinity of the receptor for the ligand). In early studies, elevated striatal D_2 expression binding density was reported in depressed inpatients (D'Haenen & Bossuyt, 1994; Shah et al., 1997), particularly in patients with psychomotor retardation (Ebert, Feistel, Loew, & Pirner, 1996). Later studies, employing nonhealthy controls or less ill outpatients identified no differences in D_2 density between patients and the comparison group (Klimke et al., 1999; Parsey et al., 2001). A major confound across these studies is that most subjects were either treated with antidepressants or had only a 1-week washout prior to imaging procedure. Additionally, as is the case in the studies of NE, variability in the level of anxiety may confound the results; anxiety has been associated with reduced D2 receptor binding (Schneier et al., 2000).

The density and function of the dopamine transporter (DAT) has also been studied in MDD, with similarly inconsistent results. The most comprehensive PET study of DAT function found reduced binding in MDD (Meyer et al., 2001). Another PET study using [^{18}F]-fluoro-DOPA uptake in the striatum to assess DA neuronal function found depressed patients with psychomotor retardation to exhibit less striatal uptake of the radioligand compared to anxious depressed inpatients and healthy volunteers (Paillere-Martinot et al., 2001).

Anhedonia is one of the two core symptoms of depression and has particular relevance to DA function because DA is critical to the processing of reward and pleasure experiences. Medication-free, severely depressed subjects experience greater reward from an oral dose of d-amphetamine (which increases DA transmission by a variety of mechanisms) than do controls and mildly depressed subjects (Tremblay, Naranjo, Cardenas, Herrmann, & Busto, 2002).

The few postmortem studies exploring the DA system in depressed patients have provided conflicting results. DA or HVA concentrations in brains of suicide victims have been found to be elevated, reduced, or unchanged in depressed subjects versus controls (Beskow, Gottfries, Roos, & Winblad, 1976; Bowden, Cheetham, et al., 1997; Crow et al., 1984). In a postmortem study of the amygdala, DAT density was reduced, and $D_{2/3}$ receptor binding density elevated in the brains of depressed subjects versus those of psychiatrically healthy controls (Klimek, Schenck, Han, Stockmeier, & Ordway, 2002), though a second study using different methods and focusing on the basal ganglia found no difference in D_2 receptor number or affinity (Bowden, Theodorou, et al., 1997).

An important persisting question regarding the role of DA in the pathogenesis of MDD is whether the psychomotor retardation is simply an epiphenomenon of more central pathophysiologic mechanisms that secondarily produce DA dysfunction, or whether there is a specific subtype of depression that derives in part due to a primary disruption in dopaminergic signaling (Dunlop & Nemeroff, 2007).

Interactions between the Hypothalamic-Pituitary-Adrenal Axis and Monoamine Systems

There are many interactions between monoamine systems and components of the HPA axis. One example is the effect of glucocorticoids to selectively facilitate DA transmission in the nucleus accumbens (Marinelli & Piazza, 2002). In healthy control subjects, cortisol concentrations are positively associated with d-amphetamine-induced DA release in the ventral striatum and dorsal putamen. Healthy individuals with higher circulating plasma cortisol concentrations report greater positive effects after administration of a stimulant drug (Oswald et al., 2005). In subjects who report poor early life maternal care, exposure to psychosocial stressors produces elevations in ventral striatal DA concentrations, and the DA increase is correlated with the increase in salivary cortisol concentrations (Pruessner, Champagne, Meaney, & Dagher, 2004). The high incidence of hypercortisolemia in MDD, particularly in severe depression, raises speculation that elevated cortisol concentrations alter dopaminergic reward systems, thereby altering hedonic responsiveness. One proposed model posits that over time, frequent bouts of stress associated with intermittent increased exposure to glucocorticoids sensitizes the mesolimbic DA system (Oswald et al., 2005). In a test of this model, dexamethasone added to the drinking water of maternal rats both pre- and postpartum resulted in a 50% greater survival rate of midbrain dopaminergic neurons in the adult offspring (McArthur, McHale, Dalley, Buckingham, & Gillies, 2005). Such a model also provides a potential explanatory framework for the high comorbidity rate between MDD and substance abuse.

Depression with psychotic features, which is associated with markedly increased glucocorticoid secretion, exemplifies another link between DA and the HPA axis. Patients with psychotic depression exhibit increased plasma DA and HVA concentrations compared to patients with nonpsychotic depression (Devanand, Bowers, Hoffman, & Nelson, 1985; Schatzberg, Rothschild, & Langlais, 1985). The elevated glucocorticoid concentrations may drive the increase in DA activity, resulting in psychotic symptoms (Posener et al., 1999; Schatzberg, Rothschild, Langlais, Bird, & Cole, 1985). This hypothesis is supported by the established ability of high-dose synthetic glucocorticoids to induce psychosis in otherwise psychiatrically healthy individuals (Lewis & Smith, 1983).

NEUROTROPHINS AND NEUROGENESIS

A particularly exciting area of current research in MDD is the study of neurotrophins and neurogenesis. The neurotrophins are a family of molecules, including brain-derived neurotrophic factor (BDNF) and vascular endothelial growth factor, involved in the maintenance, growth, and survival of neurons and their synapses. Cyclic adenosine monophosphate response element binding protein (CREB) is a protein activated via G-protein systems that increases the expression of neurotrophic and neuroprotective proteins.

Specifically, CREB increases the levels of BDNF and its receptor, tropomyosin receptor-related kinase B (TrkB). BDNF is believed to regulate the survival of neurons via its interaction with the mitogen-activated protein kinases (MAPK), which in turn can increase the expression of Bcl-2, a protein that acts to inhibit the programmed cell death of neurons. BDNF also regulates synaptic plasticity through its effects on the NMDA receptor, thus significantly affecting how networks of neurons communicate (Manji, Drevets, & Charney, 2001). The neurotrophic hypothesis of depression proposes that deficient neurotrophic activity contributes to disrupted functioning of the hippocampus in depression, and that recovery with antidepressant treatment is mediated in part by reversal of this deficit (Duman, Heninger, & Nestler, 1997).

Unlike the history of interest in the HPA axis and monoamines, the interest in the role of BDNF in MDD grew out of findings from animal research. Restraint stress in rats reduces BDNF expression in the hippocampus, implying a role for the HPA axis in suppressing BDNF levels (Smith, Makino, Kvetnansky, & Post, 1995). Direct injection of BDNF into the rat brain is efficacious in two animal models of depression (Shirayama, Chen, Nakagawa, Russell, & Duman, 2002; Siuciak, Lewis, Wiegand, & Lindsay, 1997). Many antidepressants increase CREB activity and BDNF levels in the hippocampus and prefrontal cortex of rats, which begins about 2 to 3 weeks after initiating the antidepressant, consistent with the usual time course for clinical improvement (Nestler, Terwilliger, & Duman, 1989; Nibuya, Nestler, & Duman, 1996). ECT also increases BDNF levels in the hippocampus (Vaidya, Siuciak, Du, & Duman, 1999). Surprisingly, the function of BDNF also seems required to manifest depressive states. In a mouse model of depression, BDNF was required for mice to develop social aversion in a social defeat paradigm; blockade of BDNF activity in the VTA and nucleus accumbens produced antidepressant effects in the same paradigm (Berton et al., 2006).

Although CREB can be activated and regulated by G-protein linked neurotransmitter receptors, several other intracellular signaling cascades can alter CREB activity, including those associated with growth factors and inflammatory cytokines. Subsequent work has revealed considerable complexity in the effects of antidepressants on CREB activity and BDNF levels, with variability in different brain regions and between drugs, which will require further study (Tardito et al., 2006).

The first evidence that hippocampal cell proliferation may be required for antidepressant effects was revealed in a study of mice treated with fluoxetine or imipramine, with or without prior irradiation of their hippocampus (Santarelli et al., 2003). Animals receiving irradiation prior to antidepressant administration did not develop expected antidepressant behaviors, in contrast with the control animals. Moreover, 5HT1a receptor knockout mice treated with fluoxetine did not show the expected increase in cell proliferation, whereas knockout mice treated with imipramine did. These findings suggest that 5HT1a receptor stimulation may be necessary for the behavioral and neurogenic effects of SSRIs. That antidepressants may increase neuronal proliferation is concordant with the finding that chronic antidepressant treatment increases hippocampal volume in humans (Vermetten, Vythilingam, Southwick, Charney, & Bremner, 2003).

More recent work suggests that SSRI antidepressants affect hippocampal neurogenesis and development through two separate processes. First, they can increase the proliferation of early-stage progenitor cells, but not the newborn stem-like cells, in the dentate gyrus of the hippocampus (Encinas, Vaahtokari, & Enikolopov, 2006). Second, these drugs increase the efficient survival of young neurons after they complete mitosis and migrate to the granule cell layer. BDNF signaling may play a crucial role in the new cell's formation of a dendritic tree and formation of synapses with cells in the CA3 region of the hippocampus (Sairanen, Lucas, Ernfors, Castren, & Castren, 2005; see Figure 55.3). The elimination of neurons through apoptosis

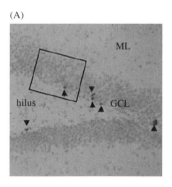

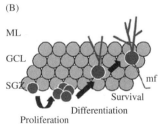

Figure 55.3 (**Figure C.54** in color section) Neurogenesis in hippocampus.

Note: (A) The dark cells indicated by arrowheads are bromodeoxy uridine-labeled newborn neurons in the rat adult hippocampus. (B) Newborn neurons in the subgranular zone (SGZ) undergo proliferation, an effect enhnaced by antidepressants. The new cells migrate to the granular cell layer (GCL), and mature to become granule cells, forming dendritic connections in the molecular layer (ML) and extending axons into the CA3 pyramidal cell layer through the mossy fiber pathway (mf). From "Hippocampal Neurogenesis: Opposing Effects of Stress and Antidepressant Treatment," by J. L. Warner-Schmidt and R. S. Duman, 2006, *Hippocampus, 16*, p. 241. Reprinted with permission.

increases concurrently with the increase in neurogenesis in the hippocampus in antidepressant-treated mice. Thus, antidepressants may act by facilitating functional neuronal connectivity and plasticity to improve information processing in neural networks involved in mood regulation (Castren, 2005). If these new synaptic networks represent a form of learning, then exposure to positive events during treatment may be necessary for recovery from depression.

The few postmortem studies measuring BDNF concentrations in the brains of depressed patients have been inconclusive, with both increases and decreases reported (Slattery, Hudson, & Nutt, 2004). Although several groups have reported reduced BDNF levels in the peripheral circulation of subjects with MDD versus controls, the degree to which plasma BDNF levels reflect brain BDNF levels remains uncertain (Karege et al., 2005).

HYPOTHALAMIC-PITUITARY-THYROID AXIS

Interest in the HPT axis in MDD emerged from observations that patients with either hyper- and hypothyroidism could develop profound depressive symptoms indistinguishable from MDD. The hypothalamic-pituitary-thyroid (HPT) axis is organized similarly to the HPA axis, starting with the release of thyrotropin-releasing hormone (TRH) from nerve terminals in the median eminence of the hypothalamus. TRH is transported in the hypothalamo-hypophoseal portal system to the anterior pituitary where it induces the release of thyroid stimulating hormone (TSH) into the peripheral circulation. TSH then acts on the thyroid gland to induce the synthesis and release of triiodothyronine (T_3) and thyroxine (T_4). Thyroid hormones provide negative feedback at the hypothalamus and pituitary to inhibit the release of TRH and TSH, respectively. In the brain, the enzyme type II 5'-deiodinase converts T_4 to T_3 (considered the active form of thyroid hormone in the CNS). The action of this enzyme can be inhibited by cortisol, thus linking the HPT and HPA axes in MDD (Hindal & Kaplan, 1988). Administration of antidepressants in rodents results in increased activity of this enzyme (Campos-Barros et al., 1994).

Approximately 20% to 30% of patients with MDD have abnormal values on one or more laboratory measures of thyroid function. TRH concentrations in CSF have been found to be elevated in depressed versus control subjects in 2 of the 3 published studies on this topic (Banki, Bissette, Arato, & Nemeroff, 1988; Kirkegaard, Faber, Hummer, & Rogowski, 1979; Roy, Wolkowitz, Bissette, & Nemeroff, 1994). The TRH stimulation test involves administering a standard dose of TRH intravenously, then measuring plasma TSH levels every 30 minutes for 2 hours after dosing. Approximately 25% to 30% of depressed patients who have no detectable thyroid dysfunction demonstrate a blunted TSH response to TRH challenge (Kastin, Ehrensing, Schalch, & Anderson, 1972; Prange, Lara, Wilson, Alltop, & Breese, 1972). A possible explanation for this is that TRH receptors in the pituitary are down-regulated in response to chronically elevated secretion of TRH into the hypophyseal-portal circulation during a depressive episode, though evidence for this hypothesis is inconclusive. Approximately 15% of patients with MDD display an enhanced TSH response to TRH stimulation (Extein, Pottash, & Gold, 1981). In two small studies, intrathecal TRH administration transiently improved mood state in patients with treatment refractory depression (Callahan et al., 1997; Marangell et al., 1997).

Transthyretin is a protein that transports and distributes thyroid hormones in the CNS. In MDD, CSF transthyretin concentrations are decreased versus controls (G. M. Sullivan et al., 1999; M. Sullivan et al., 2006). Reduced levels of transthyretin could result in a functionally hypometabolic and hypothyroid state in the CNS of affected individuals, even in the presence of normal-range serum thyroid hormone concentrations. Such a scenario could explain the observed clinical benefit of the addition of thyroid hormone to the treatment regimen of depressed patients with an inadequate antidepressant response. Another consideration in HPT function is that, unlike the HPA axis, the HPT axis can also be disrupted by anti-thyroid antibodies, that is, antithyroglobulin and antithyroid microsomal (thyroid peroxidase) antibodies. These antibodies are found more frequently in depressed subjects than in the general population (M. S. Gold, Pottash, & Extein, 1982).

Thyroid hormones may be involved in the pathophysiology of depression via their effect on serotonin function. T_3, both alone and in combination with fluoxetine, reduces transcription of the 5-HT_{1A} and 5-HT_{1B} receptors (Lifschytz et al., 2006). As previously noted, down-regulation of the 5-HT_{1A} autoreceptor may be an important mechanism of action of antidepressants. Results from treatment studies suggest that addition of thyroid hormones may enhance the speed and overall response to antidepressant treatment (Altshuler et al., 2001; Aronson, Offman, Joffe, & Naylor, 1996). Recent studies using SSRIs and large sample sizes have produced divergent results on these questions (Appelhof et al., 2004; Cooper-Kazaz et al., 2007). The effects of antidepressant treatment on thyroid hormone availability is also mixed. Severely depressed patients treated with paroxetine had a mean 11.2% reduction in circulating T_4 levels, whereas 15 depressed female inpatients treated for 24 weeks with sertraline demonstrated a 24% increase in T_3 levels, but no change in T_4 levels (Konig,

Hauger, von Hippel, Wolfersdorf, & Kaschka, 2000; Sagud et al., 2002). One study suggests that higher serum T_3 concentrations at the time of achieving remission from MDD may be protective against relapse (Joffe & Marriott, 2000).

In summary, the importance of HPT axis disruption in the pathophysiology of MDD remains unclear. It is possible that a subtype of depression exists in which abnormal HPT axis function revealed by the TRH challenge test could be separable from other forms of MDD, and warrant specific treatment with thyroid replacement. However, this remains speculative based on the current evidence.

GROWTH HORMONE AND SOMATOSTATIN

Growth hormone (GH) is an important regulator of body fuel stores, and thereby may contribute to the pathophysiology of MDD. Secretion of GH from the anterior pituitary is controlled by two hypothalamic peptides: somatostatin, which inhibits, and GHRH, which stimulates, GH release. Dopamine, NE, and tryptophan also stimulate GH secretion. In healthy individuals, GH is secreted in a circadian pattern, with peak levels occurring in the first few hours of sleep. Depressed subjects, however, show lower nocturnal GH release, and higher daylight plasma GH concentrations (Mendlewicz et al., 1985; Schilkrut et al., 1975). Dysfunction of GH secretion may be a trait marker for MDD because adolescents demonstrating lower GH levels prior to sleep onset are at greater risk of developing MDD as adults (Coplan et al., 2000). The clonidine challenge test, which stimulates GH release through clonidine's agonism at CNS α_2 receptors, is blunted in depressed patients (Matussek et al., 1980).

In addition to its effect on GH, somatostatin inhibits GABA activity and the release of CRF, ACTH, and TRH. This neuropeptide is therefore positioned to influence many of the neurotransmitters implicated in the pathophysiology of depression. CSF somatostatin concentrations have been found to be reduced in depressed patients versus controls, perhaps due to glucocorticoid inhibition of the activity of somatostatin neurons (Bissette et al., 1986; Wolkowitz et al., 1987). As is true for many hypothalamic peptides, much remains to be determined about the role of somatostatin in MDD.

FAST-ACTING NEUROTRANSMITTERS

GABA

Gamma (γ)-aminobutyric acid (GABA) is the predominant inhibitory neurotransmitter in the CNS. Approximately 20% to 40% of all neurons in the cortex and > 75% of all striatal neurons are GABAergic (Hendry, Schwark, Jones, & Yan, 1987; Tepper, Koos, & Wilson, 2004). The vast majority of GABAergic cells in the brain are interneurons, characterized by short axons that form synapses within a few hundred microns of their cell body, and which connect different neurons together to coordinate neuronal activity within local brain regions. The serotonergic neurons of the raphe nuclei are under GABAergic tonic inhibition, and 5HT-containing neurons from the raphe project to the cortex and preferentially synapse on GABA interneurons (more so than pyramidal neurons). These 5HT inputs are stimulatory to GABA interneurons, increasing their firing rate.

Indirect evidence of reduced GABAergic activity in MDD is suggested by findings of lower resting-state levels of cortical inhibition in patients undergoing transcranial magnetic stimulation (Bajbouj et al., 2006). Lower CSF and plasma GABA concentrations have been found in comparison to control patients, with the low plasma GABA levels persisting for up to 4 years after remission (B. I. Gold, Bowers, Roth, & Sweeney, 1980). Plasma GABA levels have also been reported to be lower in nondepressed individuals who have a first-degree relative with a history of major depression than in those without such a family history (Bjork et al., 2001). Although these findings suggest that low GABA concentrations may be a trait marker for MDD, the source of plasma GABA remains obscure, and it may not be derived from CNS activity. Evidence against GABA levels as a trait marker for depression emerged from recent magnetic resonance spectroscopy (MRS) studies that found that the reduced GABA concentrations in the occipital cortex in the acutely depressed state resolved after successful treatment with medication or ECT (Hasler et al., 2005; Sanacora et al., 2003; Sanacora, Mason, Rothman, & Krystal, 2002). Furthermore, reduced GABA concentrations are not specific to MDD, having also been demonstrated in alcohol dependence and mania (Petty, 1994).

GABA signaling is influenced by the neurosteroids 3-alpha, 5-alpha-tetrahydroprogesterone (THP, allopregnanolone) and 3-alpha, 5-alpha-tetrahydrodeoxycorticosterone (THDOC). These metabolites of progesterone are produced by neurons and glia in the CNS and are thought to act in a paracrine manner as positive allosteric modulators at the GABA-A receptor, enhancing GABAergic transmission (Belelli & Lambert, 2005). Administration of neurosteroids in the mouse forced swim test model of depression has demonstrated efficacy (Khisti, Chopde, & Jain, 2000). In addition, allopregnanolone exerts negative feedback on the HPA axis, decreasing plasma ACTH concentrations and CRF release (Patchev, Hassan, Holsboer, & Almeida, 1996; Patchev, Shoaib, Holsboer, & Almeida, 1994). Significantly lower serum and CSF allopregnanolone levels have been found in patients with MDD compared to healthy controls, with normalization of these concentrations after successful treatment with antidepressants, though not with ECT or transcranial magnetic stimulation (Baghai et al., 2005; Uzunova et al., 1998).

Glutamate

The N-methyl-D-aspartate (NMDA) receptor may have significance in the pathophysiology of MDD, because NMDA signaling is crucial to many forms of learning, and in high concentrations glutamate can induce neurotoxicity. NMDA receptor antagonists possess antidepressant properties in an animal model of depression (Papp & Moryl, 1994). Chronic treatment with antidepressants has also been shown to modulate NMDA receptor function (Nowak, Trullas, Layer, Skolnick, & Paul, 1993). A recent clinical trial using the NMDA antagonist ketamine reported a rapid response in treatment-refractory patients with MDD (Zarate et al., 2006). Some work suggests that MDD is associated with excessive glial cell loss (Ongur, Drevets, & Price, 1998; Rajkowska et al., 1999), which could result in increased glutamatergic transmission because glial cells remove glutamate from the synapse via glutamate transporters (Slattery et al., 2004). Finally, elevated glutamate levels have been demonstrated in the same cortical regions where GABA levels are reduced, suggesting that both fast-acting neurotransmitter systems may contribute to the pathophysiology of MDD. It is also possible that a metabolic pathway common to both systems may be responsible for these results (Sanacora et al., 2004).

FINDINGS FROM NEUROIMAGING

Structural Imaging Studies

Perhaps the most consistent structural imaging finding in MDD is the presence of smaller hippocampi in depressed versus nondepressed individuals (Neumeister et al., 2005). There is some evidence that duration of depressive illness is inversely correlated with hippocampal volume (MacQueen et al., 2003; Sheline, Sanghavi, Mintun, & Gado, 1999). To date, however, structural imaging studies have not been able to determine whether smaller hippocampal volume is a cause or consequence of MDD. To be more precise, are smaller hippocampi genetically inherited or environmentally induced, resulting in greater risk for depression, or is there shrinkage of the hippocampus as a result of a pathologic process active in the depressed patients? Smaller hippocampi are not unique to MDD; similar structural findings are present in patients with PTSD (Karl et al., 2006). Work from PTSD subjects in a twin cohort suggests that smaller hippocampi is a risk factor for the development

of the illness, rather than a consequence of the disease (Gilbertson et al., 2002), though divergent data are available (J. Douglas Bremner, personal communication). Nevertheless, the finding of smaller hippocampal volume is intriguing because the hippocampus has important roles in regulation of the HPA axis, is a site of neurogenesis, and has close functional connections to other brain structures implicated in MDD, including the amygdala and prefrontal cortex. The subgenual region of the anterior cingulate cortex (Brodmann area 25, BA 25) has also been reported to have smaller volume in depressed subjects compared to control subjects.

Functional Imaging Studies

Functional imaging studies offer the potential to better delineate specific neural networks associated with specific symptom domains of MDD. As discussed earlier, the phenotypic expression of MDD is heterogeneous, with the various symptom domains disturbed in some individuals but not others. By selecting for depressed subjects with marked symptomatic disturbances (e.g., profound anhedonia, or obvious psychomotor slowing), the neural networks underlying these symptoms may be more specifically evaluated, and may thereby contribute to a more biologically relevant categorization of MDD. For example, reduced dorsolateral prefrontal activity is correlated with impairments of psychomotor speed and executive functions (Bench, Friston, Brown, Frackowiak, & Dolan, 1993; Mayberg, 1994). Activity in the anterior cingulate cortex and its antero-medial extensions are associated with cognitive performance, emotional bias, and emotion regulation (Dolan, Bench, Brown, Scott, & Frackowiak, 1994; Elliott, Rubinsztein, Sahakian, & Dolan, 2002), and the parietal cortex and parahippocampus with anxiety (Osuch et al., 2000).

Resting state imaging studies have consistently identified differences in activity in ventral and dorsal prefrontal cortex, anterior cingulate, basal ganglia, amygdala, and hippocampal regions in depressed versus healthy controls. Across all resting state studies of depressed patients, the most consistent finding is that of reduced prefrontal cortex activity, often inversely correlated with depression severity (Ketter, George, Kimbrell, Benson, & Post, 1996).

Subgenual Anterior Cingulate Cortex

The anterior cingulate cortex (ACC), situated on the medial (mesial) wall of each cerebral hemisphere, is frequently divided into a dorsal component, involved extensively in cognitive functions, and the rostral/ventral component (Brodmann areas 25, 33, and 24), which is involved in affective processing. The affective component of the

ACC has extensive connections with the amygdala and periaqueductal grey, and parts of it project to autonomic brain stem motor nuclei. A part of the affective ACC, the subgenual ACC (BA25), is commonly identified to have altered metabolic activity at rest in depressed versus control subjects. In most studies, this region is hyperactive in depressed subjects, with partial normalization of activity with effective treatment (Figure 55.4). Although some studies have reported reduced blood flow in this region in depressed subjects, correction for volume loss (see previous discussion) indicates that overall activity here is increased (Botterton, Raichle, Drevets, Heath, & Todd, 2002; Drevets, 2000; Drevets et al., 1997). BA 25 is a component of the affective section of the ACC and receives input from many structures implicated in the pathophysiology of MDD. Induction of sadness in healthy controls activates the ventral ACC, along with the insula and amygdala among other regions, often in conjunction with reductions in dorsolateral prefrontal cortex activity (Mayberg et al., 1999). Remarkably, juvenile monkeys undergoing stimulation of BA 25 make a cry of distress similar to those heard when an animal is separated from its mother (MacLean & Newman, 1988). In humans, greater pretreatment metabolic activity in BA 25 is associated with poorer response to treatment with medication or psychotherapy. Four of six subjects with treatment-resistant severe depression demonstrated significant improvement after chronic electronic deep brain stimulation (DBS) of the white matter tracts adjacent to the subgenual ACC (Mayberg et al., 2005). The clinical improvement was associated with reduction in blood flow to the subgenual cingulate, insula, and OFC, and increases in DLPFC and dorsal ACC. It is likely that the subgenual ACC plays a fundamental role in the pathophysiology of MDD.

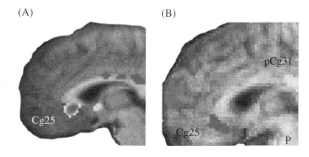

(A) (B)

Figure 55.4 (**Figure C.55** in color section) Subgenual anterior cingulate cortex activation in depressive states.

Note: (A) The subgenual cingulated cortex (Cg25) increases in activity (red) during the induction of transient sadness in healthy control subjects. (B) Chronic treatment with fluoxetine for depression induces a reduction in activity (green). From "Targeting Abnormal Neural Circuits in Mood and Anxiety Disorders: from the Laboratory to the Clinic," by K. J. Ressler and H. S. Mayberg, 2007, *Nature Neuroscience, 10*, p. 1117. Reprinted with permission.

Emotional and Cognitive Processing

So-called neuroimaging challenge paradigms involve presenting the subject with a stimulus or task designed to engage the brain in some specific manner. fMRI studies of depressed patients have identified heightened ACC and paralimbic region activity in response to negatively valenced emotional cues. Exposure to negative words results in greater and more prolonged activity of the amygdala and ventromedial prefrontal cortex in depressed patients versus controls (Elliott et al., 2002; Fossati et al., 2003). Similarly, viewing negatively valenced faces induces greater amygdala reactivity in depressed versus control subjects (Sheline et al., 2001). Through its output to the ventral PFC, this sustained amygdala response may be an important neural correlate of the common symptom of rumination in depression. The increased amygdala activity in these paradigms is reduced by effective treatment with either an SSRI (Fu et al., 2004; Sheline et al., 2001) or cognitive behavioral therapy (Siegle, Carter, & Thase, 2006). Healthy controls given an SSRI demonstrate reductions in amygdala activation in response to aversive faces (Del-Ben et al., 2005), and both SSRIs and NE reuptake inhibitors reduce the identification of negative stimuli in healthy controls (Harmer, Shelley, Cowen, & Goodwin, 2004).

A common complaint of patients with MDD is diminished concentration, often resulting from the emergence of distracting negative thoughts and feelings. fMRI studies in healthy subjects have found that as the cognitive load required to complete a task is increased, metabolic activity in cortical cognitive areas increases, along with a concomitant decrease in activity in the limbic and paralimbic regions (Pochon et al., 2002). This pattern of activity likely reflects an emotional gating that acts to inhibit emotional interference while performing cognitive work. Patients with MDD demonstrate limited ability to modulate medial prefrontal regions in the face of increasing cognitive demand, implying that the normal cortical-limbic control systems are dysfunctional, resulting in poorer performance on effortful cognitive tasks in depression (P. O. Harvey et al., 2005).

In processing information from their environment, patients with MDD demonstrate a process of automatic distortion of events in a way that emphasizes their negative aspects. These distortions can take the form of exaggerating the significance of failure, biased attention toward words that describe themselves negatively, and an exaggerated sensitivity to mistakes and negative feedback (Murphy, Michael, Robbins, & Sahakian, 2003; Wenzlaff & Grozier, 1988). The neurobiology underlying this enhanced processing of negative stimuli has been explored with fMRI and electroencephalographic monitoring (EEG). With EEG, so-called error-related negativity is detected via an electrical signal present in the midline frontocentral scalp electrodes 50 to 100 milliseconds after an incorrect response in binary choice tasks. This location is consistent with the dorsal regions of the ACC, which are thought to serve in part as error detectors. Patients with MDD demonstrate greater amplitude of the error-related negativity compared with controls (Chiu & Deldin, 2007).

SLEEP

Sleep disruption is a very common, though nonspecific, symptom of MDD. Alteration of normal sleep can occur as part of the prodrome of a depressive episode, or as a symptom of MDD, and is the most common residual symptom after recovery from depression. In depression, the amount of sleep may be excessive (hypersomnia), inhibited (insomnia), or a combination of both. Sleep onset and offset is regulated by hypothalamic systems, influenced by circadian inputs and the homeostatic sleep drive. The structure of sleep is regulated in large part by monoamines, acetylcholine, and GABA signaling, which are also implicated in the pathophysiology of MDD. The structure of sleep is disrupted in many depressed patients, with prolonged sleep initiation times, more fragmentation of sleep, smaller percentage of total sleep time spent in stage III and IV deep sleep (slow-wave sleep), and greater percentage of time spent in REM sleep (Peterson & Benca, 2006). Increased REM sleep is specifically associated with unipolar, as opposed to bipolar depression (Rao et al., 2002), and increased REM density versus controls is present in the first-degree relatives of patients with MDD (Giles, Kupfer, Rush, & Roffwarg, 1998). Because sleep disturbance is so common in MDD, understanding the nature of disrupted sleep in depression may provide insight into the pathophysiology of the illness.

Both REM and non-REM sleep are disrupted in patients with MDD versus healthy controls. Non-REM sleep is a state of reduced cortical and thalamic activity compared to the waking and REM sleep states. Depressed subjects show less of a decline in metabolic activity in the thalamus and in frontal and parietal cortical regions during the transition from waking to non-REM sleep than control subjects using PET imaging (Germain, Nofzinger, Kupfer, & Buysse, 2004) Although the function of non-REM sleep is unknown, it likely subserves a general neural restorative process, and may be important for consolidation of memories. Another PET study, this one examining REM sleep, found heightened metabolic activity in brain stem, limbic, and cortical regions in depressed patients versus controls, perhaps reflecting greater intensity of affective response to stimuli, such as dreams (Nofzinger et al., 2004). REM sleep

occurs during periods of cholinergic activation, which is usually inhibited by serotonergic projections to the cholinergic nuclei in the pons. Therefore, an alteration in the balance between monoamine and cholinergic activity, such as decreased serotonergic transmission or increased cholinergic activity, could decrease the amount of slow-wave sleep and increase REM sleep. Most antidepressants (but not nefazodone or bupropion) suppress REM sleep (Winokur et al., 2001). Increased catecholamine transmission or increased postsynaptic $5HT_{1a}$ receptor activity or may be responsible for this effect of medication (Seifritz, 2001). These alterations of sleep are consistent with the concept of depression as being a state of overarousal, and may underlie the subjective complaints of insomnia and nonrestorative sleep reported by depressed patients. Nocturnal levels of IL-6 and soluble intercellular adhesion molecule (sICAM, an endothelial activation marker) are elevated in depressed patients versus controls, and these increases are associated with difficulty initiating sleep (Motivala, Sarfatti, Olmos, & Irwin, 2005). Insufficient sleep may impact the stability networks involved in cognitive functions, particularly cortical regions involved in sustained attention, such as the medial and lateral prefrontal cortices.

SUMMARY

Despite the tremendous public health importance of MDD, our knowledge of its pathophysiology remains remarkably limited. The recent additions of powerful neuroimaging and genetics techniques to the traditional biochemical approaches offer the promise of new advances in our ability to determine and manipulate the biological forces that shape MDD and its response to treatment. The greatest advances in the neuroscience of MDD are likely to occur through the thoughtful combination of techniques in carefully selected patient populations, attempting to control some of the heterogeneity captured by the current diagnostic nomenclature.

There are several recent examples of the kind of work that can be done through the combination of investigative methods. One of the most intriguing is the emerging field of genetic neuroimaging. This paradigm uses brain-imaging techniques to evaluate how genetic polymorphisms affect neuronal processing in response to stimuli. Perhaps the most impressive examples of this kind of study have explored the effects of the SERT promoter polymorphism in healthy individuals exposed to fearful or angry facial expressions using fMRI. Individuals free of psychiatric illness, but who carry the S form of the gene, demonstrate greater amygdala reactivity to these threatening stimuli than do healthy controls with the L form (Hariri et al., 2005). This finding was subsequently extended to demonstrate that elevated amygdala reactivity in individuals with the S form was associated with impaired functional connectivity between the amygdala and the anterior cingulate regions that regulate amygdala reactivity, which may represent a risk factor for MDD in the face of stress (Pezawas et al., 2005). Another study in this paradigm using PET imaging found that subjects in remission from major depression who carry at least one copy of the L_A allele for the SERT promoter polymorphism experienced greater worsening of depressive symptoms, and increased metabolism in the amygdala, subgenual cingulate cortex, and hippocampus, than did subjects with two copies of the S allele when undergoing tryptophan depletion (Neumeister et al., 2006).

A similar study has been used linking the BDNF gene to findings on structural MRI. At coding position 66 in the BDNF gene, a single nucleotide polymorphism produces a switch in the amino acid sequence from a valine to a methionine. This switch has been inconsistently found to be associated with neuroticism and poorer cognitive performance (Sen et al., 2003). Carriers of the methionine allele for BDNF were found to have smaller hippocampal volumes than individuals homozygous for the Val allele (Frodl et al., 2007). Because smaller hippocampal volumes are associated with the development of MDD, it may be that the Met-BDNF allele conveys a risk factor for MDD via its effects on hippocampal development or plasticity. Another study explored hedonic responsiveness to d-amphetamine administration in depressed subjects, using fMRI to assess changes in neuronal processing after receipt of the stimulant. Untreated severely depressed subjects (but not mildly depressed subjects) demonstrated reduced reward experience to stimuli prior to receiving the stimulant, with subsequent hyper-responsivity to reward after ingesting the stimulant. This increase in responsivity was associated with greater activity in the VLPFC, OFC, and basal ganglia by fMRI than healthy controls (Tremblay et al., 2005). This study helps delineate a specific reward circuit deficit that may be present in severely ill, anhedonic depressed patients, versus nonseverely ill, depressed patients and healthy controls.

The few studies cited may point the way to developing a more specific and biologically based diagnostic nomenclature for the catch-all diagnosis of MDD. The outcome of this work will be improved treatment, and perhaps prevention, of depressive syndromes.

REFERENCES

Abdolmaleky, H. M., Smith, C. L., Faraone, S. V., Shafa, R., Stone, W., Glatt, S. J., et al. (2004). Methylomics in psychiatry: Modulation of gene-environment interactions may be through DNA methylation.

American Journal of Medical Genetics, Pt. B: Neuropsychiatric Genetics, 127, 51–59.

Altshuler, L. L., Bauer, M., Frye, M., Gitlin, M. J., Mintz, J., Szuba, M. P., et al. (2001). Does thyroid supplementation accelerate tricyclic antidepressant response? A review and meta-analysis of the literature. *American Journal of Psychiatry, 158,* 1617–1622.

Amsterdam, J. D., Maislin, G., Skolnick, B., Berwish, N., & Winokur, A. (1989). Multiple hormone responses to clonidine administration in depressed patients and healthy volunteers. *Biological Psychiatry, 26,* 265–278.

Anand, A., Charney, D. S., Delgado, P. L., McDougle, C. J., Heninger, G. R., & Price, L. H. (1994). Neuroendocrine and behavioral responses to intravenous m-chlorophenylpiperazine (mCPP) in depressed patients and healthy comparison subjects. *American Journal of Psychiatry, 151,* 1626–1630.

Anda, R., Williamson, D., Jones, D., Macera, C., Eaker, E., Glassman, A., et al. (1993). Depressed affect, hopelessness, and the risk of ischemic heart disease in a cohort of US adults. *Epidemiology, 4,* 285–294.

Appelhof, B. C., Brouwer, J. P., van Dyck, R., Fliers, E., Hoogendijk, W. J., Huyser, J., et al. (2004). Triiodothyronine addition to paroxetine in the treatment of major depressive disorder. *Journal of Clinical Endocrinology and Metabolism, 89,* 6271–6276.

Arana, G. W., Baldessarini, R. J., & Ornsteen, M. (1985). The dexamethasone suppression test for diagnosis and prognosis in psychiatry. *Archives of General Psychiatry, 42,* 1193–1204.

Arango, V., Ernsberger, P., Sved, A. F., & Mann, J. (1993). Quantitative autoradiography of ·1- and ·2-adrenergic receptors in the cerebral cortex of controls and suicide victims. *Brain Research, 630,* 271–282.

Arato, M., Banki, C. M., Bissette, G., & Nemeroff, C. B. (1989). Elevated CSF CRF in suicide victims. *Biological Psychiatry, 25,* 355–359.

Aronson, R., Offman, H. J., Joffe, R. T., & Naylor, C. D. (1996). Triiodothyronine augmentation in the treatment of refractory depression: A meta-analysis. *Archives of General Psychiatry, 53,* 842–848.

Asberg, M., Traskman, L., & Thoren, P. (1976). 5-HIAA in the cerebrospinal fluid: A biochemical suicide predictor? *Archives of General Psychiatry, 33,* 1193–1197.

Attar-Levy, D., Martinot, J. L., Blin, J., Dao-Castellana, M. H., Crouzel, C., Mazoyer, B., et al. (1999). The cortical serotonin2 receptors studied with positron-emission tomography. *Biological Psychiatry, 45,* 180–186.

Aubry, J.-M., Gervasoni, N., Osiek, C., Perret, G., Rossier, M. F., Bertschy, G., et al. (2007). The DEX/CRH neuroendocrine test and the prediction of depressive relapse in remitted depressed outpatients. *A Journal of Psychiatric Research, 41,* 290–294.

Baghai, T. C., di Michele, F., Schule, C., Eser, D., Zwanzger, P., Pasini, A., et al. (2005). Plasma concentrations of neuroactive steroids before and after electroconvulsive therapy in major depression. *Neuropsychopharmacology, 30,* 1181–1186.

Bajbouj, M., Lisanby, S. H., Lang, U., Danker-Hopfe, H., Heuser, I., & Neu, P. (2006). Evidence for impaired cortical inhibition in patients with unipolar major depression. *Biological Psychiatry, 59,* 395–400.

Banarjee, S. P., Kung, L. S., Riggi, S. J., & Chanda, S. K. (1977, August 4). Development of B adrenergic receptor subsensitivity by antidepressants. *Nature, 268,* 455–456.

Banki, C. M., Bissette, G., Arato, M., & Nemeroff, C. B. (1988). Elevation of immunoreactive CSF TRH in depressed patients. *American Journal of Psychiatry, 145,* 1526–1531.

Banki, C. M., Bissette, G., Arato, M., O'Connor, L., & Nemeroff, C. B. (1987). CSF corticotropin-releasing factor-like immunoreactivity in depression and schizophrenia. *American Journal of Psychiatry, 144,* 873–877.

Belelli, D., & Lambert, J. J. (2005). Neurosteroids: Endogenous regulators of the GABA(A) receptor. *Nature Reviews Neuroscience, 6,* 565–575.

Bench, C. J., Friston, K., Brown, R., Frackowiak, R., & Dolan, R. J. (1993). Regional cerebral blood flow in depression measured by positron emission tomography: The relationship with clinical dimensions. *Psychological Medicine, 23,* 579–590.

Benkelfat, C., Ellenbogen, M. A., Dean, P., Palmour, R. M., & Young, S. N. (1994). Mood-lowering effect of tryptophan depletion: Enhanced susceptibility in young men at genetic risk for major affective disorders. *Archives of General Psychiatry, 51,* 687–697.

Berman, R. M., Narasimhan, M., Miller, H. L., Anand, A., Cappiello, A., Oren, D. A., et al. (1999). Transient depressive relapse induced by catecholamine depletion. *Archives of General Psychiatry, 56,* 395–403.

Berton, O., McClung, C. A., Dileone, R. J., Krishnan, V., Renthal, W., Russo, S. J., et al. (2006, February 10). Essential role of BDNF in the mesolimbic dopamine pathway in social defeat stress. *Science, 311,* 864–868.

Beskow, J., Gottfries, C. G., Roos, B. E., & Winblad, B. (1976). Determination of monoamine and monoamine metabolites in the human brain: Post mortem studies in a group of suicides and in a control group. *Acta Psychiatrica Scandinavica, 53,* 7–20.

Bhagwagar, Z., Rabiner, E. A., Sargent, P. A., Grasby, P. M., & Cowen, P. J. (2004). Persistent reduction in brain serotonin1A receptor binding in recovered depressed men measured by positron emission tomography with. *Molecular Psychiatry, 9,* 386–392.

Bissette, G., Widerlov, E., Walleus, H., Karlsson, I., Eklund, K., Forsman, A., et al. (1986). Alterations in cerebrospinal fluid concentrations of somatostatinlike immunoreactivity in neuropsychiatric disorders. *Archives of General Psychiatry, 43,* 1148–1151.

Biver, F., Wikler, D., Lotstra, F., Damhaut, P., Goldman, S., & Mendlewicz, J. (1997). Serotonin 5-HT2 receptor imaging in major depression: Focal changes in orbito-insular cortex. *British Journal of Psychiatry, 171,* 444–448.

Bjork, J. M., Moeller, F. G., Kramer, G. L., Kram, M., Suris, A., Rush, A. J., et al. (2001). Plasma GABA levels correlate with aggressiveness in relatives of patients with unipolar depressive disorder. *Psychiatry Research, 101,* 131–136.

Blier, P., deMontigny, C., & Chaput, Y. (1990). A role for the serotonin system in the mechanism of acion of antidepressant treatment: Preclinical evidence. *Journal of Clinical Psychiatry, 51,* 14–21.

Bligh-Glover, W., Kolli, T. N., Shapiro-Kulnane, L., Dilley, G. E., Friedman, L., Balraj, E., et al. (2000). The serotonin transporter in the midbrain of suicide victims with major depression. *Biological Psychiatry, 47,* 1015–1024.

Bloch, R. G., Dooneief, A. S., Buchberg, A. S., & Spellman, S. (1954). The clinical effect of isoniazid and iproniazid in the treatment of pulmonary tuberculosis. *Annals of Internal Medicine, 40,* 881–900.

Botterton, K., Raichle, M. E., Drevets, W. C., Heath, A., & Todd, R. D. (2002). Volumetric reduction in left subgenual prefrontal cortex in early onset depression. *Biological Psychiatry, 51,* 342–344.

Bowden, C., Cheetham, S. C., Lowther, S., Katona, C. L., Crompton, M. R., & Horton, R. W. (1997). Reduced dopamine turnover in the basal ganglia of depressed suicides. *Brain Research, 769,* 135–140.

Bowden, C., Theodorou, A. E., Cheetham, S. C., Lowther, S., Katona, C. L., Crompton, M. R., et al. (1997). Dopamine D1 and D2 receptor binding sites in brain samples from depressed suicides and controls. *Brain Research, 752,* 227–233.

Bremner, J., Vythilingam, M., Ng, C. K., Vermetten, E., Nazeer, A., Oren, D. A., et al. (2003). Regional brain metabolic correlates of alpha-methylparatyrosine-induced depressive symptoms: Implications for the neural circuitry of depression. *Journal of the American Medical Association, 289,* 3125–3134.

Bunney, W. E., & Davis, J. M. (1965). Norepinephrine in depressive reactions: A review. *Archives of General Psychiatry, 13,* 483–493.

Callahan, A. M., Frye, M. A., Marangell, L. B., George, M. S., Ketter, T. A., L'Herrou, T., et al. (1997). Comparative antidepressant effects of intravenous and intrathecal thyrotropin-releasing hormone: Confounding effects of tolerance and implications for therapeutics. *Biological Psychiatry, 41,* 264–272.

Cameron, O. G., Abelson, J. L., & Young, E. A. (2004). Anxious and depressive disorders and their comorbidity: Effect on central nervous system noradrenergic function. *Biological Psychiatry, 56,* 875–883.

Campos-Barros, A., Meinhold, H., Stula, M., Muller, F., Kohler, R., Eravci, M., et al. (1994). The influence of desipramine on thyroid hormone metabolism in rat brain. *Journal of Pharmacology and Experimental Therapeutics, 268,* 1143–1152.

Carroll, B. J., Martin, F. I., & Davies, B. (1968). Pituitary-adrenal function in depression. *Lancet, 1*(7556), 1373–1374.

Caspi, A., Sugden, K., Moffitt, T. E., Taylor, A., Craig, I. W., Harrington, H., et al. (2003, July 18). Influence of life stress on depression: Moderation by a polymorphism in the 5-HTT gene. *Science, 301,* 386–389.

Castren, E. (2005). Is mood chemistry? *Nature Reviews Neuroscience, 6,* 241–246.

Chiu, P. H., & Deldin, P. J. (2007). Neural evidence for enhanced error detection in major depressive disorder. *American Journal of Psychiatry, 164,* 608–616.

Cooper-Kazaz, R., Apter, J. T., Cohen, R., Karagichev, L., Muhammed-Moussa, S., Grupper, D., et al. (2007). Combined treatment with sertraline and liothyronine in major depression: A randomized, double-blind, placebo-controlled trial. *Archives of General Psychiatry, 64,* 679–688.

Coplan, J. D., Altemus, M., Mathew, S. J., Smith, E. L. P., Scharf, B., Coplan, P. M., et al. (2005). Synchronized maternal-infant elevations of primate CSF CRF concentrations in response to variable foraging demand. *CNS Spectrums, 10,* 530–536.

Coplan, J. D., Andrews, M. W., Rosenblum, L. A., Owens, M. J., Friedman, S., Gorman, J. M., et al. (1996). Persistent elevations of cerebrospinal fluid concentrations of corticotropin-releasing factor in adult nonhuman primates exposed to early-life stressors: Implications for the pathophysiology of mood and anxiety disorders. *Proceedings of the National Academy of Sciences, USA, 93,* 1619–1623.

Coplan, J. D., Wolk, S. I., Goetz, R. R., Ryan, N. D., Dahl, R. E., Mann, J. J., et al. (2000). Nocturnal growth hormone secretion studies in adolescents with or without major depression re-examined: Integration of adult clinical follow-up data. *Biological Psychiatry, 47,* 594–604.

Coppen, A. (1967). The biochemistry of affective disorders. *British Journal of Psychiatry, 113,* 1237–1264.

Crow, T. J., Cross, A. J., Cooper, S. J., Deakin, J. F., Ferrier, I. N., Johnson, J. A., et al. (1984). Neurotransmitter receptors and monoamine metabolites in the brains of patients with Alzheimer-type dementia and depression, and suicides. *Neuropharmacology, 23,* 1561–1569.

Dantzer, R. (2004). Cytokine-induced sickness behaviour: A neuroimmune response to activation of innate immunity. *European Journal of Pharmacology, 500,* 399–411.

Davidson, R. J., Pizzagalli, D., Nitschke, J. B., & Putnam, K. M. (2002). Depression: Perspectives from affective neuroscience. *Annual Review of Psychology, 53,* 545–574.

De Bellis, M. D., Gold, P. W., Geracioti, T. D., Jr., Listwak, S. J., & Kling, M. A. (1993). Association of fluoxetine treatment with reductions in CSF concentrations of corticotropin-releasing hormone and arginine vasopressin in patients with major depression. *American Journal of Psychiatry, 150,* 656–657.

Del-Ben, C. M., Deakin, J., McKie, S., Delvai, N. A., Williams, S. R., Elliott, R., et al. (2005). The effect of citalopram pretreatment on neuronal responses to neuropsychological tasks in normal volunteers: An fMRI study. *Neuropsychopharmacology, 30,* 1724–1734.

de Paermentier, F., Cheetham, S. C., Crompton, M., Katona, C. L., & Horton, R. W. (1990). Brain -adrenoceptor binding sites in antidepressant-free depressed suicide victims. *Brain Research, 525,* 71–77.

Devanand, D. P., Bowers, M. B., Hoffman, F. J., & Nelson, J. C. (1985). Elevated plasma homovanillic acid levels in depressed females with melancholia and psychosis. *Psychiatry Research, 15,* 1–4.

D'Haenen, H. A., & Bossuyt, A. (1994). Dopamine D2 receptors in depression measured with single photon emission computed tomography. *Biological Psychiatry, 35*, 128–132.

Dolan, R. J., Bench, C. J., Brown, R. G., Scott, L. C., & Frackowiak, R. S. (1994). Neuropsychological dysfunction in depression: The relationship to regional cerebral blood flow. *Psychological Medicine, 24*, 849–857.

Drevets, W. C. (2000). Neuroimaging studies of mood disorders. *Biological Psychiatry, 48*, 813–829.

Drevets, W. C., Price, J. L., Simpson, J. R., Todd, R. D., Reich, T., Vannier, M., et al. (1997, April 24). Subgenual prefrontal cortex abnormalities in mood disorders. *Nature, 386*, 824–827.

Duman, R. S., Heninger, G. R., & Nestler, E. J. (1997). A molecular and cellular theory of depression. *Archives of General Psychiatry, 54*, 597–606.

Duman, R. S., & Nestler, E. J. (1995). Signal transduction pathways for catecholamine receptors. In F. E. Bloom & D. J. Kupfer (Eds.), *Psychopharmacology: The fourth generation of progress* (pp. 303–320). New York: Raven Press.

Dunlop, B. W., & Nemeroff, C. B. (2007). The role of dopamine in the pathophysiology of depression. *Archives of General Psychiatry, 64*, 327–337.

Ebert, D., Feistel, H., Loew, T., & Pirner, A. (1996). Dopamine and depression: Striatal dopamine D2 receptor SPECT before and after antidepressant therapy. *Psychopharmacology, 126*, 91–94.

Elliott, R., Rubinsztein, J. S., Sahakian, B. J., & Dolan, R. J. (2002). The neural basis of mood-congruent processing biases in depression. *Archives of General Psychiatry, 59*, 597–604.

Ellis, P. M., & Salmond, C. (1994). Is platelet imipramine binding reduced in depression? A meta-analysis. *Biological Psychiatry, 36*, 292–299.

Encinas, J. M., Vaahtokari, A., & Enikolopov, G. (2006). Fluoxetine targets early progenitor cells in the adult brain. *Proceedings of the National Academy of Sciences, USA, 103*, 8233–8238.

Extein, I., Pottash, A. L., & Gold, M. S. (1981). The thyrotropin-releasing hormone test in the diagnosis of unipolar depression. *Psychiatry Research, 5*, 311 316.

Extein, I., Tallman, J., Smith, C. C., & Goodwin, F. K. (1979). Changes in lymphocyte beta-adrenergic receptors in depression and mania. *Psychiatry Research, 1*, 191–197.

Fossati, P., Hevenor, S. J., Graham, S. J., Grady, C., Keightley, M. L., Craik, F., et al. (2003). In search of the emotional self: An fMRI study using positive and negative emotional words. *American Journal of Psychiatry, 160*, 1938–1945.

France, R. D., Urban, B., Krishnan, K. R., Bissett, G., Banki, C. M., Nemeroff, C., et al. (1988). CSF corticotropin-releasing factor-like immunoactivity in chronic pain patients with and without major depression. *Biological Psychiatry, 23*, 86–88.

Frodl, T., Schule, C., Schmitt, G., Born, C., Baghai, T., Zill, P., et al. (2007). Association of the brain-derived neurotrophic factor Val66Met polymorphism with reduced hippocampal volumes in major depression. *Archives of General Psychiatry, 64*, 410–416.

Fu, C. H., Williams, S. C., Cleare, A. J., Brammer, M. J., Walsh, N. D., Kim, J., et al. (2004). Attenuation of the neural response to sad faces in major depression by antidepressant treatment: A prospective, event-related functional magnetic resonance imaging study. *Archives of General Psychiatry, 61*, 877–889.

Fujita, M., Charney, D. S., & Innis, R. B. (2000). Imaging serotonergic neurotransmission in depression: Hippocampal pathophysiology may mirror global brain alterations. *Biological Psychiatry, 48*, 801–812.

Garcia-Sevilla, J., Padro, D., Giralt, T., Guimon, J., & Areso, P. (1990). 2-Adrenoceptor-mediated inhibition of platelet adenylate cyclase and induction of aggregation in major depression: Effect of long-term cyclic antidepressant drug treatment. *Archives of General Psychiatry, 47*, 125–132.

Garcia-Sevilla, J., Ulibarri, I., Ugedo, L., & Gutierrez, M. (1987). 2-Adrenoceptor-mediated inhibition of platelet adenylate cyclase activity in heroin addicts in abstinence. *Psychopharmacology, 92*, 320–323.

Germain, A., Nofzinger, E. A., Kupfer, D. J., & Buysse, D. J. (2004). Neurobiology of non-REM sleep in depression: Further evidence for hypofrontality and thalamic dysregulation. *American Journal of Psychiatry, 161*, 1856–1863.

Gershon, E. S., Hamovit, J., Guroff, J. J., Dibble, E., Leckman, J. F., Sceery, W., et al. (1982). A family study of schizoaffective bipolar, I, bipolar II, unipolar, and normal control probands. *Archives of General Psychiatry, 39*, 1157–1167.

Gibbons, J. L., & McHugh, P. R. (1962). Plasma cortisol in depressive illness. *Journal of Psychiatric Research, 1*, 162–171.

Gibbons, R. D., & Davis, J. M. (1986). Consistent evidence for a biological subtype of depression characterized by low CSF monoamine levels. *Acta Psychiatrica Scandinavica, 74*, 8–12.

Gilbertson, M. W., Shenton, M. E., Ciszewski, A., Kasai, K., Lasko, N. B., Orr, S. P., et al. (2002). Smaller hippocampal volume predicts pathologic vulnerability to psychological trauma. *Nature Neuroscience, 5*, 1242–1247.

Giles, D. E., Kupfer, D. J., Rush, A., & Roffwarg, H. P. (1998). Controlled comparison of electrophysiological sleep in families of probands with unipolar depression. *American Journal of Psychiatry, 155*, 192–199.

Glowinski, J., & Axelrod, J. (1966). Effects of drugs on the disposition of H-3-norepinephrine in the rat brain. *Pharmacological Reviews, 18*, 775–785.

Glowinski, J., Snyder, S., & Axelrod, J. (1966). Subcellular localization of H3-norepinephrine in the rat brain and the effect of drugs. *Journal of Pharmacology and Experimental Therapeutics, 152*, 282–292.

Gold, B. I., Bowers, M. B., Roth, R. H., & Sweeney, D. W. (1980). GABA levels in CSF of patients with psychiatric disorders. *American Journal of Psychiatry, 137*, 362–364.

Gold, M. S., Pottash, A. C., & Extein, I. (1982). Symptomless autoimmune thyroiditis in depression. *Psychiatry Research, 6*, 261 269.

Gurguis, G. N., Vo, S. P., Griffith, J. M., & Rush, A. (1999). Platelet alpha-sub(2A)-adrenoceptor function in major depression: G-sub(i) coupling, effects of imipramine and relationship to treatment outcome. *Psychiatry Research, 89*, 73–95.

Guze, B. H., & Barrio, J. C. (1991). The etiology of depression in Parkinson's disease patients. *Psychosomatics, 32*, 390–394.

Hariri, A. R., Drabant, E. M., Munoz, K. E., Kolachana, B. S., Mattay, V. S., Egan, M. F., et al. (2005). A susceptibility gene for affective disorders and the response of the human amygdala. *Archives of General Psychiatry, 62*, 146–152.

Harmer, C. J., Shelley, N. C., Cowen, P. J., & Goodwin, G. M. (2004). Increased positive versus negative affective perception and memory in healthy volunteers following selective serotonin and norepinephrine reuptake inhibition. *American Journal of Psychiatry, 161*, 1256–1263.

Harvey, M., Shink, E., Tremblay, M., Gagne, B., Raymond, C., Labbe, M., et al. (2004). Support for the involvement of the TPH2 gene in affective disorders. *Molecular Psychiatry, 9*, 980–981.

Harvey, P. O., Fossati, P., Pochon, J. B., Levy, R., Le Bastard, G., Lehericy, S., et al. (2005). Brain resources and cognitive effort in depression: A fMRI study using the n-back task. *NeuroImage, 26*, 860–869.

Hasler, G., Bonwetsch, R., Giovacchini, G., Toczek, M. T., Bagic, A., Luckenbaugh, D. A., et al. (2007). 5-HT1A receptor binding in temporal lobe epilepsy patients with and without major depression. *Biological Psychiatry, 62*, 1258–1264.

Hasler, G., Drevets, W. C., Manji, H. K., & Charney, D. S. (2004). Discovering endophenotypes for major depression. *Neuropsychopharmacology, 29*, 1765–1781.

Hasler, G., Neumeister, A., van der Teen, T., Tumonis, E., Bain, J., Shen, J., et al. (2005). Normal prefrontal gamma-aminobutryric acid levels in remitted depressed subjects determined by proton magnetic resonance spectroscopy. *Biological Psychiatry, 58,* 969–973.

Hauger, R. L., & Dautzenberg, F. M. (2000). Regulation of the stress response by corticotropin-releasing factor receptors. In P. M. Conn & M. E. Freedman (Eds.), *Neuroendocrinology in physiology and medicine* (pp. 261–286). Totowa, NJ: Humana Press.

Healy, D., Carney, P., O'Halloran, A., & Leonard, B. (1985). Peripheral adrenoceptors and serotonin receptors in depression: Changes associated with response to treatment with trazodone or amitriptyline. *Journal of Affective Disorders, 9,* 285–296.

Heils, A., Teufel, A., Petri, S., Stober, G., Riederer, P., Bengel, D., et al. (1996). Allelic variation of human serotonin transporter gene expression. *Journal of Neurochemistry, 66,* 2621–2624.

Heim, C., Newport, D. J., Bonsall, R., Miller, A. H., & Nemeroff, C. B. (2001). Altered pituitary-adrenal axis responses to provocative challenge tests in adult survivors of childhood abuse. *American Journal of Psychiatry, 158,* 575–581.

Heinz, A., Jones, D. W., Mazzanti, C., Goldman, D., Ragan, P., Hommer, D., et al. (2000). A relationship between serotonin transporter genotype and in vivo protein expression and alcohol neurotoxocity. *Biological Psychiatry, 47,* 643–649.

Hendry, S. H., Schwark, H. D., Jones, E. G., & Yan, J. (1987). Numbers and proportions of GABA-immunoreactive neurons in different areas of monkey cerebral cortex. *Journal of Neuroscience, 7,* 1503–1509.

Heninger, G., Delgado, P., & Charney, D. (1996). The revised monoamine theory of depression: A modulatory role for monoamines, based on new findings from monoamine depletion experiments in humans. *Pharmacopsychiatry, 29,* 2–11.

Heuser, I., Bissette, G., Dettling, M., Schweiger, U., Gotthardt, U., Schmider, J., et al. (1998). Cerebrospinal fluid concentrations of corticotropin-releasing hormone, vasopressin and somatostatin in depressed patients and healthy controls: Response to amitriptyline treatment. *Depression and Anxiety, 8,* 71–79.

Heuser, I., Yassouridis, A., & Holsboer, F. (1994). The combined dexamethasone/CRH test: A refined laboratory test for psychiatric disorders. *Journal of Psychiatric Research, 28,* 341–356.

Hindal, J. T., & Kaplan, M. M. (1988). Inhibition of thyroxine 5'-deiodination type II in cultured human placental cells by cortisol, insulin, 3', 5'-cyclic adenosine monophosphate and butyrate. *Metabolism, 37,* 664–668.

Holsboer, F., von Bardeleben, U., Wiedemann, K., Muller, O. A., & Stalla, G. K. (1987). Serial assessment of corticotropin-releasing hormone response after dexamethasone in depression: Implications for pathophysiology of DST nonsuppression. *Biological Psychiatry, 22,* 228–234.

Hu, X. Z., Zhu, G. S., Lipsky, R. H., & Goldman, D. (2004). HTTLPR allele expression is codominant, correlating with gene effects on fMRI and SPECT imaging intermediate phenotypes, and behavior. *Biological Psychiatry, 55,* S191.

Janicak, P. G., Davis, J. M., Preskorn, S. H., & Ayd, F. J. (1997). *Principles and practice of psychopharmacotherapy* (2nd ed.). Philadelphia: Lippincott, Williams, & Wilkins.

Joffe, R. T., & Marriott, M. (2000). Thyroid hormone levels and recurrence of major depression. *American Journal of Psychiatry, 157,* 1689–1691.

Jonas, B. S., & Mussolino, M. E. (2000). Symptoms of depression as a prospective risk factor for stroke. *Psychosomatic Medicine, 62,* 463–471.

Jones, M. E., & Cockrum, P. C. (2000). A critical review of published economic modeling studies in depression. *Pharmacoeconomics, 17,* 555–583.

Kapur, S., & Mann, J. J. (1992). Role of the dopaminergic system in depression. *Biological Psychiatry, 32,* 1–17.

Karege, F., Bondolfi, G., Gervasoni, N., Schwald, M., Aubry, J. M., & Bertschy, G. (2005). Low brain-derived neurotrophic factor (BDNF) levels in serum of depressed patients probably results from lowered platelet BDNF release unrelated to platelet reactivity. *Biological Psychiatry, 57,* 1068–1772.

Karl, A., Schaefer, M., Malta, L. S., Dorfel, D., Rohleder, N., & Werner, A. (2006). A meta-analysis of structural brain abnormalities in PTSD. *Neuroscience and Biobehavioral Reviews, 30,* 1004–1031.

Kastin, A. J., Ehrensing, R. H., Schalch, D. S., & Anderson, M. S. (1972). Improvement in mental depression with decreased thyrotropin response after administration of thyrotropin-releasing hormone. *Lancet, 2,* 740–742.

Kathol, R. G., Jaeckle, R. S., Lopez, J. F., & Meller, W. H. (1989). Consistent reduction of ACTH responses to stimulation with CRH, vasopressin and hypoglycaemia in patients with major depression. *British Journal of Psychiatry, 155,* 468–478.

Kavoussi, R. J., Hauger, R. L., & Coccaro, E. F. (1999). Prolactin response to d-fenfluramine in major depression before and after treatment with serotonin reuptake inhibitors. *Biological Psychiatry, 45,* 295–299.

Kendler, K. S., Gardner, C. O., & Prescott, C. A. (2002). Toward a comprehensive developmental model for major depression in women. *American Journal of Psychiatry, 159,* 1133–1145.

Kendler, K. S., Kuhn, J. W., Vittum, J., Prescott, C. A., & Riley, B. (2005). The interaction of stressful life events and a serotonin transporter polymorphism in the prediction of episodes of major depression: A replication. *Archives of General Psychiatry, 62,* 529–535.

Kendler, K. S., Neale, M. C., Kessler, R. C., Heath, A. C., & Eaves, L. J. (1993). A longitudinal twin study of personality and major depression in women. *Archives of General Psychiatry, 50,* 853–862.

Kessler, R. C., Berglund, P., Demler, O., Jin, R., Koretz, D., Merikangas, K. R., et al. (2003). The epidemiology of major depressive disorder: Results from the National Comorbidity Survey Replication (NCS-R). *Journal of the American Medical Association, 289,* 3095–3105.

Ketter, T. A., George, M. S., Kimbrell, T. A., Benson, B. A., & Post, R. M. (1996). Functional brain imaging, limbic function, and affective disorders. *Neuroscientist, 2,* 55–65.

Khisti, R. T., Chopde, C. T., & Jain, S. P. (2000). Antidepressant-like effect of the neurosteroid 3alpha-hydroxy-5alpha-pregnan-20-one in mice forced swim test. *Pharmacology, Biochemistry and Behavior, 67,* 137–143.

Kirkegaard, C., Faber, J., Hummer, L., & Rogowski, P. (1979). Increased levels of TRH in cerebrospinal fluid from patients with endogenous depression. *Psychoneuroendocrinology, 4,* 227–235.

Kirschbaum, C., Pirke, K. M., & Hellhammer, D. H. (1993). The 'Trier Social Stress Test': A tool for investigating psychobiological stress responses in a laboratory setting. *Neuropsychobiology, 28,* 76–81.

Kiss, J. Z., Martos, J., & Palkovits, M. (1991). Hypothalamic paraventricular nucleus: A quantitative analysis of cytoarchitectonic subdivisions in the rat. *Journal of Comparative Neurology, 313,* 563–573.

Klimek, V., Rajkowska, G., Luker, S. N., Dilley, G., Meltzer, H. Y., Overholser, J. C., et al. (1999). Brain noradrenergic receptors in major depression and schizophrenia. *Neuropsychopharmacology, 21,* 69–81.

Klimek, V., Schenck, J. E., Han, H., Stockmeier, C. A., & Ordway, G. A. (2002). Dopaminergic abnormalities in amygdaloid nuclei in major depression: A postmortem study. *Biological Psychiatry, 52,* 740–748.

Klimke, A., Larisch, R., Janz, A., Vosberg, H., Muller-Gartner, H. W., & Gaebel, W. (1999). Dopamine D2 receptor binding before and after treatment of major depression measured by. *Psychiatry Research, 90,* 91–101.

Konig, F., Hauger, B., von Hippel, C., Wolfersdorf, M., & Kaschka, W. P. (2000). Effect of paroxetine on thyroid hormone levels in severely depressed patients. *Neuropsychobiology, 42,* 135–138.

Krishnan, K. R., Doraiswamy, P. M., Lurie, S. N., Figiel, G. S., Husain, M. M., Boyko, O. B., et al. (1991). Pituitary size in depression. *Journal of Clinical Endocrinology and Metabolism, 72,* 256–259.

Krishnan, K. R., Hays, J. C., & Blazer, D. G. (1997). MRI-defined vascular depression. *American Journal of Psychiatry, 154*, 497–501.

Lambert, G., Johansson, M., Agren, H., & Friberg, P. (2000). Reduced brain norepinephrine and dopamine release in treatment-refractory depressive illness: Evidence in support of the catecholamine hypothesis of mood disorders. *Archives of General Psychiatry, 57*, 787–793.

Lapin, I. P., & Oxenkrug, G. F. (1969). Intensification of central serotonergic process as a possible determinant of thymoleptic effect. *Lancet, 1*(7586), 132–136.

Levinson, D. F. (2006). The genetics of depression: A review. *Biological Psychiatry, 60*, 84–92.

Lewinsohn, P. M., Allen, N. B., Seeley, J. R., & Gotlib, I. H. (1999). First onset versus recurrence of depression: Differential processes of psychosocial risk. *Journal of Abnormal Psychology, 108*, 483–489.

Lewis, D. A., & Smith, R. E. (1983). Steroid-induced psychiatric syndromes. *Journal of Affective Disorders, 5*, 319–332.

Lifschytz, T., Segman, R., Shalom, G., Lerer, B., Gur, E., Golzer, T., et al. (2006). Basic mechanisms of augmentation of antidepressant effects with thyroid hormone. *Current Drug Targets, 7*, 203–210.

Linnoila, M., & Virkkunen, M. (1992). Aggression, suicidality and serotonin. *Journal of Clinical Psychiatry, 53*(10, Suppl), 46–51.

Little, K. Y. (1988). Amphetamine, but not methylphenidate, predicts antidepressant efficacy. *Journal of Clinical Psychopharmacology, 8*, 177–183.

Lowther, S., De Paermentier, F., Crompton, M. R., Katona, C. L., & Horton, R. W. (1994). Brain 5-HT2 receptors in suicide victims: Violence of death, depression and effects of antidepressant treatment. *Brain Research, 642*, 281–289.

Maas, J. W., Fawcett, J. A., & Dekirmenjian, H. (1972). Catecholamine metabolism, depressive illness and drug response. *Archives of General Psychiatry, 26*, 252–262.

MacLean, P. D., & Newman, J. D. (1988). Role of midline frontolimbic cortex in production of the isolation call of squirrel monkeys. *Brain Research, 450*, 111–123.

MacQueen, G. M., Campbell, S., McEwen, B. S., Macdonald, K., Amano, S., Joffe, R. T., et al. (2003). Course of illness, hippocampal function, and hippocampal volume in major depression. *Proceedings of the National Academy of Sciences, USA, 100*, 1387–1392.

Maes, M., Gastel, A. V., Delmeire, L., & Meltzer, H. Y. (1999). Decreased platelet alpha-2 adrenoceptor density in major depression: Effects of tricyclic antidepressants and fluoxetine. *Biological Psychiatry, 45*, 278–284.

Maes, M., & Meltzer, H. Y. (1995). The serotonin hypothesis of major depression. In F. E. Bloom & D. J. Kupfer (Eds.), *Psychopharmacology: The fourth generation of progress* (pp. 933–944). New York: Raven Press.

Maier, W., Lichtermann, D., Minges, J., Heun, R., Hallmayer, J., & Benkert, O. (1992). Schizoaffective disorder and affective disorders with mood-incongruent psychotic features: Keep separate or combine? Evidence from a family study. *American Journal of Psychiatry, 149*, 1666–1673.

Malison, R. T., Price, L. H., Berman, R., van Dyck, C. H., Pelton, G. H., Carpenter, L., et al. (1998). Reduced brain serotonin transporter availability in major depression as measured by 123-I-2 Beta-carbomethoxy-3 beta-(4-iodophenyl)tropane and single photon emission computed tomography. *Biological Psychiatry, 44*, 1090–1098.

Manji, H. K., Drevets, W. C., & Charney, D. S. (2001). The cellular neurobiology of depression. *Nature Medicine, 7*, 541–547.

Mann, J., Stanley, M., McBride, P., & McEwen, B. S. (1986). Increased serotonin-sub-2 and β-adrenergic receptor binding in the frontal cortices of suicide victims. *Archives of General Psychiatry, 43*, 954–959.

Mann, J. J., Huang, Y. Y., Underwood, M. D., Kassir, S. A., Oppenheim, S., Kelly, T. M., et al. (2000). A serotonin transporter gene promoter polymorphism (5-HTTLPR) and prefrontal cortical binding in major depression and suicide. *Archives of General Psychiatry, 57*, 729–738.

Marangell, L. B., George, M. S., Callahan, A. M., Ketter, T. A., Pazzaglia, P. J., L'Herrou, T. A., et al. (1997). Effects of intrathecal thyrotropin-releasing hormone (protirelin) in refractory depressed patients. *Archives of General Psychiatry, 54*, 214–222.

Marinelli, M., & Piazza, P. V. (2002). Interaction between glucocorticoid hormones, stress and psychostimulant drugs. *European Journal of Neuroscience, 16*, 387–394.

Mattsubara, S., Arora, R., & Meltzer, H. (1991). Serotonergic measures in suicide brain: 5HT1a binding sites in frontal cortex of suicide victims. *Journal of Neural Transmission, 85*, 181–194.

Matussek, N., Ackenheil, M., Hippius, H., Muller, F., Schroder, H. T., Schultes, H., et al. (1980). Effects of clonidine on growth hormone release in psychiatric patients and controls. *Psychiatry Research, 2*, 25–36.

Mayberg, H. S. (1994). Frontal lobe dysfunction in secondary depression. *Journal of Neuropsychiatry and Clinical Neurosciences, 6*, 428–442.

Mayberg, H. S., Liotti, M., Brannan, S. K., McGinnis, S., Mahurin, R. K., Jerabek, P. A., et al. (1999). Reciprocal limbic-cortical function and negative mood: Converging PET findings in depression and normal sadness. *American Journal of Psychiatry, 156*, 675–682.

Mayberg, H. S., Lozano, A. M., Voon, V., McNeely, H. E., Seminowicz, D., Hamani, C., et al. (2005). Deep brain stimulation for treatment-resistant depression. *Neuron, 45*, 651–660.

McArthur, S., McHale, E., Dalley, J. W., Buckingham, C., & Gillies, G. E. (2005). Altered mesencephalic dopaminergic populations in adulthood as a consequence of brief perinatal glucocorticoid exposure. *Journal of Neuroendocrinology, 17*, 475–482.

McMahon, F. J., Buervenich, S., Charney, D., Lipsky, R., Rush, A. J., Wilson, A. F., et al. (2006). Variation in the gene encoding the serotonin 2A receptor is associated with outcome of antidepressant treatment. *American Journal of Human Genetics, 78*, 804–814.

McPherson, H., Walsh, A., & Silverstone, T. (2003). Growth hormone and prolactin response to apomorphine in bipolar and unipolar depression. *Journal of Affective Disorders, 76*, 121–125.

Meana, J., Barturen, F., & Garcia-Sevilla, J. A. (1992). A-sub-2-Adrenoceptors in the brain of suicide victims: Increased receptor density associated with major depression. *Biological Psychiatry, 31*, 471–490.

Mendlewicz, J., Linkowski, P., Kerkhofs, M., Desmedt, D., Golstein, J., Copinschi, G., et al. (1985). Diurnal hypersecretion of growth hormone in depression. *Journal of Clinical Endocrinology and Metabolism, 60*, 505–512.

Merali, Z., Kent, P., Du, L., Hrdina, P., Palkovits, M., Faludi, G., et al. (2006). Corticotropin-releasing hormone, arginine vasopressin, gastrin-releasing peptide, and neuromedin B alterations in stress-relevant brain regions of suicides and control subjects. *Biological Psychiatry, 59*, 594–602.

Merali, Z., Khan, S., Michaud, D. S., Shippy, S. A., & Anisman, H. (2004). Does amygdaloid corticotropin-releasing hormone (CRH) mediate anxiety-like behaviors? Dissociation of anxiogenic effects and CRH release. *European Journal of Neuroscience, 20*, 229–239.

Meyer, J. H., Ginovart, N., Boovariwala, A., Sagrati, S., Hussey, D., Garcia, A., et al. (2006). Elevated monoamine oxidase A levels in the brain: An explanation for the monoamine imbalance of major depression. *Archives of General Psychiatry, 63*, 1209–1216.

Meyer, J. H., Houle, S., Sagrati, S., Carella, A., Hussey, D. F., Ginovart, N., et al. (2004). Brain serotonin transporter binding potential measured with carbon 11-labeled DASB positron emission tomography: Effects of major depressive episodes and severity of dysfunctional attitudes. *Archives of General Psychiatry, 61*, 1271–1279.

Meyer, J. H., Kruger, S., Wilson, A. A., Christensen, B. K., Goulding, V. S., Schaffer, A., et al. (2001). Lower dopamine transporter binding potential in striatum during depression. *NeuroReport, 12*, 4121–4125.

Miller, A. H., Pariante, C. M., & Pearce, B. D. (1999). Effects of cytokines on glucocorticoid receptor expression and function: Glucocorticoid resistance and relevance to depression. *Advances in Experimental Medicine and Biology, , 461,* 107–116.

Miller, H. L., Delgado, P. L., Salomon, R. M., Berman, R., Krystal, J. H., Heninger, G. R., et al. (1996). Clinical and biochemical effects of catecholamine depletion on antidepressant-induced remission of depression. *Archives of General Psychiatry, 53,* 117–128.

Mineka, S., Watson, D., & Clark, L. A. (1998). Comorbidity of anxiety and unipolar mood disorders. *Annual Review of Psychology, 49,* 377–412.

Mintun, M. A., Sheline, Y. I., Moerlein, S. M., Vlassenko, A. G., Huang, Y., & Snyder, A. Z. (2004). Decreased hippocampal 5-HT2A receptor binding in major depressive disorder: In vivo measurement with. *Biological Psychiatry, 55,* 217–224.

Mitchell, P., Bearn, J., Corn, T., & Checkley, S. A. (1988). Growth hormone response to clonidine after recovery in patients with endogenous depression. *British Journal of Psychiatry, 152,* 34–38.

Mitchell, P. B., & Smythe, G. (1990). Hormonal responses to fenfluramine in depressed and control subjects. *Journal of Affective Disorders, 19,* 43–51.

Motivala, S. J., Sarfatti, A., Olmos, L., & Irwin, M. R. (2005). Inflammatory markers and sleep disturbance in major depression. *Psychosomatic Medicine, 67,* 187–194.

Mueller, I. M., Leon, A. C., Keller, M. B., Solomon, D. A., Endicott, J., Coryell, W., et al. (1999). Recurrence after recovery from major depressive disorder during 15 years of observational follow-up. *American Journal of Psychiatry, 156,* 1000–1006.

Muller, J. C., Pryer, W. W., Gibbons, J. E., & Orgain, E. (1955). Depression and anxiety occurring during Rauwolfia therapy. *Journal of the American Medical Association, 159,* 836–839.

Murphy, F., Michael, A., Robbins, T., & Sahakian, B. (2003). Neuropsychological impairment in patients with major depressive disorder: The effects of feedback on task performance. *Psychological Medicine, 33,* 455–467.

Murray, C. J. L., & Lopez, A. D. (1996). *The global burden of disease: A comprehensive assessment of mortality and disability from diseases, injuries, and risk factors in 1990 and projected to 2020.* Cambridge, MA: Harvard University Press.

Musselman, D. L., Lawson, D. H., Gumnick, J. F., Manatunga, A. K., Penna, S., Goodkin, R. S., et al. (2001). Paroxetine for the prevention of depression induced by high-dose interferon alfa [See comment]. *New England Journal of Medicine, 344,* 961–966.

Musselman, D. L., Tomer, A., Manatunga, A. K., Knight, B. T., Porter, M. R., Kasey, S., et al. (1996). Exaggerated platelet reactivity in major depression. *American Journal of Psychiatry, 153,* 1313–1317.

Nalepa, I., & Vetulani, J. (1993). The effect of calcium channel blockade on the action of chronic ECT and imipramine on responses of 1- and -adrenoreceptors in the rate cerebral cortex. *Polish Journal of Pharmacology, 45,* 201–205.

Nemeroff, C. B., Bissette, G., Akil, H., & Fink, M. (1991). Neuropeptide concentrations in the cerebrospinal fluid of depressed patients treated with electroconvulsive therapy: Corticotrophin-releasing factor, beta-endorphin and somatostatin. *British Journal of Psychiatry, 158,* 59–63.

Nemeroff, C. B., Krishnan, K. R., Reed, D., Leder, R., Beam, C., & Dunnick, N. R. (1992). Adrenal gland enlargement in major depression: A computed tomographic study. *Archives of General Psychiatry, 49,* 384–387.

Nemeroff, C. B., Owens, M. J., Bissette, G., Andorn, A. C., & Stanley, M. (1988). Reduced corticotropin releasing factor binding sites in the frontal cortex of suicide victims. *Archives of General Psychiatry, 45,* 577–579.

Nemeroff, C. B., Widerlov, E., Bissette, G., Walleus, H., Karlsson, I., Eklund, K., et al. (1984, December 14). Elevated concentrations of CSF corticotropin-releasing factor-like immunoreactivity in depressed patients. *Science, 226,* 1342–1344.

Nestler, E. J., Terwilliger, R. Z., & Duman, R. S. (1989). Chronic antidepressant administration alters the subcellular distribution of cyclic AMP-dependent protein kinase in rat frontal cortex. *Journal of Neurochemistry, 53,* 1644–1647.

Neumeister, A., Hu, X.-Z., Luckenbaugh, D. A., Schwarz, M., Nugent, A. C., Bonne, O., et al. (2006). Differential effects of 5-HTTLPR genotypes on the behavioral and neural responses to tryptophan depletion in patients with major depression and controls. *Archives of General Psychiatry, 63,* 978–986.

Neumeister, A., Wood, S., Bonne, O., Nugent, A. C., Luckenbaugh, D. A., Young, T., et al. (2005). Reduced hippocampal volume in unmedicated, remitted patients with major depression versus control subjects. *Biological Psychiatry, 57,* 935–937.

Newport, D., Stowe, Z. N., & Nemeroff, C. B. (2002). Parental depression: Animal models of an adverse life event. *American Journal of Psychiatry, 159,* 1265–1283.

Nibuya, M., Nestler, E. J., & Duman, R. S. (1996). Chronic antidepressant administration increases the expression of cAMP response element binding protein (CREB) in rat hippocampus. *Journal of Neuroscience, 6,* 2365–2372.

Nofzinger, E. A., Buysse, D. J., Germain, A., Carter, C., Luna, B., Price, J. C., et al. (2004). Increased activation of anterior paralimbic and executive cortex from waking to rapid eye movement sleep in depression. *Archives of General Psychiatry, 61,* 695–702.

Nowak, G., Trullas, R., Layer, R. T., Skolnick, P., & Paul, I. A. (1993). Adaptive changes in the N-methyl-D-aspartate receptor complex after chronic treatment with imipramine and 1-aminocyclopropanecarboxylic acid. *Journal of Pharmacology and Experimental Therapeutics, 265,* 1380–1386.

O'Keane, V., & Dinan, T. G. (1991). Prolactin and cortisol responses to d-fenfluramine in major depression: Evidence of diminished responsivity of central serotonergic function. *American Journal of Psychiatry, 148,* 1009–1015.

O'Neill, M. F., & Moore, N. A. (2003). Animal models of depression: Are there any? *Human Psychopharmacology, 18,* 239–254.

Ongur, D., Drevets, W. C., & Price, J. L. (1998). Glial reduction in the subgenual prefrontal cortex in mood disorders. *Proceedings of the National Academy of Sciences, USA, 95,* 13290–13295.

Ordway, G. A., Gambarana, C., Tejani-Butt, S. M., Areso, P., Hauptmann, M., & Frazer, A. (1991). Preferential reduction of binding of 125I-iodopindolol to beta-1 adrenoceptors in the amygdala of rat after antidepressant treatments. *Journal of Pharmacology and Experimental Therapeutics, 257,* 681–690.

Ordway, G. A., Schenk, J., Stockmeier, C. A., May, W., & Klimek, V. (2003). Elevated agonist binding to alpha2-adrenoceptors in the locus coeruleus in major depression. *Biological Psychiatry, 53,* 315–323.

Osuch, E. A., Ketter, T. A., Kimbrell, T. A., George, M. S., Benson, B. E., Willis, M. W., et al. (2000). Regional cerebral metabolism associated with anxiety symptoms in affective disorder patients. *Biological Psychiatry, 48,* 1020–1030.

Oswald, L. M., Wong, D. F., McCaul, M., Zhou, Y., Kuwabara, H., Choi, L., et al. (2005). Relationships among ventral striatal dopamine release, cortisol secretion, and subjective responses to amphetamine. *Neuropsychopharmacology, 30,* 821–832.

Owens, M. J., & Nemeroff, C. B. (1991). Physiology and pharmacology of corticotropin releasing factor. *Pharmacological Reviews, 43,* 425–473.

Pace, T. W., Hu, F., & Miller, A. H. (2007). Cytokine-effects on glucocorticoid receptor function: Relevance to glucocorticoid resistance and the pathophysiology and treatment of major depression. *Brain, Behavior, and Immunity, 21,* 9–19.

Pace, T. W., Mletzko, T. C., Alagbe, O., Musselman, D. L., Nemeroff, C. B., Miller, A. H., et al. (2006). Increased stress-induced inflammatory responses in male patients with major depression and increased early life stress. *American Journal of Psychiatry, 163,* 1630–1633.

Palliere-Martinot, M., Bragulat, V., Artiges, E., Dolle, F., Hinnen, F., Jouvent, R., et al. (2001). Decreased presynaptic dopamine function in the left caudate of depressed patients with affective flattening and psychomotor retardation. *American Journal of Psychiatry, 158*, 314–316.

Papp, M., & Moryl, E. (1994). Antidepressant activity of non-competitive and competitive NMDA receptor antagonists in a chronic mild stress model of depression. *European Journal of Pharmacology, 263*, 1–7.

Pariante, C. M., & Miller, A. H. (2001). Glucocorticoid receptors in major depression: Relevance to pathophysiology and treatment. *Biological Psychiatry, 49*, 391–404.

Parsey, R. V., Hastings, R. S., Oquendo, M. A., Huang, Y. Y., Simpson, N., Arcement, J., et al. (2006). Lower serotonin transporter binding potential in the human brain during major depressive episodes. *American Journal of Psychiatry, 163*, 52–58.

Parsey, R. V., Oquendo, M. A., Zea-Ponce, Y., Rodenhiser, J., Kegeles, L. S., Pratap, M., et al. (2001). Dopamine D2 receptor availability and amphetamine-induced dopamine release in unipolar depression. *Biological Psychiatry, 50*, 313–322.

Patchev, V. K., Hassan, A. H. S., Holsboer, F., & Almeida, O. F. X. (1996). The neurosteroid tetrahydroprogesterone attenuates the endocrine response to stress and exerts glucocorticoid-like effects on vasopressin gene transcription in the rat hypothalamus. *Neuropsychopharmacology, 15*, 533–540.

Patchev, V. K., Shoaib, M., Holsboer, F., & Almeida, O. F. (1994). The neurosteroid tetrahydroprogesterone counteracts corticotropin-releasing hormone-induced anxiety and alters the release and gene expression of corticotropin-releasing hormone in the rat hypothalamus. *Neuroscience, 62*, 265–271.

Pepin, M. C., Pothier, F., & Barden, N. (1992, February 20). Impaired type II glucocorticoid-receptor function in mice bearing antisense RNA transgene. *Nature, 355*, 725–728.

Peterson, M. J., & Benca, R. M. (2006). Sleep in mood disorders. *Psychiatric Clinics of North America, 29*, 1009–1032.

Petty, F. (1994). Plasma concentrations of GABA and mood disorders: A blood test for manic depressive disease? *Clinical Chemistry, 40*, 296–302.

Pezawas, L., Meyer-Lindenberg, A., Drabant, E. M., Verchinski, B. A., Munoz, K. E., Kolachana, B. S., et al. (2005). 5-HTTLPR polymorphism impacts human cingulate-amygdala interactions: A genetic susceptibility mechanism for depression. *Nature Neuroscience, 8*, 828–834.

Pitchot, W., Hansenne, M., Moreno, A. G., Pinto, E., Reggers, J., Fuchs, S., et al. (2001). Reduced dopamine function in depressed patients is related to suicidal behavior but not its lethality. *Psychoneuroendocrinology, 26*, 689–696.

Pitchot, W., Reggers, J., Pinto, E., Hansenne, M., Fuchs, S., Pirard, S., et al. (2001). Reduced dopaminergic activity in depressed suicides. *Psychoneuroendocrinology, 26*, 331–335.

Pochon, J. B., Levy, R., Fossati, P., Lehericy, S., Poline, J. B., Pillon, B., et al. (2002). The neural system that bridges reward and cognition in humans: An fMRI study. *Proceedings of the National Academy of Sciences, USA, 99*, 5669–5674.

Posener, J. A., Schatzberg, A. F., Williams, G. H., Samson, J. A., McHale, N. L., Bessette, M. P., et al. (1999). Hypothalamic-pituitary-adrenal axis effects on plasma homovanillic acid in man. *Biological Psychiatry, 45*, 222–228.

Potter, W., Karoum, F., & Linnoila, M. (1984). Common mechanisms of action of biochemically specific antidepressants. *Progress in Neuropsychopharmacology and Biologial Psychiatry, 8*, 153–161.

Prange, A. J., Lara, P. P., Wilson, I. C., Alltop, L. B., & Breese, G. R. (1972). Effects of thyrotropin-releasing hormone in depression. *Lancet, 2*, 999–1002.

Pruessner, J. C., Champagne, F., Meaney, M. J., & Dagher, A. (2004). Dopamine release in response to a psychological stress in humans and its relationship to early life maternal care: A positron emission tomography study using [11C] raclopride. *Journal of Neuroscience, 24*, 2825–2831.

Raison, C. L., Capuron, L., & Miller, A. H. (2006). Cytokines sing the blues: Inflammation and the pathogenesis of depression. *Trends in Immunology, 27*, 24–31.

Raison, C. L., Demetrashvili, M., Capuron, L., & Miller, A. H. (2005). Neuropsychiatric side effects of interferon-alpha: Recognition and management. *CNS Drugs, 19*, 1–19.

Raison, C. L., Marcin, M., & Miller, A. H. (2002). Antidepressant treatment of cytokine-induced depression. *Acta Neuropsychiatrica, 4*, 18–25.

Raison, C. L., & Miller, A. H. (2003). When not enough is too much: The role of insufficient glucocorticoid signaling in the pathophysiology of stress-related disorders. [Review] [114 refs]. *American Journal of Psychiatry, 160*, 1554–1565.

Rajkowska, G., Miguel-Hidalgo, J. J., Wei, J., Dilley, G., Pittman, S. D., Meltzer, H., et al. (1999). Morphometric evidence for neuronal and glial prefrontal cell pathology in major depression. *Biological Psychiatry, 48*, 486–504.

Rao, U., Dahl, R. E., Ryan, N. D., Birmaher, B., Williamson, D. E., Rao, R., et al. (2002). Heterogeneity in EEG sleep findings in adolescent depression: Unipolar versus bipolar clinical course. *Journal of Affective Disorders, 70*, 273–280.

Rausch, J. L., Johnson, M. E., Li, J., Hutcheson, J., Carr, B. M., Corley, K. M., et al. (2005). Serotonin transport kinetics correlated between human platelets and brain synaptosomes. *Psychopharmacology, 180*, 391–398.

Redmond, D., Katz, M. M., Maas, J. W., Swann, A., Casper, R., & Davis, J. M. (1986). Cerebrospinal fluid amine metabolites: Relationships with behavioral measurements in depressed, manic, and healthy control subjects. *Archives of General Psychiatry, 43*, 938–947.

Ressler, K. J., & Mayberg, H. S. (2007). Targeting abnormal neural circuits in mood and anxiety disorders: From the laboratory to the clinic. *Nature Neuroscience, 10*, 1116–1124.

Ressler, K. J., & Nemeroff, C. B. (2000). Role of serotonergic and noradrenergic systems in the pathophysiology of depression and anxiety disorders. *Depression and Anxiety, 12*(Suppl, 1), 2–19.

Reyes, B. A., Valentino, R. J., Xu, G., & Van Bockstaele, E. J. (2005). Hypothalamic projections to locus coeruleus neurons in rat brain. *European Journal of Neuroscience, 22*, 93–106.

Roy, A., De Jong, J., & Linnoila, M. (1989). Cerebrospinal fluid monoamine metabolites and suicidal behavior in depressed patients: A 5-year follow-up study. *Archives of General Psychiatry, 46*, 609–612.

Roy, A., Pickar, D., Paul, S., Doran, A., Chrousos, G. P., & Gold, P. W. (1987). CSF corticotropin-releasing hormone in depressed patients and normal control subjects. *American Journal of Psychiatry, 144*, 641–645.

Roy, A., Wolkowitz, O. M., Bissette, G., & Nemeroff, C. B. (1994). Differences in CSF concentrations of thyrotropin-releasing hormone in depressed patients and normal subjects: Negative findings. *American Journal of Psychiatry, 151*, 600–602.

Rubin, R. T., Phillips, J. J., Sadow, T. F., & McCracken, J. T. (1995). Adrenal gland volume in major depression: Increase during the depressive episode and decrease with successful treatment. *Archives of General Psychiatry, 52*, 213–218.

Sachar, E. J., Hellman, L., Fukushima, D. K., & Gallagher, T. F. (1970). Cortisol production in depressive illness. A clinical and biochemical clarification. *Archives of General Psychiatry, 23*, 289–298.

Sagud, M., Pivac, N., Muck-Seler, D., Jakovljevic, M., Mihaljevic-Peles, A., & Korsic, M. (2002). Effects of sertraline treatment on plasma cortisol, prolactin and thyroid hormones in female depressed patients. *Neuropsychobiology, 45*, 139–143.

Sairanen, M., Lucas, G., Ernfors, P., Castren, M., & Castren, E. (2005). Brain-derived neurotrophic factor and antidepressant drugs have different but coordinated effects on neuronal turnover, proliferation, and survival in the adult dentate gyrus. *Journal of Neuroscience, 25,* 1089–1094.

Salomon, R. M., Miller, H. L., Krystal, J. H., Heninger, G. R., & Charney, D. S. (1997). Lack of behavioral effects of monoamine depletion in healthy subjects. *Biological Psychiatry, 41,* 58–64.

Sanacora, G., Gueorguieva, R., Epperson, N., Wu, Y.-T., Appel, M., Rothman, D. L., et al. (2004). Subtype-specific alterations of gamma-aminobutyric acid and glutamate in patients with major depression. *Archives of General Psychiatry, 61,* 705–713.

Sanacora, G., Mason, G. F., Rothman, D. L., Hyder, F., Ciarcia, J. J., Ostroff, R. B., et al. (2003). Increased cortical GABA concentrations in depressed patients receiving ECT. *American Journal of Psychiatry, 160,* 577–579.

Sanacora, G., Mason, G. F., Rothman, D. L., & Krystal, J. H. (2002). Increased occipital cortex GABA concentrations in depressed patients after therapy with selective serotonin reuptake inhibitors. *American Journal of Psychiatry, 159,* 663–665.

Sanchez, M. M., Young, L. J., Plotsky, P. M., & Insel, T. R. (1999). Autoradiographic and in situ hybridization localization of corticotropin-releasing factor 1 and 2 receptors in nonhuman primate brain. *Journal of Comparative Neurology, 408,* 365–377.

Santarelli, L., Saxe, M., Gross, C., Surget, A., Battaglia, F., Dulawa, S., et al. (2003, August 8). Requirement of hippocampal neurogenesis for the behavioral effects of antidepressants. *Science, 301,* 805–809.

Sargent, P. A., Kjaer, K. H., Bench, C. J., Rabiner, E. A., Messa, C., Meyer, J., et al. (2000). Brain serotonin1A receptor binding measured by positron emission tomography with. *Archives of General Psychiatry, 57,* 174–180.

Schatzberg, A. F., Rothschild, A. J., & Langlais, P. J. (1985). A corticosteroid/dopamine hypothesis for psychotic depression and related states. *Journal of Psychiatric Research, 19,* 57–64.

Schatzberg, A. F., Rothschild, A. J., Langlais, P. J., Bird, E. D., & Cole, E. J. (1985). A corticosteroid/dopamine hypothesis for psychotic depression and related states. *Journal of Psychiatric Research, 19,* 57–64.

Schildkraut, J. J. (1965). The catecholamine hypothesis of affective disorders: A review of supporting evidence. *American Journal of Psychiatry, 122,* 509–522.

Schildkraut, J. J. (1973). Norepinephrine metabolites as biochemical criteria for classifying depressive disorders and predicting response to treatment: Preliminary findings. *American Journal of Psychiatry, 130,* 695–699.

Schilkrut, R., Chandra, O., Osswald, M., Ruther, E., Baafusser, B., & Matussek, N. (1975). Growth hormone release during sleep and with thermal stimulation in depressed patients. *Neuropsychobiology, 1,* 70–79.

Schneier, F. R., Liebowitz, M. R., Abi-Dargham, A., Zea-Ponce, Y., Lin, S. H., & Laruelle, M. (2000). Low dopamine D(2) receptor binding potential in social phobia. *American Journal of Psychiatry, 157,* 457–459.

Seifritz, E. (2001). Contribution of sleep physiology to depressive pathophysiology. *Neuropsychopharmacology, 25,* 85–S88.

Sen, S., Nesse, R. M., Stoltenberg, S. F., Li, S., Gleiberman, L., Chakravarti, A., et al. (2003). A BDNF coding variant associated with the NEO personality inventory domain neuroticism: A risk factor for depression. *Neuropsychopharmacology, 28,* 397–401.

Shah, P. J., Ogilvie, A. D., Goodwin, G. M., & Ebmeier, K. P. (1997). Clinical and psychometric correlates of dopamine D2 binding in depression. *Psychological Medicine, 27,* 1247–1256.

Shapira, B., Cohen, J., Newman, M. E., & Lerer, B. (1993). Prolactin response to fenfluramine and placebo challenge following maintenance pharmacotherapy withdrawal in remitted depressed patients. *Biological Psychiatry, 33,* 531–535.

Sheline, Y. I., Barch, D. M., Donnelly, J. M., Ollinger, J. M., Snyder, A. Z., & Mintun, M. A. (2001). Increased amygdala response to masked emotional faces in depressed subjects resolves with antidepressant treatment: An fMRI study. *Biological Psychiatry, 50,* 651–658.

Sheline, Y. I., Sanghavi, M., Mintun, M. A., & Gado, M. H. (1999). Depression duration but not age predicts hippocampal volume loss in medically healthy women with recurrent major depression. *Journal of Neuroscience, 19,* 5034–5043.

Shirayama, Y., Chen, A. C., Nakagawa, S., Russell, D. S., & Duman, R. S. (2002). Brain-derived neurotrophic factor produces antidepressant effects in behavioral models of depression. *Journal of Neuroscience, 22,* 3251–3261.

Shore, P. A., Silver, S. L., & Brodie, B. B. (1955, August 12). Interaction of reserpine, serotonin, and lysergic acid diethylamide in brain. *Science, 122,* 284–285.

Siegle, G. J., Carter, C. S., & Thase, M. R. (2006). FMRI predicts recovery in cognitive behavioral therapy for unipolar depression. *American Journal of Psychiatry, 163,* 735–738.

Siever, L. J., Trestman, R. L., Coccaro, E. F., Bernstein, D., Gabriel, S. M., Owen, K., et al. (1992). The growth hormone response to clonidine in acute and remitted depressed male patients. *Neuropsychopharmacology, 6,* 165–177.

Siever, L. J., Uhde, T. W., Jimerson, D. C., Lake, C., Silberman, E. R., Post, R. M., et al. (1984). Differential inhibitory noradrenergic responses to clonidine in 25 depressed patients and 25 normal control subjects. *American Journal of Psychiatry, 141,* 733–741.

Siuciak, J. A., Lewis, D. R., Wiegand, S. J., & Lindsay, R. M. (1997). Antidepressant-like effect of brain-derived neurotrophic factor (BDNF). *Pharmacology, Biochemistry and Behavior, 56,* 131–137.

Slattery, D. A., Hudson, A. L., & Nutt, D. J. (2004). The evolution of antidepressant mechanisms. *Fundamental and Clinical Pharmacology, 18,* 1–21.

Smith, M. A., Makino, S., Kvetnansky, R., & Post, R. M. (1995). Stress and glucocorticoids affect the expression of brain-derived neurotrophic factor and neurotrophin-3 mRNAs in the hippocampus. *Journal of Neuroscience, 15,* 1768–1777.

Song, C., & Leonard, B. E. (2005). The olfactory bulbectomised rat as a model of depression. *Neuroscience and Biobehavioral Reviews, 29,* 627–647.

Sullivan, G. M., Hatterer, J. A., Herbert, J., Chen, X., Roose, S. P., Attia, E., et al. (1999). Low levels of transthyretin in CSF of depressed patients. *American Journal of Psychiatry, 156,* 710–715.

Sullivan, M., Mann, J. J., Oquendo, M., Lo, E., Cooper, T., & Gorman, J. (2006). Low cerebral spinal fluid transthyretin levels in depression: Correlations with suicidal ideation and low serotonin function. *Biological Psychiatry, 60,* 500–506.

Sullivan, P. F., Neale, M. C., & Kendler, K. S. (2000). Genetic epidemiology of major depression: Review and meta-analysis. *American Journal of Psychiatry, 157,* 1552–1662.

Sulser, F., & Dingell, J. V. (1968). Adrenergic mechanisms in the central action of tricyclic antidepressants and substituted phenothiazines. *Agressologie, 9,* 281–287.

Swanson, L. W., & Kuypers, H. G. (1980). The paraventricular nucleus of the hypothalamus: Cytoarchitectonic subdivisions and organization of projections to the pituitary, dorsal vagal complex, and spinal cord as demonstrated by retrograde fluorescence double-labeling methods. *Journal of Comparative Neurology, 194,* 555–570.

Tandberg, E., Larsen, J. P., Aarsland, D., & Cummings, J. L. (1996). The occurrence of depression in Parkinson's disease. *Archives of Neurology, 53,* 175–179.

Tardito, D., Perez, J., Tiraboschi, E., Musazzi, L., Racagni, G., & Popoli, M. (2006). Signaling pathways regulating gene expression, neuroplasticity, and neurotrophic mechanisms in the action of antidepressants: A critical overview. *Pharmacological Reviews, 58,* 115–134.

Tepper, J. M., Koos, T., & Wilson, C. J. (2004). GABAergic microcircuits in the neostriatum. *Trends in Neuroscience, 11,* 662–669.

Traskman, L., Asberg, M., Bertilsson, L., & Sjostrand, L. (1981). Monoamine metabolites in CSF and suicidal behavior. *Archives of General Psychiatry, 38,* 631–636.

Tremblay, L. K., Naranjo, C. A., Cardenas, L., Herrmann, N., & Busto, U. E. (2002). Probing brain reward system function in major depression. *Archives of General Psychiatry, 59,* 409–416.

Tremblay, L. K., Naranjo, C. A., Graham, S. J., Herrmann, N., Mayberg, H. S., Hevenor, S., et al. (2005). Functional neuroanatomical substrates of altered reward processing in major depressive disorder revealed by a dopaminergic probe. *Archives of General Psychiatry, 62,* 1228–1236.

Trivedi, M. H., Rush, A., Wisniewski, S. R., Nierenberg, A. A., Warden, D., Ritz, L., et al. (2006). Evaluation of outcomes with citalopram for depression using measurement-based care in STAR*D: Implications for clinical practice. *American Journal of Psychiatry, 163,* 28–40.

Uzunova, V., Sheline, Y., Davis, J. M., Rasmusson, A., Uzunov, D. P., Costa, E., et al. (1998). Increase in the cerebrospinal fluid content of neurosteroids in patients with unipolar major depression who are receiving fluoxetine or fluvoxamine. *Proceedings of the National Academy of Sciences, USA, 95,* 3239–3244.

Vaidya, V. A., Siuciak, J. A., Du, F., & Duman, R. S. (1999). Hippocampal mossy fiber sprouting induced by chronic electroconvulsive seizures. *Neuroscience, 89,* 157–166.

van den Bogaert, A., Sleegers, K., de Zutter, S., Heyrman, L., Norrback, K.-F., Adolfsson, R., et al. (2006). Association of brain-specific tryptophan hydroxylase, TPH2, with unipolar and bipolar disorder in a northern Swedish, isolated population. *Archives of General Psychiatry, 63,* 1103–1110.

Van Pett, K., Viau, V., Bittencourt, J. C., Chan, R. K., Li, H. Y., Arias, C., et al. (2000). Distribution of mRNAs encoding CRF receptors in brain and pituitary of rat and mouse. *Journal of Comparative Neurology, 428,* 191–212.

Van Praag, H. M. (1982). Depression, suicide, and the metabolites of serotonin in the brain. *Journal of Affective Disorders, 4,* 21–29.

van Praag, H. M., Korf, J., Lakke, J. P. W. F., & Schut, T. (1975). Dopamine metabolism in depressions, psychoses and Parkinson's disease: The problem of the specificity of biological variables in behavior disorders. *Psychological Medicine, 5,* 138–146.

Veith, R. C., Lewis, N., Langohr, J. I., Murburg, M. M., Ashleigh, E. A., Castillo, S., et al. (1993). Effect of desipramine on cerebrospinal fluid concentrations of corticotropin-releasing factor in human subjects. *Psychiatry Research, 46,* 1–8.

Veith, R. C., Lewis, N., Linares, O. A., Barnes, R. F., Raskind, M. A., Villacres, E. C., et al. (1994). Sympathetic nervous system activity in major depression: Basal and desipramine-induced alterations in plasma norepinephrine kinetics. *Archives of General Psychiatry, 51,* 411–422.

Vermetten, E., Vythilingam, M., Southwick, S. M., Charney, D. S., & Bremner, J. (2003). Long-term treatment with paroxetine increases verbal declarative memory and hippocampal volume in posttraumatic stress disorder. *Biological Psychiatry, 54,* 693–702.

Weissman, M. M., Wickramaratne, P., Nomura, Y., Warner, V., Verdeli, H., Pilowsky, D. J., et al. (2005). Families at high and low risk for depression: A 3-generation study. *Archives of General Psychiatry, 62.*

Wenzlaff, R. M., & Grozier, S. A. (1988). Depression and the magnification of failure. *Journal of Abnormal Psychology, 97,* 90–93.

Williams, R. B., Marchuk, D. A., Gadde, K. M., Barefoot, J. C., Grichnik, K., Helms, M. J., et al. (2003). Serotonin-related gene polymorphisms and central nervous system serotonin function. *Neuropsychopharmacology, 28,* 533–541.

Willner, P. (1983). Dopamine and depression: A review of recent evidence. *Brain Research Reviews, 6,* 211–246.

Winokur, A., Gary, K. A., Rodner, S., Rae-Red, C., Fernando, A. T., & Szuba, M. P. (2001). Depression, sleep physiology, and antidepressant drugs. *Depression and Anxiety, 14,* 19–28.

Wolfe, N., Katz, D. I., Albert, M. L., Almozlino, A., Durso, R., Smith, M. C., et al. (1990). Neuropsychological profile linked to low dopamine: In Alzheimer's disease, major depression, and Parkinson's disease. *Journal of Neurology, Neurosurgery, and Psychiatry, 53,* 915–917.

Wolkowitz, O. M., Rubinow, D. R., Breier, A., Doran, A. R., Davis, C., & Pickar, D. (1987). Prednisone decreases CSF somatostatin in healthy humans: Implications for neuropsychiatric illness. *Life Sciences, 41,* 1929–1933.

Wong, M. L., Kling, M. A., Munson, P. J., Listwak, S., Licinio, J., Prolo, P., et al. (2000). Pronounced and sustained central hypernoradrenergic function in major depression with melancholic features: Relation to hypercortisolism and corticotropin-releasing hormone. *Proceedings of the National Academy of Sciences, USA, 97,* 325–330.

Wynn, P. C., Harwood, J. P., Catt, K. J., & Aguilera, G. (1988). Corticotropin-releasing factor (CRF) induces desensitization of the rat pituitary CRF receptor-adenylate cyclase complex. *Endocrinology, 122,* 351–358.

Yatham, L. N., Liddle, P. F., Dennie, J., Shiah, I. S., Adam, M. J., Lane, C. J., et al. (1999). Decrease in brain serotonin 2 receptor binding in patients with major depression following desipramine treatment: A positron emission tomography study with fluorine-18-labeled setoperone. *Archives of General Psychiatry, 56,* 705–711.

Yatham, L. N., Liddle, P. F., Shiah, I. S., Scarrow, G., Lam, R. W., Adam, M. J., et al. (2000). Brain serotonin2 receptors in major depression: A positron emission tomography study. *Archives of General Psychiatry, 57,* 850–858.

Young, E. A., Watson, S. J., Kotun, J., Haskett, R. F., Grunhaus, L., Murphy-Weinberg, V., et al. (1990). Beta-lipotropin-beta-endorphin response to low-dose ovine corticotropin releasing factor in endogenous depression: Preliminary studies. *Archives of General Psychiatry, 47,* 449–457.

Zammit, S., & Owen, M. J. (2006). Stressful life events, 5-HTT genotype and risk of depression. *British Journal of Psychiatry, 188,* 199–201.

Zarate, C. A., Jr., Singh, J. B., Carlson, P. J., Brutsche, N. E., Ameli, R., Luckenbaugh, D. A., et al. (2006). A randomized trial of an N-methyl-D-aspartate antagonist in treatment-resistant major depression. *Archives of General Psychiatry, 63,* 856–864.

Zhang, X., Gainetdinov, R. R., Beaulieu, J.-M., Sotinkova, T. D., Burch, L. J., Williams, R. B., et al. (2005). Loss-of-function mutation in tryptophan hydroxylase-2 identified in unipolar major depression. *Neuron, 45,* 11–16.

Zhou, Z., Roy, A., Lipsky, R., Kuchipudi, K., Zhu, G., Taubman, J., et al. (2005). Haplotype-based linkage of tryptophan hydroxylase 2 to suicide attempt, major depression, and cerebrospinal fluid 5-hydroxyindoleacetic acid in 4 populations. *Archives of General Psychiatry, 62,* 1109–1118.

Zill, P., Baghai, T. C., Zwanzger, P., Schule, C., Eser, D., Rupprecht, R., et al. (2004). SNP and haplotype analysis of a novel tryptophan hydroxylase isoform (TPH2) gene provide evidence for association with major depression. *Molecular Psychiatry, 9,* 1030–1036.

Zobel, A. W., Nickel, T., Kunzel, H. E., Ackl, N., Sonntag, A., Ising, M., et al. (2000). Effects of high-affinity corticotropin-releasing hormone receptor 1 antagonist R121919 in major depression: The first 20 patients treated. *Journal of Psychiatric Research, 34,* 171–181.

Chapter 56

The Genetics of Anxiety

KIARA R. TIMPANO, GREGOR HASLER, CHRISTINA RICCARDI, DENNIS L. MURPHY, AND NORMAN B. SCHMIDT

Anxiety-related psychopathology represents one of the most prevalent and debilitating forms of mental illness (Kessler, Berglund, et al., 2005; Weissman, 1990). Extrapolating from epidemiological studies, it may be conservatively estimated that 25% of the population will suffer from clinically significant anxiety at some point in their lives with a 12-month prevalence rate of approximately 18% (Kessler, Chiu, Demler, Merikangas, & Walters, 2005). Anxiety disorders generally maintain a chronic course when untreated (Pine, Cohen, Gurley, Brook, & Ma, 1998) and result in substantial impairment across the life span (Ferdinand, van der Reijden, Verhulst, Nienhuis, & Giel, 1995). In addition to the immense personal suffering created by clinically significant anxiety syndromes, these disorders create a considerable public expense that includes treatment costs, lost work time, and mortality. One study estimated the annual cost in the United States associated with anxiety disorders to be more than $42 billion, which is one-third of the total cost linked with the economic burden of all psychiatric disorders (Greenberg et al., 1999). Anxiety psychopathology is also associated with increased utilization of nonpsychiatric medical services (Greenberg et al., 1999), further amplifying the associated public health burden.

Despite considerable advances in elucidating the phenomenology of anxiety-related syndromes, the development of concise models of pathogenesis and the identification of definitive risk factors has remained relatively more elusive. Like most other neuropsychiatric diseases, the anxiety disorders have long been suspected of being influenced by an interaction between environmental factors and a heritable component (e.g., Cohen, 1951; Marks, 1986). Research amassed over the past few decades now provides considerable evidence for the familial aggregation of anxiety disorders. Utilizing a combination of twin and family studies, researchers have found that there is a significant association between an anxiety disorder in an individual and the occurrence of that same or genetically related disorders in their first-degree relatives (Shih, Belmonte, & Zandi, 2004). A meta-analysis of the genetic epidemiology of the anxiety disorders found that odds ratios across panic isorder (PD), generalized anxiety disorder (GAD), phobias, and obsessive compulsive disorder (OCD) ranged from 4 to 6 (Hettema, Neale, & Kendler, 2001). This same review identified estimated heritabilities for these disorders ranging from 30% to 40%. Although this estimate is rather moderate and indicates that environmental factors play a large role in the liability for the various anxiety syndromes, it does, nonetheless, point to the important role genetics may play in the pathogenesis of these conditions. These findings from genetic epidemiology have subsequently opened the road for an increasing number of investigations attempting to identify specific genetic risk factors.

We first provide a brief overview of each of the anxiety disorders, consisting of an introduction to the "landmarks" of each syndrome, including symptom presentation and associated features, followed by a review of the respective heritability and genetics research conducted to date. These summaries are not exhaustive, but rather more illustrative with regard to the most pertinent issues and research of the phenomenon being considered. PD, social anxiety disorder (SAD) and other phobias, GAD, and OCD are highlighted. We then discuss a number of broader issues relevant to interpreting past genetics research and conducting future investigations. These considerations include the importance of clearly defined phenotypes, the role of other factors such as environmental variables, and the utilization of alternative approaches, specifically the examination of endophenotypes (intermediate phenotypes more closely linked to action of genes), to studying the relationship between a disease entity and associated genetics.

GENERAL CONSIDERATIONS

Linking Neurobiology and Genetics

In searching for the origins of psychiatric disorders, it is critical to consider the different points of organization that shape a given syndrome, spanning from the macro to the micro level (Figure 56.1). That is, in conducting etiological research on vulnerability and risk factors, one should be cognizant of the different layers constituting and influencing a behavior, and how these layers work in concert. A disease phenomenon can entail neurobiological problems at the system, organ, or cellular level, which in turn can be formed from differences in the molecular underpinnings. At the same time, the disease entity is also influenced by a multitude of factors including developmental, environmental, and social/cultural variables. There is a constant bidirectional flow between these layers in the sense that at every level of the model, downstream features (e.g., environmental experiences) can subsequently influence upstream features (e.g., gene expression or neurological reactivity), or vice versa. While a specific research project may only target one organizational aspect, such as the genetics of a psychiatric disorder, it is vital to consider the consequences (e.g., neurobiology) and influencing factors (e.g., life stress).

The connection between neurobiology and genetics is important. The relationship between these two layers of organization clearly demonstrates the bidirectional flow outlined in Figure 56.1. Treatment response has often been one of the methods available to researchers who wish to pinpoint the specific neurobiological systems that may play a role in the etiology of a disorder. A specific example is the hypothesis that a disruption in the serotonin system is related to anxiety, based on the efficacy of serotonin-focused drugs in treating anxiety disorders. This knowledge has consequently led researchers to investigate genetic variations in the serotonin transporter. These genetic variations have reciprocally been associated with differential neuronal reactivity to specific stimuli. Brain regions implicated in the anxiety disorders include the prefrontal cortex, subcortical hippocampus, subgenual cingulated cortex, basal ganglia, and amygdala. Specific anxiety-related systems that cross multiple areas in the brain include the serotonergic, noradrenergic, gamma-aminobutyric acid (GABA), and dopaminergic pathways (see Figure 56.2). Given our focus on the genetics of anxiety disorders, we refer the reader to several excellent reviews on the neurology of anxiety for a more in-depth discussion (Ressler & Mayberg, 2007).

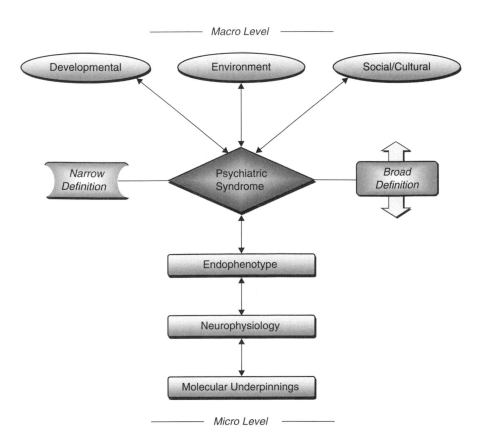

Figure 56.1   The behavior genetics viewpoint of the organizational schema of psychiatric disorders.

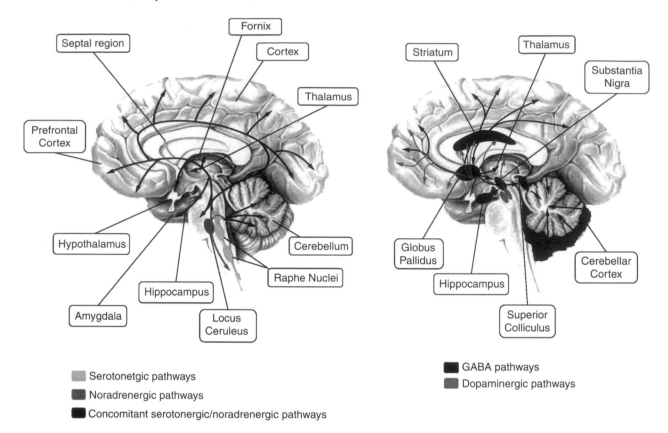

Figure 56.2   The neurobiology of anxiety disorders.

General Factors Relevant to Behavior Genetics

It may be helpful to first consider a number of general concepts relevant to studying the genetics of psychiatric disorders. Kendler and Greenspan (2006), as well as others (Lander & Schork, 1994), have identified several key aspects of the nature of genetic influence on behavior, which are reflected across species and appear to be fundamental. First of all, most behaviors, including those linked with anxiety psychopathology, represent complex phenomena with both clinical and genetic heterogeneity (Fanous, Gardner, Prescott, Cancro, & Kendler, 2002; Murphy et al., 2003). In the absence of Mendelian inheritance patterns, it is assumed that many common genetic variants contribute small effects to the macro-psychiatric phenotype. A second consideration, and one that has been supported extensively in investigations with animal models (e.g., murine), is the nonspecificity of genes as risk factors for particular traits. That is, most genes realistically influence any number of diverse phenotypes. Animal models and an increasing number of investigations with psychiatric populations have also revealed that genes interact with the environment and each other (Murphy et al., 2003). It has been found that the environment can modify genetic effects (e.g., Caspi et al., 2003), and that genes, by determining behaviors, can manipulate the environment (e.g., Lyons

et al., 1993). All of these aspects serve to complicate any attempt to tie a specific syndrome or behavior with a specific gene, and although research is making advances in that endeavor, it is important to remember that factors such as these may obscure progress.

REVIEW OF THE ANXIETY DISORDERS AND RELEVANT GENETIC FINDINGS

Panic Disorder

A central component to PD is the experience of recurrent panic attacks, which are an acute fear reaction that appears at inappropriate or unexpected times with no apparent stimulus. These attacks are accompanied by a tremendous arousal of the autonomic system, along with cognitive fears about the consequences of the attack (e.g., fear of dying or going crazy). PD is diagnosed if there is a consistent and distressing concern about experiencing panic attacks, which may be accompanied by drastic changes in behavior (e.g., agoraphobia). PD with or without agoraphobia is a highly debilitating condition with an approximately 4.7% lifetime prevalence (Kessler et al., 2006). Millions more experience panic attacks and other subsyndromal anxiety symptoms that markedly diminish quality of life. Those affected by PD suffer from negative personal, social, and economic consequences of a magnitude equal to or greater than that evidenced in major depression, alcoholism, and serious medical conditions. Other serious sequelae include increased risk for various medical conditions such as cardiovascular disease, and marked elevations in suicide attempts, as well as extremely high utilization of health services. PD is the leading cause of emergency department consultation (Weissman, 1991) and also the leading cause for seeking mental health services, ahead of both schizophrenia and mood disorders (Boyd, 1986).

Evidence from epidemiological data suggests that PD is associated with significant social and health consequences including perceptions of poor physical and emotional health, obesity, alcohol and drug abuse, increased rate of suicide attempts, increased usage of psychoactive medications, and increased marital, social, and financial problems (Markowitz, Weissman, Ouellette, Lish, & Klerman, 1989; Simon et al., 2006; Weissman, 1991). Indeed, Markowitz et al. (1989) concluded that PD confers negative social and health consequences of a magnitude equal to or greater than that for major depression.

In discussing PD, it is important to consider the distinction between the disorder and the experience of panic attacks because the two are not isomorphic. An estimated 28% of people will experience a panic attack in their lifetime, yet less than 5% develop PD (Kessler et al., 2006). The onset of panic attacks occur adolescence or early adulthood (Regier, Rae, Narrow, Kaelber, & Schatzberg, 1998) and are classified into three types: unexpected, situationally bound, and situationally predisposed. Unexpected panic attacks seem to occur out of the blue and are not associated with a particular situation or internal cue. In contrast, cued or situationally bound attacks almost always occur after exposure to or in anticipation of a particular situation. Similarly, situationally predisposed panic attacks are linked to a particular situation but do not always occur. For example, an individual may be more likely to have a panic attack when he drives, but there are times when he drives without having an attack or he may experience a panic attack only when he drive mores than 50 miles from his home. Spontaneous or uncued panic attacks are often considered to be central to the experience of PD. In fact, spontaneous panic is required for this diagnosis. However, many patients with PD experience situationally bound and predisposed panic attacks as well. Situationally bound and predisposed attacks seem to be tied to other anxiety disorders such as specific or social phobia.

Agoraphobia is one other diagnosis associated with PD. Consistent with Marks' (1970) contentions, the *DSM-III* (American Psychiatric Association, 1980) classified agoraphobia as a phobic disorder that could occur with or without panic attacks, whereas PD was considered to be a separate class of anxiety disorders called anxiety states or anxiety neuroses. In the *DSM-III,* agoraphobia received primary consideration because PD could not be diagnosed if the patient met criteria for agoraphobia. Over time, as researchers increasingly recognized that agoraphobia is often a consequence of experiencing panic attacks, the *DSM* reversed the relationship between these conditions such that in the *DSM-III-R* (American Psychiatric Association, 1987) and *DSM-IV* (American Psychiatric Association, 1994), agoraphobia is typically considered secondary to PD. In fact, in the *DSM-IV,* agoraphobia is coded only in the context of either PD or limited-symptom panic attacks (agoraphobia without history of PD). Thus, agoraphobic behaviors are now more commonly conceptualized as panic-related sequelae (Frances et al., 1993; A. J. Goldstein & Chambless, 1978).

Of all of the anxiety disorders, PD has received the most attention with regard to genetics research (for detailed review, refer to Gratacos et al., 2007). There is considerable evidence for the heritability of PD. Family aggregation studies have consistently shown a significant risk for PD in first-degree relatives of PD probands. A meta-analysis of the extant family studies revealed a summary odds ratio of 5.0 and an unadjusted aggregate risk of 10.0% for first-degree relatives, versus 2.1% in comparison relatives of probands (Hettema et al., 2001). Further support for heritability has emerged from twin studies, which have found concordance rates of 0% to 17% in dizygotic twins, in contrast to 24% to 73% concordance in monozygotic twins. That is, the concordance rates for identical twins are 2- to 3-fold higher than for fraternal twins (see Shih et al., 2004; van den Heuvel, van de Wetering, Veltman, & Pauls, 2000, for reviews). The meta-analysis conducted by Hettema et al. (2001) calculated the variance attributable to additive genetics for PD at about 30% to 40%, with a heritability estimate of .48.

The data from twin studies have also revealed information relevant to factors influencing the liability for PD. Data have failed to produce any evidence for the role of common familial environmental factors in the development of PD because it appears all variance is attributable to either genetic or individual-specific environmental factors (Hettema et al., 2001). With regard to the specific mode of genetic transmission, a series of complex segregation analyses have identified a number of best-fitting models (see van den Heuvel et al., 2000, for a review). Although consensus on specific models is lacking, the conclusions are the same: genetic liability for PD most likely is polygenic in nature, in that any number of genes with small effects might interact with one another and environmental events (Gratacos et al., 2007). Further support for this theory comes from the findings of various linkage studies.

These studies are reviewed in detail by Gratacos et al. (2007), but briefly, suggestive linkage has been found for chromosome 22q (Weissman et al., 2004), 13q (Hamilton et al., 2003; Weissman et al., 2004), 7p (Crowe et al., 2001; Knowles et al., 1998; Logue, Vieland, Goedken, & Crowe, 2003), 9q (Thorgeirsson, 2003), 1q, 11p (Gelernter et al., 2001), and 15q (Fyer et al., 2006). As Gratacos et al. (2007) discuss, the next step will be for investigators to perform fine-mapping in an attempt to identify more specific regions and/or genes. One problem is that linkage studies typically need a strong gene effect to identify a significant LOD score (Risch & Merikangas, 1996) and, based on the findings from complex segregation analyses, this is not the case for PD.

A considerable number of candidate genes have been investigated with regard to PD. They are summarized in greater detail in Gratacos et al. (2007). Broadly speaking, candidate genes for PD can be classified into two neuro-biological groups. First, there are genes relevant to the receptors and transporters of neurotransmitter pathways. Specific pathways have been targeted given pharmacological agents that are either used to treat PD (i.e., panicolytic agents) or are utilized to induce panic attacks (i.e., panico-genic agents). Polymorphisms in the dopaminergic, sero-tonergic, noradrenergic, and GABAergic, and CCKergic systems have been examined in relation to PD (Gratacos et al., 2007). The second class of genes falls within the neurodevelopmental and synaptic plasticity domain, and include genes for neurotrophic factors and their receptors. Across all studies, very few replications exist, and no gene seems to be the definitive "PD-gene"—in line with expectations from segregation and linkage analyses.

Social Anxiety Disorder and Specific Phobias

Compared to other disorders within the anxiety spectrum, social anxiety disorder (SAD) and the specific phobias (SP) have received dramatically less research on the asso-ciated genetics. As a consequence of the paucity of extant investigations, many previous reports and reviews have examined these syndromes collectively (Kendler, Neale, Kessler, Heath, & Eaves, 1992). It should be noted that although in many cases the distinction is made among the various phobic disorders (i.e., social phobia, specific phobias, agoraphobia), there are instances in the literature where they are fully combined within a general "phobia" condition (e.g., Hettema et al., 2001). From a clinical and phenomenological perspective, the latter does not seem justified because these conditions present as discrete enti-ties (Hettema, Prescott, Myers, Neale, & Kendler, 2005; Ogliari et al., 2006), and investigations that have combined them should be considered with this caveat in mind.

Social Anxiety Disorder

Social anxiety disorder (SAD), also known as social pho-bia, is characterized by an intense and often debilitating fear of social situations and inappropriate fear of negative evaluations. SAD is the second most common psychologi-cal disorder after depression (Kessler, Chiu, et al., 2005), with an estimated lifetime prevalence of 12.1% (Kessler, Berglund, et al., 2005). The negative impact of this disor-der is startling. One epidemiological study found that 50% of people with SAD failed to complete high school, 70% fell within the bottom half of socioeconomic status, and 22% received welfare benefits (Schneier, Johnson, Hornig, Liebowitz, & Weissman, 1992). SAD has also been asso-ciated with increased public health costs (Greenberg et al., 1999); impairment in occupational, school, and social endeavors; and a lower rate of marriage (Schneier et al., 1994; Stein & Kean, 2000).

SAD may be classified via two subtypes. In the case of nongeneralized SAD, social fears are specific to situ-ations (e.g., public speaking or writing), whereas with generalized SAD fear is pervasive across most social situ-ations (Heimberg, 1993). Onset of SAD typically occurs in childhood or early adolescence (Robins & Regier, 1991) and affects men and women equally (Kessler, Berglund, et al., 2005). Individuals with SAD have low rates of treat-ment presentation (Magee, Eaton, Wittchen, McGonagle, & Kessler, 1996), which is surprising given the level of impairment and chronic course associated with the dis-order (Furmark, 2002). Both behavioral inhibition and shyness in children have been linked with SAD in adult-hood. As is the case with other anxiety conditions, rates of comorbidity are high, being most pronounced with other anxiety disorders, depression, and substance use disorders (Buckner et al., in press; Regier et al., 1998).

Early etiological research on phobias and fear focused primarily on fear conditioning and learning, with particu-lar emphasis on social learning and classical conditioning models. More recent etiological research has focused on a potential genetic liability in the acquisition of fear and pho-bias, and, although the data are limited, research indicates that genes most likely also play a role in the pathogenesis of SAD (Hettema et al., 2005). A small, but growing, lit-erature points to the familial aggregation of SAD (Fyer, Mannuzza, Chapman, Liebowitz, & Klein, 1993). A con-sistent finding has been that heritability appears to play a larger role for generalized SAD and that discrete SAD does not appear to be familial (Mannuzza et al., 1995; Stein, Chartier, Hazen, et al., 1998). For example, one investigation found that only relatives of generalized SAD probands, versus those of nongeneralized SAD probands, were at a 10-fold greater risk of also being diagnosed with SAD (Stein, Chartier, Hazen, et al., 1998). Family studies have furthermore revealed that SAD in probands increases the risk in first-degree relatives only for SAD and not that of other phobias (Fyer, Mannuzza, Chapman, Martin, & Klein, 1995).

Twin studies have suggested a moderate role of genes for SAD, with one odds ratio estimate at 2.3 (Kendler, Myers, Prescott, & Neale, 2001). Of note, this study also demonstrated that monozygotic twins' SAD concordance rates were much lower than those reported for other disorders. This has led some to suggest that perhaps (a) the environment may play a larger role in determining SAD, and (b) it may be that a *susceptibility* to SAD is inherited, rather than the disorder per se (Mathew, Coplan, & Gorman, 2001). With regard to the importance of environmental factors for SAD, there are several lines of additional research supporting this notion. First, SAD is one of the anxiety disorders that evidence varying prevalence rates across cultures. Furmark (2002) has discussed the possibility that cultural variation may be explained by cultural factors influencing socializing practices. For example, Asian cultures that are more collectivist in nature also have the lowest rates of reported SAD (e.g., 0.5% to 0.6% lifetime prevalence in Korea; Lee et al., 1990), and variation can also exist within one general culture (e.g., Europe) depending on geographical and climatic regions (Furmark et al., 1999; Lecrubier et al., 2000). Although these findings do not rule out the role of genetics, they do emphasize the influence of culture as one environmental factor. Second, animal models of SAD have demonstrated that specific contexts (i.e., environment) can lead to neuroplastic changes in brain-cell production that in turn increases socially anxious behaviors (Mathew et al., 2001). Finally, research has revealed that certain types of parenting styles may influence the development of SAD (Rapee & Melville, 1997), though it is important to consider that this may be an instance through which genes can influence the environment (i.e., genes most likely contribute to parenting styles) (Perusse, Rice, Despres, Rao, & Bouchard, 1997).

With regard to the second possibility, that the genetics of SAD might confer a *susceptibility* for the disorder rather than the syndrome itself, a number of family studies have considered quantitative traits related to SAD. These include primarily harm avoidance and behavioral inhibition (Mathew et al., 2001). Preliminary data are in support of this hypothesis. For example, one family study demonstrated that the personality construct of harm avoidance is heritable in populations of SAD probands (Stein, Chartier, Lizak, & Jang, 2001). Similarly, a twin study within the general population revealed that one of the cardinal diagnostic criteria for SAD, the fear of negative evaluations, provided a heritability estimate of .42 (Stein, Jang, & Livesley, 2002). The authors concluded that perhaps these quantitative traits may reflect a more robust genetic phenotype for SAD than the disorder itself.

Only one genome scan has been conducted with SAD populations, and no complex segregation analyses could be identified. The linkage analysis of SAD found evidence of suggestive linkage on chromosome 16, which contains the gene for the norepinephrine transporter, a possible candidate gene for SAD (Gelernter, Page, Stein, & Woods, 2004). Given the general paucity of neurological work on SAD, it is perhaps not surprising that only a handful of candidate gene association studies have been completed. Pharmacological studies (Blanco, Raza, Schneier, & Liebowitz, 2003) and more imaging studies (Tiihonen et al., 1997) suggest that genes in the serotonin and dopamine neurotransmitter systems are two plausible candidates that may be involved in the etiology of SAD. In three earlier reports, genes for the dopamine transporter and receptors, as well as the serotonin system genes for 5-HT, 5-HT2A, and 5-HT1B, were investigated, with few positive results (Kennedy et al., 2001; Schneier et al., 2000; Stein, Chartier, Kozak, King, & Kennedy, 1998). An investigation by Lochner et al. (2007) suggested the 5-HT_{2A} T102C polymorphism may play a role in the etiology of SAD, though future studies are needed to replicate this finding.

Specific Phobias

An intense and irrational fear of something that possesses little actual threat is known as a specific phobia (SP). As many as 19.2 million American adults suffer from specific phobias (Kessler et al., 1994), and females are two to three times more likely to be affected than males (Magee et al., 1996). The onset of SP typically occurs in childhood or adolescence and has a persistent and chronic course. Three SP subtypes have been identified: animal, blood/injury, and situational (Muris, Schmidt, & Merckelbach, 1999). These subgroups are differentiated by symptom response, age of onset, and heritability (Fyer, 1998). Despite the availability of effective psychological and pharmacological treatments, less than 20% of individuals suffering from SPs present for treatment (Fyer, 1998). Low rates of treatment presentation most likely result from variable levels of impairment among those suffering from SP—if a feared situation can be avoided with minimal disruption of daily routine (e.g., snakes in an urban setting), it is unlikely a person will seek help.

Very little research on the potential involvement of genes in the etiology of SPs has been conducted. No candidate association studies or linkage analyses could be identified. Family and twin investigations have revealed that there appears to be a modest genetic vulnerability for SPs (Kendler et al., 1992), and furthermore, that any noted familial aggregation is largely accounted for by genetic factors (Kendler, Karkowski, & Prescott, 1999). One twin investigation with adolescence calculated a heritability estimate of approximately 0.6, though it should be noted that this is the highest heritability estimate to date (Ogliari et al., 2006). No sizeable age or gender differences have been found in the majority of family and/or twin studies (Kendler et al., 1992, 2001; Ogliari et al., 2006).

Across the twin studies investigating SPs, data indicate that in addition to genetic influences, environmental factors also play a role in the etiology. These data also provide direct evidence against classical fear conditioning and learning etiological models for SPs. It appears that while genes are related to familial aggregation, familial learning is not (e.g., Sundet, Skre, Okkenhaug, & Tambs, 2003). That is, environmental experiences that influence the acquisition of fears are largely independent from familial experiences (Hettema et al., 2001; Sundet et al., 2003). Instead, the findings from both twin and family studies point to the theory of prepared conditionability (Ohman, 1986), which states that there are certain fears hardwired (i.e., genetic predisposition) that makes conditioning more probable. For example, in their classic experiment, Mineka, Davidson, Cook, and Keir (1984) found that in response to watching individuals from their group, rhesus monkeys learned to fear snakes but not flowers. This theory is also consistent with evolutionary models of SP. One final comment reflected in this literature is that the SPs (particularly those of an animal nature, such as fears of snakes, spiders, etc.), although related to other anxiety disorders, appear to be more distinct phenomena. Specifically, a large twin study revealed that SPs were influenced by a genetic factor largely uncorrelated with a second factor that was associated with all other anxiety disorders (Hettema et al., 2005). Moreover, that same study found that animal and situational type phobias appear to be more etiologically distinct from other anxiety disorders than blood injection phobia.

Genetics of General Phobic Conditions

Although we presented data on the separate genetic findings for SAD and SPs, it should also be noted that evidence is suggestive of common genetic underpinnings for all phobic conditions. Much of this data has emerged from a series of twin studies conducted by Kendler and colleagues (1992, 2001). By assessing a range of common fears and phobias in samples of male and female twins, it was found that although there are specific genetic factors involved with each type of phobic condition (e.g., social versus animal phobia), there is also a common genetic factor. Shared environmental factors appeared to play a relatively substantial role for only agoraphobia and social phobia, while individual/unique environmental factors played a role in all other types (see discussion on genetics of SPs).

Generalized Anxiety Disorder

Generalized anxiety disorder (GAD) is characterized by chronic worry that is both excessive and unrealistic across a variety of domains. Somatic symptoms, including headaches, chest pain, muscle tenderness, and fatigue, are another hallmark feature of GAD. The onset of GAD is gradual, beginning when an individual is in his or her 20s (Rickels & Schweizer, 1990), and although the condition is chronic, symptoms fluctuate and can be exacerbated by levels of current life stress (Hidalgo & Davidson, 2001). Epidemiological investigations report a global lifetime prevalence of GAD between 4.1% and 6.6% (e.g., Kessler, Davis, & Kendler, 1997), with women approximately twice as likely than men to be diagnosed with the condition (Kessler et al., 1994; Wittchen, 2002). In addition to experiencing somatic tension, individuals with GAD are also significantly more likely to be diagnosed with somatic disorders such as osteoporosis, asthma, and diabetes (Hidalgo & Davidson, 2001). This latter fact partially explains why individuals suffering from GAD are much more likely to present for treatment in a primary care setting (Schweizer & Rickels, 1997). Indeed, after PD, GAD populations evidence the second highest utilization of medical resources among the anxiety disorders (Kessler et al., 1999).

Although comorbidity with major depressive disorder (MDD) is an important consideration across the anxiety syndromes, the specific comorbidity between GAD and depression is noteworthy. Evidence suggests that this comorbidity is particularly strong and that the genetic underpinnings for these two disorders are almost identical. Gorwood (2004) outlined three factors that support the theory that the same genes may be at play within MDD and GAD. First, there is reliable comorbidity between the two conditions. Findings from epidemiological studies demonstrate that MDD and GAD are more often comorbid with one another, than either disorder occurring individually, and that the co-occurrence of these two disorders is the most frequent "combination" of mood and anxiety disorders (Ballenger, 1999; Kessler, Foster, Saunders, & Stang, 1995). Approximately 80% of individuals diagnosed with GAD also qualify for a lifetime diagnosis of MDD (Judd et al., 1998). Similarly, an individual diagnosed with MDD has a significant odds ratio of 9.4 for a lifetime diagnosis of GAD and 17.8 for 6-month prevalence (Kessler et al., 1995). These data suggest that the comorbidity between GAD and MDD is not a matter of chance alone.

Second, the two disorders have considerable joint heritability. Family studies have found elevated rates of morbidity among first-degree relatives of individuals with GAD, and the reported aggregate risk for GAD was 19.5% contrasted with 3.5% in control subjects (Mendlewicz,

Papadimitriou, & Wilmotte, 1993). A meta-analysis of available twin studies attributed 31.6% of the variance for liability to GAD to additive genetics for both men and women (Hettema et al., 2001). Importantly and with regard to MDD, several studies have found that the genetic factors for GAD and MDD are substantial and almost completely shared (Kendler, Gardner, Gatz, & Pedersen, 2007; Kendler et al., 1992). That is, the genes at play for MDD are most likely the same genes that influence GAD.

Gorwood (2004) also notes that the two disorders must evidence similar mechanisms. For example, both GAD and MDD respond to similar treatments, whether psychological or pharmacological in nature, and similar temperamental characteristics are associated with the two conditions. Both of these factors provide an avenue for the identification of candidate genes. Genes linked with the transmission and regulation of serotonin have been the primary system investigated. In addition to polymorphisms in the serotonin transporter gene (5-HTT; O'Hara et al., 1999; You, Hu, Chen, & Zhang, 2005), researchers have considered genes coding for tryptophan hydroxylase (Fehr et al., 2001; Zhang et al., 2005), the 5-HT2A (Fehr et al., 2001), 5-HT2C (Fehr, Szegedi, et al., 2000), and 5-HTR1B (Fehr, Grintschuk, et al., 2000) receptors and MAOA (Samochowiec et al., 2004). As is the case with other disorders, findings across these candidate gene association studies are marred by few replications and many inconsistencies.

Another area of genetics research relevant to GAD and MDD is the examination of genes linked with associated temperamental characteristics. Both behavioral inhibition and neuroticism have been investigated from a genetic perspective and represent traits related to GAD/MDD. Particularly those investigations focused on neuroticism are pertinent because a recent study revealed that this factor contributes around 25% to the genetic risk for MDD and GAD (Kendler et al., 2007; Pedersen, 2007). Several linkage studies on neuroticism have found significant linkage to the following chromosomes: 1q, 4q, 7p, 8p, 12q, and 13q (Cloninger et al., 1998; Fullerton et al., 2003; Zohar et al., 2003). Candidate association studies in turn have investigated the serotonin system genes, as well as variants in the GABA, DRD4, COMT, MAOA, and BDNF genes (see Arnold, Zai, & Richter, 2004). Although investigations utilizing a continuous trait score are characterized by increased power, results generally mirror those for the disorder (i.e., no conclusive findings).

Obsessive Compulsive Disorder

Obsessive compulsive disorder (OCD) is a debilitating neuropsychiatric disease characterized by intrusive and persistent thoughts (obsessions) that evoke anxiety, followed by urges or ritualized behaviors (compulsions) meant to neutralize and relieve the distress associated with obsessions. Recent epidemiological findings indicate that OCD has a lifetime, global prevalence of approximately 2% to 3% (Angst et al., 2004; Kessler, Berglund, et al., 2005), with the greatest period of risk occurring prior to the age of 18 (Nestadt, Bienvenu, Cai, Samuels, & Eaton, 1998). This disorder represents a serious global, public health concern, due to the chronic nature and extensive personal and societal costs associated with its symptoms (Dupont, 1993). The World Health Organization included OCD as one of the top 10 leading causes of disability (Lopez & Murray, 1998).

Although obsessions and compulsions represent the hallmark features of OCD and have been consistently identified across diverse cultures (Horwath & Weissman, 2000; Rasmussen & Eisen, 1990; Weissman et al., 1994), further examination of the phenomenological, etiological, and treatment traits of OCD reveals marked heterogeneity (Miguel et al., 2005). Although the cardinal features of OCD may be consistent, the scope of symptoms classified as obsessions and compulsions diverse and includes a wide range of intrusive thoughts and preoccupations, rituals, and compulsions. Other phenomenological aspects of the disorder also reflect heterogeneity, including differences in insight, gender, age of onset, and comorbidity patterns (Leckman et al., 1997; Miguel et al., 2005; Minichiello, Baer, Jenike, & Holland, 1990). Comorbidity seems particularly relevant in any discussion of OCD. Investigations have consistently demonstrated that around 90% of individuals with OCD qualify for at least one additional, comorbid lifetime diagnosis (LaSalle et al., 2004; Pinto, Mancebo, Eisen, Pagano, & Rasmussen, 2006), and about half meet criteria for at least one additional *current* disorder (Denys, Tenney, van Megen, de Geus, & Westenberg, 2004; Pinto et al., 2006). Although major depressive disorder represents the most frequently comorbid lifetime diagnosis, other Axis I disorders, including anxiety disorders, Tourette's disorder, eating disorders, and substance use disorders, also have elevated comorbidity rates in samples of individuals with OCD (LaSalle et al., 2004).

One development within the OCD literature has been the emphasis and exploration of symptom dimensions. Extrapolating from the historical classification of patients based on phenomenology (e.g., washers; Khanna & Mukherjee, 1992), a series of exploratory factor analyses of symptom rating scales has delineated specific OCD factors. Since initial reports, over 14 factor analytic studies have been conducted on more than 2,000 patients, and similar factors have been consistently identified across investigations (Mataix-Cols, Rosario-Campos, & Leckman, 2005). The majority of analyses have suggested the existence of either four or five dimensions, including: *cleaning/contamination, checking/obsessions, symmetry/ordering,* and *hoarding* (e.g., Hasler et al., 2007). Of note, emerging research indicates that these dimensions exhibit clinically meaningful differences with regard to etiology, neurobiology, comorbidity patterns, and treatment response (Miguel et al., 2005). For example, some of the derived dimensions have been used successfully in familial analyses (Alsobrook, Leckman, Goodman, Rasmussen, & Pauls, 1999), neuroimaging experiments (Mataix-Cols et al., 2004; Rauch et al., 1998; Saxena & Maidment, 2004), treatment response (Mataix-Cols, Rauch, Manzo, Jenike, & Baer, 1999), and genetic studies (Cavallini, Di Bella, Siliprandi, Malchiodi, & Bellodi, 2002).

Given the phenotypic complexity of OCD, it should be no surprise that etiological factors, particularly those that are biological in nature, appear to be no less multifaceted. That being said, there is now growing empirical research providing substantial evidence for a heritable component for OCD and the role of genes in the pathogenesis of this syndrome (for a more detailed review, see Grados & Wilcox, 2007).

Family studies have consistently found that first-degree relatives of individuals with OCD have significantly elevated morbidity rates, such that the aggregate risk for OCD is 8.2% to 12% in the first-degree relatives, compared to less than 2% in controls (Hanna, Fischer, Chadha, Himle, & Van Etten, 2005; Hettema et al., 2001; Nestadt, Samuels, et al., 2000). One study provided evidence of specificity, in that relatives of OCD probands were significantly more likely to have OCD but not other anxiety disorders (Fyer, Lipsitz, Mannuzza, Aronowitz, & Chapman, 2005). Differences in estimates arise primarily from phenotypic considerations, such as comorbidity and age of onset. Specifically, it has been reported that both early onset and comorbidity with tics is linked with greater risk for OCD (Hanna et al., 2005; Leckman et al., 1995). Twin studies, although few in number and marked by small sample sizes, have provided further support for the notion that OCD has a hereditary element (Rasmussen & Tsuang, 1984). Twin concordance rates for OCD have ranged from 55% to 87% for monozygotic twins, and 22% to 47% for dizygotic twins. A recent cross-cultural twin study estimated that the additive genetic influence was approximately 45% to 58%, indicating that both genes and unique environmental factors play a role in the pathogenesis of OCD (Hudziak et al., 2004).

A handful of complex segregation analyses have been conducted to investigate the specific nature of OCD transmission patterns (Alsobrook et al., 1999; Cavallini, Pasquale, Bellodi, & Smeraldi, 1999; Nestadt, Lan, et al., 2000). The collective evidence is suggestive of a complex pattern of inheritance, with some genes of major effect interacting with other genes in a mixed mode of transmission (Hemmings & Stein, 2006; Wendland, Kruse, Cromer, & Murphy, 2007). This is in keeping with early results from two genome-wide scans of OCD probands that revealed regions of potential involvement on six chromosomes (Hanna et al., 2002; Shugart et al., 2006). Hanna and colleagues (2002) reported suggestive linkage on chromosome 9p24, and Shugart et al. (2006) found suggestive linkage peaks at 3q27, 1q, 6q, 7q, and 11p. The former was conducted with only seven early-onset OCD proband families, whereas the latter was based on a sample of over 200 extended sib-pair OCD families. A third linkage study utilizing the Shugart et al. sample focused on one specific phenotype, that of compulsive hoarding. This analysis found a significant linkage peak on 14q23 (Samuels et al., 2007).

Association studies are by far the primary methodology used in investigating the molecular genetics of OCD, as is true across all the anxiety disorders. It has been increasingly realized that association studies are more powerful than linkage studies for disorders with many genes and small gene effects (Risch & Merikangas, 1996). Candidate genes for OCD have revolved primarily around the serotonergic neurotransmission genes, given the therapeutic effect of SSRIs in the pharmacotherapy of OCD. The most researched gene is the serotonin transporter gene (5-HTT; SLC6A4), and an insertion-deletion polymorphism in the promoter region (5-HTTLPR). Other SERT variants, including Stin2 and the rare I425, have also been investigated (Ozaki et al., 2003). Additional serotonin system genes that have been examined are the 5-HT$_{2A}$, the 5-HT$_{1DB}$, and the 5-HT$_{2C}$ receptor genes. Across all studies investigating serotonin system genes, little consensus exists and conclusions are difficult given the number of null findings. In addition to the serotonin system, dopaminergic neurotransmission, glutaminergic neurotransmission, catechol-O-methyl transferase enzyme, monoamine oxidase A, and neurodevelopmental genes have also been examined. Candidates that have at least some positive findings include a Val158Met polymorphism in the COMT gene, a 7-repeat allele in the VNTR of the dopamine-4 receptor gene, a disruption of the Hoxb8 gene, and a Val66Met variation of the proBDNF protein gene (for a more detailed review, refer to Grados & Wilcox, 2007). As is the case with the other anxiety disorders, findings are mixed with no definitive candidate gene linked—as of yet—to the manifestation of OCD. Conclusions across investigations indicate that further analyses with increased sample sizes and more homogeneous patient samples will be necessary to identify the role a given polymorphism may play as a genetic component of OCD. Other factors that most likely need to be taken into consideration are age of onset, gender, and comorbidity patterns—particularly with regard to Tourette's disorder.

FUTURE GENETICS RESEARCH ON ANXIETY PSYCHOPATHOLOGY

Over the past several decades, improvements in molecular genetic techniques and the increasingly fine-tuned mapping of the human genome have dramatically bolstered the feasibility of identifying molecular mechanisms and gene-candidates involved in psychopathology. Given these advances, it may be surprising that the specific genes believed to function as markers for particular disorders are relatively few in number (Smoller & Tsuang, 1998). This is certainly reflected in the findings reviewed in the first part of this chapter. Despite a substantial number of hypothesized etiological candidates, definitive genes for the anxiety disorders are still not known.

As discussed briefly in the introduction to this chapter and as highlighted in the reviews of each syndrome, anxiety disorders represent complex traits. Across studies there is little to no evidence for relatively simple Mendelian inheritance patterns, and the intricacies of gene × gene × environment interactions inherent in the polygenetic nature of these disorders obscures the identification of disease and single-gene associations (Lander & Schork, 1994; Murphy et al., 2003). From a molecular perspective, additional challenges facing the successful isolation of risk genes include incomplete penetrence and the occurrence of phenocopies (Lander & Schork, 1994). Incomplete penetrance is a situation in which an individual may be a disease-causing gene carrier, but is not (at least outwardly) displaying the disorder. In this situation, investigations may be more likely to overlook a true association. Phenocopy, on the other hand, is when the disorder occurs without that individual's being a carrier for the disease-causing gene. In this instance the "copy" may be caused by random environmental factors.

One overarching challenge that influences and can interact with these molecular complications (e.g., phenocopies, gene × gene interactions) is the necessity of clearly identifying the most accurate and definitive phenotype. Tsuang, Faraone, and Lyons (1993) have identified this problem as the "rate-limiting" step of genetic investigations. Over all other impediments, this one challenge is perhaps the most central because one will never detect the association between A and C, if B is being considered rather than A. In reviewing the literature for the anxiety disorders, it may have become evident that the definition of A is still open to debate. That is, the field as a whole still lacks consensus on what the precise phenotypic definitions for each of the anxiety syndromes should be (Shih et al., 2004). As such, many genetic investigations have been complicated by trying to tie a known marker (i.e., genetic variant) to a shifting and ambiguous phenotype.

The lack of consensus on definitive phenotypes is a natural by-product of the tremendous heterogeneity inherent in each of the anxiety disorders (R. Freedman, Adler, & Leonard, 1999). Several examples of phenotypic heterogeneity reviewed in the first part of the chapter include PD with or without agoraphobia, or the various manifestations of SAD (i.e., generalized versus nongeneralized, situation specific). The anxiety disorder with perhaps the most diverse presentation is OCD, if one takes into consideration symptom dimensions, comorbidity patterns, and familiality. In all of these examples, mixed genetic findings fail to provide credence to the hypothesis that the examined constructs are homogeneous phenotypes (Pato, Pato, & Pauls, 2002). Adding another layer of complexity is the fact that in some instances researchers are still attempting to identify the most optimal means of measuring a phenomenon. For example, a study by our group found that depending on which measure was utilized, strikingly different results emerged in the association between trauma and hoarding symptoms (Cromer, Schmidt, & Murphy, 2007). Relying on a classical instrument used to tap OCD-related symptoms (i.e., the Yale-Brown Obsessive Compulsive Scale Checklist; Goodman et al., 1989), no association with trauma was revealed; yet when a more recent and empirically validated questionnaire was used to measure hoarding behaviors (i.e., Saving Inventory Revised; Frost, Steketee, & Grisham, 2004), a significant relationship emerged. There thus appear to be both conceptual and methodological obstacles, making it a challenge to settle on the "correct" phenotype, and moreover assuring that all individuals in a given sample are representatives of that "correct" phenotype.

Several frameworks have been put forth in an attempt to address the issue of phenotypic heterogeneity, with the aim of subsequently increasing the power of genetic investigations. An established approach has been to consider broad versus narrow diagnostic definitions. One classic example of this classification method can be seen in the evolution of the phenotype for schizophrenia. More recently, researchers have considered other means by which to define phenotypes, including comorbidity, the possibility of endophenotypes, and the consideration of additional, nongenetic factors such as environmental dynamics. We explore each of these approaches and how they relate to the anxiety disorders in the following sections.

One additional note in regard to the interaction between phenotypes and genetics research is that a multilevel integrative approach to the study of psychiatric phenomena key in fostering the identification of definitive etiological theories (Cacioppo & Berntson, 1992). Only by analyzing a given syndrome from various perspectives, and then integrating any gained knowledge across macro (e.g., phenotype) and micro (e.g., genetics) levels can we hope to ascertain causative pathways and outcomes (see Figure 56.1). This notion is based on the corollary that there is a bidirectional influence between the developmental, environmental, and social cultural factors associated with a psychiatric syndrome, and the underlying neurophysiological and molecular processes of that phenomenon. That is, problems in genetic research can be largely alleviated by the careful examination of a given phenotype, and by the same token, genetic investigations can provide supportive evidence for a plausible phenotype (R. Freedman et al., 1999).

It becomes increasingly clear that a necessity across research domains is for the phenotypes to be theoretically valid. In other words, for true and accurate classification (i.e., phenotypic definition), one needs an explicit theoretical foundation (Follette & Houts, 1996). Although research on the anxiety disorders in large part strives to be rooted in theory, a number of the classic definitions currently employed appear to lack a valid empirical basis. One example is the *DSM*'s characterization of OCD, with an emphasis on the distinction between obsessions and compulsions; yet research has provided clear support against this notion (Mataix-Cols et al., 2005; Summerfeldt, Richter, Antony, & Swinson, 1999). In addition to the approaches discussed in the following sections, *taxometrics* is a method for identifying theoretically based phenotypes. Taxometrics represents a data analytic tool for discerning categories from continua and establishes definitive indicators of identified categories (Schmidt, Kotov, & Joiner, 2004). We do not provide a detailed discussion of taxometrics in this chapter (for a thorough explanation of the methods and potential research applications please see Schmidt et al., 2004), but propose that this analytical approach may be extremely useful in the identification of "true" anxiety phenotypes, which in turn may be explored in genetic studies.

Narrow versus Broad Phenotypic Definitions

The heterogeneity inherent in complex psychiatric traits may be addressed by relying on two separate classification categories on opposite ends of a spectrum: those relying on discrete definitions, typically in relation to symptom presentation, and those focusing on more expansive traits that could potentially cross diagnostic boundaries.

Narrow Phenotypic Definitions

The vast majority of psychiatric genetic studies have relied on discrete diagnostic entities to define the phenotype of interest, and this is certainly true for research on the anxiety disorders (Arnold et al., 2004; Smoller & Tsuang, 1998). These definitions most often are based on the syndromal classification of a given condition as outlined by the *DSM-IV-TR* or the *ICD-10*. Although this approach has been at least partially helpful, in that twin and family studies have identified a familial and heritable component of anxiety disorders, candidate gene studies utilizing these phenotypes are highly inconsistent.

One problem is that it is unclear whether the symptoms outlined in the diagnostic manuals represent the disease process under investigation (Hayes, Wilson, Gifford, Follette, & Strosahl, 1996). A second difficulty is that our current diagnostic categories are based on consensus definitions, resulting in a certain level of arbitrariness, with obvious consequences for definitively including a given individual in a class. We address these possibilities and potential solutions in the section that follows this one. A third problem is that diagnostic categories, as supposedly homogeneous groupings, entail marked heterogeneity. That is, even within the classically narrow definitions of each diagnostic entity, any number of finer groupings is feasible. A growing number of family and candidate gene association studies have examined applying a subgrouping method in an effort to identify even more homogeneous phenotypes.

The most salient example of a factor used to create subphenotypes of a specific phenomenon is *symptom presentation*. Earlier we discussed the recent shift in our understanding of the symptomatic features of OCD, specifically the relevance of symptom dimensions. Research on the genetics, including candidate gene investigations, have been more promising, examining the possibility that these symptom dimensions may represent more homogeneous subphenotypes of OCD (Hasler, Drevets, Gould, Gottesman, & Manji, 2006; Hasler et al., 2007; Lochner et al., 2004). Another example would be the focus on *generalized* SAD, rather than considering all presentations of the disorder (i.e., exclusion of nongeneralized SAD), and again, genetic findings with this phenotype have had more relative success (Lochner et al., 2007). Family studies have also found that the specific genetic contribution to many of these subphenotypes is relatively small, as is the case, for example, with the *checking* subtype of OCD (Hasler et al., 2007). Thus, although much time and energy has been allotted to identifying subtypes of psychiatric conditions based on clinical symptoms, the overall success of tying these subtypes to specific genes has been limited.

Additional groupings that have been proposed to lessen the heterogeneity of diagnostic categories include severity, age of onset, gender, and familiality. Smoller and Tsuang (1998) have proposed ascertaining phenotypic extremes, including identifying those probands with early onset only, or those who evidence particularly severe forms of a disorder. This approach has been utilized with some success for both OCD (Leckman et al., 1995) and PD (R. B. Goldstein, Wickramaratne, Horwath, & Weissman, 1997). Identifying those individuals with a familial form of a given disorder, may furthermore be a fruitful subtyping strategy. This approach has been employed successfully in the investigation of nonpsychiatric disorders (e.g., colon and breast cancer; Lander & Schork, 1994) and is increasingly being applied to mood (Drevets et al., 1997) and anxiety disorders (Hasler et al., 2007).

Broad Phenotypic Definitions

In direct contrast to narrow phenotypic definitions, another response to the heterogeneity of psychiatric disorders has been to *broaden* the definitions of phenotypes. This approach is based on (a) the possibility that anxiety disorders may represent an extreme end of a continuum of a given phenomenon, and (b) that different syndromes may share certain genetic vulnerabilities in common. We will briefly outline means of broadening a phenotype relevant to both perspectives in following paragraphs.

As was discussed with regard to narrow phenotypes, the diagnostic entities in the *DSM* are both relatively arbitrary and atheoretical (Clark, Watson, & Reynolds, 1995). For example, if an individual meets all the criteria for GAD with the exception of endorsing two rather than three of the associated symptoms (e.g., muscle tension, fatigue, restlessness), they technically would not receive a diagnosis of GAD and would most likely be excluded from genetic investigations utilizing a narrow definition. Yet, can it be definitively concluded that this individual does not suffer from a GAD-like syndrome? The answer is no, and moreover, it is very plausible that the genetics at play for the narrow definition of GAD may also be present in this individual. Utilizing a broad definition, subclinical or subsyndromal cases may be included for analysis. Both studies for PD and OCD, as well as those for SPs have relied on this broadening technique (e.g., Crowe, Noyes, Pauls, & Slymen, 1983; Kendler et al., 2001; Shugart et al., 2006; Weissman et al., 1993).

In addition to relaxing the phenotypic definition to include subsyndromal cases, there is a growing interest in considering not only the disorders per se, but also quantifiable traits relevant to the larger diagnostic categories (Hettema et al., 2001). Assessing dimensional phenotypes can either focus on a trait relevant to a specific disorder or on a dimension that cuts across diagnostic entities. Investigations looking at disorder-specific traits are increasing in frequency, though still relatively few in number. One example would be the study on fear of negative evaluations, as

a trait relevant to SAD, conducted by Stein and colleagues (Stein et al., 2002). Other possibilities might include various cognitive vulnerabilities (e.g., anxiety sensitivity for PD, thought-action-fusion for OCD) or biological risk factors (e.g., response to CO_2 inhalation for PD). Many of these traits may be plausible endophenotypes, which will be discussed in a later section.

Focus on Comorbidity   The second approach to examining quantifiable traits—assessing dimensional phenotypes that cut across diagnostic entities—is based on the findings that different syndromes may share genetic vulnerabilities in common. As highlighted throughout the review of the anxiety disorders, comorbidity is pervasive. Some researchers have noted that a *lack* of comorbidity may constitute the exception, and that empirically exploring patterns of co-occurring disorders will be necessary for clarifying phenotypes for genetic investigations (Clark et al., 1995; Shih et al., 2004). One of the key considerations with regard to comorbidity is to determine the reasons for the co-occurrence of two or more disorders. That is, the comorbidity may be causal in nature (i.e., one disorder causes the other disorder) or an instance where the two disorders may reflect different clinical aspects of the same underlying disease or diathesis (Merikangas et al., 2003). This notion is based on the theory that commonly comorbid disorders may be comprised of independently heritable components that make up the more complex syndromes and that are shared across diagnostic entities (Grados, Walkup, & Walford, 2003). By looking across conditions at constellations of common traits, investigators may be able to identify promising and more parsimonious phenotypes for genetic analyses.

Support for pleitropy among the anxiety disorders has emerged from a series of twin and family studies. Krueger (1999) proposed grouping psychiatric disorders into internalizing and externalizing classes, and Kendler, Prescott, Myers, and Neale (2003) have also found that patterns of comorbidity (i.e., externalizing versus internalizing) were largely accounted for by genetics. In analyses conducted for both men and women, support was found for common genetic factors that play a role in the etiology of all anxiety disorders. In a series of subsequent investigations, more fine-grained investigations of potentially shared genetic factors for the anxiety disorders were conducted. Across studies, it seems that there are common shared genetic factors, along with both shared and unique environmental factors, and unique genetic factors. SPs were less strongly linked, and SAD more intermediately linked to other anxiety disorders (Hettema et al., 2005; Kendler et al., 1992, 2001). One limitation to these investigations was the noninclusion of OCD.

The next step emerging from these findings is to directly investigate potential phenotypes that might be associated with the common genetic factors. Two plausible dimensional phenotypes that cut across diagnostic entities within the anxiety spectrum are trait anxiety, or neuroticism, and behavioral inhibition (Arnold et al., 2004; Smoller & Tsuang, 1998). Genetic association studies have begun to emerge for both neuroticism and behavioral inhibition (Arnold et al., 2004). Neuroticism is of particular interest given that it may help explain the pervasive comorbidity between anxiety and depression, by representing one common characteristic that is part of a general diathesis for these disorders (Fanous et al., 2002; Hettema, Prescott, & Kendler, 2004; Jardine, Martin, & Henderson, 1984). A population-based twin study found that although the genetic correlations between each anxiety disorder and neuroticism were high, there may also be additional shared genetic factors, independent of neuroticism, between depression, GAD, and PD (Hettema, Neale, Myers, Prescott, & Kendler, 2006).

Endophenotypes

The exploration of endophenotypes is an additional strategy that has been proposed for overcoming the methodological difficulties discussed throughout this chapter with respect to elucidating the genetic basis of any given anxiety disorder. The term *endophenotype* is described as an internal phenotype (i.e., not obvious to the unaided eye) that fills the gap between available descriptors and between the gene and the elusive disease process (Gottesman & Shields, 1973), and therefore may help to resolve questions about etiological models. The endophenotype concept was based on the assumption that the number of genes involved in the variations of endophenotypes representing relatively straightforward and putatively more elementary phenomena (as opposed to behavioral macros) are fewer than those involved in producing a psychiatric diagnostic entity (Gottesman & Gould, 2003). Endophenotypes provide a means for identifying the downstream traits of clinical phenotypes, as well as the upstream consequence of genes. The methods available to identify endophenotypes include neuropsychological, cognitive, neurophysiological, neuroanatomical, and biochemical measures.

Advantages of Biological Endophenotypes

Within the broad class endophenotypes there is a gradient of proximity to the gene and gene products (geno) versus closer to the symptoms and the disease itself (pheno; Hasler et al., 2006). In twin studies, broader diagnostic definitions (e.g., schizophrenia plus mood-incongruent affective disorders plus schizotypal personality disorder plus atypical psychosis) may provide higher heritability estimates than

narrow endophenotypic diagnostic definitions (e.g., pure schizophrenia; Farmer, McGuffin, & Gottesman, 1987). Likewise, in longitudinal studies, broader diagnostic categories (e.g., mood plus anxiety disorders) showed greater stability over time than narrow diagnostic definitions (e.g., pure PD; Angst, Vollrath, Merikangas, & Ernst, 1990). This might lead one to conclude that relatively broad endophenotypes such as brain function endophenotypes (e.g., cognitive performance) are the most heritable and most appropriate for genetic studies. However, one further consideration is that although broad phenotypic constructs may show high familial transmission in twin and family studies, they may not represent alternative manifestations of a single liability distribution (McGue, Gottesman, & Rao, 1983). Genetic factors for intermediate traits that are closer to the genotype in the developmental scheme, such as biological markers, may generally be easier to identify because of the improved signal-to-noise ratio in the fraction of variance explained by any single factor (Carlson, Eberle, Kruglyak, & Nickerson, 2004).

Evaluation of Biological Endophenotypes

The evaluation of biological endophenotypes is based on the following criteria, which were structured on the seminal work by Gottesman and Shields (Hasler, Drevets, Manji, & Charney, 2004):

- *Specificity:* The endophenotype is more strongly associated with the disease of interest than with other psychiatric conditions.
- *State-independence:* The endophenotype is stable over time and not an epiphenomenon of the illness or its treatment.
- *Heritability:* Variance in the endophenotype is associated with genetic variance.
- *Familial association:* The endophenotype is more prevalent among the relatives of ill probands compared with an appropriate control group.
- *Co-segregation:* The endophenotype is more prevalent among the ill relatives of ill probands compared with the well relatives of the ill probands.
- *Biological and clinical plausibility:* The endophenotype bears some conceptual relationship to the disease.

We next discuss in detail one example of an endophenotype for the anxiety disorders, specifically focusing on PD, followed by a more general discussion of potential endophenotypes for OCD. All endophenotypes that have been proposed for PD must be seen as *putative* endophenotypes because whether they consistently meet all required endophenotype criteria is yet to be determined. In this section, we discuss the response to caffeine as a putative endophenotype because it meets many of the endophenotype criteria and has been successfully used to identify risk genes for PD.

Sensitivity to Caffeine as a Putative Endophenotype for Panic Disorder Because of its psychostimulant effects, caffeine is the most widely consumed psychotropic agent. In healthy subjects with no risk for anxiety disorders, caffeine in small and moderate doses is a mild stimulant when taken orally, although it can have marked effects when administered intravenously, including producing olfactory hallucinations. The oral intake of large amounts of caffeine in healthy subjects has been shown to produce anxiety, insomnia, and a variety of somatic symptoms, including increased blood pressure (Charney, Heninger, & Jatlow, 1985).

Considerable individual differences in the effects of caffeine (Evans & Griffiths, 1991) may point to genetic factors underlying caffeine sensitivity. Although there is little evidence for the heritability of the behavioral response to caffeine, there is increasing evidence that genetic factors influence caffeine consumption (Cornelis, El-Sohemy, & Campos, 2007), caffeine-induced anxiety (Alsene, Deckert, Sand, & de Wit, 2003), and caffeine-related reductions in sleep quality (Retey et al., 2007). There are several lines of evidence for an increased sensitivity to caffeine in subjects with PD. A study using a caffeine consumption inventory (Boulenger, Uhde, Wolff, & Post, 1984) indicated that subjects with PD, but not depressed patients or normal controls, experienced levels of anxiety that correlated with their degree of caffeine consumption. The sensitivity to caffeine was confirmed by the observation that more subjects with PD than healthy controls reported the discontinuation of coffee intake due to unwanted effects. Caffeine challenge experiments also confirmed an association between increased sensitivity to caffeine and PD (Charney et al., 1985). In the study by Charney et al. (1985), caffeine produced significantly greater increases in subject-rated anxiety, nervousness, fear, nausea, heart palpitations, restlessness, and tremors in subjects with PD than in healthy controls. In the patients, these symptoms were significantly correlated with plasma caffeine levels. In sum, there is reasonable evidence for a relatively specific elevation of caffeine sensitivity associated with PD. A pilot study in subjects with remitted PD (NIMH, unpublished data) suggests state-independence of increased caffeine sensitivity in panic disorder.

Although caffeine binding in the brain is mostly nonspecific, the stimulatory action of caffeine seems to be brought about by an inhibition of transmission via adenosine A_{2a} receptors. The central role of adenosine receptors in mediating the behavioral effects of caffeine has motivated a search for variation in genes encoding these receptors that could influence interindividual differences in caffeine response. A gene association study (Alsene et al.,

2003) found that polymorphisms in the A_1 and A_{2a} adenosine receptor genes were related to the variation in caffeine-induced anxiety. Healthy, infrequent caffeine users received either placebo or caffeine citrate (300 mg) in random order, under double-blind conditions. To determine whether genetic variations in the A_1 and the A_{2a} receptor were related to subjective or behavioral measurements, individuals were assigned to one of three genotypic groups (e.g., TT, CT, or CC) at each of the four loci of the receptor genes (716T>G, 263C>T, 1976T>C, and 2592C>Tins). The 1976T>C and 2592C>Tins polymorphisms were in nearly complete linkage disequilibrium and therefore these two linked polymorphisms formed only three genotypic groups (e.g., TT, CT, or CC). Individuals with the linked 1976 T/T and the 2592 Tins/Tins variants in the A_{2a} adenosine receptor gene reported greater increases in anxiety after caffeine challenge than did individuals in either of the other two genotypic groups. A subsequent study examined associations between the A_1 and A_{2a} adenosine receptor genes and PD. They found that subjects with PD had a significantly greater frequency of the 1976T allele and the 1976T/T genotype of the A_{2a} adenosine receptor gene than matched controls (Deckert et al., 1998). The increased sensitivity to caffeine intake in healthy first-degree relatives of panic patients (Nardi et al., 2007) suggests sheared genetic risk for caffeine sensitivity and PD.

Taken together, these studies suggest heritability, familial association, and biological plausibility for caffeine sensitivity as putative endophenotpye for PD. While there is considerable evidence for caffeine sensitivity as an endophenotype in panic, data for other biological endophenotypes are lacking. Structural imaging studies have not yielded consistent brain volumetric abnormalities in anxiety disorders. Further endophenotypes may be derived from the dysfunctions of the central serotonergic, noradrenergic, and dopaminergic systems and the hypothalamic-pituitary-adrenal axis found in patients with anxiety disorders although these dysfunctions seem to be nonspecific. Reduced binding to the benzodiazepine receptor in the prefrontal cortex has been consistently found in patients with PD (Cameron et al., 2007; Malizia et al., 1998). A recent study by Hasler et al. (unpublished data) showed specificity of this finding for PD. This literature encourages the evaluation of other endophenotype criteria, including temporal stability and familial association of this abnormality. Another putative endophenotype for PD may be derived from the respiratory system dysfunction that has been proposed as an important etiological factor in panic (Klein, 1993). Alterations of the central systems using cholecystokinin, neuropeptide Y, and dysfunctions of the thyroid axis may provide other promising leads in the discovery of endophenotypes for anxiety disorders.

Putative Endophenoyptes for Obsessive Compulsive Disorder

While the amygdala is considered as the key brain structure in the pathophysiology of anxiety disorders including PD, PTSD, and phobias, the epidemiology and the neuroanatomical model for OCD seem to be different (Fontenelle & Hasler, in press). Aberrant functioning within the cortico-striato-thalamo-cortical circuitry is the foundation of current models of OCD (de Mathis et al., 2006). Promising candidate brain function endophenotypes for OCD include (a) nonverbal recall impairments that are possibly due to the use of inappropriate organizational strategies as measured with the Rey complex figure test (Savage et al., 1999), (b) failures in decision making as measured by the Iowa Gambling Task (Bechara, Damasio, Damasio, & Anderson, 1994), (c) impaired set-shifting as measured by the object alternation test (M. Freedman, 1990), and (d) response-inhibition deficits as measured by oculomotor tests (Rosenberg et al., 1997). Chamberlain, Blackwell, Fineberg, Robbins, and Sahakian (2005) concluded that the neurobiology of the relatively specific neuropsychological deficits in OCD may be conceptualized in terms of lateral orbitofrontal loop dysfunction suggesting that functional imaging endophenotypes may be derived from such a dysfunction.

Brain structure endophenotypes may be based on anatomical alterations in the orbitofrontal cortex and the striatum frequently reported in OCD (Brambilla, Barale, Caverzasi, & Soares, 2002). Given the increasing recognition of the importance of epigenetic transformations and developmental factors in the expression of psychiatric phenotypes (Gottesman & Hanson, 2004; Hasler et al., 2005), the symptom provocation method may be necessary to achieve the endophenotype criterion state-independence. Exposure to provocative stimuli has successfully been used as a symptom provocation paradigm for neurobiological studies in OCD (Mataix-Cols et al., 2004). Studies aimed at evaluating candidate endophenotypes for OCD with respect to specificity, temporal stability, and prevalence in unaffected relatives are clearly warranted.

Given the lack of well-designed twin, family, and prospective studies evaluating putative endophenotypes in anxiety disorders, future research has the potential to considerably improve the phenotypic definition of these possibly heterogeneous entities.

Environmental Factors

Environmental factors also play an important role in genetic etiological mechanisms (Cacioppo & Berntson, 1992). Across all twin studies, a consistent finding has been the inclusion of both shared and unique environmental factors in the eti-

ological model for anxiety disorders (e.g., Hettema et al., 2006). These factors most likely help shape the trajectory a particular genotype may take, particularly in cases where disorders share common diatheses. For example, environmental factors most likely largely account for the differentiation between MDD and GAD. This type of relationship is directly in line with traditional diathesis-stress theories for psychiatric disorders (Zuckerman, 1999). A growing number of studies have found that experiences of life stress interact with genes. A seminal investigation conducted by Caspi and colleagues (2003) found that the life stress interacted with the serotonin transporter polymorphism 5-HTTLPR in the expression of depression. Furthermore, there is also evidence for gene × gene × environment interactions with psychiatric populations, involving the serotonin transporter and BDNF genes, as well as the experience of childhood abuse (Kaufman et al., 2006). To effectively study the influence of environmental factors and gene-by-environment interactions, large samples will be needed.

SUMMARY

Considering that genetic investigations of anxiety-related phenomena began less than 3 decades ago, the findings to date are quite remarkable. Across the anxiety disorders, we have extensive support for a heritable component and multiple association studies have suggested potential candidate genes. Furthermore, advances in molecular genetic techniques are empowering association, linkage, and segregation analyses, particularly with the increasing feasibility of genome-wide scans. That being said, when analyzing the data collectively, it becomes evident that the genetic picture of the anxiety construct is far from complete.

In this chapter, we set out to provide a snapshot of the anxiety-related disorders, and to discuss factors that may be contributing to the challenge of identifying specific gene and disorder (or trait) associations. Taken together, reducing the phenotypic heterogeneity is crucial for the identification of vulnerability genes. We also outlined possible alternative approaches that may provide more fruitful avenues for future investigations. These include dissecting the behavioral phenotypes into key components and simultaneously considering specific environmental risk factors. The hope is that by fine-tuning a multilevel integrative approach, we may ultimately improve phenotypic definitions and unearth the genetic diathesis of anxiety.

REFERENCES

Alsene, K., Deckert, J., Sand, P., & de Wit, H. (2003). Association between A2a receptor gene polymorphisms and caffeine-induced anxiety. *Neuropsychopharmacology, 28,* 1694–1702.

Alsobrook, I. J., Leckman, J. F., Goodman, W. K., Rasmussen, S. A., & Pauls, D. L. (1999). Segregation analysis of obsessive-compulsive disorder using symptom-based factor scores. *American Journal of Medical Genetics, 88,* 669–675.

American Psychiatric Association. (1980). *Diagnostic and Statistical Manual of Mental Disorders* (3rd ed.). Washington, DC: Author.

American Psychiatric Association. (1987). *Diagnostic and Statistical Manual of Mental Disorders* (3rd ed., revised). Washington, DC: Author.

American Psychiatric Association. (1994). *Diagnostic and Statistical Manual of Mental Disorders* (4th ed.). Washington, DC: Author.

Angst, J., Gamma, A., Endrass, J., Goodwin, R., Ajdacic, V., Eich, D., et al. (2004). Obsessive-compulsive severity spectrum in the community: Prevalence, comorbidity, and course. *European Archives of Psychiatry and Clinical Neuroscience, 254,* 156–164.

Angst, J., Vollrath, M., Merikangas, K., & Ernst, C. (1990). Comorbidity of anxiety and depression in the Zurich cohort study of young adults. In J. D. Maser & C. R. Cloninger (Eds.), *Comorbidity of mood and anxiety disorders* (pp. 123–137). Washington, DC: American Psychiatric Press.

Arnold, P. D., Zai, G., & Richter, M. A. (2004). Genetics of anxiety disorders. *Current Psychiatry Reports, 6,* 243–254.

Ballenger, J. C. (1999). Current treatments of the anxiety disorders in adults. *Biological Psychiatry, 46,* 1579–1594.

Bechara, A., Damasio, A. R., Damasio, H., & Anderson, S. W. (1994). Insensitivity to future consequences following damage to human prefrontal cortex. *Cognition, 50*(1–3), 7–15.

Blanco, C., Raza, M. S., Schneier, F. R., & Liebowitz, M. R. (2003). The evidence-based pharmacological treatment of social anxiety disorder. *International Journal of Neuropsychopharmacology, 6,* 427–442.

Boulenger, J. P., Uhde, T. W., Wolff, E. A., III, & Post, R. M. (1984). Increased sensitivity to caffeine in patients with panic disorders: Preliminary evidence. *Archives of General Psychiatry, 41,* 1067–1071.

Boyd, J. H. (1986). Use of mental health services for the treatment of panic disorder. *American Journal of Psychiatry, 143,* 1569–1574.

Brambilla, P., Barale, F., Caverzasi, E., & Soares, J. C. (2002). Anatomical MRI findings in mood and anxiety disorders. *Epidemiologia e Psichiatria Sociale, 11*(2), 88–99.

Buckner, J. D., Schmidt, N. B., Lang, A. R., Small, J., Schlauch, R. C., & Lewinsohn, P. M. (in press). Specificity of social anxiety disorder as a risk factor for alcohol and cannabis dependence. *Journal of Psychiatric Research.*

Cacioppo, J. T., & Berntson, G. G. (1992). Social psychological contributions to the decade of the brain: Doctrine of multilevel analysis. *American Psychologist, 47,* 1019–1028.

Cameron, O. G., Huang, G. C., Nichols, T., Koeppe, R. A., Minoshima, S., Rose, D., et al. (2007). Reduced [gamma]-aminobutyric acida-benzodiazepine binding sites in insular cortex of individuals with panic disorder. *Archives of General Psychiatry, 64,* 793–800.

Carlson, C. S., Eberle, M. A., Kruglyak, L., & Nickerson, D. A. (2004, May 27). Mapping complex disease loci in whole-genome association studies. *Nature, 429,* 446–452.

Caspi, A., Sugden, K., Moffitt, T. E., Taylor, A., Craig, I. W., Harrington, H., et al. (2003, July 18). Influence of life stress on depression: Moderation by a polymorphism in the 5-HTT gene. *Science, 301,* 386–389.

Cavallini, M. C., Di Bella, D., Siliprandi, F., Malchiodi, F., & Bellodi, L. (2002). Exploratory factor analysis of obsessive-compulsive patients and association with 5-HTTLPR polymorphism. *American Journal of Medical Genetics, 114,* 347–353.

Cavallini, M. C., Pasquale, L., Bellodi, L., & Smeraldi, E. (1999). Complex segregation analysis for obsessive compulsive disorder and related disorders. *American Journal of Medical Genetics, 88,* 38–43.

Chamberlain, S. R., Blackwell, A. D., Fineberg, N. A., Robbins, T. W., & Sahakian, B. J. (2005). The neuropsychology of obsessive compulsive disorder: The importance of failures in cognitive and behavioural inhibition as candidate endophenotypic markers. *Neuroscience and Biobehavioral Reviews, 29,* 399–419.

Charney, D. S., Heninger, G. R., & Jatlow, P. I. (1985). Increased anxiogenic effects of caffeine in panic disorders. *Archives of General Psychiatry, 42,* 233–243.

Clark, L. A., Watson, D., & Reynolds, S. (1995). Diagnosis and classification of psychopathology: Challenges to the current system and future directions. *Annual Review of Psychology, 46,* 121–153.

Cloninger, C. R., Van Eerdewegh, P., Goate, A., Edenberg, H. J., Blangero, J., Hesselbrock, V., et al. (1998). Anxiety proneness linked to epistatic loci in genome scan of human personality traits. *American Journal of Medical Genetics, 81,* 313–317.

Cohen, D. D. (1951). Psychotherapy and its application to anxiety states. *McGill Medical Journal, 20*(1), 28–35.

Cornelis, M. C., El-Sohemy, A., & Campos, H. (2007). Genetic polymorphism of the adenosine A2A receptor is associated with habitual caffeine consumption. *American Journal of Clinical Nutrition, 86,* 240–244.

Cromer, K. R., Schmidt, N. B., & Murphy, D. L. (2007). Do traumatic events influence the clinical expression of compulsive hoarding? *Behaviour Research and Therapy, 45,* 2581–2592.

Crowe, R. R., Goedken, R., Samuelson, S., Wilson, R., Nelson, J., & Noyes, R., Jr. (2001). Genomewide survey of panic disorder. *American Journal of Medical Genetics, 105,* 105–109.

Crowe, R. R., Noyes, R., Pauls, D. L., & Slymen, D. (1983). A family study of panic disorder. *Archives of General Psychiatry, 40,* 1065–1069.

Deckert, J., Nothen, M. M., Franke, P., Delmo, C., Fritze, J., Knapp, M., et al. (1998). Systematic mutation screening and association study of the A1 and A2a adenosine receptor genes in panic disorder suggest a contribution of the A2a gene to the development of disease. *Molecular Psychiatry, 3,* 81–85.

de Mathis, M. A., Diniz, J. B., do Rosario, M. C., Torres, A. R., Hoexter, M., Hasler, G., et al. (2006). What is the optimal way to subdivide obsessive-compulsive disorder? *CNS Spectrums, 11,* 762–776.

Denys, D., Tenney, N., van Megen, H. J., de Geus, F., & Westenberg, H. G. (2004). Axis I and II comorbidity in a large sample of patients with obsessive-compulsive disorder. *Journal of Affective Disorders, 80*(2–3), 155–162.

Drevets, W. C., Price, J. L., Simpson, J. R., Jr., Todd, R. D., Reich, T., Vannier, M., et al. (1997, April 24). Subgenual prefrontal cortex abnormalities in mood disorders. *Nature, 386,* 824–827.

Dupont, R. L. (1993). *"Town Hall" panel presentation.* Paper presented at the Anxiety Disorders of America Conference.

Evans, S. M., & Griffiths, R. R. (1991). Dose-related caffeine discrimination in normal volunteers: Individual differences in subjective effects and self-reported cues. *Behavioural Pharmacology, 2*(4/5), 345–356.

Fanous, A. H., Gardner, C. O., Prescott, C. A., Cancro, R., & Kendler, K. S. (2002). Neuroticism, major depression and gender: A population-based twin study. *Psychological Medicine, 32,* 719–728.

Farmer, A. E., McGuffin, P., & Gottesman, I. I. (1987). Twin concordance for DSM-III schizophrenia: Scrutinizing the validity of the definition. *Archives of General Psychiatry, 44,* 634–641.

Fehr, C., Grintschuk, N., Szegedi, A., Anghelescu, I., Klawe, C., Singer, P., et al. (2000). The HTR1B 861G>C receptor polymorphism among patients suffering from alcoholism, major depression, anxiety disorders and narcolepsy. *Psychiatry Research, 97,* 1–10.

Fehr, C., Schleicher, A., Szegedi, A., Anghelescu, I., Klawe, C., Hiemke, C., et al. (2001). Serotonergic polymorphisms in patients suffering from alcoholism, anxiety disorders and narcolepsy. *Progress in Neuro-Psychopharmacology and Biological Psychiatry, 25,* 965–982.

Fehr, C., Szegedi, A., Anghelescu, I., Klawe, C., Hiemke, C., & Dahmen, N. (2000). Sex differences in allelic frequencies of the 5-HT2C Cys23Ser polymorphism in psychiatric patients and healthy volunteers: Findings from an association study. *Psychiatric Genetics, 10,* 59–65.

Ferdinand, R. F., van der Reijden, M., Verhulst, F. C., Nienhuis, J., & Giel, R. (1995). Assessment of the prevalence of psychiatric disorder in young adults. *British Journal of Psychiatry: Journal of Mental Science, 166,* 480–488.

Follette, W. C., & Houts, A. C. (1996). Models of scientific progress and the role of theory in taxonomy development: A case study of the DSM. *Journal of Consulting and Clinical Psychology, 64,* 1120–1132.

Fontenelle, L. F., & Hasler, G. (in press). The analytical epidemiology of obsessive-compulsive disorder: Risk factors and correlates. *Progress in Neuro-Psychopharmacology and Biological Psychiatry.*

Frances, A., Miele, G. M., Widiger, T. A., Pincus, H. A., Manning, D., & Davis, W. W. (1993). The classification of panic disorders: From Freud to DSM-IV. *Journal of Psychiatric Research, 27*(Suppl, 1), 3–10.

Freedman, M. (1990). Object alternation and orbitofrontal system dysfunction in Alzheimer's and Parkinson's disease. *Brain and Cognition, 14,* 134–143.

Freedman, R., Adler, L. E., & Leonard, S. (1999). Alternative phenotypes for the complex genetics of schizophrenia. *Biological Psychiatry, 45,* 551–558.

Frost, R. O., Steketee, G., & Grisham, J. (2004). Measurement of compulsive hoarding: Saving inventory-revised. *Behaviour Research and Therapy, 42,* 1163–1182.

Fullerton, J., Cubin, M., Tiwari, H., Wang, C., Bomhra, A., Davidson, S., et al. (2003). Linkage analysis of extremely discordant and concordant sibling pairs identifies quantitative-trait loci that influence variation in the human personality trait neuroticism. *American Journal of Human Genetics, 72,* 879–890.

Furmark, T. (2002). Social phobia: Overview of community surveys. *Acta Psychiatrica Scandinavica, 105*(2), 84–93.

Furmark, T., Tillfors, M., Everz, P., Marteinsdottir, I., Gefvert, O., & Fredrikson, M. (1999). Social phobia in the general population: Prevalence and sociodemographic profile. *Social Psychiatry and Psychiatric Epidemiology, 34,* 416–424.

Fyer, A. J. (1998). Current approaches to etiology and pathophysiology of specific phobia. *Biological Psychiatry, 44,* 1295–1304.

Fyer, A. J., Hamilton, S. P., Durner, M., Haghighi, F., Heiman, G. A., Costa, R., et al. (2006). A third-pass genome scan in panic disorder: Evidence for multiple susceptibility loci. *Biological Psychiatry, 60,* 388–401.

Fyer, A. J., Lipsitz, J. D., Mannuzza, S., Aronowitz, B., & Chapman, T. F. (2005). A direct interview family study of obsessive-compulsive disorder Pt. I. *Psychological Medicine, 35,* 1611–1621.

Fyer, A. J., Mannuzza, S., Chapman, T. F., Liebowitz, M. R., & Klein, D. F. (1993). A direct interview family study of social phobia. *Archives of General Psychiatry, 50,* 286–293.

Fyer, A. J., Mannuzza, S., Chapman, T. F., Martin, L. Y., & Klein, D. F. (1995). Specificity in familial aggregation of phobic disorders. *Archives of General Psychiatry, 52,* 564–573.

Gelernter, J., Bonvicini, K., Page, G., Woods, S. W., Goddard, A. W., Kruger, S., et al. (2001). Linkage genome scan for loci predisposing to panic disorder or agoraphobia. *American Journal of Medical Genetics, 105,* 548–557.

Gelernter, J., Page, G. P., Stein, M. B., & Woods, S. W. (2004). Genome-wide linkage scan for loci predisposing to social phobia: Evidence for a chromosome 16 risk locus. *American Journal of Psychiatry, 161,* 59–66.

Goldstein, A. J., & Chambless, D. L. (1978). Reanalysis of agoraphobia. *Behavior Therapy, 9,* 47–59.

Goldstein, R. B., Wickramaratne, P. J., Horwath, E., & Weissman, M. M. (1997). Familial aggregation and phenomenology of "early"-onset (at or before age 20 years) panic disorder. *Archives of General Psychiatry, 54,* 271–278.

Goodman, W. K., Price, L. H., Rasmussen, S. A., Mazure, C., Fleischmann, R. L., Hill, C. L., et al. (1989). The Yale-Brown Obsessive Compulsive Scale: Pt. I. Development, use, and reliability. *Archives of General Psychiatry, 46,* 1006–1011.

Gorwood, P. (2004). Generalized anxiety disorder and major depressive disorder comorbidity: An example of genetic pleiotropy? *European Psychiatry, 19*(1), 27–33.

Gottesman, I. I., & Gould, T. D. (2003). The endophenotype concept in psychiatry: Etymology and strategic intentions. *American Journal of Psychiatry, 160,* 636–645.

Gottesman, I. I., & Hanson, D. R. (2004). Human development: Biological and genetic processes. *Annual Review of Psychology, 56,* 10.11–10.24.

Gottesman, I. I., & Shields, J. (1973). Genetic theorizing and schizophrenia. *British Journal of Psychiatry: Journal of Mental Science, 122*(566), 15–30.

Grados, M. A., Walkup, J., & Walford, S. (2003). Genetics of obsessive-compulsive disorders: New findings and challenges. *Brain and Development, 25*(Suppl, 1), S55–S61.

Grados, M. A., & Wilcox, H. C. (2007). Genetics of obsessive-compulsive disorder: A research update. *Expert Review of Neurotherapeutics, 7,* 967–980.

Gratacos, M., Sahun, I., Gallego, X., Amador-Arjona, A., Estivill, X., & Dierssen, M. (2007). Candidate genes for panic disorder: Insight from human and mouse genetic studies. *Genes, Brain, and Behavior, 6*(Suppl, 1), 2–23.

Greenberg, P. E., Sisitsky, T., Kessler, R. C., Finkelstein, S. N., Berndt, E. R., Davidson, J. R., et al. (1999). The economic burden of anxiety disorders in the 1990s. *Journal of Clinical Psychiatry, 60,* 427–435.

Hamilton, S. P., Fyer, A. J., Durner, M., Heiman, G. A., Baisre de Leon, A., Hodge, S. E., et al. (2003). Further genetic evidence for a panic disorder syndrome mapping to chromosome 13q. *Proceedings of the National Academy of Sciences, USA, 100,* 2550–2555.

Hanna, G. L., Fischer, D. J., Chadha, K. R., Himle, J. A., & Van Etten, M. (2005). Familial and sporadic subtypes of early-onset obsessive-compulsive disorder. *Biological Psychiatry, 57,* 895–900.

Hanna, G. L., Veenstra-VanderWeele, J., Cox, N. J., Boehnke, M., Himle, J. A., Curtis, G. C., et al. (2002). Genome-wide linkage analysis of families with obsessive-compulsive disorder ascertained through pediatric probands. *American Journal of Medical Genetics, 114,* 541–552.

Hasler, G., Drevets, W. C., Gould, T. D., Gottesman, II, & Manji, H. K. (2006). Toward constructing an endophenotype strategy for bipolar disorders. *Biological Psychiatry.*

Hasler, G., Drevets, W. C., Manji, H. K., & Charney, D. S. (2004). Discovering endophenotypes for major depression. *Neuropsychopharmacology, 29,* 1765–1781.

Hasler, G., Pine, D. S., Kleinbaum, D. G., Gamma, A., Luckenbaugh, D., Ajdacic, V., et al. (2005). Depressive symptoms during childhood and adult obesity: The Zurich Cohort Study. *Molecular Psychiatry, 10,* 842–850.

Hasler, G., Pinto, A., Greenberg, B. D., Samuels, J., Fyer, A. J., Pauls, D., et al. (2007). Familiality of factor analysis-derived YBOCS dimensions in OCD-affected sibling pairs from the OCD Collaborative Genetics Study. *Biological Psychiatry, 61,* 617–625.

Hayes, S. C., Wilson, K. G., Gifford, E. V., Follette, V. M., & Strosahl, K. (1996). Experimental avoidance and behavioral disorders: A functional dimensional approach to diagnosis and treatment. *Journal of Consulting and Clinical Psychology, 64,* 1152–1168.

Heimberg, R. G. (1993). Specific issues in the cognitive-behavioral treatment of social phobia. *Journal of Clinical Psychiatry, 54*(Suppl), 36–45.

Hemmings, S. M., & Stein, D. J. (2006). The current status of association studies in obsessive-compulsive disorder. *Psychiatric Clinics of North America, 29,* 411–444.

Hettema, J. M., Neale, M. C., & Kendler, K. S. (2001). A review and meta-analysis of the genetic epidemiology of anxiety disorders. *American Journal of Psychiatry, 158,* 1568–1578.

Hettema, J. M., Neale, M. C., Myers, J. M., Prescott, C. A., & Kendler, K. S. (2006). A population-based twin study of the relationship between neuroticism and internalizing disorders. *American Journal of Psychiatry, 163,* 857–864.

Hettema, J. M., Prescott, C. A., & Kendler, K. S. (2004). Genetic and environmental sources of covariation between generalized anxiety disorder and neuroticism. *American Journal of Psychiatry, 161,* 1581–1587.

Hettema, J. M., Prescott, C. A., Myers, J. M., Neale, M. C., & Kendler, K. S. (2005). The structure of genetic and environmental risk factors for anxiety disorders in men and women. *Archives of General Psychiatry, 62,* 182–189.

Hidalgo, R. B., & Davidson, J. R. (2001). Generalized anxiety disorder: An important clinical concern. *Medical Clinics of North America, 85,* 691–710.

Horwath, E., & Weissman, M. M. (2000). The epidemiology and cross-national presentation of obsessive-compulsive disorder. *Psychiatric Clinics of North America, 23,* 493–507.

Hudziak, J. J., Van Beijsterveldt, C. E., Althoff, R. R., Stanger, C., Rettew, D. C., Nelson, E. C., et al. (2004). Genetic and environmental contributions to the Child Behavior Checklist Obsessive-Compulsive Scale: A cross-cultural twin study. *Archives of General Psychiatry, 61,* 608–616.

Jardine, R., Martin, N. G., & Henderson, A. S. (1984). Genetic covariation between neuroticism and the symptoms of anxiety and depression. *Genetic Epidemiology, 1*(2), 89–107.

Judd, L. L., Kessler, R. C., Paulus, M. P., Zeller, P. V., Wittchen, H. U., & Kunovac, J. L. (1998). Comorbidity as a fundamental feature of generalized anxiety disorders: Results from the National Comorbidity Study (NCS). *Acta Psychiatrica Scandinavica, Supplementum, 393,* 6–11.

Kaufman, J., Yang, B. Z., Douglas-Palumberi, H., Grasso, D., Lipschitz, D., Houshyar, S., et al. (2006). Brain-derived neurotrophic factor-5-HTTLPR gene interactions and environmental modifiers of depression in children. *Biological Psychiatry, 59,* 673–680.

Kendler, K. S., Gardner, C. O., Gatz, M., & Pedersen, N. L. (2007). The sources of co-morbidity between major depression and generalized anxiety disorder in a Swedish national twin sample. *Psychological Medicine, 37,* 453–462.

Kendler, K. S., & Greenspan, R. J. (2006). The nature of genetic influences on behavior: Lessons from "simpler" organisms. *American Journal of Psychiatry, 163,* 1683–1694.

Kendler, K. S., Karkowski, L. M., & Prescott, C. A. (1999). Fears and phobias: Reliability and heritability. *Psychological Medicine, 29,* 539–553.

Kendler, K. S., Myers, J., Prescott, C. A., & Neale, M. C. (2001). The genetic epidemiology of irrational fears and phobias in men. *Archives of General Psychiatry, 58,* 257–265.

Kendler, K. S., Neale, M. C., Kessler, R. C., Heath, A. C., & Eaves, L. J. (1992). The genetic epidemiology of phobias in women: The interrelationship of agoraphobia, social phobia, situational phobia, and simple phobia. *Archives of General Psychiatry, 49,* 273–281.

Kendler, K. S., Prescott, C. A., Myers, J., & Neale, M. C. (2003). The structure of genetic and environmental risk factors for common psychiatric and substance use disorders in men and women. *Archives of General Psychiatry, 60,* 929–937.

Kennedy, J. L., Neves-Pereira, M., King, N., Lizak, M. V., Basile, V. S., Chartier, M. J., et al. (2001). Dopamine system genes not linked to social phobia. *Psychiatric Genetics, 11,* 213–217.

Kessler, R. C., Berglund, P., Demler, O., Jin, R., Merikangas, K. R., & Walters, E. E. (2005). Lifetime prevalence and age-of-onset distributions of DSM-IV disorders in the National Comorbidity Survey Replication. *Archives of General Psychiatry, 62,* 593–602.

Kessler, R. C., Chiu, W. T., Demler, O., Merikangas, K. R., & Walters, E. E. (2005). Prevalence, severity, and comorbidity of 12-month DSM-IV disorders in the National Comorbidity Survey Replication. *Archives of General Psychiatry, 62,* 617–627.

Kessler, R. C., Chiu, W. T., Jin, R., Ruscio, A. M., Shear, K., & Walters, E. E. (2006). The epidemiology of panic attacks, panic disorder, and agoraphobia in the National Comorbidity Survey Replication. *Archives of General Psychiatry, 63,* 415–424.

Kessler, R. C., Davis, C. G., & Kendler, K. S. (1997). Childhood adversity and adult psychiatric disorder in the US National Comorbidity Survey. *Psychological Medicine, 27,* 1101–1119.

Kessler, R. C., Foster, C. L., Saunders, W. B., & Stang, P. E. (1995). Social consequences of psychiatric disorders: Pt. I. Educational attainment. *American Journal of Psychiatry, 152,* 1026–1032.

Kessler, R. C., McGonagle, K. A., Zhao, S., Nelson, C. B., Hughes, M., Eshleman, S., et al. (1994). Lifetime and 12-month prevalence of DSM-III-R psychiatric disorders in the United States: Results from the National Comorbidity Survey. *Archive of General Psychiatry, 51,* 8–19.

Kessler, R. C., Zhao, S., Katz, S. J., Kouzis, A. C., Frank, R. G., Edlund, M., et al. (1999). Past-year use of outpatient services for psychiatric problems in the National Comorbidity Survey. *American Journal of Psychiatry, 156,* 115–123.

Khanna, S., & Mukherjee, D. (1992). Checkers and washers: Valid subtypes of obsessive compulsive disorder. *Psychopathology, 25,* 283–288.

Klein, D. F. (1993). False suffocation alarms, spontaneous panics, and related conditions: An integrative hypothesis. *Archives of General Psychiatry, 50,* 306–317.

Knowles, J. A., Fyer, A. J., Vieland, V. J., Weissman, M. M., Hodge, S. E., Heiman, G. A., et al. (1998). Results of a genome-wide genetic screen for panic disorder. *American Journal of Medical Genetics, 81,* 139–147.

Krueger, R. F. (1999). The structure of common mental disorders. *Archives of General Psychiatry, 56,* 921–926.

Lander, E. S., & Schork, N. J. (1994, September 30). Genetic dissection of complex traits. *Science, 265,* 2037–2048.

LaSalle, V. H., Cromer, K. R., Nelson, K. N., Kazuba, D., Justement, L., & Murphy, D. L. (2004). Diagnostic interview assessed neuropsychiatric disorder comorbidity in 334 individuals with obsessive-compulsive disorder. *Depression and Anxiety, 19,* 163–173.

Leckman, J. F., Goodman, W. K., Anderson, G. M., Riddle, M. A., Chappell, P. B., McSwiggan-Hardin, M. T., et al. (1995). Cerebrospinal fluid biogenic amines in obsessive compulsive disorder, Tourette's syndrome, and healthy controls. *Neuropsychopharmacology, 12*(1), 73–86.

Leckman, J. F., Grice, D. E., Boardman, J., Zhang, H., Vitale, A., Bondi, C., et al. (1997). Symptoms of obsessive-compulsive disorder. *American Journal of Psychiatry, 154*(7), 911–917.

Lecrubier, Y., Wittchen, H. U., Faravelli, C., Bobes, J., Patel, A., & Knapp, M. (2000). A European perspective on social anxiety disorder. *European Psychiatry, 15*(1), 5–16.

Lee, C. K., Kwak, Y. S., Yamamoto, J., Rhee, H., Kim, Y. S., Han, J. H., et al. (1990). Psychiatric epidemiology in Korea: Pt. I. Gender and age differences in Seoul. *Journal of Nervous and Mental Disease, 178*(4), 242–246.

Lochner, C., Hemmings, S., Seedat, S., Kinnear, C., Schoeman, R., Annerbrink, K., et al. (2007). Genetics and personality traits in patients with social anxiety disorder: A case-control study in South Africa. *European Neuropsychopharmacology, 17,* 321–327.

Lochner, C., Hemmings, S. M., Kinnear, C. J., Moolman-Smook, J. C., Corfield, V. A., Knowles, J. A., et al. (2004). Gender in obsessive-compulsive disorder: Clinical and genetic findings. *European Neuropsychopharmacology, 14,* 105–113.

Logue, M. W., Vieland, V. J., Goedken, R. J., & Crowe, R. R. (2003). Bayesian analysis of a previously published genome screen for panic disorder reveals new and compelling evidence for linkage to chromosome 7. *American Journal of Medical Genetics, Part B: Neuropsychiatric Genetics, 121,* 95–99.

Lopez, A. D., & Murray, C. C. (1998). The global burden of disease, 1990–2020. *Nature Medicine, 4,* 1241–1243.

Lyons, M. J., Goldberg, J., Eisen, S. A., True, W., Tsuang, M. T., Meyer, J. M., et al. (1993). Do genes influence exposure to trauma? A twin study of combat. *American Journal of Medical Genetics, 48,* 22–27.

Magee, W. J., Eaton, W. W., Wittchen, H. U., McGonagle, K. A., & Kessler, R. C. (1996). Agoraphobia, simple phobia, and social phobia in the National Comorbidity Survey. *Archives of General Psychiatry, 53,* 159–168.

Malizia, A. L., Cunningham, V. J., Bell, C. J., Liddle, P. F., Jones, T., & Nutt, D. J. (1998). Decreased brain GABA(A)-benzodiazepine receptor binding in panic disorder: Preliminary results from a quantitative PET study. *Archives of General Psychiatry, 55,* 715–720.

Mannuzza, S., Schneier, F. R., Chapman, T. F., Liebowitz, M. R., Klein, D. F., & Fyer, A. J. (1995). Generalized social phobia: Reliability and validity. *Archives of General Psychiatry, 52,* 230–237.

Markowitz, J. S., Weissman, M. M., Ouellette, R., Lish, J. D., & Klerman, G. L. (1989). Quality of life in panic disorder. *Archive of General Psychiatry, 46,* 984–992.

Marks, I. M. (1970). The classification of phobic disorders. *British Journal of Psychiatry: Journal of Mental Science, 116,* 377–386.

Marks, I. M. (1986). Genetics of fear and anxiety disorders. *British Journal of Psychiatry: Journal of Mental Science, 149,* 406–418.

Mataix-Cols, D., Rauch, S. L., Manzo, P. A., Jenike, M. A., & Baer, L. (1999). Use of factor-analyzed symptom dimensions to predict outcome with serotonin reuptake inhibitors and placebo in the treatment of obsessive-compulsive disorder. *American Journal of Psychiatry, 156,* 1409–1416.

Mataix-Cols, D., Rosario-Campos, M. C., & Leckman, J. F. (2005). A multidimensional model of obsessive-compulsive disorder. *American Journal of Psychiatry, 162,* 228–238.

Mataix-Cols, D., Wooderson, S., Lawrence, N., Brammer, M. J., Speckens, A., & Phillips, M. L. (2004). Distinct neural correlates of washing, checking, and hoarding symptom dimensions in obsessive-compulsive disorder. *Archive of General Psychiatry, 61,* 564–576.

Mathew, S. J., Coplan, J. D., & Gorman, J. M. (2001). Neurobiological mechanisms of social anxiety disorder. *American Journal of Psychiatry, 158,* 1558–1567.

McGue, M., Gottesman, II., & Rao, D. C. (1983). The transmission of schizophrenia under a multifactorial threshold model. *American Journal of Human Genetics, 35,* 1161–1178.

Mendlewicz, J., Papadimitriou, G. N., & Wilmotte, J. (1993). Family study of panic disorder: Comparison with generalized anxiety disorder, major depression and normal subjects. *Psychiatric Genetics, 3,* 73–78.

Merikangas, K. R., Zhang, H., Avenevoli, S., Acharyya, S., Neuenschwander, M., & Angst, J. (2003). Longitudinal trajectories of depression and anxiety in a prospective community study: The Zurich Cohort Study. *Archives of General Psychiatry, 60,* 993–1000.

Miguel, E. C., Leckman, J. F., Rauch, S. L., do Rosario-Campos, M. C., Hounie, A. G., Mercadante, M. T., et al. (2005). Obsessive-compulsive disorder phenotypes: Implications for genetic studies. *Molecular Psychiatry, 10,* 258–275.

Mineka, S., Davidson, M., Cook, M., & Keir, R. (1984). Observational conditioning of snake fear in rhesus monkeys. *Journal of Abnormal Psychology, 93,* 355–372.

Minichiello, W. E., Baer, L., Jenike, M. A., & Holland, A. (1990). Age of onset of major subtypes of obsessive-compulsive disorder. *Journal of Anxiety Disorders, 4,* 147–150.

Muris, P., Schmidt, H., & Merckelbach, H. (1999). The structure of specific phobia symptoms among children and adolescents. *Behaviour Research and Therapy, 37,* 863–868.

Murphy, D. L., Uhl, G. R., Holmes, A., Ren-Patterson, R., Hall, F. S., Sora, I., et al. (2003). Experimental gene interaction studies with SERT mutant mice as models for human polygenic and epistatic traits and disorders. *Genes, Brain, and Behavior, 2,* 350–364.

Nardi, A. E., Valenca, A. M., Nascimento, I., Freire, R. C., Veras, A. B., de-Melo-Neto, V. L., et al. (2007). A caffeine challenge test in panic disorder patients, their healthy first-degree relatives, and healthy controls. *Depression and Anxiety.*

Nestadt, G., Bienvenu, O. J., Cai, G., Samuels, J., & Eaton, W. W. (1998). Incidence of obsessive-compulsive disorder in adults. *Journal of Nervous and Mental Disease, 186,* 401–406.

Nestadt, G., Lan, T., Samuels, J., Riddle, M. A., Bienvenu, O. J., III, Liang, K. Y., et al. (2000). Complex segregation analysis provides compelling evidence for a major gene underlying obsessive-compulsive disorder and for heterogeneity by sex. *American Journal of Medical Genetics, 67,* 1611–1616.

Nestadt, G., Samuels, J., Riddle, M., Bienvenu, O. J., III, Liang, K. Y., LaBuda, M., et al. (2000). A family study of obsessive-compulsive disorder. *Archives of General Psychiatry, 57,* 358–363.

Ogliari, A., Citterio, A., Zanoni, A., Fagnani, C., Patriarca, V., Cirrincione, R., et al. (2006). Genetic and environmental influences on anxiety dimensions in Italian twins evaluated with the SCARED questionnaire. *Journal of Anxiety Disorders, 20,* 760–777.

Ohara, K., Suzuki, Y., Ochiai, M., Tsukamoto, T., Tani, K., & Ohara, K. (1999). A variable-number-tandem-repeat of the serotonin transporter gene and anxiety disorders. *Progress in Neuro-Psychopharmacology and Biological Psychiatry, 23,* 55–65.

Ohman, A. (1986). Face the beast and fear the face: Animal and social fears as prototypes for evolutionary analyses of emotion. *Psychophysiology, 23,* 123–145.

Ozaki, N., Goldman, D., Kaye, W. H., Plotnicov, K., Greenberg, B. D., Lappalainen, J., et al. (2003). Serotonin transporter missense mutation associated with a complex neuropsychiatric phenotype. *Molecular Psychiatry, 8,* 933–936.

Pato, M. T., Pato, C. N., & Pauls, D. L. (2002). Recent findings in the genetics of OCD. *Journal of Clinical Psychiatry, 63*(Suppl, 6), 30–33.

Perusse, L., Rice, T., Despres, J. P., Rao, D. C., & Bouchard, C. (1997). Cross-trait familial resemblance for body fat and blood lipids: Familial correlations in the Quebec Family Study. *Arteriosclerosis, Thrombosis, and Vascular Biology, 17,* 3270–3277.

Pine, D. S., Cohen, P., Gurley, D., Brook, J., & Ma, Y. (1998). The risk for early-adulthood anxiety and depressive disorders in adolescents with anxiety and depressive disorders. *Archives of General Psychiatry, 55,* 56–64.

Pinto, A., Mancebo, M. C., Eisen, J. L., Pagano, M. E., & Rasmussen, S. A. (2006). The Brown Longitudinal Obsessive Compulsive Study: Clinical features and symptoms of the sample at intake. *Journal of Clinical Psychiatry, 67,* 703–711.

Rapee, R. M., & Melville, L. F. (1997). Recall of family factors in social phobia and panic disorder: Comparison of mother and offspring reports. *Depression and Anxiety, 5,* 7–11.

Rasmussen, S. A., & Eisen, J. L. (1990). Epidemiology of obsessive compulsive disorder. *Journal of Clinical Psychiatry, 51*(Suppl), 10–13; discussion 14.

Rasmussen, S. A., & Tsuang, M. T. (1984). The epidemiology of obsessive compulsive disorder. *Journal of Clinical Psychiatry, 45,* 450–457.

Rauch, S. L., Dougherty, D. D., Shin, L. M., Alpert, N. M., Manzo, P., Leahy, L., et al. (1998). Neural correlates of factoranalyzed OCD symptom dimensions: A PET study. *CNS Spectrum, 3,* 37–43.

Regier, D. A., Rae, D. S., Narrow, W. E., Kaelber, C. T., & Schatzberg, A. F. (1998). Prevalence of anxiety disorders and their comorbidity with mood and addictive disorders. *British Journal of Psychiatry,* (Suppl, 34), 24–28.

Ressler, K. J., & Mayberg, H. S. (2007). Targeting abnormal neural circuits in mood and anxiety disorders: From the laboratory to the clinic. *Nature Neuroscience, 10,* 1116–1124.

Retey, J. V., Adam, M., Khatami, R., Luhmann, U. F., Jung, H. H., Berger, W., et al. (2007). A genetic variation in the adenosine A2A receptor gene

(ADORA2A) contributes to individual sensitivity to caffeine effects on sleep. *Clinical Pharmacology and Therapeutics, 81,* 692–698.

Rickels, K., & Schweizer, E. (1990). Clinical overview of serotonin reuptake inhibitors. *Journal of Clinical Psychiatry, 51*(Suppl, B), 9–12.

Risch, N., & Merikangas, K. (1996, September 13). The future of genetic studies of complex human diseases. *Science, 273,* 1516–1517.

Robins, L. R., & Regier, D. (1991). *Psychiatric disorders in America: The epidemiologic catchment area study.* New York: Free Press.

Rosenberg, D. R., Averbach, D. H., O'Hearn, K. M., Seymour, A. B., Birmaher, B., & Sweeney, J. A. (1997). Oculomotor response inhibition abnormalities in pediatric obsessive-compulsive disorder. *Archives of General Psychiatry, 54,* 831–838.

Samochowiec, J., Syrek, S., Michal, P., Ryzewska-Wodecka, A., Samochowiec, A., Horodnicki, J., et al. (2004). Polymorphisms in the serotonin transporter and monoamine oxidase A genes and their relationship to personality traits measured by the Temperament and Character Inventory and NEO Five-Factor Inventory in healthy volunteers. *Neuropsychobiology, 50,* 174–181.

Samuels, J., Shugart, Y. Y., Grados, M. A., Willour, V. L., Bienvenu, O. J., Greenberg, B. D., et al. (2007). Significant linkage to compulsive hoarding on chromosome 14 in families with obsessive-compulsive disorder: Results from the OCD Collaborative Genetics Study. *American Journal of Psychiatry, 164,* 493–499.

Savage, C. R., Baer, L., Keuthen, N. J., Brown, H. D., Rauch, S. L., & Jenike, M. A. (1999). Organizational strategies mediate nonverbal memory impairment in obsessive-compulsive disorder. *Biological Psychiatry, 45,* 905–916.

Saxena, S., & Maidment, K. M. (2004). Treatment of compulsive hoarding. *Journal of Clinical Psychology, 60,* 1143–1154.

Schmidt, N. B., Kotov, R., & Joiner, T. E. (2004). *Taxometrics: Toward a new diagnostic scheme for psychopathology* (1st ed.). Washington, DC: American Psychological Association.

Schneier, F. R., Heckelman, L. R., Garfinkel, R., Campeas, R., Fallon, B. A., Gitow, A., et al. (1994). Functional impairment in social phobia. *Journal of Clinical Psychiatry, 55,* 322–331.

Schneier, F. R., Johnson, J., Hornig, C. D., Liebowitz, M. R., & Weissman, M. M. (1992). Social phobia: Comorbidity and morbidity in an epidemiologic sample. *Archives of General Psychiatry, 49,* 282–288.

Schneier, F. R., Liebowitz, M. R., Abi-Dargham, A., Zea-Ponce, Y., Lin, S. H., & Laruelle, M. (2000). Low dopamine D(2) receptor binding potential in social phobia. *American Journal of Psychiatry, 157,* 457–459.

Schweizer, E., & Rickels, K. (1997). Strategies for treatment of generalized anxiety in the primary care setting. *Journal of Clinical Psychiatry, 58*(Suppl, 3), 27–31; discussion 32–23.

Shih, R. A., Belmonte, P. L., & Zandi, P. P. (2004). A review of the evidence from family, twin and adoption studies for a genetic contribution to adult psychiatric disorders. *International Review of Psychiatry, 16,* 260–283.

Shugart, Y. Y., Samuels, J., Willour, V. L., Grados, M. A., Greenberg, B. D., Knowles, J. A., et al. (2006). Genomewide linkage scan for obsessive-compulsive disorder: Evidence for susceptibility loci on chromosomes 3q, 7p, 1q, 15q, and 6q. *Molecular Psychiatry, 11,* 763–770.

Simon, G. E., Von Korff, M., Saunders, K., Miglioretti, D. L., Crane, P. K., van Belle, G., et al. (2006). Association between obesity and psychiatric disorders in the US adult population. *Archives of General Psychiatry, 63,* 824–830.

Smoller, J. W., & Tsuang, M. T. (1998). Panic and phobic anxiety: Defining phenotypes for genetic studies. *American Journal of Psychiatry, 155,* 1152–1162.

Stein, M. B., Chartier, M. J., Hazen, A. L., Kozak, M. V., Tancer, M. E., Lander, S., et al. (1998). A direct-interview family study of generalized social phobia. *American Journal of Psychiatry, 155,* 90–97.

Stein, M. B., Chartier, M. J., Kozak, M. V., King, N., & Kennedy, J. L. (1998). Genetic linkage to the serotonin transporter protein and 5HT2A receptor genes excluded in generalized social phobia. *Psychiatry Research, 81,* 283–291.

Stein, M. B., Chartier, M. J., Lizak, M. V., & Jang, K. L. (2001). Familial aggregation of anxiety-related quantitative traits in generalized social phobia: Clues to understanding "disorder" heritability? *American Journal of Medical Genetics, 105,* 79–83.

Stein, M. B., Jang, K. L., & Livesley, W. J. (2002). Heritability of social anxiety-related concerns and personality characteristics: A twin study. *Journal of Nervous and Mental Disease, 190,* 219–224.

Stein, M. B., & Kean, Y. M. (2000). Disability and quality of life in social phobia: Epidemiologic findings. *American Journal of Psychiatry, 157,* 1606–1613.

Summerfeldt, L. J., Richter, M. A., Antony, M. M., & Swinson, R. P. (1999). Symptom structure in obsessive-compulsive disorder: A confirmatory factor-analytic study. *Behaviour Research and Therapy, 37,* 297–311.

Sundet, J. M., Skre, I., Okkenhaug, J. J., & Tambs, K. (2003). Genetic and environmental causes of the interrelationships between self-reported fears: A study of a non-clinical sample of Norwegian identical twins and their families. *Scandinavian Journal of Psychology, 44,* 97–106.

Tiihonen, J., Kuikka, J., Bergstrom, K., Lepola, U., Koponen, H., & Leinonen, E. (1997). Dopamine reuptake site densities in patients with social phobia. *American Journal of Psychiatry, 154,* 239–242.

Tsuang, M. T., Faraone, S. V., & Lyons, M. J. (1993). Identification of the phenotype in psychiatric genetics. *European Archives of Psychiatry and Clinical Neuroscience, 243*(3–4), 131–142.

van den Heuvel, O. A., van de Wetering, B. J., Veltman, D. J., & Pauls, D. L. (2000). Genetic studies of panic disorder: A review. *Journal of Clinical Psychiatry, 61,* 756–766.

Weissman, M. M. (1990). Epidemiology of panic disorder and agoraphobia. *Psychiatric Medicine, 8*(2), 3–13.

Weissman, M. M. (1991). Panic disorder: Impact on quality of life. *Journal of Clinical Psychiatry, 52*(Suppl), 6–8, 9.

Weissman, M. M., Bland, R. C., Canino, G. J., Greenwald, S., Hwu, H. G., Lee, C. K., et al. (1994). The cross national epidemiology of obsessive compulsive disorder: The Cross National Collaborative Group. *Journal of Clinical Psychiatry, 55*(Suppl), 5–10.

Weissman, M. M., Gross, R., Fyer, A., Heiman, G. A., Gameroff, M. J., Hodge, S. E., et al. (2004). Interstitial cystitis and panic disorder: A potential genetic syndrome. *Archives of General Psychiatry, 61,* 273–279.

Weissman, M. M., Wickramaratne, P., Adams, P. B., Lish, J. D., Horwath, E., Charney, D., et al. (1993). The relationship between panic disorder and major depression: A new family study. *Archives of General Psychiatry, 50,* 767–780.

Wendland, J. R., Kruse, M. R., Cromer, K. R., & Murphy, D. L. (2007). A large case-control study of common functional SLC6A4 and BDNF variants in obsessive-compulsive disorder. *Neuropsychopharmacology.*

Wittchen, H. U. (2002). Generalized anxiety disorder: Prevalence, burden, and cost to society. *Depression and Anxiety, 16,* 162–171.

You, J. S., Hu, S. Y., Chen, B., & Zhang, H. G. (2005). Serotonin transporter and tryptophan hydroxylase gene polymorphisms in Chinese patients with generalized anxiety disorder. *Psychiatric Genetics, 15,* 7–11.

Zhang, J. S., Jin, X. M., Zhou, X. D., Shen, L. X., Huang, H., & Shen, X. M. (2005). Anxiety state and its related factors in Shanghai high school students. *Zhonghua Yu Fang Yi Xue Za Zhi, 39,* 348–351.

Zohar, A. H., Dina, C., Rosolio, N., Osher, Y., Gritsenko, I., Bachner-Melman, R., et al. (2003). Tridimensional personality questionnaire trait of harm avoidance (anxiety proneness) is linked to a locus on chromosome 8p21. *American Journal of Medical Genetics, Part B: Neuropsychiatric Genetics, 117,* 66–69.

Zuckerman, M. (1999). Diathesis-stress models. In *Vulnerability to psychopathology: A biosocial model* (pp. 3–23). Washington, DC: American Psychological Association.

Chapter 57

Neurobiology of Psychopathy: A Two Process Theory

CHRISTOPHER J. PATRICK AND EDWARD M. BERNAT

The goal of basic human neuroscience research is to understand psychological processes in terms of the structure and functioning of underlying neurobiological systems. In parallel with this, the aim of applied clinical neuroscience is to understand problem behaviors and syndromes in terms of core processes and their neurobiological substrates. A number of challenges exist to understanding traditional mental disorders in neuroscientific terms. One of the most significant is that mental disorder syndromes represent crude targets for neurobiological study: They manifest in diverse ways clinically (phenotypically) and they show frequent overlap (comorbidity) rather than occurring in isolation from one another. Here, using the syndrome of *psychopathy* (psychopathic personality) as an example, we argue that progress toward a neuroscientific understanding of mental disorders may in some cases require us to reconceptualize these disorders in terms of constituent constructs with purer neurobiological referents.

The foundation for modern empirical research on psychopathy was Cleckley's classic clinical portrayal, set forth in his book *The Mask of Sanity* (1941/1976). As Cleckley described it, psychopathy is an unusual psychiatric condition that entails an inherent dualism. On one hand, psychopathic individuals present as personable, carefree, and psychologically well adjusted. They do not exhibit the salient perceptual or thought disturbance of psychotic patients or the mood or anxiety disturbance evident among neurotic patients. On the other hand, psychopathic individuals exhibit severe behavioral problems that bring them into repeated conflict with others in society—and which result in adverse personal consequences ranging from job or relationship loss to long-term institutionalization. Along

with these behavioral problems, psychopathic individuals exhibit characteristic affective features included a striking absence of guilt, remorse, or empathic concern for others.

For many years, the dominant theoretic perspective on psychopathy has been that it is a unitary syndrome that arises from a core underlying pathology or deficit. Some etiologic models of psychopathy have proposed that a basic deficit in emotional reactivity accounts for the characteristic affective, interpersonal, and behavioral features of the disorder; other models have focused on disturbances in cognitive and attentional processing as the primary underlying cause. Here, we argue that progress in understanding this somewhat paradoxical syndrome—and, in particular, progress toward understanding its etiologic foundations—can be advanced by considering psychopathy in terms of separable dispositions with distinctive neurobiological substrates. The two dispositional constructs we focus on are *trait fearlessness* (theorized to reflect under-reactivity of the brain's defensive motivational system) and *externalizing vulnerability* (presumed to reflect impairments in frontocortical systems that mediate anticipation, planfulness, and affective/behavioral control). We present evidence in support of this model from studies employing personality trait and clinical diagnostic measures, and from studies employing peripheral and electrocortical physiological measures. We argue that a two-process perspective on psychopathy can help to advance our understanding of the causal bases of the disorder, as well as clarify our thinking about phenomena such as psychopathy subtypes and "successful" psychopathy.

CONCEPTUALIZATION AND ASSESSMENT OF PSYCHOPATHY

The dominant assessment instrument in contemporary psychopathy research is the Psychopathy Checklist—Revised (PCL-R; Hare, 1991, 2003). The PCL-R was developed to identify individuals in correctional or forensic settings who

Preparation of this chapter was supported by grants MH52384, MH65137, and MH072850 from the National Institute of Mental Health, Grant R01 AA12164 from the National Institute on Alcohol Abuse and Alcoholism, and funds from the Hathaway endowment at the University of Minnesota.

qualify as psychopathic according to the conceptualization set forth by Cleckley (1941/1976). Cleckley described psychopathy as a severe underlying pathology masked by an outward appearance of good psychological health. In contrast with other psychiatric patients who present as disoriented, anxious, dysphoric, interpersonally withdrawn, or otherwise disturbed, psychopaths appear on initial impression to be alert, poised, socially adept, and generally well adjusted. It is only through repeated observation and experience across a range of settings that the severe interpersonal and behavioral maladjustment of the psychopath becomes apparent.

Cleckley formulated a list of 16 formal criteria for diagnosing psychopathic individuals. These criteria can be grouped into three categories (Patrick, 2006): (1) The first consists of indicators of positive psychological functioning (i.e., good intelligence and social charm, absence of delusions or other irrational thinking, lack of anxiousness, and low rate of suicide). The narrative descriptions of these indicators refer not just to the absence of typical mental disorder symptoms (e.g., delusions, anxiousness, depression), but the presence of psychological hardiness and adjustment: "The surface of the psychopath . . . shows up as equal to or better than normal and gives no hint at all of a disorder within. . . . His mask is that of robust mental health." (p. 383). (2) However, in contrast with this outward social appearance, the psychopath's day-to-day behavior is marked by obvious and severe maladjustment. This behavioral maladjustment component is captured by criteria reflecting impulsive antisocial actions, unreliability (i.e., reckless irresponsibility), promiscuous sexual relations, and a general failure to plan or learn from experience. (3) And third, Cleckley's diagnostic criteria included a set of items reflecting deficient emotional experience (e.g., general poverty of affect, absence of remorse, incapacity for love) and a lack of genuine interpersonal relationships (e.g., untruthfulness, disloyalty).

Cleckley maintained that individuals with the essential disposition of a psychopath could be found in the upper echelons of society as well as among society's outcasts. He presented case illustrations of "successful psychopaths" who attained high levels of accomplishment in occupations such as medicine, academia, or business. These individuals resembled unsuccessful (persistently criminal) psychopaths in terms of their blunted capacity for emotion, lack of close personal attachments, and whimsical behavioral tendencies—but were distinguished by their ability to focus for extended periods of time on activities crucial to advancement and success.

In contrast with Cleckley's criteria for psychopathy, the 20 diagnostic items of the PCL-R focus more uniformly on deviant tendencies. Specifically, the behavioral maladjustment and affective-interpersonal features included among Cleckley's criteria are well represented in the PCL-R, but the positive psychological indicators emphasized by Cleckley are not. Even the "glibness and superficial charm" item of the PCL-R (item 1), which ostensibly resembles Cleckley's "superficial charm and good intelligence" criterion, is defined in a more deviant manner—that is, reflecting an excessively talkative, slick, and insincere demeanor. Patrick (2006) attributed the absence of positive adjustment indicators in the PCL-R to the strategy that was used to select items for the original PCL. Specifically, items were chosen from a larger pool of candidate indicators to index psychopathy as a unitary construct, using global ratings of psychopathy based on Cleckley's description as the criterion. Because the majority of Cleckley's criteria (12 of 16) reflect deviancy as opposed to adjustment, it is likely that the initial pool of candidate items for the PCL included more deviance-related indicators, and that positive adjustment indicators dropped out in the process of selecting items with desirable psychometric properties (i.e., adequate item-total correlations, high overall internal consistency).

However, despite the fact that the items of the PCL (and PCL-R) were selected to index psychopathy as a unitary entity, evidence from factor analytic and correlational studies indicates that its items nonetheless tap differentiable component constructs, or factors. In addition, recent cluster analytic studies have revealed that distinctive subgroups of high PCL-R psychopaths exist with markedly different personality profiles. The next section summarizes these findings together with evidence from other relevant literatures that challenges the view that the syndrome of psychopathy is unitary.

EMPIRICAL EVIDENCE THAT PSYCHOPATHY IS NOT UNITARY

Distinctive Factors of the PCL-R

Although the PCL/PCL-R was developed to measure psychopathy as a unitary construct, factor analytic studies have revealed that it contains distinctive subgroups of items (i.e., factors) that, while correlated, nonetheless show diverging relations with external criterion variables. Most published research on the criterion-related validity of subcomponents of the PCL-R has focused on the two factors of the original PCL structural model (Hare et al., 1990; Harpur, Hakstian, & Hare, 1988). In this model, Factor 1 encompasses the interpersonal (charm, grandiosity, and deceitfulness/conning) and affective features of psychopathy (absence of remorse, empathy, and emotional depth, and blame externalization), whereas Factor 2 encompasses the antisocial deviance features (e.g., child behavior problems, impulsivity, irresponsibility, and a lack of long-term goals). Elevations on PCL-R Factor 1 are associated with higher scores on measures reflecting selfishness and exploitativeness, such as narcissistic personality and Machiavellianism (Hare, 1991; Harpur, Hare, & Hakstian, 1989; Verona, Patrick, & Joiner, 2001), and lower scores on measures of empathy (Hare, 2003). At the same time, Factor 1—in particular, its variance that is nonredundant with Factor 2—is positively correlated with measures of social dominance (Verona et al., 2001; see also Hare, 1991; Harpur et al., 1989), and in some studies, with achievement (Verona et al., 2001) and trait positive affect (Patrick, 1994). Thus, scores on Factor 1 show some relationship with adaptive personality traits. In contrast, Factor 2 of the PCL-R shows associations mainly with indicators of deviancy and maladaptive behavior, including selective positive relations with personality traits of aggression, impulsivity, and general sensation seeking (Hare, 1991; Harpur et al., 1989) and child symptoms of *DSM* antisocial personality disorder (APD); markedly stronger correlations than Factor 1 with adult APD symptoms and criminal history variables such as onset and frequency of offending (Hare, 2003; Verona et al., 2001); and robust positive associations with measures of alcohol and drug dependence (versus null associations for Factor 1; cf. Hare, 2003).

These diverging relations with other measures are highly unusual for two variables considered to be elements of a unitary construct. Especially striking are occurrences of *cooperative suppression* (Paulhus, Robins, Trzesniewski, & Tracy, 2004) in which opposing relations of the two PCL-R factors with criterion measures become stronger once their overlapping variance is removed. For example, Hicks and Patrick (2006) reported evidence of cooperative suppressor effects in the associations of the two PCL-R factors with self-report measures of fear, anxiety, and depression. In each case, after removing overlap between the PCL-R factors, the association for Factor 1 emerged as negative whereas the association for Factor 2 was positive. Cooperative suppressor effects of this kind are notable because they signify that components of a putatively one-dimensional measurement device are actually indexing separable and distinct underlying constructs (Paulhus et al., 2004). In the case of the PCL-R, the finding of suppressor effects for its two factors fits with Cleckley's original idea that the syndrome of psychopathy reflects the atypical co-occurrence in the same individual of tendencies toward psychological resiliency on one hand, and behavioral maladjustment on the other. In particular, available evidence indicates that the items of Factor 1 contain variance that is associated with adjustment-related tendencies—including

agency (dominance and achievement); positive affectivity; and low levels of fearfulness, distress, and depression.

Alternatives to the two-factor model of the PCL-R have been proposed. Cooke and Michie (2001) advanced a three-factor model in which Factor 1 is divided into separate affective and interpersonal factors and Factor 2 is limited to items reflecting impulsive-irresponsible behavioral tendencies. Hare (2003) proposed a four-factor model in which Factor 1 is parsed into Cooke and Michie's interpersonal and affective factors, and Factor 2 is parsed into one-factor mirroring Cooke and Michie's impulsive-irresponsible factor and another reflecting overt antisocial behaviors. Research examining associations separately for the interpersonal and affective components of Factor 1 indicates that it is the interpersonal component that accounts mostly for correlations with adjustment-related constructs (Hall, Benning, & Patrick, 2004).

PCL-R Psychopathy Subtypes

The unitary conceptualization of psychopathy implies that individuals scoring high on the PCL-R should comprise a relatively homogeneous group. The dominant research strategy to date in studies of psychological and neurobiological processes in psychopathy (cf. Patrick, 2006) has been to contrast extreme high and low overall PCL-R scorers under the assumption that differences in performance or reactivity on laboratory tasks will reflect some mechanism in common among high scorers. The effort to identify etiologic mechanisms underlying PCL-R psychopathy has been characterized as a search for the "core psychopathic deficit" (Lynam & Derefinko, 2006).

However, empirical evidence challenges the view that high PCL-R scorers comprise a unitary group. Using model-based cluster analysis to classify the personality profiles of male offenders with high overall scores on the PCL-R, Hicks, Markon, Patrick, Krueger, and Newman (2004) identified two subgroups with markedly different profiles: (1) an "aggressive" subgroup with high scores on negative affective traits (especially aggression and alienation) and low scores on traits reflecting planfulness and restraint, and (2) a "stable" subgroup low in stress reactivity (anxiousness) and high on traits reflecting agency (well-being, social dominance, and achievement). The ratio of aggressive to stable psychopaths in the sample was over 2:1, reflecting the fact that the PCL-R as a whole is weighted toward the detection of high impulsive-antisocial ("externalizing") individuals. Nonetheless, individuals resembling Cleckley's psychologically well-adjusted prototype were also represented among high PCL-R scorers in this offender sample. Extrapolating beyond the prison setting, we would expect individuals with this stable profile to be even more strongly represented among "successful" psychopaths who achieve positions of stature within the community (e.g., corporate executives, political leaders; see Hall & Benning, 2006; Hare, 1993; Lykken, 1995).[1]

Distinctive Factors of Psychopathy in Noncriminals: The Psychopathic Personality Inventory

An alternative, self-report based method for assessing psychopathy, developed for use in nonincarcerated populations, is the Psychopathic Personality Inventory (PPI; Lilienfeld, 1990; Lilienfeld & Andrews, 1996; Lilienfeld & Widows, 2005). In contrast with the PCL-R, the strategy used to select items for the PPI did not rely on the assumption that psychopathy is a unitary construct. Rather, a comprehensive personality-based approach was taken with the aim of assessing the full range of trait constructs embodied in Cleckley's description of psychopathy. A review of the literature was undertaken to identify all constructs with potential relevance to psychopathy and separate unidimensional subscales were developed to assess these varying constructs. Although the PPI was developed with no specific structural model of psychopathy in mind, factor analyses of its eight subscales (Benning, Patrick, Hicks, Blonigen, & Krueger, 2003; Benning, Patrick, Salekin, & Leistico, 2005; Ross, Benning, Patrick, Thompson, & Thurston, 2009) have nonetheless revealed a clear two-factor structure in which Social Potency, Stress Immunity, and Fearlessness subscales load preferentially on one factor (PPI-I) and Impulsive Nonconformity, Blame Externalization, Machiavellian Egocentricity, and Carefree Nonplanfulness subscales load on a second factor (PPI-II). Benning, Patrick, Blonigen, Hicks, and Iacono (2005) labeled these two factors *Fearless Dominance* and *Impulsive Antisociality*. Unlike PCL-R Factors 1 and 2, which are moderately correlated, the two factors of the PPI are uncorrelated. The eighth subscale of the PPI, Coldheartedness, does not load appreciably on either PPI factor.

Validation studies have reported meaningful, diverging associations for the two factors of the PPI with a variety of external criterion measures (Benning, Patrick, Blonigen, et al., 2005; Benning et al., 2003; Benning, Patrick, Salekin, et al., 2005; Blonigen et al., 2005; Patrick, Edens, Poythress, & Lilienfeld, 2006; Ross et al., 2009). In these studies, the correlates of PPI Factors 1 and 2 have largely mirrored those of the unique variance in PCL-R Factor 1 (its interpersonal component, in particular) and of Factor 2, respectively. Specifically, high scores on PPI-I are associated with better psychological and social adaptation as well as with tendencies toward narcissism, thrill-seeking, and low empathy, whereas scores on PPI-II are more generally indicative of psychological and behavioral maladjustment—including impulsiveness and aggression, child and adult antisocial deviance, alcohol and drug problems, heightened anxiousness and somatic complaints, and suicidal ideation.

However, the two factors of the PPI are by no means identical to the two PCL-R factors (cf. Benning, Patrick, Blonigen, et al., 2005). The PPI factors are derived from self-report, whereas the PCL-R factors are derived from clinical diagnostic assessment. The PPI factors are independent of one another, whereas the PCL-R factors are moderately intercorrelated. Associations with adjustment-related variables (e.g., social dominance, resiliency) tend to be markedly stronger for PPI-I than for PCL-R Factor 1, and emerge clearly in simple (zero-order) correlations. In sum, the two factors of the PPI index major components of the psychopathy construct in a more clearly differentiated way than the two correlated factors of the PCL-R. This is probably due to differences in how the two instruments were developed: Whereas the PCL-R was developed to index a putatively unidimensional target construct, the PPI was developed to comprehensively assess the spectrum of psychopathy-related traits. In particular, PPI-I taps the positive adjustment features of psychopathy highlighted by Cleckley more robustly and distinctively than Factor 1 of the PCL-R.

Atypical Relations between Externalizing and Internalizing Tendencies in Psychopathy

An additional source of evidence regarding the nonunitary nature of the psychopathy construct comes from research examining patterns of comorbidity among diagnostic syndromes in the *DSM*. It is well known that behavior problems in children cluster around two correlated factors, labeled internalizing and externalizing (Achenbach & Edelbrock, 1978). Internalizing problems in childhood and adolescence are marked by symptoms of anxiety, dysphoria, and social withdrawal, whereas externalizing problems

---

[1]Skeem, Johansson, Andershed, Kerr, and Eno Louden (2007) also found evidence for two distinct subgroups of high PCL-R violent offenders from a model-based cluster analysis of PCL-R facet scores (Interpersonal, Affective, Lifestyle, Antisocial; Hare, 2003) along with scores on a self-report measure of trait anxiety. Although comparable in PCL-R facet score elevations, the two subgroups differed dramatically in average anxiety scale scores. The authors labeled the low- and high-anxious subgroups "primary" and "secondary," respectively, reflecting longstanding terminology in the literature (cf. Poythress & Skeem, 2006)—and made note of their resemblance to the stable and aggressive subgroups identified by Hicks et al. (2004).

are expressed in terms of impulsiveness, aggression, and delinquent acts. In parallel with this, factor analytic studies of adult mental disorders (e.g., Krueger, 1999; Vollebergh et al., 2001) have yielded evidence of internalizing and externalizing factors underlying the most prevalent disorders within the *DSM*—with the internalizing factor reflecting systematic comorbidity among mood and anxiety disorders, and the externalizing factor reflecting systematic comorbidity among APD, alcohol dependence, and drug dependence. Notably, these two broad dimensions of psychopathology—whether derived from child or adult diagnostic data—show a moderate *positive* relationship with one another, rather than being uncorrelated (orthogonal) or inversely correlated (bipolar). That is, as a general rule, children and adults who exhibit more externalizing symptomatology (rebelliousness, rule-breaking, aggression, substance use/abuse) tend also to exhibit more internalizing symptomatology (mood and anxiety disorder symptoms).

However, psychopathic individuals present a salient exception to this rule: They exhibit severe impulsive-externalizing behavior (including, in Cleckley's [1976] words, "inadequately motivated antisocial behavior" [p. 343] and "fantastic and uninviting behavior under the influence of alcohol and sometimes without" [p. 355]) without accompanying internalizing symptomatology (i.e., "absence of nervousness or psychoneurotic manifestations" [p. 340]). Scores on the PCL-R as a whole are generally uncorrelated with measures of anxiety and depression (Hare, 2003) and scores on its two factors show opposing relations with such measures, particularly after the overlapping variance between the two factors is removed (Hicks & Patrick, 2006): Consistent with Cleckley's portrayal, relations for Factor 1 are negative; in contrast, consistent with evidence that PCL-R Factor 2 indexes the broad externalizing factor of *DSM* psychopathology (Patrick, Hicks, Krueger, & Lang, 2005), relations for this factor are positive. Scores on the two corresponding factors of the PPI likewise show opposing relations with measures of anxiety and depression (Benning, Patrick, Blonigen, et al., 2005; Blonigen et al., 2005).

Why are externalizing and internalizing tendencies, in contrast with the norm, uncoupled in psychopathy? Our theoretical perspective is that the classic syndrome of psychopathy as described by Cleckley reflects the confluence within the same individual of two distinctive etiologic processes—one involving a lack of normal defensive (fear) reactivity that confers an immunity to internalizing problems, and the other a dispositional weakness in impulse control that confers a vulnerability to externalizing problems. The next section articulates this two-process conceptualization in greater detail.

TWO-PROCESS THEORY OF PSYCHOPATHY

The two-process theory of psychopathy proposes that the disorder can be understood in terms of separable etiologic processes that reflect deviations in distinct underlying neurobiological systems. The processes on which the theory focuses are trait fearlessness and externalizing vulnerability. Our position contrasts with the unitary-syndrome perspective, which posits that a single underlying deficit or impairment can account for the features of the disorder as a whole. Examples of the unitary-syndrome perspective include Lykken's low fear hypothesis (Lykken, 1957, 1995) and Newman's response modulation hypothesis (Newman, 1998; Patterson & Newman, 1993).

The two-process conceptualization of psychopathy emerged out of research investigating emotional deficits in psychopathy using picture viewing and image processing paradigms (Patrick, Bradley, & Lang, 1993; Patrick, Cuthbert, & Lang, 1994).[2] The findings of these studies suggested that the core affective-interpersonal features of psychopathy were associated with an absence of normal defensive activation in the face of explicit (visual) aversive cues, whereas the behavioral deviance features were associated with a lack of normal arousal during processing of internal (imaginal) affective representations. Subsequently, Patrick (1994) reported further evidence tying deficits in aversive startle potentiation specifically to Factor 1 of the PCL-R. Patrick and Lang (1999) posited that the affective and interpersonal features of psychopathy associated with PCL-R Factor 1 reflect an underlying weakness in the brain's core defensive motivational system—akin to the fear deficit postulated by Lykken (1995)—whereas the behavioral dyscontrol associated with PCL-R factor 2 reflects an impairment in higher representational systems that interact with primary motivational systems—akin to the impairment in higher-level processing (and affiliated behavioral disinhibition) that occurs with acute alcohol intoxication.

Levenston, Patrick, Bradley, and Lang (2000) presented evidence that the aberrant startle pattern exhibited by criminal psychopaths in the Patrick et al. (1993) study and replicated subsequently by other investigators (e.g., Herpertz et al., 2001; Pastor, Molto, Vila, & Lang, 2003; Sutton, Vitale, & Newman, 2002) arises from a heightened threshold for shifting from attentional engagement (orienting) to defensive activation. Vanman, Mejia, Dawson, Schell, and Raine (2003) reported an absence of startle potentiation specifically in relation to high scores on Factor 1 of the

---

[2]A complementary perspective, drawing on findings from the psychophysiological literature as well as concepts from the child temperament literature, was advanced by Fowles and Dindo (2006).

PCL-R in a sample of nonincarcerated individuals from the community. Similarly, Benning, Patrick, and Iacono (2005) reported a deviant pattern of startle modulation resembling that of incarcerated psychopaths in participants from the community who scored at the high extreme on the Fearless Dominance factor of the PPI (PPI-I). In contrast, individuals with extreme elevations on the Impulsive Antisociality factor (PPI-II) showed a normal affect-startle pattern.

With regard to Factor 2 of the PCL-R, Patrick, Hicks, Krueger, and Lang (2005) demonstrated a close association between this component of psychopathy and externalizing factor scores estimated from child and adult symptoms of APD, measures of alcohol and drug abuse/dependence, and scores on a broad self-report index of impulsivity and sensation seeking. The association between scores on the externalizing factor and scores on PCL-R Factor 2, controlling for variance shared with Factor 1, was extremely high, whereas the unique variance in Factor 1 was unrelated to externalizing. Paralleling this, Blonigen et al. (2005) reported a robust positive association between externalizing factor scores computed from *DSM* diagnostic variables and scores on the Impulsive Antisociality factor of the PPI in both women and men. Corresponding associations for the Fearless Dominance factor of the PPI were low, and significant only for men.

As described more fully in subsequent sections, the general propensity toward externalizing psychopathology is presumed to reflect impairments in anterior brain systems that function to regulate affect and behavior in situations involving complex or competing stimulus contingencies. Patrick (2007) postulated that the antisocial deviance features embodied in PCL-R Factor 2 reflect similar underlying impairments. Consistent with this perspective, antisocial deviance in childhood and adulthood is reliably associated with deficits on neuropsychological measures of frontal lobe function (Morgan & Lilienfeld, 2000). In addition, Molto, Poy, Segarra, Pastor, and Montanes (2007) recently demonstrated that Factor 2 of the PCL-R accounts for enhanced errors of commission in a conflict (reward-punishment) task that Newman and colleagues had used previously to infer response modulation deficits in PCL-R defined psychopaths.

Our position, emerging from the evidence reviewed in the foregoing sections, is that scientific understanding of the etiology and development of psychopathy can be advanced by focusing directly on dispositional fear and externalizing vulnerability as targets of study. The two broad factors of Hare's PCL-R, and the two somewhat parallel factors of Lilienfeld's PPI, can be viewed as imperfect manifest (phenotypic) indicators of these two underlying etiologic (genotypic) dispositions. From this perspective, a clearer understanding of etiological mechanisms underlying psychopathy can be gained by directly assessing individuals (from community as well as clinical/forensic settings) on dimensions of fear/fearlessness and externalizing, and investigating differences in psychological processing associated with varying positions along these dimensions using physiological measures. We believe this approach will also prove valuable in elucidating phenomena such as psychopathy subtypes and noncriminal ("successful") psychopaths. The remainder of this chapter reviews research work done to: (a) refine measurement of the constructs of dispositional fear and externalizing vulnerability, and (b) identify physiological response indicators of these constructs as a step toward understanding the brain processes that underlie them.

REFINING THE MEASUREMENT OF TRAIT FEAR AND EXTERNALIZING CONSTRUCTS

Evidence for a Continuous Bipolar Dimension Underlying Psychometric Measures of Fear and Fearlessness

As noted earlier, available data indicate that the two factors of Lilienfeld's (1990) PPI tap distinctive facets of the psychopathy construct. PPI-I (aka "Fearless Dominance") is negatively associated with self-report measures of fearfulness and distress (Benning, Patrick, Blonigen, et al., 2005), with diagnostic symptoms of internalizing disorders (Blonigen et al., 2005), and with fear-potentiated startle (Benning, Patrick, & Iacono, 2005). To further clarify the construct underlying PPI-I, we used principal components analysis to evaluate whether this factor of the PPI would load with other established indicators of fear and fearlessness on a common trait dimension. We utilized data from two separate samples (male and female college students, $N = 346$; male prisoners, $N = 218$) in which scores on PPI-I (estimated from scores on Tellegen's [1982] Multidimensional Personality Questionnaire; cf. Benning, Patrick, Blonigen, et al., 2005) were available along with another measure of fearlessness, the thrill and adventure seeking subscale of the Sensation Seeking Scale (SSS-tas; Zuckerman, 1979), and two measures of fearfulness, the Fear Survey Schedule (FSS; Arrindell, Emmelkamp, & van der Ende, 1984) and the fearfulness subscale of the Emotionality-Activity-Sociability Temperament Inventory (EAS-fear; Buss & Plomin, 1984). In each participant sample, an exploratory principal components analysis of these four indicators revealed a single dominant factor on which all indicators loaded substantially (from $-.63$ to $+.80$) and which accounted for over 50% of the variance across indicators. The implication is that the PPI-I construct operates as a low pole indicator of a broad individual differences dimension ranging from extreme fearlessness at one end to extreme fearfulness at the other. Given that the findings were so similar in these two distinct participant samples, we expected that this trait fear factor would likewise emerge from a structural analysis of similar indicators in other participant samples.

To address this possibility, and also to assess etiologic contributions to the broad trait fear factor, we collected data for various fear and fearlessness measures in a large, mixed-gender sample ($N = 2,572$) of identical and fraternal twins recruited from the community (Kramer, Patrick, Bayevsky, & Krueger, 2008). The following scales were administered: FSS, EAS-fear, SSS-tas, the three subscales of PPI-I (Social Potency, Stress Immunity, Fearlessness), and the four subscales (anticipatory worry; fear of uncertainty; shyness with strangers; fatigability) comprising the Harmavoidance (ha) scale of the Tridimensional Personality Questionnaire (TPQ; Cloninger, 1987). The TPQ-ha subscales were included as indicators because they are described as indexing fearfulness and sensitivity to cues for danger. Confirmatory factor analyses of these various scale measures revealed the best fit for a model of the data in which all scales loaded substantially on a general, overarching factor (trait fear), with some scales loading additionally on one of two subordinate factors (stimulation seeking, assertiveness in social situations). Consistent with expectation, fearfulness measures (FSS, EAS-fear, four TPQ-ha subscales) loaded positively ($M = +.69$) on this broad factor whereas fearlessness measures (three PPI-I scales, SSS-tas) loaded negatively ($M = -.58$).

In addition, because the participant sample for this study consisted of monozygotic (Mz) and dizygotic (Dz) twins, it was possible to estimate the proportion of variance in the broad trait fear factor that was attributable to genetic compared with environmental influences. Using standard formulae for estimating genetic and environmental contributions to a target phenotype within an Mz/Dz twin dataset (Falconer, 1989), the heritability of the broad trait fear factor (i.e., percentage of variance in scores attributable to genetic influence) was 74%, with the remaining 16% of the variance in scores attributable to nonshared environmental influence. Thus, the general disposition toward fear versus fearlessness as indexed by the broad factor underlying these various psychometric measures (which included the three subscales comprising PPI-I) appears to be a highly heritable phenotype.

Hierarchical Model of Externalizing Disorders and Traits

As noted earlier, impulse control problems of various kinds co-occur in a systematic manner such that these disorders operate as indicators of a common "externalizing" factor. Krueger et al. (2002) evaluated genetic and environmental contributions to the externalizing factor—defined as the covariance among symptoms of various *DSM* disorders (child conduct disorder, adult antisocial behavior, alcohol dependence, and drug dependence) along with a self-report measure of disinhibitory personality—in a large, mixed-gender sample of twins. More than 80% of the variance in the common externalizing factor was found to be attributable to additive genetic influence (see also: Kendler, Prescott, Myers, & Neale, 2003; Young, Stallings, Corley, Krauter, & Hewitt, 2000). The remaining variance in each primary variable not accounted for by the broad externalizing factor was attributable primarily to nonshared environmental influence—although for conduct disorder there was also a significant contribution of shared environment.

Based on these findings, Krueger et al. (2002) proposed a *hierarchical* model in which the general externalizing factor is conceptualized as a predominantly heritable vulnerability that contributes to the development of various traits and problem behaviors, with the precise phenotypic expression of this vulnerability (i.e., as subclinical disinhibitory tendencies, antisocial deviance of different sorts, or alcohol or drug problems) determined by other specific etiologic influences. Krueger, Markon, Patrick, Benning, and Kramer (2007) extended this work by developing scales to comprehensively assess the domain of externalizing problems and traits in terms of elemental constructs. Unidimensional scales were developed to measure 23 separate constructs including varying forms of impulsivity; differing types of aggression (physical, relational, and destructive); irresponsibility; rebelliousness; excitement seeking; blame externalization; and alcohol, drug, and marijuana use/problems. Confirmatory factor analyses of these 23 scales yielded evidence of a superordinate factor (externalizing) on which all subscales loaded substantially (.45 or higher), and two subordinate factors (callous aggression, addictions) that accounted for residual variance in some subscales. These findings provide further support for the idea that a common dispositional factor (externalizing) contributes to a broad spectrum of impulse control problems and affiliated traits. In addition, they suggest that separate dispositional factors shape the expression of externalizing tendencies toward callous aggression on one hand, and addictive behaviors on the other.

PHYSIOLOGICAL RESPONSE INDICATORS OF TRAIT FEAR AND EXTERNALIZING

Startle Reflex Potentiation as an Index of Trait Fear

A key method for indexing fear reactivity in both animals and humans, mentioned earlier in relation to studies of emotion in PCL-R psychopathy, is startle reflex potentiation. There is a rich literature on startle potentiation as an index of defensive reactivity in animals and humans. Davis and colleagues (e.g., Davis, 1989; Davis, Falls, Campeau, & Kim, 1993) mapped the neural circuitry of fear-potentiated startle, defined as increased magnitude of the whole-body reaction to an abrupt noise probe in the presence of a fear cue, in animals. These investigators showed that the mechanism for this effect is a pathway from the central nucleus of the amygdala to the pontine reticular node of the basic startle circuit. In unselected human participants, the startle blink response to sudden noise is reliably enhanced during viewing of aversive pictures compared with neutral pictures (Lang, 1995; Lang, Bradley, & Cuthbert, 1990). Blink potentiation is strongest for directly threatening images (e.g., aimed weapons; menacing attackers), although it also occurs to a less reliable degree for vicarious aversive scenes involving physical injury or aggression (Bernat, Patrick, & Benning, 2006; Bradley, Codispoti, Cuthbert, & Lang, 2001; Levenston et al., 2000). This effect in humans is blocked by diazepam (Patrick, Berthot, & Moore, 1996), a drug that inhibits activity in the amygdala, and which has also been shown to block fear-potentiated startle in animals (Davis, 1979). Startle reflex potentiation has also been demonstrated in other aversive cuing contexts in humans, including fear conditioning (Grillon & Davis, 1997; Hamm, Greenwald, Bradley, & Lang, 1993), stressor anticipation (Patrick & Berthot, 1995), and imagery of fearful situations (Vrana & Lang, 1990).

There is also evidence for the specificity of aversive startle potentiation as an index of fear. Davis, Walker, and Lee (1997; see also Davis, 1998) argued for the existence of two distinct systems underlying defensive reactivity: a phasic activation system, associated with the central nucleus of the amygdala, and a tonic activation system, associated with the extended amygdala—in particular, the bed nucleus of the stria terminalis (BNST). Davis et al. (1997) presented evidence that fear-potentiated startle, which involves a time-limited increase in defensive activation tied to an explicit aversive cue, is mediated by the former, whereas startle sensitization, involving a more persistent increase in negative emotional activation, is mediated by the latter. While acknowledging some interrelationship between the two systems (e.g., intense or repeated activation of the amygdala by stressful events may lead to longer-term activation of the BNST; cf. Rosen & Schulkin, 1998), Davis et al. posited that these systems play differing roles in fear and anxiety states—with the amygdala more important for cue-specific fear, and the BNST more important for nonspecific anxiety.

From this perspective, startle reflex potentiation during discrete aversive cuing holds potential as an indicator of

individual differences in fear reactivity in humans. As described earlier, research by Patrick et al. (1993) and others has demonstrated deficient startle potentiation during aversive cuing in PCL-R defined psychopaths; this deviation has been linked in particular to the affective-interpersonal (Factor 1) component of the PCL-R (Patrick, 2007), which shows negative associations with trait measures of fear and negative affectivity (Hicks & Patrick, 2006). As an illustration of this finding, subplot A of Figure 57.1 depicts average startle blink magnitude for aversive versus neutral pictures in two prisoner subgroups from the Patrick et al. (1993) study with comparably high scores on PCL-R Factor 2, but differing on PCL-R Factor 1 (i.e., low versus high).

In follow-up investigations with incarcerated male offenders, we have examined startle potentiation effects for psychopathy in relation to specific categories of aversive pictures. As noted, studies with nonclinical participants have demonstrated stronger startle potentiation effects for scenes of imminent threat or attack (e.g., guns pointed at the viewer, menacing attackers; Bernat et al., 2006; Bradley et al., 2001) than for other types of aversive scenes (e.g., snakes/spiders, physical injury, victimization). In a study of offenders, Levenston et al. (2000) reported differences between high and low PCL-R scorers in startle modulation effects for both victim scenes and threat scenes: For victim scenes, psychopaths showed startle inhibition as opposed to modest potentiation, and for threat scenes, they showed weak potentiation compared with very strong potentiation among nonpsychopaths. However, this study did not examine modulation effects in relation to the two distinct factors of the PCL-R.

Our more recent research with offenders at a state medium security prison in Minnesota (Bernat et al., 2004) has examined modulatory effects for different picture contents separately in relation to PCL-R Factor 1 and Factor 2. Test subjects were selected to represent the entire range of scores on the PCL-R, so that associations for the two PCL-R factors with startle modulation could be examined continuously and in terms of extreme groups. Participants viewed aversive pictures consisting of threat scenes and victim (physical injury, other-attack) scenes, along with neutral pictures and differing categories of pleasurable scenes. Startle potentiation scores were computed consisting of average blink magnitude for each aversive picture category (threat, victim) minus average magnitude for neutral pictures. Within the sample as a whole ($N = 107$), a significant negative relationship was found between scores on PCL-R Factor 1 and startle potentiation, for threat scenes in particular; this association was not significant for PCL-R Factor 2. Subplot B of Figure 57.1 depicts mean blink response magnitude for threat versus neutral pictures in

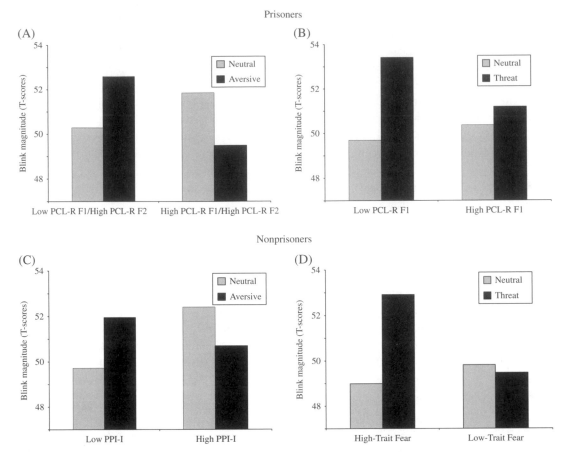

Figure 57.1   Aversive startle potentiation effects in two prisoner and two nonprisoner samples using psychopathy factor scores and trait fear scores as selection criteria for participant subgroups.

Note: **A:** Mean magnitude of startle blink responses to noise probes presented during viewing of neutral and aversive pictures in two male prisoner groups: (1) prisoners high on PCL-R Factor 2 but low on PCL-R Factor 1 ($n = 18$), and (2) prisoners high on both factors of the PCL-R ($n = 17$). Aversive pictures are of varying types (snakes, angry faces, direct threat, sickness, physical injury). Blink magnitude means are presented in T-score units ($M = 50$, $SD = 10$), based on standardization of raw magnitude scores across trials for each individual subject. Data are From "Emotion in the Criminal Psychopath: Startle Reflex Modulation," by C. J. Patrick, M. M. Bradley, and P. J. Lang, 1993, *Journal of Abnormal Psychology, 102,* 82–92. **B:** Mean blink response magnitude (in standardized T-score units) to noise probes during viewing of neutral and direct-threat (i.e., aimed weapon, menacing attacker) scenes in two male prisoner groups:

(1) prisoners low on PCL-R Factor 1, and (2) prisoners high on PCL-R Factor 1. Data are From "Exploring Mechanisms of Deviant Affect-Modulated Startle in Psychopathy," by E. M. Bernat, C. J. Patrick, B. V. Steffen, J. R. Hall, & M. Ward, 2004, *Psychophysiology, 41,* p. S40. **C:** Mean blink magnitude (in T-score units) to noise probes during viewing of neutral pictures and aversive pictures of varying types in two selected subgroups of males from the community: (1) individuals low on PPI-I, and (2) individuals high on PPI-I. Data are From "Psychopathy, Startle Blink Modulation, and Electrodermal Reactivity in Twin Men," by S. D. Benning, C. J. Patrick, and W. G. Iacono, 2005, *Psychophysiology, 42,* 753–762. **D:** Mean blink magnitude (in T-score units) to noise probes during viewing of neutral and direct-threat (weapons, attackers) scenes in two selected subgroups of college students: (1) individuals high in trait fear, and (2) individuals low in trait fear. Data are From *Startle Reflex Potentiation during Aversive Picture Viewing as an Indicator of Trait Fear,* by U. Vaidyanathan, C. J. Patrick, and E. M. Bernat, 2009, *Psychophysiology, 46,* 75–85.

offender groups comprising the lowest and highest 25% of scorers on PCL-R Factor 1 ($n = 25$ and 23, respectively). These findings provide further evidence of reductions in aversive startle potentiation specifically in relation to the affective-interpersonal (Factor 1) features of psychopathy. In addition, the fact that this association was evident especially for threat scenes supports the idea that the affective-interpersonal component of psychopathy is associated with a deficiency in cue-specific fear reactivity.

Comparable results have been reported for nonprisoner groups differing on the first (Fearless Dominance)

factor of Lilienfeld's (1990) PPI. Benning, Patrick, and Iacono (2005) examined patterns of blink reflex modulation during viewing of pleasant, neutral, and unpleasant pictures in relation to PPI factor scores in adult male participants ($N = 307$) recruited from the general community. Unpleasant pictures comprised an assortment of contents, with greater representation of victim (physical injury, disease) than threat scenes. Participants with very high scores on PPI-I showed a deviant startle pattern resembling that of offenders with high scores on PCL-R Factor 1 (i.e., an absence of fear-potentiated startle), whereas participants with very high scores on PPI-II showed no such deviation. Subplot *C* of Figure 57.1 shows mean startle blink magnitude for aversive versus neutral pictures in subgroups from this study comprising the lowest and highest 10% of PPI-I scorers ($n = 31$ per group).

Along with psychopathy, the other individual difference construct that has been associated most reliably with variations in aversive startle potentiation is fearfulness, as indexed by the Fear Survey Schedule (FSS; Arrindell et al., 1984; Wolpe & Lang, 1964). The FSS assesses reported levels of fear in relation to various specific objects and situations (e.g., insects, small animals, blood, crowds, public speaking), with total scores reflecting general fearfulness. Cook (1999) reviewed findings from six separate studies with college samples demonstrating enhanced aversive startle potentiation among individuals selected to be high on the FSS, compared with low-FSS individuals. In five of these six studies, fear-potentiated startle was assessed in a picture-viewing procedure, with the remaining study involving an imagery procedure. A related trait measure that has been examined in relation to aversive startle potentiation is the Harm Avoidance (ha) Scale of the TPQ. In two studies employing neutral and affective picture stimuli, Corr and colleagues (Corr, Kamuri, Wilson, Checkley, & Gray, 1997; Corr et al., 1995) reported that participants high on TPQ-ha showed robust startle potentiation during aversive picture viewing whereas low TPQ-ha individuals did not. This finding is especially noteworthy in light of evidence that high scores on TPQ-ha reflect tendencies opposite to those associated with high scores on PPI-I (i.e., low social dominance, high stress reactivity, and high risk aversion (Waller, Lilienfeld, Tellegen, & Lykken, 1991)).

As noted earlier, there is evidence that measures of dispositional fear and fearlessness including the FSS, TPQ-ha, and PPI-I comprise indicators of a common, bipolar trait dimension (Kramer et al., 2008). Considering this along with the aforementioned findings from startle/individual differences studies, a tenable hypothesis is that aversive startle potentiation (which has been interpreted as an index of amygdala reactivity to explicit fear cues; Davis et al., 1997; Lang et al., 1990) is a continuous physiological indicator of this bipolar trait dimension. Vaidyanathan et al. (2008) evaluated this hypothesis in a sample of undergraduate participants ($N = 88$) who were assessed with multiple trait fear and fearlessness measures (FSS, TPQ-ha subscales, EAS-fear, PPI-1 subscales, SSS-tas) and tested in an affect-startle procedure that included varying categories of aversive (threat, mutilation, victim) and pleasant pictures (erotic, action, nurturant) along with neutral pictures. Consistent with the findings of Kramer et al. (2008), a principal components analysis of these varying trait scales yielded evidence of a dominant first factor

on which all scales loaded appreciably. An omnibus index of trait fear was computed for each participant consisting of scores on the first principal component from this analysis. A robust linear association was found in the sample as a whole between trait fear and startle modulation for threat pictures in particular—the picture category, as noted earlier, that is most directly fear-relevant and yields the most reliable startle potentiation effects. Subplot *D* of Figure 57.1 shows mean startle blink magnitude for threat versus neutral pictures in subgroups comprising the lowest and highest 20% of trait fear scorers ($n = 18$ per group) from this study. The findings of this study confirm that aversive startle potentiation represents a physiological indicator of the trait fear continuum.

Brain Response Markers of Externalizing Vulnerability

Reduced P3 Amplitude

A brain response measure that has been shown to be associated with various forms of externalizing psychopathology is the P300 (or P3; see discussion that follows) component of the event-related potential (ERP). The P300 is a positive brain potential response, maximal over parietal scalp regions, that follows the occurrence of infrequent, attended targets in a stimulus sequence. It is well established that reduced amplitude of the P300 response is associated with alcohol problems and alcoholism risk. This link was first noted in work comparing abstinent alcoholics with controls (Porjesz, Begleiter, & Garozzo, 1980). Subsequent studies revealed that reduced P300 amplitude (typically assessed at parietal scalp sites) was associated not just with active symptoms, but also with risk for the development of alcohol problems. For example, children and adolescents with a paternal history of alcoholism show reliably reduced P300 compared with family negative controls (Begleiter, Porjesz, Bihari, & Kissin, 1984; Elmasian, Neville, Woods, Schuckit, & Bloom, 1982; Hill & Shen, 2002; for review, see Polich, Pollock, & Bloom, 1994). Additionally, smaller P300 amplitude prospectively predicts the later emergence of alcohol problems (Berman, Whipple, Fitch, & Noble, 1993; Hill, Steinhauer, Lowers, & Locke, 1995; Iacono, Carlson, Malone, & McGue, 2002). These results led theorists to postulate that reduced P300 response is an indicator of brain-based impairments in cognitive-executive function that confer a risk for alcohol dependence (e.g., Begleiter & Porjesz, 1999; Giancola & Tarter, 1999).

However, subsequent investigations revealed links between reduced parietal P300 response and other disorders in the externalizing spectrum besides alcohol dependence, including: drug dependence (Attou, Figiel, & Timsit-Berthier, 2001; Biggins, MacKay, Clark, & Fein,

1997; Branchey, Buydens-Branchey, & Horvath, 1993), nicotine dependence (Anokhin et al., 2000; Iacono et al., 2002), child conduct disorder (Bauer & Hesselbrock, 1999; Kim, Kim, & Kwon, 2001), and adult antisocial personality (Bauer, O'Connor, & Hesselbrock, 1994; Costa et al., 2000). In addition, reduced P300 is known to be associated with *risk* for these other disorders as well as with active symptoms (Brigham, Herning, & Moss, 1995; Iacono et al., 2002).

Taken together, findings suggest that reduced P300 amplitude reflects an underlying vulnerability not just to alcohol problems—but vulnerability to externalizing problems more generally. Patrick, Bernat et al. (2006) evaluated this hypothesis in a large sample of male twin participants (*N* = 969; median age = 17.7 years). Scores on the externalizing vulnerability factor were derived from a principal components analysis of symptoms of conduct disorder, adult antisocial behavior, alcohol dependence, drug dependence, and nicotine dependence. P300 was assessed at parietal scalp sites in a "rotated heads" visual oddball task (Begleiter et al., 1984) in which target stimuli (consisting of schematic heads) occurred on one-third of trials and nontarget stimuli (simple ovals) occurred on two-thirds of trials. Participants responded with a button press each time a head appeared and disregarded more frequently occurring ovals. Behavioral performance on the oddball task (i.e., accuracy or latency of responses to target stimuli) did not vary as a function of externalizing. However, higher scores on the externalizing factor were robustly associated with reduced amplitude of P300 to the task stimuli (see Figure 57.2). In addition, mediational analyses demonstrated that scores on the externalizing factor completely accounted for associations between individual diagnostic variables and reduced P300 amplitude.

These results indicate that P300 is an indicator of the common vulnerability that underlies antisocial syndromes and substance use disorders (i.e., the externalizing factor), rather than a marker of alcohol problems per se. Moreover, the fact that P300 amplitude, like externalizing vulnerability, is highly heritable (Katsanis, Iacono, McGue, & Carlson, 1997; O'Connor, Morzorati, Christian, & Li, 1994) raises the possibility that P300 amplitude may represent a quantitative *endophenotype* of externalizing vulnerability. An endophenotype is a biological characteristic that arises from, and thus directly reflects, an underlying genotypic predisposition (Gottesman & Shields, 1972; Iacono, 1998; John & Lewis, 1966). If reduced P300 is an endophenotype for externalizing vulnerability, it should occur at higher rates among asymptomatic individuals who are at risk for developing externalizing problems by virtue of a positive parental history of such problems (cf. Elmasian et al., 1982). Consistent with this, Iacono et al. (2002) reported

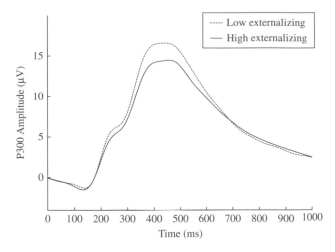

Figure 57.2 Average P300 response to visual stimuli in a two-stimulus oddball task for participants high versus low in externalizing scores.

Note: P300 waveform data are for the midline parietal (Pz) scalp site, High and low externalizing groups represent top and bottom 25% of scorers (from a sample of 969 community participants) on the first principal component derived from a PCA of DSM-III-R symptoms of conduct disorder, adult antisocial behavior, alcohol dependence, drug dependence, and nicotine dependence. Data are From "P300 Amplitude as an Indicator of Externalizing in Adolescent Males," by C. J. Patrick, E. M. Bernat, S. M. Malone, W. G. Iacono, R. F. Krueger, and M. K. McGue, 2006, *Psychophysiology, 43,* 84–92.

reduced P300 in the adolescent sons of fathers who met criteria for alcohol dependence, drug abuse/dependence, or antisocial personality, whether or not the offspring themselves met criteria for a diagnosis. In addition, they found that reduced P300 at age 17 predicted the development of externalizing problems of various kinds at age 20, even among individuals who were free from disorder at the time of P300 assessment.

Hicks et al. (2007) tested the hypothesis that reduced P300 in relation to externalizing reflects an underlying biological-genetic association by undertaking biometric (Mz/Dz twin) analyses of this association in the sample of twin participants examined by Patrick et al. (2006). The Cholesky decomposition method was used to partition the variance and covariance of P300 amplitude and externalizing scores into three sources: additive genetic (A), shared or common environment (C), and nonshared or unique environment (E). Alternative models were fit to the data using full information maximum likelihood estimation. The model that yielded the best fit to the data for each individual variable (P300, externalizing) was the AE model, indicating no shared environmental contribution to either variable. Genetic and environmental contributions to the *covariance* between P300 amplitude and externalizing were examined by comparing the fit of the AE model to that of more restrictive models. A model that required nonshared environmental factors alone to account for the association between P300 amplitude and externalizing yielded a significant reduction in fit—confirming an essential contributory role of genetic influences in the covariance between P300 amplitude and externalizing. In contrast, a model in which the covariance between P300 and externalizing was accounted for solely by genetic factors showed a slight increase in fit compared with the AE model.

The results of this study demonstrate that the association between P300 amplitude and externalizing is primarily a genetic association—implying that reduced P300 directly reflects some alteration in brain function associated with the broad, predominantly genetic vulnerability to disorders within the externalizing spectrum. What might the finding of reduced P300 response tell us about the brain mechanisms underlying this broad vulnerability? Although the P300 has been characterized for some time as a distributed brain response reflecting activity in multiple brain regions, more recent research on the neutral generators underlying P300 response supports the idea that prefrontal brain regions play a particularly important role (see, for example, Dien, Spencer, & Donchin, 2003, and Nieuwenhuis, Aston-Jones, & Cohen, 2005). In addition, follow-up research by our laboratory group has produced evidence of an enhanced relationship between externalizing scores and P300 amplitude at fronto-central compared with parietal scalp sites, particularly for novel task stimuli that are known to preferentially activate anterior brain regions.

The task procedure we have used to further investigate reduced P300 in relation to externalizing is a three-stimulus variant of the rotated heads oddball task (Bernat, Patrick, Cadwallader, van Mersbergen, & Seo, 2003). In addition to nontarget oval (70% of trials) and target "head" stimuli (15% of trials), the task includes infrequent novel stimuli (15% of trials), requiring no response. The novel stimuli consist of pleasant, neutral, and unpleasant picture stimuli selected from the International Affective Picture System (IAPS; Center for the Study of Emotion and Attention, 1999). All task stimuli occur for 100 ms, and because the primary task is to detect and respond to the target heads, the novel picture stimuli are processed incidentally. Target stimuli in a task of this kind are known to elicit a P300 response that is maximal at parietal scalp sites. In contrast, novel stimuli evoke a P300 response, termed the "novelty P3" (Courchesne, Hillyard, & Galambos, 1975) or P3a response (Squires, Squires, & Hillyard, 1975) to distinguish it from the target P300 (P3) response, that is maximal at fronto-central scalp sites. With regard to generators, evidence exists for a role of lateral prefrontal cortex in the processing of novel stimuli (see Nieuwenhuis et al., 2005) and ERP source localization work has additionally identified the anterior cingulate cortex (ACC) as contributing to the novelty P3 response (Dien et al., 2003).

Functional neuro-imaging research also implicates these two regions in novel stimulus processing, consistent with the idea that frontal brain regions are involved in the allocation of attentional resources to novel stimuli, as well as the processing of emotional cues (Fichtenholtz et al., 2004; Yamaski, LaBar, & McCarthy, 2002). The use of affective and neutral pictures as incidental, novel stimuli in this task procedure therefore provided us with an opportunity to examine automatic affective processing in relation to scores on the externalizing factor.

The strategy we have used to select subjects for recent studies of externalizing using this task procedure is to administer a 100-item screening version of the Externalizing Spectrum Inventory (Krueger et al., 2007) to students in large undergraduate classes. Scores on this screening version correlate very highly ($r = .98$) with scores on the full, 415-item Externalizing Spectrum Inventory. Individuals in the lowest and highest quartiles of the overall score distribution are over-sampled to provide low externalizing and high externalizing groups of adequate size, and in addition, individuals among the middle 50% of scorers are included to provide for supplementary correlational analyses in which the full distribution of externalizing scores is represented. Using this strategy, a total of 149 participants were selected and tested in the three-stimulus oddball task: 34 (21 female) in the low-externalizing group, 61 (34 female) in the high-externalizing group, and 54 (34 female) intermediate scorers. Brain activity was recorded from 64 scalp sites, including frontal and central as well as parietal sites.

This work has yielded a number of important findings. For ease of presentation, we focus here on results for midline anterior (FCz) and posterior (Pz) scalp sites. First, we replicated the finding of reduced P3 amplitude to target (head) stimuli in this task, both in the extreme groups analysis, and in the correlational analysis involving the full participant sample ($N = 149$). High externalizing participants showed significantly smaller P3 amplitude across scalp sites than low externalizing participants, and a significant negative correlation between externalizing scores and P3 amplitude across scalp sites was evident for the sample as a whole. This finding is important because it confirms that high scores on the Externalizing Spectrum Inventory, like high scores on the externalizing factor derived from *DSM* diagnostic symptoms, are associated with reduced P3 brain response. A second key finding was that a significant association of this kind was evident also for novel (picture) stimuli, both in the extreme (high versus low externalizing) groups analysis and in the correlational analysis employing all subjects. Also notable was the fact that the negative relationship between externalizing and P3 was stronger at anterior than at posterior sites—particularly in the case of the novel picture stimuli (see topographic

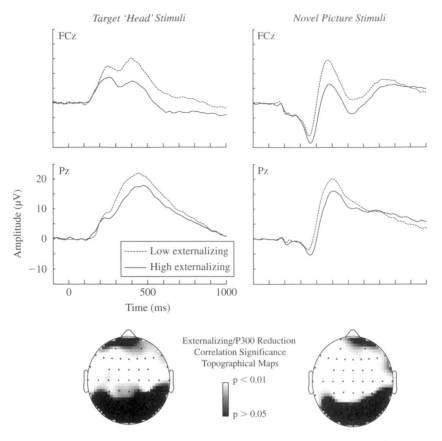

Figure 57.3 Average P3 response to target and novel stimuli in a three-stimulus visual oddball task for participants high versus low in externalizing scores.

Note: P3 waveform data are depicted for anterior (FCz; upper plots) and posterior (Pz; lower plots) scalp sites; waveforms for target (schematic 'head') and novel (affective and neutral picture) stimulus trials appear in left plots and right plots, respectively. High and low externalizing groups (*n*s = 61 and 34, respectively) were formed by oversampling from the top and bottom 25% of scorers on a 100-item version of the Externalizing Spectrum Inventory (Krueger et al., 2007) in an undergraduate screening pool. Statistical maps at the bottom depict the scalp topography distribution of the negative association between externalizing factor scores and P3 amplitude for target 'head' stimuli (left map) and novel picture stimuli (right map) in the test sample as a whole (*N* = 149). Data are from "Neurophysiological Correlates of Behavioral Disinhibition: Separable Contributions of Distinct Personality Traits," by N. C. Venables, E. M. Bernat, J. R. Hall, B. V. Steffen, M. Cadwallader, R. F. Krueger, et al., 2005, *Psychophysiology, 42*, p. S126.

maps in Figure 57.3). The enhanced magnitude of effect at anterior versus parietal scalp sites is consistent with the hypothesis that the association between reduced P3 and externalizing reflects a deviation of some kind in frontal brain processing. No moderating effects of gender were found for the association between P3 and externalizing in these analyses—indicating that the association was present for women as well as men.

A further notable finding of this study had to do with comparative brain responses to novel picture stimuli that were affective (pleasant or unpleasant) compared with neutral. Analyses of brain potential responses to affective pictures in relation to neutral pictures have consistently revealed a positive slow-wave component extending far beyond the P3 in time (e.g., Cuthbert, Schupp, Bradley, Birbaumer, & Lang, 2000; Schupp, Cuthbert, Bradley, C acioppo, Ito, & Lang., 2000). To examine effects for this affective slow-wave component separately from the P3

response, we undertook a time-frequency decomposition of brain response data in the undergraduate sample (*N* = 149) tested in the three-stimulus oddball task. Time-frequency decomposition (cf. Bernat, Williams, & Gehring, 2005) is a statistical technique that isolates ERP components through concurrent consideration of activity in both time and frequency domains; the technique provides an effective way to separate brain signals that overlap in time but have distinctive frequency characteristics. The decomposition was undertaken separately for affective picture trials and neutral picture trials. Results for the sample as a whole are presented in Figure 57.4. A slow-wave (subdelta frequency) component is evident that overlaps with the P3/delta-frequency response, but extends beyond it in time. As expected from prior work (Cuthbert et al., 2000; Schupp et al., 2000), the slow-wave component accounts for most of the positive amplitude difference between affective and neutral pictures. In Figure 57.5, these P3/delta and slow-wave/subdelta

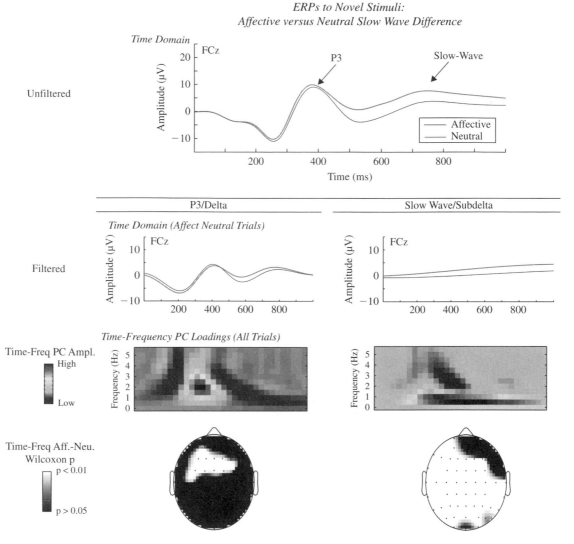

Figure 57.4 (Figure C.56 in color section) Time-frequency (TF) decomposition of average ERP responses to affective versus neutral pictures presented as novel nontargets in a three-stimulus visual oddball task.

Note: The data are for a sample of 149 undergraduate participants. Waveform plots depict results for electrode site FCz. The plot at the top depicts unfiltered ERP averages for the affective and neutral picture conditions. The waveform plots immediately below this show time-domain averages for affective versus neutral conditions that have been frequency-filtered using third-order Butterworth filters to approximate the TF components (discussed below) in a more familiar waveform representation. Activity in the delta (0.5 to 3 Hz bandpass) range corresponding to P3 response is depicted in the left plot, and activity in the subdelta (0.5 Hz lowpass) range corresponding to the ERP slow-wave response is depicted in the right plot. The two-color surface plots depict principal component scores reflecting the P3/delta and slow-wave/subdelta activity contained in the ERP signal, derived from a TF decomposition of the EEG data across all picture trials. Statistical maps at the bottom depict the scalp topography distribution of the difference in amplitude of ERP response to affective versus neutral picture stimuli in the P3/delta TF component (left map) and in the slow-wave subdelta component (right map). Data are from "Neurophysiological Correlates of Behavioral Disinhibition: Separable Contributions of Distinct Personality Traits," by N. C. Venables, E. M. Bernat, J. R. Hall, B. V. Steffen, M. Cadwallader, R. F. Krueger, et al., 2005, *Psychophysiology, 42*, p. S126.

time-frequency components are shown, but now comparing low versus high externalizing participant subgroups across all picture trials. The effect of externalizing is restricted to the P3/delta component; the slow-wave component shows no significant difference in relation to externalizing. In Figure 57.6, the affective versus neutral picture difference in the slow-wave/subdelta component is depicted for low and high externalizing groups. It can be seen that both

groups demonstrate robust slow-wave response differentiation between affective and neutral pictures.

In summary, high externalizing participants showed no reduction in brain response differentiation between pictures that were affective compared with pictures that were neutral, despite showing an overall reduction in amplitude of P3 response to novel picture stimuli (Figure 57.5). This result indicates that even though high externalizing

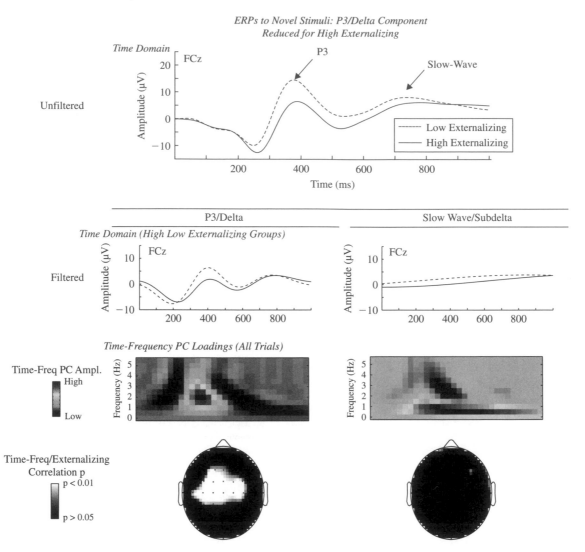

Figure 57.5 (**Figure C.57** in color section) Results from a time-frequency (TF) decomposition of average ERP responses to pictures presented as novel stimuli in a visual oddball task, displayed separately for subgroups of high versus low externalizing participants.

Note: High and low externalizing participant groups are as described in Figure 57.3. Waveform plots depict results for electrode site FCz. The plot at the top depicts unfiltered ERP averages across all novel picture trials for these high and low externalizing subgroups. The waveform plots immediately below this show time-domain averages for the two subgroups that have been frequency-filtered using third-order Butterworth

filters. Activity in the delta (0.5 to 3 Hz bandpass) range corresponding to P3 response is depicted in the left plot, and activity in the subdelta (0.5 Hz low pass) range corresponding to the ERP slow-wave response is depicted in the right plot. The two color surface plots depict principal component scores reflecting the P3/delta and slow-wave/subdelta activity contained in the ERP signal, derived from a TF decomposition of the EEG data across all picture trials. Statistical maps at the bottom depict, for the overall test sample ($N = 149$) that included these extreme subgroups, the scalp topography distribution of the negative association between externalizing scores and amplitude of ERP response to novel pictures in the P3/delta TF component (left map) and in the slow-wave subdelta component (right map).

individuals showed a generally attenuated brain response to the novel picture stimuli, these individuals nonetheless showed normal processing of the affective content of the pleasant and unpleasant pictures—suggesting an intact subcortical-affect processing system.

Diminished Error-Related Negativity

In other work employing undergraduate participants preselected according to scores on the Externalizing

Spectrum Inventory, we have examined negative-polarity scalp potentials associated with errors in responding. Hall, Bernat, and Patrick (2007) tested for an association between externalizing scores and amplitude of the response-locked error-related negativity (ERN), a negative deflection of the ERP that is observed following errors in laboratory performance tasks. The peak of the ERN typically occurs within 100 ms of the commission of an error and is maximal at fronto-central scalp sites. The ERN has

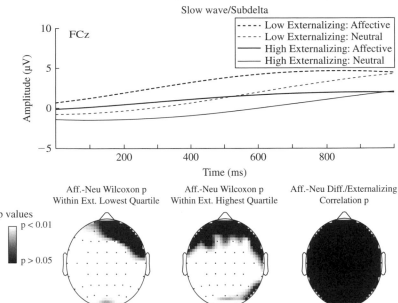

ERPs to Novel Stimuli: Affective-Neutral
Slow Wave Difference Unrelated to Externalizing

Figure 57.6 ERP slow-wave response for affective versus neutral pictures occurring as novel stimuli in a three-stimulus visual oddball task, displayed separately for subgroups of high versus low in externalizing scores.

Note: High and low externalizing groups are as described in Figure 57.3. Average time-domain ERP waveforms, depicted for electrode site FCz, are frequency (third-order Butterworth) filtered to reflect activity in the subdelta (0.5 Hz lowpass) range corresponding to the ERP slow-wave response. The left and middle statistical topographic maps at the bottom depict the scalp topography distribution of the *difference* in amplitude of slow-wave ERP response to affective versus neutral picture stimuli for the low and high externalizing subgroups, respectively; the bottom-right map depicts the lack of significant association at any scalp site between continuous scores on the externalizing factor within the test sample as a whole ($N = 149$) and the degree of affective versus neutral slow wave differentiation.

been characterized as a neurophysiological index of endogenous action monitoring—that is, the brain's automatic capacity to monitor behavioral performance on-line and to initiate corrective action as needed, either through detection of errors (Gehring, Coles, Meyers, & Donchin, 1995) or detection of conflict among competing neural response pathways (Carter et al., 1998). Consistent with this interpretation, evidence from ERP source localization studies indicates that the primary neural generator of the ERN is the anterior cingulate cortex (ACC; Dehaene, Posner, & Tucker, 1994), a brain structure that is widely believed to be involved in self-monitoring and behavioral regulation (Bush, Luu, & Posner, 2000).

The fact that externalizing psychopathology is characterized by an apparent failure to learn from experience (i.e., maladaptive behaviors are repeated despite an awareness of negative consequences for self or others) suggests the possibility of an impairment in this action monitoring capacity. In line with this hypothesis, research findings indicate that both states and traits related to behavioral disinhibition are associated with reduced amplitude of ERN responding. For instance, ERN amplitude is reduced following ingestion of moderate doses of alcohol

(Ridderinkhoff et al., 2002), a state manipulation known to produce behavioral disinhibition. In the domain of traits, Dikman and Allen (2000) found that participants low in socialization (a construct reflecting impulsivity, rebelliousness, and aggression; Gough, 1960) showed reduced ERN response within the punishment condition of a speeded reaction time task, compared with the reward condition. In a related vein, Pailing and Segalowitz (2004) reported that participants low in conscientiousness (a trait dimension reflecting tendencies toward dependability, dutifulness, and persistence) showed reduced ERN amplitude in particular when explicit performance incentives were absent. Reduced ERN amplitude has also been demonstrated in relation to trait impulsivity (Pailing, Segalowitz, Dywan, & Davies, 2002; Potts, George, Martin, & Barratt, 2006) and Eysenck's psychoticism dimension (Santesso, Segalowitz, & Schmidt, 2005). On other hand, *enhanced* ERN response has been demonstrated in participants with obsessive-compulsive disorder, a syndrome marked by excessive rumination and self-evaluation (Gehring, Himle, & Nisenson, 2000).

Collectively, these studies point to a relationship between impaired self-monitoring, as evidenced by reduced ERN response amplitude, and a variety of constructs related to externalizing. Evidence of an association with the ERN would be especially informative regarding brain mechanisms underlying externalizing vulnerability because the ERN indexes a distinctive psychological process with clear functional relevance to externalizing (i.e., online, endogenous action monitoring). Moreover, the ERN has been localized to a specific region of the brain (the ACC) that has been shown to play a key role in response monitoring processes. Using the 100-item screening version of the Externalizing Spectrum Inventory as a basis for subject selection, and oversampling high and low scorers from a large undergraduate screening pool, Hall et al. (2007) examined the association between ERN and externalizing in a sample of 92 undergraduate participants comprising 22 low-externalizing individuals, 38 high-externalizing individuals, and 32 intermediate scorers. Based on recent evidence that increases in anterior theta (4 to 7 Hz) activity account for much of the oscillatory signal comprising the ERN response (Bernat, Williams, & Gehring, 2005; Luu, Tucker, & Makieg, 2004), Hall et al. also examined the specific relationship between externalizing and brain activity within this frequency band following the commission of errors (i.e., during the ERN window). Considering these prior research findings, these investigators hypothesized that individuals high in externalizing would show a significant reduction in ERN, and a specific reduction in the anterior theta response associated with the ERN, relative to individuals low in externalizing.

The experimental task was a modified version of the Eriksen flanker task (Eriksen & Eriksen, 1974) in which participants made right- or left-hand button-press responses to indicate the middle letter in a 5-letter stimulus array. Each stimulus array was presented for 150 ms, followed by a 1,000 ms response window. Participants were instructed to respond as quickly and accurately as possible to each target array. The main task comprised a total of 600 total trials. The ERN was computed from the average response-locked ERP on trials in which performance errors occurred. There were no significant differences between high- and low-externalizing groups in indices of behavioral performance (accuracy, reaction time) on the task. However, as predicted, ERN amplitude was significantly reduced in the high-externalizing group. Figure 57.7 depicts average response-locked ERP waveforms for error trials at electrode site Cz (where ERN amplitude was maximal) for high- versus low-externalizing groups. The ERN is evident as a sharp negative deflection in the error waveform that peaks around 50 ms postresponse. The Externalizing Group × Electrode Site interaction was not significant in this analysis, indicating that group differences were evident across the three midline scalp sites. No moderating effect of gender was found for the relationship between

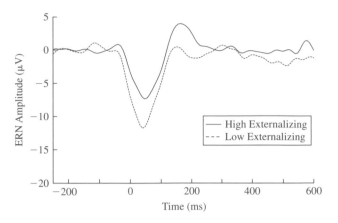

Figure 57.7   Average error-related negativity (ERN) response following performance errors in a flanker task for participants high versus low in externalizing scores

Note: ERN waveform data are for the midline central (Cz) scalp site. High and low externalizing groups (*n*s = 38 and 22, respectively) were selected from the top and bottom 25 percent of scorers on a 100-item version of the Externalizing Spectrum Inventory (Krueger et al., 2007) in a large undergraduate screening sample. Data are from "Externalizing Psychopathology and the Error-Related Negativity," by J. R. Hall, E. M. Bernat, and C. J. Patrick, 2007, *Psychological Science,18,* 326–333.

externalizing and ERN in these analyses—indicating (as for P300) that the association was present among women as well as men.

Time-frequency analysis (Bernat et al., 2005) was used to isolate distinctive components of the response-locked ERP, taking into account variations in oscillatory (frequency) elements of the ERP signal across time. A principal components decomposition of time-frequency brain response data within the ERN response window yielded a dominant first component reflecting oscillatory activity within the theta frequency band (4 to 7 Hz). The peak of this response-locked increase in theta energy coincided in time with the peak of the ERN, and had a similar midline-central scalp distribution, encouraging an interpretation of this component as the time-frequency representation of the ERN. Moreover, a source localization analysis placed the source of this component squarely within the region of the ACC. Paralleling results for the ERN, a main effect of Electrode Site indicated that the theta response to errors was maximal at electrode Cz, and theta activity was significantly attenuated in the high-externalizing group. In addition, for this specific index of brain activity, a significant Externalizing Group × Electrode Site interaction was found, indicating that group differences in theta response were maximal at electrode Cz. Consistent with this, correlational analyses revealed a significant negative association between continuous externalizing scores and theta activity at electrode site Cz, but not at sites Fz or Pz.

These findings demonstrate a relationship between reduced ERN response and the externalizing vulnerability factor.

This finding is important because it points to impairment in endogenous action monitoring processes associated with the ACC as a potential mechanism for externalizing vulnerability.[3] Despite showing reduced ERN response, high-externalizing participants nonetheless maintained a level of task performance equivalent to of the low-externalizing group—implying that within the simple processing context of the flanker task these participants were able to compensate for a lack of normal internal response monitoring to achieve adequate performance. Given a more complex experimental task, or under real world conditions, deficits in self-monitoring are likely to have more substantial consequences for performance.

SUMMARY

The two-process theory postulates that the classic syndrome of psychopathy as described by Cleckley in his book *The Mask of Sanity* can be understood in terms of two separable individual difference constructs with distinctive neurobiological underpinnings. One of these constructs is a trait dimension of fear and fearlessness that is associated with varying levels of defensive reactivity to discrete aversive cues. Fear-potentiated startle, defined as enhanced blink startle reactivity during viewing of aversive (in particular, directly threatening) visual stimuli in relation to neutral stimuli, represents one physiological indicator of this underlying trait fear dimension. The other construct is a dispositional dimension of externalizing vulnerability reflecting disinhibitory personality tendencies and liability to impulse control problems of various kinds. Variations in stimulus-locked P300 and response-locked ERN brain potential amplitude represent physiological indicators of this externalizing dimension. Available data indicate that both of these individual difference factors, trait fear, and externalizing, are substantially heritable, and biometric modeling research has established reduced P300 amplitude as an endophenotype marker of externalizing vulnerability.

The two-process theory articulated here emerged out of efforts to clarify associations between physiological response indicators of underlying neurobiological processes and phenotypic elements of the psychopathy construct as indexed by Hare's PCL-R. In studies of fear reactivity using the startle modulation paradigm, associations with PCL-R psychopathy emerged most clearly in relation to the affective-interpersonal (Factor 1) component, particularly after controlling for the behavioral deviance (Factor 2) component. Findings regarding electrocortical correlates of psychopathy have historically been mixed (cf. Raine, 1989, 1993; but see more recent work by Kiehl, Hare, Liddle, & McDonald, 1999; Kiehl, Smith, Hare, & Liddle, 2000), whereas general psychopathology studies across many years have yielded reliable associations between externalizing syndromes and brain response measures such as P300. Recent structural modeling work demonstrating a close, selective association between the behavioral deviance (Factor 2) component of the PCL-R and the broad externalizing factor of psychopathology suggests that relations between psychopathy and electrocortical response can likewise be clarified by considering the two components of the PCL-R separately. It is notable that our two-process conceptualization, derived from findings of physiological studies of psychopathy with adult participants, dovetails with recent developmental models that postulate alternative pathways to conscience formation and psychopathic tendencies in youth (Fowles & Dindo, 2006; Frick & Marsee, 2006).

A limitation of the PCL-R operationalization of psychopathy is that its affective-interpersonal and behavioral deviance components are moderately correlated, such that differential associations of these components with criterion measures are in some cases obscured (suppressed) due to their overlapping variance (cf. Hicks & Patrick, 2006). We hypothesize that differentiable facets of the psychopathy construct became partially fused in the PCL-R because the approach that was used to select items for the PCL-R favored measurement of a unidimensional construct. Lilienfeld's self-report based PPI, which was developed to assess the spectrum of psychopathy-related traits with no a priori assumptions regarding their structure, provides an alternative operationalization in which narrower content subscales map onto two broad orthogonal dimensions—one reflecting dominance, stress immunity, and fearlessness (PPI-I), and the other reflecting impulsivity, rebelliousness, alienation, and aggression (PPI-II). The available evidence indicates that these PPI dimensions, which are related to but distinct from the PCL-R factors, represent more clearly differentiated phenotypic indicators (in the domain of self-report) of the aforementioned trait fear and externalizing constructs.

However, our point in this chapter is not to advocate one approach to operationalizing psychopathy over another. Rather, our aim is to encourage a movement toward operationalizing and studying trait fear and externalizing as constructs in their own right. We believe these two constructs are important to study because they are crucial to an understanding of psychopathy, and also to an understanding of general psychopathology spectra encompassing, respectively, disorders of anxiety/mood and disorders

---

[3]However, in a separate study (Bernat, Nelson, Steele, & Patrick, 2008), we found no evidence of reduced ACC-localized negativity to *externally presented* loss feedback—suggesting that reduced ERN reactivity may reflect impairment in monitoring circuitry involving the ACC, rather than ACC impairment per se.

of impulse control. In addition, we believe these constructs are important to study because they represent purer phenotypic targets for neurobiological research. They constitute multivariate behavioral phenotypes (cf. Iacono, 1998), reflecting the overlapping variance among multiple interrelated indicators. As such, they appear to be more substantially heritable than individual phenotypic indicators—whether modeled as latent variables (e.g., Krueger et al., 2002) or extracted as manifest composite variables (e.g., Kramer et al., 2008). In addition, they account for associations between individual phenotypic indicators and physiological response measures such as fear-potentiated startle (in the case of trait fear; Vaidyanathan et al., 2008) and P300 brain potential amplitude (in the case of externalizing; Patrick et al., 2006). As such, they represent important targets in the search for endophenotype markers of psychopathology (e.g., Hicks et al., 2007) and potentially valuable referents for a neurobiologically based science of individual differences (cf. Patrick & Bernat, 2006).

The two-process model draws on two longstanding theoretical perspectives in the psychopathy literature, one emphasizing deficits in basic emotional reactivity (e.g., Blair, 2006; Lykken, 1995) and the other emphasizing deficits in inhibitory control of behavior (e.g., Gorenstein & Newman, 1980; Morgan & Lilienfeld, 2000; Newman, 1998). Our model hypothesizes that both of these processes contribute in differing ways to the phenotypic expression of the syndrome. We believe that systematic investigation of the constructs of trait fear and externalizing can help to elucidate a number of longstanding issues in the psychopathy literature, including inconsistencies in findings for cognitive and physiological measures, the role of constructs such as anxiety and aggression in psychopathy, the issue of psychopathy subtypes, and the question of how to conceptualize and identify "successful" psychopaths. More generally, we propose that to understand psychopathologic syndromes in terms of underlying brain processes, it may be necessary in some cases to reconceptualize these syndromes in alternative terms—that is, in terms of basic individual difference constructs that map more directly onto underlying neurobiological processes. We anticipate that in the future, neurobiologically based individual difference constructs will gain increasing ascendance as organizing dimensions in the domains of personality and psychopathology.

REFERENCES

Achenbach, T. M., & Edelbrock, C. S. (1978). The classification of child psychopathology: A review and analysis of empirical efforts. *Psychological Bulletin, 85,* 1275–1301.

Anokhin, A. P., Vedeniapin, A. B., Sirevaag, E. J., Bauer, L. O., O'Connor, S. J., Kuperman, S., et al. (2000). The P300 brain potential is reduced in smokers. *Psychopharmacology, 149,* 409–413.

Arrindell, W. A., Emmelkamp, P. M. G., & van der Ende, J. (1984). Phobic dimensions: Pt. I. Reliability and generalizability across samples, gender, and nations. *Advances in Behavior Research and Therapy, 6,* 207–254.

Attou, A., Figiel, C., & Timsit-Berthier, M. (2001). ERP assessment of heroin detoxification and methadone treatment in chronic heroin users. *Clinical Neurophysiology, 31,* 171–180.

Bauer, L. O., & Hesselbrock, V. M. (1999). P300 decrements in teenagers with conduct problems: Implications for substance abuse risk and brain development. *Biological Psychiatry, 46,* 263–272.

Bauer, L. O., O'Connor, S., & Hesselbrock, V. M. (1994). Frontal P300 decrements in antisocial personality disorder. *Alcoholism: Clinical and Experimental Research, 18,* 1300–1305.

Begleiter, H., & Porjesz, B. (1999). What is inherited in the predisposition toward alcoholism? A proposed model. *Alcholism: Clinical and Experimental Research, 23,* 1125–1135.

Begleiter, H., Porjesz, B., Bihari, B., & Kissin, B. (1984, September 28). Event-related brain potentials in boys at risk for alcoholism. *Science, 225,* 1493–1496.

Benning, S. D., Patrick, C. J., Blonigen, D. M., Hicks, B. M., & Iacono, W. G. (2005). Estimating facets of psychopathy from normal personality traits: A step toward community-epidemiological investigations. *Assessment, 12,* 3–18.

Benning, S. D., Patrick, C. J., Hicks, B. M., Blonigen, D. M., & Krueger, R. F. (2003). Factor structure of the Psychopathic Personality Inventory: Validity and implications for clinical assessment. *Psychological Assessment, 15,* 340–350.

Benning, S. D., Patrick, C. J., & Iacono, W. G. (2005). Psychopathy, startle blink modulation, and electrodermal reactivity in twin men. *Psychophysiology, 42,* 753–762.

Benning, S. D., Patrick, C. J., Salekin, R. T., & Leistico, A. R. (2005). Convergent and discriminant validity of psychopathy factors assessed via self-report: A comparison of three instruments. *Assessment, 12,* 270–289.

Berman, S. M., Whipple, S. C., Fitch, R. J., & Noble, E. P. (1993). P3 in young boys as a predictor of adolescent substance use. *Alcohol, 10,* 69–76.

Bernat, E. M., Nelson, L. D., Steele, V. R., & Patrick, C. J. (2008). *Externalizing psychopathology and gain/loss feedback in a simulated gambling task: Dissociable components of brain response revealed by time-frequency analysis.* Manuscript submitted for publication.

Bernat, E. M., Patrick, C. J., & Benning, S. D. (2006). Effects of picture content and intensity on affective physiological response. *Psychophysiology, 43,* 93–103.

Bernat, E. M., Patrick, C. J., Cadwallader, M., van Mersbergen, M., & Seo, D. (2003). Affective orienting responses: A novelty P3 study with emotional pictures. *Psychophysiology, 40,* S25.

Bernat, E. M., Patrick, C. J., Steffen, B. V., Hall, J. R., & Ward, M. (2004). Exploring mechanisms of deviant affect-modulated startle in psychopathy. *Psychophysiology, 41,* S40.

Bernat, E. M., Williams, W. J., & Gehring, W. J. (2005). Decomposing ERP time-frequency energy using PCA. *Clinical Neurophysiology, 116,* 1314–1334.

Biggins, C. A., MacKay, S., Clark, W., & Fein, G. (1997). Event-related potential evidence for frontal cortex effects of chronic cocaine dependence. *Biological Psychiatry, 42,* 472–485.

Blair, R. J. R. (2006). Subcortical brain systems in psychopathy: The amygdala and associated structures. In C. J. Patrick (Ed.), *Handbook of psychopathy* (pp. 296–312). New York: Guilford Press.

Blonigen, D., Hicks, B., Patrick, C., Krueger, R., Iacono, W., & McGue, M. (2005). Psychopathic personality traits: Heritability and genetic overlap with internalizing and externalizing pathology. *Psychological Medicine*, *35*, 637–648.

Bradley, M. M., Codispoti, M., Cuthbert, B. N., & Lang, P. J. (2001). Emotion and motivation: Pt. I. Defensive and appetitive reactions in picture processing. *Emotion*, *1*, 276–298.

Branchey, M. H., Buydens-Branchey, L., & Horvath, T. B. (1993). Event-related potentials in substance-abusing individuals after long-term abstinence. *American Journal of Addictions*, *2*, 141–148.

Brigham, J., Herning, R. I., & Moss, H. B. (1995). Event-related potentials and alpha synchronization in preadolescent boys at risk for psychoactive substance use. *Biological Psychiatry*, *37*, 834–846.

Bush, G., Luu, P., & Posner, M. I. (2000). Cognitive and emotional influences in anterior cingulate cortex. *Trends in Cognitive Sciences*, *4*, 215–222.

Buss, A. H., & Plomin, R. (1984). *Temperament: Early developing personality traits.* Hillsdale, NJ: Erlbaum.

Carter, C. S., Braver, T. S., Barch, D. M., Botvinick, M. M., Noll, D. N., & Cohen, J. D. (1998, May 1). Anterior cingulate cortex, error detection, and the online monitoring of performance. *Science*, *280*, 747–749.

Center for the Study of Emotion and Attention. (1999). The international affective picture system: *Digitized photographs.* Gainesville, FL: University of Florida, Center for Research in Psychophysiology.

Cleckley, H. (1976). *The mask of sanity* (5th ed.). St. Louis, MO: Mosby. (Original edition published in 1941.)

Cloninger, C. R. (1987). A systematic method for clinical description and classification of personality variants. *Archives of General Psychiatry*, *44*, 573–588.

Cook, E. W., III. (1999). *Affective individual differences, psychopathology, and startle reflex modulation.* In M. E. Dawson, A. M. Schell, & A. H. Boehmelt (Eds.), *Startle modification: Implications for clinical science, cognitive science, and neuroscience* (pp. 187–208). New York: Cambridge University Press.

Cooke, D. J., & Michie, C. (2001). Refining the construct of psychopathy: Towards a hierarchical model. *Psychological Assessment*, *13*, 171–188.

Corr, P. J., Kumari, V., Wilson, G. D., Checkley, S., & Gray, J. A. (1997). Harm avoidance and affective modulation of the startle reflex: A replication. *Personality and Individual Differences*, *22*, 591–593.

Corr, P. J., Wilson, G. D., Fotiadou, M., Kumari, V., Gray, N. S., Checkley, S., et al. (1995). Personality and affective modulation of the startle reflex. *Personality and Individual Differences*, *19*, 543–553.

Costa, L., Bauer, L., Kuperman, S., Porjesz, B., O'Connor, S., Hesselbrock, V., et al. (2000). Frontal P300 decrements, alcohol dependence, and antisocial personality disorder. *Biological Psychiatry*, *47*, 1064–1071.

Courchesne, E., Hillyard, S. A., & Galambos, R. (1975). Stimulus novelty, task relevance and the visual evoked potential in man. *Electroencephalography and Clinical Neurophysiology*, *39*, 131–143.

Cuthbert, B. N., Schupp, H. T., Bradley, M. M., Birbaumer, N., & Lang, P. J. (2000). Brain potentials in affective picture processing: Covariation with autonomic arousal and affective report. *Biological Psychology*, *52*, 95–111.

Davis, M. (1979). Diazepam and flurazepam: Effects on conditioned fear as measured with the potentiated startle paradigm. *Psychopharmacology*, *62*, 1–7.

Davis, M. (1989). *Neural systems involved in fear-potentiated startle.* In M. Davis, B. L. Jacobs, & R. I. Schoenfeld (Eds.), *Annals of the New York Academy of Sciences*, Vol. 563: *Modulation of defined neural vertebrate circuits* (pp. 165–183). New York: Author.

Davis, M. (1998). Are different parts of the extended amygdala involved in fear versus anxiety? *Biological Psychiatry*, *44*, 1239–1247.

Davis, M., Falls, W. A., Campeau, S., & Kim, M. (1993). Fear-potentiated startle: A neural and pharmacological analysis. *Behavioral and Brain Research*, *58*, 175–198.

Davis, M., Walker, D. L., & Lee, Y. (1997). Roles of the amygdala and bed nucleus of the stria terminalis in fear and anxiety measured with the acoustic startle reflex. *Annals of the New York Academy of Sciences*, *831*, 305–331.

Dehaene, S., Posner, M. I., & Tucker, D. M. (1994). Localization of a neural system for error detection and compensation. *Psychological Science*, *5*, 303–305.

Dien, J., Spencer, K. M., & Donchin, E. (2003). Localization of the event-related potential novelty response as defined by principal components analysis. *Cognitive Brain Research*, *17*(3), 637–650.

Dikman, Z. V., & Allen, J. J. B. (2000). Error monitoring during reward and avoidance learning in high- and low-socialized individuals. *Psychophysiology*, *37*, 43–54.

Elmasian, R., Neville, H., Woods, D., Schuckit, M., & Bloom, F. (1982). Event-related brain potentials are different in individuals at high and low-risk for developing alcoholism. *Proceedings of the National Academy of Sciences, USA, 79*, 7900–7903.

Eriksen, B. A., & Ericksen, C. W. (1974). Effects of noise letters upon the identification of a target letter in a nonsearch task. *Perception and Psychophysics*, *16*, 143–149.

Falconer, D. S. (1989). *Introduction to quantitative genetics* (3rd ed.). New York: Wiley.

Fichtenholtz, H. M., Dean, H. L., Dillon, D. G., Yamasaki, H., McCarthy, G., & LaBar, K. S. (2004). Emotion-attention network interactions during a visual oddball task. *Cognitive Brain Research*, *20*, 67–80.

Fowles, D. C., & Dindo, L. (2006). *A dual deficit model of psychopathy.* In C. J. Patrick (Ed.), *Handbook of psychopathy* (pp. 14–34). New York: Guilford Press.

Gehring, W. J., Coles, M. G. H., Meyer, D. E., & Donchin, E. (1995). *A brain potential manifestation of error-related processing.* In G. Karmos, M. Molnar, V. Csepe, I. Czigler, & J. E. Desmedt (Eds.), *Perspectives of event-related potentials research* (pp. 267–272). Amsterdam: Elsevier.

Gehring, W. J., Himle, J., & Nisenson, L. G. (2000). Action-monitoring dysfunction in obsessive-compulsive disorder. *Psychological Science*, *11*, 1–6.

Giancola, P. R., & Tarter, R. E. (1999). Executive cognitive functioning and risk for substance abuse. *Psychological Science*, *10*, 203–205.

Gottesman, I. I., & Shields, J. (1972). *Schizophrenia and genetics: A twin study vantage point.* New York: Academic Press.

Gorenstein, E. E., & Newman, J. P. (1980). Disinhibitory psychopathology: A new perspective and a model for research. *Psychological Review*, *87*, 301–315.

Gough, H. G. (1960). Theory and measurement of socialization. *Journal of Consulting Psychology*, *24*, 23–30.

Grillon, C., & Davis, M. (1997). Fear-potentiated startle conditioning in humans: Explicit and contextual cue conditioning following paired versus unpaired training. *Psychophysiology*, *34*, 451–458.

Hall, J. R., & Benning, S. D. (2006). The "successful" psychopath: Adaptive and subclinical manifestations of psychopathy in the general population. In C. J. Patrick (Ed.), *Handbook of psychopathy* (pp. 459–478). New York: Guilford Press.

Hall, J. R., Benning, S. D., & Patrick, C. J. (2004). Criterion-related validity of the three-factor model of psychopathy: Personality, behavior, and adaptive functioning. *Assessment*, *11*, 4–16.

Hall, J. R., Bernat, E. M., & Patrick, C. J. (2007). Externalizing psychopathology and the error-related negativity. *Psychological Science*, *18*, 326–333.

Hamm, A. O., Greenwald, M. K., Bradley, M. M., & Lang, P. J. (1993). Emotional learning, hedonic change, and the startle reflex. *Journal of Abnormal Psychology*, *102*, 453–465.

Hare, R. D. (1991). *The Hare Psychopathy Checklist-revised.* Toronto, Ontario: Multi-Health Systems.

Hare, R. D. (1993). *Without conscience: The disturbing world of the psychopaths among us.* New York: Pocket Books.

Hare, R. D. (2003). *The Hare Psychopathy Checklist-revised,* (2nd ed.). Toronto, Ontario: Multi-Health Systems.

Hare, R. D., Harpur, T. J., Hakstian, A. R., Forth, A. E., Hart, S. D., & Newman, J. P. (1990). The Revised Psychopathy Checklist: Reliability and factor structure. *Psychological Assessment, 2*, 338–341.

Harpur, T. J., Hakstian, A. R., & Hare, R. D. (1988). Factor structure of the psychopathy checklist. *Journal of Consulting and Clinical Psychology, 56*, 741–747.

Harpur, T. J., Hare, R. D., & Hakstian, A. R. (1989). Two-factor conceptualization of psychopathy: Construct validity and assessment implications. *Psychological Assessment, 1*, 6–17.

Herpertz, S. C., Werth, U., Lukas, G., Qunaibi, M., Schuerkens, A., Kunert, H., et al. (2001). Emotion in criminal offenders with psychopathy and borderline personality disorder. *Archives of General Psychiatry, 58*, 737–744.

Hicks, B. M., Bernat, E. M., Malone, S. M., Iacono, W. G., Patrick, C. J., Krueger, R. F., et al. (2007). Genes mediate the association between P3 amplitude and externalizing disorders. *Psychophysiology, 44*, 98–105.

Hicks, B. M., Markon, K. E., Patrick, C. J., Krueger, R. F., & Newman, J. P. (2004). Identifying psychopathy subtypes on the basis of personality structure. *Psychological Assessment, 16*, 276–288.

Hicks, B. M., & Patrick, C. J. (2006). Psychopathy and negative affectivity: Analyses of suppressor effects reveal distinct relations with trait anxiety, depression, fearfulness, and anger-hostility. *Journal of Abnormal Psychology, 115*, 276–287.

Hill, S. Y., & Shen, S. (2002). Neurodevelopmental patterns of visual P3b in association with familial risk for alcohol dependence and childhood diagnosis. *Biological Psychiatry, 51*, 621–631.

Hill, S. Y., Steinhauer, S., Lowers, L., & Locke, J. (1995). Eight-year longitudinal follow-up of P300 and clinical outcome in children from high-risk for alcoholism families. *Biological Psychiatry, 37*, 823–827.

Iacono, W. G. (1998). Identifying psychophysiological risk for psychopathology: Examples from substance abuse and schizophrenia research. *Psychophysiology, 35*, 621–637.

Iacono, W. G., Carlson, S. R., Malone, S. M., & McGue, M. (2002). P3 event-related potential amplitude and risk for disinhibitory disorders in adolescent boys. *Archives of General Psychiatry, 59*, 750–757.

John, B., & Lewis, K. (1966, May 6). Chromosome variability and geographic distribution in insects. *Science, 152*, 711–721.

Katsanis, J., Iacono, W. G., McGue, M., & Carlson, S. R. (1997). P300 event-related potential heritability in monozygotic and dizygotic twins. *Psychophysiology, 34*, 47–58.

Kendler, K. S., Prescott, C. A., Myers J., & Neale, M. C. (2003). The structure of genetic and environmental risk factors for common psychiatric and substance use disorders in men and women. *Archives of General Psychiatry, 60*, 929–937.

Kiehl, K. A., Hare, R. D., Liddle, P. F., & McDonald, J. J. (1999). Reduced P300 responses in criminal psychopaths during a visual oddball task. *Biological Psychiatry, 45*, 1498–1507.

Kiehl, K. A., Smith, A. M., Hare, R. D., & Liddle, P. F. (2000). An event-related potential investigation of response inhibition in schizophrenia and psychopathy. *Biological Psychiatry, 48*, 210–221.

Kim, M. S., Kim, J. J., & Kwon, J. S. (2001). Frontal P300 decrement and executive dysfunction in adolescents with conduct problems. *Child Psychiatry and Human Development, 32*, 93–106.

Knight, R. T. (1984). Decreased response to novel stimuli after prefrontal lesions in man. *Electroencephalography and Clinical Neurophysiology, 59*, 9–20.

Kramer, M. D., Patrick, C. J., Bayevsky, M., & Krueger, R. F. (2008). *Phenotypic and etiologic parallels in the structure of fear and fearlessness.* Manuscript submitted for publication.

Krueger, R. F. (1999). The structure of common mental disorders. *Archives of General Psychiatry, 56*, 921–926.

Krueger, R. F., Hicks, B., Patrick, C. J., Carlson, S., Iacono, W. G., & McGue, M. (2002). Etiologic connections among substance dependence, antisocial behavior, and personality: Modeling the externalizing spectrum. *Journal of Abnormal Psychology, 111*, 411–424.

Krueger, R. F., Markon, K. E., Patrick, C. J., Benning, S. D., & Kramer, M. (2007). Linking antisocial behavior, substance use, and personality: An integrative quantitative model of the adult externalizing spectrum. *Journal of Abnormal Psychology, 116*, 645–666.

Lang, P. J. (1995). The emotion probe: Studies of motivation and attention. *American Psychologist, 50*, 372–385.

Lang, P. J., Bradley, M. M., & Cuthbert, B. N. (1990). Emotion, attention, and the startle reflex. *Psychological Review, 97*, 377–398.

Levenston, G. K., Patrick, C. J., Bradley, M. M., & Lang, P. J. (2000). The psychopath as observer: Emotion and attention in picture processing. *Journal of Abnormal Psychology, 109*, 373–385.

Lilienfeld, S. O. (1990). *Development and preliminary validation of a self-report measure of psychopathic personality.* Unpublished doctoral dissertation, University of Minnesota.

Lilienfeld, S. O., & Andrews, B. P. (1996). Development and preliminary validation of a self-report measure of psychopathic personality traits in noncriminal populations. *Journal of Personality Assessment, 66*, 488–524.

Lilienfeld, S. O., & Widows, M. R. (2005). *Psychopathic Personality Inventory- revised (PPI-R) professional manual.* Odessa, FL: Psychological Assessment Resources.

Luu, P., Tucker, D. M., & Makeig, S. (2004). Frontal-midline theta and the error-related negativity: Neurophysiological mechanisms of action regulation. *Clinical Neurophysiology, 115*, 1821–1835.

Lykken, D. T. (1957). A study of anxiety in the sociopathic personality. *Journal of Abnormal and Clinical Psychology, 55*, 6–10.

Lykken, D. T. (1995). *The antisocial personalities.* Hillsdale, NJ: Erlbaum.

Lynam, D. R., & Derefinko, K. J. (2006). *Psychopathy and personality.* In C. J. Patrick (Ed.), *Handbook of psychopathy* (pp. 133–155). New York: Guilford Press.

Molto, J., Poy, R., Segarra, P., Pastor, M., & Montanes, S. (2007). Response perseveration in psychopaths: Interpersonal/affective or social deviance traits? *Journal of Abnormal Psychology, 3*, 632–637.

Morgan, A. B., & Lilienfeld, S. O. (2000). A meta-analytic review of the relation between antisocial behavior and neuropsychological measures of executive function. *Clinical Psychology Review, 20*, 113–136.

Nieuwenhuis, S., Aston-Jones, G., & Cohen, J. D. (2005). Decision making, the P3, and the locus coeruleus-norepinephrine system. *Psychological Bulletin, 131*, 510–532.

Newman, J. P. (1998). *Psychopathic behavior: An information processing perspective.* In D. J. Cooke, R. D. Hare, & A. Forth (Eds.), *Psychopathy: Theory, research and implications for society* (pp. 81–104). The Netherlands: Kluwer Academic.

O'Connor, S., Morzorati, S., Christian, J. C., & Li, T. K. (1994). Heritable features of the auditory oddball event-related potential: Peaks, latencies, morphology and topography. *Electroencephalography and Clinical Neurophysiology, 92*, 115–125.

Pailing, P. E., & Segalowitz, S. J. (2004). The error-related negativity as a state and trait measure: Motivation, personality, and ERPs in response to errors. *Psychophysiology, 41*, 84–95.

Pailing, P. E., Segalowitz, S. J., Dywan, J., & Davies, P. L. (2002). Error negativity and response control. *Psychophysiology, 39*, 198–206.

Pastor, M. C., Molto, J., Vila, J., & Lang, P. J. (2003). Startle reflex modulation, affective ratings and autonomic reactivity in Spanish incarcerated psychopaths. *Psychophysiology, 40*, 934–938.

Patrick, C. J. (1994). Emotion and psychopathy: Startling new insights. *Psychophysiology, 31*, 319–330.

Patrick, C. J. (2006). Back to the future: Cleckley as a guide to the next generation of psychopathy research. In C. J. Patrick (Ed.), *Handbook of psychopathy* (pp. 605–617). New York: Guilford Press.

Patrick, C. J. (2007). *Getting to the heart of psychopathy*. In H. Hervé & J. C. Yuille (Eds.), *The psychopath: Theory, research, and social implications* (pp. 207–252). Hillsdale, NJ: Erlbaum.

Patrick, C. J., & Bernat, E. M. (2006). The construct of emotion as a bridge between personality and psychopathology. In R. F. Krueger & J. Tackett (Eds.), *Personality and psychopathology* (pp. 174–209). New York: Guilford Press.

Patrick, C. J., Bernat, E. M., Malone, S. M., Iacono, W. G., Krueger, R. F., & McGue, M. K. (2006). P300 amplitude as an indicator of externalizing in adolescent males. *Psychophysiology, 43*, 84–92.

Patrick, C. J., & Berthot, B. D. (1995). Startle potentiation during anticipation of a noxious stimulus: Active versus passive response sets. *Psychophysiology, 32*, 72–80.

Patrick, C. J., Berthot, B. D., & Moore, J. D. (1996). Diazepam blocks fear-potentiated startle in humans. *Journal of Abnormal Psychology, 105*, 89–96.

Patrick, C. J., Bradley, M. M., & Lang, P. J. (1993). Emotion in the criminal psychopath: Startle reflex modulation. *Journal of Abnormal Psychology, 102*, 82–92.

Patrick, C. J., Cuthbert, B. N., & Lang, P. J. (1994). Emotion in the criminal psychopath: Fear image processing. *Journal of Abnormal Psychology, 103*, 523–534.

Patrick, C. J., Edens, J. F., Poythress, N., & Lilienfeld, S. O. (2006). Construct validity of the PPI two-factor model with offenders. *Psychological Assessment, 18*, 204–208.

Patrick, C. J., Hicks, B. M., Krueger, R. F., & Lang, A. R. (2005). Relations between psychopathy facets and externalizing in a criminal offender sample. *Journal of Personality Disorders, 19*, 339–356.

Patrick, C. J., & Lang, A. R. (1999). Psychopathic traits and intoxicated states: Affective concomitants and conceptual links. In M. E. Dawson, A. M. Schell, & A. H. Boehmelt (Eds.), *Startle modification: Implications for clinical science, cognitive science, and neuroscience* (pp. 209–230). New York: Cambridge University Press.

Patterson, C. M., & Newman, J. P. (1993). Reflectivity and learning from aversive events: Toward a psychological mechanism for the syndromes of disinhibition. *Psychological Review, 100*, 716–736.

Paulhus, D. L., Robins, R. W., Trzesniewski, K. H., & Tracy, J. L. (2004). Two replicable suppressor situations in personality research. *Multivariate Behavioral Research, 39*, 303–328.

Polich, J., Pollock, V. E., & Bloom, F. E. (1994). Meta-analysis of P300 amplitude from males at risk for alcoholism. *Psychological Bulletin, 115*, 55–73.

Porjesz, B., Begleiter, H., & Garozzo, R. (1980). Visual evoked potential correlates of information processing deficits in chronic alcoholics. In H. Begleiter (Ed.), *Biological effects of alcohol* (pp. 603–623). New York: Plenum Press.

Potts, G. F., George, M. R. M., Martin, L. E., & Barratt, E. S. (2006). Reduced punishment sensitivity in neural systems of behavior monitoring in impulsive individuals. *Neuroscience Letters, 397*, 130–134.

Poythress, N. G., & Skeem, J. L. (2006). Disaggregating psychopathy subtypes: Where and how to look for subtypes. In C. J. Patrick (Ed.), *Handbook of psychopathy* (pp. 172–192). New York: Guilford Press.

Raine, A. (1989). Evoked potentials and psychopathy. *International Journal of Psychophysiology, 8*, 1–16.

Raine, A. (1993). *The psychopathology of crime*. San Diego, CA: Academic Press.

Ridderinkhoff, K. R., de Vlugt, Y., Bramlage, A., Spaan, M., Elton, M., Snel, J., & Band, G. P. H. (2002). Alcohol consumption impairs detection of performance errors in mediofrontal cortex. *Science, 298*, 2209–2211.

Rosen, J. B., & Schulkin, J. B. (1998). From normal fear to pathological anxiety. *Psychological Review, 105*, 325–350.

Ross, S. R., Benning, S. D., Patrick, C. J., Thompson, A., & Thurston, A. (2009). Factors of the Psychopathic Personality Inventory: Criterion-related validity and relationship to the BIS/BAS and five-factor models of personality. *Assessment, 16*, 71–78.

Santesso, D. L., Segalowitz, S. J., & Schmidt, L. A. (2005). ERP correlates of error monitoring in 10 year-olds are related to socialization. *Biological Psychology, 70*, 79–87.

Schoeppner, W. L., Bernat, E. M., Scott, H., Hall, J. R., Venables, N. C., Steffen, B. V., et al. (2005). Externalizing psychopathology and brain responses to gain and loss feedback in a simulated gambling task. *Psychophysiology, 42*, S131.

Schupp, H. T., Cuthbert, B. N., Bradley, M. M., Cacioppo, J. T., Ito, T., & Lang, P. J. (2000). Affective picture processing: The late positive potential is modulated by motivational relevance. *Psychophysiology, 37*, 257–261.

Skeem, J. L., Johansson, P., Andershed, H., Kerr, M., & Eno Louden, J. (2007). Two subtypes of psychopathic violent offenders that parallel primary and secondary variants. *Journal of Abnormal Psychology, 116*, 395–409.

Squires, N. K., Squires, K. C., & Hillyard, S. A. (1975). Two varieties of long-latency positive waves evoked by unpredictable auditory stimuli in man. *Electroencephalography Clinical Neurophysiology, 38*, 387–410.

Sutton, S. K., Vitale, J. E., & Newman, J. P. (2002). Emotion among females with psychopathy during picture perception. *Journal of Abnormal Psychology, 111*, 610–619.

Tellegen, A. (1982). *Manual for the multidimensional personality questionnaire*. Unpublished manuscript. Minneapolis: University of Minnesota.

Vaidyanathan, U., Patrick, C. J., & Bernat, E. M. (2009). Startle reflex potentiation during aversive picture viewing as an indicator of trait fear. *Psychophysiology, 46*, 75–85.

Vanman, E. J., Mejia, V. Y., Dawson, M. E., Schell, A. M., & Raine, A. (2003). Modification of the startle reflex in a community sample: Do one or two dimensions of psychopathy underlie emotional processing? *Personality and Individual Differences, 35*, 2007–2021.

Venables, N. C., Bernat, E. M., Hall, J. R., Steffen, B. V., Cadwallader, M., Krueger, R. F., et al. (2005). Neurophysiological correlates of behavioral disinhibition: Separable contributions of distinct personality traits. *Psychophysiology, 42*, S126.

Verona, E., Patrick, C. J., & Joiner, T. E. (2001). Psychopathy, antisocial personality, and suicide risk. *Journal of Abnormal Psychology, 110*, 462–470.

Vollebergh, W. A. M., Iedema, J., Bijl, R. V., de Graaf, R., Smit, F., & Ormel, J. (2001). The structure and stability of common mental disorders: The NEMESIS study. *Archives of General Psychiatry, 58*, 597–603.

Vrana, S. R., & Lang, P. J. (1990). Fear imagery and the startle probe reflex. *Journal of Abnormal Psychology, 99*, 181–189.

Waller, N. G., Lilienfeld, S. O., Tellegen, A., & Lykken, D. T. (1991). The tridimensional personality questionnaire: Structural validity and comparison with the multidimensional personality questionnaire. *Multivariate Behavioral Research, 26*, 1–23.

Wolpe, J., & Lang, P. J. (1964). A fear survey schedule for use in behavior therapy. *Behaviour Research and Therapy, 2*, 27–30.

Young, S. E., Stallings, M. C., Corley, R. P., Krauter, K. S., & Hewitt, J. K. (2000). Genetic and environmental influences on behavioral disinhibition. *American Journal of Medical Genetics (Neuropsychiatric Genetics), 96*, 684–695.

Zuckerman, M. (1979). *Sensation seeking: Beyond the optimal level of arousal*. Hillsdale, NJ: Erlbaum.

Chapter 58

Addictive Processes

MARY M. TORREGROSSA AND PETER W. KALIVAS

The study of addiction involves integrating the principles and techniques of behavioral analysis, molecular biology, genetics, pharmacology, cell biology, and electrophysiology. Understanding the process of addiction also requires a close coordination between preclinical research and clinical studies of human addicts. The objective of this chapter is to familiarize the reader with the methods used to study addiction, the major findings in the field that have led to our current understanding of how addiction develops and persists, and the current state of emerging pharmacotherapeutics to treat addiction. First, we define addiction and describe the acute mechanism of action of drugs of abuse. Then, we describe how addiction is studied behaviorally, followed by descriptions of studies using neurochemical, pharmacological, cellular, and molecular techniques that have elucidated the neural changes that are thought to be critical for the development of addictive behaviors. Next, we describe the relevance of addiction research in animals to human addiction based on human imaging studies. Last, we describe how these studies have led to the discovery of new targets for the treatment of addiction that are still in the early stages of investigation.

DEFINITION OF ADDICTION: CLINICAL PERSPECTIVE

Addiction is a progressive, chronic disease that involves both biological and environmental factors. An addict generally displays several characteristic behaviors including preoccupation with the abused substance between uses, inability to control the amount of use, use despite adverse consequences, tolerance to the substance, withdrawal symptoms after use, use to control withdrawal symptoms, continued effort and failure to discontinue use, and a reduction in the participation in normal social and occupational activities in favor of use of the substance (American Psychiatric Association, *DSM-IV-TR,* 2000; Morse & Flavin, 1992). While addiction is most often

thought of as abuse of a drug or chemical such as alcohol, nicotine, cocaine, or heroin; addiction can develop to food and certain activities, including gambling, sex, shopping, work, and exercise. It is generally believed that overlapping neural systems are involved in the development of all addictions, but there may also be some important differences (Goodman, 2007). Most neuroscience research into the neural mechanisms underlying addiction has focused on drugs; therefore, this chapter focuses on the study of addiction to drugs of abuse.

In addition, it should be noted that not all drug users are addicts. There are people who control and limit drug intake, and these people are often referred to as social users. There are also people who are considered drug abusers, but not addicts from a clinical diagnostic perspective. Such an individual generally has difficulty controlling the amount of use, but can stop using when necessary, does not let his or her drug use interfere with daily activities, and adjusts his or her behavior in the face of adverse consequences. It is believed that continued exposure to a drug of abuse in a person with certain genetic predispositions and in certain psychosocial situations will eventually lead to addiction if there is no intervention. The changes in the brain that occur with chronic drug use that lead from casual use to addiction is an area of active research (Koob et al., 2004; Koob & Kreek, 2007).

Addiction is also often characterized as a cyclical disorder consisting of periods of excessive use or binges and periods of abstinence or withdrawal that can last from days to years; however, withdrawal usually refers to a specific syndrome of negative symptoms that lasts only for a few days after cessation of drug use. Unfortunately, the addict often cannot maintain abstinence from the drug and will relapse to drug taking, often repeating this cycle over and over again, often to the point where drug use becomes compulsive (Foy, 2007; Koob & LeMoal, 2001). The factors that trigger relapse and the neural mechanisms necessary for relapse are being actively investigated because preventing relapse could help many people recover from their addiction and regain a normal productive life (Kalivas & Volkow, 2005).

DEFINITION OF ADDICTION: NEUROSCIENCE PERSPECTIVE

From a neuroscience perspective, addiction can be thought of as a disorder of biological learning and reward processes (Hyman, 2005; Jones & Bonci, 2005; Kelley, 2004). Drugs usurp the neural systems responsible for normal reward learning, and after repeated exposure, can cause long-term changes in brain functioning. These long-term changes in the brain are referred to as *neuroplasticity*. Drug-induced, enduring neuroplasticity in learning processes is thought to underlie the loss of control over behavior that occurs in addiction, such that even after long periods of abstinence addicts continue to desire the drug and will often relapse. These concepts are discussed in more detail later in this chapter. Drugs of abuse alter normal brain functioning both acutely and over the long term, resulting in the symptoms of addiction. Therefore, a primary focus of addiction research is to understand the neural changes resulting from long-term exposure to drugs of abuse, and thereby identify interventions that will reverse or countermand drug-induced neuroplasticity in order to prevent craving and relapse (Hyman, Malenka, & Nestler, 2006; Kalivas & O'Brien, 2008).

PHARMACOLOGY OF DRUGS OF ABUSE

The most commonly studied drugs of abuse include alcohol; nicotine; stimulants such as cocaine, amphetamine, and MDMA; opiates such as heroin and morphine; sedative hypnotics including barbiturates; dissociative anesthetics such as ketamine and phencyclidine (PCP); hallucinogens like LSD and psilocybin; and cannabinoids (marijuana). While all of these substances bind to neurotransmitter receptors or other proteins in the brain to produce their effects, the types of receptors and proteins they bind to are very different from one another. Alcohol and the sedative hypnotics bind to different parts of the $GABA_A$ receptor to potentiate GABA-induced inhibition. Nicotine activates nicotinic acetylcholine receptors, the stimulants enhance the synaptic concentration of dopamine by preventing reuptake of dopamine by the dopamine transporter, and, in the case of amphetamine and MDMA, also enhance the release of dopamine into the synapse. MDMA also enhances the release of serotonin and has direct effects on serotonin receptors. The opiates are preferential mu opioid receptor agonists, while the dissociative anesthetics are

glutamatergic NMDA receptor antagonists. The hallucinogens are believed to produce their effects by activating serotonin (5-HT) 2A receptors, and the active ingredients in marijuana, the cannabinoids, bind and activate endogenous cannabinoid receptors. The diverse action of drugs of abuse explains some of the reported differences in the experiences these drugs produce, and the degree to which they are abused and addiction develops, but they also share downstream effects on brain systems regulating reward and learning (Johnson & North, 1992; Nestler, 2001; Ritz, Lamb, Goldberg, & Kuhar, 1987).

All drugs produce some sort of euphoric effect or "high," which is thought to reinforce repeated drug use. In addition, neurochemical studies have found that almost every drug of abuse and many natural rewards increase the release or the metabolism of the neurotransmitter dopamine in certain brain regions (DiChiara & Bassareo, 2007), and dopamine receptor antagonists can reduce the reinforcing effects of drugs of abuse (Wise, 1996). These data have led to the "dopamine hypothesis" of addiction (Adinoff, 2004; Goodman, 2007), which is discussed later in this chapter, along with caveats to this hypothesis. In summary, abused drugs have diverse actions in the brain, but they may ultimately have similar effects on specific neural systems that lead to the development of addiction.

BEHAVIORAL STUDIES OF ADDICTION

Although the primary objective of this chapter is to explain the neuroscience of drug addiction, it is impossible to explain the neural changes without first explaining the behavioral methods used to study addiction. The majority of studies in the addiction field utilize behavioral methods in combination with other techniques so that neural changes that occur with chronic exposure to drugs of abuse can be correlated with the behavioral state of the animal. In this section, we explain some of the most common behavioral assays used in the study of addiction and discuss how experiments are generally designed using these methods. In later sections of this chapter, addiction-related neurobiological changes will often be described in relation to the behavioral methods used. The behaviors described in this section are certainly not an exhaustive list, but are often used in combination with biochemical or genetic studies.

Psychomotor Sensitization

Several animal models have been developed to study different aspects of addiction from the very simple to the very complex. The simplest and possibly most common behavioral effect studied in the field of addiction is *psychomotor or locomotor sensitization.* In pharmacological terms, sensitization is any increase in drug effect that occurs after repeated exposure. Psychomotor sensitization is the phenomena that repeated, intermittent exposure to most drugs of abuse produces a progressive increase in the pyschomotor activation of an animal, which is measured as an increase in locomotor activity and/or stereotyped motor behavior. While a progressive increase in locomotor activity does not necessarily occur in humans, people do experience a progressive increase in arousal, attention, approach, and an increase in the salience of drug-related stimuli. Therefore, psychomotor sensitization provides a fairly easy way to study potentially important changes in neural circuitry that occur with chronic drug exposure. Using sensitization to study addiction has several advantages. Sensitization occurs to several drugs of abuse, including cocaine, amphetamine, morphine, nicotine, PCP, and alcohol (Kalivas & Stewart, 1991; Robinson & Berridge, 2003). Sensitization occurs after just a few days of experimenter administered drug, and the behavioral measures of locomotor activity and stereotypy can be quantified using automated systems, making sensitization studies relatively efficient to conduct. Environmental factors and stress also affect sensitization, allowing researchers to study the interaction of drugs, stress, and the environment (Badiani & Robinson, 2004; Marinelli & Piazza, 2002). Moreover, once an animal is sensitized to one type of drug, it will often show a sensitized response to a different class of drug, a phenomena known as *cross-sensitization,* which is another indication that drugs act on similar neural systems despite different primary mechanisms of action (Vezina, Giovino, Wise, & Stewart, 1989; Vezina & Stewart, 1990). Sensitization studies can be coupled to neurochemical studies using microdialysis, voltammetry, and electrophysiology, so that changes in the response of neurotransmitters or neuron firing in different brain regions can be measured alongside changes in behavior.

Conditioned Place Preference

Conditioned place preference is a relatively simple way to study some of the learning aspects of addiction and to confirm the reinforcing efficacy of a drug. The paradigm consists of exposing animals to a chamber that contains two compartments with distinct visual and tactile characteristics. Typically, an animal is first allowed to freely explore the chamber to determine if there is any bias for one compartment or the other. Then, the animal is given a reinforcer (sucrose, injection of drug) and is placed in one compartment without access to the other; on alternate trials the animal is given a control nonrewarding stimulus and is confined to the other compartment. After a few of these training sessions, if the animal is given free access to both compartments again, it will show a preference for the side paired with the reward, as measured by time spent in the reward-paired compartment. Drugs abused by humans produce a preference in this paradigm, while noxious stimuli produce a place aversion. If a compartment is paired with drug withdrawal, such as naloxone precipitated opiate withdrawal, the animal will develop conditioned aversion for that compartment. Manipulations that inhibit the development or expression of a place preference can be inferred to be interfering with the rewarding effect of the drug or the animal's ability to learn an association between reward and context, respectively. In addition, animals can have the association between drug and context extinguished by pairing the previously rewarding compartment with a neutral stimulus, and then reinstatement of place preference can be tested by re-exposing the animal to the drug (see later discussion for a description of reinstatement; Sanchis-Segura & Spanagel, 2006; Tzschentke, 2007). Conditioned place preference is an easier and more technically viable means of testing drug reward in mice, and is therefore, often the paradigm of choice to study drug reward in genetically mutated mice.

Drug Self-Administration

A more sophisticated method of studying addiction is the drug self-administration model. In self-administration studies, an animal performs a behavior that produces an administration of a drug. Usually an animal is implanted with an intravenous catheter allowing for intravenous administration of a set amount of drug after the animal performs an instrumental response. However, animals will also self-administer drugs orally, by intramuscular, intraperitoneal, intragastric, or intracranial injection, or by inhalation. All drugs known to support self-administration in laboratory animals have been abused by humans, and substances that are not abused by humans, do not support self-administration in laboratory animals. During self-administration, an animal presses a lever (or performs another instrumental response) a set number of times to receive an injection or other access to the drug. The number of times the animal has to respond to receive the drug and the drug dose can be manipulated to study different aspects of addiction. Self-administration has the advantage that the animal takes as much drug as it desires during the time it has access to the drug, and patterns of drug taking across classes of drug are similar to the pattern of intake in humans (see review by Gardner, 2000, for a detailed description of drug self-administration). Therefore, self-administration has a great deal of face validity because the animal controls its intake, as do humans. In many cases, the abuse liability of a drug is defined by its ability to support self-administration in laboratory animals.

Self-administration can be used to study many aspects of the addiction process. The acquisition of drug-taking behavior is the process of learning the association between performing an operant behavior and receiving the reinforcer. The neural substrates underlying acquisition of drug-taking behavior can be studied by comparing the amount of time (e.g., number of sessions) required for an animal to achieve stable drug intake with or without a pharmacological, genetic, or other manipulations. Acquisition studies have also been used to study the vulnerability to addiction. For example, human females have been reported to be more vulnerable to addiction and have been shown to become addicted to psychostimulants faster than males. Acquisition studies in animals have also found that a greater percentage of female rats and monkeys acquire stimulant self-administration than males, and often at a faster rate than males (Roth, Cosgrove, & Carroll, 2004).

The maintenance of self-administration is the period of time after the behavior has been acquired when the animal is taking a stable amount of drug during each session. Experimental manipulations can be made before a session to determine what factors inhibit or enhance self-administration when the behavior is already well learned. Generally, something that reduces the rewarding or reinforcing quality of a drug (e.g., a dopamine or opioid receptor antagonist for cocaine or heroin, respectively) will increase the number of responses for the drug as the animal tries to achieve the same level of drug reinforcement. An intervention that increases the reinforcing quality of the drug or that mimics the drug itself will generally reduce the amount of responding because the animal does not need as much drug to achieve the same amount of reinforcement (Koob & Weiss, 1990).

We have primarily been discussing self-administration procedures in terms of continuous reinforcement, that is, using a fixed-ratio 1 (FR1) schedule of reinforcement, where one response results in one reinforcer. Other aspects of addiction can be studied by using different schedules of reinforcement. A number of different schedules have been used, but we focus on the most common here. One of these is the progressive ratio schedule where the number of responses required to receive a single reinforcer increases progressively (e.g., 1, 2, 4, 8, 16, 32). In this paradigm, the maximum number of responses an animal is willing to make for a single reinforcer, called the *breakpoint,* is taken as a measure of the reinforcing efficacy of the drug. In other words, the more an animal is willing to work for a drug, the more reinforcing that drug must be. This procedure allows different drug classes to be compared across doses for their reinforcing efficacy, and interventions that reduce the reinforcing effect of a drug will reduce the

breakpoint, and vice versa. Alternatively, progressive ratio can be used as a measure of the motivation of the animal to seek a drug, and genetic or pharmacological manipulations that alter the breakpoint for the same dose of drug as controls, can be interpreted as altering the motivation to seek the drug (Roberts, Morgan, & Liu, 2007).

Another schedule of reinforcement that is commonly studied is the second-order schedule. Second-order schedules generally require an animal to respond under a compound schedule where a fixed ratio of responses results in the presentation of a cue previously associated with the drug, and after a fixed interval has elapsed, the animal can complete the FR for presentation of the drug. In these studies, the first interval of responding for the cue is in the drug-free state and can be used as an indication of drug-seeking behavior that is not influenced by potential rate-limiting effects of the drug. This procedure is also valuable for studying the ability of drug-associated stimuli (cues) to control behavior and the motivation for drugs. Brain lesioning and pharmacological studies have been conducted using this procedure to determine the neural substrates necessary for drug associated cues to support learning of a second-order schedule, for drug-seeking behavior itself, reinstatement (discussed next), and cue-independent drug-seeking (Everitt & Robbins, 2000).

Reinstatement

The reinstatement procedure is a model of relapse to drug taking. The procedure involves training an animal to self-administer a drug in the presence of a cue or context. After the animals have maintained stable self-administration for several days, they go into extinction, where they are placed in the chamber as they would be for self-administration, but pressing the lever no longer results in the infusion of drug or presentation of the cue. After several days of extinction training, the animals press the lever much less than they did during self-administration. However, if an animal receives a noncontingent administration of drug, if the animal is re-exposed to a cue previously associated with drug delivery, or if the animal is stressed (most commonly by foot-shock), they will reinstate lever pressing, even in the absence of any drug reinforcement. This model is very compelling because the triggers that cause reinstatement in animals, such as stress, cues, and situations previously associated with drug use, or the drug itself, are very similar to those that cause relapse in humans (de Wit & Stewart, 1981, 1983; Shaham, Shalev, Lu, de Wit, & Stewart, 2003; Shalev, Grimm, & Shaham, 2002). For example, humans often report relapsing to drug use after sampling the drug again (e.g., "just one drink"), being exposed to environmental stimuli (cues) associated with their drug use, and after experiencing stressful life events. The reinstatement model has been used to determine the neural mechanisms responsible for drug craving and relapse, and has led to the discovery of new targets for the prevention of relapse that have shown some efficacy in early clinical studies to be discussed in detail later in this chapter. As mentioned, the conditioned place preference paradigm and second-order schedules can also be used to measure reinstatement.

NEUROCIRCUITRY OF ADDICTION

Experimental Techniques

The development of animal models of addiction has allowed researchers to study the neural mechanisms underlying the development and expression of addictive behaviors. Two techniques that have been used extensively to determine the basic brain regions and neurotransmitter systems affected by addictive drugs are lesion studies and microdialysis (Torregrossa & Kalivas, 2007). Lesions can be either irreversible or reversible. An irreversible lesion involves injecting a neurotoxic chemical into a brain region, killing the neurons in that region, therefore preventing any activity or involvement of that brain region in behavior. Reversible lesions consist of injecting an inhibitory agent into a brain region such that the region is temporarily inactivated, but the neurons are not destroyed and regain function after the inhibitory agent is eliminated. GABA receptor agonists like muscimol and baclofen and voltage-dependent sodium channel blockers such as tetrodotoxin (TTX) can be used to transiently inhibit the activity of a brain region. All of these methods have advantages and disadvantages depending on the aim of the experiment (Examples of experiments using these techniques include Fuchs & See, 2002; McFarland & Kalivas, 2001; Moller, Wiklund, Hyytia, Thorsell, & Heilig, 1997). Irreversible lesions have the advantage of eliminating the activity of a brain region throughout a behavioral experiment, such that the necessity of a brain region for the acquisition of a behavior can be examined without giving repeated daily infusions of a transient inactivation agent. On the other hand, transient inactivation of a region using GABA agonists or TTX has the advantage of allowing the activity of brain region to remain intact during all phases of training except for during a specific test (e.g., reinstatement). In addition, transient inactivation can allow for within subjects analysis of behavior with or without an inactivation infusion. The advantages and disadvantages between using a voltage-dependent sodium channel blocker, such as TTX or a local anesthetic, versus GABA agonists revolves primarily around two factors. GABA agonists will not inactivate fibers of passage like

TTX or local anesthetics. Thus, GABA agonists avoid the possibility that the effect of inactivation may result from inhibiting axons passing through the nucleus in question. In contrast, GABA agonists can produce differential effects on different neuronal populations depending on the density of GABA receptors and the signaling induced by stimulating GABA receptors. While the dose of GABA agonists employed is presumed to inhibit all neurons at the injection site, it is possible that on the periphery of the injection differential neuronal sensitivity to GABA could influence the outcome of the experiment.

Microdialysis is a technique that allows a researcher to measure the amount of extracellular neurotransmitter present in a specific brain region in a behaving animal. Microdialysis consists of inserting a semi-permeable membrane into a brain region via a probe that is connected to a syringe pump perfusing artificial cerebral spinal fluid (aCSF) into the brain. Neurotransmitters present in that brain region will travel across the concentration gradient through the membrane and out tubing to be collected for later analysis. Microdialysis can be used to determine basal concentrations of neurotransmitters, and how transmitter levels change in response to drugs or during different behavioral states (Parent et al., 2001).

Neurochemical Mechanisms of Sensitization

We mentioned that despite the variety of mechanisms of action of drugs of abuse, they have been shown to have common effects on dopaminergic signaling in the brain. Some of the earliest studies using microdialysis to understand the neurochemical changes that occur in response to drugs of abuse found that almost all drugs and natural rewards increase the release of dopamine into a brain region known as the nucleus accumbens (NAc; DiChiara & Bassareo, 2007). The NAc is part of the mesocorticolimbic dopamine system, which consists of dopamine cell bodies located in a part of the midbrain known as the ventral tegmental area (VTA) that project to cortical brain regions like the medial prefrontal cortex, and limbic brain regions involved in emotional processing and learning including the NAc, hippocampus, and amygdala. In addition, the cortex, amygdala, and hippocampus communicate with the NAc via glutamatergic projections (Hyman et al., 2006). See Figure 58.1 for a diagram of dopaminergic neurocircuitry and related connections between cortical, limbic, and striatal structures.

When investigating the neurochemical mechanisms mediating psychomotor sensitization, particularly to stimulants, researchers using microdialysis techniques found that not only do drugs of abuse acutely increase dopamine release in the NAc, but after repeated administration and

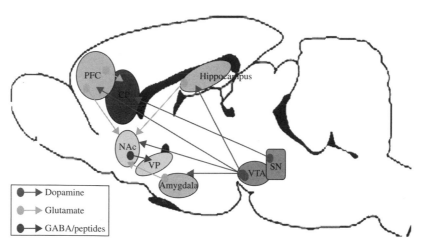

Figure 58.1 The approximate location of brain regions involved in addictive processes.

Note: The view is from a sagittal section of rat brain. The ventral tegmental area (VTA) sends dopaminergic projections to the prefrontal cortex (PFC), nucleus accumbens (NAc), amygdala, and hippocampus; and the substania nigra (SN) sends dopaminergic projections to the caudate putamen (CP), also known as the dorsal striatum. The cortical, limbic, and striatal brain regions are interconnected through glutamatergic projections, and much of the output of corticolimbicstriatal circuitry is mediated via GABA/peptide projections from the NAc to the ventral pallidum (VP).

withdrawal, a subsequent drug administration will increase dopamine release in the NAc to an even greater extent than was observed after the first administration (Kalivas & Duffy, 1993; Robinson, Jurson, Bennett, & Bentgen, 1988; Wolf, White, Nassar, Brooderson, & Khansa, 1993). These data reinforced the dopamine hypothesis of addiction (Wise, 1996); stating that reinforcement is mediated by increased dopamine signaling in the NAc, and that locomotor sensitization and addiction develop from repeated and enhanced dopamine release (Goodman, 2007). Subsequent research has found that animals expressing locomotor sensitization also show enhanced dopamine release in the medial prefrontal cortex (mPFC) and in the VTA. However, sensitization also produces an enhancement in glutamate release in the NAc and in the VTA (Kalivas & Duffy, 1998; Pierce, Bell, Duffy, & Kalivas, 1996). The enhancement of glutamate release in the NAc may be very important for sensitization as an AMPA glutamate receptor antagonist injected into the NAc prevents locomotor sensitization, and injection of AMPA itself into the NAc increases locomotor activity more effectively in cocaine-sensitized rats (Vanderschuren & Kalivas, 2000). In addition, other brain regions and/or other neurotransmitter systems have shown enhanced activity after a sensitizing regimen of drug administration, but the relative contribution of all these changes to the expression of locomotor sensitization and other addictive behaviors has not been fully elucidated. One caveat in many of the experiments mentioned here and to the "dopamine hypothesis of addiction" is that the enhanced neurotransmitter release is sometimes only seen within in a certain time period of withdrawal after the last drug administration, despite observation of behavioral sensitization at all time points. For example, some studies report that after short withdrawal times (1 to 5 days) using certain dosing regimens, there is no change in dopamine release relative to the first drug administration, but after longer withdrawal (1 to 3 weeks), sensitized dopamine release is observed, while increased locomotor activity is observed after both short and long withdrawal (Kalivas & Duffy, 1993; Wolf et al., 1993; Zhang, Loonam, Noailles, & Angulo, 2001). Therefore, enhanced dopamine release in the NAc does not fully explain the enhancement of locomotor activity after repeated drug exposure, suggesting that other mechanisms, such as increased glutamate release, are also important.

Self-Administration

Although it is useful to determine the acute and chronic effects of drugs of abuse on neurotransmission, the studies mentioned all examined the effects of experimenter-administered drug. However, a common issue in the study of addiction is that drugs can have different effects in the brain and on behavior depending on whether the drug is experimenter administered or self-administered. Therefore, some microdialysis studies have been conducted in animals self-administering a drug of abuse to verify some of the effects that have been observed with passive drug administration. A variety of neurotransmitters and brain regions have been examined. The most consistent finding has been that self-administered drugs, including cocaine, heroin, and nicotine, cause an increase in dopamine efflux preferentially in the shell subregion of the NAc rather than the core subregion, and the amount of dopamine efflux progressively increases across self-administration sessions

(Lecca et al., 2006; Lecca, Cacciapaglia, Valentini, Acquas, & Di Chiara, 2007; Lecca, Valentini, Cacciapaglia, Acquas, & Di Chiara, 2007). The importance of dopamine activity in the NAc for the development and maintenance of self-administration has been supported by studies showing that selective lesions of dopamine neurons in the NAc inhibits self-administration (Caine & Koob, 1994; Sizemore, Co, Koves, Martin, & Smith, 2004) and dopamine antagonists injected into the NAc alters self-administration behavior in a manner consistent with reduced drug reward (Bari & Pierce, 2005; Caine, Heinrichs, Coffin, & Koob, 1995). A variety of other studies have shown changes in the release of several different neurotransmitters in several brain regions during self-administration. There is evidence for increased endogenous opioid and cannabinoid signaling that may be important for drug reward and self-administration behavior (Caille, Alvarez-Jaimes, Polis, Stouffer, & Parsons, 2007; Olive, Koenig, Nannini, & Hodge, 2001), but an exhaustive list of these effects is beyond the scope of this chapter.

Reinstatement

The reinstatement of drug-seeking behavior is one model of addictive behavior where the neurocircuitry has been well elucidated. Microdialysis and reversible lesion studies have been combined to determine the brain regions and neurotransmitters critical for reinstatement induced by drug re-exposure, cues, and stress (cocaine is the only drug that has been tested across all of these modes of reinstatement). These studies have found that the mesolimbic dopamine pathway is critical for reinstatement in addition to glutamatergic projections to the NAc. Specifically, each of several brain regions was individually inactivated by a combination of the GABAa agonist muscimol and GABAb agonist baclofen before the animal was tested for reinstatement. Cocaine-primed reinstatement is prevented by inhibition of the VTA, dorsal mPFC, NAc core subregion, and the ventral pallidum, which is a region that receives GABAergic and peptide projections from the NAc and coordinates limbic and motor activity. Cocaine-primed reinstatement was not affected by inhibition of the ventral mPFC, NAc shell subregion, or the basolateral amygdala (BLA; McFarland & Kalivas, 2001). In contrast, cue-induced reinstatement behavior does require activity of the BLA, indicating the importance of the amygdala for encoding associations between cues in the environment and rewards, and inhibition of the lateral orbitofrontal cortex inhibits cue- but not cocaine-primed reinstatement (Fuchs, Evans, Parker, & See, 2004; McLaughlin & See, 2003). Stress-induced reinstatement (induced by foot-shock), on the other hand, is blocked by inhibition of the central nucleus of the amygdala (CeA), ventral bed nucleus of the

stria terminalis (vBNST), and the NAc shell. It is believed that this CeA complex activates motor circuitry through the VTA, as inhibition of the VTA, dmPFC, NAc core, and the ventral pallidum also blocks stress-induced reinstatement (McFarland, Davidge, Lapish, & Kalivas, 2004). Therefore, stress and drug-associated cues engage a richer neurocircuitry to induce reinstatement than drug priming alone, but all of these forms of reinstatement engage a common motor circuitry to produce the behavioral output (see Figure 58.2).

The neurotransmitters necessary for mediating reinstatement in this circuitry have also been determined to a great extent (see Figure 58.2). In the previous section, we mentioned that sensitization to drugs of abuse and self-administration of drugs produces increased dopamine efflux in the NAc; however, a dopamine receptor antagonist infused in the NAc core does not inhibit cocaine-primed or stress-induced reinstatement. On the other hand, a dopamine receptor antagonist infused into the dmPFC inhibits cocaine-primed reinstatement, indicating that the dopamine projection from the VTA to the dmPFC rather than the NAc mediates reinstatement (McFarland, Lapish, & Kalivas, 2003; McFarland et al., 2004). The dmPFC sends a glutamatergic projection to the NAc core, and AMPA glutamate receptor antagonists infused in the core block cocaine-primed reinstatement, while AMPA infused into the NAc produces reinstatement on its own (Cornish, Duffy, &

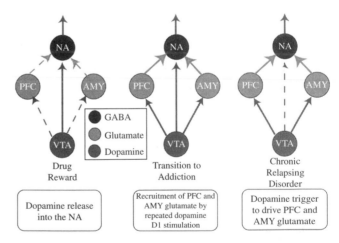

Figure 58.2 Changes in neurotransmitter regulation of corticolimbic circuitry regulating the development of addiction.

Note: Drug reward is regulated primarily by dopamine release in the projection from the ventral tegmental area (VTA) to the nucleus accumbens (NA). Repeated stimulation of this pathway by addictive drugs results in the recruitment of glutamatergic projections from the prefrontal cortex (PFC) and amygdala (AMY) to the NA. This transition corresponds to the progressive recruitment of environmental associations with drug reward. When drug use becomes a chronically relapsing disorder, it can be triggered by dopamine release as a result of a drug-associated cue, stress, or drug administration, but is ultimately driven by pathological glutamate release in the NA.

Kalivas, 1999; Cornish & Kalivas, 2000). In addition, micro-dialysis studies have shown after chronic cocaine administration and abstinence or extinction, the basal concentration of glutamate in the NAc core is reduced compared to controls. In addition, cocaine-primed reinstatement results in increased dopamine and glutamate efflux in the NAc, but by selectively preventing glutamate release by inhibition of the dmPFC, reinstatement behavior is blocked. Moreover, animals exhibiting reinstatement show an increase in NAc glutamate and dopamine, while yoked controls who are not reinstating, only show an increase in dopamine, indicating that glutamate in the NAc is the critical factor mediating drug seeking (McFarland et al., 2003). The NAc not only receives glutamatergic projections from cortex and the amygdala, but also from the hippocampus, which is a structure known to be critical for learning involving spatial and contextual cues. A few studies have examined the role of the hippocampus in reinforcement, and lesions of dorsal hippocampus impair reinstatement induced by contextual, but not discrete, cues, while lesions of the ventral hippocampus impair reinstatement induced by discrete cues or a cocaine prime (Everitt & Robbins, 2005; Rogers & See, 2007). These studies highlight the importance of glutamatergic signaling in addiction, and how chronic drug use may cause enduring changes in basal glutamate activity that underlies the compulsion to relapse to drug use after extended periods of abstinence.

Abstinence itself in human drug addicts may not be the same as extinction in the animal model of reinstatement. Extinction is a learning process that involves performing a behavior that no longer results in the presentation of a drug reward. On the other hand, in abstinence the activities and cues associated with drug use are still present, and continue to accurately predict drug reward. In humans, some forms of extinction learning can occur in a treatment program for recovering addicts, while some addicts may be placed in forced abstinence through incarceration or other means. Researchers have acknowledged this reality, and in addition to the extinction model, an abstinence model of reinstatement is also employed. In this model, animals go through self-administration, but rather than entering extinction training, the animal is kept away from the operant chamber for 2 to 3 weeks, often being placed in an alternate environment each day to control for the animal handling that would normally take place during extinction training. As in the extinction model, reinstatement testing includes pharmacological manipulations or reversible lesions immediately prior to the animal being placed in the operant chamber again, where the number of active lever presses is measured. This form of reinstatement is referred to as context-induced reinstatement after abstinence. These studies have revealed that the dorsal lateral caudate putamen (dlCP), which is also known as the dorsal lateral striatum, is critical for context reinstatement, but none of the other brain regions tested (including the BLA and dmPFC) affected context reinstatement (Fuchs, Branham, & See, 2006).

The dlCP receives dopaminergic projections like the NAc (also known as the ventral striatum), but this dopamine primarily originates from the substantia nigra rather than the VTA. In addition, the dlCP receives glutamatergic inputs from the frontal cortex. The dlCP is known to be important for habit formation (Jog, Kubota, Connolly, Hillegaart, & Graybiel, 1999), suggesting that context-induced reinstatement after abstinence may represent habitual responding that does not require cortical control, whereas, after extinction the cortex is acting to initiate behavior. This is further evidenced by the fact that animals respond more vigorously during the reinstatement test after abstinence than when tested after extinction. Several researchers have suggested that addiction develops because of pathological habit formation, to the point where behavior becomes compulsive (Everitt & Robbins, 2005).

Second-Order Schedules

Second-order schedules of reinforcement have also been used to determine the neurocircuitry underlying drug "wanting" versus drug "taking." The advantage of the second-order schedule is that responding in the first component is drug-free, representing drug wanting, while responding in the second component and later sessions can be conceived of as drug taking. These studies have helped delineate the brain regions mediating the acute rewarding effects of a drug versus those driving drug seeking or wanting. For example, inhibition of the NAc core or BLA impairs the acquisition of a second-order schedule of reinforcement for cocaine or heroin, but inhibition of these regions does not affect nondelayed (continuous reinforcement) self-administration behavior (Alderson, Robbins, & Everitt, 2000; Hutcheson, Parkinson, Robbins, & Everitt, 2001; Ito, Robbins, & Everitt, 2004; Whitelaw, Markou, Robbins, & Everitt, 1996). In addition, pharmacological studies have found that dopamine, not glutamate, antagonists in the BLA inhibit responding for cocaine on a second-order schedule, whereas glutamate, not dopamine, antagonists in the NAc core inhibit second-order responding (DiCiano & Everitt, 2001, 2004). Therefore, much like reinstatement behavior, responding on a second-order schedule requires increased glutamatergic input into the NAc that is mediated by dopamine activation in another structure (in this case the amygdala). In addition, the orbitofrontal cortex (OFC), like the NAc core, has been shown to be necessary for the acquisition of cocaine seeking on a second order schedule, but not under continuous reinforcement conditions (Everitt & Robbins, 2005). These studies provide evidence that interconnections between the OFC, BLA, and NAc are important for learning about and working for a delayed reinforcer. The OFC-BLA-NAc circuit is important for providing representations of the rewarding outcome of a series of behaviors. However, these structures are not necessary to respond for the drug when every response produces a reinforcer, indicating that these brain regions do not encode the rewarding or reinforcing effect of the drug itself.

Research into the normal mechanisms and neurocircuitry of reward learning have aided addiction researchers in determining the structures involved in the reinforcing and motivational effects of drugs and have provided clues to how drugs of abuse may "hijack" normal reward learning systems, such that drugs become favored over natural rewards. Future research may determine ways of reverting this circuit level plasticity such that the pathological changes in reward learning are reversed, and addicts can regain control over their behavior.

MOLECULAR CHANGES IN ADDICTION

Several molecular changes have been described after both acute and chronic exposure to drugs of abuse. Some of these changes are transient while others are long lasting. The transient changes may represent mechanisms involved in the basic pharmacological or rewarding effects of a drug, or initiation factors for the development of addiction. The long-lasting changes that persist during abstinence represent potential neuroplastic effects that may be responsible for craving and relapse.

Experimental Techniques

Molecular biological, genetic, and biochemical techniques provide a rich resource of methods for determining first, what molecules might be regulated by drugs of abuse, and second, which of these molecules is relevant for the development of addiction and/or is a compensatory response to drug administration. The studies outlined previously determined the neurocircuits important for addiction have provided molecular biologists a map of where in the brain they might find relevant molecular neuroplasticity. Thus, not only have the NAc and VTA been studied extensively, but in recent years the importance of other cortical and limbic brain regions has been realized, and they are beginning to receive more attention.

The techniques used to study the molecular effects of addictive drugs depend on whether one is interested in changes in gene expression, protein levels, protein modifications, or activity of entire signaling cascades. To determine changes in gene expression, scientists can utilize several different methods, including in situ hybridization, reverse transcription–polymerase chain reaction RT-PCR), northern blots, or even gene arrays. In situ hybridization is a technique that involves labeling a small piece of cDNA that is antisense to a gene of interest with a radioactive or fluorescent molecule and hybridizing the cDNA to tissue from an animal (often brain slices). The cDNA will bind to the RNA of interest and the amount of radioactivity or fluorescence can be visualized and quantified to compare treatment effects and differences between brain regions on the expression of certain genes. RT-PCR, northern blots, and gene arrays also allows for the quantification of mRNA expression, but do not allow for visualization of expression in a whole brain section. One example of the use of in situ hybridization to better understand addiction has been to determine areas of brain activation and plasticity after exposure to cocaine-associated cues. Thomas, Arroyo, and Everitt (2003) found that mRNA expression of the neural activity/plasticity related immediate early gene zif268 is up-regulated after exposure to a cocaine-associated cue in mesocorticolimbic brain regions including the VTA, NAc core and shell, and basal nucleus of the amygdala. In addition, the plasticity-related gene gamma protein kinase C was found to have increased expression in the amygdala after rats were re-exposed to a cocaine-associated cue (Thomas & Everitt, 2001), therefore, the amygdala and other parts of the mesolimbic dopamine system are likely involved in learning about drug-related stimuli. These molecular results provide further evidence for the importance of the amygdala in learning associations between environmental stimuli and rewards, as was indicated by the neurocircuitry studies discussed earlier. In situ hybridization is fairly labor-intensive, especially for determining how drug use affects several different genes or families of genes; therefore, gene arrays and RT-PCR are often used to determine differences in the expression of multiple genes. In RT-PCR, mRNA from a brain region (or other tissue) of interest is isolated and purified. The RNA is then reverse transcribed using a polymerase chain reaction (PCR) to create complementary DNA (cDNA). RNA present in high concentrations will create more cDNA than RNA for a gene that is in low concentration. The amount of cDNA for a specific gene can then be determined using primers specific for that gene and performing real-time PCR using fluorescent dyes that increase in fluorescence when double-stranded DNA is formed. Thus, the PCR cycle where fluorescence is detected above background can be used as a measure of gene quantity. A gene in high concentration will reach threshold at an earlier cycle than a gene in lower concentration. PCR is a convenient way to measure multiple genes, but gene arrays allow thousands of genes to be examined at once. Arrays consist of potentially thousands of "spots" of nucleic acids, where each spot is antisense to a specific gene. Purified RNA obtained from tissue is labeled (usually with a fluorescent marker) and allowed to hybridize to these spots producing a signal that increases with increased concentration of the gene. Gene array studies of human addicts have shown patterns of gene expression changes including decreases in genes encoding proteins involved in presynaptic neurotransmitter release in heroin abusers and decreases in myelin associated genes in cocaine abusers (Albertson, Schmidt, Kapatos, & Bannon, 2006). Gene array studies have several drawbacks, particularly with the technology that is currently available, including the high volume and complexity of data obtained and poor reproducibility. Results from gene array studies must be verified by secondary means, usually RT-PCR or in situ hybridization, and ultimately proven to be physiologically relevant through verification that the amount of protein is indeed altered by the treatment used for the array study.

Quantification of protein changes or protein modifications (e.g., phosphorylation) are most often conducted by western blotting, though techniques like immunohistochemisitry can be used to determine cell specific protein localization, and the new field of proteomics is being used to determine how multiple proteins change, including entire signaling cascades in response to drugs. Western blotting involves separating proteins from homogenized tissue on a gel into separate bands based on molecular weight, these bands of proteins are then transferred to a blot, the blot is then incubated with an antibody specific to the protein of interest, and finally incubated with a secondary antibody that allows visualization of the bands where the antibody has bound. The amount of protein can then be quantified by comparing the intensity of the band in treated animals to controls. Immunohistochemistry also uses protein-specific antibodies to visualize proteins and can be used on slices of brain to determine the cellular localization and brain region specificity of proteins. Quantification of proteins is more difficult with immunohistochemistry, but in some cases the number of cells expressing the protein can be counted and used as a measure of protein up- or down-regulation. Proteomics assays are much like gene arrays in that the presence or absence of several proteins can be determined at once. Proteomics is also used to determine if certain conditions (e.g., exposure to drug) alter the amount and type of protein modifications in a system (e.g., phosphorylation, acetylation, ubiquitination). The field of proteomics utilizes a variety of techniques, but in general proteins are separated on gels and/or by high-performance liquid chromatography

(HPLC) and the proteins and/or protein modifications present are identified by mass spectrometry. Like gene arrays, proteomics experiments generate a lot of complicated data that is not always reproducible, so other techniques, like western blotting, should be used to verify proteomics results. The advantage of using proteomics is that changes in entire categories of proteins, such as specific signaling cascades, can be determined at once, providing information on possible new targets for the treatment of addiction (see Li, Jiminez, van der Schors, Hornshaw, Schoffelmeer, & Smit, 2006, for an example of addiction-related proteomics research and Williams, Wu, Colangelo, & Nairn, 2004, for review). In all of these assays, the animal can be euthanized after acute or chronic drug exposure, differing periods of withdrawal, or after learning or performing addiction-related behaviors, allowing the researcher to determine which molecular events are relevant to which aspects of addiction.

Some of the most elegant experiments take findings from the basic biochemistry and bring it back to the animal to determine how the molecule affects addiction-related behaviors. Examples of this type of research include using transgenic mice where a candidate gene is deleted (termed a "knock-out" mouse) or mutated and the response of an animal to drug exposure in an addiction-related behavioral paradigm is determined. Alternatively, the relevance of a specific protein to addiction-related behaviors can be determined by delivering a cDNA encoding an active or dominant negative protein by viral transfection, or by transfection of a small interfering RNA (siRNA) that inhibits synthesis of the protein of interest. The cDNA or interfering RNA can be administered to an animal in a specific brain region and in different stages of the addiction cycle. In particular, these studies have increased our understanding of the effects of short-term and long-term exposure to drugs of abuse and of how the brain responds to adapt to these drug effects.

One example of a protein whose role in addiction was determined using the techniques discussed here is cyclin-dependent kinase 5 (Cdk5). First, Bibb and colleagues (2001) used in situ hybridization and western blotting to determine that chronic cocaine exposure increases Cdk5 gene expression and protein levels, respectively. In this study, inhibitors of Cdk5 were shown to enhance locomotor sensitization to cocaine, suggesting that normal Cdk5 activity is needed to restore homeostasis after chronic cocaine exposure. In a follow-up study, researchers induced specific forebrain deletion of Cdk5 using conditional knock-out mice, which also resulted in an enhancement of cocaine-induced locomotor activity, and increased progressive ratio responding for food, which further implicated Cdk5 in the effects of cocaine and reward-related processes (Benavides et al., 2007). Likewise, these researchers found that reducing

Cdk5 expression specifically in the NAc using a viral transfection technique enhanced the locomotor activating effects of cocaine and promoted conditioned place preference to cocaine (Benavides et al., 2007). This series of studies provides a powerful example of how a combination of genetic, biochemical, and behavioral techniques can be used to increase our understanding of complicated disorders like addiction. To date, fewer studies have utilized siRNA technology to study addiction in vivo; however, there are some interesting examples that highlight the potential of future siRNA experiments. In one study, researchers specifically reduced the expression of the dopamine D3 receptor in the nucleus accumbens shell and determined the resulting locomotor response to cocaine. The siRNA mediated reduction in D3 receptor expression resulted in an increase in locomotor activity in response to cocaine compared to animals that received an infusion of a control virus (Bahi, Boyer, Bussard, & Dreyer, 2005). Therefore, increased activity of D3 receptors may inhibit the effects of cocaine, and may be a potential pharmacotherapeutic target for the treatment of addiction. The following sections describe in more detail the molecular effects of acute and long-term drug exposure, and list additional studies that utilize the techniques discussed earlier.

Acute Molecular Effects

Drugs of abuse have a variety of acute molecular effects depending on their mechanism of action. For example, the psychostimulants cocaine and amphetamine bind to dopamine transporters preventing dopamine from being transported back into the cell for degradation, in addition, amphetamines reverse the transporters, such that more dopamine is released into the synapse. The increase in extracellular dopamine thus results in increased stimulation of dopamine receptors, which include members of the D1 family of receptors (D1 and D5), which are coupled to G_s G-proteins, and the D2 family of receptors (D2, D3, and D4), which are coupled to G_i G-proteins (Neve, Seamans, & Trantham-Davidson, 2004; Ron & Jurd, 2005; Sibley, Monsma, & Shen, 1993; see later discussion for a more detailed explanation of G-protein signaling). Opiates like heroin and morphine directly activate G_i coupled opioid receptors. The reinforcing effects of opiate drugs are primarily attributed to their activation of the mu opioid receptor (Contet, Kieffer, & Befort, 2004). However, because opioids indirectly increase dopaminergic activity, opioids can indirectly stimulate G_s G-proteins in certain cells, particularly in the NAc. Other drugs of abuse like alcohol and nicotine act on ligand-gated ion channels in the VTA and other brain regions, but also ultimately increase dopamine release and activation of dopamine

receptors in the NAc (Nestler, 2004). It is believed that activity at both D1 and D2 receptors in the NAc is important for the acute reinforcing effects of drugs of abuse, though the exact mechanism of reinforcement is not known (Nakajima, 1989).

One primary action of G-proteins is to regulate the activity of cyclic adenosine monophosphate (cAMP). The cAMP signaling cascade is known to be involved in many aspects of addiction and other disorders, and will be reviewed briefly here. First, cAMP is regulated by the activation of G-protein coupled receptors by neurotransmitters. Stimulatory G-proteins are called G_s proteins, while inhibitory G-proteins are called G_i proteins. The G-protein complex consists of a three subunits, α, β, and γ. The α subunit is bound to GDP and the $\beta\gamma$ complex. When a ligand activates a G_s-coupled receptor it alters the conformation of the G-protein complex such that the α-subunit is exposed to the cytosol, and the GDP is exchanged for a GTP, and it then dissociates from the $\beta\gamma$ complex. The GTP-bound α-subunit can then activate the enzyme adenylyl cyclase, which then catalyzes the production of cAMP from ATP (Siegelbaum, Schwartz, & Kandel, 2000). Increased cAMP production results in increased activity of the cAMP-dependent protein kinase (PKA), which results in increased phosphorylation of several different proteins including several known to be involved in addictive processes such as DARPP-32 and CREB (Greengard, Allen, & Nairn, 1999; Hyman et al., 2006; Kalivas and O'Brien, 2008), which will be discussed below. Unlike G_s-coupled receptors, the α-subunit of G_i G proteins inhibits the activity of adenylyl cyclase when it is bound to GTP, thus decreasing the production of cAMP and the phosphorylation of proteins by PKA (Figure 58.3). However, it should be noted that G_i-coupled receptors can activate other signaling cascades, and the $\beta\gamma$ complex of both types of G-proteins can have their own independent effects on cell signaling (Siegelbaum et al., 2000). Therefore, the acute molecular effects of drugs of abuse can be very complicated due to their activation of multiple types of receptors and intracellular signaling cascades.

One example of a possible direct effect of drug use on cAMP signaling is seen during acute withdrawal syndromes, particularly from opiate use. Opiates dampen cAMP signaling through G_i-coupled mu opioid receptors; however, during withdrawal when drug is absent, there is an up-regulation of cAMP signaling as the cellular systems "overshoot" when attempting to reestablish homeostasis (Nestler, 2001). Therefore, the negative effects of drug withdrawal may be mediated by an overproduction of cAMP. On the other hand, activation of dopamine D1 receptors in response to acute exposure to psychostimulant drugs leads to the activation of cAMP and does not

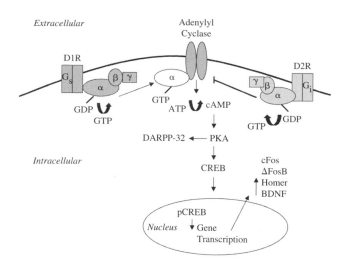

Figure 58.3   Many effects of drugs of abuse are mediated through the activation of G-protein coupled receptors.

Note: The cartoon illustrates G-protein regulation of adenylyl cyclase and the subsequent effects of cAMP activation. Arrows indicate activation or up-regulation while a straight line indicates inhibition. The D1 receptor (and many other receptors) is G_s-coupled and stimulates adenylyl cyclase and the PKA signaling cascade, while D2 receptors (and others, such as opioid receptors) are G_i-coupled and inhibit adenylyl cyclase and PKA signaling. Activation of PKA leads to phosphorylation of CREB to pCREB, which is then translocated into the nucleus to activate the transcription of several genes. The cartoon is meant to be illustrative only because D1 and D2 receptors are not necessarily located on the same cell and the genes depicted can be regulated differentially depending on the brain region, cell type, and receptors activated. Please refer to the text for abbreviation definitions.

produce a withdrawal syndrome, indicating that the acute effects of drugs on this signaling cascade is not sufficient to explain the development of addiction. However, activation of these signaling cascades in certain brain regions may be a common effect of most drugs. Moreover, the consequence of increased cAMP signaling is an up-regulation of the expression of transcription factors and other gene products that may initiate the long-term neuroplasticity that is common to all drugs of abuse (Figure 58.3). Therefore, while determining the acute effects of drugs is informative for determining the initial mechanisms of reinforcement or "reward," these effects do not necessarily explain how drug-taking becomes compulsive and impervious to negative consequences. Consequently, more recent research has examined the chronic effects of drugs.

Chronic Molecular Effects

As we described, drugs of abuse stimulate the neurocircuitry involved in natural reward learning, but do so to a greater magnitude and duration than is caused by natural rewards, like food, water, and sex. The repeated overstimulation of these circuits by drugs is thought to cause many long-term changes and adaptations in this circuitry at the

molecular level. Chronic drug use causes continued stimulation of dopamine D1 receptors. Moreover, chronic drug use up-regulates the G-protein binding protein Activator of G-protein Signaling 3 (AGS3; Bowers, McFarland, Lake, Peterson, Lapish, Gregory, et al., 2004). AGS3 selectively binds to and inhibits signaling through $G_i\alpha$ (Blumer and Lanier, 2003). In this way, after chronic drug administration dopamine release preferentially activates D1 signaling through G_s while D2 signaling through G_i is attenuated by elevated levels of AGS3 (Kalivas, Volkow, & Seamans, 2005). Accordingly, after chronic drug use there is a marked increase in cAMP activity and phosphorylation of protein kinase A (PKA). PKA phosphorylates and thus activates several other signaling molecules as described previously. One of these molecules is cAMP response element-binding protein (CREB). Phosphorylation of CREB leads to increased transcription of several genes including the immediate early genes cFos, Arc, brain-derived neurotrophic factor (BDNF) and zif/268, and other genes like Homer, dynorphin, and Narp, which have all been implicated in addictive processes (Hyman, 2005; Kalivas & O'Brien, 2008; Kelley, 2004). One particularly interesting gene up-regulated by drugs of abuse is deltaFosB. Unlike cFos, which rapidly increases for a short duration after acute drug exposure and diminishes after repeated drug administration, deltaFosB increases slowly after each drug administration and accumulates in dopamine terminal fields in the cortex and striatum upon repeated drug administration (McClung et al., 2004; Nestler, 2001; Nestler, Kelz, & Chen, 1999). The concentration of deltaFosB normalizes during abstinence, indicating that although increased deltaFosB is not an example of long-term neuroplasticity induced by addictive drugs, it may be critical in the transition from casual social use to compulsive drug use (Kalivas & O'Brien, 2008).

The role many of these proteins play in the development of addiction has been determined using transgenic mice, pharmacological, or viral overexpression studies. Activating PKA in the NAc pharmacologically diminishes the rewarding effects of cocaine, while inhibiting PKA enhances cocaine's rewarding effects as determined by progressive ratio responding, self-administration, and reinstatement (Lynch & Taylor, 2005; Self et al., 1998). Likewise, overexpression of CREB in the NAc inhibits cocaine reward, while overexpression of a dominant negative (inactive) form of CREB increases reward (as measured by conditioned place preference) (Carlezon et al., 1998). In addition, administration of an antisense oligonucleotide to CREB in the NAc reduces cocaine self-administration (Choi, Whisler, Graham, & Self, 2006). Therefore, enhancement of the PKA signaling pathway in the NAc after chronic drug exposure may be a homeostatic response. This homeostasis may be mediated by up-regulation of the preprodynorphin gene, which codes for the peptide dynorphin, an endogenous agonist at kappa opioid receptors. Kappa opioid receptor activation in the VTA inhibits dopamine neuron activity, and likely reduces reward (Margolis, Hjelmstad, Bonci, & Fields, 2003). Kappa opioid receptor agonists are known to cause dysphoric effects in humans, and therefore, increased dynorphin expression may mediate the dysphoria addicts experience during drug withdrawal (Nestler, 2001).

Increasing deltaFosB specifically in dynorphin containing neurons of the NAc using transgenic mice, increases the locomotor activating and sensitizing effects of cocaine (Colby, Whisler, Steffen, Nestler, & Self, 2003). Increased deltaFosB also increases cocaine self-administration and reinstatement behavior, while overexpression of a protein that inhibits deltaFosB in the NAc or striatum inhibits the effects of cocaine. Therefore, deltaFosB may be one of the molecular mediators for initiating the long-term effects of drugs, including sensitization and relapse (Nestler, 2001).

In addition to CREB and deltaFosB, activation of PKA results in phosphorylation of the dopamine and cAMP-dependent phosphoprotein of 32 kD (DARPP-32), specifically at threonine 34 (Thr34). Phosphorylation at this site makes DARPP-32 an inhibitor of protein-phosphatase 1 (PP-1), thus inhibiting the dephosphorylation of several proteins (Svenningsson, Nairn, & Greengard, 2005). Due to the acute ability of psychostimulants to stimulate the PKA/DARPP-32 signaling cascade the effects of cocaine in DARPP-32 knockout mice has been examined. Mice lacking the DARPP-32 gene and mice with a specific mutation to inactivate the Thr34 phosphorylation site show reduced sensitivity to the rewarding effects of cocaine in the conditioned place preference paradigm, and reduced sensitivity to the acute locomotor effects of cocaine; however, these mice displayed enhanced locomotor sensitization to cocaine (Hiroi et al., 1999; Zachariou et al., 2002, 2006). In addition, Thr34 mutated mice self-administer significantly more cocaine at lower doses compared to wild-types (Zhang et al., 2006). These results indicate that activation of DARPP-32 by PKA is important for some behavioral effects of cocaine, but that DARPP-32 activity may differentially affect cocaine-mediated behavior depending on the duration of cocaine exposure and may undergo long-term plasticity in function.

Another interesting family of proteins regulated by drugs of abuse are the Homer proteins. There are multiple Homer proteins and isoforms that are known to be involved in regulating glutamate receptor activity, calcium signaling, and synaptic remodeling. In addition, Homer genes are dynamically regulated by cocaine and environmental stimuli; specifically, abstinence from chronic cocaine decreases Homer 1b/c expression in the NAc. When a synthetic nucleic acid sequence antisense to the Homer 1b/c

gene is infused into the NAc, thus preventing the translation of the gene into protein (termed an *antisense oligonucleotide*), which recapitulates the cocaine effect, drug naïve rats have a sensitized locomotor response to cocaine (Ghasemzadeh, Permenter, Lake, Worley, & Kalivas, 2003). In addition, mice genetically modified such that the Homer1 or Homer 2 gene is knocked out (i.e., the mice no longer express the Homer proteins encoded by these genes) also display behaviors consistent with those observed after chronic cocaine and abstinence. Homer knockout mice display conditioned place preference and increased locomotor activity at lower doses of cocaine than wild-type controls. In addition, in wild-type animals exposed to chronic cocaine and abstinence, the basal extracellular concentration of glutamate in the NAc is decreased, but there is enhanced glutamate release in response to a cocaine challenge. Likewise, Homer knockout mice have a lower basal concentration of glutamate in the NAc, and an augmented glutamate (but not dopamine) release in response to cocaine. These cocaine-like effects in knock-out mice can be reversed by intra-NAc infusion of an adeno-associated virus (AAV) transfection of the Homer 2b splice variant. In other words, if Homer 2 expression is restored in the NAc of knockout mice, the sensitized effects of conditioned place preference, locomotor activity, and cocaine-induced glutamate release are reversed (Szumlinski et al., 2004). Therefore, Homer proteins are candidates for mediating the neuroplastic and behavioral effects of chronic drug use.

Another long-term neuroadaptation produced by chronic cocaine exposure and abstinence is a persistent reduction in the basal concentration of glutamate in the NAc (Baker et al., 2003; McFarland et al., 2003). The basal concentrations of amino acid neurotransmitters like glutamate are primarily controlled by activity of transporters located on glial cells, rather than by neural activity. Therefore, researchers determined whether the activity of glutamate transporters was altered after chronic cocaine. One of these transporters is the cystine/glutamate exchanger, which exchanges one extracellular cystine for one intracellular glutamate, providing cystine to the cell for glutathione synthesis, and modulating excitatory neurotransmission by providing glutamatergic tone on extrasynaptic metabotropic glutamate receptors (mGluRs). The cystine/glutamate exchanger has been shown to be down-regulated during abstinence from chronic cocaine, in which reduces extracellular glutamatergic tone on mGluRs. This glutamatergic tone normally inhibits synaptic glutamate release, and in the absence of this inhibitory regulation a relevant environmental stimulus such as an injection of cocaine or a cocaine associated cue enhances synaptic glutamate release. It is believed that this adaptation in glutamate signaling mediates the propensity to relapse during abstinence, and this hypothesis has been supported by several pieces of evidence. First, inhibitors of cystine/glutamate exchange reduce the basal concentration of glutamate similar to chronic cocaine, in drug naïve animals. Secondly, restoration of cystine/glutamate exchange by direct administration of cystine or systemic administration of the cysteine prodrug N-acetylcysteine (NAC) increases basal glutamate in cocaine abstinent animals to levels observed in controls. Finally, NAC administration prevents cocaine-priming from increasing glutamate in the NAc and prevents cocaine-primed reinstatement (Baker et al., 2003). Therefore, altered cystine/glutamate exchange is one of the enduring neuroplastic events that occurs in response to chronic cocaine. Moreover, it was recently shown that NAC blocks reinstatement in rats extinguished from heroin self-administration (Zhou & Kalivas, 2007), making altered glutamatergic signaling through the cystine/glutamate exchanger a possible mechanism for the high rates of craving and relapse in both cocaine and heroin addicts.

Another molecule that is regulated by drugs of abuse and has received a lot of attention in terms of the neuroplasticity of addiction is brain-derived neurotrophic factor (BDNF). BDNF is in the nerve growth factor family of growth factors that are important for normal neural development, but have also been shown to be important in learning processes and psychiatric disorders in adults. BDNF gene expression is regulated by CREB, and acute cocaine increases BDNF mRNA expression in the NAc (Filip et al., 2006). In addition, withdrawal from cocaine self-administration results in a progressive increase in BDNF protein in the VTA, NAc, and amygdala (Grimm et al., 2003), and a single BDNF infusion into the VTA enhances cocaine-seeking in extinction, and during reinstatement to cocaine cues for at least 30 days after infusion (Bossert, Ghitza, Lu, Epstein, & Shaham, 2005). Moreover, infusion of BDNF directly into the NAc or VTA enhances the development of sensitization to cocaine, and BDNF infused in the NAc increases the ability of a cocaine-associated stimulus to act as a conditioned reinforcer, even a month after the BDNF infusions had ceased (Corominas, Roncero, Ribases, Castells, & Casas, 2007; Horger et al., 1999). Repeated BDNF infusions into the NAc shell have been shown to increase cocaine self-administration and later reinstatement of cocaine seeking, while infusion of a neutralizing antibody to BDNF reduces cocaine self-administration and reinstatement. Likewise, inducible BDNF knock-out mice that have BDNF gene expression transiently knocked-out in the NAc show reduced cocaine self-administration (Graham et al., 2007). Heterozygous BDNF knock-out mice have also been shown to have reduced reactivity to cocaine reward in the conditioned place preference paradigm (Hall, Drgonova, Goeb, & Uhl, 2003). All of these

studies imply that BDNF is necessary for the rewarding and sensitizing effects of cocaine; however, BDNF infusion into the dorsal mPFC has been shown to inhibit all forms of reinstatement tested, suggesting that BDNF is an important regulator of addictive behavior, but that the direction of regulation is brain region dependent (Berglind et al., 2007).

Morphological Adaptations in Addiction

To this point we have been discussing changes in the expression or activity of genes and proteins that occurs with chronic drug use, but the actual structure of neurons has also been shown to change in response to drugs. The structure of neurons can be visualized by staining or filling neurons with Golgi stain or diI, respectively. Golgi staining has revealed that repeated administration of psychostimulants increases the density of dendritic spines on neurons in the PFC and NAc, while repeated morphine administration reduces spine density, suggesting that drugs can cause enduring changes in the structure of neurons. Dendritic spines are structures that protrude from neurons to receive synaptic inputs from other cells. There is some evidence of a positive correlation between the density of spines (and possibly in the shapes of spines and the degree of branching) and the number of synapses. The psychostimulant-induced increase in spine density has been shown to endure for up to several months after discontinuation of drug use. The increase in spine density may also correlate with the time period of expression of locomotor sensitization (Robinson & Kolb, 2004). While it may seem at odds to any "unified" theory of addiction that morphine has an opposite effect on spine density, there is no way to tell from these studies exactly what type of synapses (excitatory or inhibitory, cell type, etc.) are altered. Therefore, it is possible that the changes observed have the same net effect on behavioral output despite differences in the structural plasticity required to achieve it.

The molecular mechanisms underlying this drug-induced structural plasticity are poorly understood, but there have been a few studies exploring this question. One interesting finding is that chronic cocaine and abstinence results in an increase in actin cycling after a cocaine challenge (Toda, Shen, Peters, Cagle, & Kalivas, 2006). Actin cycling is the process where actin is assembled and disassembled, thereby maintaining a homeostasis between globular (G) actin and filamentous (F) actin. Actin cycling controls dendritic morphology and regulates protein insertion into the postsynaptic density. Acute cocaine increases F-actin in the NAc, as does withdrawal from chronic cocaine, amphetamine, and morphine. The increase in actin cycling can be disrupted by pharmacological means, either by preventing the polymerization of actin into filopodia-like structures using Latrunculin A or by promoting polymerization and the formation of lamellipodia-like structures with the LIM kinase inhibitor tat-cofilin. When either of these treatments is administered to the NAc prior to a cocaine-priming injection, reinstatement is enhanced. Therefore, increased actin cycling in response to cocaine appears to be an adaptation that may help the organism consume less drugs and maintain behavioral homeostasis (Toda et al., 2006).

Summary

Chronic drug exposure causes very long-lasting and possibly permanent changes in neurotransmission in neural circuits known to be important for normal reward-learning and motivated behavior. Several molecules have been identified that are modulated by chronic exposure to drugs, some of which have been shown to be adaptive effects, while others may mediate the long-term propensity to relapse observed in addicts. Current research is endeavoring to further characterize the molecular mechanisms of relapse, with an understanding that this is the most likely point of intervention for treating addiction.

HUMAN STUDIES

Neuroimaging

The advent of neuroimaging techniques has allowed researchers to directly study brain structure and function in addicts. Magnetic resonance imaging (MRI) and positron emission tomography (PET) allow researchers to visualize which brain regions are activated or inactivated when an addict receives drug or is exposed to drug-associated cues, and to determine how addicts perform on cognitive tasks. In these studies, the brains of addicts are compared to non-addicted controls or the brain activity in drug situations is compared to a neutral situation. Functional MRI or fMRI measures the disruption in the magnetic properties of brain tissue that only occurs in areas of increased activation. The temporal and spatial resolution of fMRI allows activation patterns to be determined over short time intervals (seconds) and in very specific brain regions. PET studies can be used to measure general brain activation, but also allow for neurochemical studies to be done by determining how the binding of a radioactively labeled ligand for certain proteins (e.g., receptors, transporters) changes in response to a specific manipulation. For example, a radiolabeled ligand for dopamine D2 receptors shows a strong signal at baseline conditions as it binds to dopamine receptors in

the striatum. However, if endogenous dopamine release is increased, such as when dopamine transport is blocked by cocaine, the radioactive signal will decrease as the ligand is displaced from the receptor by endogenous dopamine. Many neuroimaging studies using fMRI, PET, or their combination have been conducted in addicts, but only the most consistent findings are discussed here.

One of the most common findings in human imaging studies is that addicts have deficits in frontal cortical function. The anterior cingulate cortex of many addicts is hypoactive (Goldstein & Volkow, 2002; Volkow et al., 1992). However, when a drug associated cue or the drug itself is presented, the anterior cingulate cortex shows greater activation in addicts than in control subjects (Childress et al., 1999; Maas et al., 1998; Wexler et al., 2001). These findings provide a possible explanation for the inability of addicts to attribute the appropriate salience properties to rewards, providing a mechanism for the enhanced salience attributed to drug associated stimuli over natural rewards. The OFC region of frontal cortex is also often shown to be hypoactive in addicts, which may explain the loss of inhibitory control observed in addiction (Volkow et al., 1992). PET studies also show that addicts have lower basal binding at D2 receptors in frontal cortex, suggesting that the cortical dysfunction observed in addiction may be mediated in part by reduced signaling through D2 receptors (Volkow et al., 1993). One caveat of these studies is that in humans it is impossible to determine if the person had fewer D2 receptors before or after they became addicted, allowing the possibility that D2 abnormalities are a risk factor for addiction rather than a result of chronic drug use (Volkow, Fowler, & Wang, 2004; Volkow & Li, 2004). Recent animal studies have used imaging to determine dopamine receptor binding before drug use. Rats with reduced D2/D3 receptor binding prior to any drug exposure showed increased impulsivity and enhanced cocaine reinforcement, suggesting that dopamine receptor dysfunction increases the likelihood of becoming addicted (Dalley et al., 2007).

In addition, addicts have reduced D2 receptor binding (receptor availability) in both the dorsal and ventral striatum compared to controls, and this deficiency in striatal D2 receptors persists even after long periods of abstinence (Martinez et al., 2004; Volkow & Li, 2004). Addicts also show diminished dopamine release in response to methylphenidate exposure (a dopamine transport blocker), suggesting that addicts have reduced dopamine signaling as measured by changes in D2 receptor binding; however, the activity of D1 receptors has not been determined (Volkow, Fowler, & Wang, 1999). A few other studies have observed increased activation of the hippocampus and amygdala in response to drug-associated cues and increased activity of the thalamus based on the expectation of drug (Volkow et al., 2004). Overall, addicts show disruptions in the same mesocorticolimbic dopaminergic neurocircuitry that is observed in animal models of addiction. Several animal studies have shown that chronic drug use alters dopaminergic signaling, inhibits the ability to attribute proper salience to stimuli, and increases impulsivity while losing executive cortical control (Jentsch & Taylor, 1999). Therefore, while animal studies place a lot of emphasis on neuroplasticity in the NAc and human studies show more consistent alterations in frontal cortical function, there is significant concordance between the clinical studies of addiction and the basic science, suggesting that animal studies may lead to the development of better therapeutics to treat addiction.

Treatment of Addiction

Currently, the primary forms of treatment for addiction are agonist-based replacement therapies. These include methadone or buprenorphine for heroin addiction and the nicotine patch or gum for nicotine addiction. These therapies replace the abused drug with a drug that has the same mechanism of action (activates the same receptor), but has a less reinforcing pharmacokinetic profile, generally having a slower onset and longer duration of action. There are also antagonist therapies, such as using the mu opioid receptor antagonist naltrexone to treat opiate addiction. Long-lasting formulations of antagonist treatment seem to have lower recidivism rates than short-acting formulations. Naltrexone is also used to treat alcoholism because mu opioid receptor blockade appears to reduce multiple types of reinforcement. Nicotine addiction has also been treated successfully with the dopamine transport blocker bupropion, which has a similar mechanism of action as cocaine, but with less reinforcing pharmacokinetics. Bupropion has not been reported to be a successful treatment for cocaine or amphetamine addiction despite being pharmacologically akin to an agonist-based therapy for these drugs. In fact, few treatments have had any reported success in treating cocaine or amphetamine addiction, but there are several compounds under investigation (Volkow & Li, 2004).

One potential treatment has emerged from the type of basic neurobiological research outlined here. Chronic cocaine administration causes enduring changes in glutamatergic neurotransmission in the NAc. In rats, this dysfunction was rescued by systemic administration of the cysteine pro-drug NAC. A limited double-blind clinical trial with NAC in cocaine addicts reported less cocaine craving, desire to use, and interest in cocaine. In addition, the treated addicts spent less time viewing cocaine related cues, indicating reduced cue reactivity to cocaine. Further research is needed to determine if NAC can produce

an enduring decrease in relapse to drug taking (LaRowe et al., 2007).

In addition, GABA agonists have shown promise as a treatment for multiple types of addiction. Neuroscientists have administered GABA agonists to specific brain regions to determine whether activity of that brain region is necessary for the behavior being examined, and the ventral pallidum (VP) was among the many regions where GABA agonists inhibit the reinstatement of drug seeking. Moreover, cocaine-primed reinstatement decreases GABA release into the VP (Tang, McFarland, Cagle, & Kalivas, 2005). Therefore, increasing GABAergic activity in this region should inhibit multiple types of reinstatement behavior or relapse. Several types of compounds that increase GABAergic activity by different mechanisms are currently under investigation, but the long-term success of these treatments has not been determined (Roberts, 2005).

Several other interesting targets for the treatment of addiction have been suggested and are currently under investigation, including cannabinoid receptor (CB1) and corticotrophin-releasing factor (CRF) antagonists. CB1 antagonists block the effects of the active ingredient in marijuana and of the endogenous cannabinoids. There is some evidence that multiple drugs of abuse release endogenous cannabinoids, suggesting that CB1 antagonists may help prevent the rewarding effects of multiple drugs, and a CB1 antagonist has been shown to prevent cocaine-primed reinstatement in rats (Xi et al., 2006). In addition, the CB1 antagonist rimonabant is being investigated as a treatment for obesity, suggesting that cannabinoid receptor activity may mediate the drive to seek food in addition to drug reward. Corticotropin-releasing factor (CRF) is released when an organism experiences stress, and, in part, mediates the autonomic and central effects of stress. CRF antagonists prevent stress-induced reinstatement in animal models and are also being investigated for the treatment of depression with some success (Zoumakis, Rice, Gold, & Chrousos, 2006).

Overall, the development of new treatments for addiction has been relatively slow. However, in the past few years, basic neurobiological research has discovered new targets for the treatment of addiction, and the first clinical trials determining the efficacy of these treatments in humans are underway.

SUMMARY

Addiction is a complex, multifaceted disease that requires an interdisciplinary scientific approach and cooperation between clinical and basic science researchers. The past decade has witnessed a marked evolution in neurobiological information that has translated into lay perspectives on addiction. With this improved understanding of addiction as a pathology of neuroplasticity in neural circuits important for reward learning and as a dysfunction in cortical circuits necessary for executive control of behavior, we can better strategize treatments for addiction. While behavioral therapies are necessary to help people gain cognitive control over behavior and to rebuild adaptive relationships to the environment, pharmaceutical agents are needed to reverse the abnormal plasticity that leads to craving and compulsive drug seeking. Increased understanding of the molecular mechanisms underlying circuit level changes in the brain will continue to identify new targets for treatment. The study of addiction has also led to a better understanding of basic mechanisms of reinforcement, learning and memory, and habit formation. This has led to exciting new findings and perspectives in of the study of neuropsychiatric disorders other than addiction, including the cognitive symptoms associated with many disorders, including eating disorders, obsessive-compulsive disorder, and attention deficit disorder. Future research will undoubtedly lead to the discovery of additional neuroplasticity induced by drugs of abuse in neurocircuits, and these new mechanisms of neuroplasticity can be expected to expand our understanding of the physiology of brain function and how neuropathologies dysregulate behavioral adaptation and response to the environment.

REFERENCES

Adinoff, B. (2004). Neurobiologic processes in drug reward and addiction. *Harvard Reviews Psychiatry, 12,* 305–320.

Albertson, D. N., Schmidt, C. J., Kapatos, G., & Bannon, M. J. (2006). Distinctive profiles of gene expression in the human nucleus accumbens associated with cocaine and heroin abuse. *Neuropsychopharmacology, 31,* 2304–2312.

Alderson, H. L., Robbins, T. W., & Everitt, B. J. (2000). The effects of excitotoxic lesions of the basolateral amygdala on the acquisition of heroin-seeking behavior in rats. *Psychopharmacology, 153,* 111–119.

American Psychiatric Association. (2000). *Diagnostic and Statistical Manual of Mental Disorders* (4th ed. text revision). Washington, DC: American Psychiatric Press.

Badiani, A., & Robinson, T. E. (2004). Drug-induced neurobehavioral plasticity: The role of environmental context. *Behavioral Pharmacology, 15,* 373–376.

Bahi, A., Boyer, F., Bussard, G., & Dreyer, J. L. (2005). Silencing dopamine D3-receptors in the nucleus accumbens shell in vivo induces changes in cocaine-induced hyperlocomotion. *European Journal of Neuroscience, 21,* 3415–3426.

Baker, D. A., McFarland, K., Lake, R. W., Shen, H., Tang, X.-C., Toda, S., et al. (2003). Neuroadaptations in cystine-glutamate exchange underlie cocaine relapse. *Nature Neuroscience, 6,* 743–749.

Bari, A. A., & Pierce, R. C. (2005). D1-like and D2 dopamine receptor antagonists administered into the shell subregion of the rat nucleus accumbens decrease cocaine, but not food, reinforcement. *Neuroscience, 135,* 959–968.

Benavides, D. R., Quinn, J. J., Zhong, P., Hawasli, A. H., DiLeone, R. J., Kansy, J. W., et al. (2007). Cdk5 modulates cocaine reward, motivation, and striatal neuron excitability. *Journal of Neuroscience, 27,* 12967–12976.

Berglind, W. J., See, R. E., Fuchs, R. A., Ghee, S. M., Whitfield, T. W., Miller, S. W., et al. (2007). A BDNF infusion into the medial prefrontal cortex suppresses cocaine seeking in rats. *European Journal of Neuroscience, 26,* 757–766.

Bibb, J. A., Chen, J., Taylor, J. R., Svenningsson, P., Nishi, A., Snyder, G. L., et al. (2001, March 15). Effects of chronic exposure to cocaine are regulated by the neuronal protein Cdk5. *Nature, 410,* 376–380.

Blumer, J. B., & Lanier, S. M. (2003). Accessory proteins for G protein signaling systems: Activators of G protein signaling and other nonreceptor proteins influencing the activation state of G proteins. *Receptors and Channels, 9,* 195–204.

Bossert, J. M., Ghitza, U. E., Lu, L., Epstein, D. H., & Shaham, Y. (2005). Neurobiology of relapse to heroin and cocaine seeking: An update and clinical implications. *European Journal of Pharmacology, 526,* 36–50.

Bowers, M. S., McFarland, K., Lake, R. W., Peterson, Y. K., Lapish, C. C., Gregory, M. L., et al. (2004). Activator of G-protein signaling 3: A gatekeeper of cocaine sensitization and drug-seeking. *Neuron, 42,* 269–281.

Caille, S., Alvarez-Jaimes, L., Polis, I., Stouffer, D. G., & Parsons, L. H. (2007). Specific alterations of extracellular endocannabinoid levels in the nucleus accumbens by ethanol, heroin, and cocaine self-administration. *Journal of Neuroscience, 27,* 3695–3702.

Caine, S. B., Heinrichs, S. C., Coffin, V. L., & Koob, G. F. (1995). Effects of dopamine D-1 antagonist SCH 23390 microinjected into the accumbens, amygdala, or striatum on cocaine self-administration in the rat. *Brain Research, 692,* 47–56.

Caine, S. B., & Koob, G. F. (1994). Effects of mesolimbic dopamine depletion on responding maintained by cocaine and food. *Journal of the Experimental Analysis of Behavior, 61,* 213–221.

Carlezon, W. A., Thome, J., Olson, V. G., Lane-Ladd, S. B., Brodkin, E. S., Hiroi, N., et al. (1998, December 18). Regulation of cocaine reward by CREB. *Science, 282,* 2272–2275.

Childress, A. R., Mozley, P. D., McElgin, W., Fitzgerald, J., Reivich, M., & O'Brien, C. P. (1999). Limbic activation during cue-induced cocaine craving. *American Journal of Psychiatry, 156,* 11–18.

Choi, K. H., Whisler, K., Graham, D. L., & Self, D. W. (2006). Antisense-induced reduction in nucleus accumbens cyclic AMP response element binding protein attenuates cocaine reinforcement. *Neuroscience, 137,* 373–383.

Colby, C. R., Whisler, K., Steffen, C., Nestler, E. J., & Self, D. W. (2003). Striatal cell type-specific overexpression of DeltaFosB enhances incentive for cocaine. *Journal of Neuroscience, 23,* 2488–2493.

Contet, C., Kieffer, B. L., & Befort, K. (2004). Mu opioid receptor: A gateway to drug addiction. *Current Opinion in Neurobiology, 14,* 370–378.

Cornish, J. L., Duffy, P., & Kalivas, P. W. (1999). A role for nucleus accumbens glutamate transmission in the relapse to cocaine-seeking behavior. *Neuroscience, 93,* 1359–1367.

Cornish, J. L., & Kalivas, P. W. (2000). Glutamate transmission in the nucleus accumbens mediates relapse in cocaine addiction. *Journal of Neuroscience, 20,* RC89.

Corominas, M., Roncero, C., Ribases, M., Castells, X., & Casas, M. (2007). Brain-derived neurotrophic factor and its intracellular signaling pathways in cocaine addiction. *Neuropsychobiology, 55,* 2–13.

Dalley, J. W., Fryer, T. D., Brichard, L., Robinson, E. S., Theobald, D. E., Laane, K., et al. (2007, August 24). Nucleus accumbens D2/3 receptors predict trait impulsivity and cocaine reinforcement. *Science, 317,* 1033–1035.

de Wit, H., & Stewart, J. (1981). Reinstatement of cocaine-reinforced responding in the rat. *Psychopharmacology, 75,* 134–143.

de Wit, H., & Stewart, J. (1983). Drug reinstatement of heroin-reinforced responding in the rat. *Psychopharmacology, 79,* 29–31.

DiCiano, P., & Everitt, B. J. (2001). Dissociable effects of antagonism of NMDA and AMPA/KA receptors in the nucleus accumbens core and shell on cocaine-seeking behavior. *Neuropsychopharmacology, 25,* 341–360.

DiCiano, P., & Everitt, B. J. (2004). Direct interactions between the basolateral amygdala and nucleus accumbens core underlie cocaine-seeking behavior by rats. *Journal of Neuroscience, 24,* 7167–7173.

DiChiara, G., & Bassareo, V. (2007). Reward system and addiction: What dopamine does and doesn't do. *Current Opinion in Pharmacology, 7,* 69–76.

Everitt, B. J., & Robbins, T. W. (2000). Second-order schedules of drug reinforcement in rats and monkeys: Measurement of reinforcing efficacy and drug-seeking behaviour. *Psychopharmacology, 153,* 17–30.

Everitt, B. J., & Robbins, T. W. (2005). Neural systems of reinforcement for drug addiction: From actions to habits to compulsion. *Nature Neuroscience, 8,* 1481–1489.

Filip, M., Faron-Gorecka, A., Kusmider, M., Golda, A., Frankowska, M., & Dziedzicka-Wasylewska, M. (2006). Alterations in BDNF and trkB mRNAs following acute or sensitizing cocaine treatments and withdrawal. *Brain Research, 1071,* 218–225.

Foy, A. (2007). Circuit breakers for addiction. *Internal Medicine Journal, 37,* 320–325.

Fuchs, R. A., Branham, R. K., & See, R. E. (2006). Different neural substrates mediate cocaine seeking after abstinence versus extinction training: A critical role for the dorsolateral caudate-putamen. *Journal of Neuroscience, 26,* 3584–3588.

Fuchs, R. A., Evans, K. A., Parker, M. P., & See, R. E. (2004). Differential involvement of orbitofrontal cortex subregions in conditioned cue-induced and cocaine-primed reinstatement of cocaine seeking in rats. *Journal of Neuroscience, 24,* 6600–6610.

Fuchs, R. A., & See, R. E. (2002). Basolateral amygdala inactivation abolishes conditioned stimulus- and heroin-induced reinstatement of extinguished heroin-seeking behavior in rats. *Psychopharmacology, 160,* 425–433.

Gardner, E. L. (2000). What we have learned about addiction from animal models of drug self-administration. *American Journal of Addiction, 9,* 285–313.

Ghasemzadeh, M. B., Permenter, L. K., Lake, R., Worley, P. F., & Kalivas, P. W. (2003). Homer1 proteins and AMPA receptors modulate cocaine-induced behavioural plasticity. *European Journal of Neuroscience, 18,* 1645–1651.

Goldstein, R. Z., & Volkow, N. D. (2002). Drug addiction and its underlying neurobiological basis: Neuroimaging evidence for the involvement of the frontal cortex. *American Journal of Psychiatry, 159,* 1642–1652.

Goodman, A. (2007). Neurobiology of addiction: An integrative review. *Biochemistry and Pharmacology, 75*(1), 266–322.

Graham, D. L., Edwards, S., Bachtell, R. K., DiLeone, R. J., Rios, M., & Self, D. W. (2007). Dynamic BDNF activity in nucleus accumbens with cocaine use increases self-administration and relapse. *Nature Neuroscience, 10,* 1029–1037.

Greengard, P., Allen, P. B., & Nairn, A. C. (1999). Beyond the dopamine receptor: The DARPP-32/protein phosphatase 1 cascade. *Neuron, 23,* 435–447.

Grimm, J. W., Lu, L., Hayashi, T., Hope, B. T., Su, T. P., & Shaham, Y. (2003). Time-dependent increases in brain-derived neurotrophic factor protein levels within the mesolimbic dopamine system after withdrawal from cocaine: Implications for incubation of cocaine craving. *Journal of Neuroscience, 23,* 742–747.

Hall, F. S., Drgonova, J., Goeb, M., & Uhl, G. R. (2003). Reduced behavioral effects of cocaine in heterozygous brain-derived neurotrophic factor (BDNF) knockout mice. *Neuropsychopharmacology, 28,* 1485–1490.

Hiroi, N., Fienberg, A. A., Haile, C. N., Alburges, M., Hanson, G. R., Greengard, P., et al. (1999). Neuronal and behavioural abnormalities in striatal function in DARPP-32-mutant mice. *European Journal of Neuroscience, 11,* 1114–1118.

Horger, B. A., Iyasere, C. A., Berhow, M. T., Messer, C. J., Nestler, E. J., & Taylor, J. R. (1999). Enhancement of locomotor activity and conditioned reward to cocaine by brain-derived neurotrophic factor. *Journal of Neuroscience, 19,* 4110–4122.

Hutcheson, D. M., Parkinson, J. A., Robbins, T. W., & Everitt, B. J. (2001). The effects of nucleus accumbens core and shell lesions on intravenous heroin self-administration and the acquisition of drug-seeking behavior under a second-order schedule of heroin reinforcement. *Psychopharmacology, 153,* 464–472.

Hyman, S. E. (2005). Addiction: A disease of learning and memory. *American Journal of Psychiatry, 162,* 1414–1422.

Hyman, S. E., Malenka, R. C., & Nestler, E. J. (2006). Neural mechanisms of addiction: The role of reward-related learning and memory. *Annual Reviews Neuroscience, 29,* 565–598.

Ito, R., Robbins, T. W., & Everitt, B. J. (2004). Differential control over cocaine-seeking behavior by nucleus accumbens core and shell. *Nature Neuroscience, 7,* 389–397.

Jentsch, J. D., & Taylor, J. R. (1999). Impulsivity resulting from frontostriatal dysfunction in drug abuse: Implications for the control of behavior by reward-related stimuli. *Psychopharmacology, 146,* 373–390.

Jog, M. S., Kubota, Y., Connolly, C. I., Hillegaart, V., & Graybiel, A. M. (1999, November 26). Building neural representations of habits. *Science, 286,* 1745–1749.

Johnson, S. W., & North, R. A. (1992). Opioids excite dopamine neurons by hyperpolarization of local interneurons. *Journal of Neuroscience, 12,* 483–488.

Jones, S., & Bonci, A. (2005). Synaptic plasticity and drug addiction. *Current Opinion in Pharmacology, 5,* 20–25.

Kalivas, P. W., & Duffy, P. (1993). Time course of extracellular dopamine and behavioral sensitization to cocaine: Pt. I. Dopamine axon terminals. *Journal of Neuroscience, 13,* 266–275.

Kalivas, P. W., & Duffy, P. (1998). Repeated cocaine administration alters extracellular glutamate in the ventral tegmental area. *Journal of Neurochemistry, 70,* 1497–1502.

Kalivas, P. W., & O'Brien, C. (2008). Drug addiction as a pathology of staged neuroplasticity. *Neuropsychopharmacology, 33,* 166–180.

Kalivas, P. W., & Stewart, J. (1991). Dopamine transmission in the initiation and expression of drug- and stress-induced sensitization of motor activity. *Brain Research Brain Research Reviews, 16,* 233–244.

Kalivas, P. W., & Volkow, N. D. (2005). The neural basis of addiction: A pathology of motivation and choice. *American Journal of Psychiatry, 162,* 1403–1413.

Kalivas, P. W., Volkow, N., & Seamans, J. (2005). Unmanageable motivation in addiction: A pathology in prefrontal-accumbens glutamate transmission. *Neuron, 45,* 647–650.

Kelley, A. E. (2004). Memory and addiction: Shared neural circuitry and molecular mechanisms. *Neuron, 44,* 161–179.

Koob, G. F., Ahmed, S. H., Boutrel, B., Chen, S. A., Kenny, P. J., Markou, A., et al. (2004). Neurobiological mechanisms in the transition from drug use to drug dependence. *Neuroscience and Biobehavioral Reviews, 27,* 739–749.

Koob, G. F., & Kreek, M. J. (2007). Stress, dysregulation of drug reward pathways, and the transition to drug dependence. *American Journal of Psychiatry, 164,* 1149–1159.

Koob, G. F., & LeMoal, M. (2001). Drug addiction, dysregulation of reward, and allostasis. *Neuropsychopharmacology, 24,* 97–129.

Koob, G. F., & Weiss, F. (1990). Pharmacology of drug self-administration. *Alcohol, 7,* 193–197.

1150 Addictive Processes

LaRowe, S. D., Myrick, H., Hedden, S., Mardikian, P., Saladin, M., McRae, A., et al. (2007). Is cocaine desire reduced by N-acetylcysteine? *American Journal of Psychiatry, 164,* 1115–1117.

Lecca, D., Cacciapaglia, F., Valentini, V., Acquas, E., & Di Chiara, G. (2007). Differential neurochemical and behavioral adaptation to cocaine after response contingent and noncontingent exposure in the rat. *Psychopharmacology, 191,* 653–667.

Lecca, D., Cacciapaglia, F., Valentini, V., Gronli, J., Spiga, S., & Di Chiara, G. (2006). Preferential increase of extracellular dopamine in the rat nucleus accumbens shell as compared to that in the core during acquisition and maintenance of intravenous nicotine self-administration. *Psychopharmacology, 184,* 435–446.

Lecca, D., Valentini, V., Cacciapaglia, F., Acquas, E., & Di Chiara, G. (2007). Reciprocal effects of response contingent and noncontingent intravenous heroin on in vivo nucleus accumbens shell versus core dopamine in the rat: A repeated sampling microdialysis study. *Psychopharmacology, 194,* 103–116.

Li, K. W., Jiminez, C. R., van der Schors, R. C., Hornshaw, M. P., Schoffelmeer, A. N., & Smit, A. B. (2006). Intermittent administration of morphine alters protein expression in rat nucleus accumbens. *Proteomics, 6,* 2003–2008.

Lynch, W. J., & Taylor, J. R. (2005). Persistent changes in motivation to self-administer cocaine following modulation of cyclic AMP-dependent protein kinase A (PKA) activity in the nucleus accumbens. *European Journal of Neuroscience, 22,* 1214–1220.

Maas, L. C., Lukas, S. E., Kaufman, M. J., Weiss, R. D., Daniels, S. L., Rogers, V. W., et al. (1998). Functional magnetic resonance imaging of human brain activation during cue-induced cocaine craving. *American Journal of Psychiatry, 155,* 124–126.

Margolis, E. B., Hjelmstad, G. O., Bonci, A., & Fields, H. L. (2003). Kappa-opioid agonists directly inhibit midbrain dopaminergic neurons. *Journal of Neuroscience, 23,* 9981–9986.

Marinelli, M., & Piazza, P. V. (2002). Interaction between glucocorticoid hormones, stress, and psychostimulant drugs. *European Journal of Neuroscience, 16,* 387–394.

Martinez, D., Broft, A., Foltin, R. W., Slifstein, M., Hwang, D. R., Huang, Y., et al. (2004). Cocaine dependence and D2 receptor availability in the functional subdivisions of the striatum: Relationship with cocaine-seeking behavior. *Neuropsychopharmacology, 29,* 1190–1202.

McClung, C. A., Ulery, P. G., Perrotti, L. I., Zachariou, V., Berton, O., & Nestler, E. J. (2004). DeltaFosB: A molecular switch for long-term adaptation in the brain. *Brain Research Molecular Brain Research, 132,* 146–154.

McFarland, K., Davidge, S. B., Lapish, C. C., & Kalivas, P. W. (2004). Limbic and motor circuitry underlying footshock-induced reinstatement of cocaine-seeking behavior. *Journal of Neuroscience, 24,* 1551–1560.

McFarland, K., & Kalivas, P. W. (2001). The circuitry mediating cocaine-induced reinstatement of drug-seeking behavior. *Journal of Neuroscience, 21,* 8655–8663.

McFarland, K., Lapish, C. C., & Kalivas, P. W. (2003). Prefrontal glutamate release into the core of the nucleus accumbens mediates cocaine-induced reinstatement of drug-seeking behavior. *Journal of Neuroscience, 23,* 3531–3537.

McLaughlin, J., & See, R. E. (2003). Selective inactivation of the dorsomedial prefrontal cortex and the basolateral amygdala attenuates conditioned-cued reinstatement of extinguished cocaine-seeking behavior in rats. *Psychopharmacology, 168,* 57–65.

Moller, C., Wiklund, L., Thorsell, A., Hyytia, P., & Heilig, M. (1997). Decreased experimental anxiety and voluntary ethanol consumption in rats following central but not basolateral amygdala lesions. *Brain Research, 760,* 94–101.

Morse, R. M., & Flavin, D. K. (1992). The definition of alcoholism: The joint committee of the national council on alcoholism and drug dependence and the American society of addiction medicine to study the definition and criteria for the diagnosis of alcoholism. *Journal of the American Medical Association, 268,* 1012–1014.

Nakajima, S. (1989). Subtypes of dopamine receptors involved in the mechanism of reinforcement. *Neuroscience and Biobehavioral Reviews, 13,* 123–128.

Nestler, E. J. (2001). Molecular basis of long-term plasticity underlying addiction. *Nature Reviews Neuroscience, 2,* 119–128.

Nestler, E. J. (2004). Historical review: Molecular and cellular mechanisms of opiate and cocaine addiction. *Trends in Pharmacological Sciences, 7,* 462–466.

Nestler, E. J., Kelz, M. B., & Chen, J. (1999). DeltaFosB: A molecular mediator of long-term neural and behavioral plasticity. *Brain Research, 835,* 10–17.

Neve, K. A., Seamans, J. K., & Trantham-Davidson, H. (2004). Dopamine receptor signaling. *Journal of Receptor and Signal Transduction Research, 24,* 165–205.

Olive, M. F., Koenig, H. N., Nannini, M. A., & Hodge, C. W. (2001). Stimulation of endorphin neurotransmission in the nucleus accumbens by ethanol, cocaine, and amphetamine. *Journal of Neuroscience, 21,* RC184.

Parent, M., Bush, D., Rauw, G., Master, S., Vaccarino, F., & Baker, G. (2001). Analysis of amino acids and catecholamines, 5-hydroxytryptamine, and their metabolites in brain areas in the rat using in vivo microdialysis. *Methods, 23,* 11–20.

Pierce, R. C., Bell, K., Duffy, P., & Kalivas, P. W. (1996). Repeated cocaine augments excitatory amino acid transmission in the nucleus accumbens only in rats having developed behavioral sensitization. *Journal of Neuroscience, 16,* 1550–1560.

Ritz, M. C., Lamb, R. J., Goldberg, S. R., & Kuhar, M. J. (1987, September 4). Cocaine receptors on dopamine transporters are related to self-administration of cocaine. *Science, 237,* 1219–1223.

Roberts, D. C. S. (2005). Preclinical evidence for GABAB agonists as a pharmacotherapy for cocaine addiction. *Physiology and Behavior, 86,* 18–20.

Roberts, D. C. S., Morgan, D., & Liu, Y. (2007). How to make a rat addicted to cocaine. *Progress in Neuro-Psychopharmacology and Biological Psychiatry, 31*(8), 1614–1624.

Robinson, T. E., & Berridge, K. C. (2003). Addiction. *Annual Reviews of Psychology, 54,* 25–53.

Robinson, T. E., Jurson, P. A., Bennett, J. A., & Bentgen, K. M. (1988). Persistent sensitization of dopamine neurotransmission in ventral striatum (nucleus accumbens) produced by prior experience with (+)-amphetamine: A microdialysis study in freely moving rats. *Brain Research, 462,* 211–222.

Robinson, T. E., & Kolb, B. (2004). Structural plasticity associated with exposure to drugs of abuse. *Neuropharmacology, 47,* 33–46.

Rogers, J. L., & See, R. E. (2007). Selective inactivation of the ventral hippocampus attenuates cue-induced and cocaine-primed reinstatement of drug-seeking in rats. *Neurobiology of Learning and Memory, 87,* 688–692.

Ron, D., & Jurd, R. (2005). The "ups and downs" of signaling cascades in addiction. *Science's Signal Transduction Knowledge Environment, 2005,* re14.

Roth, M. E., Cosgrove, K. P., & Carroll, M. E. (2004). Sex differences in the vulnerability to drug abuse: A review of preclinical studies. *Neuroscience and Biobehavioral Reviews, 28,* 533–546.

Sanchis-Segura, C., & Spanagel, R. (2006). Behavioural assessment of drug reinforcement and addictive features in rodents: An overview. *Addiction Biology, 11,* 2–38.

Self, D. W., Genova, L. M., Hope, B. T., Barnhart, W. J., Spencer, J. J., & Nestler, E. J. (1998). Involvement of cAMP-dependent protein kinase in the nucleus accumbens in cocaine self-administration and relapse of cocaine-seeking behavior. *Journal of Neuroscience, 18,* 1848–1859.

Shaham, Y., Shalev, U., Lu, L., de Wit, H., & Stewart, J. (2003). The reinstatement model of drug relapse: History, methodology and major findings. *Psychopharmacology, 168,* 3–20.

Shalev, U., Grimm, J. W., & Shaham, Y. (2002). Neurobiology of relapse to heroin and cocaine seeking: A review. *Pharmacology Review, 54,* 1–42.

Sibley, D. R., Monsma, F. J., & Shen, Y. (1993). Molecular neurobiology of dopaminergic receptors. *International Review of Neurobiology, 35,* 391–415.

Siegelbaum, S. A., Schwartz, J. H., & Kandel, E. R. (2000). Modulation of synaptic transmission: Second messengers. In E. R. Kandel, J. H. Schwartz, & T. M. Jessell (Eds.), *Principles of neural science* (pp. 229–252). New York: McGraw-Hill.

Sizemore, G. M., Co, C., Koves, T. R., Martin, T. J., & Smith, J. E. (2004). Time-dependent recovery from the effects of 6-hydroxydopamine lesions of the rat nucleus accumbens on cocaine self-administration and the levels of dopamine in microdialysates. *Psychopharmacology, 171,* 413–420.

Sveninngsson P., Nairn, A. C., & Greengard, P. (2005). DARPP-32 mediates the actions of multiple drugs of abuse. *Journal of the American Association of Pharmaceutical Scientists, 7,* E353–E360.

Szumlinski, K. K., Dehoff, M. H., Kang, S. H., Frys, K. A., Lominac, K. D., Klugmann, M., et al. (2004). Homer proteins regulate sensitivity to cocaine. *Neuron, 43,* 401–413.

Tang, X.-C., McFarland, K., Cagle, S., & Kalivas, P. W. (2005). Cocaine-induced reinstatement requires endogenous stimulation of mu-opioid receptors in the ventral pallidum. *Journal of Neuroscience, 25,* 4512–4520.

Thomas, K. L., Arroyo, M., & Everitt, B. J. (2003). Induction of the learning and plasticity-associated gene Zif268 following exposure to a discrete cocaine-associated stimulus. *European Journal of Neuroscience, 17,* 1964–1972.

Thomas, K. L., & Everitt, B. J. (2001). Limbic-cortical-ventral striatal activation during retrieval of a discrete cocaine-associated stimulus: A cellular imaging study with gamma protein kinase C expression. *Journal of Neuroscience, 21,* 2526–2535.

Toda, S., Shen, H.-W., Peters, J., Cagle, S., & Kalivas, P. W. (2006). Cocaine increases actin cycling: Effects in the reinstatement model of drug seeking. *Journal of Neuroscience, 26,* 1579–1587.

Torregrossa, M. M., & Kalivas, P. W. (2007). Microdialysis and the neurochemistry of addiction. *Pharmacology Biochemistry and Behavior, 90*(2), 261–272.

Tzschentke, T. M. (2007). Measuring reward with the conditioned place preference (CPP) paradigm: Update of the last decade. *Addiction Biology, 12,* 227–462.

Vanderschuren, L. J., & Kalivas, P. W. (2000). Alterations in dopaminergic and glutamatergic transmission in the induction and expression of behavioral sensitization: A critical review of preclinical studies. *Psychopharmacology, 151,* 99–120.

Vezina, P., Giovino, A. A., Wise, R. A., & Stewart, J. (1989). Environment-specific cross-sensitization between the locomotor activating effects of morphine and amphetamine. *Pharmacology Biochemistry and Behavior, 32,* 581–584.

Vezina, P., & Stewart, J. (1990). Amphetamine administered to the ventral tegmental area but not to the nucleus accumbens sensitizes rats to systemic morphine: Lack of conditioned effects. *Brain Research, 516,* 99–106.

Volkow, N. D., Fowler, J. S., & Wang, G. J. (1999). Imaging studies on the role of dopamine in cocaine reinforcement and addiction in humans. *Journal of Psychopharmacology, 13,* 337–345.

Volkow, N. D., Fowler, J. S., & Wang, G. J. (2004). The addicted human brain viewed in light of imaging studies: Brain circuits and treatment strategies. *Neuropharmacology, 47,* 3–13.

Volkow, N. D., Fowler, J. S., Wang, G. J., Hitzemann, R., Logan, J., Schlyer, D. J., et al. (1993). Decreased dopamine D2 receptor availability is associated with reduced frontal metabolism in cocaine abusers. *Synapse, 14,* 169–177.

Volkow, N. D., Hitzemann, R., Wang, G. J., Fowler, J. S., Burr, G., Pascani, K., et al. (1992). Long-term frontal brain metabolic changes in cocaine abusers. *Synapse, 11,* 184–190.

Volkow, N. D., & Li, T.-K. (2004). Drug addiction: The neurobiology of behaviour gone awry. *Nature Reviews Neuroscience, 5,* 963–970.

Wexler, B. E., Gottschalk, C. H., Fulbright, R. K., Prohovnik, I., Lacadie, C. M., Rounsaville, B. J., et al. (2001). Functional magnetic resonance imaging of cocaine craving. *American Journal of Psychiatry, 158,* 86–95.

Whitelaw, R. B., Markou, A., Robbins, T. W., & Everitt, B. J. (1996). Excitotoxic lesions of the basolateral amygdala impair the acquisition of cocaine-seeking behavior under a second-order schedule of reinforcement. *Psychopharmacology, 127,* 213–224.

Williams, K., Wu, T., Colangelo, C., & Nairn, A. C. (2004). Recent advances in neuroproteomics and potential application to studies of drug addiction. *Neuropharmacology, 47*(Suppl. 1), 148–166.

Wise, R. A. (1996). Neurobiology of addiction. *Current Opinion Neurobiology, 6,* 243–251.

Wolf, M. E., White, F. J., Nassar, R., Brooderson, R. J., & Khansa, M. R. (1993). Differential development of autoreceptor subsensitivity and enhanced dopamine release during amphetamine sensitization. *Journal of Pharmacology and Experimental Therapeutics, 264,* 249–255.

Xi, Z.-X., Gilbert, J. G., Peng, X.-Q., Pak, A. C., Li, X., & Gardner, E. L. (2006). Cannabinoid CB1 receptor antagonist AM251 inhibits cocaine-primed relapse in rats: Role of glutamate in the nucleus accumbens. *Journal of Neuroscience, 26,* 8531–8536.

Zachariou, V., Benoit-Marand, M., Allen, P. B., Ingrassia, P., Fienberg, A. A., Gonon, F., et al. (2002). Reduction of cocaine place preference in mice lacking the protein phosphatase 1 inhibitors DARPP 32 or Inhibitor 1. *Biological Psychiatry, 51,* 612–620.

Zachariou, V., Sgambato-Faure, V., Sasaki, T., Sveninngsson, P., Berton, O., Fienberg, A. A., et al. (2006). Phosphorylation of DARPP-32 at Threonine-34 is required for cocaine action. *Neuropsychopharmacology, 31,* 555–562.

Zhang, Y., Loonam, T. M., Noailles, P. A., & Angulo, J. A. (2001). Comparison of cocaine- and methamphetamine-evoked dopamine and glutamate overflow in somatodendritic and terminal field regions of the rat brain during acute, chronic, and early withdrawal conditions. *Annals of the New York Academy of Science, 937,* 93–120.

Zhang, Y., Sveninngsson, P., Picetti, R., Schlussman, S. D., Nairn, A. C., Ho, A., et al. (2006). Cocaine self-administration in mice is inversely related to phosphorylation at Thr34 (protein kinase A site) and Ser130 (kinase CK1 site) of DARPP-32. *Journal of Neuroscience, 26,* 2645–2651.

Zhou, W., & Kalivas, P. W. (2007). N-Acetylcysteine reduces extinction responding and induces enduring reductions in cue- and heroin-induced drug-seeking. *Biological Psychiatry, 63*(3), 338–340.

Zoumakis, E., Rice, K. C., Gold, P. W., & Chrousos, G. P. (2006). Potential uses of corticotropin-releasing hormone antagonists. *Annals of the New York Academy of Science, 1083,* 239–251.

Chapter 59

Cognitive Neurology

VAUGHAN BELL AND PETER W. HALLIGAN

Cognitive neurology is a discipline that draws on cognitive neuroscience to reveal the nature of both clinical disorders and the functional architecture of the mind in an experimentally testable way (Cappa, Abutalebi, Demonet, Fletcher, & Garrard, 2008). It is informed by theories of neural and cognitive mechanisms that underlie mental processes and their behavioral manifestations and, like all bridging disciplines, comprises a broad range of methods and approaches. Central to this approach, however, is the reciprocal and ongoing relationship whereby cognitive neuroscience can inform neurology and clinical findings can enlighten cognitive research. Moreover, as a recent addition to the cognitive neurosciences, cognitive neurology is well placed to exert a powerful influence on basic science, clinical research, and rehabilitation by integrating complimentary strengths and methods from a number of key cognitive fields.

As a testament to its interdisciplinary nature, cognitive neurology connects knowledge and methods from *cognitive neuropsychology,* where patterns of performance produced by brain damage are used to develop and evaluate theories of normal function (Caramazza & Coltheart, 2006); *behavioral neurology,* a subspecialty of neurology concerned with understanding the phenomenology, pathophysiology, diagnosis, and treatment of cognitive, emotional, and behavioral disturbances in individuals with recognized neurological disorders (Silver, 2006; see Chapter 66); and *cognitive neuroscience,* including localization methods, which harness the powerful spatial and temporal resolution afforded by modern technologies such as event-related potentials (ERP), positron emission tomography (PET), functional magnetic resonance imaging (fMRI), magnetoencephalography (MEG) and transcranial magnetic stimulation (TMS) (Gazzaniga, Ivry, & Mangun, 2002).

Like its related subfields, cognitive neurology has its roots in the cognitive revolution of the 1960s and 1970s, where the success of information processing theories of the mind provided a framework for linking behavior and psychology to identifiable brain networks. From a conceptual point of view, cognitive systems are best viewed as a series of related functional systems (e.g., language, memory, attention executive) all of which can be impaired differentially (depending on age, location, and extent) following acquired brain damage. Although extensive neurological damage following stroke or head injury typically impairs several interacting cognitive systems, relatively discrete neuropathologies produce more selective impairments. The observed associations and dissociations in the patterns of impairments are subsequently used to infer the functional architecture of the brain, together with converging evidence from other behavioral and anatomical studies from normal participants and neurological patients.

Cognitive neurology is characterized by the twin focus on clinical and basic (cognitive) research questions. By considering traditional clinical and neurological syndromes in terms of damage to known cognitive systems, investigators can move beyond mere description of symptomatology and meaningfully link cognitive deficits to impaired neural processes. This was well described by Basso and Marangolo (2000, p. 228) who wrote:

> The most important contribution of cognitive neuropsychology . . . lies in the massive reduction of the theoretically motivated choices left open to the therapist. Clearly articulated and detailed hypotheses about representations and processing of cognitive functions allow rejection of all those strategies for treatment that are not theoretically justified. The more detailed the cognitive model, the narrower the spectrum of rationally motivated treatments; whereas the less fine-grained the cognitive model, the greater the number of theoretically justifiable therapeutic interventions.

Consequently, clinical terms such as *dyslexia, dysphasia, amnesia,* or *visual neglect* are not explanations in themselves but rather shorthand descriptions for different types of behavior that stand in need of a cognitive explanation. A major focus of cognitive neurology is the development of theories of how healthy systems break down with the intention of using the observed impairments to inform mechanisms, diagnosis, assessment, and potential interventions. This approach holds considerable promise for advancing the fields of functional cognition (Donovan et al., 2008), clinical diagnosis (Cappa et al., 2008), and selectively targeted interventions (Halligan & Wade, 2005).

Given that several areas related to cognitive neurology are covered elsewhere in the handbook (e.g., see chapters covering *language/language disorders, stroke and recovery, memory, attention, spatial perception and consciousness*) the aim of this chapter is provide a broad conceptual overview interspersed with several selective and in-depth considerations of common clinical conditions. For a comprehensive review the interested reader is directed to Cappa et al. (2008); Hodges (2007); Halligan, Kischka, and Marshall (2004); and Mesulam (2000).

LEARNING FROM NEUROLOGICAL DISSOCIATIONS

Cognitive neuropsychology has achieved considerable understanding of the functional architecture of cognitive systems by charting dissociations between cognitive tasks in patients with selective brain damage (Shallice, 1988). When attempting to understand complex cognitive systems, examples of robust dissociations (where neurological damage A affects cognitive process X but not cognitive process Y) provide a useful tool. Examples of double dissociation are considered evidence of two functionally independent processes.

Naturally occurring dissociations between task performances in neurological patients have provided valuable insights into the intact and damaged mechanisms in language (Margolin, 1991), amnesia (Cermak, 1982), dyslexia (Coslett & Saffran, 1989), prosopagnosia (Young, 1994), and neglect (Halligan & Marshall, 1994), to name but a few.

Some of the most striking and theoretically important dissociations in neuropsychology result from disconnections between conscious or explicit awareness (e.g., what the patient reports) and nonconscious or implicit processing (e.g., how the patient performs), and these merit particular consideration. Recording patient reports is a relatively straightforward process in most cases, but evidence for implicit psychological processing has traditionally been ascertained using a combination of at least three different methods: (1) forced choice methods—where the patient is requested to guess or indicate a preference, (2) evaluating the extent to which selective primes or cues in the affected modality modulate or interact with responses on the nonaffected side, and (3) by directly measuring the physiological or autonomic responses.

Traditionally, the method most commonly used to demonstrate dissociations involves comparing a patient's *subjective report* with their *behavioral or physiological performance*. For example, in the case of prosopagnosia (a disorder of face perception where the ability to recognize faces is impaired), some patients demonstrate differential electrical skin conductance or evoked potentials to familiar faces despite being unable to explicitly identify them (Bauer, 1984; Tranel & Damasio, 1985). In the case of memory, amnesic patients may show significant improvements in overall accuracy when a test is repeated (practice effects), despite failing to explicitly recall the test or its content. Such distinctions make it necessary to qualify amnesia as an impairment of conscious recollection rather than as a global failure to retain it (Moscovitch, Winocur, & McLachlan, 1986). In aphasia, patients who fail tests of comprehension may show normal semantic priming and semantic context effects on lexical decision tasks (Milberg, Blumstein, & Dworetsky, 1987); in dyslexia, patients who cannot read when tested explicitly can nevertheless guess correctly what the words denote using drawings (Shallice & Saffran, 1986).

Blindsight is one of the better known dissociations of consciousness reported in a small number of patients who show impressive intact visual processing in their blind visual field (at levels significantly above chance) despite a lack of phenomenological awareness for the location of stimuli when requested to guess (Stoerig, 1996; Weiskrantz, 1986). Until the 1970s, it was typically assumed that brain injury involved damage to the primary visual areas and consequently produced permanent loss of vision for selective parts of the visual field. Assessing visual field deficits involved asking the patient to report with eyes fixated on a central target, what they could see when stimuli at different locations were presented in the peripheral fields. Although demonstrably unaware of targets in their affected field, some patients were able to indicate by pointing or moving their eyes (and when requested to guess in a forced choice experiment), the location of targets in their blind field (Weiskrantz, Warrington, Sanders, & Marshall, 1974). Although such patients clearly perceive more than might be expected, blindsight does not appear to confer any functional benefit for the patient (Weiskrantz, 1991).

Evidence of blindsight has also been found using skin conductance performance (Zihl, Tretter, & Singer, 1980) and altered pupil size (Weiskrantz, 1990). Rafal, Smith, Krantz, Cohen, and Brennan (1990) demonstrated that unseen stimuli presented to the blind hemifield had the effect of inhibiting the latency of saccades to the seen stimulus in the intact field. Studies of blindsight indicate that the processing of visual stimuli can take place even though there is no phenomenological awareness by the subject. Anatomical and physiological evidence suggest that some forms of blindsight may rely on intact residual visual ability that is mediated subcortically (Stoerig, 1996; Weiskrantz, 1986). Other forms may be explained in terms of a disconnect between specialized areas in the visual cortex (Zeki, 1993).

ASSESSMENT, NEUROPSYCHOLOGICAL TESTING AND NEUROIMAGING

Central to cognitive neurology is the assessment and quantification in terms of the impact to known cognitive structures of neurological disturbance. This requires understanding how neuropsychological testing and clinical neuroimaging complement each other to inform a comprehensive clinical picture. Importantly, there is no fixed contribution that each method makes because the scope of each procedure changes with the arrival of new conceptual and technological developments. For example, neuropsychological testing is no longer the primary method for localizing brain lesions owing to the wide availability of structural and functional brain imaging, although the advent of the clinical applications of functional neuroimaging has meant that well-designed psychometric tasks are now key to uncovering meaningful functional brain networks in the latest brain scanners.

Similarly, the fact that pathology can be characterized entirely at the cognitive level (e.g., dysexecutive syndrome), the neurological level (e.g., glioma), or a mixture of both (e.g., vascular dementia) means that the contribution of each approach to the diagnosis or conceptual formulation of the disorder depends partly on the presenting clinical problem and reasons for assessment.

One of the key functions of assessment is to formulate a working hypothesis regarding the areas of intact strength and weakness in functioning that in turn provides for setting appropriate goals for effective intervention (Byng, Kay, Edmundson, & Scott, 1990; Howard & Hatfield, 1987). While this is not the sole role of assessment, the adequacy of assessments for characterizing the underlying condition in cognitive terms and informing the rehabilitation process is clearly critical. The clinical aims of both neuropsychological testing and neuroimaging typically focus on three main areas:

1. *Diagnosis* to determine the nature and extent of the underlying problem in both clinical and cognitive terms.
2. *Impact* to gauge the effect of the impairment on everyday functioning and cognitive ability.

3. *Course/outcome* to measure and predict change over time, either from premorbid levels or throughout the progression of the recovery.

When attempting to answer these questions, the clinical team will typically integrate the patient's history and presentation with the results of neuropsychology and relevant neuroimaging assessments to arrive at a well-rounded formulation based on a set of well-defined clinical questions, although clinical reality dictates that the assessment might need to be based on the best available evidence and often proceeds in an iterative manner.

Key aspects of a patient's history include their social and medical history, paying particular attention to any personal or family history concerning educational attainment, employment, developmental or idiopathic neurological disorder, dementia, or psychiatric illness. Similarly, the onset and course of the problem in an individual patient is noted alongside any results of earlier assessments and previous experience of the tests, assessments, or environment. Key aspects of presentation include the *signs* (behavioral indicators suggestive of underlying disease) and *symptoms* (subjective reports of ill health by patient), mental state, insight, other medical problems, understanding of the purpose and possible outcomes of the assessment, comprehension of the test instructions and expressive language, level of concentration, level of motivation during each test, current mood, and ongoing pain. Simple cognitive screening tests (such as the Minnesota Mental State Examination, MMSE) or simple bedside tests may be conducted by most suitably trained clinicians but more thorough cognitive testing requires the involvement of a clinical neuropsychologist. A general overview of the types of clinical assessment employed by cognitive neurologists is provided in Cappa (Chapter 2; 2001) in addition, excellent guides to neuropsychological testing are available (Hodges, 2007; Snyder, Nussbaum, & Robins, 2005) as well as more comprehensive handbooks (Lezak, Howieson, Loring, Hannay, & Fischer, 2004; Strauss, Sherman, & Spreen, 2006).

In combination with neuropsychological test results, structural scans are important for inferring links between cognitive deficits and detectable lesions in individuals (see Figure 59.1), and can also be useful for constraining test interpretation (e.g., an individual who performs poorly on an executive test but has only posterior lesions might suggest that the deficit is one that involves early vision rather than the executive system). Functional neuroimaging offers accessible reliable measures of hemodynamic changes— blood flow in the case of positron emission tomography (PET) and blood oxygenation in the case of functional magnetic resonance imaging (fMRI)—in response to selective cognitive task engagement. Both fMRI and PET

(A)   (B)

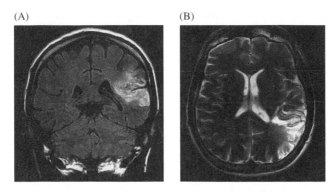

Figure 59.1   Axial **A:** and coronal **B:** slices from the MRI scans of a professional musician who suffered a stroke and experienced a selective loss in musical ability.

Note: The patient lost the ability to discriminate or reproduce rhythms but showed preserved metric judgment and normal performance in all aspects of melodic processing. The scan shows a left temporo-parietal infarct in the territory of the superior temporal gyrus, the posterior part of the middle temporal gyrus and the inferior parietal lobe. From "Receptive Amusia: Temporal Auditory Processing Deficit in a Professional Musician Following a Left Temporo-Parietal Lesion," by M. Di Pietro, M. Laganaro, B. Leemann, and A. Schnider, 2004, *Neuropsychologia, 42,* pp. 868–877. Reprinted with permission.

provide indirect measures of synaptic activity and neural firing and are extensively used to characterize the neural bases of intact and impaired neural systems underlying different sensory and cognition tasks (see Figure 59.1). Resting state functional scans (typically using positron emission tomography (PET) or single photon emission computed tomography (SPECT), and more recently perfusion MRI) can similarly provide information on whether there are disturbances of cerebral perfusion, suggesting areas which might be consistently under- or overactive. Due to individual variation in the neuroanatomical areas that support particular cognitive functions and the fact that not all neurocognitive impairments are detectable on standard clinical scans, there has been an increased interest in applying task-based functional neuroimaging, more typically used in research on normal neurocognition, for addressing clinical problems in individual patients.

Much research has focused on replacing the Wada test for establishing language lateralization and postoperative outcome assessment. The Wada test, or the intracarotid sodium amobarbital procedure (ISAP), involves neuropsychological testing of specific hemispheric functions while one, and subsequently the other, hemisphere of the brain is functionally impaired by the injection of a barbiturate into the ipsilateral carotid artery. The Wada test is also commonly used to determine likely memory impairment after a proposed unilateral temporal lobectomy in cases of intractable epilepsy. Although effective, the procedure is expensive and carries an approximate 1% morbidity risk

(Baxendale, 2000) so the development of noninvasive alternatives offers significant advantage. The application of neuroimaging methods has been promising but, so far, none are in a position to replace the Wada test. This is partly because of a lack of research data, but partly because activation patterns can be influenced by task, analysis technique, and noise in the data (Abou-Khalil, 2007).

Related difficulties affect all such attempts to apply functional neuroimaging to individual patients, which has largely been developed to determine average activation over a group of people. Data acquisition artifacts that are likely to be of minor influence when data is averaged across participants (such as head movement or minor anatomical differences) have a much larger impact when only one person is being scanned. Similarly, analyses used for groups of young healthy participants, such as the reliance on a constant blood oxygenation level dependent (BOLD) signal response, may not apply so readily to children or older patients, for whom cerebral blow flow rate is known to be significantly related to age (Ackerstaff, Keunen, van Pelt, Montauban van Swijndregt, & Stijnen, 1990; Schöning & Hartig, 1996).

To overcome similar sorts of issues, neuropsychological tests commonly employ standardized scoring and norm-referenced performance comparisons, so that an individual's performance can be seen alongside a relevant age, education, ethnicity, and/or gender matched comparison group. However, similar data for clinical function neuroimaging assessments is still rare and clinicians are encouraged to make their data available to others so these essential data sets can be created.

Although neuropsychological tests typically provide an estimate of the performance level in different cognitive domains, equally important is the process by which individuals complete the task. For example, patients with differing pathologies may not differ in their final test score, but may show remarkable differences in the way they complete the test (Kaplan, 1988). A related pattern has also been observed in functional neuroimaging studies, where a difference in behavioral measures but not activation, or vice versa, has been found (Wilkinson & Halligan, 2004). Some tests may have a measure of process built-in, and others do not. Careful observation during testing may be the key to uncovering relevant cognitive deficits in these cases.

When considering in-scanner clinical assessments, Desmond and Chen (2002) make several recommendations: (a) experimental tasks designed for research participants may be too taxing for patients, so recommend that a middle-ground compromise between collecting relevant data points and creating a valid task needs to be reached; (b) cognitive tasks may need practice outside the scanner;

(c) to draw valid clinical conclusions, the tasks need to be norm referenced; and (d) standardization of image analysis methods need to be adopted.

ACQUIRED DISORDERS OF ATTENTION

Attention—the mental process of selectively focusing on aspects of our environment including one's body while ignoring or disattending from other things—is probably one of the most important cognitive processes, given that it pervades all aspects of cognitive life and, when compromised, provides for a wide range of debilitating consequences. The range of deficits stems from the fact that attention is not a single process but rather a set of interacting, albeit relatively autonomous, subprocesses vulnerable to damage with differing consequences. As assessments have been refined over the past decade, the negative impact of impaired attention for recovery and outcome has become increasingly clear. Consequently, the development of interventions designed to enhance natural recovery in these systems remains a pressing clinical goal (Robertson & Halligan, 1999). Clearly, a framework for understanding the functional organization of attention is vital for both the clinic and research laboratory. One influential model proposed by Posner and Petersen (1990) suggests three key specific functions of attention:

1. *Spatial attention:* The capacity to distinguish incoming signals from one spatial location.
2. *Selective or focused attention:* The ability to prioritize some types of information and to restrain others on the basis of an existing planned goal or a stored representation of a target.
3. *Arousal/sustained attention:* The ability to maintain an alert, ready state.

Although these and similar taxonomies (e.g., Mirsky, Anthony, Duncan, Ahearn, & Kellam, 1991; Raz & Buhle, 2006; Van Zomeren, Brouwer, & Deelman, 1984) are capable of further fractionation, it is clear that one of the most important functional consequences is that attention modulates or "gates" activity in primary sensory areas of the brain (Desimone & Duncan, 1995) including vision (Moran & Desimone, 1985), audition (Woldorff et al., 1993), and somatoensory perception (Drevets et al., 1995).

Attention as a cognitive process cannot be observed directly but rather its presence is detected by monitoring the systematic variation in performance of different attention-demanding tasks. Posner (1980), using visual cueing paradigms, (see Figure 59.2) employed a simple but highly

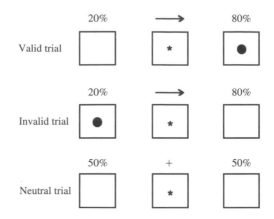

Figure 59.2 Posner's attentional cueing paradigm

Note: Participants were instructed using a symbolic central cue (the arrow) that a target stimulus (a filled circle) would occur with 80% of chance in a given spatial location. Subjects were required to fixate a central mark, not move their eyes, and to press a key as fast as possible when the filled circle appeared. Covert attention was taken as the reaction time benefit when responding to a target that appeared in the attended location (valid trials) as opposed to a response to targets appearing in unattended locations (invalid trials) or to neutral trials. From Bottini and Paulesu (2003). Adapted with permission.

influential example of this approach. Here subjects were asked to maintain their gaze at the center of a screen and only press a button when they observed a designated target to appear. Subjects had no information where on the screen this target would be, although on a number of informative trials they received a directional or spatial cue as to probable location. These attentional cues, when accurate, produced significant reductions in overall reaction time, but when inaccurate, produced significant increases. Given that all other aspects of the task remained constant, the temporal differences were attributed to the movement or allocation of spatial attention.

Attention has also been shown to operate on stimuli at differential levels of analysis depending on processing demands (Lavie, 1995). Such methods have led to clearer accounts of the capacities and limitations of normal human attention. When combined with the study of brain damaged patients, neuroimaging or neurophysiological techniques provided a working hypothesis regarding the neural basis of some cognitive abilities.

Hemi-Inattention (Visuo-spatial Neglect)

The most common and striking neurological condition to follow brain damage involving intentional processes is visuo-spatial or hemispatial neglect (Karnath, Miller, & Vallar, 2002). The neglect syndrome has become an established clinical entity that features prominently in most current texts of behavioral neurology and cognitive neuropsychology (Heilman & Valenstein, 2003). Not surprisingly, it is also the area where rehabilitation is also well developed (Luaute, Halligan, Rode, Rossetti, & Boisson, 2006).

Visual neglect refers to a person's difficulty in detecting, acting on, or even thinking about information on one side (see Robertson & Halligan, 1999). People with visual neglect often fail to notice food on the left side of their plate, fail to dress or wash the left side of their body, have difficulty in imagining the left side of familiar objects, and, in some cases, even deny ownership of their own left limbs (Figure 59.3).

A number of basic clinical observations have been established that inform our understanding of the brain's representation of space, attention, and action (Buxbaum, 2006). The condition has been reported in the visual, auditory, tactile, and olfactory modalities (Halligan & Marshall, 1993), although the most extensive investigations typically concern visuospatial neglect (Figure 59.4). Left neglect after right hemisphere lesions are more frequent, severe and long lasting than right neglect after left hemisphere lesions. Neglect can affect personal (or body) space, peripersonal space (stimuli within reaching and grasping distance), and extrapersonal space (stimuli within walking distance). Although *lateralized* (left-right) visual neglect has attracted most research interest, comparable phenomena have been observed for the other two dimensions of space (radial and altitudinal neglect). Although classically associated with lesions to the right posterior parietal cortex (Heilman & Watson, 1977; Vallar & Perani, 1986), neglect has been observed following damage to a variety of brain structures including the right prefrontal cortex and subcortical areas (Damasio, Damasio, & Chui, 1980; Mesulam, 1981; Karnath, Ferber, & Himmelbach, 2001; Samuelsson, Jensen, Ekholm, Naver, & Blomstrand, 1997).

Figure 59.3 Illustration of left-sided visual neglect when copying.

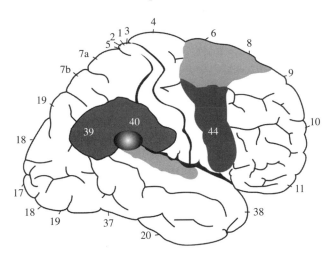

Figure 59.4 Cortical anatomical correlates of visuospatial neglect.

Note: Cortical anatomical correlates of unilateral visuospatial neglect. Most anatomo-clinical correlation studies show that the lesions responsible involve right inferior parietal lobule (Brodmann areas BA [regions of the cortex defined based on their cytoarchitecture] 39 and 40, highlighted in black) and in particular the supramarginal gyrus, at the temporoparietal junction (black–grey area). Neglect after right frontal damage although less common is usually associated with lesions to the frontal premotor cortex, particularly BA 44 and ventral BA 6. Neglect has also been associated with damage to the more dorsal and medial regions of the frontal premotor cortex, and to the superior temporal gyrus. (From Halligan, Fink, Marshall, & Vallar, 2003, reprinted with permission).

Visuospatial neglect is often diagnosed on the basis of simple (bedside) tests such as cancellation, line bisection, copying, spontaneous drawing, reading, and writing; in many patients, the verbal description of complex visual images and topographic routes (generated from long-term memory) can also show lateralized neglect (Bisiach, Brouchon, Poncet, & Rusconi, 1993). Even with such relatively simple tasks as copying or spontaneous drawing, many qualitatively distinct patterns of impairment can present as lateralized neglect (Halligan & Marshall, 2001).

Research over the past 30 years has convincingly shown that neglect is a protean disorder whose symptoms can selectively affect different sensory modalities, cognitive processes, spatial domains, and coordinated systems (Buxbaum, 2006; Halligan, Fink, Marshall, & Vallar, 2003). Deficits of attention, intention, global-local processing, spatial memory, and mental representation make it unlikely that this clinical syndrome can be traced back to the disruption of a single supramodal cognitive process (Vallar, 1998). Many of these clinical findings have been used to better understand the anatomical and functional architecture of the premorbid subsystems of spatial cognition, in particular: (a) neuropsychological structure of space, (b) relevant spatial frames of reference used prior to recognition, and (c) selective preservation of preattentive processes.

Neuropsychological Structure of Space

Although space extends seamlessly in three dimensions, it does not appear to be homogeneously represented in the brain. Embodied space can be behaviorally divided into at least three different regions: personal space, peripersonal space, and extrapersonal space (see Figure 59.5; Robertson & Halligan, 1999). *Personal space* involves the body and body surface: the space in and on where one can feel, touch, and within which one can comb one's hair or scratch an itch. *Peripersonal space* is the working space beyond the torso but within arm's reach. *Extrapersonal space* is beyond arm's reach but one can obviously bring objects within peripersonal space by moving there or by deploying a tool. One can orient the eyes toward an object in extrapersonal space, point to it, or throw something at it. Evidence for the neurobiological distinction between peripersonal (near) and extrapersonal (far) space comes from a wide range of animal and human studies (Caramazza & Hillis, 1990; Previc, 1990) but some of the clearest evidence comes from patients with left neglect after right hemisphere lesions (Buxbaum, 2006; Rizzolatti, Berti, & Gallese, 2000).

Personal Space

Neglect of left personal space can occur without neglect of left peripersonal space (Guariglia & Antonucci, 1992) and vice versa (Beschin & Robertson, 1997). One of the first demonstrations of dissociation was reported by Brain (1941) in a case of right hemisphere glioblastoma where the patient was impaired in pointing to objects in near space without comparable difficulty for objects in

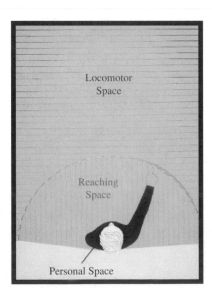

Figure 59.5 Multiple representations of space demonstrated by clinical dissociations between different spatial domains (from Robertson & Halligan, 1999).

far space. Typical manifestations of left personal neglect include failure to shave or groom the left side of the face, failure to adjust spectacles on the left side, and failure to notice the position of the left limbs and use them appropriately even when no significant motor weakness is present. By contrast, the ability to use left personal space without difficulty can be seen in the context of severe left neglect of peripersonal space as assessed by visual search tasks where the targets are displayed within arm's reach (Beschin & Robertson, 1997). This double dissociation of personal and peripersonal neglect suggested that distinct neuronal circuits underlie how the two spaces are represented in the human brain. Performance difference in different space has also been shown to include imaginal or representational space (Beschin, Basso, & Della Sala, 2000; Ortigue, Mégevand, Perren, Landis, & Blanke, 2006).

Peripersonal and Extrapersonal Space

Similar double dissociations have been discovered between left neglect in peripersonal and in extrapersonal space. When lines of constant visual angle are bisected by a laser pen in near versus far space, some patients show accurate performance in far space but a significant rightward deviation in near space (Halligan & Marshall, 1991), while other patients show the reverse dissociation: far left neglect without near left neglect (Vuilleumier, Valenza, Mayer, Reverdin, & Landis, 1998). A study by Viaud-Delmon, Brugger, and Landis (2007) shows how back space is also represented in patients suffering from spatial neglect and further underscores the distinction between motor and nonmotor space. It appears that acting in a particular spatial domain involves distinct neuronal representations of near or far space to become active. Nevertheless, a study by Pitzalis, Di Russo, Spinelli, and Zoccolotti (2001) employing both perceptual and motor versions of line bisection in near and far space argues against this view. The same patients were tested in all conditions. In both the perceptual and the motor tasks, some patients showed near left neglect without far left neglect and others the reverse dissociation. Thus, different accuracy of performance between spatial domains can be revealed by purely perceptual tasks. Furthermore, the patients showed similar degrees of impairment on the motor and the perceptual versions of line bisection.

The coding of space as extrapersonal and peripersonal is not solely determined by the hand-reaching distance and can depend on how the brain represents action capabilities. Berti and Frassinetti (2000) showed that in a patient with demonstrable peripersonal space neglect, previously intact far space bisection (using a laser light pen) became as severe as neglect in the near space when the patient performed the task using a stick as an artificial extension of the patient's body and appeared to undergo a remapping of extrapersonal space as peripersonal space.

Weiss et al. (2000) used PET to determine the functional anatomy involved when volunteers were requested to bisect lines and point to dots in peripersonal or extrapersonal space (see Figure 59.6). Twelve healthy right-handed male volunteers bisected lines or pointed to dots in near or far space using a laser pen. When performing either task in near space, subjects showed neural activity in the left dorsal occipital cortex, left intraparietal cortex, left ventral premotor cortex, and left thalamus. In far space, subjects showed activation of the ventral occipital cortex bilaterally

and the right medial temporal cortex. These findings provide physiological support for the clinically observed dissociations even when the motor components of the tasks were identical when performed in both spaces.

Spatial Frames of Reference

Systematic analysis of visual neglect over the past two decades has revealed significant insights into how attention can be allocated to object- and space-based representation in terms of differential spatial coordinate frames used in normal cognition. There is compelling evidence that egocentric space can be coded in different viewer-centered frames

(A)

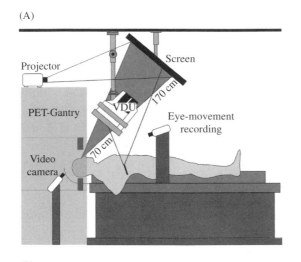

(B)

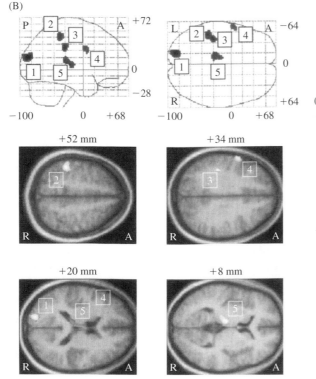

Figure 59.6 Differential neural activity when performing tasks in NEAR space (B) and FAR space (C) . From Weiss et al, Brain 2000. Reprinted with permission.
A: Experimental participant set-up. A computer monitor located within reaching range was used for visual stimulation in NEAR space .A second screen beyond reaching range was used for FAR space presentation. **B:** Sagittal and transverse views of relative rCBF increases associated with movement in NEAR space ($p < 0.001$ uncorrected). The lower rows are transverse SPM{Z} maps which have been superimposed upon the group mean MRI which was spatially normalized into the same stereotaxic space. **C:** Sagittal and transverse views of relative rCBF increases associated with movement in FAR space ($p < 0.001$ uncorrected). Actions involving FAR space resulted in activations in the ventral visuoperceptual processing stream, right medial temporal cortex (8) and bilateral ventral occipital cortex (6&7).

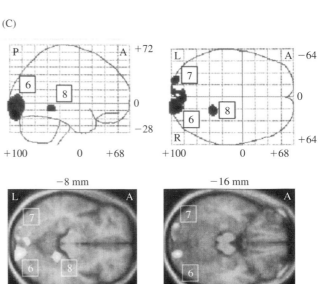

of reference, including eye, head, torso, shoulder, arm- and hand-centered coordinates (Beschin, Cubelli, Della Sala, & Spinazzola, 1997). The terms *left* or *right* are consequently relative, since they can be defined with respect to different reference points (Buxbaum, 2006).

Visuospatial attention can also operate in coordinate frameworks independent of the position of the observer. In object-based neglect, the left side of an object is ignored (Umilta, 2000). Some of the most convincing evidence for selective damage to object-based attention deployment can be found in the drawing and copying performance of neglect patients (see Figure 59.7).

By contrast, object-centered coding (Driver & Halligan, 1991) of left and right concerns the intrinsic laterality of an object (e.g., English words have an intrinsic left to right sequence of letters). Examples of this form of coding in neglect have been elegantly demonstrated by Caramazza and Hillis (1990) in a left brain damaged patient with right neglect dyslexia. When reading, her errors were always located on the right side of the word irrespective of whether the words were presented horizontally, vertically, or even mirror-reversed.

Finally, neglect findings have been used to both support and question features of Kosslyn's (1994) analogue theory of visual mental images; that is, representations that produce the experience of seeing in the absence of sensory input. Within cognitive science, the debate about the depictive representational format of visual mental imagery clearly differentiates analogue (picture-like images with intrinsically spatial representational properties) from the propositional account (linguistic descriptions without inherently spatial properties) championed by Pylyshyn (1981). Moreover, a defining assumption of the former account is that perceptual and imagery processes share the same mental

Figure 59.7 Illustrations of object-centered visual neglect in copying.

operations and neural structures (Kosslyn & Thomson, 2003). Clinical accounts of visual neglect such as those by Bisiach and Luzzatti (1978) and others involving neglect of visual images in parallel with deficits in perception (Marshall & Halligan, 2002) have been used to support the analog claims. However, subsequent case reports describing selective lateralized breakdown of imaginal representation or imagery without corresponding deficits in perceptuo-motor performance question the close functional overlap of imagery and perception processes (Bartolomeo, 2002; Behrman, Winocur, & Moscovitch, 1992).

Knowing without Knowing

Investigations of neglect have contributed to the fascinating debate regarding the processing locus of attentional selection (Kanwisher & Wojciulik, 2000). Several studies of visual neglect have shown that different levels of preattentive processing up to the level of meaning can take place in the neglected field without conscious awareness (Driver & Vuilleumier, 2001). Even on line bisection (a traditional clinical measure), patients with left neglect show implicit sensitivity to manipulations of both stimulus and the visual background (Shulman, Alexander, McGlinchey-Berroth, & Milberg, 2002) confirming that preattentive visual capacities of figure ground and stimulus can influence explicit visual motor performance.

Informally, many students of visuospatial neglect consider the condition to be a classic disorder of visual awareness— where awareness is equated to the psychological construct of attention (Posner, 1978). Unlike blindsight, which is elicited experimentally, left neglect occurs spontaneously and remains a major negative prognostic factor associated with poor performance on most functional recovery measures (Halligan & Robertson, 1992). However, with blindsight, there is considerable evidence that when tested indirectly, many patients can show some degree of information processing for the stimulus of the affected side (Berti & Rizzolatti, 1992; Marshall & Halligan, 1988; McGlinchey-Berroth, Milberg, Verfaellie, Alexander, & Kilduff, 1993; McIntosh et al., 2004).

Evidence for this possibility of nonconscious perception in the case of neglect can be traced back to Kinsbourne and Warrington (1962) who reported a length effect in neglect dyslexia; reading errors maintained the length of words presented. Moreover, A. W. Ellis, Flude, and Young (1987) who replicated this finding suggested that although neglect selectively affected the coding of the identity of the left most letters, patients are still capable of coding letter position and overall length. A clinically similar but less well known phenomenon occurs in line bisection. When requested to bisect a line located in the center of a page most patients with neglect show a displacement of absolute magnitude that is linearly related to line length (Halligan, 1995; Halligan & Marshall, 1988). This linear performance may be explained in terms of implicit processing of the visual information on the neglected side. Thus, the neglected end of the stimulus line may covertly influence the patient's performance in deciding the subjective center of the line.

In one of the first clinical cases reported by Marshall and Halligan (1988), patient PS, who had sustained a right hemisphere stroke, was presented with two line drawings of a house (see Figure 59.8) simultaneously, one of which had red flames emitting from the left side window. Requested to make same/different judgments between the two simultaneously presented pictures, PS reliably judged the two drawings identical. When asked several minutes later to select the house she would prefer to live in, she reliably chose the nonburning house with a high level of statistical significance, commenting that it was a "silly question" since both houses were identical. In other words, although PS was unable to perceive the crucial differences between the two houses (despite free movement of the head and eyes), she nevertheless appeared able to process some information in the hemispace contralateral to lesion that influenced her preference judgment (cf. Manning & Kartsounis, 1993). Later, more detailed studies by Berti and Rizzolatti (1992) and McGlinchey-Berroth et al. (1993) using cross field matching and priming experiments showed that implicit perception, up to the level of meaning, was possible in some patients with neglect. In the case of Berti and Rizzolatti (1992), patients who denied seeing anything in the left visual field nevertheless showed significantly shorter reaction times to the right field stimulus for the congruent rather than the noncongruent conditions.

Marshall and Halligan (1994) showed evidence of a further type of dissociation between two forms of conscious perceptual awareness—again in a free vision task (Figure 59.9). In a series of experiments, they showed that a patient with neglect had a selective inability to analyze and copy accurately the left contours of geometric nonsense figures. These results were present even when there was a single vertical contour (to be copied) that divided a rectangle or a circle into two subfigures. A physically identical boundary was copied more accurately when it was cued as the *right* edge of the *left* subfigure than when it was cued as the *left* edge of the *right* subfigure. The results were interpreted in terms of demonstrating the presence of intact preattentive (global) figure-ground parsing despite gross impairment when focal attention was demanded and the right side of an object was only coded as a figure.

In most cases, however, global processing of the visual world can no longer be used to direct automatic focal attention to spatial locals that require further focal analysis. Without this ability, local attention which is usually biased to the right will always represent too little of the visual

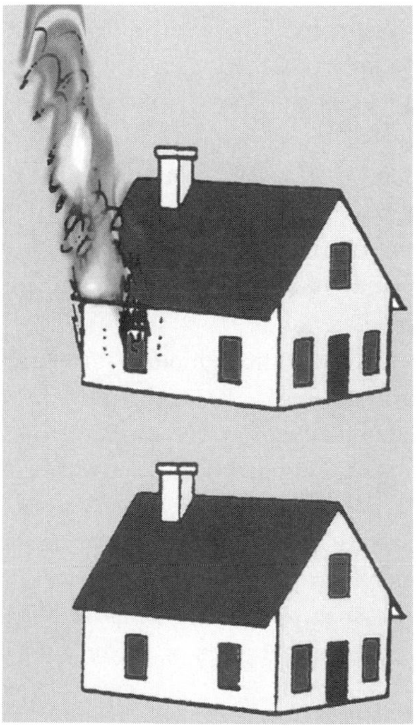

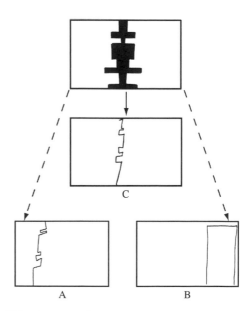

Figure 59.9   Preserved figure-ground segregation in visual neglect.
Note: When asked to copy the top display, the patient only drew the right side of the black figure (**C**). However if requested to copy the left side of the same object when cued as the right side of the left white subfigure (previously ground), the left side could be accurately copied (**A**). Copies of the left side for the same right white subfigure (previously ground) always showed neglect of the details of the contour (**B**) (see Halligan, Fink, Marshall, & Vallar, 2003).

Figure 59.8   Illustration of covert processing in visual neglect (see Marshall & Halligan, 1988).

world. However, once attention has been focused, the panoramic or global view is lost to conscious awareness. When focal attention is biased to the right as in the case of neglect, the patient is in no position to observe the absence of left-sided input. Even if selective attention can be voluntarily moved leftward, the necessary guiding framework provided by the global scale is no longer available.

Consequently, patients no longer have any reason to continue to explore leftward. In these and other examples (Marshall & Halligan, 1995) where performance within an individual patient can be normal on one aspect and grossly impaired on another involving the same stimulus seconds later, left neglect may be regarded as a partial disconnection of conscious visual awareness where residual processes of the impaired right hemisphere cannot be used to constrain the performance of the intact left hemisphere in performing the designated task.

Collectively, these findings from visual neglect highlight the danger of equating phenomenological conscious experience with the operation of the perceptual mechanisms involved. In the absence of apparent phenomenological awareness, there is evidence that many patients, when tested indirectly, may show some degree of information processing for the stimulus of the affected side in the case of neglect or blindsight.

Although adequate cognitive accounts of awareness still remain to be developed (see Clare & Halligan, 2006; Dehaene & Naccache, 2001; Farah & Feinberg, 1997), productive contributions toward the emerging cognitive neuroscience of consciousness rely on pathologies of awareness and the tasks used to reveal them (Babinski, 1914; Bisiach & Berti, 1987; Forstl, Owen, & David, 1993; Prigatano & Schacter, 1991). These have also included examples from nonvisual modalities. For example, in the tactile modality, reports of blind touch (Lahav, 1993; Paillard, Michel, & Stelmach, 1983; Rossetti, Rode, & Boisson, 1995) or "numbsense" (Perenin & Rossetti, 1996) and "deaf hearing" (Michel, Peronnet, & Schott, 1980) have also been recorded. These reports lend further support to the concept of multichanneling sensory information already well established in the visual system and the realization that perception is not a unitary process but one subserved by several separable modules.

While most theoretical studies have been concerned with showing what a patient can do *without* explicit awareness of their clinical condition using experimental task performance (Berti & Rizzolatti, 1992; Bisiach & Rusconi, 1990; Marshall & Halligan, 1988), many other clinical studies are primarily concerned with diagnostic issues (Cutting, 1978; S. J. Ellis & Small, 1994; Levine, Calvanio, & Rinn, 1991; Nathanson, Bergman, & Gordon, 1952) and characterizing the anatomical and functional consequences

of their reported and behavioral unawareness (Pia, Neppi-Modona, Ricci, & Berti, 2004; Samuelsson et al., 1997; Stone, Halligan, & Greenwood, 1993).

However, it is clear that a patient does not need to be explicitly unaware of their cognitive or neurological deficit at the level of verbal reporting to continue to demonstrate significant pathologies of awareness on formal testing. Several patients with intractable chronic neglect show what appears to be considerable conceptual and experiential insight into their deficit and its consequences while continuing to demonstrate neglect on selective tasks (Cantagallo & Della Sala, 1998). Moreover, stroke patients with anosognosia may verbally admit to being hemiplegic yet appear to ignore the consequences of such statements when planning and programming their functional motor activities (House & Hodges, 1988; Marcel, Tegnér, & Nimmo-Smith, 2004).

DISORDERS OF READING AND WRITING

Acquired Reading Disorders

Reading is a complex process that involves visual processing, access to semantics and phonology, and control of articulation. Since Marshall and Newcombe's (1966, 1973) landmark studies on two patients with reading disorders after brain injury, knowledge of both the diversity of reading deficits and of how reading occurs in the normal brain has grown exponentially. Notably, while the literature makes clear distinctions between different reading deficits, they are rarely observed as totally distinct syndromes in individual patients and are often accompanied by other language or visual processing difficulties (Patterson & Lambon Ralph, 1999). This section focuses on acquired reading disorders because they have been the focus of most research in cognitive neurology, although developmental dyslexias are now being increasingly studied in the same context (Temple, 2006).

Two neuropsychological models of normal reading currently form the basis of acquired dyslexia theories. The dual route model and its variations (Coltheart, Rastle, Perry, Langdon, & Ziegler, 2001; Rapcsak, Henry, Teague, Carnahan, & Beeson, 2007; Figure 59.10a) are largely based on observed post-brain injury dissociations between reading regular words (that follow the standard rules of pronunciation—such as 'drink'), irregular words (that are exceptions to the normal rules of pronunciation—such as 'chord'), and nonwords (pronounceable but meaningless letter strings—such as 'lart'). These models suggest that there are two main routes for determining the identity of a word or letter string. The first lexical route is where a word is recognized by matching the letter string to a directory of familiar words stored in memory, called the *visual word form system*. Once the visual word form is activated, this can activate the phonology (pronunciation) of the word either via the word's meaning (the lexical-semantic route) or direct link to its phonological representation (the direct-lexical route). Alternatively, the nonlexical route derives the pronunciation of words by working out letter-sound associations. The triangle model of reading (Plaut, 1997; Seidenberg & McClelland, 1989; Figure 59.10B) takes a radically different approach using a connectionist model with three interconnected systems that represent the recognition of orthography (vision), phonology (pronunciation), and semantics (meaning). This model suggests that both nonwords and regular words are read aloud via the vision to phonology route, while reading aloud irregular words requires both the vision to semantics route and the semantics to phonology route. This latter account is notable because it suggests that disorders of reading can be understood in terms of the disruption to one or more of these processes without the need for procedures specific to reading itself. In other words, it suggests that acquired dyslexia is not a disorder of reading per se, but the result of damage to more general cognitive processes.

Acquired dyslexia is often classified into peripheral or central types. Peripheral dyslexias are characterized by perceptual deficits that prevent the affected person from matching the visual representation of the word to the stored visual word form. Central dyslexias are where the impairment affects access to meaning or speech production after the point where the visual word form is activated.

Peripheral Dyslexias

Patients with peripheral dyslexia are impaired in reading text but have intact writing, speaking, spelling, listening comprehension, and recognition of orally spelled words. Pure alexia (also called letter-by-letter dyslexia, alexia without agraphia, spelling dyslexia, verbal dyslexia, word blindness, or letter confusability dyslexia) is a visual perceptual impairment in the processing of word and letter shapes and is often considered with the agnosias (Farah, 2004). It is typically associated with lesions centered on the left occipito-temporal junction and is often accompanied by a contralesional visual field impairment (homonymous hemianopia; Leff, Spitsyna, Plant, & Wise, 2006). It may result in letter-by-letter reading, where patients are required to identify each letter individually before comprehending the word, although even this process can be impaired in severe cases (Shallice & Rosazza, 2001).

Neglect dyslexia can result from hemispatial neglect (see section on *Attention*) where patients miss the leftmost letters of a word, and is particularly apparent when attempting to read nonwords (di Pellegrino, Ladavas, & Galletti, 2002). Attentional dyslexia (sometimes called letter position dyslexia) is where the reading of single isolated words may be relatively well preserved, but with impaired reading of words in the context of other words or letters (Friedmann & Gvion, 2001).

Central Dyslexias

Deep dyslexia is, perhaps, the most studied of the acquired reading impairments and is often the most profound and complex (Coltheart, Patterson, & Marshall, 1987). The most striking feature is the tendency to make frequent semantic errors (reading *uncle* as *cousin*, for example) although visual errors (e.g., reading *crowd* as *crown*) are also typically present, and combined visual-semantic errors have been reported (e.g., reading *earl* as *deaf*). Patients are often also impaired in reading nonwords, function words, and are worse at reading less imageable words compared with more imageable words (e.g., *trust* is more difficult than *tree*). Furthermore, nouns are typically read better than adjectives, and adjectives better than verbs. In terms of the dual route model, deep dyslexia is likely to result from reading that is reliant on the lexical-semantic route because the other pathways are impaired (Coltheart, 2006). Deep dyslexia is commonly associated with large left hemisphere lesions that cover the frontotemperoparietal area (Lambon Ralph & Graham, 2000).

Surface dyslexia is an impairment in the ability to read phonologically irregular words (such as *chord* or *ache*) while the reading of regular words (such as *book* or *tree*) and nonwords is relatively well preserved (A. W. Ellis, Lambon Ralph, Morris, & Hunter, 2000). It is most common in the dementias and particularly characteristic of semantic dementia (Hodges et al., 1999) although it is linked to left temporal damage even in acquired impairments (Vanier & Caplan, 1985).

Phonological dyslexia is a selective impairment in reading nonwords (such as *wux* or *lart*) compared with relatively intact reading of both regular and irregular real words, which suggests disruption to the nonlexical reading route that relies on working out letter-sound associations (Tree & Kay, 2006). In a review of lesion studies, Lambon, Ralph, and Graham (2000) noted that phonological dyslexia was most associated with damage focused on the anterior perisylvian regions with significant variation in size and extent.

Comparisons of patients with deep and phonological dyslexia have tended to show a continuum of impairment in phonology and semantics with no clear dividing line between the two, supporting the triangle model of reading (Crisp & Lambon Ralph, 2006). However, the model would predict that if dyslexia arises from damage to one of the three general processes (vision, semantics, or phonology), similar impairments would also be apparent in other areas that draw on the same function. In rare cases, this does not seem to be the case, as with a patient reported by Tree and Kay (2006) who presented with a clear phonological dyslexia (nonword reading impairment) despite having intact good performance on a variety of other phonological tasks. These types of cases make it unlikely that reading is based on purely general processes, although the extent to which the brain has become specialized for these relatively recently developed skills (either through selection or developmental plasticity) is still undecided. Much of the recent research is an attempt to settle this issue.

Writing Disorders

Writing is a similarly complex process involving several cognitive, linguistic, and sensorimotor processes and, although agraphia has been less studied than dyslexia, similar principles apply. Although incorporating a wide range of language processes, writing and spelling have been similarly explained using a dual route model (Rapcsak et al., 2007; Figure 59.10A) broken down into peripheral and central components (Beeson & Rapcsak, 2003): Peripheral writing processes include allographic conversion (letter representations converted to letter shapes), graphic motor programs (spatial sequences for specific letters), and graphic innervatory patterns (motor commands to control relevant muscles); central writing processes include semantic representation of word meaning, orthographical output lexicon (learned spellings), and phoneme-grapheme (sound to letter) conversion, all of which are thought to converge on a common output mechanism, termed the *graphemic buffer* (working memory for written letter output). Furthermore, a nonlexical and lexical-semantic route has been suggested to account for nonlexical phonetic spelling (creating plausible spellings from sound-to-letter conversion) and lexical-semantic retrieval of orthographic information via the activation of word meaning (Rapcsak et al., 2007).

The triangle model (Plaut, 1997) has similarly been applied to disorders of writing, suggesting that they largely arise from damage to a general three-component system of recognition of orthography (vision), phonology (pronunciation), and semantics (meaning). Recent comparisons of patients with deep dyslexia, dysgraphia, and dysphasia suggest a level of common impairment in general processes, rather than solely with task-specific abilities (Jefferies, Sage, & Ralph, 2007). Recent theories that are not so strictly tied to models of reading and which attempt more explicitly to integrate spelling processes have become more prominent (Glasspool, Shallice, & Cipolotti, 2006) partly influenced by the fact that patients

(A)

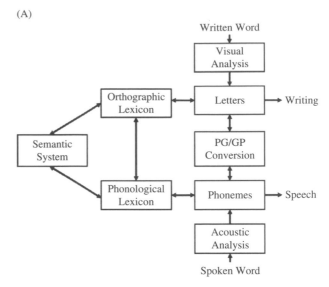

(B)

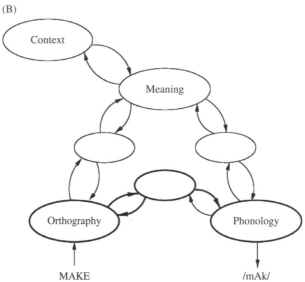

Figure 59.10   A: The dual-route model of reading and spelling and **B:** the triangle model of reading.

Note: (A) From "Do Dual-Route Models Accurately Predict Reading and Spelling Performance in Individuals with Acquired Alexia and Agraphia?" by S. Z. Rapcsak, M. L. Henry, S. L. Teague, S. D. Carnahan, and P. M. Beeson, 2007, *Neuropsychologia, 45,* 2519–2524. Reprinted with permission. (B) "A Distributed, Developmental Model of Word Recognition and Naming," by M. S. Seidenberg and J. L. McClelland, 1989, *Psychological Review, 96,* pp. 523–568. Reprinted with permission.

with both general semantic deficits and writing specific impairments (e.g., in the graphemic buffer) have been reported, which are not adequately accounted for by the existing three-factor models of central processes (e.g., Cipolotti, Bird, Glasspool, & Shallice, 2004).

Peripheral Agraphias

Impairments in the sensorimotor aspect of writing can produce peripheral agraphias that have much in common with apraxia. Apraxic agraphia with normal praxis is a selective impairment in writing while other motor functions, sensorimotor processes, and oral spelling and typing are preserved (Roeltgen & Heilman, 1983). Visuospatial agraphia (also known as constructional or afferent agraphia) is characterized by impairment to spatial orientation during writing and can result in inability to maintain writing on a line, insertion of blank space between letters, and stroke perseveration (Ardila & Rosselli, 1993). Patients with allographic writing impairment have difficulty selecting letter shapes, often selective for one case, or sometimes producing mixed case words (e.g., *HelLo*), despite having relatively intact oral spelling, praxis, and visuospatial ability (Forbes & Venneri, 2003). Writing can also be impaired following executive impairments that impact general motor planning (Ardila & Surloff, 2006) and after damage to neuromuscular control processes affected by disorders such as Parkinson's disease (Van Gemmert, Teulings, & Stelmach, 2001).

Central Agraphias

Lexical or surface agraphia is where patients are not able to access whole word spelling information and so have to rely on phoneme-to-grapheme conversion and spell words as they sound. It is most commonly linked to left posterior inferior temporal cortex damage (Rapcsak & Beeson, 2004) and is thought to arise when there is damage to the lexical-semantic route leaving spelling to rely on the relatively intact nonlexical route (Macoir & Bernier, 2002). In phonological agraphia, patients have difficulty writing nonwords in response to dictation, while writing words to dictation and oral repetition of the words and nonwords are relatively preserved. Spelling errors are often based on visual similarity reflecting the presumed deficit in the phonological system (Roeltgen, 2003) and, despite, considerable variability, the disorder is most commonly linked to lesions in the anterior-inferior part of the left supramarginal gyrus, although superior temporal damage has been reported (Kim, Chu, Lee, Kim, & Park, 2002). Patients with deep agraphia have similar trouble spelling nonwords, but also have a tendency to make semantic errors (e.g., writing *flight* instead of *propeller*), have more trouble with function words than with nouns, and words of low imageability (e.g., *love*) compared with words of high imageability (e.g., *lamb*). The syndrome is typically associated with large left hemisphere lesions (Rapcsak, Beeson, & Rubens, 1991).

OBJECT PERCEPTION AND FACE RECOGNITION

Disorders of visual perception are a relatively common result of neurological disturbance. They can include frank visual field deficits such as scotoma; acquired color-blindness (achromatopsia), motion-blindness (akinetopsia), or impairments in shape, form, or size discrimination, which can occur after visual cortex damage; or a range of visual agnosias, including object and face recognition difficulties, alexia (see earlier section on *Disorders of Reading and Writing*), and vision-for-action problems, usually caused by damage to either one or both of the ventral or dorsal streams (Pisella, Binkofski, Lasek, Toni, & Rossetti, 2006).

Less common, although admittedly, less studied, are perceptual disorders of other modalities, including auditory disorders that can impair specific frequency ranges or word or music comprehension, tactile disorders that can impair perception of simple sensations or semantic recognition through touch. In contrast to these disorders of functional deficit, frank hallucinations of varying complexity can be an equally distressing result of neurological disturbance that can occur in any of the perceptual modalities.

The visual system is heavily integrated with and reliant on other cognitive functions, which means that damage to the attentional system can lead to a similar behavioral syndrome, but with a markedly different cause (e.g., hemispatial neglect). Care must be taken to distinguish these using appropriate tests and clinicians must bear in mind that disorders of both attention and perception may co-exist.

Possibly owing to the influence of Marr's (1982) sequential computational approach to visual perception, cognitive neuroscience has been better at outlining the sequential bottom-up stages, rather than the functional neuroanatomy of top-down processing (Bly & Kosslyn, 1997). However, it has been clear from lesion studies that even early perception is heavily influenced by feedback from higher-level brain areas, as illustrated by the fact that, for example, patients with left-sided lesions typically have problems perceiving detail, while patients with right-sided lesions are more likely to have problems with perceiving perceptual wholes, even when lesions are not primarily located in the visual cortex (Robertson & Lamb, 1991). Many of the syndromes detailed in the following section have been key to understanding the components of the visual perceptual system, but have been less useful in understanding the dynamics of perception. Neuroimaging methods have been particularly useful in this regard, helping to uncover the time course of perception-related brain activity (Hopfinger, Woldorff, Fletcher, & Mangun, 2001) and how bottom-up and top-down processes interact during perceptual tasks (Mechelli, Price, Friston, & Ishai, 2004).

Disorders of the Early Visual System

Because the visual pathway from the retina via the lateral geniculate nucleus to the primary visual cortex is retinotopically organized, selective damage to any part of this pathway will lead to corresponding visual scotomas or, in severe cases, cortical blindness. The actual extent of the subjective visual field deficit may seem significantly smaller than the objective deficit, owing to the effects of visual completion (filling-in) and nystagmus (Valmaggia & Gottlob, 2002; Zur & Ullman, 2003). As well as selective impairment, visual cortex damage may also cause more diffuse problems of visual acuity.

The specialization of the primary visual cortex for the processing of color (V4) and motion (V5) means that lesions to this area can lead to selective deficits in these abilities. Color perception deficits most commonly occur after lesions to the ventral occipital cortex, although rarely affect color vision in its entirety and are typically accompanied by other perceptual difficulties including prosopagnosia, alexia, object agnosia, and spatial perception impairments (Bouvier & Engel, 2006). Reports of pure motion blindness are much rarer in the literature, although are more apparent if syndromes are included that present in only one part of the visual field (Vaina, Cowey, Eskew, LeMay, & Kemper, 2001), or are selective for a particular direction of motion (Blanke, Landis, Mermoud, Spinelli, & Safran, 2003).

Visual Agnosia

Visual agnosia is the loss of object recognition and identification in the absence of any significant damage to the early visual system and without intellectual impairment (alexia is sometimes considered among the agnosias, but is discussed earlier in the section on *Disorders of Reading and Writing*). Farah (2004) provides an excellent guide to the whole range of visual agnosias.

Following Lissauer (1890; translated in Shallice & Jackson, 1988) agnosia is typically divided into an *apperceptive* type (increasingly called *visual form agnosia*), where the problem concerns assembling a unified perceptual impression from its component parts—largely attributed to impairments in visual grouping, and an *associative* type, where the difficulty lies in attributing meaning to a correctly perceived object. Classically, the distinction between these two subtypes is made on the basis that although neither can identify objects, patients with apperceptive agnosia are additionally unable to match, copy, or distinguish between simple objects. The clinical syndromes are often indistinct, however, and agnosias with features of each major subtype have been reported (De Renzi & Lucchelli, 1993; Farah, 1990), suggesting that these are ends of spectrum rather than discrete disorders. Although a recent case has been reported (Anaki, Kaufman, Freedman, & Moscovitch, 2007), agnosia rarely presents without some

form of basic visual impairment, although these are not considered sufficient to account for the wider syndrome. More specific syndromes have also been reported, such as impaired recognition when viewed as a mirror reflection (Priftis, Rusconi, Umilta, & Zorzi, 2003), when viewed from unusual angles (Warrington & James, 1986), or intact object recognition but impaired identification of its orientation (Turnbull, Della Sala, & Beschin, 2002).

Associative visual agnosia is where an object is seemingly perceived correctly but the patient cannot name, describe, explain, or categorize the object (even in nonverbal grouping tasks), although it is possible to do so through other senses (e.g., touch). In contrast to apperceptive agnosias, visual spatial processing tends to be is relatively intact. Humphreys and Riddoch (1987) proposed that associative agnosia results from selective impairment in the integration of the largely intact high-level visual processes with memory. However, this has been challenged by Farah (1990) who reviewed the literature and found significant evidence of perceptual deficits in these cases, suggesting that the role of perception and memory in object recognition is not clearly distinct.

An illustration of an informational processing model for visual object recognition is outlined in Figure 59.11. This model charts the hypothetical information processing routes from preattentive extraction of simple structural properties, to more advanced post attentional integration of local or global processing, and finally to assignment of relevant spatial frames of reference prior to recognition and naming.

Simultanagnosia

Simultanagnosia is a related condition and involves the inability to perceive complex visual scenes, or two or more objects simultaneously, despite being able to perceive single objects without significant impairment. Farah (2004) divides the syndrome into dorsal and ventral simultanagnosia based on in which of the postoccipital visual pathways the lesion occurs. Dorsal simultanagnosia typically occurs in the context of Balint's syndrome that entails an additional inability to direct eye or hand movements to visual targets. Ventral simultanagnosia differs in that patients are somewhat less impaired and can often see multiple objects simultaneously (although do not necessarily recognize them simultaneously), can manipulate objects, and can navigate without bumping into obstacles. Nevertheless, both types typically involve grossly impaired reading ability. The condition is typically explained as a form of pathological local attentional capture, although recent studies have suggested that global scene structures or unseen objects are processed implicitly (Dalrymple, Kingstone, & Barton, 2007; Jackson, Shepherd, Mueller, Husain, & Jackson, 2006).

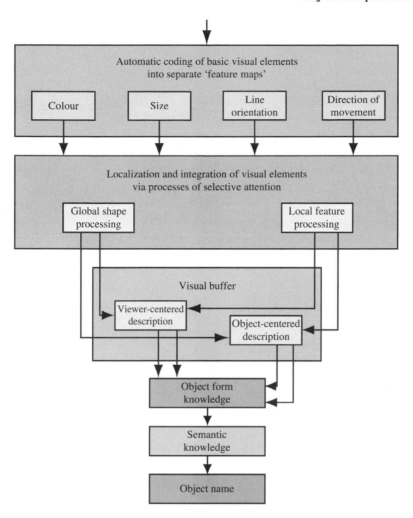

Figure 59.11   An informational processing model for visual object recognition.

Note: From p125 of "Spatial Cognition: Evidence from Visual Neglect," by P. W. Halligan, G. R. Fink, J. C. Marshall, and G. Vallar, 2003, *Trends in Cognitive Science, 7,* pp. 125–133. Reprinted with permission.

Prosopagnosia

Prosopagnosia is a form of visual agnosia that is selective or relatively selective for the recognition of faces (Figure 59.12). (See Figure 59.8 for a cognitive model of face recognition.) The condition has been classified into (1) an apperceptive type, where patients are not able to construct coherent face perceptions, and is typically detected by the inability to distinguish between faces and non-face configurations of facial pictures; and (2) an associative type involving an inability to recognize famous or previously familiar faces. Early research focused almost exclusively on the acquired type, occurring after right or bilateral fusiform gyrus lesions. It has been increasingly recognized, however that there is an idiopathic form (variously called *congenital* or *developmental prosopagnosia*) that more closely matches the associative type. There is some evidence of the syndrome running in families in an autosomal dominant pattern (Grueter et al., 2007; Kennerknecht, Plumpe,

Edwards, & Raman, 2007) and affected individuals may not be significantly impaired in everyday life because they learn to rely on non-face cues or external face features (hair, glasses etc.) for recognition. As this is an adaptive developmental strategy, people with this form of the condition often do not realize until quite late in life that they recognize people differently from others. There remains a considerable debate over whether prosopagnosia is the result of a face-specific deficit (McKone, Kanwisher, & Duchaine, 2007) or whether it is simply the most common result of damage to domain-general perceptual expertise system (Gauthier & Bukach, 2007).

Other Perceptual Disturbances

Although visual agnosias are mainly studied, agnosias are also found in other sensory modalities. Auditory agnosia has been reported—with evidence for a dissociation between

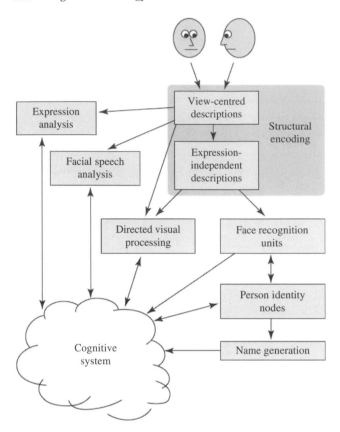

Figure 59.12   Cognitive model of face recognition.

Note: From p. 151 of "Capgras Delusion: A Window on Face Recognition," by H. D. Ellis and M. B. Lewis, 2001, *Trends in Cognitive Science, 5,* pp. 149–156. Reprinted with permission.

auditory and musical recognition deficits (Vignolo, 2003), as have gustatory (Small, Bernasconi, Bernasconi, Sziklas, & Jones-Gotman, 2005) and tactile agnosias (Caselli, 1991). Hallucinations with preserved insight into the false nature of the perceptions arise in a number of neurological conditions, including macular degeneration, migraine, epilepsy, and dementia (Manford & Andermann, 1998). Auditory verbal hallucinations (hearing voices) seem a relatively rare result of acquired brain injuries in the absence of psychosis (Lampl, Lorberboym, Gilad, Boaz, & Sadeh, 2005).

LEARNING AND MEMORY

Memory is one of the most commonly affected cognitive abilities after neurological disturbance (*cross reference—v 3-8*) and can be the source of the most disabling long-term effects. Learning occurs at all levels throughout the brain, and from this perspective, virtually all cognitive neurology is the study of how learned patterns are disrupted by neuropathology. However, decades of careful experimental

studies on both healthy participants and neurological patients have shown us that the brain has become specialized to encode, consolidate, store, and retrieve information for certain types of tasks.

Current theories of memory make functional divisions that are not necessarily mutually exclusive, although some have been shown to rely on largely independent neural systems. Sensory memory is thought to last only a matter of milliseconds and provides a lingering impression to the senses. Working memory is considered to be a limited capacity memory system where temporarily stored information (usually less than 30 s) can be manipulated by the executive system during cognitive tasks. Long-term memory is considered to represent semi-permanent or permanent storage and has been divided into semantic memory (for general knowledge, facts and words that can be recalled without access to the context in which they were learned), and episodic memory (the remembrance of episodes from our personally experienced past). Memory can also be divided into declarative or explicit memory, which we can consciously recall, reflect upon, and describe; and procedural memory, which is the ability to learn skills and actions. Implicit memory is not consciously accessible and includes skill learning (as per procedural memory), but also conditioning, associative learning, priming, and, in fact, anything down to Hebbian learning at the neural level. Memory can also be distinguished by the content that is being remembered, such as verbal, visual, or spatial memory.

Disorders of memory are usually categorized in a similar fashion and only the briefest outline will be given here. Brief reviews are available in Budson and Price (2005) and Kopelman (2002), or for a more in-depth treatment, Baddeley, Kopelman, and Wilson (2004) and Baddeley, Kopelman, and Wilson (2002) are excellent resources. The fact that the classification of memory disorders tends to pragmatically follow traditional classifications of normal memory is worth bearing in mind, particularly when data challenging the traditional models appears. For example, electrophysiological studies during tasks that are classically described as working memory tasks have been used as a basis to argue that there is no separable working memory system, only temporary activation of long-term memory stores (Ruchkin, Grafman, Cameron, & Berndt, 2003) and that short- and long-term memory stores are not separate (Cameron, Haarmann, Grafman, & Ruchkin, 2005). While this debate continues in the literature, both the clinician and researcher must be aware that there is a temptation to fit the complexity of clinical disorders into the traditional categories, rather than the more difficult task of adjusting the traditional categories to allow for the intricacy of impairment.

Working Memory Impairments

Working memory is a short-term, explicit, declarative memory system that is commonly conceptualized as having both a visual-spatial and an auditory short-term store. It uses a network of cortical and subcortical areas, although it is particularly reliant on the prefrontal cortex (Postle, 2006). It is increasingly thought that working memory is not a separate memory system, but the emergent property of a number of cognitive processes working together (D'Esposito, 2007). This means working memory is particularly sensitive to impairment after neurological disturbance that is largely caused by disruption to the executive system, rather than the short-term stores themselves (Muller & Knight, 2006). Disorders of working memory are likely to present as difficulties with concentration, following instructions, or general forgetting, with the impairment also impacting on encoding into long-term memory (Blumenfeld & Ranganath, 2007).

Long-Term Memory Impairments

Amnesia is the general name given to a range of long-term memory impairments although the classic antereograde amnesic syndrome consists of the impaired encoding of new declarative memories, intact recall of premorbid information, and intact implicit memory. Pathologies that cause anterograde amnesia typically result in a limited retrograde amnesia that follows a temporal gradient (Ribot's law), in that memories are more likely to be intact because the memories are more distant in time. Differences between antereograde amnesia caused by medial temporal lobe and diencephalon disruption have been reported in the literature but are likely to be negligible in practice, while both have faster rates of forgetfulness and benefit less well from category prompts than when the syndrome is caused by prefrontal pathology (Kopelman, 2002). Because the prefrontal cortex is involved in both encoding and retrieval of memory, pathology in this area may also lead to increased memory distortion, including false memory recall, loss of context (source amnesia), and frank confabulation (Johnson, O'Connor, & Cantor, 1997).

Posttraumatic amnesia is an amnesic syndrome that occurs in the acute stage after brain trauma. The length of the amnesia is known to reflect the severity of the brain injury and typical resolution times stretch from 1 day to several weeks (McMillan, Jongen, & Greenwood, 1996). Transient global amnesia is a dense amnesic syndrome with a sudden onset that resolves within a matter of hours. It can be triggered by physical or emotional stress, and, with the exception of headaches in affected younger people, is not reliably associated with other neurological signs (Quinette et al., 2006). Transient epileptic amnesia may present in a similar fashion, although it typically lasts for a shorter duration (less than 1 hour) and patients may experience clear seizure-related sensory and motor disturbance for the duration of the amnesia.

Specific impairments in existing semantic memory take a number of forms and are particularly common after pathology of the anterolateral temporal lobes (Levy, Bayley, & Squire, 2004). Patients may present with object identification and language difficulties and so they can sometimes erroneously be assumed to have agnosia or aphasia. A presentation of a selective semantic deficit will be in the context of normal perception and intact nonsemantic language skills such as repetition, reading aloud, and writing to dictation. Alzheimer's disease is perhaps the most common form of semantic impairment that arises from both degradation of semantic memory owing to temporal atrophy, and impairment in executive control processes due to frontal pathology (Grossman et al., 2003). Semantic dementia is a variant of frontotemporal dementia that involves focal lateral temporal atrophy and a progressive decline in semantic knowledge with little or no distortion of the phonological and syntactic aspects of language, and relative sparing of other aspects of cognition, such as episodic memory, nonverbal problem solving, and perceptual and visuospatial skills (Garrard & Hodges, 2000).

Impairments in semantic memory may be category specific, affecting knowledge of particular classes of objects. Dissociations between knowledge of animate and inanimate, living versus nonliving, and animals and plants (to name but a few) have been reported in the neurological literature (Gainotti, 2005). However, it is not clear whether these distinctions reflect the organization of knowledge within the semantic system, or whether there are other higher-level or emergent properties that could better explain the apparent category-specific effect (Borgo & Shallice, 2001).

Impairments of Procedural Memory

Procedural memory deficits can either take the form of marked impairments in acquiring new motor skills, or a loss of existing abilities. It can be spared in even the densest declarative memory amnesias allowing a considerable degree of implicit memory function and skill learning (Spiers, Maguire, & Burgess, 2001). Neuroimaging studies have indicated that procedural learning is associated with activation in the supplementary motor area, basal ganglia, and cerebellum (Daselaar, Rombouts, Veltman, Raaijmakers, & Jonker, 2003) and clinical studies have shown that damage to these areas can cause selective impairments in motor learning (Halsband & Lange, 2006). Unsurprisingly, particular impairments can be seen in degenerative disorders such as Parkinson's and Huntingdon's disease that involve circumscribe pathology to these circuits (Heindel, Salmon, Shults, Walicke, & Butters, 1989).

EXECUTIVE SYSTEM DISORDERS

The idea of an executive system as a manager of other cognitive processes is a relatively late addition to neuropsychological theory and has largely stemmed from the discovery that neurological patients often have problems with coordinating their thoughts and actions over and above any deficits that directly impact on perception, stored memories, or motor control. One of the core ideas behind the concept of an executive system is that it is primarily involved in representing and manipulating abstract concepts, an ability that supports functions such as cognitive and emotional control, initiation and inhibition of actions, behavioral flexibility, planning, introspection, perspective taking, and social cognition. Burgess (1997) has described the executive system as lacking "process-behavior correspondence" meaning, behaviorally, the operation of this system can only be measured through other cognitive processes that are managed (or mismanaged) by the system.

Lesion and neuroimaging studies have consistently indicated that the executive system relies heavily on the prefrontal cortex and its major pathways (Duncan & Owen, 2000) and damage to this system can cause a surprisingly diverse range of behavioral abnormalities, collectively labeled the *dysexecutive syndrome*. The executive system is thought to be more fully engaged in nonroutine, effortful, and online (real life) situations and so the extent of executive impairment as measured by neuropsychological testing may not always predict day-to-day disability (Burgess et al., 2006).

Executive function is closely linked to the concept of attention, although has traditionally been distinguished from perceptual and spatial attention that is more closely linked to the function of the parietal lobe However, recent work has begun to question the strict distinction between these systems and the importance of the frontoparietal network in the interaction of both is now being increasingly highlighted (Collette, Hogge, Salmon, & Van der Linden, 2006; Hon, Epstein, Owen, & Duncan, 2006).

Theories of Executive Function

Duncan, Emslie, Williams, Johnson, and Freer (1996) have argued that the executive system is involved in constructing task plans by representing and maintaining the relevant goals and requirements, and is largely synonymous with general intelligence. Executive system impairment is described as arising from goal neglect where task requirements are disregarded despite the fact that they have been remembered and understood. More recently, Duncan et al. (2008) elaborated on their theory to suggest that goal neglect reflects a limit in working memory capacity. Notably, the limiting factor is suggested to be different from the bottleneck theories of traditional capacity models of attention that concern the limits of how much perceptual or spatial information can be attended to at any one time. In this model, the limiting factor is the capacity of working memory to retain a task model—a working-memory description of relevant facts, rules, and requirements used to control current behavior. According to the theory, dysexecutive problems arise when individual task representations are lost through competition between processes that update the global task model, particularly when capacity has been limited through neurological impairment.

Norman and Shallice (1986) proposed the hugely influential supervisory attentional system (SAS) model that has two pivotal components. The contention scheduler is considered to mediate the effect of the environment (which may trigger certain actions) on the selection of automatic or routine actions. When triggered, the contention scheduling component controls the mutual inhibition of competing actions (since many actions may be triggered at once) to select the most appropriate course of action. The SAS (synonymous with the executive system in most accounts) is considered to intervene in nonroutine situations when actions have to be altered or inhibited because of a novel encounter or decision-making process. Increasingly, the supervisory system is not considered to be a single function, and there is a general consensus that it comprises of a number of anatomically and functionally independent but interrelated processes. Descriptions of the how these processes are fractionated differ and include shifting, updating, and inhibition (Miyake et al., 2000); energization, task setting, and monitoring (Stuss & Alexander, 2007) and schema selection, monitoring, memory specification, and intention setting (Shallice, 2002).

Theories of the role of reward processing in executive function have traditionally focused on the ability to respond differently to changing contingencies in the social environment (Rolls, 1996). However, more recent approaches have widened the scope of reward processing theories based on evidence that the fronto-polar cortex is involved in maintaining and prioritizing the competing demands of behavioral plans or mental tasks based on representations of reward expectations (Koechlin & Hyafil, 2007), consistent with lesion data showing that patients display decision-making impairments in open-ended situations (Burgess, Gilbert, & Dumontheil, 2007).

Problems of Affect and Social Judgment

The medial frontal cortex is known to be particularly important for social cognition (Amodio & Frith, 2006) although damage to a range of prefrontal cortex areas is known to affect the ability to perceive and make judgments on social, moral, and emotional information. Two of the most popular theories of frontally related social disability include an impairment in understanding when reward contingencies for particular social behaviors have altered (Kringelbach & Rolls, 2004); and an impairment in the perception of affect-related arousal and signaling (the somatic marker hypothesis; Bechara, 2004). Common socially relevant dysexecutive symptoms include disinhibition, inappropriate social behavior, and even mania-like states (Starkstein & Robinson, 1997). At the more serious end of the spectrum, acquired sociopathy can result from damage to the orbito-frontal cortex and involves an inability to control reactive aggression and violent impulses (Blair, 2001). Similarly, impairments in the ability to reason about the acceptability of personal moral violations have been found in patients with ventromedial lesions (Ciaramelli, Muccioli, Ladavas, and Di Pellegrino, 2007). Deficits in understanding others' emotions and mental states (Siegal & Varley, 2002) and impairments in understanding nonverbal social cues (Mah, Arnold, & Grafman, 2004) may also promote difficulties in social interaction after frontal pathology.

Deficits of Executive Memory

The executive system is most closely linked to working memory—a limited capacity memory system responsible for the temporary storage and processing of information while cognitive tasks are performed (see *Learning and Memory Impairments* section). However, the executive system is also involved in the retrieval and encoding of long-term memories and memory for intended actions in the future (prospective memory). As a result, executive impairment can have a potentially wide and varied impact. Distractibility undoubtedly impacts all parts of the memory process and is likely a significant factor in the impaired use of efficient organization strategies during both encoding and recall (Mangels, 1997; Parkin, Ward, Bindschaedler, Squires, & Powell, 1999). Although it is traditionally thought that executive impairment leads to a pattern of impaired recall with intact recognition, it is now well established that recognition difficulties are common, although less pronounced (Bastin, Van der Linden, Lekeu, Andres, & Salmon, 2006). One of the most dramatic pathologies of memory associated with executive impairment is confabulation, where patients produce fictitious stories without the apparent intent to deceive and are seemingly unaware

that they are inaccurate. While not all confabulation can be explained by executive impairment alone, they commonly present together (Schnider, 2003).

Problems of Evaluation, Judgment, and Action Planning

Despite scoring well on measures of general cognitive function, executive dysfunction is particularly associated with the inability to make competent real world decisions. Such impairments are only fully apparent in everyday situations (Goel & Grafman, 2000). Cases have been reported of patients who seem to score within the normal range during neuropsychological testing but who make obviously unwise decisions in their everyday life (Blair & Cipolotti, 2000; Elsinger & Damasio, 1985). On the level of completing specific short-term goals, impairment to the executive system has been shown to impact on action planning, so that actions sequences may be disjointed, perseverative, or contain unhelpful or irrelevant steps (Owen, 1997). Difficulties in both judgment and action planning can arise owing to problems with acquiring rule sets (Burgess & Shallice, 1996), self-monitoring and insight, making reasonable estimates (Brand, Kalbe, Fujiwara, Huber, & Markowitsch, 2003), or multitasking (Burgess, Veitch, de Lacy Costello, & Shallice, 2000). Neuroimaging evidence suggests that control implementation and performance or conflict monitoring are linked to dissociable processes in the dorsolateral prefrontal and anterior cingulate cortices, respectively (MacDonald, Cohen, Stenger, & Carter, 2000). However, lesion maps (see Figure 59.13) of cognitive control impairment after brain injury further suggest that these processes may fractionate further (Alexander, Stuss, Picton, Shallice, & Gillingham, 2007).

SUMMARY

There is little doubt that cognitive neurology continues to contribute to our understanding of established neurological, psychiatric, affective, and related pseudoneurological and or functional disorders. There is an increasing prevalence of seemingly neurological conditions for which no organic disorder can be found to explain the patient's hemipare-sis, somatosensory loss, visual field constriction, and so on (Halligan, Bass, & Marshall, 2001). Functional neuro-imaging techniques and cognitive analysis procedures have still to make a major clinical and theoretical contribution in the domain of neuropsychiatric and neurogenic disorders (Frith, 2008; Halligan & David, 2001). The rich data source of the Human Genome Project will increasingly add to our knowledge about neurological and psychiatric conditions

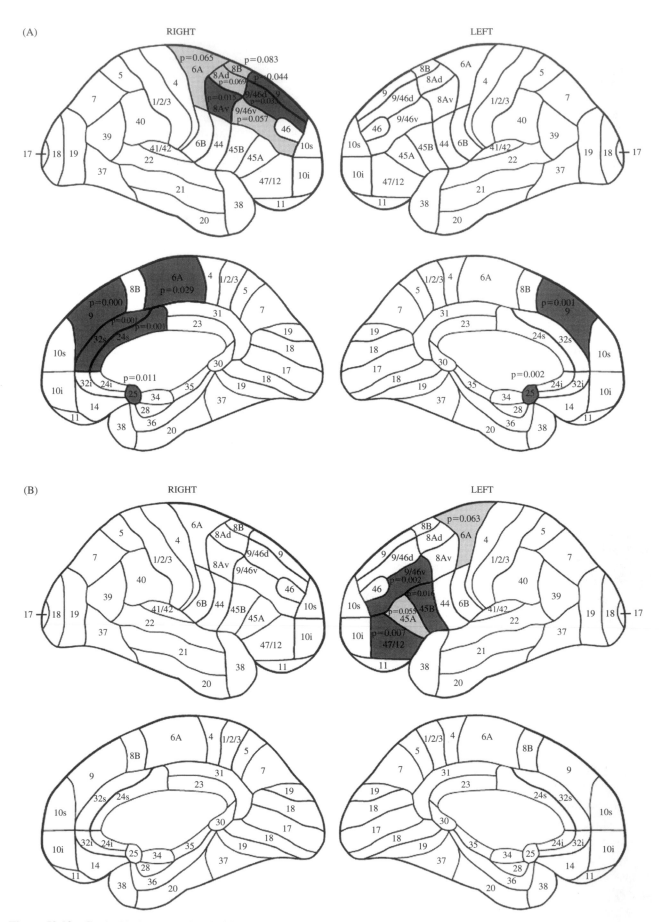

Figure 59.13 Cortical lesions associated with prolonged reaction times on Stroop task.

Note: From "Regional Frontal Injuries Cause Distinct Impairments in Cognitive Control," by M. P. Alexander, D. T. Stuss, T. Picton, T. Shallice, and S. Gillingham, 2007, *Neurology, 68,* pp. 1515–1523. Reprinted with permission.

where the onset is multiply determined by genetic susceptibility, developmental conditions, and environmental stressors. We can expect an increase in the prevalence of neurodegenerative and vascular related diseases and their associated future impact on cognitive functions and quality of life due to a growing elderly population.

New evidence about experience-dependent plasticity of the adult brain allows cautious optimism about the possibility of restitution of brain function following damage (Robertson, 2004). In 1989, Sohlberg and Mateer's book *Introduction to Cognitive Rehabilitation: Theory and Practice* helped locate cognitive rehabilitation alongside more established rehabilitation approaches. They reported an assembly of therapies that attempt to retrain, alleviate or compensate for the deficits caused by selective cognitive impairments (e.g., Basso, Cappa, & Gainotti, 2000; D. W. Ellis & Christensen, 1989; Fleminger & Powell, 1999; Ponsford; Sloan & Snow, 1995; Prigatano, 1999; Riddoch & Humphreys, 1994; Wood & Fussey, 1999). Recent progress in cognitive neuroscience provides a theoretical framework to link behaviorally mediated treatments with knowledge of underlying neurophysiological processes, where rehabilitation strategies can be tested and improved. Future developments will no doubt consider the mechanisms for neuroplasticity in the adult brain. The challenge for cognitive neurology (and sister subspecialties such as cognitive neuropsychology and neuroscience) is whether collectively they are capable of harnessing the wealth of new multidisciplinary findings offered by functional imaging to delineate the neural connectivity involved in many apparently simple cognitive functions.

REFERENCES

Abou-Khalil, B. (2007). An update on determination of language dominance in screening for epilepsy surgery: The Wada test and newer noninvasive alternatives. *Epilepsia, 48,* 442–455.

Ackerstaff, R. G., Keunen, R. W., van Pelt, W., Montauban van Swijndregt, A. D., & Stijnen, T. (1990). Influence of biological factors on changes in mean cerebral blood flow velocity in normal ageing: A transcranial Doppler study. *Neurological Research, 12,* 187–191.

Alexander, M. P., Stuss, D. T., Picton, T., Shallice, T., & Gillingham, S. (2007). Regional frontal injuries cause distinct impairments in cognitive control. *Neurology, 68,* 1515–1523.

Amodio, D. M., & Frith, C. D. (2006). Meeting of minds: The medial frontal cortex and social cognition. *Nature Reviews Neuroscience, 7,* 268–277.

Anaki, D., Kaufman, Y., Freedman, M., & Moscovitch, M. (2007). Associative (prosop)agnosia without (apparent) perceptual deficits: A case-study. *Neuropsychologia, 45,* 1658–1671.

Ardila, A., & Rosselli, M. (1993). Spatial agraphia. *Brain and Cognition, 22,* 137–147.

Ardila, A., & Surloff, C. (2006). Dysexecutive agraphia: A major executive dysfunction sign. *The International Journal of Neuroscience, 116,* 653–663.

Babinski, J. (1914). Contribution a l'étude des troubles mentaux dans l'hémiplégie organique (anosognosie). *Revue Neurologique, 27,* 845–848.

Baddeley, A. D., Kopelman, M., & Wilson, B. A. (2002). *The Handbook of Memory Disorders (2nd ed.).* London: Wiley.

Baddeley, A. D., Kopelman, M., & Wilson, B. A. (2004). *The Essential Handbook of Memory Disorders for Clinicians.* London: Wiley Ltd.

Bartolomeo, P. (2002). The relationship between visual perception and visual memtal imagery: A reappraisal of the neuropsychological evidence. *Cortex, 38,* 357–378.

Basso, A., Cappa, A., & Gainotti, G. (Eds.). (2000). *Cognitive neuropsychology and Language Rehabilitation.* Hove, England: Psychology Press.

Basso, A., & Marangolo, P. (2000). Cognitive neuropsychological rehabilitation: The emperor's new clothes? *Neuropsychological Rehabilitation, 10,* 219–230.

Bastin, C., Van der Linden, M., Lekeu, F., Andres, P., & Salmon, E. (2006). Variability in the impairment of recognition memory in patients with frontal lobe lesions. *Cortex, 42,* 983–994.

Bauer, R. M. (1984). Autonomic recognition of names and faces in prosopagnosia: A neuropsychological application of the Guilty Knowledge Test. *Neuropsychologia, 22,* 457–469.

Baxendale, S. (2000). Carotid amobarbital testing and other amobarbital procedures. In J. Oxbury, C. Polkey, & M. Duchowny (Eds.), *Intractable focal epilepsy.* London: Bailliere Tindall.

Bechara, A. (2004). The role of emotion in decision-making: Evidence from neurological patients with orbitofrontal damage. *Brain and Cognition, 55,* 30–40.

Beeson, P. M., & Rapcsak, S. Z. (2003). Neuropsychological assessment and rehabilitation of writing disorders. In P. Halligan, U. Kischka, & J. C. Marshall (Eds.), *Handbook of Clinical Neuropsychology.* Oxford: Oxford University Press.

Behrmann, M., Winocur, G., & Moscovitch, M. (1992). Dissociation between mental imagery and object recognition in a brain–damaged patient. *Nature, 359,* 636–637.

Berti, A., & Frassinetti, F. (2000). When far becomes near: Remapping of space by tool use. *Journal of Cognitive Neuroscience, 12,* 415–420.

Berti, A., & Rizzolatti, G. (1992). Visual processing without awareness: Evidence from unilateral neglect. *Journal of Cognitive Neuroscience, 4,* 345–351.

Beschin, N., Basso, A., & Della Sala S. (2000). Perceiving left and imagining right: Dissociation in neglect. *Cortex, 36,* 401–414.

Beschin, N., Cubelli, R., Della Sala, S., & Spinazzola, L. (1997). Left of what? The role of egocentric coordinates in neglect. *Journal of Neurology, Neurosurgery, and Psychiatry, 63,* 483–489.

Beschin, N., & Robertson, I. H. (1997). Personal versus extrapersonal neglect: A group study of their dissociation using a reliable clinical test. *Cortex, 33,* 379–384.

Bisiach, E. and Luzzatti, C. (1978): Unilateral neglect of representational space. *Cortex, 14,* 129–33.

Bisiach, E., & Berti, A. (1987). Dyschiria. An attempt at its systemic explanation. In M. Jeannerod (Ed.), *Neurophysiological and neuropsychological aspects of spatial neglect* (pp. 183–201). Amsterdam: Elsevier.

Bisiach, E., Brouchon, M., Poncet, M., & Rusconi, M. L. (1993). Unilateral neglect in route description. *Neuropsychologia, 31,* 1255–1262.

Bisiach, E., &. Rusconi, M. L. (1990). Break-down of perceptual awareness in unilateral neglect. *Cortex, 24,* 643–649.

Blair, R. J. R. (2001). Neurocognitive models of aggression, the antisocial personality disorders, and psychopathy. *Journal of Neurology, Neurosurgery, and Psychiatry, 71,* 727–731.

Blair, R. J. R., & Cipolotti, L. (2000). Impaired social response reversal: A case of acquired sociopathy. *Brain, 123,* 1122.

Blanke, O., Landis, T., Mermoud, C., Spinelli, L., & Safran, A. B. (2003). Direction-selective motion blindness after unilateral posterior brain damage. *European Journal of Neuroscience, 18,* 709–722.

Blumenfeld, R. S., & Ranganath, C. (2007). Prefrontal cortex and long-term memory encoding: An integrative review of findings from neuropsychology and neuroimaging. *Neuroscientist, 13,* 280–291.

Bly, B. M., & Kosslyn, S. M. (1997). Functional anatomy of object recognition in humans: Evidence from positron emission tomography and functional magnetic resonance imaging. *Current Opinion in Neurology, 10,* 5–9.

Borgo, F., & Shallice, T. (2001). When living things and other 'sensory quality' categories behave in the same fashion: A novel category specificity effect. *Neurocase, 7,* 201–220.

Bottini, G., & Paulesu, E. (2003). *Functional neuroanatomy of spatial perception, spatial processes, and attention.* In P. W. Halligan, U. Kischka, & J. C. Marshall (Eds.), *Handbook of clinical neuropsychology* (pp. 607–723). Oxford: Oxford University Press.

Bouvier, S. E., & Engel, S. A. (2006). Behavioral deficits and cortical damage loci in cerebral achromatopsia. *Cerebral Cortex, 16,* 183–191.

Brain, W. R. (1941). Visual disorientation with special reference to lesions of the right cerebral hemisphere. *Brain, 64,* 244–272.

Brand, M., Kalbe, E., Fujiwara, E., Huber, M., & Markowitsch, H. J. (2003). Cognitive estimation in patients with probable Alzheimer's disease and alcoholic Korsakoff patients. *Neuropsychologia, 41,* 575–584.

Bruce, V., & Young, A. W. (1986). Understanding face recognition. *British Journal of Psychology, 77,* 305–327.

Budson, A. E., & Price, B. H. (2005). Memory dysfunction. *New England Journal of Medicine, 352,* 692–699.

Burgess, P. W. (1997). Theory and methodology in executive function research. In P. Rabbit (Ed.), Methodology of Frontal and Executive Function. Hove, England: Psychology Press.

Burgess, P. W., Alderman, N., Forbes, C., Costello, A., Coates, L. M., Dawson, D. R., et al. (2006). The case for the development and use of "ecologically valid" measures of executive function in experimental and clinical neuropsychology. *Journal of the International Neuropsychological Society, 12,* 194–209.

Burgess, P. W., Gilbert, S. J., & Dumontheil, I. (2007). Function and localization within rostral prefrontal cortex (area 10). *Philosophical Transactions of the Royal Society of London, Series B, Biological Sciences, 362,* 887–899.

Burgess, P. W., & Shallice, T. (1996). Bizarre responses, rule detection and frontal lobe lesions. *Cortex, 32,* 241–259.

Burgess, P. W., Veitch, E., de Lacy Costello, A., & Shallice, T. (2000). The cognitive and neuroanatomical correlates of multitasking. *Neuropsychologia, 38,* 848–863.

Buxbaum, L. (2006). On the right (and left) track: Twenty years if progress in studying hemispatial neglect. *Cognitive Neuropsychology, 23,* 184–201.

Byng, S., Kay, J., Edmundson, A., & Scott, C. (1990). Aphasia tests reconsidered. *Aphasiology, 4,* 67–92.

Cameron, K. A., Haarmann, H. J., Grafman, J., & Ruchkin, D. S. (2005). Long-term memory is the representational basis for semantic verbal short-term memory. *Psychophysiology, 42,* 643–653.

Cantagallo, A., & Della Sala, S. (1998). Preserved insight in an artist with extrapersonal spatial neglect. *Cortex, 34,* 163–189.

Cappa, S. F. (2001). *Cognitive Neurology: An Introduction.* London: Imperial College Press.

Cappa, S. F., Abutalebi, J., Demonet, J., Fletcher, P., & Garrard, P. (Eds.). (2008). *Cognitive Neurology: A Clinical Textbook.* Oxford: Oxford University Press.

Caramazza, A., & Coltheart, M. (2006). Cognitive Neuropsychology Twenty Years on. *Cognitive Neuropsychology, 21,* 3–12.

Caramazza, A., & Hillis, A. E. (1990). Spatial representation of words in the brain implied by studies of a unilateral neglect patient. *Nature, 346,* 267–9.

Caselli, R. J. (1991). Rediscovering tactile agnosia. *Mayo Clinic Proceedings, 66,* 129–42.

Cermak, L. S. (1982). *Human memory and amnesia.* Hillsdale, NJ: Erlbaum.

Ciaramelli, E., Muccioli, M., Ladavas, E., & Di Pellegrino, G. (2007). Selective deficit in personal moral judgment following damage to ventromedial prefrontal cortex. *Social Cognitive and Affective Neuroscience, 2,* 84–92.

Cipolotti, L., Bird, C. M., Glasspool, D. W., & Shallice, T. (2004). The impact of deep dysgraphia on graphemic buffer disorders. *Neurocase, 10,* 405–419.

Clare, L., & Halligan, P. W. (Editorial) (2006) *Neuropsychological Rehabilitation, 16,* 353–355.

Collette, F., Hogge, M., Salmon, E., & Van der Linden, M. (2006). Exploration of the neural substrates of executive functioning by functional neuroimaging. *Neuroscience, 139,* 209–221.

Coltheart, M. (2006). Acquired dyslexias and the computational modelling of reading. *Cognitive Neuropsychology, 23,* 96–109.

Coltheart, M., Patterson, K., & Marshall, J. C. (Eds.). (1987). *Deep dyslexia* (2nd ed.). London: Routledge.

Coltheart, M., Rastle, K., Perry, C., Langdon, R., & Ziegler, J. (2001). DRC: A dual route cascaded model of visual word recognition and reading aloud. *Psychological Review, 108,* 204–256.

Coslett, H. B., & Saffran, E. M. (1989). Evidence for preserved reading in 'pure alexia'. *Brain, 112,* 327–359.

Crisp, J., & Lambon Ralph, M. A. (2006). Unlocking the nature of the phonological-deep dyslexia continuum: The keys to reading aloud are in phonology and semantics. *Journal of Cognitive Neuroscience, 18,* 348–362.

Cutting, J. (1978). Study of anosognosia. *Journal of Neurology, Neurosurgery, and Psychiatry, 41,* 548–555.

Dalrymple, K. A., Kingstone, A., & Barton, J. J. (2007). Seeing trees OR seeing forests in simultanagnosia: Attentional capture can be local or global. *Neuropsychologia, 45,* 871–875.

Damasio, A. R., Damasio, H., & Chui, H. C. (1980). Neglect following damage to frontal lobe or basal ganglia. *Neuropsychologia, 18,* 123–32.

Daselaar, S. M., Rombouts, S. A, Veltman, D. J., Raaijmakers, J. G., & Jonker, C. (2003). Similar network activated by young and old adults during the acquisition of a motor sequence. *Neurobiology of Aging, 24,* 1013–1019.

Dehaene, S., & Naccache, L. (2001). Towards a cognitive neuroscience of consciousness: Basic evidence and a workspace framework. *Cognition, 79,* 1–37.

De Renzi, E., & Lucchelli, F. (1993). The fuzzy boundaries of apperceptive agnosia. *Cortex, 29,* 187–215.

Desimone, R., & Duncan, J. (1995). Neural mechanisms of selective visual attention. *Annual Review of Neuroscience, 18,* 193–222.

Desmond, J. E., & Chen, S. H. A. (2002) Ethical issues in the clinical application of fMRI: Factors affecting the validity and interpretation of activations. *Brain and Cognition, 50,* 482–497.

D'Esposito, M. (2007). From cognitive to neural models of working memory. *Philosophical Transactions of the Royal Society of London. Series, B., Biological Sciences, 362,* 761–772.

di Pellegrino, G., Ladavas, E., & Galletti, C. (2002). Lexical processes and eye movements in neglect dyslexia. *Behavioral Neurology, 13*(1–2), 61–74.

Di Pietro, M., Laganaro, M., Leemann, B., & Schnider, A. (2004). Receptive amusia: Temporal auditory processing deficit in a professional musician following a left temporo-parietal lesion. *Neuropsychologia, 42,* 868–877.

Donovan, N. J., Kendall, D. L., Heaton, S. C., Kwon, S., Velozo, C. A., & Duncan, P. W. (2008). Conceptualizing functional cognition in stroke. *Neurorehabilitation and Neural Repair, 22,* 122–135.

Drevets, W. C., Burton, H., Videen, T. O., Snyder, A. Z., Simpson, J. R., Jr, & Raichle, M. E. (1995). Blood flow changes in human somatosensory cortex during anticipated stimulation. *Nature, 373,* 249–252.

Driver, J., & Halligan, P. W. (1991). Can visual neglect operate in object-centered co-ordinates? An affirmative single case study. *Cognitive Neuropsychology, 8,* 475–496.

Driver, J., & Vuilleumier, P. (2001). Perceptual awareness and its loss in unilateral neglect and extinction. *Cognition, 79,* 39–88.

Duncan, J., Emslie, H., Williams, P., Johnson, R., & Freer, C. (1996). Intelligence and the frontal lobe: The organization of goal-directed behavior. *Cognitive Psychology, 30,* 257–303.

Duncan, J., & Owen, A. M. (2000). Common regions of the human frontal lobe recruited by diverse cognitive demands. *Trends in Neurosciences, 23,* 475–483.

Duncan, J., Parr, A., Woolgar, A., Thompson, R., Bright, P., Cox, S., et al. (2008). Goal neglect and Spearman's g: Competing parts of a complex task. *Journal of Experimental Psychology: General, 137,* 131–148.

Ellis, A. W., Flude, B. M., & Young, A. W. (1987). "Neglect dyslexia" and the early visual processing of letters in words and nonwords. *Cognitive Neuropsychology, 4,* 439–463.

Ellis, A. W., Lambon Ralph, M. A., Morris, J., & Hunter, A. (2000). Surface dyslexia: Description, treatment, and interpretation. In E. Funnell (Ed.), *Case Studies in the Neuropsychology of Reading* (pp. 85–122). Hove, East Sussex, England: Psychology Press.

Ellis, D. W., & Christensen, A. L. (Eds.). (1989) *Neuropsychological Treatment after Brain Injury.* Boston: Kluwer Academic.

Ellis, H. D., & Lewis, M. B. (2001). Capgras delusion: A window on face recognition. *Trends in Cognitive Science, 5,* 149–156.

Ellis, S. J., & Small, M. (1994). Denial of eye closure in acute stroke. *Stroke, 25,* 1958–1962.

Elsinger, P. J., & Damasio, A. R. (1985). Severe disturbance of higher cognition after bilateral frontal lobe ablation: Patient EVR. *Neurology, 35,* 1731–1741.

Farah, M. J. (1990). *Visual Agnosia: Disorders of Object Recognition and What They Tell Us About Normal Vision.* Cambridge, MA: MIT Press.

Farah, M. J. (2004). *Visual Agnosia* (2nd ed.). Cambridge, MA: MIT Press.

Farah, M. J., & Feinberg, T.E. (1997). Perception and awareness. In T. E. Feinberg & M. J. Farah (Eds.), *Behavioral neurology and neuropsychology.* New York: McGraw-Hill.

Fleminger, S., & Powell, J. (1999). Evaluation of outcomes in brain injury rehabilitation. *Neuropsychological Rehabilitation, 9,* 225–230.

Forbes, K. E., & Venneri, A. (2003). A case for case: Handling letter case selection in written spelling. *Neuropsychologia, 41,* 16–24.

Forstl, H., Owen, A. M., & David, A. (1993). Gabriel Anton and "Anton's symptom": "On focal diseases of the brain which are not perceived by the patient" (1898). *Neuropsychiatry, Neuropsychology and Behavioral Neurology, 6,* 1–6.

Friedmann, N., & Gvion, A. (2001). Letter position dyslexia. *Cognitive Neuropsychology, 18,* 637–696.

Frith, C. (2008). Editorial: In praise of cognitive neuropsychiatry. *Cognitive Neuropsychiatry, 13,* 1–7.

Gainotti, G. (2005). The influence of gender and lesion location on naming disorders for animals, plants and artefacts. *Neuropsychologia, 43,* 1633–1644.

Garrard, P., & Hodges, J. R. (2000). Semantic dementia: Clinical, radiological and pathological perspectives. *Journal of Neurology, 247,* 409–422.

Gauthier, I., & Bukach, C. (2007). Should we reject the expertise hypothesis? *Cognition, 103,* 322–330.

Gazzaniga, M. S., Ivry, R., & Mangun, G. R. (2002). *Cognitive Neuroscience: The Biology of the Mind* (2nd ed.). New York: Norton.

Glasspool, D. W., Shallice, T., & Cipolotti, L. (2006). Towards a unified process model for graphemic buffer disorder and deep dysgraphia. *Cognitive Neuropsychology, 23,* 479–512.

Goel, V., & Grafman, J. (2000). The role of the right prefrontal cortex in ill-structured problem solving. *Cognitive Neuropsychology, 17,* 415–436.

Grossman, M., Koenig, P., Glosser, G., DeVita, C., Moore, P., Rhee, J., et al. (2003). Neural basis for semantic memory difficulty in Alzheimer's disease: An fMRI study. *Brain, 126,* 292–311.

Grueter, M., Grueter, T., Bell, V., Horst, J., Laskowski, W., Sperling, K., et al. (2007). Hereditary prosopagnosia: The first case series. *Cortex, 43,* 734–749.

Guariglia, C., & Antonucci, G. (1992). Personal and extrapersonal space: A case of neglect dissociation. *Neuropsychologia, 30,* 1001–1009.

Halligan, P. W. (1995). Drawing attention to neglect. The Psychologist, 8, 257–264.

Halligan, P. W., Bass, C., & Marshall, J. C. (Eds.). (2001). Contemporary Approaches to the Study of Hysteria. Oxford: Oxford University Press.

Halligan, P. W., & David, A. S. (2001). Cognitive neuropsychiatry: Towards a scientific psychopathology. *Nature Reviews Neuroscience,* 2, 209–215.

Halligan, P. W., Fink, G. R., Marshall, J. C., & Vallar, G. (2003). Spatial cognition: Evidence from visual neglect. *Trends in Cognitive Science,* 7, 125–133.

Halligan, P. W., Kischka, U., & Marshall, J. C. (Eds.). (2004). *Handbook of clinical neuropsychology.* Oxford University Press, UK.

Halligan, P. W., & Marshall, J. C. (1988). How long is a piece of string? A study of line bisection in a case of visual neglect. *Cortex,* 24, 321–328.

Halligan, P. W., & Marshall, J. C. (1991). Left neglect for near but not far space in man. *Nature, 350,* 498–500.

Halligan, P. W., & Marshall, J. C. (1993). When two is one: A case study of spatial parsing in visual neglect. *Perception, 22,* 309–312.

Halligan, P. W., & Marshall, J. C. (1994). Completion in visuo-spatial neglect: A case study. *Cortex, 30,* 685–694.

Halligan, P. W., & Marshall, J. C. (2001). Graphic neglect-more than the sum of the parts. *NeuroImage, 14,* S91–7.

Halligan, P. W., & Robertson, I. H. (1992). *The assessment of unilateral neglect.* Hove: Erlbaum.

Halligan, P. W., & Wade, D. T. (Eds.). (2005). *The effectiveness of rehabilitation for cognitive deficits,* Oxford University Press, UK.

Halsband, U., & Lange, R. K. (2006). Motor learning in man: A review of functional and clinical studies. *Journal of Physiology Paris, 99,* 414–424.

Heilman, K. M., & Valenstein, E. (Eds.). (2003). *Clinical neuropsychology* (4th ed.). Oxford: Oxford University Press.

Heilman, K. M., & Watson, R. T. (1977). Mechanisms underlying the unilateral neglect syndrome. *Advances in Neurology, 18,* 93–106.

Heindel, W. C., Salmon, D. P., Shults, C. W., Walicke, P. A., & Butters, N. (1989). Neuropsychological evidence for multiple implicit memory systems: A comparison of Alzheimer's, Huntington's, and Parkinson's disease patients. Journal of Neuroscience, 9, 582–587.

Hodges, J. R. (2007). *Cognitive assessment for clinicians* (2nd ed.). Oxford: Oxford University Press.

Hodges, J. R., Patterson, K., Ward, R., Garrard, P., Bak, T., Perry, R., et al. (1999). The differentiation of semantic dementia and frontal lobe dementia (temporal and frontal variants of frontotemporal dementia) from early Alzheimer's disease: a comparative neuropsychological study. *Neuropsychology, 13,* 31–40.

Hon, N., Epstein, R. A., Owen, A. M., & Duncan, J. (2006). Frontoparietal activity with minimal decision and control. *Journal of Neuroscience, 26,* 9805–9809.

Hopfinger, J. B., Woldorff, M. G., Fletcher, E. M., & Mangun, G. R. (2001). Dissociating top-down attentional control from selective perception and action. *Neuropsychologia, 39*, 1277–1291.

House, A., & Hodges, J. (1988). Persistent denial of handicap after infarction of the right basal ganglia: A case study. *Journal of neurology, neurosurgery, and psychiatry, 51*, 112–115.

Howard, D., & Hatfield, F. (1987). *Aphasia therapy: Historical and contemporary issues*. Hillsdale: Erlbaum.

Humphreys, G. W., & Riddoch, M. J. (1987). *To see but not to see: A case study of visual agnosia*. Hove: Laurence ErlbaumLtd.

Jackson, G. M., Shepherd, T., Mueller, S. C., Husain, M., & Jackson, S. R. (2006). Dorsal simultanagnosia: An impairment of visual processing or visual awareness? *Cortex, 42*, 740–749.

Jefferies, E., Sage, K., & Ralph, M. A. (2007). Do deep dyslexia, dysphasia and dysgraphia share a common phonological impairment? *Neuropsychologia, 45*, 1553–1570.

Johnson, M., O'Connor, M., & Cantor, J. (1997). Confabulation, memory deficits and frontal dysfunction. *Brain and Cognition, 34*, 189–206.

Kanwisher, N., & Wojciulik, E. (2000). Visual attention: Insights from brain imaging. *Nature Reviews Neuroscience, 1*, 91–100.

Kaplan, E. (1988). The process approach to neuropsychological assessment. *Aphasiology, 2*, 309–312.

Karnath, H. O., Ferber, S., & Himmelbach, M. (2001). Spatial awareness is a function of the temporal not the posterior parietal lobe. *Nature, 411*, 950–953.

Karnath, H. O., Miller, D., & Valar, G. (Eds.). (2002). *The cognitive and neural bases of spatial neglect*. Oxford: Oxford University Press.

Kennerknecht, I., Plumpe, N., Edwards, S., & Raman, R. (2007). Hereditary prosopagnosia (HPA): The first report outside the Caucasian population. *Journal of Human Genetics, 52*, 230–236.

Kim, H. J., Chu, K., Lee, K. M., Kim, D. W., & Park, S. H. (2002). Phonological agraphia after superior temporal gyrus infarction. *Archives of Neurology, 59*, 1314–1316.

Kinsbourne, M., & Warrington, E. K. (1962). A study of finger agnosia. *Brain, 85*, 47–66.

Koechlin, E., & Hyafil, A. (2007). Anterior prefrontal function and the limits of human decision-making. *Science, 318*, 594–598.

Kopelman, M. D. (2000). Focal retrograde amnesia and the attribution of causality: An exceptionally critical view. *Cognitive Neuropsychology, 17*, 585–621.

Kopelman, M. D. (2002). Disorders of memory. *Brain, 125*, 2152–2190.

Kosslyn, S. M. (1994). *Image and brain: The resolution of the imagery debate*. MIT: MIT Press.

Kosslyn, S. M. & Thomson, W. L. (2003). When is early visual cortex activated during visual mental imagery? *Psychological Bulletin, 129*, 723–746.

Kringelbach, M. L., & Rolls, E. T. (2004). The functional neuroanatomy of the human orbitofrontal cortex: Evidence from neuroimaging and neuropsychology. *Progress in Neurobiology, 72*, 341–372.

Lahav, H. (1993). What neuropsychology tell us about consciousness. *Philosophy of Science, 60*, 67–85.

Lambon Ralph, M. A & Graham, N. L. (2000). Previous cases: Acquired phonological and deep dyslexia. *Neurocase, 6*, 141–178.

Lampl, Y., Lorberboym, M., Gilad, R., Boaz, M., & Sadeh M. (2005). Auditory hallucinations in acute stroke. *Behavioral Neurology, 16*, 211–216.

Lavie, N. (1995). Perceptual load as a necessary condition for selective attention. *Journal of Experimental Psychology: Human Perception and Performance 21*, 451–468.

Leff, A. P., Spitsyna, G., Plant, G. T., & Wise, R. J. (2006). Structural anatomy of pure and hemianopic alexia. *Journal of Neurology, Neurosurgery, and Psychiatry, 77*, 1004–1007.

Levine, D. N., Calvanio, R., & Rinn, W. E. (1991). The pathogenesis of anosognosia for hemiplegia. *Neurology, 41*, 1770–1781.

Levy, D. A., Bayley, P. J., & Squire, L. R. (2004). The anatomy of semantic knowledge: Medial vs. lateral temporal lobe. *Proceedings of the National Academy of Sciences USA, 101*, 6710–6715.

Lezak, M. D., Howieson, D. B., Loring, D. W., Hannay, H. J., & Fischer, J. S. (2004). *Neuropsychological assessment* (4th ed.). Oxford: Oxford University Press.

Lissauer, H. (1890). Ein fall von seelenblindheit nebst einem beitrage zur theorie derselben. *Archiv Fur Psychaitrie und Nervenkrankheiten, 21*, 222–270.

Luaute, J., Halligan, P., Rode, G., Rossetti, Y., & Boisson, D. (2006). Visuospatial neglect: A systematic review of current interventions and their effectiveness. *Neuroscience and Biobehavioral Reviews, 30*, 961–982.

MacDonald, A. W. III., Cohen, J. D., Stenger, V. A., & Carter, C. S. (2000). Dissociating the role of the dorsolateral prefrontal and anterior cingulate cortex in cognitive control. *Science, 288*, 1835–1838.

Macoir, J., & Bernier, J. (2002). Is surface dysgraphia tied to semantic impairment? Evidence from a case of semantic dementia. *Brain and Cognition, 48*, 452–457.

Mah, L., Arnold, M. C., & Grafman, J. (2004). Impairment of social perception associated with lesions of the prefrontal cortex. *American Journal of Psychiatry, 161*, 1247–1255.

Manford, M., & Andermann, F. (1998). Complex visual hallucinations: Clinical and neurobiological insights. *Brain, 121*, 1819–1840.

Mangels, J. A. (1997). Strategic processing and memory for temporal order in patients with frontal lobe lesions. *Neuropsychology, 11*, 207–221.

Manning, L., & Kartsounis, L. D. (1993). Confabulations related to tacit awareness in visual neglect. *Behavioural Neurology, 6*, 211–213.

Marcel, A. J., Tegnér, R., & Nimmo-Smith, I. (2004). Anosognosia for plegia: Specificity, extension, partiality and disunity of bodily unawareness. *Cortex, 40*, 19–40.

Margolin, D. I. (1991). Cognitive neuropsychology. Resolving enigmas about Wernicke's aphasia and other higher cortical disorders. *Archives of Neurology, 48*, 751–765.

Marr, D. (1982). Vision. San Francisco: Freeman.

Marshall, J. C., & Halligan, P. W. (1988). Blindsight and insight in visuospatial neglect. *Nature, 336*, 766–767.

Marshall, J. C., & Halligan, P. W. (1994). The Yin and the Yang of visuospatial neglect: A case study. *Neuropsychologia, 32*, 1037–1057.

Marshall, J. C., & Halligan, P. W. (1995). Seeing the forest but only half the trees. *Nature, 373*, 521–523.

Marshall, J. C., & Halligan, P. W. (2002). Whoever would have imagined it? Bisiach and Luzzatti. (1978). On representational neglect in patients, I. G., & NV. In C. Code, C. W. Wallesch, Y. Joanette & A. Riche-Lecours (Eds.), *Classic Cases in Neuropsychology Vol. II* (pp. 272–274). Hove: Psychology Press.

Marshall, J. C., & Newcombe, F. (1966). Syntactic and semantic errors in paralexia. *Neuropsychologia, 4*, 181–188.

Marshall, J. C., & Newcombe, F. (1973). Patterns of paralexia: A psycholinguistic approach. *Journal of Psycholinguistic Research, 2*, 175–199.

McGlinchey-Berroth, R., Milberg, W. P., Verfaellie, M., Alexander, M., & Kilduff, P. T. (1993). Semantic processing in the neglected visual field: Evidence from a lexical decision task. *Cognitive Neuropsychology, 10*, 79–108.

McIntosh, R. D., McClements, K. I., Schindler, I., Cassidy, T. P., Birchall, D., & Milner, A.D. (2004). Avoidance of obstacles in the absence of visual awareness. *Proceedings of the Royal Society B: Biological Sciences, 271*, 15–20.

McKone, E., Kanwisher, N., & Duchaine, B. C. (2007). Can generic expertise explain special processing for faces? *Trends in Cognitive Sciences, 11*, 8–15.

McMillan, T. M., Jongen, E. L., & Greenwood, R. J. (1996). Assessment of post-traumatic amnesia after severe closed head injury: Retrospective or prospective? *Journal of Neurology, Neurosurgery, and Psychiatry, 60*, 422–427.

Mechelli, A., Price, C. J., Friston, K. J., & Ishai, A. (2004). Where bottom-up meets top-down: Neuronal interactions during perception and imagery. *Cerebral Cortex, 14*, 1256–1265.

Mesulam, M. M. (1981). A cortical network for directed attention and unilateral neglect. *Annals of Neurology, 10*, 309–325.

Mesulam, M. M. (2000). *Principles of behavioral and cognitive neurology* (2nd ed.). Oxford: Oxford University Press.

Michel, F., Peronnet, F., & Schott, B. (1980). A case of cortical deafness: Clinical and electrophysiological data. *Brain and Language, 10*, 367–377.

Milberg, W., Blumstein, S. E., & Dworetsky, B. (1987). Phonological processing and lexical access in aphasia. *Brain and Language, 34*, 279–293.

Mirsky, A. F., Anthony, B. J., Duncan, C. C., Ahearn, M. B., & Kellam, S. G. (1991). Analysis of the elements of attention: A neuropsychological approach. *Neuropsychology Review, 2*, 109–145.

Miyake, A., Friedman, N. P., Emerson, M. J., Witzki, A. H., Howerter, A., & Wager, T. D. (2000). The unity and diversity of executive functions and their contributions to complex "Frontal Lobe" tasks: A latent variable analysis. *Cognitive Psychology, 41*, 49–100.

Moran, J., & Desimone, R. (1985). Selective attention gates visual processing in the extrastriate cortex. *Science, 229*, 782–784.

Moscovitch, M., Winocur, G., & McLachlan, D. (1986). Memory as assessed by recognition and reading time in normal and memory-impaired people with Alzheimer's disease and other neurological disorders. *Journal of Experimental Psychology: Learning Memory and Cognition, 115*, 331–347.

Muller, N. G., & Knight, R. T. (2006). The functional neuroanatomy of working memory: Contributions of human brain lesion studies. *Neuroscience, 139*, 51–58.

Nathanson, M., Bergman, P., & Gordon, G. (1952). Denial of illness. Its occurrence in one hundred consecutive cases of hemiplegia. *Archives of Neurology and Psychiatry, 68*, 380–387.*Neuropsychologia, 44*, 2734–2748.

Norman, D. A., & Shallice, T. (1986). Attention to action: Willed and automatic control of behavior. In Davidson, R. J., Schwartz, G. E., & Shapiro, D. (Eds.), *Consciousness and self-regulation: Advances in research and theory* (pp. 1–18). New York: Plenum Press.

Ortigue, S., Mégevand, P., Perren, F., Landis, T., & Blanke, O. (2006). Double dissociation between representational personal and extrapersonal neglect. *Neurology, 66*, 1414–1417.

Owen, A. M. (1997). Cognitive planning in humans: Neuropsychological, neuroanatomical and neuropharmacological perspectives. *Progress in Neurobiology, 53*, 431–450.

Paillard, J., Michel, F., & Stelmach, G. (1983). Localization without content: A tactile analogue of 'blind sight'. *Archives of Neurology, 40*, 548–551.

Parkin, A. J., Ward, J., Bindschaedler, C., Squires, E. J., & Powell, G. (1999). False recognition following frontal lobe damage: The role of encoding factors. *Cognitive Neuropsychology, 16*, 243–265.

Patterson, K., & Lambon Ralph, M. A. (1999). Selective disorders of reading? *Current Opinion in Neurobiology, 9*, 235–239.

Perenin, M.-T., & Rossetti, Y. (1996). Grasping in an hemianopic field. Another instance of dissociation between perception and action. *NeuroReport, 7*, 793–897.

Pia, L., Neppi-Modona, M., Ricci, R., & Berti, A. (2004). The anatomy of anosognosia for hemiplegia: A meta-analysis. *Cortex, 40*, 367–377.

Pisella, L., Binkofski, F., Lasek, K., Toni, I., & Rossetti, Y. (2006). No double-dissociation between optic ataxia and visual agnosia: Multiple sub-streams for multiple visuo-manual integrations.

Pitzalis, S., Di Russo, F., Spinelli, D., & Zoccolotti, P. (2001). Influence of the radial and vertical dimensions on lateral neglect. *Experimental Brain Research, 136*, 281–294.

Plaut, D. C. (1997). Structure and function in the lexical system: Insights from distributed models of word reading and lexical decision. *Language and Cognitive Processes, 12*, 767–808.

Ponsford, J. L., Sloan, S., & Snow, P. (1995). *Traumatic brain injury: Rehabilitation for everyday adaptive living.* Hove: Erlbaum Ltd.

Posner, M. I. (1978). *Chronometric Explorations of Mind.* Hillsdale, NJ: Erlbaum.

Posner, M. I. (1980). Orienting of attention. *Quarterly Journal of Experimental Psychology 32*, 3–25.

Posner, M. I., & Petersen, S. E. (1990). The attention system of the human brain. *Annual Review of Neuroscience, 13*, 25–42.

Postle, B. R. (2006). Working memory as an emergent property of the mind and brain. *Neuroscience, 139*, 23–38.

Previc, F. H. (1990). Functional specialization in the lower and upper visual fields in humans: Its ecological origins and neurophysiological implications. *Behavioral and Brain Sciences, 13*, 519–575.

Priftis, K., Rusconi, E., Umilta, C., & Zorzi, M. (2003). Pure agnosia for mirror stimuli after right inferior parietal lesion. *Brain, 126*, 908–919.

Prigatano, G. P. (1999). *Principles of Neuropsychological Rehabilitation.* Oxford: Oxford University Press.

Prigatano, G. P., & Schacter, D. L. (Eds.). (1991). *Awareness of Deficit after Brain Injury.* Oxford, Oxford University Press.

Pylyshyn, Z. W. (1981). The imagery debate: Analogue media versus tacit knowledge. *Psychological Review, 87*, 16–45.

Quinette, P., Guillery-Girard, B., Dayan, J., de la Sayette, V., Marquis, S., Viader, F., et al. (2006). What does transient global amnesia really mean? Review of the literature and thorough study of 142 cases. *Brain, 129*, 1640–58.

Rafal, R., Smith, J., Krantz, J., Cohen, A., & Brennan, C. (1990). Extrageniculate vision in hemianopic humans: Saccade inhibition by signals in the blind field. *Science, 250*, 118–121.

Rapcsak, S. Z., & Beeson, P. M. (2004). The role of left posterior inferior temporal cortex in spelling. *Neurology, 62*, 2221–2229.

Rapcsak, S. Z., Beeson, P. M., & Rubens, A. B. (1991). Writing with the right hemisphere. *Brain and Language, 41*, 510–530.

Rapcsak, S. Z., Henry, M. L., Teague, S. L., Carnahan, S. D., & Beeson, P. M. (2007). Do dual-route models accurately predict reading and spelling performance in individuals with acquired alexia and agraphia? *Neuropsychologia, 45*, 2519–2524.

Raz, A., & Buhle, J. (2006). Typologies of attentional networks. *Nature Reviews Neuroscience, 7*, 367–379.

Riddoch, M. J., & Humphreys, G. W. (1994). Cognitive neuropsychology and cognitive rehabilitation: A marriage of equal partners. In M. J. Riddoch & G. W. Humphreys (Eds.), *Cognitive Neuropsychology and Cognitive Rehabilitation.* London: Erlbaum.

Rizzolatti, G., Berti, A., & Gallese, V. (2000). Spatial neglect: Neurophysiological bases, cortical circuits and theories. In F. Boller & J. Grafman (Eds.), *Handbook of neuropsychology* (pp. pp. 503–537). London: Elsevier.

Robertson, R. M. (2004). Modulation of neural circuit operation by prior environmental stress. *Integrative and Comparative Biology, 44*, 21–27.

Robertson, I. H., & Halligan, P. W. (1999). *Spatial neglect: A clinical handbook for diagnosis and treatment.* London: Erlbaum.

Robertson, L. C., & Lamb, M. R. (1991). Neuropsychological contributions to theories of part/whole organization. *Cognitive Psychology, 23,* 299–330.

Roeltgen, D. P. (2003). Agraphia. In K. M. Heilman & E. Valenstein (Eds.), *Clinical Neuropsychology* (4th ed.) (pp. 63–89). Oxford: Oxford University Press.

Roeltgen, D. P., & Heilman, K. M. (1983). Apraxic agraphia in a patient with normal praxis. *Brain and Language, 18,* 35–46.

Rolls, E. T. (1996). The orbitofrontal cortex. *Philosophic Transactions of the Royal Society of London, 351,* 1433–1444.

Rossetti, Y., Rode, G., & Boisson, D. (1995). Implicit processing of somaesthetic information: A dissociation between where and how? *NeuroReport, 6,* 506–510.

Ruchkin, D. S., Grafman, J., Cameron, K., & Berndt, R. S. (2003). Working memory retention systems: A state of activated long-term memory. *Behavioral and Brain Sciences, 26,* 709–777.

Samuelsson, H., Jensen, C., Ekholm, S., Naver, H., & Blomstrand, C. (1997). Anatomical and neurological correlates of acute and chronic visuospatial neglect following right hemisphere stroke. *Cortex, 33,* 271–285.

Schnider, A. (2003). Spontaneous confabulation and the adaptation of thought to ongoing reality. *Nature Reviews Neuroscience, 4,* 662–671.

Schöning, M., & Hartig, B. (1996). Age Dependence of Total Cerebral Blood Flow Volume from Childhood to Adulthood. *Journal of Cerebral Blood Flow and Metabolism, 16,* 827–833.

Seidenberg, M. S., & McClelland, J. L. (1989). A distributed, developmental model of word recognition and naming. *Psychological Review, 96,* 523–568.

Shallice, T. (1988). *From Neuropsychology to Mental Structure.* Cambridge: Cambridge University Press.

Shallice, T. (2002). Fractionation of the Supervisory System. In D. T. Stuss & R. T. Knight (Eds.), *Principles of Frontal Lobe Function* (pp. 261–277). Oxford: Oxford University Press.

Shallice, T., & Jackson, M. (1988). Lissauer on agnosia. *Cognitive Neuropsychology, 5,* 153–192.

Shallice, T., & Rosazza, C. (2001). Patterns of peripheral paralexia: Pure alexia and the forgotten visual dyslexia? *Cortex, 42,* 892–897.

Shallice, T., & Saffran, E. (1986). Lexical processing in the absence of explicit word identification: Evidence from a letter-by-letter reader. *Cognitive Neuropsychology, 3,* 429–458.

Shulman, M. B., Alexander, M. P., McGlinchey-Berroth, R., & Milberg, W. (2002). Triangular backgrounds shift the bias of line bisection performance in hemispatial neglect. *Journal of Neurology, Neurosurgery, and Psychiatry, 72,* 68–72.

Siegal, M., & Varley, R. (2002). Neural systems involved in "theory of mind." *Nature Reviews Neuroscience, 3,* 463–471.

Silver, J. M. (2006). Behavioral neurology and neuropsychiatry is a subspecialty. *Journal of Neuropsychiatry and Clinical Neurosciences, 18,* 146–148.

Small, D. M., Bernasconi, N., Bernasconi, A., Sziklas, V., & Jones-Gotman, M. (2005). Gustatory agnosia. *Neurology, 64,* 311–317.

Snyder, P. J., Nussbaum, P. D., & Robins, D. L. (2005). *Clinical Neuropsychology: A Pocket Handbook for Assessment* (2nd ed.). American Psychological Association.

Sohlberg, M., & Mateer, C. (1989). *Introduction to Cognitive Rehabilitation: Theory and Practice.* New York: Guilford Press.

Spiers, H. J., Maguire, E. A., & Burgess, N. (2001). Hippocampal amnesia. *Neurocase, 7,* 357–382.

Starkstein, S. E., & Robinson, R. G. (1997). Mechanism of Disinhibition After Brain Lesions. *Journal of Nervous and Mental Diseases, 185,* 108–114.

Stoerig, P. (1996). Varieties of vision: From blind responses to conscious recognition. *Trends in Neurosciences, 19,* 401–406.

Stone, S. P., Halligan, P. W., & Greenwood, R. J. (1993). The incidence of neglect phenomena and related disorders in patients with an acute right or left hemisphere stroke. *Age and Ageing, 22,* 46–52.

Strauss, E., Sherman, E. M. S., & Spreen, O. (2006). *A compendium of Neuropsychological tests administration, norms, and commentary* (3rd ed.). Oxford: Oxford University Press.

Stuss, D. T., & Alexander, M. P. (2007). Is there a dysexecutive syndrome? *Philosophical Transactions of the Royal Society of London. Series, B., Biological Sciences, 362,* 901–915.

Temple, C. M. (2006). Developmental and acquired dyslexias. *Cortex, 42,* 898–910.

Tranel, D., & Damasio, A. R. (1985). Knowledge without awareness: An autonomic index of facial recognition by prosopagnosics. *Science, 228,* 1453–1454.

Tree, J. J., & Kay, J. (2006). Phonological dyslexia and phonological impairment: An exception to the rule? *Neuropsychologia, 44,* 2861–2873.

Turnbull, O. H., Della Sala, S., & Beschin, N. (2002). Agnosia for object orientation: Naming and mental rotation evidence. *Neurocase, 8,* 296–305.

Umilta, C. (2000). Mechanisms of attention. In B. Rapp (Ed.), *Handbook of Cognitive Neuropsychology* (pp. 135–158). Hove: Psychology Press.

Vaina, L. M., Cowey, A., Eskew, R. T., Jr, LeMay, M., & Kemper, T. (2001). Regional cerebral correlates of global motion perception: Evidence from unilateral cerebral brain damage. *Brain, 124,* 310–321.

Vallar, G. (1998). Spatial hemineglect in humans. *Trends in Cognitive Science, 2,* 87–97.

Vallar, G., & Perani, D. (1986). The anatomy of unilateral neglect after right-hemisphere stroke lesions. A clinical/CT-scan correlation study in man. *Neuropsychologia, 24,* 609–622.

Valmaggia, C., & Gottlob, I. (2002). Optokinetic nystagmus elicited by filling-in in adults with central scotoma. *Investigative Ophthalmology and Visual Science, 43,* 1804–1808.

Van Gemmert, A. W., Teulings, H. L., & Stelmach, G. E. (2001). Parkinsonian patients reduce their stroke size with increased processing demands. *Brain and Cognition, 47,* 504–512.

Vanier, M., & Caplan, D. (1985). CT scan correlates of surface dyslexia. In KE Patterson (Ed.), *Surface dyslexia: Neuropsychological and cognitive analyses of phonological reading.* Hove: Psychology Press Ltd.

Van Zomeren, A. H., Brouwer, W. H., & Deelman, B. G. (1984). Attentional deficits: The riddles of selectivity, speed, and alertness. In N. Brooks (Ed.), *Closed head injury: Psychological, social and family consequences* (pp. 74–107). Oxford: Oxford University Press.

Viaud-Delmon, I., Brugger, P., & Landis, T. (2007). Hemineglect: Take a look at the back space. *Annals of Neurology, 62,* 418–422.

Vignolo, L. A. (2003). Music agnosia and auditory agnosia: Dissociations in stroke patients. *Annals of the New York Academy of Sciences, 999,* 50–57.

Vuilleumier, P., Valenza, N., Mayer, E., Reverdin, A., & Landis, T. (1998). Near and far visual space in unilateral neglect. *Annals of Neurology, 43,* 406–410.

Warrington, E. K., & James, M. (1986). Visual object recognition in patients with right hemisphere lesions: Axes or features? *Perception, 15,* 355–366.

Weiskrantz, L. (1986). *Blindsight: A case study and implications.* Oxford: Clarendon Press.

Weiskrantz, L. (1990). The Ferrier lecture, 1989. Outlooks for blindsight: explicit methodologies for implicit processes. *Proceedings of the Royal Society of London, Series B (Biology), 239,* 247–278.

Weiskrantz L. (1991). Disconnected awareness for detecting, processing, and remembering in neurological patients. *Journal of the Royal Society of Medicine, 84,* 466–470.

Weiskrantz, L., Harlow, A., & Barbur, J. L. (1991). Factors affecting visual sensitivity in a hemianopic subject. *Brain, 114,* 2269–2282.

Weiskrantz, L., Warrington, E. K., Sanders, M. D., & Marshall, J. (1974). Visual capacity in the hemianopic field following a restricted occipital ablation. *Brain, 97,* 709–728.

Weiss, P. H., Marshall, J. C., Wunderlich, G., Tellmann, L., Halligan, P. W., Freund, H. J., et al. (2000). Neural consequences of acting in near versus far space: A physiological basis for clinical dissociations. *Brain, 123,* 2531–2541.

Wilkinson, D., & Halligan, P. (2004). The relevance of behavioral measures for functional-imaging studies of cognition. *Nature Reviews Neuroscience, 5,* 67–73.

Woldorff, M. G., Gallen, C. C., Hampson, S. A., Hillyard, S. A., Pantev, C., Sobel, D., et al. (1993). Modulation of early sensory processing in human auditory cortex during auditory selective attention. *Proceedings of the National Academy of Sciences USA, 90,* 8722–6.

Wood, R. L. L., & Fussey, I. (2000). *Cognitive Rehabilitation in Perspective.* Hove, England: Psychology Press.

Young, A. (1994). Covert recognition. In M. Farah & G. Ratcliff (Eds.), *The neuropsychology of high-level vision.* Hillsdale, NJ: Erlbaum.

Zeki, S. (1993). *A vision of the brain.* Oxford: Blackwell.

Zihl, J., Tretter, F., & Singer, W. (1980). Phasic electrodermal responses after visual stimulation in the cortically blind hemifield. *Behavioural Brain Research, 1,* 197–203.

Zur, D., & Ullman, S. (2003). Filling-in of retinal scotomas. *Vision Research, 43,* 971–982.

Chapter 60

Genetics and Psychopathology

CHRISTEL M. MIDDELDORP AND DORRET I. BOOMSMA

In this chapter, we introduce the major principles of genetic research in psychopathology. To illustrate these principles, an overview of genetic studies of depression and anxiety is given. We first introduce the background of genetic epidemiology that focuses on the question to what extent a trait or disorder clusters in families and if this clustering has a genetic basis. The methods to investigate issues going beyond the question of heritability are described, including sex and age differences in the genetic architecture, gene-environment correlation, gene-environment interaction, and multivariate genetic approaches to examine the etiology of comorbidity between traits or disorders. This section is followed by a discussion of the results of these types of studies on anxiety and depression. Next, the methods of gene findings studies are introduced again followed by a discussion of the results of linkage and association studies that aim at localizing and identifying the genes underlying the genetic component in anxiety and depression. Finally, we briefly touch on some issues complicating genetics in psychopathology.

ASSESSMENT OF THE IMPORTANCE OF GENETIC VARIATION IN COMPLEX TRAITS

Individual differences in complex traits (like psychiatric disorders, intelligence, height, or blood pressure) may be due to genetic or environmental factors. These traits are called complex because their genetic architecture most likely is *complex*. They are influenced by multiple genetic as well as environmental effects and do not show a simple pattern of Mendelian inheritance. The influence of these factors

on variation in normal and abnormal human behavior may be additive or may manifest itself through more complex pathways in which the influences of genes and environment interact (Falconer & Mackay, 1996; Lynch & Walsh, 1998; Plomin, DeFries, McClearn, & McGuffin, 2008).

Genetic factors represent the effects of one or many unidentified genes. For quantitative, complex traits these effects are due to a possibly large, but unknown, number of genes (polygenes). Genes can only influence variation if they are polymorphic, that is, occur in two or more variants in the population, called *alleles*. The effect of alleles can be additive (their effects sum up) or alleles at the same or different loci can interact. Interaction, or genetic nonadditivity, between alleles within the same locus is referred to as *genetic dominance;* interaction between alleles across different loci is referred to as *epistasis*. In data from humans, genetic dominance and epistasis are difficult to distinguish. Moreover, relatives will not show a high degree of resemblance for traits that result from genetic nonadditivity. There is one exception: Identical twins will resemble each other also for traits that show dominance or epistasis. A large difference in the degree of resemblance between identical twins and first-degree relatives thus gives an indication that genetic nonadditivity plays a role.

The relative influence of genetic factors on phenotypic variation (where the phenotype stands for any observable trait), the heritability, is commonly defined as the proportion of total phenotypic variance that can be attributed to genetic variance. *Broad-sense* heritability includes all sources of genetic variance (additive and nonadditive); *narrow-sense* heritability only includes additive genetic variance.

All nongenetic influences on phenotypic variation are referred to as environmental influences and include the early influences of prenatal environment, the influence of the (early) home environment, the influence of the neighborhood, and many other, usually unidentified nongenetic effects. Environmental influences are often distinguished into two broad classes: common environmental influences that are shared among family members (e.g., siblings) who

We would like to thank Jouke-Jan Hottenga for his critical reading of this chapter.

The study was supported by the Netherlands Organization for Scientific Research NWO/ZonMW (SPI 56-464-14192, 940g-37-024, 400-05-717), CMSB (Center for Medical Systems Biology): NWO Genomics. CM was supported by the Hersenstichting Nederland (13F05(2).47).

grow up in the same family and that tend to make them alike, and unique environmental influences, that is, environmental influences that are unique to an individual and are not shared among family members. Measurement error and other sources of unreliability in a trait contribute to the unique environmental influences.

To estimate the influences of genotype and environment on phenotypic variation, it is not necessary to collect genetic material (DNA) or to measure the environment. The relative importance of both sources of variation may be estimated by statistically analyzing data that have been collected in groups of individuals who are genetically related or who do not share their genes, but who share their environment (Boomsma, Busjahn, & Peltonen, 2002; Martin, Boomsma, & Machin, 1997). For example, data from adopted children may be compared with data from their biological and adoptive parents. The resemblance between adopted children and their biological parents reinforces the importance of genetic inheritance, the resemblance of adoptive parents and their adopted children relates to the importance of cultural inheritance and shared home environment. There are some famous adoption studies on the inheritance of schizophrenia. For example, Heston (1966) looked at adopted children whose biological parents suffered from schizophrenia versus adopted children whose biological parents did not suffer from schizophrenia. All of the children studied were given up for adoption immediately after birth. Those children with a much higher chance to get the disorder had a biological parent who suffered from schizophrenia. These results clearly indicate a role for genetic factors in the development of schizophrenia.

However, adoptions are relatively rare and often neither the adopted child nor the adoptive parents are entirely representative of the general population. Therefore, the majority of studies that estimate heritability of complex traits make use of the classical twin design to unravel sources of variance. An introduction to this methodology can be found, for example, in Boomsma et al. (2002), Kendler and Eaves (2005), Plomin et al. (2008), and Posthuma et al. (2003). In the classical twin design, data from monozygotic and dizygotic twins are used to decompose the variation of a trait into genetic and environmental contributions by comparing within pair resemblance for both types of twins. Monozygotic (MZ) twins share their common environment and (nearly always) 100% of their genes. Dizygotic (DZ) twins also share their common environment and on average 50% of their segregating genes (Hall, 2003). If MZ within twin pair resemblance for a certain trait is higher than DZ within twin pair resemblance, this suggests the presence of genetic influences on that trait. A first impression of the narrow-sense heritability (a^2) of a phenotype can be calculated as twice the difference between the MZ and DZ correlations: $a^2 = 2(rMZ - rDZ)$. The expectation of the correlation in MZ twins equals: $rMZ = a^2 + c^2$ (where c^2 represents the proportion of the total variance attributable to common environment, that is, the environment shared by children raised in the same family). The expectation of the correlation in DZ twins equals: $rDZ = \frac{1}{2}a^2 + c^2$.

If there is, in addition to additive genetic influences, a contribution of genetic dominance, the expectations for the MZ correlations is: $rMZ = a^2 + d^2 + c^2$ and for the DZ correlation it is: $rDZ = \frac{1}{2}a^2 + \frac{1}{4}d^2 + c^2$. This is the situation in which the MZ correlation can be substantially higher than the DZ correlation and where the simple approach of doubling the difference between the two correlations is no longer appropriate. In this situation, the broad-sense heritability (h^2) must be estimated using different approaches, outlined below, and represents the influence of additive and nonadditive genetic factors. Although it is possible that both genetic dominance and common environment are of importance, these effects cannot be simultaneously estimated in the classical twin design if only data from MZ and DZ twins reared together are available.

If MZ within twin pair resemblance for a certain trait is similar to DZ within twin pair resemblance, or if $rMZ < 2rDZ$ this suggests the presence of common environmental influences on that trait. A first impression of the effect of common environmental influences can be calculated as $c^2 = rMZ - a^2$ (or $c^2 = 2rDZ - rMZ$). It may be important to emphasize that it is unknown what the common environment includes. One can think of parenting or socioeconomic status, but this needs to be investigated if a common environmental effect is found. A first impression of the importance of unique environmental influences can be calculated as $e^2 = 1 - rMZ$. Finally, if genetic dominance plays a role, its importance can be estimated as: $d^2 = 4rDZ - rMZ$.

If, for example, the correlation for a certain trait equals 0.60 in MZ twins and 0.45 in DZ twins, then the estimate for $a^2 = 2(0.60-0.45) = 0.30$, for $c^2 = 0.60 - 0.30 = 0.30$, and for $e^2 = 1 - 0.60 = 0.40$. If, on the other hand, the correlation in MZ twins equals 0.8 and the correlation in DZ twin pairs equals 0.3, nonadditive effects are probably present. Then, the estimate for d^2 is $1.2 - 0.8 = 0.4$ and the estimate for a^2 is also 0.4; giving a total heritability for the trait of 0.8 (note that in this case the total heritability is equal to the MZ correlation). The effect of e^2 is 0.20. The effect of c^2, *if it were present, cannot be estimated.*

Structural Equation Modeling in the Classical Twin Design

To test how well the expectations for the resemblance of relatives describe the actual data and to test which model (e.g., AE, ACE, CE, or ADE) describes the data best, parameters can be estimated by maximum likelihood or other approaches. Structural equation modeling (SEM) or genetic covariance structure modeling (GCSM) provides a general and flexible approach to analyze data gathered in genetically informative samples such as in the classical twin study. In applying GCSM to data from relatives, genotypic and environmental effects are modeled as the contribution of latent (unmeasured) variables to the (possibly multivariate) phenotypic individual differences. These latent factors represent the effects of many unidentified influences, for example, polygenes and environment. For a more detailed overview of GCSM, see Boomsma and Molenaar (1986), Boomsma and Dolan (2000), Neale (2000), and Posthuma et al. (2003). Structural relations between measured variables (phenotypes) and unmeasured variables are often graphically represented in a path diagram, which is a mathematically complete description of a structural equation model. An example of such a model for a single trait in a twin pair is shown in Figure 60.1. The variables in squares are the observed phenotypes in twin 1 and in twin 2. The variables in circles are latent (unobserved). Their influence on the phenotype is given by path coefficients a, c, and e.

Identification of structural equation models in genetics is achieved from a design that includes relatives at different degrees of relatedness, for example, by inclusion of monozygotic (MZ) and dizygotic (DZ) twins into the study. Knowledge about Mendelian inheritance patterns defines the correlations among the latent factors in Figure 60.1. The path coefficients in Figure 60.1 define the relative importance of A, C, and E on the phenotype (P): $P = aA$

$+ cC + eE$. Expressed in variance components, the phenotypic variance can be written as: $var(P) = a^2 \, var(A) + c^2 \, var(C) + e^2 \, var(E)$, under the assumption that A, C, and E are uncorrelated and do not interact. If $var(A) = var(C) = var(E) = 1$, the expression for the population variance reduces to: $var(P) = a^2 + c^2 + e^2$. Please note a possible source of confusion: In the above expression a^2, c^2, and e^2 represent variance components; often, as we did ourselves in the introduction above, they represent standardized components (i.e., the variance components divided by the variance of P).

The contributions of the latent variables are estimated as regression coefficients in the linear regression of the observed variables on the latent variables. Given an appropriate design providing sufficient information to identify these regression coefficients actual estimates may be obtained using a number of well-disseminated computer programs, such as LISREL (Jöreskog & Sörbom, 1989) or Mx (Neale, Boker, Xie, & Maes, 2006). These programs allow estimation of parameters by means of a number of estimators including normal theory maximum likelihood (ML) and weighted least squares (WLS).

These estimators can also be applied to estimate and analyze correlations among family members for discrete variables or variables that show a nonnormal distribution (Derks, Dolan, & Boomsma, 2004). Data from relatives on categorical traits (e.g., presence or absence of disorder) are analyzed within this framework by making use of a threshold model that assumes there is a continuously and normally distributed liability underlying a disorder in the populations. One or more thresholds divide the continuous distribution into discrete classes, for example, affected and unaffected (Figure 60.2; Falconer & Mackay, 1996). The tetrachoric (for dichotomous traits) or polychoric (for ordered-category data with more than two categories) correlations represent the resemblance between relatives on the unobserved liability dimension.

The significance of parameters a, c, (or d) in Figure 60.2 is tested with a likelihood ratio test. The test involves constraining the parameter of interest at zero and then testing whether the constraint leads to a significant decrease in goodness-of-fit of the model. Twice the difference between the log-likelihood of two models (e.g., an ACE model and an AE model in which the influence of C is constrained at zero) is distributed asymptotically as χ^2. The degrees of freedom for the test are equal to the difference in parameters being estimated. Utilizing the principle of parsimony, the most restrictive model is accepted as the best fitting one in case the difference between a nested and a more comprehensive model is not significant (Neale & Cardon, 1992). The e parameter cannot be dropped from the model because this also includes the measurement error.

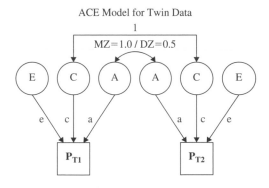

ACE Model for Twin Data

Figure 60.1 Path diagram for a single phenotype (P) assessed in twin 1 and twin 2.

Note: P is influenced by latent factors A (additive genetic influences), C (common environment shared by twins), and E (unique environment). Parameters a, c, and e represent the nonstandardized factor loadings. The latent factors are standardized. The correlation between the latent A factors depends on zygosity, and is 1 for MZ (monozygotic) and 0.5 for DZ (dizygotic) twins. The correlation between C factors is independent of zygosity as MZ and DZ twins share the same amount of environment. The correlation between A factors and between C factors may depend on sex of the twins. Especially in the presence of qualitative sex differences, in dizygotic twins of opposite sex the correlation between A factors can be lower than 0.5 or the correlation between C factors can be lower than 1 (indicating that different genes are expressed in men and women; or that different common environmental factors are of importance in the two sexes).

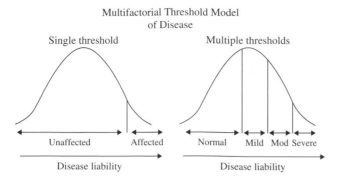

Multifactorial Threshold Model
of Disease

Figure 60.2   A threshold model assumes a normally distributed liability (or vulnerability) underlying a disorder or an ordered-category trait.

Note: The left figure shows a single threshold model with subjects scoring below the threshold on the, unobserved, liability scale being unaffected and subjects scoring above the threshold being affected. The right figure shows a model with multiple thresholds, for example mild, moderate, or severe depression. The tetrachoric correlation (for binary data) and the polychoric correlation (for ordered-category data) estimate what the correlation between family members would be if ratings for these traits were made on a continuous scale.

Beyond the Question of Heritability

Sex and Age Differences in the Genetic Architecture

The contributions of genetic factors to phenotypic variance may differ between men and women, as may the contribution of environmental factors. The expression of the genotype may also change with age. If we again denote the influence of A, C, and E on the phenotype by parameters a, c, and e, and the proportion of variance due to each of these factors as the square of these parameters, then three different models can be examined for quantitative sex differences in genetic architecture:

1. A full model in which estimates for a, c, and e are allowed to differ in magnitude between males and females. The outcome of the model can be, for example, that the genetic variance is the same in both sexes and the environmental variance larger in men than in women.

2. A scalar model in which heritabilities are constrained to be equal across sexes, but in which the total trait variance may differ in men and women. In the scalar model, all variance components for females, for example, are constrained to be equal to a scalar multiple i, of the male variance components, that is, $a_f = ia_m$, $c_f = ic_m$, and $e_f = ie_m$. As a result, the standardized variance components (such as heritabilities) are equal across sexes, even though the unstandardized components differ (Neale et al., 1992).

3. A constrained model in which parameter estimates for a, c, and e are constrained to be equal in magnitude across sexes.

If data from male and female twins are available, these quantitative sex differences models can be evaluated with standard likelihood ratio tests comparing the fit of the different models. If, for example, in males the correlation in MZ twins equals 0.60 and in DZ twins 0.30, while in females the correlation in MZ twins equals 0.70 and in DZ twins 0.40, the estimate for $a^2 = 0.60$ in males and females, but the estimate for $c^2 = 0$ in males and 0.10 in females. The estimate for e^2 is 0.40 in males and 0.30 in females. The likelihood ratio test will show whether these differences are significant. Likewise, if data are available for twins of different ages, for example, adolescent and adult twin pairs, then the significance of age differences in heritability can be tested.

If data are available for dizygotic opposite-sex (DOS) twins, a model for qualitative sex differences can be evaluated. Within this model, the test of interest is whether the same genes are expressed in men and women. This model is tested by estimating the correlation between genetic factors in the DOS pairs instead of fixing it at 0.5. If the correlation is significantly lower than 0.5, this indicates that different genes are expressed in the two sexes. A large difference between the correlation in same-sex DZ twins and DOS twins points to qualitative sex differences.

This qualitative sex differences model can also be applied in the context of an environmental hypothesis: instead of fixing the correlations between C factors at 1 in DOS twins, it can be estimated as a free parameter. If it is significantly lower than 1.0, this indicates that the influence of the shared environment differs in the two sexes. Note, however, because there is only one group of opposite-sex twins (there are no monozygotic twins of opposite sex, xcept in extremely rare cases) that a choice needs to be made to test either the genetic or the common environment correlation, but they cannot be estimated simultaneously.

Multivariate and Longitudinal Analyses

The decomposition into genetic and environmental variances for a single trait can be generalized to longitudinal and multivariate data where the variation and covariation of traits is decomposed into genetic and nongenetic sources (Boomsma et al., 2002; Boomsma & Molenaar, 1986; Martin & Eaves, 1977). In such data, the cross trait-cross twin correlations indicate how the value of twin 1 for trait A (e.g., depression) predicts the value of twin 2 for trait B (e.g., anxiety), and vice versa. The pattern of cross trait-cross

Bivariate ACE Model

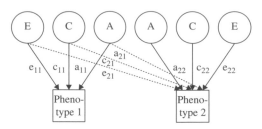

Figure 60.3   Genetic bivariate model, represented for one individual who is measured on two phenotypes.

Note: A, C, and E are the latent additive genetic, common environmental, and unique environmental factors, respectively, that influence the first phenotype (with factor loadings a_{11}, c_{11}, e_{11}), and/or the second phenotype (with factor loadings a_{21}, c_{21}, e_{21}), The second phenotype can also be influenced by a second set of independent latent factors (with factor loadings a_{22}, c_{22}, e_{22}). This model leads to the following equations for the estimates of the value of an individual's phenotype (P), the total variance (V_p), and the heritability (h^2) for phenotype 1 and phenotype 2: equations

twin correlations for MZ twins and DZ twins indicates (as described previously) to what extent the covariance between traits is influenced by genetic or environmental factors. Thus, if the cross-trait cross-twin correlation is larger in MZ twins than in DZ twins, genetic effects are likely to explain the covariance between traits.

Multivariate and longitudinal studies thus offer insight into the etiology of associations between traits, the comorbidity between disorders, and the stability of traits across time. If, for example, the same set of genes influences multiple traits, this constitutes evidence for genetic pleiotropy. If longitudinal stability is due to genetic factors, this indicates that the same set of genes is expressed across the life span. For two variables (for a single individual), the correlation between traits can be decomposed into parts caused by correlated genetic and correlated environmental factors (Figure 60.3).

Genotype Environment Correlation and Interaction

The designs discussed all assumed that genetic factors act independently from environmental factors. However, this assumption might be false. Gene-environment correlation or gene-environment interaction might play a role (Eaves, 1987; Kendler & Eaves, 1986; Rutter & Plomin, 1997). In passive gene-environment correlation the environment of an offspring depends on the genotype of parents (Eaves, 1987). For example, children who inherit the risk for depression may also grow up in a suboptimal environment because of a depressed parent. Gene-environment correlation can also arise because an individual's environment

depends on his own genotype, for example, in creating adverse life events. In other words, the exposure to a certain environment is under genetic control (Eaves, 1987; Kendler & Eaves, 1986). Gene-environment interaction reflects genetic control of sensitivity to the environment, that is, the effect of an environmental risk factor depends on the genetic make-up of an individual (Eaves, 1987; Kendler & Eaves, 1986). In the next section, methods used to investigate gene-environment correlation and interaction are described beginning with gene-environment correlation.

The classic twin design can be used to estimate to what extent the variation in exposure to a specific environment, for example, marital status or the experience of life events, is under genetic control. In other words, the twin design can be used to calculate the heritability of the "environmental" trait. Using the classical twin design, Johnson, McGue, Krueger, and Bouchard (2004) and Middeldorp, Cath, Vink, and Boomsma (2005) found that propensity to marry is heritable and McGue and Lykken (1992) found that divorce risk was, to a substantial degree, genetically mediated.

To examine whether the association between a specific environment and a trait is due to gene-environment correlation, the bivariate twin design can be applied (Purcell, 2002). This design investigates whether the genes influencing a behavioral trait also affect the chance of being exposed to a certain environment. Another approach to investigate this issue is the co-twin control design (Cederlof, Friberg, & Lundman, 1977; Kendler et al., 1993). In this design, the relative risk to have a disorder in the presence of a putative risk factor is calculated in a group of monozygotic (MZ) twins discordant for exposure to the risk factor, a group of dizygotic (DZ) twins discordant for exposure to the risk factor, and in a population consisting of unrelated subjects. If the relation between the risk factor and the disorder is causal and gene-environment correlation is absent, the relative risks will be the same in the three groups. If, on the other hand, the correlation between the risk factor and the disorder is due to genes that lead both to a higher risk for the disorder and to a higher risk of exposure to the risk factor, the relative risk will be higher in the total population than in the discordant dizygotic twins, whose relative risk will in turn be higher than the relative risk in the discordant monozygotic twins. Moreover, when gene-environment correlation entirely explains the relation between the risk factor and the disorder, the relative risk in MZ twins will be unity. This is because the unexposed member of MZ twins has the same genetic vulnerability to get the disorder as the twin who is exposed to the risk factor. Since DZ twins share on average half of their genes, the unexposed twin will share some of the genetic vulnerability to the disorder with the twin exposed to the risk factor. Unrelated subjects will show the highest relative risk.

Kendler et al. (1993) investigated whether the relation between smoking and depression was causal or due to shared genes influencing vulnerability for both traits. Although the relative risk for ever smoking given a lifetime history of depression was 1.48 in the entire sample, it was 1.18 and 0.98, respectively, in DZ and MZ twin pairs discordant for a history of depression. The relative risk for a history of depression given ever smoking was 1.60 in the entire sample, while in DZ and MZ twins discordant for smoking, it was 1.29 and 0.96, respectively. These results suggest that the association between smoking and depression in women is not a causal one but arises largely from familial factors, which are probably genetic, that predispose to both smoking and depression.

An approach to investigate gene-environment interaction is to estimate the relative influences of genotype (heritability) and environment on a trait conditional on environmental exposure (Boomsma & Martin, 2002; Eaves, 1987; Heath, Eaves, & Martin, 1998; Heath, Jardine, & Martin, 1989; Kendler & Eaves, 1986). When there is no G × E interaction, the influence of genetic and environmental factors should not differ between subjects with different degrees of exposure. If genetic effects are modified by environmental exposure, such that heritabilities differ significantly between exposure-positive and exposure-negative groups, then this constitutes evidence for gene × environment interaction. Thus, this type of interaction is detected by testing whether the amount of variance explained by genetic factors differs between exposure-positive and exposure-negative groups.

Purcell (2002) developed a model to investigate gene-environment interaction more extensively, for example, when an environmental risk factor is measured on a continuous instead of a dichotomous scale. The genetic effects are partitioned into a mean part, which is independent of the environmental moderator, and a part that is a linear function of the environmental moderator. The model also allows for a test of gene-environment interaction in the presence of gene-environment correlation.

GENETIC EPIDEMIOLOGY OF ANXIETY AND DEPRESSION

Univariate Analyses

A large number of twin studies have investigated the influence of genetic and environmental factors on depression and anxiety. The review of these studies will be limited to population-based twin studies on depression and anxiety disorders as classified by the *DSM* (American Psychiatric Association, 1980, 1987, 1994), starting with the results of single trait analyses. A meta-analysis showed that major depression is around 37% heritable with the remaining part of the variance explained by individual specific environmental factors (Sullivan, Neale, & Kendler, 2000). Environmental factors shared by family members did not seem to be of major importance. The genetic epidemiology of depression was also investigated in 42,161 twins including 15,493 complete pairs from the national Swedish Twin Registry (Kendler, Gatz, Gardner, & Pedersen, 2006). Due to the large sample, this study detected common environmental influences or differences between men and women in the etiology of depression. The heritability was estimated at 29% in men and 42% in women, which was significantly different. Common environment did not explain any of the familial clustering. The genetic correlation between men and women was 0.69 indicating the existence of sex-specific genetic factors in addition to a set of shared genes.

The amount of measurement error is reflected in the estimate of the influence of the unique environment. One study that assessed lifetime diagnosis of major depression at two occasions was able to parse out the effect of measurement error due to unreliability, resulting in a heritability estimate of 66% (Foley, Neale, & Kendler, 1998). This suggests that genetic factors might be more important for major depression than generally assumed.

Anxiety disorders have been less extensively investigated. Meta-analyses showed that genetic factors explain 43% of the variance in panic disorder and 32% in generalized anxiety disorder (GAD; Hettema, Neale, & Kendler, 2001). For phobias, the heritability estimates varied somewhat around 30% with a maximum of 48% for agoraphobia (Kendler, Jacobson, Myers, & Prescott, 2002). The findings regarding the influence of common environment were inconsistent for social phobia, animal phobia, and GAD in women (Hettema, Prescott, & Kendler, 2001; Kendler et al., 2002; Kendler, Karkowski, & Prescott, 1999b; Kendler, Neale, Kessler, Heath, & Eaves, 1992). Partly depending on the definition of the disorder, a significant influence of the common environment was found. The authors suggested that these findings were due to stochastic factors and that it is most probable that the effect of the common environment is negligible (Hettema, Prescott, et al., 2001; Kendler et al., 2002).

Regarding sex differences in the genetic architecture for anxiety disorders, no major differences were found for GAD (Hettema, Prescott, et al., 2001; Middeldorp, Birley, et al., 2005). For social phobia, one study found quantitative sex differences but another did not (Kendler et al., 2002;

Middeldorp, Birley, et al., 2005). No sex differences were found for panic syndromes (Kendler, Gardner, & Prescott, 2001), while for agoraphobia, results indicated that the genes conveying the risk are probably not entirely the same (Kendler et al., 2002). The latter finding appeared to be supported by another study that investigated panic disorder and/or agoraphobia together (Middeldorp, Birley, et al., 2005). Qualitative sex differences were also found for situational and blood/injury phobia (Kendler et al., 2002).

One study on phobias took measurement error due to unreliable assessment into account (Kendler et al., 1999b). That resulted in heritability estimates around 50% indicating that for the anxiety disorders, as well as for depression, the heritability might be higher than assumed.

Multivariate and Longitudinal Analyses

Multivariate analyses of depression and anxiety disorders address the etiology of the comorbidity between these disorders. The frequent comorbidity within anxiety disorders and between anxiety disorders and depression is an important issue: Does the comorbidity arise because of shared genetic risk factors or are there other explanations? The results of the Epidemiologic Catchment Area (ECA) Study and the National Comorbidity Survey (NCS) have shown that the occurrence of one anxiety disorder increases the risk of having an additional anxiety disorder (odds ratio on average 6.7; Kessler, 1995). The same holds for the combination of affective disorders (including dysthymia and mania) and anxiety disorders (odds ratio 7.0; Kessler, 1995). These increased odds ratios indicate that comorbidity between anxiety and depression is not only due to chance. Moreover, since the ECA and NCS studies are population based, sampling bias is highly unlikely to explain comorbidity rates. The NCS replication study showed similar results (Kessler, Chiu, Demler, Merikangas, & Walters, 2005).

The issue of comorbidity gives rise to questions at a nosological level (Neale & Kendler, 1995). Do anxiety disorders and depression reflect an arbitrary division of a single syndrome? Are the different anxiety disorders and depression distinct entities, possibly influenced by common genetic and environmental etiological factors? Are the comorbid conditions independent of the separate anxiety disorders and depression? A review of twin and family studies investigating comorbidity within anxiety disorders and between anxiety disorders and depression concluded that they are distinct disorders with comorbidity probably partly explained by shared genetic factors (Middeldorp, Cath, van Dyck, & Boomsma, 2005). Possibly, this shared genetic vulnerability is expressed in the personality trait neuroticism (Middeldorp, Cath, et al.,

2005). Most studies in this review performed bivariate analyses. Three twin studies carried out more extensive analyses (Hettema, Neale, Myers, Prescott, & Kendler, 2006; Hettema, Prescott, Myers, Neale, & Kendler, 2005; Kendler, Prescott, Myers, & Neale, 2003). Earlier factor analyses of common mental disorders showed that the latent structure of these disorders is best described by a three-factor model (Krueger, 1999; Vollebergh et al., 2001). One factor represents externalizing problems. The other two factors, which are subfactors of a higher-order factor representing internalizing problems, reflect anxious misery and fear. Kendler, Prescott, et al. (2003) aimed to extend these findings into a genetic epidemiological model. They showed that there are two genetic risk factors. One predisposes for internalizing disorders and the other for externalizing disorders. In addition, within the internalizing disorders, two genetics factors are seen that predispose to disorders dominated by anxious misery and fear.

Hettema et al. (2005, 2006) focused in more detail on the internalizing disorders. In their first study, including GAD, panic disorder, agoraphobia, social phobia, animal phobia, and situational phobia, they confirmed that two genetic factors influence these disorders (Hettema et al., 2005). In their second study, they focused on the association between neuroticism on the one hand and depression and anxiety disorders on the other. They showed that the genetic correlation between neuroticism and these disorders are high with estimates varying between 0.58 and 0.82. They also identified a second neuroticism-independent genetic factor significantly increasing the risk for major depression, generalized anxiety, and panic disorder in addition to disorder-specific genetic factors for the phobias. Comparing their results with the results of the previous studies performed in the same sample, it was hypothesized that a model with a third genetic factor influencing the phobias would provide a better fit. However, that model could not be tested due to computational problems (Hettema et al., 2006).

In all three studies, the influence of individual-specific environmental factors was largely disorder specific. The heritability estimates for depression and anxiety disorders were similar to the estimates from the univariate analyses, varying around 20% and 30%. For major depression and generalized anxiety disorder, these studies did not find an effect of the common environment. However, for panic disorder and social phobia, the common environment might explain 10% of the variance. Estimates vary somewhat for animal and situational phobia, but, in general, seem to be negligible (Hettema et al., 2005, 2006; Kendler, Prescott, et al., 2003).

Longitudinal studies on anxiety and depression are scarce. There has been one longitudinal twin study in adults with a follow-up over 10 years (Gillespie et al., 2004). Symptoms of anxiety and depression measured with self-report questionnaires were assessed in Australian twins aged 20 to 96 years at three points over a period of 16 years. For male anxiety and depression, there was no genetic innovation after age 20, thus the same genes remained to explain variation in anxiety and depression at ages 30, 40, 50, and 60. Most of the lifetime genetic variation in female anxiety and depression could also be explained by a stable set of genetic factors; however, there were also smaller age-dependent genetic innovations at age 30 for anxiety and at ages 40 and 70 for depression.

In children, a longitudinal study on anxious depression was carried out in the population-based Netherlands Twin Register (Boomsma, van Beijsterveldt, Bartels, & Hudziak, 2008). Maternal and paternal ratings for anxious depression (A/D) were available for twins at ages 3, 5, 7, 10, and 12 with over 9,025 twin pairs at age 3 and over 2,300 pairs at age 12 being assessed. The influence of genetic factors declined with increasing age. The heritability was around 60% at age 3 and declined to 40% at age 12. The decrease in heritability when children grew older was accompanied by an increase in the influence of the common environment shared by twins (8% at age 3 and 23% at age 12). These results argue for shared environmental factors playing an important role in protecting children from or putting them at risk for the expression of A/D. The contribution of nonshared environmental factors ranged between 26% and 36%. This last result indicates that nonshared environment, or environmental influences that contribute to differences between siblings, plays a substantial role across development when considering the expression of A/D. However, when comparing this estimate for e^2 with the estimates from studies in adults, it is clear that the importance of unique environmental factors increases across the life span.

The results showed that the stability of A/D was relatively low between age 3 and later ages (correlations around 0.30), but became higher after age 7 (up to 0.67 between ages 10 and 12). The genetic correlations between A/D assessed at age 3 and other ages were modest, suggesting a small overlap of genes that influence A/D in preschool children and in middle childhood (genetic correlations between 0.24 and 0.35 for A/D at age 3 with other ages). These results raise the possibility of different genetic influences of genes across development, either by variable expression patterns, variable response to environmental mediators and modifiers, or simply, evidence of developmental genetic processes. After the age of 7, the genetic correlations were larger (0.63 to 0.70), indicating that the extent to which the same genes operate across ages 7 to 12 was increased.

Across ages, the same common environmental factors were suggested because a single C factor could explain the covariance pattern across age. Family variables, such as parental conflict, negative familial environments, and separation are likely candidates for these shared environmental influences. Future genetic research should include such environmental variables (e.g., parental divorce) to specify the role of these environmental factors. Nonshared environmental factors operate mainly in a time-specific manner.

A part of the shared environment reflects parental bias. By using the same rater at two or more points, the prediction of A/D could reflect some shared rater bias. If this is the case, the observed stability is not only a reflection of stability of children's problem behavior but also a reflection of the stability of the mother's perception. However, by applying a longitudinal model to both father and mother ratings, it is possible to disentangle the effects due to real environment and the effect due to rater bias (Hewitt, Silberg, Neale, Eaves, & Erickson, 1992). The results indicated that there is still evidence for shared environmental influences on the stability of A/D when data from the father and mother are analyzed simultaneously. However, results indicate also that the rater-specific shared environment contributes to stability of A/D. This could point to possible rater bias that is persistent and affects the stability of A/D.

Conclusions

Depression and anxiety in adults are moderately heritable with genetic influences estimated mostly around 30% and 40%. These might be underestimates because studies taking measurement error into account have found that 50% to 60% of the variance could be explained by genetic factors. A common environment does not seem to play a major role in most internalizing disorders, but might be of importance in panic disorder and social phobia, although accounting for only 10% of the variance. Quantitative and qualitative sex differences in etiological factors appear to be modest. The comorbidity between major depression and anxiety disorders and within anxiety disorders is largely explained by common genetic factors. It seems that one genetic factor, expressed in the personality trait neuroticism, explains the comorbidity between internalizing disorders with two additional genetic factors influencing the risk for anxious misery and fear. Individual specific environmental factors are largely disorder specific. Although the genetic determinants of anxiety and depression appear relatively stable across the adult life span for men and women, there is some evidence to support additional mid-life and late-age gene action in women for depression. In children, the influence of genetic factors decreases with age, while the influence of the common environment becomes more important between age 7 and 12. Correlations between measures of A/D are low at younger ages, but become higher after age 7. Most of the stability across age is due to genetic stability and it appeared that other genes become important when children become older. In contrast, there is one common environmental factor influencing anxious depression in children through age 7 and 12. Unique environmental influences are largely age specific. The conclusions regarding the influences of genes and environment across life span are based on one study in adults and one study in children, so confirmation by other studies is required.

Gene-Environment Correlation and Interaction

An important indication that gene-environment correlation exists is given by a review demonstrating that several environmental factors, such as life events, parenting style, peer deviance, and social support, are modestly influenced by genetic factors (Kendler & Baker, 2006). Weighted heritabilities ranged from 7% to 39% with most estimates falling between 15% and 35%. Studies with multiple measurements of life events and social support found that temporal stability in the environment is influenced to a much greater extent by genetic factors than occasion specific events.

Gene-environment correlation has been shown to explain the association between life events and depression in some twin and family studies (Kendler, Karkowski, & Prescott, 1999a; Kendler & Karkowski-Shuman, 1997; McGuffin, Katz, & Bebbington, 1988), but not in others (Farmer et al., 2000; Romanov, Varjonen, Kaprio, & Koskenvuo, 2003). One of the studies that found support for gene-environment correlation suggested that the correlation could be explained by genes that influence personality traits associated with depression (Kendler et al., 1999a). This hypothesis was later confirmed for neuroticism, extraversion, and openness for experience (Kendler, Gardner, & Prescott, 2003; Saudino, Pedersen, Lichtenstein, McClearn, & Plomin, 1997).

One study investigated the relation between the exposure to life events and anxious depression measured with a self-report questionnaire in a longitudinal and a genetic design (Middeldorp, Cath, Beem, Willemsen, & Boomsma, 2008). The results suggested that the relation between life events and anxious depressive symptoms is due to a causal reciprocal relation. Gene-environment correlation did not seem to play a role. The personality traits neuroticism and extraversion were also included in the analyses. The latter was not related to life events at all. In contrast, neuroticism scores were increased, but to a lesser extent than depression scores, after life events. Moreover, higher neuroticism scores increased the chance of the exposure to a life event later in life. Again, gene-environment correlation did not seem to be important.

The results so far have been inconclusive. Some findings are in favor of gene-environment correlation between life events, depression, or neuroticism, but others are not. Investigating gene-environment correlation is important to get more insight into etiological mechanisms. Exclusion of gene-environment correlation is an essential step before investigating gene-environment interaction (Moffitt, Caspi, & Rutter, 2005).

Studies on gene-environment interaction for anxiety and depression with unmeasured genes have been limited to life events and marital status (Heath et al., 1998; Kendler et al., 1995; Silberg, Rutter, Neale, & Eaves, 2001). The risk for depression after a life event is higher if there are indications of a genetic vulnerability for depression, that is, a family history of depression and vice versa the genetic variance increases in the presence of life events (Kendler et al., 1995; Silberg et al., 2001). Regarding marital status, it appears that being married protects against the expression of genetic risk for depression (Heath et al., 1998).

GENE FINDING METHODS

Linkage Studies

Obtaining evidence that a trait is heritable opens up a whole new avenue of research: Where are the genes localized that influence the phenotype and can we identify them? The first question can be addressed in linkage studies, the second question in genetic association studies. Although there is a wide range of dedicated software packages to carry out genetic linkage and association studies (Abecasis, Cardon, & Cookson, 2000; Abecasis, Cherny, Cookson, & Cardon, 2002; Abecasis, Cookson, & Cardon, 2000; Almasy & Blangero, 1998; Gudbjartsson, Thorvaldsson, Kong, Gunnarsson, & Ingolfsdottir, 2005; Kruglyak, Daly, Reeve-Daly, & Lander, 1996; Purcell et al., 2007), we introduce this type of analyses within the context of genetic structural equation modeling (GCSM). GCSM can relatively easy incorporate measured genotypic information into the analysis. Genotypic information derives from polymorphic marker data that are assessed in DNA samples of subjects for whom phenotypic information is also available. If DNA markers are roughly evenly spaced along the genome, if their location is known, and if they are highly polymorphic (e.g., microsatellite markers that have multiple alleles), then they can be used in linkage studies. These studies make use of the fact that when enough DNA markers are measured, a stretch of markers will be close to the gene that influences the trait of interest.

The location of a gene that influences a complex, often quantitative trait, is called a *quantitative trait locus* (QTL).

A QTL represents a stretch of a chromosome, which includes a segregating gene, or multiple genes, that contributes to individual differences in the phenotype of interest. The segregating gene has a relatively large contribution to the phenotypic variance compared to the contributions of each polygene making up a genetic latent variable. However, compared to the total effects of the polygenetic and environmental effects, the effect of the QTL may be quite small. For instance, the QTL may account for a mere 5% or 10% of the phenotypic variance. The QTL can be treated in the same way as a polygenetic or an environmental factor, that is, as a latent variable and the relationship between the QTL and the phenotypic individual differences is modeled as a linear regression. If a set of markers is close to the QTL, then resemblance on the markers reflects resemblance for the QTL. The effect of the QTL is modeled on the covariance structure: If siblings who share more markers identical by descent (IBD) across a stretch of chromosome are more alike (their correlation for the trait is higher) than siblings who do not share any markers (Sham, 1997; Vink & Boomsma, 2002), this is evidence for linkage.

Figure 60.4 shows a path model for DZ twins or siblings that incorporates the effect of a QTL on a measured phenotype. The correlation between QTL factors of DZ twins or siblings is obtained from measured genotypic (marker) data. IBD status for the marker data determines this correlation. IBD status in sibling pairs can be 0, 1, or 2, depending on whether the two siblings inherit the same marker allele from each parent (in which case, IBD = 2), whether they receive one allele IBD from one, but not from the other parent (in which case, IBD = 1), or whether they receive a different allele from each parent (in which case, IBD = 0). Parents always share one allele

with their offspring, therefore their IBD probabilities of sharing 0, 1, or 2 alleles will be IBD0 = 0.0, IBD1 = 1.0, and IBD2 = 0.0. For two siblings, the IBD probabilities depend on their genotypes on the marker position and surrounding markers. When their parents are genotyped, the IBD status of siblings can be derived from the transmission of alleles from parents to offspring. When parents are not genotyped, the allele frequencies of markers are used in the estimation of IBD. If parents have four distinct alleles, for example, the father "A" and "B" and mother "C" and "D," the IBD status of their offspring can easily be determined (see Figure 60.5). If sibling 1 has AC and sibling 2 also has AC, the IBD probabilities will be IBD0 = 0.0, IBD1 = 0.0, and IBD2 = 1.0. If sibling 2 has AD instead, IBD0 = 0.0, IBD1 = 1.0, IBD2 = 0.0, and so on. However, if one of the parents is homozygous (e.g., AA), or if a genotype is missing, the IBD probabilities are calculated by maximum likelihood from all possible combinations of genotypes and their probabilities based on the allele frequencies of the marker, for example, IB0 = 0.0, IBD1 = 0.752, and IBD2 = 0.248. (For details on these procedures, see Haseman & Elston, 1972; Kruglyak & Lander, 1995; or Abecasis et al., 2002.) From the IBD probabilities, the correlation for the QTL marker (π) is calculated as $0 \times IBD0 + 0.5 \times IBD1 + 1 \times IBD2$ for each individual pair in each family (Sham, 1997). Within the context of genetic structural equation modeling

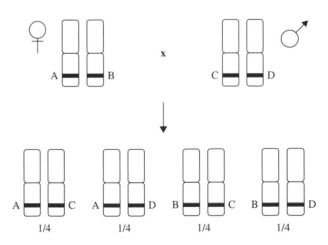

Figure 60.5 (A) Graph showing the possible allele combination for children from a mother carrying alleles A and B and a father with alleles C and D. (B) The table shows the 16 possible combinations of genotypes and the number of alleles identical by descent (IBD) for each combination for two siblings with a mother carrying alleles A and B and a father carrying alleles C and D.

Note: The chance for each combination (AC, AD, BC, and BD) in an offspring is ¼. The probability that two siblings share two parental alleles (IBD=2) is 4/16 = ¼. The probability that they do not share any parental alleles is also 4/16 = ¼, but the probability that they share one parental allele is 8/16 = ½.

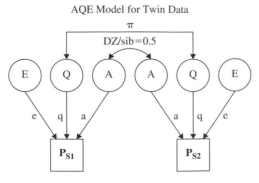

Figure 60.4 Linkage model for DZ twin or sibling data: The phenotype assessed in sibling 1 and sibling 2 (P_{S1} and P_{S2}) is influenced by additive genetic factors (A), environment (E), and a quantitative trait locus (QTL).

Note: The correlation π in two siblings for the QTL depends on the measured DNA marker data and is defined based on their identity by descent (IBD) status. If path coefficient q is significant, this is evidence for linkage, that is, the trait locus is close to the markers that defined IBD.

(see also Figure 60.4), the test for linkage involves constraining the factor loading (q) of the phenotype on the QTL factor at zero and testing if this constraint leads to a significant decrease in goodness of fit. This test is based on a likelihood ratio test and is distributed as χ^2. In classical linkage analyses of Mendelian traits (traits that are influenced by a single locus), the commonly used test statistic is the LOD score. In parametric linkage analysis, it is standard practice to summarize the results of a linkage analysis in the form of an LOD score (Morton, 1955). LOD score stands for the logarithm of the odds that the locus is linked to the trait and indicates the strength of the linkage. Evidence for linkage is present when the maximum LOD score exceeds a predefined threshold, which depends on the size of the genome and the number of markers (Lander & Kruglyak, 1995). A commonly used threshold is an LOD score of 3. This critical value can be interpreted as stating that the evidence in favor of linkage is 1,000 times more likely than the null hypothesis of no linkage. If a LOD score of 2 was observed, then the null hypothesis of no linkage is 100 times more likely than the alternative. There is a simple correspondence between χ^2 and LOD scores: LOD $= \chi^2/2\ln10$ (Sham, 1997).

Association Studies

In contrast to linkage studies that model the covariance structure in relatives, genetic association analysis models the effect of a genetic polymorphism on the trait levels. This can be done in cases and controls (e.g., dichotomous traits), in groups of unrelated individuals (for the analysis of quantitative traits), or within families. Association studies in unrelated subjects are similar in design to classic case-control studies in epidemiology. DNA collected from all participants and frequencies of the various allelic variants are compared in subjects with particular phenotypes (e.g., presence or absence of disease) to detect an association between a particular allele and the occurrence of the phenotype. The association test can be carried out for presence or absence of a particular allele or a particular genotype. For quantitative traits, the trait values are compared across the various allelic or genotypic variants of the DNA marker. The advantage of association over linkage analysis is that association studies can detect the region of a QTL that has only very small effects on the trait (Risch & Merikangas, 1996). This increase in statistical power comes from the fact that the test is carried out on first-order statistics (means or prevalences) whereas linkage tests are carried out on second-order statistics (covariances).

Provided that either the selection of cases does not introduce population stratification or that the analyses properly control for such stratification, association studies provide a good complement to the linkage strategy. However, a potential problem of association studies is the danger that a spurious association is found between the trait of interest and any locus that differs in allele frequency between subpopulations. This situation is illustrated by the chopstick gene story described by Hamer and Sirota (2000). They describe a hypothetical study in which DNA markers were assessed in American and foreign students who often used chopsticks and students who did not. One of the DNA markers showed a correlation to chopstick use. Of course, this gene had nothing to do with chopstick use, but just happened to have different allele frequencies in Asians and Caucasians, who differ in chopstick use for purely cultural rather than biological reasons. Witte, Gauderman, and Thomas (1999) have evaluated the asymptotic bias in relative risk estimates resulting from using population controls when there is confounding due to population stratification. The direction of the bias is what one would expect from the usual principles of confounding in epidemiology: If the allele frequencies and baseline risks are both higher in a population, the bias is positive; if different, the bias is negative. Case-control studies of genetic associations thus can lead to false-positive as well as to false-negative results.

To prevent significant findings due to population stratification, within-family association designs have been developed because family members are usually well matched on a number of traits that could give rise to stratification effects (Spielman, McGinnis, & Ewens, 1993). Most available family-based tests for association were initially developed for binary traits, such as the Transmission Disequilibrium Test (TDT) and the Haplotype Relative Risk test (HRR). Those tests are based on a design in which DNA is collected in affected individuals and their biological parents. Affected individuals must have received one or two susceptibility alleles from their parents. These alleles transmitted from parents to the affected individual can be viewed as a group of "case" alleles. The nontransmitted alleles from the parents can be considered as "control" alleles. In other words, those tests only need affected individuals and their parents; no other control group is required. In a different approach, the effects of genotypes on phenotypic means are partitioned into between-family and within-family components, by comparing the association of alleles and trait values across siblings from different families to the association of alleles and trait values across siblings within the same family. Sibling pairs are by definition ethnically and racially homogeneous and any difference in trait scores between siblings of different genotypes at a candidate marker, therefore, reflects true genetic association. By partitioning the mean effect of a locus into a between and a within-sibship component, spurious associations due to population stratification and admixture are controlled (Abecasis, Cookson, et al.,

2000; Fulker, Cherny, Sham, & Hewitt, 1999; Posthuma, de Geus, Boomsma, & Neale, 2004).

One problem with the candidate gene approach for most complex traits is the potentially huge number of genes that can serve as candidates. Several strategies are possible to select an optimal set of candidate genes. First, genes that are part of physiological systems known to influence the trait can be tested as candidates. Second, genes or chromosomal regions that are known to influence the trait in animals can be tested as candidate genes (or regions) in humans. Third, genes lying under a linkage signal can be the focus of research.

GENOME-WIDE ASSOCIATION STUDIES

Linkage is usually genome-wide, although until recently association studies were limited to candidate genes or candidate regions. This has changed with the possibility to assess very large numbers of genetic markers within an individual. So called Genome-Wide Association studies (GWA) assess 300,000 to 600,000 markers along the genome and test if an association between a disorder, or a quantitative trait level, and a specific allele can be detected in groups of unrelated cases (e.g., patients) and controls (e.g., healthy subjects) or within families. Association can be found either with functional genetic variants that have biological consequences, or with other variants that are in linkage disequilibrium with these variants. Linkage disequilibrium occurs when a marker allele (i.e., a single nucleotide polymorphism [SNP]) and the QTL are so close on a chromosome that they co-segregate in the population over many generations of meiotic recombination.

Gene Finding Studies in Anxiety and Depression

Linkage Studies

Seven genome-wide linkage analyses have been performed, aiming to locate genes for MDD on the genome (Camp et al., 2005; Holmans et al., 2004, 2007; McGuffin et al., 2005; Nurnberger et al., 2001; Zubenko et al., 2003). Other studies have focused on quantitative traits associated with a diagnosis of MDD, such as neuroticism (Cloninger et al., 1998; Fullerton et al., 2003; Kuo et al., 2007; Nash et al., 2004; Neale et al., 2005; Wray et al., 2008). Table 60.1 summarizes the most promising results of these studies, excluding the study of Holmans et al. (2004) because this is based on the same sample as used by Holmans et al. (2007). Several regions have shown a linkage signal with a LOD-score <3 in at least one study. The following five regions have reached a LOD-score >3 in one study and a

LOD-score > 1.5 in a second study: chromosome 1 between 126 and 137 cM (Fullerton et al., 2003; Neale et al., 2005), chromosome 8 between 8 and 38 cM (Cloninger et al., 1998; Fullerton et al., 2003), chromosome 11 between 2 and 35 cM (Camp et al., 2005; Zubenko et al., 2003), chromosome 11 between 85 and 99 cM (Fullerton et al., 2003; Zubenko et al., 2003), and chromosome 12 between 105 and 124 cM (Fullerton et al., 2003; McGuffin et al., 2005).

The most promising results of genome-wide linkage studies on anxiety phenotypes are summarized in Table 60.2 (Crowe et al., 2001; Fyer et al., 2006; Gelernter et al., 2001, 2003; Gelernter, Page, Stein, & Woods, 2004; Hamilton et al., 2003; Kaabi et al., 2006; Knowles et al., 1998; Middeldorp et al., 2008; Smoller et al., 2001; Thorgeirsson et al., 2003; Weissman et al., 2000). Three regions (chromosome 4, 9, and 13) showing significant linkage have not been replicated yet (Kaabi et al., 2006; Thorgeirsson et al., 2003; Weissman et al., 2000). Three other regions (chromosome 1, 7, and 14) have shown evidence for linkage in two studies (Crowe et al., 2001; Gelernter et al., 2001; Kaabi et al., 2006; Knowles et al., 1998; Middeldorp et al., 2008; Smoller et al., 2001). Gelernter et al. (2001, 2003, 2004) found a suggestive linkage signal on chromosome 14 for simple phobia, social phobia, and panic disorder. These three studies were performed on the same sample, thus the studies are not considered to be replications.

Only the region on chromosome 7 has been found in linkage studies on neuroticism and anxiety. No further overlap between Table 60.1 and 60.2 is seen.

Association Studies

Despite the large number of candidate gene studies, efforts to identify QTLs for depression and anxiety through this approach have met with limited success. For an overview of the results, we refer to Levinson (2006) and Stoppel, Albrecht, Pape, and Stork (2006). In this chapter, we limit the discussion of association studies to the widely investigated association between the promoter-based length polymorphism of the serotonin transporter gene (5-HTTLPR) and anxiety and depression.

The 5-HTTLPR polymorphism is located in the promoter of the gene and is defined by a length variation of a repetitive sequence with the short and the long fragment consisting of 484 and 528 base pairs, respectively. These variants are often denoted as "s" and "l." Genes involved in the serotonin system are considered likely candidates, since medication such as selective serotonin reuptake inhibitors (SSRIs),—Prozac, for example—have been proven to be effective in the treatment of patients with anxiety disorders or depression. 5-HTTLPR seemed an excellent candidate because in vitro analyses showed that the basal activity of

TABLE 60.1 Most promising linkage results in the order of the chromosomes for neuroticism, harm avoidance, MDD, or the subtypes recurrent MDD (R-MDD) and recurrent early-onset MDD (RE-MDD)

Location (Chromosome, cM)/ References	LOD	N Subjects[A]/Families	Phenotype
Chromosome 1, 42 and 90 cM (Camp et al., 2005; Nash et al., 2004).	1.7	426/90	MDD-RE
	1.6	711/283	Neuroticism
Chromosome 1, 126–137cM (Fullerton et al., 2003; Neale et al., 2005)	4.0[b]	1122/561	Neuroticism
	2.5[b]	293/129	Neuroticism
Chromosome 2, 237–248 cM (Nurnberger Jr. et al., 2001; Zubenko et al., 2003)	2.2	224 possible pairs	MDD comorbid with alcoholism
	2.5[b]	?/81	MDD
Chromosome 4, 176cM (Fullerton et al., 2003)	3.8[b]	1122/561	Neuroticism
Chromosome 7, 42 cM (Fullerton et al., 2003)	3.9[b]	1122/561	Neuroticism
Chromosome 8, 8–38 cM (Cloninger et al., 1998; Fullerton et al., 2003)	3.2	987/105	Harm avoidance
	2.9[b]	1122/561	Neuroticism
Chromosome 10, 5–9 cM (Camp et al., 2005; Wray et al., 2008)	1.6	426/90	RE-MDD
	2.0	2030/564	Neuroticism
Chromosome 10, 76 cM (Zubenko et al., 2003)	3.0	?/81	MDD
Chromosome 11, 2–35 cM (Camp et al., 2005; Zubenko et al., 2003)	1.6	426 / 90	RE-MDD and anxiety
	4.2	?/81	R-MDD
Chromosome 11, 85–99 cM (Fullerton et al., 2003; Zubenko et al., 2003)	3.7[b]	1122/561	Neuroticism
	2.5	?/81	RE-MDD
Chromosome 12, 105–124 cM (Fullerton et al., 2003; McGuffin et al., 2005)	4.7[b]	1122/561	Neuroticism
	1.6	994/497	R-MDD
Chromosome 13, 64cM (Fullerton et al., 2003)	3.8[b]	1122/561	Neuroticism
Chromosome 18, 73cM (Camp et al., 2005)	3.8	96/21	RE-MDD and anxiety
Chromosome 18, 109–117cM (Cloninger et al., 1998; Wray et al., 2008)	1.6	987/105	Harm avoidance
	1.9	8552/2509	Neuroticism

Note: Regions with a LOD $\geq$ 3 or with a LOD $\geq$ 1.5 found at least twice are shown. Sex-specific effects are not included.

[a]For the studies of MDD, the number of affected individuals is given.

[b]This is the -logP, not the LOD score.

the long variant was about threefold higher than that of the short variant, indicating that the s-l polymorphism is functional (Heils et al., 1996).

In 1996, Lesch et al. (1996) reported an association between the promoter-based length polymorphism of the serotonin transporter gene (5-HTTLPR) and the anxiety-related personality traits neuroticism and harm avoidance. The association of the short variant with higher neuroticism and harm avoidance scores was not only found in two independent groups of subjects, but also within families. The family population included 459 siblings from 210 families, of which 78 sibling pairs from 61 independent families had discordant 5-HTTLPR genotypes (one or two copies

of the short form versus homozygous for the long form). The difference in personality scores between siblings with the long form and siblings with the short form of the 5-HTTLPR genotype was statistically significant. This within-family association effect indicated that the significant associations found in the samples of unrelated individuals were not due to population stratification and could be a genuine effect.

Remarkably, subjects with the short form scored higher than subjects with the long form. This is in contrast to what would be expected considering the effect of the SSRIs on anxiety and depression, which is thought to be due to an increased serotonin concentration in the synapse. The

TABLE 60.2   Promising linkage results for anxiety phenotypes

Location/Reference	LOD	N Subjects/Families	Phenotype	Sample Ascertainment
Chromosome 1, 218–234 cM (Gelernter et al., 2001; Smoller et al., 2001)	2.04	153/20	Panic disorder	Probands with panic disorder
	2.05[a]	99/1	Aniety proneness	Probands with panic disorder
Chromosome 4, 157 cM (Kaabi et al., 2006)	4.5[b]	153/20	Broad anxiety phenotype	Probands with panic disorder
Chromosome 7, 47–57 cM (Crowe et al., 2001; Knowles et al., 1998)	1.71	–/23	Panic disorder	Probands with panic disorder
	2.23	253/23	Panic disorder	Probands with panic disorder
Chromosome 9, 105 cM (Thorgeirsson et al., 2003)	4.18	–/25	Anxiety/panic disorder	Probands with panic attacks, GAD, or phobias
Chromosome 13, 96 cM (Weissman et al., 2000)	4.2	–/34	Panic disorder combined with bladder/kidney problems	Probands with panic disorder
Chromosome 14, 36–45 cM (Gelernter et al., 2001; Gelernter et al., 2003; Gelernter et al., 2004)	3.7	129/14	Simple phobia	Probands with panic disorder
	2.93[c]	163/17	Social phobia	Probands with panic disorder
	2.38[a]	153/20	Panic disorder	Probands with panic disorder
Chromosome 14, 105 cM (Kaabi et al., 2006; Middeldorp et al., 2008)	1.7[b]	153/20	Broad anxiety phenotype	Probands with panic disorder
	3.4	1602/1566	Broad anxiety phenotype	Population based twin-family sample

Note: Regions with a LOD ≥ 3 or with a LOD ≥ 1.5 found at least twice are shown.

[a]This is the NPL score, not the LOD score.

[b]Lod score based on the nominal P-value reported by the authors.

[c]This is the Zlr score, not the LOD score.

short form of 5-HTTLPR is associated with less activity of the transporter and therefore with a higher serotonin concentration in the synapse. As a consequence, it would be expected that these subjects score lower on anxiety-related personality traits instead of higher. The authors could not explain the contradictory effect they found.

The numerous studies that have investigated the association since then showed conflicting results. Even meta-analyses on the association between 5-HTTLPR and personality traits (Munafo, Clark, & Flint, 2005a; Munafo et al., 2003; Schinka, Busch, & Robichaux-Keene, 2004; Sen, Burmeister, & Ghosh, 2004) or affective disorders (Lasky-Su, Faraone, Glatt, & Tsuang, 2005; Lotrich & Pollock, 2004) reached conflicting conclusions. This might be due to methodological differences between the meta-analyses (Munafo, Clark, & Flint, 2005b; Schinka, 2005; Sen, Burmeister, & Ghosh, 2005). Munafo et al. (2005b), therefore, stated that "Very large, well designed primary studies remain the most reliable way of obtaining reproducible results." (p. 896).

Two such studies have been performed since then. Willis-Owen et al. (2005) carried out an association study in three independent samples including, respectively, 564, 1,001, and 5,000 subjects. Subjects were selected from two general population samples based on their extreme high or low scores on neuroticism. The studies retained virtually 100% power to detect a genetic effect accounting for just 0.5% of phenotypic variance at an alpha level of .05. No significant association was found between 5-HTTLPR and neuroticism (measured with the Eysenck Personality Questionnaire; Eysenck & Eysenck, 1975) or major depression (as defined by the *DSM-IV*, American Psychiatric Association, 1994). Middeldorp et al. (2007) performed a family-based association study in a sample consisting of twins, their siblings, and parents from the Netherlands Twin Register (559 parents and 1,245 offspring). Subjects had participated between one and five times in survey studies measuring neuroticism, anxiety, and depression. Within-family and total association was tested for each time point and for the average scores across time points. Only 3 of the 36 tests showed a significant effect of 5-HTTLPR ($p < .05$). These effects were in opposite directions, that is, both negative and positive regression coefficients were found for the s allele. Offspring of these families were also approached to participate in a psychiatric interview diagnosing *DSM-IV* major depression. No additive effect of the s allele was found for *DSM-IV* depression. Three additional association analyses were carried out selecting (1) subjects aged over 30 years whose personality scores are considered to be most stable, (2) subjects scoring in the middle range at each occasion because it was suggested that the effect of 5-HTTLPR is the largest at that part of the distribution (Sirota, Greenberg, Murphy, & Hamer, 1999), and (3) families with sibling pairs scoring concordant high or low since it is conceivable that the genetic load is highest in these families. These analyses converged with the other analyses in not showing an association with 5-HTTLPR.

Notwithstanding the well-designed study of Lesch et al. (1996), there does not seem to be a straightforward association between 5-HTTLPR and neuroticism, anxiety, and depression. Caspi et al. (2003) suggested that 5-HTTLPR may not be directly associated with depression, but could moderate the serotonergic response to stress. They showed in a sample of 847 subjects that individuals with one or two copies of the short allele of 5-HTTLPR exhibited more depressive symptoms, diagnosable depression, and suicidality than individuals homozygous for the long allele in relation to stressful life events experienced in the 5 years before assessment. Uher and McGuffin (2008) reviewed the studies attempting to replicate the gene-environment interaction. They conclude that genetic moderation by 5-HTTLPR of vulnerability to adverse environment appears plausible. Findings are most consistent in young adult samples. Contradictory findings have been reported in adolescent boys and elderly people. This is in agreement with the results in a Dutch sample with a mean age of 39.2 years in which no interaction was found between 5-HTTLPR and the sensitivity to the exposure to life events regarding anxious depression scores measured with the Young Adult Self Report (Achenbach, 1990; Verhulst, Ende, & Koot, 1997; Table 60.3). In a regression analysis, including sex as a covariate, only the main effect of the number of life events was significant ($p = 0.001$). The main effect of 5-HTTLPR and the interaction did not reach significance with p values of 0.75 and 0.18, respectively.

On the whole, the candidate gene approach with the choice of genes based on the monoamine hypothesis for the etiology of depression has not been very successful.

TABLE 60.3 **Log transformed anxious depression scores (SD) per 5-HTTLPR genotype (ss, sl, and ll)**

	N	SS	SL	LL
0 life events	722	18.5 (11.2)	20.1 (10.6)	19.1 (10.4)
1 life event	295	21.6 (10.6)	21.4 (9.6)	20.1 (10.6)
2 or more life events	137	23.9 (9.1)	23.2 (10.7)	21.1 (10.3)

Note: Results for individuals who were (1) not exposed to a negative life event, such as death of a significant other, serious illness, or divorce in the previous year; (2) exposed to one life event; or (3) exposed to two or more life events. There is a significant main effect of the number of life events. The main effect of the 5-HTTLRP or the 5-HTTLPR life-events interaction effect did not reach significance.

Possibly, trying to find genes underlying the linkage peaks might be a more fruitful approach. Two studies successfully followed up on their linkage results and demonstrated a significant association of the apoptosis protease activating factor 1 (apaf-1) gene and the regulator of G-protein-signaling 2 (RGS-2) gene with depression and anxiety respectively (Harlan et al., 2006; Leygraf et al., 2006). These findings need replication, but suggest that the genes influencing the vulnerability for anxiety and depression are involved in other biological pathways than previously thought.

Genome-Wide Association Studies

We are awaiting the results of the first genome-wide association study on major depression. From the Netherlands Twin Register (NTR) and the Netherlands Study of Depression and Anxiety (NESDA), 1,862 participants with a diagnosis of depression and 1,857 controls at low liability for depression have been selected for genome-wide genotyping (Boomsma et al., 2008) by the U.S. Foundation for the National Institutes of Health Genetic Association Information Network (FNIH/GAIN; www.fnih.org/GAIN2/home_new.shtml).

Currently, two genome-wide association studies for bipolar disorder and one for neuroticism (Baum et al., 2007; Shifman et al., 2008; Welcome Trust Case Control Consortium, 2007) have been carried out. Two of these studies (Baum et al., 2007; Shifman et al., 2008) used DNA pooling instead of genotyping 500K SNPs in each individual. This approach is more cost effective, but reduces power. The results confirm the idea that complex diseases are influenced by multiple genes of small effect. Odds ratios for significant associations varied between 1.2 and 1.5. In the two studies on bipolar disorder there is one overlapping finding. Both studies found an association with an SNP in the DFNB31 gene on chromosome 9. The genome-wide association study for neuroticism was followed by a replication study in which the SNPs showing the most significant results were tested in independent samples. Ultimately, one SNP within the phosphodiesterase 4D, cAMP-specific (PDE4D) gene showed the most promising result (Shifman et al., 2008).

SUMMARY

There is clear familial clustering for anxiety and depression and the main, or even sole, reason is the genetic relatedness of biological family members. However, no chromosomal region or gene has been unequivocally identified as yet to be involved in anxiety and depression. In the near future, the results of the first genome-wide association study for depression will be published, no doubt to be followed by several other studies. The exploratory approach seems warranted as other biological pathways than those previously expected might be involved in the etiology of anxiety and depression. The findings from the two genome-wide association studies on bipolar disorder are encouraging, as are the results of the genome-wide association study on neuroticism. To distinguish between false- and true-positives, the chromosomal regions identified in linkage studies might be helpful.

This chapter provided the introductory information on commonly used methods in genetic epidemiology and gene hunting studies, some issues have been underexposed. One issue involves the definition of the phenotype in psychiatric genetics. One frequently mentioned hypothesis to explain the divergence in results from gene-finding studies is the definition of the phenotypes according to the *DSM* (American Psychiatric Association, 1980, 1987, 1994). It is possible that *DSM* categories cannot double as phenotypes when trying to discover robust genetic markers (Charney et al., 2002). The effect of a gene can, for instance, be missed when this gene leads to a different pattern of symptoms than the disorders as defined by the *DSM-IV* (for an illustration of this problem, see Hudziak, 2002).

A multivariate analysis of the entire range of symptoms instead of using a single end-diagnosis is a way to try to find genes related to psychiatric symptoms (Hottenga & Boomsma, 2008). As an alternative, Gottesman and Gould (2003) suggested focusing on endophenotypes defined as traits along the pathway between genotype and disease. Although this seems a useful approach, it has so far not yielded more conclusive results than the genetic research of the psychiatric disorders themselves. Another approach could be to refine the phenotypes in order to diminish heterogeneity. A family study on depression identified four factors: (1) mood symptoms and psychomotor retardation; (2) anxiety; (3) psychomotor agitation, guilt, and suicidality; and (4) appetite gain and hypersomnia (Korszun et al., 2004). The first three factors showed significant sibling correlations and might be interesting phenotypes for future gene-finding studies.

Other areas of research go beyond the investigation of genetic polymorphisms. A new development is the use of expression arrays or so called "gene chips." Thousands of individual gene sequences can be bound to tiny chips (glass plates). When a sample of RNA is applied, those genes actively express in the sample, bind to their embedded ligand, and the resulting interaction is visualized. This method has also been suggested to investigate depression from an epigenetic perspective (Mill & Petronis, 2007). Epigenetic factors are inherited and acquire modifications of DNA and histones that regulate various genomic functions occurring without a change in nuclear DNA sequence. These could provide a direct mechanistic route via which the environment can interact with the genome.

REFERENCES

Abecasis, G. R., Cardon, L. R., & Cookson, W. O. (2000). A general test of association for quantitative traits in nuclear families. *American Journal of Human Genetics, 66,* 279–292.

Abecasis, G. R., Cherny, S. S., Cookson, W. O., & Cardon, L. R. (2002). Merlin: Rapid analysis of dense genetic maps using sparse gene flow trees. *Nature Genetics, 30,* 97–101.

Abecasis, G. R., Cookson, W. O., & Cardon, L. R. (2000). Pedigree tests of transmission disequilibrium. *European Journal of Human Genetics, 8,* 545–551.

Achenbach, T. M. (1990). *The Young Adult Self Report.* Burlington: University of Vermont, Department of Psychiatry.

Almasy, L., & Blangero, J. (1998). Multipoint quantitative-trait linkage analysis in general pedigrees. *American Journal of Human Genetics, 62,* 1198–1211.

American Psychiatric Association. (1980). *Diagnostic and statistical manual of mental disorders* (3rd ed.). APA, Washington, DC.

American Psychiatric Association. (1987). *Diagnostic and statistical manual of mental disorders* (3rd ed., rev.). Washington, DC: Author.

American Psychiatric Association. (1994). *Diagnostic and statistical manual of mental disorders* (4th ed.). Washington, DC: Author.

Baum, A. E., Akula, N., Cabanero, M., Cardona, I., Corona, W., Klemens, B., et al. (2007). A genome-wide association study implicates diacylglycerol kinase eta (DGKH) and several other genes in the etiology of bipolar disorder. *Molecular Psychiatry.*

Boomsma, D., Busjahn, A., & Peltonen, L. (2002). Classical twin studies and beyond. *Nature Reviews.Genetics, 3,* 872–882.

Boomsma, D., & Dolan, C. V. (2000). Multivariate QTL analysis using structural equation modelling: A look at power under simple conditions. In H. S. T. D. Spector & A. M. MacGregor (Eds.), *Advances in twin and sib-pair analysis* (pp. 203–218). London: Greenwich Medical Media Ltd.

Boomsma, D. I., & Martin, N. G. (2002). Gene-environment interactions. In H. D'Haenen, J. A. Den Boer, & P. Willner (Eds.), *Biological Psychiatry* (pp. 181–187). New York: Wiley, Ltd.

Boomsma, D. I., & Molenaar, P. C. (1986). Using LISREL to analyze genetic and environmental covariance structure. *Behavior Genetics, 16,* 237–250.

Boomsma, D. I., Willemsen, G., Sullivan, P. F., de Geus, E. J., Heutink, P., Meijer, P., Sondervan, D., et al. (2008). Genome-wide association of major depression: Description of samples for the GAIN major depressive disorder study: NTR and NESDA Biobank Projects. *European Journal of Human Genetics, 16,* 335–342.

Boomsma, D. I., van Beijsterveldt, C. E. M., Bartels, M., & Hudziak, J. J. (2008). Genetic and environmental influence on anxious/depression: A longitudinal study in 3 to 12 year old children. In J. J. Hudziak (Ed.), *Genetic and environmental influences on developmental psychopathology and wellness* (pp. 161–189). Washington, DC: American Psychiatric Association.

Camp, N. J., Lowry, M. R., Richards, R. L., Plenk, A. M., Carter, C., Hensel, C. H., et al. (2005). Genome-wide linkage analyses of extended Utah pedigrees identifies loci that influence recurrent, early-onset major depression and anxiety disorders. *American Journal of Medical Genetics, Part B, Neuropsychiatric Genetics, 135,* 85–93.

Caspi, A., Sugden, K., Moffitt, T. E., Taylor, A., Craig, I. W., Harrington, H., et al. (2003). Influence of life stress on depression: Moderation by a polymorphism in the 5-HTT gene. *Science, 301,* 386–389.

Cederlof, R., Friberg, L., & Lundman, T. (1977). The interactions of smoking, environment and heredity and their implications for disease etiology. A report of epidemiological studies on the Swedish twin registries. *Acta Medica Scandinavica.Supplementum, 612,* 1–128.

Charney, D. S., Barlow, D. H., Botteron, K., Cohen, J. D., Goldman, D., Gur, R. E., et al. (2002). Neuroscience research agenda to guide development of a pathophysiologically based classification system. In D. J. Kupfer, M. B. First, & D. A. Regier (Eds.), *A research agenda for DSM-V* (pp. 31–83). Washington, DC: American Psychiatric Association.

Cloninger, C. R., Van Eerdewegh, P., Goate, A., Edenberg, H. J., Blangero, J., Hesselbrock, V., et al. (1998). Anxiety proneness linked to epistatic loci in genome scan of human personality traits. *American Journal of Medical Genetics, 81,* 313–317.

Crowe, R. R., Goedken, R., Samuelson, S., Wilson, R., Nelson, J., & Noyes, R., Jr. (2001). Genomewide survey of panic disorder. *American Journal of Medical Genetics, 105,* 105–109.

Derks, E. M., Dolan, C. V., & Boomsma, D. I. (2004). Effects of censoring on parameter estimates and power in genetic modeling. *Twin Research, 7,* 659–669.

Eaves, L. J. (1987). Including the environment in models for genetic segregation. *Journal of Psychiatric Research, 21,* 639–647.

Eysenck, H. J. & Eysenck, S. B. G. (1975). *Manual of the Eysenck Personality Questionnaire.* San Diego, CA: Educational and Industrial Testing Service.

Falconer, D. S., & Mackay, T. F. C. (1996). *Quantative genetics.* Essex: Longman Group Ltd.

Farmer, A., Harris, T., Redman, K., Sadler, S., Mahmood, A., & McGuffin, P. (2000). Cardiff depression study. A sib-pair study of life events and familiality in major depression. *British Journal of Psychiatry, 176,* 150–155.

Foley, D. L., Neale, M. C., & Kendler, K. S. (1998). Reliability of a lifetime history of major depression: Implications for heritability and co-morbidity. *Psychological Medicine, 28,* 857–870.

Fulker, D. W., Cherny, S. S., Sham, P. C., & Hewitt, J. K. (1999). Combined linkage and association sib-pair analysis for quantitative traits. *American Journal of Human Genetics, 64,* 259–267.

Fullerton, J., Cubin, M., Tiwari, H., Wang, C., Bomhra, A., Davidson, S., et al. (2003). Linkage analysis of extremely discordant and concordant sibling pairs identifies quantitative-trait loci that influence variation in the human personality trait neuroticism. *American Journal of Human Genetics, 72,* 879–890.

Fyer, A. J., Hamilton, S. P., Durner, M., Haghighi, F., Heiman, G. A., Costa, R., et al. (2006). A third-pass genome scan in panic disorder: Evidence for multiple susceptibility loci. *Biological Psychiatry, 60,* 388–401.

Gelernter, J., Bonvicini, K., Page, G., Woods, S. W., Goddard, A. W., Kruger, S., et al. (2001). Linkage genome scan for loci predisposing to panic disorder or agoraphobia. *American Journal of Medical Genetics, 105,* 548–557.

Gelernter, J., Page, G. P., Bonvicini, K., Woods, S. W., Pauls, D. L., & Kruger, S. (2003). A chromosome 14 risk locus for simple phobia: Results from a genomewide linkage scan. *Molecular Psychiatry, 8,* 71–82.

Gelernter, J., Page, G. P., Stein, M. B., & Woods, S. W. (2004). Genomewide linkage scan for loci predisposing to social phobia: Evidence for a chromosome 16 risk locus. *American Journal of Psychiatry, 161,* 59–66.

Gillespie, N. A., Kirk, K. M., Evans, D. M., Heath, A. C., Hickie, I. B., & Martin, N. G. (2004). Do the genetic or environmental determinants of anxiety and depression change with age? A longitudinal study of Australian twins. *Twin Research, 7,* 39–53.

Gottesman, I. I., & Gould, T. D. (2003). The endophenotype concept in psychiatry: Etymology and strategic intentions. *American Journal of Psychiatry, 160,* 636–645.

Gudbjartsson, D. F., Thorvaldsson, T., Kong, A., Gunnarsson, G., & Ingolfsdottir, A. (2005). Allegro version 2. *Nature Genetics, 37,* 1015–1016.

Hall, J. G. (2003). Twinning. *Lancet, 362,* 735–743.

Hamer, D., & Sirota, L. (2000). Beware the chopsticks gene. *Molecular Psychiatry, 5,* 11–13.

Hamilton, S. P., Fyer, A. J., Durner, M., Heiman, G. A., Baisre, L., Hodge, S. E., et al. (2003). Further genetic evidence for a panic disorder syndrome mapping to chromosome 13q. *Proceedings of the National Academy of Sciences of the United States of America, 100,* 2550–2555.

Harlan, J., Chen, Y., Gubbins, E., Mueller, R., Roch, J. M., Walter, K., et al. (2006). Variants in Apaf-1 segregating with major depression promote apoptosome function. *Molecular Psychiatry, 11,* 76–85.

Haseman, J. K., & Elston, R. C. (1972). The investigation of linkage between a quantitative trait and a marker locus. *Behavior Genetics, 2,* 3–19.

Heath, A. C., Eaves, L. J., & Martin, N. G. (1998). Interaction of marital status and genetic risk for symptoms of depression. *Twin Research, 1,* 119–122.

Heath, A. C., Jardine, R., & Martin, N. G. (1989). Interactive effects of genotype and social environment on alcohol consumption in female twins. *Journal of Studies on Alcohol, 50,* 38–48.

Heils, A., Teufel, A., Petri, S., Stober, G., Riederer, P., Bengel, D., et al. (1996). Allelic variation of human serotonin transporter gene expression. *Journal of Neurochemistry, 66,* 2621–2624.

Heston, L. L. (1966). Psychiatric disorders in foster home reared children of schizophrenic mothers. *British Journal of Psychiatry, 112,* 819–825.

Hettema, J. M., Neale, M. C., & Kendler, K. S. (2001). A review and meta-analysis of the genetic epidemiology of anxiety disorders. *American Journal of Psychiatry, 158,* 1568–1578.

Hettema, J. M., Neale, M. C., Myers, J. M., Prescott, C. A., & Kendler, K. S. (2006). A population-based twin study of the relationship between neuroticism and internalizing disorders. *American Journal of Psychiatry, 163,* 857–864.

Hettema, J. M., Prescott, C. A., & Kendler, K. S. (2001). A population-based twin study of generalized anxiety disorder in men and women. *Journal of Nervous and Mental Diseases, 189,* 413–420.

Hettema, J. M., Prescott, C. A., Myers, J. M., Neale, M. C., & Kendler, K. S. (2005). The structure of genetic and environmental risk factors for anxiety disorders in men and women. *Archives of General Psychiatry, 62,* 182–189.

Hewitt, J. K., Silberg, J. L., Neale, M. C., Eaves, L. J., & Erickson, M. (1992). The analysis of parental ratings of children's behavior using LISREL. *Behavior Genetics, 22,* 293–317.

Holmans, P., Weissman, M. M., Zubenko, G. S., Scheftner, W. A., Crowe, R. R., DePaulo, J. R., Jr., et al. (2007). Genetics of recurrent early-onset major depression (GenRED): final genome scan report. *American Journal of Psychiatry, 164,* 248–258.

Holmans, P., Zubenko, G. S., Crowe, R. R., DePaulo, J. R., Jr., Scheftner, W. A., Weissman, M. M., et al. (2004). Genomewide significant linkage to recurrent, early-onset major depressive disorder on chromosome 15q. *American Journal of Human Genetics, 74,* 1154–1167.

Hottenga, J. J., & Boomsma, D. I. (2008). QTL detection in multivariate data from sibling pairs. In B. M. Neale, M. A. Ferreira, S. E. Medland, & D. Posthuma (Eds.), *Statistical genetics: gene mapping through linkage and association* (pp. 239–264). Oxford: Taylor & Francis.

Hudziak, J. J. (2002). Importance of phenotype definition in genetic studies of child psychopathology. In J. E. Helzer & J. J. Hudziak (Eds.), *Defining psychopathology in the 21st century: DSM-V and beyond* (pp. 211–230). Washington, DC: American Psychiatric Publishing, Inc.

Johnson, W., McGue, M., Krueger, R. F., & Bouchard, T. J., Jr. (2004). Marriage and personality: A genetic analysis. *Journal of Personality and Social Psychology, 86,* 285–294.

Jöreskog, K. G., & Sörbom, D. (1989). *Lisrel 7: A guide to the program and applications (2nd).* Chicago: Scientific Software International.

Kaabi, B., Gelernter, J., Woods, S. W., Goddard, A., Page, G. P., & Elston, R. C. (2006). Genome scan for loci predisposing to anxiety disorders using a novel multivariate approach: Strong evidence for a chromosome 4 risk locus. *American Journal of Human Genetics, 78,* 543–553.

Kendler, K. S., & Baker, J. H. (2006). Genetic influences on measures of the environment: A systematic review. *Psychological Medicine,* 1–12.

Kendler, K. S., & Eaves, L. (2005). *Psychiatric genetics.* Arlington, VA: American Psychiatric Publishing.

Kendler, K. S., & Eaves, L. J. (1986). Models for the joint effect of genotype and environment on liability to psychiatric illness. *American Journal of Psychiatry, 143,* 279–289.

Kendler, K. S., Gardner, C. O., & Prescott, C. A. (2001). Panic syndromes in a population-based sample of male and female twins. *Psychological Medicine, 31,* 989–1000.

Kendler, K. S., Gardner, C. O., & Prescott, C. A. (2003). Personality and the experience of environmental adversity. *Psychological Medicine, 33,* 1193–1202.

Kendler, K. S., Gatz, M., Gardner, C. O., & Pedersen, N. L. (2006). A Swedish national twin study of lifetime major depression. *American Journal of Psychiatry, 163,* 109–114.

Kendler, K. S., Jacobson, K. C., Myers, J., & Prescott, C. A. (2002). Sex differences in genetic and environmental risk factors for irrational fears and phobias. *Psychological Medicine, 32,* 209–217.

Kendler, K. S., Karkowski, L. M., & Prescott, C. A. (1999a). Causal relationship between stressful life events and the onset of major depression. *American Journal of Psychiatry, 156,* 837–841.

Kendler, K. S., Karkowski, L. M., & Prescott, C. A. (1999b). Fears and phobias: reliability and heritability. *Psychological Medicine, 29,* 539–553.

Kendler, K. S., & Karkowski-Shuman, L. (1997). Stressful life events and genetic liability to major depression: Genetic control of exposure to the environment? *Psychological Medicine, 27,* 539–547.

Kendler, K. S., Kessler, R. C., Walters, E. E., MacLean, C., Neale, M. C., Heath, A. C., et al. (1995). Stressful life events, genetic liability, and onset of an episode of major depression in women. *American Journal of Psychiatry, 152,* 833–842.

Kendler, K. S., Neale, M. C., Kessler, R. C., Heath, A. C., & Eaves, L. J. (1992). Generalized anxiety disorder in women. A population-based twin study. *Archives of General Psychiatry, 49,* 267–272.

Kendler, K. S., Neale, M. C., MacLean, C. J., Heath, A. C., Eaves, L. J., & Kessler, R. C. (1993). Smoking and major depression. A causal analysis. *Archives of General Psychiatry, 50,* 36–43.

Kendler, K. S., Prescott, C. A., Myers, J., & Neale, M. C. (2003). The structure of genetic and environmental risk factors for common psychiatric and substance use disorders in men and women. *Archives of General Psychiatry, 60,* 929–937.

Kessler, R. C. (1995). Epidemiology of psychiatric comorbidity. In M. T. Tsuang, M. Tohen, & G. E. Zahner (Eds.), *Textbook in psychiatric epidemiology* (pp. 179–198). New York: John Wiley & Sons, Inc.

Kessler, R. C., Chiu, W. T., Demler, O., Merikangas, K. R., & Walters, E. E. (2005). Prevalence, severity, and comorbidity of 12-month DSM-IV disorders in the National Comorbidity Survey Replication. *Archives of General Psychiatry, 62,* 617–627.

Knowles, J. A., Fyer, A. J., Vieland, V. J., Weissman, M. M., Hodge, S. E., Heiman, G. A., et al. (1998). Results of a genome-wide genetic screen for panic disorder. *American Journal of Medical Genetics, 81,* 139–147.

Korszun, A., Moskvina, V., Brewster, S., Craddock, N., Ferrero, F., Gill, M., et al. (2004). Familiality of symptom dimensions in depression. *Archives of General Psychiatry, 61,* 468–474.

Krueger, R. F. (1999). The structure of common mental disorders. *Archives of General Psychiatry, 56,* 921–926.

Kruglyak, L., Daly, M. J., Reeve-Daly, M. P., & Lander, E. S. (1996). Parametric and nonparametric linkage analysis: A unified multipoint approach. *American Journal of Human Genetics, 58,* 1347–1363.

Kruglyak, L., & Lander, E. S. (1995). Complete multipoint sib-pair analysis of qualitative and quantitative traits. *American Journal of Human Genetics, 57,* 439–454.

Kuo, P. H., Neale, M. C., Riley, B. P., Patterson, D. G., Walsh, D., Prescott, C. A., et al. (2007). A genome-wide linkage analysis for the personality trait neuroticism in the Irish affected sib-pair study of alcohol dependence. *American Journal of Medical Genetics, Part B, Neuropsychiatric Genetics, 144,* 463–468.

Lander, E., & Kruglyak, L. (1995). Genetic dissection of complex traits: Guidelines for interpreting and reporting linkage results. *Nature Genetics, 11,* 241–247.

Lasky-Su, J. A., Faraone, S. V., Glatt, S. J., & Tsuang, M. T. (2005). Meta-analysis of the association between two polymorphisms in the serotonin transporter gene and affective disorders. *American Journal of Medical Genetics, Part B, Neuropsychiatric Genetics, 133,* 110–115.

Lesch, K. P., Bengel, D., Heils, A., Sabol, S. Z., Greenberg, B. D., Petri, S., et al. (1996). Association of anxiety-related traits with a polymorphism in the serotonin transporter gene regulatory region. *Science, 274,* 1527–1531.

Levinson, D. F. (2006). The genetics of depression: A review. *Biological Psychiatry, 60,* 84–92.

Leygraf, A., Hohoff, C., Freitag, C., Willis-Owen, S. A., Krakowitzky, P., Fritze, J., et al. (2006). Rgs 2 gene polymorphisms as modulators of anxiety in humans? *Journal of Neural Transmission, 113,* 1921–1925.

Lotrich, F. E., & Pollock, B. G. (2004). Meta-analysis of serotonin transporter polymorphisms and affective disorders. *Psychiatric Genetics, 14,* 121–129.

Lynch, M., & Walsh, B. (1998). *Genetics and analysis of quantitative traits.* Sunderland, MA: Sinauer Associates.

Martin, N., Boomsma, D., & Machin, G. (1997). A twin-pronged attack on complex traits. *Nature Genetics, 17,* 387–392.

Martin, N. G., & Eaves, L. J. (1977). The genetical analysis of covariance structure. *Heredity, 38,* 79–95.

McGue, M., & Lykken, D. T. (1992). Genetic influence on risk of divorce. *Psychological Science, 3,* 368–373.

McGuffin, P., Katz, R., & Bebbington, P. (1988). The Camberwell Collaborative Depression Study. III. Depression and adversity in the relatives of depressed probands. *British Journal of Psychiatry, 152,* 775–782.

McGuffin, P., Knight, J., Breen, G., Brewster, S., Boyd, P. R., Craddock, N., et al. (2005). Whole genome linkage scan of recurrent depressive disorder from the depression network study. *Human Molecular Genetics, 14,* 3337–3345.

Middeldorp, C. M., Birley, A. J., Cath, D. C., Gillespie, N. A., Willemsen, G., Statham, D. J., et al. (2005). Familial clustering of major depression and anxiety disorders in Australian and Dutch twins and siblings. *Twin Research and Human Genetics, 8,* 609–615.

Middeldorp, C. M., Cath, D. C., Beem, A. L., Willemsen, G., & Boomsma, D. I. (2008). The association of life events with anxious depression, neuroticism and extraversion. *Psychological Medicine, 38,* 1557–1565.

Middeldorp, C. M., Cath, D. C., van Dyck, R., & Boomsma, D. I. (2005). The co-morbidity of anxiety and depression in the perspective of genetic epidemiology. A review of twin and family studies. *Psychological Medicine, 35,* 611–624.

Middeldorp, C. M., Cath, D. C., Vink, J. M., & Boomsma, D. I. (2005). Twin and genetic effects on life events. *Twin Research and Human Genetics, 8,* 224–231.

Middeldorp, C. M., de Geus, E. J., Beem, A. L., Lakenberg, N., Hottenga, J. J., Slagboom, P. E., et al. (2007). Family based association analyses between the serotonin transporter gene polymorphism (5-HTTLPR) and neuroticism, anxiety and depression. *Behavior Genetics, 37,* 294–301.

Middeldorp, C. M., Hottenga, J. J., Slagboom, P. E., Sullivan, P. F., de Geus, E. J., Posthuma, D., et al. (2008). Linkage on chromosome 14 in a genomewide linkage study of a broad anxiety phenotype. *Molecular Psychiatry, 13,* 84–89.

Mill, J., & Petronis, A. (2007). Molecular studies of major depressive disorder: The epigenetic perspective. *Molecular Psychiatry, 12,* 799–814.

Moffitt, T. E., Caspi, A., & Rutter, M. (2005). Strategy for investigating interactions between measured genes and measured environments. *Archives of General Psychiatry, 62,* 473–481.

Morton, N. E. (1955). Sequential tests for the detection of linkage. *American Journal of Human Genetics, 7,* 277–318.

Munafo, M. R., Clark, T., & Flint, J. (2005a). Does measurement instrument moderate the association between the serotonin transporter gene and anxiety-related personality traits? A meta-analysis. *Molecular Psychiatry, 10,* 415–419.

Munafo, M. R., Clark, T., & Flint, J. (2005b). Promise and pitfalls in the meta-analysis of genetic association studies: A response to Sen and Schinka. *Molecular Psychiatry, 10,* 895–897.

Munafo, M. R., Clark, T. G., Moore, L. R., Payne, E., Walton, R., & Flint, J. (2003). Genetic polymorphisms and personality in healthy adults: A systematic review and meta-analysis. *Molecular Psychiatry, 8,* 471–484.

Nash, M. W., Huezo-Diaz, P., Williamson, R. J., Sterne, A., Purcell, S., Hoda, F., et al. (2004). Genome-wide linkage analysis of a composite index of neuroticism and mood-related scales in extreme selected sibships. *Human Molecular Genetics, 13,* 2173–2182.

Neale, B. M., Sullivan, P. F., & Kendler, K. S. (2005). A genome scan of neuroticism in nicotine dependent smokers. *American Journal of Medical Genetics, Part B, Neuropsychiatric Genetics, 132,* 65–69.

Neale, M. C. (2000). *QTL mapping with sib-pairs: The flexibility of Mx.* In H. S. T. D. Spector & A. M. MacGregor (Eds.), *Advances in twin and sib-pair analysis* (pp. 203–218). London: Greenwich Medical Media Ltd.

Neale, M. C., Boker, S. M., Xie, G., & Maes, H. H. (2006). *Mx: Statistical modeling.* Richmond (VA): Department of Psychiatry, Medical College of Virginia.

Neale, M. C., & Cardon, L. R. (1992). *Methodology for genetic studies of twins and families.* Boston: Kluwer Academic.

Neale, M. C., & Kendler, K. S. (1995). Models of comorbidity for multifactorial disorders. *American Journal of Human Genetics, 57,* 935–953.

Nurnberger, J. I., Jr., Foroud, T., Flury, L., Su, J., Meyer, E. T., Hu, K., et al. (2001). Evidence for a locus on chromosome 1 that influences vulnerability to alcoholism and affective disorder. *American Journal of Psychiatry, 158,* 718–724.

Plomin, R., DeFries, J. C., McClearn, G. E., & McGuffin, P. (2008). *Behavioral Genetics,* 5th ed. New York: Worth Publishers and Freeman and Company.

Posthuma, D., Beem, A. L., de Geus, E. J., van Baal, G. C., von Hjelmborg, J. B., Iachine, I., et al. (2003). Theory and practice in quantitative genetics. *Twin Research, 6,* 361–376.

Posthuma, D., de Geus, E. J., Boomsma, D. I., & Neale, M. C. (2004). Combined linkage and association tests in mx. *Behavior Genetics, 34,* 179–196.

Purcell, S. (2002). Variance components models for gene-environment interaction in twin analysis. *Twin Research, 5,* 554–571.

Purcell, S., Neale, B., Todd-Brown, K., Thomas, L., Ferreira, M. A., Bender, D., et al. (2007). PLINK: A Tool Set for Whole-Genome Association and Population-Based Linkage Analyses. *American Journal of Human Genetics, 81,* 559–575.

Risch, N., & Merikangas, K. (1996). The future of genetic studies of complex human diseases. *Science, 273,* 1516–1517.

Romanov, K., Varjonen, J., Kaprio, J., & Koskenvuo, M. (2003). Life events and depressiveness: The effect of adjustment for psychosocial factors, somatic health and genetic liability. *Acta Psychiatrica Scandinavica, 107,* 25–33.

Rutter, M., & Plomin, R. (1997). Opportunities for psychiatry from genetic findings. *British Journal of Psychiatry, 171,* 209–219.

Saudino, K. J., Pedersen, N. L., Lichtenstein, P., McClearn, G. E., & Plomin, R. (1997). Can personality explain genetic influences on life events? *Journal of Personality and Social Psychology, 72,* 196–206.

Schinka, J. A. (2005). Measurement scale does moderate the association between the serotonin transporter gene and trait anxiety: Comments on Munafo and colleagues. *Molecular Psychiatry, 10,* 892–893.

Schinka, J. A., Busch, R. M., & Robichaux-Keene, N. (2004). A meta-analysis of the association between the serotonin transporter gene polymorphism (5-HTTLPR) and trait anxiety. *Molecular Psychiatry, 9,* 197–202.

Sen, S., Burmeister, M., & Ghosh, D. (2004). Meta-analysis of the association between a serotonin transporter promoter polymorphism (5-HTTLPR) and anxiety-related personality traits. *American Journal of Medical Genetics, Part B, Neuropsychiatric Genetics, 127,* 85–89.

Sen, S., Burmeister, M., & Ghosh, D. (2005). 5-HTTLPR and anxiety-related personality traits meta-analysis revisited: Response to Munafo and colleagues. *Molecular Psychiatry, 10,* 893–895.

Sham, P. C. (1997). *Statistics in human genetics.* London: Arnold.

Shifman, S., Bhomra, A., Smiley, S., Wray, N. R., James, M. R., Martin, N. G., et al. (2008). A whole genome association study of neuroticism using DNA pooling. *Molecular Psychiatry, 13,* 302–312.

Silberg, J., Rutter, M., Neale, M., & Eaves, L. (2001). Genetic moderation of environmental risk for depression and anxiety in adolescent girls. *British Journal of Psychiatry, 179,* 116–121.

Sirota, L. A., Greenberg, B. D., Murphy, D. L., & Hamer, D. H. (1999). Non-linear association between the serotonin transporter promoter polymorphism and neuroticism: A caution against using extreme samples to identify quantitative trait loci. *Psychiatric Genetics, 9,* 35–38.

Smoller, J. W., Acierno, J. S., Jr., Rosenbaum, J. F., Biederman, J., Pollack, M. H., Meminger, S., et al. (2001). Targeted genome screen of panic disorder and anxiety disorder proneness using homology to murine QTL regions. *American Journal of Medical Genetics, 105,* 195–206.

Spielman, R. S., McGinnis, R. E., & Ewens, W. J. (1993). Transmission test for linkage disequilibrium: The insulin gene region and insulin-dependent diabetes mellitus (IDDM). *American Journal of Human Genetics, 52,* 506–516.

Stoppel, C., Albrecht, A., Pape, H. C., & Stork, O. (2006). Genes and neurons: Molecular insights to fear and anxiety. *Genes Brain Behavior, 5* (Suppl. 2), 34–47.

Sullivan, P. F., Neale, M. C., & Kendler, K. S. (2000). Genetic epidemiology of major depression: Review and meta-analysis. *American Journal of Psychiatry, 157,* 1552–1562.

Thorgeirsson, T. E., Oskarsson, H., Desnica, N., Kostic, J. P., Stefansson, J. G., Kolbeinsson, H., et al. (2003). Anxiety with panic disorder linked to chromosome 9q in Iceland. *American Journal of Human Genetics, 72,* 1221–1230.

Uher, R., & McGuffin, P. (2008). The moderation by the serotonin transporter gene of environmental adversity in the aetiology of mental illness: Review and methodological analysis. *Molecular Psychiatry, 13,* 131–146.

Verhulst, F. C., Ende, J. v., & Koot, H. M. (1997). *Handleiding voor de Youth Self Report.* Rotterdam: Afdeling Kinder- en Jeugdpsychiatrie,

Sophia Kinderziekenhuis/Academisch Ziekenhuis Rotterdam/Erasmus Universiteit Rotterdam.

Vink, J. M., & Boomsma, D. I. (2002). Gene finding strategies. *Biological Psychology, 61,* 53–71.

Vollebergh, W. A., Iedema, J., Bijl, R. V., De Graaf, R., Smit, F., & Ormel, J. (2001). The structure and stability of common mental disorders: The NEMESIS study. *Archives of General Psychiatry, 58,* 597–603.

Weissman, M. M., Fyer, A. J., Haghighi, F., Heiman, G., Deng, Z., Hen, R., et al. (2000). Potential panic disorder syndrome: Clinical and genetic linkage evidence. *American Journal of Medical Genetics, 96,* 24–35.

Welcome Trust Case Control Consortium. (2007). Genome-wide association study of 14, 000 cases of seven common diseases and 3,000 shared controls. *Nature, 447,* 661–678.

Willis-Owen, S. A., Turri, M. G., Munafo, M. R., Surtees, P. G., Wainwright, N. W., Brixey, R. D., et al. (2005). The serotonin transporter length polymorphism, neuroticism, and depression: A comprehensive assessment of association. *Biological Psychiatry, 58,* 451–456.

Witte, J. S., Gauderman, W. J., & Thomas, D. C. (1999). Asymptotic bias and efficiency in case-control studies of candidate genes and gene-environment interactions: Basic family designs. *American Journal of Epidemiology, 149,* 693–705.

Wray, N. R., Middeldorp, C. M., Birley, A. J., Gordon, S. D., Sullivan, P. F., Visscher, P. M., et al. (2008). Genome wide linkage analysis of multiple measures of neuroticism of two large cohorts form Australia and the Netherlands. *Archives of General Psychiatry, 65,* 649–658.

Zubenko, G. S., Maher, B., Hughes, H. B., III, Zubenko, W. N., Stiffler, J. S., Kaplan, B. B., et al. (2003). Genome-wide linkage survey for genetic loci that influence the development of depressive disorders in families with recurrent, early-onset, major depression. *American Journal of Medical Genetics, Part B, Neuropsychiatric Genetics, 123,* 1–18.

PART VIII

Health and Aging

Chapter 61

Successful Aging

DENISE C. PARK AND JOSHUA GOH

Until the advent of neuroimaging techniques, studies of cognitive aging generally showed a gradual but progressive decline across the life span, with a few areas of protected cognition. The behavioral literature demonstrated that older adults have more trouble learning new information, exhibit less efficient reasoning skills, are slower to respond on all types of cognitive tasks, and are more susceptible to disruption from interfering information than younger adults. In addition to decreased efficiency of these processes, which is characteristic of normal aging, the risk of pathological cognitive aging increases with each year of life past middle age. Of individuals aged 85 and older, an important study conducted by Unverzagt et al. (2001) indicated that only 45% of these adults were cognitively normal. A study reported by the Alzheimer's Association (2007) indicated that 42% of adults 85 and older had Alzheimer's Disease (and this statistic excludes other neurological disorders and sources of dementia).

Neuroimaging techniques have breathed new life into the study of cognitive aging, providing us with clear and optimistic evidence that demonstrates that the brain ages in a dynamic manner, with reorganization and remodeling of neural circuitry occurring in response to some of the challenges and atrophy faced by the aging brain. In this chapter, we review basic behavioral mechanisms believed to account for cognitive aging as well as basic changes that occur in brain structure with age. Then we consider theories of neural aging, resulting from behavioral, functional, and structural research, paying particular attention to the notion of the brain as a dynamic, reorganizing structure. We consider, as well, evidence suggesting that there is plasticity in the aging brain which can be exploited by a range of interventions, addressing evidence for the "use it or lose it" hypothesis, that is, the common belief that the maintenance of cognitive vitality in late adulthood can be sustained if individuals remain physically and intellectually active.

In the face of the rapidly aging population that is occurring globally, combined with the high incidence of Alzheimer's

disease and other dementing illnesses, the study of normal, healthy cognitive aging has become of increasing importance. To evaluate how neurocognitive pathology occurs, it is critically important to understand what constitutes normal, healthy cognitive function at every stage of life. Moreover, there is increasing evidence that the trajectory of cognitive aging can be delayed, and that interventions can sustain neurocognitive health. The present chapter will focus on neurocognitive theories of normal aging that are rapidly changing as a result of the truly stunning findings that have been revealed by neuroimaging technologies.

BEHAVIORAL THEORIES OF COGNITIVE AGING

Before discussing causes of cognitive aging, it is worthwhile to review findings. Figure 61.1 summarizes findings typical of the cognitive aging literature, presenting data collected by Park et al. (2002) from a large sample of older adults (350 subjects) and includes three measures of speed of processing (measured by the speed at which subjects could make simple perceptual comparisons between two items), multiple measures of visuo-spatial and verbal working memory (measured by traditional computational and visuo-spatial span measures) and long-term memory (measured by free and cued recall of both visuo-spatial and verbal stimuli), as well as measures of world knowledge (measured by different tests of vocabulary knowledge). All the measures except world knowledge show reliable differences across the life span, beginning in the twenties, and that decline does not differ as a function of process (e.g., speed, working memory, long-term memory) or format (visuospatial or verbal). Although the Park et al. data are cross-sectional, Figure 61.2 represents a blend of cross-sectional and longitudinal data from cohorts of older adults tested in the Victoria Longitudinal Study (Hultsch, Hertzog, Dixon, & Small, 1998). The findings from this study largely replicate those from the cross-sectional data depicted in

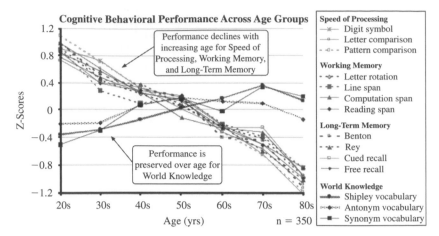

Figure 61.1   Cross-sectional aging data showing behavioral performance on measures of speed of processing, working memory, long-term memory, and world knowledge.

Note: Almost all measures of cognitive function show decline with age, except world knowledge, which may even show some improvement. From "Models of Visuo-Spatial and Verbal Memory across the Adults Life Span," by Park et al., 2002, *Psychology and Aging, 17,* pp. 299–320. Copyright 2002 by the American Psychological Association. Adapted with permission. The use of APA information does not imply endorsement by APA.

Figure 61.1, and extend the findings to other domains as well. Figure 61.2A depicts reliable increases in speed of processing (the increases represent slowing) from age 60 to 84 whereas Figure 61.2B demonstrates reliable decreases in working memory in this sample. Figure 61.2C demonstrates age invariance for measures of vocabulary, but age-related decreases when tasks that required working memory (reading comprehension) or speeded processing (verbal fluency) are used. Finally, Figure 61.2D demonstrates age-related decreases in fact and word recall, but shows age invariance when subjects recall information from a coherent story or when measures of implicit memory are used. Overall, the findings represented in Figures 61.1 and 61.2 are broadly typical of hundreds of studies that exist on cognitive aging—with age, people become slower and show decreases in working memory capacity, but generally do well on tests that measure world knowledge or implicit memory.

THEORIES OF COGNITIVE AGING

There are a range of theories that postulate the cause of age-related declines in cognitive function. Salthouse (1991, 1996) has presented the influential speed of processing theory and argued that age-related declines in the speed at which information is processed account for age differences on essentially all cognitive tasks. Baltes and Lindenberger (1997) have suggested that crude measures of sensory function (visual and auditory acuity) are even more fundamental than speed of processing in explaining age differences and provide a simple overall measure of declining neuronal

integrity, or "dedifferentiation" of function in the older adult. The view that all types of cognitive decline with age are caused by a single mechanism has been labeled the "common cause" hypothesis (Lindenberger & Baltes, 1994). Structural equation models of the data depicted in Figure 61.1 did implicate speed of processing as the most fundamental measure mediating age-related variance in the long-term memory measures (Park et al., 2002), but working memory also played a significant and intermediate role in explaining age-related variance in long-term memory. Park et al. (1996) demonstrated that age-related declines in speed of processing was the cause of declines in relatively low-effort, easy memory tasks, such as memory for spatial location of words. However, when the memory task became more demanding, as in a free or cued recall task, then speed and working memory jointly explained the age-related variance in recall that could not be explained by speed of processing declines alone.

In addition to speed and working memory as important mechanisms whose deterioration may account for cognitive aging, there is also evidence that with age there are declines in inhibitory processes (the ability to ignore irrelevant information or delete irrelevant information from working memory) and the ability to switch among tasks (see Zacks, Hasher, & Li, 2000, for reviews). It is important to recognize that speed, working memory, inhibition, and task-switching are executive functions that are used in service of many cognitive tasks including reasoning, strategic encoding, and retrieval of information in long-term memory, and many everyday or work-related tasks that require learning or responding to novel information. Our own view is that decline in all of these mechanisms are

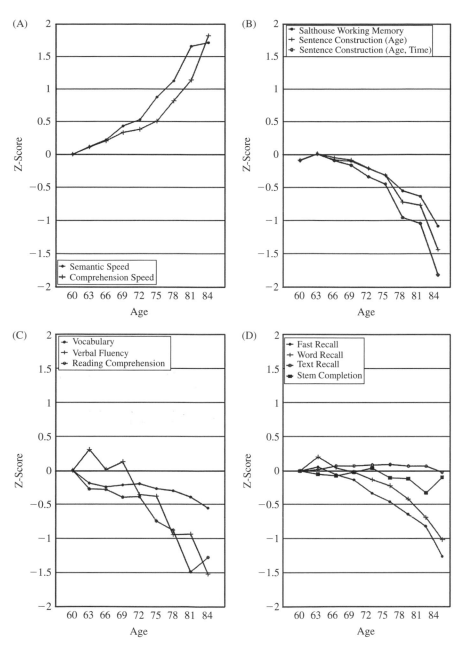

Figure 61.2 Longitudinal data from the Victoria Longitudinal Study showing cognitive performance declines with aging.

Note: Semantic and comprehension speed slows down with increasing age in **A:** (higher Z-score indicates longer response time), working memory tests also show decline with age in **B:**. In **C:** vocabulary performance is relatively preserved, however, verbal fluency (a speeded-test) and reading comprehension (involving working memory) declines. In **D:** text recall (involving retrieval from coherent context) and stem completion (involving priming) are preserved, whereas fact and word recall decline. From *Memory Change in the Aged,* by D. F. Hultsch, C. Hertzog, R. A. Dixon, and B. J. Small, 1998, New York: Cambridge University Press. Copyright 1998 by the Cambridge University Press. Reprinted with permission.

fundamental to cognitive aging, and that different individuals may decline at different rates on these mechanisms. Indeed, models of cognitive aging (Park et al., 1996, 2002) suggest a clear separation between speed and working memory, and also demonstrate that different tasks require different contributions from these mechanisms for successful performance. As we shall see, the complexity of the brain and neuroimaging findings have further constrained these theories, suggesting that it is unlikely that any single mechanism is responsible for declines in cognition associated with aging.

Both Figure 61.1 and Figure 61.2C also demonstrate that knowledge remains relatively intact and may even show growth with age, suggesting that the robust representation of knowledge in the aging cognitive system may be an important mechanism for off-setting deficits on tasks in the real world. As evidence for this, Hedden, Lautenschlager, and Park (2005) have demonstrated that a high level of verbal fluency in older people can play a compensatory role for decreased speed of processing in the free recall of words. Overall, the picture presented in Figures 61.1 and 61.2 (mirrored by many other large studies of cognitive aging across the world) is one of declines in basic mechanisms, the "hardware of the mind," but with knowledge, the "software," remaining intact with age.

Figure 61.1 also illustrates one poorly understood and little-recognized phenomenon of some importance: Both cross-sectional and longitudinal data averaged across groups suggest that decline (or at least measurement of it) results in relatively continuous decreases across the life span, beginning in young adulthood, although it is well recognized that within these groups, individuals may vary considerably in the trajectory of decline (Hultsch et al., 1998; MacDonald Hultsch, Strauss, & Dixon, 2003; Wilson et al., 2002). Because age-related decline has generally been viewed as continuous across the life span in behavioral measures, relatively little attention has been paid to the study of middle age, particularly in cross-sectional studies, because the data points associated with middle age could generally be interpolated without actual data collection. As a rule, including middle-aged adults in the behavioral study of cognitive aging provided few new insights into the process of aging, although inclusion of middle-aged adults allowed age to be treated as a continuous variable in modeling the impact of aging on cognitive function. As we shall see, neuroimaging data does not always show a continuous and gradual decline in activation with age, but rather, functional measures show dramatic changes in patterns of neural tissue engaged to performance a task as a function of age. Such findings suggest that inclusion of middle-aged adults may provide important insights to understanding neurocognitive aging, and more information about middle-aged adults is important to develop a clear understanding of the aging mind.

AGING AND BRAIN STRUCTURE

Before turning our attention to functional imaging data, which allows us to see the neural circuitry engaged to perform specific cognitive tasks, we examine what happens to neural structures with age. Structural imaging of the brain in life-span samples indicates that the brain shows volumetric changes with age, but that these changes are not equivalent across brain structures. Figure 61.3 shows both cross-sectional and longitudinal change over 5 years in brain volume (Raz et al., 2005). As shown in Figure 61.3, the greatest shrinkage across the life span occurs in the caudate, cerebellum, hippocampus, and prefrontal areas. There is minimal shrinkage in the entorhinal cortex and the visual cortex volume remains stable across the life span (Raz, 2000; Raz, Rodrigue, Head, Kennedy, & Acker, 2004). Resnick, Pham, Kraut, Zonderman, and Davatzikos (2003) reported evidence for decline in gray and white matter over a period as short as 2 years in very healthy older adults over age 59, with the frontal and parietal cortex showing greater decreases than temporal and occipital.

Other studies have focused on the characteristics of white matter—the bundles of neuronal axons underlying cortical structures. Davatzikos and Resnick (2002) reported age-related signal changes in white matter and suggested

that this reflected white matter degeneration. White matter in the corpus callosum was also studied (Head et al., 2004) using diffusion tensor imaging, which measures anisotropy and mean diffusivity of water molecules to infer white matter integrity. Results indicated greater deterioration in healthy older adults relative to young adults in anterior callosum, while individuals with mild dementia also showed greater deterioration in the posterior callosum (see Figure 61.4). The authors suggest that normal aging is characterized by decline in anterior structures and pathological aging by declines in posterior lobar regions. Reviews of the research on white matter deterioration suggest that the decline in white matter, much like cognitive behavioral declines, is generally linear from age 20, occurs at the same rate in men and women, and occurs disproportionately in frontal areas (Moseley, 2002; Sullivan & Pfefferbaum, 2006). Moreover, white matter deterioration is related to cognitive performance (Sullivan & Pfefferbaum, 2006).

Another important structural measure that appears particularly promising for the study of cognitive function is measurement of thinning in the cerebral cortex (Salat et al., 2004). Salat et al. reported that thinning of the cerebral cortex becomes apparent by middle age, with atrophy most pronounced in the frontal cortex near the primary motor area and in the calcarine cortex near the primary visual area. The measurements were highly reliable and showed sufficient variability to be useful in individual differences analyses. Moreover, this is the first technique that we are aware of that reports structural differences in the occipital cortex. This is important because functional studies (as discussed in the later sections) frequently report a shift from high levels of activation in sensory regions in young adults to high levels of activation in frontal regions in older adults on many cognitive tasks (Cabeza et al., 2004; Park et al., 2004), and it has always been somewhat surprising, given this change, that volumetric measures show invariant volume in the occipital cortex as a function of age.

NEURALLY-BASED THEORIES OF COGNITIVE AGING

Neuroimaging data have delineated the complexity and multifactorial nature of cognitive aging. At the same time, neuroimaging data have also constrained behavioral theories of cognitive aging. As our knowledge rapidly increases about the aging brain, it is now required that any behavioral theory of cognitive aging be neurally plausible. Up to this point in this discussion, the behavioral and neural data have generally been congruent with one another. As behavioral measures of cognitive aging declined (e.g., speed,

Structural Brain Changes with Age

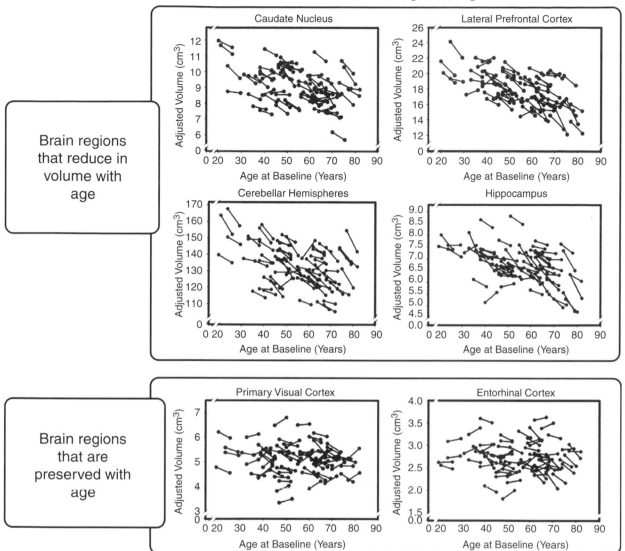

Figure 61.3 Cross-sectional age differences and longitudinal change in brain volumes across various brain regions.

Note: Each pair of connected dots represents an individual subject's first and second measurement. The caudate, hippocampal, cerebellar, and frontal regions all show both cross-sectional age differences and longitudinal shrinkage. Volume reduction in the hippocampus has a nonlinear trend; the decline accelerates with age. Entorhinal volume reduction is minimal and occipital regions are relatively preserved with age. From "Regional Brain Changes in Aging Healthy Adults: General Trends, Individual Differences, and Modifiers," by N. Raz et al., 2005, *Cerebral Cortex, 15*, pp. 1676–1689. Copyright 2005 by the Oxford University Press. Adapted with permission.

working memory, long-term memory), so did measures of neural structure (e.g., volumetric, white matter, cortical thickness measures). The picture becomes considerably more complex, however, when functional imaging data are integrated into an overall view of mechanisms of cognitive aging. Functional data provide evidence for age-related shifts in the neural structures engaged during cognitive task performance, and provide evidence for a dynamic brain that remodels in the face of the neural insults associated with aging. In this next section, we discuss theoretical views of cognitive aging that have developed primarily

from neural data, and relate the theories, as well, to behavioral theories of cognitive aging.

Dopamine Receptor Depletion Hypothesis

One emerging theory of cognitive aging that is receiving increasing support is the view that much of the behavioral change evident in cognitive aging is due to depletion of dopamine receptors. There is evidence that dopamine D_2 receptors decline at the rate of about 10% per decade (Wong, Young, Wilson, Meltzer, & Gjedde, 1997), beginning in the

White Matter Changes with Age and Alzheimer's
YNG   OLD   DAT

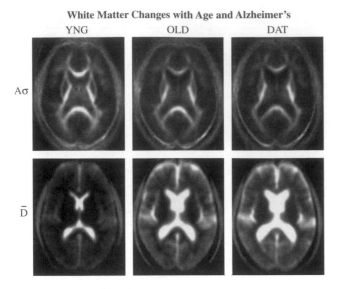

Figure 61.4   Diffusion tensor imaging data.

Note: The top row shows decrease in anisotropy (AΣ), which is a measure of white matter connectivity, from young adults (left) to older adults (middle) and Alzheimer's patients (right). The bottom row shows increase in diffusivity from young adults to older adults and Alzheimer's patients, indicating reduction in white matter fiber density. From "Differential Vulnerability of Anterior White Matter in Nondemented Aging with Minimal Acceleration in Dementia of the Alzheimer Type: Evidence from Diffusion Tensor Imaging," by D. Head et al., 2004, *Cerebral Cortex, 14,* pp. 410–423. Copyright 2004 by the Oxford University Press. Adapted with permission.

20s in both striate and extrastriatal areas. The extrastriatal declines are in areas particularly susceptible to age-related atrophy, such as the frontal cortex and hippocampus (Kaasinen et al., 2000; Li, Lindenberger, & Sikström, 2001). Dopamine receptors play a critical role in activation of cortical representations, utilization of environmental cues, and in regulation of attention—all domains that are susceptible to age-related decline. Li et al. (2001) argue that it is the loss of dopamine receptors that is responsible for many aspects of cognitive aging and the authors present striking similarities between declines in speed, working memory, and dopamine receptors (see Figure 61.5). They suggest that additional activation that occurs in functional imaging studies during cognitive tasks in older adults, primarily in the frontal cortex, is a compensatory response to less distinctive cortical representations resulting from deficient neuromodulation due to the decreased numbers of dopamine receptors. In agreement with Li et al. (2001), Wang et al. (1998) and Yang et al. (2003) used radioligands to measure dopaminergic receptors and found strong relationships among age, the number of receptors, and cognition. Backman et al. (2000) reported that literally all age-related variance on perceptual speed and episodic memory tasks was attenuated when dopamine receptor binding was statistically controlled. All of these data suggest that dopaminergic receptors play an important

D₂ Receptor Availibility in Frontal Cortex

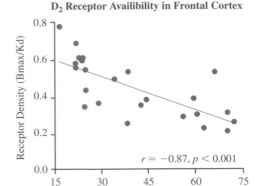

$r = -0.87, p < 0.001$

Figure 61.5   Reduction in dopamine receptor density in frontal brain regions over age.

Note: From "Age-Related Dopamine D2/D3 Receptor Loss in Extrastriatal Regions of the Human Brain," by V. Kaasinen et al., 2000, *Neurobiology of Aging, 21,* p. 686. Copyright 2000 by Elsevier Press. Reprinted with permission.

role in at least some aspects of cognitive aging. Whether the receptors are the major, or even sole, factor accounting for normal cognitive aging awaits further research. It should be noted that research in this area is hampered primarily by the high cost of radioligands that bind to dopaminergic receptors that require that PET rather than MRI be used to study this issue. Another problem is that PET requires exposure of subjects to radiation and is even more costly than MRI.

Frontal Compensation Hypotheses

Functional imaging allows us to examine neural activity in specific brain structures while a cognitive task is being performed and has provided truly surprising findings about neural activity in the aging brain. Given the declines in cognitive performance, neural structures, and dopamine receptors portrayed in Figures 61.1 through 61.5, we might intuitively expect that these declines would be accompanied by decreased activation in the aging brain. The most common finding from the cognitive neuroscience literature on aging, however, is that older adults show activation across more neural structures than young adults, although not necessarily more activation in these structures. One of the most robust findings in the emerging cognitive neuroscience of aging literature is that when performing memory or encoding tasks, activations that are highly lateralized in one hemisphere of the dorsolateral prefrontal cortex in young adults will tend to show activation in both hemispheres for older adults (reviewed in Buckner, 2004; Cabeza, 2002; Hedden & Gabrieli, 2004; Park & Gutchess, 2005; Reuter-Lorenz, 2002). As shown in Figure 61.6, this finding has been reported for both working memory (Reuter-Lorenz et al., 2000) and long-term memory (Cabeza, 2002; Cabeza et al., 1997), and has been replicated reliably in many other laboratories beyond these initial reports (Backman, 1997; Grady, Bernstein, Beig, & Siegenthaler, 2002; Madden et al., 1999; Morcom, Good, Frackowiak, & Rugg, 2003; Rosen et al., 2002). Both Reuter-Lorenz et al. (2000) and Cabeza (2002) argue that this bilateral distribution of frontal activation in old adults represents a compensatory activation that occurs in the aging brain to accommodate the decreased volume of neural tissue and declining efficiency of neural circuitry. It makes sense that the frontal cortex might somehow engage in compensatory activations for the neural degradation in volume, white matter, and dopamine receptors that occurs with age because the frontal cortex is the largest and most flexible component of the brain. It is involved in reasoning, strategies, control, and semantic processing, and plays a particularly important role in encoding and retrieval processes in memory. Cabeza (2002) presents the hemispheric asymmetry reduction in older adults (HAROLD) model, which suggests that older adults specifically recruit the contralateral hemisphere to assist in task performance that is primarily unilateral in young adults. Reuter-Lorenz & Mikels' (2006) compensation-related utilization of neural circuits (CRUNCH) model has some similarities to the HAROLD Model. CRUNCH also suggests that at lower levels of cognitive challenge, older adults will recruit more resources, but as challenge level increases, the challenge will exceed the demands of the older adult. Under high challenge, young and old may not differ, or young will show more engagement than old because the old will have already engaged maximal resources in easier conditions.

The CRUNCH model explains varying patterns of age differences in neural recruitment as a function of cognitive challenge and integrates considerable data.

One approach to assessing whether the additional contralateral frontal recruitment is compensatory for some aspect of neural degeneration with age is to examine differences in hemispheric bilaterality between groups of older adults who are either high or low performers on cognitive tasks. The presumption would be that if the additional frontal activation is compensatory, the high performers would show greater evidence of bilaterality. In examining six studies on this issue, two suggest that bilateral activation patterns are associated with good performance (Cabeza, Anderson, Locantore, & McIntosh, 2002; Rosen et al., 2002), and the other four reach the opposite conclusion (Daselaar, Veltman, Rombouts, Raaijmakers, & Jonker, 2003; Logan, Sanders, Snyder, Morris, & Buckner, 2002; Lustig et al., 2003; Stebbins et al., 2002). It is important to note that Lustig et al. contrasted old normal adults with adults who were in early stages of Alzheimer's disease and focused on parietal activations, so this study is not directly relevant to the role of prefrontal activations on cognitive function. The other studies had relatively small sample sizes, and all attempted to study neural differences based on behavioral difference, rather than sorting subjects by neural function and studying the resultant differences in behavior. Generally, little is known about patterns of activation associated with neural health, or whether specific activation patterns from individual subjects provide increased predictability of cognitive function beyond structural measures.

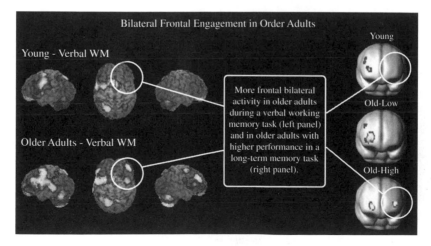

Figure 61.6 Frontal bilaterality is increased with age.

Note: The left panel shows left lateralized frontal engagement in young adults during a verbal working memory (WM) task, whereas in older adults, an additional right frontal engagement is observed. From "Age Differences in Behavior and Pet Activation Reveal Differences in Interference Resolution in Verbal Working Memory," by J., Jonides, C., Marshuetz, E., Smith, P., Reuter-Lorenz, and R., Koeppe, 2000, *Journal of Cognitive Neuroscience, 12*, pp. 188–196. Copyright 2000 from MIT Press. Reprinted with permission. The right panel shows right lateralized engagement in young adults and low-performing older adults during a long-term memory task, but bilateral frontal engagement in high-performing older adults. From "Aging Gracefully: Compensatory Brain Activity in High-Performing Older Adults," by R. Cabeza, N. D. Anderson, J. K. Locantore, and A. R. McIntosh, 2002, *NeuroImage, 17*, pp. 1394–1402. Copyright 2002 from Elsevier Press. Reprinted with permission.

Another approach to understanding whether bilaterality is compensatory in older adults is to examine neural patterns of activations uniquely associated with items that are remembered compared to items that are forgotten by older adults. There are three studies in the literature that have used such an approach by employing a subsequent memory paradigm for encoding in young and old adults. In a subsequent memory paradigm (Wagner et al., 1998), the activations associated with encoding items are recorded using an event-related fMRI design. Then, based on out-of-the-scanner recognition performance, one can determine which encoded items were actually remembered and look at the neural activations specifically associated with those items. Morcom et al. (2003) studied incidental, deep encoding of words and showed more bilateral anterior prefrontal activation for remembered items in old compared to young adults. The fact that bilaterality was uniquely associated with remembered items strongly suggests a compensatory role for bilateral activation. Gutchess et al. (2005) examined memory for complex scenes in an incidental deep-processing encoding task. Because both young and old showed bilateral activations in prefrontal areas for the pictorial task, it was not possible to find evidence for more bilaterality in old. Nevertheless, as shown in Figure 61.7, Gutchess et al. found more recruitment of the left frontal cortex in old adults compared to young for the remembered items when they subtracted activations associated with forgotten items from remembered. Moreover, Gutchess et al. also reported strong negative correlations for old adults but not young between the inferior frontal cortex and parahippocampal engagement. In old adults, the less the parahippocampus was engaged, the greater the engagement of the frontal cortex for remembered items, suggesting that greater frontal activation

was compensatory for deficient medial-temporal activations normally associated with memory.

A third approach to assessing the role of bilaterality as a compensatory mechanism is to use transcranial magnetic stimulation (TMS). In a TMS procedure, stimulation is applied to a specific area of cortex—and the stimulation interferes with the function of the brain site being stimulated. Rossi et al. (2004) applied stimulation to the left or right dorsolateral prefrontal cortex while younger and older subjects performed a spatial recognition task. In younger subjects, stimulation of the right hemisphere produced more interference in the retrieval task than left hemisphere stimulation, reflecting right lateralized processing in younger adults. In older adults, this asymmetry disappeared, suggesting that both hemispheres were facilitative for performing the task and confirming the compensatory role of bilateral activation with age.

To summarize, the research on the role of the widely observed pattern of additional frontal activation in older adults increasingly points to the probability that the additional activation is functional and enhances performance in older adults.

Medial-Temporal Function, Cognition, and Aging

Although most initial imaging work focused on the frontal cortex, there is a growing emphasis on the role of the hippocampus and other medial-temporal structures in the aging and memory literature. The hippocampus is intimately tied to episodic memory function (Brewer, Zhao, Desmond, Glover, & Gabrieli, 1998; Cohen & Eichenbaum, 1993; Gabrieli, Brewer, Desmond, & Glover, 1997; Squire et al., 1992) and also plays an important role in binding elements in complex scenes (Cohen et al., 1999). There is a literature specifically devoted to structural differences in the hippocampus and other medial-temporal structures as they relate to both normal and pathological aging. The entorhinal cortex and hippocampus are the initial brain areas attacked by Alzheimer's disease in its early stages, accounting for the memory dysfunction that is often an early symptom of the disorder. In a recent study, Rodrigue and Raz (2004) measured prefrontal, entorhinal, and hippocampal volume in 48 adults at baseline and at a 5-year follow-up period; they also measured episodic memory function. When age was covaried with structural volume, the only measure that predicted memory function was entorhinal cortical volume, suggesting that even mild shrinkage of the entorhinal cortex may be an important factor in memory function. Similarly, Rosen et al. (2003) also found a strong relationship between memory function and the entorhinal cortex volume in a small sample ($n = 14$) of older adults. Van Petten (2004) reviewed the literature relating hippocampal volume to memory ability in

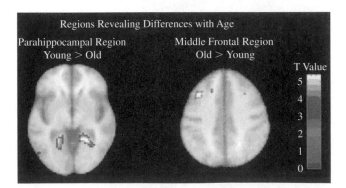

Figure 61.7   Frontal-medial-temporal age differences during an incidental encoding task involving complex scenes.

Note: Young adults engaged parahippocampal regions more than older adults, whereas older adults engaged middle frontal regions more than younger adults. From "Aging and the Neural Correlates of Successful Picture Encoding: Frontal Activations Compensate for Decreased Medial-Temporal Activity," by A. H. Gutchess et al., 2005, *Journal of Cognitive Neuroscience, 17,* pp. 84–96. Copyright 2005 from MIT Press. Reprinted with permission.

a meta-analysis and concluded that evidence for a strong relationship between hippocampus size and memory function is weak. In a study that transitions from structural imaging to functional imaging, Small, Tsai, DeLaPaz, Mayeux, and Stern (2002) developed an fMRI technique that permits segmentation of hippocampal structures into four areas: the entorhinal cortex, CA1, the subiculum, and the dentate gyrus. They reported evidence that decline in volume in the subiculum and the dentate gyrus was associated with normal aging, but that decline in the entorhinal cortex was associated with pathological decline. Although the literature relating the size of medial-temporal structures to memory have concluded that relationships are generally weak (Van Petten, 2004), the frequency with which the entorhinal cortex appears as an important structure in understanding memory function suggests that particular attention should be paid to this structure in understanding the relationship between the aging brain and neural function.

One question that naturally emerges from the compensation hypothesis is "What is it exactly that the frontal cortex is compensating for?" One possibility is under-recruitment of other key structures outside of the frontal cortex that results in compensatory frontal activations for deficient activation in these structures. Park and Gutchess (2005) provide a detailed review of the relationship between hippocampal and frontal function in the long-term memory literature. They conclude that there is strong evidence for an increased frontal/decreased hippocampal relationship across 24 functional imaging studies, a relationship that strongly suggests that increased frontal activations may be compensatory for decreased hippocampal activations. They also address the issue of hippocampal engagement in picture memory, suggesting that older adults consistently show less engagement of medial temporal areas than young adults when encoding pictures. They note that increased frontal activity in older relative to younger adults has been most likely to occur when the pictures presented are complex meaningful scenes, consistent with Cohen et al.'s (1999) view that the hippocampus plays an important role in binding scene elements, as confirmed in the imaging literature by Goh et al. (2004). In fact, Chee et al. (2006) reported deficient binding regions in the right and left parahippocampus in older adults while viewing complex meaningful scenes. Another study by Persson et al. (2006) demonstrated that age-related cognitive decline in memory was related to hippocampal volume as well as decreased white matter integrity in the interior corpus callosum, and that all of these measures were related to increased activation in the right prefrontal cortex in older subjects. This pattern of findings again confirms that additional frontal activation is compensatory and also that it is associated with decreased hippocampal volume.

Frontal versus Hippocampal Aging: Normal versus Pathological?

Thus far, the neurally based theories on aging have focused on the compensatory function of additional frontal engagement in response to reduction in medial-temporal activity with aging. An alternative to this view is proposed by Head et al. (2004). These authors noted that Alzheimer's disease patients are characterized by declining hippocampal volume whereas normal aging is characterized by white matter and frontal deterioration. They suggest that aging has two components: a normal component that is characterized by frontal decline and difficulties in executive function, and a pathological component characterized by declining volume in the medial-temporal areas, particularly the hippocampus. This view suggests frontal and hippocampal aging occur independently and is different from the notion that there is direct linkage between frontal activation and hippocampal deterioration as suggested by Park and Gutchess (2005), and confirmed by Persson et al. (2006). There is considerable support for both views. Recent work by Andrews-Hanna et al. (2007) again showed evidence for age-related disruption of default network activity associated with memory decline and white matter decline, and that the relationship was strongly independent of the amount of amyloid deposition, suggesting a normal/pathological component dissociation. Only larger studies that take integrative multimodal approaches are likely to yield more definitive evidence for these possibilities.

With this in mind, while the frontal and hippocampal regions are the subject of many aging studies, it is also important to consider other brain regions that might provide a clue as to whether the changes observed, both structural and functional, are compensatory or in fact the underlying cause for the compensatory response in complementary brain regions. One such candidate for exploration is the ventral visual areas, which we discuss the following section.

Ventral Visual Function, Memory, and Aging

There is only a modest amount of functional imaging data that specifically examines age differences in activation patterns in ventral visual cortex. Before discussing the findings, it is informative to review some very elegant behavioral work conducted by Lindenberger and Baltes (1994) and Baltes and Lindenberger (1997) that foreshadows the importance of the sensory cortex in understanding age differences in neural function. Briefly, these investigators studied a life span sample that included a large number of very old adults—up to the age of 105. They reported that measures of vision and audition explained essentially all of the age-related variance on measures of memory and reasoning, and suggested that with age, a dedifferentiation (loss of specificity) in different sensory and cognitive functions occurs, so that a loss in one domain is highly explanatory and interrelated to dysfunction in other domains. Put concisely, this work suggests that with respect to sensory cognitive function, "when it goes, it all goes together," whereas younger adults maintain some specificity and independence of function across different sensory/cognitive domains.

Some of the most specialized neural areas appear to occur in the ventral visual cortex, at least in young adults. There is evidence that in young adults, the fusiform gyrus is specialized to recognize faces (Kanwisher, McDermott, & Chun, 1997); the parahippocampus is specialized for places (Epstein & Kanwisher, 1998); the lateral occipital cortex is specialized for objects (Malach et al., 1995); and the left fusiform gyrus is specialized for letters and words (Polk et al., 2002; Puce, Allison, Asgari, Gore, & McCarthy, 1996). Park et al. (2004) examined neural specificity for faces, places, and words in young and old adults while they passively viewed pictures. They reported that voxels that were highly specialized for faces in young adults showed markedly less activation to places, chairs, and words. In contrast, old adults' "face voxels" showed substantial activation to other categories, reflecting dedifferentiation. This effect was replicated in the other categories. Young adults' "place" voxels showed specialization, but old adults also activated to faces and words, and the same was true for specialization of voxels activated to pseudowords. The results were replicated using a broad range of dependent measures, attesting to the reliability and generality of the effect. Chee et al. (2006) demonstrated decreased specificity in the object area (lateral occipital cortex) and binding area (hippocampus), confirming again the decreased specificity in this general region (Figure 61.8). Park et al. (2004) concluded that aging is accompanied by decreased selectivity in ventral visual cortex, or a dedifferentiation of neural specificity, in accord with the theorizing of Baltes and Lindenberger (1997). They consider that older adults may show increased frontal function and perceptual slowing in the behavioral domain as a result of decreased neural specialization in the ventral visual areas. The sample that Park et al. tested was quite small (13 young and 12 old), so there were insufficient subjects to correlate magnitude of neural differentiation with behavior. In accord with the Park et al. (2004) findings, a concurrent paper by Cabeza et al. (2004) demonstrated decreased occipital function with age and increased frontal function across measures of attention, working memory, and long-term memory. They suggest that the findings are "consistent with the common factor view that age-related cognitive deficits are in great part due to a decline in sensory processing, and that some

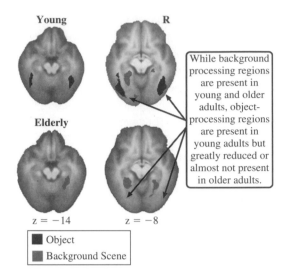

Figure 61.8 (Figure C.58 in color section) Object and background-scene processing areas identified in young and older adults during passive viewing of complex pictures.

Note: Background processing regions are present in the parahippocampal area in both young and older adults, but object regions in the lateral occipital area are greatly reduced in older adults. From "Age-Related Changes in Object Processing and Contextual Binding Revealed Using FMR Adaptation," by M. Chee et al., 2006, *Journal of cognitive Neuroscience, 18*, p. 501. Copyright 2006 from MIT Press. Reprinted with permission.

forms of compensatory prefrontal recruitment are common across tasks." Cabeza and colleagues labeled the pattern of increased frontal and decreased ventral visual/occipital findings posterior anterior shift in aging (PASA; Davis, Dennis, Daselaar, Fleck, & Cabeza, 2008). The finding of age-related cortical thinning in sensory areas by Salat et al. (2004) also adds to the plausibility of the hypothesis that sensory deficits drive much of the cognitive decline and increased frontal recruitment evidenced in cognitive aging research.

The Default Network

A relatively recent development in neuroimaging that is important to aging research is the identification of a set of brain regions termed the *default network* that is observed to be more active during periods of rest compared to when the brain is actively engaged in a task (Beer, 2007; Buckner et al., 2005; Greicius, Krasnow, Reiss, & Menon, 2003; Raichle et al., 2001; Shulman, 1997). This network involves deactivation of multiple regions when a demanding cognitive task is presented. The regions involved include the medial-frontal, inferior-parietal, posterior-cingulate, and medial-temporal structures, and deactivation of these structures during a cognitive task relative to baseline has been observed to occur in many studies across a variety of tasks. Mason et al. (2007) suggested that the default network is engaged during periods of daydreaming, or mind wandering and it becomes deactivated during a cognitive task because individuals must suppress this mind-wandering to perform the task. Mason et al. found that the frequency with which individuals reported being engaged in mind wandering was correlated with activity in the default network. This has an important relation to aging because a study by Giambra (1989) found that older adults were more likely to engage in such mind-wandering compared to younger adults, using various measures of frequency of mind wandering. As the Giambra study would predict, older adults do not deactivate these default areas as much as young adults when presented with a cognitive task. This suggests that older adults may have more trouble staying on task because the mind-wandering network fails to deactivate when a demanding task is presented. Lustig et al. (2003) reported less deactivation in the medial frontal and posterior cingulate default network regions in older adults compared to younger adults in a cognitive task. Furthermore, Alzheimer's patients showed even less default-related deactivation in these regions compared to normal older adults, a finding that was replicated by Greicius, Srivastava, Reiss, and Menon (2004). These findings suggest that older adults may find it more difficult to disengage from their default mode of processing in order to fully engage in the active task at hand. This may account in part for poorer behavioral performance in older adults across a number of tasks, just as the default network is consistently identified across a number of different tasks.

The findings on the default network reviewed here represent initial work relating default network activity to aging cognitive processes. Thus, there are many caveats to consider such as the specific nature of mind wandering and the validity of its measurements, the cognitive significance of the default network and its function, heterogeneity within the default network, and the methodological issues related to baseline comparisons in neuroimaging data. In summary, aging is associated with reduced deactivation in default network activity during active tasks. Aging is also associated with higher probability of engaging in mind wandering, which is shown to correlate with default network activity. Taken together, these suggest that at least part of the cognitive behavioral decline, as well as functional changes in brain activity observed with aging, may be related to differences in default network function in older adults.

Aging, Individual Differences and Neurocognitive Function

Age is only one of many individual differences that are important in determining cognition. A large behavioral literature examines the role of individual differences in cognitive function across the life span with evidence that (a) speed and working memory explain long-term memory function (Park et al., 2002); (b) education and social class in older adults are important in understanding the response to environmental support (Cherry & Park, 1993; Craik, Byrd, & Swanson, 1987); and (c) old individuals' variability in performance on free-recall tasks over days is an important predictor of later cognitive decline (Hultsch, MacDonald, Hunter, Levy-Bencheton, & Strauss, 2000; Li et al., 2001). A relatively unexplored area in the imaging literature that is of considerable importance to understanding neurocognitive aging is the role of individual differences in patterns of neural function in predicting cognitive performance. Equally important is the relationship between activations in different brain areas (e.g., differentiation and laterality indices) in predicting hippocampal and frontal activation on encoding tasks when the encoding data is collected on tasks independent of the differentiation and laterality indices. One of the few examples of a neuroimaging study in which a true individual differences approach has occurred, with predictors measured independently from tasks, and in which brain activation has been used to predict behavioral accuracy, is a study by Gray, Chabris, and Braver (2003). They measured general intelligence along with neural activations associated with performance on a demanding working memory task. They determined that general intelligence predicted performance on working memory accuracy. Hypothesizing that neural activation in two regions of interest (lateral prefrontal and parietal) was the mediator between general intelligence and accuracy on the working memory task, they were able to demonstrate that the activation level in these two brain sites mediated the variance associated with the relationship between intelligence and accuracy. A similar approach that integrates aging, structural, and functional variables could be very useful. Using individual differences, measures of structure along with functional indices of differentiation and laterality to predict behavioral performance could be very informative.

AGE AND CULTURE DIFFERENCES IN NEUROCOGNITIVE FUNCTION

Every individual is enmeshed in a culture, and the influences of culture on behavior are often transparent to both the individual and the society in which he or she is enmeshed. Thus, the notion that cultural influences affect cognitive and neural function may not be as obvious as findings that other life experiences affect neurocognitive function. There is a wealth of evidence that culture influences cognitive behavioral function (Nisbett, 2003; Nisbett, Peng, Choi, & Norenzayan, 2001). Nisbett (2003) proposes that beginning in ancient times, Western thought (characterized by the Greeks) and Eastern thought (characterized by Chinese) had fundamentally different philosophical views of the world that have persisted into the present and subtly shape perception, memory, and higher-order cognition, as well as social relationships (Nisbett & Masuda, 2003). Western thought is grounded in an analytic focus on objects and categories, with rules that define objects' properties and function. In contrast, Eastern thought is grounded in a holistic focus where objects are part of a larger whole, and central and contextual elements of information are given equal focus. Nisbett et al. (2001) note that the social systems of the two cultures reflect these biases because Western cultures tend to focus on the individual with an independent self that is largely unconnected to others, whereas East Asian cultures (e.g., Chinese, Japanese, Singaporean, Korean, Thai) are based on complex interdependent social relationships with the self being defined by relationships to, and function of, a social group (Markus & Kitayama, 1991). The East Asian tendency to focus on others in the group results in a tendency to monitor context and relationships, and to treat complex systems in a relatively unitary, holistic fashion. Unlike East Asians, Westerners tend to process information in an object-based, analytic fashion due to their individualistic bias and relatively unconnected self. These tendencies result in biases to prioritize different types of information for processing, with East Asians attending relatively more to contextual, relational information than Westerners, and Westerners focusing relatively more attention on objects and their properties.

Given the striking differences Park et al. (2004) found in specialization of ventral visual cortex with age, and given that culture effects in the behavioral domain are primarily perceptual (e.g., the greater attention to object stimuli in Westerners and to contextual information in East Asians), it makes sense to focus efforts to understand neurocultural differences in the ventral visual area. In an initial functional imaging study of culture, Gutchess, Welsh, Boduroglu, and Park (2006) presented young adults who were either East Asian or Western with a series of photographs (displayed in Figure 22.3) that were of three types: (1) a relatively simple target object, such as an elephant or an airplane; (2) a complex scene with no discernible central object, such as a picture of a jungle or lake; or a (3) target object against a meaningful background scene (e.g., an elephant in a jungle). Through a series of contrasts, they were able to isolate areas uniquely associated with object processing and areas uniquely associated with contextual or background processing in the ventral visual areas (Goh et al., 2004). Of central importance was the finding of evidence

for heightened activation in Americans of the middle temporal gyrus, an area used for object processing, as the culture hypothesis would predict. They saw less evidence for cultural differences in context processing, although they did observe a slight bias for more activation of context areas in East Asians, as cultural theorists would predict.

In a second study, Goh et al. (2007) compared the magnitude of adaptation in different areas in the ventral visual cortex adapted when the object and background in complex scenes were repeated. Adaptation occurs when a neural signal declines if a stimulus is repeated. There were three major findings from this study depicted in Figure 61.9. First, there were no differences in patterns of neural activation in young Asians and Americans. Second, older adults in both cultures showed evidence for a diminished object-processing area in the lateral occipital cortex. Third, this object area was significantly more diminished in the older East Asians compared to the older Americans. The older East Asians showed almost no adaptation in the object area whatsoever. Perhaps because the adaptation paradigm is comparatively subtle, cultural differences were not observed in younger adults, unlike in Gutchess et al. (2006), who reported greater neural engagement for object processing regions in young Westerners compared with young East Asians. In Goh et al. (2007), cultural differences were apparent only in older participants who have had more exposure to their respective cultural environments than younger participants. Overall, this pattern of findings provides initial neuroimaging evidence for cultural biases in perceptual processing of objects and further suggests that the long-term exposure to a particular cultural environment that occurs with aging might have a role in shaping brain function.

It is also important to note that while the evidence suggests a culture-related bias in neurocognitive processing in individuals, human beings are extremely flexible in approaching various types of situations. Indeed, even while we are steeped in our own cultural tendencies, we have the capacity to engage modes of thinking related to other cultures as well (Gardner, Gabriel, & Lee, 1999; Miyamoto, Nisbett, & Masuda, 2006). Both Gardner et al. (1999) and Miyamoto et al. (2006) have demonstrated that subjects can be primed to respond in a culturally nonpreferred manner. In a brain imaging study, Hedden, Ketay, Aron, Markus, and Gabrieli (2008) showed that such engagement of culturally nonpreferred processes requires greater attentional effort compared to when subjects were using their own cultural biases to approach a problem. Because these studies were conducted on young adults, it would be interesting to investigate this flexibility in older adults to engage different strategies to approach various situations as well.

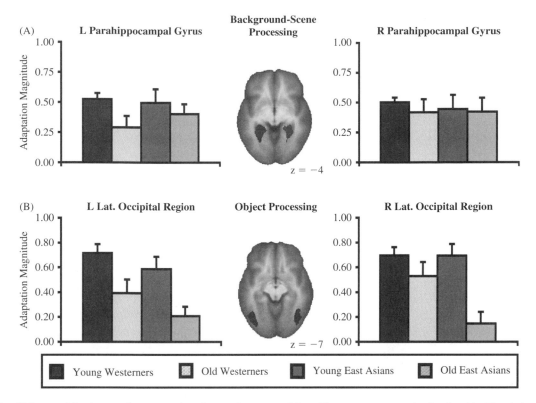

Figure 61.9 Object-and background-scene-processing regions in younger and older Westerners and East Asians.

Note: Background-processing activity in the parahippocampal region (top row) was relatively preserved across younger and older Westerners and East Asians. However, object-processing activity in the lateral occipital region (bottom row) was reduced in older adults compared to younger adults, with an even greater reduction for older East Asians compared to older Westerners. From "Age and Culture Modulate Object Processing and Object-Scene Binding in the Ventral Visual Area," by J. O. Goh et al., 2007, *Cognitive, Affective and Behavioral Neuroscience, 7,* pp. 44–52. Copyright 2007 by Psychonomic Society Publications. Adapted with permission.

One important question is whether cultural biases shape brain organization in a fundamental way or merely reflect activation patterns that can be modified by switching to other modes of thought. The data thus far argue more for the latter option. However, experience has been shown to alter brain structures in fundamental ways (see the section that follows). The cross-cultural study of neural aging provides a potential avenue to assess the possibility that culture alters structure and/or function permanently because effects of culture should be magnified with age due to the sustained exposure older adults have to culture. In addition, and at least as importantly, the cross-cultural study of neural aging allows investigators to determine what the biologically invariant aspects of neural aging are and what aspects of aging are determined by environmental and social factors. It is with this in mind that we next consider issues pertaining to neural plasticity and aging.

NEURAL PLASTICITY IN OLDER ADULTS

There is evidence from the animal literature suggesting that mental stimulation and enriched environments enhance cognition. Kempermann, Kuhn, and Gage (1998) demonstrated that old rats maintained in complex visual and play environments showed birth of new neurons in the hippocampus in old age unlike control subjects. Kobayashi, Ohashi, and Ando (2002) reported improved learning ability in rats exposed to an enriched environment, even in old age, and concluded, "These results show that aged animals still have appreciable plasticity in cognitive function and suggest that environmental stimulation could benefit aging humans as well." Kempermann, Gast, and Gage (2002) reported a similar effect and demonstrated that short-term exposure of rats to an enriched environment, even in old age, led to a fivefold increase in hippocampal neurogenesis (Figure 61.10), as well as a decrease in age-related atrophy in the dentate gyrus. The authors make a direct link of their findings to human behavior and ask, "Could this plastic response be relevant for explaining the beneficial effects of leading an 'active life' on brain function?" Is the "use it or lose it" hypothesis correct with respect to cognitive aging?

There is evidence from many correlational and longitudinal studies that individuals who lead more engaged lives have more resilient cognitive systems in late adulthood.

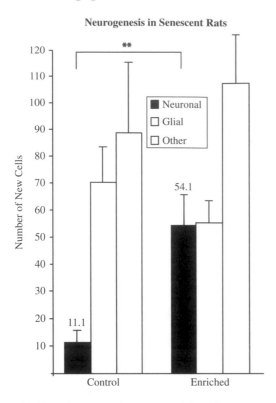

Figure 61.10 Hippocampal neurogenesis in aging rats.

Note: Rats raised in an enriched environment showed increased neurogenesis of neuronal cells compared to control rats (black bars). From "Neuroplasticity in Old Age: Sustained Fivefold Induction of Hippocampal Neurogenesis by Long-Term Environmental Enrichment," by G. Kempermann, D. Gast, and F. H. Gage, 2002, *Annals of Neurology, 52*, pp. 135–143. Copyright 2002 by John Wiley & Sons. Reprinted with permission.

For example, Schooler, Mulatu, and Oates (1999) reported that engagement in "substantively complex" work across the life span, predicted better intellectual functioning in old age than engagement in less challenging work, even after education and other related factors were controlled. Other evidence in support of the productive engagement hypothesis comes from the Maastricht Longitudinal Study. At the beginning of the study, none of the participants enrolled (aged 50 to 80) showed cognitive impairment, but 3 years later, 4% of those with low cognitively demanding jobs showed some cognitive impairment, whereas only 1.5% of those with mentally demanding jobs were impaired (Bosma et al., 2003). There are also data suggesting that individuals who self-report engagement in more intense cognitive activity across their life span show higher levels of cognitive function, as measured by text recall, perceptual speed, and the Mini-Mental Status Exam (Wilson et al., 1999). Finally, a number of studies have reported that highly educated people who tend to be involved in more cognitively stimulating activities are more cognitively resilient in the early stages of Alzheimer's disease (Bennett et al., 2003; Wilson & Bennett, 2003; Wilson, Gilley, Bennett, Beckett, & Evans, 2000), even after controlling for other

related variables. In sum, there is experimental evidence that animals raised in engaging environments show enhanced neural structure and function in old age, while correlational studies of humans indicate that productive engagement across the life span is related to higher cognitive function and resilience in the face of mild levels of brain disease.

There is also good evidence that experience changes the brains of older adults. Nyberg et al. (2003) demonstrated increased occipitoparietal activation in older adults after they had been trained in a method of loci mnemonic technique. Colcombe et al. (2004) demonstrated that several months of aerobic training in older adults increased functional activations in both the prefrontal and parietal cortices while performing a flanker task. There is rapidly growing evidence that sustained aerobic exercise provides neuroprotection for older adults, although the mechanism of improvement is still somewhat unclear. Finally, perhaps the most direct evidence that aging brains change in response to experience comes from aged stroke patients. Despite devastating brain injuries, with enormous amounts of training and practice, even very old adults show dramatic improvement from strokes, due to the residual plasticity and malleability of their brains (Hallett, 2001).

SUMMARY

Our understanding of normal cognitive aging has been radically changed by the introduction of neuroimaging tools. We now know that the aging brain is more dynamic and active than was previously thought and that despite the gradual decline of functions observed in behavior, the aging brain "does not go gently into the night." Rather, the aging brain remodels and reorganizes, activating new and increased neural circuitry in response to the declining structure and function confronting it. The past decade has resulted in tremendous increases in understanding the aging mind through the integration of structural and functional imaging techniques with behavioral data. Future direction will involve integrating even more modalities and including more studies that integrate genomics. Additionally, integration of animal and human work may provide greater understanding of mechanisms and facilitation than is currently possible. The increasing prevalence of Alzheimer's disease and other age-associated neurological disorders has become a public health crisis and a threat to the well-being, not only of older citizens, but to their families as well. Understanding normal aging and conditions that lead to a slowed rate of cognitive aging will enhance economic productivity and quality of life for citizens of all ages. The significant gains made in the past 10 years lead to optimism that we may understand the mechanisms underlying rates of cognitive aging sufficiently well to slow them in the near future.

REFERENCES

Alzheimer's Association (2007). *Alzheimer's disease facts and figures* 2007. Retrieved December 23, 2008, from http://www.alz.org/national/documents/ Report_2007FactsAndFigures.pdf

Andrews-Hanna, J. R., Snyder, A. Z., Vincent, J. L., Lustig, C., Head, D., & Raichle, M. E. (2007). Disruption of large-scale brain systems in advanced aging. *Neuron, 56*, 924–935.

Backman, L. (1997). Brain activation in young and older adults during implicit and explicit retrieval. *Journal of Cognitive Neuroscience, 9*, 378–391.

Backman, L., Ginovart, N., Dixon, R. A., Wahlin, T. B., Wahlin, A., Halldin, C., et al. (2000). Age-related cognitive deficits mediated by changes in the striatal dopamine system. *The American Journal of Psychiatry, 157*, 635–637.

Baltes, P., & Lindenberger, U. (1997). Emergence of a powerful connection between sensory and cognitive functions across the adult life span: A new window to the study of cognitive aging? *Psychology and Aging, 12*, 12–21.

Beer, J. S. (2007). The default self: Feeling good or being right? *Trends in Cognitive Sciences, 11*, 187–189.

Bennett, D. A., Wilson, R. S., Schneider, J. A., Evans, D. A., Mendes de Leon, C. F., Arnold, S. E., et al. (2003). Education modifies the relation of AD pathology to level of cognitive function in older persons. *Neurology, 60*, 1909–1915.

Bosma, H., van Boxtel, M. P., Ponds, R. W., Houx, P. J., Burdorf, A., & Jolles, J. (2003). Mental work demands protect against cognitive impairment: MAAS prospective cohort study. *Experimental Aging Research, 29*, 33–45.

Brewer, J. B., Zhao, Z., Desmond, J. E., Glover, G. H., & Gabrieli, J. D. (1998). Making memories: Brain activity that predicts how well visual experience will be remembered. *Science, 281*, 1185–1187.

Buckner, R. L. (2004). Memory and executive function in aging and AD: Multiple factors that cause decline and reserve factors that compensate. *Neuron, 44*, 195–208.

Buckner, R. L., Snyder, A. Z., Shannon, B. J., LaRossa, G., Sachs, R., Fotenos, A. F., et al. (2005). Molecular, structural, and functional characterization of alzheimer's disease: Evidence for a relationship between default activity, amyloid, and memory. *Journal of Neuroscience: Official Journal of the Society for Neuroscience, 25*, 7709–7717.

Cabeza, R. (2002). Hemispheric asymmetry reduction in older adults: The HAROLD model. *Psychology and Aging, 17*, 85–100.

Cabeza, R., Anderson, N. D., Locantore, J. K., & McIntosh, A. R. (2002). Aging gracefully: Compensatory brain activity in high-performing older adults. *NeuroImage, 17*, 1394–1402.

Cabeza, R., Daselaar, S. M., Dolcos, F., Prince, S. E., Budde, M., & Nyberg, L. (2004). Task-independent and task-specific age effects on brain activity during working memory, visual attention and episodic retrieval. *Cerebral Cortex, 14*, 364–375.

Cabeza, R., Grady, C. L., Nyberg, L., McIntosh, A. R., Tulving, E., Kapur, S., et al. (1997). Age-related differences in neural activity during memory encoding and retrieval: A positron emission tomography study. *Journal of Neuroscience: Official Journal of the Society for Neuroscience, 17*, 391–400.

Chee, M. W. L., Goh, J. O. S., Venkatraman, V., Chow Tan, J., Gutchess, A., Sutton, B., et al. (2006). Age-related changes in object processing and contextual binding revealed using fMR adaptation. *Journal of Cognitive Neuroscience, 18*, 495–507.

Cherry, K. E., & Park, D. C. (1993). Individual difference and contextual variables influence spatial memory in younger and older adults. *Psychology and Aging, 8*, 517–526.

Cohen, N. J., & Eichenbaum, H. (1993). *Memory, amnesia, and the hippocampal system.* Cambridge, MA: MIT Press.

Cohen, N., Ryan, J., Hunt, C., Romine, L., Wszalek, T., & Nash, C. (1999). The hippocampal system and declarative (relational) memory: Evidence from functional neuroimaging studies. *Hippocampus, 9*, 83–98.

Colcombe, S. J., Kramer, A. F., Erickson, K. I., Scalf, P., McAuley, E., Cohen, N. J., et al. (2004). Cardiovascular fitness, cortical plasticity, and aging. *Proceedings of the National Academy of Sciences, USA, 101*, 3316–3321.

Craik, F. I., Byrd, M., & Swanson, J. M. (1987). Patterns of memory loss in three elderly samples. *Psychology and Aging, 2*, 79–86.

Daselaar, S., Veltman, D., Rombouts, S., Raaijmakers, J., & Jonker, C. (2003). Neuroanatomical correlates of episodic encoding and retrieval in young and elderly subjects. *Brain, 126*, 43.

Davatzikos, C., & Resnick, S. M. (2002). Degenerative age changes in white matter connectivity visualized in vivo using magnetic resonance imaging. *Cerebral Cortex, 12*, 767–771.

Davis, S. W., Dennis, N. A., Daselaar, S. M., Fleck, M. S., & Cabeza, R. (2008). Que PASA? the posterior anterior shift in aging. *Cerebral Cortex, 18*, 1201–1209.

Epstein, R., & Kanwisher, N. (1998). A cortical representation of the local visual environment. *Nature, 392*, 598–601.

Gabrieli, J. D., Brewer, J. B., Desmond, J. E., & Glover, G. H. (1997). Separate neural bases of two fundamental memory processes in the human medial temporal lobe. *Science, 276*, 264–266.

Gardner, W. L., Gabriel, S., & Lee, A. Y. (1999). "I" value freedom, but "we" value relationships: Self-construal priming mirrors cultural differences in judgment. *Psychological Science, 10*, 321–326.

Giambra, L. M. (1989). Task-unrelated-thought frequency as a function of age: A laboratory study. *Psychology and Aging, 4*, 136–143.

Goh, J. O., Chee, M. W., Tan, J. C., Venkatraman, V., Hebrank, A., Leshikar, E. D., et al. (2007). Age and culture modulate object processing and object-scene binding in the ventral visual area. *Cognitive, Affective and Behavioral Neuroscience, 7*, 44–52.

Goh, J. O., Siong, S. C., Park, D., Gutchess, A., Hebrank, A., & Chee, M. W. (2004). Cortical areas involved in object, background, and object background processing revealed with functional magnetic resonance adaptation. *Journal of Neuroscience: Official Journal of the Society for Neuroscience, 24*, 10223–10228.

Grady, C. L., Bernstein, L. J., Beig, S., & Siegenthaler, A. L. (2002). The effects of encoding task on age-related differences in the functional neuroanatomy of face memory. *Psychology and Aging, 17*, 7–23.

Gray, J. R., Chabris, C. F., & Braver, T. S. (2003). Neural mechanisms of general fluid intelligence. *Nature Neuroscience, 6*, 316–322.

Greicius, M. D., Krasnow, B., Reiss, A. L., & Menon, V. (2003). Functional connectivity in the resting brain: A network analysis of the default mode hypothesis. *Proceedings of the National Academy of Sciences, USA, 100*, 253–258.

Greicius, M. D., Srivastava, G., Reiss, A. L., & Menon, V. (2004). Default-mode network activity distinguishes alzheimer's disease from healthy aging: Evidence from functional MRI. *Proceedings of the National Academy of Sciences, USA, 101*, 4637–4642.

Gutchess, A. H., Welsh, R. C., Hedden, T., Bangert, A., Minear, M., Liu, L. L., et al. (2005). Aging and the neural correlates of successful picture encoding: Frontal activations compensate for decreased medial-temporal activity. *Journal of Cognitive Neuroscience, 17*, 84–96.

Gutchess, A., Welsh, R., Boduroglu, A., & Park, D. C. (2006). Cultural differences in neural function associated with object processing. *Cognitive, Affective, and Behavioral Neuroscience, 6*, 102–109.

Hallett, M. (2001). Brain plasticity and recovery from hemiplegia. *Journal of Medical Speech-Language Pathology, 9*, 107–115.

Head, D., Buckner, R. L., Shimony, J. S., Williams, L. E., Akbudak, E., Conturo, T. E., et al. (2004). Differential vulnerability of anterior white matter in nondemented aging with minimal acceleration in dementia of the alzheimer type: Evidence from diffusion tensor imaging. *Cerebral Cortex, 14*, 410–423.

Hedden, T., Ketay, S., Aron, A., Markus, H., & Gabrieli, J. D. E. (2008). Cultural influences on neural substrates of attentional control. *Psychological Science, 19*, 12–17.

Hedden, T., & Gabrieli, J. D. E. (2004). Insights into the ageing mind: A view from cognitive neuroscience. *Nature Reviews Neuroscience, 5*, 87–96.

Hedden, T., Lautenschlager, G., & Park, D. C. (2005). Contributions of processing ability and knowledge to verbal memory tasks across the adult life-span. *The Quarterly Journal of Experimental Psychology: A, Human Experimental Psychology, 58*, 169–190.

Hultsch, D. F., Hertzog, C., Dixon, R. A., & Small, B. J. (1998). *Memory change in the aged.* New York: Cambridge University Press.

Hultsch, D. F., MacDonald, S. W., Hunter, M. A., Levy-Bencheton, J., & Strauss, E. (2000). Intraindividual variability in cognitive performance in older adults: Comparison of adults with mild dementia, adults with arthritis, and healthy adults. *Neuropsychology, 14*, 588–598.

Jonides, J., Marshuetz, C., Smith, E., Reuter-Lorenz, P., Koeppe, R. (2000). Age differences in behavior and PET activation reveal differences in interference resolution in verbal working memory. *Journal of Cognitive Neuroscience, 12*, 188–196.

Kaasinen, V., Vilkman, H., Hietala, J., Nagren, K., Helenius, H., Olsson, H., et al. (2000). Age-related dopamine D2/D3 receptor loss in extrastriatal regions of the human brain. *Neurobiology of Aging, 21*, 683–688.

Kanwisher, N., McDermott, J., & Chun, M. M. (1997). The fusiform face area: A module in human extrastriate cortex specialized for face perception. *Journal of Neuroscience, 17*, 4302–4311.

Kempermann, G., Gast, D., & Gage, F. H. (2002). Neuroplasticity in old age: Sustained fivefold induction of hippocampal neurogenesis by long-term environmental enrichment. *Annals of Neurology, 52*, 135–143.

Kempermann, G., Kuhn, H. G., & Gage, F. H. (1998). Experience-induced neurogenesis in the senescent dentate gyrus. *Journal of Neuroscience: Official Journal of the Society for Neuroscience, 18*, 3206–3212.

Kobayashi, S., Ohashi, Y., & Ando, S. (2002). Effects of enriched environments with different durations and starting times on learning capacity during aging in rats assessed by a refined procedure of the hebb-williams maze task. *Journal of Neuroscience Research, 70*, 340–346.

Li, S. C., Lindenberger, U., & Sikström, S. (2001). Aging cognition: From neuromodulation to representation. *Trends in Cognitive Sciences, 5*, 479–486.

Lindenberger, U., & Baltes, P. B. (1994). Sensory functioning and intelligence in old age: A strong connection. *Psychology and Aging, 9*, 339–355.

Logan, J. M., Sanders, A. L., Snyder, A. Z., Morris, J. C., & Buckner, R. L. (2002). Under-recruitment and nonselective recruitment dissociable neural mechanisms associated with aging. *Neuron, 33*, 827–840.

Lustig, C., Snyder, A. Z., Bhakta, M., O'Brien, K. C., McAvoy, M., Raichle, M. E., et al. (2003). Functional deactivations: Change with age and dementia of the alzheimer type. *Proceedings of the National Academy of Sciences, USA, 100*, 14504–14509.

MacDonald, S. W., Hultsch, D. F., Strauss, E., & Dixon, R. A. (2003). Age-related slowing of digit symbol substitution revisited: What do longitudinal age changes reflect? *The Journals of Gerontology, Series B, Psychological Sciences and Social Sciences, 58*, P187–P194.

Madden, D. J., Turkington, T. G., Provenzale, J. M., Denny, L. L., Hawk, T. C., Gottlob, L. R., et al. (1999). Adult age differences in the functional neuroanatomy of verbal recognition memory. *Human Brain Mapping, 7*, 115–135.

Malach, R., Reppas, J. B., Benson, R. R., Kwong, K. K., Jiang, H., Kennedy, W. A., et al. (1995). Object-related activity revealed by functional magnetic resonance imaging in human occipital cortex. *Proceedings of the National Academy of Sciences, USA, 92*, 8135–8139.

Markus, H. R., & Kitayama, S. (1991). Culture and the self: Implications for cognition, emotion, and motivation. *Psychological Review, 98*, 224–253.

Mason, M. F., Norton, M. I., Van Horn, J. D., Wegner, D. M., Grafton, S. T., & Macrae, C. N. (2007). Wandering minds: The default network and stimulus-independent thought. *Science, 315*, 393.

Miyamoto, Y., Nisbett, R. E., & Masuda, T. (2006). Culture and the Physical Environment: Holistic versus Analytic Perceptual Affordances. *Psychological Science, 14*, 113–119.

Morcom, A. M., Good, C. D., Frackowiak, R. S. J., & Rugg, M. D. (2003). Age effects on the neural correlates of successful memory encoding. *Brain, 126*, 213–229.

Moseley, M. (2002). Diffusion tensor imaging and aging: A review. *NMR in Biomedicine, 15*(7–8), 553–560.

Nisbett, R. E. (2003). The geography of thought: How asians and westerners think differently:—and why. New York: Free Press.

Nisbett, R. E., & Masuda, T. (2003). Culture and point of view. *Proceedings of the National Academy of Sciences, USA, 100*, 11163–11170.

Nisbett, R. E., Peng, K., Choi, I., & Norenzayan, A. (2001). Culture and systems of thought: Holistic versus analytic cognition. *Psychological Review, 108*, 291–310.

Nyberg, L., Sandblom, J., Jones, S., Neely, A. S., Petersson, K. M., Ingvar, M., et al. (2003). Neural correlates of training-related memory improvement in adulthood and aging. *Proceedings of the National Academy of Sciences, USA, 100*, 13728–13733.

Park, D. C., & Gutchess, A. H. (2005). Long-term memory and aging: A cognitive neuroscience perspective. In R. Cabeza, L. Nyberg, & D. C. Park (Eds.), *Cognitive neuroscience of aging: Linking cognitive and cerebral aging* (pp. 218–245). New York, USA: Oxford University Press.

Park, D. C., Polk, T. A., Park, R., Minear, M., Savage, A., & Smith, M. R. (2004). Aging reduces neural specialization in ventral visual cortex. *Proceedings of the National Academy of Sciences, USA, 101*, 13091–13095.

Park, D. C., Smith, A. D., Lautenschlager, G., Earles, J. L., Frieske, D., Zwahr, M., et al. (1996). Mediators of long-term memory performance across the life span. *Psychology and Aging, 11*, 621–637.

Park, D. C., Lautenschlager, G., Hedden, T., Davidson, N. S., Smith, A. D., & Smith, P. K. (2002). Models of visuospatial and verbal memory across the adult life span. *Psychology and Aging, 17*, 299–320.

Persson, J., Nyberg, L., Lind, J., Larsson, A., Nilsson, L., Ingvar, M., et al. (2006). Structure–function correlates of cognitive decline in aging. *Cerebral Cortex, 16*, 907–915.

Polk, T. A., Stallcup, M., Aguirre, G. K., Alsop, D. C., D'Esposito, M., Detre, J. A., et al. (2002). Neural specialization for letter recognition. *Journal of Cognitive Neuroscience, 14*, 145–159.

Puce, A., Allison, T., Asgari, M., Gore, J. C., & McCarthy, G. (1996). Differential sensitivity of human visual cortex to faces, letterstrings, and textures: A functional magnetic resonance imaging study. *Journal of Neuroscience: Official Journal of the Society for Neuroscience, 16*, 5205–5215.

Raichle, M. E., MacLeod, A. M., Snyder, A. Z., Powers, W. J., Gusnard, D. A., & Shulman, G. L. (2001). Inaugural article: A default mode of brain function. *Proceedings of the National Academy of Sciences, USA, 98*, 676.

Raz, N. (2000). Aging of the brain and its impact on cognitive performance: Integration of structural and functional findings. In F. I. M. Craik & T. A. Salthouse (Eds.), *Handbook of aging and cognition* (pp. 1–90). Mahwah, NJ: Erlbaum.

Raz, N., Lindenberger, U., Rodrigue, K. M., Kennedy, K. M., Head, D., Williamson, A., et al. (2005). Regional brain changes in aging healthy adults: General trends, individual differences and modifiers. *Cerebral Cortex, 15*, 1676–1689.

Raz, N., Rodrigue, K. M., Head, D., Kennedy, K. M., & Acker, J. D. (2004). Differential aging of the medial temporal lobe: A study of a five-year change. *Neurology, 62*, 433–438.

Resnick, S. M., Pham, D. L., Kraut, M. A., Zonderman, A. B., & Davatzikos, C. (2003). Longitudinal magnetic resonance imaging studies of older adults: A shrinking brain. *Journal of Neuroscience: Official Journal of the Society for Neuroscience, 23*, 3295–3301.

Reuter-Lorenz, P. A. (2002). New visions of the aging mind and brain. *Trends in Cognitive Sciences, 6*, 394–400.

Reuter-Lorenz, P. A., Jonides, J., Smith, E. E., Hartley, A., Miller, A., Marshuetz, C., et al. (2000). Age differences in the frontal lateralization of verbal and spatial working memory revealed by PET. *Journal of Cognitive Neuroscience, 12*, 174–187.

Reuter-Lorenz, P. A., & Mikels, J. (2006). The aging brain: Implications of enduring plasticity for behavioral and cultural change. In P. B. Baltes, P. Reuter-Lorenz, & F. Rosler (Eds.), *Lifespan development and the brain: The perspective of biocultural co-constructivism.* United Kingdom: Cambridge University Press.

Rodrigue, K. M., & Raz, N. (2004). Shrinkage of the entorhinal cortex over five years predicts memory performance in healthy adults. *Journal of Neuroscience: Official Journal of the Society for Neuroscience, 24*, 956–963.

Rosen, A. C., Prull, M. W., O'Hara, R., Race, E. A., Desmond, J. E., Glover, G. H., et al. (2002). Variable effects of aging on frontal lobe contributions to memory. *NeuroReport, 13*, 2425–2428.

Rosen, A. C., Prull, M. W., Gabrieli, J. D., Stoub, T., O'Hara, R., Friedman, L., et al. (2003). Differential associations between entorhinal and hippocampal volumes and memory performance in older adults. *Behavioral Neuroscience, 117*, 1150–1160.

Rossi, S., Miniussi, C., Pasqualetti, P., Babiloni, C., Rossini, P. M., & Cappa, S. F. (2004). Age-related functional changes of prefrontal cortex in long-term memory: A repetitive transcranial magnetic stimulation study. *Journal of Neuroscience: Official Journal of the Society for Neuroscience, 24*, 7939–7944.

Salat, D. H., Buckner, R. L., Snyder, A. Z., Greve, D. N., Desikan, R. S., Busa, E., et al. (2004). Thinning of the cerebral cortex in aging. *Cerebral Cortex, 14*, 721–730.

Salthouse, T. A. (1991). *Theoretical perspectives on cognitive aging.* Hillsdale, NJ: Lawrence Erlbaum.

Salthouse, T. A. (1996). The processing-speed theory of adult age differences in cognition. *Psychological Review, 103*, 403–428.

Schooler, C., Mulatu, M. S., & Oates, G. (1999). The continuing effects of substantively complex work on the intellectual functioning of older workers. *Psychology and Aging, 14*, 483–506.

Shulman, G. L. (1997). Common blood flow changes across visual tasks: II. Decreases in cerebral cortex. *Journal of Cognitive Neuroscience, 9*, 648–663.

Small, S. A., Tsai, W. Y., DeLaPaz, R., Mayeux, R., & Stern, Y. (2002). Imaging hippocampal function across the human life span: Is memory decline normal or not? *Annals of Neurology, 51*, 290–295.

Squire, L. R., Ojemann, J. G., Miezin, F. M., Petersen, S. E., Videen, T. O., & Raichle, M. E. (1992). Activation of the hippocampus in normal humans: A functional anatomical study of memory. *Proceedings of the National Academy of sciences, USA, 89*, 1837–1841.

Stebbins, G. T., Carrillo, M. C., Dorfman, J., Dirksen, C., Desmond, J. E., Turner, D. A., et al. (2002). Aging effects on memory encoding in the frontal lobes. *Psychology and Aging, 17*, 44–55.

Sullivan, E. V., & Pfefferbaum, A. (2006). Diffusion tensor imaging and aging. *Neuroscience and Biobehavioral Reviews, 30*, 749–761.

Unverzagt, F. W., Gao, S., Baiyewu, O., Ogunniyi, A. O., Gureje, O., Perkins, A., et al. (2001). Prevalence of cognitive impairment: Data from the Indianapolis Study of Health and Aging. *Neurology, 57*, 1655–1662.

Van Petten, C. (2004). Relationship between hippocampal volume and memory ability in healthy individuals across the lifespan: Review and meta-analysis. *Neuropsychologia, 42*, 1394–1413.

Wagner, A. D., Schacter, D. L., Rotte, M., Koutstaal, W., Maril, A., Dale, A. M., et al. (1998). Building memories: Remembering and forgetting of verbal experiences as predicted by brain activity. *Science, 281*, 1188–1191.

Wang, Y., Chan, G. L., Holden, J. E., Dobko, T., Mak, E., Schulzer, M., et al. (1998). Age-dependent decline of dopamine D1 receptors in human brain: A PET study. *Synapse, 30*(1), 56–61.

Wilson, R. S., & Bennett, D. A. (2003). Cognitive activity and risk of alzheimer's disease. *Current Directions in Psychological Science, 12*, 87–91.

Wilson, R. S., Beckett, L. A., Barnes, L. L., Schneider, J. A., Bach, J., Evans, D. A., et al. (2002). Individual differences in rates of change in cognitive abilities of older persons. *Psychology and Aging, 17*(2), 179–193.

Wilson, R. S., Bennett, D. A., Beckett, L. A., Morris, M. C., Gilley, D. W., Bienias, J. L., et al. (1999). Cognitive activity in older persons from a geographically defined population. *Journals of Gerontology. Series B, Psychological Sciences and Social Sciences, 54*(3), P155–P160.

Wilson, R. S., Gilley, D. W., Bennett, D. A., Beckett, L. A., & Evans, D. A. (2000). Person-specific paths of cognitive decline in alzheimer's disease and their relation to age. *Psychology and Aging, 15*, 18–28.

Wong, D. F., Young, D., Wilson, P. D., Meltzer, C. C., & Gjedde, A. (1997). Quantification of neuroreceptors in the living human brain: III. D2-like dopamine receptors: Theory, validation, and changes during normal aging. *Journal of Cerebral Blood Flow and Metabolism: Official Journal of the International Society of Cerebral Blood Flow and Metabolism, 17*, 316–330.

Yang, Y. K., Chiu, N. T., Chen, C. C., Chen, M., Yeh, T. L., & Lee, I. H. (2003). Correlation between fine motor activity and striatal dopamine D2 receptor density in patients with schizophrenia and healthy controls. *Psychiatry Research, 123*, 191–197.

Zacks, R. T., Hasher, L., & Li, K. Z. H. (2000). *Human memory.* In F. I. M. Craik & T. A. Salthouse (Eds.), *The handbook of aging and cognition* (pp. 293–357). Mahwah, NJ: Erlbaum.

Chapter 62

Stress and Coping

BRUCE S. McEWEN

INTRODUCTION

"Stress" is a commonly used word that generally refers to experiences that cause feelings of anxiety and frustration because they push us beyond our ability to successfully cope. "There is so much to do and so little time!" is a common expression. Besides time pressures and daily hassles at work and home, there are stressors related to economic insecurity, poor health, and interpersonal conflict. More rarely, there are life-threatening situations—accidents, natural disasters, violence—and these evoke the classical "fight-or-flight" response. In contrast to daily hassles, these stressors are acute and yet they also often lead to post-traumatic reactions and chronic stress in the aftermath of the tragic event.

The most common stressors are, therefore, ones that operate chronically, often at a low level, and cause us to behave in certain ways. Being stressed out may cause individuals to be anxious or depressed, to lose sleep at night, to eat comfort foods and take in more calories than our bodies need, and to smoke or drink alcohol excessively. Being stressed out may also cause us to neglect seeing friends, or to take time off or engage in regular physical activity as we, for example, sit at a computer and try to get out from under the burden of too much to do. Often we are tempted to take medications—anxiolytics, sleep-promoting agents—to help us cope, and with time, our bodies may increase in weight and develop other symptoms of being chronically stressed out.

Many of the long-term consequences of being stressed out have their origins in the genetic constitution and early experiences of each individual. Alleles of certain genes are increasingly recognized as contributing to vulnerability or resilience, and early life experiences have powerful effects on the ability to cope with stressors during the life course. Moreover, the social environment determines the context in which individuals cope with their own experiences, as exemplified by the well-recognized gradients of mortality and morbidity as a function of socioeconomic status (SES).

The brain is the organ that decides what is stressful and determines the behavioral and physiological responses, whether health promoting or health damaging. The brain is a biological organ that changes under acute and chronic stress and directs many systems of the body—metabolic, cardiovascular, immune—that are involved in the short- and long-term consequences of being stressed out. What does chronic stress do to the body and brain? This chapter emphasizes how the stress hormones can play both protective and damaging roles in brain and body over the life course, depending on how tightly their production is regulated. The chapter also discusses approaches for dealing with stress in a complex world at a personal as well as organizational and societal level.

CHARACTERISTICS OF HOMEOSTATIC SYSTEMS

First, it is important to understand the fundamental concept of homeostasis as the basis for the rest of this chapter. Homeostasis refers to the ability of an organism to maintain the internal environment of the body within limits that allow it to survive. Homeostasis also refers to self-regulating processes that return critical systems of the body to a set point within a narrow range of operation, consistent with survival of the organism.

Homeostasis is highly developed in warm-blooded animals living on land because they must maintain body temperature, fluid balance, blood pH, and oxygen tension within rather narrow limits, while obtaining nutrition to provide the energy to maintain homeostasis. This is because maintaining homeostasis requires the expenditure of energy. Energy is used for locomotion, as the animal seeks and consumes food and water for maintaining body temperature via the controlled release of calories from metabolism of food or fat stores, and for sustaining cell membrane function as it resorbs electrolytes in the kidney and intestine and maintains neutral blood pH.

Homeostasis also refers to the body's defensive mechanisms. These include protective reflexes against inhaling matter into the lungs, the vomiting reflex to expel toxic materials from the esophagus or stomach, the eyeblink reflex, and the withdrawal response to hot or otherwise painful skin sensations. There is also the defense against pathogens through innate and acquired immunity.

According to Walter B. Cannon (Cannon, 1932):

> Bodily homeostasis ... results in liberating those functions of the nervous systems that adapt the organism to new situations, from the necessity of paying routing attention to the management of the details of bare existence. Without homeostatic devices, we should be in constant danger of disaster, unless we were always on the alert to correct voluntarily what normally is corrected automatically. With homeostatic devices, however, that keep essential body processes steady, we as individuals are free from such slavery—free to enter into agreeable relations with our fellows, free to enjoy beautiful things, to explore and understand the wonders of the world about us, to develop new ideas and interests, and to work and play, untrammeled by the anxieties concerning our bodily affairs. (p. 323)

HISTORICAL NOTE ON THE CONCEPT OF STRESS

It is important to provide some historical perspective about the concept of stress. The late Hans Selye (1907–1983) is credited with introducing the concept of stress into popular as well as medical discussions (Selye, 1936, 1973). Before the enormous advances in biomedical research of the past 5 decades that have added more detailed knowledge of the so-called stress hormones and their actions throughout the body, Selye used the emergency reaction of the sympathetic nervous system and adrenocortical system for his classic theory of stress (Selye, 1936). This has been captured in the classic "fight-or-flight response" of a gazelle chased by a lion. Selye postulated *the general adaptation syndrome*, a stereotyped physiological response that takes the form of a series of three stages in the reaction to a stressor: (1) The *alarm reaction* in which the adrenal medulla releases epinephrine and the adrenal cortex produces glucocorticoids. The alarm reaction promotes a process of adaptation and restores homeostasis. (2) Restoration of homeostasis leads to the stage of *resistance*, in which defense and adaptation are sustained and optimal. (3) If the stress response persists, the stage of *exhaustion* follows, the adaptive responding ceases, and the consequence may be illness and death.

How has this changed in light of new information? First, Selye's general adaptation syndrome is no longer

interpreted to mean that there is a stereotyped response of stress mediators to all types of stress. Rather, there are different patterns of response of the HPA axis and the noradrenergic and adrenergic nerves that are related to the type of stressor (Chrousos, 1998; Goldstein, 1995). Another important qualification to the classic stress theory, as captured in the fight-or-flight response, is that this response most accurately characterizes the response of male animals under threat. Dr. Shelley Taylor (Taylor et al., 1998) has characterized the female response to stress as "tend-and-befriend," not fight-or-flight. Thus, although females flee from extreme danger, gender differences need to be factored into the understanding of allostasis and allostatic load. These differences include not only the different perceptions and behavioral responses to stressors, as implied in the terminology tend-and-befriend versus fight-or-flight, but also physiological differences in the regulation of mediators of allostasis. Estrogens appear to attenuate the HPA response to stress and preserve HPA regulation of cortisol release, in that postmenopausal women exhibit larger, age-related increases in cortisol secretion, higher 24-hour cortisol excretion, and a greater response to CRH stimulation than men of the same age (Van Cauter, Leproult, & Kupfer, 1996). Moreover, in response to the

---

BOX 62.1 REINTERPRETATION OF SELYE'S 3 STAGES OF THE STRESS RESPONSE

In the new terminology of allostasis, *Selye's alarm* response is reinterpreted as the process leading to adaptation, or *allostasis*, in which glucocorticoids and epinephrine, as well as other mediators, promote adaptation to the stressor. *Selye's stage of resistance* reflects the protective effects of the adaptation to the stressor. But if the alarm response is sustained and the glucocorticoids and adrenal medulla are repeatedly elevated over many days, an allostatic state may ensue leading to *allostatic load* that replaces *Selye's phase of exhaustion*, with the important distinction that this represents the almost inevitable wear and tear produced by repeated exposure to mediators of allostasis: too much of a good thing! Thus, Selye's diseases of adaptation are the result of the allostatic state leading to allostatic load and resulting in the exacerbation of pathophysiological change. As noted, examples of allostatic load include the acceleration of atherosclerosis, abdominal obesity, as well as loss of minerals from bone, and immunosuppression, as well as atrophy and damage to the brain, especially the hippocampus (McEwen, 1998; Sapolsky, 1996).

stress of a driving simulation challenge, postmenopausal women exhibited a greater HPA response than men (Seeman, Singer, & Charpentier, 1995). Furthermore, it has been shown that short-term estrogen replacement in postmenopausal women attenuates the glucocorticoid response to a psychological stress paradigm (Komesaroff, Elser, & Suhir, 1999) and physical stress (Lindheim et al., 1992).

Finally, it is Selye's "stage of exhaustion" that needs to be reinterpreted in light of newer knowledge that the stress mediators can have both protective and damaging effects depending on the time course of their secretion. Thus, rather than exhaustion of defense mechanisms, it is the stress mediators that can turn on the body and cause problems. This leads to a discussion of the concepts of allostasis and allostatic load. See Box 62.1.

Allostasis, Allostatic Load, and Allostatic Overload

Central to this discussion is a concept of how the body systems that mediate the effects of stress and promote adaptation can also contribute to pathophysiology (McEwen, 1998). Allostasis is a concept introduced by Sterling and Eyer (Sterling & Eyer, 1988) to refer to blood pressure and heart rate responses to changes in posture as well as physical activity and emotional arousal. Allostasis means "achieving stability through change" and refers to the mediators that are actively produced to achieve a new operating state and adaptation. This is all well and good as long as the system returns to a baseline after the challenge, but it is not good if it remains elevated over longer time periods (e.g., atherosclerosis and hypertension). Anticipation plays a major role, at least in the human organism, and worries about what may or may not transpire can alter brain function and physiology (Sapolsky, 2004; Schulkin, McEwen, & Gold, 1994).

McEwen and Stellar (1993) generalized the allostasis concept to include other mediators of adaptation to changes imposed on or made by the animal, and they introduced the notion of *allostatic load* referring to the wear and tear that results from prolonged operation of physiological systems in an elevated state, as well as a dysregulated state, in which the normal balance between mediators is distorted. Koob and LeMoal (2001) introduced the term *allostatic state* to refer to a state of elevated activity; a prolonged allostatic state is what leads to wear and tear on physiological systems.

The concepts of allostasis and allostatic load/overload are intended to complement and clarify ambiguities in the usage of *homeostasis* and *stress* for all situations that involve adaptation to a changing environment. In particular, they make clear that the mediators of adaptation are also involved in pathophysiology. Furthermore, they help to distinguish between the parameters that must be maintained within narrow limits to support life (e.g., pH, oxygen tension, body temperature) and those systems and mediators that maintain homeostasis.

McEwen and Wingfield (2003) suggested using "load" and "overload" to refer to different degrees of cumulative change. *Allostatic load* refers to reversible changes such as bears putting on fat for winter; whereas *allostatic overload* is intended for cumulative changes that contribute to pathophysiology such as obesity, atherosclerosis, elevated blood sugar levels, and a chronic inflammatory state.

Many people prefer the stress/homeostasis terminology, and, indeed, the popular use of stress is pervasive, even if there is ambiguity (see Box 62.1 for reinterpretation of Selye's 3 stages of the stress response). Therefore, whatever the terminology used, whether stress/homeostasis or allostasis/allostatic load, or a combination of both, the following five aspects are important for our understanding of the relationships between adaptation and pathophysiology that result from experiences or behaviors often related to being stressed out:

Key aspects of allostasis and allostatic overload

1. Same mediators—adaptation and damage
2. How experiences and behaviors interact and affect health
3. Utility of allostatic load battery in epidemiology, health psychology
4. Central role of the brain
5. Gene-environment interactions

Allostasis Involves Multiple, Interacting Mediators That Operate Nonlinearly

The mediators of allostasis and allostatic load/overload operate as a nonlinear network, with reciprocal regulation by each mediator of other mediators. It is the dysregulation of these networks of mediators that can lead to pathophysiology (see Figure 62.1). Some of these interactions are well known: Parasympathetic activity slows the heart, whereas sympathetic activity increases heart rate. Yet other interactions are less known (e.g., sympathetic activity increases proinflammatory cytokine production; Bierhaus et al., 2003), whereas parasympathetic activity is anti-inflammatory (Borovikova et al., 2000). The renin-angiotensin system also plays a role in promoting proinflammatory responses, as well as elevated blood pressure (Saavedra, Benicky, & Zhou, 2006).

One of the consequences of increased inflammatory tone is the activation of glucocorticoid secretion, which can be regarded as activating a feedback loop that reduces inflammation in many cases (Saavedra et al., 2006).

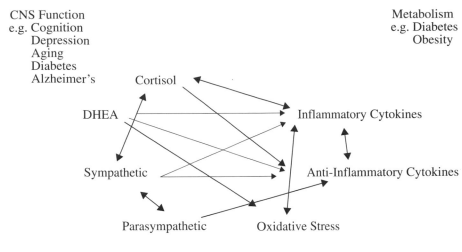

CNS Function
e.g. Cognition
     Depression
     Aging
     Diabetes
     Alzheimer's

Metabolism
e.g. Diabetes
     Obesity

Cortisol

DHEA

Sympathetic

Parasympathetic

Inflammatory Cytokines

Anti-Inflammatory Cytokines

Oxidative Stress

Cardiovascular Function
e.g. Endothelial Cell Damage
     Atherosclerosis

Immune Function
e.g. Immune Enhancement
     Immune Suppression

Figure 62.1 Nonlinear network of mediators of allostasis involved in the stress response.

Note: Arrows indicate that each system regulates the others in a reciprocal manner, creating a nonlinear network. Moreover, there are multiple pathways for regulation; inflammatory cytokine production is negatively regulated via anti-inflammatory cytokines as well as via parasympathetic and glucocorticoid pathways, whereas sympathetic activity increases inflammatory cytokine production. Parasympathetic activity, in turn, contains sympathetic activity. From "Protective and Damaging Effects of Stress Mediators: Central Role of the Brain," by B. S. McEwen, 2006a, *Dialysis in Clinical Neurosciences: Stress,* 8, pp. 286. Reprinted with permission.

BOX 62.2 STRESS SYSTEMS

Many systems in the body are involved in the response to stressors. The autonomic nervous system consists of both parasympathetic and sympathetic components. The sympathetic component involves the adrenal medulla, which releases adrenalin, and the sympathetic nerves that innervate blood vessels and many other organs. The parasympathetic nervous system is a vast, distributed neural network, with both sensory and motor components, that has many functions including the slowing of the heart and the reduction of inflammation. The hypothalamo-pituitary-adrenal axis involves the production of cortisol in response to chemical signals from the brain, namely corticotrophin-releasing factor and vasopressin, that activate the pituitary gland to release ACTH, which, in turn, causes cortisol to be produced by the adrenal cortex. Besides these systems, the pro- and anti-inflammatory cytokines produced by immune cells and also by other cells (e.g., nerve cells, microglial cells in brain) are also activated under stressful conditions. Furthermore, other hormones, such as prolactin from the pituitary gland, insulin from the pancreas and other metabolic hormones are regulated by the body's response to stressors. The complexity of these interactions is indicated in Figure 62.1.

Indeed, glucocorticoids are also anti-inflammatory but there are conditions in which glucocorticoids can have pro-inflammatory effects that are dose dependent (Sorrells & Sapolsky, 2007). A more accurate description of glucocorticoids is that they are modulators of innate and acquired immune responses (Munck, Guyre, & Holbrook, 1984; Sapolsky, Romero, & Munck, 2000). Yet glucocorticoid actions can also be modified and glucocorticoid resistance is a condition that arises in pro-inflammatory states as well as in major depressive illness (Avitsur, Stark, & Sheridan, 2001; Desouza et al., 2005; Raison, Capuron, & Miller, 2006). In conditions such as septic shock, when proinflammatory processes threaten to kill the organism, glucocorticoids may or may not be effective depending on the state of glucocorticoid resistance (Schelling et al., 1999), and parasympathetic activation (Borovikova et al., 2000) or even angiotensin receptor blockade (Saavedra et al., 2006) may be useful.

The Same Mediators Are Involved in Promoting Adaptation and Promoting Pathophysiology

Acute stress can have beneficial effects, as in the "emergency life history" stage in which the elevation of cortisol in birds during a Spring snowstorm or flood causes reproductive function to be suspended, at least temporarily, and also increases food-seeking and locomotor activity to find a safe place (McEwen & Wingfield, 2003). More generally, acute elevations of glucocorticoids enhance immune system activity (Dhabhar & McEwen, 1997), promote certain types of memory connected to emotional arousal (Roozendaal, Okuda, Van der Zee, & McGaugh, 2006), mediate energy replenishment and enhanced locomotor activity (McEwen, Sakai, & Spencer, 1993), and contribute to more efficient cardiovascular function (Ramey & Goldstein, 1957).

However, chronic cortisol elevation or exogenous treatment suppresses immune function (Munck et al., 1984), impairs certain types of memory (Lupien, 2002), promotes bone mineral loss and muscle wasting, and contributes to the metabolic syndrome (Brindley & Rolland, 1989; Chrousos, 2000). Chronic elevation of sympathetic activity is associated with hypertension, diabetes and obesity, and cardiovascular disease (Ramey & Goldstein, 1957). Chronic elevation of proinflammatory tone is associated with many disorders such as diabetes, cardiovascular disease, arthritis, and musculoskeletal disorders from repetitive motion (Barbe & Barr, 2006; Black & Garbutt, 2002; Bierhaus et al., 2001; Brami-Cherrier Lavaur, Pages, Arthur, & Cabache, 2007; Turek et al., 2005) as well as neural conditions such as depression (Raison et al., 2006) and Alzheimer's disease (McGeer & McGeer, 2001).

The transition between acute and chronic stress can lead to a reversal of direction of the effects. A single, acute restraint stress potentiates delayed-type hypersensitivity by promoting immune cell trafficking to the ear, when the antigen is applied to the ear of a rat or mouse that has formed an acquired immune response to a systemically applied antigen (Dhabhar & McEwen, 1997). However, chronic stress for 21-days has the opposite effect; it markedly suppresses immune cell trafficking to the ear (Dhabhar & McEwen, 1997). Both catecholamines and glucocorticoids are involved in the mechanism of trafficking along with locally produced cytokines such as interferon gamma (Dhabhar, 2002; Dhabhar, Satoskar, Bluethmann, David, & McEwen, 2000). There are also changes over a time course of repeated stress in the metabonomic profile of small molecules associated with lipid and energy metabolism that indicate a change in how the body handles stress with repetition (Teague et al., 2007). The chronic stress— restraint—is of the same type that causes remodeling over 21d of neuronal connections in the hippocampus, prefrontal cortex, and amygdala, whereas acute restraint stress does not produce these effects. This is discussed later in this chapter (see Boxes 62.3 and 62.4).

A major challenge is to understand how the adaptive actions associated with acute stress are permuted into dysregulation and malfunction associated with some forms of chronic stress. There are many examples of the

---

BOX 62.3 THE HIPPOCAMPUS

One of the ways that stress hormones modulate function within the brain is by changing the structure of neurons. The hippocampus is one of the most sensitive and malleable regions of the brain and is also important in cognitive function (see Figure 62.2). Within the hippocampus, the input from the entorhinal cortex to the dentate gyrus is ramified by the connections between the dentate gyrus and the CA3 pyramidal neurons. The dentate gyrus-CA3 system is believed to play a role in the memory of sequences of events, although long-term storage of memory occurs in other brain regions (Lisman & Otmakhova, 2001). But, because the DG-CA3 system is so delicately balanced between its normal function and vulnerability to damage, there is also adaptive structural plasticity, in that new neurons continue to be produced in the dentate gyrus throughout adult life, and CA3 pyramidal cells undergo a reversible remodeling of their dendrites in conditions such as hibernation and chronic stress (Magarinos, McEwen, Saboureau, & Pevet, 2006; McEwen, 1999; Popov & Bocharova, 1992; Popov, Bocharova, & Bragin, 1992). The role of this plasticity may be to protect against permanent damage, as well as to provide for renewal of memory storage processes (Leuner, Gould, & Shors, 2006).

Regarding the replacement of neurons, the subgranular layer of the dentate gyrus contains cells that have some properties of astrocytes (e.g., expression of glial fibrillary acidic protein) and which give rise to granule neurons (Kempermann & Gage, 1999; Seri, Garcia-Verdugo, McEwen, & Alvarez-Buylla, 2001). These newly born cells appear as clusters in the inner part of the granule cell layer, where a majority of them will go on to differentiate into granule neurons and establish connections with hippocampal circuitry. In the adult rat, 9,000 new neurons are estimated to be born per day and survive with a half-life of 28 days (Cameron & McKay, 2001). There are many hormonal, neurochemical, and behavioral modulators of neurogenesis and cell survival in the dentate gyrus, including estradiol, insulin-like growth factors-1 (IGF-1), antidepressants, voluntary exercise, and hippocampal-dependent learning (Aberg, Aberg, Hedbacker, Oscarsson, & Eriksson, 2000; Czeh et al., 2001; Trejo, Carro, & Torres-Aleman, 2001). With respect to stress, certain types of acute stress and many chronic stressors suppress neurogenesis or cell survival in the dentate gyrus, and the mediators of these inhibitory effects include excitatory amino acids acting via NMDA receptors and endogenous opioids (Gould, McEwen, Tanapat, Galea, & Fuchs, 1997).

BOX 62.3 (*Continued*)

Another form of structural plasticity is the remodeling of dendrites in the hippocampus. Chronic restraint stress causes retraction and simplification of dendrites in the CA3 region of the hippocampus (McEwen, 1999; Sousa, Lukoyanov, Madeira, Almeida, & Paula-Barbosa, 2000). Such dendritic reorganization is found in both dominant and subordinate rats undergoing adaptation of psychosocial stress in the visible burrow system, and it is independent of adrenal size (McKittrick et al., 2000).

What this result emphasizes is that it is not adrenal size or presumed amount of physiological stress per se that determines dendritic remodeling, but a complex set of other factors that modulate neuronal structure. Indeed, in species of mammals that hibernate, dendritic remodeling is a reversible process and occurs within hours of the onset of hibernation in European hamsters and ground squirrels, and it is also reversible within hours of wakening of the animals from torpor (Arendt et al., 2003; Magarinos et al., 2006; Popov & Bocharova, 1992; Popov et al., 1992). This implies that reorganization of the cytoskeleton is taking place rapidly and reversibly and that changes in dendrite length and branching are not damage but a form of adaptive structural plasticity.

Regarding the mechanism of structural remodeling, adrenal steroids are important mediators of remodeling of hippocampal neurons during repeated stress, and exogenous adrenal steroids can also cause remodeling in the absence of an external stressor. The role of adrenal steroids involve many interactions with neurochemical systems in the hippocampus, including serotonin, gamma amino butyric acid, and excitatory amino acids (McEwen, 1999; McEwen & Chattarji, 2004). Moreover, extracellular molecules such as polysialated neural cell adhesion molecule and tissue plasminogen activator (tPA) play a regulatory role (Pawlak, Magarinos, Melchor, McEwen, & Strickland, 2003; Pawlak, et al., 2005; Sandi, 2004), and neurotrophic factors such as brain derived neurotrophic factor (BDNF) are also implicated in maintaining dendritic shape (Govindarajan et al., 2006).

Besides endogenous factors, other hormones affect hippocampal structure and function. The hippocampus has receptors for metabolic and growth-related hormones such as insulin, IGF-1, ghrelin, and leptin, along with transport mechanisms for getting them from the blood into the brain (McEwen, 2007).

BOX 62.4 PREFRONTAL CORTEX AND AMYGDALA

Repeated stress also causes structural remodeling in other brain regions such as the prefrontal cortex and amygdala (Figure 62.2). Repeated stress causes dendritic shortening in medial prefrontal cortex (Brown, Henning, & Wellman, 2005; Cook & Wellman, 2004; Kreibich & Blendy, 2004; Liston et al., 2006; Radley, Rocher, Janssen, et al., 2005; Radley, Rocher, Miller, et al., 2005; Radley, et al., 2003, 2004; Sousa et al., 2000; Vyas, Mitra, Rao, & Chattarji, 2002; Wellman, 2001) but produces dendritic growth in neurons in amygdala (Vyas et al., 2002), as well as in orbitofrontal cortex (Liston et al., 2006). Along with many other brain regions, the amygdala and prefrontal cortex also contain adrenal steroid receptors; however, the role of adrenal steroids, excitatory amino acids, and other mediators has not yet been studied in these brain regions. Nevertheless, in the amygdala, there is some evidence regarding mechanism, in that tissue plasminogen activator (tPA) is required for acute stress not only to activate indexes of structural plasticity but also to enhance anxiety (Melchor, Pawlak, & Strickland, 2003). These effects occur in the medial and central amygdala and not in the basolateral amygdala, and the release of CRH acting via CRH1 receptors appears to be responsible (Matys et al., 2004).

Acute stress induces spine synapses in the CA1 region of the hippocampus (Shors, Chua, & Falduto, 2001), and both acute and chronic stress will increase spine synapse formation in the amygdala (Mitra, Kadhav, McEwen, Vyas, & Chattarji, 2005; Vyas et al., 2002), but chronic stress decreases it in the hippocampus (Pawlak et al., 2005). Moreover, chronic stress for 21 days or longer impairs hippocampal-dependent cognitive function (McEwen, 1999) and enhances amygdala-dependent unlearned fear and fear conditioning (Conrad, Magarinos, LeDoux, & McEwen, 1999), which are consistent with the opposite effects of stress on hippocampal and amygdala structure. Chronic stress also increases aggression between animals living in the same cage, and this is likely to reflect another aspect of hyperactivity of the amygdala (Wood, Young, Reagan, & McEwen, 2003). Behavioral correlates of remodeling in the prefrontal cortex include impairment in attention set shifting, possibly reflecting structural remodeling in the medial prefrontal cortex (Liston et al., 2006).

The Human Brain Under Stress

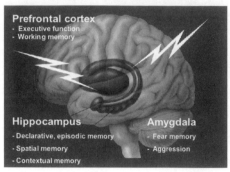

Figure 62.2   Brain regions that are involved in perception and response to stress and that show structural remodeling as a result of stress, as described in the text.

negative consequences of chronic stress, such as the shortening of telomeres associated with being a caregiver (Epel et al., 2004) or the impairment of immune function and wound healing associated with marital conflict (Kiecolt-Glaser et al., 2005), or intensely studying for an exam (Marucha, Kiecolt-Glaser, & Favagehi, 1998). There are also investigations of the effects of job strain and demand versus sense of control on cardiovascular health (Reed, Lacroix, Karasek, Miller, & MacLean, 1989; Pickering et al., 1996; Schnall et al., 1990; Theorell et al., 1998). These effects are not necessarily a matter of duration of stress but rather factors such as sense of control (Theorell, Westerlund, Alfredsson, & Oxenstierna, 2005); feelings of time pressure (Williams et al., 1997); sense of reward and accomplishment or lack thereof, as in burnout (David et al., 2005); and sense of optimism or pessimism (Folkman, 1997; Steptoe, Wardle, & Marmot, 2005). Self-esteem and locus of control play an important role and are linked to different patterns of response of mediators of allostasis and also neurological features such as the size of the hippocampus (Pruessner et al., 2005; Pruessner, Hellhammer, & Kirschbaum, 1999).

How Experiences and Behaviors Interact and Affect Health

A common experience is being stressed out, and this often involves the subjective feeling of being under time pressure or feeling a lack of control as well as anxiety. Being stressed out leads to coping behaviors such as eating excessively, smoking, drinking alcohol, and neglecting regular moderate exercise and social interactions. Sleep quality and quantity may also suffer and produce negative effects (Friedman et al., 2005; McEwen, 2006b; Spiegel, Leproult, & Van Cauter, 1999; see following list). The individual experiences that

contribute to being stressed out may not be easily identified through marked elevations of classical stress hormones such as cortisol or adrenalin, except perhaps through continuous monitoring or repeated sampling. Nevertheless, the net result is a dysregulation of networks of allostasis that often cannot be measured until it lasts for days, weeks, months, or years, and produces more easily measurable consequences such as persistent hypertension, abdominal obesity, chronically elevated blood glucose, and atherosclerotic plaques. Some of the physiological consequences of sleep deprivation are summarized in the following list:

Increased blood pressure; decreased parasympathetic tone

Elevated evening cortisol, glucose, insulin

Elevated inflammatory cytokines

Increased appetite and caloric load, which can increase physiological measures: blood pressure, cortisol, and inflammatory cytokines

Abdominal fat deposition

Depressed mood

Impaired cognitive function

Note: Adapted from "Sleep Deprivation as a Neurobiologic and Physiologic Stressor: Allostasis and Allostatic Load" B. S. McEwen, 2006b, *Metabolism,* 55, pp. S20–S23.

Physiological dysregulation can be detected and involves alterations in many of the mediators of allostasis discussed earlier; this can be illustrated for the consequences of poor sleep. Sleep deprivation is a common problem in modern life, and chronic stress and resulting changes in coping behaviors, together with the lack of adequate sleep, contribute to allostatic overload.

These factors can be assembled into an overview of what happens physiologically from being stressed out. Chronic life stressors (e.g., interpersonal conflicts, caregiving, pressure at work, crowded, noisy living and working conditions) create a sense of chaos and conflict and a lack of control. The individual may already have a preexisting history of negative or positive experiences that predispose him/her to certain types of reaction to external events. The result of chronic stress will often be chronic anxiety and depressed mood with poor quality sleep. Anxiety, mood changes, and inadequate sleep lead to self-medication through eating comfort foods, drinking alcohol, smoking, or in some cases, anorexia. These alterations in mood and anxiety, along with the distress associated with ongoing events, may cause the person to become socially isolated and to neglect regular physical activity.

Together with anxiety, depressed mood, and poor sleep, all the listed behaviors contribute to dysregulated physiological responses and contribute to an ongoing allostatic overload involving elevated cortisol, insulin, and inflammatory cytokines at night, along with increased heart rate and blood pressure and reduced parasympathetic tone. If this abnormal dysregulated state persists for months and years, there are likely to be adverse health outcomes such as hypertension, coronary disease, stroke, obesity, diabetes, arthritis, major depression, GI disorders, chronic pain, and chronic fatigue.

In contrast to the situation for human beings in modern society, in nature, eating a lot of food and putting on body mass in the autumn is an adaptive behavior in animals that hibernate and burn off the fat and excess calories during the winter; however, it is only when animals are captives in zoos that symptoms reminiscent of allostatic overload in human beings begin to appear (McEwen & Wingfield, 2003).

Central Role of the Brain in Stress, Allostasis, and Allostatic Load/Overload

As depicted in Figure 62.3, the brain is the central organ of stress, allostasis, and allostatic load because it controls behavioral and physiological responses to any change in the external world and also is part of an internal state of the individual that anticipates and worries about events and situations that may or may not take place. The brain determines if an external event is threatening and activates the fight-or-flight stress response.

As discussed later in this chapter and noted in Figure 62.3, individual differences due to genetic factors, early life experiences, and experiences in adult life determine the state of the brain and body for the response to stressors and other events. Major life events, trauma and abuse, and daily hassles of work, family, and community constitute the major categories of experiences that activate allostasis and contribute to allostatic load and overload.

What happens to the brain under acute and chronic stress? Studies in animal models have revealed that the brain responds to stressors and is capable of structural remodeling of neurons in a largely reversible way. In rats and mice, repeated restraint stress, as well as certain chronic psychosocial stressors, cause neurons in hippocampus to undergo remodeling—shortening of dendrites and reduction in synapse density—a process that is mediated by excitatory amino acids in combination with glucocorticoids and other mediators (e.g., local growth factors, extracellular proteases, insulin, and glucose). There is modest impairment of hippocampal dependent learning. The remodeling and cognitive impairment are reversible in 7–10 days with the termination of the daily stress.

A similar type of chronic stress induced remodeling occurs in the medial prefrontal cortex, whereas the basolateral amygdala and orbitofrontal cortex show expansion of dendrites and increased spine synapse density as a result of the same stress regimen. Chronic stress causes increases in anxiety and aggression and decreases in cognitive flexibility that are likely to be the result of these neuroanatomical changes.

FROM ANIMAL MODELS TO THE HUMAN BRAIN

Much of the impetus for studying the effects of stress on the structure of the human brain has come from the animal studies summarized thus far, and there is emerging information on the effects of both acute and chronic

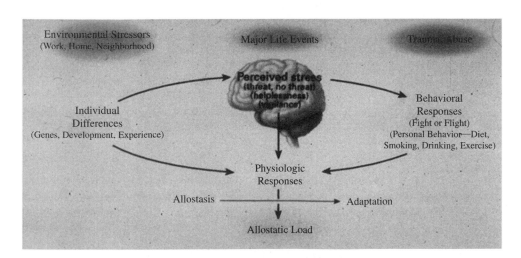

Figure 62.3 Central role of the brain in allostasis and the behavioral and physiological response to stressors.

Note: From "Protective and Damaging Effects of Stress Mediators," by B. S. McEwen, 1998, *New England Journal of Medicine, 338,* p. 172. Reprinted with permission.

stress on human brain structure and function that is consistent with the animal model findings. Functional imaging of individuals undergoing acute stressors, such as counting backward, show that there are changes in neural activity that last for many minutes after the end of the stressor and may be caused by mediators such as cortisol (Wang et al., 2005). Regarding chronic stress, a 20-year assessment of chronic perceived life stress in women has revealed a dose-response relationship, with hippocampal volume being smaller in those individuals with the highest average stress level over the 2 decades, although there were no initial volumetric measures for comparison since structural MRI did not exist at that time (Gianaros et al., 2007).

Moreover, the study of depressive illness and anxiety disorders has also provided some insights of what happens when the brain and body cannot successfully cope. Life events are known to precipitate depressive illness in individuals with certain genetic predispositions (Kendler, 1998; Caspi et al., 2003; Kessler, 1997). Moreover, brain regions such as the hippocampus, amygdala, and prefrontal cortex show altered patterns of activity in PET and fMRI and also demonstrate changes in volume with recurrent depression: that is, decreased volume of hippocampus and prefrontal cortex and amygdala (Drevets et al., 1997; Sheline, Gado, & Kraemer, 2003; Sheline, Sanghavi, Mintun, & Gado, 1999). Interestingly, amygdala volume has been reported to increase in the first episode of depression, whereas hippocampal volume is not decreased until the depression has existed for a number of years (Frodl et al., 2003; MacQueen et al., 2003). Major depressive illness is also associated with increased risk for cardiovascular disease, and abdominal obesity, as well as a comorbidity with Type 2 diabetes (Evans et al., 2005).

It has been known for some time that stress hormones, such as cortisol, are involved in psychopathology, reflecting emotional arousal and psychic disorganization rather than the specific disorder per se (Sachar et al., 1973). Indeed, we know that adrenocortical hormones enter the brain and produce a wide range of effects on it. One of the consequences, in Cushing's disease, is depressive symptoms that can be relieved by surgical correction of the hypercortisolemia (Murphy, 1991; Starkman & Schteingart, 1981). Both major depression and Cushing's disease are associated with chronic elevation of cortisol that results in gradual loss of minerals from bone and abdominal obesity (Steingart et al., 2000). In major depressive illness, as well as in Cushing's disease, the duration of the illness and not the age of the subjects predicts a progressive reduction in volume of the hippocampus, determined by structural magnetic resonance imaging (Sheline et al., 1999; Starkman, Gebarski, Berent, & Schteingart, 1992). Moreover, there

are other anxiety-related disorders, such as post-traumatic stress disorder (PTSD; Bremner, 2002; Pitman, 2001) and borderline personality disorder (Driessen et al., 2000), in which atrophy of the hippocampus has been reported, suggesting that this is a common process reflecting chronic imbalance in the activity of adaptive systems, such as the HPA axis, but also including endogenous neurotransmitters, such as glutamate.

Another important factor in hippocampal volume and function is glucose regulation. Poor glucose regulation is associated with smaller hippocampal volume and poorer memory function in individuals with Type 2 diabetes, and hippocampal volume decrease is linearly related to elevated glycosylated hemoglobin levels in blood. Moreover, prior to outright Type 2 diabetes, there is also hippocampal volume reduction related to poor glucose control in individuals in their 60s and 70s who have "mild cognitive impairment" (MCI; Convit, Wolf, Tarshish, & de Leon, 2003). Both MCI and Type 2, as well as Type 1, diabetes are recognized as risk factors for dementia (de Leon et al., 2001; Haan, 2006; Ott et al., 1996).

Linking Psychology of Coping with Neurobiology and Physiology of Adaptation

Recent studies provide linkages between the biology of allostasis and adaptation and the psychology of coping. A risk factor for poor coping ability is low self-esteem and there are now neurobiological and physiological links to the conditions that create allostatic overload. Poor self-esteem and low locus of control has been shown to cause recurrent increases in cortisol levels during a repetition of a public speaking challenge in which those individuals with good self-esteem can habituate, that is, attenuate their cortisol response after the first speech (Kirschbaum et al., 1995). Furthermore, poor self-esteem and low internal locus of control have been related to 12% to 13% smaller volume of the hippocampus, as well as higher cortisol levels during a mental arithmetic stressor (Pruessner et al., 1999, 2005). A smaller hippocampus may be a causal factor in elevated cortisol, given its role in shutting off the HPA axis in the aftermath of a stressor (Herman & Cullinan, 1997; Jacobson & Sapolsky, 1991). An important question is when and how these changes in the brain come about— whether they have a genetic component or are the result of early life experiences. Another future challenge is whether improving self-esteem would enlarge the hippocampus!

Having a positive outlook on life and good self-esteem also appear to have long-lasting health consequences (Pressman & Cohen, 2005). Positive affect, assessed by aggregating momentary experiences throughout a working or leisure day, was found to be associated with lower cortisol production and higher heart rate variability (showing higher parasympathetic activity), as well as a lower fibrinogen response to a mental stress test (Steptoe et al., 2005). Related to both positive affect and self-esteem is the role of friends and social interactions in maintaining a healthy outlook on life. Loneliness, often found in people with low self-esteem, has been associated with larger cortisol responses to wakening in the morning and higher fibrinogen and natural killer cell responses to a mental stress test, as well as sleep problems (Steptoe, Owen, Kunz-Ebrecht, & Brydon, 2004). Having three or more regular social contacts, as opposed to zero to two such contacts, is associated with lower allostatic load scores (Seeman, Singer, Ryff, Dienberg, & Levy-Storms, 2002).

Social ties and social support play a role in the beneficial effects of physical activity on physiological and cognitive health, as demonstrated in numerous studies with regard to reducing the incidence of cardiovascular disease (Bernadet, 1995; Colcombe et al., 2004) and dementia (Larson et al., 2006; Rovio et al., 2005). Regular physical activity is also an effective treatment for depression. In the Diabetes Prevention Trial, 30 minutes of walking per day sustained over a 6-year period, along with lifestyle and behavioral interventions, reduced the incidence of Type 2 diabetes by almost 60% (http://diabetes.niddk.nih.gov/dm/pubs/preventionprogram).

A similar intervention program, but lasting only 6 months, improved executive function and brain activation patterns in cerebral cortical areas linked to attention and executive function (Kramer et al., 1999, 2003). To get people to maintain a long-term program of daily physical activity, it is necessary to establish and maintain social ties and social support systems; hence, the effects of physical activity per se are difficult to distinguish from the social support (Wing, 2003). In one of the studies noted here, however, social support was similar in two groups of participants, in which one group did aerobic exercise and the other a toning program; only the aerobic exercise was found to benefit executive function (Kramer et al., 1999).

Gene-Environment Interactions and Allostasis and Allostatic Overload

Individuals differ in how they respond to stressors and this is based on at least four factors: First, experiences in adult life; second, experiences early in life; third, genetic constitution; fourth, how the experiential factors are manifested in *epigenetic effects*.

As for experiences in adult life, positive or negative experiences in school, at work, or in romantic and family interpersonal relationships can bias an individual toward either a positive or negative response in a new situation;

someone who has been treated badly in a job by an abusive supervisor or has been fired will approach a new job situation quite differently from someone who has had positive experiences in employment.

Early life experiences carry an even greater weight in terms of how an individual reacts to new situations. Animal models have been useful in providing insights into behavioral and physiological mechanisms by revealing effects of prenatal stress, postnatal abuse by mothers, and food insecurity by mothers on anxiety and attachment of offspring (see McEwen, 2007, for summary). Early life maternal care in rodents is a powerful determinant of lifelong emotional reactivity and stress hormone reactivity and increases in both are associated with earlier cognitive decline and a shorter life span (Cavigelli & McClintock, 2003; Francis, Diorio, Liu, & Meaney, 1999). Strong maternal behavior, involving licking and grooming of the offspring, produces a neophilic animal that is more exploratory of novel environments, less emotionally reactive, and produces a lower and more contained glucocorticoid stress response in novel situations. Poor maternal care leads to a neophobic phenotype with increased emotional and HPA reactivity and less exploration of a novel situation (Meaney et al., 1994).

Effects of early maternal care are transmitted across generations by the subsequent behavior of the female offspring as they become mothers, and methylation of DNA on key genes appears to play a role in this epigenetic transmission (Francis et al., 1999; Weaver et al., 2004). More generally, *epigenetics*, meaning "above the genome" was originally defined to mean the gene-environment interactions that bring about the phenotype of an individual. Now, epigenetics means something more specific in molecular terms: the methylation of cytosine bases in DNA along with modifications of histones that modify unfolding of chromatin to expose DNA sequences that can be read and transcribed (Jirtle & Skinner, 2007; see Box 62.5).

Translation to Human Physiology and Behavior

Animal models help us understand how early life experiences affect human physiology and behavior. Early life physical and sexual abuse carry with it a lifelong burden of behavioral and pathophysiological problems (Felitti et al., 1998; Heim & Nemeroff, 2001). Moreover, cold and uncaring families produce long-lasting emotional problems in children (Repetti, Taylor, & Seeman, 2002). Some of these effects are seen on brain structure and function and in the risk for later depression and post-traumatic stress disorder (Kaufman & Charney, 1999; Kaufman, Plotsky, Nemeroff, & Charney, 2000; Vermetten, Schmahl, Lindner, Loewenstein, & Bremner, 2006). Prenatal stress is believed to be a factor in causing preterm birth, as well

BOX 62.5 EPIGENETICS AND HISTONE MODIFICATIONS

The pioneering work of Allfrey, Mirsky, and colleagues in the 1960s and 1970s demonstrated the relationship of transcriptional activation of chromatin and the modification of histones by acetylation and phosphorylation (Frenster, Allfrey, & Mirsky, 1963), and presented a conceptual framework for understanding the role of histone modifications in the unfolding of DNA-protein complexes to allow transcription during states of gene activation (Allfrey, 1977). Recent work has revealed that there is a complex language of epigenetic modifications that regulate transcription, both up and down (Berger, 2007; Strahl & Allis, 2000).

Epigenetic modifications are of several types. There are genes with metastable epialleles, in which modifications that affect gene expression are reversible. The murine agouti gene is linked to altered coat color, diabetes, obesity, and tumorigenesis, and genetically identical mice can be induced to show these traits by dietary manipulations (Jirtle & Skinner, 2007). There are also imprinted genes that transfer the epigenetic state through the germline (e.g., the murine IGF2 gene, which is passed on in a modified state in the paternal genome, and the IGF2R gene that is transferred in a modified state in the maternal genome). In humans, the severe developmental disorders, Prader-Willi and Angelman syndromes, are examples of epigenetic modifications that are transmitted in the germ line (Jirtle & Skinner, 2007).

as full-term birth with low birth weight (Barker, 1997; Wadhwa, Sandman, & Garite, 2001). Low birth weight is a risk factor for cardiovascular disease and high body mass (Barker, 1997; Power, Li, Manor, & Davey Smith, 2003). Childhood experiences in emotionally cold families increase the likelihood of poor mental and physical health later in life (Repetti et al., 2002), and abuse in childhood is a well-known risk factor for depression, post-traumatic stress disorder, idiopathic chronic pain disorders, substance abuse, and antisocial behavior, as well as obesity, diabetes, and cardiovascular disease (Anda et al., 2006; Felitti et al., 1998; Heim & Nemeroff, 2001).

Chaos in the home environment is a key determinant of poor self-regulatory behaviors, a sense of helplessness, and psychological distress (Evans, Gonnella, Marcynyszyn, Gentile, & Salpekar, 2004), as well as increased body mass and elevated blood pressure (Evans, 2003). One of the lasting consequences of low socioeconomic status in childhood is an elevation in body mass as well as poor dental health (Poulton et al., 2002). Social isolation in childhood

increases the risk of cardiovascular disease later in life (Caspi, Harrington, Moffitt, Milne, & Poulton, 2006) and childhood abuse is linked to an increased pro-inflammatory tone, as measured by elevated C-reactive protein levels (McEwen & Chattarji, 2007) that were made decades later in life.

In addition to the effects of experiences, genetic differences also play an important role as part of the nature-nurture interaction. This is a vast and growing topic, and only some examples will be noted here. The short form of the serotonin transporter is associated with conditions such as alcoholism (Barr et al., 2004; Herman et al., 2005), and individuals who have this allele are more vulnerable to respond to stressful experiences by developing depressive illness (Caspi et al., 2003). In childhood, individuals with an allele of the monoamine oxidase A gene are more vulnerable to abuse in childhood and more likely themselves to become abusers and to show antisocial behaviors compared with individuals who have another commonly occurring allele (Caspi et al., 2002). Yet another example is the consequence of having the Val66Met allele of the BDNF gene on hippocampal volume, memory, and mood disorders (Chen et al., 2006; Hariri et al., 2003; Jiang et al., 2005; Pezawas et al., 2004; Szeszko et al., 2005). A mouse model of this genotype has revealed reduced dendritic branching in the hippocampus, impaired contextual fear conditioning, and increased anxiety that is less sensitive to antidepressant treatment (Chen et al., 2006). Finally, certain alleles of the glucocorticoid receptor gene that are found in the normal population confer a higher sensitivity to glucocorticoids for both negative feedback and insulin responsiveness (Huizenga et al., 1998) or glucocorticoid resistance (van Rossum et al., 2006), and there is evidence of increased likelihood of depression in several alleles and increased response to antidepressants in one of them.

SUMMARY

Given the pervasive nature of allostatic load resulting from chronic stress and altered health-related behaviors, it is important to consider briefly the most effective ways of intervening to prevent or treat these conditions. For the purposes of this overview, there are three overlapping categories to consider: (1) individual behavioral change; (2) policies of government and the private sector that provide services, create incentives, and offer opportunities for individuals to develop healthier lifestyles and behaviors; and (3) medications to treat disorders or slow down or prevent disease processes.

From the standpoint of the individual, it almost goes without saying that a major goal should be to try to improve sleep quality and quantity, have good social support and a positive outlook on life, maintain a healthy diet, avoid smoking, and engage in regular moderate physical activity. Concerning physical activity, it is not necessary to become an extreme athlete, and seemingly any amount of moderate physical activity helps (Bernadet, 1995; Rovio et al., 2005).

From the standpoint of policy of government and the private sector, the goal should be to create incentives at home and in work situations and build community services and opportunities that encourage the development of beneficial individual lifestyle practices. Providing access to affordable, healthy food, creating recreational opportunities, providing safe neighborhoods, and enhancing social cohesion are all likely to be beneficial (Sampson, Raudenbush, & Earls, 1997).

As easy as it is to say these things, finding the political will and creating effective policies is a daunting task. By the same token, for the individual, changing behavior and solving problems that cause stress at work and at home is often difficult and may require professional help on the personal level, or even a change of job or profession. Yet, these are important goals because the prevention of later disease is important for full enjoyment of life and also to reduce the financial burden on the individual and on society.

Nevertheless, many people often lack the proactive, long-term view of themselves or feel that they must maintain a stressful lifestyle, and if they deal with these issues at all, they want to treat their problems with a pill. There are many useful pharmaceutical agents: Sleep-inducing agents, anxiolytics, beta-blockers, and antidepressants are all drugs that counteract some of the problems associated with being stressed out. Likewise, drugs that reduce oxidative stress or inflammation, or block cholesterol synthesis or absorption, or treat insulin resistance or chronic pain can help deal with the metabolic and neurological consequences of being stressed out and slow down the progression of allostatic load and associated pathophysiology. All such medications are valuable to some degree, and yet each one has side effects and limitations that are based in part on the fact that all the systems that are dysregulated in allostatic overload are also systems that interact with each other and perform normal functions when properly regulated. Because of the nonlinearity of the systems of allostasis, the consequences of any drug treatment may be either to inhibit the beneficial effects of the systems in question or to perturb other systems that interact with it in a direction that promotes an unwanted side effect. So the best solution may be to avoid relying solely on such medications and to search for ways of changing lifestyle in a positive direction that reduces the need of such agents.

REFERENCES

Aberg, M. A., Aberg, N. D., Hedbacker, H., Oscarsson, J., & Eriksson, P. S. (2000). Peripheral infusion of IGF-1 selectively induces neurogenesis in the adult rat hippocampus. *Journal of Neuroscience, 20,* 2896–2903.

Allfrey, V. G. (1977). Post-synthetic modifications of histone structure. A mechanism for the control of chromosome structure by the modulation of DNA-histone interactions. In *Chromatin and Chromosome Structure* (pp. 167–199). New York: Academic Press.

Anda, R. F., Felitti, V. J., Bremner, J. D., Walker, J. D., Whitfield, C., Perry, B. D., et al. (2006). The enduring effects of abuse and related adverse experiences in childhood. *European Archives of Psychiatry and Clinical Neuroscience, 256,* 174–186.

Arendt, T., Stieler, J., Strijkstra, A. M., Hut, R. A., Rudiger, J., Van der Zee, E. A., et al. (2003). Reversible paired helical filament-like phosphorylation of tau is an adaptive process associated with neuronal plasticity in hibernating animals. *Journal of Neuroscience, 23,* 6972–6981.

Avitsur, R., Stark, J. L., & Sheridan, J. F. (2001). Social stress induces glucocorticoid resistance in subordinate animals. *Hormones and Behavior, 39,* 247–257.

Barbe, M. F., & Barr, A. E. (2006). Inflammation and the pathophysiology of work-related musculoskeletal disorders. *Brain, Behavior, and Immunity, 20,* 423–429.

Barker, D. J. P. (1997). The fetal origins of coronary heart disease. *Acta Paediatrica: Supplement, 422,* 78–82.

Barr, C. S., Newman, T. K., Lindell, S., Shannon, C., Champoux, M., Lesch, K. P., et al. (2004). Interaction between serotonin transporter gene variation and rearing condition in alcohol preference and consumption in female primates. *Archives of General Psychiatry, 61,* 1146–1152.

Berger, S. L. (2007). The complex language of chromatin regulation during transcription. *Nature, 447,* 347–412.

Bernadet, P. (1995). Benefits of physical activity in the prevention of cardiovascular disease. *Journal of Cardiovascular Pharmacology, 25* (Suppl. 1), S3–S8.

Bierhaus, A., Schiekofer, S., Schwaninger, M., Andrassy, M., Humpert, P. M., Chen, J., et al., (2001). Diabetes-associated sustained activation of the transcription factor nuclear factor-kB. *Diabetes, 50,* 2792–2808.

Bierhaus, A., Wolf, J., Andrassy, M., Rohleder, N., Humpert, P. M., Petrov, D., et al., (2003). A mechanism converting psychosocial stress into mononuclear cell activation. *Proceedings of the National Academy of Sciences, USA, 100,* 1920–1925.

Black, P. H., & Garbutt, L. D. (2002). Stress, inflammation and cardiovascular disease. *Journal of Psychosomatic Research, 52,* 1–23.

Borovikova, L. V., Ivanova, S., Zhang, M., Yang, H., Botchkina, G. I., Watkins, L. R., et al. (2000). Vagus nerve stimulation attenuates the systemic inflammatory response to endotoxin. *Nature, 405,* 458–462.

Brami-Cherrier, K., Lavaur, J., Pages, C., Arthur, J. S. C., & Caboche, J. (2007). Glutamate induces histone H3 phosphorylation but not acetylation in striatal neurons: Role of mitogen- and stress-activated kinase-1. *Journal of Neurochemistry, 101,* 697–708.

Bremner, J. D. (2002). Neuroimaging studies in post-traumatic stress disorder. *Current Psychiatry Reports, 4,* 254–263.

Brindley, D. N., & Rolland, Y. (1989). Possible connections between stress, diabetes, obesity, hypertension and altered lipoprotein metabolism that may result in atherosclerosis. *Clinical Science, 77,* 453–461.

Brown, S. M., Henning, S., & Wellman, C. L. (2005). Mild, short-term stress alters dendritic morphology in rat medial prefrontal cortex. *Cerebral Cortex, 30,* 1–9.

Cameron, H. A., & McKay, R. D. G. (2001). Adult neurogenesis produces a large pool of new granule cells in the dentate gyrus. *Journal of Comparative Neurology, 435,* 406–417.

Cannon, W. B. *The wisdom of the body.* (1932). New York: Norton and Co.

Caspi, A., Harrington, H. L., Moffitt, T. E., Milne, B. J., & Poulton, R. (2006). Socially isolated children 20 years later. Risk of cardiovascular disease. *Archives of Pediatrics and Adolescent Medicine, 160*, 805–811.

Caspi, A., McClay, J., Moffitt, T. E., Mill, J., Martin, J., Craig, I. W., et al. (2002). Role of genotype in the cycle of violence in maltreated children. *Science, 297*, 851–854.

Caspi, A., Sugden, K., Moffitt, T. E., Taylor, A., Craig, I. W., Harrington, H., et al. (2003). Influence of life stress on depression: Moderation by a polymorphism in the 5-HTT gene. *Science, 301*, 386–389.

Cavigelli, S. A., & McClintock, M. K. (2003). Fear of novelty in infant rats predicts adult corticosterone dynamics and an early death. *Proceedings of the National Academy of Sciences, USA, 100*, 16131–16136.

Chen, Z.-Y., Jing, D., Bath, K. G., Ieraci, A., Khan, T., Siao, C.-J., et al. (2006). Genetic variant BDNF (Val66Met) polymorphism alters anxiety-related behavior. *Science, 314*, 140–143.

Chrousos, G. P. (1998). Stressors, stress, and neuroendocrine integration of the adaptive response. *Annals, N. Y. Acad. Sci., 851*, 311–335.

Chrousos, G. P. (2000). The role of stress and the hypothalamic-pituitary-adrenal axis in the pathogenesis of the metabolic syndrome: Neuroendocrine and target tissue-related causes. *International Journal of Obesity, 24*, S50–S55.

Colcombe, S. J., Kramer, A. F., Erickson, K. I., Scalf, P., McAuley, E., Cohen, N. J., et al. (2004). Cardiovascular fitness, cortical plasticity, and aging. *Proceedings of the National Academy of Sciences, USA, 101*, 3316–3321.

Conrad, C. D., Magarinos, A. M., LeDoux, J. E., & McEwen, B. S. (1999). Repeated restraint stress facilitates fear conditioning independently of causing hippocampal CA3 dendritic atrophy. *Behavioral Neuroscience, 113*, 902–913.

Convit, A., Wolf, O. T., Tarshish, C., & de Leon, M. J. (2003). Reduced glucose tolerance is associated with poor memory performance and hippocampal atrophy among normal elderly. *Proceedings of the National Academy of Sciences, USA, 100*, 2019–2022.

Cook, S. C., & Wellman, C. L. (2004). Chronic stress alters dendritic morphology in rat medial prefrontal cortex. *Journal of Neurobiology, 60*, 236–248.

Czeh, B., Michaelis, T., Watanabe, T., Frahm, J., de Biurrun, G., van Kampen, M., et al. (2001). Stress-induced changes in cerebral metabolites, hippocampal volume and cell proliferation are prevented by antidepressant treatment with tianeptine. *Proceedings of the National Academy of Sciences, USA, 98*, 12796–12801.

David, S., Stegenga, S. L., Hu, P., Xiong, G., Kerr, E., Becker, K. B., et al. (2005). Expression of serum- and glucocorticoid-inducible kinase is regulated in an experience-dependent manner and can cause dendrite growth. *Journal of Neuroscience, 25*, 7048–7053.

de Leon, M. J., Convit, A., Wolf, O. T., Tarshish, C. Y., DeSanti, S., Rusinek, H., et al. (2001). Prediction of cognitive decline in normal elderly subjects with 2-[18F]fluoro-2-deoxy-D-glucose/positron-emission tomography (FDG/PET). *Proceedings of the National Academy of Sciences, USA, 98*, 10966–10971.

Desouza, L. A., Ladiwala, U., Daniel, S. M., Agashe, S., Vaidya, R. A., & Vaidya, V. A. (2005). Thyroid hormone regulates hippocampal neurogenesis in the adult rat brain. *Molecular and Cellular Neurosciences, 29*, 414–426.

Dhabhar, F. S. (2002). Stress-induced augmentation of immune function—The role of stress hormones, leukocyte trafficking, and cytokines. *Brain, Behavior, and Immunity, 16*, 785–798.

Dhabhar, F. S., & McEwen, B. S. (1997). Acute stress enhances while chronic stress suppresses cell-mediated immunity in vivo: A potential role for leukocyte trafficking. *Brain, Behavior, and Immunity, 11*, 286–306.

Dhabhar, F. S., Satoskar, A. R., Bluethmann, H., David, J. R., & McEwen, B. S. (2000). Stress-induced enhancement of skin immune function: A role for g interferon. *Proceedings of the National Academy of Sciences, USA, 97*, 2846–2851.

Drevets, W. C., Price, J. L., Simpson Jr, J. R., Todd, R. D., Reich, T., Vannier, M., et al. (1997). Subgenual prefrontal cortex abnormalities in mood disorders. *Nature, 386*, 824–827.

Driessen, M., Hermann, J., Stahl, K., Zwaan, M., Meier, S., Hill, A., et al. (2000). Magnetic resonance imaging volumes of the hippocampus and the amygdala in women with borderline personality disorder and early traumatization. *Archives of General Psychiatry, 57*, 1115–1122.

Epel, E. S., Blackburn, E. H., Lin, J., Dhabhar, F. S., Adler, N. E., Morrow, J. D., et al. (2004). Accelerated telomere shortening in response to life stress. *Proceedings of the National Academy of Sciences, USA, 101*, 17312–17315.

Evans, D. L., Charney, D. S., Lewis, L., Golden, R. N., Gorman, J. M., Krishnan, K. R. R., et al. (2005). Mood disorders in the medically ill: Scientific review and recommendation. *Biological Psychiatry, 58*, 175–189.

Evans, G. W. (2003). A multimethodological analysis of cumulative risk and allostatic load among rural children. *Developmental Psychology, 39*, 924–933.

Evans, G. W., Gonnella, C., Marcynyszyn, L. A., Gentile, L., & Salpekar, N. (2004). The role of chaos in poverty and children's socioemotional adjustment. *Psychol Science, 16*, 560–565.

Felitti, V. J., Anda, R. F., Nordenberg, D., Williamson, D. F., Spitz, A. M., Edwards, V., et al. (1998). Relationship of childhood abuse and household dysfunction to many of the leading causes of death in adults. The adverse childhood experiences (ACE) study. *American Journal of Preventive Medicine, 14*, 245–258.

Folkman, S. (1997). Positive psychological states and coping with severe stress. *Social Science and Medicine, 45*, 1207–1221.

Francis, D., Diorio, J., Liu, D., & Meaney, M. J. (1999). Nongenomic transmission across generations of maternal behavior and stress responses in the rat. *Science, 286*, 1155–1158.

Frenster, J. H., Allfrey, V. G., & Mirsky, A. E. (1963). Repressed and active chromatin isolated from interphase lymphocytes. *Proceedings of the National Academy of Sciences, USA, 50*, 1026–1032.

Friedman, E. M., Hayney, M. S., Love, G. D., Urry, H. L., Rosenkranz, M. A., Davidson, R. J., et al. (2005). Social relationships, sleep quality, and interleukin-6 in aging women. *Proceedings of the National Academy of Sciences, USA, 102*, 18757–18762.

Frodl, T., Meisenzahl, E. M., Zetzsche, T., Born, C., Jager, M., Groll, C., et al. (2003). Larger amygdala volumes in first depressive episode as compared to recurrent major depression and healthy control subjects. *Biological Psychiatry, 53*, 338–344.

Gianaros, P. J., Jennings, J. R., Sheu, L. K., Greer, P. J., Kuller, L. H., & Matthews, K. A. (2007). Prospective reports of chronic life stress predict decreased grey matter volume in the hippocampus. *NeuroImage, 35*, 795–803.

Goldstein, D. S. (1995). *Stress, catecholamines, and cardiovascular disease.* New York: Oxford University Press.

Gould, E., McEwen, B. S., Tanapat, P., Galea, L. A. M., & Fuchs, E. (1997). Neurogenesis in the dentate gyrus of the adult tree shrew is regulated by psychosocial stress and NMDA receptor activation. *Journal of Neuroscience, 17*, 2492–2498.

Govindarajan, A., Rao, B. S. S., Nair, D., Trinh, M., Mawjee, N., Tonegawa, S., et al. (2006). Transgenic brain-derived neurotrophic factor expression causes both anxiogenic and antidepressant effects. *Proceedings of the National Academy of Sciences, USA, 103*, 13208–13213.

Haan, M. N. (2006). Therapy insight: Type 2 diabetes mellitus and the risk of late-onset Alzheimer's disease. *Nature Clinical Practice: Neurology*, 2, 159–166.

Hariri, A. R., Goldberg, T. E., Mattay, V. S., Kolachana, B. S., Callicott, J. H., Egan, M. F., et al. (2003). Brain-derived neurotrophic factor val[66] met polymorphism affects human memory-related hippocampal activity and predicts memory performance. *Journal of Neuroscience*, 23, 6690–6694.

Heim, C., & Nemeroff, C. B. (2001). The role of childhood trauma in the neurobiology of mood and anxiety disorders: Preclinical and clinical studies. *Biological Psychiatry*, 49, 1023–1039.

Herman, A. I., Kaiss, K. M., Ma, R., Philbeck, J. W., Hasan, A., Dasti, H., et al. (2005). Serotonin transporter promoter polymorphism and monoamine oxidase type A VNTR allelic variants together influence alcohol binge drinking risk in young women. *American Journal of Medical Genetics: Part B, Neuropsychiatric Genetics, 133B*, 74–78.

Herman, J. P., & Cullinan, W. E. (1997). Neurocircuitry of stress: Central control of the hypothalamo-pituitary-adrenocortical axis. *Trends in Neuroscience*, 20, 78–84.

Huizenga, N. A. T. M., Koper, J. W., De Lange, P., Pols, H. A. P., Stolk, R. P., Burger, H., et al. (1998). A polymorphism in the glucocorticoid receptor gene may be associated with an increased sensitivity to glucocorticoids *in vivo*. *J. Clin. Endocrin. & Metab.*, 83, 144–151.

Jacobson, L., & Sapolsky, R. (1991). The role of the hippocampus in feedback regulation of the hypothalamic-pituitary-adrenocortical axis. *Endocrine Reviews*, 12, 118–134.

Jiang, X., Xu, K., Hoberman, J., Tian, F., Marko, A. J., Waheed, J. F., et al. (2005). BDNF variation and mood disorders: A novel functional promoter polymorphism and Val66Met are associated with anxiety but have opposing effects. *Neuropsychopharmacology*, 30, 1353–1361.

Jirtle, R. L., & Skinner, M. K. (2007). Environmental epigenomics and disease susceptibility. *Nature Reviews: Genetics*, 8, 253–262.

Kaufman, J., & Charney, D. S. (1999). Neurobiological correlates of child abuse. *Biological Psychiatry*, 45, 1235–1236.

Kaufman, J., Plotsky, P. M., Nemeroff, C. B., & Charney, D. S. (2000). Effects of early adverse experiences on brain structure and function: Clinical implications. *Biological Psychiatry*, 48, 778–790.

Kempermann, G., & Gage, F. H. (1999). New nerve cells for the adult brain. *Scientific American*, 280, 48–53.

Kendler, K. S. (1998). Major depression and the environment: A psychiatric genetic perspective. *Pharmacopsychiat. 31*, 5–9.

Kessler, R. C. (1997). The effects of stressful life events on depression. *Annual Review of Psychology*, 48, 191–214.

Kiecolt-Glaser, J. K., Loving, T. J., Stowell, J. R., Malarkey, W. B., Lemeshow, S., Dickinson, S. L., et al. (2005). Hostile marital interactions, proinflammatory cytokine production, and wound healing. *Archives of General Psychiatry*, 62, 1–8.

Kirschbaum, C., Prussner, J. C., Stone, A. A., Federenko, I., Gaab, J., Lintz, D., et al. (1995). Persistent high cortisol responses to repeated psychological stress in a subpopulation of healthy men. *Psychosomatic Medicine*, 57, 468–474.

Komesaroff, P. A., Esler, M. D., & Sudhir, K. (1999). Estrogen supplementation attenuates glucocorticoid and catecholamine responses to mental stress in perimenopausal women. *Journal of Clinical Endocrinology and Metabolism*, 84, 606–610.

Koob, G. F., & LeMoal, M. (2001). Drug addiction, dysregulation of reward, and allostasis. *Neuropsychopharmacology*, 24, 97–129.

Kramer, A. F., Colcombe, S. J., McAuley, E., Eriksen, K. I., Scalf, P., Jerome, G. J., et al. (2003). Enhancing brain and cognitive function of older adults through fitness training. *Journal of Molecular Neuroscience*, 20, 213–221.

Kramer, A. F., Hahn, S., Cohen, N. J., Banich, M. T., McAuley, E., Harrison, C. R., et al. (1999). Ageing, fitness and neurocognitive function. *Nature*, 400, 418–419.

Kreibich, A. S., & Blendy, J. A. (2004). CAMP response element-binding protein is required for stress but not cocaine-induced reinstatement. *Journal of Neuroscience*, 24, 6686–6692.

Larson, E. B., Wang, L., Bowen, J. D., McCormick, W. C., Teri, L., Crane, P., et al. (2006). Exercise is associated with reduced risk for incident dementia among persons 65 years of age or older. *Annals of Internal Medicine*, 144, 73–81.

Leuner, B., Gould, E., & Shors, T. J. (2006). Is there a link between adult neurogenesis and learning? *Hippocampus*, 26, 216–224.

Lindheim, S. R., Legro, R. S., Bernstein, L., Stanczyk, F. Z., Vijod, M. A., Presser, S. C., et al. (1992). Behavioral stress responses in premenopausal and postmenopausal women and the effects of estrogen. *American Journal of Obstetrics and Gynecology*, 167, 1831–1836.

Lisman, J. E., & Otmakhova, N. A. (2001). Storage, recall, and novelty detection of sequences by the hippocampus: Elaborating on the SOCRATIC model to account for normal and aberrant effects of dopamine. *Hippocampus*, 11, 551–568.

Liston, C., Miller, M. M., Goldwater, D. S., Radley, J. J., Rocher, A. B., Hof, P. R., et al. (2006). Stress-induced alterations in prefrontal cortical dendritic morphology predict selective impairments in perceptual attentional set-shifting. *Journal of Neuroscience*, 26, 7870–7874.

Lupien, S. J. (2002). *The neuroendocrinology of cognitive disorders*. (Vol. 15, pp. 273–282). Wiley, Ltd.

MacQueen, G. M., Campbell, S., McEwen, B. S., Macdonald, K., Amano, S., Joffe, R. T., et al. (2003). Course of illness, hippocampal function, and hippocampal volume in major depression. *Proceedings of the National Academy of Science, USA 100*, 1387–1392.

Magarinos, A. M., McEwen, B. S., Saboureau, M., & Pevet, P. (2006). Rapid and reversible changes in intrahippocampal connectivity during the course of hibernation in European hamsters. *Proceedings of the National Academy of Science, USA 103*, 18775–18780.

Marucha, P. T., Kiecolt-Glaser, J. K., & Favagehi, M. (1998). Mucosal wound healing is impaired by examination stress. *Psychosomatic Medicine, 60,* 362–365.

Matys, T., Pawlak, R., Matys, E., Pavlides, C., McEwen, B. S., & Strickland S. (2004). Tissue plasminogen activator promotes the effects of corticotropin releasing factor on the amygdala and anxiety-like behavior. *Proceedings of the National Academy of Science, USA, 101,* 16345–16350.

McEwen, B. S. (1998). Protective and damaging effects of stress mediators. *New England Journal of Medicine*, 338, 171–179.

McEwen, B. S. (1999). Stress and hippocampal plasticity. *Annual Review of Neuroscience*, 22, 105–122.

McEwen, B. S. (2006a). Protective and damaging effects of stress mediators: central role of the brain. *Dial. in Clin. Neurosci: Stress, 8,* 283–297.

McEwen, B. S. (2006b). Sleep deprivation as a neurobiologic and physiologic stressor: allostasis and allostatic load. *Metabolism, 55,* S20–S23.

McEwen, B. S. (2007). The physiology and neurobiology of stress and adaptation: Central role of the brain. *Physiological Reviews*.

McEwen, B. S., & Chattarji, S. (2004). Molecular mechanisms of neuroplasticity and pharmacological implications: The example of tianeptine. *European Neuropsychopharmacology*, 14, S497–S502.

McEwen, B. S., & Chattarji, S. (2007). Neuroendocrinology of Stress. *Handbook of Neurochemistry and Molecular Neurobiology* (3rd ed., pp. 572–593). New York: Springer-Verlag.

McEwen, B. S., Sakai, R. R., & Spencer, R. L. (1993). Adrenal steroid effects on the brain: Versatile hormones with good and bad effects, J. Schulkin. *Hormonally-induced changes in mind and brain* (pp. 157–189). San Diego, CA: Academic Press.

McEwen, B. S., & Stellar, E. (1993). Stress and the individual. Mechanisms leading to disease. *Arch Intern Med*, 153, 2093–2101.

McEwen, B. S., & Wingfield, J. C. (2003). The concept of allostasis in biology and biomedicine. *Hormones and Behavior*, *43*, 2–15.

McGeer, P. L., & McGeer, E. G. (2001). Inflammation, autotoxicity and Alzheimer disease. *Neurobiology of Aging*, *22*, 799–809.

McKittrick, C. R., Magarinos, A. M., Blanchard, D. C., Blanchard, R. J., McEwen, B. S., & Sakai, R. R. (2000). Chronic social stress reduces dendritic arbors in CA3 of hippocampus and decreases binding to serotonin transporter sites. *Synapse*, *36*, 85–94.

Meaney, M. J., Tannenbaum, B., Francis, D., Bhatnagar, S., Shanks, N., Viau, V., et al. (1994). Early environmental programming hypothalamic-pituitary-adrenal responses to stress. *Seminars in Neurosciences*, *6*, 247–259.

Melchor, J. P., Pawlak, R., & Strickland, S. (2003). The tissue plasminogen activator: Plasminogen proteolytic cascade accelerates amyloid-b (Ab) degradation and inhibits Ab-induced neurodegeneration. *Journal of Neuroscience*, *23*, 8867–8871.

Mitra, R., Jadhav, S., McEwen, B. S., Vyas, A., & Chattarji, S. (2005). Stress duration modulates the spatiotemporal patterns of spine formation in the basolateral amygdala. *Proceedings of the National Academy of Science, USA 102*, 9371–9376.

Munck, A., Guyre, P. M., & Holbrook, N. (1984). Physiological functions of glucocorticoids in stress and their relation to pharmacological actions. *Endocrine Reviews*, *5*, 25–44.

Murphy, B. E. P. (1991). Treatment of major depression with steroid suppressive drugs. *Journal of Steroid Biochemistry and Molecular Biology*, *39*, 239–244

Ott, A., Stolk, R. P., Hofman, A., van Harskamp, F., Grobbee, D. E., & Breteler, M. M. B. (1996). Association of diabetes mellitus and dementia: The Rotterdam study. *Diabetologia*, *39*, 1392–1397.

Pawlak, R., Magarinos, A. M., Melchor, J., McEwen, B., & Strickland, S. (2003). Tissue plasminogen activator in the amygdala is critical for stress-induced anxiety-like behavior. *Nature Neuroscience*, *6*, 168–174.

Pawlak, R., Rao, B. S. S., Melchor, J. P., Chattarji, S., McEwen, B., & Strickland, S. (2005). Tissue plasminogen activator and plasminogen mediate stress-induced decline of neuronal and cognitive functions in the mouse hippocampus. *Proceedings of the National Academy of Science, USA 102*, 18201–18206.

Pezawas, L., Verchinski, B. A., Mattay, V. S., Callicott, J. H., Kolachana, B. S., Straub, R. E., et al. (2004). The brain-derived neurotrophic factor val66met polymorphism and variation in human cortical morphology. *Journal of Neuroscience*, *24*, 10099–10102.

Pickering, T. G., Devereux, R. B., James, G. D., Gerin, W., Landsbergis, P., Schnall, P. L., et al. (1996). Environmental influences on blood pressure and the role of job strain. *Journal of Hypertension*, *14*, S179–S185.

Pitman, R. K. (2001). Hippocampal diminution in PTSD: More (or less?) than meets the eye. *Hippocampus*, *11*, 73–74.

Popov, V. I., & Bocharova, L. S. (1992). Hibernation-induced structural changes in synaptic contacts between mossy fibres and hippocampal pyramidal neurons. *Neuroscience*, *48*, 53–62.

Popov, V. I., Bocharova, L. S., & Bragin, A. G. (1992). Repeated changes of dendritic morphology in the hippocampus of ground squirrels in the course of hibernation. *Neuroscience*, *48*, 45–51.

Poulton, R., Caspi, A., Milne, B. J., Thomson, W. M., Taylor, A., Sears, M. R., et al. (2002). Association between children's experience of socioeconomic disadvantage and adult health: A life-course study. *Lancet*, *360*, 1640–1645.

Power, C., Li, L., Manor, O., & Davey Smith, G. (2003). Combination of low birth weight and high adult body mass index: At what age is it established and what are its determinants? *Journal of Epidemiology and Community Health*, *57*, 969–973.

Pressman, S. D., & Cohen, S. (2005). Does positive affect influence health? *Psychological Bulletin*, *131*, 925–971.

Pruessner, J. C., Baldwin, M. W., Dedovic, K., Renwick, R. M. N. K., Lord, C., Meaney, M., et al. (2005). Self-esteem, locus of control, hippocampal volume, and cortisol regulation in young and old adulthood. *NeuroImage*, *28*, 815–826.

Pruessner, J. C., Hellhammer, D. H., & Kirschbaum, C. (1999). Low self-esteem, induced failure and the adrenocortical stress response. *Personality and Individual Differences*, *27*, 477–489.

Radley, J. J., Rocher, A. B., Janssen, W. G. M., Hof, P. R., McEwen, B. S., & Morrison, J. H. (2005a). Reversibility of apical dendritic retraction in the rat medial prefrontal cortex following repeated stress. *Experimental Neurology*, *196*, 199–203.

Radley, J. J., Rocher, A. B., Miller, M., Janssen, W. G. M., Liston, C., Hof, P. R., et al. (2005b). Repeated stress induces dendritic spine loss in the rat medial prefrontal cortex. *Cerebral Cortex*.

Radley, J. J., Sisti, H. M., Hao, J., Rocher, A. B., McCall, T., Hof, P. R., et al. (2004). Chronic behavioral stress induces apical dendritic reorganization in pyramidal neurons of the medial prefrontal cortex. *Neuroscience*, *125*, 1–6.

Raison, C. L., Capuron, L., & Miller, A. H. (2006). Cytokines sing the blues: Inflammation and the pathogenesis of depression. *Trends in Immunology*, *27*, 24–31.

Ramey, E., & Goldstein, M. (1957). The adrenal cortex and sympathetic nervous system. *Physiological Review*, *37*, 155–195.

Reed, D. M., Lacroix, A. Z., Karasek, R. A., Miller, D., & MacLean, C. A. (1989). Occupational strain and the incidence of coronary heart disease. *American Journal of Epidemiology*, *129*, 495–502.

Repetti, R. L., Taylor, S. E., & Seeman, T. E. (2002). Risky families: Family social environments and the mental and physical health of offspring. *Physiological Bulletin*, *128*, 330–366.

Roozendaal, B., Okuda, S., Van der Zee, E. A., & McGaugh, J. L. (2006). Glucocorticoid enhancement of memory requires arousal-induced noradrenergic activation in the basolateral amygdala. *Proceedings of the National Academy of Sciences, USA 103*, 6741–6746.

Rovio, S., Kareholt, I., Helkala, E.-L., Viitanen, M., Winblad, B., Tuomilehto, J., et al. (2005). Leisure-time physical activity at midlife and the risk of dementia and Alzheimer's disease. *Lancet*.

Saavedra, J. M., Benicky, J., & Zhou, J. (2006). Angiotensin II: Multitasking in the brain. *Journal of Hypertension*, *24*(Suppl. 1), S131–S137.

Sachar, E. J., Hellman, L., Roffwarg, H. P., Halpern, F. S., Fukushima, D. K., & Gallagher, T. F. (1973). Disrupted 24-hour patterns of cortisol secretion in psychotic depression. *Archives of General Psychiatry*, *28*, 19–24.

Sampson, R. J., Raudenbush, S. W., & Earls, F. (1997). Neighborhoods and violent crime: A multilevel study of collective effects. *Science*, *277*, 918–924.

Sandi, C. (2004). Stress, cognitive impairment and cell adhesion molecules. *Nature Reviews: Neuroscience*, *5*, 917–930.

Sapolsky, R. M. (1996). Why stress is bad for your brain. *Science*, *273*, 749–750.

Sapolsky, R. M. (2004). *Why Zebras Don't Get Ulcers*. New York: Henry Holt.

Sapolsky, R. M., Romero, L. M., & Munck, A. U. (2000). How do glucocorticoids influence stress responses? Integrating permissive, suppressive, stimulatory, and preparative actions. *Endocrine Reviews*, *21*, 55–89.

Schelling, G., Stoll, C., Kapfhammer, H.-P., Rothenhausler, H.-B., Krauseneck, T., Durst, K., et al. (1999). The effect of stress doses of hydrocortisone during septic shock or post-traumatic stress disorder and health-related quality of life in survivors. *Critical Care Medicine*, *27*, 2678–2682.

Schnall, P. L., Pieper, C., Schwartz, J. E., Karasek, R. A., Schlussel, Y., Devereux, R. B., et al. (1990). The relationship between "job strain," workplace diastolic blood pressure, and left ventricular mass index. *Journal of American Medical Association*, *263*, 1929–1935.

Schulkin, J., McEwen, B. S., & Gold, P. W. (1994). Allostasis, amygdala, and anticipatory angst. *Neuroscience and Biobehavioral Reviews, 18,* 385–396.

Seeman, T. E., Singer, B., & Charpentier, P. (1995). Gender differences. In *Patterns of HPA axis response to challenge: MacArthur studies of successful aging. Psychoneuroendocrinology, 20,* 711–725.

Seeman, T. E., Singer, B. H., Ryff, C. D., Dienberg, G., & Levy-Storms, L. (2002). Social relationships, gender, and allostatic load across two age cohorts. *Psychosomatic Medicine, 64,* 395–406.

Selye, H. (1936). A syndrome produced by diverse nocuous agents. *Nature, 138,* 32.

Selye, H. (1973). The evolution of the stress concept. *American Scientist, 61,* 692–699.

Seri, B., Garcia-Verdugo, J. M., McEwen, B. S., & Alvarez-Buylla, A. (2001). Astrocytes give rise to new neurons in the adult mammalian hippocampus. *Journal of Neuroscience, 21,* 7153–7160.

Sheline, Y. I., Gado, M. H., & Kraemer, H. C. (2003). Untreated depression and hippocampal volume loss. *American Journal of Psychiatry, 160,* 1516–1518.

Sheline, Y. I., Sanghavi, M., Mintun, M. A., & Gado, M. H. (1999). Depression duration but not age predicts hippocampal volume loss in medically healthy women with recurrent major depression. *Journal of Neuroscience, 19,* 5034–5043.

Shors, T. J., Chua, C., & Falduto, J. (2001). Sex differences and opposite effects of stress on dendritic spine density in the male versus female hippocampus. *Journal of Neuroscience, 21,* 6292–6297.

Sorrells, S. F., & Sapolsky, R. M. (2007). An inflammatory review of glucocorticoid actions in the CNS. *Brain, Behavior, and Immunity, 21,* 259–272.

Sousa, N., Lukoyanov, N. V., Madeira, M. D., Almeida, O. F. X., & Paula-Barbosa, M. M. (2000). Reorganization of the morphology of hippocampal neurites and synapses after stress-induced damage correlates with behavioral improvement. *Neuroscience, 97,* 253–266.

Spiegel, K., Leproult, R., & Van Cauter, E. (1999). Impact of sleep debt on metabolic and endocrine function. *Lancet, 354,* 1435–1439.

Starkman, M. N., Gebarski, S. S., Berent, S., & Schteingart, D. E. (1992). Hippocampal formation volume, memory dysfunction, and cortisol levels in patients with Cushing's syndrome. *Biological Psychiatry, 32,* 756–765.

Starkman, M. N., & Schteingart, D. E. (1981). Neuropsychiatric manifestations of patients with Cushing's syndrome. *Arch Interm Medicine, 141,* 215–219.

Steingart, R. A., Silverman, W. F., Barron, S., Slotkin, T. A., Awad, Y., & Yanai, J. (2000). Neural grafting reverses prenatal drug-induced alterations in hippocampal, P. K. C., & related behavioral deficits. *Developmental Brain Research, 125,* 9–19.

Steptoe, A., Owen, N., Kunz-Ebrecht, S. R., & Brydon, L. (2004). Loneliness and neuroendocrine, cardiovascular, and inflammatory stress responses in middle-aged men and women. *Psychoneuroendocrinology, 29,* 593–611.

Steptoe, A., Wardle, J., & Marmot, M. (2005). Positive affect and health-related neuroendocrine, cardiovascular, and inflammatory processes. *Proceedings of the National Academy of Sciences of the United States of America, 102,* 6508–6512.

Sterling, P., & Eyer, J. (1988). Allostasis: A new paradigm to explain arousal pathology, S. Fisher, & J. Reason. *Handbook of life stress, cognition and health* (pp. 629–649). New York: Wiley.

Strahl, B. D., & Allis, C. D. (2000). The language of covalent histone modifications. *Nature, 403,* 41–45.

Szeszko, P. R., Lipsky, R., Mentschel, C., Robinson, D., Gunduz-Bruce, H., Sevy, S., et al. (2005). Brain-derived neurotrophic factor val66met polymorphism and volume of the hippocampal formation. *Molecular Psychiatry, 10,* 631–636.

Taylor, S. E., Klein, L. C., Lewis, B. P., Gruenewald, T. L., Gurung, R. A. R., & Updegraff, J. A. (1998). Female responses to stress: Tend-and-befriend, not fight-or-flight. *Personal Communication.*

Teague, C. R., Dhabhar, F. S., Barton, R. H., Beckwith-Hall, B., Powell, J., Cobain, M., et al. (2007). Metabonomic studies on the physiological effects of acute and chronic psychological stress in Sprague-Dawley rats. *Journal of Proteome Research, 6,* 2080–2093.

Theorell, T., Tsutsumi, A., Hallquist, J., Reuterwall, C., Hogstedt, C., Fredlund, P., et al. (1998). Decision latitude, job strain, and myocardial infarction: A study of working men in Stockholm. *American Journal of Public Health, 88,* 382–388.

Theorell, T., Westerlund, H., Alfredsson, L., & Oxenstierna, G. (2005). Coping with critical life events and lack of control: The exertion of control. *Psychoneuroendocrinology, 30,* 1027–1032.

Trejo, J. L., Carro, E., & Torres-Aleman, I. (2001). Circulating insulin-like growth factor I mediates exercise-induced increases in the number of new neurons in the adult hippocampus. *Journal of Neuroscience, 21,* 1628–1634.

Turek, F. W., Joshu, C., Kohsaka, A., Lin, E., Ivanova, G., McDearmon, E., et al. (2005). Obesity and metabolic syndrome in circadian clock mutant mice. *Science, 308,* 1043–1045.

Van Cauter, E., Leproult, R., & Kupfer, D. J. (1996). Effects of gender and age on the levels and circadian rhythmicity of plasma cortisol. *Journal of Clinical Endocrinology and Metabolism, 81,* 2468–2473.

van Rossum, E. F. C., Binder, E. B., Majer, M., Koper, J. W., Ising, M., Modell, S., et al. (2006). Polymorphisms of the glucocorticoid receptor gene and major depression. *Biological Psychiatry, 59,* 681–688.

Vermetten, E., Schmahl, C., Lindner, S., Loewenstein, R. J., & Bremner, J. D. (2006). Hippocampal and amygdalar volumes in dissociative identity disorder. *American Journal of Psychiatry, 163,* 630–636.

Vyas, A., Mitra, R., Rao, B. S. S., & Chattarji, S. (2002). Chronic stress induces contrasting patterns of dendritic remodeling in hippocampal and amygdaloid neurons. *Journal of Neuroscience, 22,* 6810–6818.

Wadhwa, P. D., Sandman, C. A., & Garite, T. J. (2001). The neurobiology of stress in human pregnancy: Implications for prematurity and development of the fetal central nervous system. *Prog in Brain Res 133* 131–142

Wang, J., Rao, H., Wetmore, G. S., Furlan, P. M., Korczykowski, M., Dinges, D. F., et al. (2005). Perfusion functional MRI reveals cerebral blood flow pattern under psychological stress. *Proceedings of the National Academy of Sciences, USA 102,* 17804–17809.

Weaver, I. C. G., Cervoni, N., Champagne, F. A., D'Alessio, A. C., Sharma, S., Seckl, J. R., et al. (2004). Epigenetic programming by maternal behavior. *Nature Neuroscience, 7,* 847–854.

Wellman, C. L. (2001). Dendritic reorganization in pyramidal neurons in medial prefrontal cortex after chronic corticosterone administration. *Journal of Neurobiology, 49,* 245–253.

Williams, R. B., Barefoot, J. C., Blumenthal, J. A., Helms, M. J., Luecken, L., Pieper, C. F., et al. (1997). Psychosocial correlates of job strain in a sample of working women. *Archives of General Psychiatry, 54,* 543.

Wing, R. R. (2003). Behavioral interventions for obesity: Recognizing our progress and future challenges. *Obesity Research, 11,* S3–S6.

Wood, G. E., Young, L. T., Reagan, L. P., & McEwen, B. S. (2003). Acute and chronic restraint stress alter the incidence of social conflict in male rats. *Hormones and Behavior, 43,* 205–213.

Chapter 63

Placebo Effects

LAUREN Y. ATLAS, TOR D. WAGER, KATHARINE P. DAHL, AND EDWARD E. SMITH

A *placebo* is a treatment that is expected to have no inherent pharmacological or physical benefit—for instance, a starch capsule given for anxiety or pain, or sham surgery in which the critical surgical procedure is not performed. Placebos are often used for comparison in clinical studies, as a baseline against which to evaluate the efficacy of investigational clinical treatments. However, placebo treatments often elicit observable improvements in signs or symptoms on their own—these are *placebo effects*. For this reason, placebos have been used as healing agents for a variety of ailments; they have had a place in the healer's repertoire for thousands of years, and they are still used as a viable treatment option by physicians in industrialized countries with surprising frequency.

Psychologists and neuroscientists today are most interested in the *placebo response*, the brain and body response to the psychosocial (and perhaps neurobiological) context surrounding treatment. The study of the placebo response reveals active processes that provide a powerful window into brain-body interactions and the brain substrates of human behavior.

Studies of drug treatments for various disorders have investigated the effects of *exogenous* regulation of neural and psychological end-points, such as reported emotion, behavioral responses, and disease-specific brain activity. The brain, however, comprises interlocking feedback mechanisms that provide powerful *endogenous* control of neural and psychological processes. These endogenous processes regulate perceptual, affective, and cognitive processes based on the evaluation of situational context. Contextual information leading to placebo responses arises from either conscious expectancies about anticipated effects of treatment, or from prior learning in the form of conditioning with active treatments. In some cases, these two sources of placebo responses can be complementary, while in other cases, they may be mutually exclusive in their influence on observed placebo effects. The context surrounding placebo administration may lead individuals to expect improvement, and positive outcomes would compose the placebo effect. Alternatively, contextual information can lead individuals

to expect worsening of symptoms; changes in the negative direction are observed as part of the *nocebo effect*. There is some evidence that the two involve separate mechanisms, although the placebo response has been much more thoroughly studied.

A literature on experimental manipulations of placebo treatments has produced substantial evidence that placebo effects result, in many cases, from active brain responses to context, rather than statistical artifacts and reporting biases. Neuroimaging and related techniques have allowed us to begin to understand the brain mechanisms by which placebos exert their effects.

PLACEBO TREATMENTS IN EXPERIMENTAL RESEARCH VERSUS CLINICAL STUDIES

The potential significance of the placebo response has led to the standard use of placebo groups in clinical trials examining the efficacy of medicine or other specific treatments on clinical conditions. Patients are assigned to receive either active treatment or placebo, and comparisons between groups are performed to test whether the active treatment elicits greater improvement than placebo. Two critical assumptions underlie the rationale behind the placebo-controlled clinical trial. First, it is assumed that psychological and nonspecific effects, such as natural course of disease, effects of being in a healing environment, and patient expectation and motivation to heal, have equal effects on outcomes in active treatment and placebo groups. Second, it is assumed that nonspecific effects and treatment effects combine additively, so that subtracting outcomes for the placebo group from the treatment group will reveal the specific effects of the drug or procedure. Although these assumptions may not always hold, the placebo-controlled randomized clinical trial is perhaps the best tool for medical practitioners and pharmaceutical companies to determine treatment efficacy.

Psychologists and neuroscientists are interested, however, in whether and how the psychological components of treatment—expectancies, appraisals, learning, context effects, and the relationship between patient and practitioner—can directly affect the bodily state: What are the effects of the treatment context, and how do they affect physiology? These questions can be answered by studying the placebo response. In the clinical context, this can be achieved through a three-arm version of the clinical trial; in addition to the active treatment and placebo groups, a subset of patients is assigned to a "natural history" comparison group that receives no treatment.[1] Comparisons between this no-treatment group and the placebo group allow researchers to avoid many potential statistical artifacts, some of which are described later in this chapter, to assess the placebo response—the active effects of psychological state.

While contrasts between the placebo and natural history arms of clinical trials allow researchers to examine the breadth of placebo effects, laboratory research on placebo allows researchers to examine the placebo response. Experimental investigations assess the psychological components of the placebo response, and the mechanisms by which these factors modulate physiological endpoints. Through mechanistic approaches to the study of the placebo response, researchers may gain insights into fundamental processes underlying mind-body interactions. These processes link placebo to many other psychological domains, as the central mechanisms supporting placebo responses involve many key concepts in psychology, including cognitive processes, such as appraisals, expectancies, learning, context effects, and valuation. Interpersonal processes also play a critical role in the placebo response; the patient-practitioner relationship may cultivate feelings of trust and "being cared for," which may not only influence patient expectancies, but may also directly contribute to the development of the placebo response (Barrett et al., 2006; Hall, Dugan, Zheng, & Mishra, 2001). Studying the placebo response offers the opportunity to increase our understanding of how these social and cognitive processes may interact with the endogenous regulatory mechanisms to control the body's physiological state.

Laboratory placebo research generally examines conditions whose onset can be controlled by experimenters, since there is no prior disease state on which to measure effects in healthy volunteers. In laboratory experiments on placebo

effects on pain, anxiety, or Parkinson's disease, experimenters can compare performance (pain response, affective ratings, motor performance) in a control condition to a condition in which placebo treatment was administered in the form of a sham medication or procedure. Improvements (decreased pain, decreased negative emotion, increased motor performance) with the placebo treatment indicate positive effects of placebo. For this reason and others, pain is a particularly well-studied domain in placebo research, as the intensity of noxious stimulation can be experimentally controlled. Placebo effects in pain are typically measured as decreases in pain ratings (or, alternatively, pain-induced physiological activity) under placebo relative to a nonplacebo control condition.

ALL PLACEBO EFFECTS ARE NOT EQUAL: ACTIVE PLACEBO RESPONSES VERSUS STATISTICAL ARTIFACTS

Many factors may influence the reporting process to resemble placebo effects on subjective outcome measures without a concomitant *active placebo response*. Active placebo responses are those processes that interact with and affect the normal processing underlying a disease or condition. True placebo effects—those that have direct impact on the course of disease—necessarily involve active placebo responses, and placebo researchers must differentiate between active placebo responses and other psychological factors that influence subjective outcome measures (Wager & Nitschke, 2005). This is not to say that subjective outcomes without a physiological basis are not desirable in and of themselves; patient quality of life is of the utmost importance in the clinic, and any treatment that eliminates suffering arguably offers great benefit to the patient, no matter whether it affects disease physiology. Nonetheless, in the interest of using the placebo response as a window into mind-body interactions, we are most interested in the breadth and extent of active placebo responses.

Statistical Artifacts

It is essential to account for the natural course of a disease in clinical studies of placebo, as numerous factors may lead to observations of clinical improvement, yet have nothing to do with actual placebo administration (and are thus not part of an active placebo response). These factors include natural symptom fluctuation, regression to the mean, spontaneous remission, and participant sampling bias; Figure 63.1 illustrates the contribution of such factors to apparent disease progression. All these factors can

---

[1] Denying patients treatment for conditions when accepted treatments do indeed exist may be viewed as unethical, so this no-treatment control group can be achieved by assigning participants with non-life-threatening conditions to waiting lists, so that they ultimately do receive treatment.

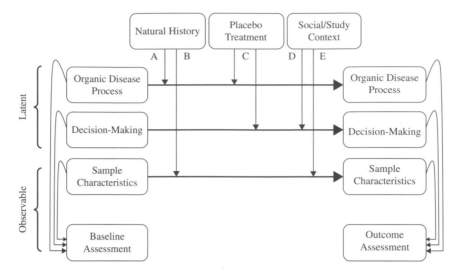

Figure 63.1   Factors that contribute to observed placebo effects in clinical trials.

Note: Improvement from baseline to outcome assessment is the measure of recovery or healing. These measures are observable outcomes based on some observable factors, such as the sample characteristics, and unobservable factors that include organic disease progression and decision-making processes about how to report signs and symptoms. Improvemen t in the average of the study sample may be influenced by factors that include effects of natural history, study context, and psychobiological responses

to placebo. **A:** Effects of time on organic disease: Natural history. **B:** Effects of time or perceived disease severity over time on sample characteristics: Sampling bias. **C:** Effects of placebo treatment on organic disease and decision-making processes: Active psychobiological placebo responses. **D:** Effects of being in the study on decision making: Hawthorne effects and demand characteristics. **E:** Effects of social factors (being cared for, implicit social contracts) on continued participation: Sampling bias. Experimental studies of placebo treatment compared with no-treatment controls can isolate active psychobiological placebo responses (C).

be adequately accounted for in clinical trials by comparing the placebo group to a natural history control group, assuming effective randomization and other standard statistical assumptions.

Natural History: Spontaneous Remission and Natural Symptom Fluctuation

Without treatment, outcomes (e.g., signs and symptoms) in all diseases follow a time course, referred to as a natural history. In many conditions, remission is part of the natural course of the illness, and with enough time, healing is likely to occur on its own. Patients are likely to eventually recover from many psychiatric illnesses, sleep disorders, and other conditions that may otherwise cause patients to seek treatment. In some other conditions, patients tend to get progressively worse. Even for conditions in which spontaneous remission is rare—such as chronic pain, Parkinson's disease, and irritable bowel syndrome—signs and symptoms fluctuate over time. The constant variation in symptomatology within an individual could easily lead to apparent improvement with a treatment if patients are enrolled when their symptoms are particularly intense or the study terminates during a relatively symptom-free period.

Regression to the Mean

It is well known that if repeated measurements are made of a variable (e.g., severity of a symptom) that is measured with error or fluctuates around a mean, extreme values tend to be

closer to the mean with each successive measurement. Thus, a subgroup of patients will appear to improve over time in virtually any study, even if there is no actual improvement. What is decreasing in these improved patients is not the underlying symptom, but the value of the measurement error. If patients tend to enroll in a study when their symptoms are relatively severe, the entire group may appear to improve, whether treated with a drug, placebo, or nothing at all. In many cases, patients are likely to seek treatment at extreme points in the course of illness, leading to a high likelihood that symptoms will have diminished by the time a second measurement is made, simply due to the natural course of disease. This phenomenon was demonstrated in a study that compared chronic pain patients who had sought treatment to a matched group who had not sought treatment (Whitney & Von Korff, 1992). The former group reported more pain at initial assessment than the latter group; both groups' reported pain levels approached the mean at a 1-year follow-up, with the group that sought treatment demonstrating steeper reductions in reported pain, demonstrating that self-selection can influence regression to the mean in a way that would affect observed treatment results.

Participant Sampling Bias

Another important potential source of artifact in clinical trials comes about because participants who experience beneficial effects over the course of the study are more likely to adhere to treatment regimens and remain enrolled in the study than participants who experience no change. Attrition rates will be higher among those receiving no benefit from treatment, and an observed improvement with treatment will actually reflect changes in the sample over time (Turk & Rudy, 1990).

Comparisons between placebo and nontreatment control groups allow researchers to control for these various artifacts and assess the efficacy of placebo administration on a given condition. To our knowledge, the efficacy of placebo treatment has been examined with comparisons between placebo and nontreatment controls in Major Depressive Disorder, heart disease/hypertension, chronic pain, nausea, erectile dysfunction, and obesity.

Placebo Effects on Decision Making

Experimental research allows researchers to differentiate between active placebo responses and placebo effects on decision making that involve no changes in the underlying physiology of the disease or condition. A recent meta-analysis of clinical trials that compared placebo and no-treatment control groups found no significant benefit of placebo administration across clinical conditions, and only found significant placebo improvement in the context of placebos for pain (Hrobjartsson & Gotzsche, 2001, 2004). The authors argued that the observed placebo effects may be an artifact of reporting bias, since pain was always measured by self-report. Placebo administration may have caused changes in participant decision making, but may have had no effect on disease processes. This study has been criticized on at least two counts. First, its conclusions are based on clinical trials that were not intended to examine placebo effects, and so strong placebo expectancies may not have been formed in many cases (Wickramasekera, 2001). Second, their main analyses averaged across many different disease processes—obesity, hypertension, pain, and marital dysfunction trials were all considered together—and there may have been too few studies within particular disorders to achieve adequate power (Kirsch & Scoboria, 2001).

Those criticisms notwithstanding, the issue of whether changes in reported experience are purely subjective is an important one. Placebo effects may reflect subjective responses in two senses. First, they may be caused by brain processes that modulate subjective experiences of emotion, pain, and suffering. Such subjective effects are clinically relevant: A treatment that affects pain and quality of life is important whether it affects an organic disease process or simply the patient's ability to cope with it. Alternatively, subjective responses may be caused by biases in the cognitive decision-making processes involved in making reports

to an experimenter or physician. In this case, the placebo does not change the organic disease and subjective suffering, but may affect decisions about how to describe the painful experiences.

In many disorders, subjective assessment is a critical component; pain is a subjective phenomenon, and there is no better way to measure pain than to ask the patient. Nonsubjective measures that are responsive to pain, such as pupillometry and skin conductance, are indirectly related to pain experience, and can be affected by other factors without a change in perceived pain. Thus, while these measures are of interest partly because they are not subject to cognitive reporting biases, they cannot entirely replace self-report as an index of the pain experience.

The problem with relying solely on self-report based measures when studying the placebo response is that they can be influenced by factors that have little to do with the disease process being studied; placebo effects may be observed with self-report measures, yet the course of disease may remain unaffected. We review sources of reporting bias and then present evidence from carefully controlled experimental placebo research demonstrating that, despite these sources of *potential* error, active placebo responses do indeed exist in many clinical and psychological domains.

Hawthorne Effects

Participants often change their behavior as a result of being observed in the study environment. This phenomenon is referred to as the Hawthorne effect, after a series of landmark studies at the Hawthorne Works of the Western Electric Company (Roethlisberger & Dickson, 1939). These studies were designed to assess how several variables—break length, work-week duration, and company subsidation of meals and beverages—affected productivity. Irrespective of these manipulations, productivity increased relative to preexperiment levels. Researchers concluded that this increased productivity resulted from the attention and special privileges that study participants received. Hawthorne effects are particularly relevant in the consideration of natural history control groups in clinical trials; to avoid Hawthorne effects, control participants should receive the same amount of attention as placebo and treatment groups.

Demand Characteristics

Demand characteristics refer to changes in participants' behavior due to expectations about how they are expected to behave or what they are expected to report. In response to hypotheses about study aims, patients may exhibit social compliance effects—patients may say what they feel *should* be said (Kelman, 1958). The question, "How much did your pain decrease?" implies that participants should have felt less pain, and they may feel pressure to report decreases despite no actual perceived changes. In the case of self-presentation biases, individuals often say what makes them look better in the eyes of others (Arkin, Gabrenya, Appelman, & Cochran, 1979); this is especially relevant if the experimenter is seen as an authority figure or relevant social figure. Finally, self-consistency biases may cause individuals to respond in ways that are consistent with past behavior or with views of the self (Wells & Sweeney, 1986).

Early research on placebo effects took advantage of then-current stage models of perception and decision making, and tested for effects of placebo treatments on measures derived from signal detection theory (SDT; Swets, Tanner, & Birdsall, 1961). The SDT characterization relied on the notion that sensory processes register a mixture of a true signal (such as a change in the strength of noxious input) and noise. The output of sensory processes is passed to a decision maker, which chooses a response ("signal present" or "signal absent") based on the perceived sensation. Thus, the likelihood of a particular decision depends not only on the perceived signal strength, but also on the relative costs of false positive decisions and missed true signals. Studies of placebo effects asked participants to provide ratings of pain with and without placebo treatment. In a classic study, the SDT measure of discriminability assessed whether participants showed a reduced tendency to rate slightly more intense stimuli with higher pain ratings (to discriminate temperatures) with placebo (Clark, 1969). The SDT measure of response bias assessed whether they rated a given stimulus as less painful with the placebo. The study found that placebo affected response bias but not discriminability, whereas an opiate drug affected both.

Though this was an important finding, the issue is complex because pain is not a two-stage sensory-decision process. The ability to discriminate stimulus intensities and the experience of pain are not the same thing; a complex network of brain circuits creates the pain experience from a combination of sensory input and internal processes, and different sensory receptors at the peripheral level may even carry different information about sensory and nociceptive (pain-related) aspects of the stimulus (Price & Dubner, 1977; Price, Greenspan, & Dubner, 2003). Thus, what is at stake in placebo research is not stimulus discriminability, but the intensity of the feeling of pain, which is likely to be captured by the response bias SDT measure.

The placebo effects on response bias observed by Clark et al. could be caused by either changes in decision-making processes—the standard interpretation in SDT—or by widespread decreases in pain processing in the brain or spinal cord, with very different implications in each alternative.

The direct measurement of brain responses to noxious stimulation can help disentangle these alternatives. Placebo shifts in reporting bias would presumably affect the pain reporting process without affecting pain processing—under placebo, neural activity would increase in decision-making circuitry (dorsolateral prefrontal cortex [DLPFC] and orbitofrontal cortex [OFC], primarily) facilitating changes in evaluative report criteria, but pain-processing activity would remain unaffected. Alternatively, finding decreases in nociceptive processing in brain regions related to pain would suggest that the second alternative is more likely to be true. We review evidence on brain placebo effects later.

In considering the various artifacts previously described, it becomes clear that experimental research manipulating placebo treatments plays a key role in testing for active placebo responses. Sound experimental designs can eliminate issues of sampling bias and regression to the mean that can plague clinical trials. In addition, sensitivity to detect active placebo responses can be enhanced by considering and minimizing cognitive biases in self-report, either by using implicit behavioral measures or physiological outcome measures that are relatively nonsusceptible to reporting biases.

Active Placebo Responses

Physiological outcome measures, including neuroimaging and electrophysiological measures of central and peripheral nervous system activity as well as peripheral outcome measures such as hormone secretion, provide powerful evidence for the existence of placebo responses beyond reporting biases. In the remainder of this chapter, we review evidence for the existence of active placebo responses in a variety of domains. We specifically examine placebo analgesia as a model system, and consider candidate central and proximal mechanisms of the placebo response.

Central Nervous System Processes in Placebo

Neuroimaging and electrophysiological methodologies provide evidence of active placebo responses in domains in which physical outcome measures may not exist or may map indirectly to stimulus processing. These methodologies—functional magnetic resonance imaging (fMRI), positron emission tomography (PET), electroencephalography (EEG), magnetoencephalography (MEG), and single-unit recording—reveal not only changes in brain-related outcomes (decreases in pain-related neural activity under placebo analgesia), but also underlying mechanisms subserving the placebo response, allowing for insights into how these mind-body interactions unfold.

Placebo responses have now been systematically studied using neuroimaging and electrophysiology techniques across several conditions and diseases, including

Parkinson's disease (Benedetti et al., 2004; de la Fuente-Fernandez et al., 2002), Major Depressive Disorder (Mayberg et al., 2002), irritable bowel syndrome (Lieberman et al., 2004; Vase, Robinson, Verne, & Price, 2005), anxiety (Petrovic et al., 2005), drug reinforcement (Volkow et al., 2003), and pain (Bingel, Lorenz, Schoell, Weiller, & Buchel, 2006; Kong et al., 2006; Lieberman et al., 2004; Price, Craggs, Verne, Perlstein, & Robinson, 2007; Wager, Matre, & Casey, 2006; Wager, Rilling, et al., 2004; Wager, Scott, & Zubieta, 2007; Watson, El-Deredy, Vogt, & Jones, 2007; Zubieta, Yau, Scott, & Stohler, 2006). Results from these studies can be combined with knowledge of the neural bases of basic cognitive processes that may be involved in the placebo response to gain synergistic insight into the mechanisms supporting placebo responses.

A central thesis of this chapter is that common effects of placebo treatment on the brain suggest the involvement of common central brain mechanisms across disorders. Other brain processes and outcomes, however, appear to be disease-specific, and we examine evidence for these domain-specific proximal mechanisms as well. In the following sections, we use pain as a model system to discuss the brain mechanisms supporting active placebo responses and use observed commonalities to compare placebo responses in pain with those in other domains.

PLACEBO ANALGESIA: PAIN AS A MODEL SYSTEM

In the laboratory context, the majority of studies of placebo have been conducted in the realm of pain. Pain is a unique domain with sensory, affective, and evaluative components, and one that has great significance for an organism's well-being. Pain is an interoceptive modality, yet can be quantitatively manipulated in the laboratory. Furthermore, the network of regions involved in the pain experience, known as the "pain matrix," has been well characterized in human and animal studies (for a detailed review, see Chapter 33, this volume). Finally, pain is known to have a strong expectancy component, and may arguably be considered more open to influence of the central nervous system than many disease processes.

Placebo analgesia occurs when (a) an individual is experiencing pain, either due to natural ongoing sources or controlled noxious stimulation (heat, cold, pressure, shock, ischemia, or other painful stimulation); (b) the individual receives placebo treatment, in the form of a cream, inert medication, or other sham procedure, often with accompanying instructions that treatment will relieve pain; (c) pain with placebo is compared with a nonplacebo control condition, and pain reports decrease under placebo.

The first powerful support for the existence of an active placebo response came in the late 1970s, when Levine and colleagues showed that placebo analgesia was reversed with administration of naloxone, a μ-opioid receptor antagonist (Levine, Gordon, Jones, & Fields, 1978). This suggested that endogenous opioids were involved in the placebo response. The known effects of opiates on pain in both humans and animals led to the conclusion that placebo painkillers may be engaging the brain's natural pain-control mechanisms. Since this initial insight, researchers have explored placebo responses in pain using a variety of methodological approaches. Contemporary neuroimaging and electrophysiological techniques offer powerful tools for investigating the brain processes affected by placebo treatments and the brain mechanisms responsible for the placebo response. Researchers now can examine placebo-induced changes in brain regions known to be involved in pain processing. This provides support for the existence of active psychobiological mechanisms underlying placebo analgesia, and offers insights into the mechanisms by which the placebo response may modulate physiological endpoints.

Pain-Related Processes Affected by Placebo Treatments

Earlier, we described potential sources of reporting bias and noted that these concerns are particularly valid in consideration of placebo effects on pain, since pain is a subjective phenomenon. We and others have used neuroimaging techniques to provide nonsubjective evidence for placebo effects on pain, and to begin an investigation of their underlying mechanisms. This approach allows us to examine differences in physiological correlates of pain processing under placebo.

In an initial study, we induced expectations of analgesia in participants using an inert cream that participants were told would have an analgesic effect (Wager, Rilling, et al., 2004). A series of thermal stimuli were delivered, and participants rated the intensity of their pain experience several seconds after the termination of each stimulus. Identical stimulation sequences were delivered on placebo- and control-treated skin regions for each participant (with locations and testing order counterbalanced). Compared with the control condition, the placebo treatment decreased the reported painfulness of both shock and heat stimulation, which replicated the placebo effect on reported pain shown in many experimental studies (Benedetti et al., 1998; Montgomery & Kirsch, 1997; Price et al., 1999; Voudouris, Peck, & Coleman, 1985). Concurrent fMRI showed decreased responsiveness to noxious stimulation in the placebo condition in rostral anterior cingulate cortex (rACC), anterior insula (aINS), and thalamus, regions of the pain matrix thought to be critical for the affective experience of pain. Furthermore, the magnitude of these decreases correlated with placebo effects in reported pain. These data are consistent with the idea that placebo treatment *directly* affects the pain experience, and suggest that the affective component of pain might be particularly important. Subsequent studies have shown differences in the brain's response to noxious stimulation under placebo (Kong et al., 2006; Price et al., 2007)—though only Price et al. reported decreases in pain-processing regions—supporting the notion that placebo effects on nociceptive processing are indeed *active* processes, and that placebo effects on reported pain reflect real changes in pain processing, rather than simple reporting biases.

This approach also allows us to examine the temporal patterns of neural activity in response to pain. If the placebo effect is due entirely to reporting bias, then activity during pain under placebo should be the same as activity during pain in control conditions; differences might be largest later on, during the pain-reporting process. Examining the time course of placebo-related effects during thermal pain suggested that the decreased activity under placebo occurred both early and late in the pain period. Placebo decreases in rACC pain activity, which were correlated with reported placebo effects, were found in the early heat period. However, the largest main effects of placebo (control placebo) appeared in the contralateral insula and thalamus only in the late phase of stimulation. One explanation is that placebo effects may require a period of pain to develop or be strongest when pain is intense; alternatively, placebo responses may be most evident during residual pain after noxious stimulation has ended. A third interpretation is that the placebo reductions during late stimulation could reflect altered evaluation of pain rather than alterations in early sensory/perceptual nociceptive processes.

To test for placebo effects on early sensory/perceptual processing, we conducted a study using laser pain-evoked event-related potentials (Wager et al., 2006) that allowed us to examine activity at a higher temporal resolution than fMRI or PET. Laser-evoked potentials (LEPs) are a reliable marker of pain processing (Bromm & Treede, 1984) and arise from nociceptive processes that occur before most decision processes begin. Thus, the cognitive biases that some have argued may influence reported placebo effects are unlikely to affect LEPs. We focused on the N2/P2 complex (200 to 300 ms; Lorenz & Garcia-Larrea, 2003), which arises from the activation of A∂ fibers and is sometimes followed by a later component thought to arise from C-fiber activation (Bromm & Treede, 1984). The P2 increases as a function of laser intensity and reported pain (Iannetti et al., 2004), and its likely source is the ACC

(Garcia-Larrea, Frot, & Valeriani, 2003; Lenz et al., 1998), a region important for both attention and pain that has been shown to be modulated by placebo in pain and emotion. P2 amplitude was indeed reduced under placebo, supporting placebo effects on early nociceptive processing. Consistent with these results, expectations of analgesia have been shown to directly modulate spinal nociceptive reflexes (Goffaux, Redmond, Rainville, & Marchand, 2007), providing direct evidence for placebo effects on even the earliest levels of nociceptive processing.

Mechanisms of Placebo Analgesia

The studies reviewed in the previous section demonstrate the existence of psychobiological placebo effects on pain processing in the central nervous system. We now turn to consideration of the mechanisms by which these effects take place. Placebo treatments may affect several aspects of the continuum from sensation to experience to reporting that comprises pain processing: sensory transmission and processing, appraisal and the generation of subjective pain, and the pain reporting process (see Figure 63.2).

The issue of which aspects are affected has been at the heart of the debate over whether placebo treatments activate physiological pain-control systems and have clinically meaningful effects. We examine the levels of the nervous system at which the placebo response can be mediated, the role of specific neurotransmitters, and central mechanisms that give rise to placebo responses in pain and other conditions; this evidence is summarized in Table 63.1. We adopt the perspective that these mechanisms may not be mutually exclusive. Finally, we examine current knowledge about central nervous system placebo responses in other domains, and placebo effects on physiological outcome measures.

Sensory Transmission and Processing: Spinal Inhibition

An important mechanism by which placebo analgesia could take place was initially put forth in Melzack and Wall's gate control theory (Melzack & Wall, 1965). This theory posits that central control mechanisms interact with afferent information to prevent nociceptive signals from reaching the central nervous system, leading to decreases in cortical nociceptive processing. It is difficult to convincingly demonstrate inhibition of signals in the human spinal cord; the reductions in P2 amplitude previously discussed are expected if nociceptive afferents are inhibited, but they could also be caused by interactions within the brain.

One approach is to test for placebo-based modulation of nociceptive effects that have been shown to be spinally mediated in animal literature. Two such effects are secondary

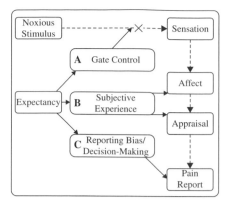

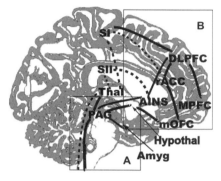

Figure 63.2 Mechanisms of placebo analgesia.

Note: There are several routes by which placebo manipulations may lead to decreases in reported pain (refer also to Table 63.1). Dashed lines in both figures represent normal stages and pathways of pain processing. Pain begins when sensory signals from the spinal cord reach the brain via the thalamus and are sent to the primary (SI) and secondary somatosensory cortex (S2). From there, signals are sent to the anterior insula (AINS) and anterior cingulate (ACC), which are involved (along with regions in the limbic system) in the subjective experience and emotional quality of pain. **A:** According to the gate control theory (Melzack & Wall, 1965), inhibition of spinal nociceptive input is possible through endogenous opioid release by the periaqueductal gray (PAG), which receives direct projections from dorsolateral prefrontal cortex (DLPFC), as well as orbitofrontal cortex (OFC), ACC, and amygdala. **B:** A second alternative is that placebo responses are a result of changes in affective appraisals and the generation of subjective pain. Appraisals are generated through interactions among the OFC, AINS, ACC, and other regions, and may be maintained in the DLPFC. **C:** Changes in decision making without a concomitant effect on pain perception are likely to involve increases in DLPFC activity and decreases in reported pain without modulating pain processing.

hyperalgesia—the tendency for skin around the site of painful stimulation to become sensitized—and the suppression of spinal nociceptive reflexes by painful stimulation of another body part. Matre, Casey, and Knardahl (2006) examined placebo effects on secondary hyperalgesia in humans by heating the skin at 46°C for five minutes. Expectation of pain relief reduced the size of the secondary hyperalgesic area, compared with a control condition in which pain relief was not expected. Sensitization of the skin area surrounding the simulation site is thought to result from sensitization in the spinal dorsal horn. These results therefore implicate a spinal mechanism in the placebo

effect. Reported pain was still the primary outcome measure in this study, leaving open the possibility that central processes as well as spinal ones may play a role in secondary hyperalgesia in humans.

Goffaux et al. (Goffaux et al., 2007) took a complementary approach by measuring spinal reflexes. They examined a leg muscle contraction reflex called R3 that is triggered by stimulation of the sural nerve, which runs along the outside of the ankle. The reflex is mediated by spinal circuits that operate at very short latency, with measurable onset in EMG at ~50 ms and a peak at ~90 ms (Dowman, 2001). Both this reflex and EEG measures of early negative (N100/150) and positive evoked cerebral potentials are dampened by painful stimulation of another limb, for example, by immersing the arm in cold water. The interaction across body parts is thought to be mediated by central pain-control circuits in the brain stem, and is termed the *diffuse noxious inhibitory control* (DNIC) *effect* (Le Bars, Dickenson, & Besson, 1979). The DNIC effect can be produced in anesthetized animals, so it is thought to be a reflexive anti-nociceptive response to noxious stimulation that involves inhibition at the spinal level. Goffaux et al. manipulated expectations about the effects of cold-water immersion: One group was told that it would reduce pain, and another that it would increase pain. Interestingly, they found that expectancy modulated the strength of the DNIC effect. Expectations for pain relief decreased the amplitude of the R3 reflex and P260 evoked potentials relative to expectations for increased pain during the cold-water immersion, but did not affect very early cortical potentials.

These findings suggest that expectancy can modulate activity at the level of the spinal cord, but that some components of cortical processing are more affected than others. If the expectancy manipulation inhibited nociceptive transmission, the R3 reflex and all cortical evoked potentials ought to have been affected. Whereas expectancy effects in early small components may be difficult to detect, it is notable that, similar to the study of Wager et al. (2006), the P260 potential showed the largest effect. This potential is thought to be localized to the anterior cingulate cortex and may overlap with the P3a or P3b potential (Dowman, 2001; Garcia-Larrea, Peyron, Laurent, & Mauguiere, 1997), and it appears to be sensitive to cognitive expectations even under conditions when pain reports are not (Dowman, 2001). These effects may reflect attentional orienting or evaluative aspects of nociceptive processing. The idea that expectancy effects influence attention-related processes does not preclude spinal inhibition, as suggested by effects on the R3 reflex. Indeed, attention has been shown to influence activity in the spinal dorsal horn in direct recordings in monkeys (Bushnell, Duncan, Dubner, & He, 1984).

TABLE 63.1 Mechanisms of placebo analgesia.

	Expected Central Nervous System Effects	Supporting Evidence
A) Gate control: Spinal inhibition of sensory transmission and processing	Widespread decreases in pain-processing regions Placebo-induced opioid release and PAG activation	Secondary hyperalgesia (Matre, Casey, & Knardahl, 2006) DNIC effects (Goffaux et al., 2007) PAG anticipatory increases (Wager, Rilling et al., 2004) PAG opioid release (Wager et al., 2007)
B) Subjective experience: Changes in appraisal and generation of subjective pain	Decreases in *select* pain-processing regions Increases in modulatory and affective regions	Reductions in pain-processing regions: insula, thalamus, ACC (Wager, Rilling et al., 2004; Price et al., 2007) OFC and rACC anticipatory increases (Wager, Rilling et al., 2004) Dopamine-opioid correlations (Scott et al., 2008) Reward-placebo correlations (Scott et al., 2007) Opioid binding and connectivity (Wager et al., 2007; Zubieta et al., 2005)
C) Reporting bias: Changes in decision making only	Changes in decision-making circuits during/after pain (pain processing decreases not expected)	Indirect evidence: Placebo modulated activity in pain matrix regions primarily during late pain period (Wager, Rilling et al., 2004) Indirect evidence: Insula is involved in decision making (Grinband, Hirsch, & Ferrara, 2006)

There is substantial evidence for centrally activated descending control systems in animals. In many (but not all) cases, these effects are mediated by endogenous opioids in the periacqueductal gray (PAG) and their projections to brain stem structures such as the rostral ventromedial medulla (RVM). The RVM, among other structures, contains neurons that exert powerful excitatory and inhibitory control (so-called On and Off cells) on spinal neurons (Fields, 2004). Thus, evidence implicating the PAG and opioids in placebo analgesia would provide further support for the spinal inhibition model.

The role of endogenous opioids in placebo analgesia is supported by studies using naloxone, an opioid antagonist that reverses placebo effects on reported pain in studies of expectancy-based placebo analgesia (Benedetti, Arduino, & Amanzio, 1999; Grevert, Albert, & Goldstein, 1983; Levine & Gordon, 1984; Levine, Gordon, & Fields, 1978; Petrovic, Kalso, Petersson, & Ingvar, 2002; Pollo, Vighetti, Rainero, & Benedetti, 2003). These results suggest that endogenous opioids indeed play a critical role in placebo analgesia.

Neuroimaging methodologies allow researchers to elaborate on the knowledge available from naloxone studies to better understand the role of endogenous opioids in the placebo response. In our early study of placebo analgesia using fMRI (Wager, Rilling et al., 2004), we observed increases in an area of the midbrain surrounding the PAG during anticipation of pain under placebo. This could be consistent with the gate control theory, in that placebo expectancy would increase opioid release by the PAG, and descending opioids would inhibit subsequent

pain at the level of the spinal cord's dorsal horn. Molecular imaging with PET provides an opportunity to understand where in the brain placebo changes opioid release. Radioactive tracers selective for μ-opioid receptors (MORs) allow researchers to infer endogenous opioid activity, as tracer binding is inversely related to endogenous MOR opioid binding. Placebo did increase opioid binding in the PAG during noxious stimulation (Wager et al., 2007). Another important observation was that placebo administration resulted in *decreased* PAG opioid binding during pain anticipation, relative to the control condition, suggesting that the placebo response may reduce the threat normally associated with noxious stimulation. Importantly, PAG was not the only region to show increases in opioid binding with placebo; placebo administration resulted in increased opioid binding during pain in many other cortical regions, particularly in frontal and limbic regions (Wager et al., 2007; Zubieta et al., 2005). Furthermore, connectivity analyses revealed that placebo increased functional integration between PAG and these regions, among other functional networks (Wager et al., 2007). These results suggest that while PAG opioid release plays an important role in placebo analgesia, it may not only induce descending inhibition of nociception, as the gate control theory would suggest, but might also facilitate changes in brain networks that lead to reduced aversion to a given noxious stimulus, by virtue of PAG correlations with opioid release in central appraisal and valuation networks (including the OFC, NAC, amygdala, insula, medial thalamus, and rACC). We consider the role of central processing in the following section.

Placebo analgesia is not always opioid-mediated, since naloxone administration does not always reverse placebo effects on reported pain. In one study, hidden naloxone administration failed to reverse placebo effects on post-surgical pain (Gracely, Dubner, Wolskee, & Deeter, 1983). Placebo significantly decreased pain regardless of naloxone administration; naloxone increased pain across placebo and control conditions; and there was no interaction between the two. Similarly, a study of placebo analgesia in patients with irritable bowel syndrome (Vase et al., 2005) found large placebo effects that were not reversible by naloxone. There are several possible explanations, including that naloxone has different effects at different doses (Levine, Gordon, & Fields, 1979) and may affect placebo analgesia without overall effects on pain only at some doses, and that irritable bowel syndrome patients may be opioid-insensitive and have developed nonopioid pain-relief mechanisms through conditioning with medication.

An intriguing possibility is that placebo effects may be opioid-mediated when central expectancy is involved. An experiment by Amanzio and Benedetti (1999) suggested placebo analgesia created by verbal instructions (and thus mediated by conscious expectancies of pain relief) was reversible by naloxone. Conditioning responses to ketorolac, a nonopioid analgesic, by repeatedly injecting the drug produced placebo analgesia as well. After repeating the injection experience-drug effect pairing, injecting saline alone reduced pain. However, this type of placebo effect was completely naloxone-insensitive. Thus, placebo analgesia may involve both opioid and nonopioid mechanisms, and this may be determined by whether there is an expectancy component to the placebo response, as well as the specific neurochemical pathways involved in the learning process.

Placebo Effects on Central Pain Processing

Though there is mounting evidence for the involvement of descending pain-control systems and endogenous opioids in placebo analgesia, there is also substantial evidence that spinal inhibition cannot provide a complete account. Wager et al. (2007) observed that placebo effects in reported pain were relatively large and persisted throughout the experimental session, whereas placebo effects in P2 amplitudes were smaller and decreased over time. We conducted a formal comparison of the actual P2 reduction versus the expected reduction if input-reduction were a complete account. The analysis revealed that reported pain effects were too large relative to P2 effects to be caused solely by input blockade, suggesting that there may be multiple sources of placebo effects on reported pain. Part of the effect may be due to spinal inhibition, and another part to changes in central pain processing and/or reporting bias.

In a classic study, Benedetti and colleagues showed that opioid-mediated placebo effects are involved with site-specific expectancies for analgesia (Benedetti, Arduino, et al., 1999). They induced specific expectations of analgesia on participants' hands or feet, and showed that naloxone reverses these specific analgesic effects. These results suggest that there is still a critical interaction with expectancy and the significance of pain that plays an important role in the ultimate pain experience. Opioid release may interact with frontal regions associated with the significance of the pain experience, rather than solely being responsible for a widespread descending inhibition.

Thus, the evidence on opioid involvement leaves ample room for central brain effects that do not involve the spinal cord. Whereas endogenous opioids are powerfully implicated in spinal inhibition, they are also known for several effects mediated largely or entirely within the brain, including their soporific and euphoric effects and their addictive potential. Opioids in DLPFC, nucleus accumbens (NAC), and insula are correlated with reported emotion during pain processing (Zubieta et al., 2006), and placebo treatments have been shown to reduce MOR binding (and thus likely increase opioid release) in brain structures implicated in the determination of affective value, including rACC, OFC, VMPFC, aINS, and NAC (Scott et al., 2007; Wager et al., 2007; Zubieta et al., 2005).

Appraisal and Subjective Pain—Changes in Pain Significance

There are several possibilities for cognitive mechanisms that would lead to changes in pain significance with placebo administration. These processes require appraisals of the significance or meaning of treatment (Moerman & Jonas, 2002), which may lead to expectancies about positive treatment outcomes, decreases in attention to pain, and changes in pain-related affect (reduced anxiety/threat; increased appetitive processing). Geers, Helfer, Weiland, and Kosbab (2006) found that reported symptoms induced by placebo treatment were greater when attention was focused on the body. Placebo-induced anxiety reduction could also lead to reduction in pain processing (Turner, Deyo, Loeser, Von Korff, & Fordyce, 1994); this is supported by research demonstrating that decreases in reported anxiety correlate with decreases in pain under placebo and lidocaine (Vase et al., 2005). Changes in affect are supported by fMRI and opioid binding studies, in which placebo effects are localized to brain systems critical for affective appraisal, evaluation of the significance of stimuli for the self, and motivation; these results and their implications are discussed in more detail later. Figure 63.3 illustrates these processes and their potential respective contributions as mediators of the relationship between noxious stimulation and reported pain under placebo.

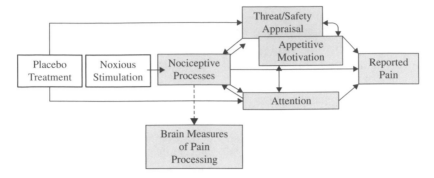

Figure 63.3   Psychological mediators of the placebo response.
Note: The effect of placebo treatment on reported pain and brain measures of pain processing may be mediated by key psychological processes, including affective appraisals and executive attention. Placebo analgesia may come about through affect modulation, by reducing threat or anxiety appraisals, or by increasing appetitive motivation. Placebo analgesia may also result from decreased attention to noxious stimulation.

While more research needs to be done to directly assess the differential contributions of these brain mechanisms, such processes are likely to be similar to those involved in executive functions—basic cognitive processes coordinating the maintenance and manipulation of information. Information about context is known to require dorsolateral prefrontal cortex (DLPFC), which interacts with working memory—a system that maintains information in an active state in the brain—to maintain expectancies induced by placebo manipulations. Placebo instructions are likely to exert their effects by changing the cognitive context in which pain stimulation is perceived, and these altered appraisals of the situation give rise to changes in expectations about pain, harm, and pain relief. Thus, maintenance of placebo context is likely to be evident through increases in DLPFC activity, which ought to inhibit pain-processing regions of cortex; indeed, DLPFC increases during pain anticipation correlated with subsequent decreases during thermal stimulation in the thalamus, insula, and rACC, and also correlated with PAG activity during anticipation (Wager, Rilling, et al., 2004). It is important to acknowledge, however, that such correlations do not conclusively determine whether the observed modulation of pain-processing regions was mediated by changes in attention, affect, or anxiety: All these require maintenance of the placebo context by DLPFC and would be expected to ultimately lead to decreases such as those observed. An approach that would allow researchers to differentiate between the contributions of these central processes would be to directly manipulate these variables to identify brain processes that mediate the relationship between DLPFC increases and subsequent pain matrix activity.

Effective placebo administration induces expectations for reduced symptomatology or diminished pain, which affects how the brain processes the condition or stimulus. The processes most likely to be altered are those that assign value and meaning (for the self, or survival) to the stimulus. Orbitofrontal cortices and rACC have been shown to be highly involved in the process of valuation. Placebo administration has been shown to result in increased opioid binding in rACC and OFC during pain in placebo relative to control (Wager et al., 2007). Increases in rACC during pain anticipation under placebo correlated with placebo effects on reported pain, and placebo-induced decreases in rACC during pain correlated with anticipatory increases in DLPFC and PAG (Wager, Rilling, et al., 2004), supporting the possible connection between executive function, descending modulation, and placebo-induced changes in pain affect. Finally, Bingel and colleagues demonstrated that rACC activity covaried with PAG and amygdala activity during placebo, but not control, conditions (Bingel et al., 2006).

An emerging model is that the largest effects of placebo are found in brain regions at the interface between nociceptive afferents and cognitive contextual processes. These regions, which include midlateral OFC, rACC, medial thalamus, and anterior insula, are part of a broader network of structures thought to be a neuroanatomical substrate for the computation of abstract reward/punishment value—or, in other terms, appraisal of the significance of a stimulus or context for the well-being and survival of the organism. This extended appraisal network includes medial prefrontal cortex (MPFC), OFC, extended amygdala, nucleus accumbens, ventral striatum, medial thalamus, and the medial temporal lobes. All these regions have shown fMRI and opioid-binding changes during placebo analgesia. More research must be done to establish how this network functions in the appraisal process and what particular roles its individual regions play. At a broad level, however, these regions are connected both anatomically—via monosynaptic and largely bidirectional projections (Price, 2000)—and functionally, as evidenced by coactivation in studies of placebo and emotional responses (Kober et al., 2008).

Expanding on the fact that placebo treatments may modulate valuation processes, some researchers have suggested that placebo analgesia may be thought of as a special case of reward processing; pain relief may be considered to be a positive outcome (Fields, 2004; Irizarry & Licinio, 2005). Scott and colleagues (Scott et al., 2007) used PET molecular imaging to examine the role of dopamine in placebo analgesia, using [^{11}C]raclopride to label dopamine binding during placebo. The authors also examined correlations between the dopamine binding results and fMRI activation during a separate session. During the fMRI session, participants performed a monetary incentive delay (MID) task (Knutson, Fong, Adams, Varner, & Hommer, 2001), and analyses focused on activity during anticipated monetary reward in the nucleus accumbens (NAC), a region rich in dopaminergic neurons. Dopamine binding levels correlated with the anticipated effectiveness of the placebo, and the magnitude of the dopamine response to pain anticipation correlated with reported placebo analgesia during pain. Furthermore, high placebo responders were found to recruit nucleus accumbens to a greater extent during reward anticipation in the MID task, and nucleus accumbens activity during reward anticipation correlated with dopamine activity during placebo analgesia.

The role of dopamine in placebo analgesia is further supported by work showing that dopamine D2 receptor agonists produce analgesia (Lin, Wu, Chandra, & Tsay, 1981; Magnusson & Fisher, 2000; Morgan & Franklin, 1991). Scott et al. (2008) used PET to image both opioid and dopamine receptor binding in the same individuals. Placebo induced both opioid and dopamine release (reduced binding) in the NAC, among other brain regions. Strikingly, endogenous dopamine increases in NAC were correlated with both opioid increases in NAC and reported placebo analgesia. Finally, pain processing and placebo treatments have been shown to involve components of the ventral striatum, a region rich in dopaminergic neurons that has been shown to be critical in reward processing and learning. Pain tolerance is correlated with drops in dopamine D2 receptor binding in the putamen (Hagelberg et al., 2002), and placebo analgesia induces increased MOR binding in the nucleus accumbens (Wager et al., 2007; Zubieta et al., 2005).

Mechanisms of the Nocebo Response

As the nocebo response involves inducing expectations for worse symptomatology or pain, its mechanisms are considerably less understood than the placebo response due to ethical constraints. However, researchers have begun to examine the nocebo response by investigating neurochemical activity in paradigms that induce expectations for increased pain, and current knowledge suggests that placebo and nocebo effects may involve similar brain mechanisms; they may involve opposite manipulations of the affective appraisal systems that evaluate the survival value of potential actions and outcomes. Scott et al. (2008) have reported that participants experiencing placebo and nocebo responses to a verbal suggestion of analgesia are at opposite ends (high and low, respectively) of a continuum of placebo-induced opioid and dopamine activity in the NAC, a key component of the brain's motivational circuitry.

There is also evidence that nocebo manipulations can affect HPA axis activity, and that they share some pharmacological similarity with placebo responses. Benedetti, Amanzio, and Maggi (1995) found that placebo responses were potentiated by proglumide, a cholecystokinin (CCK) antagonist. This was significant because CCK, in turn, blocks opioids; thus, the results suggested that proglumide disinhibited an endogenous opioid response to placebo. More recently, nocebo effects were shown to be reversed by proglumide, providing evidence for opposing effects of placebo and nocebo on the same neurochemical system. Benedetti and colleagues administered saline to postoperative patients with the instruction that it would increase pain for a short time (Benedetti, Amanzio, Casadio, Oliaro, & Maggi, 1997), which successfully induced increases in reported pain. These nocebo effects were reversed with administration of proglumide. These results were replicated in a later study, in which proglumide was found to reverse the nocebo effect in healthy subjects during ischemic arm pain (Benedetti, Amanzio, Vighetti, & Asteggiano, 2006).

Interestingly, nocebo manipulations in this latter study also induced increases in cortisol and adrenocorticotropic hormone, indexes of the hypothalamic-pituitary-adrenal (HPA) axis. The antianxiety drug diazepam reversed both HPA effects and hyperalgesia, suggesting that increased anxiety (in a general sense of the word) underlies the nocebo response (Benedetti, Lanotte, Lopiano, & Colloca, 2007). Proglumide, by contrast, reversed only the hyperalgesia, suggesting that it works on neural circuits more specific to pain processing and evaluation, and further that it is the cortisol response to *threat* that was affected by the nocebo manipulation rather than the cortisol response to *pain*. This is because one treatment (proglumide) affected pain without affecting the cortisol nocebo response; thus, the cortisol nocebo response is unlikely to be caused by the pain itself. Interestingly, placebo treatment in this study did not reliably reduce HPA axis responses, suggesting that placebo and nocebo may be dissociable. It is unknown whether the difference between placebo and nocebo responses resulted from floor effects in the cortisol response to threat; if the subjects were not substantially threatened by the pain, there would be little threat-related cortisol response to be reduced by placebo treatment.

CENTRAL VERSUS PROXIMAL MECHANISMS: PLACEBO RESPONSES ACROSS DOMAINS

Having reviewed current knowledge of mechanisms supporting placebo analgesia in depth, we now turn to placebo responses across domains. We expect that many elements of the placebo response will be domain-specific; however, neuroimaging studies of the placebo response in different modalities and conditions reveal certain commonalities that may reflect general modulatory and appraisal processes. We refer to processes involved across domains as *central mechanisms*, and domain-specific central nervous system processes as *proximal mechanisms*.

Central Mechanisms

Many neuroimaging studies of placebo reveal placebo-induced activation of rACC (Casey et al., 2000; Kong et al., 2006; Lieberman et al., 2004; Petrovic et al., 2005; Petrovic & Ingvar, 2002; Price et al., 2007; Wager, Rilling, et al., 2004; Wager et al., 2007) and lateral OFC (Lieberman et al., 2004; Petrovic et al., 2005; Wager, Rilling, et al., 2004; Wager et al., 2007), regions highly involved in affective appraisal and cognitive control; results from these studies are presented in Figure 63.4A and 63.4B. Thus, processes subserved by these regions are likely to serve as central mechanisms, supporting the etiology and maintenance of placebo responses across domains.

(A)

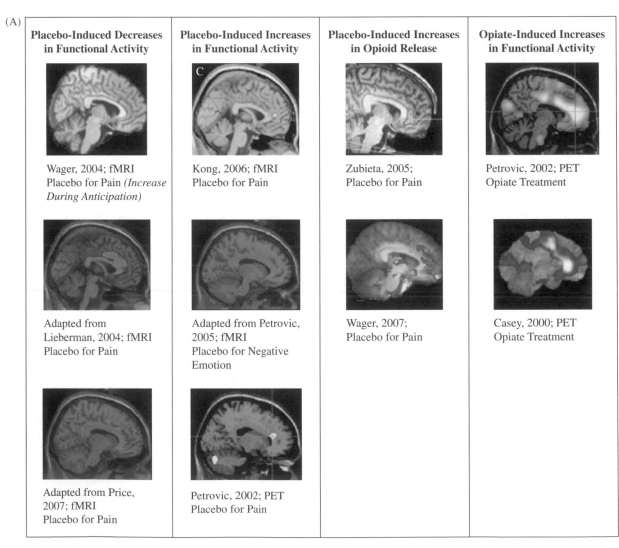

Placebo-Induced Decreases in Functional Activity	Placebo-Induced Increases in Functional Activity	Placebo-Induced Increases in Opioid Release	Opiate-Induced Increases in Functional Activity
Wager, 2004; fMRI Placebo for Pain *(Increase During Anticipation)*	Kong, 2006; fMRI Placebo for Pain	Zubieta, 2005; Placebo for Pain	Petrovic, 2002; PET Opiate Treatment
Adapted from Lieberman, 2004; fMRI Placebo for Pain	Adapted from Petrovic, 2005; fMRI Placebo for Negative Emotion	Wager, 2007; Placebo for Pain	Casey, 2000; PET Opiate Treatment
Adapted from Price, 2007; fMRI Placebo for Pain	Petrovic, 2002; PET Placebo for Pain		

Figure 63.4 (Figure C.59A in color section) Consistency of placebo results across studies.

Note: Neuroimaging studies of the placebo response and related processes reveal certain commonalities that provide synergistic insight into the mechanisms underlying the placebo response across domains.

A: Many studies reveal placebo-induced modulation of dorsal rostral anterior cingulate (rACC) a region involved in regulating affect and appraisal. **B:** Numerous studies also reveal placebo increases in lateral orbitofrontal cortex (OFC), a region highly involved in cognitive control and evaluative processing.

(B)

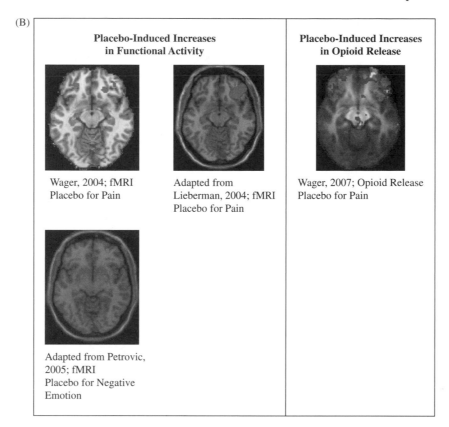

| **Placebo-Induced Increases in Functional Activity** | **Placebo-Induced Increases in Opioid Release** |

Wager, 2004; fMRI
Placebo for Pain

Adapted from
Lieberman, 2004; fMRI
Placebo for Pain

Wager, 2007; Opioid Release
Placebo for Pain

Adapted from Petrovic,
2005; fMRI
Placebo for Negative
Emotion

Figure 63.4B   (**Figure C.59B** in color section)

Placebo treatment was used to induce expectations of anxiety relief during the viewing of emotional images (Petrovic et al., 2005). Regions that exhibited increased activity under placebo during the viewing of unpleasant emotional pictures (rACC, lateral OFC) were the same that were shown to exhibit increased activity in anticipation of noxious stimulation under placebo analgesia (Wager, Rilling, et al., 2004). The specific instantiations of the placebo response, however, are modality-specific, creating differing downstream placebo effects; placebo during unpleasant picture viewing elicited decreased amygdala and extrastriate activity, while placebo during painful stimulation elicited decreased activity in rACC, aINS, and thalamus, areas responsible for pain processing. Thus, a common modulatory network may be active in maintaining positive expectancies and contextual knowledge, and may serve to downregulate whichever network of regions is responsible for producing the modality-specific appraisal of one's current state.

Lateral OFC and rACC are thus likely to influence placebo by regulating affect and appraisal. These regions are known to be an important part of a cognitive control network responsible for maintaining goals, rules, and expectations in both cognitive and affective domains. Figure 63.5 presents results from a meta-analysis of cognitive control studies, demonstrating an overlap in lateral OFC between

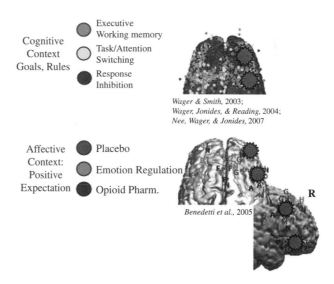

Figure 63.5   (**Figure C.60** in color section) Prefrontal regulation of pain and affect.

Note: Meta-analyses of neuroimaging studies(Benedetti, Mayberg, Wager, Stohler, & Zubieta, 2005; Nee, Wager, & Jonides, 2007; Wager, Jonides, & Reading, 2004; Wager & Smith, 2003) that examined regulation of cognitive and affective context: Each point shows results from a study. Overlap between cognitive and affective regulation can be seen in dorsolateral prefrontal cortex (DLPFC) and lateral orbitofrontal cortex (OFC). These regions likely support central modulatory mechanisms of placebo, providing placebo-induced regulation of domain-specific processes.

studies that examined cognitive context (e.g., attention switching), and studies that examined affective context (e.g., placebo).

The prominence of placebo responses in central systems for affective appraisal establishes a link between placebo analgesia and manipulations of threat and safety appraisals in other paradigms, including threats to social status and physical safety. In addition to the important role of rACC and OFC across domains, appetitive motivational shifts (involving dopamine) in the ventral striatum/NAC have also been proposed as a common mechanism for placebo effects across disorders (de la Fuente-Fernandez, Schulzer, & Stoessl, 2004), and recent studies have found that placebo analgesia is predicted by fMRI responses to anticipated monetary reward (Scott et al., 2007) and dopamine activity (Scott et al., 2008) in the nucleus accumbens. Overall, these results are promising, and more study is needed to establish the role of central appraisal systems in placebo responses across different conditions.

Proximal Mechanisms

Proximal mechanisms are the domain-specific central nervous system pathways subserving the placebo response. We briefly review current knowledge of these pathways in the domains of Parkinson's disease (PD), Major Depressive Disorder (MDD), and anxiety.

Parkinson's Disease

While the role of dopamine (DA) in placebo analgesia points to an appetitive motivational/appraisal account of placebo that may be relevant across domains, DA arguably plays a much more critical role in the placebo response in PD. PD is a debilitating movement disorder known to result from the degeneration of dopamine-producing neurons in the nigrostriatal pathway. Researchers have learned about the mechanisms of the PD-specific placebo response by examining placebo effects on motor performance, dopamine release, and single neuron activity in the substantia nigra. PET studies of dopamine D2 receptor activity have provided evidence that placebo treatments lead to dopamine release in the striatum (de la Fuente-Fernandez et al., 2001). Complementary evidence has been obtained from neurosurgical studies, in which researchers have examined placebo effects on activity in the subthalamic nucleus (STN), a stimulation site used in the treatment of Parkinson's, and have examined interactions between placebo expectancies and STN stimulation. Placebo administration directly affected STN activity in placebo responders (those who demonstrated placebo effects on muscle rigidity, a clinical sign of the disease), evidenced by decreased bursting and neuronal frequency discharge (Benedetti et al., 2004).

Researchers have also demonstrated differing effects of ventral STN stimulation on autonomic activity between hidden and open stimulation (Lanotte et al., 2005), and expectations for poor versus enhanced motor performance have been shown to modulate the effects of STN stimulation (Pollo et al., 2002). Finally, the placebo response in PD is thought to arise primarily through expectancies, as verbal instructions to induce expectations of improved motor performance were found to reverse the effects of conditioning trials in which STN stimulation was turned off, resulting in decreased motor performance (Benedetti et al., 2003).

Major Depressive Disorder

In MDD, placebo effects on the brain were examined by using PET imaging to measure baseline metabolic activity before, during, and after treatment with either placebo or fluoxetine, a common selective-serotonin reuptake inhibitor prescribed as an antidepressant (Mayberg et al., 2002). Many changes that were observed as part of successful treatment with the active drug were also observed in placebo responders, including metabolic decreases in subgenual ACC. This region has been shown to be consistently affected in depression and is a target of deep-brain stimulation in patients who do not otherwise respond to treatment. Other common sites of activity over the course of treatment with either fluoxetine or placebo included metabolic increases in prefrontal, parietal, and posterior cingulate cortex, and decreases in parahippocampus and thalamus. Importantly, these common results differ from patterns of brain activation over the course of other types of treatment, such as cognitive behavioral therapy and interpersonal psychotherapy (Brody et al., 2001; Goldapple et al., 2004), which tend to lead to metabolic decreases in prefrontal activity, rather than increases. These results suggest that both active drug and placebo treatments work in part by changing central systems involved in affective valuation and motivation. It is important to point out that this study was longitudinal, and due to ethical constraints about denying treatment to patients when successful treatments are known to exist, no natural history control group was included in these analyses. It is therefore possible that observed results in both conditions may include factors attributable to the natural course of MDD. Much more work remains to be done to unpack the brain mechanisms involved in both verum and placebo treatment for depression.

Anxiety

While studies of the placebo response in PD and MDD have generally examined effects in clinical populations, Petrovic and colleagues used emotional images and active anxiolytics to examine placebo effects on anxiety and emotion processing in healthy participants (Petrovic et al., 2005). On their first day in the laboratory, participants viewed and rated neutral and unpleasant images without treatment, then were given benzodiazepine, which decreased ratings of unpleasantness, followed by a benzodiazepine antagonist that reversed the effects of the anxiolytic. On the following visit, participants were scanned using fMRI while they were told they would undergo the same procedure. During this session, saline was administered in place of both the benzodiazepine and its antagonist, resulting in placebo and control conditions, respectively. As mentioned, this study revealed decreases in regions specific to emotion processing, and increases in regions that overlapped with modulatory regions that had been identified in studies of placebo analgesia (Petrovic et al., 2002; Wager, Rilling, et al., 2004). More specifically, placebo induced decreases in extrastriate activity and amygdala that correlated with reported placebo effects, and increases in OFC, rACC, and ventrolateral PFC activity (only rACC and vlPFC correlated with subjective placebo effects). Finally, treatment expectations on day 1 correlated with the extent of decreases in extrastriate cortex, increases in rACC, and placebo-induced activity in ventral striatum.

ETIOLOGY OF THE PLACEBO RESPONSE: EXPECTANCY VERSUS CONDITIONING

Given evidence that the placebo response does indeed involve active psychobiological mechanisms in multiple domains, the question arises of exactly how the response comes about. For about half a century, placebo researchers have focused on two possible sources: classical conditioning or conscious expectancies. Briefly, conditioning-based placebo responses result from the association between active treatment outcomes and the context or procedures surrounding treatment, regardless of the organism's awareness of the contingencies between stimuli. Expectancy-based placebo responses result from appraisals of anticipated treatment outcomes that inherently depend on the organism's beliefs about treatment. Thus, an important distinction is that only expectancy-based placebo effects can be altered by verbal instructions to participants. We assess how each factor may contribute to the development of the placebo response, and examine research directly comparing the two processes. We suggest that some placebo responses may be mediated entirely by expectancies; others may be primarily due to conditioning; and in other cases the two may not be mutually exclusive, as conditioning can serve to induce conscious expectations about placebo treatment outcomes.

Conditioning-Based Placebo Responses

Many psychologists became interested in placebo research in the 1950s, with the publication of Beecher's *The Powerful Placebo* (Beecher, 1955). This coincided with psychology's shift toward behaviorist views of psychological phenomena. Consistent with the dominant trends, the placebo response was explained in terms of classical conditioning. In the original Pavlovian stimulus-substitution model of classical conditioning, organisms learn to pair a neutral stimulus (a stimulus that elicits no response on its own) with an unconditioned stimulus (UCS) that normally elicits an unconditioned response (UCR). With repeated pairings, the neutral stimulus comes to elicit the same response as the UCS; the neutral stimulus has become a conditioned stimulus (CS), and the evoked behavior is referred to as a conditioned response (CR). Conditioning can occur in aversive contexts (in fear conditioning, a light may be paired with a shock, to elicit freezing in response to the light) or appetitive contexts (as in Pavlov's classic experiments, food can be paired with a tone and animals eventually salivate in response to the tone).

A simple classical conditioning account of placebo would propose that a pharmacological agent serves as a UCS that elicits healing effects (UCR; Montgomery & Kirsch, 1997; Wickramasekera, 1980); when the agent is delivered in pill form, the pill becomes the CS, and later administration of the pill without the pharmacological agent will elicit the active effects of the drug as the CR. Proponents of the classical conditioning view of placebo have even suggested that over a lifetime of pairings, neutral stimuli related to the medical context—doctors' offices, the procedures surrounding medicine administration, medical devices, and doctors themselves—become associated with the results of treatment, and that placebo effects are the result of conditioning to these contextual stimuli.

Several findings offer support for a classical conditioning account of the placebo response. Benedetti and colleagues showed that placebo effects following active administration of an opiate analgesic included respiratory depression, a side effect of the active medication, although participants reported no awareness of this associated side effect (Benedetti, Amanzio, Baldi, Casadio, & Maggi, 1999). In another study, participants were pretreated with pharmacological agents that elicited increases or decreases in cortisol and growth hormone release (Benedetti et al., 2003). Placebos were subsequently administered alongside verbal suggestions that treatment would produce the opposite effect, but the directionality of the physical outcomes in these two domains was not reversed. These results suggest that some placebo responses involve learning that is not modifiable by conscious expectancies.

Primary mechanistic evidence that conditioning can serve to recruit endogenous disease-related processes comes from human and animal studies of conditioned immunosuppression and conditioned induction of anti-allergic effects. Immunosuppression refers to the reduction of immune system efficacy; this may be deliberately induced in medical procedures such as organ transplants to prevent the immune system from rejecting the foreign organ. Rats that receive cyclophosphamide, an immunosuppressive agent, alongside saccharin during conditioning exhibit decreased antibodies when saccharin solution is later presented on its own, relative to rats that were not conditioned and conditioned rats that were not exposed to saccharin at test (Ader & Cohen, 1975). A later study used ß-adrenoceptor antagonists and 6-OHDA, a chemical that depletes noradrenaline, in a similar case of conditioned immunosuppression using the immunosuppressive drug cyclosporin A (CsA) and found that immunosuppressive effects in the spleen were mediated by the sympathetic nervous system (Exton et al., 2002). Finally, humans who received CsA paired with a unique beverage over repeated sessions demonstrated immunosuppression when they were exposed to the CS a week later, as indexed by lymphocyte proliferation, mRNA expression, and cytokine production and release (Goebel et al., 2002).

A similar approach was taken to induce conditioning of antiallergic effects in humans (Goebel, Meykadeh, Kou, Schedlowski, & Hengge, 2008). A unique beverage was repeatedly paired with antihistamine in patients with allergic rhinitis. Participants who received the beverage alongside a placebo pill at test exhibited levels of basophil, a white blood cell that releases histamine, that were comparable to those who received the active medication, while participants who received water alongside placebo demonstrated no basophil inhibition. These data suggest that conditioning can indeed recruit powerful endogenous mechanisms related to immune functioning, and offer preliminary windows into central nervous system pathways that may be involved in the etiology of a conditioning-based placebo response. However, while this offers some insight into the role of conditioning in endogenous processes, it is unknown how mechanisms supporting conditioned immunosuppression may generalize to other domains, such as pain and Parkinson's disease. Furthermore, participant expectancies were not assessed in these studies, and it is possible that conscious expectancies about the novel beverage and its effects on immune function may have played an important role in the observed effects.

Little is known about brain mechanisms that would specifically support a classical conditioning account of placebo, although there have been decades of research on conditioning in animal models, and aversive conditioning

mechanisms have been studied in humans using fMRI (Phelps, Delgado, Nearing, & LeDoux, 2004; Phelps et al., 2001). Different conditioning mechanisms are responsible for effects in different systems, so despite the wealth of knowledge about the specific neural circuitry involved in the realm of aversive conditioning, it is difficult to generalize across domains or infer mechanisms in domains that have not been directly examined. In eyelid conditioning, an auditory stimulus (CS) is paired with an air puff (US) to the eye, and this gradually leads to the conditioned response of an eyeblink (CR) when the tone is presented. Although these two stimuli originate in different modalities and travel through separate pathways (CS via mossy fibers, US via climbing fibers), both pathways include synapses onto the purkinje cells in the cerebellar cortex (Kim & Thompson, 1997). In fear conditioning, an auditory stimulus (CS) is paired with a shock (US), creating a startle response (CR). Again, these stimuli are processed separately (CS travels from auditory thalamus, US from brain stem), but both share common synapses in the lateral amygdala (Rogan & LeDoux, 1995; Rogan, Staubli, & LeDoux, 1997). These examples suggest that for these specific types of conditioned learning to occur, US and CS pathways must share common nuclei; furthermore, conditioning recruits unique pathways depending on stimulus and response modalities. Thus, conditioning-based placebo mechanisms are likely to involve similar neural mechanisms in principle, but our knowledge of mechanisms specific to aversive conditioning are unlikely to generalize to positive conditioning-based placebo responses.

Though little was known about the brain mechanisms of conditioned immunosuppression for many years, recent studies have begun to investigate them. An important study by Pacheco-Lopez et al. (Pacheco-Lopez et al., 2005) used a rat model to assess the effects of lesions of the insula, amygdala, and ventromedial hypothalamus on conditioned immunosuppression and taste aversion. Insula lesions disrupted both aversion to the taste paired with the immunosuppressive drug (the CS) and several peripheral markers of immunosuppression, both before the conditioning procedure and afterward, during evocation by presenting the CS. Thus, the insula is implicated in both acquisition and retrieval of the memory that leads to immunosuppression. Amygdala lesions disrupted immunosuppression only before conditioning, implicating it in the learning process but not the expression of the learned response. Conversely, hypothalamic lesions disrupted expression but not acquisition of the immunosuppressive response.

The neural mechanisms for conditioned placebo responses in pain and other domains remain unknown, and more research is needed to disentangle pathways that subserve conditioned CS-US or CS-UR learning and conscious expectancies. In one fMRI study, researchers compared brain responses to painful stimulation under opioid-based analgesia with responses to placebo analgesia (Petrovic et al., 2002). Opioid administration always preceded the placebo analgesia condition, which may have induced a conditioning-based placebo response. Brain responses to each were compared with a pain control condition, and both were associated with increased activity in rACC, and increased rACC-brain stem connectivity. While this and other brain-based studies are promising, they have not directly compared conditioning processes with nonconditioning expectancy manipulations (verbal instructions only), and the nature of the conditioning-specific placebo response remains yet to be elucidated.

Expectancy-Based Placebo Responses

A central question in cognitive neuroscience over the past 50 years concerns the processes affected by expectancies, which shape perception across virtually every sensory and affective domain. Expectancies involve appraisals of an event's significance in the context of its anticipated outcome; appraisal systems can affect brain stem and hypothalamus nuclei as part of coordinated behavioral and physiological responses that promote homeostasis. In the expectancy view of placebo, beliefs and expectations associated with treatment administration are responsible for recruitment of endogenous mechanisms to produce the requisite changes associated with the placebo response. Expectancy-based placebo effects are mediated by beliefs about upcoming experience, and do not necessitate prior exposure to an active treatment for the effect to occur.

An important distinction between expectancies and conditioning-based learning is that expectancies are generally conscious at the time when decisions are made (Stewart-Williams & Podd, 2004); if they are not conscious, they can be made conscious with directed attention (Kirsch, 2004; Kirsch & Lynn, 1999). Many conditioning theories posit that conditioning will occur regardless of the organism's awareness of the contingencies between stimuli. Thus, only expectancy effects depend on an individual's state of mind, which suggests that expectancy-based placebo effects can be altered by verbal instructions to participants, whereas conditioning-based placebo effects cannot. In the following section, we review several studies that have compared the respective contributions of expectancies and conditioning-based learning to the placebo response. In most cases, these studies suggest that expectancies provide a stronger account for observed placebo effects on reported pain.

As expectancies modulate perception across many domains, we have much to draw from in positing potential brain mechanisms underlying expectancy-based placebo effects. In many studies, expectancy mechanisms are probed by paradigms that employ novel stimuli that are predictive of different levels of stimulation. This allows researchers to examine the development of expectancies over time, as participants learn to predict stimulation based on cues. Conditioning explanations cannot account for behavior when participants have no prior experience with the predictive stimuli, or in paradigms that include contingency reversals. These paradigms allow researchers to investigate how these expectancies affect processing; and neuroimaging and electrophysiology methodologies can reveal brain mechanisms responsible for maintaining expectancies and supporting the relationship between expectancies and perceived experience. Expectancy manipulations have been shown to modulate stimulus processing in neuroimaging and electrophysiology studies of pain (Keltner et al., 2006; Koyama, McHaffie, Laurienti, & Coghill, 2005; Lorenz et al., 2005), emotion (Bermpohl et al., 2006), taste (Nitschke et al., 2006; Sarinopoulos, Dixon, Short, Davidson, & Nitschke, 2006), and reward (Hampton, Adolphs, Tyszka, & O'Doherty, 2007; Spicer et al., 2007).

As described earlier, researchers can define reasonable hypotheses about brain mechanisms supporting an expectancy-based placebo response by drawing on knowledge from brain mechanisms of cognitive control. These can be tested by contrasting anticipatory activity in a placebo condition with anticipatory activity during a control condition, so that the researcher can identify processes related to pain expectancy that are shaped by placebo treatment. This approach was used in an fMRI study of placebo analgesia (Wager, Rilling, et al., 2004) that revealed increases in DLPFC, OFC, and rACC activity during anticipation of pain with placebo. These anticipatory increases correlated with placebo effects on reported pain, and anticipatory increases in DLPFC and OFC correlated with subsequent placebo-induced reductions in pain matrix activity during thermal stimulation. Importantly, anticipatory increases in DLPFC correlated with activity in an area of the midbrain surrounding the PAG (see Figure 63.6), offering support for the interaction between expectancies and opioid release. Other studies have replicated and extended this result, showing that placebo treatments for negative emotion activate the same brain regions (Petrovic et al., 2005), and that endogenous opioids—neurochemicals linked to relaxation, euphoria, and pain relief—are released in these regions following placebo treatment (Wager et al., 2007; Zubieta et al., 2005).

Reconciling Expectancy and Conditioning Accounts of Placebo

It is difficult to resolve the relative contributions of expectancy and conditioning to placebo effects, because the two

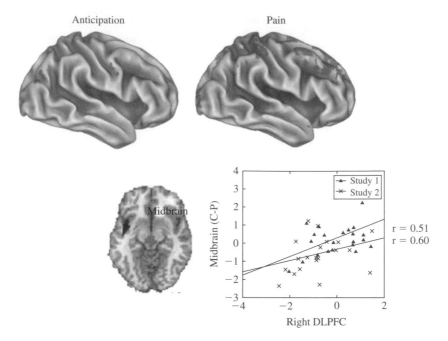

Figure 63.6   Placebo-induced activation of the cognitive/evaluative network.

Note: Contrasts between placebo and control conditions in an fMRI study of placebo analgesia (Wager, Rilling, et al., 2004) revealed increases in brain regions known to be involved in executive function and affective appraisal, including dorsolateral prefrontal cortex (DLPFC) and orbitofrontal cortex (OFC). Increases were observed both in anticipation of pain (top left) and during thermal stimulation (top right). Placebo-induced increases were also observed in an area of the midbrain surrounding the periaqueductal gray (PAG; bottom), and anticipatory activity in this region correlated with anticipatory increases in right posterior DLPFC (bottom right), offering support for the influence of expectancies on placebo-induced pain modulation.

are not always mutually exclusive; in some cases, conditioning procedures are likely to shape both learning and expectations. There are two ways to distinguish between learning and expectancy mechanisms: One relies on behavioral observations, and the other on measurement of the brain. Earlier, we suggested that conditioning results in learning that persists over time, despite expectancies; when a CS is presented without the UCS, extinction of the CR is relatively slow. Thus, effects that can be reversed in a single trial or affected by verbal instructions are not likely to be the result of conditioning, but rather expectancies. A second way to discriminate between conditioning and expectancy is by measuring brain activity. The patterns of activity increases and opioid release with placebo in OFC and rACC, and increases in DLPFC, suggest that general mechanisms of appraisal and expectancy are at work. Such effects have been found in pain and, though less well studied, depression. A difficulty, however, is that there is no way to ensure by looking at the brain that these responses are not the result of some conditioned association being activated. Another difficulty is that it is currently difficult or impossible to measure learned associations directly in the human brain; whereas synapse strength, gene expression, and other molecular markers of learning can be investigated in animal models, the techniques for probing them are invasive and cannot be used in humans—and, in addition, it is

still unknown where in the human brain cellular learning underlying placebo effects may be taking place.

Several experiments have attempted to directly compare expectancy-based and conditioning-based placebo effects in studies of placebo analgesia (Benedetti et al., 2003; de Jong, van Baast, Arntz, & Merckelbach, 1996; Montgomery & Kirsch, 1997; Voudouris et al., 1985; Voudouris, Peck, & Coleman, 1989, 1990), using variations of the same basic procedure. Verbal instructions to participants suggest that the placebo treatment is an effective analgesic drug. Some participants receive these instructions alone. Other participants are additionally exposed to an active treatment or procedure, which in most cases has involved the surreptitious reduction of painful stimulus intensity during treatment under the placebo condition. This serves as an unconditioned response (UR) or UCS with which the CS—cues associated with stimulation during placebo conditions—are associated. In some cases, a third group receives the conditioning procedure, but they are not verbally instructed that the placebo is an effective drug. The key comparisons are whether conditioning without verbal instructions reduces pain, and whether conditioning plus instructions is more effective than conditioning alone.

Voudouris and colleagues (1985, 1989, 1990) used this approach and reported that conditioning provided the stronger explanation for observed placebo effects, since conditioning plus instruction was much more effective than instruction alone. Conclusions drawn from these experiments were contested, as some argued that such studies do not compare expectancy and conditioning, but instead compare expectancies mediated by physical processes (conscious expectancies that come about as a result of the conditioning procedure) to expectancies mediated by verbal information alone (Stewart-Williams & Podd, 2004). Conscious expectancies may mediate learning in both conditions, and any observed differences may be due to the fact that physiological experiences induce stronger expectancies than verbal suggestion.

Results supporting an expectancy account of placebo analgesia were reported by de Jong and colleagues (1996), who used essentially the same experimental design, but added a group of participants who were exposed to conditioning trials with the critical addition that they were informed that noxious stimulation was being lowered during application of the cream. If the conditioning process were entirely responsible for observed placebo effects (if all that matters is the pairing of UCS and CS), then participant knowledge about the procedures would not counteract the efficacy of the conditioning manipulation on observed placebo effects; however, pain reports under placebo in this group did not differ from reported pain in the control condition. Furthermore, de Jong's group added measures for participants' conscious expectations of pain relief, which Voudouris and colleagues had not included in their original study, and found that these ratings predicted the magnitude of placebo effects. Later, Montgomery and Kirsch (1997) took a similar approach and demonstrated that although the magnitude of placebo effects seemed to offer support for a conditioning explanation of placebo, results were entirely mediated by participants' reported expectations of pain relief in the conditioning group. These studies both suggest that expectancy theory provided a better account for observed placebo effects than a conditioning explanation.

In a more expansive examination of the contributions of expectancy and conditioning to placebo effects, Benedetti and colleagues (2003) analyzed the contributions of the two potential sources to placebo effects in pain, Parkinson's disease (PD), and hormone secretion. In each modality, preconditioning with an active treatment (Keterolac for analgesia, turning off subthalamic nucleus stimulation for decreased motor performance in Parkinson's disease, and Sumatriptan for growth hormone increase and cortisol decrease) was followed by verbal instructions to induce opposing expectations in the respective groups (hyperalgesia, movement velocity increase in PD, and suggestions of GH decrease and cortisol increase). Consistent with de Jong and Montgomery and Kirsch's earlier findings, conscious expectations reversed the effects of conditioning in

pain, as well as PD. However, expectancies did not reverse the effects of preconditioning in hormonal secretion. The authors take this to suggest that placebo responses close to behavior (pain reports and motor symptoms) are mediated by expectancies, but that conditioning of some hormonal and peripheral responses can occur outside the regulation of conscious expectancies.

While the series of studies reviewed here suggest that classical conditioning and expectancies are competing explanations that must be pitted against one another to determine the true source of the placebo response, some have argued that it may not be necessary to view the two potential mechanisms as competing explanations. We framed our introduction to Pavlovian conditioning in a manner consistent with the early stimulus-substitution models of the phenomenon, which focused on contiguity, the notion that the paired presentation of stimuli is responsible for the acquisition of conditioned responses. However, computational accounts have suggested that conditioning can be explained as a *process* by which an organism learns the relationships between events, and that organisms learn to pair stimuli with subsequent *outcomes*, rather than responses (Rescorla, 1988a, 1988b). A response is generated only insofar as the stimulus provides useful information about an upcoming event, and behaviors that are performed during conditioning are performed in anticipation of the expected outcome. Some suggest that this anticipatory behavior is closely linked to expectancies. In cases in which the conditioning process allows for conscious understanding of the relationships involved, expectancies may be likely to mediate the process of learning stimulus-outcome relationships over the course of conditioning, providing a way to reconcile the two accounts.

SUMMARY

The placebo response is not only clinically relevant, but also serves as a valuable window into the powerful interaction between basic psychological processes, such as expectancies and affective appraisals, and the bodily state. Although many factors can potentially lead to observed placebo effects without affecting underlying physiology, careful experimental manipulations and supporting neuroimaging investigations provide evidence of active psychobiological placebo responses. Nearly all the studies reviewed identify a subset of participants who do not respond to the placebo manipulation (report no difference between placebo and control conditions). Early placebo researchers believed there was a true population of placebo responders, and behavioral studies sought to identify trait-level personality factors that would differentiate the placebo responder from the nonresponder. These attempts proved futile, and researchers adopted the view that anyone could demonstrate placebo reactivity under the correct circumstances (Liberman, 1964). Neuroimaging analyses, such as those reviewed earlier, generally account for responder differences through correlations between brain activity and extent of reported placebo effects, or statistical comparisons between placebo responders and nonresponders. We have reviewed specific evidence of placebo effects on pain, Parkinson's disease, Major Depressive Disorder, and anxiety, and suggest that placebo responses in these domains may share common central mechanisms, including affective appraisal, cognitive control, and factors related to the etiology of the placebo response. Much more experimental research is needed to elaborate on our knowledge of factors contributing to individual differences in the development of the placebo response, proximal placebo mechanisms in domains other than those reviewed, and to build a more comprehensive account of central and proximal mechanisms of the placebo response.

REFERENCES

Ader, R., & Cohen, N. (1975). Behaviorally conditioned immunosuppression. *Psychosomatic Medicine, 37*, 333–340.

Amanzio, M., & Benedetti, F. (1999). Neuropharmacological dissection of placebo analgesia: Expectation-activated opioid systems versus conditioning-activated specific subsystems. *Journal of Neuroscience, 19*, 484–494.

Arkin, R. M., Gabrenya, W. K., Jr., Appelman, A. S., & Cochran, S. T. (1979). Self-presentation, self-monitoring, and the self-serving bias in causal attribution. *Personality and Social Psychology Bulletin, 5*, 73–76.

Barrett, B., Muller, D., Rakel, D., Rabago, D., Marchand, L., & Scheder, J. C. (2006). Placebo, meaning, and health. *Perspectives in Biological Medicine, 49*, 178–198.

Beecher, H. K. (1955). The powerful placebo. *Journal of the American Medical Association, 159*, 1602–1606.

Benedetti, F., Amanzio, M., Baldi, S., Casadio, C., Cavallo, A., Mancuso, M., et al. (1998). The specific effects of prior opioid exposure on placebo analgesia and placebo respiratory depression. *Pain, 75*(2/3), 313–319.

Benedetti, F., Amanzio, M., Baldi, S., Casadio, C., & Maggi, G. (1999). Inducing placebo respiratory depressant responses in humans via opioid receptors. *European Journal of Neuroscience, 11*, 625–631.

Benedetti, F., Amanzio, M., Casadio, C., Oliaro, A., & Maggi, G. (1997). Blockade of nocebo hyperalgesia by the cholecystokinin antagonist proglumide. *Pain, 71*, 135–140.

Benedetti, F., Amanzio, M., & Maggi, G. (1995). Potentiation of placebo analgesia by proglumide. *Lancet, 346*, 1231.

Benedetti, F., Amanzio, M., Vighetti, S., & Asteggiano, G. (2006). The biochemical and neuroendocrine bases of the hyperalgesic nocebo effect. *Journal of Neuroscience, 26*, 12014–12022.

Benedetti, F., Arduino, C., & Amanzio, M. (1999). Somatotopic activation of opioid systems by target-directed expectations of analgesia. *Journal of Neuroscience, 19*, 3639–3648.

Benedetti, F., Colloca, L., Torre, E., Lanotte, M., Melcarne, A., Pesare, M., et al. (2004). Placebo-responsive Parkinson patients show decreased activity in single neurons of subthalamic nucleus. *Nature Neuroscience, 7*, 587–588.

Benedetti, F., Lanotte, M., Lopiano, L., & Colloca, L. (2007). When words are painful: Unraveling the mechanisms of the nocebo effect. *Neuroscience, 147*, 260–271.

Benedetti, F., Mayberg, H. S., Wager, T. D., Stohler, C. S., & Zubieta, J. K. (2005). Neurobiological mechanisms of the placebo effect. *Journal of Neuroscience, 25*, 10390–10402.

Benedetti, F., Pollo, A., Lopiano, L., Lanotte, M., Vighetti, S., & Rainero, I. (2003). Conscious expectation and unconscious conditioning in analgesic, motor, and hormonal placebo/nocebo responses. *Journal of Neuroscience, 23*, 4315–4323.

Bermpohl, F., Pascual-Leone, A., Amedi, A., Merabet, L. B., Fregni, F., Gaab, N., et al. (2006). Attentional modulation of emotional stimulus processing: An fMRI study using emotional expectancy. *Human Brain Mapping, 27*, 662–677.

Bingel, U., Lorenz, J., Schoell, E., Weiller, C., & Buchel, C. (2006). Mechanisms of placebo analgesia: RACC recruitment of a subcortical antinociceptive network. *Pain, 120*(1–2), 8–15.

Brody, A. L., Saxena, S., Stoessel, P., Gillies, L. A., Fairbanks, L. A., Alborzian, S., et al. (2001). Regional brain metabolic changes in patients with major depression treated with either paroxetine or interpersonal therapy: Preliminary findings. *Archives of General Psychiatry, 58*, 631–640.

Bromm, B., & Treede, R. D. (1984). Nerve fibre discharges, cerebral potentials and sensations induced by CO_2 laser stimulation. *Human Neurobiology, 3*, 33–40.

Bushnell, M. C., Duncan, G. H., Dubner, R., & He, L. F. (1984). Activity of trigeminothalamic neurons in medullary dorsal horn of awake monkeys trained in a thermal discrimination task. *Journal of Neurophysiology, 52*, 170–187.

Casey, K. L., Svensson, P., Morrow, T. J., Raz, J., Jone, C., & Minoshima, S. (2000). Selective opiate modulation of nociceptive processing in the human brain. *Journal of Neurophysiology, 84*, 525–533.

Clark, W. C. (1969). Sensory-decision theory analysis of the placebo effect on the criterion for pain and thermal sensitivity. *Journal of Abnormal Psychology, 74*, 363–371.

de Jong, P. J., van Baast, R., Arntz, A., & Merckelbach, H. (1996). The placebo effect in pain reduction: The influence of conditioning experiences and response expectancies. *International Journal of Behavioral Medicine, 3*, 14–29.

de la Fuente-Fernandez, R., Phillips, A. G., Zamburlini, M., Sossi, V., Calne, D. B., Ruth, T. J., et al. (2002). Dopamine release in human ventral striatum and expectation of reward. *Behavioural Brain Research, 136*, 359–363.

de la Fuente-Fernandez, R., Ruth, T. J., Sossi, V., Schulzer, M., Calne, D. B. Stoessl, A. J. (2001, August 10). Expectation and dopamine release: Mechanism of the placebo effect in Parkinson's disease. *Science, 293*, 1164–1166.

de la Fuente-Fernandez, R., Schulzer, M., & Stoessl, A. J. (2004). Placebo mechanisms and reward circuitry: Clues from Parkinson's disease. *Biological Psychiatry, 56*, 67–71.

Dowman, R. (2001). Attentional set effects on spinal and supraspinal responses to pain. *Psychophysiology, 38*, 451–464.

Exton, M. S., Gierse, C., Meier, B., Mosen, M., Xie, Y., Frede, S., et al. (2002). Behaviorally conditioned immunosuppression in the rat is regulated via noradrenaline and beta-adrenoceptors. *Journal of Neuroimmunology, 131*(1/2), 21–30.

Fields, H. (2004). State-dependent opioid control of pain. *Nature Reviews Neuroscience, 5*, 565–575.

Garcia-Larrea, L., Frot, M., & Valeriani, M. (2003). Brain generators of laser-evoked potentials: From dipoles to functional significance. *Clinical Neurophysiology, 33*, 279–292.

Garcia-Larrea, L., Peyron, R., Laurent, B., & Mauguiere, F. (1997). Association and dissociation between laser-evoked potentials and pain perception. *NeuroReport, 8,* 3785–3789.

Geers, A. L., Helfer, S. G., Weiland, P. E., & Kosbab, K. (2006). Expectations and placebo response: A laboratory investigation into the role of somatic focus. *Journal of Behavioral Medicine, 29,* 171–178.

Goebel, M. U., Meykadeh, N., Kou, W., Schedlowski, M., & Hengge, U. R. (2008). Behavioral conditioning of antihistamine effects in patients with allergic rhinitis. *Psychotherapy and Psychosomatics, 77*(4), 227–234.

Goebel, M. U., Trebst, A. E., Steiner, J., Xie, Y. F., Exton, M. S., Frede, S., et al. (2002). Behavioral conditioning of immunosuppression is possible in humans. *Federation of American Societies for Experimental Biology Journal, 16,* 1869–1873.

Goffaux, P., Redmond, W. J., Rainville, P., & Marchand, S. (2007). Descending analgesia: When the spine echoes what the brain expects. *Pain, 130*(1–2), 137–143.

Goldapple, K., Segal, Z., Garson, C., Lau, M., Bieling, P., Kennedy, S., et al. (2004). Modulation of cortical-limbic pathways in major depression: Treatment-specific effects of cognitive behavior therapy. *Archives of General Psychiatry, 61,* 34–41.

Gracely, R. H., Dubner, R., Wolskee, P. J., & Deeter, W. R. (1983, November 17). Placebo and naloxone can alter post-surgical pain by separate mechanisms. *Nature, 306,* 264–265.

Grevert, P., Albert, L. H., & Goldstein, A. (1983). Partial antagonism of placebo analgesia by naloxone. *Pain, 16,* 129–143.

Grinband, J., Hirsch, J., & Ferrara, V. P. (2006). A neural representation of categorization uncertainty in the human brain. *Neuron, 49,* 757–763.

Hagelberg, N., Martikainen, I. K., Mansikka, H., Hinkka, S., Nagren, K., Hietala, J., et al. (2002). Dopamine D2 receptor binding in the human brain is associated with the response to painful stimulation and pain modulatory capacity. *Pain, 99*(1/2), 273–279.

Hall, M. A., Dugan, E., Zheng, B., & Mishra, A. K. (2001). Trust in physicians and medical institutions: What is it, can it be measured, and does it matter? *Milbank Quarterly, 79,* 613–639.

Hampton, A. N., Adolphs, R., Tyszka, M. J., & O'Doherty, J. P. (2007). Contributions of the amygdala to reward expectancy and choice signals in human prefrontal cortex. *Neuron, 55,* 545–555.

Hrobjartsson, A., & Gotzsche, P. C. (2001). Is the placebo powerless? An analysis of clinical trials comparing placebo with no treatment. *New England Journal of Medicine, 344,* 1594–1602.

Hrobjartsson, A., & Gotzsche, P. C. (2004). Is the placebo powerless? Update of a systematic review with 52 new randomized trials comparing placebo with no treatment. *Journal of Internal Medicine, 256,* 91–100.

Iannetti, G. D., Leandri, M., Truini, A., Zambreanu, L., Cruccu, G., & Tracey, I. (2004). Adelta nociceptor response to laser stimuli: Selective effect of stimulus duration on skin temperature, brain potentials and pain perception. *Clinical Neurophysiology, 115,* 2629–2637.

Irizarry, K. J., & Licinio, J. (2005, March 4). An explanation for the placebo effect? *Science, 307,* 1411–1412.

Kelman, H. C. (1958). Compliance, identification, and internalization: Three processes of attitude change. *Journal of Conflict Resolution, 2,* 51–60.

Keltner, J. R., Furst, A., Fan, C., Redfern, R., Inglis, B., & Fields, H. L. (2006). Isolating the modulatory effect of expectation on pain transmission: A functional magnetic resonance imaging study. *Journal of Neuroscience, 26,* 4437–4443.

Kim, J. J., & Thompson, R. F. (1997). Cerebellar circuits and synaptic mechanisms involved in classical eyeblink conditioning. *Trends in Neurosciences, 20,* 177–181.

Kirsch, I. (2004). Conditioning, expectancy, and the placebo effect: Comment on Stewart-Williams and Podd. *Psychological Bulletin, 130,* 341–343; discussion 344–345.

Kirsch, I., & Lynn, S. J. (1999). Automaticity in clinical psychology. *American Psychologist, 54,* 504–515.

Kirsch, I., & Scoboria, A. (2001). Apples, oranges, and placebos: Heterogeneity in a meta-analysis of placebo effects. *Advances in Mind-Body Medicine, 17,* 307–309, 312–308.

Knutson, B., Fong, G. W., Adams, C. M., Varner, J. L., & Hommer, D. (2001). Dissociation of reward anticipation and outcome with event-related fMRI. *NeuroReport, 12,* 3683–3687.

Kober, H., Barrett, L. F., Joseph, J., Bliss-Moreau, E., Lindquist, K., Duncan, S., et al. (2008). *Networks of emotion: Functional parcelation and pathway analysis from meta-analytic data.* Submitted for publication.

Kong, J., Gollub, R. L., Rosman, I. S., Webb, J. M., Vangel, M. G., Kirsch, I., et al. (2006). Brain activity associated with expectancy-enhanced placebo analgesia as measured by functional magnetic resonance imaging. *Journal of Neuroscience, 26,* 381–388.

Koyama, T., McHaffie, J. G., Laurienti, P. J., & Coghill, R. C. (2005). The subjective experience of pain: Where expectations become reality. *Proceedings of the National Academy of Sciences, USA, 102,* 12950–12955.

Lanotte, M., Lopiano, L., Torre, E., Bergamasco, B., Colloca, L., & Benedetti, F. (2005). Expectation enhances autonomic responses to stimulation of the human subthalamic limbic region. *Brain, Behavior, and Immunity, 19,* 500–509.

Le Bars, D., Dickenson, A. H., & Besson, J. M. (1979). Diffuse noxious inhibitory controls (DNIC): Pt. I. Effects on dorsal horn convergent neurones in the rat. *Pain, 6,* 283–304.

Lenz, F. A., Rios, M., Zirh, A., Chau, D., Krauss, G., & Lesser, R. P. (1998). Painful stimuli evoke potentials recorded over the human anterior cingulate gyrus. *Journal of Neurophysiology, 79,* 2231–2234.

Levine, J. D., & Gordon, N. C. (1984, December 20). Influence of the method of drug administration on analgesic response. *Nature, 312,* 755–756.

Levine, J. D., Gordon, N. C., & Fields, H. L. (1978). The mechanism of placebo analgesia. *Lancet, 2,* 654–657.

Levine, J. D., Gordon, N. C., & Fields, H. L. (1979, April 19). Naloxone dose dependently produces analgesia and hyperalgesia in postoperative pain. *Nature, 278,* 740–741.

Levine, J. D., Gordon, N. C., Jones, R. T., & Fields, H. L. (1978, April 27). The narcotic antagonist naloxone enhances clinical pain. *Nature, 272,* 826–827.

Liberman, R. (1964). An experimental study of the placebo response under three different situations of pain. *Journal of Psychiatric Research, 2,* 233–246.

Lieberman, M. D., Jarcho, J. M., Berman, S., Naliboff, B. D., Suyenobu, B. Y., Mandelkern, M., et al. (2004). The neural correlates of placebo effects: A disruption account. *NeuroImage, 22,* 447–455.

Lin, M. T., Wu, J. J., Chandra, A., & Tsay, B. L. (1981). Activation of striatal dopamine receptors induces pain inhibition in rats. *Journal of Neural Transmission, 51*(3/4), 213–222.

Lorenz, J., & Garcia-Larrea, L. (2003). Contribution of attentional and cognitive factors to laser evoked brain potentials. *Clinical Neurophysiology, 33,* 293–301.

Lorenz, J., Hauck, M., Paur, R. C., Nakamura, Y., Zimmermann, R., Bromm, B., et al. (2005). Cortical correlates of false expectations during pain intensity judgments: A possible manifestation of placebo/nocebo cognitions. *Brain, Behavior, and Immunity, 19,* 283–295.

Magnusson, J. E., & Fisher, K. (2000). The involvement of dopamine in nociception: The role of D(1) and D(2) receptors in the dorsolateral striatum. *Brain Research, 855,* 260–266.

Matre, D., Casey, K. L., & Knardahl, S. (2006). Placebo-induced changes in spinal cord pain processing. *Journal of Neuroscience, 26,* 559–563.

Mayberg, H. S., Silva, J. A., Brannan, S. K., Tekell, J. L., Mahurin, R. K., McGinnis, S., et al. (2002). The functional neuroanatomy of the placebo effect. *American Journal of Psychiatry, 159*, 728–737.

Melzack, R., & Wall, P. D. (1965, November 19). Pain mechanisms: A new theory. *Science, 150*, 971–979.

Moerman, D. E., & Jonas, W. B. (2002). Deconstructing the placebo effect and finding the meaning response. *Annals of Internal Medicine, 136*, 471–476.

Montgomery, G. H., & Kirsch, I. (1997). Classical conditioning and the placebo effect. *Pain, 72*(1–2), 107–113.

Morgan, M. J., & Franklin, K. B. (1991). Dopamine receptor subtypes and formalin test analgesia. *Pharmacology Biochemistry and Behavior, 40*, 317–322.

Nee, D. E., Wager, T. D., & Jonides, J. (2007). Interference resolution: Insights from a meta-analysis of neuroimaging tasks. *Cognitive Affective and Behavioral Neuroscience, 7*, 1–17.

Nitschke, J. B., Dixon, G. E., Sarinopoulos, I., Short, S. J., Cohen, J. D., Smith, E. E., et al. (2006). Altering expectancy dampens neural response to aversive taste in primary taste cortex. *Nature Neuroscience, 9*, 435–442.

Pacheco-Lopez, G., Niemi, M. B., Kou, W., Harting, M., Fandrey, J., & Schedlowski, M. (2005). Neural substrates for behaviorally conditioned immunosuppression in the rat. *Journal of Neuroscience, 25*, 2330–2337.

Petrovic, P., Dietrich, T., Fransson, P., Andersson, J., Carlsson, K., & Ingvar, M. (2005). Placebo in emotional processing: Induced expectations of anxiety relief activate a generalized modulatory network. *Neuron, 46*, 957–969.

Petrovic, P., & Ingvar, M. (2002). Imaging cognitive modulation of pain processing. *Pain, 95*(1/2), 1–5.

Petrovic, P., Kalso, E., Petersson, K. M., & Ingvar, M. (2002, March 1). Placebo and opioid analgesia: Imaging a shared neuronal network. *Science, 295*, 1737–1740.

Phelps, E. A., Delgado, M. R., Nearing, K. I., & LeDoux, J. E. (2004). Extinction learning in humans: Role of the amygdala and vmPFC. *Neuron, 43*, 897–905.

Phelps, E. A., O'Connor, K. J., Gatenby, J. C., Gore, J. C., Grillon, C., & Davis, M. (2001). Activation of the left amygdala to a cognitive representation of fear. *Nature Neuroscience, 4*, 437–441.

Pollo, A., Torre, E., Lopiano, L., Rizzone, M., Lanotte, M., Cavanna, A., et al. (2002, August 7). Expectation modulates the response to subthalamic nucleus stimulation in Parkinsonian patients. *NeuroReport, 13*, 1383–1386.

Pollo, A., Vighetti, S., Rainero, I., & Benedetti, F. (2003). Placebo analgesia and the heart. *Pain, 102*(1–2), 125–133.

Price, D. D. (2000, June 9). Psychological and neural mechanisms of the affective dimension of pain. *Science, 288*, 1769–1772.

Price, D. D., Craggs, J., Verne, G. N., Perlstein, W. M., & Robinson, M. E. (2007). Placebo analgesia is accompanied by large reductions in pain-related brain activity in irritable bowel syndrome patients. *Pain, 127*(1–2), 63–72.

Price, D. D., & Dubner, R. (1977). Neurons that subserve the sensory-discriminative aspects of pain. *Pain, 3*, 307–338.

Price, D. D., Greenspan, J. D., & Dubner, R. (2003). Neurons involved in the exteroceptive function of pain. *Pain, 106*, 215–219.

Price, D. D., Milling, L. S., Kirsch, I., Duff, A., Montgomery, G. H., & Nicholls, S. S. (1999). An analysis of factors that contribute to the magnitude of placebo analgesia in an experimental paradigm. *Pain, 83*, 147–156.

Rescorla, R. A. (1988a). Behavioral studies of Pavlovian conditioning. *Annual Review of Neuroscience, 11*, 329–352.

Rescorla, R. A. (1988b). Pavlovian conditioning: It's not what you think it is. *American Psychologist, 43*, 151–160.

Roethlisberger, F. J., & Dickson, W. J. (1939). *Management and the worker.* Cambridge, MA: Harvard University Press.

Rogan, M. T., & LeDoux, J. E. (1995). LTP is accompanied by commensurate enhancement of auditory-evoked responses in a fear conditioning circuit. *Neuron, 15*, 127–136.

Rogan, M. T., Staubli, U. V., & LeDoux, J. E. (1997, December 11). Fear conditioning induces associative long-term potentiation in the amygdala. *Nature, 390*, 604–607.

Sarinopoulos, I., Dixon, G. E., Short, S. J., Davidson, R. J., & Nitschke, J. B. (2006). Brain mechanisms of expectation associated with insula and amygdala response to aversive taste: Implications for placebo. *Brain, Behavior, and Immunity, 20*, 120–132.

Scott, D. J., Stohler, C. S., Egnatuk, C. M., Wang, H., Koeppe, R. A., & Zubieta, J. K. (2007). Individual differences in reward responding explain placebo-induced expectations and effects. *Neuron, 55*, 325–336.

Scott, D. J., Stohler, C. S., Egnatuk, C. M., Wang, H., Koeppe, R. A., & Zubieta, J. K. (2008). Placebo and nocebo effects are defined by opposite opioid and dopaminergic responses. *Archives of General Psychiatry, 65*.

Spicer, J., Galvan, A., Hare, T. A., Voss, H., Glover, G., & Casey, B. (2007). Sensitivity of the nucleus accumbens to violations in expectation of reward. *Neuroimage, 34*, 455–461.

Stewart-Williams, S., & Podd, J. (2004). The placebo effect: Dissolving the expectancy versus conditioning debate. *Psychological Bulletin, 130*, 324–340.

Swets, J., Tanner, W. P., Jr., & Birdsall, T. G. (1961). Decision processes in perception. *Psychological Review, 68*, 301–340.

Turk, D. C., & Rudy, T. E. (1990). Neglected factors in chronic pain treatment outcome studies: Referral patterns, failure to enter treatment, and attrition. *Pain, 43*, 7–25.

Turner, J. A., Deyo, R. A., Loeser, J. D., Von Korff, M., & Fordyce, W. E. (1994). The importance of placebo effects in pain treatment and research. *Journal of the American Medical Association, 271*, 1609–1614.

Vase, L., Robinson, M. E., Verne, G. N., & Price, D. D. (2005). Increased placebo analgesia over time in irritable bowel syndrome (IBS) patients is associated with desire and expectation but not endogenous opioid mechanisms. *Pain, 115*, 338–347.

Volkow, N. D., Wang, G. J., Ma, Y., Fowler, J. S., Zhu, W., Maynard, L., et al. (2003). Expectation enhances the regional brain metabolic and the reinforcing effects of stimulants in cocaine abusers. *Journal of Neuroscience, 23*, 11461–11468.

Voudouris, N. J., Peck, C. L., & Coleman, G. (1985). Conditioned placebo responses. *Journal of Personality and Social Psychology, 48*, 47–53.

Voudouris, N. J., Peck, C. L., & Coleman, G. (1989). Conditioned response models of placebo phenomena: Further support. *Pain, 38*, 109–116.

Voudouris, N. J., Peck, C. L., & Coleman, G. (1990). The role of conditioning and verbal expectancy in the placebo response. *Pain, 43*, 121–128.

Wager, T. D., Jonides, J., & Reading, S. (2004). Neuroimaging studies of shifting attention: A meta-analysis. *NeuroImage, 22*, 1679–1693.

Wager, T. D., Matre, D., & Casey, K. L. (2006). Placebo effects in laser-evoked pain potentials. *Brain, Behavior, and Immunity, 20*, 219–230.

Wager, T. D., & Nitschke, J. B. (2005). Placebo effects in the brain: Linking mental and physiological processes. *Brain, Behavior, and Immunity, 19*, 281–282.

Wager, T. D., Rilling, J. K., Smith, E. E., Sokolik, A., Casey, K. L., Davidson, R. J., et al. (2004, February 20). Placebo-induced changes in fMRI in the anticipation and experience of pain. *Science, 303*, 1162–1167.

Wager, T. D., Scott, D. J., & Zubieta, J. K. (2007). Placebo effects on human μ-opioid activity during pain. *Proceedings of the National Academy of Sciences, USA, 104*, 11056–11061.

Wager, T. D., & Smith, E. E. (2003). Neuroimaging studies of working memory: A meta-analysis. *Cognitive Affective and Behavioral Neuroscience, 3*, 255–274.

Watson, A., El-Deredy, W., Vogt, B. A., & Jones, A. K. (2007). Placebo analgesia is not due to compliance or habituation: EEG and behavioural evidence. *NeuroReport, 18*, 771–775.

Wells, L. E., & Sweeney, P. D. (1986). A test of three models of bias in self-assessment. *Social Psychology Quarterly, 49*, 1–10.

Whitney, C. W., & Von Korff, M. (1992). Regression to the mean in treated versus untreated chronic pain. *Pain, 50*, 281–285.

Wickramasekera, I. (1980). A conditioned response model of the placebo effect predictions from the model. *Biofeedback and Self Regulation, 5*, 5–18.

Wickramasekera, I. (2001). The placebo efficacy study: Problems with the definition of the placebo and the mechanisms of placebo efficacy. *Advances in Mind-Body Medicine, 17*, 309–312; discussion 312–308.

Zubieta, J. K., Bueller, J. A., Jackson, L. R., Scott, D. J., Xu, Y., Koeppe, R. A., et al. (2005). Placebo effects mediated by endogenous opioid activity on μ-opioid receptors. *Journal of Neuroscience, 25*, 7754–7762.

Zubieta, J. K., Yau, W. Y., Scott, D. J., & Stohler, C. S. (2006). Belief or need? Accounting for individual variations in the neurochemistry of the placebo effect. *Brain, Behavior, and Immunity, 20*, 15–26.

Chapter 64

Psychological Influences on Neuroendocrine and Immune Outcomes

LISA M. CHRISTIAN, NATHAN T. DEICHERT, JEAN-PHILIPPE GOUIN,
JENNIFER E. GRAHAM, AND JANICE K. KIECOLT-GLASER

Over the past 25 years, substantial evidence has established that psychological factors affect clinically relevant immune and neuroendocrine outcomes. In particular, psychosocial stress reliably causes immunological changes that are not only measurable, but also meaningful in terms of health. Moreover, alterations in neuroendocrine function are primary mediators of immune changes seen in response to stress.

This chapter focuses on work linking psychosocial factors with immune function among humans in three outcome areas. We first review substantial evidence linking the psychological states of stress and depression to inflammation, a key outcome because of its clinical relevance to serious health conditions. Next, we summarize research linking stress and wound healing, a clinically vital process in which inflammation plays an important role. Finally, we review effects of stress on susceptibility to infectious illness including studies of vaccination, exposure to infectious agents, and immune control of latent viruses.

This chapter focuses primarily on the immune effects of stress, although other specific psychosocial factors (including depression, hostility, and anxiety) are also discussed. Although we emphasize human studies, we also describe key animal studies, primarily those elucidating physiological mechanisms underlying links between psychosocial factors and immune outcomes. Throughout, the role of neuroendocrine mediators is highlighted. We also describe the positive effects of social support and promising interventions that target the effects of stress.

Funding: Work on this chapter was supported by training grant T32AI55411 (L.M.C., N.T.D.), a Doctoral Research Training Award from the Fonds de la recherche en santé du Québec (J-P.G.), and grants AT002971, AG025732, AG029562, CA126857, CA131029, M01-RR-0034, and CA16058 from the National Institutes of Health.

OVERVIEW OF THE IMMUNE SYSTEM

The protective physical barrier formed by the skin provides the body's first line of defense against foreign invaders. The second line of defense is the innate immune system, which responds very rapidly (within minutes to hours) but in a nonspecific manner when exogenous antigens such as bacteria and viruses are detected. The key elements of the innate immune system are neutrophils, macrophages, natural killer (NK) cells, and complement proteins.

When the innate immune system cannot effectively eliminate or control the antigen in question, the adaptive immune system provides the third line of defense. Although the adaptive immune system may take several days to mount an optimal response, its action is highly targeted. The main cell type of the adaptive immune system is the lymphocyte, which includes T-cells and B-cells. Importantly, after the adaptive immune system is exposed to a particular antigen, certain T-cells and B-cells retain memory of that antigen, which allows a stronger and more rapid response on subsequent exposure; the ability of the adaptive immune system to form memory in this way provides the basis for vaccination (see Figure 64.1).

Cytokines are soluble proteins that are involved in communication between immune cells. Cytokines also have more far-reaching effects (e.g., effects of cytokines on the brain are key to behavioral changes related to illness). Cytokines are produced by cells of both the innate and adaptive immune systems as well as several other non-lymphoid cells in the body, such as adipocytes (fat cells). Among their multiple functions, cytokines play a key role in inflammatory immune responses, which involve the recruitment of key proteins and immune cells to an affected area. Inflammation is a critical response to infection or injury; however, chronic or excessive inflammation is linked to negative health outcomes. Thus, an adequate,

First Line of Defense
Skin
Key Features: Body's largest organ Prevents bacteria, viruses, and other exogenous antigens from entering

Second Line of Defense
Innate Immune System
Key Features: Rapid, but nonspecific response
Major components: Neutrophils, macrophages, natural killer cells, complement proteins

Third Line of Defense
Adaptive Immune System
Key Features: Slower, highly targeted response Formation of immunological memory
Major components: T-cells and B-cells

Figure 64.1   Divisions of the immune system.

but not exaggerated inflammatory response to immune challenge is optimal. For more detailed coverage of the elements of the immune system, see Chapter 7, Volume 1.

EFFECTS OF HEALTH BEHAVIORS ON IMMUNE OUTCOMES

Although this chapter focuses on neuroendocrine pathways linking psychological stress and immune outcomes, behavioral pathways are another important area of investigation. In particular, heightened distress is associated with less adaptive health behavior, including more smoking and alcohol use, poorer diet, and less sleep (Steptoe, Wardle, Pollard, Canaan, & Davies, 1996; Vitaliano, Scanlan, Zhang, Savage, & Hirsch, 2002). In turn, health behaviors affect neuroendocrine function, immune function, and related health outcomes, including wound healing and response to infectious agents (Figure 64.2).

For each of the outcomes discussed in this chapter, effects of stress remain after accounting for effects of health behaviors, indicating that more direct physiological pathways exist between psychological factors and immune outcomes. However, because health behaviors may partly explain or exacerbate the effects of stress, assessing and appropriately controlling for health behaviors is an important component of research aimed at identifying and separating physiological versus behavioral pathways linking stress and immune function. Moreover, because health behaviors are modifiable, they represent a key target for interventions. One pathway by which behavioral interventions can benefit immune function is by improving physiological responses to stress.

STRESS, DEPRESSION, AND INFLAMMATION

Inflammation is an essential immune response to infection or injury. Among multiple other functions, inflammation promotes destruction (phagocytosis) and clearance of pathogens and initiates wound healing. As described, the production of cytokines, which are soluble proteins involved in communication between immune and other cells, is an important component of the inflammatory response. Cytokines can be classified as pro- or anti-inflammatory, although some cytokines demonstrate both pro- and anti-inflammatory characteristics. As the name implies, pro-inflammatory cytokines—including interleukin (IL)-6, IL-1, and tumor necrosis factor (TNF)-α—promote inflammation. Anti-inflammatory cytokines such as interleukin-10 (IL-10) act as important regulators of the immune response, in part by inhibiting the production of pro-inflammatory cytokines (Opal & DePalo, 2000; Parham, 2005).

A local inflammatory response involves increased vascular permeability and the recruitment of key proteins and immune cells to the affected area. It can be characterized by redness, swelling, pain, and fever (Rabin, 1999). In the case of infection or injury, inflammation is beneficial, as it aids recovery. In fact, pro-inflammatory cytokines are administered therapeutically to treat hepatitis and some cancers (Capuron & Miller, 2004; Dantzer & Kelley, 2007). However, exaggerated or chronic inflammation is detrimental to health. Chronic inflammation has been implicated in serious medical conditions including cardiovascular disease, arthritis, diabetes, inflammatory bowel disease, periodontal disease, certain cancers, and age-related functional decline (Black & Garbutt, 2002; Bruunsgaard, Pedersen, & Pedersen, 2001; Ershler & Keller, 2000; Hamerman, Berman, Albers, Brown, & Silver, 1999; Ishihara & Hirano, 2002). An insufficient anti-inflammatory response can contribute to excessive inflammation. Relatedly, the administration of anti-inflammatory cytokines has been implicated as a useful therapeutic strategy for diseases marked by inflammation, particularly rheumatoid arthritis (Opal & DePalo, 2000). Excessive anti-inflammatory control can overly inhibit inflammation, resulting in increased risk for infection and illness (Opal & DePalo, 2000). Thus, an appropriate balance of inflammatory and anti-inflammatory function is necessary for optimal health.

Conceptualizing Stress and Depression

Although conceptually distinct, stress and depression are similar in that they involve negative mood, activation of the hypothalamic-pituitary-adrenal (HPA) axis, and associated negative health outcomes (Anisman & Merali, 2003;

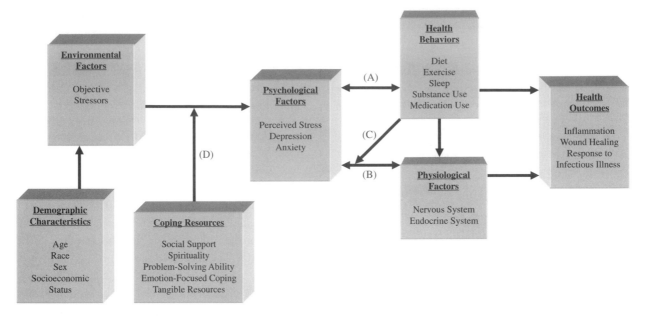

Figure 64.2 Pathways by which psychological factors affect health outcomes.

Note: An important pathway by which psychological factors affect health is health behaviors (**A**). Thus, appropriate control for health behaviors is important to research aiming to delineate physiological pathways linking psychological factors to health. Effects of psychological factors on health outcomes remain after accounting for effects of health behaviors, indicating that more direct physiological pathways between psychological factors and health outcomes exist (**B**). Importantly, health behaviors are modifiable and can moderate physiological responses to stress (**C**). Thus, health behaviors represent a key target for intervention. Another important target of interventions is coping resources, which moderate effects of environmental stressors on psychological responses (**D**).

Connor & Leonard, 1998). Stress can be defined and measured in many ways. Objective definitions generally focus on characteristics of the stressor experienced. Completing a 10-minute speech task can be defined as a mild acute stressor. In contrast, subjective measures of stress reflect an individual's perceptions of stress in their lives as well as their perceived ability to cope with that stress. In this way, subjective measures can capture important individual differences in how people react to the same stressor.

Common depressive symptoms include negative mood, loss of interest or pleasure, difficulty concentrating, changes in appetite, sleep disturbance, and thoughts of death. Importantly, psychological stress is a frequent precursor of clinical depression (Kendler, Karkowski, & Prescott, 1999). Moreover, as will be reviewed briefly, stress-associated overactivation of the sympathetic nervous system and HPA axis may play a causal role in the development of depression (also see Chapters 6 and 7, Volume 1; and Chapters 55 and 62, this volume).

Stress and Inflammation

Using various stressors, both animal and human models have demonstrated effects of stress on inflammation. In terms of animal studies, acute stress in the form of exposure to a novel environment or foot/tailshock induces increases in plasma IL-6 levels in rats (LeMay, Vander, &

Kluger, 1990; Zhou, Kusnecov, Shurin, DePaoli, & Rabin, 1993). For example, rats exposed to footshock exhibited heightened plasma IL-6. Moreover, IL-6 rose as an increasing number of footshocks were administered (Zhou et al., 1993). Notably, this physiological response to stress can be conditioned; after repeated shocking, exposure to stimuli (e.g., auditory tones) that were present when shocks were administered also elicited increases in IL-6 (Johnson et al., 2002; Zhou et al., 1993).

Pro-inflammatory cytokines also rise in response to acute stressors such as public speaking and mental arithmetic (Brydon, Edwards, Mohamed-Ali, & Steptoe, 2004; Steptoe, Willemsen, Owen, Flower, & Mohamed-Ali, 2001). Circulating IL-6 and IL-1 receptor antagonist (IL-1ra) increased two hours after completion of Stroop and mirror-tracing tasks, while control participants did not change (Steptoe et al., 2001). This time lag between acute stressors and cytokine responses in humans has been reported in other studies. Some null findings (e.g., Heesen et al., 2002; Lutgendorf, Logan, Costanzo, & Lubaroff, 2004) may be explained by the fact that samples were taken at time points that were too close to the stressor. It is also notable that the magnitude of inflammation seen in response to objective stressors is not necessarily predicted by perceived stress (e.g., Brydon et al., 2004). This is consistent with evidence that subjective evaluations are often poor predictors of cardiovascular reactivity to acute stressors (e.g., Christian & Stoney, 2006).

Importantly, repeated exposure to a stressor may not lead to habituation of inflammatory responses. A sample of 21 healthy middle-aged men completed the Trier Social Stress Test (a combined speech and mental arithmetic task; see Kirschbaum, Pirke, & Hellhammer, 1993) three times with 1-week intervals between sessions. As expected, the stressor resulted in increases in plasma IL-6. Notably, although participants demonstrated habituation of cortisol and systolic blood pressure reactivity to the task between weeks 1 and 3, they demonstrated similar stress-induced elevations in IL-6 across visits (von Kanel, Kudielka, Preckel, Hanebuth, & Fischer, 2005). If such lack of habituation also occurs in naturalistic settings, inflammatory responses to relatively minor but recurrent stress in daily life may contribute to morbidity and mortality.

Given the effects demonstrated in response to acute stress, it would be expected that chronic stress could have an even greater impact on inflammation. Caregiving provides an excellent model for assessing the effects of chronic stress on health; individuals who provide care for loved ones with chronic medical conditions, such as a spouse with dementia, commonly experience ongoing stress, significant life change, and social isolation. Relatedly, caregivers experience heightened risk of negative mental and physical health outcomes, including depressive symptoms, infectious illness, and poorer response to vaccination (Kiecolt-Glaser, Dura, Speicher, Trask, & Glaser, 1991; Pinquart & Sorensen, 2004; Vitaliano, Zhang, & Scanlan, 2003). Notably, Schulz and Beach (1999) found that strained caregivers experienced 63% greater risk of mortality over a 4-year time frame compared with noncaregiving control participants.

Inflammation from chronic stress may contribute to morbidity and mortality among caregivers. Older women caregivers had higher levels of IL-6 compared with older women undergoing moderate stress (housing relocation) and low stress (Lutgendorf et al., 1999). Additional research with caregivers has demonstrated that caregiving exacerbates typical age-related increases in IL-6; caregivers experienced fourfold greater increases in IL-6 over a 6-year follow-up period compared with controls (Kiecolt-Glaser et al., 2003). These data suggest that the experience of chronic stress can accelerate the aging process. Notably, although caregivers reported greater perceived stress, depressive symptoms, and loneliness than controls, the effects of caregiver status on inflammation were not accounted for by these factors. Thus, effects of chronic stress on inflammation were not simply a reflection of greater stress, depression, or loneliness.

Depression and Inflammation

Relationships between depression and inflammation are seen across the life span. Among young adults who were 30 years old on average, those experiencing major depression had significantly higher circulating levels of inflammatory markers than controls with no psychiatric history (Maes et al., 1995). These markers included IL-6 and the soluble receptor of IL-6 (IL-6sR), which can widen the action of IL-6 (Jones, Horiuchi, Topley, Yamamoto, & Fuller, 2001). Similarly, among middle-aged adults, those with major depression had elevated serum levels of IL-6, IL-6sr, as well as the receptor antagonist for IL-1 (IL-1ra); IL-1ra is often elevated in individuals with diseases marked by inflammation (Maes et al., 1997).

These effects are also seen in older adults. In a sample of adults over 60 years of age compared with individuals with no prior history of psychiatric disorder, those who met criteria for clinical depression had 171% higher serum levels of IL-1β (Thomas et al., 2005). Moreover, among the depressed individuals, depression severity was positively correlated with IL-1β levels. Along with other proinflammatory cytokines, IL-1β is implicated in sickness behavior. Similarly, in a study of 1,686 participants over 70 years of age, those who exceeded a clinical cutoff on the Center for Epidemiologic Studies Depression scale (CES-D) had higher levels of IL-6 compared with individuals reporting fewer depressive symptoms, a relationship that held after controlling for age, race, and gender (Dentino et al., 1999). In addition, in a sample of 3,024 adults ages 70 to 79 years, those who exceeded a clinical cutoff on the CES-D had higher levels of IL-6 as well as TNF-α and C-reactive protein (CRP; Penninx et al., 2003). CRP is an inflammatory marker that is an emerging risk factor for cardiovascular disease (Hackam & Anand, 2003). These studies demonstrate associations between depressive symptoms and inflammatory markers across the life span.

In the preceding studies that examined depressive symptoms and inflammatory markers, perceived stress was not measured or statistically controlled. This may be an important consideration, however, because perceived stress tends to covary with depressive symptoms. McDade, Hawkley, and Cacioppo (2006) found that perceived stress was a more robust predictor of CRP than depressive symptoms in a population-based study of middle-aged and older adults. Moreover, the association between depressive symptoms and CRP was attenuated after controlling for perceived stress. Future research should aim to clarify the predictive value of perceived stress versus depressive symptoms in the context of clinical depression as well as milder depressive symptomatology. Relatedly, depressive symptomatology may be an important moderator of physiological responses to objective stressors (e.g., Miller, Freedland, & Carney, 2005). Thus, the specific and interactive effects of objective stressors, perceived stress, and depressive symptomatology warrant further investigation.

Physiological Mechanisms Linking Stress, Depression, and Inflammation

The experience of life stress is a common precursor of depression and inflammatory responses to stressors may play a causal role in this relationship. Stress-induced activation of the sympathetic-adrenal-medullary (SAM) and HPA axes provokes the release of stress hormones (e.g., epinephrine and norephinephrine) that stimulate the release of inflammatory markers, including cytokines, that affect the CNS. It is well documented that cytokines elicit sickness behaviors (e.g., lethargy and withdrawal) that parallel symptoms of depression (Dantzer & Kelley, 2007).

Cytokines can affect the brain by entering from the periphery or via neural pathways that induce cytokine production within the brain. Although transfer of cytokines from peripheral circulation to the brain is largely prevented by the blood-brain barrier, cytokines can enter the brain via weaker areas of the blood-brain barrier as well as through active cytokine transporters (Raison, Capuron, & Miller, 2006). In addition, a key proposed route by which peripheral inflammation can affect the brain is via stimulation of peripheral afferent vagal nerves that innervate organs of the abdominal cavity (Konsman, Parnet, & Dantzer, 2002). Notably, cytokine receptors, including those for IL-1, IL-6, and TNF, are located throughout the brain. In particular, IL-1 has significant effects on the hypothalamus and hippocampus, which are key regulators of sickness behaviors (Bailey, Engler, Hunzeker, & Sheridan, 2003; Konsman et al., 2002).

In addition to direct action via cytokine receptors in the brain, cytokines also affect mood and behavior by altering function of neurotransmitters including dopamine, norepinephrine, and serotonin, which are known to affect depressive symptomatology. In particular, a clear causal pathway linking inflammation to decreased serotonin (5-HT) availability has been described. Specifically, heightened levels of proinflammatory cytokines reduce the availability of tryptophan (TRP), the precursor of 5-HT synthesis (Schiepers, Wichers, & Maes, 2005).

For healthy individuals, mechanisms exist that help to self-limit stress responses. Normally, cortisol, a key hormone for the regulation of inflammation and stress responses, is released by the HPA axis during stress responses and then signals back to the HPA axis, eliciting termination of HPA stress responses (Figure 64.3). In addition, cortisol has robust anti-inflammatory effects on cytokine-producing cells. However, extended exposure to elevated levels of glucocorticoids (GC), such as that seen in conditions of repeated or chronic stress, may produce GC insensitivity at the level of both cytokine-producing cells and the HPA axis (Sapolsky & McEwen, 1985; Spencer, Miller, Stein, & McEwen, 1991). GC insensitivity is marked by

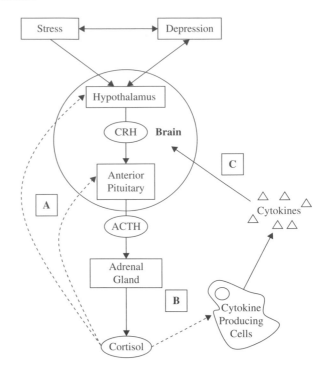

Figure 64.3 Physiological pathways linking stress, depression, and inflammation.

Note: Stress-induced activation of the HPA axis results in the release of cortisol which signals back to the hypothalamus and pituitary (**A**), eliciting termination of HPA stress responses. Cortisol also has powerful anti-inflammatory effects on cytokine-producing cells (**B**). However, extended exposure to elevated cortisol can produce glucocorticoid insensitivity in the HPA axis and cytokine-producing cells, provoking greater production of proinflammatory cytokines. Cytokines can affect the brain via transfer across the blood-brain barrier from peripheral circulation as well as via stimulation of afferent vagal nerves. In addition, inflammation can affect mood by reducing the availability of tryptophan, a precursor of serotonin (5-HT) (**C**). ACTH = Adrenocorticotropic hormone. Solid lines indicate a stimulatory association. CRH = Corticotropin-releasing hormone. Dashed lines = An inhibitory relationship.

a diminished ability of the HPA axis and cytokine producing cells to respond to cortisol, resulting in more sustained HPA axis responses and greater production of inflammatory markers. Thus, the development of GC resistance and resulting elevations in inflammatory markers has been proposed as an important pathway by which stress can contribute to depressive symptomatology (Raison & Miller, 2003). Clinical depression is frequently characterized by GC resistance, as evidenced by a reduced capacity to suppress HPA axis secretion of cortisol after administration of dexamethasone, a synthetic glucocorticoid (Modell, Yassouridis, Huber, & Holsboer, 1997).

In humans, the best evidence that inflammation can play a causal role in the development of depression comes from studies in which cytokines are administered therapeutically. In particular, the proinflammatory cytokine interferon-alpha is used with some cancers as well as some infectious illnesses (e.g., hepatitis). This treatment produces significant depressive symptomatology in a high percentage of individuals (Capuron & Miller, 2004; Dantzer & Kelley, 2007). Interferon treatment can also increase circulating IL-6 and TNF-α, alter in HPA axis function, and dysregulate serotonin metabolism (Capuron & Miller, 2004; Dantzer & Kelley, 2007). Thus, studies of interferon treatment support the proposition that inflammation can play a causal role in the development of depression. For additional coverage of physiological pathways underlying the link between stress and depression, please refer to Chapters 6 and 7, Volume 1; and Chapters 55 and 62, this volume.

Interventions Targeting Stress, Depression, and Inflammation

Certain interventions may help to break the negative cycle of stress, depression, and inflammation. For one, interventions targeting social support may be helpful. Among female cancer patients, greater social support has predicted lower levels of inflammatory markers in circulating blood and ascitic fluid (Costanzo et al., 2005; Lutgendorf, Anderson, Sorosky, Buller, & Lubaroff, 2000; Lutgendorf et al., 2002). Relatedly, religious participation, a key source of social support for many people, has predicted lower levels of IL-6 among community-based samples (Koenig et al., 1997; Lutgendorf, Russell, Ullrich, Harris, & Wallace, 2004). Interventions aimed at improving the availability and utilization of social support warrant investigation, particularly for individuals experiencing both significant stress and lack of support.

Other interventions targeting stress include yoga, tai chi, and meditation. Participation in both tai chi and yoga is associated with improved mood (Waelde, Thompson, & Gallagher-Thompson, 2004; Woolery, Myers, Sternlieb, & Zeltzer, 2004); however, limited research has attempted to link such activities with changes in inflammatory activity. One study examined effects of mindfulness-based stress reduction, which included elements of meditation and gentle yoga among breast cancer patients. Results demonstrated improvements in mood, reductions in perceived stress, and beneficial immunological changes including decreased production of interferon (IFN)—γ and increased production of IL-4, an anti-inflammatory cytokine, by stimulated T-cells (Carlson, Speca, Patel, & Goodey, 2003). Notably, regular physical activity is associated with reductions in circulating inflammatory markers (e.g., Ford, 2002). Therefore, further investigation of activities such as tai chi and yoga that involve elements of both meditation and physical activity holds promise.

In terms of clinical depression, both antidepressant medication and cognitive-behavioral therapy have been associated with reductions in inflammatory markers (Basterzi et al., 2005; Doering, Cross, Vredevoe, Martinez-Maza, & Cowan, 2007; Sharpe et al., 2001; Tuglu, Kara, Caliyurt, Vardar, & Abay, 2003). Such anti-inflammatory effects may contribute to the efficacy of these treatments. Indeed, the depressive symptoms induced by interferon treatment can largely be prevented or reversed by treatment with antidepressant medications (Hauser et al., 2002; Musselman et al., 2001).

Accumulating research also speaks to the importance of omega-3 (*n*-3) polyunsaturated fatty acids (PUFAs) for both mental health and inflammatory processes. Specifically, low plasma levels of *n*-3 PUFA as well as high omega-6 (*n*-6) to *n*-3 ratios have been associated with the presence and severity of depressive symptoms in several studies (e.g., Frasure-Smith, Lesperance, & Julien, 2004; Hibbeln, 1998; Kiecolt-Glaser et al., 2007; Maes & Smith, 1998). PUFAs inhibit the release of pro-inflammatory cytokines including IL-6, IL-1β, and TNF-α (Logan, 2003). Consistent with this evidence, higher circulating levels of *n*-3 PUFAs are related to lower levels of circulating pro-inflammatory cytokines (Ferrucci et al., 2006; Kiecolt-Glaser et al., 2007). Moreover, a number of studies have demonstrated that *n*-3 PUFA supplementation decreases depressive symptoms (for review, see Parker et al., 2006), supporting the argument that interventions targeting inflammation are a promising direction for depression treatment.

STRESS AND WOUND HEALING

Psychological stress and psychosocial factors have also been linked with wound healing (Christian, Graham, Padgett, Glaser, & Kiecolt-Glaser, 2007), a clinically critical outcome. The skin is the body's largest organ and primary immune defense, preventing bacteria, viruses, and other exogenous antigens from entering (Elias, 2005) and limiting the movement of water in and out of the body (Marks, 2004). As such, the skin's ability to heal wounds effectively is essential to good health. The effects of stress on healing have important implications in the context of surgery and naturally occurring wounds, particularly among at-risk and chronically ill populations.

The Wound-Healing Process

When tissue damage occurs in healthy individuals, healing progresses sequentially through three overlapping phases: inflammation, proliferation, and remodeling (see Baum & Arpey, 2005, figure 2; Singer & Clark, 1999). Success in later phases is highly dependent on preceding phases. The inflammatory phase, which typically lasts 5 to 7 days, is marked by vasoconstriction, blood coagulation, platelet activation, and the release of substances that attract cells to clean the area, that is, remove bacteria (Singer & Clark, 1999;

Van De Kerkhof, Van Bergen, Spruijt, & Kuiper, 1994). The proliferative phase is characterized by recruitment and replication of cells necessary for tissue regeneration and capillary regrowth. The final stage, which may continue for weeks or months, involves contraction and tissue remodeling (see Figure 64.4). The sequence and mechanisms described here apply best to acute wounds: The molecular mechanisms by which stress affects chronic wounds, such as diabetic foot ulcers, are less well understood and are complicated by other factors (Vileikyte, 2007).

A key pathway by which stress affects healing is via inflammatory processes at the site of the wound. Although prolonged or exaggerated inflammation is detrimental to health, inflammatory cytokines play a critical role in the healing cascade and a robust localized inflammatory response is ideal. Inflammatory cytokines help prevent infection, prepare injured tissue for repair, enhance recruitment and activation of additional phagocytic cells, and regulate the ability of cells to remodel damaged tissue (Lowry, 1993). Stress-induced elevations in glucocorticoids can transiently suppress pro-inflammatory cytokine production in humans (DeRijk et al., 1997). Moreover, mice treated with glucocorticoids showed impairment in the induction

of IL-1 and TNF, as well as deficient wound repair (Hübner et al., 1996). Although other mechanisms are implicated in the link between stress and healing, the interactive roles of pro-inflammatory cytokines and glucocorticoid hormones are the best delineated to date. Further evidence of their role is demonstrated in the studies described in the following subsection.

Effects of Stress on Wound Healing

The first human study to demonstrate the effects of stress on healing examined women experiencing the chronic stress of caregiving for a loved one with dementia. In this study, caregivers took 24% longer to heal a small standardized punch biopsy wound than did well-matched controls (Kiecolt-Glaser, Marucha, Malarkey, Mercado, & Glaser, 1995). Healing rate was determined using photographs to compare wound size to a standard dot. The same study revealed that circulating peripheral blood leukocytes (PBLs) from caregivers expressed less IL-1β in messenger RNA (mRNA) in response to lipopolysaccharide (LPS) stimulation than did cells from controls (Kiecolt-Glaser et al., 1995). As described earlier, a strong IL-1β response is desirable in the context of healing.

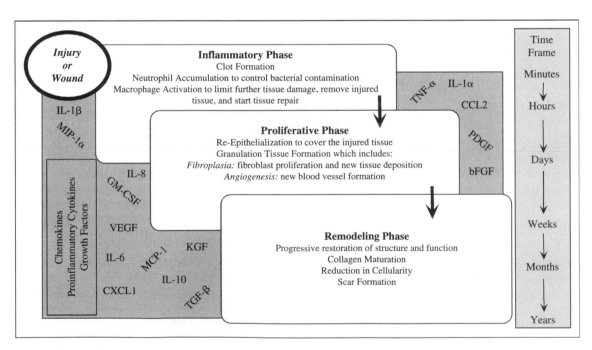

Figure 64.4 Stages of wound healing.

Note: In healthy individuals, healing progresses sequentially through three overlapping phases: (1) inflammatory phase, (2) proliferative phase, and (3) remodeling phase. Stress can affect progression through these stages via multiple immune and neuroendocrine pathways. This chapter focuses on the interactive role of glucocorticoids and cytokines (e.g., IL-8, IL-1α, IL-1β, IL-6, and TNF-α). However, additional cytokines, chemokines, and growth factors are important to healing. These include CXC-chemokine ligand 1 (CXCL1), CC-chemokine ligand 2 (CCL2), granulocyte macrophage colony-stimulating factor (GM-CSF), monocyte chemotactic protein-1 (MCP-1), macrophage inflammatory protien-1 alpha (MIP-1α), vascular endothelial growth factor (VEGF), transforming growth factor-β, (TGF-β), keratinocyte growth factor (KGF), platelet-derived growth factor (PDGF), and basic fibroblast growth factor (bFGF). For a broader review of physiological mechanisms relevant to wound healing, see Werner and Grose (2003). From "Stress and Wound Healing," by L. M. Christian, J. E. Graham, D. A. Padgett, R. Glaser, and J. K. Kiecolt-Glaser, 2007, *Neuroimmunomodulation, 13,* p. 338. Reprinted with permission.

Subsequent research demonstrated that milder stress also impairs healing. In a sample of 11 dental students, mucosal punch biopsy wounds placed in the hard palate healed an average of 40% more slowly during an examination period than during a vacation period, which was rated as less stressful by participants (Marucha, Kiecolt-Glaser, & Favagehi, 1998). This effect was remarkably reliable: Every student in the study healed more slowly during exams than during vacation. Moreover, in concordance with studies on caregiving stress, production of IL-1β mRNA by LPS-stimulated peripheral blood leukocytes (PBLs) was reduced in every student during the examination period compared with the vacation period.

Further research has examined cytokine production at the local wound site. In a study of 36 women, blister wounds were created using a suction blister device that produced 8 sterile 8 mm blister wounds (Glaser, Kiecolt-Glaser, et al., 1999). A plastic template with 8 wells was placed over the blister wounds and each well was filled with the woman's serum and a salt solution, allowing cells to migrate into the blister chambers. Women reporting greater stress had significantly lower levels of two key cytokines (IL-1α and IL-8) at the wound site (Glaser, Kiecolt-Glaser, et al., 1999). By demonstrating an association between stress and local cytokine production, this study significantly extended previous data linking stress and mechanisms associated with healing.

Dramatically, even a single 30-minute marital conflict discussion in a laboratory setting can slow wound healing: Married couples healed standardized blister wounds more slowly after a conflictive interaction than after a supportive interaction (Kiecolt-Glaser et al., 2005). Decreased production of three key cytokines—IL-6, IL-1β, and TNF-α—was observed at the wound site following conflict compared with a supportive interaction. Furthermore, couples who demonstrated consistently high levels of hostile behavior during both conflictive and supportive interactions healed wounds at 60% of the rate of low-hostile couples.

Other research has examined relationships between wound healing and subjective stress. Among healthy males, greater perceived stress predicted slower healing of a punch biopsy wound from 7 to 21 days postwounding (Ebrecht et al., 2004). Healing was also significantly related to cortisol levels: Greater morning increases in cortisol predicted slower healing. Healing in this study was assessed with ultrasound biomicroscopy, a relatively new imaging technique that uses high-resolution ultrasound scanning to measure wound depth as well as circumference. This approach provides an assessment of healing in deep tissue layers and enables measurement of wound circumference that is not impeded by scab formation (Dyson et al., 2003).

Stress also has measurable effects on healing outside a controlled laboratory setting. Depression and anxiety were associated with healing among elderly men and women with chronic leg ulcers: Those reporting greater than average symptoms of depression or anxiety were four times more likely to be categorized as slow healers compared with those reporting less distress (Cole-King & Harding, 2001). Similarly, in a sample of adults undergoing hernia surgery, self-reported worry about surgery predicted slower healing time, even after controlling for age, gender, and type of anesthetic (Broadbent, Petrie, Alley, & Booth, 2003). Moreover, greater preoperative stress predicted lower levels of IL-1 in the wound fluid, while greater worry about surgery was related to lower matrix metalloproteinase-9 (MMP-9) in the wound fluid (Broadbent et al., 2003). MMP-9, which is regulated by cytokines IL-1 and IL-6, facilitates cellular migration within the wound area, and thus aids in tissue remodeling (Pajulo et al., 1999).

Animal models support and extend findings related to causal mechanisms linking stress and healing. Mice exposed to periods of restraint stress for 3 days before and 5 days following wounding healed punch biopsy wounds 27% more slowly than did nonstressed controls (Padgett, Marucha, & Sheridan, 1998). Restraint-stressed mice also had reduced cellularity in the margins of their punch biopsy wounds, particularly early in the healing process and significantly higher levels of serum corticosterone compared with unstressed controls. Notably, when the stressed animals were treated with the glucocorticoid receptor antagonist RU40555, their healing rates were equivalent to nonstressed animals (Padgett et al., 1998). Thus, results from animal models confirm that the suppressive effects of glucocorticoids on inflammatory activity play an important role in stress-induced delays in healing.

Thus, the effects of stress on glucocorticoid functioning and subsequent effects on decreases in localized inflammatory responses to injury represent a primary pathway by which stress impairs wound healing (Figure 64.5). Glucocorticoids have multiple effects that can disrupt the inflammatory stage of healing, particularly early on. These effects include (a) suppression of immune cell differentiation and proliferation, (b) reduced expression of cell adhesion molecules that play an important role in trafficking cells to the site of the wound, (c) decreases in nuclear factor kappa B (NFκ-B) activity, which results in decreased pro-inflammatory gene expression (for review, see Glaser & Kiecolt-Glaser, 2005; Godbout & Glaser, 2006; Padgett & Glaser, 2003). In addition, disruption of inflammatory processes can prevent the proper cleaning and clearance of bacteria from a wound site, resulting in greater risk for infection, which is also associated with delayed healing.

Dysregulation of the inflammatory stage of healing is important because the stages of healing are overlapping and interdependent. Therefore, delay in the early inflammatory

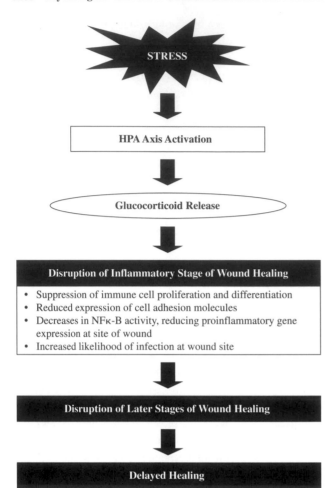

Figure 64.5 Physiological pathways linking stress to wound healing.

Note: Stress delays wound healing by affecting early inflammatory processes via glucocorticoids. Delays in the inflammatory stage of healing causes dysregulation of later stages, resulting in delayed healing.

stage disrupts progression of subsequent stages of healing, ultimately resulting in increased time to healing. This, in turn, can have important clinical implications for recovery from surgery and naturally occurring wounds.

Interventions for Enhancing Wound Healing

Exercise and social contact are two interventions that have been used to target stress or the effects of stress with the goal of improving healing. First, recent data demonstrate that regular physical activity can speed healing. Older adults who completed a 4-week exercise intervention healed standard punch biopsy wounds 25% more quickly than did their less active counterparts (Emery, Kiecolt-Glaser, Glaser, Malarkey, & Frid, 2005). These effects were notable because of the low self-reported stress across the sample; effects may be even greater among individuals reporting more distress. In this study, exercise did

not result in changes in resting cortisol levels or perceived stress over time. Further research is needed to examine mechanistic pathways by which exercise may benefit healing.

Animal work suggests that social contact may mitigate effects of stress on healing. Among hamsters subjected to restraint stress, those who were individually housed (isolated) showed significant impairment of cutaneous wound healing, whereas those who were pair-housed did not (Detillion, Craft, Glasper, Prendergast, & DeVries, 2004). The adverse effect on healing observed in isolated hamsters was driven by stress-induced increases in serum cortisol; socially housed hamsters had significantly lower serum cortisol concentrations than their isolated counterparts. The protective effects of social housing in this study appeared to be at least partly mediated by oxytocin, a hormone that is released during social contact and that may facilitate social bonding. The administration of an oxytocin antagonist to socially housed animals delayed healing and treatment of isolated animals with oxytocin, attenuated their stress-induced cortisol increases, and speeded healing (Detillion et al., 2004). Thus, these data support the notion that cortisol plays a key role in the stress-healing link.

STRESS AND INFECTIOUS AGENTS

Turning to other models used to study effects of stress on immune-relevant outcomes, stress has been linked to impaired response to infectious illness in three related areas: vaccination, experimental exposure to infectious illness, and latent viruses. Each of these models has its own strengths, and each provides clinically relevant information about immune function in a unique manner (see Figure 64.6). These models are useful, in part, because there is unexplained variability in immune responses to each type of challenge. Individuals demonstrate varying degrees of susceptibility to infection on exposure to the same infectious agent. In addition, among those who do become infected, there is a significant range of severity and duration of illness experienced. Stress contributes to such variability in response to infectious agents.

Vaccination

Measuring Immune Responses to Vaccination

Studies of immune responses to vaccination provide clinically relevant information in at least two ways. First, an adequate immune response to vaccination is required for the vaccine to provide protection against the antigen in question. Second, immune responses to vaccination serve as a proxy measure of how well an individual's immune system

Vaccination		
Outcomes	• Cellular and humoral immune responses	
Strengths	• Highly ethical model for studying immune response in humans	
Clinical relevance	• An adequate immune response is required for a vaccine to confer immunity • Responses to vaccination provide a proxy for responses to naturally occurring antigens	
Infectious Illness		
Outcomes	• Infection and clinical symptoms, cellular and humoral immune responses	
Strengths	• Laboratory exposure provides excellent control of possible confounding variables	
Clinical relevance	• Evidence of effects of stress on both susceptibility to and severity of infectious illness	
Latent Viruses		
Outcomes	• Antibody titers, cellular immune responses	
Strengths	• Study of common latent viruses does not require exposure to an infectious agent	
Clinical relevance	• Poor control of latent viruses indicates impaired cellular immune function • Latent virus reactivation contributes to morbidity and mortality among immunocompromised	

Figure 64.6 Models for studying immune responses to infectious agents.

would respond if he or she were exposed to the actual infectious agent (Kiecolt-Glaser, Glaser, Gravenstein, Malarkey, & Sheridan, 1996). Consistent with this notion, poorer immune responses to vaccination are predictive of greater likelihood of experiencing clinical illness (Plotkin, 2001). A notable strength of this methodology is that vaccination is beneficial to people, with some vaccines being highly recommended for at-risk populations (e.g., influenza vaccination among the elderly). Therefore, vaccination provides a highly ethical methodology for studying clinically relevant immune outcomes in humans.

As described, the immune system can be broadly divided into two arms: the innate immune system (the rapid nonspecific defense against an antigen), and the adaptive immune system, which mounts a slower, antigen-specific response. Studies of vaccine response examine the ability of the adaptive immunity to form and maintain immunological memory after exposure to an antigen.

Effective responses to vaccination involve activation of both the humoral and cellular arms of the adaptive immune system. The humoral immune response is governed by B-cells and marked by antibody production. Antigen-specific antibodies, produced by B-lymphocytes, can opsonize the antigen (tag it for destruction by other immune cells), and neutralize it by preventing it from further interacting with the host's cells. Therefore, it is beneficial for an individual to demonstrate a robust antibody response to vaccination that is maintained well over time. Parameters for a sufficient antibody response, referred to as seroconversion, depend on the vaccine in question. A fourfold increase in antibody titers is considered to be the standard for a sufficient response to influenza vaccine.

The cellular immune response is governed by T-cells. Cellular immune responses to vaccination are commonly quantified in terms of production of certain cytokines (e.g., IL-2, IFN-γ), that promote cell-mediated immune responses. In the context of vaccination, higher IL-2 and IFN-γ cytokine production to in vitro virus exposure is desirable because these cytokines activate virus-specific cytotoxic T-cells as well as natural killer cells.

Effects of Psychological Factors on Vaccine Response

As described above, the chronic stress of caring for a relative with dementia promotes systemic inflammation and slows wound healing. In addition, exposure to this chronic stressor impairs immune responses to vaccination. Three studies to date have demonstrated that caregivers are less likely to seroconvert following influenza vaccination compared with well-matched control subjects (Glaser, Kiecolt-Glaser, Malarkey, & Sheridan, 1998; Kiecolt-Glaser et al., 1996; Vedhara et al., 1999). For example, in a study of 32 caregivers and 32 demographically matched controls, caregivers were significantly less likely to achieve a fourfold increase in influenza-specific antibody levels 1 month after vaccination; this effect was more pronounced among older subjects (Kiecolt-Glaser et al., 1996). In addition, caregivers' peripheral blood lymphocytes produced less IL-2 in response to in vitro influenza stimulation, evidencing a poorer cellular response to vaccination.

In a similar study, caregivers showed impaired maintenance of the response to pneumoccocal pneumonia vaccination. Although caregiver and control groups demonstrated equivalent responses to the vaccine initially (at 2 weeks and 1 month), current caregivers had lower levels of antibody at 3 months and 6 months postvaccination compared with both former caregivers and controls (Glaser, Sheridan, Malarkey, MacCallum, & Kiecolt-Glaser, 2000). Notably, the immune response to influenza is largely mediated by T-lymphocytes while the immune response to pneummococcal pneumonia is not dependent on T-lymphocytes. Therefore, studies of caregivers indicate that chronic stress affects responses to both classes of vaccine.

Greater self-reported stress also predicts impaired vaccine responses among younger populations. For example, in a study of 31 college students who received influenza vaccination, those who reported less perceived stress and fewer stressful life events in the period following vaccination demonstrated significantly better maintenance of antibody levels compared with students reporting greater stress (Burns, Carroll, Drayson, Whitham, & Ring, 2003). Similarly, among 260 healthy college students, a greater number of negative life events in the previous year predicted lower hepatitis B antibody levels only among those who had been vaccinated more than 1 year prior; number of negative life events was not associated with antibody level among those who were vaccinated within the past year (Burns, Carroll, Ring, Harrison, & Drayson, 2002). These data indicate that stress affected long-term maintenance of immunological memory for the antigen.

Additional research has examined the effects of stress among college students on both T-cell dependent (influenza) and T-cell independent (meningococcal C) vaccinations. Those who reported a greater number of stressful life events in the year prior to vaccination had lower antibody responses to one strain of the influenza vaccine at both 5 weeks and 5 months. Moreover, although the final antibody response levels were similar at 5 months, students who reported greater stress mounted a slower antibody response to the meningococcal C vaccination (Phillips, Burns, Carroll, Ring, & Drayson, 2005).

It is important to consider perceived stress in the context of objectively stressful experiences. A sample of 48 medical students underwent a series of 3 hepatitis B inoculations scheduled to coincide with three major examination periods. Those who seroconverted after the first vaccination reported significantly less stress and anxiety across the three exam periods. Moreover, following the third exam period, students who reported lower anxiety and stress across exam periods demonstrated higher antibody responses to the vaccine and a stronger T-cell response to a hepatitis B challenge in vitro (Glaser et al., 1992).

A study addressed the question of which time points are most critical in terms of stress affecting immune responses to vaccination. A sample of 83 healthy young adults received influenza vaccination, and their subjective stress levels were measured for 2 days prior to vaccination, the day of vaccination, and the 10 days following vaccination. Although stress prior to or on the day of vaccination did not predict antibody responses, greater stress levels in the 10 days following vaccination were associated with poorer antibody response (Miller et al., 2004).

The studies reviewed thus far focus on chronic stress, perceived stress, and brief naturalistic stressors (e.g., exam stress). Some evidence suggests that acute stress (e.g., 2-hour restraint stress in mice; mental arithmetic or exercise stress in people) can enhance immune responses to vaccination (Edwards et al., 2006; Silberman, Wald, & Genaro, 2003). Additional research is needed to describe in better detail the processes involved in brief acute stress relative to longer-lasting stress experiences.

As reviewed, evidence for effects of stress on vaccine response is seen across a variety of vaccines and types of stressors. Variability between specific outcomes across studies may be explained in part by the different vaccines and measurement time frames used. Moreover, prior vaccination or naturalistic exposure to an antigen will affect responses to vaccination. This can cause a range restriction problem that impedes the ability to detect effects of psychosocial factors (Vedhara et al., 1999). These methodological factors should be carefully considered in research using vaccination.

Studies to date demonstrate that stressors ranging from relatively brief (e.g., academic exams) to chronic (e.g., caregiving) can significantly affect the rapidity and magnitude of antibody response as well as long-term maintenance of immunological memory conferred by vaccination. Such stress is also predictive of decreased cellular immune responses to vaccination. Although beyond the scope of this chapter, animal models demonstrate multiple effects of glucocorticoid hormones on cell-trafficking, and production of pro-inflammatory cytokines and chemokines that contribute to these effects (for review, see Glaser & Kiecolt-Glaser, 2005; Godbout & Glaser, 2006; Padgett & Glaser, 2003). Notably, effects of stress on responses to vaccination are seen in both older and younger adults, although effects tend to be stronger among older adults because of age-related decreases in immune responses to vaccination. In addition, deficits in immune response to vaccination have particular importance for older adults who are more vulnerable than younger adults to serious complications and death in the face of illness such as influenza (Yoshikawa, 1983).

Infectious Illness

Measuring Infectious Illness

Consistent with findings that stress affects immune responses to vaccination, stress also affects susceptibility, severity, and duration of infectious illnesses including influenza and rhinovirus (the common cold). In studies of infectious illness, the rates of both respiratory infection and clinical illness are of interest. Respiratory infection is defined by the presence of the virus in circulation or significant increases in virus-specific antibody titers following experimental exposure to the infectious agent. In contrast, clinical illness is typically defined by physician-judged severity of illness symptoms. Assessing both respiratory infection and clinical illness is important because among those exposed to a virus, only a portion will become infected. In turn, among those infected, only a portion will develop clinical symptoms.

Effects of Psychosocial Factors on Infectious Illness

Naturalistic studies have reported associations between stress and frequency of infectious illness. In a sample of 117 adults, the experience of stressful life events in the previous 12 months and during a 15-week observation period was assessed. During the observation period, 29 participants experienced at least one clinically verified upper respiratory illness. Risk of illness was greater among those who reported a greater number of stressful life events (Turner-Cobb & Steptoe, 1996). Although naturalistic studies provide good evidence of effects of stress on susceptibility to infectious illness, such methodology allows for limited control of important confounding variables including rates of exposure to infectious agents.

The strongest evidence of effects of stress on infectious illness comes from studies in which participants have been purposefully exposed to infectious agents that can cause upper respiratory infections (URIs) and then tracked over time in a well-controlled environment. In a key study using experimental exposure methodology, Cohen and colleagues demonstrated that self-reported stress predicted susceptibility to respiratory viruses in a dose-response manner. Specifically, 394 healthy subjects were exposed to 1 of 5 respiratory viruses, while 26 control subjects were given saline nasal drops. Participants were then quarantined and their respiratory symptoms as well as their virus-specific antibody titer levels were assessed (Cohen, Tyrrell, & Smith, 1991). Individuals reporting greater stress (as determined by a composite measure of major life events, perceptions of stress, and negative affect) showed greater likelihood of developing respiratory infections as well as clinically defined colds. This effect was found across each of the five types of virus, and the effect remained after controlling for potential confounding factors including age, sex, education, season, and personality factors.

Later research from the same laboratory focused on better delineating the importance of different types of stressful life events. In this study, 276 participants completed in-depth interviews assessing occurrence, severity,

and emotional significance of life stressors in the past year (Cohen et al., 1998). Participants were exposed to one of two rhinoviruses and kept in quarantine for the following 5 days during which their experience of infectious illness was assessed. Results indicated that acute stressors did not predict increased risk of infection or clinical colds. However, the experience of chronic stress lasting 1 month or longer was associated with significantly increased risk of developing a cold. These effects were not accounted for by differences in social network characteristics, personality, or health behaviors.

The same study explored potential endocrine mediators linking stress and virus susceptibility. In this sample, elevations in epinephrine and norepinephrine were associated with increased risk of developing colds. However, unexpectedly, the experience of chronic stress was not associated with higher levels of these stress hormones. This could be due in part to the stress and novelty of the experimental situation, which may have caused acute stress in all participants and masked effects of chronic stressors on these endocrine markers (Cohen et al., 1998).

Other research indicates that variability in physiological responses to stress affects stress-induced susceptibility to infection. In a sample of 115 healthy individuals, those who showed larger cortisol responses to laboratory stressors experienced greater risk of developing clinically verified colds under conditions of higher stress (Cohen et al., 2002). Stress level was unrelated to URI risk among those showing smaller cortisol responses to acute stress. Thus, individuals who experience greater physiological reactivity to stress may be more vulnerable to infectious illness in conditions of stress.

Subsequent research, also from the same laboratory, explored the role of inflammation in explaining the link between stress and symptom severity. In a study of 55 subjects who were exposed to an influenza virus, those reporting higher stress experienced greater symptoms of illness and greater mucous weight, as well as greater inflammatory responses to the infection, as indicated by higher IL-6 levels in nasal secretions (Cohen, Doyle, & Skoner, 1999). These data suggest that stress may contribute to an exaggerated local inflammatory response to infection, contributing to illness severity. However, in the context of infectious illness, effects of stress may differ for the production of other cytokines and at other sites (e.g., lungs). In mice exposed to influenza virus, restraint stress reduced the production of the pro-inflammatory cytokine IL-1α, but did not affect the production of IL-6 in the lungs (Konstantinos & Sheridan, 2001). In another animal study, restraint stress resulted in reduced production of IL-6 from splenocytes, but enhanced production of IL-6 from regional lymph nodes (Dobbs, Feng, Beck, & Sheridan, 1996). Thus, the effects of stress on inflammatory mediators during viral infection are complex and may best be understood as dysregulated, rather than enhanced or suppressed. Moreover, the clinical relevance of noted alterations may differ for susceptibility versus severity of illness.

In sum, several well-controlled laboratory studies have demonstrated a relationship between stress and susceptibility, severity, and duration of infectious illness (see Figure 64.7). Naturalistic studies report parallel findings. Human models implicate glucocorticoids and local cytokine production in the link between stress and illness susceptibility and severity. Animal models support and extend these findings, providing evidence for effects of glucocorticoids, dysregulated cytokine production, alterations in cell trafficking, and dysregulated antibody responses (Bonneau, Padgett, & Sheridan, 2001; Konstantinos & Sheridan, 2001). A continued focus on physiological pathways will help to better delineate the role of specific immune alterations in affecting the susceptibility, duration, and severity of infectious illness.

Latent Viruses

Measuring Immune Control of Latent Viruses

Normally, viruses are eliminated from the host when infection is resolved. However, some viruses are maintained in the body in a latent state in asymptomatic individuals after primary infection. Such viruses include those from the herpesviruses family, such as herpes simplex virus (HSV) I and II, varicella-zoster virus (VZV), Epstein-Barr virus (EBV), and cytomegalovirus (CMV). After primary infection, latent viruses are maintained within certain cells (e.g., B-lymphocytes for EBV). Although the immune system is typically quite effective in controlling latent viruses, reactivation of the opportunistic virus can occur when cellular immunity wanes. During reactivation, the virus produces greater quantities of viral proteins. This elicits cellular and humoral immune responses and results in the production of virus-specific antibody. Thus, higher levels of antigen-specific antibody can be used as an indicator of impaired cell-mediated control of a latent virus.

One strength of examining immune control of latent viruses is that some forms are ubiquitous and can therefore be studied in a variety of populations. More than 95% of the adult population is infected with EBV (Wolf & Morag, 1998). Therefore, the study of such latent viruses does not require experimental exposure to an antigen, a clear benefit for human studies.

Ineffective control of latent viruses can have important clinical implications among immunosuppressed individuals. Reactivation of latent viruses predicts increased mortality and morbidity among organ transplant recipients (Gray et al., 1995) and individuals infected with HIV (Cruess et al., 2000). Although reactivation of EBV typically causes no symptoms in healthy individuals (Hess, 2004), reactivation of HSV I or II can cause cold sores (Bystricka & Russ, 2005), and VZV reactivation can cause shingles (Quinlivan & Breuer, 2006). Even in the absence of clinical disease, reactivation of a latent virus provides a sensitive marker of impairment in cell-mediated immunity. Thus, studies of viral latency provide clinically relevant information even among asymptomatic individuals.

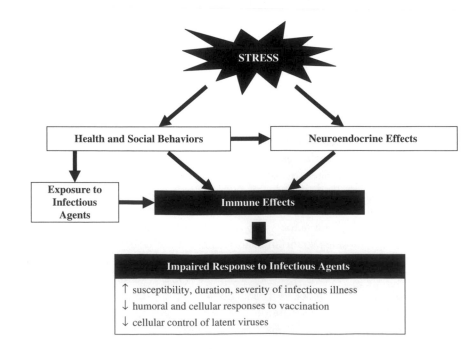

Figure 64.7 Behavioral and neuroendocrine pathways linking stress and response to infectious agents.

Note: By affecting health behaviors, social behaviors, and neuroendocrine function, stress can impair both humoral and cellular immune responses to infectious agents. This has important clinical implications for immune responses to exposure to infectious illnesses, vaccination, and control of latent viruses. (Although social support can buffer negative effects of stress, contact with a diverse social network can result in greater exposure to infectious agents.)

Effects of Psychosocial Factors on Immune Control of Latent Viruses

Given the effects of chronic stress on other aspects of immune function, it is not surprising that chronic stress impairs immune control of latent viruses. Individuals who are caregivers for a family member with dementia exhibited higher EBV (Kiecolt-Glaser et al., 1991) and HSV-1 (Glaser & Kiecolt-Glaser, 1997) antibody levels compared with well-matched controls. In addition, individuals experiencing the enduring stress of living near the Three Mile Island damaged nuclear plant showed higher HSV-1 antibody levels, compared with matched community controls living 80 miles away from the nuclear plant (McKinnon, Weisse, Reynolds, Bowles, & Baum, 1989).

Stress from disrupted significant relationships also affects immune function (Graham, Christian, & Kiecolt-Glaser, 2006a), including immune control of latent viruses. Women who had been divorced or separated for 1 year or less showed higher levels of EBV antibody compared with demographically matched women who were currently married (Kiecolt-Glaser et al., 1987). Similarly, men who were unsatisfied in their marriage had higher levels of EBV antibody than their happily married counterparts (Kiecolt-Glaser et al., 1988).

More transient stressors also affect viral latency. In prospective studies of examination stress, medical students exhibited higher EBV, HSV-1, and CMV antibody titers on the day of an academic examination, compared with several weeks before or after the exam (Glaser, Friedman, et al., 1999; Glaser, Kiecolt-Glaser, Speicher, & Holliday, 1985; Sarid, Anson, Yaari, & Margalith, 2001). Other research has shown that the intense stress of space flight (Mehta, Stowe, Feiveson, Tyring, & Pierson, 2000, 2004; Payne, Mehta, Tyring, Stowe, & Pierson, 1999; Pierson, Stowe, Phillips, Lugg, & Mehta, 2005) and Antarctic expeditions (Mehta, Pierson, Cooley, Dubow, & Lugg, 2000) resulted in higher EBV- and CMV-specific antibody titers and decreased EBV-specific T-cell responses. This is not surprising, given that effects of stress on viral latency are seen in response to much less significant stressors (e.g., examinations).

In addition to effects of objective stressors, other psychological factors have also been associated with poorer control of latent virus. Higher levels of EBV-specific antibodies have been found in students who reported a greater tendency to repress their emotions (Esterling, Antoni, Kumar, & Schneiderman, 1990), higher levels of anxiety (Esterling, Antoni, Kumar, & Schneiderman, 1993), and greater loneliness (Glaser et al., 1985). Similarly, patients with syndromal or subsyndromal symptoms of depression have shown higher levels of HSV-1 antibody and poorer VZV-specific T-cell immunity than those without depressive

symptoms (Delisi et al., 1986; Irwin et al., 1998; Robertson et al., 1993) Conversely, older women reporting higher vigor during housing relocation had lower EBV-antibody titers compared with women who reported lower levels of vigor (Lutgendorf et al., 2001). Thus, in addition to objective stressors, certain psychological characteristics (e.g., mood, ways of coping) may be associated with impaired control of latent viruses.

Other research has addressed physiological mechanisms by which stress may impair control of latent viruses. In studies of examination stress, students exhibited poorer cytotoxic and proliferative T-cell responses to in vitro EBV exposure on examination days compared with non-examination days (Glaser et al., 1987, 1993). In addition, exam stress predicted suppression of leukocyte migration inhibition factor (MIF), a condition associated with HSV-2 lesions (Sheridan, Donnenberg, Aurelian, & Elpern, 1982). Glucocorticoids may also play a role in stress-induced reactivation of latent viruses; indeed, glucocorticoids can induce latent EBV and CMV replication in vitro (Tanaka et al., 1984). However, some human studies have failed to find an association between basal cortisol levels and control of latent viruses (Cruess et al., 2000; Glaser, Pearl, Kiecolt-Glaser, & Malarkey, 1994). Cacioppo et al. (2002) observed that increased tonic plasma concentration of synthetic glucocorticoid hormone did not lead to enhanced in vitro EBV replication. However, when the synthetic glucocorticoid hormone was administered in a pulsative manner with varying concentration, mimicking a dysregulation of its diurnal variation, increased EBV replication occurred. Thus, assessments of patterns of cortisol release may be key to understanding the role of glucocorticoids in stress-induced virus reactivation.

Interventions to Improve Response to Infectious Agents

A variety of factors have been demonstrated to reduce stress and benefit immune response to infectious agents. As emphasized throughout this chapter, social support can serve as an important stress buffer. College students who reported greater social support showed stronger antibody responses to influenza vaccination (Phillips et al., 2005) as well as better cellular and humoral immune responses to hepatitis B vaccination (Glaser et al., 1992). Similarly, when exposed to infectious agents in a controlled laboratory environment, participants reporting more social ties were less likely to develop colds than those reporting fewer social ties (Cohen, Doyle, Skoner, Rabin, & Gwaltney, 1997). Although social support may buffer the effects of stress, having a diverse social network may also result in greater exposure to a broader diversity of viruses. In fact, in a naturalistic study, greater social network diversity was associated with fewer URIs only under conditions of low stress (Hamrick, Cohen, & Rodriguez, 2002).

A key beneficial component of social support may be that it provides an outlet for emotional disclosure. Indeed, interventions designed to encourage disclosure benefit immune function. In a sample of 40 students, those who completed a writing task involving emotional disclosure prior to receiving hepatitis B vaccination had higher antibody titers at 6 months postvaccination than did control participants (Petrie, Booth, Pennebaker, Davison, & Thomas, 1995). Similarly, college students who were randomly assigned to write or talk about a traumatic event had lower EBV antibody titers at the end of the 4-week intervention while students in a control condition showed no such reduction (Esterling, Antoni, Fletcher, Margulies, & Schneiderman, 1994).

Other studies have examined stress management groups that involved elements of social support and emotional disclosure, as well as a focus on coping or problem solving. In a study of caregivers, those who participated in a stress management group for an hour per week for 8 weeks and subsequently received influenza vaccination were more likely to achieve a fourfold increase in antibody titer than caregivers who did not receive the intervention (Vedhara et al., 2003). A number of studies have examined effects of cognitive-behavioral stress management interventions among HIV-infected and at-risk gay men. Such interventions have resulted in decreases in HSV-2 and EBV antibody titers, indicating improved control of latent viruses (Carrico et al., 2005; Esterling et al., 1992; Lutgendorf et al., 1997).

Stress reduction through relaxation and meditation has also been examined. In a study of 45 older adults, those randomized to relaxation training (3 practices/week for 1 month) exhibited decreased HSV-1 antibody titers and less distress at the end of the intervention, whereas no such changes were seen among control participants (Kiecolt-Glaser et al., 1985). Reductions seen in HSV-1 were maintained at 1-month follow-up. A more recent study demonstrated that meditation is a promising intervention strategy. In a study of 48 healthy adults, those who completed an 8-week meditation intervention prior to receiving influenza vaccination exhibited better antibody responses to vaccination compared with a waiting-list control group. The meditation group also demonstrated decreased trait anxiety and increased left-sided brain activation, presumably reflecting more positive affect (Davidson et al., 2003).

In addition, a recent study examined effects of tai chi, which involves physical activity as well as meditation (Irwin, Olmstead, & Oxman, 2007). A group of 112 older adults completed either a 16-week tai chi intervention or a health education group. At the end of the intervention, participants in both groups received a varicella-zoster virus (VZV) vaccine. VZV antibody levels were measured at the conclusion of the intervention, and following vaccination. Remarkably, tai chi alone resulted in increases in VZV-specific immunity equivalent to that conferred by vaccination. Moreover, tai chi in combination with vaccination had an additive effect. Thus, participants in the tai chi intervention group exhibited greater VZV-specific cell-mediated immunity than the health education group both at the end of the 16-week intervention and 9 weeks after the vaccination. Participants in the tai chi intervention group also showed significant improvements in mental health as measured by the SF-36, a quality-of-life index.

SUMMARY

Stressors ranging in magnitude and duration affect clinically meaningful health outcomes including inflammation, wound healing, and responses to viruses. Effects of stress on neuroendocrine parameters via the SAM and HPA axes play a primary mechanistic role in the link between stress and immune variables. In addition, mediators that are beyond the scope of this chapter are also implicated in this complex system (e.g., opioids, growth hormones, neuropeptides). Future studies should aim to more clearly delineate the multiple and complex neuroendocrine pathways linking stress to immune outcomes.

We have focused on physiological mediators in the link between psychological factors and immune outcomes. However, behavior change resulting from stress also plays an important role. The appropriate measurement and control of health behaviors will continue to be important for studies seeking to elucidate physiological pathways linking psychological factors with neuroendocrine and immune function. This is especially true for research with patients experiencing chronic illness as they may show considerable variability in terms of health behaviors including medication adherence, sleep, and diet.

Research to date indicates that age and stress interact to produce more significant immunological and neuroendocrine changes among older adults. An important area of future research is the examination of how early developmental experiences may set the stage for vulnerability in later life; psychosocial stressors during fetal development and early life can have lasting effects on physiology (Graham, Christian, & Kiecolt-Glaser, 2006b). A continued emphasis on understanding the interactive effects of stress and age throughout the life span will contribute to our understanding of the clinical significance of stress-related immune dysregulation.

There have been successful attempts to intervene in stress processes to benefit immune-related health outcomes. Such interventions include stress management, meditation, yoga, tai chi, exercise, dietary changes, psychotherapy, and antidepressant medications. In addition, social support can provide an important buffer from the effects of stress on health. In future research, an increased emphasis on the identification of physiological mechanisms underlying successful interventions would be of great value.

Over the past 25 years, research examining effects of stress on immune outcomes has grown dramatically. A continued emphasis on appropriately controlling for behavioral variables, delineating physiological mechanisms, and demonstrating the clinical significance of noted physiological alterations will contribute to future advances.

REFERENCES

Anisman, H., & Merali, Z. (2003). Cytokines, stress, and depressive illness: Brain-immune interaction. *Annals of Medicine, 35*, 2–11.

Bailey, M., Engler, H., Hunzeker, J., & Sheridan, J. F. (2003). The hypothalamic-pituitary-adrenal axis and viral infection. *Viral Immunology, 16*, 141–157.

Basterzi, A. D., Aydemir, C., Kisa, C., Aksaray, S., Tuzer, V., Yazici, K., et al. (2005). Il-6 levels decrease with ssri treatment in patients with major depression. *Human Psychopharmacology, 20*, 473–476.

Baum, C. L., & Arpey, C. J. (2005). Normal cutaneous wound healing: Clinical correlation with cellular and molecular events. *Dermatologic Surgery, 31*, 674–686.

Black, P. H., & Garbutt, L. D. (2002). Stress, inflammation and cardiovascular disease. *Journal of Psychosomatic Research, 52*, 1–23.

Bonneau, R. H., Padgett, D. A., & Sheridan, J. F. (2001). Psychoneuroimmune interactions in infectious disease: Studies in animals. In R. Ader, D. L. Felten, & N. Cohen (Eds.), *Psychoneuroimmunology* (3rd ed., Vol. 2, pp. 483–498). San Diego, CA: Academic Press.

Broadbent, E., Petrie, K. J., Alley, P. G., & Booth, R. J. (2003). Psychological stress impairs early wound repair following surgery. *Psychosomatic Medicine, 65*, 865–869.

Bruunsgaard, H., Pedersen, M., & Pedersen, B. K. (2001). Aging and proinflammatory cytokines. *Current Opinion in Hematology, 8*, 131–136.

Brydon, L., Edwards, S., Mohamed-Ali, V., & Steptoe, A. (2004). Socioeconomic status and stress-induced increases in interleukin-6. *Brain, Behavior, and Immunity, 18*, 281–290.

Burns, V. E., Carroll, D., Drayson, M., Whitham, M., & Ring, C. (2003). Life events, perceived stress and antibody response to influenza vaccination in young, healthy adults. *Journal of Psychosomatic Research, 55*, 569–572.

Burns, V. E., Carroll, D., Ring, C., Harrison, L. K., & Drayson, M. (2002). Stress, coping, and hepatitis b antibody status. *Psychosomatic Medicine, 64*, 287–293.

Bystricka, M., & Russ, G. (2005). Immunity in latent herpes simplex virus infection. *Acta Virologica, 49*, 59–67.

Cacioppo, J., Kiecolt-Glaser, J. K., Malarkey, W. B., Laskowski, B. F., Rozlog, L. A., Poehlmann, K. M., et al. (2002). Autonomic and glucocorticoid associations with steady-state expression of latent Epstein-Barr virus. *Hormones and Behavior, 42*, 32–41.

Capuron, L., & Miller, A. H. (2004). Cytokines and psychopathology: Lessons from interferon-α. *Biological Psychiatry, 56*, 819–824.

Carlson, L. E., Speca, M., Patel, K. D., & Goodey, E. (2003). Mindfulness-based stress reduction in relation to quality of life, mood, symptoms of stress, and immune parameters in breast and prostate cancer outpatients. *Psychosomatic Medicine, 65*, 571–581.

Carrico, A. W., Antoni, M. H., Pereira, D. B., Fletcher, M. A., Klimas, N., Lechner, S. C., et al. (2005). Cognitive behavioral stress management effects on mood, social support, and a marker of antiviral immunity are maintained up to 1 year in HIV-infected gay men. *International Journal of Behavioral Medicine, 12*, 218–226.

Christian, L. M., Graham, J. E., Padgett, D. A., Glaser, R., & Kiecolt-Glaser, J. K. (2007). Stress and wound healing. *Neuroimmunomodulation, 13*, 337–346.

Christian, L. M., & Stoney, C. M. (2006). Social support versus social evaluation: Unique effects on vascular and myocardial response patterns. *Psychosomatic Medicine, 68*, 914–921.

Cohen, S., Doyle, W. J., & Skoner, D. P. (1999). Psychological stress, cytokine production, and severity of upper respiratory illness. *Psychosomatic Medicine, 61*, 175–180.

Cohen, S., Doyle, W. J., Skoner, D. P., Rabin, B. S., & Gwaltney, J. M. (1997). Social ties and susceptibility to the common cold. *Journal of the American Medical Association, 277*, 1940–1944.

Cohen, S., Frank, E., Doyle, W. J., Skoner, D. P., Rabin, B. S., & Gwaltney, J. M. (1998). Types of stressors that increase susceptibility to the common cold in healthy adults. *Health Psychology, 17*, 214–223.

Cohen, S., Harmrick, N., Rodriguez, M. S., Fedman, P. J., Rabin, B. S., & Manuck, S. B. (2002). Reactivity and vulnerability to stress-associated risk for upper respiratory illness. *Psychosomatic Medicine, 64*, 302–312.

Cohen, S., Tyrrell, D. A., & Smith, A. P. (1991). Psychological stress and susceptibility to the common cold. *New England Journal of Medicine, 325*, 606–612.

Cole-King, A., & Harding, K. G. (2001). Psychological factors and delayed healing in chronic wounds. *Psychosomatic Medicine, 63*, 216–220.

Connor, T. J., & Leonard, B. E. (1998). Depression, stress and immunological activation: The role of cytokines in depressive disorders. *Life Sciences, 62*, 583–606.

Costanzo, E. S., Lutgendorf, S. K., Sood, A. K., Anderson, B., Sorosky, J., & Lubaroff, D. M. (2005). Psychosocial factors and interleukin-6 among women with advanced ovarian cancer. *Cancer, 104*, 305–313.

Cruess, S., Antoni, M., Cruess, D., Fletcher, M. A., Ironson, G., Kumar, M., et al. (2000). Reductions in herpes simplex virus type 2 antibody titers after cognitive behavioral stress management and relationships with neuroendocrine function, relaxation skills, and social support in HIV-positive men. *Psychosomatic Medicine, 62*, 828–837.

Dantzer, R., & Kelley, K. W. (2007). Twenty years of research on cytokine-induced sickness behavior. *Brain, Behavior, and Immunity, 21*, 153–160.

Davidson, R. J., Kabat-Zinn, J., Schumacher, J., Rosenkranz, M., Muller, D., Santorelli, S. F., et al. (2003). Alterations in brain and immune function produced by mindfulness meditation. *Psychosomatic Medicine, 65*, 564–570.

Delisi, L. E., Smith, S. B., Hamovit, J. R., Maxwell, M. E., Glodwin, L. R., Dingman, C. W., et al. (1986). Herpes simplex virus, cytomegalovirus and Epstein-Barr virus antibody titres in sera from schizophrenic patients. *Psychological Medicine, 16*, 757–763.

Dentino, A. N., Pieper, C. F., Rao, M. K., Currie, M. S., Harris, T., Blazer, D. G., et al. (1999). Association of interleukin-6 and other biologic variables with depression in older people living in the community. *Journal of the American Geriatrics Society, 47*, 6–11.

DeRijk, R., Michelson, D., Karp, B., Petrides, J., Galliven, E., Deuster, P., et al. (1997). Exercise and circadian rhythm-induced variations in plasma cortisol differentially regulate interleukin-1β (il-1β), il-6, and tumor necrosis factor-α (tnf-α) production in humans: High sensitivity of tnf-α and resistance of il-6. *Journal of Clinical Endocrinology and Metabolism, 82,* 2182–2192.

Detillion, C. E., Craft, T. K. S., Glasper, E. R., Prendergast, B. J., & DeVries, A. C. (2004). Social facilitation of wound healing. *Psychoneuroendocrinology, 29,* 1004–1011.

Dobbs, C. M., Feng, N., Beck, F. M., & Sheridan, J. F. (1996). Neuroendocrine regulation of cytokine production during experimental influenza viral infection: Effects of restraint stress-induced elevation in endogenous corticosterone. *Journal of Immunology, 157,* 1870–1877.

Doering, L. V., Cross, R., Vredevoe, D., Martinez-Maza, O., & Cowan, M. J. (2007). Infection, depression, and immunity in women after coronary artery bypass: A pilot study of cognitive behavioral therapy. *Alternative Therapies in Health and Medicine, 13,* 18–21.

Dyson, M., Moodley, S., Verjee, L., Verling, W., Wienman, J., & Wilson, P. (2003). Wound healing assessment using 20 mhz ultrasound and photography. *Skin Research and Technology, 9,* 116–121.

Ebrecht, M., Hextall, J., Kirtley, L.-G., Taylor, A., Dyson, M., & Weinman, J. (2004). Perceived stress and cortisol levels predict speed of wound healing in healthy male adults. *Psychoneuroendocrinolgy, 29,* 798–809.

Edwards, K. M., Burns, V. E., Reynolds, T., Carroll, D., Drayson, M., & Ring, C. (2006). Acute stress exposure prior to influenza vaccination enhances antibody response in women. *Brain, Behavior, and Immunity, 20,* 159–168.

Elias, P. M. (2005). Stratum corneum defensive functions: An integrated view. *Journal of Investigative Dermatology, 125,* 183–200.

Emery, C. F., Kiecolt-Glaser, J. K., Glaser, R., Malarkey, W. B., & Frid, D. J. (2005). Exercise accelerates wound healing among healthy older adults: A preliminary investigation. *Journals of Gerontology Series A: Biological Sciences and Medical Sciences, 60,* 1432–1436.

Ershler, W., & Keller, E. (2000). Age-associated increased interleukin-6 gene expression, late-life diseases, and frailty. *Annual Review of Medicine, 51,* 245–270.

Esterling, B. A., Antoni, M. H., Fletcher, M. A., Margulies, S., & Schneiderman, N. (1994). Emotional disclosure through writing or speaking modulates latent Epstein-Barr virus antibody titers. *Journal of Consulting and Clinical Psychology, 62,* 130–140.

Esterling, B. A., Antoni, M. H., Kumar, M., & Schneiderman, N. (1990). Emotional repression, stress disclosure responses, and Epstein-Barr viral capsid antigen titers. *Psychosomatic Medicine, 52,* 397–410.

Esterling, B. A., Antoni, M. H., Kumar, M., & Schneiderman, N. (1993). Defensiveness, trait anxiety, and Epstein-Barr viral capsid antigen antibody titers in healthy college students. *Health Psychology, 12,* 132–139.

Esterling, B. A., Antoni, M. H., Schneiderman, N., Carver, C. S., LaPerriere, A., Ironson, G., et al. (1992). Psychosocial modulation of antibody to Epstein-Barr viral capsid antigen and human herpesvirus type-6 in HIV-1-infected and at-risk gay men. *Psychosomatic Medicine, 54,* 354–371.

Ferrucci, L., Cherubini, A., Bandinelli, S., Bartali, B., Corsi, A., Lauretani, F., et al. (2006). Relationship of plasma polyunsaturated fatty acids to circulating inflammatory markers. *Journal of Clinical Endocrinology and Metabolism, 91,* 439–446.

Ford, E. S. (2002). Does exercise reduce inflammation? Physical activity and c-reactive protein among US adults. *Epidemiology, 13,* 561–568.

Frasure-Smith, N., Lesperance, F., & Julien, P. (2004). Major depression is associated with lower omega-3 fatty acid levels in patients with recent acute coronary syndromes. *Biological Psychiatry, 55,* 891–896.

Glaser, R., Friedman, S. B., Smyth, J., Ader, R., Bijur, P., Brunell, P., et al. (1999). The differential impact of training stress and final examination stress on herpesvirus latency at the United States military academy at West Point. *Brain, Behavior, and Immunity, 13,* 240–251.

Glaser, R., & Kiecolt-Glaser, J. K. (1997). Chronic stress modulates the virus-specific immune response to latent herpes simplex virus type 1. *Annals of Behavioral Medicine, 19,* 78–82.

Glaser, R., & Kiecolt-Glaser, J. K. (2005). Stress-induced immune dysfunction: Implications for health. *Nature Reviews Immunology, 5,* 243–251.

Glaser, R., Kiecolt-Glaser, J. K., Bonneau, R. H., Malarkey, W., Kennedy, S., & Hughes, J. (1992). Stress-induced modulation of the immune response to recombinant hepatitis b vaccine. *Psychosomatic Medicine, 54,* 22–29.

Glaser, R., Kiecolt-Glaser, J. K., Malarkey, W. B., & Sheridan, J. F. (1998). The influence of psychological stress on the immune response to vaccines. *Annals of the New York Academy of Sciences, 840,* 656–663.

Glaser, R., Kiecolt-Glaser, J. K., Marucha, P. T., MacCallum, R. C., Laskowski, B. F., & Malarkey, W. B. (1999). Stress-related changes in proinflammatory cytokine production in wounds. *Archives of General Psychiatry, 56,* 450–456.

Glaser, R., Kiecolt-Glaser, J. K., Speicher, C. E., & Holliday, J. E. (1985). Stress, loneliness, and changes in herpesvirus latency. *Journal of Behavioral Medicine, 8,* 249–260.

Glaser, R., Pearl, D. K., Kiecolt-Glaser, J. K., & Malarkey, W. B. (1994). Plasma cortisol levels and reactivation of latent Epstein-Barr virus in response to examination stress. *Psychoneuroendocrinology, 19,* 765–772.

Glaser, R., Pearson, G. R., Bonneau, R. H., Esterling, B. A., Atkinson, C., & Kiecolt-Glaser, J. K. (1993). Stress and the memory t-cell response to Epstein-Barr virus in healthy medical students. *Health Psychology, 12,* 435–442.

Glaser, R., Rice, J., Sheridan, J., Fertel, R., Stout, J., Speicher, C. E., et al. (1987). Stress-related immune suppression: Health implications. *Brain, Behavior, and Immunity, 1,* 7–20.

Glaser, R., Sheridan, J. F., Malarkey, W. B., MacCallum, R. C., & Kiecolt-Glaser, J. K. (2000). Chronic stress modulates the immune response to a pneumococcal pneumonia vaccine. *Psychosomatic Medicine, 62,* 804–807.

Godbout, J. P., & Glaser, R. (2006). Stress-induced immune dysregulation: Implications for wound healing, infectious disease, and cancer. *Journal of Neuroimmune Pharmacology, 1,* 421–427.

Graham, J. E., Christian, L. M., & Kiecolt-Glaser, J. K. (2006a). *Close relationships and immunity.* In R. Ader (Ed.), *Psychoneuroimmunology* (4th ed., Vol. 2, pp. 781–798). Burlington, MA: Elsevier Academic Press.

Graham, J. E., Christian, L. M., & Kiecolt-Glaser, J. K. (2006b). Stress, age, and immune function: Toward a lifespan approach. *Journal of Behavioral Medicine, 29.*

Gray, J., Wreghitt, T. G., Pavel, P., Smyth, R. L., Parameshwar, J., Stewart, S., et al. (1995). Epstein-Barr virus infection in heart and heart-lung transplant recipients: Incidence and clinical impact. *Journal of Heart and Lung Transplantation, 14,* 640–646.

Hackam, D. G., & Anand, S. S. (2003). Emerging risk factors for atherosclerotic vascular disease: A critical review of the evidence. *Journal of the American Medical Association, 290,* 932–940.

Hamerman, D., Berman, J. W., Albers, G. W., Brown, D. L., & Silver, D. (1999). Emerging evidence for inflammation in conditions frequently affecting older adults: Report of a symposium. *Journal of the American Geriatrics Society, 47,* 1016–1025.

Hamrick, N., Cohen, S., & Rodriguez, M. S. (2002). Being popular can be healthy or unhealthy: Stress, social network diversity, and incidence of upper respiratory infection. *Health Psychology, 21,* 294–298.

Hauser, P., Khosla, J., Aurora, H., Laurin, J., Kling, M. A., Hill, J., et al. (2002). A prospective study of the incidence and open-label treatment of interferon-induced major depressive disorder in patients with hepatitis C. *Molecular Psychiatry, 7,* 942–947.

Heesen, C., Schulz, H., Schmidt, M., Gold, S., Tessmer, W., & Schulz, K. H. (2002). Endocrine and cytokine responses to acute psychological stress in multiple sclerosis. *Brain, Behavior, and Immunity, 16,* 282–287.

Hess, R. D. (2004). Routine Epstein-Barr virus diagnostics from the laboratory perspective: Still challenging after 35 years. *Journal of Clinical Microbiology, 42,* 3381–3387.

Hibbeln, J. R. (1998). Fish consumption and major depression. *Lancet, 351,* 1213.

Hübner, G., Brauchle, M., Smola, H., Madlener, M., Fassler, R., & Werner, S. (1996). Differential regulation of pro-inflammatory cytokines during wound healing in normal and glucocorticoid-treated mice. *Cytokine, 8,* 548–556.

Irwin, M., Costlow, C., Williams, H., Artin, K. H., Chan, C. Y., Stinson, D. L., et al. (1998). Cellular immunity to varicella-zoster virus in patients with major depression. *Journal of Infectious Diseases, 178,* S104–S108.

Irwin, M., Olmstead, R., & Oxman, M. N. (2007). Augmenting immune responses to varicella zoster virus in older adults: A randomized, controlled trial of tai chi. *Journal of the American Geriatrics Society, 55,* 511–517.

Ishihara, K., & Hirano, T. (2002). Il-6 in autoimmune disease and chronic inflammatory proliferative disease. *Cytokine and Growth Factor Reviews, 13,* 357–368.

Johnson, J. D., O'Connor, K. A., Deak, T., Stark, M., Watkins, L. R., & Maier, S. F. (2002). Prior stressor exposure sensitizes lps-induced cytokine production. *Brain, Behavior, and Immunity, 16,* 461–476.

Jones, S. A., Horiuchi, S., Topley, N., Yamamoto, N., & Fuller, G. M. (2001). The soluble interleukin 6 receptor: Mechanisms of production and implications in disease. *FASEB Journal, 15,* 43–58.

Kendler, K. S., Karkowski, L. M., & Prescott, C. A. (1999). Causal relationship between stressful life events and the onset of major depression. *American Journal of Psychiatry, 156,* 837–841.

Kiecolt-Glaser, J. K., Belury, M. A., Porter, K., Beversdorf, D., Lemeshow, S., & Glaser, R. (2007). Depressive symptoms, omega-6: Omega-3 fatty acids, and inflammation in older adults. *Psychosomatic Medicine, 69,* 217–224.

Kiecolt-Glaser, J. K., Dura, J. R., Speicher, C. E., Trask, O. J., & Glaser, R. (1991). Spousal caregivers of dementia victims: Longitudinal changes in immunity and health. *Psychosomatic Medicine, 53,* 345–362.

Kiecolt-Glaser, J. K., Fisher, L. D., Ogrocki, P., Stout, J. C., Speicher, C. E., & Glaser, R. (1987). Marital quality, marital disruption, and immune function. *Psychosomatic Medicine, 49,* 31–34.

Kiecolt-Glaser, J. K., Glaser, R., Gravenstein, S., Malarkey, W. B., & Sheridan, J. (1996). Chronic stress alters the immune response to influenza virus vaccine in older adults. *Proceedings of the National Academy of Sciences, USA, 93,* 3043–3047.

Kiecolt-Glaser, J. K., Glaser, R., Williger, D., Stout, J., Messick, G., Sheppard, S., et al. (1985). Psychosocial enhancement of immunocompetence in a geriatric population. *Health Psychology, 4,* 25–41.

Kiecolt-Glaser, J. K., Kennedy, S., Malkoff, S., Fisher, L., Speicher, C. E., & Glaser, R. (1988). Marital discord and immunity in males. *Psychosomatic Medicine, 50,* 213–229.

Kiecolt-Glaser, J. K., Loving, T. J., Stowell, J. R., Malarkey, W. B., Lemeshow, S., Dickinson, S. L., et al. (2005). Hostile marital interactions, proinflammatory cytokine production, and wound healing. *Archives of General Psychiatry, 62,* 1377–1384.

Kiecolt-Glaser, J. K., Marucha, P. T., Malarkey, W. B., Mercado, A. M., & Glaser, R. (1995). Slowing of wound healing by psychological stress. *Lancet, 346,* 1194–1196.

Kiecolt-Glaser, J. K., Preacher, K. J., MacCallum, R. C., Atkinson, C., Malarkey, W. B., & Glaser, R. (2003). Chronic stress and age-related increases in the proinflammatory cytokine il-6. *Proceedings of the National Academy of Sciences, USA, 100,* 9090–9095.

Kirschbaum, C., Pirke, K. M., & Hellhammer, D. H. (1993). The "trier social stress test": A tool for investigating psychobiological stress responses in a laboratory setting. *Neuropsychobiology, 28,* 76–81.

Koenig, H. G., Cohen, H. J., George, L. K., Hays, J. C., Larson, D. B., & Blazer, D. G. (1997). Attendance at religious services, interleukin-6, and other biological parameters of immune function in older adults. *International Journal of Psychiatry in Medicine, 27,* 233–250.

Konsman, J. P., Parnet, P., & Dantzer, R. (2002). Cytokine-induced sickness behavior: Mechanisms and implications. *Trends in Neurosciences, 25,* 154–159.

Konstantinos, A. P., & Sheridan, J. F. (2001). Stress and influenza viral infection: Modulation of proinflammatory cytokine responses in the lung. *Respiration Physiology, 128,* 71–77.

LeMay, L. G., Vander, A. J., & Kluger, M. J. (1990). The effects of psychological stress on plasma interleukin-6 activity in rats. *Physiology and Behavior, 47,* 957.

Logan, A. C. (2003). Neurobehavioral aspects of omega-3 fatty acids: Possible mechanisms and therapeutic value in major depression. *Alternative Medicine Review: Journal of Clinical Therapeutic, 8,* 410–425.

Lowry, S. F. (1993). Cytokine mediators of immunity and inflammation. *Archives of Surgery, 28,* 1235–1241.

Lutgendorf, S. K., Anderson, B., Sorosky, J. I., Buller, R. E., & Lubaroff, D. M. (2000). Interleukin-6 and use of social support in gynecologic cancer patients. *International Journal of Behavioral Medicine, 7,* 127–142.

Lutgendorf, S. K., Antoni, M. H., Ironson, G., Klimas, N., McCabe, P., Cleven, K., et al. (1997). Cognitive-behavioral stress management decreases dysphoric mood and herpes simplex virus-type 2 antibody titers in symptomatic HIV-seropositive gay men. *Journal of Consulting and Clinical Psychology, 65,* 31–43.

Lutgendorf, S. K., Garand, L., Buckwalter, K. C., Reimer, T. T., Hong, S., & Lubaroff, D. M. (1999). Life stress, mood disturbance, and elevated interleukin-6 in healthy older women. *Journals of Gerontology, Series A: Biological Sciences and Medical Sciences, 54,* M434–M439.

Lutgendorf, S. K., Johnsen, E. L., Cooper, B., Anderson, B., Sorosky, J. I., Buller, R. E., et al. (2002). Vascular endothelial growth factor and social support in patients with ovarian carcinoma. *Cancer, 95,* 808–815.

Lutgendorf, S. K., Logan, H., Costanzo, E., & Lubaroff, D. (2004). Effects of acute stress, relaxation, and a neurogenic inflammatory stimulus on interleukin-6 in humans. *Brain, Behavior, and Immunity, 18,* 55–64.

Lutgendorf, S. K., Reimer, T. T., Harvey, J. H., Marks, G., Hong, S. Y., Hillis, S. L., et al. (2001). Effects of housing relocation on immunocompetence and psychosocial functioning in older adults. *Journals of Gerontology, Series A: Biological Sciences and Medical Sciences, 56,* M97–M105.

Lutgendorf, S. K., Russell, D., Ullrich, P., Harris, T. B., & Wallace, R. (2004). Religious participation, interleukin-6, and mortality in older adults. *Health Psychology, 23,* 465–475.

Maes, M., Bosmans, E., De Jongh, R., Kenis, G., Vandoolaeghe, E., & Neels, H. (1997). Increased serum il-6 and il-1 receptor antagonist concentrations in major depression and treatment resistant depression. *Cytokine, 9,* 853–858.

Maes, M., Meltzer, H. Y., Bosmans, E., Bergmans, R., Vandoolaeghe, E., Ranjan, R., et al. (1995). Increased plasma concentrations of interleukin-6, soluble interleukin-6, soluble interleukin-2 and transferrin receptor in major depression. *Journal of Affective Disorders, 34,* 301–309.

Maes, M., & Smith, R. S. (1998). Fatty acids, cytokines, and major depression. *Biological Psychiatry, 43,* 313–314.

Marks, R. (2004). The stratum corneum barrier: The final frontier. *Journal of Nutrition, 134,* S2071–S2021.

Marucha, P. T., Kiecolt-Glaser, J. K., & Favagehi, M. (1998). Mucosal wound healing is impaired by examination stress. *Psychosomatic Medicine, 60,* 362–365.

McDade, T. W., Hawkley, L. C., & Cacioppo, J. T. (2006). Psychosocial and behavioral predictors of inflammation in middle-aged and older adults: The Chicago health, aging, and social relations study. *Psychosomatic Medicine, 68,* 376–381.

McKinnon, W., Weisse, C. S., Reynolds, C. P., Bowles, C. A., & Baum, A. (1989). Chronic stress, leukocyte subpopulations, and humoral response to latent viruses. *Health Psychology, 8,* 389–402.

Mehta, S. K., Pierson, D. L., Cooley, H., Dubow, R., & Lugg, D. (2000). Epstein-Barr virus reactivation associated with diminished cell-mediated immunity in Antarctic expeditioners. *Journal of Medical Virology, 61,* 235–240.

Mehta, S. K., Stowe, R. P., Feiveson, A. H., Tyring, S. K., & Pierson, D. L. (2000). Reactivation and shedding of cytomegalovirus in astronauts during spaceflight. *Journal of Infectious Diseases, 182,* 1761–1764.

Mehta, S. K., Stowe, R. P., Feiveson, A. H., Tyring, S. K., & Pierson, D. L. (2004). Stress-induced subclinical reactivation of varicella zoster virus in astronauts. *Journal of Medical Virology, 72,* 174–179.

Miller, G. E., Cohen, S., Pressman, S., Barkin, A., Rabin, B. S., & Treanor, J. J. (2004). Psychological stress and antibody response to influenza vaccination: When is the critical period for stress, and how does it get inside the body? *Psychosomatic Medicine, 66,* 215–223.

Miller, G. E., Freedland, K. E., & Carney, R. M. (2005). Depressive symptoms and the regulation of proinflammatory cytokine expression in patients with coronary heart disease. *Journal of Psychosomatic Research, 59,* 231–236.

Modell, S., Yassouridis, A., Huber, J., & Holsboer, F. (1997). Corticosteroid receptor function is decreased in depressed patients. *Neuroendocrinology, 65,* 216–222.

Musselman, D. L., Lawson, D. H., Gumnick, J. F., Manatunga, A. K., Penna, S., Goodkin, R. S., et al. (2001). Paroxetine for the prevention of depression induced by high-dose interferon alfa. *New England Journal of Medicine, 344,* 961–966.

Opal, S. M., & DePalo, V. A. (2000). Anti-inflammatory cytokines. *Chest, 117,* 1162–1172.

Padgett, D. A., & Glaser, R. (2003). How stress influences the immune response. *Trends in Immunology, 24,* 444–448.

Padgett, D. A., Marucha, P. T., & Sheridan, J. F. (1998). Restraint stress slows cutaneous wound healing in mice. *Brain, Behavior, and Immunity, 12,* 64–73.

Pajulo, O. T., Pulkki, K. J., Alanen, M. S., Reunanen, M. S., Lertola, K. K., Mattila-Vuori, A. I., et al. (1999). Correlation between interleukin-6 and matrix metalloproteinase-9 in early wound healing in children. *Wound Repair and Regeneration, 7,* 453–457.

Parham, P. (2005). *The immune system* (2nd ed.). New York: Garland Science.

Parker, G., Gibson, N. A., Brotchie, H., Heruc, G., Rees, A. M., & Hadzi-Pavlovic, D. (2006). Omega-3 fatty acids and mood disorders. *American Journal of Psychiatry, 163,* 969–978.

Payne, D. A., Mehta, S. K., Tyring, S. K., Stowe, R. P., & Pierson, D. L. (1999). Incidence of Epstein-Barr virus in astronaut saliva during spaceflight. *Aviation Space and Environmental Medicine, 70,* 1211–1213.

Penninx, B. W. J. H., Kritchevsky, S. B., Yaffe, K., Newman, A. B., Simonsick, E. M., Rubin, S., et al. (2003). Inflammatory markers and depressed mood in older persons: Results from the health, aging, and body composition study. *Biological Psychiatry, 54,* 566–572.

Petrie, K. J., Booth, R. J., Pennebaker, J. W., Davison, K. P., & Thomas, M. G. (1995). Disclosure of trauma and immune response to a hepatitis b vaccination program. *Journal of Consulting and Clinical Psychology, 63,* 787–792.

Phillips, A. C., Burns, V. E., Carroll, D., Ring, C., & Drayson, M. (2005). The association between life events, social support, and antibody status following thymus-dependent and thymus-independent vaccinations in healthy young adults. *Brain, Behavior, and Immunity, 19,* 325–333.

Pierson, D. L., Stowe, R. P., Phillips, T. M., Lugg, D. J., & Mehta, S. K. (2005). Epstein-Barr virus shedding by astronauts during space flight. *Brain, Behavior, and Immunity, 19,* 235–242.

Pinquart, M., & Sorensen, S. (2004). Associations of caregiver stressors and uplifts with subjective well-being and depressive mood: A meta-analytic comparison. *Aging and Mental Health, 8,* 438–449.

Plotkin, S. A. (2001). Immunologic correlates of protection induced by vaccination. *Pediatric Infectious Disease, 20,* 73–75.

Quinlivan, M., & Breuer, J. (2006). Molecular studies of varicella zoster virus. *Reviews in Medical Virology, 16,* 225–250.

Rabin, B. S. (1999). *Stress, immune function, and health: The connection.* New York: Wiley-Liss.

Raison, C. L., Capuron, L., & Miller, A. H. (2006). Cytokines sing the blues: Inflammation and the pathogenesis of depression. *Trends in Immunology, 27,* 24–31.

Raison, C. L., & Miller, A. H. (2003). When not enough is too much: The role of insufficient glucocorticoid signaling in the pathophysiology of stress-related disorders. *American Journal of Psychiatry, 160,* 1554–1565.

Robertson, K. R., Wilkins, J. W., Handy, J., Van Der Horst, C., Robertson, W. T., Fryer, J. G., et al. (1993). Psychoimmunology and aids: Psychological distress and herpes simplex virus in human immunodeficiency virus infected individuals. *Psychology and Health, 8,* 317–327.

Sapolsky, R. M., & McEwen, B. S. (1985). Down-regulation of neural corticosterone receptors by corticosterone and dexamethasone. *Brain Research, 339,* 161–165.

Sarid, O., Anson, O., Yaari, A., & Margalith, M. (2001). Epstein-Barr virus specific salivary antibodies as related to stress caused by examinations. *Journal of Medical Virology, 64,* 149–156.

Schiepers, O. J. G., Wichers, M. C., & Maes, M. (2005). Cytokines and major depression. *Progress in Neuro-psychopharmacology and Biological Psychiatry, 29,* 201–217.

Schulz, R., & Beach, S. R. (1999). Caregiving as a risk factor for mortality: The caregiver health effects study. *Journal of the American Medical Association, 282,* 2215–2219.

Sharpe, L., Sensky, T., Timberlake, N., Ryan, B., Brewin, C. R., & Allard, S. (2001). A blind, randomized, controlled trial of cognitive-behavioural intervention for patients with recent onset rheumatoid arthritis: Preventing psychological and physical morbidity. *Pain, 89,* 275–283.

Sheridan, J. F., Donnenberg, A. D., Aurelian, L., & Elpern, D. J. (1982). Immunity to herpes simplex virus type 2: Pt. IV. Impaired lymphokine production during recrudescence correlates with an imbalance in t lymphocyte subsets. *Journal of Immunology, 129,* 326–331.

Silberman, D. M., Wald, M. R., & Genaro, A. M. (2003). Acute and chronic stress exert opposing effects on antibody responses associated with changes in stress hormone regulation of t-lymphocyte reactivity. *Journal of Neuroimmunology, 144,* 53–60.

Singer, A. J., & Clark, R. A. (1999). Cutaneous wound healing. *New England Journal of Medicine, 341,* 738–746.

Spencer, R. L., Miller, A. H., Stein, M., & McEwen, B. S. (1991). Corticosterone regulation of type I and type II adrenal steroid receptors in brain, pituitary, and immune tissue. *Brain Research, 549,* 236–246.

Steptoe, A., Wardle, J., Pollard, T. M., Canaan, L., & Davies, G. J. (1996). Stress, social support and health-related behavior: A study of smoking, alcohol consumption and physical exercise. *Journal of Psychosomatic Research, 41,* 171–180.

Steptoe, A., Willemsen, G., Owen, N., Flower, L., & Mohamed-Ali, V. (2001). Acute mental stress elicits delayed increases in circulating inflammatory cytokine levels. *Clinical Science, 101,* 185–192.

Tanaka, J., Ogura, T., Kamiya, S., Sato, H., Yoshie, T., Ogura, H., et al. (1984). Enhanced replication of human cytomegalovirus in human fibroblasts treated with dexamethasone. *Journal of General Virology, 65,* 1759–1767.

Thomas, A. J., Davis, S., Morris, C., Jackson, E., Harrison, R., & O'Brien, J. T. (2005). Increase in interleukin-1beta in late-life depression. *American Journal of Psychiatry, 162,* 175–177.

Tuglu, C., Kara, S. H., Caliyurt, O., Vardar, E., & Abay, E. (2003). Increased serum tumor necrosis factor-alpha levels and treatment response in major depressive disorder. *Psychopharmacology, 170,* 429–433.

Turner-Cobb, J. M., & Steptoe, A. (1996). Psychosocial stress and susceptibility to upper respiratory tract illness in and adult population sample. *Psychosomatic Medicine, 58,* 404–412.

Van De Kerkhof, P. C. M., Van Bergen, B., Spruijt, K., & Kuiper, J. P. (1994). Age-related changes in wound healing. *Clinical and Experimental Dermatology, 19,* 369–374.

Vedhara, K., Bennett, P. D., Clark, S., Lightman, S. L., Shaw, S., Perks, P., et al. (2003). Enhancement of antibody responses to influenza vaccination in the elderly following a cognitive-behavioural stress management intervention. *Psychother Psychosom, 72,* 245–252.

Vedhara, K., Cox, N. K. M., Wilcock, G. K., Perks, P., Hunt, M., Anderson, S., et al. (1999). Chronic stress in elderly carers of dementia patients and antibody response to influenza vaccination. *Lancet, 353,* 627–631.

Vileikyte, L. (2007). Stress and wound healing. *Clinics in Dermatology, 25,* 49–55.

Vitaliano, P. P., Scanlan, J. M., Zhang, J., Savage, M. V., & Hirsch, I. B. (2002). A path model of chronic stress, the metabolic syndrome, and coronary heart disease. *Psychosomatic Medicine, 64,* 418–435.

Vitaliano, P. P., Zhang, J., & Scanlan, J. M. (2003). Is caregiving hazardous to one's physical health? A meta-analysis. *Psychological Bulletin, 129,* 946–972.

von Kanel, R., Kudielka, B. M., Preckel, D., Hanebuth, D., & Fischer, J. E. (2005). Delayed response and lack of habituation in plasma interleukin-6 to acute mental stress in men. *Brain, Behavior, and Immunity, 20,* 40–48.

Waelde, L. C., Thompson, L., & Gallagher-Thompson, D. (2004). A pilot study of a yoga and meditation intervention for dementia caregiver stress. *Journal of Clinical Psychology, 60,* 677–687.

Werner, S., Grose, R. (2003). Regulation of wound healing by growth factors and cytokines. *Physiological Reviews, 83,* 835–870.

Wolf, H. J., & Morag, A. J. (1998). *Epstein-Barr virus vaccines.* In P. G. Medveczky, M. Bendinelli, & H. Friedman (Eds.), *Herpesviruses and immunity* (pp. 231–246). New York: Plenum Press.

Woolery, A., Myers, H., Sternlieb, B., & Zeltzer, L. (2004). A yoga intervention for young adults with elevated symptoms of depression. *Alternative Therapies in Health and Medicine, 10,* 60–63.

Yoshikawa, T. T. (1983). Geriatric infectious diseases: An emerging problem. *Journal of the American Geriatrics Society, 31,* 34–39.

Zhou, D., Kusnecov, A. W., Shurin, M. R., DePaoli, M., & Rabin, B. S. (1993). Exposure to physical and psychological stressors elevates plasma interleukin 6: Relationship to the activation of hypothalamic-pituitary-adrenal axis. *Endocrinology, 133,* 2523–2530.

Chapter 65

Telomeres, Telomerase, Stress, and Aging

JUE LIN, ELISSA S. EPEL, AND ELIZABETH H. BLACKBURN

Why should a behavioral scientist study telomeres? Maintenance of telomeres, the natural ends of linear chromosomes, is a fundamental biological mechanism of all eukaryotic cells, from protozoa to humans. Gradual shortening of telomeres after each cell division eventually can lead to loss of cellular division capacity and cell death, and contribute to genomic instability, a characteristic of cancer. Telomeres and telomerase, the enzyme that adds nucleotides to telomere ends, have been linked to human aging and aging-related diseases (Aubert & Lansdorp, 2008). Further, lifestyle and psychological state are increasingly being associated with telomere length and telomerase activity changes. Thus, telomere length and telomerase activity emerge as new biomarkers for cellular aging and may serve as surrogate markers for factors that contribute to aging and aging-related diseases. Therefore, scientists interested in understanding early onset of aging-related diseases, as well as longevity, may want to include this measure of cell aging.

This chapter gives the behavioral scientist a general understanding of the telomere/telomerase maintenance system, from its molecular basis, to clinical observations, to measurement. It addresses such questions as: Why do telomeres shorten? What are the consequences of telomere shortening? How are telomeres and telomerase related to cancer and diseases of aging? And, lastly and most relevant to behavioral scientists, what environmental (nongenetic) factors modulate telomere length? For detailed discussion of each topic, readers are encouraged to read the literature cited in this chapter.

TELOMERE MAINTENANCE AND THE AGING OF CELLS AND ORGANISMS

Telomeres Defined

First named by Hermann Muller in 1938, telomeres are the natural ends of eukaryotic chromosomes. Muller used X-rays to break chromosomes, thus generating mutants of the fruit fly. The mutants recovered often had chromosome fragments that rejoined. However, it appeared that the rejoining did not occur between two natural free chromosomal ends or between one broken end and one natural free end. Barbara McClintock had independently made comparable observations while studying chromosomes in maize. Muller called the natural free ends of chromosomes "telomeres." Telomeres thus behave differently from a broken chromosome end in that they are refractory to the molecular machinery that joins the broken ends.

The first telomeric DNA sequence was determined from the abundant minichromosomes of the ciliated protozoan *Tetrahymena thermophila*. This telomeric DNA consists of approximately 50 tandem repeats of the sequence TTGGGG, with each 3'-OH end of the duplex chromosomal DNA molecule being the G-rich strand (Blackburn et al., 1983; Blackburn & Gall, 1978). Since then, telomeric sequences from many organisms have been determined, including those of many species of yeast, plants, ciliates, birds, and mammals. Human telomeres contain 5 to 10 kilobases of TTAGGG repeats (Moyzis et al., 1989), while the lab strain of mouse *Mus musculus* has telomeres over 40 to 80 kb long of the same sequence as human (Blasco et al., 1997). Interestingly, the fruit fly *Drosophila melanogaster* that Muller used to discover the unusual properties of telomeres lacks the canonical repetitive telomeric sequences characteristic of most eukaryotes. Instead, Drosophila telomeres contain arrays of retrotransposon elements (evolutionarily related to retroviruses such as HIV viruses, Pardue & DeBaryshe, 2003). Nevertheless, telomeres in Drosophila are still protected from being recognized as broken ends.

Telomeres are organized into a high-order DNA-protein complex by the binding of multiple telomeric proteins. Evidence for a higher order structure called a T-loop has been found, in which the 3' overhang of the telomeric end is tucked into the double-stranded portion of the telomere sequence to form a loop structure (Figure 65.1). Overall, this higher order structure protects telomeres from being recognized as broken ends. Furthermore, the concerted

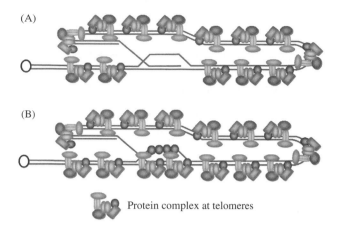

(A)

(B)

Protein complex at telomeres

Figure 65.1   Telomeres: A DNA-protein complex at the end of chromosomes, showing the "T-loop" structure.

Note: **A:** shows the 3' end of the single stranded region tucked into the double-stranded region to form the "T-loop." **B:** shows that the T-loop is bound by a multiprotein complex. From "Structure and Variability of Human Chromosome Ends," by de Lange et al., 1990, *Molecular and Cellular Biology*, 10, pp. 518–527. Adapted with permission.

actions of telomeric proteins and other factors determine the length of telomeres under different conditions.

Why Do Telomeres Shorten? The DNA End Replication Problem and Telomerase

As conventional DNA polymerases need a primer from which nucleotide extension occurs, the removal of the RNA primer at the lagging DNA synthesis strand will result in a 5'-terminal gap after DNA replication (Figure 65.2). Due to this end-replication problem (Watson, 1972), telomeric sequences are lost in each cell division. For immortal single-cell organisms and germ cells, an active cellular mechanism is needed to prevent the loss of telomeres. Since the presentation of the replication problem in the 1970s and early 1980s, many models have been put forward to explain this fundamental phenomenon (for a historical view of this, see Blackburn, 1984). This end-replication problem is solved for eukaryotic chromosomes by the cellular enzyme telomerase, a specialized ribonucleoprotein reverse transcriptase that uses its integral RNA molecule as the template to synthesize telomeric sequences (Greider & Blackburn, 1985, 1987; Figure 65.3).

Telomere Shortening Leads to Cellular Senescence

Hayflick and colleagues first described the limited proliferation capacity of normal human fibroblasts when cultured in vitro (Hayflick & Moorhead, 1961). The term *cellular senescence* refers to this state of irreversible cell cycle arrest. Since it is predicted that gradual shortening of telomeres will lead to eventual cell cycle arrest due to the end replication problem,

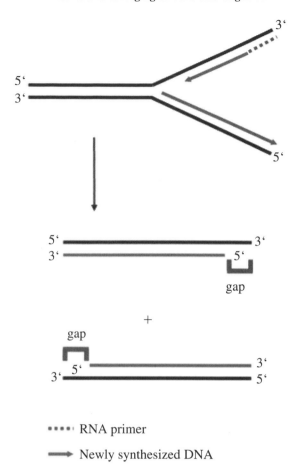

gap

+

gap

••••• RNA primer

→ Newly synthesized DNA

Figure 65.2   The DNA end replication problem.

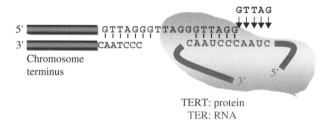

Chromosome terminus

TERT: protein
TER: RNA

Figure 65.3   Telomerase: the enzyme that adds nucleotides to and protects telomeric ends.

Telomerase activity was originally discovered in *Tetrahymena*, using extracts from freshly mated cells (Greider & Blackburn, 1985). This developmental stage was carefully chosen because soon after mating, in the somatic nucleus the chromosomes are fragmented, and hundreds of new telomeres are generated de novo, which requires especially high telomerase activity formation. Telomerase activity was subsequently identified in a variety of organisms, including yeast (Cohn & Blackburn, 1995) and human (Morin, 1989). The gene for the RNA component of human telomerase (TER or TERC) was cloned in 1995 (Feng et al., 1995), while the gene for the core protein component (TERT) was cloned in 1997 (Counter, Meyerson, Eaton, & Weinberg, 1997; Lingner et al., 1997; Nakamura et al., 1997). We now know that only the RNA and this protein component are required for minimal enzymatic activity by the telomerase ribonucleoprotein (RNP) enzyme. However, in vivo addition of telomeric DNA onto chromosomal ends requires the collaboration and coordination of dozens of proteins (reviewed in Cong, Wright, & Shay, 2002; Smogorzewska & de Lange, 2004).

the finite doubling capacity of mammalian cells described by Hayflick is proposed to be caused by attrition of telomeric sequence down to a critically short length. Soon after the identification of human telomere sequences, Harley and colleagues reported that telomeres progressively shorten during in vitro culturing of human primary fibroblasts (Harley, Futcher, & Greider, 1990). Furthermore, when fibroblasts directly taken from donors were examined for their telomere length, a loose negative correlation between the age of the donor and their telomere length was reported (Harley et al., 1990). Since then, the correlation between telomere shortening and cellular senescence has been supported by a large body of literature.

Although cellular senescence can be induced by critically shortened telomeres, other cellular signals can induce cellular senescence as well. Current models postulate that two major pathways can lead to cellular senescence (Campisi, 2005). The replicative senescence pathway caused by erosion of telomeres and their dysfunction is dependent on the tumor suppressor p53 (Campisi, 2005). Other cellular stresses, including oxidative stress and overexpression of oncogenes, can lead to stress-induced premature senescence, which is dependent on the p16/pRB pathway (Campisi, 2005). PRB and p16 are tumor suppressor proteins; on activation by cellular stress signals, they cause a chain of reactions that leads to cell-cycle arrest, therefore inhibiting cell proliferation (reviewed in Kim & Sharpless, 2006).

Senescent cells, whether caused by telomere dysfunction or cellular stress, display distinct characteristics. A hallmark of senescent cells is the irreversibility of cell cycle arrest. Senescent cells do not respond to growth stimuli, although they remain metabolically active for long periods. Morphologically, senescent cells are larger than their young counterparts and appear to be flat. They stain positive for the enzyme ß-galactosidase (Senescence-Associated ß-gal, SA-ß-gal) and express p53/p21 (telomere dependent senescence only) and p16 (stress-induced premature senescence). In telomere dependent senescence, DNA damage foci—cytologically visible clusters of proteins involved in DNA damage responses, including histone λ-H_2AX and 53BP1—colocalize with telomeres (d'Adda di Fagagna et al., 2003; Herbig, Ferreira, Condel, Carey, & Sedivy, 2004; Takai, Smogorzewska, & de Lange, 2003). An interesting feature of senescence is that cells are now more resistant to apoptosis; they do not respond to signals that cause apoptosis in normal cells. This may have physiological significance for the mechanism of immunosenescence, the aging of the immune system (discussed later). The gene expression profile of senescent cells is distinctively different from that of young cells. Two cell-cycle inhibitors, p21 and p16, are predominantly expressed in senescent cells. p21 expression is upregulated by the tumor suppressor p53, and p16 is induced by pRB. In addition, senescent fibroblasts express proteins that remodel the extracellular matrix, including metallo-matrix proteases and pro-inflammatory cytokines. These proteins are thought to contribute to carcinogenesis by creating a microenvironment advantageous for cancer cell growth (Campisi & d'Adda di Fagagna, 2007).

It is worth pointing out that for rodents, telomere-dependent replication senescence is not the primary pathway for cellular senescence of in vitro cell cultures; rodent telomeres are long and telomerase expression is generally higher than in the comparable normal human cell types (Chadeneau, Siegel, Harley, Muller, & Bacchetti, 1995; Prowse & Greider, 1995). The observed limited proliferation for mouse cells cultured in vitro is mainly due to insult from high oxidative stress under in vitro culture conditions, which triggers a p53 dependent DNA damage response. Despite this difference, as discussed later in this chapter, telomerase knockout mice, with telomere length similar to that of humans, have proved to be useful in vivo models to examine the potential roles of telomeres and telomerase in human diseases including cancer and other aging-related diseases.

Although the cellular senescence observed for in vitro cultured cells has been proposed to reflect in vivo organismal aging, there has been much controversy about what cellular senescence really means. The relevance of cellular senescence to aging became apparent when markers of cellular senescence were observed in vivo. Telomeres shorten during aging in many tissues that can be renewed throughout life, including peripheral blood, liver, kidney, spleen dermal fibroblasts, and keratinocytes, but not in postmitotic cells (e.g., neurons and cardiomyocytes; Djojosubroto, Choi, Lee, & Rudolph, 2003, and reference therein). This is consistent with the idea that in older organisms, the cells in the self-renewing tissues have gone through more divisions than younger people. Staining of the senescence associated enzyme ß-galactosidase (SA-ß-gal) has been reported in senescent fibroblast and keratinocytes in aging human skin (Dimri et al., 1995) as well as in damaged tissues in various diseases (reviewed in Erusalimsky & Kurz, 2005). Furthermore, expression of the senescence marker protein p16 was also reported (Krishnamurthy et al., 2004). Localization of DNA damage proteins at telomeres was also observed in skin cells of aging baboons and was taken as evidence of replicative senescence in vivo during aging (Herbig et al., 2006). In addition, the link between telomere dysfunction and pathological conditions has now been well established (to be discussed later).

Regulation of Telomerase

Human telomerase activity is highly regulated, both during development and tissue-specifically. Telomerase activity is expressed in embryonic stem cells and germ lines, but is decreased later in development (Forsyth, Wright, & Shay, 2002; Wright, Piatyszek, Rainey, Byrd, & Shay, 1996). In adults, low levels of telomerase activity were found in stem cells and progenitor cells including hematopoietic stem cells and neuronal, skin, intestinal crypt, mammary epithelial, pancreas, adrenal cortex, kidney, and mesenchymal stem cells (reviewed in E. Hiyama & Hiyama, 2007). Also, very low levels of telomerase activity have been detected in proliferating smooth muscle cells (Cao et al., 2002; Haendeler et al., 2004) and fibroblasts (Masutomi et al., 2003). However, telomerase activity in the adult progenitor cells is not high enough to prevent telomere attrition, as progenitor cells were shown to lose telomeric DNA length as the organism ages. This suggests that modulating telomerase activity in these cells may alter the rates of telomere shortening, thus affecting their proliferation capacity.

The regulation of telomerase activity in lymphocytes has been extensively studied. Telomerase activity is high in early stages of T and B cell development, but decreased at later stages. Only very low activity was detected in mature resting circulating T and B cells from peripheral blood mononuclear cells (K. Hiyama et al., 1995; Weng, Levine, June, & Hodes, 1996). However, telomerase activity is upregulated in T and B cells on stimulation by mitogens or antigens (Broccoli, Young, & de Lange, 1995; K. Hiyama et al., 1995); and this upregulation is required for clonal expansion of T and B cells during an immune response. Upregulated telomerase activity in lymphocytes is still not enough to compensate for telomere loss during proliferation, as telomere shortening was observed during in vitro culturing of activated T and B cells and these cells have a finite life span (Perillo, Walford, Newman, & Effros, 1989; Son, Murray, Yanovski, Hodes, & Weng, 2000). In vivo, memory T cells were found to have shorter telomeres than naive cells, indicating that their telomeres were shortened during clonal expansion. Since a proper adaptive immune response requires extensive and rapid clonal expansion of T and B cells, limited proliferation capacity may lead to compromised immune functions over the long term.

A host of environmental factors regulate telomerase activity (Figure 65.4). Reactive oxidative species (ROS) are reported to decrease telomerase activity in both cancer cells and human umbilical vein endothelial cells (Haendeler, Hoffmann, Brandes, Zeiher, & Dimmeler, 2003; Haendeler, Hoffmann, Rahman, Zeiher, & Dimmeler, 2003; Haendeler et al., 2004). Estrogen upregulates telomerase activity, while progesterone activates telomerase activity transiently, but inhibits activity in longer term experiments. Androgen activates telomerase activity in prostate cancer cells while inhibiting it in normal cells (reviewed in Bayne & Liu, 2005). Many growth hormones

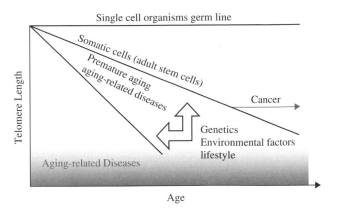

Figure 65.4 Telomere length can be modulated by various factors.

Note: From "The Common Biology of Cancer and Aging," by T. Finkel, M. Serrano, and M. A. Blasco, 2007, *Nature*, 448, pp. 767–774. Adapted with permission.

also play important roles in telomerase activity regulation. Insulin, IGF-1, VEGF and EGF upregulate telomerase activity, while TGF-ß inhibits it (Maida et al., 2002; Torella et al., 2004; Wetterau, Francis, Ma, & Cohen, 2003; Zaccagnini et al., 2005). Many cytokines, including IL-2, IL-6, IL-15, TNF-α and IFN-α, ß, and γ were also reported to regulate telomerase activity (Akiyama et al., 2004; Das, Banik, & Ray, 2007; Kawauchi, Ihjima, & Yamada, 2005; Li, Zhi, Wareski, & Weng, 2005; Xu et al., 2000; Yamagiwa, Meng, & Patel, 2006).

Regulation of telomerase activity is often executed at the level of transcriptional regulation of TERT. Several transcriptional factors have been reported to activate or repress telomerase activity through the hTERT promoter (Flores, Benetti, & Blasco, 2006). Modulations of alternative splicing, posttranslational modification, and subcellular localization and epigenetic modifications have also been reported (Anderson, Hoare, Ashcroft, Bilsland, & Keith, 2006; Flores et al., 2006; Jalink et al., 2007; Liu, Hodes, & Weng, 2001; Saeboe-Larssen, Fossberg, & Gaudernack, 2006).

Telomere Length-Independent Role(s) of Telomerase

There is now evidence suggesting that telomerase may have roles independent of its telomere lengthening function. Constitutive overexpression of hTERT in cancer cells that otherwise maintain their telomere length by telomerase-independent pathways (ALT cells) facilitates malignant transformation, suggesting that this cancer-promoting effect does not rely on extension of telomere length (Stewart et al., 2002). Furthermore, in normal fibroblast cells, further suppression of the already low amount of hTERT in these cells by RNA interference using a shRNA (small hairpin RNA) impairs the DNA damage response (Masutomi et al., 2003). Telomerase RNA knockdown by shRNAs or ribozymes in malignant cancer cells—rapidly causes a change in gene expression profile (Li et al., 2004; Li & Blackburn, 2005). In postmitotic cells, telomerase may protect against neurotoxicity: PC 12 cells overexpressing hTERT become more resistant to amyloid ß-peptide induced apoptosis (Zhu, Fu, & Mattson, 2000) and to DNA damaging drugs (Lu, Fu, & Mattson, 2001). Along the same lines, TERT mRNA is induced in cortical neurons after ischemic injury in mice, and transgenic mice overexpressing TERT are more resistant to neurotoxicity caused by NMDA (Kang et al., 2004). Although these experiments do not directly address whether it was telomere lengthening or telomerase activity that contributed to these effects, given the short period in which the effects are seen in cultured cells, they suggest that telomerase, as opposed to telomere length change, is the cause mechanistically.

Most convincingly, transgenic mice that overexpress TERT in their skin epithelium have grossly increased proliferation of their hair follicle stem cells. Since this effect is also seen in a telomerase RNA knockout background, this demonstrated that the enzymatic activity (telomere extension function) is not required (Sarin et al., 2005). The mechanisms of telomere length-independent telomerase function(s) remain unknown. A possible pathway is through the maintenance of the very tip of telomeres, that is, the capping function of telomerase. The physical presence of a telomerase complex that includes its RNA component may serve this purpose. An alternative, but not mutually exclusive mechanism is suggested by microarray gene-profiling data, where overexpression of hTERT is shown to upregulate growth-controlling genes (Smith, Coller, & Roberts, 2003). Consistent with this, a recent publication showed that TERT facilitates activation of progenitor cells in the skin and hair follicle by triggering a change in gene expression that significantly overlaps the program controlling natural hair follicle cycling (Choi et al., 2008).

TELOMERE MAINTENANCE AND HUMAN DISEASES

Telomeres and Aging-Related Diseases

The possibility that cellular senescence is associated with organismal aging is consistent with observations that in vivo, senescent cells accumulate with aging (Dimri et al., 1995). Whether replicative senescence caused by telomere erosion is relevant to organismal aging is under debate (Patil, Mian, & Campisi, 2005). However, several lines of evidence

strongly suggest a link between telomere dysfunction and aging and aging-related diseases. First, numerous clinical studies link short telomere length in white blood cells (specifically, peripheral blood mononuclear cells, PBMCs) to aging-related disease or preclinical conditions of diseases. A short list of them includes increased mortality from cardiovascular disease and infectious disease (Cawthon, Smith, O'Brien, Sivatchenko, & Kerber, 2003), coronary atherosclerosis (Samani, Boultby, Butler, Thompson, & Goodall, 2001), premature myocardial infarction (Brouilette, Singh, Thompson, Goodall, & Samani, 2003), vascular dementia (von Zglinicki, Pilger, & Sitte, 2000), hypertension with carotid atherosclerosis (Benetos et al., 2004), age-related calcific aortic stenosis (Kurz et al., 2004), increased pulse pressure (Jeanclos et al., 2000), obesity and smoking (Valdes et al., 2005), Alzheimer's disease (Panossian et al., 2003; Zhang et al., 2003), and insulin-resistance, a preclinical condition for diabetes (Brouilette et al., 2007; Collerton et al., 2007). The main findings of these and several other clinical studies that examined the relationship between telomere length and aging-related diseases are summarized in Table 65.1 and Appendix 65.1 on page 1295.

Second, evidence for in vivo cellular senescence was found in affected tissues of cardiovascular patients. Telomere shortening is accelerated in the atherosclerosis-prone areas compared with control areas (Chang & Harley, 1995; Okuda et al., 2000) and telomeres are shorter in diseased coronary arteries than nondiseased age-matched specimens (Ogami et al., 2004). Similarly, putative endothelial cell senescence was observed in human atherosclerosis (Minamino et al., 2002) and vascular smooth muscle cells (VSMCs) with cells in the diseased area containing shorter telomeres than in nondiseased areas in the same patient (Matthews et al., 2006).

Third, in vitro studies with cultured cells have recapitulated some aspects of cellular senescence in vivo regarding cardiovascular diseases. Briefly, stimuli and conditions that affect endothelial and vascular smooth muscle (VSMC) cell function in vitro appear to correlate with telomerase and telomere length maintenance: Oxidative stress reduced telomerase activity and accelerated telomere shortening in EC and VSMC, whereas hypoxia and antioxidants induced telomerase activity and promoted proliferation. Furthermore, overexpression of telomerase in endothelial cells and VSMC extended proliferation life span and improves functional properties (Edo & Andres, 2005).

Fourth, the most compelling evidence for the role of telomeres and telomerase in aging and aging-related diseases came from studies of the genetic disease dyskeratosis congenita (DC) and other related diseases, as discussed in a later section.

TABLE 65.1   Studies linking telomere maintenance to diseases.

Study	Main Findings	Authors
Telomere shortening and prostate cancer	Telomere attrition in the high-grade prostatic, intraepithelial neoplastia and surrounding stroma is predicative of prostate cancer.	Joshua et al. (2007)
Telomere shortening and breast cancer	Short telomeres in PBMCs are associated with breast cancer risk.	Shen et al. (2007)
Telomere shortening and bladder cancer	Short telomeres appear to be associated with increased risks for human bladder, head and neck, lung, and renal cell cancers.	Wu et al. (2003)
Telomere shortening and bladder cancer	Short telomeres in buccal cells associated with bladder cancer risk.	Broberg, Bjork, Paulsson, Hoglund, & Albin (2005)
Telomere dysfunction and renal cancer	Telomere length in lymphocytes is associated with renal cancer.	Shao et al. (2007)
598 participants of the Leiden 85-plus study (average age = 89.8)	Telomere length in leucocytes is not associated with morbidity or mortality in the oldest old.	Martin-Ruiz, Gussekloo, van Heemst, von Zglinicki, & Westendorp (2005)
812 participants (652 twins) 73–101 years of age	In twin pairs, the twin with shorter telomere died first. No association between telomere length and survival in this study.	Bischoff et al. (2006)
Lothian Birth Cohort	Telomere length is not associated with age-related physical and cognitive decline or mortality.	Harris et al. (2006)
Scottish Mental Survey (n = 190, born 1921)	Short telomere length is associated with heart disease in old people.	Starr et al. (2007)
183 healthy controls and 620 chronic heart failure patients	Telomere length in PBMCs is shorter in chronic heart failure patients and related to severity of the disease.	van der Harst et al. (2007)
West Scotland Coronary Prevention Study (n = 484)	Short telomere length is associated the risk of coronary heart disease. Statin treatment attenuates the association.	Brouilette et al. (2007)
Newcastle 85+ study	Telomere length is associated with left ventricular function in the oldest old.	Collerton et al. (2007)
Chennai Urban Rural Epidemiology Study (India)	Short telomere length is associated with impaired glucose and diabetic macroangiopathy.	Adaikalakoteswari, Balasubramanyam, Ravikumar, Deepa, & Mohan (2007)
Cardiovascular Health Study	Short telomere length associated with diabetes, diastolic blood pressure, carotid intima-media thickness, and IL-6.	Fitzpatrick et al. (2007)
2509 Caucasian of Askelpios study (n = 35–55 free of overt CVD)	No association between telomere length and cholesterol and blood pressure. Short telomeres are associated with levels of inflammation and oxidative stress markers. Shorter telomere length is associated with unhealthy lifestyle in men.	Bekaert et al. (2007)
Women ages 18–79 (N = 2150)	Telomere length in leukocytes positively correlates with bone mineral density. Shorter telomere length is correlated with osteoporosis.	Valdes et al. (2007)
1086 from TwinsUK Adult Twin Registry	Short telomeres in leukocytes is associated with radiographic hand osteoarthritis.	Zhai et al. (2006)
Caucasian men ages 40–89 from the Framingham Heart Study (N = 327)	Shorter telomere length associated with hypertension, increased insulin resistance, and oxidative stress.	Demissie et al. (2006)
Women ages 18–79 (N = 1517)	Insulin resistance, leptin, and C-reactive protein levels are inversely related to leucocyte telomere length in premenopausal women, but not in postmenopausal women.	Aviv et al. (2006)
Type II diabetes (N = 21) and control (N = 29)	Mean monocyte telomere length in the diabetic group is lower than in control, without significant differences in lymphocyte telomere length.	Sampson, Winterbone, Hughes, Dozio, & Hughes (2006)
Young adults of the Bogalusa Heart Study	Telomere attrition is correlated with insulin resistance and changes in the body mass index.	Gardner et al. (2005)
Women ages 18–76 (N = 1122)	Shorter telomere length is associated with obesity and cigarette smoking.	Valdes et al. (2005)

(continues)

TABLE 65.1   *(Contineud)*

Study	Main Findings	Authors
Hypertensive men (N = 163)	Telomeres are shorter in hypertensive men with carotid artery plaques than hypertensive men without carotid artery plaques	Benetos et al. (2004)
N = 143	Short telomeres associated with high rates of mortality from cardiovascular disease and infection.	Cawthon, Smith, O'Brien, Sivatchenko, & Kerber (2003)
Premature myocardial infarction (N = 203) and control (N = 180)	Telomeres are shorter in leucocytes in premature myocardial infarction than controls.	Brouilette, Singh, Thompson, Goodall, & Samani (2003)
10 patients and 20 controls	Telomere length in white blood cells shorter in patients with severe coronary artery disease.	Samani, Boultby, Butler, Thompson, & Goodall (2001)
49 twin pairs from the Danish Twin Register	Short telomere length in leucocytes correlates with high pulse pressure.	Jeanclos et al. (2000)

Note: From *de Lange, T. (2005) Shelterin.* The protein complex that shapes and safeguards human telomeres. *Genes & Development, 19, 2100–2110*

Telomerase and Cancer

The finite life span of somatic cells in multicellular organisms has been suggested to be an antitumor mechanism to prevent accumulation of mutations that leads to cancer. However, the secretion of cancer-promoting factors by senescent human cells, as described earlier, argues against this notion. Therefore, it is uncertain whether replicative senescence, caused by critically short telomeres, is a tumor suppression mechanism in humans. Telomerase activity is essential for tumor growth since in over 90% of human cancers, telomerase becomes upregulated during tumorigenesis (Kim et al., 1994), while the rest adopt recombination pathways to maintain their telomere length (ALT for alternative lengthening of telomeres; Bryan, Englezou, Dalla-Pozza, Dunham, & Reddel, 1997). Yet cancer cells often have shorter telomeres than adjacent normal cells (de Lange et al., 1990; Joshua et al., 2007). A commonly invoked model for tumorigenesis, although unproven in humans, is that in normal cells, short telomeres induce replicative senescence, a p53-dependent DNA damage response that results in cell cycle arrest, to serve as antitumor mechanism. Rare events of inactivation of p53 allow cells to bypass this short telomere-induced arrest, known as M1, and continue to grow. Further shortening of telomeres leads to a second cell cycle arrest, M2, also known as crisis. At M2, most cells die from apoptosis, but a few escape by reactivation of telomerase, thereby become cancer cells (Figure 65.5).

Recent clinical studies have also linked short telomeres in PBMCs or, in some cases, buccal cells to greater risk factors for various cancers, including bladder, head and neck, lung, breast and renal cancer (Broberg, Bjork, Paulsson, Hoglund, & Albin, 2005; Shao et al., 2007; Shen et al., 2007; Wu et al., 2003). It is not clear whether the short telomeres in PBMCs and buccal cells reflect genetic predisposition to cancer and/or environmental factors thought to contribute to high cancer risks (e.g., oxidative stress and chronic inflammation).

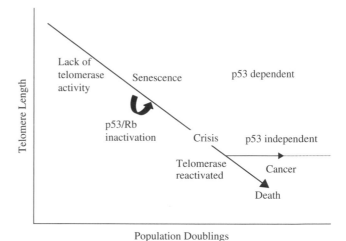

Figure 65.5 One model for telomere maintenance and tumorigenesis.

Telomerase Knockout and TERT Overexpression Mice as Models for Roles of Telomere and Telomerase in Aging-Related Diseases

Studies using telomerase knockout mice have provided essential evidence for the role of telomere and telomerase in health. The first telomerase knockout mouse was created by deleting the RNA component of telomerase mTER (Blasco et al., 1997). As this lab strain of *Mus musculus* normally has over 50 kb-long telomeres (Prowse & Greider, 1995), it was not surprising that the first three generations of TERC-/- did not show any early cytogenetic, morphologic, or physiological phenotypes, despite the expected telomere shortening due to the lack of telomerase activity. However, a notable phenotype is that G1 knockout mice have shorter life span despite their still-long telomeres, indicating that telomerase may have telomere-length independent roles in longevity. Successive breeding of the mTERC-/- mice resulted in phenotypes characterized by deficiencies in tissue renewal. At the sixth generation (G6), TERC-/- mice are sterile, with males exhibiting testicular atrophy and declined spermatogenesis, while the females have a decreased number of oocytes. In the hematopoietic system, reduced progenitor cell numbers, spleen atrophy, and decreased proliferation of T and B cells on induction by mitogens were reported (reviewed in Blasco, 2005). Thus the phenotypes exhibited in late generation mTERC-/- mouse support the role of telomerase in maintaining telomere length required for cell proliferation for tissue renewal.

The phenotypes of mTERC-/- mouse with regard to cancer seem to be complicated. Chromosomal end-to-end fusions of critically short telomeres, which lead to massive genome instability, were observed in late generation mTERC-/- mice. In addition, gross chromosomal rearrangements, such as nonreciprocal translocations, a common feature of human cancer, were also found. This is consistent with the proposal that for human cancers, critically short telomeres lead to chromosome fusion and breakage—fusion-bridge cycles. Consistent with the role of short telomeres in promoting cancer, these mice have higher incidences of tumors. However, the growth of tumors derived from mTERC-/- mice is decreased compared with wild type, in agreement with the notion that upregulation of telomerase is required for cancer cell growth. Thus telomerase appears to have antagonistic effects on tumorigenesis.

Mice overexpressing the telomerase core protein gene, mTERT, had increased death risk during the first half of their life due to increased tumorigenesis, but had extended life span in the second half of life. These long-lived mice had decreased degenerative lesions in testis, uterus and ovary, and kidney (Gonzalez-Suarez, Flores, & Blasco, 2002; Gonzalez-Suarez, Geserick, Flores, & Blasco, 2005; Gonzalez-Suarez et al., 2001). Notably, kidney dysfunction is a common cause of death in elderly humans.

These findings in telomerase knockout and TERT overexpression mice strengthen the idea that a delicate balance is important to ensure just the right amount of telomerase activity. When the activity is too low, it is not sufficient to allow proliferation of renewable tissues or full protection from cancer, thus contributing to premature aging and aging-related diseases. However, at least in mice, too much telomerase activity predisposes the organism to higher cancer incidence.

Telomerase and Human Genetic Diseases

The strongest evidence suggesting a direct role of telomerase and telomere maintenance in human aging and aging-related diseases came from studies of the rare multisystem disorder *dyskeratosis congenita* (Vulliamy et al., 2006). Classically, dyskeratosis congenita (DC) is characterized by a triad of mucoctaneous symptoms: abnormal skin pigmentation, nail dystrophy, and mucosal leukoplakia. However, a host of other symptoms, including hair graying and loss, pulmonary disease, and predisposition to cancer, were also reported. Patients die of eventual failure of the hematopoietic system (bone marrow failure). Three genetic forms of DC were reported: most DC patients have the X-linked recessive form, caused by mutations in the gene for dyskerin, a protein required for pseudo-uridylation of ribosomal RNA, which is also a component of the mammalian cellular telomerase RNP complex. Of interest here, a more rare genetic type of DC is autosomal-dominant and is caused by mutations in the RNA or protein component of telomerase (TERC or TERT). The apparent autosomal-dominant inheritance mode is due to haploinsufficiency for telomerase activity. Most recently, the genetic cause for one subtype of the autosomal recessive DC is reported to be mutations in another telomerase-associated protein, NOP 10 (Walne et al., 2007).

It has now become clear that the primary molecular basis for the defects in all forms of DC studied so far lies in a deficiency for telomerase activity, which leads to shorter telomeres, especially in the affected tissues. Over a dozen hTER deletion or point mutations have now been reported in DC patients. Using a reconstituted cell-free system that expresses the DC-forms of hTER, or by introducing the DC mutant copy of hTER into a cell line that does not have endogenous hTER, several labs have demonstrated that mutant hTER found in DC patients leads to reduced telomerase activity (Comolli, Smirnov, Xu, Blackburn, & James, 2002; Fu & Collins, 2003; Ly et al., 2005; Marrone, Stevens, Vulliamy, Dokal, & Mason, 2004). Similarly, mutations in the protein subunit of telomerase were also reported in DC patients (Marrone et al., 2007). Retroviral expression of hTER and/or hTERT extended telomere length and rescued DC cells from premature senescence (Westin et al., 2007).

Interestingly, even in the X-linked form of DC caused by dyskerin mutations, telomerase RNA level appears to be the limiting factor for telomere length maintenance (Wong & Collins, 2006), as reintroduction of the wild type hTER and hTERT into cells from DC patients restores the cells to normal rRNA processing and proliferation. DC patients have shorter telomere length than unaffected family members and patients with the severest phenotypes have shorter telomeres than patients with milder symptoms (Vulliamy et al., 2006). Furthermore, autosomal-dominant DC families show an earlier age of onset and more severe disease phenotypes in succeeding generations (Armanios et al., 2005), a phenomenon called *disease anticipation*. This is consistent with the progressive shortening of telomeres over generations.

Analysis of the immune system of a large family with autosomal dominant DC caused by a TERC mutation revealed immune abnormalities including severe B lymphopenia and decreased immunoglobulin M (IgM) levels, and T cells that overexpressed senescent cell surface markers. In vitro culturing of the cells from these DC patients showed their lymphocytes had reduced proliferative capacity and increased basal apoptotic rate (Knudson, Kulkarni, Ballas, Bessler, & Goldman, 2005).

Diseases caused by deficient telomerase activity are not limited to family histories of hereditary disorders. Sporadic cases of bone marrow failure syndromes including aplastic anemia (Ly et al., 2005; Xin et al., 2007), melodysplastic syndrome (Field et al., 2006; Ortmann et al., 2006; Yamaguchi, 2006, 2007), and essential thrombocytemia (Ly et al., 2005) were also found to have mutations in hTERC or hTERT. The spectrum of diseases caused by telomerase mutations has now been broadened to include idiopathic pulmonary fibrosis (Armanios et al., 2007).

What Does the Length of Telomeres in Humans Really Reflect?

The length of telomeres is determined by several factors: telomeres that were inherited (genetic), level of telomerase, environmental factors that influence the rate of attrition and telomerase activity, and number of cell divisions (history of division). In the following subsections, we discuss common genetic variations, replicative history, and biochemical environment factors that contribute to person-to-person variation in telomere length and rate of telomere shortening.

Genetic Transmission

A study in 115 twin pairs, 2 to 63 years of age, indicated a 78% heritability for mean telomere length in this age cohort (Slagboom, Droog, & Boomsma, 1994). In 2,050 unselected women aged 18 to 80 years, comprising 1,025 complete dizygotic twin pairs, telomere length was reported to have 36% to 90% heritability (Andrew et al., 2006). In another study of 383 adults including 258 twin pairs, the heritability of telomere length was reported to be 81.9% ± 11.8% (Vasa-Nicotera et al., 2005). While the preceding studies suggested autosomal genes contribute to telomere length heritability, some reports also suggest X-linked modes of inheritance (between fathers and daughters, between mothers and sons and daughters; and among siblings, but not between father and son). A paternal inheritance (father-son and father-daughter) of telomere length was found in Old Order Amish people (Njajou et al., 2007). However, a study examining telomere length in an elderly population of 686 males including monozygotic (MZ) and dizygotic (DZ) twins reported no evidence of heritable effects, but rather that telomere length was largely associated with shared environmental factors (Huda et al., 2007). While it is still not known why there are discrepancies

among findings from different groups, it is likely that it is due to different populations and different ages when the telomeres were measured. It seems plausible that the older the general population, the more environmental impacts might override genetic influences. Further, while there is strong genetic transmission of telomere length, it is not known whether maternal telomere length (e.g., in immune cells) is transmitted to offspring through nongenetic means. In other words, can short telomeres due to environmental exposures in mothers be transmitted through nongenetic or epigenetic means (Epel, in press).

Replication History

Examination of telomere length in various human tissues has suggested that the rate of telomere length attrition roughly reflects the rate of cell turnover in the tissue. A rapid telomere shortening in peripheral blood cells was seen in the first year of life (Frenck, Blackburn, & Shannon, 1998; Rufer et al., 1999), although it is not clear that this reflects higher cell turnover rates. The rate of telomere attrition in adults is estimated to be 31 to 62 bp/year (Takubo et al., 2002). Telomeres are shorter in patients with diseases characterized by high cell turnover rates compared with their age-matched peers, including chronic viral infection: HIV, CMV, lupus, and rheumatoid arthritis (Nakajima et al., 2006; Steer et al., 2007). In brain tissues, no evidence for telomere shortening was seen in a cross-sectional study comparing adults of different ages (Allsopp et al., 1995). However, human adrenocortical cells, which divide continuously throughout life, showed a strong age-related decline in telomere length (Yang, Suwa, Wright, Shay, & Hornsby, 2001). The average rate of telomere attrition in PBMCs in women is lower than in men, when measured in cross-sectional studies. It is not clear why, but it has been suggested that estrogen, which is known to upregulate telomerase, may play a role in slowing telomere attrition.

Lifestyle Factors

Lifestyle factors may affect telomere length, such as factors that promote obesity, which is linked to shorter telomeres (Valdes et al., 2005). Cigarette smoking is linked to both shorter telomere length (Valdes et al., 2005) and lower telomerase (Epel et al., 2006). Exercise has been associated with longer leukocyte telomere length (Cherkas et al., 2008). No studies have examined other health behaviors such as alcohol use, although given their relations with insulin and obesity, it is likely that nutrition, dysregulated eating patterns, and overeating would all affect cell aging. Dietary restraint, which is linked to stress, cortisol, and dysregulated eating patterns, is linked to shorter telomere length (Kiefer, Lin, Blackburn, & Epel, 2008). It appears that nutrition in early life may affect telomeres, at least in certain tissues such as kidney (Jennings, Ozanne, & Hales, 2000). Protein restriction while in utero was related to shorter telomeres, whereas protein restriction during early life was related to longer kidney telomeres (Jennings et al., 2000).

Lastly, psychological stress is related to shorter PBMC telomeres. Our group has found this both in young maternal caregivers (Epel et al., 2004) and in elderly dementia caregivers (unpublished data). Others have now replicated this finding in dementia caregivers (Damjanovic et al., 2007), in major depression (Simon et al., 2006), and in stressed mice (Kotrschal, Ilmonen, & Penn, 2007). The mediating pathways are unknown, but likely involve many of the pathways described earlier; both behavioral (such as poor nutrition and fitness, and insufficient sleep) and biochemical pathways are affected by stress. Telomere length is not equivalent to a biological measure of stress, which becomes obvious when we take into account the myriad other factors that modulate telomere length. Telomere length is, however, reflective of stress, as well as of a multitude of other biological, and environmental factors, extending from early in life to throughout the life span.

Possible Mechanisms Relating Telomere Maintenance to Aging-Related Diseases

With the growing body of literature demonstrating the link between telomere dysfunction and aging-related diseases, we might start to ask how mechanistically telomere dysfunction is related to, and contributes to, aging-related diseases. As discussed, telomere shortening is the end result of a multitude of pathways, making attribution of cause and effect difficult. In a notable exception, our group has found evidence that chronicity of psychological stress is quantitatively associated with the degree of telomere shortness, thus implicating chronic psychological stress in a causative role in telomere shortening. Beyond that, the causality of the relationships between telomere shortness and disease and disease risk factors is likely to be challenging to unravel.

In human studies, telomere shortness in leukocytes has been studied extensively. As well as having the practical advantage of being readily obtained, these cells may be closely linked to disease processes. Here we consider three possible, nonmutually exclusive, mechanisms that could link leukocyte aging to risk for aging-related diseases—in particular, cardiovascular diseases:

Mechanism 1: cellular aging in leukocytes simply reflects the same process that is ongoing in cells of other tissues, but does not directly contribute to the aging or disease development of those tissues. Just like cells of the immune system, accumulation of senescent cells limits the proliferation capacity of other tissues that require self-renewal and repair, including tissue stem and progenitor cells. It has been shown in recent years that even in organs that are believed to be postmitotic, progenitor cells are involved in repair after damage or even normal functions. Cardiac stem cells are involved in repair from ischemic injury (Anversa, Kajstura, Leri, & Bolli, 2006; Leri, Kajstura, & Anversa, 2005), and neuronal progenitor cells in the hippocampus may be involved in memory (Kempermann & Gage, 2000).

Mechanism 2: The same detrimental factors (e.g., stress hormones, oxidative stress, pro-inflammatory cytokines and other risk factors) that cause telomere dysfunction in leukocytes cause damage to cells of other organs through different mechanisms. Therefore, leukocyte telomere dysfunction is not the contributing factor, but rather, it serves as a cellular readout for these damaging factors (telomere dysfunction may be a surrogate marker of other damaging factors that cause aging-related disease). Telomere length thus reflects the cumulative assault the cells receive over the cause of life; particular candidates of interest are oxidative stress and pro-inflammatory cytokines, as they are known to be associated with CVD. Results from clinical studies are now showing a consensus that PBMC telomere length is linked to the family of biochemical factors reflecting metabolic stress, such as oxidative stress, pro-inflammatory cytokines, insulin and leptin (Aviv et al., 2006; Bekaert et al., 2007; Demissie et al., 2006; Fitzpatrick et al., 2007). Telomere length in PBMCs may therefore be predictive of morbidity and mortality, in that it reflects cumulative effects, as opposed to the current status.

Mechanism 3: Senescent cells of the immune system secrete proteins detrimental to the surrounding cells. Immunosenescent $CD8^+CD28^-$ cells are known to produce high levels of proinflammatory cytokines IL-6 and TNF-α. Since local inflammation plays a pivotal role in some aging-related disease including atherosclerosis (Tedgui & Mallat, 2006), the senescent cells of the immune system may contribute to cardiovascular disease through this pathway. In addition, senescent fibroblasts were shown to secrete growth factors that promoted cancer cell growth, providing another potential contributor to the increased risk of cancer with age.

MEASUREMENT OF CELL AGING AND POTENTIAL CONFOUNDING FACTORS

Accurate measurement of telomere length and telomerase activity is crucial, but prone to pitfalls with current techniques. So for the immediate future, behavioral researchers will need to rely on expertise specifically in these measurements, as well as expert study design to obtain interpretable results.

Telomere Length Measurement

As with any assay, a new lab should test their measure and its reliability against a gold standard lab. Small differences in blood or other tissue collection, reagent solution freshness, DNA quality, and storage conditions have all been found to affect telomere length measurement accuracy. Currently, Southern blot analysis, quantitative-PCR based (Cawthon, 2002) and q-FISH (quantitative fluorescence in situ hybridization (Poon and Lansdorp, 2001) methods are used to measure telomere length. A detailed review of these methods can be found in a recent review (Canela, Klatt, & Blasco, 2007).

Telomerase Detection

The most commonly used method to detect telomerase activity is Telomere Repeat Amplification Protocol (TRAP), developed by Kim and colleagues (Kim et al., 1994; Kim & Wu, 1997). A commercial kit, called TRAPeze, based on the design of the TRAP method, is available from Chemicon, Inc. The TRAP method has been adapted to run on quantitative PCR platforms. Nonetheless, the sensitivity of the method does not reach that of the gel-TRAP method and this lack of sensitivity has to date precluded its use in quantitative measures of telomerase activity in clinical samples of normal human cells such as PBMCs. In the future, further development of this method may render it (or an adaptation) usable for such clinical samples. A detailed review of methods to detect telomerase activity can be found (e.g., Fajkus, 2006).

A second important consideration is that interpretations of telomere length will be affected by subject selection and sample collection. Because measuring cell aging in vivo, in humans, is a new field, we know relatively little about effects of hormones, medications, certain diseases, current infections, and lifestyle factors. Therefore, it is essential either to carefully rule out or to measure these confounding factors. Large studies that have not carefully quantified such health history factors that may leave imprints in telomere length or affect telomerase activity regulation may only pick up the largest effects. For example, the effects of smoking, a large source of oxidative stress, and medications like statins, which are known to alter telomerase, would likely override effects of psychosocial factors, which are typically of smaller magnitude.

SUMMARY AND CONCLUSIONS

The telomere/telomerase maintenance system will be an important focus of behavioral neuroscience research in the coming years. Telomere length and telomerase together appear to be cellular indicators of the potential for viability and self-renewal of cells. We have reviewed the multitude of factors that influence telomere length throughout the life span, including genetics and early nutrition, as well as adulthood obesity, chronic life stress, and biochemical factors. With an in-depth understanding of telomere length and of telomere maintenance by telomerase; their fundamental biological, environmental, and behavioral modifiers; and accurate measurement, behavioral scientists have a valuable role to play in shedding further light on the interwoven environmental, psychological and behavioral modifiers of cell aging.

REFERENCES

Adaikalakoteswari, A., Balasubramanyam, M., Ravikumar, R., Deepa, R., & Mohan, V. (2007). Association of telomere shortening with impaired glucose tolerance and diabetic macroangiopathy. *Atherosclerosis, 195*, 83–89.

Akiyama, M., Yamada, O., Hideshima, T., Yanagisawa, T., Yokoi, K., Fujisawa, K., et al. (2004). TNFalpha induces rapid activation and nuclear translocation of telomerase in human lymphocytes. *Biochemical and Biophysical Research Communications, 316*, 528–532.

Allsopp, R. C., Chang, E., Kashefi-Aazam, M., Rogaev, E. I., Piatyszek, M. A., Shay, J. W., et al. (1995). Telomere shortening is associated with cell division in vitro and in vivo. *Experimental Cell Research, 220*, 194–200.

Anderson, C. J., Hoare, S. F., Ashcroft, M., Bilsland, A. E., & Keith, W. N. (2006). Hypoxic regulation of telomerase gene expression by transcriptional and post-transcriptional mechanisms. *Oncogene, 25*, 61–69.

Andrew, T., Aviv, A., Falchi, M., Surdulescu, G. L., Gardner, J. P., Lu, X., et al. (2006). Mapping genetic loci that determine leukocyte telomere length in a large sample of unselected female sibling pairs. *American Journal of Human Genetics, 78*, 480–486.

Anversa, P., Kajstura, J., Leri, A., & Bolli, R. (2006). Life and death of cardiac stem cells: A paradigm shift in cardiac biology. *Circulation, 113*, 1451–1463.

Armanios, M., Chen, J. L., Chang, Y. P., Brodsky, R. A., Hawkins, A., Griffin, C. A., et al. (2005). Haploinsufficiency of telomerase reverse transcriptase leads to anticipation in autosomal dominant dyskeratosis congenita. *Proceedings of the National Academy of Sciences, USA, 102*, 15960–15964.

Armanios, M., Chen, J. J., Cogan, J. D., Alder, J. K., Ingersoll, R. G., Markin, C., et al. (2007). Telomerase mutations in families with idiopathic pulmonary fibrosis. *New England Journal of Medicine, 356*, 1317–1326.

Aubert, G., & Lansdorp, P. M. (2008). Telomeres and aging. *Physiology Review, 88*, 557–579.

Aviv, A., Valdes, A., Gardner, J. P., Swaminathan, R., Kimura, M., & Spector, T. D. (2006). Menopause modifies the association of leukocyte telomere length with insulin resistance and inflammation. *Journal of Clinical Endocrinology and Metabolism, 91*, 635–640.

Bayne, S., & Liu, J. P. (2005). Hormones and growth factors regulate telomerase activity in ageing and cancer. *Molecular and Cellular Endocrinology, 240,* 11–22.

Bekaert, S., De Meyer, T., Rietzschel, E. R., De Buyzere, M. L., De Bacquer, D., Langlois, M., et al. (2007). Telomere length and cardiovascular risk factors in a middle-aged population free of overt cardiovascular disease. *Aging Cell, 6,* 639–647.

Benetos, A., Gardner, J. P., Zureik, M., Labat, C., Xiaobin, L., Adamopoulos, C., et al. (2004). Short telomeres are associated with increased carotid atherosclerosis in hypertensive subjects. *Hypertension, 43,* 182–185.

Bischoff, C., Petersen, H. C., Graakjaer, J., Andersen-Ranberg, K., Vaupel, J. W., Bohr, V. A., et al. (2006). No association between telomere length and survival among the elderly and oldest old. *Epidemiology, 17,* 190–194.

Blackburn, E. H. (1984). The molecular structure of centromeres and telomeres. *Annual Review of Biochemistry, 53,* 163–194.

Blackburn, E. H., Budarf, M. L., Challoner, P. B., Cherry, J. M., Howard, E. A., Katzen, A. L., et al. (1983). DNA termini in ciliate macronuclei. *Cold Spring Harbor Symposia on Quantitative Biology, 47*(Pt. 2), 1195–1207.

Blackburn, E. H., & Gall, J. G. (1978). A tandemly repeated sequence at the termini of the extrachromosomal ribosomal RNA genes in Tetrahymena. *Journal of Molecular Biology, 120,* 33–53.

Blasco, M. A. (2005). Mice with bad ends: Mouse models for the study of telomeres and telomerase in cancer and aging. *European Molecular Biology Organization Journal, 24,* 1095–1103.

Blasco, M. A., Lee, H. W., Hande, M. P., Samper, E., Lansdorp, P. M., DePinho, R. A., et al. (1997). Telomere shortening and tumor formation by mouse cells lacking telomerase RNA. *Cell, 91,* 25–34.

Broberg, K., Bjork, J., Paulsson, K., Hoglund, M., & Albin, M. (2005). Constitutional short telomeres are strong genetic susceptibility markers for bladder cancer. *Carcinogenesis, 26,* 1263–1271.

Broccoli, D., Young, J. W., & de Lange, T. (1995). Telomerase activity in normal and malignant hematopoietic cells. *Proceedings of the National Academy of Sciences, USA, 92,* 9082–9086.

Brouilette, S., Moore, J. S., McMahon, A. D., Thompson, J. R., Ford, I., Shepherd, J., et al. (2007). Telomere length, risk of coronary heart disease, and statin treatment in the West of Scotland Primary Prevention Study: A nested case-control study. *Lancet, 369,* 107–114.

Brouilette, S., Singh, R. K., Thompson, J. R., Goodall, A. H., & Samani, N. J. (2003). White cell telomere length and risk of premature myocardial infarction. *Arteriosclerosis, Thrombosis, and Vascular Biology, 23,* 842–846.

Bryan, T. M., Englezou, A., Dalla-Pozza, L., Dunham, M. A., & Reddel, R. R. (1997). Evidence for an alternative mechanism for maintaining telomere length in human tumors and tumor-derived cell lines. *Nature Medicine, 3,* 1271–1274.

Campisi, J. (2005). Senescent cells, tumor suppression, and organismal aging: Good citizens, bad neighbors. *Cell, 120,* 513–522.

Campisi, J., & d'Adda di Fagagna, F. (2007). Cellular senescence: When bad things happen to good cells. *Nature Reviews: Molecular Cell Biology, 8,* 729–740.

Canela, A., Klatt, P., & Blasco, M. A. (2007). Telomere length analysis. *Methods in Molecular Biology, 371,* 45–72.

Cao, Y., Li, H., Mu, F. T., Ebisui, O., Funder, J. W., & Liu, J. P. (2002). Telomerase activation causes vascular smooth muscle cell proliferation in genetic hypertension. *Federation of American Societies for Experimental Biology Journal, 16,* 96–98.

Cawthon, R. M. (2002). Telomere measurement by quantitative PCR. *Nucleic Acids Research, 30,* e47.

Cawthon, R. M., Smith, K. R., O'Brien, E., Sivatchenko, A., & Kerber, R. A. (2003). Association between telomere length in blood and mortality in people aged 60 years or older. *Lancet, 361,* 393–395.

Chadeneau, C., Siegel, P., Harley, C. B., Muller, W. J., & Bacchetti, S. (1995). Telomerase activity in normal and malignant murine tissues. *Oncogene, 11,* 893–898.

Chang, E., & Harley, C. B. (1995). Telomere length and replicative aging in human vascular tissues. *Proceedings of the National Academy of Sciences, USA, 92,* 11190–11194.

Cherkas, L. F., Hunkin, J. L., Kato, B. S., Richards, B., Gardner, J. P., Surdulescu, G. L., et al. (2008). The association between physical activity in leisure time and leukocyte telomere length. *Archives of Internal Medicine, 168,* 154–158.

Choi, J., Southworth, L. K., Sarin, K. Y., Venteicher, A. S., Ma, W., Chang, W., et al. (2008). TERT promotes epithelial proliferation through transcriptional control of a Myc- and Wnt-related developmental program. *PLoS Genetics, 4,* e10.

Cohn, M., & Blackburn, E. H. (1995, July 21). Telomerase in yeast. *Science, 269,* 396–400.

Collerton, J., Martin-Ruiz, C., Kenny, A., Barrass, K., von Zglinicki, T., Kirkwood, T., et al. (2007). Telomere length is associated with left ventricular function in the oldest old: The Newcastle 85+ study. *European Heart Journal, 28,* 172–176.

Comolli, L. R., Smirnov, I., Xu, L., Blackburn, E. H., & James, T. L. (2002). A molecular switch underlies a human telomerase disease. *Proceedings of the National Academy of Sciences, USA, 99,* 16998–17003.

Cong, Y. S., Wright, W. E., & Shay, J. W. (2002). Human telomerase and its regulation. *Microbiology and Molecular Biology Reviews, 66,* 407–425.

Counter, C. M., Meyerson, M., Eaton, E. N., & Weinberg, R. A. (1997). The catalytic subunit of yeast telomerase. *Proceedings of the National Academy of Sciences, USA, 94,* 9202–9207.

d'Adda di Fagagna, F., Reaper, P. M., Clay-Farrace, L., Fiegler, H., Carr, P., Von Zglinicki, T., et al. (2003, November 13). A DNA damage checkpoint response in telomere-initiated senescence. *Nature, 426,* 194–198.

Damjanovic, A. K., Yang, Y., Glaser, R., Kiecolt-Glaser, J. K., Nguyen, H., Laskowski, B., et al. (2007). Accelerated telomere erosion is associated with a declining immune function of caregivers of Alzheimer's disease patients. *Journal of Immunology, 179,* 4249–4254.

Das, A., Banik, N. L., & Ray, S. K. (2007). Differentiation decreased telomerase activity in rat glioblastoma c6 cells and increased sensitivity to IFN-gamma and taxol for apoptosis. *Neurochemical Research, 32,* 2167–2183.

de Lange, T., Shiue, L., Myers, R. M., Cox, D. R., Naylor, S. L., Killery, A. M., et al. (1990). Structure and variability of human chromosome ends. *Molecular and Cellular Biology, 10,* 518–527.

Demissie, S., Levy, D., Benjamin, E. J., Cupples, L. A., Gardner, J. P., Herbert, A., et al. (2006). Insulin resistance, oxidative stress, hypertension, and leukocyte telomere length in men from the Framingham Heart Study. *Aging Cell, 5,* 325–330.

Dimri, G. P., Lee, X., Basile, G., Acosta, M., Scott, G., Roskelley, C., et al. (1995). A biomarker that identifies senescent human cells in culture and in aging skin in vivo. *Proceedings of the National Academy of Sciences, USA, 92,* 9363–9367.

Djojosubroto, M. W., Choi, Y. S., Lee, H. W., & Rudolph, K. L. (2003). Telomeres and telomerase in aging, regeneration and cancer. *Molecules and Cells, 15,* 164–175.

Edo, M. D., & Andres, V. (2005). Aging, telomeres, and atherosclerosis. *Cardiovascular Research, 66,* 213–221.

Epel, E. S. (in press). Telomeres in a lifespan perspective: A new psychobiomarker? *Current Directions in Psychological Science.*

Epel, E. S., Blackburn, E. H., Lin, J., Dhabhar, F. S., Adler, N. E., Morrow, J. D., et al. (2004). Accelerated telomere shortening in response to life stress. *Proceedings of the National Academy of Sciences, USA, 101,* 17312–17315.

Epel, E. S., Lin, J., Wilhelm, F. H., Wolkowitz, O. M., Cawthon, R., Adler, N. E., et al. (2006). Cell aging in relation to stress arousal and cardiovascular disease risk factors. *Psychoneuroendocrinology, 31*, 277–287.

Erusalimsky, J. D., & Kurz, D. J. (2005). Cellular senescence in vivo: Its relevance in ageing and cardiovascular disease. *Experimental Gerontology, 40*, 634–642.

Fajkus, J. (2006). Detection of telomerase activity by the TRAP assay and its variants and alternatives. *Clinica Chimica Acta, 371*, 25–31.

Feng, J., Funk, W. D., Wang, S. S., Weinrich, S. L., Avilion, A. A., Chiu, C. P., et al. (1995, September 1). The RNA component of human telomerase. *Science, 269*, 1236–1241.

Field, J. J., Mason, P. J., An, P., Kasai, Y., McLellan, M., Jaeger, S., et al. (2006). Low frequency of telomerase RNA mutations among children with aplastic anemia or myelodysplastic syndrome. *American Journal of Pediatric Hematology/Oncology, 28*, 450–453.

Finkel, T., Serrano, M., & Blasco, M. A. (2007, August 16). The common biology of cancer and aging. *Nature, 448*, 767–774.

Fitzpatrick, A. L., Kronmal, R. A., Gardner, J. P., Psaty, B. M., Jenny, N. S., Tracy, R. P., et al. (2007). Leukocyte telomere length and cardiovascular disease in the cardiovascular health study. *American Journal of Epidemiology, 165*, 14–21.

Flores, I., Benetti, R., & Blasco, M. A. (2006). Telomerase regulation and stem cell behaviour. *Current Opinion in Cell Biology, 18*, 254–260.

Forsyth, N. R., Wright, W. E., & Shay, J. W. (2002). Telomerase and differentiation in multicellular organisms: Turn it off, turn it on, and turn it off again. *Differentiation, 69*, 188–197.

Frenck, R. W., Jr., Blackburn, E. H., & Shannon, K. M. (1998). The rate of telomere sequence loss in human leukocytes varies with age. *Proceedings of the National Academy of Sciences, USA, 95*, 5607–5610.

Fu, D., & Collins, K. (2003). Distinct biogenesis pathways for human telomerase RNA and H/ACA small nucleolar RNAs. *Molecules and Cells, 11*, 1361–1372.

Gardner, J. P., Li, S., Srinivasan, S. R., Chen, W., Kimura, M., Lu, X., et al. (2005). Rise in insulin resistance is associated with escalated telomere attrition. *Circulation, 111*, 2171–2177.

Gonzalez-Suarez, E., Flores, J. M., & Blasco, M. A. (2002). Cooperation between p53 mutation and high telomerase transgenic expression in spontaneous cancer development. *Molecular and Cellular Biology, 22*, 7291–7301.

Gonzalez-Suarez, E., Geserick, C., Flores, J. M., & Blasco, M. A. (2005). Antagonistic effects of telomerase on cancer and aging in K5-mTert transgenic mice. *Oncogene, 24*, 2256–2270.

Gonzalez-Suarez, E., Samper, E., Ramirez, A., Flores, J. M., Martin-Caballero, J., Jorcano, J. L., et al. (2001). Increased epidermal tumors and increased skin wound healing in transgenic mice overexpressing the catalytic subunit of telomerase, mTERT, in basal keratinocytes. *European Molecular Biology Organization Journal, 20*, 2619–2630.

Greider, C. W., & Blackburn, E. H. (1985). Identification of a specific telomere terminal transferase activity in Tetrahymena extracts. *Cell, 43*, 405–413.

Greider, C. W., & Blackburn, E. H. (1987). The telomere terminal transferase of Tetrahymena is a ribonucleoprotein enzyme with two kinds of primer specificity. *Cell, 51*, 887–898.

Haendeler, J., Hoffmann, J., Brandes, R. P., Zeiher, A. M., & Dimmeler, S. (2003). Hydrogen peroxide triggers nuclear export of telomerase reverse transcriptase via Src kinase family-dependent phosphorylation of tyrosine 707. *Molecular and Cellular Biology, 23*, 4598–4610.

Haendeler, J., Hoffmann, J., Diehl, J. F., Vasa, M., Spyridopoulos, I., Zeiher, A. M., et al. (2004). Antioxidants inhibit nuclear export of telomerase reverse transcriptase and delay replicative senescence of endothelial cells. *Circulation Research, 94*, 768–775.

Haendeler, J., Hoffmann, J., Rahman, S., Zeiher, A. M., & Dimmeler, S. (2003). Regulation of telomerase activity and anti-apoptotic function

by protein-protein interaction and phosphorylation. *Federation of European Biochemical Societies Letters, 536*, 180–186.

Harley, C. B., Futcher, A. B., & Greider, C. W. (1990, May 31). Telomeres shorten during ageing of human fibroblasts. *Nature, 345*, 458–460.

Harris, S. E., Deary, I. J., MacIntyre, A., Lamb, K. J., Radhakrishnan, K., Starr, J. M., et al. (2006). The association between telomere length, physical health, cognitive ageing, and mortality in non-demented older people. *Neuroscience Letters, 406*, 260–264.

Hayflick, L., & Moorhead, P. S. (1961). The serial cultivation of human diploid cell strains. *Experimental Cell Research, 25*, 585–621.

Herbig, U., Ferreira, M., Condel, L., Carey, D., & Sedivy, J. M. (2006, March 3). Cellular senescence in aging primates. *Science, 311*, 1257.

Hiyama, E., & Hiyama, K. (2007). Telomere and telomerase in stem cells. *British Journal of Cancer, 96*, 1020–1024.

Hiyama, K., Hirai, Y., Kyoizumi, S., Akiyama, M., Hiyama, E., Piatyszek, M. A., et al. (1995). Activation of telomerase in human lymphocytes and hematopoietic progenitor cells. *Journal of Immunology, 155*, 3711–3715.

Huda, N., Tanaka, H., Herbert, B. S., Reed, T., & Gilley, D. (2007). Shared environmental factors associated with telomere length maintenance in elderly male twins. *Aging Cell, 6*, 709–713.

Jalink, M., Ge, Z., Liu, C., Bjorkholm, M., Gruber, A., & Xu, D. (2007). Human normal T lymphocytes and lymphoid cell lines do express alternative splicing variants of human telomerase reverse transcriptase (hTERT) mRNA. *Biochemical and Biophysical Research Communications, 353*, 999–1003.

Jeanclos, E., Schork, N. J., Kyvik, K. O., Kimura, M., Skurnick, J. H., & Aviv, A. (2000). Telomere length inversely correlates with pulse pressure and is highly familial. *Hypertension, 36*, 195–200.

Jennings, B. J., Ozanne, S. E., & Hales, C. N. (2000). Nutrition, oxidative damage, telomere shortening, and cellular senescence: Individual or connected agents of aging? *Molecular Genetics and Metabolism, 71*, 32–42.

Joshua, A. M., Vukovic, B., Braude, I., Hussein, S., Zielenska, M., Srigley, J., et al. (2007). Telomere attrition in isolated high-grade prostatic intraepithelial neoplasia and surrounding stroma is predictive of prostate cancer. *Neoplasia, 9*, 81–89.

Kang, H. J., Choi, Y. S., Hong, S. B., Kim, K. W., Woo, R. S., Won, S. J., et al. (2004). Ectopic expression of the catalytic subunit of telomerase protects against brain injury resulting from ischemia and NMDA-induced neurotoxicity. *Journal of Neuroscience, 24*, 1280–1287.

Kawauchi, K., Ihjima, K., & Yamada, O. (2005). IL-2 increases human telomerase reverse transcriptase activity transcriptionally and post-translationally through phosphatidylinositol 3'-kinase/Akt, heat shock protein 90, and mammalian target of rapamycin in transformed NK cells. *Journal of Immunology, 174*, 5261–5269.

Kempermann, G., & Gage, F. H. (2000). Neurogenesis in the adult hippocampus. *Novartis Foundation Symposium, 231*, 220–235; discussion 235–241, 302–226.

Kiefer, A., Lin, J., Blackburn, E., & Epel, E. (2008). Dietary restraint and telomere length in pre- and postmenonpausal women. *Psychosom Med., 70*, 845–849.

Kim, N. W., Piatyszek, M. A., Prowse, K. R., Harley, C. B., West, M. D., Ho, P. L., et al. (1994, December 23). Specific association of human telomerase activity with immortal cells and cancer. *Science, 266*, 2011–2015.

Kim, N. W., & Wu, F. (1997). Advances in quantification and characterization of telomerase activity by the telomeric repeat amplification protocol (TRAP). *Nucleic Acids Research, 25*, 2595–2597.

Kim, W. Y., & Sharpless, N. E. (2006). The regulation of INK4/ARF in cancer and aging. *Cell, 127*, 265–275.

Knudson, M., Kulkarni, S., Ballas, Z. K., Bessler, M., & Goldman, F. (2005). Association of immune abnormalities with telomere shortening in autosomal-dominant dyskeratosis congenita. *Blood*, *105*, 682–688.

Kotrschal, A., Ilmonen, P., & Penn, D. J. (2007). Stress impacts telomere dynamics. *Biology Letters*, *3*, 128–130.

Krishnamurthy, J., Torrice, C., Ramsey, M. R., Kovalev, G. I., Al-Regaiey, K., Su, L., et al. (2004). Ink4a/Arf expression is a biomarker of aging. *Journal of Clinical Investigation*, *114*, 1299–1307.

Kurz, D. J., Decary, S., Hong, Y., Trivier, E., Akhmedov, A., & Erusalimsky, J. D. (2004). Chronic oxidative stress compromises telomere integrity and accelerates the onset of senescence in human endothelial cells. *Journal of Cell Science*, *117*, 2417–2426.

Leri, A., Kajstura, J., & Anversa, P. (2005). Cardiac stem cells and mechanisms of myocardial regeneration. *Physiological Reviews*, *85*, 1373–1416.

Li, S., & Blackburn, E. H. (2005). Cellular and gene expression responses involved in the rapid growth inhibition of human cancer cells by RNA interference-mediated depletion of telomerase RNA. *Journal of Biological Chemistry*, *280*, 23709–23717.

Li, S., Rosenberg, J. E., Donjacour, A. A., Botchkina, I. L., Hom, Y. K., Cunha, G. R., et al. (2004). Rapid inhibition of cancer cell growth induced by lentiviral delivery and expression of mutant-template telomerase RNA and anti-telomerase short-interfering RNA. *Cancer Research*, *64*, 4833–4840.

Li, Y., Zhi, W., Wareski, P., & Weng, N. P. (2005). IL-15 activates telomerase and minimizes telomere loss and may preserve the replicative life span of memory CD81 T cells in vitro. *Journal of Immunology*, *174*, 4019–4024.

Lingner, J., Hughes, T. R., Shevchenko, A., Mann, M., Lundblad, V., & Cech, T. R. (1997, April 25). Reverse transcriptase motifs in the catalytic subunit of telomerase. *Science*, *276*, 561–567.

Liu, K., Hodes, R. J., & Weng, N. (2001). Cutting edge: Telomerase activation in human T lymphocytes does not require increase in telomerase reverse transcriptase (hTERT) protein but is associated with hTERT phosphorylation and nuclear translocation. *Journal of Immunology*, *166*, 4826–4830.

Lu, C., Fu, W., & Mattson, M. P. (2001). Telomerase protects developing neurons against DNA damage-induced cell death. *Brain Research: Developmental Brain Research*, *131*, 167–171.

Ly, H., Calado, R. T., Allard, P., Baerlocher, G. M., Lansdorp, P. M., Young, N. S., et al. (2005). Functional characterization of telomerase RNA variants found in patients with hematologic disorders. *Blood*, *105*, 2332–2339.

Maida, Y., Kyo, S., Kanaya, T., Wang, Z., Yatabe, N., Tanaka, M., et al. (2002). Direct activation of telomerase by EGF through Ets-mediated transactivation of TERT via MAP kinase signaling pathway. *Oncogene*, *21*, 4071–4079.

Marrone, A., Stevens, D., Vulliamy, T., Dokal, I., & Mason, P. J. (2004). Heterozygous telomerase RNA mutations found in dyskeratosis congenita and aplastic anemia reduce telomerase activity via haploinsufficiency. *Blood*, *104*, 3936–3942.

Marrone, A., Walne, A., Tamary, H., Masunari, Y., Kirwan, M., Beswick, R., et al. (2007). Telomerase reverse transcriptase homozygous mutations in autosomal recessive dyskeratosis congenita and Hoyeraal-Hreidarsson syndrome. *Blood*, *110*, 4198–4205.

Martin-Ruiz, C. M., Gussekloo, J., van Heemst, D., von Zglinicki, T., & Westendorp, R. G. (2005). Telomere length in white blood cells is not associated with morbidity or mortality in the oldest old: A population-based study. *Aging Cell*, *4*, 287–290.

Masutomi, K., Yu, E. Y., Khurts, S., Ben-Porath, I., Currier, J. L., Metz, G. B., et al. (2003). Telomerase maintains telomere structure in normal human cells. *Cell*, *114*, 241–253.

Matthews, C., Gorenne, I., Scott, S., Figg, N., Kirkpatrick, P., Ritchie, A., et al. (2006). Vascular smooth muscle cells undergo telomere-based senescence in human atherosclerosis: Effects of telomerase and oxidative stress. *Circulation Research*, *99*, 156–164.

Minamino, T., Miyauchi, H., Yoshida, T., Ishida, Y., Yoshida, H., & Komuro, I. (2002). Endothelial cell senescence in human atherosclerosis: Role of telomere in endothelial dysfunction. *Circulation*, *105*, 1541–1544.

Morin, G. B. (1989). The human telomere terminal transferase enzyme is a ribonucleoprotein that synthesizes TTAGGG repeats. *Cell*, *59*, 521–529.

Moyzis, R. K., Torney, D. C., Meyne, J., Buckingham, J. M., Wu, J. R., Burks, C., et al. (1989). The distribution of interspersed repetitive DNA sequences in the human genome. *Genomics*, *4*, 273–289.

Muller, H. J. (1938). The remaking of chromosomes. *Collecting Net*, *8*, 182–195.

Nakajima, T., Moriguchi, M., Katagishi, T., Sekoguchi, S., Nishikawa, T., Takashima, H., et al. (2006). Premature telomere shortening and impaired regenerative response in hepatocytes of individuals with NAFLD. *Liver International*, *26*, 23–31.

Nakamura, T., Morin, G. B., Chapman, K. B., Weinrich, S. L., Andrews, W. H., Lingner, J., et al. (1997, August 15). Telomerase catalytic subunit homologs from fission yeast and human. *Science*, *277*, 955–959.

Njajou, O. T., Cawthon, R. M., Damcott, C. M., Wu, S. H., Ott, S., Garant, M. J., et al. (2007). Telomere length is paternally inherited and is associated with parental lifespan. *Proceedings of the National Academy of Sciences, USA*, *104*, 12135–12139.

Ogami, M., Ikura, Y., Ohsawa, M., Matsuo, T., Kayo, S., Yoshimi, N., et al. (2004). Telomere shortening in human coronary artery diseases. *Arteriosclerosis, Thrombosis, and Vascular Biology*, *24*, 546–550.

Okuda, K., Khan, M. Y., Skurnick, J., Kimura, M., Aviv, H., & Aviv, A. (2000). Telomere attrition of the human abdominal aorta: Relationships with age and atherosclerosis. *Atherosclerosis*, *152*, 391–398.

Ortmann, C. A., Niemeyer, C. M., Wawer, A., Ebell, W., Baumann, I., & Kratz, C. P. (2006). TERC mutations in children with refractory cytopenia. *Haematologica*, *91*, 707–708.

Panossian, L. A., Porter, V. R., Valenzuela, H. F., Zhu, X., Reback, E., Masterman, D., et al. (2003). Telomere shortening in T cells correlates with Alzheimer's disease status. *Neurobiology of Aging*, *24*, 77–84.

Pardue, M. L., & DeBaryshe, P. G. (2003). Retrotransposons provide an evolutionarily robust non-telomerase mechanism to maintain telomeres. *Annual Review of Genetics*, *37*, 485–511.

Patil, C. K., Mian, I. S., & Campisi, J. (2005). The thorny path linking cellular senescence to organismal aging. *Mechanisms of Ageing and Development*, *126*, 1040–1045.

Perillo, N. L., Walford, R. L., Newman, M. A., & Effros, R. B. (1989). Human T lymphocytes possess a limited in vitro life span. *Experimental Gerontology*, *24*, 177–187.

Poon, S. S., & Lansdorp, P. M. (2001). Quantitative fluorescence in situ hybridization (Q-FISH). Current Protocols in Cell Biology, Chapter 18: Unit 18.4.

Prowse, K. R., & Greider, C. W. (1995). Developmental and tissue-specific regulation of mouse telomerase and telomere length. *Proceedings of the National Academy of Sciences, USA*, *92*, 4818–4822.

Rufer, N., Brummendorf, T. H., Kolvraa, S., Bischoff, C., Christensen, K., Wadsworth, L., et al. (1999). Telomere fluorescence measurements in granulocytes and T lymphocyte subsets point to a high turnover of hematopoietic stem cells and memory T cells in early childhood. *Journal of Experimental Medicine*, *190*, 157–167.

Saeboe-Larssen, S., Fossberg, E., & Gaudernack, G. (2006). Characterization of novel alternative splicing sites in human telomerase reverse transcriptase (hTERT): Analysis of expression and mutual correlation in mRNA isoforms from normal and tumour tissues. *BMC Molecular Biology*, *7*, 26.

Samani, N. J., Boultby, R., Butler, R., Thompson, J. R., & Goodall, A. H. (2001). Telomere shortening in atherosclerosis. *Lancet, 358,* 472–473.

Sampson, M. J., Winterbone, M. S., Hughes, J. C., Dozio, N., & Hughes, D. A. (2006). Monocyte telomere shortening and oxidative DNA damage in type 2 diabetes. *Diabetes Care, 29,* 283–289.

Sarin, K. Y., Cheung, P., Gilison, D., Lee, E., Tennen, R. I., Wang, E., et al. (2005, August 18). Conditional telomerase induction causes proliferation of hair follicle stem cells. *Nature, 436,* 1048–1052.

Shao, L., Wood, C. G., Zhang, D., Tannir, N. M., Matin, S., Dinney, C. P., et al. (2007). Telomere dysfunction in peripheral lymphocytes as a potential predisposition factor for renal cancer. *Journal of Urology, 178,* 1492–1496.

Shen, J., Terry, M. B., Gurvich, I., Liao, Y., Senie, R. T., & Santella, R. M. (2007). Short telomere length and breast cancer risk: A study in sister sets. *Cancer Research, 67,* 5538–5544.

Simon, N. M., Smoller, J. W., McNamara, K. L., Maser, R. S., Zalta, A. K., Pollack, M. H., et al. (2006). Telomere shortening and mood disorders: Preliminary support for a chronic stress model of accelerated aging. *Biological Psychiatry, 60,* 432–435.

Slagboom, P. E., Droog, S., & Boomsma, D. I. (1994). Genetic determination of telomere size in humans: A twin study of three age groups. *American Journal of Human Genetics, 55,* 876–882.

Smith, L. L., Coller, H. A., & Roberts, J. M. (2003). Telomerase modulates expression of growth-controlling genes and enhances cell proliferation. *Nature Cell Biology, 5,* 474–479.

Smogorzewska, A., & de Lange, T. (2004). Regulation of telomerase by telomeric proteins. *Annual Review of Biochemistry, 73,* 177–208.

Son, N. H., Murray, S., Yanovski, J., Hodes, R. J., & Weng, N. (2000). Lineage-specific telomere shortening and unaltered capacity for telomerase expression in human T and B lymphocytes with age. *Journal of Immunology, 165,* 1191–1196.

Starr, J. M., McGurn, B., Harris, S. E., Whalley, L. J., Deary, I. J., & Shiels, P. G. (2007). Association between telomere length and heart disease in a narrow age cohort of older people. *Experimental Gerontology, 42,* 571–573.

Steer, S. E., Williams, F. M., Kato, B., Gardner, J. P., Norman, P. J., Hall, M. A., et al. (2007). Reduced telomere length in rheumatoid arthritis is independent of disease activity and duration. *Annals of the Rheumatic Diseases, 66,* 476–480.

Stewart, S. A., Hahn, W. C., O'Connor, B. F., Banner, E. N., Lundberg, A. S., Modha, P., et al. (2002). Telomerase contributes to tumorigenesis by a telomere length-independent mechanism. *Proceedings of the National Academy of Sciences, USA, 99,* 12606–12611.

Takai, H., Smogorzewska, A., & de Lange, T. (2003). DNA damage foci at dysfunctional telomeres. *Current Biology, 13,* 1549–1556.

Takubo, K., Izumiyama-Shimomura, N., Honma, N., Sawabe, M., Arai, T., Kato, M., et al. (2002). Telomere lengths are characteristic in each human individual. *Experimental Gerontology, 37,* 523–531.

Tedgui, A., & Mallat, Z. (2006). Cytokines in atherosclerosis: Pathogenic and regulatory pathways. *Physiological Reviews, 86,* 515–581.

Torella, D., Rota, M., Nurzynska, D., Musso, E., Monsen, A., Shiraishi, I., et al. (2004). Cardiac stem cell and myocyte aging, heart failure, and insulin-like growth factor-1 overexpression. *Circulation Research, 94,* 514–524.

Valdes, A. M., Andrew, T., Gardner, J. P., Kimura, M., Oelsner, E., Cherkas, L. F., et al. (2005). Obesity, cigarette smoking, and telomere length in women. *Lancet, 366,* 662–664.

Valdes, A. M., Richards, J. B., Gardner, J. P., Swaminathan, R., Kimura, M., Xiaobin, L., et al. (2007). Telomere length in leukocytes correlates with bone mineral density and is shorter in women with osteoporosis. *Osteoporosis International, 18,* 1203–1210.

van der Harst, P., van der Steege, G., de Boer, R. A., Voors, A. A., Hall, A. S., Mulder, M. J., et al. (2007). Telomere length of circulating leukocytes is decreased in patients with chronic heart failure. *Journal of the American College of Cardiology, 49,* 1459–1464.

Vasa-Nicotera, M., Brouilette, S., Mangino, M., Thompson, J. R., Braund, P., Clemitson, J. R., et al. (2005). Mapping of a major locus that determines telomere length in humans. *American Journal of Human Genetics, 76,* 147–151.

von Zglinicki, T., Pilger, R., & Sitte, N. (2000). Accumulation of single-strand breaks is the major cause of telomere shortening in human fibroblasts. *Free Radical Biology and Medicine, 28,* 64–74.

Vulliamy, T. J., Marrone, A., Knight, S. W., Walne, A., Mason, P. J., & Dokal, I. (2006). Mutations in dyskeratosis congenita: Their impact on telomere length and the diversity of clinical presentation. *Blood, 107,* 2680–2685.

Walne, A. J., Vulliamy, T., Marrone, A., Beswick, R., Kirwan, M., Masunari, Y., et al. (2007). Genetic heterogeneity in autosomal recessive dyskeratosis congenita with one subtype due to mutations in the telomerase-associated protein NOP10. *Human Molecular Genetics, 16,* 1619–1629.

Watson, J. D. (1972). Origin of concatemeric T7 DNA. *New Biology, 239,* 197–201.

Weng, N. P., Levine, B. L., June, C. H., & Hodes, R. J. (1996). Regulated expression of telomerase activity in human T lymphocyte development and activation. *Journal of Experimental Medicine, 183,* 2471–2479.

Westin, E. R., Chavez, E., Lee, K. M., Gourronc, F. A., Riley, S., Lansdorp, P. M., et al. (2007). Telomere restoration and extension of proliferative lifespan in dyskeratosis congenita fibroblasts. *Aging Cell, 6,* 383–394.

Wetterau, L. A., Francis, M. J., Ma, L., & Cohen, P. (2003). Insulin-like growth factor I stimulates telomerase activity in prostate cancer cells. *Journal of Clinical Endocrinology and Metabolism, 88,* 3354–3359.

Wong, J. M., & Collins, K. (2006). Telomerase RNA level limits telomere maintenance in X-linked dyskeratosis congenita. *Genes and Development, 20,* 2848–2858.

Wright, W. E., Piatyszek, M. A., Rainey, W. E., Byrd, W., & Shay, J. W. (1996). Telomerase activity in human germline and embryonic tissues and cells. *Developmental Genetics, 18,* 173–179.

Wu, X., Amos, C. I., Zhu, Y., Zhao, H., Grossman, B. H., Shay, J. W., et al. (2003). Telomere dysfunction: A potential cancer predisposition factor. *Journal of the National Cancer Institute, 95,* 1211–1218.

Xin, Z. T., Beauchamp, A. D., Calado, R. T., Bradford, J. W., Regal, J. A., Shenoy, A., et al. (2007). Functional characterization of natural telomerase mutations found in patients with hematologic disorders. *Blood, 109,* 524–532.

Xu, D., Erickson, S., Szeps, M., Gruber, A., Sangfelt, O., Einhorn, S., et al. (2000). Interferon alpha down-regulates telomerase reverse transcriptase and telomerase activity in human malignant and nonmalignant hematopoietic cells. *Blood, 96,* 4313–4318.

Yamagiwa, Y., Meng, F., & Patel, T. (2006). Interleukin-6 decreases senescence and increases telomerase activity in malignant human cholangiocytes. *Life Sciences, 78,* 2494–2502.

Yamaguchi, H. (2006). Bone marrow failure due to telomerase complex gene mutations. *Rinsho Ketsueki, 47,* 1431–1437.

Yamaguchi, H. (2007). Mutations of telomerase complex genes linked to bone marrow failures. *Journal of Nippon Medical School, 74,* 202–209.

Yang, L., Suwa, T., Wright, W. E., Shay, J. W., & Hornsby, P. J. (2001). Telomere shortening and decline in replicative potential as a function of donor age in human adrenocortical cells. *Mechanisms of Ageing and Development, 122,* 1685–1694.

Zaccagnini, G., Gaetano, C., Della Pietra, L., Nanni, S., Grasselli, A., Mangoni, A., et al. (2005). Telomerase mediates vascular endothelial growth factor-dependent responsiveness in a rat model of hind limb ischemia. *Journal of Biological Chemistry, 280,* 14790–14798.

Zhai, G., Aviv, A., Hunter, D. J., Hart, D. J., Gardner, J. P., Kimura, M., et al. (2006). Reduction of leucocyte telomere length in radiographic hand osteoarthritis: A population-based study. *Annals of the Rheumatic Diseases, 65,* 1444–1448.

Zhang, J., Kong, Q., Zhang, Z., Ge, P., Ba, D., & He, W. (2003). Telomere dysfunction of lymphocytes in patients with Alzheimer disease. *Cognitive and Behavioral Neurology, 16,* 170–176.

Zhu, H., Fu, W., & Mattson, M. P. (2000). The catalytic subunit of telomerase protects neurons against amyloid beta-peptide-induced apoptosis. *Journal of Neurochemistry, 75,* 117–124.

APPENDIX 65.1   Updates to Table 65.1 Studies linking telomere maintenance to diseases.

Study	Main Findings	Reference
1067 breast cancer cases and 1110 controls in the Long Island Breast Cancer Study project	In premenopausal women short telomere associated with risk for breast cancer.	Shen, J., Gammon, M. D., Terry, M. B., Wang, Q., Bradshaw, P., Teitelbaum, S. L., Neugut, A. I., & Santella, R. M. (2009). Telomere length, oxidative damage, antioxidants and breast cancer risk. *Int J Cancer 124,* 1637-1643.
105 patients (61 men and 44 women)	Clear cell renal cell carcinoma patients with long telomeres had a worse prognosis than patients with short telomeres. TL in kidney cortex and tumor tissue did not predict survival.	Svenson, U., Ljungberg, B., & Roos, G. (2009). Telomere length in peripheral blood predicts survival in clear cell renal cell carcinoma. *Cancer Res 69,* 2896-2901.
265 newly diagnosed breast cancer and 446 female controls	Patients have longer telomeres than controls. Patients with short telomeres have increased survival	Svenson, U., Nordfjall, K., Stegmayr, B., Manjer, J., Nilsson, P., Tavelin, B., Henriksson, R., Lenner, P., & Roos, G. (2008). Breast cancer survival is associated with telomere length in peripheral blood cells. *Cancer Res 68,* 3618-3623.
388 hypertensive patients and 379 controls in Chinese population	Telomeres are shorter in patients. After 5 year follow up, subjects with short telomeres are at high risk of developing coronary artery diseases	Yang, Z., Huang, X., Jiang, H., Zhang, Y., Liu, H., Qin, C., Eisner, G. M., Jose, P., Rudolph, L., & Ju, Z. (2009). Short telomeres and prognosis of hypertension in a chinese population. *Hypertension 53,* 639-645.
1203 Framingham Study participants (mean age, 59 years; 51% women).	LTL was shorter in individuals with a higher renin-to-aldosterone ratio, especially in participants with hypertension.	Vasan, R. S., Demissie, S., Kimura, M., Cupples, L. A., Rifai, N., White, C., Wang, T. J., Gardner, J. P., Cao, X., Benjamin, E. J., et al. (2008). Association of leukocyte telomere length with circulating biomarkers of the renin-angiotensin-aldosterone system: the Framingham Heart Study. *Circulation 117,* 1138-1144.
1062 individuals (496 men, 566 women) aged 33 to 86 years in the Framingham Offspring Study	In obese men, shortened LTL is a powerful marker of increased carotid intimal medial thickness	O'Donnell, C. J., Demissie, S., Kimura, M., Levy, D., Gardner, J. P., White, C., D'Agostino, R. B., Wolf, P. A., Polak, J., Cupples, L. A., & Aviv, A. (2008). Leucocyte telomere length and carotid artery intimal medial thickness: the Framingham Heart Study. Arterioscler *Thromb Vasc Biol 28,* 1165-1171.
41 subjects with nonaffective psychosis (prior to antipsychotic drugs) and 41 controls	Patients have decreased telomere content (as measured by dotblot) and increased pulse pressure	Fernandez-Egea, E., Bernardo, M., Heaphy, C. M., Griffith, J. K., Parellada, E., Esmatjes, E., Conget, I., Nguyen, L., George, V., Stoppler, H., & Kirkpatrick, B. (2009). Telomere length and pulse pressure in newly diagnosed, antipsychotic-naive patients with nonaffective psychosis. *Schizophr Bull 35,* 437-442.
62 participants in the Nurses' Health study	Short telomere associated with preclinical dementia states and decreasing hippocampal volume	Grodstein, F., van Oijen, M., Irizarry, M. C., Rosas, H. D., Hyman, B. T., Growdon, J. H., & De Vivo, I. (2008). Shorter telomeres may mark early risk of dementia: preliminary analysis of 62 participants from the nurses' health study. *PLoS ONE 3, e1590.*
National Institute of Environmental Health Science Sister Study, n=647 women	High BMI and hip circumference associated with shorter telomeres.	Kim, S., Parks, C. G., DeRoo, L. A., Chen, H., Taylor, J. A., Cawthon, R. M., & Sandler, D. P. (2009). Obesity and weight gain in adulthood and telomere length. *Cancer Epidemiol Biomarkers Prev 18,* 816-820.
National Institute of Environmental Health Science Sister Study, n=647 women	High stress and urinary stress catecholamine associated with shorter telomeres. Short telomeres associated with increase age, obesity and current smoking	Parks, C. G., Miller, D. B., McCanlies, E. C., Cawthon, R. M., Andrew, M. E., DeRoo, L. A., & Sandler, D. P. (2009). Telomere length, current perceived stress, and urinary stress hormones in women. *Cancer Epidemiol Biomarkers Prev 18,* 551-560.
134 healthy seniors over 85 years with no disease and 47 random 40-50 olds	Healthy seniors have reduced telomere length variations compared to the random mid-age group	Halaschek-Wiener, J., Vulto, I., Fornika, D., Collins, J., Connors, J. M., Le, N. D., Lansdorp, P. M., & Brooks-Wilson, A. (2008). Reduced telomere length variation in healthy oldest old. *Mech Ageing Dev 129,* 638-641.
24 men with biopsy-diagnosed low-risk prostate cancer who made comprehensive lifestyle changes.	PBMC telomerase activity increased from baseline to 3 month. The increases in telomerase activity were significantly associated with decreases in low-density lipoprotein (LDL) cholesterol and decreases in psychological distress.	Ornish, D., Lin, J., Daubenmier, J., Weidner, G., Epel, E., Kemp, C., Magbanua, M. J., Marlin, R., Yglecias, L., Carroll, P. R., & Blackburn, E. H. (2008). Increased telomerase activity and comprehensive lifestyle changes: a pilot study. *Lancet Oncol 9,* 1048-1057.

Chapter 66

Constraint-Induced Movement Therapy: A Paradigm for Translating Advances in Behavioral Neuroscience into Rehabilitation Treatments

EDWARD TAUB AND GITENDRA USWATTE

After injury to the central nervous system (CNS), the initial deficit in behavior, perception, or cognitive ability is frequently followed by spontaneous recovery of function. One might characterize this resiliency as a type of behavioral plasticity. In apparent contrast, the traditional view in neuroscience during the first three quarters of the twentieth century was that the mature CNS has little capacity to reorganize and repair itself in response to injury. This view extends well back into the nineteenth century, influenced initially by Broca's studies of localization of function within the brain (Broca, 1861); it emphasized the constancy of organization of the mature CNS even after substantial injury. Though contrary views were expressed (e.g., Fleurens, 1842; Fritsch & Hitzig, 1870; Lashley, 1938; Munk, 1881), the mature CNS was generally believed (Kaas, 1995) to exhibit little or no plasticity (Hubel & Wiesel, 1970; Ruch, 1960). Hughlings Jackson's hierarchical view that lower centers of the brain substituted in function for higher damaged centers after CNS insult (Jackson, 1873, 1884) and other related formulations influenced thought concerning recovery of function for most of the twentieth century. However, the phenomenon of spontaneous recovery of function was never fully explained and received little experimental attention, largely because the techniques to explore this process had not yet been developed. Beginning in the 1970s, research from laboratories, including those of Merzenich (Merzenich et al., 1983, 1984), Kaas (Kaas, Merzenich, & Killackey, 1983), and Wall (Dostrovsky, Millar, & Wall, 1976; Wall & Egger, 1971), showed that, contrary to the established belief, the adult mammalian nervous system does have some capacity to reorganize itself functionally after injury. This phenomenon was referred to as cortical reorganization but is now more commonly termed *brain plasticity*. The question

naturally arises whether there is some relation between the spontaneous recovery or behavioral plasticity that occurs after CNS damage and brain plasticity, and ultimately whether this relationship can be manipulated to improve the potential for recovery of function so that it can help a patient who has suffered neurological injury.

Research involving somatosensory deafferentation in monkeys provides a paradigm for answering this question. After the surgical abolition of somatic sensation from a single forelimb in monkeys, the animals never use that extremity in the free situation. However, they can be induced to use the affected limb by one of two general techniques: prolonged restraint of the unaffected forelimb and repetitive training of the affected limb (Taub, 1977a). The application of these procedures produces a substantial rehabilitation of movement or plasticity of behavior where this was not thought to be possible. The same protocol has been successfully translated from the primate laboratory to humans, where it has also been shown to result in a substantial rehabilitation of function in patients with stroke for the upper extremity (Taub, 1980; Taub et al., 1993; Taub, Uswatte, King, et al., 2006; Wolf et al., 2006), lower extremity (Taub, Uswatte, & Pidikiti, 1999), multiple sclerosis (Mark et al., 2008), speech (Pulvermüller et al., 2001), and cerebral palsy (Taub, Griffin, et al., 2006; Taub, Ramey, DeLuca, & Echols, 2004). These techniques, which constitute a new approach to the rehabilitation of movement after neurological damage, have been termed *constraint-induced movement therapy* (CI therapy). Derivations of this approach have also been used successfully for the treatment of such formerly intractable conditions as focal hand dystonia (Candia et al., 1999) and phantom limb pain (Weiss, Miltner, Adler, Bruckner, & Taub, 1999).

In a parallel line of investigation, Pons and coworkers (1991) showed that after somatosensory deafferentation of an upper extremity in monkeys, "massive cortical reorganization" takes place over the entire cortical arm area. This work was significant because the area of cortical reorganization was sufficiently large to promise relevance for recovery of function after CNS damage. This experiment led directly to a series of studies employing magnetoencepholograpy which showed that "massive cortical reorganization" takes place in human beings after amputation (Elbert et al., 1994) and that cortical reorganization has a strong correlation with such perceptual phenomena as phantom limb pain (N. P. Birbaumer et al., 1997; Flor et al., 1995; Taub, Flor, Knecht, & Elbert, 1995), tinnitus (Mühlnickel, Elbert, Taub, & Flor, 1998) and focal hand dystonia (Elbert et al., 1998). Other work in this line of investigation followed the seminal research of Recanzone, Merzenich, Jenkins, and coworkers (Jenkins, Merzenich, Ochs, Allard, & Guic-Robles, 1990; Recanzone, Jenkins, & Merzenich, 1992; Recanzone, Merzenich, & Jenkins, 1992; Recanzone, Merzenich, Jenkins, Grajski, & Dinse, 1992) on use-dependent cortical reorganization in monkeys that showed that increased use of a body part leads to an enlargement of its cortical representation. Elbert, Taub, and coworkers, elaborating on these observations, demonstrated that the same type of cortical reorganization occurs in humans (Elbert, Pantev, Wienbruch, Rockstroh, & Taub, 1995; Elbert et al., 1997, 1998; Sterr, Mueller, Elbert, & Rockstroh, et al., 1998; Sterr, Mueller, Elbert, & Taub, 1998). There are thus two types of brain plasticity that our group and other investigators have studied. One kind follows injuries to the nervous system that result in a reduction in somatosensory input and may be characterized as input-decrease cortical reorganization; the other type results from increased use of a body part or sensory system and may be termed input-increase cortical reorganization (Elbert et al., 1997). Input-decrease cortical reorganization seems to be correlated with the presence of adverse symptoms, while input-increase or use-dependent cortical reorganization generally appears to be related to the development of skills and with results that are advantageous to the individual. This is a general characterization and there are important exceptions.

Stroke and the consequent reduced use or nonuse of the upper extremity on the more-affected side of the body has been shown to be associated with a marked reduction of the cortical representation of that extremity (Liepert, Bauder, Miltner, Taub, & Weiller, 2000; Liepert et al., 1998). As noted, CI therapy enhances recovery of function in many patients after stroke. Work from two laboratories has shown that this substantial plasticity of behavior is associated with a massive increase in the cortical representation of the more-affected arm following CI therapy (Bauder, Balzer, Miltner, & Taub, 1999; Kopp et al., 1999; Liepert et al., 1998, 2000). One might hypothesize, therefore, that the use-dependent brain plasticity produced by CI therapy counteracts the injury-related contraction of the cortical representation zone of the arm and is importantly involved in the rehabilitative effect produced by this intervention. A significant question that remains now is whether brain plasticity and functional recovery after CNS damage can be further enhanced by pharmacological and additional behavioral means.

BEHAVIORAL PLASTICITY AFTER SOMATOSENSORY DEAFFERENTATION IN MONKEYS

When somatic sensation is surgically abolished from a single forelimb by severing all dorsal spinal nerve roots innervating that limb, the animal does not make use of it in the free situation (Knapp, Taub, & Berman, 1958, 1963; Lassek, 1953; Mott & Sherrington, 1885; Twitchell, 1954). This is the case even though the motor outflow over the ventral roots remains intact. However, monkeys can be induced to use the deafferented extremity by restricting movement of the intact limb (Knapp et al., 1963; Taub & Berman, 1963, 1968). The monkey may not have used the affected extremity for several years, but the application of this simple technique results in a striking conversion of the useless forelimb into a limb that is used for a wide variety of purposes, usually within a period of hours (Taub, 1977b, 1980). The movements are not normal; they are clumsy since somatic sensation has been abolished, but they are extensive and effective. This may be characterized as a substantial rehabilitation of movement, though the term is not usually applied to monkeys. If the restraint device is left in place for a period of 1 week or more, this reversal in use of the limb is permanent, persisting for the animal's entire life.

Training procedures are another means of overcoming the inability to use a single deafferented limb in primates (Knapp et al., 1958, 1963; Taub, 1976, 1977b, 1980; Taub, Bacon, & Berman, 1965; Taub & Berman, 1963, 1968; Taub, Ellman, & Berman, 1966; Taub, Goldberg, & Taub, 1975; Taub, Williams, Barro, & Steiner, 1978). Transfer from the experimental to the life situation was never observed when using conditioned response techniques to train limb use. However, when shaping was employed, there was substantial improvement in the motor ability of the deafferented limb in the life situation (Taub, 1976, 1977b; Taub & Berman, 1968; Taub, Goldberg, et al., 1975). Shaping is an operant training method in which a desired motor or behavioral objective is approached in small steps, by "successive approximations," so that the improvement required for successful performance at any one point in the training is small (Morgan, 1974; Panyan, 1980; Risley & Baer, 1973; Skinner, 1938, 1968; Taub et al., 1994). The actions shaped included (a) pointing at visual targets (Taub, Goldberg, et al., 1975) and (b) prehension in juveniles deafferented on day of birth (Taub, Perrella, & Barro, 1973) and prenatally (Taub, Perrella, Miller, & Barro, 1975) who had never exhibited any prehension previously. In both cases, shaping produced an almost complete reversal of the motor disability, which progressed from total absence of the target behavior to very good (although not normal) performance.

During the course of this century, several other investigators have found that a behavioral technique could be employed in animals to substantially improve a motor deficit resulting from neurological damage (Chambers, Konorski, Liu, Yu, & Anderson, 1972; Lashley, 1924; Ogden & Franz, 1917; Tower, 1940). However, none of these observations was embedded in a formal theoretical context that permitted prediction nor was the generality of the mechanisms recognized. Consequently, these findings remained a set of disconnected observations that received little attention.

A Possible Mechanism: Learned Nonuse

Several converging lines of evidence suggest that nonuse of a single deafferented limb is a learning phenomenon involving a conditioned suppression of movement termed *learned nonuse*. The restraint and training techniques appear to be effective because they overcome learned nonuse. We offer the following explanation for further empirical test and hypothesis formation and recognize that important modulating influences have not been taken into consideration, such as the site of the CNS lesion and interactions with other reinforcement mechanisms. However, if the learned nonuse hypothesis is proven incorrect, this development would not negate the clinical efficacy of CI therapy, which has been demonstrated in multiple experiments that are described in later sections.

Substantial neurological injury usually leads to a depression in motor and/or perceptual function that is considerably worse than the level of function that will be attained after spontaneous recovery has taken place. The processes responsible for the initial depression of function and the later gradual recovery that occurs at the level of both the spinal cord and the brain is, at present, incompletely understood. Whatever the mechanism, however, recovery processes come into operation following deafferentation so that after a period of time movements can be once again,

at least potentially, be expressed. In monkeys the initial period of depressed function lasts from 2 to 6 months following forelimb deafferentation (Taub, 1977b, 1980).

Thus, immediately after surgical deafferentation of a limb, monkeys cannot use that extremity; recovery from the initial depression of function requires considerable time. Animals with one deafferented limb are unsuccessful in attempts to use that extremity during this period. Efforts to use the deafferented limb often lead to painful and otherwise aversive consequences, such as incoordination and falling, loss of food objects, and in general, failure of any activity attempted with the deafferented limb. Many learning experiments have demonstrated that punishment has the effect of suppressing the behavior associated with it (Azrin & Holz, 1966; Catania, 1998; Estes, 1944); in addition, individuals learn to avoid performance of the punished behavior. The monkeys, meanwhile, get along quite well in the laboratory environment on three limbs and are therefore positively reinforced for this pattern of behavior which, as a result, is strengthened. Thus, the response tendency to not use the affected limb persists and, consequently, monkeys never learn that the limb has become potentially useful several months after surgery. The mechanism by which learned nonuse develops is depicted schematically in Figure 66.1 and can best be appreciated as sequential processes that proceed from left to right in the diagram.

When the movements of the intact limb are restricted several months after unilateral deafferentation, the situation is changed dramatically. Animals either use the deafferented limb, or cannot with any degree of efficiency feed themselves, locomote, or carry out large portions of their daily activities. This new constraint on behavior increases the drive to use the deafferented limb, thereby inducing monkeys to use it and overcoming the learned nonuse. However, current ongoing environmental contingencies, such as the relative inefficiency of the affected upper extremity compared with the unaffected arm, continue to affect the contingencies of reinforcement for use of the affected extremity. If the movement-restriction device is removed a short while after the early display of purposive movement, the newly learned use of the deafferented limb acquires little strength and is quickly overwhelmed by the well-learned tendency to not use the limb. However, ongoing environmental factors, such as the relative inefficiency of the affected upper extremity compared with the unaffected arm, continue to affect the contingencies of reinforcement for use of the affected extremity. If the movement-restriction device is left on for several days or longer, use of the deafferented limb acquires strength and then when the device is removed can compete successfully with the strongly overlearned nonuse of that limb. The

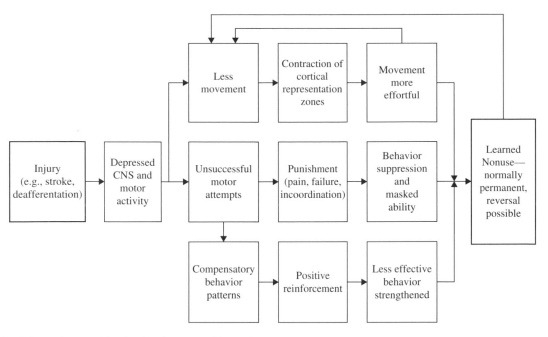

Figure 66.1 Schematic model for the development of learned nonuse.

counterconditioning of learned nonuse is depicted schematically in Figure 66.2.

The conditioned response and shaping conditions described in the previous section, just like the restriction of the intact limb, place major constraints on the animals' behavior. In the conditioned response situation, if the monkeys do not perform the required response with the deafferented limb, they are either punished or do not receive food pellets or liquid when hungry or thirsty, respectively. Similarly, during shaping, reward is contingent on making an improved movement with the deafferented limb. The monkeys cannot get by using just the intact forelimb as they can in the colony environment. These new sets of conditions, just as the movement-restriction device, constrain the animals to use their deafferented limb to avoid punishment or obtain reward and thereby induce the animals to use their deafferented limb and overcome the learned nonuse.

As noted, use of the deafferented limb does not transfer from the conditioned response situation to the life situation of the monkeys. This lack of transfer may be due to the restriction of training in the conditioning paradigm to a few specific movements within a narrow context; training of arm use is not generalized to a variety of movements or situations. The shaping situation, however, is more flexible and free-form; it appears to provide a bridge from the training to the life situation. What is learned in the shaping situation transfers to the colony environment and even generalizes to movement categories other than those trained.

The movement restriction, conditioned response, and shaping situations share a common feature; each involves

a constraint-induced (CI) facilitation of impaired movement that has the effect of overcoming the learned nonuse of the deafferented limb. Thus, the induction of movement by CI therapy would appear to be the agent responsible in each case for the rehabilitation of motor ability. The term *constraint* in the name of the treatment used with humans conveys the meaning that physical restraint of the less affected arm and training or shaping procedures both constitute forms of constraint, the training situation no less so than physical restraint of the less affected arm. In addition, all three of these situations involved massed or repetitive practice in using the deafferented extremity for prolonged periods over a set of consecutive days (for a more detailed description of these experiments, see Taub, 1977b, 1980).

Direct Test of the Learned Nonuse Hypothesis

An experiment was carried out to test the learned nonuse formulation directly (Taub, 1977b, 1980). Movement of a unilaterally deafferented forelimb was prevented with a restraining device in several animals so that they could not attempt to use that extremity for a period of 3 months following surgery. Restraint was begun while the animals were still under anesthesia. The reasoning was that by preventing animals from trying to use the deafferented limb during the period before spontaneous recovery of function had taken place, they would be unable to learn that the limb could not be used during that interval. Learned nonuse of the affected extremity should therefore not develop. In addition, the intact limb was restrained for the same period so that the animals could not receive reinforcement for use of that extremity alone. In conformity with the prediction,

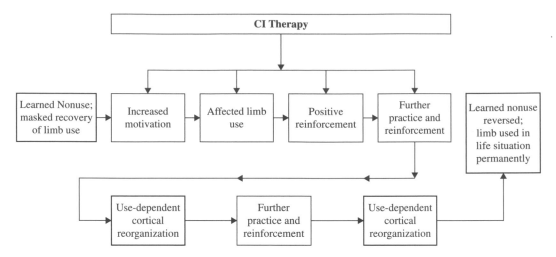

Figure 66.2 Schematic model of mechanism for overcoming learned nonuse.

the animals were able to use their deafferented extremity in the free situation after the restraint was removed 3 months after operation, and this was permanent, persisting for the rest of the animals' lives. Suggestive evidence in support of the operation of the learned nonuse mechanism was also obtained during deafferentation experiments carried out prenatally (Taub et al., 1973; Taub, Perrella, et al., 1975). Life in the physically restricted uterine environment imposes major constraints on the ability to use the forelimbs (while not preventing use of the limbs entirely), thereby functioning like a sling or a protective safety mitt in a CI therapy experiment (to be discussed later). Four animals were studied that had received unilateral forelimb deafferentation during the prenatal period; three when two-thirds the way through gestation and one when two-fifths of the way through gestation. These animals exhibited purposive use of the deafferented extremity from the first day of extrauterine life, at which time they all employed the limb for postural support during "sprawling" and for pushing into a sitting position. Subsequently, though the intact limb was never restrained, the ability to use the deafferented limb continued to develop in ontogeny until it was similar to that of animals given unilateral deafferentation when mature. This, then, constitutes a second direct line of evidence supporting the learned nonuse formulation.

Bilateral Forelimb Deafferentation

One of the most striking features of the primate somatosensory deafferentation literature is the diametrically opposed result produced by deafferentation of just one forelimb versus deafferentation of both forelimbs. Until this point in the discussion, attention has been focused on the fact that following unilateral forelimb deafferentation, monkeys never use the affected extremity in the free situation;

this demonstration has been replicated (Lassek, 1953; Twitchell, 1954) and was accorded considerable theoretical significance (Sherrington, 1910, 1913, 1931). In contrast, we found that after bilateral forelimb deafferentation, a lesion of twice the extent, monkeys made extensive use of their upper extremities after a period of gradual recovery of function. It would appear that bilateral forelimb deafferentation, by affecting both extremities, has the effect of constraining an animal to use its deafferented forelimbs to carry out daily activities, much like placing a movement-restriction device on the intact forelimb of an unilaterally deafferented animal constrains it to use the deafferented forelimb. As in monkeys who receive unilateral deafferentation and wear the movement-restriction device on their intact limb or receive shaping of the deafferented limb, the bilaterally deafferented monkeys achieve clumsy, but effective control of their forelimb movements. Research on bilateral forelimb deafferentation has theoretical significance because it provides evidence, in addition to the work described in the two previous sections, that somatosensory feedback and spinal reflexes are not necessary in the performance of purposive movement and learning (Taub, 1977b; Taub & Berman, 1968).

Applicability of the Model to Humans after Stroke

Given the general nature of the learned nonuse mechanism proposed by the formulation, it was reasoned that the constraint-induced techniques developed in the experiments with monkeys might be an appropriate approach to the rehabilitation of motor disability due to nervous system injury in humans. For example, stroke often leaves patients with an apparently permanent loss of function in an upper extremity, although the limb is not paralyzed.

Additionally, the motor impairment is preponderantly unilateral. These factors are similar to those that pertain after unilateral forelimb deafferentation in monkeys. Therefore, it seemed reasonable to formulate a protocol that simply transferred the techniques used for overcoming learned nonuse of a deafferented limb in monkeys to humans who had experienced a cerebrovascular accident (Taub, 1980).

A question might arise whether a mechanism that leads to rehabilitation of movement after somatosensory deafferentation would have relevance to the rehabilitation of movement after stroke since the two injuries involve very different types of damage to the nervous system. Somatosensory deafferentation interrupts afferent neurons at spinal cord level, whereas a stroke damages motor and other neurons at cortical level. However, both deafferentation and stroke provide the necessary circumstances for learned nonuse to develop; both result in an initial period of inability to use an affected extremity followed by a slow spontaneous recovery of function. The initial depression of motor ability creates contingencies of reinforcement (punishment for attempted use of the initially useless or seriously impaired extremity, and reward for use of the intact extremity) that lead to a conditioned nonuse of the affected body part. This nonuse is overlearned so that it persists and suppresses motor behavior even when the potential for more extensive use of a limb returns as a result of spontaneous recovery of function. Thus, the final motor disability is in excess of the eventual, true level of motor impairment. As learned nonuse is a function of the punishments and rewards that result from attempted activity after an injury, it should operate whatever the location and type of nervous system injury.

The model does not at present incorporate some modifiers, such as comorbid disorders, self-generated discipline in practicing use of an extremity, or psychosocial support, that could potentially influence the mechanisms underlying the development of learned nonuse and those that overcome it. Moreover, in the case of stroke, the model also does not in any way minimize the possible general correlation between the location of neural damage following stroke and the amount of motor function that is spontaneously recovered on the more-affected side. Such a correlation could be a sufficient explanation for the observed differences in the actual use of a more-affected extremity among many patients. However, the fact that some patients with a given extent and locus of lesion exhibit greater use of a more-affected extremity than other patients having similar lesions suggests that additional factors may be involved. One of these factors might be the operation of a learned nonuse mechanism. The validity of this analysis can be assessed empirically. If two functional deficits that

are similar in nature but different in anatomic origin can be overcome by the same techniques, we would have suggestive evidence that the same mechanism is involved in their remediation. It would still be possible that the resemblance was just phenotypic and that different mechanisms were involved in the two cases. However, the more parsimonious explanation would be that the same mechanism was involved in each case, especially if there was a strong conceptual basis for this hypothesis.

A LINKED, BUT INDEPENDENT, MECHANISM: USE-DEPENDENT PLASTIC BRAIN REORGANIZATION

New findings in neuroscience suggested an additional mechanism responsible for the effectiveness of CI therapy. Cortical reorganization involves changes in the area and location of the cortex devoted to the representation of a particular sensory or motor function. The general principles of cortical reorganization as they can be understood on the basis of current research are as follows:

- *Deafferentation, as produced by amputation or dorsal rhizotomy, results in the invasion of the cortical representation zone of the affected body part by adjacent cortical representations of intact parts of the body.* T. Pons and coworkers found that massive cortical reorganization had occurred in monkeys that had received somatosensory deafferentation of an entire forelimb in Taub's laboratory some years earlier (Pons et al., 1991). Tactile stimulation of the monkeys' face gave rise not only to evoked single unit responses in the somatosensory face area, but also to responses in the somatosensory cortical zone formerly representing the now-deafferented arm. The cortical zone representing the deafferented arm had been invaded by the face area. In several more recent studies in humans, we determined that invasion of deafferented representational zones is strongly correlated with amount of symptomatology in pathological conditions such as phantom limb pain (Birbaumer et al., 1997; Flor et al., 1995) and tinnitus (Mühlnickel et al., 1998). Prior to our findings, these conditions were enigmatic entities in that they had no agreed-on etiology. CNS correlates of these conditions had been long sought; however, it was not possible to identify them until our group (Elbert et al., 1994) and a group in San Diego (Yang et al., 1994) showed in 1994 that massive cortical reorganization takes place in humans after CNS injury.
- *Increased use of a limb leads to an expansion of the cortical representation zone of that body part and*

to a reduction in the size of the receptive fields of the neurons in that representation zone. Following the seminal work of Recanzone, Merzenich, and coworkers on use-dependent cortical reorganization in monkeys (Jenkins et al., 1990; Recanzone, Jenkins, et al., 1992; Recanzone, Merzenich, & Jenkins, 1992; Recanzone, Merzenich, Jenkins, Grajski, et al., 1992), neuroimaging studies by Elbert, Taub, and coworkers among others showed that the same phenomenon occurs in humans (Braun, Schweizer, Elbert, Birbaumer, & Taub, 2000; Elbert et al., 1997). For example, it was found that the cortical somatosensory representation of the digits of the left hand was larger in string players, who use their left hand for the dexterity-demanding task of fingering the strings, than in nonmusician controls (Elbert et al., 1995).

- *Training of extremity use after a CNS injury affecting the cortical tissue representing that body part results in improved extremity function and reorganization in brain activity.* Intensive, extended training (see following bullet on massed practice), in producing a use-dependent cortical reorganization, may constitute a countervailing influence that reverses the adverse consequences of alterations in the functional organization of the brain (injury-related cortical reorganization) that occur consequent to stroke. Nudo and coworkers carried out a groundbreaking intracortical microstimulation study demonstrating that in adult squirrel monkeys that were surgically given an ischemic infarct in the cortical area controlling the movements of a hand, training of the affected limb resulted in improved behavioral function and in cortical reorganization. Specifically, the area surrounding the infarct, which would not normally be involved in control of the hand, came to participate in that function (Nudo, Wise, SiFuentes, & Milliken, 1996).

- *Massing or intensity of practice: Plastic brain reorganization emerges in response to a heavy training schedule (e.g., several hours a day for several successive days).* CI therapy, which involves repetitive practice of tasks for multiple hours per day for 10 or 15 consecutive weekdays, has been found to produce "massive" cortical reorganization. Our data also show that CI therapy is highly effective when administered several hours a day over a limited period, though not necessarily on consecutive days. The optimal amount of massing or intensity of practice for producing maximal plastic brain change or CI therapy treatment effect has yet to be determined (Dettmers et al., 2005; Page, Sisto, Levine, & McGrath, 2004; Sterr et al., 2002; Taub, Lum, Hardin, Mark, & Uswatte, 2005).

- *Use-dependent cortical reorganization requires a high motivational drive.* The behavioral relevance of sensory experience has been found to determine whether cortical reorganization will occur (Jenkins et al., 1990). Projections from the basal forebrain signal the importance of sensory stimuli to the individual, enhancing the CNS response to relevant events and diminishing it to others. "Absorption" in focus on a task may be the operative factor in "behavioral relevance" and, thus, may be important in determining the amount of use-dependent cortical reorganization that will occur with repetitive stimulation.

Several collaborative neurophysiological studies have now shown that CI therapy produces a large use-dependent cortical reorganization in humans with stroke-related paresis of an upper limb similar to that observed by Nudo et al. (1996) in monkeys. In one study, Liepert and coworkers (1998) used focal transcranial magnetic stimulation to map the area of the motor cortex that controls an important muscle of the hand (abductor pollicis brevis) in six patients with a chronic upper extremity hemiparesis (mean chronicity = 6 years) before and after CI therapy. We first replicated the clinical result that CI therapy produces a very large increase in patients' amount of arm use in the home over a 2-week treatment period. Over the same interval, the cortical region from which electromyography responses of the abductor pollicis brevis muscle could be elicited by transcranial magnetic stimulation was greatly increased. In a follow-up study with nine additional subjects (total $N = 15$), we found that both the motor rehabilitation effect and the alteration in brain function persisted for the 6 months tested (Liepert et al., 2000). CI therapy had led to an increase in the excitability and recruitment of a large number of neurons in the innervation of movements of the more-affected limb adjacent to those originally involved in control of the extremity prior to treatment. The effect was sufficiently large that it represented a return to normal size of the motor output area for the abductor pollicis brevis muscle in the infarcted side of the brain, though it was the size of excitable cortical area that had become normal, not its function; the affected hand, though much improved after CI therapy, was not normal in function. In a third study, Kopp et al. (1999) carried out dipole modeling of steady-state movement-related cortical potentials (EEG) of patients before and after CI therapy. We found that 3 months after treatment the motor cortex ipsilateral to the affected arm, which normally controls movements of the contralateral (less-affected) arm, had been recruited to generate movements of the affected arm. This effect was not in evidence immediately after treatment and was presumably due to the sustained increase in more-affected arm use in the life situation produced by CI therapy over the 3-month follow-up period.

This experimental evidence that CI therapy is associated with substantial changes in brain activity has been confirmed by convergent data from two other neurophysiological studies using two additional techniques in association with the administration of CI therapy. Bauder, Sommer, Taub, and Miltner (1999) showed that there is a large increase in the amplitude of the late components of the Bereitschaftspotential (a movement-related cortical potential) after CI therapy, suggesting that an enhanced neuronal excitability is induced in the damaged hemisphere; this is consistent with the results of Liepert et al. (1998, 2000). We also found that after CI therapy there was a large increase in the activation of the (usually little-activated) healthy, ipsilateral hemisphere with more-affected hand movement. The increased activity of an ipsilateral source or generator after CI therapy confirms the findings of Kopp et al. (1999). In addition, Wittenberg et al. (2003) found in a positron emission tomography study that before CI therapy there was a larger activation in bilateral primary sensorimotor cortices with more-affected side movement compared to healthy control subjects. This excessive activation diminished after CI therapy. The preliminary interpretation of this result is that less effort is required to produce movements after CI therapy than before treatment.

Since these initial studies, there have been approximately 20 other studies demonstrating an alteration in brain structure or function associated with a CI therapy-induced improvement in movement after CNS damage. By providing a physiological basis for the treatment effect reported for CI therapy, these results have tended to increase confidence in the clinical results.

The findings suggest that CI therapy produces a long-term increase in arm use by two linked but independent mechanisms (Kopp et al., 1999; Liepert et al., 1998; Taub & Uswatte, 2000). As noted, CI therapy changes the contingencies of reinforcement (provides opportunities for reinforcement of use of the more-affected arm and aversive consequences for its nonuse) by three techniques: (1) intensive training procedures, (2) a set of techniques that promote transfer of therapeutic gains made in the laboratory to the life situation, and (3) restraint of the less-affected arm so that the nonuse of the more-affected arm learned in the acute and early subacute periods is counter-conditioned or lifted. The consequent increase in more-affected arm use, involving sustained and repeated practice of functional arm movements in both the laboratory and home environments, induces expansion of the contralateral cortical area controlling movement of the more-affected arm and recruitment of new ipsilateral areas. This use-dependent brain plasticity

may serve as the neural basis for the long-term increase in use of the affected arm.

APPLICATION OF THE LEARNED NONUSE MODEL TO HUMANS AFTER STROKE

Initial Studies on the Application of CI Therapy to the Rehabilitation of Paretic Arm Use

The initial studies of the application of CI therapy to humans were carried out by Ince (1969) and Halberstam, Zaretsky, Brucker, and Guttman (1971). Ince transferred the conditioned response techniques used with the deafferented monkeys that he had observed in Taub's laboratory (e.g., Taub & Berman, 1968) directly to the rehabilitation of movement of the paretic upper extremity of three patients with chronic stroke. He tied the less-affected upper extremity of the patients to the arm of a chair, while asking the patients to flex their more-affected arm to avoid an electric shock. The motor status of two of the patients did not change; the third patient, however improved substantially in the training and life situations (Ince, 1969). Halberstam et al. (1971), from a nearby institution, used a similar treatment protocol with a sample of 20 elderly patients and 20 age-matched controls. The treatment group was asked to either flex their more-affected arm or to make a lateral movement at the elbow to avoid electric shock; the less-affected arm was not tied down. Most of the patients in the treatment group increased the amplitude of their movements in the two conditioned response tasks; some showed very large improvements (Halberstam et al., 1971). There was no report of whether this improvement transferred to the life situation.

Steven Wolf and coworkers (Ostendorf & Wolf, 1981; Wolf, Lecraw, Barton, & Jann, 1989) applied the less-affected limb constraint portion, but not the more-affected limb training component, of the CI therapy protocol published by Taub (1980) to the rehabilitation of movement in persons with a chronic upper extremity hemiparesis. The study included 25 stroke and traumatic brain injury patients who were more than 1 year postinjury and who possessed a minimum of 10 degrees extension at the metacarpophalangeal and interphalangeal joints and 20 degrees extension at the wrist of the more-affected arm. The patients were asked to wear a sling on the less-affected arm all day for 2 weeks, except during a half-hour exercise period and sleeping hours. The patients demonstrated significant but small improvements in speed or force of movement, depending on the task, on 19 out of 21 tasks on the Wolf Motor Function Test (WMFT), a laboratory test involving simple upper extremity movements. There was no report of whether the improvements transferred to the life situation. Though the effect size was small (.2), it was reliable. The results appeared promising, especially since training had not been used and there was some question of compliance with the instruction to wear the sling for most of waking hours during the intervention period for some subjects. This type of intervention involving only use of a restraint device is now termed *Forced Use* therapy and not CI therapy.

Demonstration of Efficacy of CI Therapy for Paretic Arm Rehabilitation at the University of Alabama at Birmingham (UAB) Laboratory

Taub et al. (1993) applied both the paretic arm training and contralateral arm restraint portions of the CI therapy protocol and also a set of behavioral techniques termed the *Transfer Package* (Morris, Taub, & Mark, 2006; Taub, Uswatte, King, et al., 2006; Taub, Uswatte, Mark, & Morris, 2006) to the rehabilitation of persons with a chronic upper extremity hemiparesis in a study that employed an attention-placebo control group and emphasized transfer of therapeutic gains in the laboratory to the life situation. Patients with chronic stroke were selected as subjects for this study because according to the research literature (Bard & Hirschberg, 1965; Parker, Wade, & Langton-Hewer, 1986; Twitchell, 1951), and clinical experience, motor recovery usually reaches a plateau within 1 year after stroke. Therefore, any marked improvement in the motor function of individuals with chronic stroke would be of increased therapeutic significance. After a long-standing plateau, the probability would be very low that an abrupt, large improvement in motor ability could be due to spontaneous recovery.

Four treatment subjects signed a behavioral contract in which they agreed to wear a sling on their less-affected arm for 90% of waking hours for 14 days. On 10 of those days, the treatment subjects received 6 hours of supervised task practice using their more-affected arm (e.g., eating lunch, throwing a ball, playing dominoes, Chinese checkers or card games, writing, pushing a broom, and using the Purdue Pegboard and Minnesota Rate of Manipulation Test) interspersed with one hour of rest. Five control subjects were told they had much greater movement in their more-affected limb than they were exhibiting, were led through a series of passive movement exercises in the treatment center, and were given passive movement exercises to perform at home. All experimental and control subjects were at least 1 year poststroke (M = 4.4 yr) and had passed the minimum motor criterion employed by Wolf et al. (1989) before intake into the study. This kind of motor deficit could be characterized as mild/moderate

or Grade 2 in the UAB system of classifying motor deficit at the impairment level based on active range of motion at each of the upper extremity joints. Treatment efficacy was evaluated by the WMFT (Morris, Uswatte, Crago, Cook, & Taub, 2001; Taub et al., 1993; Wolf et al., 1989, 2005), the Arm Motor Ability Test (Kopp et al., 1997; McCulloch et al., 1988), and the Motor Activity Log (Taub et al., 1993; Uswatte, Taub, Morris, Light, & Thompson, 2006; Uswatte, Taub, Morris, Vignolo, & McCulloch, 2005; van der Lee, Beckerman, Knol, de Vet, & Bouter, 2004), a structured scripted interview tracking arm use in a variety of activities of daily living (ADL). The treatment group demonstrated a significant increase in motor ability as measured by both laboratory motor tests (WMFT, Arm Motor Ability Test) over the treatment period, whereas the control subjects showed no change or a decline in arm motor ability. On the Motor Activity Log (MAL), the treatment group showed a large increase in real-world arm use over the 2-week period and no decrease in retention of the treatment gain in real-world use when tested 2 years after treatment. In other experiments, we have found a 20% decrement in retention over a 2-year posttreatment period in patients with a similar, mild/moderate deficit as the patients in this experiment. The control subjects exhibited no change or a decline in real-world arm use over the 2-week treatment period.

These results have since been confirmed in an experiment using less-affected arm constraint and shaping (Morgan, 1974; Panyan, 1980; Skinner, 1938, 1968) of the more-affected arm, instead of task practice. This experiment also had a larger sample (N = 41) and a more credible control procedure than in the first study. The shaping procedure involved requiring that improvements in performance be made in small steps (successive approximations), providing explicit feedback and verbal reinforcement for small improvements in task performance, and selecting tasks that were tailored to address the motor deficits of the individual patient (Taub, Burgio, et al., 1994; Taub, Pidikiti, DeLuca, & Crago, 1996). Modeling and prompting of task performance were also used. The control group was designed to control for the duration and intensity of the therapist–patient interaction and the duration and intensity of the therapeutic activities. The control procedure was a general fitness program in which subjects performed strength, balance, and stamina training exercises, played games that stimulated cognitive activity, and practiced relaxation skills for 10 days. Both experimental and control subjects were at least 1-year poststroke (M = 4.5 yr) and exceeded the minimum motor criterion used in the first experiment prior to entry into the study. In addition, all subjects exhibited a substantial lack of spontaneous use of their more affected arm in their daily life, as defined by a score of less than 2.5 on the MAL (half as much use of the more impaired arm as before the stroke in the life situation). The motor deficit and amount of arm use of subjects in the two groups prior to treatment was not significantly different (Taub, Pidikiti, Uswatte, Shaw, & Yakley, 1998; Taub & Uswatte, 2000; Taub, Uswatte, King, et al., 2006). As in the first experiment, the treatment group demonstrated a significant increase in motor ability on the WMFT and a large increase in real-world arm use over the intervention, whereas the control subjects did not. Control subjects' answers to an expectancy and self-efficacy questionnaire about their expectations for rehabilitation prior to the control intervention and their reported increase in quality of life after the intervention, as measured by the Medical Outcomes Study 36-Item Short-Form Health Survey (Ware & Sherbourne, 1992), suggested that they found the control intervention to be credible.

CI Therapy: A Family of Treatments

Other experiments carried out at UAB have indicated that there is a family of techniques that can overcome learned nonuse (Taub, Crago, & Uswatte, 1998; Taub et al., 1996; Taub & Uswatte, 2000; Uswatt, Taub, Morris, Barman, & Crago, 2006). The other interventions that have been tested are (a) placement of a half-glove on the less-affected arm as a reminder not to use it and shaping of the paretic arm, (b) shaping of the paretic arm only, and (c) intensive physical therapy (aquatic therapy, neurophysiological facilitation, and task practice) of the paretic arm for 5 hours a day for 10 consecutive weekdays (Uswatt, Taub, Morris, Barman, et al., 2006). The half-glove intervention was designed so that CI therapy could be employed with patients who have balance problems and might be at risk for falls when wearing a sling; this intervention expands the population of stroke patients amenable to CI therapy threefold. Currently, a "padded or protective safety mitt" is used instead of the half glove for patients with balance problems. This restraint leaves the less-affected arm free so as not to compromise safety, but prevents use of the hand and fingers in ADL. The shaping-only intervention was tested to evaluate the relative importance of the constraint and task practice components of the intervention. The intensive physical therapy intervention did not involve physical constraint of the less-affected arm; however, subjects were asked not to use their less-affected arm and this regimen was monitored. To our knowledge, such a concentrated application of physical therapy had not been evaluated before this trial. All three of these groups showed very large increases in arm use in the life situation over the treatment period equivalent to that observed for the sling plus task practice and the sling plus shaping groups. Two

years after treatment, each of the groups retained approximately 80% of their original treatment effect.

Effect Size

Several hundred subjects with mild/moderate stroke motor symptoms (Grade 2; approximately 25% to 35% of the stroke population) have been given upper extremity CI therapy to date in this laboratory. The mean effect size (ES) for the WMFT, a laboratory motor function test, in all of these studies was .9; the mean ES for the MAL, which records ADL in the life situation, was 3.3. The much larger ES for the MAL than for the WMFT indicates that CI therapy has its greatest effect on increasing the actual amount of use of a more-affected upper extremity in the real-world setting, though the improvement in quality of movement as indexed by the WMFT is still substantial. In the meta-analysis literature, an ES (d') of .2 is considered small, a .4 to .6 ES is moderate, while ESs of .8 and above are large (Cohen, 1988). Thus, the ES of CI therapy for real-world outcome in patients with chronic stroke from the upper quartile of motor functioning is extremely large.

Replications in Other Laboratories

Over 400 patients with stroke in the UAB laboratory have been given one variant or another of CI therapy and all but three of these patients have demonstrated substantial improvement in motor ability (improvement greater than a Minimum Clinically Important Difference; defined in Lum et al., 2004; Uswatte & Taub, 2005; van der Lee et al. 2004). This laboratory's results have been replicated quantitatively with patients with chronic stroke in published studies from four laboratories; the therapists were trained in this laboratory and monitored by one of us (ET) twice yearly (Dettmers et al., 2005; Kunkel et al., 1999; Miltner, Bauder, Sommer, Dettmers, & Taub, 1999; Sterr et al., 2002).

There have been over 200 other papers on adult and pediatric CI therapy published to date. To our knowledge all the studies up to now have reported positive results. Some of the papers report outcomes as large as those obtained in this and related laboratories. Many studies, however, have results that are significant, but one half to one third as large as those obtained here. The likely reasons for this disparity are twofold: (1) There was incomplete or lack of use of the procedures of the transfer package (to be described), which, though reported in the papers from this laboratory, had been largely unremarked and underemphasized. We have replicated the reduced treatment effect obtained by others by duplicating everything that is normally done in treatment here except implementing the transfer package. (2) A protocol with attenuated intensity (movement per unit time) was used, such as in van der Lee, Beckerman, Lankhorst, & Bouter (1999).

Massing of Practice as a Therapeutic Factor

The question arises as to what is the common factor or factors underlying the therapeutic effect in the different CI therapy interventions tested to date. Although most of the techniques involve restraining movement of the less-affected arm, the shaping-only and intensive physical therapy interventions do not. There is thus nothing talismanic about use of a sling or other restraining device on the less-affected extremity. Until recently, the common and most important factor appeared to be repeatedly practicing use of the paretic arm. It was thought that any technique that induced a patient to use an affected extremity intensively for an extended duration should be therapeutically efficacious. Butefisch, Hummelsheim, Kenzler, and Mauritz (1995) have also shown that repetitive practice is an important factor in stroke rehabilitation. However, we have found that there is a factor more important still in producing increased spontaneous use of a more affected arm in the free situation—a set of techniques referred to collectively as the transfer package. These techniques are discussed in the following section. However, this finding does not vitiate the importance of massing of practice as an independent therapeutic factor. Studies that make use of restraint of the less-affected arm but do not give concentrated, extended practice in use of the more-affected arm cannot be said to have administered CI therapy (Taub & Uswatte, 2000). Wolf et al.'s (1989) study provided evidence that this type of procedure yields a markedly reduced treatment effect. In a more recent study (van der Lee, Wagenaar, et al., 1999), investigators who trained in the UAB laboratory were counseled before they left that the practice schedule incorporating activities modeled on hobbies they were planning to use would not work well because of its relaxed, attenuated nature. Subjects were treated in groups of four with one or two therapists in attendence, in contrast to the much more intensive one-on-one therapy administered in the UAB laboratory. Not surprisingly, their attenuated intervention did not produce treatment effects as large as those obtained in the UAB laboratory. It should also be noted that in the van der Lee et al. (1999) study an intensive conventional physical therapy intervention, which concentrated the administration of therapy far beyond the schedule with which conventional therapy is usually delivered, was contrasted with the attenuated form of CI therapy they used. This procedure would not provide a meaningful control for evaluating the efficacy of CI therapy even if CI therapy was administered correctly. We had already shown with our intensive physical therapy group (Taub, Crago, et al., 1998; Uswatt, Taub, Morris, Barman, et al., 2006) that massing practice of conventional therapy gives results as good as those achieved with restraint of the less-affected arm combined with intensive task practice or shaping.

In apparent contradiction to the identification of massed practice as an important therapeutic factor in CI therapy, the motor learning literature indicates that massed practice has only a neutral or negative effect on the learning of continuous tasks and a variable effect on the learning of discrete tasks (Schmidt & Lee, 1999). However, CI therapy employs massed practice to increase the tendency of patients to use their more-impaired limb and overcome learned nonuse. There is little evidential basis for believing that operant learning resulting in the increased frequency of already learned and previously performed movement and the lifting of the conditioned inhibition associated with learned nonuse is governed by the same principles as the acquisition of new types of skilled movement that is the focus of the motor learning approach. Although both processes involve learning, they would appear to be of different types. Therefore, it is no surprise that findings from the motor learning literature concerning massed versus spaced practice do not apply to the effectiveness demonstrated for massed practice in CI therapy.

The Transfer Package

In recent work, we unexpectedly found that a set of techniques now termed the *transfer package* (TP) made a much more important contribution to the treatment effect produced by CI therapy than had been anticipated. The purpose of the TP techniques is to promote transfer of the therapeutic gains from the laboratory to the real-world environment. They are behavioral procedures that are used routinely in behavioral interventions. We had previously viewed the TP as a transparent aspect of CI therapy. It was something we had routinely done, but not directed much attention toward, though several rehabilitation professionals on joining our research team had remarked that the procedures were radically different from those generally carried out in rehabilitation treatment centers. The TP includes the following seven components: (1) *daily administration of the MAL,* which collects information about use of the more affected arm in 30 important ADL; (2) *a patient-kept daily diary* that details what a patient did when out of the laboratory overnight and the extent to which there was compliance with an agreed-on amount of use of the more affected arm; (3) *problem solving* to help patients overcome perceived barriers to real-world use of the more affected arm reported during monitoring; (4) *behavioral contracts* for patients and caregivers specifying agreed-on real-world activities for which the more affected arm would be used exclusively (items 1, 2, and 4 are *monitoring and accountability components*); (5) *home practice* of specified exercises; (6) *restraint* of the less affected arm in a padded mitt; and (7) *weekly telephone contacts with patients for the first month after the end of treatment* in which the MAL is administered and problem solving is carried out. (For a more detailed description of the elements of the TP, see Morris et al., 2006; Taub, Uswatte, Mark, et al., 2006). In most physical rehabilitation regimens, there is a passive element; the patient is responsible primarily for carrying out the therapist's instructions only during treatment sessions. A major difference in CI therapy is the involvement of the patient as an active participant in all requirements of the therapy not only during the treatment sessions but also at home during the treatment period and for the first month after laboratory therapy has been completed (and afterward though it is not checked on). The TP makes patients responsible for adhering to the requirements of the therapy, and therefore in effect they become responsible for their own improvement.

The study population was chronic stroke patients with mild/moderate upper extremity hemiparesis (Grade 2). Half the patients were given intensive training for 3 hr/day for 10 consecutive weekdays and also received the TP. The remaining subjects were treated in exactly the same way but received no TP. On a laboratory motor function test (WMFT) where patients are asked to use the more affected arm as rapidly and as well as they can, the two groups showed an equivalent significant improvement after treatment. The subjects without the TP performed just as well in the laboratory as the subjects with the TP. The results were very different for spontaneous use of the more affected arm in ADL in the life situation. Though the subjects without the TP showed a significant and clinically meaningful improvement in amount of use of the more affected arm in the life situation, the subjects given the TP had 2.5 to 3 times greater real-world limb use than the subjects without the TP. However, the TP by itself does not have a therapeutic effect. In a placebo-controlled experiment (Taub, Uswatte, King, et al., 2006), use of the TP with a placebo treatment did not result in a significant effect.

Confirmation of this result was obtained from a separate group of 10 subjects who were given no TP during training. However, two TP components, the MAL and problem solving about perceived barriers to the use of the arm in ADL in the home, were administered by telephone on a weekly basis for a month after treatment. Participants in this group showed the same modest improvement from pre- to posttreatment in spontaneous real-world use of the more affected extremity as the other subjects who did not receive the TP during training, but they showed a substantial increase in real-world use of their more impaired arm after the end of treatment when the four weekly MAL follow-ups were introduced. At the end of this process, the MAL scores, though still much lower than those of the TP subjects, had increased so that they were approximately 75% greater than those of the subjects who did not receive the TP at any time. It was felt that the results of this group were particularly suggestive as to the therapeutic power of the elements of the TP. In addition, it seems likely that the TP can be separated from CI therapy and used with other rehabilitation interventions.

The TP makes patients active participants, in fact the critical factors, in their own improvement. What then is the importance of massed, intensive practice? The data indicate that it is critical. It is a precondition for the operation of the TP. Thus, when it was used in conjunction with a placebo intervention, there was no treatment effect. However, once massed extensive practice is employed, the TP becomes the dominant factor. It increases the real-world treatment effect by 2.5 times; and numerous commentators agree that improvement of use of an extremity in the life situation is the primary purpose of rehabilitation.

Structural Imaging Studies with CI Therapy and Brain Plasticity

We have described studies showing that alterations in afferent input could alter the *function and organization* of specific brain regions, but until recently there was no evidence that environmental stimuli could measurably alter brain *structures* in adult humans. It has now been shown that seasoned taxi drivers have significantly expanded hippocampi (Maguire et al., 2000), jugglers acquire significantly increased temporal lobe density (Draganski et al., 2004), and thalamic density significantly declines after limb amputation (Draganski et al., 2006). Moreover, in an animal model of stroke, CI therapy combined with exercise reduced tissue loss associated with stroke (DeBow, Davies, Clarke, & Colbourne, 2003). Accordingly, structural imaging studies became a logical initial step toward understanding whether there are anatomical changes following the administration of CI therapy and whether these are correlated with clinical improvements. Moreover, anatomical studies making use of structural MRI have advantages over fMRI studies, including the fact that there is no need to control specific, restricted movements during scanning.

Longitudinal voxel-based morphometry (pre- vs. posttreatment) was performed on subjects enrolled in our study of the contribution made by the TP to CI therapy outcome (Gauthier et al., 2008). It was found that structural brain changes paralleled changes in amount of use of the impaired extremity for activities of daily living. Groups receiving the TP showed profuse increases in grey matter tissue in sensorimotor cortices both contralateral and ipsilateral to the affected arm, as well as in bilateral hippocampi. The aforementioned sensorimotor clusters were bilaterally symmetrical and encompassed the hand/arm regions of primary sensory and motor cortices as well as the anterior supplementary motor area and portions of Brodmann's area 6 (Figure 66.3). In contrast, the groups that did not receive the TP showed relatively small improvements in real-world arm use and failed to demonstrate grey matter increases. Moreover, the increase in grey matter from pre- to posttreatment differed significantly between groups. It was of importance that increases in grey matter were significantly correlated with increases on the MAL for the sensorimotor clusters on both sides of the brain and the predefined hippocampus region of interest (r's $>$ .45). Thus, this change in the brain's morphology is directly related to administration of the TP which in turn substantially increases the amount of real-world use of the affected arm. The fact that this anatomical change is directly related to the TP both lends increased credibility to the importance of the TP and provides a mechanism for its operation.

Increases were also observed in the grey matter of the hippocampus, which may have included the adjacent subventricular zone. The hippocampus is known to be involved in learning and memory and these two processes are associated with the improved limb use that occurs with CI therapy. Evidence also indicates that stem cells are located at this site in the adult mammalian brain (Eriksson et al., 1998; Yamashima et al., 2004) and simulated stroke in animals can increase the quantity of these cells (Yamashima et al., 2004). One might speculate that the increases in grey matter observed in the hippocampal region and sensory and motor areas of the brain are mediated in part by increased production of neuronal or glial stem cells that might participate in the migratory repair of an infarcted area (Kolb et al., 2007). Alternatively, or in addition, grey matter increases may result from rehabilitation-induced increases in dendritic arborization and synaptic density (Briones, Suh, Jozsa, & Woods, 2006), and possibly gliosis or angiogenesis. Notably, the grey matter increases that we observed occurred over the course of just 2 weeks of therapy, emphasizing the rapid time course in which structural neuroplastic changes can take place.

Application of CI Therapy to the Lower Extremity

The UAB laboratory has applied CI therapy techniques to the rehabilitation of the lower extremity of patients with chronic CVA with substantial success (Taub et al., 1999). The 38 patients treated to date have had a wide range of disability extending from being close to nonambulatory to having moderately impaired coordination. The treatment consisted of massed or repetitive practice of lower extremity tasks (e.g., treadmill walking with and without a partial body weight support harness, over-ground walking, sit-to-stand, lie-to-sit, step climbing, various balance and support exercises) for 6 hours/day with interspersed rest intervals as needed over 3 weeks and 0.5 hours/day devoted to TP procedures. Task performance was shaped as in our upper extremity work. Training was enhanced through the use of force feedback (limb load monitor) and joint angle feedback (electric goniometer) devices. No restraining device was placed on the less-affected leg. The lower-extremity procedure is considered to be a form of CI therapy because of the use of the TP, the strong massed practice element, and because the reinforcement of adaptive patterns of ambulation over maladaptive patterns in our training procedure constitutes a significant form of constraint. Control data were provided by the general fitness control group (procedure described later in this chapter), who received the same battery of lower-extremity tests as the lower-extremity treatment subjects. Among the 38 lower extremity patients, five minimally ambulatory patients who required support from a person to walk improved to the status of fully independent (but impaired) ambulation in two cases and ambulation with minimal assistance in three other cases. An additional minimally ambulatory patient improved, but not a great deal. Each of the 32 subjects with a moderate level of impairment improved substantially on most

(A)   (B)
CI Therapy Group   **Comparison Group**

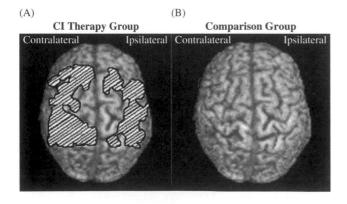

Figure 66.3 Cortical surface-rendered images of grey matter change.

Note: Grey matter increases displayed on a standard brain for (A) participants who received the CI therapy transfer package and (B) those who did not. Surface rendering was performed with a depth of 20 mm. Regions in which significant changes in grey matter were clustered are indicated by hatch marks.

or all our measures. On a group basis, the lower-extremity patients showed a significantly greater improvement than the fitness control subjects both on laboratory motor tests and real-world measures of lower-extremity use.

The treatment gain obtained for the upper extremity and the lower limb interventions is difficult to compare because different instruments are used to measure upper- and lower- function. The effect sizes (ESs) for real-world lower extremity use (MAL) have been above 2.0 in all the upper extremity CI therapy studies in which the intervention was properly administered. The effect size (ES) on the measure of real-world extremity use for the lower extremity after treatment is somewhat smaller (ES = 1.6). However, since 0.8 is considered a large ES, the lower-extremity ES we have obtained is still very large.

Approximately 90% of patients with chronic CVA ambulate but may do so with a degraded pattern of coordination. These disordered patterns may be partly due to the persistence of movements learned in the early postinjury period before spontaneous recovery of function would have permitted an improved mode of ambulation. This phenomenon may be viewed as *learned misuse* rather than *learned nonuse*. Initially, we thought that it might be more difficult to overcome learned misuse than learned nonuse, if it was possible at all. In the case of learned misuse, bad habits of coordination need to be overcome before more appropriate patterns of coordination can be substituted. In the case of learned nonuse, as with the upper extremity after stroke, there is simply an absence or greatly reduced amount of extremity use in the life situation; surmounting improper coordination as an initial step is not a primary problem. We were surprised that our expectation of a substantially reduced lower-extremity treatment outcome proved to be incorrect.

Data obtained concerning long-term retention are of interest. Over a 2-year period of follow-up, there was virtually no loss in retention of the treatment effect even in patients with substantial deficits. This is in contrast to the case for the upper extremity, where there is some loss over 2 years that is greater as the pretreatment amount of deficit increases. The lack of loss of treatment gains over time for the lower-extremity therapy may relate to the fact that if patients are not to be helpless, they must ambulate, and while doing so, they presumably keep practicing the improved patterns of coordination learned during their lower-extremity CI therapy. This is not the case for the upper extremity. If patients become depressed, otherwise ill, or experience a life crisis, they may lose the motivation or attentional focus to expend the extra effort to use the more affected extremity before it becomes habitual. This would have the effect of reducing retention recorded for a group of subjects.

Consistency of CI Therapy Efficacy with General Clinical Experience

In 1979, Andrews and Stewart published an article entitled "Stroke Recovery: He Can But Does He?" in which they reported, "a difference in what the patients could do in the unit and what they did do at home. *Each* activity of daily living was less well performed in the home situation in 25% to 45% of cases" (p. 43; emphasis added). Most clinicians recognize the veracity of this statement. Indeed, decrement in performance outside the clinic environment is frequently reported as a source of intense frustration. Clinicians often work with patients intensively for one or more sessions, with the result that there is a substantial improvement in some aspect of movement. However, by the time of the next therapy session, there have been varying degrees of regression. In fact, some clinicians report that they sometimes see degradation in motor patterns as soon as the patient crosses the threshold into the corridor just outside the therapy room.

Very little explicit attention is paid to this dimension of treatment. A reasonably intensive search of the literature failed to reveal a single reference to this phenomenon. Similarly, very little attention has been paid to the Andrews and Stewart (1979) paper, which has been virtually "lost in the literature." For many stroke and other types of patients we have worked with, there is undeniably a gap between performance in the clinic on laboratory motor tests when specific activities are requested and the actual amount of lower extremity use in the home. This gap may be viewed as an index of learned nonuse; CI therapy operates in this window. It establishes a bridge between the laboratory or clinic and the life setting so that the therapeutic gains made in the clinic transfer maximally and contribute to the functional independence of the patient in the real world. Thus, many patients, though exhibiting a pronounced deficit in spontaneous real-world more affected limb use, might have a considerable latent capacity for motor improvement that could be brought to expression by CI therapy.

APPLICATION OF CI THERAPY TO THE TREATMENT OF OTHER NEUROLOGICAL AND ORTHOPEDIC DISORDERS

The range of disorders for which CI therapy might be an effective treatment encompasses conditions in which motor disability is in apparent excess of the underlying pathology. A possible explanation for the excess motor disability in some of these cases might be that it is being maintained by learned nonuse (Taub, 1980, 1994). The research with deafferented monkeys suggests that learned nonuse is established whenever (a) organic damage results in an initial inability to use a body part so that an individual is punished for attempts to use that part of the body and rewarded for use of other parts of the body, and (b) there is recovery from or healing of the organic damage so that the person recovers the ability to use that body part, but the suppression of use conditioned in the acute phase remains in force. Thus, in the most general terms, CI therapy may be viewed as a treatment for excess motor disability. Clinicians know that there is a very large amount of excess motor disability. It costs the health care system billions of dollars each year, and yet there is no treatment. For example, a woman breaks her hip, the bone heals, but the woman never gets out of bed; or if she does, she does not resume normal activity. Why? The usual explanation is muscular deconditioning from a prolonged period in bed or psychological problems, that is, it is all in her head. In any case, nothing that can be treated very easily. The advantage of the learned nonuse or CI therapy approach is that there is something you can try to do to remediate the situation. It does not involve a therapeutic philosophy of despair. In this section, we summarize our initial work on applying CI therapy to rehabilitate arm use in persons with traumatic brain injury, progressive multiple sclerosis, speech in persons with aphasia consequent to stroke, ambulation in persons with spinal cord injury or fractured hip, and in finger coordination in musicians with focal hand dystonia. An additional application is the alleviation of phantom limb pain in persons with an upper extremity amputation. This work, however, does not exhaust the conditions that appear to involve considerable learned nonuse for which there is at present no effective treatment.

Upper Extremity Use in Persons with Traumatic Brain Injury (TBI)

TBI patients with predominantly unilateral upper limb motor deficits show gains in motor function after CI therapy are similar to those shown by stroke patients with equivalent initial deficits (Morris, Shaw, et al., 2006; Shaw et al., 2005; Shaw, Morris, Yakley, McKay, & Taub, 2000). Two Iraq War veterans with TBI whom we have treated had better than average success. They approached the treatment exercises with focused attention and military discipline. They were ideal patients.

Upper Extremity Use in Persons with Progressive Multiple Sclerosis (MS)

Few therapeutic approaches have been shown to benefit real-world disability in MS. A preliminary trial from our laboratory of CI therapy in progressive MS patients with chronic upper extremity hemiparesis suggests gains that are similar to those for stroke patients after CI therapy (Mark et al., 2008). The findings suggest the possibility that other slowly progressive neurological disorders may benefit from CI therapy and involve learned nonuse.

Cerebral Palsy

The origin of this work was in some research carried out with infant monkeys given somatosensory deafferentation of one or both forelimbs on their day of birth or prenatally (Taub et al., 1973; Taub, Perrella, et al., 1975). The same techniques that had been used successfully with monkeys with mature nervous systems were also found to be effective with infant monkeys. Consequently, after the initial work with adult stroke survivors (Taub et al., 1993), it was suggested that CI therapy ought to be at least as effective with children who have suffered damage to the CNS because the immature nervous system is so much more plastic than the nervous system of adults (Taub & Crago, 1995). We have carried out two randomized controlled trials of CI therapy with young children, the first with children with asymmetric upper extremity motor deficits of varied etiologies from 8 months to 8 years of age and the second with children with hemiparesis consequent to prenatal, perinatal, or early antenatal stroke from 2 to 6 years old (Taub et al., 2004). The procedures used with children were similar to those used with adults and diverged simply to make the basic techniques age-appropriate. Posttreatment gains in the children were better than those obtained in adults. Marked changes were observed in (a) quality of movement in the laboratory scored by masked observers from videotapes, (b) actual amount of use of the more affected arm in the life situation, (c) active range of motion, and (d) emergence of new classes of behavior never performed before, such as in individual cases, fine thumb-forefinger grasp, supination, and use of the more affected extremity in crawling with palmar placement and rhythmic alteration. CI therapy does not make movement normal in children with cerebral palsy with asymmetric upper extremity motor disorders. However, it can produce a substantial improvement in a large majority of cases.

Ambulation in Persons with Spinal Cord Injury or Fractured Hip

Six incomplete spinal cord injury patients have been treated with the same lower extremity protocol used with patients with stroke (King, Willcutt, & Taub, 1999). The patients were ambulatory but with severe initial deficits: They spent most of their time in a wheelchair and reported that they never ambulated over distances greater than 5 feet. All six subjects improved substantially; their results were just as good as those of patients with chronic stroke after lower-extremity CI therapy.

In addition, five subjects with residual motor deficit after fractured hip and having no apparent organic basis for their disability were treated with the CI therapy lower extremity intervention. All five subjects improved substantially. This work shows that CI therapy has applicability not only after CNS damage but after substantial injury to any other system in the body, such as the skeletal system, where healing or recovery is sufficiently slow so that learned nonuse can supervene.

Speech in Persons with Aphasia

Aphasia arises as a consequence of focal brain damage, often in association with stroke. The demonstration that motor behavior is modifiable in patients with chronic stroke led us to believe that another consequence of stroke, language impairment (which often has an important motor component), might be sufficiently plastic to be rehabilitated by an appropriate modification of the CI therapy techniques used for rehabilitating movement of the extremities. In the first study (Pulvermüller et al., 2001), aphasic subjects with chronic stroke who had previously received extensive conventional speech therapy and had reached an apparent maximum in recovery of language function received CI aphasia therapy (CIAT) or perhaps more appropriately CI language therapy (CILT). They were induced to talk and improve their language skills three hours each weekday over a 2-week period. Groups of three patients and a therapist participated in language game activities in which success was achieved by progressively improving the naming of pictured objects and explicitly requesting that other participants conform to the rules of the game (Pulvermüller, 1990; Pulvermüller & Schonle, 1993). CILT patients in a randomized controlled trial improved significantly both in performance on laboratory tests of language ability and in the amount of talking they did in the life situation (Pulvermüller et al., 2001). The procedures employed in this work that were developed on the basis of the CI therapy model in motor rehabilitation were massing of practice, constraining patients to communicate using speech during the language game, shaping patients' speech during the game, and emphasis on measuring the patients' real-world behavior. This study has since been replicated and expanded on in a series of studies by Meinzer, Elbert, and coworkers (Meinzer et al., 2007) and by Maher and coworkers (2006).

Digital Coordination in Musicians with Focal Hand Dystonia

Focal hand dystonia is a condition involving manual incoordination that occurs in individuals, including musicians,

who engage in extensive and forceful use of the digits. To date, no treatments have been found to be effective on more than a temporary basis. Using magnetic source imaging, we found that musicians with focal hand dystonia exhibit a use-dependent overlap or smearing of the representational zones of the digits of the dystonic hand in the somatosensory cortex (Elbert et al., 1998; Elbert, Candia, Rockstroh, & Taub, 2000). Another laboratory has obtained similar results (Bara-Jimenez, Catalan, Hallett, & Gerloff, 1998). Digital overuse had previously been found to produce a similar phenomenon in monkeys in the laboratory of M. Merzenich. Since behavioral mechanisms apparently underlie both the cortical disorder and the involuntary incoordination of movement, we hypothesized that a behavioral intervention could reduce or eliminate both of these correlated abnormalities. The procedures employed in our treatment approach to focal hand dystonia (Candia et al., 1999, 2002) were derived in part from CI therapy.

Eight professional musicians (six pianists and two guitarists) with long-standing symptoms were studied. Our therapy involved immobilization by splint(s) of one or more of the digits other than the focal dystonic finger. The musicians were required to carry out repetitive exercises with the focal dystonic finger in coordination with one or more of the other digits for 1.5 to 2.5 hours daily (depending on patient fatigue) over a period of 8 consecutive days (14 days in one case) under therapist supervision. The practice was thus massed; practice of this intensity and duration was very taxing and was at the limit of the patients' capacity. After the end of the primary period of treatment, the patients continued practicing the exercises with the splint for 1 hour every day or every other day at home in combination with progressively longer periods of repertoire practice without the splint.

All patients showed significant and substantial improvements without the splint at the end of treatment in the smoothness of finger movement, as determined by a device that measured finger displacement, and self-reported dystonia symptoms. The improvement persisted for the 2 years of follow-up in all the patients but one who did not comply with home practice regimen prescribed. Half of the subjects have returned to the normal or almost normal range of digit function in music performance. The treatment is characterized as a form of CI therapy because it has all its main components: massed practice, the main elements of the TP, frequent feedback during exercises and shaping of improved finger movements, and restraint of a body part.

Phantom Limb Pain in Persons with an Upper Extremity Amputation

Weiss et al. (1999) studied the experience of phantom limb pain, nonpainful phantom limb sensation, and telescoping by questionnaire in a group of persons with upper extremity amputation wearing a functionally effective prosthesis that allowed extensive use of the residual limb, and in a group of patients wearing a cosmetic prosthesis that did little to increase the utilization of the amputation stump. We found that the functionally effective prosthesis group reported a significant and very large decrease in phantom limb pain. After obtaining the prosthesis, 9 of 11 patients reported a disappearance of phantom limb pain by the time of the study. In contrast, the cosmetic prosthesis group displayed a trend toward an increase in phantom limb pain over time. Neither group experienced a decrease in non-painful phantom limb sensation or telescoping.

As noted, work in collaboration with H. Flor and others had shown that the amount of phantom limb pain is strongly correlated with the amount of injury-related, afferent-decrease cortical reorganization (Birbaumer et al., 1997; Flor et al., 1995). It is possible that the increased use of the residual limb induced by wearing a functionally effective prosthesis produced a countervailing use-dependent afferent-increase type of cortical reorganization. This would have the effect of reducing the injury-related afferent-decrease cortical reorganization and would thereby reverse the phantom limb pain.

These preliminary results require replication and direct experimental test. Phantom limb pain has proved to be refractory to all the many therapeutic approaches tested to date. If the preliminary observations reported in this study are confirmed, the findings would suggest that it might be of value to fit persons with upper extremity amputation with functional prostheses to reduce the occurrence of phantom limb pain.

AN IMPENDING PARADIGM SHIFT

The relative dearth of effective interventions in neurorehabilitation may be attributable to the weak contribution from basic sciences such as behavioral psychology and neuroscience. These two disciplines arguably should have been the parent sciences of rehabilitation. Behavioral psychology has contributed much to the treatment of chronic pain (Fordyce, 1976), but has little or no place in the curriculum of physical therapy schools or in developing treatments for movement disorders. Neuroscience holds an important place in the curriculum of physical therapy schools, but its influence has been largely didactic and has had little bearing on clinical practice.

Other reasons for this lack of development have been discussed by investigators from within this field (Duncan, 1997; Horak, 1992; Shumway-Cook & Woollacott, 1995). In other health-related fields, basic research has been of inestimable value in enabling the development of new therapeutic interventions. CI therapy is a new approach to the rehabilitation of movement that, as noted at the beginning of this chapter, emerged directly from basic research in behavioral science and neuroscience. The success of this clinical technique is probably based importantly on its firm grounding in a body of replicated and generally accepted basic research.

However, CI therapy is not alone in this regard. Research involving CI therapy may constitute part of the leading edge of an impending paradigm shift in which other advances in behavioral science and neuroscience are employed for the development of new strategies in the fields of rehabilitation and remediation. An important case in point is the intervention for children with specific language impairments (SLI) and dyslexia developed by Merzenich, Tallal, and coworkers (Merzenich et al., 1996; Tallal et al., 1996). Children with SLI show limitations in a wide range of expressive and/or receptive oral language abilities revealed by poor vocabulary and deficits in syntax production or comprehension. Generally, children with SLI develop difficulties in reading, writing, and spelling (become dyslexic) despite having normal intellectual capacity and educational resources. The remedial treatment for SLI is derived in important part from basic research studies investigating language functions in SLI and dyslexic children. Psychoacoustic studies have revealed that auditory phoneme processing is deficient in many children with SLI and dyslexia (Reed, 1989; Stark & Heinz, 1996; Tallal & Piercy, 1974, 1975; Tallal & Stark, 1981; Tallal, Stark, & Mellits, 1985; for reviews, see Farmer & Klein, 1995; Tallal, Miller, & Fitch, 1993). SLI children have greater difficulty than children with normal language development in integrating brief and rapidly changing sounds, and therefore experience difficulties in discriminating stop consonant-vowel syllables with their short (40 ms) transitional periods. That this may constitute a basic impairment is supported by the fact that deficits in stop consonant perception are, in fact, highly correlated with language comprehension scores of SLI children (Tallal et al., 1985). The impairment can be overcome by synthetically extending the brief transitional periods (Tallal & Piercy, 1975).

Using the principles underlying neuroplasticity and cortical reorganization, Merzenich and Tallal designed a computer-based training program (FastForward) and demonstrated that impaired processing of rapidly changing sounds could be greatly improved in 5- to 10-year-old children with SLI (Merzenich et al., 1996; Tallal et al., 1996). Children were trained for about 100 min/day, 5 days a week for 20 training days with audiovisual games. Rapid transitional speech and nonspeech stimuli were initially made more discriminable by extending them in time and amplifying them. As training progressed and the children demonstrated success, the modified acoustic stimuli were presented in progressively less modified form until the stimuli approximated sounds as they occur in natural speech. Thus, as in the case of CI therapy, the training protocol involved a shaping procedure. Other training principles included in the therapy were that it had to be "applied with a heavy schedule" on successive days and "would require intense practice schedules" (massed practice, again as in CI therapy), and "high motivational drive" (Merzenich et al., 1996, p. 89). These elements originated in neuroplasticity studies, many of them carried out in Merzenich's own laboratory (Jenkins et al., 1990; Recanzone, Jenkins, et al., 1992; Recanzone, Merzenich, & Jenkins, 1992; Recanzone, Merzenich, Jenkins, et al., 1992). Seven percent of preschool children are estimated to suffer from SLI (Tomblin et al., 1997); prevalence estimates for dyslexia vary between 4% to 9% (Shaywitz, Shaywitz, Fletcher, & Escobar, 1990). Therefore, this treatment may be of benefit to large numbers of children (Merzenich, personal communication, November, 1998; Tallal, personal communication, March, 2000).

Both CI therapy and the intervention of Merzenich, Tallal, and coworkers for dyslexia depend in part on manipulations that produce a use-dependent alteration in task-related portions of the brain through the massed repetition of appropriate experiences. The potential for extending this approach to other conditions for which effective treatments do not at present exist has only begun to be tapped. It could well be a major new wave, just beginning to gather force, that may sweep the field of rehabilitation.

Another potentially significant therapeutic development derived from basic research is the development of devices that enable people to control their environment by biofeedback-aided self-regulation of the electrical activity of the brain. Birbaumer and coworkers have recently trained totally paralyzed "locked-in" individuals with amyotrophic lateral sclerosis (ALS) to first construct individual words and then complete messages, letter-by-letter, using a computer-based spelling program; a computer interface permitted the detection of self-regulated amplitude increases in the individual's slow cortical potentials (SCP) and triggered the execution of a command when the SCP amplitude exceeded a criterion level. The individuals with ALS were trained to regulate their brain activity using EEG biofeedback and shaping techniques (Birbaumer et al., 1999; Kuebler et al., 1999). The first report of this type of approach was from the laboratory of E. Donchin with healthy subjects in which letters were selected on the basis of the appearance of an enhanced P300 wave in the slow cortical potential elicited by the presentation of the desired letter in an alphabet set (Farwell & Donchin, 1988). Wolpaw and colleagues worked with the self-regulation of the sensorimotor rhythm in healthy and partially paralyzed subjects with ALS who still had extensive

control of their striate musculature (Wolpaw, Flotzinger, Pfurtscheller, & McFarland, 1997; Wolpaw & McFarland, 1994; Wolpaw, McFarland, Neat, & Forneris, 1991). A group at Johns Hopkins University has worked on techniques for enabling the self-regulation of electrical activity recorded from an electrode implanted directly in the brain (Kennedy & Bakay, 1998). These emerging techniques for controlling the environment by the self-regulation of brain activity have implications that are broader than providing a means of communication for individuals with total paralysis, as important as that goal is.

Another development stems from animal research in the laboratory of D. Feeney in which it was found that dextroamphetamine improves the recovery of function in rats after motor cortex lesions (Feeney, 1997; Feeney & Baron, 1986; Feeney, Gonzalez, & Law, 1982). Of particular interest is that this pharmacological intervention has an effect on recovery of function primarily when it is used in conjunction with one or another behavioral training paradigm. There are several studies in which an attempt has been made to use d-amphetamine to improve the rehabilitation of limb movement (Crisostomo, Duncan, Propst, Dawson, & Davis, 1988) or language function in aphasic patients (Walker-Batson, Smith, Curtis, Unwin, & Greenlee, 1995; Walker-Batson et al., 1992) after stroke. Other pharmacological approaches include the administration of methylphenidate in animals (Kline, Chen, Tso-Oliveras, & Feeney, 1994) and humans (Grade, Redford, Chrostowski, Toussaint, & Blackwell, 1998); glycine to enhance weight bearing and stepping in spinal cats (de Leon, Tamaki, Hodgson, Roy, & Edgerton, 1999); noradrenergic agonists to help initiate locomotion or increase treadmill speed in animals (Barbeau, Chau, & Rossignol, 1993; Barbeau & Rossignol, 1991) and humans with spinal cord injuries (Norman, Pepin, & Barbeau, 1998; Stewart, Barbeau, & Gauthier, 1991); serotonergic antagonists to increase weight bearing and treadmill speed in persons with SCI (Norman et al., 1998; Wainberg, Barbeau, & Gauthier, 1990); and combinations of drugs to enhance ambulatory activity (e.g., serotonin and N-methyl-D-L-aspartate in neonatal rats, Bertrand & Cazalets, 1998; and clonidine and cyproheptadine in persons with SCI, Fung, Stewart, & Barbeau, 1990).

These studies are mainly preliminary; they involve small numbers of patients and do not include the controls that will be appropriate when this field is more mature. However, taken together and in conjunction with the animal research, these early results are suggestive and exciting. CI therapy has potential value in this type of experimental enterprise. It is one of the few rehabilitation treatments for which there is controlled evidence of efficacy (Duncan, 1997; Wolf et al., 2006, 2008), and the animal research shows that an effective behavioral method for improving function is of importance as a substrate, so to speak, for the effectiveness of the pharmacological intervention.

There has been a long history of research on enabling the regeneration of neural tissue within the mammalian CNS after neurological injury so that new and functional synaptic connections could be formed that would provide a basis for improved function. The work in this area has now entered a very promising phase. Here, again, the improvements in function that have been observed in animals come largely in connection with the concomitant use of behavioral techniques. The recent discovery that undifferentiated stem cells exist in the mature mammalian nervous system that are capable of assuming the role of many different types of CNS cell types, during learning, exercise, and after loss due to injury, opens up new vistas in this area.

The investigation of the effect of enriched environments on the central nervous system is another area of research that has a long history with promise of important practical applications for remediation and rehabilitation. Most of the basic animal research has been on the ways in which environmental enrichment can greatly enhance the development of the immature nervous system. The work of C. T. and S. L. Ramey has shown that use of a comprehensively enriched environment starting at an early age (e.g., 1 year) can increase IQ by a mean of 15 points in children from disadvantaged homes compared with control children (Ramey & Ramey, 1998a, 1998b). In the area of rehabilitation, Fischer and Peduzzi (1997) have shown that enriching the environment of rats with novel objects and pathways to explore can substantially improve hind-limb function after spinal cord injury.

From this brief summary, it is evident that most of these new or promising treatments in the fields of rehabilitation and remediation either (a) emerge from behavioral research or research in behavior and neuroscience, (b) involve behavioral techniques in conjunction with other types of interventions, or (c) make use of behavioral methods to produce an advantageous effect on the nervous system. These approaches are not entirely new, but their explicit formulation and the effectiveness with which they are currently being applied to the enhancement of impaired human abilities are new. It is this development that we feel justifies the designation of these approaches as an impending paradigm shift in the field of rehabilitation.

REFERENCES

Andrews, K., & Stewart, J. (1979). Stroke recovery: He can but does he? *Rheumatology and Rehabilitation, 18*, 43–48.

Azrin, N. H., & Holz, W. C. (1966). Punishment. In W. K. Honig (Ed.), *Operant behavior: Areas of research and application* (pp. 380–447). New York: Appleton-Century-Crofts.

Bara-Jimenez, W., Catalan, M. J., Hallett, M., & Gerloff, C. (1998). Abnormal somatosensory homunculus in dystonia of the hand. *Annals of Neurology, 44*, 828–831.

Barbeau, H., Chau, C., & Rossignol, S. (1993). Noradrenergic agonists and locomotor training affect locomotor recovery after cord transection in adult cats. *Brain Research Bulletin, 30*, 387–393.

Barbeau, H., & Rossignol, S. (1991). Initiation and modulation of the locomotor pattern in the adult chronic spinal cat by noradrenergic, serotonergic, and dopaminergic drugs. *Brain Research, 546*, 250–260.

Bard, G., & Hirschberg, G. G. (1965). Recovery of voluntary movement in upper extremity following hemiplegia. *Archives of Physical Medicine and Rehabilitation, 46*, 567–572.

Bauder, H., Balzer, C., Miltner, W. H. R., & Taub, E. (1999). *Change in movement-related cortical potentials following CI therapy after stroke.* Manuscript submitted for publication.

Bauder, H., Sommer, M., Taub, E., & Miltner, W. H. R. (1999). Effect of CI therapy on movement-related brain potentials. *Psychophysiology, 36*(Suppl, 1), S31 (Abstract).

Bertrand, S., & Cazalets, J.-R. (1998). GABA-A and GABA-B modulations of synaptic transmission between L1–L2 locomotor network and the motorneurons in the newborn rat isolated spinal cord. *Annals of the New York Academy of Sciences, 860*, 470–471.

Birbaumer, N., Ghanayim, N., Hinterberger, T., Iverson, S., Kotchoubey, B., Kubler, A., et al. (1999, March 25). A spelling device for the paralyzed. *Nature, 398*, 297–298.

Birbaumer, N., Lutzenberger, W., Montoya, P., Larbig, W., Unertl, K., Topfner, S., et al. (1997). Effects of regional anesthesia on phantom limb pain are mirrored in changes in cortical reorganization. *Journal of Neuroscience, 17*, 5503–5508.

Braun, C., Schweizer, R., Elbert, T., Birbaumer, N., & Taub, E. (2000). Differential activation in somatosensory cortex for different discrimination tasks. *Journal of Neuroscience, 20*, 446–450.

Briones, T. L., Suh, E., Jozsa, L., & Woods, J. (2006). Behaviorally induced synaptogenesis and dendritic growth in the hippocampal region following transient global cerebral ischemia are accompanied by improvement in spatial learning. *Experimental Neurology, 198*, 530–538.

Broca, P. (1861). Nouvelle observation d'aphemie produite par une lesion de la motie posterieure des deuxieme et troisieme circonvulutions frontales [New observations on aphasia produced by a lesion of the posterior portion of the second and third frontal gyri]. *Bulletin de la Societe Anatomique de Paris, 6*, 398–407.

Butefisch, C., Hummelsheim, H., Kenzler, P., & Mauritz, K.-H. (1995). Repetitive training of isolated movements improves the outcome of motor rehabilitation of the centrally paretic hand. *Journal of Neurological Sciences, 130*, 59–68.

Candia, V., Elbert, T., Altenmüller, E., Rau, H., Schäfer, T., & Taub, E. (1999). Constraint-induced movement therapy for focal hand dystonia in musicians. *Lancet, 353*, 42.

Candia, V., Schafer, T., Taub, E., Rau, H., Altenmuller, E., Rockstroh, B., et al. (2002). Sensory motor retuning: A behavioral treatment for focal hand dystonia of pianists and guitarists. *Archives of Physical Medicine and Rehabilitation, 83*, 1342–1348.

Catania, A. C. (1998). *Learning* (4th ed.). Upper Saddle River, NJ: Prentice-Hall.

Chambers, W. W., Konorski, J., Liu, C. N., Yu, J., & Anderson, R. (1972). The effects of cerebellar lesions upon skilled movements and instrumental conditioned reflexes. *Acta Neurobiologiae Experimentalis, 32*, 721–732.

Cohen, J. (1988). *Statistical power analysis for the behavioral sciences* (2nd ed.). Hillsdale, NJ: Erlbaum.

Crisostomo, E. A., Duncan, P. W., Propst, M. A., Dawson, D. V., & Davis, J. N. (1988). Evidence that amphetamine with physical therapy promotes recovery of motor function in stroke patients. *Annals of Neurology, 23*, 94–97.

DeBow, S. B., Davies, M. L. A., Clarke, H. L., & Colbourne, F. (2003). Constraint-induced movement therapy and rehabilitation exercises lessen motor deficits and volume of brain injury after striatal hemorrhagic stroke in rats. *Stroke, 34*, 1021–1026.

de Leon, R. D., Tamaki, H., Hodgson, J. A., Roy, R. R., & Edgerton, V. R. (1999). Hindlimb locomotor and postural training modulates glycinergic inhibition in the spinal cord of the adult spinal cat. *Journal of Neurophysiology, 82*, 359–369.

Dettmers, C., Teske, U., Hamzei, F., Uswatte, G., Taub, E., & Weiller, C. (2005). Distributed form of constraint-induced movement therapy improves functional outcome and quality of life after stroke. *Archives of Physical Medicine and Rehabilitation, 86*, 204–209.

Dostrovsky, J. O., Millar, J., & Wall, P. D. (1976). The immediate shift of afferent drive to dorsal column nucleus cells following deafferentation: A comparison of acute and chronic deafferentation in gracile nucleus and spinal cord. *Experimental Neurology, 52*, 480–495.

Draganski, B., Gaser, C., Busch, V., Schuierer, G., Bogdahn, U., & May, A. (2004, January 22). Changes in grey matter induced by training. *Nature, 427*, 311–312.

Draganski, B., Moser, T., Lummel, N., Ganssbauer, S., Bogdahn, U., Haas, F., et al. (2006). Decrease of thalamic gray matter following limb amputation. *NeuroImage, 31*, 951–957.

Duncan, P. W. (1997). Synthesis of intervention trials to improve motor recovery following stroke. *Topics in Stroke Rehabilitation, 3*, 1–20.

Elbert, T., Candia, B., Altenmuller, E., Rau, H., Sterr, A., Rockstroh, B., et al. (1998). Alteration of digital representations in somatosensory cortex in focal hand dystonia. *NeuroReport, 9*, 3571–3575.

Elbert, T., Candia, V., Rockstroh, B., & Taub, E. (2000, March). *Maladaptive use-dependent cortical reorganization: Smearing of the somatotopy in individuals with focal hand dystonia reverses after successful treatment.* Paper presented at the Third Berlin Workshop on Cortical Plasticity, Berlin, Germany.

Elbert, T., Flor, H., Birbaumer, N., Knecht, S., Hampson, S., Larbig, W., et al. (1994). Extensive reorganization of the somatosensory cortex in adult humans after nervous system injury. *NeuroReport, 5*, 2593–2597.

Elbert, T., Pantev, C., Wienbruch, C., Rockstroh, B., & Taub, E. (1995, October 13). Increased cortical representation of the fingers of the left hand in string players. *Science, 270*, 305–307.

Elbert, T., Sterr, A., Flor, H., Rockstroh, B., Knecht, S., Pantev, C., et al. (1997). Input-increase and input-decrease types of cortical reorganization after upper extremity amputation in humans. *Experimental Brain Research, 117*, 161–164.

Eriksson, P. S., Perfilieva, E., Bjork-Eriksson, T., Alborn, A. M., Nordborg, C., & Peterson, D. A. (1998). Neurogenesis in the adult human hippocampus. *Natural Medicine, 4*, 1313–1317.

Estes, W. K. (1944). An experimental study of punishment. *Psychological Monographs, 57*(Serial No. 263).

Farmer, M. E., & Klein, R. M. (1995). The evidence for a temporal processing deficit linked to dyslexia: A review. *Psychonomic Bulletin and Review, 2*, 460–493.

Farwell, L. A., & Donchin, E. (1988). Talking off the top of your head: Toward a mental prosthesis utilizing event-related brain potentials. *Electroencephalography and Clinical Neurophysiology, 70*, 510–523.

Feeney, D. M. (1997). From laboratory to clinic: Noradrenergic enhancement of physical therapy for stroke or trauma patients. In H. J. Freund, B. A. Sabel, & O. W. Witte (Eds.), *Brain plasticity: Advances in neurology* (Vol. 73, pp. 383–394). Philadelphia: Lippencott-Raven.

Feeney, D. M., & Baron, J. (1986). Diaschisis. *Stroke, 17*, 817–830.

Feeney, D. M., Gonzalez, A., & Law, W. A. (1982). Amphetamine, haloperidol and experience interact to affect rate of recovery after motor cortex injury. *Science, 217*, 855–857.

Fischer, F. R., & Peduzzi, J. D. (1997). Functional improvement in rats with chronic spinal cord injuries after exposure to an enriched environment [Abstract]. *Society for Neuroscience Abstracts, 23*, 2188.

Fleurens, P. (1842). *Recherches experimentales sur les propietes et les functions du systeme neurveux dans les animaux [Experiments on the properties and functions of the nervous system of animals]* (2nd ed.). Paris: Belliere.

Flor, H., Elbert, T., Knecht, S., Wienbruch, C., Pantev, C., Birbaumer, N., et al. (1995, June 8). Phantom limb pain as a perceptual correlate of massive reorganization in upper limb amputees. *Nature, 375*, 482–484.

Fordyce, W. E. (1976). *Behavioral methods for chronic pain and illness.* St. Louis, MO: Mosby.

Fritsch, G., & Hitzig, E. (1870). Über die electrische erregbarkeit des grosshirns [On the electrical excitability of the cerebral cortex]. *Archiv für Anatomie und Physiologie, 37*, 300–332.

Fung, J., Stewart, J. E., & Barbeau, H. (1990). The combined effects of clonidine and cyproheptadine with interactice training on the modulation of locomotion in spinal cord injured subjects. *Journal of the Neurological Sciences, 100*, 85–93.

Gauthier, L. V., Taub, E., Perkins, C., Ortmann, M., Mark, V. W., & Uswatte, G. (2008). Remodeling the brain: Plastic structural brain changes produced by different motor therapies after stroke. *Stroke, 39*, 1520–1525.

Grade, C., Redford, B., Chrostowski, J., Toussaint, L., & Blackwell, B. (1998). Methylphenidate in early poststroke recovery: A double-blind, placebo-control study. *Archives of Physical Medicine and Rehabilitation, 79*, 1047–1050.

Halberstam, J. L., Zaretsky, H. H., Brucker, B. S., & Guttman, A. (1971). Avoidance conditioning of motor responses in elderly brain-damaged patients. *Archives of Physical Medicine and Rehabilitation, 52*, 318–328.

Horak, K. (1992). Assumptions underlying motor control for neurologic rehabilitation. In *Contemporary management of motor control problems: Proceedings of the II step conference* (pp. 11–28). Alexandria, VA: American Physical Therapy Association.

Hubel, D. H., & Wiesel, T. N. J. (1970). The period of susceptibility to the physiological effects of unilateral eye closure in kittens. *Journal of Physiology, 206*, 419–436.

Ince, L. P. (1969). Escape and avoidance conditioning of response in the plegic arm of stroke patients: A preliminary study. *Psychonomic Science, 16*, 49–50.

Jackson, J. H. (1873). On the anatomical and physiological localization of movements in the brain. *Lancet, 1*, 84–85, 162–164, 232–234.

Jackson, J. H. (1884). Evolution and dissolution of the nervous system (the Croonian Lectures). *British Medical Journal, 1*, 591–754.

Jenkins, W. M., Merzenich, M. M., Ochs, M. T., Allard, T., & Guic-Robles, E. (1990). Functional reorganization of primary somatosensory cortex in adult owl monkeys after behaviorally controlled tactile stimulation. *Journal of Neurophysiology, 63*, 82–104.

Kaas, J. H. (1995, June 29). Neurobiology: How cortex reorganizes [news; comment]. *Nature, 375*, 735–736.

Kaas, J. H., Merzenich, M. M., & Killackey, H. P. (1983). The reorganization of somatosensory cortex following peripheral nerve damage in adult and developing mammals. *Annual Review of Neuroscience, 6*, 325–356.

Kennedy, P. R., & Bakay, R. A. E. (1998). Restoration of neural output from a paralyzed patient by a direct brain connection. *NeuroReport, 9*, 1707–1711.

King, D. K., Willcutt, C., & Taub, E. (1999). [CI therapy: Application to the lower extremities in spinal cord injury patients]. Unpublished raw data.

Kline, A. E., Chen, M. J., Tso-Oliveras, D. Y., & Feeney, D. M. (1994). Methylphenidate treatment following ablation induced hemiplegia: Experience during drug action alters effects on recovery of function. *Phamacology, Biochemistry and Behavior, 48*, 773–779.

Knapp, H. D., Taub, E., & Berman, A. J. (1958, October 10). Effects of deafferentation on a conditioned avoidance response. *Science, 128*, 842–843.

Knapp, H. D., Taub, E., & Berman, A. J. (1963). Movements in monkeys with deafferented limbs. *Experimental Neurology, 7*, 305–315.

Kolb, B., Morshead, C., Gonzalez, C., Kim, M., Gregg, C., Shingo, T., et al. (2007). Growth factor-stimulated generation of new cortical tissue and functional recovery after stroke damage to the motor cortex of rats. *Journal of Cerebral Blood Flow and Metabolism, 27*, 983–997.

Kopp, B., Kunkel, A., Flor, H., Platz, T., Rose, U., Mauritz, K.-H., et al. (1997). The Arm Motor Ability Test (AMAT): Reliability, validity, and sensitivity to change of an instrument for assessing ADL disability. *Archives of Physical Medicine and Rehabilitation, 78*, 615–620.

Kopp, B., Kunkel, A., Mühlnickel, W., Villringer, K., Taub, E., & Flor, H. (1999). Plasticity in the motor system related to therapy-induced improvement of movement after stroke. *NeuroReport, 10*, 807–810.

Kuebler, A., Kotchoubey, B., Hinterberger, T., Ghanayim, N., Perelmouter, J., Schauer, M., et al. (1999). The thought translation device: A neurophysiological approach to communication in total motor paralysis. *Experimental Brain Research, 124*, 223–232.

Kunkel, A., Kopp, B., Muller, G., Villringer, K., Villringer, A., Taub, E., et al. (1999). Constraint-induced movement therapy for motor recovery in stroke patients. *Archives of Physical Medicine and Rehabilitation, 80*, 624–628.

Lashley, K. S. (1924). Studies of cerebral function in learning: Pt. V. The retention of motor areas in primates. *Archives of Neurological Psychiatry, 12*, 249–276.

Lashley, K. S. (1938). Factors limiting recovery after central nervous lesions. *Journal of Nervous and Mental Diseases, 88*, 733–755.

Lassek, A. M. (1953). Inactivation of voluntary motor function following rhizotomy. *Journal of Neuropathology and Experimental Neurology, 3*, 83–87.

Liepert, J., Bauder, H., Miltner, W. H. R., Taub, E., & Weiller, C. (2000). Treatment-induced cortical reorganization after stroke in humans. *Stroke, 31*, 1210–1216.

Liepert, J., Bauder, H., Sommer, M., Miltner, W. H. R., Dettmers, C., Taub, E., et al. (1998). Motor cortex plasticity during Constraint-induced movement therapy in chronic stroke patients. *Neuroscience Letters, 250*, 5–8.

Lum, P. S., Taub, E., Schwandt, D., Postman, M., Hardin, P., & Uswatte, G. (2004). Automated constraint-induced therapy extension (AutoCITE) for movement deficits after stroke. *Journal of Rehabilitation Research and Development, 41*, 249–258.

Maguire, E. A., Gadian, D. G., Johnsrude, I. S., Good, C. D., Ashburner, J., Frackowiak, R. S. J., et al. (2000). Navigation-related structural change in the hippocampi of taxi drivers. *Proceedings of the National Academy of Sciences, USA, 97*, 4398–4403.

Maher, L. M., Kendall, D., Swearengin, J. A., Rodriguez, A., Leon, S. A., Pingel, K., et al. (2006). A pilot study of use-dependent learning in the context of constraint induced language therapy. *Journal of the International Neuropsychological Society, 12*, 843–852.

Mark, V., Taub, E., Bashir, K., Uswatte, G., Delgado, A., Bowman, M. H., et al. (2008). Constraint-induced movement therapy for hemiparetic progressive multiple sclerosis: Preliminary results. *Multiple Sclerosis, 14*, 992–994.

McCulloch, K., Cook, E. W., III., Fleming, W. C., Novack, T. A., Nepomuceno, C. S., & Taub, E. (1988). A reliable test of upper extremity ADL function [Abstract]. *Archives of Physical Medicine and Rehabilitation, 69*, 755.

Meinzer, M., Elbert, T., Barthel, G., Djundja, D., Taub, E., & Rockstroh, B. (2007). Extending the constraint-induced movement therapy (CIMT) approach to cognitive functions: Constraint-induced aphasia therapy (CIAT) of chronic aphasia. *Neurorehabilitation, 22*, 311–318.

Merzenich, M. M., Jenkins, W. M., Johnston, P., Schreiner, C., Miller, S. L., & Tallal, P. (1996, January 5). Temporal processing deficits of language-learning impaired children ameliorated by training. *Science, 271*, 77–80.

Merzenich, M. M., Kaas, J. H., Wall, J., Nelson, R. J., Sur, M., & Felleman, D. (1983). Topographic reorganization of somatosensory cortical areas 3b and 1 in adult monkeys following restricted deafferentation. *Neuroscience, 8*, 33–55.

Merzenich, M. M., Nelson, R. J., Stryker, M. P., Cynader, M. S., Schoppman, A., & Zook, J. M. (1984). Somatosensory cortical map changes following digit amputation in adult monkeys. *Journal of Comparative Neurology, 224*, 591–605.

Miltner, W. H. R., Bauder, H., Sommer, M., Dettmers, C., & Taub, E. (1999). Effects of constraint-induced movement therapy on chronic stroke patients: A replication. *Stroke, 30*, 586–592.

Morgan, W. G. (1974). The shaping game: A teaching technique. *Behavior Therapy, 5*, 271–272.

Morris, D., Shaw, S., Mark, V., Uswatte, G., Barman, J., & Taub, E. (2006). The influence of neuropsychological characteristics on the use of CI therapy with persons with traumatic brain injury. *Neurorehabilitation, 21*, 131–137.

Morris, D., Taub, E., & Mark, V. (2006). Constraint-induced movement therapy (CI therapy): Characterizing the intervention protocol. *Europa Medicophysica, 42*, 257–268.

Morris, D., Uswatte, G., Crago, J., Cook, E. W., III., & Taub, E. (2001). The reliability of the Wolf Motor Function Test for assessing upper extremity motor function following stroke. *Archives of Physical Medicine and Rehabilitation, 82*, 750–755.

Mott, F. W., & Sherrington, C. S. (1885). Experiments upon the influence of sensory nerves upon movement and nutrition of the limbs. *Proceedings of the Royal Society of London, 57*, 481–488.

Mühlnickel, W., Elbert, T., Taub, E., & Flor, H. (1998). Reorganization of primary auditory cortex in tinnitus. *Proceedings of the National Academy of Sciences, USA, 95*, 10340–10343.

Munk, H. (1881). *Über die funktionen der grosshirnrinde, gesammelte mitteilungen aus den jahren 1877–1880 [On the functions of the cerebral cortex, collected writing from the years 1877–1880].* Berlin, Germany: Hirshwald.

Norman, K. E., Pepin, A., & Barbeau, H. (1998). Effects of drugs on walking after spinal cord injury. *Spinal Cord, 36*, 699–715.

Nudo, R. J., Wise, B. M., SiFuentes, F., & Milliken, G. W. (1996, June 21). Neural substrates for the effects of rehabilitative training on motor recovery after ischemic infarct. *Science, 272*, 1791–1794.

Ogden, R., & Franz, S. I. (1917). On cerebral motor control: The recovery from experimentally produced hemiplegia. *Psychobiology, 1*, 33–47.

Ostendorf, C. G., & Wolf, S. L. (1981). Effect of forced use of the upper extremity of a hemiplegic patient on changes in function: A single-case design. *Physical Therapy, 61*, 1022–1028.

Page, S., Sisto, S., Levine, P., & McGrath, E. (2004). Efficacy of modified constraint-induced movement therapy in chronic stroke: A single-blinded randomized controlled trial. *Archives of Physical Medicine and Rehabilitation, 85*, 14–18.

Panyan, M. V. (1980). *How to use shaping.* Lawrence, KS: H & H Enterprises.

Parker, V. M., Wade, D. T., & Langton-Hewer, R. (1986). Loss of arm function after stroke: Measurement, frequency, and recovery. *International Journal of Rehabilitation Medicine, 8*, 69–73.

Pons, T. P., Garraghty, A. K., Ommaya, A. K., Kaas, J. H., Taub, E., & Mishkin, M. (1991, June 28). Massive cortical reorganization after sensory deafferentation in adult macaques. *Science, 252*, 1857–1860.

Pulvermüller, F. (1990). *Aphasische kommunikation: Grundfragen ihrer analyse und therapie [Communication in aphasics: Basic questions and therapeutic approaches].* Tuebingen, Germany: Gunter Narr Verlag.

Pulvermüller, F., Neininger, B., Elbert, T., Mohr, B., Rockstroh, B., Köbbel, P., et al. (2001). Constraint-induced therapy of chronic aphasia following stroke. *Stroke, 32,* 1621–1626.

Pulvermüller, F., & Schonle, P. (1993). Behavioral and neuronal changes during treatment of mixed transcortical aphasia. *Cognition, 48,* 139–161.

Ramey, C. T., & Ramey, S. L. (1998a). Early intervention and early experience. *American Psychologist, 53,* 109–120.

Ramey, C. T., & Ramey, S. L. (1998b). Prevention of intellectual disabilities: Early interventions to improve cognitive development. *Preventive Medicine, 27,* 224–232.

Recanzone, G. H., Jenkins, W. M., & Merzenich, M. M. (1992). Progressive improvement in discriminative abilities in adult owl monkeys performing a tactile frequency discrimination task. *Journal of Neurophysiology, 67,* 1015–1030.

Recanzone, G. H., Merzenich, M. M., & Jenkins, W. M. (1992). Frequency discrimination training engaging a restricted skin surface results in an emergence of a cutaneous response zone in cortical area 3a. *Journal of Neurophysiology, 67,* 1057–1070.

Recanzone, G. H., Merzenich, M. M., Jenkins, W. M., Grajski, A., & Dinse, H. R. (1992). Topographic reorganization of the hand representation in area 3b of owl monkeys trained in a frequency discrimination task. *Journal of Neurophysiology, 67,* 1031–1056.

Reed, M. A. (1989). Speech perception and the discrimination of brief auditory cues in reading disabled children. *Journal of Experimental Child Psychology, 48,* 270–292.

Risley, T. R., & Baer, D. M. (1973). Operant behavior modification: The deliberate development of behavior. In M. Caldwell & H. N. Riccuiti (Eds.), *Review of child development research: Development and social action* (Vol. 3, pp. 283–329). Chicago: University of Chicago Press.

Ruch, T. C. (1960). The cerebral cortex: Its structure and motor functions. In T. C. Ruch & J. F. Fulton (Eds.), *Medical physiology and biophysics* (18th ed., pp. 249–276). Philadelphia: Saunders.

Schmidt, R. A., & Lee, T. D. (1999). Conditions of practice. *Motor control and learning: A behavioral emphasis* (3rd ed., pp. 285–321). Champaign, IL: Human Kinetics.

Shaw, S. E., Morris, D. M., Uswatte, G., McKay, S., Meythaler, J. M., & Taub, E. (2005). Constraint-induced movement therapy for recovery of upper-limb function following traumatic brain injury. *Journal of Rehabilitation Research and Development, 42,* 769–778.

Shaw, S. E., Morris, D. M., Yakley, S. R., McKay, S. B., & Taub, E. (2000, June). *Constraint induced movement therapy to improve upper extremity function in subjects following traumatic brain injury: A case study.* Paper presented at Physical Therapy 2000: APTA Scientific Meeting and Exposition, Indianapolis, IN.

Shaywitz, S. E., Shaywitz, B. A., Fletcher, J. M., & Escobar, M. D. (1990). Prevalence of reading disability in boys and girls: Results of the Connecticut Longitudinal Study. *Journal of the American Medical Association, 264,* 998–1002.

Sherrington, C. S. (1910). Remarks on the reflex mechanism of the step. *Brain, 33,* 1–25.

Sherrington, C. S. (1913). Further observations on the production of reflex stepping by combination of reflex excitation with reflex inhibition. *Journal of Physiology, 47,* 196–214.

Sherrington, C. S. (1931). Quantitative management of contraction in lowest level coordination. *Brain, 54,* 1–28.

Shumway-Cook, A., & Woollacott, M. H. (1995). *Motor control: Theory and practical applications.* Baltimore: Williams & Wilkins.

Skinner, B. F. (1938). *The behavior of organisms.* New York: Appleton-Century-Crofts.

Skinner, B. F. (1968). *The technology of teaching.* New York: Appleton-Century-Crofts.

Stark, R. E., & Heinz, J. M. (1996). Perception of stop consonants in children with expressive and receptive-expressive language impairments. *Journal of Speech and Hearing Research, 39,* 676–686.

Sterr, A., Elbert, T., Berthold, I., Kölbel, S., Rockstroh, B., & Taub, E. (2002). CI therapy in chronic hemiparesis: The more the better? *Archives of Physical Medicine and Rehabilitation, 83,* 1374–1377.

Sterr, A., Mueller, M., Elbert, T., Rockstroh, B., Pantev, C., & Taub, E. (1998, January 8). Changed perceptions in braille readers. *Nature, 391,* 134–135.

Sterr, A., Mueller, M., Elbert, T., & Taub, E. (1998). Perceptual correlates of use-dependent changes in cortical representation of the fingers in blind braille readers. *Journal of Neuroscience, 18,* 4417–4423.

Stewart, J. E., Barbeau, H., & Gauthier, S. (1991). Modulation of locomotor patterns and spasticity with clonidine in spinal cord injured patients. *Canadian Journal of Neurological Sciences, 18,* 321–332.

Tallal, P., Miller, S., Bedi, G., Byma, G., Wang, X., Srikantan, S., et al. (1996, January 5). Language comprehension in language-learning impaired children improved with acoustically modified speech. *Science, 271,* 81–84.

Tallal, P., Miller, S., & Fitch, R. H. (1993). Untitled. In P. Tallal, A. M. Galaburda, R. R. Llinas, & C. von Euler (Eds.), *Temporal information processing in the nervous system: Special reference to dyslexia and dysphagia* (pp. 27–47). New York: New York Academy of Sciences.

Tallal, P., & Piercy, M. (1974). Developmental aphasia: Rate of auditory processing and selective impairment of consonant perception. *Neuropsychologia, 12,* 83–93.

Tallal, P., & Piercy, M. (1975). Developmental aphasia: The perception of brief vowels and extended stop consonants. *Neuropsychologia, 13,* 69–74.

Tallal, P., & Stark, R. E. (1981). Speech acoustic-cue discrimination abilities of normally developing and language impaired children. *Journal of the Acoustical Society of America, 69,* 568–574.

Tallal, P., Stark, R. E., & Mellits, E. D. (1985). Identification of language-impaired children on the basis of rapid perception and production skills. *Brain and Language, 25,* 314–322.

Taub, E. (1976). Motor behavior following deafferentation in the developing and motorically mature monkey. In R. Herman, S. Grillner, H. J. Ralston, P. S. G. Stein, & D. Stuart (Eds.), *Neural control of locomotion* (pp. 675–705). New York: Plenum Press.

Taub, E. (1977a). Deafferentation techniques in the investigation of sensory-motor integration. In D. M. Landers & R. W. Christina (Eds.), *Motor behavior* (Vol. 1, pp. 207–213). Champaign, IL: Human Kinetics.

Taub, E. (1977b). Movement in nonhuman primates deprived of somatosensory feedback. In *Exercise and sports science reviews* (Vol. 4, pp. 335–374).

Taub, E. (1980). Somatosensory deafferentation research with monkeys: Implications for rehabilitation medicine. In L. P. Ince (Ed.), *Behavioral psychology in rehabilitation medicine: Clinical applications* (pp. 371–401). New York: Williams & Wilkins.

Taub, E. (1994). Overcoming learned nonuse: A new behavioral medicine approach to physical medicine. In J. G. Carlson, S. R. Seifert, & N. Birbaumer (Eds.), *Clinical applied psychophysiology* (pp. 185–220). New York: Plenum Press.

Taub, E., Bacon, R., & Berman, A. J. (1965). The acquisition of a trace-conditioned avoidance response after deafferentation of the responding limb. *Journal of Comparative and Physiological Psychology, 58,* 275–279.

Taub, E., & Berman, A. J. (1963). Avoidance conditioning in the absence of relevant proprioceptive and exteroceptive feedback. *Journal of Comparative and Physiological Psychology, 56,* 1012–1016.

Taub, E., & Berman, A. J. (1968). Movement and learning in the absence of sensory feedback. In S. J. Freedman (Ed.), *The neuropsychology of spatially oriented behavior* (pp. 173–192). Homewood, IL: Dorsey Press.

Taub, E., Burgio, L., Miller, N. E., Cook, E. W., Groomes, T., DeLuca, S., et al. (1994). An operant approach to overcoming learned nonuse after CNS damage in monkeys and man: The role of shaping. *Journal of the Experimental Analysis of Behavior, 61,* 281–293.

Taub, E., & Crago, J. (1995). Behavioral plasticity following central nervous system damage in monkeys and man. In B. Julesz & I. Kovacs (Eds.), *Maturational windows and adult cortical plasticity: SFI studies in the sciences of complexity* (Vol. 23, pp. 201–215). Redwood City, CA: Addison-Wesley.

Taub, E., Crago, J., & Uswatte, G. (1998). Constraint-induced movement therapy: A new approach to treatment in physical rehabilitation. *Rehabilitation Psychology, 43,* 152–170.

Taub, E., Ellman, S. J., & Berman, A. J. (1966, February 4). Deafferentation in monkeys: Effect on conditioned grasp response. *Science, 151,* 593–594.

Taub, E., Flor, H., Knecht, S., & Elbert, T. (1995). Correlation between phantom limb pain and cortical reorganization. *Journal of NIH Research, 7,* 49–50.

Taub, E., Goldberg, I. A., & Taub, P. B. (1975). Deafferentation in monkeys: Pointing at a target without visual feedback. *Experimental Neurology, 46,* 178–186.

Taub, E., Griffin, A., Gammons, K., Nick, J., Uswatte, G., & Law, C. R. (2006, October). *CI therapy for young children with congenital hemiparesis.* Paper presented at the Society for Neuroscience, Atlanta, GA.

Taub, E., Lum, P. S., Hardin, P., Mark, V., & Uswatte, G. (2005). AutoCITE: Automated delivery of CI therapy with reduced effort by therapists. *Stroke, 36,* 1301–1304.

Taub, E., Miller, N. E., Novack, T. A., Cook, E. W., Fleming, W. C., Nepomuceno, C. S., et al. (1993). Technique to improve chronic motor deficit after stroke. *Archives of Physical Medicine and Rehabilitation, 74,* 347–354.

Taub, E., Perrella, P. N., & Barro, G. (1973, September 7). Behavioral development following forelimb deafferentation on day of birth in monkeys with and without blinding. *Science, 181,* 959–960.

Taub, E., Perrella, P. N., Miller, D., & Barro, G. (1975). Diminution of early environmental control through perinatal and prenatal somatosensory deafferentation. *Biological Psychiatry, 10,* 609–626.

Taub, E., Pidikiti, R., DeLuca, S., & Crago, J. (1996). Effects of motor restriction of an unimpaired upper extremity and training on improving functional tasks and altering brain/behaviors. In J. Toole (Ed.), *Imaging and neurologic rehabilitation* (pp. 133–154). New York: Demos.

Taub, E., Pidikiti, R., Uswatte, G., Shaw, S., & Yakley, S. (1998). Constraint-induced (CI) movement therapy: Application to lower functioning stroke patients [Abstract]. *Society for Neuroscience Abstracts, 24,* 1769.

Taub, E., Ramey, S. L., DeLuca, S., & Echols, E. (2004). Efficacy of constraint-induced (CI) movement therapy for children with cerebral palsy with asymmetric motor impairment. *Pediatrics, 113,* 305–312.

Taub, E., & Uswatte, G. (2000). Constraint-induced movement therapy: Rehabilitation based on behavioral neuroscience. In R. G. Frank & T. R. Elliott (Eds.), *Handbook of rehabilitation psychology* (pp. 475–496). Washington, DC: American Psychological Association.

Taub, E., Uswatte, G., King, D. K., Morris, D., Crago, J., & Chatterjee, A. (2006). A placebo controlled trial of constraint-induced movement therapy for upper extremity after stroke. *Stroke, 37,* 1045–1049.

Taub, E., Uswatte, G., Mark, V., & Morris, D. (2006). The learned nonuse phenomenon: Implications for rehabilitation. *Europa Medicophysica, 42,* 241–255.

Taub, E., Uswatte, G., & Pidikiti, R. (1999). Constraint-induced movement therapy: A new family of techniques with broad application to physical rehabilitation: A clinical review. *Journal of Rehabilitation Research and Development, 36,* 237–251.

Taub, E., Williams, E., Barro, G., & Steiner, S. S. (1978). Comparison of the performance of deafferented and intact monkeys on continuous and fixed ratio schedules of reinforcement. *Experimental Neurology, 58,* 1–13.

Tomblin, J. B., Records, N. L., Buckwalter, P., Zhang, X., Smith, E., & O'Brien, M. (1997). Prevalence of specific language impairment in kindergarten children. *Journal of Speech, Language, and Hearing Research, 40,* 1245–1260.

Tower, S. S. (1940). Pyramidal lesions in the monkey. *Brain, 63,* 36–90.

Twitchell, T. E. (1951). The restoration of motor function following hemiplegia in man. *Brain, 74,* 443–480.

Twitchell, T. E. (1954). Sensory factors in purposive movement. *Journal of Neurophysiology, 17,* 239–254.

Uswatte, G., & Taub, E. (2005). Implications of the learned nonuse formulation for measuring rehabilitation outcomes: Lessons from constraint-induced movement therapy. *Rehabilitation Psychology, 50,* 34–42.

Uswatte, G., Taub, E., Morris, D., Barman, J., & Crago, J. (2006). Contribution of the shaping and restraint components of constraint-induced movement therapy to treatment outcome. *Neurorehabilitation, 21,* 147–156.

Uswatte, G., Taub, E., Morris, D., Light, K., & Thompson, P. (2006). The motor activity log-28: A method for assessing daily use of the hemiparetic arm after stroke. *Neurology, 67,* 1189–1194.

Uswatte, G., Taub, E., Morris, D., Vignolo, M., & McCulloch, K. (2005). Reliability and validity of the upper-extremity motor activity log-14 for measuring real-world arm use. *Stroke, 36,* 2493–2496.

van der Lee, J., Beckerman, H., Knol, D., de Vet, H., & Bouter, L. (2004). Clinimetric properties of the Motor Activity Log for the assessment of arm use in hemiparetic patients. *Stroke, 35,* 1–5.

van der Lee, J., Beckerman, H., Lankhorst, G., & Bouter, L. (1999). Constraint-induced movement therapy [Letter to the Editor]. *Archives of Physical Medicine and Rehabilitation, 80,* 1606.

van der Lee, J., Wagenaar, R., Lankhorst, G., Vogelaar, T., Deville, W., & Bouter, L. (1999). Forced use of the upper extremity in chronic stroke patients: Results from a single-blind randomized clinical trial. *Stroke, 30,* 2369–2375.

Wainberg, M., Barbeau, H., & Gauthier, S. (1990). The effects of cyproheptadine on locomotion and spasticity in patients with spinal cord injuries. *Journal of Neurology, Neurosurgery, and Psychiatry, 53,* 754–763.

Walker-Batson, D., Smith, P., Curtis, S., Unwin, H., & Greenlee, R. (1995). Amphetamine paired with physical therapy accelerates motor recovery after stroke: Further evidence. *Stroke, 26,* 2254–2259.

Walker-Batson, D., Unwin, H., Curtis, S., Allan, E., Wood, M., Devous, M., et al. (1992). Use of amphetamine in the treatment of aphasia. *Restorative Neurology and Neuroscience, 4,* 47–50.

Wall, P. D., & Egger, M. D. (1971, August 20). Formation of new connections in adult rat brains following partial deafferentation. *Nature, 232,* 542–545.

Ware, J. E., & Sherbourne, C. D. (1992). The MOS 36-item Short-Form Health Survey (SF-36): Pt. I. Conceptual framework and item selection. *Medical Care, 30,* 473–483.

Weiss, T., Miltner, W. H. R., Adler, T., Bruckner, L., & Taub, E. (1999). Decrease in phantom limb pain associated with prosthesis-induced increased use of an amputation stump in humans. *Neuroscience Letters, 272,* 131–134.

Wittenberg, G. F., Chen, R., Ishii, K., Bushara, K. O., Eckloff, S., Croarkin, E., et al. (2003). Constraint-induced therapy in stroke: Magnetic-stimulation motor maps and cerebral activation. *Neurorehabilitation and Neural Repair, 17,* 48–57.

Wolf, S., Lecraw, D., Barton, L., & Jann, B. (1989). Forced use of hemiplegic upper extremities to reverse the effect of learned nonuse among chronic stroke and head-injured patients. *Experimental Neurology, 104*, 125–132.

Wolf, S., Thompson, P., Morris, D., Rose, D., Winstein, C., Taub, E., et al. (2005). The EXCITE trial: Attributes of the Wolf Motor Function Test in patients with subacute stroke. *Neurorehabilitation and Neural Repair, 19*, 194–205.

Wolf, S., Winstein, C., Miller, J., Taub, E., Uswatte, G., Morris, D., et al. (2006). Effect of constraint-induced movement therapy on upper extremity function 3–9 months after stroke: The EXCITE randomized clinical trial. *Journal of the American Medical Association, 296*, 2095–2104.

Wolf, S., Winstein, C., Miller, J., Thompson, P., Taub, E., Uswatte, G., et al. (2008). Upper limb function in stroke survivors who have received constraint-induced movement therapy: Follow-up of the EXCITE randomized trial. *Lancet Neurology, 7*, 33–40.

Wolpaw, J. R., Flotzinger, D., Pfurtscheller, G., & McFarland, D. (1997). Timing of EEG-based cursor control. *Journal of Clinical Neurophysiology, 14*, 529–538.

Wolpaw, J. R., & McFarland, D. J. (1994). Multichannel EEG-based brain-computer communication. *Electroencephalography and Clinical Neurophysiology, 78*, 314–317.

Wolpaw, J. R., McFarland, D. J., Neat, G. W., & Forneris, C. A. (1991). An EEG-based brain-computer interface for cursor control. *Electroencephalography and Clinical Neurophysiology, 78*, 252–259.

Yamashima, T., Tonchev, A. B., Vachkov, I. H., Popivanova, B. K., Seki, T., Sawamoto, K., et al. (2004). Vascular adventitia generates neuronal progenitors in the monkey hippocampus after ischemia. *Hippocampus, 14*, 861–875.

Yang, T. T., Gallen, C., Schwartz, B., Bloom, F. E., Ramachandran, V. S., & Cobb, S. (1994, April 14). Sensory maps in the human brain. *Nature, 368*, 592–593.

Author Index

Subject Index

A

Abstinence model, of reinstatement, 1139
Abstract constructs, 10
Abstraction. *See* Categorization of visual
    objects
Abyssinian tea, 90
ACC. *See* Anterior cingulate cortex (ACC)
ACE. *See* Angiotensin converting
    enzyme (ACE)
Acetaminophen, tramadol with, 652
Acetylcholine, 84–87, 91, 106, 109
    receptors, 793
    and thirst, 695
Acid transduction, 270
Acoustic stimuli, 332, 464–465, 518
ACSF. *See* Artificial cerebral spinal
    fluid (aCSF)
Actin cycling, defined, 1145–1146
Activation overlap equals *process
    overlap*, 162
Activator of G-protein Signaling 3
    (AGS3), 1143
Active placebo response, 1240
    defined, 1237
    vs. statistical artifacts, 1237–1241
Active sleep. *See* Rapid eye-movement
    (REM) sleep
Activity dependent facilitation (ADF), 719
Acute pain, 638
    in animals, pain measurement, 647
Acute - phase response, 121
Acute stress, 1223–1224. *See also* Stress
A/D. *See* Anxious depression (A/D)
Adaptation, psychology of. *See also* Stress
    coping and, 1228–1229
Adaptation-specific (emotional) systems, 710
Adaptive immune system, 120, 126
Adaptive significance, of circadian system, 59,
    60–61
Addiction
    behavioral methods
        conditioned place preference, 1134
        drug self-administration model,
            1134–1135
        psychomotor sensitization, 1133–1134
        reinstatement procedure, 1135–1136
    clinical perspective, 1132–1133
    defined, 1132
    dopamine hypothesis of, 1137

drugs of abuse, pharmacology of, 1133
molecular changes in
    acute effects, 1142–1143
    chronic effects, 1143–1145
    experimental techniques, 1140–1142
    morphological adaptations, 1145–1146
morphological adaptations in, 1145–1146
neurocircuitry of
    experimental techniques, 1136
    reinstatement, 1138–1139
    second-order schedules, 1139–1140
    self-administration, 1137–1138
    sensitization, neurochemical mechanisms
        of, 1136–1137
neuroimaging and, 1146–1147
neuroscience perspective, 1133
and reward system, 796–798
treatment of, 1147
Addiction Research Center Inventory, 781
Adenosine, 95, 467
Adenosine triphosphate (ATP), 122
Adenylyl cyclase, 1142
ADF. *See* Activity dependent facilitation (ADF)
ADHD. *See* Attention- deficit/hyperactivity
    disorder (ADHD)
Adipocyte hormone, 661
Admiration, 870–871
Adolescence
    circadian rhythmicity in, 470–471
    internalizing and externalizing problems in,
        1113–1114
ADOS. *See* Autism diagnostic observational
    scale (ADOS)
Adrenalectomy, 71
β-adrenergic receptors, 834, 1072–1073
Adult ADHD, 1030. *See also* Attention- deficit/
    hyperactivity disorder (ADHD)
Adult affiliative behavior, 49
Adult antisocial behavior, reduced P300
    response and, 1120
Affect
    prefrontal regulation of, 1249
2 - AG (2 - arachidonoyl - glycerol), 93
Aggression, 5, 36, 39, 48. *See also* Offensive
    aggression
    and anger, 963–965
    antecedents to offensive, 965–969
    gender and, 105
    genes effect on, 105

nature of, 105
neural system for, 970–972
seasonal changes in, 66, 70–72
Aging, 93. *See also* Cognitive aging
    of cells and organisms, 1280–1284
    energy metabolism associated with, 94
    in immune-brain relationships, 128–131
    thirst with, 699–700
Aging-related diseases
    mechanisms relating telomere maintenance
        to, 1289
    models for roles of telomere and telomerase
        in, 1286–1287
    and telomeres, 1284
Agnosia, and face perception, 841–842
Agonists, 83
Agoraphobia, 1008
Agouti gene- related transcript (AgRP),
    673–674
Agraphias
    central, 1165
    peripheral, 1164–1165
AgRP. *See* Agouti gene- related transcript
    (AgRP)
AGS3. *See* Activator of G-protein Signaling 3
    (AGS3)
Air pressure, 251–253, 256
Akinetic mutism, 926
    defined, 484
Alarm reaction, 1221
Alcohol
    and ADHD, 1031. *See also* Attention- deficit/
        hyperactivity disorder (ADHD)
    dependence, reduced P300 response and,
        1119–1120
    GABA$_A$ receptor and, 1133
    treatment, naltrexone and, 1147
Alcohol fetal syndrome, 1023
Alert attention network, 364
Alerting
    definition of, 376
    functions in, 363, 376
    measure of, 378
    network, 364
    sign of, 371
    tasks, 365
Alexia without agraphia. *See* Pure alexia
ALFRED (allele frequency database), 1031
Alkyloids, 268

M